LARC

DICCIONARIO

ESPAÑOL–INGLÉS
INGLÉS–ESPAÑOL

SPANISH–ENGLISH
ENGLISH–SPANISH

DICTIONARY

LAROUSSE

Dirección editorial

Ralf Brockmeier

Coordinación de la obra

Sinda López Fuentes

Redacción

Joaquín Blasco, Dileri Borunda Johnston,
José A. Gálvez y Patrick Goldsmith

Lengua y cultura

Lydia Goldsmith y Patrick Goldsmith

Edición

Marc Chabrier
con Lucy Bove y Dominique Chevalier

Diseño

Sophie Rivoire

Informática editorial y preimpresión

Dalila Abdelkader y Monika Al Mourabit

© Larousse, 2010

21, rue du Montparnasse, 75283 Paris Cedex 06, France

Published in the United States of America and Canada by
Publicado en Estados Unidos y Canadá por
Éditions LAROUSSE, 21, rue du Montparnasse, 75283 Paris Cedex 06, France
www.larousse.fr

ISBN 978-2-03-541037-5

Distribución/Sales: Houghton Mifflin Harcourt, Boston
Library of Congress CIP Data has been applied for

Índice
Contents

Guía de pronunciación

Las siguientes letras y combinaciones de letras no se pronuncian igual que en español:

a puede pronunciarse:
[ɑː] como en *after*,
[eɪ] como en *name*,
[ɒ] como en *wash*,
[ə] como en el artículo *a*,
[æ] como en *manage*,
[eə] como en *care*.

e puede pronunciarse:
[e] como en *ten*,
[iː] como en *she* o puede ser muda,
como en *finished* ['fɪnɪʃt].

g puede pronunciarse:
[g] como en *give*,
[dʒ] como en *page* o puede ser muda,
como en *night* [naɪt].

h es aspirada en la mayoría de las palabras
como en *hat* [hæt] o puede ser muda
como en *hour* ['aʊər].

i puede pronunciarse:
[ɪ] como en *pig*,
[aɪ] como en *nice*,
[ɜː] como en *bird*.

j se pronuncia [dʒ] como en *John*.

l puede pronunciarse:
[l] como en *leg* o puede ser muda,
como en *half* [hɑːf].

o puede pronunciarse:
[ɒ] como en *coffee*,
[əʊ] como en *no*,
[uː] como en *move*,
[ʌ] como en *love*,
[ə] como en *tomato*.

q puede pronunciarse:
[kw] como en *question*,
[k] como en *technique*.

r puede pronunciarse:
[r] como en *rich* o puede ser muda,
como en *farm* [fɑːm].

s puede pronunciarse:
[s] como en *miss*,
[z] como en *rose*.

La *s* final de los sustantivos en plural y la *s* de los verbos en la tercera persona del singular puede pronunciarse:
[s] como en *cats*, *works*,
[z] como en *dogs*, *lives*,
[ɪz] como en *houses*, *rises*.

u puede pronunciarse:
[juː] como en *music*,
[ʌ] como en *but*,
[ə] como en *surprise*.

w puede pronunciarse:
[w] como en *wet* o puede ser muda,
como en *two* [tuː].

y puede pronunciarse:
[j] como en *yes*,
[aɪ] como en *cry*,
[ɪ] como en *fifty*.

La combinación *ai* puede pronunciarse:
[eə] como en *chair*,
[eɪ] como en *wait*.

La combinación *au* puede pronunciarse:
[ɒ] como en *because*,
[ɔː] como en *daughter*.

La combinación *aw* puede pronunciarse:
[ɒ] como en *saw*,
[ɔː] como en *law*.

La combinación *ee* puede pronunciarse:
[iː] como en *three*,
[ɪə] como en *deer*.

La combinación *ea* puede pronunciarse:
[iː] como en *tea*,
[ɪə] como en *ear*.

La combinación *ow* puede pronunciarse:
[əʊ] como en *blow*,
[aʊ] como en *cow*.

La combinación *oo* puede pronunciarse:
[uː] como en *food*,
[ɔː] como en *door*,
[ʌ] como en *blood*.

La combinación *oy* se pronuncia [ɔɪ] como en *boy*.

La combinación *ou* puede pronunciarse:
[aʊ] como en *mouse*,
[ɔː] como en *of course*,
[ʌ] como en *enough*,
[uː] como en *through*.

Algunos sonidos no tienen equivalente o son raros en español, como:

– las letras *th* que se pronuncian:
[ð] como en *the*, *this*, *mother*,
[θ] como en *three*, *think*, *thank you*.

– las letras *ng* al final que se pronuncian:
[ŋ] como en *song* y *morning*.

Cómo usar este diccionario

1. Elementos básicos de las entradas

○ Lemas

Los lemas, así como la numeración y los indicadores, aparecen en azul en ambos lados para facilitar la búsqueda de información. Las categorías gramaticales de la entrada aparecen indicadas por un rombo y las varias acepciones van indicadas con un número en un círculo azul.

dig [dɪg] ◆ *vt* ❶ cavar; escarbar ❷ cavar en ❸ excavar ◆ *vi* ❶ cavar ❷ escarbar ◆ *s* ❶ pulla ❷ Arqueología excavación

pegatina *sf* sticker

○ Pronunciación

La fonética de cada lema inglés va entre corchetes, para indicar cómo pronunciar correctamente cada palabra.

destination [ˌdestɪ'neɪʃn] *s* destino

○ Traducciones

En el lado inglés-español cuando las traducciones no necesitan clarificación, éstas se dan sin indicadores.

slant [slɑːnt] *s* ❶ inclinación ❷ enfoque

En el lado español-inglés cuando hay más de una traducción, las traducciones irán diferenciadas o bien mediante un indicador o bien mediante una etiqueta señalando un ámbito.

revelar *vt* ❶ [*declarar*] to reveal ❷ [*evidenciar*] to show ❸ Fotografía to develop

En los casos en los que no hay un equivalente exacto se da una explicación que va resaltada en azul o un equivalente cultural, precedida por el símbolo ≃.

pesero *sm* ▶ *para explicar lo que es puedes decir:* it's a fixed-rate taxi service

savings bank *s* ≃ caja de ahorros

○ Indicadores

Cuando hay más de una traducción y una aclaración es necesaria, se emplean indicadores o etiquetas que indican el ámbito.

portal *sm* ❶ [*entrada*] entrance hall ❷ [*puerta*] main door ❸ Informática portal

○ Ejemplos

Los ejemplos de uso corriente ayudan a entender y expresarse en un inglés usual.

borrow ['bɒrəʊ] *vt* • to borrow something from somebody tomar algo prestado a alguien • can I borrow your bike? ¿me prestas tu bici?

○ Palabras compuestas

Las palabras compuestas aparecen en azul al final del sentido correspondiente.

partida *sf* ❶ [*marcha*] departure • ❷ [*documento*] certificate ▶ **partida de defunción** death certificate ▶ **partida de matrimonio** marriage certificate ▶ **partida de nacimiento** birth certificate

● Expresiones

Las expresiones idiomáticas aparecen agrupadas al final de cada categoría gramatical, precedidas de la etiqueta **expresión** o **expresiones**.

loop [lu:p] *s* ❶ lazo ❷ *INFORMÁTICA* bucle
expresión **to be out of the loop** no estar al corriente

● Verbos en inglés con partícula (phrasal verbs)

Los verbos en inglés con partícula, o sea, los verbos que van seguidos de una preposición como *down, in, out,* etc., van en orden alfabético al final de la entrada precedidos por un cuadratín. En cada caso van seguidos de una nota indicando donde se coloca el complemento.

■ **light up** *vt* 💡 *El objeto se puede colocar antes o después de la preposición.* iluminar

● Verbos pronominales

Los verbos pronominales van al final de la entrada precedidos por un cuadratín.

atemorizar *vt* to frighten
■ **atemorizarse** *v pronominal* to get frightened

● Reenvíos

Hay dos tipos de reenvíos, y van indicados por los símbolos → o =. En ambos casos hay que consultar la entrada indicada.

blest [blest] *pretérito & participio pasado* → **bless**

pasapurés *sm invariable* = **pasapuré**

2. Información lingüística y gramatical

● Gramática

En todo el diccionario hay breves notas precedidas de una explicación que da información gramatical básica sobre el inglés.

rencoroso, sa *adj* resentful 💡 *Los adjetivos ingleses son invariables.*

linguistics [lɪŋ'ɡwɪstɪks] *s* 💡 *incontable* lingüística

Las dificultades gramaticales de ciertas palabras vienen explicadas en recuadros azules al final de la entrada.

bit [bɪt] ...

a bit

A bit puede ser un adverbio (he's **a bit** shy *es un poco tímido*) o un pronombre (would you like some cake? — yes, just **a bit** *¿quieres pastel? — sí, un poco*). Cuando va delante de un sustantivo se añade of (**a bit of** air *un poco de aire*).

A bit y a bit of significan lo mismo que a little, pero en un lenguaje menos formal.

Las palabras gramaticales en ambos lados aparecen en un recuadro azul con varios ejemplos de uso.

> **ought** [ɔt]
> ◆ *v modal*
> ❶ [*para realizar una recomendación*]
> • **you ought to see a doctor** deberías ver a un médico
> • **I really ought to go** realmente me tengo que ir
> ❷ [*para realizar un reproche*]
> • **you ought not to have done that** no deberías haber hecho eso

○ Formas irregulares

Las formas irregulares de las palabras inglesas van indicadas en una nota al final de la entrada resaltada en azul.

> **schoolchild** [ˈskuːltʃaɪld] *s* colegial, la
> El plural de **schoolchild** es **schoolchildren** [ˈskuːltʃɪldrən].

En el lado español-inglés se dan las formas plurales y femeninas irregulares, y éstas aparecen subrayadas.

> **pescador, ra** *sm, f* fisherman, *plural* fishermen, *femenino* fisherwoman, *plural* fisherwomen

En el lado inglés-español se incluye la traducción femenina (en forma abreviada).

> **amazed** [əˈmeɪzd] *adj* asombrado, da

○ Falsos amigos

Los falsos amigos, o sea aquellos términos que, pese a tener una forma parecida en español y en inglés, tienen un significado muy distinto, van explicados en recuadros azules al final del lema.

> **restar** *vt*
>
> ### restar ≠ rest
> • La palabra inglesa **rest** es un falso amigo que significa **descansar**. **Restar** se traduce al inglés por **to subtract**.

○ Listas temáticas

Estas listas ofrecen glosarios temáticos para ayudar a adquirir vocabulario.

> **naturaleza** *sf*
>
> ### la naturaleza
>
>
> | | |
> |---|---|
> | el acantilado | the cliff |
> | el bosque | the forest |
> | el campo | the countryside |
> | un campo | a field |

⊙ Cómo expresarse

Recuadros con ejemplos genuinos con vistas a dominar el inglés.

asombro ...

expresar su asombro

- **What a surprise!** ¡Qué sorpresa!
- **Who'd have thought it?** ¿Quién lo hubiera creído?
- **What a coincidence!** ¡Qué casualidad!
- **I'm amazed.** Me extraña.
- **That's really strange!** ¡Qué curioso!
- **I'd never have believed that.** Nunca me lo hubiera imaginado.

3. Información cultural

En el lado inglés-español de este diccionario hay recuadros azules marcados con el símbolo de un libro en el que se explican algunos aspectos de la vida y la cultura de los Estados Unidos.

Broadway

BROADWAY

Broadway es el nombre de una calle de Nueva York, en Manhattan, donde se encuentran muchos teatros. Centro de la cultura teatral estadounidense, Broadway se destaca sobre todo por sus obras musicales.

Formas abreviadas y símbolos

adj	adjetivo
adv	adverbio
f	femenino
m	masculino
pl	plural
pp	participio pasado
s	sustantivo
sf	sustantivo femenino
sm	sustantivo masculino
sm,f	sustantivo masculino, sustantivo femenino
smf	sustantivo masculino y femenino
v	verbo
vi	verbo intransitivo
vt	verbo transitivo

ESPAÑOL–INGLÉS

a¹, A *sf* [*letra*] a ; A

a²

◆ *preposición*

❶ [*indica a donde va alguien*] to
• **voy a San Diego/a África/al Japón** I'm going to San Diego/to Africa/to Japan
• **llegó a Córdoba/a la fiesta** he arrived in Córdoba/at the party
• **llegó a México** he arrived in Mexico

❷ [*indica donde está alguien*]
• **está a más de cien kilómetros** it's more than a hundred kilometers
• **está a la derecha/a la izquierda** it's on the right/on the left

❸ [*indica un momento preciso*] at
• **a las siete** at seven o'clock
• **a la salida del cine** at the entrance to the theater
• **a los once años** at eleven

❹ [*indica el tiempo que ha pasado*]
• **a las pocas semanas** a few weeks later
• **al mes de casados** a month after getting married

❺ [*expresa la simultaneidad*] when
• **al oír la noticia se desmayó** he fainted when he heard the news

❻ [*indica un precio*]
• **¿a cuánto están las peras?** how much are the pears?
• **vende las manzanas a diez pesos** she sells the apples for ten pesos

❼ [*indica una cantidad*]
• **cuarenta horas a la semana** forty hours a week
• **a cien kilómetros por hora** at fifty kilometers per hour
• **a cientos/miles** by the hundred/thousand

❽ [*antes de un complemento directo*]
• **quiere a su padre/gato** he loves his father/cat

❾ [*antes de un complemento indirecto*] to
• **dáselo a Juan** give it to Juan

❿ [*para expresar la manera, el método*] by
• **lavar a máquina/a mano** machine wash/wash by hand

• **a la antigua** (in) the old-fashioned way
• **a escondidas** secretly

⓫ [*indica el objetivo*]
• **entró a pagar** he went in to pay
• **vino a buscar un libro** he came in to look for a book
• **aprende a nadar** he's learning to swim

⓬ [*expresa una suposición*]
• **a no ser por mí, hubieras fracasado** if it hadn't been for me, you would have failed

⓭ [*para dar una orden*]
• **¡a comer!** dinner's ready!
• **¡niños, a callar!** be quiet, children!

■ **a que**

◆ *locución conjuntiva*
[*expresa un desafío*]
• **¿a que no lo haces?** I bet you'll do it!

abad, esa *sm, f* abbot, *femenino* abbess
abadía *sf* abbey
abajo ◆ *adv* ❶ [*posición - generalmente*] below ; [*- en edificio*] downstairs • **vive (en el piso de) abajo** she lives downstairs • **más abajo** further down ❷ [*dirección*] down • **ve abajo** [*en edificio*] go downstairs • **hacia/para abajo** down ; downwards • **calle/escaleras abajo** down the street/stairs • **río abajo** downstream ❸ [*en un texto*] below
◆ *exclamación* • **¡abajo la dictadura!** down with the dictatorship!
abanderado *sm* literal & figurado standard-bearer
abandonado, da *adj* ❶ [*desierto*] deserted ❷ [*desamparado*] abandoned ❸ [*descuidado - jardín, casa*] neglected • **dejar abandonado** to abandon ⚲ *Los adjetivos ingleses son invariables.*
abandonar *vt* ❶ [*generalmente*] to abandon • **no podemos abandonar a los cachorros, tenemos que alimentarlos** we can't abandon the puppies, we have to feed them • **¡abandonen el barco!** abandon ship! ❷ [*lugar, profesión, cónyuge*] to leave • **abandonó su ciudad** she left her town ❸ [*desatender - obligaciones, estudios*] to neglect ; [*- trabajo*] to quit • **no puedo abandonar el trabajo ahora** I can't quit my job now

A

abandono *sm* ❶ [*acción - generalmente*] abandonment; [*- de lugar, profesión, cónyuge*] leaving; [*- de obligaciones, estudios*] neglect ❷ [*estado*] state of abandon ❸ DEPORTE • **ganar por abandono** to win by default

abanicar *vt* to fan

abanico *sm* [*para dar aire*] fan

abaratar *vt* to reduce the price of

abarcar *vt* to cover • **el curso de historia abarca desde el siglo XVI hasta el presente** the history course covers from the 16th century to the present

abarrotado, da *adj* • **abarrotado (de) a)** [*teatro, camión*] packed (with) **b)** [*desván, baúl*] crammed (with). ♀ *Los adjetivos ingleses son invariables.*

abarrotar *vt* • **abarrotar algo (de** o **con) a)** [*teatro, camión*] to pack something (with) **b)** [*desván, baúl*] to cram something full (of)

abarrote *sm* bundle

abarrotería *sf* grocery store

abarrotero, ra *sm, f* grocer

abastecer *vt* • **abastecer algo/a alguien (de)** to supply something/somebody (with)

abastecimiento *sm* ❶ [*cantidad*] supply ❷ [*acción*] supplying

abasto *sm*
expresión **no darse abasto para hacer algo** to be unable to cope with doing something ▶ **no me doy abasto con tanto trabajo** I can't cope with all this work

abatido, da *adj* dejected. ♀ *Los adjetivos ingleses son invariables.*

abatir *vt* ❶ [*derribar - muro*] to knock down; [*- avión*] to shoot down ❷ [*desanimar*] to depress

abdicar *vi* to abdicate • **abdicar de algo** *figurado* to renounce something

abdomen *sm* abdomen

abdominal *adj* abdominal. ♀ *Los adjetivos ingleses son invariables.*

abecé *sm* *literal & figurado* ABC

abecedario *sm* [*alfabeto*] alphabet

abeja *sf* bee

abejorro *sm* bumblebee

aberración *sf* aberration
expresión **eso es una aberración** that's absurd

abertura *sf* opening

abeto *sm* fir (tree)

abierto, ta ◆ *participio pasado*→ **abrir**
◆ *adj* [*generalmente*] open • **la puerta está abierta** the door is open • **dejar la llave abierta** to leave the faucet on • **bien** o **muy abierto** wide open. ♀ *Los adjetivos ingleses son invariables.*

abismal *adj* colossal. ♀ *Los adjetivos ingleses son invariables.*

abismo *sm* [*profundidad*] abyss

ablandar *vt* [*material*] to soften • **el agua ablandó la pasta** the water softened the pasta

■ **ablandarse** *v pronominal* [*material*] to soften • **la mantequilla se ablandó con el calor** the butter softened in the heat

abofetear *vt* to slap

abogacía *sf* legal profession

abogado, da *sm, f* lawyer; attorney • **mi madre es abogada** my mother is a lawyer ▶ **abogado defensor** counsel for the defense ▶ **abogado del estado** public prosecutor

abogar *vi* *figurado* [*defender*] • **abogar por algo** to advocate something • **abogar por alguien** to stand up for somebody

abolición *sf* abolition

abolir *vt* to abolish • **abolieron la pena de muerte** they abolished the death penalty

abollado, a *adj* ❶ dented ❷ *familiar* [*sin dinero*] penniless; broke

abolladura *sf* dent

abollar *vt* to dent

abominable *adj* abominable. ♀ *Los adjetivos ingleses son invariables.*

abonado, da *sm, f* ❶ [*de teléfono, revista*] subscriber ❷ [*al fútbol, teatro, transporte*] season-ticket holder

abonar *vt* ❶ [*pagar*] to pay • **ayer aboné los primeros cien pesos por la mesa** I paid the first 100 pesos for the table yesterday • **abonar algo en la cuenta de alguien** to credit somebody's account with something ❷ [*tierra*] to fertilize • **abonamos la tierra para que la planta crezca fuerte y sana** we fertilized the soil so the plant will grow strong and healthy

abono *sm* ❶ [*fertilizante*] fertilizer • **el abono natural no daña el medio ambiente** natural fertilizer doesn't damage the environment ❷ [*pago*] payment • **tengo que hacer un abono de 100 pesos** I have to make a payment of 100 pesos ❸ [*plazo*] installment • **pagué el primer abono al carpintero** I paid the first installment to the carpenter

abordar *vt* ❶ [*embarcación*] to board ❷ *figurado* [*tema, tarea*] to tackle

aborrecer *vt* ❶ [*actividad*] to abhor ❷ [*persona*] to loathe

abortar *vi* MEDICINA [*espontáneamente*] to have a miscarriage; [*intencionadamente*] to have an abortion

aborto *sm* MEDICINA [*espontáneo*] miscarriage; [*intencionado*] abortion

abotonar *vt* to button up

■ **abotonarse** *v pronominal* ❶ to do your buttons up ❷ [*abrigo, camisa*] to button up • **abotónese el abrigo, que se va a resfriar** button up your coat or you'll catch a cold

abrazar *vt* [*con los brazos*] to hug • **antes de subir al avión, abrazamos a la familia** we hugged our relatives before getting on the plane • **abrazar fuerte a alguien** to hold somebody tight

■ **abrazarse** *v pronominal* to hug (each other) • **los amigos se abrazaron afectuosamente** the two friends hugged each other affectionately

abrazo *sm* embrace; hug • **dale un abrazo a tu abuelo** give your grandfather a hug

abrebotellas *sm invariable* bottle opener

abrecartas *sm invariable* letter opener

abrelatas *sm invariable* can opener

abreviar *vt* ❶ [*generalmente*] to shorten ❷ [*texto*] to abridge ❸ [*palabra*] to abbreviate ❹ [*viaje, estancia*] to cut short

abreviatura *sf* abbreviation • **"Sr." es la abreviatura de "señor"** "Sr." is the abbreviation of "señor"

abridor *sm* ❶ [*abrebotellas*] (bottle) opener ❷ [*abrelatas*] (can) opener

abrigar *vt* ❶ [*arropar - sujeto: persona*] to wrap up • **abriga bien al niño** wrap the baby up warm; [*- sujeto: ropa*] to keep warm • **estas mallas abrigan demasiado** this pantyhose is too warm ❷ *figurado* [*albergar esperanza*] to cherish; [*sospechas, malas intenciones*] to harbor

■ **abrigarse** *v pronominal* [*arroparse*] to wrap up • **nos abrigamos con cobijas de lana** we wrapped ourselves up in wool blankets

abrigo *sm* ❶ [*prenda*] coat; overcoat ❷ [*refugio*] shelter

abril *sm* April ver también **septiembre**

abrillantar *vt* to polish

abrir ◆ *vt* ❶ [*generalmente*] to open • **no puedo abrir esta caja** I can't open this box ❷ [*alas*] to spread ❸ [*melón*] to cut open ❹ [*puerta*] to unlock; to open ❺ [*pestillo*] to pull back ❻ [*llave del agua*] to turn on ❼ [*cierre*] to undo ❽ [*túnel*] to dig ❾ [*canal, camino*] to build ❿ [*agujero, surco*] to make
◆ *vi* [*establecimiento*] to open

abrochar *vt* ❶ [*camisa, botón*] to button up ❷ [*cinturón*] to fasten

■ **abrocharse** *v pronominal* ❶ to button ❷ [*cinturón*] to fasten • **abróchense los cinturones de seguridad** fasten your seat belts

abrupto, ta *adj* ❶ [*escarpado*] sheer ❷ [*accidentado*] rugged ⚠ *Los adjetivos ingleses son invariables.*

ábside *sm* apse

absolución *sf* ❶ DERECHO acquittal ❷ RELIGIÓN absolution

absoluto, ta *adj* ❶ [*generalmente*] absolute ❷ [*silencio, obediencia*] total ⚠ *Los adjetivos ingleses son invariables.*

absolver *vt* • **absolver a alguien (de algo) a)** DERECHO to acquit somebody (of something) **b)** RELIGIÓN to absolve somebody (of something)

absorbente *adj* ❶ [*que empapa*] absorbent ❷ [*actividad*] absorbing ⚠ *Los adjetivos ingleses son invariables.*

absorber *vt* ❶ [*generalmente*] to absorb ❷ [*consumir, gastar*] to soak up

absorción *sf* absorption

abstemio, mia *adj* teetotal ⚠ *Los adjetivos ingleses son invariables.*

abstención *sf* abstention

abstenerse *v pronominal* • **abstenerse (de algo/de hacer algo)** to abstain (from something/from doing something) • **en la votación, 20 legisladores se abstuvieron** 20 legislators abstained from voting • **le han recomendado que se abstenga del alcohol** she has been advised to stay away from alcohol • **se abstuvo de hacer cualquier comentario** she refrained from commenting

abstinencia *sf* abstinence

abstracción *sf* abstraction

abstracto, ta *adj* abstract ⚠ *Los adjetivos ingleses son invariables.*

absurdo, da *adj* absurd ⚠ *Los adjetivos ingleses son invariables.*

■ **absurdo** *sm* • **decir/hacer un absurdo** to say/do something ridiculous

abuchear *vt* to boo

abuelo, la *sm, f* [*familiar*] grandfather, *femenino* grandmother

abultar ◆ *vt* ❶ [*hinchar*] to swell ❷ [*exagerar*] to blow up
◆ *vi* [*ser muy grande*] to be bulky

abundancia *sf* ❶ [*gran cantidad*] abundance • **había comida en abundancia** there was an abundance of food ❷ [*riqueza*] plenty; prosperity • **vivir en la abundancia** to be well-off

abundante *adj* abundant ⚠ *Los adjetivos ingleses son invariables.*

abundar *vi* [*ser abundante*] to abound • **en los pueblos de mar abundan las gaviotas** seagulls abound in coastal towns

aburrido, da ◆ *adj* ❶ [*harto, fastidiado*] bored • **estar aburrido de hacer algo** to be fed up with doing something ❷ [*que aburre*] boring • **la película que vi ayer estuvo muy aburrida** the movie I saw yesterday was very boring ⚠ *Los adjetivos ingleses son invariables.*
◆ *sm, f* bore

aburrimiento *sm* boredom • **¡qué aburrimiento!** what a bore!

aburrir *vt* to bore • **me aburre** I'm bored of it

■ **aburrirse** *v pronominal* ❶ to get bored • **nos aburrimos mucho en la fiesta** we got really bored at the party ❷ [*estar aburrido*] to be bored • **¡me aburro!** I'm bored!

abusado, da *adj* astute; shrewd ⚠ *Los adjetivos ingleses son invariables.*

abusar *vi* ❶ [*excederse*] to go too far • **abusar de algo** to abuse something • **abusar del alcohol** to drink too much ❷ [*aprovecharse*] • **abusar de alguien** to take advantage of somebody • **estás abusando de mí** you're taking advantage of me • **no quiero abusar de su hospitalidad** I don't want to take advantage of your hospitality • **no abuses de mi paciencia** don't try my patience ❸ [*forzar sexualmente*] • **abusar de alguien** to sexually abuse somebody

abusivo, va *adj* ❶ [*trato*] very bad ❷ [*precio*] extortionate ⚠ *Los adjetivos ingleses son invariables.*

A

abuso sm [uso excesivo] • **abuso (de)** abuse (of) • **es muy difícil combatir el abuso de las drogas** it's very hard to combat drug abuse • **¡esto es un abuso!** this is an outrage! • **los precios de este restaurante son un abuso** the prices in this restaurant are outrageous ▶ **abuso de confianza** breach of confidence ▶ **abusos deshonestos** sexual abuse ⚲ *incontable*

a. C. (abreviatura escrita de antes de Cristo) BC

acá adv❶ [lugar] here • **acá están las llaves que buscabas** here are the keys you were looking for • **de acá para allá** back and forth ❷ [tiempo] • **de una semana acá** during the last week

acabar
◆ *vt*
❶ [terminar] to finish
• **cuando acabe este capítulo, me iré a dormir** when I finish this chapter, I'll go to bed
• **¿ya acabaste el trabajo?** have you finished your work?
❷ [utilizar completamente]
• **primero hay que acabar todos los recursos a tu alcance** first you have to exhaust all possibilities
• **ya se les acabó el tiempo, entreguen el examen** time's up, turn in your tests
◆ *vi*
❶ [terminar] to finish
• **¿ya se acabó?** has it finished?
❷ [terminar de cierta manera] to end
• **acabar bien/mal** to end well/badly
❸ [pasar de un estado a otro]
• **acabar loco** to go mad
• **acabó sola** she ended up all alone
• **acabamos agotados** we ended up exhausted
❹ [seguido por un gerundio]
• **acabó cediendo** he ended up giving in
■ **acabar de**
◆ *v + preposición*
❶ [expresa el pasado reciente] to have just
• **acabo de llegar ahora mismo** I only just got here
❷ [en frases negativas]
• **no acabo de entender su reacción** I can't understand his reaction
❸ [en expresiones]
• **de nunca acabar** never-ending; endless
■ **acabar con**
◆ *v + preposición*
❶ [dar fin a]
• **hay que acabar con el problema de la droga** we must solve the drug problem once and for all
• **estás acabando con mi paciencia** don't make me lose my patience
• **una enfermedad acabó con su salud** an illness ruined his health
❷ [vencer a alguien o deshacerse de alguien]
• **acabaron con el enemigo** they annihilated the enemy

■ **acabar en**
◆ *v + preposición*
end in
• **las palabras que acaban en "n"** words that end in "n"
■ **acabar por**
◆ *v + preposición*
• **acabaron por venir** they ended up coming
■ **acabarse**
◆ *v pronominal*
❶ [terminarse]
• **las vacaciones se acabaron** vacation is over
• **se acabó la comida** there's nothing to eat
• **¡se acabó!** that's enough!
❷ [terminar]
• **acábate la sopa** finish your soup
• **se nos acabó la gasolina** we're out of gas

acabose sm
expresión **¡es el acabose!** familiar it really is the limit!

academia sf❶ [para aprender] school • **María va tres veces por semana a la academia de danza** María goes to dance school three times a week ❷ [institución] academy • **la Real Academia Española se creó en 1713** the Royal Academy of the Spanish Language was founded in 1713

académico, ca adj academic ⚲ *Los adjetivos ingleses son invariables.*

acalorado, da adj❶ [por calor] hot ❷ [apasionado - debate] heated ⚲ *Los adjetivos ingleses son invariables.*

acampar vi to camp

acantilado sm cliff

acaparar vt❶ [monopolizar] to monopolize ❷ [mercado] to corner ❸ [guardarse] to hoard

acariciar vt❶ [persona] to caress ❷ [animal] to stroke • **al niño le encanta acariciar al gato** the boy loves stroking the cat ❸ figurado [idea, proyecto] to cherish

acarrear vt❶ [transportar] to carry ❷ figurado [ocasionar] to bring; to give rise to

acaso adv perhaps • **¿acaso no lo sabías?** are you trying to tell me you didn't know? • **por si acaso** (just) in case • **¿acaso es culpa mía?** is it my fault?

acatar vt to respect; to comply with

acatarrarse v pronominal to catch a cold

acceder vi❶ [consentir] • **acceder (a algo/hacer algo)** to agree (to something/to do something) • **al final el maestro accedió al pedido de los alumnos** in the end the teacher agreed to the students' request ❷ [tener acceso] • **acceder a** • **no tiene las calificaciones exigidas para acceder a la universidad** he doesn't have the grades required to get into college • **el estudio permite acceder a mejores puestos de trabajo** education can allow you to obtain better jobs ❸ [alcanzar] • **acceder a a)** [trono] to accede to **b)** [poder] to come to **c)** [cargo] to obtain

accesible adj❶ [lugar] accessible ❷ [persona] approachable • **la nueva maestra es muy accesible** the new teacher is very approachable ·❄: *Los adjetivos ingleses son invariables.*

acceso *sm* ❶ [*entrada*] • **acceso (a)** entrance (to) ❷ [*paso*] • **acceso (a)** access (to) • **éste es el acceso principal al edificio** this is the main access to the building • **acceso a Internet** Internet access ▶ **acceso remoto** remote access ❸ [*carretera*] access road ; ramp ❹ MEDICINA [*de tos*] fit ❺ MEDICINA [*de fiebre, gripa*] bout

accidentado, da ◆ *adj* ❶ [*vida, viaje*] eventful ❷ [*terreno, camino*] rough ·❄: *Los adjetivos ingleses son invariables.*
◆ *sm, f* injured person

accidental *adj* ❶ [*imprevisto*] accidental ❷ [*encuentro*] chance ·❄: *Los adjetivos ingleses son invariables.*

accidente *sm* ❶ [*desgracia*] accident • **un conductor distraído provocó el accidente** a careless driver caused the accident • **sufrir un accidente** to have an accident ▶ **accidente laboral/mortal** industrial/fatal accident ▶ **accidente de tráfico** car accident ·❄: *generalmente pl* [*del terreno*] unevenness ·❄: *incontable*

acción *sf* ❶ [*generalmente*] action • **ponerse en acción** to go into action ❷ [*hecho*] deed • **hizo una buena acción** she performed a good deed ❸ FINANZAS share

accionar *vt* to activate

accionista *smf* shareholder

acechar *vt* ❶ [*vigilar*] to keep under surveillance ❷ [*sujeto: cazador*] to stalk ❸ [*amenazar*] to be lying in wait for • **el gato está siempre acechando al ratón** the cat is always lying in wait for the mouse

acecho *sm* • **estar al acecho de a)** to lie in wait for **b)** *figurado* to be on the lookout for

aceite *sm* oil ▶ **aceite de oliva** olive oil

aceitera *sf* oil can

aceitero, a ◆ *adj* oil
◆ *sm, f* oil vendor
■ **aceitero** *sf* oil cruet

aceituna *sf* olive ▶ **aceituna negra** black olive ▶ **aceituna verde** green olive

aceleración *sf* acceleration

acelerador, ra *adj* accelerating ·❄: *Los adjetivos ingleses son invariables.*
■ **acelerador** *sm* gas pedal • **vas muy rápido, no aprietes más el acelerador** you're going too fast, stop pressing the gas pedal

acelerar ◆ *vt* ❶ [*avivar*] to speed up ❷ TECNOLOGÍA to accelerate
◆ *vi* to accelerate • **tendrás que acelerar si lo quieres alcanzar** you'll have to accelerate if you want to catch him

acelga *sf* chard

acento *sm* ❶ [*generalmente*] accent • **"café" lleva acento en la "e"** "café" has an accent on the "e" • **el acento paraguayo es diferente al acento venezolano** the Paraguayan accent is different from the Venezuelan accent ❷ [*intensidad*] stress ; accent • **¿cuál es la sílaba con acento en la palabra "silla"?** what syllable does the stress fall on in the word "silla"?

acentuación *sf* accentuation

acentuar *vt* ❶ [*palabra, letra - al escribir*] to put an accent on • **no sé muy bien cuándo acentuar las palabras** I'm not sure when to put an accent on a word ; [*- al hablar*] to stress ❷ *figurado* [*realzar*] to accentuate • **el vestido acentuaba su cintura** the dress accentuated her waist
■ **acentuarse** *v pronominal* ❶ [*intensificarse*] to deepen • **la crisis se acentuó** the crisis deepened ❷ [*llevar acento*] to have an accent on • **"café" se acentúa en la última sílaba** "café" has an accent on the last syllable

acepción *sf* meaning ; sense

aceptable *adj* acceptable ·❄: *Los adjetivos ingleses son invariables.*

aceptación *sf* ❶ [*aprobación*] acceptance ❷ [*éxito*] success ; popularity

aceptar *vt* to accept • **Juan aceptó el trabajo que le ofrecieron** Juan accepted the job they offered him

acequia *sf* irrigation channel

acera *sf* [*para peatones*] sidewalk
expresión **ser de la otra acera, ser de la acera de enfrente** *familiar & despectivo* to bat for the other team

acerca ■ **acerca de** *locución adverbial* about • **la historia es acerca de una familia de extraterrestres** the story is about a family of aliens

acercar *vt* to move closer • **acerca la silla a la mesa** move your chair closer to the table • **¡acércame el pan!** could you pass me the bread?
■ **acercarse** *v pronominal* [*arrimarse - viniendo*] to move closer ; [*- yendo*] to go up to • **me acerqué al fuego para entrar en calor** I moved closer to the fire to warm up • **se acercó a la ventana** she went up to the window • **no te acerques al perro** don't get too close to the dog

acero *sm* steel ▶ **acero inoxidable** stainless steel

acertar ◆ *vt* ❶ [*adivinar*] to guess (correctly) • **¿a que no aciertas cuántas páginas tiene este libro?** I bet you can't guess how many pages this book has ❷ [*el blanco*] to hit • **acerté el blanco** I hit the target
◆ *vi* ❶ [*atinar*] • **acertar (al hacer algo)** to be right (to do something) • **acertaste al decírselo** you were right to tell her ❷ [*conseguir*] • **acertar a hacer algo** to manage to do something • **los científicos no acertaron a dar una explicación racional del fenómeno** scientists couldn't manage to find a rational explanation for the phenomenon ❸ [*hallar*] • **acertar con** to find • **acertó con la respuesta** he got the answer right

acertijo *sm* riddle

achaque *sm* ailment

achatado, da *adj* flattened ·❄: *Los adjetivos ingleses son invariables.*

achicar *vt* ❶ [*tamaño*] to make smaller ❷ [*agua - de barco*] to bale out ❸ *figurado* [*acobardar*] to intimidate

achicharrar *vt* [*chamuscar*] to burn

acicalar *vt* [*arreglar*] to dress up

A

acidez *sf* ❶ [*cualidad*] acidity ❷ Medicina ▸ **acidez (de estómago)** heartburn

ácido, da *adj* ❶ Química acidic ❷ [*bebida, sabor, carácter*] acid; sour ◌̇ *Los adjetivos ingleses son invariables.*

■ **ácido** *sm* Química acid ▸ **ácido clorhídrico/desoxirribonucleico/ribonucleico/sulfúrico** hydrochloric/deoxyribonucleic/ribonucleic/sulfuric acid

acierto *sm* ❶ [*a pregunta*] correct answer ❷ [*habilidad, tino*] good o sound judgment ❸ [*éxito*] success

aclamación *sf* [*ovación*] acclamation; acclaim • **por aclamación** unanimously • **entre aclamaciones** to great acclaim

aclamar *vt* to acclaim

aclaración *sf* explanation

aclaratorio, ria *adj* explanatory ◌̇ *Los adjetivos ingleses son invariables.*

acné *sm* acne

acogedor, ra *adj* ❶ [*país, persona*] welcoming ❷ [*casa, ambiente*] cozy ◌̇ *Los adjetivos ingleses son invariables.*

acoger *vt* ❶ [*recibir*] to welcome ❷ [*dar refugio*] to take in

acogida *sf* reception • **acogida familiar** fostering

acometer ◆ *vt* ❶ [*atacar*] to attack ❷ [*emprender*] to undertake
◆ *vi* [*embestir*] • **acometer contra** to hurtle into • **el toro acometió contra la barrera** the bull hurtled into the barrier

acomodado, da *adj* [*rico*] well-off ◌̇ *Los adjetivos ingleses son invariables.*

acomodador, ra *sm, f* usher, *femenino* usherette

acomodar *vt* ❶ [*instalar - persona*] to seat; to instal; [- *cosa*] to place ❷ [*adaptar*] to fit
■ **acomodarse** *v pronominal* [*instalarse*] to make yourself comfortable • **acomódese** make yourself comfortable • **acomodarse en** to settle down in • **se acomodó en el sillón** he settled down in the armchair

acompañamiento *sm* Cocina & Música accompaniment

acompañante *smf* ❶ [*compañero*] companion ❷ Música accompanist

acompañar *vt* ❶ [*ir con*] • **acompañar a alguien a)** [*generalmente*] to go with somebody **b)** [*a la puerta*] to show somebody out **c)** [*a casa*] to walk somebody home • **¿quiere acompañarme al supermercado?** do you want to go to the supermarket with me? • **te acompaño** I'll come with you ❷ [*estar con*] • **acompañar a alguien** to keep somebody company • **la acompañé un rato en el hospital** I kept her company in the hospital for a while ❸ [*adjuntar*] to enclose • **acompaño una copia del documento** I enclose a copy of the document ❹ Música to accompany

acomplejar *vt* to give a complex

acondicionado, da *adj* equipped ▸ **aire acondicionado** air conditioning ◌̇ *Los adjetivos ingleses son invariables.*

aconsejar *vt* [*dar consejos*] • **aconsejar a alguien (que haga algo)** to advise somebody (to do something) • **te aconsejo que vayas al médico** I'd advise you to see a doctor

acontecimiento *sm* event • **su llegada fue un gran acontecimiento** her arrival was a great event

acopio *sm* stock

acoplar *vt* ❶ [*encajar*] to attach ❷ Ferrocarril to couple

acordar *vt* • **acordar algo/hacer algo** to agree on something/to do something • **los enemigos acordaron firmar el tratado de paz** the enemies agreed to sign the peace treaty
■ **acordarse** *v pronominal* • **acordarse (de algo/de hacer algo)** to remember (something/to do something) • **siempre me acuerdo de ustedes cuando voy ahí** I always remember you when I go there • **acuérdate de llevar el traje a la tintorería** remember to take your suit to the dry cleaner's

acorde ◆ *adj* [*en consonancia*] • **acorde con** in keeping with ◌̇ *Los adjetivos ingleses son invariables.*
◆ *sm* Música chord

acordeón *sm* accordion

acordonar *vt* [*lugar*] to cordon off

acorralar *vt* literal & figurado to corner • **acorralaron al conejo para meterlo en la jaula** they cornered the rabbit to put him in the cage

acortar *vt* ❶ [*falda, pantalón* etc] to take up ❷ [*cable*] to shorten ❸ [*plazo, vacaciones*] to cut short ❹ [*extensión*] to shorten

acosar *vt* ❶ [*hostigar*] to harass ❷ [*perseguir*] to pursue relentlessly

acoso *sm* [*hostigamiento*] harassment ▸ **acoso sexual** sexual harassment

acostar *vt* [*en la cama*] to put to bed • **ya es hora de acostar a los niños** it's time to put the kids to bed
■ **acostarse** *v pronominal* ❶ [*irse a la cama*] to go to bed • **se acostaron tarde, por eso están tan cansados** they went to bed late, that's why they're so tired ❷ [*tumbarse*] to lie down ❸ *familiar* [*tener relaciones sexuales*] • **acostarse con alguien** to sleep with somebody

acostumbrado, da *adj* ❶ [*habitual*] usual ❷ [*habituado*] • **estar acostumbrado a** to be used to • **estoy acostumbrado al calor** I'm used to the heat ◌̇ *Los adjetivos ingleses son invariables.*

acostumbrar ◆ *vt* [*habituar*] • **acostumbrar a alguien a algo/a hacer algo** to get somebody used to something/to doing something • **hay que acostumbrar al niño a que se duerma temprano** you have to get the baby used to going to sleep early
◆ *vi* [*soler*] • **acostumbrar a hacer algo** to be in the habit of doing something • **acostumbro a levantarme temprano** I usually get up early
■ **acostumbrarse** *v pronominal* [*habituarse*] • **acostumbrarse a algo/a hacer algo** to get used to something/to doing something • **al cabo de los años se acostumbraron al frío** they got used to the cold after a few years

acotamiento *sm* [*arcén*] shoulder

acreedor, ra ◆ *adj* • **hacerse acreedor de algo** to earn something ᵠ *Los adjetivos ingleses son invariables.*

◆ *sm, f* creditor

acribillar *vt* [*herir*] • **acribillar (a)** to pepper o riddle (with) • **acribillar a balazos** to riddle with bullets

acrílico, ca *adj* acrylic ᵠ *Los adjetivos ingleses son invariables.*

acrobacia *sf* [*en circo*] acrobatics *pl*

acróbata *smf* acrobat

acta *sf* ❶ [*de junta, reunión*] minutes *pl* • **levantar acta** to take the minutes ❷ [*de defunción* ᴇᴛᴄ] certificate ▶ **acta notarial** affidavit

actitud *sf* [*disposición de ánimo*] attitude

activar *vt* ❶ [*generalmente*] to activate ❷ [*explosivo*] to detonate

actividad *sf* ❶ [*acción*] activity ▶ **actividades extraescolares** extracurricular activities ❷ [*trabajo*] work

activo, va *adj* ❶ [*generalmente*] ɢʀᴀᴍáᴛɪᴄᴀ active ❷ [*trabajador*] hard-working ᵠ *Los adjetivos ingleses son invariables.*

■ **activo** *sm* ꜰɪɴᴀɴᴢᴀꜱ assets *pl* ▶ **activo fijo/líquido/ financiero** fixed/liquid/financial assets • **activo y pasivo** assets and liabilities

acto *sm* ❶ [*acción*] act • **un acto terrorista** a terrorist act • **los adultos son responsables de sus actos** adults are responsible for their actions • **hacer acto de presencia** to show your face ▶ **acto de solidaridad** show of solidarity ❷ [*ceremonia*] ceremony • **fuimos al acto de inauguración del museo** we went to the museum's opening ceremony ❸ ᴛᴇᴀᴛʀᴏ act

actor, triz *sm, f* actor, *femenino* <u>actress</u>

actuación *sf* ❶ [*conducta, proceder*] conduct; behavior ❷ [*interpretación*] performance

actual *adj* ❶ [*existente*] current • **mi vecina actual no es la misma del año pasado** my current neighbor isn't the same one from last year ❷ [*de moda*] modern • **no les gusta mucho la música actual** they don't like modern music ❸ [*de actualidad*] topical • **ese es un tema muy actual** that's a very topical issue ᵠ *Los adjetivos ingleses son invariables.*

actual ≠ actual
- La palabra inglesa **actual** es un falso amigo que significa *real*.
- *Actual* se traduce al inglés por **current** o **modern**.

actualidad *sf* ❶ [*momento presente*] current situation • **de actualidad a)** [*moderno*] in fashion **b)** [*de interés actual*] topical • **en la actualidad** currently • **en la actualidad, mucha gente usa computadoras** currently, a lot of people use computers ❷ [*noticia*] news ᵠ *incontable* • **ser actualidad** to be making the news

actualizar *vt* ❶ [*información*] to update ❷ [*tecnología, industria*] to modernize ❸ ɪɴꜰᴏʀᴍáᴛɪᴄᴀ to upgrade

actualmente *adv* [*hoy día*] nowadays • **actualmente, mucha gente tiene celular** nowadays a lot of people have cell phones

actualmente ≠ actually
- La palabra inglesa **actually** es un falso amigo que significa *en realidad*.
- *Actualmente* se traduce al inglés por **nowadays**.

actuar *vi* [*generalmente*] to act • **actuaron rápidamente y evitaron un accidente** they acted quickly and avoided an accident • **actuar de** to act as • **las puertas actúan de separadores móviles** the doors act as movable partitions

acuarela *sf* watercolor

acuario *sm* ❶ [*pequeño*] fish tank • **me regalaron un acuario para mi cumpleaños** I was given a fish tank for my birthday ❷ [*edificio*] aquarium • **el domingo fuimos a visitar el acuario** we went to the aquarium on Sunday

■ **acuario** ◆ *sm* [*zodiaco*] Aquarius

◆ *smf* [*persona*] Aquarius

acuático, ca *adj* aquatic • **en este lago hay muchas plantas acuáticas** there are many aquatic plants in the lake ᵠ *Los adjetivos ingleses son invariables.*

acuatizar *vi* to land on water

acudir *vi* ❶ [*ir*] to go ❷ [*venir*] to come ❸ [*recurrir*] • **acudir a** to go o turn to ❹ [*presentarse*] • **acudir (a) a)** [*escuela, iglesia*] to attend **b)** [*cita, examen*] to turn up (for) **c)** *figurado* [*memoria, mente*] to come (to) • **no se disculpó por no haber acudido a la reunión** he didn't apologize for not attending the meeting • **más de 20 millones de electores acudieron a las urnas** over 20 million voters turned up to vote

acueducto *sm* aqueduct

acuerdo *sm* agreement • **los presidentes firmaron un acuerdo** the presidents signed an agreement • **de acuerdo** all right, O.K. • **de acuerdo con** [*conforme a*] in accordance with • **estar de acuerdo (con alguien/en hacer algo)** to agree (with somebody/to do something)

acumular *vt* to accumulate

acunar *vt* to rock

acuñar *vt* ❶ [*moneda*] to mint ❷ [*palabra*] to coin

acupuntura *sf* acupuncture

acusación *sf* [*inculpación*] charge

acusado, da ◆ *adj* [*marcado*] marked ᵠ *Los adjetivos ingleses son invariables.*

◆ *sm, f* [*procesado*] accused; defendant • **la acusada se declaró culpable** the defendant pled guilty

acusar *vt* ❶ [*culpar*] to accuse • **lo acusaron sin razón** they accused him for no reason ❷ ᴅᴇʀᴇᴄʜᴏ to charge • **acusar a alguien de algo a)** [*generalmente*] to accuse

A

somebody of something **b)** Derecho to charge somebody with something ❸ [*mostrar*] to show

acusativo *sm* accusative

acuse ■ **acuse de recibo** *sm* acknowledgement of receipt

acústico, ca *adj* acoustic:💡*Los adjetivos ingleses son invariables.*

■ **acústica** *sf* [*de local*] acoustics *pl*

adaptación *sf* ❶ [*aclimatación*] • **adaptación (a)** adjustment (to) ❷ [*modificación*] adaptation

adaptar *vt* ❶ [*acomodar, ajustar*] to adjust ❷ [*modificar*] to adapt

■ **adaptarse** *v pronominal* • **adaptarse (a)** to adjust (to) • **después de varios años, se adaptaron al frío** they adapted to the cold after a few years

adecuado, da *adj* appropriate • **ese vestido no es adecuado para el funeral** that dress isn't appropriate for the funeral:💡*Los adjetivos ingleses son invariables.*

adecuar *vt* to adapt

adefesio *sm familiar* [*persona fea*] fright

a. de JC., a. C. (*abreviatura escrita de* antes de Jesucristo) BC

adelantamiento *sm* Automóviles overtaking

adelantar ◆ *vt* ❶ [*dejar atrás*] to overtake • **adelantó un camión** he overtook a bus ❷ [*ficha*] to move forward ❸ [*pie, reloj*] to put forward • **tuvimos que adelantar los relojes una hora** we had to put the clocks forward by an hour ❹ [*en el tiempo - trabajo, viaje*] to bring forward • **adelantaron la boda un mes** they brought the wedding forward by a month; [*- dinero*] to pay in advance • **tuvimos que adelantar 1.000 pesos** we had to pay 1,000 pesos in advance

◆ *vi* ❶ [*progresar*] to make progress • **hace dos horas que estás leyendo, ¿cuánto adelantaste?** you've been reading for two hours, how much progress have you made? ❷ [*reloj*] to gain time • **este reloj adelanta** this clock gains time

■ **adelantarse** *v pronominal* ❶ [*en el tiempo*] to be early ❷ [*frío, verano*] to arrive early • **este año el invierno se adelantó** winter arrived early this year ❸ [*reloj*] to gain • **adelantarse a alguien** to beat somebody to it ❹ [*en el espacio*] to go on ahead • **me adelanté para reservar lugar** I went ahead to save a place

adelante ◆ *adv* forward; ahead • **(de ahora) en adelante** from now on, in future • **de ahora en adelante no quiero más discusiones** from now on I don't want any more arguments • **adelante de** in front of • **iba adelante de mí** he was in front of me • **más adelante a)** [*en el tiempo*] later (on) **b)** [*en el espacio*] further on

◆ *exclamación* • **¡adelante! a)** [*¡siga!*] go ahead! **b)** [*¡pase!*] come in!

adelanto *sm* advance

adelgazar ◆ *vi* to lose weight

◆ *vt* to lose • **adelgazó cinco kilos en un mes** she lost five kilos in a month

además *adv* ❶ [*con énfasis*] besides • **además, llegaste tarde** besides, you were late ❷ [*también*] also • **además de** as well as, in addition to • **además de**

traductora, es intérprete as well as being a translator, she's an interpreter • **la casa es grande y además tiene un jardín precioso** in addition to being very big, the house has a beautiful yard

adentrarse *v pronominal* • **adentrarse en a)** [*jungla* etc] to enter the heart of **b)** [*tema* etc] to study in depth

adentro *adv* inside • **fíjate adentro de la caja** look inside the box • **tierra adentro** inland • **mar adentro** out to sea

adepto, ta *sm, f* • **adepto (a)** follower (of)

aderezo *sm* [*aliño - de ensalada*] dressing; [*- de comida*] seasoning

adeudar *vt* ❶ [*deber*] to owe ❷ Comercio to debit

adherir *vt* to stick • **asegúrate de adherir bien la estampilla** make sure to stick the stamp on well

adhesión *sf* [*apoyo*] support

adhesivo, va *adj* adhesive:💡*Los adjetivos ingleses son invariables.*

■ **adhesivo** *sm* [*pegatina*] sticker

adicción *sf* • **adicción (a)** addiction (to)

adición *sf* addition

adicional *adj* additional:💡*Los adjetivos ingleses son invariables.*

adicto, ta ◆ *adj* • **adicto (a)** addicted (to):💡*Los adjetivos ingleses son invariables.*

◆ *sm, f* • **adicto (a)** addict (of)

adiestrar *vt* to train • **adiestrar a alguien en algo/ para hacer algo** to train somebody in something/to do something

adinerado, da *adj* wealthy:💡*Los adjetivos ingleses son invariables.*

adiós ◆ *sm* goodbye

◆ *exclamación* ❶ • **¡adiós!** goodbye! ❷ [*al cruzarse con alguien*] hello!

adivinanza *sf* riddle • **jugar a las adivinanzas** to play at guessing riddles

adivinar *vt* ❶ [*predecir*] to foretell ❷ [*el futuro*] to tell ❸ [*acertar*] to guess (correctly) • **¡adivina lo que tengo para ti!** guess what I have for you!

adivino, na *sm, f* fortune-teller

adjudicar *vt* [*asignar*] to award

adjuntar *vt* to enclose

adjunto, ta ◆ *adj* [*incluido*] enclosed • '**adjunto le remito…**' please find enclosed…:💡*Los adjetivos ingleses son invariables.*

◆ *sm, f* [*auxiliar*] assistant

administración *sf* ❶ [*suministro*] supply ❷ [*de medicamento, justicia*] administering ❸ [*gestión*] administration ❹ [*gerentes*] management ❺ [*oficina*] manager's office

■ **Administración** *sf* [*gobierno*] administration ▶ **Administración local** local government ▶ **Administración pública** civil service

administrador, ra *sm, f* [*de empresa*] manager ▶ **administrador de Web** Webmaster ❷ [*de bienes ajenos*] administrator

administrar *vt* ❶ [*gestionar - empresa, rancho* ETC] to manage ; to run ; [- *casa*] to run ❷ [*país*] to run the affairs of ❸ [*suministrar*] to administer

administrativo, va *adj* administrative • **se ocupa de las tareas administrativas** he's in charge of the administrative work ·ℚ· *Los adjetivos ingleses son invariables.*

admirable *adj* admirable ·ℚ· *Los adjetivos ingleses son invariables.*

admiración *sf* ❶ [*sentimiento*] admiration • **tiene gran admiración por su hermano mayor** he has a great deal of admiration for his older brother • **causar admiración** to be admired • **sentir admiración por alguien** to admire somebody ❷ [*signo ortográfico*] exclamation mark • **signo de admiración** exclamation mark

admirar *vt* ❶ [*generalmente*] to admire ❷ [*sorprender*] to amaze

admisible *adj* acceptable ·ℚ· *Los adjetivos ingleses son invariables.*

admisión *sf* ❶ [*de persona*] admission ❷ [*de solicitudes* ETC] acceptance • **examen de admisión** entrance exam

admitir *vt* ❶ [*acoger, reconocer*] to admit • **al final admitió que le gustaba Pedro** she finally admitted that she likes Pedro • **mi madre no admite que le grite** my mother doesn't allow me to shout at her • **admitir a alguien en** to admit somebody to ❷ [*aceptar*] to accept • **nos acaban de admitir al club** we've just been accepted into the club

ADN (*abreviatura de* ácido desoxirribonucleico) *sm* DNA

adolescencia *sf* adolescence

adolescente *adj* & *smf* adolescent ·ℚ· *Los adjetivos ingleses son invariables.*

adonde *adv* where • **la ciudad adonde vamos** the city we are going to, the city where we are going • **adonde vayas, cuídate mucho** wherever you go, take care of yourself

expresión adonde fueres, haz lo que vieres when in Rome, do as the Romans do

adónde *adv* where • **¿adónde vas?** where are you going?

adopción *sf* ❶ [*de hijo, propuesta*] adoption ❷ [*de ley*] passing

adoptar *vt* ❶ [*hijo, propuesta*] to adopt • **mis amigos han decidido adoptar un bebé** my friends have decided to adopt a baby ❷ [*ley*] to pass

adoptivo, va *adj* ❶ [*hijo, país*] adopted ❷ [*padre*] adoptive ·ℚ· *Los adjetivos ingleses son invariables.*

adorable *adj* ❶ [*persona*] adorable ❷ [*ambiente, película*] wonderful ·ℚ· *Los adjetivos ingleses son invariables.*

adoración *sf* adoration • **sentir adoración por alguien** to worship somebody

adorar *vt* ❶ [*dios, ídolo*] to worship • **los mexicas adoraban a Tláloc** the Mexicas worshiped Tláloc ❷ [*persona, comida*] to adore • **Juan y María adoran a sus padres** Juan and María adore their parents

adormecer *vt* [*producir sueño*] to lull to sleep

adornar *vt* to decorate • **adornamos la casa para la fiesta** we decorated the house for the party

adorno *sm* decoration • **las calles están llenas de adornos de Navidad** the streets are full of Christmas decorations • **de adorno a)** [*árbol, figura*] decorative, ornamental **b)** [*person*] serving no useful purpose

adosar *vt* ❶ to place o lean against ❷ [*unir*] to join ❸ [*agregar*] to attach

adquirir *vt* ❶ [*comprar*] to acquire ; to purchase • **la escuela adquirió más computadoras** the school acquired more computers ❷ [*conseguir - conocimientos, hábito, cultura*] to acquire ; [- *éxito, popularidad*] to achieve • **adquirió mucha experiencia trabajando en esa oficina** she gained a lot of experience working in that office ; [- *compromiso*] to undertake

adquisición *sf* ❶ [*compra, cosa comprada*] purchase • **ser una buena/mala adquisición** to be a good/bad buy ❷ [*obtención*] acquisition ❸ [*de costumbres*] adoption

adquisitivo, va *adj* purchasing ·ℚ· *Sólo se usa delante del sustantivo.*

adrede *adv* on purpose • **no creo que lo haya hecho adrede** I don't think she did it on purpose

adrenalina *sf* adrenalin

aduana *sf* [*administración*] customs *pl* • **pasar por la aduana** to go through customs

adulterar *vt* [*alimento*] to adulterate

adulterio *sm* adultery

adúltero, ra ◆ *adj* adulterous ·ℚ· *Los adjetivos ingleses son invariables.*
◆ *sm, f* adulterer, *femenino* adulteress

adulto, ta *adj* & *sm, f* adult • **los adultos deben responsabilizarse por sus actos** adults have to take responsibility for their actions ·ℚ· *Los adjetivos ingleses son invariables.*

adverbio *sm* adverb ▶ **adverbio de cantidad/lugar/modo/tiempo** adverb of degree/place/manner/time

adversario, ria *sm, f* ❶ [*enemigo*] adversary ❷ [*en concurso*] opponent

adversidad *sf* adversity

adverso, sa *adj* ❶ [*generalmente*] adverse ❷ [*destino*] unkind ❸ [*suerte*] bad ❹ [*viento*] unfavorable ·ℚ· *Los adjetivos ingleses son invariables.*

advertencia *sf* warning • **advertencia: no entre a la obra sin casco protector** warning: hard hats must be worn on building site • **servir de advertencia** to serve as a warning • **hacer una advertencia a alguien** to warn somebody

advertir *vt* ❶ [*notar*] to notice • **no advertí la presencia del ladrón** I didn't notice the thief's presence ❷ [*prevenir, avisar*] to warn • **el maestro advirtió que no tolerará tramposos** the teacher warned that he would not put up with cheaters • **te advierto que no deberías hacerlo** I'd advise against you doing it • **te advierto que no me sorprende** mind you, it doesn't surprise me

adyacente *adj* adjacent:♀ *Los adjetivos ingleses son invariables.*

aéreo, a *adj* ❶ [*del aire*] aerial • **una fotografía aérea** an aerial photograph ❷ AERONÁUTICA air:♀ *Sólo se usa delante del sustantivo.* • **te lo enviaré por correo aéreo** I'll send it by air mail

aerodeslizador *sm* hovercraft

aerodinámico, ca *adj* ❶ FÍSICA aerodynamic ❷ [*forma, línea*] streamlined:♀ *Los adjetivos ingleses son invariables.*

aeródromo *sm* airfield

aeroespacial *adj* aerospace:♀ *Sólo se usa delante del sustantivo.*

aerolínea *sf* airline

aeromozo, za *sm, f* flight attendant

aeronaval *adj* air and sea:♀ *Sólo se usa delante del sustantivo.*

aeronave *sf* ❶ [*generalmente*] aircraft ❷ [*dirigible*] airship

aeroplano *sm* aeroplane

aeropuerto *sm* airport

aerosol *sm* aerosol • **prefiero usar el desodorante en aerosol** I prefer aerosol deodorant

afable *adj* affable:♀ *Los adjetivos ingleses son invariables.*

afamado, da *adj* famous:♀ *Los adjetivos ingleses son invariables.*

afán *sm* ❶ [*esfuerzo*] hard work:♀ *incontable* ❷ [*anhelo*] urge • **tener afán de algo** to be eager for something • **afán de conocimiento** thirst for knowledge

afanar *vt* familiar [*robar*] to pinch

afear *vt* to make ugly

afectar *vt* ❶ [*generalmente*] to affect ❷ [*afligir*] to upset; to affect badly

afectísimo, ma *adj* [*en cartas*] • **'suyo afectísimo'** yours sincerely:♀ *Los adjetivos ingleses son invariables.*

afecto *sm* affection • **el afecto es muy importante para la amistad** affection is very important in friendship • **sentir afecto por alguien, tenerle afecto a alguien** to be fond of somebody

afectuoso, sa *adj* affectionate; loving:♀ *Los adjetivos ingleses son invariables.*

afeitar *vt* [*pelo, barba*] to shave

■ **afeitarse** *v pronominal* to shave • **mi hermano se afeita todas las mañanas** my brother shaves every morning

afeminado, da *adj* effeminate:♀ *Los adjetivos ingleses son invariables.*

aferrarse *v pronominal* • **aferrarse a** *literal & figurado* to cling to

Afganistán *nombre propio* Afghanistan

afiche *sm* poster

afición *sf* ❶ [*inclinación*] fondness; liking • **tener afición a algo** to be keen on something ❷ [*en tiempo libre*] hobby • **por afición** as a hobby ❸ [*aficionados*] fans *pl*

aficionado, da ◆ *adj* ❶ [*interesado*] keen • **ser aficionado a algo** to be keen on something ❷ [*no profesional*] amateur:♀ *Los adjetivos ingleses son invariables.*
◆ *sm, f* ❶ [*interesado*] fan • **aficionado al cine** movie buff ❷ [*amateur*] amateur

afiebrarse *v pronominal* to become feverish

afilado, da *adj* ❶ [*borde, filo*] sharp ❷ [*dedos*] pointed:♀ *Los adjetivos ingleses son invariables.*

afilar *vt* to sharpen • **hay que afilar el cuchillo antes de usarlo** you should sharpen the knife before using it

afiliado, da *sm, f* • **afiliado (a)** member (of)

afiliarse *v pronominal* • **afiliarse a** to join • **quisiera afiliarme a un club de golf** I'd like to join a golf club

afín *adj* [*semejante*] similar • **Pedro es muy afín de su hermano** Pedro is very similar to his brother:♀ *Los adjetivos ingleses son invariables.*

afinar *vt* ❶ MÚSICA [*instrumento*] to tune • **los músicos afinaron los instrumentos** the musicians tuned their instruments • **afinar la voz** to sing in tune ❷ [*perfeccionar, mejorar*] to fine-tune ❸ [*pulir*] to refine

afinidad *sf* [*generalmente*] QUÍMICA affinity

afirmación *sf* statement

afirmar *vt* ❶ [*confirmar*] to confirm ❷ [*decir*] to say ❸ [*consolidar*] to reaffirm ❹ CONSTRUCCIÓN to reinforce

afirmativo, va *adj* affirmative:♀ *Los adjetivos ingleses son invariables.*

afligir *vt* ❶ [*afectar*] to afflict ❷ [*causar pena*] to distress

aflojar ◆ *vt* ❶ [*destensar*] to loosen • **no puedo aflojar este nudo** I can't loosen this knot ❷ [*cuerda*] to slacken
◆ *vi* ❶ [*disminuir*] to die down ❷ *figurado* [*ceder*] to ease off

afluencia *sf* stream; volume

afluente *sm* tributary

afónico, ca *adj* • **quedarse afónico** to lose your voice

aforo *sm* [*cabida*] seating capacity

afortunadamente *adv* fortunately

afortunado, da *adj* ❶ [*agraciado*] lucky ❷ [*oportuno*] happy:♀ *Los adjetivos ingleses son invariables.*

afrenta *sf* [*ofensa, agravio*] affront

África *nombre propio* Africa

africano, na *adj* & *sm, f* African:♀ *Los adjetivos ingleses son invariables.*

afrontar *vt* [*hacer frente a*] to face

afuera *adv* outside • **vamos para afuera** let's go outside • **por (la parte de) afuera** on the outside

■ **afueras** *sfpl* • **las afueras** the outskirts • **las industrias están en las afueras de la ciudad** the factories are on the outskirts of town

afuerita *adv* familiar right outside

afusilar *vt* familiar to shoot

agachar *vt* ❶ to lower ❷ [*la cabeza*] to bow
■ **agacharse** *v pronominal* ❶ [*acuclillarse*] to crouch
down • **me agaché para estar a la misma altura que
los niños** I crouched down to be on the same level as
the children ❷ [*inclinar la cabeza*] to stoop

agalla *sf* Zoología gill

agarradera *sf* handle ; holder

agarrar *vt* ❶ [*asir*] to grab ❷ [*pillar - ladrón, resfriado*]
to catch ; [*- tomar*] to take • **en pocas horas la policía agarró al ladrón** the police caught the thief in
just a few hours • **agarra al niño de la mano para
cruzar la calle** hold the child's hand when you cross
the street
■ **agarrarse** *v pronominal* [*sujetarse*] to hold on • **¡agá-
rrate bien!** hold on tight! • **agarrarse de** o **a algo** to
hold on to o clutch something

agarrón *sm* [*tirón*] pull ; tug

agencia *sf* ❶ [*empresa*] agency ▶ **agencia de viajes**
travel agency ❷ [*sucursal*] branch

agenda *sf* ❶ [*de notas, fechas*] diary ❷ [*de teléfonos,
direcciones*] address book ❸ [*de trabajo*] agenda

agente ◆ *sm, f* [*persona*] agent ▶ **agente de aduanas** customs officer ▶ **agente de la policía** o **de la autoridad** policeman, *femenino* policewoman ▶ **agente
secreto** secret agent ▶ **agente de tráfico** traffic cop
▶ **agente de viajes** travel agent
◆ *sm* [*causa activa*] agent

ágil *adj* [*movimiento, persona*] agile • **las gimnastas
son ágiles y flexibles** gymnasts are agile and flexible ☞ *Los adjetivos ingleses son invariables.*

agilidad *sf* agility

agilizar *vt* to speed up

agitar *vt* ❶ [*mover - botella*] to shake • **agita el envase antes de servir el jugo** shake the carton before
pouring the juice ; [*- líquido*] to stir ; [*- brazos*] to wave
❷ [*inquietar*] to perturb ; to worry ❸ [*alterar, perturbar*] to stir up

aglomeración *sf* ❶ build-up ❷ [*de gente*] crowd • **se
produjo una aglomeración** a crowd formed

aglomerar *vt* to bring together

agnóstico, ca *adj & sm, f* agnostic ☞ *Los adjetivos
ingleses son invariables.*

agobiado, da *adj* • **agobiado (de) a)** [*trabajo*]
snowed under (with) **b)** [*problemas*] weighed down
(with) ☞ *Los adjetivos ingleses son invariables.*

agobiar *vt* to overwhelm

agonía *sf* ❶ [*pena*] agony ❷ [*del moribundo*] death
throes *pl*

agonizar *vi* [*expirar*] to be dying

agosto *sm* [*mes*] August
expresión hacer su agosto to line your pockets ver
también **septiembre**

agotado, da *adj* ❶ [*cansado*] • **agotado (de)** exhausted (from) ❷ [*producto*] out of stock ; sold out
❸ [*pila, batería*] dead ☞ *Los adjetivos ingleses son
invariables.*

agotador, ra *adj* exhausting ☞ *Los adjetivos ingleses son invariables.*

agotar *vt* ❶ [*generalmente*] to exhaust ❷ [*producto*]
to sell out of ❸ [*agua*] to drain
■ **agotarse** *v pronominal* ❶ [*cansarse*] to tire yourself out • **me agoté subiendo las escaleras** I tired myself out climbing the stairs ❷ [*acabarse*] to run out
• **se agotó el azúcar** we've run out of sugar ❸ [*libro,
disco, entradas*] to be sold out • **se agotaron todas las
entradas** all the tickets are sold out ❹ [*pila, batería*]
to go flat • **se agotó la batería del celular** the cellphone's battery died

agraciado, da *adj* ❶ [*atractivo*] attractive ❷ [*afortunado*] • **agraciado con algo** lucky enough to win something ☞ *Los adjetivos ingleses son invariables.*

agraciar *vt* [*embellecer*] to make more attractive

agradable *adj* pleasant • **en primavera, la temperatura es más agradable que en invierno** the temperature is more pleasant in the spring than in the
winter ☞ *Los adjetivos ingleses son invariables.*

agradar *vt* to please

agradecer *vt* [*sujeto: persona*] • **agradecer algo a alguien a)** [*dar las gracias*] to thank somebody for something **b)** [*estar agradecido*] to be grateful to somebody
for something • **los novios agradecieron los regalos**
the newlyweds thanked their guests for the presents • **agradecemos la ayuda que nos han dado** we
are grateful for the help you've given us

agradecido, da *adj* ❶ [*ser*] grateful ❷ [*estar*] appreciative ☞ *Los adjetivos ingleses son invariables.*

agradecimiento *sm* gratitude

agrario, ria *adj* ❶ [*reforma*] agrarian ❷ [*producto,
política*] agricultural ☞ *Los adjetivos ingleses son
invariables.*

agravar *vt* ❶ [*situación*] to aggravate ❷ [*impuestos*
ETC] to increase (the burden of)

agredir *vt* to attack • **agredió al árbitro** he attacked
the referee

agregar *vt* • **agregar (algo a algo)** to add (something
to something) • **agrega la leche después de la harina**
add the milk after the flour

agresión *sf* [*ataque*] attack

agresividad *sf* aggression

agresivo, va *adj* literal & figurado aggressive • **es
muy agresiva** she's very aggressive ☞ *Los adjetivos
ingleses son invariables.*

agresor, ra *sm, f* attacker

agriar *vt* [*vino, leche*] to (turn) sour

agrícola *adj* ❶ agricultural ❷ [*pueblo*] farming
☞ *Sólo se usa delante del sustantivo.*

agricultor, ra *sm, f* farmer • **el agricultor trabaja
en el campo** the farmer works in the fields

agricultura *sf* agriculture ▶ **agricultura ecológica**
organic farming

agridulce *adj* ❶ bittersweet ❷ Cocina sweet and
sour ☞ *Los adjetivos ingleses son invariables.*

agrio, agria *adj* ❶ [*ácido*] sour • **la leche está agria**
the milk turned sour ❷ figurado [*discusión*] bitter ☞ *Los
adjetivos ingleses son invariables.*

agronomía *sf* agronomy

A

agropecuario, ria *adj* farming and livestock ·ໍ֯·: *Sólo se usa delante del sustantivo.*

agrupar *vt* to group (together)

agua *sf* water ▶ **agua bendita** holy water ▶ **agua corriente** running water ▶ **agua de colonia** eau de cologne ▶ **agua dulce** fresh water ▶ **agua mineral** mineral water ▶ **agua oxigenada** hydrogen peroxide ▶ **agua potable** drinking water ▶ **agua salada** salt water ▶ **aguas residuales** sewage ·ໍ֯·: *incontable*

expresión **venir como agua de mayo** to be a godsend

aguacate *sm* [*fruto*] avocado

aguacero *sm* shower

aguado, da *adj* ❶ [*con demasiada agua*] watery ❷ [*diluido a propósito*] watered-down ·ໍ֯·: *Los adjetivos ingleses son invariables.*

aguafiestas *smf invariable* spoilsport

aguafuerte *sm* etching

aguamiel *sf* ❶ [*bebida*] *para explicar lo que es puedes decir:* it's water mixed with honey or cane syrup ❷ [*jugo*] maguey juice

aguantador, ra *adj familiar* patient

aguantar *vt* ❶ [*sostener*] to hold ❷ [*peso*] to take · **la bolsa no aguantó el peso de las naranjas** the bag couldn't take the weight of the oranges ❸ [*tolerar, soportar*] to stand · **no aguanto más el ruido de esa sirena** I can't stand the noise of that siren · **no sé cómo la aguantas** I don't know how you put up with her ❹ [*contener - risa*] to contain; [*- respiración*] to hold · **yo no puedo aguantar la respiración más que 30 segundos** I can only hold my breath for 30 seconds

aguardar *vt* to wait for · **aguardaremos cinco minutos el próximo tren** we'll wait five minutes for the next train

aguardiente *sm* spirit; liquor

aguarrás *sm* turpentine

agudo, da *adj* ❶ [*generalmente*] sharp · **sentí un dolor agudo en una muela** I felt a sharp pain in my tooth ❷ [*crisis, problema, enfermedad*] serious · **estamos atravesando una crisis aguda** we're going through a serious crisis ❸ *figurado* [*ingenioso*] witty ❹ MÚSICA [*nota, voz*] high ·ໍ֯·: *Los adjetivos ingleses son invariables.*

aguijón *sm* ❶ [*de insecto*] sting ❷ *figurado* [*estímulo*] spur

águila *sf* ❶ [*ave*] eagle ❷ *figurado* [*vivo, listo*] sharp person

expresión **¿águila o sol?** heads or tails?

aguinaldo *sm* Christmas bonus

aguja *sf* ❶ [*de coser, jeringa*] needle ❷ [*de tejer*] knitting needle ❸ [*de reloj*] hand ❹ [*de brújula*] pointer ❺ [*de iglesia*] spire ❻ FERROCARRIL point ❼ [*de tocadiscos*] stylus; needle

agujerear *vt* to make a hole o holes in

agujero *sm* hole ▶ **agujero negro** ASTRONOMÍA black hole

agujetas *sfpl* shoelaces

ah *exclamación* · **¡ah! a)** [*admiración*] ooh! **b)** [*sorpresa*] oh! **c)** [*pena*] ah!

ahí *adv* there · **vino por ahí** he came that way · **¿quién está ahí?** who's there? · **yo ahí no voy** I'm not going there · **la solución está ahí** that's where the solution lies · **ahí mismo** right there · **¡ahí tienes!** here you are!; there you go! · **ahí fue cuando me acordé** that was when I remembered · **de ahí en adelante** from then on · **de ahí que** [*por eso*] and consequently; so · **está por ahí a)** [*en lugar indefinido*] he/she is around (somewhere) **b)** [*en la calle*] he/she is out

expresión **por ahí, por ahí** *figurado* something like that ▶ **por ahí va la cosa** you're not too far wrong

ahijado, da *sm, f* [*de padrinos*] godson, *femenino* goddaughter

ahogar *vt* ❶ [*en el agua*] to drown ❷ [*asfixiar*] to suffocate ❸ [*estrangular*] to strangle ❹ [*extinguir*] to put out ❺ *figurado* [*controlar levantamiento*] to quell; [*pena*] to hold back ❻ [*motor*] to flood

■ **ahogarse** *v pronominal* ❶ [*en el agua*] to drown · **se ahogó en el mar** he drowned in the ocean ❷ [*asfixiarse*] to suffocate · **me ahogo con tanto humo** I'm suffocating with all this smoke

ahora ✦ *adv* ❶ [*en el presente*] now · **ahora no está lloviendo** it's not raining now · **hasta ahora todo va bien** so far, so good · **ahora mismo** right now · **ahora mismo no está** she's not here right now · **de ahora en adelante** from now on · **de ahora en adelante él es el jefe** from now on he is the boss · **por ahora** for the time being ❷ [*pronto*] in a second o moment · **ahora voy** I'll be there in a second

✦ *conjunción* [*pero*] but; however · **ahora que** but; though · **ahora bien** but; however

ahorcar *vt* to hang

■ **ahorcarse** *v pronominal* to hang yourself · **se ahorcó con un cinturón** he hanged himself with his belt

ahorita, ahoritita *adv familiar* right now · **ahorita no está lloviendo** it's not raining now · **ahorita lo hago** I'll do it in a minute · **acaba de llamar ahorita** he called just a moment ago

ahorrador, ra ✦ *adj* thrifty; careful with money ·ໍ֯·: *Los adjetivos ingleses son invariables.*

✦ *sm, f* thrifty person

ahorrar *vt* to save · **ahorra tiempo y dinero** it saves you time and money

ahorro *sm* ❶ [*generalmente*] saving ❷ ·ໍ֯·: *generalmente pl* [*cantidad ahorrada*] savings *pl*

ahumado, da *adj* smoked ·ໍ֯·: *Los adjetivos ingleses son invariables.*

ahuyentar *vt* ❶ [*espantar, asustar*] to scare away ❷ *figurado* [*apartar*] to drive away

airado, da *adj* angry ·ໍ֯·: *Los adjetivos ingleses son invariables.*

aire *sm* ❶ [*fluido*] air · **el aire que respiramos** the air we breathe ▶ **aire acondicionado** air conditioning ❷ [*viento*] wind · **soplaba un aire frío** a cold wind was blowing · **hoy hace (mucho) aire** it's (very) windy today ❸ [*corriente*] draft ❹ *figurado* [*aspecto*] air; appearance

expresiones **al aire** exposed ▶ **al aire libre** outdoors

• **pasan mucho tiempo al aire libre** they spend a lot of time outdoors • **una piscina al aire libre** an outdoor swimming pool ▶ **estar en el aire** to be in the air ▶ **saltar o volar por los aires** to be blown sky high; to explode ▶ **tomar el aire** to go for a breath of fresh air

airear *vt figurado* [*contar*] to air (publicly)

airoso, sa *adj* ❶ [*garboso*] graceful ❷ [*triunfante*] • **salir airoso de algo** to come out of something with flying colors ♀ *Los adjetivos ingleses son invariables.*

aislado, da *adj* ❶ [*generalmente*] isolated ❷ TecNOLOGÍA insulated ♀ *Los adjetivos ingleses son invariables.*

aislar *vt* ❶ [*generalmente*] to isolate • **tuvieron que aislar al enfermo** they had to isolate the patient ❷ TecNOLOGÍA to insulate • **hay que aislar el techo** we need to insulate the roof

ajá *exclamación* ❶ [*sorpresa*] aha! ❷ *familiar* [*aprobación*] great!

ajedrez *sm invariable* ❶ [*juego*] chess • **jugar al ajedrez** to play chess ❷ [*piezas*] chess set • **el ajedrez está guardado en el cajón** the chess set is in the drawer

ajeno, na *adj* ❶ [*de otro*] of others • **las cosas ajenas** other people's things • **jugar en campo ajeno** to play away from home ❷ [*extraño*] • **ajeno a** having nothing to do with • **ajeno a nuestra voluntad** beyond our control ♀ *Los adjetivos ingleses son invariables.*

ajetreo *sm* ❶ [*tarea*] running around; hard work ❷ [*animación*] (hustle and) bustle

ajo *sm* garlic

expresión andar **o** estar en el ajo *figurado* to be in on it

ajustado, da *adj* [*ceñido - ropa*] tight-fitting • **unos pantalones ajustados** a pair of tight-fitting pants • **estos pantalones me quedan muy ajustados** these pants are too tight on me; [- *tuerca, pieza*] tight; [- *resultado, final*] close ♀ *Los adjetivos ingleses son invariables.*

ajustar *vt* ❶ [*arreglar*] to adjust • **el mecánico ajustó el motor** the mechanic adjusted the engine ❷ [*apretar*] to tighten • **hay que ajustar estos tornillos** I have to tighten these screws ❸ [*encajar - piezas de motor*] to fit; [- *puerta, ventana*] to push to ❹ [*pactar - matrimonio*] to arrange; [- *pleito*] to settle; [- *paz*] to negotiate; [- *precio*] to fix; to agree

ajuste *sm* ❶ [*de pieza*] fitting ❷ [*de mecanismo*] adjustment ❸ [*de salario*] agreement

al *preposición* → **a**

ala *sf* ❶ Zoología & Política wing • **las alas del cóndor** the wings of the condor • **el ala izquierda del avión** the plane's left wing ▶ **ala delta** hang glider • **hacer ala delta** to hang glide ❷ [*parte lateral - de tejado*] eaves *pl*; [- *de sombrero*] brim • **un sombrero de ala ancha** a wide-brimmed hat ❸ Deporte winger; wing

alabanza *sf* praise

alacrán *sm* [*animal*] scorpion

alambre *sm* wire ▶ **alambre de púas** barbed wire

alameda *sf* ❶ [*sitio con álamos*] poplar grove ❷ [*paseo*] tree-lined avenue

álamo *sm* poplar

alarde *sm* • **alarde (de)** show o display (of) • **hacer alarde de algo** to brag about something

alardear *vi* • **alardear de** to brag about • **alardea de que sus padres son inmensamente ricos** he brags about his parents being filthy rich

alargar *vt* ❶ [*ropa*] to lengthen • **quiero alargar estos pantalones** I want to lengthen these pants ❷ [*viaje, visita, plazo*] to extend • **van a alargar las vacaciones** they're going to extend their vacation

■ **alargarse** *v pronominal* [*hacerse más largo - reunión*] to be prolonged; [- *días*] to get longer • **en esta época los días se van alargando** the days get longer at this time of year

alarido *sm* shriek; howl

alarma *sf* [*generalmente*] alarm • **empezó a sonar la alarma** the alarm went off • **dar la alarma** to raise the alarm ▶ **alarma antirrobo** antitheft alarm ▶ **alarma contra incendios** fire alarm ▶ **alarma de coche** car alarm

alarmante *adj* alarming ♀ *Los adjetivos ingleses son invariables.*

alarmar *vt* ❶ [*avisar*] to alert ❷ *figurado* [*asustar*] to alarm • **no queremos alarmar a nadie** we don't want to alarm anyone

■ **alarmarse** *v pronominal* [*inquietarse*] to be alarmed • **no hay por qué alarmarse** there's no need to be alarmed

alba *sf* [*amanecer*] dawn • **al alba** at dawn

albahaca *sf* basil

Albania *nombre propio* Albania

albañil *sm* bricklayer

alberca *sf* [*piscina*] swimming pool

albergue *sm* ❶ accommodation ♀ *incontable*; lodgings *pl* ❷ [*de montaña*] shelter; refuge ▶ **albergue de juventud o juvenil** youth hostel

albóndiga *sf* meatball

alborotar ◆ *vi* to be noisy o rowdy
◆ *vt* [*amotinar*] to stir up; to rouse

alboroto *sm* ❶ [*ruido*] din ❷ [*jaleo*] fuss; to-do • **armar un alboroto** to cause a commotion

álbum *sm* album

ALCA (*abreviatura de* Área de Libre Comercio de América) *sf* LAFTA

alcachofa *sf* Botánica artichoke

alcalde, esa *sm, f* mayor

alcaldía *sf* [*oficina*] city o town hall

alcance *sm* ❶ [*de arma, misil, emisora*] range • **de corto/largo alcance** short-/long-range • **un telescopio de largo alcance** a long-range telescope ❷ [*de persona*] reach • **no lo dejes al alcance de los niños** don't leave it within the children's reach • **a mi/a tu etc alcance** within my/your etc reach • **al alcance de la vista** within sight • **fuera del alcance de** beyond the reach of ❸ [*de reformas etc*] scope; extent

alcanfor *sm* camphor

alcantarilla *sf* ❶ sewer ❷ [*boca*] drain

alcantarillado *sm* sewers *pl*

alcanzar ♦ *vt* ❶ [*llegar a*] to reach • **no alcanzo el estante de arriba** I can't reach the top shelf ❷ [*igualarse con*] to catch up with • **si te apuras, lo alcanzas** if you hurry you can catch up with him ❸ [*entregar*] to pass • **me alcanzó la sal** he passed me the salt ❹ [*sujeto: bala* ETC] to hit ❺ [*autobús, tren*] to manage to catch

♦ *vi* ❶ [*ser suficiente*] • **alcanzar para algo/hacer algo** to be enough for something/to do something ❷ [*poder*] • **alcanzar a hacer algo** to be able to do something

alcaparra *sf* caper

alcohol *sm* alcohol • **una bebida sin alcohol** a nonalcoholic drink

alcohólico, ca *adj & sm, f* alcoholic ۞ **Los adjetivos ingleses son invariables.**

alcoholímetro *sm* [*para la sangre*] breathalyzer

alcoholismo *sm* alcoholism

alcornoque *sm* ❶ [*árbol*] cork oak ❷ *figurado* [*persona*] idiot; fool

aldea *sf* small village

aldeano, na *sm, f* villager

aleatorio, ria *adj* ❶ [*número*] random ❷ [*suceso*] chance ۞ **Sólo se usa delante del sustantivo.**

alegación *sf* ❶ allegation ❷ argument

alegar *vt* [*motivos, pruebas*] to put forward • **alegar que** to claim (that)

alegoría *sf* allegory

alegórico, ca *adj* allegorical ۞ **Los adjetivos ingleses son invariables.**

alegrar *vt* ❶ [*persona*] to cheer up • **sus nietos siempre lo alegran** his grandchildren always cheer him up • **me alegró mucho recibir tu carta** your letter really cheered me up • **me alegra que me lo preguntes** I'm glad you asked me that • **me alegra que hayas podido venir** I'm so glad you could come ❷ [*fiesta*] to liven up

■ **alegrarse** *v pronominal* [*sentir alegría*] • **alegrarse (de algo/por alguien)** to be pleased (about something/for somebody) • **¡cuánto me alegro!** I'm so pleased! • **anda, ¡alégrate!** come on, cheer up! • **me alegro muchísimo por ti** I'm very happy for you

alegre *adj* ❶ [*contento*] happy; cheerful • **¡qué alegre estás hoy!** you're very cheerful today ❷ [*que da alegría*] bright • **usa ropa de colores alegres** he wears bright clothes ❸ *familiar* [*borracho*] tipsy ۞ **Los adjetivos ingleses son invariables.**

alegría *sf* ❶ [*gozo*] happiness; joy • **los niños brincaban de alegría** the children jumped for joy • **¡qué alegría!** how wonderful! • **sentí mucha alegría al verlo** I was so happy to see him ❷ [*motivo de gozo*] joy

---

expresar su alegría

• **I'm glad we saw each other.** Me alegro de que nos hayamos visto.
• **I'm really looking forward to my vacation.** Me alegro tan sólo con pensar en las vacaciones.

• **I'm glad you're feeling better.** Me alegra que estés mejor.
• **It's really nice to see you!** ¡Es un placer verte!
• **What a nice surprise!** ¡Qué agradable sorpresa!

alejar *vt* ❶ [*poner más lejos*] to move away ❷ *figurado* [*ahuyentar*] to drive out

■ **alejarse** *v pronominal* • **alejarse (de)** [*ponerse más lejos*] to go o move away (from) • **aléjense de la orilla** move away from the edge • **no se alejen demasiado** don't go too far

aleluya *exclamación* • **¡aleluya!** Hallelujah!

alemán, ana *adj & sm, f* German • **los alemanes** the Germans ۞ **Los adjetivos ingleses son invariables.**

■ **alemán** *sm* [*lengua*] German

Alemania *nombre propio* Germany

alergia *sf* literal & figurado allergy • **tener alergia a algo** to be allergic to something • **tengo alergia al polen** I'm allergic to pollen ▶ **alergia primaveral** hay fever

alérgico, ca *adj* literal & figurado allergic (to) • **alérgico (a)** allergic (to) • **soy alérgico a los gatos** I'm allergic to cats ۞ **Los adjetivos ingleses son invariables.**

alero *sm* ❶ [*del tejado*] eaves *pl* ❷ DEPORTE winger; wing

alerta ♦ *adj invariable & adv* alert ۞ **Los adjetivos ingleses son invariables.**

♦ *sf* alert

expresión **dar la alerta** to raise the alarm • **alguien dio la alerta** somebody raised the alarm

alertar *vt* to alert

aleta *sf* ❶ [*de pez*] fin ▶ **aleta dorsal** dorsal fin ❷ [*de buzo, foca*] flipper ❸ [*de coche*] fender

alevín *sm* ❶ [*cría de pez*] fry; young fish ❷ *figurado* [*persona*] beginner

alfabetizar *vt* ❶ [*personas*] to teach to read and write ❷ [*ordenar*] to put into alphabetical order

alfabeto *sm* alphabet

alfalfa *sf* alfalfa

alfarería *sf* [*técnica*] pottery

alfil *sm* bishop

alfiler *sm* ❶ [*aguja*] pin ❷ [*joya*] brooch; pin

alfombra *sf* ❶ [*grande*] carpet • **una alfombra de pared a pared** wall-to-wall carpeting ❷ [*pequeña*] rug • **una alfombra persa** a Persian rug

alforja *sf* ۞ **generalmente pl** [*de caballo*] saddlebag

alga *sf* ❶ [*de mar*] seaweed ۞ **incontable** • **algunos peces se alimentan de algas** some fish eat seaweed ❷ [*microscópica*] algae *pl*

álgebra *sf* algebra

algo ♦ *pronombre* ❶ [*alguna cosa*] something • **compré algo para ti** I bought something for you • **¿quieres tomar algo?** do you want something to drink? • **o algo así** • **su apellido es Laren o algo así** her last name is Laren or something like that • **si algo sale**

mal, es por su culpa if anything goes wrong it's her fault • **algo es algo** something is better than nothing • **por algo lo habrá dicho** he must have said it for a reason ❷ [*en interrogativas*] anything • **¿te pasa algo?** is anything the matter? • **¿le dijiste algo a la maestra?** did you say anything to the teacher? ❸ [*cantidad pequeña*] a bit ; a little • **algo de** a little • **hablo algo de inglés** I speak a little English ❹ *figurado* [*cosa importante*] something • **se cree que es algo** he thinks he's something (special)

♦ *adv* [*un poco*] rather ; somewhat

♦ *sm* • **tiene un algo** there's something attractive about him

algodón *sm* cotton • **unos calcetines de algodón** cotton socks • **se limpió la herida con un algodón** she cleaned her wound with a cotton ball

algoritmo *sm* INFORMÁTICA algorithm

alguien *pronombre* ❶ [*alguna persona*] someone ; somebody • **alguien preguntó por ti** somebody was asking for you • **si alguien pregunta, dile que no sabes** if anybody asks tell them you don't know ❷ [*en interrogativas*] anyone ; anybody • **¿hay alguien ahí?** is anyone there? • **¿ha llamado alguien?** did anybody call? • **¿puede alguien cerrar la puerta?** can somebody close the door? ❸ *figurado* [*persona de importancia*] somebody • **se cree alguien** she thinks she's somebody (special)

---

alguno, na

♦ *adj*

❶ [*indeterminado*]

• **algún día** one day

• **vinieron algunas amigas** some friends came over

• **¿haces algún deporte?** do you do any sports?

• **si tienen alguna pregunta, hacerla al final de la clase** if you have any questions please ask them at the end of class

• **¿has estado alguna vez en México?** have you ever been to Mexico?

• **algún tiempo después** some time later

• **algunas veces** sometimes

• **en alguna parte** somewhere

• **en algún sitio** somewhere

• **en algunos casos** in some cases

• **alguno que otro** some

• **¿alguna cosa más?** anything else?

❷ [*después de un sustantivo, con sentido negativo*] no

• **no tengo duda alguna** I have no doubt at all

• **no hay mejora alguna** there's no improvement at all

⚲ *Los adjetivos ingleses son invariables.*

♦ *pronombre*

• **¿te gustó alguno?** did you like any of them?

• **algunos de sus amigos no vinieron** some of his friends didn't come

• **algunos de ellos se fueron a esquiar** a few of them went skiing

• **compra alguno barato** buy a cheap one

• **alguna de ellas lo sabe** one of them should know

• **algunas tienen techo de madera** some of them have wooden roofs

alhaja *sf* [*joya*] jewel • **¿por qué no le regalas una alhaja?** why don't you get her a piece of jewelry?

alhajera *sf* jewelry box

aliado, da *adj* allied ⚲ *Los adjetivos ingleses son invariables.*

alianza *sf* ❶ [*pacto, parentesco*] alliance ❷ [*anillo*] wedding ring

aliar *vt* [*naciones*] to ally

■ **aliarse** *v pronominal* to form an alliance • **se aliaron con los aztecas** they formed an alliance with the Aztecs

alias ♦ *adv* alias

♦ *sm invariable* ❶ alias ❷ [*entre amigos*] nickname

alicates *smpl* pliers

aliento *sm* [*respiración*] breath • **tiene mal aliento** he has bad breath • **llegué arriba sin aliento** I was out of breath when I got upstairs • **cobrar aliento** to catch your breath • **dar aliento a alguien** to encourage somebody • **lo que nos dijo nos dio aliento para seguir** what he said encouraged us to keep going

alimentación *sf* ❶ [*acción*] feeding • **yo me hago cargo de la alimentación de mi perro** I'm in charge of feeding my dog ❷ [*comida*] food • **el sector de la alimentación** the food industry ❸ [*régimen alimenticio*] diet • **es importante una alimentación equilibrada** a balanced diet is important

alimentar *vt* ❶ [*generalmente*] to feed • **tienen problemas para alimentar a su familia** they are having problems feeding their family • **come cosas que no alimentan** he eats things that aren't nutritious • **deben alimentarse bien** you should try to eat well ❷ [*motor, coche*] to fuel

■ **alimentarse** *v pronominal* [*comer*] • **alimentarse de** to live on • **se alimentan de hierbas** they live on plants

alimenticio, cia *adj* nourishing ▶ **productos alimenticios** foodstuffs ▶ **valor alimenticio** food value ⚲ *Los adjetivos ingleses son invariables.*

alimento *sm* ❶ [*generalmente*] food • **alimentos ricos en proteínas** foods high in protein ▶ **alimento chatarra** junk food ▶ **alimentos congelados** frozen foods ▶ **alimentos transgénicos** genetically engineered foods ❷ [*valor nutritivo*] nourishment

alineación *sf* ❶ [*en el espacio*] alignment ❷ DEPORTE line-up

alinear *vt* ❶ [*en el espacio*] to line up ❷ DEPORTE to select

aliñar *vt* ❶ [*ensalada*] to dress ❷ [*carne*] to season

aliño *sm* ❶ [*para ensalada*] dressing ❷ [*para carne*] seasoning

alisar *vt* to smooth (down)

alistar *vt* to get ready

■ **alistarse** *v pronominal* [*prepararse*] to get ready • **se alistaron para salir** they got ready to go out

aliviar *vt* ❶ [*atenuar*] to soothe • **tómate ésto para aliviar el dolor** take this to soothe the pain • **esto te aliviará** this will make you feel better • **esa pastilla me alivió el dolor de cabeza** that pill got rid of my headache ❷ [*aligerar - persona*] to relieve; [- *carga*] to lighten

■ **aliviarse** *v pronominal* ❶ [*mejorar*] to give birth • **no me he podido aliviar de este resfrío** I haven't been able to get over this cold ❷ [*dar a luz*] to give birth • **se alivió la semana pasada** she gave birth last week

alivio *sm* relief • **¡qué alivio!** what a relief!

expresar alivio

• **Fortunately, we'll make it in time** Menos mal, llegaremos a tiempo
• **Phew, the vase didn't break!** ¡Uf, el jarrón no se rompió!
• **There you are at last!** ¡Por fin estás aquí!
• **I'm so relieved that...** Me alivia mucho que....

allá *adv* ❶ [*espacio*] over there • **allá están los demás** the others are over there • **ya van para allá** they're on their way over • **allá abajo/arriba** down/up there • **allá fuera** out there • **allá lejos** way over there • **más allá** further on • **más allá de** beyond • **¡allá voy!** I'm coming! ❷ [*tiempo*] • **allá por los años cincuenta** back in the 50s • **allá para el mes de agosto** around August some time

expresión **allá él/ella** ETC that's his/her ETC problem • **allá tú si no quieres estudiar** it's your problem if you don't want to study

allanar *vt* ❶ [*terreno*] to flatten ❷ [*irrumpir en*] to break into

allegado, da *sm, f* ❶ [*familiar*] relative ❷ [*amigo*] close friend

allí *adv* there • **estuvieron allí toda la mañana** they were there all morning • **allí abajo/arriba** down/up there • **allí mismo** right there • **está por allí** it's around there somewhere • **hasta allí** up until then

alma *sf* ❶ [*generalmente*] soul • **el cuerpo y el alma** body and soul • **te lo agradezco en el alma** I'm very grateful • **siento en el alma no poder ir** I'm so sorry I can't go ❷ [*de bastón, ovillo*] core

almacén *sm* warehouse

almacenar *vt* ❶ [*generalmente*] INFORMÁTICA to store ❷ [*reunir*] to collect

almendra *sf* almond

almendro *sm* almond (tree)

almíbar *sm* syrup • **duraznos en almíbar** peaches in syrup

almidón *sm* starch

almirante *sm* admiral

almohada *sf* pillow

expresión **consultarlo con la almohada** *figurado* to sleep on it

almohadilla *sf* ❶ [*generalmente*] TECNOLOGÍA & ZOO-LOGÍA pad ❷ [*cojín*] small cushion

almorzar ◆ *vt* [*al mediodía*] to have for brunch • **almorcé fruta y un pan** I had fruit and a roll as a mid-morning snack

◆ *vi* [*a media mañana*] to have brunch • **almorzamos en la terraza** we had brunch on the terrace

almuerzo *sm* [*a media mañana*] brunch

alojamiento *sm* accommodation • **encontraron alojamiento en un albergue juvenil** they found accommodations at a youth hostel • **buscar alojamiento** to look for accommodations

alojar *vt* to put up

■ **alojarse** *v pronominal* ❶ [*hospedarse*] to stay • **nos alojamos en un hotel de lujo** we stayed at a luxury hotel ❷ [*introducirse*] to lodge

alpargata *sf* ☼ *generalmente pl* espadrille

Alpes *smpl* • **los Alpes** the Alps

alpinismo *sm* mountaineering • **hacer alpinismo** to go mountain climbing

alpinista *smf* mountaineer

alquilar *vt* ❶ [*casa, TV, oficina*] to rent • **le alquila el cuarto a un estudiante** she rents the room to a student • **alquilé una bicicleta** I rented a bicycle • **'se alquila'** for rent ❷ [*coche*] to rent

alquiler *sm* ❶ [*acción - de casa, TV, oficina*] renting; **de alquiler a)** [*casa*] rented **b)** [*coche*] rental ☼ *Sólo se usa delante del sustantivo.* • **tenemos departamentos en alquiler** we have apartments to rent • **alquiler de autos** car rental ❷ [*precio - de casa, oficina*] rent • **¿cuánto pagan de alquiler?** how much is your rent?; [- *de televisión*] rental; [- *de coche*] rental

alquimia *sf* alchemy

alquitrán *sm* tar

alrededor *adv* ❶ [*en torno*] around • **los niños se sentaron a su alrededor** the children sat around him • **mira a tu alrededor** look around you • **de alrededor** surrounding ❷ [*aproximadamente*] • **alrededor de** around; about • **corrimos alrededor de la fuente** we ran around the fountain • **estudió inglés alrededor de tres años** she studied English for about three years

■ **alrededores** *smpl* surrounding area *sing* • **en los alrededores de Londres** in the area around London • **vive en los alrededores de la ciudad** she lives in the outskirts of the city

alta *sf* [*del hospital*] discharge • **dar de alta a alguien** to discharge somebody • **lo dieron de alta en el hospital** they discharged him from the hospital

altar *sm* altar

expresión **conducir** o **llevar a alguien al altar** *figurado* to lead somebody down the aisle

altavoz *sm* ❶ [*generalmente*] speaker ❷ [*para anuncios*] loudspeaker

alteración *sf* ❶ [*cambio*] alteration ❷ [*excitación*] agitation ❸ [*alboroto*] disturbance ▶ **alteración del orden público** disturbing the peace

alterar *vt* ❶ [*cambiar*] to change • **tuvimos que alterar los planes** we had to change our plans ❷ [*perturbar - persona*] to disturb • **no debes alterar a la abuela** you shouldn't disturb your grandmother; [*orden público*] to disturb

■ **alterarse** *v pronominal* [*perturbarse*] to get agitated o flustered

altercado *sm* argument

alternar ◆ *vt* to alternate

◆ *vi* ❶ [*relacionarse*] • **alternar (con)** to mix (with); to socialize (with) • **prefiere no alternar con los compañeros fuera del trabajo** he prefers not to socialize with colleagues outside work ❷ [*sucederse*] • **alternar con** to alternate with • **su locura alterna con períodos de lucidez** her madness alternates with lucid periods

alternativa *sf* [*opción*] alternative • **no tiene más alternativa que aceptar la propuesta** he has no alternative but to accept the offer

alternativamente *adv* [*moverse*] alternately

alternativo, va *adj* ❶ [*movimiento*] alternating ❷ [*posibilidad*] alternative ✍ *Los adjetivos ingleses son invariables.*

alterno, na *adj* ❶ alternate ❷ ELECTRICIDAD alternating ✍ *Los adjetivos ingleses son invariables.*

alteza *sf* figurado [*de sentimientos*] loftiness

altibajos *smpl* figurado [*de vida* ETC] ups and downs

altiplano *sm* high plateau

altitud *sf* altitude

alto, ta *adj* ❶ [*generalmente*] high • **una de las montañas más altas del continente** one of the highest mountains on the continent • **es un avión que vuela muy alto** it's a plane that flies very high • **ponen el volumen muy alto** they turn the volume up too high • **en alta mar** on the high seas ▶ **alta fidelidad** high fidelity ▶ **altos hornos** blast furnace ❷ [*persona, árbol, edificio*] tall • **es muy alto para su edad** he's very tall for his age ❸ [*ruidoso*] loud • **no hablen tan alto** don't talk so loud ❹ [*avanzado*] late • **a altas horas de la noche** late at night; in the small hours ✍ *Los adjetivos ingleses son invariables.*

■ **alto** ◆ *sm* ❶ [*altura*] height • **tiene dos metros de alto** it's two meters high ❷ [*interrupción*] stop • **hicieron un alto para descansar** they made a rest stop • **pasarse un alto** to run a red light ❸ [*lugar elevado*] height • **en lo alto de** at the top of ❹ MÚSICA alto

expresiones **el alto al fuego** the ceasefire ▶ **pasar por alto algo** to pass over something ▶ **por todo lo alto a)** [*lujoso*] grand ; luxurious **b)** [*a lo grande*] in (great) style

◆ *adv* ❶ [*arriba*] high (up) ❷ [*hablar* ETC] loud

◆ *exclamación* • **¡alto!** halt!; stop!

altura *sf* ❶ [*generalmente*] height • **esos aviones pueden volar a mucha altura** those planes can fly at great heights • **el Aconcagua tiene cerca de 7.000 metros de altura** the Aconcagua is nearly 7,000 meters high ▶ **a estas alturas** at this point • **a estas alturas no hay nada que podamos hacer** at this point there's nothing we can do ❷ [*en el mar*] depth • **ganar altura** to climb

❸ [*nivel*] level • **está a la altura del ayuntamiento** it's next to the town hall ❹ [*latitud*] latitude

alucinado, da *adj* ❶ MEDICINA hallucinating ❷ familiar [*sorprendido*] shocked ✍ *Los adjetivos ingleses son invariables.*

alucinante *adj* ❶ MEDICINA hallucinatory ❷ familiar [*extraordinario*] mind-blowing ✍ *Los adjetivos ingleses son invariables.*

alucinar *vi* MEDICINA to hallucinate

alud *sm* literal & figurado avalanche

aludido, da *sm, f* • **el aludido** the aforesaid • **darse por aludido a)** [*ofenderse*] to take it personally **b)** [*reaccionar*] to take the hint

aludir *vi* • **aludir a a)** [*sin mencionar*] to allude to **b)** [*mencionando*] to refer to

alumbrar *vt* ❶ [*iluminar*] to light up • **lleven una linterna para alumbrar el camino** take a flashlight to light the way ❷ [*instruir*] to enlighten ❸ [*dar a luz*] to give birth to

aluminio *sm* aluminum

alumnado *sm* students *pl*

alumno, na *sm, f* student

alusión *sf* ❶ [*sin mencionar*] allusion ❷ [*mencionando*] reference

alusivo, va *adj* allusive ✍ *Los adjetivos ingleses son invariables.*

alza *sf* rise • **habrá un alza en el precio de los boletos** ticket prices will rise • **en alza** on the rise • **el índice de criminalidad está en alza** the crime rate is on the rise

expresión **jugar al alza** FINANZAS to bull the market

alzar *vt* ❶ [*levantar*] to raise • **si quieren hacer una pregunta, alcen la mano** raise your hand if you have a question ❷ [*voz*] to raise • **¡no me alces la voz!** don't raise your voice at me! ❸ [*vela*] to hoist ❹ [*cuello de abrigo*] to turn up ❺ [*mangas*] to pull up ❻ [*aumentar*] to raise

■ **alzarse** *v pronominal* ❶ [*levantarse*] to rise ❷ [*sublevarse*] to rise up ; to revolt

a.m. (*abreviatura escrita de* ante meridiem) a.m.

amabilidad *sf* kindness • **¿tendría la amabilidad de...?** would you be so kind as to...?

amable *adj* kind • **la secretaria es muy amable** the secretary is very kind • **¿sería tan amable de abrir la ventana?** would you be so kind as to open the window? ✍ *Los adjetivos ingleses son invariables.*

amamantar *vt* ❶ [*animal*] to suckle ❷ [*bebé*] to nurse

amanecer ◆ *sm* dawn • **al amanecer** at dawn

◆ *v impersonal* • **amaneció a las siete** dawn broke at seven • **en esta época amanece más temprano** it gets light early at this time of year • **amaneció enfermo** he woke up sick • **hoy amaneció lloviendo** it was raining when we got up

amante *smf* ❶ [*querido*] lover ❷ figurado [*aficionado*] • **ser amante de algo/hacer algo** to be keen on something/doing something • **los amantes del arte** art lovers

amañar *vt* ❶ [falsear] to fix ❷ [elecciones, resultado] to rig ❸ [documento] to doctor

amapola *sf* poppy

amar *vt* to love

amargado, da *adj* [resentido] bitter • **es una persona muy amargada** she's a very bitter person • **están amargados porque perdieron** they're sore because they lost. Los adjetivos ingleses son invariables.

amargar *vt* to spoil • **eso nos amargó el paseo** it spoiled our outing • **le amarga la vida a sus padres** he makes his parents' life miserable

amargo, ga *adj* literal & figurado bitter. Los adjetivos ingleses son invariables.

amarillo, lla *adj* [color] yellow. Los adjetivos ingleses son invariables.

■ **amarillo** *sm* [color] yellow

amarra *sf* mooring rope o line • **largar** o **soltar amarras** to cast off

amarrar *vt* ❶ NÁUTICA to moor ❷ [atar] to tie (up) • **amarrar algo/a alguien a algo** to tie something/somebody to something • **amarró el perro a un árbol** he tied the dog to a tree

■ **amarrarse** *v pronominal* ❶ [pelo] to tie up ❷ [zapatos] to tie • **se amarró los zapatos** he tied his shoelaces

amasar *vt* ❶ [masa] to knead ❷ [yeso] to mix ❸ familiar & figurado [riquezas] to amass

amatista *sf* amethyst

Amazonas *sm* • **el Amazonas** the Amazon

ámbar *sm* amber

ambición *sf* ambition

ambicioso, sa *adj* ambitious. Los adjetivos ingleses son invariables.

ambientador *sm* air freshener

ambiente *sm* ❶ [aire] air • **este ambiente es irrespirable** you can't breathe in this air • **abran las ventanas, el ambiente está muy viciado** open the windows, it's very stuffy in here ❷ [circunstancias] atmosphere • **es un ambiente ideal para los niños** it's an ideal atmosphere for children • **un cambio de ambiente le haría bien** a change of scenery will do him good ❸ [ámbito] world; circles *pl* ❹ [animación] atmosphere • **en este bar no hay ambiente** there is no atmosphere in this bar • **una fiesta con mucho ambiente** a really happening party

ambigüedad *sf* ambiguity

ambiguo, gua *adj* [generalmente] ambiguous. Los adjetivos ingleses son invariables.

ámbito *sm* ❶ [espacio, límites] confines *pl* • **una ley de ámbito provincial** an act which is provincial in its scope ❷ [ambiente] world; circles *pl*

ambivalente *adj* ambivalent. Los adjetivos ingleses son invariables.

ambos, bas ◆ *adj pl* both • **los alumnos de ambos colegios** the students from both schools. Los adjetivos ingleses son invariables.

◆ *pronombre pl* both (of them) • **ambos pasaron de año** they both passed • **los castigaron a ambos** they were both punished

ambulancia *sf* ambulance

ambulante *adj* ❶ traveling ❷ [biblioteca] mobile. Los adjetivos ingleses son invariables.

amén *adv* [en plegaria] amen

expresión **decir amén a** *figurado* to accept unquestioningly

amenaza *sf* threat ▶ **amenaza de bomba** bomb scare ▶ **amenaza de muerte** death threat

expresar una amenaza

• If you don't stop that racket at once, I'm calling the police! ¡Si no dejan de hacer tanto escándalo, llamo a la policía!
• Leave that woman alone or I'll call the police! ¡Deje a esta señora en paz o llamo a la policía!
• I won't tell you again, stop that immediately! No te lo volveré a decir, ¡deja de hacer eso inmediatamente!
• That's enough now! ¡Ya basta!

amenazar *vt* to threaten • **amenazar a alguien con hacerle algo** to threaten to do something to somebody • **me amenazó con dejarme castigado** she threatened to ground me • **amenazar a alguien con hacer algo** to threaten somebody with doing something • **amenazar a alguien de muerte/con el despido** to threaten to kill/fire somebody • **amenaza lluvia** it's threatening to rain

ameno, na *adj* [entretenido] entertaining. Los adjetivos ingleses son invariables.

América *nombre propio* America ▶ **América Central** Central America ▶ **América del Norte** North America ▶ **América del Sur** South America ▶ **América Latina** Latin America

americano, na *adj* & *sm, f* American. Los adjetivos ingleses son invariables.

ameritar *vt* to deserve

ametralladora *sf* machine gun

ametrallar *vt* to machinegun

amigo, ga ◆ *adj* [generalmente] friendly. Los adjetivos ingleses son invariables.

◆ *sm, f* ❶ [persona] friend • **es mi mejor amigo** he's my best friend • **son muy amigos** they're good friends • **hacerse amigo de alguien** to make friends with somebody • **hacer amigos** to make friends • **hacerse amigos** to become friends ▶ **amigo íntimo** close friend ❷ familiar [compañero, novio] partner ❸ [amante] lover

aminoácido *sm* amino acid

aminorar *vt* to reduce

amistad *sf* ❶ friendship • **valoro mucho tu amistad** I really value your friendship ❷ • **las amistades** friends • **vinieron todas sus amistades** all her friends came

A

amistoso, sa *adj* friendly ☼ *Los adjetivos ingleses son invariables.*

amnesia *sf* amnesia

amnistía *sf* amnesty

amo, ama *sm, f* ❶ [*generalmente*] owner • **lo abandonó su amo** it was abandoned by its owner ❷ [*de criado, situación* ETC] master, *femenino* mistress ▶ **ama de casa** homemaker ▶ **ama de llaves** housekeeper

amoldar *vt* [*adaptar*] • **amoldar (a)** to adapt (to)

amoníaco, amoniaco *sm* [*gas*] ammonia

amontonar *vt* ❶ [*apilar*] to pile up • **amontonaron los libros en el piso** they piled the books up on the floor ❷ [*reunir*] to accumulate

■ **amontonarse** *v pronominal* ❶ [*personas*] to form a crowd ❷ [*problemas, trabajo*] to pile up ❸ [*ideas, solicitudes*] to come thick and fast

amor *sm* love

expresión **hacer el amor** to make love ▶ **por amor al arte** for the love of it

■ **amor propio** *sm* pride

amoratado, da *adj* ❶ [*de frío*] blue ❷ [*por golpes*] bruised ☼ *Los adjetivos ingleses son invariables.*

amoratar *vt* ❶ [*por frío*] to make blue ❷ [*por golpes*] to bruise

■ **amoratarse** *v pronominal* ❶ [*por frío*] to turn blue ❷ [*por golpes*] to bruise

amortiguar *vt* ❶ [*ruido*] to muffle ❷ [*golpe*] to soften

amparar *vt* ❶ [*proteger*] to protect ❷ [*dar cobijo a*] to give shelter to

amperio *sm* amp

ampliación *sf* ❶ [*aumento*] expansion ❷ [*de edificio, plazo*] extension ▶ **ampliación de capital** ECONOMÍA increase in capital ❸ FOTOGRAFÍA enlargement

ampliar *vt* ❶ [*generalmente*] to expand • **van a ampliar el gimnasio** they're going to expand the gym ❷ [*plazo*] to extend • **ampliaron el plazo de inscripciones** they extended the registration period ❸ FOTOGRAFÍA to enlarge • **quiero ampliar esta foto** I want to enlarge this picture

amplificador *sm* ELECTRÓNICA amplifier

amplio, plia *adj* ❶ [*sala* ETC] spacious ❷ [*avenida, gama*] wide ❸ [*ropa*] loose ❹ [*explicación* ETC] comprehensive • **en el sentido más amplio de la palabra** in the broadest sense of the word ☼ *Los adjetivos ingleses son invariables.*

ampolla *sf* ❶ [*en piel*] blister ❷ [*para inyecciones*] ampoule ❸ [*frasco*] vial

amputar *vt* to amputate

amueblar *vt* to furnish • **amueblaron el cuarto** they furnished the room • **un departamento sin amueblar** an unfurnished apartment

anacronismo *sm* anachronism

anagrama *sm* anagram

analfabetismo *sm* illiteracy

analfabeto, ta *adj & sm, f* illiterate ☼ *Los adjetivos ingleses son invariables.*

analgésico, ca *adj* analgesic ☼ *Los adjetivos ingleses son invariables.*

■ **analgésico** *sm* painkiller

análisis *sm invariable* analysis ▶ **análisis de sangre** blood test

analizar *vt* to analyse

analogía *sf* similarity • **por analogía** by analogy

analógico, ca *adj* INFORMÁTICA & TECNOLOGÍA analog ☼ *Los adjetivos ingleses son invariables.*

anarquía *sf* [*falta de gobierno*] anarchy

anarquista *adj & smf* anarchist ☼ *Los adjetivos ingleses son invariables.*

anatomía *sf* anatomy

anca *sf* haunch ▶ **ancas de rana** frogs' legs

ancho, cha *adj* [*generalmente*] wide • **una avenida muy ancha** a very wide avenue • **ser ancho de espaldas** to have broad shoulders ☼ *Los adjetivos ingleses son invariables.*

expresión **a mis/tus** ETC **anchas** *figurado* at ease ▶ **quedarse tan ancho** not to care less

■ **ancho** *sm* width • **mide el ancho de la ventana** measure the width of the window • **¿cuánto mide de ancho?** how wide is it? • **tiene dos metros de ancho** it's two meters wide • **a lo ancho** crosswise • **cinco metros de ancho** five meters wide • **a lo ancho de** across (the width of) ▶ **ancho de banda** bandwidth

anchoa *sf* anchovy *(salted)*

anchura *sf* [*medida*] width

anciano, na ◆ *adj* old ☼ *Los adjetivos ingleses son invariables.*

◆ *sm, f* old person ; old man, *femenino* old woman

ancla *sf* anchor • **echar/levar anclas** to drop/weigh anchor

anclar *vi* to anchor

andadas *sfpl*

expresión **volver a las andadas** *familiar & figurado* to return to your evil ways

ándale *exclamación* *familiar* come on!

andamio *sm* scaffold

andar ◆ *vi* ❶ [*caminar*] to walk • **vine andando** I walked here ❷ [*moverse*] to move ❸ [*funcionar*] to work • **mi reloj no anda** my watch isn't working • **las cosas andan mal** things are going badly ❹ [*estar*] to be • **andar preocupado** to be worried • **ando muy ocupado** I am very busy • **¿cómo anda tu papá?** how is your father? • **ando buscando a la profesora** I'm looking for the teacher • **hay que andarse con cuidado** you should be careful • **andar tras algo/alguien** *figurado* to be after something/somebody ❺ ☼ *antes de gerundio* • **andar haciendo algo** to be doing something • **anda repartiendo las invitaciones** he's handing out the invitations • **anda buscando algo** he's looking for something ❻ [*ocuparse*] • **andar en** (*asuntos, líos*) to be involved in ❼ [*papeleos, negocios*] to be busy with ❽ [*hurgar*] • **andar en** to rummage around in ❾ [*alcanzar, rondar*] • **anda por los 60** he's about sixty ❿ [*desplazarse*] • **andar en bicicleta** to ride a bicycle • **andar a caballo** to go horseback riding

◆ *vt* [*recorrer*] to go ; to travel
◆ *sm* walk
■ **anda** *exclamación* • **¡anda! a)** [*sorpresa, desilusión*] oh! **b)** [*¡vamos!*] come on! **c)** [*¡por favor!*] go on! • **¡anda! que vamos a llegar tarde** come on! we're going to be late • **¡anda! mira lo que encontré** hey! look what I found! • **¡anda ya!** [*incredulidad*] come off it!
andén *sm* FERROCARRIL platform
Andes *smpl* • **los Andes** the Andes
anécdota *sf* anecdote
anecdótico, ca *adj* ❶ [*con historietas*] anecdotal ❷ [*no esencial*] incidental ҉ *Los adjetivos ingleses son invariables.*
anegar *vt* [*inundar*] to flood
anemia *sf* anemia
anémona *sf* anemone
anestesia *sf* anesthesia ❱ **anestesia general/local** general/local anesthesia
anexión *sf* annexation
anfetamina *sf* amphetamine
anfibio, bia *adj* literal & figurado amphibious ҉ *Los adjetivos ingleses son invariables.*
anfiteatro *sm* ❶ CINE & TEATRO circle ❷ [*edificio*] amphitheater
anfitrión, ona *sm, f* host, *femenino* hostess
ángel *sm* literal & figurado angel ❱ **ángel de la guarda** guardian angel
expresión **tener ángel** to have something special
angina *sf* ҉ *generalmente pl* tonsils • **tener anginas** to have a sore throat
anglicano, na *adj* & *sm, f* Anglican ҉ *Los adjetivos ingleses son invariables.*
anglosajón, ona *adj* & *sm, f* Anglo-Saxon ҉ *Los adjetivos ingleses son invariables.*
Angola *nombre propio* Angola
angosto, ta *adj* culto narrow • **un pasillo angosto** a narrow hallway ҉ *Los adjetivos ingleses son invariables.*
anguila *sf* eel
ángulo *sm* ❶ [*generalmente*] angle ❱ **ángulo de tiro** [*para disparar*] elevation ❱ **ángulo recto** right angle ❷ [*rincón*] corner
angustia *sf* [*aflicción*] anxiety
angustiar *vt* to distress
angustioso, sa *adj* ❶ [*espera, momentos*] anxious ❷ [*situación, noticia*] distressing ҉ *Los adjetivos ingleses son invariables.*
anhelar *vt* to long o wish for • **anhelar hacer algo** to long to do something
anhelo *sm* longing
anhídrido *sm* anhydride ❱ **anhídrido carbónico** carbon dioxide
anilla *sf* ring
anillo *sm* [*generalmente*] ASTRONOMÍA ring ❱ **anillo de boda** wedding ring ❱ **anillo de compromiso** engagement ring

animación *sf* ❶ [*alegría*] liveliness ❷ [*bullicio*] hustle and bustle ; activity ❸ CINE animation
animado, da *adj* ❶ [*con buen ánimo*] cheerful • **¡qué animado estás hoy!** you're very cheerful today! ❷ [*divertido*] lively • **las playas tienen un ambiente muy animado** the beaches have a very lively atmosphere ❸ CINE animated ҉ *Los adjetivos ingleses son invariables.*
animador, ra *sm, f* ❶ [*en espectáculo*] host ❷ [*en fiesta de niños*] children's entertainer ❸ [*en béisbol* ETC] cheerleader
animadversión *sf* animosity
animal ◆ *adj* ❶ [*reino, funciones*] animal ҉ *Sólo se usa delante del sustantivo.* • **el reino animal** the animal kingdom ❷ familiar [*persona basto*] rough ; [*ignorante*] ignorant
◆ *smf* familiar & figurado [*persona*] animal ; brute
◆ *sm* animal ❱ **animal doméstico a)** [*de granja* ETC] domestic animal **b)** [*de compañía*] pet ❱ **animal de tiro** draught animal

los animales

la ardilla	the squirrel
la ballena	the whale
el burro	the donkey
el caballo	the horse
la cabra	the goat
el canguro	the kangaroo
la cebra	the zebra
el cerdo	the pig
el chango	the monkey
el cocodrilo	the crocodile
el conejo	the rabbit
el delfín	the dolphin
el elefante	the elephant
la gallina	the hen
el gato	the cat
el hipopótamo	the hippopotamus
la jirafa	the giraffe
el león	the lion
la llama	the llama
el lobo	the wolf
el murciélago	the bat
el oso	the bear
la oveja	the sheep
el pájaro	the bird
el pato	the duck
el perico	the parrot
el perro	the dog
el pez	the fish
el pingüino	the penguin
la rana	the frog
el ratón	the mouse
el rinoceronte	the rhinoceros
la serpiente	the snake
el tiburón	the shark
el tigre	the tiger
la tortuga	the turtle

la tortuga marina	the sea turtle
la vaca	the cow
el venado	the deer

los sonidos de los animales

el burro rebuzna	the donkey brays
el caballo relincha	the horse whinnies
la cabra bala	the goat bleats
el cerdo gruñe	the pig grunts
el elefante brama	the elephant trumpets
la gallina cloquea	the hen clucks
el gato maulla	the cat miaows
la golondrina trina	the swallow chirps
el león ruge	the lion roars
el lobo aúlla	the wolf howls
la oveja bala	the sheep bleats
el pájaro canta	the bird sings
el pato parpa	the duck quacks
el perro ladra	the dog barks
la rana croa	the frog croaks
la serpiente silba	the snake hisses
la vaca muge	the cow lows
el venado brama	the stag bellows

animar *vt* ❶ [*estimular*] to encourage • **animar a alguien a** o **para hacer algo** to encourage somebody to do something • **hay que animarlo para que siga estudiando** we have to encourage him to stay in school ❷ [*alegrar - persona*] to cheer up • **fuimos para animarlo un poco** we went to try to cheer him up a little • **gritaban para animar al equipo** they yelled to cheer on the team ❸ [*avivar - fuego, diálogo, fiesta*] to liven up ❹ [*comercio*] to stimulate
■ **animarse** *v pronominal* ❶ [*alegrarse - persona*] to cheer up • **¡anda, anímate!** come on, cheer up!; [- *fiesta* ETC] to liven up ❷ [*decidir*] • **animarse (a hacer algo)** to finally decide (to do something) • **vamos a nadar ¿quién más se anima?** we're going swimming — who else is up for it? • **no me animo a decírselo a la profesora** I don't dare tell the teacher about it

ánimo ◆ *sm* ❶ [*valor*] courage ❷ [*aliento*] encouragement • **dar ánimos a alguien** to encourage somebody ❸ [*humor*] disposition
◆ *exclamación* [*para alentar*] • **¡ánimo!** come on! • **¡ánimo! que ya casi terminamos** come on! we're nearly finished • **¡ánimo! todo se va a arreglar** cheer up! it'll all work out

aniquilar *vt* to annihilate; to wipe out

anís (pl anises) *sm* ❶ [*grano*] anise ❷ [*licor*] anisette

aniversario *sm* ❶ [*generalmente*] anniversary • **es el aniversario de boda de mis papás** it's my parents' wedding anniversary ❷ [*cumpleaños*] birthday

ano *sm* anus

anoche *adv* last night • **anoche fuimos al cine** we went to the movies last night • **antes de anoche** the night before last

anochecer ◆ *sm* dusk; nightfall • **al anochecer** at dusk
◆ *v impersonal* to get dark • **en esta época anochece más temprano** it gets dark early at this time of year

anomalía *sf* anomaly

anómalo, la *adj* anomalous ֎ *Los adjetivos ingleses son invariables.*

anónimo, ma *adj* anonymous ֎ *Los adjetivos ingleses son invariables.*
■ **anónimo** *sm* anonymous letter

anorexia *sf* anorexia

anormal *adj* [*anómalo*] abnormal ֎ *Los adjetivos ingleses son invariables.*

anotación *sf* ❶ [*generalmente*] note ▶ **anotación al margen** marginal note ❷ [*en registro*] entry ▶ **anotación contable** COMERCIO book entry

anotar *vt* ❶ [*apuntar*] to write down • **anotó las tareas en el cuaderno** she wrote down the homework assignment in her notebook ❷ [*marcar*] to score • **anotó el gol ganador** she scored the winning goal

anquilosarse *v pronominal* ❶ [*estancarse*] to stagnate ❷ MEDICINA to become paralyzed

ansia *sf* ❶ [*afán*] • **ansia de** longing o yearning for ❷ [*ansiedad*] anxiousness ❸ [*angustia*] anguish

ansiedad *sf* ❶ [*inquietud*] anxiety • **con ansiedad** anxiously ❷ PSICOLOGÍA nervous tension

ansioso, sa *adj* [*impaciente*] impatient • **estar ansioso por** o **de hacer algo** to be impatient to do something ֎ *Los adjetivos ingleses son invariables.*

antártico, ca *adj* Antarctic ֎ *Los adjetivos ingleses son invariables.*

Antártida *sf* • **la Antártida** the Antarctic

ante¹ *sm* ❶ [*piel*] suede ❷ [*animal*] elk

ante² *preposición* ❶ [*delante de, en presencia de*] before • **tiene que presentarse ante el director** she has to appear before the manager ❷ [*frente a - hecho, circunstancia*] in the face of • **no sabía qué hacer ante una situación tan complicada** he didn't know what to do in the face of such a complicated situation • **estamos ante un grave problema** we are facing a serious problem

anteanoche *adv* the night before last

anteayer *adv* the day before yesterday

antebrazo *sm* forearm

antecedente ◆ *adj* preceding; previous ֎ *Los adjetivos ingleses son invariables.*
◆ *sm* [*precedente*] precedent
■ **antecedentes** *smpl* ❶ [*de persona*] record *sing* • **una persona sin antecedentes** a person with a clean record • **tiene muy buenos antecedentes** he has a good record ▶ **antecedentes penales** police record ❷ [*de asunto*] background *sing* • **poner a alguien en antecedentes de** [*informar*] to fill somebody in on

antecesor, ra *sm, f* [*predecesor*] predecessor

antelación *sf* • **con antelación** in advance; beforehand • **con dos horas de antelación** two hours in advance

A

antena *sf* ❶ RADIO & TELEVISIÓN antenna • **la antena de la tele está descompuesta** the tv antenna is broken ❱ **antena parabólica** satellite dish ❷ ZOOLOGÍA antenna

anteojo *sm* telescope ❱ **anteojo de larga vista** binoculars
■ **anteojos** *smpl* ❶ [*gafas*] glasses • **lleva anteojos** he wears glasses ❱ **anteojos de sol** sunglasses ❷ [*anteojeras*] blinders ❸ DEPORTE goggles

antepasado, da *sm, f* ancestor • **estoy orgulloso de mis antepasados** I'm proud of my ancestors

antepenúltimo, ma *adj & sm, f* second to last ⚡ *Los adjetivos ingleses son invariables.*

anteponer *vt* • **anteponer algo a algo** to put something before something

anterior *adj* ❶ [*previo*] • **anterior (a)** previous (to) • **mi colegio anterior era mucho mejor** my previous school was much better ❱ **el día anterior** the day before ❷ [*delantero*] front ⚡ *Sólo se usa delante del sustantivo.* • **las piernas anteriores** the front legs

anterioridad *sf* • **con anterioridad** beforehand • **con anterioridad a** before; prior to

anteriormente *adv* previously

---

antes
◆ *preposición*
❶ [*en el tiempo*] before
• **esto lo deberías haber hecho antes** you should have done this before
• **la inscripción es gratuita pero antes debe llenar un formulario** enrollment is free but you have to fill out a form first
• **antes de** before
• **antes de salir, limpiemos la cocina** let's clean the kitchen before we go out
❷ [*en el espacio*] before
• **el correo está antes de la farmacia** the post office is before the drugstore
❸ [*primero*] first
• **yo estaba antes** I was here first
• **ella llegó antes** she got here first
• **llegaron antes que yo** they arrived before me
❹ [*indica una preferencia*]
• **antes ir a la cárcel que mentir** better to go to prison than lie
• **prefiero el mar antes que la montaña** I prefer the sea to the mountains
expresiones **antes que nada** first of all ❱ **cuanto antes mejor** the sooner, the better ❱ **lo antes posible** as soon as possible ❱ **poco antes** a short time before
◆ *adj*
• **el año antes** the year before
• **el mes antes** the month before
• **el día antes** the day before
⚡ *Los adjetivos ingleses son invariables.*

---

antesala *sf* anteroom
expresión **hacer antesala** [*esperar*] to wait

antiadherente *adj* non-stick ⚡ *Los adjetivos ingleses son invariables.*

antiaéreo, a *adj* anti-aircraft ⚡ *Los adjetivos ingleses son invariables.*

antibiótico, ca *adj* antibiotic ⚡ *Los adjetivos ingleses son invariables.*
■ **antibiótico** *sm* antibiotic

anticiclón *sm* anticyclone

anticipado, da *adj* ❶ [*elecciones*] early ❷ [*pago*] advance • **por anticipado** in advance ⚡ *Los adjetivos ingleses son invariables.*

anticipar *vt* ❶ [*prever*] to anticipate • **no habíamos anticipado tantos problemas** we hadn't anticipated so many problems ❷ [*adelantar*] to bring forward • **estamos considerando anticipar nuestro viaje** we're thinking of bringing our trip forward
■ **anticiparse** *v pronominal* ❶ [*suceder antes*] to arrive early • **se anticipó el invierno** winter has come early • **se anticipó a su tiempo** he was ahead of his time ❷ [*adelantarse*] • **anticiparse a alguien** to get in before somebody • **se me anticipó y contestó la pregunta de la profesora** she got in before me and answered the teacher's question

anticipo *sm* [*de dinero*] advance

anticonceptivo, va *adj* contraceptive ⚡ *Los adjetivos ingleses son invariables.*
■ **anticonceptivo** *sm* contraceptive

anticongelante *adj & sm* antifreeze ⚡ *Los adjetivos ingleses son invariables.*

anticuado, da *adj* old-fashioned ⚡ *Los adjetivos ingleses son invariables.*

anticuario, ria *sm, f* ❶ [*comerciante*] antique dealer ❷ [*experto*] antiquarian

anticuerpo *sm* antibody

antidoping *adj* doping ⚡ *Sólo se usa delante del sustantivo.*

antídoto *sm* antidote

antier *adv* familiar the day before yesterday

antifaz *sm* mask

antiguamente *adv* ❶ [*hace mucho*] long ago ❷ [*previamente*] formerly

antigüedad *sf* ❶ [*generalmente*] antiquity ❷ [*veteranía*] seniority • **recibe una bonificación de antigüedad** he gets a seniority bonus
■ **antigüedades** *sfpl* [*objetos*] antiques ❱ **tienda de antigüedades** antique store

antiguo, gua *adj* ❶ [*viejo*] old • **un antiguo amigo** an old friend ❷ [*inmemorial*] ancient • **las civilizaciones antiguas** ancient civilizations ❸ [*anterior, previo*] former • **el antiguo presidente** the former president ⚡ *Los adjetivos ingleses son invariables.*

antihigiénico, ca *adj* unhygienic ⚡ *Los adjetivos ingleses son invariables.*

antihistamínico *sm* antihistamine

antiinflamatorio *sm* anti-inflammatory drug

antílope *sm* antelope

antiniebla → **faro**

A

antipatía *sf* dislike • **no pude disimular mi antipatía hacia ella** I couldn't hide my dislike for her • **tener antipatía a alguien** to dislike somebody

antipático, ca *adj* unpleasant • **¡qué mujer más antipática!** what an unpleasant woman! ☞ *Los adjetivos ingleses son invariables.*

antípodas *sfpl* • **las antípodas** the Antipodes

antítesis *sf invariable* antithesis

antitetánico, ca *adj* anti-tetanus ☞ *Sólo se usa delante del sustantivo.*

antivirus *sm invariable* INFORMÁTICA antivirus system

antojarse *v pronominal* ❶ [capricho] • **se le antojaron esos zapatos** he liked those shoes • **se le ha antojado ir al cine** he felt like going to the movies • **cuando se me antoje** when I feel like it ❷ [posibilidad] • **se me antoja que...** I have a feeling that...

antojitos *smpl* snacks; appetizers

antología *sf* anthology

antorcha *sf* torch

anual *adj* annual • **el promedio anual** the annual average ☞ *Los adjetivos ingleses son invariables.*

anualidad *sf* yearly payment

anuario *sm* yearbook

anulación *sf* ❶ [cancelación] cancellation ❷ [de ley] repeal ❸ [de matrimonio, contrato] annulment

anular¹ *sm* → dedo

anular² *vt* ❶ [cancelar - generalmente] to cancel • **no será fácil anular el contrato** it won't be easy to cancel the contract; [- ley] to repeal; [- matrimonio, contrato] to annul ❷ DEPORTE [gol] to disallow • **el árbitro anuló el gol** the referee disallowed the goal; [resultado] to declare void

anunciación *sf* announcement

anunciante *smf* advertiser

anunciar *vt* ❶ [notificar] to announce • **el gobierno anunció una baja de impuestos** the government announced a tax cut ❷ [hacer publicidad de] to advertise • **anuncian el producto en televisión** the product is advertised on TV ❸ [presagiar] to herald

anuncio *sm* ❶ [notificación] announcement ❷ [cartel, aviso] notice ❸ [póster] poster ❹ [publicitario] advertisement; advert • **puedes poner un anuncio en el diario** you can put an advert in the paper • **cada día hay más anuncios en la tele** there are more commercials on TV every day ▶ **anuncios clasificados** classified ads ▶ **anuncio publicitario** advertisement; ad ❺ [presagio] sign; herald

añadir *vt* to add • **le añadió un poco de pimienta a la salsa** he added a little pepper to the sauce

añicos *smpl* • **hacerse añicos** to shatter

expresión **estoy hecho añicos** I'm beat

año *sm* year • **en el año 1939** in 1939 • **el año que viene** next year • **¿cuántos años tienes? — tengo 14 años** how old are you? — I'm fourteen • **cumplo 15 años este marzo** I'll be 15 this March • **estoy cursando quinto año** I'm in 5th grade • **los años 30** the thirties ▶ **año académico** academic year ▶ **año bisiesto** leap

year ▶ **año escolar** school year ▶ **año fiscal** tax year ▶ **año nuevo** New Year • **¡Feliz Año Nuevo!** Happy New Year! ▶ **año solar** solar year

anzuelo *sm* [para pescar] (fish) hook

apacible *adj* ❶ [generalmente] mild; gentle ❷ [lugar, ambiente] pleasant ☞ *Los adjetivos ingleses son invariables.*

apaciguar *vt* ❶ [tranquilizar] to calm down ❷ [aplacar - dolor ETC] to soothe

apagado, da *adj* ❶ [luz, fuego] out ❷ [aparato] off ❸ [color, persona] subdued ❹ [sonido] muffled ❺ [voz] quiet ☞ *Los adjetivos ingleses son invariables.*

apagar *vt* ❶ [extinguir - fuego] to put out; [- luz] to turn off; [- vela] to extinguish ❷ [desconectar] to turn o switch off • **apaga la televisión antes de subir** turn the TV off before going upstairs ❸ [aplacar - sed] to quench ❹ [rebajar - sonido] to muffle

expresión **apaga y vámonos** *figurado* we have nothing more to talk about

apagón *sm* power cut

apañar *vt* familiar ❶ [apoderarse] to seize ❷ to excuse; to forgive

apapachar *vt* ❶ [mimar] to cuddle ❷ [consentir] to spoil

aparador *sm* [mueble] sideboard

aparato *sm* ❶ [máquina] machine ❷ [de laboratorio] apparatus ☞ *incontable* ❸ [electrodoméstico] appliance ▶ **aparato de radio** radio ▶ **aparato de televisión** television set ▶ **aparatos electrodomésticos** household appliances ❹ [dispositivo] device ❺ MEDICINA [prótesis] aid; [para dientes] brace ❻ ANATOMÍA system ▶ **aparato circulatorio** circulatory system ❼ POLÍTICA machinery ❽ [ostentación] pomp; ostentation

aparatoso, sa *adj* ❶ [ostentoso] ostentatious ❷ [espectacular] spectacular ☞ *Los adjetivos ingleses son invariables.*

aparecer *vi* ❶ [generalmente] to appear ❷ [acudir] • **aparecer por (un lugar)** to turn up at (a place) ❸ [ser encontrado] to turn up

aparejo *sm* ❶ [de caballerías] harness ❷ MECÁNICA block and tackle ❸ NÁUTICA rigging

aparentar ♦ *vt* ❶ [fingir] to pretend to be • **aparentó estar triste** he pretended to be sad ❷ [edad] to look • **aparenta más de sus 16 años** she looks older than 16

♦ *vi* [presumir] to show off • **le gusta aparentar** she likes to show off

aparente *adj* [falso, supuesto] apparent ☞ *Los adjetivos ingleses son invariables.*

aparición *sf* ❶ [generalmente] appearance ❷ [de ser sobrenatural] apparition

apariencia *sf* [aspecto] appearance • **deberías preocuparte más de tu apariencia** you should take more care of your appearance • **guardar las apariencias** to keep up appearances • **las apariencias engañan** appearances can be deceptive

apartado, da *adj* ❶ [separado] • **apartado de** away from • **se mantiene apartado de su familia** he stays away from his family ❷ [*alejado*] remote ☼ *Los adjetivos ingleses son invariables.*

■ **apartado** *sm* ❶ [*párrafo*] paragraph • **la respuesta está en el apartado 2** the answer is in paragraph 2 ❷ [*sección*] section • **contesta las preguntas en el apartado A** answer the questions in section A ▸ **apartado de correos** P.O. Box ▸ **apartado postal** P.O. Box

apartamento *sm* apartment

apartar *vt* ❶ [*alejar*] to move away • **aparta esa basura de ahí** move that garbage out of the way ❷ [*quitar*] to remove ❸ [*separar*] to separate • **te apartaré un pedazo de pastel** I'll set aside a piece of cake for you ❹ [*escoger*] to take; to select

■ **apartarse** *v pronominal* ❶ [*hacerse a un lado*] to move to one side • **¡apártate!** stand aside! ❷ [*separarse*] to separate • **apartarse de a)** [*generalmente*] to move away from **b)** [*tema*] to get away from **c)** [*mundo, sociedad*] to cut yourself off from • **no se aparta ni un momento de su hermano gemelo** he's never apart from his twin brother • **no te apartes del hilo del razonamiento** don't lose the thread of the argument • **decidió apartarse del mundo y vivir en un monasterio** he decided to cut himself off from the world and go and live in a monastery

aparte ◆ *adv* ❶ [*en otro lugar, a un lado*] aside; to one side • **voy a dejar tus cosas aparte** I'll put your things to one side • **bromas aparte** joking apart • **dejar algo aparte** to leave something aside • **poner algo aparte** to put something aside • **impuestos aparte** before tax ❷ [*además*] besides • **y aparte él me dijo que lo hiciera** besides, he told me to do it • **aparte de fea...** besides being ugly... ❸ [*por separado*] separately

◆ *sm* ❶ [*párrafo*] new paragraph ❷ TEATRO aside

apasionado, da ◆ *adj* passionate ☼ *Los adjetivos ingleses son invariables.*

◆ *sm, f* lover; enthusiast

apasionante *adj* fascinating ☼ *Los adjetivos ingleses son invariables.*

apasionar *vt* to fascinate • **me apasiona el arte** I'm fascinated by art • **le apasiona la música** he's crazy about music

apatía *sf* apathy

apear *vt* [*bajar*] to take down

apedrear *vt* ❶ [*persona*] to stone ❷ [*cosa*] to throw stones at

apego *sm* fondness; attachment • **tener/tomar apego a** to be/become fond of

apelar *vi* ❶ DERECHO to (lodge an) appeal • **apelar ante/contra** to appeal to/against • **las víctimas apelaron ante el Tribunal de Apelaciones** the victims appealed to the Court of Appeals • **los inculpados han apelado contra la sentencia** the accused have appealed against the sentence ❷ [*recurrir*] • **apelar a a)** [*persona*] to go to **b)** [*sentido común, bondad*] to appeal to **c)** [*violencia*] to resort to • **apelar a la violencia no es una solución** resorting to violence isn't a solution • **el presidente se dirigió a los huelguistas y apeló a su sentido común** the president addressed the strikers and appealed to their common sense

apelativo *sm* name

apellido *sm* last name

apenado, da *adj* [*avergonzado*] ashamed; embarrassed ☼ *Los adjetivos ingleses son invariables.*

apenas *adv* ❶ [*casi no*] hardly • **apenas me puedo mover** I can hardly move • **apenas podía respirar por el calor** I could hardly breathe because of the heat ❷ [*tan sólo*] only • **apenas hace dos minutos** only two minutes ago • **hace apenas dos semanas que nos conocemos** we met barely two weeks ago ❸ [*tan pronto como*] as soon as • **apenas había llegado cuando empezaron con las preguntas** they started asking questions as soon as I walked in • **apenas llegó, sonó el teléfono** no sooner had he arrived than the phone rang

apéndice *sm* appendix

apendicitis *sf invariable* appendicitis

apercibir *vt* [*amonestar*] to reprimand

aperitivo *sm* ❶ [*bebida*] aperitif ❷ [*comida*] appetizer

apertura *sf* ❶ [*generalmente*] opening ❷ [*de año académico, temporada*] start

apestar *vi* • **apestar (a)** to stink (of) • **¡tu ropa apesta a puros!** your clothes stink of cigars!

apetecer *vi* • **¿te apetece un café?** would you like some coffee? • **me apetece salir** I feel like going out

apetecible *adj* ❶ [*comida*] appetizing; tempting ❷ [*vacaciones* ETC] desirable ☼ *Los adjetivos ingleses son invariables.*

apetito *sm* appetite • **abrir el apetito** to whet your appetite • **perder el apetito** to lose your appetite • **tener apetito** to be hungry

apetitoso, sa *adj* [*comida*] appetizing ☼ *Los adjetivos ingleses son invariables.*

apicultura *sf* beekeeping

apilar *vt* to pile up

apiñar *vt* to pack o cram together

apio *sm* celery

aplacar *vt* ❶ to placate ❷ [*hambre*] to satisfy ❸ [*sed*] to quench

aplanar *vt* to level

aplastante *adj* [*apabullante*] overwhelming; devastating ☼ *Los adjetivos ingleses son invariables.*

aplastar *vt* ❶ [*por el peso*] to flatten ❷ [*derrotar*] to crush

aplaudir *vt & vi* to applaud • **el público aplaudió su discurso** the public applauded his speech

aplauso *sm* ❶ [*ovación*] round of applause • **aplausos** applause ☼ *incontable* ❷ figurado [*alabanza*] applause

aplazamiento *sm* postponement

aplazar *vt* [*retrasar*] to postpone

aplicación *sf* [*generalmente*] INFORMÁTICA application

aplicado, da *adj* [*estudioso*] diligent ☼ *Los adjetivos ingleses son invariables.*

aplicar *vt* ❶ [*generalmente*] to apply • **primero, aplicamos la pintura** first, we apply the paint • **ahora vamos a aplicar lo que hemos aprendido** now we'll put what we've learned into practice ❷ [*nombre, calificativo*] to give ❸ [*postular*] to apply • **ambos aplicamos al mismo trabajo** we both applied for the same job

aplomo *sm* composure • **perder el aplomo** to lose your composure

apocalipsis *sm invariable* apocalypse

apodar *vt* to nickname

apoderado, da *sm, f* ❶ [*representante*] (official) representative ❷ TAUROMAQUIA agent ; manager

apoderar *vt* ❶ [*generalmente*] to authorize ❷ DERECHO to grant power of attorney to

apodo *sm* nickname

apogeo *sm figurado* height ; apogee • **estar en (pleno) apogeo** to be at its height

apolítico, ca *adj* apolitical ☿ *Los adjetivos ingleses son invariables.*

apología *sf* apology ; eulogy

aportación *sf* [*contribución*] contribution

aportar *vt* [*contribuir con*] to contribute

aporte *sm* contribution ; donation

aposento *sm* ❶ [*habitación*] room • **retirarse a sus aposentos** *desusado & humorístico* to withdraw (to your chamber) ❷ [*alojamiento*] lodgings *pl*

aposta *adv* on purpose

apostar ◆ *vt* ❶ [*jugarse*] to bet ❷ [*emplazar*] to post

◆ *vi* • **apostar (por)** to bet (on) • **aposté por el caballo ganador** I bet on the winning horse • **apuesto a que no viene** I bet he won't come

apóstol *sm literal & figurado* apostle

apóstrofo *sm* GRAMÁTICA apostrophe

apoteósico, ca *adj* tremendous ☿ *Los adjetivos ingleses son invariables.*

apoyar *vt* ❶ [*inclinar*] to rest • **apoya tus piernas en la mesa de centro** rest your legs on the coffee table ❷ *figurado* [*basar, respaldar*] to support • **yo apoyo al candidato progresista** I'm supporting the progressive candidate

■ **apoyarse** *v pronominal* ❶ [*sostenerse*] • **apoyarse en** to lean on • **se apoyó en la pared** he leaned against the wall ❷ *figurado* [*basarse*] • **apoyarse en a)** [*sujeto: tesis, conclusiones*] to be based on ; to rest on **b)** [*sujeto: persona*] to base your arguments on • **sus conclusiones se apoyan en los resultados de años de investigación** his conclusions are based on the results of years of investigation ❸ [*respaldarse*] to support one another

apoyo *sm literal & figurado* support

apreciable *adj* ❶ [*perceptible*] appreciable ❷ *figurado* [*estimable*] worthy ☿ *Los adjetivos ingleses son invariables.*

apreciación *sf* ❶ [*consideración*] appreciation ❷ [*estimación*] evaluation

apreciar *vt* ❶ [*valorar*] to appreciate ❷ [*sopesar*] to evaluate ❸ [*sentir afecto por*] to think highly of ❹ [*percibir*] to tell ; to make out

aprecio *sm* esteem

aprehender *vt* [*coger - persona*] to apprehend ; [- *alijo, mercancía*] to seize

aprehensión *sf* ❶ [*de persona*] arrest ; capture ❷ [*de alijo, mercancía*] seizure

apremiante *adj* urgent ☿ *Los adjetivos ingleses son invariables.*

apremiar ◆ *vt* [*meter prisa*] • **apremiar a alguien para que haga algo** to urge somebody to do something • **nos apremiaron para que viniéramos cuanto antes** we were urged to come as soon as possible

◆ *vi* [*ser urgente*] to be pressing

apremio *sm* [*urgencia*] urgency

aprender ◆ *vt* ❶ [*estudiar*] to learn ❷ [*memorizar*] to memorize

◆ *vi* • **aprender (a hacer algo)** to learn (to do something) • **hoy aprendí a nadar** I learned to swim today

aprendiz, za *sm, f* ❶ [*ayudante*] apprentice ; trainee ❷ [*novato*] beginner

aprendizaje *sm* ❶ [*acción*] learning ❷ [*tiempo, situación*] apprenticeship

aprensión *sf* • **aprensión (por) a)** [*miedo*] apprehension (about) **b)** [*escrúpulo*] squeamishness (about)

aprensivo, va *adj* ❶ [*miedoso*] apprehensive ❷ [*hipocondríaco*] hypochondriac ☿ *Los adjetivos ingleses son invariables.*

apresar *vt* ❶ [*sujeto: animal*] to catch ❷ [*sujeto: persona*] to capture

apretado, da *adj* ❶ [*generalmente*] tight ❷ [*triunfo*] narrow ❸ [*carrera*] close ❹ [*caligrafía*] cramped ❺ [*apiñado*] packed ☿ *Los adjetivos ingleses son invariables.*

apretar ◆ *vt* ❶ [*oprimir - botón, tecla*] to press ; [- *gatillo*] to pull ; [- *nudo, tuerca, cinturón*] to tighten • **apriete el botón rojo** press the red button • **el zapato me aprieta** my shoe is pinching ❷ [*estrechar*] to squeeze • **¡me estás apretando la mano muy fuerte!** you're squeezing my hand too tightly! ❸ [*abrazar*] to hug ❹ [*comprimir - ropa, objetos*] to pack tight ❺ [*juntar - dientes*] to grit ; [- *labios*] to press together

◆ *vi* [*calor, lluvia*] to intensify

apretón *sm* [*estrechamiento*] squeeze ❱ **apretón de manos** handshake

aprieto *sm figurado* fix ; difficult situation • **poner en un aprieto a alguien** to put somebody in a difficult position • **verse** o **estar en un aprieto** to be in a fix

aprisa *adv* quickly

aprobación *sf* approval

aprobar *vt* ❶ [*proyecto, moción, medida*] to approve • **me aprobaron las vacaciones** they approved my vacation request ❷ [*ley*] to pass ❸ [*comportamiento* ETC] to approve of ❹ [*examen, asignatura*] to pass • **me aprobaron en matemática** I passed math class

aprobar de alguien

- **Yes, exactly!** ¡Sí, eso es!
- **I think so too!** ¡Pienso lo mismo!

- **That's what I believe too!** ¡Pienso lo mismo!
- **Good idea!** ¡Buena idea!
- **That's a really good idea!** ¡Es una excelente idea!
- **Fantastic!** ¡Estupendo!

apropiado, da *adj* suitable ; appropriate ⚲ *Los adjetivos ingleses son invariables.*

aprovechable *adj* usable ⚲ *Los adjetivos ingleses son invariables.*

aprovechado, da *adj* ❶ [*oportunista*] • **es muy aprovechado** he's always taking advantage of other people ❷ [*bien empleado - tiempo*] well-spent ; [- *espacio*] well-planned ⚲ *Los adjetivos ingleses son invariables.*

aprovechamiento *sm* [*utilización*] use

aprovechar ◆ *vt* ❶ [*generalmente*] to make the most of • **aprovéchalo mientras puedas** make the most of it while you can ❷ [*oferta, ocasión*] to take advantage of ❸ [*conocimientos, experiencia*] to use ; to make use of ❹ [*lo inservible*] to put to good use
◆ *vi* [*ser provechoso*] to be beneficial

aprox. (*abreviatura escrita de* aproximadamente) approx.

aproximación *sf* ❶ [*acercamiento*] approach ❷ [*en cálculo*] approximation

aproximadamente *adv* approximately

aproximado, da *adj* approximate ⚲ *Los adjetivos ingleses son invariables.*

aproximar *vt* to move closer

aptitud *sf* ability ; aptitude • **tener aptitud para algo** to have an aptitude for something

apto, ta *adj* ❶ [*adecuado, conveniente*] • **apto (para)** suitable (for) ❷ [*capacitado - intelectualmente*] able ; [- *físicamente*] fit ❸ CINE • **apto/no apto para menores** appropriate/inappropriate for children • **no es apto para niños** it's not appropriate for children ⚲ *Los adjetivos ingleses son invariables.*

apto. (*abreviatura escrita de* apartamento) Apt.

apuesta *sf* bet • **hicimos una apuesta** we made a bet

apuesto, ta *adj* dashing ⚲ *Los adjetivos ingleses son invariables.*

apuntalar *vt* literal & figurado to underpin

apuntar *vt* ❶ [*anotar*] to write down • **déjame apuntar tu teléfono** let me write down your number • **apuntar a alguien** [*en lista*] to put somebody down ❷ [*dirigir - dedo*] to point • **no apuntes con el dedo, que es mala educación** don't point, it's rude ; [- *arma*] to aim • **apuntar a alguien a)** [*con el dedo*] to point at somebody **b)** [*con un arma*] to aim at somebody ❸ TEATRO to prompt ❹ figurado [*indicar*] to point out

apunte *sm* [*nota*] note
■ **apuntes** *smpl* EDUCACIÓN notes • **tomar apuntes** to take notes

apuñalar *vt* to stab

apurado, da *adj* ❶ [*necesitado*] in need • **apurado de** short of ❷ [*avergonzado*] embarrassed ❸ [*difícil*] awkward ❹ [*con prisa*] • **estar apurado** to be in a hurry ⚲ *Los adjetivos ingleses son invariables.*

apurar *vt* ❶ [*agotar*] to finish off ❷ [*existencias, la paciencia*] to exhaust ❸ [*meter prisa*] to hurry ❹ [*preocupar*] to trouble ❺ [*avergonzar*] to embarrass
■ **apurarse** *v pronominal* ❶ [*preocuparse*] • **apurarse (por)** to worry (about) ❷ [*darse prisa*] to hurry • **¡apúrate!** hurry up!

apuro *sm* ❶ [*dificultad*] fix • **estar en apuros** to be in a tight spot • **nos vimos en apuros anoche** we found ourselves in a jam last night ❷ [*penuria*] hardship ⚲ *incontable* ❸ [*vergüenza*] embarrassment • **me da apuro (decírselo)** I'm embarrassed (to tell her)

aquel *adj demostrativo* that, *plural* those • **está en aquel cajón** it's in that drawer • **en aquellos días vivía en México** in those days he lived in Mexico

aquél *pronombre demostrativo* ❶ [*ése*] that (one) ; those (ones) *pl* • **este cuadro me gusta pero aquél del fondo no** I like this picture, but I don't like that one at the back • **pásame aquél, por favor** pass me that one, please • **aquél fue mi último día en Londres** that was my last day in London ❷ [*nombrado antes*] the former ❸ [*con oraciones relativas*] whoever ; anyone who • **aquél que quiera hablar que levante la mano** whoever wishes o anyone wishing to speak should raise their hand • **aquéllos que...** those who...

aquello *pronombre demostrativo* that • **aquello de su mujer es una mentira** all that about his wife is a lie • **¿qué fue aquello que me dijiste hace un rato?** what was that you told me a while ago?

aquí *adv* ❶ [*generalmente*] here • **no eres de por aquí, ¿verdad?** you're not from around here, are you? • **aquí abajo/arriba** down/up here • **aquí dentro/fuera** in/out here • **aquí mismo** right here • **de aquí para allá** [*de un lado a otro*] to and fro • **por aquí** over here ❷ [*ahora*] now • **de aquí a mañana** between now and tomorrow • **de aquí a poco** shortly ; soon • **de aquí a un mes** a month from now ; in a month

árabe ◆ *adj* Arab ; Arabian ⚲ *Los adjetivos ingleses son invariables.*
◆ *smf* [*persona*] Arab
◆ *sm* [*lengua*] Arabic

Arabia Saudí, Arabia Saudita *nombre propio* Saudi Arabia

arábigo, ga *adj* ❶ [*de Arabia*] Arab ; Arabian ❷ [*numeración*] Arabic ⚲ *Los adjetivos ingleses son invariables.*

arado *sm* plow

arancel *sm* tariff

arándano *sm* blueberry ▶ **arándano rojo/agrio** cranberry

arandela *sf* TECNOLOGÍA washer

araña *sf* [*animal*] spider

arañar *vt* [*generalmente*] to scratch • **el gato arañó la mejilla de la niña** the cat scratched the little girl's cheek

arañazo *sm* scratch

arar *vt* to plow

arbitraje *sm* ❶ DEPORTE [*en futbol* ETC] refereeing; [*en tenis*] umpiring ❷ DERECHO arbitration

arbitrar ◆ *vt* ❶ DEPORTE [*en futbol* ETC] to referee; [*en tenis*] to umpire ❷ DERECHO to arbitrate

◆ *vi* ❶ DEPORTE [*en futbol* ETC] to referee; [*en tenis*] to umpire ❷ DERECHO to arbitrate

arbitrariedad *sf* [*cualidad*] arbitrariness

arbitrario, ria *adj* arbitrary ⚲ *Los adjetivos ingleses son invariables.*

árbitro *sm* ❶ DEPORTE [*en futbol* ETC] referee • **el árbitro le mostró una tarjeta amarilla** the referee gave him a yellow card • **es árbitra de tenis** she's a tennis umpire ❱ **árbitro asistente** assistant referee; [*en tenis*] umpire ❷ DERECHO arbitrator

árbol *sm* ❶ BOTÁNICA tree ❱ **árbol genealógico** family tree ❱ **árbol de Navidad** Christmas tree ❷ TECNOLOGÍA shaft ❱ **árbol de levas** camshaft ❸ NÁUTICA mast

los árboles

el abeto	the fir tree
el arce	the maple
el bambú	the bamboo
el cerezo	the cherry tree
el chabacano	the apricot tree
el durazno	the peach tree
el haya	the beech tree
el manzano	the apple tree
el naranjo	the orange tree
el olivo	the olive tree
la palmera	the palm tree
el peral	the pear tree
el pino	the pine tree
el plátano	the banana tree
el roble	the oak tree

arboleda *sf* grove

arbusto *sm* bush; shrub

arca *sf* [*arcón*] chest

arcaico, ca *adj* archaic ⚲ *Los adjetivos ingleses son invariables.*

arcén *sm* ❶ [*de autopista*] shoulder ❷ [*de carretera*] verge

archiduque, esa *sm, f* archduke, *femenino* archduchess

archipiélago *sm* archipelago

archivar *vt* [*guardar - documento, fichero* ETC] to file • **lo voy a archivar en la T** I'll file it under "T"

archivo *sm* ❶ [*lugar*] archive ❷ [*documentos*] archives *pl* • **los archivos históricos** the historical archives ❸ [*informe, ficha*] file ❹ INFORMÁTICA file • **este archivo sólo ocupa 30Kb** this file is only 30Kb

arcilla *sf* clay

arco *sm* ❶ GEOMETRÍA arc ❱ **arco iris** rainbow ❷ ARQUITECTURA arch ❱ **arco de herradura** horseshoe arch ❱ **arco triunfal** o **de triunfo** triumphal arch ❸ MILITAR & MÚSICA bow • **puso una flecha en el arco** he placed an

arrow in the bow ❹ [*en futbol*] goal • **pateó el balón hacia el arco** he kicked the ball toward the goal

arder *vi* ❶ to burn ❷ [*sin llama*] to smolder • **arder de** *figurado* to burn with

expresión **está que arde a)** [*persona*] he's fuming **b)** [*reunión*] it's getting pretty heated

ardiente *adj* ❶ [*generalmente*] burning ❷ [*líquido*] scalding ❸ [*admirador, defensor*] ardent ⚲ *Los adjetivos ingleses son invariables.*

ardilla *sf* squirrel

ardor *sm* ❶ [*quemazón*] burning (sensation) ❱ **ardor de estómago** heartburn ❷ *figurado* [*entusiasmo*] fervor

arduo, dua *adj* arduous ⚲ *Los adjetivos ingleses son invariables.*

área *sf* ❶ [*generalmente*] area ❱ **área de libre cambio** ECONOMÍA free trade area ❱ **área metropolitana** metropolitan area ❷ DEPORTE ❱ **área (de castigo** o **penalti)** (penalty) area

arena *sf* ❶ [*de playa* ETC] sand • **hicimos un castillo de arena** we built a sand castle ❱ **arenas movedizas** quicksand ⚲ *incontable* ❷ [*para luchar*] arena ❸ TAUROMAQUIA bullring

arenal *sm* sandy ground ⚲ *incontable*

arenoso, sa *adj* sandy ⚲ *Los adjetivos ingleses son invariables.*

arenque *sm* herring

arete *sm* earring

argamasa *sf* mortar

Argelia *nombre propio* Algeria

Argentina *nombre propio* Argentina

argentino, na *adj* & *sm, f* Argentinian ⚲ *Los adjetivos ingleses son invariables.*

argolla *sf* [*aro*] (large) ring • **una argolla de oro** a gold ring

argot *sm* ❶ [*popular*] slang ❷ [*técnico*] jargon

argumentación *sf* line of argument

argumentar *vt* ❶ [*teoría, opinión*] to argue ❷ [*razones, excusas*] to allege

argumento *sm* ❶ [*razonamiento*] argument • **presentó sus argumentos en contra de la nueva ley** he presented his arguments against the new law ❷ [*trama*] plot • **el argumento de la película** the plot of the movie

aridez *sf* ❶ [*generalmente*] dryness ❷ [*de zona, clima*] aridity

árido, da *adj* ❶ [*generalmente*] dry ❷ [*zona, clima*] arid ⚲ *Los adjetivos ingleses son invariables.*

Aries ◆ *sm* [*zodiaco*] Aries

◆ *smf* [*persona*] Aries

arisco, ca *adj* surly ⚲ *Los adjetivos ingleses son invariables.*

arista *sf* edge

aristocracia *sf* aristocracy

aristócrata *smf* aristocrat

aritmético, ca *adj* arithmetic ⚲ *Los adjetivos ingleses son invariables.*

■ **aritmética** *sf* arithmetic

arma *sf* ❶ [*instrumento*] weapon ▶ **arma biológica** biological weapon ▶ **arma blanca** blade ▶ **arma de fuego** firearm ▶ **arma homicida** murder weapon ▶ **arma nuclear** nuclear weapon ▶ **arma química** chemical weapon ▶ **armas de destrucción masiva** weapons of mass destruction ❷ *figurado* [*medio*] weapon

armada *sf* ❶ [*marina*] navy ❷ [*escuadra*] fleet

armadillo *sm* armadillo

armado, da *adj* ❶ [*con armas*] armed ❷ [*con armazón*] reinforced ⚲ *Los adjetivos ingleses son invariables.*

armadura *sf* ❶ [*de barco, tejado*] framework ❷ [*de gafas*] frame ❸ [*de guerrero*] armor

armamento *sm* [*armas*] arms *pl*

armar *vt* ❶ [*montar - mueble* ETC] to assemble • **ayúdame a armar el escritorio** help me assemble the desk; [- *tienda*] to pitch ❷ [*ejército, personas*] to arm • **armaron a la población** they armed the population ❸ *familiar & figurado* [*provocar*] to cause • **armarla** *familiar* to cause trouble

■ **armarse** *v pronominal* ❶ [*con armas*] to arm yourself • **se armaron para la guerra** they armed themselves for war ❷ [*prepararse*] • **armarse de** [*valor, paciencia*] to summon up • **¡hay que armarse de paciencia!** you have to summon up all your patience!

expresión **se armó la gorda** o **la de San Quintín** o **la de Dios es Cristo** *familiar* all hell broke loose

armario *sm* [*para ropa, objetos*] closet ▶ **armario empotrado** fitted closet • **salir del armario** *familiar* to come out of the closet

armatoste *sm* ❶ [*mueble, objeto*] unwieldy object ❷ [*máquina*] contraption

armazón *sf* ❶ [*generalmente*] frame ❷ [*de avión, coche*] chassis ❸ [*de edificio*] skeleton

armiño *sm* ❶ [*piel*] ermine ❷ [*animal*] stoat

armisticio *sm* armistice

armonía *sf* harmony • **estar en armonía** to be in harmony

armónico, ca *adj* harmonic ⚲ *Los adjetivos ingleses son invariables.*

■ **armónica** *sf* harmonica

armonioso, sa *adj* harmonious ⚲ *Los adjetivos ingleses son invariables.*

armonizar ◆ *vt* ❶ [*concordar*] to match ❷ MÚSICA to harmonize

◆ *vi* [*concordar*] • **armonizar con** to match

arnés *sm* armor

aro *sm* ❶ [*círculo*] hoop • **el león pasó por el aro** the lion jumped through the hoop ❷ TECNOLOGÍA ring ▶ **los aros olímpicos** the Olympic rings ❸ [*pendiente*] earring • **lleva un aro** he wears an earring

expresión **entrar** o **pasar por el aro** to knuckle under

aroma *sm* ❶ [*generalmente*] aroma • **el intenso aroma del café** the intense aroma of coffee • **el aroma dulce de las flores** the sweet scent of the flowers ❷ [*de vino*] bouquet ❸ COCINA flavoring

aromático, ca *adj* aromatic ⚲ *Los adjetivos ingleses son invariables.*

aromatizador *sm* atomizer

arpa *sf* harp

arpón *sm* harpoon

arquear *vt* ❶ [*generalmente*] to bend ❷ [*cejas, espalda, lomo*] to arch

arqueología *sf* archeology

arqueólogo, ga *sm, f* archeologist

arquero *sm* ❶ DEPORTE & MILITAR archer ❷ [*portero de futbol*] goalkeeper • **el arquero paró el penal** the goalkeeper saved the penalty

arquetipo *sm* archetype

arquitecto, ta *sm, f* architect • **mi padre es arquitecto** my father is an architect

arquitectura *sf* architecture

arraigado, da *adj* ❶ [*costumbre, idea*] deeply rooted ❷ [*persona*] established ⚲ *Los adjetivos ingleses son invariables.*

arraigar *vi* literal & figurado to take root

arraigo *sm* roots *pl* • **tener mucho arraigo** to be deeply rooted

arrancar ◆ *vt* ❶ [*desarraigar - árbol*] to uproot; [- *malas hierbas, flor*] to pull up • **trata de no arrancar las flores** try not to pull up the flowers ❷ [*quitar, separar*] to tear o rip off ❸ [*cable, página, pelo*] to tear out • **arranqué todas las páginas del libro** I tore out all the pages of the book ❹ [*cartel, cortinas*] to tear down ❺ [*muela*] to pull out ❻ [*ojos*] to gouge out ❼ [*arrebatar*] • **arrancar algo a alguien** to grab o snatch something from somebody ❽ AUTOMÓVILES & TECNOLOGÍA to start ❾ INFORMÁTICA to start up ❿ figurado [*obtener*] • **arrancar algo a alguien a)** [*confesión, promesa, secreto*] to extract something from somebody **b)** [*sonrisa, dinero, ovación*] to get something out of somebody **c)** [*suspiro, carcajada*] to bring something from somebody

◆ *vi* ❶ [*partir*] to leave • **el tren arranca en un minuto** the train leaves in one minute ❷ [*sujeto: máquina, coche*] to start • **el coche no arranca** the car won't start ❸ [*provenir*] • **arrancar de** to stem from

arranque *sm* ❶ [*comienzo*] start ❷ AUTOMÓVILES starter motor ❸ figurado [*arrebato*] fit

arrasar *vt* to devastate

arrastrar ◆ *vt* ❶ [*generalmente*] to drag along • **Pedro arrastró su mochila por el suelo** Pedro dragged his backpack on the floor ❷ [*pies*] to drag ❸ [*carro, vagón*] to pull ❹ [*sujeto: corriente, aire*] to carry away ❺ figurado [*convencer*] to win over • **arrastrar a alguien a algo/a hacer algo** to lead somebody into something/to do something • **dejarse arrastrar por algo/alguien** to allow yourself to be swayed by something/somebody ❻ INFORMÁTICA to drag • **arrastrar y soltar algo** to drag and drop something ❼ figurado [*producir*] to bring

◆ *vi* [*rozar el suelo*] to drag (along) the ground

arrastre *sm* ❶ [*acarreo*] dragging ❷ [*pesca*] trawling

arrebatar *vt* ❶ [*arrancar*] • **arrebatar algo a alguien** to snatch something from somebody ❷ *figurado* [*cautivar*] to captivate

arrebato *sm* ❶ [*arranque*] fit • **un arrebato de amor** a crush ❷ [*furia*] rage

arreciar *vi* ❶ [*temporal* ETC] to get worse ❷ *figurado* [*críticas* ETC] to intensify

arrecife *sm* reef

arreglado, da *adj* ❶ [*reparado*] fixed ❷ [*ropa*] mended ❸ [*ordenado*] tidy ❹ [*bien vestido*] smart ❺ [*solucionado*] sorted out ❻ *figurado* [*precio*] reasonable ⚲ *Los adjetivos ingleses son invariables.*

arreglar *vt* ❶ [*reparar*] to fix • **Bruno arregló mi reloj** Bruno fixed my watch ❷ [*ordenar*] to tidy (up) • **arreglemos la casa antes de que lleguen** let's tidy up the house before they arrive ❸ [*solucionar*] to sort out • **no te preocupes, he arreglado todo** don't worry, I've sorted everything out ❹ [*ropa*] to mend ❺ MÚSICA to arrange ❻ [*acicalar*] to smarten up ❼ [*cabello*] to do

■ **arreglarse** *v pronominal* ❶ [*apañarse*] • **arreglarse (con algo)** to make do (with something) • **arreglárselas (para hacer algo)** to manage (to do something) • **yo me las arreglo solo** I'll manage on my own ❷ [*acicalarse*] to smarten up • **lleva dos horas en el baño arreglándose** she's been in the bathroom getting ready for two hours ❸ [*solucionarse*] • **las cosas no se arreglan solas** things don't just sort themselves out

arreglo *sm* ❶ [*reparación*] repair • **el coche requiere bastantes arreglos** the car needs a lot of repairs ❷ [*de ropa*] mending ❸ [*solución*] solution • **tener arreglo** to have a solution • **esto no tiene arreglo** there's no solution to this problem ❹ MÚSICA (musical) arrangement ❺ [*acuerdo*] agreement • **tengo un arreglo con uno de los guardias** I have a little arrangement with one of the guards • **llegar a un arreglo** to reach agreement

arremetida *sf* attack

arrendar *vt* ❶ [*dar en arriendo*] to let ❷ [*tomar en arriendo*] to rent

arrendatario, ria *sm, f* tenant

arrepentido, da ◆ *adj* repentant ⚲ *Los adjetivos ingleses son invariables.*

◆ *sm, f* POLÍTICA *person who renounces terrorist activities*

arrepentimiento *sm* regret ; repentance

arrepentirse *v pronominal* to repent • **me arrepiento de no haberlo hecho antes** I regret not having done it sooner

arrestar *vt* to arrest • **queda arrestado** you're under arrest

arriar *vt* to lower

arriba ◆ *adv* ❶ [*posición - encima de*] above; [- *en edificio*] upstairs • **mira en el cajón de arriba** look in the top drawer • **vive (en el departamento de) arriba** she lives upstairs • **está aquí/allí arriba** it's up here/there • **tu hermano está arriba** your brother is upstairs • **arriba del todo** right at the top • **más arriba** further up ❷ [*dirección*] up • **ve arriba** [*en edificio*] go upstairs • **hacia/para arriba** up ; upwards • **calle/escaleras arriba** up the street/stairs • **río arriba** upstream ❸ [*en un texto*] above • **'el arriba mencionado...'** the above-mentioned...

expresión **de arriba abajo a)** [*cosa*] from top to bottom **b)** [*persona*] from head to toe ▶ **mirar a alguien de arriba abajo** [*con desdén*] to look somebody up and down

◆ *preposición* • **arriba (de)** [*encima de*] on top of

◆ *exclamación* • **¡arriba...!** up (with)...! • **¡arriba los mineros!** up (with) the miners! • **¡arriba las manos!** hands up!

arriesgado, da *adj* [*peligroso*] risky ⚲ *Los adjetivos ingleses son invariables.*

arriesgar *vt* ❶ to risk • **arriesgó su vida para salvarme** she risked her life to save me • **no se arriesgó a provocarla** he didn't risk provoking her ❷ [*hipótesis*] to suggest

■ **arriesgarse** *v pronominal* to risk • **no queremos arriesgarnos** we don't want to risk it • **los expertos no se arriesgaron a realizar un pronóstico de la situación** experts wouldn't risk forecasting the situation

arrimar *vt* [*acercar*] to move o bring closer • **arrima tu silla para que te pueda ver mejor** bring your chair closer so I can see you better • **arrimar algo a** [*pared, mesa*] to move something up against

■ **arrimarse** *v pronominal* to move closer • **si tienes frío, arrímate al fuego** if you're cold, move closer to the fire

arrinconar *vt* ❶ [*apartar*] to put in a corner ❷ [*abandonar*] to discard ❸ *figurado* [*persona dar de lado a*] to cold-shoulder; [*acorralar*] to corner

arrodillarse *v pronominal* ❶ to kneel down • **nos arrodillamos frente al altar** we kneeled down in front of the altar ❷ *figurado* to go down on your knees

arrogancia *sf* arrogance

arrogante *adj* arrogant • **tu esposa es muy arrogante** your wife is very arrogant ⚲ *Los adjetivos ingleses son invariables.*

arrojar *vt* ❶ [*lanzar*] to throw • **arrojaron la basura por la ventana** they threw the trash out the window ❷ [*con violencia*] to hurl ❸ [*despedir - humo*] to send out; [- *olor*] to give off; [- *lava*] to spew out ❹ [*echar*] • **arrojar a alguien de** to throw somebody out of • **lo arrojaron de la fiesta** he was thrown out of the party ❺ [*resultado*] to produce ❻ [*vomitar*] to throw up

arrojo *sm* courage

arrollador, ra *adj* ❶ overwhelming ❷ [*belleza, personalidad*] dazzling ⚲ *Los adjetivos ingleses son invariables.*

arrollar *vt* ❶ [*atropellar*] to run over ❷ [*tirar - sujeto: agua, viento*] to sweep away ❸ [*vencer*] to crush

arropar *vt* ❶ [*con ropa*] to wrap up ❷ [*en cama*] to tuck up

arrorró, arrorrú *sm* familiar lullaby

arroyo *sm* [*riachuelo*] stream • **tomamos agua de un pequeño arroyo** we drank water from a small stream

arroz *sm* rice ▶ **arroz blanco** white rice ▶ **arroz con leche** rice pudding ▶ **arroz integral** brown rice

arruga *sf* ❶ [*en ropa, papel*] crease • **su camisa estaba llena de arrugas** his shirt was really creased ❷ [*en piel*] wrinkle • **tiene muchas arrugas en la frente** he has a lot of wrinkles on his forehead

arrugar *vt* ❶ [*ropa, papel*] to crease ❷ [*piel*] to wrinkle

arruinar *vt* literal & figurado to ruin • **la lluvia arruinó la fiesta** the rain ruined the party

arsenal *sm* ❶ [*de barcos*] shipyard ❷ [*de armas*] arsenal ❸ [*de cosas*] array

arsénico *sm* arsenic

art. (*abreviatura escrita de* artículo) art

arte *sm o sf* ☺ *en singular generalmente m; en plural f* ❶ [*generalmente*] art • **las artes** the arts • **el arte moderno** modern art ▶ **arte abstracto** abstract art ▶ **arte dramático** drama ▶ **arte figurativo** figurative art ▶ **artes marciales** martial arts ❷ [*don*] artistry ❸ [*astucia*] cunning • **malas artes** trickery ☺ *incontable*

artefacto *sm* ❶ [*aparato*] device ❷ [*máquina*] machine

arteria *sf* literal & figurado artery

artesanal *adj* [*hecho a mano*] handmade ☺ *Los adjetivos ingleses son invariables.*

artesanía *sf* craftsmanship • **de artesanía** [*producto*] handmade

artesano, na *sm, f* craftsman, *femenino* craftswoman

ártico, ca *adj* arctic • **el océano Glacial Ártico** the Arctic Ocean ☺ *Los adjetivos ingleses son invariables.*

■ **Ártico** *sm* • **el Ártico** the Arctic

articulación *sf* ❶ ANATOMÍA & TECNOLOGÍA joint ❷ LINGÜÍSTICA articulation

articulado, da *adj* articulated ☺ *Los adjetivos ingleses son invariables.*

articular *vt* [*palabras, piezas*] to articulate

artículo *sm* [*generalmente*] article • **tienes que leer este artículo** you have to read this article ▶ **artículo básico** ECONOMÍA basic product ▶ **artículo de fondo** editorial; leader ▶ **artículo de primera necesidad** basic commodity

artífice *smf* figurado architect

artificial *adj* artificial ☺ *Los adjetivos ingleses son invariables.*

artificio *sm* ❶ figurado [*falsedad*] artifice ❷ [*artimaña*] trick

artillería *sf* artillery

artillero *sm* artilleryman

artilugio *sm* gadget

artimaña *sf* trick

artista *smf* ❶ [*generalmente*] artist • **cada cuadro va firmado por el artista** each painting is signed by the artist ❷ [*de espectáculos*] artiste ▶ **artista de cine** movie actor, *femenino* actress

artístico, ca *adj* artistic ☺ *Los adjetivos ingleses son invariables.*

artritis *sf* arthritis

arzobispo *sm* archbishop

as *sm* ❶ [*carta, dado*] ace • **el as de picas** the ace of spades ❷ [*campeón*] • **un as del volante** an ace driver

expresión **ser un as** to be brilliant

asa *sf* handle • **levántalo de las asas** lift it by the handles

asado, da *adj* roasted • **castañas asadas** roasted chestnuts ☺ *Los adjetivos ingleses son invariables.*

■ **asado** *sm* [*carne*] roast • **asado de cordero** roast lamb

asador *sm* ❶ [*aparato*] roaster ❷ [*varilla*] spit

asalariado, da ◆ *adj* wage-earning ☺ *Los adjetivos ingleses son invariables.*

◆ *sm, f* wage earner

asaltante *smf* ❶ [*agresor*] attacker ❷ [*atracador*] robber

asaltar *vt* ❶ [*atacar*] to attack • **me asaltaron a dos cuadras de mi casa** I was attacked two blocks from my house ❷ [*castillo, ciudad* ETC] to storm ❸ [*robar*] to rob • **asaltaron el banco** they robbed the bank

asalto *sm* ❶ [*ataque*] attack ❷ [*de castillo, ciudad*] storming ❸ [*robo*] robbery ❹ DEPORTE round

asamblea *sf* ❶ assembly • **la asamblea legislativa entra en sesión** the legislative assembly is in session ❷ POLÍTICA meeting • **resolvieron el problema en asamblea** they solved the problem in a meeting

asar *vt* ❶ [*al horno*] to bake ❷ [*a la parrilla*] to grill ❸ [*en asador*] to roast

expresión **¡me estoy asando!** I'm boiling!

ascendencia *sf* ❶ [*linaje*] descent ❷ [*extracción social*] extraction ❸ figurado [*influencia*] ascendancy

ascender ◆ *vi* ❶ [*subir*] to climb • **ascendimos la montaña lentamente** we climbed the mountain slowly ❷ [*aumentar, elevarse*] to rise • **ascendieron las temperaturas** the temperatures rose ❸ [*en empleo, deportes*] • **ascender (a)** to be promoted (to) • **ascendió a gerente** he was promoted to manager ❹ [*totalizar*] • **ascender a** to come to • **los daños causados por el terremoto ascienden a cientos de millones de dólares** the damage done by the earthquake comes to hundreds of millions of dollars

◆ *vt* • **ascender a alguien (a)** to promote somebody (to) • **lo ascendieron a gerente** he was promoted to manager

ascendiente *smf* [*antepasado*] ancestor

ascensión *sf* ascent

ascenso *sm* ❶ [*en empleo, deportes*] promotion ❷ [*escalada*] ascent ❸ [*de precios, temperaturas*] rise

ascensor *sm* elevator

asco *sm* [*sensación*] disgust • **me dan asco los cigarros** I find cigarettes disgusting • **siento asco** I feel sick • **¡qué asco de tiempo!** what foul weather! • **me da asco** I find it disgusting • **¡qué asco!** how disgusting!

expresión **hacer ascos a** to turn your nose up at

A

ascua *sf* ember

expresión en o sobre ascuas on tenterhooks

aseado, da *adj* ❶ [*limpio*] clean ❷ [*arreglado*] smart ♀: *Los adjetivos ingleses son invariables.*

asear *vt* to clean • **los sábados aseamos la casa** on Saturdays we clean the house

asediar *vt* ❶ to lay siege to ❷ *figurado* to pester

asedio *sm* ❶ siege ❷ *figurado* pestering

asegurar *vt* ❶ [*fijar*] to secure • **mejor asegurarlo con candado** it's better to secure it with a padlock ❷ [*garantizar*] to assure • **le aseguro que no fue así** I can assure you that it didn't happen like that • **te lo aseguro** I assure you • **asegurar a alguien que...** to assure somebody that... ❸ COMERCIO • **asegurar (contra)** to insure (against) • **aseguré mi casa contra incendios** I insured my house against fire • **asegurar algo en** [*cantidad*] to insure something for

■ **asegurarse** *v pronominal* [*cerciorarse*] • **asegurarse de que...** to make sure that... • **asegúrate de que cerraste la puerta** make sure you locked the door • **se aseguró de que nadie la hubiera seguido hasta allí** she made sure no one had followed her there

asemejar ■ **asemejar a** *vi* to be similar to ■ **asemejarse** *v pronominal* to be similar • **asemejarse a** to be similar to

asentamiento *sm* [*campamento*] settlement

asentar *vt* ❶ [*empresa, campamento*] to set up ❷ [*comunidad, pueblo*] to settle ❸ [*cimientos*] to lay

aseo *sm* ❶ [*acción*] cleaning ❷ [*cualidad*] cleanliness • **el aseo es muy importante** cleanliness is very important • **aseo personal** personal hygiene

■ **aseos** *smpl* restroom *sing*

aséptico, ca *adj* MEDICINA aseptic ♀: *Los adjetivos ingleses son invariables.*

asequible *adj* ❶ [*accesible, comprensible*] accessible ❷ [*precio, producto*] affordable ♀: *Los adjetivos ingleses son invariables.*

aserrar *vt* to saw

asesinar *vt* ❶ to murder • **asesinaron al gángster** the gangster was murdered ❷ [*rey, jefe de estado*] to assassinate • **asesinaron al presidente** the president was assassinated

asesinato *sm* ❶ murder ❷ [*de rey, jefe de estado*] assassination

asesino, na *sm, f* ❶ murderer, *femenino* murderess ❷ [*de rey, jefe de estado*] assassin ▸ **asesino en serie** serial killer

asesor, ra *sm, f* ❶ adviser ❷ FINANZAS consultant ▸ **asesor fiscal** tax consultant

asesorar *vt* ❶ to advise ❷ FINANZAS to provide with consultancy services

asesoría *sf* [*oficina*] consultant's office

asestar *vt* ❶ [*golpe*] to deal ❷ [*tiro*] to fire

asfalto *sm* asphalt

asfixia *sf* suffocation ; asphyxiation *culto*

asfixiar *vt* to suffocate • **casi me asfixio** I nearly suffocated

■ **asfixiarse** *v pronominal* to suffocate

así

◆ *adv*

❶ [*de esta manera*]

• **así es/fue como empezó todo** that's how it all began

• **era así de largo** it was this long

• **¡no seas así!** don't be like that!

• **me dijo que lo hiciera así** she told me to do it like this

• **algo así** something like that

• **y así todos los días** and that's the way it is every day

• **y así sucesivamente** and so on

• **¡así es!** that's it

• **¡así de fácil!** it's that easy!

• **así, así** so-so

• **así como así** just like that

• **¡así me gusta!** that's what I like to see!

❷ [*de este tipo*]

• **quiero uno así** I'd like one like that

◆ *conjunción*

• **no lo haré así me paguen** I wouldn't do it even if you paid me

◆ *adj invariable*

[*de este tipo*] like that

• **con vecinos así, uno vive más tranquilo** with neighbors like that, you can rest easy

♀ *Los adjetivos ingleses son invariables.*

■ **así como**

◆ *locución adverbial*

❶ [*tanto como*] as well as

• **habló de Lorca así como de poetas contemporáneos** he spoke about Lorca and also about contemporary poets

• **estaban sus padres así como sus hermanas** his parents were there as well as his sisters

❷ [*tan pronto como*] as soon as

• **llámame así como llegues** call me as soon as you get there

■ **así no más**

◆ *locución adverbial* familiar

❶ [*sin razón*]

• **ocurrió así no más** it happened just like that

❷ [*regular*]

• **¿cómo estás? — así no más** how are you? — not great

■ **así pues**

◆ *locución adverbial*

[*expresa la consecuencia*] so

• **no lo necesito, así pues, te lo devuelvo** I don't need it, so you can have it back

■ **así que**

◆ *locución conjuntiva*

❶ [*expresa la consecuencia*] so

• **estoy enferma así que no voy a ir** I'm ill, so I won't be going

A

• **así que te habló mal de mí** so, he spoke badly of me

❷ [*tan pronto como*] once
• **me iré así que haya terminado** I'll leave once I've finished

■ **así y todo**
♦ *locución adverbial*
even so
• **no tienen dinero, y así y todo, han ido a esquiar** they don't have any money, and even so, they've gone skiing

Asia *nombre propio* Asia

asiático, ca *adj & sm, f* Asian ☼ *Los adjetivos ingleses son invariables.*

asiduidad *sf* frequency

asiduo, dua *adj & sm, f* regular ☼ *Los adjetivos ingleses son invariables.*

asiento *sm* [*en casa, teatro*] seat • **tome asiento** take a seat

asignación *sf* ❶ [*atribución*] allocation ❷ [*sueldo*] salary

asignar *vt* ❶ [*atribuir*] • **asignar algo a alguien** to assign something to somebody ❷ [*destinar*] • **asignar a alguien a** to send somebody to

asilado, da *sm, f* ▶ resident in a retirement home, convalescent home ETC

asilo *sm* ❶ [*hospicio*] home ▶ **asilo de ancianos** retirement home ❷ *figurado* [*amparo*] asylum ▶ **asilo político** political asylum ❸ [*hospedaje*] accommodation

asimilación *sf* assimilation

asimilar *vt* to take in • **es difícil asimilar tanta información** it's hard to take in so much information

asimismo *adv* ❶ [*también*] also ❷ ☼ *a principio de frase* likewise

asir *vt* to grasp

asistencia *sf* ❶ [*presencia - acción*] attendance ; [*- hecho*] presence ❷ [*ayuda*] assistance ▶ **asistencia jurídica** legal advice ▶ **asistencia médica** medical attention ▶ **asistencia sanitaria** health care ▶ **asistencia técnica** technical assistance ❸ [*afluencia*] audience ❹ DEPORTE assist

asistente *smf* ❶ [*ayudante*] assistant • **mandó a su asistente por el café** she sent her assistant out for coffee ▶ **asistente personal** INFORMÁTICA personal digital assistant ; PDA ▶ **asistente social** social worker ❷ [*presente*] person present • **los asistentes** the people present

asistido, da *adj* ❶ AUTOMÓVILES power ☼ *Sólo se usa delante del sustantivo.* • **dirección asistida** power steering ❷ INFORMÁTICA computer-assisted

asistir ♦ *vt* to attend to
♦ *vi* • **asistir a** to attend • **¿cuántas personas asistieron a la boda?** how many people attended the wedding?

asma *sf* asthma

asno *sm* literal & figurado ass

asociación *sf* association • **estamos trabajando en asociación con la policía** we're working in association with the police ▶ **asociación de padres de alumnos** parent-teacher association ▶ **asociación de vecinos** residents' association

asociar *vt* to associate • **asocio ese olor con mi niñez** I associate that smell with my childhood

■ **asociarse** *v pronominal* ❶ [*relacionarse*] • **asociarse con alguien** to go into partnership with somebody ❷ [*unirse*] to join • **se asoció al gimnasio** she joined the gym

asolar *vt* to devastate

asomar ♦ *vi* ❶ [*generalmente*] to peep up ❷ [*del interior de algo*] to peep out
♦ *vt* to stick • **asomar la cabeza por la ventana** to stick your head out of the window • **asómate por la ventana para que lo puedas ver** lean out the window so you can see it

asombrar *vt* ❶ [*causar admiración*] to amaze ❷ [*causar sorpresa*] to surprise

asombro *sm* ❶ [*admiración*] amazement ❷ [*sorpresa*] surprise

expresar su asombro

• **What a surprise!** ¡Qué sorpresa!
• **Who'd have thought it?** ¿Quién lo hubiera creído?
• **What a coincidence!** ¡Qué casualidad!
• **I'm amazed.** Me extraña.
• **That's really strange!** ¡Qué curioso!
• **I'd never have believed that.** Nunca me lo hubiera imaginado.

asombroso, sa *adj* ❶ [*sensacional*] amazing ❷ [*sorprendente*] surprising ☼ *Los adjetivos ingleses son invariables.*

asomo *sm* ❶ [*indicio*] hint ❷ [*de esperanza*] glimmer

aspecto *sm* ❶ [*apariencia*] appearance • **tiene un aspecto muy refinado** he has a very refined appearance ❷ [*faceta*] aspect • **me interesa más el aspecto creativo** I'm more interested in the creative aspect • **en todos los aspectos** in every respect

aspereza *sf* ❶ roughness ❷ figurado sourness

áspero, ra *adj* ❶ [*rugoso*] rough • **tengo la piel áspera** my skin feels rough ❷ [*voz*] harsh • **¡qué voz más áspera!** what a harsh voice! ❸ figurado [*desagradable*] sharp ☼ *Los adjetivos ingleses son invariables.*

aspersor *sm* ❶ [*para jardín*] sprinkler ❷ [*para cultivos*] sprayer

aspiración *sf* ❶ [*ambición*] LINGÜÍSTICA aspiration • **tengo aspiraciones de ser músico** my aspiration is to become a musician ❷ [*de aire - por una persona*] breathing in ; [*- por una máquina*] suction

aspiradora *sf* vacuum cleaner ▶ **pasar la aspiradora** to vacuum

aspirante *smf* • **aspirante (a) a)** candidate (for) **b)** [*en deportes, concursos*] contender (for)

aspirar ◆ *vt* to breathe in
◆ *vi* • **aspirar a algo** to aspire to something • **la película aspira al máximo galardón en el certamen** the movie aspires to the highest award in the competition

aspirina *sf* aspirin

asquear *vt* to disgust

asqueroso, sa *adj* disgusting • **es asqueroso cómo come** the way he eats is disgusting 💡 *Los adjetivos ingleses son invariables.*

asta *sf* ❶ [*de bandera*] flagpole ❷ [*de lanza*] shaft ❸ [*de brocha*] handle ❹ [*de toro*] horn

asterisco *sm* asterisk

astigmatismo *sm* astigmatism

astilla *sf* splinter • **tengo una astilla en el dedo** I have a splinter in my finger • **hacer astillas** *figurado* to smash to smithereens

astillero *sm* shipyard

astro *sm* ❶ ASTRONOMÍA heavenly body ❷ *figurado* star

astrofísica *sf* astrophysics 💡 *incontable*

astrología *sf* astrology

astrólogo, ga *sm, f* astrologer

astronauta *smf* astronaut • **cuando sea grande quiero ser astronauta** when I grow up I want to be an astronaut

astronomía *sf* astronomy

astrónomo, ma *sm, f* astronomer

astucia *sf* ❶ [*picardía*] cunning ❷ 💡 *generalmente pl* [*treta*] cunning trick

astuto, ta *adj* ❶ [*ladino, tramposo*] cunning ❷ [*sagaz, listo*] astute 💡 *Los adjetivos ingleses son invariables.*

asumir *vt* ❶ [*generalmente*] to assume • **hay que asumir que están bien** we have to assume they're fine • **asumió el papel de malo** he took on the role of bad guy • **no quiero asumir esa responsabilidad** I don't want to take on that responsibility ❷ [*aceptar*] to accept • **me cuesta asumir que se fue** I can't accept that she left

asunción *sf* assumption

asunto *sm* ❶ [*tema - general*] subject; [*- específico*] matter; • **estos son asuntos para la policía** these are matters for the police • **no es asunto tuyo** it's none of your business ▶ **asuntos a tratar** agenda *sing* ❷ [*de obra, libro*] theme ❸ [*cuestión, problema*] issue ❹ [*negocio*] business 💡 *incontable*

asustado, da *adj* frightened 💡 *Los adjetivos ingleses son invariables.*

asustar *vt* to frighten • **lo asustaron esos ruidos** those noises frightened him
■ **asustarse** *v pronominal* • **asustarse (de)** to be frightened o scared (of) • **si se asusta, llámeme** if you get scared, call me • **no se asusta de nada ni de nadie** she's not frightened of anything or anyone

atacar *vt* [*generalmente*] to attack • **nos atacaron con palos** they attacked us with sticks • **me ataca los nervios** *figurado* it gets on my nerves

atadura *sf* literal & figurado tie

atajar ◆ *vi* [*acortar*] • **atajar (por)** to take a short cut (through)
◆ *vt* ❶ [*contener*] to put a stop to ❷ [*hemorragia, inundación*] to stem

atajo *sm* ❶ [*camino corto, medio rápido*] short cut • **tomar un atajo** to take a short cut ❷ *despectivo* [*panda*] bunch

ataque *sm* ❶ [*generalmente*] DEPORTE attack • **el ataque nos tomó por sorpresa** the attack took us by surprise ❷ *figurado* [*acceso*] fit ▶ **ataque cardíaco** o **al corazón** heart attack ▶ **ataque de nervios** nervous breakdown

atar *vt* ❶ [*unir*] to tie (up) • **te ves bien con el pelo atado** you look good with your hair tied back • **átate los zapatos** tie your shoelaces ❷ *figurado* [*constreñir*] to tie down

atardecer ◆ *sm* dusk • **al atardecer** at dusk
◆ *v impersonal* to get dark • **apúrate que está atardeciendo** hurry up, it's getting dark

atareado, da *adj* busy 💡 *Los adjetivos ingleses son invariables.*

atascar *vt* to block (up)

atasco *sm* ❶ [*obstrucción*] blockage ❷ AUTOMÓVILES traffic jam

ataúd *sm* coffin

ataviar *vt* ❶ [*cosa*] to deck out ❷ [*persona*] to dress up

ate *sm* quince jelly

atemorizar *vt* to frighten
■ **atemorizarse** *v pronominal* to get frightened

atención ◆ *sf* ❶ [*interés*] attention • **prestar atención** to pay attention ▶ **atención al cliente** customer service department ▶ **atención personalizada** personalized service ▶ **atención psiquiátrica** psychiatric treatment ❷ [*cortesía*] attentiveness 💡 *incontable*
◆ *exclamación* • **¡atención (por favor)!** [*en aeropuerto, conferencia*] your attention please!

atender ◆ *vt* ❶ [*satisfacer - petición, ruego*] to attend to; [*- consejo, instrucciones*] to heed; [*- propuesta*] to agree to ❷ [*cuidar de - necesitados, invitados*] to look after; [*- enfermo*] to care for; [*- cliente*] to serve • **¿le atienden?** are you being served? • **¿lo puedo atender?** may I help you? • **atiende muy bien a sus pacientes** he takes good care of his patients • **ahora tengo que atender a un cliente** I have to attend to a client now
◆ *vi* [*estar atento*] • **atender (a)** to pay attention (to) • **atiende a lo que te digo** pay attention to what I'm saying • **no me estás atendiendo** you're not paying attention to me

atentado *sm* attack • **un atentado terrorista** a terrorist attack • **atentado contra alguien** attempt on somebody's life • **atentado contra algo** crime against something • **un atentado contra el presidente** an assassination attempt on the president

atentamente *adv* [*en cartas*] Sincerely

atentar *vi* • **atentar contra (la vida de) alguien** to make an attempt on somebody's life • **atentar contra algo** [*principio* ETC] to be a crime against something • **han atentado varias veces contra su vida** several attempts have been made on his life

atento, ta *adj* ❶ [*pendiente*] attentive • **es una estudiante muy atenta** she's a very attentive student • **estar atento a a)** [*explicación, programa, lección*] to pay attention to **b)** [*ruido, sonido*] to listen out for **c)** [*acontecimientos, cambios, avances*] to keep up with ❷ [*cortés*] thoughtful • **¡qué atento!** that's very thoughtful of you! ‍:💡: *Los adjetivos ingleses son invariables.*

atenuante *sm* DERECHO extenuating circumstance

atenuar *vt* ❶ [*generalmente*] to diminish ❷ [*dolor*] to ease ❸ [*luz*] to filter

ateo, a ◆ *adj* atheistic :💡: *Los adjetivos ingleses son invariables.*
◆ *sm, f* atheist

aterrador, ra *adj* terrifying :💡: *Los adjetivos ingleses son invariables.*

aterrar *vt* to terrify • **me aterra con sólo pensar en eso** it terrifies me just to think about it

aterrizaje *sm* landing • **el aterrizaje fue muy suave** the landing was very smooth ▶ **aterrizaje de emergencia** o **forzoso** emergency landing

aterrizar *vi* to land • **aterrizaremos en veinte minutos** we will be landing in twenty minutes

aterrorizar *vt* ❶ to terrify ❷ [*sujeto: agresor*] to terrorize • **esos dos matones aterrorizan a todos los otros niños** those two bullies terrorize all the other children

atiborrar *vt* to stuff full

ático *sm* ❶ [*para vivir*] penthouse ❷ [*desván*] attic

atípico, ca *adj* atypical :💡: *Los adjetivos ingleses son invariables.*

atisbar *vt* ❶ [*divisar, prever*] to make out ❷ [*acechar*] to observe

atisbo *sm* :💡: *generalmente pl* ❶ hint ❷ [*de esperanza*] glimmer

atlántico, ca *adj* Atlantic • **el océano Atlántico** the Atlantic Ocean :💡: *Los adjetivos ingleses son invariables.*
■ **Atlántico** *sm* • **el Atlántico** the Atlantic

atlas *sm invariable* atlas

atleta *smf* athlete

atlético, ca *adj* athletic :💡: *Los adjetivos ingleses son invariables.*

atletismo *sm* athletics :💡: *incontable*

atmósfera *sf* literal & figurado atmosphere

atole *sm* ▶ drink made of corn meal

atolladero *sm* fix

atómico, ca *adj* ❶ atomic ❷ [*central, armas*] nuclear :💡: *Los adjetivos ingleses son invariables.*

átomo *sm* literal & figurado atom
expresión **ni un átomo de** without a trace of

atónito, ta *adj* astonished :💡: *Los adjetivos ingleses son invariables.*

atontado, da *adj* ❶ [*aturdido*] dazed ❷ [*tonto*] stupid :💡: *Los adjetivos ingleses son invariables.*

atontar *vt* [*aturdir*] to daze

atormentar *vt* ❶ to torture ❷ figurado to torment • **¿por qué me estás atormentando con tantas preguntas?** why are you tormenting me with all these questions?

atornillar *vt* to screw

atorón *sm* traffic jam

atosigar *vt* figurado to harass

atracador, ra *sm, f* ❶ [*de banco*] armed robber ❷ [*en la calle*] mugger

atracar ◆ *vi* NÁUTICA • **atracar (en)** to dock (in) • **el buque atracó en el puerto** the ship docked in the port
◆ *vt* ❶ [*banco*] to rob ❷ [*persona*] to mug

atracción *sf* ❶ [*generalmente*] attraction • **la atracción entre ellos era obvia** the attraction between them was palpable ▶ **atracciones turísticas** tourist attractions ❷ [*espectáculo*] act ❸ figurado [*centro de atención*] center of attention ❹ :💡: *generalmente pl* [*atracción de feria*] fairground attraction

atraco *sm* robbery

atracón *sm* familiar feast • **darse un atracón** to stuff your face

atractivo, va *adj* attractive • **el candidato es joven y atractivo** the candidate is young and attractive :💡: *Los adjetivos ingleses son invariables.*
■ **atractivo** *sm* ❶ [*de persona*] attractiveness ❷ [*de cosa*] attraction

atraer *vt* [*generalmente*] to attract • **ese bar atrae gente bohemia** that bar attracts an artsy crowd • **no me atrae para nada el esquí** skiing doesn't appeal to me at all

atrapar *vt* [*agarrar, alcanzar*] to catch • **atraparon al fugitivo** they caught the fugitive

atrás *adv* ❶ [*detrás - posición*] behind • **el parque está atrás de ese edificio** the park is behind that building; [*- movimiento*] back • **hazte para atrás** move back • **¡atrás!** get back! ❷ [*antes*] earlier
expresión **quedarse atrás** to fall behind

atrasado, da *adj* ❶ [*en el tiempo*] delayed • **su vuelo salió atrasado** his flight was delayed • **estoy atrasado para mi clase** I'm late for my class • **el proyecto está atrasado** the project is behind schedule ❷ [*reloj*] slow • **mi reloj está atrasado diez minutos** my watch is ten minutes slow ❸ [*pago*] overdue ❹ [*número, copia*] back :💡: *Sólo se usa delante del sustantivo.* • **busco un número atrasado de esa revista** I'm looking for a back issue of that magazine ❺ [*en evolución, capacidad*] backward • **una región atrasada** a backward region • **va atrasada en la escuela** she's behind in school

atrasar ◆ *vt* to put back
◆ *vi* to be slow

atraso *sm* [*de evolución*] backwardness

A

atravesar *vt* ❶ [*interponer*] to put across ❷ [*cruzar*] to cross • **el río atraviesa el país entero** the river crosses the entire country • **atravesamos la calle sin esperar la luz verde** we crossed the street without waiting for the light ❸ [*perforar*] to go through • **el clavo atravesó la madera** the nail went through the piece of wood ❹ *figurado* [*vivir*] to go through

atrayente *adj* attractive ❀ *Los adjetivos ingleses son invariables.*

atreverse *v pronominal* • **atreverse (a hacer algo)** to dare (to do something) • **no me atrevo a decírselo** I don't dare tell him • **se atreve con todo** she's not afraid of anything

atrevido, da *adj* ❶ [*osado*] daring ❷ [*caradura*] cheeky ❀ *Los adjetivos ingleses son invariables.*

atrevimiento *sm* ❶ [*osadía*] daring ❷ [*insolencia*] nerve • **¡qué atrevimiento!** what a nerve!

atribución *sf* ❶ [*imputación*] attribution ❷ [*competencia*] responsibility

atribuir *vt* [*imputar*] • **atribuir algo a** to attribute something to

atributo *sm* attribute

atrocidad *sf* [*crueldad*] atrocity

atropellar *vt* ❶ [*sujeto: vehículo*] to run over • **¡casi me atropellaste!** you nearly ran me over ❷ *figurado* [*sujeto: persona*] to trample on

atropello *sm* ❶ [*por vehículo*] running over ❷ *figurado* [*moral*] abuse

atroz *adj* ❶ atrocious ❷ [*dolor*] awful ❀ *Los adjetivos ingleses son invariables.*

atte. *abreviatura escrita de* **atentamente**

atuendo *sm* attire

atún *sm* tuna • **un sandwich de atún** a tuna fish sandwich

audacia *sf* [*intrepidez*] daring

audaz *adj* [*intrépido*] daring • **un piloto audaz** a daring pilot ❀ *Los adjetivos ingleses son invariables.*

audición *sf* ❶ [*generalmente*] hearing ❷ Música & Teatro audition

audiencia *sf* ❶ [*público, recepción*] audience ▸ **índice de audiencia** audience ratings ❷ Derecho [*juicio*] hearing ❸ Derecho [*tribunal, edificio*] court

audífono *sm* hearing aid • **mi abuelo usa audífono** my grandfather wears a hearing aid

audiovisual *adj* audiovisual ❀ *Los adjetivos ingleses son invariables.*

auditivo, va *adj* ear ❀ *Sólo se usa delante del sustantivo.*

auditor, ra *sm, f* Finanzas auditor

auditorio *sm* ❶ [*público*] audience ❷ [*lugar*] auditorium

auge *sm* [*generalmente*] Economía boom

augurio *sm* omen

aula *sf* ❶ [*de escuela*] classroom ❷ [*de universidad*] lecture room

aullar *vi* to howl

aullido *sm* howl • **los aullidos de los perros no me dejaron dormir** the dogs' howls kept me awake

aumentar ♦ *vt* ❶ [*generalmente*] to increase • **han aumentado los impuestos** taxes have been increased ❷ [*peso*] to put on • **aumentar de peso** to put on weight ❸ [*en óptica*] to magnify ❹ [*sonido*] to amplify

♦ *vi* ❶ to increase ❷ [*precios*] to rise

aumento *sm* ❶ [*incremento*] increase • **los precios han visto un aumento del 5%** prices have increased by 5% ❷ [*de sueldo, precios*] rise • **ir en aumento** to be on the increase ❸ [*en óptica*] magnification

aun ♦ *adv* even

♦ *conjunción* • **aun estando cansado, lo hizo** even though he was tired, he did it • **ni aun puesta de puntillas llega** she can't reach, even on tiptoe • **aun cuando** even though • **aun así** even so • **aun así, no lo creo** even so, I don't believe it

aún *adv* ❶ [*todavía*] still; [*- en negativas*] yet ❷ • **no ha llegado aún** he hasn't arrived yet; he still hasn't arrived • **aún no me dice qué va a hacer** she still hasn't told me what she's going to do • **aún no he terminado** I haven't finished yet • **¡eres aún más bella de lo que me imaginaba!** you're even more beautiful than I imagined!

---

aunque

♦ *conjunción*

❶ [*seguido por el indicativo*] although

• **aunque está enfermo, sigue trabajando** although he's sick, he's still working

• **se me antoja el filete, aunque normalmente no como carne** the steak sounds good, although I don't usually eat meat

• **te ayudo, aunque estoy agotado** I'll help you even though I'm exhausted

❷ [*seguido por el subjuntivo*] even if

• **aunque esté enfermo, tendrá que seguir trabajando** even if he's sick, he'll have to keep working

• **tenemos que ir aunque no quieras** we have to go even if you don't want to

---

aúpa *exclamación* • **¡aúpa!** [*¡levántate!*] get up!

aupar *vt* ❶ to help up ❷ *figurado* [*animar*] to cheer on

aureola *sf* ❶ Astronomía & Religión halo ❷ *figurado* [*fama*] aura

auricular *sm* [*de teléfono*] receiver

aurora *sf* first light of dawn

auscultar *vt* to sound *(with a stethoscope)*

ausencia *sf* absence • **no había cambiado nada en mi ausencia** nothing had changed during my absence
expresión brillar por su ausencia to be conspicuous by your/its absence

ausente ♦ *adj* ❶ [*no presente*] absent • **has estado ausente demasiadas veces** you've been absent too many times ❷ [*fuera*] away • **estará ausente todo el día** he'll be away all day ❸ [*distraído*] distracted • **te ves ausente hoy** you look distracted today ❀ *Los adjetivos ingleses son invariables.*

◆ *smf* ❶ [*no presente*] • **criticó a los ausentes** he criticized the people who weren't there ❷ Derecho missing person

auspiciar *vt* to sponsor

austeridad *sf* austerity

austero, ra *adj* [*generalmente*] austere ·👁️· *Los adjetivos ingleses son invariables.*

austral ◆ *adj* southern ·👁️· *Los adjetivos ingleses son invariables.*

◆ *sm* [*moneda*] austral

Australia *nombre propio* Australia

australiano, na *adj* & *sm, f* Australian ·👁️· *Los adjetivos ingleses son invariables.*

Austria *nombre propio* Austria

austriaco, ca *adj* & *sm, f* Austrian ·👁️· *Los adjetivos ingleses son invariables.*

auténtico, ca *adj* ❶ [*verdadero*] genuine • **es un tío auténtico** he's a genuine guy • **un cuadro auténtico** a genuine painting ❷ [*para dar énfasis*] real • **un auténtico imbécil** a real idiot ·👁️· *Los adjetivos ingleses son invariables.*

auto *sm familiar* car

autoadhesivo, va *adj* self-adhesive ·👁️· *Los adjetivos ingleses son invariables.*

autobiografía *sf* autobiography

autobús *sm* bus

autocontrol *sm* self-control

autóctono, na *adj* indigenous ·👁️· *Los adjetivos ingleses son invariables.*

autodefensa *sf* self-defense

autodidacta *adj* self-taught ·👁️· *Los adjetivos ingleses son invariables.*

autoescuela *sf* driving school

autoestop *sm* hitch-hiking • **hacer autoestop** to hitch-hike

autoestopista *smf* hitch-hiker

autógrafo *sm* autograph

automático, ca *adj* automatic ·👁️· *Los adjetivos ingleses son invariables.*

■ **automático** *sm* [*botón*] press-stud

automóvil *sm* automobile • **la industria del automóvil** the automobile industry

automovilismo *sm* ❶ motoring ❷ Deporte motor racing

automovilista *smf* motorist

automovilístico, ca *adj* ❶ motor ·👁️· *Sólo se usa delante del sustantivo.* ❷ Deporte motor-racing ·👁️· *Sólo se usa delante del sustantivo.*

autonomía *sf* [*facultad*] autonomy

autopista *sf* freeway ▶ **autopista de cuota** toll road

autopsia *sf* autopsy

autor, ra *sm, f* ❶ Literatura author • **es la autora del poema** she's the author of the poem • **el autor de la música** the composer • **el autor del cuadro** the painter ❷ [*de crimen*] perpetrator • **los autores del crimen** the perpetrators

autoridad *sf* ❶ [*generalmente*] authority • **no tiene ninguna autoridad sobre los alumnos** she doesn't have any authority over the students ❷ [*ley*] • **la autoridad** the authorities *pl* • **las autoridades** the authorities *pl*

autoritario, ria *adj* & *sm, f* authoritarian ·👁️· *Los adjetivos ingleses son invariables.*

autorización *sf* authorization • **necesito la autorización del director** I need authorization from the manager

autorizado, da *adj* ❶ [*permitido*] authorized ❷ [*digno de crédito*] authoritative ·👁️· *Los adjetivos ingleses son invariables.*

autorizar *vt* ❶ [*dar permiso*] to allow • **autorizar a alguien para que haga algo** to authorize somebody to do something • **nos autorizaron para salir más temprano** we were authorized to leave early ❷ [*en situaciones oficiales*] to authorize ❸ [*capacitar*] to entitle

autorretrato *sm* self-portrait

autoservicio *sm* ❶ [*tienda*] self-service shop ❷ [*restaurante*] self-service restaurant

autosuficiencia *sf* self-sufficiency

auxiliar ◆ *adj* [*generalmente*] Gramática auxiliary ·👁️· *Los adjetivos ingleses son invariables.*

◆ *smf* assistant ▶ **auxiliar administrativo** office clerk

◆ *vt* to assist

auxilio *sm* help • **pedir/prestar auxilio** to call for/give help • **los primeros auxilios** first aid ·👁️· *incontable* • **¡socorro, auxilio!** help! help!

aval *sm* ❶ [*persona*] guarantor ❷ [*documento*] guarantee

avalancha *sf* literal & figurado avalanche

avalar *vt* to endorse

avance *sm* ❶ [*generalmente*] advance ❷ Finanzas [*anticipo*] advance payment ❸ Radio & Televisión [*meteorológico* etc] summary; [*de futura programación*] preview ▶ **avance informativo** news in brief

avanzar ◆ *vi* ❶ *en el espacio*] to move forward ❷ [*progresar*] to make progress • **ha avanzado mucho en sus estudios** he has made a lot of progress at school

◆ *vt* ❶ [*adelantar*] to move forward ❷ [*anticipar*] to tell in advance

avaricia *sf* greed

avaricioso, sa *adj* avaricious ·👁️· *Los adjetivos ingleses son invariables.*

avaro, ra *adj* mean ·👁️· *Los adjetivos ingleses son invariables.*

avasallar *vt* to overwhelm

avda. ave.

ave *sf* [*generalmente*] bird ▶ **ave de rapiña** bird of prey ▶ **aves de corral** poultry ·👁️· *incontable*

expresión **ser un ave pasajera** *figurado* to be a rolling stone

avellana *sf* hazelnut

avemaría *sf* [*oración*] Hail Mary

avena *sf* [*grano*] oats *pl*

avenida *sf* avenue

aventajado, da *adj* outstanding.♀ *Los adjetivos ingleses son invariables.*

aventajar *vt* ❶ [*rebasar*] to overtake ❷ [*estar por delante de*] to be ahead of • **aventajar a alguien en algo** to surpass somebody in something

aventar *vt* [*echar al aire*] to throw • **me aventó la pelota** she threw me the ball

aventón *sm* • **dar aventón a alguien** to give somebody a lift • **nos dio un aventón al colegio** he gave us a ride to school • **pedir aventón** to hitchhike

aventura *sf* ❶ [*generalmente*] adventure ❷ [*relación amorosa*] affair

aventurero, ra ◆ *adj* adventurous.♀ *Los adjetivos ingleses son invariables.*

◆ *sm, f* adventurer, *femenino* adventuress

avergonzar *vt* ❶ [*deshonrar*] to shame ❷ [*abochornar*] to embarrass • **me avergonzó delante de la clase** he embarrassed me in front of the class • **¿no te avergüenza andar con esa ropa?** aren't you ashamed to go around dressed like that?

■ **avergonzarse** *v pronominal* • **avergonzarse (de) a)** [*por culpa*] to be ashamed (of) **b)** [*por timidez*] to be embarrassed (about) • **avergonzarse de algo** to be ashamed of something • **me avergüenzo de haberlo acusado** I'm ashamed of accusing him

avería *sf* ❶ [*de máquina*] fault ❷ Automóviles breakdown • **su coche tuvo una avería en el camino** their car had a breakdown on the way

averiado, da *adj* ❶ [*máquina*] out of order ❷ [*coche*] broken down.♀ *Los adjetivos ingleses son invariables.*

averiar *vt* to damage

averiguación *sf* investigation

averiguar *vt* to find out • **tengo que averiguar la fecha exacta** I have to find out the exact date

aversión *sf* aversion

avestruz *sm* ostrich

aviación *sf* ❶ [*navegación*] aviation • **quiere estudiar aviación civil** he wants to study civil aviation • **un accidente de aviación** a plane crash ❷ [*ejército*] air force • **es teniente de la aviación** he's a lieutenant in the air force

aviador, ra *sm, f* aviator

avicultura *sf* poultry farming

ávido, da *adj* • **ávido de** eager for.♀ *Los adjetivos ingleses son invariables.*

avión *sm* plane ; airplane • **le encantan los aviones** she loves airplanes • **en avión** by plane • **por avión** [*correo*] by airmail ▶ **avión a reacción** jet ▶ **avión de papel** paper airplane

avioneta *sf* light aircraft

avisar *vt* ❶ [*informar*] • **avisar a alguien** to let somebody know • **¿le avisaste que no ibas a ir?** did you let her know you weren't going? • **avísame con tiempo** let

me know in advance ❷ [*advertir*] • **avisar (de)** to warn (of) • **te aviso que vas a tener problemas** I'm warning you, you'll have problems ❸ [*llamar*] to call • **siempre llega sin avisar** he always comes without calling

aviso *sm* ❶ [*advertencia, amenaza*] warning ❷ [*anuncio*] advertisement ; ad *familiar* • **puso un aviso en el periódico** she put an ad in the paper • **los avisos de la televisión** tv commercials ▶ **aviso clasificado** classified ad ❸ [*notificación*] notice • **el aviso daba información acerca del cambio de dirección** the notice informed us of the change of address ❹ [*en teatros, aeropuertos*] call • **hasta nuevo aviso** until further notice • **sin previo aviso** without notice

avispa *sf* wasp

avispero *sm* [*nido*] wasp's nest

avivar *vt* ❶ [*sentimiento*] to rekindle ❷ [*color*] to brighten ❸ [*fuego*] to stoke up

axila *sf* armpit

axioma *sm* axiom

ay (pl ayes) *exclamación* • **¡ay! a)** [*dolor físico*] ouch! **b)** [*sorpresa, pena*] oh!

expresión **¡ay de ti si te cojo!** Heaven help you if I catch you!

ayer *adv* ❶ yesterday • **ayer la vi** I saw her yesterday • **ayer (por la) noche** last night • **ayer por la mañana** yesterday morning ▶ **antes de ayer** the day before yesterday ❷ *figurado* in the past

ayuda *sf* ❶ help • **¿necesitas ayuda?** do you need help? • **me pidió ayuda** she asked me for help ❷ Economía & Política aid ▶ **ayuda en carretera** breakdown service ▶ **ayuda humanitaria** humanitarian aid

ofrecer su ayuda

• **Can I help you?** ¿Te/Le puedo ayudar?
• **What can I do for you?** ¿En qué te/le puedo ayudar?
• **If you like, I'll see to it.** Si quiere, me ocupo de ello.

ayudante *adj* & *smf* assistant.♀ *Los adjetivos ingleses son invariables.*

ayudar *vt* to help • **me ha ayudado mucho** it's helped me a lot • **ayudar a alguien a hacer algo** to help somebody (to) do something • **mi papá me ayudó a hacer las tareas** my dad helped me do my homework • **¿en qué puedo ayudarle?** how can I help you?

ayunar *vi* to fast

ayunas *sfpl* • **en ayunas a)** [*sin comer*] without having eaten **b)** *figurado* [*sin enterarse*] in the dark

ayuno *sm* fast • **hacer ayuno** to fast

ayuntamiento *sm* ❶ [*corporación*] ≃ City Hall • **un curso organizado por el ayuntamiento** a course organized by City Hall ❷ [*edificio*] city hall • **vivo cerca del ayuntamiento** I live near City Hall

azabache *sm* jet

expresión **negro como el azabache** jet-black

azada *sf* hoe

azafrán *sm* saffron

azalea *sf* azalea

azar *sm* chance • **al azar** at random • **escoge una carta al azar** pick a card at random • **por (puro) azar** by (pure) chance • **me enteré por azar** I only found out by chance

azotar *vt* ❶ [*sujeto: persona*] to beat ❷ [*en el trasero*] to smack ❸ [*con látigo*] to whip

azote *sm* ❶ [*golpe*] blow ❷ [*en el trasero*] smack ❸ [*latigazo*] lash ❹ *figurado* [*calamidad*] scourge

azotea *sf* terraced roof

expresión estar mal de la azotea *familiar & figurado* to be funny in the head

azteca *adj* & *smf* Aztec ☀ *Los adjetivos ingleses son invariables.*

azúcar *sm* sugar • **no le pongo azúcar al café** I don't have sugar in my coffee ▶ **azúcar moreno** brown sugar

azucarado, da *adj* sweet ☀ *Los adjetivos ingleses son invariables.*

azucarar *vt* ❶ [*endulzar*] to sugar-coat ❷ [*suavizar*] to sweeten

azucarero, ra *adj* sugar ☀ *Sólo se usa delante del sustantivo.* • **la cosecha azucarera** the sugar crop
■ **azucarero** *sm* sugar bowl

azucena *sf* white lily

azufre *sm* sulfur

azul *adj* & *sm* blue • **un vestido azul** a blue dress • **es de color azul** it's blue ☀ *Los adjetivos ingleses son invariables.*

azulejo *sm* (glazed) tile

B

b, B *sf* [*letra*] b; B

baba *sf* ❶ [*de adulto*] saliva ❷ [*de niño*] dribble ❸ [*de perro*] slobber

expresión **echar babas** to drool

babear *vi* ❶ [*niño*] to dribble ❷ [*adulto, animal*] to slobber ❸ *figurado* to drool

babero *sm* bib

babor *sm* • **a babor** to port

baca *sf* luggage rack

bacalao *sm* ❶ [*fresco*] cod ❷ [*salado*] dried salted cod

expresión **partir** o **cortar el bacalao** *familiar & figurado* to be the boss

bache *sm* ❶ [*en carretera*] pothole • **hay muchos baches en el camino** there are a lot of potholes in the road ❷ *figurado* [*dificultades*] bad patch • **están pasando por un mal bache** they're going through a bad patch ❸ [*en un vuelo*] air pocket

bacteria *sf* germ • **bacterias** bacteria

bádminton *sm invariable* badminton

bafle *sm* loudspeaker

bagatela *sf* trifle

bagazo *sm* bagasse

bagre *sm* catfish

Bahamas *sfpl* • **las Bahamas** the Bahamas

bahía *sf* bay

bailar ◆ *vt* to dance • **estoy aprendiendo a bailar salsa** I'm taking salsa lessons
◆ *vi* [*danzar*] to dance • **anoche fuimos a bailar** we went out dancing last night

bailarín, ina *sm, f* ❶ dancer • **quiere ser bailarina** she wants to be a dancer ❷ [*de ballet*] ballet dancer ▶ **prima bailarina** prima ballerina

baile *sm* ❶ [*generalmente*] dance • **la rumba es un baile cubano** the rumba is a Cuban dance • **tiene clases de baile** she takes dance lessons • **lo van a celebrar con un baile** they're going to celebrate with a dance ▶ **baile clásico** ballet • **baile de salón** ballroom dancing ❷ [*fiesta*] ball ▶ **un baile de etiqueta** a ball

bailongo *sm* public dance

baja *sf* ❶ [*descenso*] drop • **una brusca baja de la temperatura** a sudden drop in temperature ❷ [*cese*] • **dar de baja a alguien** a) [*en una empresa*] to lay somebody off b) [*en un club, sindicato*] to expel somebody • **darse de baja (de)** a) [*dimitir*] to resign (from) b) [*salirse*] to drop out (of) ❸ [*por enfermedad - permiso*] sick leave ❓ *incontable* • **estar/darse de baja** to be on/to take sick leave; [- *documento*] sick note ▶ **baja por maternidad/paternidad** maternity/paternity leave

bajada *sf* ❶ [*descenso*] descent • **una bajada muy empinada** a steep descent • **la bajada es siempre más fácil** the way down is always easier ▶ **bajada de bandera** [*de taxi*] minimum fare ❷ [*pendiente*] (downward) slope ❸ [*disminución*] drop

bajamar *sf* low tide

bajar ◆ *vt* ❶ [*poner abajo - libro, cuadro* ETC] to take/bring down • **voy a bajar el teléfono a la cocina** I'm going to take the phone down to the kitchen • **por favor, bájame un suéter que aquí hace frío** please bring me down a sweater, it's cold here • **baja el diccionario del estante** get the dictionary down from the shelf; [- *telón, ventanilla, mano*] to lower ❷ [*descender - montaña, escaleras*] to go/come down ❸ [*precios, inflación, hinchazón*] to lower • **han bajado el precio de la entrada** they've lowered ticket prices ❹ [*música, volumen, radio*] to turn down • **baja la música, por favor** please turn down the music • **¡bajen la voz, que no puedo estudiar!** keep your voices down, I'm trying to study! ❺ [*fiebre*] to bring down ❻ [*ojos, cabeza, voz*] to lower ❼ [*de Internet*] to download • **acabo de bajar esta canción** I just downloaded this song
◆ *vi* ❶ [*descender*] to go/come down • **voy a bajar por las escaleras** I'll go down the stairs • **baja que quiero decirte algo** come down here, I need to tell you something • **ya bajo** I'm coming down • **bajar por algo** to go/come down to get something • **bajar corriendo** to run down ❷ [*disminuir*] to fall ❸ [*fiebre, hinchazón*] to go down ❹ [*Bolsa*] to suffer a fall

bajeza *sf* ❶ [*cualidad*] baseness ❷ [*acción*] nasty deed

bajo, ja *adj* ❶ [*generalmente*] low • **la silla es muy baja** the chair is very low • **saqué notas muy bajas** I got very low grades • **alimentos bajos en calorías** low-calorie foods ❷ [*persona*] short • **José es muy bajo** José

bala

is very short ❸ [*planta*] ground ☼ ***Sólo se usa delante del sustantivo.*** ❹ [*sonido*] soft • **hablen más bajo** please lower your voices • **en voz baja** in a low voice ❺ [*territorio, época*] lower • **el bajo Amazonas** the lower Amazon ❻ [*pobre*] lower-class ❼ [*vil*] base

■ **bajo** ◆ *sm* MÚSICA [*instrumento, cantante*] bass; [*instrumentista*] bassist

◆ *adv* ❶ [*generalmente*] low ❷ [*hablar*] quietly ❸ [*volar*] low • **iba volando muy bajo** it was flying very low

◆ *preposición* ❶ [*generalmente*] under • **bajo el gobierno anterior** under the previous government • **escribe bajo un seudónimo** she writes under a pseudonym • **bajo tierra** underground • **estacionamientos construidos bajo tierra** underground parking lots ❷ [*con temperaturas*] below • **bajo cero** below zero • **tres grados bajo cero** three degrees below zero

bala *sf* ❶ [*proyectil*] bullet ❷ [*fardo*] bale

balacear *vt* to shoot

balada *sf* ballad

balance *sm* ❶ COMERCIO [*operación*] balance; [*documento*] balance sheet ❷ [*resultado*] outcome • **hacer balance (de)** to take stock (of)

balancear *vt* ❶ [*cuna*] to rock ❷ [*columpio*] to swing

balanza *sf* ❶ [*báscula*] scales *pl* ❷ COMERCIO ▶ **balanza comercial/de pagos** balance of trade/payments

balazo *sm* ❶ [*disparo*] shot • **oímos unos balazos** we heard some shots • **lo mataron de un balazo** he was shot to death ❷ [*herida*] bullet wound

Balcanes *smpl* • **los Balcanes** the Balkans

balcón *sm* balcony

balde *sm* bucket • **un balde de agua** a bucket of water

baldosa *sf* ❶ [*en casa, edificio*] floor tile ❷ [*en la acera*] paving stone

baldosín *sm* tile

balero *sm* ❶ bullet mold ❷ cup and ball

balido *sm* bleat

balístico, ca *adj* ballistic ☼ ***Los adjetivos ingleses son invariables.***

baliza *sf* ❶ NÁUTICA marker buoy ❷ AERONÁUTICA beacon

ballena *sf* [*animal*] whale

ballet (pl ballets) *sm* ballet

balneario *sm* ❶ [*con baños termales*] spa ❷ [*con piscinas*, ETC] ≃ lido

balompié *sm* soccer

balón *sm* [*pelota*] ball ▶ **balón de reglamento** regulation ball

balón ≠ balloon

• La palabra inglesa **balloon** es un falso amigo que significa *globo*.
• *Balón* se traduce al inglés por **ball**.

baloncesto *sm* basketball

balonmano *sm* handball

balonvolea *sm* volleyball

balsa *sf* ❶ [*embarcación*] raft ❷ [*estanque*] pool

bálsamo *sm* ❶ [*medicamento*] balsam ❷ [*alivio*] balm

Báltico *sm* • **el (mar) Báltico** the Baltic (Sea)

baluarte *sm* ❶ [*fortificación*] bulwark ❷ *figurado* [*bastión*] stronghold

bambú *sm* bamboo

banana *sf* banana

banca *sf* ❶ [*actividad*] banking ▶ **banca por Internet** Internet banking ▶ **banca en línea** online banking ▶ **banca telefónica** telephone banking ❷ [*institución*] • **la banca** the banks *pl* ❸ [*en juegos*] bank

bancario, ria *adj* banking ☼ ***Sólo se usa delante del sustantivo.*** • **el sector bancario** the banking sector

bancarrota *sf* bankruptcy • **en bancarrota** bankrupt

banco *sm* ❶ [*asiento*] bench • **me senté en un banco de la plaza** I sat on a bench in the square ❷ [*de iglesia*] pew • **los bancos de la iglesia** the pews ❸ FINANZAS bank • **depositó el cheque en el banco** he deposited the check at the bank ❹ [*de peces*] shoal ❺ [*de carpintero, artesano* ETC] workbench ❻ MEDICINA bank ▶ **banco de sangre** blood bank ❼ [*al lado de río, mar*] ▶ **banco de arena** sandbank

banda *sf* ❶ [*cuadrilla*] gang • **detuvieron a una banda de ladrones** they caught a gang of thieves ▶ **banda terrorista** terrorist organization ❷ MÚSICA band • **toca en la banda del colegio** she plays in the school band ❸ [*faja*] sash • **llevaba una banda con el nombre de su país** she wore a sash with her country's name on it ❹ [*cinta*] ribbon ❺ [*franja*] stripe ❻ INFORMÁTICA band ▶ **banda ancha** broadband ❼ RADIO waveband ❽ [*margen*] side ❾ [*en billar*] cushion ❿ [*en futbol*] touchline • **fuera de banda** out of play • **sacar de banda** to throw the ball in ⓫ MÚSICA ▶ **banda sonora** soundtrack

bandeja *sf* tray ▶ **bandeja de entrada** INFORMÁTICA inbox ▶ **bandeja de salida** INFORMÁTICA outbox

expresión **servir** o **dar algo a alguien en bandeja** to hand something to somebody on a plate

bandera *sf* flag • **jurar bandera** to swear allegiance (to the flag)

expresión **estar hasta la bandera** to be packed

banderín *sm* pennant

bandido, da *sm, f* ❶ [*delincuente*] bandit ❷ [*granuja*] rascal

bando *sm* ❶ [*facción*] side • **pasarse al otro bando** to change sides ❷ [*de alcalde*] edict

bandolero, ra *sm, f* bandit

■ **bandolera** *sf* [*correa*] bandoleer • **en bandolera** slung across your chest

banjo *sm* banjo

banquero, ra *sm, f* banker • **su padre es banquero** his father is a banker

banqueta *sf* ❶ [*asiento*] stool ❷ [*acera*] sidewalk

banquete *sm* [*comida*] banquet • **los invitaron a un banquete** they were invited to a banquet ▶ **banquete de bodas** wedding reception

banquillo *sm* ❶ [*asiento*] low stool ❷ DEPORTE bench

bañar *vt* ❶ [*asear*] to bath ❷ MEDICINA to bathe ❸ [*sumergir*] to soak ❹ [*revestir*] to coat
■ **bañarse** *v pronominal* ❶ [*en el baño*] to take a bath ❷ [*en playa, alberca*] to go swimming • **nos bañamos en el mar** we swam in the sea

bañera *sf* bathtub

baño *sm* ❶ [*en bañera*] bath • **darse un baño** to take a bath ❷ [*en playa, piscina*] swim ❸ [*bañera*] bathtub • **llenó el baño de agua** she filled the bathtub ❹ [*cuarto de aseo*] bathroom • **¿dónde está el baño, por favor?** can you tell me where the bathroom is, please? • **una casa con tres baños** a house with three bathrooms ❺ [*capa*] coat

bar *sm* bar

baraja *sf* deck (of cards)

barajar *vt* ❶ [*cartas*] to shuffle ❷ [*considerar - nombres, posibilidades*] to consider ; [*- datos, cifras*] to marshal

barata *sf* sale • **lo compré en una barata** I bought it on sale

baratija *sf* trinket

barato, ta *adj* cheap • **¿cuál es más barato?** which one is cheaper? ☼ *Los adjetivos ingleses son invariables.*
■ **barato** *adv* cheaply ; cheap • **aquí podemos comer barato** we can eat cheaply here • **el viaje nos costó barato** our trip was pretty cheap

barba *sf* beard • **barba incipiente** stubble • **dejarse barba** to grow a beard • **se está dejando barba** he's growing a beard

expresión **por barba** [*cada uno*] per head

barbacoa *sf* barbecue • **hacer una barbacoa** to have a barbecue

barbaridad *sf* ❶ [*cualidad*] cruelty • **¡qué barbaridad!** how terrible! • **¡qué barbaridad! mira qué tarde es** oh my God! look how late it is! ❷ [*disparate*] nonsense ☼ *incontable* • **no digas tantas barbaridades** don't talk such nonsense ❸ [*montón*] • **una barbaridad (de)** tons (of) • **se gastó una barbaridad** she spent a fortune

barbarie *sf* ❶ [*cualidad*] cruelty ❷ [*acción*] atrocity

barbería *sf* barber's (shop)

barbero, ra *sm, f* barber

barbilla *sf* chin

barbudo, da *adj* bearded ☼ *Los adjetivos ingleses son invariables.*

barca *sf* small boat ▶ **barca de remos** rowboat

barcaza *sf* barge

barco *sm* ❶ [*generalmente*] boat ❷ [*de gran tamaño*] ship • **en barco** by boat ▶ **barco cisterna** tanker ▶ **barco de guerra** warship ▶ **barco mercante** cargo ship ▶ **barco de vapor** steamer ; steamboat ▶ **barco de vela** sailboat

barítono *sm* baritone

barman (pl barmans) *sm* bartender

barniz *sm* ❶ [*para madera*] varnish ▶ **barniz de uñas** nail polish ❷ [*para loza, cerámica*] glaze

barnizar *vt* ❶ [*madera*] to varnish ❷ [*loza, cerámica*] to glaze

barómetro *sm* barometer

barón, onesa *sm, f* baron, *femenino* baroness

barquero, ra *sm, f* boatman, *femenino* boatwoman

barquillo *sm* COCINA cone

barra *sf* ❶ [*generalmente*] bar • **una barra de metal** a metal bar • **una barra de jabón** a bar of soap ▶ **barra de labios** lipstick ▶ **barra de pan** baguette ❷ [*de bar, café*] bar (counter) • **tomamos unas bebidas en la barra** we had drinks at the bar ▶ **barra libre** *para explicar lo que es puedes decir:* it's unlimited drinks for a fixed price ❸ [*signo gráfico*] slash ❹ INFORMÁTICA • **barra de estado** status bar • **barra de herramientas** tool bar • **barra de menús** menu bar ❺ DERECHO • **la barra** the bar

barranco *sm* ❶ [*precipicio*] precipice ❷ [*cauce*] ravine

barrendero, ra *sm, f* street sweeper

barreño *sm* washing-up bowl

barrer *vt* ❶ [*con escoba, reflectores*] to sweep • **tengo que barrer el patio** I have to sweep the patio ❷ [*sujeto: viento, olas*] to sweep away

barrera *sf* ❶ [*generalmente*] barrier ▶ **la barrera del sonido** the sound barrier ▶ **barreras arancelarias** tariff barriers ❷ FERROCARRIL crossing gate ❸ [*de campo, casa*] fence ❹ DEPORTE wall

barricada *sf* barricade

barriga *sf* stomach • **me duele la barriga** I have stomach ache

barril *sm* barrel • **un barril de petróleo** an oil barrel • **de barril** [*bebida*] draught

barrio *sm* [*vecindario*] neighborhood • **un barrio residencial** a residential neighborhood • **va a un colegio del barrio** she goes to a neighborhood school

barriobajero, ra *adj* despectivo lowlife ☼ *Sólo se usa delante del sustantivo.* • **actividades barriobajeras** lowlife activities

barro *sm* ❶ [*arcilla*] clay • **una olla de barro** a clay pot ❷ [*grano*] blackhead

barrote *sm* bar

bártulos *smpl* things

barullo *sm* familiar ❶ [*ruido*] racket • **tenían un barullo en la clase** there was a racket in the classroom • **armar barullo** to raise hell ❷ [*desorden*] mess • **se me armó un barullo con las cuentas** I got into a real mess with the accounts • **en el barullo perdí el libro** I lost my book in the confusion

basar *vt* to base • **basar algo en algo** to base something on something

B

■ **basarse en** *v pronominal* ❶ [sujeto: teoría, obra ETC] to be based on ❷ [sujeto: persona] to base your argument on

báscula *sf* scales *pl*

base *sf* ❶ [generalmente] MATEMÁTICAS & MILITAR base • **la base de la pirámide** the base of the pyramid • **corrió a la tercera base** she ran to third base ▶ **base de datos** INFORMÁTICA database ▶ **base naval** naval base ❷ [de edificio] foundations *pl* • **sentar las bases para** to lay the foundations of ❸ [fundamento, origen] basis • **la base de su éxito fue el estudio** studying was the basis for his success ❹ [de partido, sindicato] • **las bases** the grass roots *pl*

expresiones **a base de** through • **a base de trabajar mucho** through hard work ▶ **vivir a base de algo** to live on something • **vivo a base de verduras** I live on vegetables ▶ **a base de bien** extremely well

básico, ca *adj* basic • **lo básico de** the basics of.☿ *Los adjetivos ingleses son invariables.*

basílica *sf* basilica

basta *exclamación* • **¡basta!** that's enough! • **¡basta de chistes/tonterías!** that's enough jokes/of this nonsense!

bastante ◆ *adv* ❶ [suficientemente] enough • **no estudian bastante** they don't study enough • **es lo bastante lista para...** she's smart enough to... ❷ [considerablemente] quite • **son bastante caras** they're quite expensive • **me gustó bastante** I quite enjoyed it
◆ *adj* ❶ [suficiente] enough • **hay bastante comida para todos** there's enough food for everyone • **no tengo dinero bastante** I haven't enough money ❷ [mucho] quite • **había bastante gente** there were quite a lot of people • **tengo bastante frío** I'm quite cold • **mañana tengo bastantes cosas que hacer** I have quite a lot to do tomorrow.☿ *Los adjetivos ingleses son invariables.*
◆ *pronombre* ❶ [suficiente] enough • **no tengo bastante** I don't have enough ❷ [mucho] quite a lot • **éramos bastantes** there were quite a lot of us.☿ *Los adjetivos ingleses son invariables.*

bastar *vi* to be enough • **basta con que se lo digas** it's enough for you to tell her • **bastaba con decirlo** you should have just said • **con ocho basta** eight is enough • **baste decir que...** suffice it to say that...

expresión **con la intención basta** it's the thought that counts

bastidor *sm* frame

basto, ta *adj* coarse.☿ *Los adjetivos ingleses son invariables.*

bastón *sm* ❶ [para andar] walking stick ❷ [de mando] baton ❸ [para esquiar] ski stick

expresión **empuñar el bastón** *figurado* to take the helm

basura *sf* literal & figurado garbage • **pasan a recoger la basura los lunes** they pick up the garbage on Monday • **tirar algo a la basura** to throw something away ▶ **basura radioactiva** radioactive waste

basurero *sm* ❶ [persona] garbage man ❷ [vertedero] Dumpster • **lo encontró en el basurero** she found it in the Dumpster

bata *sf* ❶ [de casa] housecoat ❷ [para baño, al levantarse] robe ▶ **bata de baño** bathrobe ❸ [de médico] white coat ❹ [de laboratorio] lab coat

batacazo *sm* bump

batalla *sf* battle

batallar *vi* to fight

batallón *sm* MILITAR battalion

bate *sm* DEPORTE bat

batear ◆ *vt* to hit
◆ *vi* to bat

batería *sf* ❶ ELECTRICIDAD & MILITAR battery • **necesito una nueva batería para mi coche** my car needs a new battery ❷ MÚSICA drums *pl* • **estoy aprendiendo a tocar la batería** I'm learning to play the drums ❸ [conjunto] set ▶ **batería de cocina** pots and pans *pl* ❹ [de preguntas] barrage

batidor, ra *adj* beating

■ **batidor** *sm* ❶ COCINA beater ❷ MILITAR scout

batidora *sf* mixer

batir *vt* ❶ [generalmente] to beat • **bate los huevos ligeramente** beat the eggs lightly ❷ [crema] to whip • **hay que batir la crema primero** you have to whip the cream first ❸ [récord] to break • **Woods ha batido todos los récords** Woods has beaten all the records ❹ [sujeto: olas, lluvia, viento] to beat against ❺ [derribar] to knock down

batuta *sf* baton

expresión **llevar la batuta** to call the tune

baúl *sm* [cofre] trunk

bautismo *sm* baptism

bautizar *vt* ❶ RELIGIÓN to christen • **la bautizan el sábado** she's being christened on Saturday • **la bautizaron con el nombre de la abuela** she was named after her grandmother ❷ *familiar & figurado* [aguar] to dilute

bautizo *sm* RELIGIÓN christening

bayeta *sf* ❶ [tejido] flannel ❷ [para fregar] cloth ❸ [de gamuza] chamois

bayoneta *sf* bayonet

baza *sf* [en cartas] trick

expresión **no pude meter baza (en la conversación)** I couldn't get a word in edgeways ▶ **no jugó bien su baza** he didn't play his cards right

bazar *sm* bazaar

bazo *sm* ANATOMÍA spleen

be *sf* ▶ **be larga** o **grande** b

beatificar *vt* to beatify

beato, ta *adj* ❶ [beatificado] blessed ❷ [piadoso] devout ❸ *figurado* [santurrón] sanctimonious.☿ *Los adjetivos ingleses son invariables.*

bebé *sm* baby ▶ **bebé probeta** test-tube baby

bebedor, ra *sm, f* heavy drinker

beber ◆ *vt* [líquido] to drink • **no bebas esa agua** don't drink that water • **se bebieron todo el vino** they drank all the wine • **tienes que bebértelo todo** you

have to drink all of it • **bebimos a la salud de los novios** we drank to the bride and grooms' health
◆ *vi* [*tomar líquido*] to drink

bebida *sf* drink ▶ **bebida alcohólica** alcoholic drink

expresión **darse** o **entregarse a la bebida** to take to the bottle

bebido, da *adj* drunk ⚲ *Los adjetivos ingleses son invariables.*

beca *sf* ❶ [*del gobierno*] grant • **recibimos una beca del gobierno** we got a government grant ❷ [*de organización privada*] scholarship • **se ganó una beca para asistir a Harvard** she won a scholarship to go to Harvard

becar *vt* ❶ [*sujeto: gobierno*] to award a grant to ❷ [*sujeto: organización privada*] to award a scholarship to

becerro, rra *sm, f* calf

bechamel = besamel

bedel *sm* janitor

béisbol *sm* baseball

belén *sm* crib

belga *adj* & *smf* Belgian ⚲ *Los adjetivos ingleses son invariables.*

Bélgica *nombre propio* Belgium

Belice *nombre propio* Belize

bélico, ca *adj* ❶ [*generalmente*] war ⚲ *Sólo se usa delante del sustantivo.* ❷ [*actitud*] warlike

belicoso, sa *adj* ❶ bellicose ❷ *figurado* aggressive ⚲ *Los adjetivos ingleses son invariables.*

beligerante *adj* & *smf* belligerent ⚲ *Los adjetivos ingleses son invariables.*

belleza *sf* beauty

bello, lla *adj* beautiful ⚲ *Los adjetivos ingleses son invariables.*

bellota *sf* acorn

bendecir *vt* to bless

bendición *sf* blessing • **el sacerdote realizó la bendición de los anillos** the priest performed the blessing of the rings

bendito, ta *adj* ❶ [*santo*] holy ❷ [*alma*] blessed ❸ [*dichoso*] lucky ❹ [*para enfatizar*] damned ⚲ *Los adjetivos ingleses son invariables.*

benefactor, ra *sm, f* benefactor, *femenino* benefactress

beneficiar *vt* to benefit • **la nueva ley beneficia a todos** the new law benefits everybody

beneficio *sm* ❶ [*bien*] benefit • **a beneficio de** [*gala, concierto*] in aid of • **en beneficio de** for the good of • **en beneficio de todos** in everyone's interest • **en beneficio propio** for your own good ❷ [*ganancia*] profit • **la empresa tuvo un beneficio de 2.000 dólares** the company made a profit of $2,000 ▶ **beneficio bruto/neto** gross/net profit

beneficioso, sa *adj* • **beneficioso (para)** beneficial (to) ⚲ *Los adjetivos ingleses son invariables.*

benéfico, ca *adj* ❶ [*favorable*] beneficial ❷ [*función*] charity ⚲ *Sólo se usa delante del sustantivo.* • **una rifa benéfica** a charity raffle • **cena benéfica** benefit dinner ❸ [*organización*] charitable

bengala *sf* ❶ [*para pedir ayuda, iluminar* ETC] flare ❷ [*fuego artificial*] sparkler

benigno, na *adj* ❶ [*generalmente*] benign • **un tumor benigno** a benign tumor ❷ [*clima, temperatura*] mild • **un clima benigno** a mild climate ⚲ *Los adjetivos ingleses son invariables.*

berenjena *sf* eggplant

bermudas *sfpl* Bermuda shorts

berrido *sm* ❶ [*del becerro*] bellow ❷ [*de persona*] howl

berrinche *sm* *familiar* tantrum • **agarrarse un berrinche** to have a tantrum

berro *sm* watercress

besamel, bechamel *sf* béchamel sauce

besar *vt* to kiss

■ **besarse** *v pronominal* to kiss • **se estaban besando** they were kissing

beso *sm* kiss • **dar un beso a alguien** to give somebody a kiss

bestia ◆ *adj* ❶ [*ignorante*] thick ❷ [*torpe*] clumsy ❸ [*maleducado*] rude ⚲ *Los adjetivos ingleses son invariables.*
◆ *smf* [*ignorante, torpe*] brute
◆ *sf* [*animal*] beast ▶ **bestia de carga** beast of burden

bestial *adj* ❶ [*brutal*] animal ❷ [*apetito*] tremendous ❸ *familiar* [*formidable*] terrific ⚲ *Los adjetivos ingleses son invariables.*

bestialidad *sf* ❶ [*brutalidad*] brutality ❷ *familiar* [*tontería*] rubbish ⚲ *incontable* ❸ *familiar* [*montón*] • **una bestialidad** de stacks *pl* of

besugo *sm* ❶ [*pez*] sea bream ❷ *familiar* [*persona*] idiot

besuquear *vt* *familiar* to smother with kisses

betabel *sm* beet

betún *sm* ❶ [*para calzado*] shoe polish ❷ QUÍMICA bitumen

biberón *sm* (baby's) bottle • **dar el biberón a** to bottle-feed

Biblia *sf* Bible

bibliografía *sf* bibliography

biblioteca *sf* ❶ [*generalmente*] library • **la biblioteca de la escuela** the school library ❷ [*mueble*] bookcase

bibliotecario, ria *sm, f* librarian

bicarbonato *sm* [*medicamento*] bicarbonate of soda

bíceps *sm invariable* biceps

bicho *sm* ❶ [*animal*] animal ❷ [*insecto*] bug

bici *sf* *familiar* bike

bicicleta *sf* bicycle • **montar en bicicleta** to ride a bicycle • **no sabe montar en bicicleta** he doesn't know how to ride a bicycle ▸ **bicicleta de montaña** mountain bike

bicolor *adj* two-colored:💡 *Los adjetivos ingleses son invariables.*

bidé *sm* bidet

bidimensional *adj* two-dimensional:💡 *Los adjetivos ingleses son invariables.*

bidón *sm* ❶ drum *(for oil* ETC*)* ❷ [*lata*] canister ❸ [*de plástico*] (large) bottle

bien

◆ *adv*

❶ [*correctamente, de manera satisfactoria*] well
• **habla bien el inglés** he speaks English well
• **encontrarse bien** to feel well
• **¿seguro que estás bien? te veo un poco pálida...** are you sure you're feeling well? you look a little pale
• **has hecho bien** you've done the right thing
• **este vestido te sienta muy bien** this dress really suits you
• **¡cierra bien la puerta!** close the door properly!

❷ [*de buena calidad*]
• **este libro está muy bien** this book is very good
• **tu tarea no está bien** your homework isn't right

❸ [*sabor, olor*] good
• **saber bien** to taste good
• **oler bien** to smell good

❹ [*expresa acuerdo*] OK
• **está bien: te dejo el coche** it's all right: I'm leaving you the car
• **¿nos vamos? — ¡bien!** shall we go now? — OK!
• **¡bien, vamos al cine!** great, let's go to the movies!
• **¡está bien!** ok!

❺ [*en expresiones*]
• **nos lo pasamos muy bien en la fiesta** we had a lot of fun at the party
• **como bien le parezca** as you wish

expresión **¡muy bien!** very good! • **¡ya está bien!** that's enough, now!

◆ *adj invariable*
well-to-do
• **es gente bien** they're well-to-do
• **un chavo bien** a well-to-do kid

💡 *Los adjetivos ingleses son invariables.*

◆ *conjunción*
[*expresa una alternativa*]
• **puede pagar bien en efectivo bien con tarjeta** you can either pay in cash or with a card

◆ *sm*
❶ [*sentido moral*] good
• **el bien y el mal** good and evil
• **hacer el bien** to do good

❷ [*propiedad*] bien
• **un bien público** public property

❸ [*interes propio*] good
• **es por tu bien** it's for your own good

❹ EDUCACIÓN ≈ good

■ **más bien**
◆ *locución adverbial*
[*indica una tendencia*] quite
• **el clima de esta región es más bien húmedo** the climate in that area is quite damp

bienal *sf* biennial exhibition

bienestar *sm* wellbeing

bienhechor, ra *sm, f* benefactor, *femenino* benefactress

bienio *sm* two years *pl*

bienvenido, da ◆ *adj* welcome:💡 *Los adjetivos ingleses son invariables.*
◆ *exclamación* • **¡bienvenido!** welcome! • **bienvenido a nuestra casa** welcome to our home
■ **bienvenida** *sf* welcome • **dar la bienvenida a alguien** to welcome somebody

bífido, da *adj* forked:💡 *Los adjetivos ingleses son invariables.*

bifurcación *sf* ❶ [*entre calles*] fork ❷ TECNOLOGÍA bifurcation

bigote *sm* mustache

bikini = **biquini**

bilateral *adj* bilateral:💡 *Los adjetivos ingleses son invariables.*

bilingüe *adj* bilingual:💡 *Los adjetivos ingleses son invariables.*

bilis *sf invariable* literal & figurado bile

billar *sm* ❶ [*juego*] billiards :💡 *incontable* ❷ [*sala*] billiard hall

billete *sm* ❶ [*dinero*] bill • **un billete de 100 pesos** a 100-peso bill ❷ [*de lotería*] lottery ticket

billetera *sf* wallet • **una billetera de cuero** a leather wallet

billón *numeral* trillion ver también **seis**

bingo *sm* ❶ [*juego*] bingo ❷ [*sala*] bingo hall ❸ [*premio*] (full) house

binóculo *sm* pince-nez

biocombustible *sm* biofuel

biodegradable *adj* biodegradable:💡 *Los adjetivos ingleses son invariables.*

bioética *sf* bioethics *pl*

biografía *sf* biography

biográfico, ca *adj* biographical:💡 *Los adjetivos ingleses son invariables.*

biógrafo, fa *sm, f* biographer

biología *sf* biology

biológico, ca *adj* biological:💡 *Los adjetivos ingleses son invariables.*

biólogo, ga *sm, f* biologist

biombo *sm* (folding) screen

biopsia *sf* biopsy

bioquímico, ca ◆ *adj* biochemical:💡 *Los adjetivos ingleses son invariables.*
◆ *sm, f* biochemist

B

- **bioquímica** *sf* [*ciencia*] biochemistry
biorritmo *sm* biorhythm
biotecnología *sf* biotechnology
biquini, bikini *sm* bikini
Birmania *nombre propio* Burma
birria *sf familiar* ❶ [*persona*] sight ❷ [*cosa*] monstrosity
bisabuelo, la *sm, f* great-grandfather, *femenino* great-grandmother
bisagra *sf* hinge
bisexual *adj* & *smf* bisexual ❖ *Los adjetivos ingleses son invariables.*
bisiesto → **año**
bisnieto, ta *sm, f* great-grandchild; great-grandson, *femenino* great-granddaughter
bisonte *sm* bison
bisoño, ña *sm, f* novice
bistec *sm* steak
bisturí (pl bisturíes o bisturís) *sm* scalpel
bisutería *sf* imitation jewelry
bit (pl bits) *sm* INFORMÁTICA bit
bizco, ca *adj* cross-eyed ❖ *Los adjetivos ingleses son invariables.*
bizcocho *sm* sponge
blanco, ca ◆ *adj* white • **una pared blanca** a white wall ❖ *Los adjetivos ingleses son invariables.*
◆ *sm, f* [*persona*] white (person)
■ **blanco** *sm* ❶ [*color*] white • **el blanco es mi color preferido** white is my favorite color • **el blanco del ojo** the white of the eye ❷ [*diana*] target • **el ciervo fue el blanco de los cazadores** the deer was the target of the hunters • **dar en el blanco a)** DEPORTE & MILITAR to hit the target **b)** *figurado* to hit the nail on the head ❸ *figurado* [*objetivo*] target • **fue el blanco de todas las críticas** he was the target of all the criticism ❹ [*de miradas*] object ❺ [*espacio vacío*] blank (space)
■ **blanca** *sf* MÚSICA half note
expresión **estar** o **quedarse sin blanca** *figurado* to be flat broke
blancura *sf* whiteness
blandengue *adj literal & figurado* weak ❖ *Los adjetivos ingleses son invariables.*
blando, da *adj* ❶ [*generalmente*] soft • **una superficie blanda** a soft surface ❷ [*carne*] tender • **mi filete estaba muy tierno** my steak was really tender ❸ *figurado* [*personadébil*] weak; [*indulgente*] lenient • **es muy blando con sus hijos** he's very lenient with his children ❖ *Los adjetivos ingleses son invariables.*
blanquear *vt* ❶ [*ropa*] to whiten ❷ [*con lejía*] to bleach ❸ [*con cal*] to whitewash ❹ *figurado* [*dinero*] to launder
blanquecino, na *adj* off-white ❖ *Los adjetivos ingleses son invariables.*
blanqueo *sm* ❶ [*de ropa*] whitening ❷ [*con lejía*] bleaching ❸ [*encalado*] whitewashing ❹ *figurado* [*de dinero*] laundering
blanquillo *sm* [*huevo*] egg

blasfemar *vi* RELIGIÓN • **blasfemar (contra)** to blaspheme (against)
blasfemia *sf* RELIGIÓN blasphemy
bledo *sm*
expresión **me importa un bledo (lo que diga)** *familiar* I don't give a damn (about what he says)
blindado, da *adj* ❶ armor-plated ❷ [*coche*] armored ❖ *Los adjetivos ingleses son invariables.*
bloc (pl blocs) *sm* pad ▸ **bloc de dibujo** sketchpad ▸ **bloc de notas** notepad
bloque *sm* ❶ [*generalmente*] INFORMÁTICA block • **un bloque de cemento** a cement block ❷ POLÍTICA bloc ❸ MECÁNICA cylinder block
bloquear *vt* ❶ [*generalmente*] DEPORTE to block • **el camión bloqueaba la entrada** the truck was blocking the entrance ❷ [*aislar - sujeto: ejército, barcos*] to blockade; [*- sujeto: nieve, inundación*] to cut off ❸ FINANZAS to freeze
bloqueo *sm* ❶ [*generalmente*] DEPORTE blocking ▸ **bloqueo mental** mental block ❷ ECONOMÍA & MILITAR blockade ❸ FINANZAS freeze
blusa *sf* blouse
blusón *sm* ❶ [*camisa*] long shirt ❷ [*de pintor*] smock
boa *sf* ZOOLOGÍA boa
bobada *sf familiar* • **decir bobadas** to talk nonsense
bobina *sf* ❶ [*generalmente*] reel ❷ [*en máquina de coser*] bobbin ❸ ELECTRICIDAD coil
bobo, ba ◆ *adj* ❶ [*tonto*] daft ❷ [*ingenuo*] naïve ❖ *Los adjetivos ingleses son invariables.*
◆ *sm, f* ❶ [*tonto*] idiot ❷ [*ingenuo*] simpleton
boca *sf* ❶ [*generalmente*] mouth • **una boca pequeña** a small mouth • **boca arriba/abajo** face up/down ❷ [*entrada*] opening ❸ [*de cañón*] muzzle ▸ **boca de metro** subway entrance
expresión **quedarse con la boca abierta** to be dumbfounded ▸ **se me hace la boca agua** it makes my mouth water
bocacalle *sf* side street • **la tienda está en una bocacalle de la plaza** the store is in a side street off the square • **gire en la tercera bocacalle** take the third turning
bocado *sm* ❶ [*comida*] mouthful • **no probar bocado a)** [*por estar desganado*] not to touch your food **b)** [*no haber podido comer*] not to have a thing to eat • **no hemos probado bocado** we haven't had a thing to eat ❷ [*mordisco*] bite • **probé un bocado del pastel** I tried a bite of the cake
bocanada *sf* ❶ [*de líquido*] mouthful ❷ [*de humo*] puff ❸ [*de viento*] gust
boceto *sm* sketch
bochorno *sm* ❶ [*calor*] stifling heat ❷ [*vergüenza*] embarrassment
bochornoso, sa *adj* ❶ [*tiempo*] muggy ❷ [*vergonzoso*] embarrassing ❖ *Los adjetivos ingleses son invariables.*

bocina *sf* ❶ AUTOMÓVILES & MÚSICA horn • **el conductor tocó la bocina** the driver honked the horn ❷ [*megáfono*] megaphone

bocón, ona *sm, f familiar* bigmouth

boda *sf* ❶ [*ceremonia*] wedding ❷ [*convite*] reception ▶ **bodas de diamante/oro/plata** diamond/golden/silver wedding *sing*

bodega *sf* ❶ [*cava*] wine cellar • **una bodega de vino** a wine cellar ❷ [*tienda*] wine shop ❸ [*bar*] bar ❹ [*en buque, avión*] hold • **el equipaje está en la bodega del barco** the luggage is in the ship's hold

bodegón *sm* ARTE still life

bodrio *sm* ❶ *familiar & despectivo* [*generalmente*] rubbish ☼: *incontable* ❷ [*comida*] pigswill ☼: *incontable*

body (pl bodies) *sm* body

bofetada *sf* slap (in the face) • **le dio una bofetada fuerte** she gave him a hard slap

bofetón *sm* hard slap (in the face)

boga *sf*
expresión **estar en boga** to be in vogue

bogavante *sm* lobster

Bogotá *nombre propio* Bogotá

bohemio, mia *adj* ❶ [*vida* ETC] bohemian ❷ [*de Bohemia*] Bohemian ☼: *Los adjetivos ingleses son invariables.*

boicot (pl boicots) *sm* boycott

boicotear *vt* to boycott

bóiler *sm* boiler

boina *sf* beret

bol (pl boles) *sm* bowl

bola *sf* ball • **pásame la bola** pass me the ball ▶ **bola de cristal** crystal ball ▶ **bolas de naftalina** mothballs
expresión **convertirse en una bola de nieve** to snowball ▶ **se corrió la bola** the rumor has spread

bolear *vt* to shine • **boleo mis zapatos todas las semanas** I shine my shoes every week

bolería *sf* shoeshine stand

bolero, ra *sm, f* shoeshine • **hay muchos boleros en la ciudad** there are many shoeshines in the city

boleta *sf* ❶ [*recibo*] receipt • **reclama siempre tu boleta de compra** always ask for your receipt ❷ [*para voto*] voting slip ❸ [*de calificaciones*] report card

boletero, ra *sm, f* box office attendant

boletín *sm* bulletin ▶ **boletín de noticias** o **informativo** news bulletin ▶ **boletín meteorológico** weather forecast ▶ **boletín de prensa** press release

boleto *sm* ❶ [*de rifa, cine*] ticket ❷ [*para medio de transporte*] ticket • **compré un boleto de autobús** I bought a bus ticket ▶ **un boleto de ida y vuelta** a round-trip ticket ▶ **un boleto de viaje redondo** a round-trip ticket

boliche *sm* ❶ [*en la petanca*] jack ❷ [*bolos*] bowling • **le gusta jugar boliche** he likes to go bowling ❸ [*bolera*] bowling alley

bólido *sm* racing car
expresión **ir como un bólido** to go like the clappers

bolígrafo *sm* pen • **marca las correcciones con un bolígrafo rojo** mark the corrections with a red pen

bolillo *sm* bread roll

Bolivia *nombre propio* Bolivia

boliviano, na *adj* & *sm, f* Bolivian ☼: *Los adjetivos ingleses son invariables.*

bollo *sm* ❶ [*para comer - de pan*] (bread) roll; [*- dulce*] bun ❷ [*abolladura*] dent ❸ [*abultamiento*] bump

bolo *sm* ❶ DEPORTE [*pieza*] skittle ❷ [*actuación*] show

bolsa *sf* ❶ [*generalmente*] bag • **traje las compras en una bolsa de papel** I carried the shopping in a paper bag • **mi hermana compró una bolsa roja** my sister bought a red purse ▶ **bolsa de agua caliente** hot-water bottle ▶ **bolsa de aire** air pocket ▶ **bolsa de basura** bin liner ▶ **bolsa de deportes** sports bag ▶ **bolsa de dormir** sleeping bag ▶ **bolsa de papas fritas** bag of chips ▶ **bolsa de plástico** plastic bag ▶ **bolsa de viaje** travel bag ❷ FINANZAS ▶ **bolsa (de valores)** stock market • **la bolsa ha subido/bajado** share prices have gone up/down • **jugar a la bolsa** to speculate on the stock market

bolsillo *sm* pocket • **lo pagué de mi bolsillo** I paid for it out of my own pocket • **de bolsillo** pocket ☼: *Sólo se usa delante del sustantivo.* • **una edición de bolsillo** a pocket edition

bolsista *smf* ❶ stockbroker ❷ pickpocket

bolso *sm* ❶ bag • **un bolso de cuero** a leather bag ❷ [*de mujer*] purse

bomba *sf* ❶ [*explosivo*] bomb • **estalló una bomba en una tienda** a bomb exploded in a store ▶ **bomba atómica** atom o nuclear bomb ▶ **bomba de mano** (hand) grenade ❷ [*máquina*] pump • **usamos una bomba para sacar el agua** we used a pump to get the water out ❸ *figurado* [*acontecimiento*] bombshell

bombardear *vt literal & figurado* to bombard

bombardeo *sm* bombardment

bombardero *sm* bomber

bombear *vt* [*generalmente*] DEPORTE to pump • **los voluntarios bombearon el agua del pozo** the volunteers pumped out the water from the well

bombero, ra *sm, f* [*de incendios*] fireman, *femenino* firewoman

bombilla *sf* [*de lámpara*] light bulb

bombillo *sm* light bulb

bombo *sm* ❶ MÚSICA bass drum ❷ *familiar & figurado* [*elogio*] hype ❸ MECÁNICA drum
expresión **estar con bombo** *familiar* to be in the family way ▶ **a bombo y platillo** with a lot of hype

bombón *sm* chocolate

bombona *sf* cylinder ▶ **bombona de butano** (butane) gas cylinder

bonachón, ona *adj familiar* kindly ☼: *Los adjetivos ingleses son invariables.*

bonanza *sf* ❶ [*de tiempo*] fair weather ❷ [*de mar*] calm at sea ❸ *figurado* [*prosperidad*] prosperity

B

bondad *sf* ❶ [*cualidad*] goodness ❷ [*inclinación*] kindness • **tener la bondad de hacer algo** to be kind enough to do something

bondadoso, sa *adj* kind ☼: *Los adjetivos ingleses son invariables.*

bonito, ta *adj* ❶ pretty • **esta blusa es muy bonita** this blouse is very pretty ❷ [*bueno*] nice • **¡qué día tan bonito!** what a nice day! ☼: *Los adjetivos ingleses son invariables.*

■ **bonito** *sm* bonito (tuna)

bono *sm* ❶ [*vale*] voucher • **me dieron un bono por el 10% de mi compra** they gave me a voucher for 10% off my purchase ❷ COMERCIO bond ▶ **bono del Estado/ del tesoro** government/treasury bond

boquete *sm* hole

boquiabierto, ta *adj* ❶ open-mouthed ❷ figurado astounded ☼: *Los adjetivos ingleses son invariables.*

boquilla *sf* ❶ [*para fumar*] cigarette holder ❷ [*de pipa, instrumento musical*] mouthpiece ❸ [*de tubo, aparato*] nozzle

borda *sf* NÁUTICA gunwale

expresión **tirar** o **echar algo por la borda** to throw something overboard

bordado, da *adj* embroidered ☼: *Los adjetivos ingleses son invariables.*

■ **bordado** *sm* embroidery

bordar *vt* to embroider

borde *sm* ❶ [*generalmente*] edge • **es peligroso asomarse al borde del barranco** it's dangerous to get close to the edge of the ravine ❷ [*de carretera*] side ❸ [*del mar*] shore ❹ [*de río*] bank ❺ [*de vaso, botella*] rim • **al borde de** figurado on the verge of • **está al borde de una crisis nerviosa** he's on the verge of a nervous breakdown

bordear *vt* ❶ [*estar alrededor de*] to border ❷ [*moverse alrededor de*] to skirt (round)

bordillo *sm* curb

bordo ■ **a bordo** locución adverbial on board • **subimos a bordo de la lancha** we got on board the boat

borrachera *sf* ❶ [*embriaguez*] drunkenness ☼: incontable • **coger una borrachera** to get drunk ❷ figurado [*emoción*] intoxication

borracho, cha *adj* & *sm, f* drunk ☼: *Los adjetivos ingleses son invariables.*

■ **borracho** *sm* [*bizcocho*] ≃ rum baba

borrador *sm* ❶ [*de escrito*] rough draft • **es un borrador** it's a rough draft ❷ [*de dibujo*] sketch ❸ [*goma de borrar*] eraser • **la maestra pidió un borrador nuevo** the teacher asked for a new eraser

borrar *vt* ❶ [*con goma, en casete*] to erase ❷ [*en computadora*] to delete ❸ [*tachar*] to cross out ❹ figurado [*de lista* ETC] to remove ❺ figurado [*olvidar*] to erase

borrasca *sf* area of low pressure

borrego, ga *sm, f* lamb

borrón *sm* ❶ blot ❷ figurado blemish

expresión **hacer borrón y cuenta nueva** to wipe the slate clean

borroso, sa *adj* ❶ [*foto, visión*] blurred ❷ [*escritura, texto*] smudgy ❸ [*recuerdo*] vague ☼: *Los adjetivos ingleses son invariables.*

Bosnia *nombre propio* Bosnia

bosnio, nia *adj* & *sm, f* Bosnian ☼: *Los adjetivos ingleses son invariables.*

bosque *sm* ❶ [*pequeño*] wood ❷ [*grande*] forest

bostezar *vi* to yawn

bostezo *sm* yawn

bota *sf* ❶ [*calzado*] boot • **compré botas de cuero** I bought leather boots ▶ **botas vaqueras/de montar** cowboy/riding boots ❷ [*de vino*] small leather container in which wine is kept

botado, a ◆ *adj* ❶ [*expulsado*] fired ❷ [*barato*] cheap ◆ *sm, f* foundling

botana *sf* snack • **es un lugar ideal para comer botanas** it's an ideal place to eat snacks

botánico, ca ◆ *adj* botanical ☼: *Los adjetivos ingleses son invariables.*
◆ *sm, f* [*persona*] botanist
■ **botánica** *sf* [*ciencia*] botany

botar ◆ *vt* ❶ NÁUTICA to launch ❷ familiar [*despedir*] to throw out ❸ [*pelota*] to bounce ❹ [*tirar*] to throw • **está prohibido botar papeles al suelo** it's prohibited to throw paper on the ground ◆ *vi* ❶ [*saltar*] to jump ❷ [*pelota*] to bounce

bote *sm* ❶ [*tarro*] jar • **no queda mermelada en el bote** there's no jam left in the jar ❷ [*lata*] can • **compramos un bote de pintura** we bought a can of paint ❸ [*barca*] boat • **hay muchos botes en el lago hoy** there are lots of boats in the lake today • **pasear en bote** to go sailing ▶ **bote salvavidas** lifeboat ❹ [*salto*] jump • **dar botes a)** [*generalmente*] to jump up and down **b)** [*en tren, coche*] to bump up and down ❺ [*de pelota*] bounce • **dar botes** to bounce

botella *sf* bottle • **una botella de vidrio** a glass bottle ▶ **de botella** bottled

botellín *sm* small bottle

botín *sm* ❶ [*de guerra, atraco*] loot ❷ [*calzado*] ankle boot

botiquín *sm* ❶ [*caja*] first-aid kit ❷ [*mueble*] first-aid cupboard ❸ [*enfermería*] first-aid post

botón *sm* button • **perdió dos botones de la blusa** she lost two buttons off her blouse ▶ **botón de marcado abreviado** TELECOMUNICACIONES speed-dial button
■ **botones** *sm invariable* ❶ [*de hotel*] bellhop ❷ [*de oficinas* ETC] errand boy

boutique *sf* boutique

bóveda *sf* ARQUITECTURA vault

box (pl boxes) *sm* boxing • **el box es un deporte muy rudo** boxing is a very rough sport

boxeador, ra *sm, f* boxer

boxear *vi* to box

boxeo *sm* boxing

bóxer (pl boxers) *sm* boxer

braille *sm* Braille

brandy *sm* brandy

brasa *sf* ember • **a la brasa** Cocina barbecued

brasero *sm* brazier

brasier, brassier *sm* bra

Brasil *nombre propio* Brazil

brassier = brasier

braveza *sf* bravery

bravo, va *adj* ❶ [*valiente*] brave ❷ [*animal*] wild ❸ [*mar*] rough ☼ *Los adjetivos ingleses son invariables.*

■ **bravo** ◆ *sm* [*aplauso*] cheer
◆ *exclamación* • ¡bravo! bravo!

bravuconear *vi despectivo* to brag

bravura *sf* ❶ [*de persona*] bravery ❷ [*de animal*] ferocity

brazada *sf* stroke

brazalete *sm* ❶ [*en la muñeca*] bracelet ❷ [*en el brazo*] armband

brazo *sm* ❶ [*generalmente*] Anatomía arm • **Ricardo se fracturó el brazo** Ricardo broke his arm • **cogidos del brazo** arm in arm • **en brazos** in your arms ❷ [*de animal*] foreleg ❸ [*de árbol, río, candelabro*] branch ▸ *expresión* **luchar a brazo partido** to fight tooth and nail ▸ **ser el brazo derecho de alguien** to be somebody's right-hand man, *femenino* woman

brea *sf* ❶ [*sustancia*] tar ❷ [*para barco*] pitch

brebaje *sm* concoction

brecha *sf* ❶ [*abertura*] hole ❷ Militar breach ❸ *figurado* [*impresión*] impression

breve ◆ *adj* brief • **una breve pausa** a brief pause • **en breve a)** [*pronto*] shortly **b)** [*en pocas palabras*] in short ☼ *Los adjetivos ingleses son invariables.*
◆ *sf* Música breve

brevedad *sf* shortness • **con la mayor brevedad** as soon as possible

bribón, ona *sm, f* scoundrel

brigada ◆ *sm* Militar ≃ warrant officer
◆ *sf* ❶ Militar brigade ❷ [*equipo*] squad

brillante ◆ *adj* ❶ [*reluciente - luz, astro*] shining; [*- metal, zapatos, pelo*] shiny; [*- ojos, sonrisa, diamante*] sparkling ❷ [*magnífico*] brilliant • **es una estudiante brillante** she's a brilliant student ☼ *Los adjetivos ingleses son invariables.*
◆ *sm* diamond

brillantina *sf* brilliantine; Brylcreem®

brillar *vi* ❶ [*estrellas, sol*] to shine • **las estrellas brillan** the stars are shining ❷ [*ojos, diamante*] to sparkle • **sus ojos brillaban** his eyes sparkled

brillo *sm* ❶ [*de sol, estrellas*] brilliance ❷ [*de zapatos*] shine ❸ [*lucimiento*] splendor

brilloso, sa *adj* shining • **los zapatos estaban brillosos** the shoes were shining ☼ *Los adjetivos ingleses son invariables.*

brincar *vi* to skip (about) • **brincar de alegría** to jump for joy • **el niño brincaba de emoción** the boy was jumping up and down in excitement

brinco *sm* jump
expresión **en un brinco** in a second ▸ **pegar un brinco** to jump • **pegué un brinco al verla** seeing her made me jump

brindar ◆ *vi* to drink a toast • **brindar por algo/alguien** to drink to something/somebody • **en la fiesta brindamos por los novios** at the party we drank a toast to the bride and groom
◆ *vt* to offer • **te brindo mi amor** I offer you my love
■ **brindarse** *v pronominal* • **brindarse a hacer algo** to offer to do something • **me brindé a lavar los platos** I offered to do the dishes

brindis *sm invariable* toast • **hagamos un brindis por los novios** let's drink a toast to the bride and groom

brío *sm* spirit

brisa *sf* breeze • **hay una brisa muy agradable** there's a very pleasant breeze

británico, ca ◆ *adj* British ☼ *Los adjetivos ingleses son invariables.*
◆ *sm, f* British person; Briton • **los británicos** the British

broca *sf* (drill) bit

brocha *sf* brush ▸ **brocha de afeitar** shaving brush

brochazo *sm* brushstroke

broche *sm* ❶ [*cierre*] fastener • **se rompió el broche del collar** the fastener of the necklace broke ▸ **broche de oro** *figurado* final flourish ❷ [*joya*] brooch • **me gusta usar un broche en la solapa** I like to wear a brooch in my lapel ❸ [*para el cabello*] barrette

broma *sf* ❶ [*ocurrencia, chiste*] joke ❷ [*jugarreta*] practical joke • **lo decía en broma** I was just joking • **gastar una broma a alguien** to play a joke on somebody

bromear *vi* to joke • **sólo estábamos bromeando** we were only joking

bromista *smf* joker

bronca *sf* fight • **se armó una bronca terrible en el partido** there was a terrible fight during the game

bronce *sm* bronze

bronceado, da *adj* tanned • **su piel estaba bronceada** his skin was tanned • **ponerse bronceado** to get a tan • **me pongo bronceado después de sólo una hora en el sol** I get a tan after only one hour in the sun ☼ *Los adjetivos ingleses son invariables.*
■ **bronceado** *sm* tan

broncear *vt* to tan

bronquio *sm* bronchial tube

bronquitis *sf invariable* bronchitis

brotar *vi* ❶ [*planta*] to sprout ❷ [*agua, sangre* etc] • **brotar de** to well up out of ❸ *figurado* [*esperanza, sospechas, pasiones*] to stir ❹ [*en la piel*] • **le brotó un sarpullido** he broke out in a rash

brote *sm* ❶ [*de planta*] bud ❷ *figurado* [*inicios*] sign

bruja ◆ *sf* ❶ [*hechicera*] witch ❷ [*mujer fea*] hag ❸ [*mujer mala*] cow
◆ *adj invariable* ▶ **estar bruja** *familiar* to be broke ⚲ *Los adjetivos ingleses son invariables.*
brujería *sf* witchcraft
brujo, ja *adj* ❶ [*hechicero*] enchanting ❷ *familiar* [*sin dinero*] ▶ **estar brujo** to be broke • **a esta altura del mes estamos brujos** at this point of the month we're broke ⚲ *Los adjetivos ingleses son invariables.*
■ **brujo** *sm* wizard
brújula *sf* compass
bruma *sf* ❶ [*niebla*] mist ❷ [*en el mar*] sea mist
brusco, ca *adj* ❶ [*repentino, imprevisto*] sudden ❷ [*tosco, grosero*] brusque ⚲ *Los adjetivos ingleses son invariables.*
brusquedad *sf* ❶ [*imprevisión*] suddenness ❷ [*grosería*] brusqueness
brutal *adj* brutal ⚲ *Los adjetivos ingleses son invariables.*
brutalidad *sf* brutality
bruto, ta ◆ *adj* ❶ [*torpe*] clumsy ❷ [*ignorante*] thick ❸ [*maleducado*] rude ❹ [*sin tratar*] • **en bruto a)** [*diamante*] uncut **b)** [*petróleo*] crude ❺ [*sueldo, peso* etc] gross • **las ganancias brutas** gross profits ⚲ *Los adjetivos ingleses son invariables.*
◆ *sm, f* brute
bucear *vi* [*en agua*] to dive
buceo *sm* (underwater) diving
bucle *sm* [*rizo*] curl
budismo *sm* Buddhism
bueno, na *adj* ❶ [*generalmente*] good • **sacó muy buenas notas en el examen** he got very good grades on the test ❷ [*bondadoso*] kind • **ser bueno con alguien** to be good to somebody ❸ [*curado, sano*] well ❹ [*tiempo, clima*] fine ❺ [*aprovechable*] all right ❻ [*comida*] fresh ❼ [*uso enfático*] • **ese buen hombre** that good man • **un buen día** one fine day ⚲ *Los adjetivos ingleses son invariables.*
expresiones **de buen ver** good-looking ▶ **de buenas a primeras a)** [*de repente*] all of a sudden **b)** [*a simple vista*] at first sight ▶ **estar bueno** *familiar* [*persona*] to be hot ▶ **estar de buenas** to be in a good mood ▶ **lo bueno es que...** the best thing about it is that...
■ **bueno** ◆ *sm* CINE • **el bueno** the goody
◆ *adv* ❶ [*vale, de acuerdo*] O.K. • **bueno, comamos pizza** OK, let's eat pizza ❷ [*pues*] well
◆ *exclamación* [*al teléfono*] • **¡bueno!** hello • **¡bueno! ¿quién habla?** hello! who's speaking?
Buenos Aires *nombre propio* Buenos Aires
buey (pl bueyes) *sm* ox
búfalo *sm* buffalo
bufanda *sf* scarf
bufé, buffet (pl buffets) *sm* [*en restaurante*] buffet
bufón *sm* buffoon
buhardilla *sf* attic
búho *sm* owl
buitre *sm* literal & figurado vulture

bujía *sf* AUTOMÓVILES spark plug
bulbo *sm* ANATOMÍA & BOTÁNICA bulb
bulevar (pl bulevares) *sm* boulevard
Bulgaria *nombre propio* Bulgaria
bulla *sf* racket ; uproar • **armar bulla** to make a racket
bullicio *sm* ❶ [*de ciudad, mercado*] hustle and bustle ❷ [*de multitud*] hubbub
bullicioso, sa *adj* ❶ [*agitado - reunión, multitud*] noisy ; [*- calle, mercado*] busy ❷ [*inquieto*] rowdy ⚲ *Los adjetivos ingleses son invariables.*
bulto *sm* ❶ [*volumen*] bulk ❷ [*en cabeza, rodilla*] bump ❸ [*en bolsillo*] bulge • **la cartera te hace un bulto en el bolsillo** your wallet makes a bulge in your pocket ❹ [*forma imprecisa*] blurred shape • **sólo puedo distinguir dos bultos grandes en este cuarto oscuro** I can only distinguish two large shapes in this dark room ❺ [*paquete*] package ❻ [*maleta*] bag • **viajan con cuatro bultos** they're traveling with four bags ▶ **bulto de mano** item of hand luggage ❼ [*fardo*] bundle
expresión **escurrir el bulto a)** [*trabajo*] to shirk **b)** [*cuestión*] to evade the issue
bungalow (pl bungalows) *sm* bungalow
búnquer (pl búnquers), **bunker** (pl bunkers) *sm* [*refugio*] bunker
buñuelo *sm* COCINA [*dulce*] sweet fritter ; [*de bacalao* etc] ≃ dumpling
buque *sm* ship ▶ **buque nodriza** supply ship ▶ **buque de vapor** steamer
burbuja *sf* bubble • **hacer burbujas** to bubble • **con burbujas** fizzy
burbujear *vi* to bubble
burdel *sm* brothel
burdo, da *adj* ❶ [*generalmente*] crude ❷ [*tela*] coarse ⚲ *Los adjetivos ingleses son invariables.*
burgués, esa *adj* ❶ middle-class ❷ HISTORIA & POLÍTICA bourgeois ⚲ *Los adjetivos ingleses son invariables.*
burguesía *sf* ❶ middle class ❷ HISTORIA & POLÍTICA bourgeoisie
burla *sf* ❶ [*mofa*] taunt • **las burlas de sus compañeros fueron crueles** the taunts of his colleagues were cruel • **hacer burla de** to mock ❷ [*broma*] joke ❸ [*engaño*] trick
expresión **burlas aparte** joking aside
■ **burlas** *sfpl* ridicule ⚲ *incontable*
burlar *vt* ❶ [*esquivar*] to evade ❷ [*ley*] to flout
expresión **burla burlando** without anyone noticing
burlón, ona *adj* mocking ⚲ *Los adjetivos ingleses son invariables.*
buró *sm* bedside table
burocracia *sf* bureaucracy
burócrata *smf* bureaucrat
burrada *sf* [*acción, dicho*] • **hacer burradas** to act stupidly • **decir burradas** to talk nonsense
burrito *sm* burrito
burro, rra *sm, f* ❶ [*animal*] donkey ❷ *familiar* [*necio*] dimwit

expresión apearse o **bajarse del burro** *familiar* to back down ▶ **no ver tres en un burro** *familiar* to be as blind as a bat

■ **burro** *sm* ❶ [*escalera*] stepladder ❷ [*tabla de planchar*] ironing board

bursátil *adj* stock-market ☼: *Sólo se usa delante del sustantivo.* • **inversiones bursátiles** stock-market investments

bus (pl buses) *sm* AUTOMÓVILES & INFORMÁTICA bus • **tomamos el bus para ir al museo** we took the bus to the museum

buscar ◆ *vt* ❶ [*generalmente*] to look for • **estoy buscando trabajo** I'm looking for work • **'se busca camarero'** waiter wanted ❷ [*recoger*] to get • **voy a buscar el periódico** I'm going to get the paper • **ir a buscar a alguien** to pick somebody up • **va a buscar a los niños al colegio todos los días** she goes to pick up the children from school every day ❸ [*en diccionario, índice, horario*] to look up • **busqué la palabra en el diccio-** nario I looked up the word in the dictionary ❹ INFORMÁTICA to search for

◆ *vi* to look • **sigamos buscando** let's keep looking
■ **buscarse** *v pronominal* • **buscársela** to be asking for it

buscón, ona *sm, f* swindler

búsqueda *sf* search • **la búsqueda de la niña duró dos días** the search for the girl lasted two days

busto *sm* [*pecho, escultura*] bust

butaca *sf* ❶ [*mueble*] armchair ❷ [*en cine*] seat

butano *sm* butane (gas)

buzo *sm* [*persona*] diver

buzón *sm* mailbox • **encontré dos cartas en el buzón** I found two letters in the mailbox • **echar algo al buzón** to mail something ▶ **buzón electrónico** electronic mailbox ▶ **buzón de sugerencias** suggestion box ▶ **buzón de voz** voice mail

byte *sm* INFORMÁTICA byte

C

c, c *sf* [*letra*] c ; C

c/ ❶ (*abreviatura escrita de* calle) St. **❷** (*abreviatura escrita de* cuenta) a/c

cabalgar *vi* to ride

cabalgata *sf* cavalcade

caballa *sf* mackerel

caballada *sf* **❶** herd of horses **❷** asinine remark o action

caballería *sf* **❶** [*animal*] mount **❷** [*cuerpo militar*] cavalry

caballero ♦ *adj* [*cortés*] gentlemanly ⚬ *Los adjetivos ingleses son invariables.*

♦ *sm* **❶** [*generalmente*] gentleman • **ser todo un caballero** to be a real gentleman **❷** [*al dirigir la palabra*] sir **❸** [*miembro de una orden*] knight

caballete *sm* **❶** [*de lienzo*] easel **❷** [*de mesa*] trestle **❸** [*de nariz*] bridge

caballito *sm* small horse

caballo *sm* **❶** [*animal*] horse • **montar a caballo** to ride **▶ caballo de Troya** Trojan horse **❷** [*pieza de ajedrez*] knight **❸** [*naipe*] ≃ queen **❹** MECÁNICA **▶ caballo (de fuerza o de vapor)** horsepower

cabaña *sf* **❶** [*choza*] cabin **❷** [*ganado*] livestock ⚬ *incontable*

cabaré *sm* cabaret

cabecear *vi* **❶** [*persona - negando*] to shake your head ; [- *afirmando*] to nod your head **❷** [*caballo*] to toss its head **❸** [*dormir*] to nod (off) • **el viejo cabeceaba frente a la tele** the old man was nodding off in front of the TV **❹** [*en futbol*] to head the ball • **el jugador cabeceó y marcó un gol** the player headed the ball and scored a goal

cabecera *sf* **❶** [*generalmente*] head • **el invitado se sentó a la cabecera de la mesa** the guest sat down at the head of the table **❷** [*de cama*] headboard **❸** [*de texto*] heading **❹** [*de periódico*] headline **❺** [*de río*] headwaters *pl*

cabecilla *smf* ringleader

cabellera *sf* long hair ⚬ *incontable*

cabello *sm* hair ⚬ *incontable* • **tiene un cabello suave y brilloso** she has smooth, glossy hair

caber *vi* **❶** [*generalmente*] to fit • **en esta habitación caben diez personas** ten people fit in this room • **no cabe nadie más** there's no room for anyone else • **no me cabe en el dedo** it won't fit my finger • **estos pantalones ya no me caben** these pants don't fit me anymore **❷** [*ser posible*] to be possible • **cabe destacar que...** it's worth pointing out that...

cabestrillo ■ en cabestrillo *locución adjetiva* in a sling

cabeza *sf* **❶** [*generalmente*] head • **me duele la cabeza** I have a headache • **por cabeza** per person • **tirarse de cabeza (a)** *literal & figurado* to dive (into) • **venir a la cabeza** to come to mind **▶ cabeza (lectora)** head **▶ cabeza de ajo** head of garlic **❷** [*pelo*] hair **❸** [*posición*] front • **a la cabeza** at the head • **el sacerdote iba a la cabeza de la procesión** the priest was at the head of the procession

expresiones alzar o **levantar cabeza** to get back on your feet **▶ se le ha metido en la cabeza que...** he has got it into his head that... **▶ obrar con cabeza** to use your head **▶ perder la cabeza** to lose your head **▶ romperse la cabeza** to rack your brains **▶ sentar la cabeza** to settle down

■ cabeza de familia *sm, f* head of the household

cabezada *sf* **❶** [*de sueño*] nod • **dar cabezadas** to nod off **❷** [*golpe*] butt

cabezal *sm* [*de aparato*] head

cabezón, ona *adj* [*terco*] pigheaded ⚬ *Los adjetivos ingleses son invariables.*

cabida *sf* capacity • **dar cabida a, tener cabida para** to hold ; to have room for

cabina *sf* **❶** [*locutorio*] booth **▶ cabina de prensa** press box **❷** **▶ cabina telefónica** phone booth **❸** [*de avión*] cockpit **▶ cabina de mandos** flight deck **❹** [*de camión*] cab

cabizbajo, ja *adj* crestfallen ⚬ *Los adjetivos ingleses son invariables.*

cable *sm* cable • **se tropezó con un cable** he tripped on a cable • **tengo cable en casa** I have cable television at home

expresión echar un cable *familiar & figurado* to help out ; to lend a hand

cabo *sm* ❶ GEOGRAFÍA cape ❷ NÁUTICA rope ❸ MILITAR corporal ❹ [*trozo*] bit ❺ [*trozo final*] stub ❻ [*de cuerda*] end ▶ **cabo suelto** loose end

expresiones **atar cabos** to put two and two together • **el inspector ató cabos hasta dar con el asesino** the inspector put two and two together and found the murderer ▶ **llevar algo a cabo** to carry something out • **la empresa llevó a cabo un proyecto original** the company carried out an original project

cabra *sf* [*animal*] goat

expresión **estar como una cabra** *familiar* to be off your head ▶ **la cabra siempre tira al monte** *proverbio* you can't make a leopard change his spots

cabrito *sm* [*animal*] kid (goat)

cabrón, ona *vulgar* ◆ *adj* • **¡qué cabrón eres!** you bastard!:♀: *Los adjetivos ingleses son invariables.*
◆ *sm, f* bastard, *femenino* bitch

caca *sf familiar* ❶ [*excremento*] pooh ❷ [*cosa sucia*] dirty thing

cacahuate *sm* peanut

cacao *sm* ❶ [*bebida*] cocoa ❷ [*árbol*] cacao

cacarear *vi* [*gallo*] to cluck

cacatúa *sf* cockatoo

cacería *sf* hunt

cacerola *sf* pan

cachalote *sm* sperm whale

cacharro *sm* ❶ [*recipiente*] pot • **fregar los cacharros** to do the dishes ❷ *familiar* [*trasto*] junk:♀: *incontable* • **el sótano está lleno de cacharros viejos** the basement is full of old junk ❸ [*máquina*] crock ❹ [*coche*] jalopy

cachear *vt* to frisk

cacheo *sm* frisk

cachet *sm* ❶ [*distinción*] cachet ❷ [*cotización de artista*] fee

cachetada *sf familiar* slap • **le pegó una tremenda cachetada** she gave him a hard slap

cachete *sm* ❶ [*moflete*] cheek • **se le pusieron los cachetes rojos de vergüenza** his cheeks turned red in shame ❷ [*bofetada*] slap • **el padre le pegó un cachete al niño** the father gave the boy a slap

cachetear *vt* to slap

cachivache *sm familiar* knick-knack

cacho *sm familiar* piece

cachorro, rra *sm, f* ❶ [*de perro*] puppy ❷ [*de león, lobo, oso*] cub

cacique *sm* ❶ [*persona influyente*] local political boss ❷ [*jefe indio*] chief

caco *sm familiar* thief

cacto, cactus (*pl* cactus) *sm* cactus

cada *adj invariable* ❶ [*generalmente*] each • **cada alumno trajo su propio cuaderno** each student brought his own notebook • **cada cual** each one; every one • **cada uno de** each of ❷ [*con números, tiempo*] every • **viene a casa cada quince días** he comes home every two weeks • **cada cosa a su tiempo** one thing

at a time ❸ [*valor progresivo*] • **cada vez más** more and more • **cada vez menos** less and less • **cada vez más largo** longer and longer • **cada día más** more and more each day ❹ [*valor enfático*] such • **¡se pone cada sombrero!** she wears such hats! • **¡dices cada cosa!** you say the funniest things:♀: *Los adjetivos ingleses son invariables.*

cadáver *sm* corpse

cadena *sf* ❶ [*generalmente*] chain • **me regalaron una cadena de plata** they gave me a silver chain • **el magnate compró una cadena de hoteles** the magnate bought a chain of hotels ❷ TELEVISIÓN channel • **una sola cadena de televisión transmitirá el partido** only one television channel will show the game ❸ RADIO [*emisora*] station; [*red de emisoras*] network ❹ [*de proceso industrial*] line ▶ **cadena de montaje** assembly line ❺ [*aparato de música*] sound system ❻ GEOGRAFÍA range

■ **cadena perpetua** *sf* life imprisonment • **lo condenaron a cadena perpetua** they sentenced him to life imprisonment

cadencia *sf* rhythm

cadera *sf* hip

cadete *sm* cadet

caducar *vi* ❶ [*carné, ley, pasaporte* ETC] to expire ❷ [*medicamento*] to pass its use-by date ❸ [*alimento*] to pass its sell-by date

caducidad *sf* expiry • **fecha de caducidad** expiration date

caduco, ca *adj* ❶ [*viejo*] decrepit ❷ [*idea*] outmoded ❸ [*desfasado*] no longer valid:♀: *Los adjetivos ingleses son invariables.*

caer *vi* ❶ [*generalmente*] to fall • **cayó un meteorito** a meteorite fell • **cayó la dictadura** the dictatorship fell ❷ [*diente, pelo*] to fall out • **dejar caer algo** to drop something ❸ [*al perder equilibrio*] to fall over • **caer de un tejado/caballo** to fall from a roof/horse ❹ *figurado* [*sentar*] • **caer bien/mal (a alguien)** [*comentario, noticia* ETC] to go down well/badly (with somebody) ❺ *figurado* [*mostrarse*] • **me cae bien/mal** I like/don't like him • **Antonio me cae muy bien** I really like Antonio ❻ *figurado* [*estar situado*] • **cae cerca de aquí** it's not far from here ❼ *figurado* [*recordar*] • **caer (en algo)** to be able to remember (something) • **ahora caigo** now I remember

expresiones **al caer la noche** at nightfall ▶ **caer bajo** to sink (very) low ▶ **estar al caer** to be about to arrive

■ **caerse** *v pronominal* ❶ [*persona*] to fall over • **me caí** I fell over • **se cayó por la escalera** she fell down the stairs ❷ [*objetos*] to drop ❸ [*desprenderse - diente, pelo* ETC] to fall out; [*- botón*] to fall off; [*- cuadro*] to fall down

expresión **caerse de ingenuo/listo** to be incredibly naive/clever

café *sm* ❶ [*generalmente*] coffee ▶ **café solo/con leche** black/white coffee ❷ [*establecimiento*] cafe

cafeína *sf* caffeine

cafetera *sf* ❶ [*generalmente*] coffee pot ❷ [*en bares*] expresso machine ❸ [*eléctrica*] coffee machine

cafetería *sf* cafe

cafetero, ra *sm, f* ❶ [*cultivador*] coffee grower ❷ [*comerciante*] coffee merchant

caído, da *adj* [*árbol, hoja*] fallen ⚡ *Los adjetivos ingleses son invariables.*

■ **caída** *sf* ❶ [*generalmente*] fall • **como consecuencia de una caída, se fracturó una pierna** because of a fall, he broke his leg • **los precios sufrieron una fuerte caída** prices suffered a sharp fall • **caída (de)** [*de paro, precios, terreno*] drop (in) ❷ [*de diente, pelo*] loss ❸ [*de falda, vestido* ETC] drape

caimán *sm* ❶ [*animal*] alligator ❷ *figurado* [*persona*] sly fox

caja *sf* ❶ [*generalmente*] box • **me regalaron una caja de madera** they gave me a wooden box ▶ **caja de zapatos** shoebox ▶ **caja negra** black box ❷ [*para transporte, embalaje*] crate ▶ **caja de cervezas** crate of beer ▶ **caja torácica** thorax ❸ [*de reloj*] case ❹ [*de engranajes* ETC] housing ▶ **caja de cambios** gearbox ❺ [*ataúd*] coffin ❻ [*de dinero*] cash box ▶ **caja fuerte** o **de caudales** safe; strongbox ▶ **caja registradora** cash register ❼ [*en tienda, supermercado*] checkout • **tenemos que pagar en la caja** we have to pay at the checkout ❽ [*en banco*] cashier's desk ❾ [*banco*] ▶ **caja (de ahorros)** savings bank, ≈ savings and loan association ❿ [*hueco - de chimenea, ascensor*] shaft ⓫ IMPRENTA case ⓬ [*de instrumento musical*] body ▶ **caja de resonancia** sound box ▶ **caja de ritmos** drum machine

cajero, ra *sm, f* ❶ [*en tienda*] cashier • **el cajero me cobró de menos** the cashier undercharged me ❷ [*en banco*] teller

■ **cajero** *sm* ▶ **cajero (automático)** ATM

cajetilla *sf* ❶ [*de cigarros*] pack ❷ [*de cerillos*] box

cajón *sm* ❶ [*caja grande*] case ❷ [*gaveta*] drawer ❸ [*ataúd*] coffin

expresión **de cajón** *familiar* customary

cajuela *sf* trunk

cal *sf* lime

cala *sf* ❶ [*bahía pequeña*] cove ❷ [*del barco*] hold

calabacita *sm* zucchini

calabaza *sf* squash

calabozo *sm* cell

calamar *sm* squid

calambre *sm* ❶ [*descarga eléctrica*] (electric) shock ❷ [*contracción muscular*] cramp ⚡ *incontable* • **me dio un fuerte calambre en la pierna** I got a strong cramp in my leg

calamidad *sf* calamity • **ser una calamidad** *figurado* to be a dead loss

calaña *sf* • **de esa calaña** *despectivo* of that ilk

calar ◆ *vt* ❶ [*empapar*] to soak • **la tormenta nos caló** the storm soaked us ❷ *figurado* [*persona*] to see through ❸ [*gorro, sombrero*] to jam on ❹ [*sandía, melón*] to cut a sample of ❺ [*perforar*] to pierce

◆ *vi* ❶ NÁUTICA to draw ❷ *figurado* [*penetrar*] • **calar en** to have an impact on • **su mensaje no acaba de calar en la opinión pública** his message hasn't really had an impact on public opinion

calavera *sf* [*cráneo*] skull

■ **calaveras** *sfpl* [*luces*] tail lights • **no están funcionando bien estas calaveras** these rear car lights aren't working well

calcar *vt* ❶ [*dibujo*] to trace ❷ [*imitar*] to copy

calcetín *sm* sock

calcinar *vt* to char

calcio *sm* calcium

calco *sm* ❶ [*reproducción*] tracing ❷ *figurado* [*imitación*] carbon copy

calcomanía *sf* transfer

calculador, ra *adj* literal & figurado calculating ⚡ *Los adjetivos ingleses son invariables.*

■ **calculadora** *sf* calculator

calcular *vt* ❶ [*cantidades*] to calculate • **calcula el monto total y multiplícalo por dos** calculate the total amount and multiply it by two ❷ [*suponer*] to reckon • **calculo que este trabajo no nos conviene** I reckon that this job doesn't suit us

cálculo *sm* ❶ [*operación, evaluación*] calculation • **según mis cálculos, estaremos en la capital antes del mediodía** according to my calculations, we will be in the capital before noon ❷ [*ciencia*] calculus • **el cálculo es realmente difícil** calculus is really difficult ❸ MEDICINA stone • **me operé de unos cálculos en el riñón** I was operated on for some kidney stones

caldear *vt* ❶ [*calentar*] to heat (up) ❷ *figurado* [*excitar*] to warm up

caldera *sf* ❶ [*recipiente*] cauldron ❷ [*máquina*] boiler

calderilla *sf* small change

caldero *sm* cauldron

caldo *sm* ❶ [*sopa*] broth ❷ [*caldillo*] stock ❸ [*vino*] wine

calefacción *sf* heating • **esta casa tiene muy buena calefacción** this house has very good heating ▶ **calefacción central** central heating

calefactor *sm* heater

calendario *sm* ❶ [*sistema*] calendar ▶ **calendario escolar/laboral** school/working year ▶ **calendario solar** solar calendar ❷ [*programa*] schedule • **marca los feriados en el calendario** mark the holidays on the schedule

calentador *sm* ❶ [*aparato*] heater ❷ [*prenda*] legwarmer

calentar ◆ *vt* [*subir la temperatura de*] to heat (up) • **calienta la comida** heat up the food

◆ *vi* [*entrenarse*] to warm up • **necesito calentar antes del partido** I need to warm up before the match

calentura *sf* ❶ [*fiebre*] fever • **el niño tiene calentura** the boy has a fever ❷ [*herida*] cold sore

calibración *sf* calibration

calibrar *vt* ❶ [*medir*] to calibrate ❷ [*arma*] to bore ❸ *figurado* [*juzgar*] to gauge

calibre *sm* ❶ [*diámetro - de pistola*] calibre; [- *de alambre*] gauge; [- *de tubo*] bore ❷ [*instrumento*] gauge ❸ *figurado* [*tamaño*] size

calidad *sf* ❶ [*generalmente*] quality • **este mueble es de muy buena calidad** this furniture is very good quality • **de calidad** quality 💡 *Sólo se usa delante del sustantivo.* • **ropa de calidad** quality clothing ▸ **calidad de vida** quality of life ❷ [*clase*] class ❸ [*condición*] • **en calidad de** in your capacity as

cálido, da *adj* warm 💡 *Los adjetivos ingleses son invariables.*

caliente *adj* ❶ [*generalmente*] hot • **la plancha está muy caliente** the iron is very hot ❷ [*templado*] warm ❸ *figurado* [*acalorado*] heated • **es una discusión caliente** it's a heated discussion 💡 *Los adjetivos ingleses son invariables.*

expresión en caliente in the heat of the moment

calificación *sf* ❶ [*de película*] rating ❷ EDUCACIÓN grade

calificar *vt* ❶ [*denominar*] • **calificar a alguien de algo** to describe somebody as something ❷ EDUCACIÓN to grade ❸ GRAMÁTICA to qualify

caligrafía *sf* ❶ [*arte*] calligraphy ❷ [*tipo de letra*] handwriting

cáliz *sm* RELIGIÓN chalice

callado, da *adj* quiet 💡 *Los adjetivos ingleses son invariables.*

callar ◆ *vi* ❶ [*no hablar*] to keep quiet • **en estas circunstancias prefiero callar** in these circumstances I prefer to keep quiet ❷ [*dejar de hablar*] to be quiet
◆ *vt* ❶ [*ocultar*] to keep quiet about ❷ [*secreto*] to keep ❸ [*acallar*] to silence
■ **callarse** *v pronominal* ❶ [*no hablar*] to keep quiet ❷ [*dejar de hablar*] to be quiet • **¡cállate!** shut up! • **callarse la boca** to shut up ❸ [*ocultar*] to keep quiet about ❹ [*secreto*] to keep

calle *sf* ❶ [*vía de circulación*] street • **calle arriba/abajo** up/down the street ▸ **calle de dirección única** one-way street ▸ **calle peatonal** pedestrian precinct ▸ **calle sin salida** dead end ❷ DEPORTE lane

expresión dejar a alguien en la calle to put somebody out of a job ▸ **traer o llevar a alguien por la calle de la amargura** to make somebody's life a misery

callejear *vi* to wander the streets

callejón *sm* ❶ alley ▸ **callejón sin salida** cul-de-sac ❷ *figurado* impasse

callejuela *sf* backstreet

callista *smf* chiropodist

callo *sm* ❶ [*dureza*] callus • **tengo un callo en la mano izquierda** I have a callus on my left hand ❷ [*en el pie*] corn • **tengo un callo en el pie derecho** I have a corn on my right foot

expresión dar el callo *familiar & figurado* to slog

calma *sf* ❶ [*sin ruido o movimiento*] calm • **disfruto mucho la calma del campo** I really enjoy the calm of the countryside • **mantengan la calma** keep calm ❷ [*sosiego*] tranquility • **tómatelo con calma** take it easy ❸ [*apatía*] indifference

calmante ◆ *adj* soothing 💡 *Los adjetivos ingleses son invariables.*

◆ *sm* ❶ [*para tranquilizar*] sedative • **el té de tilo es un calmante muy eficaz** lime tea is a very effective sedative ❷ [*para el dolor*] painkiller • **tomé un calmante para el dolor de cabeza** I took a painkiller for my headache

calmar *vt* ❶ [*mitigar*] to relieve • **la aspirina calma el dolor de cabeza** aspirin relieves headaches ❷ [*tranquilizar*] to calm • **la niña calmó a su hermano con palabras suaves** the girl calmed her brother with gentle words
■ **calmarse** *v pronominal* ❶ to calm down • **cálmate, que ya vamos a llegar** calm down, we're nearly there ❷ [*dolor, tempestad*] to abate

calor *sm* ❶ [*generalmente*] heat • **no aguanto este calor** I can't stand this heat ❷ [*sin quemar*] warmth • **entrar en calor a)** [*generalmente*] to get warm **b)** [*público, deportista*] to warm up • **hacer calor** to be warm o hot • **tener calor** to be warm o hot

caloría *sf* calorie

calumnia *sf* ❶ [*oral*] slander ❷ [*escrita*] libel

calumniar *vt* ❶ [*oralmente*] to slander ❷ [*por escrito*] to libel

calumnioso, sa *adj* ❶ [*de palabra*] slanderous ❷ [*por escrito*] libelous 💡 *Los adjetivos ingleses son invariables.*

caluroso, sa *adj* ❶ [*generalmente*] hot ❷ [*templado*] warm ❸ *figurado* [*afectuoso*] warm 💡 *Los adjetivos ingleses son invariables.*

calva *sf* bald patch

calvicie *sf* baldness

calvo, va *adj* bald 💡 *Los adjetivos ingleses son invariables.*

calzado, da *adj* shod 💡 *Los adjetivos ingleses son invariables.*

■ **calzado** *sm* footwear • **aquí el calzado es de muy buena calidad** footwear is good quality here
■ **calzada** *sf* road

calzar *vt* ❶ [*poner calzado*] to put shoes on • **los niños están descalzos, cálzalos** the children are barefoot, put shoes on them ❷ [*llevar un calzado*] to wear • **¿qué número calza?** what size do you take? ❸ [*poner cuña a*] to wedge
■ **calzarse** *v pronominal* to put on • **cálzate, que ya vamos a salir** put your shoes on, we're going out

calzo *sm* [*cuña*] wedge

calzón *sm* chaps *pl*

expresión a calzón quitado *familiar* boldly

calzoncillo *sm* 💡 *generalmente pl* underpants *pl* • **unos calzoncillos** a pair of underpants

cama *sf* bed • **estar en cama** to be in bed • **hacer la cama** to make the bed

expresión hacerle o ponerle la cama a alguien to plot against somebody

camada *sf* litter

camaleón *sm literal & figurado* chameleon

cámara ◆ *sf* ❶ [*generalmente*] TECNOLOGÍA chamber ▸ **cámara alta/baja** upper/lower house ❷ CINE, FOTOGRAFÍA & TELEVISIÓN camera ▸ **cámara digital** digital cam-

era ▶ **cámara de seguridad** security camera ▶ **cámara de vídeo** video camera ❸ [*de balón, neumático*] inner tube ❹ [*habitáculo*] cabin
◆ *smf* [*persona*] cameraman, *femenino* camerawoman

camarada *smf* POLÍTICA comrade

camarero, ra *sm, f* ❶ [*de restaurante*] waiter, *femenino* waitress ❷ [*de hotel*] steward, *femenino* chambermaid

camarilla *sf* ❶ clique ❷ POLÍTICA lobby

camarón *sm* shrimp

camarote *sm* cabin

cambiante *adj* changeable ☼ *Los adjetivos ingleses son invariables.*

cambiar ◆ *vt* ❶ [*generalmente*] to change • **ayúdame a cambiar las sábanas** help me change the sheets • **¿dónde puedo cambiar dinero?** where can I change money? • **cambiar pesos por dólares** to change pesos into dollars ❷ [*canjear*] • **cambiar algo (por)** to trade something (for) • **te cambio mis medias rojas por las tuyas verdes** I'll trade my red stockings for your green ones
◆ *vi* ❶ [*generalmente*] to change • **Pedro cambió mucho desde que llegó aquí** Pedro has changed a lot since he arrived here • **cambiar de** [*generalmente*] to change • **cambiar de casa** to move jobs • **cambiar de idea** to change your mind • **cambiar de ropa** to change clothes • **cambiar de trabajo** to move jobs ❷ AUTOMÓVILES • **cambiar de marcha** to change gear
■ **cambiarse** *v pronominal* • **cambiarse (de) a)** [*ropa*] to change **b)** [*casa*] to move • **cambiarse de vestido** to change your dress • **cambiarse de casa** to move

cambio *sm* ❶ [*generalmente*] change • **en las sociedades modernas, los cambios suceden muy rápido** in modern societies, changes happen very rapidly • **el cajero me dio mal el cambio** the cashier gave me the wrong change • **no tengo cambio para el camión** I don't have small change for the bus ▶ **cambio climático** climate change ▶ **cambio de domicilio** change of address ▶ **cambio de guardia** changing of the guard ❷ [*trueque*] exchange • **no se admiten cambios ni devoluciones** exchanges and refunds are not permitted • **a cambio (de)** in exchange (for) ❸ FINANZAS [*de acciones*] price; [*de divisas*] exchange rate • **'cambio'** bureau de change ❹ AUTOMÓVILES • **este coche es automático, no tiene cambios** this car is automatic, it doesn't have a manual gearshift ▶ **cambio de marchas** o **velocidades** gearshift • **cambio de sentido** U-turn
■ **libre cambio** *sm* ❶ ECONOMÍA [*librecambismo*] free trade ❷ FINANZAS [*de divisas*] floating exchange rates *pl*

camelar *vt familiar* to butter up

camelia *sf* camellia

camello, lla *sm, f* [*animal*] camel
■ **camello** *sm familiar* [*traficante*] drug dealer

camellón *sm* median (strip)

camerino *sm* dressing room

camilla *sf* ❶ [*generalmente*] stretcher ❷ [*de psiquiatra, dentista*] couch

caminante *smf* walker

caminar ◆ *vi* ❶ [*a pie*] to walk ❷ *figurado* [*ir*] • **caminar (hacia)** to head (for)
◆ *vt* [*una distancia*] to travel

caminata *sf* long walk

camino *sm* ❶ [*sendero*] path • **el camino no es muy ancho** the path is not very wide • **fuimos a mi casa y por el camino compramos una pizza** we went to my house and on the way we bought a pizza ❷ [*carretera*] road ▶ **camino de montaña** mountain path ❸ [*ruta*] way • **a medio camino** halfway • **estar a medio camino** to be halfway there • **camino de** on the way to • **en el** o **de camino** on the way • **ir camino de** to be heading for ❹ [*viaje*] journey • **ponerse en camino** to set off ❺ *figurado* [*medio*] way
expresiones abrir camino a to clear the way for ▶ **abrirse camino** to get on o ahead ▶ **quedarse a medio camino** to stop halfway through

camión *sm* ❶ [*de mercancías*] truck ▶ **camión articulado** semi-trailer truck ▶ **camión cisterna** tanker ▶ **camión de la mudanza** moving van ❷ [*bus*] bus

camionero, ra ◆ *adj* bus ☼ *Los adjetivos ingleses son invariables.*
◆ *sm, f* trucker

camioneta *sf* van

camisa *sf* shirt ▶ **camisa de fuerza** straitjacket
expresión meterse en camisa de once varas to complicate matters unnecessarily

camiseta *sf* ❶ [*prenda interior*] undershirt ❷ [*de verano*] T-shirt ❸ DEPORTE [*de tirantes*] tank (top); [*de mangas*] shirt

camisola *sf* camisole

camisón *sm* nightdress

campamento *sm* camp • **armaron el campamento junto al río** they set up camp next to the river • **estuvimos de campamento una semana** we went camping for a week

campana *sf* bell ▶ **campana de buzo** o **de salvamento** diving bell ▶ **campana extractora de humos** extractor hood

campanada *sf* ❶ [*de campana*] peal • **son las dos, acaban de sonar dos campanadas** it's two o'clock, two peals just rang out ❷ [*de reloj*] stroke ❸ *figurado* [*suceso*] sensation

campanario *sm* bell tower

campanilla *sf* ❶ [*de la puerta*] (small) bell ❷ [*con mango*] handbell ❸ [*flor*] bellflower

campante *adj*
expresión estar o **quedarse tan campante** *familiar* to remain unbothered

campaña *sf* ❶ MILITAR & POLÍTICA campaign • **la campaña contra el tabaquismo durará todo un mes** the campaign against tobacco use will last a whole month • **hacer campaña (de/contra)** to campaign (for/against) ▶ **campaña electoral** electoral campaign ▶ **campaña publicitaria** advertising campaign → **tienda** ❷ countryside

campechano, na *adj familiar* good-natured ☼ *Los adjetivos ingleses son invariables.*

campeón, ona *sm, f* champion

campeonato *sm* championship • **de campeonato** *figurado* terrific

campesino, na *sm, f* ❶ [*generalmente*] farmer ❷ [*muy pobre*] peasant

campestre *adj* country ☼ *Sólo se usa delante del sustantivo.* • **la vida campestre** country life

camping (pl campings) *sm* ❶ [*actividad*] camping • **ir de camping** to go camping ❷ [*lugar de acampada*] campsite

campo *sm* ❶ [*generalmente*] INFORMÁTICA field • **el campo de deportes está junto a la escuela** the playing field is next to the school ▸ **campo de aviación** airfield ▸ **campo de batalla** battlefield ▸ **campo de concentración** concentration camp ▸ **campo de tiro** firing range ❷ [*campiña*] country • **mis abuelos viven en el campo** my grandparents live in the country • **el campo está muy bonito en este momento** the countryside looks very pretty right now • **a campo traviesa** cross country ❸ DEPORTE [*de futbol*] field; [*de golf*] course

camuflaje *sm* camouflage

cana *sf* grey hair

expresión **echar una cana al aire** to let your hair down

Canadá *nombre propio* • **(el) Canadá** Canada

canadiense *adj & smf* Canadian ☼ *Los adjetivos ingleses son invariables.*

En inglés, los adjetivos que se refieren a un país o una región se escriben con mayúscula.

canal *sm* ❶ [*cauce artificial*] ANATOMÍA canal ▸ **canal de riego** irrigation channel ❷ [*medio, vía*] GEOGRAFÍA channel • **los canales oficiales** the official channels ▸ **el canal de Panamá** the Panama Canal ❸ RADIO & TELEVISIÓN channel • **la programación de este canal es muy mala** the programming of this channel is very poor ▸ **canal por cable** cable channel ❹ [*de agua, gas*] conduit

canalizar *vt* ❶ [*territorio*] to canalize ❷ [*agua*] to channel

canalla *smf* swine

canapé *sm* ❶ COCINA canapé ❷ [*sofá*] sofa

canario *sm* [*pájaro*] canary, *plural* <u>canaries</u>

canasta *sf* basket

canasto *sm* large basket

cancelación *sf* cancellation

cancelar *vt* ❶ [*anular*] to cancel ❷ [*deuda*] to pay

cáncer *sm figurado* MEDICINA cancer • **la lucha contra el cáncer** the fight against cancer

■ **Cáncer** ♦ *sm* [*zodiaco*] Cancer

♦ *smf* [*persona*] Cancer

cancerígeno, na *adj* carcinogenic ☼ *Los adjetivos ingleses son invariables.*

canceroso, sa *adj* ❶ [*úlcera, tejido*] cancerous ❷ [*enfermo*] suffering from cancer ☼ *Los adjetivos ingleses son invariables.*

cancha *sf* ❶ [*de tenis*] court ❷ [*de futbol*] field

canciller *sm* ❶ [*de gobierno, embajada*] chancellor ❷ [*de asuntos exteriores*] foreign minister

canción *sf* song ▸ **canción de cuna** lullaby

expresión **la misma canción** the same old story

cancionero *sm* songbook

candado *sm* padlock

candelabro *sm* candelabra

candelero *sm* candlestick

candente *adj* ❶ [*incandescente*] red-hot ❷ *figurado* [*actual*] burning ☼ *Sólo se usa delante del sustantivo.*

candidato, ta *sm, f* candidate • **ser candidato a la presidencia** to be a candidate for the presidency

candidatura *sf* [*para un cargo*] candidacy

cándido, da *adj* ingenuous ☼ *Los adjetivos ingleses son invariables.*

candil *sm* ❶ [*lámpara*] oil lamp ❷ [*araña*] chandelier

canelón *sm* COCINA cannelloni *pl*

cangrejo *sm* crab

canguro *sm* ❶ [*animal*] kangaroo ❷ [*para bebé*] sling

caníbal *smf* cannibal

canica *sf* [*pieza*] marble

■ **canicas** *sfpl* [*juego*] marbles • **jugar a las canicas** to play marbles

canijo, ja *adj* ❶ sickly ❷ tough ☼ *Los adjetivos ingleses son invariables.*

canilla *sf* ❶ [*espinilla*] shinbone ❷ [*pierna*] leg

canino, na *adj* canine ☼ *Los adjetivos ingleses son invariables.*

■ **canino** *sm* [*diente*] canine tooth, *plural* <u>canine teeth</u>

canjear *vt* to exchange

cano, na *adj* grey ☼ *Los adjetivos ingleses son invariables.*

canoa *sf* canoe

canódromo *sm* greyhound track

canon *sm* ❶ [*norma*] canon ❷ [*modelo*] ideal ❸ [*impuesto*] tax ❹ MÚSICA canon

expresión **como mandan los cánones** according to the rules

canónigo *sm* canon

canonizar *vt* to canonize

canoso, sa *adj* ❶ [*pelo*] grey ❷ [*persona*] grey-haired ☼ *Los adjetivos ingleses son invariables.*

cansado, da *adj* ❶ [*agotado*] tired • **estoy cansado** I'm tired • **estar cansado de algo/de hacer algo** to be tired of something/of doing something ❷ [*pesado, cargante*] tiring ☼ *Los adjetivos ingleses son invariables.*

C

cansancio *sm* tiredness • **¡qué cansancio tengo!** I'm exhausted!

cansar ◆ *vt* to tire (out) • **estudiar muchas horas seguidas me cansa** studying for many hours in a row tires me
◆ *vi* to be tiring

cantaleta *sf* nagging • **estoy harta de sus cantaletas** I'm tired of her nagging

cantante ◆ *adj* singing:ᗱ *Los adjetivos ingleses son invariables.*
◆ *smf* singer

cantar ◆ *vt* ❶ [*canción*] to sing ❷ [*bingo, línea, el gordo*] to call (out)
expresión **cantar victoria** to claim victory ▶ **cantar a alguien las cuarenta** to give somebody a piece of your mind
◆ *vi* ❶ [*persona, ave*] to sing ❷ [*gallo*] to crow ❸ [*grillo*] to chirp ❹ *familiar & figurado* [*confesar*] to talk

cántaro *sm* large pitcher
expresión **llover a cántaros** to rain cats and dogs

cantera *sf* [*de piedra*] quarry

cantidad *sf* ❶ [*medida*] quantity, *plural* quantities • **hay que considerar la calidad más que la cantidad** you must consider quality above quantity ❷ [*abundancia*] abundance • **en cantidad** in abundance • **cantidad de** lots of ❸ [*número*] number ❹ [*suma de dinero*] sum (of money)

cantimplora *sf* water bottle

cantina *sf* ❶ [*de soldados*] mess ❷ [*en fábrica*] canteen ❸ [*bar*] bar

canto *sm* ❶ [*acción, arte*] singing • **María estudia canto, quiere ser soprano** María studies singing; she wants to be a soprano ❷ [*canción*] song • **es hermoso el canto de ese canario** that canary's song is beautiful ❸ [*lado, borde*] edge • **de canto** edgeways ❹ [*de cuchillo*] blunt edge ❺ [*guijarro*] pebble ▶ **canto rodado a)** [*pequeño*] pebble **b)** [*grande*] boulder

cantor, ra *sm, f* singer

canturrear *vt & vi familiar* to sing softly

canuto *sm* tube

caña *sf* BOTÁNICA cane ▶ **caña de azúcar** sugarcane ▶ **caña de pescar** fishing rod

cáñamo *sm* hemp

cañería *sf* pipe

caño *sm* ❶ [*de fuente*] jet ❷ [*tubería*] pipe

cañón *sm* ❶ [*arma*] gun ❷ HISTORIA cannon ▶ **cañón de nieve** snow cannon ❸ ▶ **cañón antiaéreo** anti-aircraft gun ❹ [*de fusil*] barrel ❺ [*de chimenea*] flue ❻ [*de órgano*] pipe ❼ GEOGRAFÍA canyon • **el Gran Cañón** the Grand Canyon

caoba *sf* mahogany

caos *sm invariable* chaos • **los niños sembraron el caos en casa de sus abuelos** the children created chaos at their grandparents' house

caótico, ca *adj* chaotic:ᗱ *Los adjetivos ingleses son invariables.*

capa *sf* ❶ [*manto*] cloak • **Caperucita llevaba una capa roja** Little Red Riding Hood wore a red cloak ❷ [*baño - de barniz, pintura*] coat; [*- de chocolate* ETC] coating ❸ [*estrato*] layer ❹ GEOLOGÍA stratum ▶ **capa de hielo** sheet of ice ▶ **capa de ozono** ozone layer ❺ [*grupo social*] class ❻ TAUROMAQUIA cape
expresión **andar de capa caída** to be in a bad way ▶ **de capa y espada** cloak and dagger

capacidad *sf* ❶ [*generalmente*] capacity • **la capacidad de esta jarra es un litro** the capacity of this jar is one liter • **con capacidad para 500 personas** with a capacity of 500 people ❷ [*aptitud*] talent • **tiene mucha capacidad para las ciencias** she has a lot of talent for sciences • **no tener capacidad para algo/para hacer algo** to be no good at something/at doing something

capacitación *sf* training

capacitar *vt* • **capacitar a alguien para algo a)** [*habilitar*] to qualify somebody for something **b)** [*formar*] to train somebody for something

capar *vt* to castrate

caparazón *sm literal & figurado* shell

capataz *sm, f* foreman, *femenino* forewoman

capaz *adj* ❶ [*generalmente*] capable • **es un alumno muy capaz** he's a very capable student • **capaz de algo/de hacer algo** capable of something/of doing something • **Pedro no sería capaz de algo así** Pedro wouldn't be capable of something like that ❷ [*atrevido*] • **ser capaz** to dare ▶ **ser capaz de hacer algo** to bring yourself to do something ❸ [*espacioso*] • **muy/poco capaz** with a large/small capacity • **capaz para** with room for:ᗱ *Los adjetivos ingleses son invariables.*

capazo *sm* large wicker basket

capellán *sm* chaplain

caperuza *sf* hood

capicúa *adj invariable* reversible:ᗱ *Los adjetivos ingleses son invariables.*

capilla *sf* chapel ▶ **capilla ardiente** funeral chapel

cápita ■ **per cápita** *locución adjetiva* per capita

capital ◆ *adj* ❶ [*importante*] supreme ❷ [*principal*] main:ᗱ *Los adjetivos ingleses son invariables.*
◆ *sm* ECONOMÍA capital • **el capital necesario para abrir una panadería es muy grande** the capital necessary to open a bakery is a lot
◆ *sf* [*ciudad*] capital • **Lima es la capital de Perú** Lima is the capital of Peru • **soy de Guadalajara capital** I'm from the city of Guadalajara

capitalismo *sm* capitalism

capitalista *adj & smf* capitalist:ᗱ *Los adjetivos ingleses son invariables.*

capitalizar *vt* ❶ ECONOMÍA to capitalize ❷ *figurado* [*sacar provecho*] to capitalize on

capitán, ana *sm, f* captain

capitanear *vt* DEPORTE & MILITAR to captain

capitel *sm* capital

capitulación *sf* surrender

capitular *vi* to surrender

C

capítulo *sm* ❶ [*sección, división*] chapter ❷ *figurado* [*tema*] subject

caporal *sm* ❶ MILITAR ≃ corporal ❷ foreman

capota *sf* top

capote *sm* ❶ [*capa*] cape with sleeves ❷ [*militar*] greatcoat ❸ TAUROMAQUIA cape

capricho *sm* ❶ [*antojo*] whim • **la tía le consiente todos los caprichos** her aunt caters to all her whims • **darse un capricho** to treat yourself ❷ MÚSICA & ARTE caprice

caprichoso, sa *adj* capricious ♀ *Los adjetivos ingleses son invariables.*

Capricornio ♦ *sm* [*zodiaco*] Capricorn
♦ *smf* [*persona*] Capricorn

cápsula *sf* ❶ [*generalmente*] ANATOMÍA capsule ▶ **cápsula espacial** space capsule ❷ [*tapón*] cap

captar *vt* ❶ [*atraer - simpatía*] to win; [*- interés*] to gain ❷ [*entender*] to grasp • **no capté lo que me dijiste** I didn't grasp what you told me ❸ [*sintonizar*] to receive • **el televisor está roto, no capta las imágenes** the television is broken; it doesn't receive the pictures ❹ [*aguas*] to collect

captura *sf* capture

capturar *vt* to capture

capucha *sf* hood

capuchón *sm* cap

caqui *adj invariable* khaki ♀ *Los adjetivos ingleses son invariables.*

cara *sf* ❶ [*rostro, aspecto*] face • **ve a lavarte la cara** go wash your face • **cara a cara** face to face ❷ [*lado*] side • **la otra cara de un problema** the other side of a problem ❸ GEOMETRÍA face ❹ [*de moneda*] heads ♀ *incontable* • **cara o cruz** heads or tails • **echar algo a cara o cruz** to toss (a coin) for something ❺ *familiar* [*osadía*] cheek • **¡qué cara!** what cheek!
expresiones **dar la cara** to face the consequences of your actions ▶ **de cara a** with a view to ▶ **decir algo a alguien en** o **a la cara** to say something to somebody's face ▶ **echar en cara algo a alguien** to reproach somebody for something ▶ **por su linda cara, por su cara bonita** because his/her face fits ▶ **verse las caras a)** [*pelearse*] to have it out **b)** [*enfrentarse*] to fight it out

carabina *sf* ❶ [*arma*] rifle ❷ *familiar & figurado* [*mujer*] chaperone

Caracas *nombre propio* Caracas

caracol *sm* ❶ [*animal*] snail ❷ [*concha*] shell ❸ [*rizo*] curl

caracola *sf* conch

carácter (pl caracteres) *sm* ❶ [*de persona*] character • **una mujer de carácter** a woman of character • **tener buen/mal carácter** to be good-natured/bad-tempered ❷ [*índole*] nature • **con carácter de urgencia** as a matter of urgency • **una reunión de carácter privado/oficial** a private/official meeting ❸ INFORMÁTICA character ▶ **carácter alfanumérico** alphanumeric character ▶ **caracteres de imprenta** typeface *sing* ❹ BIOLOGÍA trait

característico, ca *adj* characteristic ♀ *Los adjetivos ingleses son invariables.*
■ **característica** *sf* characteristic

caracterización *sf* ❶ [*generalmente*] characterization ❷ [*maquillaje*] make-up

caracterizar *vt* ❶ [*definir*] to characterize ❷ [*representar*] to portray ❸ [*maquillar*] to make up

caradura *adj familiar* cheeky ♀ *Los adjetivos ingleses son invariables.*

carajo *exclamación muy familiar* • **¡carajo!** damn it!

caramba *exclamación* • **¡caramba! a)** [*sorpresa*] good heavens! **b)** [*enfado*] for heaven's sake!

carambola *sf* ❶ [*en billar*] cannon ❷ [*fruta*] starfruit

caramelo *sm* ❶ [*golosina*] candy ❷ [*azúcar fundido*] caramel

carátula *sf* ❶ [*de libro*] front cover ❷ [*de disco*] sleeve ❸ [*máscara*] mask ❹ [*de reloj*] face

caravana *sf* ❶ [*generalmente*] trailer ❷ [*de coches*] back-up

caray *exclamación* • **¡caray! a)** [*sorpresa*] good heavens! **b)** [*enfado*] damn it!

carbón *sm* coal ▶ **carbón de leña** charcoal ▶ **carbón mineral** o **de piedra** coal

carboncillo *sm* charcoal • **al carboncillo** in charcoal

carbonizar *vt* to char

carbono *sm* carbon

carburador *sm* carburettor

carburante *sm* fuel

carca *despectivo adj familiar* old-fashioned ♀ *Los adjetivos ingleses son invariables.*

carcajada *sf* guffaw • **reír a carcajadas** to roar with laughter • **nos reímos a carcajadas con los cuentos de Pablo** we roared with laughter at Pablo's stories

cárcel *sf* prison • **aún no salió de la cárcel** he still hasn't gotten out of prison • **estar en la cárcel** to be in prison

carcelero, ra *sm, f* warder

carcoma *sf* ❶ [*insecto*] woodworm ❷ [*polvo*] wood dust

carcomer *vt literal & figurado* to eat away at

cardar *vt* ❶ [*lana*] to card ❷ [*pelo*] to tease

cardenal *sm* RELIGIÓN cardinal • **los cardenales eligen al Papa** the cardinals elect the Pope

cardiaco, ca, cardíaco, ca *adj* cardiac • **un paro cardiaco** a cardiac arrest ♀ *Los adjetivos ingleses son invariables.*

cardinal *adj* cardinal • **los puntos cardinales** the cardinal points ♀ *Los adjetivos ingleses son invariables.*

cardiólogo, ga *sm, f* cardiologist

cardo *sm* thistle

carecer *vi* • **carecer de algo** to lack something • **la región carece de interés turístico** the area lacks any tourist attractions

C

carencia *sf* ❶ [*ausencia*] lack ❷ [*defecto*] deficiency

carente *adj* • carente de lacking (in) ᐧ⬩*Los adjetivos ingleses son invariables.*

carestía *sf* shortage

careta *sf* ❶ [*máscara*] mask ▸ **careta antigás** gas mask ❷ *figurado* [*engaño*] front

carga *sf* ❶ [*acción*] loading • **de carga frontal** front-loading • **carga y descarga** loading and unloading ❷ [*cargamento - de avión, barco*] cargo ; [- *de tren*] freight ; [- *de camión*] load • **la carga de manzanas se cayó del camión** the load of apples fell from the truck ❸ [*peso*] load ❹ *figurado* [*sufrimiento*] burden • **puedes quedarte en casa, no eres ninguna carga** you can stay in my home, you're not a burden ❺ [*ataque, explosivo*] charge ❻ [*de batería, condensador*] charge ❼ [*para mechero, bolígrafo*] refill ❽ [*impuesto*] tax ▸ **carga fiscal** tax burden

expresión **volver a la carga** to persist

cargado, da *adj* ❶ [*abarrotado*] • **cargado (de)** laden (with) • **un árbol cargado de fruta** a tree laden with fruit ❷ [*arma*] loaded ❸ [*bebida*] strong ❹ [*bochornoso - habitación*] stuffy ; [- *tiempo*] sultry ; close ; [- *cielo*] overcast ❺ ▸ **cargado de hombros** round-shouldered ᐧ⬩*Los adjetivos ingleses son invariables.*

cargamento *sm* cargo

cargante *adj familiar & figurado* annoying ᐧ⬩*Los adjetivos ingleses son invariables.*

cargar ◆ *vt* ❶ [*generalmente*] to load • **cargamos las valijas en el coche y salimos hacia la estación** we loaded the suitcases into the car and left for the station • **cargó el rifle y empezó a disparar** he loaded the rifle and began to shoot ❷ [*pluma, encendedor*] to refill ❸ [*peso encima*] to throw over your shoulder ❹ ELECTRICIDAD to charge • **necesito cargar la batería del celular** I need to charge the cell phone battery ❺ INFORMÁTICA [*archivo*] [*por internet*] to upload ; [*con disco*] to load ❻ *figurado* [*responsabilidad, tarea*] to give • **cargar a alguien de deudas** to encumber somebody with debts ❼ [*producir pesadez - sujeto: humo*] to make stuffy ; [- *sujeto: comida*] to bloat ❽ [*gravar*] • **cargar un impuesto a algo/alguien** to tax something/somebody ❾ [*importe, factura, deuda*] • **cargar algo (a)** to charge something (to) • **cárguelo a mi cuenta** charge it to my account

◆ *vi* [*atacar*] • **cargar (contra)** to charge

cargo *sm* ❶ [*generalmente*] ECONOMÍA & DERECHO charge • **sin cargo** free of charge • **correr a cargo de** to be borne by • **estar a cargo de algo, tener algo a cargo de uno** to be in charge of something • **las personas a mi cargo** the people in my care ❷ [*empleo*] post ▸ **cargo público** public office

expresión **hacerse cargo de a)** [*asumir el control de*] to take charge of **b)** [*ocuparse de*] to take care of **c)** [*comprender*] to understand

carguero *sm* cargo boat

Caribe *sm* • **el (mar) Caribe** the Caribbean (Sea)

caribeño, ña *adj* Caribbean ᐧ⬩*Los adjetivos ingleses son invariables.*

caricatura *sf* ❶ [*de personaje, situación*] caricature ❷ [*dibujos animados*] cartoon

caricia *sf* ❶ [*a persona*] caress • **una tierna caricia** a gentle caress • **hacerle una caricia a alguien** to caress somebody • **le hizo una caricia a su hijo** she caressed her son ❷ [*a perro, gato* ETC] stroke

caridad *sf* charity, *plural* charities

caries *sf invariable* tooth decay • **esta pasta dental previene las caries** this toothpaste prevents tooth decay • **tengo dos caries** I have two cavities

cariño *sm* ❶ [*afecto*] affection • **había mucho cariño en ese hogar** there was a lot of affection in that home • **tomar cariño a** to grow fond of • **con mucho cariño** with great affection • **hacerle cariños a alguien** to caress somebody ❷ [*cuidado*] loving care ❸ [*apelativo*] love

cariñoso, sa *adj* affectionate ᐧ⬩*Los adjetivos ingleses son invariables.*

carisma *sm* charisma

carismático, ca *adj* charismatic ᐧ⬩*Los adjetivos ingleses son invariables.*

caritativo, va *adj* charitable ᐧ⬩*Los adjetivos ingleses son invariables.*

cariz *sm* look • **tomar mal/buen cariz** to take a turn for the worse/better

carmín ◆ *adj* [*color*] carmine ᐧ⬩*Los adjetivos ingleses son invariables.*
◆ *sm* ❶ [*color*] carmine ❷ [*lápiz de labios*] lipstick

carnada *sf literal & figurado* bait

carnal ◆ *adj* ❶ [*de la carne*] carnal ❷ [*pariente*] • **primo carnal** first cousin ᐧ⬩*Los adjetivos ingleses son invariables.*
◆ *sm* ❶ [*hermano*] brother ❷ [*amigo*] buddy

carnaval *sm* carnival

carnaza *sf literal & figurado* bait

carne *sf* ❶ [*de persona, fruta*] flesh • **en carne viva** raw ❷ [*alimento*] meat • **carne de cerdo** pork ▸ **carne de cordero** lamb ▸ **carne molida** ground beef ▸ **carne de puerco** pork ▸ **carne de res** beef ▸ **carne de ternera** veal ▸ **carne de vaca** beef

expresiones **entrado** o **metido en carnes** plump ▸ **ser carne de cañón** to be cannon fodder ▸ **ser de carne y hueso** to be human ▸ **poner toda la carne en el asador** to go for broke ▸ **poner la carne de gallina a alguien a)** [*de frío*] to give somebody goose bumps **b)** [*de miedo*] to give somebody the creeps

carnicería *sf* ❶ [*tienda*] butcher shop ❷ *figurado* [*masacre*] carnage ᐧ⬩*incontable*

carnicero, ra *sm, f literal & figurado* butcher

carnitas *sfpl* ▸ *para explicar lo que es puedes decir:* it's small pieces of braised pork

caro, ra *adj* [*precio*] expensive • **siempre compra ropa cara** she always buys expensive clothes ᐧ⬩*Los adjetivos ingleses son invariables.*

■ **caro** *adv* • **costar caro a)** to be expensive **b)** *figurado* to cost an arm and a leg • **pagar caro algo** *figurado* to pay dearly for something • **salir caro a)** to be expensive **b)** *figurado* to cost an arm and a leg • **ven-**

der **caro** algo **a)** to sell something at a high price **b)** *figurado* not to give something up easily

carpa *sf* ❶ [*pez*] carp ❷ [*de circo*] big top ❸ [*para acampar, fiestas* ETC] tent

carpeta *sf* folder

carpintería *sf* ❶ [*arte*] carpentry ❷ [*de puertas y ventanas*] woodwork ❸ [*taller*] carpenter's shop

carpintero, ra *sm, f* ❶ carpenter ❷ [*de puertas y ventanas*] joiner

carraspear *vi* to clear your throat

carrera *sf* ❶ [*acción de correr*] run ❷ *figurado* DEPORTE race • **con mucho esfuerzo gané la carrera** with a lot of effort I won the race ▸ **carrera ciclista** cycle race ▸ **carrera de coches** motor race ▸ **carrera de obstáculos** steeplechase ❸ [*trayecto*] route ❹ [*de taxi*] ride ❺ [*estudios*] university course • **hacer la carrera de derecho** to study law (at university) ❻ [*profesión*] career • **mi carrera me es muy importante** my career is very important to me ❼ [*en medias*] run

carreta *sf* cart

carrete *sm* ❶ [*de hilo*] bobbin ❷ [*de alambre*] coil ❸ FOTOGRAFÍA roll (of film) ❹ [*para pescar*] reel ❺ [*de máquina de escribir*] spool

carretera *sf* road • **viaje por carretera** road trip ▸ **carretera de circunvalación** ring road ▸ **carretera de cuota** toll road ▸ **carretera nacional** ≃ interstate

carretero, a *adj* road ϟ *Sólo se usa delante del sustantivo.* • **un accidente carretero** a road accident • **tráfico carretero** road traffic

carretilla *sf* wheelbarrow

carril *sm* ❶ [*de carretera*] lane ▸ **carril bici** cycle lane ▸ **carril bus** bus lane ❷ [*de vía de tren*] rail

carrillo *sm* cheek

expresión comer a dos carrillos to cram your face with food

carrito *sm* cart

carro *sm* ❶ [*vehículo*] cart • **voy a buscar un carro para las valijas** I'm going to look for a cart for the suitcases ▸ **carro de supermercado** shopping cart ❷ [*de máquina de escribir*] carriage ❸ [*automóvil*] car • **compramos un carro nuevo** we bought a new car ▸ **carro de carreras** race car ❹ ▸ **carro comedor** [*en tren*] dining car

carrocería *sf* body

carromato *sm* [*carro*] wagon

carroña *sf* carrion

carroza *sf* carriage

carruaje *sm* carriage

carrusel *sm* carousel

carta *sf* ❶ letter • **recibí una carta de mi prima** I received a letter from my cousin • **echar una carta** to post a letter ▸ **carta certificada/urgente** registered/ express letter ▸ **carta de ajuste** test card ▸ **carta de presentación** letter of introduction ▸ **carta de recomendación** reference (letter) ❷ [*naipe*] (playing) card • **jugamos a las cartas toda la tarde** we played cards all afternoon • **echar las cartas a alguien** to tell

somebody's fortune *(with cards)* ❸ [*en restaurante*] menu ❹ [*mapa*] map ❺ NÁUTICA chart ❻ [*documento*] charter ▸ **Carta Magna** Constitution ▸ **carta verde** green card

expresión dar carta blanca a alguien to give somebody carte blanche ▸ **jugarse todo a una carta** to put all your eggs in one basket

cartabón *sm* set square

cartapacio *sm* folder

cartel *sm* ❶ [*póster*] poster • **'prohibido fijar carteles'** billposters will be prosecuted ❷ [*letrero*] sign • **ahí hay un cartel de "Pare"** there's a stop sign there

cártel *sm* cartel

cartelera *sf* ❶ [*tablón*] billboard ❷ PRENSA entertainments page • **estar en cartelera** to be showing • **lleva un año en cartelera** it's been running for a year

cárter *sm* AUTOMÓVILES housing

cartera *sf* ❶ [*para dinero*] wallet ❷ [*para documentos*] briefcase ❸ [*sin asa*] portfolio ❹ COMERCIO, FINANZAS & POLÍTICA portfolio ❺ [*bolsillo*] pocket flap

carterista *smf* pickpocket

cartero, ra *sm, f* letter carrier

cartílago *sm* cartilage

cartilla *sf* ❶ [*documento*] book ▸ **cartilla (de ahorros)** savings book ❷ [*para aprender a leer*] primer

cartón *sm* ❶ [*material*] cardboard ▸ **cartón piedra** papier mâché ❷ [*de cigarros, leche*] carton ❸ [*de huevos*] box

cartucho *sm* [*de arma*] cartridge

expresión quemar el último cartucho *figurado* to play your last card

cartulina *sf* cardstock ▸ **cartulina amarilla/roja** FÚTBOL yellow/red card

casa *sf* ❶ [*edificio*] house ▸ **casa de campo** country house ❷ [*hogar*] home • **bienvenido a casa** welcome home • **en casa** at home • **ir a casa** to go home • **pásate por mi casa** come round to my place • **jugar en casa/fuera de casa** to play at home/away ❸ [*empresa*] company • **vino de la casa** house wine ❹ [*organismo*] ▸ **casa de huéspedes** guesthouse ▸ **casa de juego** gambling house

expresión se le cae la casa encima it's the end of the world for him ▸ **en casa del herrero cuchillo de palo** *proverbio* the shoemaker's wife is always worst shod

la casa

el balcón	the balcony
el baño	the bathroom
el camino	the driveway
el césped	the lawn
la chimenea (exterior)	the chimney
la chimenea (interior)	the fireplace
la cocina	the kitchen
el comedor	the dining room
la contraventana	the shutter
el despacho	the study

el desván	the attic
la entrada	the hall
las escaleras	the stairs
el garaje	the garage
el macizo de flores	the flower bed
la pared	the wall
el pasillo	the hall
la persiana	the blind
la puerta	the door
la recámara	the bedroom
la regadera	the shower
la sala	the living room
el sótano	the basement
el tejado	the roof
la terraza	the terrace
la ventana	the window

casado, da *adj* • casado (con) married (to) ☼ *Los adjetivos ingleses son invariables.*

casamiento *sm* wedding

casar ◆ *vt* ❶ [*en matrimonio*] to marry ❷ [*unir*] to fit together
◆ *vi* to match
■ **casarse** *v pronominal* • casarse (con) to get married (to) • se casaron hace tres años they got married three years ago • Ana se casó con Pedro Ana married Pedro

cascabel *sm* (small) bell

cascanueces *sm invariable* nutcracker

cascar *vt* ❶ [*romper*] to crack ❷ *familiar* [*pegar*] to thump

cáscara *sf* ❶ [*de almendra, huevo* ETC] shell ❷ [*de limón, naranja*] peel ❸ [*de plátano*] skin

cascarón *sm* eggshell
expresión salir del cascarón *figurado* to leave the nest

cascarrabias *smf invariable* grouch

casco *sm* ❶ [*para la cabeza*] helmet • siempre lleva casco he always wears a helmet ❷ [*de motorista*] crash helmet ❸ [*de barco*] hull ❹ [*de ciudad*] ▶ casco antiguo old (part of) town ▶ casco urbano city center ❺ [*de caballo*] hoof ❻ [*envase*] empty bottle

casero, ra ◆ *adj* ❶ [*de casa - comida*] homemade; [*- trabajos*] domestic; [*- reunión, velada*] at home • remedios caseros home remedies ❷ [*hogareño*] home-loving ☼ *Los adjetivos ingleses son invariables.*
◆ *sm, f* [*propietario*] landlord, *femenino* landlady

caseta *sf* ❶ booth ❷ ▶ caseta de cobro tollbooth ▶ caseta telefónica phone booth

casete *sm* cassette

casi *adv* almost • casi me muero I almost died • son casi las once, vamos a dormir it's almost eleven o'clock, let's go to sleep • casi no dormí I hardly slept at all • casi, casi almost; just about • casi nada hardly anything • casi nunca hardly ever

casilla *sf* ❶ [*de caja, armario*] compartment ❷ [*para cartas*] pigeonhole ❸ [*en un impreso*] box ❹ [*de ajedrez* ETC] square ❺ [*de votación*] voting booth

casillero *sm* ❶ [*mueble*] set of pigeonholes ❷ [*casilla*] pigeonhole ❸ [*locker*] locker

casino *sm* casino

caso *sm* ❶ [*generalmente*] DERECHO & GRAMÁTICA case • el caso es que... the fact is (that)... • en el mejor/peor de los casos at best/worst ▶ caso clínico clinical case ❷ [*ocasión*] occasion • en caso de in the event of • en caso de que if • (en) caso de que venga should she come • en cualquier o todo caso in any event o case • hacer caso a to pay attention to • hazle caso a tu madre pay attention to your mother
expresión ni caso • ya se lo dije pero ni caso I've already told him but he didn't take any notice

caspa *sf* dandruff

casquete *sm* skullcap

casquillo *sm* case ▶ casquillo de bala bullet shell

casta *sf* ❶ [*linaje*] lineage ❷ [*especie, calidad*] breed ❸ [*en la India*] caste

castañetear *vi* [*dientes*] to chatter

castellano, na *adj* & *sm, f* Castilian ☼ *Los adjetivos ingleses son invariables.*
■ **castellano** *sm* [*lengua*] Spanish • estamos aprendiendo castellano we're learning Spanish
En inglés los nombres de los idiomas se escriben con mayúscula.

castidad *sf* chastity

castigar *vt* ❶ [*imponer castigo*] to punish ❷ DEPORTE to penalize ❸ [*maltratar*] to damage

castigo *sm* ❶ [*sanción*] punishment • como castigo, lavarás los platos hasta fin de mes as punishment, you will wash the dishes until the end of the month ❷ [*sufrimiento*] suffering ☼ *incontable* ❸ [*daño*] damage ☼ *incontable* ❹ DEPORTE penalty

castillo *sm* [*edificio*] castle ▶ castillo de naipes house of cards
expresión castillos en el aire castles in the air

castizo, za *adj* pure ☼ *Los adjetivos ingleses son invariables.*

casto, ta *adj* chaste ☼ *Los adjetivos ingleses son invariables.*

castor *sm* beaver

castrar *vt* ❶ [*animal, persona*] to castrate ❷ [*gato*] to doctor

casual *adj* chance ☼ *Los adjetivos ingleses son invariables.*

casualidad *sf* coincidence • fue pura casualidad it was sheer coincidence • de casualidad by coincidence • nos encontramos en el parque de casualidad we met in the park by coincidence • dio la casualidad de que... it so happened that... • por casualidad by chance • ¿por casualidad viste a mi perro? did you see my dog by any chance? • ¡qué casualidad! what a coincidence!

casualmente *adv* by chance

cataclismo *sm* cataclysm

catador, ra *sm, f* taster

catalejo *sm* telescope

C

catalogar *vt* ❶ [*en catálogo*] to catalogue ❷ [*clasificar*] • **catalogar a alguien (de)** to class somebody (as)

catálogo *sm* catalogue

catamarán *sm* catamaran

catapulta *sf* catapult

catar *vt* to taste

catarata *sf* ❶ [*de agua*] waterfall • **visitamos las cataratas del Iguazú** we visited the Iguazú waterfalls ❷ MEDICINA cataract • **a la abuela la operaron de cataratas** they operated on my grandmother's cataracts

catarro *sm* cold

catástrofe *sf* ❶ catastrophe ❷ [*accidente*] disaster ▶ **catástrofe aérea** air disaster ▶ **catástrofe natural** natural disaster

catastrófico, ca *adj* catastrophic. ☼ *Los adjetivos ingleses son invariables.*

catchup, ketchup *sm invariable* ketchup

catecismo *sm* catechism

cátedra *sf* ❶ [*cargo - en universidad*] chair; [- *en instituto*] post of head of department ❷ [*departamento*] department

catedral *sf* cathedral

catedrático, ca *sm, f* ❶ [*de universidad*] professor ❷ [*de instituto*] head of department

categoría *sf* ❶ [*generalmente*] category ▶ **categoría gramatical** part of speech ❷ [*posición social*] standing • **de categoría** important ❸ [*calidad*] quality • **es un hotel de categoría** it's a quality hotel • **de (primera) categoría** first-class

categórico, ca *adj* categorical. ☼ *Los adjetivos ingleses son invariables.*

catequesis *sf invariable* catechesis

cateto, ta *sm, f* *despectivo* country bumpkin

catolicismo *sm* Catholicism

católico, ca ◆ *adj* Catholic. ☼ *Los adjetivos ingleses son invariables.*
En inglés las religiones y los miembros de una religión se escriben con mayúscula.
◆ *sm, f* Catholic

catorce *numeral* fourteen ver también **seis**

catorceavo, va *numeral* fourteenth

catrín, ina *sm, f* *familiar* dandy

cauce *sm* ❶ *figurado* AGRICULTURA channel ❷ [*de río*] river bed • **el cauce del río se secó** the river bed dried up
expresión **volver a su cauce** to return to normal

caucho *sm* [*sustancia*] rubber ▶ **caucho vulcanizado** vulcanized rubber

caudaloso, sa *adj* ❶ [*río*] with a large flow ❷ [*persona*] wealthy. ☼ *Los adjetivos ingleses son invariables.*

caudillo *sm* leader

causa *sf* ❶ [*origen, ideal*] cause • **descubrieron la causa del incendio** they discovered the cause of the fire • **por una buena causa** for a good cause ❷ [*razón*] reason • **a causa de** because of ❸ DERECHO case

causalidad *sf* causality

causante *adj* • **la razón causante** the cause. ☼ *Los adjetivos ingleses son invariables.*

causar *vt* ❶ [*generalmente*] to cause • **un cortocircuito causó el incendio** a short circuit caused the fire ❷ [*impresión*] to make ❸ [*placer*] to give • **causar asombro a alguien** to amaze somebody

cáustico, ca *adj literal & figurado* caustic. ☼ *Los adjetivos ingleses son invariables.*

cautela *sf* caution

cauteloso, sa *adj* cautious. ☼ *Los adjetivos ingleses son invariables.*

cautivador, ra ◆ *adj* captivating. ☼ *Los adjetivos ingleses son invariables.*
◆ *sm, f* charmer

cautivar *vt* ❶ [*apresar*] to capture ❷ [*seducir*] to captivate

cautiverio *sm* captivity

cautividad *sf* = **cautiverio**

cautivo, va *adj & sm, f* captive. ☼ *Los adjetivos ingleses son invariables.*

cauto, ta *adj* cautious. ☼ *Los adjetivos ingleses son invariables.*

cavar *vt & vi* ❶ [*generalmente*] to dig ❷ [*con azada*] to hoe

caverna *sf* ❶ cave ❷ [*más grande*] cavern

cavernícola *smf* caveman, *femenino* cavewoman

caviar *sm* caviar

cavidad *sf* ❶ cavity ❷ [*formada con las manos*] cup

caza ◆ *sf* ❶ [*acción de cazar*] hunting • **aún hoy se practica la caza** even today people go hunting • **dar caza a** to hunt down ▶ **caza de brujas** *figurado* witchhunt ❷ [*animales, carne*] game
◆ *sm* fighter (plane)

cazabombardero *sm* fighter bomber

cazador, ra *sm, f* [*persona*] hunter ▶ **cazador furtivo** poacher
■ **cazadora** *sf* [*prenda*] bomber jacket

cazar *vt* ❶ [*animales* ETC] to hunt ❷ *figurado* [*pillar, atrapar*] to catch ❸ [*en matrimonio*] to trap

cazo *sm* saucepan

cazuela *sf* ❶ [*recipiente*] pot ❷ [*de barro*] earthenware pot ❸ [*para el horno*] casserole (dish) • **a la cazuela** casseroled ❹ [*guiso*] stew • **comimos una cazuela de mariscos deliciosa** we ate a delicious seafood stew

cc ❶ (*abreviatura escrita de* centímetro cúbico) cc *(cubic centimeter)* ❷ (*abreviatura escrita de* copia de carbón) cc *(carbon copy)*

c/c (*abreviatura escrita de* cuenta corriente) a/c

CD *sm* ❶ (*abreviatura de* compact disc) CD ❷ (*abreviatura de* club deportivo) sports club ❸ [*en futbol*] FC

CE *sf* ❶ (*abreviatura de* Comunidad Europea) EC ❷ (*abreviatura de* Comisión Europea) EC

cebada *sf* barley

cebar *vt* ❶ [*sobrealimentar*] to fatten (up) ❷ [*máquina, arma*] to prime ❸ [*anzuelo*] to bait

cebo *sm* ❶ [*para cazar*] bait ❷ *figurado* [*para atraer*] incentive

cebolla *sf* onion

cebolleta *sf* ❶ BOTÁNICA spring onion ❷ [*en vinagre*] pickled onion ❸ [*muy pequeña*] silverskin onion

cebollino *sm* ❶ BOTÁNICA chive ❷ [*cebolleta*] spring onion ❸ *familiar* [*necio*] idiot

cebra *sf* zebra

cecear *vi* to lisp

ceceo *sm* lisp

ceder ◆ *vt* ❶ [*traspasar, transferir*] to hand over ❷ [*conceder*] to give up • **ceder la palabra a alguien** to give the floor to somebody • **'ceda el paso'** give way ◆ *vi* ❶ [*venirse abajo*] to give way • **el televisor era demasiado pesado y la mesa cedió** the television was too heavy and the table gave way ❷ [*destensarse*] to give ❸ [*disminuir*] to abate ❹ [*rendirse*] to give up • **ceder a** to give in to • **el gobierno acabó cediendo a la presión de los sindicatos** the government ended up giving in to pressure from the labor unions ❺ [*ensancharse*] to stretch

cedro *sm* cedar

cédula *sf* document ▸ **cédula de identidad** identity card ▸ **cédula hipotecaria** mortgage bond

cegar *vt* ❶ [*generalmente*] to blind ❷ [*tapar - ventana*] to block off; [- *tubo*] to block up

cegato, ta *adj familiar* short-sighted ☿ *Los adjetivos ingleses son invariables.*

ceguera *sf literal & figurado* blindness

ceja *sf* ANATOMÍA eyebrow

expresión **quemarse las cejas** *familiar* to burn the midnight oil ▸ **tener a alguien entre ceja y ceja** *familiar* not to be able to stand the sight of somebody

cejar *vi* • **cejar en** to give up on • **no cejaba en sus intentos por convencernos** he wouldn't give up trying to convince us • **no cejaré en mi empeño** I'll never give up

celda *sf* cell ▸ **celda de castigo** solitary confinement cell

celebración *sf* ❶ [*festejo*] celebration ❷ [*realización*] holding

celebrar *vt* ❶ [*festejar*] to celebrate • **celebró su cumpleaños con una fiesta** he celebrated his birthday with a party • **celebraron la reunión en el salón de actos** they held the meeting in the assembly hall ❷ [*llevar a cabo*] to hold ❸ [*oficio religioso*] to celebrate ❹ [*alegrarse de*] to be delighted with ❺ [*alabar*] to praise

célebre *adj* famous ☿ *Los adjetivos ingleses son invariables.*

celebridad *sf* ❶ [*fama*] fame ❷ [*persona famosa*] celebrity

celeridad *sf* speed

celeste *adj* celestial ☿ *Los adjetivos ingleses son invariables.*

celestial *adj* celestial ☿ *Los adjetivos ingleses son invariables.*

celibato *sm* celibacy

célibe *adj* & *smf* celibate ☿ *Los adjetivos ingleses son invariables.*

celo *sm* ❶ [*esmero*] zeal ❷ [*devoción*] devotion ❸ [*de animal*] heat • **en celo** on heat; in season

■ **celos** *smpl* jealousy ☿ *incontable* • **lo hizo por celos** she did it out of jealousy • **dar celos a alguien** to make somebody jealous • **tener celos de alguien** to be jealous of somebody

celofán *sm* Cellophane®

celoso, sa *adj* ❶ [*con celos*] jealous • **es muy celosa** she's a jealous person • **está celoso de Lupe** he's jealous of Lupe ❷ [*cumplidor*] keen ☿ *Los adjetivos ingleses son invariables.*

celta ◆ *adj* Celtic ☿ *Los adjetivos ingleses son invariables.*
◆ *smf* [*persona*] Celt
◆ *sm* [*lengua*] Celtic

célula *sf* cell ▸ **célula fotoeléctrica** photoelectric cell ▸ **célula madre** stem cell

celular *sm* cellphone

celulitis *sf invariable* cellulitis

celulosa *sf* cellulose

cementerio *sm* ❶ [*para personas*] cemetery ❷ [*de cosas inutilizables*] dump ▸ **cementerio de automóviles** junkyard ▸ **cementerio nuclear** o **radioactivo** nuclear dumping ground

cemento *sm* ❶ [*generalmente*] cement ❷ [*hormigón*] concrete ▸ **cemento armado** reinforced concrete

cena *sf* dinner ▸ **cena de despedida** farewell dinner ▸ **cena de negocios** business dinner

cenagal *sm* bog

cenar ◆ *vt* to have for dinner • **sólo cené pescado** I only had fish for dinner
◆ *vi* to have dinner • **cenamos a las nueve** we have dinner at nine o'clock

cencerro *sm* cowbell

expresión **estar como un cencerro** *familiar & figurado* to be as mad as a hatter

cenicero *sm* ashtray

cenit, zenit *sm literal & figurado* zenith

censar *vt* to take a census of

censo *sm* ❶ [*padrón*] census ▸ **censo de población** population census ▸ **censo electoral** electoral roll ❷ [*tributo*] tax

censor, ra *sm, f* censor

censura *sf* ❶ [*prohibición*] censorship ❷ [*organismo*] censors *pl* ❸ [*reprobación*] severe criticism

censurar *vt* ❶ [*prohibir*] to censor ❷ [*reprobar*] to censure

centavo, va *numeral* hundredth

■ **centavo** *sm* cent

expresión no tengo ni un centavo I'm broke

centella *sf* ❶ [*rayo*] flash ❷ [*chispa*] spark

centellear *vi* ❶ [*luz*] to sparkle ❷ [*estrella*] to twinkle

centena *sf* hundred • **una centena de** a hundred

centenar *sm* hundred • **a centenares** by the hundred

centeno *sm* rye

centésimo, ma *numeral* hundredth

centígrado, da *adj* centigrade ☼: *Los adjetivos ingleses son invariables.*

centigramo *sm* centigram

centilitro *sm* centiliter

centímetro *sm* centimeter

céntimo *sm* [*moneda*] cent

expresión estar sin un céntimo to be flat broke

centinela *sm* sentry

centrado, da *adj* ❶ [*basado*] • **centrado en** based on ❷ [*equilibrado*] stable ❸ [*rueda, cuadro* ETC] centered ☼: *Los adjetivos ingleses son invariables.*

central ◆ *adj* central ☼: *Los adjetivos ingleses son invariables.*

◆ *sf* ❶ [*oficina*] head office ❷ [*de correos, comunicaciones*] main office ❸ [*de energía*] power station ▶ **central camionera** bus station ▶ **central hidroeléctrica** o **hidráulica** hydroelectric power station ▶ **central nuclear** nuclear power station ▶ **central térmica** thermal power station

centralita *sf* switchboard

centralización *sf* centralization

centralizar *vt* to centralize

centrar *vt* ❶ [*generalmente*] DEPORTE to center ❷ [*arma*] to aim ❸ [*persona*] to steady ❹ [*atención, interés*] to be the center of

■ **centrarse** *v pronominal* ❶ [*concentrarse*] • **centrarse en** to concentrate on • **céntrate en lo que realmente es importante** concentrate on what is really important ❷ [*equilibrarse*] to find your feet

céntrico, ca *adj* central ☼: *Los adjetivos ingleses son invariables.*

centrifugadora *sf* [*para secar ropa*] spin-dryer

centrifugar *vt* [*ropa*] to spin-dry

centrista *adj* center ☼: *Sólo se usa delante del sustantivo.* • **un partido centrista** a center party

centro *sm* ❶ [*generalmente*] center • **vivo en el centro de Acapulco** I live in the center of Acapulco ▶ **centro comercial** shopping mall ▶ **centro de desintoxicación** detoxification center ▶ **centro de mesa** centerpiece ▶ **centro de planificación familiar** family planning clinic ▶ **centro de salud** health center ▶ **centro nervioso/óptico** nerve/optic center ▶ **centro social** community center ❷ [*de ciudad*] town center • **me voy al centro** I'm going to town • **las tiendas del centro** the downtown stores ▶ **centro urbano** town center

Centroamérica *sf* Central America

centroamericano, na *adj* Central American ☼: *Los adjetivos ingleses son invariables.*

centrocampista *smf* DEPORTE midfielder

ceñir *vt* ❶ [*apretar*] to be tight on ❷ [*abrazar*] to embrace

ceño *sm* frown • **frunció el ceño** he frowned • **lo miró con el ceño fruncido** she frowned at him

cepa *sf* literal & figurado stock

expresión de pura cepa a) [*auténtico*] real ; genuine b) [*pura sangre*] thoroughbred

cepillar *vt* ❶ [*ropa, pelo, dientes*] to brush • **se cepilló los dientes** he brushed his teeth ❷ [*madera*] to plane

cepillo *sm* ❶ [*para limpiar*] brush ❷ [*para pelo*] hairbrush ▶ **cepillo de dientes** toothbrush ❸ [*de carpintero*] plane

cepo *sm* ❶ [*para cazar*] trap ❷ [*para vehículos*] wheel clamp ❸ [*para sujetar*] clamp

cera *sf* ❶ [*generalmente*] wax ❷ [*de abeja*] beeswax • **hacerse la cera en las piernas** to wax your legs ▶ **cera depilatoria** hair-removing wax

cerámica *sf* ❶ [*arte*] pottery • **mi mamá estudia cerámica** my mom studies pottery ❷ [*objeto*] piece of pottery • **una cerámica** a piece of pottery

ceramista *smf* potter

cerca ◆ *sf* fence

◆ *adv* near ; close • **queda cerca de la escuela** it's near the school • **mi casa está muy cerca** my house is very close • **los exámenes ya están cerca** the exams are already coming up soon • **¿hay una farmacia cerca?** is there a pharmacy nearby? • **por aquí cerca** nearby • **de cerca a)** [*examinar, ver*] closely b) [*afectar, vivir*] deeply

cercado *sm* ❶ [*valla*] fence ❷ [*lugar*] enclosure

cercanía *sf* nearness

cercano, na *adj* ❶ [*pueblo, lugar*] nearby • **los pueblos cercanos** the nearby towns • **la zona cercana a la estación** the area close to the station ❷ [*tiempo*] near ❸ [*pariente, fuente de información*] • **cercano (a)** close (to) • **un pariente cercano** a close relative ☼: *Los adjetivos ingleses son invariables.*

cercar *vt* ❶ [*vallar*] to fence (off) ❷ [*rodear, acorralar*] to surround

cerco *sm* ❶ [*generalmente*] circle ❷ [*de puerta, ventana*] frame ❸ [*asedio*] siege • **poner cerco a** to lay siege to ❹ [*valla*] fence

cerdo, da *sm, f* ❶ [*animal*] pig, *femenino* <u>sow</u> • **crían cerdos** they raise pigs ❷ [*carne*] pork • **ayer comimos cerdo** yesterday we ate pork ❸ *familiar & figurado* [*persona*] pig • **comí como un cerdo** I ate like a pig

cereal *sm* cereal • **cereales** (breakfast) cereal ☼: *incontable*

cerebro *sm* ❶ [*generalmente*] brain ❷ *figurado* [*cabecilla*] brains *sing* ❸ *figurado* [*inteligencia*] brains *pl*

ceremonia *sf* ceremony, *plural* <u>ceremonies</u>

ceremonial *adj* & *sm* ceremonial ☼: *Los adjetivos ingleses son invariables.*

ceremonioso, sa *adj* ceremonious ᪻ *Los adjetivos ingleses son invariables.*

cereza *sf* cherry, *plural* <u>cherries</u>

cerezo *sm* cherry tree

cerillo *sm* match

cero ◆ *adj invariable* zero ᪻ *Los adjetivos ingleses son invariables.*

◆ *sm* ❶ [*signo*] Meteorología zero • **el primer número es cero** the first number is zero • **cero coma dos** zero point two • **tenemos dos grados bajo cero** it's two degrees below zero ❷ [*en futbol*] nil • **dos goles a cero** two nil • **fue un empate a cero** it was a no-score tie ❸ [*en tenis*] love • **cuarenta cero** forty-love ❹ [*cantidad*] nothing

expresión ser un cero a la izquierda a) *familiar* [*un inútil*] to be useless b) [*un don nadie*] to be a nobody ▶ **partir de cero** to start from scratch ver también **seis**

cerrado, da *adj* ❶ [*al exterior*] closed • **la tienda estaba cerrada** the store was closed • **cerrado a** closed to ❷ [*con llave, pestillo* etc] locked • **está cerrado con llave** it's locked ❸ [*tiempo, cielo*] overcast • **era noche cerrada** it was completely dark ❹ [*agua, gas*] off • **deja la llave cerrada** leave the faucet off ❺ [*rodeado*] surrounded ❻ [*por montañas*] walled in ❼ Electrónica • **circuito cerrado** closed circuit ❽ [*curva*] sharp ❾ [*vocal*] close ❿ [*acento, deje*] broad ᪻ *Los adjetivos ingleses son invariables.*

cerradura *sf* lock

cerrajero, ra *sm, f* locksmith

cerrar ◆ *vt* ❶ [*generalmente*] to close • **cerró la ventana** he closed the window • **la biblioteca cierra a las cinco** the library closes at five ❷ [*puerta, cajón, boca*] to shut; to close ❸ [*puños*] to clench ❹ [*con llave, pestillo* etc] to lock • **¿cerraste la puerta con llave?** did you lock the door? ❺ [*tienda, negocio - definitivamente*] to close down ❻ [*apagar*] to turn off • **cierra bien la llave** turn the faucet off completely ❼ [*bloquear - sujeto: accidente, inundación* etc] to block; [- *sujeto: policía* etc] to close off ❽ [*tapar - agujero, hueco*] to fill; [- *bote*] to put the lid on ❾ [*cercar*] to fence (off) ❿ [*cicatrizar*] to heal ⓫ [*ir último en*] to bring up the rear of ⓬ • **cerrar un trato** to seal a deal

◆ *vi* ❶ to close; to shut ❷ [*con llave, pestillo* etc] to lock up

■ **cerrarse** *v pronominal* ❶ [*al exterior*] to close; to shut • **la ventana se cerró con el viento** the window closed with the wind • **se me cerraban los ojos** I couldn't keep my eyes open ❷ [*incomunicarse*] to clam up • **cerrarse a** to close your mind to • **no hay que cerrarse a ninguna posibilidad** we must keep an open mind about things ❸ [*herida*] to heal ❹ [*acto, debate, discusión* etc] to (come to a) close

cerro *sm* hill

expresión irse por los cerros de Úbeda to stray from the point

cerrojo *sm* bolt

certamen *sm* competition

certero, ra *adj* ❶ [*tiro*] accurate ❷ [*opinión, respuesta* etc] correct ᪻ *Los adjetivos ingleses son invariables.*

certeza *sf* certainty

certidumbre *sf* certainty

certificación *sf* ❶ [*hecho*] certification ❷ [*documento*] certificate

certificado, da *adj* ❶ [*generalmente*] certified ❷ [*carta, paquete*] registered ᪻ *Los adjetivos ingleses son invariables.*

■ **certificado** *sm* certificate ▶ **certificado de depósito** Banca certificate of deposit ▶ **certificado de estudios** school-leaving certificate ▶ **certificado de origen** Comercio certificate of origin

certificar *vt* ❶ [*constatar*] to certify ❷ [*en correos*] to register

cerumen *sm* earwax

cervecería *sf* ❶ [*fábrica*] brewery ❷ [*bar*] bar

cervecero, ra *sm, f* brewer

cerveza *sf* beer • **fueron a tomar unas cervezas** they went to have a few beers ▶ **cerveza de barril** draft beer ▶ **cerveza negra** stout ▶ **cerveza rubia** lager

cesante *adj* ❶ [*destituido*] fired ❷ [*ministro*] removed from office ❸ [*en paro*] unemployed ᪻ *Los adjetivos ingleses son invariables.*

cesar ◆ *vt* ❶ [*destituir*] to fire ❷ [*ministro*] to remove from office

◆ *vi* [*parar*] • **cesar (de hacer algo)** to stop o cease (doing something) • **no cesaba de llorar** he didn't stop crying • **no cesa de intentarlo** she keeps trying • **sin cesar** non-stop; incessantly

cesárea *sf* caesarean (section)

cese *sm* ❶ [*detención, paro*] stopping ❷ [*destitución*] firing ❸ [*de ministro*] removal from office

cesión *sf* cession ▶ **cesión de bienes** surrender of property

césped *sm* lawn • **'prohibido pisar el césped'** keep off the lawn

cesta *sf* basket ▶ **cesta de Navidad** Christmas hamper

■ **cesta de la compra** *sf* ❶ *figurado* cost of living ❷ [*para compras en Internet*] shopping basket

cesto *sm* (large) basket • **el cesto de los papeles** the wastepaper basket

ceviche *sm* ▶ *para explicar lo que es puedes decir:* <u>it's a dish with raw, marinated fish</u>

cg (*abreviatura escrita de* centigramo) cg

chacal *sm* jackal

chacha *sf* maid

chafar *vt* ❶ [*aplastar*] to flatten ❷ *figurado* [*estropear*] to spoil

chalado, da *adj familiar* crazy ᪻ *Los adjetivos ingleses son invariables.*

chalán, ana *familiar* ◆ *adj* horse-trading

◆ *sm, f* ❶ [*comerciante*] horse dealer ❷ horse trainer

chalé *sm* ❶ [*generalmente*] detached house (with garden) ‣ **chalé pareado** semi-detached house ❷ [*en el campo*] cottage ❸ [*de alta montaña*] chalet

chaleco *sm* vest ‣ **chaleco salvavidas** life jacket

chalina *sf* ❶ [*corbata*] cravat ❷ [*chal*] narrow shawl

chalupa *sf* ❶ [*barca*] boat ❷ [*canoa*] small canoe ❸ [*plato*] *para explicar lo que es puedes decir:* it's a small tortilla with a raised rim to contain a filling

chamaco, ca *sm, f familiar* kid

chamarra *sf* jacket

chamba *sf familiar* job

chambero, ra *sm, f* itinerant worker

chamizar *vt* to thatch (with chamiso)

champán *sm* champagne

champiñón *sm* mushroom

champú (pl champús o champúes) *sm* shampoo

champurrado *sm* ❶ hodgepodge ❷ hot, corn-based chocolate drink

chamuscar *vt* ❶ [*tierra*] to scorch ❷ [*cabello, barba, tela*] to singe

chamusquina *sf* scorch

expresión **me huele a chamusquina** *familiar* it smells a bit fishy to me

chance ◆ *sf* opportunity
◆ *adv* maybe

chanchullo *sm familiar* fiddle

chancleta *sf* ❶ [*sandalia*] low sandal ❷ [*para la playa*] flip-flop

changarro *sm* small store

chango, ga *sm, f* monkey

chantaje *sm* blackmail • **hacer chantaje a alguien** to blackmail somebody ‣ **chantaje emocional** emotional blackmail

chantajear *vt* to blackmail • **lo chantajearon por mucho dinero** they blackmailed him for a lot of money

chao *exclamación* • **¡chao!** *familiar* bye!; see you!

chapa *sf* ❶ [*lámina - de metal*] sheet; [*- de madera*] board • **de tres chapas** three-ply ❷ [*tapón*] top ❸ [*insignia*] badge ❹ [*ficha de guardarropa*] metal token ❺ [*cerradura*] lock

chapar *vt* ❶ [*con metal*] to plate ❷ [*con madera*] to veneer

chaparro, rra ◆ *adj* short and squat ☼: *Los adjetivos ingleses son invariables.*
◆ *sm, f* [*persona*] short person

chaparrón *sm* ❶ downpour ❷ *familiar* [*gran cantidad*] torrent

chapata *sf* ciabatta

chapear *vt* ❶ [*con metal*] to plate ❷ [*con madera*] to veneer ❸ [*terreno*] to clear

chapopote *sm* asphalt

chapotear *vi* to splash around • **los niños chapotearon en la piscina** the children splashed around in the swimming pool

chapucero, ra ◆ *adj* ❶ [*trabajo*] shoddy ❷ [*persona*] bungling ☼: *Los adjetivos ingleses son invariables.*
◆ *sm, f* bungler

chapulín *sm* ❶ [*saltamontes*] grasshopper ❷ *familiar* [*niño*] kid

chapurrear *vt* to speak badly

chapuza *sf* ❶ [*trabajo mal hecho*] botch (job) ❷ [*trabajo ocasional*] odd job

chapuzón *sm* dip • **darse un chapuzón** to go for a dip

chaqueta *sf* ❶ jacket ‣ **chaqueta de fuerza** straitjacket ❷ [*de punto*] cardigan

chaquetón *sm* short coat

charca *sf* pool

charco *sm* puddle

expresión **cruzar el charco** to cross the pond

charcutería *sf* ❶ [*tienda*] *para explicar lo que es puedes decir:* it's a shop selling cold cooked meats and cheeses, ≃ delicatessen ❷ [*productos*] cold cuts *pl* and cheese

charla *sf* ❶ [*conversación*] chat • **estaban de charla** they were having a chat ❷ [*conferencia*] talk • **dio una charla sobre el medio ambiente** she gave a talk about the environment

charlar *vi* to chat • **charlaron de sus novios** they chatted about their boyfriends

charlatán, ana ◆ *adj* talkative ☼: *Los adjetivos ingleses son invariables.*
◆ *sm, f* ❶ [*hablador*] chatterbox ❷ [*mentiroso*] trickster

charola *sf* tray

charro, rra *adj* ❶ [*tosco*] unsophisticated ❷ *familiar* [*de mal gusto*] gaudy ❸ [*diestro*] skilled in horsemanship ❹ [*pintoresco*] picturesque
■ **charro** *sm* cowboy

chárter *adj invariable* charter ☼: *Sólo se usa delante del sustantivo.* • **vuelo chárter** charter flight

chasco *sm* disappointment • **¡qué chasco!** what a disappointment! • **llevarse un chasco** to be disappointed

chasquear ◆ *vt* ❶ [*látigo*] to crack ❷ [*la lengua*] to click
◆ *vi* [*madera*] to crack

chasquido *sm* ❶ [*de látigo, madera, hueso*] crack ❷ [*de lengua, arma*] click ❸ [*de dedos*] snap

chatarra *sf* ❶ [*metal*] scrap (metal) ❷ [*objetos, piezas*] junk

chato, ta ◆ *adj* ❶ [*nariz*] snub ❷ [*persona*] snub-nosed ❸ [*aplanado*] flat ☼: *Los adjetivos ingleses son invariables.*
◆ *sm, f familiar* [*apelativo*] love

chauvinista = chovinista

chaval, la *sm, f familiar* kid

chavo, va *sm, f familiar* guy, *femenino* girl

cheque *sm* check • **extender un cheque** to make out a check ‣ **cheque en blanco/sin fondos** blank/bad check ‣ **cheque nominativo** check in favor of a specific person ▶ **cheque al portador** check payable to the bearer ▶ **cheque de viaje** o **de viajero** traveler's check ▶ **cheque regalo** gift certificate

chequear *vt* ❶ MEDICINA • **chequear a alguien** to give somebody a checkup ❷ [*comprobar*] to check

chequeo *sm* ❶ MEDICINA checkup ❷ [*comprobación*] check

chica *sf* ❶ [*criada*] maid ❷ → **chico**

chícharo *sm* pea

chicharra *sf* ❶ ZOOLOGÍA cicada ❷ [*timbre*] buzzer

chicharro *sm* [*pez*] horse mackerel

chicharrones *smpl* [*embutido*] *para explicar lo que es puedes decir:* it's cold processed meat made from pork

chichón *sm* bump • **tiene un chichón en la cabeza** he has a bump on his head

chicle *sm* chewing gum • **le gusta mascar chicle** she likes to chew gum • **¿me das un chicle?** may I have a piece of chewing gum?

chico, ca ◆ *adj* ❶ [*pequeño*] small • **el baño es muy chico** the bathroom is very small • **estos pantalones me quedan chicos** these pants are too small for me ❷ [*joven*] young • **cuando era chica jugaba con él** when she was young she played with him ☿ *Los adjetivos ingleses son invariables.*
◆ *sm, f* ❶ [*joven*] boy, *femenino* girl ❷ [*tratamiento - hombre*] sonny; [*- mujer*] darling
■ **chico** *sm* [*recadero*] messenger; office-boy

chicotazo *sm* whiplash

chicote *sm* [*látigo*] whip

chiflado, da *adj familiar* crazy ☿ *Los adjetivos ingleses son invariables.*

chiflar ◆ *vt familiar* [*encantar*] • **me chiflan las papas fritas** I'm mad about chips
◆ *vi* [*silbar*] to whistle

chiflido *sm* whistling

chilango, ga *adj* of/from Mexico City

chile *sm* chili (pepper) ▶ **chile con carne** COCINA chili con carne

Chile *nombre propio* Chile

chileno, na *adj* & *sm, f* Chilean ☿ *Los adjetivos ingleses son invariables.*
En inglés, los adjetivos que se refieren a un país o una región se escriben con mayúscula.

chillar ◆ *vi* ❶ [*gritar - personas*] to scream; [*- ave, mono*] to screech; [*- cerdo*] to squeal; [*- ratón*] to squeak ❷ [*chirriar*] to screech ❸ [*puerta, madera*] to creak ❹ [*bisagras*] to squeak
◆ *vt familiar* [*reñir*] to yell at

chillido *sm* ❶ [*de persona*] scream ❷ [*de ave, mono*] screech ❸ [*de cerdo*] squeal ❹ [*de ratón*] squeak

chillón, ona *adj* ❶ [*voz*] piercing ❷ [*persona*] noisy ❸ [*color*] gaudy ☿ *Los adjetivos ingleses son invariables.*

chimenea *sf* ❶ [*hogar*] fireplace • **nos sentamos frente a la chimenea** we sat down in front of the fire-

place ❷ [*en tejado*] chimney • **las chimeneas de la fábrica** the factory chimneys

chimpancé *sm* chimpanzee

china *sf* ❶ [*piedra*] pebble ❷ [*porcelana*] china

China *nombre propio* • **(la) China** China

chinampa *sf* ▶ *para explicar lo que es puedes decir:* it's a floating garden near Mexico City

chinchar *vt familiar* to pester

chinche ◆ *adj familiar* & *figurado* annoying ☿ *Los adjetivos ingleses son invariables.*
◆ *sf* [*insecto*] bedbug

chincheta *sf* thumbtack

chinchín *sm* [*brindis*] toast • **¡chinchín!** cheers!

chinchorro *sm* ❶ [*red*] sweep net ❷ [*bote de remos*] dinghy ❸ small herd

chip (pl chips) *sm* INFORMÁTICA chip

chipotle *sm* ▶ *para explicar lo que es puedes decir:* it's a smoked jalapeño chili

chiqueo *sm* show of affection

chiquilín *sm familiar* small boy

chiquillo, lla *sm, f* kid

chiripa *sf familiar* & *figurado* fluke • **de** o **por chiripa** by luck

chirriar *vi* ❶ [*generalmente*] to screech ❷ [*puerta, madera*] to creak ❸ [*bisagra, muelles*] to squeak

chirrido *sm* ❶ [*generalmente*] screech ❷ [*de puerta, madera*] creak ❸ [*de bisagra, muelles*] squeak

chis *exclamación* • **¡chis!** ssh!

chisguete *sm* ❶ *familiar* [*trago*] swig ❷ [*chorro*] jet

chisme *sm* ❶ [*cotilleo*] rumor ❷ *familiar* [*cosa*] thingamajig

chismorrear *vi* to gossip

chismoso, sa ◆ *adj* • **es muy chismoso** he's a real gossip ☿ *Los adjetivos ingleses son invariables.*
◆ *sm, f* gossip

chispa *sf* ❶ [*de fuego, electricidad*] spark • **saltaron chispas del fuego** sparks popped out of the fire ❷ [*de lluvia*] spot (of rain) ❸ *figurado* [*pizca*] bit ▶ **una chispa de sal** a pinch of salt ❹ *figurado* [*agudeza*] sparkle
▐ *expresión* ▌ **echar chispas** *familiar* to be hopping mad

chispear ◆ *vi* ❶ [*chisporrotear*] to spark ❷ [*relucir*] to sparkle
◆ *v impersonal* [*llover*] to spit (with rain)

chisporrotear *vi* ❶ [*fuego, leña*] to crackle ❷ [*aceite*] to splutter ❸ [*comida*] to sizzle

chistar *vi* • **me fui sin chistar** I left without a word

chiste *sm* joke • **contar chistes** to tell jokes ▶ **chiste colorado** dirty joke ▶ **chiste picante** dirty joke ▶ **chiste verde** dirty joke

chistoso, sa *adj* funny ☿ *Los adjetivos ingleses son invariables.*

chiva *sf* [*barba*] goatee
■ **chivas** *sfpl* odds and ends

chivar *vt familiar* to tell secretly

chivatazo *sm familiar* tip-off • **dar el chivatazo** to grass

chivato, ta *sm, f* ❶ *familiar* [*delator*] informer ❷ [*acusica*] telltale

chivo, va *sm, f* kid; young goat

expresión **ser el chivo expiatorio** to be the scapegoat

chocante *adj* startling ☿ *Los adjetivos ingleses son invariables.*

chocar ◆ *vi* ❶ [*colisionar*] • **chocar (contra)** to crash (into) • **chocó contra un árbol** he crashed into a tree • **chocaron de frente** they collided head on • **choqué con él a la salida** I bumped into him on the way out ❷ *figurado* [*enfrentarse*] to clash

◆ *vt figurado* [*sorprender*] to shock • **me choca el vocabulario que usan** the vocabulary that they use shocks me • **me choca cuando hace eso** it bothers me when he does that

expresión **¡chócala!** give me five!

chochear *vi* [*viejo*] to be senile

chocho, cha *adj* ❶ [*viejo*] senile ❷ *familiar & figurado* [*encariñado*] soft ☿ *Los adjetivos ingleses son invariables.*

chocolate *sm* ❶ [*para comer*] chocolate • **me encanta el chocolate** I love chocolate • **me dio un chocolate** she gave me a chocolate ▶ **chocolate blanco** white chocolate ▶ **chocolate con leche** milk chocolate ❷ [*para beber*] hot chocolate • **me tomé un chocolate** I drank a hot chocolate ▶ **chocolate (a la taza)** thick drinking chocolate

chofer (pl choferes) *smf* ❶ [*como oficio - de automóvil*] chauffeur; [*- de autobús*] driver ❷ [*conductor*] driver

chompipe *sm* turkey

chongo *sm* bun

choque *sm* ❶ [*impacto*] impact ❷ [*de coche, avión* ETC] crash • **hubo un choque frente al colegio** there was a crash in front of the school ▶ **choque frontal** head-on collision ❸ *figurado* [*enfrentamiento*] clash ▶ **choque cultural** culture shock

chorizo *sm* ❶ [*embutido*] chorizo ❷ *familiar* [*ladrón*] thief

chorrear *vi* ❶ [*gotear - gota a gota*] to drip; [*- en un hilo*] to trickle ❷ [*brotar*] to spurt (out)

chorro *sm* ❶ [*de líquido - borbotón*] spurt; [*- hilo*] trickle • **salir a chorros** to gush out ▶ **chorro de vapor** steam jet ❷ *figurado* [*de luz, gente* ETC] stream • **tiene un chorro de dinero** she has loads of money

expresión **a chorros** in abundance ▶ **me gusta un chorro ese cantante** *familiar* I like that singer a lot

chovinista, chauvinista ◆ *adj* chauvinistic ☿ *Los adjetivos ingleses son invariables.*

◆ *smf* chauvinist

choza *sf* hut

chubasco *sm* shower

chubasquero *sm* raincoat

chuchería *sf* ❶ [*golosina*] candy ❷ [*objeto*] trinket

chucho *sm familiar* mutt

chueco, ca *adj* ❶ [*torcido*] crooked • **esta raya está chueca** this line is crooked ❷ *familiar* [*proyecto, razonamiento*] shady ❸ [*patizambo*] bowlegged ☿ *Los adjetivos ingleses son invariables.*

chulear *vi familiar* [*fanfarronear*] • **chulear (de)** to be cocky (about)

chulería *sf* [*descaro*] cockiness

chuleta *sf* [*de carne*] chop ▶ **chuleta de cordero** lamb chop

chulo, la *adj familiar* [*bonito*] lovely • **mira, ¡qué vestido tan chulo!** look, what a cute dress! • **tu hermana es muy chula** your sister is very pretty ☿ *Los adjetivos ingleses son invariables.*

chumbo → **higo**

chupado, da *adj* ❶ [*delgado*] skinny ❷ *familiar* [*fácil*] • **estar chupado** to be dead easy o a piece of cake ☿ *Los adjetivos ingleses son invariables.*

chupar *vt* ❶ [*succionar*] to suck • **no te chupes el dedo** don't suck your finger ❷ [*fumando*] to puff at ❸ [*absorber*] to soak up ❹ [*quitar*] • **chuparle algo a alguien** to milk somebody for something

expresión **chuparle la sangre a alguien** to bleed somebody dry

chupete *sm* pacifier

chupón *sm* ❶ [*chupete*] pacifier ❷ [*de biberón*] nipple

chusma *sf* rabble

chut (pl chuts) *sm* kick

chutar *vi* to shoot

CIA (*abreviatura de* Central Intelligence Agency) *sf* CIA

cía. Co.

cianuro *sm* cyanide

ciático, ca *adj* sciatic ☿ *Los adjetivos ingleses son invariables.*

■ **ciática** *sf* sciatica

cibercafé *sm* Internet cafe

ciberespacio *sm* cyberspace

cicatriz *sf literal & figurado* scar • **le va a quedar una cicatriz en la frente** she's going to have a scar on her forehead

cicatrizar ◆ *vi* to heal (up)

◆ *vt figurado* to heal

cíclico, ca *adj* cyclical ☿ *Los adjetivos ingleses son invariables.*

ciclismo *sm* cycling • **el ciclismo es un deporte bastante popular** cycling is a pretty popular sport

ciclista *smf* cyclist

ciclo *sm* ❶ [*generalmente*] cycle • **el ciclo de las estaciones** the cycle of the seasons ▶ **ciclo vital** life cycle ❷ [*de conferencias, actos*] series ❸ [*de enseñanza*] stage

ciclocrós *sm* cyclo-cross

ciclomotor *sm* moped

ciclón *sm* cyclone

cicuta *sf* hemlock

C

ciego, ga ◆ *adj* **❶** [*invidente*] blind • **es ciega** she's blind • **es ciego de nacimiento** he's blind from birth • **quedarse ciego** to go blind • **a ciegas** *literal & figurado* blindly **❷** *figurado* [*enloquecido*] • **ciego (de)** blinded (by) **❸** [*pozo, tubería*] blocked (up):♡: *Los adjetivos ingleses son invariables.*
◆ *sm, f* [*invidente*] blind person • **los ciegos** the blind

cielo *sm* **❶** [*generalmente*] sky • **el cielo estaba despejado** the sky was clear **❷** [*mina*] opencast **❸** RELIGIÓN heaven • **dice que su perro está en el cielo** she says that her dog is in heaven **❹** [*nombre cariñoso*] darling
expresión **clamar al cielo** to be outrageous ❱ **ser un cielo** to be an angel

ciempiés *sm invariable* centipede

cien → **ciento**

ciénaga *sf* marsh

ciencia *sf* science • **la ciencia moderna** modern science ❱ **ciencia ficción** science fiction
expresión **a ciencia cierta** for certain

cieno *sm* mud

científico, ca ◆ *adj* scientific:♡: *Los adjetivos ingleses son invariables.*
◆ *sm, f* scientist

ciento, cien *numeral* a o one hundred • **ciento cincuenta pesos** a hundred and fifty pesos • **vinieron cerca de cien personas** around a hundred people came • **cien mil** a hundred thousand • **a cientos** by the hundred • **cientos de** hundreds of • **por ciento** per cent • **ciento por ciento, cien por cien** a hundred per cent • **cientos de veces** hundreds of times ver también **seis**

cierre *sm* **❶** [*generalmente*] closing **❷** [*con llave*] locking ❱ **cierre patronal** lockout **❸** [*de fábrica*] shutdown **❹** RADIO & TELEVISIÓN closedown **❺** [*mecanismo*] fastener ❱ **cierre metálico** [*de tienda* ETC] metal shutter ❱ **cierre relámpago** [*cremallera*] zipper

cierto, ta *adj* **❶** [*verdadero*] true • **¡eso no es cierto!** that's not true! • **estar en lo cierto** to be right • **lo cierto es que...** the fact is that... **❷** [*seguro*] certain • **ciertas personas piensan que es culpable** certain people think that he's guilty **❸** [*algún*] certain • **cierto hombre** a certain man • **en cierta ocasión** once; on one occasion • **durante cierto tiempo** for a while:♡: *Los adjetivos ingleses son invariables.*
■ **cierto** *adv* right; certainly

ciervo, va *sm, f* deer, *plural* deer

cifra *sf* [*generalmente*] figure • **un número de dos cifras** a two-figure number ❱ **cifra de negocios** ECONOMÍA turnover ❱ **cifra de ventas** sales figures

cifrar *vt* **❶** [*codificar*] to code **❷** *figurado* [*centrar*] to concentrate

cigarra *sf* cicada

cigarrillo *sm* cigarette

cigarro *sm* **❶** [*habano*] cigar **❷** [*cigarrillo*] cigarette

cigüeña *sf* stork

cilindrada *sf* cylinder capacity

cilíndrico, ca *adj* cylindrical:♡: *Los adjetivos ingleses son invariables.*

cilindro *sm* **❶** [*generalmente*] cylinder **❷** [*de imprenta*] roller

cima *sf* **❶** [*punta - de montaña*] summit; [*- de árbol*] top **❷** *figurado* [*apogeo*] peak

cimentar *vt* **❶** [*edificio*] to lay the foundations of **❷** [*ciudad*] to found **❸** *figurado* [*idea, paz, fama*] to cement

cimiento *sm* CONSTRUCCIÓN foundation • **echar los cimientos** *literal & figurado* to lay the foundations

cinc, zinc *sm* zinc

cincho *sm* **❶** [*faja*] belt **❷** [*zuncho*] metal hoop **❸** [*de rueda*] iron rim **❹** [*de caballo*] girth

cinco *numeral* five
expresión **¡choca esos cinco!** put it there! ❱ **estar sin cinco** to be broke ver también **seis**

cincuenta *numeral* fifty • **los (años) cincuenta** the fifties ver también **seis**

cincuentón, ona *sm, f* fifty-year-old

cine *sm* **❶** [*arte*] cinema • **el cine mexicano** Mexican cinema • **un artista de cine** a movie actor • **hacer cine** to make movies ❱ **cine de terror** horror movies **❷** [*lugar*] movie theater • **ir al cine** to go to the movies ❱ **cine de barrio** local movie theater ❱ **cine de estreno** premiere movie theater ❱ **cine de verano** open-air movie theater

cineasta *smf* movie maker

cineclub *sm* [*asociación*] movie club

cinéfilo, la *sm, f* movie buff

cinematografía *sf* cinematography

cinematográfico, ca *adj* movie:♡: *Sólo se usa delante del sustantivo.* • **el mundo cinematográfico** the movie world

cínico, ca ◆ *adj* cynical • **es muy cínico** he's very cynical:♡: *Los adjetivos ingleses son invariables.*
◆ *sm, f* cynic

cinismo *sm* cynicism

cinta *sf* **❶** [*tira - de plástico, papel*] strip; [*- de tela*] ribbon • **se amarró el pelo con una cinta** she tied her hair back with a ribbon • **cinta adhesiva** adhesive tape ❱ **cinta Dúrex®** Scotch tape® ❱ **cinta métrica** tape measure **❷** [*de imagen, sonido, ordenadores*] tape ❱ **cinta digital** digital tape ❱ **cinta limpiadora** head-cleaning tape ❱ **cinta magnética** magnetic tape ❱ **cinta magnetofónica** recording tape ❱ **cinta de video** videotape ❱ **cinta virgen** blank tape **❸** [*mecanismo*] belt ❱ **cinta transportadora** conveyor belt ❱ **cinta de equipajes** baggage carousel

cintura *sf* waist • **me aprieta en la cintura** it's too tight in the waist

cinturón *sm* **❶** [*cinto*] belt ❱ **cinturón de castidad** chastity belt ❱ **cinturón de miseria** slum on the city outskirts ❱ **cinturón salvavidas** life preserver ❱ **cinturón de seguridad** safety belt **❷** AUTOMÓVILES beltway **❸** [*cordón*] cordon
expresión **apretarse el cinturón** to tighten your belt

ciprés *sm* cypress

circo *sm* circus

circuito *sm* ❶ DEPORTE & ELECTRÓNICA circuit ▶ **circuito cerrado de televisión** closed-circuit television ❷ [*recorrido*] tour

circulación *sf* ❶ [*generalmente*] circulation • **tengo muy buena circulación** I have very good circulation ▶ **circulación de la sangre** circulation of the blood ▶ **circulación fiduciaria** o **monetaria** paper currency ❷ [*tráfico*] traffic • **una calle de mucha circulación** a street with a lot of traffic

circular ◆ *adj* & *sf* circular ⚲ *Los adjetivos ingleses son invariables.*

◆ *vi* ❶ [*de mano en mano*] to circulate • **abran la puerta para que circule el aire** open the window so that the air will circulate ❷ [*moneda*] to be in circulation ❸ [*difundirse*] to go round • **son rumores que circulan en el colegio** they're rumors that go around the school ❹ [*manejar*] to drive • **en ese país circulan por la izquierda** in that country they drive on the left side of the road

círculo *sm* literal & figurado circle • **nos sentamos en círculo** we sat down in a circle ▶ **círculo polar** polar circle ▶ **el círculo polar ártico/antártico** the Arctic/Antarctic Circle ▶ **círculo vicioso** vicious circle

circuncisión *sf* circumcision

circundante *adj* surrounding ⚲ *Los adjetivos ingleses son invariables.*

circundar *vt* to surround

circunferencia *sf* circumference

circunloquio *sm* circumlocution

circunscribir *vt* ❶ [*limitar*] to restrict ❷ GEOMETRÍA to circumscribe

circunscripción *sf* ❶ [*distrito*] district ❷ MILITAR division ❸ POLÍTICA constituency

circunscrito, ta ◆ *participio pasado* → **circunscribir**

◆ *adj* limited ⚲ *Los adjetivos ingleses son invariables.*

circunstancia *sf* circumstance • **bajo ninguna circunstancia** under no circumstance • **dadas las circunstancias** given the circumstances • **en estas circunstancias** under the circumstances

circunstancial *adj* chance ⚲ *Sólo se usa delante del sustantivo.* • **una visita circunstancial** a chance visit

circunvalar *vt* to go round

cirio *sm* (wax) candle

expresión **montar un cirio** to make a row

cirrosis *sf invariable* cirrhosis

ciruela *sf* plum ▶ **ciruela pasa** prune

cirugía *sf* surgery ▶ **cirugía estética** o **plástica** cosmetic o plastic surgery • **se hizo la cirugía plástica** she had plastic surgery

cirujano, na *sm, f* surgeon

cisma *sm* ❶ [*separación*] schism ❷ [*discordia*] split

cisne *sm* swan

cisterna *sf* [*de retrete*] cistern

cistitis *sf invariable* cystitis

cita *sf* ❶ [*entrevista*] appointment • **mi mamá tiene una cita con el director** my mom has an appointment with the director • **concertar una cita** to make an appointment • **darse cita** to meet ❷ [*de novios*] date • **tiene una cita con su novio** she has a date with her boyfriend ❸ [*referencia*] quotation • **una cita de Rubén Darío** a quotation from Rubén Darío

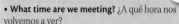

hacer una cita

• **What time are we meeting?** ¿A qué hora nos volvemos a ver?

• **Where are we going to meet?** ¿En dónde nos vemos?

• **Do you want to meet up this evening?** ¿Quieres/Quiere que nos juntemos esta noche?

• **Do you have anything planned for tomorrow?** ¿Tienes/Tiene ya plan para mañana?

• **I can't tomorrow, but I'm free all weekend.** Mañana no puedo, pero no tengo nada planeado para el fin de semana.

citación *sf* DERECHO summons *sing*

citar *vt* ❶ [*convocar*] • **lo citaron a las nueve** they gave her an appointment for nine o'clock ❷ [*aludir*] to mention ❸ [*textualmente*] to quote • **citó un pasaje de la Biblia** he quoted a passage from the Bible ❹ DERECHO to summons

citología *sf* ❶ [*análisis*] smear test ❷ BIOLOGÍA cytology

cítrico, ca *adj* citric ⚲ *Los adjetivos ingleses son invariables.*

ciudad *sf* ❶ [*localidad*] city, *plural* cities • **en ciudades como Buenos Aires** in cities like Buenos Aires ▶ **ciudad balneario** coastal resort ▶ **ciudad perdida** shanty town ▶ **ciudad universitaria** university campus ❷ [*pequeña*] town • **vive en una ciudad de muy pocos habitantes** he lives in a town with very few inhabitants

■ **Ciudad del Cabo** *sf* Cape Town
■ **Ciudad de México** *sf* Mexico City
■ **Ciudad del Vaticano** *sf* Vatican City

la ciudad

la ambulancia	the ambulance
el ayuntamiento	the city hall
la banqueta	the sidewalk
la calle	the street
la calzada	the avenue
el cine	the movies *pl*
el edificio	the building
los escaparates	the window displays
el estacionamiento	the parking lot
el hospital	the hospital
el kiosko	the newsstand
la parada de autobús	the bus stop

la parada de taxis	the taxi rank
el paso de peatones	the crosswalk
el peatón	the pedestrian
la plaza	the square
el semáforo	the traffic lights *pl*
el taxi	the taxi
la tienda	the store
la tienda (departamental)	the department store

ciudadanía *sf* ❶ [*nacionalidad*] citizenship ❷ [*población*] citizens *pl*

ciudadano, na *sm, f* citizen • **es ciudadano mexicano** he's a Mexican citizen

cívico, ca *adj* ❶ civic ❷ [*conducta*] public-spirited ♀ *Los adjetivos ingleses son invariables.*

civil ♦ *adj* literal & figurado civil ▶ **derechos civiles** civil rights ♀ *Los adjetivos ingleses son invariables.*

♦ *sm* [*no militar*] civilian

civilización *sf* civilization

civilizado, da *adj* civilized ♀ *Los adjetivos ingleses son invariables.*

civilizar *vt* to civilize

civismo *sm* ❶ [*urbanidad*] community spirit ❷ [*cortesía*] civility

cizaña *sf* BOTÁNICA darnel

cl (*abreviatura escrita de* centilitro) cl

clamar ♦ *vt* ❶ [*expresar*] to exclaim ❷ [*exigir*] to cry out for

♦ *vi* ❶ [*implorar*] to appeal ❷ [*protestar*] to cry out

clamor *sm* clamor

clamoroso, sa *adj* ❶ [*rotundo*] resounding ❷ [*vociferante*] loud ♀ *Los adjetivos ingleses son invariables.*

clan *sm* ❶ [*tribu, familia*] clan ❷ [*banda*] faction

clandestino, na *adj* ❶ clandestine ❷ POLÍTICA underground ♀ *Los adjetivos ingleses son invariables.*

claqueta *sf* clapperboard

clara *sf* [*de huevo*] white • **hay que batir las claras** you have to beat the egg whites

claraboya *sf* skylight

clarear *v impersonal* ❶ [*amanecer*] • **empezaba a clarear** dawn was breaking ❷ [*despejarse*] to clear up

claridad *sf* ❶ [*transparencia*] clearness ❷ [*luz*] light ❸ [*franqueza*] candidness ❹ [*lucidez*] clarity • **explicar algo con claridad** to explain something clearly

clarificar *vt* ❶ [*gen*] to clarify ❷ [*misterio*] to clear up ❸ [*purificar*] to refine

clarín *sm* [*instrumento*] bugle

clarinete *sm* [*instrumento*] clarinet

clarividencia *sf* farsightedness

claro, ra *adj* ❶ [*generalmente*] clear • **su explicación fue muy clara** his explanation was very clear • **está claro que miente** it's clear that he's lying • **claro está que...** of course... ❷ [*luminoso*] bright ❸ [*color*] light • **prefiere los colores claros** she prefers light colors • **tiene los ojos verde claro** he has light green eyes

❹ [*diluido - té, café*] weak ♀ *Los adjetivos ingleses son invariables.*

expresiones **a las claras** clearly ▶ **dejar algo claro** to make something clear ▶ **pasar una noche en claro** to spend a sleepless night ▶ **poner algo en claro** to get something clear ; to clear something up ▶ **sacar algo en claro (de)** to make something out (from) ▶ **tener algo claro** to be sure of something

■ **claro** ♦ *sm* ❶ [*en bosque*] clearing ❷ [*en multitud, texto*] space ❸ METEOROLOGÍA bright spell

♦ *adv* clearly • **no lo veo muy claro** I don't see it very clearly • **tienes que hablarle claro** you have to be frank with him

♦ *exclamación* • **¡claro!** of course! • **¡claro que no!** of course not! • **¡claro que sí!** yes, of course

clase *sf* ❶ [*generalmente*] class ▶ **clase alta** upper class ▶ **clase baja** lower class ▶ **clase media** middle class ▶ **clase obrera** o **trabajadora** working class ▶ **clase salón** FERROCARRIL first class ▶ **clase social** social class ▶ **primera clase** first class ❷ [*tipo*] sort ; kind • **toda clase de** all sorts o kinds of ❸ [*materia, alumnos*] class • **esa niña está en mi clase** that girl is in my class • **hoy tuvimos clase de historia** today we had history class • **dar clases a)** [*en un colegio*] to teach **b)** [*en una universidad*] to lecture ▶ **clases particulares** private lessons ❹ [*aula*] classroom • **los alumnos estaban en la clase cuando llegó el maestro** the students were in the classroom when the teacher arrived

clásico, ca ♦ *adj* ❶ [*de la Antigüedad*] classical ❷ [*ejemplar, prototípico*] classic ❸ [*peinado, estilo, música* ETC] classical ❹ [*habitual*] customary ❺ [*peculiar*] • **clásico de** typical of ♀ *Los adjetivos ingleses son invariables.*

♦ *sm, f* [*persona*] classic

clasificación *sf* ❶ classification ❷ DEPORTE (league) table

clasificar *vt* to classify • **en la clase de biología clasificamos varias plantas** in biology class we classified a number of plants

clasista *adj* ❶ class-conscious ❷ despectivo snobbish ♀ *Los adjetivos ingleses son invariables.*

claudicar *vi* to give in

claustro *sm* ❶ ARQUITECTURA & RELIGIÓN cloister ❷ [*de universidad*] senate

claustrofobia *sf* claustrophobia

cláusula *sf* clause

clausura *sf* ❶ [*acto solemne*] closing ceremony ❷ [*cierre*] closing down ❸ RELIGIÓN religious seclusion

clausurar *vt* ❶ [*acto*] to close ❷ [*local*] to close down

clavadista *smf* diver

clavado *adj* ❶ [*en punto - hora*] on the dot ❷ [*parecido*] almost identical • **ser clavado a alguien** to be the spitting image of somebody ♀ *Los adjetivos ingleses son invariables.*

clavar *vt* ❶ [*clavo, estaca* ETC] to drive ❷ [*cuchillo*] to thrust ❸ [*chincheta, alfiler*] to stick ❹ [*cartel, placa* ETC] to nail ❺ figurado [*mirada, atención*] to fix

C

C

clave ◆ *adj invariable* key ▶ **palabra clave** keyword ⋅ *Los adjetivos ingleses son invariables.*
◆ *sm* Música harpsichord
◆ *sf* ❶ [*código*] code • **en clave** in code ❷ *figurado* [*solución*] key • **la clave del problema** the key to the problem ❸ Música clef ▶ **clave de sol** treble clef ❹ Informática key

clavel *sm* carnation

clavícula *sf* collar bone

clavija *sf* ❶ Electricidad & Tecnología pin ❷ [*de auriculares, teléfono*] jack ❸ Música peg

clavo *sm* ❶ [*pieza metálica*] nail ❷ Botánica & Cocina clove ❸ Medicina [*para huesos*] pin
expresiones **agarrarse a un clavo ardiendo** to clutch at straws ▶ **dar en el clavo** to hit the nail on the head ▶ **¡por los clavos de Cristo!** for heaven's sake

claxon® (pl cláxones) *sm* horn • **tocar el claxon** to sound the horn

clemencia *sf* mercy

clérigo *sm* ❶ [*católico*] priest ❷ [*anglicano*] clergyman

clero *sm* clergy

clic *sm* Informática click • **hacer clic en algo** to click on something

cliché *sm* ❶ Fotografía negative ❷ Imprenta plate ❸ *figurado* [*tópico*] cliché

cliente, ta *sm, f* ❶ [*de tienda, garaje, bar*] customer ▶ **cliente habitual** regular customer ❷ [*de banco, abogado* etc] client ❸ [*de hotel*] guest

clientela *sf* ❶ [*de tienda, garaje*] customers pl ❷ [*de banco, abogado* etc] clients pl ❸ [*de hotel*] guests pl ❹ [*de bar, restaurante*] clientele

clima *sm literal & figurado* climate ▶ **clima mediterráneo/tropical** Mediterranean/tropical climate

climatizado, da *adj* air-conditioned ⋅ *Los adjetivos ingleses son invariables.*

climatizar *vt* to air-condition

climatología *sf* ❶ [*tiempo*] weather ❷ [*ciencia*] climatology

clímax *sm invariable* climax

clínico, ca *adj* clinical ⋅ *Los adjetivos ingleses son invariables.*
■ **clínica** *sf* clinic

clip *sm* [*para papel*] paper clip

cloaca *sf* sewer

cloro *sm* Química chlorine

cloruro *sm* chloride ▶ **cloruro de sodio** o **sódico** sodium chloride

clóset, closets *sm* closet

club (pl clubes o clubs) *sm* club ▶ **club de fans** fan club ▶ **club de futbol** soccer club ▶ **club náutico** yacht club ▶ **club nocturno** nightclub

cm (*abreviatura escrita de* centímetro) cm

Co. (*abreviatura escrita de* compañía) Co.

coacción *sf* coercion

coaccionar *vt* to coerce

coagular *vt* ❶ [*generalmente*] to coagulate ❷ [*sangre*] to clot ❸ [*leche*] to curdle
■ **coagularse** *v pronominal* ❶ [*generalmente*] to coagulate ❷ [*sangre*] to clot ❸ [*leche*] to curdle

coágulo *sm* clot

coalición *sf* coalition • **formar una coalición** to form a coalition

coartada *sf* alibi

coba *sf familiar* [*halago*] flattery • **dar coba a alguien a)** [*hacer la pelota*] to suck up o crawl to somebody **b)** [*aplacar*] to soft-soap somebody

cobarde ◆ *adj* cowardly • **¡no seas cobarde!** don't be a coward! ⋅ *Los adjetivos ingleses son invariables.*
◆ *smf* coward

cobardía *sf* cowardice

cobertizo *sm* ❶ [*tejado adosado*] lean-to ❷ [*barracón*] shed

cobertura *sf* ❶ [*generalmente*] cover ❷ [*de un edificio*] covering ❸ Prensa ▶ **cobertura informativa** news coverage ❹ Telecomunicaciones • **no tengo cobertura** I can't get a signal

cobija *sf* [*manta*] blanket

cobijar *vt* ❶ [*albergar*] to house ❷ [*proteger*] to shelter

cobra *sf* cobra

cobrador, ra *sm, f* ❶ [*del autobús*] conductor ❷ [*de deudas, recibos*] collector

cobrar ◆ *vt* ❶ Comercio [*dinero*] to charge ; [*cheque*] to cash ; [*deuda*] to collect • **me cobraron 100 pesos por el almuerzo** they charged me 100 pesos for lunch • **viene todos los meses a cobrar el alquiler** he comes every month to collect the rent • **¿me cobra, por favor?** how much do I owe you? ❷ [*en el trabajo*] to earn • **cobra 10.000 pesos de sueldo mensual** she earns 10,000 pesos as a monthly salary ❸ [*adquirir - importancia*] to acquire • **cobrar fama** to become famous ❹ [*sentir - cariño, afecto*] to start to feel
◆ *vi* [*en el trabajo*] to get paid

cobre *sm* copper
expresión **no tener un cobre** to be flat broke

cobro *sm* ❶ [*de talón*] cashing ❷ [*de pago*] collection • **llamar a cobro revertido** to call collect • **llamada a cobro revertido** collect call

coca *sf* ❶ [*planta*] coca ❷ *familiar* [*cocaína*] coke

cocaína *sf* cocaine

cocción *sf* ❶ [*generalmente*] cooking ❷ [*en agua*] boiling ❸ [*en horno*] baking

cóccix, coxis *sm invariable* coccyx

cocer *vt* ❶ [*generalmente*] to cook • **cuece el pescado cuarenta minutos en la cacerola** you cook the fish forty minutes in the pan ❷ [*hervir*] to boil • **cuece las zanahorias quince minutos** you boil the carrots fifteen minutes ❸ [*en horno*] to bake ❹ [*cerámica, ladrillos*] to fire

coche *sm* ❶ [*automóvil*] car ; automobile • **ir en coche a)** [*montado*] to go by car **b)** [*conduciendo*] to drive • **coche de alquiler** rental car ▶ **coche blindado** armored car ▶ **coche bomba** car bomb ▶ **coche**

de bomberos fire engine ▶ **coche de carreras** race car ❷ [*de tren*] car ▶ **coche cama** sleeping car ▶ **coche restaurante** dining car ❸ [*de caballos*] carriage

cochera *sf* ❶ [*para coches*] garage ❷ [*de autobuses, tranvías*] depot

cochinilla *sf* ❶ [*crustáceo*] woodlouse ❷ [*insecto*] cochineal

cochinillo *sm* sucking pig

cochino, na ◆ *adj* ❶ [*persona*] filthy • **estás cochino, ¡ve a lavarte!** you're filthy, go wash up! ❷ [*tiempo, dinero*] lousy ⦂Ḟ *Los adjetivos ingleses son invariables.*
◆ *sm, f* [*animal - macho*] pig; [*- hembra*] sow

cocido *sm* stew

cociente *sm* quotient ▶ **cociente intelectual** intelligence quotient; I.Q.

cocina *sf* ❶ [*habitación*] kitchen • **esta casa tiene una cocina muy amplia** this house has a very spacious kitchen ❷ [*electrodoméstico*] cooker • **ayer compramos una cocina nueva** yesterday we bought a new cooker ▶ **cocina eléctrica/de gas** electric/gas cooker ❸ [*arte*] cooking • **alta cocina** haute cuisine • **cocina casera** home cooking • **cocina mexicana** Mexican cuisine • **libro/clase de cocina** cookery book/class

cocinar *vt* & *vi* to cook

cocinero, ra *sm, f* cook

expresión **haber sido cocinero antes que fraile** to know what you are talking about

coco *sm* ❶ [*árbol*] coconut palm ❷ [*fruto*] coconut

cocodrilo *sm* crocodile

cocotero *sm* coconut palm

cóctel *sm* ❶ [*bebida, comida*] cocktail ▶ **cóctel de gambas** prawn cocktail ▶ **cóctel molotov** Molotov cocktail ❷ [*reunión*] cocktail party

codazo *sm* nudge • **abrirse paso a codazos** to elbow your way through • **dar un codazo a alguien a)** [*con disimulo*] to give somebody a nudge **b)** [*con fuerza*] to elbow somebody

codera *sf* elbow patch

codicia *sf* greed

codiciar *vt* to covet

codicioso, sa *adj* greedy ⦂Ḟ *Los adjetivos ingleses son invariables.*

codificar *vt* ❶ [*ley*] to codify ❷ [*un mensaje*] to encode ❸ INFORMÁTICA to code

código *sm* INFORMÁTICA code ▶ **código civil/penal** civil/penal code ▶ **código de barras/de señales** bar/signal code ▶ **código de circulación** highway code ▶ **código máquina** machine code ▶ **código postal** zip code

codo *sm* elbow • **se lastimó el codo** he hurt his elbow • **estaba con los codos sobre la mesa** she was leaning (with her elbows) on the table • **dar con el codo** to nudge

codorniz *sf* quail

coeficiente *sm* ❶ [*generalmente*] coefficient ▶ **coeficiente intelectual** o **de inteligencia** intelligence quotient, I.Q. ❷ [*índice*] rate

coexistir *vi* to coexist

cofre *sm* ❶ [*arca*] chest ❷ [*para joyas*] jewelry box

coger *vt* ❶ [*asir, agarrar*] to take • **coger a alguien de** o **por la mano** to take somebody by the hand ❷ [*atrapar - ladrón, pez, pájaro*] to catch ❸ [*recoger - frutos, flores*] to pick ❹ [*sentir - manía, odio, afecto*] to start to feel

cogote *sm* nape

coherencia *sf* [*de razonamiento*] coherence

coherente *adj* coherent ⦂Ḟ *Los adjetivos ingleses son invariables.*

cohesión *sf* cohesion

cohete *sm* rocket

cohibido, da *adj* inhibited ⦂Ḟ *Los adjetivos ingleses son invariables.*

COI (*abreviatura de* Comité Olímpico Internacional) *sm* IOC

coincidencia *sf* coincidence • **¡qué coincidencia!** what a coincidence!

coincidir *vi* ❶ [*superficies, versiones, gustos*] to coincide • **su cumpleaños coincide con Navidad** his birthday coincides with Christmas ❷ [*personas - encontrarse*] to meet; [*- estar de acuerdo*] to agree • **coincidimos en una fiesta** we saw each other at a party • **en eso coincido contigo** I agree with you on that

cojear *vi* ❶ [*persona*] to limp • **la vieja cojea mucho** the old woman limps a lot ❷ [*mueble*] to wobble • **esa mesa cojea** that table wobbles

cojera *sf* ❶ [*acción*] limp ❷ [*estado*] lameness

cojín *sm* cushion

cojinete *sm* ❶ [*en eje*] bearing ❷ [*en un riel de ferrocarril*] chair

cojo, ja ◆ *adj* ❶ [*persona*] lame ❷ [*mueble*] wobbly ⦂Ḟ *Los adjetivos ingleses son invariables.*
◆ *sm, f* cripple
◆ *v* → **coger**

col *sf* cabbage ▶ **col de Bruselas** Brussels sprout

expresión **entre col y col, lechuga** variety is the spice of life

cola *sf* ❶ [*de animal, avión*] tail ❷ [*fila*] line • **¡a la cola!** get in line! • **hacer cola** to stand in line • **ponerse en la cola** to join the end of the line ❸ [*de clase, lista*] bottom ❹ [*de desfile*] end ❺ [*pegamento*] glue ❻ [*peinado*] ▶ **cola (de caballo)** pony tail ❼ *familiar* [*nalgas*] butt

colaboración *sf* ❶ [*generalmente*] collaboration ❷ [*de prensa*] contribution

colaborador, ra *sm, f* ❶ [*generalmente*] collaborator ❷ [*de prensa*] contributor

colaborar *vi* ❶ [*ayudar*] to collaborate • **se negó a colaborar con la policía** he refused to collaborate with the police • **varios laboratorios colaboran en la investigación sobre la enfermedad de Alzheimer** several laboratories are collaborating on the research into Alzheimer's • **colabora con la limpieza, no tires**

C

papeles al piso help with the cleaning, don't throw paper on the floor ❷ [*en prensa*] • **colaborar en** o **con** to write for ❸ [*contribuir*] to contribute

colación *sf*
expresión sacar o **traer algo a colación** [*tema*] to bring something up

colador *sm* ❶ [*para líquidos*] strainer ❷ [*para verdura*] colander

colapsar ♦ *vt* to bring to a halt
♦ *vi* to come o grind to a halt

colapso *sm* ❶ MEDICINA collapse • **sufrir un colapso** to collapse ▶ **colapso nervioso** nervous breakdown ❷ [*de actividad*] stoppage ❸ [*de tráfico*] traffic jam

colar ♦ *vt* ❶ [*verdura, té*] to strain ❷ [*café*] to filter
♦ *vi familiar* [*pasar por bueno*] • **esto no colará** this won't wash
■ **colarse** *v pronominal* ❶ [*líquido*] • **colarse por** to seep through ❷ [*persona*] to slip ❸ [*en una cola*] • **presta atención, siempre hay alguien que se cuela en la fila** pay attention, there is always somebody who slips into the line • **colarse en una fiesta** to gatecrash a party

colateral *adj* [*lateral*] on either side ☼ *Los adjetivos ingleses son invariables.*

colcha *sf* bedspread

colchón *sm* mattress ▶ **colchón inflable** air bed

colchoneta *sf* ❶ [*para playa*] beach mat ❷ [*en gimnasio*] mat

cole *sm familiar* school

colear *vi* [*animal*] to wag its tail

colección *sf literal & figurado* collection • **tiene una colección de estampillas de todo el mundo** he has a collection of stamps from all over the world

coleccionable ♦ *adj* collectable ☼ *Los adjetivos ingleses son invariables.*
♦ *sm* special issue

coleccionar *vt* to collect

coleccionista *smf* collector

colecta *sf* collection

colectividad *sf* community

colega *smf* ❶ [*compañero profesional*] colleague ❷ [*homólogo*] counterpart ❸ *familiar* [*amigo*] mate

colegial, la *sm, f* schoolboy, *femenino* schoolgirl

colegio *sm* ❶ [*escuela*] school ▶ **colegio de curas** school run by priests ▶ **colegio de monjas** convent school ❷ [*de profesionales*] ▶ **colegio (profesional)** professional association
■ **colegio electoral** *sm* ❶ [*lugar*] polling station ❷ [*votantes*] ward

cólera ♦ *sm* MEDICINA cholera
♦ *sf* [*ira*] anger • **montar en cólera** to get angry

colérico, ca *adj* [*carácter*] bad-tempered ☼ *Los adjetivos ingleses son invariables.*

colesterol *sm* cholesterol

coleta *sf* pigtail

coletilla *sf* postscript

colgado, da *adj* ❶ [*cuadro, jamón* ETC] • **colgado (de)** hanging (from) ❷ [*teléfono*] on the hook ☼ *Los adjetivos ingleses son invariables.*

colgador *sm* hanger

colgante ♦ *adj* hanging ☼ *Los adjetivos ingleses son invariables.*
♦ *sm* pendant

colgar ♦ *vt* ❶ [*suspender, ahorcar*] to hang • **cuelga tu chaqueta en esa percha** hang your jacket on that rack • **colgar el teléfono** to hang up ❷ [*imputar*] • **colgar algo a alguien** to blame something on somebody
♦ *vi* ❶ [*pender*] • **colgar (de)** to hang (from) • **¡no te cuelgues de esa rama, que se puede romper!** don't hang off that branch, it might break! ❷ [*hablando por teléfono*] to hang up • **colgó sin despedirse** he hung up without saying goodbye

colibrí *sm* hummingbird

cólico *sm* stomachache

coliflor *sf* cauliflower

colilla *sf* (cigarette) butt

colina *sf* hill

colisión *sf* ❶ [*de automóviles*] crash ❷ [*de ideas, intereses*] clash

colisionar *vi* [*coche*] • **colisionar (contra)** to crash (into)

collar *sm* ❶ [*de personas*] necklace ❷ [*para animales*] collar

collarín *sm* surgical collar

colmar *vt* ❶ [*recipiente*] to fill (to the brim) ❷ *figurado* [*aspiración, deseo*] to fulfill • **colmar a alguien de regalos** to shower gifts on somebody

colmena *sf* beehive

colmillo *sm* ❶ [*de persona*] eye-tooth ❷ [*de perro*] fang ❸ [*de elefante*] tusk

colmo *sm* height • **¡eso es el colmo!** that's the last straw! • **para colmo de desgracias** to crown it all • **es el colmo de la locura** it's sheer madness

colocación *sf* ❶ [*acción*] placing ❷ [*situación*] place ❸ [*empleo*] position

colocado, da *adj* ❶ [*generalmente*] placed • **estar muy bien colocado** to have a very good job ❷ *familiar* [*borracho*] legless ☼ *Los adjetivos ingleses son invariables.*

colocar *vt* ❶ [*en su sitio*] to place ❷ [*en un empleo*] to find a job for ❸ [*invertir*] to place
■ **colocarse** *v pronominal* [*en un trabajo*] to get a job

colofón *sm* [*remate, fin*] climax

Colombia *nombre propio* Colombia

colombiano, na *adj* & *sm, f* Colombian ☼ *Los adjetivos ingleses son invariables.*
En inglés, los adjetivos que se refieren a un país o una región se escriben con mayúscula.

colon *sm* colon

colonia *sf* ❶ [*generalmente*] colony • **España tenía colonias en América y África** Spain had colonies in

America and Africa ❷ [*perfume*] eau de cologne ❸ [*barrio*] neighborhood • **viven en la colonia Obregón** they live in the Obregón neighborhood ▶ **colonia proletaria** shanty town

colonial *adj* colonial ☿:*Los adjetivos ingleses son invariables.*

colonización *sf* colonization

colonizador, ra *sm, f* colonist

colonizar *vt* to colonize

colono *sm* settler

coloquial *adj* colloquial ☿:*Los adjetivos ingleses son invariables.*

coloquio *sm* ❶ [*conversación*] conversation ❷ [*debate*] discussion

color *sm* [*generalmente*] color • **¿de qué color?** what color? • **una falda de color rosa** a pink skirt • **a todo color** in full color • **color rojo** red • **color azul** blue • **de color** [*persona*] colored

los colores

amarillo	yellow
azul	blue
azul claro	light blue
blanco	white
café	brown
granate	burgundy
gris	gray
malva	mauve
naranja	orange
negro	black
rojo	red
rosa	pink
rosa vivo	bright pink
verde	green
verde claro	light green
verde oscuro	dark green
violeta	violet

colorado, da *adj* red • **ponerse colorado** to go red ☿:*Los adjetivos ingleses son invariables.*

colorante *sm* coloring

colorear *vt* to color (in) • **ahora que dibujaste el paisaje, coloréalo** now that you've drawn the landscape, color it

colorete *sm* rouge

colorido *sm* colors *pl*

colosal *adj* ❶ [*estatura, tamaño*] colossal ❷ [*extraordinario*] enormous ☿:*Los adjetivos ingleses son invariables.*

coloso *sm* ❶ [*estatua*] colossus ❷ *figurado* [*cosa, persona*] giant

columna *sf* ❶ [*generalmente*] column • **la fachada está adornada con columnas** the façade is adorned with columns ❷ *figurado* [*pilar*] pillar ❸ ANATOMÍA spine • **el ortopedista trata los problemas de la columna** the orthopedist treats problems of the spine ▶ **columna vertebral** spinal column

columnista *smf* columnist

columpiar *vt* to swing

columpio *sm* swing

coma ◆ *sm* MEDICINA coma • **estar en coma** to be in a coma

◆ *sf* GRAMÁTICA comma • **en esa oración no hay que poner coma allí** that sentence doesn't require a comma there

comadre *sf* ❶ godmother ❷ [*relación*] mother of the child ❸ [*partera*] midwife ❹ [*amiga*] friend

comadreja *sf* weasel

comadrona *sf* midwife

comandante *sm* ❶ MILITAR [*rango*] major; [*de un puesto*] commander ❷ [*de avión*] captain

comandar *vt* MILITAR to command

comando *sm* MILITAR commando

comarca *sf* region

comba *sf* ❶ [*juego*] skipping ❷ [*cuerda*] skipping rope

combar *vt* to bend

combate *sm* ❶ [*generalmente*] fight • **hay que empeñarse en el combate a las drogas** we have to get involved in the fight against drugs ❷ [*batalla*] battle • **el combate fue largo y dejó varios heridos** the battle was long and left a number of wounded people

expresión dejar a alguien fuera de combate a) [*en boxeo*] to knock somebody out b) *figurado* to put somebody out of the running

combatiente *smf* combatant

combatir ◆ *vt* to combat • **es importante combatir la desnutrición** it's important to combat malnutrition

◆ *vi* • **combatir (contra)** to fight (against) • **estos soldados combatieron en la última guerra** these soldiers fought in the last war

combativo, va *adj* combative ☿:*Los adjetivos ingleses son invariables.*

combinación *sf* ❶ [*generalmente*] combination ❷ [*de bebidas*] cocktail ❸ [*prenda*] slip ❹ [*de medios de transporte*] connections *pl*

combinar *vt* ❶ [*generalmente*] to combine ❷ [*bebidas*] to mix ❸ [*colores*] to match

combustible ◆ *adj* combustible ☿:*Los adjetivos ingleses son invariables.*

◆ *sm* fuel • **este carro precisa combustible urgentemente** this car needs fuel urgently

combustión *sf* combustion

comecocos *sm invariable* familiar • **este panfleto es un comecocos** this pamphlet is designed to brainwash you

comedia *sf* ❶ [*obra, película, género*] comedy, *plural* comedies ❷ *figurado* [*engaño*] farce • **hacer la comedia** to pretend

comediante, ta *sm, f* ❶ actor, *femenino* actress ❷ *figurado* [*farsante*] fraud

comedor *sm* ❶ [*de casa*] dining room ❷ [*de fábrica*] canteen

C

comensal *smf* fellow diner

comentar *vt* ❶ [*opinar sobre*] to comment on • **comentó que hacía mucho frío afuera** he commented that it was very cold outside ❷ [*hablar de*] to discuss • **en clase comentamos los textos que leemos en casa** in class we discuss the texts that we read at home

comentario *sm* ❶ [*observación*] comment ❷ [*crítica*] commentary

comentarista *smf* commentator

comenzar ◆ *vt* to start; to begin • **comenzar a hacer algo** to start doing something • **comenzar diciendo que...** to begin by saying that... • **de repente comenzó a llover** it suddenly started raining

◆ *vi* to start; to begin • **las clases comienzan a las ocho** classes begin at eight o'clock

comer ◆ *vi* ❶ [*generalmente*] to eat • **¿comiste suficiente?** did you eat enough? ❷ [*al mediodía*] to have lunch • **comemos normalmente a las dos** we usually eat lunch at two

◆ *vt* ❶ [*generalmente*] to eat ❷ [*al mediodía*] to have for lunch • **comimos pollo** we had chicken for lunch ❸ [*en juegos de tablero*] to take ❹ *figurado* [*consumir*] to eat up

comercial ◆ *adj* commercial ☞ *Los adjetivos ingleses son invariables.*

◆ *sm* [*anuncio*] commercial

comercializar *vt* to market

comerciante *smf* ❶ tradesman, *femenino* tradeswoman ❷ [*tendero*] storekeeper

comerciar *vi* to trade in • **comercia con piedras preciosas** he trades in precious stones

comercio *sm* ❶ [*de productos*] trade ▶ **comercio electrónico** e-business ▶ **comercio exterior/interior** foreign/domestic trade ▶ **comercio justo** fair trade ▶ **libre comercio** free trade ❷ [*actividad*] business ❸ [*tienda*] shop

comestible *adj* edible ☞ *Los adjetivos ingleses son invariables.*

cometa ◆ *sm* ASTRONOMÍA comet

◆ *sf* kite

cometer *vt* ❶ [*crimen*] to commit • **cometió muchos crímenes antes de morir** he commited many crimes before he died ❷ [*error*] to make • **cometí un error muy grave** I made a very serious error

comezón *sf* [*picor*] itching ☞ *incontable* • **los piquetes de mosquitos dan comezón** mosquito bites cause itching

cómic (pl comics) *sm* (adult) comic

comicios *smpl* elections

cómico, ca ◆ *adj* ❶ [*de la comedia*] comedy ☞ *Sólo se usa delante del sustantivo.* ❷ [*gracioso*] comic

◆ *sm, f* ❶ [*actor de teatro*] actor, *femenino* actress ❷ [*humorista*] comedian, *femenino* comedienne

comida *sf* ❶ [*alimento*] food ☞ *incontable* ▶ **comida basura** junk food ▶ **comida chatarra** junk food ▶ **comida rápida** fast food ❷ [*almuerzo, cena* ETC] meal • **tomar un comprimido antes de cada comida** take one pill before each meal • **me gusta preparar la co-** mida con productos frescos I like to prepare meals with fresh produce ❸ [*al mediodía*] lunch ▶ **comida de negocios** business lunch

la comida

el agua con gas	the sparkling water
el agua sin gas	the still water
el agua de la llave	the tap water
el agua mineral	the mineral water
el café	the coffee
la carne	the meat
la cerveza	the beer
la charola	the tray
los cubiertos	the cutlery
los embutidos	the cold cuts
la entrada	the appetizer
la fruta	the fruit
la infusión	the herbal tea
la jarra de agua	the water pitcher
el jugo de manzana	the apple juice
el jugo de naranja	the orange juice
el pan	the bread
el pastel	the cake
el pastel de cumpleaños	the birthday cake
el plato	a) [*pieza*] the plate b) [*comida*] the dish
el postre	the dessert
el primer plato	the appetizer
el queso	the cheese
el segundo plato	the main course
la tabla de quesos	the cheese board
la tarta	the tart
el té	the tea
el vaso	the glass
las verduras	the vegetables
las verduras crudas	the crudités
el vino	the wine
el yogurt	the yogurt

comienzo *sm* start • **a comienzos de los años 50** in the early 1950s • **dar comienzo** to start

comillas *sfpl* quotation marks • **entre comillas** in quotation marks

comilona *sf* familiar [*festín*] blow-out

comino *sm* [*planta*] cumin

expresión **me importa un comino** *familiar* I don't give a damn

comisaría *sf* precinct

comisario, ria *sm, f* ❶ ▶ **comisario (de policía)** police superintendent ❷ [*delegado*] commissioner

comisión *sf* ❶ [*de un delito*] perpetration ❷ COMERCIO commission • **(trabajar) a comisión** (to work) on a commission basis ▶ **comisión fija** ECONOMÍA flat fee ❸ [*delegación*] commission ▶ **Comisión Europea** European Commission ▶ **comisión investigadora** committee of inquiry ▶ **comisión permanente** standing commission

comité *sm* committee

comitiva *sf* retinue

como ◆ *adv* ❶ ⚲ *comparativo* • **tan... como...** as... as... • **eres tan inteligente como ella** you're as intelligent as her • **es (tan) negro como el carbón** it's as black as coal • **ser como algo** to be like something • **tu bicicleta es como la mía** your bicycle is like mine • **vive como un rey** he lives like a king • **lo que dijo fue como para ruborizarse** his words were enough to make you blush ❷ [*de la manera que*] as • **lo he hecho como es debido** I did it as o the way it should be done • **me encanta como bailas** I love the way you dance ❸ [*según*] as • **como te decía ayer...** as I was telling you yesterday... ❹ [*en calidad de*] as • **trabaja como bombero** he works as a fireman • **dieron el dinero como anticipo** they gave the money as an advance ❺ [*aproximadamente*] about • **me quedan como cien pesos** I have about a hundred pesos left • **tiene un sabor como a naranja** it tastes a bit like an orange • **llegaron como a las diez** they arrived around ten o'clock

◆ *conjunción* ❶ [*ya que*] as; since • **como no llegabas, nos fuimos** as o since you didn't arrive, we left ❷ [*si*] if • **como no me hagas caso, lo pasarás mal** if you don't listen to me, there will be trouble

cómo *adv* ❶ [*de qué modo, por qué motivo*] how • **¿cómo lo has hecho?** how did you do it? • **¿cómo son?** what are they like? • **no sé cómo has podido decir eso** I don't know how you could say that • **¿cómo que no la has visto nunca?** what do you mean you've never seen her? • **¿a cómo están los tomates?** how much are the tomatoes? • **¿cómo es eso?** *familiar* [*¿por qué?*] how come? ❷ [*exclamativo*] how • **¡cómo pasan los años!** how time flies!

expresión **¡cómo no!** of course! • **está lloviendo, ¡y cómo!** it sure is raining!

cómoda *sf* chest of drawers

comodidad *sf* convenience ⚲ *incontable* • **para su comodidad** for your convenience

comodín *sm* ❶ comfort lover ❷ [*naipe*] joker ❸ INFORMÁTICA wild card

cómodo, da *adj* ❶ [*confortable*] comfortable • **ponte cómodo** make yourself comfortable • **sentirse cómodo con alguien** to feel comfortable with somebody ❷ [*útil*] convenient ❸ [*oportuno, fácil*] easy ⚲ *Los adjetivos ingleses son invariables.*

comoquiera *adv* • **comoquiera que a)** [*de cualquier manera que*] whichever way, however **b)** [*dado que*] since; seeing as

compactar *vt* to compress

compacto, ta *adj* compact ⚲ *Los adjetivos ingleses son invariables.*

compadecer *vt* to pity

compadre *sm* *familiar* [*amigo*] friend; buddy

compaginar *vt* [*combinar*] to reconcile

compañerismo *sm* comradeship

compañero, ra *sm, f* ❶ [*acompañante*] companion ❷ [*pareja*] partner • **compañero sentimental** partner ❸ [*colega*] colleague • **compañero de clase** classmate • **compañero de piso** flatmate

compañía *sf* company • **trabaja en una compañía francesa** she works for a French company • **le perdieron las malas compañías** he was led astray by the bad company he kept • **en compañía de** accompanied by, in the company of • **hacer compañía a alguien** to keep somebody company • **mis amigos me hicieron compañía toda la tarde** my friends kept me company all afternoon • **compañía de seguros** insurance company • **compañía de teatro** theater company

comparación *sf* comparison • **en comparación con** in comparison with, compared to

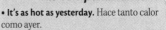

las comparaciones

• **It's as hot as yesterday.** Hace tanto calor como ayer.

• **It's not as hot as in May.** Hace menos calor que en mayo.

• **We're the same age.** Tenemos la misma edad.

• **The red bike is half the price of the blue one.** La bicicleta roja cuesta la mitad de la azul.

• **Compared with you, your sister's short.** Comparada contigo, tu hermana es chaparra.

• **She sings better than me.** Ella canta mejor que yo.

comparar *vt* • **comparar algo (con)** to compare something (to) • **no le gusta que la comparen con la hermana** she doesn't like to be compared with her sister

comparativo, va *adj* comparative ⚲ *Los adjetivos ingleses son invariables.*

comparecer *vi* to appear

comparsa ◆ *sf* TEATRO extras *pl*
◆ *smf* ❶ TEATRO extra ❷ *figurado* [*en carreras, competiciones*] also-ran ❸ [*en organizaciones, empresas*] nobody

compartimento, compartimiento *sm* compartment • **compartimento de fumadores** smoking compartment

compartir *vt* ❶ [*ganancias*] to share (out) • **compartió con sus amigos los dulces que le regalaron** he shared the candy they gave him with his friends ❷ [*piso, ideas*] to share

compás *sm* ❶ [*instrumento*] pair of compasses ❷ MÚSICA [*periodo*] bar; [*ritmo*] rhythm; beat • **al compás (de la música)** in time (with the music) • **llevar el compás** to keep time • **perder el compás** to lose the beat

compasión *sf* pity • **¡por compasión!** for pity's sake! • **tener compasión de** to feel sorry for

expresar compasión

• **That's really bad luck!** ¡Eso sí que es tener mala suerte!

• **I'm really sorry.** Lo siento muchísimo.

• **You poor thing!** ¡Pobre!

• **Please accept my deepest sympathy.** Mi más sentido pésame.

C

compatibilizar *vt* to make compatible

compatible *adj* INFORMÁTICA compatible ⚲ *Los adjetivos ingleses son invariables.*

compatriota *smf* fellow countryman, *femenino* fellow countrywoman

compendio *sm* ❶ [*libro*] compendium ❷ *figurado* [*síntesis*] epitome

compenetración *sf* mutual understanding

compenetrarse *v pronominal* to understand each other

compensación *sf* [*generalmente*] compensation • **en compensación (por)** in return (for) • **compensación económica** financial compensation

compensar *vt* ❶ [*valer la pena*] to make up for • **no me compensa (perder tanto tiempo)** it's not worth my while (wasting all that time) ❷ [*indemnizar*] • **compensar a alguien (de o por)** to compensate somebody (for)

competencia *sf* ❶ [*entre personas, empresas*] competition • **hacer la competencia a** to compete with ▶ **competencia desleal** ECONOMÍA unfair competition ❷ [*incumbencia*] field ❸ [*aptitud, atribuciones*] competence ❹ [*en deportes*] competition • **la competencia de natación empieza mañana** the swimming competition begins tomorrow

competente *adj* competent • **competente en materia de** responsible for ⚲ *Los adjetivos ingleses son invariables.*

competición *sf* competition

competidor, ra *sm, f* competitor

competir *vi* • **competir (con/por)** to compete (with/for) • **compite mañana por la medalla de oro** she competes tomorrow for the gold medal • **esos dos supermercados compiten entre sí** those two supermarkets compete against each other

competitividad *sf* competitiveness

competitivo, va *adj* competitive ⚲ *Los adjetivos ingleses son invariables.*

compilar *vt* to compile

compinche *smf familiar* crony

complacer *vt* to please • **es difícil complacer a todo el mundo** it's difficult to please everybody • **me complace presentarles a este cantante** it is my pleasure to introduce this singer to you

complaciente *adj* ❶ [*amable*] obliging ❷ [*indulgente*] indulgent ⚲ *Los adjetivos ingleses son invariables.*

complejo, ja *adj* complex ⚲ *Los adjetivos ingleses son invariables.*

■ **complejo** *sm* complex • **por aquí se va al complejo deportivo de la universidad** this is the way to the university's sports complex • **tiene complejo porque es muy alto** he has a complex because he's very tall ▶ **complejo de Edipo** Oedipus complex • **complejo hotelero** hotel complex ▶ **complejo industrial** industrial park ▶ **complejo de inferioridad/de superioridad** inferiority/superiority complex ▶ **complejo turístico** tourist development ▶ **complejo vitamínico** vitamin complex

complementar *vt* to complement

complementario, ria *adj* complementary ⚲ *Los adjetivos ingleses son invariables.*

complemento *sm* ❶ [*añadido*] complement ❷ GRAMÁTICA object ▶ **complemento directo/indirecto** direct/indirect object

completamente *adv* completely

completar *vt* ❶ [*generalmente*] to complete ❷ [*formulario*] to fill in • **complete este formulario, por favor** fill in this form, please

completo, ta *adj* ❶ [*entero, perfecto*] complete • **acabo de comprar las obras completas de Rulfo** I just bought the complete works of Rulfo • **por completo** completely • **un deportista muy completo** an all-round sportsman ❷ [*lleno*] full • **el avión venía completo** the airplane was full ⚲ *Los adjetivos ingleses son invariables.*

complexión *sf* build • **de complexión atlética** with an athletic build • **de complexión fuerte** well-built

complicación *sf* ❶ [*generalmente*] complication ❷ [*complejidad*] complexity

complicado, da *adj* ❶ [*difícil*] complicated ❷ [*implicado*] • **complicado (en)** involved (in) ⚲ *Los adjetivos ingleses son invariables.*

complicar *vt* to complicate

cómplice *smf* accomplice

complicidad *sf* complicity

complot, compló *sm* plot

componente ◆ *sm* component
◆ *smf* [*persona*] member

componer *vt* ❶ [*constituir, ser parte de*] to make up • **estos diez jugadores componen el equipo** these ten players make up the team ❷ [*música, versos*] to compose • **Beethoven compuso nueve sinfonías** Beethoven composed nine symphonies ❸ [*arreglar*] to repair • **este televisor no funciona, hay que componerlo** this television doesn't work, we have to repair it

comportamiento *sm* behavior

comportar *vt* to involve

composición *sf* composition

compositor, ra *sm, f* composer

compostura *sf* ❶ [*reparación*] repair ❷ [*de persona, rostro*] composure ❸ [*en comportamiento*] restraint

compota *sf* COCINA stewed fruit ⚲ *incontable*

compra *sf* purchase • **la última compra que hice ayer fue este libro** the last purchase that I made yesterday was this book • **ir de compras** to go shopping • **ir a o hacer la compra** to do the shopping ▶ **compra al contado** cash purchase ▶ **compra a plazos** hire purchase

comprador, ra *sm, f* ❶ [*generalmente*] buyer ❷ [*en una tienda*] shopper

comprar *vt* ❶ [*adquirir*] to buy • **antes de comprar conviene comparar precios** before buying, it's good to compare prices • **comprar algo a alguien** to buy something from somebody ❷ [*sobornar*] to buy (off)

comprender *vt* ❶ [*incluir*] to include • **el curso comprende los más recientes descubrimientos de la astronomía** the course includes astronomy's most recent discoveries ❷ [*entender*] to understand • **no comprendí la lección** I didn't understand the lesson • **hacerse comprender** to make yourself understood

comprensión *sf* understanding

comprensivo, va *adj* understanding • **María es una persona muy comprensiva** María is a very understanding person ♀: *Los adjetivos ingleses son invariables.*

comprimir *vt* to compress

comprobante *sm* ❶ [*documento*] supporting document ❷ [*recibo*] receipt

comprobar *vt* ❶ [*averiguar*] to check • **comprueba que la puerta esté bien cerrada** check that the door is closed properly ❷ [*demostrar*] to prove

comprometer *vt* ❶ [*poner en peligro - éxito* ETC] to jeopardize; [*- persona*] to compromise ❷ [*avergonzar*] to embarrass

■ **comprometerse** *v pronominal* ❶ [*hacerse responsable*] • **comprometerse (a hacer algo)** to commit yourself (to doing something) • **no quiso comprometerse, porque no sabía cuándo podría entregar el trabajo** he refused to commit himself, because he didn't know when he would be able to turn in the paper • **se comprometió a entregar el trabajo mañana** he promised to turn in the paper tomorrow ❷ [*ideológicamente, moralmente*] • **comprometerse (en algo)** to become involved (in something)

comprometido, da *adj* ❶ [*con una idea*] committed ❷ [*difícil*] compromising ♀: *Los adjetivos ingleses son invariables.*

compromiso *sm* ❶ [*obligación*] commitment • **es una persona confiable, que respeta sus compromisos** she's a trustworthy person who honors her commitments ❷ [*acuerdo*] agreement ❸ [*cita*] engagement • **no podré verte mañana porque tengo varios compromisos** I can't see you tomorrow because I have several engagements • **sin compromiso** without obligation ❹ [*de matrimonio*] engagement • **compromiso matrimonial** engagement ❺ [*dificultad, aprieto*] compromising o difficult situation • **me pones en un compromiso** you're putting me in an awkward position

compuerta *sf* sluice

compuesto, ta ◆ *participio pasado* → **componer**
◆ *adj* ❶ GRAMÁTICA compound • **"mediodía" es una palabra compuesta** "mediodía" is a compound word ❷ [*formado*] • **compuesto de** composed of ♀: *Los adjetivos ingleses son invariables.*
■ **compuesto** *sm* GRAMÁTICA & QUÍMICA compound

computadora *sf* computer ▶ **computadora de mesa** desktop computer ▶ **computadora personal** personal computer ▶ **computadora portátil** laptop

la computadora

la alfombrilla del ratón	the mouse pad
el buscador	the search engine
la computadora	the computer
la computadora portátil	the laptop
la conexión ADSL	the ADSL connection
la conexión a Internet	the Internet connection
el correo electrónico	the email
la dirección de Internet	the Internet address
el escáner	the scanner
la impresora	the printer
el módem	the modem
la pantalla	the screen
la pantalla plana	the flat screen
el proveedor de acceso al Internet	the Internet Service Provider
el ratón	the mouse
la red	the network
el sitio de Internet	the Internet site
el teclado	the keyboard
la unidad central	the central processing unit

cómputo *sm* calculation

comulgar *vi* RELIGIÓN to take communion

común *adj* ❶ [*generalmente*] common • **los alumnos cuentan con una sala de lectura común** there is a common reading room for students • **es común que haga calor en esta época** it's normal for it to be hot at this time of year • **en común** in common • **tenemos varios intereses en común** we have several things in common • **por lo común** generally • **poco común** unusual ❷ [*compartido - amigo, interés*] mutual; [*- bienes, pastos*] communal ❸ [*ordinario - vino* ETC] ordinary ; average • **común y corriente** perfectly ordinary ♀: *Los adjetivos ingleses son invariables.*

comunicación *sf* ❶ [*generalmente*] communication • **se cortó la comunicación** we were cut off • **ponerse en comunicación con alguien** to get in touch with somebody ❷ [*escrito oficial*] communiqué ❸ [*informe*] report

comunicar ◆ *vt* ❶ [*transmitir - sentimientos, ideas*] to convey; [*- movimiento, virus*] to transmit ❷ [*información*] • **comunicar algo a alguien** to inform somebody of something • **nos comunicó su proyecto de casarse** he informed us of his plan to get married
◆ *vi* ❶ [*hablar - generalmente*] to communicate; [*- al teléfono*] to get through ❷ [*escribir*] to get in touch ❸ [*dos lugares*] • **comunicar con algo** to connect with something

■ **comunicarse** *v pronominal* ❶ [*hablarse*] to communicate (with each other) • **las líneas están cortadas, por eso no hemos podido comunicarnos** the lines are down so we haven't been able to communicate with them ❷ [*dos lugares*] to be connected • **la habitación se comunica con el baño** the bedroom is connected to the bathroom

comunidad *sf* community • **la comunidad latina es numerosa en esta región** there is a large Latin community in this area ▶ **Comunidad Económica Europea** HISTORIA European Economic Community

comunión *sf* communion • **hacer la primera comunión** to take your First Communion

comunismo *sm* communism

comunista *adj* & *smf* communist ☼: *Los adjetivos ingleses son invariables.*

comunitario, ria *adj* [*de la comunidad*] community ☼: *Sólo se usa delante del sustantivo.* • **un servicio comunitario** a community service

---

con
◆ *preposición*
❶ [*indica acompañamiento*] with
• **¿quieres venir con nosotros?** do you want to come with us?
• **rellené las empanadas con queso** I filled the turnovers with cheese
❷ [*en lo que se refiere a*] to
• **fueron muy amables con ella** they were very kind to her
❸ [*indica la manera*]
• **la miró con atención** he looked at her carefully
• **hablaba con calma** she spoke calmly
• **lo ha conseguido con su esfuerzo** he's got where he has by his own efforts
❹ [*indica el método, el instrumento*]
• **bebía con un popote** he was drinking through a straw
• **corta la carne con un cuchillo filoso** cut the meat with a sharp knife
❺ [*indica una característica*]
• **la chica con el suéter rojo/con los ojos azules** the girl in the red sweater/with blue eyes
❻ [*indica el contenido*]
• **un portafolios con varios documentos** a briefcase with several documents inside
❼ [*a pesar de*] in spite of
• **con lo estudiosa que es la suspendieron** in spite of being so studious, she failed
❽ [*seguido por el infinitivo, indica una condición*] if
• **con salir a las diez vale** if we can leave by ten, that'll be OK
❾ [*a pesar de*]
• **¡mira que perder con lo bien que jugaste!** I can't understand how you lost when you played so well!

■ **con (tal) que**
◆ *locución conjuntiva*
[*seguido por el subjuntivo, indica una condición*] as long as
• **con que llegue a tiempo me conformo** as long as it arrives in time I'll be happy
• **con tal de verte, voy adonde sea** as long as I can see you I'll go anywhere
• **con tal de que te aplaudan es capaz de hacer cualquier cosa** he'll do anything in order to get the applause

---

conato *sm* attempt • **un conato de robo** an attempted robbery • **un conato de incendio** the beginnings of a fire

cóncavo, va *adj* concave ☼: *Los adjetivos ingleses son invariables.*

concebir ◆ *vt* ❶ [*plan, hijo*] to conceive ❷ [*imaginar*] to imagine
◆ *vi* to conceive

conceder *vt* ❶ [*dar*] to grant • **el hada madrina le concedió tres deseos** her fairy godmother granted her three wishes ❷ [*premio*] to award ❸ [*asentir*] to admit

concejal, la *sm, f* (town) councillor

concentración *sf* ❶ [*generalmente*] concentration • **estudiar requiere mucha concentración** studying requires a lot of concentration ❷ [*de gente*] gathering ▶ **concentración parcelaria** ECONOMÍA land consolidation

concentrado *sm* concentrate

concentrar *vt* ❶ [*generalmente*] to concentrate ❷ [*reunir - gente*] to bring together; [*- tropas*] to assemble
■ **concentrarse** *v pronominal* ❶ [*mentalmente*] to concentrate • **no logro concentrarme porque están haciendo demasiado ruido** I can't concentrate because you're making too much noise • **concéntrate en lo que haces** concentrate on what you are doing ❷ [*reunirse*] to gather • **varias personas se concentraron en la puerta del teatro** several people gathered at the theater doors

concéntrico, ca *adj* concentric ☼: *Los adjetivos ingleses son invariables.*

concepción *sf* conception

concepto *sm* ❶ [*idea*] concept ❷ [*opinión*] opinion • **te tiene en muy buen concepto** she thinks highly of you ❸ [*motivo*] • **bajo ningún concepto** under no circumstances • **en concepto de** by way of; as

concernir *v impersonal* to concern • **la droga es un problema que nos concierne a todos** drugs are a problem that concerns us all • **en lo que concierne a** as regards • **por lo que a mí me concierne** as far as I'm concerned

concertar ◆ *vt* ❶ [*precio*] to agree on ❷ [*cita*] to arrange ❸ [*pacto*] to reach
◆ *vi* [*concordar*] • **concertar (con)** to tally (with); to fit in (with)

concesión *sf* ❶ [*de préstamo* ETC] granting ❷ [*de premio*] awarding ❸ *figurado* COMERCIO concession

concesionario, ria *sm, f* ❶ [*persona con derecho exclusivo de venta*] licensed dealer ❷ [*titular de una concesión*] licensee

concha *sf* ❶ [*de los animales*] shell ❷ [*material*] tortoiseshell

conchabarse *v pronominal* • **conchabarse (contra)** *familiar* to gang up (on)

conciencia, consciencia *sf* ❶ [*conocimiento*] consciousness • **tener/tomar conciencia de** to be/become aware of • **no tiene conciencia del daño que ha hecho**

he's not aware of the damage he's done • **conciencia de clase** class consciousness • **conciencia social** social conscience ❷ [*moral, integridad*] conscience • **la voz de la conciencia** the voice of conscience • **a conciencia** conscientiously • **me remuerde la conciencia** I have a guilty conscience • **tener la conciencia tranquila** to have a clear conscience

concienciar *vt* to make aware

concientizar *vt* • **concientizar a alguien de algo** to make somebody aware of something

concierto *sm* ❶ [*actuación*] concert • **fuimos a un concierto de rock** we went to a rock concert ❷ [*composición*] concerto

conciliar *vt* to reconcile • **conciliar el sueño** to get to sleep

concisión *sf* conciseness

conciso, sa *adj* concise ☝ *Los adjetivos ingleses son invariables.*

concluir ◆ *vt* ❶ [*deducir*] to conclude • **concluyo que no te interesa participar en el proyecto** I can only conclude that you're not interested in participating in the project • **concluir haciendo o por hacer algo** to end up doing something ❷ [*acabar*] to finish • **concluimos el trabajo a tiempo** we finished the work on time
◆ *vi* to (come to an) end

conclusión *sf* conclusion • **llegar a una conclusión** to come to o to reach a conclusion • **en conclusión** in conclusion

concordancia *sf* agreement

concordar ◆ *vt* to reconcile
◆ *vi* ❶ [*estar de acuerdo*] • **concordar (con)** to agree o tally (with) ❷ Gramática • **concordar (con)** to agree (with)

concretar *vt* [*precisar*] to specify

concreto, ta *adj* specific • **quiero un ejemplo concreto** I want a specific example • **en concreto a)** [*en resumen*] in short **b)** [*específicamente*] specifically • **nada en concreto** nothing definite ☝ *Los adjetivos ingleses son invariables.*

■ **concreto armado** *sm* reinforced concrete

concurrencia *sf* ❶ [*asistencia*] attendance ❷ [*espectadores*] crowd ❸ [*de sucesos*] concurrence

concurrido, da *adj* ❶ [*bar, calle*] crowded ❷ [*espectáculo*] well-attended ☝ *Los adjetivos ingleses son invariables.*

concurrir *vi* ❶ [*reunirse*] • **concurrir a algo** to go to something; to attend something ❷ [*participar*] • **concurrir a a)** [*concurso*] to take part in **b)** [*examen*] to take

concursante *smf* ❶ [*en concurso*] contestant ❷ [*en oposiciones*] candidate

concursar *vi* ❶ [*competir*] to compete ❷ [*en oposiciones*] to be a candidate

concurso *sm* ❶ [*prueba - literaria, deportiva*] competition; [*- de televisión*] game show • **fuera de concurso** out of the running ❷ [*para una obra*] tender

• **salir a concurso** to be put out to tender ❸ [*ayuda*] cooperation

conde, esa *sm, f* count, *femenino* countess

condecorar *vt* to decorate

condena *sf* sentence

condenado, da *adj* ❶ [*a una pena*] convicted ❷ [*a un sufrimiento*] condemned ❸ *familiar* [*maldito*] damned ☝ *Los adjetivos ingleses son invariables.*

condenar *vt* ❶ [*declarar culpable*] to convict ❷ [*castigar*] • **condenar a alguien a algo** to sentence somebody to something • **lo condenaron a diez años en prisión** he was sentenced to ten years in prison ❸ [*recriminar*] to condemn

condensar *vt* to condense

condición *sf* ❶ [*generalmente*] condition • **condiciones de un contrato** terms of a contract • **con una sola condición** on one condition • **te lo presto, con la condición de que me lo devuelvas mañana** I'll lend it to you on condition that you give it back to me tomorrow ❷ [*naturaleza*] nature ❸ [*clase social*] social class

■ **condiciones** *sfpl* ❶ [*aptitud*] talent ☝ *incontable* ❷ [*circunstancias*] conditions ▶ **condiciones atmosféricas/de vida** weather/living conditions ❸ [*estado*] condition ☝ *incontable* • **estar en condiciones de** o **para hacer algo a)** [*físicamente*] to be in a fit state to do something **b)** [*por la situación*] to be in a position to do something • **estar en buenas condiciones a)** [*casa, coche*] to be in good condition **b)** [*carne, pescado*] to be fresh • **estar en malas condiciones a)** [*casa, coche*] to be in bad condition **b)** [*carne, pescado*] to be off

condicional *adj* & *sm* conditional ☝ *Los adjetivos ingleses son invariables.*

condicionar *vt* • **condicionar algo a algo** to make something dependent on something

condimento *sm* seasoning ☝ *incontable*

condolencia *sf* condolence

condón *sm* condom

cóndor *sm* condor

conducción *sf* [*de vehículo*] driving

conducir ◆ *vt* ❶ [*vehículo*] to drive ❷ [*dirigir - empresa*] to manage; [*- ejército*] to lead; [*- asunto*] to handle ❸ [*a una persona a un lugar*] to lead
◆ *vi* ❶ [*en vehículo*] to drive ❷ [*a sitio, situación*] • **conducir a** to lead to

conducta *sf* behavior

conducto *sm* ❶ [*de fluido*] pipe ❷ *figurado* [*vía*] channel ❸ Anatomía duct

conductor, ra *sm, f* ❶ [*de vehículo*] driver ❷ Física conductor

conductor ≠ conductor
• La palabra inglesa **conductor** es un falso amigo que significa *cobrador*.
• *Conductor* se traduce al inglés por **driver**.

conectar *vt* to connect • **sólo falta conectar el teléfono** we just have to connect the phone • **conectar algo (a** o **con)** to connect something (to o up to) • **esa carretera conecta mi pueblo con la capital** this road connects my town to the capital

conejillo ■ **conejillo de Indias** *sm* guinea pig

conejo, ja *sm, f* rabbit, *femenino* doe

conexión *sf* ❶ [*generalmente*] connection ❷ RADIO & TELEVISIÓN link-up▶ **conexión a Internet** Internet connection▶ **conexión vía satélite** satellite link

confección *sf* ❶ [*de ropa*] tailoring ❷ [*de comida*] preparation ❸ [*de lista*] drawing up

confeccionar *vt* ❶ [*ropa*] to make (up) ❷ [*lista*] to draw up ❸ [*plato*] to prepare ❹ [*bebida*] to mix

confederación *sf* confederation

conferencia *sf* ❶ [*charla*] lecture • **dar una conferencia** to give a lecture ❷ [*reunión*] conference • **fue a una conferencia médica** he went to a medical conference ❸ [*por teléfono*] (long-distance) call

conferir *vt* ❶ • **conferir algo a alguien a)** [*honor, dignidad*] to confer o bestow something upon somebody **b)** [*responsabilidades*] to give something to somebody ❷ [*cualidad*] to give

confesar *vt* ❶ [*generalmente*] to confess • **el ladrón confesó el crimen** the thief confessed to the crime ❷ [*debilidad*] to admit • **Pablo me confesó que está enamorado de Ana** Pablo admitted he's in love with Ana

confesión *sf* ❶ [*generalmente*] confession ❷ [*credo*] religion

confesionario *sm* confessional

confeti *sm* confetti ☼: *incontable*

confiado, da *adj* ❶ [*seguro*] confident ❷ [*crédulo*] trusting ☼: *Los adjetivos ingleses son invariables.*

confianza *sf* ❶ [*seguridad*] • **confianza (en)** confidence (in) • **confianza en uno mismo** self-confidence ❷ [*fe*] trust • **nunca me ha mentido, le tengo total confianza** he's never lied to me, I trust him completely • **de confianza** trustworthy • **ser digno de confianza** to be trustworthy ❸ [*familiaridad*] familiarity • **nos trata con confianza porque nos conocemos hace mucho** he treats us with familiarity because we've known each other a long time • **con toda confianza** in all confidence • **puedes hablar con toda confianza** you can talk quite freely • **en confianza** in confidence • **en confianza, no creo que apruebe** don't tell anyone I said this, but I doubt she'll pass

confiar *vt* ❶ [*secreto*] to confide ❷ [*responsabilidad, persona, asunto*] • **confiar algo a alguien** to entrust something to somebody • **su padre le confió el cuidado de la tienda** his father entrusted him with the running of the store

confidencia *sf* confidence • **hacer confidencias a alguien** to confide in somebody

confidencial *adj* confidential ☼: *Los adjetivos ingleses son invariables.*

confidente *smf* ❶ [*amigo*] confidant, *femenino* confidante ❷ [*soplón*] informer

configurar *vt* to shape

confinar *vt* ❶ [*detener*] • **confinar (en)** to confine (to) ❷ [*desterrar*] • **confinar (en)** to banish (to)

confirmación *sf* confirmation • **la confirmación de la reserva** the booking confirmation

confirmar *vt* to confirm • **antes de viajar, es importante confirmar el vuelo** it's important to confirm your flights before your trip

confiscar *vt* to confiscate

confitería *sf* candy store

confitura *sf* preserves

conflictivo, va *adj* ❶ [*asunto*] controversial ❷ [*situación*] troubled ❸ [*trabajador*] difficult ☼: *Los adjetivos ingleses son invariables.*

conflicto *sm* ❶ [*generalmente*] conflict ❷ [*de intereses, opiniones*] clash • **estar en conflicto** to be in conflict ▶ **conflicto armado** armed conflict ▶ **conflicto generacional** generation gap ▶ **conflicto laboral** industrial dispute

confluir *vi* ❶ [*corriente, cauce*] • **confluir (en)** to converge (at) ❷ [*personas*] • **confluir (en)** to come together (in)

conformarse con *v pronominal* ❶ [*suerte, destino*] to resign yourself to ❷ [*apañárselas con*] to make do with ❸ [*contentarse con*] to settle for • **nuestro equipo tuvo que conformarse con un empate** our team had to settle for a tie

conforme ◆ *adj* ❶ [*acorde*] • **conforme a** in accordance with ❷ [*de acuerdo*] • **conforme (con)** in agreement (with) ❸ [*contento*] • **conforme (con)** happy (with) ☼: *Los adjetivos ingleses son invariables.*
◆ *adv* [*generalmente*] as • **conforme envejecía** as he got older • **conforme vayan terminando la prueba, pueden salir** you may leave as you finish the test

conformista *adj & smf* conformist ☼: *Los adjetivos ingleses son invariables.*

confort (pl conforts) *sm* comfort • **'todo confort'** all mod cons

confortable *adj* comfortable ☼: *Los adjetivos ingleses son invariables.*

confortar *vt* to console

confrontar *vt* ❶ [*enfrentar*] to confront ❷ [*comparar*] to compare

confundir *vt* ❶ [*trastocar*] • **confundir una cosa con otra** to mistake one thing for another • **el perdón no debe confundirse con el olvido** forgiveness shouldn't be mistaken for forgetfulness • **confundir dos cosas** to get two things mixed up ❷ [*liar*] to confuse • **con esa jugada lograste confundir a tu rival** you managed to confuse your opponent with that move ❸ [*mezclar*] to mix up • **siempre confundo a las dos gemelas** I always mix up the twins
■ **confundirse** *v pronominal* ❶ [*equivocarse*] to make a mistake • **confundirse de piso** to get the wrong floor ❷ [*liarse*] to get confused • **me confundí en el camino porque no había señales** I got confused on the way because there were no signs ❸ [*mezclarse - colores, siluetas*] • **confundirse (en)** to merge (into); [*- personas*] • **confundirse entre la gente** to lose yourself

in the crowd • **el ladrón huyó y se confundió entre la multitud** the thief escaped and disappeared into the crowd

confusión *sf* ❶ [*generalmente*] confusion • **en la confusión de la mañana se me olvidaron las llaves** I forgot my keys in all the confusion this morning ❷ [*error*] mix-up

confuso, sa *adj* ❶ [*incomprensible - estilo, explicación*] obscure ❷ [*poco claro - rumor*] muffled; [- *clamor, griterío*] confused; [- *contorno, forma*] blurred ❸ [*turbado*] confused ✿ *Los adjetivos ingleses son invariables.*

congelación *sf* ❶ [*de alimentos*] freezing ❷ ECONOMÍA [*de precios, salarios*] freeze

congelador *sm* freezer

congelar *vt* [*generalmente*] ECONOMÍA to freeze

congénito, ta *adj* ❶ [*enfermedad*] congenital ❷ [*talento*] innate ✿ *Los adjetivos ingleses son invariables.*

congestión *sf* congestion

congestionar *vt* to block

congregación *sf* congregation

congregar *vt* to assemble

congresista *smf* ❶ [*en un congreso*] delegate ❷ [*político*] congressman, *femenino* congresswoman

congreso *sm* ❶ [*de una especialidad*] congress • **fue a un congreso de cirugía en Costa Rica** he went to a surgical conference in Costa Rica ❷ [*asamblea nacional*] • **el Congreso** [*en Estados Unidos*] Congress • **lo eligieron para el congreso** he was elected to Congress

conjetura *sf* conjecture • **hacer conjeturas, hacerse una conjetura** to conjecture

conjugación *sf* GRAMÁTICA conjugation

conjugar *vt* ❶ GRAMÁTICA to conjugate ❷ [*opiniones*] to bring together ❸ [*esfuerzos, ideas*] to pool

conjunción *sf* ASTRONOMÍA & GRAMÁTICA conjunction

conjunto, ta *adj* ❶ [*generalmente*] joint ❷ [*hechos, acontecimientos*] combined ✿ *Los adjetivos ingleses son invariables.*

■ **conjunto** *sm* ❶ [*generalmente*] set • **un conjunto de circunstancias** a number of reasons ❷ [*de ropa*] outfit • **compré un conjunto de pantalón y chaqueta** I bought an outfit with a jacket and matching pants ❸ MÚSICA [*de rock*] band; [*de música clásica*] ensemble ❹ [*totalidad*] whole • **en conjunto** overall; as a whole ❺ MATEMÁTICAS set

conjuro *sm* spell

conllevar *vt* [*implicar*] to entail

conmemoración *sf* commemoration

conmemorar *vt* to commemorate

conmigo *pronombre personal* with me • **ayer vino conmigo al cine** she went to the movies with me yesterday • **siempre fue muy buena conmigo** she was always very good to me • **conmigo mismo** with myself

conmoción *sf* ❶ [*física o psíquica*] shock ▶ **conmoción cerebral** concussion ❷ *figurado* [*trastorno, disturbio*] upheaval

conmocionar *vt* ❶ [*psíquicamente*] to shock ❷ [*físicamente*] to concuss

conmovedor, ra *adj* moving ✿ *Los adjetivos ingleses son invariables.*

conmover *vt* ❶ [*emocionar*] to move ❷ [*sacudir*] to shake

conmutador *sm* ❶ ELECTRICIDAD switch ❷ [*de teléfonos*] switchboard

cono *sm* cone

conocedor, ra *sm, f* • **conocedor (de) a)** [*generalmente*] expert (on) **b)** [*de vinos*] connoisseur (of)

conocer *vt* ❶ [*generalmente*] to know • **a Juan lo conozco hace más de diez años** I've known Juan for over ten years • **darse a conocer** to make yourself known • **conocer bien un tema** to know a lot about a subject • **conocer alguien de vista** to know somebody by sight • **conocer a alguien de oídas** to have heard of somebody ❷ [*descubrir - lugar, país*] to get to know • **no conozco Egipto** I have never been to Egypt ❸ [*a una persona - por primera vez*] to meet • **quiero que conozcas a mi hermana** I'd like you to meet my sister ❹ [*reconocer*] • **conocer a alguien (por algo)** to recognize somebody (by something)

conocido, da ◆ *adj* well-known ✿ *Los adjetivos ingleses son invariables.*
◆ *sm, f* acquaintance

conocimiento *sm* ❶ [*generalmente*] knowledge • **el conocimiento del sistema solar** knowledge of the solar system ❷ MEDICINA [*sentido*] consciousness **expresión** perder/recobrar el conocimiento to lose/regain consciousness

conque *conjunción* so • **¿conque te has cansado?** so you're tired, are you?

conquista *sf* [*de tierras, persona*] conquest

conquistador, ra *sm, f* ❶ [*de tierras*] conqueror ❷ HISTORIA conquistador

conquistar *vt* [*tierras*] to conquer • **conquistamos la cima** we conquered the summit • **la conquisté con flores** I won her over with flowers

consabido, da *adj* ❶ [*conocido*] well-known ❷ [*habitual*] usual ✿ *Los adjetivos ingleses son invariables.*

consagrar *vt* ❶ RELIGIÓN to consecrate ❷ [*dedicar*] • **consagrar algo a algo/alguien a)** [*tiempo, espacio*] to devote something to something/somebody **b)** [*monumento, lápida*] to dedicate something to something/somebody ❸ [*acreditar, confirmar*] to confirm

consciencia = conciencia

consciente *adj* conscious • **ser consciente de** to be aware of • **estar consciente** [*físicamente*] to be conscious ✿ *Los adjetivos ingleses son invariables.*

conscripción *sf* conscription

conscripto *sm* conscript

consecución *sf* ❶ [*de un deseo*] realization ❷ [*de un objetivo*] attainment ❸ [*de un premio*] winning

consecuencia *sf* [*resultado*] consequence • **tendrá que pagar las consecuencias** she'll have to pay the consequences • **a** o **como consecuencia de** as a consequence o result of • **atenerse a las consecuencias** to accept the consequences • **traer como consecuencia** to result in

consecuente *adj* consistent·Ⓥ *Los adjetivos ingleses son invariables.*

consecutivo, va *adj* consecutive·Ⓥ *Los adjetivos ingleses son invariables.*

conseguir *vt* ❶ [*generalmente*] to obtain ❷ [*un objetivo*] to achieve • **si te dedicas, puedes conseguir cualquier cosa** you can achieve anything if you make the effort • **¡lo conseguiste!** you did it! • **conseguir hacer algo** to manage to do something • **conseguir que alguien haga algo** to get somebody to do something

consejero, ra *sm, f* ❶ [*en asuntos personales*] counselor ❷ [*en asuntos técnicos*] adviser ❸ [*de un consejo de administración*] board member

consejo *sm* ❶ [*advertencia*] advice·Ⓥ *incontable* • **dar un consejo** to give some advice ❷ [*organismo*] council ▶ **consejo de administración** board of directors ▶ **consejo de ministros** cabinet ❸ [*reunión*] meeting ▶ **consejo de guerra** court martial

---

dar o pedir un consejo

- **What should I do?** ¿Qué hago?
- **What do you think?** ¿Qué piensas?
- **If I were you, I'd call the doctor.** Si fuera tú, llamaría al médico.
- **You'd be better off staying at home.** Más te valdría quedarte en casa.

---

consenso *sm* ❶ [*acuerdo*] consensus ❷ [*consentimiento*] consent

consentimiento *sm* consent

consentir ♦ *vt* ❶ [*tolerar*] to allow • **les consienten todo** they are allowed to do whatever they want ❷ [*mimar*] to spoil • **su padre siempre la ha consentido** her father has always spoiled her

♦ *vi* • **consentir en algo/en hacer algo** to agree to something/to do something • **el gobierno acabó consintiendo en que el tema fuera sometido a referéndum** the government ended up agreeing to a referendum on the subject

conserje *smf* ❶ [*portero*] porter ❷ [*encargado*] caretaker

conserjería *sf* ❶ [*de un hotel*] reception desk ❷ [*de un edificio público o privado*] porter's lodge

conserva *sf* • **conserva de carne** tinned meat • **en conserva** tinned; canned

conservación *sf* ❶ [*generalmente*] conservation ❷ [*de alimentos*] preservation

conservacionista ♦ *adj* conservation·Ⓥ *Sólo se usa delante del sustantivo.*

♦ *smf* conservationist

conservante *smf* preservative

conservar *vt* ❶ [*generalmente*] Cocina to preserve • **quieren conservar sus tradiciones** they want to preserve their traditions ❷ [*amistad*] to keep up ❸ [*salud*] to look after ❹ [*calor*] to retain ❺ [*guardar - libros, cartas, secreto*] to keep

conservatorio *sm* conservatoire

considerable *adj* ❶ [*generalmente*] considerable ❷ [*importante, eminente*] notable·Ⓥ *Los adjetivos ingleses son invariables.*

consideración *sf* ❶ [*valoración*] consideration ❷ [*respeto*] respect • **tratar a alguien con consideración** to be nice to somebody • **tratar a alguien sin consideración** to show no consideration to somebody • **en consideración a algo** in recognition of something ❸ [*importancia*] • **de consideración** serious

considerado, da *adj* ❶ [*atento*] considerate • **debería ser más considerado con nosotros** he should be more considerate toward us ❷ [*respetado*] highly regarded • **está muy bien considerado entre otros músicos** he is highly regarded by other musicians·Ⓥ *Los adjetivos ingleses son invariables.*

considerar *vt* ❶ [*valorar*] to consider • **la profesora consideró que valía la pena** the teacher considered it worthwhile • **considerar los pros y los contras** to weigh up the pros and cons • **tenemos que considerar que ha faltado** we have to take into account that he's been absent ❷ [*juzgar, estimar*] to think

consigna *sf* ❶ [*órdenes*] instructions *pl* ❷ [*para el equipaje*] checkroom

consignar *vt* ❶ [*poner por escrito*] to record ❷ [*enviar - mercancía*] to dispatch ❸ [*equipaje*] to deposit in the checkroom

consigo *pronombre personal* ❶ with him/her; with them *pl* • **Luis llevó su tienda consigo** Luis brought his tent with him • **María trajo su traje de baño consigo** María brought her bathing suit with her ❷ [*con usted*] with you • **traiga consigo lo que necesite** bring with you whatever you need ❸ [*con uno mismo*] with yourself • **consigo mismo/misma** with himself/herself • **hablar consigo mismo** to talk to yourself

consiguiente *adj* consequent • **por consiguiente** consequently; therefore·Ⓥ *Los adjetivos ingleses son invariables.*

consistencia *sf* literal & figurado consistency

consistente *adj* ❶ [*sólido - material*] solid ❷ [*coherente - argumento*] sound ❸ [*compuesto*] • **consistente en** consisting of·Ⓥ *Los adjetivos ingleses son invariables.*

consistir ▪ **consistir en** *vi* ❶ [*generalmente*] to consist of • **la obra consiste en dos actos** the play consists of two acts • **¿en qué consiste este juego?** what does this game involve? ❷ [*deberse a*] to be based on

consola *sf* ❶ [*mesa*] console table ❷ Informática & Tecnología console ▶ **consola de videojuegos** video console

consolación *sf* consolation

consolar *vt* to console

consolidar *vt* to consolidate

consonancia *sf* harmony • **en consonancia con** in keeping with

consonante *sf* consonant

conspiración *sf* plot

conspirar *vi* to plot

constancia *sf* ❶ [*perseverancia - en una empresa*] perseverance; [*- en las ideas, opiniones*] steadfastness ❷ [*testimonio*] record • **dejar constancia de algo a)** [*registrar*] to put something on record **b)** [*probar*] to demonstrate something

constante ◆ *adj* ❶ [*persona - en una empresa*] persistent • **ser constante** to persevere • **para tener éxito hay que ser constante** you have to persevere to be successful ❷ [*acción*] constant • **tengo un dolor de cabeza constante** I have a constant headache:♀: *Los adjetivos ingleses son invariables.*
◆ *sf* constant

constar *vi* ❶ [*una información*] • **constar (en)** to appear (in); to figure (in) • **constarle a alguien** to be clear to somebody • **me consta que...** I am quite sure that... • **que conste que...** let it be clearly understood that... • **hacer constar** to put on record • **hacer constar por escrito** to confirm in writing ❷ [*estar constituido por*] • **constar de** to consist of • **el curso consta de dos módulos** the course consists of two modules

constelación *sf* constellation

consternación *sf* consternation

constiparse *v pronominal* to catch a cold

constitución *sf* constitution

constitucional *adj* constitutional:♀: *Los adjetivos ingleses son invariables.*

constituir *vt* ❶ [*componer*] to make up ❷ [*ser*] to be ❸ [*crear*] to set up

constituyente *adj* & *sm* constituent:♀: *Los adjetivos ingleses son invariables.*

construcción *sf* ❶ [*generalmente*] construction • **una empresa de construcción** a construction company • **en construcción** under construction ❷ [*edificio*] building

construir *vt* ❶ [*edificio, barco*] to build ❷ [*aviones, coches*] to manufacture ❸ [*frase, teoría*] to construct

consuelo *sm* consolation

cónsul, consulesa *sm, f* consul

consulado *sm* ❶ [*oficina*] consulate ❷ [*cargo*] consulship

consulta *sf* ❶ [*pregunta*] consultation • **hacer una consulta a alguien** to seek somebody's advice ▶ **consulta popular** referendum ❷ [*despacho de médico*] consulting room • **el doctor está en su consulta de 9 a 3** the doctor is in his office from 9 to 3 • **horas de consulta** office hours ▶ **consulta a domicilio** house call

consultar ◆ *vt* ❶ [*dato, fecha*] to look up ❷ [*libro, persona*] to consult • **consultar un libro** to look something up in a book
◆ *vi* • **consultar con** to consult • **mejor consulta con el médico** you should consult your doctor

consultor, ra *sm, f* consultant

consultorio *sm* ❶ [*de un médico*] consulting room ❷ [*en periódico*] problem page ❸ [*en radio*] *para explicar lo que es puedes decir:* it's a phone-in program that answers listeners' questions ❹ [*asesoría*] advice bureau

consumar *vt* ❶ [*generalmente*] to complete ❷ [*un crimen*] to perpetrate ❸ [*el matrimonio*] to consummate

consumición *sf* ❶ [*acción*] consumption • **está prohibida la consumición de bebidas alcohólicas** the consumption of alcohol is prohibited ❷ [*bebida*] drink ❸ [*comida*] food ▶ **consumición mínima** cover charge

consumidor, ra *sm, f* ❶ [*generalmente*] consumer ❷ [*en un bar, restaurante*] patron

consumir ◆ *vt* ❶ [*generalmente*] to consume • **consumieron los refrescos en el bar** they had their drinks at the bar • **consumir preferentemente antes de...** best before... ❷ [*gastar*] to use • **su coche consume mucha gasolina** his car uses a lot of gas ❸ [*destruir - sujeto: fuego*] to destroy
◆ *vi* to consume

consumismo *sm* consumerism

consumo *sm* consumption • **cómprate un coche de bajo consumo** buy a car with low gas consumption • **el consumo de drogas** drug use • **no apto para el consumo** unfit for human consumption • **una sociedad de consumo** a consumer society ▶ **bienes de consumo** consumer goods

contabilidad *sf* ❶ [*oficio*] accountancy ❷ [*de persona, empresa*] accounting • **estudiar contabilidad** to study accounting • **llevar la contabilidad** to do the accounts

contable *smf* accountant

contacto *sm* ❶ [*generalmente*] contact • **echo de menos el contacto humano** I miss human contact • **ponerse en contacto con alguien** to get in touch with somebody • **perder el contacto** to lose touch ❷ AUTOMÓVILES ignition

contado, da *adj* [*raro*] rare • **contadas veces** very rarely:♀: *Los adjetivos ingleses son invariables.*

contador, ra *sm, f* accountant ▶ **contador público** certified public accountant
■ **contador** *sm* [*aparato*] meter

contaduría *sf* accounting ▶ **contaduría general** audit office

contagiar *vt* ❶ [*persona*] to infect ❷ [*enfermedad*] to transmit

contagio *sm* infection

contagioso, sa *adj* ❶ [*enfermedad*] contagious • **esa enfermedad es muy contagiosa** it's a very contagious disease ❷ [*risa* ETC] infectious • **tu risa es muy contagiosa** you have an infectious laugh:♀: *Los adjetivos ingleses son invariables.*

contaminación *sf* ❶ [*generalmente*] contamination ❷ [*del medio ambiente*] pollution

contaminar *vt* ❶ [*generalmente*] to contaminate ❷ [*el medio ambiente*] to pollute

contar ◆ *vt* ❶ [*enumerar, incluir*] to count • **cuenta hasta diez** count to ten ❷ [*narrar*] to tell • **¿te cuento un cuento?** do you want me to tell you a story? • **¡a mí me lo vas a contar!** you're telling me!
◆ *vi* to count • **ese gol no cuenta** that goal doesn't count

contemplar *vt* to contemplate

contemporáneo, a *adj* & *sm, f* contemporary ۞ *Los adjetivos ingleses son invariables.*

contener *vt* ❶ [*encerrar*] to contain • **el paquete contiene libros** the package contains books ❷ [*detener, reprimir*] to restrain
■ **contenerse** *v pronominal* to contain yourself • **no pudo contenerse de alegría** she could hardly contain herself she was so happy

contenido *sm* ❶ [*generalmente*] contents *pl* • **el contenido del sitio web** the contents of the website ❷ [*de discurso, redacción*] content

contentar *vt* to please

contento, ta *adj* ❶ [*alegre*] happy • **está muy contento con sus notas** he's very happy with his grades ❷ [*satisfecho*] pleased • **estar contento con alguien/ algo** to be pleased with sb/something • **tener contento a alguien** to keep somebody happy ۞ *Los adjetivos ingleses son invariables.*

contestación *sf* answer

contestador ■ **contestador (automático)** *sm* answering machine

contestar ◆ *vt* to answer • **contestó que vendría** she answered that she'd come
◆ *vi* ❶ [*responder*] to answer • **no contestan** there's no answer ❷ [*replicar*] to talk back • **no contestes a tu madre** don't talk back to your mother

contestatario, ria *adj* anti-establishment ۞ *Los adjetivos ingleses son invariables.*

contexto *sm* context

contienda *sf* ❶ [*competición, combate*] contest ❷ [*guerra*] conflict

contigo *pronombre personal* with you • **¿puedo ir contigo?** can I come with you? • **contigo mismo/ misma** with yourself. • **¿estás contento contigo mismo?** are you pleased with yourself?

contiguo, gua *adj* adjacent ۞ *Los adjetivos ingleses son invariables.*

continental *adj* continental ۞ *Los adjetivos ingleses son invariables.*

continente *sm* GEOGRAFÍA continent

contingente ◆ *adj* unforeseeable ۞ *Los adjetivos ingleses son invariables.*
◆ *sm* ❶ [*grupo*] contingent ❷ COMERCIO quota

continuación *sf* continuation • **a continuación** next; then

continuar ◆ *vt* to continue • **podemos continuar la discusión después de la comida** we can continue this discussion after lunch
◆ *vi* to continue • **no puedes continuar así** you can't go on like this • **continuar haciendo algo** to continue

doing o to do something • **continúa lloviendo** it's still raining • **'continuará'** to be continued

continuidad *sf* ❶ [*en una sucesión*] continuity ❷ [*permanencia*] continuation

continuo, nua *adj* ❶ [*ininterrumpido*] continuous ❷ [*constante, perseverante*] continual ۞ *Los adjetivos ingleses son invariables.*

contorno *sm* ❶ GEOGRAFÍA contour ❷ [*línea*] outline ❸ [*de una ciudad*] outskirts *pl*

contra ◆ *preposición* against • **un jarabe contra la tos** a cough syrup • **en contra** against • **estar en contra de algo** to be opposed to something • **en contra de** [*a diferencia de*] contrary to
◆ *sm* • **los pros y los contras** the pros and cons

contraataque *sm* counterattack

contrabajo *sm* ❶ [*instrumento*] double-bass ❷ [*voz, cantante*] low bass

contrabandista *smf* smuggler

contrabando *sm* ❶ [*acto*] smuggling ❷ [*mercancías*] contraband • **pasar algo de contrabando** to smuggle something in ▶ **contrabando de armas** gunrunning

contracción *sf* contraction

contradecir *vt* to contradict • **siempre me contradices** you're always contradicting me

contradicción *sf* contradiction • **estar en contradicción con** to be in (direct) contradiction to

contradictorio, ria *adj* contradictory ۞ *Los adjetivos ingleses son invariables.*

contraer *vt* ❶ [*generalmente*] to contract ❷ [*costumbre, acento* ETC] to acquire ❸ [*enfermedad*] to catch

contraindicación *sf* • **'contraindicaciones:...'** not to be taken with...

contraloría *sf* office controlling public spending

contraluz *sm* • **a contraluz** against the light

contrapartida *sf* compensation • **como contrapartida** to make up for it

contrapesar *vt* [*físicamente*] to counterbalance

contrapeso *sm* ❶ [*en ascensores, poleas*] counterweight ❷ *figurado* [*fuerza que iguala*] counterbalance

contraponer *vt* [*oponer*] • **contraponer (a)** to set up (against)

contraportada *sf* ❶ [*de periódico, revista*] back page ❷ [*de libro, disco*] back cover

contraproducente *adj* counterproductive ۞ *Los adjetivos ingleses son invariables.*

contrariar *vt* ❶ [*contradecir*] to go against ❷ [*disgustar*] to upset

contrariedad *sf* ❶ [*dificultad*] setback ❷ [*disgusto*] annoyance

contrario, ria *adj* ❶ [*opuesto - dirección, sentido*] opposite; [- *parte*] opposing; [- *opinión*] contrary • **vamos en sentido contrario** we're going in the opposite direction • **el equipo contrario no es muy bueno** the opposing team isn't very good • **ser contrario a algo** to

be opposed to something ❷ [*perjudicial*] • **contrario a** contrary to:♀:*Los adjetivos ingleses son invariables.*
■ **contrario** *sm* ❶ [*rival*] opponent ❷ [*opuesto*] opposite
expresiones **al contrario, por el contrario** on the contrary ▶ **de lo contrario** otherwise • **de lo contrario, te verás en problemas** otherwise, you'll be in trouble ▶ **todo lo contrario** quite the contrary

contrarreloj *adj invariable* • **etapa contrarreloj** time trial:♀:*Los adjetivos ingleses son invariables.*

contrasentido *sm* nonsense :♀: *incontable* • **es un contrasentido hacer eso** it doesn't make sense to do that

contraseña *sf* password

contrastar ♦ *vi* to contrast
♦ *vt* ❶ [*probar - hechos*] to check ❷ [*resistir*] to resist

contraste *sm* contrast • **la tele tiene demasiado contraste** there's too much contrast on the TV • **hacer constraste con algo** to contrast with something • **en contraste con** in contrast to • **por contraste** in contrast

contratar *vt* ❶ [*obreros, personal, detective*] to hire ❷ [*deportista*] to sign ❸ [*servicio, obra, mercancía*] • **contratar algo a alguien** to contract for something with somebody

contratiempo *sm* ❶ [*accidente*] mishap ❷ [*dificultad*] setback

contrato *sm* contract • **firmó el contrato ayer** she signed the contract yesterday • **bajo contrato** under contract • **contrato matrimonial** marriage contract

contribución *sf* ❶ [*generalmente*] contribution • **hice una contribución voluntaria** I made a voluntary contribution ❷ [*impuesto*] tax • **la contribución federal** federal tax

contribuir *vi* ❶ [*generalmente*] • **contribuir (a)** to contribute (to) • **contribuir con algo para** to contribute something towards • **cada uno contribuyó al regalo con diez dólares** everyone contributed ten dollars to the present ❷ [*pagar impuestos*] to pay taxes

contribuyente *smf* taxpayer

contrincante *smf* opponent

control *sm* ❶ [*generalmente*] control • **bajo control** under control • **fuera de control** out of control • **perder el control** to lose your temper ▶ **control de calidad** quality control ▶ **control del estrés** stress management ▶ **control de natalidad** birth control ▶ **control remoto** remote control ❷ [*verificación*] examination • **(bajo) control médico** (under) medical supervision ▶ **control antidoping** dope test ❸ [*puesto policial*] checkpoint ▶ **control de pasaportes** passport control

controlador, ra *sm, f* [*generalmente*] INFORMÁTICA controller ▶ **controlador aéreo** air traffic controller

controlar *vt* ❶ [*generalmente*] to control • **deberías aprender a controlarte mejor** you should learn to control yourself ❷ [*cuentas*] to audit ❸ [*comprobar*] to check

controversia *sf* controversy

contundente *adj* ❶ [*arma, objeto*] blunt ❷ [*golpe*] thudding ❸ *figurado* [*razonamiento, argumento*] forceful:♀:*Los adjetivos ingleses son invariables.*

convalidar *vt* ❶ [*estudios*] to recognize ❷ [*asignaturas*] to validate

convencer *vt* to convince • **su argumento no me convenció** his argument didn't convince me • **convencer a alguien de algo** to convince somebody of something • **no la pude convencer para que viniera** I couldn't persuade her to come

C

convencer a alguien

• **Trust me!** ¡Créeme!
• **Believe me!** ¡Créeme!
• **You won't regret it!** ¡No te arrepentirás/se arrepentirá!
• **Forget it!** ¡Déjalo!
• **Don't be so pig-headed!** ¡Mira que eres terco!

convención *sf* convention

convencional *adj* conventional:♀:*Los adjetivos ingleses son invariables.*

conveniencia *sf* ❶ [*utilidad*] usefulness ❷ [*oportunidad*] suitability ❸ [*interés*] convenience • **sólo mira su conveniencia** he only looks after his own interests

conveniente *adj* ❶ [*útil*] useful ❷ [*oportuno*] suitable ❸ [*lugar, hora*] convenient • **no me resulta conveniente** it's not convenient for me ❹ [*aconsejable*] advisable • **sería conveniente asistir** it would be a good idea to go:♀:*Los adjetivos ingleses son invariables.*

convenio *sm* agreement

convenir *vi* ❶ [*ser aconsejable*] to be a good idea • **conviene analizar la situación** it would be a good idea to examine the situation • **no te conviene hacerlo** it's not a good idea for you to do it • **no sabes lo que te conviene** you don't know what's good for you ❷ [*venir bien*] to be convenient • **me conviene más a las once** eleven o'clock is more convenient for me ❸ [*acordar*] • **convenir en** to agree on • **convenimos en reunirnos** we agreed to have a meeting

convento *sm* ❶ [*de monjas*] convent ❷ [*de monjes*] monastery

conversación *sf* conversation • **tuvimos una buena conversación** we had a good conversation • **cambiar de conversación** to change the subject • **trabar conversación con alguien** to strike up a conversation with somebody

empezar una conversación

• **Listen,...** Oye,...
• **Hey,...** Oye,...
• **Do you have a minute?** ¿Tiene un momentito?
• **Excuse me, but I have a question.** Disculpe, pero tengo una pregunta.

C

conversar *vi* to talk

conversión *sf* conversion

convertir *vt* ❶ RELIGIÓN to convert ❷ [*transformar*] • **convertir algo/a alguien en** to turn something/somebody into • **convirtieron la bodega en una discoteca** they turned the warehouse into a disco

■ **convertirse** *v pronominal* ❶ RELIGIÓN • **convertirse (a)** to convert (to) • **se convirtió al budismo** she converted to Buddhism ❷ [*transformarse*] • **convertirse en** to turn into • **se convirtió en un pesado** he turned into a jerk

convexo, xa *adj* convex ⚡ *Los adjetivos ingleses son invariables.*

convicción *sf* conviction • **tener la convicción de que** to be convinced that

convidar *vt* to invite • **¿vas a convidarlos a la fiesta?** are you going to invite them to the party?

convincente *adj* convincing ⚡ *Los adjetivos ingleses son invariables.*

convite *sm* ❶ [*invitación*] invitation ❷ [*fiesta*] banquet

convivencia *sf* living together

convivir *vi* to live together • **convivir con** to live with

convocar *vt* ❶ [*reunión*] to convene ❷ [*huelga, elecciones*] to call

convocatoria *sf* ❶ [*anuncio, escrito*] notice ❷ [*de examen*] diet

convulsión *sf* ❶ [*de músculos*] convulsion ❷ [*política, social*] upheaval ⚡ *incontable*

conyugal *adj* conjugal • **vida conyugal** married life ⚡ *Los adjetivos ingleses son invariables.*

cónyuge *smf* spouse • **los cónyuges** husband and wife

coñac (pl coñacs) *sm* brandy; cognac

cooperación *sf* cooperation • **la cooperación entre países** cooperation between countries

cooperar *vi* • **cooperar (con alguien en algo)** to cooperate (with somebody in something) • **esperamos que cooperes con nosotros** we hope you'll cooperate with us

coordinador, ra ◆ *adj* coordinating ⚡ *Los adjetivos ingleses son invariables.*
◆ *sm, f* coordinator

coordinar *vt* ❶ [*movimientos, gestos*] to coordinate • **le cuesta coordinar sus movimientos** he has trouble coordinating his movements ❷ [*esfuerzos, medios*] to combine

copa *sf* ❶ [*vaso*] glass • **ir de copas** to go out drinking • **¿quieres (tomar) una copa?** would you like (to have) a drink? • **lleva unas copas de más** she's had one too many ❷ [*de árbol*] top • **es un profesional como la copa de un pino** *familiar* he's a consummate professional • **es una mentira como la copa de un pino** *familiar* it's a whopper of a lie ❸ [*en deporte*] cup • **ganaron la Copa Mundial** they won the World Cup

copia *sf* [*reproducción*] copy • **sacar una copia** to make a copy ▶ **copia de seguridad** INFORMÁTICA backup

• **hacer una copia de seguridad de algo** to back something up

copiar ◆ *vt* ❶ [*generalmente*] to copy ❷ [*al dictado*] to take down
◆ *vi* [*en examen*] to cheat

copiloto *smf* copilot

copión, ona *sm, f* ❶ [*imitador*] copycat ❷ [*en examen*] cheat

copo *sm* [*de nieve, cereales*] flake • **un copo de nieve** a snowflake ▶ **copos de avena** rolled oats ▶ **copos de maíz** cornflakes

copropietario, ria *sm, f* co-owner

copulativo, va *adj* copulative ⚡ *Los adjetivos ingleses son invariables.*

coquetear *vi* to flirt

coqueto, ta *adj* ❶ [*que flirtea*] flirtatious ❷ [*que se arregla mucho*] concerned with your appearance ⚡ *Los adjetivos ingleses son invariables.*

coraje *sm* ❶ [*valor*] courage • **hay que tener mucho coraje para hacer eso** it takes a lot of courage to do that ❷ [*rabia*] anger • **me da mucho coraje** that makes me very angry

coral ◆ *adj* choral ⚡ *Los adjetivos ingleses son invariables.*
◆ *sm* coral
◆ *sf* ❶ [*coro*] choir ❷ [*composición*] chorale

Corán *sm* • **el Corán** the Koran

corazón *sm* ❶ [*órgano*] heart • **el ejercicio es bueno para el corazón** exercise is good for the heart • **Pepe es un hombre de buen corazón** Pepe is a kind-hearted man ❷ [*centro - de ciudad, alcachofa*] heart ; [- *de manzana*] core ❸ → **dedo**

corazonada *sf* ❶ [*presentimiento*] hunch ❷ [*impulso*] sudden impulse

corbata *sf* tie • **lleva corbata** he wears a tie ▶ **corbata de moño** bowtie

corchete *sm* ❶ [*broche*] hook and eye ❷ [*signo ortográfico*] square bracket

corcho *sm* cork

cordel *sm* cord

cordero, ra *sm, f* literal & figurado lamb

cordial *adj* cordial ⚡ *Los adjetivos ingleses son invariables.*

cordialidad *sf* cordiality

cordillera *sf* mountain range • **tuvieron que atravesar la cordillera** they had to cross the mountain range • **la cordillera de los Andes** the Andes

cordón *sm* ❶ [*generalmente*] ANATOMÍA cord • **necesitamos un cordón más fuerte** we need a stronger cord ❷ [*de zapato*] lace • **átate los cordones** tie your shoelaces ▶ **cordón umbilical** umbilical cord ❸ [*cable eléctrico*] (power) cord ❹ figurado [*para protección, vigilancia*] cordon ▶ **cordón sanitario** cordon sanitaire

cordura *sf* ❶ [*juicio*] sanity ❷ [*sensatez*] sense

Corea *nombre propio* ▶ **Corea del Norte/Sur** North/South Korea

corear *vt* to chorus

coreógrafo, fa *sm, f* choreographer

córner *sm* corner (kick) • **lanzar un córner** to take a corner

corneta *sf* bugle

cornisa *sf* ARQUITECTURA cornice

coro *sm* ❶ [*generalmente*] choir • **Lucía canta en el coro** Lucía sings in the choir • **contestar a coro** to answer all at once ❷ [*de obra musical*] chorus

corona *sf* ❶ [*generalmente*] crown ❷ [*de flores*] garland ◗ **corona fúnebre/de laurel** funeral/laurel wreath ❸ [*de santos*] halo

coronación *sf* coronation

coronar *vt* ❶ [*persona*] to crown ❷ *figurado* [*terminar*] to complete ❸ [*culminar*] to crown

coronel *sm* colonel

coronilla *sf* crown (of the head)

expresión **estar hasta la coronilla (de)** to be sick and tired (of)

corporación *sf* corporation

corporal *adj* corporal • **el castigo corporal** corporal punishment • **el trabajo corporal** physical labor • **la temperatura corporal** body temperature ☞ *Los adjetivos ingleses son invariables.*

corporativo, va *adj* corporate ☞ *Los adjetivos ingleses son invariables.*

corpulento, ta *adj* corpulent ☞ *Los adjetivos ingleses son invariables.*

corral *sm* ❶ [*generalmente*] yard ❷ [*para cerdos, ovejas*] pen

correa *sf* ❶ [*de bolso, reloj*] strap • **se me rompió la correa del reloj** my watch strap broke ❷ [*de pantalón*] belt ❸ [*de perro*] leash • **ponle la correa al perro** put the dog's leash on ❹ TECNOLOGÍA belt ◗ **correa del ventilador** fan belt

corrección *sf* ❶ [*de errores*] correction ❷ [*de exámenes*] marking ❸ [*de texto*] revision ❹ [*de comportamiento*] correctness

correcto, ta *adj* ❶ [*resultado, texto, respuesta*] correct • **la mayoría de sus respuestas fueron correctas** most of her answers were correct • **¡correcto!** that's right! ❷ [*persona*] polite • **es un niño muy correcto** he's a very polite boy ❸ [*conducta*] proper ☞ *Los adjetivos ingleses son invariables.*

corredor, ra ◆ *adj* running ☞ *Los adjetivos ingleses son invariables.*

◆ *sm, f* ❶ [*deportista*] runner ❷ [*intermediario*] ◗ **corredor de bolsa** stockbroker ◗ **corredor de comercio** COMERCIO registered broker ◗ **corredor de seguros** COMERCIO insurance broker

■ **corredor** *sm* [*pasillo*] corridor

corregir *vt* ❶ [*generalmente*] to correct • **me corrigió las faltas de ortografía** she corrected my spelling mistakes ❷ [*exámenes*] to grade • **estuvo horas corrigiendo los exámenes** she spent hours grading tests

correo *sm* mail • **mándamelo por correo** send it to me by mail • **echar al correo** to mail • **a vuelta de correo** by return mail • **el correo** the mail ◗ **correo aéreo** air mail ◗ **correo basura** INFORMÁTICA spam ◗ **correo**

certificado certified mail ◗ **correo comercial** direct mail ◗ **correo electrónico** e-mail ◗ **correo urgente** special delivery ◗ **correo de voz** voice mail

correr ◆ *vi* ❶ [*andar de prisa*] to run • **corre muy rápido** he runs very fast • **le dije que corriera para no llegar tarde** I told him to hurry up so he wouldn't be late • **a todo correr** at full speed o pelt ❷ [*conducir de prisa*] to drive fast • **no corras tanto que vas a chocar** don't drive so fast or you'll crash ❸ [*pasar por - río*] to flow; [*- camino, agua del grifo*] to run • **el río corre de norte a sur** the river runs from north to south • **deja correr el agua de la llave** leave the faucet running ❹ [*el tiempo, las horas*] to pass ❺ [*propagarse - noticia* ETC] to spread

expresión **(ella) corre que se las pela** she runs like the wind

◆ *vt* ❶ [*recorrer - una distancia*] to cover • **corrió los 100 metros** he ran the 100 meters ❷ [*deslizar - mesa, silla*] to move o pull up ❸ [*cortinas*] to draw • **correr el pestillo** to bolt the door ❹ [*experimentar - aventuras, vicisitudes*] to have; [*- riesgo*] to run ❺ [*despedir*] to throw out

correspondencia *sf* ❶ [*generalmente*] correspondence • **no hay correspondencia entre sonidos y letras** there is no correspondence between sounds and letters • **curso por correspondencia** correspondence course ❷ [*cartas*] mail • **le llega mucha correspondencia** he gets a lot of mail ❸ [*de metro, tren*] connection

corresponder *vi* ❶ [*compensar*] • **corresponder (con algo) a alguien/algo** to repay somebody/something (with something) • **me invitó para corresponder a mi favor** she paid to repay the favor I'd done for her ❷ [*pertenecer*] to belong • **ponlo donde corresponde** put it where it belongs ❸ [*coincidir*] • **corresponder (a/con)** to correspond (to/with) ❹ [*tocar*] • **corresponderle a alguien hacer algo** to be somebody's responsibility to do something ❺ [*a un sentimiento*] to reciprocate

correspondiente *adj* ❶ [*generalmente*] • **correspondiente (a)** corresponding (to) ❷ [*respectivo*] respective ☞ *Los adjetivos ingleses son invariables.*

corresponsal *smf* PRENSA correspondent

corretear *vi* to run about

corrido, da *adj* [*avergonzado*] embarrassed ☞ *Los adjetivos ingleses son invariables.*

■ **corrida** *sf* ❶ TAUROMAQUIA bull fight ❷ [*acción de correr*] run • **dar una corrida** to make a dash • **en una corrida** in a flash

corriente ◆ *adj* ❶ [*normal*] common • **un nombre muy corriente** a very common name • **corriente y moliente** run-of-the-mill ❷ [*agua*] running ❸ [*mes, año, cuenta*] current ☞ *Los adjetivos ingleses son invariables.*

◆ *sf* ❶ [*de río, electricidad*] current • **no parece haber corriente** there doesn't seem to be any power • **se cortó la corriente** there was a power cut ◗ **corriente eléctrica** electric current ❷ [*de aire*] draft • **cierra la ventana que entra una corriente** close the window, there's a draft ❸ *figurado* [*tendencia*] trend ❹ [*de opinión*] tide

expresiones dejarse llevar de o **por la corriente** to follow the crowd ▸ **ir contra corriente** to go against the tide ▸ **llevarle la corriente a alguien** to humor somebody
◆ *sm* • **estar al corriente de** to be up to date with • **poner al corriente** to bring up to date • **ponerse al corriente** to bring yourself up to date • **tener a alguien al corriente** to keep somebody informed

corro *sm* circle • **en corro** in a circle

corroer *vt* ❶ [*generalmente*] to corrode ❷ GEOLO-GÍA to erode

corromper *vt* ❶ [*pudrir - madera*] to rot; [- *alimentos*] to turn bad ❷ [*pervertir*] to corrupt • **el poder corrompe** power corrupts

corrosivo, va *adj* literal & figurado corrosive: ☼: *Los adjetivos ingleses son invariables.*

corrupción *sf* ❶ [*generalmente*] corruption ▸ **corrupción de menores** corruption of minors ❷ [*de una substancia*] decay

cortado, da *adj* ❶ [*labios, manos*] chapped • **tengo los labios cortados** my lips are chapped ❷ [*leche*] sour, off ❸ [*salsa*] curdled • **la crema está cortada** the cream is curdled ❹ [*calle, carretera*] closed • **la calle está cortada por obras** the street is closed due to roadwork ❺ *familiar* & *figurado* [*tímido*] inhibited: ☼: *Los adjetivos ingleses son invariables.*
■ **cortado** *sm* [*café*] *para explicar lo que es puedes decir:* it's a small coffee with a splash of milk

cortafuegos *sm invariable* INFORMÁTICA firewall

cortante *adj* ❶ [*afilado*] sharp ❷ figurado [*frase*] cutting ❸ [*viento*] biting ❹ [*frío*] bitter: ☼: *Los adjetivos ingleses son invariables.*

cortar ◆ *vt* ❶ [*seccionar - pelo, uñas*] to cut; [- *papel*] to cut up; [- *ramas*] to cut off; [- *árbol*] to cut down • **Ana sabe cortar pelo** Ana knows how to cut hair • **cortaron la escena porque era demasiado violenta** they cut the scene because it was too violent • **me cortaron el teléfono** my phone was cut off ❷ [*amputar*] to cut off ❸ [*tela, figura de papel*] to cut out ❹ [*interrumpir - retirada, luz, teléfono*] to cut off; [- *carretera*] to block (off); [- *hemorragia*] to stop; [- *discurso, conversación*] to interrupt ❺ [*labios, piel*] to chap
◆ *vi* ❶ [*producir un corte*] to cut ❷ [*cesar una relación*] to break o split up • **he cortado con mi novio** I've split up with my boyfriend
■ **cortarse** *v pronominal* ❶ [*herirse*] to cut yourself • **me corté con un cuchillo** I cut myself with a knife • **cortarse el pelo** to have a haircut ❷ [*alimento*] to curdle ❸ *familiar* [*turbarse*] to become tongue-tied

cortaúñas *sm invariable* nail clippers *pl*

corte ◆ *sm* ❶ [*raja*] cut • **tengo un corte en la mano** I've got a cut on my hand • **un corte de pelo** a haircut ❷ [*en pantalones, camisa* ETC] tear ▸ **corte y confección a)** [*para mujeres*] dressmaking **b)** [*para hombres*] tailoring ❸ [*interrupción*] ▸ **corte de digestión** stomach cramps ❹ [*sección*] section ❺ [*concepción, estilo*] style ❻ *familiar* [*vergüenza*] embarrassment
◆ *sf* [*palacio*] court • **la corte del rey** the royal court ▸ **Corte Suprema** Supreme Court

cortejo *sm* retinue ▸ **cortejo fúnebre** funeral cortège

cortés *adj* polite • **un caballero muy cortés** a very polite gentleman: ☼: *Los adjetivos ingleses son invariables.*

expresión lo cortés no quita lo valiente politeness isn't a sign of weakness

cortesía *sf* courtesy • **le falta cortesía al manejar** he lacks courtesy when he's driving • **de cortesía** complimentary • **por cortesía de** courtesy of

corteza *sf* ❶ [*del árbol*] bark • **la corteza del árbol** the tree bark ❷ [*de pan*] crust • **me gusta la corteza del pan** I like the bread's crust ❸ [*de queso*] rind ❹ [*de naranja, limón*] peel ❺ [*terrestre*] crust ❻ ANATOMÍA cortex • **corteza cerebral** cerebral cortex

cortina *sf* ❶ [*de tela*] curtain ❷ figurado • **cortina de agua** sheet of water

corto, ta *adj* ❶ [*generalmente*] short • **te ves bien con el pelo corto** you look good with short hair ❷ [*escaso - raciones*] meager; [- *disparo*] short of the target • **corto de** [*dinero* ETC] short of ❸ figurado [*bobo*] dim: ☼: *Los adjetivos ingleses son invariables.*

expresiones ni corto ni perezoso as bold as brass ▸ **quedarse corto** [*al calcular*] to underestimate • **decir que es bueno es quedarse corto** it's an understatement to call it good ▸ **ser corto de vista** to be nearsighted

cortocircuito *sm* short circuit

cortometraje *sm* short (movie)

cosa *sf* ❶ [*generalmente*] thing • **pásame esa cosa verde** pass me that green thing • **¿queréis alguna cosa?** is there anything you want? • **no es gran cosa** it's not important, it's no big deal • **poca cosa** nothing much • **cualquier cosa** anything ❷ [*asunto*] matter • **esto es otra cosa** that's another matter • **no es cosa de risa** it's no laughing matter

expresiones ¡a otra cosa, mariposa! let's change the subject! ▸ **decir cuatro cosas a alguien** to give somebody a piece of your mind ▸ **eso es cosa mía** that's my affair o business ▸ **no es cosa tuya** it's none of your business ▸ **hacer algo como quien no quiere la cosa a)** [*disimuladamente*] to do something as if you weren't intending to **b)** [*sin querer*] to do something almost without realizing it ▸ **son cosas de la vida** that's life ▸ **son cosas de mamá** that's just the way mom is

coscorrón *sm* bump on the head

cosecha *sf* ❶ [*generalmente*] harvest • **es época de cosecha** it's harvest time • **el granizo arruinó la cosecha** hail ruined the crop ❷ [*del vino*] vintage

expresión ser de la (propia) cosecha de alguien to be made up by somebody

cosechar ◆ *vt* ❶ [*cultivar*] to grow ❷ [*recolectar*] to harvest
◆ *vi* to (bring in the) harvest

coser ◆ *vt* [*con hilo*] to sew
◆ *vi* to sew • **si supiera coser, te arreglaría la camisa** if I knew how to sew I'd mend your shirt

expresión coser a cuchilladas to stab repeatedly ▸ **ser cosa de coser y cantar** to be child's play

cosido *sm* stitching

cosmético, ca *adj* cosmetic ⚲ *Sólo se usa delante del sustantivo.*
- **cosmético** *sm* cosmetic
- **cosmética** *sf* cosmetics ⚲ *incontable*

cosmopolita *adj* & *smf* cosmopolitan ⚲ *Los adjetivos ingleses son invariables.*

cosquillas *sfpl* • **hacer cosquillas** to tickle • **¡no me hagas cosquillas!** stop tickling me! • **tener cosquillas** to be ticklish
expresión **buscarle las cosquillas a alguien** to wind somebody up

costa *sf* GEOGRAFÍA coast • **tiene una casa en la costa** he has a house on the coast

costado *sm* side • **me gusta dormir de costado** I like to sleep on my side • **es francés por los cuatro costados** he's French through and through

costar ◆ *vt* ❶ [*dinero*] to cost • **¿cuánto cuesta?** how much does it cost? ❷ [*tiempo*] to take • **me costó tres días acabarlo** it took me three days to finish it ◆ *vi* [*ser difícil*] • **me está costando aprender alemán** I'm finding it hard to learn German • **costar caro a alguien** to cost somebody dear

Costa Rica *nombre propio* Costa Rica

costarricense, costarriqueño, ña *adj* & *sm, f* Costa Rican ⚲ *Los adjetivos ingleses son invariables.*
En inglés, los adjetivos que se refieren a un país o a una región se escriben con mayúscula.

costear *vt* [*pagar*] to pay for

costilla *sf* ❶ [*de persona, barco*] rib ❷ [*de animal*] cutlet

costo *sm* ❶ [*de una mercancía*] price ❷ [*de un producto, de la vida*] cost • **el costo humano de la guerra** the human cost of war

costoso, sa *adj* [*operación, maquinaria*] expensive ⚲ *Los adjetivos ingleses son invariables.*

costra *sf* [*de herida*] scab

costumbre *sf* habit • **una mala costumbre** a bad habit • **una costumbre local** a local custom • **tener/perder la costumbre de hacer algo** to be in/get out of the habit of doing something • **como de costumbre** as usual • **por costumbre** out of habit

costura *sf* ❶ [*labor*] sewing • **a Jimena le gusta la costura** Jimena likes sewing ❷ [*puntadas*] seam • **una costura mal hecha** a badly-sewn seam ❸ [*oficio*] dressmaking • **alta costura** haute couture

costurero *sm* [*caja*] sewing box

cotidiano, na *adj* daily ⚲ *Los adjetivos ingleses son invariables.*

cotización *sf* ❶ [*valor*] price ❷ [*en Bolsa*] quotation

cotizar ◆ *vt* ❶ [*valorar*] to quote ❷ [*pagar*] to pay ◆ *vi* to pay contributions

coto *sm* preserve • **coto de caza** game preserve
expresión **poner coto a** to put a stop to

cotorra *sf* parrot

covacha *sf* ❶ [*cueva*] small cave ❷ [*vivienda*] shack

coxis = cóccix

coyote *sm* ❶ [*animal*] coyote ❷ *familiar* [*guía*] guide ❸ *familiar* [*intermediario*] fixer

coyuntura *sf* ❶ [*situación*] moment ❷ ANATOMÍA joint

coz *sf* kick

crac (pl cracs) *sm* FINANZAS crash

cráneo *sm* skull

cráter *sm* crater

creación *sf* creation

creador, ra ◆ *adj* creative ⚲ *Los adjetivos ingleses son invariables.* ◆ *sm, f* creator • **creador gráfico** creator (of cartoon etc)

crear *vt* ❶ [*generalmente*] to create • **crearon una base de datos** they created a database • **crear falsas expectativas** to raise false hopes • **crear problemas** to cause problems ❷ [*fundar - una academia*] to found

creatividad *sf* creativity

creativo, va *adj* creative ⚲ *Los adjetivos ingleses son invariables.*

crecer *vi* ❶ [*persona, planta*] to grow • **has crecido mucho** you've grown a lot • **creció en Nueva York** she grew up in New York ❷ [*días, noches*] to grow longer ❸ [*río, marea, precios*] to rise • **ha crecido la inflación y el desempleo** inflation and unemployment have risen ❹ [*aumentar - animosidad* etc] to increase; [*- rumores*] to spread

creces ■ **con creces** *adv* with interest

crecido, da *adj* ❶ [*cantidad*] large ❷ [*hijo*] grown-up ⚲ *Los adjetivos ingleses son invariables.*
- **crecida** *sf* flood

creciente *adj* ❶ [*generalmente*] growing ❷ [*luna*] crescent ⚲ *Los adjetivos ingleses son invariables.*

crecimiento *sm* ❶ [*generalmente*] growth • **crecimiento económico** economic growth ❷ [*de precios*] rise

credibilidad *sf* credibility

crédito *sm* ❶ [*préstamo*] credit • **¿crees que te darán un crédito?** do you think they'll give you credit? • **a crédito** on credit • **comprar algo a crédito** to buy something on credit • **crédito personal** personal loan ❷ [*confianza*] trust • **digno de crédito** trustworthy ❸ [*en universidad*] credit
expresión **dar crédito a algo** to believe something

creencia *sf* belief

creer *vt* ❶ [*generalmente*] to believe • **no lo puedo creer** I can't believe it • **¡ya lo creo!** of course! ❷ [*suponer*] to think • **creo que tienes razón** I think you're right • **creo que no** I don't think so • **creo que sí** I think so • **según creo** to the best of my knowledge ❸ [*estimar*] to think • **lo creo muy capaz de hacerlo** I think he's quite capable of doing it

creído, da *adj*, conceited

crema *sf* ❶ [*generalmente*] cream • **la crema le gusta a los gatos** cats like cream • **la crema del mundo literario** the cream of the literary world ❿ **crema batida** whipped cream ❿ **crema de champiñones** mushroom soup ❷ [*cosmético, betún*] cream ❿ **crema de afeitar** shaving cream ❿ **crema dental** toothpaste ❿ **crema depilatoria** hair remover ❿ **crema facial** face cream ❿ **crema hidratante** moisturizer ❿ **crema para las manos** hand cream ❸ [*licor*] crème ❹ [*dulce, postre*] custard

cremallera *sf* zipper

cremoso, sa *adj* creamy◌ *Los adjetivos ingleses son invariables.*

crepa *sf* crepe

crepúsculo *sm* ❶ [*al amanecer*] first light ❷ [*al anochecer*] twilight

cresta *sf* ❶ [*generalmente*] crest ❷ [*del gallo*] comb *expresión* **estar en la cresta (de la ola)** to be riding high

cretino, na *sm, f* cretin

creyente *smf* believer

cría *sf* ❶ [*hijo del animal*] young • **los animales y sus crías** animals and their young • **una cría de elefante** a baby elephant • **una cría de león** a lion cub ❷ [*crianza - de animales*] breeding; [*- de plantas*] growing

criadero *sm* ❶ [*de animales*] farm ❷ [*de árboles, plantas*] nursery

criado, da *sm, f* servant, *femenino* maid

criador, ra *sm, f* ❶ [*de animales*] breeder ❷ [*de vinos*] grower

crianza *sf* ❶ [*de animales, personas*] breeding ❷ [*del vino*] vintage ❸ [*de personas*] upbringing

criar *vt* ❶ [*amamantar - sujeto: mujer*] to breastfeed; [*- sujeto: animal*] to suckle ❷ [*animales*] to breed • **crían perros** they breed dogs ❸ [*flores, árboles*] to grow ❹ [*vino*] to make ❺ [*educar*] to bring up • **sus padres la criaron bien** her parents brought her up well

■ **criarse** *v pronominal* to grow up • **nos criamos juntos** we grew up together

criatura *sf* ❶ [*niño*] child ❷ [*bebé*] baby ❸ [*ser vivo*] creature

criba *sf* ❶ [*tamiz*] sieve ❷ [*selección*] screening

crimen *sm* crime • **cometer un crimen** to commit murder ❿ **crimen de guerra** war crime ❿ **crimen organizado** organized crime

criminal *adj* & *smf* criminal ❿ **criminal de guerra** war criminal◌ *Los adjetivos ingleses son invariables.*

crin *sf* mane

crío, cría *sm, f* kid

criollo, lla *adj* ❶ [*persona*] native to Latin America ❷ [*comida, lengua*] creole◌ *Los adjetivos ingleses son invariables.*

crisantemo *sm* chrysanthemum

crisis *sf invariable* [*generalmente*] crisis • **una crisis económica** an economic crisis • **crisis de los cuarenta** midlife crisis ❿ **crisis cardíaca** cardiac arrest ❿ **crisis económica** o **financiera** credit crunch ❿ **crisis nerviosa** nervous breakdown

crisma *sf familiar* head • **romperle la crisma a alguien** to bash somebody's head in

crispar *vt* ❶ [*los nervios*] to set on edge ❷ [*los músculos*] to tense ❸ [*las manos*] to clench

cristal *sm* ❶ [*material*] glass ◌ *incontable* ❷ [*vidrio fino*] crystal • **cristal de roca** rock crystal ❸ [*en la ventana*] (window) pane ❹ [*en mineralogía*] crystal

cristalera *sf* ❶ [*puerta*] French window ❷ [*techo*] glass roof ❸ [*armario*] glass-fronted cabinet

cristalizar *vt* ❶ [*una sustancia*] to crystallize ❷ *figurado* [*un asunto*] to bring to a head

cristianismo *sm* Christianity

cristiano, na *adj* & *sm, f* Christian◌ *Los adjetivos ingleses son invariables.*

cristo *sm* crucifix

■ **Cristo** *sm* Christ

expresión **estar hecho un Cristo** *familiar* to be a pitiful sight

criterio *sm* ❶ [*norma*] criterion ❷ [*juicio*] taste ❸ [*opinión*] opinion

crítica *sf* ❶ [*juicio - sobre arte, literatura*] review • **voy a escribir una crítica del libro** I'm going to write a review of the book ❷ [*conjunto de críticos*] • **la crítica** the critics *pl* ❸ [*ataque*] criticism • **no aguantó tanta crítica y se fue** he couldn't stand so much criticism so he left

criticar *vt* ❶ [*enjuiciar - literatura, arte*] to review • **criticar una película** to review a movie ❷ [*censurar*] to criticize • **la critica constantemente** he's constantly criticizing her

crítico, ca ✦ *adj* critical◌ *Los adjetivos ingleses son invariables.*
✦ *sm, f* [*persona*] critic • **un crítico de cine** a movie critic

criticón, ona ✦ *adj* nit-picking◌ *Los adjetivos ingleses son invariables.*
✦ *sm, f* nitpicker

Croacia *nombre propio* Croatia

croar *vi* to croak

croata ✦ *adj* Croatian◌ *Los adjetivos ingleses son invariables.*
✦ *smf* Croat

crol *sm* DEPORTE crawl

cromo *sm* ❶ [*metal*] chrome ❷ [*estampa*] picture card
expresión **ir hecho un cromo** to be dressed up to the nines

cromosoma *sm* chromosome

crónico, ca *adj* chronic◌ *Los adjetivos ingleses son invariables.*

■ **crónica** *sf* ❶ [*de la historia*] chronicle ❷ [*de un periódico*] column ❸ [*de la televisión*] feature

cronista *smf* ❶ [*historiador*] chronicler ❷ [*periodista*] columnist

cronología *sf* chronology

cronometrar *vt* to time

cronómetro *sm* ❶ DEPORTE stopwatch ❷ TECNOLO-GÍA chronometer

croqueta *sf* croquette

croquis *sm invariable* sketch

cruasán, croissant (pl croissants) *sm* croissant

cruce *sm* ❶ [*de líneas*] crossing • **un cruce fronterizo** a border crossing ❷ [*de carreteras*] crossroads • **un cruce de carreteras** a crossroads ❸ [*paso*] crossing ▶ **cruce a nivel** grade crossing ▶ **cruce de peatones** (pedestrian) crosswalk ❹ [*de animales*] cross

crucero *sm* ❶ [*viaje*] cruise ❷ [*barco*] cruiser ❸ [*de iglesias*] transept

crucial *adj* crucial:💡*Los adjetivos ingleses son invariables.*

crucificar *vt* [*en una cruz*] to crucify

crucifijo *sm* crucifix

crucifixión *sf* crucifixion

crucigrama *sm* crossword (puzzle)

crudeza *sf* ❶ [*generalmente*] harshness • **con crudeza** harshly ❷ [*de descripción, imágenes*] brutality

crudo, da *adj* ❶ [*natural*] raw • **carne cruda** raw meat ❷ [*petróleo*] crude ❸ [*sin cocer completamente*] undercooked • **el pollo está crudo** the chicken's undercooked ❹ [*realidad, clima, tiempo*] harsh ❺ [*novela*] hard-hitting ❻ [*cruel*] cruel ❼ *familiar* [*con resaca*] • **estar crudo** to be hung over:💡*Los adjetivos ingleses son invariables.*

■ **crudo** *sm* crude (oil)

cruel *adj* cruel:💡*Los adjetivos ingleses son invariables.*

crueldad *sf* ❶ [*generalmente*] cruelty ❷ [*acción cruel*] act of cruelty

crujido *sm* ❶ [*de madera*] creak ❷ [*de hojas secas*] crackle

crujiente *adj* ❶ [*madera*] creaky ❷ [*hojas secas*] rustling ❸ [*patatas fritas*] crunchy:💡*Los adjetivos ingleses son invariables.*

crujir *vi* ❶ [*madera*] to creak • **la cama crujía cada vez que me movía** the bed creaked every time I moved ❷ [*papas fritas, nieve*] to crunch • **la nieve crujía bajo nuestros pies** the snow crunched under our feet ❸ [*hojas secas*] to rustle • **las hojas secas crujían con el viento** the dry leaves rustled in the wind ❹ [*dientes*] to grind • **le crujen los dientes** he grinds his teeth

cruz *sf* ❶ [*generalmente*] cross ▶ **cruz gamada** swastika ▶ **la Cruz Roja** the Red Cross ❷ [*de una moneda*] tails:💡*incontable* ❸ *figurado* [*aflicción*] burden

cruza *sf* cross

cruzado, da *adj* ❶ [*cheque, piernas, brazos*] crossed ❷ [*animal*] crossbred ❸ [*abrigo, chaqueta*] double-breasted:💡*Los adjetivos ingleses son invariables.*

■ **cruzada** *sf* literal & figurado crusade

cruzar *vt* ❶ [*generalmente*] to cross • **ten cuidado al cruzar la calle** be careful when you cross the street • **cruzar los brazos** to fold your arms • **cruzar los dedos** to cross your fingers ❷ [*unas palabras*] to exchange

cuaderno *sm* ❶ [*generalmente*] notebook • **un cuaderno de espiral** a spiral notebook ❷ [*en el colegio*] exercise book

cuadra *sf* ❶ [*de caballos*] stable ❷ [*en calle*] block • **queda a tres cuadras** it's three blocks from here

cuadrado, da *adj* square • **diez kilómetros cuadrados** ten square kilometers • **tu hermano es muy cuadrado** your brother is really square • **al cuadrado** MATEMÁTICAS squared • **tres al cuadrado** three squared • **elevar al cuadrado** MATEMÁTICAS to square:💡*Los adjetivos ingleses son invariables.*

■ **cuadrado** *sm* square

cuadragésimo, ma *numeral* fortieth

cuadrar ◆ *vi* ❶ [*información, hechos*] • **cuadrar (con)** to square o agree (with) ❷ [*números, cuentas*] to add up

◆ *vt* [*generalmente*] to square

cuadrícula *sf* grid

cuadrilátero *sm* ❶ GEOMETRÍA quadrilateral ❷ DE-PORTE ring

cuadrilla *sf* ❶ [*de amigos, trabajadores*] group ❷ [*de maleantes*] gang

cuadro *sm* ❶ [*pintura*] painting • **colecciona cuadros** she collects paintings ❷ [*escena*] scene ❸ [*descripción*] portrait ❹ [*cuadrado*] square • **a cuadros** check ❺ [*equipo*] team ▶ **cuadros medios** middle management:💡*incontable* ❻ [*gráfico*] chart ❼ [*de la bicicleta*] frame ❽ TEATRO scene

expresión **quedarse a cuadros** *familiar* to be gobsmacked ▶ **quedarse en cuadros** to be down to a skeleton staff

cuádruple *sm* quadruple

cuajar ◆ *vt* ❶ [*leche*] to curdle ❷ [*huevo*] to set ❸ [*sangre*] to clot

◆ *vi* ❶ [*lograrse - acuerdo*] to be settled; [*- negocio*] to take off ❷ [*ser aceptado - persona*] to fit in; [*- moda*] to catch on ❸ [*nieve*] to settle

cuajo *sm* rennet

---

cual

◆ *pronombre relativo*

❶ [*sujeto*] [*- persona*] who; [*- cosa*] which
• **llamé a Juan, el cual dormía** I called Juan, who was sleeping
• **han sacado un nuevo producto, el cual es muy eficaz** they've released another product, which is very effective

❷ [*complemento directo*] who
• **el libro el cual te presté** the book (which) I lent you
• **Jorge es el hermano de Ana, a la cual por cierto veo a menudo** Jorge is the brother of Ana, who I actually see quite often

❸ [*complemento indirecto*] who; whom
• **un amigo al cual confío mis secretos** a friend (who) I confide in
• **la chica a la cual regalé el libro** the girl I gave the book to

• **la película a la cual hago referencia** the movie I refer to

❹ [*complemento de manera, objetivo, etc*]
• **la computadora con la cual trabajo** the computer I work with
• **el puesto para el cual me contrataron** the post they hired me for
• **la amiga con la cual fui al cine** the girl I went to the movies with

❺ [*complemento de lugar*]
• **la cabina desde la cual te llamo** the phone booth I'm calling you from

❻ [*antes de la preposición "de"*]
• **el club del cual soy socio** the club I'm a member of
• **el libro/el actor del cual te hablé** the book/the actor I was talking to you about
• **una noticia de la cual me alegro** some good news

❼ [*en expresiones*]
• **sea cual sea el resultado** whatever the result
■ **lo cual**
◆ *pronombre indefinido*
• **vendrán atletas de todas partes del mundo, lo cual requiere mucha organización** athletes will be coming from all over the world, which will require a lot of organization
• **está muy enfadada, lo cual comprendo perfectamente** she's very angry, which I understand perfectly

cuál *pronombre* ⊙ *interrogativo* ❶ what ❷ [*en concreto, especificando*] which one • **¿cuál es tu nombre?** what is your name? • **¿cuál es la diferencia?** what's the difference? • **no sé cuáles son mejores** I don't know which are best • **¿cuál prefieres?** which one do you prefer?

cualidad *sf* quality

cualificado, da *adj* skilled ⊙ *Los adjetivos ingleses son invariables.*

cualitativo, va *adj* qualitative ⊙ *Los adjetivos ingleses son invariables.*

cualquiera (pl cualesquiera) ◆ *adj* any • **cualquier día vendré a visitarte** I'll drop by one of these days • **este examen lo puede aprobar cualquier alumno** any student can pass this exam • **a cualquier hora** any time • **en cualquier lugar** anywhere • **en cualquier momento** at any time ⊙ *Los adjetivos ingleses son invariables.*

◆ *pronombre* anyone • **cualquiera te lo dirá** anyone will tell you • **cualquiera puede aprobar el examen si estudia** anyone can pass the test if they study • **cualquiera que a)** [*persona*] anyone who **b)** [*cosa*] whatever • **cualquiera que sea la razón** whatever the reason (may be)
◆ *sm, f* [*don nadie*] nobody

cuan *adv* [*todo lo que*] • **se desplomó cuan largo era** he fell flat on the ground

cuán *adv* how

cuando ◆ *adv* when • **ven cuando puedas** come when you can • **de cuando en cuando** from time to time • **de vez en cuando** now and again
◆ *conjunción* ❶ [*de tiempo*] when • **cuando llegue el verano iremos de viaje** when summer comes we'll go traveling ❷ [*si*] if • **cuando tú lo dices será verdad** it must be true if you say so ❸ [*aunque*] • **no mentiría aun cuando le fuera en ello la vida** she wouldn't lie even if her life depended on it

cuándo *adv* when • **¿cuándo vas a venir?** when are you coming? • **quisiera saber cuándo sale el tren** I'd like to know when o at what time the train leaves

cuantía *sf* ❶ [*suma*] quantity ❷ [*alcance*] extent

cuantificar *vt* to quantify

cuantioso, sa *adj* large ⊙ *Los adjetivos ingleses son invariables.*

cuantitativo, va *adj* quantitative ⊙ *Los adjetivos ingleses son invariables.*

cuanto, ta

◆ *adj*
❶ [*indica la totalidad*]
• **despilfarra cuanto dinero gana** he wastes all the money he earns
❷ [*introduce una correlación*]
• **cuantas más mentiras digas, menos te creerán** the more lies you tell, the less you'll be believed
• **cuanto menos pienses en ello, mejor será** the less you think of her, the better it will be

⊙ *Los adjetivos ingleses son invariables.*

◆ *pronombre*
❶ [*indica un grupo determinado*]
• **dio las gracias a todos cuantos la ayudaron** she thanked everybody who had helped her
• **es la mejor versión entre todas cuantas conozco** it's the best version of all the ones I know
❷ [*indica la totalidad*]
• **comprendo cuanto dice** I understand everything he says
• **me gustaron cuantas vi** I liked all the ones I saw
• **come cuanto quieras** eat as much as you want
❸ [*introduce una correlación*]
• **cuanto más se tiene, más se quiere** the more you have, the more you want
• **cuanto más la conozco, más me gusta** the more I get to know her, the more I like her

cuánto, ta

◆ *adj*
❶ [*en frases interrogativas - con incontables*] how much; [*- con contables*] how many
• **¿cuánto dinero tienes?** how much money do you have?
• **no sé cuántas horas tardaré en hacerlo** I don't know how many hours it will take me to do it
❷ [*en frases exclamativas*]
• **¡cuánta gente hay!** what a lot of people there are!

• **¡cuánto tiempo sin verte!** it's been such a long time since we last met!

Los adjetivos ingleses son invariables.

◆ *pronombre*

❶ [*en frases interrogativas*] how much ; how many • **¿cuánto has ganado este mes?** how much have you earnt this month?
• **dime cuántas necesitas** tell me how many you need

❷ [*en frases exclamativas*]
• **¡cuánto me gusta este cuadro!** I really like this picture!
• **¡cuánto han cambiado las cosas!** how things have changed!
• **hablando de cómics, ¡cuántos tienes!** speaking of comic books, what a lot you have!

cuarenta *numeral* forty • **los (años) cuarenta** the forties ver también **seis**

cuarentena *sf* [*por epidemia*] quarantine • **poner en cuarentena a)** [*enfermos*] to (put in) quarantine **b)** [*noticia*] to put on hold

cuartel *sm* MILITAR barracks *pl* ▶ **cuartel general** headquarters *pl*

cuarteto *sm* quartet

cuarto, ta *numeral* fourth • **eres la cuarta persona en llegar** you're the fourth person to arrive • **la cuarta parte** a quarter
■ **cuarto** *sm* ❶ [*parte*] quarter • **un cuarto de hora** a quarter of an hour • **son las dos y cuarto** it's a quarter after two • **son las dos menos cuarto** it's a quarter of two ❷ [*habitación*] room • **la casa tiene cinco cuartos** the house has five rooms ▶ **cuarto de baño** bathroom ▶ **cuarto de estar** living room ▶ **cuarto de huéspedes** guestroom ▶ **cuarto oscuro** FOTOGRAFÍA darkroom
■ **cuarta** *sf* [*palmo*] span

cuarzo *sm* quartz

cuate, ta *sm, f familiar* ❶ [*amigo*] buddy • **fui al cine con unos cuates** I went to the movies with my buddies • **¿conoces a ese cuate?** do you know that guy? ❷ [*gemelo*] twin • **sus hijos son cuates** her kids are twins

cuatro ◆ *numeral* four • **más de cuatro** quite a few
◆ *adj figurado* [*poco*] a few • **hace cuatro días** a few days ago. *Los adjetivos ingleses son invariables.* ver también **seis**

cuatrocientos, tas *numeral* four hundred ver también **seis**

cuba *sf* barrel
beber como una cuba to drink like a fish ▶ **estar como una cuba** to be blind drunk

Cuba *nombre propio* Cuba

cuba libre *sm* rum and coke

cubano, na *adj & sm, f* Cuban. *Los adjetivos ingleses son invariables.*

En inglés, los adjetivos que se refieren a un país o a una región se escriben con mayúscula.

cubeta *sf* bucket

cúbico, ca *adj* cubic • **diez metros cúbicos** ten cubic meters. *Los adjetivos ingleses son invariables.*

cubierto, ta ◆ *participio pasado* → **cubrir**
◆ *adj* ❶ [*generalmente*] • **cubierto (de)** covered (with) ❷ [*cielo*] overcast. *Los adjetivos ingleses son invariables.*
estar a cubierto a) [*protegido*] to be under cover **b)** [*con saldo acreedor*] to be in the black ▶ **ponerse a cubierto** to take cover
■ **cubierto** *sm* ❶ [*pieza de cubertería*] piece of cutlery • **cubiertos** cutlery. *incontable* • **cubiertos de plata** silver cutlery ❷ [*para cada persona*] place setting
■ **cubierta** *sf* ❶ [*generalmente*] cover • **un libro con cubiertas de cuero** a book with leather covers ❷ [*de neumático*] tyre ❸ [*de barco*] deck • **voy a subir a la cubierta para ver el mar** I'm going up on deck to look at the sea

cubilete *sm* cup

cubito *sm* ❶ [*de hielo*] ice cube ❷ [*de caldo*] stock cube

cubo *sm* ❶ [*recipiente*] bucket • **un cubo de agua** a bucket of water ❷ GEOMETRÍA & MATEMÁTICAS cube • **un cubo de hielo** an ice cube • **elevar al cubo** to cube

cubrir *vt* ❶ [*generalmente*] to cover ❷ [*proteger*] to protect ❸ [*disimular*] to cover up ❹ [*puesto, vacante*] to fill

cucaracha *sf* roach

cuchara *sf* [*para comer*] spoon • **cuchara de palo** wooden spoon • **cuchara de postre** dessert spoon
meter la cuchara *familiar* to butt in

cucharada *sf* spoonful • **una cucharada de azúcar** a spoonful of sugar

cucharilla *sf* teaspoon

cucharón *sm* ladle

cuchichear *vi* to whisper • **cuchicheó algo al oído de Sonia** she whispered something into Sonia's ear

cuchilla *sf* blade ▶ **cuchilla de afeitar** razor blade

cuchillo *sm* knife ▶ **cuchillo de cocina** kitchen knife ▶ **cuchillo de trinchar** carving knife

cuchitril *sm* hovel

cuclillas ■ **en cuclillas** *locución adverbial* squatting • **ponerse en cuclillas** to squat (down)

cucurucho *sm* ❶ [*de papel*] paper cone ❷ [*para helado*] cone

cuello *sm* ❶ [*generalmente*] neck • **me duele el cuello** my neck hurts • **alargar el cuello** to stretch your neck ▶ **cuello de botella** bottleneck ▶ **cuello uterino** cervix ❷ [*de prendas*] collar • **el cuello de la camisa me queda apretado** the shirt collar is too tight for me ▶ **cuello en V** V-neck ▶ **cuello alto** turtleneck ▶ **cuello de tortuga** turtleneck
hablar para el cuello de su camisa *familiar* to talk to yourself

cuenca *sf* ❶ [*de río*] basin ❷ [*del ojo*] (eye) socket ❸ [*región minera*] coalfield

cuenco *sm* earthenware bowl

cuenta *sf* ❶ [*acción de contar*] count • **perder la cuenta** to lose count • **echar cuentas** to reckon up • **llevar/perder la cuenta de** to keep/lose count of ▶ **cuenta atrás** countdown ❷ [*cálculo*] sum ❸ *Banca & Comercio* account • **abonar algo en cuenta a alguien** to credit something to somebody's account • **pagar mil dólares a cuenta** to pay a thousand dollars down ▶ **cuenta de ahorros** savings account ▶ **cuenta corriente** checking account ▶ **cuenta de crédito** checking account with overdraft protection ▶ **cuenta deudora** overdrawn account ▶ **cuenta a plazo fijo** deposit account ❹ [*factura*] bill • **la cuenta del teléfono** the phone bill • **la cuenta, por favor** can I have the check, please • **pasar la cuenta** to send the bill ▶ **cuenta por cobrar/pagar** account receivable/payable ❺ [*bolita de collar, rosario*] bead

expresiones **a fin de cuentas** in the end ▶ **ajustarle a alguien las cuentas** to settle a score with somebody ▶ **caer en la cuenta de algo** to realize something ▶ **darse cuenta de algo** to realize something ▶ **más de la cuenta** too much ▶ **por mi/tu** *etc* **cuenta** on my/your *etc* own ▶ **tener en cuenta algo** to bear something in mind

cuentagotas *sm invariable* dropper
expresión **a** o **con cuentagotas** in dribs and drabs

cuentakilómetros *sm invariable* ❶ [*de distancia recorrida*] ≃ milometer ❷ [*de velocidad*] speedometer

cuentarrevoluciones *sm invariable* rev counter

cuento *sm* ❶ [*fábula*] tale ▶ **cuento de hadas** fairy tale ❷ [*narración*] short story • **cuéntame un cuento** tell me a story ❸ [*mentira, exageración*] story • **¡no me vengas con cuentos!** I don't want to hear your excuses • **¡puro cuento!** what nonsense! ▶ **cuento chino** tall story

expresión **ser el cuento de la lechera** to be wishful thinking ▶ **tener cuento** to put it on

cuerda *sf* ❶ [*para atar - fina*] string; [*- más gruesa*] rope • **afloja la cuerda** loosen the rope • **amarra el paquete con una cuerda** tie the package with some string • **saltar la cuerda** to jump rope ▶ **cuerda floja** tightrope ❷ [*de instrumento*] string • **se me rompió una cuerda de la guitarra** I broke a guitar string ❸ [*de reloj*] spring • **dar cuerda a un reloj** to wind a watch ❹ *Geometría* chord

cuerno *sm* ❶ [*generalmente*] horn ❷ [*de ciervo*] antler

expresión **saber a cuerno quemado** *familiar* to be fishy ▶ **¡vete al cuerno!** *familiar* go to hell!

cuero *sm* ❶ [*piel de animal*] skin ❷ [*piel curtida*] hide ▶ **cuero cabelludo** scalp • **en cueros, en cueros vivos** stark naked ❸ [*material*] leather • **guantes de cuero** leather gloves

cuerpo *sm* ❶ [*generalmente*] body • **el cuerpo humano** the human body • **cuerpo celeste** heavenly body • **a cuerpo** without a coat on • **luchar cuerpo a cuerpo** to fight hand-to-hand ❷ [*tronco*] trunk ❸ [*corporación consular, militar* etc] corps ▶ **cuerpo de bomberos** fire brigade ▶ **cuerpo diplomático** diplomatic corps

expresión **tomar cuerpo** to take shape ▶ **en cuerpo y alma** body and soul

el cuerpo humano

la arteria	the artery
la barbilla	the chin
la barriga	the stomach
la boca	the mouth
el brazo	the arm
el cabello	the hair
la cabeza	the head
la cadera	the hip
la ceja	the eyebrow
el cerebro	the brain
la cintura	the waist
el codo	the elbow
la columna vertebral	the spine
el corazón	the heart
la costilla	the rib
el cráneo	the skull
el cuello	the neck
el dedo	the finger
el dedo del pie	the toe
el diente	the tooth
el esófago	the esophagus
la espalda	the back
el estómago	the stomach
la frente	the forehead
el hígado	the liver
el hombro	the shoulder
el intestino	the intestine
la lengua	the tongue
la mandíbula	the jaw
la mano	the hand
la mejilla	the cheek
la muñeca	the wrist
el muslo	the thigh
las nalgas	the buttocks
la nariz	the nose
el ojo	the eye
el ombligo	the navel
la oreja	the ear
la pantorrilla	the calf
el párpado	the eyelid
el pecho	the chest
la pestaña	the eyelash
el pie	the foot
la pierna	the leg
el pulmón	the lung
el riñón	the kidney
la rodilla	the knee
el talón	the heel
el tobillo	the ankle
la uña	the nail
la vena	the vein
la vértebra	the vertebra

cuervo *sm* crow

cuesta *sf* slope • **esta cuesta es muy empinada** this is a very steep slope • **a cuestas** on your back • **cuesta arriba** uphill • **cuesta abajo** downhill • **ir cuesta abajo** to go downhill • **¿qué tal llevas la cuesta de enero?** are you managing to get through January?

cuestión *sf* ❶ [*pregunta*] question ❷ [*problema*] problem ❸ [*asunto*] issue • **en cuestión** at issue • **ser cuestión de** to be a question of

cuestionar *vt* to question

cuestionario *sm* questionnaire

cueva *sf* cave • **cueva de ladrones** den of thieves

cuidado ◆ *sm* care • **el cuidado de la piel** skin care • **con cuidado a)** [*con esmero*] carefully **b)** [*con cautela*] cautiously • **tener cuidado con** to be careful with • **ten cuidado al cruzar la calle** be careful crossing the street ◗ **cuidados intensivos** intensive care ⚲*incontable*

expresión eso me tiene o **trae sin cuidado** I couldn't care less about that

◆ *exclamación* • **¡cuidado!** careful!; look out!

cuidadoso, sa *adj* careful⚲*Los adjetivos ingleses son invariables.*

cuidar *vt* ❶ [*generalmente*] to look after • **¿quién va a cuidar del perro cuando estemos de vacaciones?** who is going to look after the dog while we're on vacation? ❷ [*estilo* ETC] to take care over • **deberías cuidar tu salud más** you should take better care of your health ❸ [*detalles*] to pay attention to

cuitlacoche *sm* corn smut

culata *sf* ❶ [*de arma*] butt ❷ [*de motor*] cylinder head

culebra *sf* snake

culinario, ria *adj* culinary⚲*Los adjetivos ingleses son invariables.*

culminar *vi* to finish • **el acto conmemorativo culminó con un baile popular** the commemorative ceremony finished with a popular dance

culo *sm familiar* ❶ [*de personas*] backside ❷ [*de objetos*] bottom

expresiones caerse de culo to be flabbergasted ◗ estar en el culo del mundo to be in the back of beyond ◗ ser un culo de mal asiento to be fidgety

culpa *sf* fault • **tener la culpa de algo** to be to blame for something • **yo tengo la culpa** it's my fault • **echar la culpa a alguien (de)** to blame somebody (for) • **por culpa de** because of

culpable ◆ *adj* • **culpable (de)** guilty (of) • **declararse culpable** to plead guilty⚲*Los adjetivos ingleses son invariables.*

◆ *smf* DERECHO guilty party • **tú eres el culpable** you're to blame

culpar *vt* • **culpar a alguien (de) a)** [*atribuir la culpa*] to blame somebody (for) **b)** [*acusar*] to accuse somebody (of)

cultivar *vt* ❶ [*tierra*] to farm • **cultivar la tierra** to farm the land ❷ [*plantas*] to grow • **cultiva lechugas en su jardín** she grows lettuce in her garden

cultivo *sm* ❶ [*de tierra*] farming • **el cultivo intensivo** intensive farming ❷ [*de plantas*] growing ❸ [*plantación*] crop

culto, ta *adj* ❶ [*persona*] educated • **una persona muy culta** a well-educated person ❷ [*estilo*] refined ❸ [*palabra*] literary⚲*Los adjetivos ingleses son invariables.*

■ **culto** *sm* ❶ [*devoción*] worship • **el culto al sol** sun worship • **libertad de culto** freedom of worship ❷ [*religión*] cult

cultura *sf* ❶ [*de sociedad*] culture • **la cultura popular** popular culture ❷ [*sabiduría*] knowledge • **cultura general** general knowledge

cultural *adj* cultural⚲*Los adjetivos ingleses son invariables.*

cumbre *sf* ❶ [*de montaña*] summit ❷ *figurado* [*punto culminante*] peak ❸ POLÍTICA summit (conference)

cumpleaños *sm invariable* birthday • **¡feliz cumpleaños!** happy birthday!

cumplido, da *adj* ❶ [*completo, lleno*] full ❷ [*cortés*] courteous⚲*Los adjetivos ingleses son invariables.*

■ **cumplido** *sm* compliment • **le hice un cumplido** I gave her a compliment • **andarse con cumplidos** to stand on ceremony • **visita de cumplido** courtesy call

cumplidor, ra *adj* reliable⚲*Los adjetivos ingleses son invariables.*

cumplimiento *sm* ❶ [*de un deber*] performance ❷ [*de contrato, promesa*] fulfillment ❸ [*de la ley*] observance ❹ [*de órdenes*] carrying out ❺ [*de condena*] completion ❻ [*de plazo*] expiry

cumplir ◆ *vt* ❶ [*orden*] to carry out ❷ [*promesa*] to keep • **no cumple sus promesas** she doesn't keep her promises ❸ [*ley*] to observe ❹ [*contrato*] to fulfill ❺ [*años*] to reach • **mañana cumplo los 20** it's my 20th birthday tomorrow ❻ [*condena*] to serve • **le faltan dos años para cumplir su condena** he has two years left to serve on his sentence ❼ [*servicio militar*] to do

◆ *vi* ❶ [*plazo, garantía*] to expire ❷ [*realizar el deber*] to do your duty • **considero haber cumplido contigo** I think I've done my duty by you • **cumplió con la tarea que le di** he carried out the task I gave him • **para o por cumplir** out of politeness • **cumplir con el deber** to do your duty • **cumplir con la palabra** to keep your word

cúmulo *sm* ❶ [*de objetos*] pile ❷ *figurado* [*de asuntos, acontecimientos*] series

cuna *sf* [*para dormir*] cradle

cundir *vi* ❶ [*propagarse*] to spread ❷ [*dar de sí - comida, reservas, tiempo*] to go a long way

cuneta *sf* ❶ [*de una carretera*] ditch ❷ [*de una calle*] gutter

cuña *sf* ❶ [*pieza*] wedge ❷ [*de publicidad*] commercial break

cuñado, da *sm, f* brother-in-law, *femenino* <u>sister-in-law</u>

cuota *sf* ❶ [*contribución - a entidad, club*] membership fee • **la cuota de socio anual** the yearly membership fee❷ [*cupo*] quota • **la cuota de exportación** the export quota ❸ [*peaje*] toll • **una carretera de cuota** a toll road

cupo ◆ *sm*❶ [*cantidad máxima*] quota ❷ [*cantidad proporcional*] share ❸ [*de una cosa racionada*] ration ❹ [*cabida*] capacity
◆ *v* → **caber**

cupón *sm* ❶ [*generalmente*] coupon ❷ [*de lotería, rifa*] ticket

cúpula *sf*❶ ARQUITECTURA dome ❷ *figurado* [*mandos*] leaders *pl*

cura ◆ *sm* priest
◆ *sf*❶ [*curación*] recovery ❷ [*tratamiento*] cure • **esa enfermedad no tiene cura** that illness doesn't have a cure ▶ **cura de emergencia** first aid ▶ **cura de reposo** rest cure

curación *sf*❶ [*de un enfermo - recuperación*] recovery; [*- tratamiento*] treatment ❷ [*de una herida*] healing ❸ [*de jamón*] curing

curado, da *adj* ❶ [*alimento*] cured ❷ [*pieles*] tanned ☼ *Los adjetivos ingleses son invariables.*
expresión **curado de espanto** unshockable

curandero, ra *sm, f* quack

curar ◆ *vt*❶ [*generalmente*] to cure ❷ [*herida*] to dress ❸ [*pieles*] to tan
◆ *vi*❶ [*enfermo*] to recover ❷ [*herida*] to heal up
■ **curarse** *v pronominal*❶ [*sanar*] • **curarse (de)** to recover (from) • **José tardó dos meses en curarse** José took two months to recover • **se curó de su enfermedad sin recurrir a ningún tratamiento** she recovered from her illness without having any treatment • **se me curó la herida rápidamente** my wound healed quickly ❷ [*alimento*] to cure

curiosear ◆ *vi*❶ [*fisgonear*] to nose around ❷ [*por una tienda*] to browse round
◆ *vt* [*libros, revistas*] to browse through

curiosidad *sf* curiosity • **sentir** o **tener curiosidad por** to be curious about

curioso, sa ◆ *adj*❶ [*por saber, averiguar*] inquisitive • **los alumnos son bastante curiosos** the students are pretty inquisitive ❷ [*raro*] strange • **¡qué curioso!** how strange ☼ *Los adjetivos ingleses son invariables.*
◆ *sm, f* onlooker

curita *sf* Band-Aid®

cursillo *sm* short course

cursiva → **letra**

curso *sm*❶ [*año académico*] year ❷ [*lecciones*] course • **quiero tomar un curso de francés** I want to take a French course ▶ **curso intensivo** crash course ▶ **curso por correspondencia** correspondence course ❸ [*dirección - de río, acontecimientos*] course; [*- de la economía*] trend • **seguir su curso** to go on; to continue • **el resfriado debe seguir su curso** you should allow the cold to run its course

cursor *sm* INFORMÁTICA cursor

curva *sf*❶ [*generalmente*] curve ❷ [*en carretera*] bend • **curva cerrada** sharp bend ▶ **curva de nivel** contour line

custodiar *vt*❶ [*vigilar*] to guard ❷ [*proteger*] to look after

cutáneo, a *adj* skin ☼ *Sólo se usa delante del sustantivo.*

cutícula *sf* cuticle

cutis *sm invariable* complexion

cutter (pl cutters) *sm* (artist's) scalpel *(with retractable blade)*

cuyo, ya *adj* [*posesión - por parte de personas*] whose; [*- por parte de cosas*] of which; whose • **esos son los amigos en cuya casa nos hospedamos** those are the friends in whose house we spent the night • **ese señor, cuyo hijo conociste ayer** that man, whose son you met yesterday • **un equipo cuya principal estrella...** a team the star player of which o whose star player... • **en cuyo caso** in which case ☼ *Los adjetivos ingleses son invariables.*

CV (*abreviatura de* currículum vitae) *sm* CV

D

d, D *sf* [*letra*] d ; D

D. *abreviatura escrita de* **don**

dactilar → **huella**

dado, da *adj* given • **en un momento dado** at a certain point • **ser dado a** to be fond of: ☀: *Los adjetivos ingleses son invariables.*

■ **dado** *sm* dice, *plural* <u>dice</u> • **echar o tirar los dados** to roll the dice • **jugar a los dados** to play dice

dálmata *adj* & *smf* [*perro*] Dalmatian: ☀: *Los adjetivos ingleses son invariables.*

daltónico, ca *adj* color-blind: ☀: *Los adjetivos ingleses son invariables.*

dama *sf* ❶ [*mujer*] lady • **damas y caballeros** ladies and gentlemen ▶ **primera dama a)** TEATRO leading lady **b)** POLÍTICA first lady ❷ [*en damas*] king ❸ [*en ajedrez, naipes*] queen

danta *sf* [*anta*] elk

danza *sf* ❶ [*generalmente*] dancing ❷ [*baile*] dance • **una danza tradicional** a traditional dance

dañar *vt* ❶ [*vista, cosecha*] to damage • **el tabaco daña la salud** tobacco damages your health ❷ [*persona*] to hurt ❸ [*pieza, objeto*] to damage • **dañó la mercancía** he damaged the merchandise

danzar *vi* ❶ [*bailar*] to dance ❷ *figurado* [*ir de un sitio a otro*] to run about

dañino, na *adj* harmful: ☀: *Los adjetivos ingleses son invariables.*

daño *sm* ❶ [*dolor*] hurt • **hacer daño a alguien** to hurt somebody • **hacerse daño** to hurt yourself ❷ [*perjuicio - a algo*] damage: ☀: *incontable*; [*- a persona*] harm • **el daño que el barco sufrió es leve** the damage that the boat suffered is slight ▶ **daños colaterales** collateral damage ▶ **daños y perjuicios** damages

---

dar

◆ *vt*

❶ [*ofrecer*] to give
• **dame un caramelo** give me a candy
• **¿te gusta? te lo doy** do you like it? you can have it
• **¿me da un kilo de papas?** could I have a kilogram of potatoes?

• **nos dio un beso a cada uno** he gave us all a kiss
• **dar una fiesta** to have a party

❷ [*comunicar un dato, relatar información*] to give
• **¿podrías darme un ejemplo?** could you give me an example?
• **¿quién te dio mi número de teléfono?** who gave you my phone number?

❸ [*ofrecer algo a alguien*] to give
• **me dio un buen consejo** he gave me a good piece of advice
• **no nos dio permiso para ir** he gave us permission to go

❹ [*producir*] to produce
• **esta tierra da mucho trigo** this land produces a lot of wheat
• **esta fuente ya no da agua** this fountain doesn't work any more

❺ [*indica la hora*] to strike
• **el reloj ha dado las dos** the clock struck two

❻ [*provocar un estado, una emoción, o una reacción*]
• **dar gusto/miedo/pena** to please/frighten/embarrass
• **dar risa** to make somebody laugh
• **dar escalofríos** to make somebody shiver

❼ *familiar* [*hacer que alguien pase un mal rato*]
• **me dio la tarde con sus preguntas** he didn't stop asking me questions until it was the afternoon

❽ [*con sustantivos*]
• **dar los buenos días** to say good morning
• **dar las gracias** to say thank you ; to thank
• **dar un paseo** to go for a walk
• **dar un grito** to shout
• **dar un empujón a alguien** to push somebody
• **dar prisa** to hurry

expresión **dar la lata** to bug ▶ **da lo mismo** it doesn't matter

◆ *vi*

❶ [*indica la hora*] to strike
• **acaban de dar las tres** it's just struck three

❷ [*seguido por un sustantivo, indica un estado*]
• **le dio un mareo/un ataque de nervios** he got seasick/an attack of nerves

expresión **dar de sí** to stretch • **la falda ha dado**

mucho de sí the skirt has stretched a lot ▶ **(que)**
dale *familiar* • **te digo que pares y tú ¡dale !** I told you to stop but you kept right on going

■ **dar a**
◆ *v + preposición*
[*estar orientado hacia*]
• **la fachada principal da al este** the front of the building faces east
• **la ventana da al patio** the window looks out onto the patio
• **la puerta da a la calle** the door opens onto the street

■ **dar con**
◆ *v + preposición*
• **he dado con la solución** I've found the solution
• **di con él al salir de aquí** I bumped into him on my way out of here

■ **dar contra**
◆ *v + preposición*
to hit
• **la piedra dio contra el cristal** the stone hit the glass

■ **dar de**
◆ *v + preposición*
❶ [*seguido por un infinitivo*] to give
• **¿les dieron de comer?** did they give you anything to eat?
• **le da de mamar a sus crías** it suckles its young
❷ [*seguido por un sustantivo*]
• **dar de golpes** to hit something repeatedly

■ **dar para**
◆ *v + preposición*
❶ [*ser suficiente*]
• **esa tela no da para una falda** there isn't enough cloth to make a skirt
❷ [*en expresiones*]
• **esta tarjeta de teléfono no da para más** there's no credit left on this phone card
• **no doy para más** I'm exhausted

■ **dar por**
◆ *v + preposición*
❶ [*adoptar una costumbre, una manía*]
• **le ha dado por dejarse la barba** he's suddenly decided that he wants to grow a beard
• **le ha dado por creerse Napoleón** he's taken to believing he's Napoleon
❷ [*considerar a algo o alguien como*]
• **con estas palabras dio la conversación por terminada** with these words he ended the conversation
• **lo doy por hecho** I'm taking it as a given
• **lo dieron por muerto** they thought he was dead

■ **dar que**
◆ *locución conjuntiva*
[*seguido por el infinitivo*]
• **esa historia dio mucho que hablar** that story led to a lot of discussion

■ **darse a**
◆ *v pronominal + preposición*

[*dedicarse a algo*]
• **darse a la bebida** to turn to drink

■ **darse de**
◆ *v pronominal + preposición*
[*considerarse como*]
• **se las da de listo** he thinks he's very clever
• **se las da de valiente** he pretends he's brave

■ **darse por**
◆ *v pronominal + preposición*
[*considerar*]
• **puedes darte por satisfecho** you can be pleased you were right
• **puedes darte por suspendido** you can consider yourself suspended

dardo *sm* dart

dátil *sm* date

dato *sm* [*generalmente*] piece of information • **un dato interesante** an interesting piece of information • **datos a)** [*generalmente*] information ⚡ *incontable* **b)** INFORMÁTICA data ⚡ *incontable* ▶ **datos personales** personal details ▶ **datos bancarios** bank details

dcha. (*abreviatura escrita de* derecha) rt.

d. de JC., d. C. AD

de
◆ *preposición*
❶ [*indica la pertenencia*]
• **el coche de mi padre** my father's car
• **esto es de Pepe** this is Pepe's
❷ [*indica la materia*]
• **un reloj de oro** a gold watch
❸ [*indica el contenido*]
• **una taza de té** a cup of tea
• **bebió un vaso de agua** he drank a glass of water
• **los libros de historia** history books
• **la clase de matemáticas** the math class
❹ [*indica una característica*]
• **un aparato de fácil manejo** a piece of equipment that's easy to use
• **un sello de veinte pesos** a twenty peso stamp
• **la señora de verde** the lady in green
❺ [*indica el objetivo*]
• **una bici de carreras** a racing bike
❻ [*indica la causa*]
• **llorar de alegría** to cry for joy
❼ [*indica la manera*]
• **de una sola vez** in one go
❽ [*indica el origen*] from
• **vengo de mi casa** I've come here from my house
• **salgo de mi casa muy temprano** I leave home very early
• **soy de Bilbao** I'm from Bilbao
• **es de buena familia** she's from a good family
❾ [*indica el momento*]
• **a las tres de la tarde** at three in the afternoon
• **llegamos de madrugada** we arrived very early in the morning
• **trabaja de noche y duerme de día** he works at night and sleeps during the day

• **de pequeño, comía muchos caramelos** when I was small, I used to eat lots of candy
❿ [*indica un punto de partida en el tiempo*]
• **de nueve a cinco** from nine to five
⓫ [*indica la profesión*]
• **trabaja de bombero** he's a firefighter
• **trabaja de mesero en un restaurante** he works as a waiter in a restaurant
⓬ [*indica el autor*] by
• **una película de Spielberg** a movie by Spielberg
⓭ [*en frases superlativas*] of
• **el mejor de todos** the best of them all
⓮ [*seguido por el infinitivo, expresa una condición*]
• **de haber querido ayudarme, lo habría hecho** if he had wanted to help me, he would have done
⓯ [*con valor enfático*]
• **el idiota de tu hermano** your idiot brother

debajo *adv* underneath • **debajo de** under • **ponte algo debajo de la chaqueta** put something on under your jacket • **pasar por debajo** to go under • **por debajo de lo normal** below normal

debate *sm* debate

debatir *vt* to debate

debe *sm* debit (side)

deber
◆ *vt*
❶ [*tener que pagar o proporcionar*] to owe
• **¿cuánto le debo?** how much do I owe you?
• **me debes al menos una explicación** at the very least, you owe me an explanation
❷ [*expresa una obligación moral, una necesidad*] must; should
• **debo hacerlo** I must do it
• **debes dominar tus impulsos** you must learn to control yourself
• **deberían abolir esa ley** they should abolish that law
• **deberías hacerlo** you should do it
◆ *sm*
duty
■ **deber de**
◆ *v + preposición*
[*expresa una suposición*]
• **deben de ser las siete** it must be seven o'clock
• **no debe de haber nadie en casa** there can't be anybody at home
• **debe de tener más de sesenta años** she must be over sixty
■ **deberes**
◆ *smpl*
homework ⚲ ː **incontable**

debidamente *adv* properly

debido, da *adj* [*justo, conveniente*] due • **a su debido tiempo** in due course • **como es debido** properly ⚲ː **Los adjetivos ingleses son invariables.**

débil *adj* ❶ [*persona - sin fuerzas*] weak ❷ [*voz, sonido*] faint ❸ [*luz*] dim ⚲ː **Los adjetivos ingleses son invariables.**

debilidad *sf* weakness • **la debilidad del puente lo hace peligroso** the weakness of the bridge makes it dangerous • **tener debilidad por** to have a soft spot for

debilitar *vt* to weaken

debutar *vi* to make your debut

década *sf* decade • **la década de los sesenta** the sixties

decadencia *sf* decadence

decaer *vi* ❶ [*generalmente*] to decline ❷ [*enfermo*] to get weaker ❸ [*salud*] to fail ❹ [*entusiasmo*] to flag ❺ [*restaurante* ETC] to go downhill

decaído, da *adj* ❶ [*desalentado*] gloomy ❷ [*débil*] frail ⚲ː **Los adjetivos ingleses son invariables.**

decena *sf* ten • **una decena de veces** about ten times

decencia *sf* ❶ [*generalmente*] decency ❷ [*en el vestir*] modesty ❸ [*dignidad*] dignity

decenio *sm* decade

decente *adj* ❶ [*generalmente*] decent ❷ [*en el comportamiento*] proper ❸ [*en el vestir*] modest ❹ [*limpio*] clean ⚲ː **Los adjetivos ingleses son invariables.**

decepción *sf* disappointment • **llevarse una decepción** to be disappointed

expresar su decepción

• **What a shame!** ¡Qué lástima!
• **It's a shame the concert's been cancelled.** Lástima que haya cancelado el concierto.
• **That's really bad luck!** ¡Eso sí que es tener mala suerte!
• **I wasn't expecting that.** No me lo esperaba.
• **I'd never have believed that of him.** Nunca me lo hubiera podido imaginar de él.

decepcionar *vt* to disappoint

decidido, da *adj* determined • **un hombre muy decidido** a very determined man • **está decidido a pasar el examen** he's determined to pass the exam ⚲ː **Los adjetivos ingleses son invariables.**

decidir ◆ *vt* ❶ [*generalmente*] to decide • **decidir hacer algo** to decide to do something • **decidió hacerlo después de todo** he decided to do it after all ❷ [*determinar*] to determine
◆ *vi* to decide

decimal *adj* [*sistema*] decimal ⚲ː **Los adjetivos ingleses son invariables.**

decir *vt* ❶ [*generalmente*] to say • **¿cómo se dice "estación" en inglés?** how do you say "estación" in English? • **¿que quiere decir esto?** what does this mean? • **dijo que no** he said no • **¿diga?, ¿dígame?** [*al teléfono*] hello? • **dime como te va** tell me how you're doing • **decir a alguien que haga algo** to tell somebody to do something • **se dice**

que they o people say (that) • **decir la verdad** to tell the truth ❸ *figurado* [*revelar*] to tell • **eso lo dice todo** that says it all ✦ *expresiones* **como quien dice, como si dijéramos** so to speak ▶ **decir para sí** to say to yourself ▶ **es decir** that is; that's to say ▶ **(o) mejor dicho** or rather ▶ **¡no me digas!** no way! ▶ **por así decir** so to speak ▶ **querer decir** to mean

decisión *sf* ❶ [*dictamen, resolución*] decision • **tomar una decisión** to make o take a decision ❷ [*empeño, tesón*] determination ❸ [*seguridad, resolución*] decisiveness

decisivo, va *adj* decisive ✧ *Los adjetivos ingleses son invariables.*

declaración *sf* ❶ [*generalmente*] statement ❷ [*de amor, guerra*] declaration • **una declaración de amor** a declaration of love • **prestar declaración** to give evidence ▶ **declaración de derechos** bill of rights ❸ [*de impuestos*] tax return • **tengo que hacer la declaración** I have to do my tax return • **declaración conjunta** joint tax return ▶ **declaración del impuesto sobre la renta** income tax return

declarar ✦ *vt* ❶ [*generalmente*] to declare • **acaban de declarar la guerra** they've just declared war ❷ [*afirmar*] to announce • **declaró que era inocente** he announced he was innocent • **declarar culpable/inocente a alguien** to find somebody guilty/not guilty • **lo declararon inocente** they found him not guilty

✦ *vi* Derecho to testify

declinar ✦ *vt* ❶ [*generalmente*] Gramática to decline ❷ [*responsabilidad*] to disclaim

✦ *vi* ❶ [*día, tarde*] to draw to a close ❷ [*fiebre*] to subside ❸ [*economía*] to decline

declive *sm* ❶ [*decadencia*] decline • **en declive** in decline ❷ [*pendiente*] slope

decodificador = **descodificador**

decoración *sf* ❶ [*acción*] decoration ❷ [*efecto*] décor ❸ [*adorno*] decorations *pl*

decorado *sm* Cine & Teatro set

decorar *vt* to decorate • **decoraron la sala para la Navidad** they decorated the room for Christmas

decorativo, va *adj* decorative ✧ *Los adjetivos ingleses son invariables.*

decreto *sm* decree ▶ **decreto ley** decree

dedal *sm* thimble

dedicación *sf* dedication

dedicar *vt* ❶ [*tiempo, dinero, energía*] to devote • **deberías dedicar más tiempo al estudio** you should devote more time to studying ❷ [*libro, monumento*] to dedicate • **le dedicó el poema a su hija** she dedicated the poem to her daughter

dedicatoria *sf* dedication • **le pedí que me escribiera una dedicatoria en su libro** I asked him to write a dedication to me in his book

dedo *sm* ❶ [*de la mano*] finger • **se cortó el dedo** he cut his finger • **contar con los dedos** to count on your fingers • **dos dedos de whisky** two fingers of whisky • **meterse el dedo en la nariz** to pick your

nose ▶ **dedo anular** ring finger ▶ **dedo corazón** middle finger ▶ **dedo gordo** o **pulgar** thumb ❷ [*del pie*] toe • **el dedo gordo del pie** the big toe ✦ *expresiones* **estar a dos dedos de** to be within an inch of ▶ **hacer dedo** *familiar* to hitchhike ▶ **no mover un dedo** not to lift a finger ▶ **nombrar a alguien a dedo** to handpick somebody ▶ **pillarse los dedos** *figurado* to get your fingers burnt ▶ **poner el dedo en la llaga** to put your finger on it

deducir *vt* ❶ [*inferir*] to guess ❷ [*descontar*] to deduct

defecto *sm* ❶ [*físico*] defect • **tu abrigo tiene un defecto en la manga** your coat has a defect on the sleeve ❷ [*moral*] fault • **es un defecto de su personalidad** it's a personality fault of his • **defecto de pronunciación** speech defect

defectuoso, sa *adj* ❶ [*mercancía*] faulty ❷ [*trabajo*] inaccurate ✧ *Los adjetivos ingleses son invariables.*

defender *vt* ❶ [*generalmente*] to defend ❷ [*amigo* Etc] to stand up for

defensa ✦ *sf* ❶ defense • **salió en mi defensa** he came to my defense • **defensa personal** self-defense ❷ bumper

✦ *smf* Deporte defender • **defensa central** centerback

defensivo, va *adj* defensive ✧ *Los adjetivos ingleses son invariables.*

■ **defensiva** *sf* • **ponerse/estar a la defensiva** to go/be on the defensive

defensor, ra ✦ *adj* → **abogado**

✦ *sm, f* ❶ [*generalmente*] defender ❷ [*abogado*] counsel for the defense ❸ [*adalid*] champion ▶ **defensor del pueblo** ≃ ombudsman

deficiente *adj* ❶ [*defectuoso - generalmente*] deficient • **una dieta deficiente en calcio** a diet deficient in calcium ❷ [*audición, vista*] defective ✧ *Los adjetivos ingleses son invariables.*

■ **deficiente (mental)** *smf* mentally handicapped person

déficit *sm invariable* Economía deficit

deficitario, ria *adj* ❶ [*empresa, operación*] lossmaking ❷ [*balance*] negative ✧ *Los adjetivos ingleses son invariables.*

definición *sf* ❶ [*generalmente*] definition • **por definición** by definition ❷ [*en televisión*] resolution

definir *vt* to define

definitivamente *adv* ❶ [*sin duda*] definitely ❷ [*para siempre*] for good

definitivo, va *adj* ❶ [*texto* Etc] definitive ❷ [*respuesta*] definite • **en definitiva** in short; anyway ✧ *Los adjetivos ingleses son invariables.*

deforestación *sf* deforestation

deformación *sf* ❶ [*de huesos, objetos* Etc] deformation ❷ [*de la verdad* Etc] distortion • **deformación física** (physical) deformity • **deformación profesional** • **soy profesor, es deformación profesional** I'm a teacher; I can't help myself

deformar *vt* ❶ [*huesos, objetos* ETC] to deform
• **quedó deformado después del accidente** he was left deformed after the accident ❷ *figurado* [*la verdad* ETC] to distort • **el espejo deforma la imagen** the mirror distorts the image

deforme *adj* ❶ [*cuerpo*] deformed ❷ [*imagen*] distorted ❸ [*objeto*] misshapen ❖ *Los adjetivos ingleses son invariables.*

defraudar *vt* ❶ [*decepcionar*] to disappoint ❷ [*estafar*] to defraud • **defraudar a Hacienda** to evade tax

degenerar *vi* • **degenerar (en)** to degenerate (into)
• **la manifestación degeneró en enfrentamientos con la policía** the demonstration degenerated into clashes with police

degradar *vt* ❶ [*moralmente*] to degrade ❷ [*de un cargo*] to demote

degustación *sf* tasting (of wines ETC)

dejadez *sf* ❶ [*abandono*] neglect ❷ [*en aspecto*] slovenliness

dejado, da *adj* ❶ [*abandonado*] careless ❷ [*aspecto*] slovenly ❖ *Los adjetivos ingleses son invariables.*

---

dejar
◆ *vt*
❶ [*depositar*] to leave
• **deja el libro en la mesa** leave the book on the table
• **dejé el abrigo en la entrada** I left my coat in the hall
• **dejaré la llave en la recepción** I'll leave the key at reception
❷ [*dar, confiar*]
• **dejarle algo a alguien** to leave somebody something
• **su abuelo le dejó mucho dinero** his grandfather left him a lot of money
❸ [*reservar*] to leave
• **deja un poco de café para mí** leave a bit of coffee for me
❹ [*prestar*] to leave
• **¿puedes dejarme la pluma/cien pesos?** can you lend me a pen/a hundred pesos?
❺ [*autorizar, permitir*]
• **deja que tu hijo venga con nosotros** let your son come with us
• **sus gritos no me dejaron dormir** their shouting didn't let me sleep
❻ [*abandonar*]
• **está triste porque su novia lo dejó** he's sad because his girlfriend left him
• **se negó a dejar a sus hijos** he refused to leave his children
• **lo obligaron a dejar el país** they forced him to leave the country
• **tuvo que dejar los estudios y ponerse a trabajar** he had to give up his studies and go out to work
❼ [*cesar de*]
• **ha dejado la bebida** he's stopped drinking
• **sin dejar de hablar** without stopping talking

❽ [*no molestar a alguien*]
• **¡déjame!, que tengo trabajo** stop interrupting! I have work to do
❾ [*no preocuparse por algo*]
• **déjalo, no importa** forget it, it's not important
❿ [*llevar a alguien a algún sitio*]
• **¿te puedo dejar en algún sitio? — sí, déjame en la estación, por favor** can I drop you off somewhere? — yes, drop me at the station, please
⓫ [*no omitir*]
• **lo copió todo, sin dejar una coma** he copied everything, without missing out even a comma
⓬ [*no hacer algo*]
• **dejó la cama sin hacer** he didn't make his bed
• **dejaron varias cuestiones por resolver** they've left a lot unanswered
⓭ [*cambiar el estado de algo o alguien*]
• **me dejó los zapatos como nuevos** he left my shoes looking like new again
• **con lo que me dijiste, me dejaste preocupado** what you said worried me
⓮ [*posponer, diferir una acción*]
• **dejó que terminara de llover para salir** he waited for it to stop raining before he went out
• **dejaremos la fiesta para cuando se encuentre bien** we'll postpone the party until he's feeling better
expresión **más vale dejarlo correr** just let it go
◆ *vi*
to leave
• **esta traducción deja mucho que desear** this translation leaves a lot to be desired
■ **dejar de**
◆ *v + preposición*
❶ [*cesar de hacer algo*] to stop
• **he decidido dejar de fumar** I've decided to stop smoking
• **¡deja de gritar!** stop shouting!
❷ [*asegurarse de hacer algo*]
• **¡no dejes de escribirme!** don't forget to write to me!
• **no dejaremos de venir a verte** we won't forget to come and visit you
■ **dejarse de**
◆ *v pronominal + preposición*
stop ❖ + *gerundio*
• **¡déjate de tonterías!** stop talking nonsense!

---

del → de

delantal *sm* apron

delante *adv* ❶ [*en primer lugar, en la parte delantera*] in front • **vaya delante** go in front • **el de delante** the one in front • **el asiento de delante** the seat in front ❷ [*enfrente*] opposite ❸ [*presente*] present

delantero, ra ◆ *adj* front • **la rueda delantera** the front wheel ❖ *Los adjetivos ingleses son invariables.*
◆ *sm, f* DEPORTE forward ▸ **delantero centro** center forward
■ **delantera** *sf* DEPORTE forwards *pl*
expresiones **coger** o **tomar la delantera** to take the lead

D

D

▶ **coger** o **tomar la delantera a alguien** to beat somebody to it ▶ **llevar la delantera** to be in the lead

delatar *vt* ❶ to denounce ❷ *figurado* [*sujeto: sonrisa, ojos* ETC] to betray

delator, ra *sm, f* informer

delegación *sf* ❶ [*autorización, embajada*] delegation • **delegación de poderes** devolution (of power) ❷ [*sucursal*] branch ❸ [*oficina pública*] local office ❹ [*comisaría*] precinct

delegado, da *sm, f* ❶ [*generalmente*] delegate • **delegado de curso** class representative ❷ COMERCIO representative

delegar *vt* • **delegar algo (en** o **a)** to delegate something (to)

deletrear *vt* to spell (out)

delfín *sm* dolphin

delgado, da *adj* ❶ [*generalmente*] thin ❷ [*esbelto*] slim ☝ *Los adjetivos ingleses son invariables.*

delicadeza *sf* ❶ [*miramiento - con cosas*] care; [- *con personas*] thoughtfulness • **tener la delicadeza de** to be thoughtful enough to ❷ [*finura - de perfume, rostro*] delicacy; [- *de persona*] sensitivity ❸ [*de un asunto, situación*] delicacy

delicado, da *adj* ❶ [*generalmente*] delicate • **¡que manos tan delicadas!** what delicate hands! ❷ [*perfume, gusto*] subtle ❸ [*paladar*] refined ❹ [*persona - sensible*] sensitive; [- *muy exigente*] fussy; [- *educado*] polite • **tengo la piel muy delicada** my skin is very sensitive • **tienes que aprender a ser más delicado** you should learn to be more tactful • **estar delicado de salud** to be very weak ☝ *Los adjetivos ingleses son invariables.*

delicia *sf* delight

delicioso, sa *adj* ❶ [*comida*] delicious ❷ [*persona*] lovely ☝ *Los adjetivos ingleses son invariables.*

delincuencia *sf* crime • **la delincuencia es un problema en este barrio** crime is a problem in this area ▶ **delincuencia juvenil** juvenile delinquency

delincuente *smf* criminal ▶ **delincuente habitual** habitual offender ▶ **delincuente juvenil** juvenile delinquent

delirar *vi* ❶ [*un enfermo*] to be delirious ❷ [*desbarrar*] to talk nonsense

delirio *sm* ❶ [*por la fiebre*] delirium ❷ [*de un enfermo mental*] ravings *pl* ▶ **delirios de grandeza** delusions of grandeur • **con delirio** madly

delito *sm* crime; offence • **lo que estoy haciendo no es un delito** what I'm doing isn't a crime ▶ **delito común** common law offence ▶ **delito ecológico** ecological crime ▶ **delito fiscal** tax offence ▶ **delito informático** computer crime

delta *sm, f* delta

demanda *sf* ❶ [*petición*] request ❷ [*reivindicación*] demand • **en demanda de** asking for ▶ **demanda salarial** wage claim ❸ ECONOMÍA demand • **ese juguete tiene mucha demanda** that toy is in great demand ❹ DERECHO lawsuit ❺ [*por daños y perjuicios*] claim • **presentar una demanda contra** to take legal action against

demandar *vt* ❶ DERECHO • **demandar a alguien (por)** to sue somebody (for) ❷ [*pedir*] to demand • **la música demanda mucha práctica** music demands a lot of practice

demás ◆ *adj* other • **los demás invitados** the other guests ☝ *Los adjetivos ingleses son invariables.*
◆ *pronombre* • **lo demás** the rest • **lo demás es para mañana** the rest is for tomorrow • **todo lo demás** everything else • **estudia esto e ignora todo lo demás** study this and ignore everything else • **los/las demás** the others • **por lo demás** apart from that • **y demás** and so on

demasiado, da ◆ *adj* too much, *plural* too many • **demasiada comida** too much food • **le pusiste demasiada sal** you put too much salt on it • **demasiados niños** too many children • **siempre hay demasiada gente** there are always too many people ☝ *Los adjetivos ingleses son invariables.*
◆ *adv* ❶ [*generalmente*] too much ❷ ☝ *antes de adj o adv* too • **habla demasiado** she talks too much • **hablas francés demasiado rápido para mí** you speak French too quickly for me • **iba demasiado rápido** he was going too fast

democracia *sf* democracy, *plural* democracies

demócrata ◆ *adj* democratic ☝ *Los adjetivos ingleses son invariables.*
◆ *smf* democrat

democrático, ca *adj* democratic ☝ *Los adjetivos ingleses son invariables.*

demografía *sf* demography

demoler *vt* ❶ [*edificio*] to demolish ❷ *figurado* to destroy

demolición *sf* demolition

demonio *sm literal & figurado* devil • **estos alumnos son unos pequeños demonios** these students are little devils

expresión **de mil demonios** a hell of a... • **un pesado de mil demonios** one hell of a bore ▶ **¿qué/dónde demonios...?** what/where the hell...?

demora *sf* delay • **tenemos que hacerlo sin demora** we have to do it without delay

demorar ◆ *vt* ❶ [*retrasar*] to delay ❷ [*tardar*] • **demoraron tres días en hacerlo** it took them three days to do it • **demora una hora para vestirse** it takes her one hour to get dressed
◆ *vi* [*tardar*] • **¡no demores!** don't be late! • **nos estamos demorando mucho** we're taking too long

demostración *sf* ❶ [*generalmente*] demonstration • **tenían varios aparatos de demostración** they had several pieces of equipment for demonstration • **hacer una demostración a)** [*de cómo funciona algo*] to demonstrate **b)** [*de gimnasia* ETC] to put on a display • **demostración de afecto** show of affection ❷ [*de un teorema*] proof ❸ [*exhibición*] display ❹ [*señal*] sign ❺ [*prueba*] proof

demostrar *vt* ❶ [*hipótesis, teoría, verdad*] to prove • **ha demostrado su habilidad** she's proven her ability ❷ [*alegría, impaciencia, dolor*] to show • **demostró interés** she showed interest ❸ [*funcionamiento,* *procedimiento*] to demonstrate • **ahora vamos a demostrar cómo funciona** now we shall demonstrate how it works

denominador *sm* denominator ▸ **denominador común** *figurado* MATEMÁTICAS common denominator

densidad *sf* density ▸ **densidad de población** population density

denso, sa *adj* ❶ [*generalmente*] dense • **un libro denso** a heavy book ❷ [*líquido*] thick • **un líquido denso** a thick liquid

dentadura *sf* teeth *pl* • **tiene la dentadura muy buena** she has very good teeth ▸ **dentadura postiza** false teeth *pl*

dentera *sf* • **dar dentera a alguien** to set somebody's teeth on edge

dentífrico, ca *adj* • **pasta dentífrica** toothpaste ■ **dentífrico** *sm* toothpaste

dentista *smf* dentist

dentro *adv* ❶ inside • **no sé que hay dentro** I don't know what's inside • **está ahí dentro** it's in there • **hacia / para dentro** inwards • **por dentro** (on the) inside • **límpialo por dentro** clean it on the inside ❷ *figurado* inside; deep down

denuncia *sf* ❶ [*acusación*] accusation ❷ [*condena*] denunciation ❸ [*a la policía*] complaint • **presentar una denuncia contra** to file a complaint against

denunciar *vt* ❶ to condemn • **denunciaron el abuso de poder** they condemned the abuse of power ❷ [*delito*] to report • **denunció el crimen a las 3:15** he reported the crime at 3:15

departamento *sm* ❶ [*generalmente*] department ❷ [*división territorial*] administrative district ❸ [*de maleta, cajón, tren*] compartment

dependencia *sf* ❶ [*de una persona*] dependence ❷ [*de país, drogas, alcohol*] dependency ❸ [*departamento*] section ❹ [*sucursal*] branch

depender *vi* to depend • **depende…** it depends…

dependiente ◆ *adj* dependent • **un organismo dependiente del gobierno central** a body which forms part of the central government ۞ *Los adjetivos ingleses son invariables.*
◆ *sm* salesperson

depilar *vt* ❶ [*generalmente*] to remove the hair from ❷ [*cejas*] to pluck ❸ [*con cera*] to wax

deplorable *adj* ❶ [*suceso, comportamiento*] deplorable ❷ [*aspecto*] sorry ۞ *Los adjetivos ingleses son invariables.*

deponer *vt* ❶ [*abandonar - actitud*] to drop; to set aside ❷ [*las armas*] to lay down ❸ [*destituir - ministro, secretario*] to remove from office; [*- líder, rey*] to depose

deportar *vt* to deport

deporte *sm* sport • **mi deporte preferido es el futbol** my favorite sport is soccer • **hacer deporte** to do o practice sports • **hacer deporte es bueno para la salud** sport is good for your health • **practicar un deporte** to practice a sport ▸ **deportes de competición** competitive sports ▸ **deportes extremos** extreme sports ▸ **deportes naúticos** water sports

los deportes

el atletismo	track and field
el basquetbol	basketball
el béisbol	baseball
el boxeo	boxing
la equitación	horseriding
la esgrima	fencing
el esquí	skiing
el futbol	soccer
el futbol americano	football
el golf	golf
el hockey sobre hielo	hockey
el judo	judo
la natación	swimming
el patinaje sobre hielo	ice-skating
el piragüismo	canoeing
el rugby	rugby
el tenis	tennis
el tenis de mesa	table-tennis
la vela	sailing
el voleibol	volleyball
el windsurf	windsurfing

deportista *sm, f* sportsman, *femenino* sportswoman

depositar *vt* ❶ [*generalmente*] to leave • **deposite su basura aquí** leave your garbage here ❷ [*en el banco* ETC] to deposit • **tienes que depositar el dinero antes de las tres** you have to deposit the money before three o'clock

depósito *sm* ❶ [*almacén - de mercancías*] store; warehouse; [*- de armas*] dump ▸ **depósito de cadáveres** morgue; mortuary ❷ [*recipiente*] tank ▸ **depósito de agua a)** [*cisterna*] water tank **b)** [*embalse*] reservoir ❸ [*de dinero*] deposit

depreciar *vt* to (cause to) depreciate

depredador, ra ◆ *adj* predatory ۞ *Los adjetivos ingleses son invariables.*
◆ *sm, f* predator

depresión *sf* depression ▸ **depresión nerviosa** nervous breakdown ▸ **depresión posparto** postnatal depression

depresivo, va ◆ *adj* ❶ PSICOLOGÍA depressive ❷ [*deprimente*] depressing ۞ *Los adjetivos ingleses son invariables.*
◆ *sm, f* depressive

deprimido, da *adj* depressed ۞ *Los adjetivos ingleses son invariables.*

deprimir *vt* to depress

deprisa, de prisa *adv* quickly • **hazlo deprisa** do it quickly • **¡deprisa!** quick!

depuración *sf* ❶ [*de agua, metal, gas*] purification ❷ *figurado* [*de organismo, sociedad*] purge

depurar *vt* ❶ [*agua, metal, gas*] to purify ❷ *figurado* [*organismo, sociedad*] to purge

derecha *sf* ❶ [*contrario de izquierda*] right • **a la derecha** to the right • **tienes que doblar a la derecha** you have to turn to the right • **María está sentada a la derecha de Juan** María is seated to the right of Juan • **de la derecha** on the right • **abre esa puerta, la de la derecha** open that door, the one on the right ❷ POLÍTICA right (wing) • **ser de derechas** to be right-wing

derecho, cha ◆ *adj* ❶ [*diestro*] right • **el margen derecho** the right-hand margin ❷ [*vertical*] upright • **siempre anda muy derecha** she always walks with a very upright posture ❸ [*recto*] straight: ♀ *Los adjetivos ingleses son invariables.*

◆ *adv* ❶ [*en posición vertical*] upright ❷ [*en línea recta*] straight • **todo derecho** straight ahead • **siga todo derecho y llegará al museo** continue straight ahead and you'll come to the museum ❸ [*directamente*] straight • **se fue derecha a casa** she went straight home

■ **derecho** *sm* ❶ [*leyes, estudio*] law • **un estudiante de derecho** a law student ▶ **derecho canónico/fiscal** canon/tax law ❷ [*prerrogativa*] right • **con derecho a** with a right to • **de pleno derecho** fully-fledged • **hacer valer sus derechos** to exercise your rights • **¡no hay derecho!** it's not fair! • **reservado el derecho de admisión** the management reserves the right of admission ▶ **derecho de asilo** right of asylum ▶ **derecho de réplica** right to reply ▶ **el derecho al voto** the right to vote ▶ **los derechos humanos** human rights ❸ [*de una tela, prenda*] right side • **del derecho** right side out

deriva *sf* drift • **a la deriva** adrift • **ir a la deriva** to drift

derivar ◆ *vt* ❶ [*desviar*] to divert ❷ MATEMÁTICAS to derive

◆ *vi* [*desviarse*] to change direction

derramamiento *sm* spilling • **derramamiento de sangre** bloodshed

derramar *vt* ❶ [*por accidente*] to spill ❷ [*verter*] to pour

derrame *sm* ❶ MEDICINA discharge ❷ [*de líquido*] spilling ❸ [*de sangre*] shedding

derrapar *vi* to skid

derretir *vt* ❶ [*generalmente*] to melt ❷ [*nieve*] to thaw

derribar *vt* ❶ [*construcción*] to demolish • **derribaron un edificio viejo** they demolished an old building • **derribé a otro niño porque no lo vi** I knocked down another boy because I didn't see him ❷ [*hacer caer - árbol*] to fell • [- *avión*] to bring down ❸ [*gobierno, gobernante*] to overthrow • **quieren derribar al gobierno** they want to overthrow the government

derrocar *vt* ❶ [*gobierno*] to overthrow ❷ [*ministro*] to oust

derrochar *vt* to squander

derroche *sm* waste

derrota *sf* defeat

derrotar *vt* to defeat

derrumbamiento *sm* ❶ [*de puente, edificio - por accidente*] collapse; [- *intencionado*] demolition ❷ *figurado* [*de imperio*] fall ❸ [*de empresa* ETC] collapse

derrumbar *vt* [*puente, edificio*] to demolish

desabotonar *vt* to unbutton

desabrochar *vt* to undo • **tienes los pantalones desabrochados** your pants are undone

desaconsejar *vt* • **desaconsejar algo (a alguien)** to advise (somebody) against something • **desaconsejar a alguien que haga algo** to advise somebody not to do something

desactivar *vt* to defuse

desacuerdo *sm* disagreement

expresar su desacuerdo

• **I (completely) disagree with you.** No estoy (en absoluto) de acuerdo contigo.
• **I don't agree.** Pienso diferente.
• **Whatever!** ¡Qué disparate!
• **You can't be serious!** ¿No lo estás diciendo en serio?
• **I don't believe it.** ¡No es verdad!
• **I'm afraid you can't compare the two cases.** Me temo que ambos casos no son comparables.

desafiar *vt* ❶ [*persona*] to challenge • **el héroe desafió a su enemigo** the hero challenged his enemy • **desafiar a alguien a algo/a que haga algo** to challenge somebody to something/to do something ❷ [*peligro*] to defy • **los bomberos desafían a la muerte todos los días** firefighters defy death every day

desafinar *vi* MÚSICA to be out of tune

desafío *sm* challenge

desafortunadamente *adv* unfortunately

desafortunado, da *adj* ❶ [*generalmente*] unfortunate ❷ [*sin suerte*] unlucky: ♀ *Los adjetivos ingleses son invariables.*

desagradable *adj* unpleasant • **¡no seas tan desagradable!** don't be so unpleasant! ♀ *Los adjetivos ingleses son invariables.*

desagradar *vi* to displease • **su actitud le desagradó** he was displeased at her attitude

desagradecido, da *sm, f* ungrateful person

desagüe *sm* ❶ [*vaciado*] drain ❷ [*cañería*] drainpipe

desahogado, da *adj* ❶ [*de espacio*] spacious ❷ [*de dinero*] well-off: ♀ *Los adjetivos ingleses son invariables.*

desahogar *vt* ❶ [*ira*] to vent • **Esther desahogó todos sus problemas con su madre** Esther vented all her problems to her mother ❷ [*pena*] to relieve

desahogo *sm* ❶ [*moral*] relief ❷ [*de espacio*] space ❸ [*económico*] ease

desahuciar *vt* ❶ [*inquilino*] to evict ❷ [*enfermo*] • **desahuciar a alguien** to give up all hope of saving somebody

desajuste *sm* ❶ [*de piezas*] misalignment ❷ [*de máquina*] breakdown ❸ [*de declaraciones*] inconsistency ❹ [*económico* ETC] imbalance

desalojar *vt* ❶ [*edificio, personas*] to evacuate ❷ [*inquilinos*] to evict ❸ [*por propia voluntad*] to abandon

desangrar *vt* ❶ [*animal, persona*] to bleed ❷ *figurado* [*económicamente*] to bleed dry

desanimado, da *adj* [*persona*] downhearted ℹ *Los adjetivos ingleses son invariables.*

desanimar *vt* to discourage • **la falta de dinero nos desanimó** the lack of money discouraged us

desánimo *sm* ❶ [*generalmente*] dejection ❷ [*depresión*] depression

desapacible *adj* unpleasant ℹ *Los adjetivos ingleses son invariables.*

desaparecer *vi* ❶ [*generalmente*] to disappear ❷ [*en guerra, accidente*] to go missing

desaparecido, da *sm, f* missing person

desaparición *sf* disappearance

desapercibido, da *adj* • **pasar desapercibido** to go unnoticed ℹ *Los adjetivos ingleses son invariables.*

desaprensivo, va *sm, f* unscrupulous person

desaprobar *vt* ❶ [*generalmente*] to disapprove of ❷ [*un plan* ETC] to reject

desaprovechar *vt* to waste

desarmador *sm* ❶ [*herramienta*] screwdriver ❷ [*cóctel*] vodka and orange

desarmar *vt* ❶ [*generalmente*] to disarm • **el policía desarmó con facilidad al pistolero** the police officer easily disarmed the gunman ❷ [*desmontar*] to take apart • **desarmamos el juguete para arreglarlo** we took the toy apart in order to fix it

desarme *sm* MILITAR disarmament

desarreglar *vt* ❶ [*armario, pelo*] to mess up ❷ [*planes, horario*] to upset

desarreglo *sm* ❶ [*de cuarto, persona*] untidiness ❷ [*de vida*] disorder

desarrollado, da *adj* developed ℹ *Los adjetivos ingleses son invariables.*

desarrollar *vt* ❶ [*mejorar - crecimiento, país*] to develop • **desarrolló los músculos de sus brazos** he developed his arm muscles ❷ [*exponer - teoría, tema, fórmula*] to expound ❸ [*realizar - actividad, trabajo*] to carry out • **desarrolla un trabajo indispensable** she carries out indispensable work

desarrollo *sm* ❶ [*mejora*] development • **países en vías de desarrollo** developing countries ❷ [*crecimiento*] development • **el desarrollo de las niñas comienza antes que el de los niños** girls' development begins before that of boys ❸ [*de idea, argumento, acontecimiento*] development

desarticular *vt* ❶ [*huesos*] to dislocate ❷ *figurado* [*organización, banda*] to break up ❸ [*plan*] to foil

desastre *sm* disaster • **su madre es un desastre** her mother is hopeless • **¡vas hecho un desastre!** you look a mess ▸ **desastre natural** natural disaster

desastroso, sa *adj* disastrous ℹ *Los adjetivos ingleses son invariables.*

desatar *vt* ❶ [*nudo, lazo*] to untie • **desatamos al perro** we untied the dog • **ayúdame a desatar este nudo** help me undo this knot ❷ [*paquete*] to undo ❸ [*animal*] to unleash ❹ *figurado* [*tormenta, iras, pasión*] to unleash ❺ [*entusiasmo*] to arouse ❻ [*lengua*] to loosen

■ **desatarse** *v pronominal* ❶ [*nudo, lazo*] to come undone • **se desató el nudo** the knot came undone ❷ [*tormenta*] to break • **se desató una tormenta muy violenta** a very violent storm broke ❸ [*ira, cólera*] to erupt

desatascar *vt* to unblock

desautorizar *vt* ❶ [*desmentir - noticia*] to deny ❷ [*prohibir - manifestación, huelga*] to ban ❸ [*desacreditar*] to discredit

desayunar ✦ *vi* to have breakfast • **ya es hora de desayunar** it's time to have breakfast

✦ *vt* to have for breakfast • **¿quieres desayunar algo?** would you like to have some breakfast?

desayuno *sm* breakfast ▸ **desayuno continental** continental breakfast ▸ **desayuno de trabajo** working breakfast

desbancar *vt figurado* to oust

desbandada *sf* breaking up • **a la desbandada** in great disorder

desbarajuste *sm* disorder

desbloquear *vt* ❶ [*cuenta*] to unfreeze ❷ [*país*] to lift the blockade on ❸ [*negociación*] to end the deadlock in

desbordar *vt* ❶ [*cauce, ribera*] to overflow ❷ [*límites, previsiones*] to exceed ❸ [*paciencia*] to push beyond the limit

descabalgar *vi* to dismount

descabellado, da *adj* crazy ℹ *Los adjetivos ingleses son invariables.*

descalabro *sm* setback

descalificar *vt* ❶ [*en una competición*] to disqualify ❷ [*desprestigiar*] to discredit

descalzar *vt* • **descalzar a alguien** to take somebody's shoes off

■ **descalzarse** *v pronominal* to take off your shoes • **por favor descálzense antes de entrar** please take your shoes off before entering

descalzo, za *adj* barefoot • **me gusta correr descalzo por la playa** I like to run barefoot on the beach ℹ *Los adjetivos ingleses son invariables.*

descaminado, da *adj figurado* • **ir descaminado** to be on the wrong track ℹ *Los adjetivos ingleses son invariables.*

descampado *sm* open country

descansar ✦ *vi* ❶ [*reposar*] to rest • **descansamos durante las vacaciones** we rested during our vacation ❷ [*dormir*] to sleep • **¡que descanses!** sleep well!

✦ *vt* ❶ to rest • **descansar la vista** to rest your eyes • **descansa la cabeza en mi hombro** rest your head on my shoulder ❷ [*dormir*] to sleep

descansillo *sm* landing

descanso *sm* ❶ [*reposo*] rest • **necesito un buen descanso** I need a good rest • **tomarse un descanso** to take a rest ▶ **día de descanso** day off ❷ [*pausa*] break • **vamos a hacer un descanso de diez minutos** we're going to take a ten minute break ❸ CINE & TEATRO intermission • **esta obra de teatro tiene un descanso de cinco minutos** this play has a five minute intermission ❹ DEPORTE half-time ❺ [*de escalera*] landing • **hay una papelera en el descanso de la escalera** there is a wastepaper basket on the staircase landing ❻ *figurado* [*alivio*] relief

descapotable *adj* & *sm* convertible ☿ *Los adjetivos ingleses son invariables.*

descarado, da *adj* ❶ [*desvergonzado*] cheeky ❷ [*flagrante*] barefaced ☿ *Los adjetivos ingleses son invariables.*

descarga *sf* ❶ [*de mercancías*] unloading ❷ [*de electricidad*] shock ❸ [*disparo*] shots *pl* ❹ INFORMÁTICA download

descargar *vt* ❶ [*vaciar - mercancías, pistola*] to unload • **descargaron la mercadería** they unloaded the merchandise ❷ [*disparar - munición, arma, ráfaga*] • **descargar (sobre)** to fire (at) • **descargó su arma sobre víctimas inocentes** he fired his weapon at innocent victims ❸ ELECTRICIDAD to run down ❹ INFORMÁTICA to download • **descarga muchos programas de Internet** she downloads many programs from the Internet

■ **descargarse** *v pronominal* ❶ [*desahogarse*] • **descargarse con alguien** to take it out on somebody ❷ ELECTRICIDAD to go flat • **se descargó la batería del coche** the car battery went flat

descaro *sm* cheek

descarrilamiento *sm* derailment

descarrilar *vi* to be derailed

descartar *vt* ❶ [*ayuda*] to refuse ❷ [*posibilidad*] to rule out

descendencia *sf* ❶ [*hijos*] offspring ❷ [*linaje*] lineage

descender *vi* ❶ [*en estimación*] to go down • **descender a segunda** to be relegated to the second division ❷ [*cantidad, valor, temperatura, nivel*] to drop • **descendió la temperatura** the temperature dropped

descenso *sm* ❶ [*en el espacio*] descent • **el descenso de esta montaña es muy peligroso** the descent from this mountain is very dangerous ❷ [*de cantidad, temperatura, nivel*] fall • **un fuerte descenso de los precios** a sharp fall in prices

descentralizar *vt* to decentralize

descentrar *vt* ❶ [*sacar del centro*] to knock off-center ❷ *figurado* [*desconcentrar*] to distract

descifrar *vt* ❶ [*clave, mensaje*] to decipher ❷ [*motivos, intenciones*] to work out ❸ [*misterio*] to solve ❹ [*problemas*] to puzzle out

descodificador, decodificador *sm* decoder

descolgar *vt* ❶ [*una cosa colgada*] to take down • **descolgamos todos los cuadros** we took down all the pictures ❷ [*teléfono*] to pick up • **descuelga el teléfono** pick up the telephone

■ **descolgarse** *v pronominal* [*bajar*] • **descolgarse (por algo)** to slide down (something)

descolorido, da *adj* faded ☿ *Los adjetivos ingleses son invariables.*

descomponer *vt* ❶ [*pudrir - fruta*] to rot; [- *cadáver*] to decompose ❷ [*dividir*] to break down • **descomponer algo en** to break something down into ❸ [*desordenar*] to mess up ❹ [*estropear*] to damage

■ **descomponerse** *v pronominal* ❶ [*pudrirse - fruta*] to rot; [- *cadáver*] to decompose ❷ [*averiarse*] to break down

descomposición *sf* ❶ [*de elementos*] decomposition ❷ [*putrefacción - de fruta*] rotting; [- *de cadáver*] decomposition ❸ [*alteración*] distortion

descompostura *sf* ❶ [*falta de mesura*] lack of respect; rudeness ❷ [*avería*] breakdown

descompuesto, ta ◆ *participio pasado* → **descomponer**

◆ *adj* ❶ [*putrefacto - fruta*] rotten; [- *cadáver*] decomposed ❷ [*alterado - rostro*] distorted ❸ [*mecanismo, máquina*] broken ☿ *Los adjetivos ingleses son invariables.*

descomunal *adj* enormous ☿ *Los adjetivos ingleses son invariables.*

desconcentrar *vt* to distract

desconcertante *adj* disconcerting ☿ *Los adjetivos ingleses son invariables.*

desconcertar *vt* to disconcert

desconcierto *sm* ❶ [*desorden*] disorder ❷ [*desorientación, confusión*] confusion

desconectar *vt* ❶ [*aparato*] to switch off ❷ [*línea*] to disconnect ❸ [*desenchufar*] to unplug

desconfianza *sf* distrust

desconfiar ■ **desconfiar de** *vi* ❶ [*sospechar de*] to distrust • **desconfío de sus palabras** I distrust his words • **desconfía hasta de su propia sombra** he doesn't even trust his own shadow ❷ [*no confiar en*] to have no faith in

descongelar *vt* ❶ [*producto*] to thaw ❷ [*nevera*] to defrost ❸ *figurado* [*precios*] to free ❹ [*créditos, salarios*] to unfreeze

descongestionar *vt* ❶ MEDICINA to clear ❷ *figurado* [*calle, centro de ciudad*] to make less congested • **descongestionar el tráfico** to reduce congestion

desconocer *vt* ❶ [*ignorar*] to be unfamiliar with • **desconocen el tema** they are unfamiliar with the subject ❷ [*no conocer*] not to recognize • **la desconocí con esa ropa moderna** I didn't recognize her in those trendy clothes

desconocido, da ◆ *adj* [*no conocido*] unknown • **una actriz desconocida ganó el premio** an unknown actress won the award ☿ *Los adjetivos ingleses son invariables.*

◆ *sm, f* stranger

desconocimiento *sm* ignorance

desconsiderado, da *adj* inconsiderate ☿ *Los adjetivos ingleses son invariables.*

desconsolar *vt* to distress

desconsuelo *sm* distress

descontado, da *adj* discounted ☼ *Los adjetivos ingleses son invariables.*

descontar *vt* ❶ [*una cantidad*] to deduct • **desconté 100 pesos de la deuda** I deducted 100 pesos from the debt ❷ COMERCIO to discount

desconvocar *vt* to cancel

descorazonador, ra *adj* discouraging ☼ *Los adjetivos ingleses son invariables.*

descorchar *vt* to uncork

descortés *adj* rude ☼ *Los adjetivos ingleses son invariables.*

descremado, da *adj* skimmed ☼ *Los adjetivos ingleses son invariables.*

describir *vt* to describe

descripción *sf* description

descubierto, ta ✦ *participio pasado* → descubrir

✦ *adj* ❶ [*generalmente*] uncovered ❷ [*coche*] open ❸ [*cielo*] clear ❹ [*sin sombrero*] bareheaded ☼ *Los adjetivos ingleses son invariables.*

■ **descubierto** *sm* FINANZAS [*de empresa*] deficit; [*de cuenta bancaria*] overdraft

descubrimiento *sm* ❶ [*de continentes, invenciones*] discovery ❷ [*de placa, busto*] unveiling ❸ [*de complots*] uncovering ❹ [*de asesinos*] detection

descubrir *vt* ❶ [*generalmente*] to discover • **descubrieron una isla desierta** they discovered a desert island ❷ [*petróleo*] to strike ❸ [*complot*] to uncover • **descubrí el desfalco** I uncovered the embezzlement ❹ [*destapar - estatua, placa*] to unveil • **la novia descubrió su rostro** the bride unveiled her face ❺ [*vislumbrar*] to spot ❻ [*delatar*] to give away

descuento *sm* discount • **un descuento del 10%** a 10% discount • **hacer descuento** to give a discount • **me hicieron un 15% de descuento** they gave me a 15% discount • **con descuento** at a discount

descuidado, da *adj* ❶ [*desaseado - persona, aspecto*] untidy; [- *jardín*] neglected ❷ [*negligente*] careless ❸ [*distraído*] off your guard ☼ *Los adjetivos ingleses son invariables.*

descuidar ✦ *vt* [*desatender*] to neglect • **el alumno descuidó sus notas** the student neglected his grades

✦ *vi* [*no preocuparse*] not to worry • **descuida, que yo me encargo** don't worry, I'll take care of it

descuido *sm* ❶ [*falta de aseo*] carelessness ❷ [*olvido*] oversight ❸ [*error*] slip • **en un descuido** by mistake

desde *preposición* ❶ [*tiempo*] since • **no lo veo desde el mes pasado/desde ayer** I haven't seen him since last month/yesterday • **vivo en este país desde 1998** I have lived in this country since 1998 • **vivo aquí desde hace cuatro meses** I've lived here for four months • **desde ahora** from now on • **desde hace mucho/un mes** for ages/a month • **desde... hasta...** from... until... • **desde el lunes hasta el viernes** from Monday till Friday • **desde entonces** since then • **desde que** since • **desde que murió mi madre** since my mother died

❷ [*espacio*] from • **viajamos desde Córdoba a Mendoza** we traveled from Córdoba to Mendoza • **vi el volcán desde el tren** I saw the volcano from the train • **desde... hasta...** from... to... • **desde aquí hasta el centro** from here to the center

desdén *sm* disdain

desdeñar *vt* to scorn

desdicha *sf* [*desgracia - situación*] misery; [- *suceso*] misfortune • **por desdicha** unfortunately

desdichado, da *adj* ❶ [*decisión, situación*] unfortunate ❷ [*persona - sin suerte*] unlucky; [- *sin felicidad*] unhappy ☼ *Los adjetivos ingleses son invariables.*

desdoblar *vt* ❶ [*servilleta, carta*] to unfold ❷ [*alambre*] to straighten out

desear *vt* ❶ [*querer*] to want ❷ [*anhelar*] to wish • **te deseo toda la suerte del mundo** I wish you all the luck in the world • **deseo hablar con el encargado** I wish to speak with the person in charge • **¿qué desea?** [*en tienda*] what can I do for you? • **desearía estar allí** I wish I was there ❸ [*sexualmente*] to desire

expresión **dejar mucho que desear** to leave much to be desired

desechable *adj* disposable ☼ *Los adjetivos ingleses son invariables.*

desechar *vt* ❶ [*tirar - ropa, piezas*] to throw out; to discard ❷ [*rechazar - ayuda, oferta*] to refuse; to turn down ❸ [*desestimar - idea*] to reject; [- *plan, proyecto*] to drop

desecho *sm* ❶ [*objeto usado*] unwanted object ❷ [*ropa*] castoff • **material de desecho a)** [*generalmente*] waste products *pl* **b)** [*metal*] scrap

desembalar *vt* to unpack

desembarazar *vt* to clear

desembarcar ✦ *vt* ❶ [*pasajeros*] to disembark • **los viajeros desembarcaron al llegar al puerto** the travelers disembarked upon arriving at the port ❷ [*mercancías*] to unload • **desembarcaron el equipaje de los pasajeros** they unloaded the passengers' luggage

✦ *vi* ❶ [*de barco, avión*] to disembark ❷ [*de autobús, tren*] to get off

desembarco *sm* ❶ [*de pasajeros*] disembarkation ❷ MILITAR landing

desembarque *sm* [*de mercancías*] unloading

desembocadura *sf* ❶ [*de río*] mouth ❷ [*de calle*] opening

desembocar ■ **desembocar en** *vi* ❶ [*río*] to flow into • **desembocar en** to lead into • **esta calle desemboca en la avenida principal** this street leads into the main avenue ❷ [*asunto*] to result in

desembolso *sm* payment • **desembolso inicial** down payment

desempaquetar *vt* ❶ [*paquete*] to unwrap ❷ [*caja*] to unpack

desempatar *vi* to decide the contest • **jugar para desempatar** to have a play-off

desempate *sm* final result • **partido de desempate** decider

desempeñar *vt* ❶ [*función, misión*] to carry out ❷ [*cargo, puesto*] to hold ❸ [*papel*] to play ❹ [*joyas*] to redeem

desempeño *sm* ❶ [*de función*] carrying out ❷ [*de papel*] performance ❸ [*de objeto*] redemption

desempleado, da *adj* unemployed ⋅ *Los adjetivos ingleses son invariables.*

desempleo *sm* ❶ [*falta de empleo*] unemployment ⋅ **el desempleo ha aumentado mucho** unemployment has increased a lot ❷ [*subsidio*] unemployment benefit ⋅ **cobrar el desempleo** to receive unemployment benefit

desencadenar *vt* ❶ [*preso, perro*] to unchain ❷ *figurado* [*suceso, polémica*] to give rise to ❸ [*pasión, furia*] to unleash

desencajar *vt* ❶ [*mecanismo, piezas - sin querer*] to knock out of place; [*- intencionadamente*] to take apart ❷ [*hueso*] to dislocate

desenchufar *vt* to unplug

desenfadado, da *adj* ❶ [*persona, conducta*] relaxed ❷ [*comedia, programa de TV*] light-hearted ❸ [*estilo*] light ❹ [*en el vestir*] casual ⋅ *Los adjetivos ingleses son invariables.*

desenfocado, da *adj* ❶ [*imagen*] out of focus ❷ [*visión*] blurred ⋅ *Los adjetivos ingleses son invariables.*

desenfrenado, da *adj* ❶ [*ritmo, baile*] frantic ❷ [*comportamiento*] uncontrolled ❸ [*apetito*] insatiable ⋅ *Los adjetivos ingleses son invariables.*

desenfreno *sm* ❶ [*generalmente*] lack of restraint ❷ [*vicio*] debauchery

desenfundar *vt* [*pistola*] to draw

desenganchar *vt* ❶ [*vagón*] to uncouple ❷ [*caballo*] to unhitch ❸ [*pelo, jersey*] to free

desengaño *sm* disappointment ⋅ **llevarse un desengaño con alguien** to be disappointed in somebody

desenlace *sm* outcome

desenmascarar *vt* [*descubrir*] to unmask

desenredar *vt* ❶ [*hilos, pelo*] to untangle ❷ *figurado* [*asunto*] to sort out ❸ [*problema*] to resolve

desenrollar *vt* ❶ [*hilo, cinta*] to unwind ❷ [*persiana*] to roll down ❸ [*pergamino, papel*] to unroll

desenroscar *vt* to unscrew

desenterrar *vt* ❶ [*cadáver*] to disinter ❷ [*tesoro, escultura*] to dig up ❸ *figurado* [*recordar*] ⋅ **desenterrar algo (de)** to recall o revive something (from)

desentonar *vi* ❶ MÚSICA [*cantante*] to sing out of tune; [*instrumento*] to be out of tune ❷ [*color, cortinas, edificio*] ⋅ **desentonar (con)** to clash (with)

desenvoltura *sf* ❶ [*al moverse, comportarse*] ease ❷ [*al hablar*] fluency

desenvolver *vt* to unwrap

■ **desenvolverse** *v pronominal* ❶ [*asunto, proceso*] to progress ❷ [*trama*] to unfold ❸ [*persona*] to cope

desenvuelto, ta ◆ *participio pasado* → desenvolver

◆ *adj* ❶ [*al moverse, comportarse*] natural ❷ [*al hablar*] fluent ⋅ *Los adjetivos ingleses son invariables.*

deseo *sm* ❶ [*anhelo*] wish ⋅ **su deseo se hizo realidad** her wish came true ⋅ **buenos deseos** good intentions ⋅ **pedir un deseo** to make a wish ❷ [*apetito sexual*] desire

expresar un deseo

- **I'd like to go to the movies.** Me gustaría ir al cine.
- **I really want to buy this sweater.** Tengo muchas ganas de comprarme este suéter.
- **I wish it was a little warmer!** ¡Si al menos hiciera un poco más de calor!
- **I really feel like a hot bath.** Tengo muchas ganas de un baño caliente.
- **I'd really like you two to meet!** ¡Me gustaría tanto que se conocieran!

deseoso, sa *adj* ⋅ **estar deseoso de algo/hacer algo** to long for something/to do something ⋅ *Los adjetivos ingleses son invariables.*

desequilibrado, da *adj* ❶ [*persona*] unbalanced ❷ [*balanza, eje*] off-center ⋅ *Los adjetivos ingleses son invariables.*

desequilibrio *sm* ❶ [*mecánico*] lack of balance ❷ [*mental*] mental instability

desertar *vi* to desert

desértico, ca *adj* ❶ [*del desierto*] desert ⋅ *Sólo se usa delante del sustantivo.* ❷ [*despoblado*] deserted

desertización *sf* ❶ [*del terreno*] desertification ❷ [*de la población*] depopulation

desesperación *sf* [*falta de esperanza*] despair ⋅ **con desesperación** in despair

desesperado, da *adj* ❶ [*persona, intento*] desperate ❷ [*estado, situación*] hopeless ❸ [*esfuerzo*] furious ⋅ *Los adjetivos ingleses son invariables.*

desesperante *adj* infuriating ⋅ *Los adjetivos ingleses son invariables.*

desesperar ◆ *vt* to exasperate

◆ *vi* to despair

■ **desesperarse** *v pronominal* ❶ [*perder la esperanza*] to be driven to despair ❷ [*irritarse, enojarse*] to get exasperated

desestabilizar *vt* to destabilize

desfachatez *sf familiar* cheek

desfallecer *vi* ❶ [*debilitarse*] to be exhausted ❷ [*desmayarse*] to faint ⋅ **desfallecer de** to feel faint from ⋅ **desfallecíamos de cansancio** we felt faint with exhaustion

desfasado, da *adj* ❶ [*persona*] out of touch ❷ [*libro, moda*] out of date ⋅ *Los adjetivos ingleses son invariables.*

desfase *sm* [*diferencia*] gap ⋅ **desfase horario** jet lag

desfavorable *adj* unfavorable.ϙ: *Los adjetivos ingleses son invariables.*

desfiladero *sm* narrow mountain pass

desfilar *vi* MILITAR to parade

desfile *sm* ❶ MILITAR parade ▶ **desfile de modelos** fashion parade ❷ [*de carrozas*] procession

desgana *sf* ❶ [*falta de hambre*] lack of appetite ❷ [*falta de ánimo*] lack of enthusiasm • **con desgana** unwillingly; reluctantly

desganado, da *adj* [*sin apetito*] • **estar desganado** to be off your food.ϙ: *Los adjetivos ingleses son invariables.*

desgarrar *vt* to rip • **desgarrar el corazón** to break your heart

■ **desgarrarse** *v pronominal* [*músculo*] to tear • **me desgarré un músculo de la pierna** I tore a muscle in my leg

desgarro *sm* tear

desgastar *vt* to wear out

■ **desgastarse** *v pronominal* [*persona*] to wear yourself out • **las suelas de las botas se han desgastado** the soles of the boots have gotten worn out

desgaste *sm* ❶ [*de tela, muebles* ETC] wear and tear ❷ [*de roca*] erosion ❸ [*de pilas*] running down ❹ [*de cuerdas*] fraying ❺ [*de metal*] corrosion ❻ [*de persona*] wear and tear • **desgaste político** erosion of voter confidence

desgracia *sf* ❶ [*mala suerte*] misfortune • **por desgracia** unfortunately • **tener la desgracia de** to be unfortunate enough to ❷ [*catástrofe*] disaster • **desgracias personales** casualties • **es una desgracia que...** it's a terrible shame that...

ᴇxᴘʀᴇsɪóɴ caer en desgracia to fall into disgrace ▶ **las desgracias nunca vienen solas** it never rains but it pours

desgraciado, da *adj* ❶ [*generalmente*] unfortunate ❷ [*sin suerte*] unlucky ❸ [*infeliz*] unhappy.ϙ: *Los adjetivos ingleses son invariables.*

desguace *sm* ❶ [*de coches*] scrapping ❷ [*de buques*] breaking

deshabitado, da *adj* uninhabited.ϙ: *Los adjetivos ingleses son invariables.*

deshacer *vt* ❶ [*costura, nudo, paquete*] to undo ❷ [*maleta*] to unpack ❸ [*castillo de arena*] to destroy ❹ [*disolver - helado, mantequilla*] to melt; [- *pastilla, terrón de azúcar*] to dissolve ❺ [*poner fin a - contrato, negocio*] to cancel; [- *pacto, tratado*] to break; [- *plan, intriga*] to foil; [- *organización*] to dissolve ❻ [*destruir - enemigo*] to rout; [- *matrimonio*] to ruin ❼ INFORMÁTICA to undo

■ **deshacerse** *v pronominal* ❶ [*desvanecerse*] to disappear ❷ [*disolverse*] to melt • **el buen chocolate se deshace en la boca** good chocolate melts in your mouth ❸ [*nudo*] to come undone • **el nudo se deshizo** the knot came undone ❹ figurado [*librarse*] • **deshacerse de** to get rid of • **el capitán se deshizo de la carga más pesada** the captain got rid of the heaviest cargo ❺ figurado • **deshacerse en algo (con** o **hacia alguien) a)** [*cumplidos*] to lavish something (on somebody) **b)**

[*insultos*] to heap something (on somebody) • **deshacerse en elogios** to shower with praise

deshecho, cha ◆ *participio pasado* → **deshacer**

◆ *adj* ❶ [*costura, nudo, paquete*] undone ❷ [*cama*] unmade ❸ [*maleta*] unpacked ❹ [*enemigo*] destroyed ❺ [*tarta, matrimonio*] ruined ❻ [*derretido - pastilla, terrón de azúcar*] dissolved; [- *helado, mantequilla*] melted ❼ [*afligido*] devastated ❽ [*cansado*] tired out.ϙ: *Los adjetivos ingleses son invariables.*

desheredar *vt* to disinherit

deshidratar *vt* to dehydrate

deshielo *sm* thaw

deshinchar *vt* ❶ [*globo, rueda*] to let down ❷ [*hinchazón*] to reduce the swelling in

deshojar *vt* ❶ [*árbol*] to strip the leaves off ❷ [*flor*] to pull the petals off ❸ [*libro*] to pull the pages out of

deshonesto, ta *adj* ❶ [*sin honradez*] dishonest ❷ [*sin pudor*] indecent.ϙ: *Los adjetivos ingleses son invariables.*

deshonor *sm* dishonor

deshonra *sf* = **deshonor**

deshonrar *vt* to dishonor

desierto, ta *adj* ❶ [*generalmente*] deserted ❷ [*vacante - premio*] deferred.ϙ: *Los adjetivos ingleses son invariables.*

■ **desierto** *sm* desert

designar *vt* ❶ [*nombrar*] to appoint ❷ [*fijar, determinar*] to name

desigual *adj* ❶ [*diferente*] different ❷ [*terreno*] uneven ❸ [*tiempo, persona, humor*] changeable ❹ [*alumno, actuación*] inconsistent ❺ [*lucha*] unequal ❻ [*tratamiento*] unfair.ϙ: *Los adjetivos ingleses son invariables.*

desilusión *sf* disappointment • **llevarse una desilusión** to be disappointed

desilusionar *vt* ❶ [*desengañar*] to reveal the truth to ❷ [*decepcionar*] to disappoint • **me has desilusionado con tus malas calificaciones** you've disappointed me with your bad grades

■ **desilusionarse** *v pronominal* ❶ [*decepcionarse*] to be disappointed • **se desilusionó al ver la reacción de su novio** she was disappointed to see the reaction of her boyfriend ❷ [*desengañarse*] to realize the truth

desinfección *sf* disinfection

desinfectar *vt* to disinfect

desinflar *vt* to deflate

desinstalar *vt* INFORMÁTICA uninstall

desintegración *sf* ❶ [*de objetos*] disintegration ❷ [*de grupos, organizaciones*] breaking up

desintegrar *vt* ❶ [*objetos*] to disintegrate ❷ [*átomo*] to split ❸ [*grupos, organizaciones*] to break up

desinterés *sm* ❶ [*indiferencia*] lack of interest • **hay un gran desinterés de los jóvenes por la política** there's a huge lack of interest in politics among young people ❷ [*generosidad*] unselfishness • **me ayudó con total desinterés** he helped me with total unselfishness

desinteresado, da *adj* unselfish ☼ *Los adjetivos ingleses son invariables.*

desistir *vi* • **desistir (de hacer algo)** to give up (doing something) • **desistió de la idea de entrar al seminario** he gave up the idea of entering the priesthood

deslave *sm* landslide • **el deslave provocó la muerte de muchas personas** the landslide caused the death of many people

desleal *adj* [*competencia*] unfair • **desleal (con)** disloyal (to) ☼ *Los adjetivos ingleses son invariables.*

desliz *sm* slip • **cometer un desliz** to slip up

deslizar *vt* [*mano, objeto*] • **deslizar algo en** to slip something into • **deslizar algo por algo** to slide something along something • **deslizó un billete entre sus manos** he slipped a bill into her hands

■ **deslizarse** *v pronominal* [*resbalar*] • **deslizarse por** to slide along • **el carro se deslizó por la pendiente** the car slid down the slope

deslucido, da *adj* ❶ [*sin brillo*] faded ❷ [*plata*] tarnished ❸ [*sin gracia - acto, ceremonia*] dull; [- *actuación*] lacklustre ☼ *Los adjetivos ingleses son invariables.*

deslumbrar *vt* literal & figurado to dazzle • **me deslumbró con su belleza** she dazzled me with her beauty

desmadre *sm* familiar chaos

desmantelar *vt* ❶ [*casa, fábrica*] to clear out ❷ [*organización*] to disband ❸ [*arsenal, andamio*] to dismantle ❹ [*barco*] to unrig

desmaquillador *sm* make-up remover

desmayar *vi* to lose heart

■ **desmayarse** *v pronominal* to faint • **se desmayó en medio de la competencia** she fainted in the middle of the competition • **se desmayó de dolor** he fainted from pain

desmayo *sm* [*físico*] fainting fit • **le dio un desmayo** she fainted

desmedido, da *adj* excessive ☼ *Los adjetivos ingleses son invariables.*

desmentir *vt* ❶ [*negar*] to deny ❷ [*no corresponder*] to belie

desmenuzar *vt* ❶ [*trocear - pan, pastel, roca*] to crumble; [- *carne*] to chop up; [- *papel*] to tear up into little pieces ❷ figurado [*examinar, analizar*] to scrutinize

desmerecer ♦ *vt* to be unworthy of

♦ *vi* to lose value • **desmerecer (en algo) de alguien** to be inferior to somebody (in something)

desmesurado, da *adj* ❶ [*excesivo*] excessive ❷ [*enorme*] enormous ☼ *Los adjetivos ingleses son invariables.*

desmitificar *vt* to demythologize

desmontar *vt* ❶ [*desarmar - máquina*] to take apart o to pieces; [- *motor*] to strip down; [- *piezas*] to dismantle; [- *rueda*] to remove; to take off; [- *tienda de campaña*] to take down; [- *arma*] to uncock ❷ [*jinete - sujeto: caballo*] to unseat; [- *sujeto: persona*] to help down

desmoralizar *vt* to demoralize

desmoronar *vt* [*edificios, rocas*] to cause to crumble

desnatado, da *adj* skimmed ☼ *Los adjetivos ingleses son invariables.*

desnivel *sm* [*del terreno*] irregularity

desnivelar *vt* ❶ to make uneven ❷ [*balanza*] to tip

desnudar *vt* to undress

desnudez *sf* ❶ [*de persona*] nudity ❷ [*de cosa*] bareness

desnudo, da *adj* ❶ [*persona, cuerpo*] naked ❷ figurado [*salón, hombro, árbol*] bare ❸ [*verdad*] plain ❹ [*paisaje*] barren ☼ *Los adjetivos ingleses son invariables.*

■ **desnudo** *sm* nude

desnutrición *sf* malnutrition

desobedecer *vt* to disobey

desobediencia *sf* disobedience ▸ **desobediencia civil** civil disobedience

desobediente *adj* disobedient ☼ *Los adjetivos ingleses son invariables.*

desocupado, da *adj* ❶ [*persona - ocioso*] free; unoccupied; [- *sin empleo*] unemployed ❷ [*lugar*] vacant ☼ *Los adjetivos ingleses son invariables.*

desocupar *vt* ❶ [*edificio*] to vacate ❷ [*habitación, mesa*] to leave

desodorante *sm* deodorant

desolación *sf* ❶ [*destrucción*] desolation ❷ [*desconsuelo*] distress

desolar *vt* ❶ [*destruir*] to devastate ❷ [*afligir*] to cause anguish to

desorbitado, da *adj* ❶ [*generalmente*] disproportionate ❷ [*precio*] exorbitant ❸ • **con los ojos desorbitados** pop-eyed ☼ *Los adjetivos ingleses son invariables.*

desorden *sm* ❶ [*confusión*] chaos ❷ [*falta de orden*] mess • **tienes que acomodar el desorden de tu cuarto** you have to clean up the mess in your room • **en desorden** topsy-turvy • **poner en desorden** to upset ❸ [*disturbio*] disturbance • **cometieron desórdenes públicos** they caused public disturbances

desordenado, da *adj* ❶ [*habitación, persona*] untidy ❷ [*documentos, fichas*] jumbled (up) ☼ *Los adjetivos ingleses son invariables.*

desorganización *sf* disorganization

desorganizar *vt* to disrupt

desorientar *vt* ❶ [*en el espacio*] to disorientate • **el fuerte sol los desorientó** the strong sunlight disoriented them ❷ figurado [*aturdir*] to confuse • **me desorientó su actitud** his attitude confused me

despachar ♦ *vt* ❶ [*mercancía*] to dispatch ❷ [*en tienda - cliente*] to serve; [- *entradas, bebidas* ETC] to sell ❸ familiar & figurado [*terminar - trabajo, discurso*] to finish off ❹ [*asunto, negocio*] to settle

♦ *vi* [*en una tienda*] to serve

despacho *sm* ❶ [*oficina*] office ❷ [*en casa*] study ❸ [*comunicación oficial*] dispatch ❹ [*venta*] sale

D

❺ [*lugar de venta*] • **despacho de billetes/localidades** ticket/box office

despacio *adv* slowly

desparramar *vt* ❶ [*líquido*] to spill ❷ [*objetos*] to spread

despectivo, va *adj* ❶ [*despreciativo*] contemptuous ❷ GRAMÁTICA pejorative ۞ *Los adjetivos ingleses son invariables.*

despedazar *vt* ❶ [*físicamente*] to tear apart ❷ *figurado* [*moralmente*] to shatter

despedida *sf* [*adiós*] farewell

despedir *vt* ❶ [*decir adiós a*] to say goodbye to • **fuimos a despedirlo en la estación** we went to see him off at the station ❷ [*echar - de un empleo*] to fire ; [*- de un club*] to throw out • **despidieron a cuatro obreros** they fired four workers ❸ [*lanzar, arrojar*] to fling • **salir despedido hacia algo** to fly out towards something ❹ *figurado* [*difundir, desprender*] to give off

■ **despedirse** *v pronominal* ❶ **despedirse (de)** to say goodbye (to) • **se despidieron en la estación** they said goodbye at the station • **nos despedimos de nuestros padres en el aeropuerto** we said goodbye to our parents at the airport • **si no apruebas, despídete de la moto** if you fail your exams, you can say goodbye to the motorcycle

al despedirse

- **Goodbye!** ¡Hasta luego!
- **Bye!** ¡Adiós!
- **See you later!** ¡Nos vemos luego!
- **See you tonight!** ¡Hasta la noche!
- **See you Tuesday!** ¡Hasta el martes!
- **Good night!** ¡Buenas noches!
- **Sorry, I've got to go.** Lo siento, pero tengo que irme.
- **I'm in a hurry.** Tengo prisa.
- **OK, see you.** Bueno, ¡hasta la próxima!
- **It was nice meeting you.** Ha sido un placer conocerte/lo.
- **I really enjoyed meeting you.** Encantado de conocerte/lo.
- **Good luck!** ¡Ánimo!
- **Have a good journey** o **trip!** ¡Buen viaje!

despegar ♦ *vt* to unstick
♦ *vi* [*avión*] to take off

despegue *sm* takeoff • **despegue vertical** vertical takeoff

despeinar *vt* [*pelo*] to ruffle • **despeinar a alguien** to mess up somebody's hair

despejado, da *adj* ❶ [*tiempo, día*] clear ❷ *figurado* [*persona, mente*] alert ❸ [*espacio - ancho*] spacious ; [*- sin estorbos*] clear ; uncluttered ۞ *Los adjetivos ingleses son invariables.*

despejar *vt* to clear

despensa *sf* pantry, *plural* pantries

despeñadero *sm* precipice

despeñar *vt* to throw over a cliff

desperdiciar *vt* ❶ [*tiempo, comida*] to waste ❷ [*dinero*] to squander ❸ [*ocasión*] to throw away • **desperdició muy buenas oportunidades** he threw away very good opportunities

desperdicio *sm* [*acción*] waste • **es un desperdicio no comer esa carne** it's a waste not to eat that meat ❷ [*residuo*] • **desperdicios** scraps

desperdigar *vt* to scatter

desperfecto *sm* ❶ [*deterioro*] damage ۞ *incontable* ❷ [*defecto*] flaw

despertador *sm* alarm clock • **mi despertador suena a las seis de la mañana** my alarm clock goes off at six in the morning

despertar ♦ *vt* ❶ [*persona, animal*] to wake (up) • **desperté a mi hijo temprano** I woke my son early ❷ *figurado* [*reacción*] to arouse • **su actitud despertó sospechas** his attitude aroused suspicion ❸ *figurado* [*recuerdo*] to awaken
♦ *vi* to wake up
♦ *sm* awakening

■ **despertarse** *v pronominal* to wake up • **me desperté con el ruido de la calle** I woke up with the noise of the street

despido *sm* dismissal • **despido colectivo** collective dismissal

despierto, ta *adj* ❶ [*sin dormir*] awake • **no estoy despierto todavía** I'm not awake yet ❷ *figurado* [*espabilado, listo*] sharp • **es una niña muy despierta** she's a very sharp child ۞ *Los adjetivos ingleses son invariables.*

despilfarrar *vt* ❶ [*dinero*] to squander ❷ [*electricidad, agua* ETC] to waste

despilfarro *sm* ❶ [*de dinero*] squandering ❷ [*de energía, agua* ETC] waste

despistado, da *adj* absent-minded ۞ *Los adjetivos ingleses son invariables.*

despistar *vt* ❶ [*dar esquinazo a*] to throw off the scent ❷ *figurado* [*confundir*] to mislead

despiste *sm* ❶ [*distracción*] absent-mindedness ❷ [*error*] slip

desplante *sm* rude remark • **hacer un desplante a alguien** to snub somebody

desplazamiento *sm* ❶ [*viaje*] journey ❷ [*traslado*] move ❸ NÁUTICA displacement

desplazar *vt* ❶ [*trasladar*] to move ❷ *figurado* [*desbancar*] to take the place of • **el avión ha desplazado al barco** the airplane has taken the place of the ship

■ **desplazarse** *v pronominal* [*viajar*] to travel • **me desplazo por la ciudad en coche** I travel about the city by car

desplegar *vt* ❶ [*tela, periódico, mapa*] to unfold ❷ [*alas*] to spread ❸ [*bandera*] to unfurl ❹ [*cualidad*] to display ❺ MILITAR to deploy

despliegue *sm* ❶ [*de cualidad*] display ❷ MILITAR deployment

despoblado, da *adj* deserted:♀: *Los adjetivos ingleses son invariables.*

despojar *vt* • **despojar a alguien de algo** to strip somebody of something

■ **despojarse** *v pronominal* • **despojarse de algo a)** [*bienes, alimentos*] to give something up **b)** [*abrigo, chandal*] to take something off • **se despojó de todas sus riquezas** she renounced all her wealth • **se despojó de la ropa** he took his clothes off

déspota *smf* despot

despreciar *vt* ❶ [*desdeñar*] to scorn ❷ [*rechazar*] to spurn

desprecio *sm* contempt

desprender *vt* ❶ [*lo que estaba fijo*] to detach ❷ [*olor, luz*] to give off • **ese calentador desprende gas** that heater gives off gas

■ **desprenderse** *v pronominal* ❶ [*caerse, soltarse*] to peel off • **el papel pintado se desprende fácilmente de la pared** wallpaper peels off the wall easily ❷ *figurado* [*deducirse*] • **de sus palabras se desprende que...** from his words it is clear o it can be seen that... ❸ [*librarse*] • **desprenderse de** to get rid of ❹ [*apartarse*] • **desprenderse de** to let go of • **no se desprende nunca de sus hijos** she will never let go of her children

desprendimiento *sm* [*separación*] detachment ▶ **desprendimiento de tierras** landslide

despreocupado, da *adj* ❶ [*libre de preocupaciones*] unconcerned ❷ [*en el vestir*] casual:♀: *Los adjetivos ingleses son invariables.*

desprevenido, da *adj* unprepared • **está desprevenido, no va a asimilar lo que le vas a decir** he's unprepared, he won't be able to accept what you're going to tell him • **pillar desprevenido a alguien** to catch somebody unawares ; to take somebody by surprise:♀: *Los adjetivos ingleses son invariables.*

desproporcionado, da *adj* disproportionate:♀: *Los adjetivos ingleses son invariables.*

despropósito *sm* stupid remark

desprovisto, ta *adj* • **desprovisto de** lacking in ; devoid of:♀: *Los adjetivos ingleses son invariables.*

después *adv* ❶ [*en el tiempo - más tarde*] afterwards ; later ; [*- entonces*] then ; [*- justo lo siguiente*] next • **primero le pones la sal, y después le pones la pimienta** first you put in the salt and then you put in the pepper • **poco después** soon after • **años después** years later • **después, iremos a bailar** afterward, we'll go dancing • **ellos llegaron después** they arrived later • **llamé primero y después entré** I knocked first and then I went in • **yo voy después** it's my turn next ❷ [*en el espacio*] next ; after • **¿qué viene después?** what comes next o after? • **hay una farmacia y después está mi casa** there's a chemist's and then there's my house ❸ [*en una lista*] further down

desquiciar *vt* ❶ *figurado* [*desequilibrar*] to derange ❷ [*sacar de quicio*] to drive mad

desquite *sm* revenge

destacamento *sm* detachment • **destacamento de tropas** task force

destacar ◆ *vt* ❶ [*poner de relieve*] to emphasize • **cabe destacar que...** it is important to point out that... ❷ MILITAR to detach

◆ *vi* [*sobresalir*] to be remarkable • **la región destaca por su patrimonio histórico y artístico** the area is remarkable for its history and artistic heritage

■ **destacarse** *v pronominal* • **destacarse (de/por)** to stand out (from/because of) • **se destaca por su altura** he stands out because of his height

destajo *sm* piecework • **trabajar a destajo a)** [*por trabajo hecho*] to do piecework **b)** *figurado* [*afanosamente*] to work flat out

destapador *sm* bottle opener

destapar *vt* ❶ [*abrir - caja, botella*] to open ❷ [*olla*] to take the lid off ❸ [*descorchar*] to uncork ❹ [*descubrir*] to uncover

destartalado, da *adj* ❶ [*viejo, deteriorado*] dilapidated ❷ [*desordenado*] untidy:♀: *Los adjetivos ingleses son invariables.*

destello *sm* ❶ [*de luz, brillo*] sparkle ❷ [*de estrella*] twinkle ❸ *figurado* [*manifestación momentánea*] glimmer

desteñir ◆ *vt* to fade

◆ *vi* to run

desterrar *vt* [*persona*] to banish

destierro *sm* exile • **en el destierro** in exile

destilar *vt* [*agua, petróleo*] to distil

destilería *sf* distillery • **destilería de petróleo** oil refinery

destinar *vt* ❶ • **destinar algo a o para a)** [*cantidad, edificio*] to set something aside for **b)** [*empleo, cargo*] to assign something to **c)** [*carta*] to address something to **d)** [*medidas, programa, publicación*] to aim something at ❷ • **destinar a alguien a a)** [*cargo, empleo*] to appoint somebody to **b)** [*plaza, lugar*] to post somebody to

destinatario, ria *sm, f* addressee

destino *sm* ❶ [*sino*] destiny • **mi destino es ayudar a los demás** my destiny is to help others ❷ [*rumbo*] destination • **los pasajeros cuyo destino es Perú deben embarcar a la brevedad** the passengers whose destination is Peru must get on board as soon as possible • **(ir) con destino a** (to be) bound for o going to • **un vuelo con destino a...** a flight to... ❸ [*empleo, plaza*] position ❹ [*finalidad*] function

destitución *sf* dismissal

destituir *vt* to dismiss

destornillador *sm* screwdriver

destornillar *vt* to unscrew

destreza *sf* skill

destrozar *vt* ❶ [*físicamente - romper*] to smash ; [*- estropear*] to ruin ❷ [*moralmente - persona*] to shatter ; [*- vida*] to ruin

destrozo *sm* damage:♀: *incontable* • **ocasionar grandes destrozos** to cause a lot of damage

destrucción *sf* destruction

destruir *vt* ❶ [*generalmente*] to destroy ❷ [*casa, argumento*] to demolish ❸ [*proyecto*] to ruin ❹ [*ilusión*] to dash

desuso *sm* disuse • **caer en desuso** to become obsolete

desvalijar *vt* ❶ [*casa*] to burglarize ❷ [*persona*] to rob

desván *sm* attic

desvanecer *vt* ❶ [*humo, nubes*] to dissipate ❷ [*sospechas, temores*] to dispel

desvanecimiento *sm* [*desmayo*] fainting fit

desvariar *vi* ❶ [*delirar*] to be delirious ❷ [*decir locuras*] to talk nonsense

desvelar *vt* ❶ [*quitar el sueño a*] to keep awake • **el café me desvela** coffee keeps me awake ❷ [*noticia, secreto* ETC] to reveal • **me desveló la verdad** he revealed the truth to me

desvelo *sm* [*esfuerzo*] effort

desvencijado, da *adj* ❶ [*silla, mesa*] rickety ❷ [*camión, coche*] battered. Los adjetivos ingleses son invariables.

desventaja *sf* disadvantage • **en desventaja** at a disadvantage

desvergonzado, da *adj* shameless. Los adjetivos ingleses son invariables.

desvergüenza *sf* [*atrevimiento, frescura*] shamelessness

desvestir *vt* to undress

desviación *sf* ❶ [*de dirección, cauce, norma*] deviation ❷ [*en la carretera*] detour • **tuvimos que tomar una desviación en el camino** we had to take a detour on the way

desviar *vt* ❶ [*río, carretera, tráfico*] to divert ❷ [*dirección*] to change ❸ [*golpe*] to parry ❹ [*pelota, disparo*] to deflect ❺ [*pregunta*] to evade ❻ [*conversación*] to change the direction of ❼ [*mirada, ojos*] to avert

■ **desviarse** *v pronominal* [*cambiar de dirección - conductor*] to take a detour; [*- avión, barco*] to go off course • **desviarse de** to turn off • **nos desviamos de la ruta principal** we turned off from the main route

desvío *sm* detour

desvirtuar *vt* ❶ [*generalmente*] to detract from ❷ [*estropear*] to spoil ❸ [*verdadero sentido*] to distort

detallado, da *adj* detailed. Los adjetivos ingleses son invariables.

detallar *vt* ❶ [*historia, hechos*] to detail ❷ [*cuenta, gastos*] to itemize

detalle *sm* ❶ [*generalmente*] detail • **me contó los detalles de la historia** he told me the details of the story • **con detalle** in detail • **entrar en detalles** to go into detail ❷ [*atención*] kind gesture o thought • **¡qué detalle!** what a kind gesture! • **tener un detalle con alguien** to be thoughtful o considerate to somebody

detallista *smf* COMERCIO retailer

detectar *vt* to detect

detective *smf* detective

detener *vt* ❶ [*arrestar*] to arrest ❷ [*parar*] to stop ❸ [*retrasar*] to hold up

■ **detenerse** *v pronominal* ❶ [*pararse*] to stop ❷ [*demorarse*] to linger

detenidamente *adv* carefully

detenido, da ♦ *adj* ❶ [*detallado*] thorough ❷ [*arrestado*] • **(estar) detenido** (to be) under arrest. Los adjetivos ingleses son invariables.

♦ *sm, f* prisoner

detenimiento ■ **con detenimiento** *locución adverbial* carefully; thoroughly

detergente *sm* detergent

deteriorar *vt* to damage

■ **deteriorarse** *v pronominal* figurado [*empeorar*] to deteriorate

deterioro *sm* ❶ [*daño*] damage ❷ [*empeoramiento*] deterioration

determinación *sf* ❶ [*fijación - de precio* ETC] settling; fixing ❷ [*resolución*] determination ❸ [*decisión*] decision • **tomar una determinación** to take a decision

determinado, da *adj* ❶ [*concreto*] specific ❷ [*en particular*] particular ❸ [*resuelto*] determined ❹ GRAMÁTICA definite. Los adjetivos ingleses son invariables.

determinar *vt* ❶ [*fijar - fecha, precio*] to settle ❷ [*averiguar*] to determine ❸ [*motivar*] to bring about • **el excelente trabajo de los empleados determinó el éxito del negocio** the excellent work of the employees brought about the success of the business ❹ [*decidir*] to decide • **determinar hacer algo** to decide to do something • **determinamos seguir con el viaje** we decided to continue with the trip

detestar *vt* to detest

detrás *adv* ❶ [*en el espacio*] behind • **tus amigos vienen detrás** your friends are coming behind us • **el interruptor está detrás** the switch is at the back • **siéntate detrás** sit at the back ❷ [*en el orden*] then • **Portugal y detrás Puerto Rico** Portugal and then Puerto Rico • **uno detrás de otro** one after another

deuda *sf* debt • **tengo una deuda con el banco** I owe a debt to the bank ▶ **deuda pública** ECONOMÍA public debt

deudor, ra ♦ *adj* ❶ [*saldo*] debit. Sólo se usa delante del sustantivo. ❷ [*entidad*] indebted

♦ *sm, f* debtor

devaluación *sf* devaluation

devaluar *vt* to devalue

devastar *vt* to devastate

devoción *sf* • **devoción (por)** devotion (to)

devolución *sf* ❶ [*generalmente*] return ❷ [*de dinero*] refund

devolver ♦ *vt* ❶ [*restituir*] • **devolver algo (a) a)** [*coche, dinero* ETC] to give something back (to) **b)** [*producto defectuoso, carta*] to return something (to) ❷ [*restablecer, colocar en su sitio*] • **devolver algo a** to return something to • **ya he devuelto los libros a la biblioteca** I've already returned the books to the library ❸ [*favor, agravio*] to pay back for ❹ [*visita*] to return

❺ [*vomitar*] to throw up • **el bebe devolvió la comida** the baby threw up the food

◆ *vi* to throw up

■ **devolverse** *v pronominal* to come back • **nos devolvimos a los quince días** we returned after two weeks

devorar *vt* to devour • **el jabalí devoró al cordero** the wild boar devoured the lamb • **el fuego devoró la bodega** the fire consumed the warehouse

dg (*abreviatura escrita de* decigramo) dg

día *sm* ❶ [*generalmente*] day • **marzo tiene 31 días** March has 31 days • **me voy el día ocho** I'm going on the eighth • **¿a qué día estamos?** what day is it today? • **¿qué tal día hace?** what's the weather like today? • **de día en día** from day to day; day by day • **del día** fresh • **hoy (en) día** nowadays • **todo el (santo) día** all day long • **el día de mañana** in the future • **al día siguiente** on the following day • **un día sí y un día no** every other day • **todos los días** every day ▶ **día de los enamorados** St Valentine's Day ▶ **día festivo** (public) holiday ▶ **día de los Inocentes** 28th December, ≃ April Fools' Day ▶ **día de las madres** Mother's Day ▶ **día de los Muertos** All Souls' Day ▶ **día de pago** payday ❷ [*luz*] day • **los días son más largos en verano** the days are longer in the summer • **es de día** it's daytime • **hacer algo de día** to do something in the daytime o during the day • **hacer buen día** to be a fine day • **día y noche** day and night

expresiones **estar/ponerse al día (de)** to be/get up to date (with) ▶ **poner algo/a alguien al día** to update something/somebody ▶ **vivir al día** to live from hand to mouth

los días de la semana

lunes Monday	**viernes** Friday
martes Tuesday	**sábado** Saturday
miércoles Wednesday	**domingo** Sunday
jueves Thursday	

En inglés, los días de la semana se escriben con mayúscula.

diabético, ca *adj* & *sm, f* diabetic:💡 *Los adjetivos ingleses son invariables.*

diablo *sm literal* & *figurado* devil • **pobre diablo** poor devil

diablura *sf* prank

diabólico, ca *adj* ❶ [*del diablo*] diabolic ❷ *figurado* [*muy malo, difícil*] diabolical:💡 *Los adjetivos ingleses son invariables.*

diadema *sf* [*para el pelo*] hairband

diáfano, na *adj* ❶ [*transparente*] transparent ❷ *figurado* [*claro*] clear:💡 *Los adjetivos ingleses son invariables.*

diafragma *sm* diaphragm

diagnosticar *vt* to diagnose

diagnóstico *sm* diagnosis • **el médico dio un diagnóstico alentador** the doctor gave an encouraging diagnosis • **diagnóstico precoz** early diagnosis

diagonal *adj* & *sf* diagonal:💡 *Los adjetivos ingleses son invariables.*

diagrama *sm* diagram ▶ **diagrama de flujo** INFORMÁTICA flow chart o diagram

dial *sm* dial

dialecto *sm* dialect

dialogar *vi* • **dialogar (con) a)** [*hablar*] to have a conversation (with); to talk (to) **b)** [*negociar*] to hold a dialogue o talks (with)

diálogo *sm* ❶ [*conversación*] conversation • **mantuvimos un diálogo muy interesante** we had a very interesting conversation ❷ LITERATURA & POLÍTICA dialogue • **el diálogo condujo a una solución pacífica** the dialogue led to a peaceful solution

diamante *sm* [*piedra preciosa*] diamond • **me regaló un anillo con un diamante** he gave me a diamond ring ▶ **diamante en bruto** uncut diamond

expresión **ser un diamante en bruto** to have a lot of potential

diámetro *sm* diameter

diana *sf* ❶ [*en blanco de tiro*] bull's-eye ❷ [*en cuartel*] reveille

diapositiva *sf* slide

diario, ria *adj* daily • **hago tres comidas diarias** I have three meals daily • **a diario** every day • **de diario** daily; everyday • **ropa de diario** everyday clothes:💡 *Los adjetivos ingleses son invariables.*

■ **diario** *sm* ❶ [*periódico*] newspaper • **pásame el diario de la mañana** pass me the morning newspaper ❷ [*relación día a día*] diary • **escribo en mi diario todos los días** I write in my diary every day ▶ **diario de sesiones** parliamentary report ▶ **diario de vuelo** flight log

diarrea *sf* diarrhea

dibujante *sm, f* ❶ [*generalmente*] sketcher ❷ [*de dibujos animados*] cartoonist ❸ [*de dibujo técnico*] draftsman

dibujar *vt* & *vi* to draw

dibujo *sm* ❶ [*generalmente*] drawing • **no se le da bien el dibujo** he's no good at drawing • **hizo un dibujo de la madre** he did a drawing of his mother • **dibujo al natural** drawing from life ▶ **dibujo artístico** art ▶ **dibujo lineal** technical drawing ▶ **dibujos animados** cartoons ❷ [*de tela, prenda* ETC] pattern

diccionario *sm* dictionary

dicho, cha ◆ *participio pasado* → **decir**

◆ *adj* said • **dichos hombres** the said men; these men • **lo dicho** what I/we ETC said • **o mejor dicho** or rather:💡 *Los adjetivos ingleses son invariables.*

expresión **dicho y hecho** no sooner said than done

■ **dicho** *sm* saying

expresión **del dicho al hecho hay un gran** o **mucho trecho** it's easier said than done

diciembre *sm* December ver también **septiembre**

dictado *sm* dictation • **la maestra pone un dictado todas las semanas** the teacher gives us a dictation every week • **escribir al dictado** to take dictation

dictador, ra *sm, f* dictator

dictadura *sf* dictatorship

dictar *vt* **❶** [*texto*] to dictate • **el jefe le dictó una carta a la secretaria** the boss dictated a letter to his secretary **❷** [*emitir - sentencia, fallo*] to pronounce; [*-ley*] to enact; [*- decreto*] to issue • **el juez dictó sentencia** the judge pronounced the sentence

didáctico, ca *adj* didactic ⚲: *Los adjetivos ingleses son invariables.*

diecinueve *numeral* nineteen ver también **seis**

dieciocho *numeral* eighteen ver también **seis**

dieciséis *numeral* sixteen ver también **seis**

diecisiete *numeral* seventeen ver también **seis**

diente *sm* tooth, *plural* teeth • **está echando** o **le están saliendo los dientes** she's teething ▶ **diente de ajo** clove of garlic ▶ **diente de leche** milk tooth ▶ **dientes postizos** false teeth

expresiones **armado hasta los dientes** armed to the teeth ▶ **hablar entre dientes** to mumble; to mutter ▶ **reírse entre dientes** to chuckle

diéresis *sf invariable* diaeresis

diesel, diésel *adj* diesel ⚲: *Los adjetivos ingleses son invariables.*

diestro, tra *adj* [*hábil*] • **diestro (en)** skillful (at) • **es muy diestro manejando los caballos** he's very skillful at handling the horses ⚲: *Los adjetivos ingleses son invariables.*

expresión **a diestro y siniestro** *figurado* left, right and center, all over the place

dieta *sf* MEDICINA diet • **estar/ponerse a dieta** to be/go on a diet • **dieta blanda** soft-food diet • **dieta equilibrada** balanced diet • **dieta mediterránea** Mediterranean diet

dietético, ca *adj* dietetic ⚲: *Los adjetivos ingleses son invariables.*

diez ◆ *numeral* ten

◆ *sm* [*en la escuela*] A; top marks *pl* ver también **seis**

difamar *vt* **❶** [*verbalmente*] to slander **❷** [*por escrito*] to libel

diferencia *sf* difference • **tiene una gran diferencia de edad con su hermano** there's a big age difference between him and his brother • **los socios tuvieron graves diferencias** the partners had serious differences • **con diferencia** by far • **es, con diferencia, el más listo** he's the smartest by far • **partir la diferencia** to split the difference ▶ **diferencia horaria** time difference

diferenciar ◆ *vt* • **diferenciar (de)** to distinguish (from)

◆ *vi* • **diferenciar (entre)** to distinguish (between)

diferente ◆ *adj* • **diferente (de** o **a)** different (from o to) • **sus hijos son muy diferentes** his children are very different ⚲: *Los adjetivos ingleses son invariables.*

◆ *adv* differently • **Ana come diferente porque está a dieta** Ana is eating differently because she's on a diet

diferido ■ **en diferido** *locución adverbial* TELEVISIÓN recorded

difícil *adj* difficult • **difícil de hacer** difficult to do • **es difícil que ganen** they are unlikely to win ⚲: *Los adjetivos ingleses son invariables.*

dificultad *sf* **❶** [*calidad de difícil*] difficulty, *plural* difficulties **❷** [*obstáculo*] problem

dificultar *vt* **❶** [*estorbar*] to hinder **❷** [*obstruir*] to obstruct

difuminar *vt* to blur

difundir *vt* **❶** [*noticia, doctrina, epidemia*] to spread **❷** [*luz, calor*] to diffuse **❸** [*emisión radiofónica*] to broadcast

D

difunto, ta *sm, f* • **el difunto** the deceased

difusión *sf* **❶** [*de cultura, noticia, doctrina*] dissemination **❷** [*de programa*] broadcasting

digerir *vt* **❶** to digest **❷** *figurado* [*hechos*] to assimilate

digestión *sf* digestion • **hacer la digestión** to digest your food

digestivo, va *adj* digestive ⚲: *Los adjetivos ingleses son invariables.*

digital *adj* INFORMÁTICA & TECNOLOGÍA digital ⚲: *Los adjetivos ingleses son invariables.*

dígito *sm* digit

dignidad *sf* [*cualidad*] dignity

digno, na *adj* **❶** [*noble - actitud, respuesta*] dignified; [*- persona*] honorable; noble **❷** [*merecedor*] • **digno de** worthy of • **digno de elogio** praiseworthy • **digno de mención/de ver** worth mentioning/seeing **❸** [*adecuado*] • **digno de** appropriate for; fitting for **❹** [*decente - sueldo, actuación* ETC] decent ⚲: *Los adjetivos ingleses son invariables.*

dilatar *vt* **❶** [*extender*] to expand **❷** [*retina, útero*] to dilate **❸** [*prolongar*] to prolong **❹** [*demorar*] to delay

dilema *sm* dilemma

diligencia *sf* **❶** [*esmero, cuidado*] diligence **❷** [*trámite, gestión*] business ⚲: *incontable* • **hacer una diligencia** to run an errand **❸** [*vehículo*] stagecoach

diluir *vt* to dilute

diluvio *sm literal & figurado* flood ▶ **el Diluvio Universal** the Flood

dimensión *sf* dimension • **es una casa de grandes dimensiones** it's a house of large dimensions • **las dimensiones de la tragedia** the extent of the tragedy • **las dimensiones del armario son...** the measurements of the closet are...

diminutivo *sm* diminutive

diminuto, ta *adj* tiny ⚲: *Los adjetivos ingleses son invariables.*

dimisión *sf* resignation • **presentar la dimisión** to hand in your resignation

dimitir *vi* • **dimitir (de)** to resign (from)

Dinamarca *nombre propio* Denmark

dinámico, ca *adj* dynamic ⚲: *Los adjetivos ingleses son invariables.*

dinamismo *sm* dynamism

dinamita *sf* dynamite

dinamo, dínamo *sf* dynamo

dinastía *sf* dynasty

dineral *sm familiar* fortune

dinero *sm* money • **andar bien/mal de dinero** to be well off for/short of money • **hacer dinero** to make money • **tirar el dinero** to throw money away ▶ **dinero en metálico** cash

dinosaurio *sm* dinosaur

dios, osa *sm, f* god, *femenino* goddess • **en su religión adoran a más de un dios** in their religion they worship more than one god

■ **Dios** *sm* God

expresiones a la buena de Dios any old how ▶ **Dios los cría y ellos se juntan** *proverbio* birds of a feather flock together *proverbio* ▶ **Dios mediante, si Dios quiere** God willing ▶ **¡Dios me libre!** God o heaven forbid! ▶ **¡Dios mío!** good God!; (oh) my God! ▶ **Dios sabe, sabe Dios** God (alone) knows ▶ **¡por Dios!** for God's sake! ▶ **¡que Dios se lo pague!** God bless you! ▶ **¡vaya por Dios!** for Heaven's sake!; honestly!

diploma *sm* diploma

diplomacia *sf* [*generalmente*] diplomacy

diplomado, da *adj* qualified. ☝ *Los adjetivos ingleses son invariables.*

diplomático, ca ◆ *adj literal & figurado* diplomatic. ☝ *Los adjetivos ingleses son invariables.*

◆ *sm, f* diplomat

diptongo *sm* diphthong

diputado, da *sm, f* representative

dique *sm* ❶ [*en río*] dike ❷ [*en puerto*] dock
expresión estar en (el) dique seco to be out of action

dirección *sf* ❶ [*sentido, rumbo*] direction • **estamos yendo en dirección norte** we are going in a northerly direction • **al perdernos pedimos direcciones para volver al camino principal** when we got lost we asked for directions to return to the main road • **en dirección a** towards ❷ [*domicilio*] address • **tengo la dirección de la fiesta** I have the address of the party ▶ **dirección comercial** business address ▶ **dirección electrónica** o **de correo electrónico** e-mail address ▶ **dirección particular** home address ❸ [*mando - de empresa, hospital*] management; [*- de partido*] leadership; [*- de colegio*] headship; [*- de periódico*] editorship; [*- de película*] direction; [*- de obra de teatro*] production; [*- de orquesta*] conducting • **lo mandaron en castigo a la dirección** they sent him to management for punishment ❹ [*junta directiva*] management ❺ [*de vehículo*] steering • **está fallando la dirección del coche** the car's steering is failing ▶ **dirección asistida** power steering

directivo, va ◆ *adj* managerial. ☝ *Los adjetivos ingleses son invariables.*

◆ *sm, f* [*jefe*] manager

■ **directiva** *sf* [*junta*] board (of directors)

directo, ta *adj* ❶ [*generalmente*] direct • **tengo órdenes directas del jefe** I have direct orders from the

boss • **este es un vuelo directo a Buenos Aires** this is a non-stop flight to Buenos Aires ❷ [*derecho*] straight • **fui directo a casa** I went straight home. ☝ *Los adjetivos ingleses son invariables.*

■ **directo** *adv* straight • **directo a** straight to

■ **directa** *sf* AUTOMÓVILES top gear

director, ra *sm, f* ❶ [*de empresa*] director ❷ [*de hotel, hospital*] manager, *femenino* manageress ❸ [*de periódico*] editor ❹ [*de cárcel*] governor ❺ [*de obra artística*] ▶ **director de cine** film director ▶ **director de orquesta** conductor ❻ [*de colegio*] headmaster, *femenino* headmistress ❼ [*de tesis, trabajo de investigación*] supervisor

directorio *sm* directory, *plural* directories • **tengo muchos directorios en mi computadora** I have many directories in my computer ▶ **directorio telefónico** phone book

directriz *sf* GEOMETRÍA directrix

dirigente *smf* ❶ [*de partido político*] leader ❷ [*de empresa*] manager

dirigir *vt* ❶ [*conducir - coche, barco*] to steer; [*- avión*] to pilot; *figurado* [*mirada*] to direct ❷ [*llevar - empresa, hotel, hospital*] to manage; [*- colegio, cárcel, periódico*] to run; [*- partido, revuelta*] to lead; [*- expedición*] to head ❸ [*película, obra de teatro*] to direct ❹ [*orquesta*] to conduct ❺ [*carta, paquete*] to address • **esta carta está dirigida a mi jefe** this letter is addressed to my boss ❻ [*guiar - persona*] to guide ❼ [*dedicar*] • **dirigir algo a** to aim something at

■ **dirigirse** *v pronominal* ❶ [*encaminarse*] • **dirigirse a** o **hacia** to head for • **venía de Nicaragua y se dirigía a Guatemala** it was on its way from Nicaragua and heading for Guatemala • **nos dirigimos hacia el oeste** we headed towards the west ❷ [*hablar*] • **dirigirse a** to address; to speak to • **se dirigió a los estudiantes** he addressed the students ❸ [*escribir*] • **dirigirse a** to contact • **sírvanse dirigirse al servicio de reclamaciones** please contact the complaints department

discapacidad *sf* disability

disciplina *sf* discipline

discípulo, la *sm, f* disciple

disco *sm* ❶ ANATOMÍA, ASTRONOMÍA & GEOMETRÍA disc ❷ [*de música*] record ▶ **disco compacto** compact disc ▶ **disco de larga duración** LP; long-playing record ❸ [*semáforo*] (traffic) light ❹ DEPORTE discus ❺ INFORMÁTICA disk ▶ **disco duro** hard disk
expresión parecer un disco rayado *familiar* to go on like a cracked record

discografía *sf* records previously released *(by an artist or group)*

discoteca *sf* [*local*] disco

discreción *sf* discretion

discrepar *vi* • **discrepar (de) a)** [*diferenciarse*] to differ (from) **b)** [*disentir*] to disagree (with)

discreto, ta *adj* ❶ [*prudente*] discreet ❷ [*cantidad*] moderate ❸ [*normal - actuación*] fair. ☝ *Los adjetivos ingleses son invariables.*

discriminación *sf* discrimination ▶ **discriminación racial/sexual** racial/sexual discrimination

discriminar *vt* **❶** [*cosa*] • **discriminar algo de** to distinguish something from • **tienes que discriminar entre lo que está bien y lo que está mal** you have to distinguish between what's good and what's bad **❷** [*persona, colectividad*] to discriminate against • **hay leyes que discriminan según el color de la piel** there are laws that discriminate according to skin color

disculpa *sf* **❶** [*pretexto*] excuse **❷** [*excusa, perdón*] apology • **su disculpa no fue suficiente** his apology was not enough • **dar disculpas** to make excuses • **pedir disculpas a alguien (por)** to apologize to somebody (for)

---

presentar y aceptar una disculpa

• **Excuse me!** ¡Perdona!/¡Perdone!
• **Sorry!** ¡Perdón!
• **Sorry for disturbing you/for being late!** ¡Perdone que lo moleste/por el retraso!
• **I'm (really) sorry!** Lo siento (muchísimo).
• **Not at all.** No hay de qué.
• **It doesn't matter.** No tiene importancia.
• **Don't worry about it.** No es nada.
• **These things happen.** Son cosas que pasan.
• **It can happen to anyone.** Esto le puede ocurrir a cualquiera.

---

disculpar ◆ *vt* to excuse • **disculpar a alguien (de o por algo)** to forgive somebody (for something) ◆ *vi* • **disculpe, ¿podría pasar?** excuse me, may I get by?
■ **disculparse** *v pronominal* • **disculparse (de o por algo)** to apologize (for something) • **el profesor se disculpó por haber llegado tarde** the professor apologized for having arrived late

discurrir *vi* **❶** [*pasar - personas*] to wander; to walk; [- *tiempo, vida, sesión*] to go by; to pass; [- *río, tráfico*] to flow **❷** [*pensar*] to think

discurso *sm* speech

discusión *sf* **❶** [*conversación*] discussion • **la discusión sobre el tema se hizo interminable** the discussion of the subject became endless **❷** [*pelea*] argument • **tuvimos una discusión con el encargado del restaurante** we had an argument with the manager of the restaurant

discutible *adj* debatable: ◌̣̈ *Los adjetivos ingleses son invariables.*

discutir ◆ *vi* **❶** [*hablar*] to discuss • **discutimos el tema de la crisis financiera** we discussed the subject of the financial crisis **❷** [*pelear*] • **discutir (de)** to argue (about) • **discutieron con el encargado del restaurante** they argued with the manager of the restaurant ◆ *vt* **❶** [*hablar*] to discuss **❷** [*contradecir*] to dispute

diseminar *vt* **❶** [*semillas*] to scatter **❷** [*ideas*] to disseminate

diseñar *vt* to design

diseño *sm* design • **ropa de diseño** designer clothes ▶ **diseño asistido por ordenador** INFORMÁTICA computer-aided design ▶ **diseño gráfico** graphic design

disertación *sf* **❶** [*oral*] lecture **❷** [*escrita*] dissertation

disfraz *sm* **❶** [*generalmente*] disguise **❷** [*para baile, fiesta* ETC] fancy dress: ◌̣̈ *incontable*

disfrazar *vt* **❶** [*generalmente*] to disguise **❷** [*para baile, fiesta* ETC] to dress up • **disfrazó al hijo para el carnaval** she dressed her son up for the carnival
■ **disfrazarse** *v pronominal* to disguise yourself • **disfrazarse de** to dress up as • **los niños se disfrazaron de indios y vaqueros** the children dressed up as cowboys and indians

disfrutar ◆ *vi* **❶** [*sentir placer*] to enjoy yourself • **disfruté en la fiesta** I enjoyed myself at the party **❷** [*disponer de*] • **disfrutar de algo** to enjoy something • **disfrutamos de unas merecidas vacaciones** we enjoyed a well-deserved holiday • **disfruta de una envidiable salud para su edad** he is in enviable good health for his age ◆ *vt* to enjoy

disgustar *vt* [*sujeto: comentario, críticas, noticia*] to upset • **a los clientes les disgustan estas respuestas** these answers upset the clients
■ **disgustarse** *v pronominal* • **disgustarse (con alguien/por algo)** a) [*sentir enfado*] to get upset (with somebody/about something) b) [*enemistarse*] to fall out (with somebody/over something) • **el jefe se disgustó con uno de los empleados** the boss got upset with one of the employees

disgusto *sm* **❶** [*enfado*] annoyance **❷** [*pesadumbre*] sorrow • **dar un disgusto a alguien** to upset somebody • **llevarse un disgusto** to be upset **❸** [*pelea*] • **tener un disgusto con alguien** to have a quarrel with somebody

disidente *smf* **❶** [*político*] dissident **❷** [*religioso*] dissenter

disimular ◆ *vt* to hide • **disimularon su enojo** they hid their anger ◆ *vi* to pretend

disimulo *sm* pretence

dislexia *sm* dyslexia

disminución *sf* decrease

disminuido, da *adj* handicapped: ◌̣̈ *Los adjetivos ingleses son invariables.*

disminuir ◆ *vt* to decrease • **disminuye la velocidad en la curva** decrease your speed on the curve ◆ *vi* **❶** [*generalmente*] to decrease • **la inflación disminuyó el 1%** inflation decreased by 1% **❷** [*precios, temperatura*] to drop **❸** [*vista, memoria*] to fail **❹** [*días*] to get shorter **❺** [*beneficios*] to fall off

disolución *sf* **❶** [*en un líquido*] dissolving **❷** [*de matrimonio, sociedad, partido*] dissolution **❸** [*mezcla*] solution

disolvente *adj* & *sm* solvent: ◌̣̈ *Los adjetivos ingleses son invariables.*

disolver *vt* ❶ [*generalmente*] to dissolve • **tuvimos que disolver la pastilla en el agua** we had to dissolve the tablet in the water ❷ [*reunión, manifestación, familia*] to break up • **la policía disolvió la manifestación** the police broke up the demonstration

■ **disolverse** *v pronominal* ❶ [*generalmente*] to dissolve • **el medicamento se disuelve en el agua** the medicine dissolves in water ❷ [*reunión, manifestación, familia*] to break up

disparar ◆ *vt* ❶ to shoot ❷ [*pedrada*] to throw
◆ *vi* to fire • **la policía disparó sobre los prófugos** the police fired on the fugitives

disparatado, da *adj* absurd ۞ *Los adjetivos ingleses son invariables.*

disparate *sm* ❶ [*acción*] silly thing ❷ [*comentario*] foolish remark ❸ [*idea*] crazy idea • **hacer disparates** to do silly things • **decir disparates** to talk nonsense • **lo que dices es un disparate** what you're saying is nonsense

disparo *sm* shot • **disparo de advertencia** warning shot • **disparo de salida** starting shot

dispersar *vt* ❶ [*esparcir - objetos*] to scatter ❷ [*disolver - gentío*] to disperse ; [*- manifestación*] to break up

disponer ◆ *vt* ❶ [*generalmente*] to arrange • **dispusimos las sillas junto a las mesas** we arranged the chairs close to the tables ❷ [*cena, comida*] to lay on ❸ [*decidir - sujeto: persona*] to decide ❹ [*sujeto: ley*] to stipulate
◆ *vi* ❶ [*poseer*] • **disponer de** to have • **el hotel dispone de todas las comodidades** the hotel has all the amenities ❷ [*usar*] • **disponer de** to make use of

disponibilidad *sf* [*generalmente*] availability

disponible *adj* ❶ [*generalmente*] available ❷ [*tiempo*] free ۞ *Los adjetivos ingleses son invariables.*

disposición *sf* ❶ [*colocación*] arrangement • **no me gusta la disposición de las sillas en esta sala** I don't like the arrangement of the chairs in this room ❷ [*orden*] order ❸ [*de ley*] provision • **la disposición del gobierno regula el comercio interno** the provision of the government regulates internal commerce ❹ [*uso*] • **a disposición de** at the disposal of • **pasar a disposición policial** to be brought before the judge

dispositivo *sm* device ▸ **dispositivo intrauterino** intrauterine device ; IUD

disputa *sf* dispute

disputar *vt* ❶ [*cuestión, tema*] to argue about ❷ [*trofeo, puesto*] to compete for ❸ [*carrera, partido*] to compete in

disquete *sm* INFORMÁTICA floppy disk

distancia *sf* ❶ [*generalmente*] distance • **hay una distancia de 100 km entre las dos ciudades** there's a distance of 100 km between the two cities • **¿a qué distancia está la tienda?** how far away is the store? • **a dos millas de distancia** two miles away • **recorrer una gran distancia** to cover a lot of ground • **a distancia** from a distance • **mantener a distancia** to keep at a distance • **mantener las distancias** to keep your distance ❷ [*en el tiempo*] gap

distanciar *vt* ❶ [*generalmente*] to drive apart ❷ [*rival*] to forge ahead of

distante *adj* ❶ [*en el espacio*] • **distante (de)** far away (from) • **vive en una zona distante de la capital** he lives in an area far away from the capital ❷ [*en el trato*] distant • **tiene una actitud distante con respecto al problema** she has a distant attitude regarding the problem ۞ *Los adjetivos ingleses son invariables.*

distar *vi* [*hallarse a*] • **ese sitio dista varios kilómetros de aquí** that place is several kilometers away from here

distendido, da *adj* [*informal*] relaxed ۞ *Los adjetivos ingleses son invariables.*

distensión *sf* ❶ [*entre países*] détente ❷ [*entre personas*] easing of tension ❸ MEDICINA strain

distinción *sf* ❶ [*diferencia*] distinction • **a distinción de** in contrast to ; unlike • **sin distinción** alike ❷ [*privilegio*] privilege ❸ [*elegancia*] refinement

distinguido, da *adj* ❶ [*notable*] distinguished ❷ [*elegante*] refined ۞ *Los adjetivos ingleses son invariables.*

distinguir *vt* ❶ [*diferenciar*] to distinguish • **no puedo distinguir a un mellizo del otro** I can't distinguish one twin from the other • **no distingue lo que dice aquel cartel** he can't make out what that sign says ❷ [*separar*] to pick out ❸ [*caracterizar*] to characterize • **las rayas blancas distinguen a las cebras** zebras are characterized by their white stripes ❹ [*premiar*] to honor • **lo distinguieron con el primer premio** they honored him with first prize

distinto, ta *adj* [*diferente*] different ۞ *Los adjetivos ingleses son invariables.*

distracción *sf* ❶ [*entretenimiento*] entertainment ❷ [*pasatiempo*] hobby ❸ [*despiste*] slip ❹ [*falta de atención*] absent-mindedness

distraer *vt* ❶ [*divertir*] to entertain • **las películas me distraen** movies entertain me ❷ [*despistar*] to distract • **el ruido me distrae cuando estudio** noise distracts me when I'm studying

■ **distraerse** *v pronominal* ❶ [*divertirse*] to enjoy yourself • **me distraigo viendo televisión** I enjoy myself watching television ❷ [*pasar el tiempo*] to pass the time ❸ [*despistarse*] to let your mind wander • **el niño se distrae fácilmente en clase** the boy lets his mind wander in class

distraído, da *adj* ❶ [*entretenido*] entertaining ❷ [*despistado*] absent-minded ۞ *Los adjetivos ingleses son invariables.*

distribución *sf* ❶ [*generalmente*] distribution • **distribución de premios** prizegiving ❷ [*de correo, mercancías*] delivery ❸ [*de casa, habitaciones*] layout

distribuir *vt* ❶ [*generalmente*] to distribute ❷ [*carga, trabajo*] to spread ❸ [*pastel, ganancias*] to divide up ❹ [*correo, mercancías*] to deliver ❺ [*casa, habitaciones*] to arrange

distrito *sm* district ▸ **distrito federal** federal district • **México es un Distrito Federal** Mexico City is a Federal District

disturbio *sm* ❶ disturbance ❷ [*violento*] riot • **disturbios raciales** race riots

disuadir *vt* • **disuadir (de)** to dissuade (from)

disuasión *sf* deterrence

diurno, na *adj* ❶ [*generalmente*] daytime ❖ *Sólo se usa delante del sustantivo.* • **me tocó el turno diurno en el trabajo** I got the day shift at work ❷ [*planta, animal*] diurnal

diván *sm* ❶ divan ❷ [*de psiquiatra*] couch

divergencia *sf* ❶ [*de líneas*] divergence ❷ [*de opinión*] difference of opinion

diversidad *sf* diversity

diversificar *vt* to diversify

diversión *sf* amusement • **le dedica más tiempo a la diversión que al trabajo** he dedicates more time to amusement than to work • **el cine es mi diversión preferida** movies are my favorite pastime

> ### *diversión ≠ diversion*
> • La palabra inglesa **diversion** es un falso amigo que significa *desvío*
> • *Diversión* se traduce al inglés por **amusement** o **pastime**.

diverso, sa *adj* [*diferente*] different ❖ *Los adjetivos ingleses son invariables.*

divertido, da *adj* ❶ [*entretenido - película, libro*] entertaining; [*- fiesta*] enjoyable ❷ [*que hace reír*] funny ❖ *Los adjetivos ingleses son invariables.*

divertir *vt* to amuse • **los payasos no me divierten en absoluto** clowns don't amuse me at all

dividir *vt* • **dividir (en)** to divide (into) • **un tabique dividía el ambiente en dos** a partition divided the room in two • **dividir entre a)** [*generalmente*] to divide between **b)** MATEMÁTICAS to divide by • **dividimos los caramelos entre todos los niños** we divided up the candy between all the children • **divide 464 entre cuatro** divide 464 by four

divino, na *adj literal & figurado* divine ❖ *Los adjetivos ingleses son invariables.*

divisa *sf* ❶ ❖ *generalmente pl* [*moneda*] foreign currency ❷ [*distintivo*] emblem

divisar *vt* to make out

división *sf* division • **la división de los bienes fue problemática** the division of the possessions was problematic • **su niño ya hace divisiones en la escuela** her son is already doing division at school • **su equipo pertenece a la segunda división** his team belongs to the second division

divorciado, da ◆ *adj* divorced ❖ *Los adjetivos ingleses son invariables.*

◆ *sm, f* divorcé, *femenino* <u>divorcée</u>

divorciar *vt literal & figurado* to divorce

■ **divorciarse** *v pronominal* to get divorced • **se divorciaron después de diez años de casados** they got divorced after being married for ten years

divorcio *sm* DERECHO divorce

divulgar *vt* ❶ [*noticia, secreto*] to reveal ❷ [*rumor*] to spread ❸ [*cultura, ciencia, doctrina*] to popularize

dizque *adv* apparently

Dña *abreviatura escrita de* **doña**

do *sm* ❶ MÚSICA C ❷ [*en solfeo*] doh

expresión **dar el do de pecho** *familiar* to give your all

doblado, da *adj* ❶ [*papel, camisa*] folded ❷ [*voz, película*] dubbed ❖ *Los adjetivos ingleses son invariables.*

D

doblar ◆ *vt* ❶ [*duplicar*] to double • **le doblaron el sueldo** they doubled his salary ❷ [*plegar*] to fold • **doblé la ropa antes de guardarla en el ropero** I folded the clothes before putting them in the wardrobe ❸ [*torcer*] to bend ❹ [*esquina*] to turn ❺ [*voz, actor*] to dub • **doblaron la película al español** they dubbed the movie into Spanish

◆ *vi* ❶ [*girar*] to turn • **doblamos en la primera esquina** we turned at the first corner ❷ [*campanas*] to toll

doble ◆ *adj* double • **reservé una habitación doble** I reserved a double room • **tiene doble número de habitantes** it has double o twice the number of inhabitants • **es doble de ancho** it's twice as wide • **una frase de doble sentido** a phrase with a double meaning • **doble clic** INFORMÁTICA double click ❖ *Los adjetivos ingleses son invariables.*

◆ *smf* [*generalmente*] CINE double

◆ *sm* [*duplo*] • **el doble** twice as much • **gana el doble que yo** she earns twice as much as I do; she earns double what I do

◆ *adv* double • **como había perdido la entrada, tuvo que pagar doble** since he had lost the ticket, he had to pay double • **trabajar doble** to work twice as hard

doce *numeral* twelve *ver también* **seis**

doceavo, va *numeral* twelfth

docena *sf* dozen • **por docenas** by the dozen

docente *adj* teaching • **centro docente** educational institution ❖ *Los adjetivos ingleses son invariables.*

dócil *adj* obedient ❖ *Los adjetivos ingleses son invariables.*

doctor, ra *sm, f* • **doctor (en)** doctor (of) • **la doctora me dio de alta** the doctor pronounced me fit

doctrina *sf* doctrine

documentación *sf* [*identificación personal*] papers *pl*

documentado, da *adj* [*informado - película, informe*] researched; [*- persona*] informed ❖ *Los adjetivos ingleses son invariables.*

documental *adj & sm* documentary ❖ *Los adjetivos ingleses son invariables.*

documentar *vt* ❶ [*evidenciar*] to document ❷ [*informar*] to brief

documento *sm* ❶ [*escrito*] document ▶ **documento nacional de identidad** identity card ❷ [*testimonio*] record

dólar *sm* dollar

doler *vi* to hurt • **me duele la pierna** my leg hurts • **me duelen las muelas** my teeth ache • **¿te duele?** does it hurt? • **le dolió mucho que la novia lo abandonara** it hurt him a lot that his girlfriend left him

dolido, da *adj* hurt.💡 *Los adjetivos ingleses son invariables.*

dolor *sm*❶ [*físico*] pain • **siento un dolor en el brazo** I have a pain in my arm▶ **dolor de cabeza** headache • **tengo dolor de cabeza** I have a headache▶ **dolor de estómago** stomachache▶ **dolor de muelas** toothache❷ [*moral*] sorrow

dolorido, da *adj*❶ [*físicamente*] sore❷ [*moralmente*] sorrowing.💡 *Los adjetivos ingleses son invariables.*

doloroso, sa *adj*❶ [*físicamente*] painful❷ [*moralmente*] distressing.💡 *Los adjetivos ingleses son invariables.*

domador, ra *sm, f*❶ [*de caballos*] breaker❷ [*de leones*] tamer

domar *vt*❶ [*generalmente*] to tame❷ [*caballo*] to break in❸ *figurado* [*personas*] to control

domesticar *vt* *literal & figurado* to tame

doméstico, ca *adj* domestic • **las tareas domésticas** household chores • **compramos un lavaplatos de uso doméstico** we bought a dishwasher for home use.💡 *Los adjetivos ingleses son invariables.*

domicilio *sm*❶ [*vivienda*] residence; home▶ **domicilio particular** private residence❷ [*dirección*] address • **escriba su nombre y domicilio en este formulario** write your name and address on this form • **sin domicilio fijo** of no fixed abode▶ **domicilio social** head office

dominante *adj*❶ [*nación, religión, tendencia*] dominant❷ [*vientos*] prevailing❸ [*persona*] domineering.💡 *Los adjetivos ingleses son invariables.*

dominar ◆ *vt*❶ [*controlar - país, territorio*] to rule (over); [- *pasión, nervios, caballo*] to control; [- *situación*] to be in control of; [- *incendio*] to bring under control; [- *rebelión*] to put down❷ [*divisar*] to overlook❸ [*conocer - técnica, tema*] to master; [- *lengua*] to be fluent in
◆ *vi* [*predominar*] to predominate

domingo *sm* Sunday▶ **domingo de Resurrección** o **de Pascua** Easter Sunday ver también **sábado**

dominguero, ra *sm, f* Sunday tripper/driver ETC

dominical *adj* Sunday.💡 *Sólo se usa delante del sustantivo.*

dominicano, na *adj & sm, f* Dominican.💡 *Los adjetivos ingleses son invariables.*

En inglés, los adjetivos que se refieren a un país o a una región se escriben con mayúscula.

dominio *sm*❶ [*dominación, posesión*] • **dominio (sobre)** control (over) • **tiene un dominio total de la situación** he has total control over the situation • **dominio de**❷ **sobre sí mismo** self-control❷ [*autoridad*] authority❸ *figurado* [*territorio*] domain❹ [*ámbito*] realm❺ [*conocimiento - de arte, técnica*] mastery; [- *de idiomas*] command • **tiene un dominio excelente del español** he has an excellent command of Spanish❻ INFORMÁTICA domain

dominó *sm*❶ [*juego*] dominoes.💡 *incontable*❷ [*fichas*] set of dominoes

don *sm*❶.💡 *En inglés no se usa un título con el nombre de pila, sólo con el apellido que en el caso de "don" sería "Mr.". En correspondencia oficial también se puede usar la forma abreviada de Esquire "Esq.".* [*tratamiento*] • **don Luis García a)** [*generalmente*] Mr Luis García **b)** [*en cartas*] Luis García Esquire❷ [*habilidad*] gift • **el don de la palabra** the gift of the gab • **tiene un don para los idiomas** he has a gift for languages

donante *smf* donor▶ **donante de sangre** blood donor

donar *vt* to donate

donativo *sm* donation

donde ◆ *adv* where • **el bolso está donde lo dejaste** the bag is where you left it • **puedes marcharte donde quieras** you can go wherever you want • **de donde** from which • **hasta donde** as far as; up to where • **por donde** wherever
◆ *pronombre* where • **la casa donde nací** the house where I was born • **la ciudad de donde viene** the town (where) she comes from; the town from which she comes

dónde *adv*.💡 *interrogativo* where • **¿dónde está el niño?** where's the child? • **no sé dónde se habrá metido** I don't know where she can be • **¿de dónde eres?** where are you from? • **¿hacia dónde vas?** where are you heading? • **¿por dónde?** whereabouts? • **¿por dónde se va al teatro?** how do you get to the theater from here?

dondequiera ■ **dondequiera que** *adv* wherever

doña *sf*.💡 *En inglés no se usa un título con el nombre de pila, sólo con el apellido que en el caso de "doña" sería "Mrs.".* • **doña Luisa García** Mrs Luisa García

dopado, da *adj* • **un jugador dopado** a player who has taken performance-enhancing drugs

doping *sm* doping

dorado, da *adj* *literal & figurado* golden.💡 *Los adjetivos ingleses son invariables.*

dorar *vt*❶ [*cubrir con oro*] to gild❷ [*alimento*] to brown

dormilón, ona *sm, f* *familiar* [*persona*] sleepyhead

dormir ◆ *vt*❶ [*niño, animal*] to put to bed • **dormir la siesta** to have an afternoon nap❷ MEDICINA to anesthetize • **te duermen únicamente la zona que te van a operar** they anesthetize only the area they're going to operate on
◆ *vi* to sleep • **durmió profundamente toda la noche** he slept deeply all night • **dormimos en un hotel 5 estrellas** we stayed in a five-star hotel

dormitorio *sm*❶ [*de casa*] bedroom❷ [*de colegio*] dormitory

dorsal ◆ *adj* dorsal.💡 *Los adjetivos ingleses son invariables.*
◆ *sm* number *(on player's back)*

dorso *sm* back • **al dorso, en el dorso** on the back • **firme al dorso del documento** sign on the back of the document • **'véase al dorso'** see overleaf • **dorso de la mano** back of your hand

dos *numeral* two

expresión cada dos por tres every five minutes; continually ver también **seis**

doscientos, tas *numeral* two hundred ver también **seis**

dosificar *vt figurado* [*fuerzas, palabras*] to use sparingly

dosis *sf invariable literal & figurado* dose • **en pequeñas dosis** in small doses

dossier *sm invariable* dossier

dote *sf* [*en boda*] dowry

Dr. (*abreviatura escrita de* doctor) Dr.

Dra. (*abreviatura escrita de* doctora) Dr.

dragón *sm* dragon

drama *sm* ❶ [*generalmente*] drama ❷ [*obra*] play

dramático, ca *adj* dramatic ☼: *Los adjetivos ingleses son invariables.*

dramaturgo, ga *sm, f* playwright

drástico, ca *adj* drastic ☼: *Los adjetivos ingleses son invariables.*

drenar *vt* to drain

driblar *vt* DEPORTE to dribble

droga *sf* drug • **la droga** drugs *pl* ▶ **droga blanda** soft drug ▶ **droga de diseño** designer drug ▶ **droga dura** hard drug

drogadicto, ta *sm, f* drug addict

drogar *vt* to drug

dromedario *sm* dromedary

dto. *abreviatura escrita de* **descuento**

Dublín *nombre propio* Dublin

ducha *sf* shower • **la ducha de este baño es demasiado pequeña** the shower in this bathroom is too small • **me di una ducha antes de acostarme** I took a shower before going to bed ▶ **ducha de teléfono** hand-held shower

expresión una ducha de agua fría a bucket of cold water

duchar *vt* to shower

■ **ducharse** *v pronominal* to take a shower • **me ducho siempre de mañana** I always take a shower in the morning

duda *sf* doubt • **tengo dudas sobre la honestidad de su respuesta** I have doubts about the honesty of his reply • **la profesora preguntó si alguien tenía alguna duda sobre el tema** the professor asked if anybody had any questions about the topic • **poner algo en duda** to call something into question • **salir de dudas** to set your mind at rest • **sin duda** undoubtedly

expresiones no cabe duda there is no doubt about it ▶ **sin la menor duda** without the slightest doubt ▶ **sin sombra de duda** beyond the shadow of a doubt

dudar ◆ *vi* ❶ [*desconfiar*] • **dudar de algo/alguien** to have your doubts about something/somebody ❷ [*no estar seguro*] • **dudar sobre algo** to be unsure about something ❸ [*vacilar*] to hesitate • **dudar entre hacer una cosa u otra** to hesitate between one thing or another • **dudo entre ir al cine o ir al teatro** I am hesitating between going to the movies and going to the theater

◆ *vt* to doubt • **dudo que venga** I doubt whether he'll come • **duda de todo y de todos** he doubts everything and everyone

dudoso, sa *adj* ❶ [*improbable*] • **ser dudoso (que)** to be doubtful (whether); to be unlikely (that) ❷ [*vacilante*] hesitant ❸ [*sospechoso*] suspect ☼: *Los adjetivos ingleses son invariables.*

duelo *sm* ❶ [*combate*] duel • **batirse en duelo** to fight a duel ❷ [*sentimiento*] grief

duende *sm* [*personaje*] goblin

dueño, ña *sm, f* ❶ [*generalmente*] owner ❷ [*de piso* ETC] landlord, *femenino* landlady • **cambiar de dueño** to change hands

dulce ◆ *adj* ❶ [*generalmente*] sweet ❷ [*agua*] fresh ❸ [*mirada*] tender ☼: *Los adjetivos ingleses son invariables.*

◆ *sm* ❶ [*caramelo, golosina*] candy ❷ [*postre*] dessert

expresión a nadie le amarga un dulce anything's better than nothing

dulzura *sf* [*generalmente*] sweetness

duna *sf* dune

dúo *sm* ❶ MÚSICA duet ❷ [*pareja*] duo • **a dúo** together

duodécimo, ma *numeral* twelfth

duplicar *vt* ❶ [*cantidad*] to double ❷ [*documento*] to duplicate

duque, esa *sm, f* duke, *femenino* duchess

duración *sf* length • **de larga duración a)** [*pila, foco*] long-life **b)** [*huelga*] long-term **c)** [*disco*] long-playing

duradero, ra *adj* ❶ [*generalmente*] lasting ❷ [*ropa, zapatos*] hard-wearing ☼: *Los adjetivos ingleses son invariables.*

durante *preposición* during • **le escribí durante las vacaciones** I wrote to him during vacation • **estuve escribiendo durante una hora** I was writing for an hour • **durante toda la semana** all week

durar *vi* ❶ [*generalmente*] to last • **estos zapatos nuevos me duraron sólo dos meses** these new shoes lasted me only two months ❷ [*permanecer, subsistir*] to remain ❸ [*ropa*] to wear well • **aún dura la fiesta** the party's still going on

duraznero *sm* peach tree

durazno *sm* peach

dúrex *sm* Scotch® tape

dureza *sf* ❶ [*de objeto, metal* ETC] hardness ❷ [*de clima, persona*] harshness

duro, ra *adj* ❶ [*generalmente*] hard • **este tipo de madera es más duro que el otro** this type of wood is

duro

harder than the other ❷ [*carne*] [*material*] tough • **un material duro** a tough material ❸ [*palabras, clima*] harsh.💡 *Los adjetivos ingleses son invariables.*

expresión a duras penas with great difficulty • **a duras penas gana para vivir** with great difficulty he makes a living

■ **duro** *adv* hard • **estudio duro para el examen** I am studying hard for the exam

E

e¹, E *sf* [letra] e ; E
■ **E** *sm* (*abreviatura de* este) E

e² *conjunción* and • **María e Inés son compañeras de clase** María and Inés are classmates

ebrio, ebria *adj* [borracho] drunk ☼: *Los adjetivos ingleses son invariables.*

ebullición *sf* boiling • **punto de ebullición** boiling point

eccema *sm* eczema

---

echar
◆ *vt*

❶ [aventar, lanzar algo]
• **échame la pelota** throw me the ball
• **échalo a la basura** throw it away

❷ [depositar algo en un sitio determinado]
• **eché la carta al buzón** I posted the letter
• **echar azúcar en el café** to put some sugar in your coffee

❸ [cerrar]
• **echar la llave** to lock the door
• **echar el cerrojo** to bolt the door

❹ [despedir algo]
• **echar vapor/chispas** to steam/spark
• **echar humo** to smoke
• **echar lágrimas** to cry

❺ [correr a alguien]
• **lo echaron del colegio** he's been expelled from his school
• **la empresa echó a catorce empleados** the company sacked fourteen employees

❻ [imponer un castigo]
• **le echaron diez años de prisión** they sentenced him to ten years

❼ [dar de comer]
• **fue a echar comida a las gallinas** he went to feed the hens

❽ [producir algo, refiriéndose a un organismo]
• **los rosales echan flores** roses flower

❾ *familiar* [hacer una suposición]
• **¿cuántos años me echas?** how old do you reckon I am?

• **¿qué precio le echas?** what do you reckon I paid for this?

expresiones **echar abajo** demolish ▶ **echar cuentas** to settle up ▶ **echo de menos aquella época** I miss that time ▶ **echo de menos a mis hijos** I miss my children ▶ **las lluvias echaron a perder la cosecha** the rains ruined the crops ▶ **echó a perder todos nuestros planes** he ruined all our plans ▶ **vas a echar a perder a la niña con tantos regalos** you're going to spoil the girl with so many gifts

■ **echar a**
◆ *v + preposición*

[empezar a realizar una acción] to start
• **echó a correr** he started running

■ **echarse**
◆ *v pronominal*

❶ [acostarse en algún sitio] to lie down
• **me voy a echar un ratito** I'm going to lie down for a while

❷ [lanzarse sobre algo o alguien] to throw yourself at
• **al vernos se nos echó encima** when he saw us, he threw himself at us

❸ [en expresiones]
• **echarse a un lado** to move aside
• **me eché atrás para que pasaran** I moved aside to let them by
• **¡ahora ya no te puedes echar atrás!** now you can't get out of it!
• **toda la comida se ha echado a perder** all the food has gone bad
• **con la lluvia la fiesta se echó a perder** the party was ruined by the rain

■ **echarse a**
◆ *v pronominal + preposición*

[empezar a realizar una acción] to start to
• **se echó a llorar** he burst into tears

---

eclipse *sm* eclipse • **eclipse lunar** lunar eclipse • **eclipse solar** solar eclipse • **eclipse total** total eclipse

E

eco *sm* echo • **en esta habitación hay eco** there's an echo in this room

ecología *sf* ecology

ecológico, ca *adj* ❶ [*generalmente*] ecological ❷ [*alimentos*] organic ❖ *Los adjetivos ingleses son invariables.*

ecologista ◆ *adj* environmental ❖ *Los adjetivos ingleses son invariables.*

◆ *smf* environmentalist

economía *sf* ❶ [*generalmente*] economy • **la economía no anda muy bien** the economy is not doing very well ▶ **economía sumergida** black economy ❷ [*estudio*] economics ❖ *incontable* • **es profesor de economía** he's a professor of economics ▶ **economía familiar** home economics ❸ [*ahorro*] saving

económico, ca *adj* ❶ [*problema, doctrina* ETC] economic ❷ [*barato*] cheap ❸ [*que gasta poco - motor* ETC] economical; [*- persona*] thrifty ❖ *Los adjetivos ingleses son invariables.*

economista *smf* economist

economizar *vt* to save

ecosistema *sm* ecosystem

ecotasa *sf* ecotax

ecoturismo *sm* ecotourism

ecuación *sf* equation

ecuador *sm* equator

expresión **pasar el ecuador** to pass the halfway mark

Ecuador *nombre propio* Ecuador

ecuatoriano, na *adj* & *sm, f* Ecuadorian ❖ *Los adjetivos ingleses son invariables.*

En inglés, los adjetivos que se refieren a un país o una región se escriben con mayúscula.

edad *sf* age • **a la edad de tres años** at the age of three • **¿qué edad tienes?** how old are you? • **tiene 25 años de edad** she's 25 (years old) • **una persona de edad** an elderly person • **edad avanzada** old age ▶ **edad adulta** adulthood ▶ **edad del juicio** ∩ **de la razón** age of reason ▶ **edad escolar** school age ▶ **Edad Media** Middle Ages *pl* ▶ **edad mental** mental age ▶ **edad del pavo** awkward age

edecán *sm* assistant

edición *sf* ❶ [*acción* IMPRENTA publication; INFORMÁTICA, RADIO & TELEVISIÓN editing ❷ *ejemplares*] edition

edificar *vt* [*construir*] to build

edificio *sm* building

editar *vt* ❶ [*libro, periódico*] to publish ❷ [*disco*] to release ❸ INFORMÁTICA, RADIO & TELEVISIÓN to edit

editor, ra ◆ *adj* publishing ❖ *Sólo se usa delante del sustantivo.*

◆ *sm, f* ❶ [*de libro, periódico*] publisher ❷ RADIO & TELEVISIÓN editor

editorial ◆ *adj* publishing ❖ *Sólo se usa delante del sustantivo.*

◆ *sm* editorial

◆ *sf* publishing house

edredón *sm* comforter ▶ **edredón nórdico** duvet

educación *sf* ❶ [*enseñanza*] education ▶ **educación física/sexual** physical/sex education ▶ **educación primaria/secundaria** primary/secondary education ❷ [*crianza*] upbringing • **este niño ha tenido una muy buena educación** this boy has had a very good upbringing ❸ [*modales*] good manners *pl* • **¡qué poca educación!** how rude! ▶ **mala educación** bad manners *pl*

educado, da *adj* well-mannered • **mal educado** rude ; ill-mannered ❖ *Los adjetivos ingleses son invariables.*

educador, ra *sm, f* teacher

educar *vt* ❶ [*enseñar*] to educate • **educaron a sus hijos en los mejores colegios** they educated their children in the best secondary schools ❷ [*criar*] to bring up • **no han educado a su hija de una manera muy tradicional** they haven't brought up their daughter in a very traditional manner ❸ [*cuerpo, voz, oído*] to train

edulcorante *sm* sweetener

EE UU (*abreviatura escrita de* Estados Unidos) *smpl* USA

efectivamente *adv* [*en respuestas*] precisely

efectividad *sf* effectiveness

efectivo, va *adj* ❶ [*útil*] effective ❷ [*real*] actual • **hacer efectivo a)** [*generalmente*] to carry out **b)** [*promesa*] to keep **c)** [*dinero, crédito*] to pay **d)** [*cheque*] to cash ❖ *Los adjetivos ingleses son invariables.*

■ **efectivo** *sm* [*dinero*] cash • **en efectivo** in cash • **efectivo en caja** cash in hand

efecto *sm* ❶ [*generalmente*] effect • **el medicamento me hizo efecto en pocos minutos** the medicine took effect on me in just a few minutes • **de efecto retardado** delayed-action ▶ **efecto dominó** domino effect ▶ **efecto invernadero** greenhouse effect ▶ **efecto óptico** optical illusion ▶ **efectos especiales** special effects ▶ **efectos personales** personal possessions ▶ **efectos secundarios** side effects ▶ **efectos sonoros/visuales** sound/visual effects ❷ [*finalidad*] aim • **a tal efecto** to that end • **a efectos** ∩ **para los efectos de algo** as far as something is concerned ❸ [*impresión*] impression • **producir buen/mal efecto** to make a good/bad impression ❹ [*de balón, bola*] spin • **dar efecto a** to put spin on ❺ COMERCIO [*documento*] bill

efectuar *vt* ❶ [*generalmente*] to carry out ❷ [*compra, pago, viaje*] to make

efervescente *adj* [*bebida*] fizzy ❖ *Los adjetivos ingleses son invariables.*

eficacia *sf* ❶ [*eficiencia*] efficiency ❷ [*efectividad*] effectiveness

eficaz *adj* ❶ [*eficiente*] efficient • **es un empleado muy eficaz** he's a very efficient employee ❷ [*efectivo*] effective • **este medicamento es muy eficaz para curar los dolores de cabeza** this medicine is very effective for curing headaches ❖ *Los adjetivos ingleses son invariables.*

eficiencia *sf* efficiency

eficiente *adj* efficient ☼ *Los adjetivos ingleses son invariables.*

egipcio, cia *adj* & *sm, f* Egyptian ☼ *Los adjetivos ingleses son invariables.*

Egipto *nombre propio* Egypt

egoísmo *sm* selfishness

egoísta ◆ *adj* selfish ☼ *Los adjetivos ingleses son invariables.*
◆ *smf* selfish person

egresado, da *sm, f* graduate

egresar *vi* to graduate • **Francisco egresó de una universidad pública** Francisco graduated from a public university

egreso *sm* graduation

eh *exclamación* • **¡eh!** hey!

ej. *abreviatura escrita de* **ejemplo**

eje *sm* ❶ [*de rueda*] axle • **se rompió uno de los ejes de la rueda** one of the axles of the wheel broke ❷ [*de máquina*] shaft ❸ GEOMETRÍA axis • **el eje de la Tierra es una línea imaginaria** the earth's axis is an imaginary line ❹ *figurado* [*idea central*] basis • **el eje de sus conversaciones siempre es el dinero** the basis of their conversations is always money

ejecución *sf* ❶ [*realización*] carrying out ❷ [*de condenado*] execution ❸ [*de concierto*] performance

ejecutar *vt* ❶ [*realizar*] to carry out ❷ [*condenado*] to execute ❸ [*concierto*] to perform ❹ INFORMÁTICA [*programa*] to run

ejem *exclamación* • **¡ejem! a)** [*expresa duda*] um! **b)** [*expresa ironía*] ahem!

ejemplar ◆ *adj* exemplary • **comportamiento ejemplar** exemplary behavior ☼ *Los adjetivos ingleses son invariables.*
◆ *sm* ❶ [*de libro*] copy ❷ [*de revista*] issue ❸ [*de moneda*] example ❹ [*de especie, raza*] specimen • **ejemplar de muestra** specimen copy

ejemplo *sm* example • **siguieron el buen ejemplo de su madre** they followed their mother's good example • **por ejemplo** for example
expresión **predicar con el ejemplo** to practise what you preach

ejercer ◆ *vt* ❶ [*profesión*] to practise ❷ [*cargo*] to hold ❸ [*poder, derecho*] to exercise ❹ [*influencia, dominio*] to exert • **ejercer presión sobre** to put pressure on
◆ *vi* to practise (your profession) • **ejercer de** to practise • **ejerce de abogado** he practices law

ejercicio *sm* ❶ [*generalmente*] exercise • **la maestra puso varios ejercicios de geometría** the teacher assigned several geometry exercises • **hacer ejercicio** to (do) exercise • **ejercicio escrito** written exercise • **ejercicio físico** physical exercise • **ejercicios de calentamiento** warm-up exercises • **ejercicios de mantenimiento** keep-fit exercises ❷ [*de profesión*] practising ❸ [*de cargo, funciones*] carrying out

ejército *sm* army

ejote *sm* green bean

el, la (mpl los, fpl las) *artículo* ❶ [*en sentido genérico*] the • **el coche** the car • **la casa** the house • **los niños** the children • **el agua/hacha/águila** the water/axe/eagle • **fui a recoger a los niños** I went to pick up the children • **los niños imitan a los adultos** children copy adults ❷ [*con sustantivo abstracto*] • **el amor** love • **la vida** life ❸ [*indica posesión, pertenencia*] • **se partió la pierna** he broke his leg • **se quitó los zapatos** she took her shoes off • **tiene el pelo oscuro** he has dark hair ❹ [*con días de la semana*] • **vuelven el sábado** they're coming back on Saturday ❺ [*con nombres propios geográficos*] the • **el Sena** the (River) Seine • **el Everest** (Mount) Everest ❻ [*con complemento de nombre, especificativo*] • **el de** the one • **he perdido el tren, cogeré el de las nueve** I've missed the train, I'll get the nine o'clock one • **el de azul** the one in blue ❼ [*con complemento de nombre, posesivo*] • **mi hermano y el de Juan** my brother and Juan's ❽ [*antes de frase*] • **el que a)** [*cosa*] the one; whichever **b)** [*persona*] whoever • **coge el que quieras** take whichever you like • **el que más corra** whoever runs fastest ❾ [*antes de adjetivo*] • **prefiero el rojo al azul** I prefer the red one to the blue one

él, ella *pronombre personal* ❶ [*sujeto, predicado - persona*] he, *femenino* she; [- *animal, cosa*] it • **mi hermana es ella** she's the one who is my sister ❷ ☼ *después de preposición* [*complemento*] him, *femenino* her • **voy a ir de vacaciones con ella** I'm going on holiday with her • **díselo a ella** tell her it ❸ [*posesivo*] • **de él** his • **de ella** hers

elaborar *vt* ❶ [*producto*] to make ❷ [*idea*] to work out ❸ [*plan, informe*] to draw up

elástico, ca *adj* [*generalmente*] elastic ☼ *Los adjetivos ingleses son invariables.*
■ **elástico** *sm* [*cinta*] elastic

elección *sf* ❶ [*nombramiento*] election • **tuvimos una elección para escoger el presidente del club** we had an election to choose the president of the club ❷ [*opción*] choice • **por lo menos tienes elección** at least you have a choice

elector, ra *sm, f* voter

electorado *sm* electorate

electoral *adj* electoral ☼ *Los adjetivos ingleses son invariables.*

electricidad *sf* electricity ▸ **electricidad estática** static electricity

electricista *smf* electrician

eléctrico, ca *adj* electric ☼ *Los adjetivos ingleses son invariables.*

electrocutar *vt* to electrocute

electrodoméstico *sm* ☼ *generalmente pl* electrical household appliance

electrón *sm* electron

electrónico, ca *adj* [*de la electrónica*] electronic ☼ *Los adjetivos ingleses son invariables.*
■ **electrónica** *sf* electronics ☼ *incontable*

elefante, ta *sm, f* elephant

elegancia *sf* elegance

E

elegante *adj* ❶ [*persona, traje, estilo*] elegant ❷ [*conducta, actitud, respuesta*] dignified ⚲ *Los adjetivos ingleses son invariables.*

elegantoso, sa *adj* elegant ⚲ *Los adjetivos ingleses son invariables.*

elegir *vt* ❶ [*escoger*] to choose • **elegimos esta casa por el precio** we chose this house because of the price ❷ [*por votación*] to elect

elemental *adj* ❶ [*básico*] basic ❷ [*obvio*] obvious ⚲ *Los adjetivos ingleses son invariables.*

elemento ◆ *sm* ❶ [*generalmente*] element ❷ [*factor*] factor ❸ [*persona - en equipo, colectivo*] individual
◆ *smf familiar* • **una elementa de cuidado** a bad lot • **¡menudo elemento está hecho tu sobrino!** your nephew is a real tearaway!

elevación *sf* ❶ [*de pesos, objetos* ETC] lifting ❷ [*de nivel, altura, precios*] rise ❸ [*de terreno*] elevation

elevado, da *adj* ❶ [*alto*] high ❷ figurado [*sublime*] lofty ⚲ *Los adjetivos ingleses son invariables.*

elevador *sm* ❶ [*montacargas*] hoist ❷ [*ascensor*] elevator

elevadorista *smf* elevator operator

elevalunas *sm invariable* window winder

elevar *vt* ❶ [*generalmente*] MATEMÁTICAS to raise ❷ [*peso, objeto*] to lift ❸ [*ascender*] • **elevar a alguien (a)** to elevate somebody (to)

eliminar *vt* ❶ [*generalmente*] to eliminate • **un equipo rival eliminó a mi equipo de futbol en la final** a rival team eliminated my soccer team in the finals ❷ [*contaminación, enfermedad*] to get rid of • **el agua ayuda a eliminar las sustancias tóxicas del cuerpo** water helps to get rid of the body's toxic substances

eliminatorio, ria *adj* qualifying ⚲ *Sólo se usa delante del sustantivo.*
■ **eliminatoria** *sf* ❶ [*generalmente*] qualifying round ❷ [*en atletismo*] heat

élite, elite *sf* elite

elitista *adj & smf* elitist ⚲ *Los adjetivos ingleses son invariables.*

elixir, elíxir *sm* ❶ [*producto medicinal*] ▶ **elixir bucal** mouthwash ❷ figurado [*remedio milagroso*] elixir

ello *pronombre personal* it • **no quiero hablar de ello** I don't want to talk about it • **por ello** for that reason

ellos, ellas *pronombre personal* ❶ [*sujeto, predicado*] they • **los invitados son ellos** they are the guests; it is they who are the guests ❷ ⚲ *después de preposición* [*complemento*] them • **me voy al bar con ellas** I'm going with them to the bar • **díselo a ellos** tell them it ❸ [*posesivo*] • **de ellos/ellas** theirs • **esta es la casa de ellas** this is their house

elogiar *vt* to praise

elogio *sm* praise

elote *sm* corncob

El Salvador *nombre propio* El Salvador

embadurnar *vt* • **embadurnar algo** to smear something

embajada *sf* [*edificio*] embassy

embajador, ra *sm, f* ambassador

embalaje *sm* [*acción*] packing

embalar *vt* to pack

embalsamar *vt* to embalm

embalse *sm* reservoir

embarazada ◆ *adj f* pregnant • **está embarazada de tres meses** she's three months pregnant • **dejar embarazada a alguien** to get somebody pregnant • **quedarse embarazada** to get pregnant ⚲ *Los adjetivos ingleses son invariables.*
◆ *sf* pregnant woman

embarazada ≠ embarrassed

• La palabra inglesa **embarrassed** es un falso amigo que significa *avergonzado*.
• *Embarazada* se traduce al inglés por **pregnant**.

embarazo *sm* ❶ [*preñez*] pregnancy, *plural* pregnancies • **el embarazo ha sido difícil** the pregnancy has been difficult • **interrumpir un embarazo** to terminate a pregnancy • **prueba del embarazo** pregnancy test ❷ [*timidez*] embarrassment

embarazoso, sa *adj* embarrassing ⚲ *Los adjetivos ingleses son invariables.*

embarcación *sf* [*barco*] boat ▶ **embarcación pesquera** fishing boat ▶ **embarcación de recreo** pleasure boat

embarcadero *sm* jetty

embarcar ◆ *vt* ❶ [*personas*] to board ❷ [*mercancías*] to ship
◆ *vi* to board

embargo *sm* ❶ DERECHO seizure ❷ ECONOMÍA embargo

embarque *sm* ❶ [*de personas*] boarding ❷ [*de mercancías*] embarkation

embarrancar *vi* to run aground

embellecer *vt* to adorn

embestida *sf* ❶ [*generalmente*] attack ❷ [*de toro*] charge

embestir *vt* ❶ [*generalmente*] to attack ❷ [*toro*] to charge

emblema *sm* ❶ [*divisa, distintivo*] emblem ❷ [*símbolo*] symbol

embolia *sf* embolism

émbolo *sm* AUTOMÓVILES piston

embonar *vt familiar* ❶ [*ajustar*] to suit ❷ [*abonar*] to manure ❸ [*ensamblar*] to join

emborrachar *vt* to make drunk
■ **emborracharse** *v pronominal* to get drunk

emborronar *vt* ❶ [*garabatear*] to scribble on ❷ [*manchar*] to smudge

emboscada *sf literal & figurado* ambush

embotellado, da *adj* bottled ⚲: *Los adjetivos ingleses son invariables.*

embotellamiento *sm* [*de tráfico*] traffic jam

embotellar *vt* [*líquido*] to bottle

embragar *vi* to engage the clutch

embrague *sm* clutch • **suelta el embrague despacio** let up on the clutch slowly

embriaguez *sf* ❶ [*borrachera*] drunkenness ❷ [*éxtasis*] intoxication

embrión *sm* embryo

embrollo *sm* ❶ [*de hilos*] tangle ❷ *figurado* [*lío*] mess ❸ [*mentira*] lie

embromar *vt* ❶ [*burlarse de*] to make fun of ❷ [*engañar*] to cheat ❸ [*fiesta, vacaciones*] to ruin

embrujar *vt literal & figurado* to bewitch

embrujo *sm* ❶ [*maleficio*] curse ❷ *figurado* [*de ciudad, ojos*] charm

embrutecer *vt* to brutalize

embudo *sm* funnel

embuste *sm* lie

embustero, ra ◆ *adj* lying ⚲: *Los adjetivos ingleses son invariables.*
◆ *sm, f* liar

embutido *sm* [*comida*] cold cured meat

emergencia *sf* ❶ [*urgencia*] emergency, *plural* <u>emergencies</u> • **llámame si ocurre alguna emergencia** call me if there is an emergency • **en caso de emergencia** in case of emergency ❷ [*brote*] emergence

emerger *vi* ❶ [*salir del agua*] to emerge ❷ [*aparecer*] to appear

emigración *sf* ❶ [*de personas*] emigration ❷ [*de aves*] migration

emigrante *adj* & *smf* emigrant ⚲: *Los adjetivos ingleses son invariables.*

emigrar *vi* ❶ [*persona*] to emigrate • **mi abuelo emigró de Europa a principios del siglo XX** my grandfather emigrated from Europe at the beginning of the 20th century ❷ [*ave*] to migrate • **muchos pájaros emigran al sur antes del invierno** many birds migrate to the south before the winter

eminencia *sf* [*persona*] leading light

eminente *adj* [*distinguido*] eminent ⚲: *Los adjetivos ingleses son invariables.*

emirato *sm* emirate

Emiratos Árabes Unidos *smpl* • **los Emiratos Árabes Unidos** United Arab Emirates

emisión *sf* ❶ [*de energía, rayos* ETC] emission ❷ RADIO & TELEVISIÓN [*transmisión*] broadcasting ; [*programa*] program; broadcast

emisor, ra *adj* transmitting ⚲: *Sólo se usa delante del sustantivo.*

■ **emisora** *sf* radio station • **emisora pirata** pirate radio station

emitir ◆ *vt* ❶ [*rayos, calor, sonidos*] to emit • **la televisión emitía un sonido raro** the television was emitting a strange sound ❷ [*moneda, sellos, bonos*] to issue

• **el Gobierno emitirá nuevos billetes** the government will issue new bills ❸ [*expresar - juicio, opinión*] to express; [*- fallo*] to pronounce ❹ RADIO & TELEVISIÓN to broadcast
◆ *vi* to broadcast

emoción *sf* ❶ [*conmoción, sentimiento*] emotion • **no puedo expresar la emoción que sentía** I can't express the emotion I felt ❷ [*expectación*] excitement • **¡qué emoción!** how exciting!

emocionante *adj* ❶ [*conmovedor*] moving ❷ [*apasionante*] exciting ⚲: *Los adjetivos ingleses son invariables.*

emocionar *vt* ❶ [*conmover*] to move ❷ [*excitar, apasionar*] to thrill

emotivo, va *adj* ❶ [*persona*] emotional ❷ [*escena, palabras*] moving ⚲: *Los adjetivos ingleses son invariables.*

empacar *vi* to pack

empachar *vt* to give indigestion to

empacho *sm* [*indigestión*] upset stomach

empadronarse *v pronominal* ≃ to register on the electoral roll

empalagoso, sa *adj* sickly ⚲: *Los adjetivos ingleses son invariables.*

empalmar ◆ *vt* [*tubos, cables*] to connect
◆ *vi* ❶ [*autocares, trenes*] to connect ❷ [*carreteras*] to link o join (up)

empalme *sm* ❶ [*entre cables, tubos*] joint ❷ [*de líneas férreas, carreteras*] junction

empanada *sf* pasty

empanadilla *sf* small pasty

empanar *vt* COCINA to coat in breadcrumbs

empantanar *vt* to flood

empañar *vt* ❶ [*cristal*] to mist o steam up ❷ *figurado* [*reputación*] to tarnish

empapar *vt* ❶ [*mojar*] to soak ❷ [*absorber*] to soak up

■ **empaparse** *v pronominal* ❶ [*mojarse*] to get soaked • **me empapé con el chaparrón** I got soaked in the downpour ❷ [*enterarse bien*] to soak up • **fui allí a vivir una temporada para empaparme del ambiente** I went to live there a while to soak up the atmosphere • **se empapó de sociología antes de dar la conferencia** she did a lot of reading up about sociology before giving her speech • **¡para que te empapes!** *familiar* so there!

empapelar *vt* [*pared*] to paper

empaquetar *vt* to pack

emparejar *vt* [*aparejar - personas*] to pair off; [*- zapatos* ETC] to match (up)

emparentar *vi* • **emparentar con** to marry into

empastar *vt* to fill

empaste *sm* filling

empatar *vi* ❶ DEPORTE to draw ❷ [*en elecciones* ETC] to tie • **empatar a cero** to draw nil-nil

empate *sm* [*resultado*] draw • **un empate a cero/dos** a goalless/two-all draw

empedernido, da adj**❶** [bebedor, fumador] heavy **❷** [criminal, jugador] hardened.☼: *Los adjetivos ingleses son invariables.*

empeine sm [de pie, zapato] instep

empeñar vt [joyas ETC] to pawn

■ **empeñarse** v pronominal **❶** [obstinarse] to insist • **empeñarse en hacer algo a)** [obstinarse] to insist on doing something **b)** [persistir] to persist in doing something • **se empeña en seguir haciendo deporte** he insists on continuing to play sports • **no te empeñes en convencerme, no vale la pena** don't keep trying to convince me, you're wasting your time **❷** [endeudarse] to get into debt

empeño sm **❶** [de joyas ETC] pawning • **casa de empeños** pawnshop **❷** [obstinación] determination • **poner mucho empeño en algo** to put a lot of effort into something • **tener empeño en hacer algo** to be determined to do something

empeorar vi to get worse

emperador, emperatriz sm, f emperor, *femenino* empress

■ **emperador** sm [pez] swordfish

empezar ♦ vt to begin; to start

♦ vi • **ya empezó la clase** class already began • **empezar (a hacer algo)** to begin o start (to do something) • **empezar (por hacer algo)** to begin o start (by doing something) • **para empezar** to begin o start with • **por algo se empieza** you've got to start somewhere

empinado, da adj steep.☼: *Los adjetivos ingleses son invariables.*

empinar vt [levantar] to raise

empírico, ca adj empirical.☼: *Los adjetivos ingleses son invariables.*

emplazamiento sm [ubicación] location

emplazar vt**❶** [situar] to locate**❷** MILITAR to position **❸** [citar] to summon**❹** DERECHO to summons

empleado, da sm, f**❶** [generalmente] employee **❷** [de banco, administración, oficina] clerk

emplear vt**❶** [usar - objetos, materiales ETC] to use; [- tiempo] to spend • **emplean materiales reciclados** they use recycled materials • **emplear algo en hacer algo** to use something to do something **❷** [contratar] to employ

empleo sm**❶** [uso] use • **modo de empleo** instructions for use **❷** [trabajo] employment **❸** [puesto] job • **me ofrecieron empleo en una escuela** they offered me a job at a school • **estar sin empleo** to be out of work

empobrecer vt to impoverish

■ **empobrecerse** v pronominal to get poorer

empollar vt [huevo] to incubate

empotrado, da adj fitted.☼: *Los adjetivos ingleses son invariables.*

empotrar vt to fit

emprendedor, ra adj enterprising.☼: *Los adjetivos ingleses son invariables.*

emprender vt**❶** [trabajo] to start **❷** [viaje, marcha] to set off on • **emprender vuelo** to fly off

EXPRESIÓN emprenderla con alguien to take it out on somebody ▶ **emprenderla a golpes con alguien** to start hitting somebody

empresa sf [sociedad] company • **pequeña y mediana empresa** small and medium-sized business ▶ **empresa privada** private company ▶ **empresa de trabajo temporal** temping agency

empresarial adj management.☼: *Sólo se usa delante del sustantivo.*

empresario, ria sm, f**❶** [patrono] employer **❷** [hombre, mujer de negocios] businessman, *femenino* businesswoman **❸** [de teatro] impresario

empujar vt to push • **empujamos el carro unos metros** we pushed the car a few meters • **empujar a alguien a que haga algo** to push somebody into doing something

empuje sm**❶** [presión] push • **le dimos un fuerte empuje a este proyecto** we gave this project a strong push **❷** [energía] drive • **siempre tuvo empuje para trabajar** he always had the drive to work

empujón sm [empellón] push • **le dieron un empujón tan grande que se cayó por la escalera** they gave him such a hard push that he fell down the stairs • **abrirse paso a empujones** to push your way through

empuñadura sf**❶** handle **❷** [de espada] hilt

empuñar vt to take hold of

emulsión sf emulsion

---

en

♦ *preposición*

❶ [en el interior de] in; into
• **lo guardé en el cajón** I put it away in the drawer
• **entraron en la habitación** they went into the room

❷ [indica el lugar donde se encuentra algo o alguien] in; at
• **viven en París** they live in Paris
• **en la calle** in the street
• **en casa** at home
• **en el trabajo** at work

❸ [indica la posición de algo] on
• **en la mesa/el estante** on the table/shelf

❹ [indica un momento preciso] in
• **llegará en mayo** it will arrive in May
• **nació en 1967** he was born in 1967
• **en Navidad/invierno** at Christmas/in winter
• **en aquella época** at that time
• **en la antigüedad** in antiquity

❺ [indica la duración] in
• **lo hizo en dos días** he did it in two days

❻ [indica el medio de transporte] en
• **ir en tren/coche/avión/barco** to go by train/car/plane/boat

❼ [indica la manera]
• **pagar en metálico** to pay cash
• **pagar en dólares** to pay in dollars
• **fabricar en serie** to mass produce
• **lo dijo en inglés** he said it in English

• **en voz baja** in a low voice
• **lo conocí en su forma de hablar** I recognized him by the way he spoke
❽ [*indica el destino de algo*] on
• **todo se lo gasta en ropa** he spends all his money on clothes
❾ [*seguido por una cifra*]
• **te lo dejo en 200 pesos** I can let you have it for 200 pesos
• **las ganancias se calculan en millones** their profits are in the millions
❿ [*indica una cualidad*]
• **es un experto en la materia** he's an expert in the field
• **es doctor en medicina** she's a doctor of medicine
• **le supera en inteligencia** she's cleverer than he is

enagua *sf* petticoat

enamorado, da ◆ *adj* • **enamorado (de)** in love (with) ☼: *Los adjetivos ingleses son invariables.*
◆ *sm, f* lover

enamorar *vt* to win the heart of
■ **enamorarse** *v pronominal* • **enamorarse (de)** to fall in love (with) • **se enamora fácilmente** she falls in love easily • **se enamoró de Catalina** he fell in love with Catalina

enano, na *adj & sm, f* dwarf ☼: *Los adjetivos ingleses son invariables.*
expresión **disfrutar como un enano** *familiar* to have a whale of a time

encabezamiento *sm* ❶ [*de carta, escrito*] heading ❷ [*de artículo periodístico*] headline ❸ [*preámbulo*] foreword

encabezar *vt* ❶ [*artículo de periódico*] to headline ❷ [*libro*] to write the foreword for ❸ [*lista, carta*] to head ❹ [*marcha, expedición*] to lead

encadenar *vt* ❶ [*atar*] to chain (up) • **encadené la bicicleta a un árbol** I chained the bicycle to a tree ❷ [*enlazar*] to link (together)

encajar ◆ *vt* ❶ [*meter ajustando*] • **encajar (en)** to fit (into) ❷ [*meter con fuerza*] • **encajar (en)** to push (into) ❸ [*hueso dislocado*] to set ❹ [*recibir - golpe, noticia, críticas*] to take
◆ *vi* ❶ [*piezas, objetos*] to fit ❷ [*hechos, declaraciones, datos*] • **encajar (con)** to square (with)

encallar *vi* [*barco*] to run aground

encaminar *vt* ❶ [*persona, pasos*] to direct ❷ [*medidas, leyes, actividades*] to aim • **encaminado a** aimed at

encantado, da *adj* ❶ [*contento*] delighted • **estar encantado con algo/alguien** to be delighted with something/somebody • **encantado de conocerle** pleased to meet you ❷ [*hechizado - casa, lugar*] haunted; [*- persona*] bewitched ☼: *Los adjetivos ingleses son invariables.*

encantador, ra *adj* charming ☼: *Los adjetivos ingleses son invariables.*

encantar *vt* ❶ [*gustar*] • **encantarle a alguien algo/hacer algo** to love something/doing something • **me encanta el chocolate** I love chocolate • **le encanta bailar** she loves dancing ❷ [*embrujar*] to cast a spell on

encanto *sm* ❶ [*atractivo*] charm • **ser un encanto** to be a treasure o a delight ❷ [*hechizo*] spell

encapuchado, da *adj* hooded ☼: *Los adjetivos ingleses son invariables.*

encaramar *vt* to lift up

encarcelar *vt* to imprison

encarecer *vt* [*productos, precios*] to make more expensive

encarecidamente *adv* earnestly

encarecimiento *sm* [*de producto, coste*] increase in price

encargado, da ◆ *adj* • **encargado (de)** responsible (for); in charge (of) ☼: *Los adjetivos ingleses son invariables.*
◆ *sm, f* ❶ [*generalmente*] person in charge ❷ COMERCIO manager, *femenino* manageress • **hablé con la encargada de la tienda** I spoke with the manager of the store ▶ **encargado de negocios** POLÍTICA chargé d'affaires

encargar *vt* ❶ [*poner al cargo*] • **encargar a alguien de algo** to put somebody in charge of something • **encargar a alguien que haga algo** to tell somebody to do something ❷ [*pedir*] to order • **encargamos dos libros por Internet** we ordered two books on the Internet
■ **encargarse** *v pronominal* [*ocuparse*] • **encargarse de** to take care of • **yo me encargaré de eso** I'll take care of that

encargo *sm* ❶ [*pedido*] order • **por encargo** to order ❷ [*recado*] errand ❸ [*tarea*] task

encarnación *sf* [*personificación - cosa*] embodiment; [*- persona*] personification

encarnado, da *adj* ❶ [*personificado*] incarnate ❷ [*color*] red ☼: *Los adjetivos ingleses son invariables.*

encarnizado, da *adj* bloody ☼: *Los adjetivos ingleses son invariables.*

encarrilar *vt* figurado [*negocio, situación*] to put on the right track

encasillar *vt* ❶ [*clasificar*] to pigeonhole ❷ TEATRO to typecast

encasquetar *vt* ❶ [*imponer*] • **encasquetar algo a alguien a)** [*idea, teoría*] to drum something into somebody **b)** [*discurso, lección*] to force somebody to sit through something ❷ [*sombrero*] to pull on

encendedor *sm* lighter

encender *vt* ❶ [*vela, cigarro, chimenea*] to light • **encendimos la chimenea** we lit the fire ❷ [*aparato*] to turn on • **encendió la luz** he turned on the light • **encendió el motor** she started up the engine ❸ figurado [*avivar - entusiasmo, ira*] to arouse; [*pasión, discusión*] to inflame

encerar *vt* to wax

encerrar *vt* ❶ [*recluir - generalmente*] to shut (up o in); [*- con llave*] to lock (up o in); [*- en la cárcel*] to lock away o up ❷ [*contener*] to contain
■ **encerrarse** *v pronominal* ❶ [*generalmente*] to shut yourself away ❷ [*con llave*] to lock yourself away

encestar *vt* & *vi* to score *(in basketball)*

enceste *sm* basket

encharcar *vt* to waterlog

enchilada *sf* ▸ *filled tortilla*

enchilado, da *adj* ❶ seasoned with chili ❷ [*rojo*] (bright) red

enchilarse *v pronominal* familiar [*enfadarse*] to get angry • **se enchiló con sus cuates** he got angry with his friends

enchufado, da *adj* familiar • **estar enchufado** to get where your are through connections.☿ *Los adjetivos ingleses son invariables.*

enchufar *vt* ❶ [*aparato*] to plug in • **enchufó la impresora** he plugged in the printer ❷ familiar [*a una persona*] to pull strings for

enchufe *sm* ❶ Electricidad [*macho*] plug; [*hembra*] socket • **enchufe múltiple** adapter ❷ familiar [*recomendación*] connections *pl* • **obtener algo por enchufe** to get something by pulling strings

encía *sf* gum

enciclopedia *sf* encyclopedia

encierro *sm* [*protesta*] sit-in

encima *adv* ❶ [*arriba*] on top • **por encima** [*superficialmente*] superficially ❷ [*en el piso de arriba*] upstairs • **yo vivo encima** I live upstairs ❸ [*en el tiempo*] • **ya tenemos encima el periodo de exámenes** the exam period is upon us ❹ [*además*] on top of that • **es feo y encima caro** it's ugly and on top of that expensive ❺ [*sobre sí*] • **lleva un abrigo encima** she has a coat on • **¿llevas dinero encima?** have you got any money on you?

encinta *adj f* pregnant.☿ *Los adjetivos ingleses son invariables.*

encoger ✦ *vt* ❶ [*ropa*] to shrink ❷ [*miembro, músculo*] to contract
✦ *vi* to shrink • **este pantalón encogió con el lavado** these pants shrank when washed
■ **encogerse** *v pronominal* ❶ [*ropa*] to shrink ❷ [*músculos* etc] to contract • **encogerse de hombros** to shrug your shoulders ❸ figurado [*apocarse*] to cringe

encomendar *vt* to entrust

encomienda *sf* [*encargo*] assignment; mission

encontrar *vt* ❶ [*generalmente*] to find ❷ [*dificultades*] to encounter ❸ [*persona*] to meet
■ **encontrarse** *v pronominal* ❶ [*hallarse*] to be • **se encuentra en París** she's in Paris • **la farmacia se encuentra en esta calle** the pharmacy is located on this street ❷ [*coincidir*] • **encontrarse (con alguien)** to meet (somebody) • **me encontré con Juan** I met Juan ❸ [*de ánimo*] to feel • **¿cómo te encuentras?** how are you feeling? • **encontrarse bien/mal** to feel fine/ill ❹ [*chocar*] to collide

encrucijada *sf* literal & figurado crossroads *sing*

encuadernación *sf* binding • **encuadernación en cuero** leather binding • **encuadernación en tela** cloth binding

encuadernar *vt* to bind

encuadrar *vt* ❶ [*enmarcar - cuadro, tema*] to frame ❷ [*encerrar*] to contain ❸ [*encajar*] to fit

encubierto, ta ✦ *participio pasado* → encubrir
✦ *adj* ❶ [*intento*] covert ❷ [*insulto, significado*] hidden.☿ *Los adjetivos ingleses son invariables.*

encubrir *vt* ❶ [*delito*] to conceal ❷ [*persona*] to harbor

encuentro *sm* ❶ [*acción*] meeting • **el encuentro de ex-alumnos es el sábado** the alumni meeting is Saturday • **salir al encuentro de alguien a)** [*para recibir*] to go to meet somebody **b)** [*para atacar*] to confront somebody ❷ Deporte game • **ayer se realizó el encuentro deportivo más popular del año** yesterday the most popular game of the year took place ❸ [*hallazgo*] find

encuesta *sf* ❶ [*de opinión*] survey ; opinion poll ❷ [*investigación*] inquiry

encuestador, ra *sm, f* pollster

encuestar *vt* to poll

endeble *adj* ❶ [*persona, argumento*] feeble ❷ [*objeto*] fragile.☿ *Los adjetivos ingleses son invariables.*

endémico, ca *adj* Medicina endemic.☿ *Los adjetivos ingleses son invariables.*

endemoniado, da *adj* ❶ familiar [*molesto - niño*] wicked; [*- trabajo*] very tricky ❷ [*desagradable*] terrible ❸ [*poseído*] possessed (of the devil).☿ *Los adjetivos ingleses son invariables.*

enderezar *vt* ❶ [*poner derecho*] to straighten ❷ [*poner vertical*] to put upright ❸ figurado [*corregir*] to set right

endeudamiento *sm* debt

endiablado, da *adj* ❶ [*persona*] wicked ❷ [*tiempo, genio*] foul ❸ [*problema, crucigrama*] fiendishly difficult.☿ *Los adjetivos ingleses son invariables.*

endibia, endivia *sf* endive

endosar *vt* ❶ [*tarea, trabajo*] • **endosar algo a alguien** to lumber somebody with something ❷ Comercio to endorse

endulzar *vt* ❶ [*con azúcar*] to sweeten ❷ figurado [*hacer agradable*] to ease

endurecer *vt* ❶ [*generalmente*] to harden ❷ [*fortalecer*] to strengthen

enemigo, ga ✦ *adj* enemy.☿ *Sólo se usa delante del sustantivo.* • **el ejército enemigo invadió la ciudad** the enemy army invaded the city • **ser enemigo de algo** to hate something
✦ *sm, f* enemy • **pasarse al enemigo** to go over to the enemy

enemistad *sf* enmity

enemistarse *v pronominal* • **enemistarse (con)** to fall out (with)

energético, ca *adj* energy ☼ *Sólo se usa delante del sustantivo.*

energía *sf* ❶ [*generalmente*] energy • **el sol es una fuente importante de energía** the sun is an important source of energy ❿ **energía atómica** nuclear power ❿ **energía eléctrica** electric power ❿ **energía eólica** wind power ❿ **energía hidráulica** water power ❿ **energía nuclear** nuclear power ❿ **energía solar** solar energy o power ❷ [*fuerza*] strength • **hay que empujar con energía** you have to push hard • **no tengo energías para salir** I don't have the energy to go out

enérgico, ca *adj* ❶ [*generalmente*] energetic ❷ [*carácter*] forceful ❸ [*gesto, medida*] vigorous ❹ [*decisión, postura*] emphatic ☼ *Los adjetivos ingleses son invariables.*

energúmeno, na *sm, f* madman, *femenino* madwoman • **gritaba como un energúmeno** he was screaming like one possessed

enero *sm* January ver también **septiembre**

enésimo, ma *adj* MATEMÁTICAS nth ❷ *figurado* umpteenth • **por enésima vez** for the umpteenth time ☼ *Los adjetivos ingleses son invariables.*

enfadado, da *adj* angry ☼ *Los adjetivos ingleses son invariables.*

enfadar *vt* to anger

■ **enfadarse** *v pronominal* • **enfadarse (con)** to get angry (with) • **se enfadó con los niños por sus travesuras** she got angry with the children because of their pranks

enfado *sm* anger

énfasis *sm invariable* emphasis • **poner énfasis en algo** to emphasize something

enfático, ca *adj* emphatic ☼ *Los adjetivos ingleses son invariables.*

enfatizar *vt* to emphasize

enfermar ◆ *vt* [*causar enfermedad a*] to make ill ◆ *vi* to fall ill • **enfermar del pecho** to develop a chest complaint

enfermedad *sf* disease; illness • **se recupera de una enfermedad muy grave** she's recovering from a very serious illness • **contraer una enfermedad** to catch a disease ❿ **enfermedad contagiosa** contagious disease • **enfermedad infecciosa** infectious disease ❿ **enfermedad mental** mental illness ❿ **enfermedad profesional** occupational disease ❿ **enfermedad terminal** terminal illness • **enfermedad venérea** venereal disease

enfermería *sf* sick bay

enfermero, ra *sm, f* male nurse, *femenino* nurse

enfermizo, za *adj* literal & figurado unhealthy ☼ *Los adjetivos ingleses son invariables.*

enfermo, ma ◆ *adj* sick; ill • **mi maestro estuvo enfermo esta semana** my teacher was sick this week • **está gravemente enferma** she's seriously ill • **caer enfermo** to fall ill ☼ *Los adjetivos ingleses son invariables.*

◆ *sm, f* ❶ [*generalmente*] sick person ❷ [*en el hospital*] patient • **enfermo terminal** terminally ill patient

enfocar *vt* ❶ [*imagen, objetivo*] to focus ❷ [*sujeto: luz, foco*] to shine on ❸ [*tema, asunto*] to approach

enfoque *sm* ❶ [*de imagen*] focus ❷ [*de asunto*] approach • **dar un enfoque nuevo a algo** to adopt a new approach to something

enfrentar *vt* ❶ [*hacer frente a*] to face • **enfrenta cargos por difamación** he faces charges for slander ❷ [*poner frente a frente*] to bring face to face

■ **enfrentarse** *v pronominal* ❶ [*encontrarse*] to meet ❷ [*oponerse*] • **enfrentarse con alguien** to confront somebody ❸ [*pelearse*] to clash • **grupos de jóvenes se enfrentaron con las fuerzas del orden** groups of youths clashed with police

enfrente *adv* ❶ [*delante*] opposite • **mis amigos estaban sentados enfrente** my friends were sitting opposite • **la tienda de enfrente** the shop across the road • **enfrente de** opposite ❷ [*en contra*] • **tiene a todos enfrente** everyone's against her

enfriamiento *sm* ❶ [*catarro*] cold ❷ [*acción*] cooling

enfriar *vt* literal & figurado to cool • **esta heladera no enfría bien** this refrigerator doesn't cool well • **dejar enfriar** this refrigerator doesn't cool well • **dejó enfriar la salsa** he let the sauce cool

■ **enfriarse** *v pronominal* ❶ [*líquido, pasión, amistad*] to cool down ❷ [*quedarse demasiado frío*] to go cold • **se enfrió la comida** the food went cold ❸ MEDICINA to catch a cold • **me enfrié por salir cuando llovía** I caught a cold going out while it was raining

enfurecer *vt* to infuriate

enganchar *vt* ❶ [*agarrar - vagones*] to couple; [*- remolque, caballos*] to hitch up; [*- pez*] to hook ❷ [*colgar de un gancho*] to hang up

enganche *sm* ❶ [*de trenes*] coupling ❷ [*gancho*] hook ❸ [*depósito*] down payment • **pagamos un enganche del 20%** we paid 20% as a down payment

engañar *vt* ❶ [*generalmente*] to deceive • **Sofía engaña a su esposo** Sofía is deceiving her husband ❷ [*estafar*] to cheat; to swindle

engaño *sm* ❶ [*generalmente*] deceit ❷ [*estafa*] swindle

engañoso, sa *adj* ❶ [*persona, palabras*] deceitful ❷ [*aspecto, apariencia*] deceptive ❸ [*consejo*] misleading ☼ *Los adjetivos ingleses son invariables.*

engordar ◆ *vt* ❶ [*cebar*] to fatten up ❷ *figurado* [*aumentar*] to swell

◆ *vi* ❶ [*persona*] to put on weight • **engordé este mes** I put on weight this month ❷ [*comida*] to be fattening • **la mayonesa engorda** mayonnaise is fattening

engranaje *sm* ❶ [*piezas - de reloj, piñón*] cogs *pl* ❷ AUTOMÓVILES gears *pl* ❸ [*aparato - político, burocrático*] machinery

engrapador *sm* stapler

engrapar *vt* to staple

engrasar *vt* ❶ [*generalmente*] to lubricate ❷ [*bisagra, mecanismo*] to oil ❸ [*eje, bandeja*] to grease

engreído, da *adj* conceited ☼ *Los adjetivos ingleses son invariables.*

E

engullir *vt* to gobble up

enhorabuena ✦ *sf* congratulations *pl* • **dar la enhorabuena a alguien** to congratulate somebody
✦ *exclamación* • **¡enhorabuena (por...)!** congratulations (on...)!

enigma *sm* enigma

enigmático, ca *adj* enigmatic:☼ *Los adjetivos ingleses son invariables.*

enjabonar *vt* [con jabón] to soap

enjambre *sm* literal & figurado swarm

enjaular *vt* ❶ [en jaula] to cage ❷ familiar [en prisión] to jail

enjuagar *vt* to rinse

enjugar *vt* ❶ [secar] to dry ❷ [pagar - deuda] to pay off; [- déficit] to cancel out

enlace *sm* ❶ [acción] link • **hay enlace entre los dos crímenes** there's a connection between the two crimes ❷ [persona] go-between ▶ **enlace sindical** shop steward ❸ [casamiento] • **enlace (matrimonial)** marriage ❹ [de trenes] connection • **estación de enlace** junction • **vía de enlace** crossover ❺ INFORMÁTICA link • **sigue el enlace para encontrar la otra página web** follow the link to find the other web page • **enlace de datos** data link • **enlace hipertextual** o **de hipertexto** hypertext link

enlatar *vt* to can; to tin

enlazar ✦ *vt* • **enlazar algo a a)** [atar] to tie something up to **b)** [trabar, relacionar] to link o connect something with
✦ *vi* • **enlazar en** [trenes] to connect at

enlodar *vt* to cover with mud

enloquecer ✦ *vt* ❶ [volver loco] to drive mad ❷ figurado [gustar mucho] to drive crazy
✦ *vi* to go mad

enmarcar *vt* to frame

enmascarado, da *adj* masked:☼ *Los adjetivos ingleses son invariables.*

enmascarar *vt* ❶ [rostro] to mask ❷ figurado [encubrir] to disguise

enmienda *sf* ❶ [en un texto] corrections *pl* ❷ POLÍTICA amendment

enmudecer ✦ *vt* to silence
✦ *vi* ❶ [callarse] to go quiet ❷ [perder el habla] to be struck dumb

enojar *vt* ❶ [enfadar] to anger ❷ [molestar] to annoy
■ **enojarse** *v pronominal* • **enojarse (con) a)** [enfadarse] to get angry (with) **b)** [molestarse] to get annoyed (with) • **se enojó sin razón** he got angry for no reason

enojo *sm* ❶ [enfado] anger ❷ [molestia] annoyance

enojoso, sa *adj* ❶ [molesto] annoying ❷ [delicado, espinoso] awkward:☼ *Los adjetivos ingleses son invariables.*

enorgullecer *vt* to fill with pride

enorme *adj* ❶ [en tamaño] enormous ❷ [en gravedad] monstrous:☼ *Los adjetivos ingleses son invariables.*

enormidad *sf* [de tamaño] enormity

enredadera *sf* creeper

enredar *vt* ❶ [madeja, pelo] to tangle up ❷ [situación, asunto] to complicate ❸ [implicar] • **enredar a alguien (en)** to embroil somebody (in); to involve somebody (in)
■ **enredarse** *v pronominal* ❶ [plantas] to climb ❷ [madeja, pelo] to get tangled up • **se me enreda el pelo frecuentemente** my hair gets tangled frequently ❸ [situación, asunto] to become confused

enredo *sm* ❶ [maraña] tangle ❷ [lío] mess ❸ [asunto ilícito] shady affair ❹ [amoroso] (love) affair

enriquecer *vt* ❶ [hacer rico] to make rich ❷ figurado [engrandecer] to enrich
■ **enriquecerse** *v pronominal* to get rich • **se enriqueció con su trabajo** he got rich with his work

enrojecer ✦ *vt* ❶ [generalmente] to redden ❷ [rostro, mejillas] to cause to blush
✦ *vi* ❶ [por calor] to flush ❷ [por turbación] to blush

enrolar *vt* to enlist

enrollar *vt* [arrollar] to roll up

enroscar *vt* ❶ [enrollar] to roll up ❷ [cuerpo, cola] to curl up

ensalada *sf* [de lechuga ETC] salad ▶ **ensalada de frutas** fruit salad ▶ **ensalada mixta** mixed salad ▶ **ensalada César** Caesar salad

ensalzar *vt* to praise

ensanchar *vt* ❶ [orificio, calle] to widen ❷ [ropa] to let out ❸ [ciudad] to expand

ensartar *vt* ❶ [perlas] to string ❷ [aguja] to thread ❸ [atravesar - torero] to gore ❹ [puñal] to plunge

ensayar *vt* ❶ [generalmente] to test ❷ TEATRO to rehearse

ensayista *smf* essayist

ensayo *sm* ❶ TEATRO rehearsal • **ayer fui al ensayo de un concierto** yesterday I went to the concert rehearsal ▶ **ensayo general** dress rehearsal ❷ [prueba] test ▶ **ensayo nuclear** nuclear test ❸ LITERATURA essay ❹ [en rugby] try

enseguida *adv* ❶ [inmediatamente] right away • **enseguida comienza la función** the performance will begin right away ❷ [pronto] very soon • **llegará enseguida** he'll be here very soon • **enseguida vuelvo** I'll be right back

ensenada *sf* cove

enseñanza *sf* ❶ [generalmente] education ▶ **enseñanza primaria** elementary education ▶ **enseñanza secundaria** secondary education ▶ **enseñanza superior** higher education ▶ **enseñanza universitaria** university education ❷ [instrucción] teaching

enseñar *vt* ❶ [instruir, aleccionar] to teach • **enseñar a alguien a hacer algo** to teach somebody (how) to do something • **en este colegio nos enseñan a razonar** at this school they teach us to reason ❷ [mos-

trar] to show • **me enseñó su computadora nueva** he showed me his new computer

ensillar *vt* to saddle up

ensordecer ◆ *vt* [*sujeto: sonido*] to deafen
◆ *vi* to go deaf

ensuciar *vt* ❶ to (make) dirty • **ensució el mantel con vino** he dirtied the tablecloth with wine ❷ *figurado* [*desprestigiar*] to tarnish

■ **ensuciarse** *v pronominal* to get dirty • **me ensucié en el jardín** I got dirty in the garden

ensueño *sm literal & figurado* dream • **de ensueño** dream ⚡ *Sólo se usa delante del sustantivo.*

entablar *vt* ❶ [*iniciar - conversación, amistad*] to strike up ❷ [*entablillar*] to put in a splint

ente *sm* [*ser*] being

entender ◆ *vt* ❶ [*generalmente*] to understand • **no entiendo lo que dices** I don't understand what you're saying • **¿tú qué entiendes por "amistad"?** what do you understand by "friendship"? • **dar algo a entender** to imply something ❷ [*darse cuenta*] to realize ❸ [*oír*] to hear ❹ [*juzgar*] to think • **yo no lo entiendo así** I don't see it that way

◆ *vi* ❶ [*comprender*] to understand • **hacerse entender** to make yourself understood • **no se hace entender con claridad** he doesn't make himself clearly understood ❷ [*saber*] • **entender de** o **en algo** to be an expert on something • **entender poco/algo de** to know very little/a little about • **¿tú entiendes de informática?** do you know anything about computers?

◆ *sm* • **a mi entender...** the way I see it...

■ **entenderse** *v pronominal* ❶ [*comprenderse - uno mismo*] to know what you mean; [*- dos personas*] to understand each other ❷ [*llevarse bien*] to get along • **mi novia y yo nos entendemos muy bien** my girlfriend and I get along very well together ❸ [*ponerse de acuerdo*] to reach an agreement ❹ [*comunicarse*] to communicate (with each other)

---

no entiendo ⟳

• **Sorry?/Excuse me?** ¿Perdón?
• **Can you say that again, please?** ¿Puedes/Puede repetir eso, por favor?
• **Sorry, I don't understand.** Lo siento, no entiendo.
• **How do you write that, please?** ¿Cómo se escribe eso, por favor?
• **Do you mean that...?** ¿Quieres/Quiere decir que...?
• **What do you mean by that?** ¿Qué quieres/quiere decir con eso?
• **Have I understood properly?** ¿Lo he entendido bien?

---

entendimiento *sm* ❶ [*comprensión*] understanding • **falta entendimiento entre las partes** there's a lack of understanding between the parties ❷ [*juicio*] judgment ❸ [*inteligencia*] mind ❹ [*acuerdo*] un-

derstanding • **llegar a un entendimiento** to come to o reach an understanding

enterarse *v pronominal* • **enterarse (de)** to find out (about) • **me enteré de que vas a cursar química** I found out that you're going to take chemistry • **como se entere de esto, te va a matar** if he finds out about this, he'll kill you • **no quiero que se enteren de lo nuestro** I don't want them to hear about us • **¿te has enterado de lo que ha pasado en Madagascar?** have you heard what's happened in Madagascar?

entereza *sf* ❶ [*serenidad*] composure ❷ [*honradez*] integrity ❸ [*firmeza*] firmness

entero, ra *adj* ❶ [*completo*] whole ❷ [*sereno*] composed ❸ [*honrado*] upright ⚡ *Los adjetivos ingleses son invariables.*

enterrar *vt* [*generalmente*] to bury • **lo enterraron en un cementerio privado** they buried him in a private cemetery

entidad *sf* ❶ [*corporación*] body ❷ [*empresa*] firm ❸ FILOSOFÍA entity ❹ [*importancia*] importance

entierro *sm* ❶ [*acción*] burial ❷ [*ceremonia*] funeral

entlo. *abreviatura escrita de* **entresuelo**

entonación *sf* intonation

entonar ◆ *vt* ❶ [*cantar*] to sing ❷ [*tonificar*] to pick up
◆ *vi* ❶ [*al cantar*] to sing in tune ❷ [*armonizar*] • **entonar (con algo)** to match (something)

entonces ◆ *adv* then • **hablé con la maestra y entonces me dijo que había perdido el examen** I spoke with the teacher and then she told me that I had failed the exam • **entonces lo mejor que puedes hacer es pedir perdón** so the best that you can do is to say sorry • **desde entonces** since then • **en** o **por aquel entonces** at that time • **para entonces** by then
◆ *exclamación* • **¡entonces!** well, then!

entornar *vt* to half-close

entorno *sm* ❶ [*ambiente*] environment ❷ INFORMÁTICA environment • **entorno gráfico** graphic environment • **entorno de programación** programming environment

entorpecer *vt* ❶ [*debilitar - movimientos*] to hinder; [*- mente*] to cloud ❷ [*dificultar*] to obstruct

entrada *sf* ❶ [*acción*] entry, *plural* entries ❷ [*llegada*] arrival • **'prohibida la entrada'** no entry ❸ [*lugar*] entrance ❹ [*puerta*] doorway • **'entrada'** way in • **entrada principal** main entrance • **entrada de servicio** tradesman's entrance ❺ TECNOLOGÍA intake • **entrada de aire** air intake ❻ [*en espectáculos - boleto*] ticket; [*- recaudación*] receipts *pl*; takings *pl* • **compramos cinco entradas para el recital** we bought five tickets for the recital • **entrada gratuita** admission free • **entrada libre** admission free ❼ [*público*] audience ❽ DEPORTE attendance ❾ [*pago inicial*] down payment ❿ [*en contabilidad*] income ⓫ [*plato*] starter ⓬ [*en la frente*] • **tener entradas** to have a receding hairline ⓭ [*en un diccionario*] entry ⓮ [*principio*] • **de entrada** right from the beginning o the word go

entrante ◆ *adj* ❶ [*año, mes*] coming ❷ [*presidente, gobierno*] incoming ☼ *Los adjetivos ingleses son invariables.*
◆ *sm* ❶ [*plato*] starter ❷ [*hueco*] recess
entraña *sf* ☼ *generalmente pl* ❶ [*víscera*] entrails *pl* ❷ *figurado* [*centro, esencia*] heart
entrañable *adj* intimate ☼ *Los adjetivos ingleses son invariables.*
entrañar *vt* to involve

entrar
◆ *vi*
❶ [*ir al interior de un sitio*] to go in
• **está prohibido entrar** you're not allowed to go in
• **¡no te quedes ahí en la puerta, entra!** don't stay there in the doorway, come in!
• **entré por la ventana** I climbed in through the window
❷ [*quedar*]
• **los jeans del año pasado no me entran** I don't fit in last year's jeans
• **este anillo no te entra** this ring is too small for you
❸ [*empezar*]
• **entró el año con buen tiempo** the year started with good weather
❹ [*empezar a sentir*]
• **le entraron ganas de hablar** he suddenly wanted to talk
• **le entró pánico** he was seized by fear
• **me está entrando frío** I'm starting to feel cold
• **me entró una flojera terrible** I felt horribly lazy
❺ *familiar* [*entender, asimilar*]
• **no le entra la geometría** he can't understand geometry
❻ [*velocidad*]
• **no entra la tercera** it won't go into third gear
■ **entrar a**
◆ *v + preposición*
to start
• **entró a trabajar aquí el mes pasado** he started working here last month
■ **entrar de**
◆ *v + preposición*
[*empezar un trabajo en calidad de*] to start as
• **entró de telefonista y ahora es director** he started working as a receptionist and now he's a director
■ **entrar en**
◆ *v + preposición*
❶ [*ir al interior de un lugar*] to enter
• **entró en la casa** he entered the house
• **entraron en la tienda de enfrente** they went in the store across the way
• **entró en la universidad el año pasado** he began at the university last year
❷ [*pasar a un estado nuevo*] to enter
• **entramos en un período de cambios** we are entering a period of change

• **con este vino entramos en calor rápidamente** we got warm quickly with this wine
❸ [*empezar a ejercer una profesión*] to join
• **decidió entrar en el ejército** he decided to join the army
❹ [*estar en, incluir en*]
• **no entramos todos en tu coche** we don't all fit in your car
• **esto no entraba en mis cálculos** this wasn't a part of my calculations
• **esto no entra en el precio** this isn't included in the price
entre *preposición* ❶ [*generalmente*] between • **llegará entre las cuatro y las cinco** he'll arrive between four and five o'clock • **la escuela queda entre tu casa y la mía** the school is between your house and mine • **entre nosotros** [*en confianza*] between you and me ; between ourselves • **entre una cosa y otra** what with one thing and another ❷ [*en medio de muchos*] among • **acampamos entre los árboles** we camped among the trees • **estaba entre los asistentes** she was among those present • **entre sí** amongst themselves • **discutían entre sí** they were arguing with each other • **entre todos** together • **lo pueden hacer entre todos** together they can do it
entreabrir *vt* to half-open
entrecortado, da *adj* ❶ [*voz, habla*] faltering ❷ [*respiración*] labored ❸ [*señal, sonido*] intermittent ☼ *Los adjetivos ingleses son invariables.*
entrecot, entrecote *sm* ribeye
entredicho *sm* • **estar en entredicho** to be in doubt • **poner en entredicho** to question ; to call into question
entrega *sf* ❶ [*generalmente*] handing over ❷ [*pedido, paquete*] delivery ▶ **entrega a domicilio** home delivery ❸ [*de premios*] presentation • **la entrega de premios fue muy emotiva** the award presentation was very moving ❹ [*dedicación*] entrega (a) devotion (to) • **su entrega hacia los demás es totalmente desinteresada** her devotion to others is totally unselfish ❺ [*fascículo*] instalment • **publicar por entregas** to serialize
entregar *vt* ❶ [*generalmente*] to hand over ❷ [*pedido, paquete*] to deliver ❸ [*examen, informe*] to hand in ❹ [*persona*] to turn over
■ **entregarse** *v pronominal* [*rendirse - soldado, ejército*] to surrender ; [*- criminal*] to turn yourself in • **los delincuentes se entregaron a la policía** the criminals surrendered to the police
entrelazar *vt* to interlace
entremés *sm* ☼ *generalmente pl* COCINA hors d'œuvres
entrenador, ra *sm, f* ❶ coach ❷ [*seleccionador*] manager
entrenamiento *sm* training
entrenar *vt & vi* to train
entrepierna *sf* crotch
entresacar *vt* to pick out

entresijos *smpl* ins and outs

entresuelo *sm* mezzanine

entretanto *adv* meanwhile

entretener *vt* ❶ [*despistar*] to distract ❷ [*retrasar*] to hold up ❸ [*divertir*] to entertain
■ **entretenerse** *v pronominal* ❶ [*despistarse*] to get distracted ❷ [*divertirse*] to amuse yourself • **me entretengo mucho con los dibujos animados** I amuse myself a lot with cartoons ❸ [*retrasarse*] to be held up

entretenido, da *adj* entertaining ⚲ *Los adjetivos ingleses son invariables.*

entretenimiento *sm* ❶ [*acción*] entertainment ❷ [*pasatiempo*] pastime

entrevista *sf* ❶ [*periodística, de trabajo*] interview • **hoy tuve una entrevista de trabajo** today I had a job interview • **hacer una entrevista a alguien** to interview somebody ❷ [*reunión*] meeting

entrevistar *vt* to interview

entristecer *vt* to make sad

entrometido, da *sm, f* meddler

entusiasmar *vt* ❶ [*animar*] to fill with enthusiasm ❷ [*gustar*] • **le entusiasma la música** he loves music

entusiasmo *sm* enthusiasm • **el entusiasmo del público era increíble** the enthusiasm of the public was incredible • **con entusiasmo** enthusiastically

entusiasta ◆ *adj* enthusiastic ⚲ *Los adjetivos ingleses son invariables.*
◆ *smf* enthusiast

enumeración *sf* listing

enumerar *vt* to list

enunciar *vt* to formulate

envasado *sm* ❶ [*en botellas*] bottling ❷ [*en latas*] canning ❸ [*en paquetes*] packing

envasar *vt* ❶ [*en botellas*] to bottle ❷ [*en latas*] to can ❸ [*en paquetes*] to pack

envase *sm* ❶ [*envasado - en botellas*] bottling ; [*- en latas*] canning ; [*- en paquetes*] packing ❷ [*recipiente*] container ❸ [*botella*] bottle ▶ **envase desechable** disposable container ▶ **envase retornable** returnable bottle ▶ **envase sin retorno** non-returnable bottle

envejecer ◆ *vi* ❶ [*hacerse viejo*] to grow old ❷ [*parecer viejo*] to age
◆ *vt* to age

envejecimiento *sm* ageing

envenenamiento *sm* poisoning

envenenar *vt* to poison

envergadura *sf* ❶ [*importancia*] size ❷ [*complejidad*] complexity • **de gran envergadura** wide-ranging • **una reforma de gran envergadura** a wide-ranging reform ❸ [*anchura*] span

enviado, da *sm, f* ❶ POLÍTICA envoy ❷ PRENSA correspondent

enviar *vt* to send • **enviamos el cheque por correo** we sent the check by mail • **enviar a alguien a hacer algo** to send somebody to do something

envidia *sf* envy • **la envidia puede destruir una relación** envy can destroy a relationship • **era la envidia de todos** it was the envy of everyone • **dar envidia a alguien** to make somebody jealous o envious • **tener envidia de alguien/algo** to envy somebody/something • **morirse de envidia alguien** to be green with envy

envidiar *vt* to envy

envidioso, sa *adj* envious ⚲ *Los adjetivos ingleses son invariables.*

envío *sm* ❶ COMERCIO dispatch ❷ [*de correo*] delivery ❸ [*de víveres, mercancías*] consignment • **gastos de envío** shipping and handling ▶ **envío a domicilio** home delivery ▶ **envío contra reembolso** C.O.D. ❹ [*paquete*] package

enviudar *vi* to be widowed

envoltorio *sm* wrapper

envoltura *sf* = **envoltorio**

envolver *vt* ❶ [*embalar*] to wrap (up) ❷ [*enrollar*] to wind ❸ [*implicar*] • **envolver a alguien en** to involve somebody in

enyesar *vt* ❶ MEDICINA to put in plaster ❷ CONSTRUCCIÓN to plaster

enzarzar *vt* to embroil

enzima *sf* enzyme

épico, ca *adj* epic ⚲ *Los adjetivos ingleses son invariables.*

epidemia *sf* epidemic

epígrafe *sm* heading

epilepsia *sf* epilepsy

epílogo *sm* epilogue

episodio *sm* [*generalmente*] episode

epitafio *sm* epitaph

epíteto *sm* epithet

época *sf* ❶ [*periodo histórico*] era • **la época victoriana** the Victorian era • **de época** period ⚲ *Sólo se usa delante del sustantivo.* • **época dorada** golden age ❷ [*de la vida*] time • **en aquella época** at that time • **estas cosas no pasaban en mi época** these things didn't happen in my time ❸ [*estación*] season • **la época de las lluvias** the rainy season • **es la época más calurosa del año** it's the hottest time of the year

epopeya *sf* ❶ [*generalmente*] epic ❷ figurado [*hazaña*] feat

equidistante *adj* equidistant ⚲ *Los adjetivos ingleses son invariables.*

equilibrado, da *adj* ❶ [*generalmente*] balanced ❷ [*sensato*] sensible ⚲ *Los adjetivos ingleses son invariables.*

equilibrar *vt* to balance

equilibrio *sm* balance • **perdió el equilibrio y cayó al piso** he lost his balance and fell to the floor
expresión **hacer equilibrios** figurado to perform a balancing act

equilibrista *smf* ❶ [*trapecista*] trapeze artist ❷ [*funambulista*] tightrope walker

equinoccio *sm* equinox

E

equipaje *sm* baggage• **llevo mucho equipaje** I'm carrying a lot of baggage• **hacer el equipaje** to pack ▶ **equipaje de mano** hand luggage

equipar *vt*• **equipar (de o con)a)** [*generalmente*] to equip (with)**b)** [*ropa*] to fit out (with)• **equiparon la escuela con tecnología moderna** they equipped the school with modern technology

equiparar *vt* to compare

equipo *sm*❶ [*equipamiento*] equipment❷ [*personas, jugadores*] team• **los mejores equipos de basquetbol compiten hoy** the best basketball teams compete today• **equipo de rescate** rescue team❸ [*de música*] system▶ **equipo de música** sound system

expresión **caerse con todo el equipo** *familiar* to get it in the neck

equis *adj* X• **un número equis de personas** x number of people ❢ *Los adjetivos ingleses son invariables.*

equitación *sf*❶ [*arte*] equestrianism❷ [*actividad*] horse riding

equitativo, va *adj* fair • **repartieron el dinero de manera equitativa** they divided up the money in a fair manner ❢ *Los adjetivos ingleses son invariables.*

equivalente *adj* & *sm* equivalent ❢ *Los adjetivos ingleses son invariables.*

equivaler ■ **equivaler a** *vi*❶ to be equivalent to ❷ *figurado* [*significar*] to amount to• **eso equivaldría a reconocer tu error** that would amount to admitting your mistake

equivocación *sf* mistake• **cometí varias equivocaciones en mi vida** I made several mistakes in my life• **por equivocación** by mistake

equivocado, da *adj* mistaken ❢ *Los adjetivos ingleses son invariables.*

equivocar *vt* to choose wrongly • **equivocar algo con algo** to mistake something for something
■ **equivocarse** *v pronominal* to be wrong• **equivocarse en** to make a mistake in• **se equivocó de nombre** he got the wrong name• **me equivoqué con él, en realidad es simpatiquísimo** I was wrong about him, he's actually really funny• **debes admitirlo cuando te equivocas** you must admit it when you make a mistake• **me equivoqué de salida en la autopista** I took the wrong exit on the highway

era *sf* [*periodo*] era→ **ser**

erario *sm* funds *pl*

erección *sf* erection

erecto, ta *adj* erect ❢ *Los adjetivos ingleses son invariables.*

erguir *vt* to raise

erigir *vt* [*construir*] to erect

erizar *vt* to cause to stand on end

erizo *sm*❶ [*mamífero*] hedgehog❷ [*pez*] globefish ▶ **erizo de mar** sea urchin

ermita *sf* hermitage

erosionar *vt* to erode

erótico, ca *adj* erotic ❢ *Los adjetivos ingleses son invariables.*

erotismo *sm* eroticism

erradicación *sf* eradication

erradicar *vt* to eradicate• **el gobierno intenta erradicar la pobreza** the government is trying to eradicate poverty

errar ◆ *vt*❶ [*vocación, camino*] to choose wrongly ❷ [*disparo, golpe*] to miss
◆ *vi*❶ [*vagar*] to wander❷ [*equivocarse*] to make a mistake❸ [*al disparar*] to miss

errata *sf* misprint

erróneo, a *adj* mistaken ❢ *Los adjetivos ingleses son invariables.*

error *sm* mistake• **cometer un error** to make a mistake• **estar en un error** to be mistaken• **por error** by mistake • **me lleve tu lápiz por error** I took your pencil by mistake• **salvo error u omisión** errors and omissions excepted▶ **error de cálculo** miscalculation ▶ **error humano** human error▶ **error de imprenta** misprint▶ **error judicial** miscarriage of justice▶ **error tipográfico** typo

eructar *vi* to belch

eructo *sm* belch

erudito, ta *adj* erudite ❢ *Los adjetivos ingleses son invariables.*

erupción *sf*❶ GEOLOGÍA eruption• **la erupción del volcán mató a tres personas** the eruption of the volcano killed three people• **en erupción** erupting• **entrar en erupción** to erupt❷ MEDICINA rash• **le salió una erupción en la cara** a rash broke out on his face

esbelto, ta *adj* slender ❢ *Los adjetivos ingleses son invariables.*

esbozar *vt*❶ to outline❷ [*sonrisa*] to give a hint of

esbozo *sm* outline

escabeche *sm* COCINA marinade

escala *sf*❶ [*generalmente*] scale• **sacó ocho en una escala del uno al diez** he got an eight on a scale of one to ten • **a escala** [*gráfica*] to scale• **hicieron el mapa a escala** they made the map to scale• **a escala mundial** *figurado* on a worldwide scale • **a gran escala** on a large scale• **a pequeña escala** small-scale • **en pequeña escala** on a small scale▶ **escala salarial** salary scale❷ [*de colores*] range❸ [*en un viaje*] stopover• **hacer escala** to stop over▶ **escala técnica** refueling stop

escalada *sf*❶ [*de montaña*] climb▶ **escalada libre** free climbing❷ [*de violencia, precios*] escalation

escalador, ra *sm, f* [*alpinista*] climber

escalafón *sm* scale

escalar *vt* to climb

escaldar *vt* to scald

escalera *sf*❶ [*generalmente*] stairs *pl*; staircase• **la casa tiene una escalera de madera** the house has a wooden staircase▶ **escalera automática** escalator ▶ **escalera de caracol** spiral staircase▶ **escalera de incendios** fire escape▶ **escalera mecánica** escalator ❷ [*de mano*] ladder▶ **escalera de mano** stepladder ❸ [*en naipes*] run

escalinata *sf* staircase

escalofriante *adj* spine-chilling ·§· *Los adjetivos ingleses son invariables.*

escalofrío *sm* ·§· *generalmente pl* shiver • **dar escalofríos a alguien** to give somebody the shivers • **tener escalofríos** to have the shivers

escalón *sm* ❶ [*en escalera*] step • **cuidado con el escalón** careful of the step ❷ *figurado* grade

escalonar *vt* ❶ [*generalmente*] to spread out ❷ [*terreno*] to terrace

escalope *sm* escalope

escama *sf* ❶ [*de peces, reptiles*] scale ❷ [*de jabón, en la piel*] flake

escamar *vt familiar & figurado* [*mosquear*] to make suspicious

escamotear *vt* • **escamotear algo a alguien a)** [*estafar*] to swindle somebody out of something **b)** [*hurtar*] to rob somebody of something

escandalizar *vt* to shock

escándalo *sm* ❶ [*inmoralidad*] scandal • **un escándalo de corrupción** a corruption scandal ❷ [*indignación*] outrage • **la película provocó un escándalo** the movie caused an outrage ❸ [*alboroto*] uproar • **armar un escándalo** to kick up a fuss

escandaloso, sa *adj* ❶ [*inmoral*] outrageous ❷ [*ruidoso*] very noisy ·§· *Los adjetivos ingleses son invariables.*

escanear *vt* to scan

escáner (pl escaners) *sm* ❶ [*aparato*] scanner ❷ [*exploración*] scan • **hacerse un escáner** to have a scan

escaño *sm* ❶ [*cargo*] seat (in parliament) ❷ [*asiento*] bench (in parliament)

escapada *sf* ❶ [*huida*] escape ❷ DEPORTE breakaway ❸ [*viaje*] quick trip

escapar *vi* [*huir*] • **escapar (de)** to escape (from) • **escaparon de la policía** they escaped from the police ■ **escaparse** *v pronominal* ❶ [*huir*] • **escaparse (de)** to escape (from) • **se escapó de la cárcel** he escaped from prison • **escaparse de casa** to run away from home ❷ [*salir - gas, agua* ETC] to leak ❸ [*sin querer*] • **se me escapó un grito** I let out a scream

escaparate *sm* [*de tienda*] (shop) window

escapatoria *sf* [*fuga*] escape • **no tener escapatoria** to have no way out

escape *sm* ❶ [*de gas* ETC] leak ❷ [*de coche*] exhaust

escarabajo *sm* beetle

escaramuza *sf figurado* MILITAR skirmish

escarbar *vt* to scratch

escarcha *sf* frost

escarlata *adj & sm* scarlet ·§· *Los adjetivos ingleses son invariables.*

escarmentar *vi* to learn (your lesson) • **¡no escarmienta!** he never learns! • **¡para que escarmientes!** that'll teach you!

escarmiento *sm* lesson • **servir de escarmiento** to serve as a lesson

escarola *sf* endive

escasear *vi* to be scarce

escasez *sf* ❶ [*insuficiencia*] shortage ❷ [*pobreza*] poverty

escaso, sa *adj* ❶ [*insuficiente - conocimientos, recursos*] limited; [*- tiempo*] short; [*- cantidad, número*] low; [*- víveres, trabajo*] scarce; [*- visibilidad, luz*] poor • **el platino es un metal muy escaso** platinum is a very scarce metal • **andar escaso de** to be short of • **siempre anda escaso de tiempo** he is always short of time ❷ [*casi completo*] • **un metro escaso** barely a metre ·§· *Los adjetivos ingleses son invariables.*

escatimar *vt* ❶ [*gastos, comida*] to be sparing with ❷ [*esfuerzo, energías*] to use as little as possible • **no escatimar gastos** to spare no expense

escayola *sf* ❶ CONSTRUCCIÓN plaster of Paris ❷ MEDICINA plaster

escena *sf* ❶ [*generalmente*] scene ❷ [*escenario*] stage • **llevar a la escena** to dramatize • **poner en escena** to stage • **salir a escena** to go on stage
expresión hacer una escena to make a scene

escenario *sm* ❶ [*tablas, escena*] stage • **los actores salieron al escenario** the actors went out on stage ❷ CINE & TEATRO [*lugar de la acción*] setting ❸ *figurado* [*de suceso*] scene

escenificar *vt* ❶ [*novela*] to dramatize ❷ [*obra de teatro*] to stage

escenografía *sf* set design

escepticismo *sm* scepticism

escéptico, ca ◆ *adj* [*incrédulo*] sceptical ·§· *Los adjetivos ingleses son invariables.*
◆ *sm, f* sceptic

escisión *sf* ❶ [*del átomo*] splitting ❷ [*de partido político*] split

esclarecer *vt* to clear up

esclavitud *sf literal & figurado* slavery

esclavizar *vt literal & figurado* to enslave

esclavo, va *sm, f literal & figurado* [*persona*] slave • **es un esclavo del trabajo** he's a slave to his work

esclerosis *sf invariable* MEDICINA sclerosis ▸ **esclerosis múltiple** multiple sclerosis

esclusa *sf* ❶ [*de canal*] lock ❷ [*compuerta*] floodgate

escoba *sf* broom • **pasar la escoba** to sweep (up)

escocer *vi literal & figurado* to sting

Escocia *nombre propio* Scotland

escoger *vt* to choose • **es difícil escoger entre los dos** it's difficult to choose between the two

escogido, da *adj* ❶ [*elegido*] chosen ❷ [*selecto*] choice ·§· *Los adjetivos ingleses son invariables.*

escolar ◆ *adj* school ·§· *Sólo se usa delante del sustantivo.* • **el autobús escolar** the school bus
◆ *sm, f* schoolboy, *femenino* schoolgirl

escolarizar *vt* to provide with schooling

escollo *sm* ❶ [*en el mar*] reef ❷ *figurado* stumbling block

E

escolta *sf* escort

escoltar *vt* to escort

escombros *smpl* rubble ⚕️ *incontable*

esconder *vt* to hide

■ **esconderse** *v pronominal* • **esconderse (de)** to hide (from) • **se escondió detrás de la puerta** he hid behind the door

escondido, da *adj* [*lugar*] secluded ⚕️ *Los adjetivos ingleses son invariables.*

escondite *sm* ❶ [*lugar*] hiding place • **el escondite de los ladrones** the thieves' hiding place ❷ [*juego*] hide-and-seek • **jugar al escondite** to play hide-and-seek

escondrijo *sm* hiding place

escopeta *sf* shotgun ▶ **escopeta de aire comprimido** air gun

escoria *sf* figurado scum

Escorpio, Escorpión ◆ *sm* [*zodiaco*] Scorpio • **ser Escorpio** to be (a) Scorpio
◆ *smf* [*persona*] Scorpio

escorpión *sm* scorpion

■ **Escorpión** *sm* = **Escorpio**

escote *sm* ❶ [*de prendas*] neckline ❷ [*de persona*] neck ▶ **escote en pico** V-neck ▶ **escote redondo** round neck

escotilla *sf* hatch

escribir *vt* & *vi* to write • **ha escrito varios libros** she's written several books • **nos escribe muy seguido** he writes us often • **escribir a lápiz** to write in pencil • **escribir a mano** to write by hand • **escribir a máquina** to type

■ **escribirse** *v pronominal* ❶ [*personas*] to write to one another • **han dejado de escribirse** they have stopped writing each other ❷ [*palabras*] to spell • **se escribe con "h"** it is spelt with an "h" • **¿cómo se escribe su nombre?** how do you spell her name?

escrito, ta ◆ *participio pasado* → **escribir**
◆ *adj* written • **un examen escrito** a written test • **una nota escrita a mano** a hand-written note • **por escrito** in writing • **tienes que pedirlo por escrito** you have to request it in writing ⚕️ *Los adjetivos ingleses son invariables.*

■ **escrito** *sm* ❶ [*generalmente*] text ❷ [*documento*] document ❸ [*obra literaria*] writing; work

escritor, ra *sm, f* writer

escritorio *sm* [*mueble*] desk • **lo dejé encima del escritorio** I left it on the desk

el escritorio

el atlas	the atlas
el bolígrafo	the pen
el cajón	the drawer
la carpeta	the ring binder
el compás	the compass
la computadora	the computer
el cuaderno	the notebook
el escritorio	the desk
la escuadra	the set square
el estuche	the pencil case
la goma	the eraser
la lámpara	the lamp
el lápiz	the pencil
el libro	the book
el mouse	the mouse
la pantalla	the screen
el pegamento	the glue
la pluma	the fountain pen
la regla	the ruler
el sacapuntas	the pencil sharpener
la silla	the chair
el tapete del mouse	the mousepad
el teclado	the keyboard
las tijeras	the scissors
la unidad central	the central processing unit

escritura *sf* ❶ [*arte*] writing ❷ [*sistema de signos*] script ❸ DERECHO deed

escrúpulo *sm* ❶ [*duda, recelo*] scruple ❷ [*minuciosidad*] scrupulousness ❸ [*aprensión*] qualm • **le da escrúpulo** he has qualms about it

escrupuloso, sa *adj* ❶ [*generalmente*] scrupulous ❷ [*aprensivo*] fussy ⚕️ *Los adjetivos ingleses son invariables.*

escrutinio *sm* count *(of votes)*

escuadra *sf* ❶ GEOMETRÍA square ❷ [*de buques*] squadron ❸ [*de soldados*] squad

escuadrilla *sf* squadron

escuadrón *sm* squadron ▶ **escuadrón de la muerte** death squad

escuálido, da *adj* culto emaciated ⚕️ *Los adjetivos ingleses son invariables.*

escucha *sf* • **estar a la escucha** to listen in ▶ **escuchas telefónicas** telephone tapping ⚕️ *incontable*

escuchar ◆ *vt* to listen to • **me encanta escuchar música** I love to listen to music • **no escucha a nadie** he doesn't listen to anybody
◆ *vi* to listen • **¡escuchen! alguien viene** listen! somebody's coming

escudería *sf* team *(in motor racing)*

escudo *sm* ❶ [*arma*] shield ❷ [*emblema*] coat of arms ❸ [*de club, equipo*] badge

escuela *sf* school • **no pudo ir a la escuela** he couldn't go to school ▶ **escuela de manejo** driving school ▶ **escuela normal** teacher training college ▶ **escuela nocturna** night school ▶ **escuela parroquial** parish school ▶ **escuela privada** private school ▶ **escuela pública** public school

expresión **ser de la vieja escuela** to be of the old school

la escuela

el alumno/la alumna	the student
el bote de basura	the wastepaper basket

la cafetería	the cafeteria
el calendario	the schedule
la clase	the class
el gis	the chalk
el mapa	the map
la mochila	the school bag
el patio	the schoolyard
el pizarrón	the blackboard
el pizarrón blanco	the whiteboard
el pizarrón interactivo	the interactive board
el profesor/la profesora	the teacher
el pupitre	the desk
la silla	the chair

escueto, ta *adj* ❶ [*sucinto*] concise ❷ [*sobrio*] plain ҉ *Los adjetivos ingleses son invariables.*

escuincle, cla *sm, f familiar* [*muchacho*] kid

escultor, ra *sm, f* sculptor, *femenino* sculptress

escultura *sf* sculpture

escupir ◆ *vi* to spit • **escupió en el suelo** he spit on the floor
◆ *vt* ❶ [*sujeto: persona, animal*] to spit out ❷ [*sujeto: volcán, chimenea* ETC] to belch out

escupitajo *sm* gob

escurreplatos *sm invariable* dish rack

escurridizo, za *adj literal & figurado* slippery ҉ *Los adjetivos ingleses son invariables.*

escurridor *sm* colander

escurrir ◆ *vt* ❶ [*generalmente*] to drain ❷ [*ropa*] to wring out ❸ [*en lavadora*] to spin-dry
◆ *vi* [*gotear*] to drip

ese¹ *sf* [*figura*] zigzag
expresión hacer eses a) [*en carretera*] to zigzag b) [*al andar*] to stagger about

ese² (pl esos)**, esa** (pl esas) *adj demostrativo* ❶ [*generalmente*] that, *plural* those • **María vive en esa casa** María lives in that house • **¿quién es ese muchacho que preguntó por ti?** who is that guy who's asking for you? ❷ ҉ *después de sustantivo familiar & despectivo* that, *plural* those • **el hombre ese no me inspira confianza** I don't trust that guy

ése (pl ésos)**, ésa** (pl ésas) *pronombre demostrativo* ❶ [*generalmente*] that one, *plural* those ones • **me gusta ése** I like that one • **ése es el que compramos** that's the one we bought ❷ [*mencionado antes*] the former ❸ *familiar & despectivo* • **ése fue el que me pegó** that's the guy who hit me
expresión ¡a ése! stop that man! ▶ **ni por ésas** not even then

esencia *sf* essence ▶ **quinta esencia** quintessence

esencial *adj* essential • **la lectura es algo esencial** reading is something that's essential • **lo esencial** the main thing • **lo esencial es entender** the main thing is to understand ҉ *Los adjetivos ingleses son invariables.*

esfera *sf* ❶ [*generalmente*] sphere • **esfera de influencia** sphere of influence ▶ **esfera de arrastre o de**

desplazamiento INFORMÁTICA trackball ▶ **esfera terrestre** (terrestrial) globe ❷ [*círculo social*] circle

esférico, ca *adj* spherical ҉ *Los adjetivos ingleses son invariables.*

esfinge *sf* sphinx
expresión parecer una esfinge to be inscrutable

esforzar *vt* [*voz*] to strain

esfuerzo *sm* effort • **no lo hacen porque es mucho esfuerzo** they don't do it because it takes a lot of effort • **saltó sin ningún esfuerzo** he jumped effortlessly • **hacer un esfuerzo** to make an effort

esgrima *sf* fencing

esguince *sm* sprain

eslabón *sm* link ▶ **el eslabón perdido** the missing link

eslogan (pl eslóganes)**, slogan** (pl slogans) *sm* slogan

eslora *sf* NÁUTICA length

esmalte *sm* [*sustancia - en dientes, cerámica* ETC] enamel; [- *de uñas*] (nail) varnish o polish

esmeralda *sf* emerald

esmero *sm* great care

eso *pronombre demostrativo* that • **eso es la Torre Eiffel** that's the Eiffel Tower • **¿para qué sirve eso?** what is that for? • **eso es lo que yo pienso** that's just what I think • **eso que propones es irrealizable** what you're proposing is impossible • **eso de vivir solo no me gusta** I don't like the idea of living on my own • **para eso es mejor no ir** if that's all it is, you might as well not go
expresiones ¡eso, eso! that's right!; yes! ▶ ¡eso es! that's it ▶ ¿cómo es eso?, ¿y eso? [*¿por qué?*] how come? ▶ **por eso vine** that's why I came ▶ **por eso** that's why • **por eso vine** that's why I came

esófago *sm* oesophagus

espabilar *vt* ❶ [*despertar*] to wake up ❷ [*avispar*] • **espabilar a alguien** to sharpen somebody's wits

espacial *adj* space ҉ *Sólo se usa delante del sustantivo.* • **construyeron una estación espacial** they built a space station • **una nave espacial** a spaceship

espacio *sm* ❶ [*generalmente*] space • **hay que dejar espacio para las correcciones** you have to leave space for the corrections • **deja un espacio entre las dos palabras** leave a space between the two words • **no tengo mucho espacio** I don't have much room • **no hay suficiente espacio para una cama** there's not enough room for a bed • **esto ocupa demasiado espacio** this takes up too much room • **el espacio** space • **el primer hombre en el espacio** the first man in space • **a doble espacio** double-spaced • **espacio en blanco** blank • **llena los espacios en blanco** fill in the blanks • **por espacio de** over a period of ▶ **espacio aéreo** air space ❷ RADIO & TELEVISIÓN program

espacioso, sa *adj* spacious ҉ *Los adjetivos ingleses son invariables.*

espada *sf* [*arma*] sword ▶ **espada de dos filos** *figurado* double-edged sword

E

---

espada ≠ spade

• La palabra inglesa **spade** es un falso amigo que significa *pala*.
• *Espada* se traduce al inglés por **sword**.

---

espagueti *sm* spaghetti ☞ *incontable*

espalda *sf* ❶ [*generalmente*] back • **me duele la espalda** my back hurts • **cargado de espaldas** round-shouldered • **por la espalda a)** from behind **b)** *figurado* behind your back • **echarse de espaldas** to lie on your back ❷ [*en natación*] backstroke
expresión **echarse algo sobre las espaldas** to take something on ▸ **tirar** o **tumbar de espaldas** to be amazing o stunning

espantapájaros *sm invariable* scarecrow

espantar *vt* ❶ [*ahuyentar*] to frighten away ❷ [*asustar*] to frighten

espanto *sm* fright

espantoso, sa *adj* ❶ [*terrorífico*] horrific • **hubo un choque espantoso** there was a horrific crash ❷ [*enorme*] terrible • **el calor era espantoso** the heat was terrible ❸ [*feísimo*] dreadful • **¡qué color más espantoso!** what a dreadful color! ☞ *Los adjetivos ingleses son invariables.*

España *nombre propio* Spain

español, la ◆ *adj* Spanish ☞ *Los adjetivos ingleses son invariables.*
◆ *sm, f* [*persona*] Spaniard • **los españoles** Spaniards
■ **español** *sm* [*lengua*] Spanish

esparcido, da *adj* scattered ☞ *Los adjetivos ingleses son invariables.*

esparcir *vt* ❶ [*generalmente*] to spread ❷ [*semillas, papeles, objetos*] to scatter

espárrago *sm* asparagus ☞ *incontable*
expresión **mandar a alguien a freír espárragos** *familiar* to tell somebody to get lost

espátula *sf* ❶ COCINA & MEDICINA spatula ❷ ARTE palette knife ❸ CONSTRUCCIÓN bricklayer's trowel ❹ [*de empapelador*] stripping knife

especia *sf* spice

especial *adj* ❶ [*generalmente*] special • **lo uso sólo en ocasiones especiales** I use it only on special occasions • **la película no tiene nada de especial** the movie is nothing special • **especial para** specially for • **en especial** especially • **son todos inteligentes, en especial Carlos** they're all intelligent, especially Carlos ❷ [*peculiar - carácter, gusto, persona*] peculiar ☞ *Los adjetivos ingleses son invariables.*

especialidad *sf* specialty, *plural* specialties ▸ **especialidad de la casa** house specialty

especialista *sm, f* ❶ [*experto*] • **especialista (en)** specialist (in) ❷ CINE stuntman, *femenino* stuntwoman

especializado, da *adj* • **especializado en** specialized (in) ☞ *Los adjetivos ingleses son invariables.*

especializar *vt* to specialize

especie *sf* ❶ BIOLOGÍA species *sing* • **una especie en vías de extinción** a species in the process of extinction • **especie protegida** protected species ❷ [*clase*] kind; sort • **una especie de** a type of • **llevaba una especie de turbán en la cabeza** he was wearing a type of turban on his head

especificar *vt* to specify

específico, ca *adj* specific ☞ *Los adjetivos ingleses son invariables.*

espectacular *adj* spectacular ☞ *Los adjetivos ingleses son invariables.*

espectáculo *sm* ❶ [*diversión*] entertainment ❷ [*función*] show • **un espectáculo para gente joven** a show for young people ▸ **espectáculo de variedades** variety show ❸ [*suceso, escena*] sight • **un espectáculo muy lamentable** a very pitiful sight • **dar un espectáculo** to make a scene • **deja de gritar que estás dando un espectáculo** stop screaming, you're making a scene

espectador, ra *sm, f* ❶ TELEVISIÓN viewer ❷ CINE & TEATRO member of the audience • **hicieron salir del cine a un espectador** they made an audience member leave • **los espectadores** the audience ❸ DEPORTE spectator • **un espectador saltó a la cancha** a spectator jumped onto the field • **los espectadores** the spectators ❹ [*de suceso, discusión*] onlooker

especulación *sf* speculation

especular *vi* • **especular (sobre)** to speculate (about)

espejismo *sm* ❶ mirage ❷ *figurado* illusion

espejo *sm literal & figurado* mirror • **se miró al espejo** he looked at himself in the mirror ▸ **espejo retrovisor** rear-view mirror

espeluznante *adj* hair-raising ☞ *Los adjetivos ingleses son invariables.*

espera *sf* [*acción*] wait

esperanza *sf* ❶ [*deseo, ganas*] hope ❷ [*confianza, expectativas*] expectation • **dar esperanzas** to give hope to • **eso me ha dado esperanzas** that's given me hope • **perder las esperanzas** to lose hope • **tener esperanza de hacer algo** to hope to be able to do something

esperar ◆ *vt* ❶ [*aguardar*] to wait for • **¿qué estás esperando?** what are you waiting for? • **estoy esperando el tren** I'm waiting for the train • **está esperando un hijo** [*embarazada*] she's expecting a child • **esperar a que alguien haga algo** to wait for somebody to do something ❷ [*tener esperanza de*] • **esperar que** to hope that • **espero que sí** I hope so • **esperar hacer algo** to hope to do something • **espero volverlo a ver** I hope to see him again ❸ [*tener confianza en*] to expect • **esperar que** to expect (that) ❹ [*ser inminente para*] to await
◆ *vi* [*aguardar*] to wait • **voy a esperar hasta mañana** I'm going to wait until tomorrow • **espere en la sala, por favor** wait in the room, please • **espera y verás** wait and see • **como era de esperar** as was to be expected • **no estudió nada — bueno, eso era de esperar** he didn't study at all — well, that was to be expected

esperma *sm* o *sf* BIOLOGÍA sperm

espeso, sa *adj* ❶ [*generalmente*] thick ❷ [*bosque, niebla*] dense ❸ [*nieve*] deep:💡 *Los adjetivos ingleses son invariables.*

espesor *sm* ❶ [*grosor*] thickness • **tiene 2 metros de espesor** it's 2 metres thick ❷ [*densidad - de niebla, bosque*] density; [*- de nieve*] depth

espesura *sf* ❶ [*vegetación*] thicket ❷ [*grosor*] thickness ❸ [*densidad*] density

espía *smf* spy

espiar *vt* to spy on

espiga *sf* ❶ [*de trigo* ETC] ear ❷ [*en telas*] herringbone ❸ [*pieza - de madera*] peg; [*- de hierro*] pin

espina *sf* ❶ [*de pez*] bone • **un pescado con muchas espinas** a fish with a lot of bones ▶ **espina bífida** spina bifida ▶ **espina dorsal** spine ❷ [*de planta*] thorn • **las espinas de los rosales** the thorns of the rosebushes **expresiones** **me da mala espina** it makes me uneasy, there's something fishy about it ▶ **sacarse la espina** to get even ▶ **tener una espina clavada** to bear a great burden

espinaca *sf* 💡 *generalmente pl* spinach 💡 *incontable*

espinilla *sf* ❶ [*hueso*] shin ❷ [*grano*] blackhead

espinoso, sa *adj* literal & figurado thorny:💡 *Los adjetivos ingleses son invariables.*

espionaje *sm* espionage

espiral *sf* literal & figurado spiral • **una escalera en espiral** a spiral staircase

espíritu *sm* ❶ [*generalmente*] spirit ▶ **espíritu de equipo** team spirit ❷ [*fantasma*] ghost • **dicen que aquí hay muchos espíritus** they say that there are a lot of ghosts here ❸ RELIGIÓN soul ▶ **Espíritu Santo** Holy Ghost

espiritual *adj* & *sm* spiritual:💡 *Los adjetivos ingleses son invariables.*

espléndido, da *adj* ❶ [*magnífico*] splendid ❷ [*generoso*] generous:💡 *Los adjetivos ingleses son invariables.*

esplendor *sm* ❶ [*magnificencia*] splendour ❷ [*apogeo*] greatness

esponja *sf* sponge ▶ **esponja vegetal** vegetable sponge **expresión** **beber como una esponja** familiar to drink like a fish ▶ **tirar la esponja** to throw in the towel

esponjoso, sa *adj* spongy:💡 *Los adjetivos ingleses son invariables.*

espontaneidad *sf* spontaneity

espontáneo, a *adj* spontaneous:💡 *Los adjetivos ingleses son invariables.*

esporádico, ca *adj* sporadic:💡 *Los adjetivos ingleses son invariables.*

esposar *vt* to handcuff

esposo, sa *sm, f* [*persona*] husband, *femenino* wife

espray (pl esprays)**, spray** *sm* spray

esprint (pl esprints)**, sprint** *sm* sprint

espuela *sf* [*generalmente*] spur

espuma *sf* ❶ [*generalmente*] foam ❷ [*de cerveza*] head ❸ [*de jabón*] lather ❹ [*de olas*] surf • **la espuma de las olas** the surf ❺ [*de caldo*] scum • **hacer espuma** to foam ▶ **espuma de afeitar** shaving foam ▶ **espuma seca** carpet shampoo ❻ [*para pelo*] (styling) mousse **expresión** **crecer como la espuma** to mushroom

espumoso, sa *adj* ❶ [*generalmente*] foamy ❷ [*vino*] sparkling ❸ [*jabón*] lathery:💡 *Los adjetivos ingleses son invariables.*

esqueleto *sm* [*de persona*] skeleton **expresión** **menear el esqueleto** familiar to boogie (on down)

esquema *sm* ❶ [*gráfico*] diagram • **les hice un esquema de mi casa** I drew them a diagram of my house ❷ [*resumen*] outline • **hice un esquema de lo que iba a escribir** I made an outline of what I was going to write ▶ **su respuesta me rompe los esquemas** her answer has thrown all my plans up in the air

esquemático, ca *adj* schematic:💡 *Los adjetivos ingleses son invariables.*

esquí (pl esquís) *sm* ❶ [*tabla*] ski • **un par de esquís** a pair of skis ❷ [*deporte*] skiing • **el esquí es su deporte favorito** skiing is his favorite sport ▶ **esquí de fondo** cross-country skiing ▶ **esquí acuático** water skiing • **hacer esquí acuático** to go water skiing

esquiador, ra *sm, f* skier

esquiar *vi* to ski

esquimal *adj* & *smf* Eskimo:💡 *Los adjetivos ingleses son invariables.*

esquina *sf* corner • **a la vuelta de la esquina** just round the corner • **doblar la esquina** to turn the corner

esquivar *vt* ❶ [*generalmente*] to avoid ❷ [*golpe*] to dodge

esquizofrenia *sf* schizophrenia

estabilidad *sf* stability

estabilizar *vt* to stabilize

estable *adj* ❶ [*firme*] stable ❷ [*permanente - huésped*] permanent; [*- cliente*] regular:💡 *Los adjetivos ingleses son invariables.*

establecer *vt* ❶ [*generalmente*] to establish • **han establecido relaciones diplomáticas** they've established diplomatic relations • **estableció el récord mundial en jabalina** he established the world record in the javelin ❷ [*récord*] to set ❸ [*negocio, campamento*] to set up ❹ [*inmigrantes* ETC] to settle

■ **establecerse** *v pronominal* ❶ [*instalarse*] to settle • **se establecieron en la Ciudad de México** they settled in Mexico City ❷ [*poner un negocio*] to set up a business

establecimiento *sm* ❶ [*generalmente*] establishment ❷ [*de récord*] setting ❸ [*de negocio, colonia*] setting up

establo *sm* cowshed

estaca *sf* ❶ [*para clavar, delimitar*] stake ❷ [*de tienda de campaña*] peg ❸ [*garrote*] cudgel

E

E

estacada *sf* ❶ [*valla*] picket fence ❷ MILITAR stockade

expresión **dejar a alguien en la estacada** to leave somebody in the lurch

estación *sf* ❶ [*generalmente*] INFORMÁTICA station • **se baja en la siguiente estación** he gets off at the next station ▸ **estación de autocares** coach/railway station ▸ **estación de esquí** ski resort ▸ **estación de gasolina** petrol station ▸ **estación meteorológica** weather station ▸ **estación de servicio** service station ▸ **estación de trabajo** workstation ▸ **estación de tren** railway station ❷ [*del año, temporada*] season • **la estación de las lluvias** the rainy season

las estaciones del año

el invierno	the winter
el otoño	the fall
la primavera	the spring
el verano	the summer

estacionamiento *sm* ❶ [*acción*] parking • **es una zona de estacionamiento prohibido** it's a no parking zone ▸ **estacionamiento indebido** parking offence ❷ [*lugar*] parking area • **el edificio tiene un estacionamiento subterráneo** the building has an underground parking area

estacionar *vt* AUTOMÓVILES to park • **nunca hay dónde estacionar** there's never a place to park

estacionario, ria *adj* ❶ [*generalmente*] stationary ❷ ECONOMÍA stagnant ⚲ *Los adjetivos ingleses son invariables.*

estadio *sm* ❶ DEPORTE stadium, *plural* stadia o stadiums ❷ [*fase*] stage

estadista *smf* statesman, *femenino* stateswoman

estadístico, ca *adj* statistical ⚲ *Los adjetivos ingleses son invariables.*

■ **estadística** *sf* ❶ [*ciencia*] statistics ⚲ *incontable* ❷ [*datos*] statistics *pl*

estado *sm* state • **¿en qué estado quedó la moto?** what state was the motorcycle in? • **en uno de los estados del norte** in one of the northern states • **su estado es grave** his condition is serious • **estar en buen/mal estado a)** [*coche, terreno* ETC] to be in good/bad condition **b)** [*alimento, bebida*] to be fresh/off ▸ **estado de ánimo** state of mind ▸ **estado civil** marital status ▸ **estado de bienestar** welfare state ▸ **estado de excepción** o **emergencia** state of emergency ▸ **estado de salud** (state of) health

expresión **estar en estado (de buena esperanza)** to be expecting

■ **Estado** *sm* [*gobierno*] State • **tiene una beca del Estado** she has a scholarship from the state ▸ **Estado Mayor** MILITAR general staff

■ **Estados Unidos (de América)** *nombre propio* United States (of America)

estadounidense ◆ *adj* United States ⚲ *Sólo se usa delante del sustantivo.*

En inglés, los adjetivos que se refieren a un país o una región se escriben con mayúscula.

◆ *smf* United States citizen

estafa *sf* ❶ [*generalmente*] swindle ❷ COMERCIO fraud

estafador, ra *sm, f* swindler

estafar *vt* ❶ [*generalmente*] to swindle • **estafaron al banco** they swindled the bank ❷ [*en comercio*] to rip off • **en esa tienda me estafaron** they ripped me off in that store

estallar *vi* ❶ [*reventar - bomba*] to explode; [*- neumático*] to burst ❷ [*guerra, epidemia* ETC] to break out

estallido *sm* ❶ [*de bomba*] explosion ❷ [*de trueno*] crash ❸ [*de látigo*] crack ❹ [*de guerra* ETC] outbreak

estampa *sf* ❶ [*imagen, tarjeta*] print ❷ [*aspecto*] appearance

estampar *vt* ❶ [*imprimir - generalmente*] to print; [*- metal*] to stamp ❷ [*escribir*] • **estampar la firma** to sign your name

estampida *sf* stampede

estampido *sm* bang

estampilla *sf* ❶ [*para marcar*] rubber stamp ❷ [*sello de correos*] stamp

estancado, da *adj* ❶ [*agua*] stagnant ❷ [*situación, proyecto*] at a standstill ⚲ *Los adjetivos ingleses son invariables.*

estancia *sf* ❶ [*tiempo*] stay • **durante nuestra estancia en el extranjero** during our stay out of the country ❷ [*habitación*] room

estándar (*pl* estándares), **standard** (*pl* standards) *adj invariable* & *sm* standard ⚲ *Los adjetivos ingleses son invariables.*

estandarizar *vt* to standardize

estandarte *sm* standard

estanque *sm* pond

estante *sm* shelf

estantería *sf* ❶ [*generalmente*] shelves *pl* ❷ [*para libros*] bookcase

estaño *sm* tin

estar

◆ *vi*

❶ [*indica un estado transitorio*] to be
• **¿cómo estás?** how are you?
• **estoy enfermo/cansado** I'm sick/tired
• **¡estás loco!** you're mad!
• **esta calle está sucia** this street is filthy!
❷ [*estar en un sitio determinado*] to be
• **estoy aquí** I'm here
• **¿está María?** is Maria in?
❸ [*estar en una posición determinada*] to be
• **el cuadro está torcido** the picture's crooked
❹ [*quedarse en un sitio un tiempo determinado*] to stay
• **estaré un par de horas y me iré** I'll be there a couple of hours and I'll leave
• **estuvo toda la tarde en casa** he spent all the afternoon at home

❺ [*estar listo*]
• **la comida estará a las dos** lunch will be ready at two
◆ *v auxiliar*
❶ [*seguido por un gerundio, indica que una acción está sucediendo*]
• **estoy pintando** I'm painting
❷ [*seguido por un gerundio, expresa la duración*]
• **estuvieron trabajando día y noche** they were working night and day
❸ [*antes de un participio pasado, forma pasiva*]
• **la exposición está organizada por el ayuntamiento** the exhibition has been organized by the city government
■ **estar a**
◆ *v + preposición*
❶ [*para indicar un valor, un precio*] to be
• **¿a cuánto está el dólar?** what's the dollar at?
❷ [*para ubicar en el tiempo*] to be
• **¿a qué estamos hoy?** what's the date today?
• **hoy estamos a 13 de julio** today's July thirteenth
❸
• **estar a régimen** to be on a diet
■ **estar de**
◆ *v + preposición*
❶ [*ocupar un puesto*] to be
• **está de director de la agencia** he's director of the agency
❷ [*indica un estado*] to be
• **hoy estoy de buen/mal humor** I'm in a good/bad mood today
❸
• **estar de viaje** to be traveling
■ **estar en**
◆ *v + preposición*
❶ [*indica el lugar donde se encuentra algo o alguien*] to be
• **toda su familia está en Buenos Aires** all his family is in Buenos Aires
• **estoy aquí** I'm here
• **la llave está en la cerradura** the key is in the lock
• **el Museo de Arte Moderno está en Chapultepec** the Museum of Modern Art is in Chapultepec
❷ [*se encuentra*] to be
• **el problema está en la fecha** it's the date that's the problem
■ **estar en que**
◆ *v + conjunción*
[*expresa una opinion*]
• **estoy en que no vendrá** I'm thinking he won't turn up
■ **estar para**
◆ *v + preposición*
❶ [*indica el humor, el estado de ánimo*] to be
• **no estoy para bromas** I'm in no mood for jokes
• **no estoy para jugar** I'm not fit to play
❷ [*indica la función*] to be
• **para eso están los amigos** that's what friends are for

■ **estar por**
◆ *v + preposición*
❶ [*indica que una acción aun no se ha terminado*]
• **el trabajo más difícil todavía está por hacer** the most difficult task is still ahead of us
• **eso está por ver** that remains to be seen
❷ [*indica que una acción es inminente*]
• **estaba por irme cuando llegaste** I was just about to leave when you arrived
• **estuve por pegarle** I was about to hit him
• **estoy por llamarlo** I'm tempted to call him
■ **estar que**
◆ *v + conjunción*
• **estoy que no sé qué hacer** I really don't know what to do
• **hoy el jefe está que muerde** the boss is in a terrible mood today

estárter (pl estárters), **starter** (pl starters) *sm* starter

estatal *adj* state ☿ *Sólo se usa delante del sustantivo.*

estático, ca *adj* [*inmóvil*] stock-still ☿ *Los adjetivos ingleses son invariables.*

estatua *sf* statue

estatura *sf* height • **de estatura media** ○ **mediana** of average ○ medium height • **mide casi dos metros de estatura** he's almost two meters tall

estatus, status *sm invariable* status

estatuto *sm* ❶ [*generalmente*] statute ❷ [*de empresa*] article (of association) ❸ [*de ciudad*] by-law

este¹ ◆ *adj* ❶ [*posición, parte*] east ❷ [*dirección, viento*] easterly ☿ *Los adjetivos ingleses son invariables.*
◆ *sm* east • **el sol aparece por el este** the sun rises in the east • **el este de la ciudad** the east part of the city • **al este** to the east • **los países del Este** the Eastern bloc countries

este² (pl estos), **esta²** *adj demostrativo* ❶ [*generalmente*] this, *plural* these • **esta camisa** this shirt • **este año** this year ❷ [*familiar & despectivo*] that, *plural* those • **no soporto a la niña esta** I can't stand that girl

éste (pl éstos), **ésta** *pronombre demostrativo* ❶ [*generalmente*] this one, *plural* these ones • **dame otro boli; éste no funciona** give me another pen; this one doesn't work • **aquellos cuadros no están mal, aunque éstos me gustan más** those paintings aren't bad, but I like these (ones) better • **ésta es mi casa** this is my house • **ésta ha sido la semana más feliz de mi vida** this has been the happiest week of my life • **éste no es el que yo quería** this is not the one that I wanted ❷ [*recién mencionado*] the latter • **entraron Juan y Pedro, éste con un abrigo verde** Juan and Pedro came in, the latter wearing a green coat ❸ *familiar & despectivo* • **éste es el que me pegó** this is the guy who hit me

estela *sf* ❶ [*de barco*] wake ❷ [*de avión, estrella fugaz*] trail ❸ [*figurado*] [*rastro*] trail

estelar *adj* ❶ ASTRONOMÍA stellar ❷ CINE & TEATRO star ☿ *Sólo se usa delante del sustantivo.*

estepa *sf* steppe

estéreo, stereo *adj invariable* & *sm* stereo.⚲ *Los adjetivos ingleses son invariables.*

estereotipo *sm* stereotype

estéril *adj* ❶ [*persona, terreno, imaginación*] sterile ❷ [*inútil*] futile.⚲ *Los adjetivos ingleses son invariables.*

esterilizar *vt* to sterilize

esterlina → **libra**

esternón *sm* breastbone

estero *sm* ❶ [*pantano*] marsh ❷ [*charco*] puddle

esteroides *smpl* steroids

esteticista *sf* beautician

estético, ca *adj* aesthetic.⚲ *Los adjetivos ingleses son invariables.*

estiércol *sm* ❶ [*excrementos*] dung ❷ [*abono*] manure

estilarse *v pronominal* familiar to be in (fashion) • *esa clase de peinado ya no se estila* that type of hairstyle is no longer in fashion

estilo *sm* ❶ [*generalmente*] style • *es típico de su estilo* it's typical of his style • *al estilo de* in the style of • *algo por el estilo* something of the sort • *salen a caminar, andar en bicicleta y cosas por el estilo* they go out for walks, bike rides and that sort of thing ▶ *estilo de vida* lifestyle ❷ [*en natación*] stroke ❸ GRAMÁTICA speech ▶ *estilo directo/indirecto* direct/indirect speech

estilográfica *sf* fountain pen

estima *sf* esteem

estimación *sf* ❶ [*aprecio*] esteem ❷ [*valoración*] valuation ❸ [*en impuestos*] assessment

estimado, da *adj* [*querido*] esteemed • *Estimado señor* Dear Sir.⚲ *Los adjetivos ingleses son invariables.*

estimar *vt* ❶ [*valorar - generalmente*] to value; [*- valor*] to estimate ❷ [*apreciar*] to think highly of ❸ [*creer*] to consider

estimulante ◆ *adj* [*que excita*] stimulating.⚲ *Los adjetivos ingleses son invariables.*
◆ *sm* stimulant

estimular *vt* ❶ [*animar*] to encourage • *nos estimulan para que leamos más* they encourage us to read more ❷ [*excitar*] to stimulate • *un tónico para estimular el apetito* a tonic to stimulate the appetite

estímulo *sm* ❶ [*aliciente*] incentive ❷ [*ánimo*] encouragement ❸ [*de un órgano*] stimulus

estirado, da *adj* [*persona - altanero*] haughty; [*- adusto*] uptight.⚲ *Los adjetivos ingleses son invariables.*

estirar ◆ *vt* ❶ [*alargar - generalmente*] to stretch; [*- cuello*] to crane • *salí a estirar las piernas un poco* I went out to stretch my legs a little ❷ [*desarrugar*] to straighten ❸ figurado [*dinero* ETC] to make last ❹ [*discurso, tema*] to spin out
◆ *vi* • *estirar (de)* to pull • *no estires de la cuerda* don't pull on the rope

estirón *sm* [*acción*] tug

estival *adj* summer.⚲ *Sólo se usa delante del sustantivo.*

esto *pronombre demostrativo* this thing • *esto es tu regalo de cumpleaños* this is your birthday present • *esto que acabas de decir no tiene sentido* what you just said doesn't make sense • *esto de trabajar de noche no me gusta* I don't like this business of working at night • *esto es* that is (to say)

estofado *sm* stew

estomacal *adj* ❶ [*dolencia*] stomach.⚲ *Sólo se usa delante del sustantivo.* ❷ [*bebida*] digestive

estómago *sm* stomach • *me duele el estómago* my stomach hurts

expresión **revolver el estómago a alguien** to turn somebody's stomach ▶ **tener buen estómago** to be tough

estorbar ◆ *vt* ❶ [*obstaculizar*] to hinder ❷ [*molestar*] to bother
◆ *vi* [*estar en medio*] to be in the way • *estas cajas estorban* these boxes are in the way

estorbo *sm* ❶ [*obstáculo*] hindrance ❷ [*molestia*] nuisance

estornudar *vi* to sneeze

estrado *sm* platform

estrafalario, ria *adj* outlandish.⚲ *Los adjetivos ingleses son invariables.*

estrambótico, ca *adj* outlandish.⚲ *Los adjetivos ingleses son invariables.*

estrangular *vt* ❶ [*ahogar*] to strangle ❷ MEDICINA to strangulate

estratagema *sf* ❶ MILITAR stratagem ❷ figurado [*astucia*] artifice

estrategia *sf* strategy

estratégico, ca *adj* strategic.⚲ *Los adjetivos ingleses son invariables.*

estrato *sm* figurado GEOLOGÍA stratum

estrechar *vt* ❶ [*hacer estrecho - generalmente*] to narrow; [*- ropa*] to take in ❷ figurado [*relaciones*] to make closer ❸ [*apretar*] to squeeze • *estrechar la mano a alguien* to shake somebody's hand

estrechez *sf* ❶ [*falta de anchura*] narrowness ❷ [*falta de espacio*] lack of space ❸ [*de ropa*] tightness ▶ *estrechez de miras* narrow-mindedness ❹ figurado [*falta de dinero*] hardship • *pasar estrecheces* to be hard up ❺ [*intimidad*] closeness

estrecho, cha *adj* ❶ [*no ancho - generalmente*] narrow; [*- ropa*] tight; [*- habitación*] cramped • *es una calle muy estrecha* it's a very narrow street • *le gustan los suéteres estrechos* she likes tight sweaters • *estrecho de miras* narrow-minded ❷ figurado [*íntimo*] close.⚲ *Los adjetivos ingleses son invariables.*
■ **estrecho** *sm* GEOGRAFÍA strait ▶ *el Estrecho de Magallanes* the Strait of Magellan

estrella *sf* ❶ [*generalmente*] star • *un hotel de tres estrellas* a three-star hotel ▶ *estrella de cine* movie star ▶ *estrella de mar* starfish ▶ *estrella fugaz* shooting star ❷ figurado [*destino*] fate

estrellar *vt* [*arrojar*] to smash

estrellón *sm* crash

estremecer *vt* to shake

estrenar *vt* ❶ [*generalmente*] to use for the first time ❷ [*ropa*] to wear for the first time ❸ [*departamento*] to move into ❹ CINE to release ❺ TEATRO to premiere

■ **estrenarse** *v pronominal* [*persona*] to make your debut

estreno *sm* ❶ [*de espectáculo*] premiere ❷ [*de cosa*] first use ❸ [*en un empleo*] debut

estreñido, da *adj* constipated ‿Q: *Los adjetivos ingleses son invariables.*

estreñimiento *sm* constipation • **tener estreñimiento** to be constipated

estrépito *sm* ❶ [*ruido*] racket ❷ *figurado* [*ostentación*] fanfare

estrepitoso, sa *adj* ❶ [*generalmente*] noisy ❷ [*aplausos*] deafening ❸ [*derrota*] resounding ❹ [*fracaso*] spectacular ‿Q: *Los adjetivos ingleses son invariables.*

estrés, stress *sm invariable* stress

estría *sf* ❶ [*generalmente*] groove ❷ [*en la piel*] stretch mark

estribillo *sm* ❶ MÚSICA chorus ❷ LITERATURA refrain

estribo *sm* ❶ [*de montura*] stirrup ❷ [*de coche, tren*] step

expresión estar con un pie en el estribo to be ready to leave ▶ **perder los estribos** to fly off the handle

estribor *sm* starboard

estricto, ta *adj* strict ‿Q: *Los adjetivos ingleses son invariables.*

estridente *adj* ❶ [*ruido*] strident ❷ [*color*] garish ‿Q: *Los adjetivos ingleses son invariables.*

estrofa *sf* stanza

estropajo *sm* ❶ scourer ❷ loofah

estropear *vt* ❶ [*averiar*] to break • **si sigues jugando con eso lo vas a estropear** if you keep on playing with that you're going to break it ❷ [*dañar*] to damage ❸ [*echar a perder*] to ruin • **la lluvia nos estropeó el picnic** the rain ruined our picnic

■ **estropearse** *v pronominal* ❶ [*máquina*] to break down • **se nos estropeó la tele** our television broke ❷ [*comida*] to spoil • **se estropeó la comida con el calor** the food spoiled with the heat ❸ [*piel*] to get damaged ❹ [*plan*] to fall through

estropicio *sm* • **hacer un estropicio** to wreak havoc

estructura *sf* structure ▶ **estructura profunda/superficial** deep/surface structure

estruendo *sm* ❶ [*estrépito*] din ❷ [*de trueno*] crash ❸ [*alboroto*] uproar

estrujar *vt* ❶ [*limón*] to squeeze ❷ [*trapo, ropa*] to wring (out) ❸ [*papel*] to screw up ❹ [*caja*] to crush ❺ [*abrazar - persona, mano*] to squeeze ❻ *figurado* [*sacar partido de*] to bleed dry

estuche *sm* ❶ [*caja*] case • **un estuche para lápices** a pencil case ❷ [*de joyas*] jewellery box ❸ [*utensilios*] set

estudiante *smf* student

estudiantil *adj* student ‿Q: *Sólo se usa delante del sustantivo.*

estudiar ◆ *vt* to study • **le gustaría estudiar arquitectura** she'd like to study architecture

◆ *vi* to study • **estudiar para médico** to be studying to be a doctor

estudio *sm* ❶ [*generalmente*] study • **ha dedicado su vida al estudio de la fauna** he's dedicated his life to the study of animals • **tengo dos horas de estudio entre las clases** I have a two-hour study break between classes • **dedica muy poco tiempo al estudio** she devotes very little time to her studies • **estar en estudio** to be under consideration ▶ **estudio de mercado a)** [*técnica*] market research **b)** [*investigación*] market survey ❷ [*oficina*] study ❸ [*de fotógrafo, pintor*] studio ❹ [*apartamento*] studio apartment • **vive en un estudio** she lives in a studio apartment ❺ CINE, RADIO & TELEVISIÓN studio • **un estudio de televisión** a television studio

■ **estudios** *smpl* ❶ [*serie de cursos*] studies • **terminó sus estudios a los veinte años** he completed his studies when he was twenty ❷ [*educación*] education ‿Q: *incontable* • **dar estudios a alguien** to pay for somebody's education • **tener estudios** to be well-educated ▶ **estudios primarios/secundarios** primary/secondary education

estudioso, sa *adj* studious ‿Q: *Los adjetivos ingleses son invariables.*

estufa *sf* stove • **una olla de agua hervía en la estufa** a pot of water boiled on the stove

estupefaciente *sm* narcotic

estupendamente *adv* wonderfully • **estoy estupendamente** I feel wonderful

estupidez *sf* stupidity • **decir/hacer una estupidez** to say/do something stupid

estúpido, da *adj* stupid • **¡qué pregunta más estúpida!** what a stupid question! ‿Q: *Los adjetivos ingleses son invariables.*

etapa *sf* stage • **por etapas** in stages

etc. (*abreviatura escrita de* etcétera) etc.

etcétera *adv* etcetera

eternidad *sf* eternity

expresión hace una eternidad que... it's ages since... • **hace una eternidad que no la veo** it's ages since I last saw her

eterno, na *adj* ❶ [*vida, amor*] eternal ❷ *familiar* [*larguísimo*] never-ending ‿Q: *Los adjetivos ingleses son invariables.*

ético, ca *adj* ethical ‿Q: *Los adjetivos ingleses son invariables.*

■ **ética** *sf* [*moralidad*] ethics *pl*

etílico, ca *adj* QUÍMICA ethyl ‿Q: *Sólo se usa delante del sustantivo.* • **intoxicación etílica** alcohol poisoning

etimología *sf* etymology

Etiopía *nombre propio* Ethiopia

etiqueta *sf* ❶ [*generalmente*] INFORMÁTICA label ▶ **etiqueta adhesiva o autoadhesiva** sticky label ▶ **etiqueta del precio** price tag ❷ [*ceremonial*] etiquette

E

• **de etiqueta** formal• **vestir de etiqueta** to wear formal dress

etiquetar *vtliteral & figurado* to label• **etiquetar a alguien de algo** to label somebody something

étnico, ca *adj* ethnic.⚲ *Los adjetivos ingleses son invariables.*

EUA (*abreviatura escrita de* Estados Unidos de América) *smpl* USA

eucalipto *sm* eucalyptus

eucaristía *sf*• **la Eucaristía** the Eucharist

eufemismo *sm* euphemism

euforia *sf* euphoria

eufórico, ca *adj* euphoric.⚲ *Los adjetivos ingleses son invariables.*

euro *sm* [*unidad monetaria*] euro

Europa *nombre propio* Europe

europeo, a *adj & sm, f* European.⚲ *Los adjetivos ingleses son invariables.*

En inglés, los adjetivos que se refieren a un país o una región se escriben con mayúscula.

evacuación *sf* evacuation

evacuar *vt***①** [*generalmente*] to evacuate **②** [*vientre*] to empty

evadir *vt***①** to evade **②** [*respuesta, peligro*] to avoid

evaluación *sf***①** [*generalmente*] evaluation **②** EDUCACIÓN [*examen*] assessment

evaluar *vt* to evaluate

evangelio *sm* gospel

evaporar *vt* to evaporate

■ **evaporarse** *v pronominal* [*líquido* ETC] to evaporate • **el agua se evaporó con el calor del sol** the water evaporated with the heat of the sun

evasión *sf***①** [*huida*] escape **②** [*de dinero*] ▶ **evasión de capitales** o **divisas** capital flight ▶ **evasión fiscal** tax evasion **③** [*entretenimiento*] amusement **④** [*escapismo*] escapism • **de evasión** escapist

evento *sm* event

eventual *adj***①** [*no fijo - trabajador*] temporary; [- *gastos*] incidental **②** [*posible*] possible.⚲ *Los adjetivos ingleses son invariables.*

eventualidad *sf***①** [*temporalidad*] temporariness **②** [*hecho incierto*] eventuality **③** [*posibilidad*] possibility

evidencia *sf***①** [*prueba*] evidence • **negar la evidencia** to refuse to accept the obvious • **rendirse ante la evidencia** to bow to the evidence **②** [*claridad*] obviousness • **poner algo en evidencia** to demonstrate something • **poner a alguien en evidencia** to show somebody up

evidenciar *vt* to show

evidente *adj* obvious • **es evidente que no ha estudiado** it's obvious he hasn't studied.⚲ *Los adjetivos ingleses son invariables.*

evitar *vt***①** [*generalmente*] to avoid • **a esa hora evitamos el tráfico** we can avoid traffic at that time • **eso**

nos habría evitado muchas molestias that would have saved us a lot of trouble• **no lo pude evitar** I couldn't help it **②** [*desastre, accidente*] to prevent • **lo hacen para evitar accidentes** they do it to prevent accidents • **evitar hacer algo** to avoid doing something • **evitar que alguien haga algo** to prevent somebody from doing something

evolución *sf***①** [*generalmente*] evolution • **la teoría de la evolución** the theory of evolution **②** [*de enfermedad*] development **③** MILITAR manoeuvre

evolucionar *vi***①** [*generalmente*] to evolve **②** [*enfermedad*] to develop **③** [*cambiar*] to change **④** MILITAR to carry out manoeuvres

ex *preposición* ex • **el ex presidente** the ex-president; the former president

exactitud *sf* precision • **la exactitud de un test** the precision of a test • **no lo recuerdo con exactitud** I can't remember precisely

exacto, ta *adj***①** [*justo - cálculo, medida*] exact • **tres metros exactos** exactly three meters • **¿me puedes dar la hora exacta?** can you tell me the exact time? • **el avión salió a la hora exacta** the plane left right on time **②** [*preciso*] precise **③** [*correcto*] correct **④** [*idéntico*] • **exacto (a)** exactly the same (as).⚲ *Los adjetivos ingleses son invariables.*

■ **exacto** *exclamación* ¡**exacto!** exactly!; precisely!

exageración *sf* exaggeration • **este precio es una exageración** this price is over the top

exagerado, da *adj***①** [*generalmente*] exaggerated **②** [*persona*] overly dramatic **③** [*precio*] exorbitant **④** [*gesto*] flamboyant.⚲ *Los adjetivos ingleses son invariables.*

exagerar *vt & vi* to exaggerate • **no exageres** don't exaggerate

exaltado, da *adj***①** [*jubiloso*] elated **②** [*acalorado - persona*] worked up; [- *discusión*] heated **③** [*excitable*] hotheaded.⚲ *Los adjetivos ingleses son invariables.*

exaltar *vt***①** [*elevar*] to promote **②** [*glorificar*] to exalt

examen *sm***①** [*ejercicio*] exam • **tengo que estudiar para el examen de inglés** I have to study for my English exam • **presentarse a un examen** to sit an exam ▶ **examen final** final (exam) ▶ **examen de manejar** driving test ▶ **examen oral** oral (exam) ▶ **examen parcial** ≃ end-of-term exam **②** [*indagación*] examination • **someter algo a examen** to examine something

examinar *vt* to examine

exasperar *vt* to exasperate

excavación *sf* [*lugar*] dig

excavar *vt***①** [*generalmente*] to dig **②** [*en arqueología*] to excavate

excedencia *sf***①** leave (of absence) **②** EDUCACIÓN sabbatical ▶ **excedencia por maternidad** maternity leave

excedente ◆ *adj* [*producción* ETC] surplus.⚲ *Los adjetivos ingleses son invariables.*

◆ *sm* COMERCIO surplus

exceder *vt* to exceed

excelencia *sf* [*cualidad*] excellence • **por excelencia** par excellence

excelente *adj* excellent ❖ *Los adjetivos ingleses son invariables.*

excéntrico, ca *adj & sm, f* eccentric ❖ *Los adjetivos ingleses son invariables.*

excepción *sf* exception • **hacer una excepción** to make an exception • **hicieron una excepción con él** they made an exception for him • **con excepción de** except • **estudié todo con excepción de esto** I studied everything except this • **de excepción** exceptional ▸ *expresión* **la excepción confirma la regla** *proverbio* the exception proves the rule

excepcional *adj* exceptional ❖ *Los adjetivos ingleses son invariables.*

excepto *adv* except (for) • **todos llevaron algo excepto yo** everybody except me brought something

exceptuar *vt* • **exceptuar (de) a)** [*excluir*] to exclude (from) **b)** [*eximir*] to exempt (from) • **exceptuando a...** excluding...

excesivo, va *adj* excessive ❖ *Los adjetivos ingleses son invariables.*

exceso *sm* [*demasía*] excess • **en exceso** to excess • **hay gente que bebe en exceso** some people drink to excess ▸ **exceso de equipaje** excess baggage ▸ **exceso de peso** [*obesidad*] excess weight

excitado, da *adj* ❶ [*nervioso*] agitated ❷ [*por enfado, sexo*] aroused ❖ *Los adjetivos ingleses son invariables.*

excitante *sm* stimulant

excitar *vt* ❶ [*inquietar*] to upset ❷ [*estimular - sentidos*] to stimulate; [*- apetito*] to whet; [*- pasión, curiosidad, persona*] to arouse

■ **excitarse** *v pronominal* to get worked up • **se excita mucho cuando discute** he gets very worked up when he argues

exclamación *sf* ❶ [*interjección*] exclamation • **signo de exclamación** exclamation mark ❷ [*grito*] cry

exclamar *vt & vi* to exclaim

excluir *vt* ❶ [*dejar fuera*] to exclude • **excluir a alguien de algo** to exclude somebody from something • **lo excluyeron del equipo** he was excluded from the team • **fueron todos, excluyendo Pepe** they all went except for Pepe ❷ [*hipótesis, opción*] to rule out ❸ [*hacer imposible*] to preclude

exclusión *sf* exclusion

exclusivo, va *adj* exclusive ❖ *Los adjetivos ingleses son invariables.*

■ **exclusiva** *sf* ❶ PRENSA exclusive ❷ COMERCIO exclusive o sole right

excombatiente *smf* war veteran

excomulgar *vt* to excommunicate

excomunión *sf* excommunication

excremento *sm* ❖ *generalmente pl* excrement ❖ *incontable*

excursión *sf* trip • **hicimos una excursión a un pueblo cercano** we made a trip to a nearby town • **ir de excursión** to go on a trip • **el martes vamos de ex-**

cursión con el colegio we're going on a school field trip on Tuesday

excursionista *smf* ❶ [*en la ciudad*] sightseer ❷ [*en el campo*] rambler ❸ [*en la montaña*] hiker

excusa *sf* ❶ [*generalmente*] excuse • **¡nada de excusas!** no excuses! • **buscar una excusa** to look for an excuse • **dar excusas** to make excuses ❷ [*petición de perdón*] apology • **presentar uno sus excusas** to apologize

excusar *vt* ❶ [*disculpar a*] to excuse ❷ [*disculparse por*] to apologize for

exento, ta *adj* exempt • **exento de a)** [*sin*] free from; without **b)** [*eximido de*] exempt from • **exento de impuestos** tax free ❖ *Los adjetivos ingleses son invariables.*

exhaustivo, va *adj* exhaustive ❖ *Los adjetivos ingleses son invariables.*

exhausto, ta *adj* exhausted ❖ *Los adjetivos ingleses son invariables.*

exhibición *sf* ❶ [*demostración*] display • **tienen reptiles en exhibición** they have reptiles on display ❷ [*deportiva, artística* ETC] exhibition • **una exhibición de arte africano** an exhibition of African art ❸ [*de películas*] showing

exhibir *vt* ❶ [*exponer - cuadros, fotografías*] to exhibit; [*- modelos*] to show; [*- productos*] to display ❷ [*lucir - joyas, cualidades* ETC] to show off • **le encanta exhibirse** she loves to show off ❸ [*película*] to show

exigencia *sf* ❶ [*obligación*] demand ❷ [*capricho*] fussiness ❖ *incontable*

exigente *adj* demanding ❖ *Los adjetivos ingleses son invariables.*

exigir *vt* ❶ [*generalmente*] to demand • **la profesora nos exige mucho** the teacher demands a great deal from us • **exigir algo de** o **a alguien** to demand something from somebody ❷ [*requerir, necesitar*] to require

exiliado, da ✦ *adj* exiled ❖ *Los adjetivos ingleses son invariables.*

✦ *sm, f* exile • **un exiliado político** a political exile

exiliar *vt* to exile

exilio *sm* exile

existencia *sf* existence

existir *vi* to exist • **existe mucha pobreza** there is a lot of poverty

éxito *sm* ❶ [*generalmente*] success • **con éxito** successfully • **tener éxito** to be successful • **su libro ha tenido mucho éxito** her book has been very successful ❷ [*libro*] bestseller ❸ [*canción*] hit

> **éxito ≠ exit**
> • La palabra inglesa **exit** es un falso amigo que significa *salida*.
> • *Éxito* se traduce al inglés por **success**.

exitoso, sa *adj* successful ❖ *Los adjetivos ingleses son invariables.*

éxodo *sm* exodus

exorbitante *adj* exorbitant·👁️ *Los adjetivos ingleses son invariables.*

exótico, ca *adj* exotic·👁️ *Los adjetivos ingleses son invariables.*

expandir *vt* to expand

expansión *sf* ❶ [*generalmente*] expansion ❷ Economía growth • **en expansión** expanding ❸ [*recreo*] relaxation

expansivo, va *adj* ❶ [*generalmente*] expansive ❷ [*persona*] open·👁️ *Los adjetivos ingleses son invariables.*

expectación *sf* expectancy

expectativa *sf* ❶ [*espera*] expectation ❷ [*esperanza*] hope ❸ [*perspectiva*] prospect • **estar a la expectativa** to wait and see • **estar a la expectativa de a)** [*atento*] to be on the lookout for **b)** [*a la espera*] to be hoping for ▶ **expectativa de vida** life expectancy

expedición *sf* [*viaje, grupo*] expedition • **expedición militar** military expedition • **expedición de salvamento** rescue mission

expediente *sm* ❶ [*documentación*] documents *pl* ❷ [*ficha*] file ❸ [*historial*] record ▶ **expediente académico** transcript ❹ [*investigación*] inquiry • **abrir expediente a alguien a)** [*castigar*] to take disciplinary action against somebody **b)** [*investigar*] to start proceedings against somebody

expedir *vt* ❶ [*carta, pedido*] to dispatch ❷ [*pasaporte, decreto*] to issue ❸ [*contrato, documento*] to draw up

expendio *sm* ❶ expense; outlay ❷ [*tienda*] store; shop ❸ [*venta al por menor*] retailing

expensas *sfpl* [*gastos*] expenses

experiencia *sf* [*generalmente*] experience • **no es necesario tener experiencia previa** no previous experience is necessary • **necesitan a una persona con experiencia** they need an experienced person • **por (propia) experiencia** from (your own) experience

experimentado, da *adj* ❶ [*persona*] experienced ❷ [*método*] tried and tested·👁️ *Los adjetivos ingleses son invariables.*

experimentar *vt* ❶ [*generalmente*] to experience • **nunca había experimentado algo así** I'd never experienced anything like it ❷ [*derrota, pérdidas*] to suffer ❸ [*probar*] to test ❹ [*hacer experimentos con*] to experiment on • **experimentan con conejos** they experiment on rabbits

experimento *sm* experiment

experto, ta *adj* & *sm, f* expert • **ser experto en la materia** to be a specialist in the subject • **ser experto en hacer algo** to be an expert at doing something·👁️ *Los adjetivos ingleses son invariables.*

expirar *vi* to expire

explicación *sf* explanation • **debe haber una explicación para todo esto** there has to be an explanation for all of this • **dar/pedir explicaciones** to give/demand an explanation

explicar *vt* ❶ [*generalmente*] to explain • **no lo pudo explicar** she couldn't explain it • **explicarle algo a alguien** to explain something to somebody ❷ [*teoría*] to expound

explícito, ta *adj* explicit·👁️ *Los adjetivos ingleses son invariables.*

exploración *sf* [*generalmente*] Medicina exploration

explorador, ra *sm, f* explorer

explorar *vt* ❶ [*generalmente*] to explore ❷ Militar to scout ❸ Medicina to examine ❹ [*internamente*] to probe

explosión *sf* literal & figurado explosion • **hubo una gran explosión** there was a big explosion • **hacer explosión** to explode

explosivo, va *adj* [*generalmente*] explosive·👁️ *Los adjetivos ingleses son invariables.*

■ **explosivo** *sm* explosive

explotación *sf* ❶ [*acción*] exploitation ❷ [*de fábrica* etc] running ❸ [*de yacimiento minero*] mining ❹ [*agrícola*] farming ▶ **explotación agrícola** farm ❺ [*de petróleo*] drilling

explotar ◆ *vt* ❶ [*generalmente*] to exploit • **dice que la explotan en su trabajo** she says they exploit her at work • **han explotado los recursos al máximo** they've exploited their resources to the full ❷ [*fábrica*] to run ❸ [*terreno*] to farm ❹ [*mina*] to work

◆ *vi* to explode • **la bomba va explotar en 10 minutos** the bomb will explode in 10 minutes

exponente *sm* ❶ Matemáticas exponent ❷ [*ejemplo*] example • **un magnífico exponente** a magnificent example

exponer *vt* ❶ [*generalmente*] to expose ❷ [*teoría*] to expound ❸ [*ideas, propuesta*] to set out ❹ [*cuadro, obra*] to exhibit • **van a exponer sus cuadros en una galería** they're going to exhibit her paintings in a gallery ❺ [*objetos en vitrinas*] to display ❻ [*vida, prestigio*] to risk • **exponen su vida para salvar a otros** they risk their lives to save others

■ **exponerse** *v pronominal* [*arriesgarse*] • **exponerse (a) a)** [*generalmente*] to run the risk (of) **b)** [*a la muerte*] to expose yourself (to) • **no deben exponerse demasiado al sol** you shouldn't expose yourself to the sun too much

exportación *sf* ❶ [*acción*] export ❷ [*mercancías*] exports *pl*

exportar *vt* Comercio & Informática to export

exposición *sf* ❶ [*generalmente*] Fotografía exposure ❷ [*de arte* etc] exhibition ❸ [*de objetos en vitrina*] display ▶ **exposición universal** world fair ❹ [*de teoría*] exposition ❺ [*de ideas, propuesta*] setting out

expositor, ra *sm, f* ❶ [*de arte*] exhibitor ❷ [*de teoría*] exponent

exprés ◆ *adj* ❶ [*tren*] express ❷ [*café*] espresso·👁️ *Los adjetivos ingleses son invariables.*

◆ *sm* expresso

expresamente *adv* ❶ [*a propósito*] expressly ❷ [*explícitamente*] explicitly

expresar *vt* ❶ to express • **le cuesta expresar lo que siente** he has trouble expressing his feelings ❷ [*sujeto: rostro*] to show
■ **expresarse** *v pronominal* to express yourself • **no sabe expresarse muy bien** she's not very good at expressing herself

expresión *sf* expression • **tenía una expresión de tristeza en la cara** she had a sad expression on her face • **es una expresión que se usa en México** it's an expression used in Mexico

expresivo, va *adj* ❶ expressive ❷ [*cariñoso*] affectionate ◌̣: *Los adjetivos ingleses son invariables.*

exprimidor *sm* squeezer

exprimir *vt* ❶ [*fruta*] to squeeze ❷ [*zumo*] to squeeze out

expropiar *vt* to expropriate

expuesto, ta ◆ *participio pasado* → **exponer**
◆ *adj* ❶ [*dicho*] stated ❷ [*desprotegido*] • **expuesto (a)** exposed (to) ❸ [*arriesgado*] dangerous ❹ [*exhibido*] on display ◌̣: *Los adjetivos ingleses son invariables.*

expulsar *vt* ❶ [*persona - de colegio*] to expel • **lo expulsaron del colegio** he was expelled from school; [*- de clase, local, asociación*] to throw out ❷ DEPORTE to eject ❸ [*humo*] to emit

expulsión *sf* ❶ [*generalmente*] expulsion ❷ DEPORTE ejection

exquisitez *sf* exquisiteness

exquisito, ta *adj* ❶ exquisite ❷ [*comida*] delicious ◌̣: *Los adjetivos ingleses son invariables.*

éxtasis *sm invariable* ecstasy

extender *vt* ❶ [*desplegar - tela, plano, alas*] to spread (out); [*- brazos, piernas*] to stretch out • **extendió la sábana sobre la cama** she spread the sheet on the bed • **hay que extender bien el protector solar por todo el cuerpo** you have to spread the sun block all over your body ❷ [*esparcir - mantequilla*] to spread; [*- pintura*] to smear; [*- objetos*] ETC] to spread out ❸ [*ampliar - castigo, influencia* ETC] to extend ❹ [*documento*] to draw up ❺ [*cheque*] to make out ❻ [*pasaporte, certificado*] to issue

extensión *sf* ❶ [*superficie - de terreno* ETC] expanse • **es dueño de una gran extensión de terreno** he owns a vast expanse of land ❷ [*amplitud - de país* ETC] size; [*- de conocimientos*] extent ❸ [*duración*] duration ❹ [*sentido - de concepto, palabra*] range of meaning • **en toda la extensión de la palabra** in every sense of the word ❺ INFORMÁTICA & TELECOMUNICACIONES extension • **¿sabes el número de su extensión?** do you know her extension?

extensivo, va *adj* extensive ◌̣: *Los adjetivos ingleses son invariables.*

extenso, sa *adj* ❶ extensive ❷ [*país*] vast ❸ [*libro, película*] long ◌̣: *Los adjetivos ingleses son invariables.*

extenuar *vt* to exhaust completely

exterior ◆ *adj* ❶ [*de fuera*] outside ❷ [*capa*] outer • **hay que subir por la escalera exterior** you have to climb up the outside ladder • **la parte exterior es más antigua** the outside is older ❸ [*visible*] outward

❹ [*extranjero*] foreign • **el comercio exterior** foreign trade ◌̣: *Los adjetivos ingleses son invariables.*
◆ *sm* ❶ [*superficie*] outside ❷ [*extranjero*] foreign countries *pl* • **en el exterior** abroad ❸ [*aspecto*] appearance

exteriorizar *vt* to reveal

exterminar *vt* to exterminate

exterminio *sm* extermination

externo, na *adj* ❶ [*generalmente*] external • **la pomada es de uso externo** the ointment is for external use ❷ [*parte, capa*] outer • **la parte externa de una flor** the outside of the flower ❸ [*influencia*] outside ❹ [*signo, aspecto*] outward ❺ [*alumno*] day ◌̣: *Sólo se usa delante del sustantivo.* • **un colegio sólo para alumnos externos** a day school

extinción *sf* ❶ [*generalmente*] extinction • **¿qué provocó la extinción de los dinosaurios?** what caused the extinction of dinosaurs? • **especies en vías de extinción** endangered species ❷ [*de esperanzas*] loss

extinguir *vt* ❶ [*incendio*] to put out • **luchaban por extinguir el fuego** they fought to put out the fire ❷ [*raza*] to wipe out ❸ [*afecto, entusiasmo*] to put an end to

extinto, ta *adj* ❶ [*fuego*] extinguished ❷ [*animal, volcán*] extinct ◌̣: *Los adjetivos ingleses son invariables.*

extintor *sm* fire extinguisher

extirpar *vt* ❶ [*tumor*] to remove ❷ [*muela*] to extract ❸ *figurado* to eradicate

extorsión *sf* ❶ [*molestia*] trouble ❷ DERECHO extortion

extra ◆ *adj* ❶ [*adicional*] extra • **pueden poner una cama extra** they can set up an extra bed • **trabajar horas extras** to work overtime • **tiempo extra** overtime ❷ [*de gran calidad*] top quality ◌̣: *Los adjetivos ingleses son invariables.*
◆ *smf* CINE extra
◆ *sm* [*gasto* ETC] extra

extracción *sf* ❶ [*generalmente*] extraction ❷ [*en sorteos*] draw ❸ [*de carbón*] mining

extracto *sm* ❶ [*resumen*] summary ▸ **extracto de cuentas** statement (of account) ❷ [*concentrado*] extract

extraditar *vt* to extradite

extraer *vt* • **extraer (de) a)** [*generalmente*] to extract (from) **b)** [*sangre, conclusiones*] to draw (from) **c)** [*carbón*] to mine (from)

extranjero, ra ◆ *adj* foreign • **un visitante extranjero** a foreign visitor ◌̣: *Los adjetivos ingleses son invariables.*
◆ *sm, f* [*persona*] foreigner • **muchos extranjeros viven en esta zona** a lot of foreigners live in this area
■ **extranjero** *sm* [*territorio*] foreign countries *pl* • **estar en el/ir al extranjero** to be/go abroad • **le gustaría viajar por el extranjero** she'd like to travel abroad

extrañar *vt* ❶ [*sorprender*] to surprise • **me extraña (que digas esto)** I'm surprised (that you should say that) • **me extrañó no verte en clases** I was surprised that you weren't in class ❷ [*echar de menos*] to miss

• **extraña mucho a su familia** he misses his family a lot

■ **extrañarse** *v pronominal* to be surprised • **a mi edad ya no me extraño de nada** at my age, nothing surprises me anymore

extrañeza *sf* surprise

extraño, ña ♦ *adj* ❶ [*raro*] strange • **una costumbre muy extraña** a strange custom • **¡qué extraño!** how odd o strange! • **¡qué cosa más extraña!** how strange! ❷ [*ajeno*] detached ❸ Medicina foreign ᬀ̣̌ *Los adjetivos ingleses son invariables.*

♦ *sm, f* stranger

extraoficial *adj* unofficial ᬀ̣̌ *Los adjetivos ingleses son invariables.* **extraordinario, ria** *adj* ❶ [*generalmente*] extraordinary • **no tiene nada de extraordinario** there's nothing extraordinary about that ❷ [*gastos*] additional ❸ [*edición, suplemento*] special ᬀ̣̌ *Los adjetivos ingleses son invariables.*

■ **extraordinario** *sm* PRENSA special edition

extrapolar *vt* to generalize about

extrarradio *sm* outskirts *pl*

extraterrestre *adj* & *smf* extraterrestrial ᬀ̣̌ *Los adjetivos ingleses son invariables.*

extravagancia *sf* eccentricity

extravagante *adj* eccentric ᬀ̣̌ *Los adjetivos ingleses son invariables.*

extravertido, da, extrovertido, da *adj* & *sm, f* extrovert ᬀ̣̌ *Los adjetivos ingleses son invariables.*

extraviado, da *adj* ❶ [*perdido*] lost ❷ [*animal*] stray ᬀ̣̌ *Los adjetivos ingleses son invariables.*

extraviar *vt* ❶ [*objeto*] to lose ❷ [*excursionista*] to mislead

extravío *sm* [*pérdida*] loss

extremar *vt* to maximize

extremidad *sf* [*extremo*] end

extremista *adj* & *smf* extremist ᬀ̣̌ *Los adjetivos ingleses son invariables.*

extremo, ma *adj* ❶ [*generalmente*] extreme • **tienen temperaturas extremas en el desierto** they have extreme temperatures in the desert ❷ [*en el espacio*] far • **la extrema derecha** the far right ᬀ̣̌ *Los adjetivos ingleses son invariables.*

■ **extremo** *sm* ❶ [*punta*] end • **amarró los dos extremos del cordel** he tied the two ends of the rope • **recorrió el país de extremo a extremo** he traveled from one end of the country to the other ❷ [*límite*] extreme • **en último extremo** as a last resort

expresión **ir** o **pasar de un extremo al otro** to go from one extreme to the other ▸ **ser el extremo opuesto** to be the complete opposite

extrovertido, da = extravertido

exuberancia *sf* exuberance

exuberante *adj* exuberant ᬀ̣̌ *Los adjetivos ingleses son invariables.*

F

f, F *sf* [*letra*] f; F

fa *sm* ❶ MÚSICA F ❷ [*en solfeo*] fa

fábrica *sf* factory ▸ **fábrica de automóviles** car factory ▸ **fábrica de cerveza** brewery ▸ **fábrica de conservas** canning plant ▸ **fábrica de papel** paper mill

> ## *fábrica* ≠ *fabric*
> • La palabra inglesa **fabric** es un falso amigo que significa *tela*.
> • *Fábrica* se traduce al inglés por **factory**.

fabricación *sf* manufacture • **de fabricación casera** home-made ▸ **fabricación en serie** mass production

fabricante *smf* manufacturer

fabricar *vt* ❶ [*producir*] to manufacture • **fabrican zapatos de niños** they manufacture children's shoes • **fabricado en Corea** made in Korea • **fabricar en serie** to mass-produce ❷ [*construir*] to build ❸ [*figurado*] [*inventar*] to fabricate

fábula *sf* ❶ LITERATURA fable ❷ [*leyenda*] legend

fabuloso, sa *adj* ❶ [*ficticio*] mythical ❷ [*muy bueno*] fabulous ❖ *Los adjetivos ingleses son invariables.*

facción *sf* POLÍTICA faction

faceta *sf* facet

facha *sf* ❶ [*aspecto*] look • **ese muchacho tiene facha de estudiante** that guy has the look of a student ❷ [*mamarracho*] mess • **vas hecho una facha** you look a mess • **no quiero que nadie me vea en esta facha** I don't want anyone to see me looking like this

fachada *sf* ARQUITECTURA façade

facial *adj* facial ❖ *Los adjetivos ingleses son invariables.*

fácil *adj* ❶ [*generalmente*] easy • **una tarea fácil** an easy homework assignment • **es muy fácil equivocarse** it's very easy to make a mistake • **fácil de hacer** easy to do ❷ [*probable*] likely • **lleva paraguas porque es fácil que llueva** bring an umbrella because it's likely to rain ❖ *Los adjetivos ingleses son invariables.*

facilidad *sf* ❶ [*simplicidad*] ease • **con facilidad** easily • **ganaron con facilidad** they won easily • **con la mayor facilidad** with the greatest of ease ❷ [*aptitud*] aptitude • **tener facilidad para algo** to have a gift for something

facilitar *vt* ❶ [*simplificar*] to facilitate ❷ [*posibilitar*] to make possible ❸ [*proporcionar*] to provide • **facilitar algo a alguien** to provide o supply somebody with something

factible *adj* feasible ❖ *Los adjetivos ingleses son invariables.*

factor *sm* [*generalmente*] factor • **el clima es un factor importante** weather is an important factor ▸ **factor humano** human factor ▸ **factor de riesgo** risk factor

factura *sf* ❶ [*por mercancías, trabajo realizado*] invoice ▸ **factura pro forma** o **proforma** COMERCIO proforma invoice ❷ [*en tienda, hotel*] bill

facturación *sf* [*ventas*] net revenue

facturar *vt* ❶ [*cobrar*] • **facturarle a alguien algo** to invoice o bill somebody for something ❷ [*vender*] to turn over

facultad *sf* ❶ [*capacidad*] faculty ▸ **facultades mentales** mental faculties • **tiene todas sus facultades mentales** he's in full possession of his mental faculties ❷ UNIVERSIDAD school • **la Facultad de Medicina** the medical school ❸ [*poder*] power

facultativo, va ◆ *adj* ❶ [*voluntario*] optional ❷ [*médico*] medical ❖ *Los adjetivos ingleses son invariables.*
◆ *sm, f* doctor

faena *sf* [*tarea*] work ❖ *incontable* • **estar en plena faena** to be hard at work

faenar *vi* to fish

fagot *sm* [*instrumento*] bassoon

faisán *sm* pheasant

faja *sf* ❶ [*prenda*] corset ❷ [*banda*] sash ❸ [*de terreno - pequeña*] strip ; [*- grande*] belt

fajo *sm* ❶ [*de billetes, papel*] wad • **un fajo de billetes** a wad of cash ❷ [*de leña, cañas*] bundle

falda *sf* ❶ [*prenda*] skirt ▸ **falda escocesa** kilt ▸ **falda pantalón** culottes *pl* ▸ **falda plisada** o **tableada** pleated skirt ❷ [*de montaña*] slope ; mountainside

F

expresión **estar pegado a las faldas de su madre** to to be tied to your mother's apron strings

faldón *sm* ❶ [*de ropa*] tail ❷ [*de cortina, mesa camilla*] folds *pl*

falla *sf* ❶ GEOLOGÍA fault ❷ [*error*] error ▶ **falla humana** human error

fallar ◆ *vt* ❶ [*sentenciar*] to pass sentence on ❷ [*premio*] to award ❸ [*equivocar - respuesta*] to get wrong; [*- tiro*] to miss

◆ *vi* ❶ [*equivocarse*] to get it wrong ❷ [*no acertar*] to miss • **fallar un tiro** to miss a shot ❸ [*fracasar, flaquear*] to fail • **le está fallando la memoria** her memory is failing her • **le fallaron los frenos** his brakes failed ❹ [*plan*] to go wrong ❺ [*decepcionar*] • **fallarle a alguien** to let somebody down • **cuento contigo, no me vayas a fallar** I'm counting on you, don't let me down ❻ [*sentenciar*] • **fallar a favor/en contra de** to find in favour of/against

fallecer *vi* to pass away

fallecimiento *sm* death

fallo *sm* ❶ [*error*] mistake • **¡qué fallo!** what a stupid mistake! • **fallo humano** human error ❷ DEPORTE miss ❸ [*sentencia - de juez, jurado*] verdict

falsear *vt* ❶ [*hechos, historia*] to falsify ❷ [*moneda, firma*] to forge

falsedad *sf* ❶ [*falta de verdad, autenticidad*] falseness ❷ [*mentira*] falsehood

falsificar *vt* to forge • **le falsificó la firma** he forged her signature

falso, sa *adj* ❶ [*rumor, excusa* ETC] false • **lo que dijo es falso** what he said is false • **usaba un nombre falso** she was using a false name • **una falsa alarma** a false alarm • **jurar en falso** to commit perjury ❷ [*dinero, firma, cuadro*] forged ❸ [*joyas*] fake ❹ [*hipócrita*] deceitful.ᗐ: **Los adjetivos ingleses son invariables.**

falta *sf* ❶ [*carencia*] lack • **por falta de** for lack of • **por falta de experiencia** due to lack of experience • **es por mi falta de costumbre** it's because I'm not used to it ❷ • **hace falta** • **me hace falta un buen diccionario** I need a good dictionary • **hace falta que llueva** we need some rain ❸ [*escasez*] shortage ❹ [*ausencia*] absence • **he tenido cuatro faltas en el mes** I've been absent four times this month • **echar en falta algo/a alguien a)** [*notar la ausencia de*] to notice that something/somebody is missing **b)** [*echar de menos*] to miss something/somebody ❺ [*imperfección*] fault ❻ [*error*] mistake ▶ **falta de educación** bad manners *pl* ▶ **falta de ortografía** spelling mistake ▶ **falta de respeto** disrespect ❼ DEPORTE foul • **el árbitro no marcó la falta** the referee didn't call the foul ❽ [*en tenis*] fault • **doble falta** double fault ❾ DERECHO offence

faltante *sm* deficit

faltar *vi* ❶ [*no haber*] to lack • **le falta experiencia** he lacks experience • **me falta tiempo** I lack time • **falta aire** there's not enough air • **le falta sal** it needs a bit of salt ❷ [*estar ausente*] to be missing • **falta Elena** Elena is missing • **a este libro le falta una página** this book is missing a page ❸ [*hacer falta*] to be necessary ❹ [*quedar*] • **falta un mes para las vacaciones** there's a month to go till summer vacation • **sólo te falta fir-**

mar all you have to do is sign • **¿cuánto falta para Laredo?** how much further is it to Laredo? • **falta mucho por hacer** there is still a lot to be done • **falta poco para que llegue** it won't be long till he arrives • **falta poco para terminar** we're almost finished

expresión **¡era lo único que nos faltaba!** that's all we needed! ▶ **¡no faltaba** o **faltaría más! a)** [*asentimiento*] of course! **b)** [*rechazo*] that tops it all!

fama *sf* ❶ [*renombre*] fame • **alcanzó la fama con su primer disco** she shot to fame with her first record • **tener fama** to be famous ❷ [*reputación*] reputation • **tiene fama de flojo** he has a reputation for being lazy • **tiene muy mala fama** he has a bad reputation

expresión **cría fama y échate a dormir** *proverbio* once you're famous, you can sit back and enjoy the benefits

familia *sf* family • **fue a visitar a su familia** she went to visit her family • **celebramos la Navidad en familia** we celebrated Christmas with the family • **ser de buena familia** to come from a good family • **ser como de la familia** to be like one of the family ▶ **familia de acogida** host family ▶ **familia monoparental** one-parent family ▶ **familia política** in-laws *pl* ▶ **familia real** royal family

la familia

la abuela	the grandmother
el abuelo	the grandfather
los abuelos	the grandparents
la bisabuela	the great-grandmother
el bisabuelo	the great-grandfather
los bisabuelos	the great-grandparents
la cuñada	the sister-in-law
el cuñado	the brother-in law
la familia extensa	the extended family
la hermana	the sister
la hermanastra	the stepsister, the half- sister
el hermano	the brother
los hermanos	the brothers and sisters
el hermanastro	the stepbrother, the half-brother
la hija	the daughter
los hijastros	the stepchildren
el hijo	the son
los hijos	the children
la madrastra	the stepmother
la madre	the mother
la nuera	the daughter-in-law
el padrastro	the stepfather
los padrastros	the step-parents
el padre	the father
los padres	the parents
la prima	the cousin
el primo	the cousin
los primos	the cousins
la suegra	the mother-in-law
el suegro	the father-in-law

los suegros	the parents-in-law
el tío	the uncle
la tía	the aunt
los tíos	the aunts and uncles
el yerno	the son-in-law

familiar ◆ *adj* ❶ [*de familia*] family ☼ *Sólo se usa delante del sustantivo.* • **hay un ambiente familiar en este restaurante** this restaurant has a family atmosphere ❷ [*en el trato - agradable*] friendly ; [*- en demasía*] overly familiar ❸ [*lenguaje, estilo*] informal ❹ [*tamaño*] family-size • **viene en envase familiar** it comes in a family-size pack ❺ [*conocido*] familiar • **su cara le era familiar** her face was familiar to him
◆ *smf* relative

familiaridad *sf* familiarity

familiarizar *vt* • **familiarizar (con)** to familiarize (with)

famoso, sa *adj* famous ☼ *Los adjetivos ingleses son invariables.*

fanático, ca ◆ *adj* fanatical ☼ *Los adjetivos ingleses son invariables.*
◆ *sm, f* ❶ [*generalmente*] fanatic • **es una fanática de la música pop** she's a pop music fanatic ❷ DEPORTE fan

fanatismo *sm* fanaticism

fanfarrón, ona *adj* boastful ☼ *Los adjetivos ingleses son invariables.*

fango *sm* mud

fantasía *sf* ❶ [*imaginación*] imagination ❷ [*cosa imaginada*] fantasy • **un mundo de fantasía** a fantasy world • **de fantasía** [*ropa*] fancy

fantasma *sm* [*espectro*] ghost

fantástico, ca *adj* fantastic ☼ *Los adjetivos ingleses son invariables.*

fardo *sm* bundle

faringitis *sf invariable* sore throat

farmacéutico, ca ◆ *adj* pharmaceutical ☼ *Los adjetivos ingleses son invariables.*
◆ *sm, f* chemist

farmacia *sf* drugstore

fármaco *sm* drug

faro *sm* ❶ [*para barcos*] lighthouse • **podíamos ver el faro en la distancia** we could see the lighthouse in the distance ❷ [*de coche*] headlight • **encendí los faros del carro** I switched on the car's headlights ▶ **faro antiniebla** foglamp

farol *sm* ❶ [*farola*] street light • **los faroles se encendieron al atardecer** the streetlights came on as the sun went down ❷ [*linterna*] lantern • **un farol alumbraba la entrada** a lantern lit up the doorway

farola *sf* ❶ [*farol*] street light ❷ [*poste*] lamppost

farra *sf* binge

farsa *sf* literal & figurado farce • **fuimos al teatro a ver una farsa** we went to the theater to see a farce • **¿elecciones con un solo candidato? ¡eso es una farsa!** an election with just one candidate? what a farce!

farsante *adj* deceitful ☼ *Los adjetivos ingleses son invariables.*

fascículo *sm* instalment *(of serialization)*

fascinante *adj* fascinating ☼ *Los adjetivos ingleses son invariables.*

fascinar *vt* to fascinate • **me fascinan sus pinturas** his paintings fascinate me

fase *sf* phase • **las fases de la luna son cuatro** the moon has four phases • **en fase terminal** in terminal phase

fastidiar *vt* ❶ [*estropear - fiesta* ETC] to spoil ; [*- máquina, objeto* ETC] to break ❷ [*molestar*] to annoy • **me fastidia que los vecinos hagan tanto ruido** it really annoys me that the neighbors make so much noise • **no fastidies a tu hermana, que está haciendo su tarea** don't bother your sister, she's doing her homework

fastidio *sm* ❶ [*molestia*] nuisance • **¡qué fastidio!** what a nuisance! • **¡qué fastidio tener que salir con esta lluvia!** what a nuisance to have to go out in this rain! ❷ [*enfado*] annoyance

fatal ◆ *adj* ❶ [*mortal*] fatal • **el accidente fue fatal** it was a fatal accident ❷ [*muy malo*] awful • **hoy fue un día fatal, todo lo que hice me salió mal** today was awful, everything I did went wrong ❸ [*inevitable*] inevitable ☼ *Los adjetivos ingleses son invariables.*
◆ *adv* terribly • **pasarlo fatal** to have an awful time • **sentirse fatal** to feel terrible

fatalidad *sf* ❶ [*destino*] fate ❷ [*desgracia*] misfortune

fatídico, ca *adj* fateful ☼ *Los adjetivos ingleses son invariables.*

fatiga *sf* [*cansancio*] tiredness

fatigar *vt* to tire
■ **fatigarse** *v pronominal* to get tired

fauna *sf* fauna

favor *sm* favor • **hacerle un favor a alguien** to do somebody a favor • **me han hecho varios favores y por eso les estoy agradecida** they've done me a few favors so I'm grateful to them • **pedir un favor a alguien** to ask somebody a favor • **a favor de** in favor of • **tener a o en su favor a alguien** to enjoy somebody's support

favorable *adj* favorable • **ser favorable a algo** to be in favor of something ☼ *Los adjetivos ingleses son invariables.*

favorecer *vt* ❶ [*generalmente*] to favor • **esa ley favorece a los ricos** that law favors the rich ❷ [*ayudar*] to help ❸ [*sentar bien*] to suit

favoritismo *sm* favoritism

favorito, ta *adj & sm, f* favorite ☼ *Los adjetivos ingleses son invariables.*

fax *sm invariable* ❶ [*aparato*] fax (machine) • **acabo de instalar el nuevo fax** I just set up the new fax machine • **mandar algo por fax** to fax something ❷ [*documento*] fax • **llegó un fax con la información que faltaba** we got a fax with the missing information

fe *sf* ❶ [*generalmente*] faith • **hacer algo de buena fe** to do something in good faith • **tener fe en** to have

F

faith in • **tengo fe en que todo va a salir bien** I have faith that everything will turn out all right ❷ [*documento*] certificate▶ **fe de bautismo** certificate of baptism▶ **fe de erratas** errata *pl*

expresión **dar fe de que** to testify that

fealdad *sf* [*de rostro* ETC] ugliness

febrero *sm* February ver también **septiembre**

febril *adj* ❶ feverish ❷ *figurado* [*actividad*] hectic:ᄝ *Los adjetivos ingleses son invariables.*

fecha *sf* date • **hasta la fecha** to date • **a partir de esta fecha** from today▶ **fecha de caducidad a)** [*de alimentos*] sell-by date **b)** [*de carné, pasaporte*] expiry date **c)** [*de medicamento*] "use before" date▶ **fecha de nacimiento** date of birth▶ **fecha tope** o **límite** deadline

fechoría *sf* misdemeanor

fécula *sf* starch *(in food)*

fecundación *sf* fertilization▶ **fecundación artificial** artificial insemination▶ **fecundación asistida** assisted fertilization▶ **fecundación in vitro** in vitro fertilization

fecundar *vt* ❶ [*fertilizar*] to fertilize ❷ [*hacer productivo*] to make fertile

federación *sf* federation

federal *adj* & *smf* federal:ᄝ *Los adjetivos ingleses son invariables.*

federar *vt* to federate

felicidad *sf* happiness • **el dinero no compra la felicidad** money can't buy you happiness

desear felicidades a alguien

- **Good luck!** ¡(Buena) suerte!
- **Have a good time!** ¡Diviértete!/¡Diviértanse!
- **Happy Birthday!** ¡Feliz cumpleaños!
- **Merry Christmas!** ¡Feliz Navidad!
- **Happy holidays!** ¡Felices fiestas!
- **Happy New Year!** ¡Feliz Año Nuevo!

felicitación *sf* ❶ [*acción*] • **felicitaciones** congratulations ❷ [*postal*] greetings card • **felicitación de Navidad** Christmas card

felicitar *vt* to congratulate • **¡te felicito!** congratulations! • **felicitar a alguien por algo** to congratulate somebody on something • **vamos a felicitarlo por sus buenos resultados** let's congratulate him on his good grades • **llamamos a nuestros amigos para felicitarlos por Navidad** we called our friends to wish them a merry Christmas

felicitar a alguien

- **I'd like to congratulate you on doing so well in your exam.** Te/Lo felicito por el examen.
- **Congratulations on getting your license!** ¡Felicitaciones por haber sacado la licencia!

felino, na *adj* feline:ᄝ *Los adjetivos ingleses son invariables.*

feliz *adj* ❶ [*dichoso*] happy • **hacer feliz a alguien** to make somebody happy • **¡feliz cumpleaños!** happy birthday! ❷ [*afortunado*] lucky ❸ [*oportuno*] timely:ᄝ *Los adjetivos ingleses son invariables.*

felpa *sf* ❶ [*de seda*] plush ❷ [*de algodón*] towelling

felpudo *sm* doormat

femenino, na *adj* ❶ [*generalmente*] feminine ❷ BOTÁNICA & ZOOLOGÍA female:ᄝ *Los adjetivos ingleses son invariables.*

■ **femenino** *sm* GRAMÁTICA feminine

feminismo *sm* feminism

feminista *adj* & *smf* feminist:ᄝ *Los adjetivos ingleses son invariables.*

fémur (pl fémures) *sm* thighbone

fenomenal *adj* [*magnífico*] wonderful:ᄝ *Los adjetivos ingleses son invariables.*

fenómeno ◆ *sm* [*generalmente*] phenomenon
◆ *adv* familiar brilliantly • **pasarlo fenómeno** to have a great time
◆ *exclamación* • **¡fenómeno!** great!; terrific!

feo, a *adj* ❶ [*persona*] ugly • **ese cuadro no me gusta nada, es muy feo** I don't like that picture at all, it's so ugly ❷ [*aspecto, herida, conducta*] rude • **es feo escupir** it's rude to spit:ᄝ *Los adjetivos ingleses son invariables.*

expresión **le tocó bailar con la más fea** he drew the short straw▶ **ser más feo que Picio** to be as ugly as sin

féretro *sm* coffin

feria *sf* ❶ [*generalmente*] fair • **me gané el muñeco en la feria** I won the doll at the fair • **mañana se inaugura la feria del juguete** the toy fair opens tomorrow ▶ **feria (de muestras)** trade fair ❷ [*fiesta popular*] festival ❸ [*cambio*] small change • **necesito feria para el teléfono** I need some small change for the phone

fermentación *sf* fermentation

fermentar *vt* & *vi* to ferment

feroz *adj* ❶ [*animal, bestia*] fierce ❷ *figurado* [*criminal, asesino*] cruel ❸ *figurado* [*dolor, angustia*] terrible:ᄝ *Los adjetivos ingleses son invariables.*

férreo, a *adj* literal & figurado iron:ᄝ *Sólo se usa delante del sustantivo.*

ferretería *sf* hardware store

ferrocarril *sm* ❶ [*sistema, medio*] railroad ❷ [*tren*] train • **por ferrocarril** by train

ferry *sm* ferry

fértil *adj* literal & figurado fertile:ᄝ *Los adjetivos ingleses son invariables.*

fertilidad *sf* literal & figurado fertility

fertilizante *sm* fertilizer

fertilizar *vt* to fertilize

ferviente *adj* fervent:ᄝ *Los adjetivos ingleses son invariables.*

fervor *sm* fervor

festejar *vt* to celebrate

festejo *sm* [*fiesta*] party

festín *sm* banquet

festival *sm* festival • **festival de cine** film festival

festividad *sf* festivity

festivo, va *adj* ❶ [*de fiesta*] festive ❱ **día festivo** (public) holiday ❷ [*alegre*] cheerful ❸ [*chistoso*] funny · ϙ̣· **Los adjetivos ingleses son invariables.**

feto *sm* foetus

fiable *adj* ❶ [*máquina*] reliable ❷ [*persona*] trustworthy · ϙ̣· **Los adjetivos ingleses son invariables.**

fiambre *sm* [*comida*] cold cuts *pl*

fianza *sf* ❶ [*depósito*] deposit ❷ DERECHO bail • **bajo fianza** on bail ❸ [*garantía*] security

fiar ◆ *vt* COMERCIO to sell on credit
◆ *vi* COMERCIO to sell on credit
expresión ser de fiar to be trustworthy
■ **fiarse** *v pronominal* • **¡no te fíes!** don't be too sure (about it)! • **fiarse de algo/alguien** to trust something/somebody • **no te fíes de todos los que vengan a ofrecerte ayuda** don't trust everyone that offers to help you • **no te fíes de todo lo que oyes** don't believe everything you hear

fibra *sf* ❶ [*generalmente*] fiber • **el pan integral contiene mucha fibra** wholewheat bread contains a lot of fiber ❷ [*de madera*] grain ❱ **fibra de vidrio** fiberglass

ficción *sf* fiction

ficha *sf* ❶ [*tarjeta*] (index) card • **en esta ficha anotaré tus datos** I'll write your details on this card ❷ [*con detalles personales*] file ❱ **ficha médica** medical records *pl* ❱ **ficha policial** police record ❸ [*de guardarropa, estacionamiento*] ticket ❹ [*de teléfono*] token ❺ [*de juego - generalmente*] counter ❻ [*en ajedrez*] piece • **faltan algunas fichas** some of the pieces are missing ❼ [*en casino*] chip ❽ INFORMÁTICA card

fichaje *sm* ❶ DEPORTE [*contratación*] signing (up) ❷ [*importe*] transfer fee

fichar ◆ *vt* ❶ [*archivar*] to file ❷ [*sujeto: policía*] to put on police records ❸ DEPORTE to sign up
◆ *vi* ❶ [*suj: trabajador - al entrar*] to clock in; [- *al salir*] to clock out ❷ DEPORTE • **fichar (por)** to sign up (for)

fichero *sm* ❶ [*mueble*] filing cabinet • **guardo los informes en el fichero** I keep the reports in the filing cabinet ❷ INFORMÁTICA file • **un fichero informático** a computer file

ficticio, cia *adj* [*imaginario*] fictitious · ϙ̣· **Los adjetivos ingleses son invariables.**

fidelidad *sf* ❶ [*lealtad*] loyalty ❷ [*de cónyuge, perro*] faithfulness ❸ [*precisión*] accuracy ❱ **alta fidelidad** high fidelity

fideo *sm* noodle
expresión quedarse como un fideo to be as thin as a rake

fiebre *sf* fever • **le di una aspirina para bajarle la fiebre** I gave her an aspirin to lower the fever • **tener fiebre** to have a temperature ❱ **fiebre aftosa** foot-and-

mouth disease ❱ **fiebre amarilla/de Malta** yellow/Malta fever ❱ **fiebre del heno** hay fever

fiel *adj* ❶ [*leal - amigo, seguidor*] loyal; [- *cónyuge, perro*] faithful • **Juan siempre ha sido fiel a sus amigos** Juan has always been loyal to his friends ❷ [*preciso*] accurate · ϙ̣· **Los adjetivos ingleses son invariables.**

fieltro *sm* felt

fiero, ra *adj* ferocious · ϙ̣· **Los adjetivos ingleses son invariables.**
■ **fiera** *sf* [*animal*] wild animal
expresión ponerse como una fiera to fly into a rage

fierro *sm* iron

fiesta *sf* ❶ [*reunión*] party • **hicimos una fiesta para su cumpleaños** we threw a party for his birthday • **estar de fiesta** to be celebrating • **la familia está de fiesta por el nacimiento del niño** the family is celebrating the birth of the baby ❷ [*de pueblo* ETC] (local) festivities *pl* ❱ **fiesta de disfraces** costume party ❱ **fiesta mayor** *para explicar lo que es puedes decir:* it's the local festival of a town's patron saint ❱ **fiesta patria** independence day ❸ [*día*] public holiday • **ser fiesta** to be a public holiday
expresión no estar para fiestas to be in no mood for joking

figura *sf* ❶ [*generalmente*] figure • **dibujamos figuras de diferentes tamaños** we drew different size figures ❷ [*forma*] shape • **tener buena figura** to have a good figure ❸ [*en naipes*] picture card

figurado, da *adj* figurative · ϙ̣· **Los adjetivos ingleses son invariables.**

figurar ◆ *vi* ❶ [*aparecer*] • **figurar (en)** to appear (in); to figure (in) • **tu nombre no figura en esta lista** your name doesn't appear on this list ❷ [*ser importante*] to be prominent
◆ *vt* ❶ [*representar*] to represent ❷ [*simular*] to feign

fijador *sm* [*líquido*] fixative ❱ **fijador de pelo a)** [*crema*] hair gel **b)** [*espray*] hair spray

fijar *vt* ❶ [*generalmente*] to fix ❷ [*fecha*] to set ❸ [*asegurar*] to fasten ❹ [*cartel*] to stick up ❺ [*sello*] to stick on ❻ [*significado*] to establish • **fijar el domicilio** to take up residence • **fijar la mirada/la atención en** to fix your gaze/attention on
■ **fijarse** *v pronominal* ❶ • **fijarse en algo** [*darse cuenta*] to notice something • **no me fijé en qué llevaba puesto** I didn't really notice what she was wearing ❷ [*prestar atención*] to pay attention to • **en el supermercado tienes que fijarte en la fecha de caducidad de los productos** at the supermarket, you have to pay attention to the use-by dates on products

fijo, ja *adj* ❶ [*generalmente*] fixed ❷ [*sujeto*] secure ❸ [*cliente*] regular ❹ [*fecha*] definite ❺ [*empleado, trabajo*] permanent · ϙ̣· **Los adjetivos ingleses son invariables.**

fila *sf* ❶ [*de personas*] line • **la fila en el banco era larguísima** the line at the bank was really long • **en fila, en fila india** in line; in single file • **ponerse en fila** to line up ❷ [*de asientos*] row • **conseguimos asientos en tercera fila** we got seats in the third row

filatelia *sf* stamp collecting; philately *culto*

filete *sm* ❶ Cocina [*grueso*] (fillet) steak; [*delgado*] fillet ❷ [*solomillo*] sirloin

filial ◆ *adj* ❶ [*de hijo*] filial ❷ [*de empresa*] subsidiary:🔾 *Los adjetivos ingleses son invariables.*
◆ *sf* subsidiary

Filipinas *sfpl* • (las) **Filipinas** the Philippines *sing*

filmar *vt* to film • **Pedro filmó el nacimiento de su hijo** Pedro filmed the birth of his son

filmoteca *sf* ❶ [*archivo*] film library ❷ [*sala de cine*] film institute

filo *sm* (cutting) edge • **de doble filo, de dos filos** *literal & figurado* double-edged • **sacarle filo a algo** to sharpen something

filón *sm* ❶ [*de carbón* etc] seam ❷ *figurado* [*mina*] gold mine

filoso, sa *adj* sharp:🔾 *Los adjetivos ingleses son invariables.*

filosofía *sf* philosophy

filósofo, fa *sm, f* philosopher

filtración *sf* ❶ [*de agua*] filtration ❷ *figurado* [*de noticia* etc] leak

filtrar *vt* ❶ [*tamizar*] to filter ❷ *figurado* [*datos, noticia*] to leak
■ **filtrarse** *v pronominal* ❶ [*penetrar*] • **se está filtrando agua del techo** the roof is leaking • **filtrarse (por)** to filter (through) ❷ *figurado* [*datos, noticia*] to be leaked

filtro *sm* filter ▸ **filtro del aceite** oil filter

fin *sm* ❶ [*final*] end • **se acerca el fin del año escolar** we're approaching the end of the school year • **'fin'** [*en película*] the end • **poner fin a algo** to put an end to something • **tocar a su fin** to come to a close • **a fines de** at the end of • **al fin** at last • **a fin de cuentas** after all • **al fin y al cabo** after all ▸ **fin de semana** weekend ▸ **el fin de año** New Year's Eve ❷ [*objetivo*] aim
expresión **el fin justifica los medios** *proverbio* the end justifies the means

final ◆ *adj* final:🔾 *Los adjetivos ingleses son invariables.*
◆ *sm* end • **final feliz** happy ending • **a finales de** at the end of
◆ *sf* final

finalidad *sf* aim

finalista *smf* finalist

finalizar ◆ *vt* to finish
◆ *vi* • **finalizar (con)** to end (in)

financiación *sf* financing

financiar *vt* to finance

financiero, ra ◆ *adj* financial:🔾 *Los adjetivos ingleses son invariables.*
◆ *sm, f* [*persona*] financier
■ **financiera** *sf* [*firma*] finance company

finanzas *sfpl* finance:🔾 *incontable* • **las finanzas de una empresa** a company's finances

finca *sf* ❶ [*generalmente*] property ❷ [*casa de campo*] country residence

fincar *vi* ❶ [*comprar propiedades*] to acquire real estate ❷ [*establecerse*] to settle

fingir ◆ *vt* to pretend • **no finjas que duermes, sé que estás despierta** stop pretending you're asleep, I know you're awake
◆ *vi* to pretend

Finlandia *nombre propio* Finland

fino, na *adj* ❶ [*generalmente*] fine ❷ [*delgado*] thin ❸ [*cintura*] slim ❹ [*cortés*] refined ❺ [*agudo*] sharp:🔾 *Los adjetivos ingleses son invariables.*
■ **fino** *sm* dry sherry

finura *sf* ❶ [*generalmente*] fineness ❷ [*delgadez*] thinness ❸ [*cortesía*] refinement ❹ [*de oído, humor*] sharpness

firma *sf* ❶ [*rúbrica*] signature ❷ [*acción*] signing ❸ [*empresa*] firm

firmamento *sm* firmament

firmar *vt* to sign • **firme aquí, por favor** sign here please
expresión **firmar algo en blanco** *figurado* to rubber-stamp something

firme *adj* ❶ [*generalmente*] firm ❷ [*mueble, andamio, edificio*] stable ❸ [*argumento, base*] solid ❹ [*carácter, actitud, paso*] resolute:🔾 *Los adjetivos ingleses son invariables.*

firmeza *sf* ❶ [*generalmente*] firmness ❷ [*de mueble, edificio*] stability ❸ [*de argumento*] solidity ❹ [*de carácter, actitud*] resolution

fiscal ◆ *adj* tax:🔾 *Sólo se usa delante del sustantivo.*
◆ *smf* district attorney

fisco *sm* treasury

fisgar *vi* ❶ [*generalmente*] to pry ❷ [*escuchando*] to eavesdrop

fisgón, ona *sm, f* nosy parker

físico, ca ◆ *adj* physical • **el niño no tiene ningún problema físico** the child has no physical problems • **educación física** physical education:🔾 *Los adjetivos ingleses son invariables.*
◆ *sm, f* [*persona*] physicist
■ **físico** *sm* [*complexión*] physique
■ **física** *sf* [*ciencia*] physics:🔾 *incontable*

fisiológico, ca *adj* physiological:🔾 *Los adjetivos ingleses son invariables.*

fisioterapeuta *smf* physiotherapist

fisonomía *sf* features *pl*

fisura *sf* fissure

flácido, da *adj* flaccid:🔾 *Los adjetivos ingleses son invariables.*

flaco, ca *adj* thin:🔾 *Los adjetivos ingleses son invariables.*

flagrante *adj* flagrant:🔾 *Los adjetivos ingleses son invariables.*

flamante *adj* ❶ [*vistoso*] resplendent ❷ [*nuevo*] brand-new:🔾 *Los adjetivos ingleses son invariables.*

flan *sm* crème caramel

expresión estar hecho un flan to be shaking like a jelly

flanquear *vt* to flank

flaquear *vi* ❶ to weaken ❷ *figurado* to flag

flaqueza *sf* weakness

flash (pl flashes) *sm* ❶ FOTOGRAFÍA flash ❷ [*informativo*] newsflash

flato *sm* • tener flato to have a stitch

flauta *sf* flute • toca muy bien la flauta he plays the flute very well ▶ **flauta dulce** recorder

flecha *sf* ❶ [*generalmente*] arrow ❷ ARQUITECTURA spire

expresión salir como una flecha to shoot out

flechazo *sm* • fue un flechazo it was love at first sight

fleco *sm* ❶ [*adorno*] fringe ❷ [*cabello*] bangs *pl*

flema *sf* phlegm

flemático, ca *adj* [*tranquilo*] phlegmatic ☼: *Los adjetivos ingleses son invariables.*

flemón *sm* gumboil

fletar *vt* to hire

flexible *adj* flexible ☼: *Los adjetivos ingleses son invariables.*

flexo *sm* adjustable table lamp

flirtear *vi* to flirt

flojear *vi* ❶ [*piernas, fuerzas* ETC] to weaken ❷ [*memoria*] to be failing ❸ [*película, libro*] to flag ❹ [*calor, trabajo*] to ease off ❺ [*ventas*] to fall off

flojera *sf* lethargy

flojo, ja *adj* ❶ [*suelto*] loose ❷ [*débil - persona, bebida*] weak; [- *sonido*] faint; [- *tela*] thin; [- *salud*] poor; [- *viento*] light ❸ [*inactivo - mercado, negocio*] slack ☼: *Los adjetivos ingleses son invariables.*

flor *sf* BOTÁNICA flower • de flores floral

expresiones echar flores a alguien to pay somebody compliments ▶ **estar en la flor de la edad** to be in the prime of life ▶ **ser flor de un día** to be a flash in the pan ▶ **ser la flor (y nata)** to be la crème de la crème

las flores

la amapola	the poppy
el cardo	the thistle
el clavel	the carnation
el geranio	the geranium
el girasol	the sunflower
la lila	the lilac
el lirio	the iris
la margarita	the daisy
el muguete	the lily of the valley
la orquídea	the orchid
la rosa	the rose
el tulipán	the tulip
la violeta	the violet

flora *sf* flora

florecer *vi* ❶ to flower ❷ *figurado* to flourish

floreciente *adj* *figurado* flourishing ☼: *Los adjetivos ingleses son invariables.*

florero *sm* vase

florido, da *adj* ❶ [*con flores*] flowery ❷ [*estilo, lenguaje*] florid ☼: *Los adjetivos ingleses son invariables.*

florista *smf* florist

floristería *sf* florist's (shop)

flota *sf* fleet

flotador *sm* ❶ [*para nadar*] rubber ring ❷ [*de caña de pescar*] float

flotar *vi* ❶ [*generalmente*] ECONOMÍA to float ❷ [*banderas*] to flutter

flote ■ a flote *locución adverbial* afloat

expresión sacar algo a flote to get something back on its feet • **salir a flote** to get back on your feet

flotilla *sf* flotilla

fluctuar *vi* to fluctuate

fluidez *sf* ❶ [*generalmente*] fluidity ❷ [*del tráfico*] free flow ❸ [*de relaciones*] smoothness ❹ *figurado* [*en el lenguaje*] fluency

fluir *vi* to flow

flujo *sm* flow ▶ **flujo de caja** cash flow

flúor *sm* fluorine

fluorescente *sm* strip light

fluvial *adj* river ☼: *Sólo se usa delante del sustantivo.*

FM (*abreviatura de* frecuencia modulada) *sf* FM

FMI (*abreviatura de* Fondo Monetario Internacional) *sm* IMF

fobia *sf* phobia

foca *sf* seal

foco *sm* ❶ *figurado* [*centro*] focal point ❷ [*lámpara - para un punto*] spotlight; [- *para una zona*] floodlight • el foco brillaba sobre ella the spotlight shone upon her • los focos iluminaron el campo the floodlights lit up the field ❸ FÍSICA & GEOMETRÍA focus • fuera de foco out of focus ❹ [*bombilla*] light bulb • necesito un foco nuevo para esta lámpara I need a new lightbulb for this lamp

fofo, fa *adj* flabby ☼: *Los adjetivos ingleses son invariables.*

fogata *sf* bonfire

fogón *sm* [*para cocinar*] stove

fogoso, sa *adj* passionate ☼: *Los adjetivos ingleses son invariables.*

fogueo *sm* • de fogueo blank

foie-gras *sm* (pâté de) foie-gras

folclore *sm* folklore

fólder *sm* folder

folio *sm* ❶ [*hoja*] sheet ❷ [*tamaño*] folio

follaje *sm* foliage

folleto *sm* ❶ [*turístico, publicitario*] brochure ❷ [*explicativo, de instrucciones*] leaflet

fomentar *vt* to encourage

fomento *sm* encouragement

fondear *vi* to anchor

fondo *sm* ❶ [*de recipiente, mar, piscina*] bottom • **están explorando el fondo del mar** they are exploring the bottom of the sea • **tocar fondo a)** [*embarcación*] to scrape along the sea/river bed **b)** *figurado* to hit rock bottom • **doble fondo** false bottom ❷ [*de habitación* ETC] back • **al fondo de a)** [*calle, pasillo*] at the end of **b)** [*sala*] at the back of • **el baño está al fondo del corredor** the bathroom is at the end of the hall ❸ [*dimensión*] depth ❹ [*de tela, cuadro, foto*] background • **el retrato tenía un fondo azul** the portrait had a blue background • **al fondo** in the background ❺ [*de asunto, tema*] heart ❻ ECONOMÍA fund • **a fondo perdido** nonreturnable ▸ **fondo común** kitty ❼ [*de biblioteca, archivo*] catalog ❽ DEPORTE stamina ❾ [*combinación*] slip • **se te ve el fondo** your slip is showing

■ **fondos** *smpl* ECONOMÍA [*capital*] funds • **recaudar fondos** to raise funds

fonético, ca *adj* phonetic ❖ *Los adjetivos ingleses son invariables.*

■ **fonética** *sf* phonetics ❖ *incontable*

fontanero, ra *sm, f* plumber

footing *sm* jogging • **hacer footing** to go jogging

forajido, da *sm, f* outlaw

foráneo, a *adj* foreign ❖ *Los adjetivos ingleses son invariables.*

forastero, ra *sm, f* stranger

forcejear *vi* to struggle

fórceps *sm invariable* forceps

forense ◆ *adj* forensic ❖ *Los adjetivos ingleses son invariables.*

◆ *smf* pathologist

forestal *adj* forest ❖ *Sólo se usa delante del sustantivo.* • **el guardia forestal detectó el incendio** the forest ranger spotted the fire

forja *sf* ❶ [*fragua*] forge ❷ [*forjadura*] forging

forjar *vt* ❶ [*metal*] to forge ❷ *figurado* [*inventarse*] to invent ❸ [*crear*] to build up

forma *sf* ❶ [*generalmente*] shape • **encuentra todas las formas circulares** find all the circular shapes • **dar forma a** to shape • **en forma de** in the shape of • **tomar forma** to take shape ❷ [*manera*] way • **este ejercicio puede resolverse de diferentes formas** this problem can be solved several ways • **no me gusta su forma de ser, siempre está de mal humor** I don't like the way she acts; she's always in a bad mood • **de cualquier forma** anyway • **de esta forma** in this way • **de forma que** so that • **de todas formas** anyway • **de todas formas tendrás que limpiar tu cuarto** you'll have to clean your room anyway ❸ ARTE & LITERATURA form ❹ [*condición física*] fitness • **estar en forma** to be fit • **estar en baja forma** to be in poor shape • **mantenerse en forma** to stay in shape ❺ [*formulario*] form • **llene esta forma y entréguesela a la señorita** fill out this form and hand it to the young lady

formación *sf* ❶ [*generalmente*] MILITAR formation ❷ [*educación*] training ▸ **formación profesional** vocational training ❸ [*conjunto*] grouping

formal *adj* ❶ [*generalmente*] formal • **nos mandaron una invitación formal** they sent us a formal invitation ❷ [*que se porta bien*] well-behaved ❸ [*de confianza*] reliable • **necesitamos trabajadores más formales** we need more reliable workers ❹ [*serio*] serious ❖ *Los adjetivos ingleses son invariables.*

formalidad *sf* ❶ [*generalmente*] formality ❷ [*educación*] (good) manners *pl* ❸ [*fiabilidad*] reliability ❹ [*seriedad*] seriousness

formalizar *vt* to formalize

formar ◆ *vt* ❶ [*generalmente*] to form • **Juan y sus amigos formaron una banda musical** Juan and his friends formed a band • **si unes los puntos formarás la figura de un elefante** if you connect the dots you'll make an elephant ❷ [*educar*] to train • **la universidad se ocupa de formar a los profesionales liberales** it's the university's job to train professionals

◆ *vi* MILITAR to fall in

formatear *vt* INFORMÁTICA to format

formato *sm* format

formica® *sf* Formica®

formidable *adj* ❶ [*enorme*] tremendous ❷ [*extraordinario*] amazing ❖ *Los adjetivos ingleses son invariables.*

fórmula *sf* formula • **es difícil recordar todas las fórmulas matemáticas** it's hard to remember all the mathematical formulas • **una fórmula mágica** a magic formula ▸ **fórmula de cortesía** polite set expression • **tienes que empezar la carta con una fórmula de cortesía** you should start the letter with a polite set expression ▸ **fórmula uno** formula one

formular *vt* to formulate

formulario *sm* form

fornido, da *adj* well-built ❖ *Los adjetivos ingleses son invariables.*

foro *sm* ❶ [*tribunal*] court (of law) ❷ TEATRO back of the stage ❸ [*debate*] forum ▸ **foro de discusión** INFORMÁTICA forum

expresión **desaparecer por el foro** to slip away unnoticed

forraje *sm* fodder

forrar *vt* • **forrar (de) a)** [*libro*] to cover (with) **b)** [*ropa*] to line (with) **c)** [*asiento*] to upholster (with)

forro *sm* ❶ [*de libro*] cover ❷ [*de ropa*] lining ❸ [*de asiento*] upholstery

fortalecer *vt* to strengthen

fortaleza *sf* ❶ [*generalmente*] strength • **su fortaleza lo ayudó a recuperarse pronto** his strength helped him recover quickly ❷ [*recinto*] fortress • **a lo largo de la costa hay varias fortalezas antiguas** there are several old fortresses along the coast

fortificación *sf* fortification

fortuito, ta *adj* chance ❖ *Sólo se usa delante del sustantivo.*

fortuna *sf* ❶ [*suerte*] luck • **probar fortuna** to try your luck • **tuvo la fortuna de conocer personalmente a su actor favorito** he had the good fortune to meet his favorite actor • **por fortuna** fortunately ❷ [*ri-*

queza] fortune • **su fortuna personal es de cerca de diez millones de dólares** her personal fortune comes to nearly ten million dollars ❸ [*destino*] fate

forzado, da *adj* forced ❂ *Los adjetivos ingleses son invariables.*

forzar *vt* ❶ [*generalmente*] to force • **el mal tiempo nos forzó a quedarnos en casa todo el fin de semana** the bad weather forced us to stay home all weekend • **forzar la vista** to strain your eyes ❷ [*violar*] to rape

forzoso, sa *adj* ❶ [*obligatorio*] compulsory ❷ [*inevitable*] inevitable ❸ [*necesario*] necessary ❂ *Los adjetivos ingleses son invariables.*

fosa *sf* ❶ [*sepultura*] grave ❷ ANATOMÍA cavity ▶ **fosas nasales** nostrils ❸ [*hoyo*] pit ▶ **fosa marina** ocean trough

fosfato *sm* phosphate

fosforescente *adj* phosphorescent ❂ *Los adjetivos ingleses son invariables.*

fósforo *sm* ❶ QUÍMICA phosphorus ❷ [*cerillo*] match

fósil *sm* GEOLOGÍA fossil

foso *sm* ❶ [*hoyo*] ditch ❷ [*de fortaleza*] moat ❸ DEPORTE & TEATRO pit

foto *sf* photo

fotocopia *sf* [*objeto*] photocopy

fotocopiadora *sf* photocopier

fotocopiar *vt* to photocopy

fotoeléctrico, ca *adj* photoelectric ❂ *Los adjetivos ingleses son invariables.*

fotogénico, ca *adj* photogenic ❂ *Los adjetivos ingleses son invariables.*

fotografía *sf* ❶ [*arte*] photography ❷ [*imagen*] photograph ; photo *familiar* • **hacer una fotografía de alguien** to take a photo of somebody

fotografiar *vt* to photograph

fotógrafo, fa *sm, f* photographer

fotosíntesis *sf invariable* photosynthesis

fracasar *vi* to fail • **nuestros planes de viaje fracasaron por falta de dinero** our travel plans failed due to lack of money • **fracasar (en/como)** to fail (at/as)

fracaso *sm* failure • **el espectáculo fue un fracaso, no vino nadie** the show was a failure, nobody came • **todo fue un fracaso** the whole thing was a disaster

fracción *sf* ❶ [*generalmente*] fraction • **en la clase de hoy estudiamos las fracciones** we studied fractions in class today • **en una fracción de segundo** in a split second ❷ POLÍTICA faction

fraccionadora *sf* estate agent

fraccionamiento *sm* [*urbanización*] housing development

fractura *sf* fracture • **la caída le produjo varias fracturas** she sustained several fractures from the fall

fragancia *sf* fragrance

fraganti ■ **in fraganti** *locución adverbial* • **coger a alguien in fraganti** to catch somebody in the act

fragata *sf* frigate

frágil *adj* ❶ [*objeto*] fragile ❷ [*persona*] frail ❂ *Los adjetivos ingleses son invariables.*

fragilidad *sf* ❶ [*de objeto*] fragility ❷ [*de persona*] frailty

fragmentar *vt* ❶ [*romper*] to fragment ❷ [*dividir*] to divide

fragmento *sm* ❶ [*trozo*] piece ❷ [*de obra*] excerpt

frambuesa *sf* raspberry, *plural* raspberries

Francia *nombre propio* France

franco, ca *adj* ❶ [*sincero*] frank • **te voy a ser franco, no confío en él** I'll be frank, I don't trust him • **para serte franco** to be honest ❷ [*directo*] frank ❸ [*sin obstáculos, gastos*] free ❂ *Los adjetivos ingleses son invariables.*

francotirador, ra *sm, f* MILITAR sniper

franja *sf* ❶ strip ❷ [*en bandera, uniforme*] stripe ▶ **franja horaria** time zone

franquear *vt* ❶ [*paso, camino*] to clear ❷ [*río, montaña* ETC] to cross ❸ [*correo*] to frank

franqueo *sm* postage

franqueza *sf* frankness

franquicia *sf* exemption

frasco *sm* bottle • **el perfume viene en un frasco muy bonito** the perfume comes in a pretty bottle • **no puedo abrir el frasco de la mayonesa** I can't open the mayonnaise jar

frase *sf* ❶ [*oración*] sentence ❷ [*locución*] expression ▶ **frase hecha a)** [*modismo*] set phrase **b)** [*tópico*] cliché

fraterno, na *adj* brotherly ❂ *Los adjetivos ingleses son invariables.*

fraude *sm* fraud ▶ **fraude electoral** election o electoral fraud ▶ **fraude fiscal** tax evasion

fraudulento, ta *adj* fraudulent ❂ *Los adjetivos ingleses son invariables.*

frazada *sf* blanket ▶ **frazada eléctrica** electric blanket

frecuencia *sf* frequency • **las ondas de una frecuencia tan alta no se oyen** you can't hear waves of such a high frequency • **¿con qué frecuencia visitas a tus abuelos?** how often do you visit your grandparents? • **con frecuencia** often • **somos buenas amigas y nos vemos con frecuencia** we're good friends and see each other frequently ▶ **frecuencia modulada** frequency modulation

frecuentar *vt* ❶ [*lugar*] to frequent ❷ [*persona*] to see

frecuente *adj* ❶ [*reiterado*] frequent ❷ [*habitual*] common ❂ *Los adjetivos ingleses son invariables.*

fregadero *sm* (kitchen) sink

fregón, ona ◆ *adj* annoying ◆ *sm, f* pest

freidora *sf* deep fat fryer

frenar ◆ *vt* ❶ AUTOMÓVILES to brake ❷ [*contener*] to check

F

◆ *vi* ❶ to stop ❷ AUTOMÓVILES to brake

frenazo *sm* ❶ AUTOMÓVILES • **dar un frenazo** to brake hard ❷ *figurado* [*parón*] sudden stop

frenesí (pl frenesíes O frenesís) *sm* frenzy

frenético, ca *adj* ❶ [*colérico*] furious ❷ [*enloquecido*] frantic:👁️ *Los adjetivos ingleses son invariables.*

freno *sm* ❶ AUTOMÓVILES brake❱ **freno de mano** handbrake ❷ [*de caballerías*] bit ❸ *figurado* [*contención*] check • **poner freno a** to put a stop to

frente ◆ *sf* forehead • **arrugar la frente** to knit your brow • **frente a frente** face to face

expresión **con la frente muy alta** with your head held high

◆ *sm* front • **el frente de la casa estaba pintado de blanco** the front of the house was painted white • **estar al frente (de)** to be at the head (of) • **hacer frente a** to face up to • **pasar al frente** to go up to the front❱ **frente de batalla** battle front❱ **frente cálido/frío** warm/cold front

fresa *sf* [*planta, fruto*] strawberry

fresco, ca ◆ *adj* ❶ [*generalmente*] fresh • **es importante comer verduras y frutas frescas** it's important to eat fresh fruit and vegetables ❷ [*temperatura*] cool • **los días están más frescos últimamente** the days are growing cooler lately ❸ [*pintura, tinta*] wet • **'cuidado, pintura fresca'** wet paint ❹ [*descarado*] nervy • **¡qué fresco!** he's got some nerve!:👁️ *Los adjetivos ingleses son invariables.*

◆ *sm, f* [*caradura*] nervy person

■ **fresco** *sm* ❶ ARTE fresco • **al fresco** in fresco ❷ [*frescor*] coolness • **hace fresco** it's chilly • **tomar el fresco** to get a breath of fresh air

frescor *sm* coolness

frescura *sf* ❶ [*generalmente*] freshness ❷ [*descaro*] nerve

fresón *sm* large strawberry

frialdad *sf* literal & *figurado* coldness

fricción *sf* ❶ [*generalmente*] friction • **la fricción entre las dos piezas provocó un desgaste** friction between the two pieces caused them to wear down ❷ [*friega*] rub • **¿quieres fricciones en la espalda?** do you want a back rub?

frigorífico, ca *adj* ❶ [*camión*] refrigerator:👁️ *Sólo se usa delante del sustantivo.* ❷ [*cámara*] cold

frijol *sm* bean

frío, a *adj* ❶ [*generalmente*] cold • **la sopa está fría** the soup is cold ❷ [*inmutable*] cool • **dejar a alguien frío** to leave somebody cold:👁️ *Los adjetivos ingleses son invariables.*

■ **frío** *sm* cold • **pillar frío** to catch a cold • **hace frío** it's cold • **hace un frío que pela** *familiar* it's freezing • **tener frío** to be cold

expresión **no darle a alguien ni frío ni calor** to leave somebody cold

friolento, ta ◆ *adj* sensitive to the cold:👁️ *Los adjetivos ingleses son invariables.*

◆ *sm, f* • **es un friolento** he really feels the cold

frito, ta *adj* ❶ [*alimento*] fried • **preparé un pescado frito** I made some fried fish ❷ *familiar* & *figurado* [*persona*] [*- harta*] fed up (to the back teeth); [*- dormida*] flaked out:👁️ *Los adjetivos ingleses son invariables.*

■ **fritos** *smpl* 👁️ *generalmente pl* fried food 👁️ *incontable*

frondoso, sa *adj* leafy:👁️ *Los adjetivos ingleses son invariables.*

frontal *adj* frontal:👁️ *Los adjetivos ingleses son invariables.*

frontera *sf* ❶ [*de un país*] border ❷ [*límite*] bounds *pl*

fronterizo, za *adj* border:👁️ *Sólo se usa delante del sustantivo.*

frotar *vt* to rub

frustración *sf* frustration

frustrar *vt* to frustrate

■ **frustrarse** *v pronominal* ❶ [*persona*] to get frustrated ❷ [*ilusiones*] to be thwarted ❸ [*proyecto*] to fail

fruta *sf* fruit❱ **fruta confitada** candied fruit❱ **fruta de estación** seasonal fruit❱ **fruta de la pasión** passion fruit❱ **fruta del tiempo** seasonal fruit❱ **fruta seca** nuts and dried fruits *pl*

las frutas

el aguacate	the avocado
el albaricoque	the apricot
el arándano	the blueberry
el arándano rojo	the cranberry
la cereza	the cherry
la ciruela	the plum
la clementina	the clementine
el coco	the coconut
la frambuesa	the raspberry
la fresa	the strawberry
la granada	the pomegranate
la grosella	the redcurrant
la grosella negra	the blackcurrant
la guayaba	the guava
el higo	the fig
el kiwi	the kiwi
el limón	the lemon
la lima	the lime
el mango	the mango
la manzana	the apple
el maracuyá	the passion fruit
el melocotón	the peach
el melón	the melon
la mora	the blackberry
la naranja	the orange
la pera	the pear
la piña	the pineapple
el plátano	the banana
la sandía	the watermelon
la uva	the grape

frutal *sm* fruit tree

frutería *sf* fruit shop

fruto *sm* ❶ [*naranja, plátano* ETC] fruit ❷ [*nuez, avellana* ETC] nut ▶ **frutos secos** dried fruit and nuts ❸ [*resultado*] fruit • **dar fruto** to bear fruit • **sacar fruto de algo** to profit from something

fucsia *sf* fuchsia

fuego *sm* ❶ [*generalmente*] MILITAR fire • **no consiguieron controlar el fuego** they couldn't control the fire • **pegar fuego a algo** to set something on fire ▶ **fuegos artificiales** fireworks ❷ [*de cocina, fogón*] ring ❸ [*para fumador*] • **pedir/dar fuego** to ask for/give a light • **¿tiene fuego?** have you got a light? ❹ [*apasionamiento*] passion

fuente *sf* ❶ [*manantial*] spring ▶ **fuente de sodas** snack bar ❷ [*construcción*] fountain ❸ [*bandeja*] (serving) dish ❹ [*origen*] source ▶ **fuente de información/ingresos** source of information/income ▶ **fuentes oficiales** official sources

fuera ◆ *adv* ❶ [*en el exterior*] outside • **el perro duerme fuera de la casa** the dog sleeps outside the house • **le echó fuera** she threw him out • **hacia fuera** outwards • **por fuera** (on the) outside ❷ [*en otro lugar*] away ❸ [*en el extranjero*] abroad • **de fuera** [*extranjero*] from abroad ❹ *figurado* [*alejado*] • **fuera de a)** [*alcance, peligro*] out of **b)** [*cálculos, competencia*] outside ❺ DEPORTE • **fuera de juego** offside
expresión **estar fuera de sí** to be beside yourself (with rage)
◆ *exclamación* • **¡fuera! a)** [*generalmente*] (get) out! **b)** [*en el teatro*] (get) off! → **ir,** → **ser**

fueraborda *sm invariable* outboard motor

fuerte ◆ *adj* ❶ [*generalmente*] strong • **ese pescado tiene un olor muy fuerte** that fish has a very strong smell • **un carácter fuerte** a strong character ❷ [*frío, dolor*] intense ❸ [*color*] bold • **prefiero los colores fuertes** I prefer bold colors ❹ [*lluvia*] heavy ❺ [*ruido*] loud • **la música está muy fuerte para platicar** the music is too loud for conversation ❻ [*golpe, pelea*] hard • **se dio un golpe tan fuerte que empezó a llorar** he hit himself so hard he started to cry ❼ [*comida, salsa*] rich ❽ [*nudo*] tight ❾ *Los adjetivos ingleses son invariables.*
◆ *adv* ❶ [*intensamente - generalmente*] hard; [*- abrazar, agarrar*] tight ❷ [*abundantemente*] a lot ❸ [*en voz alta*] loudly
◆ *sm* ❶ [*fortificación*] fort ❷ [*punto fuerte*] strong point

fuerza *sf* ❶ [*generalmente*] strength • **vamos a descansar para recuperar fuerzas** let's have a break to recover our strength • **cobrar fuerza** to gather strength • **a fuerza de** by dint of • **por fuerza** of necessity • **tener fuerza** to be strong • **tener fuerzas para** to have the strength to ▶ **fuerza mayor a)** DERECHO force majeure **b)** [*en seguros*] act of God • **no llegué por un caso de fuerza mayor** I didn't make it due to circumstances beyond my control ▶ **fuerza de voluntad** willpower ❷ [*violencia*] force • **a la fuerza a)** [*contra la voluntad*] by force **b)** [*por necesidad*] of necessity • **por la fuerza** by force • **fuerza bruta** brute force ❸ [*de sonido*] loudness ❹ [*de dolor*] intensity ❺ FÍSICA & MILITAR force ▶ **fuerza aérea** airforce ▶ **fuerza disuasoria** deterrent ▶ **fuerza de la gravedad** force of gravity ▶ **fuerza motriz a)** [*generalmente*] motive power **b)** *figurado* driving force ❻ ELECTRICIDAD power ▶ **fuerza hidráulica** water power
expresión **írsele a alguien la fuerza por la boca** to be all talk and no action

fuga *sf* ❶ [*huida*] escape • **los prisioneros planearon su fuga** the prisoners planned their escape ▶ **fuga de capitales** flight of capital ❷ [*escape*] leak • **encontramos una fuga de gas en la cocina** we found a gas leak in the kitchen ❸ MÚSICA fugue

fugarse *v pronominal* to escape • **se fugó de la cárcel** he escaped from prison • **fugarse de casa** to run away from home • **fugarse con alguien** to run off with somebody

fugaz *adj* fleeting ❀ *Los adjetivos ingleses son invariables.*

fugitivo, va *sm, f* fugitive

fulano, na *sm, f* what's his/her name
■ **fulana** *sf* [*prostituta*] tart

fulminante *adj* ❶ *figurado* [*despido, muerte*] sudden ❷ [*enfermedad*] devastating ❸ [*mirada*] withering ❀ *Los adjetivos ingleses son invariables.*

fumador, ra *sm, f* smoker • **no fumador** nonsmoker ▶ **fumador empedernido** chain-smoker ▶ **fumador pasivo** passive smoker

fumar *vt* & *vi* to smoke • **fumar en pipa** to smoke a pipe • **'prohibido fumar'** no smoking

función *sf* ❶ [*generalmente*] function ❷ [*trabajo*] duty • **director en funciones** acting director • **entrar en funciones** to take up your duties ❸ CINE & TEATRO show

funcional *adj* functional ❀ *Los adjetivos ingleses son invariables.*

funcionamiento *sm* operation

funcionar *vi* to work • **la licuadora ya no funciona por que es muy vieja** the blender doesn't work any more because it's so old • **funcionar con gasolina** to run on petrol • **'no funciona'** out of order

funcionario, ria *sm, f* civil servant

funda *sf* ❶ [*de sofá, máquina de escribir*] cover ❷ [*de almohada*] case ❸ [*de disco*] sleeve ❹ [*de pistola*] sheath

fundación *sf* foundation

fundador, ra *sm, f* founder

fundamental *adj* fundamental ❀ *Los adjetivos ingleses son invariables.*

fundamentar *vt* ❶ *figurado* [*basar*] to base ❷ CONSTRUCCIÓN to lay the foundations of

fundamento *sm* ❶ [*base*] foundation ❷ [*razón*] grounds *pl* • **sin fundamento** groundless

fundar *vt* ❶ [*crear*] to found ❷ [*basar*] • **fundar (en)** to base (on)

fundición *sf* ❶ [*fusión - de vidrio*] melting; [*- de metal*] smelting ❷ [*taller*] foundry

F

fundir

fundir *vt* ❶ [*metalurgia*] [*- plomo*] to melt; [*- hierro*] to smelt ❷ ELECTRICIDAD to fuse ❸ [*bombilla, fusible*] to blow ❹ COMERCIO to merge

■ **fundirse** *v pronominal* ❶ ELECTRICIDAD to blow • **el foco de la lámpara se fundió** the bulb in the lamp has blown ❷ [*derretirse*] to melt • **la manteca se funde si la dejas al calor** lard will melt if you leave it out in the heat ❸ *figurado* to merge • **durante la crisis económica, varias empresas se fundieron** several companies merged during the economic crisis ❹ [*arruinarse*] to go bust

fúnebre *adj* funeral ❀ *Sólo se usa delante del sustantivo.*

funeral *sm* ❀ *generalmente pl* funeral

funerario, ria *adj* funeral ❀ *Sólo se usa delante del sustantivo.*

■ **funeraria** *sf* funeral home

funesto, ta *adj* fateful ❀ *Los adjetivos ingleses son invariables.*

fungir *vi* ▸ **fungir (de** o **como)** to act (as)

funicular *sm* ❶ [*por tierra*] funicular ❷ [*por aire*] cable car

furgón *sm* FERROCARRIL wagon ▸ **furgón de cola** caboose

furia *sf* fury • **estar hecho una furia** to be furious

furioso, sa *adj* furious ❀ *Los adjetivos ingleses son invariables.*

furor *sm* [*enfado*] rage • **hacer furor** to be all the rage

furtivo, va *adj* [*mirada, sonrisa*] furtive ❀ *Los adjetivos ingleses son invariables.*

fusible *sm* fuse

fusil *sm* rifle

fusilar *vt* [*ejecutar*] to shoot

fusión *sf* ❶ [*agrupación*] merging ❷ [*de empresas, bancos*] merger ❸ [*derretimiento*] melting ❹ FÍSICA fusion

fusionar *vt* ❶ [*generalmente*] ECONOMÍA to merge ❷ FÍSICA to fuse

fusta *sf* riding crop

futbol *sm* soccer • **un jugador de futbol** a soccer player ▸ **futbol americano** football

futbolista *smf* ❶ soccer player ❷ football player

futuro, ra *adj* future • **las generaciones futuras** future generations • **la futura mamá** the mother-to-be ❀ *Los adjetivos ingleses son invariables.*

■ **futuro** *sm* [*generalmente*] GRAMÁTICA future • **en un futuro próximo** in the near future

G

g, G *sf* [*letra*] g; G

gabardina *sf* [*prenda*] raincoat

gabinete *sm* ❶ [*gobierno*] cabinet ❷ [*despacho*] office ▸ **gabinete de prensa** press office ❸ [*sala*] study

gacela *sf* gazelle

gachas *sfpl* COCINA (corn) porridge ⚐ *incontable*

gafas *sfpl* sunglasses ▸ **gafas de sol** sunglasses

gaita *sf* bagpipes *pl*

gajes *smpl* ▸ **gajes del oficio** occupational hazards

gajo *sm* segment

gala *sf* ❶ [*fiesta*] gala • **ropa/uniforme de gala** [*ropa*] full dress/uniform • **cena de gala** black tie dinner; formal dinner ❷ [*ropa*] • **galas** best clothes ❸ [*actuación*] show

expresión **hacer gala de algo a)** [*preciarse*] to be proud of something **b)** [*exhibir*] to demonstrate something

galán *sm* TEATRO leading man

galantería *sf* ❶ [*cualidad*] politeness ❷ [*acción*] gallantry

galápago *sm* turtle

galardón *sm* award

galaxia *sf* galaxy

galería *sf* ❶ [*generalmente*] gallery • **una galería de arte** an art gallery • **una galería comercial** a shopping mall ❷ [*corredor descubierto*] verandah ❸ *figurado* [*vulgo*] masses *pl*

Gales *nombre propio* • **(el país de) Gales** Wales

galgo *sm* greyhound

expresión **¡échale un galgo!** you can forget it!

galimatías *sm invariable* ❶ [*lenguaje*] gibberish ⚐ *incontable* ❷ [*lío*] jumble

galleta *sf* COCINA cookie • **compré un paquete de galletas** I bought a pack of cookies • **galleta salada** cracker

gallina ◆ *sf* [*ave*] hen ▸ **la gallina ciega** blind man's bluff

expresión **acostarse con las gallinas** to go to bed early ▸ **estar como gallina en corral ajeno** to be like a fish out of water

◆ *smf* familiar [*persona*] chicken

gallinero *sm* ❶ [*corral*] henhouse ❷ *familiar* TEATRO gods *sing*

gallo *sm* ❶ [*ave*] rooster ❷ [*al cantar*] false note ❸ [*al hablar*] squeak ❹ [*pez*] John Dory

expresión **en menos que canta un gallo** in no time at all ▸ **otro gallo cantaría** things would be very different

galón *sm* ❶ [*adorno*] braid ❷ MILITAR stripe ❸ [*medida*] gallon

galopar *vi* to gallop

galope *sm* gallop • **al galope** at a gallop • **a galope tendido** at full gallop

galpón *sm* shed

gama *sf* ❶ [*generalmente*] range ❷ MÚSICA scale

gana *sf* ❶ [*afán*] • **gana (de)** desire (to) • **de buena gana** willingly • **se ofreció a acompañarla de buena gana** he willingly offered to go with her • **de mala gana** reluctantly • **me contestó de mala gana** he answered reluctantly • **me da/no me da la gana hacerlo** I damn well feel like/don't damn well feel like doing it ❷ [*apetito*] appetite

ganadería *sf* ❶ [*actividad*] livestock farming ❷ [*ganado*] livestock

ganado *sm* livestock ▸ **ganado porcino** pigs *pl* ▸ **ganado vacuno** cattle *pl*

ganador, ra ◆ *adj* winning ⚐ *Los adjetivos ingleses son invariables.*

◆ *sm, f* winner

ganancia *sf* ❶ [*rendimiento*] profit ❷ [*ingreso*] earnings *pl* ▸ **ganancias y pérdidas** profit and loss ▸ **ganancia líquida** net profit

ganar ◆ *vt* ❶ [*generalmente*] to win • **nuestra escuela ganó el campeonato de futbol** our school won the soccer championship ❷ [*sueldo, dinero*] to earn • **gana seis mil pesos al mes** she earns six thousand pesos a month ❸ [*peso, tiempo, terreno*] to gain ❹ [*derrotar*] to beat • **la tenista rusa le ganó a la francesa** the Russian tennis player beat the French one • **ganar a alguien a algo** to beat somebody at something ❺ [*aventajar*] • **ganar a alguien en algo** to be better than somebody as regards something

◆ *vi* ❶ [*vencer*] to win ❷ [*lograr dinero*] to earn money ❸ [*mejorar*] • **ganar en algo** to gain in something

■ **ganarse** *v pronominal* ❶ [*conquistar - simpatía, respeto*] to earn ; [*- persona*] to win over • **se gana la vida como mesero** he earns a living as a waiter • **se ganó la confianza de todos** she earned everybody's trust ❷ [*merecer*] to deserve • **se ganó el castigo** he deserved the punishment

ganchillo *sm* ❶ [*aguja*] crochet hook ❷ [*labor*] crochet • **hacer ganchillo** to crochet

gancho *sm* ❶ [*generalmente*] hook • **lo colgó de un gancho** he hung it on a hook ❷ [*de percha*] peg ❸ [*percha*] hanger • **colgamos la ropa en ganchos de plástico** we hung up the clothes on plastic hangers ❹ [*cómplice - de estafador*] decoy ; [*- de vendedor*] person who attracts buyers

ganga *sf familiar* bargain

gángster (pl gángsters) *sm* gangster

ganso, sa *sm, f* [*ave - hembra*] goose ; [*- macho*] gander

garabatear *vi* & *vt* to scribble

garabato *sm* scribble

garaje *sm* garage

garantía *sf* ❶ [*generalmente*] guarantee • **este equipo de música tiene garantía por un año** this stereo system has a one-year guarantee • **de garantía** reliable • **ser garantía de algo** to guarantee something ▶ **garantías constitucionales** constitutional rights ❷ [*fianza*] surety

garantizar *vt* ❶ [*generalmente*] to guarantee • **garantizan la calidad del producto** they guarantee the quality of the product • **te garantizo que llegaremos a tiempo** I guarantee you we'll get there on time ❷ [*avalar*] to vouch for

garbanzo *sm* chickpea
expresión ser el garbanzo negro de la familia to be the black sheep of the family

garbo *sm* ❶ [*de persona*] grace ❷ [*de escritura*] style

gargajo *sm* phlegm

garganta *sf* ❶ ANATOMÍA throat • **me duele la garganta** I have a sore throat ❷ [*desfiladero*] gorge
expresión lo tengo atravesado en la garganta *figurado* he sticks in my gullet ▶ **tener buena garganta** to have a good voice

gargantilla *sf* choker

gárgaras *sfpl* • **hacer gárgaras** to gargle
expresión mandar a alguien a hacer gárgaras *familiar* to send somebody packing ▶ **¡vete a hacer gárgaras!** *familiar* get lost!

garita *sf* ❶ [*generalmente*] cabin ❷ [*de conserje*] porter's lodge ❸ MILITAR sentry box

garra *sf* ❶ [*de animal*] claw • **el lobo lo lastimó con sus garras** the wolf scratched him with his claws ❷ [*de ave de rapiña*] talon • **las garras del cóndor son muy peligrosas** the condor's talons are very dangerous ❸ *despectivo* [*de persona*] paw
expresión caer en las garras de alguien to fall into somebody's clutches ▶ **tener garra a)** [*persona*] to have charisma **b)** [*novela, canción* ETC] to be gripping

garrafa *sf* carafe

garrafal *adj* monumental ☀ *Los adjetivos ingleses son invariables.*

garrapata *sf* tick

garrote *sm* ❶ [*palo*] club ❷ [*instrumento*] garotte

garza *sf* heron ▶ **garza real** grey heron

gas *sm* gas • **la explosión se produjo por un escape de gas** the explosion was caused by a gas leak • **con gas a)** [*agua*] sparkling ; carbonated **b)** [*refresco*] fizzy ; carbonated ▶ **gas butano** butane (gas) ▶ **gas licuado de petróleo** liquified petroleum gas ▶ **gas natural** natural gas ▶ **gas lacrimógeno** tear gas

■ **gases** *smpl* [*en el estómago*] gas ☀ *incontable* • **el niño está con gases** the child has a lot of gas

gasa *sf* gauze

gaseoducto *sm* gas pipeline

gaseoso, sa *adj* ❶ gaseous ❷ [*bebida*] fizzy ☀ *Los adjetivos ingleses son invariables.*

gasóleo *sm* diesel oil

gasolina *sf* gas • **poner gasolina** to fill up (with gas)

gasolinera *sf* gas station

gastado, da *adj* ❶ [*ropa, pieza* ETC] worn out ❷ [*frase, tema*] hackneyed ❸ [*persona*] burnt out ☀ *Los adjetivos ingleses son invariables.*

gastar ◆ *vt* ❶ [*consumir - dinero, tiempo*] to spend ; [*- gasolina, electricidad*] to use (up) ; [*- ropa, zapatos*] to wear out • **gastamos mucho dinero en la reforma de la cocina** we spent a lot of money redoing the kitchen • **este carro gasta demasiado** this car uses too much gas • **este niño gasta mucho la ropa** this child really wears out his clothes ❷ *figurado* [*usar - generalmente*] to use ; [*- ropa*] to wear ; [*- número de zapatos*] to take • **gastar una broma (a alguien)** to play a joke (on somebody) ❸ [*malgastar*] to waste ◆ *vi* [*despilfarrar*] to spend (money)

■ **gastarse** *v pronominal* ❶ [*deteriorarse*] to wear out ❷ [*terminarse*] to run out

gasto *sm* ❶ [*acción de gastar*] outlay ❷ [*cosa que pagar*] expense • **el gasto más importante en nuestra casa es la comida** our biggest household expense is on food • **cubrir gastos** to cover costs ▶ **gasto deducible** ECONOMÍA tax-deductible expense ▶ **gasto público** public expenditure ▶ **gastos de envío** postage and packing ▶ **gastos fijos a)** COMERCIO fixed costs **b)** [*en una casa*] overheads ▶ **gastos generales** overheads ▶ **gastos de mantenimiento** maintenance costs ▶ **gastos de representación** entertainment allowance *sing* ❸ [*de energía, gasolina*] consumption ❹ [*despilfarro*] waste • **el gasto de energía es exagerado en este país** the waste of energy in this country is ridiculous

gastritis *sf invariable* gastritis

gastronomía *sf* gastronomy

gatas ■ **a gatas** *locución adverbial* on all fours

gatear *vi* to crawl • **mi hija gatea por toda la casa** my daughter crawls all over the house

gatillo *sm* trigger • **apretar el gatillo** to pull the trigger

gato, ta *sm, f* cat • **le encantan los gatos** she loves cats

expresiones **aquí hay gato encerrado** there's something fishy going on here▸ **buscar tres pies al gato** to overcomplicate matters▸ **dar gato por liebre a alguien** to cheat somebody▸ **el gato escaldado del agua fría huye** *proverbio* once bitten twice shy▸ **jugar al gato y al ratón** to play cat and mouse▸ **llevarse el gato al agua** to pull it off

■ **gato** *sm* AUTOMÓVILES jack • **no tenemos un gato para cambiar el neumático** we don't have a jack for changing the tire

gaviota *sf* seagull

gay *adj invariable* & *smf* gay (homosexual)☼: *Los adjetivos ingleses son invariables.*

géiser (pl géiseres) *sm* geyser

gel *sm* gel

gelatina *sf*❶ [de carne] gelatine❷ [de fruta] jelly

gema *sf* gem

gemelo, la ◆ *adj* twin☼: *Sólo se usa delante del sustantivo.* • **tiene un hermano gemelo** she has a twin brother
◆ *sm, f* [persona] twin

gemido *sm*❶ [de persona] moan❷ [de animal] whine

Géminis ◆ *sm* [zodiaco] Gemini
◆ *smf* [persona] Gemini

gemir *vi*❶ [persona] to moan • **gemir de dolor** to moan with pain❷ [animal] to whine❸ [viento] to howl

genealogía *sf* genealogy

generación *sf* generation

generador, ra *adj* generating☼: *Los adjetivos ingleses son invariables.*

■ **generador** *sm* generator

general ◆ *adj*❶ [generalmente] general • **por lo general, en general** generally • **por lo general comemos fuera los domingos** we generally eat out on Sundays❷ [usual] usual☼: *Los adjetivos ingleses son invariables.*
◆ *sm* MILITAR general▸ **general de brigada** brigadier general▸ **general de división** major general

generalidad *sf*❶ [mayoría] majority❷ [vaguedad] generalization

generalizar ◆ *vt* to make widespread
◆ *vi* to generalize • **la profesora generalizó cuando dijo que todos habíamos copiado** the teacher was generalizing when she said we had all cheated

generalmente *adv* generally

generar *vt*❶ [generalmente] to generate❷ [engendrar] to create

genérico, ca *adj* [común] generic☼: *Los adjetivos ingleses son invariables.*

género *sm*❶ [clase] type • **también tengo problemas de ese género** I also have that type of problem❷ GRAMÁTICA gender • **género masculino** masculine gender • **muchos sustantivos de género masculino**

terminan con la letra "o" many masculine nouns end in "o"❸ LITERATURA genre• **el género policial me gusta mucho** I really enjoy the detective genre❹ BIOLOGÍA genus▸ **el género humano** the human race❺ [productos] merchandise❻ [tejido] cloth▸ **géneros de punto** knitwear☼: *incontable*

generosidad *sf* generosity

generoso, sa *adj* generous • **es una persona muy generosa con los demás** she's very generous to other people☼: *Los adjetivos ingleses son invariables.*

genético, ca *adj* genetic☼: *Los adjetivos ingleses son invariables.*

■ **genética** *sf* genetics☼: *incontable*

genial *adj*❶ [autor, compositor ETC] of genius❷ [estupendo] brilliant; great☼: *Los adjetivos ingleses son invariables.*

genio *sm*❶ [talento] genius• **fue un verdadero genio de la literatura** he was a true literary genius❷ [carácter] nature❸ [mal carácter] bad temper • **estar de/tener mal genio** to be in a mood/bad-tempered❹ [ser sobrenatural] genie • **no creo en el genio de la lámpara** I don't believe in genies in bottles

genital *adj* genital☼: *Los adjetivos ingleses son invariables.*

genocidio *sm* genocide

genoma *sm* genome▸ **genoma humano** human genome

gente *sf*❶ [generalmente] people *pl* • **había mucha gente en la fiesta** there were a lot of people at the party▸ **gente bien** well-to-do people▸ **gente de bien** good people▸ **gente menuda** kids *pl*❷ familiar [familia] folks *pl*

gentileza *sf* courtesy

gentío *sm* crowd

gentuza *sf* riffraff

genuflexión *sf* genuflection

genuino, na *adj* genuine☼: *Los adjetivos ingleses son invariables.*

geografía *sf*❶ geography▸ **geografía física** physical geography▸ **geografía política** political geography❷ figurado • **varios puntos de la geografía nacional** several parts of the country

geógrafo, fa *sm, f* geographer

geología *sf* geology

geólogo, ga *sm, f* geologist

geometría *sf* geometry▸ **geometría del espacio** solid geometry

geranio *sm* geranium

gerencia *sf* management

gerente *smf* manager

germen *sm* germ▸ **germen de trigo** wheat germ

gerundio *sm* present participle

gestar *vi* to gestate

gesticular *vi*❶ to gesticulate❷ [con la cara] to pull faces

gestión *sf*❶ [diligencia] • **tengo que hacer unas gestiones** I have a few things to do❷ [administración] management ▶ **gestión de cartera** ECONOMÍA portfolio management ▶ **gestión de datos** INFORMÁTICA data management ▶ **gestión de ficheros** INFORMÁTICA file management

gestionar *vt* ❶ [*tramitar*] to negotiate ❷ [*administrar*] to manage

gesto *sm* ❶ [*generalmente*] gesture • **un gesto simbólico** a symbolic gesture • **hacer gestos** to gesture • **hacer un gesto** to gesture • **me hizo un gesto para que me acercara** he gestured for me to come closer ❷ [*mueca*] face • **torcer el gesto** to pull a face

gestor, ra ◆ *adj* managing ☼: *Sólo se usa delante del sustantivo.*

◆ *sm, f* manager

giba *sf* [*de camello*] hump

gigabyte *sm* INFORMÁTICA gigabyte

gigahercio *sm* INFORMÁTICA gigahertz

gigante, ta *sm, f* giant

■ **gigante** *adj* gigantic ☼: *Los adjetivos ingleses son invariables.*

gigantesco, ca *adj* gigantic ☼: *Los adjetivos ingleses son invariables.*

gimnasia *sf* gymnastics ☼: *incontable* • **hacer gimnasia** to do gymnastics

gimnasio *sm* gymnasium

gimnasta *smf* gymnast

gimotear *vi* to whine

gin ■ **gin tonic** *sm* gin and tonic

ginebra *sf* gin

ginecología *sf* gynaecology

ginecólogo, ga *sm, f* gynaecologist

gira *sf* tour

girar ◆ *vi* ❶ [*dar vueltas, torcer*] to turn • **giró hacia la derecha** he turned to the right • **la tierra gira alrededor del sol** the earth revolves around the sun ❷ [*rápidamente*] to spin ❸ figurado [*centrarse*] • **girar en torno de** to be centred around

◆ *vt* ❶ [*hacer dar vueltas a*] to turn ❷ [*rápidamente*] to spin ❸ COMERCIO to draw ❹ [*dinero - por correo, telégrafo*] to transfer

girasol *sm* sunflower

giratorio, ria *adj* ❶ revolving ❷ [*silla*] swivel ☼: *Sólo se usa delante del sustantivo.*

giro *sm* ❶ [*generalmente*] turn • **un giro a la izquierda** a turn to the left • **la situación tuvo un giro inesperado** the situation took an unexpected turn ▶ **giro de 180 grados** literal & figurado U-turn ❷ [*postal, telegráfico*] money order ▶ **giro postal** postal order ❸ [*de letras, órdenes de pago*] draft ▶ **giro en descubierto** overdraft ❹ [*expresión*] turn of phrase

gis *sm* chalk

gitano, na *sm, f* gypsy

glacial *adj* ❶ [*periodo*] glacial ❷ [*viento, acogida*] icy ☼: *Los adjetivos ingleses son invariables.*

glaciar ◆ *adj* glacial ☼: *Los adjetivos ingleses son invariables.*

◆ *sm* glacier

glándula *sf* gland ▶ **glándula endocrina** endocrine gland ▶ **glándula sebácea** sebaceous gland

global *adj* global ☼: *Los adjetivos ingleses son invariables.*

globalización *sf* globalization

globo *sm* ❶ [*Tierra*] globe ▶ **globo terráqueo** globe ❷ [*aeróstato, juguete*] balloon • **trajimos globos de colores para los niños** we brought colored balloons for the kids • **mi sueño es viajar en globo** my dream is to travel in a hot-air balloon ❸ [*esfera*] sphere

glóbulo *sm* MEDICINA corpuscle ▶ **glóbulo blanco/ rojo** white/red corpuscle

gloria *sf* ❶ [*generalmente*] glory ❷ [*placer*] delight

glorificar *vt* to glorify

glorioso, sa *adj* [*importante*] glorious ☼: *Los adjetivos ingleses son invariables.*

glosa *sf* marginal note

glosario *sm* glossary

glotón, ona ◆ *adj* greedy ☼: *Los adjetivos ingleses son invariables.*

◆ *sm, f* glutton

glúcido *sm* carbohydrate

glucosa *sf* glucose

gluten *sm* gluten

gobernación *sf* government

expresión **Secretaría de Gobernación** Department of Homeland Security

gobernador, ra *sm, f* governor

gobernante ◆ *adj* ruling ☼: *Sólo se usa delante del sustantivo.*

◆ *smf* leader

gobernar *vt* ❶ [*generalmente*] to govern ❷ [*casa, negocio*] to run ❸ [*barco*] to steer ❹ [*avión*] to fly

gobierno *sm* ❶ [*generalmente*] government • **el gobierno tomó drásticas medidas económicas** the government took drastic economic measures ❷ [*administración, gestión*] management • **el presidente anunció su plan de gobierno** the president announced his management plan ❸ [*control*] control

goce *sm* pleasure

gol (pl goles) *sm* goal • **marcar** o **meter un gol** to score a goal ▶ **gol del empate** equalizer ▶ **gol de penalti** penalty goal ▶ **gol en propia meta** own goal

expresión **meter un gol a alguien** to put one over on somebody

goleador, ra *sm, f* goalscorer

golear *vt* to score a lot of goals against

golf *sm* golf

golfista *smf* golfer

golfo, fa *sm, f* ❶ [*gamberro*] lout ❷ [*vago*] layabout

■ **golfo** *sm* GEOGRAFÍA gulf ▶ **el Golfo Pérsico** the Persian Gulf

golondrina *sf* swallow

golosina *sf* ❶ [*dulce*] candy • **compré golosinas para los niños** I bought some candy for the children ❷ [*exquisitez*] delicacy

goloso, sa *adj* sweet-toothed ·☼· *Los adjetivos ingleses son invariables.*

golpe *sm* ❶ [*generalmente*] bump • **darse un golpe en la cabeza/la pierna** to bump your head/leg • **a golpes a)** by force **b)** *figurado* in fits and starts • **lo agarraron a golpes** they beat him up • **un golpe bajo** *figurado* DEPORTE a blow below the belt • **un golpe de suerte** a stroke of luck • **un golpe de tos** a coughing fit • **un golpe de viento** a gust of wind • **un golpe de vista** a glance • **al primer golpe de vista** at a glance ▶ **golpe de castigo** [*en rugby*] penalty (kick) ▶ **golpe de gracia** coup de grâce ▶ **golpe franco** free kick ❷ [*bofetada*] smack ❸ [*con puño*] punch ❹ [*en puerta* ETC] knock ❺ [*en tenis, golf*] shot ❻ [*entre coches*] bump ❼ [*disgusto*] blow • **las bajas calificaciones fueron un golpe para Pedro** his low grades were a blow to Pedro ❽ [*atraco*] heist ❾ POLÍTICA ▶ **golpe (de Estado)** coup (d'état)

expresiones **dar el golpe** to cause a sensation ▶ **errar el golpe** to miss the mark ▶ **no dar** o **pegar golpe** not to lift a finger

golpear *vt* & *vi* ❶ [*generalmente*] to hit • **se golpeó el codo contra la mesa** he hit his elbow on the table ❷ [*puerta*] to bang ❸ [*con puño*] to punch

golpista *smf* person involved in military coup

golpiza *sf* beating

goma *sf* ❶ [*sustancia viscosa, pegajosa*] glue • **usa la goma para pegar los dibujos** use the glue to stick down the pictures ▶ **goma arábiga** gum arabic ▶ **goma de mascar** chewing gum ▶ **goma de pegar** glue ❷ [*tira elástica*] rubber band ▶ **goma elástica** elastic ❸ [*caucho*] rubber • **la goma es un material impermeable** rubber is a waterproof material ❹ [*de borrar*] eraser • **necesito una goma para borrar los errores** I need an eraser to erase my mistakes ▶ **goma de borrar** eraser

gomina *sf* hair gel

gordinflón, ona *sm, f* fatty

gordo, da ◆ *adj* ❶ [*persona*] fat ❷ [*grueso*] thick ❸ [*grande*] big ❹ [*grave*] serious ·☼· *Los adjetivos ingleses son invariables.*

expresión **me cae gordo** I can't stand him

◆ *sm, f* ❶ [*persona obesa*] fat man, *femenino* fat woman ❷ [*querido*] dear • **¿cómo estás, gordo?** how are you, dear?

expresión **armar la gorda** to create a scene

■ **gordo** *sm* [*en lotería*] first prize

gordura *sf* fatness

gorila *sm* ❶ ZOOLOGÍA gorilla ❷ [*guardaespaldas*] bodyguard ❸ [*en discoteca* ETC] bouncer

gorra *sf* (peaked) cap • **siempre uso una gorra cuando estoy al sol** I always wear a cap in the sun ▶ **una gorra de baño** a shower cap

expresión **de gorra** for free • **vivir de gorra** to scrounge

gorrión *sm* sparrow

gorro *sm* ❶ [*generalmente*] cap ❷ [*de niño*] bonnet • **gorro de baño a)** [*para ducha*] shower cap **b)** [*para piscina*] swimming cap

gorrón, ona *sm, f* familiar sponger

gorronear *vt* & *vi* familiar to sponge

gota *sf* ❶ [*de agua, leche, sangre*] drop • **tienes que tomar cinco gotas de este medicamento** you have to take five drops of this medicine ❷ [*de sudor*] bead ❸ [*cantidad pequeña*] • **una gota de** a (tiny) drop of ❹ [*enfermedad*] gout • **la gota es una enfermedad muy dolorosa** gout is a very painful illness

expresiones **caer cuatro gotas** to spit (with rain) ▶ **ni gota** • **no se veía ni gota** you couldn't see a thing • **no tienes ni gota de sentido común** you haven't got an ounce of common sense ▶ **ser la gota que colma el vaso** to be the last straw ▶ **sudar la gota gorda** to sweat blood and tears

■ **gotas** *sfpl* [*medicamento*] drops

gotear ◆ *vi* ❶ [*líquido*] to drip • **esta llave gotea** this faucet drips ❷ [*techo, depósito* ETC] to leak ❸ *figurado* to trickle through

◆ *v impersonal* [*chispear*] to spit

gotera *sf* [*filtración*] leak

gótico, ca *adj* Gothic ·☼· *Los adjetivos ingleses son invariables.*

gozar *vi* to enjoy yourself • **gozar de algo** to enjoy something • **un cantante que goza de gran popularidad entre los jóvenes** a singer who enjoys enormous popularity among the young • **gozar con** to relish • **gozaba con la idea de encontrarse cerca de su amada** he was relishing the idea of being near his loved one

gozo *sm* joy

grabación *sf* recording • **hicieron una nueva grabación de la canción** they made a new recording of the song • **grabación digital** digital recording • **grabación en video** video recording

grabado *sm* ❶ [*generalmente*] engraving • **este grabado reproduce la imagen de una ciudad colonial** this engraving shows a colonial city ❷ [*en madera*] carving ❸ [*en papel - acción*] printing; [*- lámina*] print

grabar *vt* ❶ [*generalmente*] to engrave • **grabaron sus nombres en los anillos de casamiento** they engraved their names on the wedding rings ❷ [*en madera*] to carve ❸ [*en papel*] to print ❹ [*sonido, cinta*] to record • **acaba de grabar un disco nuevo** she just recorded a new album • **grabé en video la fiesta de cumpleaños** I taped the birthday party

gracia *sf* ❶ [*humor, comicidad*] humor • **hacer gracia a alguien** to amuse somebody • **sus chistes me hacen mucha gracia** his jokes really amuse me • **no me hizo gracia** I didn't find it funny • **¡maldita la gracia!** it's not a bit funny • **¡qué gracia!** how funny! • **tener gracia** to be funny ❷ [*arte, habilidad*] skill ❸ [*encanto*] grace ❹ [*chiste*] joke • **hacer una gracia a alguien** to play a prank on somebody • **no le rías las gracias** don't laugh when he says something silly

expresión **caer en gracia** to be liked ▶ **caerle en gracia a alguien** to take a liking to somebody

G

■ **gracias** *sfpl* thank you ; thanks • **muchas gracias** thank you ; thanks very much • **gracias — de nada** thanks — you're welcome • **gracias a Dios** thank God • **¡gracias por el regalo!** thanks for the present! • **dar las gracias a alguien (por)** to thank somebody (for) • **le dimos las gracias a Pedro por su ayuda** we thanked Pedro for his help

gracioso, sa ♦ *adj* [*divertido*] funny • **contó unos chistes muy graciosos** she told some very funny jokes • **¡qué gracioso!** how funny! • **es gracioso que...** it's funny how...:🔍 *Los adjetivos ingleses son invariables.*
♦ *sm, f* comedian • **hacerse el gracioso** to try to be funny

---

gracioso ≠ gracious

• La palabra inglesa **gracious** es un falso amigo que significa *cortés*.
• **Gracioso** se traduce al inglés por *funny*.

---

grada *sf* ❶ [*peldaño*] step ❷ TEATRO row
gradería *sf* = **graderío**
graderío *sm* ❶ TEATRO rows *pl* ❷ DEPORTE bleachers *pl*
grado *sm* ❶ [*generalmente*] degree • **este ángulo tiene 60 grados** this is a 60 degree angle • **grados bajo cero** degrees below zero ❷ [*fase*] stage ❸ [*índice, nivel*] level • **en grado sumo** greatly ❹ EDUCACIÓN grade • **Ana está en tercer grado** Ana is in third grade ❺ MILITAR rank
expresiones a tal grado so • **se enojó a tal grado, que acabó a los golpes** he got so mad they came to blows ▸ **hacer algo de buen/mal grado** to do something willingly/unwillingly
graduación *sf* ❶ [*acción*] grading ❷ [*de la vista*] eyetest ❸ EDUCACIÓN graduation ❹ [*de bebidas*] strength, ≃ proof ❺ MILITAR rank
graduado, da *sm, f* [*persona*] graduate
■ **graduado** *sm* [*título*] certificate
gradual *adj* gradual:🔍 *Los adjetivos ingleses son invariables.*
graduar *vt* ❶ [*medir*] to gauge ❷ [*regular*] to regulate ❸ [*vista*] to test ❹ [*escalonar*] to stagger ❺ EDUCACIÓN to confer a degree on ❻ MILITAR to commission
■ **graduarse** *v pronominal* • **graduarse (en)** to graduate (in) • **me gradué el mes pasado y ya estoy trabajando** I graduated last month and I'm already working • **se graduó en ciencias políticas** she graduated in political science
gráfico, ca *adj* graphic:🔍 *Los adjetivos ingleses son invariables.*
■ **gráfico** *sm* ❶ [*gráfica*] chart ▸ **gráfico de barras** bar chart ❷ [*dibujo*] diagram
■ **gráfica** *sf* chart
gral. (*abreviatura escrita de* general) gen.
gramática *sf* [*disciplina, libro*] grammar
gramatical *adj* grammatical:🔍 *Los adjetivos ingleses son invariables.*

gramático, ca *adj* grammatical:🔍 *Los adjetivos ingleses son invariables.*
gramo *sm* gram
gran → **grande**
granada *sf* ❶ [*fruta*] pomegranate ❷ [*proyectil*] grenade
granate ♦ *sm* garnet
♦ *adj invariable* garnet-colored:🔍 *Los adjetivos ingleses son invariables.*
Gran Bretaña *sf* Great Britain
grande ♦ *adj* 🔍 *Sólo se usa delante del sustantivo.* ❶ [*de tamaño*] big • **un hombre grande** a big man • **este traje me está grande** this suit is too big for me • **es un libro para gente grande** it's a book for adults ❷ [*de altura*] tall ❸ [*de intensidad, importancia*] great • **un gran hombre** a great man:🔍 *Los adjetivos ingleses son invariables.*
expresiones hacer algo a lo grande to do something in style ▸ **pasarlo en grande** *familiar* to have a great time ▸ **vivir a lo grande** to live in style
♦ *sm* [*noble*] grandee
grandeza *sf* ❶ [*de tamaño*] (great) size ❷ [*de sentimientos*] generosity
grandioso, sa *adj* grand:🔍 *Los adjetivos ingleses son invariables.*
grandullón, ona *sm, f* big boy, *femenino* big girl
granel ■ **a granel** *locución adverbial* [*sin envase - generalmente*] loose; [*- en gran cantidad*] in bulk
granero *sm* granary
granito *sm* granite
granizada *sf* METEOROLOGÍA hailstorm
granizado *sm* iced drink
granizar *v impersonal* to hail • **granizó de madrugada** it was hailing at dawn
granizo *sm* hail • **el granizo estropeó la cosecha** the hail ruined the crop • **caer granizo** to hail
granja *sf* farm ▸ **granja avícola** poultry farm
granjero, ra *sm, f* farmer
grano *sm* ❶ [*semilla - de cereales*] grain • **se alimenta a base de granos** his diet is based on grains ▸ **grano de café** coffee bean ▸ **grano de pimienta** peppercorn ❷ [*partícula*] grain • **se me metió un grano de arena en el ojo** I got a grain of sand in my eye ❸ [*en la piel*] pimple • **tiene un grano en la nariz** she has a pimple on her nose
expresiones apartar el grano de la paja to separate the wheat from the chaff ▸ **ir al grano** to get to the point ▸ **poner uno su grano de arena** to do your bit
granuja *smf* ❶ [*pillo*] rogue ❷ [*canalla*] trickster
grapa *sf* ❶ [*para papeles* ETC] staple ❷ [*para heridas*] stitch
grasa *sf* ❶ [*en comestibles*] fat • **con alto contenido de grasa** high in fat ▸ **grasa animal** animal fat ▸ **grasa saturada** saturated fat ❷ [*de cerdo*] lard ❸ [*lubricante*] grease • **las manos del mecánico estaban cubiertas de grasa** the mechanic's hands were covered in grease ❹ [*suciedad*] grease

grasiento, ta *adj* greasy:ϙ *Los adjetivos ingleses son invariables.*

graso, sa *adj* ❶ [*generalmente*] greasy ❷ [*con alto contenido en grasas*] fatty:ϙ *Los adjetivos ingleses son invariables.*

gratificación *sf* ❶ [*moral*] reward ❷ [*monetaria*] bonus

gratificante *adj* rewarding:ϙ *Los adjetivos ingleses son invariables.*

gratificar *vt* ❶ [*complacer*] to reward ❷ [*retribuir*] to give a bonus to ❸ [*dar propina a*] to tip

gratis ◆ *adj* free • **tengo dos entradas gratis para el cine** I have two free tickets to the movies
◆ *adv* free • **los menores entran gratis al concierto** children can attend the concert for free

gratitud *sf* gratitude

grato, ta *adj* pleasant • **nos es grato comunicarle que...** we are pleased to inform you that...:ϙ *Los adjetivos ingleses son invariables.*

gratuito, ta *adj* ❶ [*sin dinero*] free • **la entrada es gratuita los lunes** admission is free on Mondays ❷ [*arbitrario*] gratuitous • **su comentario fue totalmente gratuito** her comment was completely gratuitous ❸ [*infundado*] unfair:ϙ *Los adjetivos ingleses son invariables.*

grava *sf* gravel

gravar *vt* [*con impuestos*] to tax

grave *adj* ❶ [*generalmente*] serious • **éste es un problema muy grave** this is a very serious problem • **cometió un delito grave** he committed a serious crime ❷ [*paciente*] seriously ill • **tuvo un accidente y está grave** he was in an accident and is seriously ill ❸ [*sonido, voz*] deep • **el abuelo tiene una voz muy grave** grandfather has a very deep voice:ϙ *Los adjetivos ingleses son invariables.*

gravedad *sf* ❶ [*cualidad*] seriousness • **no nos habíamos imaginado la gravedad del asunto** we hadn't realized the seriousness of the situation ❷ FÍSICA gravity • **Newton definió las leyes de la gravedad** Newton defined the laws of gravity

Grecia *nombre propio* Greece

gremio *sm* ❶ [*sindicato*] (trade) union ❷ [*profesión*] trade • **ser del gremio** to be in the trade ❸ HISTORIA guild

griego, ga *adj & sm, f* Greek:ϙ *Los adjetivos ingleses son invariables.*
■ **griego** *sm* [*lengua*] Greek

grieta *sf* ❶ [*en pared, piel*] crack ❷ [*entre montañas*] crevice ❸ [*que deja pasar luz*] chink

grillete *sm* shackle

grillo *sm* cricket

grima *sf* [*dentera*] • **dar grima** to set your teeth on edge

gringo, ga *adj & sm, f* despectivo gringo:ϙ *Los adjetivos ingleses son invariables.*

gripa *sf* flu • **no fui a la escuela por que tenía gripa** I didn't go to school because I had the flu

gris ◆ *adj* ❶ [*color*] grey ❷ [*triste*] gloomy:ϙ *Los adjetivos ingleses son invariables.*
◆ *sm* grey

gritar ◆ *vi* ❶ [*hablar alto*] to shout ❷ [*chillar*] to scream • **gritar de alegría** to scream with joy • **gritar de dolor** to scream with pain
◆ *vt* • **gritar (algo) a alguien** to shout (something) at somebody • **un cliente le gritó al empleado de la tienda** a customer shouted at one of the salesclerks

griterío *sm* shouting

grito *sm* ❶ [*generalmente*] shout ❷ [*de dolor, miedo*] scream ❸ [*de sorpresa, de animal*] cry • **dar un grito** to scream (out) ❹ • **el grito** *para explicar lo que es puedes decir:* it's the custom of commemorating Mexico's independence on September 15
▶ **expresiones a grito limpio** at the top of your voice ▶ **pedir algo a gritos** to be crying out for something ▶ **poner el grito en el cielo** to hit the roof ▶ **ser el último grito** to be the latest fashion

grogui *adj* groggy:ϙ *Los adjetivos ingleses son invariables.*

grosella *sf* redcurrant ▶ **grosella negra** blackcurrant

grosería *sf* ❶ [*cualidad*] rudeness ❷ [*acción*] rude thing ❸ [*palabrota*] swear word

grosero, ra *adj* ❶ [*maleducado*] rude ❷ [*tosco*] coarse:ϙ *Los adjetivos ingleses son invariables.*

grosor *sm* thickness

grotesco, ca *adj* grotesque:ϙ *Los adjetivos ingleses son invariables.*

grúa *sf* ❶ CONSTRUCCIÓN crane ❷ AUTOMÓVILES breakdown truck ❸ [*de la policía*] tow truck

grueso, sa *adj* ❶ [*espeso*] thick ❷ [*corpulento*] thickset ❸ [*grande*] large ❹ [*mar*] stormy:ϙ *Los adjetivos ingleses son invariables.*
■ **grueso** *sm* thickness

grumo *sm* ❶ [*generalmente*] lump ❷ [*de sangre*] clot

gruñido *sm* ❶ [*generalmente*] growl ❷ [*de cerdo*] grunt • **dar gruñidos** to grunt ❸ [*de persona*] grumble

gruñir *vi* ❶ [*generalmente*] to growl ❷ [*cerdo*] to grunt ❸ [*persona*] to grumble

gruñón, ona *adj* familiar grumpy:ϙ *Los adjetivos ingleses son invariables.*

grupo *sm* ❶ [*generalmente*] group • **formamos un grupo de seis personas** we form a group of six people • **en grupo** in a group ▶ **grupo de discusión** INFORMÁTICA forum ▶ **grupo electrógeno** generator ▶ **grupo de noticias** INFORMÁTICA newsgroup ▶ **grupo sanguíneo** blood group ❷ [*de árboles*] cluster ❸ TECNOLOGÍA unit

gruta *sf* grotto

guaca *sf* ❶ [*sepultura*] Indian tomb ❷ [*tesoro*] hidden treasure ❸ [*hucha*] money box

guacal *sm* ❶ [*caja*] slatted crate ❷ [*calabaza*] gourd

guacamole *sm* guacamole

G

guachinango *sm* [*pez*] red snapper

guajiro, ra ✦ *adj* rustic
✦ *sm, f* peasant

guajolote *sm* ❶ [*pavo*] turkey • **criamos guajolotes en este terreno** we raise turkeys on this land ❷ [*tonto*] fool • **estos hombres parecen unos guajolotes** these men look like fools

guano *sm* [*abono*] guano

guantazo *sm familiar* slap

guante *sm* glove

expresión echar el guante a algo to get hold of something ▸ echar el guante a alguien to nab somebody

guantera *sf* glove compartment

guapo, pa *adj* ❶ [*generalmente*] good-looking ❷ [*hombre*] handsome ❸ [*mujer*] pretty ۞ *Los adjetivos ingleses son invariables.*

guaracha *sf* [*bulla*] noise

guarache *sm* sandal

guarda ✦ *smf* [*vigilante*] guard • **los guardas vigilaban la costa** the guards were watching the coast ▸ **guarda jurado** security guard
✦ *sf* ❶ [*tutela*] guardianship ❷ [*de libros*] flyleaf

guardabosque *smf* forest ranger

guardacostas *sm invariable* [*barco*] coastguard boat

guardaespaldas *smf invariable* bodyguard

guardameta *smf* goalkeeper

guardar *vt* ❶ [*generalmente*] to keep • **no guardé el documento necesario** I didn't keep the necessary document ❷ [*en su sitio*] to put away • **guardé la ropa en el armario** I put the clothes away in the closet ❸ [*vigilar*] to keep watch over ❹ [*proteger*] to guard ❺ [*reservar, ahorrar*] • **guardar algo (a o para alguien)** to save something (for somebody) • **guárdame un poco de cena** save me a little supper ❻ [*cumplir - ley*] to observe; [*- secreto, promesa*] to keep • **no sabe guardar un secreto** he can't keep a secret

guardarropa *sm* ❶ [*generalmente*] wardrobe ❷ [*de cine, discoteca* ETC] cloakroom

guardería *sf* ❶ nursery ❷ [*en el lugar de trabajo*] crèche

guardia ✦ *sf* ❶ [*generalmente*] guard ❷ [*vigilancia*] guard • **montar (la) guardia** to mount guard ▸ **guardia municipal** urban police ❸ [*turno*] duty • **estar de guardia** to be on duty • **hicimos un turno de guardia nocturna** we took a turn on the night shift
✦ *sm, f* [*policía*] policeman, *femenino* policewoman ▸ **guardia de tráfico** traffic warden

guardián, ana *sm, f* ❶ [*de persona*] guardian ❷ [*de cosa*] watchman

guarecer *vt* • **guarecer (de)** to protect (from)

guarida *sf* ❶ lair • **los lobos se refugiaron en una guarida** the wolves took shelter in a lair ❷ *figurado* hideout • **la policía descubrió la guarida de los ladrones** the police discovered the thieves' hideout

guarnición *sf* ❶ COCINA garnish ❷ MILITAR garrison

guarura *sm familiar* bodyguard

Guatemala *nombre propio* ❶ [*país*] Guatemala ❷ [*ciudad*] Guatemala City

guatemalteco, ca, guatemaltés, esa *adj* & *sm, f* Guatemalan ۞ *Los adjetivos ingleses son invariables.*
En inglés, los adjetivos que se refieren a un país o una región se escriben con mayúscula.

guau *sm* woof

guepardo *sm* cheetah

güero, ra *adj familiar* blond, *femenino* blonde ۞ *Los adjetivos ingleses son invariables.*

guerra *sf* ❶ [*conflicto*] war • **declarar la guerra** to declare war • **en guerra** at war • **hacer la guerra** to wage war ▸ **guerra espacial** o **de las galaxias** star wars ▸ **guerra fría** cold war ▸ **guerra a muerte** fight to the death ❷ [*refiriéndose al tipo de conflicto*] warfare ▸ **guerra bacteriológica/química** germ/chemical warfare ▸ **guerra de guerrillas** guerrilla warfare ▸ **guerra psicológica** psychological warfare ❸ [*de intereses, ideas*] conflict

expresión dar guerra to be a pain

guerrear *vi* to (wage) war

guerrero, ra ✦ *adj* warlike ۞ *Los adjetivos ingleses son invariables.*
✦ *sm, f* warrior

guerrilla *sf* [*grupo*] guerrilla group

guerrillero, ra *sm, f* guerrilla

gueto *sm* ghetto

guía ✦ *smf* [*persona*] guide ▸ **guía turístico** tourist guide
✦ *sf* ❶ [*indicación*] guidance ❷ [*libro*] guide (book) ▸ **guía de carreteras** road atlas ▸ **guía de ferrocarriles** train timetable ▸ **guía telefónica** telephone book

guiar *vt* ❶ [*indicar dirección a*] to guide ❷ [*aconsejar*] to direct ❸ AUTOMÓVILES to drive ❹ NÁUTICA to steer

guijarro *sm* pebble

guillotina *sf* guillotine

guinche, güinche *sm* winch

guinda *sf* morello cherry

guindar *vt* to hang high

guindilla *sf* chilli (pepper)

guiño *sm* wink • **Luis le hizo un guiño a María** Luis gave a wink to María

guiñol *sm* puppet theater

guion *sm* ❶ CINE & TELEVISIÓN script • **el guión de la película es excelente** the movie's script is excellent ❷ GRAMÁTICA [*signo*] hyphen

guionista *smf* scriptwriter

guirnalda *sf* garland

güiro *sm* gourd

guisa *sf* way • **a guisa de** by way of

guisado *sm* stew

guisante *sm* pea

guisar *vt* & *vi* to cook

guiso *sm* dish

guitarra *sf* guitar ▸ **guitarra acústica** acoustic guitar

guitarrista *smf* guitarist

gula *sf* gluttony

gusanillo *sm familiar*

expresiones **el gusanillo de la conciencia** conscience ▸ **entrarle a uno el gusanillo de los videojuegos** to be bitten by the videogame bug▸ **matar el gusanillo a)** [*bebiendo*] to have a drink on an empty stomach **b)** [*comiendo*] to have a snack between meals▸ **sentir un gusanillo en el estómago** to have butterflies (in your stomach)

gusano *sm* worm • **hay un gusano en la manzana** there's a worm in the apple▸ **un gusano de seda** a silkworm

---

gustar

◆ *vi*

:◌: *gustar corresponde al verbo "to like" pero en inglés el sujeto de la oración española se convierte en objeto*

❶ [*refiriéndose a una persona*] to like
• **me gusta esa muchacha** I like that girl
• **a Pedro le gusta María** Pedro likes María

❷ [*refiriéndose a una cosa*] to love
• **me gusta el deporte** I love sports
• **a mi hermano le gustan mucho las motos** my brother loves motorbikes
• **¿te gusta ir al cine?** do you like going to the movies?
• **no me gustó que me gritaran** I didn't like them shouting at me

■ **gustar de**

◆ *v + preposición*

to like
• **gusto de viajar** I like traveling

---

gustazo *sm familiar* great pleasure • **darse el gustazo de algo/hacer algo** to allow yourself the pleasure of something/doing something

gusto *sm* ❶ [*generalmente*] taste • **el gusto es uno de los sentidos más importantes** taste is one of the most important senses • **esta pareja tiene gustos incompatibles** this couple has incompatible tastes ❷ [*sabor*] taste • **esta leche tiene gusto a podrido** this milk has a spoiled taste • **de buen/mal gusto** in good/bad taste • **tener buen gusto** to have good taste • **tener mal gusto** to have bad taste ❸ [*placer*] pleasure• **con mucho gusto** with pleasure • **da gusto estar aquí** it's a real pleasure to be here • **dar gusto a alguien** to please somebody • **mucho gusto** pleased to meet you • **le presento a mi jefe — mucho gusto en conocerlo** allow me to introduce you to my boss — it's a pleasure to meet you • **tener el gusto de** to have the pleasure of • **tengo el gusto de invitarle** I have the pleasure of inviting you • **tomar gusto a algo** to take a liking to something ❹ [*capricho*] whim

---

hablar de sus gustos

• **I like fish.** Me gusta el pescado.
• **I really like trout.** Me gusta mucho la trucha.
• **I love smoked salmon.** Me encanta el salmón ahumado.
• **I hate raw meat.** Me choca la carne cruda.
• **It's disgusting.** Me da asco.
• **I like swimming.** Me gusta nadar.
• **I prefer dancing.** Prefiero bailar.
• **What I like best is listening to music.** Lo que prefiero más que nada es escuchar música.
• **I hate getting up early.** ¡Odio levantarme temprano!

---

gustoso, sa *adj* ❶ [*sabroso*] tasty ❷ [*con placer*] • **hacer algo gustoso** to do something gladly :◌: *Los adjetivos ingleses son invariables.*

gutural *adj* guttural :◌: *Los adjetivos ingleses son invariables.*

h, H *sf* [*letra*] h ; H

haba *sf* broad bean

haber

◆ *v auxiliar*

> 💡 *La traducción general de "haber" es "to have" pero también se usa para formar otros tiempos verbales.*

❶ [*con un verbo transitivo, para formar los tiempos compuestos*] to have
- **no lo he hecho** I haven't done it
- **no se lo había dicho** I hadn't told told him
- **no han sido identificados** they haven't been identified
- **no he querido verla** I haven't wanted to see her

❷ [*con un verbo de movimiento o estado, para formar los tiempos compuestos*] to have
- **no ha salido** he hasn't been out
- **no lo hemos hecho** we haven't done it

❸ [*con un verbo pronominal, para formar los tiempos compuestos*] to have
- **niños, ¿no se han lavado las manos?** children, haven't you washed your hands?

❹ [*estar, existir*]
- **hay** [*en singular*] there is
- **hay** [*en plural*] there are
- **hay una sola persona en el cine** there is only one person in the movie theater
- **hay mucha gente en la calle** there are a lot of people in the street
- **en la manifestación había dos mil personas** there were two thousand people at the demonstration
- **hubo muchos problemas** there were lots of problems
- **¿quién habrá en la fiesta?** who will be at the party?

❺ [*expresar un reproche*]
- **haber venido a la reunión** you should have come to the meeting

> **expresiones ¡hay que ver qué malo es!** you wouldn't believe how bad he is!❱ **no hay de qué**

don't mention it❱ **¿qué hubo?** *familiar* how are things?

◆ *vt*
to occur
- **los accidentes habidos este verano** the accidents that have occurred this summer

■ **haber de**
◆ *v + preposición*

❶ [*expresa una obligación*] must
- **has de trabajar más** you must work more

❷ [*expresa una suposición*] must
- **ha de ser su hermano** it must be his brother
- **han de ser las tres** it must be three o'clock

■ **haber que**
◆ *v + conjunción*

[*expresa una obligación*] must
- **habrá que encontrar una solución** we must find a solution

■ **haberse**
◆ *v pronominal*
to have it out
- **para esto tendrás que habértelas con el director** for that, you'll have to have it out with the director

habichuela *sf* bean

hábil *adj* **❶** [*diestro*] skilful **❷** [*inteligente*] clever **❸** [*utilizable - lugar*] suitable ; fit **❹** DERECHO **•** **días hábiles** working days 💡 *Los adjetivos ingleses son invariables.*

habilidad *sf* **❶** [*destreza*] skill **❷** [*inteligencia*] cleverness **•** **tener habilidad para algo** to be good at something

habilitar *vt* **❶** [*acondicionar*] to fit out **❷** [*autorizar*] to authorize

habitación *sf* **❶** [*generalmente*] room **❷** [*dormitorio*] bedroom❱ **habitación doble a)** [*con cama de matrimonio*] double room **b)** [*con dos camas*] twin room ❱ **habitación individual** o **simple** single room **•** **habitación para invitados** guest room

habitante *sm* **❶** [*de ciudad, país*] inhabitant **❷** [*de barrio*] resident

habitar ◆ *vi* to live

♦ *vt* to live in

hábitat (pl hábitats) *sm* habitat

hábito *sm* habit • **tener el hábito de hacer algo** to be in the habit of doing something

habitual *adj* ❶ [*acción*] habitual ❷ [*cliente, lector*] regular ❄️ *Los adjetivos ingleses son invariables.*

habituar *vt* • **habituar a alguien a** to accustom somebody to

habla *sf* ❶ [*idioma*] language ❷ [*dialecto*] dialect • **de habla española** Spanish-speaking ❸ [*facultad*] speech • **dejar a alguien sin habla** to leave somebody speechless • **quedarse sin habla** to be left speechless ❹ LINGÜÍSTICA discourse ❺ [*al teléfono*] • **estar al habla con alguien** to be on the line to somebody

hablado, da *adj* spoken • **bien hablado** well-spoken • **mal hablado** foul-mouthed • **cine hablado** talking pictures

■ **habladas** *sfpl* gossip ❄️ *incontable*

hablador, ra *adj* talkative ❄️ *Los adjetivos ingleses son invariables.*

hablante ♦ *adj* speaking ❄️ *Los adjetivos ingleses son invariables.*
♦ *smf* speaker

hablar ♦ *vi* • **hablar (con)** to talk (to); to speak (to) • **el niño todavía no habla** the boy doesn't talk yet • **hablar de** to talk about • **hablamos de todo y de nada** we talked about everything and nothing • **hablar bien/mal de** to speak well/badly of • **hablar en español/inglés** to speak Spanish/English
expresiones **¡ni hablar!** no way! ▶ **¡mira quién fue a hablar!** look who's talking! ▶ **hablar por los codos** to talk too much
♦ *vt* ❶ [*idioma*] to speak • **mis amigos hablan ruso** my friends speak Russian ❷ [*asunto*] • **hablar algo (con)** to discuss something (with)

hacendado, da *sm, f* landowner

---

hacer
♦ *vt*

❄️ *"hacer" suele traducirse por "to make" pero con algunas actividades se usa "to do". También tiene un uso impersonal con el tiempo donde en inglés se usa "to be". Mira los ejemplos en la entrada.*

❶ [*fabricar, crear*] to make
• **hacer un vestido/un pastel** to make a dress/cake
• **hacer una fotocopia** to make a photocopy
❷ [*realizar un gesto, una acción*] to make
• **le hice señas** I waved at him
• **hacer planes** to make plans
❸ [*cama*] to make
• **no he hecho la cama** I haven't made the bed
❹ [*someter algo a una acción particular*]
• **voy a hacer teñir este traje** I'm going to have this outfit dyed
❺ [*llevar a cabo una actividad*] to do
• **hacer un crucigrama** to do a crossword
• **debes hacer deporte** you must do some sport

❻ [*producir, ser el origen de*] to make
• **el árbol hace sombra** the tree provides shade
• **no hagas ruido** don't make a noise
❼ [*actuar como*]
• **deja de hacer el tonto** stop acting the fool
• **hace el papel de detective** he plays the role of a detective
❽ [*provocar un estado*]
• **me hizo daño** it hurt me
• **me hizo reír** it made me laugh
• **te hará feliz** it will make you happy
❾ [*transformar a alguien en algo*] to make
• **hizo de ella una buena cantante** he made her into a good singer
❿ [*dar cierta impresión*]
• **este espejo te hace gordo** this mirror makes you look fat
• **este peinado la hace más joven** this hairstyle makes her look younger
⓫ [*imaginar, pensar*]
• **yo te hacía en París** I thought you were in Paris
♦ *vi*
[*intentar*] to have a go
• **déjame hacer a mí** let me have a go
♦ *v impersonal*
❶ [*para indicar la temperatura, el tiempo*] to be
• **hace frío** it's cold
• **hace calor** it's hot
• **hace buen tiempo** it's a fine day
❷ [*para indicar un punto de partida en el tiempo*]
• **hace una semana** a week ago
• **hace mucho** a long time ago
• **mañana hará un mes que estoy aquí** tomorrow I'll have been here for a month
■ **hacer como si** o **como que**
♦ *v + conjunción*
• **hace como si no nos viera** he acts as if we weren't here
• **hace como que no entiende** he acts as if he doesn't understand
■ **hacer de**
♦ *v + preposición*
❶ [*servir de*]
• **un sofá que también hace de cama** a sofa that also serves as a bed
❷ [*representar el papel de*]
• **en su última película hace de vampiro** in his latest film he appears as a vampire
■ **hacerse a**
♦ *v pronominal + preposición*
[*acostumbrarse a*] to get used to
• **no me hago a esta casa** I can't get used to this house
■ **hacerse con**
♦ *v pronominal + preposición*
❶ [*apropiarse*]
• **se hicieron con todo el dinero** they got hold of all the money

• los rebeldes se han hecho con el poder the rebels have taken power

❷ [*conseguir*]

• habrá que hacerse con víveres para la expedición we will need to get hold of some food for the expedition

hacha *sf* axe

expresión **enterrar el hacha de guerra** to bury the hatchet

hachís *sm* hashish

hacia *preposición* ❶ [*dirección, tendencia, sentimiento*] towards **• caminó hacia la salida** he walked towards the exit **• hacia aquí/allí** this/that way **• hacia abajo** downwards **• hacia arriba** upwards **• hacia adelante** forwards **• hacia atrás** backwards ❷ [*tiempo*] around **• hacia finales de diciembre terminan las clases** they finish classes around the end of December **• hacia las diez** around ten o'clock

hacienda *sf* ❶ [*finca*] country estate ❷ [*bienes*] property ▶ **hacienda pública** public purse

■ **Hacienda** *sf* ▶ **Ministerio de Hacienda** the Internal Revenue Service

hada *sf* fairy ▶ **hada madrina** fairy godmother

Haití *nombre propio* Haiti

halagar *vt* to flatter **• me halagan tus comentarios** your comments flatter me

halago *sm* flattery

halagüeño, ña *adj* promising ☀ *Los adjetivos ingleses son invariables.*

halcón *sm* ❶ ZOOLOGÍA hawk ❷ *familiar* [*matón*] government-paid killer

hall (pl halls) *sm* foyer

hallar *vt* ❶ [*generalmente*] to find **• hallaron un tesoro escondido** they found a hidden treasure ❷ [*averiguar*] to find out

hallazgo *sm* ❶ [*descubrimiento*] discovery ❷ [*objeto*] find

halterofilia *sf* weightlifting

hamaca *sf* hammock

hambre *sf* ❶ [*apetito*] hunger **• tener hambre** to be hungry ❷ [*inanición*] starvation **• matar de hambre a alguien** to starve somebody to death **• morirse de hambre** to be starving **• pasar hambre** to starve ❸ [*epidemia*] famine ❹ *figurado* [*deseo*] **• hambre de** hunger o thirst for

expresión **matar el hambre** to satisfy your hunger

hambriento, ta *adj* starving ☀ *Los adjetivos ingleses son invariables.*

hamburguesa *sf* hamburger

hardware *sm* INFORMÁTICA hardware

harina *sf* flour

expresión **estar metido en harina** to be right in the middle of something

harinoso, sa *adj* ❶ floury ❷ [*manzana*] mealy ☀ *Los adjetivos ingleses son invariables.*

hartar *vt* ❶ [*atiborrar*] to stuff (full) ❷ [*fastidiar*] **• hartar a alguien** to annoy somebody

■ **hartarse** *v pronominal* ❶ [*atiborrarse*] to stuff yourself **• se hartaron de dulces** they stuffed themselves with candy ❷ [*cansarse*] **• hartarse (de)** to get fed up (with) **• me harté de esperar y me fui** I got fed up of waiting and left ❸ [*no parar*] **• hartarse de algo** to have your fill of something

harto, ta *adj* ❶ [*de comida*] full ❷ [*cansado*] **• harto (de)** tired (of); fed up (with) **• estoy harta del estudio** I'm fed up with studying ❸ [*mucho*] a lot of **• tiene harto dinero** she has a lot of money **• de este aeropuerto salen hartos aviones** a lot of planes fly from this airport **• tiene harta paciencia** she has a lot of patience ☀ *Los adjetivos ingleses son invariables.*

■ **harto** *adv* ❶ somewhat ❷ *familiar* [*mucho*] a lot ❸ [*muy*] very

hasta ◆ *preposición* ❶ [*en el espacio*] up to **• llene el tanque hasta la mitad** fill the tank up to the middle **• fueron conmigo hasta la playa** they went with me as fas as the beach **• desde aquí hasta allí** from here to there **• ¿hasta dónde va este tren?** where does this train go? ❷ [*en el tiempo*] until **• lo cuidó hasta que se curó** she took care of him until he got better **• hasta ahora** (up) until now; so far **• hasta el final** right up until the end **• hasta luego** o **pronto** o **la vista** see you (later) ❸ [*con cantidades*] up to

◆ *adv* ❶ [*incluso*] even **• hasta un ignorante puede aprender esto** even an ignorant person can learn this ❷ [*no antes de*] **• no pintaremos la casa hasta fin de mes** we won't start painting the house until the end of the month

hastiar *vt* ❶ [*aburrir*] to bore ❷ [*asquear*] to sicken

haz *sm* ❶ [*de leña*] bundle ❷ [*de cereales*] sheaf ❸ [*de luz*] beam → **hacer**

hazaña *sf* feat

hazmerreír *sm* laughing stock

hebilla *sf* buckle

hechicero, ra *sm, f* wizard, *femenino* witch

hechizar *vt* ❶ to cast a spell on ❷ *figurado* to bewitch

hechizo *sm* ❶ [*maleficio*] spell ❷ *figurado* [*encanto*] magic

hecho, cha ◆ *participio pasado* → **hacer**

◆ *adj* ❶ [*acabado, realizado*] done **• bien/mal hecho** well/badly done ❷ [*manufacturado*] made **• hecho a mano** handmade **• hecho a máquina** machine-made ❸ [*convertido en*] **• estás hecho un artista** you've become quite an artist ❹ [*carne*] done ☀ *Los adjetivos ingleses son invariables.*

expresión **hecho y derecho • es un hombre hecho y derecho** he's a grown man **• es una mujer hecha y derecha** she's a grown woman

■ **hecho** *sm* ❶ [*obra*] action **• prefiero hechos y no palabras** I prefer actions to words ❷ [*suceso*] event **• el periodista destacó los hechos más importantes de la semana** the reporter highlighted the most important events of the week ❸ [*realidad, dato*] fact

H

hectárea *sf* hectare

hediondo, da *adj* [*pestilente*] stinking. Los adjetivos ingleses son invariables.

hedor *sm* stink

hegemonía *sf* ❶ [*generalmente*] dominance ❷ POLÍTICA hegemony

helada *sf* frost • **anoche cayó una helada** there was a frost last night

heladería *sf* ❶ [*tienda*] ice-cream parlor ❷ [*puesto*] ice-cream stand

helado, da *adj* ❶ [*hecho hielo - agua*] frozen; [*- lago*] frozen over ❷ [*muy frío - manos, agua*] freezing • **esta habitación está helada** this room is freezing. Los adjetivos ingleses son invariables.

■ **helado** *sm* ice-cream

helar ◆ *vt* [*líquido*] to freeze

◆ *v impersonal* • **ayer heló** there was a frost last night

■ **helarse** *v pronominal* ❶ to freeze • **este lago se hiela en invierno** this lake freezes in winter ❷ [*plantas*] to be frostbitten

hélice *sf* ❶ TECNOLOGÍA propeller ❷ [*espiral*] spiral

helicóptero *sm* helicopter

helio *sm* helium

hematoma *sm* MEDICINA hematoma

hembra *sf* ❶ BIOLOGÍA female ❷ [*mujer*] woman ❸ [*niña*] girl ❹ [*del enchufe*] socket

hemisferio *sm* hemisphere

hemorragia *sf* haemorrhage ▶ **hemorragia nasal** nosebleed

hemorroides *sfpl* haemorrhoids

hendidura *sf* ❶ [*en carne, piel*] cut ❷ [*en piedra, madera*] crack

heno *sm* hay

hepatitis *sf invariable* hepatitis. incontable

herbicida *sm* weedkiller

hercio, hertz *sm* hertz

heredar *vt* • **heredar (de)** to inherit (from) • **heredamos una gran fortuna** we inherited a large fortune • **Juan heredó el carácter del padre** Juan inherited his father's character

heredero, ra *sm, f* heir, *femenino* heiress ▶ **heredero forzoso** heir apparent ▶ **heredero universal** residuary legatee

hereditario, ria *adj* hereditary. Los adjetivos ingleses son invariables.

hereje *smf* heretic

herejía *sf* heresy

herencia *sf* ❶ [*de bienes*] inheritance ❷ [*de características*] legacy ❸ BIOLOGÍA heredity

herida *sf* ❶ [*lesión*] injury ❷ [*en lucha, atentado*] wound • **herida superficial** flesh wound • **heridas múltiples** multiple injuries

herido, da ◆ *adj* ❶ [*generalmente*] injured • **resultó herido de gravedad** he turned out to be seriously injured ❷ [*en lucha, atentado*] wounded • **fue herido en la batalla** he was wounded in the battle ❸ [*sentimentalmente*] hurt. Los adjetivos ingleses son invariables.

◆ *sm, f* ❶ [*generalmente*] injured person ❷ [*en lucha, atentado*] wounded person • **no hubo heridos** there were no casualties • **los heridos** the wounded

herir *vt* ❶ [*físicamente*] to injure • **lo hirieron gravemente en la pelea** they injured him seriously in the fight ❷ [*en lucha, atentado*] to wound • **la explosión hirió a varias personas** the explosion wounded several people ❸ [*vista*] to hurt • **con su negativa lo hirió en lo más profundo** with her refusal, she hurt him deeply ❹ [*oído*] to pierce ❺ [*sentimentalmente*] to hurt

hermanastro, tra *sm, f* stepbrother, *femenino* stepsister

hermandad *sf* ❶ [*asociación*] association ❷ RELIGIÓN [*de hombres*] brotherhood; [*de mujeres*] sisterhood

hermano, na *sm, f* brother, *femenino* sister ▶ **hermano gemelo** twin brother ▶ **hermano mayor** older brother ; big brother *familiar* ▶ **hermano menor** younger brother ; little brother *familiar* ▶ **hermano de sangre** blood brother

hermético, ca *adj* ❶ [*al aire*] airtight ❷ [*al agua*] watertight ❸ *figurado* [*persona*] inscrutable. Los adjetivos ingleses son invariables.

hermoso, sa *adj* ❶ [*generalmente*] beautiful • **¡qué hermoso día!** what a beautiful day! ❷ [*hombre*] handsome ❸ [*excelente*] wonderful. Los adjetivos ingleses son invariables.

hermosura *sf* ❶ [*generalmente*] beauty ❷ [*de hombre*] good looks *pl*

hernia *sf* hernia ▶ **hernia discal** slipped disc

héroe *sm* hero, *plural* heroes

heroico, ca *adj* heroic. Los adjetivos ingleses son invariables.

heroína *sf* ❶ [*mujer*] heroine ❷ [*droga*] heroin

heroísmo *sm* heroism

herpes *sm invariable* herpes. incontable

herradura *sf* horseshoe

herramienta *sf* tool

herrumbre *sf* [*óxido*] rust

hertz = hercio

hervidero *sm* ❶ [*de pasiones, intrigas*] hotbed ❷ [*de gente - muchedumbre*] swarm; [*- sitio*] place throbbing with people

hervir ◆ *vt* to boil

◆ *vi* ❶ [*líquido*] to boil ❷ *figurado* [*lugar*] • **hervir de** to swarm with

hervor *sm* boiling • **dar un hervor a algo** to blanch something

heterodoxo, xa *adj* unorthodox. Los adjetivos ingleses son invariables.

heterogéneo, a *adj* heterogeneous. Los adjetivos ingleses son invariables.

heterosexual *adj* & *smf* heterosexual. Los adjetivos ingleses son invariables.

hexágono *sm* hexagon

hez *sf* literal & figurado dregs *pl*

hibernar *vi* to hibernate

híbrido, da *adj* literal & figurado hybrid. ☼ *Los adjetivos ingleses son invariables.*

■ **híbrido** *sm* [animal, planta] hybrid

hidratante *sm* moisturizing cream

hidratar *vt* ❶ [piel] to moisturize ❷ QUÍMICA to hydrate

hidrato *sm* ▶ **hidrato de carbono** carbohydrate

hidráulico, ca *adj* hydraulic. ☼ *Los adjetivos ingleses son invariables.*

hidroavión *sm* seaplane

hidroeléctrico, ca *adj* hydroelectric. ☼ *Los adjetivos ingleses son invariables.*

hidrógeno *sm* hydrogen

hielo *sm* ice • **con hielo** [whisky] with ice ; on the rocks

expresión **romper el hielo** figurado to break the ice ▶ **ser más frío que el hielo** to be as cold as ice

hiena *sf* hyena

hierba, yerba *sf* ❶ [planta] herb • **condimenté el pollo con hierbas** I seasoned the chicken with herbs • **mala hierba** weed ❷ [césped] grass • **tomamos sol en la hierba** we sunbathed in the grass ❸ *familiar* [droga] grass

hierbabuena *sf* mint

hierro *sm* [metal] iron • **de hierro** [severo] iron ☼ *Sólo se usa delante del sustantivo.* ▶ **hierro forjado** wrought iron ▶ **hierro fundido** cast iron ▶ **hierro laminado** sheet metal

hígado *sm* liver

higiene *sf* hygiene • **es increíble la falta de higiene de este lugar** this place's lack of hygiene is incredible ▶ **higiene corporal** personal hygiene ▶ **higiene dental** dental hygiene ▶ **higiene personal** personal hygiene

higiénico, ca *adj* hygienic • **papel higiénico** toilet paper. ☼ *Los adjetivos ingleses son invariables.*

higienizar *vt* to sterilize

higo *sm* fig ▶ **higo chumbo** prickly pear

expresión **de higos a brevas** once in a blue moon ▶ **me importa un higo** familiar I couldn't care less

higuera *sf* fig tree

expresión **estar en la higuera** to live in a world of your own

hijastro, tra *sm, f* stepson, *femenino* stepdaughter

hijo, ja *sm, f* [descendiente] son, *femenino* daughter • **tienen un hijo y una hija** they have a son and a daughter ▶ **hijo de papá** familiar daddy's boy

expresión **cualquier** o **todo hijo de vecino** familiar any Tom, Dick or Harry

■ **hijo** *sm* [hijo o hija] child • **van a tener un hijo** they're going to have a baby ▶ **hijo adoptivo** adopted child ▶ **hijo ilegítimo** o **natural** illegitimate child ▶ **hijo no deseado** unwanted child ▶ **hijo único** only child

hilar *vt* ❶ [hilo, tela] to spin ❷ [ideas, planes] to think up

hilera *sf* row • **hay una hilera de árboles en la entrada a la casa** there's a row of trees at the house's entrance • **los niños formaron una hilera** the children formed a line

hilo *sm* ❶ [fibra, hebra] thread • **necesito hilo para coser este dobladillo** I need thread in order to sew this hem ❷ [tejido] linen ❸ [de metal, teléfono] wire • **sin hilos** wireless ❹ [de agua, sangre] trickle • **de su boca salía un hilo de sangre** a trickle of blood came out of his mouth ❺ [de pensamiento] train ❻ [de discurso, conversación] thread

expresiones **colgar** o **pender de un hilo** to be hanging by a thread ▶ **mover los hilos** to pull some strings ▶ **perder el hilo** to lose the thread ▶ **seguir el hilo** to follow (the thread)

hilvanar *vt* ❶ [ropa] to baste ❷ [coordinar - ideas] to piece together

himno *sm* hymn ▶ **himno nacional** national anthem

hincapié *sm* • **hacer hincapié en a)** [insistir] to insist on **b)** [subrayar] to emphasize ; to stress

hincar *vt* • **hincar algo en** to stick something into

■ **hincarse** *v pronominal* • **hincarse de rodillas** to fall to your knees

hinchado, da *adj* ❶ [rueda, globo] inflated ❷ [cara, tobillo] swollen ❸ figurado [persona] bigheaded ❹ [lenguaje, estilo] bombastic. ☼ *Los adjetivos ingleses son invariables.*

hinchar *vt* to blow up

■ **hincharse** *v pronominal* ❶ [pierna, mano] to swell (up) • **se le hinchó la cara después del accidente** her face swelled after the accident ❷ figurado [de comida] • **hincharse (a)** to stuff yourself (with) • **nos hinchamos de marisco** we stuffed ourselves with seafood

hinchazón *sf* swelling

hindú (pl hindúes o hindús) *adj & smf* ❶ [de la India] Indian ❷ RELIGIÓN Hindu. ☼ *Los adjetivos ingleses son invariables.*

híper *sm* familiar hypermarket

hiperactivo, va *adj* hyperactive. ☼ *Los adjetivos ingleses son invariables.*

hipérbola *sf* hyperbola

hiperenlace *sm* INFORMÁTICA hyperlink

hipermercado *sm* hypermarket

hipertensión *sf* high blood pressure

hipertexto *sm* INFORMÁTICA hypertext

hípico, ca *adj* ❶ [de las carreras] horseracing. ☼ *Sólo se usa delante del sustantivo.* ❷ [de la equitación] showjumping. ☼ *Sólo se usa delante del sustantivo.*

■ **hípica** *sf* ❶ [carreras de caballos] horseracing ❷ [equitación] showjumping

hipnosis *sf invariable* hypnosis

hipnótico, ca *adj* hypnotic. ☼ *Los adjetivos ingleses son invariables.*

hipnotismo *sm* hypnotism

hipnotizador, ra *adj* ❶ hypnotic ❷ figurado mesmerizing. ☼ *Los adjetivos ingleses son invariables.*

H

hipnotizar *vt* ❶ to hypnotize ❷ *figurado* to mesmerize

hipo *sm* hiccups *pl* • **tener hipo** to have (the) hiccups

expresión quitar el hipo a uno *figurado* to take your breath away

hipocondriaco, ca *adj* & *sm, f* hypochondriac ஜ *Los adjetivos ingleses son invariables.*

hipocresía *sf* hypocrisy

hipócrita ♦ *adj* hypocritical ஜ *Los adjetivos ingleses son invariables.*

♦ *smf* hypocrite

hipodérmico, ca *adj* hypodermic ஜ *Los adjetivos ingleses son invariables.*

hipódromo *sm* racetrack

hipopótamo *sm* hippopotamus

hipoteca *sf* mortgage

hipotecar *vt* [*bienes*] to mortgage

hipotecario, ria *adj* mortgage ஜ *Sólo se usa delante del sustantivo.*

hipotenusa *sf* hypotenuse

hipótesis *sf invariable* hypothesis

hipotético, ca *adj* hypothetical ஜ *Los adjetivos ingleses son invariables.*

hippy, hippie (pl hippies) *adj* & *smf* hippy ஜ *Los adjetivos ingleses son invariables.*

hiriente *adj* [*palabras*] hurtful ஜ *Los adjetivos ingleses son invariables.*

hispánico, ca *adj* & *sm, f* Hispanic ஜ *Los adjetivos ingleses son invariables.*

En inglés los gentilicios se escriben con mayúscula.

hispanidad *sf* ❶ [*cultura*] Spanishness ❷ [*pueblos*] Spanish-speaking world

hispano, na ♦ *adj* ❶ [*español*] Spanish • **los países de habla hispana** Spanish-speaking countries ❷ [*hispanoamericano*] Spanish-American ❸ [*en Estados Unidos*] Hispanic • **la población hispana** the Hispanic population ஜ *Los adjetivos ingleses son invariables.*

En inglés, los adjetivos que se refieren a un país o una región se escriben con mayúscula.

♦ *sm, f* ❶ [*español*] Spaniard ❷ [*estadounidense*] Hispanic

hispanoamericano, na ♦ *adj* Spanish-American ஜ *Los adjetivos ingleses son invariables.*

♦ *sm, f* Spanish American

hispanohablante ♦ *adj* Spanish-speaking ஜ *Los adjetivos ingleses son invariables.*

♦ *smf* Spanish speaker

histeria *sf figurado* MEDICINA hysteria

histérico, ca *adj figurado* MEDICINA hysterical • **ponerse histérico** to get hysterical ஜ *Los adjetivos ingleses son invariables.*

histerismo *sm figurado* MEDICINA hysteria

historia *sf* ❶ [*generalmente*] history, *plural* histories • **hacer historia** to make history • **pasar a la historia** to go down in history ▸ **historia antigua/universal** ancient/world history ▸ **historia del arte** art history ❷ [*narración, chisme*] story • **una historia de amor** a love story

expresión dejarse de historias to stop beating about the bush

historiador, ra *sm, f* historian

historial *sm* ❶ [*generalmente*] record ❷ [*profesional*] résumé

histórico, ca *adj* ❶ [*de la historia*] historical ❷ [*verídico*] factual ❸ [*importante*] historic ஜ *Los adjetivos ingleses son invariables.*

historieta *sf* ❶ [*chiste*] funny story ❷ [*tira cómica*] comic strip

hito *sm literal* & *figurado* milestone

Hno. (*abreviatura de* hermano) Br.

hobby (pl hobbies) *sm* hobby, *plural* hobbies • **los colecciona por hobby** he collects them as a hobby

hocico *sm* ❶ [*de perro*] muzzle ❷ [*de gato*] nose ❸ [*de cerdo*] snout

hockey *sm* hockey ▸ **hockey sobre hielo/patines** ice/roller hockey ▸ **hockey sobre pasto** field hockey

hogar *sm* ❶ [*de chimenea*] fireplace ❷ [*de horno, cocina*] grate ❸ [*domicilio*] home • **tuvo un hogar feliz** he had a happy home life • **la gente sin hogar** the homeless • **artículos para el hogar** household goods • **labores del hogar** housework ▸ **hogar de ancianos** old people's home

expresión hogar, dulce hogar home, sweet home

hogareño, ña *adj* ❶ [*generalmente*] family ஜ *Sólo se usa delante del sustantivo.* ❷ [*amante del hogar*] home-loving

hoguera *sf* bonfire • **morir en la hoguera** to be burned at the stake

hoja *sf* ❶ [*de plantas*] leaf, *plural* leaves • **de hoja caduca** deciduous • **de hoja perenne** evergreen ❷ [*de flor*] petal ❸ [*de hierba*] blade ❹ [*de papel*] sheet (of paper) • **escríbelo en esta hoja** write it on this sheet • **una hoja en blanco** a blank sheet ▸ **hoja de cálculo** spreadsheet ❺ [*de libro*] page • **está en la hoja siguiente** it's on the next page ❻ [*de cuchillo*] blade ▸ **hoja de afeitar** razor blade ❼ [*de puertas, ventanas*] leaf

hojalata *sf* tinplate

hojaldre *sm* puff pastry

hojear *vt* to leaf through

hola *exclamación* • **¡hola!** hello! • **hola ¿qué tal?** hello, how are things?

Holanda *nombre propio* Holland

holgado, da *adj* ❶ [*ropa*] baggy ❷ [*habitación, espacio*] roomy ❸ [*victoria, situación económica*] comfortable ஜ *Los adjetivos ingleses son invariables.*

holgazán, ana ♦ *adj* idle ஜ *Los adjetivos ingleses son invariables.*

♦ *sm, f* good-for-nothing

holgazanear *vi* to laze about

holgura *sf* ❶ [*anchura - de espacio*] room; [*- de ropa*] looseness; [*- entre piezas*] give ❷ [*bienestar*] comfort

holocausto *sm* holocaust

hombre ◆ *sm* man, *plural* men• **es un hombre inteligente** he's an intelligent man • **¡pobre hombre!** poor guy!▶ **el hombre de la calle** o **de a pie** the man in the street▶ **hombre de las cavernas** caveman▶ **hombre de negocios** businessman▶ **hombre orquesta** one-man band▶ **hombre de palabra** man of his word▶ **hombre rana** frogman

expresiones **de hombre a hombre** man to man▶ **ser un hombre hecho y derecho** to be a grown man▶ **hombre precavido vale por dos** *proverbio* forewarned is forearmed*proverbio*

◆ *exclamación*• **¡hombre! ¡qué alegría verte!** (hey,) how nice to see you!

hombrera *sf*❶ [*de traje, vestido*] shoulder pad❷ [*de uniforme*] epaulette

hombro *sm* shoulder • **a hombros** over your shoulders• **hombro con hombro** shoulder to shoulder• **encogerse de hombros** to shrug your shoulders

expresión **arrimar el hombro** to lend a hand▶ **mirar por encima del hombro a alguien** to look down your nose at somebody

homenaje *sm*❶ [*generalmente*] tribute❷ [*al soberano*] homage • **partido (de) homenaje** testimonial (match)• **en homenaje a** in honor of• **rendir homenaje a** to pay tribute to• **la multitud rindió homenaje a su ídolo** the masses paid tribute to their idol

homenajeado, da *sm, f* guest of honor

homenajear *vt* to pay tribute to

homeopatía *sf* homeopathy

homicida ◆ *adj* [*mirada* ETC] murderous • **arma homicida** murder weapon❀ *Los adjetivos ingleses son invariables.*
◆ *smf* murderer

homicidio *sm* murder • **homicidio frustrado** attempted murder

homogéneo, a *adj* homogenous❀ *Los adjetivos ingleses son invariables.*

homologar *vt*❶ [*equiparar*] • **homologar (con)** to bring into line (with); to make comparable (with) ❷ [*dar por válido - producto*] to authorize officially; [*- récord*] to confirm officially

homólogo, ga ◆ *adj* [*semejante*] equivalent❀ *Los adjetivos ingleses son invariables.*
◆ *sm, f* counterpart

homosexual *adj & smf* homosexual❀ *Los adjetivos ingleses son invariables.*

honda *sf* sling

hondo, da *adj* literal & figurado [*generalmente*] deep • **yo no me meto en la parte honda** I don't go in the deep end• **tiene tres metros de hondo** it's three meters deep• **lo hondo** the depths *pl*• **calar hondo en** to strike a chord with• **en lo más hondo de** in the depths of❀ *Los adjetivos ingleses son invariables.*

hondonada *sf* hollow

Honduras *nombre propio* Honduras

hondureño, ña *adj & sm, f* Honduran❀ *Los adjetivos ingleses son invariables.*

En inglés, los adjetivos que se refieren a un país o una región se escriben con mayúscula.

honestidad *sf*❶ [*honradez*] honesty • **la honestidad es su mayor virtud** honesty is his greatest virtue • **dímelo con toda honestidad** be completely honest with me❷ [*decencia*] modesty❸ [*justicia*] fairness

honesto, ta *adj*❶ [*honrado*] honest❷ [*decente*] modest❸ [*justo*] fair❀ *Los adjetivos ingleses son invariables.*

hongo *sm*❶ [*planta - comestible*] mushroom; [*- no comestible*] toadstool❷ [*enfermedad*] fungus, *plural* fungi

honor *sm* honor

expresión **en honor a la verdad** to be (quite) honest ▶ **hacer honor a** to live up to

honorable *adj* honorable❀ *Los adjetivos ingleses son invariables.*

honorario, ria *adj* honorary❀ *Los adjetivos ingleses son invariables.*

honorífico, ca *adj* honorific❀ *Los adjetivos ingleses son invariables.*

honra *sf* honor • **¡y a mucha honra!** and proud of it!

■ **honras fúnebres** *sfpl* funeral *sing*

honradez *sf* honesty

honrado, da *adj* honest❀ *Los adjetivos ingleses son invariables.*

honrar *vt* to honor

honroso, sa *adj* ❶ [*que da honra*] honorary ❷ [*respetable*] honorable❀ *Los adjetivos ingleses son invariables.*

hora *sf*❶ [*del día*] hour • **media hora** half an hour• **a altas horas de la noche** in the small hours • **a primera hora** first thing in the morning • **a última hora a)** [*al final del día*] at the end of the day **b)** [*en el último momento*] at the last moment • **dar la hora** to strike the hour• **de última hora a)** [*noticia*] latest; up-to-the-minute **b)** [*preparativos*] last-minute • **'última hora'** stop press • **(pagar) por horas** (to pay) by the hour • **hora de dormir** bedtime▶ **horas de oficina/trabajo** office/working hours▶ **hora local/oficial** local/official time▶ **hora pico** rush hour▶ **horas extraordinarias** overtime❀ *incontable* ▶ **horas libres** free time❀ *incontable* • **¿qué haces en tus horas libres?** what do you do in your free time?▶ **horas de visita** visiting hours ▶ **horas de vuelo** flying time *sing*❷ [*momento determinado*] time • **¿qué hora es?** what time is it? • **¿tienes la hora?** do you have the time? • **¿a qué hora sale?** what time❶ when does it leave? • **es hora de irse** it's time to go • **es hora de cenar** it's time for supper • **a la hora** on time• **cada hora** hourly • **en su hora** when the time comes▶ **hora de cerrar** closing time

expresiones **en mala hora** unluckily▶ **la hora de la verdad** the moment of truth▶ **¡ya era hora!** and about time too!

horario, ria *adj* time ❖ *Sólo se usa delante del sustantivo.*

■ **horario** *sm* schedule • **según mi horario, tengo inglés mañana** according to my schedule, I have English tomorrow • **no sé el horario de los trenes** I don't know the train schedule ◗ **horario de atención al público** opening hours ◗ **horario comercial/laboral** opening/working hours *pl* ◗ **horario intensivo** *para explicar lo que es puedes decir:* it's a working day without a lunch break so you can finish earlier ◗ **horario de visitas** visiting hours *pl*

horca *sf* ❶ [*patíbulo*] gallows *pl* ❷ AGRICULTURA pitchfork

horizontal *adj* horizontal ❖ *Los adjetivos ingleses son invariables.*

horizonte *sm* horizon • **el sol aparece por el horizonte** the sun appears on the horizon

horma *sf* ❶ [*generalmente*] mould ❷ [*para arreglar zapatos*] last ❸ [*para conservar zapatos*] shoe tree ❹ [*de sombrero*] hat block

hormiga *sf* ant

expresión **ser una hormiga** to be hard-working and thrifty

hormigón *sm* concrete ◗ **hormigón armado** reinforced concrete

hormigueo *sm* pins and needles *pl*

hormiguero *sm* ants' nest → **oso**

hormona *sf* hormone

hornada *sf literal & figurado* batch

hornear *vt* to bake

hornillo *sm* ❶ [*para cocinar*] camping stove ❷ [*de laboratorio*] small furnace

horno *sm* ❶ COCINA oven • **pollo al horno** roasted chicken • **papas al horno** baked potatoes ◗ **horno eléctrico** electric oven ◗ **horno de gas** gas oven ◗ **horno microondas** microwave (oven) ❷ TECNOLOGÍA furnace ❸ [*de cerámica, ladrillos*] kiln ◗ **altos hornos** [*factoría*] iron and steelworks

expresión **ser un horno** to be like an oven

horóscopo *sm* ❶ [*signo zodiacal*] star sign ❷ [*predicción*] horoscope

horquilla *sf* [*para el pelo*] bobby pin

horrendo, da *adj* ❶ [*generalmente*] horrendous ❷ [*muy malo*] awful ❖ *Los adjetivos ingleses son invariables.*

horrible *adj* ❶ [*generalmente*] horrible ❷ [*muy malo*] awful ❖ *Los adjetivos ingleses son invariables.*

horripilante *adj* horrifying ❖ *Los adjetivos ingleses son invariables.*

horror *sm* ❶ [*miedo*] horror • **escuchó un grito de horror** he heard a scream of horror • **una película de horror** a horror movie • **¡qué horror!** how awful! ❷ ❖ *generalmente pl* [*atrocidad*] atrocity, *plural* atrocities • **los horrores de la guerra** the horrors of war

horrorizado, da *adj* horrified ❖ *Los adjetivos ingleses son invariables.*

horrorizar *vt* to horrify

horroroso, sa *adj* ❶ [*generalmente*] awful • **el tiempo estuvo horroroso** the weather was awful ❷ [*muy feo*] horrible • **¡qué cuadro más horroroso!** what a horrible painting! ❖ *Los adjetivos ingleses son invariables.*

hortaliza *sf* (garden) vegetable

hortensia *sf* hydrangea

horticultura *sf* horticulture

hospedar *vt* ❶ to put up ❷ INFORMÁTICA to host

■ **hospedarse** *v pronominal* to stay • **se hospedaron en albergues juveniles** they stayed in youth hostels

hospicio *sm* ❶ [*para niños*] children's home ❷ [*para pobres*] poorhouse

hospital *sm* hospital

hospitalario, ria *adj* hospitable ❖ *Los adjetivos ingleses son invariables.*

hospitalidad *sf* hospitality

hospitalizar *vt* to hospitalize

hostal *sm* guesthouse

hostelería *sf* catering

hostia *sf* RELIGIÓN host • **la hostia sagrada** the sacred host

hostigar *vt* ❶ [*acosar*] to pester ❷ MILITAR to harass

hostil *adj* hostile ❖ *Los adjetivos ingleses son invariables.*

hostilidad *sf* [*sentimiento*] hostility

hotel *sm* hotel

hotelero, ra *adj* hotel ❖ *Sólo se usa delante del sustantivo.*

hoy *adv* ❶ [*en este día*] today • **hoy es su cumpleaños** today is her birthday • **el diario de hoy** today's newspaper • **de hoy en adelante** from now on • **hoy mismo** this very day • **por hoy** for now ❷ [*en la actualidad*] nowadays • **hoy es posible curar muchas enfermedades** nowadays it's possible to cure many diseases • **hoy día, hoy en día, hoy por hoy** nowadays

hoyo *sm* ❶ [*generalmente*] hole ❷ [*de golf*] hole

hoyuelo *sm* dimple

hoz *sf* sickle • **la hoz y el martillo** the hammer and sickle

HTML (*abreviatura de* hypertext markup language) *sm* INFORMÁTICA HTML

huacal *sm* [*caja*] slatted crate

hucha *sf* moneybox

hueco, ca *adj* ❶ [*vacío*] hollow ❷ [*sonido*] hollow ❸ [*sin ideas*] empty. ♀ *Los adjetivos ingleses son invariables.*
■ **hueco** *sm* ❶ [*cavidad - generalmente*] hole; [*- en pared*] recess ❷ [*tiempo libre*] spare moment • **hacer un hueco a alguien** to fit somebody in • **está muy ocupada pero va a hacer un hueco para recibirme** she's very busy but she's going to set aside some time to see me ❸ [*espacio libre*] space • **hay que hacer un hueco para poner este libro** we have to make a space for this book ❹ [*de escalera*] well ❺ [*de ascensor*] shaft

huelga *sf* strike • **estar/declararse en huelga** to be/to go on strike ▶ **huelga de brazos caídos** o **cruzados** sit-down (strike) ▶ **huelga de celo** work-to-rule ▶ **huelga de hambre** hunger strike ▶ **huelga general** general strike ▶ **huelga salvaje** wildcat strike

huelguista *smf* striker

huella *sf* ❶ [*de persona*] footprint • **había huellas en la nieve** there were footprints in the snow ❷ [*de animal, rueda*] track • **íbamos siguiendo la huella del jeep** we were following the jeep's tracks ▶ **huella digital** o **dactilar** fingerprint ❸ *figurado* [*vestigio*] trace • **sin dejar huella** without (a) trace ❹ *figurado* [*impresión profunda*] mark • **dejar huella** to leave your mark

huérfano, na *adj* & *sm, f* orphan • **quieren adoptar a un niño huérfano** they want to adopt an orphan • **es huérfano de madre** his mother is dead • **quedó huérfano** he was orphaned. ♀ *Los adjetivos ingleses son invariables.*

huerta *sf* truck farm

huerto *sm* ❶ [*de hortalizas*] vegetable garden ❷ [*de frutales*] orchard

hueso *sm* ❶ [*del cuerpo*] bone • **encontraron un hueso de dinosaurio** they found a dinosaur bone ❷ [*de fruto*] pit • **el hueso del durazno** the peach pit ❸ *familiar* [*enchufe*] contacts *pl* ❹ *familiar* [*trabajo fácil*] cushy job
expresión **estar calado hasta los huesos** to be soaked to the skin ▶ **ser un hueso duro de roer** to be a hard nut to crack

huésped, da *sm, f* guest

hueva *sf* roe

huevo *sm* [*de animales*] egg ▶ **huevo cocido** hard-boiled egg ▶ **huevo estrellado** fried egg ▶ **huevo pasado por agua** soft-boiled egg ▶ **huevo de Pascua** Easter egg ▶ **huevos revueltos** scrambled eggs ▶ **huevo tibio** soft-boiled egg

huida *sf* escape

huir *vi* ❶ [*escapar*] • **huir (de) a** [*generalmente*] to flee (from) **b)** [*de cárcel* ETC] to escape (from) • **huyeron cuando vieron que venía la policía** they fled when they saw that the police were coming • **la famosa actriz huía de los periodistas** the famous actress was fleeing from the press • **varios presos huyeron de la cárcel** several prisoners escaped from prison • **cuando sonó la alarma salieron huyendo** when the alarm went off they ran away • **huir del país** to flee the country ❷ [*evitar*] • **huir de algo** to avoid something

hule *sm* rubber

humanidad *sf* humanity • **fue una gran muestra de humanidad** it was a great demonstration of humanity • **la humanidad** humankind

humanitario, ria *adj* humanitarian. ♀ *Los adjetivos ingleses son invariables.*

humanizar *vt* to humanize

humano, na *adj* ❶ [*del hombre*] human • **el cuerpo humano** the human body ❷ [*compasivo*] humane • **recibieron un tratamiento muy humano** they received very humane treatment. ♀ *Los adjetivos ingleses son invariables.*
■ **humano** *sm* human being • **los humanos** mankind. ♀ *incontable*

humareda *sf* cloud of smoke

humear *vi* ❶ [*salir humo*] to (give off) smoke ❷ [*salir vapor*] to steam

humedad *sf* ❶ [*generalmente*] dampness ❷ [*de atmósfera* ETC] humidity • **el calor y la humedad eran insoportables** the heat and humidity were insufferable • **no hace mucho calor pero hay mucha humedad** it's not very hot but it's very humid ▶ **humedad absoluta/relativa** absolute/relative humidity ❸ [*en pared, techo*] damp ❹ [*de algo chorreando*] wetness ❺ [*de piel, ojos* ETC] moistness

humedecer *vt* to moisten

húmedo, da *adj* ❶ [*generalmente*] damp • **esta ropa está húmeda** these clothes are damp • **la casa es muy húmeda en invierno** the house is very damp in the winter ❷ [*chorreando*] wet ❸ [*piel, ojos* ETC] moist ❹ [*aire, clima, atmósfera*] humid • **es una ciudad con un clima húmedo** it's a city with a humid climate. ♀ *Los adjetivos ingleses son invariables.*

humildad *sf* humility

humilde *adj* humble • **debería ser un poco más humilde** he should be a little more humble • **alumnos que provienen de zonas humildes** students that come from poor areas. ♀ *Los adjetivos ingleses son invariables.*

humillación *sf* humiliation

humillado, da *adj* humiliated. ♀ *Los adjetivos ingleses son invariables.*

humillante *adj* humiliating. ♀ *Los adjetivos ingleses son invariables.*

humillar *vt* to humiliate

humo *sm* ❶ [*generalmente*] smoke • **el humo de un cigarro** cigarette smoke ❷ [*vapor*] steam ❸ [*de coches* ETC] fumes *pl* • **el humo de los tubos de escape** exhaust fumes • **echar humo a)** [*generalmente*] to smoke **b)** *figurado* to be fuming • **estaba que echaba humo** he was fuming • **tragarse el humo** [*al fumar*] to inhale
expresión **hacerse humo** to disappear

humor *sm* ❶ [*estado de ánimo*] mood ❷ [*carácter*] temperament • **estar de buen/mal humor** to be in a good/bad mood ❸ [*gracia*] humor • **no entiendo esa clase de humor** I don't understand that kind of humor • **tiene mucho sentido del humor** he has a good sense of humor • **un programa de humor** a comedy show ▶ **humor negro** black comedy ❹ [*ganas*] mood • **no**

estoy de humor I'm not in the mood • **no estaba de humor para explicar nada** she wasn't in the mood to explain anything

humorista *smf* ❶ humorist ❷ *TEATRO & TELEVISIÓN* comedian, *femenino* comedienne

humorístico, ca *adj* humorous ⚲ *Los adjetivos ingleses son invariables.*

hundimiento *sm* ❶ [*naufragio*] sinking ❷ [*ruina*] collapse

hundir *vt* ❶ [*generalmente*] to sink • **hundir algo en el agua** to put something underwater ❷ [*afligir*] to devastate ❸ [*hacer fracasar*] to ruin

■ **hundirse** *v pronominal* ❶ [*sumergirse*] to sink • **el lugar donde se hundió el barco** the place where the boat sank • **se me hundían los pies en el lodo** my feet sank in the mud ❷ [*intencionadamente*] to dive ❸ [*derrumbarse*] to collapse • **el techo se hundió con el peso de la nieve** the roof collapsed with the weight of the snow ❹ [*techo*] to cave in ❺ [*fracasar*] to be ruined

Hungría *nombre propio* Hungary

huracán *sm* hurricane

hurgar *vi* • **hurgar (en) a)** [*generalmente*] to rummage around (in) **b)** [*con el dedo, un palo*] to poke around (in)

hurón *sm* *ZOOLOGÍA* ferret

hurra *exclamación* • **¡hurra!** hurray!

hurtadillas ■ **a hurtadillas** *locución adverbial* on the sly

hurtar *vt* to steal

hurto *sm* theft

husmear ◆ *vt* [*olfatear*] to sniff out • **el perro le husmeaba los zapatos** the dog sniffed his shoes

◆ *vi* [*curiosear*] to snoop • **lo encontré husmeando en mi clóset** I found him snooping in my closet

huy *exclamación* • **¡huy! a)** [*dolor*] ouch! **b)** [*sorpresa*] gosh!

H

i, I *sf* [*letra*] i ; I

iberoamericano, na *adj* & *sm, f* Latin American ⚲ *Los adjetivos ingleses son invariables.*

iceberg (pl icebergs) *sm* iceberg

icono *sm* icon

ida *sf* outward journey • **la ida la hicimos sin problemas** the outward journey was fine • **la ida sola sale más cara** one-way costs more • **es mejor comprar ida y vuelta** it's better to buy a round trip ▶ **(boleto de) ida y vuelta** round-trip(ticket)

idea *sf* ❶ [*generalmente*] idea • **creo que es una buena idea** I think it's a good idea • **¿tienes idea de cómo funciona esto?** do you have any idea how this works? • **cuando se le mete una idea en la cabeza...** when he gets an idea into his head... • **cambiar de idea** to change your mind • **hacerse a la idea de que...** to get used to the idea that... • **hacerse una idea de algo** to get an idea of something • **no tener ni idea (de)** not to have a clue (about) • **¡ni idea!** *familiar* I haven't got a clue! ▶ **idea fija** obsession ▶ **idea preconcebida** preconception ❷ [*propósito*] intention • **con la idea de** with the intention of • **mi idea era ir al cine** my idea was to go to the movies ❸ [*opinión*] opinion

ideal *adj* & *sm* ideal • **es el lugar ideal para un picnic** it's an ideal place for a picnic • **lo ideal sería hacerlo mañana** ideally, we would do it tomorrow ⚲ *Los adjetivos ingleses son invariables.*

idealista ◆ *adj* idealistic ⚲ *Los adjetivos ingleses son invariables.*
◆ *smf* idealist

idear *vt* ❶ [*planear*] to devise • **idearon una manera de copiar las respuestas** they devised a way to copy the answers ❷ [*inventar*] to invent • **idearon un sistema diferente** they invented a different system

ideario *sm* ideology

ídem *pronombre* ditto

idéntico, ca *adj* identical • **los dos cuadros son idénticos** the two paintings are identical • **idéntico a algo** identical to something • **tengo una falda idéntica a la tuya** I have a skirt identical to yours • **Pedro es idéntico a su padre** Pedro's the image of his father ⚲ *Los adjetivos ingleses son invariables.*

identidad *sf* identity, *plural* identities

identificación *sf* identification • **es necesario llevar una identificación** it's necessary to carry some ID

identificar *vt* to identify • **identificaron al asaltante** they identified the attacker

ideología *sf* ideology

idílico, ca *adj* idyllic ⚲ *Los adjetivos ingleses son invariables.*

idilio *sm* love affair

idioma *sm* language

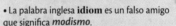

idioma ≠ idiom

- La palabra inglesa **idiom** es un falso amigo que significa *modismo*.
- *Idioma* se traduce al inglés por **language**.

idiota ◆ *adj despectivo* [*tonto*] stupid ⚲ *Los adjetivos ingleses son invariables.*
◆ *smf* idiot

idiotez *sf* stupid thing

ídolo *sm* idol

idóneo, a *adj* • **idóneo (para)** suitable (for) ⚲ *Los adjetivos ingleses son invariables.*

iglesia *sf* church • **va poco a la iglesia** he seldom goes to church • **se casaron por la iglesia** they got married in the church ▶ **la Iglesia Católica** the Catholic Church

iglú (pl iglúes O iglús) *sm* igloo

ignorancia *sf* ignorance

ignorante ◆ *adj* ignorant ⚲ *Los adjetivos ingleses son invariables.*
◆ *smf* ignoramus

ignorar *vt* ❶ [*desconocer*] not to know • **ignoraba que era sacerdote** she didn't know that he was a priest ❷ [*no tener en cuenta*] to ignore • **está tratando de molestarte, así que ignóralo** he's trying to bother you, so ignore him

igual ◆ *adj* ❶ [*idéntico*] • **igual (que)** the same (as) • **llevan jerseys iguales** they're wearing the same jumper • **son iguales** they're the same • **es igual a su padre** he's like his father • **son iguales de largo** they are the same length❷ [*parecido*] • **igual (que)** similar (to)❸ [*equivalente*] • **igual (a)** equal (to) • **todos somos iguales ante la ley** we're all equal before the law❹ [*liso*] even❺ [*constante - velocidad*] constant; [*- clima, temperatura*] even❻ MATEMÁTICAS • **A más B es igual a C** A plus B equals C ¤: *Los adjetivos ingleses son invariables.*

◆ *smf* equal • **sin igual** without equal; unrivaled

◆ *adv* ❶ [*de la misma manera*] the same • **yo pienso igual** I think the same; I think so too • **al igual que** just like • **por igual** equally❷ [*posiblemente*] perhaps • **igual llueve** it could well rain • **igual vino y no estábamos** maybe he came and we weren't there❸ DEPORTE • **van iguales** the score is tied • **quince iguales** [*en tenis*] fifteen all

expresión **dar o ser igual a alguien** to be all the same to somebody • **es o da igual** it doesn't matter; it doesn't make any difference

igualado, da *adj* level ¤: *Los adjetivos ingleses son invariables.*

igualar *vt* ❶ [*generalmente*] to make equal❷ DEPORTE to equalize • **igualar algo a o con** to equate something with❸ [*persona*] to be equal to • **nadie le iguala en generosidad** nobody is as generous as he is❹ [*terreno*] to level❺ [*superficie*] to smooth

igualdad *sf* ❶ [*equivalencia*] equality • **la igualdad ante la ley** equality before the law • **en igualdad de condiciones** on equal terms • **igualdad de oportunidades** equal opportunities *pl* • **igualdad de sexos** gender equality❷ [*identidad*] sameness

igualmente *adv* ❶ [*también*] also❷ [*fórmula de cortesía*] the same to you

ilegal *adj* illegal ¤: *Los adjetivos ingleses son invariables.*

ilegible *adj* illegible ¤: *Los adjetivos ingleses son invariables.*

ilegítimo, ma *adj* illegitimate ¤: *Los adjetivos ingleses son invariables.*

ileso, sa *adj* unharmed • **salir o resultar ileso** to escape unharmed ¤: *Los adjetivos ingleses son invariables.*

ilícito, ta *adj* illicit ¤: *Los adjetivos ingleses son invariables.*

ilimitado, da *adj* unlimited ¤: *Los adjetivos ingleses son invariables.*

iluminación *sf* ❶ [*generalmente*] lighting❷ [*acción*] illumination❸ RELIGIÓN enlightenment

iluminar *vt* [*generalmente*] to light up • **la luz que ilumina la entrada** the light that lights the entrance • **esta linterna ilumina muy poco** this lantern doesn't give much light

ilusión *sf* ❶ [*esperanza - generalmente*] hope; [*- infundada*] delusion; illusion • **empezó con mucha ilusión** he began with a lot of hope • **su gran ilusión es ser bailarina** her big dream is to be a dancer • **hacerse o forjarse ilusiones** to build up your hopes • **hacerse la ilusión de** to imagine that • **tener ilusión por** to look forward to❷ [*emoción*] thrill; excitement ¤: *incontable* • **¡qué ilusión!** how exciting! • **me hace mucha**

ilusión I'm really looking forward to it❸ [*espejismo*] illusion • **el color crea la ilusión de que la sala es más grande** the color creates the illusion that the room is bigger • **ilusión óptica** optical illusion

ilusionar *vt* ❶ [*esperanzar*] • **ilusionar a alguien (con algo)** to raise somebody's hopes (about something) • **la ilusionaron para después decirle que no** they raised her hopes only to later tell her no❷ [*emocionar*] to excite • **no me ilusiona mucho la idea** the idea doesn't excite me much

■ **ilusionarse** *v pronominal* [*emocionarse*] • **ilusionarse (con)** to get excited (about) • **se ilusiona fácilmente con todo** he easily gets excited about everything • **se había ilusionado tanto y todo fracasó** he had built up his hopes so much and everything fell through

ilusionista *smf* conjurer

iluso, sa *adj* gullible ¤: *Los adjetivos ingleses son invariables.*

ilustración *sf* ❶ [*estampa*] illustration❷ [*cultura*] learning

■ **Ilustración** *sf* HISTORIA • **la Ilustración** the Enlightenment

ilustrado, da *adj* ❶ [*publicación*] illustrated❷ [*persona*] learned❸ HISTORIA enlightened ¤: *Los adjetivos ingleses son invariables.*

ilustrar *vt* ❶ [*explicar*] to illustrate❷ [*publicación*] to illustrate

ilustre *adj* [*generalmente*] illustrious ¤: *Los adjetivos ingleses son invariables.*

imagen *sf* ❶ [*generalmente*] image • **es la imagen que la gente tiene de mí** it's the image that people have of me • **el grupo quiere cambiar de imagen** the group wants to change its image • **imagen corporativa** corporate identity❷ TELEVISIÓN picture • **imagen borrosa** blur • **imagen congelada** freeze frame

expresión **ser la viva imagen de alguien** to be the spitting image of somebody

imaginación *sf* ❶ [*facultad*] imagination • **no tiene imaginación para nada** he doesn't have any imagination at all • **se deja llevar por la imaginación** he lets his imagination run away with him • **pasar por la imaginación de alguien** to cross somebody's mind • **ni se me pasó por la imaginación contárselo** it didn't cross my mind to tell him❷ [*idea falsa*] • **es pura imaginación tuya** it's all in your mind • **son imaginaciones tuyas** you're imagining things

imaginar *vt* ❶ [*generalmente*] to imagine❷ [*idear*] to think up

■ **imaginarse** *v pronominal* to imagine • **imagínate que estás en una playa desierta** imagine that you're on a deserted beach • **no te imaginas lo furioso que estaba** you can't imagine how furious he was • **me lo imaginaba más alto** I imagined him to be taller • **¡imagínate!** can you imagine? • **me imagino que sí** I suppose so

imán *sm* [*para atraer*] magnet

imbécil ◆ *adj* stupid ¤: *Los adjetivos ingleses son invariables.*

◆ *smf* idiot

imbecilidad *sf* stupidity • **decir/hacer una imbecilidad** to say/do something stupid

imborrable *adj* ❶ *figurado* indelible ❷ [*recuerdo*] unforgettable ۞ *Los adjetivos ingleses son invariables.*

imitación *sf* ❶ imitation • **hay que tener cuidado con las imitaciones** you have to be careful with imitations • **a imitación de** in imitation of • **aprenden por imitación** they learn by imitation • **piel de imitación** imitation leather ❷ [*de humorista*] impression • **le encanta hacer imitaciones** he loves to do impressions

imitador, ra *sm, f* ❶ [*que imita*] imitator ❷ [*humorista*] impersonator

imitar *vt* ❶ [*generalmente*] to imitate • **trata de imitar a su padre** he tries to imitate his father • **te imita muy bien el acento** she imitates your accent very well ❷ [*a personajes famosos*] to impersonate • **imita a casi todos los profesores** he impersonates almost all of the teachers ❸ [*producto, material*] to simulate

impaciencia *sf* impatience

impacientar *vt* to make impatient

impaciente *adj* impatient • **no seas tan impaciente** don't be so impatient • **impaciente por hacer algo** impatient to do something • **estaba impaciente por saber quién ganó** he was impatient to know who won ۞ *Los adjetivos ingleses son invariables.*

impactante *adj* ❶ [*imagen*] hard-hitting ❷ [*belleza*] striking ۞ *Los adjetivos ingleses son invariables.*

impactar ♦ *vt* [*sujeto: noticia*] to have an impact on
♦ *vi* [*bala*] to hit

impacto *sm* ❶ [*generalmente*] impact ❷ [*de bala*] hit ❸ [*señal*] (impact) mark • **impacto de bala** bullethole

impar *adj* MATEMÁTICAS odd • **un número impar** an odd number ۞ *Los adjetivos ingleses son invariables.*

imparable *adj* unstoppable ۞ *Los adjetivos ingleses son invariables.*

imparcial *adj* impartial ۞ *Los adjetivos ingleses son invariables.*

impartir *vt* to give

impecable *adj* impeccable ۞ *Los adjetivos ingleses son invariables.*

impedido, da *adj* disabled • **estar impedido de un brazo** to have the use of only one arm ۞ *Los adjetivos ingleses son invariables.*

impedimento *sm* ❶ [*generalmente*] obstacle ❷ [*contra un matrimonio*] impediment

impedir *vt* ❶ [*imposibilitar*] to stop • **no lo pueden impedir** they can't stop it • **impedir a alguien hacer algo** to stop somebody from doing something • **quisieron impedir que reclamáramos** they wanted to stop us from protesting • **si quieres ir nadie te lo está impidiendo** if you want to go nobody is stopping you • **no impidan el paso** don't block the way ❷ *figurado* [*dificultar*] to hinder

impensable *adj* unthinkable ۞ *Los adjetivos ingleses son invariables.*

imperar *vi* to prevail

imperceptible *adj* imperceptible ۞ *Los adjetivos ingleses son invariables.*

imperdible *sm* safety pin

imperdonable *adj* unforgivable ۞ *Los adjetivos ingleses son invariables.*

imperfección *sf* ❶ [*cualidad*] imperfection ❷ [*defecto*] flaw

imperfecto, ta *adj* ❶ [*generalmente*] imperfect ❷ [*defectuoso*] faulty ۞ *Los adjetivos ingleses son invariables.*

■ **imperfecto** *sm* GRAMÁTICA imperfect

imperial *adj* imperial ۞ *Los adjetivos ingleses son invariables.*

imperio *sm* ❶ [*territorio*] empire ❷ [*dominio*] rule

imperioso, sa *adj* ❶ [*autoritario*] imperious ❷ [*apremiante*] urgent ۞ *Los adjetivos ingleses son invariables.*

impermeable ♦ *adj* waterproof ۞ *Los adjetivos ingleses son invariables.*
♦ *sm* raincoat

impersonal *adj* impersonal ۞ *Los adjetivos ingleses son invariables.*

impertinencia *sf* ❶ [*generalmente*] impertinence ❷ [*comentario*] impertinent remark

impertinente *adj* impertinent ۞ *Los adjetivos ingleses son invariables.*

imperturbable *adj* imperturbable ۞ *Los adjetivos ingleses son invariables.*

ímpetu *sm* ❶ [*brusquedad*] force ❷ [*energía*] energy ❸ FÍSICA impetus

impetuoso, sa *adj* ❶ [*olas, viento, ataque*] violent ❷ [*persona*] impulsive ۞ *Los adjetivos ingleses son invariables.*

implacable *adj* implacable ۞ *Los adjetivos ingleses son invariables.*

implantar *vt* ❶ [*establecer*] to introduce ❷ MEDICINA to insert

implicación *sf* ❶ [*participación*] involvement ❷ ۞ *generalmente pl* [*consecuencia*] implication

implicar *vt* ❶ [*involucrar*] • **implicar (en)** to involve (in) ❷ DERECHO to implicate (in) ❸ [*significar*] to mean

implícito, ta *adj* implicit ۞ *Los adjetivos ingleses son invariables.*

implorar *vt* to implore

imponente *adj* ❶ [*impresionante*] imposing ❷ [*estupendo*] sensational ۞ *Los adjetivos ingleses son invariables.*

imponer ♦ *vt* ❶ • **imponer algo (a alguien) a)** [*generalmente*] to impose something (on somebody) **b)** [*respeto*] to command something (from somebody) • **le impusieron un castigo muy severo** they imposed a very severe punishment on him • **le impusieron una multa** they imposed a fine on him • **el director sabe imponer respeto** the director knows how to command respect❷ [*moda*] to set❸ [*costumbre*] to introduce

◆ *vi* to be imposing

■ **imponerse** *v pronominal*❶ [*hacerse respetar*] to assert yourself• **la profesora no sabe imponerse** the teacher doesn't know how to assert herself❷ [*prevalecer*] to prevail• **es una moda que se impuso en los sesenta** it's a fashion that prevailed in the sixties❸ [*ser necesario*] to be necessary❹ DEPORTE to win

impopular *adj* unpopular.♀: *Los adjetivos ingleses son invariables.*

importación *sf*❶ [*acción*] importing • **prohibieron la importación de transgénicos** they prohibited the importing of genetically modified articles❷ [*artículo*] import

importador, ra *sm, f* importer

importancia *sf* importance • **la importancia de una buena educación** the importance of a good education• **un acontecimiento de gran importancia** an event of great importance • **dar importancia a algo** to attach importance to something• **quitar importancia a algo** to play something down• **tener importancia** to be important

expresión **darse importancia** to be full of yourself

importante *adj*❶ [*generalmente*] important• **sus amigos lo más importante para él** his friends are what's most important for him• **es una persona muy importante** he's a very important person• **lo importante es prepararse con tiempo** the important thing is to prepare yourself ahead of time❷ [*lesión*] serious❸ [*cantidad*] considerable.♀: *Los adjetivos ingleses son invariables.*

importar ◆ *vt*❶ [*generalmente*] INFORMÁTICA to import• **tienen que importar muchos productos** they have to import many products❷ [*sujeto: factura, coste*] to amount to

◆ *vi*❶ [*preocupar*] to matter• **no me importa** I don't care• **eso es lo único que le importa** that's the only thing that matters to her• **¿y a ti qué te importa?** what's it to you?• **no me importa caminar hasta el colegio** I don't mind walking to school❷ [*en preguntas*] to mind• **¿le importa que me siente?** do you mind if I sit down?• **¿te importa si se lo cuento?** do you mind if I tell him?• **¿te importaría acompañarme?** would you mind coming with me?

expresión **me importa un bledo** o **comino** o **pito** *familiar* I couldn't care less

◆ *v impersonal* to matter• **no importa** it doesn't matter• **no importa si no tienes experiencia** it doesn't matter if you don't have experience

importe *sm* ❶ [*generalmente*] cost❷ [*de factura*] total

imposibilitado, da *adj* disabled • **estar imposibilitado para hacer algo** to be unable to do something.♀: *Los adjetivos ingleses son invariables.*

imposible *adj*❶ [*irrealizable*] impossible • **es imposible estudiar con tanto ruido** it's impossible to study with so much noise• **es imposible que lo haya sabido** it's impossible for him to have found it out❷ [*insoportable*] impossible • **son unos niños imposibles** they're impossible children.♀: *Los adjetivos ingleses son invariables.*

imposición *sf*❶ [*obligación*] imposition❷ [*impuesto*] tax❸ BANCA deposit • **hacer** o **efectuar una imposición** to make a deposit

impostor, ra *sm, f* impostor

impotencia *sf* impotence

impotente *adj* impotent.♀: *Los adjetivos ingleses son invariables.*

impracticable *adj*❶ [*irrealizable*] impracticable❷ [*intransitable*] impassable.♀: *Los adjetivos ingleses son invariables.*

imprecisión *sf* imprecision

impreciso, sa *adj* imprecise.♀: *Los adjetivos ingleses son invariables.*

impredecible *adj*❶ unforeseeable❷ [*variable*] unpredictable.♀: *Los adjetivos ingleses son invariables.*

impregnar *vt* • **impregnar (de)** to impregnate (with)

imprenta *sf*❶ [*arte*] printing❷ [*máquina*] (printing) press❸ [*establecimiento*] printing house

imprescindible *adj* essential.♀: *Los adjetivos ingleses son invariables.*

impresentable *adj* unpresentable.♀: *Los adjetivos ingleses son invariables.*

impresión *sf*❶ [*generalmente*] impression• **causar (una) buena/mala impresión** to make a good/bad impression• **le causó muy buena impresión a la profesora** he made a very good impression on the teacher • **dar la impresión de** to give the impression of• **da la impresión de ser muy estudioso** he gives the impression of being very studious • **tengo la impresión de haber estado aquí antes** I have the feeling that I've been here before❷ [*huella*] imprint❸ IMPRENTA [*acción*] printing; [*edición*] edition

impresionante *adj*❶ [*generalmente*] impressive • **tiene una cantidad de videos impresionante** he has an impressive number of videos• **el parecido es impresionante** the similarity is striking❷ [*error*] enormous.♀: *Los adjetivos ingleses son invariables.*

impresionar ◆ *vt*❶ [*maravillar*] to impress • **impresionó al público con sus acrobacias** he impressed the public with his acrobatics• **impresiona lo rápido que aprende** it's impressive how fast he learns❷ [*conmocionar*] to move❸ [*horrorizar*] to shock • **me impresionó ver tanta pobreza** it shocked me to see so much poverty❹ FOTOGRAFÍA to expose

◆ *vi* [*maravillar*] to make an impression

■ **impresionarse** *v pronominal*❶ [*maravillarse*] to be impressed• **los niños se impresionan con mucha facilidad** children are easily impressed❷ [*conmocionarse*] to be moved❸ [*horrorizarse*] to be shocked

imprevisible *adj*❶ unforeseeable❷ [*variable*] unpredictable.♀: *Los adjetivos ingleses son invariables.*

imprevisto, ta *adj* unexpected.♀: *Los adjetivos ingleses son invariables.*

■ **imprevisto** *sm* [*hecho*] • **no pudo ir porque surgió un imprevisto** he couldn't go because something unexpected came up • **tienen un fondo para imprevis-**

tos they have a fund for unexpected expenses • **salvo imprevistos** barring accidents

imprimir *vt* ❶ [*generalmente*] to print ❷ [*huella, paso*] to leave ❸ *figurado* [*transmitir*] • **imprimir algo a** to impart o bring something to

improbable *adj* unlikely ☌ *Los adjetivos ingleses son invariables.*

improcedente *adj* ❶ [*inoportuno*] inappropriate ❷ DERECHO inadmissible ☌ *Los adjetivos ingleses son invariables.*

impropio, pia *adj* • **impropio (de)** improper (for); unbecoming (to) ☌ *Los adjetivos ingleses son invariables.*

improvisado, da *adj* ❶ [*generalmente*] improvised ❷ [*discurso, truco*] impromptu ❸ [*comentario*] ad-lib ❹ [*cama* ETC] makeshift ☌ *Los adjetivos ingleses son invariables.*

improvisar ✦ *vt* ❶ [*generalmente*] to improvise • **improvisar una cama** to make (up) a makeshift bed ❷ [*comida*] to rustle up
✦ *vi* ❶ [*generalmente*] to improvise ❷ MÚSICA to extemporize

improviso ◼ **de improviso** *locución adverbial* unexpectedly • **coger a alguien de improviso** to catch somebody unawares

imprudencia *sf* ❶ [*en los actos*] carelessness ☌ *incontable* ❷ [*en los comentarios*] indiscretion

imprudente *adj* ❶ [*en los actos*] careless • **muchos manejan en forma imprudente** many people drive in a careless manner • **sería imprudente tomar una decisión ahora** it would be unwise to make a decision now ❷ [*en los comentarios*] indiscreet • **es muy imprudente, todo lo cuenta** he's very indiscreet, he tells everything ☌ *Los adjetivos ingleses son invariables.*

impuesto, ta *participio pasado* → **imponer**
◼ **impuesto** *sm* tax • **todos deben pagar impuestos** everybody has to pay taxes • **lo compró en la tienda libre de impuestos** he bought it in the duty-free shop ❱ **impuesto de circulación** road tax ❱ **impuesto sobre el valor añadido** value-added tax ❱ **impuesto sobre la renta** ≃ income tax

impulsar *vt* ❶ [*empujar*] to drive • **dos motores impulsan el vehículo** two motors drive the vehicle • **no sabe qué lo impulsó a hacerlo** she doesn't know that she drove him to do it ❷ [*promocionar*] to stimulate

impulsivo, va *adj* impulsive ☌ *Los adjetivos ingleses son invariables.*

impulso *sm* ❶ [*progreso*] stimulus ❷ [*fuerza*] momentum • **hay que tomar bastante impulso antes de saltar** you have to get up enough momentum before jumping ❸ [*motivación*] impulse • **mi primer impulso fue esconderme** my first impulse was to hide • **casi siempre actúa por impulso** he almost always acts on impulse

impulsor, ra *sm, f* dynamic force

impune *adj* unpunished ☌ *Los adjetivos ingleses son invariables.*

impunidad *sf* impunity

impureza *sf* impurity, *plural* impurities

impuro, ra *adj* impure ☌ *Los adjetivos ingleses son invariables.*

inacabable *adj* endless ☌ *Los adjetivos ingleses son invariables.*

inaccesible *adj* inaccessible ☌ *Los adjetivos ingleses son invariables.*

inaceptable *adj* unacceptable ☌ *Los adjetivos ingleses son invariables.*

inactividad *sf* inactivity

inactivo, va *adj* inactive ☌ *Los adjetivos ingleses son invariables.*

inadecuado, da *adj* inappropriate ☌ *Los adjetivos ingleses son invariables.*

inadmisible *adj* inadmissible ☌ *Los adjetivos ingleses son invariables.*

inadvertido, da *adj* unnoticed • **pasar inadvertido** to go unnoticed ☌ *Los adjetivos ingleses son invariables.*

inagotable *adj* inexhaustible ☌ *Los adjetivos ingleses son invariables.*

inaguantable *adj* unbearable • **este calor es inaguantable** this heat is unbearable ☌ *Los adjetivos ingleses son invariables.*

inalámbrico, ca *adj* ❶ cordless ❷ INFORMÁTICA wireless ☌ *Los adjetivos ingleses son invariables.*

inalcanzable *adj* unattainable ☌ *Los adjetivos ingleses son invariables.*

inalterable *adj* ❶ [*generalmente*] unalterable ❷ [*salud*] stable ❸ [*amistad*] undying ❹ [*color*] fast ❺ [*rostro, carácter*] impassive ❻ [*resultado, marcador*] unchanged ☌ *Los adjetivos ingleses son invariables.*

inamovible *adj* fixed ☌ *Los adjetivos ingleses son invariables.*

inanimado, da *adj* inanimate ☌ *Los adjetivos ingleses son invariables.*

inapreciable *adj* ❶ [*incalculable*] invaluable ❷ [*insignificante*] imperceptible ☌ *Los adjetivos ingleses son invariables.*

inapropiado, da *adj* inappropriate ☌ *Los adjetivos ingleses son invariables.*

inaudito, ta *adj* unheard-of ☌ *Los adjetivos ingleses son invariables.*

inauguración *sf* opening • **mañana es la inauguración de la biblioteca** tomorrow is the opening of the library • **la ceremonia de inauguración** the opening ceremony

inaugurar *vt* to inaugurate • **mañana inauguran la nueva biblioteca** tomorrow they inaugurate the new library

inca *adj* & *smf* Inca ☌ *Los adjetivos ingleses son invariables.*

incalculable *adj* incalculable ☌ *Los adjetivos ingleses son invariables.*

incalificable *adj* unspeakable ☌ *Los adjetivos ingleses son invariables.*

incandescente *adj* incandescent ☌ *Los adjetivos ingleses son invariables.*

incansable *adj* tireless:☿ *Los adjetivos ingleses son invariables.*

incapacidad *sf* ❶ [*imposibilidad*] inability • **su absoluta incapacidad para expresarse con corrección** his absolute inability to express himself correctly ❷ [*inaptitud*] incompetence • **la incapacidad de algunos políticos es impresionante** the incompetence of some politicians is amazing ❸ DERECHO incapacity

incapaz *adj* ❶ [*generalmente*] • **incapaz de** incapable of • **es incapaz de hacer una cosa así** he's incapable of doing something like that ❷ [*sin talento*] • **incapaz para** incompetent at; no good at ❸ DERECHO incompetent:☿ *Los adjetivos ingleses son invariables.*

incauto, ta *adj* gullible:☿ *Los adjetivos ingleses son invariables.*

incendiar *vt* to set fire to • **quisieron incendiar el local** they tried to set fire to the place

■ **incendiarse** *v pronominal* to catch fire • **se le incendió la casa al vecino** the neighbor's house caught fire

incendiario, ria ◆ *adj* ❶ [*bomba* ETC] incendiary ❷ [*artículo, libro* ETC] inflammatory:☿ *Los adjetivos ingleses son invariables.*

◆ *sm, f* arsonist

incendio *sm* fire • **no pudieron apagar el incendio** they couldn't put out the fire ▶ **incendio forestal** forest fire ▶ **incendio provocado** arson • **creen que fue un incendio provocado** they believe that it was arson

incentivo *sm* incentive ▶ **incentivo fiscal** tax incentive

incertidumbre *sf* uncertainty, *plural* uncertainties

---

expresar su incertidumbre

• **Do you really think so?** ¿Estás seguro?
• **I'm not so sure.** No estoy muy convencida.
• **Who knows? Maybe he changed his mind.** ¿Quién sabe?, quizás ha cambiado de opinión.
• **I don't really know.** No estoy seguro del todo.
• **I wonder whether I've done the right thing.** Me pregunto si he hecho bien.

---

incidencia *sf* ❶ [*repercusión*] impact ❷ [*suceso*] event

incidente *sm* incident • **el partido terminó sin incidentes** the match ended without incident • **incidente diplomático** diplomatic incident

incienso *sm* incense

incierto, ta *adj* ❶ [*dudoso*] uncertain ❷ [*falso*] untrue:☿ *Los adjetivos ingleses son invariables.*

incineración *sf* ❶ [*de cadáver*] cremation ❷ [*de basura*] incineration

incinerar *vt* ❶ [*cadáver*] to cremate ❷ [*basura*] to incinerate

incipiente *adj* ❶ incipient ❷ [*estado, etapa*] early:☿ *Los adjetivos ingleses son invariables.*

incisión *sf* incision

incisivo, va *adj* ❶ [*instrumento*] sharp ❷ figurado [*mordaz*] incisive:☿ *Los adjetivos ingleses son invariables.*

incitar *vt* • **incitar a alguien a algo** [*violencia, rebelión* ETC] to incite somebody to something • **incitar a alguien a la fuga/venganza** to urge somebody to flee/avenge himself • **incitar a alguien a hacer algo a)** [*rebelarse* ETC] to incite somebody to do something **b)** [*fugarse, vengarse*] to urge somebody to do something

inclinación *sf* ❶ [*desviación*] inclination ❷ [*de terreno*] slope ❸ figurado [*afición*] • **inclinación (a o por)** penchant (for) ❹ [*cariño*] • **inclinación hacia alguien** fondness towards somebody ❺ [*saludo*] bow

inclinar *vt* ❶ [*doblar*] to bend ❷ [*ladear*] to tilt ❸ [*cabeza*] to bow

■ **inclinarse** *v pronominal* ❶ [*doblarse*] to lean • **me incliné sobre la cuna para darle un beso** I leaned over the cradle to give him a kiss • **inclínate hacia adelante** lean forward • **se inclinó para recoger el libro** he bent down to pick up the book ❷ [*para saludar*] • **inclinarse (ante)** to bow (before)

incluir *vt* ❶ [*generalmente*] to include • **el premio incluye el viaje de ida y vuelta y la estadía** the prize includes the round trip and the stay • **se me olvidó incluirlo en la lista** I forgot to include him on the list ❷ [*adjuntar - en cartas*] to enclose

inclusive *adv* • **hay que estudiar hasta el capítulo tres inclusive** we have to study up and including chapter three • **abren todos los días, inclusive días festivos** they're open every day, including holidays

incluso, sa *adj* enclosed:☿ *Los adjetivos ingleses son invariables.*

■ **incluso** *adv* & *preposición* even • **cualquiera lo puede hacer, incluso un niño** anybody can do it, even a child • **incluso nos fue a dejar a la casa** he even left us at the house

incógnito, ta *adj* unknown:☿ *Los adjetivos ingleses son invariables.*

■ **incógnita** *sf* ❶ MATEMÁTICAS unknown quantity ❷ [*misterio*] mystery

incoherencia *sf* ❶ [*cualidad*] incoherence ❷ [*comentario*] nonsensical remark

incoherente *adj* ❶ [*inconexo*] incoherent ❷ [*inconsecuente*] inconsistent:☿ *Los adjetivos ingleses son invariables.*

incoloro, ra *adj* literal & figurado colorless:☿ *Los adjetivos ingleses son invariables.*

incomodar *vt* ❶ [*causar molestia*] to bother ❷ [*enfadar*] to annoy

■ **incomodarse** *v pronominal* [*enfadarse*] • **incomodarse (por)** to get annoyed (about)

incomodidad *sf* ❶ [*de silla* ETC] uncomfortableness ❷ [*de situación, persona*] awkwardness

incómodo, da *adj* ❶ [*silla* ETC] uncomfortable • **las camas son un poco incómodas** the beds are a little uncomfortable • **es muy incómodo estar sin teléfono** it's very inconvenient to be without a telephone ❷ [*situación, persona*] awkward • **sentirse incómodo** to feel awkward:☿ *Los adjetivos ingleses son invariables.*

incomparable *adj* incomparable.💡: *Los adjetivos ingleses son invariables.*

incompatible *adj* • **incompatible (con)** incompatible (with).💡: *Los adjetivos ingleses son invariables.*

incompetencia *sf* incompetence

incompetente *adj* incompetent.💡: *Los adjetivos ingleses son invariables.*

incompleto, ta *adj* ❶ [*generalmente*] incomplete ❷ [*inacabado*] unfinished.💡: *Los adjetivos ingleses son invariables.*

incomprendido, da *adj* misunderstood.💡: *Los adjetivos ingleses son invariables.*

incomprensible *adj* incomprehensible.💡: *Los adjetivos ingleses son invariables.*

incomprensión *sf* lack of understanding

incomunicado, da *adj* ❶ [*generalmente*] isolated ❷ [*por la nieve* ETC] cut off ❸ [*preso*] in solitary confinement.💡: *Los adjetivos ingleses son invariables.*

inconcebible *adj* inconceivable.💡: *Los adjetivos ingleses son invariables.*

incondicional ♦ *adj* ❶ unconditional ❷ [*ayuda*] wholehearted ❸ [*seguidor*] staunch.💡: *Los adjetivos ingleses son invariables.*
♦ *smf* staunch supporter

inconformista *adj* & *smf* nonconformist.💡: *Los adjetivos ingleses son invariables.*

inconfundible *adj* ❶ unmistakable ❷ [*prueba*] irrefutable.💡: *Los adjetivos ingleses son invariables.*

inconsciencia *sf* ❶ [*generalmente*] unconsciousness ❷ *figurado* [*falta de juicio*] thoughtlessness

inconsciente *adj* ❶ [*generalmente*] unconscious • **está vivo pero inconsciente** he's alive but unconscious • **cayó inconsciente al suelo** he fell unconscious to the floor ❷ *figurado* [*irreflexivo*] thoughtless • **¡cómo pueden ser tan inconscientes!** how can you be so thoughtless!.💡: *Los adjetivos ingleses son invariables.*

inconsistente *adj* ❶ [*tela, pared* ETC] flimsy ❷ [*salsa*] runny ❸ [*argumento, discurso* ETC] lacking in substance.💡: *Los adjetivos ingleses son invariables.*

inconstancia *sf* ❶ [*en el trabajo, la conducta*] unreliability ❷ [*de opinión, ideas*] changeability

inconstante *adj* ❶ [*en el trabajo, la conducta*] unreliable ❷ [*de opinión, ideas*] changeable.💡: *Los adjetivos ingleses son invariables.*

incontable *adj* countless.💡: *Los adjetivos ingleses son invariables.*

incontinencia *sf* incontinence

incontrolable *adj* uncontrollable.💡: *Los adjetivos ingleses son invariables.*

inconveniente ♦ *adj* ❶ [*inoportuno*] inappropriate ❷ [*descortés*] rude.💡: *Los adjetivos ingleses son invariables.*
♦ *sm* ❶ [*dificultad*] problem • **surgieron algunos inconvenientes** some problems came up • **el inconveniente es que está en el tercer piso** the problem is that it's on the third floor • **no tener inconveniente en hacer algo** to have no objection to doing something ❷ [*desventaja*] drawback

incordiar *vt familiar* to pester

incorporación *sf* • **incorporación (a) a)** [*generalmente*] incorporation (into) **b)** [*a un puesto*] induction (into)

incorporar *vt* ❶ [*añadir*] • **incorporar (a) a)** [*generalmente*] to incorporate (into) **b)** COCINA to mix (into) ❷ [*levantar*] to sit up

incorrección *sf* ❶ [*inexactitud*] incorrectness ❷ [*error gramatical*] mistake ❸ [*descortesía*] lack of courtesy

incorrecto, ta *adj* ❶ [*equivocado*] incorrect ❷ [*descortés*] rude.💡: *Los adjetivos ingleses son invariables.*

incorregible *adj* incorrigible.💡: *Los adjetivos ingleses son invariables.*

incredulidad *sf* incredulity

expresar su incredulidad

- **It's not possible!** ¡No puede ser!
- **Really?** ¿De veras?
- **No way!** ¡No es cierto!
- **It's absolutely unbelievable!** ¡Parece mentira!
- **Who'd have thought it?** ¿Quién lo hubiera creído?
- **It's inconceivable!** ¡Es impensable!

incrédulo, la *adj* ❶ [*desconfiado*] skeptical ❷ RELIGIÓN unbelieving.💡: *Los adjetivos ingleses son invariables.*

increíble *adj* ❶ [*inconcebible*] unbelievable • **es increíble que pasen cosas así** it's hard to believe that such things can happen ❷ [*extraordinario*] incredible • **nos pasó algo increíble** something incredible happened to us.💡: *Los adjetivos ingleses son invariables.*

incrementar *vt* to increase

incremento *sm* ❶ increase ❷ [*de temperatura*] rise ▶ **incremento salarial** pay increase

incriminar *vt* to accuse

incubar *vt* ❶ [*huevo*] to incubate ❷ [*enfermedad*] to be sickening for

inculpar *vt* • **inculpar a alguien (de) a)** [*generalmente*] to accuse somebody (of) **b)** DERECHO to charge somebody (with)

inculto, ta ♦ *adj* [*persona*] uneducated.💡: *Los adjetivos ingleses son invariables.*
♦ *sm, f* ignoramus

incumplimiento *sm* ❶ [*de deber*] failure to fulfil ❷ [*de orden, ley*] non-compliance ▶ **incumplimiento de contrato** breach of contract ❸ [*de promesa*] failure to keep

incumplir *vt* ❶ [*deber*] to fail to fulfil ❷ [*orden, ley*] to fail to comply with ❸ [*promesa*] to break ❹ [*contrato*] to breach

incurable *adj* incurable.💡: *Los adjetivos ingleses son invariables.*

incursión *sf* incursion

G

I

indecencia *sf* ❶ [*cualidad*] indecency ❷ [*acción*] outrage

indecente *adj* ❶ [*impúdico*] indecent ❷ [*indigno*] miserable:🔆 *Los adjetivos ingleses son invariables.*

indecisión *sf* indecisiveness

indeciso, sa ◆ *adj* ❶ [*persona - inseguro*] indecisive; [*- que está dudoso*] undecided • **siempre ha sido muy indecisa** she's always been very indecisive • **está indeciso, no sabe si ir o no** he can't make up his mind, he doesn't know whether to go or not ❷ [*pregunta, respuesta*] hesitant ❸ [*resultado*] undecided:🔆 *Los adjetivos ingleses son invariables.*

◆ *sm, f* undecided voter

indefenso, sa *adj* defenceless:🔆 *Los adjetivos ingleses son invariables.*

indefinido, da *adj* ❶ [*ilimitado*] indefinite • **se lo prestó por tiempo indefinido** she loaned it to him for an indefinite period of time ❷ [*contrato*] open-ended ❸ [*impreciso*] indeterminate • **tiene los ojos de un color indefinido** his eyes are an indeterminate color ❹ GRAMÁTICA indefinite • **el artículo indefinido** the indefinite article:🔆 *Los adjetivos ingleses son invariables.*

indeleble *adj culto* indelible:🔆 *Los adjetivos ingleses son invariables.*

indemnización *sf* ❶ [*generalmente*] compensation ❷ [*por despido*] severance pay▶ **indemnización por daños y perjuicios** DERECHO damages *pl*

indemnizar *vt* • **indemnizar a alguien (por)** to compensate somebody (for)

independencia *sf* independence • **con independencia de** independently of

independiente *adj* ❶ [*generalmente*] independent ❷ [*aparte*] separate:🔆 *Los adjetivos ingleses son invariables.*

independizar *vt* to grant independence to

■ **independizarse** *v pronominal* • **independizarse (de)** to become independent (of) • **es natural que quieran independizarse de los padres** it's natural that they want to become independent from their parents

indeseable *adj* undesirable:🔆 *Los adjetivos ingleses son invariables.*

indeterminación *sf* indecisiveness

indeterminado, da *adj* ❶ [*sin determinar*] indeterminate • **el boleto es válido para un número indeterminado de viajes** the ticket is valid for an indeterminate number of trips • **por tiempo indeterminado** indefinitely ❷ [*impreciso*] vague:🔆 *Los adjetivos ingleses son invariables.*

indexar *vt* INFORMÁTICA to index

India *nombre propio* • **(la) India** India

indiano, na *sm, f* ❶ [*indígena*] (Latin American) Indian ❷ [*emigrante*] *para explicar lo que es puedes decir:* it's someone from Spain who emigrated to Latin America and went back after making their fortune

indicación *sf* ❶ [*señal, gesto*] sign ❷ [*instrucción*] instruction ❸ [*para llegar a un sitio*] • **indicaciones** directions *pl* ❹ [*nota, corrección*] note

indicado, da *adj* suitable:🔆 *Los adjetivos ingleses son invariables.*

indicar *vt* ❶ [*señalar*] to show • **me indicó en el mapa cómo llegar** he showed me on the map how to get there ❷ [*señal, instrumento*] to indicate • **el barómetro indica mal tiempo** the barometer indicates bad weather • **con un gesto nos indicó que nos sentáramos** with a gesture he signaled for us to sit down ❸ [*prescribir*] to advise • **el médico me indicó que tomara tres al día** the doctor advised me to take three a day

índice *sm* ❶ [*generalmente*] index • **lo busqué en el índice** I looked it up in the index ▶ **índice alfabético** alphabetical index ▶ **índice del coste de la vida** cost of living index ▶ **índice de materias** o **temático** table of contents ❷ [*proporción*] rate ▶ **índice de natalidad** birth rate ▶ **índice de mortalidad** mortality rate ❸ [*señal*] indicator ▶ **índice económico** economic indicator ❹ [*catálogo*] catalogue ❺ [*dedo*] index finger • **lo indicó con el índice** he pointed to it with his index finger

indicio *sm* ❶ sign • **la fiebre es un mal indicio** fever is a bad sign ❷ [*pista*] clue ❸ [*cantidad pequeña*] trace

Índico *sm* • **el (océano) Índico** the Indian Ocean

indiferencia *sf* indifference

expresar su indiferencia

- **I don't mind either way.** Me da igual.
- **It's all the same to me.** Me da igual.
- **It has nothing to do with me.** ¡Esto no es asunto mío!
- **Bad luck!** ¡Mala suerte!
- **It doesn't matter.** ¡Qué importa!
- **That's your business.** Es cosa tuya.
- **If you like.** Si tú lo dices.

indiferente *adj* indifferent • **son indiferentes a todo lo que pasa en el mundo** they're indifferent to everything that happens in the world • **es indiferente que sea blanco o negro** it makes no difference whether it's white or black:🔆 *Los adjetivos ingleses son invariables.*

indígena ◆ *adj* indigenous:🔆 *Los adjetivos ingleses son invariables.*

◆ *smf* native

indigente *adj* destitute:🔆 *Los adjetivos ingleses son invariables.*

indigestión *sf* indigestion

indigesto, ta *adj* [*comida, libro*] heavy:🔆 *Los adjetivos ingleses son invariables.*

indignación *sf* indignation

indignar *vt* to anger • **le indigna que ponga la música tan fuerte** it angers him that they play the music so loud

■ **indignarse** *v pronominal* • **indignarse (por)** to get angry (about) • **se indigna cuando le mienten** she gets angry when they lie to her • **numerosos son los que se indignan por el maltrato dado a los emigran-**

tes many people are outraged by the ill-treatment of emigrants

indigno, na *adj* ❶ [*generalmente*] • **indigno (de)** unworthy (of) ❷ [*impropio*] wrong ❸ [*vergonzoso*] contemptible ஃ *Los adjetivos ingleses son invariables.*

indio, dia ◆ *adj* Indian ஃ *Los adjetivos ingleses son invariables.*

◆ *sm, f* Indian ▶ **indio americano** Native American ***expresión*** **hacer el indio** to play the fool

indirecto, ta *adj* indirect ஃ *Los adjetivos ingleses son invariables.*

■ **indirecta** *sf* hint • **lanzar una indirecta a alguien** to drop a hint to somebody

indisciplina *sf* lack of discipline

indiscreción *sf* ❶ [*cualidad*] indiscretion ❷ [*comentario*] indiscreet remark • **si no es indiscreción** if you don't mind my asking

indiscreto, ta *adj* ❶ [*sin discreción*] indiscreet • **fue una pregunta muy indiscreta** it was a very indiscreet question ❷ [*sin tacto*] tactless • **fue muy indiscreto al hacerle esa pregunta** he was very tactless to ask her that question ஃ *Los adjetivos ingleses son invariables.*

indiscutible *adj* ❶ [*generalmente*] indisputable ❷ [*poder*] undisputed ஃ *Los adjetivos ingleses son invariables.*

indispensable *adj* indispensable • **es indispensable tener experiencia** it's indispensable to have experience • **traigan sólo lo indispensable** bring only the essentials ஃ *Los adjetivos ingleses son invariables.*

indispuesto, ta *adj* unwell ஃ *Los adjetivos ingleses son invariables.*

indistinto, ta *adj* ❶ [*indiferente*] • **es indistinto** it makes no difference ❷ [*cuenta, cartilla*] joint ❸ [*perfil, figura*] indistinct ஃ *Los adjetivos ingleses son invariables.*

individual *adj* ❶ [*generalmente*] individual • **nos sirvieron porciones individuales** they served us individual portions ❷ [*habitación, cama*] single • **mi casa tiene un dormitorio individual y dos dobles** my house has one single bedroom and two doubles ❸ [*despacho*] personal ❹ [*prueba, competición*] singles ஃ *Sólo se usa delante del sustantivo.* • **competición individual** singles competition

individualizar *vi* to single people out

individuo, dua *sm, f* individual • **todo individuo tiene derecho a la vida** every individual has a right to life

indocumentado, da *adj* ❶ [*sin documentación*] without identity papers ❷ [*ignorante*] ignorant ஃ *Los adjetivos ingleses son invariables.*

Indonesia *nombre propio* Indonesia

inducir *vt* • **inducir a alguien a algo/a hacer algo** to lead somebody into something/into doing something • **inducir a error** to mislead

indudable *adj* undoubted ஃ *Los adjetivos ingleses son invariables.*

indultar *vt* to pardon

indulto *sm* pardon

industria *sf* industry, *plural* industries

industrial ◆ *adj* industrial ஃ *Los adjetivos ingleses son invariables.*

◆ *smf* industrialist

industrializar *vt* to industrialize

inédito, ta *adj* ❶ [*no publicado*] unpublished ❷ [*sorprendente*] unprecedented ஃ *Los adjetivos ingleses son invariables.*

ineficaz *adj* ❶ [*de bajo rendimiento*] inefficient ❷ [*de baja efectividad*] ineffective ஃ *Los adjetivos ingleses son invariables.*

ineficiente *adj* ❶ [*de bajo rendimiento*] inefficient ❷ [*de baja efectividad*] ineffective ஃ *Los adjetivos ingleses son invariables.*

ineludible *adj* unavoidable ஃ *Los adjetivos ingleses son invariables.*

inepto, ta *adj* inept ஃ *Los adjetivos ingleses son invariables.*

inequívoco, ca *adj* ❶ [*apoyo, resultado*] unequivocal ❷ [*señal, voz*] unmistakeable ஃ *Los adjetivos ingleses son invariables.*

inercia *sf* inertia

inesperado, da *adj* unexpected ஃ *Los adjetivos ingleses son invariables.*

inestable *adj* unstable • **esta mesa es un poco inestable** this table is a little unstable • **el tiempo ha estado muy inestable** the weather has been very changeable ஃ *Los adjetivos ingleses son invariables.*

inevitable *adj* inevitable ஃ *Los adjetivos ingleses son invariables.*

inexacto, ta *adj* ❶ [*impreciso*] inaccurate ❷ [*erróneo*] incorrect ஃ *Los adjetivos ingleses son invariables.*

inexistente *adj* nonexistent ஃ *Los adjetivos ingleses son invariables.*

inexperiencia *sf* inexperience

inexperto, ta *adj* ❶ [*falto de experiencia*] inexperienced ❷ [*falto de habilidad*] unskilful ஃ *Los adjetivos ingleses son invariables.*

inexpresivo, va *adj* expressionless ஃ *Los adjetivos ingleses son invariables.*

infalible *adj* infallible ஃ *Los adjetivos ingleses son invariables.*

infancia *sf* [*periodo*] childhood

infante, ta *sm, f* ❶ [*niño*] infant ❷ [*hijo del rey*] prince, *femenino* princess

infantería *sf* infantry ▶ **infantería ligera** light infantry

infantil *adj* ❶ [*para niños*] children's ஃ *Sólo se usa delante del sustantivo.* • **un cuento infantil** a children's story ❷ [*de niños*] child ஃ *Sólo se usa delante del sustantivo.* • **psicología infantil** child psychology ❸ *figurado* [*inmaduro*] childish • **es muy infantil para su edad** he's very childish for his age

infarto *sm* heart attack • **le dio un infarto** she had a heart attack ▶ **infarto cerebral** stroke

expresión de infarto *familiar* heart-stopping

infatigable *adj* tireless. ☼ *Los adjetivos ingleses son invariables.*

infección *sf* infection • **tiene una infección en la garganta** she has a throat infection

infeccioso, sa *adj* infectious. ☼ *Los adjetivos ingleses son invariables.*

infectar *vt* to infect • **se le infectó la herida** his wound became infected

■ **infectarse** *v pronominal* to become infected • **mi computadora se infectó con un virus** my computer became infected with a virus

infeliz *adj* ❶ [*desgraciado*] unhappy ❷ *figurado* [*ingenuo*] gullible. ☼ *Los adjetivos ingleses son invariables.*

inferior ◆ *adj* lower • **la parte inferior de la pantalla** the lower part of the screen • **el párpado inferior** the lower eyelid • **productos de calidad inferior** inferior-quality products • **inferior (a) a)** [*en espacio, cantidad*] lower (than) **b)** [*en calidad*] inferior (to) • **temperaturas inferiores a lo normal** lower than normal temperatures • **se siente inferior a su hermano** he feels inferior to his brother • **un número inferior a cincuenta** a number below fifty. ☼ *Los adjetivos ingleses son invariables.*
◆ *smf* inferior

inferioridad *sf* inferiority • **estar en inferioridad de condiciones** to be at a disadvantage

infernal *adj* literal & figurado infernal. ☼ *Los adjetivos ingleses son invariables.*

infestar *vt* ❶ to infest ❷ [*sujeto: carteles, propaganda* ETC] to be plastered across

infidelidad *sf* ❶ [*conyugal*] infidelity ❷ [*a la patria, un amigo*] disloyalty

infiel ◆ *adj* ❶ [*desleal - cónyuge*] unfaithful; [*- amigo*] disloyal ❷ [*inexacto*] inaccurate. ☼ *Los adjetivos ingleses son invariables.*
◆ *smf* RELIGIÓN infidel

infierno *sm* literal & figurado hell

expresión en el quinto infierno in the middle of nowhere ▸ ¡vete al infierno! go to hell!

infiltrado, da *sm, f* infiltrator

infiltrar *vt* to infiltrate

ínfimo, ma *adj* ❶ [*calidad, categoría*] extremely low ❷ [*precio*] giveaway ❸ [*importancia*] minimal. ☼ *Los adjetivos ingleses son invariables.*

infinidad *sf* ❶ • **una infinidad de** an infinite number of ❷ *figurado* masses of • **tengo una infinidad de cosas que hacer** I have masses of things to do

infinitivo *sm* infinitive

infinito, ta *adj* infinite • **tiene una paciencia infinita** she has infinite patience. ☼ *Los adjetivos ingleses son invariables.*
■ **infinito** *sm* infinity

inflación *sf* ECONOMÍA inflation ▸ **inflación subyacente** underlying inflation

inflamable *adj* inflammable. ☼ *Los adjetivos ingleses son invariables.*

inflamación *sf* MEDICINA inflammation

inflamar *vt* figurado MEDICINA to inflame

inflamatorio, ria *adj* inflammatory. ☼ *Los adjetivos ingleses son invariables.*

inflar *vt* ❶ [*soplando*] to blow up • **hay que inflar los globos** you have to blow up the balloons ❷ [*con bomba*] to pump up • **paramos para inflar una rueda** we stopped in order to pump up a tire ❸ *figurado* [*exagerar*] to blow up • **inflar una situación** to blow up a situation

inflexible *adj* literal & figurado inflexible • **el profesor es muy inflexible con los alumnos** the professor is very inflexible with the students. ☼ *Los adjetivos ingleses son invariables.*

infligir *vt* ❶ [*dolor*] to inflict ❷ [*castigo*] to impose

influencia *sf* influence • **tiene mucha influencia sobre los alumnos** she has a lot of influence over her students • **una persona de mucha influencia** a very influential person • **bajo la influencia del alcohol** under the influence of alcohol

influenciar *vt* to influence

influir ◆ *vt* to influence
◆ *vi* to have influence • **influir en** to influence • **las personas que más han influido en mí** the people that have influenced me most

influyente *adj* influential. ☼ *Los adjetivos ingleses son invariables.*

infografía *sf* computer graphics *pl*

información *sf* ❶ [*conocimiento*] information. ☼ *incontable* • **hay mucha información sobre becas** there is a lot of information about scholarships • **es una información muy valiosa** it's a very valuable piece of information ❷ PRENSA [*noticias*] news. ☼ *incontable*; [*noticia*] report; piece of news; [*sección*] section • **me leí sólo la información internacional** I read only the international news ▸ **información meteorológica** weather report ❸ [*oficina*] information office ❹ [*mostrador*] information desk • **preguntemos en información a qué hora llega** let's ask at the information desk when it's arriving ❺ TELECOMUNICACIONES directory assistance • **en información te pueden dar el número** directory assistance can give you the number

---

pedir información

• **Excuse me, please!** ¡Disculpe, por favor!

• **Can you tell me where the market is?** ¿Me sabría decir dónde se encuentra el mercado?

• **Do you know what time the train to Boston leaves?** ¿Sabe a qué hora sale el tren para Boston?

• **What's the time, please?** Por favor, ¿qué hora tiene?

• **What time are you open until today?** ¿Hasta qué hora están abiertos hoy?

• **Could you give me change for 50 pesos?** ¿Tiene cambio de 50 pesos?

informal *adj* ❶ [*desenfadado*] informal • **un ambiente muy informal** a very informal atmosphere • **había gente vestida de fiesta y con ropa informal** there were people dressed for a party and in casual clothes ❷ [*irresponsable*] unreliable • **Pepe es muy informal** Pepe is very unreliable ☼ *Los adjetivos ingleses son invariables.*

informante *smf* informant

informar ◆ *vt* • **informar a alguien (de)** to inform somebody (about) • **nos informaron que el avión venía atrasado** they informed us that the airplane was late • **informaron la hora de llegada por los altoparlantes** they announced the time of arrival on the loudspeakers • **¿me podría informar sobre el programa de becas?** could I get some information about the scholarship program? • **me informaron mal** they misinformed me
◆ *vi* ❶ to inform ❷ PRENSA to report

informático, ca ◆ *adj* computer ☼ *Sólo se usa delante del sustantivo.*
◆ *sm, f* [*persona*] computer expert
■ **informática** *sf* [*ciencia*] information technology

informatizar *vt* to computerize

informe ◆ *adj* shapeless ☼ *Los adjetivos ingleses son invariables.*
◆ *sm* ❶ [*generalmente*] report • **según un informe de la policía** according to a police report ❷ DERECHO plea

infracción *sf* ❶ infringement ❷ [*de circulación*] offence • **lo multaron por una infracción de tráfico** they fined him for a traffic offense

infraestructura *sf* infrastructure

infrahumano, na *adj* subhuman ☼ *Los adjetivos ingleses son invariables.*

infranqueable *adj* ❶ impassable ❷ *figurado* insurmountable ☼ *Los adjetivos ingleses son invariables.*

infrarrojo, ja *adj* infrared ☼ *Los adjetivos ingleses son invariables.*

infravalorar *vt* to undervalue

infringir *vt* [*reglas*] to infringe

infundado, da *adj* unfounded ☼ *Los adjetivos ingleses son invariables.*

infusión *sf* infusion • **infusión de manzanilla** camomile tea

ingeniería *sf* engineering

ingeniero, ra *sm, f* engineer • **es ingeniero** he's an engineer ▶ **ingeniero de caminos, canales y puertos** civil engineer

ingenio *sm* ❶ [*inteligencia*] ingenuity • **gracias al ingenio de Pepe** thanks to Pepe's ingenuity ❷ [*agudeza*] wit ❸ [*máquina*] device • **ingenio nuclear** nuclear device ▶ **ingenio azucarero** sugar refinery

ingenioso, sa *adj* ❶ [*inteligente*] clever • **es un muchacho muy ingenioso** he's a very clever guy • **siempre tiene ideas ingeniosas** she always has clever ideas ❷ [*agudo*] witty • **hizo un comentario muy ingenioso** he made a very witty comment ☼ *Los adjetivos ingleses son invariables.*

ingenuidad *sf* naivety

ingenuo, nua *adj* naive ☼ *Los adjetivos ingleses son invariables.*

ingerir *vt* to ingest

Inglaterra *nombre propio* England

ingle *sf* groin

inglés, esa ◆ *adj* English ☼ *Los adjetivos ingleses son invariables.*
En inglés, los adjetivos que se refieren a un país o una región se escriben con mayúscula.
◆ *sm, f* [*persona*] Englishman, *femenino* Englishwoman • **los ingleses** the English
■ **inglés** *sm* [*lengua*] English

ingrediente *sm* ingredient

ingresar ◆ *vt* BANCA to pay in
◆ *vi* • **ingresar (en) a)** [*asociación, ejército*] to join **b)** [*hospital*] to be admitted (to) **c)** [*universidad*] to start **d)** [*convento*] to enter • **me gustaría ingresar al nuevo club de tenis** I would like to join the new tennis club • **ingresó ayer al hospital** he was admitted to hospital yesterday • **el próximo año ingresa a la universidad** he starts college next year • **ingresar cadáver** to be dead on arrival

ingreso *sm* ❶ [*generalmente*] entry ❷ [*en asociación, ejército*] joining ❸ [*en hospital, universidad*] admission ❹ BANCA deposit • **hacer un ingreso** to make a deposit
■ **ingresos** *smpl* ❶ [*sueldo* ETC] income ☼ *incontable* • **tienen muy poco ingresos** they have very little income ▶ **ingresos brutos/netos** gross/net income ❷ [*recaudación*] revenue ☼ *incontable*

inhalador *sm* inhaler

inhalar *vt* to inhale

inherente *adj* • **inherente (a)** inherent (in) ☼ *Los adjetivos ingleses son invariables.*

inhibir *vt* to inhibit

inhumano, na *adj* ❶ [*despiadado*] inhuman ❷ [*desconsiderado*] inhumane ☼ *Los adjetivos ingleses son invariables.*

iniciación *sf* ❶ [*generalmente*] initiation ❷ [*de suceso, curso*] start

inicial *adj* & *sf* initial • **pon tus iniciales aquí** put your initials here ☼ *Los adjetivos ingleses son invariables.*

inicializar *vt* INFORMÁTICA to initialize

iniciar *vt* ❶ [*generalmente*] to start ❷ [*debate, discusión*] to start off

iniciativa *sf* initiative • **no tener iniciativa** to lack initiative • **por iniciativa propia** on your own initiative • **iniciativa de paz** peace initiative

inicio *sm* start

inigualable *adj* unrivalled ☼ *Los adjetivos ingleses son invariables.*

injertar *vt* to graft

injerto *sm* graft

injusticia *sf* injustice • **hay muchas injusticias en el mundo** there are many injustices in the world • **¡es una injusticia!** that's unfair! • **es una injusticia que**

lo hayan castigado it's an injustice that they've punished him • **cometer una injusticia con alguien** to do somebody an injustice

injustificado, da *adj* unjustified.🔧 *Los adjetivos ingleses son invariables.*

injusto, ta *adj* unfair • **es un castigo injusto** it's an unfair punishment • **han sido muy injustos con él** they've been very unfair to him.🔧 *Los adjetivos ingleses son invariables.*

inmadurez *sf* immaturity

inmaduro, ra *adj* immature.🔧 *Los adjetivos ingleses son invariables.*

inmediatamente *adv* immediately

inmediato, ta *adj* ❶ [*generalmente*] immediate • **el alivio fue inmediato** the relief was immediate • **de inmediato** immediately • **do it immediately** do it immediately ❷ [*contiguo*] next.🔧 *Los adjetivos ingleses son invariables.*

inmejorable *adj* unbeatable.🔧 *Los adjetivos ingleses son invariables.*

inmenso, sa *adj* immense • **tiene un jardín inmenso** he has an immense garden • **la inmensa mayoría de los estudiantes** the vast majority of the students.🔧 *Los adjetivos ingleses son invariables.*

inmersión *sf* ❶ immersion▸ **inmersión lingüística** language immersion ❷ [*de submarinista*] dive

inmerso, sa *adj* • **inmerso (en)** immersed (in).🔧 *Los adjetivos ingleses son invariables.*

inmigración *sf* immigration

inmigrante *smf* immigrant

inmigrar *vi* to immigrate

inminente *adj* imminent.🔧 *Los adjetivos ingleses son invariables.*

inmobiliario, ria *adj* real estate.🔧 *Sólo se usa delante del sustantivo.*

■ **inmobiliaria** *sf* real estate office

inmoral *adj* immoral.🔧 *Los adjetivos ingleses son invariables.*

inmortal *adj* immortal.🔧 *Los adjetivos ingleses son invariables.*

inmortalizar *vt* to immortalize

inmóvil *adj* ❶ motionless • **se quedó inmóvil** he remained motionless ❷ [*coche, tren*] stationary.🔧 *Los adjetivos ingleses son invariables.*

inmovilizar *vt* to immobilize

inmueble ◆ *adj* • **bienes inmuebles** real estate.🔧 *incontable Los adjetivos ingleses son invariables.*

◆ *sm* [*edificio*] building

inmune *adj* MEDICINA immune • **con la vacuna estoy inmune al contagio** with the vaccine I am immune to the infection.🔧 *Los adjetivos ingleses son invariables.*

inmunidad *sf* immunity▸ **inmunidad diplomática/parlamentaria** diplomatic/parliamentary immunity

inmunizar *vt* to immunize

innecesario, ria *adj* unnecessary.🔧 *Los adjetivos ingleses son invariables.*

innovación *sf* innovation

innovador, ra ◆ *adj* innovative.🔧 *Los adjetivos ingleses son invariables.*

◆ *sm, f* innovator

innovar *vt* [*método, técnica*] to improve on

innumerable *adj* countless.🔧 *Los adjetivos ingleses son invariables.*

inocencia *sf* innocence

inocente *adj* ❶ [*generalmente*] DERECHO innocent • **un niño inocente** an innocent child • **declarar inocente a alguien** to find somebody not guilty ❷ [*ingenuo - persona*] naive • **¡no seas inocente!** don't be naïve! ❸ [*sin maldad - persona*] harmless.🔧 *Los adjetivos ingleses son invariables.*

inofensivo, va *adj* harmless.🔧 *Los adjetivos ingleses son invariables.*

inolvidable *adj* unforgettable.🔧 *Los adjetivos ingleses son invariables.*

inoportuno, na *adj* ❶ [*en mal momento*] inopportune ❷ [*molesto*] inconvenient ❸ [*inadecuado*] inappropriate.🔧 *Los adjetivos ingleses son invariables.*

inoxidable *adj* [*acero*] stainless.🔧 *Los adjetivos ingleses son invariables.*

inquebrantable *adj* ❶ unshakeable ❷ [*lealtad*] unswerving.🔧 *Los adjetivos ingleses son invariables.*

inquietar *vt* to worry

inquieto, ta *adj* ❶ [*preocupado*] • **inquieto (por)** worried (about) • **están inquietos porque no ha escrito** they're worried because he hasn't written ❷ [*agitado, emprendedor*] restless • **mi hermano menor es muy inquieto** my little brother is very restless.🔧 *Los adjetivos ingleses son invariables.*

inquietud *sf* worry

inquilino, na *sm, f* tenant

insaciable *adj* insatiable.🔧 *Los adjetivos ingleses son invariables.*

insatisfecho, cha *adj* ❶ [*descontento*] dissatisfied ❷ [*no saciado*] unsatisfied.🔧 *Los adjetivos ingleses son invariables.*

inscribir *vt* ❶ [*grabar*] • **inscribir algo (en)** to engrave something (on) ❷ [*apuntar*] • **inscribir algo/a alguien (en)** to register something/somebody (on)

■ **inscribirse** *v pronominal* • **inscribirse (en) a)** [*generalmente*] to enroll (in) **b)** [*asociación*] to join **c)** [*concurso*] to enter • **me inscribí en el curso de inglés** I enrolled in the English course • **se inscribió en un club de golf** he joined a golf club • **se ha inscrito en la lista de espera** he's put his name down on the waiting list

inscripción *sf* ❶ EDUCACIÓN enrollment; registration • **mañana abren la inscripción** enrollment starts tomorrow ❷ [*en censo, registro*] registration ❸ [*en partido* ETC] enrollment ❹ [*en concursos* ETC] entry ❺ [*escrito*] inscription • **a la entrada hay una inscripción con la fecha** at the entrance there is an inscription with the date

insecticida *sm* insecticide

insecto *sm* insect

inseguridad *sf* ❶ [*falta de confianza*] insecurity, *plural* insecurities • **se esfuerza por superar su inseguridad** he strives to overcome his insecurity ❷ [*duda*] uncertainty ❸ [*peligro*] lack of safety

inseguro, ra *adj* ❶ [*sin confianza*] insecure ❷ [*dudoso*] uncertain ❸ [*peligroso*] unsafe ❖ *Los adjetivos ingleses son invariables.*

inseminación *sf* insemination ▶ **inseminación artificial** artificial insemination

insensatez *sf* foolishness • **hacer/decir una insensatez** to do/say something foolish

insensato, ta ◆ *adj* foolish ❖ *Los adjetivos ingleses son invariables.*
◆ *sm, f* fool

insensibilidad *sf* ❶ [*emocional*] insensitivity ❷ [*física*] numbness

insensible *adj* ❶ [*indiferente*] • **insensible (a)** insensitive (to) • **es una persona muy insensible** he's a very insensitive person • **son insensibles al frío** they're not sensitive to the cold ❷ [*entumecido*] numb • **el brazo derecho le quedó insensible** his right arm became numb ❸ [*imperceptible*] imperceptible ❖ *Los adjetivos ingleses son invariables.*

insertar *vt* [*generalmente*] INFORMÁTICA • **insertar (en)** to insert (into)

inservible *adj* useless • **tiene tantas cosas inservibles en su escritorio** he has so many useless things in his desk • **lo metió en lavadora y quedó inservible** he put it in the washer and it came out unusable ❖ *Los adjetivos ingleses son invariables.*

insignia *sf* ❶ [*distintivo*] badge ❷ MILITAR insignia ❸ [*bandera*] flag

insignificante *adj* insignificant ❖ *Los adjetivos ingleses son invariables.*

insinuar *vt* • **insinuar algo (a)** to insinuate something (to) • **insinuó que yo había copiado** he insinuated that I had copied • **insinuó que le gustaría venir** she hinted that she would like to come

insípido, da *adj* literal & figurado insipid ❖ *Los adjetivos ingleses son invariables.*

insistencia *sf* insistence

insistir *vi* to insist • **por más que insista no le van a dar permiso** however much he insists, they are not going to give him permission • **insistir (en)** to insist (on) • **insiste en que quiere hacerlo él solo** he insists that he wants to do it by himself

insolación *sf* MEDICINA sunstroke ❖ *incontable* • **le dio una insolación** she got sunstroke

insolencia *sf* insolence • **no sé cómo toleran su insolencia** I don't know how they tolerate his insolence • **fue una insolencia hablarle así a tu abuela** it was rude to speak to your grandmother that way

insolente *adj* ❶ [*descarado*] insolent ❷ [*orgulloso*] haughty ❖ *Los adjetivos ingleses son invariables.*

insolidario, ria *adj* lacking in solidarity ❖ *Los adjetivos ingleses son invariables.*

insólito, ta *adj* very unusual ❖ *Los adjetivos ingleses son invariables.*

insoluble *adj* insoluble ❖ *Los adjetivos ingleses son invariables.*

insolvencia *sf* insolvency

insolvente *adj* insolvent ❖ *Los adjetivos ingleses son invariables.*

insomnio *sm* insomnia

insonorizar *vt* to soundproof

insoportable *adj* unbearable ❖ *Los adjetivos ingleses son invariables.*

insostenible *adj* untenable ❖ *Los adjetivos ingleses son invariables.*

inspección *sf* ❶ inspection ▶ **inspección ocular** visual inspection ❷ [*policial*] search

inspeccionar *vt* ❶ to inspect ❷ [*sujeto: policía*] to search

inspector, ra *sm, f* inspector ▶ **inspector de aduanas** customs official ▶ **inspector de Hacienda** tax inspector

inspiración *sf* ❶ [*generalmente*] inspiration ❷ [*respiración*] inhalation

inspirar *vt* ❶ [*generalmente*] to inspire • **inspira respeto** he inspires respect • **no me inspira confianza** he doesn't inspire my confidence ❷ [*respirar*] to inhale • **inspire por favor** inhale please

instalación *sf* ❶ [*generalmente*] installation • **la instalación es gratis** installation is free ▶ **instalación eléctrica** wiring ❷ [*de gente*] settling

instalar *vt* ❶ [*montar - antena* ETC] to install; [*- local, puesto* ETC] to set up • **instalaron un sistema de seguridad** they installed a security system • **no puede instalar el programa** he can't install the program ❷ [*situar - objeto*] to place; [*- gente*] to settle
■ **instalarse** *v pronominal* [*establecerse*] • **instalarse en a)** to settle (down) in **b)** [*nueva casa*] to move into • **se instalaron en el extranjero** they settled out of the country

instancia *sf* ❶ [*solicitud*] application (form) ❷ [*ruego*] request • **a instancias de** at the request o bidding of • **en última instancia** as a last resort

instantáneo, a *adj* ❶ [*momentáneo*] momentary ❷ [*rápido*] instant • **la muerte sería instantánea** death would be instant • **café instantáneo** instant coffee ❖ *Los adjetivos ingleses son invariables.*
■ **instantánea** *sf* snapshot

instante *sm* moment • **en ese mismo instante sonó el teléfono** at that same moment the telephone rang • **hace un instante estaba aquí** he was here a moment ago • **a cada instante** constantly • **a cada instante me preguntaba la hora** he was constantly asking me what time it was • **al instante** instantly; immediately • **en un instante** in a second

instaurar *vt* to establish

instigar *vt* • **instigar a alguien (a que haga algo)** to instigate somebody (to do something) • **instigar a algo** to incite to something

instintivo, va *adj* instinctive ☼ *Los adjetivos ingleses son invariables.*

instinto *sm* instinct • **reaccionó por instinto** he reacted out of instinct ▶ **instinto maternal** maternal instinct ▶ **instinto de supervivencia** survival instinct

institución *sf* ❶ [*generalmente*] institution ❷ [*de ley, sistema*] introduction ❸ [*de organismo*] establishment ❹ [*de premio*] foundation

expresión **ser una institución** to be an institution

instituir *vt* ❶ [*gobierno*] to establish ❷ [*premio, sociedad*] to found ❸ [*sistema, reglas*] to introduce

instituto *sm* [*corporación*] institute ▶ **instituto de belleza** beauty salon

instrucción *sf* ❶ [*conocimientos*] education ❷ [*docencia*] instruction ❸ DERECHO [*investigación*] preliminary investigation; [*curso del proceso*] proceedings *pl*

■ **instrucciones** *sfpl* [*de uso*] instructions • **tiene instrucciones de no comentarlo con nadie** he has instructions to not discuss it with anybody

instructivo, va *adj* ❶ [*generalmente*] instructive ❷ [*juguete, película*] educational ☼ *Los adjetivos ingleses son invariables.*

instructor, ra ◆ *adj* training ☼ *Los adjetivos ingleses son invariables.*

◆ *sm, f* ❶ [*generalmente*] instructor ❷ DEPORTE coach

instrumental *sm* instruments *pl*

instrumentista *smf* ❶ MÚSICA instrumentalist ❷ MEDICINA surgical technologist

instrumento *sm* ❶ *figurado* MÚSICA instrument ❷ [*herramienta*] tool

---

los instrumentos musicales

la armónica	the harmonica
la batería	the drums
el clarinete	the clarinet
el contrabajo	the double bass
la flauta dulce	the recorder
la flauta travesera	the flute
la guitarra	the guitar
la pandereta	the tambourine
el piano	the piano
el platillo	the cymbal
el saxofón	the saxophone
el trombón	the trombone
la trompeta	the trumpet
el violín	the violin
el violoncelo	the cello
el xilófono	the xylophone

---

insuficiencia *sf* ❶ [*escasez*] lack ❷ MEDICINA failure ▶ **insuficiencia cardiaca/renal** heart/kidney failure

insuficiente ◆ *adj* insufficient ☼ *Los adjetivos ingleses son invariables.*

◆ *sm* [*nota*] fail

insulina *sf* insulin

insultar *vt* to insult

insulto *sm* insult

insuperable *adj* ❶ [*inmejorable*] unsurpassable ❷ [*sin solución*] insurmountable ☼ *Los adjetivos ingleses son invariables.*

intacto, ta *adj* ❶ untouched ❷ *figurado* intact ☼ *Los adjetivos ingleses son invariables.*

integral *adj* ❶ [*total*] total ❷ [*sin refinar - pan, harina, pasta*] whole-grain; [*- arroz*] brown ☼ *Los adjetivos ingleses son invariables.*

integrante ◆ *adj* integral ☼ *Los adjetivos ingleses son invariables.*

◆ *smf* member

integrar *vt* ❶ [*generalmente*] MATEMÁTICAS to integrate ❷ [*componer*] to make up

integridad *sf* ❶ [*generalmente*] integrity ❷ [*totalidad*] wholeness

íntegro, gra *adj* ❶ [*completo*] whole ❷ [*versión* ETC] unabridged ❸ [*honrado*] honorable ☼ *Los adjetivos ingleses son invariables.*

intelecto *sm* intellect

intelectual *adj & smf* intellectual ☼ *Los adjetivos ingleses son invariables.*

inteligencia *sf* intelligence ▶ **inteligencia artificial** artificial intelligence ▶ **inteligencia emocional** emotional intelligence

inteligente *adj* intelligent ☼ *Los adjetivos ingleses son invariables.*

inteligible *adj* intelligible ☼ *Los adjetivos ingleses son invariables.*

intemperie *sf* • **a la intemperie** in the open air

intempestivo, va *adj* ❶ [*clima, comentario*] harsh ❷ [*hora*] ungodly ❸ [*proposición, visita*] inopportune ☼ *Los adjetivos ingleses son invariables.*

intención *sf* intention • **mi intención no era causar problemas** it was not my intention to cause problems • **lo que vale es la intención** it's the thought that counts • **con la intención de hacer algo** with the intention of doing something • **lo hizo con la intención de ayudar** he did it with the intention of helping • **no tenía la más mínima intención de obedecer** he didn't have the least intention of obeying • **con intención** intentionally • **sin intención** without meaning to • **tener la intención de** to intend to • **tenía intenciones de ir mañana** I intended to go tomorrow • **tener malas intenciones** to be up to no good • **buena/mala intención** good/bad intentions *pl* • **segunda intención** underhandedness

expresión **de buenas intenciones está el infierno lleno** *proverbio* the road to hell is paved with good intentions

intencionado, da *adj* deliberate • **el cabezazo fue intencionado** the headbutt was deliberate • **bien intencionado a)** [*acción*] well-meant **b)** [*persona*] well-meaning • **es una persona bien intencionada** she's a well-meaning person ☼ *Los adjetivos ingleses son invariables.*

intensidad *sf* ❶ [*generalmente*] intensity ❷ [*de lluvia*] heaviness ❸ [*de luz, color*] brightness ❹ [*de amor*] passion

intensificar *vt* to intensify

intensivo, va *adj* intensive. ֎ *Los adjetivos ingleses son invariables.*

intenso, sa *adj* ❶ [*generalmente*] intense ❷ [*lluvia*] heavy ❸ [*luz, color*] bright ❹ [*amor*] passionate. ֎ *Los adjetivos ingleses son invariables.*

intentar *vt* to try • **ya lo ha intentado varias veces** he's already tried it several times • **intentar hacer algo** to try to do something • **intenta concentrarte más en clase** try to concentrate more in class • **intenta que sea lo más claro posible** try to make it as clear as possible

intento *sm* attempt • **pasó el examen al segundo intento** he passed the exam on his second attempt ▶ **intento de golpe/robo** attempted coup/robbery ▶ **intento de suicidio** suicide attempt

interactivo, va *adj* INFORMÁTICA interactive. ֎ *Los adjetivos ingleses son invariables.*

intercalar *vt* to insert

intercambiable *adj* interchangeable. ֎ *Los adjetivos ingleses son invariables.*

intercambio *sm* exchange • **hacer un intercambio** to go on an exchange program • **intercambio comercial** trade

interceder *vi* • **interceder (por alguien)** to intercede (on somebody's behalf) • **nunca podré agradecerle lo bastante haber intercedido por mí en tan delicado asunto** I'll never be able to thank her enough for having interceded on my behalf in such a delicate matter

interceptar *vt* ❶ [*detener*] to intercept ❷ [*obstruir*] to block

interés *sm* ❶ [*generalmente*] FINANZAS interest • **tienes que poner más interés en lo que haces** you have to take more of an interest in what you do • **escuchaba con interés** she was listening with interest • **tengo interés en que venga pronto** it's in my interest that he should come soon • **de interés** interesting • **esperar algo con interés** to await something with interest • **tener interés por** to be interested in ▶ **interés acumulado** accrued interest ▶ **interés compuesto** compound interest ▶ **interés simple** simple interest ▶ **intereses creados** vested interests ❷ [*egoísmo*] self-interest • **por interés** out of selfishness

interesado, da ◆ *adj* ❶ [*generalmente*] • **interesado (en** o **por)** interested (in) ❷ [*egoísta*] selfish. ֎ *Los adjetivos ingleses son invariables.*

◆ *sm, f* [*deseoso*] interested person • **los interesados** those interested

interesante *adj* interesting • **hacerse el/la interesante** to try to draw attention to yourself. ֎ *Los adjetivos ingleses son invariables.*

interesar *vi* to interest • **le interesa el arte** she's interested in art • **siempre me han interesado ese tipo de cosas** that type of thing has always interested me

• **¿te interesaría saber más del tema?** would it interest you to know more on the subject?

interfaz *sf* INFORMÁTICA interface

interferencia *sf* interference

interferir ◆ *vt* ❶ TELECOMUNICACIONES, RADIO & TELEVISIÓN to jam ❷ [*interponerse*] to interfere with

◆ *vi* • **interferir (en)** to interfere (in) • **no quiero que nada interfiera en mis planes** I don't want anything interfering with my plans • **no interfieras en mis asuntos** don't meddle in my affairs

interfono *sm* intercom

interino, na ◆ *adj* ❶ [*generalmente*] temporary ❷ [*presidente, director* ETC] acting ❸ [*gobierno*] interim. ֎ *Los adjetivos ingleses son invariables.*

◆ *sm, f* ❶ [*generalmente*] stand-in ❷ [*médico, juez*] locum ❸ [*profesor*] supply teacher

interior ◆ *adj* ❶ [*generalmente*] inner • **la parte interior es roja** the inner part is red ❷ [*patio, jardín* ETC] inside • **en el bolsillo interior de la chaqueta** in the inside pocket of the jacket ❸ [*habitación, vida*] inner ❹ POLÍTICA domestic ❺ GEOGRAFÍA inland. ֎ *Los adjetivos ingleses son invariables.*

◆ *sm* ❶ [*parte de dentro*] inside ❷ GEOGRAFÍA interior ❸ [*de una persona*] inner self • **en mi interior** deep down

interiorismo *sm* interior design

interiorizar *vt* to internalize

interjección *sf* interjection

interlocutor, ra *sm, f* • **su interlocutor** the person she was speaking to

intermediario, ria *sm, f* ❶ [*generalmente*] intermediary ❷ COMERCIO middleman ❸ [*en disputas*] mediator

intermedio, dia *adj* ❶ [*etapa*] intermediate • **está en el nivel intermedio** he's at intermediate level ❷ [*calidad*] average ❸ [*tamaño*] medium • **el tamaño intermedio te quedaría mejor** the medium size would fit you better ❹ [*tiempo*] intervening ❺ [*espacio*] in between. ֎ *Los adjetivos ingleses son invariables.*

■ **intermedio** *sm* ❶ [*generalmente*] TEATRO interval ❷ CINE intermission

interminable *adj* endless. ֎ *Los adjetivos ingleses son invariables.*

intermitente ◆ *adj* intermittent. ֎ *Los adjetivos ingleses son invariables.*

◆ *sm* indicator

internacional *adj* international. ֎ *Los adjetivos ingleses son invariables.*

internado, da *adj* ❶ [*en manicomio*] confined ❷ [*en colegio*] boarding ❸ POLÍTICA interned. ֎ *Los adjetivos ingleses son invariables.*

■ **internado** *sm* [*colegio*] boarding school

internar *vt* • **internar (en) a)** [*internado*] to send to boarding school (at) **b)** [*manicomio*] to commit (to) **c)** [*campo de concentración*] to intern (in)

internauta *smf* Internet user

Internet *sf* Internet • **en Internet** on the Internet

interno, na ◆ *adj* ❶ [*generalmente*] internal • **son problemas internos del colegio** they are internal problems of the school ❷ POLÍTICA domestic ❸ [*alumno*] • **está interna en un colegio de monjas** she's a boarder at a convent school • **si no mejora las notas lo van a poner interno** if he doesn't improve his grades they're going to send him to boarding school ❄ *Los adjetivos ingleses son invariables.*
◆ *sm, f* ❶ [*alumno*] boarder ❷ → **médico** ❸ [*preso*] prisoner

interponer *vt* ❶ [*generalmente*] to interpose ❷ DERECHO to lodge

interpretación *sf* ❶ [*explicación*] interpretation • **cada uno le dio una interpretación distinta** each one gave her a different interpretation • **mala interpretación** misinterpretation ❷ [*artística*] performance • **lo que más me gustó fue la interpretación del pianista** what I most liked was the pianist's performance ❸ [*traducción*] interpreting

interpretar *vt* ❶ [*generalmente*] to interpret • **lo puedes interpretar de diferentes maneras** you can interpret it in different ways • **me interpretaste mal** you misunderstood me ❷ [*artísticamente*] to play • **interpretó una pieza al piano** she played a piece on the piano

intérprete *smf* ❶ [*traductor*] INFORMÁTICA interpreter ❷ [*artista*] performer

interrogación *sf* ❶ [*acción*] questioning ❷ [*signo*] question mark

interrogante *sm o sf* [*incógnita*] question mark

interrogar *vt* ❶ [*generalmente*] to question ❷ [*con amenazas* ETC] to interrogate • **la policía lo quiere interrogar** the police want to interrogate him

interrogatorio *sm* ❶ [*generalmente*] questioning ❷ [*con amenazas*] interrogation

interrumpir ◆ *vt* ❶ [*generalmente*] to interrupt • **no le gusta que lo interrumpan** he doesn't like to be interrupted ❷ [*circulación*] to block • **un árbol caído interrumpía el tráfico** a fallen tree was blocking traffic • **no interrumpas el paso** don't block the way ❸ [*viaje, vacaciones*] to cut short • **tuvieron que interrumpir las vacaciones** they had to cut their vacation short
◆ *vi* to interrupt • **no interrumpas cuando alguien está hablando** don't interrupt when somebody is talking

interrupción *sf* ❶ [*generalmente*] interruption • **no ha podido estudiar con tanta interrupción** she hasn't been able to study with so much interruption ▶ **interrupción (voluntaria) del embarazo** termination of pregnancy ❷ [*de discurso, trabajo*] breaking-off ❸ [*de viaje, vacaciones*] cutting-short

interruptor *sm* switch

intersección *sf* intersection

interurbano, na *adj* ❶ inter-city ❷ TELECOMUNICACIONES long-distance ❄ *Los adjetivos ingleses son invariables.*

intervalo *sm* ❶ [*generalmente*] MÚSICA interval • **a intervalos** at intervals • **a intervalos de diez minutos**

at ten minute intervals ❷ [*duración*] • **en el intervalo de un mes** in the space of a month

intervención *sf* ❶ [*generalmente*] intervention ❷ [*discurso*] speech ❸ [*interpelación*] contribution ❹ COMERCIO auditing ❺ MEDICINA operation ❻ TELECOMUNICACIONES tapping

intervenir ◆ *vi* ❶ [*participar*] • **intervenir (en) a)** [*generalmente*] to take part (in) **b)** [*pelea*] to get involved (in) **c)** [*discusión* ETC] to make a contribution (to) ❷ [*dar un discurso*] to make a speech ❸ [*interferir*] • **intervenir (en)** to intervene (in) ❹ MEDICINA to operate
◆ *vt* ❶ MEDICINA to operate on ❷ TELECOMUNICACIONES to tap ❸ [*incautar*] to seize ❹ COMERCIO to audit

interventor, ra *sm, f* COMERCIO auditor

intestino, na *adj* internecine ❄ *Los adjetivos ingleses son invariables.*
■ **intestino** *sm* intestine ▶ **intestino delgado/grueso** small/large intestine

intimidad *sf* ❶ [*vida privada*] private life ❷ [*privacidad*] privacy • **mis hermanos no respetan mi intimidad** my brothers don't respect my privacy • **en la intimidad** in private • **lo que pase en la intimidad es cosa de ellos** what happens in private is their business ❸ [*amistad*] intimacy

íntimo, ma ◆ *adj* ❶ [*vida, fiesta*] private ❷ [*ambiente, restaurante*] intimate ❸ [*relación, amistad*] close ❹ [*sentimiento* ETC] innermost • **en lo (más) íntimo de su corazón/alma** deep down in her heart/soul ❄ *Los adjetivos ingleses son invariables.*
◆ *sm, f* close friend

intolerable *adj* ❶ intolerable ❷ [*dolor, ruido*] unbearable ❄ *Los adjetivos ingleses son invariables.*

intolerancia *sf* [*actitud*] intolerance

intoxicación *sf* poisoning ❄ *incontable* ▶ **intoxicación alimenticia** food poisoning ▶ **intoxicación etílica** alcohol poisoning

intranquilizar *vt* to worry

intranquilo, la *adj* ❶ [*preocupado*] worried • **está muy intranquilo porque ha estudiado muy poco** he's very worried because he has studied very little ❷ [*nervioso*] restless ❄ *Los adjetivos ingleses son invariables.*

intransigente *adj* intransigent ❄ *Los adjetivos ingleses son invariables.*

intrascendente *adj* insignificant ❄ *Los adjetivos ingleses son invariables.*

intrépido, da *adj* intrepid ❄ *Los adjetivos ingleses son invariables.*

intriga *sf* ❶ [*curiosidad*] curiosity • **de intriga** suspense ❄ *Sólo se usa delante del sustantivo.* ❷ [*maquinación*] intrigue ❸ [*trama*] plot

intrigar *vt & vi* to intrigue

intrínseco, ca *adj* intrinsic ❄ *Los adjetivos ingleses son invariables.*

introducción *sf* • **introducción (a)** introduction (to)

introducir *vt* **❶** [*meter - llave, carta* ETC] to insert • **hay que introducir una moneda en la ranura** you have to insert a coin into the slot **❷** [*mercancías* ETC] to bring in **❸** [*datos*] to enter • **introdujo los datos en la computadora** he entered the data into the computer **❹** [*medidas, sistema*] to introduce • **introdujeron el sistema métrico** they introduced the metric system **❺** [*dar a conocer*] • **introducir a alguien en** to introduce somebody to • **introducir algo en** to introduce something to • **quieren introducir algunos cambios en el horario** they want to introduce some changes in the schedule

intromisión *sf* meddling

introvertido, da *adj* & *sm, f* introvert ⚲ *Los adjetivos ingleses son invariables.*

intruso, sa *sm, f* intruder

intuición *sf* intuition • **la intuición me dice que no deberíamos tomar ese avión** intuition tells me that we shouldn't take that airplane

intuir *vt* to sense

intuitivo, va *adj* intuitive ⚲ *Los adjetivos ingleses son invariables.*

inundación *sf* flood • **las últimas inundaciones obligaron a evacuar varias casas** the last floods forced the evacuation of several houses

inundar *vt* **❶** to flood • **la lluvia inundó las regiones más bajas del pueblo** the rain flooded the lowest areas of the town **❷** *figurado* to inundate

■ **inundarse** *v pronominal* to flood • **las regiones más bajas del pueblo se inundaron con las últimas lluvias** the lowest areas of the town were flooded with the last rains • **inundarse de** *figurado* to be inundated with

inútil *adj* **❶** [*generalmente*] useless • **su secretaria es inútil** his secretary is useless • **es inútil, no lo vamos a lograr** it's useless, we're not going to manage it **❷** [*intento, esfuerzo*] unsuccessful **❸** [*inválido*] disabled ⚲ *Los adjetivos ingleses son invariables.*

inutilidad *sf* **❶** [*generalmente*] uselessness **❷** [*falta de sentido*] pointlessness

inutilizar *vt* **❶** [*generalmente*] to make unusable **❷** [*máquinas, dispositivos*] to disable

invadir *vt* to invade • **el ejército enemigo invadió la ciudad** the enemy army invaded the city • **la invade la tristeza** she's overcome by sadness

invalidez *sf* **❶** MEDICINA disability ▸ **invalidez permanente/temporal** permanent/temporary disability **❷** DERECHO invalidity

inválido, da ◆ *adj* **❶** MEDICINA disabled • **su tío quedó inválido después del accidente** his uncle became disabled after the accident **❷** DERECHO invalid ⚲ *Los adjetivos ingleses son invariables.*

◆ *sm, f* disabled person • **los inválidos** the disabled

invariable *adj* invariable ⚲ *Los adjetivos ingleses son invariables.*

invasión *sf* invasion

invasor, ra ◆ *adj* invading ⚲ *Los adjetivos ingleses son invariables.*

◆ *sm, f* invader

invención *sf* invention

inventar *vt* **❶** [*generalmente*] to invent • **Alexander Graham Bell inventó el teléfono** Alexander Graham Bell invented the telephone **❷** [*narración, falsedades*] to make up • **le gusta inventar historias para entretener a sus hijos** he likes to make up stories to entertain his children

inventario *sm* inventory

inventiva *sf* inventiveness

invento *sm* **❶** [*generalmente*] invention • **el teléfono fue un invento de Alexander Graham Bell** the telephone was an invention of Alexander Graham Bell **❷** [*narración, falsedad*] fabrication • **ya estoy cansada de tus inventos** I'm tired of your fabrications

inventor, ra *sm, f* inventor

invernadero *sm* greenhouse

invernar *vi* **❶** [*pasar el invierno*] to (spend the) winter **❷** [*hibernar*] to hibernate

inverosímil *adj* improbable ⚲ *Los adjetivos ingleses son invariables.*

inversión *sf* **❶** [*del orden*] inversion **❷** [*de dinero, tiempo*] investment

inverso, sa *adj* opposite • **en sentido inverso** in the opposite direction • **a la inversa** the other way around • **en orden inverso** in reverse order ⚲ *Los adjetivos ingleses son invariables.*

inversor, ra *sm, f* COMERCIO & FINANZAS investor

invertido, da *adj* **❶** [*al revés*] reversed **❷** [*sentido, dirección*] opposite ⚲ *Los adjetivos ingleses son invariables.*

invertir *vt* **❶** [*generalmente*] to reverse • **si invertimos el orden de los números, obtendremos otro resultado** if we reverse the order of the numbers, we will obtain a different result **❷** [*poner boca abajo*] to turn upside down **❸** [*dinero, tiempo, esfuerzo*] to invest • **hay varios empresarios interesados en invertir en el país** there are several businessmen interested in investing in the country **❹** [*tardar - tiempo*] to spend

investigación *sf* **❶** [*estudio*] research • **mi amigo se dedica a la investigación en biología** my friend is dedicated to research in biology ▸ **investigación y desarrollo** research and development **❷** [*indagación*] investigation • **al cabo de dos días de investigación policial, capturaron al ladrón** at the end of two days of police investigation, they captured the thief • **investigación judicial** judicial inquiry

investigador, ra *sm, f* **❶** [*estudioso*] researcher • **el investigador descubrió una nueva reacción química** the researcher discovered a new chemical reaction **❷** [*detective*] investigator • **los investigadores capturaron al ladrón en un par de días** the investigators captured the thief in a couple of days

investigar ◆ *vt* **❶** [*estudiar*] to research • **los científicos están investigando la nueva enfermedad** scientists are researching the new disease **❷** [*indagar*] to investigate • **la policía investiga el caso hace una semana** the police have been investigating the case for a week

♦ *vi* ❶ [*estudiar*] to do research ❷ [*indagar*] to investigate

inviable *adj* impractical.♀: *Los adjetivos ingleses son invariables.*

invidente *smf* blind person • **los invidentes** the blind

invierno *sm* winter • **el próximo invierno** next winter • **en invierno** in winter ▶ **invierno nuclear** nuclear winter

invisible *adj* invisible.♀: *Los adjetivos ingleses son invariables.*

invitación *sf* invitation

invitado, da *sm, f* guest

invitar ♦ *vt* ❶ [*convidar*] • **invitar a alguien (a algo/a hacer algo)** to invite somebody (to something/to do something) ❷ [*pagar*] • **os invito** it's my treat • **te invito a cenar fuera** I'll take you out for dinner
♦ *vi* to pay • **invita la casa** it's on the house

involucrar *vt* • **involucrar a alguien (en)** to involve somebody (in)

involuntario, ria *adj* ❶ [*espontáneo*] involuntary ❷ [*sin querer*] unintentional.♀: *Los adjetivos ingleses son invariables.*

inyección *sf* injection

inyectar *vt* to inject

ion *sm* ion

ir
♦ *vi*
❶ [*desplazarse hacia un sitio determinado*] to go
• **no quiero ir** I don't want to go
• **iremos en coche/en tren/a pie** we'll go by car/train/on foot
• **¡vamos!** let's go
❷ [*extenderse de un punto a otro*] to go
• **nuestro terreno va de aquí hasta el mar** our piece of land goes from here to the sea
• **el nuevo camino irá del pueblo a la ciudad** the new road will go from the town to the city
❸ [*antes de un gerundio, indica que una acción se realiza poco a poco*]
• **voy mejorando mi estilo** I'm gradually improving my style
• **su estado va empeorando** he's getting worse and worse
❹ [*funcionar, andar*]
• **tu coche va muy bien** your car runs very well
• **sus negocios van mal** his business is going badly
❺ [*estar*]
• **iba muy borracho** he was very drunk
• **iba hecho un pordiosero** he was dressed in rags
❻ [*quedarle bien a alguien, refiriéndose a ropa, colores*] to suit
• **te van muy bien estos lentes** these glasses suit you perfectly
• **le va fatal el color negro** black doesn't suit her

❼ [*en una apuesta*]
• **van cien pesos a que no lo haces** I bet you a hundred pesos you wouldn't do it
❽ [*con valor enfático, indica que una acción se realiza de manera imprevista o repentina*]
• **fue y se puso a llorar** all of a sudden, he burst into tears
• **fue y se lo contó todo** he went and told her everything
❾ [*en expresiones*]
• **¿cómo te va?** how are you?
• **¡qué va!** you're not joking!
• **unas vacaciones te harían bien** you need a vacation
■ **ir a**
♦ *v + preposición*
❶ [*desplazarse hacia un sitio determinado*] to go to
• **voy a Mérida/al cine** I'm going to Mérida/to the movies
• **todavía va al colegio** he's still at school
❷ [*seguido por el infinitivo, expresa el futuro inmediato*] to go
• **voy a llamarlo ahora mismo** I'm going to call him straight away
• **va a llover** it's going to rain
■ **ir con**
♦ *v + preposición*
❶ [*llevar puesto*] to wear
• **ir con corbata** to wear a tie
❷ [*estar en harmonía con*] to go with
• **el color del sofá no va con el de las cortinas** the color of the sofa doesn't go with the drapes
■ **ir en**
♦ *v + preposición*
[*estar vestido de*] to be in
• **ir en camiseta** to be in a t-shirt
■ **irse**
♦ *v pronominal*
[*dejar un sitio, partir*] to leave
• **nos vamos porque ya es tarde** we're leaving because it's late now
• **como sigas así me voy** if you keep on like this, I'm leaving
• **se ha ido de viaje/a comer** he's gone on a trip/for lunch
• **esta mancha no se va** this spot won't come out
• **¡vete!** buzz off!

ira *sf* anger • **tuvo un arrebato de ira** he had a fit of anger

Irán *nombre propio* • **(el) Irán** Iran

iraní (pl **iraníes o iranís**) *adj* & *smf* Iranian.♀: *Los adjetivos ingleses son invariables.*

Iraq *nombre propio* • **(el) Iraq** Iraq

iraquí (pl **iraquíes o iraquís**) *adj* & *smf* Iraqi.♀: *Los adjetivos ingleses son invariables.*

iris *sm invariable* iris

Irlanda *nombre propio* Ireland

ironía *sf* irony

irónico, ca *adj* ironic ⠴ *Los adjetivos ingleses son invariables.*

irracional *adj* irrational ⠴ *Los adjetivos ingleses son invariables.*

irreal *adj* unreal ⠴ *Los adjetivos ingleses son invariables.*

irreconocible *adj* unrecognizable ⠴ *Los adjetivos ingleses son invariables.*

irrecuperable *adj* irretrievable ⠴ *Los adjetivos ingleses son invariables.*

irreflexivo, va *adj* rash ⠴ *Los adjetivos ingleses son invariables.*

irregular *adj* ❶ [*generalmente*] irregular ❷ [*terreno, superficie*] uneven ⠴ *Los adjetivos ingleses son invariables.*

irrelevante *adj* irrelevant ⠴ *Los adjetivos ingleses son invariables.*

irremediable *adj* irremediable ⠴ *Los adjetivos ingleses son invariables.*

irreparable *adj* irreparable ⠴ *Los adjetivos ingleses son invariables.*

irresistible *adj* irresistible • **esos chocolates son irresistibles** those chocolates are irresistible • **el dolor de muelas es irresistible** toothache is unbearable ⠴ *Los adjetivos ingleses son invariables.*

irrespetuoso, sa *adj* disrespectful ⠴ *Los adjetivos ingleses son invariables.*

irrespirable *adj* unbreathable ⠴ *Los adjetivos ingleses son invariables.*

irresponsable *adj* irresponsible ⠴ *Los adjetivos ingleses son invariables.*

irreversible *adj* irreversible ⠴ *Los adjetivos ingleses son invariables.*

irrevocable *adj* irrevocable ⠴ *Los adjetivos ingleses son invariables.*

irritable *adj* irritable ⠴ *Los adjetivos ingleses son invariables.*

irritar *vt* to irritate • **esa crema te está irritando la piel** that cream is irritating your skin

■ **irritarse** *v pronominal* ❶ [*enfadarse*] to get angry ❷ [*sujeto: piel* ETC] to become irritated

irrompible *adj* unbreakable ⠴ *Los adjetivos ingleses son invariables.*

isla *sf* island

islam *sm* Islam

islamismo *sm* Islam

Islandia *nombre propio* Iceland

isleño, ña ♦ *adj* island ⠴ *Sólo se usa delante del sustantivo.*

♦ *sm, f* islander

islote *sm* small island

Israel *nombre propio* Israel

israelí (pl israelíes o israelís) *adj* & *smf* Israeli ⠴ *Los adjetivos ingleses son invariables.*

Italia *nombre propio* Italy

itálico, ca *adj* → letra

itinerante *adj* ❶ itinerant ❷ [*embajador*] roving ⠴ *Los adjetivos ingleses son invariables.*

itinerario *sm* route

izar *vt* to raise

izda (*abreviatura escrita de* izquierda) L; l

izquierda *sf* ❶ [*lado*] left • **a la izquierda (de)** to the left (of) • **María está sentada a la izquierda de Juan** María is seated to the left of Juan • **girar a la izquierda** to turn left • **de la izquierda** on the left • **abre esa puerta, la de la izquierda** open that door, the one on the left ❷ [*mano*] left hand ❸ POLÍTICA left • **la izquierda** the left • **de izquierdas** left-wing

izquierdo, da *adj* left • **la pierna izquierda** the left leg ⠴ *Los adjetivos ingleses son invariables.*

j, J *sf* [*letra*] j ; J

ja *exclamación* • ¡ja! ha!

jabalí (pl jabalíes o jabalís) *sm* wild boar

jabalina *sf* DEPORTE javelin

jabón *sm* soap

jactarse *v pronominal* • **jactarse (de)** to brag (about) • **se jacta de ser el mejor de la clase** he brags about being the best in the class

jadear *vi* to pant

jaguar (pl jaguars) *sm* jaguar

jaibol *sm* highball

jalar ◆ *vt* [*tirar*] to pull • **si me jalas el pelo, te pego** if you pull my hair, I'll hit you • **jala una silla y siéntate** pull up a seat and sit down
◆ *vi* to pull • **'jale'** pull • **no vi que decía "jale", por eso estaba empujando** I didn't see that it said "pull", that's why I was pushing

jalea *sf* jelly, *plural* jellies ▸ **jalea real** royal jelly

jalear *vt* to cheer on

jalón *sm* ❶ [*tirón*] pull ❷ [*trecho*] stretch

Jamaica *nombre propio* Jamaica

jamás *adv* never • **no lo he visto jamás** I've never seen him • **la mejor película que jamás se haya hecho** the best film ever made
expresión jamás de los jamases never ever

jamón *sm* ham ▸ **jamón cocido** cooked ham ▸ **jamón dulce** boiled ham ▸ **jamón (de) York** boiled ham ▸ **jamón serrano** cured ham, ≃ Parma ham

Japón *nombre propio* • **(el) Japón** Japan

jaque *sm* ▸ **jaque mate** checkmate

jaqueca *sf* migraine

jarabe *sm* syrup ▸ **jarabe para la tos** cough mixture o syrup

jardín *sm* garden ▸ **jardín botánico** botanical garden ▸ **jardín zoológico** zoological garden

jardinera *sf* flowerpot stand

jardinería *sf* gardening

jardinero, ra *sm, f* gardener

jarra *sf* ❶ [*para servir*] jug ❷ [*para beber*] tankard

jarro *sm* jug

jarrón *sm* vase

jaula *sf* cage

jazmín *sm* jasmine

jazz *sm* jazz

JC (abreviatura escrita de Jesucristo) JC

je *exclamación* • ¡je! ha!

jeep (pl jeeps) *sm* jeep

jefatura *sf* ❶ [*cargo*] leadership ❷ [*organismo*] headquarters

jefe, fa *sm, f* ❶ [*generalmente*] boss ▸ **jefe de cocina** chef ▸ **jefe de estación** stationmaster ▸ **jefe de Estado** head of state ▸ **jefe de redacción** editor-in-chief ❷ COMERCIO manager, *femenino* manageress ▸ **jefe de producción/ventas** production/sales manager ❸ [*líder*] leader ❹ [*de tribu, ejército*] chief • **en jefe** MILITAR in-chief ❺ [*de departamento* ETC] head ▸ **jefe de estudios** deputy head

jengibre *sm* ginger

jeque *sm* sheikh

jerarquía *sf* [*organización*] hierarchy

jerárquico, ca *adj* hierarchical 🔍 *Los adjetivos ingleses son invariables.*

jerez *sm* sherry

jerga *sf* ❶ jargon ❷ [*argot*] slang

jeringa *sf* syringe

jeringuilla *sf* syringe

Jerusalén *nombre propio* Jerusalem

jesuita *adj* & *sm* Jesuit 🔍 *Los adjetivos ingleses son invariables.*

jesús *exclamación* • ¡jesús! **a)** [*sorpresa*] good heavens! **b)** [*tras estornudo*] bless you!

jet (pl jets) *sm* jet

jet-set *sf* jet set

jícara *sf* gourd bowl

jinete *smf* ❶ rider ❷ [*yóquey*] jockey
jinetear *vi* to ride on horseback
jirafa *sf* ZOOLOGÍA giraffe
jitomate *sm* tomato, *plural* tomatoes
JJ OO (*abreviatura escrita de* juegos olímpicos) *smpl* Olympic Games
jocoso, sa *adj* jocular ☞ *Los adjetivos ingleses son invariables.*
jolgorio *sm* merrymaking
jornada *sf* ❶ [*de trabajo*] working day • **media jornada** half day ▶ **jornada laboral** working day ❷ [*de viaje*] day's journey ❸ DEPORTE round of matches
jornal *sm* day's wage
jornalero, ra *sm, f* day laborer
joroba *sf* hump
jorobado, da ◆ *adj* [*con joroba*] hunchbacked ☞ *Los adjetivos ingleses son invariables.* ◆ *sm, f* hunchback
jorongo *sm* ❶ [*manta*] blanket ❷ [*poncho*] poncho
joven ◆ *adj* young ☞ *Los adjetivos ingleses son invariables.* ◆ *smf* young man, *femenino* young woman • **los jóvenes** young people
jovial *adj* cheerful ☞ *Los adjetivos ingleses son invariables.*
joya *sf* ❶ jewel ❷ *figurado* gem
joyería *sf* ❶ [*tienda*] jeweller's (shop) ❷ [*arte, comercio*] jewellery
juanete *sm* bunion
jubilación *sf* [*retiro*] retirement ▶ **jubilación anticipada** early retirement ▶ **jubilación forzosa** compulsory retirement ▶ **jubilación voluntaria** voluntary retirement
jubilado, da ◆ *adj* retired ☞ *Los adjetivos ingleses son invariables.* ◆ *sm, f* senior citizen
jubilar *vt* • **jubilar a alguien (de)** to pension somebody off o retire somebody (from)
judía *sf* bean
judicial *adj* judicial ☞ *Los adjetivos ingleses son invariables.*
judío, a ◆ *adj* Jewish ☞ *Los adjetivos ingleses son invariables.* ◆ *sm, f* Jew, *femenino* Jewess
judo = **yudo**
juego *sm* ❶ [*generalmente*] DEPORTE game • **tiene muchísimos juegos de computadora** he has many computer games • **abrir/cerrar el juego** to begin/finish the game • **estar (en) fuera de juego a)** DEPORTE to be offside **b)** *figurado* not to know what's going on • **hacer juego (con)** to match • **esa corbata hace juego con la camisa** that tie matches your shirt ▶ **juego de azar** game of chance ▶ **juego de manos** conjuring trick ▶ **juego de mesa** board game ▶ **juego de palabras** play on words ▶ **juego sucio/limpio** foul/clean play ❷ [*acción*] play ❸ [*con dinero*] gambling ❹ [*conjunto de objetos*] set ▶ **juego de herramientas** tool kit ▶ **juego de llaves** set of keys ▶ **juego de sábanas** set of sheets
expresión **descubrirle el juego a alguien** to see through somebody
■ **Juegos Olímpicos** *smpl* Olympic Games
juerga *sf* familiar rave-up
juerguista *smf* familiar reveller
jueves *sm invariable* Thursday ▶ **Jueves Santo** Maundy Thursday ver también **sábado**
juez *smf* ❶ DERECHO judge • **cuando el juez entró a la sala todos se pararon** when the judge came into the room everybody stood up ▶ **juez de paz** Justice of the Peace ❷ DEPORTE [*generalmente*] referee; [*en atletismo*] official ▶ **juez de línea a)** [*futbol*] linesman **b)** [*rugby*] touch judge ▶ **juez de salida** starter ▶ **juez de silla** umpire
jugada *sf* ❶ DEPORTE period of play ❷ [*en tenis, ping-pong*] rally ❸ [*en futbol, rugby* ETC] move ❹ [*en ajedrez* ETC] move ❺ [*en billar*] shot ❻ [*treta*] dirty trick • **hacer una mala jugada a alguien** to play a dirty trick on somebody
jugador, ra *sm, f* ❶ [*generalmente*] player ❷ [*de juego de azar*] gambler
jugar ◆ *vi* ❶ [*generalmente*] to play • **jugar al ajedrez** to play chess • **jugar en un equipo** to play for a team • **te toca jugar** it's your turn • **jugar limpio/sucio** to play clean/dirty • **jugar con algo** to play with something • **jugar contra alguien** to play (against) somebody ❷ [*con dinero*] • **jugar (a)** to gamble (on) • **jugar a la Bolsa** to speculate on the Stock Exchange ◆ *vt* ❶ [*generalmente*] to play ❷ [*ficha, pieza*] to move ❸ [*dinero*] • **jugar algo (a algo)** to gamble something (on something)
jugarreta *sf* familiar dirty trick
jugo *sm* ❶ [*generalmente*] ANATOMÍA juice ❷ BOTÁNICA sap ▶ **jugos gástricos** gastric juices ❸ [*interés*] meat • **sacar jugo a algo/alguien** to get the most out of something/somebody
jugoso, sa *adj* ❶ [*con jugo*] juicy ❷ *figurado* [*picante*] juicy ❸ [*sustancioso*] meaty ☞ *Los adjetivos ingleses son invariables.*
juguete *sm* literal & figurado toy • **de juguete** toy ☞ *Sólo se usa delante del sustantivo.* ▶ **juguete educativo** educational toy
juguetear *vi* to play (around) • **juguetear con algo** to toy with something
juguetería *sf* toy shop
juguetón, ona *adj* playful ☞ *Los adjetivos ingleses son invariables.*
juicio *sm* ❶ DERECHO trial • **Elena está en medio de un juicio para resolver su divorcio** Elena is in the middle of a trial to resolve her divorce ▶ **juicio civil** civil action ▶ **juicio criminal** criminal trial ❷ [*sensatez*] (sound) judgement ❸ [*cordura*] reason • **estar/no estar en su (sano) juicio** to be/not to be in your right mind • **perder el juicio** to lose your reason ❹ [*opinión*] opinion • **a mi juicio** in my opinion

■ **Juicio Final** *sm* • **el Juicio Final** the Last Judgement

juicioso, sa *adj* sensible ◌̊: *Los adjetivos ingleses son invariables.*

julio *sm* ❶ [*mes*] July ❷ FÍSICA joule ver también **septiembre**

jungla *sf* jungle

junio *sm* June ver también **septiembre**

júnior (pl juniors) *adj invariable* ❶ DEPORTE under-21 ❷ [*hijo*] junior ◌̊: *Los adjetivos ingleses son invariables.*

junta *sf* ❶ [*generalmente*] committee ❷ [*de empresa, examinadores*] board ▶ **junta directiva** board of directors ▶ **junta militar** military junta ❸ [*reunión*] meeting • **el presidente está en junta y no puede atenderlo ahora** the president is in a meeting and cannot attend to you now ❹ [*juntura*] joint • **el motor pierde aceite por esa junta mal apretada** the motor is losing oil because of that joint that's not tightened well ▶ **junta de culata** gasket

juntar *vt* ❶ [*generalmente*] to put together • **junta los pies** put your feet together ❷ [*fondos*] to raise ❸ [*personas*] to bring together

■ **juntarse** *v pronominal* ❶ [*reunirse - personas*] to get together; [*- ríos, caminos*] to meet • **nos juntamos para celebrar los 80 años del abuelo** we got together to celebrate our grandfather's 80th birthday ❷ [*arrimarse*] to draw o move closer ❸ [*convivir*] to live together

junto, ta ◆ *adj* ❶ [*generalmente*] together • **Cecilia y su esposo llegaron juntos a la fiesta** Cecilia and her husband arrived together at the party ❷ [*próximo*] close together • **pon los pies juntos** put your feet close together ◌̊: *Los adjetivos ingleses son invariables.*
◆ *adv* • **todo junto a)** [*ocurrir* ETC] all at the same time **b)** [*escribirse*] as one word

Júpiter *sm* Jupiter

jurado, da *adj* ❶ [*declaración* ETC] sworn ❷ → **guarda** ◌̊: *Los adjetivos ingleses son invariables.*

■ **jurado** *sm* ❶ [*tribunal*] jury, *plural* juries • **el jurado concluyó que el acusado es culpable del asesinato** the jury concluded that the accused is guilty of the murder ❷ [*miembro*] member of the jury

juramento *sm* ❶ [*promesa*] oath ❷ [*blasfemia*] oath

jurar ◆ *vt* ❶ to swear • **te lo juro** I swear it • **jurar por... que** to swear by... that ❷ [*constitución* ETC] to pledge allegiance to
expresión **tenérsela jurada a alguien** to have it in for somebody
◆ *vi* [*blasfemar*] to swear

jurídico, ca *adj* legal ◌̊: *Los adjetivos ingleses son invariables.*

jurisdicción *sf* jurisdiction

jurista *smf* jurist

justamente *adv* ❶ [*con justicia*] justly ❷ [*exactamente*] exactly

justicia *sf* ❶ [*generalmente*] justice • **los manifestantes reclamaban justicia** the demonstrators were demanding justice • **hacer justicia** to do justice ❷ [*organización*] • **la justicia** the law
expresión **ser de justicia** to be only fair

justiciero, ra *adj* righteous ◌̊: *Los adjetivos ingleses son invariables.*

justificación *sf* [*generalmente*] IMPRENTA justification

justificante *sm* documentary evidence ◌̊: *incontable*

justificar *vt* ❶ [*generalmente*] IMPRENTA to justify • **no intentes justificar tu grosería** don't try to justify your rudeness ❷ [*excusar*] • **justificar a alguien** to make excuses for somebody

justo, ta *adj* ❶ [*equitativo*] fair • **tomaron una decisión justa** they made a fair decision ❷ [*merecido - recompensa, victoria*] deserved; [*- castigo*] just ❸ [*exacto - medida, hora*] exact • **aquí tienes 300 pesos justos** here you have exactly 300 pesos ❹ [*idóneo*] right ❺ [*apretado*] tight • **esa blusa te queda demasiado justa** that blouse is too tight • **estar justo** to be a tight fit ◌̊: *Los adjetivos ingleses son invariables.*

■ **justo** *adv* just • **justo iba a llamarte** I was just about to ring you • **justo en medio** right in the middle • **llegué justo antes de que el tren se fuera** I arrived right before the train left • **la comida dio justo para todos** the food was just enough for everybody

juvenil *adj* ❶ youthful ❷ DEPORTE youth ◌̊: *Sólo se usa delante del sustantivo.*

juventud *sf* ❶ [*edad*] youth ❷ [*conjunto*] young people *pl*
expresión **¡juventud, divino tesoro!** what it is to be young!

juzgado *sm* [*tribunal*] court

juzgar *vt* ❶ [*enjuiciar*] to judge • **no juzgues por las apariencias** don't judge by appearances • **lo juzgaron inocente** they judged him innocent ❷ DERECHO to try • **juzgar mal a alguien** to misjudge somebody • **a juzgar por (como)** judging by (how) ❸ [*estimar*] to consider

k *sf* [*letra*] k; K

kárate *sm* karate

kart (pl karts) *sm* go-kart

Kazajstán *nombre propio* Kazakhstan

Kenia *nombre propio* Kenya

ketchup *sm* ketchup

kg (*abreviatura escrita de* kilogramo) kg

kibutz (pl kibutzim) *sm* kibbutz

kilo *sm* [*peso*] kilo

kilogramo *sm* kilogram

kilometraje *sm* ≃ mileage distance in kilometers

kilométrico, ca *adj* [*distancia*] kilometric ✧: *Los adjetivos ingleses son invariables.*

kilómetro *sm* kilometer • **kilómetros por hora** kilometers per hour ▶ **kilómetro cuadrado** square kilometer

kilovatio *sm* kilowatt

kiosco = **quiosco**

kiwi *sm* [*fruto*] kiwi (fruit)

km (*abreviatura escrita de* kilómetro) km

km/h (*abreviatura escrita de* kilómetro por hora) km/h

KO (*abreviatura de* knockout) *sm* KO

Kuwait *nombre propio* Kuwait

l, L *sf* [*letra*] l; L

la¹ *sm* ❶ MÚSICA A ❷ [*en solfeo*] lah

la² ◆ *artículo* → **el** ◆ *pronombre* → **lo**

laberinto *sm* literal & figurado labyrinth

labia *sf* familiar smooth talk • **tener mucha labia** to have the gift of the gab

labio *sm* ❶ ANATOMÍA lip • **leer los labios** to lip-read ❷ [*borde*] edge

labor *sf* ❶ [*trabajo*] work • **siempre está ocupado en sus labores** he's always busy with his work ❷ [*tarea*] task ▶ **labores domésticas** household chores ❸ [*de costura*] needlework ▶ **labores de punto** knitting
expresión **ser de profesión sus labores** to be a housewife ▶ **no estar por la labor a)** [*distraerse*] not to have your mind on the job **b)** [*ser reacio*] not to be keen on the idea

laboral *adj* ❶ labor ❷ [*semana, condiciones*] working ☼ *Sólo se usa delante del sustantivo.* • **la semana laboral** the working week

laboratorio *sm* laboratory, *plural* <u>laboratories</u> ▶ **laboratorio espacial** space laboratory ▶ **laboratorio fotográfico** photographic laboratory ▶ **laboratorio de idiomas** o **lenguas** language laboratory

labrador, ra *sm, f* ❶ [*agricultor*] farmer ❷ [*trabajador*] farm worker

labrar *vt* ❶ [*campo - cultivar*] to cultivate; [*- arar*] to plough ❷ [*piedra, metal* ETC] to work ❸ figurado [*desgracia* ETC] to bring about ❹ [*porvenir, fortuna*] to carve out

labriego, ga *sm, f* farmworker

laca *sf* ❶ [*generalmente*] lacquer ❷ [*para cuadros*] lake ❸ [*para el pelo*] hairspray

lacónico, ca *adj* laconic ☼ *Los adjetivos ingleses son invariables.*

lacra *sf* scourge

lacrar *vt* to seal with sealing wax

lacre *sm* sealing wax

lacrimógeno, na *adj* ❶ [*novela* ETC] weepy ❷ → **gas** ☼ *Los adjetivos ingleses son invariables.*

lacrimoso, sa *adj* ❶ [*ojos* ETC] tearful ❷ [*historia* ETC] weepy ☼ *Los adjetivos ingleses son invariables.*

lactancia *sf* lactation ▶ **lactancia artificial** bottle-feeding ▶ **lactancia materna** breastfeeding

lactante *smf* breast-fed baby

lácteo, a *adj* ❶ [*generalmente*] milk ☼ *Sólo se usa delante del sustantivo.* ❷ [*industria, productos*] dairy

ladear *vt* to tilt

ladera *sf* slope

lado *sm* ❶ [*generalmente*] side • **el triángulo tiene tres lados** the triangle has three sides • **a ambos lados** on both sides • **en el lado de arriba/abajo** on the top/bottom • **al otro lado de** on the other side of • **de lado** [*torcido*] crooked • **dormir de lado** to sleep on your side • **de lado a lado** from side to side • **echar a un lado** to push aside • **echarse** o **hacerse a un lado** to move aside ❷ [*lugar*] • **debe estar en otro lado** it must be somewhere else • **¿vamos a pasear a algún lado?** are we going to go out somewhere? • **de un lado para** o **a otro** to and fro • **por todos lados** on all sides
expresiones **dar de lado a alguien** to cold-shoulder somebody ▶ **ponerse del lado de alguien** to side with somebody ▶ **por un lado** on the one hand ▶ **por otro lado** on the other hand • **por un lado me llevaría éste, pero por otro lado me parece demasiado caro** on the one hand I would take this one, but on the other hand it seems too expensive to me

ladrar *vi* to bark

ladrido *sm* bark • **a lo lejos se oían los ladridos del perro** the dog's barks were heard in the distance

ladrillo *sm* CONSTRUCCIÓN brick

ladrón, ona *sm, f* [*persona*] thief, *plural* <u>thieves</u> ■ **ladrón** *sm* [*para varios enchufes*] adapter

lagartija *sf* (small) lizard

lagarto, ta *sm, f* ZOOLOGÍA lizard

lago *sm* lake

lágrima *sf* tear
expresión **deshacerse en lágrimas** to dissolve into tears ▶ **llorar a lágrima viva** to cry buckets

lagrimal *sm* corner of the eye

laguna *sf* ❶ [*lago*] lagoon ❷ figurado [*en colección, memoria*] gap ❸ [*en leyes, reglamento*] loophole

La Habana *nombre propio* Havana

laico, ca *adj* lay:ϙ *Los adjetivos ingleses son invariables.*

lama *sm* lama

lamber *vt familiar* to lick

La Meca *nombre propio* Mecca

lamentable *adj* ❶ [*triste*] terribly sad ❷ [*malo*] deplorable:ϙ *Los adjetivos ingleses son invariables.*

lamentar *vt* to be sorry about • **lamento que ustedes dos no se entiendan** I'm sorry that you two don't understand each other • **lo lamento** I'm very sorry

lamento *sm* moan

lamer *vt* to lick

lámina *sf* ❶ [*plancha*] sheet ❷ [*placa*] plate ❸ [*rodaja*] slice ❹ [*plancha grabada*] engraving ❺ [*dibujo*] plate

lámpara *sf* ❶ [*aparato*] lamp ▶ **lámpara de mesa** table lamp ▶ **lámpara de pie** standard lamp ▶ **lámpara de soldar** blowtorch ▶ **lámpara de techo** ceiling lamp ❷ [*bombilla*] bulb ❸ TECNOLOGÍA valve

lana *sf* wool • **de lana** woollen • **pura lana virgen** pure new wool

expresión **ir a por lana y volver trasquilado** *proverbio* to be hoist by your own petard ▶ **unos cardan la lana y otros llevan la fama** *proverbio* some do all the work and others get all the credit

lance *sm* ❶ [*en juegos, deportes*] incident ❷ [*acontecimiento*] event ❸ [*riña*] dispute

lancha *sf* [*embarcación - grande*] launch; [*- pequeña*] boat • **lancha motora** motorboat ▶ **lancha salvavidas** lifeboat

langosta *sf* ❶ [*crustáceo*] lobster ❷ [*insecto*] locust

langostino *sm* king prawn

lánguido, da *adj* ❶ [*débil*] listless ❷ [*falto de ánimo*] disinterested:ϙ *Los adjetivos ingleses son invariables.*

lanza *sf* [*arma - arrojadiza*] spear; [*- en justas, torneos*] lance

expresión **estar lanza en ristre** to be ready for action ▶ **romper una lanza por alguien** to fight for somebody

lanzagranadas *sm invariable* grenade launcher

lanzamiento *sm* ❶ [*de objeto*] throwing ❷ [*de cohete*] launching ❸ DEPORTE [*con la mano*] throw; [*con el pie*] kick; [*en béisbol*] pitch ▶ **lanzamiento de peso** shot put ❹ [*de producto, artista*] launch ❺ [*de disco*] release

lanzamisiles *sm invariable* rocket launcher

lanzar *vt* ❶ [*generalmente*] to throw ❷ [*con fuerza*] to hurl ❸ [*de una patada*] to kick ❹ [*bomba*] to drop ❺ [*flecha, misil*] to fire ❻ [*cohete*] to launch ❼ [*proferir*] to let out ❽ [*acusación, insulto*] to hurl ❾ [*suspiro*] to heave ❿ COMERCIO [*producto, artista, periódico*] to launch; [*disco*] to release

La Paz *nombre propio* La Paz

lapicero *sm* pencil

lápida *sf* memorial stone ▶ **lápida mortuoria** tombstone

lápiz (pl **lápices**) *sm* pencil • **escribir algo a lápiz** to write something in pencil ▶ **lápiz de cejas** eyebrow pencil ▶ **lápices de colores** crayons ▶ **lápiz de labios** lipstick ▶ **lápiz de ojos** eyeliner ▶ **lápiz óptico** light pen

lapso *sm* space • **lapso de tiempo** space of time

lapsus *sm invariable* lapse

largar *vt* ❶ [*aflojar*] to pay out ❷ *familiar* [*dar, decir*] to give • **le largué un bofetón** I gave him a smack

largo, ga *adj* ❶ [*en espacio, tiempo*] long • **caminaron una distancia larga para llegar al pueblo** they walked a long distance to arrive at the town ❷ [*alto*] tall ❸ [*sobrado*] • **media hora larga** a good half hour:ϙ *Los adjetivos ingleses son invariables.*

■ **largo** ◆ *sm* length • **el largo de la cuadra es 100 metros** the length of the block is 100 meters • **a lo largo** lengthwise • **tiene dos metros de largo** it's two meters long • **pasar de largo** to pass by • **a lo largo de a)** [*en el espacio*] along **b)** [*en el tiempo*] throughout

expresión **¡largo de aquí!** go away! ▶ **para largo** a long time

◆ *adv* at length • **hacía tiempo que no se veían y hablaron largo** it had been a while since they had seen each other and they talked at great length • **largo y tendido** at great length

largometraje *sm* feature film

larguero *sm* ❶ CONSTRUCCIÓN main beam ❷ DEPORTE crossbar

largura *sf* length

laringe *sf* larynx

laringitis *sf invariable* laryngitis

larva *sf* larva

las ◆ *artículo* → **el**
◆ *pronombre* → **lo**

lasaña *sf* lasagna

láser ◆ *adj invariable* → **rayo**
◆ *sm invariable* laser

lástima *sf* ❶ [*compasión*] pity ❷ [*pena*] shame • **es una lástima que** it's a shame that • **¡qué lástima!** what a shame! • **da lástima ver gente así** it's sad to see people in that state • **tener** o **sentir lástima de** to feel sorry for

expresión **quedarse hecho una lástima** to be a sorry o pitiful sight

lastimar *vt* to hurt • **ten cuidado, no lastimes a tu hermano** be careful, don't hurt your brother

■ **lastimarse** *v pronominal* to hurt yourself • **se lastimó al caerse de la bicicleta** he hurt himself falling off the bicycle

lastre *sm* ❶ [*peso*] ballast ❷ *figurado* [*estorbo*] burden

lata *sf* ❶ [*envase*] can • **tenemos varias latas de atún** we have several cans of tuna ❷ [*de bebidas*] can • **en lata** canned ❸ *familiar* [*fastidio*] pain • **¡qué lata!** what a pain!

expresión **dar lata a alguien** to pester somebody

latente *adj* latent ⓘ *Los adjetivos ingleses son invariables.*

lateral ◆ *adj* [*del lado - generalmente*] lateral; [*- puerta, pared*] side ⓘ *Los adjetivos ingleses son invariables.*
◆ *sm* [*lado*] side

latido *sm* ❶ [*del corazón*] beat ❷ [*en dedo* ETC] throb

latifundio *sm* large rural estate

latigazo *sm* ❶ [*golpe*] lash ❷ [*chasquido*] crack (of the whip)

látigo *sm* whip

latín *sm* Latin ▸ **latín macarrónico** dog Latin
expresión **saber (mucho) latín** *figurado* to be sharp ; to be on the ball

latino, na *adj* & *sm, f* Latin ⓘ *Los adjetivos ingleses son invariables.*

latinoamericano, na *adj* & *sm, f* Latin American ⓘ *Los adjetivos ingleses son invariables.*
En inglés, los adjetivos que se refieren a un país o una región se escriben con mayúscula.

latir *vi* [*sujeto: corazón*] to beat

latitud *sf* GEOGRAFÍA latitude • **Buenos Aires está a 37 grados de latitud sur** Buenos Aires is at 37 degrees latitude south

latón *sm* brass

latoso, sa *adj familiar* tiresome ⓘ *Los adjetivos ingleses son invariables.*

laureado, da *adj* prize-winning ⓘ *Los adjetivos ingleses son invariables.*

laurel *sm* ❶ BOTÁNICA laurel ❷ COCINA bay leaf

lava *sf* lava

lavabo *sm* [*objeto*] sink

lavadero *sm* ❶ [*en casa*] laundry o utility sink ❷ washboard

lavado *sm* wash • **lavado a mano** hand-wash ▸ **lavado de cerebro** brainwashing ▸ **lavado de dinero** money-laundering ▸ **lavado en seco** dry cleaning

lavadora *sf* washing machine ▸ **lavadora secadora** washer-drier ▸ **lavadora de trastes** dishwasher

lavamanos *sm invariable* sink

lavanda *sf* lavender

lavandería *sf* ❶ [*de hotel*] laundry ❷ [*automática*] laundromat

lavar *vt* to wash • **¿quién va a lavar los platos?** who's going to wash the dishes? • **lavar a mano** to wash by hand • **lavar en seco** to dry-clean • **lavar y marcar** shampoo and set

■ **lavarse** *v pronominal* ❶ [*generalmente*] to wash yourself ❷ [*cara, manos, pelo*] to wash • **hoy tienes que lavarte el pelo** today you have to wash your hair ❸ [*dientes*] to brush • **¿ya te lavaste los dientes?** did you already brush your teeth?

laxante *sm* laxative

lazo *sm* ❶ [*atadura*] bow • **el paquete tenía un lazo celeste** the package had a blue bow • **hacer un lazo** to tie a bow ❷ [*trampa*] snare ❸ [*de vaquero*] lasso

• **el caballo estaba atado a la cerca con un lazo** the horse was tied to the fence with a lasso ❹ *figurado* [*vínculo*] tie

Lda. *(abreviatura escrita de* licenciada) → **licenciado**

Ldo. *abreviatura escrita de* **licenciado**

le *pronombre personal* ❶ ⓘ *complemento indirecto* [*hombre*] (to) him ❷ [*mujer*] (to) her ❸ [*cosa*] to it ❹ [*usted*] to you ❺ ⓘ *complemento directo* him • **le dije que me esperara, pero se fue** I told him to wait for me, but he left • **le expliqué el motivo** I explained the reason to him/her ❻ [*usted*] you • **ya le dije lo que pasaría** *a usted* I told you what would happen

leal *adj* • **leal (a)** loyal (to) ⓘ *Los adjetivos ingleses son invariables.*

lealtad *sf* • **lealtad (a)** loyalty (to)

lección *sf* lesson • **es mejor que estudies la lección antes de ir a clase** it's better for you to study the lesson before going to class • **aprenderse la lección** to learn your lesson

leche *sf* ❶ [*generalmente*] milk ▸ **leche esterilizada** sterilized milk ▸ **leche homogeneizada** homogenized milk ▸ **leche merengada** *para explicar lo que puedes decir:* it's a drink made from milk, egg whites, sugar and cinnamon ❷ *muy familiar* [*mal humor*] • **estar de mala leche** to be in a real bad mood • **tener mala leche** to have a real temper

lechería *sf* dairy, *plural* dairies

lechero, ra ◆ *adj* milk ⓘ *Sólo se usa delante del sustantivo.*
◆ *sm, f* [*persona*] milkman, *femenino* milkwoman

lecho *sm* bed • **lecho de muerte** deathbed

lechón *sm* sucking pig

lechuga *sf* lettuce ▸ **lechuga iceberg** iceberg lettuce ▸ **lechuga romana** cos lettuce
expresión **ser más fresco que una lechuga** to be a cheeky devil

lechuza *sf* (barn) owl

lectivo, va *adj* school ⓘ *Sólo se usa delante del sustantivo.*

lector, ra *sm, f* ❶ [*generalmente*] reader ❷ EDUCACIÓN language assistant
■ **lector** *sm* [*de microfilms* ETC] reader

lectura *sf* ❶ [*generalmente*] reading • **todos los días dedica dos horas a la lectura** every day he devotes two hours to reading • **en esa clase hacemos tres lecturas por semana** in that class we do three readings a week • **dar lectura a algo** to read something out loud ❷ [*escrito*] reading (matter) ⓘ *incontable* ❸ [*de tesis*] viva voce ❹ [*de datos*] scanning ▸ **lectura óptica** optical scanning

leer ◆ *vt* [*generalmente*] INFORMÁTICA to read
◆ *vi* to read • **¿sabes leer?** do you know how to read? • **leer de corrido** to read fluently

legado *sm* ❶ [*herencia*] legacy ❷ [*representante - persona*] legate

legal *adj* ❶ [*generalmente*] legal ❷ [*hora*] standard ⓘ *Los adjetivos ingleses son invariables.*

legalidad *sf* legality

L

legalizar *vt* to legalize

legendario, ria *adj* legendary⚲ *Los adjetivos ingleses son invariables.*

legible *adj* legible⚲ *Los adjetivos ingleses son invariables.*

legión *sf* literal & figurado legion

legislación *sf* legislation

legislar *vi* to legislate

legislatura *sf* [periodo] period of office

legitimar *vt* ❶ [legalizar] to legitimize ❷ [certificar] to authenticate

legítimo, ma *adj* ❶ [generalmente] legitimate ❷ [auténtico] real ❸ [oro] pure⚲ *Los adjetivos ingleses son invariables.*

lego, ga ✦ *adj* ❶ [generalmente] lay ❷ [ignorante] ignorant⚲ *Los adjetivos ingleses son invariables.*
✦ *sm, f* [generalmente] layman, *femenino* laywoman

legumbre *sf* ⚲ *generalmente pl* ❶ [garbanzo] pulse • **las habas y las lentejas son legumbres** beans and lentils are pulses ❷ [hortaliza] vegetable • **las lechugas y las papas son legumbres** lettuce and tomatoes are vegetables

lejanía *sf* distance

lejano, na *adj* distant • **se fue a vivir a un país muy lejano** she went to live in a very distant country • **no está lejano** it's not far (away)⚲ *Los adjetivos ingleses son invariables.*

lejía *sf* bleach

lejos *adv* ❶ [en el espacio] far • **podemos ir a pie, no es lejos de aquí** we can walk, it's not far from here • **¿está lejos?** is it far? • **a lo lejos** in the distance • **de lejos** from a distance ❷ [en el pasado] long ago • **eso queda ya lejos** that happened a long time ago ❸ [en el futuro] far in the future
expresiones **ir demasiado lejos** to go too far ▶ **llegar lejos** to go far ▶ **sin ir más lejos** indeed

lema *sm* ❶ [norma] motto ❷ [político, publicitario] slogan ❸ LINGÜÍSTICA & MATEMÁTICAS lemma

lencería *sf* ❶ [ropa] linen ❷ [tienda] draper's

lengua *sf* ❶ [generalmente] tongue • **el médico me pidió que le mostrara la lengua** the doctor asked me to show him my tongue • **sacarle la lengua a alguien** to stick your tongue out at somebody • **con la lengua de fuera** out of breath ▶ **lengua de gato** COCINA ≃ ladyfinger ▶ **lengua de fuego** tongue of flame ▶ **lengua de tierra** tongue of land ▶ **lengua de víbora** o **viperina** malicious tongue ❷ [idioma, lenguaje] language • **habla tres lenguas** she speaks three languages ▶ **lengua materna** mother tongue ▶ **lengua oficial** official language
expresiones **¿te ha comido la lengua el gato?** has the cat got your tongue? ▶ **darle a la lengua** *familiar* to chatter ▶ **irse de la lengua** to let the cat out of the bag ▶ **las malas lenguas dicen que...** according to the gossip... ▶ **morderse la lengua** to bite your tongue ▶ **tirar a alguien de la lengua** to draw somebody out

lenguado *sm* sole

lenguaje *sm* [generalmente] INFORMÁTICA language ▶ **lenguaje coloquial/comercial** colloquial/business language ▶ **lenguaje cifrado** code ▶ **lenguaje corporal** body language ▶ **lenguaje gestual** gestures *pl* ▶ **lenguaje máquina** machine language ▶ **lenguaje de alto nivel/de bajo nivel** high-level/low-level language ▶ **lenguaje de programación** programming language ▶ **lenguaje de los sordomudos** sign language

lengüeta *sf* MÚSICA tongue

lente *sf* lens • **los telescopios funcionan con un sistema de lentes** telescopes function with a system of lenses ▶ **lente de aumento** magnifying glass ▶ **lentes de contacto** contact lenses
■ **lentes** *smpl* glasses • **mi papá usa lentes desde hace años** my dad has been wearing glasses for years

lenteja *sf* lentil

lentitud *sf* slowness • **habla con una lentitud exasperante** he speaks with an exasperating slowness • **con lentitud** slowly

lento, ta *adj* ❶ [generalmente] slow ❷ [veneno] slow-working ❸ [agonía, enfermedad] lingering⚲ *Los adjetivos ingleses son invariables.*

leña *sf* [madera] firewood
expresión **echar leña al fuego** to add fuel to the flames o fire ▶ **llevar leña al monte** to carry coals to Newcastle

leñador, ra *sm, f* woodcutter

leño *sm* [de madera] log
expresión **dormir como un leño** to sleep like a log

Leo ✦ *sm* [zodiaco] Leo
✦ *smf* [persona] Leo

león, ona *sm, f* ❶ [africano] lion, *femenino* lioness ▶ **león marino** sea lion ❷ [puma] puma
expresión **ponerse como un león** to get furious ▶ **no es tan fiero el león como lo pintan** *proverbio* he/it ETC is not as bad as he/it ETC is made out to be

leonino, na *adj* [contrato, condiciones] one-sided⚲ *Los adjetivos ingleses son invariables.*

leopardo *sm* leopard

leotardo *sm* ❶ [medias] • **leotardos** stockings *pl* ❷ [de gimnasta ETC] leotard

leproso, sa *sm, f* leper

les *pronombre personal pl* ❶ ⚲ *complemento indirecto* (to) them • **les expliqué el motivo** I explained the reason to them • **les tengo miedo** I'm afraid of them • **Juan y Ana todavía no llegaron, aunque les pedí que pasaran por aquí a las ocho** Juan and Ana still haven't come, even though I asked them to come by here at eight o'clock ❷ [ustedes] you • **ya les dije lo que pasaría** [a ustedes] I told you what would happen • **¿no me oyeron? les pedí que no hicieran ruido** you didn't hear me? I asked you not to make noise

lesión *sf* ❶ [herida] injury • **los accidentados se están recuperando de las lesiones** the injured are recuperating from their injuries ▶ **lesión cerebral** brain damage ❷ DERECHO ▶ **lesión grave** grievous bodily harm

lesionado, da ✦ *adj* injured⚲ *Los adjetivos ingleses son invariables.*

◆ *sm, f* injured person

lesionar *vt* ❶ to injure ❷ *figurado* to damage

letal *adj* lethal:᷉ *Los adjetivos ingleses son invariables.*

letargo *sm* ZOOLOGÍA hibernation

letra *sf* ❶ [*signo*] letter • **la "a" es la primera letra del alfabeto** "a" is the first letter of the alphabet ▶ **letra mayúscula/minúscula** capital/small letter ❷ [*caligrafía*] handwriting • **tu letra es ilegible** your handwriting is illegible ❸ IMPRENTA typeface ▶ **letra bastardilla** o **cursiva** o **itálica** italic type; italics *pl* ▶ **letra de imprenta** o **molde a)** IMPRENTA print **b)** [*en formularios* ETC] block capitals *pl* ▶ **letra negrita** o **negrilla** bold (face) ▶ **letra versalita** small capital ❹ [*de canción*] lyrics *pl* ❺ COMERCIO • **letra (de cambio)** bill of exchange

expresiones **la letra con sangre entra** *proverbio* spare the rod and spoil the child ▶ **leer la letra pequeña** to read the small print ▶ **mandar cuatro letras a alguien** to drop somebody a line

letrado, da ◆ *adj* learned:᷉ *Los adjetivos ingleses son invariables.*
◆ *sm, f* lawyer

letrero *sm* sign ▶ **letrero luminoso** neon sign

letrina *sf* latrine

leucemia *sf* leukaemia

levadura *sf* yeast ▶ **levadura de cerveza** brewer's yeast ▶ **levadura en polvo** baking powder

levantamiento *sm* ❶ [*sublevación*] uprising ❷ [*elevación*] raising ▶ **levantamiento de pesas** DEPORTE weightlifting ❸ [*supresión*] lifting

levantar *vt* ❶ [*generalmente*] to raise • **el que esté de acuerdo, que levante la mano** those who agree, raise your hands ❷ [*peso, capó, trampilla*] to lift • **el campeón de pesas levanta 200 kilos** the weightlifting champion lifts 200 kilos • **levantar el ánimo** to cheer up • **levantar la vista** o **mirada** to look up ❸ [*pintura, venda, tapa*] to remove ❹ [*recoger - campamento*] to strike; [- *tienda de campaña, puesto*] to take down; [- *mesa*] to clear ❺ [*protestas, polémica*] to stir up • **levantar a alguien contra** to stir somebody up against ❻ [*suspender - embargo, prohibición*] to lift; [- *pena, castigo*] to suspend; [- *sesión*] to adjourn ❼ [*redactar - acta, atestado*] to draw up

■ **levantarse** *v pronominal* ❶ [*ponerse de pie*] to stand up ❷ [*de la cama*] to get up • **me levanto a las siete** I get up at seven o'clock • **levantarse tarde** to sleep in ❸ [*elevarse - avión* ETC] to take off; [- *niebla*] to lift ❹ [*sublevarse*] to rise up ❺ [*empezar - viento, oleaje*] to get up; [- *tormenta*] to gather

levar *vt* to weigh

leve *adj* ❶ [*generalmente*] light • **los pájaros son muy leves y eso les permite volar** birds are very light and that allows them to fly ❷ [*olor, sabor, temblor*] slight ❸ [*pecado, falta, herida*] minor ❹ [*enfermedad*] slight:᷉ *Los adjetivos ingleses son invariables.*

levedad *sf* ❶ lightness ❷ [*de temblor* ETC] slightness ❸ [*de pecado, falta, herida*] minor nature

ley *sf* ❶ [*generalmente*] law • **todos los ciudadanos son iguales ante la ley** all citizens are equal before the law

• **aprobar una ley** to pass a law ▶ **ley del embudo** one law for yourself and another for everyone else ▶ **ley de la gravedad** law of gravity ▶ **ley marcial** martial law ▶ **ley de la oferta y de la demanda** law of supply and demand ▶ **ley de la ventaja** DEPORTE advantage (law) ❷ [*parlamentaria*] act ❸ [*regla*] rule ❹ [*de un metal*] • **de ley a)** [*oro*] pure **b)** [*plata*] sterling

expresión **con todas las de la ley** in due form

leyenda *sf* legend • **según la leyenda...** according to the legend...

liar *vt* ❶ [*atar*] to tie up ❷ [*envolver - cigarrillo*] to roll • **liar algo en a)** [*papel*] to wrap something up in **b)** [*toalla* ETC] to roll something up in ❸ [*involucrar*] • **liar a alguien (en)** to get somebody mixed up (in) ❹ [*complicar - asunto* ETC] to confuse • **¡ya me has liado!** now you've really got me confused!

Líbano *sm* • **el Líbano** the Lebanon

libélula *sf* dragonfly

liberación *sf* ❶ [*generalmente*] liberation ❷ [*de preso*] release

liberado, da *adj* ❶ [*generalmente*] liberated ❷ [*preso*] freed:᷉ *Los adjetivos ingleses son invariables.*

liberal *adj* & *smf* liberal:᷉ *Los adjetivos ingleses son invariables.*

liberar *vt* ❶ [*generalmente*] to liberate ❷ [*preso*] to free • **las autoridades liberaron al acusado** the authorities freed the accused • **liberar de algo a alguien** to free somebody from something

libertad *sf* freedom • **tienes total libertad para tomar la decisión que te parezca mejor** you have complete freedom to make the decision that seems the best to you • **tener libertad para hacer algo** to be free to do something • **tomarse la libertad de hacer algo** to take the liberty of doing something ▶ **libertad de circulación de capitales/trabajadores** ECONOMÍA free movement of capital/workers ▶ **libertad de conciencia** freedom of conscience ▶ **libertad condicional** probation ▶ **libertad de cultos** religious freedom ▶ **libertad de expresión** freedom of speech ▶ **libertad de prensa** freedom of the press

libertar *vt* ❶ [*generalmente*] to liberate ❷ [*preso*] to set free

Libia *nombre propio* Libya

libido *sf* libido

libra *sf* [*peso, moneda*] pound • **una libra equivale aproximadamente a medio quilo** one pound equals approximately half a kilo ▶ **libra esterlina** pound sterling

■ **Libra** ◆ *sm* [*zodiaco*] Libra
◆ *smf* [*persona*] Libran

librar ◆ *vt* ❶ [*eximir*] • **librar a alguien (de algo/de hacer algo) a)** [*generalmente*] to free somebody (from something/from doing something) **b)** [*pagos, impuestos*] to exempt somebody (from something/from doing something) ❷ [*entablar - pelea, lucha*] to engage in; [- *batalla, combate*] to join; to wage ❸ COMERCIO to draw
◆ *vi* [*no trabajar*] to be off work

■ **librarse** *v pronominal* ❶ [*salvarse*] • **librarse (de hacer algo)** to escape (from doing something) • **gracias a su abogado se libró de la cárcel** thanks to his attorney, he escaped a jail sentence • **de buena te libraste** you had a narrow escape • **como está enfermo, se libró de limpiar la casa** since he's sick, he got out of cleaning the house ❷ [*deshacerse*] • **librarse de algo/alguien** to get rid of something/somebody • **no conseguí librarme de aquel pesado en toda la noche** I didn't manage to get rid of that pain all night

libre *adj* ❶ [*generalmente*] free • **no aguantaba ver al pájaro en una jaula, así que lo dejé libre** I couldn't stand seeing the bird in a cage, so I let it go free • **ser libre de hacer algo** to be free to do something ❷ [*rato, tiempo*] spare ❸ [*camino, vía*] clear ❹ [*espacio, departamento*] empty • **libre de a)** [*generalmente*] free from **b)** [*exento*] exempt from • **libre de franqueo** postage-paid • **libre de impuestos** tax-free ❺ [*alumno*] external:ℚ: *Los adjetivos ingleses son invariables.*

expresión **ir por libre** to go it alone ▶ **estudiar por libre** to be an external student

librería *sf* [*tienda*] bookstore ▶ **librería de ocasión** second-hand bookstore

> ## librería ≠ library
> • La palabra inglesa **library** es un falso amigo que significa **biblioteca**.
> • *Librería* se traduce al inglés por **bookstore**.

librero, ra ◆ *sm, f* [*persona*] bookseller ◆ *sm* [*mueble*] bookcase

libreta *sf* ❶ [*para escribir*] notebook • **libreta de direcciones** address book ❷ [*del banco*] ▶ **libreta (de ahorros)** savings book

libro *sm* book • **un libro de viajes** a travel book • **llevar los libros** to keep the books ▶ **libro de bolsillo** paperback ▶ **libro de contabilidad** accounts book ▶ **libro de ejercicios** workbook ▶ **libro de reclamaciones** complaints book ▶ **libro de texto** textbook ▶ **libro de visitas** visitor's book

expresión **colgar los libros** to give up your studies ▶ **ser como un libro abierto** to be an open book

Lic. *abreviatura escrita de* **licenciado**

licencia *sf* ❶ [*documento*] licence • **para conducir automóviles necesitas una licencia** in order to drive a car you need a license ❷ [*autorización*] permission • **a los 16 años le dieron licencia para llegar a medianoche** when he was 16 years old they gave him permission to get home at midnight ▶ **licencia de exportación/importación** export/import license ▶ **licencia de obras** planning permission ❸ [*en el trabajo*] leave • **tengo 20 días de licencia anual** I have 20 days of annual leave ▶ **licencia por enfermedad** sick leave ❹ MILITAR discharge ❺ [*confianza*] license ▶ **licencia poética** poetic license

licenciado, da *sm, f* EDUCACIÓN graduate • **mi hermana es licenciada en biología** my sister is a biology graduate • **licenciado en economía** economics grad-

uate ❷ MILITAR discharged soldier ❸ [*forma de tratamiento*] • **el licenciado González** Mr. González

licenciar *vt* MILITAR to discharge

licenciatura *sf* degree • **hizo la licenciatura en la Universidad Veracruzana** he got his degree at the University of Veracruz

lícito, ta *adj* ❶ [*legal*] lawful ❷ [*correcto*] right ❸ [*justo*] fair:ℚ: *Los adjetivos ingleses son invariables.*

licor *sm* liquor

licuado *sm* milk shake

licuadora *sf* blender

licuar *vt* COCINA to blend or purée

líder ◆ *adj* leading:ℚ: *Los adjetivos ingleses son invariables.*
◆ *smf* leader

liderato, liderazgo *sm* ❶ [*primer puesto*] lead ❷ [*en liga*] first place ❸ [*dirección*] leadership

lidiar *vi* [*luchar*] • **lidiar (con)** to struggle (with)

liebre *sf* ZOOLOGÍA hare

lienzo *sm* ❶ [*para pintar*] canvas ❷ [*cuadro*] painting

lifting (pl liftings) *sm* facelift

liga *sf* ❶ [*generalmente*] league • **el campeón de la liga de primavera fue el mismo que el año pasado** the champion of the spring league was the same as last year's ❷ [*de medias*] garter • **necesito una liga para la media** I need a garter for my stocking

ligadura *sf* ❶ MEDICINA & MÚSICA ligature ❷ [*atadura*] bond

ligamento *sm* ANATOMÍA ligament

ligar ◆ *vt* ❶ [*generalmente*] COCINA to bind ❷ [*atar*] to tie (up)
◆ *vi* ❶ [*coincidir*] • **ligar (con)** to tally (with) ❷ *familiar* [*conquistar*] • **ligar (con)** to hook up (with)

ligereza *sf* ❶ [*levedad*] lightness ❷ [*agilidad*] agility ❸ [*irreflexión - cualidad*] rashness; [*- acto*] rash act • **con ligereza** in a superficial manner

ligero, ra *adj* ❶ [*generalmente*] light • **la ropa de lino es ligera** linen clothing is light ❷ [*dolor, rumor, descenso*] slight ❸ [*traje, tela*] thin ❹ [*ágil*] agile ❺ [*rápido*] quick • **ese caballo es muy ligero** that horse is very quick:ℚ: *Los adjetivos ingleses son invariables.*

expresiones **hacer algo a la ligera** to do something without much thought ▶ **juzgar a alguien a la ligera** to be quick to judge somebody ▶ **tomarse algo a la ligera** not to take something seriously

light *adj invariable* ❶ [*comida*] low-calorie ❷ [*refresco*] diet:ℚ: *Sólo se usa delante del sustantivo.* ❸ [*cigarrillos*] light

lija *sf* [*papel*] sandpaper

lila ◆ *sf* [*flor*] lilac
◆ *adj invariable* & *sm* [*color*] lilac • **el lila es mi color favorito** lilac is my favorite color:ℚ: *Los adjetivos ingleses son invariables.*

lima *sf* ❶ [*utensilio*] file ▶ **lima de uñas** nail file ❷ BOTÁNICA lime

limar *vt* ❶ [*pulir*] to file down ❷ [*perfeccionar*] to polish

limitación *sf* ❶ [*restricción*] limitation ❷ [*distrito*] boundaries *pl*

limitado, da *adj* ❶ [*generalmente*] limited ❷ [*poco inteligente*] dim-witted. ♀: *Los adjetivos ingleses son invariables.*

limitar ◆ *vt* ❶ [*generalmente*] to limit ❷ [*terreno*] to mark out ❸ [*atribuciones, derechos* ETC] to set out
◆ *vi* • limitar (con) to border (on)

límite ◆ *adj invariable* ❶ [*precio, velocidad, edad*] maximum ❷ [*situación*] extreme ❸ [*caso*] borderline. ♀: *Los adjetivos ingleses son invariables.*
◆ *sm* ❶ [*tope*] limit • **se esforzó hasta el límite para ganar** he exerted himself to the limit in order to win • **dentro de un límite** within limits • **su pasión no tiene límite** her passion knows no bounds ▸ **límite de velocidad** speed limit ❷ [*confín*] boundary, *plural* boundaries • **el balón salió de los límites del campo** the ball went out of the field's boundaries

limítrofe *adj* ❶ [*país, territorio*] bordering ❷ [*terreno, finca*] neighboring. ♀: *Los adjetivos ingleses son invariables.*

limón *sm* lemon

limonada *sf* lemonade

limonero, ra *adj* lemon. ♀: *Sólo se usa delante del sustantivo.*
■ **limonero** *sm* lemon tree

limosna *sf* alms *pl* • **pedir limosna** to beg

limosnero, ra ◆ *adj* charitable
◆ *sm, f* beggar

limpia *sf* cleaning

limpiabotas *smf invariable* shoeshine

limpiacristales *sm invariable* window-cleaning fluid

limpiamente *adv* ❶ [*con destreza*] cleanly ❷ [*honradamente*] honestly

limpiaparabrisas *sm invariable* windshield wiper

limpiar *vt* ❶ [*generalmente*] to clean • **tú limpia la cocina y yo limpiaré el baño** you clean the kitchen and I'll clean the bathroom • **limpiar en seco** to dry-clean ❷ [*con trapo*] to wipe • **¿tienes un trapo para limpiar la mesa?** do you have a rag to wipe the table? ❸ [*mancha*] to wipe away ❹ [*zapatos*] to polish ❺ *figurado* [*desembarazar*] • **limpiar algo de algo** to clear something of something

limpieza *sf* ❶ [*cualidad*] cleanliness • **la limpieza es primordial en los hospitales** cleanliness is essential in hospitals ❷ [*acción*] cleaning • **hoy la limpieza me llevó cuatro horas** today the cleaning took me four hours ▸ **limpieza en seco** dry cleaning ❸ [*destreza*] skill ❹ [*honradez*] honesty

limpio, pia *adj* ❶ [*generalmente*] clean ❷ [*pulcro*] neat ❸ [*cielo, imagen*] clear ❹ [*sueldo*] net ❺ [*honrado*] honest ❻ [*intenciones*] honorable ❼ [*juego*] clean ❽ [*sin culpa*] • **estar limpio** to be in the clear. ♀: *Los adjetivos ingleses son invariables.*

■ **limpio** *adv* • **pasar** O **poner en limpio** to make a clean copy of • **jugar limpio** to play fair

linaje *sm* lineage

lince *sm* lynx

expresión **ser un lince para algo** to be very sharp at something

linchar *vt* to lynch

lindar ■ lindar con *vi* ❶ [*terreno*] to adjoin ❷ [*conceptos, ideas*] to border on

lindo, da *adj* pretty • **se compró un lindo vestido blanco para la fiesta** she bought herself a pretty white dress for the party • **es una linda película, vale la pena verla** it's a nice movie, it's worth seeing. ♀: *Los adjetivos ingleses son invariables.*

expresión **de lo lindo** a great deal

línea *sf* ❶ [*generalmente*] DEPORTE & TELECOMUNICACIONES line • **la distancia más corta entre dos puntos es una línea recta** the shortest distance between two points is a straight line • **hay varias líneas de ómnibus para ir al centro** there are several bus lines that go downtown • **había leído apenas diez líneas cuando tuve que interrumpir** he had scarcely read ten lines when I had to interrupt ▸ **línea aérea** airline ▸ **línea de conducta** course of action ▸ **línea continua** AUTOMÓVILES solid white line ▸ **línea de mira** O **tiro** line of fire ▸ **línea de puntos** dotted line ▸ **línea telefónica** telephone line • **cortar la línea (telefónica)** to cut off the phone ❷ [*de un coche* ETC] lines *pl* ❸ [*silueta*] figure • **guardar la línea** to watch your figure ❹ [*estilo*] style • **de línea clásica** classical ❺ [*categoría*] class • **de primera línea** first-rate ❻ INFORMÁTICA • **en línea** on-line • **fuera de línea** off-line

expresiones **en líneas generales** in broad terms ▸ **en toda la línea** [*completamente*] all along the line ▸ **leer entre líneas** to read between the lines

lineamientos *smpl* ❶ [*generalidades*] outline ❷ [*directrices*] guidelines

lingote *sm* ingot

lingüista *smf* linguist

lingüístico, ca *adj* linguistic. ♀: *Los adjetivos ingleses son invariables.*
■ **lingüística** *sf* linguistics. ♀: *incontable*

linier (pl liniers) *sm* linesman

lino *sm* ❶ [*planta*] flax ❷ [*tejido*] linen

linterna *sf* ❶ [*de pilas*] flashlight ❷ [*farol*] lantern

lío *sm* ❶ [*paquete*] bundle ❷ *familiar* [*enredo*] mess • **¡qué lío hay en esta habitación!** what a mess this room is! • **hacerse un lío** to get muddled up • **meterse en líos** to get into trouble ❸ *familiar* [*jaleo*] racket ❹ *familiar* [*amorío*] affair

liposucción *sf* liposuction

liquidación *sf* ❶ [*pago*] settlement ❷ [*rebaja*] clearance sale ❸ [*fin*] liquidation

liquidar *vt* ❶ [*pagar - deuda*] to pay; [*- cuenta*] to settle ❷ [*rebajar*] to sell off ❸ [*malgastar*] to throw away ❹ [*acabar - asunto*] to settle; [*- negocio, sociedad*] to wind up

líquido, da *adj* ❶ [*generalmente*] liquid ❷ ECONOMÍA [*neto*] net ⚬ *Los adjetivos ingleses son invariables.*

■ **líquido** *sm* ❶ [*generalmente*] liquid ❷ ECONOMÍA liquid assets *pl* ❸ MEDICINA fluid

lira *sf* MÚSICA lyre

lírico, ca *adj* LITERATURA lyrical ⚬ *Los adjetivos ingleses son invariables.*

■ **lírica** *sf* lyric poetry

lirio *sm* iris

lirón *sm* ZOOLOGÍA dormouse

expresión **dormir como un lirón** to sleep like a log

liso, sa *adj* ❶ [*llano*] flat ❷ [*sin asperezas*] smooth • **la piel de los bebés es lisa y suave** babies' skin is smooth and soft ❸ [*pelo*] straight • **los 400 metros lisos** the 400 meters ❹ [*no estampado*] plain • **me gusta más esta blusa lisa que aquella floreada** I like this plain blouse more than that flowered one ⚬ *Los adjetivos ingleses son invariables.*

expresión **lisa y llanamente** quite simply

lista *sf* ❶ [*enumeración*] list • **¿dónde está la lista de invitados?** where's the invitation list? • **pasar lista** to call the register ❷ [*tela, madera*] strip ❸ [*de papel*] slip ❹ [*de color*] stripe

listado, da *adj* striped ⚬ *Los adjetivos ingleses son invariables.*

listo, ta *adj* ❶ [*inteligente, hábil*] smart • **Marcos es un niño listo, va a tener buenas calificaciones** Marcos is a smart boy, he's going to have good grades ❷ [*preparado*] ready • **cuando llegué a casa de Marisa, ya estaba lista** when I arrived at Marisa's house, she was already ready • **¿estáis listos?** are you ready? ⚬ *Los adjetivos ingleses son invariables.*

expresiones **dárselas de listo** to make yourself out to be clever ▶ **pasarse de listo** to be too clever by half ▶ **ser más listo que el hambre** to be nobody's fool

listón *sm* ❶ lath ❷ DEPORTE bar

expresión **poner el listón muy alto** to set very high standards

litera *sf* ❶ [*cama*] bunk (bed) ❷ [*de barco*] berth ❸ [*de tren*] sleeping berth (on train) ❹ [*vehículo*] litter

literal *adj* literal ⚬ *Los adjetivos ingleses son invariables.*

literario, ria *adj* literary ⚬ *Los adjetivos ingleses son invariables.*

literatura *sf* literature

litigio *sm* ❶ DERECHO litigation ⚬ *incontable* ❷ *figurado* dispute • **en litigio** in dispute

litoral ◆ *adj* coastal ⚬ *Los adjetivos ingleses son invariables.*
◆ *sm* coast

litro *sm* liter

liviano, na *adj* ❶ [*ligero - blusa*] thin ; [*- carga*] light ❷ [*sin importancia*] slight ⚬ *Los adjetivos ingleses son invariables.*

lívido, da *adj* ❶ [*pálido*] very pale ❷ [*amoratado*] livid ⚬ *Los adjetivos ingleses son invariables.*

llaga *sf* literal & figurado wound

llama *sf* ❶ [*de fuego, pasión*] flame • **en llamas** ablaze ❷ ZOOLOGÍA llama

llamada *sf* ❶ [*generalmente*] call ❷ [*a la puerta*] knock ❸ [*con timbre*] ring ❹ TELECOMUNICACIONES phone call • **hacer una llamada** to make a phone call • **devolver una llamada** to phone back ▶ **llamada internacional** international call

llamado, da *adj* so-called ⚬ *Los adjetivos ingleses son invariables.*

■ **llamado** *sm* [*al público*] call

llamamiento *sm* appeal

llamar ◆ *vt* ❶ [*generalmente*] to call • **la mamá de Julio lo llamaba para que entrara a comer** Julio's mom was calling him to come in and eat • **su nombre es Inés, pero la llaman Ina** her name is Inés, but they call her Ina ❷ [*por teléfono*] to phone ; to call • **mañana te llamo antes de pasar a buscarte** I'll call tomorrow before coming to get you ❸ [*convocar*] to call • **el presidente llamó a los ministros para pedirles su opinión** the president called upon the ministers to ask them their opinions • **llamar (a filas)** MILITAR to call up ❹ [*atraer*] to attract

◆ *vi* ❶ [*a la puerta* ETC *- con golpes*] to knock ; [*- con timbre*] to ring • **están llamando** there's somebody at the door • **están llamando a la puerta** somebody's knocking at the door ❷ [*por teléfono*] to phone

■ **llamarse** *v pronominal* [*tener por nombre*] to be called • **¿cómo se llama su último disco?** what's his latest record called? • **¿cómo te llamas?** what's your name? • **me llamo Pepe** my name's Pepe

llamarada *sf* [*de fuego, ira* ETC] blaze

llamativo, va *adj* ❶ [*color*] bright ❷ [*ropa*] showy ⚬ *Los adjetivos ingleses son invariables.*

llano, na *adj* ❶ [*campo, superficie*] flat ❷ [*trato, persona*] natural ❸ [*pueblo, clase*] ordinary ❹ [*lenguaje, expresión*] simple ⚬ *Los adjetivos ingleses son invariables.*

■ **llano** *sm* [*llanura*] plain

llanta *sf* [*neumático*] tire ▶ **llanta de refacción** spare tire

llanto *sm* tears *pl*

llanura *sf* plain

llave *sf* ❶ [*generalmente*] key • **puedes dejar la llave debajo del felpudo** you can leave the key under the doormat • **bajo llave** under lock and key • **cerrar con llave** to lock • **echar la llave** to lock up • **llave en mano** [*vivienda*] ready for immediate occupation ▶ **llave de contacto** ignition key ▶ **llave maestra** master key ❷ [*del agua, gas*] faucet • **cierra la llave para no desperdiciar agua** turn off the faucet in order to not waste water ❸ [*de la electricidad*] switch ▶ **cerrar la llave de paso** to turn the water/gas off at the mains ❹ [*herramienta*] wrench ▶ **llave de périco** adjustable wrench ❺ [*de judo* ETC] hold ❻ [*signo ortográfico*] curly bracket

llavero *sm* keyring

llegada *sf* ❶ [*generalmente*] arrival ❷ DEPORTE finish

llegar *vi* ❶ [*a un sitio*] • **llegar (de)** to arrive (from) • **llegué a la capital al final del día** I arrived in the capital at the end of the day • **llegar a un hotel/una ciudad** to arrive at a hotel/in a city • **llegaré pronto** I'll be there early ❷ [*un tiempo, la noche* ETC] to come ❸ [*durar*] • **llegar a** o **hasta** to last until ❹ [*alcanzar*] • **llegar a** to reach • **llegar a un acuerdo** to reach an agreement • **no llego al techo** I can't reach the ceiling • **llegar hasta** to reach up to ❺ [*ser suficiente*] • **llegar (para)** to be enough (for) ❻ [*lograr*] • **llegar a (ser) algo** to get to be something; to become something • **si llego a saberlo** if I'd known

llenar *vt* ❶ [*ocupar*] • **llenar algo (de) a)** [*vaso, hoyo, habitación*] to fill something (with) **b)** [*pared, suelo*] to cover something (with) ❷ [*satisfacer*] to satisfy ❸ [*rellenar - impreso*] to fill in o out ❹ [*colmar*] • **llenar a alguien de** to fill somebody with

■ **llenarse** *v pronominal* ❶ [*ocuparse*] to fill up • **el estadio se llenó de aficionados** the stadium filled up with fans ❷ [*saciarse*] to be full • **no puedo comer más, ya me llené** I can't eat any more, I'm already full ❸ [*cubrirse*] • **llenarse de** to get covered in • **se le llenó la cara de granos** his face got covered in pimples

lleno, na *adj* ❶ [*generalmente*] full • **el teatro está lleno, no vamos a poder entrar** the theater is full, we're not going to be able to get in • **estas medias están llenas de agujeros** these stockings are full of holes • **no me sirvas más, por favor, estoy lleno** don't serve me more, please, I'm full ❷ [*cubierto*] covered • **lleno de a)** [*generalmente*] full of **b)** [*manchas, pósters*] covered in • **lleno hasta los topes** full to bursting ❸ *familiar* [*regordete*] chubby ♀ *Los adjetivos ingleses son invariables.*

llevadero, ra *adj* bearable ♀ *Los adjetivos ingleses son invariables.*

---

llevar
◆ *vt*

❶ [*tener un peso, una carga*] to carry
• **llevaba un costal en la espalda** he was carrying a sack on his back
• **el avión llevaba carga** the plane was carrying cargo

❷ [*tener en su persona*]
• **no llevo dinero** I haven't got any cash on me

❸ [*tener en su persona, refiriéndose a la ropa*] to wear
• **lleva un vestido azul** she's wearing a blue dress
• **lleva un traje nuevo/lentes** she's wearing a new suit/glasses

❹ [*indica un estado transitorio*] to have
• **lleva el pelo corto/recogido** she has short hair/she wears her hair up
• **llevas las manos sucias** your hands are dirty

❺ [*de un lugar a otro*] to take
• **Elena llevó los platos a la mesa** Elena took the plates to the table
• **le llevé un regalo** I took him a present
• **llevo a Diego a su casa** I'll take Diego home

• **nos llevó al teatro** he took us to the theater
• **llévenos al hospital** take us to hospital

❻ [*conducir alguien a algo/ a hacer algo*] to lead to
• **una estrategia que los llevó a la victoria** a strategy that led us to victory
• **ese éxito juvenil lo llevó a dejar los estudios** that early success led him to abandon his studies
• **el juego te va a llevar a la ruina** the game is going to ruin you

❼ [*para expresar la duración*]
• **lleva dos años aquí** he's been here two years
• **llevo una hora esperándote** I've been waiting an hour for you
• **me llevó un día hacer este pastel** it took me a day to make this cake

❽ [*dirigir*]
• **lleva bien su negocio** he manages his business well
• **el matrimonio que lleva el restaurante** the couple who manage the restaurant

❾ [*encargarse de*]
• **es ella quien lleva la casa** she's the one who manages everything at home
• **llevar las cuentas** to keep the accounts

❿ [*soportar*]
• **lleva su enfermedad con resignación** she's resigned to her illness
• **lleva mal su descalificación** he's not handling his disqualification well

⓫ [*rebasar en edad, estatura*]
• **mi hijo me lleva dos centímetros** my son is two centimeters taller than me

⓬ [*mantener*]
• **llevar el paso** walk in step

◆ *vi*

❶ [*antes de un gerundio, expresa la continuidad*]
• **llevan saliendo juntos desde el pasado verano** they've been going out together since last summer

❷ [*antes de un participio pasado, para constatar algo*]
• **lleva leída media novela** he's half-way through the novel
• **llevamos andados 20 kilómetros** we've walked 20 kilometers so far

■ **llevarse**

◆ *v pronominal*

❶ [*tomar, transportar*]
• **los ladrones se llevaron todo** the thieves took everything
• **¡alguien se ha llevado mi bolso!** somebody's taken my bag!
• **el río se llevó la carretera** the floods washed away the road

❷ [*ganar*] to take
• **se llevó el premio a la mejor actriz** she took the prize for best actress

❸ [*desplazar un lugar a otro*]
• **se llevó la copa a los labios** she raised the glass to her lips

❹ [*tener una sensación*] to have
• **¡me llevé un susto!** I had a real scare!

❺ [*tener una buena o mala relación con alguien*]
• **llevarse bien/mal (con alguien)** to get on well/badly (with sb)
• **los tres hermanos se llevan muy bien** the three brothers get along very well

❻ [*estar de moda*]
• **la minifalda ya no se lleva** miniskirts are not fashionable any more

❼ [*en matemáticas*]
• **menos dos, más tres y me llevo seis...** take away two, add three and carry six

llorar *vi* to cry

lloriquear *vi* to whine

lloro *sm* tears *pl*

llorón, ona *sm, f* crybaby

lloroso, sa *adj* tearful:☝ *Los adjetivos ingleses son invariables.*

llover *v impersonal* to rain • **está lloviendo** it's raining

expresión **está lloviendo a cántaros** it's raining cats and dogs

llovizna *sf* drizzle

lloviznar *v impersonal* to drizzle

lluvia *sf* Meteorología rain • **lluvia torrencial** torrential rain • **bajo la lluvia** in the rain ▶ **lluvia ácida** acid rain ▶ **lluvia radiactiva** (nuclear) fallout

lluvioso, sa *adj* rainy:☝ *Los adjetivos ingleses son invariables.*

lo, la (mpl los, fpl las) *pronombre personal* **❶**:☝ *complemento directo* [*cosa*] it, *plural* them • **¿tu libro? hace días que no lo veo** your book? I haven't seen it in days **❷** [*persona*] him, *femenino* her, *plural* them • **¿a tu hermano? hace mucho que no lo veo** your brother? I haven't seen him in a long time **❸** [*usted*] you • **venga conmigo, lo llevaré hasta la oficina de su esposa** come with me, I'll take you to your wife's office

■ lo **◆** *pronombre personal* it • **su hermana es muy guapa pero él no lo es** his sister is very good-looking, but he isn't • **es muy bueno aunque no lo parezca** it's very good, even if it doesn't look it

◆ *artículo determinado* • **lo antiguo me gusta más que lo moderno** I like old things better than modern things • **lo mejor/peor** the best/worst part • **no te imaginas lo grande que era** you can't imagine how big it was • **lo bueno es que nos reconciliamos** the good thing is we made up • **prefiero lo dulce** I prefer sweet things

lobato *sm* wolf cub

lobby (pl lobbies) *sm* lobby

lobo, ba *sm, f* wolf

■ lobo de mar *sm* [*marinero*] sea dog

lóbulo *sm* lobe

local **◆** *adj* local:☝ *Los adjetivos ingleses son invariables.*

◆ *sm* [*edificio*] premises *pl* • **'alquilo local comercial'** commercial premises for rent

localidad *sf* **❶** [*población*] town • **la gente de la localidad es muy simpática** the people in town are very nice **❷** [*asiento*] seat **❸** [*entrada*] ticket • **¡qué lástima! ya se agotaron las localidades** what a shame! the tickets are sold out • **'no hay localidades'** sold out

localizar *vt* **❶** [*encontrar*] to locate **❷** [*circunscribir*] to localize

loción *sf* lotion

loco, ca **◆** *adj* **❶** [*generalmente*] crazy • **volverse loco por** to be crazy about • **loco de atar** o **remate** stark raving mad **❷** [*extraordinario - interés, ilusión*] tremendous; [*- amor, alegría*] wild:☝ *Los adjetivos ingleses son invariables.*

◆ *sm, f* literal & figurado madman, *femenino* madwoman • **conduce como un loco** he drives like a madman

locomoción *sf* [*de tren*] locomotion

locomotor, ra, triz *adj* locomotive:☝ *Los adjetivos ingleses son invariables.*

■ locomotora *sf* engine

locución *sf* phrase

locura *sf* **❶** [*demencia*] madness **❷** [*imprudencia*] folly • **hacer locuras** to do crazy things • **ser una locura** to be madness

locutor, ra *sm, f* **❶** [*de radio*] announcer **❷** [*de televisión*] presenter

locutorio *sm* **❶** Telecomunicaciones phone box **❷** Radio & Televisión studio

lodo *sm* mud

logaritmo *sm* logarithm

lógico, ca *adj* logical • **es lógico que se enfade** it stands to reason that he should get angry:☝ *Los adjetivos ingleses son invariables.*

■ lógica *sf* [*ciencia*] logic

logístico, ca *adj* logistic:☝ *Los adjetivos ingleses son invariables.*

■ logística *sf* logistics *pl*

logopeda *smf* speech therapist

logotipo *sm* logo

logrado, da *adj* [*bien hecho*] accomplished:☝ *Los adjetivos ingleses son invariables.*

lograr *vt* **❶** [*generalmente*] to achieve • **siempre logra lo que se propone** he always achieves what he sets out to do **❷** [*puesto, beca, divorcio*] to get **❸** [*resultado*] to obtain **❹** [*perfección*] to attain **❺** [*victoria, premio*] to win **❻** [*deseo, aspiración*] to fulfil • **lograr hacer algo** to manage to do something • **lograr que alguien haga algo** to manage to get somebody to do something • **no logro entender este artículo en inglés** I can't seem to understand this article in English

logro *sm* achievement • **tiene miedo de volar así que fue un logro subirla al avión** she's afraid of flying so it was quite an achievement to get her on the plane

loma *sf* hillock

lombriz *sf* earthworm

lomo *sm* **❶** [*espalda*] back • **el lomo de un caballo** the back of a horse **❷** [*carne*] loin **❸** [*de libro*] spine

• **en el lomo del libro puedes ver el título** you can read the title on the spine of the book

lona *sf* canvas • **me compré zapatos azules de lona** I bought some blue canvas shoes

lonchería *sf* snack bar

londinense ◆ *adj* London ⚐ *Sólo se usa delante del sustantivo.*

◆ *smf* Londoner

Londres *nombre propio* London

longitud *sf* ❶ [*dimensión*] length • **la piscina tiene 50 metros de longitud** the pool is 50 meters in length ▶ **longitud de onda** wavelength ❷ ASTRONOMÍA & GEOGRAFÍA longitude • **la longitud se mide a partir del meridiano de Greenwich** longitude is measured from the Greenwich meridian

lonja *sf* love handle

loquera *sf* madness

loro *sm* parrot

los ◆ *artículo* → **el**

◆ *pronombre* → **lo**

losa *sf* ❶ [*generalmente*] paving stone ❷ [*de tumba*] tombstone

lote *sm* ❶ [*parte*] share ❷ [*conjunto*] batch ❸ [*de tierra*] plot (of land)

lotería *sf* ❶ [*generalmente*] lottery • **le tocó la lotería** she won the lottery • **jugar a la lotería** to play the lottery ❷ [*juego de mesa*] lotto

loza *sf* ❶ [*material*] earthenware ❷ [*porcelana*] china ❸ [*objetos*] crockery

lubricante, lubrificante ◆ *adj* lubricating ⚐ *Los adjetivos ingleses son invariables.*

◆ *sm* lubricant

lubricar, lubrificar *vt* to lubricate

lucha *sf* ❶ [*combate*] fight ❷ figurado struggle • **abandonar la lucha** to give up the struggle ▶ **lucha armada** armed struggle ▶ **lucha libre** all-in wrestling

luchar *vi* ❶ [*combatir*] to fight • **el regimiento luchó con valentía hasta el fin** the regiment fought bravely to the end ❷ figurado struggle • **luchar contra/por** to fight against/for • **los diputados lucharon por imponer sus ideas** the representatives struggled to enforce their ideas

lucidez *sf* lucidity

lúcido, da *adj* lucid ⚐ *Los adjetivos ingleses son invariables.*

luciérnaga *sf* glow-worm

lucimiento *sm* ❶ [*de ceremonia* ETC] sparkle ❷ [*de actriz* ETC] brilliant performance

lucir ◆ *vi* ❶ [*generalmente*] to shine ❷ [*llevar puesto*] to wear • **Ana lució con orgullo su vestido nuevo** Ana wore her new dress proudly ❸ [*parecer*] to look • **trabaja demasiado, por eso luce cansada** she works too much, that's why she looks tired

◆ *vt* ❶ [*generalmente*] to show off ❷ [*ropa*] to sport

■ **lucirse** *v pronominal* ❶ [*destacar*] • **lucirse (en)** to shine (at) ❷ familiar & irónico [*quedar mal*] to mess things up

lucrativo, va *adj* lucrative • **no lucrativo** non profit-making ⚐ *Los adjetivos ingleses son invariables.*

lucro *sm* profit

lúdico, ca *adj* [*del juego*] game ⚐ *Sólo se usa delante del sustantivo.*

luego ◆ *adv* ❶ [*justo después*] then • **primero arreglé el jardín y luego me senté a disfrutar del sol** first I did the gardening and then sat down to enjoy the sunshine • **primero aquí y luego allí** first here and then there ❷ [*más tarde*] later • **el primer grupo irá a las tres y el segundo llegará luego** the first group will go at three and the second will arrive later • **¡hasta luego!** see you! • **hazlo luego** do it later ❸ [*pronto*] soon

◆ *conjunción* ❶ [*así que*] so ❷ • **luego luego a)** familiar [*inmediatamente*] immediately ; right away

lugar *sm* ❶ [*generalmente*] place • **queremos comprar una casa en algún lugar con muchos árboles** we want to buy a house in a place with a lot of trees • **fuera de lugar** out of place • **en primer lugar** in the first place • **en último lugar** lastly • **ponte en mi lugar** put yourself in my place • **yo en tu lugar** if I were you • **tener lugar** to take place ▶ **lugar común** platitude ▶ **lugar de nacimiento** birthplace ▶ **lugar de trabajo** workplace ❷ [*localidad*] place ❸ [*espacio*] room • **¿hay lugar para mí en el carro?** is there room for me in the car? • **no hay lugar a duda** there's no room for doubt • **sin lugar a dudas** without a doubt ; undoubtedly ❹ [*del crimen, accidente* ETC] scene ❺ [*asiento*] seat • **llegamos tarde y ya no encontramos lugares** we were late and couldn't find seats ❻ [*para acampar, merendar* ETC] spot ❼ [*motivo*] cause • **dar lugar a** to cause ❽ [*puesto*] position

expresión dejar a alguien en buen/mal lugar to make somebody look good/bad ▶ **poner las cosas en su lugar** to set things straight

lugareño, ña *sm, f* villager

lúgubre *adj* gloomy ⚐ *Los adjetivos ingleses son invariables.*

lujo *sm* luxury • **viven rodeados de lujo** they live in the lap of luxury • **permitirse el lujo de hacer algo** to be able to afford to do something

lujoso, sa *adj* luxurious ⚐ *Los adjetivos ingleses son invariables.*

lujuria *sf* lust

lumbago *sm* lumbago

lumbre *sf* [*fuego*] fire • **no pongas las salchichas directamente en la lumbre que se van a quemar** don't put the hot dogs directly on the fire, they'll burn • **dar lumbre a alguien** to give somebody a light

lumbrera *sf* familiar leading light

luminoso, sa *adj* bright ⚐ *Los adjetivos ingleses son invariables.*

luna *sf* ❶ [*astro*] moon ▶ **luna llena** full moon ▶ **luna de miel** honeymoon ❷ [*cristal*] window (pane)
expresión estar en la luna to be miles away

lunar ◆ *adj* lunar ⚐ *Los adjetivos ingleses son invariables.*

L

◆ *sm* ❶ [*en la piel*] mole • **Alicia tiene un lunar en la mejilla izquierda** Alicia has a mole on her left cheek ❷ [*en telas*] spot • **a lunares** spotted

lunático, ca *sm, f* lunatic

lunes *sm invariable* Monday ver también **sábado**

luneta *sf* [*de coche*] windscreen ▶ **luneta térmica** demister

lupa *sf* magnifying glass

lustro *sm* five-year period

luto *sm* mourning • **estar de luto** to be in mourning

luxación *sf* dislocation

luz *sf* ❶ [*generalmente*] light • **apagar la luz** to switch off the light • **encender la luz** to switch on the light • **se ha ido la luz** the lights have gone out • **a plena luz del día** in broad daylight ▶ **luz eléctrica** electric light ▶ **luz solar** sunlight ❷ [*electricidad*] electricity • **cortar la luz** to cut off the electricity supply • **pagar (el recibo de) la luz** to pay the electricity (bill) ❸ [*destello*] flash (of light)

expresiones a la luz de a) [*una vela, la luna* ETC] by the light of **b)** [*los acontecimientos* ETC] in the light of ▶ **arrojar luz sobre** to shed light on ▶ **dar a luz (un niño)** to give birth (to a child) ▶ **sacar algo a la luz a)** [*secreto*] to bring to light **b)** [*obra*] to bring out; to publish ▶ **salir a la luz a)** [*descubrirse*] to come to light **b)** [*publicarse*] to come out ▶ **ver la luz** to see the light

■ **luces** *sfpl* AUTOMÓVILES lights • **poner las luces de carretera** o **largas** to put (your headlights) on full beam ▶ **luces de tráfico** o **de señalización** traffic lights

lycra® *sf* Lycra®

m, M *sf* [letra] m ; M

macabro, bra *adj* macabre ◌: *Los adjetivos ingleses son invariables.*

macarrón *sm* [tubo] sheath *(of cable)*

macedonia *sf* salad ▸ **macedonia de frutas** fruit salad

maceta *sf* [tiesto] flowerpot

macetero *sm* flowerpot holder

machacar ◆ *vt* ❶ [triturar] to crush ❷ *figurado* [insistir] to keep going on about
◆ *vi* *figurado* • **machacar (sobre)** to go on (about)

machete *sm* machete

machista *adj* & *smf* male chauvinist ◌: *Los adjetivos ingleses son invariables.*

macho ◆ *adj* ❶ BIOLOGÍA male ❷ *figurado* [hombre] macho ◌: *Los adjetivos ingleses son invariables.*
◆ *sm* ❶ BIOLOGÍA male ❷ *figurado* [hombre] he-man ❸ TECNOLOGÍA male part ❹ [de enchufe] pin

macizo, za *adj* solid • **le regalaron una pulsera de oro macizo** they gave her a solid gold bracelet ◌: *Los adjetivos ingleses son invariables.*
expresión estar macizo a) *familiar* [hombre] to be hunky b) [mujer] to be gorgeous
■ **macizo** *sm* ❶ GEOGRAFÍA massif ❷ BOTÁNICA ▸ **macizo de flores** flowerbed

macro *sf* INFORMÁTICA macro

macrobiótico, ca *adj* macrobiotic ◌: *Los adjetivos ingleses son invariables.*

macuto *sm* backpack

madeja *sf* hank
expresión enredar la madeja to complicate matters

madera *sf* ❶ [generalmente] wood • **esa mesa es de madera maciza, por eso pesa tanto** the table is made of solid wood, that's why it's so heavy • **de madera** wooden ▸ **madera contrachapada** plywood ❷ CONSTRUCCIÓN timber ❸ [tabla] piece of wood
expresión tener madera de algo to have the makings of something ▸ **tocar madera** to knock on wood

madrastra *sf* stepmother

madrazo *sm* hard blow

madre *sf* mother • **es madre de tres niños** she's a mother of three ▸ **madre adoptiva/de alquiler** foster/surrogate mother ▸ **madre biológica** biological mother ▸ **madre de familia** mother ▸ **madre política** mother-in-law ▸ **madre soltera** single mother ▸ **madre superiora** mother superior

madriguera *sf* ❶ [escondrijo] den ❷ [de conejo] burrow

madrileño, ña *sm, f* native/inhabitant of Madrid

madrina *sf* ❶ [generalmente] patroness ❷ [de boda] bridesmaid ❸ [de bautizo] godmother

madrugada *sf* ❶ [amanecer] dawn • **de madrugada** at daybreak ❷ [noche] early morning • **siempre se levanta de madrugada para tomar agua** she always gets up early in the morning to drink some water • **las tres de la madrugada** three in the morning

madrugador, ra *adj* early-rising ◌: *Los adjetivos ingleses son invariables.*

madrugar *vi* ❶ to get up early • **detesto madrugar** I hate getting up early ❷ *figurado* to be quick off the mark
expresión no por mucho madrugar amanece más temprano *proverbio* time must take its course

madurar ◆ *vt* ❶ [generalmente] to mature ❷ [fruta, mies] to ripen ❸ [idea, proyecto etc] to think through
◆ *vi* ❶ [generalmente] to mature ❷ [fruta] to ripen

madurez *sf* ❶ [cualidad - generalmente] maturity; [- de fruta, mies] ripeness ❷ [edad adulta] adulthood

maduro, ra *adj* ❶ [generalmente] mature • **su marido es joven, pero muy maduro** her husband is young but very mature • **su padre es un hombre maduro, pero rebosante de salud** his father is older, but in very good health ❷ [fruta] ripe • **los duraznos maduros tienen un delicioso perfume** ripe peaches have a delicious scent • **de edad madura** middle-aged ◌: *Los adjetivos ingleses son invariables.*

maestría *sf* ❶ [habilidad] mastery ❷ [título] master's degree

maestro, tra ◆ *adj* ❶ [perfecto] masterly ❷ [principal] main ❸ [llave] master ◌: *Sólo se usa delante del sustantivo.*

♦ *sm, f* ❶ [*profesor*] teacher ❷ [*de universidad*] professor ❸ [*sabio*] master ❹ MÚSICA maestro ❺ [*director*] ▶ **maestro de ceremonias** master of ceremonies ▶ **maestro de cocina** chef ▶ **maestro de obras** foreman ▶ **maestro de orquesta** conductor

mafia *sf* mafia

mafioso, sa *sm, f* mafioso

magdalena *sf* fairy cake

magia *sf* magic ▶ **magia blanca/negra** white/black magic

mágico, ca *adj* ❶ [*con magia*] magic ❷ [*atractivo*] magical ᛫Ọ᛫ **Los adjetivos ingleses son invariables.**

magisterio *sm* ❶ [*enseñanza*] teaching ❷ [*profesión*] teaching profession

magistrado, da *sm, f* [*juez*] judge

magistral *adj* ❶ [*de maestro*] magisterial ❷ [*genial*] masterly ᛫Ọ᛫ **Los adjetivos ingleses son invariables.**

magistratura *sf* ❶ [*jueces*] magistrature ❷ [*tribunal*] tribunal ▶ **magistratura de trabajo** industrial tribunal

magnate *sm* magnate ▶ **magnate del petróleo** oil baron ▶ **magnate de la prensa** press baron

magnesia *sf* magnesia

magnesio *sm* magnesium

magnético, ca *adj* magnetic ᛫Ọ᛫ **Los adjetivos ingleses son invariables.**

magnificencia *sf* magnificence

magnitud *sf* magnitude

mago, ga *sm, f* ❶ [*prestidigitador*] magician ❷ [*en cuentos* ETC] wizard

magulladura *sf* bruise

magullar *vt* to bruise

magullón *sm* bruise

mahometano, na *adj* & *sm, f* Muslim ᛫Ọ᛫ **Los adjetivos ingleses son invariables.**

maicena® *sf* cornstarch

maíz *sm* corn • **desde aquí se ven los campos de maíz** you can see the corn fields from here ▶ **maíz dulce** sweet corn

majadero, ra ♦ *sm, f* rude person

♦ *adj* rude ᛫Ọ᛫ **Los adjetivos ingleses son invariables.**

majestad *sf* majesty

majestuoso, sa *adj* majestic ᛫Ọ᛫ **Los adjetivos ingleses son invariables.**

mal ♦ *adj* → **malo**

♦ *sm* ❶ [*perversión*] • **el mal** evil • **un mal necesario** a necessary evil ❷ [*daño*] harm ; damage ❸ [*enfermedad*] illness ▶ **mal de montaña** altitude sickness ▶ **mal de ojo** evil eye ❹ [*inconveniente*] bad thing

♦ *adv* ❶ [*incorrectamente*] wrong • **esto está mal hecho** this has been done wrong • **has escrito mal esta palabra** you've spelt that word wrong ❷ [*inadecuadamente*] badly • **mi sobrino sigue portándose mal** my nephew is still behaving badly • **la fiesta salió mal** the party went off badly • **oigo/veo mal** I can't hear/see very well • **encontrarse mal a)** [*enfermo*] to feel ill **b)** [*incómodo*] to feel uncomfortable • **oler mal** [*tener mal*

olor] to smell bad ❸ *familiar* [*tener mal cariz*] to smell fishy • **sentar mal a alguien a)** [*ropa*] not to suit somebody **b)** [*comida*] to disagree with somebody ❹ [*comentario, actitud*] to upset somebody • **tomar algo a mal** to take something the wrong way ❺ [*difícilmente*] hardly • **mal puede saberlo si no se lo cuentas** he's hardly going to know it if you don't tell him

expresiones **estar a mal con alguien** to have fallen out with somebody ▶ **ir de mal en peor** to go from bad to worse ▶ **no estaría mal que...** it would be nice if...

malabarismo *sm* literal & figurado juggling ᛫Ọ᛫ *incontable*

malabarista *smf* juggler

malacate *sm* spindle

malacostumbrado, da *adj* spoiled ᛫Ọ᛫ **Los adjetivos ingleses son invariables.**

malagradecido, da *adj* ungrateful

malaria *sf* malaria

malcriadez *sf* bad manners

malcriado, da *adj* spoiled ᛫Ọ᛫ **Los adjetivos ingleses son invariables.**

maldad *sf* ❶ [*cualidad*] evil ❷ [*acción*] evil thing

maldecir ♦ *vt* to curse

♦ *vi* to curse

maldición *sf* curse

maldito, ta *adj* ❶ [*embrujado*] cursed ❷ *familiar* [*para enfatizar*] damned ᛫Ọ᛫ **Los adjetivos ingleses son invariables.**

expresión **¡maldita sea!** *familiar* damn it!

maleante *smf* crook

malecón *sm* [*atracadero*] jetty

maleducado, da *adj* rude ᛫Ọ᛫ **Los adjetivos ingleses son invariables.**

maleficio *sm* curse

malentendido *sm* misunderstanding

malestar *sm* ❶ [*dolor*] upset • **su decisión causó malestar** her decision caused upset • **siento un malestar en el estómago** I've got an upset stomach • **sentir malestar general** to feel unwell ❷ [*inquietud*] uneasiness

maleta *sf* suitcase • **preparar la maleta** to pack (your bags)

maletín *sm* briefcase

maleza *sf* ❶ [*arbustos*] undergrowth ❷ [*malas hierbas*] weeds *pl*

malformación *sf* malformation ▶ **malformación congénita** congenital malformation

malgastar *vt* ❶ [*dinero, tiempo*] to waste ❷ [*salud*] to ruin

malhablado, da *adj* foul-mouthed ᛫Ọ᛫ **Los adjetivos ingleses son invariables.**

malhechor, ra *adj* & *sm, f* criminal ᛫Ọ᛫ **Los adjetivos ingleses son invariables.**

malhumorado, da *adj* ❶ bad-tempered ❷ [*enfadado*] in a bad mood ᛫Ọ᛫ **Los adjetivos ingleses son invariables.**

malicia *sf* ❶ [*maldad*] wickedness ❷ [*mala intención*] malice

malicioso, sa *adj* ❶ [*malo*] wicked ❷ [*malintencionado*] malicious ̣♀̣ *Los adjetivos ingleses son invariables.*

maligno, na *adj* malignant ̣♀̣ *Los adjetivos ingleses son invariables.*

malla *sf* ❶ [*tejido*] mesh ▶ **malla de alambre** wire mesh ❷ [*red*] net

malo, la *adj* ❶ [*generalmente*] bad • **la película estuvo malísima** the movie was really bad • **es un muchacho malo, que pelea con todo el mundo** he's a bad boy, always fighting with everyone • **lo malo fue que...** the problem was (that)... ❷ [*calidad*] poor ❸ [*malicioso*] wicked ❹ [*enfermo*] ill • **estar/ponerse malo** to be/fall ill ❺ [*travieso*] naughty ̣♀̣ *Los adjetivos ingleses son invariables.*

expresión **más vale malo conocido que bueno por conocer** *proverbio* better the devil you know (than the devil you don't)

■ **malo, la** *sm,f* [*de película* ETC] villain

malograr *vt* to waste

malparado, da *adj* • **salir malparado de algo** to come out of something badly ̣♀̣ *Los adjetivos ingleses son invariables.*

malpensado, da *adj* evil-minded ̣♀̣ *Los adjetivos ingleses son invariables.*

malsano, na *adj* unhealthy ̣♀̣ *Los adjetivos ingleses son invariables.*

malsonante *adj* rude ̣♀̣ *Los adjetivos ingleses son invariables.*

malteada *sf* [*batido*] milkshake

maltratar *vt* ❶ [*pegar, insultar*] to mistreat ❷ [*estropear*] to damage

maltrecho, cha *adj* battered • **dejar maltrecho a alguien** to leave somebody in a bad way ̣♀̣ *Los adjetivos ingleses son invariables.*

malvado, da *adj* evil ̣♀̣ *Los adjetivos ingleses son invariables.*

malversación *sf* ▶ **malversación (de fondos)** embezzlement (of funds)

malversar *vt* to embezzle

mama *sf* ❶ [*órgano - de mujer*] breast; ZOOLOGÍA udder ❷ *familiar* [*madre*] mum

mamá *sf familiar* mom ▶ **mamá grande** grandma

mamar ✦ *vt* ❶ [*sujeto: bebé*] to suckle ❷ [*aprender*] • **lo mamó desde pequeño** he was immersed in it as a child
✦ *vi* to suckle • **los gatitos están mamando** the kittens are suckling • **el bebé recién nacido mama cada tres horas** a newborn baby feeds every three hours

mamarracho *sm* [*fantoche*] mess

mamífero, ra *adj* mammal ̣♀̣ *Los adjetivos ingleses son invariables.*

■ **mamífero** *sm* mammal

mamografía *sf* ❶ MEDICINA [*técnica*] breast scanning ❷ MEDICINA [*resultado*] breast scan

mamotreto *sm* ❶ *despectivo* [*libro*] hefty tome ❷ [*objeto grande*] monstrosity

mampara *sf* screen

manada *sf* ZOOLOGÍA [*generalmente*] herd; [*de lobos*] pack; [*de ovejas*] flock; [*de leones*] pride

manager (pl managers) *sm* manager

manantial *sm* ❶ spring ❷ *figurado* source

manar *vi literal & figurado* • **manar (de)** to flow (from)

manazas *adj invariable* clumsy ̣♀̣ *Los adjetivos ingleses son invariables.*

mancha *sf* ❶ [*generalmente*] stain • **su blusa tenía una mancha en el cuello** her blouse had a stain on the collar ❷ [*de tinta*] blot ❸ [*de color*] mark • **Paloma tiene una mancha de nacimiento en la mejilla izquierda** Paloma has a birthmark on her left cheek ❹ ASTRONOMÍA spot ❺ [*deshonra*] blemish • **sin mancha** unblemished

expresión **extenderse como una mancha de aceite** to spread like wildfire

manchar *vt* ❶ [*ensuciar*] • **manchar algo (de** o **con) a)** [*generalmente*] to make something dirty (with) **b)** [*con manchas*] to stain something (with) **c)** [*emborronar*] to smudge something (with) ❷ [*deshonrar*] to tarnish

manco, ca *adj* ❶ [*sin una mano*] one-handed ❷ [*sin manos*] handless ❸ [*sin un brazo*] one-armed ❹ [*sin brazos*] armless ̣♀̣ *Los adjetivos ingleses son invariables.*

expresión **no ser manco para** o **en** to be a dab hand at

mancuernilla *sf* cufflink

mandamás (pl mandamases) *smf* bigwig

mandamiento *sm* ❶ [*orden - militar*] order; command; [*- judicial*] writ ❷ RELIGIÓN commandment • **los diez mandamientos** the Ten Commandments

mandar ✦ *vt* ❶ [*dar órdenes a*] to order • **el general mandó que las tropas avanzaran** the general ordered the troops to advance • **mandar a alguien hacer algo** to order somebody to do something • **mandar hacer algo** to have something done ❷ [*enviar*] to send • **mi hermana me mandó un paquete por correo** my sister sent me a package in the mail ❸ [*dirigir, gobernar*] to be in charge of ❹ [*país*] to rule
✦ *vi* ❶ [*generalmente*] to be in charge ❷ [*jefe de estado*] to rule • **aquí mando yo** I'm in charge here • **mandar en algo** to be in charge of something ❸ *despectivo* [*dar órdenes*] to order people around

expresión **¿mande?** *familiar* yes? • **disculpe, señorita — ¿mande?** excuse me, miss? — yes?

mandarina *sf* mandarin

mandato *sm* ❶ [*generalmente*] order ❷ [*poderes de representación, disposición*] mandate ▶ **mandato judicial** warrant ❸ POLÍTICA term of office ❹ [*reinado*] period of rule

mandíbula *sf* jaw

mando *sm* ❶ [*poder*] command • **entregar el mando** to hand over command • **al mando de** in charge of ❷ [*periodo en poder*] term of office ❸ ̣♀̣ **ge-**

M

M

neralmente pl [autoridades] leadership ☼*incontable*
❹ MILITAR command ☼*incontable* ▶ **alto mando** MI-
LITAR high command ▶ **mandos intermedios** middle
management *sing* ❺ [dispositivo] control ▶ **mando
automático/a distancia** automatic/remote control
mandón, ona ✦ adj bossy ☼*Los adjetivos ingleses son invariables.*
✦ sm, f bossy-boots
manecilla sf [del reloj] hand
manejable adj ❶ [generalmente] manageable ❷ [herramienta] easy to use ☼*Los adjetivos ingleses son
invariables.*
manejar ✦ vt ❶ [conocimientos, datos] to use ❷ [máquina, mandos] to operate ❸ [caballo, bicicleta] to handle ❹ [arma] to wield ❺ [negocio ETC] to manage
• **Alberto maneja la empresa con mucha habilidad**
Alberto manages the business skillfully ❻ [gente] to
handle ❼ [vehículo] to drive
✦ vi [conducir] to drive • **mi hija está aprendiendo a
manejar** my daughter is learning to drive
manejo sm ❶ [de máquina, mandos] operation ❷ [de
armas, herramientas] use • **de fácil manejo** user-friendly
❸ [de conocimientos, datos] marshaling ❹ [de idiomas]
command ❺ [de caballo, bicicleta] handling ❻ [de negocio ETC] management ❼ ☼*generalmente pl* figurado [intriga] intrigue
manera sf way • **Juan tiene una manera de caminar inconfundible** Juan has an unmistakeable way of
walking • **lo haremos a mi manera** we'll do it my way
• **¡qué manera de…!** what a way to…! • **a mi manera
de ver** the way I see it • **de cualquier manera a)** [sin
cuidado] any old how **b)** [de todos modos] anyway • **de
esta manera** in this way • **de la misma manera** similarly • **de ninguna manera a)** [refuerza negación] by
no means; under no circumstances **b)** [respuesta ex-
clamativa] no way! • **de todas maneras** anyway • **en
cierta manera** in a way • **de manera que** [para] so
(that) • **no hay manera** there is no way; it's impossible ▶ **manera de ser** way of being; nature
manga sf ❶ [de prenda] sleeve • **llevaba una camisa de manga corta** he wore a short-sleeved shirt
• **en mangas de camisa** in shirtsleeves • **sin mangas**
sleeveless ▶ **manga raglán** o **ranglán** raglan sleeve
❷ [manguera] hosepipe ❸ [de pastelería] forcing bag
❹ DEPORTE round
expresión **andar manga por hombro** to be a mess
▶ **ser de manga ancha, tener manga ancha** to be
over-indulgent
mango sm ❶ [asa] handle • **¡cuidado! el mango de
la cacerola está caliente** careful! the pan's handle is
hot ❷ [fruta] mango • **cuando están maduros, los
mangos son muy perfumados** ripe mangoes have a
lovely scent ❸ [árbol] mango tree
manguera sf ❶ hosepipe ❷ [de bombero] fire
hose
manía sf ❶ [idea fija] obsession • **mi hermana tiene
la manía de limpiar constantemente** my sister has
an obsession with cleaning all the time ❷ [peculiaridad] idiosyncracy ❸ [mala costumbre] bad habit

❹ [afición exagerada] mania ❺ familiar [ojeriza] dislike ❻ PSICOLOGÍA mania
maniaco, ca, maníaco, ca ✦ adj manic ☼*Los
adjetivos ingleses son invariables.*
✦ sm, f maniac
maniático, ca ✦ adj fussy ☼*Los adjetivos ingleses son invariables.*
✦ sm, f fussy person • **es un maniático del futbol**
he's football-crazy
manicomio sm insane asylum
manifestación sf ❶ [de alegría, dolor ETC] show ❷ [de
opinión] declaration ❸ [indicio] sign • **la fiebre es una
manifestación de que el cuerpo tiene alguna infección**
fever is a sign that the body is fighting an infection
❹ [por la calle] demonstration • **hoy habrá una manifestación de los maestros desocupados** the unemployed teachers will be holding a demonstration today
• **hacer una manifestación** to hold a demonstration
manifestar vt ❶ [alegría, dolor ETC] to show ❷ [opinión ETC] to express
■ **manifestarse** v pronominal ❶ [por la calle] to demonstrate • **los maestros se manifestaron contra la
guerra** the teachers demonstrated against the war
❷ [hacerse evidente] to become apparent • **las consecuencias de la inundación se manifestaron pocos
días después** the consequences of the flood became
apparent a few days later
maniobra sf ❶ [generalmente] maneuver • **tuvo
que hacer varias maniobras para estacionarse en un
sitio muy pequeño** it took him some maneuvers to
get into a tight parking space • **estar de maniobras**
MILITAR to be on maneuvers ❷ [treta] trick
maniobrar vi to maneuver
manipulación sf ❶ [generalmente] handling ❷ [engaño] manipulation
manipular vt ❶ [manejar] to handle ❷ [mangonear - información, resultados] to manipulate; [- negocios, asuntos] to interfere in
maniquí ✦ sm dummy
✦ sm, f [modelo] model
manitas smf invariable handy person
manito sm familiar buddy
manivela sf crank
manjar sm delicious food ☼*incontable*
mano ✦ sf ❶ [generalmente] hand • **lávate las manos**
wash your hands • **a mano** by hand • **estos suéteres
son caros porque se hacen a mano** these sweaters
are expensive because they're made by hand • **dar**
o **estrechar la mano a alguien** to shake hands with
somebody • **darse** o **estrecharse la mano** to shake
hands • **a mano armada** armed • **echar/tender una
mano** to give/offer a hand • **¡manos arriba!, ¡arriba
las manos!** hands up! ▶ **mano de obra a)** [capacidad
de trabajo] labor **b)** [trabajadores] workforce ❷ ZOO-
LOGÍA [generalmente] forefoot; [de perro, gato] (front)
paw; [de cerdo] (front) trotter ❸ [lado] • **a mano dere-
cha/izquierda** on the right/left ❹ [de pintura ETC] coat
• **a esta pared le falta una mano de pintura** this wall

needs a coat of paint ❺ [*influencia*] influence ❻ [*partida de naipes*] game ❼ [*serie, tanda*] series
expresiones **bajo mano** secretly ▶ **caer en manos de alguien** to fall into somebody's hands ▶ **con las manos cruzadas** sitting around doing nothing ▶ **coger a alguien con las manos en la masa** to catch somebody red-handed o in the act ▶ **dar una mano a alguien** to give somebody a hand ▶ **de primera mano a)** [*coche* ETC] brand new **b)** [*noticias* ETC] first-hand ▶ **de segunda mano** second-hand ▶ **mano a mano** tête-à-tête ▶ **mano sobre mano** sitting around doing nothing ▶ **¡manos a la obra!** let's get down to it! ▶ **tener buena mano para algo** to have a knack for something
◆ *sm* buddy

manojo *sm* bunch

manopla *sf* mitten

manosear *vt* ❶ [*generalmente*] to handle roughly ❷ [*papel, tela*] to rumple ❸ [*persona*] to fondle

manotazo *sm* slap

mansalva ■ **a mansalva** *locución adverbial* [*en abundancia*] in abundance

mansión *sf* mansion

manso, sa *adj* ❶ [*apacible*] calm ❷ [*domesticado*] tame.👁️ *Los adjetivos ingleses son invariables.*

manta *sf* [*para abrigarse*] blanket ▶ **manta de viaje** travel rug
expresión **liarse la manta a la cabeza** to take the plunge

manteca *sf* ❶ [*grasa*] fat ❷ lard ❸ [*mantequilla*] butter ▶ **manteca de cacao** cocoa butter ▶ **manteca de cerdo** lard

mantecado *sm* ❶ [*pastel*] almond shortcake ❷ [*helado*] fresh ice cream

mantel *sm* tablecloth

mantener *vt* ❶ [*sustentar, aguantar*] to support • **cuando me case voy a seguir trabajando, no quiero que mi marido me mantenga** I'm going to keep working when I get married, I don't want my husband to have to support me ❷ [*conservar*] to keep ❸ [*en buen estado*] to maintain ❹ [*tener - relaciones, conversación*] to have ❺ [*defender - opinión*] to stick to; to maintain; [*- candidatura*] to refuse to withdraw

mantenimiento *sm* ❶ [*sustento*] sustenance ❷ [*conservación*] maintenance

mantequilla *sf* butter

manto *sm* [*generalmente*] cloak

mantón *sm* shawl

manual ◆ *adj* [*con las manos*] manual.👁️ *Los adjetivos ingleses son invariables.*
◆ *sm* manual

manubrio *sm* handlebars *pl*

manufacturar *vt* to manufacture

manutención *sf* ❶ [*sustento*] maintenance ❷ [*alimento*] food

maña *sf* ❶ [*destreza*] skill • **tener maña para** to have a knack for ❷ [*astucia*] wits *pl*

mañana ◆ *sf* morning • **a la mañana siguiente** the next morning • **a las dos de la mañana** at two in the morning • **por la mañana** in the morning
◆ *sm* • **el mañana** tomorrow; the future
◆ *adv* tomorrow • **mañana iremos a comprarte ropa** we'll go buy you some clothes tomorrow • **a partir de mañana** starting tomorrow • **¡hasta mañana!** see you tomorrow! • **mañana por la mañana** tomorrow morning • **pasado mañana** the day after tomorrow

manzana *sf* ❶ [*fruta*] apple • **acabo de comerme una deliciosa manzana** I just ate a delicious apple ❷ [*grupo de casas*] block (of houses) • **fuimos a dar la vuelta a la manzana** we went for a walk around the block

manzanilla *sf* ❶ [*planta*] camomile ❷ [*infusión*] camomile tea

mañanitas *sfpl* birthday song *sing*

manzano *sm* apple tree

mapa *sm* map • **está en el mapa** it's on the map ▶ **mapa de carreteras** road map

mapamundi *sm* world map

maqueta *sf* ❶ [*reproducción a escala*] (scale) model ❷ [*de libro*] dummy

maquila *sf* ❶ [*de máquinas*] assembly ❷ [*de ropas*] making-up

maquiladora *sf* assembly plant

maquillaje *sm* ❶ [*producto*] make-up ❷ [*acción*] making-up

maquillar *vt* [*pintar*] to make up
■ **maquillarse** *v pronominal* to make yourself up

máquina *sf* ❶ [*generalmente*] machine • **coser a máquina** to machine-sew • **escribir a máquina** to type • **hecho a máquina** machine-made ▶ **máquina de afeitar** electric razor ▶ **máquina de coser** sewing machine ▶ **máquina de escribir** typewriter ▶ **máquina fotográfica** camera ▶ **máquina tragaperras** slot machine ❷ [*locomotora*] engine ▶ **máquina de vapor** steam engine ❸ [*mecanismo*] mechanism ❹ [*de estado, partido etc*] machinery.👁️ *incontable*
expresión **a toda máquina** at full pelt

maquinaria *sf* ❶ [*generalmente*] machinery • **esa fábrica cuenta con maquinaria muy moderna** that factory has very modern machinery ❷ [*de reloj etc*] mechanism • **la maquinaria de un reloj digital es muy precisa** the mechanism in a digital watch is very precise

maquinilla *sf* ▶ **maquinilla de afeitar** razor ▶ **maquinilla eléctrica** electric razor

maquinista *smf* engineer

mar *sm o sf* literal & figurado sea • **alta mar** high seas *pl* ▶ **mar de fondo** literal & figurado groundswell ▶ **mar gruesa** heavy sea ▶ **el Mar Caribe** the Caribbean Sea ▶ **el mar del Norte** the North Sea
expresión **llover a mares** to rain buckets

marabunta *sf* crowd

maraca *sf* maraca

maracuyá *sf* passion fruit

maraña *sf* ❶ [*maleza*] thicket ❷ figurado [*enredo*] tangle

M

maratón *sm o sf* marathon

maravilla *sf* wonder • **el faro de Alejandría era una de las siete maravillas del mundo antiguo** the lighthouse at Alexandria was one of the seven wonders of the ancient world • **es una maravilla** it's wonderful • **es una maravilla ver lo rápido que se recuperó después del accidente** it's wonderful to see how quickly he recovered after the accident

expresiones **a las mil maravillas, de maravilla** wonderfully ▶ **hacer maravillas** to do o work wonders ▶ **venir de maravilla** to be just the thing o ticket

maravillar *vt* to amaze

maravilloso, sa *adj* wonderful ☿ *Los adjetivos ingleses son invariables.*

marca *sf* ❶ [*señal*] mark • **hay varias marcas en la pared, ¿de qué serán?** there are several marks on the wall, I wonder what they're from ▶ **marca de nacimiento** birthmark ❷ [*de rueda, animal*] track ❸ [*en ganado*] brand ❹ [*en papel*] watermark ❺ Comercio [*de tabaco, café etc*] brand; [*de carro, ordenador etc*] make • **¿qué marca de detergente usas?** what brand of detergent do you use? • **en cuanto a carros, prefiero las marcas japonesas** I prefer Japanese makes when it comes to cars • **de marca** designer ☿ *Sólo se usa delante del sustantivo.* ▶ **marca de fábrica** trademark ▶ **marca registrada** registered trademark ❻ [*etiqueta*] label ❼ Deporte [*generalmente*] performance; [*en carreras*] time; [*plusmarca*] record

marcador, ra *adj* marking ☿ *Los adjetivos ingleses son invariables.*

■ **marcador** *sm* ❶ [*tablero*] scoreboard ❷ Deporte [*defensor*] marker; [*goleador*] scorer ❸ [*rotulador*] marker ❹ [*fluorescente*] highlighter

marcapasos *sm invariable* pacemaker

marcar ◆ *vt* ❶ [*generalmente*] to mark • **marqué todos mis útiles escolares para reconocerlos** I marked all my school supplies so I can tell them apart ❷ [*poner precio a*] to price ❸ [*indicar*] to indicate ❹ [*resaltar*] to emphasize ❺ [*número de teléfono*] to dial • **¿cuál es el número de teléfono que hay que marcar?** which phone number do I need to dial? ❻ [*sujeto: termómetro, contador etc*] to read ❼ [*sujeto: reloj*] to say ❽ Deporte [*tanto*] to score • **mi equipo marcó tres goles** my team scored three goals ❾ Deporte [*a un jugador*] to mark ❿ [*cabello*] to set

◆ *vi* ❶ [*dejar secuelas*] to leave a mark ❷ Deporte [*anotar un tanto*] to score

marcha *sf* ❶ [*partida*] departure ❷ [*ritmo*] speed • **en marcha** [*motor*] running ❸ [*plan*] underway • **poner en marcha a)** [*generalmente*] to start ▶ [*dispositivo, alarma*] to activate • **ponerse en marcha a)** [*persona*] to start off **b)** [*máquina*] to start • **hacer algo sobre la marcha** to do something as you go along ❹ Automóviles gear ▶ **marcha atrás** reverse ❺ Militar & Política march • **organizaron una marcha en defensa de la educación pública** they organized a march in defense of public education ❻ Música march ❼ [*transcurso*] course • **la marcha de los acontecimientos fue inesperada** the course of events was unexpected ❽ [*progreso*] progress ❾ Deporte walk

marchar *vi* ❶ [*andar*] to walk ❷ [*partir*] to leave ❸ [*funcionar*] to work ❹ [*desarrollarse*] to progress • **el negocio marcha** business is going well

■ **marcharse** *v pronominal* to leave • **se marchó del pueblo hace un año** he left town a year ago

marchitar *vt literal & figurado* to wither

■ **marchitarse** *v pronominal* ❶ [*planta*] to fade ❷ [*figurado*] [*persona*] to languish

marcial *adj* martial ☿ *Los adjetivos ingleses son invariables.*

marco *sm* ❶ [*cerco*] frame • **el marco de la puerta es de madera** the door frame is made of wood ❷ [*ambiente, paisaje*] setting ❸ [*ámbito*] framework • **su comportamiento es inadmisible en un marco legal** her behavior is unacceptable in a legal framework ❹ [*portería*] goalmouth

marea *sf* [*del mar*] tide • **la marea está subiendo** the tide is rising ▶ **marea alta** high tide ▶ **marea baja** low tide ▶ **marea negra** oil slick

marear *vt* ❶ [*provocar náuseas a*] to make nauseous ❷ [*en carro, avión etc*] to cause motion sickness ❸ [*en barco*] to make seasick ❹ [*aturdir*] to make dizzy ❺ *familiar* [*fastidiar*] to annoy

■ **marearse** *v pronominal* ❶ [*tener náuseas*] to feel nauseous ❷ [*en coche, avión etc*] to get motion sickness ❸ [*en barco*] to get seasick ❹ [*estar aturdido*] to get dizzy ❺ [*emborracharse*] to get drunk

maremoto *sm* tidal wave

mareo *sm* ❶ [*náuseas*] nausea ❷ [*en coche, avión etc*] motion sickness ❸ [*en barco*] seasickness ❹ [*aturdimiento*] dizziness

marfil *sm* ivory

margarina *sf* margarine

margarita *sf* daisy

expresión **echar margaritas a los cerdos** to cast pearls before swine

margen *sm o sf* ❶ [*de río*] bank ❷ [*de camino*] side ❸ [*de página*] margin • **la maestra puso algunos comentarios en el margen** the teacher wrote some comments in the margin ❹ [*límite*] Comercio margin • **nuestro equipo ganó por un amplio margen** our team won by a wide margin • **dejar al margen** to exclude • **estar al margen de** to have nothing to do with • **mantenerse al margen de** to keep out of ▶ **margen de error** margin of error ❺ [*ocasión*] • **dar margen a alguien para hacer algo** to give somebody the chance to do something

marginación *sf* exclusion

marginado, da ◆ *adj* excluded ☿ *Los adjetivos ingleses son invariables.*

◆ *sm, f* outcast

Maricastaña → **tiempo**

marido *sm* husband

marihuana *sf* marijuana

marimacho *sm* ❶ *familiar* mannish woman ❷ *despectivo* butch woman

marimba *sf* [*xilófono*] xylophone

marina *sf* MILITAR navy • **entró en la marina el año pasado** he joined the navy last year ▶ **marina de guerra** navy

marinero, ra *adj* ❶ [*generalmente*] sea ᷆: *Sólo se usa delante del sustantivo.* ❷ [*buque*] seaworthy ❸ [*pueblo*] seafaring
■ **marinero** *sm* sailor

marino, na *adj* sea ᷆: *Sólo se usa delante del sustantivo.*
■ **marino** *sm* sailor

marioneta *sf* puppet

mariposa *sf* ❶ [*insecto*] butterfly ❷ [*en natación*] butterfly

mariquita *sf* ladybug

marisco *sm* seafood ᷆: *incontable*

marítimo, ma *adj* ❶ [*del mar*] maritime ❷ [*cercano al mar*] seaside ᷆: *Sólo se usa delante del sustantivo.*

marketing *sm* marketing ▶ **marketing directo** direct marketing

mármol *sm* marble

marmota *sf* marmot

maromero, ra *sm, f* tightrope walker

marqués, esa *sm* marquis, *femenino* marchioness

marquesina *sf* ❶ glass canopy ❷ [*parada de autobús*] bus-shelter

marrano, na *sm, f* ❶ [*animal*] pig ❷ *familiar* [*sucio*] (filthy) pig

marro *sm* mallet

marrón *adj & sm* brown ᷆: *Los adjetivos ingleses son invariables.*

Marte *sm* Mars

martes *sm invariable* Tuesday ▶ **martes trece** ≃ Friday the 13th ver también **sábado**

martillear, martillar *vt* to hammer

martillo *sm* hammer

mártir *smf* martyr

martirio *sm* ❶ RELIGIÓN martyrdom ❷ [*sufrimiento*] torment
expresión **ser un martirio chino** to be torture

marzo *sm* March ver también **septiembre**

mas *conjunción* but

más
◆ *adv*
❶ [*comparativo*] more
• **Gabriel es más alto** Gabriel is taller
• **hace más calor que ayer** it's hotter than yesterday
• **necesito más tiempo** I need more time
• **tengo más de cien dólares** I have more than a hundred dollars
• **Lucía es más joven que tú** Lucía is younger than you
• **Mercedes tiene más experiencia que tú** Mercedes has more experience than you

• **tiene dos años más que yo** she's two years older than me
❷ [*superlativo*] most
• **el más alto** the tallest
• **la más guapa** the prettiest
• **lo más importante** the most important
• **es la más lista de la clase** she's the cleverest in the class
• **lo más posible** as much as possible
❸ [*otra cantidad de*] more
• **quiero más pastel** I want some more cake
❹ [*en frases negativas, para indicar que uno no quiere continuar*] (any) more
• **no quiero más** I don't want any more
• **¡no puedo comer ni una cucharada más!** I can't eat one more spoonful
❺ [*con un pronombre interrogatvo o un pronombre indefinido*]
• **¿qué más?** what else?
• **¿alguien más quiere?** does anybody else want some?
• **no vendrá nadie más** nobody else will come
❻ [*indica una preferencia*] better
• **más vale que nos vayamos** we'd better leave
❼ [*en frases exclamativas, para intensificar*]
• **¡es más tonto!** he's so silly!
• **¡qué día más bonito!** what a beautiful day!
❽ [*en sumas*] plus; and
• **uno más uno son dos** one and o plus one is two
❾ [*en expresiones*]
• **más bien** rather
• **no fue un accidente, más bien lo hizo a propósito** it wasn't an accident, rather he did it on purpose
• **más o menos** more or less
• **el que más y el que menos** everybody
• **más y más** more and more
• **sin más (ni más)** just like that, for no reason
• **¿qué más da?** what does it matter?
• **no estaba contento, es más, estaba furioso** he wasn't happy, what's more, he was furious
• **no trabaja bien, es más, el jefe lo ha llamado a su despacho** he doesn't do his work properly, and what's more, the boss has called him into his office
◆ *sm invariable*
❶ [*lo máximo*]
• **es lo más que puedo hacer** it's the most I can do
❷ [*signo de suma*] plus
• **el más es el signo de la suma** the plus sign is the sign for addition
■ **de más**
◆ *locución adverbial*
over
• **hay cinco pesos de más** there are five pesos more than there should be

masa *sf* ❶ [*generalmente*] mass • **una masa enfurecida tomó las calles** a crazed mass of people took to the streets ❷ COCINA dough • **esta masa está cruda** the dough is raw

masacre *sf* massacre

masaje *sm* massage • **Pedro le dio un masaje a Adela en la espalda** Pedro gave Adela a back massage

masajista *smf* masseur, *femenino* masseuse

mascar *vt* & *vi* to chew

máscara *sf* mask ▶ **máscara antigás** gas mask ▶ **máscara de oxígeno** oxygen mask

mascarilla *sf* ❶ MEDICINA mask ❷ [*cosmética*] face pack

mascota *sf* mascot • **la mascota del equipo es un oso** the team's mascot is a bear • **no se permiten mascotas en este apartamento** pets aren't allowed in this apartment

masculino, na *adj* ❶ BIOLOGÍA male • **la población masculina ha aumentado en esta ciudad** the city's male population has increased ❷ [*varonil*] manly ❸ GRAMÁTICA masculine ☆ *Los adjetivos ingleses son invariables.*

masificación *sf* overcrowding

masivo, va *adj* mass ☆ *Sólo se usa delante del sustantivo.*

máster (pl masters) *sm* Master's (degree)

masticar *vt* to chew

mástil *sm* ❶ NÁUTICA mast ❷ [*palo*] pole ❸ MÚSICA neck

mata *sf* ❶ [*arbusto*] bush • **matas** scrub ❷ [*matojo*] tuft ▶ **mata de pelo** mop of hair

matadero *sm* slaughterhouse

matamoscas *sm invariable* ❶ [*pala*] flyswat ❷ [*espray*] flyspray

matanza *sf* [*masacre*] slaughter

matar *vt* ❶ [*generalmente*] to kill • **mataron a personas inocentes** they killed innocent people • **me mata tener que madrugar** it kills me having to get up so early ❷ [*apagar - sed*] to quench; [*- hambre*] to stay **expresión** **matarlas callando** to be up to something on the quiet

matasellos *smf invariable* postmark

mate ◆ *adj* matt ☆ *Los adjetivos ingleses son invariables.*
◆ *sm* ❶ [*en ajedrez*] mate ❷ [*en baloncesto*] dunk ❸ [*en tenis*] smash

matemático, ca ◆ *adj* mathematical ☆ *Los adjetivos ingleses son invariables.*
◆ *sm, f* [*científico*] mathematician
■ **matemáticas** *sfpl* [*ciencia*] mathematics ☆ *incontable*

materia *sf* ❶ [*sustancia*] matter • **estudia la transformación de la materia** he's studying the transformation of matter ▶ **materia gris** gray matter ❷ [*material*] material ▶ **materia prima** raw material ❸ [*tema, asignatura*] subject • **la materia que más me gusta es química** my favorite subject is chemistry • **en materia de** on the subject of, concerning

material ◆ *adj* ❶ [*generalmente*] physical ❷ [*daños, consecuencias*] material ❸ [*real*] actual ☆ *Los adjetivos ingleses son invariables.*

◆ *sm* ❶ [*generalmente*] material • **trajeron los materiales para construir la casa** they brought all the materials for building the house • **el material que contiene esta revista es muy interesante** the subject matter in this magazine is very interesting ❷ [*instrumentos*] equipment ▶ **material bélico** o **de guerra** military equipment ▶ **material de oficina** office stationery

materializar *vt* ❶ [*idea, proyecto*] to realize ❷ [*hacer tangible*] to produce

maternal *adj* maternal • **tiene fuertes sentimientos maternales** she has strong maternal instincts ☆ *Los adjetivos ingleses son invariables.*

maternidad *sf* ❶ [*cualidad*] motherhood • **la maternidad es su verdadera vocación** motherhood is her true calling ❷ [*hospital*] maternity ward • **llegó a la maternidad de madrugada** she arrived in the maternity ward at dawn

materno, na *adj* ❶ maternal • **mi abuelo materno era arquitecto** my maternal grandfather was an architect ❷ [*lengua*] • **lengua materna** mother tongue ☆ *Los adjetivos ingleses son invariables.*

matinal *adj* morning ☆ *Sólo se usa delante del sustantivo.*

matiz *sm* ❶ [*variedad - de color, opinión*] shade; [*- de sentido*] nuance ❷ [*atisbo*] trace

matizar *vt* ❶ [*teñir*] • **matizar (de)** to tinge (with) ❷ *figurado* [*distinguir - rasgos, aspectos*] to distinguish; [*- tema*] to explain in detail ❸ *figurado* [*dar tono especial*] to tinge ❹ ARTE to blend

matón, ona *sm, f* familiar bully

matorral *sm* thicket

matrícula *sf* ❶ [*inscripción*] registration ❷ [*documento*] registration document ❸ AUTOMÓVILES number plate ❹ [*en universidad*] ▶ **matrícula de honor** top marks *pl*

matricular *vt* to register

matrimonial *adj* ❶ marital ❷ [*vida*] married ☆ *Los adjetivos ingleses son invariables.*

matrimonio *sm* ❶ [*generalmente*] marriage • **éste es su segundo matrimonio** it's his second marriage • **fuera del matrimonio** out of wedlock ▶ **matrimonio civil** civil wedding ▶ **matrimonio de conveniencia** marriage of convenience ▶ **matrimonio religioso** church wedding ❷ [*pareja*] married couple • **salimos con un matrimonio de ingenieros** we went out with a couple who are both engineers

matriz ◆ *sf* ❶ ANATOMÍA womb ❷ [*de talonario*] (cheque) stub ❸ [*molde*] mould ❹ MATEMÁTICAS matrix
◆ *adj* ❶ [*empresa*] parent ☆ *Sólo se usa delante del sustantivo.* ❷ [*casa*] head ☆ *Sólo se usa delante del sustantivo.* ❸ [*iglesia*] mother ☆ *Sólo se usa delante del sustantivo.*

matutino, na *adj* morning ☆ *Sólo se usa delante del sustantivo.* • **trabajo en horario matutino** I work the morning shift

maullar *vi* to miaow

maxilar *sm* jaw

máxime *adv* especially

máximo, ma ✦ *superlativo* = **grande**

✦ *adj* ❶ maximum • **hay un plazo máximo de tres meses** the maximum period is three months ❷ [*galardón, puntuación*] highest • **fue el máximo goleador del campeonato** he was the highest scorer in the championship ⚲: *Los adjetivos ingleses son invariables.*

■ **máximo** *sm* maximum • **al máximo** to the utmost • **llegar al máximo** to reach the limit • **como máximoa)** [*a más tardar*] at the latest **b)** [*como mucho*] at the most

mayo *sm* May ver también **septiembre**
En inglés los nombres de los meses se escriben con mayúscula.

mayonesa, mahonesa *sf* mayonnaise

mayor ✦ *adj* ❶ ⚲: *comparativo* • **mayor (que)a)** [*de tamaño*] bigger (than) **b)** [*de importancia etc*] greater (than) **c)** [*de edad*] older (than) **d)** [*de número*] higher (than) • **la casa nueva tiene un tamaño mayor que la vieja** the new house is bigger than the old one • **mi hermano mayor es soltero** my older brother is single ❷ ⚲: *superlativo* • **el/la mayor... a)** [*de tamaño*] the biggest... **b)** [*de importancia etc*] the greatest... **c)** [*de edad*] the oldest... **d)** [*de número*] the highest... • **es uno de los mayores músicos de su época** he's one of the greatest musicians of his era ❸ [*adulto*] grown-up • **hacerse mayor** to grow up ❹ [*anciano*] elderly • **mi abuelo ya es una persona mayor** my grandfather is an elderly man ❺ MÚSICA • **en do mayor** in C major ⚲: *Los adjetivos ingleses son invariables.*

expresión **al por mayor** COMERCIO wholesale

✦ *smf* • **el/la mayor** [*hijo, hermano*] the eldest

■ *sm* MILITAR major

mayordomo *sm* butler

mayoreo *sm* wholesale • **al mayoreo** wholesale

mayoría *sf* majority • **el partido de derecha obtuvo la mayoría en el parlamento** the right-wing party obtained a majority in congress • **la mayoría de** most of • **la mayoría de los mexicanos** most Mexicans • **la mayoría de las veces** usually • **en su mayoría** in the main ▶ **mayoría simple** simple majority

■ **mayoría de edad** *sf* • **llegar a la mayoría de edad** to come of age

mayorista *smf* wholesaler

mayoritario, ria *adj* majority ⚲: *Sólo se usa delante del sustantivo.*

mayúscula → **letra**

mayúsculo, la *adj* tremendous ⚲: *Los adjetivos ingleses son invariables.*

maza *sf* ❶ [*arma*] mace ❷ [*del bombo*] drumstick

mazmorra *sf* dungeon

mazo *sm* ❶ [*martillo*] mallet ❷ [*de mortero*] pestle ❸ [*de naipes*] balance (of the deck)

me *pronombre personal* ❶ [*complemento directo*] me • **le gustaría verme** she'd like to see me • **préstame tu libro** lend me your book ❷ [*complemento indirecto*] (to) me • **me lo dio** he gave it to me • **me tiene miedo** he's afraid of me ❸ [*reflexivo*] myself • **me voy a lavar las manos** I'm going to wash my hands • **me**

peiné rápidamente I combed my hair quickly • **me dormí una buena siesta** I took a good nap

mear *vi* familiar to pee

mecánico, ca ✦ *adj* mechanical ⚲: *Los adjetivos ingleses son invariables.*

✦ *sm, f* [*persona*] mechanic

■ **mecánica** *sf* ❶ [*ciencia*] mechanics ⚲: *incontable* ❷ [*funcionamiento*] mechanics *pl*

mecanismo *sm* mechanism

mecanografía *sf* typing

mecanógrafo, fa *sm, f* typist

mecapal *sm* porter's leather harness

mecedora *sf* rocking chair

mecenas *smf invariable* patron

mecer *vt* to rock

mecha *sf* ❶ [*de vela*] wick ❷ [*de explosivos*] fuse ❸ [*de pelo*] streak

mechón *sm* ❶ [*de pelo*] lock ❷ [*de lana*] tuft

medalla *sf* medal • **lo premiaron con una medalla** he was rewarded with a medal ▶ **medalla de bronce** bronze medal ▶ **medalla de oro** gold medal ▶ **medalla de plata** silver medal

expresión **ponerse medallas** to show off

medallón *sm* ❶ [*joya*] medallion ❷ [*rodaja*] médaillon ▶ **medallón de pescado** [*empanado*] fishcake

media *sf* ❶ [*promedio*] average • **tienes que calcular la media entre estos números** you have to figure out the average of these numbers ❷ ⚲: *generalmente pl* [*prenda*] pantyhose ❸ [*hora*] • **al dar la media** on the half-hour ❹ DEPORTE midfielders *pl*

mediación *sf* mediation • **por mediación de** through

mediado, da *adj* half-full • **mediada la película** halfway through the film ⚲: *Los adjetivos ingleses son invariables.*

mediano, na *adj* ❶ [*intermedio - de tamaño*] medium; [*- de calidad*] average • **esta caja es de tamaño mediano** this is a medium-sized box • **de mediana edad** middle-aged • **de mediana estatura** of medium height ❷ [*mediocre*] average • **es una persona de mediana inteligencia** he is a person of average intelligence ⚲: *Los adjetivos ingleses son invariables.*

medianoche (pl **mediasnoches**) *sf* midnight • **a medianoche** at midnight

mediante *preposición* by means of • **lograron curar la enfermedad mediante tecnología innovadora** they managed to cure the disease by means of a technological innovation

mediar *vi* ❶ [*llegar a la mitad*] to be halfway through • **mediaba julio** it was mid-July ❷ [*estar en medio - tiempo, distancia, espacio*] • **mediar entre** to be between • **media un jardín entre las dos casas** there is a garden between the two houses • **medió una semana** a week passed by ❸ [*intervenir*] • **mediar (en/entre)** to mediate (in/between) ❹ [*interceder*] • **mediar (en favor de o por)** to intercede (on behalf of o for)

medicación *sf* medication

M

medicamento *sm* medicine

medicar *vt* to give medicine to

medicina *sf* medicine • **estudia medicina** she's studying medicine • **le recetaron una nueva medicina** he was prescribed a new medicine

medicinal *adj* medicinal ☿ *Los adjetivos ingleses son invariables.*

medición *sf* measurement

médico, ca ♦ *adj* medical ☿ *Los adjetivos ingleses son invariables.*
♦ *sm, f* doctor ❱ **médico de cabecera** general practitioner ❱ **médico de familia** family doctor ❱ **médico de guardia** on-call doctor ❱ **médico interno** intern

medida *sf* ❶ [*generalmente*] measure • **tomar medidas** to take measures • **a medida que** as • **a medida que entraban** as they were coming in ❱ **medida cautelar** precautionary measure ❱ **medidas de seguridad** security measures ❷ [*medición*] measurement • **el sastre le tomó las medidas al cliente** the tailor took his client's measurements • **a la medida** custom-made • **se mandó hacer un traje a la medida** he ordered a custom-made suit ❸ [*grado*] extent • **en cierta/gran medida** to some/a large extent • **en la medida de lo posible** as far as possible • **en mayor/menor medida** to a greater/lesser extent

medidor *sm* meter

medieval *adj* medieval ☿ *Los adjetivos ingleses son invariables.*

medio, dia *adj* ❶ [*generalmente*] half • **media docena/hora** half a dozen/an hour • **un kilo y medio** one and a half kilos • **la niña estaba medio dormida cuando llegamos** the little girl was half asleep when we arrived • **son (las dos) y media** it's half past (two) • **a medio camino a)** [*en viaje*] halfway there **b)** [*en trabajo etc*] halfway through • **medio pueblo estaba allí** half the town was there • **a media luz** in the half-light • **hacer algo a medias** to half-do something • **pagar a medias** to go halves, to share the cost ❷ [*intermedio - estatura, tamaño*] medium; [*- posición, punto*] middle ❸ [*de promedio - temperatura, velocidad*] average • **la temperatura media es 25 grados centígrados** the average temperature is 25 degrees Celsius ☿ *Los adjetivos ingleses son invariables.*
■ **medio** ♦ *adv* half • **medio borracho** half drunk • **a medio hacer** half done
♦ *sm* ❶ [*mitad*] half ❷ [*centro*] middle • **en medio (de)** in the middle (of) • **estar por (en) medio** to be in the way ❸ [*sistema, manera*] means • **un medio de transporte** a means of transportation • **por medio de** by means of ❱ **los medios de comunicación** the media ❹ [*elemento físico*] environment ❱ **medio ambiente** environment ❺ [*ambiente social*] circle • **en medios bien informados** in well-informed circles ❻ DEPORTE midfielder
expresión **meterse** o **ponerse de por medio a)** to get in the way **b)** *figurado* to interfere ❱ **quitar de en medio a alguien** to get rid of somebody

medioambiental *adj* environmental ☿ *Los adjetivos ingleses son invariables.*

mediocre *adj* mediocre ☿ *Los adjetivos ingleses son invariables.*

mediodía (pl mediodías) *sm* midday ; noon • **al mediodía** at midday o noon

medir *vt* ❶ [*generalmente*] to measure • **medí el tamaño de la cocina** I measured the kitchen • **la mesa mide más de un metro** the table is more than a meter across • **¿cuánto mides?** how tall are you? • **mido 1,80** ≃ I'm 6 foot (tall) • **mide diez metros** it's ten meters long ❷ [*pros, contras etc*] to weigh up ❸ [*palabras*] to weigh carefully

meditar ♦ *vi* • **meditar (sobre)** to meditate (on) • **le gusta meditar todas las mañanas** he likes to meditate in the morning • **meditó antes de responder** she thought before answering
♦ *vt* ❶ [*generalmente*] to meditate ❷ [*planear*] to plan

mediterráneo, a *adj* Mediterranean ☿ *Los adjetivos ingleses son invariables.*
■ **Mediterráneo** *sm* • **el (mar) Mediterráneo** the Mediterranean (Sea)

médula *sf* ANATOMÍA (bone) marrow ❱ **médula espinal** spinal cord ❱ **médula ósea** bone marrow ❷ [*esencia*] core • **hasta la médula** to the core

medusa *sf* jellyfish

megafonía *sf* public-address system • **llamar por megafonía a alguien** to page somebody

megáfono *sm* megaphone

mejilla *sf* cheek

mejillón *sm* mussel

mejor ♦ *adj* ❶ ☿ *comparativo* better • **mejor (que)** better (than) • **tiene un carro mejor que el mío** she has a better car than I do ❷ ☿ *superlativo* • **el/la mejor...** the best... • **Susana es mi mejor amiga** Susana is my best friend ☿ *Los adjetivos ingleses son invariables.*
♦ *smf* • **el/la mejor (de)** the best (in) • **el mejor de todos** the best of all • **lo mejor fue que...** the best thing was that...
♦ *adv* ❶ ☿ *comparativo* • **mejor (que)** better (than) • **ahora veo mejor** I can see better now • **es mejor que no vengas** it would be better if you didn't come ❷ [*recuperado*] to be better ❸ ☿ *superlativo* best • **el que la conoce mejor** the one who knows her best

mejora *sf* improvement

mejorar ♦ *vt* ❶ [*generalmente*] to improve ❷ [*enfermo*] to make better
♦ *vi* to improve • **el tiempo mejoró** the weather improved

mejoría *sf* improvement

melancolía *sf* melancholy

melaza *sf* molasses *pl*

melena *sf* ❶ [*de persona*] long hair ☿ *incontable* ❷ [*de león*] mane
expresión **soltarse la melena** to let your hair down

melenudo, da *despectivo adj* with a mop of hair ☿ *Los adjetivos ingleses son invariables.*

mellizo, za *adj* & *sm, f* twin ☿ *Los adjetivos ingleses son invariables.*

melocotón *sm* peach

melodía *sf* ❶ Música melody ❷ [*de celular*] ring tone

melódico, ca *adj* melodic ♀ *Los adjetivos ingleses son invariables.*

melodrama *sm* melodrama

melón *sm* melon

membrana *sf* membrane

membresía *sf* membership• **la membresía de este club es muy cara** membership at this club is very expensive

membrete *sm* letterhead

membrillo *sm* ❶ [*fruto*] quince ❷ [*dulce*] quince jelly

memorable *adj* memorable ♀ *Los adjetivos ingleses son invariables.*

memoria *sf* ❶ [*generalmente*] Informática memory • **Augusto tiene una memoria increíble** Augusto has an incredible memory • **quiero ampliar la memoria de mi computadora** I want to expand my computer's memory • **¡qué memoria la mía!** what a memory I have! • **si la memoria no me falla** if my memory serves me right • **de memoria** by heart • **sabe de memoria las tablas de multiplicar** she knows the multiplication tables by heart • **falta de memoria** forgetfulness • **hacer memoria** to try to remember • **tener buena/mala memoria** to have a good/bad memory • **traer a la memoria** to call to mind • **venir a la memoria** to come to mind ❷ [*recuerdo*] remembrance • **ser de feliz/ingrata memoria** to be a happy/an unhappy memory ❸ [*disertación*] (academic) paper ❹ [*informe*] • **memoria (anual)** (annual) report

memorizar *vt* to memorize

mención *sf* mention ▸ **mención honorífica** honorable mention

mencionar *vt* to mention

mendigar ◆ *vt* to beg for ◆ *vi* to beg

mendigo, ga *sm, f* beggar

menear *vt* [*mover - generalmente*] to move; [- *cabeza*] to shake; [- *cola*] to wag; [- *caderas*] to wiggle

menestra *sf* vegetable stew

mengano, na *sm, f* so-and-so

menguante *adj* [*luna*] waning ♀ *Los adjetivos ingleses son invariables.*

menguar ◆ *vi* ❶ [*disminuir*] to decrease ❷ [*luna*] to wane ◆ *vt* [*disminuir*] to diminish

menopausia *sf* menopause

menor ◆ *adj* ❶ ♀ *comparativo* • **menor (que)a)** [*de tamaño*] smaller (than) **b)** [*de edad*] younger (than) **c)** [*de importancia etc*] lesser (than) **d)** [*de número*] lower (than) ❷ ♀ *superlativo* • **el/la menor...a)** [*de tamaño*] the smallest... **b)** [*de edad*] the youngest... **c)** [*de importancia*] the slightest... **d)** [*de número*] the lowest... ❸ [*de poca importancia*] minor • **un problema menor** a minor problem ❹ [*joven*] • **ser menor de edad a)** [*para votar, conducir etc*] to be under age **b)** Derecho to

be a minor ❺ Música • **en do menor** in C minor ♀ *Los adjetivos ingleses son invariables.*

expresión **al por menor** Comercio retail

◆ *smf* ❶ ♀ *superlativo* • **el/la menor** [*hijo, hermano*] the youngest ❷ Derecho [*niño*] minor

menorista *smf* retailer

menos
◆ *adv*
❶ [*comparativo*] less
• **Tomás es menos gordo** Tomás is less fat
• **hace menos frío que ayer** it's less cold than yesterday
• **menos manzanas** less/fewer apples
• **tengo menos de diez dólares** I have less than ten dollars
• **Teresa tiene menos libros que tú** Teresa has less/fewer books than you
• **tengo dos años menos que tú** I'm two years younger than you
❷ [*superlativo*] least
• **el menos alto** the least tall
• **la menos guapa** the least pretty
• **lo menos importante** the least important
• **es la menos lista de la clase** she's the least intelligent in the class
• **lo menos posible** the least possible
❸ [*excepto*] but
• **todo menos eso** everything but that
• **fuimos todos menos Ricardo** we all went except for Ricardo
❹ [*en matemáticas*] minus; take away
• **diez menos cinco es cinco** ten minus five is five
• **diez menos dos son ocho** ten take away two is eight
❺ [*en expresiones*]
• **¡menos mal!** just as well!
• **menos mal que dejó de llover** just as well it stopped raining
• **venir a menos** to come down in the world
◆ *sm invariable*
❶ [*lo mínimo*] least
• **es lo menos que puedo hacer** it's the least I could do
❷ [*signo de resta*] minus
• **el menos es el signo de la resta** the minus is the sign for subtraction
■ **al menos, por lo menos**
◆ *locución adverbial*
❶ [*indica el límite inferior en el cálculo aproximado de una cantidad*] at least
• **por lo menos llamaron veinte personas** at least twenty people have called
• **pesa por lo menos 80 kilos** he weighs at least 80 kilos
❷ [*introduce una explicación que limita el alcance de una declaración*] at least
• **estamos en pleno agosto, pero al menos, no hace tanto calor como temíamos** we're in the

middle of August, but at least it isn't as hot as we feared

❸ [*como mínimo*] at least
• **explícame, al menos, qué hacías allí** at least explain to me what you were doing there

menospreciar *vt* ❶ [*despreciar*] to scorn ❷ [*infravalorar*] to undervalue

mensaje *sm* message • **dejé el mensaje en el contestador** I left a message on the answering machine ▶ **mensaje de texto** text message

mensajero, ra *sm, f* ❶ [*generalmente*] messenger ❷ [*de mensajería*] courier

menso, sa *adj* stupid • **Álvaro es tan menso que me cansa** Álvaro is so stupid it's annoying

menstruación *sf* menstruation

menstruar *vi* to menstruate

mensual *adj* monthly • **es una revista mensual** it's a monthly magazine • **1.000 dólares mensuales** 1.000 dollars a month ☼ *Los adjetivos ingleses son invariables.*

mensualidad *sf* ❶ [*sueldo*] monthly salary ❷ [*pago*] monthly payment

menta *sf* mint

mental *adj* mental ☼ *Los adjetivos ingleses son invariables.*

mentalidad *sf* mentality

mentalizar *vt* to put into a frame of mind

mente *sf* mind • **Lucía tiene una mente brillante** Lucía has a brilliant mind • **quedarse la mente en blanco** to go blank • **tener en mente** to have in mind • **traer a la mente** to bring to mind

mentir *vi* to lie • **no me mientas más** don't lie to me anymore

mentira *sf* lie • **lo castigaron por decir mentiras** he was punished for telling lies • **aunque parezca mentira** strange as it may seem • **de mentira** pretend, false • **parece mentira (que...)** it hardly seems possible (that...) ▶ **mentira piadosa** white lie

mentiroso, sa ◆ *adj* ❶ [*que miente*] • **es la persona más mentirosa que conozco** she's the biggest liar I know ❷ [*engañoso*] deceptive ☼ *Los adjetivos ingleses son invariables.*
◆ *sm, f* liar

mentón *sm* chin

menú (pl menús) *sm* ❶ [*lista*] INFORMÁTICA menu ❷ [*comida*] food ▶ **menú del día** set meal

menudeo *sm* COMERCIO retailing • **al menudeo** retail • **esta tienda vende al menudeo** this is a retail store

menudo, da *adj* ❶ [*pequeño*] small • **pica la cebolla muy menudita** chop the onion very small ❷ [*insignificante*] insignificant ❸ ☼ *Sólo se usa delante del sustantivo.* [*para enfatizar*] what! • **¡menudo lío/gol!** what a mess/goal!

meollo *sm* heart
expresión **llegar al meollo de la cuestión** to come to the heart of the matter

mercadería *sf* merchandise; goods *pl*

mercado *sm* market • **hicimos las compras en el mercado** we did our shopping in the market ▶ **mercado común** Common Market ▶ **mercado libre** free market ▶ **mercado negro** black market ▶ **mercado de valores** stock market

mercancía *sf* goods *pl* • **nos vendieron mercancía dañada** they sold us damaged goods

mercante *adj* merchant ☼ *Los adjetivos ingleses son invariables.*

mercantil *adj* mercantile ☼ *Los adjetivos ingleses son invariables.*

mercenario, ria *adj & sm, f* mercenary ☼ *Los adjetivos ingleses son invariables.*

mercería *sf* [*tienda*] notions store

mercurio *sm* mercury

Mercurio *sm* Mercury

merecedor, ra *adj* • **merecedor de** worthy of ☼ *Los adjetivos ingleses son invariables.*

merecer ◆ *vt* to be worthy of • **la isla merece una visita** the island is worth a visit • **no merece la pena** it's not worth it
◆ *vi* to be worthy

merecido *sm* • **recibir su merecido** to get your just deserts

merendar ◆ *vi* to have supper
◆ *vt* to have for supper

merengue *sm* ❶ COCINA meringue ❷ [*baile*] merengue

meridiano, na *adj* ❶ [*hora* ETC] midday ❷ *figurado* [*claro*] crystal-clear ☼ *Los adjetivos ingleses son invariables.*
■ **meridiano** *sm* meridian

merienda *sf* supper

mérito *sm* ❶ [*cualidad*] merit ❷ [*valor*] value; worth • **tiene mucho mérito** it's no mean achievement • **de mérito** worthy

merluza *sf* [*pez, pescado*] hake

mermelada *sf* jam ▶ **mermelada de naranja** marmalade

mes *sm* ❶ [*del año*] month • **el mes que más me gusta es diciembre** my favorite month is December • **pagamos un mes por adelantado** we paid a month in advance • **estar de tres meses** to be three months pregnant ❷ [*salario*] monthly salary

los meses del año

enero January	**julio** July
febrero February	**agosto** August
marzo March	**septiembre** September
abril April	**octubre** October
mayo May	**noviembre** November
junio June	**diciembre** December

En inglés, los meses se escriben con mayúscula.

mesa *sf* ❶ [*generalmente*] table • **compré una mesa nueva para el comedor** I bought a new table for the dining room • **bendecir la mesa** to say grace • **poner la mesa** to set the table ▶ **mesa de billar** billiard table ▶ **mesa de mezclas** mixing desk ▶ **mesa plegable** folding table ▶ **mesa redonda** [*coloquio*] round table ❷ [*de oficina, despacho*] desk ❸ [*comité*] board ▶ **mesa directiva** executive board ❹ [*en un debate* ETC] panel

mesero, ra *sm, f* waiter, *femenino* waitress

meseta *sf* plateau

mesías *sm figurado* Messiah

mesilla *sf* small table ▶ **mesilla de noche** bedside table

mestizo, za ◆ *adj* ❶ [*persona*] half-caste ❷ [*animal, planta*] cross-bred ⚲ *Los adjetivos ingleses son invariables.*

◆ *sm, f* half-caste

meta *sf* ❶ DEPORTE [*llegada*] finishing line; [*portería*] goal • **el deportista colombiano fue el primero en cruzar la meta** the Colombian athlete was the first to cross the finishing line • **metió la pelota en la meta** he put the ball in the goal ❷ [*objetivo*] goal • **su meta es hacer mucho dinero** his goal is to make a lot of money

metabolismo *sm* metabolism

metáfora *sf* metaphor

metal *sm* ❶ [*material*] metal ❷ MÚSICA brass

metálico, ca ◆ *adj* ❶ [*sonido, color*] metallic ❷ [*objeto*] metal ⚲ *Los adjetivos ingleses son invariables.*

◆ *sm* • **pagar en metálico** to pay (in) cash

metalizado, da *adj* [*pintura*] metallic ⚲ *Los adjetivos ingleses son invariables.*

metamorfosis *sf invariable* metamorphosis

metate *sm* grinding stone

metedura ■ **metedura de pata** *sf* blunder

meteorito *sm* meteorite

meteoro *sm* meteor

meteorología *sf* meteorology

meteorológico, ca *adj* meteorological ⚲ *Los adjetivos ingleses son invariables.*

meteorólogo, ga *sm, f* ❶ meteorologist ❷ RADIO & TELEVISIÓN weatherman, *femenino* weatherwoman

---

meter

◆ *vt*

❶ [*poner en un sitio determinado*] to put
• **metí los calcetines en el cajón de arriba** I put the socks in the top drawer
• **metió la llave en la cerradura** he put the key in the lock
• **mete todo el dinero en el banco** put all the money in the bank
• **lo metieron en la cárcel** they put him in prison

❷ [*poner en una situación particular*]
• **¡en menudo lío nos ha metido!** he's got us into a real mess!

❸ [*hacer a alguien entrar a algo*] to get sb into
• **me metió en la asociación** he got me into the organization

• **metieron al niño en una escuela privada** they put the boy in a private school

❹ [*producir un efecto determinado sobre alguien*]
• **¡le vas a meter miedo al niño!** you're going to scare the kid!
• **¡no me metas prisa!** don't hurry me!

❺ [*hacer participar en una actividad*]
• **nos metió a todos a inflar globos para la fiesta** he made us all blow up balloons for the party

❻ [*marcar*] to score
• **metió el gol ganador** she scored the winning goal

❼ *familiar* [*dar un golpe*]
• **me metió un puñetazo** he got a punch in
• **metió una patada a la máquina de bebidas** he kicked the drink machine

■ **meterse**

◆ *v pronominal*

❶ [*colocarse, instalarse*]
• **no sabía dónde meterme** I didn't know where to put myself
• **me metí en la cama a las diez** I went to bed at ten

❷ [*ir a alguna parte, entrar en un lugar*]
• **¿dónde se metió?** where's he gone?
• **se metió en el cine** he went into the movie theater
• **no se metan en el agua después de comer** don't go in the water after eating

❸ [*dedicarse*] to become
• **se metió de periodista** he became a journalist
• **su hijo se ha metido de cura** her son has become a priest

❹ *familiar* [*entrometerse en algo que no le concierne*]
• **¡no te metas !** stay out of it!
• **¿y tú por qué te metes?** and why are you poking your nose in?
• **no te metas donde no te llaman** don't meddle in other people's business

■ **meterse en**

◆ *v pronominal + preposición*

❶ *familiar* [*entrar en una situación dada*]
• **siempre te estás metiendo en problemas** you're always getting yourself into difficulties

❷ *familiar* [*entrometerse en algo que no le concierne*]
• **no te metas en los asuntos de los demás** don't meddle in other people's business
• **se mete en todo** he sticks his nose in everything

metiche *smf familiar* busybody

metida de pata *sf* blunder

método *sm* [*sistema*] method

metralleta *sf* submachine gun

métrico, ca *adj* [*del metro*] metric ⚲ *Los adjetivos ingleses son invariables.*

metro *sm* ❶ [*generalmente*] meter • **José mide casi dos metros** José is nearly two meters tall ▶ **metro cuadrado** square meter ❷ [*transporte*] subway • **to-**

M

mamos el metro para ir al centro de la ciudad we took the subway into the city ➌ [cinta métrica] tape measure

metrópoli sf [ciudad] metropolis

metrópolis sf invariable = **metrópoli**

metropolitano, na adj metropolitan ☆ Los adjetivos ingleses son invariables.

mexicano, na adj & sm, f Mexican ☆ Los adjetivos ingleses son invariables.

En inglés, los adjetivos que se refieren a un continente o a un país se escriben con mayúscula.

México nombre propio Mexico

mezcla sf ➊ [generalmente] mixture ➋ [tejido] blend ➌ [de grabación] mix ➍ [acción] mixing

mezclar vt ➊ [generalmente] to mix • **mezcló los ingredientes en un bol** she mixed the ingredients in a bowl ➋ [combinar, armonizar] to blend ➌ [confundir, desordenar] to mix up ➍ [implicar] • **mezclar a alguien en** to get somebody mixed up in

mezclilla sm denim

mezquita sf mosque

mg (abreviatura escrita de miligramo) mg

mi¹ sm ➊ MÚSICA E ➋ [en solfeo] mi

mi² (pl mis) adj posesivo my • **mi casa** my house • **mis libros** my books

mí pronombre personal ☆ después de preposición ➊ [generalmente] me • **este trabajo no es para mí** this job isn't for me • **no se fía de mí** he doesn't trust me ➋ [reflexivo] myself • **me gusta reflexionar sobre mí misma** I like to think about myself

expresiones ¡a mí qué! so what?; why should I care? ▶ **para mí** [yo creo] as far as I'm concerned; in my opinion ▶ **por mí** as far as I'm concerned • **por mí, no hay inconveniente** it's fine by me

miau sm miaow

microbio sm germ

microbús sm ➊ minibus ➋ [taxi] (collective) taxi

micrófono sm microphone

microondas sm invariable microwave (oven)

microprocesador sm INFORMÁTICA microprocessor

microscópico, ca adj microscopic ☆ Los adjetivos ingleses son invariables.

microscopio sm microscope ▶ **microscopio electrónico** electron microscope

miedo sm fear • **coger miedo a algo** to develop a fear of something • **dar miedo** to be frightening • **me da miedo manejar** I'm afraid of driving • **por miedo de que...** for fear that... • **temblar de miedo** to tremble with fear • **tener miedo** to be afraid

expresión de miedo familiar • **esta película está de miedo** this film is brilliant • **lo pasamos de miedo** we had a whale of a time

expresar miedo o temor

• **I'm afraid of spiders.** Tengo miedo a las arañas.

• **I'm really frightened there are going to be more attacks.** Tengo miedo que vaya a haber más atentados.

• **I'm worried about you.** Me preocupo por ti.

miedoso, sa adj fearful ☆ Los adjetivos ingleses son invariables.

miel sf honey

miembro sm ➊ [generalmente] member • **es miembro de un club deportivo** he's a member of a sports club ➋ [extremidad] limb • **los miembros inferiores del ser humano son las piernas** the legs are a human being's lower limbs • **miembros superiores/inferiores** upper/lower limbs ▶ **miembro (viril)** penis

miércoles sm Wednesday ▶ **miércoles de ceniza** Ash Wednesday ver también **sábado**

miga sf [de pan] crumb

expresión tener miga a) familiar [ser sustancioso] to have a lot to it **b)** [ser complicado] to have more to it than meets the eye

migra sf despectivo familiar • **la migra** para explicar lo que es puedes decir: it's the US police border patrol

migración sf migration

migrar vi to migrate

migratorio, ria adj migratory ☆ Los adjetivos ingleses son invariables.

mil numeral thousand • **dos mil** two thousand • **mil pesos** a thousand pesos • **acudieron miles de personas** thousands of people came ver también **seis**

milagro sm miracle • **es un milagro que sobreviviera al accidente** it's a miracle she survived the accident • **de milagro** miraculously • **sobrevivió de milagro** she miraculously survived

milagroso, sa adj ➊ miraculous ➋ figurado amazing ☆ Los adjetivos ingleses son invariables.

milenio sm millennium

milésimo, ma numeral thousandth

miligramo sm milligram

milímetro sm millimeter

militante adj & smf militant ☆ Los adjetivos ingleses son invariables.

militar ◆ adj military • **ingresó a la escuela militar** he enrolled in military school ☆ Los adjetivos ingleses son invariables.
◆ smf soldier • **los militares** the military
◆ vi • **militar (en)** to be active (in)

milla sf mile ▶ **milla (marina)** nautical mile

millar sm thousand • **un millar de personas** a thousand people

millón numeral million • **dos millones** two million • **un millón de personas** a million people • **gastó millones en la reforma de la casa** he spent millions on alterations to the house

expresión un millón de cosas que hacer a million things to do ▶ **un millón de gracias** thanks a million

millonario, ria *sm, f* millionaire, *femenino* millionairess

millonésimo, ma *numeral* millionth

milpa *sf* cornfield

mimado, da *adj* spoilt ⋅♡⋅ *Los adjetivos ingleses son invariables.*

mimar *vt* to spoil

mímica *sf* ❶ [*mimo*] mime ❷ [*lenguaje*] sign language

mimo *sm* ❶ [*zalamería*] mollycoddling ❷ [*cariño*] show of affection ❸ TEATRO mime

mina *sf* ❶ GEOLOGÍA & MILITAR mine • **la mina está abandonada** the mine is abandoned ▶ **mina de carbón** coalmine ❷ [*de lápiz*] lead • **se me rompió la mina del lápiz** the pencil's lead broke

mineral ◆ *adj* mineral ⋅♡⋅ *Los adjetivos ingleses son invariables.*
◆ *sm* ❶ GEOLOGÍA mineral ❷ [*en mineralogía*] ore

minería *sf* ❶ [*técnica*] mining ❷ [*sector*] mining industry

minero, ra ◆ *adj* ❶ mining ⋅♡⋅ *Sólo se usa delante del sustantivo.* ❷ [*producción, riqueza*] mineral
◆ *sm, f* miner

miniatura *sf* miniature

minicadena *sf* midi system

minifalda *sf* mini skirt

minigolf (pl minigolfs) *sm* [*juego*] crazy golf

mínimo, ma ◆ *superlativo* = **pequeño**
◆ *adj* ❶ [*lo más bajo posible o necesario*] minimum • **paga la tarifa mínima** he pays the minimum fare ❷ [*lo más bajo temporalmente*] lowest ❸ [*muy pequeño - efecto, importancia* ETC] minimal; very small; [*- protesta, ruido* ETC] slightest • **no tengo la más mínima idea** I haven't the slightest idea • **como mínimo** at the very least • **en lo más mínimo** in the slightest ⋅♡⋅ *Los adjetivos ingleses son invariables.*
■ **mínimo** *sm* [*límite*] minimum • **quieren reducir los gastos al mínimo** they want to cut costs to the minimum
■ **mínima** *sf* METEOROLOGÍA lowest temperature

ministerio *sm* ❶ POLÍTICA department ❷ RELIGIÓN ministry

ministro, tra *sm, f* POLÍTICA secretary ▶ **primer ministro** prime minister

minoría *sf* minority • **una minoría de la población es analfabeta** a minority of the population is illiterate • **estar en minoría** to be in a o the minority ▶ **minorías étnicas** ethnic minorities

minorista ◆ *adj* retail ⋅♡⋅ *Los adjetivos ingleses son invariables.*
◆ *smf* retailer

minoritario, ria *adj* minority ⋅♡⋅ *Sólo se usa delante del sustantivo.*

minucioso, sa *adj* ❶ [*meticuloso*] meticulous ❷ [*detallado*] highly detailed ⋅♡⋅ *Los adjetivos ingleses son invariables.*

minúsculo, la *adj* ❶ [*tamaño*] minute ❷ [*letra*] small ❸ IMPRENTA lower-case ⋅♡⋅ *Los adjetivos ingleses son invariables.*
■ **minúscula** *sf* ❶ small letter ❷ IMPRENTA lower-case letter

minusvalía *sf* [*física*] handicap

minusválido, da ◆ *adj* handicapped ⋅♡⋅ *Los adjetivos ingleses son invariables.*
◆ *sm, f* handicapped person

minutero *sm* minute hand

minuto *sm* minute • **espera un minuto, por favor** wait a minute, please • **guardar un minuto de silencio** to observe a minute's silence

mío, mía ◆ *adj posesivo* mine • **este libro es mío** this book is mine • **un amigo mío** a friend of mine • **no es asunto mío** it's none of my business
◆ *pronombre posesivo* • **el mío** mine • **el mío es rojo** mine is red
expresiones **esta es la mía** *familiar* this is the chance I've been waiting for ▶ **lo mío es el teatro** [*lo que me va*] theater is what I should be doing ▶ **los míos a)** *familiar* [*mi familia*] my folks **b)** [*mi bando*] my lot; my side

miope *adj* shortsighted ⋅♡⋅ *Los adjetivos ingleses son invariables.*

miopía *sf* shortsightedness

mira ◆ *sf* ❶ [*en arma*] sight ❷ [*intención*] intention • **con miras a** with a view to
◆ *exclamación* • **¡mira!** look!

mirador *sm* ❶ [*balcón*] enclosed balcony ❷ [*para ver un paisaje*] viewpoint

miramiento *sm* circumspection • **andarse con miramientos** to stand on ceremony • **sin miramientos** just like that

mirar ◆ *vt* ❶ [*generalmente*] to look at • **¡mírala!** look at her! • **mirar algo de cerca/lejos** to look at something closely/from a distance • **mirar algo por encima** to have a quick look at something ❷ [*observar*] to watch • **el jefe miraba cómo trabajaban los empleados** the boss watched his employees work ❸ [*fijamente*] to stare at ❹ [*fijarse en*] to keep an eye on ❺ [*examinar, averiguar*] to check • **me miraron las valijas en la aduana** they checked my bags at customs • **mira si tienes dinero suficiente** look and see if you have enough money • **le miraron todas las maletas** they searched all her luggage • **mira si ha llegado la carta** go and see if the letter has arrived ❻ [*considerar*] to consider • **¡mira lo que haces!** watch what you're doing!
◆ *vi* ❶ [*generalmente*] to look • **miraba por la ventana** she was looking out the window • **miraron por un agujero** they peeked through a hole • **mira hacia adelante cuando camines** look in front of you when you're walking • **el niño miró hacia arriba en busca de su globo** the boy looked up in search of his balloon ❷ [*observar*] to watch ❸ [*fijamente*] to stare • **mira, yo creo que...** look, I think that... ❹ [*buscar*] to look • **he mirado en todas partes** I've looked everywhere ❺ [*orientarse*] • **mirar a** to face ❻ [*cuidar*] • **mirar por alguien/algo** to look after somebody/something

M

■ **mirarse** *v pronominal* [*uno mismo*] to look at yourself • **se miró en el espejo del cuarto** she looked at herself in the room's mirror • **se miraron con complicidad** they looked at each other complicitly

mirilla *sf* spyhole

mirón, ona *sm, f* familiar ❶ [*espectador*] onlooker ❷ [*curioso*] nosy parker ❸ [*voyeur*] peeping Tom

misa *sf* mass • **decir/oír misa** to say/hear mass

miscelánea *sf* [*tienda*] small general store

miserable ✦ *adj* ❶ [*pobre*] poor ❷ [*vivienda*] wretched ❸ [*penoso, insuficiente*] miserable ❹ [*vil*] contemptible ❺ [*tacaño*] stingy *Los adjetivos ingleses son invariables.*
✦ *smf* [*ruin*] wretch

miseria *sf* ❶ [*pobreza*] poverty • **vivir en la miseria** to live in poverty ❷ [*cantidad muy pequeña*] pittance • **gana una miseria** she earns a pittance ❸ [*desgracia*] misfortune ❹ [*tacañería*] meanness

misericordia *sf* compassion • **pedir misericordia** to beg for mercy

mísero, ra *adj* [*pobre*] wretched • **ni un mísero...** not even a miserable... *Los adjetivos ingleses son invariables.*

misil (pl misiles) *sm* missile ▶ **misil de crucero** cruise missile

misión *sf* ❶ [*generalmente*] mission ❷ [*cometido*] task ❸ [*expedición científica*] expedition

misionero, ra *adj & sm, f* missionary *Los adjetivos ingleses son invariables.*

mismo, ma ✦ *adj* ❶ [*igual*] same • **el mismo departamento** the same apartment • **tengo puesta la misma camisa que ayer** I'm wearing the same shirt I wore yesterday • **María ya no es la misma de antes** María just isn't the same anymore • **del mismo color que** the same color as ❷ [*para enfatizar*] • **yo mismo** I myself • **yo misma lo vi** I saw him myself • **repetí sus mismas palabras** I repeated her exact words • **ahora mismo vuelvo** I'll be right back • **en este mismo cuarto** in this very room • **en su misma calle** right in the street where he lives • **por mí/ti mismo** by myself/yourself • **¡tú mismo!** it's up to you *Los adjetivos ingleses son invariables.*
✦ *pronombre* • **el mismo** the same • **el mismo que vi ayer** the same one I saw yesterday • **terminé el trabajo e hice una copia del mismo** I finished the assignment and made a copy of it • **lo mismo** the same (thing) • **lo mismo que** the same as
expresión **da o es lo mismo** it doesn't matter ▶ **me da lo mismo** I don't care
■ **mismo** *adv* *después de sustantivo* ❶ [*para enfatizar*] • **lo vi desde mi casa mismo** I saw it from my own house • **ahora/aquí mismo** right now/here • **ayer mismo** only yesterday • **por eso mismo** precisely for that reason ❷ [*por ejemplo*] • **escoge uno — cualquiera este mismo** choose any — this one, for instance

misterio *sm* mystery

misterioso, sa *adj* mysterious *Los adjetivos ingleses son invariables.*

místico, ca *adj* mystical *Los adjetivos ingleses son invariables.*

mitad *sf* ❶ [*generalmente*] half • **comimos la mitad del postre** we ate half the dessert • **a mitad de precio** at half price • **a mitad del camino** halfway there • **a mitad de la película** halfway through the film • **la mitad de** half (of) • **la mitad del tiempo no está** half the time she's not in • **mitad y mitad** half and half ❷ [*centro*] middle • **en mitad de** in the middle of • **(cortar algo) por la mitad** (to cut something) in half

mítico, ca *adj* mythical *Los adjetivos ingleses son invariables.*

mitin (pl mítines) *sm* rally

mito *sm* [*generalmente*] myth

mitología *sf* mythology

mitote *sm* familiar [*bulla*] racket

mixto, ta *adj* ❶ mixed • **comí una ensalada mixta** I ate a mixed salad ❷ [*comisión*] joint ❸ [*colegio*] coed • **es una escuela mixta** it's a coed school *Los adjetivos ingleses son invariables.*

ml (*abreviatura escrita de* mililitro) ml

mm (*abreviatura escrita de* milímetro) mm

mobiliario *sm* furniture ▶ **mobiliario urbano** street furniture

mochila *sf* ❶ backpack ❷ bookbag

moción *sf* motion

moco *sm* familiar ❶ snot *incontable* • **limpiarse los mocos** to wipe your nose • **sorberse los mocos** to sniffle • **tener mocos** to have a runny nose ❷ MEDICINA mucus *incontable*

mocoso, sa *sm, f* familiar & despectivo brat

moda *sf* fashion • **el mundo de la moda** the fashion world • **estar de moda** to be in fashion • **estar a la moda** to be fashionable • **estar pasado de moda** to be out of fashion • **ponerse de moda** to come into fashion • **moda pasajera** fad

modal *adj* modal *Los adjetivos ingleses son invariables.*
■ **modales** *smpl* manners • **tiene muy buenos modales** he has very nice manners

modalidad *sf* ❶ form ❷ DEPORTE discipline

modelar *vt* ❶ to model ❷ figurado to shape

modelo ✦ *adj* model *Los adjetivos ingleses son invariables.*
✦ *smf* model
✦ *sm* ❶ [*generalmente*] model ▶ **modelo económico** ECONOMÍA economic model ❷ [*prenda de vestir*] outfit

módem (pl modems) *sm* INFORMÁTICA modem
expresión **módem fax** fax modem

moderación *sf* moderation

moderado, da *adj & sm, f* moderate *Los adjetivos ingleses son invariables.*

moderador, ra *sm, f* chair

moderar *vt* ❶ [*generalmente*] to moderate ❷ [*velocidad*] to reduce ❸ [*debate*] to chair

modernizar *vt* to modernize

moderno, na *adj* modern ⚙ *Los adjetivos ingleses son invariables.*

modestia *sf* modesty

modesto, ta *adj* modest • **es un hombre modesto que no presume de sí mismo** he's a modest man who doesn't show off • **compramos un apartamento modesto** we bought a modest apartment ⚙ *Los adjetivos ingleses son invariables.*

modificar *vt* ❶ [*variar*] to alter • **modificamos el frente de la casa** we altered the house's façade ❷ GRAMÁTICA to modify • **los adjetivos modifican a los sustantivos** adjectives modify nouns

modista *sm, f* ❶ [*diseñador*] fashion designer ❷ [*que cose*] tailor, *femenino* dressmaker

modisto *sm* ❶ [*diseñador*] fashion designer ❷ [*sastre*] tailor

modo *sm* ❶ [*manera, forma*] way • **tiene un modo especial de caminar** he has a special way of walking • **a modo de** by way of • **a mi modo** (in) my own way • **de ese modo** in that way • **de ningún modo** in no way • **de todos modos** in any case • **de un modo u otro** one way or another • **en cierto modo** in some ways • ▶ **modo de empleo** instructions *pl* for use ▶ **modo de pensar** way of thinking ▶ **modo de ser** way of being ▶ **modo de vida** way of life • **de modo que a)** [*de manera que*] in such a way that **b)** [*así que*] so ❷ GRAMÁTICA mood • **estuvimos practicando el modo subjuntivo en clase de español** we practiced the subjunctive mood in Spanish class

módulo *sm* ❶ [*generalmente*] module ▶ **módulo lunar** lunar module ❷ [*de muebles*] unit

mofa *sf* mockery

moflete *sm* chubby cheek

moho *sm* ❶ [*hongo*] mould • **criar moho** to go mouldy ❷ [*herrumbre*] rust

mojado, da *adj* ❶ wet ❷ [*húmedo*] damp ⚙ *Los adjetivos ingleses son invariables.*

mojar *vt* ❶ [*sin querer*] to get wet ❷ [*a propósito*] to wet • **mojé el suelo de la cocina** I wetted the kitchen floor ❸ [*humedecer*] to dampen ❹ [*comida*] to dunk • **el niño mojó el pan en la sopa** the boy dunked his bread in his soup • **moja el pan en la salsa** dip your bread in the sauce
■ **mojarse** *v pronominal* [*con agua*] to get wet • **nos mojamos con la lluvia** we got wet in the rain

molcajete *sm* mortar

molde *sm* mould

moldeado *sm* ❶ [*del pelo*] soft perm ❷ [*de figura, cerámica*] moulding

moldear *vt* ❶ [*generalmente*] to mould ❷ [*modelar*] to cast ❸ [*cabello*] to give a soft perm to

mole ◆ *sf* hulk
◆ *sm* ❶ [*salsa*] thick chili sauce ❷ [*guiso*] chili stew

molécula *sf* molecule

moler *vt* ❶ [*generalmente*] to grind ❷ [*aceitunas*] to press ❸ [*trigo*] to mill ❹ *familiar* [*cansar*] to wear out

molestar *vt* ❶ [*perturbar*] to annoy • **me molesta la impuntualidad de la gente** people who aren't punctual annoy me • **no molesten a Juan mientras está trabajando** don't bother Juan while he's working • **¿le molesta que fume?** do you mind if I smoke? • **perdone que le moleste...** I'm sorry to bother you... ❷ [*doler*] to hurt • **le molestan los zapatos nuevos** his new shoes are hurting him ❸ [*ofender*] to offend
■ **molestarse** *v pronominal* ❶ [*incomodarse*] to bother • **molestarse en hacer algo** to bother to do something • **ni se molestó en mirar quién entraba** she didn't even bother to see who was coming in • **molestarse por alguien/algo** to put yourself out for somebody/something ❷ [*ofenderse*] • **molestarse (por algo)** to take offence (at something)

molestia *sf* ❶ [*incomodidad*] nuisance • **es una molestia tener invitados en casa** having houseguests is a nuisance • **disculpen las molestias** we apologize for any inconvenience • **si no es demasiada molestia** if it's not too much trouble • **tomarse la molestia** to take the trouble ❷ [*malestar*] discomfort • **¿sientes alguna molestia?** do you feel any discomfort? • **siento una molestia en el estómago** my stomach doesn't feel too good • **siento algunas molestias en la pierna** I have some pains in my leg

molesto, ta *adj* ❶ [*incordiante*] annoying ❷ [*visita*] inconvenient ❸ [*irritado*] • **molesto (con)** annoyed (with) ❹ [*con malestar*] in discomfort ⚙ *Los adjetivos ingleses son invariables.*

molido, da *adj familiar* [*cansado*] worn out • **estar molido de** to be worn out from ⚙ *Los adjetivos ingleses son invariables.*

molinillo *sm* grinder ▶ **molinillo de café** coffee grinder

molino *sm* mill ▶ **molino de viento** windmill

molusco *sm* mollusc

momentáneo, a *adj* ❶ [*de un momento*] momentary ❷ [*pasajero*] temporary ⚙ *Los adjetivos ingleses son invariables.*

momento *sm* ❶ [*generalmente*] moment • **en el momento en que yo salía, ella entraba** she walked in the moment I left • **fueron momentos de mucha angustia** they were very anguished moments • **a cada momento** all the time • **al momento** straightaway • **a partir de este momento** from this moment (on) • **de momento, por el momento** for the time being • **de un momento a otro** any minute now • **dentro de un momento** in a moment • **desde el momento (en) que... a)** [*tiempo*] from the moment that... **b)** [*causa*] seeing as... • **en algún momento** sometime • **momentos después** moments later • **¡un momento!** just a minute! • **momento decisivo** turning point ❷ [*periodo*] time • **llegó un momento en que...** there came a time when... • **del momento** [*actual*] of the day

momia *sf* mummy

monada *sf* ❶ [*persona*] • **su novia es una monada** his girlfriend is gorgeous • **¡qué monada de bebé!** what a cute baby! ❷ [*cosa*] • **¡qué monada de falda!** what a lovely skirt!

monarca *sm* monarch

M

monarquía *sf* monarchy ▸ **monarquía absoluta/constitucional/parlamentaria** absolute/constitutional/parliamentary monarchy

monárquico, ca *adj* monarchic ☼: *Los adjetivos ingleses son invariables.*

monasterio *sm* ❶ [*de monjes*] monastery ❷ [*de monjas*] convent

moneda *sf* ❶ [*pieza*] coin • **necesito cambio en monedas** I need some change in coins ❷ [*divisa*] currency • **la moneda de México es el peso** the currency of Mexico is the peso

expresión **pagar a alguien con la misma moneda** to pay somebody back in kind ▸ **ser moneda corriente** to be commonplace

monedero *sm* coin purse ▸ **monedero electrónico** electronic wallet

monetario, ria *adj* monetary ☼: *Los adjetivos ingleses son invariables.*

mongólico, ca *sm, f* MEDICINA person with Down's syndrome

monigote *sm* ❶ [*muñeco*] rag doll ❷ [*dibujo*] doodle ❸ [*figurado*] [*persona*] puppet

monja *sf* nun

monje *sm* monk

mono, na ◆ *adj* [*bonito*] lovely ☼: *Los adjetivos ingleses son invariables.*

◆ *sm, f* [*animal*] monkey

expresiones **aunque la mona se vista de seda, mona se queda** *proverbio* you can't make a silk purse out of a sow's ear *proverbio* ▸ **mandar a alguien a freír monas** *familiar* to tell somebody to get lost ▸ **ser el último mono** to be bottom of the heap

■ **mono** *sm* [*prenda - con peto*] dungarees *pl*; [*- con mangas*] overalls *pl* • **los mecánicos usan un mono azul** the mechanics wear blue coveralls

monolingüe *adj* monolingual ☼: *Los adjetivos ingleses son invariables.*

monólogo *sm* ❶ monologue ❷ TEATRO soliloquy

monopatín *sm* skateboard

monopolio *sm* monopoly

monopolizar *vt* to monopolize

monotonía *sf* [*uniformidad*] monotony

monótono, na *adj* monotonous ☼: *Los adjetivos ingleses son invariables.*

monovolumen *sm* people carrier

monstruo ◆ *adj invariable* [*grande*] enormous ☼: *Los adjetivos ingleses son invariables.*

◆ *sm* ❶ [*generalmente*] monster ❷ [*prodigio*] giant

monstruosidad *sf* ❶ [*crueldad*] monstrosity ❷ [*fealdad*] hideousness ❸ [*anomalía*] freak

monstruoso, sa *adj* ❶ [*cruel*] monstrous ❷ [*feo*] hideous ❸ [*enorme*] enormous ❹ [*deforme*] terribly deformed ☼: *Los adjetivos ingleses son invariables.*

monta *sf* [*importancia*] importance • **de poca monta** of little importance

montacargas *sm invariable* forklift

montaje *sm* ❶ [*de máquina*] assembly ❷ TEATRO staging ❸ FOTOGRAFÍA montage ❹ CINE editing

montaña *sf* mountain • **ir de excursión a la montaña** to go on a trip to the mountains ▸ **montaña rusa** roller coaster

expresión **hacer una montaña de un grano de arena** to make a mountain out of a molehill

montañero, ra *sm, f* mountaineer

montañismo *sm* mountaineering

montañoso, sa *adj* mountainous ☼: *Los adjetivos ingleses son invariables.*

montar ◆ *vt* ❶ [*ensamblar - máquina, estantería*] to assemble; [*- tienda de campaña, tenderete*] to put up ❷ [*encajar*] • **montar algo en algo** to fit something into something ❸ [*organizar - negocio, departamento*] to set up ❹ [*cabalgar*] to ride ❺ [*poner encima*] • **montar a alguien en** to lift somebody onto ❻ TEATRO to stage ❼ CINE to edit

◆ *vi* ❶ [*subir*] to get on ❷ [*en coche*] to get in • **montar en a)** [*generalmente*] to get onto **b)** [*coche*] to get into **c)** [*animal*] to mount ❸ [*ir montado*] to ride • **montar en bicicleta/a caballo** to ride a bicycle/a horse

monte *sm* ❶ [*elevación*] mountain ❷ [*terreno*] woodland ▸ **monte bajo** scrub

expresión **no todo el monte es orégano** *proverbio* life's not a bowl of cherries

montículo *sm* hillock

montón *sm* ❶ [*pila*] pile ❷ [*muchos*] loads • **había montones de gente en el concierto** there were loads of people at the concert • **un montón de** loads of

expresión **del montón** ordinary

montura *sf* ❶ [*cabalgadura*] mount ❷ [*arreos*] harness ❸ [*silla*] saddle ❹ [*soporte - de gafas*] frame

monumental *adj* ❶ [*ciudad, lugar*] famous for its monuments ❷ [*fracaso etc*] monumental ☼: *Los adjetivos ingleses son invariables.*

monumento *sm* monument

moño *sm* [*lazo*] bow • **amarró el paquete con un moño** she tied the package with a bow

expresión **agarrarse del moño** [*pegarse*] to pull each other's hair out ▸ **estar hasta el moño (de)** to be sick to death (of)

monzón *sm* monsoon

mora *sf* ❶ [*de la zarzamora*] blackberry ❷ [*del moral*] mulberry

morado, da *adj* purple ☼: *Los adjetivos ingleses son invariables.*

■ **morado** *sm* [*color*] purple

moral ◆ *adj* moral ☼: *Los adjetivos ingleses son invariables.*

◆ *sf* ❶ [*ética*] morality ❷ [*ánimo*] morale • **no hay que dejar que decaiga la moral del grupo** we have to keep up the group's morale

moraleja *sf* moral

morbo *sm familiar* [*placer malsano*] morbid pleasure

morboso, sa *adj* morbid ☼: *Los adjetivos ingleses son invariables.*

morcilla *sf* COCINA ≈ blood sausage

expresión ¡que te/os den morcilla! *muy familiar* you can stuff it, then!

mordaz *adj* caustic ♀ *Los adjetivos ingleses son invariables.*

mordaza *sf* gag

mordedura *sf* bite

morder ◆ *vt* ❶ [*con los dientes*] to bite • **el cachorro me mordió el tobillo** the puppy bit me on the ankle ❷ [*gastar*] to eat into ◆ *vi* to bite

expresión estar que muerde to be hopping mad

mordida *sf* ❶ bite • **le dio una mordida al sándwich** he took a bite out of the sandwich ❷ *familiar* [*soborno*] bribe • **tuvimos que darle una mordida para conseguir el permiso** we had to give him a bribe to get the permit

mordisco *sm* bite

mordisquear *vt* to nibble (at)

moreno, na ◆ *adj* ❶ [*pelo, piel*] dark • **Luis es de piel morena** Luis has dark skin ❷ [*por el sol*] tanned • **ponerse moreno** to get a tan • **mi hermana tiene la piel morena por el sol** my sister's skin is tan from the sun ❸ [*pan, azúcar*] brown • **cocino con azúcar morena** I cook with brown sugar ♀ *Los adjetivos ingleses son invariables.*
◆ *sm, f* ❶ [*de pelo*] dark-haired person ❷ [*de piel*] dark-skinned person

morera *sf* white mulberry

moretón *sm* bruise

morfina *sf* morphine

moribundo, da *adj* dying ♀ *Los adjetivos ingleses son invariables.*

morir *vi* ❶ [*generalmente*] to die • **su tío murió en un accidente** her uncle died in an accident • **morir de algo** to die of something • **me moría de aburrimiento en la clase** I was dying of boredom in class ❷ [*río, calle*] to come out ❸ [*fuego*] to die down ❹ [*luz*] to go out ❺ [*día*] to come to a close

mormón, ona *adj & sm, f* Mormon ♀ *Los adjetivos ingleses son invariables.*

moro, ra *adj* HISTORIA Moorish ♀ *Los adjetivos ingleses son invariables.*

moronga *sf* blood sausage

moroso, sa ◆ *adj* COMERCIO defaulting ♀ *Los adjetivos ingleses son invariables.*
◆ *sm, f* COMERCIO defaulter

morralla *sf* [*suelto*] loose change

morro *sm* ❶ [*hocico*] snout ❷ *familiar* [*de coche, avión*] nose

morsa *sf* walrus

morse *sm* ♀ *en aposición invariable* Morse (code)

mortadela *sf* Mortadella

mortal ◆ *adj* ❶ [*no inmortal*] mortal • **todos somos seres mortales** we're all mortal ❷ [*caída, enfermedad*] fatal • **tiene una enfermedad mortal** she has a fatal disease ❸ [*aburrimiento, susto, enemigo*] deadly • **la película es de un aburrimiento mortal** the movie was deadly boring ♀ *Los adjetivos ingleses son invariables.*
◆ *smf* mortal

mortalidad *sf* mortality

mortandad *sf* mortality

mortero *sm* mortar

mortífero, ra *adj* deadly ♀ *Los adjetivos ingleses son invariables.*

mosca *sf* fly

expresiones no se oía ni una mosca you could have heard a pin drop ▶ por si las moscas just in case ▶ ¿qué mosca te ha picado? what's up with you?

■ mosca muerta *smf* slyboots

moscardón *sm* ZOOLOGÍA blowfly

moscón *sm* ZOOLOGÍA bluebottle

mosquero *sm* swarm of flies

mosquitero *sm* mosquito net

mosquito *sm* mosquito

mostaza *sf* mustard

mostrador *sm* ❶ [*en tienda*] counter ❷ [*en bar*] bar

mostrar *vt* to show • **la vendedora nos mostró una camisa carísima** the saleswoman showed us a very expensive shirt • **un policía me mostró cómo llegar al museo** a policeman showed me how to get to the museum

mota *sf* ❶ [*de polvo*] speck ❷ [*en tela*] dot

mote *sm* nickname • **poner un mote a alguien** to nickname somebody

motel *sm* motel

motín *sm* ❶ [*del pueblo*] uprising ❷ [*de las tropas*] mutiny

motivación *sf* motivation ♀ *incontable*

motivar *vt* ❶ [*causar*] to cause ❷ [*impulsar*] to motivate • **no se sabe qué lo motivó a tomar esa decisión** we don't know what motivated him to make that decision • **la maestra motiva a los alumnos a trabajar en clase** the teacher motivates her students to work in class

motivo *sm* ❶ [*causa*] reason • **la maestra explicó el motivo de su ausencia** the teacher explained the reason for her absence • **bajo ningún motivo** under no circumstances • **con motivo de** for • **viajó a Perú con motivo de un congreso** he traveled to Peru for a conference • **dar motivo a** to give reason to • **tener motivos para** to have reason to ❷ [*de crimen*] motive ❸ ARTE, LITERATURA & MÚSICA motif • **dibujó unos motivos navideños** she drew some Christmassy motifs

moto *sf* motorcycle

motocicleta *sf* motorcycle

motociclismo *sm* motorcycling

motociclista *smf* motorcyclist

motoneta *sf* (motor) scooter

motonetista *smf* scooter rider

M

motor, a, motriz *adj* motor ☼ *Los adjetivos ingleses son invariables.*

■ **motor** *sm* ❶ [*aparato*] engine • **se rompió el motor del carro** the car's engine died ▶ **motor fuera borda** outboard motor ❷ [*fuerza*] dynamic force

■ **motora** *sf* motorboat

motorismo *sm* motorcycling

motorista *smf* motorcyclist

mousse *sm invariable* Cocina mousse

mover *vt* ❶ [*generalmente*] INFORMÁTICA to move • **movió la silla** he moved the chair • **empezamos a mover el asunto** we put the matter in motion • **mueven grandes cantidades de dinero** they handle large sums of money ❷ [*mecánicamente*] to drive ❸ [*cabeza - afirmativamente*] to nod; [- *negativamente*] to shake ❹ [*suscitar*] to provoke ❺ *figurado* [*empujar*] • **mover a alguien a algo/a hacer algo** to drive somebody to something/to do something

■ **moverse** *v pronominal* ❶ [*generalmente*] to move • **muévete un poco hacia acá** move this way a little • **el barco se movió durante todo el trayecto** the boat swayed during the whole trip ❷ [*en la cama*] to toss and turn ❸ [*darse prisa*] to get a move on

movido, da *adj* ❶ [*debate, torneo*] lively ❷ [*persona*] active ❸ [*jornada, viaje*] hectic ❹ FOTOGRAFÍA blurred ☼ *Los adjetivos ingleses son invariables.*

móvil ◆ *adj* mobile ☼ *Los adjetivos ingleses son invariables.*
◆ *sm* ❶ [*motivo*] motive ❷ [*juguete*] mobile

movilidad *sf* mobility

movilizar *vt* to mobilize

movimiento *sm* ❶ [*generalmente*] POLÍTICA movement • **hizo un movimiento con la mano** he made a movement with his hand ▶ **movimiento obrero/pacifista** working-class/pacifist movement ❷ FÍSICA & TECNOLOGÍA motion ▶ **movimiento continuo/de rotación** perpetual/rotational motion ▶ **movimiento sísmico** earth tremor ❸ [*circulación - generalmente*] activity; [- *de personal, mercancías*] turnover; [- *de vehículos*] traffic • **hay mucho movimiento en la calle** there is a lot of activity on the street ❹ MÚSICA [*parte de la obra*] movement

mozo, za ◆ *adj* ❶ [*joven*] young ❷ [*soltero*] single ☼ *Los adjetivos ingleses son invariables.*
◆ *sm, f* young boy, *femenino* young girl
■ **mozo** *sm* ❶ [*trabajador*] assistant (worker) ▶ **mozo de cordel** o **de cuerda** porter ▶ **mozo de estación** (station) porter ❷ [*recluta*] conscript

MP3 (*abreviatura de* MPEG-1 Audio Layer-3) *sm* INFORMÁTICA MP3

mu *sm* [*mugido*] moo

expresión no decir ni mu not to say a word

muchachada *sf* group of youngsters

muchacho, cha *sm, f* boy, *femenino* girl
■ **muchacha** *sf* [*sirvienta*] maid

muchedumbre *sf* ❶ [*de gente*] crowd ❷ [*de cosas*] great number

mucho, cha ◆ *adj* ❶ [*gran cantidad*] a lot of • **como mucha fruta** I eat a lot of fruit • **tengo muchos lápices de colores** I have a lot of colored pencils ❷ ☼ *en interrogativas y negativas* [*con singular*] much • **no tuvo mucha suerte** he didn't have much luck; [*con plural*] many • **¿había muchos chavos en la fiesta?** were there many kids at the party? ☼ *Los adjetivos ingleses son invariables.*
◆ *pronombre* ❶ ☼ *en sing* a lot • **sabe mucho de filosofía** he knows a lot about philosophy ❷ ☼ *pl* many; a lot • **tengo mucho que contarte** I have a lot to tell you • **¿queda dinero? — no mucho** is there any money left? — not much o not a lot • **muchos piensan igual** a lot of people think the same
■ **mucho** *adv* ❶ [*generalmente*] a lot • **habla mucho** he talks a lot • **me canso mucho** I get really o very tired • **me gusta mucho** I like it a lot o very much • **no me gusta mucho** I don't like it much • **soy mucho mayor que mi hermana** I'm much older than my sister • **(no) mucho más tarde** (not) much later ❷ [*largo tiempo*] • **hace mucho que no vienes** I haven't seen you for a long time • **¿dura mucho la obra?** is the play long? • **mucho antes/después** long before/after ❸ [*frecuentemente*] • **¿vienes mucho por aquí?** do you come here often?

expresiones como mucho at the most ▶ con mucho by far; easily ▶ ni con mucho not by a long chalk ▶ ni mucho menos by no means • no está ni mucho menos decidido it is by no means decided ▶ por mucho que however much • por mucho que insistas however much you insist

muda *sf* [*ropa interior*] change of underwear

mudanza *sf* move • **estar de mudanza** to be moving

mudar ◆ *vt* ❶ [*generalmente*] to change ❷ [*casa*] to move • **cuando mude la voz** when his voice breaks ❸ [*piel, plumas*] to moult
◆ *vi* [*cambiar*] • **mudar de a)** [*opinión, color*] to change **b)** [*domicilio*] to move • **los camaleones pueden mudar de color** chameleons can change color
■ **mudarse** *v pronominal* • **mudarse (de casa)** to move (house) • **se mudaron para la ciudad** they moved to the city • **mudarse (de ropa)** to change • **me mudé de ropa antes de salir** I changed clothes before going out

mudo, da *adj* ❶ [*sin habla*] dumb • **se quedó muda como consecuencia de un golpe en la cabeza** she went mute after a blow to the head ❷ [*callado*] silent • **se quedó mudo** he was left speechless ❸ [*sin sonido*] silent • **la "h" es la única letra muda del español** "h" is the only silent letter in Spanish ☼ *Los adjetivos ingleses son invariables.*

mueble *sm* piece of furniture • **un mueble bonito** a very nice piece of furniture • **los muebles** the furniture ☼ *incontable* • **compré muebles nuevos** I bought new furniture

expresión salvar los muebles to save face

mueca *sf* ❶ [*generalmente*] face ❷ [*de dolor*] grimace

muela *sf* [*diente - generalmente*] tooth ; [- *molar*] molar • **tengo un fuerte dolor de muelas** I have a strong toothache ▶ **muela del juicio** wisdom tooth

muelle *sm* ❶ [*de colchón, reloj*] spring ❷ [*en el puerto*] dock ❸ [*en el río*] wharf

muerte *sf* ❶ [*generalmente*] death • **muchas personas creen que hay vida después de la muerte** many people believe there is life after death • **fueron condenados a muerte** they were condemned to death • **un susto de muerte** a terrible shock ▶ **muerte natural/ violenta** natural/violent death ▶ **muerte súbita a)** [*de bebé*] cot death **b)** [*en tenis*] tiebreak ; tiebreaker ❷ [*homicidio*] murder

expresión estar de muerte a)** *familiar* [*comida*] to be yummy **b)** [*persona*] to be gorgeous

muerto, ta ✦ *participio pasado* → **morir**

✦ *adj* [*generalmente*] dead • **encontramos un perro muerto en la carretera** we found a dead dog on the road • **caer muerto** to drop dead ۞ *Los adjetivos ingleses son invariables.*

expresiones estar muerto (de cansancio) to be dead tired ▶ **estar muerto de miedo/frío** to be scared/ freezing to death ▶ **no tener donde caerse muerto** not to have a penny to your name

✦ *sm, f* ❶ [*persona*] dead person ❷ [*cadáver*] corpse

expresión cargar con el muerto a)** [*trabajo, tarea*] to be left holding the baby **b)** [*culpa*] to get the blame

muestra *sf* ❶ [*pequeña cantidad*] sample • **nos regalaron una muestra de perfume** they gave us a perfume sample • **se sacó una muestra de sangre** they took a blood sample ❷ [*señal*] sign ❸ [*prueba*] proof ❹ [*de cariño, aprecio*] token ❺ [*modelo*] pattern • **usaron mi vestido como muestra** they used my dress as a pattern ❻ [*exposición*] show ; exhibition

expresión para muestra (basta) un botón one example is enough

mugido *sm* ❶ [*de vaca*] moo ❷ [*de toro*] bellow

mugir *vi* ❶ [*vaca*] to moo ❷ [*toro*] to bellow

mugre *sf* filth

mugriento, ta *adj* filthy ۞ *Los adjetivos ingleses son invariables.*

mujer *sf* ❶ woman • **las mujeres de la familia organizaron una fiesta** the women in the family organized a party ▶ **mujer fatal** femme fatale ▶ **mujer de la limpieza** cleaning lady ▶ **mujer policía** policewoman ❷ [*cónyuge*] wife • **Gonzalo me presentó a su mujer** Gonzalo introduced me to his wife

mulato, ta *adj* & *sm, f* mulatto ۞ *Los adjetivos ingleses son invariables.*

muleta *sf* ❶ [*para andar*] crutch ❷ *figurado* prop

mullido, da *adj* soft ۞ *Los adjetivos ingleses son invariables.*

mulo, la *sm, f* ZOOLOGÍA mule

multa *sf* fine • **poner una multa a alguien** to fine somebody

multar *vt* to fine

multiconfesional *adj* [*sociedad, organización*] multifaith ۞ *Los adjetivos ingleses son invariables.*

multimedia *adj invariable* INFORMÁTICA multimedia ۞ *Los adjetivos ingleses son invariables.*

multimillonario, ria *sm, f* multimillionaire

multinacional *adj* & *sf* multinational ۞ *Los adjetivos ingleses son invariables.*

múltiple *adj* [*variado*] multiple • **ya ha sucedido en múltiples ocasiones** it has happened before on multiple occasions ۞ *Los adjetivos ingleses son invariables.*

multiplicación *sf* multiplication • **el niño es muy bueno haciendo multiplicaciones** the boy is very good at multiplication

multiplicar *vt* & *vi* to multiply • **multiplica 48 por 2** multiply 48 by 2

multitud *sf* [*de personas*] crowd • **una multitud de admiradores fue al concierto** a crowd of fans attended the concert • **una multitud de cosas** loads of things

multitudinario, ria *adj* [*manifestación*] mass ۞ *Sólo se usa delante del sustantivo.*

multiuso *adj invariable* multipurpose ۞ *Los adjetivos ingleses son invariables.*

mundial ✦ *adj* ❶ [*política, economía, guerra*] world ۞ *Sólo se usa delante del sustantivo.* • **una guerra mundial** a world war ❷ [*tratado, organización, fama*] worldwide • **el hambre es un problema de escala mundial** hunger is a problem on a worldwide scale

✦ *sm* ❶ World Championships *pl* ❷ [*en futbol*] World Cup

mundo *sm* [*generalmente*] world • **quieren dar la vuelta alrededor del mundo** they want to go around the world • **me atrae el mundo del deporte** I'm attracted to the world of sports • **el otro mundo** the next world ; the hereafter • **todo el mundo** everyone • **todo el mundo se enteró del secreto de Adriana** everyone found out about Adriana's secret

expresiones irse al otro mundo to pass away ▶ **por nada del mundo** not for (all) the world ▶ **se le cayó el mundo encima** his world fell apart ▶ **venir al mundo** to come into the world ▶ **ver** o **correr mundo** to see life

munición *sf* ammunition

municipal ✦ *adj* ❶ town ۞ *Sólo se usa delante del sustantivo.* ❷ [*elecciones*] local ❸ [*instalaciones*] public

✦ *smf* → **guardia**

municipio *sm* ❶ [*corporación*] town council ❷ [*territorio*] town

muñequera *sf* wristband

mural ✦ *adj* ❶ [*pintura*] mural ❷ [*mapa*] wall ۞ *Los adjetivos ingleses son invariables.*

✦ *sm* mural

muralla *sf* wall

murciélago *sm* bat

murmullo *sm* ❶ [*generalmente*] murmur • **a lo lejos se oía el murmullo de las olas** you could hear the far-off murmur of the waves ❷ [*de hojas*] rustle ❸ [*de insectos*] buzz

murmurar ✦ *vt* to murmur • **se enojó y salió de casa murmurando algo que no entendí** he got angry and left the house murmuring something I didn't catch ✦ *vi* ❶ [*susurrar - persona*] to murmur; to whisper; [- *agua, viento*] to murmur; to gurgle ❷ [*rezongar, quejarse*] to grumble

muro *sm* wall ❱ **muro de las lamentaciones** Wailing Wall

musaraña *sf* ZOOLOGÍA shrew

expresión **pensar en las musarañas** to have your head in the clouds

muscular *adj* muscular ☼ *Los adjetivos ingleses son invariables.*

musculatura *sf* muscles *pl*

músculo *sm* muscle

musculoso, sa *adj* muscular ☼ *Los adjetivos ingleses son invariables.*

museo *sm* museum • **museo de ciencias naturales** natural history museum

musgo *sm* moss

música *sf* music • **poner música a algo** to set something to music ❱ **música ambiental** background music ❱ **música clásica** classical music ❱ **música de fondo** background music ❱ **música ligera/pop** light/pop music

músico, ca ✦ *adj* musical ☼ *Los adjetivos ingleses son invariables.*
✦ *sm, f* [*persona*] musician • **músico callejero** street musician

muslo *sm* ❶ thigh ❷ [*de pollo*] drumstick

mustio, tia *adj* ❶ [*flor, planta*] withered ❷ [*persona*] gloomy ☼ *Los adjetivos ingleses son invariables.*

musulmán, ana *adj* & *sm, f* Muslim ☼ *Los adjetivos ingleses son invariables.*

mutación *sf* ❶ [*cambio*] sudden change ❷ BIOLOGÍA mutation

mutante *adj* & *smf* mutant ☼ *Los adjetivos ingleses son invariables.*

mutar *vt* to mutate

mutilado, da *adj* mutilated ☼ *Los adjetivos ingleses son invariables.*

mutilar *vt* ❶ [*generalmente*] to mutilate ❷ [*estatua*] to deface

mutuo, tua *adj* mutual ☼ *Los adjetivos ingleses son invariables.*

muy *adv* ❶ [*mucho*] very • **muy bueno/cerca** very good/near • **muy de mañana** very early in the morning • **¡muy bien! a)** [*vale*] OK!; all right! **b)** [*qué bien*] very good!; good job! • **es muy hombre** he's a real man • **eso es muy de ella** that's just like her • **eso es muy de los americanos** that's typically American • **¡el muy idiota!** what an idiot! ❷ [*demasiado*] too • **es muy joven para votar** she's too young to vote

M

N

n *sf* [*letra*] n ; N

n.° (*abreviatura escrita de* número) no

nabo *sm* turnip

nácar *sm* mother-of-pearl

nacer *vi* ❶ [*venir al mundo - niño, animal*] to be born ; [*- planta*] to sprout ; [*- pájaro*] to hatch (out) • **Diana nació en 1992** Diana was born in 1992 • **nacer de familia humilde** to be born into a poor family • **nacer para algo** to be born to be something • **ha nacido cantante** she's a born singer ❷ [*surgir - pelo*] to grow ; [*- río*] to rise ; [*- costumbre, actitud, duda*] to have its roots
expresión **volver a nacer** to have a lucky escape

nacido, da ◆ *adj* born ☿ *Los adjetivos ingleses son invariables.*

◆ *sm, f* • **los nacidos hoy** those born today • **recién nacido** new-born baby
expresión **ser un mal nacido** to be a vile person

naciente *adj* ❶ [*día*] dawning ❷ [*sol*] rising ❸ [*gobierno, estado*] new ❹ [*interés*] growing ☿ *Los adjetivos ingleses son invariables.*

nacimiento *sm* ❶ [*generalmente*] birth • **el nacimiento del bebé llenó de alegría a la familia** the birth of the baby filled the family with joy • **fecha de nacimiento** date of birth ❷ [*de planta*] sprouting ❸ [*de río*] source ❹ [*origen*] origin ❺ [*belén*] Nativity scene

nación *sf* ❶ [*generalmente*] nation ▸ **Naciones Unidas** United Nations ❷ [*territorio*] country

nacional *adj* ❶ national ❷ [*asuntos*] home ☿ *Sólo se usa delante del sustantivo.* ❸ [*mercado, vuelo*] domestic

nacionalidad *sf* nationality • **¿cuál es tu nacionalidad?** what is your nationality? ▸ **doble nacionalidad** dual nationality

nacionalismo *sm* nationalism

nacionalista *adj* & *smf* nationalist ☿ *Los adjetivos ingleses son invariables.*

nacionalizar *vt* ❶ [*banca, bienes*] to nationalize ❷ [*persona*] to naturalize

nada ◆ *pronombre* ❶ nothing • **nada más** nothing else • **¿qué compraste? — nada** what did you buy? — nothing ❷ ☿ *en negativas* anything • **no he leído nada de este autor** I haven't read anything by

this author • **no quiero nada más** I don't want anything else • **¿no compraste nada?** didn't you buy anything? • **vamos a almorzar afuera porque en casa no hay nada de comer** we're going out for lunch because there isn't anything to eat at home
expresiones **de nada a)** [*respuesta a "gracias"*] you're welcome **b)** [*pequeño*] little • **te he traído un regalito de nada** I've brought you a little something ▸ **eso no es nada** that's nothing

◆ *adv* ❶ [*en absoluto*] at all • **la película no me ha gustado nada** I didn't like the movie at all • **no es nada extraño** it's not at all strange ❷ [*poco*] a little • **no hace nada que salió** he left just a minute ago • **nada menos que a)** [*cosa*] no less than **b)** [*persona*] none other than

◆ *sf* • **la nada** nothingness ; the void • **salir de la nada** to appear out of nowhere

nadador, ra *sm, f* swimmer

nadar *vi* ❶ [*generalmente*] to swim ❷ [*flotar*] to float

nadie *pronombre* nobody • **no ha llamado nadie** nobody phoned • **casi nadie** hardly anybody • **no se lo dije a nadie** I didn't tell anybody • **¿ya llegó alguien? — no, nadie** is anybody here yet? — no, no one • **¿todavía no llegó nadie?** has anybody arrived yet?

nailon, nylon° *sm* nylon

naipe *sm* (playing) card

nalga *sf* buttock

nana *sf* [*niñera*] nanny

naranja ◆ *adj invariable* orange ☿ *Los adjetivos ingleses son invariables.*

◆ *sm* [*color*] orange

◆ *sf* [*fruto*] orange

■ **media naranja** *sf* familiar other half

naranjo *sm* [*árbol*] orange tree

narcotraficante *smf* drug trafficker

narcotráfico *sm* drug trafficking

nariz *sf* ❶ [*órgano*] nose • **suénate la nariz** blow your nose • **hablar por la nariz** to talk through your nose • **tener la nariz tapada** to have a blocked nose ❷ [*orificio*] nostril ❸ [*olfato*] sense of smell
expresiones **de narices** familiar [*estupendo*] great ▸ **estar**

hasta las narices (de algo) *familiar* to be fed up to the back teeth (with something) ▶ **meter las narices en algo** *familiar* to stick your nose into something

narración *sf* ❶ [*cuento, relato*] narrative ❷ [*acción*] narration

narrador, ra *sm, f* narrator

narrar *vt* [*contar*] to tell

narrativo, va *adj* narrative ☼ *Los adjetivos ingleses son invariables.*

■ **narrativa** *sf* narrative

nasal *adj* nasal ☼ *Los adjetivos ingleses son invariables.*

nata *sf* [*de leche hervida*] skin

natación *sf* swimming • **me encanta la natación** I love swimming

natal *adj* ❶ [*país*] native ❷ [*ciudad, pueblo*] home ☼ *Sólo se usa delante del sustantivo.* • **mi ciudad natal** my home town

natalidad *sf* birth rate

natillas *sfpl* custard ☼ *incontable*

nativo, va *adj & sm, f* native • **Laura es hablante nativa de español** Laura is a native Spanish speaker ☼ *Los adjetivos ingleses son invariables.*

natural ◆ *adj* ❶ [*generalmente*] natural ❷ [*flores, fruta, leche*] fresh • **soy rubia natural** I'm a natural blonde • **al natural a)** [*persona*] in your natural state **b)** [*fruta*] in its own juice • **ser natural en alguien** to be natural for somebody ❸ [*nativo*] native • **ser natural de** to come from ☼ *Los adjetivos ingleses son invariables.*
◆ *smf* [*nativo*] native
◆ *sm* [*talante*] nature

naturaleza *sf* ❶ [*generalmente*] nature • **pasamos los fines de semana en el campo, en contacto con la naturaleza** we spend weekends in the country, in touch with nature • **por naturaleza** by nature ❷ [*complexión*] constitution

la naturaleza

el acantilado	the cliff
el bosque	the forest
el campo	the countryside
un campo	a field
la colina	the hill
la granja	the farm
la isla	the island
el mar	the sea
la montaña	the mountain
el peñasco	the rock
la planicie	the plain
la playa	the beach
el río	the river
el valle	the valley
el volcán	the volcano

naturalidad *sf* naturalness • **con naturalidad** naturally

naturalizar *vt* to naturalize

naufragar *vi* ❶ [*barco*] to sink ❷ [*persona*] to be shipwrecked

naufragio *sm* shipwreck

náufrago, ga *sm, f* castaway

náusea *sf* ☼ *generalmente pl* nausea ☼ *incontable* • **me da náuseas** it makes me feel nauseous

nauseabundo, da *adj* nauseating ☼ *Los adjetivos ingleses son invariables.*

náutico, ca *adj* nautical ☼ *Los adjetivos ingleses son invariables.*

■ **náutica** *sf* navigation

navaja *sf* ❶ [*cuchillo - pequeño*] penknife; [- *más grande*] jackknife ❷ [*molusco*] razor-shell

naval *adj* naval ☼ *Los adjetivos ingleses son invariables.*

nave *sf* ❶ [*barco*] ship ▶ **nave espacial** spaceship ❷ [*vehículo*] craft ❸ [*de iglesia*] nave

expresión **quemar las naves** to burn your bridges

navegación *sf* navigation

navegador *sm* INFORMÁTICA browser

navegante *smf* navigator

navegar ◆ *vi* ❶ [*barco*] to sail • **salimos a navegar en su nuevo velero** we went sailing on his new sailboat ❷ [*avión*] to fly • **navegar por Internet** INFORMÁTICA to surf the Net
◆ *vt* ❶ [*barco*] to sail ❷ [*avión*] to fly

Navidad *sf* ❶ [*día*] Christmas (Day) ❷ [*periodo*] Christmas (time) • **feliz Navidad** Merry Christmas

navideño, ña *adj* Christmas ☼ *Sólo se usa delante del sustantivo.*

navío *sm* large ship

nazi *adj & smf* Nazi ☼ *Los adjetivos ingleses son invariables.*

nazismo *sm* Nazism

neblina *sf* mist

nebuloso, sa *adj* ❶ [*con nubes*] cloudy ❷ [*de niebla*] foggy ❸ [*idea, mirada*] vague ☼ *Los adjetivos ingleses son invariables.*

■ **nebulosa** *sf* ASTRONOMÍA nebula

necesario, ria *adj* necessary • **haremos lo que sea necesario** we will do whatever is necessary • **es necesario hacerlo** it needs to be done • **no es necesario que lo hagas** you don't need to do it • **si fuera necesario** if need be • **un mal necesario** a necessary evil ☼ *Los adjetivos ingleses son invariables.*

neceser *sm* toilet case

necesidad *sf* ❶ [*generalmente*] need • **tener necesidad de algo** to need something ❷ [*obligación*] necessity • **por necesidad** out of necessity ❸ [*hambre*] hunger

expresión **hacer de la necesidad virtud** to make a virtue of necessity ▶ **la necesidad aguza el ingenio** *proverbio* necessity is the mother of invention *proverbio*

necesitado, da ◆ *adj* needy ☼ *Los adjetivos ingleses son invariables.*

◆ *sm, f* poor person • **los necesitados** the poor

necesitar *vt* to need • **si somos cuatro para la cena, necesitamos un pollo entero** if there's four of us having dinner we'll need a whole chicken • **necesito que me lo digas** I need you to tell me

necio, cia *adj* ❶ foolish ❷ [*fastidioso*] annoying ☼ *Los adjetivos ingleses son invariables.*

néctar *sm* nectar

nectarina *sf* nectarine

nefasto, ta *adj* ❶ [*funesto*] ill-fated ❷ [*dañino*] bad ❸ [*pésimo*] terrible ☼ *Los adjetivos ingleses son invariables.*

negación *sf* ❶ [*desmentido*] denial ❷ [*negativa*] refusal ❸ [*lo contrario*] antithesis ❹ GRAMÁTICA negative

negado, da *adj* useless ☼ *Los adjetivos ingleses son invariables.*

negar *vt* ❶ [*rechazar*] to deny • **le pregunté si había roto el vidrio y lo negó** I asked if he had broken the window and he denied it ❷ [*denegar*] to refuse • **negarle algo a alguien** to refuse somebody something • **la abuela malcría a los nietos, nunca les niega nada** grandma is spoiling her grandchildren, she never refuses them anything

■ **negarse** *v pronominal* • **negarse (a)** to refuse (to) • **Juan se negó a que lo ayudara y dijo que él haría la tarea solo** Juan refused my help and said he would do his homework by himself

negativo, va *adj* [*generalmente*] negative ☼ *Los adjetivos ingleses son invariables.*

■ **negativo** *sm* FOTOGRAFÍA negative

■ **negativa** *sf* ❶ [*rechazo*] refusal • **una negativa rotunda** a flat refusal ❷ [*mentís*] denial

negligencia *sf* negligence

negligente *adj* negligent ☼ *Los adjetivos ingleses son invariables.*

negociable *adj* negotiable ☼ *Los adjetivos ingleses son invariables.*

negociación *sf* negotiation

negociante *sm, f* [*comerciante*] businessman, *femenino* businesswoman

negociar ◆ *vi* ❶ [*comerciar*] to do business • **negociar con** to deal with ❷ [*discutir*] to negotiate

◆ *vt* to negotiate • **los presidentes se reunieron para negociar un acuerdo** the presidents gathered to negotiate an agreement

negocio *sm* ❶ [*generalmente*] business • **trabaja en un negocio familiar** he works in a family business • **mi tío se dedica a los negocios** my uncle is a businessman • **el mundo de los negocios** the business world ❷ [*transacción*] deal ▶ **negocio sucio** shady deal ❸ [*operación ventajosa*] good deal • **hacer negocio** to do well ❹ [*tienda*] store • **vivimos en un barrio residencial donde hay pocos negocios** we live in a residential area with few stores

negrita → **letra**

negro, gra ◆ *adj* ❶ [*generalmente*] black ❷ [*furioso*] furious • **ponerse negro** to get mad ❸ CINE • **cine negro** film noir ☼ *Los adjetivos ingleses son invariables.*

◆ *sm, f* black man, *femenino* black woman

■ **negro** *sm* black • **el negro es mi color favorito** black is my favorite color

nene, na *sm, f* familiar [*niño*] baby

nenúfar *sm* water lily

neón *sm* neon

neoyorquino, na ◆ *adj* New York ☼ *Sólo se usa delante del sustantivo.*

◆ *sm, f* New Yorker

nervio *sm* ❶ ANATOMÍA nerve ▶ **nervio óptico** optic nerve ❷ [*de carne*] sinew ❸ [*vigor*] energy • **sus niños son puro nervio** her kids never sit still for five minutes

■ **nervios** *smpl* [*estado mental*] nerves • **cálmate, no permitas que los nervios te afecten durante la prueba** calm down, don't let nerves get to you during the test • **tener nervios** to be nervous

expresión **poner los nervios de punta a alguien** to get on somebody's nerves ▶ **tener los nervios de punta** to be on edge

nerviosismo *sm* nervousness

nervioso, sa *adj* ❶ ANATOMÍA [*sistema, enfermedad*] nervous; [*tejido, célula, centro*] nerve ☼ *Sólo se usa delante del sustantivo.* ❷ [*inquieto*] nervous • **es un niño muy nervioso que distrae a toda la clase** he's a nervous boy who distracts the whole class • **mamá está nerviosa porque papá tarda en llegar** Mom's nervous because Dad is late • **ponerse nervioso** to get nervous ❸ [*irritado*] worked-up • **ponerse nervioso** to get uptight

neto, ta *adj* ❶ [*claro*] clear ❷ [*verdad*] simple ❸ [*peso, sueldo*] net ☼ *Los adjetivos ingleses son invariables.*

N

neumático, ca *adj* pneumatic ☼ *Los adjetivos ingleses son invariables.*

■ **neumático** *sm* tire ▶ **neumático de repuesto** spare tire

neumonía *sf* pneumonia

neurálgico, ca *adj* ❶ MEDICINA neuralgic ❷ [*importante*] critical ☼ *Los adjetivos ingleses son invariables.*

neurona *sf* neuron

neurosis *sf invariable* neurosis

neurótico, ca *adj & sm, f* neurotic ☼ *Los adjetivos ingleses son invariables.*

neutral *adj & smf* neutral ☼ *Los adjetivos ingleses son invariables.*

neutralidad *sf* neutrality

neutralizar *vt* to neutralize

neutro, tra *adj* ❶ [*generalmente*] neutral ❷ BIOLOGÍA & GRAMÁTICA neuter ☼ *Los adjetivos ingleses son invariables.*

neutrón *sm* neutron

nevado, da *adj* snowy ☼ *Los adjetivos ingleses son invariables.*

■ **nevada** *sf* snowfall

nevar *v impersonal* to snow

nevería *sf* [heladería] ice cream parlor

nexo *sm* link

ni ◆ *conjunción* • **ni... ni...** neither... nor... • **ni mañana ni pasado** neither tomorrow nor the day after • **no... ni...** neither... nor...; not... or... (either) • **no es alto ni bajo** he's neither tall nor short; he's not tall or short (either) • **no es rojo ni verde ni azul** it's neither red nor green nor blue • **ni un/una...** not a single... • **no me quedaré ni un minuto más** I'm not staying a minute longer • **ni uno/una** not a single one • **no he aprobado ni una** I haven't passed a single one • **ni que** as if • **¡ni que yo fuera tonto!** as if I were that stupid!

◆ *adv* not even • **anda tan atareado que ni tiene tiempo para comer** he's so busy he doesn't even have time to eat

Nicaragua *nombre propio* Nicaragua

nicaragüense *adj & smf* Nicaraguan ☼ *Los adjetivos ingleses son invariables.*

En inglés, los adjetivos que se refieren a un país o una región se escriben con mayúscula.

nicho *sm* niche ▶ **nicho ecológico** ecological niche

nicotina *sf* nicotine

nido *sm* nest

niebla *sf* ❶ [densa] fog • **hay niebla** it's foggy ❷ [neblina] mist

nieto, ta *sm, f* grandson, *femenino* granddaughter

nieve *sf* ❶ METEOROLOGÍA snow ❷ COCINA • **a punto de nieve** beaten stiff ❸ [helado de leche] ice cream ❹ [helado de agua] sorbet

Nilo *sm* • **el Nilo** the (river) Nile

ninfa *sf* nymph

ninfómana *sf* nymphomaniac

ninguno, na ◆ *adj* no • **no dieron ninguna respuesta** no answer was given • **no tengo ningún interés en hacerlo** I've no interest in doing it; I'm not at all interested in doing it • **no tengo ningún hijo/ninguna buena idea** I don't have any children/good ideas • **no encontramos ninguna película interesante** we couldn't find any interesting movies • **no tiene ninguna gracia** it's not funny • **ningún lado** anywhere • **no vi a tu hermana por ningún lado** I didn't see your sister anywhere • **ningún momento** never • **en ningún momento me dijo que se sentía mal** she never said she felt bad ☼ *Los adjetivos ingleses son invariables.*

◆ *pronombre* ❶ [cosa] none ❷ [persona] nobody • **ninguno lo sabrá** nobody will know • **ninguno funciona** none of them works • **no hay ninguno** there aren't any; there are none • **ninguno de** none of • **ninguno de ellos** none of them • **ninguno de los niños sabía japonés** none of the children knew Japanese • **ninguno de los dos** neither of them

niña *sf* ❶ [del ojo] pupil ❷ → **niño**

niñería *sf* ❶ [cualidad] childishness ☼ *incontable* ❷ [tontería] childish thing

niñero, ra *adj* fond of children ☼ *Los adjetivos ingleses son invariables.*

■ **niñera** *sf* ❶ [empleada] nanny, *plural* nannies ❷ [ocasional] babysitter

niñez *sf* childhood

niño, ña ◆ *adj* young ☼ *Los adjetivos ingleses son invariables.*

◆ *sm, f* [crío] boy, *femenino* girl • **un niño de cinco años** a five year old boy • **los niños** the children • **esa película no la pueden ver los niños** this movie isn't for children ▶ **niño prodigio** child prodigy ❷ [bebé] baby

expresión **ser el niño bonito de alguien** to be somebody's blue-eyed boy

níquel *sm* nickel

níspero *sm* medlar

nitidez *sf* ❶ clarity ❷ [de imágenes, colores] sharpness

nítido, da *adj* ❶ clear ❷ [imágenes, colores] sharp ☼ *Los adjetivos ingleses son invariables.*

nitrato *sm* nitrate

nitrógeno *sm* nitrogen

nivel *sm* ❶ [generalmente] level ❷ [altura] height • **al nivel de** level with • **al nivel del mar** at sea level ❸ [grado] level • **al mismo nivel (que)** on a level (with) • **a nivel europeo** at a European level ▶ **nivel de vida** standard of living ▶ **niveles de audiencia** ratings

nivelador, ra *adj* leveling ☼ *Los adjetivos ingleses son invariables.*

nivelar *vt* ❶ [allanar] to level ❷ [equilibrar] to even out ❸ FINANZAS to balance

no ◆ *adv* ❶ [expresa negación - generalmente] not; [- en respuestas] no; [- con sustantivos] non- • **no sé** I don't know • **no veo nada** I can't see anything • **no es fácil** it's not easy; it isn't easy • **no tiene dinero** he has no money; he hasn't got any money • **todavía no** not yet • **¿no vienes? — no, no creo** aren't you coming? — no, I don't think so • **no fumadores** non-smokers • **no bien** as soon as • **no ya... sino que...** not only... but (also)... • **¡a que no lo haces!** I bet you don't do it! • **¿cómo no?** of course • **eso sí que no** certainly not • **pues no** certainly not • **¡que no!** I said no! ❷ [expresa duda, extrañeza] • **¿no irás a venir?** you're not coming, are you? • **estamos de acuerdo, ¿no?** we're agreed then, are we? • **es español, ¿no?** he's Spanish, isn't he?

◆ *sm* no

noble *adj & smf* noble • **los nobles** the nobility ☼ *Los adjetivos ingleses son invariables.*

nobleza *sf* nobility

noche *sf* ❶ night • **llovió toda la noche** it rained all night • **ayer por la noche** last night • **esta noche** tonight • **al caer la noche** at nightfall • **hacer noche en** to stay the night in • **hacerse de noche** to get dark • **por la noche, de noche** at night • **buenas noches a)** [despedida] good night **b)** [saludo] good evening • **es noche cerrada** it's completely dark ▶ **noche de bodas** wedding night ▶ **noche del estreno** first o opening night ▶ **noche toledana** sleepless night ❷ [*atardecer*] evening

expresión **de la noche a la mañana** overnight

Nochebuena *sf* Christmas Eve

Nochevieja *sf* New Year's Eve

noción *sf* [*concepto*] notion • **tener noción (de)** to have an idea (of)

nocivo, va *adj* ❶ [*generalmente*] harmful • **fumar es nocivo para la salud** smoking is harmful to your health ❷ [*gas*] noxious ⋮Ö⋮ *Los adjetivos ingleses son invariables.*

nocturno, na *adj* ❶ [*club, tren, vuelo*] night ⋮Ö⋮ *Sólo se usa delante del sustantivo.* • **tomaremos el tren nocturno** we'll take the night train ❷ [*clase*] evening ⋮Ö⋮ *Sólo se usa delante del sustantivo.* • **tengo una clase nocturna** I have an evening class ❸ [*animales, plantas*] nocturnal • **el búho es un ave nocturna** owls are nocturnal birds

nodriza *sf* wet nurse

nómada ◆ *adj* nomadic ⋮Ö⋮ *Los adjetivos ingleses son invariables.*

◆ *smf* nomad

nombramiento *sm* appointment

nombrar *vt* ❶ [*citar*] to mention • **no me nombró a su padre en toda la conversación** he didn't mention his father in the whole conversation ❷ [*designar*] to appoint • **a mi hermano lo nombraron gerente de ese banco** my brother was appointed manager of that bank

nombre *sm* ❶ [*generalmente*] name • **conocer a alguien de nombre** to know somebody by name • **poner nombre a** to name • **sin nombre** nameless ▶ **nombre artístico/comercial** stage/trade name ▶ **nombre y apellidos** full name ▶ **nombre compuesto** compound name ▶ **nombre de dominio** [*INFORMÁTICA*] domain name ▶ **nombre de pila** first o Christian name ▶ **nombre de soltera** maiden name ❷ [*fama*] reputation • **hacerse un nombre** to make a name for yourself • **tener mucho nombre** to be renowned ❸ *GRAMÁTICA* noun ▶ **nombre abstracto/colectivo** abstract/collective noun

expresión **en nombre de** on behalf of ▶ **lo que hizo no tiene nombre** what he did is outrageous

nomenclatura *sf* nomenclature

nómina *sf* ❶ [*lista de empleados*] payroll ❷ [*hoja de salario*] payslip

nominal *adj* nominal ⋮Ö⋮ *Los adjetivos ingleses son invariables.*

nominar *vt* to nominate

non *sm* odd number

nonagésimo, ma *numeral* ninetieth

nordeste = noreste

nórdico, ca *adj* ❶ [*del norte*] northern ❷ [*escandinavo*] Nordic ⋮Ö⋮ *Los adjetivos ingleses son invariables.*

noreste, nordeste ◆ *adj* ❶ [*posición, parte*] northeast ❷ [*dirección, viento*] northeasterly ⋮Ö⋮ *Los adjetivos ingleses son invariables.*

◆ *sm* north-east

noria *sf* ❶ [*para agua*] water wheel ❷ [*de feria*] Ferris wheel

norma *sf* ❶ [*patrón*] standard ❷ [*regla*] rule • **para poder cumplir las normas, hay que saberlas** you have to know the rules to follow them • **tener por norma hacer algo** to make it a rule to do something • **es la norma hacerlo así** it's usual to do it this way ▶ **normas de seguridad** safety regulations

normal *adj* normal • **es normal que extrañes si es la primera vez que estás lejos de tu familia** it's normal to be homesick if it's the first time you've been away from home • **normal y corriente** run-of-the-mill • **es una persona normal y corriente** he's a perfectly ordinary person ⋮Ö⋮ *Los adjetivos ingleses son invariables.*

normalidad *sf* normality

normalizar *vt* ❶ [*volver normal*] to return to normal ❷ [*estandarizar*] to standardize

normativo, va *adj* normative ⋮Ö⋮ *Los adjetivos ingleses son invariables.*

■ **normativa** *sf* regulations *pl*

noroeste ◆ *adj* ❶ [*posición, parte*] northwest ❷ [*dirección, viento*] northwesterly ⋮Ö⋮ *Los adjetivos ingleses son invariables.*

◆ *sm* northwest

norte ◆ *adj* ❶ [*posición, parte*] north ❷ [*dirección, viento*] northerly ⋮Ö⋮ *Los adjetivos ingleses son invariables.*

◆ *sm* *GEOGRAFÍA* north • **el norte de la ciudad** the north part of the city • **al norte** to the north

norteamericano, na *adj* & *sm, f* North American ⋮Ö⋮ *Los adjetivos ingleses son invariables.*

En inglés, los adjetivos que se refieren a un país o una región se escriben con mayúscula.

Noruega *nombre propio* Norway

nos *pronombre personal* ❶ ⋮Ö⋮ *complemento directo* us • **todavía no nos entregaron las calificaciones** they haven't given us our grades yet • **le gustaría vernos** she'd like to see us ❷ ⋮Ö⋮ *complemento indirecto* (to) us • **nos lo dio** he gave it to us • **nos tiene miedo** he's afraid of us ❸ ⋮Ö⋮ *reflexivo* ourselves ❹ ⋮Ö⋮ *recíproco* each other • **no nos conocíamos, pero mi hermano nos presentó en la fiesta** we didn't know each other but my brother introduced us at the party • **nos enamoramos** we fell in love (with each other)

nosocomio *sm* hospital

nosotros, tras *pronombre personal* ❶ ⋮Ö⋮ *sujeto* we • **ellos quieren helado pero nosotros preferimos fruta** they want ice cream but we prefer fruit ❷ ⋮Ö⋮ *predicado* • **somos nosotros** it's us ❸ ⋮Ö⋮ *después de preposición, complemento* us • **vente a comer con nosotros** come and eat with us

expresión **entre nosotros** between you and me

nostalgia *sf* ❶ [*del pasado*] nostalgia ❷ [*de país, amigos*] homesickness

nota *sf* ❶ [*generalmente*] *MÚSICA* note • **vamos a dejarle una nota avisando que fuimos al cine** we'll leave her a note to let her know we went to the movies

N

• **"do" es la primera nota de la escala musical** "do" is the first note on the musical scale • **tomar nota de algo a)** [*apuntar*] to note something down **b)** [*fijarse*] to take note of something • **tomar notas** to take notes ◗ **nota al margen** marginal note ◗ **nota dominante** prevailing mood ❷ [*cuenta*] bill

expresión **dar la nota** to make yourself conspicuous

notable ◆ *adj* remarkable ҉ *Los adjetivos ingleses son invariables.*

◆ *sm* EDUCACIÓN merit

notar *vt* ❶ [*advertir*] to notice • **¿notaste que trae un calcetín café y otro verde?** did you notice she's wearing one brown sock and one green? • **te noto cansado** you look tired to me • **hacer notar algo** to point something out ❷ [*sentir*] to feel • **noto un dolor raro** I can feel a strange pain

■ **notarse** *v pronominal* • **se nota que...** you can tell (that...) • **se nota que le gusta** you can tell she likes it • **se nota ¿o no?** can you tell or not? • **se nota algo preocupado** he seems a bit worried

notario, ria *sm, f* notary (public)

noticia *sf* news ҉ *incontable* • **una noticia** a piece of news • **tengo una noticia para darte: el año que viene no vendré más a esta escuela** I have some news for you: I won't be going to this school next year • **¿tienes noticias suyas?** have you heard from him?

notoriedad *sf* [*fama*] fame

notorio, ria *adj* ❶ [*evidente*] obvious ❷ [*conocido*] widely-known ҉ *Los adjetivos ingleses son invariables.*

novato, ta ◆ *adj* inexperienced ҉ *Los adjetivos ingleses son invariables.*

◆ *sm, f* beginner

novecientos, tas *numeral* nine hundred ver también **seis**

novedad *sf* ❶ [*cualidad - de nuevo*] newness; [*- de novedoso*] novelty • **como nunca había visto una jirafa, para ella era una novedad** since she'd never seen a giraffe before it was quite a novelty for her • **ahora la novedad es combinar verde con anaranjado** the latest thing is to combine green and orange ❷ [*cambio*] change ❸ [*noticia*] news ҉ *incontable* • **al volver de viaje, quiso enterarse de las novedades del país** when she returned from her trip she wanted to catch up on the country's news • **sin novedad a)** without incident **b)** MILITAR all quiet

novedoso, sa *adj* novel ҉ *Los adjetivos ingleses son invariables.*

novela *sf* novel ◗ **novela policíaca** detective story

novelista *smf* novelist

noveno, na *numeral* ninth

noventa *numeral* ninety • **los (años) noventa** the nineties ver también **seis**

noviar *vi* • **noviar con alguien** to date somebody • **están noviando** they are dating

noviazgo *sm* engagement

noviembre *sm* November ver también **septiembre**

novio, via *sm, f* ❶ [*compañero*] boyfriend, *femenino* girlfriend ❷ [*prometido*] fiancé, *femenino* fiancée ❸ [*recién casado*] bridegroom, *femenino* bride • **los novios** the newly-weds

nubarrón *sm* storm cloud

nube *sf* ❶ [*generalmente*] cloud ◗ **nube atómica** mushroom cloud ◗ **nube de tormenta** thundercloud ❷ [*de personas, moscas*] swarm

expresión **poner algo/a alguien por las nubes** to praise something/somebody to the skies ◗ **por las nubes** [*caro*] sky-high; terribly expensive

nublado, da *adj* ❶ [*encapotado*] cloudy ❷ *figurado* [*turbado*] clouded ҉ *Los adjetivos ingleses son invariables.*

nublar *vt literal & figurado* to cloud

nubosidad *sf* clouds *pl*

nuca *sf* back of the neck

nuclear *adj* nuclear ҉ *Los adjetivos ingleses son invariables.*

núcleo *sm* ❶ [*centro*] nucleus • **el núcleo de la célula contiene información genética** the cell's nucleus contains genetic information ❷ *figurado* center ◗ **núcleo de población** population center ❸ [*grupo*] core

nudillo *sm* knuckle

nudismo *sm* nudism

nudo *sm* ❶ [*generalmente*] knot ❷ [*cruce*] junction ❸ [*vínculo*] tie ❹ [*punto principal*] crux

expresión **se le hizo un nudo en la garganta** she got a lump in her throat

nuera *sf* daughter-in-law

nuestro, tra ◆ *adj posesivo* our • **nuestro coche** our car • **este libro es nuestro** this book is ours; this is our book • **un amigo nuestro** a friend of ours • **no es asunto nuestro** it's none of our business

◆ *pronombre posesivo* • **el nuestro** ours • **el nuestro es rojo** ours is red

expresiones **ésta es la nuestra** *familiar* this is the chance we have been waiting for ◗ **lo nuestro es el teatro** [*lo que nos va*] theater is what we should be doing ◗ **los nuestros a)** *familiar* [*nuestra familia*] our folks **b)** [*nuestro bando*] our lot; our side

Nueva York *nombre propio* New York

Nueva Zelanda *nombre propio* New Zealand

nueve *numeral* nine ver también **seis**

nuevo, va ◆ *adj* ❶ [*generalmente*] new • **llegó en su coche nuevo** she arrived in her new car • **esto es nuevo para mí, no lo sabía** that's news to me; I didn't know it • **ser nuevo en** to be new to ❷ [*vino*] young ҉ *Los adjetivos ingleses son invariables.*

expresión **estar/quedar como nuevo** to be as good as new

◆ *sm, f* newcomer

nuez *sf* ❶ BOTÁNICA [*generalmente*] nut ◗ **nuez moscada** nutmeg ❷ [*de nogal*] pecan ❸ ANATOMÍA Adam's apple

nulidad *sf* ❶ [*no validez*] nullity ❷ [*ineptitud*] incompetence

nulo, la *adj* ❶ [*sin validez*] null and void ❷ *familiar* [*incapacitado*] • **nulo (para)** useless (at) ⌇ *Los adjetivos ingleses son invariables.*

núm. (*abreviatura escrita de* número) No

numeración *sf* ❶ [*acción*] numbering ❷ [*sistema*] numerals *pl*

numeral *adj* numeral ⌇ *Los adjetivos ingleses son invariables.*

numerar *vt* to number

numérico, ca *adj* numerical ⌇ *Los adjetivos ingleses son invariables.*

número *sm* ❶ [*generalmente*] number • **¿cuál es tu número favorito?** what's your favorite number? • **los sustantivos en español tienen género y número** in Spanish, nouns have number and gender ▶ **número de fax** fax number ▶ **número de identificación personal** PIN ▶ **número de licencia** Automóviles license plate number ▶ **número redondo** round number ▶ **número de serie** serial number ▶ **número de teléfono** telephone number ❷ [*tamaño, talla*] size • **¿qué número calzas?** what size shoe do you wear? ❸ [*de publicación*] issue ▶ **número atrasado** back issue ❹ [*de lotería*] ticket

expresiones **en números rojos** in the red ▶ **hacer números** to reckon up ▶ **montar el número** *familiar* to make o cause a scene

numeroso, sa *adj* numerous • **un grupo numeroso** a large group ⌇ *Los adjetivos ingleses son invariables.*

nunca *adv* ❶ ⌇ *en frases afirmativas* never • **nunca me llama** he never calls me ❷ ⌇ *en frases negativas* ever • **casi nunca viene** he almost never comes ; he hardly ever comes • **¿nunca le has visto?** have you never seen her? ; haven't you ever seen her? • **más que nunca** more than ever • **nunca jamás** never again

nupcial *adj* wedding ⌇ *Sólo se usa delante del sustantivo.*

nutria *sf* otter

nutrición *sf* nutrition

nutricionista *smf* dietician

nutrido, da *adj* ❶ [*alimentado*] nourished • **mal nutrido** undernourished ❷ [*numeroso*] large ⌇ *Los adjetivos ingleses son invariables.*

nutrir *vt* ❶ [*alimentar*] • **nutrir (con o de)** to nourish (with) ❷ [*fomentar*] to feed ❸ [*suministrar*] • **nutrir (de)** to supply (with)

nutritivo, va *adj* nutritious ⌇ *Los adjetivos ingleses son invariables.*

nylon® = nailon

ñ *sf* [*letra*] ñ ; Ñ

ñoñería, ñoñez *sf* inanity

ñoño, ña *adj* ❶ [*remilgado*] squeamish ❷ [*quejica*] whining ❸ [*soso*] dull ⌇ *Los adjetivos ingleses son invariables.*

Ñ

o¹, O *sf* [*letra*] o ; O

o² *conjunción* or • **¿cuáles prefieres: los rojos o los blancos?** which ones do you prefer: the red ones or the white ones? • **o... o** either... or • **el doctor puede atenderte o mañana o la semana que viene** the doctor can see you either tomorrow or next week • **o sea (que)** in other words

o/ *abreviatura escrita de* **orden**

O *sm* (*abreviatura escrita de* oeste) W

oasis *sm invariable* literal & figurado oasis

obedecer ♦ *vt* • **obedecer (a alguien)** to obey (somebody) • **generalmente obedezco a mi madre** generally I obey my mother
♦ *vi* ❶ [*acatar*] to obey • **hacerse obedecer** to command obedience ❷ [*someterse*] • **obedecer a** to respond to ❸ [*estar motivado*] • **obedecer a** to be due to • **un comportamiento que obedece a un instinto natural de defensa** behavior which is due to a natural instinct to defend yourself

obediencia *sf* obedience

obediente *adj* obedient ☼: *Los adjetivos ingleses son invariables.*

obertura *sf* overture

obesidad *sf* obesity

obeso, sa *adj* obese ☼: *Los adjetivos ingleses son invariables.*

obispo *sm* bishop

objeción *sf* objection • **poner objeciones a** to raise objections to • **tener objeciones** to have objections

objetar *vt* to object to • **no tengo nada que objetar** I have no objection

objetivo, va *adj* objective ☼: *Los adjetivos ingleses son invariables.*

■ **objetivo** *sm* ❶ [*finalidad*] objective ❷ MILITAR target ❸ FOTOGRAFÍA lens

objeto *sm* ❶ [*generalmente*] object • **ser objeto de** to be the object of ▶ **objeto volador no identificado** unidentified flying object ▶ **objetos de valor** valuables ▶ **objetos perdidos** lost property ☼: *incontable* ❷ [*propósito*] purpose • **sin objeto** [*inútilmente*] to no purpose • **al o con objeto de** [*para*] in order to

obligación *sf* ❶ [*generalmente*] obligation • **los padres tienen la obligación de cuidar a sus hijos** parents have the obligation of caring for their children • **por obligación** out of a sense of duty ❷ ☼: *generalmente pl* FINANZAS bond

obligar *vt* • **obligar a alguien (a hacer algo)** to oblige o force somebody (to do something)

obligatorio, ria *adj* obligatory ☼: *Los adjetivos ingleses son invariables.*

obra *sf* ❶ [*generalmente*] ARTE work • **en este museo hay varias obras de Frida Kahlo** there are several works by Frida Kahlo in this museum • **es obra suya** it's his doing • **poner en obra** to put into effect • **por obra (y gracia) de** thanks to ▶ **obra de caridad** [*institución*] charity ▶ **obras completas** complete works ▶ **obras sociales** community work ☼: *incontable* ❷ TEATRO play • **en ese teatro están dando una obra sensacional** they're putting on a sensational play at that theater ❸ LITERATURA book ❹ MÚSICA opus ▶ **obra maestra** masterpiece ❺ CONSTRUCCIÓN [*lugar*] construction site • **con el ruido de la obra de al lado, no puedo concentrarme** I can't concentrate with the noise from the construction site next door ❻ [*reforma*] alteration • **'obras'** [*en carretera*] roadworks ▶ **obras públicas** public works

expresión **obras son amores y no buenas razones** *proverbio* actions speak louder than words

obrar ♦ *vi* ❶ [*actuar*] to act ❷ [*causar efecto*] to work ❸ [*estar en poder*] • **obrar en manos de** to be in the possession of
♦ *vt* to work

obrero, ra ♦ *adj* ❶ [*clase*] working ❷ [*movimiento*] labor ☼: *Sólo se usa delante del sustantivo.*
♦ *sm, f* worker ▶ **obrero cualificado** skilled worker ▶ **obrero de la construcción** a construction worker

obscenidad *sf* obscenity

obsceno, na *adj* obscene ☼: *Los adjetivos ingleses son invariables.*

obsequiar *vt* • **obsequiar a alguien con algo** to present somebody with something

obsequio *sm* gift

observación *sf* ❶ [*generalmente*] observation • **bajo observación** under observation ❷ [*comentario*] remark

• **hacer una observación** to make a remark ❸ [*nota*] note ❹ [*cumplimiento*] observance

observador, ra ♦ *adj* observant ☼ *Los adjetivos ingleses son invariables.*

♦ *sm, f* observer

observar *vt* ❶ [*contemplar, comentar*] to observe • **se dedicó a observar y estudiar a los monos en la selva** he devoted himself to observing and studying monkeys in the jungle • **este dibujo está excelente, observó la maestra** this drawing is excellent, remarked the teacher ❷ [*advertir*] to notice ❸ [*acatar - ley, normas*] to observe; [*- conducta, costumbre*] to follow

observatorio *sm* observatory

obsesión *sf* obsession

obsesionar *vt* to obsess

obsesivo, va *adj* obsessive ☼ *Los adjetivos ingleses son invariables.*

obseso, sa ♦ *adj* obsessed ☼ *Los adjetivos ingleses son invariables.*

♦ *sm, f* obsessed person

obstaculizar *vt* to hinder

obstáculo *sm* obstacle • **pese a los obstáculos, Javier logró terminar su carrera** in spite of the obstacles, Javier managed to finish his studies • **un obstáculo para** an obstacle to • **poner obstáculos a algo/alguien** to hinder something/somebody

obstante ■ **no obstante** *locución adverbial* nevertheless

obstinado, da *adj* ❶ [*persistente*] persistent ❷ [*terco*] obstinate ☼ *Los adjetivos ingleses son invariables.*

obstrucción *sf* obstruction

obstruir *vt* ❶ [*bloquear*] to block ❷ [*obstaculizar*] to obstruct

obtener *vt* ❶ [*beca, cargo, puntos*] to get ❷ [*premio, victoria*] to win ❸ [*ganancias*] to make ❹ [*satisfacción*] to gain

obús (pl **obuses**) *sm* [*proyectil*] shell

obvio, via *adj* obvious ☼ *Los adjetivos ingleses son invariables.*

oca *sf* [*ave*] goose

ocasión *sf* ❶ [*oportunidad*] opportunity, *plural* opportunities • **todavía no tuve ocasión de conocerla** I still haven't had the opportunity to meet her ❷ [*momento*] moment ❸ [*vez*] occasion • **me prestó el carro en varias ocasiones** he loaned me his car on several occasions • **en dos ocasiones** on two occasions • **en alguna ocasión** sometimes • **en cierta ocasión** once • **en otra ocasión** some other time ❹ [*motivo*] • **con ocasión de** on the occasion of • **dar ocasión para algo/ hacer algo** to give cause for something/to do something ❺ [*ganga*] bargain • **de ocasión** [*precio, artículos* ETC] bargain ☼ *Sólo se usa delante del sustantivo.*

ocasional *adj* ❶ [*accidental*] accidental ❷ [*irregular*] occasional ☼ *Los adjetivos ingleses son invariables.*

ocasionar *vt* to cause

ocaso *sm* ❶ [*puesta del sol*] sunset ❷ [*decadencia*] decline

occidental *adj* western ☼ *Los adjetivos ingleses son invariables.*

occidente *sm* west

■ **Occidente** *sm* [*bloque de países*] the West

Oceanía *nombre propio* Oceania

océano *sm* ❶ ocean ▶ **el océano Atlántico** the Atlantic Ocean ▶ **el océano Pacífico** the Pacific Ocean ❷ [*inmensidad*] sea

ochenta *numeral* eighty • **los (años) ochenta** the eighties ver también **seis**

ocho *numeral* eight • **de aquí en ocho días** [*en una semana*] a week today ver también **seis**

ochocientos, tas *numeral* eight hundred ver también **seis**

ocio *sm* ❶ [*tiempo libre*] leisure ❷ [*inactividad*] idleness

ocioso, sa *adj* ❶ [*inactivo*] idle ❷ [*innecesario*] unnecessary ❸ [*inútil*] pointless ☼ *Los adjetivos ingleses son invariables.*

ocre ♦ *sm* ochre

♦ *adj invariable* ochre ☼ *Los adjetivos ingleses son invariables.*

octágono *sm* octagon

octano *sm* octane

octavilla *sf* ❶ [*de propaganda política*] pamphlet ❷ [*tamaño*] octavo

octogenario, ria *adj* & *sm, f* octogenarian ☼ *Los adjetivos ingleses son invariables.*

octubre *sm* October ver también **septiembre**

ocular *adj* eye ☼ *Sólo se usa delante del sustantivo.*

oculista *smf* ophthalmologist

ocultar *vt* ❶ [*generalmente*] to hide • **no me ocultes la verdad** don't hide the truth from me ❷ [*delito*] to cover up

oculto, ta *adj* hidden ☼ *Los adjetivos ingleses son invariables.*

ocupación *sf* ❶ [*generalmente*] occupation ▶ **ocupación ilegal de viviendas** squatting ❷ [*empleo*] job

ocupado, da *adj* ❶ [*persona*] busy ❷ [*teléfono, lavabo* ETC] engaged ❸ [*lugar - gen, por ejército*] occupied ❹ [*plaza*] taken ☼ *Los adjetivos ingleses son invariables.*

ocupante *smf* occupant ▶ **ocupante ilegal de viviendas** squatter

ocupar *vt* ❶ [*generalmente*] to occupy • **¿quién está ocupando ese asiento?** who's occupying that seat? • **durante la guerra, el ejército enemigo ocupó la capital** during the war, the enemy army took control of the capital ❷ [*superficie, espacio*] to take up • **este ropero es muy grande, ocupa todo el cuarto** the wardrobe is too big, it takes up the whole room ❸ [*habitación, departamento*] to live in • **nosotros ocupamos el cuarto del fondo, el del frente está libre** we live in the room at the back, the one at the front is available ❹ [*mesa*] to sit at ❺ [*sillón*] to sit in ❻ [*actividad*] to take up ❼ [*cargo*] to hold ❽ [*dar trabajo a*] to employ • **esta**

fábrica ocupa a cientos de obreros this factory employs hundreds of workers ❾ [*usar*] to use

■ **ocuparse** *v pronominal* [*encargarse*] • **ocuparse de a)** [*generalmente*] to deal with **b)** [*niños, enfermos, finanzas*] to look after • **ocúpate de tus cosas** you deal with your own things • **los abuelos se van a ocupar de los niños este fin de semana** their grandparents are going to look after the children this weekend • **¡ocúpate de lo tuyo!** mind your own business!

ocurrencia *sf* ❶ [*idea*] bright idea ❷ [*dicho gracioso*] witty remark

ocurrir *vi* ❶ [*acontecer*] to happen • **la historia cuenta lo que ocurrió en el pasado** history tells what happened in the past ❷ [*pasar, preocupar*] • **¿qué le ocurre a Juan?** what's up with Juan?

■ **ocurrirse** *v pronominal* [*venir a la cabeza*] • **no se me ocurre ninguna solución** I can't think of a solution • **¿se te ocurre algo para regalarle a mamá el día de su cumpleaños?** can you think of something to give Mom for her birthday? • **¡ni se te ocurra!** don't even think about it! • **se me ocurre que...** it occurs to me that...

ODECA *sf* (*abreviatura de* Organización de Estados Centroamericanos) OCAS

odiar *vt & vi* to hate

odio *sm* hatred

odioso, sa *adj* hateful ☞ *Los adjetivos ingleses son invariables.*

odontólogo, ga *sm, f* dentist

OEA (*abreviatura de* Organización de Estados Americanos) *sf* OAS

oeste ◆ *adj* ❶ [*posición, parte*] west ❷ [*dirección, viento*] westerly ☞ *Los adjetivos ingleses son invariables.*

◆ *sm* west • **el sol se oculta por el oeste** the sun sets in the west • **el oeste de la ciudad** the west of the city • **al oeste** to the west

ofender *vt* ❶ [*injuriar*] to insult ❷ [*palabras*] to offend

■ **ofenderse** *v pronominal* • **ofenderse (por)** to take offence (at)

ofensa *sf* ❶ [*acción*] • **ofensa (a)** offence (against) ❷ [*injuria*] insult

ofensivo, va *adj* offensive ☞ *Los adjetivos ingleses son invariables.*

■ **ofensiva** *sf* offensive

oferta *sf* ❶ [*generalmente*] offer • **recibí dos ofertas de trabajo** I received two job offers • **'ofertas de trabajo'** situations vacant ❷ ECONOMÍA [*suministro*] supply • **la oferta y la demanda** supply and demand ▸ **oferta monetaria** money supply ❸ [*rebaja*] bargain • **de oferta** bargain ☞ *Sólo se usa delante del sustantivo*, on offer • **en oferta** on sale ❹ FINANZAS [*proposición*] bid ▸ **oferta pública de adquisición** COMERCIO takeover bid

oficial *adj* official

oficialismo *sm* • **el oficialismo a)** [*gobierno*] the Government **b)** [*partidarios del gobierno*] government supporters

oficialista *adj* pro-government ☞ *Los adjetivos ingleses son invariables.*

oficiar *vt* to officiate at

oficina *sf* office ▸ **oficina de turismo** tourist office

oficinista *smf* office worker

oficio *sm* ❶ [*profesión manual*] trade • **¿qué oficio te gustaría aprender?** what trade would you like to learn? • **de oficio** by trade ❷ [*trabajo*] job ❸ RELIGIÓN service

expresión **tener mucho oficio** to be very experienced

los oficios

el abogado/la abogada	the lawyer
el actor/la actriz	the actor/the actress
el arquitecto/la arquitecta	the architect
el banquero/la banquera	the banker
el bombero/la bombera	the firefighter
el cartero/la cartera	the letter carrier
el fotógrafo/la fotógrafa	the photographer
el ingeniero/la ingeniera	the engineer
el juez/la jueza	the judge
el mecánico/la mecánica	the mechanic
el médico/la médica	the doctor
el peluquero/la peluquera	the hairdresser
el/la periodista	the journalist
el/la piloto	the pilot
el pintor/la pintora	the painter
el/la policía	the police officer
el profesor/la profesora	the teacher
el vendedor/la vendedora	the salesperson

Por lo general, en inglés se usa el mismo nombre para los oficios tanto para el masculino como el femenino. Los que sí cambian son los que acaban en **-man** o **-woman**

oficioso, sa *adj* unofficial ☞ *Los adjetivos ingleses son invariables.*

ofimática *sf* office automation

ofrecer *vt* ❶ [*generalmente*] to offer • **ofrecerle algo a alguien** to offer somebody something • **la vendedora me ofreció varios vestidos y compré el verde** the saleswoman offered me several dresses and I bought the green one ❷ [*aspecto*] to present

■ **ofrecerse** *v pronominal* [*presentarse*] to offer • **ofrecerse a o para hacer algo** to offer to do something • **el vecino se ofreció para ayudarnos con la mudanza** the neighbor offered to help us with the move

ofrecimiento *sm* offer

ofrenda *sf* ❶ RELIGIÓN offering ❷ [*por gratitud, amor*] gift

oftalmología *sf* ophthalmology

ogro *sm* ogre

oh *exclamación* • **¡oh!** oh!

oído *sm* ❶ [*órgano*] ear • **tengo una infección en el oído derecho** I have an infection in my right ear ❷ [*sentido*] (sense of) hearing • **el oído es uno de los cinco sentidos** hearing is one of the five senses

expresiones de oído by ear ▶ hacer oídos sordos to turn a deaf ear ▶ ser duro de oído to be hard of hearing

oír ◆ *vt* ❶ [*generalmente*] to hear • habla más fuerte, no te oigo speak louder, I can't hear you ❷ [*atender*] to listen to • anoche oí la radio durante dos horas last night I listened to the radio for two hours
◆ *vi* to hear • ¡oiga, por favor! excuse me! • ¡oye! *familiar* hey!

ojal *sm* buttonhole

ojalá *exclamación* • ¡ojalá! if only (that were so)! • ¡ojalá lo haga! I hope she does it! • ¡ojalá fuera ya domingo! I wish it were Sunday! • ¡ojalá que pare llover! I hope it stops raining!

ojeada *sf* look • echar una ojeada a algo/alguien to take a quick look at something/somebody

ojear *vt* to have a look at

ojera *sf* ☀: *generalmente pl* bags *pl* under the eyes

ojo ◆ *sm* ❶ ANATOMÍA eye • ojos saltones popping eyes ❷ [*agujero - de aguja*] eye; [*- de puente*] span ▶ ojo de la cerradura keyhole
expresiones a ojo (de buen cubero) roughly; approximately ▶ andar con (mucho) ojo to be (very) careful ▶ comerse con los ojos a alguien *familiar* to drool over somebody ▶ echar el ojo a algo to have your eye on something ▶ en un abrir y cerrar de ojos in the twinkling of an eye ▶ estar ojo alerta o avizor to be on the lookout ▶ mirar algo con buenos/malos ojos to look favourably/unfavourably on something ▶ no pegar ojo not to get a wink of sleep ▶ tener (buen) ojo to have a good eye ▶ ojos que no ven, corazón que no siente *proverbio* what the eye doesn't see, the heart doesn't grieve over
◆ *exclamación* • ¡ojo! be careful!

ola *sf* wave • ola de calor heatwave • ola de frío cold spell

ole, olé *exclamación* • ¡ole! bravo!

oleada *sf* ❶ [*del mar*] swell ❷ *figurado* [*avalancha*] wave

oleaje *sm* swell

óleo *sm* oil (painting)

oleoducto *sm* oil pipeline

oler ◆ *vt* to smell • acércate y huele las rosas come near and smell the roses
◆ *vi* ❶ [*despedir olor*] to smell • oler a to smell of • la habitación huele a tabaco the room smells of smoke • huele a perfume, ¿quién estuvo aquí? it smells like perfume, who was here? • oler bien to smell good • oler mal to smell bad ❷ *familiar* [*indicando sospecha*] • oler a to smack of

olfatear *vt* ❶ [*olisquear*] to sniff ❷ [*barruntar*] to smell

olfato *sm* ❶ [*sentido*] (sense of) smell • el olfato es uno de los cinco sentidos smell is one of the five senses ❷ *figurado* [*sagacidad*] nose • tener olfato para algo to be a good judge of something

olimpiada, olimpíada *sf* Olympic Games *pl* • las olimpiadas the Olympics

oliva *sf* olive • aceite de oliva olive oil

olivo *sm* olive tree

olla *sf* pot ▶ olla exprés o a presión pressure cooker ▶ olla podrida COCINA stew

olor *sm* smell • olor a smell of

olvidadizo, za *adj* forgetful ☀: *Los adjetivos ingleses son invariables.*

olvidar *vt* ❶ [*generalmente*] to forget • olvidaste llamar a tu madre you forgot to call your mother ❷ [*dejarse*] to leave • olvidé las llaves en la oficina I left my keys at the office • olvidé el horno prendido I left the oven on

olvido *sm* ❶ [*de un nombre, hecho* ETC] • caer en el olvido to fall into oblivion • al principio tuvo éxito pero después cayó en el olvido at the beginning he was successful but then he fell into oblivion ❷ [*descuido*] oversight • ¿no felicitaste a tu hijo el día de su cumpleaños? ¡qué olvido imperdonable! you didn't wish your son a happy birthday? what an unforgiveable oversight!

ombligo *sm* ANATOMÍA navel

omnipotente *adj* omnipotent ☀: *Los adjetivos ingleses son invariables.*

omnívoro, ra *adj* omnivorous ☀: *Los adjetivos ingleses son invariables.*

omoplato, omóplato *sm* shoulder-blade

once *numeral* eleven ver también seis

onceavo, va *numeral* eleventh

onda *sf* wave ▶ onda eléctrica o hertziana Hertzian wave ▶ onda expansiva shock wave ▶ onda luminosa/sonora light/sound wave
expresión estar en la onda *familiar* to be on the ball ▶ ¿qué onda? *familiar* how's it going?

ondear *vi* to ripple

ondulado, da *adj* wavy ☀: *Los adjetivos ingleses son invariables.*

ondular ◆ *vi* ❶ [*agua*] to ripple ❷ [*terreno*] to undulate
◆ *vt* to wave

ONG (*abreviatura de* organización no gubernamental) *sf* NGO

ONU (*abreviatura de* Organización de las Naciones Unidas) *sf* UN

onza *sf* [*unidad de peso*] ounce

OPA (*abreviatura de* oferta pública de adquisición) *sf* takeover bid

opaco, ca *adj* opaque ☀: *Los adjetivos ingleses son invariables.*

opción *sf* ❶ [*elección*] option • tienes varias opciones, elige la que te parezca mejor you have several options, choose the one that seems best to you • no hay opción there is no alternative ▶ opciones sobre acciones stock options ❷ [*derecho*] right • dar opción a to give the right to • tener opción a [*empleo, cargo*] to be eligible for

opcional *adj* optional ☀: *Los adjetivos ingleses son invariables.*

OPEP (*abreviatura de* Organización de Países Exportadores de Petróleo) *sf* OPEC

ópera *sf* opera ▶ **ópera bufa** comic opera

operación *sf* ❶ [*generalmente*] operation ▶ **operación quirúrgica** (surgical) operation ❷ COMERCIO transaction

operar ◆ *vt* ❶ [*enfermo*] • **operar a alguien (de algo)** [*enfermedad*] to operate on somebody (for something) • **el oculista la va a operar de cataratas** the eye doctor is going to operate on her for cataracts • **lo operaron del hígado** they've operated on his liver ❷ [*cambio* ETC] to bring about

◆ *vi* ❶ [*generalmente*] to operate ❷ [*actuar*] to act ❸ COMERCIO & FINANZAS to deal

■ **operarse** *v pronominal* ❶ [*enfermo*] to have an operation • **me voy a operar del hígado** I'm going to have an operation on my liver • **mañana se opera de cataratas** tomorrow she's having an operation for cataracts ❷ [*cambio* ETC] to occur

operario, ria *sm, f* worker

opinar ◆ *vt* to think • **¿qué opinas de los grupos ecológicos?** what do you think of ecological groups?

◆ *vi* to give your opinion • **es mejor no opinar cuando uno no conoce el tema** it's better to not give your opinion when you are not familiar with the topic

opinión *sf* [*parecer*] opinion • **¿cuál es tu opinión sobre los grupos ecológicos?** what's your opinion about ecological groups? ▶ **la opinión pública** public opinion

opio *sm* opium

oponente *smf* opponent

oponer *vt* ❶ [*resistencia*] to put up ❷ [*argumento, razón*] to put forward

■ **oponerse** *v pronominal* ❶ [*no estar de acuerdo*] to be opposed • **oponerse a algo a)** [*desaprobar*] to be opposed to something **b)** [*contradecir*] to contradict something • **nuestro grupo se opone a la tala indiscriminada en los bosques** our group is opposed to indiscriminate tree felling in the forests • **me opongo a creerlo** I refuse to believe it ❷ [*obstaculizar*] • **oponerse a** to impede

oportunidad *sf* [*ocasión*] opportunity, *plural* opportunities • **tuvo la oportunidad de irse a pasar el verano a la playa** she had the opportunity to go spend the summer at the beach • **darle una oportunidad a alguien** to give somebody a chance

oportunismo *sm* opportunism

oportunista *smf* opportunist

oportuno, na *adj* ❶ [*pertinente*] appropriate ❷ [*propicio*] timely • **el momento oportuno** the right time ҉ *Los adjetivos ingleses son invariables.*

oposición *sf* ❶ [*generalmente*] opposition • **la iniciativa de la maestra se chocó con la oposición de los alumnos** the teacher's plans collided with the students' opposition ❷ [*resistencia*] resistance ❸ ҉ *generalmente pl* [*examen*] public entrance examination • **preparar oposiciones** to be studying for a public entrance examination ▶ **oposición a profesor** public examination to be a teacher

opresión *sf* oppression

opresivo, va *adj* oppressive ҉ *Los adjetivos ingleses son invariables.*

opresor, ra *sm, f* oppressor

oprimir *vt* ❶ [*apretar - botón* ETC] to press; [*- garganta, brazo* ETC] to squeeze ❷ [*zapatos, cinturón*] to pinch ❸ *figurado* [*reprimir*] to oppress ❹ *figurado* [*angustiar*] to weigh down on

optar *vi* [*escoger*] • **optar (por algo)** to choose (something) • **optar por hacer algo** to choose to do something • **optaste por quedarte, ahora no te quejes** you chose to stay, now don't complain • **optar entre** to choose between

optativo, va *adj* optional ҉ *Los adjetivos ingleses son invariables.*

óptico, ca ◆ *adj* optic ҉ *Los adjetivos ingleses son invariables.*

◆ *sm, f* [*persona*] optician

■ **óptica** *sf* ❶ FÍSICA optics ҉ *incontable* ❷ [*tienda*] optician's (shop) ❸ *figurado* [*punto de vista*] point of view

optimismo *sm* optimism

optimista ◆ *adj* optimistic ҉ *Los adjetivos ingleses son invariables.*

◆ *smf* optimist

óptimo, ma ◆ *superlativo* = **bueno**

◆ *adj* optimum ҉ *Los adjetivos ingleses son invariables.*

opuesto, ta ◆ *participio pasado* → **oponer**

◆ *adj* ❶ [*contrario*] conflicting • **opuesto a** opposed to ❷ [*de enfrente*] opposite • **vivimos en direcciones opuestas** we live in opposite directions ҉ *Los adjetivos ingleses son invariables.*

oración *sf* ❶ [*rezo*] prayer • **algunas personas dicen una oración antes de la comida** some people say a prayer before the meal ❷ GRAMÁTICA sentence • **la segunda oración** the second sentence

orador, ra *sm, f* speaker

oral ◆ *adj* oral • **al final del curso de inglés tendremos un examen oral** at the end of the English course we'll have an oral exam • **en la caja de este medicamento dice "administrar por vía oral"** on this medicine's box it says "administer orally" ҉ *Los adjetivos ingleses son invariables.*

◆ *sm* → **examen**

órale *exclamación familiar* ❶ [*de acuerdo*] right! ❷ [*¡venga!*] come on!

orangután *sm* orangutang

orar *vi* to pray

órbita *sf* ❶ ASTRONOMÍA orbit • **la Luna describe una órbita ovalada alrededor de la Tierra** the moon travels in an oval orbit around the earth • **entrar/poner en órbita** to go/put into orbit ❷ [*de ojo*] eye socket

orca *sf* killer whale

orden ◆ *sm* ❶ [*generalmente*] order • **hay que poner un poco de orden en esta oficina** we have to put a little order in this office • **por orden** in order • **pónganse en fila, por orden de altura** get in line, in order

O

of height • **las fuerzas del orden** the forces of law and order ▶ **orden del día** agenda ▶ **orden de compra** COMERCIO purchase order ▶ **orden público** law and order ❷ [*tipo*] type ; order • **problemas de orden económico** economic problems

◆ *sf* order • **por orden de** by order of
expresión **¡a la orden!** MILITAR (yes) sir! ▶ **estar a la orden del día** to be the order of the day

dar una orden

- **Silence!** ¡Silencio!
- **Stop! OK?** ¡Basta!, ¿entendido?
- **Step back, please!** Retroceda, por favor.
- **Put the box down here!** ¡Pon esa caja aquí!

ordenado, da *adj* [*lugar, persona*] neat • **es muy ordenada, siempre tiene la casa impecable** she's very neat, her house is always tidy ❖ *Los adjetivos ingleses son invariables.*

ordenar *vt* ❶ [*poner en orden - generalmente*] to arrange ; [*- habitación, armario* ETC] to straighten (up) ❷ [*mandar*] to order ❸ RELIGIÓN to ordain ❹ [*solicitar*] to order

ordeñar *vt* to milk

ordinario, ria *adj* ❶ [*común*] ordinary ❷ [*vulgar*] common ❸ [*no selecto*] unexceptional ❹ [*no especial - presupuesto, correo*] daily ; [*- tribunal*] of first instance ❖ *Los adjetivos ingleses son invariables.*

orégano *sm* oregano

oreja *sf* ANATOMÍA ear

orfanato *sm* orphanage

orgánico, ca *adj* organic ❖ *Los adjetivos ingleses son invariables.*

organigrama *sm* [*generalmente*] INFORMÁTICA flowchart

organismo *sm* ❶ BIOLOGÍA organism ❷ ANATOMÍA body ❸ *figurado* [*entidad*] organization

organización *sf* organization • **la organización es importante para poder estudiar con eficiencia** organization is important to be able to study efficiently ▶ **Organización Mundial del Comercio** COMERCIO World Trade Organization ▶ **organización no gubernamental** non-governmental organization

organizar *vt* to organize

órgano *sm* organ • **el corazón es el órgano principal del cuerpo humano** the heart is the main organ of the human body • **ese músico escribió varias piezas para órgano** that musician wrote several pieces for the organ

orgasmo *sm* orgasm

orgía *sf* orgy

orgullo *sm* pride

orgulloso, sa *adj* proud ❖ *Los adjetivos ingleses son invariables.*

orientación *sf* ❶ [*dirección - acción*] guiding ; [*- rumbo*] direction • **no tiene sentido de la orientación** he has no sense of direction ❷ [*posicionamiento*

- acción] positioning ; [*- lugar*] position ❸ *figurado* [*información*] guidance ▶ **orientación profesional** careers guidance

oriental ◆ *adj* ❶ [*generalmente*] eastern ❷ [*del Lejano Oriente*] oriental ❖ *Los adjetivos ingleses son invariables.*

◆ *smf* oriental

orientar *vt* ❶ [*dirigir*] to direct • **el maestro orientó a sus alumnos en el trabajo** the teacher directed her students in their work ❷ [*casa*] to build facing ❸ *figurado* [*medidas* ETC] • **orientar hacia** to direct towards o at ❹ *figurado* [*aconsejar*] to give advice to

■ **orientarse** *v pronominal* ❶ [*dirigirse - foco* ETC] • **orientarse a** to point towards o at ❷ [*encontrar el camino*] to get your bearings • **deja que me oriente** let me get my bearings ❸ *figurado* [*encaminarse*] • **orientarse hacia** to be aiming at

oriente *sm* east

■ **Oriente** *sm* • **el Oriente** the East • **Lejano** o **Extremo Oriente** Far East ▶ **Oriente Medio/Próximo** Middle/Near East

orificio *sm* ❶ hole ❷ TECNOLOGÍA opening

origen *sm* ❶ [*generalmente*] origin • **el origen de esta costumbre es un antiguo rito maya** the origin of this custom is an ancient Mayan ceremony ❷ [*ascendencia*] origins *pl* • **de origen español** of Spanish origin ❸ [*causa*] cause • **dar origen a** to give rise to

original ◆ *adj* ❶ [*generalmente*] original • **éste es el texto original, ¿dónde están las copias?** this one is the original text, where are the copies? • **es un artista muy original** he's a very original artist ❷ [*raro*] eccentric ❖ *Los adjetivos ingleses son invariables.*

◆ *sm* original

originalidad *sf* ❶ [*generalmente*] originality ❷ [*extravagancia*] eccentricity

originar *vt* to cause

originario, ria *adj* [*inicial, primitivo*] original • **ése no era el plan originario** that wasn't the original plan • **ser originario de** to come from • **el maíz es originario de América** corn comes from America ❖ *Los adjetivos ingleses son invariables.*

orilla *sf* ❶ [*ribera - de río*] bank ; [*- de mar*] shore • **a orillas de** [*río*] on the banks of • **a orillas del mar** by the sea ❷ [*borde*] edge ❸ [*acera*] pavement

orina *sf* urine

orinal *sm* chamberpot

orinar *vi* & *vt* to urinate

■ **orinarse** *v pronominal* to wet yourself

ornitología *sf* ornithology

oro *sm* ❶ [*metal*] gold • **oro 18 quilates** 18 carat gold • **bañado en oro** gold-plated • **le regalamos una pulsera bañada en oro** we gave her a gold-plated bracelet ▶ **oro negro** oil ❷ *figurado* riches *pl*
expresión **hacerse de oro** to make your fortune ▶ **pedir el oro y el moro** to ask the earth

orografía *sf* terrain

orquesta *sf* ❶ [*músicos*] orchestra ▸ **orquesta de cámara/sinfónica** chamber/symphony orchestra ❷ [*lugar*] orchestra pit

orquestar *vt* to orchestrate

orquídea *sf* orchid

ortiga *sf* (stinging) nettle

ortodoxia *sf* orthodoxy

ortodoxo, xa *adj* orthodox ☿ *Los adjetivos ingleses son invariables.*

ortografía *sf* spelling

ortográfico, ca *adj* spelling ☿ *Sólo se usa delante del sustantivo.*

ortopedia *sf* orthopedics ☿ *incontable*

ortopédico, ca *adj* orthopedic ☿ *Los adjetivos ingleses son invariables.*

ortopedista *smf* orthopedist

oruga *sf* caterpillar

osadía *sf* ❶ [*valor*] boldness ❷ [*descaro*] audacity

osado, da *adj* ❶ [*valeroso*] bold ❷ [*descarado*] cheeky ☿ *Los adjetivos ingleses son invariables.*

osar *vi* to dare ▸ **no osé decirle la verdad** I didn't dare tell her the truth

oscilación *sf* ❶ [*movimiento*] swinging ❷ FÍSICA oscillation ❸ *figurado* [*variación*] fluctuation

oscilar *vi* ❶ [*moverse*] to swing ❷ FÍSICA to oscillate ❸ *figurado* [*variar*] to fluctuate

oscurecer ◆ *vt* ❶ [*privar de luz*] to darken ▸ **si no oscureces la habitación no vas a poder dormir la siesta** if you don't darken the room you're not going to be able to take a nap ❷ *figurado* [*mente*] to confuse ◆ *v impersonal* [*anochecer*] to get dark ▸ **en invierno, oscurece a las cuatro de la tarde** in the winter, it gets dark at four o'clock in the afternoon

oscuridad *sf* ❶ [*falta de luz*] darkness ▸ **el apagón nos dejó en la oscuridad** the blackout left us in darkness ▸ **¿le tienes miedo a la oscuridad?** are you afraid of the dark? ❷ *figurado* [*falta de claridad*] obscurity

oscuro, ra *adj* ❶ [*generalmente*] dark ▸ **aquí está muy oscuro, no puedo leer** it's very dark here, I can't read ▸ **llevaba anteojos oscuros** he was wearing dark glasses ▸ **verde oscuro** dark green ▸ **a oscuras** in the dark ❷ [*nublado*] overcast ❸ *figurado* [*inusual*] obscure ❹ *figurado* [*intenciones, asunto*] shady ☿ *Los adjetivos ingleses son invariables.*

óseo, a *adj* bone ☿ *Sólo se usa delante del sustantivo.*

oso, osa *sm, f* bear, *femenino* she-bear ▸ **oso de peluche** teddy bear ▸ **oso hormiguero** anteater ▸ **oso panda** panda ▸ **oso pardo** brown bear ▸ **oso polar** polar bear

ostensible *adj* evident ☿ *Los adjetivos ingleses son invariables.*

ostentación *sf* ostentation

osteópata *smf* osteopath

ostión *sm* oyster

ostra *sf* oyster
expresión aburrirse como una ostra *familiar* to be bored to death

OTAN (*abreviatura de* Organización del Tratado del Atlántico Norte) *sf* NATO

OTI (*abreviatura de* Organización de Televisiones Iberoamericanas) *sf* ▸ *para explicar lo que es puedes decir:* it's an association of all Spanish-speaking television networks

otitis *sf invariable* inflammation of the ear

otoñal *adj* fall ☿ *Sólo se usa delante del sustantivo.*

otoño *sm literal & figurado* fall ▸ **el próximo otoño** next fall ▸ **en otoño** in the fall

otorgar *vt* ❶ to grant ❷ [*premio*] to award ❸ DERECHO to execute

otorrino, na *sm, f familiar* ear, nose and throat specialist

otro, tra ◆ *adj* ❶ [*distinto*] another; other ▸ **otro chico** another boy ▸ **el otro chico** the other boy ▸ **quiero otro pedazo de torta** I want another piece of cake ▸ **me gustan más las otras clases** I like the other classes more ▸ **(los) otros chicos** (the) other boys ▸ **no hacer otra cosa que llorar** to do nothing but cry ▸ **yo me refería a otra cosa** I was referring to something else ▸ **si no lo encuentras aquí, debe estar en otra parte** if you don't find it here, it must be somewhere else ▸ **el otro día** [*pasado*] the other day ❷ [*nuevo*] another ▸ **estamos ante otro Dalí** this is another Dalí ▸ **otros tres goles** another three goals ☿ *Los adjetivos ingleses son invariables.*
◆ *pronombre* ☿ *sing* another (one), ☿ *pl* others ▸ **dame otro** give me another (one) ▸ **¿puedo servirme otro?** can I have another one? ▸ **el otro** the other one ▸ **este no me gusta, prefiero el otro** I don't like this one, I prefer the other one ▸ **no pedí estos, quiero los otros** I didn't order these, I want the others ▸ **(los) otros** (the) others ▸ **yo no lo hice, fue otro** it wasn't me, it was somebody else ▸ **otro habría abandonado, pero no él** anyone else would have given up, but not him ▸ **¡otra!** [*en conciertos*] encore!; more!

ovación *sf* ovation

ovacionar *vt* to give an ovation to

oval *adj* oval ☿ *Los adjetivos ingleses son invariables.*

ovalado, da *adj* oval ☿ *Los adjetivos ingleses son invariables.*

ovario *sm* ovary

oveja *sf* sheep, *plural* sheep ▸ **oveja negra** black sheep

overol, overoles *sm* [*ropa - con peto*] overalls *pl*; [*- para bebé*] romper

ovillo *sm* ball ▸ **tengo dos ovillos de lana** I have two balls of yarn
expresión hacerse un ovillo to curl up into a ball

ovino, na *adj* sheep ☿ *Sólo se usa delante del sustantivo.*

ovni *sm* (*abreviatura de* objeto volador no identificado) UFO

ovulación *sf* ovulation

ovular ◆ *adj* ovular ☼ *Los adjetivos ingleses son invariables.*

◆ *vi* to ovulate

oxidación *sf* rusting

oxidar *vt* ❶ to rust ❷ QUÍMICA to oxidize

■ **oxidarse** *v pronominal* to get rusty

óxido *sm* ❶ QUÍMICA oxide ❷ [*herrumbre*] rust

oxigenado, da *adj* ❶ QUÍMICA oxygenated ❷ [*cabello*] peroxided ☼ *Sólo se usa delante del sustantivo.*

oxigenar *vt* QUÍMICA to oxygenate

oxígeno *sm* oxygen

oyente *smf* ❶ RADIO listener ❷ [*alumno*] unregistered student

ozono *sm* ozone

p *sf* [*letra*] p; P

pabellón *sm* ❶ [*edificio*] pavilion ❷ [*parte de un edificio*] block ❸ [*en parques, jardines*] summerhouse ❹ [*tienda de campaña*] bell tent ❺ [*bandera*] flag

pachanga *sf familiar* rowdy celebration

pachorra *sf familiar* calmness

pachucho, cha *adj familiar* under the weather ☞ *Los adjetivos ingleses son invariables.*

paciencia *sf* patience • **perder la paciencia** to lose your patience • **tener paciencia** to be patient

paciente *adj & smf* patient ☞ *Los adjetivos ingleses son invariables.*

pacificación *sf* pacification

pacificar *vt* ❶ [*país*] to pacify ❷ [*ánimos*] to calm

pacífico, ca *adj* ❶ [*generalmente*] peaceful ❷ [*persona*] peaceable ☞ *Los adjetivos ingleses son invariables.*

Pacífico *sm* • **el (océano) Pacífico** the Pacific (Ocean)

pacifismo *sm* pacifism

pacifista *adj & smf* pacifist ☞ *Los adjetivos ingleses son invariables.*

pacotilla *sf*

expresión **de pacotilla** trashy; third-rate

pactar ◆ *vt* to agree to
◆ *vi* • **pactar (con)** to strike a deal (with)

pacto *sm* ❶ [*generalmente*] pact ❷ [*entre países*] treaty

padecer ◆ *vt* ❶ to suffer • **el país está padeciendo una crisis económica** the country is suffering an economic crisis ❷ [*enfermedad*] to suffer from
◆ *vi* ❶ to suffer ❷ [*enfermedad*] • **padecer de** to suffer from • **padece del corazón** he suffers from a heart complaint

padecimiento *sm* suffering

padrastro *sm* ❶ [*pariente*] stepfather ❷ [*pellejo*] hangnail

padre ◆ *sm* [*generalmente*] RELIGIÓN father • **Juan salió a pasear con su padre** Juan went out for a walk with his father • **el párroco de mi iglesia es el padre Luis** the parish priest of my church is Father Luis ▶ **padre de familia** family man
◆ *adj invariable familiar* [*estupendo*] great ☞ *Los adjetivos ingleses son invariables.*

padrenuestro (pl padrenuestros) *sm* Lord's Prayer

padrino *sm* ❶ [*de bautismo*] godfather ❷ [*de boda*] best man ❸ [*en duelos, torneos* ETC] second ❹ *figurado* [*protector*] patron

padrísimo *adj familiar* great ☞ *Los adjetivos ingleses son invariables.*

padrón *sm* ❶ [*censo*] census ❷ [*para votar*] electoral roll

padrote *sm familiar* pimp

paella *sf* paella

pág. p

paga *sf* ❶ payment ❷ [*salario*] salary ❸ [*de niño*] pocket money

pagar ◆ *vt* ❶ [*generalmente*] to pay • **tengo que pasar por la caja a pagar esta fruta** I have to go by the cash register to pay for this fruit ❷ [*deuda*] to pay off ❸ [*ronda, gastos, delito*] to pay for ❹ [*ayuda, favor*] to repay

expresión **me las pagarás** *familiar* you'll pay for this ▶ **pagar el pato** o **los platos rotos** *familiar* to pay for it

◆ *vi* to pay • **me dijeron que no tengo que pagar** they told me that I don't have to pay • **pagar en efectivo** o **metálico** to pay (in) cash

página *sf* page ▶ **página inicial** o **de inicio** INFORMÁTICA home page ▶ **página Web** Web page ▶ **las páginas amarillas** the Yellow Pages

pago *sm* ❶ [*con dinero*] payment • **tengo que mandarle los pagos al banco cada mes** I have to send the payments to the bank every month ▶ **pago anticipado/inicial** advance/down payment ▶ **pago por visión** pay-per-view ❷ *figurado* reward • **en pago de a)** [*en recompensa por*] as a reward for **b)** [*a cambio de*] in return for

paisaje *sm* ❶ [*generalmente*] landscape ❷ [*vista panorámica*] scenery ☞ *incontable*

Países Bajos *smpl* • **los Países Bajos** the Netherlands
paja *sf* [*generalmente*] straw
pajar *sm* hay loft
pájaro *sm* Zoología bird ▸ **pájaro bobo** penguin ▸ **pájaro carpintero** woodpecker ▸ **pájaro de mal agüero** bird of ill omen
expresiones **más vale pájaro en mano que ciento volando** *proverbio* a bird in the hand is worth two in the bush ▸ **matar dos pájaros de un tiro** to kill two birds with one stone ▸ **tener pájaros en la cabeza** to be scatterbrained o empty-headed
pala *sf* ❶ [*herramienta*] spade ❷ [*para recoger*] shovel ❸ Cocina spatula ❹ [*de remo, hélice*] blade
palabra *sf* ❶ [*generalmente*] word • **de palabra** by word of mouth ▸ **palabra de Dios** word of God ▸ **palabra de honor** word of honor ❷ [*habla*] speech ❸ [*derecho de hablar*] right to speak • **dar la palabra a alguien** to give the floor to somebody
expresiones **en cuatro** o **dos palabras** in a few words ▸ **en una palabra** in a word ▸ **no tener palabra** to go back on your word
palabrería *sf familiar* hot air
palabrota *sf* swearword • **decir palabrotas** to swear
palacete *sm* small palace
palacio *sm* palace
paladar *sm* palate
paladear *vt* to savor
palanca *sf* [*barra, mando*] lever ▸ **palanca de cambio** gearshift ▸ **palanca de mando** joystick
palco *sm* box *(at theater)* ▸ **palco de autoridades** VIP box
Palestina *nombre propio* Palestine
palestino, na *adj* & *sm, f* Palestinian 💡 ***Los adjetivos ingleses son invariables.***
paleta *sf* ❶ [*generalmente*] small shovel ❷ [*llana*] trowel ❸ Cocina slice ❹ Arte palette • **el pintor preparó su paleta para empezar a pintar** the painter prepared his palette to start painting ❺ [*de ping-pong*] bat ❻ [*helado*] Popsicle® • **la paleta de mango que me comí estaba deliciosa** the mango Popsicle I ate was delicious
paliar *vt* [*atenuar*] to ease
palidecer *vi* to go pale
palidez *sf* paleness
pálido, da *adj* ❶ pale ❷ *figurado* dull 💡 ***Los adjetivos ingleses son invariables.***
palillero *sm* toothpick holder
palillo *sm* ❶ [*mondadientes*] toothpick ❷ [*baqueta*] drumstick ❸ [*para comida china*] chopstick
paliza *sf* ❶ [*golpes, derrota*] beating ❷ [*esfuerzo*] hard grind
palma *sf* ❶ [*de mano*] palm ❷ [*palmera*] palm (tree) ❸ [*hoja de palmera*] palm leaf
palmada *sf* ❶ [*golpe*] pat ❷ [*más fuerte*] slap ❸ [*aplauso*] clap • **palmadas** clapping 💡 ***incontable***

P

palmarés *sm* ❶ [*historial*] record ❷ [*lista*] list of winners
palmera *sf* ❶ [*árbol*] palm (tree) ❷ [*datilera*] date palm
palmito *sm* ❶ [*árbol*] palmetto ❷ Cocina palm heart
palmo *sm* handspan
expresión **palmo a palmo** bit by bit ▸ **dejar a alguien con un palmo de narices** to let somebody down
palo *sm* ❶ [*generalmente*] stick ❷ [*de golf*] club ❸ [*de portería*] post ❹ [*de la escoba*] handle ❺ [*mástil*] mast ❻ [*golpe*] blow *(with a stick)* ❼ [*de baraja*] suit ❽ *figurado* [*pesadez*] bind
expresión **a palo seco a)** [*generalmente*] without anything else **b)** [*bebida*] neat
paloma *sf* ❶ dove; pigeon ▸ **paloma mensajera** carrier pigeon ❷ moth
palomita *sf* • **palomitas** popcorn 💡 ***incontable***
palpar ◆ *vt* ❶ [*tocar*] [*percibir*] to feel • **Rosaura palpó la tela para ver si era de fibra natural** Rosaura felt the cloth to see if it was made of natural fibers ❷ Medicina to palpate
◆ *vi* to feel around
palpitación *sf* ❶ [*del corazón*] beat ❷ [*con fuerza*] throb
palpitar *vi* ❶ [*latir*] to beat • **el corazón palpita rápidamente cuando uno está nervioso** the heart beats quickly when one is nervous ❷ [*con fuerza*] to throb
paludismo *sm* malaria
palurdo, da *sm, f* hick
pampa *sf* • **la pampa** the pampas *pl*
pan *sm* ❶ [*alimento*] bread • **no le gusta comer mucho pan** she doesn't like to eat a lot of bread ▸ **pan integral** wholewheat bread ▸ **pan molido** breadcrumbs *pl* ❷ [*hogaza*] loaf of bread, *plural* loaves of bread • **pasé por la panadería y compré tres panes chicos** I went by the bakery and bought three small loaves of bread
expresiones **contigo pan y cebolla** I'll go through thick and thin with you ▸ **llamar al pan pan y al vino vino** to call a spade a spade ▸ **ser pan comido** to be a piece of cake ▸ **ser el pan nuestro de cada día** to be a regular occurrence; to be commonplace ▸ **ser más bueno que el pan** to be kindness itself ▸ **no sólo de pan vive el hombre** man cannot live on bread alone
PAN *sm* (*abreviatura de* Partido Acción Nacional) *Mexican political party*
pana *sf* corduroy
panacea *sf literal & figurado* panacea
panadería *sf* bakery, *plural* bakeries
panadero, ra *sm, f* baker
panal *sm* honeycomb
Panamá *nombre propio* Panama
panameño, ña *adj* & *sm, f* Panamanian 💡 ***Los adjetivos ingleses son invariables.***
En inglés los gentilicios se escriben con mayúscula.

pancarta *sf* placard

páncreas *sm invariable* pancreas

panda *sm* → **oso**

pandereta *sf* tambourine

pandero *sm* MÚSICA tambourine

pandilla *sf* gang

panel *sm* ❶ [*generalmente*] panel ▸ **panel solar** solar panel ❷ [*pared, biombo*] screen ❸ [*tablero*] board

panfleto *sm* pamphlet

pánico *sm* panic • **los ladrones sembraron el pánico en la ciudad** the thieves caused panic in the city

panorama *sm* ❶ [*vista*] panorama ❷ *figurado* [*situación*] overall state ❸ [*perspectiva*] outlook

panorámico, ca *adj* panoramic ☼ *Los adjetivos ingleses son invariables.*

■ **panorámica** *sf* panorama

panque *sm* pound cake

pantaletas *sfpl* [*calzones*] panties

pantalla *sf* ❶ [*generalmente*] INFORMÁTICA screen • **como no tenían pantalla, proyectaban la película en una pared blanca** since they didn't have a screen, they projected the film onto a white wall • **la pequeña pantalla** the small screen ▸ **pantalla ancha** widescreen ▸ **pantalla de cristal líquido** liquid crystal display ❷ [*de lámpara*] lampshade • **hay que ponerle una pantalla a esa lámpara, para que no dé luz directa** you have to put a shade on that lamp, so that it doesn't give direct light

pantallazo *sm* screenshot

pantalón *sm* ☼ *generalmente pl* pants *pl* ▸ **pantalón vaquero** o **de mezclilla** jeans *pl*

pantano *sm* ❶ [*ciénaga*] marsh ❷ [*laguna*] swamp ❸ [*embalse*] reservoir

pantanoso, sa *adj* ❶ [*cenagoso*] marshy ❷ *figurado* [*difícil*] tricky ☼ *Los adjetivos ingleses son invariables.*

panteón *sm* ❶ pantheon ❷ [*familiar*] mausoleum

pantera *sf* panther

pantimedias *sfpl* pantyhose

pantorrilla *sf* calf, *plural* calves

pantufla *sf* ☼ *generalmente pl* slipper

panty (pl pantys) *sm* tights *pl*

panza *sf* belly, *plural* bellies

panzazo *sm* belly flop

pañal *sm* diaper

expresión **estar en pañales a)** [*en sus inicios*] to be in its infancy **b)** [*sin conocimientos*] not to have a clue

paño *sm* ❶ [*tela*] cloth ❷ [*trapo*] cloth ❸ [*para polvo*] duster ❹ [*de cocina*] tea towel ❺ [*lienzo*] panel

pañuelo *sm* ❶ [*de nariz*] handkerchief • **como siempre está resfriada, no va a ningún lado sin un pañuelo** since he's always got a cold, he doesn't go anywhere without a handkerchief ▸ **pañuelo de papel** tissue ❷ [*para el cuello*] scarf, *plural* scarves • **había tanto viento, que decidí usar un pañuelo para no despeinarme** there was so much wind that I decided to

wear a scarf to not mess up my hair ❸ [*para la cabeza*] headscarf, *plural* headscarves

papa *sf* potato, *plural* potatoes ▸ **papas fritas** French fries

expresión **no saber ni papa** *familiar* not to have a clue

■ **Papa** *sm* Pope

papá *sm familiar* dad

papachador, ra *adj* comforting ☼ *Los adjetivos ingleses son invariables.*

papachar *vt* to cuddle

papagayo *sm* [*pájaro*] parrot

papal ◆ *adj* papal
◆ *sm* potato field

papalote *sm* kite

papaya *sf* papaya

papel *sm* ❶ [*generalmente*] paper • **estos cuadernos son de papel reciclado** these notebooks are made of recycled paper ▸ **papel celofán** Cellophane ▸ **papel continuo** INFORMÁTICA continuous paper ▸ **papel de envolver** wrapping paper ▸ **papel de fumar** cigarette paper ▸ **papel de lija** sandpaper ▸ **papel higiénico** toilet paper ▸ **papel cuadriculado** graph paper ▸ **papel tapiz** wallpaper ▸ **papel reciclado** recycled paper ▸ **papel tapiz** INFORMÁTICA wallpaper ❷ [*hoja*] piece of paper • **saquen un papel y escriban su nombre** take out a piece of paper and write your name ❸ *figurado* CINE & TEATRO role • **es el protagonista de la película, tiene el papel principal** he's the star of the film; he has the main role • **hacer el papel de** to play the role of ▸ **papel principal/secundario** main/minor part ❹ FINANZAS stocks and shares *pl* ▸ **papel moneda** paper money; bills *pl*

papeleo *sm* paperwork

papelera *sf* ❶ [*en oficina, casa*] wastepaper basket ❷ [*en la calle*] garbage can

papelería *sf* stationery store

papeleta *sf* ❶ [*boleto*] ticket ❷ [*de votación*] ballot paper ❸ EDUCACIÓN *para explicar lo que es puedes decir:* slip of paper with university exam results

paperas *sfpl* mumps

papi *sm familiar* daddy

papilla *sf* [*para niños*] baby food

expresión **echar** o **arrojar la primera papilla** *familiar* to be as sick as a dog ▸ **hecho papilla a)** *familiar* [*cansado*] shattered **b)** [*cosa*] smashed to bits

papiro *sm* papyrus

paquete *sm* ❶ [*de libros, regalos* ETC] package • **tengo que pasar al correo a recoger un paquete** I have to go by the post office to pick up a package ▸ **paquete bomba** mail bomb ▸ **paquete postal** package ❷ [*de cigarrillos, klínex, folios* ETC] pack • **¿me podrías traer un paquete de galletitas del supermercado?** could you bring me a pack of cookies from the supermarket? ❸ [*de azúcar, arroz*] bag ❹ [*de medidas*] package ▸ **paquete turístico** package tour ❺ INFORMÁTICA package

P

par ◆ *adj* ❶ MATEMÁTICAS even • **2, 4 y 6 son números pares** 2, 4 and 6 are even numbers ❷ [*igual*] equal.♀ *Los adjetivos ingleses son invariables.*

expresión echar algo a pares o **nones** *para explicar lo que es puedes decir:*it's a way of deciding something by guessing the number of fingers the other person is holding out behind his or her back

◆ *sm* ❶ [*pareja - de zapatos* ETC] pair ❷ [*dos - veces* ETC] couple ❸ [*número indeterminado*] couple • **un par de copas** a couple of drinks ❹ [*en golf*] par ❺ [*noble*] peer

para

◆ *preposición*

❶ [*indica el destinatario*] for
• **es para ti** it's for you

❷ [*indica el objetivo*]
• **sale para distraerse** she goes out to take her mind off things
• **me estoy preparando para correr en la maratón** I'm preparing to run the marathon
• **lo hice para agradarte** I did it to please you
• **¿para qué?** what for?
• **¿para qué sirve esto?** what is this for?
• **no sirve para nada** it's no use for anything
• **es malo para la salud** it's bad for your health

❸ [*indica el destino, la dirección*]
• **salieron para Morelia** they set off for Morelia
• **vete para casa** go home
• **échate para el lado** go towards that side

❹ [*indica un momento, una duración*]
• **tiene que estar hecho para mañana** it must be ready by tomorrow
• **queda leche para dos días** there's enough milk left for two days
• **faltan dos semanas para las vacaciones** it's two weeks till the vacation
• **¿para cuándo tendrá pronta la traducción?** when will he have the translation ready?
• **para siempre** forever

❺ [*en comparaciones*] for
• **está muy espabilado para su edad** he's very advanced for his age

❻ [*indica el punto de vista*]
• **para mí, no es la respuesta correcta** in my view, that's not the right answer
• **para mí, no debería habérselo dicho** in my view, he shouldn't have told him

❼ [*antes de un infinitivo, indica que algo está por pasar*]
• **la cena está lista para servir** dinner's ready to be served

■ **para que**
◆ *locución conjuntiva*
[*indica el objetivo*] so (that)
• **te lo digo para que lo sepas** I'm telling you just so you know

parábola *sf* ❶ [*alegoría*] parable ❷ GEOMETRÍA parabola

parabólico, ca *adj* parabolic.♀ *Los adjetivos ingleses son invariables.*

parabrisas *sm invariable* windshield

paracaídas *sm invariable* parachute

paracaidista *smf* ❶ parachutist ❷ MILITAR paratrooper

parada *sf* ❶ [*detención*] stop • **a las dos horas hicimos una parada para descansar** after two hours we stopped for a rest ❷ DEPORTE save ❸ [*de autobús*] (bus) stop ❹ [*de taxi*] (taxi) stand ❺ [*de metro*] (subway) station ❻ MILITAR parade

paradero *sm* [*de persona*] whereabouts *pl*

paradisiaco, ca, paradisíaco, ca *adj* heavenly.♀ *Los adjetivos ingleses son invariables.*

parado, da *adj* [*inmóvil - coche*] standing; [*- persona*] still; [*- fábrica, proyecto*] at a standstill • **¿qué haces ahí parada? ven a ayudarme** what are you doing standing there? come help me • **hay un tren parado en el andén, pero no sé si es el que va al centro** there's a train stopped at the platform, but I don't know if it's the one that's going downtown.♀ *Los adjetivos ingleses son invariables.*

expresión salir bien/mal parado de algo to come off well/badly out of something

paradoja *sf* paradox

paraguas *sm invariable* umbrella

Paraguay *nombre propio* • **(el) Paraguay** Paraguay

paraguayo, ya *adj* & *sm, f* Paraguayan.♀ *Los adjetivos ingleses son invariables.*

paragüero *sm* umbrella stand

paraíso *sm* ❶ RELIGIÓN Paradise ❷ *figurado* paradise

paraje *sm* spot

paralelismo *sm* ❶ GEOMETRÍA parallelism ❷ [*semejanza*] similarity

paralelo, la *adj* parallel • **las ruedas del carro dejaron dos líneas paralelas en la arena** the car's wheels left two parallel lines in the sand • **paralelo a** parallel to.♀ *Los adjetivos ingleses son invariables.*

■ **paralelo** *sm* GEOGRAFÍA parallel

■ **paralela** *sf* GEOMETRÍA parallel (line)

parálisis *sf invariable* paralysis ▶ **parálisis cerebral** cerebral palsy

paralítico, ca *adj* & *sm, f* • **quedó paralítico a causa del accidente** he became paralyzed because of the accident.♀ *Los adjetivos ingleses son invariables.*

paralizar *vt* to paralyze • **un derrame le paralizó la mitad del cuerpo** a hemorrhage paralyzed half of his body

parámetro *sm* parameter

paranoia *sf* paranoia

parapente *sm* ❶ [*deporte*] paragliding ❷ [*paracaídas*] parapente

parapléjico, ca *adj* & *sm, f* paraplegic.♀ *Los adjetivos ingleses son invariables.*

parar ◆ *vi* ❶ [*generalmente*] to stop • **parar de hacer algo** to stop doing something • **sin parar** non-stop • **en esta fábrica trabajan sin parar** in this factory they work nonstop ❷ [*alojarse*] to stay • **cuando viene a la ciudad, para en mi casa** when he comes to town, he stays at my house ❸ [*recaer*] • **parar en manos de alguien** to come into the possession of somebody ❹ [*acabar*] to end up • **¿en qué parará este lío?** where will it all end?

◆ *vt* ❶ [*generalmente*] to stop • **paré el carro** I stopped the car ❷ [*golpe*] to parry ❸ [*preparar*] to prepare ❹ [*levantar*] to raise

■ **pararse** *v pronominal* ❶ [*detenerse*] to stop • **¿por qué te paraste? sigue caminando** why did you stop? keep walking ❷ [*ponerse de pie*] to stand up • **cuando entró la directora, los músicos se pararon** when the conductor came in, the musicians stood up ❸ [*salir de la cama*] to get up

pararrayos *sm invariable* lightning conductor

parásito, ta *adj* BIOLOGÍA parasitic ☿ *Los adjetivos ingleses son invariables.*

■ **parásito** *sm figurado* BIOLOGÍA parasite

parasol *sm* parasol

parcela *sf* ❶ [*de tierra*] plot (of land) ❷ [*de saber*] area

parche *sm* ❶ [*generalmente*] patch ❷ [*chapuza - para salir de un problema*] makeshift solution

parchís *sm invariable* parcheesi

parcial *adj* ❶ [*no total*] partial ❷ [*no ecuánime*] biased ☿ *Los adjetivos ingleses son invariables.*

parcialidad *sf* [*tendenciosidad*] bias

parecer ◆ *sm* ❶ [*opinión*] opinion ❷ [*apariencia*] • **de buen parecer** good-looking

◆ *vi* ☿ *Sólo se usa delante del sustantivo.* to look like • **parece un palacio** it looks like a palace

◆ *v copulativo* to look • **pareces cansado** you look tired

◆ *v impersonal* ❶ [*opinar*] • **me parece que...** I think that... • **me parece que sí/no** I think/don't think so • **¿qué te parece?** what do you think (of it)? ❷ [*tener aspecto de*] • **parece que va a llover** it looks like it's going to rain • **parece que le gusta** it looks as if o it seems that she likes it • **eso parece** so it seems • **al parecer** apparently

■ **parecerse** *v pronominal* ❶ • **parecerse (en)** to be alike (in) • **parecerse a alguien** [*físicamente*] to look like somebody ❷ [*en carácter*] to be like somebody

parecido, da *adj* similar • **bien parecido** [*atractivo*] good-looking ☿ *Los adjetivos ingleses son invariables.*

■ **parecido** *sm* • **parecido (con/entre)** resemblance (to/between)

pared *sf* ❶ [*generalmente*] wall ❷ [*de montaña*] side

expresión **las paredes oyen** walls have ears ▶ **subirse por las paredes** to hit the roof

parejo, ja *adj* • **parejo (a)** similar (to) • **Diego y Andrés son parejos en altura** Diego and Andrés

are similar in height ☿ *Los adjetivos ingleses son invariables.*

■ **pareja** *sf* ❶ [*generalmente*] pair • **por parejas** in pairs • **el tenis se puede jugar en parejas** tennis can be played in pairs ❷ [*de novios*] couple • **Virginia y Antonio hacen una linda pareja** Virginia and Antonio make a nice couple ▶ **pareja de hecho** common-law couple • **son una pareja de hecho** they live together ❸ [*miembro del par*] partner

parentela *sf familiar* relations *pl*

parentesco *sm* relationship

paréntesis *sm invariable* ❶ [*signo*] parenthesis • **entre paréntesis** in parenthesis ❷ [*intercalación*] digression ❸ [*interrupción*] break

pariente, ta *sm, f* [*familiar*] relative • **un pariente cercano/lejano** a close/distant relative

parir ◆ *vi* to give birth ◆ *vt* to give birth to

París *nombre propio* Paris

parlamentar *vi* to negotiate

parlamentario, ria ◆ *adj* parliamentary ☿ *Los adjetivos ingleses son invariables.* ◆ *sm, f* member of parliament

parlamento *sm* POLÍTICA parliament

parlanchín, ina *familiar* ◆ *adj* chatty ☿ *Los adjetivos ingleses son invariables.* ◆ *sm, f* chatterbox

parlante *sm* speaker

parlotear *vi familiar* to chatter

paro *sm* ❶ [*cesación - acción*] shutdown; [*- estado*] stoppage ▶ **paro cardíaco** cardiac arrest ❷ [*huelga*] strike • **ayer no fui a la escuela porque había paro de maestros** yesterday I didn't go to school because there was a teacher strike

parodia *sf* parody

parodiar *vt* to parody

parpadear *vi* ❶ [*pestañear*] to blink • **me entró una basurita en el ojo y por eso parpadeo tanto** a piece of dirt got in my eye and that's why I'm blinking so much ❷ [*centellear*] to flicker • **la luz está parpadeando, va a haber un apagón** the light is flickering, there's going to be a blackout

párpado *sm* eyelid

parque *sm* ❶ [*generalmente*] park ▶ **parque acuático** waterpark ▶ **parque de atracciones** amusement park ▶ **parque eólico** wind farm ▶ **parque nacional** national park ▶ **parque tecnológico** science park ▶ **parque temático** theme park ▶ **parque zoológico** zoo ❷ [*vehículos*] fleet ❸ [*para niños*] playpen

parqué *sm* parquet (floor)

parquímetro *sm* parking meter

parra *sf* grapevine

parrafada *sf* lecture

párrafo *sm* paragraph

parranda *sf familiar* [*juerga*] • **irse de parranda** to go out on the town

parrilla *sf* [*utensilio*] grill • **a la parrilla** grilled

párroco *sm* parish priest

parroquia *sf* ❶ [*iglesia*] parish church ❷ [*jurisdicción*] parish ❸ [*clientela*] clientele

parte ◆ *sm* report • **dar parte (a alguien de algo)** to report (something to somebody) ❿ **parte facultativo** o **médico** medical report ❿ **parte meteorológico** weather forecast

◆ *sf* ❶ [*generalmente*] part • **vivo en la parte oeste del pueblo** I live in the west part of town • **hay que dividir el pastel en ocho partes** we have to divide the cake into eight portions • **la mayor parte de la gente** most people • **la tercera parte de** a third of • **en alguna parte** somewhere • **no lo veo por ninguna parte** I can't find it anywhere • **de parte de alguien** from • **mándale saludos a tu mamá de mi parte** say hello to your mom from me • **¿de parte de (quién)?** TELECOMUNICACIONES who is calling, please? • **en parte** partly • **todo lo que ha pasado es en parte culpa tuya** everything that's happened is partly your fault • **por mi parte** for my part • **por parte de padre/madre** on your father's/mother's side • **por partes** bit by bit • **por otra parte** besides • **por una parte... por la otra...** on the one hand... on the other (hand)... • **tomar parte en algo** to take part in something ❷ [*bando*] side • **tenemos que averiguar quién está de nuestra parte** we have to find out who's on our side ❸ DERECHO party

participación *sf* ❶ [*colaboración*] participation ❷ [*de lotería*] share of a lottery ticket ❸ [*comunicación*] notice

participante *smf* participant

participar ◆ *vi* ❶ [*colaborar*] • **participar (en)** to take part in • **miles de personas participaron en la maratón** thousands of people took part in the marathon • **numerosos científicos han participado en el proyecto** many scientists have participated in the project ❷ FINANZAS • **participar (en)** to have a share in • **los empleados participan en los beneficios de la empresa** the employees have a share in the company's profits

◆ *vt* • **participar algo a alguien** to notify somebody of something

partícipe ◆ *adj* • **partícipe (de)** involved (in) • **hacer partícipe de algo a alguien a)** [*notificar*] to notify somebody of something **b)** [*compartir*] to share something with somebody ଼: *Los adjetivos ingleses son invariables.*

◆ *smf* participant

partícula *sf* particle

particular ◆ *adj* ❶ [*generalmente*] particular • **tiene su sabor particular** it has its own particular taste • **en particular** in particular ❷ [*no público - domicilio, clases* ETC] private • **el hotel tiene una playa particular para los huéspedes** the hotel has a private beach for the guests ❸ [*no corriente - habilidad* ETC] special • **tiene un talento particular para la pintura** he has a special talent for painting ଼: *Los adjetivos ingleses son invariables.*

◆ *smf* [*persona*] member of the public

◆ *sm* [*asunto*] matter

partida *sf* ❶ [*marcha*] departure • **la partida del tren está prevista para las ocho en punto** the train's departure is planned for eight o'clock on the dot ❷ [*en juego*] game • **me ganaste dos partidas de póquer** you beat me at two games of poker ❸ COMERCIO [*mercancía*] consignment ; [*entrada*] item ; entry

partidario, ria ◆ *adj* • **partidario de** in favor of ଼: *Los adjetivos ingleses son invariables.*

◆ *sm, f* supporter

partidista *adj* partisan ଼: *Los adjetivos ingleses son invariables.*

partido *sm* ❶ POLÍTICA party, *plural* parties • **en política es independiente: no pertenece a ningún partido** in politics he's independent: he doesn't belong to any party ❷ DEPORTE match • **espero que mi equipo gane el partido del domingo** I hope that my team wins the match on Sunday ❿ **partido amistoso** friendly (match)

EXPRESIÓN **sacar partido de** to make the most of ❿ **tomar partido por** to side with

partir ◆ *vt* ❶ [*dividir*] to divide • **mamá partió el pollo en ocho trozos** Mom divided the chicken into eight pieces ❷ [*repartir*] to share out ❸ [*romper*] to break open ❹ [*cascar*] to crack • **necesito ayuda para partir este coco** I need help to crack this coconut ❺ [*tronco, loncha* ETC] to cut

◆ *vi* ❶ [*marchar*] to leave • **el tren partió hace cinco minutos** the train left five minutes ago ❷ [*basarse*] • **partir de** to start from

■ **partirse** *v pronominal* ❶ [*romperse*] to split ❷ [*rajarse*] to crack

partitura *sf* score

parto *sm* birth • **estar en trabajo de parto** to be in labor ❿ **parto natural/prematuro** natural/premature birth

pasa *sf* [*fruta*] raisin ❿ **pasa de Corinto** currant ❿ **pasa de Esmirna** sultana

pasable *adj* passable ଼: *Los adjetivos ingleses son invariables.*

pasadizo *sm* passage

pasado, da *adj* ❶ [*generalmente*] past • **pasado un año** a year later ❷ [*último*] last • **el año pasado** last year ❸ [*podrido*] off ❹ [*hecho - filete, carne*] well done ଼: *Los adjetivos ingleses son invariables.*

EXPRESIÓN **lo pasado, pasado está** let bygones be bygones

■ **pasado** *sm* ❶ [*generalmente*] past • **la historia estudia el pasado** history studies the past ❷ GRAMÁTICA past (tense)

pasaje *sm* ❶ [*boleto*] ticket ❷ [*pasajeros*] passengers *pl* ❸ [*calle*] passage ❹ [*fragmento*] passage

pasajero, ra ◆ *adj* passing ଼: *Los adjetivos ingleses son invariables.*

◆ *sm, f* passenger

pasamanos *sm invariable* ❶ [*de escalera interior*] bannister ❷ [*de escalera exterior*] handrail

pasamontañas *sm invariable* balaclava (helmet)

pasaporte *sm* passport
pasapuré *sm* food mill
pasapurés *sm invariable* = **pasapuré**

---

pasar
♦ *vt*
❶ [*dar*] to pass
• **pásame la sal** pass me the salt
• **me ha pasado su catarro** he's given me his cold
❷ [*tiempo*] to spend
• **pasó dos años en Roma** she spent two years in Rome
• **durante el verano pasamos unos días en la playa** during the summer we spend some days at the beach
• **ya pasó la Navidad** Christmas is over
❸ [*cruzar, atravesar*] to cross
• **pasar la frontera** to cross the frontier
❹ [*hacer atravesar un filtro*]
• **pasar la harina por el tamiz** sift the flour
❺ [*en la tele, en el cine*] to show
• **pasar una película** to show a movie
❻ [*en el teatro*] to be on
• **¿qué pasan actualmente en el Rex?** what's on at the Rex?
❼ [*conducir*]
• **me pasó a la sala** he showed me into the living room
❽ [*cambiar algo de lugar*]
• **pasar algo de un sitio a otro** move sth from one place to another
❾ [*soportar, aguantar*]
• **está pasando una depresión** she's going through a bout of depression
• **están pasando problemas económicos** they have money problems at the moment
• **pasar frío/hambre** to be cold/hungry
❿ [*aprobar*] to show
• **pasó el examen de historia con muy buena nota** he passed his History exam with a very good grade
⓫ [*rebasar*]
• **un coche nos pasó por la derecha** a car overtook us on the right
• **ya ha pasado los treinta** he's over thirty
⓬
• **pasarla bien/mal** to have a good/bad time
• **la pasamos muy bien en la fiesta** we had a great time at the party
• **la pasó muy mal** he had a very bad time
♦ *vi*
❶ [*transcurrir, refiriéndose al tiempo*] to go by
• **pasan los días** the days go by
• **pasaron 20 minutos y decidí que no esperaba más** 20 minutes went by and I decided that I wasn't waiting any more
❷ [*cambiar de estado*]
• **pasa fácilmente de la alegría a la tristeza** he switches easily from happiness to sadness

❸ [*cambiar de función*]
• **pasó de secretario a tesorero** he went from being a secretary to being the treasurer
❹ [*terminar*] to be over
• **pasó el frío** the cold weather is over
• **cuando pasó el terremoto, muchas casas estaban destruidas** when the earthquake was over, many houses were destroyed
❺ [*ir de un sitio a otro*] to go
• **ese tren pasa por varias estaciones antes de llegar al centro** that train goes through several stations before arriving downtown
• **pasar de largo** to walk past
• **¡pase!** come in!
❻ [*suceder*] to happen
• **cuéntame lo que pasó** tell me what happened
• **no sé qué pasó en la clase de ayer** I don't know what happened in yesterday's class
• **¿cómo pasó?** what happened?
• **pase lo que pase** whatever happens
■ **pasar a**
♦ *v + preposición*
to move on to
• **pasemos a otra cosa** let's move on to something else
■ **pasar de**
♦ *v + preposición*
❶ [*haber más, tener más*]
• **pasan de veinte** there are over twenty
• **no pasa de los cuarenta** he's not a day over forty
❷ *familiar* [*no interesarse*]
• **paso de ir al cine** I'm not interested in going to the movies
• **paso de política** I'm not into politics
• **dice que pasa de él** she's not interested in him
■ **pasar por**
♦ *v + preposición*
❶ [*ser considerado como*] to seem
• **pasar por tonto** to seem like an idiot
❷ [*tener que aguantar*] to go through
• **está pasando por un momento difícil** he's going through a difficult time
❸ [*sitio, mente*]
• **si puedo pasaré por tu casa** I'll drop by if I can
• **ni se me había pasado por la imaginación** it hadn't even occurred to me
■ **pasar sin**
♦ *v + preposición*
[*vivir sin*]
• **pasar sin carne** to go without meat
• **no puedo pasar sin hablar** I have to talk
■ **pasarse**
♦ *v pronominal*
❶ [*no durar, irse*] to pass
• **¿se te ha pasado el dolor?** has the pain passed?
❷ [*gastar el tiempo*] to spend
• **se pasaron el día hablando** they spent the day talking

P

❸ [*perderse*] to miss
• **se nos acaba de pasar una magnífica oportunidad** we've just missed an excellent opportunity
❹ [*pudrirse, echarse a perder*]
• **hay que comer el pescado antes de que se pase** the fish needs to be eaten before it goes off
• **hay que comerse estas manzanas antes de que se pasen** you have to eat these apples before they get overripe
• **estas conservas se han pasado** these cans are past their sell-by date
❺ [*olvidar*] to forget
• **se me pasó decirle que no era preciso reservar** I forgot to tell her that you don't need to reserve
• **no se le pasa nada** nothing escapes him
❻ *familiar* [*exagerar, ir demasiado lejos*] to go too far
• **deberías pedirle perdón a Carmen, ¡esta vez te has pasado!** you should apologize to Carmen. You've gone too far this time!
❼ [*divertirse*]
• **pasársela bien/mal** to enjoy/not enjoy yourself
• **¿qué tal te la estás pasando?** are you enjoying yourself?
• **se la pasó muy mal en la fiesta** she didn't enjoy the party at all
• **nos la pasamos muy bien en el zoológico** we had a great time at the zoo
■ **pasarse a**
◆ *v pronominal + preposición*
[*cambiarse de bando*]
• **algunos se pasaron al enemigo** some went over to the enemy
• **pasarse al otro bando** to change sides
■ **pasarse de**
◆ *v pronominal + preposición*
[*exagerar, ir demasiado lejos*]
• **a veces te pasas de bueno** sometimes you're too nice
• **¡no te pases de listo!** don't try and be clever!

pasarela *sf* ❶ [*puente*] footbridge ❷ [*para desembarcar*] gangway ❸ [*en un desfile*] catwalk

pasatiempo *sm* [*hobby*] hobby

Pascua *sf* ❶ [*de los judíos*] Passover ❷ [*de los cristianos*] Easter
expresión **hacer la Pascua a alguien** *familiar* **a)** [*ser pesado*] to pester somebody **b)** [*poner en apuros*] to land somebody in it

pase *sm* ❶ [*generalmente*] DEPORTE & TAUROMAQUIA pass ❷ [*desfile*] parade ▶ **pase de modelos** fashion parade

pasear ◆ *vi* ❶ [*a pie*] to go for a walk • **después del almuerzo, el abuelo sale a pasear por el jardín** after lunch, my grandfather goes for a walk in the garden ❷ [*en carro*] to go for a drive • **los domingos salimos a pasear con mi tío en el auto** on Sundays we go for a drive in the car with my uncle ❸ [*en bici*] to go for a ride • **como el día estaba lindo, agarré la bicicleta y salí a pasear** since it was a nice day, I got my bicycle and I went for a ride

◆ *vt* ❶ to take for a walk ❷ [*perro*] to walk • **¿a quién le toca pasear al perro hoy?** whose turn is it to walk the dog today? ❸ *figurado* to show off

paseo *sm* ❶ [*acción - a pie*] walk; [*- en coche*] drive; [*- a caballo*] ride; [*- en barca*] row • **dar un paseo** [*a pie*] to go for a walk • **después del almuerzo, el abuelo sale a dar un paseo por el jardín** after lunch my grandfather goes out for a walk through the garden • **como el día estaba lindo, agarré la bicicleta y salí de paseo** since it was a nice day, I grabbed my bicycle and went out for a ride • **los domingos salimos de paseo con mi tío en el carro** on Sundays we go for a drive in the car with my uncle • **dos veces por año toda la escuela hace un paseo** twice a year the whole school goes on an outing ❷ [*lugar*] avenue ▶ **paseo marítimo** promenade

pasillo *sm* corridor

pasión *sf* passion
■ **Pasión** *sf* RELIGIÓN • **la pasión** the Passion

pasmoso, sa *adj* astonishing ⊠ *Los adjetivos ingleses son invariables.*

paso *sm* ❶ [*generalmente*] step • **la niña recién aprendió a caminar y da pasos cortos** the little girl recently learned to walk and she takes short steps • **los pasos en el tango son largos y lentos** the steps are long and slow in the tango ❷ [*huella*] footprint ❸ [*acción*] passing ❹ [*cruce*] crossing ▶ **paso elevado** flyover ▶ **paso a nivel** level crossing ▶ **paso de cebra** zebra crossing ❺ [*camino de acceso*] way through • **abrir paso a alguien** *literal & figurado* to make way for somebody • **ceder el paso (a alguien) a)** to let somebody past **b)** AUTOMÓVILES to give way (to somebody) • **'ceda el paso'** give way • **'prohibido el paso'** no entry ❻ [*forma de andar*] walk ❼ [*ritmo*] pace ❽ GEOGRAFÍA [*en montaña*] pass; [*en el mar*] strait ❾ ⊠ *generalmente pl* [*gestión*] step • **dar los pasos necesarios** to take the necessary steps ❿ [*progreso*] advance
expresiones **a cada paso** every other minute ▶ **está a dos o cuatro pasos** it's just down the road ▶ **estar de paso** to be passing through ▶ **paso a paso** step by step ▶ **salir del paso** to get out of trouble

pasta *sf* ❶ [*masa*] paste ▶ **pasta dentífrica** toothpaste ❷ [*de papel*] pulp ❸ COCINA [*espagueti* ETC] pasta; [*de pasteles*] pastry; [*de pan*] dough • **los ravioles son mis pastas preferidas** ravioli is my favorite pasta • **tienes que amasar bien la pasta** you have to knead the dough well ❹ [*pastelillo*] pastry ❺ [*encuadernación*] • **en pasta** hardback

pastar *vi* to graze

pastel *sm* ❶ COCINA cake; • **a Beatriz le prepararon un pastel de chocolate para su cumpleaños** they made a chocolate cake for Beatriz's birthday ❷ ARTE pastel • **me gusta pintar con pasteles** I like to paint with pastels

pastelería *sf* ❶ [*establecimiento*] bakery ❷ [*repostería*] pastries *pl*

pastilla *sf* ❶ MEDICINA pill • **el médico me recetó unas pastillas para la tos** the doctor prescribed me some pills for my cough ❷ [*de jabón, chocolate*] bar • **hay que traer seis pastillas de jabón del supermer-**

cado you have to bring six bars of soap from the supermarket ❸ [*de caldo*] cube

pasto *sm* ❶ [*sitio*] pasture ❷ [*hierba*] fodder ❸ [*hierba*] lawn

expresión **ser pasto de las llamas** to go up in flames

pastor, ra *sm, f* [*de ganado*] shepherd, *femenino* shepherdess • **el pastor cuida las ovejas** the shepherd cares for the sheep

■ **pastor** *sm* ❶ [*sacerdote*] minister • **el pastor de mi iglesia siempre habla de la caridad** the minister in my church always talks about charity ❷ → **perro**

pastoso, sa *adj* ❶ [*blando*] pasty ❷ [*arroz*] sticky ❸ [*seco*] dry ☼ *Los adjetivos ingleses son invariables.*

pata *sf* ❶ [*pierna*] leg ❷ [*pie - generalmente*] foot; [*- de perro, gato*] paw; [*- de vaca, caballo*] hoof ▶ **pata de gallo** [*en la cara*] crow's feet *pl* ❸ *familiar* [*de persona*] leg • **a cuatro patas** on all fours ❹ [*de mueble*] leg ❺ [*de gafas*] arm

expresiones **ir a la pata coja** to hop ▶ **meter la pata** to put your foot in it ▶ **poner/estar patas arriba** to turn/be upside down ▶ **tener mala pata** to be unlucky

patada *sf* ❶ kick • **dar una patada a alguien** to kick somebody ❷ [*en el suelo*] stamp

expresión **tratar a alguien a patadas** to treat somebody like dirt

patalear *vi* ❶ to kick about ❷ [*en el suelo*] to stamp your feet

pataleta *sf* tantrum

paté *sm* paté

patear ◆ *vt* ❶ [*dar un puntapié*] to kick ❷ [*pisotear*] to stamp on

◆ *vi* [*patalear*] to stamp your feet

paternal *adj* fatherly ☼ *Los adjetivos ingleses son invariables.*

paternidad *sf* ❶ fatherhood ❷ DERECHO paternity

paterno, na *adj* paternal ☼ *Los adjetivos ingleses son invariables.*

patético, ca *adj* pathetic ☼ *Los adjetivos ingleses son invariables.*

patidifuso, sa *adj familiar* stunned ☼ *Los adjetivos ingleses son invariables.*

patilla *sf* ❶ [*de pelo*] sideburn • **¿te estás dejando crecer las patillas?** are you letting your sideburns grow? ❷ [*de lentes*] arm • **se me rompió una patilla de los lentes** one of the arms on my glasses broke

patín *sm* [*calzado - de cuchilla*] ice skate; [*- de ruedas*] roller skate; [*- en línea*] roller blade ▶ **patín del diablo** scooter

patinaje *sm* skating ▶ **patinaje sobre hielo** ice skating

patinar *vi* ❶ [*sobre hielo*] to skate • **patina muy bien** she skates very well ❷ [*sobre ruedas*] to roller-skate ❸ [*resbalar - coche*] to skid; [*- persona*] to slip • **patiné con una cáscara de plátano y casi me quiebro un brazo** I slipped on a banana peel and almost broke my arm ❹ *familiar* [*meter la pata*] to put your foot in it

patinazo *sm* ❶ [*de coche*] skid ❷ [*de persona*] slip ❸ *familiar* [*planchazo*] blunder

patinete *sm* scooter

patio *sm* ❶ [*generalmente*] patio ❷ [*de escuela*] playground ❸ [*de cuartel*] parade ground

pato, ta *sm, f* duck

expresión **pagar el pato** to carry the can

patria *sf* native country

patriarca *sm* patriarch

patrimonio *sm* ❶ [*bienes - heredados*] inheritance; [*- propios*] wealth ❷ [*cultural*] heritage

patriota *smf* patriot

patriotismo *sm* patriotism

patrocinador, ra *sm, f* sponsor

patrocinar *vt* to sponsor

patrocinio *sm* sponsorship

patrón, ona *sm, f* ❶ [*de obreros*] boss ❷ [*de criados*] master, *femenino* mistress ❸ [*de pensión* ETC] landlord, *femenino* landlady ❹ [*santo*] patron saint

■ **patrón** *sm* ❶ [*de barco*] skipper ❷ [*en costura*] pattern

patronal ◆ *adj* [*empresarial*] management ☼ *Sólo se usa delante del sustantivo.*

◆ *sf* ❶ [*de empresa*] management ❷ [*de país*] employers' organization

patrono, na *sm, f* ❶ [*de empresa - encargado*] boss; [*- empresario*] employer ❷ [*santo*] patron saint

patrulla *sf* patrol • **los policías vigilan el barrio en sus patrullas** the police guard watch over the area on their patrols ▶ **patrulla urbana** vigilante group

patrullar *vt* & *vi* to patrol

paulatino, na *adj* gradual ☼ *Los adjetivos ingleses son invariables.*

pausa *sf* ❶ [*descanso*] pause • **después de una pausa dijo: "estoy muy cansado"** after a pause he said: "I'm very tired" • **hacer una pausa** to pause • **con pausa** unhurriedly ▶ **pausa publicitaria** commercial break ❷ MÚSICA rest

pausado, da *adj* slow ☼ *Los adjetivos ingleses son invariables.*

pauta *sf* ❶ [*generalmente*] standard • **marcar la pauta** to set the standard ❷ [*en un papel*] guideline

pavimentación *sf* ❶ [*de carretera*] road surfacing ❷ [*de acera*] paving ❸ [*de suelo*] flooring

pavimento *sm* ❶ [*de carretera*] road surface ❷ [*de banqueta*] paving ❸ [*de suelo*] flooring

pavo, va *sm, f* [*ave*] turkey ▶ **pavo real** peacock, *femenino* peahen

pavor *sm* terror

pay *sm* pie

payasada *sf* • **hacer payasadas** to clown around

payasear *vi* to clown around

payaso, sa *sm, f* clown

paz *sf* ❶ [*ausencia de violencia*] peace • **no queremos la guerra, queremos vivir en paz** we don't want war, we want to live in peace • **dejar a alguien en paz** to

leave somebody alone • **deja a tu hermano en paz, que está haciendo su tarea** leave your brother alone, he's doing his homework • **estar o quedar en paz** to be quits • **hacer las paces** to make peace • **estuvieron peleadas varios días pero al final hicieron las paces** they fought for several days but in the end they made peace • **poner paz entre** to make peace between ❷ [*tranquilidad*] peacefulness
expresión **que en paz descanse, que descanse en paz** may he/she rest in peace

PC *sm* (*abreviatura de* personal computer) PC

PD (*abreviatura escrita de* posdata) PS

peaje *sm* toll

peatón *sm* pedestrian

peca *sf* freckle

pecado *sm* sin • **la pereza es uno de los siete pecados capitales** laziness is one of the seven deadly sins • **sería un pecado tirar este vestido** it would be a crime to throw out this dress • **estar en pecado** to be in sin • **morir en pecado** to die unrepentant ▶ **pecado mortal** mortal sin

pecador, ra *sm, f* sinner

pecar *vi* RELIGIÓN to sin

pecera *sf* ❶ [*rectangular*] fish tank ❷ [*redonda*] fish bowl

pecho *sm* ❶ [*tórax*] chest ❷ [*de mujer*] bosom ❸ [*mama*] breast • **dar pecho a** to breastfeed • **ya es hora de darle otra vez el pecho al bebé** now it's time to breastfeed the baby again ❹ [*en natación*] breaststroke • **nadar de pecho** to swim the breaststroke
expresión **a lo hecho, pecho** it's no use crying over spilt milk ▶ **tomarse algo a pecho** to take something to heart

pechuga *sf* [*de ave*] breast • **¿qué parte del pollo prefieres: la pata o la pechuga?** what part of the chicken do you prefer: the leg or the breast?

pecoso, sa *adj* freckly ☞ *Los adjetivos ingleses son invariables.*

peculiar *adj* ❶ [*característico*] typical ❷ [*curioso*] peculiar ☞ *Los adjetivos ingleses son invariables.*

peculiaridad *sf* ❶ [*cualidad*] uniqueness ❷ [*detalle*] particular feature

pedagogía *sf* education

pedagogo, ga *sm, f* ❶ [*especialista*] educator ❷ [*profesor*] teacher

pedal *sm* pedal ▶ **pedal de embrague** clutch (pedal) ▶ **pedal de freno** brake pedal

pedalear *vi* to pedal

pedante *adj* pompous ☞ *Los adjetivos ingleses son invariables.*

pedazo *sm* piece • **a pedazos** in pieces • **caerse a pedazos** to fall to pieces

pedestal *sm* pedestal
expresión **poner a alguien en un pedestal** to put somebody on a pedestal

pedestre *adj* on foot ☞ *Los adjetivos ingleses son invariables.*

pediatra *smf* pediatrician

pedido *sm* COMERCIO order • **hacer un pedido** to place an order

pedir ♦ *vt* ❶ [*generalmente*] to ask for • **pedir a alguien que haga algo** to ask somebody to do something • **te pedí que vinieras porque necesito ayuda** I asked you to come because I need help • **pedir prestado algo a alguien** to borrow something from somebody • **pedir a alguien (en matrimonio)** to ask for somebody's hand (in marriage) ❷ [*en comercios, restaurantes*] to order • **pedí dos pollos y ensalada para cinco** I ordered two chickens and salad for five ❸ [*exigir*] to demand ❹ [*requerir*] to call for ❺ [*poner precio*] • **pedir (por)** to ask (for) • **pide un millón por la moto** he's asking a million for the motorbike
♦ *vi* [*mendigar*] to beg

pedo *sm* familiar [*ventosidad*] fart • **tirarse un pedo** to fart

pedrada *sf* [*golpe*] • **a pedradas** by stoning • **matar a alguien a pedradas** to stone somebody to death

pegadizo, za *adj* ❶ [*música*] catchy ❷ [*contagioso*] catching ☞ *Los adjetivos ingleses son invariables.*

pegajoso, sa *adj* ❶ [*adhesivo*] sticky • **tengo las manos pegajosas, me las voy a lavar** I have sticky hands, I'm going to wash them ❷ despectivo [*persona*] clinging ☞ *Los adjetivos ingleses son invariables.*

pegamento *sm* glue

pegar ♦ *vt* ❶ [*adherir*] to stick ❷ [*con pegamento*] to glue • **pegué la taza rota con pegamento especial para cerámica** I glued the broken cup with special glue for ceramics ❸ [*póster, cartel*] to fix ❹ [*botón*] to sew on ❺ [*arrimar*] • **pegar algo a** to put something against • **pega la silla a la pared** put the chair against the wall ❻ [*golpear*] to hit • **a ese animal le deben haber pegado mucho, por eso es tan asustadizo** they must have hit that animal a lot, that's why it's so skittish ❼ [*dar - bofetada, paliza* ETC] to give; [*- golpe*] to deal • **pegar un salto** to jump • **pegué un salto cuando sonó el teléfono** I jumped when the telephone rang • **pegar un susto a alguien** to scare somebody • **el gato le pegó un susto cuando saltó sobre su falda** the cat scared her when it jumped on her skirt • **¡Qué susto me pegaste!** You made me jump! ❽ [*contagiar*] • **pegar algo a alguien** to give somebody something • **Susana me pegó su gripe cuando fui a visitarla** Susana gave me her flu when I went to visit her
♦ *vi* ❶ [*adherir*] to stick ❷ [*golpear*] to hit ❸ [*armonizar*] to go together • **pegar con** to go with ❹ [*sol*] to beat down
■ **pegarse** *v pronominal* ❶ [*adherirse*] to stick ❷ [*agredirse*] to fight ❸ [*golpearse*] • **pegarse (un golpe) con algo** to hit yourself against something ❹ [*contagiarse - enfermedad*] to be transmitted

pegatina *sf* sticker

peinado *sm* [*estilo, tipo*] hairstyle

peinar *vt* literal & figurado to comb

peine *sm* comb • **pasarse el peine** to comb your hair
expresión **enterarse de lo que vale un peine** familiar to find out what's what

p.ej. *(abreviatura escrita de* por ejemplo) e.g

Pekín *nombre propio* Peking; Beijing

peladilla *sf* sugared almond

pelado, da *adj* ❶ [*cabeza*] shorn ❷ [*piel, cara* ETC] peeling ❸ [*fruta*] peeled ❹ [*habitación, monte, árbol*] bare ❺ [*número*] exact; round ❻ *familiar* [*sin dinero*] broke ⚲ *Los adjetivos ingleses son invariables.*

pelaje *sm* ❶ [*de gato, oso, conejo*] fur ❷ [*de perro, caballo*] coat

pelar *vt* ❶ [*persona*] to cut the hair of ❷ [*fruta, papas*] to peel ❸ [*guisantes, marisco*] to shell ❹ [*aves*] to pluck ❺ [*conejos* ETC] to skin
expresión **hace un frío que pela** it's bitterly cold

peldaño *sm* ❶ step ❷ [*de escalera de mano*] rung

pelea *sf* ❶ [*a golpes*] fight • **le quedó un ojo morado después de una pelea en la escuela** he had a black eye after a fight at school ❷ [*riña*] row • **Luisa tuvo otra pelea con el novio** Luisa had another row with her boyfriend

pelear *vi* ❶ [*a golpes*] to fight • **los pueblos hispanoamericanos pelearon por conseguir su independencia** the Hispanic Americans fought to gain their independence ❷ [*a gritos*] to have a row ❸ [*esforzarse*] to struggle

peliagudo, da *adj* tricky ⚲ *Los adjetivos ingleses son invariables.*

película *sf* [*generalmente*] movie • **echar una película** to show a movie ▶ **película de dibujos animados** feature-length cartoon ▶ **película muda** silent movie ▶ **película del Oeste** western ▶ **película de terror** horror movie
expresión **de película** amazing

peligro *sm* danger • **correr peligro (de)** to be in danger (of) • **estar/poner en peligro** to be/put at risk • **en peligro de extinción** [*especie, animal*] endangered • **fuera de peligro** out of danger • **el paciente está fuera de peligro** the patient is out of danger • **peligro de incendio** fire hazard • **¡peligro de muerte!** danger!

peligroso, sa *adj* dangerous ⚲ *Los adjetivos ingleses son invariables.*

pelirrojo, ja ✦ *adj* red-headed ⚲ *Los adjetivos ingleses son invariables.*
✦ *sm, f* redhead

pellizcar *vt* [*generalmente*] to pinch

pellizco *sm* pinch • **dar un pellizco a alguien** to give somebody a pinch

pelo *sm* ❶ [*generalmente*] hair • **me lavo el pelo todos los días** I wash my hair every day ❷ [*de oso, conejo, gato*] fur ❸ [*de perro, caballo*] coat ❹ [*de una tela*] nap
expresiones **con pelos y señales** with all the details ▶ **no tener pelos en la lengua** *familiar* not to mince your words ▶ **poner a alguien los pelos de punta** *familiar* to make somebody's hair stand on end ▶ **por los pelos** by the skin of your teeth ▶ **tomar el pelo a alguien** *familiar* to pull somebody's leg

pelota *sf* ❶ [*generalmente*] DEPORTE ball • **jugar a la pelota** to play ball ▶ **pelota vasca** pelota ❷ *familiar* [*cabeza*] nut

pelotón *sm* ❶ [*de soldados*] squad ❷ [*de gente*] crowd ❸ DEPORTE pack

peluca *sf* wig

peluche *sm* plush

peludo, da *adj* hairy ⚲ *Los adjetivos ingleses son invariables.*

peluquería *sf* ❶ [*establecimiento*] hairdresser's (shop) ❷ [*oficio*] hairdressing

peluquero, ra *sm, f* hairdresser

peluquín *sm* toupee
expresión **¡ni hablar del peluquín!** *familiar* it's out of the question!

pelusa *sf* ❶ [*de tela*] fluff ❷ [*vello*] down

pelvis *sf invariable* pelvis

Pemex *smpl* (*abreviatura de* Petróleos Mexicanos) Mexican Oil

pena *sf* ❶ [*lástima*] shame; pity • **¡qué pena!** what a shame! • **dar pena** • **el pobre me da pena** I feel sorry for the poor thing ❷ [*tristeza*] sadness ❸ ⚲ *generalmente pl* [*desgracia*] problem ❹ ⚲ *generalmente pl* [*dificultad*] struggle ⚲ *incontable* • **a duras penas** with great difficulty ❺ [*castigo*] punishment • **so** o **bajo pena de** under penalty of ▶ **pena capital** o **de muerte** death penalty ❻ [*vergüenza*] embarrassment • **me da pena** I'm ashamed of it • **le da pena hablar en público** he's embarrassed to speak in public
expresión **vale la pena** it's worth it

penal ✦ *adj* criminal ⚲ *Los adjetivos ingleses son invariables.*
✦ *sm* prison

penalidad *sf* ⚲ *generalmente pl* suffering ⚲ *incontable*

penalti, penalty *sm* DEPORTE penalty

pendejo, ja *familiar* ✦ *adj* [*tonto*] stupid
✦ *sm, f* [*tonto*] jerk

pendiente ✦ *adj* ❶ [*por resolver*] pending • **hay varios asuntos pendientes** there are several matters pending ❷ [*deuda*] outstanding • **estar pendiente de a)** [*atento a*] to keep an eye on **b)** [*a la espera de*] to be waiting for ❸ [*asignatura*] failed ⚲ *Los adjetivos ingleses son invariables.*
✦ *sm* earring
✦ *sf* slope • **bajamos esquiando por la pendiente** we went skiing down the slope

pene *sm* penis

penetración *sf* ❶ [*generalmente*] penetration ▶ **penetración de mercado** ECONOMÍA market penetration ❷ [*sagacidad*] astuteness

penetrante *adj* ❶ [*intenso - dolor*] acute; [- *olor*] sharp; [- *frío*] biting; [- *mirada*] penetrating; [- *voz, sonido* ETC] piercing ❷ [*sagaz*] sharp ⚲ *Los adjetivos ingleses son invariables.*

penetrar ✦ *vi* • **penetrar en a)** [*internarse en*] to enter **b)** [*filtrarse por*] to get into; to penetrate **c)** [*perforar*] to pierce **d)** [*llegar a conocer*] to get to the bottom of
✦ *vt* ❶ [*introducirse en - arma, sonido* ETC] to pierce; to penetrate; [- *humedad, líquido*] to permeate; [- *emoción,*

P

sentimiento] to pierce ❷ [*llegar a conocer - secreto* ETC] to get to the bottom of ❸ [*sexualmente*] to penetrate

penicilina *sf* penicillin

península *sf* peninsula

peninsular *adj* peninsular ♀ *Los adjetivos ingleses son invariables.*

penitencia *sf* penance

penitenciaría *sf* penitentiary

penoso, sa *adj* ❶ [*trabajoso*] laborious ❷ [*lamentable*] distressing ❸ [*aspecto, espectáculo*] sorry ❹ [*vergonzoso*] shy ♀ *Los adjetivos ingleses son invariables.*

pensador, ra *sm, f* thinker

pensamiento *sm* ❶ [*generalmente*] thought ❷ [*mente*] mind ❸ [*idea*] idea ❹ BOTÁNICA pansy

pensar ✦ *vi* to think • **pensar en algo/en alguien/en hacer algo** to think about something/about somebody/about doing something • **piensa en un número** think of a number • **pensar sobre algo** to think about something • **pensar bien/mal de alguien** to think well/ill of somebody

expresión **dar que pensar a alguien** to give somebody food for thought

✦ *vt* ❶ [*reflexionar*] to think about • **voy a pensarlo y mañana te respondo** I'm going to think about it and tomorrow I'll give you an answer ❷ [*opinar, creer*] to think • **pensar algo de alguien/algo** to think something of somebody/something • **pienso que no vendrá** I don't think she'll come ❸ [*idear*] to think up ❹ [*tener la intención de*] • **pensar hacer algo** to intend to do something

pensativo, va *adj* pensive ♀ *Los adjetivos ingleses son invariables.*

pensión *sf* ❶ [*dinero*] pension ▶ **pensión de jubilación/de viudedad** retirement/widow's pension ❷ [*de huéspedes*] ≃ guest house • **media pensión** [*en hotel*] half board • **estar a media pensión** [*en colegio*] to have school dinners • **pensión completa** full board

pensionista *smf* [*jubilado*] pensioner

pentágono *sm* pentagon

pentagrama *sm* MÚSICA stave

penúltimo, ma *adj & sm, f* penultimate ♀ *Los adjetivos ingleses son invariables.*

penumbra *sf* half-light

peña *sf* ❶ [*grupo de amigos*] circle ❷ [*club*] club

peñasco *sm* large crag

peñón *sm* rock

peón *sm* ❶ [*obrero*] unskilled laborer ❷ farmhand ❸ [*en ajedrez*] pawn

peor ✦ *adj* ❶ ♀ *comparativo* • **peor (que)** worse (than) • **peor para él** that's his problem ❷ ♀ *superlativo* • **el/la peor...** the worst... ♀ *Los adjetivos ingleses son invariables.*

✦ *pronombre* • **el/la peor (de)** the worst (in) • **de las tres películas malas que vimos esta semana, la de hoy fue la peor de todas** out of the three bad movies we saw this week, today's was the worst of all • **el peor de todos** the worst of all • **lo peor fue que...** the worst thing was that...

✦ *adv* ❶ ♀ *comparativo* • **peor (que)** worse (than) • **la película de hoy fue peor que la que vimos ayer** today's movie was worse than the one we saw yesterday • **ahora veo peor** I see worse now • **estar peor** [*enfermo*] to get worse ❷ ♀ *superlativo* worst • **el que lo hizo peor** the one who did it (the) worst

pepinillo *sm* gherkin

pepino *sm* BOTÁNICA cucumber

expresión **me importa un pepino** I couldn't care less

pepita *sf* ❶ [*de fruta*] pip ❷ [*de oro*] nugget

pequeño, ña *adj* ❶ [*en tamaño*] small • **el paquete es pequeño** the package is small • **cuando era pequeña me encantaba jugar con muñecas** when I was little I loved to play with dolls • **me queda pequeño** it's too small for me ❷ [*hermano*] little ❸ [*posibilidad*] slight ❹ [*ingresos, cifras* ETC] low ♀ *Los adjetivos ingleses son invariables.*

pera *sf* ❶ [*fruta*] pear ❷ [*para ducha* ETC] (rubber) bulb

expresión **pedir peras al olmo** to ask (for) the impossible ▶ **ser una pera en dulce** to be a gem

percepción *sf* [*de los sentidos*] perception ▶ **percepción extrasensorial** extrasensory perception

percha *sf* ❶ [*de armario*] (coat) hanger ❷ [*de pared*] coat rack ❸ [*para pájaros*] perch

perchero *sm* ❶ [*de pared*] coat rack ❷ [*de pie*] coat stand

percibir *vt* ❶ [*con los sentidos*] to perceive ❷ [*por los oídos*] to hear ❸ [*ver*] to see ❹ [*cobrar*] to receive

percusión *sf* percussion

perdedor, ra *sm, f* loser

perder ✦ *vt* ❶ [*generalmente*] to lose • **perdí las llaves** I lost the keys • **llevas las de perder** you can't hope to win • **salir perdiendo** to come off worst ❷ [*desperdiciar*] to waste • **perder tiempo** to waste time ❸ [*tren, oportunidad*] to miss • **si no salimos ya mismo, vas a perder el avión** if we don't leave right now, you're going to miss the plane

✦ *vi* [*salir derrotado*] to lose • **está triste porque su equipo perdió** he's sad because his team lost

expresión **echar algo a perder** to spoil something ▶ **echarse a perder** [*alimento*] to go off

■ **perderse** *v pronominal* ❶ [*generalmente*] to get lost • **quiero irme antes de que oscurezca, para evitar perderme** I want to go before it gets dark, to avoid getting lost • **¡piérdete!** get lost! ❷ [*desaparecer*] to disappear ❸ [*desperdiciarse*] to be wasted ❹ [*desaprovechar*] • **¡no te lo pierdas!** don't miss it! ❺ *figurado* [*por los vicios*] to be beyond salvation

perdición *sf* undoing

pérdida *sf* ❶ [*generalmente*] loss • **no ha logrado recuperarse de la pérdida de su madre** she hasn't been able to recover from the loss of her mother • **por la sequía, los agricultores sufrieron pérdidas graves** because of the drought, the farmers suffered severe losses ❷ [*de tiempo, dinero*] waste • **qué pérdida de tiempo** what a waste of time ❸ [*escape*] leak

expresión **no tiene pérdida** you can't miss it

perdidamente *adv* hopelessly

perdido, da *adj* ❶ [*extraviado*] lost • **dar algo por perdido** to give something up for lost ❷ [*animal, bala*] stray ❸ [*sucio*] filthy ❹ *familiar* [*de remate*] complete:🔆 *Los adjetivos ingleses son invariables.*

expresión estar perdido to be done for

perdiz *sf* partridge

perdón *sm* ❶ [*generalmente*] • **pedir perdón** to apologize • **nos pidió perdón por no haber venido a visitarnos** he apologized for not having come to visit us • **no tener perdón** to be unforgivable • **¡perdón!** I'm sorry! • **te pisé sin querer, perdón** I accidentally stepped on you, I'm sorry • **perdón, ¿me deja pasar?** excuse me, could you let me through? ❷ DERECHO pardon ❸ RELIGIÓN forgiveness

perdonar ◆ *vt* ❶ [*generalmente*] to forgive • **lo hice sin querer, espero que me perdones** I did it unintentionally, I hope that you forgive me • **perdóname, te pisé sin querer** excuse me, I stepped on you accidentally • **perdonarle algo a alguien** to forgive somebody for something • **perdone que le moleste** sorry to bother you ❷ [*eximir de - deuda, condena*] • **perdonar algo a alguien** to let somebody off something • **perdonarle la vida a alguien** to spare somebody their life

◆ *vi* • **perdone, ¿cómo ha dicho?** excuse me, what did you say?

perdurar *vi* ❶ [*durar mucho*] to endure ❷ [*persistir*] to persist

perecedero, ra *adj* ❶ [*productos*] perishable ❷ [*naturaleza*] transitory:🔆 *Los adjetivos ingleses son invariables.*

perecer *vi* to perish

peregrinación *sf* RELIGIÓN pilgrimage

peregrino, na ◆ *adj* ❶ [*ave*] migratory ❷ *figurado* [*extraño*] strange:🔆 *Los adjetivos ingleses son invariables.*

◆ *sm, f* [*persona*] pilgrim

perejil *sm* parsley

perenne *adj* BOTÁNICA perennial:🔆 *Los adjetivos ingleses son invariables.*

pereza *sf* laziness • **sentir pereza** to feel lazy • **darle pereza a alguien : me da pereza ponerme a estudiar** I don't feel like starting to study now

perezoso, sa *adj* lazy:🔆 *Los adjetivos ingleses son invariables.*

perfección *sf* perfection • **habla tres idiomas a la perfección** she speaks three languages to perfection • **es de una gran perfección** it's exceptionally good

perfeccionar *vt* ❶ [*redondear*] to perfect ❷ [*mejorar*] to improve

perfeccionista *adj & smf* perfectionist:🔆 *Los adjetivos ingleses son invariables.*

perfecto, ta *adj* perfect:🔆 *Los adjetivos ingleses son invariables.*

perfil *sm* ❶ [*contorno*] outline ❷ [*de cara, cuerpo*] profile • **de perfil** in profile ❸ *figurado* [*característica*] characteristic ❹ *figurado* [*retrato moral*] profile ❺ GEOMETRÍA cross section

perforar *vt* ❶ [*horadar*] to perforate ❷ [*agujero*] to drill ❸ INFORMÁTICA to punch

perfume *sm* perfume • **los perfumes franceses son apreciados en todo el mundo** French perfumes are esteemed throughout the world • **me fascina el perfume de los jazmines** the scent of jasmine fascinates me

perfumería *sf* ❶ [*tienda, arte*] perfumery ❷ [*productos*] perfumes *pl*

pergamino *sm* parchment

periferia *sf* ❶ periphery ❷ [*alrededores*] outskirts *pl*

periférico, ca *adj* ❶ peripheral ❷ [*barrio*] outlying:🔆 *Los adjetivos ingleses son invariables.*

perífrasis *sf invariable* • **perífrasis (verbal)** compound verb

perilla *sf* goatee

expresión venir de perilla(s) to be just the right thing

perímetro *sm* perimeter

periódico, ca *adj* periodic • **es importante hacer visitas periódicas al dentista** it's important to make periodic visits to the dentist:🔆 *Los adjetivos ingleses son invariables.*

■ **periódico** *sm* newspaper ▶ **periódico dominical** Sunday paper

periodismo *sm* journalism

periodista *smf* journalist

periodo, período *sm* ❶ [*de tiempo*] period ❷ DEPORTE half

periquete *sm* • **en un periquete** *familiar* in a jiffy

periquito *sm* parakeet

perjudicar *vt* to damage • **es mejor que no fumes, el tabaco perjudica la salud** it's better that you don't smoke, smoking damages your health • **esta sequía va a perjudicar a los productores rurales** this drought is going to hurt farmers

perjudicial *adj* • **perjudicial (para)** harmful (to) • **fumar es perjudicial para la salud** smoking is harmful to your health:🔆 *Los adjetivos ingleses son invariables.*

perjuicio *sm* harm :🔆 *incontable*

perla *sf* ❶ pearl ▶ **perla de cultivo** cultured pearl ❷ *figurado* [*maravilla*] gem

expresión de perlas great ; fine ▶ **me viene de perlas** it's just the right thing

permanecer *vi* ❶ [*en un lugar*] to stay ❷ [*en un estado*] to remain

permanencia *sf* ❶ [*en un lugar*] staying ❷ [*en un estado*] continuation

permanente ◆ *adj* ❶ permanent ❷ [*comisión*] standing:🔆 *Los adjetivos ingleses son invariables.*

◆ *sf* perm • **hacerse la permanente** to have a perm

permiso *sm* ❶ [*autorización*] permission • **dar permiso para hacer algo** to give permission to do something • **le dieron permiso para faltar tres días** they gave him permission to miss three days • **con permiso** excuse me • **con permiso, ¿puedo pasar?** excuse me, can I get by? ❷ [*documento*] licence • **permiso de armas** gun licence • **permiso de conducir** driver's license ▶ **permiso de residencia** residence permit ❸ [*vacaciones*] leave

permitir *vt* to allow • **permitir a alguien hacer algo** to allow somebody to do something • **no les permitieron entrar porque el concierto ya había empezado** they didn't allow them to enter because the concert had already started • **¿me permite?** may I?

pero ◆ *conjunción* but • **la casa es vieja pero céntrica** the house may be old, but it's central • **el modelo de ese vestido es lindo, pero no me gusta el color** the style of that dress is pretty, but I don't like the color • **pero ¿qué es tanto ruido?** but what on earth is all this noise about? • **pero ¿yo no te había dado las instrucciones para llegar a mi casa?** but, hadn't I given you directions to get to my house?
◆ *sm* fault • **poner peros a todo** to find fault with everything

perpendicular *adj* perpendicular • **ser perpendicular a algo** to be at right angles to something ⚲ *Los adjetivos ingleses son invariables.*

perpetrar *vt* to perpetrate

perpetuar *vt* to perpetuate

perpetuo, tua *adj* ❶ [*generalmente*] perpetual ❷ [*para toda la vida*] lifelong ❸ DERECHO life ⚲ *Sólo se usa delante del sustantivo.*

perplejo, ja *adj* perplexed ⚲ *Los adjetivos ingleses son invariables.*

perrera *sf* ❶ [*lugar*] kennels *pl* ❷ [*vehículo*] dogcatcher's van

perrería *sf familiar* • **hacer perrerías a alguien** to play dirty tricks on somebody

perro, rra *sm, f* [*animal*] dog, *femenino* bitch ▶ **perro callejero** stray dog ▶ **perro de caza** hunting dog ▶ **perro de compañía** pet dog ▶ **perro faldero** lapdog ▶ **perro lazarillo** guide dog ▶ **perro lobo** German shepherd ▶ **perro pastor** sheepdog ▶ **perro policía** police dog
expresión echar los perros a alguien to have a go at somebody ▶ **ser perro viejo** to be an old hand

persecución *sf* ❶ [*seguimiento*] pursuit ❷ [*acoso*] persecution

perseguir *vt* ❶ [*seguir, tratar de obtener*] to pursue ❷ [*acosar*] to persecute ❸ [*mala suerte, problema* ETC] to dog

perseverante *adj* persistent ⚲ *Los adjetivos ingleses son invariables.*

persiana *sf* shade

persistente *adj* persistent ⚲ *Los adjetivos ingleses son invariables.*

persistir *vi* • **persistir (en)** to persist (in)

persona *sf* ❶ [*individuo*] person, *plural* people • **de persona a persona** person to person • **cien personas** a hundred people • **muchas personas son partidarias del reciclaje** many people are in favor of recycling • **en persona** in person • **por persona** per head • **ser buena persona** to be nice ▶ **persona mayor** adult; grown-up ❷ DERECHO party ❸ GRAMÁTICA person

personaje *sm* ❶ [*persona importante*] important person ❷ [*de obra*] character • **el personaje principal de una película es el protagonista** the main character of a film is the protagonist
expresión ser todo un personaje *familiar* to be a real big shot

personal ◆ *adj* ❶ [*generalmente*] personal ❷ [*teléfono, dirección*] private ⚲ *Los adjetivos ingleses son invariables.*
◆ *sm* [*trabajadores*] staff

personalidad *sf* ❶ [*características*] personality, *plural* personalities • **tiene una personalidad muy abierta** she has a very open personality ❷ [*persona famosa*] celebrity, *plural* celebrities ❸ [*persona importante*] figure • **es una personalidad de la política** he's a political figure

personalizar *vi* [*nombrar*] to name names

personificar *vt* to personify

perspectiva *sf* ❶ [*generalmente*] perspective ❷ [*paisaje*] view ❸ [*futuro*] prospect • **en perspectiva** in prospect

perspicacia *sf* perceptiveness

perspicaz *adj* perceptive ⚲ *Los adjetivos ingleses son invariables.*

persuadir *vt* to persuade • **persuadir a alguien para que haga algo** to persuade somebody to do something

persuasión *sf* persuasion

persuasivo, va *adj* persuasive ⚲ *Los adjetivos ingleses son invariables.*

pertenecer *vi* • **pertenecer a** to belong to • **este reloj de bolsillo perteneció a mi abuelo** this pocket watch belonged to my grandfather • **¿a quién pertenece este paraguas?** who does this umbrella belong to? • **¿todavía perteneces al club de coleccionadores de sellos?** do you still belong to the stamp collectors club?

pertenencia *sf* ❶ [*propiedad*] ownership ❷ [*afiliación*] membership
■ **pertenencias** *sfpl* [*enseres*] belongings

pértiga *sf* ❶ [*vara*] pole ❷ DEPORTE pole-vault

pertinente *adj* ❶ [*adecuado*] appropriate ❷ [*relativo*] relevant ⚲ *Los adjetivos ingleses son invariables.*

perturbar *vt* ❶ [*trastornar*] to disrupt ❷ [*inquietar*] to disturb ❸ [*enloquecer*] to perturb

Perú *nombre propio* • **(el) Perú** Peru

peruano, na *adj* & *sm, f* Peruvian ⚲ *Los adjetivos ingleses son invariables.*

perversión *sf* perversion

perverso, sa *adj* depraved ⚲ *Los adjetivos ingleses son invariables.*

pervertido, da *sm, f* pervert

pervertir *vt* to corrupt

pesa *sf* ❶ [*generalmente*] weight ❷ ⚲ *generalmente pl* DEPORTE weights *pl* • **alzar pesas** to lift weights

pesadez *sf* ❶ [*peso*] weight ❷ [*sensación*] heaviness ❸ [*molestia, fastidio*] drag ❹ [*aburrimiento*] ponderousness

pesadilla *sf* nightmare

pesado, da ◆ *adj* ❶ [*generalmente*] heavy • **este baúl es muy pesado** this trunk is very heavy • **es mejor evitar comidas pesadas antes de irse a dormir** it's best to avoid heavy foods before going to sleep ❷ [*caluroso*] sultry ❸ [*lento*] sluggish ❹ [*duro*] difficult ❺ [*aburrido*] boring ❻ [*molesto*] annoying • **¡qué pesado eres!** you're so annoying! ☀ *Los adjetivos ingleses son invariables.*

◆ *sm, f* bore

pésame *sm* condolences *pl* • **dar el pésame** to offer your condolences • **mi más sentido pésame** my deepest sympathies

pesar ◆ *sm* ❶ [*tristeza*] grief ❷ [*arrepentimiento*] remorse

expresión **a pesar mío** against my will

◆ *vt* ❶ [*determinar el peso de*] to weigh • **por favor, ¿me podría pesar esta bolsa de naranjas?** please, could you weigh this bag of oranges for me? ❷ [*examinar*] to weigh up

◆ *vi* ❶ [*tener peso*] to weigh • **el bebé pesa siete kilos** the baby weighs seven kilos ❷ [*ser pesado*] to be heavy ❸ [*importar*] to play an important part ❹ [*entristecer*] • **me pesa tener que decirte esto** I'm sorry to have to tell you this

---

expresar un pesar

- **It really upsets me.** Me apena muchísimo.
- **Unfortunately, I couldn't get in touch with him.** Desgraciadamente no lo he podido localizar.
- **It's a real shame that we can't see each other any more.** Es una verdadera pena que no podamos continuar viéndonos.

---

pesca *sf* ❶ [*acción*] fishing • **ir de pesca** to go fishing ❷ **pesca con caña** angling ❷ **pesca con red** net fishing ❷ [*lo pescado*] catch

pescadería *sf* fishmonger

pescadilla *sf* whiting

pescado *sm* fish • **el pescado asado es mi plato favorito** grilled fish is my favorite dish

pescador, ra *sm, f* fisherman, *plural* fishermen, femenino fisherwoman, *plural* fisherwomen

pescar ◆ *vt* ❶ [*peces*] to catch • **en un solo día pescamos 25 truchas** in only one day we caught 25 trout ❷ *figurado* [*enfermedad*] to catch ❸ *familiar & figurado* [*conseguir*] to land ❹ *familiar & figurado* [*atrapar*] to catch • **¡te pesqué con las manos en la masa!** I caught you red-handed!

◆ *vi* to go fishing • **salimos a pescar con el abuelo** we went fishing with our grandfather

pescuezo *sm* neck

pesebre *sm* ❶ [*para los animales*] manger ❷ [*belén*] Nativity scene

pesero *sm* ▶ *para explicar lo que es puedes decir:* it's a fixed-rate taxi service

pesimismo *sm* pessimism

pesimista ◆ *adj* pessimistic ☀ *Los adjetivos ingleses son invariables.*

◆ *smf* pessimist

pésimo, ma ◆ *superlativo* = **malo**

◆ *adj* terrible ☀ *Los adjetivos ingleses son invariables.*

peso *sm* ❶ [*generalmente*] weight • **¿tiene idea del peso de esa valija?** do you have any idea what the weight of that suitcase is? • **tiene un kilo de peso** it weighs a kilo ▶ **peso atómico/molecular** atomic/molecular weight ▶ **peso bruto/neto** gross/net weight ▶ **peso muerto** dead weight ❷ [*moneda*] peso • **¿a cuántos pesos chilenos equivale un peso mexicano?** how many Chilean pesos equal a Mexican peso? ❸ [*de atletismo*] shot ❹ [*balanza*] scales *pl*

pestaña *sf* [*de párpado*] eyelash ▶ **pestañas postizas** false eyelashes

expresión **quemarse las pestañas** to burn the midnight oil

pestañear *vi* to blink

expresión **sin pestañear** without batting an eyelid

peste *sf* ❶ [*enfermedad, plaga*] plague • **en Europa hubo varias pestes que diezmaron a la población** in Europe there were several plagues that decimated the population ▶ **peste bubónica** bubonic plague ❷ *familiar* [*mal olor*] stink • **¡qué peste!** what a stink!

expresión **decir pestes de alguien** to heap abuse on somebody

pesticida *sm* pesticide

pestillo *sm* ❶ [*cerrojo*] bolt • **echar el pestillo** to shoot the bolt ❷ [*mecanismo, en verjas*] latch

petaca *sf* ❶ [*para cigarrillos*] cigarette case ❷ [*para tabaco*] tobacco pouch ❸ [*para bebidas*] flask ❹ [*maleta*] suitcase

pétalo *sm* petal

petardo *sm* firecracker

petición *sf* ❶ [*acción*] request • **hicimos una petición al alcalde** we made a request to the mayor • **a petición de** at the request of ❷ DERECHO [*escrito*] petition • **entregaron una petición al patrón** they delivered a petition to the boss

petrificar *vt* literal & figurado to petrify

petrodólar *sm* petrodollar

petróleo *sm* oil

petrolífero, ra *adj* oil ☀ *Sólo se usa delante del sustantivo.*

peyorativo, va *adj* pejorative ☀ *Los adjetivos ingleses son invariables.*

pez *sm* fish, *plural* fish • **hay muchos peces en este río** there are many fish in this river ▶ **pez de colores** goldfish ▶ **pez de río** freshwater fish ▶ **pez espada** swordfish ▶ **pez gordo** familiar & figurado big shot

pezón *sm* [*de pecho*] nipple

pezuña *sf* hoof, *plural* hooves

pianista *smf* pianist

piano *sm* piano

piar *vi* to cheep

PIB (*abreviatura de* producto interior bruto) *sm* GDP

pica *sf* ❶ [*naipe*] spade ❷ [*lanza*] pike
expresión **poner una pica en Flandes** to do the impossible

picadero *sm* [*de caballos*] riding school

picadillo *sm* ❶ [*de carne*] mince ❷ [*de verdura*] chopped vegetables *pl*
expresión **hacer picadillo a alguien** *familiar* to beat somebody to a pulp

picado, da *adj* [*marcado - piel*] pockmarked; [*fruta*] bruised ❷ [*agujereado*] perforated ❸ [*triturado - alimento*] chopped; [*- tabaco*] cut ❹ [*diente*] decayed ❺ [*mar*] choppy ❻ *figurado* [*enfadado*] annoyed 🔆 *Los adjetivos ingleses son invariables.*

picadora *sf* grinder

picadura *sf* ❶ [*de mosquito, serpiente*] bite ❷ [*de avispa, ortiga, escorpión*] sting ❸ [*tabaco*] (cut) tobacco 🔆 *incontable*

picante ♦ *adj* ❶ [*comida* ETC] spicy ❷ *figurado* [*obsceno*] saucy 🔆 *Los adjetivos ingleses son invariables.*
♦ *sm* ❶ [*comida*] spicy food ❷ [*sabor*] spiciness

picar ♦ *vt* ❶ [*sujeto: mosquito, serpiente*] to bite • **estaba en el jardín al anochecer y me picaron los mosquitos** I was in the yard at nightfall and the mosquitos bit me ❷ [*sujeto: avispa, escorpión, ortiga*] to sting ❸ [*escocer*] to itch • **me pican los ojos** my eyes are stinging ❹ [*triturar - verdura*] to chop; [*- carne*] to mince • **para esa sopa, hay que picar las verduras en pedazos chicos** for that soup, you have to chop up the vegetables into small pieces ❺ [*sujeto: ave*] to peck ❻ [*aperitivo*] to pick at ❼ [*tierra, piedra, hielo*] to hack at ❽ *figurado* [*enojar*] to irritate ❾ *figurado* [*estimular - persona, caballo*] to spur on; [*- curiosidad*] to prick ❿ [*perforar - boleto, ficha*] to punch
♦ *vi* ❶ [*alimento*] to be hot • **ten cuidado, que esta salsa pica mucho** be careful, this salsa is very hot ❷ [*pez*] to bite • **los peces demoraron varias horas en picar** the fish took several hours to bite ❸ [*escocer*] to itch ❹ [*ave*] to peck ❺ [*tomar un aperitivo*] to nibble ❻ [*sol*] to burn ❼ [*dejarse engañar*] to take the bait

pichón *sm* ❶ [*paloma*] young pigeon ❷ [*novato*] novice

picnic (pl picnics) *sm* picnic

pico *sm* ❶ [*de ave*] beak ❷ [*punta, saliente*] corner ❸ [*herramienta*] pick ❹ [*cumbre*] peak ❺ [*cantidad indeterminada*] • **cincuenta y pico** fifty-odd • **llegó a las cinco y pico** he got there just after five ❻ *familiar* [*boca*] gob
expresión **ser** o **tener un pico de oro** to be a smooth talker

picor *sm* ❶ [*del calor*] burning ❷ [*que irrita*] itch

picoso, sa *adj* spicy 🔆 *Los adjetivos ingleses son invariables.*

picotear *vt* [*sujeto: ave*] to peck

pie *sm* ❶ [*generalmente*] ANATOMÍA foot, *plural* feet • **a pie** on foot • **estar de** o **en pie** to be standing • **ponerse de** o **en pie** to stand up • **de pies a cabeza** *figurado* from head to toe • **seguir en pie** [*vigente*] to be still valid • **en pie de igualdad** on an equal footing • **en pie de guerra** at war ▶ **pie de foto** caption ❷ [*de micrófono, lámpara* ETC] stand ❸ [*de copa*] stem
expresiones **al pie de la letra** to the letter; word for word ▶ **andar con pies de plomo** to tread carefully ▶ **buscarle (los) tres pies al gato** to split hairs ▶ **dar pie a alguien para que haga algo** to give somebody cause to do something ▶ **no tener ni pies ni cabeza** to make no sense at all ▶ **no tenerse de** o **en pie a)** [*por cansancio*] not to be able to stand up a minute longer **b)** *figurado* [*por ser absurdo*] not to stand up ▶ **pararle los pies a alguien** to put somebody in their place ▶ **tener un pie en la tumba** to have one foot in the grave

piedad *sf* ❶ [*compasión*] pity • **por piedad** for pity's sake • **tener piedad de alguien** to take pity on somebody ❷ [*religiosidad*] piety

piedra *sf* ❶ [*generalmente*] stone ▶ **piedra angular** *literal & figurado* cornerstone ▶ **piedra pómez** pumice stone ▶ **piedra preciosa** precious stone ▶ **piedra de toque** touchstone ❷ [*de mechero*] flint

piel *sf* ❶ ANATOMÍA skin • **los bebés tienen la piel suave y delicada** babies have soft, delicate skin ▶ **piel de gallina** goose bumps ❷ [*cuero*] leather • **la piel se utiliza para fabricar zapatos** leather is used to make shoes ❸ [*pelo*] fur • **los abrigos de piel han pasado de moda** fur coats have gone out of style ❹ [*cáscara*] skin

pierna *sf* leg
expresión **estirar las piernas** to stretch your legs

pieza *sf* ❶ [*generalmente*] piece • **acabo de comprar un rompecabezas de 1.000 piezas** I just bought a 1,000 piece puzzle ❷ [*de mecanismo*] part ▶ **piezas de recambio** spare parts ❸ [*obra dramática*] play ❹ [*habitación*] room • **mis dos hermanos comparten una pieza y mi hermana y yo tenemos otra** my two brothers share one room and my sister and I have another
expresión **dejar/quedarse de una pieza** to leave/be thunderstruck

pigmento *sm* pigment

pijama *sm* pyjamas *pl*

pila *sf* ❶ [*generador*] battery, *plural* batteries • **esta radio funciona con electricidad o a pila** this radio works with electricity or with batteries ❷ [*montón*] pile • **una pila de libros** a pile of books • **tiene una pila de deudas** he's up to his neck in debt ❸ [*fregadero*] sink

pilar *sm* *literal & figurado* pillar

píldora *sf* ❶ pill ❷ [*anticonceptivo*] • **la píldora** the pill ▶ **píldora del día siguiente** morning after pill
expresión **dorar la píldora** to sugar the pill

pillar ♦ *vt* ❶ [*generalmente*] to catch ❷ [*chiste, explicación*] to get ❸ [*atropellar*] to knock down
♦ *vi* *familiar* [*hallarse*] • **me pilla lejos** it's out of the way for me • **me pilla de camino** it's on my way • **no me pilla de nuevas** it doesn't surprise me

pillo, lla *familiar* ◆ *adj* ❶ [*travieso*] mischievous ❷ [*astuto*] crafty ☼ *Los adjetivos ingleses son invariables.*
◆ *sm, f* [*pícaro*] rascal
pilotar *vt* ❶ [*avión*] to fly ❷ [*coche*] to drive ❸ [*barco*] to steer
piloto ◆ *smf* ❶ [*generalmente*] pilot ▶ **piloto automático** automatic pilot ❷ [*de coche*] driver
◆ *sm* [*luz - de coche*] tail light ; [*- de aparato*] pilot lamp
◆ *adj invariable* pilot ☼ *Sólo se usa delante del sustantivo.*
pimentón *sm* ❶ [*dulce*] paprika ❷ [*picante*] cayenne pepper
pimienta *sf* pepper ▶ **pimienta blanca/negra** white/ black pepper
pimiento *sm* pepper ▶ **pimiento morrón** bell pepper
pinacoteca *sf* art gallery
pinar *sm* pine wood
pincel *sm* ❶ [*para pintar*] paintbrush ❷ [*para maquillar* ETC] brush
pinchar *vt* ❶ [*punzar - generalmente*] to prick ❷ [*penetrar*] to pierce
pinche ◆ *sm, f* kitchen boy, *femenino* kitchen maid
◆ *adj familiar* lousy ☼ *Los adjetivos ingleses son invariables.*
ping-pong® *sm* ping-pong
pingüino *sm* penguin
pino *sm* pine
expresión en el quinto pino in the middle of nowhere
pintado, da *adj* ❶ [*coloreado*] colored • **'recién pintado'** wet paint ❷ [*maquillado*] made-up ❸ [*moteado*] speckled ☼ *Los adjetivos ingleses son invariables.*
pintar ◆ *vt* ❶ [*con pintura*] to paint • **le pidieron que pintara un retrato de la familia** they asked him to paint a family portrait • **si quieres ahorrar dinero, podemos pintar nosotros mismos la casa** if you want to save money, we can paint the house ourselves • **pintar algo de negro** to paint something black ❷ [*significar, importar*] • **aquí no pinto nada** there's no place for me here • **¿qué pinto yo en este asunto?** where do I come in?
◆ *vi* [*con pintura*] to paint
■ **pintarse** *v pronominal* [*maquillarse*] to make yourself up
pintor, ra *sm, f* painter
pintoresco, ca *adj* ❶ [*bonito*] picturesque ❷ [*extravagante*] colorful ☼ *Los adjetivos ingleses son invariables.*
pintura *sf* ❶ ARTE painting • **Irma presentó sus primeras pinturas en una galería de la ciudad** Irma showed her first paintings in a gallery in the city ▶ **pintura a la acuarela** watercolor ▶ **pintura al óleo** oil painting ❷ [*materia*] paint • **para pintar toda la casa necesi-**

tamos muchas latas de pintura in order to paint the whole house we need a lot of cans of paint
pinza *sf* ☼ *generalmente pl* ❶ [*generalmente*] tweezers *pl* ❷ [*de tender ropa*] clothespin ❸ [*de animal*] pincer ❹ [*pliegue*] fold
piña *sf* ❶ [*del pino*] pine cone ❷ [*ananás*] pineapple
piñata *sf* ▶ *para explicar lo que es puedes decir*: it's a decorated figure full of candy which blindfolded children try to break open with sticks at parties
piñón *sm* ❶ [*fruto*] pine nut ❷ [*rueda dentada*] pinion
piojo *sm* louse, *plural* lice
pionero, ra *sm, f* pioneer
pipa *sf* [*para fumar*] pipe
expresión pasarlo pipa *familiar* to have a whale of a time
pipí *sm familiar* wee-wee • **hacer pipí** to have a wee-wee
pique *sm* ❶ [*enfado*] grudge ❷ [*rivalidad*] rivalry
expresión irse a pique a) [*barco*] to sink **b)** [*negocio*] to go under **c)** [*plan*] to fail
piquete *sm* [*grupo*] ▶ **piquete de ejecución** firing squad ▶ **piquete (de huelga)** picket
piragua *sf* canoe
piragüismo *sm* canoeing
pirámide *sf* pyramid
piraña *sf* piranha
pirata ◆ *adj* ❶ pirate ☼ *Sólo se usa delante del sustantivo.* • **el mercado de CDs y videos piratas aumenta día a día** the pirate CD and video market grows daily ❷ [*disco*] bootleg
◆ *smf literal & figurado* pirate ▶ **pirata informático** hacker
piratear ◆ *vi* ❶ [*generalmente*] to be involved in piracy ❷ INFORMÁTICA to hack
◆ *vt* INFORMÁTICA to hack into
pírex *sm* Pyrex®
pirómano, na *sm, f* pyromaniac
piropo *sm familiar* flirtatious remark, ≃ wolf whistle
pirotecnia *sf* pyrotechnics ☼ *incontable*
pirueta *sf* pirouette
piruleta *sf* lollipop
pirulí (pl pirulís) *sm* lollipop
pis (pl pises) *sm familiar* pee
pisada *sf* ❶ [*acción*] footstep • **lo oigo cuando llega porque sus pisadas son muy fuertes** I hear him when he arrives because his footsteps are very loud ❷ [*huella*] footprint • **en la luna ha habido pisadas humanas desde 1969** there have been human footprints on the moon since 1969
expresión seguir las pisadas de alguien to follow in somebody's footsteps
pisar *vt* ❶ [*con el pie*] to tread on ❷ [*uvas*] to tread ❸ *figurado* [*llegar a*] to set foot in ❹ *figurado* [*despre-*

ciar] to trample on ❺ *figurado* [*anticiparse*] • **pisar un contrato a alguien** to beat somebody to a contract • **pisar una idea a alguien** to think of something before somebody

expresión **pisar fuerte** *figurado* to be firing on all cylinders

piscina *sf* swimming pool ▶ **piscina al aire libre** open air swimming pool ▶ **piscina climatizada** heated swimming pool

Piscis ◆ *sm* [*zodiaco*] Pisces
◆ *smf* [*persona*] Pisces

piso *sm* ❶ [*planta*] floor ❷ [*suelo - de carretera*] surface; [*- de edificio*] floor ❸ [*capa*] layer

pisotear *vt* ❶ [*con el pie*] to trample on ❷ [*humillar*] to scorn

pista *sf* ❶ [*generalmente*] track ▶ **pista de aterrizaje** runway ▶ **pista de baile** dance floor ▶ **pista cubierta** indoor track ▶ **pista de esquí** ski slope ▶ **pista de hielo** ice rink ❷ *figurado* [*indicio*] clue • **te voy a dar una pista para ayudarte a encontrar el tesoro escondido** I'm going to give you a clue to help you find the hidden treasure

pistacho *sm* pistachio

pistola *sf* ❶ [*arma - con cilindro*] gun; [*- sin cilindro*] pistol ❷ [*pulverizador*] spraygun • **pintar a pistola** to spray-paint

pistolero, ra *sm, f* [*persona*] gunman

pistón *sm* ❶ MECÁNICA piston ❷ MÚSICA [*corneta*] cornet; [*llave*] key

pitar ◆ *vt* [*abuchear*] • **pitar a alguien** to whistle at somebody in disapproval
◆ *vi* ❶ [*tocar el pito*] to blow a whistle ❷ [*del coche*] to toot your horn

pitido *sm* whistle

pito *sm* ❶ [*silbato*] whistle ❷ [*claxon*] horn

pitón¹ ◆ *sm* ❶ [*cuerno*] horn ❷ [*pitorro*] spout ❸ [*del árbol*] shoot ❹ nozzle
◆ *sf* ZOOLOGÍA python

pitonisa *sf* fortune-teller

piyama *sm o sf* pajamas ▶ **unas piyamas** a pair of pyjamas

pizarra *sf* ❶ [*roca, material*] slate ❷ [*encerado*] blackboard

pizarrón *sm* blackboard

pizca *sf* familiar ❶ [*generalmente*] tiny bit ❷ [*de sal*] pinch ❸ [*cosecha*] harvest

pizza *sf* pizza

pizzería *sf* pizzeria

placa *sf* ❶ [*lámina*] plate • **desde que se fracturó el cráneo, lleva una placa de metal en la cabeza** since he fractured his skull, he has a metal plate in his head ▶ **placa solar** solar panel ❷ [*de madera*] sheet ❸ [*inscripción*] plaque ❹ [*de policía*] badge ❺ [*matrícula*] number plate ❻ [*de cocina*] ring ❼ ELECTRÓNICA board ❽ ▶ **placa dental** dental plaque

placenta *sf* placenta

placentero, ra *adj* pleasant ❢ *Los adjetivos ingleses son invariables.*

placer *sm* pleasure • **ha sido un placer (conocerle)** it has been a pleasure meeting you

plácido, da *adj* ❶ [*persona*] placid ❷ [*día, vida, conversación*] peaceful ❢ *Los adjetivos ingleses son invariables.*

plaga *sf* ❶ [*generalmente*] plague ❷ AGRICULTURA blight ❸ [*animal*] pest ❹ [*epidemia*] epidemic

plagado, da *adj* • **plagado (de)** infested (with) ❢ *Los adjetivos ingleses son invariables.*

plagiar *vt* to plagiarize

plagio *sm* plagiarism

plan *sm* ❶ [*proyecto, programa*] plan • **no tenemos planes para mañana** we don't have any plans for tomorrow ❷ *familiar* [*ligue*] date ❸ *familiar* [*modo, forma*] • **lo dijo en plan serio** he was serious about it • **¡vaya plan de vida!** what a life! • **si te pones en ese plan...** if you're going to be like that about it...

plana *sf* page • **en primera plana** on the front page

expresión **enmendarle la plana a alguien** to find fault with somebody

plancha *sf* ❶ [*para planchar*] iron ▶ **plancha de vapor** steam iron ❷ [*para cocinar*] grill • **a la plancha** grilled ❸ [*placa*] plate ❹ [*de madera*] sheet ❺ IMPRENTA plate

planchar *vt* to iron • **¿quién me va a planchar estas camisas?** who is going to iron these shirts for me? • **detesto planchar** I hate to do the ironing

planeador *sm* glider

planear ◆ *vt* to plan
◆ *vi* ❶ [*hacer planes*] to plan ❷ [*en el aire*] to glide

planeta *sm* planet

planicie *sf* plain

planificación *sf* planning ▶ **planificación familiar** family planning

planificar *vt* to plan

planilla *sf* [*formulario*] form

plano, na *adj* flat ❢ *Los adjetivos ingleses son invariables.*

■ **plano** *sm* ❶ [*diseño, mapa*] plan • **el arquitecto presentó los planos de la casa** the architect presented the house plans • **¿tienes un plano de la ciudad?** do you have a map of the city? ❷ [*nivel, aspecto*] level ❸ CINE shot ▶ **primer plano** close-up ❹ GEOMETRÍA plane

expresión **en segundo plano** *figurado* in the background

planta *sf* ❶ BOTÁNICA plant • **tiene tantas plantas que la casa parece una selva en miniatura** she has so many plants that her house looks like a miniature jungle ❷ [*fábrica*] plant • **hay varias plantas industriales en las afueras del pueblo** there are several industrial plants on the outskirts of town ▶ **planta depuradora** purification plant ▶ **planta de envase** o **envasado** packaging plant ❸ [*piso*] floor • **el edificio donde trabajo tiene cuatro plantas** the building where I work has four floors ▶ **planta baja** ground floor

❹ [*del pie*] sole • **no me gusta andar descalza porque me da miedo clavarme algo en la planta de un pie** I don't like to go barefoot because I'm afraid of something sticking the sole of my foot

plantación *sf* ❶ [*terreno*] plantation ❷ [*acción*] planting

plantado, da *adj* standing ✎ *Los adjetivos ingleses son invariables.*

expresión **dejar plantado a alguien a)** *familiar* [*cortar la relación*] to walk out on somebody **b)** [*no acudir*] to stand somebody up ▶ **ser bien plantado** to be good-looking

plantar *vt* ❶ [*sembrar*] • **plantar algo (de)** to plant something (with) ❷ [*fijar - tienda de campaña*] to pitch; [*- poste*] to put in ❸ *familiar* [*asestar*] to land

planteamiento *sm* ❶ [*exposición*] raising ❷ [*enfoque*] approach

plantear *vt* ❶ [*exponer - problema*] to pose; [*- posibilidad, dificultad, duda*] to raise ❷ [*enfocar*] to approach

plantilla *sf* ❶ [*de empresa*] staff ❷ [*suela interior*] insole ❸ [*patrón*] pattern

plasmar *vt* ❶ *figurado* [*reflejar*] to give shape to ❷ [*modelar*] to shape

plástico, ca *adj* plastic ✎ *Los adjetivos ingleses son invariables.*

■ **plástico** *sm* [*generalmente*] plastic • **muchos artículos que antes eran de vidrio hoy son de plástico** many things that used to be made of glass are made of plastic nowadays

plastificar *vt* to plasticize

plastilina® *sf* ≃ **Plasticine®**

plata *sf* ❶ [*metal*] silver • **una mina de plata** a silver mine ▶ **plata de ley** sterling silver ❷ [*objetos de plata*] silverware

expresión **hablar en plata** *familiar* to speak bluntly

plataforma *sf* ❶ [*generalmente*] platform ▶ **plataforma espacial** space station • **plataforma petrolífera** oil rig ❷ *figurado* [*punto de partida*] launching pad ❸ GEOLOGÍA shelf

plátano *sm* ❶ [*fruta*] banana ❷ [*banano*] banana tree ❸ [*árbol platanáceo*] plane tree

platea *sf* stalls *pl*

plateado, da *adj* ❶ [*con plata*] silver-plated ❷ *figurado* [*color*] silvery ✎ *Los adjetivos ingleses son invariables.*

■ **pleno** *sm* [*reunión*] plenary meeting

plática *sf* talk

platicar *vi* to talk

platillo *sm* ❶ [*plato pequeño*] small plate ❷ [*de taza*] saucer ❸ [*de una balanza*] pan ❹ ✎ *generalmente pl* MÚSICA cymbal

platino *sm* [*metal*] platinum

plato *sm* ❶ [*recipiente*] plate • **hay que poner cinco platos en la mesa** we have to put five plates on the table • **lavar los platos** to do the dishes ❷ [*parte de una comida*] course • **primer plato** appetizer • **de primer plato** for the appetizer • **segundo plato** entrée ▶ **plato del día** special of the day ▶ **plato fuerte a)**

[*en una comida*] main course **b)** *figurado* main part ▶ **plato principal** main course ❸ [*comida*] dish • **su especialidad son los platos peruanos** his specialty is Peruvian dishes

expresión **pagar los platos rotos** to carry the can

platónico, ca *adj* Platonic ✎ *Los adjetivos ingleses son invariables.*

plausible *adj* ❶ [*admisible*] acceptable ❷ [*posible*] plausible ✎ *Los adjetivos ingleses son invariables.*

playa *sf* [*en el mar*] beach • **en esta playa hay que tener cuidado porque las olas son muy grandes** you have to be careful because the waves are very big on this beach • **ir a la playa de vacaciones** to go on vacation to the beach

plaza *sf* ❶ [*en una población*] square ▶ **plaza mayor** main square ❷ [*sitio*] place ❸ [*asiento*] seat • **de dos plazas** two-seater ✎ *Sólo se usa delante del sustantivo.* ❹ [*puesto de trabajo*] position • **plaza vacante** vacancy ❺ [*mercado*] market ❻ TAUROMAQUIA ▶ **plaza (de toros)** bullring

plazo *sm* ❶ [*de tiempo*] period • **hay un plazo de dos semanas** there is a period of two weeks • **en un plazo de un mes** within a month • **mañana termina el plazo de inscripción** the deadline for registration is tomorrow • **a corto/largo plazo a)** [*generalmente*] in the short/long term **b)** ECONOMÍA short/long term ❷ [*de dinero*] installment • **a plazos** in installments

plegable *adj* ❶ [*cama*] foldaway ❷ [*silla*] folding ✎ *Los adjetivos ingleses son invariables.*

plegar *vt* ❶ [*papel*] to fold ❷ [*mesita, hamaca*] to fold away

pleito *sm* ❶ DERECHO [*litigio*] lawsuit • **al final ganó el pleito** in the end she won the lawsuit ❷ [*discusión*] argument • **ya estoy cansada de estos pleitos, no puede ser que dos hermanos se lleven tan mal** I'm tired of these arguments, it's not possible that two brothers get along so badly

plenitud *sf* [*totalidad*] completeness

pleno, na *adj* full • **me siento plena de energía** I feel full of energy • **en plena actuación, el actor tropezó y se cayó** in the middle of the performance, the actor tripped and fell • **le dio en plena cara** she hit him right in the face • **en pleno día** in broad daylight • **en plena guerra** in the middle of the war • **en pleno uso de sus facultades** in full command of his faculties • **en plena forma** on top form ✎ *Los adjetivos ingleses son invariables.*

■ **pleno** *sm* [*reunión*] plenary meeting

pliegue *sm* ❶ [*generalmente*] GEOLOGÍA fold ❷ [*en un plisado*] pleat

plomería *sf* plumbing store

plomero *sm* plumber

plomizo, za *adj* [*color*] leaden ✎ *Los adjetivos ingleses son invariables.*

plomo *sm* ❶ [*metal*] lead ❷ [*pieza de metal*] lead weight ❸ [*fusible*] fuse

expresión **caer a plomo** to fall like a stone

pluma ◆ *sf* ❶ [*de ave*] feather • **este bebé es más ligero que una pluma** this baby is lighter than a feather

P

❷ [*para escribir*] pen • **¿me prestas una pluma para escribir una carta?** will you lend me a pen to write a letter? ▸ **pluma estilográfica** fountain pen ▸ **pluma fuente** fountain pen ❸ HISTORIA quill ❹ [*bolígrafo*] ballpoint pen

◆ *adj invariable* DEPORTE featherweight:🔆 *Los adjetivos ingleses son invariables.*

plumero *sm* feather duster

expresión **vérsele a alguien el plumero** *familiar* to see through somebody

plumón *sm* ❶ [*de ave*] down ❷ [*marcador*] marker

plural *adj* & *sm* plural:🔆 *Los adjetivos ingleses son invariables.*

pluralidad *sf* diversity

pluralismo *sm* pluralism

pluralizar *vi* to generalize

plus (pl pluses) *sm* bonus

pluscuamperfecto *adj* & *sm* pluperfect:🔆 *Los adjetivos ingleses son invariables.*

plusmarca *sf* record

plusvalía *sf* ECONOMÍA appreciation

Plutón *nombre propio* Pluto

p.m. (*abreviatura escrita de* post merídiem) p.m

PNB (*abreviatura de* producto nacional bruto) *sm* GNP

población *sf* ❶ [*ciudad*] town ; city ❷ [*pueblo*] village ❸ [*habitantes*] population

poblado, da *adj* ❶ [*habitado*] inhabited • **una zona muy poblada** a densely populated area ❷ *figurado* [*lleno*] full • **poblado de algo** full of something ❸ [*barba, cejas*] bushy:🔆 *Los adjetivos ingleses son invariables.*

■ **poblado** *sm* settlement

poblador, ra *sm, f* settler

poblar *vt* ❶ [*establecerse en*] to populate • **a lo largo de los siglos, diferentes olas de inmigrantes poblaron América** through the centuries, different waves of immigrants populated America ❷ *figurado* [*llenar*] • **poblar (de) a)** [*plantas, árboles*] to plant (with) **b)** [*peces* ETC] to stock (with) ❸ [*habitar*] to inhabit • **cuando los españoles colonizaron América, los aztecas poblaban lo que hoy es México** when the Spanish colonized America, the Aztecs inhabited what is today Mexico

■ **poblarse** *v pronominal* ❶ [*colonizarse*] to be settled with ❷ *figurado* [*llenarse*] to fill up • **poblarse (de)** to fill up (with) • **con la llegada de la primavera, los campos se poblaron de flores** with the arrival of spring, the fields became filled with flowers

pobre ◆ *adj* poor • **vivíamos en un barrio pobre** we used to live in a poor area • **¡pobre hombre!** poor man! • **¡pobre de mí!** poor me!:🔆 *Los adjetivos ingleses son invariables.*

◆ *smf* [*generalmente*] poor person • **los pobres** the poor • **¡el pobre!** poor thing!

pobreza *sf* [*escasez*] poverty

pochismo *sm* *familiar para explicar lo que es puedes decir:* it's a language mistake caused by English influence

pocho, cha *adj* ❶ [*fruta*] over-ripe ❷ *familiar* [*americanizado*] Americanized:🔆 *Los adjetivos ingleses son invariables.*

pocilga *sf* literal & figurado pigsty

pócima *sf* [*poción*] potion

poción *sf* potion

poco, ca ◆ *adj* little, *plural* few; not much, *plural* not many • **poca agua** not much water • **de poca importancia** of little importance • **hay pocos árboles** there aren't many trees • **pocas personas lo saben** few people know it • **tenemos poco tiempo** we don't have much time • **hace poco tiempo** not long ago • **dame unos pocos días** give me a few days:🔆 *Los adjetivos ingleses son invariables.*

◆ *pronombre* little, *plural* few; not much, *plural* not many • **queda poco** there's not much left • **tengo muy pocos** I don't have very many; I have very few • **pocos hay que sepan tanto** not many people know so much • **un poco** a bit • **¿me dejas un poco?** can I have a bit? • **¿quieres flan? queda un poco** do you want some flan? there's a little left • **un poco de** a bit of • **un poco de sentido común** a bit of common sense • **unos pocos** a few • **de poca (madre)** *familiar* bloody cool

■ **poco** *adv* ❶ [*escasamente*] not much • **este niño come poco** this boy doesn't eat much • **estás cansada porque anoche dormiste muy poco** you're tired because you slept very little last night • **me queda muy poca dinero, no va a ser suficiente** I have very little money left, it's not going to be enough • **es poco común** it's not very common • **es un poco triste** it's rather sad • **por poco** almost; nearly ❷ [*brevemente*] • **tardaré muy poco** I won't be long • **al poco de...** shortly after... • **dentro de poco** soon; in a short time • **hace poco** a little while ago • **poco a poco** [*progresivamente*] little by little • **¡poco a poco!** [*despacio*] steady on!

podar *vt* to prune

poder¹ *sm* ❶ [*generalmente*] power • **estar en/hacerse con el poder** to be in/to seize power ▸ **poder adquisitivo** purchasing power ▸ **poderes fácticos** *para explicar lo que es puedes decir:* it's the church, the military and the press ❷ [*posesión*] • **estar en poder de alguien** to be in somebody's hands ❸ 🔆 *generalmente pl* [*autorización*] • **dar poderes a alguien para que haga algo** to authorize somebody to do something • **por poderes** by proxy

poder²
◆ *vt*
❶ [*tener la posibilidad de*] to be able to
• **no podré venir a tu boda** I won't be able to come to your wedding
• **¿puedes venir un momento, por favor?** could you come here a minute, please?
• **puedo pagarme el viaje** I can pay for my own trip

• **¿puedo llevarme este libro? — sí, claro** can I take this book? — yes, of course

❷ [*tener el derecho de*]
• **no podemos abandonarlo** we can't just leave him

❸ [*expresa una posibilidad, una eventualidad*]
• **puede estallar la guerra** war could break out
• **podías habérmelo dicho** you could have told me

◆ *vi*

• **no puedo más** I can't take any more
• **disfrutamos hasta más no poder** we had a fantastic time
• **es avaro a más no poder** he's as mean as they come

◆ *v impersonal*

[*expresa una posibilidad, una eventualidad*]
• **puede ser** maybe
• **no puede ser** it can't be
• **puede que llueva** it might rain
• **¿vendrás mañana? — puede** are you coming tomorrow? — maybe
• **¿se puede?** can I come in?

■ **poder a**

◆ *v + preposición*

[*ser capaz de enfrentar*]
• **a mí no hay quien me pueda** no one can take me on

■ **poder con**

◆ *v + preposición*

❶ [*ser capaz de encarar una situación*]
• **poder con algo/con alguien** to cope with something/somebody
• **ella sola no podrá con la corrección de pruebas** she won't be able to manage the proofs all by herself
• **por mucho que lo intento, no puedo con las matemáticas** however hard I try, I just can't do math

❷ *familiar* [*ser capaz de aguantar a alguien*]
• **de verdad, ¡no puedo con Roberto!** honestly, I can't stand Roberto!

poderío *sm* [*poder*] power

poderoso, sa *adj* powerful ♡ *Los adjetivos ingleses son invariables.*

podíatra, podiatra *smf* podiatrist

podio, podium *sm* podium

podólogo, ga *sm, f* chiropodist

podrido, da ◆ *participio pasado* → **pudrir**

◆ *adj* rotten ♡ *Los adjetivos ingleses son invariables.*

poema *sm* poem

poesía *sf* ❶ [*género literario*] poetry • **se me hace muy difícil leer poesía** I find it very difficult to read poetry ❷ [*poema*] poem • **Laura leyó sus poesías en la fiesta de la escuela** Laura read her poems at the school party

poeta *smf* poet

poético, ca *adj* poetic ♡ *Los adjetivos ingleses son invariables.*

poetisa *sf* female poet

polar *adj* polar ♡ *Los adjetivos ingleses son invariables.*

polarizar *vt* figurado [*miradas, atención, esfuerzo*] to concentrate

polea *sf* pulley

polémico, ca *adj* controversial ♡ *Los adjetivos ingleses son invariables.*

■ **polémica** *sf* controversy

polen *sm* pollen

poli *familiar* ◆ *smf* cop

◆ *sf* • **la poli** the cops

policía ◆ *sm, f* policeman, *plural* <u>policemen</u>, *femenino* <u>policewoman</u>, *plural* <u>policewomen</u>

◆ *sf* • **la policía** the police

policiaco, ca, policíaco, ca *adj* ❶ police ♡ *Sólo se usa delante del sustantivo.* ❷ [*novela, película*] detective ♡ *Sólo se usa delante del sustantivo.*

policial *adj* police ♡ *Sólo se usa delante del sustantivo.*

poliéster *sm invariable* polyester

polietileno *sm* polyethylene

polifacético, ca *adj* multifaceted ♡ *Los adjetivos ingleses son invariables.*

polilla *sf* moth

politécnico, ca *adj* polytechnic ♡ *Los adjetivos ingleses son invariables.*

político, ca *adj* ❶ [*de gobierno*] political • **un partido político** a political party ❷ [*pariente*] • **la esposa de mi tío es mi tía política** my uncle's wife is my aunt by marriage • **hermano político** brother-in-law • **familia política** in-laws *pl* ♡ *Los adjetivos ingleses son invariables.*

■ **político** *sm* politician

■ **política** *sf* ❶ [*arte de gobernar*] politics ♡ *incontable* ❷ [*modo de gobernar, táctica*] policy

polivalente *adj* ❶ [*vacuna, suero*] polyvalent ❷ [*edificio, sala*] multipurpose ♡ *Los adjetivos ingleses son invariables.*

póliza *sf* ❶ [*de seguro*] (insurance) policy ❷ [*sello*] *para explicar lo que es puedes decir*: it's a stamp on a document showing that a tax has been paid

polizón *sm* stowaway

pollito *sm* chick

pollo, lla *sm, f* ZOOLOGÍA chick

■ **pollo** *sm* COCINA chicken

polo *sm* ❶ [*generalmente*] pole ❷ ELECTRICIDAD terminal ▶ **polo negativo/positivo** negative/positive terminal ❸ [*helado*] ice lolly ❹ [*jersey*] polo shirt ❺ DEPORTE polo

Polonia *nombre propio* Poland

polución *sf* [*contaminación*] pollution

polvareda *sf* dust cloud

expresión **levantar una gran polvareda** to cause a commotion

polvo *sm* ❶ [*en el aire*] dust • **hay que limpiar aquí porque está lleno de polvo** you have to clean here because it's covered in dust • **limpiar** o **quitar el polvo** to do the dusting ❷ [*de un producto*] powder • **en polvo** powdered ▶ **polvos de talco** talcum powder ▶ **polvos picapica** itching powder

expresiones estar hecho polvo *familiar* to be knackered ▶ **hacer polvo algo** to smash something ▶ **limpio de polvo y paja** including all charges

pólvora *sf* [*sustancia explosiva*] gunpowder

expresión correr como la pólvora to spread like wildfire

polvoriento, ta *adj* ❶ [*superficie*] dusty ❷ [*sustancia*] powdery ּ֍֯ *Los adjetivos ingleses son invariables.*

polvorín *sm* munitions dump

pomada *sf* ointment

pomelo *sm* [*fruto*] grapefruit, *plural* grapefruit

pómez → **piedra**

pomo *sm* [*de puerta*] handle • **el pomo de esta puerta está pegajoso** this door's handle is sticky

pompa *sf* ❶ [*suntuosidad*] pomp ❷ [*ostentación*] show

pompón *sm* pompom

pomposo, sa *adj* ❶ [*suntuoso*] sumptuous ❷ [*ostentoso*] showy ❸ [*lenguaje*] pompous ּ֍֯ *Los adjetivos ingleses son invariables.*

pómulo *sm* [*hueso*] cheekbone

ponche *sm* punch

poncho *sm* poncho

ponderar *vt* ❶ [*alabar*] to praise ❷ [*considerar*] to weigh up

ponencia *sf* ❶ [*conferencia*] lecture ❷ [*informe*] report

poner
♦ *vt*
❶ [*colocar*] to put
• **¿dónde has puesto el libro?** where did you put the book?
• **pon vinagre en la ensalada** add some vinegar to the salad
❷ [*colocar en el cuerpo, vestir*] to put on
• **ponle el abrigo/los guantes** put his coat/gloves on
❸ [*encender*] to put on
• **pon el radio/la calefacción** put the radio/heating on
❹ [*preparar*] to set
• **pon la mesa mientras yo preparo la ensalada** set the table while I make the salad
❺ [*contribuir*]
• **puso toda su voluntad en ello** he gave it his all
• **podrías poner un poco de tu parte** you could help a bit
• **ya he puesto mi parte** I've already done my bit

❻ [*instalar*]
• **nos están poniendo el gas y la luz en el departamento nuevo** we're having the gas and power hooked up at our new apartment
• **han puesto su casa con mucho gusto** they've done their house really tastefully
❼ [*abrir*] to open
• **pusieron una tienda de comestibles** they opened a new grocery store
❽ [*provocar un estado*]
• **lo que le dije la puso furiosa** she was furious about what I said to her
• **poner triste a alguien** to make somebody sad
• **lo pones de mal humor** you put him in a bad mood
❾ [*dar*] to give
• **este profesor siempre nos pone mucha tarea** this teacher always gives us too much homework
❿ [*en el teatro*] to do
• **¿qué obra ponen en el Insurgentes?** what play are they doing at the Insurgentes?
⓫ [*dar un nombre*] to name
• **le pusieron Mario** they named him Mario
• **¿qué nombre le van a poner al bebé?** what are they going to call the baby?
⓬ [*tratar como*]
• **no aceptaré que me pongan de mentiroso** I won't let them call me a liar
⓭ [*suponer*]
• **pongamos que...** let's suppose (that)...
⓮ [*en matemáticas*]
• **pongo 6 y llevo 3** I'll add 6 and carry 3
⓯ [*telecomunicaciones*]
• **nos puso un fax** he sent us a fax
⓰ [*huevo*] to lay
• **las gallinas ponen huevos** hens lay eggs
⓱ [*en expresiones*]
• **poner de comer** to serve
• **poner a régimen** to put on a diet
• **poner impedimentos a algo** to put obstacles in the way of something
• **¡no pongas esa cara!** don't pull that face!
• **poner a mal tiempo buena cara** to put on a brave face
♦ *vi*
[*huevo*] to lay
• **las gallinas ponen** hens lay
■ **ponerse**
♦ *v pronominal*
❶ [*adoptar cierta posición*]
• **ponerse cómodo** to make yourself comfortable
• **ponerse de pie** to stand up
❷ [*colocarse en el cuerpo, vestirse*] to put on
• **¡ponte el abrigo!** put your coat on!
• **se puso un poco de colorete** she put on some blush
❸ [*pasar de un estado a otro*]
• **se puso rojo de ira** she went red with anger
• **a menudo se ponía melancólica** she'd often get sad

• **¡no te pongas así!** don't be like that!
• **¿con quién has quedado que te has puesto tan guapa!** who are you meeting to have made such an effort?
❹ [*salud*]
• **ponerse enfermo** to get sick
• **ponerse bien** to get well
❺ [*sol*] to set
• **el sol se pone por el oeste** the sun sets in the West
❻ [*en expresiones*]
• **ponerse al tanto** to get up to date
expresión **ponérselas** *familiar* [*emborracharse*] to get wasted
■ **ponerse a**
◆ *v pronominal + preposición*
[*seguido por el infinitivo: empezar a*] to start ☼ + *infinitivo*
• **se puso a llorar** he started crying

pontífice *sm* Pope

pop *adj* pop ☼ *Los adjetivos ingleses son invariables.*

popa *sf* stern

popote *sm* drinking straw

popular *adj* ❶ [*del pueblo, famoso*] of the people
• **es un cantante muy popular** he's a very popular singer ❷ [*arte, música*] folk • **estudia la cultura popular** he studies folk culture ☼ *Los adjetivos ingleses son invariables.*

popularidad *sf* popularity • **su popularidad ha aumentado en los últimos años** his popularity has increased in the last few years • **gozar de popularidad** to be popular

popularizar *vt* to popularize

póquer *sm* [*juego*] poker

por
◆ *preposición*
❶ [*indica el objetivo*] to
• **lo hizo por complacerte** she did it to please you
❷ [*a favor de*] for
• **lo hizo por ella** she did it for her
• **votó por mí** she voted for me
❸ [*indica la manera*] by
• **lo cogieron por el brazo** they took him by the arm
• **por escrito** in writing
❹ [*indica el medio*] by
• **por mensajero/fax** by courier/fax
❺ [*indica la causa*] because of
• **cerraron el aeropuerto por mal tiempo** they closed the airport because of bad weather
• **se enfadó por tu culpa** it was your fault she got annoyed
❻ [*introduce el complemento agente*] by
• **el récord fue batido por el atleta** the record was broken by the athlete

❼ [*indica un momento*]
• **por abril** throughout April
❽ [*indica un momento del día*]
• **por la mañana/tarde/noche** in the morning/afternoon/at night
❾ [*indica la duración*]
• **por unos días** for a few days
❿ [*indica la posición, el lugar*]
• **había papeles por el suelo** there were papers all over the floor
• **había niños por todas partes** there were children everywhere
• **¿por dónde vive?** whereabouts does he live?
⓫ [*indica el lugar por donde uno pasa*]
• **sólo pasaba por aquí** I was just passing
• **viajamos por varios países** we traveled through several countries
• **entramos en África por Tánger** we arrived in Africa via Tangiers
• **pasar por la aduana** to go through customs
• **los ladrones entraron por la ventana** the burglars went in through the window
⓬ [*indica el precio*] for
• **lo ha comprado por poco dinero** he bought it cheap
• **lo tuve por 10 pesos** I got it for 10 pesos
⓭ [*indica un cambio*] for
• **cambió el carro por la moto** he exchanged his car for the motorbike
⓮ [*en lugar de*] for
• **él lo hará por mí** he'll do it for me
⓯ [*indica la distribución, el reparto*]
• **tocan a dos por cabeza** there are two each
• **100 km por hora** 100 km per hour
• **huevos por docenas** eggs by the dozen
⓰ [*en matemáticas*] times
• **tres por tres son nueve** three times three is nine
⓱ [*ir a buscar*]
• **baja por leche** go out and get some milk
• **vino por los libros** he came to get the books
⓲ [*indica que una acción está a punto de ser completada*]
• **estaba por salir** I was about to go out
• **la mesa está por poner** the table hasn't been set yet
• **estuve por llamarte** I was about to call you
⓳ [*en expresiones*]
• **no me cae bien, por (muy) simpático que te parezca** I don't like him, however nice you think he is
• **por mucho que llores, no arreglarás nada** crying won't solve anything

porcelana *sf* [*material*] porcelain

porcentaje *sm* percentage

porche *sm* ❶ [*soportal*] arcade ❷ [*entrada*] porch

porción *sf* portion

pordiosero, ra *sm, f* beggar

pormenor *sm* ☼ *generalmente pl* detail • **entrar en pormenores** to go into detail

pornografía *sf* pornography

pornográfico, ca *adj* pornographic ☼ *Los adjetivos ingleses son invariables.*

poro *sm* ❶ [*piel*] pore • **la piel respira por los poros** skin breathes through the pores ❷ [*puerro*] leek • **mi sopa favorita es la de poros** my favorite kind of soup is leek

poroso, sa *adj* porous ☼ *Los adjetivos ingleses son invariables.*

porque *conjunción* ❶ [*debido a que*] because • **no vino porque estaba enfermo** he didn't come because he was sick • **¿por qué lo hiciste? — porque sí** why did you do it? — just because ❷ [*para que*] so that

porqué *sm* reason • **el porqué de** the reason for • **quiero saber el porqué de este escándalo** I want to know the reason for this commotion

porquería *sf* ❶ [*suciedad*] filth ❷ [*cosa de mala calidad*] rubbish ☼ *incontable*

porra *sf* ❶ [*palo*] club ❷ [*de policía*] truncheon ❸ DEPORTE [*grito*] cheer

expresión **mandar a alguien a la porra** *familiar* to tell somebody to go to hell ▶ **¡y una porra!** *familiar* like hell!

porrazo *sm* ❶ [*golpe*] bang ❷ [*caída*] bump

portaaviones *sm invariable* aircraft carrier

portada *sf* ❶ [*de libro*] title page ❷ [*de revista*] (front) cover ❸ [*de periódico*] front page ❹ [*de disco*] sleeve

portador, ra *sm, f* bearer • **al portador** COMERCIO to the bearer

portal *sm* ❶ [*entrada*] entrance hall ❷ [*puerta*] main door ❸ INFORMÁTICA portal

portamonedas *sm invariable* purse

portar *vt* to carry

portátil *adj* portable ☼ *Los adjetivos ingleses son invariables.*

portavoz *sm, f* [*persona*] spokesman, *femenino* spokeswoman

portazo *sm* • **la puerta se cerró de un portazo** the door slammed shut • **desde aquí oí el portazo** I heard the door slam from here • **dar un portazo** to slam the door

porte *sm* ❶ ☼ *generalmente pl* [*gasto de transporte*] carriage ▶ **porte debido/pagado** COMERCIO carriage due/paid ❷ [*transporte*] carriage ❸ [*aspecto*] bearing

portento *sm* wonder

portentoso, sa *adj* wonderful ☼ *Los adjetivos ingleses son invariables.*

porteño, ña *adj* from the city of Buenos Aires ☼ *Los adjetivos ingleses son invariables.*

portería *sf* ❶ [*de edificio, departamentos*] doorman's desk o office ❷ DEPORTE goal • **un saque de portería** a goal kick

portero, ra *sm, f* ❶ [*en la puerta*] doorman ❷ [*encargado del edificio*] super (intendant) ❸ DEPORTE goalkeeper • **el portero atajó el balón** the goalkeeper intercepted the ball

pórtico *sm* ❶ [*fachada*] portico ❷ [*arcada*] arcade

portuario, ria *adj* port ☼ *Sólo se usa delante del sustantivo.* ❷ [*de los muelles*] dock ☼ *Sólo se usa delante del sustantivo.* • **trabajador portuario** docker

Portugal *nombre propio* Portugal

portugués, esa *adj & sm, f* Portuguese • **los portugueses** the Portuguese ☼ *Los adjetivos ingleses son invariables.*

En inglés, los adjetivos que se refieren a un país o una región se escriben con mayúscula.

■ **portugués** *sm* [*lengua*] Portuguese

posar ◆ *vt* ❶ to put down ❷ [*mano, mirada*] to rest

◆ *vi* to pose

posavasos *sm invariable* ❶ [*de madera*] coaster ❷ [*de cartón*] beer mat

posdata, postdata *sf* postscript

pose *sf* pose • **adoptar una pose** to strike a pose

poseedor, ra *sm, f* ❶ [*propietario*] owner ❷ [*de cargo, acciones, récord*] holder

poseer *vt* ❶ [*ser dueño de*] to own ❷ [*estar en poder de*] to have

poseído, da *adj* • **poseído por** possessed by ☼ *Los adjetivos ingleses son invariables.*

posesión *sf* possession

posesivo, va *adj* possessive ☼ *Los adjetivos ingleses son invariables.*

posgraduado, da *adj & sm, f* postgraduate ☼ *Los adjetivos ingleses son invariables.*

posguerra *sf* post-war period

posibilidad *sf* possibility, *plural* possibilities • **no había pensado en esa posibilidad** I hadn't thought about that possibility • **eso le da la posibilidad de ir a la universidad** that gives him the chance to go to college • **tiene muchas posibilidades de llegar a la final** he has a good chance of making it to the finals • **cabe la posibilidad de que...** there is a chance that...

posibilitar *vt* to make possible

posible *adj* possible • **¿es posible cambiar los boletos?** is it possible to change the tickets? • **lo siento, pero no es posible** I'm sorry, but it's not possible • **es posible que llueva** it could rain • **dentro de lo posible, en lo posible** as far as possible • **de ser posible** if possible • **hacer (todo) lo posible** to do everything possible • **lo antes posible** as soon as possible • **¡no es posible!** surely not! ☼ *Los adjetivos ingleses son invariables.*

posición *sf* ❶ [*generalmente*] position • **hay que mantenerlo en posición vertical** we have to keep it in a vertical position • **en posición de descanso** standing at ease ❷ [*categoría - social*] status ☼ *incontable* • **de buena posición** of high social status; [*- económica*] situation ❸ DEPORTE position

positivo, va *adj* [*generalmente*] ELECTRICIDAD positive • **el análisis dio positivo** the test was positive ☼ *Los adjetivos ingleses son invariables.*

P

poso *sm* ❶ [*sedimento*] sediment ❷ *figurado* trace

posponer *vt* ❶ [*relegar*] to put behind ❷ [*aplazar*] to postpone

posta ■ **a posta** *locución adverbial* on purpose

postal ◆ *adj* postal.☼. *Los adjetivos ingleses son invariables.*

◆ *sf* postcard

postdata = **posdata**

poste *sm* ❶ [*madero*] pole ▶ **poste de alta tensión** electricity pylon ▶ **poste telegráfico** telegraph pole ❷ DEPORTE post • **el balón dio en el poste derecho del arco** the ball hit the right goal post

póster (pl posters) *sm* poster

postergar *vt* ❶ [*retrasar*] to postpone ❷ [*relegar*] to put behind

posteridad *sf* ❶ [*generación futura*] posterity ❷ [*futuro*] future

posterior *adj* ❶ [*en el espacio*] rear ❷ [*en el tiempo*] subsequent.☼. *Los adjetivos ingleses son invariables.*

posterioridad *sf* • **con posterioridad** later

postizo, za *adj* [*falso*] false.☼. *Los adjetivos ingleses son invariables.*

■ **postizo** *sm* hairpiece

postor, ra *sm, f* bidder

postre *sm* dessert • **¿qué hay de postre?** what's for dessert?

expresión **para postre** to cap it all

postrimerías *sfpl* final stages

póstumo, ma *adj* posthumous.☼. *Los adjetivos ingleses son invariables.*

postura *sf* ❶ [*posición*] position ❷ [*actitud*] attitude • **tomar postura** to adopt an attitude ❸ [*uso*] • **tienen dos posturas y ya se rompieron** they've been worn twice and they already broke

potable *adj* [*bebible*] drinkable • **agua potable** drinking water.☼. *Los adjetivos ingleses son invariables.*

potaje *sm* COCINA [*guiso*] vegetable stew; [*sopa*] vegetable soup

potasio *sm* potassium

pote *sm* pot

potencia *sf* [*generalmente*] MATEMÁTICAS & POLÍTICA power • **un motor de mucha potencia** a high power motor • **tiene mucha potencia** it's very powerful • **en potencia** in the making • **es un gran músico en potencia** he's a great musician in the making

potencial ◆ *adj* [*generalmente*] FÍSICA potential.☼. *Los adjetivos ingleses son invariables.*

◆ *sm* ❶ [*fuerza*] power ❷ [*posibilidades*] potential ❸ GRAMÁTICA conditional

potenciar *vt* ❶ [*fomentar*] to encourage ❷ [*reforzar*] to boost

potente *adj* powerful.☼. *Los adjetivos ingleses son invariables.*

potrero *sm* [*prado*] field

pozo *sm* ❶ well • **un pozo de petróleo** an oil well ❷ [*de mina*] shaft

ppp (*abreviatura escrita de* puntos por pulgada) INFORMÁTICA dpi

práctica *sf* ❶ [*generalmente*] practice • **llevar algo a la práctica, poner algo en práctica** to put something into practice • **puso su idea en práctica** he put his idea into practice • **en la práctica** in practice • **en la práctica la gente confunde esas dos palabras** in practice people confuse those two words ▶ **prácticas de tiro** target practice ❷ [*clase no teórica*] practical

practicante ◆ *adj* practising.☼. *Los adjetivos ingleses son invariables.*

◆ *smf* ❶ [*de deporte*] practitioner ❷ MEDICINA medical assistant

practicar ◆ *vt* ❶ [*generalmente*] to practice • **necesitas practicar más tu inglés** you need to practice your English more ❷ [*deporte*] to play • **¿practicas algún deporte?** do you play a sport? ❸ [*realizar*] to carry out

◆ *vi* to practice

práctico, ca *adj* practical • **es una persona muy práctica** he's a very practical person.☼. *Los adjetivos ingleses son invariables.*

pradera *sf* prairie

prado *sm* meadow

pragmático, ca ◆ *adj* pragmatic.☼. *Los adjetivos ingleses son invariables.*

◆ *sm, f* [*persona*] pragmatist

pral. *abreviatura escrita de* **principal**

PRD *sm* (*abreviatura de* Partido de la Revolución Democrática) Mexican political party

preámbulo *sm* [*introducción - de libro*] foreword; preface; [*- de congreso, conferencia*] introduction

precalentar *vt* ❶ COCINA to pre-heat ❷ DEPORTE to warm up

precario, ria *adj* precarious.☼. *Los adjetivos ingleses son invariables.*

precaución *sf* ❶ [*prudencia*] caution ❷ [*medida*] precaution • **tomar precauciones** to take precautions • **hay que tomar precauciones cuando tomamos el sol** we have to take precautions when we sunbathe

precaver *vt* to guard against

precavido, da *adj* ❶ [*cauto*] cautious • **es muy precavido** he's very cautious ❷ [*prevenido*] well-prepared • **como persona precavida, trajo el paraguas** like the well-prepared person she is, she brought an umbrella.☼. *Los adjetivos ingleses son invariables.*

precedente ◆ *adj* previous.☼. *Los adjetivos ingleses son invariables.*

◆ *sm* precedent

preceder *vt* to go before

preciado, da *adj* valuable.☼. *Los adjetivos ingleses son invariables.*

precintar *vt* to seal

precinto *sm* seal

precio *sm* price • **van a subir los precios otra vez** prices are going to go up again • **a cualquier precio** at any price • **poner precio a la cabeza de alguien** to put a price on somebody's head • **¿qué precio tiene**

P

esto? how much is this? • **subir/bajar los precios** to raise/lower prices • **al precio de** *figurado* at the cost of ▶ **precio de salida** starting price ▶ **precio de venta (al público)** retail price

preciosidad *sf* [*cosa bonita*] • **¡es una preciosidad!** it's lovely! • **¡qué preciosidad de niña!** what a lovely girl!

precioso, sa *adj* ❶ [*valioso*] precious ❷ [*bonito*] lovely ⚲ *Los adjetivos ingleses son invariables.*

preciosura *sf* beauty

precipicio *sm* precipice

precipitación *sf* ❶ [*apresuramiento*] haste ❷ [*lluvia*] rainfall ⚲ *incontable*

precipitado, da *adj* hasty ⚲ *Los adjetivos ingleses son invariables.*

precipitar *vt* ❶ [*arrojar*] to throw down ❷ [*acelerar*] to speed up

■ **precipitarse** *v pronominal* ❶ [*caer*] to plunge (down) ❷ [*acelerarse - acontecimientos* ETC] to speed up ❸ [*apresurarse*] • **precipitarse (hacia)** to rush (towards) ❹ [*obrar irreflexivamente*] to be too hasty • **no se precipiten y elijan con calma** don't be too hasty and choose carefully • **parece que me precipité al juzgarlo** it seems that I was hasty in judging him

precisamente *adv* [*justamente*] • **¡precisamente!** exactly! • **precisamente por eso** for that very reason • **precisamente tú lo sugeriste** in fact it was you who suggested it

precisar *vt* ❶ [*determinar*] to fix ❷ [*aclarar*] to specify exactly

precisión *sf* accuracy

preciso, sa *adj* ❶ [*determinado, conciso*] precise • **me dio indicaciones precisas de cómo llegar** he gave me precise directions for how to get there ❷ [*instrumento*] accurate • **un instrumento muy preciso** a very accurate instrument ❸ [*necesario*] • **ser preciso (para algo/hacer algo)** to be necessary (for something/to do something) • **no es preciso que te lo aprendas de memoria** it's not necessary for you to memorize it • **es preciso que vengas** you must come • **si es preciso, pide ayuda** if necessary, ask for help ❹ [*justo*] just • **en este preciso momento** at this very moment ⚲ *Los adjetivos ingleses son invariables.*

preconcebido, da *adj* ❶ [*idea*] preconceived ❷ [*plan*] drawn up in advance ⚲ *Los adjetivos ingleses son invariables.*

preconcebir *vt* to draw up in advance

precoz *adj* [*persona*] precocious ⚲ *Los adjetivos ingleses son invariables.*

precursor, ra *sm, f* precursor

predecesor, ra *sm, f* predecessor

predecir *vt* to predict

predestinado, da *adj* • **predestinado (a)** predestined (to) ⚲ *Los adjetivos ingleses son invariables.*

predestinar *vt* to predestine

predeterminar *vt* to predetermine

predicado *sm* GRAMÁTICA predicate

predicador, ra *sm, f* preacher

predicar *vt* & *vi* to preach

predicción *sf* ❶ prediction ❷ [*del tiempo*] forecast

predilección *sf* • **predilección (por)** preference (for)

predilecto, ta *adj* favorite ⚲ *Los adjetivos ingleses son invariables.*

predio *sm* ❶ [*edificio*] building ❷ [*terreno*] lot

predisponer *vt* • **predisponer (a)** to predispose (to)

predisposición *sf* ❶ [*aptitud*] • **predisposición para** aptitude for ❷ [*tendencia*] • **predisposición a** predisposition to

predispuesto, ta ◆ *participio pasado* → **predisponer**

◆ *adj* • **predispuesto (a)** predisposed (to) ⚲ *Los adjetivos ingleses son invariables.*

predominante *adj* ❶ predominant ❷ [*viento, actitudes*] prevailing ⚲ *Los adjetivos ingleses son invariables.*

predominar *vi* • **predominar (sobre)** to predominate o prevail (over)

predominio *sm* preponderance

preescolar *adj* pre-school ⚲ *Los adjetivos ingleses son invariables.*

prefabricado, da *adj* prefabricated ⚲ *Los adjetivos ingleses son invariables.*

prefacio *sm* preface

preferencia *sf* preference • **de preferencia** preferably • **el martes, de preferencia en la mañana** Tuesday, preferably in the morning • **dar preferencia (a)** to give priority (to) • **dan preferencia a los estudiantes con mejores calificaciones** they give priority to the students with better grades • **tener preferencia** AUTOMÓVILES to have right of way • **tienen preferencia los que vienen por la derecha** the ones coming from the right have the right of way • **tener preferencia por** to prefer • **tiene preferencia por los colores brillantes** she prefers bright colors

preferente *adj* preferential ⚲ *Los adjetivos ingleses son invariables.*

preferentemente *adv* preferably

preferible *adj* • **preferible (a)** preferable (to) ⚲ *Los adjetivos ingleses son invariables.*

preferido, da *adj* favorite ⚲ *Los adjetivos ingleses son invariables.*

preferir *vt* • **preferir algo (a algo)** to prefer something (to something) • **prefiere estudiar solo en su casa** he prefers to study alone in his house • **prefiero que vengas** I'd rather you came • **prefiero no saber** I'd rather not know

prefijo *sm* ❶ GRAMÁTICA prefix ❷ TELECOMUNICACIONES area code

pregunta *sf* question • **no contestó mi pregunta** he didn't answer my question • **hacer una pregunta** to ask a question

expresión **andar a la cuarta** o **última pregunta** to be broke

preguntar ✦ *vt* to ask • **pregúntale a la profesora** ask the teacher • **preguntar algo a alguien** to ask somebody something • **le pregunté la hora** I asked him what time it was

✦ *vi* • **preguntar por** to ask for • **cuando llegues allá, pregunta por Ana** when you get there, ask for Ana • **siempre pregunta por él para saber cómo está** she always asks about him to know how he is • **Isabel me ha preguntado por ti** Isabel asked me how you were

prehistoria *sf* prehistory

prehistórico, ca *adj* prehistoric◌*Los adjetivos ingleses son invariables.*

prejuicio *sm* prejudice • **tener prejuicios** to be prejudiced • **no tiene prejuicios contra nadie** he's not prejudiced toward anybody ❯ **prejuicios raciales** racial prejudices

preliminar ✦ *adj* preliminary◌*Los adjetivos ingleses son invariables.*

✦ *sm* ◌*generalmente pl* preliminary

premamá *adj invariable* maternity◌*Los adjetivos ingleses son invariables.*

prematrimonial *adj* premarital◌*Los adjetivos ingleses son invariables.*

prematuro, ra *adj* premature◌*Los adjetivos ingleses son invariables.*

premeditación *sf* premeditation

premeditar *vt* to think out in advance

premiar *vt* ❶ [*recompensar*] to reward • **hay que premiar el esfuerzo** we have to reward the effort ❷ [*dar un premio a*] to give an award to • **premiaron al mejor alumno** they gave an award to the best student

premier (pl premiers) *sm* British prime minister

premio *sm* ❶ [*en competición*] prize • **se ganó el primer premio** he won the first prize • **le dieron el Premio Nobel** they gave him the Nobel Prize ❯ **premio gordo** first prize ❷ [*recompensa*] reward • **en premio a su buen trabajo** in reward for his good work

premonición *sf* premonition

prenatal *adj* prenatal◌*Los adjetivos ingleses son invariables.*

prenda *sf* ❶ [*vestido*] garment ❯ **prenda de vestir** garment ❯ **prendas de lana** woolen garments ❷ [*garantía*] pledge • **dejar algo en prenda** to leave something as a pledge ❸ [*de un juego*] forfeit • **jugar a las prendas** to play forfeits

expresión **no soltar prenda** not to say a word

prender ✦ *vt* ❶ [*sujetar*] to fasten ❷ [*enchufar*] to turn on • **prende el televisor** turn on the television • **prendió la luz** he turned the light on ❸ [*encender*] to light • **prendió un cerillo** he lit a match • **prenderle fuego a algo** to set fire to something ❹ [*agarrar*] to grip

✦ *vi* [*arder*] to light • **este carbón no prende** this charcoal won't light

prensa *sf* ❶ [*generalmente*] press • **la prensa nacional** the national press • **lo leí en la prensa de hoy** I read it in today's news ❯ **prensa del corazón** romantic magazines *pl* ❷ [*imprenta*] printing press

expresión **tener buena/mala prensa** *figurado* to have a good/bad press

prensar *vt* to press

preñado, da *adj* [*mujer*] pregnant • **quedarse preñada** to get pregnant◌*Los adjetivos ingleses son invariables.*

preocupación *sf* worry, *plural* worries • **tienen muchas preocupaciones** they have a lot of worries • **es un motivo de preocupación para sus padres** it's a cause for concern for his parents

preocupado, da *adj* • **preocupado (por)** worried(about)◌*Los adjetivos ingleses son invariables.*

preocupar *vt* to worry • **no preocupes a tus padres** don't worry your parents • **me preocupa mucho el examen de mañana** tomorrow's exam worries me a lot

■ **preocuparse** *v pronominal* ❶ [*inquietarse*] • **preocuparse (por)** to worry (about) • **mi mamá se preocupa por todo** my mom worries about everything • **no se preocupen** don't worry ❷ [*encargarse*] • **preocuparse de algo** to take care of something • **preocuparse de hacer algo** to see to it that something is done • **preocuparse de que...** to make sure that...

preparación *sf* ❶ [*generalmente*] preparation • **la preparación de los informes lleva tiempo** the reports' preparation takes time ❷ [*conocimientos*] training • **le falta preparación** he lacks training

preparar *vt* ❶ [*generalmente*] to prepare • **nos están preparando para el examen de admisión** they're preparing us for the entrance exam • **el profesor no preparó la clase** the professor didn't prepare for class ❷ [*comida, bebida*] to make • **prepara unos postres exquisitos** he makes the most delicious desserts • **voy a preparar el té** I'm going to make tea ❸ [*trampa*] to set ❹ [*maletas*] to pack ❺ [*examen*] to prepare for ❻ DEPORTE to train

■ **prepararse** *v pronominal* • **prepararse (para algo)** to get ready (for something) • **prepararse para hacer algo** to get ready to do something • **se preparó para salir** he got ready to leave • **tienen que prepararse para el examen** they have to prepare for the exam • **se están preparando para el maratón** they're training for the marathon • **prepárate para una gran sorpresa** prepare yourself for a big surprise

preparativos *smpl* preparations

preposición *sf* preposition

prepotente *adj* [*arrogante*] domineering◌*Los adjetivos ingleses son invariables.*

presa *sf* ❶ [*captura - de cazador*] catch; [*- de animal*] prey • **tiburones en busca de una presa** sharks in search of prey • **hacer presa en alguien** to seize somebody • **ser presa del pánico** to be panic-stricken ❷ [*dique*] dam • **van a construir una presa** they're going to build a dam

presagiar *vt* ❶ [*felicidad, futuro*] to foretell ❷ [*tormenta, problemas*] to warn of

presagio *sm* ❶ [*premonición*] premonition ❷ [*señal*] omen

prescindir ■ **prescindir de** *vi* ❶ [*renunciar a*] to do without • **vivo en el campo y no puedo prescindir del**

coche I live in the country and I can't do without a car ❷ [*omitir*] to leave aside • **prescindiendo de un par de detalles, el resto me parece perfecto** aside from a couple of details, the rest looks great ❸ [*no tener en cuenta*] to disregard

prescribir ◆ *vt* to prescribe
◆ *vi* ❶ [*ordenar*] to prescribe ❷ Derecho to expire

prescripción *sf* prescription

presencia *sf* [*asistencia, aspecto*] presence • **en presencia de** in the presence of • **lo hizo en mi presencia** he did it in my presence

presencial → **testigo**

presenciar *vt* ❶ [*asistir*] to be present at ❷ [*ser testigo de*] to witness

presentación *sf* ❶ [*generalmente*] presentation • **me puso una calificación por la presentación** he gave me a grade for the presentation ❷ [*entre personas*] introduction • **hacer las presentaciones** to introduce people to each other • **mi papá se encargó de hacer las presentaciones** my father took care of the introductions

las presentaciones

• **Let me introduce myself: my name is...** Me presento: me llamo...
• **My name is Smith.** Me llamo Smith.
• **This is Mrs. Thomas.** Te presento a la señora Thomas.
• **It's a pleasure!** ¡Encantado!
• **Pleased to meet you!** ¡Encantado de conocerlo!

presentador, ra *sm, f* presenter • **el presentador del noticiero de las seis** the presenter of the six o'clock news • **el nuevo presentador del programa** the new host of the program

presentar *vt* ❶ [*generalmente*] to present ❷ [*dimisión*] to tender ❸ [*tesis, pruebas, propuesta*] to submit ❹ [*solicitud, recurso, denuncia*] to lodge ❺ [*moción*] to propose ❻ [*libro, disco*] to launch • **va a presentar su nuevo disco** he's going to launch his new album ❼ [*ofrecer - ventajas, novedades*] to offer; [*- disculpas, excusas*] to make; [*- respetos*] to pay ❽ [*persona, amigos* etc] to introduce • **me presentó a su hermana** he introduced me to his sister • **te presento a mi hermano** this is my brother ❾ [*enseñar*] to show ❿ [*tener - aspecto* etc] to have; to show • **presenta difícil solución** it's going to be difficult to solve ⓫ [*proponer*] • **presentar a alguien para** to propose somebody for
■ **presentarse** *v pronominal* ❶ [*aparecer*] to turn up • **se presentó tarde y sin las tareas** he turned up late and without his homework ❷ [*en juzgado, comisaría*] • **presentarse (en)** to report (to) • **presentarse a un examen** to sit an exam ❸ [*darse a conocer*] to introduce yourself • **se presentó como el nuevo director** he introduced himself as the new director ❹ [*para un cargo*] • **presentarse (a)** to stand o run (for) ❺ [*futuro*] to appear ❻ [*problema* etc] to arise

presente ◆ *adj* ❶ [*generalmente*] present • **había sólo tres alumnos presentes** there were only three students present • **¡presente!** here! • **aquí presente** here present • **en las presentes circunstancias** in present circumstances • **tener algo presente** to remember something • **tenía tan presente traerlo y se me olvidó** I had remembered that I was supposed to bring it, but then I forgot it ❷ [*en curso*] current • **del presente mes** of this month ☞ *Los adjetivos ingleses son invariables.*
◆ *smf* [*escrito*] • **por la presente le informo...** I hereby inform you...
◆ *sm* ❶ [*generalmente*] Gramática present ❷ [*regalo*] gift ❸ [*corriente*] • **el presente a)** [*mes*] the current month **b)** [*año*] the current year

presentimiento *sm* feeling

presentir *vt* to foresee • **presentir que algo va a pasar** to have a feeling that something is going to happen • **presentir lo peor** to fear the worst

preservar *vt* to protect

preservativo *sm* condom

presidencia *sf* ❶ [*de nación*] presidency ❷ [*de asamblea, empresa*] chairmanship

presidenciable *smf* potential presidential candidate

presidente, ta *sm, f* ❶ [*de nación*] president • **el Presidente de la República** the President of the Republic ▶ **presidente del gobierno** ≃ prime minister ❷ [*de asamblea, empresa*] chairman, *femenino* chairwoman

presidiario, ria *sm, f* convict

presidio *sm* prison

presidir *vt* ❶ [*ser presidente de*] to preside over ❷ [*reunión*] to chair ❸ [*predominar*] to dominate

presión *sf* pressure • **tiene la presión alta** he has high blood pressure ▶ **presión fiscal** Economía tax burden

presionar *vt* ❶ [*apretar*] to press ❷ figurado [*coaccionar*] to pressurize

preso, sa *sm, f* prisoner

prestación *sf* [*de servicio - acción*] provision; [*- resultado*] service

prestado, da *adj* on loan • **dar prestado algo** to lend something • **vivir de prestado** to live off other people ☞ *Los adjetivos ingleses son invariables.*

prestamista *smf* moneylender

préstamo *sm* ❶ [*acción - de prestar*] lending; [*- de pedir prestado*] borrowing ❷ [*cantidad*] loan • **pidió un préstamo** he asked for a loan

prestar *vt* ❶ [*dejar - dinero* etc] to lend • **un amigo me prestó su bicicleta** a friend lent me his bicycle • **¿me prestas los patines?** can I borrow the skates? ❷ [*dar - ayuda* etc] to give; to offer; [*- servicio*] to provide; [*- atención*] to pay; [*- declaración, juramento*] to make • **prestar atención** to pay attention • **presta más atención a lo que dice la profesora** pay more attention to what the professor says

prestidigitador, ra *sm, f* conjurer

prestigio *sm* prestige • **el prestigio del primer ministro está cayendo** the prime minister's prestige is falling • **de prestigio** prestigious

prestigioso, sa *adj* prestigious ᐅ *Los adjetivos ingleses son invariables.*

presumido, da *adj* conceited ᐅ *Los adjetivos ingleses son invariables.*

presumir ♦ *vt* [*suponer*] to presume • **es de presumir que irán** presumably they'll go
♦ *vi* ❶ [*jactarse*] to show off • **lo hace sólo para presumir** he only does it to show off • **Tito presume de inteligente** Tito thinks he's really intelligent ❷ [*ser vanidoso*] to be conceited

presunto, ta *adj* ❶ [*supuesto*] presumed ❷ [*criminal, robo* ETC] alleged ᐅ *Los adjetivos ingleses son invariables.*

presuponer *vt* to presuppose

prêt-à-porter *sm* off-the-peg clothing

pretender *vt* ❶ [*intentar*] • **pretender hacer algo** to try to do something ❷ [*aspirar a*] • **pretender hacer algo** to want to do something • **pretender que alguien haga algo** to want somebody to do something • **¿qué pretendes decir?** what do you mean? • **no sé lo que pretenden con eso** I don't know what they're trying to achieve with that • **pretenden hacernos estudiar más** they intend to make us study more • **no pretenderán que me estudie todo esto** they won't expect me to study all this • **¿pretendes que yo te crea?** do you expect me to believe you? ❸ [*afirmar*] to claim ❹ [*cortejar*] to court

> *pretender ≠ pretend*
> • La palabra inglesa **pretend** es un falso amigo que significa *fingir*.
> • **Pretender** se traduce al inglés por **to intend**.

pretendiente ♦ *smf* ❶ [*aspirante*] • **pretendiente (a)** candidate (for) ❷ [*a un trono*] • **pretendiente (a)** pretender (to)
♦ *sm* [*a una mujer*] suitor

pretensión *sf* ❶ [*intención*] aim ❷ [*aspiración*] aspiration ❸ [*supuesto derecho*] • **pretensión (a o sobre)** claim (to) ❹ [*afirmación*] claim ❺ ᐅ *generalmente pl* [*exigencia*] demand ❻ ᐅ *generalmente pl* [*presuntuosidad*] pretentiousness • **sin pretensiones** unpretentious

pretexto *sm* pretext

prevalecer *vi* • **prevalecer (sobre)** to prevail (over) • **soñaba con una sociedad en que la justicia prevaleciera sobre los intereses económicos** he dreamt of a society in which justice prevailed over financial concerns

prevención *sf* ❶ [*acción*] prevention • **la prevención de accidentes** accident prevention ❷ [*medida*] precaution

prevenido, da *adj* ❶ [*previsor*] • **ser prevenido** to be cautious ❷ [*avisado, dispuesto*] • **estar prevenido** to be prepared ᐅ *Los adjetivos ingleses son invariables.*

prevenir *vt* ❶ [*evitar*] to prevent • **ayuda a prevenir los resfriados** it helps to prevent colds ❷ [*avisar*] to warn • **me previnieron lo que podría pasar** they warned me what could happen ❸ [*predisponer*] • **prevenir a alguien contra algo/alguien** to prejudice somebody against something/somebody

expresión **más vale prevenir que curar** *proverbio* prevention is better than cure *proverbio*

preventivo, va *adj* ❶ [*medicina, prisión*] preventive ❷ [*medida*] precautionary ᐅ *Los adjetivos ingleses son invariables.*

prever ♦ *vt* ❶ [*conjeturar*] to foresee • **prevén un aumento de las temperaturas a nivel mundial** they foresee an increase in temperatures worldwide ❷ [*planear*] to plan • **prevén finalizar las obras este año** they plan to finish the repairs this year ❸ [*predecir*] to forecast
♦ *vi* • **como era de prever** as was to be expected

previo, via *adj* previous • **no es necesario tener experiencia previa** it's not necessary to have previous experience • **previo pago de multa** on payment of a fine • **sin previo aviso** without warning ᐅ *Los adjetivos ingleses son invariables.*

previsible *adj* foreseeable ᐅ *Los adjetivos ingleses son invariables.*

previsión *sf* ❶ [*predicción*] forecast ❷ [*visión de futuro*] foresight

previsor, ra *adj* prudent ᐅ *Los adjetivos ingleses son invariables.*

previsto, ta ♦ *participio pasado* → **prever**
♦ *adj* [*planeado*] planned • **la salida está prevista a las dos** the departure is planned for two o'clock • **un cambio que no estaba previsto** an unanticipated change • **resultó tal como estaba previsto** it came out as expected • **no tenía previsto gastar tanto** he didn't plan to spend so much • **tiene prevista la llegada a las dos** she's due in at two o'clock ᐅ *Los adjetivos ingleses son invariables.*

prieto, ta *adj familiar* [*moreno*] dark-skinned ᐅ *Los adjetivos ingleses son invariables.*

prima *sf* ❶ [*paga extra*] bonus ❷ [*de un seguro*] premium

primario, ria *adj* ❶ [*básico*] primary ❷ [*primitivo*] primitive ᐅ *Los adjetivos ingleses son invariables.*

primavera *sf* [*estación*] spring • **en primavera** in spring

primaveral *adj* spring ᐅ *Sólo se usa delante del sustantivo.*

primer → **primero**

primerizo, za *sm, f* beginner

primero, ra ♦ *adj numeral* ❶ [*para ordenar*] first • **el primero de mayo** the first of May • **en la primera página** on the first page • **en primer lugar, nos dio a todos las gracias** first, he thanked all of us • **se sienta en la primera fila** he sits in the first row ❷ [*en importancia*] main • **lo primero** the main thing ᐅ *Los adjetivos ingleses son invariables.*
♦ *sm, f* ❶ [*en orden*] • **el primero** the first one • **fue el primero en terminar** he was the first one to finish

P

• **llegó el primero** he came first • **es el primero de la clase** he's top of the class • **a primeros de mes** at the beginning of the month ❷ [*mencionado antes*] • **vinieron Pedro y Juan, el primero con...** Pedro and Juan arrived, the former with...
■ **primero** ◆ *adv* ❶ [*en primer lugar*] first ❷ [*antes, todo menos*] • **primero morir que traicionarle** I'd rather die than betray him
◆ *sm* ❶ [*piso*] first floor ❷ [*año escolar*] first grade
primicia *sf* scoop
primitivo, va *adj* ❶ primitive ❷ [*original*] original ⚗ *Los adjetivos ingleses son invariables.*
primo, ma *sm, f* ❶ [*pariente*] cousin • **primo hermano** first cousin ❷ *familiar* [*tonto*] sucker
expresión **hacer el primo** to be taken for a ride
primogénito, ta *adj* & *sm, f* first-born ⚗ *Los adjetivos ingleses son invariables.*
primordial *adj* fundamental ⚗ *Los adjetivos ingleses son invariables.*
princesa *sf* princess
principal *adj* ❶ [*más importante*] main • **una de las principales causas de accidentes** one of the main causes of accidents • **lo principal es ser honesto** the main thing is to be honest ❷ [*puerta*] front ⚗ *Los adjetivos ingleses son invariables.*
príncipe *sm* prince
principiante ◆ *adj* inexperienced ⚗ *Los adjetivos ingleses son invariables.*
◆ *smf* novice
principio *sm* ❶ [*comienzo*] beginning • **el principio de la película es muy original** the beginning of the movie is very original • **al principio** at first • **al principio dijo que no** at first he said no • **a principios de** at the beginning of • **a principios de mes** at the beginning of the month • **a principios de siglo** at the turn of the century • **en un principio** at first ❷ [*fundamento, ley*] principle • **se basa en un principio moral** it's based on a moral principle • **en principio** in principle • **en principio, parecía bueno** in principle, it seemed good • **por principio** on principle ❸ [*origen*] origin; source ❹ [*elemento*] element
pringar *vt* ❶ [*ensuciar*] to make greasy ❷ [*mojar*] to dip
pringoso, sa *adj* ❶ [*grasiento*] greasy ❷ [*pegajoso*] sticky ⚗ *Los adjetivos ingleses son invariables.*
prioridad *sf* ❶ priority ❷ AUTOMÓVILES right of way
prioritario, ria *adj* priority ⚗ *Sólo se usa delante del sustantivo.*
prisa *sf* hurry • **¿a qué tanta prisa?** what's the hurry? • **correr prisa** to be urgent • **darse prisa** to hurry (up) • **meter prisa a alguien** to hurry somebody • **tener prisa** to be in a hurry
prisión *sf* ❶ [*cárcel*] prison ❷ [*encarcelamiento*] imprisonment
prisionero, ra *sm, f* prisoner • **hacer prisionero a alguien** to take somebody prisoner
prisma *sm* ❶ FÍSICA & GEOMETRÍA prism ❷ [*perspectiva*] perspective

prismáticos *smpl* binoculars
privación *sf* ❶ [*generalmente*] deprivation ❷ [*de libertad*] loss
privado, da *adj* private • **un colegio privado** a private school • **su vida privada** his private life • **en privado** in private ⚗ *Los adjetivos ingleses son invariables.*
privar *vt* [*quitar*] • **privar a alguien/algo de** to deprive somebody/something of
privilegiado, da *adj* ❶ [*favorecido*] privileged ❷ [*excepcional*] exceptional ⚗ *Los adjetivos ingleses son invariables.*
privilegio *sm* privilege • **es un gran privilegio** it's a great privilege
pro ◆ *preposición* for • **una asociación pro derechos humanos** a human rights organization
◆ *sm* ▶ **los pros y los contras** the pros and cons
proa *sf* ❶ NÁUTICA prow ❷ AERONÁUTICA nose
probabilidad *sf* ❶ [*posibilidad, oportunidad*] chance • **no tiene ninguna probabilidad de ganar** he doesn't have any chance of winning • **¿cuáles son las probabilidades?** what are the chances? • **si no estudian hay menos probabilidades de que aprueben** if you don't study there's less chance that you'll pass • **con toda probabilidad** in all probability ❷ MATEMÁTICAS probability, *plural* probabilities
probable *adj* likely • **tal vez se perdieron — es muy probable** maybe they got lost — it's very likely • **me parece muy poco probable** it seems very unlikely to me • **es probable que llueva** it'll probably rain • **es probable que se haya olvidado** it's likely that he forgot ⚗ *Los adjetivos ingleses son invariables.*
probador *sm* fitting room
probar ◆ *vt* ❶ [*demostrar, indicar*] to prove • **puedo probar que miente** I can prove that he's lying ❷ [*comprobar*] to test • **están probando una nueva vacuna** they're testing a new vaccine ❸ [*experimentar*] to try • **prueba esto, que te va a gustar** try this, you'll like it ❹ [*degustar*] to taste • **pruébala por si le falta aliño** taste it and see if it needs seasoning
◆ *vi* • **probar a hacer algo** to try to do something • **prueba a hacerlo tú mismo** try to do it yourself
probeta *sf* test tube
problema *sm* problem • **tiene muchos problemas** he has many problems • **tiene problemas del corazón** he has heart problems • **nunca pude resolver el problema** I never managed to solve the problem • **está viejo y ya empieza a darme problemas** it's old and it's now beginning to give me trouble • **siempre se está metiendo en problemas** he's always getting into trouble
problemático, ca *adj* problematic ⚗ *Los adjetivos ingleses son invariables.*
procedencia *sf* ❶ [*origen*] origin ❷ [*punto de partida*] point of departure • **con procedencia de** (arriving) from
procedente *adj* ❶ [*originario*] • **procedente de a)** [*generalmente*] originating in **b)** AERONÁUTICA & FERROCARRIL (arriving) from ❷ [*oportuno*] appropriate ❸ DE-

RECHO right and proper ·❦· *Los adjetivos ingleses son invariables.*

proceder *vi* ❶ [*originarse*] • **proceder de** to come from • **la energía de las estrellas procede de la fusión termonuclear** the energy of the stars comes from thermonuclear fusion ❷ [*ser nativo de*] • **proceder de** to be from • **sus abuelos procedían de Galicia** her grandparents were from Galicia ❸ [*actuar*] • **proceder (con)** to act (with) ❹ [*empezar*] to begin • **procedieron a contar los votos** they began counting the votes ❺ [*ser oportuno*] to be appropriate

procedimiento *sm* ❶ [*método*] procedure ❷ DERECHO proceedings *pl*

procesado, da *sm, f* accused

procesador *sm* INFORMÁTICA processor ▶ **procesador Pentium®** Pentium® processor ▶ **procesador de textos** word processor

procesar *vt* ❶ DERECHO to prosecute ❷ INFORMÁTICA to process

procesión *sf* figurado RELIGIÓN procession

proceso *sm* ❶ [*generalmente*] process • **el proceso de paz** the peace process ❷ [*desarrollo, intervalo*] course ❸ DERECHO [*juicio*] trial ; [*causa*] lawsuit

proclamar *vt* ❶ [*nombrar*] to proclaim ❷ [*anunciar*] to declare

procurador, ra *sm, f* DERECHO attorney

procuraduría *sf* justice department

procurar *vt* ❶ [*intentar*] • **procurar hacer algo** to try to do something • **procurar que...** to make sure that... ❷ [*proporcionar*] to get

prodigio *sm* ❶ [*suceso*] miracle ❷ [*persona*] prodigy

prodigioso, sa *adj* ❶ [*sobrenatural*] miraculous ❷ [*extraordinario*] wonderful ·❦· *Los adjetivos ingleses son invariables.*

producción *sf* ❶ [*generalmente*] CINE production ❷ [*productos*] products *pl*

producir *vt* ❶ [*generalmente*] CINE to produce • **la región produce café** the region produces coffee ❷ [*causar*] to cause • **el accidente produjo un gran atasco** the accident caused a major traffic jam • **el polen me produce alergia** pollen gives me allergies ❸ [*interés, fruto*] to yield

productividad *sf* productivity

productivo, va *adj* ❶ productive ❷ [*que da beneficio*] profitable ·❦· *Los adjetivos ingleses son invariables.*

producto *sm* ❶ [*generalmente*] MATEMÁTICAS product ❷ AGRICULTURA produce ·❦· *incontable* ▶ **producto acabado/manufacturado** finished/manufactured product ▶ **producto de belleza** beauty product ▶ **producto interior/nacional bruto** gross domestic/national product ▶ **producto químico** chemical ▶ **productos alimenticios** foodstuffs ❸ figurado [*resultado*] result

productor, ra ✦ *adj* producing ·❦· *Los adjetivos ingleses son invariables.*
✦ *sm, f* CINE [*persona*] producer
■ **productora** *sf* CINE [*firma*] production company

profecía *sf* [*predicción*] prophecy

profesión *sf* profession

profesional *adj* & *smf* professional ·❦· *Los adjetivos ingleses son invariables.*

profesionista *smf* professional

profesor, ra *sm, f* ❶ [*generalmente*] teacher • **la profesora de inglés** the English teacher ❷ [*de universidad*] professor • **profesor universitario** university professor ❸ [*de autoescuela, esquí* ETC] instructor • **la profesora de natación** the swimming instructor

profesorado *sm* ❶ [*plantilla*] faculty ❷ [*profesión*] teaching profession

profeta *sm* prophet

profundidad *sf* depth • **a una profundidad de tres metros** at a depth of three meters • **en profundidad** in depth • **tiene dos metros de profundidad** it's two meters deep

profundizar ✦ *vt* figurado to study in depth
✦ *vi* to go into detail • **profundizar en** to study in depth

profundo, da *adj* ❶ [*generalmente*] deep • **la parte más profunda de la piscina** the deepest part of the swimming pool • **un pozo poco profundo** a shallow well ❷ figurado [*respeto, libro, pensamiento*] profound ❸ [*dolor*] intense ·❦· *Los adjetivos ingleses son invariables.*

programa *sm* ❶ [*generalmente*] programme ❷ [*de actividades*] schedule ❸ [*de estudios*] syllabus • **el programa de estudios** the syllabus ❹ INFORMÁTICA program • **un programa informático** a computer program

programación *sf* ❶ INFORMÁTICA programming ❷ TELEVISIÓN scheduling • **la programación del lunes** Monday's programmes

programador, ra *sm, f* programmer

programar *vt* ❶ [*vacaciones, reforma* ETC] to plan • **no he programado nada para el sábado** I haven't planned anything for Saturday ❷ CINE & TELEVISIÓN to put on ❸ TECNOLOGÍA & INFORMÁTICA to program

progresar *vi* to progress

progresión *sf* ❶ [*generalmente*] MATEMÁTICAS progression ▶ **progresión aritmética/geométrica** arithmetic/geometric progression ❷ [*mejora*] progress

progresista *adj* & *smf* progressive ·❦· *Los adjetivos ingleses son invariables.*

progresivo, va *adj* progressive ·❦· *Los adjetivos ingleses son invariables.*

progreso *sm* progress • **el progreso de la ciencia** scientific progress • **hacer progresos** to make progress

prohibición *sf* ban

P

expresar una prohibición
• **No smoking** Prohibido fumar
• **Running in the corridors is strictly forbidden.** Queda terminantemente prohibido correr en los pasillos
• **It's out of the question!** ¡Ni pensarlo!
• **I won't stand for it!** ¡No lo consentiré!

prohibido, da *adj* banned • **un medicamento prohibido en ese país** a drug banned in that country • **eso está absolutamente prohibido** that is absolutely forbidden • **'prohibido estacionarse/fumar'** no parking/smoking • **'prohibida la entrada'** no entry:💡 *Los adjetivos ingleses son invariables.*

prohibir *vt* ❶ [*generalmente*] to forbid • **le prohibieron los alimentos grasos** they forbade him from eating fatty foods • **prohibir a alguien hacer algo** to forbid somebody to do something • **'se prohíbe el paso'** no entry ❷ [*por ley - de antemano*] to prohibit; [*- a posteriori*] to ban

prohibitivo, va *adj* prohibitive:💡 *Los adjetivos ingleses son invariables.*

prójimo *sm* fellow human being

proliferación *sf* proliferation

proliferar *vi* to proliferate

prólogo *sm* ❶ [*de libro*] preface ❷ *figurado* prelude

prolongación *sf* extension

prolongado, da *adj* ❶ [*alargado*] long ❷ *figurado* [*dilatado*] lengthy:💡 *Los adjetivos ingleses son invariables.*

prolongar *vt* ❶ [*generalmente*] to extend ❷ [*espera, visita, conversación*] to prolong ❸ [*cuerda, tubo*] to lengthen

promedio *sm* average • **como promedio** on average

promesa *sf* [*compromiso*] promise • **siempre cumple sus promesas** she always keeps her promises • **hacer una promesa** to make a promise • **romper una promesa** to break a promise

hacer una promesa

- **It's a promise!** ¡Prometido!
- **You can count on me.** Cuenta conmigo.
- **I'll see to it.** Y me encargo de ello.
- **No problem. It's OK.** No hay problema, está bien.

prometer ◆ *vt* to promise • **prometió estudiar más** he promised to study more • **¿me lo prometes?** do you promise?
◆ *vi* [*tener futuro*] to show promise

prometido, da ◆ *sm, f* fiancé, *femenino* fiancée ◆ *adj* [*para casarse*] engaged:💡 *Los adjetivos ingleses son invariables.*

promoción *sf* ❶ [*generalmente*] DEPORTE promotion ❷ [*curso*] class

promocionar *vt* to promote

promotor, ra *sm, f* ❶ [*de una rebelión*] instigator ❷ COMERCIO promoter ▸ **promotor inmobiliario** real estate developer

promover *vt* ❶ [*iniciar - fundación* ETC] to set up; [*- rebelión*] to stir up ❷ [*impulsar*] to stimulate ❸ [*ocasionar*] to cause ❹ [*ascender*] • **promover a alguien a** to promote somebody to

pronombre *sm* pronoun

pronosticar *vt* to forecast

pronóstico *sm* ❶ [*predicción*] forecast ▸ **pronóstico del tiempo** weather forecast ❷ MEDICINA prognosis • **de pronóstico grave** serious

pronto, ta *adj* ❶ [*rápido*] quick ❷ [*respuesta*] prompt ❸ [*curación, tramitación*] speedy:💡 *Los adjetivos ingleses son invariables.*
■ **pronto** ◆ *adv* ❶ [*rápidamente*] quickly ❷ [*temprano*] early • **salimos pronto** we left early ❸ [*dentro de poco*] soon • **tan pronto como** as soon as • **¡hasta pronto!** see you soon!
◆ *sm familiar* sudden impulse

pronunciación *sf* pronunciation

pronunciamiento *sm* ❶ [*sublevación*] uprising ❷ DERECHO pronouncement

pronunciar *vt* [*decir - palabra*] to pronounce; [*- discurso*] to make

propagación *sf* ❶ [*generalmente*] spreading:💡 *incontable* ❷ BIOLOGÍA & FÍSICA propagation

propaganda *sf* ❶ [*publicidad*] advertising:💡 *incontable* • **hay mucha propaganda en la televisión** there's a lot of advertising on television ❷ [*política, religiosa*] propaganda

propagar *vt* ❶ [*generalmente*] to spread ❷ [*razas, especies*] to propagate

propensión *sf* propensity

propenso, sa *adj* • **propenso a algo/a hacer algo** prone to something/doing something:💡 *Los adjetivos ingleses son invariables.*

propicio, cia *adj* ❶ [*favorable*] favorable ❷ [*adecuado*] suitable:💡 *Los adjetivos ingleses son invariables.*

propiedad *sf* ❶ [*derecho*] ownership ❷ [*bienes*] property ▸ **propiedad privada** private property ▸ **propiedad pública** public ownership ❸ [*facultad*] property, *plural* properties ❹ [*exactitud*] accuracy • **usar una palabra con propiedad** to use a word properly

propietario, ria *sm, f* [*de bienes*] owner

propina *sf* tip • **¿dejaste propina?** did you leave a tip? • **le di propina la taxista** I tipped the taxi driver

propio, pia *adj* ❶ [*generalmente*] own • **tiene coche propio** she has a car of her own • **por tu propio bien** for your own good ❷ [*peculiar*] • **propio de** typical of • **es muy propio de la gente de esa edad** it's very typical of people of that age • **no es propio de él** it's not like him ❸ [*apropiado*] • **propio (para)** suitable o right (for) ❹ [*en persona*] himself, *femenino* herself • **el propio compositor** the composer himself:💡 *Los adjetivos ingleses son invariables.*

proponer *vt* ❶ [*sugerir*] to suggest • **propongo que nos vayamos** I suggest that we leave • **propuso ir al cine** he suggested going to the movies ❷ [*candidato*] to put forward

proponer algo

- **Why don't we all go the movies together?** Propongo que vayamos todos juntos al cine.

• **Do you feel like going to a restaurant?**
¿Tienes/Tiene ganas de ir al restaurante?
• **What about going for a swim?** ¿Y si fuéramos
a nadar?
• **Would you like to go to the museum?** ¿Te/Le
gustaría ir al museo?

proporción *sf* ❶ [*generalmente*] MATEMÁTICAS proportion • **en proporción a** in proportion to ❷ ☼: *generalmente pl* [*importancia*] extent

proporcionado, da *adj* • **proporcionado (a) a)**
[*estatura, sueldo*] commensurate (with) **b)** [*medidas*]
proportionate (to) • **bien proporcionado** well-propor-
tioned ☼: *Los adjetivos ingleses son invariables.*

proporcionar *vt* ❶ [*facilitar*] • **proporcionar algo
a alguien** to provide somebody with something ❷ *figurado* [*conferir*] to lend

proposición *sf* [*propuesta*] proposal

propósito *sm* ❶ [*intención*] intention • **sus pro-
pósitos son buenos** his intentions are good ❷ [*objetivo*] purpose • **su único propósito es ganar** his only
purpose is to win

propuesta *sf* ❶ proposal • **a propuesta de** at the
suggestion of ❷ [*de empleo*] offer

propulsar *vt* ❶ [*impeler*] to propel ❷ *figurado* [*promover*] to promote

propulsión *sf* propulsion • **propulsión a chorro**
jet propulsion

prórroga *sf* ❶ [*generalmente*] extension ❷ [*de estudios, servicio militar*] deferment ❸ DEPORTE extra time

prorrogar *vt* ❶ [*alargar*] to extend ❷ [*aplazar*] to
defer

prosa *sf* LITERATURA prose

proseguir ◆ *vt* to continue
◆ *vi* to go on

prospección *sf* ❶ [*generalmente*] exploration ❷ [*petrolífera, minera*] prospecting

prospecto *sm* ❶ leaflet ❷ COMERCIO & EDUCACIÓN
prospectus

prosperar *vi* [*mejorar*] to prosper

prosperidad *sf* ❶ [*mejora*] prosperity ❷ [*éxito*]
success

próspero, ra *adj* prosperous ☼: *Los adjetivos ingleses son invariables.*

prostitución *sf* prostitution

prostituta *sf* prostitute

protagonista *sm, f* ❶ [*generalmente*] main character ❷ TEATRO lead

protagonizar *vt* ❶ [*obra, película*] to play the lead in
❷ *figurado* [*hazaña*] to play a leading part in

protección *sf* protection • **bajo la protección de
alguien** under the protection of somebody ❿ **protección de datos** INFORMÁTICA data protection

proteccionismo *sm* protectionism

protector, ra ◆ *adj* protective ☼: *Los adjetivos ingleses son invariables.*

◆ *sm, f* [*persona*] protector

proteger *vt* [*generalmente*] to protect • **proteger
algo de algo** to protect something from something
• **la sombrilla nos protege del sol** the sunshade is pro-
tecting us from the sun

protegeslip *sm* panty liner

protegido, da *sm, f* protégé, *femenino* protégée

proteína *sf* protein • **rico en proteínas** rich in
protein

prótesis *sf invariable* ❶ MEDICINA prosthesis
❷ [*miembro*] artificial limb

protesta *sf* [*queja*] protest • **una manifestación de
protesta** a protest demonstration

protestante *adj & smf* Protestant ☼: *Los adjetivos
ingleses son invariables.*

protestar *vi* ❶ [*quejarse*] • **protestar (por/con-
tra)** to protest (about/against) • **protestan por la
subida de los precios** they're protesting the increase
in prices • **¡protesto!** DERECHO objection! ❷ [*refunfuñar*] to grumble

protocolo *sm* ❶ [*generalmente*] INFORMÁTICA protocol ❷ [*ceremonial*] etiquette

prototipo *sm* ❶ [*modelo*] archetype ❷ [*primer ejemplar*] prototype

provecho *sm* [*generalmente*] benefit • **sacar provecho de algo** to benefit from something • **no sacó
ningún provecho de su estadía en Europa** he didn't
benefit at all from his stay in Europe • **¡buen provecho!** enjoy your meal!

provechoso, sa *adj* ❶ [*ventajoso*] beneficial
❷ [*lucrativo*] profitable ☼: *Los adjetivos ingleses son
invariables.*

proveedor, ra *sm, f* provider ❿ **proveedor de servicios** service provider ❿ **proveedor de acceso a Internet** Internet access provider

proveer *vt* ❶ [*abastecer*] to supply ❷ [*puesto, cargo*]
to fill

provenir *vi* • **provenir de** to come from

proverbio *sm* proverb

providencial *adj* providential ☼: *Los adjetivos ingleses son invariables.*

provincia *sf* province

provinciano, na *adj & sm, f* *despectivo* provincial ☼: *Los adjetivos ingleses son invariables.*

provisión *sf* ☼: *generalmente pl* [*suministro*]
supply

provisional *adj* provisional ☼: *Los adjetivos ingleses son invariables.*

provisorio, ria *adj* provisional ☼: *Los adjetivos ingleses son invariables.*

provocación *sf* [*hostigamiento*] provocation

provocar *vt* ❶ [*incitar*] to incite • **provocar a alguien
a hacer algo a)** [*generalmente*] to cause somebody to
do something **b)** [*matar, luchar* ETC] to provoke somebody to do something ❷ [*irritar*] to provoke • **déja de
provocar a tu hermano** stop provoking your brother
❸ [*ocasionar - generalmente*] to cause • **las inunda-**

ciones han provocado el cierre de varios caminos the floods have caused the closing of several roads ❹ [*excitar sexualmente*] to arouse

provocativo, va *adj* provocative ҉ *Los adjetivos ingleses son invariables.*

próximamente *adv* ❶ [*pronto*] soon ❷ CINE coming soon

proximidad *sf* [*cercanía*] proximity

próximo, ma *adj* ❶ [*cercano*] close • **próximo a algo** close to something ❷ [*casa, ciudad*] nearby • **en fecha próxima** shortly ❸ [*siguiente*] next • **el próximo año** next year ҉ *Los adjetivos ingleses son invariables.*

proyección *sf* ❶ [*generalmente*] GEOMETRÍA projection ❷ CINE screening ❸ figurado [*trascendencia*] importance

proyectar *vt* ❶ [*dirigir - focos* ETC] to shine; to direct ❷ [*mostrar - película*] to screen; [*- sombra*] to cast; [*- diapositivas*] to show ❸ [*planear - viaje, operación, edificio*] to plan; [*- puente, obra*] to design ❹ [*arrojar*] to throw forwards

proyectil *sm* projectile

proyecto *sm* ❶ [*intención*] project • **trabaja en un proyecto de desarrollo** he works on a development project ❷ [*plan*] plan • **están haciendo proyectos para las vacaciones** they're making vacation plans ❸ [*diseño -* ARQUITECTURA] design; [*- TECNOLOGÍA*] plan ❹ [*borrador*] draft ▶ **proyecto de ley** bill

proyector *sm* [*de cine, diapositivas*] projector

prudencia *sf* ❶ [*cuidado*] caution ❷ [*previsión, sensatez*] prudence ❸ [*moderación*] moderation • **con prudencia** in moderation

prudente *adj* ❶ [*cuidadoso*] careful ❷ [*previsor, sensato*] sensible ❸ [*razonable*] reasonable ҉ *Los adjetivos ingleses son invariables.*

prueba ♦ *v* → **probar**
♦ *sf* ❶ [*demostración*] DERECHO proof • **es prueba de que lo puede hacer** it's proof that he can do it • **no tengo pruebas** I have no proof • **como prueba de** in o as proof of ❷ [*manifestación*] token • **es una prueba de cariño** it's a token of affection ❸ EDUCACIÓN & MEDICINA test • **tengo dos pruebas esta semana** I have two tests this week ▶ **prueba de alcoholemia** Breathalyzer®test ▶ **prueba de admisión** entrance exam ▶ **prueba de aptitud** aptitude test ▶ **prueba del embarazo** pregnancy test ❹ [*comprobación*] test • **a** o **de prueba a)** [*trabajador*] on trial **b)** [*producto comprado*] on approval • **poner a prueba** to (put to the) test ❺ DEPORTE event • **las pruebas de atletismo** the track events

PS (*abreviatura escrita de* post scriptum) PS

psicoanálisis *sm invariable* psychoanalysis

psicoanalista *smf* psychoanalyst

psicodélico, ca *adj* psychedelic ҉ *Los adjetivos ingleses son invariables.*

psicología *sf* psychology

psicológico, ca *adj* psychological ҉ *Los adjetivos ingleses son invariables.*

psicólogo, ga *sm, f* psychologist

psicópata *smf* psychopath

psicosis *sf invariable* psychosis

psicosomático, ca *adj* psychosomatic ҉ *Los adjetivos ingleses son invariables.*

psiquiatra *smf* psychiatrist

psiquiátrico, ca *adj* psychiatric ҉ *Los adjetivos ingleses son invariables.*

psíquico, ca *adj* psychic ҉ *Los adjetivos ingleses son invariables.*

púa *sf* ❶ [*de planta*] thorn ❷ [*de peine*] tooth ❸ [*de tenedor*] prong ❹ MÚSICA plectrum

pubertad *sf* puberty

publicación *sf* publication

publicar *vt* ❶ [*editar*] to publish ❷ [*aviso*] to issue

publicidad *sf* ❶ [*difusión*] publicity • **ha tenido muy mala publicidad** he's had very bad publicity • **dar publicidad a algo** to publicize something ❷ COMERCIO advertising • **una campaña de publicidad** an advertising campaign ❸ TELEVISIÓN adverts *pl*

publicitario, ria *adj* advertising ҉ *Sólo se usa delante del sustantivo.*

público, ca *adj* public • **un colegio público** a public school • **ser público** [*conocido*] to be common knowledge • **en público** in public ҉ *Los adjetivos ingleses son invariables.*

■ **público** *sm* ❶ CINE, TEATRO & TELEVISIÓN audience • **el público en el cine empezó a aplaudir** the audience in the movie theater began to applaud ❷ DEPORTE crowd ❸ [*comunidad*] public • **todavía no está abierto al público** it's still not open to the public • **hablar en público lo pone nervioso** speaking in public makes him nervous ▶ **el gran público** the (general) public

pudding = **pudin**

púdico, ca *adj* ❶ [*recatado*] modest ❷ [*tímido*] bashful ҉ *Los adjetivos ingleses son invariables.*

pudin (pl **púdines**), **pudding** (pl **puddings**) *sm* (plum) pudding

pudor *sm* ❶ [*recato*] (sense of) shame ❷ [*timidez*] bashfulness

pudrir *vt* ❶ [*descomponerse*] to rot ❷ [*fastidiar*] to be fed up

■ **pudrirse** *v pronominal* to rot

pueblerino, na *adj* despectivo provincial ҉ *Los adjetivos ingleses son invariables.*

pueblo *sm* ❶ [*población - pequeña*] village; [*- grande*] town ❷ [*nación*] people • **el pueblo de América Latina** the people of Latin America

puente *sm* ❶ [*generalmente*] bridge ▶ **puente peatonal** footbridge ❷ [*días festivos*] • **hacer puente** to take a long weekend • **el puente del veinte de noviembre** the long weekend for the November 20th holiday
expresión tender un puente to build bridges
■ **puente aéreo** *sm* ❶ [*civil*] air shuttle ❷ [*militar*] airlift

puenting *sm* bungee-jumping

puerco, ca ♦ *adj* filthy ҉ *Los adjetivos ingleses son invariables.*
♦ *sm, f* [*animal*] pig, *femenino* <u>sow</u>

◆ *sm* [*carne*] pork • **no come puerco** she doesn't eat pork

puercoespín *sm* porcupine

puerta *sf* **❶** [*de casa*] door • **de puerta en puerta** from door to door • **llamar a la puerta** to knock on the door ▶ **puerta blindada/de vidrio** reinforced/glass door **❷** [*de jardín, ciudad* ETC] gate ▶ **puerta de embarque** boarding gate **❸** DEPORTE goalmouth
expresión **a las puertas de** on the verge of

puerto *sm* **❶** [*de mar*] port ▶ **puerto deportivo** marina ▶ **puerto franco** o **libre** free port ▶ **puerto pesquero** fishing port **❷** [*de montaña*] pass **❸** INFORMÁTICA port ▶ **puerto USB** USB port **❹** *figurado* [*refugio*] haven

Puerto Rico *nombre propio* Puerto Rico

pues *conjunción* **❶** [*dado que*] since **❷** [*por lo tanto*] therefore • **creo, pues, que...** I think that... **❸** [*así que*] so • **querías verlo, pues ahí está** you wanted to see it, so here it is **❹** [*enfático*] • **¡pues ya está!** well, that's it! • **¡pues claro!** but of course!

puesto, ta ◆ *participio pasado* → **poner**
◆ *adj* • **ir muy puesto** to be all dressed up ☞ *Los adjetivos ingleses son invariables.*
■ **puesto** *sm* **❶** [*lugar*] place • **le reservé un puesto en la mesa** I saved her a place at the table **❷** [*empleo*] post ▶ **puesto de trabajo** job **❸** [*en fila, clasificación* ETC] place **❹** [*tenderete*] stand • **un puesto de fruta** a fruit stand **❺** MILITAR post ▶ **puesto de mando/vigilancia** command/sentry post ▶ **puesto de policía** police station ▶ **puesto de primeros auxilios** first-aid post
■ **puesta** *sf* [*acción*] ▶ **puesta a punto a)** [*de una técnica*] perfecting **b)** [*de un motor*] tuning ▶ **puesta al día** updating ▶ **puesta en escena** staging; production ▶ **puesta en marcha a)** [*de máquina*] starting; start-up **b)** [*de acuerdo, proyecto*] implementation ▶ **puesta en práctica** implementation
■ **puesta de sol** *sf* sunset

púgil *sm* boxer

pulga *sf* flea

pulgada *sf* inch

pulgar → **dedo**

pulgón *sm* greenfly

pulir *vt* to polish

pulmón *sm* lung
expresión **a pleno pulmón a)** [*gritar*] at the top of one's voice **b)** [*respirar*] deeply ▶ **tener buenos pulmones** to have a powerful voice

pulmonía *sf* pneumonia

púlpito *sm* pulpit

pulpo *sm* [*animal*] octopus

pulque *sm* fermented maguey juice

pulquería *sf* "pulque" bar

pulsación *sf* **❶** [*del corazón*] beat **❷** [*en máquina de escribir*] keystroke

pulsador *sm* button

pulsar *vt* **❶** [*botón, timbre* ETC] to press **❷** [*teclas de ordenador*] to hit **❸** [*teclas de piano*] to play

pulsera *sf* bracelet • **una pulsera de oro** a gold bracelet

pulso *sm* **❶** [*latido*] pulse • **le tomó el pulso** she took his pulse **❷** [*firmeza*] • **tener buen pulso** to have a steady hand • **a pulso** unaided
expresión **ganarse algo a pulso** to deserve something ▶ **tomar el pulso a algo** to sound something out

pulverizar *vt* **❶** [*líquido*] to spray **❷** [*sólido*] to reduce to dust **❸** TECNOLOGÍA to pulverize **❹** *figurado* [*aniquilar*] to pulverize

puma *sm* puma

punta *sf* **❶** [*extremo - generalmente*] point; [*- de pan, pelo*] end; [*- de dedo, cuerno*] tip • **de punta a punta** from one end to the other • **en punta** pointed • **queda en la otra punta de la ciudad** it's at the other end of the city • **sacar punta a (un lápiz)** to sharpen (a pencil) **❷** [*de sal*] pinch
expresión **a punta (de) pala** by the dozen ▶ **tener algo en la punta de la lengua** to have something on the tip of one's tongue

puntapié *sm* kick • **le dio un puntapié a la pelota** he gave the ball a kick • **dar un puntapié a alguien** to kick somebody
expresión **tratar a alguien a puntapiés** to be nasty to somebody

puntería *sf* **❶** [*destreza*] marksmanship **❷** [*orientación*] aim • **hacer puntería** to take aim

puntiagudo, da *adj* pointed ☞ *Los adjetivos ingleses son invariables.*

puntilla *sf* point lace
expresión **dar la puntilla** to give the coup de grâce

puntilloso, sa *adj* **❶** [*susceptible*] touchy **❷** [*meticuloso*] punctilious ☞ *Los adjetivos ingleses son invariables.*

punto *sm* **❶** [*generalmente*] point • **ganaron por un punto** they won by one point • **es uno de los puntos que van a tratar** it's one of the points that they're going to discuss ▶ **punto débil/fuerte** weak/strong point ▶ **punto de vista** point of view **❷** [*signo ortográfico*] dot • **el punto sobre la "i"** the dot on the "i" • **hay que terminar la frase con un punto** you have to end the sentence with a period ▶ **punto y coma** semi-colon ▶ **puntos suspensivos** dots ▶ **dos puntos** colon **❸** [*marca, lugar*] spot **❹** [*momento*] point • **estar a punto** to be ready • **estoy a punto de terminar** I'm just about to finish • **estuvo a punto de llorar** he was on the verge of tears • **estuve a punto de decírselo** I nearly told her **❺** [*estado*] state • **llegar a un punto en que...** to reach the stage where... **❻** [*puntada - en costura, cirugía*] stitch • **le pusieron cinco puntos en la frente** they gave her five stitches on her forehead • **hacer punto** to knit **❼** [*estilo de tejer*] knitting ▶ **punto de ganchillo** crochet
expresión **poner punto final a algo** to bring something to a close ▶ **estar en su punto a)** [*generalmente*] to be just right **b)** [*comida*] to be done to a turn
■ **punto muerto** *sm* **❶** AUTOMÓVILES neutral **❷** [*en un proceso*] deadlock
expresión **estar en un punto muerto** to be deadlocked

P

puntuación *sf* ❶ [*calificación*] mark ❷ [*en concursos, competiciones*] score ❸ [*ortográfica*] punctuation

puntual *adj* ❶ [*en el tiempo*] punctual • **ser muy puntual** to be very punctual ❷ [*exacto, detallado*] detailed ❸ [*aislado*] isolated ☀: *Los adjetivos ingleses son invariables.*

puntualidad *sf* [*en el tiempo*] punctuality

puntualizar *vt* to specify

puntuar ◆ *vt* ❶ [*calificar*] to mark ❷ Deporte to award marks to ❸ [*escrito*] to punctuate
◆ *vi* ❶ [*calificar*] to mark ❷ [*entrar en el cómputo*] • **puntuar (para)** to count (toward)

punzada *sf* [*dolor intenso*] stabbing pain ☀: *incontable*

puñado *sm* handful

puñal *sm* dagger

puñalada *sf* [*herida*] stab wound • **recibió varias puñaladas** he received several stab wounds

puñetazo *sm* punch • **le dio un puñetazo en el ojo** he punched him in the eye • **lo derribó de un puñetazo** he knocked him to the ground

puño *sm* ❶ [*mano cerrada*] fist • **luchó con los puños** he fought with his fists ❷ [*de manga*] cuff • **una manga con puño** a sleeve with a cuff ❸ [*empuñadura - de espada*] hilt ; [*- de paraguas*] handle

expresión **de su puño y letra** in his/her own handwriting

punzón *sm* punch

pupila *sf* pupil

pupilo, la *sm, f* [*discípulo*] pupil

pupitre *sm* desk

puré *sm* ❶ Cocina purée ▶ **puré de papas** mashed potatoes ❷ [*sopa*] thick soup

expresión **hacer puré a alguien** to beat somebody to a pulp

pureza *sf* purity

purificar *vt* ❶ to purify ❷ [*mineral, metal*] to refine

puritano, na *adj* & *sm, f* puritan ☀: *Los adjetivos ingleses son invariables.*

puro, ra *adj* ❶ [*generalmente*] pure • **es plata pura** it's pure silver • **por pura casualidad** by pure chance ❷ [*oro*] solid ❸ [*conducta, persona*] innocent ❹ [*mero*] sheer ❺ [*verdad*] plain ☀: *Los adjetivos ingleses son invariables.*

■ **puro** *sm* cigar

púrpura ◆ *adj invariable* purple ☀: *Los adjetivos ingleses son invariables.*

◆ *sm* purple

pus *sm* pus

putrefacción *sf* rotting

pza. (*abreviatura escrita de* plaza) Sq

q *sf* [*letra*] q ; Q

que

◆ *pronombre relativo*

❶ [*sujeto*] that
• **la moto que me gusta** the motorbike (that) I like
• **ese hombre es el que me lo compró** that's the man who bought it from me

❷ [*complemento directo*] that
• **el hombre que conociste ayer** the man (that) you met yesterday
• **¿no ha leído el libro que le presté?** haven't you read the book I lent you?
• **la señora a la que fuiste a ver** the lady you went to see

❸ [*complemento indirecto*]
• **el joven al que di la propina** the young man I tipped
• **la mujer a la que se lo regalé** the woman I gave it to

❹ [*precedido por una preposición, al hablar de una persona*]
• **la amiga con la que fui al cine** the friend I went to the movies with
• **ése es el chico al que hablé** that's the boy I spoke to
• **la chica con que sueño a menudo** the girl I often dream about

❺ [*precedido por una preposición, al hablar de una cosa*]
• **el coche con el que participé en la carrera** the car I drove in the race
• **es algo sin lo que no puedo vivir** it's something I can't live without

❻ [*introduce un complemento de lugar o de tiempo*]
• **la playa a la que fui de vacaciones** the beach I went to on vacation
• **nunca olvidaré el día (en) que te conocí** I'll never forget the day I met you

◆ *conjunción*

❶ [*introduce una cláusula subordinada*] that
• **es importante que me escuches** it's important that you listen to me

• **me ha confesado que me quiere** he's confessed he loves me
• **quiero que lo hagas** I want you to do it
• **espero que te diviertas** I hope you enjoy yourself

❷ [*introduce una comparación*] than
• **es más rápido que tú** he's faster than you

❸ [*introduce el objetivo*] so
• **ven aquí que te vea** come here so I can see you

❹ [*introduce la consecuencia*] that
• **me lo pidió tantas veces que se lo di** he asked me for it so many times that I ended up giving it to him

❺ [*expresa la causa*]
• **déjalo que está durmiendo** leave him, he's asleep

❻ [*en frases exclamativas, para expresar un deseo*]
• **¡que te diviertas!** have fun!
• **¡que tengas mucha suerte!** good luck!

❼ [*introduce una suposición*]
• **que no quieres, pues no pasa nada** no problem if you don't want to

❽ [*para insistir*]
• **estaban habla que habla** they were chatting non-stop

qué ◆ *adj* ❶ [*generalmente*] what • **¿qué hora es?** what's the time? • **¿qué día es hoy?** what day is today? • **¿a qué distancia?** how far away? • **¿a qué colegio vas?** which school do you go to? ❷ [*al elegir, al concretar*] which • **¿qué coche prefieres?** which car do you prefer? ⚲ *Los adjetivos ingleses son invariables.*

◆ *pronombre* ⚲ *interrogativo* what • **¿qué te dijo?** what did he tell you? • **no sé qué hacer** I don't know what to do • **¿qué?** [*¿cómo?*] sorry?

◆ *adv* ❶ [*exclamativo*] how • **¡qué horror!** how awful! • **¡qué tonto eres!** how stupid you are! • **¡qué casa más bonita!** what a lovely house! ❷ [*expresa gran cantidad*] • **¡qué de...!** what a lot of...! • **¡qué de gente hay aquí!** what a lot of people there are here!

expresión **¡y qué!** so what?

quebradero ■ **quebradero de cabeza** *sm* headache

quebrar ◆ *vt* [*romper*] to break
◆ *vi* FINANZAS to go bankrupt
■ **quebrarse** *v pronominal* ❶ [*romperse*] to break
• **me caí y me quebré una pierna** I fell and broke a leg ❷ [*voz*] to break

---

quedar
◆ *vi*

❶ [*continuar existiendo*] to be left
• **quedan tres manzanas** there are three apples left
• **no queda leche** there's no milk left
• **nos quedan dos días para inscribirnos** we have two days left to register

❷ [*continuar estando en el mismo estado*]
• **el cuadro quedó sin acabar** the painting wasn't finished
• **queda mucho por hacer** there's a lot to be done still

❸ [*dar cierta impresión*]
• **quedó como un imbécil** he just looked like an idiot
• **quedar bien/mal (con alguien)** to make a good/bad impression(on somebody)
• **quedar en ridículo** to look stupid

❹ [*indica un resultado*] to turn out
• **el pastel te quedó perfecto** the cake turned out perfectly

❺ [*irle bien a alguien, refiriéndose a ropa, colores*]
• **ese color te queda muy bien** that color really suits you
• **la nueva falda te queda fatal** that new skirt doesn't fit you at all

❻ [*tener cita*]
• **hemos quedado en el cine** we've arranged to meet at the movie theater
• **he quedado con Luisa a las diez delante del teatro** I've arranged to meet Luisa at ten outside the theater
• **hemos quedado para el lunes** we arranged to meet on Monday

❼ [*encontrarse, estar*]
• **queda lejos** it's far
• **el colegio queda muy cerca** the school is very close by
• **¿por dónde queda eso?** whereabouts is that?

❽ [*permanecer*]
• **por mí que no quede** I don't need him to stay on my account
• **que no quede por falta de dinero** he shouldn't not go because of money

■ **quedar en**
◆ *v + preposición*
[*decidir que*]
• **habíamos quedado en que vendrías a buscarme** we said you'd come and get me
• **¿en qué quedamos?** what shall we do then?

■ **quedarse**
◆ *v pronominal*

❶ [*indica un cambio de estado provisional*]
• **se quedó callado/sorprendido** he was quiet/surprised
• **se quedó embarazada** she got pregnant

❷ [*indica un cambio de estado permanente*] to go
• **se quedó ciego** he went blind

❸ [*permanecer en alguna parte*]
• **me quedé en el colegio estudiando** I stayed at school studying
• **Alfonso se quedó a dormir en mi casa** Alfonso slept over at my house

queja *sf* ❶ [*lamento*] moan ❷ [*protesta*] complaint
• **presentar una queja** to make a complaint

quejarse *v pronominal* [*protestar*] to complain
• **¡no te quejes!** don't complain! • **quejarse de** to complain about • **se quejó del frío** to complain about something

quejica *despectivo* *adj* whining ☀ *Los adjetivos ingleses son invariables.*

quejido *sm* cry

quemado, da *adj* ❶ [*generalmente*] burned • **oler a quemado** to smell burning ❷ [*por agua hirviendo*] scalded ❸ [*por electricidad*] burned-out ❹ [*fusible*] blown ❺ [*por sol*] sunburned ❻ [*bronceado*] tanned ☀ *Los adjetivos ingleses son invariables.*
expresión **estar quemado a)** [*agotado*] to be burned-out **b)** [*harto*] to be fed up

quemador *sm* burner

quemadura *sf* ❶ [*por fuego*] burn • **tiene una quemadura en la mano** she has a burn on her hand • **una crema para las quemaduras de sol** a cream for sunburn • **quemadura en tercer grado** third-degree burn ❷ [*por agua hirviendo*] scald

quemar ◆ *vt* ❶ [*generalmente*] to burn ❷ [*sujeto: agua hirviendo*] to scald ❸ [*sujeto: electricidad*] to blow ❹ figurado [*malgastar*] to fritter away ❺ figurado [*desgastar*] to burn out ❻ figurado [*hartar*] to make fed up
◆ *vi* [*estar caliente*] to be (scalding) hot
■ **quemarse** *v pronominal* ❶ [*por fuego*] to burn down • **se les quemó la casa** their house burned down ❷ [*por agua hirviendo*] to get scalded ❸ [*por calor*] to burn • **me quemé la mano** I burned my hand ❹ [*por electricidad*] to blow ❺ [*por el sol*] to get burned ❻ figurado [*desgastarse*] to burn out ❼ figurado [*hartarse*] to get fed up

quemazón *sf* ❶ burning ❷ [*picor*] itch

queque *sm* sponge cake

---

querer
◆ *vt*

❶ [*tener ganas de, desear*] to want
• **quiero pan** I want some bread
• **no quiso ir** he didn't want to go
• **¿tú quieres que me enfade?** do you want me to get cross?
• **quiere hacerse abogado** he wants to become a lawyer
• **no sé qué ha querido decir con eso** I'm not sure what he meant by that

• **lo hizo queriendo** he meant to do it
• **lo he roto sin querer** I didn't mean to break it
❷ [*pedir como precio*] to want
• **¿cuánto quiere por el coche?** how much do you want for the car?
❸ [*exigir*] to want
• **querer que alguien haga algo** to want somebody to do something
• **quiero que seas tú quien se lo diga** I want it to be you who tells her
• **¿quieres que lave los platos?** do you want me to do the dishes?
❹ [*sentir afecto o amor*] to love
• **te quiere mucho** he loves you very much
❺ [*seguido por el infinitivo, introduce una suposición*]
• **parece que quiere llover** it looks like it's going to rain
expresión **querer es poder** where there's a will there's a way ▶ **quien bien te quiere te hará llorar** you have to be cruel to be kind

querido, da ✦ *adj* dear ☞ *Los adjetivos ingleses son invariables.*
✦ *sm, f* [*apelativo afectuoso*] darling
quesadilla *sf* ▶ *para explicar lo que es puedes decir:* it's a tortilla filled with melted cheese or other fillings
queso *sm* cheese ▶ **queso gruyère/parmesano/roquefort** Gruyère/Parmesan/Roquefort (cheese) ▶ **queso de bola** Dutch cheese ▶ **queso para untar** cheese spread ▶ **queso rallado** grated cheese
quicio *sm* jamb
expresión **estar fuera de quicio** to be out of kilter ▶ **sacar de quicio a alguien** to drive somebody mad
quiebra *sf* ❶ [*ruina*] bankruptcy • **ir a la quiebra** to go bankrupt ❷ [*en bolsa*] crash
quien *pronombre* ❶ ☞ *relativo* [*sujeto*] who • **fue mi hermano quien me lo explicó** it was my brother who explained it to me ❷ [*complemento*] whom • **era Pepe a quien vi/de quien no me fiaba** it was Pepe (whom) I saw/didn't trust ❸ ☞ *indefinido* • **quienes quieran verlo que se acerquen** whoever wants to see it will have to come closer • **hay quien lo niega** there are those who deny it
expresión **quien más quien menos** everyone
quién *pronombre* ❶ ☞ *interrogativo* [*sujeto*] who • **¿quién es ese hombre?** who's that man? ❷ [*complemento*] who • **no sé quién viene** I don't know who is coming • **¿a quiénes has invitado?** who have you invited? • **¿de quién es?** whose is it? • **¿quién es? a)** [*en la puerta*] who is it? **b)** [*al teléfono*] who's calling?
quienquiera (pl quienesquiera) *pronombre* whoever • **quienquiera que venga** whoever comes • **quienquiera que sea, dile que no estoy** whoever it is, tell him I'm not here
quieto, ta *adj* [*parado*] still • **¡estáte quieto!** keep still! • **¡quieto ahí!** don't move! ☞ *Los adjetivos ingleses son invariables.*
quilate *sm* carat

quilla *sf* NÁUTICA keel
químico, ca ✦ *adj* chemical ☞ *Los adjetivos ingleses son invariables.*
✦ *sm, f* [*científico*] chemist
■ **química** *sf* [*ciencia*] chemistry
quince *numeral* fifteen • **quince días** a fortnight ver también **seis**
quinceañero, ra *sm, f* teenager
quinceavo, va *numeral* fifteenth
quincena *sf* fortnight
quincenal *adj* fortnightly ☞ *Los adjetivos ingleses son invariables.*
quincuagésimo, ma *numeral* fiftieth
quinientos, tas *numeral* five hundred ver también **seis**
quinquenio *sm* [*periodo*] five-year period
quinteto *sm* quintet
quinto, ta *numeral* fifth • **fue la quinta persona en entrar** he was the fifth person to enter • **la quinta parte** a fifth
■ **quinto** *sm* [*parte*] fifth • **un quinto** a fifth
expresión **no tienen ni un quinto** *familiar* they're broke
quintuplicar *vt* to increase fivefold
quiosco, kiosco *sm* [*de periódicos*] newspaper stand ▶ **quiosco de música** bandstand
quirófano *sm* operating theater
quirúrgico, ca *adj* surgical ☞ *Los adjetivos ingleses son invariables.*
quisquilloso, sa *adj* ❶ [*detallista*] pernickety ❷ [*susceptible*] touchy ☞ *Los adjetivos ingleses son invariables.*
quiste *sm* cyst
quitaesmalte *sm* nail-polish remover
quitamanchas *sm invariable* stain remover
quitanieves *sm invariable* snow plough
quitar *vt* ❶ [*generalmente*] to remove ❷ [*ropa, zapatos* ETC] to take off • **quitarle algo a alguien** to take something away from somebody ❸ [*dolor, ansiedad*] to take away ❹ [*sed*] to quench ❺ [*tiempo*] to take up ❻ [*robar*] to take ❼ [*impedir*] • **esto no que sea un vago** that doesn't change the fact that he's a layabout ❽ [*exceptuar*] • **quitando el queso, me gusta todo** apart from cheese, I'll eat anything ❾ [*desconectar*] to switch off
expresión **de quita y pon a)** removable **b)** [*capucha*] detachable
■ **quitarse** *v pronominal* ❶ [*apartarse*] to get out of the way ❷ [*ropa*] to take off • **se quitó los zapatos** she took off her shoes ❸ [*sujeto: mancha*] to come out
expresión **quitarse a alguien de encima** to get rid of somebody
quitasol *sm* parasol
quizá, quizás *adv* perhaps • **quizá llueva mañana** it might rain tomorrow • **quizá vaya al cine** perhaps I'll go to the movies • **quizá no lo creas** you may not believe it • **quizá sí** maybe • **quizá no** maybe not

Q

r *sf* [*letra*] r ; R

rábano *sm* radish

expresión **coger el rábano por las hojas** to get the wrong end of the stick ❱ **me importa un rábano** I couldn't care less ; I don't give a damn

rabia *sf* ❶ [*ira*] rage • **lloraba de pura rabia** she was crying out of pure rage • **me da rabia** it makes me mad • **le tengo rabia** I have a grudge against him ❷ [*enfermedad*] rabies • **lo vacunaron contra la rabia** they vaccinated him against rabies

rabieta *sf familiar* tantrum • **tener una rabieta** to throw a tantrum

rabillo *sm* corner • **mirar algo con el rabillo del ojo** to look at something out of the corner of one's eye

rabioso, sa *adj* ❶ [*furioso*] furious ❷ [*excesivo*] terrible ❸ [*enfermo de rabia*] rabid ❹ [*chillón*] loud ❖ *Los adjetivos ingleses son invariables.*

rabo *sm* ❶ [*de animal*] tail ❷ [*de hoja, fruto*] stem

expresión **salir con el rabo entre las piernas** to go off with one's tail between one's legs

rácano, na *adj familiar* [*tacaño*] mean ❖ *Los adjetivos ingleses son invariables.*

racha *sf* ❶ [*ráfaga*] gust • **una racha de viento** a gust of wind ❷ [*época*] spell • **están pasando por una buena racha** they're going through a lucky spell • **tuvo una mala racha** he had a piece of bad luck

expresión **a rachas** in fits and starts

racial *adj* racial ❖ *Los adjetivos ingleses son invariables.*

racimo *sm* [*de frutos*] bunch

raciocinio *sm* [*razón*] (power of) reason

ración *sf* ❶ [*porción*] portion ❷ [*en bar, restaurante*] *para explicar lo que es puedes decir:* it's a large portion of a dish served as a snack

racional *adj* rational ❖ *Los adjetivos ingleses son invariables.*

racismo *sm* racism

racista *adj* & *smf* racist ❖ *Los adjetivos ingleses son invariables.*

radar (pl radares) *sm* radar

radiación *sf* radiation

radiactivo, va, radioactivo, va *adj* radioactive ❖ *Los adjetivos ingleses son invariables.*

radiador *sm* radiator

radiante *adj* radiant • **estaba radiante de alegría** she was radiant with happiness • **lucía un sol radiante** it was brilliantly sunny ❖ *Los adjetivos ingleses son invariables.*

radical *adj* & *smf* radical ❖ *Los adjetivos ingleses son invariables.*

radicar *vi* • **radicar en a)** [*sujeto: problema* ETC] to lie in **b)** [*sujeto: población*] to be (situated) in

radio ◆ *sm* ❶ ANATOMÍA & GEOMETRÍA radius ❷ [*de rueda*] spoke ❸ QUÍMICA radium

◆ *sf* radio • **oír algo por la radio** to hear something on the radio ❱ **radio digital** digital radio ❱ **radio pirata** pirate radio station

radioactivo = **radiactivo**

radioaficionado, da *sm, f* radio ham

radiocasete *sm* radio cassette (player)

radiodespertador *sm* clock radio

radiodifusión *sf* broadcasting

radiofónico, ca *adj* radio ❖ *Sólo se usa delante del sustantivo.*

radiografía *sf* [*fotografía*] X-ray • **hacerse una radiografía** to be X-rayed

radiorreloj *sm* clock radio

radiotaxi *sm* taxi (with radio link)

radioterapia *sf* radiotherapy

radioyente *smf* listener

ráfaga *sf* ❶ [*de aire, viento*] gust ❷ [*de disparos*] burst ❸ [*de luces*] flash

raíl *sm* rail

raíz (pl raíces) *sf* [*generalmente*] MATEMÁTICAS root ❱ **raíz cuadrada/cúbica** square/cube root • **a raíz de** as a result of

expresión **echar raíces** to put down roots

raja *sf* ❶ [*porción*] slice • **una raja de melón** a slice of melon • **una raja de canela** a stick of cinnamon ❷ [*grieta*] crack • **este plato tiene una raja** this plate has a crack

rajar *vt* ❶ [*partir*] to crack ❷ [*melón*] to slice ❸ *muy familiar* [*apuñalar*] to slash

■ **rajarse** *v pronominal* [*partirse*] to crack • **la pared se rajó** the wall cracked • **se le rajaron los pantalones** her pants tore

rajatabla ■ **a rajatabla** *locución adverbial* to the letter

ralentí *sm* neutral

rallado, da *adj* grated ☞ *Los adjetivos ingleses son invariables.*

rallador *sm* grater

ralladura *sf* ☞ *generalmente pl* grating

rallar *vt* to grate

rally (pl rallies) *sm* rally

RAM (*abreviatura de* random access memory) *sf* IN-FORMÁTICA RAM

rama *sf* branch

expresión andarse por las ramas *familiar* to beat about the bush ▸ **irse por las ramas** *familiar* to go off at a tangent

ramal *sm* [*de carretera, ferrocarril*] branch

ramificación *sf* ❶ [*generalmente*] ramification ❷ [*de carretera, ferrocarril, ciencia*] branch

ramificarse *v pronominal* [*bifurcarse*] to branch out • **el movimiento artístico se ramificó en dos escuelas** the artistic movement branched out into two schools of thought

ramillete *sm* bunch

ramo *sm* ❶ [*de flores*] bouquet • **un ramo de rosas** a bouquet of roses ❷ [*rama*] branch ❸ [*sector*] industry • **el ramo de la construcción** the building industry

rampa *sf* ❶ [*para subir y bajar*] ramp ❷ [*cuesta*] steep incline

rana *sf* frog

ranchero, ra *sm, f* rancher

■ **ranchera** *sf* ❶ MÚSICA popular Mexican song ❷ AU-TOMÓVILES estate car

rancho *sm* [*granja*] ranch • **un rancho ganadero** a cattle ranch

rancio, cia *adj* ❶ [*pasado*] rancid ❷ [*antiguo*] ancient ❸ [*añejo - vino*] mellow ☞ *Los adjetivos ingleses son invariables.*

rango *sm* ❶ [*social*] standing ❷ [*jerárquico*] rank

ranking (pl rankings) *sm* ranking

ranura *sf* ❶ [*surco*] groove ❷ [*de máquina tragaperras, cabina telefónica*] slot

rapapolvo *sm familiar* ticking-off • **echar un rapapolvo a alguien** to tick somebody off

rapar *vt* ❶ [*barba, bigote*] to shave off ❷ [*cabeza*] to shave ❸ [*persona*] to shave the hair of

rape *sm* monkfish

rapero, ra *sm, f* rapper

rápidamente *adv* quickly

rapidez *sf* speed

rápido, da *adj* ❶ [*veloz*] quick; fast ❷ [*carro*] fast ❸ [*beneficio, decisión*] quick ☞ *Los adjetivos ingleses son invariables.*

■ **rápido** ◆ *adv* quickly • **más rápido** quicker • **¡ven, rápido!** come, quick!

◆ *sm* [*tren*] express train

raptar *vt* to kidnap

rapto *sm* ❶ [*secuestro*] kidnapping ❷ [*ataque*] fit

raqueta *sf* [*para jugar - al tenis*] racquet; [- *al ping pong*] bat

raquítico, ca *adj* ❶ MEDICINA rachitic ❷ [*insuficiente*] miserable ☞ *Los adjetivos ingleses son invariables.*

rareza *sf* ❶ [*poco común, extraño*] rarity ❷ [*extravagancia*] eccentricity

raro, ra *adj* ❶ [*extraño*] strange • **me pasó algo muy raro** something very strange happened to me • **¡qué raro!** how strange! ❷ [*excepcional*] rare • **es una pieza muy rara y valiosa** it's a very rare and valuable piece ❸ [*visita*] infrequent ❹ [*extravagante*] odd ❺ [*escaso*] rare • **rara vez** rarely ☞ *Los adjetivos ingleses son invariables.*

ras *sm* • **a ras de** level with • **a ras de tierra** at ground level • **volar a ras de tierra** to fly low

rasante *sf* [*de carretera*] gradient

rascacielos *sm invariable* skyscraper

rascar ◆ *vt* ❶ [*con uñas, clavo*] to scratch ❷ [*con espátula*] to scrape (off) ❸ [*con cepillo*] to scrub

◆ *vi* to be rough

rasgar *vt* ❶ to tear • **rasgó la tela** he tore the cloth ❷ [*sobre*] to tear open

rasgo *sm* ❶ [*característica*] trait ❷ [*trazo*] flourish

■ **rasgos** *smpl* ❶ [*del rostro*] features • **tiene los rasgos muy finos** she has very delicate features ❷ [*letra*] handwriting ☞ *incontable*

rasguño *sm* scratch

raspa *sf* backbone (of fish)

raspar *vt* ❶ [*rascar*] to scrape (off) ❷ [*rasar*] to graze

raspón *sm* [*desolladura*] scratch

rastras ■ **a rastras** *locución adverbial* • **llevar algo/a alguien a rastras** *literal & figurado* to drag something/somebody along

rastreador, ra *sm, f* tracker

rastrear *vt* [*seguir las huellas de*] to track

rastrero, ra *adj* despicable ☞ *Los adjetivos ingleses son invariables.*

rastrillo *sm* ❶ [*en jardinería*] rake ❷ [*para afeitarse*] safety razor

rastro *sm* ❶ [*pista*] trail • **perder el rastro de alguien** to lose track of somebody ❷ [*vestigio*] trace • **sin dejar rastro** without a trace ❸ [*matadero*] slaughterhouse

rastrojo *sm* stubble

rata *sf* rat

ratificar *vt* to ratify

rato *sm* while • **estuvimos hablando mucho rato** we were talking for quite a while • **el avión viene atrasado así es que tenemos para rato** the airplane is late so we still have some time • **al poco rato (de)** shortly after • **pasar el rato** to kill time • **pasar un mal rato** to have a hard time of it • **ratos libres** spare time ☀*incontable*
expresión **a ratos** at times ▸ **un rato (largo)** *figurado* really

ratón *sm* mouse, *plural* mice

ratonera *sf* ❶ [*para ratas*] mousetrap ❷ *figurado* [*trampa*] trap

raudal *sm* ❶ [*de agua*] torrent ❷ *figurado* [*montón*] abundance • **a raudales** in abundance

ravioli *sm* ☀*generalmente pl* ravioli ☀*incontable*

raya *sf* ❶ [*línea*] line • **haz una raya vertical** draw a vertical line ❷ [*en tejido*] stripe • **una blusa con rayas azules y blancas** a blouse with blue and white stripes • **a rayas** striped ❸ [*de pantalón*] crease ❹ [*señal - en disco, pintura* ETC] scratch ❺ [*pez*] ray ❻ [*guión*] dash • **una raya precedida de un punto** a dash preceded by a dot
expresión **mantener a raya a alguien** to keep somebody in line ▸ **pasarse de la raya** to overstep the mark

rayar ◆ *vt* ❶ [*marcar*] to scratch ❷ [*trazar rayas*] to rule lines on
◆ *vi* ❶ [*aproximarse*] • **rayar en algo** to border on something • **raya en lo ridículo** it's bordering on the ridiculous • **raya en los cuarenta** he's pushing forty ❷ [*alba*] to break

rayo *sm* ❶ [*de luz*] ray • **un rayo de luz** a ray of light ▸ **rayo solar** sunbeam ❷ FÍSICA ray ▸ **rayo láser** laser beam ▸ **rayos infrarrojos/ultravioleta/uva** infrared/ultraviolet/UVA rays ▸ **rayos X** X-rays ❸ METEOROLOGÍA lightning bolt • **cayó un rayo en el campanario** a lightning bolt struck the bell tower • **rayos** lightning ☀*incontable* • **¿viste los rayos anoche?** did you see the lightning last night?
expresión **caer como un rayo** *figurado* to be a bombshell

raza *sf* ❶ [*humana*] race • **la raza humana** the human race ❷ [*animal*] breed • **no sé de qué raza es su perro** I don't know what breed her dog is

razón *sf* ❶ [*generalmente*] reason • **no hay ninguna razón para que falte a clases** there's no reason for him to miss classes • **con razón no vino** no wonder he didn't come • **dar la razón a alguien** to say that somebody is right • **en razón de** in view of • **tener razón (en hacer algo)** to be right (to do something) • **no tener razón** to be wrong • **razón de más para hacer algo** all the more reason to do something • **y con razón** and quite rightly so ▸ **razón de ser** raison d'être ❷ [*información*] • **no me pudo dar razón de Silvia** he couldn't tell me anything about Silvia ❸ MATEMÁTICAS ratio

razonable *adj* reasonable ☀*Los adjetivos ingleses son invariables.*

razonamiento *sm* reasoning ☀*incontable*

razonar ◆ *vt* [*argumentar*] to reason out
◆ *vi* [*pensar*] to reason

re *sm* ❶ MÚSICA D ❷ [*en solfeo*] re

reacción *sf* reaction ▸ **reacción alérgica** allergic reaction ▸ **reacción en cadena** chain reaction

reaccionar *vi* to react • **reaccionó muy mal** he reacted badly • **reaccionar a algo** to react to something

reaccionario, ria *adj* & *sm, f* reactionary ☀*Los adjetivos ingleses son invariables.*

reacio, cia *adj* reluctant ☀*Los adjetivos ingleses son invariables.*

reactor *sm* ❶ [*propulsor*] reactor ❷ [*avión*] jet (plane)

readmitir *vt* to allow back

reafirmar *vt* to confirm

reajuste *sm* ECONOMÍA [*de precios, impuestos*] increase; [*de salarios*] reduction ▸ **reajuste ministerial** cabinet reshuffle ▸ **reajuste de plantilla** lay-offs *pl*

real *adj* ❶ [*verdadero*] real • **vive en un mundo que no es real** she lives in a world that isn't real ❷ [*de monarquía*] royal • **la familia real** the royal family ☀*Los adjetivos ingleses son invariables.*

realce *sm* [*esplendor*] glamour • **dar realce a algo/alguien** to enhance something/somebody

realeza *sf* [*monarcas*] royalty

realidad *sf* ❶ [*mundo real*] reality • **una mezcla de realidad y ficción** a mix of reality and fiction ▸ **realidad virtual** virtual reality ❷ [*verdad*] • **mis deseos se hicieron realidad** my dreams came true • **en realidad** actually • **en realidad no sé la respuesta** actually, I don't know the answer

realista ◆ *adj* realistic ☀*Los adjetivos ingleses son invariables.*
◆ *smf* ARTE realist

realización *sf* ❶ [*ejecución*] carrying-out ❷ [*de proyecto, medidas*] implementation ❸ [*de sueños, deseos*] fulfilment ❹ [*obra*] achievement ❺ CINE production

realizador, ra *sm, f* CINE & TELEVISIÓN director

realizar *vt* ❶ [*ejecutar - esfuerzo, viaje, inversión*] to make; [*- operación, experimento, trabajo*] to perform; [*- encargo, plan, reformas*] to carry out; [*- plan, reformas*] to implement ❷ [*hacer real*] to fulfill ❸ CINE to produce

realmente *adv* ❶ [*en verdad*] in fact ❷ [*muy*] really

realzar *vt* ❶ [*resaltar*] to enhance ❷ [*en pintura*] to highlight

reanimar *vt* ❶ [*físicamente*] to revive ❷ [*moralmente*] to cheer up ❸ MEDICINA to resuscitate

reanudar *vt* ❶ [*conversación, trabajo*] to resume ❷ [*amistad*] to renew

reaparición *sf* reappearance

rearme *sm* rearmament

reavivar *vt* to revive

rebaja *sf* ❶ [*acción*] reduction ❷ [*descuento*] discount • **hacer una rebaja** to give a discount • **me hicieron una rebaja del diez por ciento** they gave me a ten percent discount

rebajado, da *adj* ❶ [*precio*] reduced ❷ [*humillado*] humiliated ᷂᷂ *Los adjetivos ingleses son invariables.*

rebajar *vt* ❶ [*precio*] to reduce • **los rebajaron un diez por ciento** they reduced them by ten percent • **te lo rebajo 2 dólares** I'll knock 2 dollars off for you ❷ [*persona*] to humiliate ❸ [*intensidad*] to tone down

rebanada *sf* slice

rebaño *sm* ❶ [*de ovejas*] flock ❷ [*de vacas*] herd

rebasar *vt* ❶ [*sobrepasar*] to exceed ❷ [*agua*] to overflow ❸ Automóviles to overtake

rebelarse *v pronominal* to rebel • **se rebelan contra la autoridad** they're rebelling against authority

rebelde ◆ *adj* ❶ [*sublevado*] rebel ᷂᷂ *Sólo se usa delante del sustantivo.* ❷ [*desobediente*] rebellious ◆ *smf* [*sublevado, desobediente*] rebel

rebeldía *sf* [*cualidad*] rebelliousness

rebelión *sf* rebellion

rebosar ◆ *vt* to overflow with ◆ *vi* to overflow • **rebosar de a)** [*recipiente*] to be overflowing with **b)** [*persona*] to burst with • **los niños rebosan de energía** the children are bursting with energy

rebotar *vi* • **rebotar (en)** to bounce (off); to rebound (off)

rebote *sm* ❶ [*bote*] bounce ❷ Deporte rebound

rebozado, da *adj* Cocina coated in batter o breadcrumbs ᷂᷂ *Los adjetivos ingleses son invariables.*

rebozar *vt* Cocina to coat in batter o breadcrumbs

rebuznar *vi* to bray

recadero, ra *sm, f* messenger

recado *sm* ❶ [*mensaje*] message • **le dejé un recado con la secretaria** I left her a message with her secretary • **mandar recado de que...** to send word that... ❷ [*encargo*] errand • **hacer recados** to run errands

recaer *vi* ❶ [*enfermo*] to have a relapse ❷ [*ir a parar*] • **recaer sobre** to fall on • **las sospechas recayeron inmediatamente sobre un vecino de la víctima** suspicion immediately fell on one of the victim's neighbors ❸ [*reincidir*] • **recaer en** to relapse into • **lo más difícil es evitar recaer en la droga** the most difficult thing is to avoid relapsing into taking drugs

recaída *sf* relapse

recalentar *vt* ❶ [*volver a calentar*] to reheat ❷ [*calentar demasiado*] to overheat

recámara *sf* ❶ [*de arma de fuego*] chamber ❷ [*dormitorio*] bedroom

recamarera *sf* chambermaid

recambio *sm* ❶ [*repuesto*] spare (part) ❷ [*para pluma*] refill

recapacitar *vi* to think • **recapacitar sobre** to think about

recargado, da *adj* [*estilo* etc] overelaborate ᷂᷂ *Los adjetivos ingleses son invariables.*

recargar *vt* ❶ [*volver a cargar - encendedor, recipiente*] to refill; [*- batería, pila*] to recharge; [*- fusil, camión*] to reload; [*- teléfono celular*] to top up ❷ [*cargar demasiado*] to overload ❸ [*adornar en exceso*] to overelab-

orate ❹ [*cantidad*] • **recargar 20 dólares a alguien** to charge somebody 20 dollars extra ❺ [*poner en exceso*] • **recargar algo de algo** to put too much of something in something

recargo *sm* extra charge

recaudación *sf* ❶ [*acción*] collection ❷ [*cantidad*] takings *pl* ❸ Deporte gate ❹ [*de un cine*] box-office takings

recaudador, ra *sm, f* ▸ **recaudador (de impuestos)** tax collector

recaudar *vt* to collect

recelo *sm* mistrust

receloso, sa *adj* mistrustful ᷂᷂ *Los adjetivos ingleses son invariables.*

recepción *sf* reception

recepcionista *smf* receptionist

receptivo, va *adj* receptive ᷂᷂ *Los adjetivos ingleses son invariables.*

receptor, ra *sm, f* [*persona*] recipient ■ **receptor** *sm* [*aparato*] receiver

recesión *sf* recession

receta *sf* ❶ Cocina recipe • **¿me das la receta del postre?** will you give me the recipe for the dessert? ❷ Medicina prescription • **sólo lo venden con receta** it's only available by prescription

rechazar *vt* ❶ [*generalmente*] Medicina to reject ❷ [*oferta*] to turn down ❸ [*repeler - a una persona*] to push away ❹ Militar to repel

rechazo *sm* ❶ [*generalmente*] Medicina rejection ❷ [*hacia una ley, un político*] disapproval ❸ [*negación*] denial

rechistar *vi* to answer back

rechoncho, cha *adj* familiar chubby ᷂᷂ *Los adjetivos ingleses son invariables.*

rechupete ■ **de rechupete** *locución adverbial* familiar ❶ [*generalmente*] brilliant ❷ [*comida*] scrumptious

recibidor *sm* entrance hall

recibimiento *sm* reception

recibir ◆ *vt* ❶ [*generalmente*] to receive ❷ [*clase, instrucción*] to have ❸ [*dar la bienvenida a*] to welcome ❹ [*ir a buscar*] to meet ◆ *vi* [*atender visitas*] to receive visitors ■ **recibirse** *v pronominal* ▸ **recibirse** to graduate • **recibirse de algo** to get a degree in something

recibo *sm* receipt • **acusar recibo de** to acknowledge receipt of *expresión* **no ser de recibo** to be unacceptable

reciclaje *sm* ❶ [*de residuos*] recycling ❷ [*de personas*] retraining

reciclar *vt* [*residuos*] to recycle

recién *adv* ❶ [*hace poco*] newly • **el recién casado** the newly-wed • **los recién llegados** the newcomers • **el recién nacido** the newborn baby • **está recién pintado** it's just been painted ❷ [*hace poco*] just • **recién llegó** he just arrived • **recién lo vi** I just saw him

reciente *adj* ❶ [*acontecimiento* ETC] recent ❷ [*pintura, pan* ETC] fresh ☿ *Los adjetivos ingleses son invariables.*

recientemente *adv* recently

recinto *sm* ❶ [*zona cercada*] enclosure ❷ [*área*] place ❸ [*alrededor de edificios*] grounds *pl* ▶ **recinto ferial** fairground *(of trade fair)*

recio, cia *adj* ❶ [*persona*] robust ❷ [*voz*] gravelly ❸ [*objeto*] solid ❹ [*material, tela*] tough ☿ *Los adjetivos ingleses son invariables.*

recipiente *sm* container

reciprocidad *sf* reciprocity

recíproco, ca *adj* mutual ☿ *Los adjetivos ingleses son invariables.*

recital *sm* ❶ [*de música clásica*] recital ❷ [*de rock*] concert ❸ [*de lectura*] reading

recitar *vt* to recite

reclamación *sf* ❶ [*petición*] claim ❷ [*queja*] complaint • **hacer una reclamación** to lodge a complaint

reclamar ◆ *vt* [*pedir, exigir*] to demand • **reclaman una solución a sus problemas** they're demanding a solution to their problems

◆ *vi* [*protestar*] • **reclamar (contra)** to protest (against); to complain (about)

reclamo *sm* ❶ [*para atraer*] inducement ❷ [*queja*] complaint ❸ [*reivindicación*] claim

reclinar *vt* • **reclinar algo (sobre)** to lean something (on)

reclusión *sf* ❶ [*encarcelamiento*] imprisonment ❷ *figurado* [*encierro*] seclusion

recluso, sa *sm, f* [*preso*] prisoner

recluta *sm* ❶ [*obligatorio*] conscript ❷ [*voluntario*] recruit

reclutamiento *sm* [*de soldados - obligatorio*] conscription; [*- voluntario*] recruitment

recobrar *vt* ❶ [*generalmente*] to recover ❷ [*conocimiento*] to regain ❸ [*tiempo perdido*] to make up for

recogedor *sm* dustpan

recoger *vt* ❶ [*coger*] to pick up • **recoja el papel del suelo** pick the paper up off the floor ❷ [*ordenar, limpiar - mesa*] to clear; [*- habitación, cosas*] to tidy up ❸ [*ir a buscar*] to pick up ❹ [*cosechar*] to gather ❺ [*fruta*] to pick

recolección *sf* ❶ [*cosecha*] harvest ❷ [*recogida*] collection

recolector, ra *sm, f* ❶ [*de cosecha*] harvester ❷ [*de fruta*] picker

recomendación *sf* ☿ *generalmente pl* ❶ [*generalmente*] recommendation ❷ [*referencia*] reference

recomendar *vt* to recommend • **recomendar a alguien que haga algo** to recommend that somebody do something

recompensa *sf* reward • **ofrecen una recompensa** they're offering a reward • **en recompensa por** in return for

recompensar *vt* [*premiar*] to reward

reconciliación *sf* reconciliation

reconciliar *vt* to reconcile

reconfortar *vt* ❶ [*anímicamente*] to comfort ❷ [*físicamente*] to revitalize

reconfortar a alguien

- **Don't worry!** No te preocupes.
- **Hang on in there!** ¡Ánimo!
- **Don't give in.** No te des por vencido.
- **Don't be discouraged!** ¡Ánimo!

reconocer *vt* ❶ [*generalmente*] to recognize • **no lo reconocí con la barba** I didn't recognize him with a beard ❷ [*admitir*] to admit • **reconoció que se había equivocado** he admitted that he was wrong ❸ MEDICINA to examine ❹ [*terreno*] to survey

reconocimiento *sm* ❶ [*generalmente*] recognition ▶ **reconocimiento del habla** INFORMÁTICA speech recognition ❷ [*agradecimiento*] gratitude ❸ MEDICINA examination ❹ MILITAR reconnaissance

reconquista *sf* reconquest

reconstruir *vt* ❶ [*edificio, país* ETC] to rebuild ❷ [*suceso*] to reconstruct

recopilación *sf* ❶ [*de poemas, artículos*] compilation ❷ [*de leyes*] code

recopilar *vt* ❶ [*recoger*] to collect ❷ [*escritos, leyes*] to compile

récord (*pl* records) ◆ *sm* record • **el récord mundial de los 100 metros** the 100 meter world record • **batir un récord** to break a record

◆ *adj invariable* record ☿ *Los adjetivos ingleses son invariables.*

recordar ◆ *vt* ❶ [*acordarse de*] to remember • **no recuerdo su nombre** I can't remember his name • **recuerdo que te lo pedí** I remember asking you for it • **recordar a alguien algo/que haga algo** to remind somebody to do something • **recuérdame que lo llame** remind me to call him ❷ [*traer a la memoria*] to remind • **me recuerda a un amigo mío** he reminds me of a friend of mine

◆ *vi* to remember • **si mal no recuerdo** as far as I can remember

recordatorio *sm* [*aviso*] reminder

recordman (*pl* recordmen O recordmans) *sm* record holder

recorrer *vt* ❶ [*atravesar - lugar, país*] to travel through; [*- ciudad*] to go round ❷ [*distancia*] to cover ❸ *figurado* [*con la mirada*] to look over

recorrida *sf* ❶ [*ruta, itinerario*] route ❷ [*viaje*] journey

recorrido *sm* ❶ [*trayecto*] route ❷ [*viaje*] journey

recortar *vt* ❶ [*cortar - lo que sobra*] to cut off; [*- figuras de un papel*] to cut out ❷ [*pelo, fleco*] to trim ❸ *figurado* [*reducir*] to cut

■ **recortarse** *v pronominal* [*figura* ETC] to stand out • **recortarse sobre algo** to stand out against something

R

recorte *sm* ❶ [*pieza cortada*] cut ❷ [*de periódico, revista*] cutting ❸ [*reducción*] cut • **recortes presupuestarios** budget cuts

recostar *vt* to lean (back)

recreativo, va *adj* recreational ☼ *Los adjetivos ingleses son invariables.*

recreo *sm* ❶ [*entretenimiento*] recreation ❷ EDUCACIÓN recess

recriminar *vt* to reproach

recta *sf* straight line

rectángulo *sm* rectangle

rectificar *vt* ❶ [*error*] to rectify ❷ [*conducta, actitud* ETC] to improve ❸ [*ajustar*] to put right

recto, ta *adj* [*sin curvas, vertical*] straight ☼ *Los adjetivos ingleses son invariables.*
■ **recto** ◆ *sm* ANATOMÍA rectum
◆ *adv* straight ahead

recuadro *sm* box

recubrir *vt* ❶ [*generalmente*] to cover ❷ [*con pintura, barniz*] to coat

recuento *sm* recount

recuerdo *sm* ❶ [*rememoración*] memory • **tengo muy buenos recuerdos de mi primer colegio** I have very good memories of my first school ❷ [*de viaje*] souvenir • **lo compré de recuerdo** I bought it as a souvenir

recuperación *sf* recovery

recuperar *vt* ❶ [*lo perdido*] to recover ❷ [*tiempo*] to make up • **tengo que recuperar el tiempo perdido** I have to make up for lost time ❸ [*conocimiento*] to regain

recurrir *vi* ❶ [*buscar ayuda*] • **recurrir a alguien** to turn to somebody • **recurrir a algo** to resort to something ❷ DERECHO to appeal • **recurrir contra algo** to appeal against something

recurso *sm* ❶ [*medio*] resort • **como último recurso** as a last resort ❷ DERECHO appeal

red *sf* ❶ [*malla*] net • **una red de pesca** a fishing net • **la pelota tocó la red** the ball touched the net ❷ [*para cabello*] hairnet ❸ [*sistema*] network ▶ **red viaria** road network ❹ [*de electricidad, agua*] mains *sing* ❺ [*organización - de espionaje*] ring ; [*- de tiendas*] chain ❻ INFORMÁTICA network ▶ **red local/neuronal** local/neural network • **la Red** the Net • **navegar por la Red** to surf the Net

redacción *sf* ❶ [*acción - generalmente*] writing ; [*- de periódico* ETC] editing ❷ [*estilo*] wording ❸ [*equipo de redactores*] editorial team ❹ [*oficina*] editorial office ❺ EDUCACIÓN essay • **tengo que hacer una redacción sobre mis vacaciones** I have to write an essay about my vacation

redactar *vt* to write

redactor, ra *sm, f* PRENSA [*escritor*] writer ; [*editor*] editor ▶ **redactor jefe** editor-in-chief

redada *sf* [*de policía - en un solo lugar*] raid ; [*- en varios lugares*] round-up

redoblar ◆ *vt* to redouble

◆ *vi* to roll

redondear *vt* ❶ [*hacer redondo*] to make round ❷ [*negocio, acuerdo*] to round off ❸ [*cifra, precio*] to round up/down

redondel *sm* circle

redondo, da *adj* ❶ [*circular, esférico*] round • **tiene la cara redonda** she has a round face • **girar en redondo** to turn around ❷ [*perfecto*] excellent ☼ *Los adjetivos ingleses son invariables.*
expresión **caerse redondo** to collapse in a heap

reducción *sf* reduction • **reducción de gastos** reduction in costs

reducido, da *adj* ❶ [*pequeño*] small ❷ [*limitado*] limited ❸ [*estrecho*] narrow ☼ *Los adjetivos ingleses son invariables.*

reducir *vt* ❶ [*generalmente*] to reduce ❷ [*someter - país, ciudad*] to suppress ; [*- sublevados, atracadores*] to bring under control ❸ MATEMÁTICAS [*convertir*] to convert

reducto *sm* ❶ [*fortificación*] redoubt ❷ *figurado* [*refugio*] stronghold

redundancia *sf* redundancy • **y valga la redundancia** if you'll excuse the repetition

redundante *adj* redundant ☼ *Los adjetivos ingleses son invariables.*

reelección *sf* reelection

reemplazar *vt* to replace • **reemplazar algo/alguien por algo/alguien** to replace something/somebody with something/somebody • **reemplaza esta palabra por una menos formal** replace this word with a less formal one

reemplazo *sm* replacement

reemprender *vt* to start again

reencarnación *sf* reincarnation

reencuentro *sm* reunion

reestructurar *vt* to restructure

ref. (*abreviatura escrita de* referencia) ref

refacción *sf* ❶ [*reparación*] renovation ❷ [*recambio*] spare part

referencia *sf* reference • **con referencia a** with reference to

referéndum (pl referendos O referéndum) *sm* referendum • **convocar un referéndum** to call a referendum

referente *adj* • **referente a** concerning • **en lo referente a** regarding ☼ *Los adjetivos ingleses son invariables.*

referir *vt* ❶ [*remitir*] • **referir a alguien a** to refer somebody to ❷ [*relacionar*] • **referir algo a** to relate something to

refilón ■ **de refilón** *locución adverbial* ❶ [*de lado*] sideways • **mirar algo de refilón** to look at something out of the corner of your eye ❷ *figurado* [*de pasada*] briefly

refinado, da *adj* refined ☼ *Los adjetivos ingleses son invariables.*

refinamiento *sm* refinement

refinar *vt* to refine

refinería *sf* refinery

reflector *sm* ❶ ᴇʟᴇᴄᴛʀɪᴄɪᴅᴀᴅ spotlight ❷ ᴍɪʟɪᴛᴀʀ searchlight

reflejar *vt* to reflect

reflejo, ja *adj* [movimiento, dolor] reflex ☼: **Sólo se usa delante del sustantivo.** • **un acto reflejo** a reflex action

■ **reflejo** *sm* ❶ [generalmente] reflection • **el reflejo del sol en el agua** the reflection of the sun in the water ❷ ᴀɴᴀᴛᴏᴍíᴀ reflex • **tiene muy buenos reflejos** he has very good reflexes

■ **reflejos** *smpl* [de peluquería] highlights

reflexión *sf* reflection

reflexionar *vi* to think • **reflexionar sobre algo** to think about something

reflexivo, va *adj* ❶ [que piensa] thoughtful ❷ ɢʀᴀᴍáᴛɪᴄᴀ reflexive ☼: **Los adjetivos ingleses son invariables.**

reflujo *sm* ebb (tide)

reforestación *sf* reforestation

reforma *sf* ❶ [modificación] reform ▶ **reforma agraria** agrarian reform ❷ [en local, casa ᴇᴛᴄ] alterations *pl* • **hicieron algunas reformas en su casa** they made some alterations to the house

■ **Reforma** *sf* • **la Reforma** ʀᴇʟɪɢɪóɴ the Reformation

reformar *vt* ❶ [generalmente] ʀᴇʟɪɢɪóɴ to reform ❷ [local, casa ᴇᴛᴄ] to renovate

■ **reformarse** *v pronominal* to mend your ways • **se ha reformado y ahora es muy responsable** he's mended his ways and is very responsible now

reformatorio *sm* reform school ; reformatory

reforzar *vt* to reinforce

refractario, ria *adj* [material] refractory ☼: **Los adjetivos ingleses son invariables.**

refrán *sm* proverb

refregar *vt* ❶ [frotar] to scrub ❷ figurado [reprochar] • **refregar algo a alguien** to reproach somebody for something

refrenar *vt* to curb

refrescante *adj* refreshing ☼: **Los adjetivos ingleses son invariables.**

refrescar ✦ *vt* ❶ [generalmente] to refresh ❷ [bebidas] to chill ❸ figurado [conocimientos] to brush up ✦ *vi* ❶ [tiempo] to cool down ❷ [bebida] to be refreshing

■ **refrescarse** *v pronominal* ❶ [tomar aire fresco] to get a breath of fresh air ❷ [beber algo] to have a drink ❸ [mojarse con agua fría] to splash yourself down

refresco *sm* soft drink

refrigeración *sf* ❶ [aire acondicionado] air-conditioning ❷ [de alimentos] refrigeration ❸ [de máquinas] cooling

refrigerador, ra *adj* cooling ☼: **Los adjetivos ingleses son invariables.**

■ **refrigerador** *sm* [de alimentos] refrigerator

refrigerar *vt* ❶ [alimentos] to refrigerate ❷ [local] to air-condition ❸ [máquina] to cool

refuerzo *sm* reinforcement

refugiado, da *sm, f* refugee

refugiar *vt* to give refuge to

■ **refugiarse** *v pronominal* to take refuge • **se refugiaron en una iglesia** they took refuge in a church • **refugiarse de algo** to shelter from something

refugio *sm* ❶ [lugar] shelter • **un refugio para los damnificados** a shelter for the victims ▶ **refugio atómico** nuclear bunker ❷ figurado [amparo, consuelo] refuge

refunfuñar *vi* to grumble

regadera *sf* ❶ [para regar] watering can ❷ [ducha] shower

regadío *sm* irrigated land

regalado, da *adj* ❶ [muy barato] dirt cheap ❷ [agradable] comfortable ☼: **Los adjetivos ingleses son invariables.**

regalar *vt* [dar - de regalo] to give (as a present) ; [- gratis] to give away • **no sé qué regalarle para su cumpleaños** I don't know what to give him for his birthday • **me regaló un reloj** she gave me a watch • **me queda chico así es que no lo voy a regalar** it's too small for me so I'm going to give it away • **me regalaron una guitarra para Navidad** I was given a guitar for Christmas

regaliz *sm* liquorice

regalo *sm* [obsequio] present • **es un regalo de cumpleaños** it's a birthday present • **hacerle un regalo a alguien** to give somebody a present • **una tienda de regalos** a gift shop • **un regalo del cielo** a godsend

regañadientes ■ **a regañadientes** *locución adverbial familiar* unwillingly

regañar *vt* [reprender] to scold

regañiza *sf* [reprimenda] scolding

regar *vt* ❶ [con agua - planta] to water ; [- calle] to hose down ❷ [sujeto: río] to flow through

regata *sf* ɴáᴜᴛɪᴄᴀ yacht race

regatear ✦ *vt* ❶ [escatimar] to be sparing with • **no ha regateado esfuerzos** he has spared no effort ❷ ᴅᴇᴘᴏʀᴛᴇ to beat ❸ [precio] to haggle over ✦ *vi* ❶ [negociar el precio] to barter ❷ ɴáᴜᴛɪᴄᴀ to race

regateo *sm* bartering

regazo *sm* lap

regeneración *sf* ❶ [recuperación] regeneration ❷ [moral] reform

regenerar *vt* ❶ [recuperar] to regenerate ❷ [moralmente] to reform

regente ✦ *adj* regent ☼: **Los adjetivos ingleses son invariables.**

✦ *sm, f* ❶ [de un país] regent ❷ [administrador - de tienda] manager ; [- de colegio] governor ❸ [alcalde] mayor

régimen (pl regímenes) *sm* ❶ [sistema político] regime • **un régimen democrático** a democratic re-

R

gime ❷ [*dieta*] diet • **estar/ponerse a régimen** to be/go on a diet ❸ [*de vida, lluvias* ETC] pattern

regimiento *sm* regiment

región *sf* region

regir ◆ *vt* ❶ [*reinar en*] to rule ❷ [*administrar*] to run ❸ *figurado* [*determinar*] to govern
◆ *vi* [*ley*] to be in force
■ **regirse por** *v pronominal* to trust in

registrado, da *adj* [*correspondencia*] registered

registrar *vt* ❶ [*inspeccionar - zona, vivienda*] to search; [*- persona*] to frisk • **le registraron el equipaje** they searched his luggage ❷ [*nacimiento, temperatura* ETC] to register • **los sismógrafos registraron el temblor** the seismographs registered the tremor
■ **registrarse** *v pronominal* ❶ [*suceder*] to occur ❷ [*observarse*] to be recorded ❸ [*en hotel*] to check in

registro *sm* ❶ [*oficina*] registry (office) ▶ **registro civil** registry (office) ❷ [*libro*] register ❸ [*inspección*] search ❹ INFORMÁTICA record ❺ LINGÜÍSTICA & MÚSICA register

regla *sf* ❶ [*para medir*] ruler • **usó una regla para medir la línea** she used a ruler to measure the line ❷ [*norma*] rule • **es una regla en mi colegio** it's a rule in my school • **en regla** in order • **por regla general** as a rule ❸ MATEMÁTICAS operation ❹ *familiar* [*menstruación*] period • **tener la regla** to have your period

reglamento *sm* regulations *pl* • **el reglamento del colegio** the school's regulations

regresar ◆ *vi* ❶ [*yendo*] to go back • **regresaron a su país** they went back to their country ❷ [*viniendo*] to come back • **tienes que regresar temprano** you have to come back early
◆ *vt* [*devolver*] to return • **tengo que regresar el libro a la biblioteca** I have to return the book to the library

regresivo, va *adj* regressive ❖ *Los adjetivos ingleses son invariables.*

regreso *sm* return • **nuestro regreso al colegio se acercaba** our return to school was drawing near • **'no se aceptan regresos sin recibo'** no returns without a receipt • **de regreso** on the way back • **de regreso paramos en una playa del Caribe** on the way back we stopped at a Caribbean beach • **el vuelo de regreso** the return flight • **estar de regreso** to be back

reguero *sm* ❶ [*de sangre, agua*] trickle ❷ [*de harina* ETC] trail
expresión **correr como un reguero de pólvora** to spread like wildfire

regular ◆ *adj* ❶ [*generalmente*] regular • **viene a intervalos regulares** he comes at regular intervals • **por lo regular** usually • **por lo regular, me levanto a las siete** I usually get up at seven • **de un modo regular** regularly ❷ [*de tamaño*] medium ❸ [*mediocre*] average ❹ [*normal*] normal ❖ *Los adjetivos ingleses son invariables.*
◆ *adv* [*de salud*] so-so
◆ *vt* ❶ [*generalmente*] to control ❷ [*mecanismo*] to adjust

regularidad *sf* regularity • **con regularidad** regularly

regularizar *vt* [*legalizar*] to regularize

regusto *sm* ❶ [*sabor*] aftertaste ❷ [*semejanza, aire*] flavor

rehabilitación *sf* ❶ [*de personas*] rehabilitation ❷ [*en un puesto*] reinstatement ❸ [*de local*] restoration

rehabilitar *vt* ❶ [*personas*] to rehabilitate ❷ [*en un puesto*] to reinstate ❸ [*local*] to restore

rehacer *vt* ❶ [*volver a hacer*] to redo ❷ [*reconstruir*] to rebuild ❸ INFORMÁTICA redo

rehén (pl rehenes) *sm* hostage • **tomar como rehén** to take hostage

rehogar *vt* to fry over a low heat

rehuir *vt* to avoid

reina *sf* [*monarca*] queen ▶ **reina de belleza** beauty queen ▶ **reina madre** queen mother

reinado *sm* reign

reinante *adj* ❶ [*monarquía, persona*] ruling ❷ [*viento*] prevailing ❸ [*frío, calor*] current ❖ *Los adjetivos ingleses son invariables.*

reinar *vi* to reign

reincidir *vi* • **reincidir en a)** [*falta, error*] to relapse into; to fall back into **b)** [*delito*] to repeat

reincorporar *vt* to reincorporate

reino *sm* ❶ BIOLOGÍA & POLÍTICA kingdom ▶ **el reino animal** the animal kingdom ▶ **el Reino Unido** the United Kingdom ❷ [*ámbito*] realm

reinstalar *vt* re-install

reintegrar *vt* ❶ [*a un puesto*] to reinstate ❷ [*dinero*] to reimburse

reintegro *sm* [*de dinero*] reimbursement

reír ◆ *vi* to laugh • **no me hagas reír** don't make me laugh • **se echó a reír** he burst out laughing
◆ *vt* to laugh at
■ **reírse** *v pronominal* • **reírse (de)** to laugh (at) • **se ríen de él** they're laughing at him

reiterar *vt* to reiterate

reivindicación *sf* ❶ [*de derechos*] claim ❷ [*de atentado*] claiming of responsibility

reivindicar *vt* ❶ [*derechos, salario* ETC] to claim ❷ [*atentado*] to claim responsibility for

reja *sf* ❶ [*generalmente*] bars *pl* ❷ [*en el suelo*] grating ❸ [*celosía*] grille

rejego, ga *adj familiar* [*terco*] stubborn ❖ *Los adjetivos ingleses son invariables.*

rejilla *sf* ❶ [*enrejado*] grid ❷ [*de ventana*] grille ❸ [*de cocina*] grill (on stove) ❹ [*de horno*] gridiron ❺ [*para sillas, muebles*] wickerwork ❻ [*para equipaje*] luggage rack

rejuvenecer *vt* & *vi* to rejuvenate

relación *sf* ❶ [*nexo*] relation • **tener relación con algo** to bear relation to something • **con relación a, en relación con** in relation to ▶ **relación precio-calidad** value for money ❷ [*comunicación, trato*] relationship • **tiene una buena relación con los alumnos** she has a good relationship with the students ❸ [*lista*] list ❹ ❖ *generalmente pl* [*noviazgo*] relationship ❺ MATE-

MÁTICAS ratio • **en una relación de tres a uno** in a ratio of three to one

relacionar *vt* [*vincular*] to relate

relajación *sf* relaxation

relajar *vt* to relax

relajo *sm familiar* [*alboroto*] racket

relámpago *sm* ➊ [*descarga*] lightning ⚲ *incontable* • **los relámpagos iluminaron el cielo** lightning lit up the sky ➋ [*destello*] flash

relampaguear *vi figurado* to flash

relatar *vt* ➊ [*suceso*] to relate ➋ [*historia*] to tell

relatividad *sf* relativity

relativo, va *adj* [*generalmente*] relative • **todo es relativo** it's all relative ⚲ *Los adjetivos ingleses son invariables.*

relato *sm* ➊ [*exposición*] account ➋ [*cuento*] tale

relax *sm invariable* [*relajación*] relaxation

relevante *adj* outstanding ⚲ *Los adjetivos ingleses son invariables.*

relevar *vt* ➊ [*sustituir*] to relieve ➋ [*destituir*] • **relevar (de)** to dismiss (from) ➌ DEPORTE [*en partidos*] to substitute ; [*en relevos*] to take over from

relevo *sm* ➊ MILITAR relief ➋ DEPORTE [*acción*] relay **expresión tomar el relevo** to take over

relieve *sm* ➊ [*generalmente*] ARTE & GEOGRAFÍA relief ▸ **bajo relieve** bas-relief ➋ [*importancia*] importance • **poner de relieve** to underline

religión *sf* religion

religioso, sa ◆ *adj* religious ⚲ *Los adjetivos ingleses son invariables.*

◆ *sm, f* [*monje*] monk, *femenino* nun

relinchar *vi* to neigh

reliquia *sf* ➊ [*restos*] relic ➋ [*familiar*] heirloom

rellano *sm* [*de escalera*] landing

rellenar *vt* ➊ [*volver a llenar*] to refill ➋ [*documento, formulario*] to fill in ➌ [*pollo, cojín* ETC] to stuff • **rellenó los aguacates con camarones** she stuffed the avocados with shrimp ➍ [*tarta, pastel*] to fill • **lo voy a rellenar con crema** I'm going to fill it with cream

relleno, na *adj* ➊ [*generalmente*] stuffed ➋ [*tarta, pastel*] filled ⚲ *Los adjetivos ingleses son invariables.*

■ **relleno** *sm* ➊ [*de pollo*] stuffing • **el relleno del pollo está delicioso** the stuffing for the chicken is delicious ➋ [*de pastel*] filling • **el relleno es de chocolate** the filling is chocolate

reloj *sm* ➊ [*de pared*] clock • **ese reloj está adelantado** the clock is fast ▸ **reloj despertador** alarm clock ➋ [*de pulsera*] watch • **mi reloj se atrasa** my watch is losing time ▸ **reloj analógico/digital** analog/digital watch ▸ **reloj de arena** hourglass ▸ **reloj de pulsera** wristwatch

expresión hacer algo contra reloj to do something against the clock ▸ **ser como un reloj** to be like clockwork

relojero, ra *sm, f* watchmaker

reluciente *adj* shining ⚲ *Los adjetivos ingleses son invariables.*

relucir *vi* to shine

expresión sacar algo a relucir to bring something up ▸ **salir a relucir** to come to the surface

remangar *vt* to roll up

remar *vi* to row

rematado, da *adj* utter ⚲ *Los adjetivos ingleses son invariables.*

rematar ◆ *vt* ➊ [*acabar*] to finish ➋ [*matar - persona*] to finish off ; [*- animal*] to put out of its misery ➌ [*subastar*] to auction

expresión y para rematarla *familiar* to top it all off

◆ *vi* ➊ [*en futbol*] to shoot ➋ [*de cabeza*] to head at goal

remate *sm* ➊ [*fin, colofón*] end ➋ [*en futbol*] shot ➌ [*de cabeza*] header at goal

expresión para remate [*colmo*] to cap it all

remediar *vt* ➊ [*daño*] to remedy ➋ [*problema*] to solve ➌ [*peligro*] to avoid

expresión no lo puedo remediar I can't help it

remedio *sm* ➊ [*alternativa*] alternative • **no tener más remedio** to have no alternative • **no hay** o **queda más remedio que...** there's no alternative but to... • **¡tú no tienes remedio!** you're hopeless! • **como último remedio** as a last resort ➋ [*medicamento*] remedy • **un remedio natural** a natural remedy

remendar *vt* to mend ; to darn

remero, ra *sm, f* [*persona*] rower

remesa *sf* ➊ [*de productos*] consignment ➋ [*de dinero*] remittance

remiendo *sm* [*parche*] mend

remite *sm* sender's name and address

remitente *smf* sender

remitir ◆ *vt* ➊ [*enviar*] to send ➋ [*traspasar*] • **remitir algo a** to refer something to

◆ *vi* ➊ [*en texto*] • **remitir a** to refer to ➋ [*disminuir*] to subside

remo *sm* ➊ [*pala*] oar ➋ [*deporte*] rowing

remodelar *vt* ➊ [*generalmente*] to redesign ➋ [*gobierno*] to reshuffle

remojar *vt* [*humedecer*] to soak

remojo *sm* • **poner en remojo** to leave to soak • **estar en remojo** to be soaking

remolacha *sf* beet ▸ **remolacha azucarera** sugar beet

remolcar *vt* ➊ [*coche*] to tow ➋ [*barco*] to tug

remolino *sm* ➊ [*de agua*] whirlpool ➋ [*de viento*] whirlwind ➌ [*de humo*] swirl ➍ [*de gente*] throng ➎ [*de pelo*] cowlick

remolón, ona *adj* lazy ⚲ *Los adjetivos ingleses son invariables.*

remolque *sm* ➊ [*acción*] towing ➋ [*vehículo*] trailer

expresión ir a remolque a) [*voluntariamente*] to go in tow ; to tag along **b)** [*obligado*] to be dragged along

R

remontar *vt* ❶ [*pendiente, río*] to go up ❷ [*obstáculo*] to overcome

remorder *vt figurado* • **remorderle a alguien** to fill somebody with remorse

remordimiento *sm* remorse • **no siente el más mínimo remordimiento** he doesn't feel a bit of remorse • **tener remordimientos de conciencia** to suffer pangs of conscience

remoto, ta *adj* remote • **en lugares muy remotos** in remote places • **no tengo ni la más remota idea** I haven't got the faintest idea.⚲ *Los adjetivos ingleses son invariables.*

remover *vt* ❶ [*agitar - sopa, café*] to stir; [- *ensalada*] to toss; [- *bote, frasco*] to shake; [- *tierra*] to dig up ❷ [*reavivar - recuerdos, pasado*] to rake up ❸ [*despedir*] to dismiss

remuneración *sf* remuneration

remunerar *vt* [*pagar*] to remunerate

renacer *vi* ❶ [*generalmente*] to be reborn ❷ [*flores, hojas*] to grow again ❸ [*alegría, esperanza*] to return

renacimiento *sm* ❶ [*generalmente*] rebirth ❷ [*de flores, hojas*] budding

renacuajo *sm* ❶ [*animal*] tadpole ❷ *familiar* [*niño*] tiddler

renal *adj* kidney ⚲ *Sólo se usa delante del sustantivo.*

rencilla *sf* quarrel

rencor *sm* resentment • **no debe haber rencor entre los hermanos** there shouldn't be any resentment among siblings • **guardarle rencor a alguien** to hold a grudge against somebody

rencoroso, sa *adj* resentful ⚲ *Los adjetivos ingleses son invariables.*

rendición *sf* surrender

rendido, da *adj* [*agotado*] exhausted • **estoy rendido** I'm exhausted • **caer rendido** to collapse ⚲ *Los adjetivos ingleses son invariables.*

rendija *sf* crack

rendimiento *sm* ❶ [*de inversión, negocio*] yield ❷ [*de trabajador, fábrica*] productivity • **a pleno rendimiento** at full capacity ❸ [*de tierra, cosecha*] yield ❹ [*de motor*] performance

rendir ◆ *vt* ❶ [*cansar*] to tire out ❷ [*rentar*] to yield ❸ [*vencer*] to defeat ❹ [*ofrecer*] to give
◆ *vi* ❶ [*máquina*] to perform well ❷ [*negocio*] to be profitable ❸ [*fábrica, trabajador*] to be productive
■ **rendirse** *v pronominal* ❶ [*entregarse*] to surrender • **se rindieron al enemigo** they surrendered to the enemy ❷ [*ceder*] • **rendirse a** to give in to ❸ [*desanimarse*] to give up • **me rindo ¿cuál es la solución?** I give up, what's the answer?

renegar *vi* ❶ [*repudiar*] • **renegar de a)** [*ideas*] to renounce **b)** [*familia*] to disown ❷ *familiar* [*gruñir*] to grumble

renglón *sm* line
expresión **a renglón seguido** in the same breath

renguear *vi* to limp

reno *sm* reindeer

renombrar *vt* INFORMÁTICA to rename

renombre *sm* fame • **de renombre** famous

renovación *sf* ❶ [*de carné, contrato*] renewal ❷ [*de mobiliario, local*] renovation

renovar *vt* ❶ [*cambiar - mobiliario, local*] to renovate; [- *vestuario*] to clear out; [- *personal, plantilla*] to shake out ❷ [*rehacer - carné, contrato, ataques*] to renew ❸ [*restaurar*] to restore ❹ [*innovar*] to rethink ❺ POLÍTICA to reform

renta *sf* ❶ [*ingresos*] income ▶ **renta fija** fixed income ▶ **renta variable/vitalicia** variable/life annuity ❷ [*importe del alquiler*] rent ❸ [*beneficios*] return ❹ [*intereses*] interest ❺ [*alquiler*] rental • **renta de bicicletas** bicycle rental

rentable *adj* profitable ⚲ *Los adjetivos ingleses son invariables.*

rentar ◆ *vt* ❶ [*rendir*] to produce ❷ [*alquilar*] to rent
◆ *vi* to be profitable

renuncia *sf* ❶ [*abandono*] giving up ❷ [*dimisión*] resignation • **presentó su renuncia** he handed in his resignation

renunciar *vi* ❶ [*abandonar*] to give up ❷ [*dimitir*] to resign

reñido, da *adj* ❶ [*enfadado*] • **reñido (con)** on bad terms (with) • **están reñidos** they've fallen out ❷ [*disputado*] hard-fought ❸ [*incompatible*] • **estar reñido con** to be incompatible with ⚲ *Los adjetivos ingleses son invariables.*

reñir ◆ *vt* [*disputar*] to fight
◆ *vi* [*enfadarse*] to argue

reo, a *sm, f* ❶ [*culpado*] offender ❷ [*acusado*] accused

reojo *sm* • **mirar algo de reojo** to look at something out of the corner of your eye

reparación *sf* [*arreglo*] repair • **en reparación** under repair

reparador, ra *adj* [*descanso, sueño*] refreshing ⚲ *Los adjetivos ingleses son invariables.*

reparar ◆ *vt* ❶ [*coche* ETC] to repair ❷ [*error, daño* ETC] to make amends for ❸ [*fuerzas*] to restore
◆ *vi* [*advertir*] • **reparar en algo** to notice something • **reparé en este detalle mucho más tarde** I only noticed that detail later on • **no reparar en gastos** to spare no expense

reparo *sm* ❶ [*objeción*] objection ❷ [*apuro*] • **no tener reparos en** not to be afraid to

repartidor, ra *sm, f* ❶ [*generalmente*] distributor ❷ [*de butano, carbón*] deliveryman, *femenino* deliverywoman ❸ [*de leche*] milkman, *femenino* milklady ❹ [*de periódicos*] paperboy, *femenino* papergirl

repartir *vt* ❶ [*dividir - generalmente*] to share out ❷ [*distribuir - leche, periódicos, correo*] to deliver; [- *naipes*] to deal ❸ [*asignar - trabajo, órdenes*] to give out; [- *papeles*] to assign

reparto *sm* ❶ [*división*] division ❷ [*distribución - de leche, periódicos, correo*] delivery • **no cobran por el reparto** they don't charge for delivery • **reparto a domi-**

cilio home delivery ❸ [asignación] allocation ▸ **reparto de premios** prizegiving ❹ CINE & TEATRO cast • **tiene un excelente reparto** it has an excellent cast

repasar *vt* ❶ [revisar] to go over • **repasa bien las sumas** go over your sums carefully ❷ [lección] to review • **están repasando para los exámenes** they're reviewing for their exams

repaso *sm* [estudio] revision • **darle un repaso a algo** to review something • **curso de repaso** refresher course

repelente *adj* ❶ [desagradable, repugnante] repulsive ❷ [ahuyentador] repellent 💡 ***Los adjetivos ingleses son invariables.***

repeler *vt* ❶ [rechazar] to repel ❷ [repugnar] to repulse

repente *sm* [arrebato] fit

repentino, na *adj* sudden 💡 ***Los adjetivos ingleses son invariables.***

repercusión *sf* [consecuencia] repercussion

repercutir *vi figurado* [afectar] • **repercutir en** to have repercussions on • **la subida del petróleo repercute en el precio de venta** the increase in oil prices has repercussions on the sale price

repertorio *sm* ❶ [obras] repertoire ❷ *figurado* [serie] selection

repetición *sf* ❶ [de acción] repetition ❷ [de una jugada] action replay

repetir ◆ *vt* ❶ [acción] to repeat ❷ [ataque] to renew ❸ [en comida] to have seconds of

◆ *vi* ❶ [alumno] to repeat a year ❷ [sabor, alimento] • **repetir (a alguien)** to repeat (on somebody) ❸ [comensal] to have seconds

repisa *sf* ❶ [estante] shelf ❷ [sobre chimenea] mantelpiece

replegar *vt* [ocultar] to retract

repleto, ta *adj* • **repleto (de)** packed (with) • **el estadio estaba repleto** the stadium was packed 💡 ***Los adjetivos ingleses son invariables.***

réplica *sf* ❶ [respuesta] reply ❷ [copia] replica

replicar ◆ *vt* ❶ [responder] to answer ❷ [objetar] to answer back

◆ *vi* [objetar] to answer back

repliegue *sm* [retirada] withdrawal

repoblación *sf* ❶ [con gente] repopulation ❷ [con peces] restocking ▸ **repoblación forestal** reafforestation

repoblar *vt* ❶ [con gente] to repopulate ❷ [con peces] to restock ❸ [con árboles] to replant

repollo *sm* cabbage

reponer *vt* ❶ [generalmente] to replace ❷ CINE & TEATRO to rerun ❸ TELEVISIÓN to repeat ❹ [replicar] • **reponer que** to reply that

reportaje *sm* ❶ RADIO & TELEVISIÓN report • **apareció en el reportaje sobre la juventud actual** it appeared in the report on today's youth ❷ PRENSA article • **su reportaje salió publicado en la revista** his article was published in the magazine

reportar *vt* ❶ [traer] to bring ❷ [denunciar] to report ❸ [informar] to report

■ **reportarse** *v pronominal* ▸ **reportarse (a)** to report (to)

reporte *sm* ❶ [informe] report ❷ [noticia] news item

reportero, ra, repórter *sm, f* reporter

reposado, da *adj* relaxed 💡 ***Los adjetivos ingleses son invariables.***

reposar *vi* ❶ [descansar] to (have a) rest ❷ [sedimentarse] to stand

reposición *sf* ❶ CINE rerun ❷ TEATRO revival ❸ TELEVISIÓN repeat ❹ [de existencias, pieza ETC] replacement

reposo *sm* [descanso] rest

repostar ◆ *vi* ❶ [coche] to fill up ❷ [avión] to refuel

◆ *vt* ❶ [gasolina] to fill up with ❷ [provisiones] to stock up on

repostería *sf* [oficio, productos] confectionery

reprender *vt* ❶ [a niños] to tell off ❷ [a empleados] to reprimand

represalia *sf* 💡 ***generalmente pl*** reprisal • **tomar represalias** to retaliate

representación *sf* ❶ [generalmente] COMERCIO representation • **en representación de** on behalf of ❷ TEATRO performance

representante ◆ *adj* representative 💡 ***Los adjetivos ingleses son invariables.***

◆ *smf* ❶ [generalmente] COMERCIO representative • **el representante de la empresa** the company representative • **representante de la ley** officer of the law ❷ [de artista] agent • **el representante de la cantante** the singer's agent

representar *vt* ❶ [generalmente] COMERCIO to represent • **representó a México en las Olimpíadas** she represented Mexico in the Olympics ❷ [aparentar] to look • **representa unos 40 años** she looks about 40 ❸ [significar] to mean • **representa el 50% del consumo interno** it accounts for 50% of domestic consumption ❹ TEATRO [función] to perform; [papel] to play • **esa obra es muy difícil de representar** that play is very difficult to perform

representativo, va *adj* ❶ [simbolizador] • **ser representativo de** to represent ❷ [característico, relevante] • **representativo (de)** representative (of) 💡 ***Los adjetivos ingleses son invariables.***

represión *sf* repression

reprimenda *sf* reprimand

reprimir *vt* ❶ [generalmente] to suppress ❷ [minorías, disidentes] to repress

reprobar *vt* ❶ [condenar] to condemn • **hay que reprobar el uso de las drogas** we must condemn the use of drugs ❷ [no pasar] to fail • **si no estudias vas a reprobar el examen** you'll fail the test if you don't study

reprochar *vt* • **reprochar algo a alguien** to reproach somebody for something

reproche *sm* reproach

reproducción *sf* reproduction

reproducir *vt* ❶ [*generalmente*] ARTE to reproduce ❷ [*gestos*] to copy

reptil *sm* reptile

república *sf* republic

República Checa *sf* Czech Republic

República Dominicana *sf* Dominican Republic

republicano, na *adj* & *sm, f* republican ☝ *Los adjetivos ingleses son invariables.*

repudiar *vt* ❶ [*condenar*] to repudiate ❷ [*rechazar*] to disown

repuesto, ta ◆ *participio pasado* → **reponer** ◆ *adj* • **repuesto (de)** recovered (from) ☝ *Los adjetivos ingleses son invariables.* ■ **repuesto** *sm* ❶ [*generalmente*] reserve ❷ AUTOMÓVILES spare part • **¿venden repuestos para el carro?** do you sell spare auto parts?

repugnancia *sf* disgust

repugnante *adj* disgusting ☝ *Los adjetivos ingleses son invariables.*

repugnar *vt* • **me repugna ese olor/su actitud** I find that smell/his/her attitude disgusting • **me repugna hacerlo** I'm loath to do it

repulsivo, va *adj* repulsive ☝ *Los adjetivos ingleses son invariables.*

reputación *sf* reputation • **esa tienda tiene mala reputación** that store has a bad reputation

requerir *vt* ❶ [*necesitar*] to require ❷ [*ordenar*] to demand ❸ [*pedir*] • **requerir a alguien (para) que haga algo** to ask somebody to do something

requesón *sm* ▶ *para explicar lo que es puedes decir:* it's a ricotta-type cheese

requisito *sm* requirement • **requisito previo** prerequisite

res *sf* ❶ [*animal*] beast ❷ ▶ **carne de res** beef

resaca *sf* ❶ [*de las olas*] undertow ❷ *familiar* [*de borrachera*] hangover

resaltar ◆ *vi* ❶ [*destacar*] to stand out ❷ [*en edificios - decoración*] to stand out ◆ *vt* [*destacar*] to highlight

resarcir *vt* • **resarcir a alguien (de)** to compensate somebody (for)

resbalada *sf familiar* slip

resbaladilla *sf* slide

resbaladizo, za *adj* slippery ☝ *Los adjetivos ingleses son invariables.*

resbalar *vi* ❶ [*deslizarse*] to slide ❷ [*estar resbaladizo*] to be slippery ■ **resbalarse** *v pronominal* to slip • **se resbaló en el piso mojado** he slipped on the wet floor

resbalón *sm* slip • **dar un resbalón** to slip

rescatar *vt* ❶ [*liberar, salvar*] to rescue ❷ [*pagando rescate*] to ransom ❸ [*recuperar - herencia* ETC] to recover

rescate *sm* ❶ [*liberación, salvación*] rescue ❷ [*dinero*] ransom ❸ [*recuperación*] recovery

rescindir *vt* to rescind

rescisión *sf* cancellation

resecar *vt* [*piel*] to dry out

reseco, ca *adj* ❶ [*piel, garganta, pan*] very dry ❷ [*tierra*] parched ❸ [*flaco*] emaciated ☝ *Los adjetivos ingleses son invariables.*

resentido, da *adj* resentful • **estar resentido con alguien** to be really upset with somebody ☝ *Los adjetivos ingleses son invariables.*

resentimiento *sm* resentment

reseña *sf* [*de libro, concierto*] review

reseñar *vt* [*libro, concierto*] to review

reserva *sf* ❶ [*de hotel, avión* ETC] reservation ❷ [*provisión*] reserves *pl* • **tener algo de reserva** to keep something in reserve ❸ [*objeción*] reservation ❹ [*de indígenas*] reservation ❺ [*de animales*] MILITAR reserve ▶ **reserva natural** nature reserve

reservación *sf* [*de hotel, avión* ETC] reservation

reservar *vt* ❶ [*habitación, asiento* ETC] to reserve • **quisiera reservar una mesa para dos** I'd like to reserve a table for two ❷ [*guardar - dinero, pasteles* ETC] to set aside; [*- sorpresa*] to keep ❸ [*callar - opinión, comentarios*] to reserve

resfriado, da *adj* • **estar resfriado** to have a cold ☝ *Los adjetivos ingleses son invariables.* ■ **resfriado** *sm* cold • **pescar un resfriado** to catch a cold • **me vas a pegar tu resfriado** you're going to give me your cold

resfriar ■ **resfriarse** *v pronominal* [*constiparse*] to catch a cold • **te vas a resfriar** you're going to catch a cold

resguardar *vt* & *vi* • **resguardar de** to protect against

resguardo *sm* ❶ [*documento*] receipt ❷ [*protección*] protection

residencia *sf* ❶ [*localidad, domicilio*] residence • **fijó residencia en Veracruz** he took up residence in Veracruz • **segunda residencia** second home ▶ **residencia canina** kennels ❷ [*establecimiento - de estudiantes*] dormitory; [*- de ancianos*] nursing home; [*- de oficiales*] residence ❸ [*permiso para extranjeros*] residence permit

residencial *adj* residential ☝ *Los adjetivos ingleses son invariables.*

residente *adj* & *smf* resident • **es residente en México** he is resident in Mexico ☝ *Los adjetivos ingleses son invariables.*

residir *vi* ❶ [*vivir*] to live • **residió ocho años en el extranjero** she lived abroad for eight years ❷ [*radicar*] • **residir en** to lie in • **la clave de su éxito reside en su facilidad de manejo** the key to its success lies in that it's easy to use

residuo *sm* ☝ *generalmente pl* [*material inservible*] waste ▶ **residuos nucleares** nuclear waste ☝ *incontable* ▶ **residuos tóxicos** toxic waste ☝ *incontable*

resignación *sf* resignation • **aceptó su castigo con resignación** he accepted his punishment with resignation

resignarse *v pronominal* • **resignarse (a hacer algo)** to resign yourself (to doing something) • **se resignó a su destino** he resigned himself to his fate

resina *sf* resin

resistencia *sf* ❶ [*generalmente*] ELECTRICIDAD & POLÍTICA resistance • **ofrecer resistencia** to put up resistance ❷ [*de puente, cimientos*] strength ❸ [*física - para correr* ETC] stamina • **tiene gran resistencia física** he has great stamina

resistente *adj* [*generalmente*] tough ; strong • **resistente al calor** heat-resistant ☼ *Los adjetivos ingleses son invariables.*

resistir ✦ *vt* ❶ [*dolor, peso, críticas*] to withstand ❷ [*tentación, impulso, deseo*] to resist ❸ [*tolerar*] to tolerate ❹ [*ataque*] to resist

✦ *vi* ❶ [*ejército, ciudad* ETC] • **resistir (a algo/a alguien)** to resist (something/somebody) ❷ [*corredor* ETC] to keep going • **resistir a algo** to stand up to something ❸ [*mesa, dique* ETC] to take the strain • **resistir a algo** to withstand something ❹ [*mostrarse firme - ante tentaciones* ETC] to resist (it) • **resistir a algo** to resist something

resolución *sf* ❶ [*solución - de una crisis*] resolution; [- *de un crimen*] solution ❷ [*firmeza*] determination ❸ [*decisión*] decision ❹ [*de Naciones Unidas* ETC] resolution

resolver *vt* ❶ [*solucionar - duda, crisis*] to resolve; [- *problema, caso*] to solve ❷ [*decidir*] • **resolver hacer algo** to decide to do something ❸ [*partido, disputa, conflicto*] to settle

resonancia *sf* ❶ [*generalmente*] FÍSICA resonance ☼ *incontable* ❷ *figurado* [*importancia*] repercussions *pl*

resonar *vi* to resound

resoplar *vi* ❶ [*de cansancio*] to pant ❷ [*de enfado*] to snort

resorte *sm* ❶ [*muelle*] spring • **saltar como movido por un resorte** to spring up ❷ [*medio*] means *pl* ❸ [*elástico*] elastic • **la falda tiene resorte en la cintura** the skirt has an elastic waistband

expresión **tocar todos los resortes** to pull out all the stops

respaldar *vt* to support

respaldo *sm* ❶ [*de asiento*] back • **una silla sin respaldo** a chair without a back ❷ *figurado* [*apoyo*] support • **expresó su respaldo a la idea** he expressed his support for the idea

respectar *v impersonal* • **por lo que respecta a alguien/a algo, en lo que respecta a alguien/a algo** as far as somebody/something is concerned

respectivo, va *adj* respective • **en lo respectivo a** with regard to ☼ *Los adjetivos ingleses son invariables.*

respecto *sm* • **al respecto, a este respecto** in this respect • **no sé nada al respecto** I don't know anything about it

respetable *adj* ❶ [*venerable*] respectable ❷ [*bastante*] considerable ☼ *Los adjetivos ingleses son invariables.*

respetar *vt* ❶ [*generalmente*] to respect ❷ [*la palabra*] to honor

respeto *sm* • **respeto (a o por)** respect (for) • **es una falta de respeto** it shows a lack of respect • **por respeto a** out of consideration for

respetuoso, sa *adj* • **respetuoso (con)** respectful (of) ☼ *Los adjetivos ingleses son invariables.*

respiración *sf* [*de ser vivo*] breathing • **tiene la respiración irregular** her breathing is irregular

expresión **quedarse sin respiración** [*asombrado*] to be stunned

respirar ✦ *vt* [*aire*] to breathe

✦ *vi* ❶ [*aire*] to breathe ❷ *figurado* [*sentir alivio*] to breathe again

expresión **no dejar respirar a alguien** not to allow somebody a moment's peace ▶ **sin respirar a)** [*sin descanso*] without a break **b)** [*atentamente*] with great attention

respiratorio, ria *adj* respiratory • **el aparato respiratorio** the respiratory system ☼ *Los adjetivos ingleses son invariables.*

respiro *sm* ❶ [*descanso*] rest ❷ [*alivio*] relief • **dar un respiro a alguien** to give somebody a break

resplandecer *vi* ❶ [*brillar*] to shine ❷ *figurado* [*destacar*] to shine

resplandeciente *adj* ❶ [*sonrisa*] beaming ❷ [*época*] glittering ❸ [*vestimenta, color*] resplendent ☼ *Los adjetivos ingleses son invariables.*

responder ✦ *vt* to answer

✦ *vi* ❶ [*contestar*] • **responder (a algo)** to answer (something) • **no pudo responder a la pregunta de la maestra** she couldn't answer the teacher's question • **gracias por responder a mi e-mail** thank you for replying to my e-mail ❷ [*reaccionar*] • **responder (a)** to respond (to) • **el enfermo respondió bien al tratamiento** the patient responded well to the treatment ❸ [*responsabilizarse*] • **responder de algo/por alguien** to answer for something/for somebody ❹ [*replicar*] to answer back

respondón, ona *adj* insolent ☼ *Los adjetivos ingleses son invariables.*

responsabilidad *sf* ❶ [*obligación*] responsibility, *plural* responsibilities • **le han dado mucha responsabilidad** they've given her a lot of responsibility • **tener la responsabilidad de algo** to be responsible for something • **exigir responsabilidades a alguien** to hold somebody accountable ❷ DERECHO liability ▶ **responsabilidad civil/penal** DERECHO civil/criminal liability

responsabilizar *vt* • **responsabilizar a alguien (de algo)** to hold somebody responsible (for something)

responsable ✦ *adj* responsible • **María es muy responsable** María is very responsible • **responsable de** responsible for • **ella es responsable del bienestar de los niños** she's responsible for the children's well-being ☼ *Los adjetivos ingleses son invariables.*

✦ *smf* ❶ [*culpable*] person responsible ❷ [*encargado*] person in charge

R

respuesta *sf* ❶ [*generalmente*] answer; reply • **espero tu respuesta** I'll await your reply ❷ [*en exámenes*] answer • **en respuesta a** in reply to ❸ *figurado* [*reacción*] response

resquebrajar *vt* to crack

resta *sf* MATEMÁTICAS subtraction

restablecer *vt* to reestablish

restante *adj* • **lo restante** the rest ☿ *Los adjetivos ingleses son invariables.*

restar ◆ *vt* ❶ MATEMÁTICAS to subtract ❷ [*disminuir*] • **restar importancia a algo** to play down the importance of something
◆ *vi* [*faltar*] to be left

> **restar ≠ rest**
>
> • La palabra inglesa **rest** es un falso amigo que significa *descansar*. **Restar** se traduce al inglés por **to subtract**.

restaurante *sm* restaurant

restaurar *vt* to restore

resto *sm* • **el resto a)** [*generalmente*] the rest **b)** MATEMÁTICAS the remainder

restricción *sf* restriction

restringir *vt* to limit

resucitar ◆ *vt* ❶ [*person*] to bring back to life ❷ [*costumbre*] to revive
◆ *vi* [*persona*] to rise from the dead

resuelto, ta ◆ *participio pasado* → **resolver**
◆ *adj* [*decidido*] determined ☿ *Los adjetivos ingleses son invariables.*

resultado *sm* result • **el resultado del sorteo** the results of the drawing • **el resultado del partido** the game's score • **dar buen/mal resultado** to be a success/failure

resultar ◆ *vi* ❶ [*acabar siendo*] • **resultar (ser)** to turn out (to be) • **el cuarto resultó ser muy pequeño** the room turned out to be very small • **resultó ileso** he was uninjured • **nuestro equipo resultó vencedor** our team came out on top ❷ [*salir bien*] to work (out) • **no le resultaron sus planes** his plans didn't work out ❸ [*ser*] to be • **resulta sorprendente** it's surprising • **me resultó imposible terminar antes** I was unable to finish earlier
◆ *v impersonal* [*suceder*] • **resultar que** to turn out that • **ahora resulta que no quiere alquilarlo** now it seems that she doesn't want to rent it

resumen *sm* summary • **el resumen es demasiado largo** the summary is too long • **en resumen** in short

resumir *vt* ❶ [*abreviar*] to summarize • **tuvimos que resumir la película en dos párrafos** we had to summarize the movie in two paragraphs • **resumiendo** in short ❷ [*discurso*] to sum up

resurrección *sf* resurrection

retén *sm* [*de policía,ejército*] roadblock

retener *vt* ❶ [*detener*] to hold back ❷ [*en comisaría*] to detain ❸ [*hacer permanecer*] to keep ❹ [*contener - impulso, ira*] to hold back ❺ [*conservar*] to retain ❻ [*quedarse con*] to hold on to ❼ [*memorizar*] to remember ❽ [*deducir del sueldo*] to deduct

reticente *adj* [*reacio*] unwilling ☿ *Los adjetivos ingleses son invariables.*

retina *sf* retina

retirado, da *adj* ❶ [*jubilado*] retired ❷ [*solitario, alejado*] isolated ☿ *Los adjetivos ingleses son invariables.*

■ **retirada** *sf* ❶ MILITAR retreat • **batirse en retirada** to beat a retreat ❷ [*de fondos, moneda*] withdrawal ❸ [*de competencia, actividad*] withdrawal

retirar *vt* ❶ [*quitar - generalmente*] to remove; [*- dinero, moneda, carné*] to withdraw; [*- nieve*] to clear ❷ [*jubilar - a deportista*] to force to retire; [*- a empleado*] to retire ❸ [*retractarse de*] to take back

■ **retirarse** *v pronominal* ❶ [*generalmente*] to retire ❷ [*de competición, elecciones*] to withdraw ❸ [*de reunión*] to leave ❹ [*de campo de batalla*] to retreat ❺ [*apartarse*] to move away

retiro *sm* ❶ [*jubilación*] retirement ❷ [*pensión*] pension ❸ [*refugio, ejercicio*] retreat

reto *sm* challenge

retocar *vt* to touch up

retoque *sm* ❶ [*toque*] touching-up ☿ *incontable* • **dar los últimos retoques a** to put the finishing touches to ❷ [*de prenda de vestir*] alteration

retorcer *vt* [*torcer - brazo, alambre*] to twist; [*- ropa, cuello*] to wring

retorcido, da *adj* ❶ [*torcido - brazo, alambre*] twisted ❷ *figurado* [*rebuscado*] complicated ☿ *Los adjetivos ingleses son invariables.*

retornable *adj* returnable • **no retornable** non-returnable ☿ *Los adjetivos ingleses son invariables.*

retornar *vt* & *vi* to return

retorno *sm* [*generalmente*] INFORMÁTICA return ▸ **retorno de carro** carriage return

retortijón *sm* ☿ *generalmente pl* stomach cramp

retransmisión *sf* broadcast ▸ **retransmisión en directo/diferido** live/recorded broadcast

retransmitir *vt* to broadcast

retrasado, da *adj* ❶ [*país, industria*] backward • **una sociedad retrasada** a backward society ❷ [*reloj*] slow • **mi reloj está retrasado por cinco minutos** my watch is five minutes slow ❸ [*tren*] late ❹ [*en el pago, los estudios*] behind • **va un poco retrasado en el colegio** he's a little behind in school ❺ MEDICINA learning-disabled ☿ *Los adjetivos ingleses son invariables.*

retrasar *vt* ❶ [*aplazar*] to postpone • **retrasaron la fiesta una semana** they postponed the party for a week ❷ [*demorar*] to delay • **todos los trenes están retrasados** all the trains are delayed ❸ [*hacer más lento*] to slow down ❹ [*en el pago, los estudios*] to set back ❺ [*reloj*] to put back • **este fin de semana hay que retrasar los relojes** we have to put back the clocks this weekend

■ **retrasarse** *v pronominal* ❶ [*llegar tarde*] to be late • **me retrasé por el tráfico** I was late because of traffic ❷ [*quedarse atrás*] to fall behind ❸ [*aplazarse*] to be put off ❹ [*reloj*] to lose time

retraso *sm* ❶ [*por llegar tarde*] delay • **hubo un retraso de dos horas** there was a two-hour delay • **llegar con (15 minutos de) retraso** to be (15 minutes) late ❷ [*por sobrepasar una fecha*] • **llevo en mi trabajo un retraso de 20 páginas** I'm 20 pages behind with my work ❸ [*subdesarrollo*] backwardness ❹ MEDICINA mental deficiency

retratar *vt* ❶ [*fotografiar*] to photograph ❷ [*dibujar*] to do a portrait of ❸ *figurado* [*describir*] to portray

retrato *sm* ❶ [*dibujo*] portrait ❷ [*fotografía*] photograph ▶ **retrato robot** photofit picture ❸ *figurado* [*reflejo*] portrayal

expresión **ser el vivo retrato de alguien** to be the spitting image of somebody

retrete *sm* toilet

retribuir *vt* ❶ [*pagar*] to pay ❷ [*recompensar*] to reward ❸ [*favor, obsequio*] to return

retro *adj* old-fashioned ☞ *Los adjetivos ingleses son invariables.*

retroactivo, va *adj* ❶ [*ley*] retroactive ❷ [*pago*] backdated ☞ *Los adjetivos ingleses son invariables.*

retroceder *vi* ❶ [*hacia atrás*] to go back ❷ *figurado* to back down

retroceso *sm* [*regresión - generalmente*] backward movement ; [*- en negociaciones*] setback ; [*- en la economía*] recession

retrógrado, da *adj* & *sm, f* reactionary ☞ *Los adjetivos ingleses son invariables.*

retroproyector *sm* overhead projector

retrospectivo, va *adj* retrospective ☞ *Los adjetivos ingleses son invariables.*

retrovisor *sm* rear-view mirror

retumbar *vi* [*resonar*] to resound

reuma, reúma *sm o sf* rheumatism

reumatismo *sm* rheumatism

reunión *sf* meeting

reunir *vt* ❶ [*público, accionistas* ETC] to bring together ❷ [*objetos, textos* ETC] to collect ❸ [*fondos*] to raise ❹ [*requisitos*] to meet ❺ [*cualidades*] to possess

revalidar *vt* [*estudios, diploma*] to validate

revancha *sf* ❶ [*venganza*] revenge ❷ DEPORTE return match

revelación *sf* revelation

revelar *vt* ❶ [*declarar*] to reveal ❷ [*evidenciar*] to show ❸ FOTOGRAFÍA to develop

reventar ◆ *vt* ❶ [*explotar*] to burst ❷ [*echar abajo*] to break down ❸ [*con explosivos*] to blow up ❹ [*fastidiar*] to bug • **su actitud me revienta** his attitude really bugs me

◆ *vi* [*explotar*] to burst

■ **reventarse** *v pronominal* ❶ [*explotar*] to explode ❷ [*rueda*] to burst ❸ *familiar* to party

reventón *sm* [*fiesta*] party

reverencia *sf* ❶ [*respeto*] reverence ❷ [*saludo - inclinación*] bow ; [*- flexión de piernas*] curtsy

reversa *sf* reverse • **meter reversa** to put the car in reverse

reversible *adj* reversible ☞ *Los adjetivos ingleses son invariables.*

reverso *sm* back

revertir *vi* ❶ [*volver, devolver*] to revert ❷ [*resultar*] • **revertir en** to result in • **revertir en beneficio de** to be to the advantage of

revés *sm* ❶ [*parte opuesta - de papel, mano*] back ; [*- de tela*] other side • **al revés a)** [*en sentido contrario*] the wrong way round **b)** [*en forma opuesta*] the other way round • **del revés a)** [*lo de detrás, delante*] the wrong way round **b)** [*lo de dentro, fuera*] inside out **c)** [*lo de arriba, abajo*] upside down ❷ [*bofetada*] slap ❸ DEPORTE backhand ❹ [*contratiempo*] setback

revestimiento *sm* covering

revestir *vt* ❶ [*recubrir*] • **revestir (de) a)** [*generalmente*] to cover (with) **b)** [*pintura*] to coat (with) **c)** [*forro*] to line (with) ❷ [*poseer - solemnidad, gravedad* ETC] to take on ; to have

revisar *vt* ❶ [*repasar*] to go over again ❷ [*inspeccionar*] to inspect ❸ [*cuentas*] to audit ❹ [*modificar*] to revise

revisión *sf* ❶ [*repaso*] revision ❷ [*inspección*] inspection ▶ **revisión de cuentas** audit ▶ **revisión médica** check-up ❸ AUTOMÓVILES service

revisor, ra *sm, f* [*en tren, autobús*] conductor

revista *sf* ❶ [*publicación*] magazine ▶ **revista del corazón** gossip magazine ▶ **revista de modas** fashion magazine ❷ [*sección de periódico*] section ❸ [*espectáculo teatral*] revue ❹ [*inspección*] inspection • **pasar revista a a)** MILITAR to inspect **b)** [*examinar*] to examine

revistero *sm* [*mueble*] magazine rack

revivir ◆ *vi* to revive
◆ *vt* [*recordar*] to revive memories of

revolcar *vt* to upend

revolotear *vi* to flutter (about)

revoltijo, revoltillo *sm* jumble

revoltoso, sa *adj* ❶ [*travieso*] mischievous ❷ [*sedicioso*] rebellious ☞ *Los adjetivos ingleses son invariables.*

revolución *sf* revolution

revolucionar *vt* [*transformar*] to revolutionize

revolucionario, ria *adj* & *sm, f* revolutionary ☞ *Los adjetivos ingleses son invariables.*

revolver *vt* ❶ [*dar vueltas*] to turn around ❷ [*líquido*] to stir ❸ [*mezclar*] to mix ❹ [*ensalada*] to toss ❺ [*desorganizar*] to mess up ❻ [*cajones*] to turn out ❼ [*irritar*] to upset

revólver *sm* revolver

revuelo *sm* [*agitación*] commotion • **armar un gran revuelo** to cause a great stir

rey *sm* king ▶ **los Reyes Magos** the Three Wise Men

R

rezagado, da *adj* • **ir rezagado** to lag behind ◌̣ *Los adjetivos ingleses son invariables.*

rezar *vi* ❶ [*orar*] • **rezar (a)** to pray (to) • **rezar por algo/alguien** to pray for something/somebody ❷ [*decir*] to read

rezo *sm* [*oración*] prayer

riachuelo *sm* brook

riada *sf* flood

ribera *sf* ❶ [*del río*] bank ❷ [*del mar*] shore

rico, ca ◆ *adj* ❶ [*generalmente*] rich ❷ [*abundante*] • **rico (en)** rich (in) • **un país rico en petróleo** a country rich in oil ❸ [*sabroso*] delicious ❹ [*simpático*] cute ◌̣ *Los adjetivos ingleses son invariables.*

◆ *sm, f* rich person • **los ricos** the rich

ridiculez *sf* ❶ [*payasada*] silly thing ❷ [*nimiedad*] trifle • **cuesta una ridiculez** it costs next to nothing

ridiculizar *vt* to ridicule

ridículo, la *adj* ❶ [*ropa*] ridiculous ❷ [*precio, suma*] laughable ◌̣ *Los adjetivos ingleses son invariables.*

■ **ridículo** *sm* ridicule • **hacer el ridículo** to make a fool of yourself • **dejar en ridículo a alguien** to make somebody look stupid • **quedar en ridículo** to look like a fool

riego *sm* ❶ [*de campo*] irrigation ❷ [*de jardín*] watering

rienda *sf* [*de caballería*] rein

expresión **dar rienda suelta a** to give free rein to

riesgo *sm* risk • **corres el riesgo de perderlo todo** you run the risk of losing it all

riesgoso, sa *adj* risky ◌̣ *Los adjetivos ingleses son invariables.*

rifa *sf* raffle

rifar *vt* to raffle

rifle *sm* rifle

rigidez *sf* ❶ [*de un cuerpo, objeto* ETC] rigidity ❷ [*del rostro*] stoniness ❸ *figurado* [*severidad*] strictness

rígido, da *adj* ❶ [*cuerpo, objeto* ETC] rigid ❷ [*rostro*] stony ❸ [*severo - normas* ETC] harsh; [*- carácter*] inflexible ◌̣ *Los adjetivos ingleses son invariables.*

rigor *sm* ❶ [*severidad*] strictness ❷ [*exactitud*] accuracy ❸ [*inclemencia*] harshness

riguroso, sa *adj* ❶ [*severo*] strict ❷ [*exacto*] rigorous ❸ [*inclemente*] harsh ◌̣ *Los adjetivos ingleses son invariables.*

rimar *vt* & *vi* to rhyme • **rimar con algo** to rhyme with something

rímel, rimmel° *sm* mascara

rincón *sm* corner *(inside)*

ring (pl rings) *sm* (boxing) ring

rinoceronte *sm* rhinoceros

riña *sf* ❶ [*disputa*] quarrel ❷ [*pelea*] fight

riñón *sm* kidney

expresión **tener el riñón bien cubierto** to be well-heeled

río *sm* river • **río arriba** upstream • **río abajo** downstream

expresión **a río revuelto, ganancia de pescadores** *proverbio* it's an ill wind that blows nobody any good *proverbio* ▶ **cuando el río suena, agua lleva** *proverbio* there's no smoke without fire *proverbio*

riqueza *sf* ❶ [*fortuna*] wealth • **la concentración de la riqueza** the concentration of wealth ❷ [*abundancia*] richness • **la riqueza de la vegetación** the richness of the vegetation

risa *sf* laugh • **tiene una risa muy contagiosa** she has a very infectious laugh • **me da risa** I find it funny • **¡qué risa!** how funny! • **de risa** funny

risueño, ña *adj* [*alegre*] smiling ◌̣ *Los adjetivos ingleses son invariables.*

ritmo *sm* ❶ [*generalmente*] rhythm • **el ritmo de la música** the rhythm of the music • **al ritmo de** to the rhythm of • **llevar el ritmo** to keep time • **perder el ritmo** to get out of time ❷ [*cardíaco*] beat ❸ [*velocidad*] pace • **no puedo caminar a tu ritmo** I can't walk at your pace

rito *sm* ❶ RELIGIÓN rite ❷ [*costumbre*] ritual

ritual *adj* & *sm* ritual ◌̣ *Los adjetivos ingleses son invariables.*

rival *adj* & *smf* rival • **sin rival** unrivalled ◌̣ *Los adjetivos ingleses son invariables.*

rivalidad *sf* rivalry

rivalizar *vi* • **rivalizar (con)** to compete (with) • **nuestros productos no pueden rivalizar con los asiáticos** our products cannot compete with Asian ones

rizado, da *adj* ❶ [*pelo*] curly ❷ [*mar*] choppy ◌̣ *Los adjetivos ingleses son invariables.*

■ **rizado** *sm* [*en peluquería*] • **hacerse un rizado** to have your hair curled

rizar *vt* [*pelo*] to curl

rizo *sm* ❶ [*de pelo*] curl ❷ [*del agua*] ripple ❸ [*de avión*] loop

expresión **rizar el rizo** to split hairs

robar *vt* ❶ [*generalmente*] to steal • **me robaron la cartera** my wallet was stolen ❷ [*casa*] burglarize ❸ [*banco*] to rob ❹ [*en cartas*] to draw ❺ [*cobrar caro*] to rob

roble *sm* oak

expresión **más fuerte que un roble** as strong as an ox

robo *sm* ❶ [*delito*] robbery • **el robo de un banco** a bank robbery ❷ [*hurto*] theft • **el robo de una televisión** the theft of a TV set ❸ [*en casa*] burglary • **el robo en una casa** a burglary

expresión **ser un robo** [*precios* ETC] to be daylight robbery

robot (pl robots) *sm* INFORMÁTICA robot

robótica *sf* robotics ◌̣ *incontable*

robustecer *vt* to strengthen

robusto, ta *adj* robust ◌̣ *Los adjetivos ingleses son invariables.*

roca *sf* rock

expresión **firme como una roca** solid as a rock

roce *sm* ❶ [*rozamiento - generalmente*] rub ; [*- suave*] brush ❷ Física friction ❸ [*desgaste*] wear ❹ [*rasguño - en piel*] graze ; [*- en zapato, puerta*] scuffmark ; [*- en metal*] scratch ❺ [*trato*] close contact ❻ [*desavenencia*] brush • **tener un roce con alguien** to have a brush with somebody

rociar *vt* ❶ [*arrojar gotas*] to sprinkle ❷ [*con espray*] to spray ❸ [*con vino*] to wash down

rocío *sm* dew

rock, rock and roll *sm invariable* rock and roll

rocoso, sa *adj* rocky ⚬: *Los adjetivos ingleses son invariables.*

rodaja *sf* slice

rodapié *sm* skirting board

rodar ◆ *vi* ❶ [*deslizar*] to roll ❷ [*circular*] to travel ❸ [*caer*] • **rodar (por)** to tumble (down) ❹ [*ir de un lado a otro*] to go around ❺ Cine to shoot
◆ *vt* ❶ Cine to shoot ❷ [*automóvil*] to run in

rodear *vt* ❶ [*generalmente*] to surround • **los admiradores del cantante lo rodearon** the singer's fans surrounded him • **rodear algo de algo** to surround something with something • **le rodeó el cuello con los brazos** she put her arms around his neck ❷ [*dar la vuelta a*] to go around ❸ [*eludir*] to skirt around

rodeo *sm* ❶ [*camino largo*] detour • **dar un rodeo** to make a detour ❷ ⚬: *generalmente pl* [*evasiva*] evasiveness ⚬: *incontable* ❸ [*espectáculo*] rodeo

rodilla *sf* knee • **de rodillas** on your knees

rodillera *sf* [*protección*] knee pad

rodillo *sm* ❶ [*generalmente*] roller ❷ [*para repostería*] rolling pin

roer *vt* ❶ [*con dientes*] to gnaw (at) ❷ figurado [*gastar*] to eat away (at)

rogar *vt* [*implorar*] to beg • **rogar a alguien que haga algo** to beg somebody to do something • **le ruego me perdone** I beg your pardon • **les rogamos disculpen estas molestias** we ask that you forgive these disruptions • **'se ruega silencio'** silence, please

rojizo, za *adj* reddish ⚬: *Los adjetivos ingleses son invariables.*

rojo, ja *adj* red • **ponerse rojo a)** [*generalmente*] to turn red **b)** [*ruborizarse*] to blush ⚬: *Los adjetivos ingleses son invariables.*

■ **rojo** *sm* [*color*] red • **al rojo vivo a)** [*en incandescencia*] red hot **b)** figurado heated

rol (pl roles) *sm* [*papel*] role

rollizo, za *adj* chubby ⚬: *Los adjetivos ingleses son invariables.*

rollo *sm* ❶ [*cilindro*] roll ▶ **rollo de primavera** Cocina spring roll ❷ Cine roll ❸ familiar [*discurso*] • **el rollo de costumbre** the same old story ❹ familiar [*embuste*] tall story ❺ familiar [*pelmazo, pesadez*] bore

romance *sm* ❶ Lingüística Romance language ❷ [*idilio*] romance

románico, ca *adj* ❶ Arquitectura & Arte Romanesque ❷ Lingüística Romance ⚬: *Los adjetivos ingleses son invariables.*

romano, na *sm, f* Roman

romanticismo *sm* ❶ Arte & Literatura Romanticism ❷ [*sentimentalismo*] romanticism

romántico, ca *adj* & *sm, f* ❶ Arte & Literatura Romantic ❷ [*sentimental*] romantic ⚬: *Los adjetivos ingleses son invariables.*

rombo *sm* Geometría rhombus

romería *sf* [*peregrinación*] pilgrimage

rompecabezas *sm invariable* ❶ [*juego*] jigsaw ❷ familiar [*problema*] puzzle

rompeolas *sm invariable* breakwater

romper ◆ *vt* ❶ [*generalmente*] to break ❷ [*hacer añicos*] to smash ❸ [*rasgar*] to tear ❹ [*interrumpir - monotonía, silencio, hábito*] to break ; [*- hilo del discurso*] to break off ; [*- tradición*] to put an end to ❺ [*terminar - relaciones* etc] to break off
◆ *vi* ❶ [*terminar una relación*] to break up • **rompieron después de tres años juntos** they broke up after three years • **romper (con alguien)** to break (with somebody) ❷ [*olas, el día*] to break ❸ [*hostilidades*] to break out • **al romper el día** at daybreak ❹ [*empezar*] • **romper a hacer algo** to suddenly start doing something • **romper a llorar** to burst into tears • **romper a reír** to burst out laughing

rompimiento *sm* ❶ breaking ❷ [*de relaciones*] breaking-off ❸ [*de relaciones, conversaciones*] breaking-off ❹ [*de pareja*] break-up ❺ [*de contrato*] breach

ron *sm* rum

roncar *vi* to snore

ronco, ca *adj* ❶ [*afónico*] hoarse • **se quedó ronco de tanto gritar** he shouted himself hoarse ❷ [*bronco*] harsh ⚬: *Los adjetivos ingleses son invariables.*

ronda *sf* ❶ [*de vigilancia, visitas*] rounds *pl* • **hacer la ronda** to do your rounds ❷ [*de bebidas, en el juego* etc] round

rondar ◆ *vt* ❶ [*vigilar*] to patrol ❷ [*rayar - edad*] to be around
◆ *vi* [*merodear*] • **rondar (por)** to wander around

ronquera *sf* hoarseness

ronquido *sm* snore

ronronear *vi* to purr

ronroneo *sm* purr

roña ◆ *adj* familiar [*tacaño*] stingy ⚬: *Los adjetivos ingleses son invariables.*
◆ *sf* [*suciedad*] filth

roñoso, sa ◆ *adj* ❶ [*sucio*] dirty ❷ [*tacaño*] mean ⚬: *Los adjetivos ingleses son invariables.*
◆ *sm, f* miser

ropa *sf* clothes *pl* ▶ **ropa blanca** linen ▶ **ropa de abrigo** warm clothes *pl* ▶ **ropa de cama** bed linen ▶ **ropa interior** underwear • **ropa sucia** laundry
expresión **nadar y guardar la ropa** to cover your back

la ropa	
el abrigo	the coat
la bata	the bathrobe
la blusa	the blouse

R

la bota	the boot
el brasier	the bra
la bufanda	the scarf
los calzones	the panties
el calcetín	the sock
los calzoncillos	the underpants
la camisa	the shirt
la camiseta	the t-shirt
el camisón	the nightdress
la chamarra	the jacket
la chamarra de cuero	the leather jacket
la falda	the skirt
las gafas de sol	the sunglasses
el gorro	the cap
el gorro de baño	the swimming cap
el guante	the glove
el impermeable	the raincoat
los jeans	the jeans
las medias	the pantyhose
la minifalda	the miniskirt
el pantalón	the pants
el pantalón corto	the shorts
los pants	the sweatpants
la piyama	the pyjamas
la sandalia	the sandal
el suéter	the sweater
el suéter abierto	the cardigan
los tenis	the sneakers
el traje de baño	the bathing suit, the swimsuit
el vestido	the dress
la zapatilla	the slipper
el zapato	the shoe

ropaje *sm* robes *pl*

ropero *sm* ❶ [*armario*] wardrobe ❷ [*habitación*] walk-in wardrobe ❸ TEATRO cloakroom

roquero, ra *sm, f* ❶ [*músico*] rock musician ❷ [*fan*] rock fan

rosa ◆ *sf* [*flor*] rose
expresión **estar (fresco) como una rosa** to be as fresh as a daisy ▶ **no hay rosa sin espinas** there's no rose without a thorn
◆ *sm* [*color*] pink
◆ *adj invariable* [*color*] pink ᛜᵻ *Los adjetivos ingleses son invariables.*
expresión **verlo todo de color (de) rosa** to see everything through rose-tinted spectacles

rosado, da ◆ *adj* pink ᛜᵻ *Los adjetivos ingleses son invariables.*
◆ *sm* [*vino*] rosé

rosal *sm* [*arbusto*] rose bush

rosario *sm* ❶ RELIGIÓN rosary • **rezar el rosario** to say your rosary ❷ [*sarta*] string

rosca *sf* ❶ [*de tornillo*] thread ❷ [*forma - de anillo*] ring; [- *espiral*] coil ❸ COCINA ring doughnut

rosquilla *sf* ring doughnut

rostro *sm* face
expresión **tener (mucho) rostro** *familiar* to have a real nerve

rotación *sf* [*giro*] rotation • **el movimiento de la rotación de la Tierra** the Earth's rotation ▶ **rotación de cultivos** crop rotation

roto, ta ◆ *participio pasado* → **romper**
◆ *adj* ❶ [*generalmente*] broken • **este plato está roto** this plate is broken ❷ [*tela, papel*] torn • **tus libros siempre están rotos** your books are always torn ❸ *figurado* [*deshecho - vida* ETC] destroyed; [- *corazón*] broken ❹ *figurado* [*exhausto*] shattered ᛜᵻ *Los adjetivos ingleses son invariables.*
■ **roto** *sm* [*en tela*] tear

rotonda *sf* ❶ [*glorieta*] traffic circle ❷ [*plaza*] circus

rótula *sf* kneecap

rótulo *sm* ❶ [*letrero*] sign ❷ [*encabezamiento*] headline

rotundo, da *adj* ❶ [*categórico - negativa, persona*] categorical; [- *lenguaje, estilo*] emphatic ❷ [*completo*] total ᛜᵻ *Los adjetivos ingleses son invariables.*

rotura *sf* ❶ [*generalmente*] break ❷ [*de hueso*] fracture

rozadura *sf* ❶ [*señal*] scratch ❷ [*herida*] graze ❸ diaper rash

rozamiento *sm* ❶ [*fricción*] rub ❷ FÍSICA friction ᛜᵻ *incontable*

rozar *vt* ❶ [*generalmente*] to rub • **los zapatos nuevos me están rozando los talones** these new shoes are rubbing against my heels ❷ [*suavemente*] to brush • **tu beso apenas me rozó la mejilla** your kiss barely brushed my cheek ❸ [*sujeto: zapato*] to graze ❹ [*pasar cerca de*] to skim

Rte. *abreviatura escrita de* **remitente**

rubeola, rubéola *sf* German measles ᛜᵻ *incontable*

rubí (pl rubíes O rubís) *sm* ruby

rubio, bia ◆ *adj* ❶ [*pelo, persona*] blond, *femenino* blonde • **tiene el pelo rubio** he has blond hair • **teñirse de rubio** to dye your hair blond ❷ [*cerveza*] lager ᛜᵻ *Sólo se usa delante del sustantivo.*
◆ *sm, f* [*persona*] blond, *femenino* blonde ▶ **rubia platino** platinum blonde

rubor *sm* ❶ [*vergüenza*] embarrassment • **causar rubor** to embarrass ❷ [*sonrojo*] blush

ruborizar *vt* [*avergonzar*] to embarrass

rudeza *sf* ❶ [*tosquedad*] roughness ❷ [*grosería*] coarseness

rudimentario, ria *adj* rudimentary ᛜᵻ *Los adjetivos ingleses son invariables.*

rudo, da *adj* ❶ [*tosco*] rough ❷ [*brusco*] sharp ❸ [*grosero*] rude ᛜᵻ *Los adjetivos ingleses son invariables.*

rueda *sf* ❶ [*pieza*] wheel ▶ **rueda delantera/trasera** front/rear wheel ▶ **rueda de repuesto** spare wheel ❷ [*corro*] circle ▶ **rueda de prensa** press conference
expresión **comulgar con ruedas de molino** to be very gullible ▶ **ir sobre ruedas** to go smoothly

R

ruedo *sm* Tauromaquia bullring

ruego *sm* request • **ruegos y preguntas** any other business

rufián *sm* villain

rugby *sm* rugby

rugido *sm* ❶ [*generalmente*] roar ❷ [*de persona*] bellow

rugir *vi* ❶ [*generalmente*] to roar ❷ [*persona*] to bellow

rugoso, sa *adj* ❶ [*áspero - material, terreno*] rough ❷ [*con arrugas - rostro* etc] wrinkled ; [*- tejido*] crinkled ·ᛞ· *Los adjetivos ingleses son invariables.*

ruido *sm* ❶ [*generalmente*] noise ❷ [*escándalo*] racket • **hacer ruido** to make a racket

expresión **mucho ruido y pocas nueces** much ado about nothing

ruidoso, sa *adj* [*que hace ruido*] noisy ·ᛞ· *Los adjetivos ingleses son invariables.*

ruin *adj* ❶ [*vil*] low ❷ [*avaro*] mean ·ᛞ· *Los adjetivos ingleses son invariables.*

ruina *sf* ❶ [*generalmente*] ruin • **dejar en la ruina a alguien** to ruin somebody • **ser una ruina** to cost a fortune ❷ [*destrucción*] destruction ❸ [*fracaso - persona*] wreck • **estar hecho una ruina** to be a wreck

ruinoso, sa *adj* ❶ [*poco rentable*] ruinous ❷ [*edificio*] ramshackle ·ᛞ· *Los adjetivos ingleses son invariables.*

ruiseñor *sm* nightingale

ruleta *sf* roulette

ruletear *vi familiar* to drive a taxi

ruletero *sm familiar* taxi driver

rulo *sm* [*para el pelo*] roller

rumbo *sm* ❶ [*dirección*] direction • **caminar sin rumbo fijo** to walk aimlessly • **ir con rumbo a** to be heading for • **tomar otro rumbo** to take a different tack ❷ *figurado* [*camino*] path

expresión **perder el rumbo a)** [*barco*] to go off course **b)** *figurado* [*persona*] to lose your way

rumiante *adj* & *sm* ruminant ·ᛞ· *Los adjetivos ingleses son invariables.*

rumiar ◆ *vt* ❶ [*sujeto: rumiante*] to chew ❷ *figurado* to chew over

◆ *vi* [*masticar*] to ruminate

rumor *sm* ❶ [*ruido sordo*] murmur • **el rumor del gentío** the murmur of the crowd ❷ [*chisme*] rumor • **han oído algunos rumores acerca de eso** I've heard some rumors about that • **corre el rumor de que** there's a rumor going around that

rupestre *adj* cave ·ᛞ· *Sólo se usa delante del sustantivo.*

ruptura *sf* ❶ [*generalmente*] break ❷ [*de relaciones, conversaciones*] breaking-off ❸ [*de contrato*] breach

rural *adj* rural ·ᛞ· *Los adjetivos ingleses son invariables.*

Rusia *nombre propio* Russia

rústico, ca *adj* ❶ [*del campo*] country ·ᛞ· *Sólo se usa delante del sustantivo.* ❷ [*tosco*] rough

ruta *sf* ❶ [*itinerario*] route ❷ *figurado* way

rutina *sf* routine

rutinario, ria *adj* routine ·ᛞ· *Los adjetivos ingleses son invariables.*

R

S

s, S *sf* [*letra*] s ; S

s. (*abreviatura escrita de* siglo) c (*century*)

SA (*abreviatura de* sociedad anónima) *sf* ≃ corporation

sábado *sm* Saturday • **¿qué día es hoy? — (es) sábado** what day is it (today)? — (it's) Saturday • **cada sábado, todos los sábados** every Saturday • **cada dos sábados, un sábado sí y otro no** every other Saturday • **caer en sábado** to be on a Saturday • **te llamo el sábado** I'll call you on Saturday • **el próximo sábado, el sábado que viene** next Saturday • **el sábado pasado** last Saturday • **el sábado por la mañana/tarde/noche** Saturday morning/afternoon/night • **en sábado** on Saturdays • **nací en sábado** I was born on a Saturday • **este sábado a)** [*pasado*] last Saturday **b)** [*próximo*] this (coming) Saturday • **¿trabajas los sábados?** do you work (on) Saturdays? • **un sábado cualquiera** on any Saturday

En inglés, los días de la semana se escriben con mayúscula.

sábana *sf* sheet

sabandija *sf* figurado [*persona*] worm

saber ♦ *sm* knowledge

♦ *vt* ❶ [*conocer*] to know • **ya lo sé** I know • **hacer saber algo a alguien** to inform somebody of something; to tell somebody something • **¿se puede saber qué haces?** would you mind telling me what you are doing? ❷ [*ser capaz de*] • **saber hacer algo** to know how to do something; to be able to do something • **sabe hablar inglés** she can speak English ❸ [*enterarse*] to find out • **lo supe ayer** I only found out yesterday ❹ [*entender de*] to know about • **sabe mucha física** he knows a lot about physics

♦ *vi* ❶ [*tener sabor*] • **saber (a)** to taste (of) • **saber bien/mal** to taste good/bad ❷ [*entender*] • **saber de algo** to know about something ❸ [*tener noticia*] • **saber de alguien** to hear from somebody • **no supe nada de él por más de un año** I didn't hear from him for over a year • **saber de algo** to learn of something ❹ [*parecer*] • **eso me sabe a disculpa** that sounds like an excuse to me

expresiones **saber mal a alguien** to upset o annoy somebody ▶ **que yo sepa** as far as I know ▶ **¡quién sabe!, ¡vete a saber!** who knows!

sabiduría *sf* ❶ [*conocimientos*] knowledge ❷ [*prudencia*] wisdom ▶ **sabiduría popular** popular wisdom

sabio, bia *adj* ❶ [*sensato, inteligente*] wise ❷ [*docto*] learned ⚲ *Los adjetivos ingleses son invariables.*

sabiondo, da *adj* & *sm, f* know-it-all ⚲ *Los adjetivos ingleses son invariables.*

sable *sm* sabre

sablear *vi* familiar to scrounge money

sabor *sm* ❶ [*gusto*] taste • **tener sabor a algo** to taste of something ❷ figurado [*estilo*] flavor

expresión **dejar mal/buen sabor (de boca)** figurado to leave a nasty taste in your mouth/a warm feeling

saborear *vt* literal & figurado to savor

sabotaje *sm* sabotage

sabotear *vt* to sabotage

sabroso, sa *adj* ❶ [*gustoso*] tasty ❷ figurado [*substancioso*] tidy ; considerable ⚲ *Los adjetivos ingleses son invariables.*

sabrosura *sf* delicious thing

sacacorchos *sm invariable* corkscrew

sacapuntas *sm invariable* pencil sharpener

---

sacar

♦ *vt*

❶ [*retirar*] to take out
• **sacó el coche del garaje** he took the car out of the garage
• **saca a pasear al perro** take the dog out for a walk
• **sacó un papel del bolsillo** he took a note out of his pocket
• **tengo que pasar por un cajero a sacar dinero** I have to go by an ATM to take some money out
• **lo han sacado del colegio** they've taken him out of school
• **le van a sacar una muela** he's going to have a molar taken out

❷ [*provenir de*]
• **sacar vino de la uva** to produce wine from grapes
• **sacar una película de una novela** to make a movie from a novel

❸ [*recibir un beneficio económico*] to make
• **ha sacado mucho dinero de sus cuadros** he's made a lot of money from his paintings
❹ [*ganarse un premio*] to win
• **sacar el gordo** to win the lottery
❺ [*hacer los trámites necesarios para obtener un documento*]
• **saqué el pasaporte en París** my passport was issued in Paris
❻ [*foto, copia*] to take
• **sacar una foto** to take a photo
• **sacar una fotocopia** to take a photocopy
❼ [*poner algo a la disposición de alguien*] to give
• **nos sacó algo de comer** she gave us something to eat
❽ [*solucionar un problema después de reflexionar*]
• **sacar un problema de matemáticas/una ecuación** to solve a math problem/an equation
• **sacar algo en claro** to bring something out in the open
• **no saques conclusiones demasiado rápidas** don't jump to conclusions
❾ [*hacer que alguien dé algo a la fuerza o por engaño*] to take
• **me despachó sin miramientos después de haberme sacado el dinero** he got rid of me without a second thought having taken my money
❿ [*crear, promover un producto*]
• **la fábrica ha sacado un nuevo modelo** the factory has a new model out
⓫ [*mostrar una parte del cuerpo*]
• **sacar el pecho/la lengua** to stick your chest/tongue out
⓬ [*obtener*] to have
• **este año Guillermo ha sacado buenas calificaciones** Guillermo has had good grades this year
⓭ [*invitar*]
• **sacar a bailar** to ask to dance
⓮ [*en la televisión*] to show
• **lo sacaron en televisión** they showed it on television
⓯ [*llevar una ventaja*]
• **sacó tres minutos a su rival** he took a three-minute lead over his opponent
⓰ [*en expresiones*]
• **sacar adelante un negocio** to get a business off the ground
• **sacar adelante a los hijos** to give your children a good start in life
• **sacar de banda** DEPORTE to take a throw in
◆ *vi*
❶ [*una pelota*]
• **le toca sacar al equipo contrario** it's the other team's turn to start
❷ [*en tenis*] to serve
• **Javier saca con mucha fuerza** Javier has a big serve
■ **sacarse**
◆ *v pronominal*
[*quitarse algo que se lleva encima*] to take off
• **sácate los zapatos** take your shoes off

sacarina *sf* saccharine
saciar *vt* [*satisfacer - sed*] to quench ; [*- hambre*] to satisfy
saco *sm* ❶ [*bolsa*] sack • **un saco de carbón** a sack of coal ▸ **saco de dormir** sleeping bag ❷ [*chaqueta*] jacket
expresión **entrar a saco en** to sack ▸ **no echar algo en saco roto** to take good note of something
sacramento *sm* sacrament
sacrificar *vt* ❶ [*generalmente*] to sacrifice • **sacrificar algo a** *literal & figurado* to sacrifice something to ❷ [*animal - para consumo*] to slaughter
sacrificio *sm* *literal & figurado* sacrifice
sacristía *sf* sacristy
sacudida *sf* ❶ [*generalmente*] shake ❷ [*de la cabeza*] toss ❸ [*de tren, coche*] jolt • **dar sacudidas** to jolt ▸ **sacudida eléctrica** electric shock ❹ [*terremoto*] tremor
sacudir *vt* ❶ [*agitar, hacer temblar*] to shake ❷ [*golpear - alfombra* ETC] to beat ❸ [*conmover*] to shake ❹ *familiar* [*pegar*] to smack
saeta *sf* arrow
safari *sm* [*expedición*] safari • **ir de safari** to go on safari
saga *sf* saga
sagacidad *sf* astuteness
sagaz *adj* astute ☼ *Los adjetivos ingleses son invariables.*
Sagitario ◆ *sm* [*zodiaco*] Sagittarius
◆ *smf* [*persona*] Sagittarian
sagrado, da *adj* ❶ [*en religión*] holy • **la Meca es la ciudad más sagrada del Islam** Mecca is the holiest city of Islam ❷ *figurado* sacred • **la amistad es algo sagrado** friendship is sacred ☼ *Los adjetivos ingleses son invariables.*
sal *sf* COCINA & QUÍMICA salt • **la sal de la vida** *figurado* the spark of life
sala *sf* ❶ [*habitación - generalmente*] room ; [*- de una casa*] living room ; [*- de hospital*] ward • **la sala de mi casa no es muy grande** my living room isn't very large ▸ **sala de embarque** departure lounge ▸ **sala de espera** waiting room ▸ **sala de estar** lounge ; living room ▸ **sala de partos** delivery room ▸ **sala de profesores** staffroom ❷ [*local - de conferencias, conciertos*] hall ; [*- de cine, teatro*] auditorium ▸ **sala de conciertos** concert hall ▸ **sala de fiestas** discothèque
salado, da *adj* ❶ [*con sal*] salted ❷ [*agua*] salt ☼ *Sólo se usa delante del sustantivo.* ❸ [*con demasiada sal*] salty ❹ *figurado* [*gracioso*] witty ❺ [*desgraciado*] unfortunate
salamandra *sf* [*animal*] salamander
salarial *adj* wage ☼ *Sólo se usa delante del sustantivo.*
salario *sm* ❶ salary • **gana un salario enorme** he is paid a huge salary ❷ [*semanal*] wage ▸ **el salario mínimo** the minimum wage
salchicha *sf* sausage

salchichón *sm* ≃ salami

salchichonería *sf* delicatessen

saldar *vt* ❶ [*pagar - cuenta*] to close ; [*- deuda*] to settle ❷ *figurado* [*poner fin a*] to settle ❸ COMERCIO to sell off

saldo *sm* ❶ [*de cuenta*] balance ❷ [*de deudas*] settlement ❸ ⚡*generalmente pl* [*restos de mercancías*] remnant ❹ [*rebajas*] sale • **de saldo** bargain ❺ *figurado* [*resultado*] balance

salero *sm* ❶ [*recipiente*] salt shaker ❷ [*gracia*] wit ❸ [*donaire*] charm

salida *sf* ❶ [*acción de partir - generalmente*] leaving ; [*- de tren, avión*] departure ▸ **salidas nacionales/internacionales** domestic/international departures ❷ DEPORTE start • **dar la salida** to start the race ❸ [*lugar*] exit ▸ **salida de emergencia/incendios** emergency/fire exit ❹ [*momento*] • **quedamos a la salida del trabajo** we agreed to meet after work ❺ [*viaje*] trip ❻ [*aparición - de sol, luna*] rise ; [*- de revista, nuevo modelo*] appearance ❼ COMERCIO [*posibilidades*] market ; [*producción*] output ❽ *figurado* [*solución*] solution • **este problema no tiene salida** this problem has no solution • **si no hay otra salida** if there's no alternative ❾ *figurado* [*futuro, de carreras etc*] opening ; opportunity

salido, da *adj* ❶ [*saliente*] projecting ❷ [*ojos*] bulging ⚡*Los adjetivos ingleses son invariables.*

saliente ◆ *adj* POLÍTICA outgoing ⚡*Los adjetivos ingleses son invariables.*
◆ *sm* projection

---

salir

◆ *vi*

❶ [*dejar un sitio para ir afuera o a otro lugar*] to go out
• **salió a la calle** he's gone out
• **Juan sale mucho con sus amigos** Juan goes out with his friends a lot
• **como castigo no me dejaron salir por un mes** I'm not allowed to go out for a month as punishment

❷ [*emprender un viaje*] to leave
• **el tren/el barco sale a las dos** the train/boat leaves in two hours
• **el avión saldrá con retraso** the plane's departure will be delayed
• **mañana saldremos para Guadalajara** we're leaving for Guadalajara tomorrow
• **salir corriendo** to rush out
• **salir de viaje** to go on a trip

❸ [*sobresalir*] to stick out
• **esta cornisa sale demasiado** this cornice sticks out too much

❹ [*obtener un resultado*]
• **salir bien/mal** to work/not work
• **el pastel te ha salido muy bien** the cake's really worked
• **el plan les ha salido mal** their plan didn't work
• **el postre me ha salido mal** my dessert didn't turn out very well

❺ [*para presentar un resultado*]
• **salir elegido** to be voted
• **salió elegida mejor actriz** she was voted best actress
• **su billete salió premiado** he had the winning ticket
• **salir ganando/perdiendo** to come out winning/losing

❻ [*lograr hacer*]
• **el problema no me sale** I can't solve the problem
• **nunca me salen los crucigramas** I can never do crosswords

❼ [*tener una relación amorosa con alguien*] to date
• **María y Pedro están saliendo** María and Pedro are dating
• **sale con su vecina** he's dating his neighbor

❽ [*ser publicada*] to come out
• **una revista que sale los miércoles** a magazine that comes out on Wednesdays
• **la novela sale en junio** the novel's coming out in June

❾ [*ponerse a la venta*]
• **el nuevo modelo saldrá el año que viene** the new model will come out next year

❿ [*aparecer en público, en los medios de comunicación*]
• **mi vecina salió en la tele** my neighbor was on tv
• **salió en los periódicos** it was in the papers
• **¡qué bien sales en la foto!** it's a really good picture of you!

⓫ [*surgir, presentarse*]
• **nos ha salido una oportunidad estupenda** we have a golden opportunity
• **le ha salido un empleo muy bien pagado** he's found a really well-paid job

⓬ [*brotar*]
• **los tulipanes empiezan a salir** the tulips are starting to bloom

⓭ [*sol*] to rise
• **el sol sale por el este** the sun rises in the East

⓮ [*decir algo inesperado*] to come out with
• **nunca se sabe por dónde va a salir** you never know what he's going to come out with

⓯ INFORMÁTICA to exit
• **sal del programa y apaga la computadora** exit the program and switch off the computer

⓰ [*en expresiones*]
• **no consigo salir adelante** I can't seem to get ahead
• **el proyecto acabó saliendo adelante** the project ended up going ahead successfully

■ **salir a**
◆ *v + preposición*
to look like
• **este niño ha salido a su padre** this boy looks like his father

■ **salir a, salir por**
◆ *v + preposición*

[*costar*]

• **la cena nos salió por 50 pesos cada uno** the meal came out at 50 pesos per person

expresión salir caro to work out expensive

■ **salir de**

◆ *v + preposición*

❶ [*dejar un sitio para ir afuera o a otro lugar*] to leave

• **salgo del hospital** I'm leaving the hospital
• **nunca salgo de mi casa sin un paraguas** I never leave home without an umbrella

❷ [*dejar un estado, una situación*] to emerge from

• **salir de la crisis** to emerge from the crisis

■ **salirse**

◆ *v pronominal*

[*desbordarse*]

• **se está saliendo el agua del tanque** the water tank is overflowing

expresión salirse con la suya to get your own way

■ **salirse de**

◆ *v pronominal + preposición*

❶ [*irse fuera de un lugar particular*]

• **se salió de la autopista** it came off the freeway
• **el tren se salió de la vía** the train went off the track
• **salirse de la carretera** to go off the road
• **salirse de los límites** to go overboard

❷ [*irse de un grupo*]

• **salirse de una asociación** to leave an association

❸ [*alejarse*]

• **salirse del tema** to go off the subject

❹ [*desbordarse*]

• **el agua se salió de la tina** the bathtub overflowed

■ **salirse por**

◆ *v pronominal + preposición*

[*gas, líquido*] to escape

• **el aire sale por los poros** air escapes through the pores

saliva *sf* saliva

expresión tragar saliva to bite your tongue

salmo *sm* psalm

salmón ◆ *sm* [*pez*] salmon

◆ *adj* & *sm invariable* [*color*] salmon (pink) ☝ *Los adjetivos ingleses son invariables.*

salobre *adj* salty ☝ *Los adjetivos ingleses son invariables.*

salón *sm* ❶ [*habitación - en casa*] sitting room ▶ **salón comedor** living room-dining room; [- *en residencia, edificio público*] reception hall ❷ [*local - de sesiones etc*] hall ▶ **salón de actos** assembly hall ❸ [*feria*] show ▶ **salón de exposiciones** exhibition hall ❹ [*establecimiento*] ▶ **salón de belleza/masaje** beauty/massage parlor ▶ **salón de té** tea-room

salpicadera *sf* fender

salpicadero *sm* dashboard

salpicar *vt* [*rociar*] to splash

salsa *sf* ❶ COCINA [*generalmente*] sauce; [*de carne*] gravy ▶ **salsa bernesa** bearnaise sauce ▶ **salsa rosa** thousand island dressing ▶ **salsa tártara** tartar sauce ▶ **salsa de tomate** tomato sauce ❷ *figurado* [*interés*] spice ❸ MÚSICA salsa

expresión en su propia salsa in your element

saltamontes *sm invariable* grasshopper

saltar ◆ *vt* ❶ [*obstáculo*] to jump (over) ❷ [*omitir*] to skip

◆ *vi* ❶ [*generalmente*] to jump • **saltar de alegría** to jump for joy ❷ [*a la comba*] to skip ❸ [*al agua*] to dive • **saltar sobre alguien** [*abalanzarse*] to set upon somebody • **saltar de un tema a otro** to jump (around) from one subject to another ❹ [*levantarse*] to jump up • **saltar de la silla** to jump out of your seat ❺ [*salir para arriba - objeto*] to jump (up); [- *champán, aceite*] to spurt (out); [- *corcho, válvula*] to pop out ❻ [*explotar*] to explode ❼ [*romperse*] to break ❽ [*reaccionar violentamente*] to explode

■ **saltarse** *v pronominal* ❶ [*omitir*] to skip ❷ [*salir despedido*] to pop off ❸ [*no respetar - cola, semáforo*] to jump; [- *ley, normas*] to break

salteado, da *adj* ❶ COCINA sautéed ❷ [*espaciado*] unevenly spaced ☝ *Los adjetivos ingleses son invariables.*

saltear *vt* COCINA to sauté

salto *sm* ❶ [*generalmente*] DEPORTE jump • **dar** o **pegar un salto a)** to jump **b)** [*grande*] to leap • **levantarse de un salto** to leap to somebody's feet ▶ **salto alto** high jump ▶ **salto con garrocha** pole vault ▶ **salto de agua** waterfall ▶ **salto largo** long jump ▶ **salto mortal** somersault ❷ [*grande*] leap ❸ [*al agua*] dive

saltón, ona *adj* ❶ [*ojos*] bulging ❷ [*dientes*] sticking out ☝ *Los adjetivos ingleses son invariables.*

salud ◆ *sf* health • **es malo para la salud** it's bad for your health

◆ *exclamación* • **¡salud! a)** [*para brindar*] cheers! **b)** [*después de estornudar*] bless you!

saludable *adj* ❶ [*sano*] healthy ❷ [*provechoso*] beneficial ☝ *Los adjetivos ingleses son invariables.*

saludar *vt* ❶ [*por cortesía*] to greet • **ni siquiera me saludó** he didn't even say hello to me • **saluda a Ana de mi parte** give my regards to Ana • **lo saluda atentamente** yours sincerely • **saludar con la mano a alguien** to wave to somebody • **lo saludé desde lejos** I waved to him from a distance ❷ MILITAR to salute

saludar a alguien

• **Hi!/Hey!** ¡Hola!
• **Good morning!** ¡Buenos días!
• **Hello!** ¡Hola!
• **How are you?** ¿Qué tal?
• **Good evening!** *culto* ¡Buenas tardes!

saludo *sm* ❶ [*por cortesía*] greeting • **nos recibió con un cálido saludo** he greeted us warmly • **retirarle el saludo a alguien** to stop speaking to somebody • **saludos** best regards • **Ana te manda saludos a)** [*en cartas*] Ana sends you her regards **b)** [*al teléfono*] Ana

S

says hello • **un saludo afectuoso** [*en cartas*] yours sincerely ❷ Militar salute

salva *sf* • **una salva de aplausos** a round of applause

salvador, ra *sm, f* [*persona*] savior

■ **Salvador** *sm* Geografía • **El Salvador** El Salvador

salvadoreño, ña *adj* & *sm, f* Salvadoran ☆ *Los adjetivos ingleses son invariables.*

En inglés, los adjetivos que refieren a un país o a una región se escriben con mayúscula.

salvaje ◆ *adj* ❶ [*generalmente*] wild ❷ [*pueblo, tribu*] savage ☆ *Los adjetivos ingleses son invariables.*
◆ *smf* ❶ [*primitivo*] savage ❷ [*bruto*] maniac

salvamanteles *sm invariable* ❶ [*llano*] table mat ❷ [*con pies*] trivet

salvamento *sm* rescue • **equipo de salvamento** rescue team

salvar *vt* ❶ [*generalmente*] Informática to save • **le salvó la vida su hermano** he saved his brother's life • **salvar algo/a alguien de algo** to save something/somebody from something ❷ [*rescatar*] to rescue ❸ [*superar - moralmente*] to overcome ; [*- físicamente*] to go over ❹ [*recorrer*] to cover ❺ [*exceptuar*] • **salvando algunos detalles** except for a few details

salvavidas ◆ *adj invariable* life ☆ *Sólo se usa delante del sustantivo.* ▶ **chaleco salvavidas** lifejacket
◆ *sm* ❶ [*chaleco*] lifejacket ❷ [*flotador*] lifebelt

salvo, va *adj* safe • **estar a salvo** to be safe • **poner algo a salvo** to put something in a safe place ☆ *Los adjetivos ingleses son invariables.*
■ **salvo** *adv* except • **todos vinieron salvo Eduardo** everyone came except Eduardo • **salvo que** unless • **salvo que se especifique a lo contrario** unless otherwise specified

san *adj* Saint • **san José** Saint Joseph ☆ *Los adjetivos ingleses son invariables.*

sanar ◆ *vt* ❶ [*persona*] to cure ❷ [*herida*] to heal
◆ *vi* ❶ [*persona*] to get better ❷ [*herida*] to heal

sanatorio *sm* sanatorium

sanción *sf* ❶ [*castigo*] punishment ❷ Economía sanction

sancionar *vt* [*castigar*] to punish

sandalia *sf* sandal

sandía *sf* watermelon

sándwich (pl sándwiches) *sm* ❶ [*con pan de molde*] sandwich ❷ [*con pan de barra*] filled baguette

sanear *vt* ❶ [*higienizar - tierras*] to drain ; [*- un edificio*] to disinfect ❷ *figurado* Finanzas [*moneda*] to stabilize ; [*economía*] to put back on a sound footing

sangrar *vi* to bleed • **su herida sangraba mucho** her wound was bleeding profusely

sangre *sf* blood
expresión **a sangre fría** in cold blood ▶ **no llegó la sangre al río** it didn't get too nasty

sangriento, ta *adj* [*ensangrentado, cruento*] bloody ☆ *Los adjetivos ingleses son invariables.*

sanguijuela *sf* literal & figurado leech

sanguinario, ria *adj* bloodthirsty ☆ *Los adjetivos ingleses son invariables.*

sanguíneo, a *adj* blood ☆ *Sólo se usa delante del sustantivo.* ▶ **vaso sanguíneo** blood vessel

sanidad *sf* ❶ [*salubridad*] health ❷ [*servicio*] public health ❸ [*ministerio*] health department

sanitario, ria *adj* health ☆ *Sólo se usa delante del sustantivo.*

San José *nombre propio* San José

sano, na *adj* ❶ [*saludable*] healthy • **es un muchacho fuerte y sano** he's a strong and healthy boy • **sano y salvo** safe and sound ❷ [*positivo - principios, persona etc*] sound ; [*- ambiente, educación*] wholesome ❸ [*entero*] intact ☆ *Los adjetivos ingleses son invariables.*

San Salvador *nombre propio* San Salvador

santería *sf* [*tienda*] *para explicar lo que es puedes decir:* it's a store selling religious mementos such as statues of saints

Santiago (de Chile) *nombre propio* Santiago

santiamén ■ **en un santiamén** *locución adverbial familiar* in a flash

santiguarse *v pronominal* to cross yourself

santo, ta ◆ *adj* ❶ [*sagrado*] holy ❷ [*virtuoso*] saintly ❸ *familiar* [*dichoso*] damn • **todo el santo día** all day long ☆ *Los adjetivos ingleses son invariables.*
◆ *sm, f* Religión saint
■ **santo** *sm* [*onomástica*] saint's day
expresión **¿a santo de qué?** why on earth?

Santo Domingo *nombre propio* Santo Domingo

santuario *sm* ❶ [*templo*] shrine ❷ *figurado* [*refugio*] sanctuary

sapo *sm* toad
expresión **echar sapos y culebras** to rant and rave

saque *sm* ❶ [*en futbol*] ▶ **saque de banda** throw-in ▶ **saque inicial** o **de centro** kick-off ❷ [*en tenis etc*] serve

saquear *vt* ❶ [*rapiñar - ciudad*] to sack ; [*- tienda etc*] to loot ❷ *familiar* [*vaciar*] to ransack

saqueo *sm* ❶ [*de ciudad*] sacking ❷ [*de tienda etc*] looting

sarcasmo *sm* sarcasm

sarcástico, ca *adj* sarcastic ☆ *Los adjetivos ingleses son invariables.*

sarcófago *sm* sarcophagus

sardina *sf* sardine
expresión **como sardinas en lata** like sardines

sargento *smf* Militar ≃ sergeant

sarpullido *sm* rash

sarro *sm* [*de dientes*] tartar

sartén *sm* frying pan
expresión **tener el sartén por el mango** to be in control

sastre *sm* tailor

Satanás *sm* Satan

satélite *sm* satellite

S

sátira *sf* satire

satírico, ca ♦ *adj* satirical ⚬ **Los adjetivos ingleses son invariables.**

♦ *sm, f* satirist

satisfacción *sf* satisfaction

satisfacer *vt* ❶ [*generalmente*] to satisfy ❷ [*sed*] to quench ❸ [*deuda, pago*] to pay ❹ [*ofensa, daño*] to redress ❺ [*duda, pregunta*] to answer ❻ [*cumplir - requisitos, exigencias*] to meet

satisfactorio, ria *adj* satisfactory ⚬ **Los adjetivos ingleses son invariables.**

satisfecho, cha ♦ *participio pasado* → **satisfacer**

♦ *adj* satisfied • **la profesora está muy satisfecha con sus alumnos** the teacher is very pleased with her students • **darse por satisfecho** to be satisfied • **satisfecho de sí mismo** self-satisfied ⚬ **Los adjetivos ingleses son invariables.**

saturar *vt* to saturate

Saturno *nombre propio* Saturn

sauce *sm* willow ▶ **sauce llorón** weeping willow

sauna *sf* sauna

savia *sf* ❶ [*de planta*] sap ❷ [*vitalidad*] vitality ▰**expresión**▰ **savia nueva** *figurado* new blood

saxo *sm* [*instrumento*] sax

saxofón = **saxófono**

saxófono, saxofón *sm* [*instrumento*] saxophone

---

se

♦ *pronombre personal*

❶ [*uso reflexivo*]
• **se pasea** he goes for a walk
• **se divierte** she enjoys herself
• **hay que lavarse todos los días** you should wash every day
• **se está bañando** he's having a bath
• **siéntese** have a seat
• **¡que se diviertan!** have fun!

❷ [*uso recíproco*]
• **se quieren** they love each other

❸ [*equivalente de la forma pasiva*]
• **se ha suspendido la reunión** the meeting has been called off
• **este producto sólo se vende aquí** this product is only sold here
• **'se alquilan habitaciones'** rooms for rent

❹ [*impersonal*]
• **se dice que el golf es un deporte elitista** people think of golf as an elitist sport
• **desde aquí se ve bien** you can see well from here
• **se rumorea que el presidente va a dimitir** the rumor is that the president is going to resign
• **'se habla inglés'** We speak English
• **'se prohíbe fumar'** no smoking

❺ [*reemplaza los complementos indirectos "el" y "los"*]
• **cómpraselo** buy it for him

• **se lo dije, pero no me hicieron caso** I told them but they didn't take any notice
• **si usted quiere, yo se las mandaré** I'll send them to you if you like

---

SE *sf* (*abreviatura de* Secretaría de Economía) *para explicar lo que es puedes decir:* it's the Mexican Department of Economy

sebo *sm* ❶ [*grasa*] fat ❷ [*para jabón, velas*] tallow

secador *sm* dryer ▶ **secador de pelo** hair-dryer

secadora *sf* ❶ [*de ropa*] clothes dryer ❷ [*de pelo*] hair dryer

secar *vt* ❶ [*desecar*] to dry ❷ [*enjugar*] to wipe away ❸ [*con fregona*] to mop up

■ **secarse** *v pronominal* ❶ [*generalmente*] to dry up ❷ [*ropa, vajilla, suelo*] to dry

sección *sf* ❶ [*generalmente*] GEOMETRÍA section ❷ [*departamento*] department

seccionar *vt* ❶ [*cortar*] to cut ❷ TECNOLOGÍA to section ❸ [*dividir*] to divide (up)

seco, ca *adj* ❶ [*generalmente*] dry • **el desierto es un lugar seco** the desert is a dry place • **lavar en seco** to dry-clean ❷ [*plantas, flores*] withered ❸ [*higos, pasas*] dried • **higos secos** dried figs ❹ [*tajante*] brusque ⚬ **Los adjetivos ingleses son invariables.**

▰**expresión**▰ **dejar a alguien seco a)** [*matar*] to kill somebody stone dead **b)** [*pasmar*] to stun somebody ▶ **parar en seco** to stop dead

secretaría *sf* ❶ [*oficina, lugar*] secretary's office ❷ [*organismo*] secretariat • **secretaría general** general secretariat ❸ [*ministerio*] department • **la Secretaría de Relaciones Exteriores** State Department

secretario, ria *sm, f* ❶ secretary ❷ [*ministro*] secretary

secreto, ta *adj* ❶ [*generalmente*] secret • **en secreto** in secret ❷ [*tono*] confidential ⚬ **Los adjetivos ingleses son invariables.**

■ **secreto** *sm* ❶ [*generalmente*] secret • **guardar un secreto** to keep a secret ▶ **secreto bancario** banking confidentiality ❷ [*sigilo*] secrecy

secta *sf* sect

sector *sm* ❶ [*generalmente*] sector ❷ [*grupo*] group ❸ [*zona*] area

secuaz *smf* *despectivo* minion

secuela *sf* consequence

secuencia *sf* sequence

secuestrador, ra *sm, f* ❶ [*de persona*] kidnapper ❷ [*de avión*] hijacker

secuestrar *vt* ❶ [*raptar*] to kidnap ❷ [*avión*] to hijack ❸ [*embargar*] to seize

secuestro *sm* ❶ [*rapto*] kidnapping ❷ [*de avión, barco*] hijack ❸ [*de bienes etc*] seizure

secular *adj* ❶ [*seglar*] secular ❷ [*centenario*] age-old ⚬ **Los adjetivos ingleses son invariables.**

secundario, ria *adj* secondary ⚬ **Los adjetivos ingleses son invariables.**

■ **secundaria** *sf* secondary education

sed ♦ *v* → **ser**

◆ *sf* thirst • **saciar la sed** to quench your thirst • **el calor da sed** heat makes you thirsty • **tener sed** to be thirsty

seda *sf* silk

sedal *sm* fishing line

sedante ◆ *adj* ❶ MEDICINA sedative ❷ [*música*] soothing ☿ *Los adjetivos ingleses son invariables.*
◆ *sm* sedative

sede *sf* ❶ [*emplazamiento*] headquarters *pl* ▶ **sede social** head office ❷ [*de gobierno*] seat ❸ [*de campeonato*] host

■ **Santa Sede** *sf* • **la Santa Sede** the Holy See

sedentario, ria *adj* sedentary ☿ *Los adjetivos ingleses son invariables.*

sediento, ta *adj* ❶ [*de agua*] thirsty ❷ figurado [*deseoso*] • **sediento de** hungry for ☿ *Los adjetivos ingleses son invariables.*

sedimentar *vt* to deposit

sedimento *sm* ❶ [*poso*] sediment ❷ GEOLOGÍA deposit

sedoso, sa *adj* silky ☿ *Los adjetivos ingleses son invariables.*

seducción *sf* ❶ [*cualidad*] seductiveness ❷ [*acción - generalmente*] attraction; [*- sexual*] seduction

seducir *vt* ❶ [*atraer*] to attract ❷ [*sexualmente*] to seduce ❸ [*persuadir*] • **seducir a alguien para que haga algo** to tempt somebody to do something

seductor, ra ◆ *adj* ❶ [*generalmente*] charming ❷ [*sexualmente*] seductive ❸ [*persuasivo*] tempting ☿ *Los adjetivos ingleses son invariables.*
◆ *sm, f* seducer

segmento *sm* ❶ GEOMETRÍA & ZOOLOGÍA segment ❷ [*trozo*] piece ❸ [*sector*] sector

segregación *sf* [*separación, discriminación*] segregation • **segregación racial** racial segregation

segregar *vt* ❶ [*separar, discriminar*] to segregate ❷ [*secretar*] to secrete

seguido, da *adj* ❶ [*consecutivo*] consecutive • **diez años seguidos** ten years in a row • **ganó el torneo tres veces seguidas** she won the tournament three consecutive times • **estornudé cinco veces seguidas** I sneezed five times in a row ❷ [*sin interrupción - generalmente*] one after the other; [*- línea, pitido etc*] continuous ☿ *Los adjetivos ingleses son invariables.*

■ **seguido** *adv* ❶ [*inmediatamente después*] right after ❷ [*en línea recta*] straight ahead ❸ [*frecuentemente*] often • **voy bastante seguido** I go there pretty often

seguidor, ra *sm, f* follower

seguimiento *sm* ❶ [*de noticia*] following ❷ [*de clientes*] follow-up

seguir ◆ *vt* ❶ [*generalmente*] to follow • **sígueme a mí** follow me • **seguir de cerca algo** to follow something closely • **seguir de cerca a alguien** to tail somebody ❷ [*perseguir*] to chase ❸ [*reanudar*] to continue
◆ *vi* ❶ [*sucederse*] • **seguir a algo** to follow something • **a la tormenta siguió la lluvia** the storm was followed by rain ❷ [*continuar*] to go on • **¡sigue! ¡no te pares!** go on, don't stop! • **seguir adelante** to carry

on • **sigo trabajando en la fábrica** I'm still working at the factory • **debes seguir haciéndolo** you should keep on doing it • **sigo pensando que está mal** I still think it's wrong • **sigue enferma/en el hospital** she's still sick/in the hospital

según ◆ *preposición* ❶ [*de acuerdo con*] according to • **según su opinión, ha sido un éxito** according to him, it was a success • **según yo/tú** ETC in my/your ETC. opinion ❷ [*dependiendo de*] depending on • **según la hora que sea** depending on the time
◆ *adv* ❶ [*como*] (just) as • **todo permanecía según lo recordaba** everything was just as she remembered it • **actuó según se le recomendó** he did as he had been advised ❷ [*a medida que*] as • **entrarás en forma según vayas entrenando** you'll get in shape as you train ❸ [*dependiendo*] • **¿te gusta la música? — según** do you like music? — it depends • **lo intentaré según esté de tiempo** I'll try to do it, depending on how much time I have

segundero *sm* second hand

segundo, da ◆ *adj numeral* second • **llegó en el segundo tren** she arrived on the second train ☿ *Los adjetivos ingleses son invariables.*
◆ *sm, f* ❶ [*en orden*] • **el segundo** the second one • **llegó el segundo** he came second ❷ [*mencionado antes*] • **vinieron Pedro y Juan, el segundo con...** Pedro and Juan arrived, the latter with... ❸ [*ayudante*] number two ▶ **segundo de abordo** NÁUTICA first mate

■ **segundo** *sm* ❶ [*generalmente*] second ❷ [*piso*] second floor

seguramente *adv* probably • **seguramente iré, pero aún no lo sé** I'll probably go, but I'm not sure yet

seguridad *sf* ❶ [*fiabilidad, ausencia de peligro*] safety • **la seguridad personal** personal safety ❷ [*protección, estabilidad*] security • **de seguridad a)** [*cinturón, cierre*] safety ☿ *Sólo se usa delante del sustantivo.* **b)** [*puerta, guardia*] security ☿ *Sólo se usa delante del sustantivo.* ▶ **seguridad ciudadana** public safety ▶ **seguridad vial** road safety ❸ [*certidumbre*] certainty • **con seguridad** for sure ❹ [*confianza*] confidence • **seguridad en sí mismo** self-confidence

■ **Seguridad Social** *sf* Social Security

seguro, ra *adj* ❶ [*fiable, sin peligro*] safe • **es bastante seguro comprar en Internet** it's quite safe to buy on the Internet ❷ [*protegido, estable*] secure ❸ [*infalible - prueba, negocio etc*] reliable ❹ [*confiado*] sure • **¿estás seguro?** are you sure? • **estar seguro de algo** to be sure about something • **tener por seguro que** to be sure that ❺ [*indudable - nombramiento, fecha etc*] definite ❻ [*con aplomo*] self-confident • **estar seguro de sí mismo** to be self-confident ☿ *Los adjetivos ingleses son invariables.*

■ **seguro** ◆ *sm* ❶ [*contrato*] insurance ☿ *incontable* ▶ **seguro a todo riesgo/a terceros** comprehensive/third party insurance ▶ **seguro de incendios/de vida** fire/life insurance ▶ **seguro de auto** car insurance ▶ **seguro de invalidez** o **incapacidad** disability insurance ▶ **seguro de vida** life insurance ❷ [*dispositivo*] safety device ❸ [*de armas*] safety catch ❹ [*imperdible*] safety pin

S

◆ *adv* definitely • **seguro que vendrá** she'll definitely come

seis ◆ *adj numeral* ❶ [*para contar*] six • **tiene seis años** she's six (years old) ❷ [*para ordenar*] (number) six • **la página seis** page six ☼ *Los adjetivos ingleses son invariables.*

◆ *sm* ❶ [*número*] six • **el seis** number six • **doscientos seis** two hundred and six • **treinta y seis** thirty-six ❷ [*en fechas*] sixth • **el seis de agosto** the sixth of August ❸ [*en direcciones*] • **calle Mayor (número) seis** number six calle Mayor ❹ [*en naipes*] six • **el seis de diamantes** the six of diamonds • **echar un seis** to play a six

◆ *smpl* ❶ [*referido a grupos*] • **invité a diez y sólo vinieron seis** I invited ten and only six came along • **somos seis** there are six of us • **de seis en seis** in sixes • **los seis** the six of them ❷ [*en temperaturas*] • **estamos a seis bajo cero** the temperature is six below zero ❸ [*en puntuaciones*] • **empatar a seis** to draw six all • **seis a cero** six-nil

◆ *sfpl* [*hora*] • **las seis** six o'clock • **son las seis** it's six o'clock

seiscientos, tas *numeral* six hundred ver también **seis**

seísmo *sm* earthquake

selección *sf* ❶ [*generalmente*] selection ❷ [*de personal*] recruitment ❸ [*equipo*] team ▶ **selección nacional** national team

seleccionador, ra *sm, f* ❶ DEPORTE selector, ≈ manager ❷ [*de personal*] recruiter

seleccionar *vt* to pick

selectivo, va *adj* selective ☼ *Los adjetivos ingleses son invariables.*

selecto, ta *adj* ❶ [*excelente*] fine ❷ [*escogido*] exclusive ☼ *Los adjetivos ingleses son invariables.*

self-service *sm invariable* self-service restaurant

sellar *vt* ❶ [*timbrar*] to stamp ❷ [*lacrar*] to seal

sello *sm* ❶ [*generalmente*] stamp ❷ [*tampón*] rubber stamp ❸ [*lacre*] seal ❹ *figurado* [*carácter*] hallmark

selva *sf* ❶ [*generalmente*] jungle ▶ **selva tropical** tropical rain forest ❷ [*bosque*] forest

semáforo *sm* traffic lights *pl*

semana *sf* week • **entre semana** during the week • **la semana próxima/que viene** next week ▶ **semana laboral** working week

■ **Semana Santa** *sf* ❶ [*de vacaciones*] Easter ❷ RELIGIÓN Holy Week

semanal *adj* weekly ☼ *Los adjetivos ingleses son invariables.*

semanario, ria *adj* weekly ☼ *Los adjetivos ingleses son invariables.*

■ **semanario** *sm* [*publicación semanal*] weekly

sembrar *vt* ❶ [*plantar*] to sow • **sembrar algo de algo** to sow something with something ❷ *figurado* [*confusión, pánico etc*] to sow

semejante ◆ *adj* ❶ [*parecido*] • **semejante (a)** similar (to) • **descubrieron un sistema solar semejante al nuestro** they discovered a solar system similar to ours ❷ [*tal*] such • **jamás aceptaría semejante invitación** I would never accept such an invitation ☼ *Los adjetivos ingleses son invariables.*

◆ *sm* fellow (human) being

semejanza *sf* similarity • **a semejanza de** similar to

semen *sm* semen

semental *sm* ❶ [*animal*] stud ❷ [*caballo*] stallion

semestral *adj* half-yearly ☼ *Los adjetivos ingleses son invariables.*

semestre *sm* semester • **cada semestre** every six months

semifinal *sf* semifinal

semilla *sf* seed

seminario *sm* ❶ [*escuela para sacerdotes*] seminary ❷ EDUCACIÓN [*curso, conferencia*] seminar; [*departamento*] department

sémola *sf* semolina

senado *sm* senate

senador, ra *sm, f* senator

sencillez *sf* ❶ [*facilidad*] simplicity ❷ [*modestia*] unaffectedness ❸ [*discreción*] plainness

sencillo, lla *adj* ❶ [*fácil, sin lujo, llano*] simple ❷ [*campechano*] unaffected ❸ [*boleto, unidad etc*] one-way ☼ *Los adjetivos ingleses son invariables.*

■ **sencillo** *sm* [*disco*] single

senda *sf* = **sendero**

sendero *sm* path

sendos, das *adj pl* each • **llegaron los dos con sendos paquetes** they each arrived carrying a package ☼ *Los adjetivos ingleses son invariables.*

sénior (pl **seniores**) *adj invariable* & *sm* senior ☼ *Los adjetivos ingleses son invariables.*

seno *sm* ❶ [*pecho*] breast ❷ [*pechera*] bosom ❸ [*útero*] ▶ **seno (materno)** womb ❹ *figurado* [*amparo, cobijo*] refuge • **en el seno de** within ❺ ANATOMÍA [*de la nariz*] sinus

sensación *sf* ❶ [*percepción*] feeling ❷ [*efecto*] sensation ❸ [*premonición*] feeling

sensacional *adj* sensational ☼ *Los adjetivos ingleses son invariables.*

sensacionalista *adj* sensationalist ☼ *Los adjetivos ingleses son invariables.*

sensatez *sf* wisdom

sensato, ta *adj* sensible ☼ *Los adjetivos ingleses son invariables.*

sensibilidad *sf* ❶ [*perceptibilidad*] feeling ❷ [*sentimentalismo*] sensitivity • **tener la sensibilidad a flor de piel** to be very sensitive ❸ [*de emulsión fotográfica, balanza etc*] sensitivity

sensibilizar *vt* [*concienciar*] to raise the awareness of

sensible *adj* ❶ [*generalmente*] sensitive ❷ [*evidente*] perceptible ❸ [*pérdida*] significant ☼ *Los adjetivos ingleses son invariables.*

sensible ≠ sensible

• La palabra inglesa **sensible** es un falso amigo que significa *sensato*. *Sensible* se traduce al inglés por **sensitive**.

sensitivo, va *adj* ❶ [*de los sentidos*] sensory ❷ [*receptible*] sensitive ⚲ *Los adjetivos ingleses son invariables.*

sensor *sm* sensor ▶ **sensor de humo** smoke detector

sensorial *adj* sensory ⚲ *Los adjetivos ingleses son invariables.*

sensual *adj* sensual ⚲ *Los adjetivos ingleses son invariables.*

sentado, da *adj* ❶ [*en asiento*] seated • **estar sentado** to be sitting down ❷ [*establecido*] • **dar algo por sentado** to take something for granted • **dejar sentado que...** to make it clear that... ⚲ *Los adjetivos ingleses son invariables.*

sentar ◆ *vt* ❶ [*en asiento*] to seat ❷ [*establecer*] to establish

◆ *vi* ❶ [*ropa, color*] to suit • **ese peinado le sienta muy bien** that haircut really suits her ❷ [*comida*] • **sentar bien/mal a alguien** to agree/disagree with somebody ❸ [*vacaciones, medicamento*] • **sentar bien a alguien** to do somebody good ❹ [*comentario, consejo*] • **le sentó mal** it upset her • **le sentó bien** she appreciated it

■ **sentarse** *v pronominal* to sit down • **siéntate ahí si quieres** sit down there if you want

sentencia *sf* ❶ DERECHO sentence ❷ [*proverbio, máxima*] maxim

sentenciar *vt* DERECHO • **sentenciar (a alguien a algo)** to sentence (somebody to something)

sentido, da *adj* [*profundo*] heartfelt ⚲ *Los adjetivos ingleses son invariables.*

■ **sentido** *sm* ❶ [*generalmente*] sense • **no tiene sentido del ritmo** he has no sense of rhythm • **los cinco sentidos** the five senses • **en cierto sentido** in a sense • **en sentido literal** in a literal sense • **tener sentido** to make sense ▶ **sentido común** common sense ▶ **sentido del humor** sense of humor ▶ **sexto sentido** sixth sense ❷ [*conocimiento*] consciousness • **perder el sentido** to lose consciousness ❸ [*significado*] meaning ▶ **doble sentido** double meaning ❹ [*dirección*] direction • **ir en sentido contrario** to go the wrong way • **de sentido único** one-way

sentimental *adj* sentimental ⚲ *Los adjetivos ingleses son invariables.*

sentimiento *sm* ❶ [*generalmente*] feeling ❷ [*pena, aflicción*] • **le acompaño en el sentimiento** my deepest sympathy

sentir *vt* ❶ [*generalmente*] to feel • **siento un aire frío** I feel a cold breeze • **siento un olor a gas** I can smell gas ❷ [*lamentar*] to be sorry about • **siento que no puedas venir** I'm sorry you can't come • **lo siento (mucho)** I'm (really) sorry ❸ [*oír*] to hear • **¿sentiste ese ruido afuera?** did you hear that noise outside?

seña *sf* [*gesto, indicio, contraseña*] sign • **te doy una seña cuando esté listo** I'll give you a sign when I'm ready

señal *sf* ❶ [*generalmente*] TELECOMUNICACIONES signal • **la señal es muy débil** the signal is very weak ▶ **señal de alarma/salida** alarm/starting signal ❷ [*de teléfono*] tone • **señal de ocupado** busy signal ❸ [*indicio, símbolo*] sign • **es una señal positiva** it's a positive sign • **en señal de** as a sign of • **dar señales de vida** to show signs of life ▶ **señal de la Cruz** sign of the Cross ▶ **señal de tráfico** road sign ❹ [*marca, huella*] mark ❺ [*cicatriz*] scar ❻ [*fianza*] deposit

expresión **no dejó ni señal** she didn't leave a trace

señalado, da *adj* [*importante - fecha*] special; [*- personaje*] distinguished ⚲ *Los adjetivos ingleses son invariables.*

señalar *vt* ❶ [*marcar, denotar*] to mark ❷ [*hora, temperatura etc*] to indicate ❸ [*indicar - con el dedo, con un comentario*] to point out • **¿puedes señalar dónde está?** can you point out where it is? • **no señales a la gente con el dedo** don't point at people ❹ [*fijar*] to set

señalización *sf* ❶ [*conjunto de señales*] signs *pl* ▶ **señalización vial** roadsigns *pl* ❷ [*colocación de señales*] signposting

señalizar *vt* to signpost

señor, ra *sm* ❶ [*tratamiento - antes de nombre, cargo*] Mr.; [*- al dirigir la palabra*] Sir • **el señor López** Mr. López • **¡señor presidente!** Mr. President! • **¿qué desea el señor?** what would you like, Sir? • **Muy señor mío** [*en cartas*] Dear Sir ❷ [*hombre*] man ❸ [*caballero*] gentleman ❹ [*dueño*] owner ❺ [*amo - de criado*] master

■ **señora** *sf* ❶ [*tratamiento - antes de nombre, cargo*] Mrs.; [*- al dirigir la palabra*] Madam • **la señora López** Mrs. López • **¡señora presidenta!** Madam President! • **¿qué desea la señora?** what would you like, Madam? • **¡señoras y señores! ...** Ladies and Gentlemen! ... • **Estimada señora** [*en cartas*] Dear Madam ❷ [*mujer*] lady • **señora de la limpieza** cleaning woman ❸ [*dama*] lady ❹ [*dueña*] owner ❺ [*esposa*] wife

señoría *sf* lordship, *femenino* ladyship • **su señoría a)** [*generalmente*] his lordship **b)** [*a un noble*] your lordship **c)** [*a un parlamentario*] the right honorable gentleman/lady **d)** [*a un juez*] your Honor

separación *sf* ❶ [*generalmente*] separation ❷ [*espacio*] space

separado, da *adj* ❶ [*generalmente*] separate • **mantén los ingredientes separados** keep the ingredients separate • **está muy separado de la pared** it's too far away from the wall • **por separado** separately ❷ [*del cónyuge*] separated • **sus padres están separados** his parents are separated ⚲ *Los adjetivos ingleses son invariables.*

separar *vt* ❶ [*generalmente*] to separate • **separa a los niños, por favor** separate the children, please • **separar algo de** to separate something from ❷ [*desunir*] to take off ❸ [*apartar - silla* ETC] to move away ❹ [*reservar*] to put aside

■ **separarse** *v pronominal* ❶ [*apartarse*] to move apart ❷ [*ir por distinto lugar*] to part company ❸ [*matrimonio*] • **separarse (de alguien)** to separate (from

S

somebody) • **se separaron después de diez años** they separated after ten years **❹** [*desprenderse*] to come away

separo *sm* (prison) cell

septiembre *sm* September • **el 1 de septiembre** the 1st of September • **uno de los septiembres más lluviosos de la última década** one of the rainiest Septembers in the last decade • **a principios/mediados/finales de septiembre** at the beginning/in the middle/at the end of September • **el pasado/próximo (mes de) septiembre** last/next September • **en septiembre** in September • **en pleno septiembre** in mid-September • **este (mes de) septiembre a)** [*pasado*] (this) last September **b)** [*próximo*] next September; this coming September • **para septiembre** by September

En inglés los nombres de los meses se escriben con mayúscula.

séptimo, ma *numeral* seventh

sepulcral *adj* [*profundo - voz, silencio*] lugubrious ☼ *Los adjetivos ingleses son invariables.*

sepulcro *sm* tomb

sepultar *vt* to bury

sepultura *sf* **❶** [*enterramiento*] burial • **dar sepultura a alguien** to bury somebody **❷** [*fosa*] grave

sequedad *sf* **❶** [*falta de humedad*] dryness **❷** [*antipatía*] brusqueness

sequía *sf* drought

séquito *sm* [*comitiva*] retinue

ser
◆ *sm*
being
• **los seres humanos** human beings
◆ *vi*

☼ *"Ser" se traduce por "to be" pero mira las varias acepciones para ver los diferentes usos del verbo.*

❶ [*antes de un adjetivo, indica una característica permanente*] to be
• **es muy guapo** he's very good looking
• **son muy simpáticos** they're really nice
❷ [*para insistir en una característica*] to be
• **lo que me explicó era muy interesante** what he told me was very interesting
• **lo importante es decidirse** the important thing is to make your mind up
• **allí fue donde nació** that's where he was born
❸ [*antes de un sustantivo*] to be
• **soy abogado** I'm a lawyer
• **es un amigo** he's a friend
❹ [*antes de un participio pasado, para formar la voz pasiva*] to be
• **fue visto por un testigo** he was seen by a witness
❺ [*para indicar la hora*] to be
• **¿qué hora es?** what's the time?
• **son las tres de la tarde** it's 3 pm

❻ [*para indicar la fecha*] to be
• **hoy es martes** it's Tuesday today
• **mañana es 15 de julio** tomorrow it's July 15
❼ [*en expresiones temporales*] to be
• **es muy tarde** it's very late
❽ [*para indicar un precio, una cantidad*] to be
• **¿cuánto es?** how much is it?
• **somos tres** there are three of us
❾ [*suceder*]
• **la conferencia era esta mañana** the conference took place this morning
• **¿cómo fue el accidente?** how did the accident happen?
❿ [*en matemáticas*] to be
• **dos y dos son cuatro** two plus two are four
⓫ [*seguido por "que", para insistir*]
• **es que ayer no vine porque estaba enfermo** I couldn't come yesterday because I was sick
expresiones **a no ser que** unless ▶ **como sea** however ▶ **de no ser por** if it wasn't for you • **de no ser por ti me hubiera ahogado** if it wasn't for you, I'd have drowned ▶ **no es nada** it's nothing • **se ha dado un golpe, pero no es nada** he had a bump but it's nothing ▶ **¡no es para menos!** and with good reason! ▶ **por si fuera poco** as if that weren't enough • **se nos ponchó la llanta y por si fuera poco nos quedamos sin gasolina** we had a flat tire and as if that weren't enough, we ran out of gas
■ **ser de**
◆ *v + preposición*
❶ [*indica el origen*] to be from
• **yo soy de Tijuana** I'm from Tijuana
❷ [*indica la pertenencia*]
• **ese libro es de mi hermano** that's my brother's book
• **él es del Consejo de Seguridad** he's from the Security Council
• **Pedro es como de la familia** Pedro is like a member of the family
❸ [*indica la materia*] to be made of
• **el reloj es de oro** the watch is made of gold
expresiones **es de día** it's daytime ▶ **es de desear que** we can only hope that • **es de desear que la situación se mejore** we can only hope that the situation improves ▶ **era de esperar** it was to be expected ▶ **es de suponer que** we can only assume that • **es de suponer que han tomado las precauciones necesarias** we can only assume that they took the relevant precautions ▶ **¿qué es de ti?** what are you up to?
■ **ser para**
◆ *v + preposición*
❶ [*servir para*]
• **este trapo es para limpiar los cristales** this cloth is for cleaning the windows
❷ [*indicado para*]
• **este libro no es para niños** this isn't a children's book

serenarse *v pronominal* [*calmarse*] to calm down

serenata *sf* MÚSICA serenade

serenidad *sf* ❶ [*tranquilidad*] calm ❷ [*quietud*] tranquility

serie *sf* ❶ [*generalmente*] TELEVISIÓN series *sing* ❷ [*de hechos, sucesos*] chain ❸ [*de mentiras*] string
expresión **ser un fuera de serie** to be unique
■ **de serie** *locución adjetiva* [*equipamiento*] (fitted) as standard
■ **en serie** *locución adverbial* [*fabricación*] • **fabricar en serie** to mass-produce

seriedad *sf* ❶ [*gravedad*] seriousness ❷ [*responsabilidad*] sense of responsibility ❸ [*formalidad - de persona*] reliability

serio, ria *adj* ❶ [*generalmente*] serious • **estar serio** to look serious ❷ [*responsable, formal*] responsible ❸ [*sobrio*] sober ☿ *Los adjetivos ingleses son invariables.*

sermón *sm* ❶ [*religioso*] sermon ❷ [*bronca*] lecture • **echar un sermón a alguien por algo** to give somebody a lecture for something

seropositivo, va ◆ *adj* MEDICINA HIV-positive ☿ *Los adjetivos ingleses son invariables.*
◆ *sm, f* MEDICINA HIV-positive person

serpiente *sf* snake

serrar *vt* to saw (up)

serrín *sm* sawdust

serrucho *sm* handsaw

servicial *adj* attentive ☿ *Los adjetivos ingleses son invariables.*

servicio *sm* ❶ [*generalmente*] service • **ofrecen un servicio muy bueno** they offer very good service • **fuera de servicio** out of order ❱ **servicio a domicilio** delivery service ❱ **servicio de inteligencia** o **secreto** intelligence o secret service ❱ **servicio de mesa** dinner service ❱ **servicio militar** military service ❱ **servicio de té** tea set ❷ [*servidumbre*] servants *pl* ❸ DEPORTE serve

servil *adj* servile ☿ *Los adjetivos ingleses son invariables.*

servilleta *sf* napkin

servilletero *sm* napkin ring

servir ◆ *vt* to serve • **ya sirvieron la cena** they've already served dinner • **sírvanos dos cervezas** bring us two beers • **¿te sirvo más papas?** would you like some more papas? • **¿en qué puedo servirle?** what can I do for you?
◆ *vi* [*valer, ser útil*] to be useful for • **esto no sirve para nada** this is no use for anything • **la máquina todavía sirve** the machine still works • **no sirve para estudiar** he's no good at studying • **de nada sirve que se lo digas** it's no use telling him • **servir de algo** to serve as something

sésamo *sm* sesame

sesenta *numeral* sixty • **los (años) sesenta** the sixties ver también **seis**

sesión *sf* ❶ [*reunión*] meeting ❷ [*proyección, representación*] showing • **la última sesión** the last showing ❱ **sesión continua** continuous showing ❱ **sesión matinal** matinée ❱ **sesión de tarde** afternoon matinée ❱ **sesión de noche** evening showing

seso ☿ *generalmente pl sm* ❶ [*cerebro*] brain ❷ [*sensatez*] brains *pl*
expresión **calentarse** o **devanarse los sesos** to rack your brains ❱ **sorber el seso** o **los sesos a alguien** to brainwash somebody

set (pl sets) *sm* DEPORTE set

seta *sf* mushroom • **algunas setas son venenosas** some mushrooms are poisonous

setecientos, tas *numeral* seven hundred ver también **seis**

setenta *numeral* seventy • **los (años) setenta** the seventies ver también **seis**

seto *sm* fence ❱ **seto vivo** hedge

seudónimo *sm* pseudonym

severidad *sf* ❶ [*rigor*] severity ❷ [*intransigencia*] strictness

severo, ra *adj* ❶ [*castigo*] harsh • **el castigo fue demasiado severo** the punishment was too harsh ❷ [*persona*] strict • **esa profesora es muy severa** that teacher is very strict ☿ *Los adjetivos ingleses son invariables.*

sexagésimo, ma *numeral* sixtieth

sexista *adj* & *smf* sexist ☿ *Los adjetivos ingleses son invariables.*

sexo *sm* sex

sexto, ta *numeral* sixth

sexual *adj* ❶ [*generalmente*] sexual ❷ [*educación, vida*] sex ☿ *Sólo se usa delante del sustantivo.*

sexualidad *sf* sexuality

shorts *smpl* shorts

show (pl shows) *sm* show
expresión **montar un show** to cause a scene

si¹ (pl sis) *sm* ❶ MÚSICA B ❷ [*en solfeo*] ti

si² *conjunción* ❶ ☿ *condicional* if • **si viene él yo me voy** if he comes, then I'm going • **si hubieses venido te habrías divertido** if you had come, you would have enjoyed yourself ❷ ☿ *en oraciones interrogativas indirectas* if; whether • **ignoro si lo sabe** I don't know if she knows • **pregúntale si va a venir o no** ask her whether she's coming or not ❸ [*expresa protesta*] but • **¡si te dije que no lo hicieras!** but I told you not to do it!

sí (pl síes) ◆ *adv* ❶ [*afirmación*] yes • **¿vendrás? — sí, iré** will you come? — yes, I will • **claro que sí** of course • **creo que sí** I think so • **¿están de acuerdo? — algunos sí** do they agree? — some do • **¿sí?** [*incredulidad*] really? ❷ [*uso enfático*] • **sí que** really • **sí que me gusta** I really like it
expresión **no creo que puedas hacerlo — ¡a que sí!** I don't think you can do it — I bet I can!
◆ *pronombre personal* ❶ ☿ *reflexivo* [*de personas*] himself, *femenino* herself, *plural* themselves ❷ [*usted*] yourself, *plural* yourselves ❸ [*de cosas, animales*] itself,

plural themselves • **lo quiere todo para sí (misma)** she wants everything for herself • **se acercó la silla hacia sí** he drew the chair nearer (himself) • **de (por) sí** [*cosa*] in itself ❹ ☿ *reflexivo impersonal* yourself • **cuando uno piensa en sí mismo** when you think about yourself
◆ *sm* consent
expresión **dar el sí** to give your consent

sida (*abreviatura de* síndrome de inmunodeficiencia adquirida) *sm* AIDS

sidra *sf* cider

siempre *adv* [*generalmente*] always • **esa tienda siempre está cerrada** that store is always closed • **somos amigos de siempre** we've always been friends • **como siempre** as usual • **lo de siempre** the usual • **es así desde siempre** it has always been that way • **para siempre (jamás)** for ever and ever

sierra *sf* ❶ [*herramienta*] saw ❷ [*cordillera*] mountain range ❸ [*región montañosa*] mountains *pl*

siesta *sf* nap • **echarse la siesta** to have an afternoon nap

siete *numeral* seven ver también **seis**

sifón *sm* siphon

sigilo *sm* ❶ [*generalmente*] secrecy ❷ [*al robar, escapar*] stealth

sigiloso, sa *adj* ❶ [*discreto*] secretive ❷ [*al robar, escapar*] stealthy ☿ *Los adjetivos ingleses son invariables.*

siglas *sfpl* acronym

siglo *sm* ❶ [*cien años*] century • **el siglo XX** the 20th century • **el siglo III antes de Cristo** the third century before Christ ❷ [*mucho tiempo*] • **hace siglos que no la veo** I haven't seen her for ages

significado *sm* [*sentido*] meaning

significar ◆ *vt* [*generalmente*] to mean • **¿qué significa esta palabra?** what does this word mean? • **¿qué significa S.A.?** what does S.A. stand for?
◆ *vi* [*tener importancia*] • **no significa nada para mí** it means nothing to me

significativo, va *adj* significant ☿ *Los adjetivos ingleses son invariables.*

signo *sm* ❶ [*generalmente*] sign • **¿de qué signo eres?** what sign are you? ▸ **signo de multiplicar/dividir** multiplication/division sign ▸ **signo del zodiaco** sign of the zodiac ❷ [*en la escritura*] mark ▸ **signo de admiración/interrogación** exclamation/question mark ❸ [*símbolo*] symbol

siguiente ◆ *adj* ❶ [*en el tiempo, espacio*] next • **deja todo preparado para el día siguiente** she leaves everything ready for the next day ❷ [*a continuación*] following • **los siguientes alumnos** the following students ☿ *Los adjetivos ingleses son invariables.*
◆ *smf* ❶ [*el que sigue*] • **el siguiente** the next one • **¡el siguiente!** next, please! ❷ [*lo que sigue*] • **lo siguiente** the following

sílaba *sf* syllable

silbar ◆ *vt* ❶ [*generalmente*] to whistle ❷ [*abuchear*] to hiss
◆ *vi* ❶ [*generalmente*] to whistle ❷ [*abuchear*] to hiss ❸ *figurado* [*oídos*] to ring

silbato *sm* whistle

silbido *sm* ❶ [*generalmente*] whistle ❷ [*para abuchear, de serpiente*] hiss

silenciar *vt* to keep quiet

silencio *sm* silence • **necesito silencio para estudiar** I need silence when I study • **en silencio** silently • **escuchamos en silencio** we listened silently • **¡silencio, por favor!** quiet, please! • **guardar silencio (sobre algo)** to keep silent (about something) • **reinaba el silencio más absoluto** there was complete silence • **romper el silencio** to break the silence

silencioso, sa *adj* silent ☿ *Los adjetivos ingleses son invariables.*

silicona *sf* silicone

silla *sf* ❶ [*generalmente*] chair ▸ **silla de ruedas** wheelchair ▸ **silla eléctrica** electric chair ❷ [*de caballo*] ▸ **silla (de montar)** saddle

sillín *sm* saddle

sillón *sm* armchair

silueta *sf* ❶ [*cuerpo*] figure ❷ [*contorno*] outline ❸ [*dibujo*] silhouette

silvestre *adj* wild ☿ *Los adjetivos ingleses son invariables.*

simbólico, ca *adj* symbolic ☿ *Los adjetivos ingleses son invariables.*

simbolizar *vt* to symbolize

símbolo *sm* symbol

simetría *sf* symmetry

similar *adj* • **similar (a)** similar (to) ☿ *Los adjetivos ingleses son invariables.*

similitud *sf* similarity

simio, mia *sm, f* simian

simpatía *sf* ❶ [*cordialidad*] friendliness ❷ [*cariño*] affection • **inspirar simpatía** to inspire affection • **coger simpatía a alguien** to take a liking to somebody • **sentir simpatía por alguien** to like somebody

simpático, ca *adj* ❶ [*generalmente*] nice • **Ana es muy simpática** Ana is very nice • **estuvo muy simpático con nosotros** he was very nice to us ❷ [*abierto, cordial*] friendly • **Juan me cae simpático** I like Juan ❸ [*anécdota, comedia* ETC] amusing ❹ [*reunión, velada* ETC] pleasant ☿ *Los adjetivos ingleses son invariables.*

simpático ≠ sympathetic

• La palabra inglesa **sympathetic** es un falso amigo que significa *comprensivo*. *Simpático* se traduce al inglés por *nice*.

simpatizante *smf* sympathizer

simpatizar *vi* • **simpatizar (con) a)** [*persona*] to hit it off (with) **b)** [*cosa*] to sympathize (with)

simple ◆ *adj* ❶ [*generalmente*] simple • **es un ejercicio muy simple** it's a very simple exercise ❷ [*fácil*] easy ❸ [*único, sin componentes*] single • **dame una simple razón** give me one single reason ❹ [*mero*] mere • **no soy más que un simple principiante** I'm a mere beginner • **por simple estupidez** through sheer stupidity ❈ *Los adjetivos ingleses son invariables.*
◆ *smf* [*persona*] simpleton

simplemente *adv* simply

simpleza *sf* ❶ [*de persona*] simple-mindedness ❷ [*tontería*] trifle

simplicidad *sf* simplicity

simplificar *vt* to simplify

simplista *adj* simplistic ❈ *Los adjetivos ingleses son invariables.*

simulacro *sm* simulation • **simulacro de combate** mock battle ▶ **simulacro de incendio** fire drill

simular *vt* ❶ [*sentimiento, desmayo* ETC] to pretend • **simuló que no me había visto** he pretended not to have seen me ❷ [*enfermedad*] to fake ❸ [*combate, salvamento*] to simulate

simultáneo, nea *adj* simultaneous ❈ *Los adjetivos ingleses son invariables.*

sin *preposición* without • **salió sin paraguas** she went out without an umbrella • **sin alcohol** alcohol-free • **estoy sin un peso** I'm penniless • **ha escrito cinco libros sin (contar) las novelas** he has written five books, not counting his novels • **está sin hacer** it hasn't been done yet • **estamos sin vino** we're out of wine • **sin que** ❈ + *subjuntivo* without ❈ + *gerundio* • **sin que nadie se enterara** without anyone noticing

sinagoga *sf* synagogue

sinceridad *sf* ❶ sincerity ❷ [*llaneza, franqueza*] frankness • **con toda sinceridad** frankly

sincero, ra *adj* ❶ sincere ❷ [*abierto, directo*] frank • **para ser sincero** to be honest ❈ *Los adjetivos ingleses son invariables.*

sincronizar *vt* [*regular*] to synchronize

sindical *adj* (trade) union ❈ *Sólo se usa delante del sustantivo.*

sindicalista *smf* trade unionist

sindicato *sm* labor union

síndrome *sm* syndrome ▶ **síndrome de abstinencia** withdrawal symptoms *pl* ▶ **síndrome de clase turista** economy-class syndrome ▶ **síndrome de Down** Down's syndrome ▶ **síndrome de inmunodeficiencia adquirida** acquired immune deficiency syndrome ▶ **síndrome premenstrual** premenstrual syndrome

sinfín *sm* • **un sinfín de problemas** no end of problems

sinfonía *sf* symphony

sinfónico, ca *adj* symphonic ❈ *Los adjetivos ingleses son invariables.*

■ **sinfónica** *sf* symphony orchestra

singular ◆ *adj* ❶ [*raro*] peculiar ❷ [*único*] unique ❸ GRAMÁTICA singular ❈ *Los adjetivos ingleses son invariables.*
◆ *sm* GRAMÁTICA singular • **en singular** in the singular

siniestro, tra *adj* ❶ [*perverso*] sinister ❷ [*desgraciado*] disastrous ❈ *Los adjetivos ingleses son invariables.*

■ **siniestro** *sm* ❶ disaster ❷ [*accidente de coche*] accident ❸ [*incendio*] fire

sinnúmero *sm* • **un sinnúmero de** countless • **un sinnúmero de veces** countless times

sino *conjunción* ❶ [*para contraponer*] but • **no sólo es listo, sino también trabajador** he's not only clever but also hardworking • **no lo hizo él, sino ella** he didn't do it, she did ❷ [*para exceptuar*] but • **¿quién sino tú lo haría?** who else but you would do it? • **no quiero sino que se haga justicia** I only want justice to be done

sinónimo, ma *adj* synonymous • **ser sinónimo de algo** to be synonymous with something ❈ *Los adjetivos ingleses son invariables.*

■ **sinónimo** *sm* synonym

síntesis *sf invariable* synthesis • **en síntesis** in short

sintético, ca *adj* [*artificial*] synthetic ❈ *Los adjetivos ingleses son invariables.*

sintetizador *sm* synthesizer

sintetizar *vt* ❶ [*resumir*] to summarize ❷ [*fabricar artificialmente*] to synthesize

síntoma *sm* symptom

sintonía *sf* ❶ [*música*] signature tune ❷ [*conexión*] tuning ❸ *figurado* [*compenetración*] harmony • **en sintonía con** in tune with

sintonizar ◆ *vt* [*conectar*] to tune in to
◆ *vi* ❶ [*conectar*] • **sintonizar (con)** to tune in (to) ❷ *figurado* [*compenetrarse*] • **sintonizar en algo (con alguien)** to be on the same wavelength (as somebody) about something

sinuoso, sa *adj* ❶ [*camino*] winding ❷ [*movimiento*] sinuous ❈ *Los adjetivos ingleses son invariables.*

sinvergüenza *smf* ❶ [*canalla*] rogue ❷ [*fresco, descarado*] insolent person

sinvergüenzada *sf* familiar dirty trick

siquiera ◆ *conjunción* [*aunque*] even if • **ven siquiera por pocos días** do come, even if it's only for a few days
◆ *adv* [*por lo menos*] at least • **dime siquiera tu nombre** (you could) at least tell me your name

sirena *sf* ❶ MITOLOGÍA mermaid ❷ [*señal*] siren

sirviente, ta *sm, f* servant

sísmico, ca *adj* seismic ❈ *Los adjetivos ingleses son invariables.*

sistema *sm* ❶ [*generalmente*] INFORMÁTICA system ▶ **sistema métrico (decimal)** metric (decimal) system ▶ **sistema monetario europeo** European Monetary System ▶ **sistema monetario/nervioso/solar** monetary/nervous/solar system ▶ **sistema montañoso** mountain chain ▶ **sistema nervioso** nervous system ▶ **sistema periódico de los elementos** periodic table of elements ▶ **sistema solar** solar system ❷ [*método, orden*] method

S

sistemático, ca *adj* systematic ☼ *Los adjetivos ingleses son invariables.*

sistematizar *vt* to systematize

sitiar *vt* [*cercar*] to besiege

sitio *sm* ❶ [*lugar*] place • **está en un sitio seguro** it's in a safe place • **cambiar de sitio (con alguien)** to change places (with somebody) • **en otro sitio** elsewhere • **poner a alguien en su sitio** to put somebody in his/her place ▶ **sitio de taxis** taxi stand ❷ [*espacio*] room • **no hay suficiente sitio** there's not enough room • **hacer sitio a alguien** to make room for somebody • **ocupar sitio** to take up space ❸ [*cerco*] siege ❹ INFORMÁTICA ▶ **sitio Web** Web site

situación *sf* ❶ [*circunstancias*] situation ❷ [*legal, social*] status ❸ [*condición, estado*] state ❹ [*ubicación*] location

situado, da *adj* ❶ [*ubicado*] located ❷ [*acomodado*] • **estar bien situado** to be well off ☼ *Los adjetivos ingleses son invariables.*

situar *vt* ❶ [*colocar*] to place ❷ [*edificio, ciudad*] to locate ❸ [*en clasificación*] to place

SL (*abreviatura de* sociedad limitada) *sf* ≃ Ltd

slip *sm* briefs *pl*

slogan = **eslogan**

s/n (*abreviatura escrita de* sin número) ▶ *para explicar lo que es puedes decir:* it's an abbreviation used in addresses, where the building has no number

snowboard *sm* snowboard *m*

so ♦ *preposición* under • **so pretexto de** under • **so pena de** under penalty of
♦ *adv* • **¡so tonto!** you idiot!
♦ *exclamación* • **¡so!** whoa!

sobaco *sm* armpit

sobar *vt* ❶ [*tocar*] to finger ❷ *despectivo* [*acariciar, besar*] to touch up

soberanía *sf* sovereignty

soberano, na ♦ *adj* ❶ [*independiente*] sovereign ❷ *figurado* [*grande*] massive ❸ [*paliza*] thorough ❹ [*belleza, calidad*] unrivalled ☼ *Los adjetivos ingleses son invariables.*
♦ *sm, f* sovereign

soberbio, bia *adj* ❶ [*arrogante*] proud ❷ [*magnífico*] superb ☼ *Los adjetivos ingleses son invariables.*
■ **soberbia** *sf* ❶ [*arrogancia*] pride ❷ [*magnificencia*] grandeur

sobornar *vt* to bribe

soborno *sm* ❶ [*acción*] bribery ❷ [*dinero, regalo*] bribe

sobra *sf* • **de sobra** enough • **tenemos tiempo de sobra** we have enough of time • **lo sabemos de sobra** we know it only too well • **¿alguien tiene una entrada de sobra?** does anybody have a spare ticket?
■ **sobras** *sfpl* [*de comida*] leftovers

sobrado, da *adj* ❶ [*de sobra*] more than enough ❷ [*de dinero*] well off ☼ *Los adjetivos ingleses son invariables.*

sobrante *adj* remaining ☼ *Los adjetivos ingleses son invariables.*

sobrar *vi* ❶ [*quedar, restar*] to be left over • **nos sobró comida** we had some food left over ❷ [*haber de más*] to be more than enough • **parece que van a sobrar bocadillos** it looks like there are going to be too many sandwiches ❸ [*estar de más*] to be superfluous • **lo que dices sobra** that goes without saying

sobre¹ *sm* ❶ [*para cartas*] envelope ❷ [*para alimentos*] sachet

---

sobre²
♦ *preposición*

❶ [*indica una posición superior con contacto directo*] on
• **el libro está sobre la mesa** the book is on the table
❷ [*indica una posición superior sin contacto directo*] over
• **hay un cuadro sobre la chimenea** there's a picture over the fireplace
• **el pato vuela sobre el lago** the duck is flying over the lake
❸ [*indica un tema*] on
• **una conferencia sobre el desarme** a conference on disarmament
❹ [*indica una aproximación*] around
• **llegarán sobre las diez** they'll arrive around ten
❺ [*indica la repetición de algo*] after
• **fracaso sobre fracaso** failure after failure

---

sobrecarga *sf* ❶ [*exceso de carga*] excess weight ❷ [*saturación*] overload

sobrecargo *sm* [*de avión*] purser

sobrecoger *vt* ❶ [*asustar*] to startle ❷ [*impresionar*] to move

sobredosis *sf invariable* overdose

sobreentender = **sobrentender**

sobremesa *sf* after-dinner period • **de sobremesa** [*programación* ETC] mid-afternoon ☼ *Sólo se usa delante del sustantivo.*

sobrenatural *adj* [*extraordinario*] supernatural ☼ *Los adjetivos ingleses son invariables.*

sobrenombre *sm* nickname

sobrentender, sobreentender *vt* to understand

sobrepasar *vt* ❶ [*exceder*] to exceed ❷ [*aventajar*] • **sobrepasar a alguien** to overtake somebody

sobrepeso *sm* excess weight

sobresaliente ♦ *adj* [*destacado*] outstanding ☼ *Los adjetivos ingleses son invariables.*
♦ *sm* ❶ [*en escuela*] excellent, ≃ A ❷ [*en universidad*] ≃ first class

sobresalir *vi* ❶ [*en tamaño*] to jut out ❷ [*en importancia*] to stand out

sobresaltar *vt* to startle

sobresalto *sm* start

sobreviviente = **superviviente**

sobrevivir *vi* to survive • **sobrevivieron al accidente** they survived the accident • **sobrevivió a sus dos hijos** he outlived his two sons

sobrevolar *vt* to fly over

sobrino, na *sm, f* nephew, *femenino* niece

sobrio, bria *adj* ❶ [*moderado*] restrained ❷ [*no excesivo*] simple ❸ [*austero, no borracho*] sober ☼ *Los adjetivos ingleses son invariables.*

socavar *vt* ❶ [*excavar por debajo*] to dig under ❷ *figurado* [*debilitar*] to undermine

socavón *sm* ❶ [*hoyo*] hollow ❷ [*en la carretera*] pothole

sociable *adj* sociable ☼ *Los adjetivos ingleses son invariables.*

social *adj* ❶ [*generalmente*] social ❷ COMERCIO company ☼ *Sólo se usa delante del sustantivo.*

socialismo *sm* socialism

socialista *adj & smf* socialist ☼ *Los adjetivos ingleses son invariables.*

sociedad *sf* ❶ [*generalmente*] society, *plural* societies ▶ **sociedad de consumo** consumer society ▶ **sociedad deportiva** sports club ▶ **sociedad literaria** literary society ❷ COMERCIO [*empresa*] company ▶ **sociedad anónima** corporation ▶ **sociedad (de responsabilidad) limitada** private limited company

socio, cia *sm, f* ❶ COMERCIO partner ❷ [*miembro*] member

sociología *sf* sociology

sociólogo, ga *sm, f* sociologist

socorrer *vt* to help

socorrista *smf* ❶ [*sanitario*] first aid worker ❷ [*en la playa*] lifeguard

socorro ◆ *sm* help • **oímos unos gritos pidiendo socorro** we heard some cries for help
◆ *exclamación* • **¡socorro!** help!

soda *sf* [*bebida*] soda

sodio *sm* sodium

sofá *sm* sofa ▶ **sofá cama** sofa bed

sofisticación *sf* sophistication

sofisticado, da *adj* sophisticated ☼ *Los adjetivos ingleses son invariables.*

sofocar *vt* ❶ [*ahogar*] to suffocate ❷ [*incendio*] to put out ❸ *figurado* [*rebelión*] to quell

sofoco *sm* ❶ [*ahogo*] breathlessness ☼ *incontable* ❷ [*sonrojo, bochorno*] hot flush ❸ *figurado* [*vergüenza*] mortification ❹ *figurado* [*disgusto*] • **llevarse un sofoco** to have a fit

sofreír *vt* to fry lightly over a low heat

software *sm* INFORMÁTICA software

soga *sf* ❶ [*cuerda*] rope ❷ [*para ahorcar*] noose

soja *sf* soya

sol *sm* ❶ [*astro*] sun • **a pleno sol** in the sun • **al salir/ponerse el sol** at sunrise/sunset • **hace sol** it's sunny • **tomar el sol** to sunbathe ❷ MÚSICA G ❸ [*en solfeo*] so ❹ [*moneda*] sol

expresión **no dejar a alguien ni a sol ni a sombra** not to give somebody a moment's peace

solamente *adv* only • **vino solamente él** only he came

solapa *sf* ❶ [*de prenda*] lapel ❷ [*de libro, sobre*] flap

solar ◆ *adj* solar ☼ *Los adjetivos ingleses son invariables.*
◆ *sm* undeveloped plot (of land)

soldado *sm* soldier ▶ **soldado raso** private

soleado, da *adj* sunny ☼ *Los adjetivos ingleses son invariables.*

soledad *sf* loneliness • **sufren de pobreza y soledad** they suffer from poverty and loneliness • **en soledad** alone

solemne *adj* ❶ [*con pompa*] formal ❷ [*grave*] solemn ❸ *figurado* [*enorme*] utter ☼ *Los adjetivos ingleses son invariables.*

solemnidad *sf* [*suntuosidad*] pomp • **de solemnidad** extremely

soler *vi* • **soler hacer algo** to do something usually • **aquí suele llover mucho** it usually rains a lot here • **solíamos ir a la playa cada día** we used to go to the beach every day

solfeo *sm* MÚSICA music reading

solicitar *vt* ❶ [*pedir*] to request • **escribí solicitando información** I wrote requesting information ❷ [*un empleo*] to apply for • **voy a solicitar una beca** I'm going to apply for a scholarship • **solicitar algo a o de alguien** to request something of somebody ❸ [*persona*] to pursue • **estar muy solicitado** to be very popular

solicitud *sf* ❶ [*petición*] request • **presentar una solicitud** to submit a request ❷ [*documento*] application • **rechazaron mi solicitud** they rejected my application ❸ [*atención*] care

solidaridad *sf* solidarity • **en solidaridad con** in solidarity with

solidario, ria *adj* [*adherido*] • **solidario (con)** supporting (of) ☼ *Los adjetivos ingleses son invariables.*

solidez *sf* [*física*] solidity

solidificar *vt* to solidify

sólido, da *adj* ❶ [*generalmente*] solid ❷ [*cimientos, fundamento*] firm ❸ [*argumento, conocimiento, idea*] sound ☼ *Los adjetivos ingleses son invariables.*
■ **sólido** *sm* solid

solista ◆ *adj* solo ☼ *Los adjetivos ingleses son invariables.*
◆ *smf* soloist

solitario, ria ◆ *adj* ❶ [*sin compañía*] solitary ❷ [*lugar*] lonely ☼ *Los adjetivos ingleses son invariables.*
◆ *sm, f* [*persona*] loner
■ **solitario** *sm* [*juego*] solitaire • **le gusta hacer solitarios** he likes to play solitaire

solo, la *adj* ❶ [*sin nadie*] alone • **dejar solo a alguien** to leave somebody alone • **se quedó solo a temprana edad** he was on his own from an early age • **a solas** alone • **quiere hablar a solas conmigo** he wants to speak to me alone ❷ [*sin nada*] on its own ❸ [*café*]

S

black ❹ [*whisky*] neat ❺ [*único*] single • **ni una sola gota** not a (single) drop • **dame una sola cosa** give me just one thing ❻ [*solitario*] lonely • **se siente solo** he feels lonely ☼ *Los adjetivos ingleses son invariables.*
■ **solo** *sm* Música solo

sólo *adv* only • **sólo quería un vaso de agua** I only wanted a glass of water • **no sólo... sino (también)...** not only... but (also)... • **con sólo, sólo con** just by • **sólo que...** only...

solomillo *sm* sirloin

soltar *vt* ❶ [*desasir*] to let go of • **no le sueltes la mano** don't let go of his hand • **¡suéltame!** let go of me! ❷ [*desatar - generalmente*] to unfasten; [*- nudo*] to untie; [*- hebilla, cordones*] to undo • **no puedo soltar este nudo** I can't untie this knot ❸ [*dejar libre*] to release • **soltaron a los sospechosos** they released the suspects ❹ [*desenrollar - cable* ETC] to let out ❺ [*patada, grito, suspiro* ETC] to give ❻ [*decir bruscamente*] to come out with

soltero, ra ◆ *adj* single • **padres solteros** single parents ☼ *Los adjetivos ingleses son invariables.*
◆ *sm, f* bachelor, *femenino* single woman

soltura *sf* ❶ [*generalmente*] fluency ❷ [*seguridad de sí mismo*] assurance

soluble *adj* ❶ [*que se disuelve*] soluble ❷ [*que se soluciona*] solvable ☼ *Los adjetivos ingleses son invariables.*

solución *sf* solution

solucionar *vt* ❶ [*dificultad*] to solve • **no solucionas nada con llorar** you don't solve anything by crying ❷ [*disputa*] to resolve • **al final todo se solucionó** in the end everything was resolved

solvente *adj* ❶ [*económicamente*] solvent ❷ *figurado* [*fuentes* ETC] reliable ☼ *Los adjetivos ingleses son invariables.*

sombra *sf* ❶ [*proyección - fenómeno*] shadow; [*- zona*] shade • **su sombra se proyectaba en la pared** her shadow was cast on the wall • **sentémonos a la sombra** let's sit in the shade • **dar sombra a** to cast a shadow over ▶ **sombra de ojos** eyeshadow ❷ [*en pintura*] shade
expresión **tener mala sombra** to be a nasty swine ▶ **permanecer en la sombra** to stay out of the limelight

sombrero *sm* [*prenda*] hat
expresión **quitarse el sombrero** to take your hat off

sombrilla *sf* parasol
expresión **me vale sombrilla** I couldn't care less

sombrío, bría *adj* ❶ [*oscuro*] gloomy ❷ *figurado* [*triste*] sombre ☼ *Los adjetivos ingleses son invariables.*

someter *vt* ❶ [*a rebeldes*] to subdue ❷ [*presentar*] • **someter algo a la aprobación de alguien** to submit something for somebody's approval • **someter algo a votación** to put something to the vote ❸ [*subordinar*] to subordinate ❹ [*a operación, interrogatorio* ETC] • **someter a alguien a algo** to subject somebody to something

sonajero *sm* rattle

sonámbulo, la *sm, f* sleepwalker

sonar¹ *sm* sonar

sonar² *vi* ❶ [*generalmente*] to sound • **suena a falso/chiste** it sounds false/like a joke ❷ [*timbre*] to ring • **el teléfono no ha parado de sonar** the telephone hasn't stopped ringing • **el despertador no sonó** the alarm clock didn't go off ❸ [*hora*] • **sonaron las doce** the clock struck twelve ❹ [*ser conocido, familiar*] to sound familiar • **esto me suena conocido** this sounds familiar • **me suena** it rings a bell • **no me suena su nombre** I don't remember hearing her name before ❺ [*pronunciarse - letra*] to be pronounced ❻ [*rumorearse*] to be rumored
expresión **(así o tal) como suena** literally

sonda *sf* ❶ Medicina & Tecnología probe ❷ Náutica sounding line ❸ [*en una mina*] drill

sondear *vt* ❶ [*indagar*] to sound out ❷ [*terreno*] to test; [*roca*] to drill

sondeo *sm* ❶ [*encuesta*] (opinion) poll ❷ [*de un terreno*] drilling ☼ *incontable* ❸ Náutica sounding

sonido *sm* sound

sonoro, ra *adj* ❶ [*generalmente*] sound ☼ *Sólo se usa delante del sustantivo.* ❷ [*película*] talking ❸ [*ruidoso, resonante, vibrante*] resonant

sonreír *vi* [*reír levemente*] to smile • **me sonrió** he smiled at me

sonriente *adj* smiling ☼ *Los adjetivos ingleses son invariables.*

sonrisa *sf* smile

sonrojarse *v pronominal* to blush

sonrosado, da *adj* rosy ☼ *Los adjetivos ingleses son invariables.*

sonsear *vi* to fool around

soñador, ra *sm, f* dreamer

soñar ◆ *vt* literal & figurado to dream • **soñé que ganábamos el partido** I dreamed that we were winning the game
expresión **¡ni soñarlo!** not on your life!
◆ *vi* literal & figurado • **soñar (con)** to dream (of) • **sueña con ser famoso** he dreams of being famous • **anoche soñé con él** last night I dreamt about him

sopa *sf* soup • **sopa de verduras** vegetable soup

sopapo *sm familiar* slap

sope *sm* ▶ *para explicar lo que es puedes decir*: it's a fried corn tortilla, with beans and cheese or other toppings

sopero, ra *adj* soup ☼ *Sólo se usa delante del sustantivo.*
■ **sopera** *sf* [*recipiente*] soup tureen

sopesar *vt* [*ventajas y desventajas*] to weigh up

sopetón ■ **de sopetón** *locución adverbial* suddenly

soplar ◆ *vt* ❶ [*vela, fuego*] to blow out ❷ [*ceniza, polvo*] to blow off ❸ [*globo* ETC] to blow up ❹ [*vidrio*] to blow ❺ *figurado* [*pregunta, examen*] to prompt
◆ *vi* [*generalmente*] to blow

soplete *sm* blowtorch

soplido *sm* blow • **tienes que apagarlas de un so-plido** you have to blow them out with one blow

soplo *sm* ❶ [*soplido*] blow ❷ MEDICINA murmur ❸ *familiar* [*chivatazo*] tip-off

soplón, ona *sm, f familiar* grass

soponcio *sm familiar* • **le dio un soponcio a)** [*desmayo*] she passed out **b)** [*ataque*] she had a fit

soporífero, ra *adj literal & figurado* soporific ⚲*Los adjetivos ingleses son invariables.*

soportar *vt* ❶ [*sostener*] to support • **esta columna soporta todo el peso** this column supports all the weight ❷ [*resistir, tolerar*] to stand • **¡no le soporto!** I can't stand him!

soporte *sm* ❶ [*apoyo*] support ❷ INFORMÁTICA medium ▸ **soporte físico** hardware ▸ **soporte lógico** software

soprano *smf* soprano

sor *sf* RELIGIÓN sister

sorber *vt* ❶ [*beber*] to sip ❷ [*haciendo ruido*] to slurp ❸ [*absorber*] to soak up ❹ [*atraer*] to draw in

sorbete *sm* sorbet

sorbo *sm* ❶ [*acción*] gulp • **se lo tomó de un sorbo** he drank it in one gulp ❷ [*pequeño*] sip • **apenas le dio un sorbo a la sopa** he barely had a sip of the soup • **beber a sorbos** to sip

sordera *sf* deafness

sórdido, da *adj* ❶ [*miserable*] squalid ❷ [*obsceno, perverso*] sordid ⚲*Los adjetivos ingleses son invariables.*

sordo, da ◆ *adj* ❶ [*que no oye*] deaf • **es sordo** he's deaf • **se quedó sordo** he went deaf ❷ [*ruido, dolor*] dull ⚲*Los adjetivos ingleses son invariables.*
◆ *sm, f* [*persona*] deaf person • **los sordos** the deaf

sordomudo, da ◆ *adj* deaf and dumb ⚲*Los adjetivos ingleses son invariables.*
◆ *sm, f* deaf-mute

sorprendente *adj* surprising ⚲*Los adjetivos ingleses son invariables.*

sorprender *vt* ❶ [*asombrar*] to surprise • **ya nada me sorprende** nothing surprises me these days • **no me sorprendería que lo volviera a hacer** it would not surprise me if he did it again ❷ [*atrapar*] • **sorprender a alguien (haciendo algo)** to catch somebody (doing something) • **lo sorprendieron copiando** they caught him copying

sorprendido, da *adj* surprised • **quedarse sorprendido** to be surprised ⚲*Los adjetivos ingleses son invariables.*

sorpresa *sf* surprise • **su pregunta me tomó por sorpresa** his question took me by surprise

sortear *vt* ❶ [*rifar*] to raffle ❷ [*echar a suertes*] to draw lots for ❸ *figurado* [*esquivar*] to dodge

sorteo *sm* ❶ [*lotería*] draw ❷ [*rifa*] raffle

sortija *sf* ring

sosegado, da *adj* calm ⚲*Los adjetivos ingleses son invariables.*

soso, sa *adj* ❶ [*sin sal*] bland ❷ [*sin gracia*] dull ⚲*Los adjetivos ingleses son invariables.*

sospecha *sf* suspicion • **despertar sospechas** to arouse suspicion

sospechar ◆ *vt* [*creer, suponer*] to suspect • **sospecho que mis vecinos lo hicieron** I suspect that my neighbors did it • **sospecho que no la terminará** I doubt whether she'll finish it
◆ *vi* • **sospechar de** to suspect • **sospechan del jardinero** they suspect the gardener

sospechoso, sa ◆ *adj* suspicious ⚲*Los adjetivos ingleses son invariables.*
◆ *sm, f* suspect

sostén *sm* ❶ [*apoyo*] support ❷ [*sustento*] main support ❸ [*alimento*] sustenance ❹ [*sujetador*] bra

sostener *vt* ❶ [*sujetar*] to support • **estas dos vigas sostienen el techo** these two beams support the roof ❷ [*defender - idea, opinión, tesis*] to defend; [- *promesa, palabra*] to stand by; to keep • **sostener que...** to maintain that... • **siempre ha sostenido que él no lo hizo** he's always maintained that he didn't do it ❸ [*tener - conversación*] to hold; to have; [- *correspondencia*] to keep up
■ **sostenerse** *v pronominal* ❶ to hold yourself up ❷ [*en pie*] to stand up ❸ [*en el aire*] to hang

sostenido, da *adj* ❶ [*persistente*] sustained ❷ MÚSICA sharp ⚲*Los adjetivos ingleses son invariables.*

sotana *sf* cassock

sótano *sm* basement

spanglish *sm* Spanglish

spray = espray

sprint = esprint

squash *sm invariable* squash

Sr. (*abreviatura escrita de* señor) Mr

Sra. (*abreviatura escrita de* señora) Mrs

Sres. (*abreviatura escrita de* señores) Messrs

Srta. (*abreviatura escrita de* señorita) Miss

Sta. (*abreviatura escrita de* santa) St

standard = estándar

starter = estárter

status = estatus

stereo = estéreo

stock *sm* stock

stop *sm* AUTOMÓVILES stop sign

stress = estrés

su (pl sus) *adj posesivo* ❶ [*de él*] his • **vino con su novia** he came with his girlfriend ❷ [*de ella*] her • **conozco a su marido** I know her husband ❸ [*de cosa, animal*] its • **viene en su propia caja** it comes in its own box ❹ [*de ellos, ellas*] their • **trajeron sus bicicletas** they brought their bicycles ❺ [*de usted, ustedes*] your • **su nombre, por favor** your name, please • **no dejen sus cosas tiradas** don't leave your things lying around

suave *adj* ❶ [*generalmente*] soft • **tocaban una música muy suave** they were playing very soft music ❷ [*liso*] smooth • **es suave al tacto** it's smooth to the

S

suavidad

touch ❸ [*sabor, olor, color*] delicate ❹ [*apacible - persona, carácter*] gentle ; [- *clima*] mild • **tiene un clima suave** it has a mild climate ❺ [*fácil - cuesta, tarea, ritmo*] gentle ; [- *dirección de un coche*] smooth ☼ *Los adjetivos ingleses son invariables.*

suavidad *sf* ❶ [*generalmente*] softness ❷ [*lisura*] smoothness ❸ [*de sabor, olor, color*] delicacy ❹ [*de carácter*] gentleness ❺ [*de clima*] mildness ❻ [*de cuesta, tarea, ritmo*] gentleness ❼ [*de la dirección de un coche*] smoothness

suavizante *sm* conditioner ▶ **suavizante para la ropa** fabric conditioner

suavizar *vt* ❶ [*generalmente*] to soften ❷ [*ropa, cabello*] to condition ❸ [*ascensión, conducción, tarea*] to ease ❹ [*clima*] to make milder ❺ [*sabor, olor, color*] to tone down ❻ [*alisar*] to smooth

subalquilar *vt* to sublet

subalterno, na *sm, f* [*empleado*] subordinate

subasta *sf* ❶ [*venta pública*] auction • **sacar algo a subasta** to put something up for auction ❷ [*contrata pública*] tender • **sacar algo a subasta** to put something out to tender

subastar *vt* to auction

subcampeón, ona *sm, f* runner-up

subconsciente *adj* & *sm* subconscious ☼ *Los adjetivos ingleses son invariables.*

subdesarrollado, da *adj* underdeveloped ☼ *Los adjetivos ingleses son invariables.*

subdesarrollo *sm* underdevelopment

subdirector, ra *sm, f* assistant manager

subdirectorio *sm* INFORMÁTICA subdirectory

súbdito, ta *sm, f* ❶ [*subordinado*] subject ❷ [*ciudadano*] citizen

subestimar *vt* ❶ to underestimate ❷ [*infravalorar*] to underrate

subir ◆ *vi* ❶ [*a piso, azotea*] to go/come up • **voy a subir por las escaleras** I'm going to go up the stairs • **sube que quiero decirte algo** come up, I want to tell you something ❷ [*a montaña, cima*] to climb • **subió la montaña** she climbed the mountain ❸ [*aumentar - precio, temperatura*] to go up ; to rise ; [- *cauce, marea*] to rise ❹ [*montar - en avión, barco*] to get on ; [- *en coche*] to get in • **sube al coche** get into the car ❺ [*cuenta, importe*] • **subir a** to come o amount to ❻ [*de categoría*] to be promoted

◆ *vt* ❶ [*ascender - calle, escaleras*] to go/come up ; [- *pendiente, montaña*] to climb ❷ [*poner arriba*] to lift up ❸ [*llevar arriba*] to take/bring up • **voy a subir la televisión a mi cuarto** I'm going to take the television up to my room • **por favor, súbeme el suéter que dejé en la cocina** please bring me up the sweater that I left in the kitchen ❹ [*aumentar - precio, peso*] to put up ; to increase ; [- *volumen de radio* ETC] to turn up ❺ [*montar*] • **subir algo/a alguien a** to lift something/somebody onto ❻ [*alzar - mano, bandera, voz*] to raise ; [- *persiana*] to roll up ; [- *ventanilla*] to wind up

■ **subirse** *v pronominal* ❶ [*ascender*] • **subirse a a)** [*árbol*] to climb up **b)** [*mesa*] to climb onto **c)** [*piso*] to go/come up to ❷ [*montarse*] • **subirse a a)** [*tren,*

avión] to get on ; to board **b)** [*caballo, bicicleta*] to mount **c)** [*coche*] to get into • **el taxi paró y me subí** the taxi stopped and I got in ❸ [*alzarse - pantalón, mangas*] to roll up ; [- *zíper*] to zip up ; [- *pantalones, calcetines*] to pull up

súbito, ta *adj* sudden • **de súbito** suddenly ☼ *Los adjetivos ingleses son invariables.*

subjetivo, va *adj* subjective ☼ *Los adjetivos ingleses son invariables.*

subjuntivo, va *adj* subjunctive ☼ *Los adjetivos ingleses son invariables.*

■ **subjuntivo** *sm* subjunctive

sublevación *sf* uprising

sublevamiento *sm* = **sublevación**

sublevar *vt* ❶ [*amotinar*] to stir up ❷ [*indignar*] to infuriate

sublime *adj* sublime ☼ *Los adjetivos ingleses son invariables.*

submarinismo *sm* skin-diving

submarinista *smf* skin-diver

submarino, na *adj* underwater ☼ *Los adjetivos ingleses son invariables.*

■ **submarino** *sm* submarine

subnormal ◆ *adj* ❶ despectivo [*minusválido*] subnormal ❷ despectivo [*imbécil*] moronic ☼ *Los adjetivos ingleses son invariables.*

◆ *smf* despectivo [*imbécil*] moron

suboficial *sm* MILITAR non-commissioned officer

subordinado, da *adj* & *sm, f* subordinate ☼ *Los adjetivos ingleses son invariables.*

subordinar *vt* [*generalmente*] GRAMÁTICA to subordinate • **subordinar algo a algo** to subordinate something to something

subrayar *vt* literal & figurado to underline

subsanar *vt* ❶ [*solucionar*] to resolve ❷ [*corregir*] to correct

subsecretario, ria *sm, f* ❶ [*de secretario*] assistant secretary ❷ [*de ministro*] undersecretary

subsidio *sm* benefit ▶ **subsidio de desempelo** unemployment benefit ▶ **subsidio de invalidez** disability allowance

subsistencia *sf* [*vida*] subsistence

subsistir *vi* ❶ [*vivir*] to live ❷ [*sobrevivir*] to survive

substancia = **sustancia**

substituir = **sustituir**

subsuelo *sm* subsoil

subterráneo, a *adj* underground ☼ *Los adjetivos ingleses son invariables.*

■ **subterráneo** *sm* basement

subtítulo *sm* [*generalmente*] CINE subtitle

suburbio *sm* suburb

subvención *sf* subsidy

subvencionar *vt* to subsidize

subversión *sf* subversion

subversivo, va *adj* subversive ·𝕺· *Los adjetivos ingleses son invariables.*

suceder ◆ *v impersonal* [*ocurrir*] to happen • **suceda lo que suceda** whatever happens

◆ *vi* [*venir después*] • **suceder a** to follow • **a la guerra sucedieron años muy tristes** the war was followed by years of misery

sucesión *sf* [*generalmente*] succession

sucesivamente *adv* successively • **y así sucesivamente** and so on

sucesivo, va *adj* ❶ [*consecutivo*] successive ❷ [*siguiente*] • **en días sucesivos les informaremos** we'll let you know over the next few days • **en lo sucesivo** in future ·𝕺· *Los adjetivos ingleses son invariables.*

suceso *sm* ❶ [*acontecimiento*] event ❷ ·𝕺· *generalmente pl* [*hecho delictivo*] crime • **sección de sucesos** accident and crime reports ❸ [*incidente*] incident

sucesor, ra *sm, f* successor

suciedad *sf* ❶ [*cualidad*] dirtiness ·𝕺· *incontable* ❷ [*porquería*] dirt

sucinto, ta *adj* [*conciso*] succinct ·𝕺· *Los adjetivos ingleses son invariables.*

sucio, cia *adj* ❶ [*generalmente*] dirty ❷ [*al comer, trabajar*] messy ❸ [*juego*] dirty ❹ [*borrador*] • **en sucio** in rough ·𝕺· *Los adjetivos ingleses son invariables.*

suculento, ta *adj* tasty ·𝕺· *Los adjetivos ingleses son invariables.*

sucumbir *vi* ❶ [*rendirse, ceder*] • **sucumbir (a)** to succumb (to) • **era difícil no sucumbir a su encanto** it was difficult not to succumb to her charms ❷ [*fallecer*] to die

sucursal *sf* branch

sudadera *sf* [*prenda*] sweatshirt

Sudáfrica *nombre propio* South Africa

sudafricano, na *adj & sm, f* South African ·𝕺· *Los adjetivos ingleses son invariables.*

sudar *vi* [*generalmente*] to sweat

sudeste, sureste ◆ *adj* ❶ [*posición, parte*] southeast ❷ [*dirección, viento*] southeasterly ·𝕺· *Los adjetivos ingleses son invariables.*

◆ *sm* southeast

sudoeste, suroeste ◆ *adj* ❶ [*posición, parte*] southwest ❷ [*dirección, viento*] southwesterly ·𝕺· *Los adjetivos ingleses son invariables.*

◆ *sm* southwest

sudor *sm* sweat • **sudor frío** cold sweat

sudoroso, sa *adj* sweaty ·𝕺· *Los adjetivos ingleses son invariables.*

Suecia *nombre propio* Sweden

suegro, gra *sm, f* father-in-law, *femenino* mother-in-law

suela *sf* sole

expresión no llegarle a alguien a la suela del zapato not to hold a candle to somebody

sueldo *sm* ❶ salary, *plural* salaries ❷ [*semanal*] wage

suelo *sm* ❶ [*pavimento - en interiores*] floor ; [*- en el exterior*] ground • **caerse al suelo** to fall over ❷ [*terreno, territorio*] soil ❸ [*para edificar*] land ❹ [*base*] bottom

expresiones besar el suelo to fall flat on your face ◗ echar por el suelo un plan to ruin a project ◗ estar por los suelos a) [*persona, precio*] to be at rock bottom b) [*productos*] to be dirt cheap ◗ poner por los suelos to run down → **soler**

suelto, ta *adj* ❶ [*generalmente*] loose • **llevaba una blusa suelta** she wore a loose shirt • **te queda bien el pelo suelto** you look good with your hair loose ❷ [*botón, cordón* ETC] loose • **este tornillo está suelto** this screw is loose • **andar suelto a)** [*en libertad*] to be free b) [*en fuga*] to be at large ❸ [*separado*] separate • **no los vendemos sueltos** we don't sell them separately ❹ [*lenguaje, estilo*] fluent ❺ [*desenvuelto*] comfortable ·𝕺· *Los adjetivos ingleses son invariables.*

sueño *sm* ❶ [*ganas de dormir*] • **¡qué sueño!** I'm really sleepy! • **tener sueño** to be sleepy ❷ [*estado*] sleep • **es falta de sueño** it's lack of sleep • **coger el sueño** to get to sleep ❸ [*imagen mental, objetivo, quimera*] dream • **tuve un sueño muy raro** I had a very strange dream • **en sueños** in a dream • **ni en sueños** *figurado* no way

suero *sm* ❶ MEDICINA serum ❷ [*de la leche*] whey

suerte *sf* [*fortuna*] luck • **desear suerte a alguien** to wish somebody luck • **tocar en suerte a alguien** to fall to somebody's lot • **echar algo a suertes** to draw lots for something • **estar de suerte** to be in luck • **por suerte** luckily • **¡qué suerte!** that was lucky! • **tener (buena) suerte** to be lucky • **tener mala suerte** to be unlucky • **traer mala suerte** to bring bad luck

expresiones de suerte que in such a way that ◗ la suerte está echada the die is cast ◗ toda suerte de all manner of

desearle suerte a alguien

- **Best of luck!** ¡Te deseo mucha suerte!
- **Good luck.** ¡(Buena) suerte!
- **I wish you all the best.** Te deseo muchas cosas buenas.
- **Fingers crossed.** Toco madera.

suéter (pl suéteres) *sm* sweater

suficiente ◆ *adj* [*bastante*] enough • **no había suficiente comida** there wasn't enough food • **no llevo (dinero) suficiente** I don't have enough (money) on me • **no tienes la estatura suficiente** you're not tall enough ·𝕺· *Los adjetivos ingleses son invariables.*

◆ *sm* [*calificación*] pass

sufragio *sm* suffrage

sufrimiento *sm* suffering

sufrir ◆ *vt* ❶ [*generalmente*] to suffer • **no hagas sufrir a tu mamá** don't make your mom suffer ❷ [*accidente*] to have ❸ [*soportar*] to put up with • **tengo que sufrir sus manías** I have to put up with his idiosyncrasies ❹ [*experimentar - cambios* ETC] to undergo

S

◆ *vi* [*padecer*] to suffer • **ha sufrido mucho** he has suffered a lot • **sufrir de** [*enfermedad*] to suffer from • **sufre de asma** she suffers from asthma • **sufre del estómago** he has a stomach complaint • **sufre del corazón** he suffers from a heart condition

sugerencia *sf* suggestion • **hacer una sugerencia** to make a suggestion

sugerente *adj* evocative:☿ *Los adjetivos ingleses son invariables.*

sugerir *vt* ❶ [*proponer*] to suggest • **sugerir a alguien que haga algo** to suggest that somebody should do something ❷ [*evocar*] to evoke

sugestión *sf* suggestion

sugestionar *vt* to influence

sugestivo, va *adj* ❶ [*atrayente*] attractive ❷ [*que sugiere*] stimulating:☿ *Los adjetivos ingleses son invariables.*

suicida ◆ *adj* suicidal:☿ *Los adjetivos ingleses son invariables.*

◆ *smf* ❶ [*por naturaleza*] suicidal person ❷ [*suicidado*] person who has committed suicide

suicidarse *v pronominal* to commit suicide

suicidio *sm* suicide

Suiza *nombre propio* Switzerland

suizo, za *adj* & *sm, f* Swiss:☿ *Los adjetivos ingleses son invariables.*

sujetador *sm* bra

sujetar *vt* ❶ [*sostener*] to hold ❷ [*agarrar*] to hold down ❸ [*papeles*] to fasten together ❹ [*someter*] to subdue

sujeto, ta *adj* ❶ [*agarrado - objeto*] fastened ❷ [*expuesto*] • **sujeto a** subject to:☿ *Los adjetivos ingleses son invariables.*

■ **sujeto** *sm* ❶ [*generalmente*] Gramática subject ❷ [*individuo*] individual

sultán *sm* sultan

suma *sf* ❶ Matemáticas [*acción*] addition; [*resultado*] total ❷ [*conjunto - de conocimientos, datos*] total; sum; [*- de dinero*] sum ❸ [*resumen*] • **en suma** in short

sumamente *adv* extremely

sumar *vt* ❶ Matemáticas to add together • **sumar algo a algo** to add something to something • **cuatro y cuatro suman ocho** four plus four equals eight ❷ [*costar*] to come to

sumergible *adj* waterproof:☿ *Los adjetivos ingleses son invariables.*

sumergir *vt* ❶ [*hundir*] to submerge ❷ [*con fuerza*] to plunge ❸ [*bañar*] to dip

suministrador, ra *sm, f* supplier

suministrar *vt* to supply • **suministrar algo a alguien** to supply somebody with something

suministro *sm* ❶ [*generalmente*] supply ❷ [*acto*] supplying

sumir *vt* • **sumir a alguien en** to plunge somebody into

sumo, ma *adj* ❶ [*supremo*] highest ❷ [*gran*] extreme:☿ *Los adjetivos ingleses son invariables.*

suntuoso, sa *adj* sumptuous:☿ *Los adjetivos ingleses son invariables.*

súper ◆ *sm* familiar supermarket

◆ *sf* ❶ (gasolina) súper ≃ premium gas

superable *adj* surmountable:☿ *Los adjetivos ingleses son invariables.*

superar *vt* ❶ [*mejorar*] to beat ❷ [*récord*] to break • **superó la marca mundial** he broke the world record • **superar algo/a alguien en algo** to beat something/somebody in something ❸ [*ser superior*] to surpass • **los supera a todos en agilidad** she surpasses them all in agility ❹ [*adelantar - corredor*] to overtake ❺ [*época, técnica*] • **estar superado** to have been superseded ❻ [*vencer - dificultad* etc] to overcome • **tiene que superar su timidez** he has to overcome his shyness

superávit *sm invariable* surplus

superdotado, da *sm, f* extremely gifted person

superficial *adj* superficial:☿ *Los adjetivos ingleses son invariables.*

superficie *sf* ❶ [*generalmente*] surface • **la superficie del lago está congelada** the lake's surface is frozen • **salir a la superficie** to surface ❷ [*área*] area • **abarca una superficie de cuatro kilómetros cuadrados** it covers an area of four kilometers squared

superfluo, flua *adj* ❶ superfluous ❷ [*gasto*] unnecessary:☿ *Los adjetivos ingleses son invariables.*

superior, ra *sm, f* Religión superior, *femenino* mother superior

■ **superior** ◆ *adj* ❶ [*de arriba*] top ❷ [*mayor*] • **superior (a)** higher (than) ❸ [*mejor*] • **superior (a)** superior (to) ❹ [*excelente*] excellent ❺ Anatomía & Geografía upper ❻ Educación higher:☿ *Los adjetivos ingleses son invariables.*

◆ *sm* :☿ *generalmente pl* [*jefe*] superior

superioridad *sf* superiority • **superioridad sobre algo/alguien** superiority over something/somebody

superlativo, va *adj* ❶ [*belleza* etc] exceptional ❷ Gramática superlative:☿ *Los adjetivos ingleses son invariables.*

supermercado *sm* supermarket

superpoblación *sf* overpopulation

superponer, sobreponer *vt* figurado [*anteponer*] • **superponer algo a algo** to put something before something

superpotencia *sf* superpower

superpuesto, ta ◆ *adj* superimposed:☿ *Los adjetivos ingleses son invariables.*

◆ *participio pasado* → **superponer**

supersónico, ca *adj* supersonic:☿ *Los adjetivos ingleses son invariables.*

superstición *sf* superstition

supersticioso, sa *adj* superstitious:☿ *Los adjetivos ingleses son invariables.*

supervisar *vt* to supervise

supervisor, ra *sm, f* supervisor

supervivencia *sf* survival

superviviente, sobreviviente ✦ *adj* surviving ·�· *Los adjetivos ingleses son invariables.*
✦ *smf* survivor
suplementario, ria *adj* supplementary ·�· *Los adjetivos ingleses son invariables.*
suplemento *sm* ❶ [*generalmente*] PRENSA supplement ❷ [*complemento*] attachment
suplente *smf* ❶ [*generalmente*] stand-in ❷ TEATRO understudy ❸ DEPORTE substitute
súplica *sf* [*ruego*] plea
suplicar *vt* [*rogar*] • **suplicar algo (a alguien)** to plead for something (with somebody) • **suplicar a alguien que haga algo** to beg somebody to do something
suplicio *sm* torture
suplir *vt* ❶ [*sustituir*] • **suplir algo/a alguien (con)** to replace something/somebody (with) ❷ [*compensar*] • **suplir algo (con)** to compensate for something (with)
suponer *vt* ❶ [*creer, presuponer*] to suppose • **supongo que no has hecho la tarea** I suppose that you haven't done the homework • **supongo que sí** I suppose so ❷ [*implicar*] to involve ❸ [*significar*] to mean • **eso supone tener que levantarme más temprano** that means I'll have to get up earlier ❹ [*conjeturar*] • **lo suponía** I guessed as much • **te suponía mayor** I thought you were older
suposición *sf* assumption

hacer una suposición

• **I suppose he's away.** Supongo que está de viaje.
• **Maybe he did it deliberately.** Tal vez lo ha hecho a propósito.
• **If I'm not mistaken, it's her birthday soon.** Si no me equivoco, pronto va a ser su cumpleaños.
• **She'll probably come tomorrow.** Sin duda vendrá mañana.

supositorio *sm* suppository
supremo, ma *adj* supreme ·☽· *Los adjetivos ingleses son invariables.*
supresión *sf* ❶ [*de ley, impuesto, derecho*] abolition ❷ [*de sanciones, restricciones*] lifting ❸ [*de palabras, texto*] deletion ❹ [*de puestos de trabajo, proyectos*] axing
suprimir *vt* ❶ [*ley, impuesto, derecho*] to abolish ❷ [*sanciones, restricciones*] to lift ❸ [*palabras, texto*] to delete ❹ [*puestos de trabajo, proyectos*] to axe
supuesto, ta ✦ *participio pasado* → **suponer**
✦ *adj* ❶ [*hipotético*] supposed ❷ [*culpable, asesino*] alleged ❸ [*nombre*] false ·☽· *Los adjetivos ingleses son invariables.*
■ **por supuesto** *locución adverbial* of course • **por supuesto que no** of course not
■ **supuesto** *sm* assumption • **partimos del supuesto de que...** we work on the assumption that... • **en el supuesto de que...** assuming...

sur ✦ *adj* ❶ [*posición, parte*] south ❷ [*dirección, viento*] southerly ·☽· *Los adjetivos ingleses son invariables.*
✦ *sm* south
surcar *vt* ❶ [*tierra*] to plough ❷ [*aire, agua*] to cut through
surco *sm* ❶ [*zanja*] furrow ❷ [*señal - de disco*] groove; [*- de rueda*] rut ❸ [*arruga*] line
sureste = **sudeste**
surf, surfing *sm* surfing
surgir *vi* ❶ [*brotar*] to spring forth ❷ [*aparecer*] to appear ❸ *figurado* [*producirse*] to arise
suroeste = **sudoeste**
surrealista *adj* & *smf* surrealist ·☽· *Los adjetivos ingleses son invariables.*
surtidor *sm* ❶ [*de gasolina*] pump ❷ [*de un chorro*] spout
surtir *vt* [*proveer*] • **surtir a alguien (de)** to supply somebody (with)
susceptible *adj* ❶ [*sensible*] sensitive ❷ [*propenso a ofenderse*] touchy ❸ [*posible*] • **susceptible de** liable to ·☽· *Los adjetivos ingleses son invariables.*
suscitar *vt* [*interés, dudas, sospechas*] to arouse
suscribir *vt* ❶ [*firmar*] to sign ❷ [*ratificar*] to endorse
■ **suscribirse, subscribirse** *v pronominal* PRENSA • **suscribirse (a)** to subscribe (to) • **me suscribí a una revista** I subscribed to a magazine
suscripción *sf* subscription
suscriptor, ra *sm, f* subscriber
susodicho, cha *adj* above-mentioned ·☽· *Los adjetivos ingleses son invariables.*
suspender *vt* ❶ [*colgar*] to hang (up) • **suspender algo de algo** to hang something from something ❷ [*interrumpir*] to suspend ❸ [*aplazar*] to postpone
suspensión *sf* ❶ [*generalmente*] AUTOMÓVILES suspension ❷ [*aplazamiento*] postponement
suspenso, sa *adj* ❶ [*colgado*] • **suspenso de** hanging from ❷ *figurado* [*interrumpido*] • **en suspenso** pending ·☽· *Los adjetivos ingleses son invariables.*
■ **suspenso** *sm* suspense • **una historia llena de suspenso** a story filled with suspense • **una película de suspenso** a thriller
suspicacia *sf* suspicion
suspicaz *adj* suspicious ·☽· *Los adjetivos ingleses son invariables.*
suspirar *vi* [*dar suspiros*] to sigh
suspiro *sm* [*aspiración*] sigh
sustancia, substancia *sf* ❶ [*generalmente*] substance • **sin sustancia** lacking in substance ❷ [*esencia*] essence ❸ [*de alimento*] nutritional value
sustancial *adj* substantial ·☽· *Los adjetivos ingleses son invariables.*
sustancioso, sa *adj* substantial ·☽· *Los adjetivos ingleses son invariables.*
sustantivo, va *adj* GRAMÁTICA noun ·☽· *Sólo se usa delante del sustantivo.*

■ **sustantivo** *sm* Gʀᴀᴍᴀ́ᴛɪᴄᴀ noun

sustentar *vt* ❶ [*generalmente*] to support ❷ *figurado* [*mantener - argumento, teoría*] to defend

sustento *sm* ❶ [*alimento*] sustenance ❷ [*mantenimiento*] livelihood ❸ [*apoyo*] support

sustitución *sf* [*cambio*] replacement • **la sustitución de Elena por Luis** the replacement of Elena by Luis

sustituir, substituir *vt* • **sustituir (por)** to replace (with) • **sustituir a Elena por Luis** to replace Elena with Luis • **sustituir algo por algo** to substitute something with something • **puedes sustituir el azúcar por sacarina** you can substitute the sugar with saccharine

sustituto, ta *sm, f* replacement

susto *sm* fright • **pegarse un susto** to get a fright • **¡qué susto me diste!** what a scare you gave me!

sustracción *sf* ❶ [*robo*] theft ❷ Mᴀᴛᴇᴍᴀ́ᴛɪᴄᴀs subtraction

sustraer *vt* ❶ [*robar*] to steal ❷ Mᴀᴛᴇᴍᴀ́ᴛɪᴄᴀs to subtract

susurrar *vt* & *vi* to whisper • **le susurró algo al oído** he whispered something to her

susurro *sm* ❶ [*palabras*] whisper ❷ [*del agua, viento*] murmur

sutil *adj* ❶ [*generalmente*] subtle ❷ [*velo, tejido*] delicate ❸ [*brisa*] gentle ❹ [*hilo, línea*] fine ❂ *Los adjetivos ingleses son invariables.*

sutileza *sf* ❶ [*generalmente*] subtlety ❷ [*de velo, tejido*] delicacy ❸ [*de brisa*] gentleness ❹ [*de hilo, línea*] fineness

suyo, ya ♦ *adj posesivo* ❶ [*de él*] his • **este libro es suyo** this book is his • **no es asunto suyo** it's none of his business ❷ [*de ella*] hers • **un amigo suyo** a friend of hers • **no es asunto suyo** it's none of her business ❸ [*de ellos, ellas*] theirs • **¿es ésta su calle? — no, la suya es la próxima** is this their street? — no, theirs is the next one ❹ [*de usted, ustedes*] yours

expresión es muy suyo *familiar* he/she is really selfish

♦ *pronombre posesivo* ❶ • **el suyo** [*de él*] his ❷ • **el suyo** [*de ella*] hers ❸ • **el suyo** [*de cosa, animal*] its (own) ❹ • **el suyo** [*de ellos, ellas*] theirs ❺ • **el suyo** [*de usted, ustedes*] yours

expresiones de suyo in itself ❯ **hacer de las suyas** to be up to his/her ᴇᴛᴄ usual tricks ❯ **hacer suyo** to make your own ❯ **lo suyo es el teatro** he/she ᴇᴛᴄ should be on the stage ❯ **lo suyo sería volver** the proper thing to do would be to go back

T

t, T *sf* [*letra*] t ; T

tabacalero, ra *adj* tobacco ◌ *Sólo se usa delante del sustantivo.*

tabaco *sm* ❶ [*planta*] tobacco plant ❷ [*picadura*] tobacco ▶ **tabaco negro/rubio** dark/Virginia tobacco ❸ [*cigarrillos*] cigarettes *pl*

tábano *sm* horsefly

tabique *sm* [*pared*] partition (wall)

tabla *sf* ❶ [*plancha*] board • **con un par de tablas hizo una mesa** with a couple of boards he made a table ❷ [*lista, gráfico*] table ▶ **tabla de multiplicación** multiplication table ▶ **tabla periódica** o **de los elementos** periodic table ❸ NÁUTICA [*de surf, vela* ETC] board ▶ **tabla de planchar** ironing board ❹ ARTE panel

tablado *sm* ❶ [*de teatro*] stage ❷ [*de baile*] dance-floor ❸ [*plataforma*] platform

tablero *sm* ❶ [*generalmente*] board ▶ **tablero de ajedrez** chessboard ▶ **tablero de damas** checkerboard ❷ [*en baloncesto*] backboard ❸ • **tablero (de mandos)** [*de avión*] instrument panel ❹ • **tablero (de mandos)** [*de carro*] dashboard

tableta *sf* ❶ MEDICINA tablet ❷ [*de chocolate*] bar

tablón *sm* plank ▶ **tablón de anuncios** notice board

tabú (pl tabúes O tabús) *adj* & *sm* taboo ◌ *Los adjetivos ingleses son invariables.*

taburete *sm* stool

tacaño, ña *adj* mean ◌ *Los adjetivos ingleses son invariables.*

tachar *vt* ❶ [*lo escrito*] to cross out • **taché su nombre de la lista** I crossed her name from the list ❷ [*acusar*] • **tachar a alguien de algo** to accuse somebody of being something • **los tachan de machistas** they accused them of being chauvinists

tachón *sm* [*tachadura*] correction

tachuela *sf* tack

taco *sm* ❶ [*tarugo*] plug ❷ [*cuña*] wedge ❸ [*de billar*] cue ❹ [*tortilla de maíz*] taco

tacón *sm* heel • **zapatos de tacón** high-heeled shoes

táctico, ca *adj* tactical ◌ *Los adjetivos ingleses son invariables.*

■ **táctica** *sf* tactics *pl* • **van a tener que cambiar de táctica** they're going to have to change tactics

tacto *sm* ❶ [*sentido*] (sense of) touch • **es suave al tacto** it's soft to the touch ❷ [*textura*] feel ❸ *figurado* [*delicadeza*] tact • **le falta tacto** she's lacking tact

tajante *adj* [*categórico*] categorical ◌ *Los adjetivos ingleses son invariables.*

tal

◆ *adj*

❶ [*indica la intensidad*] such
• **lo dijo con tal seguridad que todos lo creyeron** he said it with such assurance that everyone believed him

❷ [*para designar, sin definir con precisión*] such
• **mañana a tal hora** tomorrow at such a time

❸ [*de este tipo*]
• **tal cosa jamás se ha visto** we've never seen anything like it
• **en tales condiciones** in such conditions

❹ [*antes de un nombre propio*]
• **te ha llamado un tal Pérez** somebody called Pérez called for you

◌ *Los adjetivos ingleses son invariables.*

◆ *pronombre*

expresiones **son tal para cual** they're made for each other ▶ **que si tal que si cual tal y tal** this and that ▶ **y tal** and so on

■ **qué tal**

◆ *locución adverbial*

[*para preguntar sobre el estado o alguna novedad*]
• **¿qué tal?** how are you?
• **¿qué tal la entrevista?** how did your interview go?
• **¿qué tal estuvieron las vacaciones?** how did your vacation go?

■ **tal cual**

◆ *locución adverbial*

• **se lo dije tal cual, sin añadir ningún comentario** I told him straight without adding anything

■ **tal vez**

◆ *locución adverbial* maybe

taladrar *vt* ❶ [*agujerear*] to drill ❷ *figurado* [*sujeto: sonido*] to pierce

taladro *sm* ❶ [*taladradora*] drill ❷ [*agujero*] drill hole

talar *vt* to fell

talco *sm* talcum powder

talento *sm* ❶ [*don natural*] talent • **tiene talento para el dibujo** he has a talent for drawing • **de talento** talented ❷ [*inteligencia*] intelligence

talibán ◆ *adj* taliban ⚲ *Los adjetivos ingleses son invariables.*

◆ *sm* taliban

talismán *sm* talisman

talla *sf* ❶ [*medida*] size • **¿qué talla usas?** what size are you? ❷ [*estatura*] height ❸ *figurado* [*capacidad*] stature ❹ ARTE [*en madera*] carving; [*en piedra*] sculpture

expresión **dar la talla** to be up to it

tallado, da *adj* ❶ [*madera*] carved ❷ [*piedras preciosas*] cut ⚲ *Los adjetivos ingleses son invariables.*

tallar *vt* ❶ [*madera*] to carve ❷ [*piedras preciosas*] to cut

tallarín *sm* ⚲ *generalmente pl* noodle

taller *sm* ❶ [*generalmente*] workshop ❷ AUTOMÓVILES garage ❸ ARTE studio

tallo *sm* ❶ stem ❷ [*brote*] sprout

talón *sm* ❶ [*generalmente*] ANATOMÍA heel ▶ **talón de Aquiles** *figurado* Achilles' heel ❷ [*cheque*] check ▶ **talón bancario** cashier's check ▶ **talón devuelto/en blanco** bounced/blank check ❸ [*matriz*] stub

expresión **pisarle a alguien los talones** to be hot on somebody's heels

talonario *sm* ❶ [*de cheques*] check book ❷ [*de recibos*] receipt book

tamal *sm* tamale

tamaño, ña *adj* such • **¡cómo pudo decir tamaña estupidez!** how could he say such a stupid thing! ⚲ *Los adjetivos ingleses son invariables.*

■ **tamaño** *sm* size • **¿qué tamaño tiene?** what size is he? • **de gran tamaño** large • **de tamaño familiar** family-size • **de tamaño natural** life-size

también *adv* also; too • **a mí también me regalaron uno** they also gave me one; they gave me one too • **canta y también toca el piano** he sings and he also plays the piano • **yo también** me too • **Juan está enfermo — Elena también** Juan is sick — so is Elena • **quiero ir — nosotros también** I want to go — we do too • **también a mí me gusta** I like it too; I also like it

tambor *sm* ❶ MÚSICA & TECNOLOGÍA drum ❷ [*de pistola*] cylinder ❸ ANATOMÍA eardrum

tampoco *adv* neither • **ella no va y tú tampoco** she's not going and neither are you • **no puedo hacerlo — yo tampoco** I can't do it — me neither • **no sabía que tenía un hermano — nosotros tampoco** she didn't know that he had a brother — neither did we • **yo tampoco lo sé** I don't know either • **no estu-**

dió ni tampoco hizo la tarea he didn't study and he didn't do his homework either

tampón *sm* ❶ [*sello*] stamp ❷ [*almohadilla*] inkpad ❸ [*para la menstruación*] tampon

tan *adv* ❶ [*mucho*] so • **tan grande/deprisa** so big/quickly • **¡qué película tan larga!** what a long film! • **tan... que...** so... that... • **lo pusiste tan arriba que no lo puedo alcanzar** you put it so high up that I can't reach it • **tan es así que...** so much so that... ❷ [*en comparaciones*] • **tan... como...** as... as... • **no es tan inteligente como su hermano** he's not as intelligent as his brother

tanda *sf* ❶ [*grupo, lote*] group ❷ [*serie*] series ❸ [*de inyecciones*] course

tándem (*pl* tándemes O tándems O tándem) *sm* ❶ [*bicicleta*] tandem ❷ [*pareja*] duo

tangente *sf* tangent

expresión **salirse por la tangente** to change the subject

tango *sm* tango

tanque *sm* ❶ MILITAR tank ❷ [*vehículo cisterna*] tanker ❸ [*depósito*] tank

tantear ◆ *vt* ❶ [*sopesar - peso, precio, cantidad*] to try to guess; [- *problema, posibilidades, ventajas*] to weigh up ❷ [*probar, sondear*] to test (out)

◆ *vi* [*andar a tientas*] to feel your way

tanteo *sm* ❶ [*prueba, sondeo*] testing out ❷ [*de posibilidades, ventajas*] weighing up ❸ [*de contrincante, puntos débiles*] sizing up ❹ [*puntuación*] score

---

tanto, ta

◆ *adj*

❶ [*indica una gran cantidad, una intensidad*] so many

• **¡tiene tantos libros!** she has so many books
• **¡tengo tantas ganas de verte!** I'm really looking forward to seeing you

❷ [*indica una cantidad indeterminada*] so much

• **nos daban tanto dinero al día** they gave us so much money per day

❸ [*introduce una comparación*]

• **no tengo tanto dinero como tú** I don't have as much money as you

• **tenemos tanta hambre como vosotros** we're just as hungry as you are

❹ [*después de un nombre, indica una adición insignificante*]

• **tiene cincuenta y tantos años** she's fifty something

⚲ *Los adjetivos ingleses son invariables.*

◆ *pronombre*

❶ [*en comparaciones*] as much; as many

• **tienes muchos vestidos, yo no tantos** you have a lot of dresses, I don't have as many

• **había mucha gente aquí, allí no tanta** there were a lot of people here, not so many there

- **otro tanto** as much again
- **le ocurrió otro tanto** the same happened to her
❷ [*indica una cantidad o una fecha indeterminada*] so many
- **supongamos que vengan tantos...** let's say so many come...
- **a tantos de febrero** on such and such a date in August
■ **tanto**
◆ *sm*
❶ [*punto ganado en una competencia*]
- **marcar un tanto** to score a point
❷ [*en futbol*] to score a goal
❸ *familiar* [*ventaja*]
- **es un tanto a su favor** that's something in his favor
- **apuntarse un tanto (a favor)** to notch up a point
❹ [*indica una suma indeterminada*]
- **le pagan un tanto por página** she gets paid so much per page
❺ [*en expresiones*]
▸ **tanto por ciento** percentage
- **intento ponerme al tanto de las novedades** I try and keep up with the latest things
- **hay que estar bien al tanto, por aquí hay carteristas** you have to keep your wits about you because there are pickpockets around
expresión **márcate un tanto y déjame salir** you'll get some brownie points if you let me go out
◆ *adv*
❶ [*indica el límite de la intensidad*] so much
- **no me sirvas tanto** don't give me so much
❷ [*indica la intensidad*]
- **la quiere tanto que no podría vivir sin ella** he loves her so much he couldn't live without her
- **de eso hace tanto que ni me acuerdo** it's been so long since that that I don't even remember it
❸ [*introduce una comparación*] as much as
- **trabajo tanto como él** I work as much as he does
expresión **¡y tanto!** you bet!
■ **tanto como**
◆ *locución conjuntiva*
[*en comparaciones*] as much
- **de eso sé tanto como él** I know about as much about that as he does

tapa *sf*❶ [*de caja, baúl, recipiente*] lid ❷ [*de libro*] cover ❸ [*de zapato*] heel plate ❹ [*de frasco*] stopper
expresión **volarse la tapa de los sesos** *familiar* to blow your brains out

tapa ≠ tap

- La palabra inglesa **tap** es un falso amigo que significa *grifo*. *Tapa* se traduce al inglés por **lid**.

tapadera *sf*❶ [*tapa*] lid ❷ [*para encubrir*] front

tapar *vt*❶ [*cerrar - ataúd, cofre*] to close (the lid of); [*- olla, caja*] to put the lid on; [*- botella*] to put the top on ❷ [*ocultar, cubrir*] to cover ❸ [*no dejar ver*] to block out ❹ [*obstruir*] to block ❺ [*abrigar - con ropa*] to wrap up; [*- en la cama*] to tuck in ❻ [*empaste*] to fill • **me taparon una muela** I had a tooth filled
■ **taparse** *v pronominal*❶ [*cubrirse*] to cover (up) • **se tapó la boca con la mano** she covered her mouth with her hand ❷ [*abrigarse - con ropa*] to wrap up; [*- en la cama*] to tuck yourself in • **tápate bien** wrap yourself up well

tapete *sm*❶ [*paño*] runner ❷ [*de billar, para cartas*] baize ❸ [*alfombra*] rug • **un tapete persa** a Persian rug

tapia *sf* (stone) wall

tapiar *vt*❶ [*cercar*] to wall in ❷ [*enladrillar*] to brick up

tapiz *sm*❶ [*para la pared*] tapestry ❷ *figurado* [*de nieve, flores*] carpet

tapizado *sm*❶ [*de mueble*] upholstery ❷ [*de pared*] tapestries *pl*

tapizar *vt*❶ [*mueble*] to upholster ❷ *figurado* [*campos, calles*] to carpet

tapón *sm*❶ [*para tapar - botellas, frascos*] stopper; [*- de corcho*] cork; [*- de metal, plástico*] cap; [*- de bañera, lavabo*] plug ❷ [*en el oído - de cerumen*] wax · ❂ *incontable* in the ear; [*- de algodón*] earplug ❸ [*en baloncesto*] block ❹ [*fusible*] fuse

taponar *vt*❶ [*lavadero*] to put the plug in ❷ [*salida*] to block ❸ [*tubería*] to stop up

taquería *sf*❶ [*quiosco*] taco stand ❷ [*restaurante*] taco restaurant

taquilla *sf*❶ [*ventanilla - generalmente*] ticket office; CINE & TEATRO box office • **en taquilla** at the ticket/box office ❷ [*recaudación*] takings *pl* ❸ [*armario*] locker

taquillero, ra ◆ *adj* • **es un espectáculo taquillero** the show is a box-office hit · ❂ *Los adjetivos ingleses son invariables.*
◆ *sm, f* ticket clerk

tara *sf*❶ [*defecto*] defect ❷ [*peso*] tare

tarántula *sf* tarantula

tararear *vt* to hum

tardanza *sf* lateness

tardar *vi*❶ [*llevar tiempo*] to take • **esto va a tardar** this will take time • **tardó un año en hacerlo** she took a year to do it • **¿cuánto tardarás (en hacerlo)?** how long will it take you (to do it)? ❷ [*retrasarse*] to be late ❸ [*ser lento*] • **¡no tardéis!** don't be long! • **tardar en hacer algo** to take a long time to do something • **no tardaron en hacerlo** they were quick to do it • **a más tardar** at the latest

tarde ◆ *sf*❶ [*hasta las cinco*] afternoon ❷ [*después de las cinco*] evening • **por la tarde a)** [*hasta las cinco*] in the afternoon **b)** [*después de las cinco*] in the evening • **buenas tardes a)** [*hasta las cinco*] good afternoon **b)** [*después de las cinco*] good evening • **muy de tarde en tarde** very occasionally
expresión **de tarde en tarde** from time to time

T

◆ *adv* ❶ [*generalmente*] late • **¡apúrate!, que vamos a llegar tarde** hurry! we're going to arrive late • **tarde o temprano** sooner or later ❷ [*en exceso*] too late • **ya es tarde para eso** it's too late for that now

tardío, a *adj* ❶ [*generalmente*] late ❷ [*intento, decisión*] belated ᄋ̣̈: *Los adjetivos ingleses son invariables.*

tarea *sf* ❶ [*generalmente*] task • **tienen la tarea de cuidar los parques** they have the task of looking after the parks ❷ EDUCACIÓN homework • **no ha hecho las tareas** she hasn't done the homework ▶ **tareas de la casa** housework ᄋ̣̈: *incontable*

tarifa *sf* ❶ [*precio*] charge ❷ COMERCIO tariff ❸ [*por servicio*] rate ▶ **tarifa plana** flat rate ❹ [*en transportes*] fare ❺ ᄋ̣̈: *generalmente pl* [*lista*] price list

tarjeta *sf* [*generalmente*] INFORMÁTICA card ▶ **tarjeta amarilla/roja** DEPORTE yellow/red card ▶ **tarjeta regalo** gift card ▶ **tarjeta de crédito/débito** credit/debit card ▶ **tarjeta de felicitación** greetings card ▶ **tarjeta postal** postcard ▶ **tarjeta recargable** rechargeable card ▶ **tarjeta de sonido/video** sound/video card ▶ **tarjeta telefónica** phonecard ▶ **tarjeta de visita** calling card

tarrina *sf* tub

tarro *sm* [*recipiente*] jar

tarta *sf* tart

tartamudear *vi* to stammer

tartamudo, da ◆ *adj* stammering ᄋ̣̈: *Los adjetivos ingleses son invariables.*
◆ *sm, f* stammerer

tasa *sf* ❶ [*índice*] rate ▶ **tasa de desempleo** unemployment rate ▶ **tasa de mortalidad** death rate ▶ **tasa de natalidad** birth rate ❷ [*impuesto*] tax ▶ **tasas de aeropuerto** airport tax ❸ EDUCACIÓN • **tasas** fees

tata *sm familiar* daddy

tatarabuelo, la *sm, f* great-great-grandfather, *femenino* grandmother

tatuaje *sm* [*dibujo*] tattoo

tatuar *vt* to tattoo

tauro ◆ *sm* [*zodiaco*] Taurus
◆ *smf* [*persona*] Taurean

tauromaquia *sf* bullfighting

taxi *sm* taxi

taxímetro *sm* taximeter

taxista *smf* taxi driver

taza *sf* ❶ [*para beber*] cup • **una taza de té a)** [*recipiente*] a teacup **b)** [*contenido*] a cup of tea ❷ [*de excusado*] bowl

tazón *sm* bowl

te *pronombre personal* ❶ ᄋ̣̈: *complemento directo* you • **te llamó ayer** she called you yesterday • **le gustaría verte** she'd like to see you ❷ ᄋ̣̈: *complemento indirecto* (to) you • **te lo dio** he gave it to you • **te tiene miedo** he's afraid of you ❸ ᄋ̣̈: *reflexivo* yourself • **sólo si te portas bien** only if you behave yourself ❹ ᄋ̣̈: *valor impersonal familiar* • **si te dejas pisar, estás perdido** if you let people walk all over you, you've had it

té (pl tés) *sm* tea • **¿quieres té?** do you want some tea?

teatral *adj* ❶ [*de teatro - generalmente*] theater ᄋ̣̈: *Sólo se usa delante del sustantivo.* ; [*- grupo*] drama ᄋ̣̈: *Sólo se usa delante del sustantivo.* ❷ [*exagerado*] theatrical

teatro *sm* ❶ [*generalmente*] theater • **fuimos al teatro** we went to the theater ▶ **teatro de la ópera** opera house ❷ *figurado* [*fingimiento*] playacting

techo *sm* ❶ [*generalmente*] roof • **había palomas encima del techo** there were pigeons on the roof • **bajo techo** under cover ▶ **techo solar** AUTOMÓVILES sun roof ❷ [*dentro de casa*] ceiling • **dos lámparas colgaban del techo** two light fixtures hung from the ceiling ❸ *figurado* [*límite*] ceiling

techumbre *sf* roof

tecla *sf* [*generalmente*] INFORMÁTICA & MÚSICA key

teclado *sm* [*generalmente*] MÚSICA keyboard

teclear *vt* & *vi* ❶ [*en computador* ETC] to type ❷ [*en piano*] to play

técnico, ca ◆ *adj* technical ᄋ̣̈: *Los adjetivos ingleses son invariables.*
◆ *sm, f* ❶ [*mecánico*] technician ❷ [*experto*] expert ❸ DEPORTE [*entrenador*] coach
■ **técnica** *sf* ❶ [*generalmente*] technique ❷ [*tecnología*] technology

tecnócrata *smf* technocrat

tecnología *sf* technology, *plural* technologies ▶ **tecnologías de la información** information technology ▶ **tecnología punta** state-of-the-art technology

tecnológico, ca *adj* technological ᄋ̣̈: *Los adjetivos ingleses son invariables.*

tecolote *sm* ❶ [*búho*] owl ❷ [*policía*] cop *(on night patrol)*

tedio *sm* boredom

tedioso, sa *adj* tedious ᄋ̣̈: *Los adjetivos ingleses son invariables.*

Tegucigalpa *nombre propio* Tegucigalpa

teja *sf* [*de tejado*] tile

tejado *sm* roof

tejano, na ◆ *adj* [*de Texas*] Texan ᄋ̣̈: *Los adjetivos ingleses son invariables.*
◆ *sm, f* [*persona*] Texan

tejemaneje *sm familiar* ❶ [*maquinación*] intrigue ❷ [*ajetreo*] to-do

tejer ◆ *vt* ❶ [*generalmente*] to weave ❷ [*labor de punto*] to knit ❸ [*telaraña*] to spin
◆ *vi* ❶ [*hacer gano*] to crochet ❷ [*hacer punto*] to knit

tejido *sm* ❶ [*tela*] fabric ❷ [*en industria*] textile ❸ ANATOMÍA tissue ❹ [*labor de punto*] knitting

tejón *sm* badger

tel. tel.

tela *sf* ❶ [*tejido*] fabric ❷ [*retal*] piece of material ▶ **tela de araña** cobweb ▶ **tela metálica** wire netting ❸ ARTE [*lienzo*] canvas
expresión **poner en tela de juicio** to call into question

T

telar *sm* ❶ [*máquina*] loom ❷ ☿ *generalmente pl* [*fábrica*] textiles mill

telaraña *sf* cobweb • **el desván está lleno de telarañas** the attic is full of cobwebs • **había un insecto atrapado en la telaraña** there was an insect trapped in the spiderweb ▶ **la telaraña mundial** INFORMÁTICA the (World Wide) Web

tele *sf familiar* TV

telecomedia *sf* sitcom

telecomunicación *sf* [*medio*] telecommunication

teledirigido, da *adj* remote-controlled ☿ *Los adjetivos ingleses son invariables.*

teleférico *sm* cable-car

telefilme, telefilm (pl telefilms) *sm* TV movie

telefonear *vt* & *vi* to phone

telefónico, ca *adj* telephone ☿ *Sólo se usa delante del sustantivo.*

telefonista *smf* telephonist

teléfono *sm* ❶ [*generalmente*] telephone • **no tiene teléfono** he doesn't have a telephone • **contestar el teléfono** to answer the phone • **hablar por teléfono** to talk on the phone • **llamar por teléfono** to call ▶ **teléfono celular** cell phone ▶ **teléfono fijo/inalámbrico** land line/cordless phone • **teléfono público** public phone ❷ ▶ **(número de) teléfono** telephone number • **¿me das tu teléfono?** will you give me your telephone number?

telegrama *sm* telegram

telemando *sm* remote control

telenovela *sf* television soap opera

telepatía *sf* telepathy

telescópico, ca *adj* telescopic ☿ *Los adjetivos ingleses son invariables.*

telescopio *sm* telescope

telesilla *sm* chair lift

telespectador, ra *sm, f* viewer

telesquí *sm* ski lift

teletexto *sm* Teletext®

teletrabajo *sm* telecommuting

televenta *sf* ❶ [*por teléfono*] telesales pl ❷ [*por televisión*] teleshopping

televidente *smf* viewer

televisar *vt* to televise

televisión *sf* ❶ [*sistema, empresa*] television • **lo vimos por la televisión** we saw it on television ▶ **televisión digital** digital television ▶ **televisión a color** color television ▶ **televisión privada/pública** commercial/public television ❷ [*televisor*] television (set)

televisor *sm* television (set) ▶ **televisor de pantalla plana** flatscreen television

telón *sm* [*de escenario - delante*] curtain ; [*- detrás*] backcloth ▶ **el telón de acero** HISTORIA the Iron Curtain ▶ **telón de fondo** backdrop

tema *sm* ❶ [*asunto*] subject • **¿qué opinas del tema?** what's your opinion on the subject? ❷ MÚSICA [*de composición, película*] theme • **un tema musical** a mu-

sical theme ❸ [*canción*] song ❹ EDUCACIÓN [*de asignatura, oposiciones*] topic • **el tema de mi proyecto es el medioambiente** the topic of my project is the environment ❺ [*en libro de texto*] unit

temario *sm* [*de asignatura*] curriculum

temático, ca *adj* thematic ☿ *Los adjetivos ingleses son invariables.*

■ **temática** *sf* subject matter

temblar *vi* ❶ [*tiritar*] • **temblar (de) a)** [*generalmente*] to tremble (with) **b)** [*de frío*] to shiver (with) • **temblaba de miedo** she was trembling with fear • **estaba temblando de frío** he was shivering with cold • **tiemblo por lo que pueda pasarle** I shudder to think what could happen to him ❷ [*vibrar - suelo, edificio, vehículo*] to shudder ; [*- voz*] to tremble • **le temblaban las manos** her hands were trembling

temblor *sm* ▶ **un temblor de tierra** an earth tremor

tembloroso, sa *adj* trembling ☿ *Los adjetivos ingleses son invariables.*

temer ◆ *vt* ❶ [*tener miedo de*] to fear • **todos le temen al director** everybody fears the director ❷ [*sospechar*] to fear
◆ *vi* to be afraid • **no temas, nada te va a pasar** don't be afraid, nothing's going to happen to you • **temer por** to fear for • **temen por su vida** they fear for their lives

temerario, ria *adj* ❶ rash ❷ [*conducción*] reckless ☿ *Los adjetivos ingleses son invariables.*

temeridad *sf* ❶ [*cualidad*] recklessness ❷ [*acción*] folly ☿ *incontable*

temeroso, sa *adj* [*receloso*] fearful ☿ *Los adjetivos ingleses son invariables.*

temible *adj* fearsome ☿ *Los adjetivos ingleses son invariables.*

temor *sm* fear • **el temor a lo desconocido** the fear of the unknown • **por temor a** ○ **de** for fear of • **no salen de noche por temor a los asaltos** they don't go out at night for fear of assault

temperamental *adj* ❶ [*cambiante*] temperamental ❷ [*impulsivo*] impulsive ☿ *Los adjetivos ingleses son invariables.*

temperamento *sm* temperament

temperatura *sf* temperature • **¿qué temperatura hace?** what's the temperature? • **le tomó la temperatura** she took his temperature

tempestad *sf* storm

tempestuoso, sa *adj literal & figurado* stormy ☿ *Los adjetivos ingleses son invariables.*

templado, da *adj* ❶ [*tibio - agua, bebida, comida*] lukewarm ❷ GEOGRAFÍA [*clima, zona*] temperate ❸ [*nervios*] steady ❹ [*persona, carácter*] calm ☿ *Los adjetivos ingleses son invariables.*

templar *vt* ❶ [*lo frío*] to warm (up) ❷ [*lo caliente*] to cool down ❸ [*nervios, ánimos*] to calm ❹ [*ira*] to restrain

templete *sm* pavilion

T

templo *sm literal* & *figurado* temple
expresión **como un templo** huge

temporada *sf* ❶ [*periodo concreto*] season • **de temporada** [*fruta, trabajo*] seasonal ▸ **temporada alta/baja** high/low season ▸ **temporada media** mid-season ❷ [*de exámenes*] period ❸ [*periodo indefinido*] (period of) time • **pasé una temporada en el extranjero** I spent some time abroad

temporal ◆ *adj* ❶ [*provisional*] temporary ❷ [*del tiempo*] time ❸ *sustantivo* ANATOMÍA & RELIGIÓN temporal:♀: *Los adjetivos ingleses son invariables.*
◆ *sm* [*tormenta*] storm
expresión **capear el temporal** to ride out the storm

temporario, ria *adj* temporary:♀: *Los adjetivos ingleses son invariables.*

temporizador *sm* timing device

temprano, na *adj* early:♀: *Los adjetivos ingleses son invariables.*
■ **temprano** *adv* early

tenacidad *sf* tenacity

tenaz *adj* [*perseverante*] tenacious:♀: *Los adjetivos ingleses son invariables.*

tenaza *sf*:♀: *generalmente pl* ❶ [*herramienta*] pliers *pl* ❷ [*pinzas*] tongs *pl* ❸ ZOOLOGÍA pincer

tendedero *sm* ❶ [*cuerda*] clothes line ❷ [*armazón*] clothes horse

tendencia *sf* ❶ [*inclinación*] tendency, *plural* tendencies • **tener tendencia a algo** tendency to something • **tiene tendencia a la gordura** he has a tendency toward being fat ❷ [*corriente*] trend • **nuevas tendencias** new trends

tendencioso, sa *adj* tendentious:♀: *Los adjetivos ingleses son invariables.*

tender *vt* ❶ [*colgar - ropa*] to hang out • **la tendió al sol** she hung it out in the sun ❷ [*tumbar*] to lay (out) • **tendió la toalla en el suelo** he laid the towel out on the floor ❸ [*extender*] to stretch (out) ❹ [*mantel*] to spread ❺ [*dar - cosa*] to hand; [*- mano*] to hold out ❻ [*entre dos puntos - cable, vía*] to lay; [*- puente*] to build ❼ *figurado* [*preparar - trampa* ETC] to lay ❽ [*cama*] to make ❾ [*mesa*] to set
■ **tenderse** *v pronominal* to stretch out • **se tendió en la arena** she stretched out in the sand

tenderete *sm* [*puesto*] stall

tendero, ra *sm, f* shopkeeper

tendón *sm* tendon ▸ **el tendón de Aquiles** Achilles' heel

tenedor[1] *sm* [*utensilio*] fork

tenencia *sf* possession ▸ **tenencia ilícita de armas** illegal possession of arms

tener
◆ *vt*
❶ [*indica la posesión*] to have
• **tiene un coche/mucho dinero** she has a car/a lot of money
• **tengo un hermano mayor** I have a brother
• **van a tener un niño** they're having a baby

• **tener huéspedes** to have guests
• **¿tiene algo que decirnos?** do you have something to tell us?
❷ [*indica una característica*] to have
• **tiene los ojos azules** he has blue eyes
• **tiene buen corazón** he has a big heart
❸ [*indica la edad*] to be
• **¿cuántos años tienes?** how old is he?
❹ [*indica una sensación, un estado*] to be
• **tengo hambre** I'm hungry
• **le tiene lástima** she feels sorry for him
• **tendrá una sorpresa** he's in for a surprise
❺ [*indica una actividad*] to have
• **hoy tengo clase** I have class today
❻ [*llevar en las manos, en los brazos*] to hold
• **tener un niño en brazos** to hold a baby in your arms
❼ [*medir*] to be
• **la sala tiene cuatro metros de largo** the living room is four meters long
❽ [*para designar*]
• **aquí tiene su cambio** here's your change
• **aquí me tienes** here I am
❾ [*en frases exclamativas, para expresar un deseo*]
• **¡que tengas un buen viaje!** have a good trip!
• **que tengan unas felices Navidades** happy holidays!
❿ [*considerar*]
• **me tiene por tonto, pero yo me entero de todo** he thinks I'm stupid but I know everything that's going on
• **ten por seguro que lloverá** you can be sure it'll rain
⓫ [*en expresiones*]
• **tener lugar** to happen
• **tener presente algo/alguien** to remember somebody/something
• **hay que tener presente que la situación internacional es muy tensa** we mustn't forget that the international situation is very tense
• **tener que ver con algo/alguien** to have something to do with somebody/something
• **yo no tengo nada que ver con ese asunto/ese individuo** that matter/person is nothing to do with me
• **¿conque esas tenemos? ¿te niegas a hacerlo?** so that's the game, is it? are you refusing to do it?
• **no las tiene todas consigo** he's a bit dubious
• **le ruego tenga a bien mandarme toda la información disponible** please send me any information you have
◆ *v auxiliar*
❶ [*antes de un participio pasado, indica un resultado*]
• **ya tengo hecha la mitad** I've done half already
• **tengo leído medio libro** I've read half the book
• **teníamos pensado ir al teatro** we were thinking of going to the theater
❷ [*antes de un participio o un adjetivo, mantener un estado particular*]

• **el ruido me ha tenido despierto toda la noche** the noise kept me awake all night
• **eso la tiene entretenida** that keeps her busy
■ **tener que**
◆ *v + conjunción*
❶ [*indica una obligación*]
• **tengo que irme** I have to go
❷ [*indica un deber moral o una intención*]
• **tenemos que salir a cenar juntos** we should go out for dinner together
■ **tenerse por**
◆ *v pronominal + preposición*
[*considerarse como*]
• **se tiene por muy listo** he thinks he's very clever

teniente *sm* lieutenant ❱ **teniente coronel/general** lieutenant colonel/general

tenis *sm invariable* tennis ❱ **tenis de mesa** table tennis

tenista *smf* tennis player

tenor *sm* MÚSICA tenor

tensar *vt* ❶ [*cable, cuerda*] to tauten ❷ [*arco*] to draw

tensión *sf* ❶ [*generalmente*] tension ❱ **tensión nerviosa** nervous tension ❷ TECNOLOGÍA [*estiramiento*] stress ❸ ELECTRICIDAD voltage • **alta tensión** high voltage

tenso, sa *adj* ❶ [*cuerda, cable*] taut • **el ambiente estaba muy tenso** the atmosphere was very tense ❷ [*situación, ambiente*] tense • **la cuerda no está suficientemente tensa** the cord is not taut enough ☼ *Los adjetivos ingleses son invariables.*

tentación *sf* temptation • **caer en la tentación** to give in to temptation • **tener la tentación de** to be tempted to • **estos bombones son una tentación** these chocolates are really tempting

tentáculo *sm* tentacle

tentador, ra *adj* tempting ☼ *Los adjetivos ingleses son invariables.*

tentar *vt* [*atraer, incitar*] to tempt • **no me tientes con eso** don't tempt me with that

tentativa *sf* attempt ❱ **tentativa de asesinato** attempted murder ❱ **tentativa de suicidio** suicide attempt

tentempié (pl tentempiés) *sm* snack

teñir *vt* [*ropa, pelo*] • **teñir algo (de rojo** ETC**)** to dye something (red ETC) • **tiñó la camiseta de azul** she dyed the T-shirt blue

teología *sf* theology ❱ **teología de la liberación** liberation theology

teólogo, ga *sm, f* theologian

teorema *sm* theorem

teoría *sf* theory, *plural* theories • **en teoría** in theory

teórico, ca *adj* theoretical • **clase teórica** theory class ☼ *Los adjetivos ingleses son invariables.*

teorizar *vi* to theorize

tepache *sm* ❱ *para explicar lo que es puedes decir:* it's a mildly alcoholic drink made from fermented pineapple peelings and unrefined sugar

tequila *sm o sf* tequila

terapéutico, ca *adj* therapeutic ☼ *Los adjetivos ingleses son invariables.*

terapia *sf* therapy, *plural* therapies ❱ **terapia de grupo** group therapy ❱ **terapia intensiva** intensive care

tercermundista *adj* third-world ☼ *Sólo se usa delante del sustantivo.*

tercero, ra *numeral* third • **vive en el tercer piso** he lives on the third floor • **llegó tercero** he came in third • **una tercera parte de los estudiantes** a third of the students
■ **tercero** *sm* ❶ [*piso*] third floor ❷ [*curso*] third year ❸ [*mediador, parte interesada*] third party

tercio *sm* [*tercera parte*] third • **un tercio de la población** a third of the population

terciopelo *sm* velvet

terco, ca *adj* stubborn ☼ *Los adjetivos ingleses son invariables.*

tergiversar *vt* to distort

termal *adj* thermal ☼ *Los adjetivos ingleses son invariables.*

térmico, ca *adj* thermal ☼ *Los adjetivos ingleses son invariables.*

terminación *sf* ❶ [*finalización*] completion ❷ [*parte final*] and ❸ GRAMÁTICA ending

terminal ◆ *adj* ❶ [*generalmente*] final ❷ [*enfermo*] terminal ☼ *Los adjetivos ingleses son invariables.*
◆ *sm* ELECTRICIDAD & INFORMÁTICA terminal
◆ *sf* ❶ [*de aeropuerto*] terminal ❷ [*de autobuses*] terminus ❱ **terminal de camiones** bus station

terminante *adj* ❶ [*prohibición*] categorical ❷ [*prueba*] conclusive ☼ *Los adjetivos ingleses son invariables.*

terminar ◆ *vt* to finish • **ya terminé las tareas** I've already finished my homework
◆ *vi* ❶ [*acabar*] to end • **la clase no ha terminado todavía** class hasn't ended yet ❷ [*tren*] to stop • **terminar en** [*objeto*] to end in ❸ [*ir a parar*] • **terminar (de/en)** to end up (as/in) • **terminé aceptando la invitación** I ended up accepting the invitation • **la discusión terminó en pelea** the argument ended up in a fight • **terminar por hacer algo** to end up doing something • **terminó por convencerme** he ended up convincing me
■ **terminarse** *v pronominal* ❶ [*finalizar*] to finish ❷ [*agotarse*] to run out • **se nos ha terminado la sal** we have run out of salt

término *sm* ❶ [*fin, extremo*] end • **poner término a algo** to put an end to something ❷ [*plazo*] period • **en el término de un mes** within (the space of) a month ❸ [*lugar, posición*] place • **en primer término** ARTE & FOTOGRAFÍA in the foreground • **en último término a)** ARTE & FOTOGRAFÍA in the background **b)** figurado [*si es necesario*] as a last resort ❹ [*situación, punto*] point ❱ **término medio a)** [*media*] average **b)** [*compromiso*] compro-

T

mise; happy medium • **por término medio** on average • **¿qué término quiere la carne?** how would you like your meat done? ❺ Lingüística & Matemáticas term • **es un término técnico** it's a technical term • **los términos del contrato** the terms of the contract • **a mí no me hables en esos términos** don't talk to me like that • **en términos generales** generally speaking

terminología *sf* terminology

termo *sm* Thermos®(flask)

termómetro *sm* thermometer • **poner el termómetro a alguien** to take somebody's temperature

termostato *sm* thermostat

ternero, ra *sm, f* [*animal*] calf
■ **ternera** *sf* [*carne*] veal

ternura *sf* tenderness

terraplén *sm* embankment

terráqueo, a *adj* Earth ☼ *Sólo se usa delante del sustantivo.*

terrateniente *smf* landowner

terraza *sf* ❶ [*balcón*] balcony, *plural* balconies ❷ [*de café*] terrace • **un bar con terraza** a terrace bar ❸ [*azotea*] terrace roof ❹ [*bancal*] terrace

terremoto *sm* earthquake

terrenal *adj* earthly ☼ *Los adjetivos ingleses son invariables.*

terreno *sm* ❶ [*suelo - generalmente*] land; Geología terrain; Agricultura soil • **la casa tiene mucho terreno** the house has a lot of land • **es un terreno muy fértil** it's very fertile land ❷ [*solar*] plot (of land) ❸ Deporte • **terreno (de juego)** field ❹ *figurado* [*ámbito*] field

terrestre *adj* ❶ [*del planeta*] terrestrial ❷ [*de la tierra*] land ☼ *Sólo se usa delante del sustantivo.*

terrible *adj* ❶ [*enorme, insoportable*] terrible ❷ [*aterrador*] terrifying ☼ *Los adjetivos ingleses son invariables.*

terrícola *smf* earthling

territorial *adj* territorial ☼ *Los adjetivos ingleses son invariables.*

territorio *sm* territory, *plural* territories • **por todo el territorio nacional** across the country

terrón *sm* ❶ [*de tierra*] clod of earth ❷ [*de harina* Etc] lump • **un terrón de azúcar** a sugar lump

terror *sm* ❶ [*miedo, persona terrible*] terror • **el temblor causó terror en el pueblo** the tremor caused terror in the village • **les tiene terror a las arañas** she's terrified of spiders ❷ Cine horror • **película de terror** horror movie • **dar terror** to terrify

terrorífico, ca *adj* ❶ [*enorme, insoportable*] terrible ❷ [*aterrador*] terrifying ☼ *Los adjetivos ingleses son invariables.*

terrorismo *sm* terrorism

terrorista *adj* & *smf* terrorist • **un atentado terrorista** a terrorist attack ☼ *Los adjetivos ingleses son invariables.*

tesina *sf* (undergraduate) dissertation

tesis *sf invariable* [*generalmente*] Universidad thesis, *plural* theses

tesorero, ra *sm, f* treasurer

tesoro *sm* ❶ [*botín*] treasure • **un tesoro escondido** a hidden treasure ❷ [*apelativo*] darling • **¿cómo estás tesoro?** how are you darling?
■ **Tesoro** *sm* Economía • **el Tesoro (Público)** the Treasury

test (pl tests) *sm* test

testamento *sm* ❶ [*documento*] will • **hacer testamento** to write your will ❷ *figurado* [*artístico, intelectual*] legacy

testar *vt* [*probar*] to test

testarudo, da *adj* stubborn ☼ *Los adjetivos ingleses son invariables.*

testículo *sm* testicle

testificar ◆ *vt* ❶ [*dar testimonio de*] to testify ❷ *figurado* [*probar*] to testify to
◆ *vi* to testify

testigo ◆ *smf* [*persona*] witness • **fuimos testigos del accidente** we witnessed the accident ▶ **testigo de cargo/descargo** witness for the prosecution/defence ▶ **testigo de Jehová** Jehovah's Witness ▶ **testigo ocular** o **presencial** eyewitness
◆ *sm* Deporte baton

testimonial *adj* [*documento, prueba* Etc] testimonial ☼ *Los adjetivos ingleses son invariables.*

testimoniar *vt* [*ser testigo de*] to testify to

testimonio *sm* ❶ [*relato*] account ❷ Derecho testimony • **prestar testimonio** to give evidence ❸ [*prueba*] proof • **como testimonio de** as proof of • **dar testimonio de** to prove

teta *sf* ❶ *familiar* [*de mujer*] tit ❷ [*de animal*] teat

tétanos *sm invariable* tetanus

tetera *sf* teapot

tetilla *sf* ❶ [*de hombre, animal*] nipple ❷ [*de biberón*] teat

tetina *sf* teat

tetrapléjico, ca *adj* & *sm, f* quadriplegic ☼ *Los adjetivos ingleses son invariables.*

tétrico, ca *adj* gloomy ☼ *Los adjetivos ingleses son invariables.*

textil *adj* & *sm* textile ☼ *Los adjetivos ingleses son invariables.*

texto *sm* ❶ [*generalmente*] text • **un libro de texto** a textbook • **el Sagrado Texto** the Holy Scripture ❷ [*pasaje*] passage

textual *adj* ❶ [*del texto*] textual ❷ [*exacto*] exact ☼ *Los adjetivos ingleses son invariables.*

textura *sf* texture

ti *pronombre personal* ☼ *después de preposición* ❶ [*generalmente*] you • **siempre pienso en ti** I'm always thinking about you • **me acordaré de ti** I'll remember you • **lo compré para ti** I bought it for you ❷ [*reflexivo*] yourself • **sólo piensas en ti (mismo)** you only think about yourself

tianguis *sm invariable* open-air market

tibia *sf* shinbone

tibio, bia *adj* ❶ [*cálido*] warm ❷ [*falto de calor*] tepid ❸ *figurado* [*frío*] lukewarm ⚲ *Los adjetivos ingleses son invariables.*

tiburón *sm* shark

tic *sm* tic ❱ **tic nervioso** nervous tic

tictac *sm* tick tock

tiempo *sm* ❶ [*generalmente*] time • **no me dio tiempo a terminarlo** I didn't have (enough) time to finish it • **a tiempo parcial** part-time • **a tiempo (de hacer algo)** in time (to do something) • **al poco tiempo** soon afterwards • **con el tiempo** in time • **estar a** o **tener tiempo de** to have time to • **fuera de tiempo** at the wrong moment • **ganar tiempo** to save time • **perder el tiempo** to waste time ❱ **tiempo libre** o **de ocio** spare time ❷ [*periodo largo*] long time • **con tiempo** in good time • **en los últimos tiempos** recently • **hace tiempo que** it is a long time since • **hace tiempo que no vive aquí** he hasn't lived here for some time • **tomarse uno su tiempo** to take your time ❸ [*edad*] age • **¿qué tiempo tiene?** how old is he? ❹ METEOROLOGÍA weather • **hizo buen/mal tiempo** the weather was good/bad • **si el tiempo lo permite** o **no lo impide** weather permitting ❺ DEPORTE half ❻ GRAMÁTICA tense ❼ MÚSICA [*compás*] time; [*ritmo*] tempo

expresiones **en tiempos de Maricastaña** donkey's years ago ❱ **matar el tiempo** to kill time ❱ **hace un tiempo de perros** it's a foul day

el tiempo

el granizo	the hail
la lluvia	the rain
la niebla	the fog
la nieve	the snow
la nube	the cloud
el relámpago	the lightning
el sol	the sun
la tormenta	the storm
el viento	the wind

hablar del tiempo

• **What's the weather like?** ¿Cómo está el tiempo/clima?

• **It's nice.** Hace buen tiempo.

• **The sun's out.** Brilla el sol.

• **The weather's bad.** Hace mal tiempo.

• **It's overcast and it looks like rain.** Está nublado y seguramente va a llover.

• **It's warm/hot/cold** Hace (mucho) calor/frío.

• **What's the weather forecast?** ¿Qué dice el pronóstico (del tiempo)?

• **The forecast's for snow tomorrow.** El pronóstico meteorológico anunció nieve para mañana.

tienda *sf* ❶ [*establecimiento*] store • **ir de tiendas** to go shopping ❱ **tienda de abarrotes** grocery store ❱ **tienda de departamentos** department store ❱ **tienda virtual** online retailer ❷ [*para acampar*] ❱ **tienda (de campaña)** tent

la tienda

el billete	the bill
el billete de 10 pesos	the 10 peso bill
la caja	the checkout
la cartera	the wallet
el celular	the cell phone
el cliente/la clienta	the customer
el elevador	the elevator
la escalera eléctrica	the escalator
el gancho	the clothes hanger
la llave	the key
la moneda	the coin
el monedero	the coin purse
el probador	the fitting room

tierno, na *adj* ❶ [*blando, cariñoso*] tender • **es una persona muy tierna** she's a very tender person • **la carne estaba muy tierna** the meat was very tender ❷ [*del día*] fresh • **pan tierno** fresh bread ⚲ *Los adjetivos ingleses son invariables.*

tierra *sf* ❶ [*generalmente*] land • **cultivan la tierra** they cultivate the land • **tierra adentro** inland ❱ **tierra firme** terra firma ❱ **tierra prometida** Promised Land ❷ [*materia inorgánica*] soil • **aquí la tierra es muy fértil** the soil is very fertile here • **un camino de tierra** a dirt track • **pista de tierra batida** clay court ❸ [*suelo*] ground • **caer a tierra** to fall to the ground • **quedarse en tierra** [*pasajero*] to miss the plane/boat/train • **tomar tierra** to touch down ❹ [*patria*] homeland • **extraña su tierra** she misses her homeland • **de la tierra** [*vino, queso*] local ❺ ELECTRICIDAD ground • **conectado a tierra** grounded

■ **Tierra** *sf* • **la Tierra** the Earth

tieso, sa *adj* ❶ [*rígido*] stiff ❷ [*erguido*] erect ❸ *familiar* [*muerto*] stone dead ❹ *familiar* [*sin dinero*] broke ❺ *figurado* [*engreído*] haughty ⚲ *Los adjetivos ingleses son invariables.*

tiesto *sm* flowerpot

tifón *sm* typhoon

tifus *sm invariable* typhus

tigre *sm* tiger

tijera *sf* ⚲ *generalmente pl* ❶ [*para cortar*] scissors *pl* • **unas tijeras** a pair of scissors ❷ [*de jardinero, esquilador*] shears *pl* • **unas tijeras** a pair of shears • **de tijera** [*escalera, silla*] folding

expresión **meter la tijera** to cut

tilde *sf* ❶ [*signo ortográfico*] tilde ❷ [*acento gráfico*] accent

tiliches *smpl familiar* stuff

timar *vt* [*estafar*] • **timar a alguien** to swindle somebody • **timar algo a alguien** to swindle somebody out of something

timbre *sm* ❶ [*aparato*] bell • **tocar el timbre** to ring the bell ❷ [*de voz, sonido*] tone ❸ [*de correos*] stamp

T

timidez *sf* shyness

tímido, da *adj* shy ҉ *Los adjetivos ingleses son invariables.*

timo *sm* [*estafa*] swindle

timón *sm* ❶ AERONÁUTICA & NÁUTICA rudder ❷ *figurado* [*gobierno*] helm • **llevar el timón de** to be at the helm of

timonel, timonero *sm* NÁUTICA helmsman

tímpano *sm* ANATOMÍA eardrum

tina *sf* ❶ [*tinaja*] pitcher ❷ [*gran cuba*] vat ❸ [*bañera*] bathtub

tinaja *sf* (large) pitcher

tinglado *sm* ❶ [*cobertizo*] shed ❷ [*armazón*] platform ❸ *figurado* [*lío*] fuss ❹ *figurado* [*maquinación*] plot

tinta *sf* ink • **una mancha de tinta** an ink stain ▸ **tinta china** Indian ink

expresiones **andarse con medias tintas** to be wishy-washy ▸ **recargar las tintas** to exaggerate ▸ **saberlo de buena tinta** to have it on good authority ▸ **sudar tinta** to sweat blood

tinte *sm* ❶ [*sustancia*] dye ❷ [*tintorería*] dry cleaner's ❸ *figurado* [*tono*] shade

tintinear *vi* to jingle

tinto, ta *adj* [*vino*] red ҉ *Los adjetivos ingleses son invariables.*

■ **tinto** *sm* [*vino*] red wine

tintorería *sf* dry cleaner's

tío, a *sm, f* [*familiar*] uncle, *femenino* aunt • **el tío Juan** Uncle Juan • **un regalo de mis tíos** a present from my aunt and uncle ▸ **el tío Sam** *figurado* Uncle Sam

típico, ca *adj* ❶ [*característico*] typical • **el típico mexicano** the typical Mexican • **típico de** typical of • **eso es típico de él** that's typical of him ❷ [*traje, restaurante* ETC] traditional • **un baile típico del centro del país** a traditional dance from the center of the country ҉ *Los adjetivos ingleses son invariables.*

tipo, pa *sm, f* familiar guy, *femenino* woman • **¿quién es ese tipo?** who's that guy?

■ **tipo** *sm* ❶ [*clase*] type • **el tipo de música preferida por los jóvenes** the type of music preferred by teens • **todo tipo de** all sorts of ❷ [*cuerpo - de mujer*] figure; [*- de hombre*] build • **tiene muy buen tipo** she has a very good figure ❸ ECONOMÍA rate ❹ IMPRENTA & ZOOLOGÍA type

tipografía *sf* [*procedimiento*] printing

tíquet (pl tiquets) *sm* ticket

tira *sf* ❶ [*banda cortada*] strip ❷ [*de viñetas*] comic strip

expresión **la tira** *familiar* [*la policía*] the cops ▸ **la tira de** *familiar* loads *pl* of

tirachinas *sm invariable* catapult

tiradero *sm* garbage dump

tirado, da *adj* ❶ *familiar* [*barato*] dirt cheap ❷ *familiar* [*fácil*] dead easy ҉ *Los adjetivos ingleses son invariables.*

expresión **dejar tirado a alguien** *familiar* to leave somebody in the lurch

■ **tirada** *sf* ❶ [*lanzamiento*] throw • **sacó dos seises a la primera tirada de los dados** he rolled two sixes with the first throw of the dice ❷ IMPRENTA print run

expresión **de una tirada** in one stretch

tiraje *sm* print run

tiranía *sf* tyranny

tirano, na ◆ *adj* tyrannical ҉ *Los adjetivos ingleses son invariables.*
◆ *sm, f* tyrant

tirante ◆ *adj* ❶ [*estirado*] taut ❷ *figurado* [*violento, tenso*] tense ҉ *Los adjetivos ingleses son invariables.*
◆ *sm* [*de tela*] strap • **un vestido con tirantes** a dress with straps

■ **tirantes** *smpl* [*para pantalones*] suspenders

tirar ◆ *vt* ❶ [*lanzar*] to throw • **tirar algo a alguien/algo** [*para hacer daño*] to throw something at somebody/something • **les tiraban piedras a los policías** they were throwing rocks at the police • **tírame una manzana** throw me an apple • **tírale un beso** blow him a kiss ❷ [*dejar caer*] to drop • **tiré el florero sin querer** I accidentally dropped the vase ❸ [*derramar*] to spill ❹ [*volcar*] to knock over ❺ [*desechar, malgastar*] to throw away • **deberías tirar esto, ya no sirve** you should throw this away, it's no good anymore • **qué manera de tirar el dinero** what a way to waste money ❻ [*disparar*] to fire ❼ [*bomba*] to drop ❽ [*petardo, cohete*] to let off ❾ [*foto*] to take ❿ [*derribar*] to knock down ⓫ [*jugar - carta*] to play; [*- dado*] to throw ⓬ DEPORTE [*falta, penalti* ETC] to take; [*balón*] to pass
◆ *vi* ❶ [*estirar, arrastrar*] • **tirar (de algo)** to pull (something) ❷ [*disparar*] to shoot ❸ *familiar* [*atraer*] • **me tira la vida del campo** I feel drawn towards life in the country ❹ [*chimenea*] to draw ❺ [*dirigirse*] to go ❻ *familiar* [*apañárselas*] to get by • **voy tirando** I'm O.K. ❼ [*parecerse*] • **tira a gris** it's grayish • **tira a su abuela** she takes after her grandmother • **tirando a** approaching ❽ [*tender*] • **tirar para algo** [*persona*] to have the makings of something • **este programa tira a (ser) cursi** this programme is a bit on the tacky side • **el tiempo tira a mejorar** the weather looks as if it's getting better ❾ DEPORTE [*con el pie*] to kick; [*con la mano*] to throw; [*a meta, canasta* ETC] to shoot

■ **tirarse** *v pronominal* ❶ [*lanzarse*] • **tirarse (a) a)** [*al agua*] to dive (into) **b)** [*al vacío*] to jump (into) • **se tiró al agua** she dove into the water • **se tiró de cabeza** he dove in headfirst • **tirarse sobre alguien** to jump on top of somebody ❷ [*tumbarse*] to stretch out ❸ [*pasar tiempo*] to spend

tiritar *vi* to shiver • **tiritaba de frío** he was shivering with cold

tiro *sm* ❶ [*generalmente*] shot • **disparó un tiro** he fired a shot • **pegar un tiro a alguien** to shoot somebody • **pegarse un tiro** to shoot yourself ❷ [*acción*] shooting ▸ **tiro al blanco a)** [*deporte*] target shooting **b)** [*lugar*] shooting range ▸ **tiro con arco** archery ❸ [*huella, marca*] bullet mark ❹ [*herida*] gunshot wound ❺ [*alcance*] range • **a tiro de** within the range of • **a tiro de piedra** a stone's throw away • **ponerse/estar a tiro a)** [*de arma*] to come/be within range **b)** *figurado* [*de persona*] to come/be within your reach ❻ [*de chimenea, horno*] draw

expresión **ni a tiros** never in a million years ▶ **le salió el tiro por la culata** it backfired on him

tiroides *sm o sf invariable* thyroid (gland)

tirón *sm* ❶ [*estirón*] pull ❷ [*robo*] bagsnatching ❸ MEDICINA ▶ **tirón (muscular)** strained muscle ❹ *familiar* [*popularidad*] pull

tirotear *vt* to fire at

tiroteo *sm* ❶ [*tiros*] shooting ❷ [*intercambio de disparos*] shootout

títere *sm literal & figurado* puppet

titipuchal *sm familiar* • **un titipuchal** a ton • **tenemos un titipuchal de tarea** we have a ton of homework • **hace un titipuchal de años** many years ago

titiritero, ra *sm, f* ❶ [*de títeres*] puppeteer ❷ [*acróbata*] acrobat

titubeante *adj* ❶ [*actitud*] hesitant ❷ [*voz*] stuttering ❸ [*al andar*] tottering ❧ *Los adjetivos ingleses son invariables.*

titubear *vi* ❶ [*dudar*] to hesitate ❷ [*al hablar*] to stutter

titulado, da *sm, f* ❶ [*diplomado*] holder of a qualification ❷ [*licenciado*] graduate

titular ◆ *adj* [*profesor, médico*] official ❧ *Los adjetivos ingleses son invariables.*
◆ *smf* [*poseedor*] holder
◆ *sm* ❧ *generalmente pl* PRENSA headline
◆ *vt* [*llamar*] to title

título *sm* ❶ [*generalmente*] title • **no me acuerdo del título de la canción** I don't remember the title of the song • **a título de** as ▶ **título de propiedad** title deed ▶ **títulos de crédito** CINE credits ❷ [*licenciatura*] degree • **acaba de recibir su título universitario** she just received her university degree ❸ [*diploma*] diploma • **tenía su título colgado en la pared** he had his diploma hanging on the wall

tlapalería *sf* hardware store

TLC, TLCAN *sm* (*abreviatura de* Tratado de Libre Comercio de América del Norte) NAFTA

toalla *sf* [*para secarse*] towel ▶ **toalla de baño/manos** bath/hand towel ▶ **toalla femenina** sanitary pad ▶ **toalla higiénica** o **sanitaria** sanitary pad
expresión **arrojar** o **tirar la toalla** to throw in the towel

toallero *sm* towel rail

tobillo *sm* ankle • **me torcí el tobillo** I twisted my ankle

tobogán *sm* ❶ [*rampa*] slide ❷ [*en parque de atracciones*] helter-skelter ❸ [*en piscina*] flume

tocador *sm* ❶ [*mueble*] dressing table ❷ [*habitación - en lugar público*] powder room; [*- en casa*] boudoir

tocar ◆ *vt* ❶ [*generalmente*] to touch • **no toques la computadora** don't touch the computer ❷ [*palpar*] to feel ❸ [*instrumento, canción*] to play • **¿sabes tocar la guitarra?** do you know how to play the guitar? ❹ [*sirena, alarma*] to sound ❺ [*campana, timbre*] to ring • **el reloj tocó las doce** the clock struck twelve ❻ [*abordar - tema* ETC] to touch on ❼ *figurado* [*conmover*] to touch

◆ *vi* ❶ [*entrar en contacto*] to touch ❷ [*estar próximo*] • **tocar (con) a)** [*generalmente*] to be touching **b)** [*país, jardín*] to border (on) ❸ [*llamar - a la puerta, ventana*] to knock ❹ [*corresponder en reparto*] • **tocar a alguien** to be due to somebody • **tocamos a mil cada uno** we're due a thousand each • **le tocó la mitad** he got half of it ❺ [*caer en suerte*] • **me ha tocado la lotería** I've won the lottery • **le ha tocado sufrir mucho** he has had to suffer a lot ❻ [*llegar el momento*] • **nos toca pagar ahora** it's time (for us) to pay now • **me toca a mí jugar** it's my turn to play

tocayo, ya *sm, f* namesake

tocino *sm* ❶ [*para cocinar*] lard ❷ [*para comer*] bacon

todavía *adv* ❶ [*aún*] still • **todavía la quiere** he still loves her ❷ [*con negativo*] still • **todavía no lo he recibido** I still haven't got it • **todavía ayer** as late as yesterday • **todavía no** not yet ❸ [*incluso*] even • **ahí hace todavía más calor** it's even hotter there • **todavía mejor** even better

todo, da ◆ *adj* ❶ [*generalmente*] all • **todo el día** all day • **todo el tiempo** all the time • **todo el mundo** everybody • **todo el libro** the whole book ❷ [*cada, cualquier*] • **todos los días/lunes** every day/Monday • **todo español** every Spaniard ❸ [*para enfatizar*] • **es todo un hombre** he's every bit a man • **ya es toda una mujer** she's a big girl now • **fue todo un éxito** it was a great success ❧ *Los adjetivos ingleses son invariables.*
◆ *pronombre* ❶ [*todas las cosas*] everything • **lo vendió todo** he sold everything • **todos están rotos** they're all broken • **ante todo a)** [*principalmente*] above all **b)** [*en primer lugar*] first of all • **con todo** despite everything • **sobre todo** above all ❷ [*todas las personas*] • **todos** everybody • **todas vinieron** everybody came
expresión **está en todo** he/she always makes sure everything is just so ▶ **todo lo más** at (the) most
■ **todo** ◆ *sm* whole
◆ *adv* all

todopoderoso, sa *adj* almighty ❧ *Los adjetivos ingleses son invariables.*

todoterreno *sm* all-terrain vehicle

toldo *sm* ❶ [*de tienda*] awning ❷ [*de playa*] sunshade

tolerancia *sf* tolerance

tolerante *adj* tolerant ❧ *Los adjetivos ingleses son invariables.*

tolerar *vt* ❶ [*consentir, aceptar*] to tolerate • **no voy a tolerar una cosa así** I'm not going to tolerate something like that • **tolerar que alguien haga algo** to tolerate somebody doing something ❷ [*aguantar*] to stand • **no tolero a la gente mal educada** I can't stand rude people

toma *sf* ❶ [*de biberón, papilla*] feed ❷ [*de medicamento*] dose ❸ [*de ciudad* ETC] capture ❹ [*de agua, aire*] inlet ▶ **toma de corriente** ELECTRICIDAD socket ▶ **toma de tierra** ELECTRICIDAD earth ❺ CINE [*de escena*] take

tomador, ra ◆ *adj* drinking
◆ *sm, f* [*bebedor*] drinker

T

tomar ✦ *vt* ❶ [*generalmente*] to take • **me voy a tomar el día libre** I'm going to take the day off • **me tomó la mano** he took my hand • **tomé apuntes en la clase** I took notes in class ❷ [*actitud, costumbre*] to adopt ❸ [*comida, bebida*] to have • **¿qué quieres tomar?** what would you like (to drink)? ❹ [*autobús, tren* ETC] to take ❺ [*taxi*] to take • **tomamos un taxi** we took a taxi ❻ [*considerar, confundir*] • **tomar a alguien por algo/alguien** to take somebody for something/somebody

expresiones **tomarla con alguien** *familiar* to have it in for somebody ▶ **¡toma!** a) [*al dar algo*] here you are! b) [*expresando sorpresa*] well I never! ▶ **¡toma (ésa)!** *familiar* [*expresa venganza*] take that!

✦ *vi* ❶ [*encaminarse*] to go ❷ [*beber alcohol*] to drink

tomate *sm* [*fruto*] tomato, *plural* <u>tomatoes</u>

tómbola *sf* tombola

tomo *sm* [*volumen*] volume

tonalidad *sf* [*de color*] tone

tonel *sm* [*recipiente*] barrel

tonelada *sf* tonne

tono *sm* ❶ [*generalmente*] tone • **me di cuenta por el tono de su voz** I realized by the tone of his voice • **el tono de marcar** the dial tone ❷ MÚSICA [*tonalidad*] key; [*altura*] pitch ❸ [*de color*] shade • **siempre se viste con tonos claros** she always dresses in light shades ▶ **tono de piel** complexion

expresión **fuera de tono** out of place

tontear *vi* [*hacer el tonto*] to fool about

tontería *sf* ❶ [*estupidez*] stupid thing • **decir una tontería** to talk nonsense • **hacer una tontería** to do something foolish ❷ [*cosa sin importancia o valor*] trifle

tonto, ta ✦ *adj* stupid • **¡qué excusa más tonta!** what a stupid excuse! ▶ **tonto de capirote** o **remate** daft as a brush ᠅ *Los adjetivos ingleses son invariables.*

✦ *sm, f* idiot • **hacer el tonto** to play the fool • **hacerse el tonto** to act innocent

top (pl tops) *sm* [*prenda*] short top

topacio *sm* topaz

topar *vi* [*encontrarse*] • **topar con alguien** to bump into somebody • **topar con algo** to come across something

tope ✦ *adj invariable* ❶ [*máximo*] top ❷ [*fecha*] last ᠅ *Los adjetivos ingleses son invariables.*

✦ *sm* ❶ [*pieza*] block ❷ [*para puerta*] doorstop ❸ [*límite máximo*] limit ❹ [*para velocidad*] speed bump

expresión **estar hasta los topes** to be bursting at the seams ▶ **poner tope a** to rein in; to curtail

topo *sm* ❶ *figurado* ZOOLOGÍA mole ❷ [*lunar*] polka dot

topónimo *sm* place name

toque *sm* ❶ [*generalmente*] touch • **dar los últimos toques a algo** to put the finishing touches to something ❷ [*aviso*] warning ❸ [*sonido - de campana*] chime; chiming ᠅ *incontable*; [- *de sirena* ETC] blast ▶ **toque de diana** reveille ▶ **toque de difuntos** death knell ▶ **toque de queda** curfew

toquetear *vt* [*manosear - cosa*] to fiddle with; [- *persona*] to fondle

tórax *sm invariable* thorax

torbellino *sm* ❶ [*remolino - de aire*] whirlwind; [- *de agua*] whirlpool; [- *de polvo*] dustcloud ❷ *figurado* [*mezcla confusa*] spate

torcedura *sf* [*esguince*] sprain

torcer ✦ *vt* ❶ [*generalmente*] to twist ❷ [*doblar*] to bend ❸ [*girar*] to turn

✦ *vi* [*girar*] to turn

torcido, da *adj* ❶ [*enroscado*] twisted ❷ [*doblado*] bent ❸ [*cuadro, corbata*] crooked ᠅ *Los adjetivos ingleses son invariables.*

torear ✦ *vt* ❶ [*lidiar*] to fight *(bulls)* ❷ *figurado* [*eludir*] to dodge

✦ *vi* [*lidiar*] to fight bulls

toreo *sm* bullfighting

torero, ra *sm, f* bullfighter

tormenta *sf* storm

tormento *sm* torment • **ser un tormento** a) [*persona*] to be a torment b) [*cosa*] to be torture

tormentoso, sa *adj* ❶ [*cielo, día*] stormy ❷ [*sueño*] troubled ᠅ *Los adjetivos ingleses son invariables.*

tornado *sm* tornado

tornar *culto* ✦ *vt* [*convertir*] • **tornar algo en (algo)** to turn something into (something)

✦ *vi* ❶ [*regresar*] to return ❷ [*volver a hacer*] • **tornar a hacer algo** to do something again

torneo *sm* tournament

tornillo *sm* ❶ [*con punta*] screw ❷ [*con tuerca*] bolt

expresión **le falta un tornillo** *familiar* he has a screw loose

torniquete *sm* MEDICINA tourniquet

torno *sm* [*de alfarero*] (potter's) wheel

toro *sm* bull

toronja *sf* grapefruit

torpe *adj* ❶ [*generalmente*] clumsy ❷ [*necio*] slow ᠅ *Los adjetivos ingleses son invariables.*

torpedear *vt* to torpedo

torpedo *sm* [*proyectil*] torpedo

torpeza *sf* ❶ [*generalmente*] clumsiness • **fue una torpeza hacerlo** it was a clumsy thing to do ❷ [*falta de inteligencia*] slowness

torre *sf* ❶ [*construcción*] tower ▶ **torre (de apartamentos)** apartment building ▶ **torre de control** control tower ▶ **torre de marfil** *figurado* ivory tower ▶ **torre de perforación** oil derrick ❷ ELECTRICIDAD pylon ❸ [*en ajedrez*] rook

torreja *sf* French toast ᠅ *incontable*

torrencial *adj* torrential ᠅ *Los adjetivos ingleses son invariables.*

torrente *sm* torrent • **un torrente de** a) *figurado* [*gente, palabras* ETC] a stream of b) [*dinero, energía*] masses of

tórrido, da *adj* torrid ☼ *Los adjetivos ingleses son invariables.*

torso *sm* torso

torta *sf* ❶ [*sándwich*] sandwich • **no tuve tiempo de sentarme a almorzar, sólo comí una torta** I didn't have time to sit down and eat lunch, I only ate a sandwich ❷ *familiar* [*bofetada*] thump

tortazo *sm familiar* [*bofetada*] thump

tortícolis *sf invariable* crick in the neck

tortilla *sf* ❶ [*de maíz*] tortilla ❷ [*de huevo*] omelette ❿ **tortilla (a la) española** Spanish omelette ❿ **tortilla (a la) francesa** French omelette

expresión se dio la vuelta la tortilla the tables turned

tortuga *sf* ❶ [*terrestre*] tortoise ❷ [*marina*] turtle ❸ [*fluvial*] terrapin ❹ *familiar* [*persona o cosa lenta*] snail

tortura *sf* torture

torturar *vt* to torture

tos *sf* cough • **está resfriada y tiene mucha tos** she has a cold and a bad cough ❿ **tos ferina** whooping cough

toser *vi* to cough

tostado, da *adj* ❶ [*pan, almendras*] toasted ❷ [*color*] brownish ❸ [*piel*] tanned ☼ *Los adjetivos ingleses son invariables.*

■ **tostada** *sf* ❿ *para explicar lo que es puedes decir:* it's a fried corn tortilla, served with beans, meat, ETC

tostador *sm* toaster

tostadora *sf* = tostador

tostar *vt* ❶ [*dorar, calentar - pan, almendras*] to toast ; [*- carne*] to brown ❷ [*broncear*] to tan

■ **tostarse** *v pronominal* to get brown • **tostarse (al sol)** to sunbathe

tostón *sm familiar* [*rollo, aburrimiento*] bore

total ◆ *adj* ❶ [*absoluto, completo*] total ❷ *familiar* [*estupendo*] brill ☼ *Los adjetivos ingleses son invariables.*

◆ *sm* ❶ [*suma*] total • **el total de sumar 10 más 10 es 20** the total from adding 10 plus 10 is 20 ❷ [*totalidad, conjunto*] whole • **el total del grupo** the whole group • **en total** in all

◆ *adv* anyway • **total que me marché** so anyway, I left

totalidad *sf* whole • **en su totalidad** as a whole

totalitario, ria *adj* totalitarian ☼ *Los adjetivos ingleses son invariables.*

totalizar *vt* to amount to

tóxico, ca *adj* toxic ☼ *Los adjetivos ingleses son invariables.*

■ **tóxico** *sm* poison

toxicómano, na *sm, f* drug addict

toxina *sf* toxin

tozudo, da *adj* stubborn ☼ *Los adjetivos ingleses son invariables.*

trabajador, ra ◆ *adj* hard-working ☼ *Los adjetivos ingleses son invariables.*

◆ *sm, f* worker

trabajar ◆ *vi* ❶ [*generalmente*] to work • **trabajar de/en** to work as/in • **trabajar en una empresa** to work for a firm ❷ CINE & TEATRO to act

◆ *vt* ❶ [*hierro, barro, tierra*] to work ❷ [*masa*] to knead ❸ [*mejorar*] to work on

trabajo *sm* ❶ [*generalmente*] work • **si quieres hablar con ella ahora, puedes llamarla al trabajo** if you want to talk with her now, you can call her at work • **hacer un buen trabajo** to do a good job ❿ **trabajo intelectual/físico** mental/physical effort ❿ **trabajo manual** manual labor ❿ **trabajos forzados** o **forzosos** hard labor ☼ *incontable* ❿ **trabajos manuales** [*en el colegio*] arts and crafts ❷ [*empleo*] job • **tardó sólo un par de semanas en encontrar trabajo** he only took a couple of weeks to find a job • **no tener trabajo** to be out of work ❸ [*estudio escrito*] essay • **¿cuándo tenemos que entregar el trabajo de historia?** when do we have to turn in the history essay?

trabajoso, sa *adj* ❶ [*difícil*] hard ❷ [*molesto*] tiresome ☼ *Los adjetivos ingleses son invariables.*

trabalenguas *sm invariable* tongue-twister

tracción *sf* traction ❿ **tracción a las cuatro ruedas** four-wheel drive

tractor *sm* tractor

tradición *sf* tradition

tradicional *adj* traditional ☼ *Los adjetivos ingleses son invariables.*

traducción *sf* translation ❿ **traducción directa/inversa** translation into/out of your own language

traducir ◆ *vt* [*a otro idioma*] to translate

◆ *vi* to translate • **traducir (de/a)** to translate (from/ into) • **hay que traducir estos ejemplos al inglés** you have to translate these examples into English

■ **traducirse** *v pronominal* [*a otro idioma*] • **traducirse (por)** to be translated (by)

traductor, ra *sm, f* translator

traer *vt* ❶ [*trasladar, provocar*] to bring • **tengo frío, por favor tráeme una manta** I'm cold, please bring me a blanket ❷ [*consecuencias*] to carry • **traer consigo** [*implicar*] to mean ❸ [*llevar*] to carry • **¿qué traes ahí?** what have you got there? ❹ [*llevar adjunto, dentro*] to have • **trae un artículo interesante** it has an interesting article in it ❺ [*llevar puesto*] to wear • **mi madre trae las sandalias que le regalé** my mother is wearing the sandals I gave her

traficante *smf* [*de drogas, armas* ETC] trafficker

traficar *vi* • **traficar (en** o **con algo)** to traffic (in something)

tráfico *sm* ❶ [*de vehículos*] traffic ❷ [*de drogas, armas*] trafficking

tragar ◆ *vt* ❶ [*ingerir, creer*] to swallow ❷ [*absorber*] to swallow up ❸ [*soportar*] to put up with

◆ *vi* ❶ [*ingerir*] to swallow ❷ [*aguantar*] to grin and bear it ❸ [*acceder, ceder*] to give in

tragedia *sf* tragedy, *plural* tragedies

trágico, ca *adj* tragic ☼ *Los adjetivos ingleses son invariables.*

T

trago sm ❶ [de líquido] • **dar un trago de algo** to take a swig of something • **de un trago** in one gulp ❷ familiar [copa] drink

expresión **ser un trago para alguien** familiar [disgusto] to be tough on somebody

tragón, ona familiar ◆ adj greedy ❓ *Los adjetivos ingleses son invariables.*

◆ sm, f pig

traición sf ❶ [infidelidad] betrayal ❷ DERECHO treason

traicionar vt [persona, país, ideales] to betray

traidor, ra ◆ adj ❶ [desleal] treacherous ❷ DERECHO treasonous ❓ *Los adjetivos ingleses son invariables.*

◆ sm, f traitor

tráiler (pl trailers) sm ❶ CINE trailer ❷ AUTOMÓVILES semi-trailer truck ❸ [caravana] trailer

traje sm ❶ [con chaqueta] suit ❷ [de una pieza] dress ▶ **ir de traje** to wear a suit ▶ **traje de baño** swimsuit ▶ **traje de ceremonia** o **de gala** dress suit ; formal dress ❓ *incontable* ❸ [regional, de época ETC] costume ❹ [ropa] clothes pl

trama sf ❶ [argumento] plot ❷ [conspiración] intrigue

tramar vt ❶ [planear] to plot ❷ [complot] to hatch • **estar tramando algo** to be up to something

tramitar vt ❶ [suj: autoridades - solicitud, dimisión] to process ❷ [sujeto: solicitante] • **tramitar un permiso/visado** to be in the process of applying for a licence/visa

trámite sm [gestión] formal step • **de trámite** routine

tramo sm ❶ [espacio] section ❷ [de escalera] flight (of stairs)

trampa sf ❶ [para cazar] trap ❷ figurado [engaño] trick • **tender una trampa a alguien** to set o lay a trap for somebody • **hacer trampas** to cheat

trampilla sf [en el suelo] trapdoor

trampolín sm ❶ [de piscina] diving board ❷ [en gimnasia] springboard

tramposo, sa ◆ adj [fullero] cheating ❓ *Los adjetivos ingleses son invariables.*

◆ sm, f [fullero] cheat

tranquilidad sf peacefulness • **para mayor tranquilidad** to be on the safe side

tranquilizante sm MEDICINA tranquilizer

tranquilizar vt ❶ [calmar] to calm (down) ❷ [dar confianza] to reassure

tranquilizar a alguien

• **You'll see: it'll be all right.** Ya verás, todo saldrá bien.
• **Don't worry!** No te preocupes.
• **Don't worry about it!** ¡No es nada!

tranquilo, la adj ❶ [sosegado - lugar, música] peaceful ; [- persona, tono de voz, mar] calm • **¡(tú) tranquilo!**

familiar don't you worry! ❷ [velada, charla, negocio] quiet ❸ [mente] untroubled ❹ [conciencia] clear ❺ [despreocupado] casual ❓ *Los adjetivos ingleses son invariables.*

transacción sf COMERCIO transaction

transar vi ❶ [negociar] to come to an arrangement ❷ [transigir] to compromise

transbordador sm ❶ NÁUTICA ferry ❷ AERONÁUTICA ▶ **transbordador (espacial)** space shuttle

transbordo sm • **hacer transbordo** to change (trains ETC)

transcurrir vi ❶ [tiempo] to pass • **ya transcurrieron dos años desde que llegué a esta ciudad** two years have already passed since I arrived in this city ❷ [ocurrir] to take place • **la historia de Drácula transcurre en Transilvania** the story of Dracula takes place in Transylvania

transcurso sm ❶ [paso de tiempo] passing ❷ [periodo de tiempo] • **en el transcurso de** in the course of

transeúnte smf [viandante] passer-by

transexual adj & smf transsexual ❓ *Los adjetivos ingleses son invariables.*

transferencia sf transfer

transferir vt to transfer

transformación, trasformación sf [cambio, conversión] transformation

transformador sm ELECTRÓNICA transformer

transformar vt ❶ [cambiar radicalmente] to transform • **la tecnología está transformando los métodos educativos** technology is transforming educational methods • **transformar algo/a alguien (en)** to transform something/somebody (into) ❷ [convertir] • **transformar algo (en)** to convert something (into) ■ **transformarse** v pronominal ❶ [cambiar radicalmente] to be transformed ❷ [convertirse] • **transformarse en algo** to be converted into something • **en esta represa, la fuerza del agua se transforma en energía eléctrica** at this dam, the force of the water is converted into electric energy

transfusión sf transfusion

transición sf transition • **periodo de transición** transition period

transitar vi to go (along)

tránsito sm [de vehículos] traffic • **accidente de tránsito** traffic accident • **pasajeros en tránsito a...** passengers with connecting flights to...

transitorio, ria adj ❶ [generalmente] transitory ❷ [residencia] temporary ❸ [régimen, medida] transitional ❓ *Los adjetivos ingleses son invariables.*

translúcido, da adj translucent ❓ *Los adjetivos ingleses son invariables.*

transmisión sf ❶ [generalmente] AUTOMÓVILES transmission ❷ RADIO & TELEVISIÓN broadcast

transmisor, ra adj transmission ❓ *Sólo se usa delante del sustantivo.*

■ **transmisor** sm transmitter

transmitir, trasmitir *vt* ❶ [*generalmente*] to transmit ❷ [*saludos, noticias*] to pass on • **le transmitiré a mi familia tus saludos** I will pass your greetings on to my family ❸ RADIO & TELEVISIÓN to broadcast ❹ [*ceder*] to transfer

transparencia *sf* transparency, *plural* transparencies

transparente *adj* ❶ [*generalmente*] transparent ❷ [*tela*] see-through ۞: *Los adjetivos ingleses son invariables.*

transpiración *sf* perspiration

transpirar *vi* to perspire

transportador *sm* ❶ [*para trasladar*] transporter ❷ [*para medir ángulos*] protractor

transportar *vt* [*trasladar*] to transport

transporte *sm* transportation • **medio de transporte** means of transportation ❱ **transporte público** o **colectivo** public transportation

los medios de transporte

el autobús	the bus
el avión	the plane
el barco	the boat
la bicicleta	the bicycle
el camión	the bus
el camión (de carga)	the truck
la camioneta	the van
el coche	the car
el helicóptero	the helicopter
el metro	the subway
la moto	the motorcycle
los patines en línea	the rollerblades
la patineta	the skateboard
el tren	the train
el tranvía	the streetcar

transportista *smf* carrier

transversal *adj* transverse ۞: *Los adjetivos ingleses son invariables.*

tranvía *sm* streetcar

trapeador *sm* mop

trapear *vt* to mop

trapecio *sm* [*de gimnasia*] trapeze

trapecista *smf* trapeze artist

trapo *sm* ❶ [*trozo de tela*] rag • **¿dónde hay un trapo para limpiar la mesa?** where is there a rag to clean the table? ❷ [*gamuza, bayeta*] cloth • **pasar el trapo a algo** to wipe something with a cloth ❱ **trapo de cocina** dishcloth

expresión **poner a alguien como un trapo** to tear somebody to shreds

tráquea *sf* windpipe

traqueteo *sm* [*ruido*] rattling

tras *preposición* ❶ [*detrás de*] behind ❷ [*después de, en pos de*] after • **uno tras otro** one after the other

• **día tras día** day after day • **andar tras algo** to be after something

trascendencia *sf* significance • **esta decisión tendrá una gran trascendencia** this decision will be of major significance

trascendental *adj* ❶ [*importante*] momentous ❷ [*meditación*] transcendental ۞: *Los adjetivos ingleses son invariables.*

trascendente *adj* momentous ۞: *Los adjetivos ingleses son invariables.*

trasero, ra *adj* back ۞: *Sólo se usa delante del sustantivo.* • **el asiento trasero del auto** the back seat of the car

■ **trasero** *sm familiar* butt

trasformación = **transformación**

traslación *sf* ASTRONOMÍA passage

trasladar *vt* ❶ [*desplazar*] to move ❷ [*a empleado, funcionario*] to transfer ❸ [*reunión, fecha*] to postpone

traslado *sm* ❶ [*de casa, empresa, muebles*] move ❷ [*de trabajo*] transfer ❸ [*de personas*] movement

trasluz *sm* • **al trasluz** against the light

trasmitir = **transmitir**

trasnochar *vi* to stay up late

traspapelar *vt* to mislay

traspasar *vt* ❶ [*perforar, atravesar*] to go through ❷ [*sujeto: líquido*] to soak through ❸ [*puerta*] to pass through ❹ [*cambiar de sitio*] to move ❺ [*vender - jugador*] to transfer ; [- *negocio*] to sell (as a going concern)

traspaso *sm* [*venta - de jugador*] transfer ; [- *de negocio*] sale (as a going concern)

traspié (*pl* traspiés) *sm* ❶ [*resbalón*] trip • **dar un traspié** to trip up ❷ [*error*] slip

trasplantar *vt* to transplant

trasplante *sm* transplant

traste *sm* ❶ MÚSICA fret ❷ • **trastes** utensils • **lavar los trastes** to do the dishes

expresión **dar al traste con algo** to ruin something ❱ **irse al traste** to fall through

trastero *sm* junk room

trastienda *sf* backroom

trasto *sm* ❶ [*utensilio inútil*] junk ۞: *incontable* • **el sótano está lleno de trastos** the basement is full of junk ❷ *familiar* [*persona traviesa*] menace

trastornado, da *adj* disturbed ۞: *Los adjetivos ingleses son invariables.*

trastornar *vt* ❶ [*volver loco*] to drive mad ❷ [*inquietar*] to worry ❸ [*alterar*] to turn upside down ❹ [*planes*] to disrupt

trastorno *sm* ❶ [*mental*] disorder ❱ **trastorno bipolar** bipolar disorder ❷ [*digestivo*] upset ❸ [*alteración - por huelga, nevada*] disruption ۞: *incontable* ; [- *por guerra* ETC] upheaval

tratado *sm* [*convenio*] treaty, *plural* treaties

T

tratamiento *sm* ❶ [*generalmente*] MEDICINA treatment ❷ [*título*] title ❸ INFORMÁTICA processing ▶ **tratamiento de datos/textos** data/word processing ▶ **tratamiento por lotes** batch processing

tratar ◆ *vt* ❶ [*generalmente*] MEDICINA to treat • **son excelentes anfitriones, nos trataron muy bien** they are excellent hosts, they treated us very well • **necesito un médico que me trate esta alergia** I need a doctor to treat this allergy for me ❷ [*discutir*] to discuss ❸ INFORMÁTICA to process ❹ [*dirigirse a*] • **tratar a alguien de** [*usted, tú* ETC] to address somebody as • **en algunas regiones de América, los amigos se tratan de "vos"** in some regions of Latin America, friends address each other as "vos"
◆ *vi* ❶ [*intentar*] • **tratar de hacer algo** to try to do something • **no trates de engañarme porque no tardaré en descubrir la verdad** don't try to deceive me because I won't take long to discover the truth ❷ [*versar*] • **tratar de/sobre** to deal with • **la película trata de problemas muy actuales** the movie deals with very current problems ❸ [*tener relación*] • **tratar con alguien** to mix with somebody ❹ [*comerciar*] • **tratar en** to deal in

trato *sm* ❶ [*comportamiento*] treatment • **de trato agradable** pleasant ▶ **malos tratos** beating ☞ *incontable (of child, wife)* ❷ [*acuerdo*] deal • **cerrar** o **hacer un trato** to do a deal • **¡trato hecho!** it's a deal!

trauma *sm* trauma

traumatólogo, ga *sm, f* traumatologist

través ■ **a través de** *locución preposicional* ❶ [*de un lado a otro de*] across ❷ [*por, por medio de*] through

travesaño *sm* ❶ ARQUITECTURA crosspiece ❷ DEPORTE crossbar ❸ [*de escalera*] rung

travesía *sf* ❶ [*viaje - por mar*] voyage ❷ [*calle*] cross street

travestido, da, travestí (pl travestís) *sm, f* transvestite

travesura *sf* [*acción*] prank • **hacer travesuras** to play pranks

travieso, sa *adj* mischievous ☞ *Los adjetivos ingleses son invariables.*

trayecto *sm* ❶ [*distancia*] distance ❷ [*viaje*] journey ❸ [*ruta*] route • **dile al taxista que elija el trayecto más corto** tell the taxi driver to choose the shortest route • **final de trayecto** end of the line

trayectoria *sf* ❶ [*recorrido*] trajectory ❷ *figurado* [*evolución*] path

trazado *sm* ❶ [*trazo*] outline ❷ [*diseño*] plan ❸ [*recorrido*] route

trazar *vt* ❶ [*dibujar*] to draw ❷ [*ruta*] to plot ❸ [*indicar, describir*] to outline ❹ [*idear*] to draw up

trazo *sm* ❶ [*de dibujo, rostro*] line ❷ [*de letra*] stroke

trébol *sm* [*planta*] clover

trece *numeral* thirteen ver también **seis**

treceavo, va *numeral* thirteenth

trecho *sm* ❶ [*espacio*] distance ❷ [*tiempo*] time

tregua *sf* ❶ [*entre combatientes*] truce ❷ *figurado* [*descanso*] respite

treinta *numeral* thirty • **los (años) treinta** the Thirties ver también **seis**

treintena *sf* thirty

tremendo, da *adj* [*enorme*] tremendous ☞ *Los adjetivos ingleses son invariables.*

tren *sm* [*ferrocarril*] train • **ir en tren** to go by train ▶ **tren de aterrizaje** undercarriage
expresión **estar como (para parar) un tren** to be really gorgeous ▶ **subirse al tren** to climb on the bandwagon

trenza *sf* braid

trepar ◆ *vt* to climb
◆ *vi* ❶ [*subir*] to climb ❷ *familiar* [*medrar*] to be a social climber

trepidar *vi* to shake

tres *numeral* three
expresión **ni a la de tres** for anything in the world, no way ver también **seis**

trescientos, tas *numeral* three hundred ver también **seis**

tresillo *sm* [*sofá*] three-piece suite

triangular *adj* triangular ☞ *Los adjetivos ingleses son invariables.*

triángulo *sm* GEOMETRÍA & MÚSICA triangle ▶ **triángulo equilátero/rectángulo** equilateral/right-angled triangle

triates *smpl* triplets

tribu *sf* tribe

tribuna *sf* ❶ [*estrado*] platform ❷ [*del jurado*] jury box ❸ DEPORTE [*localidad*] stand; [*graderío*] grandstand ❹ PRENSA ▶ **tribuna de prensa** press box

tribunal *sm* ❶ [*generalmente*] court ❷ [*de examen*] board of examiners ❸ [*de concurso*] panel

tributo *sm* ❶ [*impuesto*] tax ❷ [*homenaje*] tribute

triciclo *sm* tricycle

tridimensional *adj* three-dimensional ☞ *Los adjetivos ingleses son invariables.*

trigésimo, ma *numeral* thirtieth

trigo *sm* wheat

trigonometría *sf* trigonometry

trillizo, za *sm, f* triplet

trillón *sm* quintillion

trilogía *sf* trilogy

trimestral *adj* ❶ [*revista*] quarterly ❷ [*exámenes, calificaciones*] end-of-term ☞ *Sólo se usa delante del sustantivo.*

trimestre *sm* ❶ [*tres meses*] trimester ❷ [*en escuela, universidad*] ≃ quarter

trinar *vi* to chirp
expresión **está que trina** she's fuming

trinchera *sf* MILITAR trench

trineo *sm* ❶ [*pequeño*] sledge ❷ [*grande*] sleigh

Trinidad *sf* • **la (Santísima) Trinidad** the (Holy) Trinity

trino *sm* [*de pájaros*] chirp

trío *sm* trio

tripa *sf* ➊ [*vientre*] stomach ➋ *familiar* [*barriga*] belly

triple ◆ *adj* triple ☿ *Los adjetivos ingleses son invariables.*
◆ *sm* ➊ [*tres veces*] • **el triple** three times as much • **el triple de gente** three times as many people ➋ [*en baloncesto*] three-pointer

triplicado *sm* second copy

triplicar *vt* to triple

trípode *sm* tripod

tripulación *sf* crew

tripulante *smf* crew member

tripular *vt* to man

triste *adj* ➊ [*generalmente*] sad • **me dijeron que esa película es muy triste** they told me that that movie is very sad • **es triste que** it's a shame that ➋ [*día, tiempo, paisaje*] gloomy ➌ *figurado* [*color, vestido, luz*] pale ➍ [*humilde*] poor ☿ *Sólo se usa delante del sustantivo.* ➎ [*sueldo*] miserable
expresión **ni un triste** not a single

tristeza *sf* ➊ [*generalmente*] sadness ➋ [*de paisaje, día*] gloominess

triturador *sm* ➊ [*de basura*] waste-disposal unit ➋ [*de papeles*] shredder

triturar *vt* ➊ [*moler, desmenuzar*] to crush ➋ [*papel*] to shred ➌ [*masticar*] to chew

triunfador, ra *sm, f* winner

triunfal *adj* triumphant ☿ *Los adjetivos ingleses son invariables.*

triunfar *vi* ➊ [*vencer*] to win ➋ [*tener éxito*] to succeed

triunfo *sm* ➊ [*generalmente*] triumph ➋ [*en encuentro, elecciones*] victory, *plural* victories

trocar *vt* ➊ [*transformar*] • **trocar algo (en algo)** to change something (into something) ➋ [*intercambiar*] to swap

trocear *vt* to cut up (into pieces)

trofeo *sm* trophy, *plural* trophies

troglodita *smf* ➊ [*cavernícola*] cave dweller ➋ *familiar* [*bárbaro, tosco*] roughneck

trolebús *sm* trolleybus

trombón *sm* [*instrumento*] trombone

trombosis *sf invariable* thrombosis

trompa *sf* ➊ [*de elefante*] trunk ➋ [*de oso hormiguero*] snout ➌ [*de insecto*] proboscis ➍ MÚSICA horn

trompazo *sm familiar* bang • **darse un trompazo con** to bang into

trompeta *sf* trumpet

trompetista *smf* trumpeter

trompicón *sm* [*tropezón*] stumble
expresión **a trompicones** in fits and starts

tronar ◆ *v impersonal* & *vi* ➊ to thunder ➋ *familiar* [*negocio*] to fail ➌ *familiar* [*relación*] to break up ➍ *familiar* [*examen*] to flunk
◆ *vt familiar* [*reprobar*] to flunk

tronco *sm* ➊ ANATOMÍA & BOTÁNICA trunk ➋ [*talado y sin ramas*] log
expresión **dormir como un tronco** to sleep like a log

trono *sm* throne • **subir al trono** to ascend the throne

tropa *sf* MILITAR • **las tropas** troops

tropecientos, tas *adj familiar* loads of

tropel *sm* [*de personas*] mob

tropezar *vi* ➊ [*con el pie*] • **tropezar (con)** to stumble (on) • **tropecé con el escalón** I stumbled on the stairs ➋ [*problema, persona*] • **tropezar con** to encounter • **el proyecto tropezó con numerosas dificultades** the project encountered many difficulties

tropezón *sm* ➊ [*con el pie*] stumble • **dar un tropezón** to stumble ➋ *figurado* [*desacierto*] slip-up

tropical *adj* tropical ☿ *Los adjetivos ingleses son invariables.*

trópico *sm* tropic ▶ **el trópico de Cáncer** the Tropic of Cancer ▶ **el trópico de Capricornio** the Tropic of Capricorn

tropiezo *sm* ➊ [*con el pie*] stumble • **dar un tropiezo** to stumble ➋ *figurado* [*equivocación*] slip-up ➌ [*revés*] setback

trotamundos *smf invariable* globe-trotter

trotar *vi* ➊ [*caballo*] to trot ➋ *familiar* [*de aquí para allá*] to rush around

trote *sm* [*de caballo*] trot • **al trote** at a trot

trozar *vt* to cut up

trozo *sm* ➊ [*generalmente*] piece • **cortar algo en trozos** to cut something into pieces • **hacer algo a trozos** to do something in bits ➋ [*de sendero, camino*] stretch ➌ [*de obra, película*] extract

trucha *sf* [*pez*] trout

truco *sm* ➊ [*trampa, engaño*] trick ▶ **truco de magia** magic trick ▶ **truco publicitario** advertising gimmick ➋ [*habilidad, técnica*] knack • **coger el truco** to get the knack

truculento, ta *adj* horrifying ☿ *Los adjetivos ingleses son invariables.*

trueno *sm* METEOROLOGÍA clap of thunder • **truenos** thunder

trueque *sm* ➊ COMERCIO & HISTORIA barter ➋ [*intercambio*] exchange

trufa *sf* [*hongo, bombón*] truffle

trunco, a *adj* [*incompleto*] incomplete

tu (pl tus) *adj posesivo* ☿ *Sólo se usa delante del sustantivo.* your

tú *pronombre personal* you • **es más alta que tú** she's taller than you • **tratar de tú a alguien** to address somebody as "tú"
expresión **de tú a tú** [*lucha*] evenly matched

tubérculo *sm* tuber

tuberculosis *sf invariable* tuberculosis

T

tubería *sf* [*tubo*] pipe

tubo *sm* ❶ [*tubería*] pipe ▶ **tubo del desagüe** drain-pipe ❷ [*recipiente*] tube ▶ **tubo de ensayo** test tube ▶ **tubo de escape** AUTOMÓVILES exhaust (pipe) ❸ ANATOMÍA tract ▶ **tubo digestivo** digestive tract

tuerca *sf* nut

tuerto, ta *adj* ❶ [*sin un ojo*] one-eyed ❷ [*ciego de un ojo*] blind in one eye ⚲ *Los adjetivos ingleses son invariables.*

tuétano *sm* ANATOMÍA (bone) marrow

tufo *sm* [*mal olor*] stench

tulipán *sm* tulip

tumba *sf* grave

expresión **ser (como) una tumba** to be as silent as the grave

tumbar *vt* [*derribar*] to knock over

■ **tumbarse** *v pronominal* to lie down • **llegó cansadísima y se tumbó en el sofá** she arrived extremely tired and lay down on the sofa

tumbo *sm* jolt

expresión **ir dando tumbos** [*persona*] to have a lot of ups and downs

tumbona *sf* ❶ [*en la playa*] deck chair ❷ [*en el jardín*] (sun) lounger

tumor *sm* tumor

tumulto *sm* ❶ [*disturbio*] riot ❷ [*alboroto*] uproar

tumultuoso, sa *adj* ❶ [*conflictivo*] tumultuous ❷ [*turbulento*] rough ⚲ *Los adjetivos ingleses son invariables.*

túnel *sm* tunnel ▶ **túnel de lavado** car wash

expresión **salir del túnel** to turn the corner

túnica *sf* tunic

tuntún ■ **al tuntún** *locución adverbial* without thinking

tupé *sm* [*cabello*] quiff

tupido, da *adj* dense ⚲ *Los adjetivos ingleses son invariables.*

turba *sf* ❶ [*combustible*] peat ❷ [*muchedumbre*] mob

turbante *sm* turban

turbina *sf* turbine

turbio, bia *adj* ❶ [*agua* ETC] cloudy ❷ [*vista*] blurred ❸ *figurado* [*negocio* ETC] shady ❹ *figurado* [*época* ETC] turbulent ⚲ *Los adjetivos ingleses son invariables.*

turbulencia *sf* ❶ [*de fluido*] turbulence ❷ [*alboroto*] uproar

turbulento, ta *adj* ❶ [*generalmente*] turbulent ❷ [*revoltoso*] unruly ⚲ *Los adjetivos ingleses son invariables.*

turco, ca ◆ *adj* Turkish ⚲ *Los adjetivos ingleses son invariables.*

◆ *sm, f* [*persona*] Turk

■ **turco** *sm* [*lengua*] Turkish

turismo *sm* ❶ [*generalmente*] tourism • **hacer turismo (por)** to go touring (around) ❷ AUTOMÓVILES private car

turista *smf* tourist

turístico, ca *adj* tourist ⚲ *Sólo se usa delante del sustantivo.*

turnarse *v pronominal* • **turnarse (con alguien)** to take turns (with somebody) • **cuando la abuela estuvo enferma, nos turnábamos para acompañarla** when our grandmother was sick, we took turns keeping her company

turno *sm* ❶ [*tanda*] turn • **le ha llegado el turno de hacerlo** it's his turn to do it ❷ [*de trabajo*] shift • **trabajar por turnos** to work shifts ▶ **turno de día/noche** day/night shift

turquesa ◆ *sf* [*mineral*] turquoise

◆ *adj invariable* [*color*] turquoise ⚲ *Los adjetivos ingleses son invariables.*

◆ *sm* [*color*] turquoise

Turquía *nombre propio* Turkey

turrón *sm* ▶ *para explicar lo que es puedes decir:* it's a type of almond nougat eaten at Christmas

tutor, ra *sm, f* ❶ DERECHO guardian ❷ [*profesor - privado*] tutor ; [*- de un curso*] form teacher

tutoría *sf* ❶ DERECHO guardianship ❷ [*en colegio*] tutorial

tuyo, ya ◆ *adj posesivo* yours • **este libro es tuyo** this book is yours • **un amigo tuyo** a friend of yours • **no es asunto tuyo** it's none of your business

◆ *pronombre posesivo* • **el tuyo** yours • **el tuyo es rojo** yours is red

expresiones **ésta es la tuya** *familiar* this is the chance you've been waiting for ▶ **lo tuyo es el teatro** [*lo que haces bien*] you should be on the stage ▶ **los tuyos a)** *familiar* [*tu familia*] your folks **b)** [*tu bando*] your lot

TV (*abreviatura de* televisión) *sf* TV

T

U

u¹, U *sf* [*letra*] u; U

u² *conjunción* or • **pídele a Miguel u Omar que te ayuden** ask Miguel or Omar to help you → **o**

ubicación *sf* location

ubicar *vt* ❶ [*persona, objeto*] to put • **ubicó a los niños en el asiento trasero** she put the children in the back seat ❷ [*edificio* ETC] to locate ❸ [*encontrar*] to find • **no logro ubicarlo** I can't find him

■ **ubicarse** *v pronominal* [*edificio* ETC] to be situated • **las Américas se ubican entre el océano Pacífico y el Atlántico** the Americas are situated between the Pacific and the Atlantic Oceans

ubre *sf* udder

UCI (*abreviatura de* unidad de cuidados intensivos) *sf* ICU

Ud., Vd. *abreviatura escrita de* **usted**

Uds., Vds. *abreviatura escrita de* **usted**

UE (*abreviatura de* Unión Europea) *sf* EU

UHF (*abreviatura de* ultra high frequency) *sf* UHF

újule *exclamación* • **¡újule!** wow!

úlcera *sf* MEDICINA ulcer

ulcerar *vt* to ulcerate

ultimador, ra *sm, f* killer

últimamente *adv* recently

ultimar *vt* ❶ [*generalmente*] to conclude ❷ [*matar*] to kill

ultimátum (pl ultimatos O ultimátum) *sm* ultimatum

último, ma ◆ *adj* ❶ [*generalmente*] last • **es mi último año de estudios** it's my last year of studies • **por último** lastly • **ser lo último a)** [*lo final*] to come last **b)** [*el último recurso*] to be a last resort **c)** [*el colmo*] to be the last straw ❷ [*más reciente*] latest ❸ [*más remoto*] furthest ❹ [*más bajo*] bottom ❺ [*más alto*] top • **viven en el último piso** they live on the top floor ❻ [*de más atrás*] back • **se sentó en la última fila** she sat down in the back row ⚲ *Los adjetivos ingleses son invariables.*

◆ *sm, f* ❶ [*en fila, carrera* ETC] • **el último** the last (one) • **llegar el último** to come last ❷ [*en comparaciones, enumeraciones*] • **éste último...** the latter...

ultra *smf* POLÍTICA right-wing extremist

ultrasonido *sm* ultrasound

ultratumba *sf* • **de ultratumba** from beyond the grave

ultravioleta *adj invariable* ultraviolet ⚲ *Los adjetivos ingleses son invariables.*

umbilical → **cordón**

umbral *sm* ❶ [*generalmente*] threshold ❷ *figurado* [*límite*] bounds *pl*

un, una ◆ *artículo* a; an ⚲ *ante sonido vocálico* • **un hombre/coche** a man/car • **una mujer/mesa** a woman/table • **un águila/hacha** an eagle/axe • **una hora** an hour

◆ *adj* → **uno** ⚲ *Los adjetivos ingleses son invariables.*

unánime *adj* unanimous ⚲ *Los adjetivos ingleses son invariables.*

unanimidad *sf* unanimity • **por unanimidad** unanimously

undécimo, ma *numeral* eleventh

ungüento *sm* ointment

únicamente *adv* only

único, ca *adj* ❶ [*sólo*] only • **es el único par de zapatos que me gusta** it's the only pair of shoes that I like • **es lo único que quiero** it's all I want ❷ [*excepcional*] unique • **este pintor es originalísimo, su obra es única** this painter is very original, his work is unique ❸ [*precio, función, razón*] single ⚲ *Los adjetivos ingleses son invariables.*

unidad *sf* ❶ [*generalmente*] MATEMÁTICAS & MILITAR unit • **la caja de 20 unidades cuesta el doble que la de 10** the box with 20 units costs twice as much as the one with 10 • **25 pesos la unidad** 25 pesos each ▶ **unidad central de proceso** INFORMÁTICA central processing unit ▶ **unidad de disco** INFORMÁTICA disk drive ▶ **unidad de terapia intensiva** intensive care unit ▶ **unidad monetaria** monetary unit ❷ [*cohesión, acuerdo*] unity • **es importante que haya unidad entre los miembros de la familia** it's important that there be unity among family members

unido, da *adj* ❶ [*junto*] united ❷ [*familia, amigo*] close ⚲ *Los adjetivos ingleses son invariables.*

unifamiliar *adj* detached • **vivienda unifamiliar** house *(detached or terraced)* ⚙️ *Los adjetivos ingleses son invariables.*

unificar *vt* ❶ [*unir*] to unite ❷ [*países*] to unify ❸ [*uniformar*] to standardize

uniformar *vt* ❶ [*igualar*] to standardize ❷ [*poner uniforme*] to put into uniform

uniforme ◆ *adj* ❶ uniform ❷ [*superficie*] even ⚙️ *Los adjetivos ingleses son invariables.*

◆ *sm* uniform

uniformidad *sf* ❶ [*de movimiento*] uniformity ❷ [*de superficie*] evenness

unión *sf* ❶ [*generalmente*] union • **en unión con** together with ▶ **la Unión Europea** the European Union ❷ [*cohesión*] unity • **es importante que haya unión entre los hermanos** it's important that there be unity between the brothers

unir *vt* ❶ [*pedazos, habitaciones* ETC] to join • **si unimos estos dos tubos, obtendremos uno más largo** if we join these two tubes, we'll get a longer one ❷ [*empresas, estados, facciones*] to unite • **las dificultades económicas unieron a la familia** the economic difficulties united the family ❸ [*comunicar - ciudades* ETC] to link ❹ [*sujeto: amistad, circunstancias* ETC] to bind ❺ [*casar*] to join ❻ [*combinar*] to combine • **unir algo a algo** to combine something with something

unisexo, unisex *adj invariable* unisex ⚙️ *Los adjetivos ingleses son invariables.*

universal *adj* ❶ [*generalmente*] universal ❷ [*mundial*] world ⚙️ *Sólo se usa delante del sustantivo.* • **de fama universal** world famous

universidad *sf* university, *plural* universities

universitario, ria ◆ *adj* university ⚙️ *Sólo se usa delante del sustantivo.* • **un estudiante universitario** a university student

◆ *sm, f* [*estudiante*] university student

universo *sm* ❶ ASTRONOMÍA universe ❷ *figurado* [*mundo*] world

uno, una
◆ *adj*
❶ [*artículo indefinido*] one
• **un día volveré** I'll be back one day
• **un hombre, un voto** one man, one vote
❷ [*en plural, indica una cantidad indeterminada*]
• **había unos coches mal estacionados** there were some badly-parked cars
❸ [*en plural, indica una aproximación*]
• **me voy unos días a Guadalajara** I'm off to Guadalajara for a few days
• **vinieron unas diez personas** about ten people came
• **cuesta unos 45 pesos** it costs about 45 pesos

⚙️ *Los adjetivos ingleses son invariables.*

◆ *pronombre*
❶ [*designa un elemento indeterminando entre muchos*] one
• **coge uno** take one
• **uno de ellos** one of them
• **uno de tantos** one of many
• **como uno más** like everyone else
• **unos cuantos** a few
• **más de uno** more than one
❷ [*designa un elemento indeterminando entre pocos*] some
• **tienes muchas manzanas, dame unas** you have a lot of apples, let me have some
• **unas son buenas, otras malas** some are good, some are bad
❸ *familiar* [*designa una persona determinada de manera imprecisa*]
• **ayer hablé con uno que te conoce** I spoke to somebody who knows you yesterday
• **lo sé porque me lo han contado unos** I know because some people told me
❹ [*para hablar de sí mismo de manera impersonal*] you
• **entonces es cuando se da uno cuenta de ya no es tan joven como antes** that's when you realize you're not as young as you used to be

expresiones **uno a uno** one by one ▶ **de uno en uno** o **uno por uno** one by one ▶ **uno tras otro** one after the other ▶ **uno a otro** one to another

■ **uno**
◆ *sm*
[*número*] one
• **uno y uno son dos** one plus one is two ver también **seis**

untar *vt* ❶ [*pan, tostada*] • **untar (con)** to spread (with) ❷ [*piel, cara* ETC] to smear (with) ❸ [*máquina, bisagra* ETC] to grease

uña *sf* ❶ [*de mano*] fingernail ❷ [*de pie*] toenail ❸ [*garra*] claw

expresión **ser uña y carne** to be as thick as thieves ▶ **enseñar las uñas** to get your claws out

uranio *sm* uranium

Urano *nombre propio* Uranus

urbanismo *sm* town planning

urbanización *sf* ❶ [*acción*] urbanization ❷ [*zona residencial*] (housing) estate

urbanizar *vt* to develop

urbano, na *adj* urban ⚙️ *Los adjetivos ingleses son invariables.*

urbe *sf* large city

urdir *vt* ❶ [*planear*] to plot ❷ [*hilos*] to warp

urgencia *sf* ❶ [*cualidad*] urgency ❷ MEDICINA emergency, *plural* emergencies • **de urgencia** emergency • **los médicos siempre reciben llamadas de urgencia** doctors always receive emergency calls • **en caso de urgencia** in case of emergency

urgente *adj* ❶ [*apremiante*] urgent ❷ MEDICINA emergency ⚙️ *sustantivo* ❸ [*correo*] express ⚙️ *Los adjetivos ingleses son invariables.*

urgir *vi* • **me urge hacerlo** I urgently need to do it • **urgir a alguien a que haga algo** to urge somebody to do something

URL (*abreviatura de* uniform resource locator) *sf* INFORMÁTICA URL

urna *sf* ❶ [*vasija*] urn ❷ [*caja de cristal*] glass case ❸ [*para votar*] ballot box

urraca *sf* magpie

Uruguay *nombre propio* • **(el) Uruguay** Uruguay

uruguayo, ya *adj* & *sm, f* Uruguayan ☼ *Los adjetivos ingleses son invariables.*
En inglés, los adjetivos que se refieren a un país o una región se escriben con mayúscula.

usado, da *adj* ❶ [*utilizado*] used • **muy usado** widely used ❷ [*de segunda mano*] second-hand ❸ [*gastado*] worn-out ☼ *Los adjetivos ingleses son invariables.*

usanza *sf* • **a la vieja usanza** in the old way

usar *vt* ❶ [*generalmente*] to use • **el carro está usando mucho aceite porque tiene una falla** the car is using a lot of oil because there's something wrong with it • **usar algo/a alguien de algo** to use something/somebody as something ❷ [*prenda*] to wear • **no me gusta usar ropa negra, me parece demasiado triste** I don't like to wear black clothes, they seem too gloomy to me
■ **usarse** *v pronominal* ❶ [*emplearse*] to be used ❷ [*estar de moda*] to be worn

USB (*abreviatura de* universal serial bus) *sm* INFORMÁTICA USB

uso *sm* ❶ [*generalmente*] use • **creo que este aparato tiene otros usos, además de abrir latas** I think this appliance has other uses, besides opening cans • **al uso** fashionable • **al uso mexicano** in the Mexican style • **'de uso externo'** MEDICINA for external use only ❷ LINGÜÍSTICA usage ❸ [*desgaste*] wear and tear

usted *pronombre personal* ❶ [*tratamiento de respeto - sing*] you ; [*- pl*] • **ustedes** you *pl* • **¿cómo está usted?** how are you? • **contesten ustedes a las preguntas** please answer the questions • **me gustaría hablar con usted** I'd like to talk to you • **¡oiga, usted!** hey, you! • **tratar a alguien de usted** to address somebody using the 'usted' form ❷ [*tratamiento de respeto - posesivo*] • **de usted/ustedes** yours

usual *adj* usual ☼ *Los adjetivos ingleses son invariables.*

usuario, ria *sm, f* user

usurero, ra *sm, f* usurer

usurpar *vt* to usurp

utensilio *sm* ❶ [*generalmente*] tool ▶ **utensilios de pesca** fishing tackle ❷ COCINA utensil

útero *sm* womb

útil ◆ *adj* [*beneficioso, aprovechable*] useful ☼ *Los adjetivos ingleses son invariables.*
◆ *sm* ❶ ☼ *generalmente pl* [*herramienta*] tool ▶ **útiles de jardinería** gardening tools ❷ AGRICULTURA implement ▶ **útiles de labranza** agricultural implements

utilidad *sf* ❶ [*cualidad*] usefulness ❷ [*beneficio*] profit

utilización *sf* use

utilizar *vt* [*generalmente*] to use

utopía *sf* utopia

utópico, ca *adj* utopian ☼ *Los adjetivos ingleses son invariables.*

UV (*abreviatura de* ultravioleta) UV

uva *sf* grape ▶ **uva de mesa** dessert grape ▶ **uva moscatel** muscatel grape ▶ **uva pasa** raisin
expresión **estar de mala uva** to be in a bad mood ▶ **tener mala uva** to be a nasty piece of work

uy *exclamación* • **¡uy!** ahh!

U

v *sf* [*letra*] v ; V

vaca *sf* **❶** [*animal*] cow ▶ **vaca lechera/sagrada** dairy/ sacred cow **❷** [*carne*] beef

vacaciones *sfpl* vacation *sing* • **estar/irse de vacaciones** to be/go on vacation

vacacionista *sm, f* tourist

vacante ◆ *adj* vacant ᛫᛫ *Los adjetivos ingleses son invariables.*

◆ *sf* vacancy

vaciar *vt* **❶** [*generalmente*] to empty • **hay que vaciar estos cajones para limpiarlos bien** you have to empty those boxes to clean them well • **vaciar algo de** to empty something of **❷** [*dejar hueco*] to hollow (out)

vacilante *adj* **❶** [*generalmente*] hesitant **❷** [*al elegir*] indecisive **❸** [*luz*] flickering **❹** [*pulso*] irregular ᛫᛫ *Los adjetivos ingleses son invariables.*

vacilar *vi* **❶** [*dudar*] to hesitate **❷** [*al elegir*] to be indecisive **❸** [*luz*] to flicker **❹** [*pulso*] to be irregular

vacío, a *adj* empty ᛫᛫ *Los adjetivos ingleses son invariables.*

■ **vacío** *sm* ▶ FÍSICA vacuum • **envasar al vacío** to vacuum-pack ▶ **vacío de poder** power vacuum **❷** [*abismo, carencia*] void • **perdió el equilibrio y cayó al vacío** he lost his balance and fell into the void **❸** [*hueco*] space

vacuna *sf* vaccine • **la vacuna antitetánica hay que dársela cada diez años** the vaccine against tetanus has to be given every ten years • **poner una vacuna a alguien** to vaccinate somebody

vacunar *vt* to vaccinate • **vacunar contra algo** to vaccinate against something

vacuno, na *adj* bovine ᛫᛫ *Los adjetivos ingleses son invariables.*

vagabundo, da ◆ *adj* **❶** [*persona*] vagrant **❷** [*perro*] stray ᛫᛫ *Los adjetivos ingleses son invariables.*

◆ *sm, f* bum

vagar *vi* • **vagar (por)** to wander (around) • **vagando por ese barrio, encontré un museo muy interesante** wandering around that neighborhood, I found a very interesting museum

vagina *sf* vagina

vago, ga ◆ *adj* **❶** [*flojo*] lazy **❷** [*impreciso*] vague ᛫᛫ *Los adjetivos ingleses son invariables.*

◆ *sm, f* bum

vagón *sm* **❶** [*de pasajeros*] car ▶ **vagón restaurante** dining car **❷** [*de mercancías*] freight car

vagoneta *sf* station wagon

vaguedad *sf* **❶** [*cualidad*] vagueness **❷** [*dicho*] vague remark

vaho *sm* **❶** [*vapor*] steam **❷** [*aliento*] breath

vaina *sf* BOTÁNICA pod

vainilla *sf* vanilla • **helado de vainilla** vanilla ice cream

vaivén *sm* **❶** [*balanceo - de barco*] swaying ; [- de péndulo, columpio*] swinging **❷** [*altibajo*] ups-and-downs *pl*

vajilla *sf* • **una vajilla** a dinner service • **entre las tres podemos lavar la vajilla en 15 minutos** between the three of us we can wash the dishes in 15 minutes

vale *sm* **❶** [*bono*] coupon **❷** [*comprobante*] receipt

valemadrista *adj* **❶** [*apático*] apathetic **❷** [*cínico*] cynical

valentía *sf* bravery

valer ◆ *vt* **❶** [*costar - precio*] to cost • **¿cuánto vale?** [*de precio*] how much does it cost? **❷** [*tener un valor de*] to be worth **❸** [*ocasionar*] to earn **❹** [*merecer*] to deserve **❺** [*equivaler*] to be equal to

◆ *vi* **❶** [*merecer aprecio*] to be worthy **❷** [*servir*] • **eso aún vale** you can still use that • **¿para qué vale?** what's it for? **❸** [*ser válido*] to be valid • **la prueba no valió porque muchos copiaron** the test wasn't valid because many people copied **❹** [*en juegos*] to be allowed **❺** [*tener calidad*] to be of worth • **no valer nada** to be worthless **❻** [*equivaler*] • **valer por** to be worth

expresiones **hacerse valer** to show your worth ▶ **más vale tarde que nunca** better late than never ▶ **más vale que te calles** it would be better if you shut up ▶ **¿vale?** okay? ▶ **¡vale!** okay!

■ **valerse** *v pronominal* **❶** [*servirse*] • **valerse de algo/ alguien** to use something/somebody • **se ha valido de sus conocidos para obtener un empleo** she used her contacts to get a job **❷** [*desenvolverse*] • **valerse (por sí mismo)** to manage on your own

expresión ¡no se vale! that's not fair!

valeroso, sa *adj* brave ҉: *Los adjetivos ingleses son invariables.*

válido, da *adj* valid ҉: *Los adjetivos ingleses son invariables.*

valiente *adj* [*valeroso*] brave ҉: *Los adjetivos ingleses son invariables.*

valija *sf* suitcase

valioso, sa *adj* ❶ [*generalmente*] valuable ❷ [*intento, esfuerzo*] worthy ҉: *Los adjetivos ingleses son invariables.*

valla *sf* ❶ fence ▶ **valla publicitaria** billboard ❷ DEPORTE hurdle

vallar *vt* to put a fence round

valle *sm* valley

valor *sm* ❶ [*generalmente*] MATEMÁTICAS & MÚSICA value • **Julieta tiene muchos valores, entre ellos, la honestidad** Julieta has many values, among them, honesty • **joyas por valor de...** jewels worth... • **sin valor** worthless ❷ [*importancia*] importance • **dar valor a algo** to give importance to something • **quitar valor a algo** to take away from something ❸ [*valentía*] bravery • **Luis se lanzó con valor para salvar al niño** Luis rushed in bravely to save the child

■ **valores** *smpl* ❶ [*principios*] values ❷ FINANZAS securities

valoración *sf* ❶ [*de precio, pérdidas*] valuation ❷ [*de mérito, cualidad, ventajas*] evaluation

valorar *vt* ❶ [*tasar, apreciar*] to value ❷ [*evaluar*] to evaluate

vals (pl valses) *sm* waltz

válvula *sf* valve ▶ **válvula de escape** *figurado* means of letting off steam

vampiro *sm* vampire

vandalismo *sm* vandalism

vanguardia *sf* ❶ MILITAR vanguard ❷ [*cultural*] avant-garde • **de vanguardia** avant-garde

expresión ir a la vanguardia de to be at the forefront of

vanidad *sf* ❶ [*orgullo*] vanity ❷ [*inutilidad*] futility

vanidoso, sa *adj* vain ҉: *Los adjetivos ingleses son invariables.*

vano, na *adj* ❶ [*generalmente*] vain • **en vano** in vain • **los esfuerzos por salvarlo fueron en vano** the efforts to save him were in vain ❷ [*vacío, superficial*] shallow ҉: *Los adjetivos ingleses son invariables.*

vapor *sm* ❶ [*emanación*] vapor ❷ [*de agua*] steam • **plancha a vapor** steam iron • **al vapor** COCINA steamed • **de vapor** [*máquina* ETC] steam ҉: *Sólo se usa delante del sustantivo.* ❸ [*barco*] steamship

expresión a todo vapor at full speed

vapulear *vt* ❶ [*golpear*] to beat ❷ [*criticar*] to slate

vaquero, ra ◆ *adj* cowboy ҉: *Sólo se usa delante del sustantivo.*

◆ *sm, f* [*persona*] cowboy, *femenino* cowgirl

vara *sf* ❶ [*rama, palo*] stick ❷ [*de metal* ETC] rod ❸ [*insignia*] staff

variable *adj* changeable ҉: *Los adjetivos ingleses son invariables.*

variación *sf* ❶ [*cambio*] variation ❷ [*del tiempo*] change

variado, da *adj* ❶ [*diverso*] varied ❷ [*galletas, bombones*] assorted ҉: *Los adjetivos ingleses son invariables.*

variante ◆ *adj* variant ҉: *Los adjetivos ingleses son invariables.*

◆ *sf* ❶ [*variación*] variation ❷ [*carretera*] by-pass

variar ◆ *vt* ❶ [*modificar*] to alter • **a media estación, las temperaturas varían entre 15 y 20 grados** at mid-season, the temperatures vary between 15 and 20 degrees ❷ [*dar variedad*] to vary

◆ *vi*

expresión para variar *irónico* [*cambiara*] (just) for a change

varicela *sf* chickenpox

variedad *sf* variety, *plural* varieties

varilla *sf* ❶ [*barra larga*] rod ❷ [*tira larga - de abanico, paraguas*] spoke; [*- de gafas*] arm

variopinto, ta *adj* diverse ҉: *Los adjetivos ingleses son invariables.*

varita *sf* wand ▶ **varita mágica** magic wand

variz *sf* ҉: *generalmente pl* varicose vein

varón *sm* ❶ [*hombre*] man, *plural* men ❷ [*chico*] boy

varonil *adj* masculine ҉: *Los adjetivos ingleses son invariables.*

vasectomía *sf* vasectomy

vaselina® *sf* Vaseline®

vasija *sf* vessel

vaso *sm* ❶ [*recipiente, contenido*] glass • **quiero un vaso de agua, por favor** I want a glass of water, please ▶ **vaso de plástico** plastic cup ❷ ANATOMÍA vessel ▶ **vasos sanguíneos** blood vessels

vaso ≠ vase

• La palabra inglesa **vase** es un falso amigo que significa *florero*. *Vaso* se traduce al inglés por **glass**.

vasto, ta *adj* vast ҉: *Los adjetivos ingleses son invariables.*

váter (pl váteres)**, water** (pl wateres) *sm* toilet

vatio, watio *sm* watt

vaya *exclamación* ❶ [*sorpresa*] • **¡vaya!** well! ❷ [*énfasis*] • **¡vaya moto!** what a motorbike! → **ir**

VB *abreviatura escrita de* **visto bueno**

Vd. (*abreviatura escrita de* usted) = **Ud.**

Vda. (*abreviatura escrita de* viuda) → **viudo**

Vds. (*abreviatura escrita de* ustedes) = **Uds.**

véase → **ver**

vecindad *sf* ❶ [*vecindario*] neighborhood ❷ [*alrededores*] vicinity ❸ [*vivienda*] tenement house

vecindario *sm* ❶ [*de barrio*] neighborhood ❷ [*de población*] community

vecino, na ♦ *adj* [*cercano*] neighboring ☼ *Los adjetivos ingleses son invariables.*

♦ *sm, f* ❶ [*de la misma casa, calle*] neighbor ❷ [*de un barrio*] resident ❸ [*de una localidad*] inhabitant

vegetación *sf* vegetation

vegetal ♦ *adj* ❶ BIOLOGÍA plant ☼ *Sólo se usa delante del sustantivo.* ❷ [*sandwich*] salad ☼ *Sólo se usa delante del sustantivo.*

♦ *sm* vegetable

vegetar *vi* to vegetate

vegetariano, na *adj & sm, f* vegetarian ☼ *Los adjetivos ingleses son invariables.*

vehículo *sm* ❶ [*generalmente*] vehicle ❷ [*de infección*] carrier

veinte *numeral* twenty • **los (años) veinte** the twenties ver también **seis**

veinteavo, va *numeral* twentieth

veintena *sf* • **una veintena de** about twenty

vejación *sf* humiliation

vejamen *sm* = vejación

vejez *sf* old age

vejiga *sf* bladder

vela *sf* ❶ [*para dar luz*] candle ❷ [*de barco*] sail ❸ DEPORTE sailing • **hacer vela** to go sailing

expresiones estar a dos velas not to have two halfpennies to rub together ▶ ¿quién le ha dado vela en este entierro? who asked you to stick your oar in? ▶ pasar la noche en vela a) [*adrede*] to stay awake all night b) [*desvelado*] to have a sleepless night

velada *sf* evening

velado, da *adj* ❶ [*oculto*] veiled ❷ FOTOGRAFÍA fogged ☼ *Los adjetivos ingleses son invariables.*

velar ♦ *vi* ❶ [*cuidar*] • **velar por** to look after ❷ [*no dormir*] to stay awake

♦ *vt* [*muerto*] to keep a vigil over

■ **velarse** *v pronominal* FOTOGRAFÍA to get fogged

velero *sm* sailing boat

veleta *sf* weather vane

vello *sm* ❶ [*pelusilla*] down ❷ [*pelo*] hair ▶ vello púbico pubic hair

velo *sm* literal & figurado veil

expresión correr un (tupido) velo sobre algo to draw a veil over something

velocidad *sf* ❶ [*generalmente*] speed • **a toda velocidad** at full speed • **de alta velocidad** high-speed • **cobrar velocidad** to pick up speed • **perder velocidad** to lose speed ▶ velocidad máxima top speed ▶ velocidad punta top speed ❷ TECNOLOGÍA velocity ❸ AUTOMÓVILES [*marcha*] gear • **cambiar de velocidad** to change gear

velocímetro *sm* speedometer

velódromo *sm* cycle track

veloz *adj* fast ☼ *Los adjetivos ingleses son invariables.*

vena *sf* ❶ [*generalmente*] ANATOMÍA & GEOLOGÍA vein ❷ [*inspiración*] inspiration ❸ [*don*] • **tener vena de algo** to have a gift for doing something

venado *sm* ❶ ZOOLOGÍA deer, *plural* deer ❷ COCINA venison

vencedor, ra ♦ *adj* winning ☼ *Los adjetivos ingleses son invariables.*

♦ *sm, f* winner

vencer ♦ *vt* ❶ [*ganar*] to beat • **el nadador chino venció a los demás en la primera prueba** the Chinese swimmer beat the others in the first round • **el ejército nacional venció a las fuerzas extranjeras** the national army defeated the foreign forces ❷ [*derrotar - sujeto: sueño, cansancio, emoción*] to overcome • **estaba muy cansada y finalmente la venció el sueño** she was very tired and finally sleep overcame her ❸ [*aventajar*] • **vencer a alguien a** o **en algo** to outdo somebody at something ❹ [*superar - miedo, obstáculos*] to overcome; [*- tentación*] to resist

♦ *vi* ❶ [*ganar*] to win ❷ [*caducar - garantía, contrato, plazo*] to expire; [*- deuda, pago*] to fall due ❸ [*prevalecer*] to prevail

■ **vencerse** *v pronominal* [*estante* ETC] to give way

vencido, da *adj* ❶ [*derrotado*] defeated • **darse por vencido** to give up ❷ [*caducado - garantía, contrato, plazo*] expired; [*- pago, deuda*] due ☼ *Los adjetivos ingleses son invariables.*

vencimiento *sm* [*término - de garantía, contrato, plazo*] expiry; [*- de pago, deuda*] due date

venda *sf* bandage • **venda de gasa** gauze bandage • **los secuestradores le pusieron una venda en los ojos** the kidnappers put a blindfold over his eyes

expresión tener una venda en o delante de los ojos to be blind

vendaje *sm* dressing • **poner un vendaje** to put on a dressing

vendar *vt* to bandage • **le vendaron el tobillo que se torció** they bandaged the ankle that he twisted • **vendar los ojos a alguien** to blindfold somebody

vendaval *sm* gale

vendedor, ra *sm, f* ❶ [*generalmente*] seller ▶ vendedor ambulante street vendor ❷ [*en tienda*] sales assistant ❸ [*de coches, seguros*] salesman, *femenino* saleswoman

vender *vt* to sell • **los vecinos venden su casa** the neighbors are selling their house • **vender algo por** to sell something for

■ **venderse** *v pronominal* ❶ [*ser vendido*] to be sold o on sale • **'se vende'** for sale ❷ [*dejarse sobornar*] to sell yourself

vendimia *sf* grape harvest

veneno *sm* ❶ [*generalmente*] poison ❷ [*de serpiente, insecto*] venom

venenoso, sa *adj* ❶ [*generalmente*] poisonous ❷ figurado [*malintencionado*] venomous ☼ *Los adjetivos ingleses son invariables.*

V

venerable *adj* venerable ·ᄋ̣· *Los adjetivos ingleses son invariables.*

venerar *vt* to venerate

venezolano, na *adj* & *sm, f* Venezuelan ·ᄋ̣· *Los adjetivos ingleses son invariables.*

En inglés, los adjetivos que se refieren a un país o una región se escriben con mayúscula.

Venezuela *nombre propio* Venezuela

venganza *sf* vengeance

vengar *vt* to avenge

■ **vengarse** *v pronominal* • **vengarse (de)** to take revenge (on) • **las víctimas prometieron que se vengarían del estafador** the victims promised that they would take revenge on the swindler

vengativo, va *adj* vengeful ·ᄋ̣· *Los adjetivos ingleses son invariables.*

venia *sf* ❶ [*permiso*] permission ❷ DERECHO [*perdón*] pardon • **con la venia** [*tomando la palabra*] by your leave

venidero, ra *adj* future • **en los años venideros** in future years ·ᄋ̣· *Los adjetivos ingleses son invariables.*

venir
◆ *vi*
❶ [*ir hacia el sitio donde se encuentra el que habla*] to come
• **¿vienes tú o voy yo?** are you coming here or shall I go there?
• **vinieron a las doce** they came at midday
• **ya vienen los turistas** the tourists are about to arrive
• **no quiero que Laura venga** I don't want Laura to come
• **¿has venido en coche o andando?** did you drive or walk?
• **¿quién vino a la fiesta?** who went to the party?
❷ [*indica una característica*]
• **el texto viene en inglés** the text is in English
• **desde unos quince días, viene muy preocupado** he's been very worried for the last couple of weeks
• **los cambios vienen motivados por la presión de la oposición** the changes are the result of pressure from the opposition
❸ [*antes de un gerundio, indica que la acción comienza en el pasado y continua hasta el momento en que se describe*]
• **las peleas vienen sucediéndose desde hace tiempo** these fights have been going on for a while already
❹ [*aparecer*]
• **su foto viene en primera página** her photo's on the front page
❺ [*sentir*]
• **me viene sueño** I'm feeling sleepy
• **le vinieron ganas de reír** he felt like laughing
❻ [*refiriéndose a la ropa*]
• **¿qué tal te viene?** how does it fit you?
• **el abrigo le viene pequeño** the coat's too small for her

• **venir clavado a alguien** to be made for somebody

expresión **venir bien/mal** it suits me/it doesn't suit me • **¿te viene bien el martes?** how does Tuesday suit you? • **mañana no me viene bien** tomorrow doesn't work for me ❱ **el año/mes que viene** next year/month

■ **venir a**
◆ *v + preposición*
[*seguido por el infinitivo, ser equivalente a*] to come to
• **venir a ser** to come to
• **el viaje nos vino a costar unos 2.000 pesos** the trip came to around 2.000 pesos
• **viene a ser lo mismo** it's the same thing

expresiones **¿a qué viene esto?** what's all this about? ❱ **venir a menos** to go downhill • **el negocio vino a menos** the business went downhill • **una familia venida a menos** a family who has gone down in the world ❱ **venir a parar en** to end in ❱ **venir al pelo** *familiar* to go smoothly

■ **venir con**
◆ *v + preposición*
• **no me vengas con historias** don't come telling tales

■ **venir de**
◆ *v + preposición*
[*originarse en*] to come from
• **esta palabra viene del latín** this word comes from Latin

venta *sf* ❶ [*acción*] sale • **'en venta'** for sale • **estar en venta** to be for sale ❱ **venta al contado** cash sale ❱ **venta a plazos** sale by instalments ❷ [*cantidad*] • **ventas** sales *pl* • **las ventas siempre aumentan en diciembre** sales always increase in December

ventaja *sf* ❶ [*hecho favorable*] advantage • **tiene la ventaja de saber inglés y francés** she has the advantage of knowing English and French ❷ [*en competición*] lead • **llevar ventaja a alguien** to have a lead over somebody

ventajoso, sa *adj* advantageous ·ᄋ̣· *Los adjetivos ingleses son invariables.*

ventana *sf* [*generalmente*] INFORMÁTICA window

ventanilla *sf* ❶ [*de vehículo, sobre*] window ❷ [*taquilla*] counter

ventilación *sf* ventilation

ventilador *sm* fan

ventilar *vt* ❶ [*airear*] to air ❷ [*resolver*] to clear up ❸ [*discutir*] to air

ventolera *sf* gust of wind

ventosa *sf* sucker

ventosidad *sf* wind

ventoso, sa *adj* windy ·ᄋ̣· *Los adjetivos ingleses son invariables.*

ventrílocuo, cua *sm, f* ventriloquist

Venus *nombre propio* Venus

ver

◆ *vt*

❶ [*percibir con los ojos*] to see
• **desde casa vemos el mar** we can see the sea from our house
• **hacía mucho tiempo que no te veía por aquí** it's been ages since I saw you around here

❷ [*asistir como espectador*]
• **¿has visto esa película?** have you seen that film?
• **Pablo se pasa el día viendo la tele** Pablo spends his day watching tv

❸ [*visitar a alguien*] to see
• **fue a ver a unos amigos** he went to see some friends

❹ [*darse cuenta*] to see
• **ya veo lo que quieres decir** I see what you mean now
• **veo que estás de mal humor** I can see you're in a bad mood
• **veo que tendré que irme sola** I can see I'm going to have to go on my own

❺ [*hacerse una opinión de*] to look
• **cada cual tiene su manera de ver las cosas** everyone has their own way of looking at things
• **esto lo veremos más adelante** we can look at this later on

expresiones **¡hay que ver lo tonto que es!** can you believe how stupid he is? ▶ **no poder ver algo/a alguien (ni en pintura)** *familiar* not to be able to stand (the sight of)somebody/something ▶ **por lo visto** o **que se ve** apparently ▶ **¡te he visto venir!** I saw you coming!

◆ *vi*

[*con los ojos*] to see
• **no veo bien, necesito lentes** I don't see well, I need glasses

expresiones **a ver** • **¿qué es esto ? ¿a ver?** what's this? Let's see. • **¡a ver, niños! ¿qué pasa aquí?** come on, guys! What's going on here? • **¿y encima te ha invitado al restaurante? — ¡a ver!** and on top of that he's invited you the restaurant? — looks like it! • **a ver qué pasa** we'll see what happens ▶ **eso está por ver** that remains to be seen ▶ **ya veremos** we'll see

◆ *sm*

[*apariencia*]
• **estar de buen ver** to be good-looking

■ **verse**

◆ *v pronominal*

❶ [*frecuentarse*] to see each other
• **nos vemos a veces** we see each other occasionally

❷ [*imaginarse a sí mismo*] to see yourself
• **él ya se ve instalado en el despacho del presidente** he can see himself in the president's office already

• **ya me veo haciendo su maleta** I can already see myself packing his bag

❸ [*en frases impersonales*]
• **nunca se ha visto nada igual** we've never seen anything like this before
• **¡habráse visto!** *familiar* can you believe it?
• **se ve que no sabe nada de inglés** it's obvious that he doesn't know any English

❹ [*instrucciones en un libro, un documento*] see
• **'véase anexo 1'** see attachment 1

veracidad *sf* truthfulness

veranear *vi* • **veranear en** to spend your summer vacation in

veraneo *sm* summer vacation • **de veraneo** vacation ⚲ *Sólo se usa delante del sustantivo.*

veraniego, ga *adj* summer ⚲ *Sólo se usa delante del sustantivo.*

verano *sm* summer • **el próximo verano** next summer

veras ■ **de veras** *locución adverbial* ❶ [*verdaderamente*] really ❷ [*en serio*] seriously

veraz *adj* truthful ⚲ *Los adjetivos ingleses son invariables.*

verbal *adj* verbal ⚲ *Los adjetivos ingleses son invariables.*

verbo *sm* GRAMÁTICA verb

verdad *sf* ❶ [*generalmente*] truth • **a decir verdad** to tell the truth ❷ [*principio aceptado*] fact ❸ [*buscando confirmación*] • **no te gusta, ¿verdad?** you don't like it, do you? • **está bueno, ¿verdad?** it's good, isn't it?

■ **de verdad** ◆ *locución adverbial* ❶ [*en serio*] seriously ❷ [*realmente*] really
◆ *locución adjetiva* [*auténtico*] real

verdadero, ra *adj* [*cierto, real*] real • **fue un verdadero lío** it was a real mess ⚲ *Los adjetivos ingleses son invariables.*

verde ◆ *adj* ❶ [*generalmente*] green ❷ [*fruta*] unripe ❸ *figurado* [*obsceno*] blue ❹ *figurado* [*inmaduro-proyecto* ETC] in its early stages ⚲ *Los adjetivos ingleses son invariables.*

expresión **estar verde de envidia** to be green with envy ▶ **poner verde a alguien** to criticize somebody
◆ *sm* [*color*] green • **mi color preferido es el verde** my favorite color is green

verdugo *sm* ❶ [*de preso*] executioner ❷ [*que ahorca*] hangman

verdulería *sf* fruit and vegetable store

verdulero, ra *sm, f* fruit and vegetable seller

verdura *sf* vegetables *pl*

---

las verduras

el ajo	the garlic
la alcachofa	the artichoke
el apio	the celery
la berenjena	the eggplant
el brécol	the broccoli

V

el brote de soja	the beansprout
el calabacín	the zucchini
la calabaza	the pumpkin
la cebolla	the onion
el champiñón	the mushroom
el chícharo	the pea
la col de Bruselas	the brussels sprout
la coliflor	the cauliflower
el espárrago	the asparagus
las espinacas	the spinach
la judía verde	the string bean
la lechuga	the lettuce
el maíz	the corn
el nabo	the turnip
la patata	the patato
el pepino	the cucumber
el pimiento	the pepper
el puerro	the leek
el rábano	the radish
la remolacha	the beet
el tomate	the tomato
la zanahoria	the carrot

vereda *sf* path

expresión hacer entrar a alguien en vereda to bring somebody into line

veredicto *sm* verdict

vergonzoso, sa *adj* ❶ [*deshonroso*] shameful ❷ [*tímido*] bashful ⚲ *Los adjetivos ingleses son invariables.*

vergüenza *sf* ❶ [*turbación*] embarrassment • **morir de vergüenza** to die of embarrassment • **dar vergüenza** to embarrass • **¡qué vergüenza!** how embarrassing! • **sentir vergüenza** to feel embarrassed ❷ [*timidez*] bashfulness ❸ [*remordimiento*] shame • **sentir vergüenza** to feel ashamed ❹ [*deshonra, escándalo*] disgrace • **¡es una vergüenza!** it's disgraceful!

verídico, ca *adj* [*cierto*] true ⚲ *Los adjetivos ingleses son invariables.*

verificar *vt* [*comprobar, examinar*] to check

verja *sf* ❶ [*puerta*] iron gate ❷ [*valla*] railings *pl* ❸ [*enrejado*] grille

vermú, vermut (pl vermuts) *sm* [*bebida*] vermouth

verosímil *adj* ❶ [*creíble*] believable ❷ [*probable*] likely ⚲ *Los adjetivos ingleses son invariables.*

verruga *sf* wart

versar *vi* • **versar sobre algo** to be on something • **su último ensayo versa sobre el arte africano** his latest essay is on African art

versátil *adj* ❶ [*voluble*] fickle ❷ [*polifacético*] versatile ⚲ *Los adjetivos ingleses son invariables.*

versículo *sm* verse

versión *sf* ❶ [*generalmente*] version • **el testigo dio su versión de los hechos** the witness gave his version of the facts ▸ **versión original** CINE original (version) ❷ [*en música pop*] cover version

verso *sm* ❶ [*género*] verse ❷ [*unidad rítmica*] line (*of poetry*) ❸ [*poema*] poem • **sabe de memoria algunos versos de Neruda** he knows some of Neruda's poems by heart

vértebra *sf* vertebra, *plural* vertebrae

vertebrado, da *adj* vertebrate ⚲ *Los adjetivos ingleses son invariables.*

vertedero *sm* ❶ [*de basuras*] dump ❷ [*de agua*] overflow

verter *vt* ❶ [*derramar*] to spill ❷ [*vaciar - líquido*] to pour (out); [*- recipiente*] to empty ❸ [*tirar - basura, residuos*] to dump

vertical ◆ *adj* ❶ GEOMETRÍA vertical ❷ [*derecho*] upright ⚲ *Los adjetivos ingleses son invariables.*
◆ *sf* GEOMETRÍA vertical

vértice *sm* ❶ [*generalmente*] vertex ❷ [*de cono*] apex

vertido *sm* ❶ ⚲ *generalmente pl* [*residuo*] waste ⚲ *incontable* ❷ [*acción*] dumping

vertiente *sf* ❶ [*pendiente*] slope ❷ figurado [*aspecto*] side

vertiginoso, sa *adj* ❶ [*mareante*] dizzy ❷ figurado [*raudo*] giddy ⚲ *Los adjetivos ingleses son invariables.*

vértigo *sm* ❶ [*enfermedad*] vertigo • **no puedo subir muy alto porque tengo vértigo** I can't go up very high because I have vertigo ❷ [*mareo*] dizziness • **trepar me da vértigo** climbing makes me dizzy

vesícula *sf* ▸ vesícula biliar gall bladder

vespertino, na *adj* evening ⚲ *Sólo se usa delante del sustantivo.*

vestíbulo *sm* ❶ [*de casa*] (entrance) hall ❷ [*de hotel, oficina*] lobby

vestido, da *adj* dressed • **ir vestido** to be dressed • **iba vestido de negro** he was dressed in black ⚲ *Los adjetivos ingleses son invariables.*
■ **vestido** *sm* ❶ [*indumentaria*] clothes *pl* ❷ [*prenda femenina*] dress ▸ **vestido de noche** evening dress ▸ **vestido de novia** wedding dress

vestimenta *sf* clothes *pl*

vestir ◆ *vt* ❶ [*generalmente*] to dress • **Luisa y Juana se entretienen vistiendo a las muñecas** Luisa and Juana entertain themselves dressing their dolls ❷ [*llevar puesto*] to wear
◆ *vi* [*llevar ropa*] to dress
■ **vestirse** *v pronominal* ❶ [*ponerse ropa*] to get dressed • **¿cuánto tardas en vestirte?** how long will it take you to get dressed? • **vestirse de** to wear ❷ [*adquirir ropa*] • **vestirse en** to buy your clothes at

vestuario *sm* ❶ [*vestimenta*] clothes *pl* ❷ TEATRO costumes *pl* ❸ [*para cambiarse*] changing room ❹ [*de actores*] dressing room

veta *sf* [*filón*] vein

vetar *vt* to veto

veterano, na *adj & sm, f* veteran ⚲ *Los adjetivos ingleses son invariables.*

veterinario, ria ◆ *adj* veterinary ⚲ *Los adjetivos ingleses son invariables.*

◆ *sm, f* [*persona*] vet

■ **veterinaria** *sf* [*ciencia*] veterinary science

veto *sm* veto • **poner veto a algo** to veto something

vez *sf* ❶ [*generalmente*] time • **ya te pedí cien veces que te callaras** I already asked you a hundred times to be quiet • **una vez** once • **dos veces** twice • **tres veces** three times • **¿has estado allí alguna vez?** have you ever been there? • **a mi/tu** ETC **vez** in my/your ETC turn • **a la vez (que)** at the same time (as) • **escribía una carta a la vez que escuchaba música** she was writing a letter at the same time that she was listening to music • **cada vez (que)** every time • **cada vez más** more and more • **cada vez menos** less and less • **cada vez la veo más feliz** she seems happier and happier • **de una vez** in one go • **de una vez para siempre** o **por todas** once and for all • **muchas veces** often, a lot • **otra vez** again • **no puedo creer que estés aquí otra vez** I can't believe that you're here again • **pocas veces, rara vez** rarely, seldom • **por última vez** for the last time • **una** o **alguna que otra vez** occasionally • **una vez más** once again • **una y otra vez** time and again • **érase una vez** once upon a time ❷ [*turno*] • **pedir la vez** to ask who is last

■ **a veces, algunas veces** *locución adverbial* sometimes • **a veces pienso que no debería haber venido** sometimes I think that I shouldn't have come

■ **de vez en cuando** *locución adverbial* from time to time

■ **en vez de** *locución preposicional* instead of • **en vez de ir al parque, podríamos ir a la playa, ¿no?** instead of going to the park, we could go to the beach, don't you think?

VHF (*abreviatura de* very high frequency) *sf* VHF

VHS (*abreviatura de* video home system) *sm* VHS

vía ◆ *sf* ❶ [*medio de transporte*] route • **por vía aérea a)** [*generalmente*] by air **b)** [*correo*] (by) airmail • **por vía marítima** by sea • **por vía terrestre** by land ▶ **vía fluvial** waterway ❷ [*calzada, calle*] road ▶ **vía pública** public thoroughfare ❸ FERROCARRIL [*raíl*] rails *pl*; track ; [*andén*] platform ▶ **vía férrea** [*ruta*] railway line ❹ [*proceso*] • **estar en vías de** to be in the process of • **país en vías de desarrollo** developing country • **una especie en vías de extinción** an endangered species ❺ ANATOMÍA tract ❻ [*opción*] channel • **por vía oficial/judicial** through official channels/the courts

expresión **dar vía libre a)** [*dejar paso*] to give way **b)** [*dar libertad de acción*] to give a free rein

◆ *preposición* via

■ **Vía Láctea** *sf* Milky Way

viabilidad *sf* viability

viable *adj* [*posible*] viable ☿ *Los adjetivos ingleses son invariables.*

viaducto *sm* viaduct

viajar *vi* to travel • **como no le gusta viajar en avión, usa el tren o el barco** since he doesn't like to travel by plane, he goes by train or by boat

viaje *sm* ❶ [*generalmente*] trip • **vamos a hacer un viaje por América del Sur** we're going to take a trip through South America • **¡buen viaje!** have a good trip!

• **estar/ir de viaje** to be/go away (on a trip) • **hay 11 días de viaje** it's an 11-day journey ▶ **viaje de ida/de vuelta** outward/return trip ▶ **viaje de ida y vuelta** round trip ▶ **viaje de negocios** business trip ▶ **viaje de bodas** honeymoon ▶ **viaje organizado** package tour ❷ [*en barco*] voyage

viajero, ra ◆ *adj* ❶ [*persona*] traveling ❷ [*ave*] migratory ☿ *Los adjetivos ingleses son invariables.*

◆ *sm, f* ❶ [*generalmente*] traveler ❷ [*en transporte público*] passenger

víbora *sf* viper

vibración *sf* vibration

vibrante *adj* ❶ [*oscilante*] vibrating ❷ *figurado* [*emocionante*] vibrant ❸ [*trémulo*] quivering ☿ *Los adjetivos ingleses son invariables.*

vibrar *vi* ❶ [*oscilar*] to vibrate ❷ *figurado* [*voz, rodillas* ETC] to shake ❸ *figurado* [*público*] to get excited

vicepresidente, ta *sm, f* ❶ [*de país, asociación*] vice-president ❷ [*de comité, empresa*] vice-chairman

viceversa *adv* vice versa

viciado, da *adj* ❶ [*aire*] stuffy ❷ [*estilo*] marred ☿ *Los adjetivos ingleses son invariables.*

viciar *vt* [*pervertir*] to corrupt

vicio *sm* ❶ [*mala costumbre*] bad habit ❷ [*libertinaje*] vice ❸ [*defecto físico, de dicción* ETC] defect

expresión **quejarse de vicio** to complain for no (good) reason

vicioso, sa ◆ *adj* dissolute ☿ *Los adjetivos ingleses son invariables.*

◆ *sm, f* dissolute person

víctima *sf* ❶ [*por mala suerte o negligencia*] victim • **la inundación produjo cien víctimas** there were a hundred victims from the flood ❷ [*en accidente, guerra*] casualty • **ser víctima de** to be the victim of

victimar *vt* to kill

victoria *sf* victory, *plural* victories

expresión **cantar victoria** to claim victory

victorioso, sa *adj* victorious ☿ *Los adjetivos ingleses son invariables.*

vid *sf* vine

vida *sf* life • **de por vida** for life • **en vida de** during the life o lifetime of • **en mi/tu** ETC **vida** never (in my/your ETC) life • **estar con vida** to be alive • **ganarse la vida** to earn a living • **pasar a mejor vida** to pass away • **pasarse la vida haciendo algo** to spend your life doing something • **perder la vida** to lose your life • **quitar la vida a alguien** to kill somebody ▶ **vida nocturna** night life

expresión **¡así es la vida!** that's life!

vidente *smf* clairvoyant

video *sm* video

videocámara *sf* camcorder

videocasete *sm* video

videoclip (pl videoclips) *sm* (pop) video

videoclub (pl videoclubes o videoclubs) *sm* video club

videojuego *sm* video game

V

vidriero, ra *sm, f* ❶ [*que fabrica cristales*] glass merchant ❷ [*que coloca cristales*] glazier
■ **vidriera** *sf* ❶ [*puerta*] glass door ❷ [*ventana*] glass window ❸ [*en catedrales*] stained glass window

vidrio *sm* ❶ [*material*] glass ❷ [*de vehículo*] window

viejo, ja ◆ *adj* old • **estos zapatos están muy viejos, tengo que comprar otros** these shoes are very old, I have to buy some others • **hacerse viejo** to grow old ❡ *Los adjetivos ingleses son invariables.*
◆ *sm, f* ❶ [*anciano*] old man, *femenino* old lady • **los viejos** the elderly ▶ **viejo verde** dirty old man, *femenino* dirty old woman ❷ *familiar* [*padres*] old man, *femenino* old lady • **mis viejos** my folks ❸ *familiar* [*amigo*] pal

viento *sm* [*aire*] MÚSICA wind • **hace viento** it's windy
expresiones **contra viento y marea** in spite of everything ▶ **echar a alguien con viento fresco** to send somebody packing ▶ **mis esperanzas se las llevó el viento** my hopes flew out of the window ▶ **viento en popa** splendidly

vientre *sm* ANATOMÍA stomach

viernes *sm invariable* Friday ver también **sábado**
■ **Viernes Santo** *sm* RELIGIÓN Good Friday

viga *sf* ❶ [*de madera*] beam ❷ [*de metal*] girder

vigencia *sf* ❶ [*de ley* ETC] validity • **estar/entrar en vigencia** to be in/come into force ❷ [*de costumbre*] use

vigente *adj* ❶ [*ley* ETC] in force ❷ [*costumbre*] in use ❡ *Los adjetivos ingleses son invariables.*

vigésimo, ma *numeral* twentieth

vigía *smf* lookout

vigilancia *sf* ❶ [*cuidado*] vigilance ❷ [*control*] surveillance • **estar bajo vigilancia** to be under surveillance

vigilante ◆ *adj* vigilant ❡ *Los adjetivos ingleses son invariables.*
◆ *smf* guard ▶ **vigilante nocturno** night watchman

vigilar ◆ *vt* ❶ [*enfermo*] to watch over ❷ [*presos, banco*] to guard ❸ [*niños, bolso*] to keep an eye on ❹ [*proceso*] to oversee
◆ *vi* to keep watch

vigor *sm* vigor • **entrar en vigor** to come into force

vigoroso, sa *adj* [*generalmente*] vigorous ❡ *Los adjetivos ingleses son invariables.*

vil *adj* vile ❡ *Los adjetivos ingleses son invariables.*

villa *sf* ❶ [*población*] small town ❷ [*casa*] villa

villancico *sm* [*navideño*] Christmas carol

villano, na *sm, f* villain

vinagre *sm* vinegar

vinagrera *sf* vinegar bottle

vinagreta *sf* vinaigrette

vinculación *sf* link

vincular *vt* ❶ [*enlazar*] to link • **vincular algo con algo** to link something with o to something ❷ [*por obligación*] to tie

vínculo *sm* ❶ [*entre hechos, países*] link ❷ [*personal, familiar*] tie

vinícola *adj* ❶ [*país, región*] wine-producing ❡ *Sólo se usa delante del sustantivo.* ❷ [*industria*] wine ❡ *Sólo se usa delante del sustantivo.*

vinicultura *sf* wine production

vino *sm* wine ▶ **vino blanco/tinto** white/red wine ▶ **vino rosado** rosé → **venir**

viña *sf* vineyard

viñedo *sm* (large) vineyard

viñeta *sf* ❶ [*de tebeo*] (individual) cartoon ❷ [*de libro*] vignette

viola *sf* viola

violación *sf* ❶ [*de ley, derechos*] violation ❷ [*de persona*] rape

violador, ra *adj & sm, f* rapist ❡ *Los adjetivos ingleses son invariables.*

violar *vt* ❶ [*ley, derechos, domicilio*] to violate ❷ [*persona*] to rape

violencia *sf* ❶ [*agresividad*] violence ▶ **violencia doméstica** domestic violence ❷ [*fuerza - de viento, pasiones*] force

violentar *vt* ❶ [*incomodar*] to embarrass ❷ [*forzar - domicilio*] to break into

violento, ta *adj* ❶ [*generalmente*] violent ❷ [*goce*] intense ❸ [*incómodo*] awkward ❡ *Los adjetivos ingleses son invariables.*

violeta ◆ *sf* [*flor*] violet
◆ *adj invariable & sm* [*color*] violet ❡ *Los adjetivos ingleses son invariables.*

violín *sm* violin

violonchelo, violoncelo *sm* cello

virar ◆ *vt* [*girar*] to turn (round)
◆ *vi* [*girar*] to turn (round)

virgen ◆ *adj* ❶ [*generalmente*] virgin ❷ [*cinta*] blank ❡ *Los adjetivos ingleses son invariables.*
◆ *smf* [*persona*] virgin
◆ *sf* ARTE Madonna
■ **Virgen** *sf* • **la Virgen** RELIGIÓN the (Blessed) Virgin ▶ **¡Virgen santa!** good heavens!

virgo *sm* [*virginidad*] virginity
■ **Virgo** ◆ *sm* [*zodiaco*] Virgo
◆ *smf* [*persona*] Virgo

viril *adj* manly ❡ *Los adjetivos ingleses son invariables.*

virilidad *sf* virility

virtual *adj* ❶ [*posible*] possible ❷ [*casi real*] virtual ❡ *Los adjetivos ingleses son invariables.*

virtud *sf* ❶ [*cualidad*] virtue • **la honestidad es una de sus virtudes** honesty is one of his virtues ❷ [*poder*] power • **tener la virtud de** to have the power to

virtuoso, sa ◆ *adj* [*honrado*] virtuous ❡ *Los adjetivos ingleses son invariables.*

◆ *sm, f* [genio] virtuoso

viruela *sf* ❶ [enfermedad] smallpox ❷ [pústula] pockmark • **picado de viruelas** pockmarked

virulencia *sf figurado* MEDICINA virulence

virus *sm invariable* [generalmente] INFORMÁTICA virus ◗ **virus informático** computer virus

viruta *sf* shaving

visa *sf* visa

visado *sm* visa

visceral *adj figurado* ANATOMÍA visceral ☿ *Los adjetivos ingleses son invariables.*

vísceras *sfpl* entrails • **el corazón y el estómago son vísceras** the heart and the stomach are entrails

viscoso, sa *adj* ❶ [generalmente] viscous ❷ [baboso] slimy ☿ *Los adjetivos ingleses son invariables.*

visera *sf* ❶ [de gorra] peak ❷ [de casco, suelta] visor ❸ [de automóvil] sun visor

visibilidad *sf* visibility

visible *adj* visible • **la cerradura tenía marcas visibles: habían tratado de forzarla** the lock had visible marks: they had tried to force it • **estar visible** [presentable] to be decent ☿ *Los adjetivos ingleses son invariables.*

visillo *sm* net curtain

visión *sf* ❶ [sentido, lo que se ve] sight ❷ [alucinación, lucidez] vision • **no hay nadie ahí, ves visiones** there's not anybody there, you're seeing visions

visionario, ria *adj* & *sm, f* visionary ☿ *Los adjetivos ingleses son invariables.*

visita *sf* ❶ [generalmente] visit • **después de la visita de mis sobrinos, la casa es un caos** after my nieces' and nephews' visit, the house is chaos • **hacer una visita a alguien** to pay somebody a visit ❷ [visitante] visitor • **anoche las visitas se quedaron hasta tardísimo** last night the visitors stayed until very late • **tener visitas** to have visitors ❸ [a página web] hit

visitante *smf* visitor

visitar *vt* ❶ [generalmente] to visit ❷ [sujeto: médico] to call on

vislumbrar *vt* ❶ [entrever] to make out ❷ [adivinar] to have an inkling of

visón *sm* mink

víspera *sf* eve • **la víspera del viaje no pude dormir por la emoción** I couldn't sleep on the eve of the trip because of the excitement • **en vísperas de** on the eve of

vistazo *sm* glance

visto, ta ◆ *participio pasado* → **ver**

◆ *adj* • **estar bien/mal visto** to be considered good/frowned upon ☿ *Los adjetivos ingleses son invariables.*

■ **vista** ◆ *v* → **vestir**

◆ *sf* ❶ [sentido] sight • **la vista es uno de los cinco sentidos** sight is one of the five senses • **a primera vista** [aparentemente] at first sight • **estar a la vista a)** [visible] to be visible **b)** [muy cerca] to be staring one in the face ❷ [ojos] eyes *pl* • **fijar la vista en** to fix your

eyes on ❸ [mirada] gaze • **alzar/bajar la vista** to look up/down ❹ [panorama] view • **compramos una preciosa casa con vista al mar** we bought a lovely house with a view of the sea

expresiones **conocer a alguien de vista** to know somebody by sight ◗ **hacer la vista gorda** to turn a blind eye ◗ **¡hasta la vista!** see you! ◗ **no perder de vista a alguien/algo a)** [vigilar] not to let somebody/something out of your sight **b)** [tener en cuenta] not to lose sight of somebody/something ◗ **perder de vista a)** [dejar de ver] to lose sight of **b)** [perder contacto] to lose touch with ◗ **saltar a la vista** to be blindingly obvious

■ **vistas** *sfpl* [panorama] view *sing* • **con vistas al mar** with a sea view

■ **visto bueno** *sm* • **el visto bueno** the go-ahead • **'visto bueno'** approved

vistoso, sa *adj* eye-catching ☿ *Los adjetivos ingleses son invariables.*

visual *adj* visual ☿ *Los adjetivos ingleses son invariables.*

visualizar *vt* ❶ [generalmente] to visualize ❷ INFORMÁTICA to display

vital *adj* ❶ [generalmente] vital ❷ [ciclo] life ☿ *Sólo se usa delante del sustantivo.* ❸ [persona] full of life

vitalidad *sf* vitality

vitamina *sf* vitamin

vitaminado, da *adj* vitamin-enriched ☿ *Los adjetivos ingleses son invariables.*

vitamínico, ca *adj* vitamin ☿ *Sólo se usa delante del sustantivo.*

viticultor, ra *sm, f* wine grower

viticultura *sf* wine growing

vitorear *vt* to cheer

vitrina *sf* ❶ [en casa] display cabinet ❷ [en tienda] store window

vitro ■ **in vitro** *locución adverbial* in vitro

viudo, da *sm, f* widower, *femenino* <u>widow</u> • **se quedó viuda pocos meses después del casamiento** she became a widow only a few months after the wedding

viva ◆ *sm* cheer • **dar vivas** to cheer

◆ *exclamación* • **¡viva!** hurrah! • **¡viva el rey!** long live the King!

vivacidad *sf* liveliness

vivamente *adv* ❶ [relatar, describir] vividly ❷ [afectar, emocionar] deeply

vivencia *sf* experience

víveres *smpl* supplies

vivero *sm* ❶ [de plantas] nursery, *plural* <u>nurseries</u> ❷ [de peces] fish farm ❸ [de moluscos] bed

viveza *sf* ❶ [de colorido, descripción] vividness ❷ [de persona, discusión, ojos] liveliness ❸ [de ingenio, inteligencia] sharpness

vívido, da *adj* vivid ☿ *Los adjetivos ingleses son invariables.*

vividor, ra *sm, f despectivo* scrounger

vivienda *sf* ❶ [*alojamiento*] housing ❷ [*morada*] dwelling

vivir ◆ *vt* [*experimentar*] to experience

◆ *vi* ❶ [*generalmente*] to live • **vive en un apartamento muy grande, en el centro de la ciudad** she lives in a very big apartment, in the middle of the city • **desde muy joven vive de su propio trabajo** from very young he's lived by his own labor ❷ [*estar vivo*] to be alive • **el perro quedó malherido, pero aún vive** the dog was badly wounded, but he's still alive

expresión vivir para ver who'd have thought it?

vivito *adj*

expresión vivito y coleando *familiar* alive and kicking

vivo, va *adj* ❶ [*existente - ser, lengua* ETC] living • **estar vivo** [*persona, costumbre, recuerdo*] to be alive ❷ [*dolor, deseo, olor*] intense ❸ [*luz, color, tono*] bright ❹ [*gestos, ojos, descripción*] lively ❺ [*activo - ingenio, niño*] quick; sharp; [*- ciudad*] lively·🔆 *Los adjetivos ingleses son invariables.*

vocablo *sm* word

vocabulario *sm* vocabulary

vocación *sf* vocation

vocal ◆ *adj* vocal·🔆 *Los adjetivos ingleses son invariables.*

◆ *sf* vowel

vocalizar *vi* to vocalize

voceador, ra *sm, f* newspaper vendor

vocear ◆ *vt* [*mercancía*] to hawk

◆ *vi* [*gritar*] to shout

vociferar *vi* to shout

vodka *sm o sf* vodka

vol. (*abreviatura escrita de* volumen) vol.

volante ◆ *adj* flying·🔆 *Los adjetivos ingleses son invariables.*

◆ *sm* ❶ [*para conducir*] (steering) wheel • **estar** o **ir al volante** to be at the wheel ❷ [*del médico*] (referral) note ❸ [*en bádminton*] shuttlecock

volar ◆ *vt* ❶ [*en guerras, atentados*] to blow up ❷ [*caja fuerte, puerta*] to blow open ❸ [*edificio en ruinas*] to demolish *(with explosives)* ❹ [*en cantera*] to blast

◆ *vi* ❶ [*generalmente*] to fly • **volar a) a)** [*una altura*] to fly at **b)** [*un lugar*] to fly to • **echar(se) a volar** to fly away o off ❷ [*papeles* ETC] to blow away ❸ *familiar* [*desaparecer*] to disappear

volátil *adj* figurado QUÍMICA volatile·🔆 *Los adjetivos ingleses son invariables.*

volcán *sm* volcano, *plural* volcanoes

volcánico, ca *adj* volcanic·🔆 *Los adjetivos ingleses son invariables.*

volcar ◆ *vt* ❶ [*tirar*] to knock over ❷ [*carretilla*] to tip up ❸ [*vaciar*] to empty out

◆ *vi* ❶ [*coche, camión*] to overturn ❷ [*barco*] to capsize

■ **volcarse** *v pronominal* [*esforzarse*] • **volcarse (con/en)** to throw yourself (into) • **después de la muerte de su marido, se volcó en su trabajo** after her husband's death, she threw herself into her work

volea *sf* volley

voleibol *sm* volleyball

voleo *sm* volley

expresión al voleo randomly

voltaje *sm* voltage

voltear ◆ *vt* ❶ [*heno, crepa, torero*] to toss ❷ [*tortilla - con plato*] to turn over ❸ [*mesa, silla*] to turn upside-down ❹ [*derribar*] to knock over ❺ [*volver*] to turn

◆ *vi* [*torcer*] to turn

■ **voltearse** *v pronominal* [*volverse*] to turn around

voltereta *sf* ❶ [*en el suelo*] handspring ❷ [*en el aire*] somersault

voltio *sm* volt

voluble *adj* changeable·🔆 *Los adjetivos ingleses son invariables.*

volumen *sm* volume • **la maestra pidió que calculáramos el volumen de un cubo** the teacher asked us to calculate the volume of a cube • **esa novela es muy larga, se publicó en tres volúmenes** that novel is very long, it was published in three volumes • **¿podrías bajar el volumen del radio, por favor?** could you lower the radio's volume, please? • **a todo volumen** at full blast ▸ **volumen de negocio** o **ventas** turnover

voluminoso, sa *adj* bulky·🔆 *Los adjetivos ingleses son invariables.*

voluntad *sf* ❶ [*determinación, deseo*] will • **contra la voluntad de alguien** against somebody's will • **a voluntad** [*cuanto se quiere*] as much as you like • **por voluntad propia** of your own free will • **voluntad de hierro** iron will ❷ [*intención*] intention • **buena voluntad** goodwill • **mala voluntad** ill will

voluntariado *sm* voluntary enlistment

voluntario, ria ◆ *adj* voluntary·🔆 *Los adjetivos ingleses son invariables.*

◆ *sm, f* volunteer

voluntarioso, sa *adj* [*esforzado*] willing·🔆 *Los adjetivos ingleses son invariables.*

---

volver

◆ *vt*

❶ [*voltear*] to turn over

• **volved la hoja del examen** turn the exam paper over

• **volvió la carta y... ¡era un as!** he turned the card over and... it was an ace!

❷ [*una parte del cuerpo*] to turn

• **volver la cabeza/la espalda** to turn your head/back

❸ [*transformar de manera definitiva*] to make

• **aquello lo volvió loco** that made him go mad

• **el éxito lo ha vuelto orgulloso** success has made him proud

◆ *vi*

[*regresar al sitio de donde vino*]

• **vuelve, no te vayas** come back, don't go

• **no pienso volver allí** I'm never going back there again

• **espérame un minuto que enseguida vuelvo** wait for me a minute, I'll be right back

• **ahora tengo que volver a la escuela, pero más tarde paso por tu casa** I have to go back to school now, but I'll come by your house later
expresión **volver en sí** to come to
■ **volverse**
◆ *v pronominal*
❶ [*cuerpo*] to turn round
• **me volví para verla mejor** I turned round to see her better
❷ [*transformarse de manera definitiva*] to become
• **se ha vuelto muy antipática** she's become really unpleasant
❸ [*regresar al sitio de donde vino*] to go back
• **me volví porque me olvidé de la llave** I went back because I forgot the key
• **me di cuenta de que había olvidado la cartera y tuve que volverme atrás** I realized I'd left my wallet and had to go back
❹ [*en expresiones*]
• **llegados a este punto del proyecto no es posible volverse atrás** at this point in the project, there's no turning back
■ **volverse a**
◆ *v pronominal + preposición*
❶ [*regresar al sitio de donde vino*] to return
• **me vuelvo a casa** I'm going home
❷ [*retomar el hilo de un relato, de un sujeto*]
• **volvamos a nuestro tema** let's get back to the subject
■ **volverse (contra)**
◆ *v pronominal + preposición*
to turn against
• **la opinión pública se volvió contra él** public opinion is turning against him

vomitar ◆ *vt* [*devolver*] to vomit
◆ *vi* to vomit
vómito *sm* vomit ⚲ *incontable*
vos *pronombre personal* [*tú - sujeto*] you; [*- objeto*] you
votación *sf* vote • **decidir algo por votación** to put something to the vote ❱ **votación a mano alzada** show of hands
votante *smf* voter
votar ◆ *vt* ❶ [*partido, candidato*] to vote for ❷ [*ley*] to vote on ❸ [*aprobar*] to pass
◆ *vi* to vote • **aquí se puede votar a partir de los 18 años** here you can vote starting at 18 years of age
• **votar por a)** [*emitir un voto por*] to vote for **b)** *figurado* [*estar a favor de*] to be in favor of • **votar por que...** to vote (that)... • **votar en blanco** to return a blank ballot paper
voto *sm* ❶ [*generalmente*] vote ❷ RELIGIÓN vow
voz *sf* ❶ [*generalmente*] GRAMÁTICA voice • **a media voz** in a low voice • **aclarar** o **aclararse la voz** to clear your throat • **alzar** o **levantar la voz a alguien** to raise

your voice to somebody • **en voz alta** aloud • **en voz baja** softly ❱ **voz en off** CINE voice-over ❷ [*grito*] shout • **a voces** shouting • **dar voces** to shout ❸ [*vocablo*] word ❹ [*derecho a expresarse*] say • **no tener ni voz ni voto** to have no say in the matter
vudú *sm* voodoo
vuelco *sm* • **dar un vuelco a)** [*coche*] to overturn **b)** [*relaciones*] to change completely **c)** [*empresa*] to go to ruin
expresión **me dio un vuelco el corazón** my heart missed a beat
vuelo *sm* flight • **es entretenido observar el vuelo de los pájaros** it's entertaining to observe birds' flight • **alzar** o **levantar el vuelo a)** [*despegar*] to take flight **b)** *figurado* [*irse de casa*] to fly the nest • **coger algo al vuelo a)** [*en el aire*] to catch something in flight **b)** *figurado* [*rápido*] to catch on to something very quickly • **remontar el vuelo** to soar ❱ **vuelo libre** hang gliding ❱ **vuelo sin motor** gliding
vuelta *sf* ❶ [*generalmente*] turn • **este paso de baile incluye varias vueltas** this dance step includes several turns • **dar una vuelta (a algo)** [*recorriéndolo*] to go round (something) • **dar la vuelta al mundo** to go around the world • **darse la vuelta** to turn round • **dar vueltas (a algo) a)** [*girándolo*] to turn (something) round **b)** [*pensándolo*] to turn something over in your mind ❷ DEPORTE lap ❱ **vuelta (ciclista)** tour ❸ [*regreso, devolución*] round-trip • **boleto de ida y vuelta** round-trip ticket • **a la vuelta a)** [*volviendo*] on the way back **b)** [*al llegar*] on your return • **estar de vuelta** to be back ❹ [*paseo*] • **dar una vuelta a)** [*a pie*] to go for a walk **b)** [*en carro*] to go for a ride • **¿vamos a dar una vuelta por el parque?** are we going to go for a walk around the park? • **salimos a dar una vuelta en el carro nuevo de mi tío** we went out for a ride in my uncle's new car ❺ [*dinero sobrante*] change ❻ [*ronda, turno*] round ❼ [*parte opuesta*] back • **a la vuelta de la esquina** *literal & figurado* round the corner
expresiones **a vuelta de correo** by return of post ❱ **dar la vuelta a la tortilla** *familiar* to turn the tables ❱ **dar una vuelta/dos** ETC **vueltas de campana** [*coche*] to turn over once/twice ETC ❱ **estar de vuelta de algo** to be blasé about something ❱ **no tiene vuelta de hoja** there are no two ways about it
vuelto, ta ◆ *participio pasado* → **volver**
◆ *adj* turned ⚲ *Los adjetivos ingleses son invariables.*
■ **vuelto** *sm* change
vulgar *adj* ❶ [*no refinado*] vulgar ❷ [*corriente, ordinario*] ordinary • **vulgar y corriente** ordinary ⚲ *Los adjetivos ingleses son invariables.*
vulgaridad *sf* [*grosería*] • **hacer/decir una vulgaridad** to do/say something vulgar
vulnerable *adj* vulnerable ⚲ *Los adjetivos ingleses son invariables.*
vulnerar *vt* ❶ [*prestigio* ETC] to harm ❷ [*ley, pacto* ETC] to violate
vulva *sf* vulva

V

W

w, W *sf* [*letra*] w ; W

walkie-talkie (pl walkie-talkies) *sm* walkie-talkie

walkman® (pl walkmans) *sm* Walkman®

water (pl wateres) = **váter**

waterpolo *sm* water polo

watio = **vatio**

WC (*abreviatura de* water closet) *sm* WC

web *sf* • **la (World Wide) Web** the (World Wide) Web

windsurf, windsurfing *sm* windsurfing • **me gusta hacer windsurf** I like to windsurf

WWW (*abreviatura escrita de* World Wide Web) *sf* WWW

X

x, X *sf* [*letra*] x ; X

xenofobia *sf* xenophobia

xilofón, xilófono *sm* xylophone

Y

y¹, Y *sf* [*letra*] y ; Y

y² conjunción ❶ [*generalmente*] and • **una computadora y una impresora** a computer and a printer • **horas y horas de espera** hours and hours of waiting • **son las ocho y veinte** it's eight twenty **❷** [*pero*] and yet • **sabía que no lo conseguiría y seguía intentándolo** she knew she wouldn't manage it and yet she kept on trying **❸** [*en preguntas*] what about • **¿y tu mujer?** what about your wife? • **¿y qué?** so what? • **el coche no funciona — ¿y qué?** **podemos ir en taxi** the car's not working — so what? we can go by taxi

ya ◆ *adv* **❶** [*en el pasado*] already • **ya me lo habías contado** you had already told me • **ya en 1926** as long ago as 1926 **❷** [*ahora*] now • **ya me voy** I'm off now • **engordé y este vestido ya no me sirve** I got heavier and this dress isn't any use to me now **❸** [*inmediatamente*] at once • **hay que hacer algo ya** something has to be done at once • **bueno, yo ya me voy** right, I'm off now • **ya no es así** it's no longer like that **❹** [*en el futuro*] • **ya te llamaré** I'll give you a ring some time • **ya hablaremos** we'll talk later • **ya nos habremos ido** we'll already have gone • **ya verás** you'll (soon) see **❺** [*refuerza al verbo*] • **ya entiendo/lo sé** I understand/know

◆ *conjunción* [*distributiva*] • **ya (sea) por... ya (sea) por...** whether for... or...

◆ *exclamación* • **¡ya! a)** [*expresa asentimiento*] right! **b)** [*expresa comprensión*] yes!

expresión ¡ya, ya! *irónico* sure!

yacer *vi* to lie

yacimiento *sm* **❶** [*minero*] deposit ▶ **yacimiento de petróleo** oilfield **❷** [*arqueológico*] site

yanqui *smf* *familiar* yank

yate *sm* yacht

yegua *sf* mare

yema *sf* **❶** [*de huevo*] yolk **❷** [*de planta*] bud **❸** [*de dedo*] fingertip

yerba = **hierba**

yermo, ma *adj* [*estéril*] barren ۞ *Los adjetivos ingleses son invariables.*

yerno *sm* son-in-law

yeso *sm* **❶** GEOLOGÍA gypsum **❷** CONSTRUCCIÓN plaster **❸** ARTE gesso

yo *pronombre personal* **❶** [*sujeto*] I • **yo me llamo Luis** I'm called Luis • **¿quién quiere ir al parque? — ¡yo!** who wants to go to the park? — me! • **Rosa y yo queremos ser bailarinas** Rosa and I want to be dancers **❷** [*predicado*] • **soy yo** it's me

expresión yo que tú/él ETC if I were you/him ETC

yodo *sm* iodine

yoga *sm* yoga

yogur (pl yogures)**, yogurt** (pl yogurts) *sm* yoghurt

yonqui *smf familiar* junkie

yoyó *sm* yoyo

yuca *sf* ❶ BOTÁNICA yucca ❷ COCINA cassava

yudo *sm* judo

yugular *adj* & *sf* jugular ·💡 *Los adjetivos ingleses son invariables.*

Z

z, Z *sf* [*letra*] z ; Z

zacate *sm* fodder

zafarse *v pronominal* ANATOMÍA to become dislocated

zafio, fia *adj* rough ·💡 *Los adjetivos ingleses son invariables.*

zafiro *sm* sapphire

zaga *sf* DEPORTE defence • **a la zaga** behind
expresión **no irle a la zaga a alguien** to be every bit as good as somebody

zaguán *sm* (entrance) hall

zambullir *vt* to dip

■ **zambullirse** *v pronominal* • **zambullirse (en) a)** [*agua*] to dive (into) **b)** [*actividad*] to immerse yourself (in)

zampar *vi familiar* to gobble

zanahoria *sf* carrot

zanca *sf* [*de ave*] leg

zancada *sf* stride

zancadilla *sf* trip
expresión **poner la zancadilla a alguien a)** [*hacer tropezar*] to trip somebody up **b)** [*engañar*] to trick somebody

zancadillear *vt* to trip up

zanco *sm* stilt

zancudo *sm* mosquito

zanja *sf* ditch

zanjar *vt* ❶ [*poner fin a*] to put an end to ❷ [*resolver*] to settle

zapata *sf* [*de freno*] shoe

zapatear *vi* to stamp your feet

zapatería *sf* ❶ [*tienda*] shoe store ❷ [*taller*] shoemaker's

zapatero, ra *sm, f* ❶ [*vendedor*] shoe seller ❷ [*fabricante*] shoemaker

zapatilla *sf* ❶ [*de baile*] shoe ❷ [*de estar en casa*] slipper ❸ [*de deporte*] sneaker

zapato *sm* shoe ▶ **zapato de piso** flat shoe ▶ **zapato de tacón** high heeled shoe

zapping *sm invariable* channel-hopping • **hacer zapping** to channel-hop

zarandear *vt* ❶ [*cosa*] to shake ❷ [*persona*] to jostle

zarpa *sf* ❶ [*uña*] claw ❷ [*mano*] paw

zarpar *vi* to set sail • **zarpar rumbo a** to set sail for

zarpazo *sm* • **me acerqué a los gatitos y la gata me dio un zarpazo** I got close to the kittens and the mother cat gave me a scratch

zarza *sf* bramble

zarzal *sm* bramble patch

zarzamora *sf* blackberry, *plural* blackberries

zas *exclamación* • **¡zas!** wham!

zenit = cenit

zigzag (pl zigzags O zigzagues) *sm* zigzag • **caminar en zigzag** to walk in a zigzag

zigzaguear *vi* to zigzag

zinc = cinc

zíper *sm* zipper

zócalo *sm* ❶ [*de edificio, pedestal*] plinth ❷ [*plaza*] main square

zoclo *sm* baseboard

zodiaco, zodíaco *sm* zodiac

zona *sf* zone • **la zona comercial de la ciudad está en el centro** the commercial zone of the city is downtown ▶ **zona de exclusión** exclusion zone ▶ **zona verde a)** [*grande*] park **b)** [*pequeño*] lawn

zoo *sm* zoo

zoología *sf* zoology

zoológico, ca *adj* zoological ·💡 *Los adjetivos ingleses son invariables.*

■ **zoológico** *sm* zoo

zoólogo, ga *sm, f* zoologist

zoquete *smf* blockhead

zorra *sf* ❶ [*animal*] vixen ❷ *familiar* [*borrachera*] drunkenness

zorrillo *sm* skunk

zorro, rra *sm, f literal & figurado* fox

■ **zorro** *sm* [*piel*] fox (fur)

zozobrar *vi* ❶ [*naufragar*] to be shipwrecked ❷ *figurado* [*fracasar*] to fall through

zueco *sm* clog

zumbar *vi* ❶ [*generalmente*] to buzz • **me zumban los oídos** my ears are buzzing ❷ [*máquinas*] to whirr

zumbido *sm* ❶ [*generalmente*] buzz ❷ [*de máquinas*] whirr

zurcido *sm* ❶ [*acción*] darning ❷ [*remiendo*] darn

zurcir *vt* to darn

zurdo, da *adj* ❶ [*mano* ETC] left ❷ [*persona*] left-handed ·💡 *Los adjetivos ingleses son invariables.*

■ **zurda** *sf* [*mano*] left hand

zurrar *vt* [*pegar*] to beat

zutano, na *sm, f* so-and-so

Lengua y cultura

Comunicarse en inglés

Los saludos

1. Saludar a alguien

Las fórmulas que se utilicen variarán según el momento del día. Las expresiones usuales son:

Good morning.
Buenos días.

Good afternoon.
Buenas tardes.

Good evening.
Buenas noches.

💡 No es indispensable mencionar después del saludo el nombre de la persona a quien se saluda, pero si es alguien conocido, puede agregarse "*Mr*", "*Mrs*" o "*Miss*" seguido del apellido.

Good evening, Mr Watts.
Buenas noches, Sr. (Watts.)

Si conocemos bien a la persona, podemos utilizar su nombre de pila:

Good morning, Chris.
Buenos días, Chris.

En un ámbito más familiar basta con decir:

Hi (there)!
¡Hola!

Hello!
Buenos días/Buenas tardes.

Para saludar a un grupo de personas se dice:

(Good) morning everyone!
¡Buenos días a todos!

💡 El uso de "*Good*" no es obligatorio, un simple "*Morning*" puede bastar para los saludos familiares.

Con frecuencia, después del saludo sigue alguna fórmula ritual como:

Hello. How are you?
Hola. ¿Cómo estás?

How are you doing?
¿Cómo te va?

All right?/O.K.?
¿Qué tal?

💡 En teoría, "*Good morning*" se utiliza antes del mediodía y "*Good afternoon*" después. En la práctica, su uso depende de la hora de la comida, que va del mediodía a las dos de la tarde. De igual modo, la hora en que comienza a decirse "*Good evening*" varía según las estaciones y la hora en que cae la tarde, hacia las cinco en invierno, pero mucho más tarde en verano. En caso de duda, es mejor utilizar simplemente "*Hello*".

2. Cómo responder

Pueden utilizarse las siguientes fórmulas, que son las más comunes:

Very well, thank you. And you?
Muy bien, gracias. ¿Y tú?

Fine/Fine, thank you/Fine, thanks.
Bien (gracias).

Not (too) bad.
Ahí la llevo.

💡 Fíjate en que la contracción "*thanks*" se emplea sobre todo de manera familiar.

3. Reunirse con un conocido

Si la persona a quien nos dirigimos es un conocido a quien no hemos visto hace algún tiempo, podemos emplear fórmulas como:

I haven't seen you for ages!
¡Hace siglos que no te veo!

Long time no see!
¡Cuánto tiempo!

Las presentaciones

1. Presentarse a sí mismo

Cuando debemos presentarnos a nosotros mismos, la forma más común de hacerlo es:

Hi, I'm Isabel.
Hola, soy Isabel.

My name's Enrique Gómez.
Me llamo Enrique Gómez.

I'm María Cortés from the Los Pinos School.
Soy María Cortés, del Colegio Los Pinos.

2. Presentar a dos personas entre sí

Do you know everybody?
¿Conoces a todos?

This is Emma.
Te presento a Emma.

Do you know George?
¿Conoces a George?

3. Cómo responder

Para responder a alguien que acabamos de conocer, existen varias respuestas posibles. Es necesario elegir la más adecuada según la naturaleza de la relación que tenemos con nuestro interlocutor.

Los siguientes ejemplos incluyen fórmulas que van de la más familiar a la más tradicional:

Hello/Hi!
Buenos días/¡Hola!

How do you do?
Encantado/Encantada (de conocerlo).

Pleased to meet you.
Mucho gusto.

Para corroborar lo que ha dicho nuestro interlocutor, podemos pedirle aclaraciones de esta forma:

I'm sorry, I didn't catch your name.
Perdón, no oí su nombre.

4. Cómo presentarse por teléfono

Cuando le hablamos a un amigo, la fórmula es de este tipo:

Hello! It's Karen/It's me.
¡Hola! Soy Karen/Soy yo.

Observación

Durante las presentaciones, se acostumbra responder simplemente *"Pleased to meet you!"* antes del saludo con la mano. En general, este *"handshake"* es exclusivo del primer encuentro.

Despedirse

1. Fórmulas comunes

Para despedirse, por lo general basta con decir:

Goodbye/Bye (Bye)!
Adiós.

Cuando nos despedimos de alguien por la noche, también podemos decir:

Good night, Jane.
Buenas noches, Jane.

En tiendas o en llamadas oficiales escucharás mucho:

Have a nice day!
¡Qué tengas un buen día!

> Tanto *"Good night"* como *"Good evening"* pueden traducirse como "**Buenas noches**", pero la primera expresión se utiliza cuando nos despedimos, y la segunda sólo cuando saludamos a alguien.

2. Fórmulas de cortesía

Cuando nos despedimos de alguien que acabamos de conocer, se acostumbra agregar esta fórmula:

It was nice meeting you.
Encantado/Encantada de conocerlo.

3. Fórmulas familiares

Pueden emplearse las siguientes expresiones:

See you soon.
Hasta pronto.

See you later.
Hasta luego.

See you on Sunday.
Hasta el domingo.

See you next week.
Hasta la próxima semana.

4. Cómo despedirse por teléfono

Por teléfono es preferible elegir:

Talk to you soon.
Hasta pronto.

390 · Comunicarse en inglés

5. Cómo terminar una carta

Las fórmulas para concluir una carta son más sencillas que en español. Si comenzamos nuestra carta con: **"To whom it may concern"**, podemos terminar con: **"Yours truly"** ("Reciba un cordial saludo").

De igual manera:

Dear Mr/Mrs/Ms Jones
Estimado Sr./Estimada Sra./Srta. Jones (...)

Sincerely (yours),
Reciba mis más sinceros saludos,

En una carta dirigida a una persona más conocida:

Dear Ann,
Querida Ann, (...)

(Kind) Regards,
Saludos,

Según el grado de familiaridad con nuestro destinatario, podemos elegir entre varias fórmulas:

Best wishes,
Te deseo lo mejor,

(Lots of) Love,
un (gran) abrazo,

6. En un correo electrónico

La elección de las fórmulas de saludo es muy libre y las formas más cortas son las mejores; las más populares son las siguientes:

Hi Gemma!
¡Hola, Gemma!

Dear Paul
Querido Paul

La fórmula usual para terminar nuestro correo electrónico es:

Regards
Saludos

Si nuestro destinatario es conocido, podemos emplear las mismas fórmulas familiares que en una carta, como por ejemplo:

Love
Besos/un abrazo

💡 Fíjate en que **"love"**, que significa **"amor"** y corresponde a **"besos"** o **"un abrazo"**, es la fórmula preferida para terminar un mensaje

dirigido a miembros de la familia o amigos cercanos.

Observación

"Ms" se utiliza cuando no conocemos el estado civil de una mujer. Es importante saber que en Estados Unidos algunas mujeres, sobre todo si conservan su apellido de solteras aun estando casadas, prefieren que se les llame empleando esta fórmula.

Los agradecimientos

1. Agradecer

Para agradecer algo a alguien, puede decirse simplemente:

Thank you (very much).
(Muchas) gracias.

En un ámbito más familiar, basta con la sencilla expresión:

Thanks.
Gracias.

2. Responder a un agradecimiento

Es común responder a los agradecimientos con una fórmula como:

Not at all.
De nada.

Don't mention it.
No hay de qué.

3. Otras fórmulas de agradecimiento

Podemos agradecer de manera más concreta agregando una observación personal:

It's great/cool, thanks!
¡Gracias, es padre!

Thanks, it was awesome!
¡Gracias, estuvo genial!

It was delicious!
¡Estaba delicioso!

He aquí algunos ejemplos de situaciones que podemos llegar a encontrarnos:

> *Thank you for the present. It's just what I wanted.*
> Gracias por el regalo. Es justo lo que quería.

> *I'm glad you like it.*
> Me alegra que te guste.

> *I'm glad you enjoyed it.*
> Me alegra que te haya gustado.

> *It was nice of you to invite us.*
> Fue muy amable de tu parte habernos invitado.

Si queremos transmitir el agradecimiento de otra persona:

> *Thank you for the birthday present you gave my brother.*
> Gracias por el regalo de cumpleaños que le diste a mi hermano.

> *My Mom asked me to thank you for the concert tickets.*
> Mi mamá me pidió que te diera las gracias por los boletos para el concierto.

4. Agradecer un favor

He aquí algunas expresiones que sirven para darle las gracias a alguien por un favor:

> *Thank you for your help.*
> Gracias por tu ayuda.

> *It's very nice of you to give me a ride to the mall.*
> Es muy amable de tu parte llevarme al centro comercial.

🔆 La expresión *"Thank you for..."* debe ir seguida por el gerundio (por ejemplo *"being"*), mientras que la expresión *"It is kind/nice of you to"* va seguida por la forma infinitiva del verbo (por ejemplo *"give"*).

5. Expresar gratitud

Para expresar una profunda gratitud, pueden utilizarse fórmulas como:

> *I'm really grateful for what you've done.*
> Estoy realmente agradecido por lo que hiciste.

> *I don't know how to thank you.*
> No sé cómo agradecértelo.

6. Expresar gratitud por correspondencia

En una carta puede escribirse:

> *I would like to thank you for your gift.*
> Me gustaría agradecerle su regalo.

> *I am very grateful to you for your help during my work experience.*
> Estoy muy agradecido por la ayuda que me brindó durante mis prácticas de trabajo.

🔆 Deben evitarse fórmulas abreviadas como *"I'd like"* o *"I'm grateful"* en las cartas; sí pueden utilizarse en los correos electrónicos.

Felicitar

1. Las felicitaciones

Cuando alguien logra algo, puede felicitársele con fórmulas sencillas como:

> *Congratulations!*
> ¡Felicidades!

> *Good job!*
> ¡Bien hecho!

> *I'm really pleased to hear your good news!*
> Me alegra mucho oír esa noticia tan buena.

> *Congratulations on passing your exams.*
> Felicidades por aprobar los exámenes.

2. Los buenos deseos

En numerosas ocasiones tendremos que presentar nuestros buenos deseos. Los siguientes ejemplos pueden ayudarnos:

> *Happy birthday!*
> ¡Feliz cumpleaños!

> *Merry Christmas and a Happy New Year!*
> ¡Feliz Navidad y próspero Año Nuevo!

Disculparse

1. Fórmulas sencillas

Es fácil disculparse con mayor o menor efusión utilizando fórmulas sencillas como:

Sorry!
¡Perdón!

I'm sorry.
Lo siento.

I'm very/really sorry.
Lo siento mucho.

2. Precisar el motivo

Después puede precisarse el motivo de la disculpa:

I'm sorry I forgot to call you.
Perdón, se me olvidó hablarte.

Excuse me. I have to go.
Disculpe. Tengo que irme.

I apologize for arriving late.
Por favor, disculpe mi retraso.

I didn't mean to do that!
¡No lo hice a propósito!

> 💡 Cuando es complemento de objeto, el pronombre relativo *"that"* (**"que"**) puede omitirse, tanto al escribir como al hablar. Por lo demás, casi siempre se omite en la lengua hablada.

Citas e invitaciones

1. Concertar una cita con un amigo

En el ámbito de las relaciones familiares, puede elegirse entre un gran número de fórmulas:

Why don't we play soccer after school?
¿Qué tal si jugamos futbol después de la escuela?

How about a game of basketball?
¿Jugamos un partido de basquetbol?

What about going to the movies?
¿Qué tal si vamos al cine?

Do you want to come to my house?
¿Te gustaría venir a mi casa?

> 💡 Para expresar una sugerencia, puede utilizarse la pregunta *"why"* + *"don´t"* + una base verbal. También puede utilizarse la interrogación *"what/how about"* seguida por un sustantivo o gerundio.

2. Confirmar una cita

Podemos inspirarnos en los siguientes ejemplos:

Right, that's settled then.
Sale.

Next Friday evening, outside the movie theater at six o'clock.
El próximo viernes, afuera del cine a las seis.

3. Formular una invitación

Existen fórmulas sencillas para hacer una invitación:

Would you like to play baseball after school?
¿Te gustaría jugar beisbol después de la escuela?

Do you want to come and eat at our house?
Quieres venir a comer en nuestra casa?

We're going to the mall later, do you want to come too?
¿Vamos al centro comercial más tarde, quieres acompañarnos?

Herramientas esenciales de la comunicación

1. Solicitar una explicación

Si tenemos que pedir brevemente a nuestro interlocutor que aclare lo que acaba de decir:

I'm sorry, I didn't (quite) understand.
Perdón, no entendí (muy bien).

Can you explain what you mean?
¿Podría explicar lo que quiere decir?

Can you repeat that, please?
¿Podría repetirlo, por favor?

💡 En inglés, *"please"* se emplea con mucha mayor frecuencia que **"por favor"** en español. Al escribir se traduce como **"Podría..."** o **"Le ruego..."**. Al hablar puede omitirse si la pregunta es lo suficientemente amable.

Oralmente, en un ámbito más familiar, pueden emplearse las siguientes expresiones:

Sorry I didn't catch that.
Perdona, no te entendí.

What was that (you said)?
¿Qué (dijiste)?

I don't get it.
No entiendo.

2. Pedir información

Para corroborar la hora, la fecha o los horarios de apertura, pueden utilizarse las siguientes fórmulas:

What time is it?
¿Qué horas son?

What's the date today?
¿Qué día es hoy?

What time does the movie start?
¿A qué horas empieza la película?

3. Pedir un favor

Cuando debemos recurrir a un compañero o vecino:

Could you look after my cat while I'm away?
¿Podrías cuidar a mi gato cuando estoy fuera?

En caso de problemas, podemos pedir ayuda a un desconocido:

Excuse me, could you tell me the way to the mall please?
Perdone, ¿podría indicarme cómo llegar al centro comercial, por favor?

4. Pedir permiso

Puede elegirse entre las siguientes fórmulas usuales:

Do you mind if I phone home?
¿Podría llamar a casa (por teléfono)?

Would you mind if I borrowed your cell phone?
¿Podría usar su celular?

Si debemos pedir permiso en nombre de otra persona:

Could Susie stay for the weekend?
¿Podría quedarse Susie el fin de semana?

Do you mind if Jake comes over for supper?
¿Te importa si viene Jake a cenar?

5. Hacer una propuesta

Para hacer una sugerencia, puede decirse simplemente:

Can I make a suggestion?
¿Puedo hacer una sugerencia?

May I suggest something?
¿Podría sugerir algo?

6. Dar un consejo

Para dar un consejo, a menudo se emplean fórmulas como:

Why don't you do your homework later?
¿Por qué no haces la tarea después?

You'd better not tell your Dad.
Más vale que no se lo digas a tu papá.

7. Persuadir a alguien

Las expresiones usuales para persuadir a alguien son las siguientes:

Couldn't you stay a little longer?
¿No podrías quedarte un poco más?

Please wait until Simon gets home.
Por favor espera a que Simon vuelva (a casa).

Have another taco.
Toma otro taco.

💡 Pueden emplearse fórmulas como *"What/How about...?"* o *"Why don't you...?"* y después precisar de qué se trata utilizando respectivamente el gerundio *"What about coming on holiday with us?"* ("¿Qué tal si vienes de vacaciones con nosotros?") o el infinitivo *"Why don't you come to Guanajuato with us?"* ("¿Por qué no vienes a Guanajuato con nosotros?").

8. Responder a una propuesta

Si estamos de acuerdo, podemos decir simplemente:

All right then.
Bueno, de acuerdo.

OK, if you're sure your parents will let us.
OK, si estás seguro que tus papás nos darán permiso.

Si no estamos de acuerdo, las posibles respuestas son:

Sorry I can't.
Lo siento, pero no puedo.

I'd rather not.
Mejor no.

9. Expresar deseos

Para expresar deseos que difícilmente se cumplirán:

I wish I didn't have to do any homework.
¡Ojalá no tuviera que hacer tarea!

I wish it would stop raining.
Ojalá dejara de llover.

I wish I had more friends.
¡Ojalá tuviera más amigos!

10. Confirmar

Cuando debemos confirmar algo podemos simplemente utilizar los siguientes ejemplos:

Yes, of course.
Sí, por supuesto.

Yes, that's fine.
Sí, está bien.

That's right.
Está bien.

No problem.
Claro que sí.

11. Asegurar

Según las circunstancias, puede agregarse un detalle tranquilizante:

I'll be there.
Allí estaré.

Leave it to me.
Confía en mí.

I'll take care of it.
Yo me ocupo de eso.

Don't worry about it.
No te preocupes.

12. Aceptar hacer un favor

Si alguien nos pide un favor, podemos indicarle que estamos dispuestos a ayudar mediante fórmulas simples:

Yes of course.
Sí, por supuesto.

No trouble at all.
No es ninguna molestia.

13. Rechazar

Las siguientes fórmulas podrán ayudarnos si debemos rechazar una oferta:

It's very kind of you, but no thanks.
Es muy amable de su parte, pero no gracias.

No, I'd rather not.
No, preferiría no hacerlo.

No, it's all right thank you.
No, está bien, gracias.

I'm sorry, but I really don't like chile.
De verdad que lo siento, pero no me gusta el chile.

No, maybe another time.
No, quizás en otra ocasión.

14. Negarse a cumplir una petición o una solicitud

Si debemos responder de forma negativa a una petición, podemos responder simplemente:

No, I'm sorry I can't.
Lo siento, pero no puedo.

Sorry, I don't know the answer.
Lo siento, no conozco la respuesta.

Observación

Fíjate en que es mejor evitar el uso de *"no"* solo. No obstante, sí se usa en carteles y señales para indicar una prohibición. Por ejemplo, el letrero *"No Parking"* quiere decir "Prohibido estacionarse" y *"No smoking"* significa "Prohibido fumar".

15. Oponerse a un interlocutor

Para indicarle a alguien que está equivocado:

No, you're wrong.
No, te equivocas.

No, you've got it all wrong.
No, no has entendido nada.

16. Afirmar algo con certeza

Podemos expresar nuestra certeza de manera sencilla:

Yes I'm sure.
Sí, estoy seguro.

I'm certain about that.
Estoy seguro/segura de ello.

17. Expresar reservas

La incertidumbre puede expresarse de manera sencilla y personal:

No, I'm not sure.
No, no estoy seguro.

No, I don't think that's right.
No, no creo que eso esté bien.

Temas de conversación

1. La salud

Para hablar de la salud en términos generales:

How are you?
¿Cómo estás?

How have you been?
¿Cómo has estado últimamente?

Seguramente recibiremos como respuesta una de las siguientes expresiones:

Very well, thank you.
Muy bien, gracias.

I'm fine.
Bien.

Not bad, thanks.
Bien, gracias.

OK/So-so.
Más o menos.

Por nuestra parte, podemos informarnos sobre la salud de nuestro interlocutor agregando:

And how are you?
¿Y tú cómo estás?

He aquí los problemas de salud benignos más comunes que pueden mencionarse:

I have a bad cold.
Tengo un catarro espantoso.

My throat's really sore.
Me duele mucho la garganta.

Informarse acerca de un tercero:

What about your Dad?
¿Y tu papá?

How's your sister?
¿Cómo está tu hermana?

2. Las vacaciones y los viajes

Una conversación sobre este tema puede iniciarse de la siguiente manera:

Have you been on holiday yet this year?
¿Ya saliste de vacaciones este año?

Do you enjoy traveling?
¿Te gusta viajar?

Las respuestas variarán de acuerdo con la pregunta:

I've been to Canada with my parents.
Estuve en Canadá con mis papás.

We're going to San Diego in July.
Vamos a San Diego en julio.

Yes, we love camping in the mountains.
Sí, nos encanta ir de camping en las montañas.

Podemos informarnos acerca del desarrollo de un viaje utilizando las siguientes expresiones:

Did you have a good journey?
¿Te fue bien en el viaje?

Did you have a good time?
¿La pasaste bien?

Did everything go according to plan?
¿Todo salió de acuerdo con lo planeado?

Y para responder:

> *It was fine. Everything went smoothly.*
> Me fue muy bien. Todo salió bien.
>
> *It was awful. Everything went wrong.*
> Fue horrible. Todo salió mal.

3. El entretenimiento

Una conversación sobre este tema puede comenzarse preguntando:

> *What do you like doing in your spare time?*
> ¿Qué te gusta hacer en tu tiempo libre?
>
> *What are you interested in?*
> ¿Cuáles son tus intereses?
>
> *Do you like sports?*
> ¿Te gusta el deporte?

Las siguientes respuestas son las más comunes:

> *I like listening to music.*
> Me gusta escuchar música.
>
> *I'm interested in American literature.*
> Me interesa la literatura estadounidense.
>
> *I don't like sports much, but I enjoy Ultimate Frisbee.*
> No me gusta mucho el deporte, pero me gusta jugar al Frisbee.

La conversación puede mantenerse con observaciones como:

> *That's nice.*
> Qué bien.
>
> *That must be fun/tiring.*
> Debe ser divertido/cansado.

Observación

En inglés se utilizan mucho los adjetivos *"nice"* y *"great"*, que pueden traducirse de diversas formas según lo que califiquen. Así pues, ambos pueden significar, según el caso: "hermoso", "bueno", o incluso "amable", "simpático".

Hablar de nuestra situación personal

1. Hablar de nosotros en un ámbito familiar

Cuando visitamos a personas conocidas o recibimos visitas que ya conocemos:

> *Hello everyone! How are you all?*
> Hola a todos. ¿Cómo están?

Si se trata de la primera visita:

> *Hello! You must be Susan.*
> ¡Hola! Debes ser Susan.
>
> *Nice to meet you, Jan.*
> Encantado de conocerte, Jan.
>
> *I'm Julie and this is my brother Martin.*
> Soy Julie y éste es mi hermano Martin.

Para asegurarnos de que nuestros invitados están bien podemos preguntar:

> *Do you need anything?*
> ¿Necesitan algo?

En caso contrario, puede responderse:

> *No thank you. I'm fine.*
> No gracias. Estoy bien.
>
> *Not for the moment thanks.*
> Por ahora no, gracias.

Podemos mostrar un interés más preciso por la vida de nuestros invitados preguntándoles sobre su lugar de residencia habitual:

> *Do you live in a house or an apartment?*
> ¿Viven en una casa o en un departamento?
>
> *Are you far from downtown?*
> ¿Viven lejos del centro?
>
> *What's your house like?*
> ¿Cómo es su casa?
>
> *Do you have a yard?*
> ¿Tienen jardín?

Algunas posibles respuestas:

> *We live in an apartment.*
> Vivimos en un departamento.
>
> *We're five minutes from downtown/ the station.*
> Vivimos a cinco minutos del centro/de la estación.

It's fairly new/old.
Es relativamente nuevo/viejo.

It's about the same size as yours.
Es más o menos del mismo tamaño que el de ustedes.

We have four bedrooms.
Tenemos cuatro recámaras.

Our yard is smaller.
Nuestro jardín es más pequeño.

También puede hablarse de las mascotas:

We have a cat and a dog.
Tenemos un gato y un perro.

We don't have any pets.
No tenemos mascotas.

Si tú eres el invitado, las siguientes fórmulas pueden serte útiles:

Can I have a towel?
¿Puedes traerme una toalla?

Could I use the bathroom please?
¿Podría utilizar el baño, por favor?

May I have a drink?
¿Podría tomar algo?

2. Carta a un amigo por correspondencia

Podemos presentarnos de la siguiente manera:

My name is Claudio.
Me llamo Claudio.

I am fifteen years old.
Tengo quince años.

I have an older brother, Simón, and a sister called Ana.
Tengo un hermano mayor, Simón, y una hermana que se llama Ana.

We have a sheep dog called Zulu.
Tenemos un perro pastor que se llama Zulu.

Podemos continuar hablando de nuestro lugar de residencia:

I live in a small village near Puebla with my parents and grandparents.
Vivo en un pueblito cerca de Puebla con mis padres y abuelos.

También, podemos describir nuestra apariencia física:

I am tall and slim.
Soy alto y delgado.

I have blue eyes.
Tengo ojos azules.

I have red hair and freckles.
Soy pelirrojo y tengo pecas.

Después podemos hablar de nuestros intereses :

I don't like going to museums.
No me gusta ir a los museos.

Clubs and discos are cool.
Me gustan los bares y los antros.

I have lots of CDs and DVDs.
Tengo un montón de CDs y DVDs.

I love Justin Timberlake's music.
Me encanta la música de Justin Timberlake.

Finalmente, podemos hablar de la profesión u ocupación de los demás miembros de la familia:

> Para hablar del oficio o la profesión de una persona, es necesario utilizar el artículo indefinido *"a/an"*: *"She is a physical therapist"*; *"I'm an architect"*.

My sister is in her last year at school. She's going to take her final exams.
Mi hermana está a punto de terminar el bachillerato y hacer sus exámenes.

My father is self-employed. He owns a small factory in Celaya.
Mi padre es autónomo. Tiene una pequeña fábrica en Celaya.

My mother is a physical therapist. She works in a local hospital.
Mi madre es fisioterapeuta. Trabaja en un hospital local.

My brother is nineteen.
At the moment he works as a mechanic.
Mi hermano tiene diecinueve años. Actualmente trabaja como mecánico en un taller.

> En inglés existen numerosas maneras de expresar que nos gusta hacer algo. La fórmula más común es *"I like"*, pero podemos variarla diciendo *"I enjoy"* o *"I love"*. En cualquier caso, es necesario utilizar la construcción verbo + *"ing"*.

La cultura estadounidense

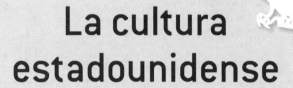

La educación

El gobierno central de los EE UU ejerce muy poco control directo sobre la educación, y los sistemas educativos difieren de una región a otra. La mayoría de las escuelas e institutos de enseñanza superior son centros mixtos regidos por los propios estados. Los estudios son generalmente obligatorios, y se extienden desde los 5 o 6 años de edad hasta los 16 o 18.

Educación Preescolar

Aproximadamente el 35% de los niños de 3 y 4 años concurre a guarderías, y casi todos los niños entre 4 y 5 años concurren al kinder.

Escuela Primaria y Escuela Secundaria

Por lo general, los niños van a la escuela primaria de 6 a 13 años y a la secundaria hasta los 18 años. La cantidad de años de estudios de cada una varía de estado en estado. Las siguientes pautas son las mas corrientes:

Grade school	Junior high school	Senior high school
6 años	3 años	3 años
Grade school	Middle school	High school
5 años	3 años	4 años
Grade school	High school	
8 años	4 años	

Plan de Estudios

No hay un plan nacional de estudios. La mayoría de los estudiantes de los colegios secundarios debe estudiar algunas materias clave, y en los cursos superiores pueden elegir materias optativas.

Escuelas Privadas

Aproximadamente el 12% de los niños estadounidenses concurre a escuelas de pago. Siguen el sistema de cursos de las escuelas estatales, pero su plan de estudios se concentra en asegurar la admisión a las mejores universidades.

Exámenes

Los estudiantes toman exámenes al final de cada curso semestral, pero no hay ningún examen nacional para finalizar los estudios secundarios como en otros países. En cambio, los estudiantes tienen evaluaciones contínuas a lo largo de sus años escolares. Los estudiantes que aspiran a ir a la universidad hacen exámenes nacionales, como el *ACT* (*American College Test*) y el *SAT* (*Scholastic Aptitude Test*).

Graduación

Todos los estudiantes aspiran a tener una ceremonia de graduación de la escuela secundaria. Los estudiantes visten un birrete y una toga especiales, y se les otorga un diploma.

Glosario	
class ring	anillo conmemorativo
commencement	ceremonia de graduación
prom	baile formal
yearbook	anuario

Enseñanza Superior

Mas del 50% de los graduados de la escuela secundaria pasa a hacer estudios de enseñanza superior (de 18 a 26 años). La tabla de abajo indica los cursos y títulos ofrecidos por cada institución. Las cuotas son pagadas por cada estudiante (o por sus padres), aunque alrededor del 50% de los estudiantes consigue apoyo económico.

Instituciones		
	curso	**título**
Community o Junior colleges	2 años	Associate's
College/University	4 años	Bachelor's
Graduate schools	1-2 años	Master's
	2-6 años	Doctorate
Ivy League	Así se llama el grupo de prestigiosas universidades que comprende *Brown, Columbia, Cornell, Dartmouth, Harvard, Pensilvania, Princeton* y *Yale*.	

Educación de Adultos

Millones de adultos estadounidenses concurren a universidades y otros centros de enseñanza superior con cursos de tiempo completo o tiempo parcial. El 40% de los estudiantes universitarios tiene mas de 25 años.

Medios de comunicación

Canales de televisión

Existen cuatro cadenas comerciales a nivel nacional:

- *American Broadcasting Company (ABC)*
- *Nacional Broadcasting Company (NBC)*
- *Columbia Broadcasting Service (CBS)*
- *Fox TV*

Existen aproximadamente 1,300 canales comerciales, y 400 canales no comerciales del estado y canales educativos.

Canal	Programación
Programas en cadena	concursos televisivos, programas de entrevistas, comedias de situación, películas
Vía satélite y Cable *canales dedicados a temas particulares*	deportes, películas, religión, noticias (p. ej. *CNN*), compras, música (p. ej. *MTV*)
Servicio Público de Televisión (PBS) *sustentada por fondos federales, auspicios de empresas y donaciones de particulares*	programas culturales y educativos

Radio

Los EE UU tienen más de 10,000 estaciones de radio, y en las ciudades principales suele haber entre 50 y 100 estaciones locales. Muchas estaciones de radio están afiliadas a cadenas nacionales como ABC, NBC y CBS. También existen más de 100 cadenas regionales.

Estaciones principales	Programación
National Public Radio (NPR)	noticias y temas de actualidad
American Public Radio (APR) *sustentadas por subsidios y auspicios privados*	programas de entretenimiento

Periódicos

La mayoría de los periódicos de los EE UU es de carácter regional. *USA Today* es el diario popular más destacado y vende más de 5 millones de copias diarias. El *Wall Street Journal* se imprime en varias ciudades, y tiene cuatro ediciones regionales.

Nacionales	*Christian Science Monitor, Los Angeles Times, New York Times, USA Today, Wall Street Journal, Washington Post*
Regionales	*Boston Globe, Chicago Tribune, Denver Post, Miami Herald, San Francisco Herald*

Semanales	*National Enquirer, Globe, Star* Estos tres se concentran en temas de entretenimiento, escándalos y deportes.
Dominicales	La mayoría de los diarios publica una edición dominical con varias secciones.
Revistas de noticias	*Newsweek, Time, US News, World Report* Son muy populares y proveen una buena cobertura informativa.

La recreación

Los estadounidenses gozan de relativamente poco tiempo libre pero abajo se ve una lista de las fiestas principales.

Fiestas nacionales		
1º de enero	*New Year's Day* (Día de Año Nuevo)	Se celebra el año nuevo.
Tercer lunes de enero	*Martin Luther King* (Día de Martin Luther King)	Se conmemora el cumpleaños de Martin Luther King.
Tercer lunes de febrero	*Presidents' Day* (Día de los Presidentes)	Se conmemoran los aniversarios de nacimiento de Lincoln y de Washington.
Último lunes de mayo	*Memorial Day* (conmemoración de los caídos)	Se conmemoran los caídos en las guerras.
4 de julio	*Independence Day* (Día de la Independencia)	Se conmemoran la fecha en que los EE UU declaró su independencia de Inglaterra en 1776.
Primer lunes de septiembre	*Labor Day* (Día del Trabajo)	Día feriado en honor de los trabajadores.
Segundo lunes de octubre	*Columbus Day* (Día de la Raza)	Se conmemora la llegada de Cristóbal Colón a las Américas.
11 de noviembre	*Armistice Day* (Día del Armisticio)	Se conmemora el fin de la primera guerra mundial.
Cuarto jueves de noviembre	*Thanksgiving* (Día de Acción de Gracias)	Se conmemora la cosecha recogida por la Colonia de Plymouth en 1621, tras un invierno de grandes privaciones. Las familias se reúnen para disfrutar de una comida tradicional que consiste en pavo relleno, papas, salsa de arándano, y pay de calabaza o de manzana.
25 de diciembre	*Christmas Day* (Día de Navidad)	En muchos hogares se pone un árbol de Navidad (*Christmas tree*) con luces y adornos, la gente se obsequia regalos de Navidad (*Christmas presents*) y se hace una comida de Navidad (*Christmas dinner*) con pavo o jamón asado, papas y verduras.

Deportes

Los estadounidenses toman el deporte muy en serio. La lista de abajo indica algunos de los deportes más populares.

Deportes nacionales	Deportes participativos populares
beisbol	natación
futbol (americano)	ciclismo
basquetbol	esquí

Geografía

Estadísticas

Área	9,159.070 km² (el cuarto país más grande del mundo)
Población	295,269,000 (el tercer país más populoso del mundo, después de China e India)
Extensión de oeste a este	4,000 km
Extensión de norte a sur	1,930 km

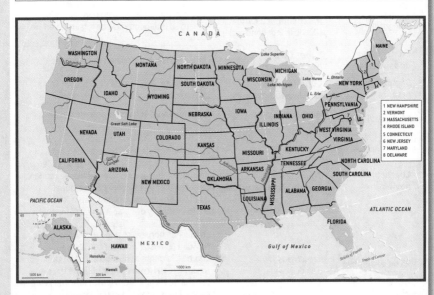

Regiones

Los EE UU se dividen en cuatro regiones geográficas:

Noreste (the East Coast)	Nueva Inglaterra (formada por Connecticut, Nuevo Hampshire, Maine, Massachusetts, Rhode Island y Vermont), Nueva Jersey, Nueva York, Pensilvania, Maryland, Delaware y Washington DC
Región Central (the Midwest)	Illinois, Indiana, Iowa, Kansas, Michigan, Minnesota, Missouri, Nebraska, Dakota del Norte, Ohio, Dakota del Sur y Wisconsin
Sur (the South)	Alabama, Arkansas, Florida, Georgia, Kentucky, Louisiana, Mississippi, Carolina del Norte, Oklahoma, Carolina del Sur, Tennessee, Texas, Virginia y Virginia Occidental
Oeste (the West Coast)	Alaska, Arizona, California, Colorado, Hawai, Idaho, Montana, Nevada, Nuevo Mexico, Oregon, Utah, Washington y Wyoming

Gobierno Federal y del Estado

Estados Unidos es una república federal formada por 50 estados y el Distrito de Columbia, territorio entre los estados de Maryland y Virginia donde se encuentra la capital de la nación, Washington DC. El poder se divide entre el gobierno federal, el del Estado, y el local.

Los Gobiernos	Constituido por	Resposabilidades
El Gobierno Federal	• el Presidente • el Congreso *(formado por la Cámara de Representantes y el Senado)* • la Suprema Corte	defensa, asuntos exteriores, la emisión de la moneda, y la regulación del comercio
Los Gobiernos del Estado	• el Gobernador • el Congreso del Estado	impuestos, la salud pública, la educación, y la legislación civil y penal
Los Estados	• administración local • el alcalde • el ayuntamiento	escuelas, hospitales, servicios de urgencia, eliminación de resíduos, carreteras, y leyes de regulación de actividad comercial

La gramática inglesa

Los sustantivos

1. El género

En inglés, los sustantivos no tienen género gramatical y los artículos definidos (*the*) e indefinidos (*a/an*) son invariables. Algunos sustantivos tienen una forma masculina y una femenina (*host/hostess*).

2. El plural

En general, la marca del plural es una *–s*.
> *pen/pens, house/houses, car/cars*

En algunos casos debe modificarse el sustantivo para formar su plural.
> *(wo)man/(wo)men, child/children, tooth/teeth, mouse/mice*

Algunos sustantivos conservan la misma forma en singular y en plural.
> *sheep, deer, fish, aircraft, series, species*

3. Contables e incontables

Los sustantivos contables son aquellos que poseen un singular y un plural, y que pueden contarse. Pueden estar precedidos por *a/an, the, some* o por un número.

Singular: *a book, the book, one book*

Plural: *some books, the books, three books*

Los sustantivos incontables no tienen plural. Se refieren a un conjunto de objetos, a materiales, a nociones abstractas o a estados. Pueden estar precedidos por *some*:
> *water, furniture, money, food, work, happiness.*

Los artículos

1. El artículo indefinido

○ *¿a o an?*

El artículo *a* se utiliza antes de una consonante: *a car, a job, a year.*

También se utiliza delante de un nombre que comience con una vocal pronunciada [j] o [w], o delante de una "h" aspirada: *a university, a one-way ticket, a house, a husband.*

El artículo *an* se utiliza delante de una vocal o una "h" muda: *an animal, an architect, an hour, an honor.*

2. El artículo definido

○ <u>Uso</u>

The es el artículo definido que se utiliza para todos los nombres, tanto en singular como en plural. Corresponde a **el, la, los, las** en español. Se utiliza para indicar que se está hablando de algo o alguien específico o único.
> *I can't find the dictionary.*
> No encuentro el diccionario.

○ <u>Ausencia de artículo</u>

La ausencia de artículo delante de los sustantivos indefinidos y de los definidos en plural destaca la naturaleza "genérica" del sustantivo.
> *I hate fish.*
> Detesto el pescado.

Los adjetivos

Los adjetivos son invariables: *a tall man/a tall woman, a friendly dog/friendly dogs.*

Los adjetivos calificativos se colocan siempre delante del sustantivo que califican: *a beautiful house, expensive shoes.*

¡Atención!
Los gentilicios se escriben con mayúscula.
French wine, American movies

El comparativo y el superlativo

1. El comparativo

Existen tres categorías de comparativos:
• el comparativo de superioridad (más... que);
• el comparativo de inferioridad (menos... que);
• el comparativo de igualdad (tan... como).

He is taller than you.
Él es más alto que tú.

She is more intelligent than her sister.
Ella es más inteligente que su hermana.

The silver one is less expensive than the gold one.
El de plata es menos caro que el de oro.

The bag is as expensive as the jacket.
La bolsa es tan cara como el saco.

El comparativo de superioridad puede construirse de dos formas. En general, se agrega *–er* a los adjetivos cortos y se antepone *more* a los adjetivos largos.

taller, shorter, quicker, pero *more intelligent, more expensive, more beautiful*

2. El superlativo

Existen dos categorías de superlativos:
• el superlativo de superioridad (el/la/los/las más...);
• el superlativo de inferioridad (el/la/los/las menos...).

Los superlativos se construyen agregando *–est* a los adjetivos cortos y anteponiendo *most* (de superioridad) o *least* (de inferioridad) a los adjetivos largos. En ambos casos, el adjetivo va precedido por *the*.

The tallest man.
El hombre más alto.

The most expensive book.
El libro más caro.

¡Atención!

El comparativo y el superlativo de algunos adjetivos son irregulares.

adjetivo	comparativo	superlativo
bad	*worse*	*the worst*
far	*farther/ further*	*the farthest/furthest*
good	*better*	*the best*

Los pronombres personales

	Pronombre sujeto	Pronombre objeto
Singular		
1ª persona	*I*	*me*
2ª persona	*you*	*you*
3ª persona		
-masculino	*he*	*him*
-femenino	*she*	*her*
-indefinido	*one/you*	*one/you*
-neutro	*it*	*it*
Plural		
1ª persona	*we*	*us*
2ª persona	*you*	*you*
3ª persona	*they*	*them*

El posesivo

1. El caso posesivo

En español, un vínculo de posesión se indica mediante la cosa poseída + de + el poseedor; en inglés, el nombre del poseedor va seguido por *–'s* + el nombre de la cosa poseída.

Paul's mother.
La madre de Paul.

The girl's bag.
La bolsa de la muchacha.

¡Atención!

Cuando los nombres en plural terminan en **–s**, el nombre del poseedor va seguido por el apóstrofo y después el nombre de la cosa poseída. *My parents' car.* El coche de mis padres.

2. Los adjetivos y pronombres posesivos

	Adjetivo posesivo	Pronombre posesivo
Singular		
1ª persona	*my*	*mine*
2ª persona	*your*	*yours*
3ª persona masculino	*his*	*his*
femenino	*her*	*hers*
indefinido	*one's* /your	
neutro	*its*	
Plural		
1ª persona	*our*	*ours*
2ª persona	*your*	*yours*
3ª persona	*their*	*theirs*

El adjetivo posesivo se coloca antes del sustantivo. El pronombre posesivo se utiliza en lugar de la construcción adjetivo posesivo + sustantivo cuando este último ya ha sido mencionado o no es necesario repetirlo.

That's his book and this is mine.
Ése es su libro y éste es el mío.

Expresar el presente

Existen dos formas de presente:

1. El presente simple

○ Formación

Se utiliza la base verbal en todas las personas a excepción de la tercera del singular, a la cual se le agrega una **–s**.

Forma base: *work*

singular: *I/you work; he/she/it works*

plural: *we/you/they work*

El verbo *to be* (ser o estar) es irregular:

I am (yo soy/estoy); *you are* (tú eres/estás); *he/she/it is* (él/ella/ello es/está); *we are* (nosotros somos/estamos); *you are* (ustedes son/están); *they are* (ellos/ellas son/están).

○ Uso

Por lo general, el presente simple corresponde al presente de indicativo en español.

2. El presente continuo

○ Formación

El presente continuo se construye con el auxiliar *to be* en presente + la base verbal terminada en *-ing*.

I am; you are; he/she is; we are; you are; they are + studying IT (Yo estudio/él/ella estudia informática).

¡Atención!

En inglés, las subordinadas introducidas por *if, when* o *after* con valor de futuro utilizan el presente simple.

I'll go to Six Flags when I have enough money.
Iré a Six Flags cuando tenga suficiente dinero.

○ Uso

El presente continuo se emplea para hablar de un acontecimiento que sucede durante un periodo limitado que incluye el momento presente:

At the moment I am taking extra
English classes.
Por el momento estoy tomando clases extras
de inglés.

También se utiliza para expresar un acontecimiento que está sucediendo o se está llevando a cabo.

She is talking to a friend.
Está hablando con una amiga.

Indica que la acción se produce en el momento presente:

It is raining.
Llueve/Está lloviendo.

Puede tener un valor de futuro cuando se trata de un proyecto que no tardará en realizarse:

We're moving next Friday.
Nos cambiamos de casa el viernes que entra.

Expresar el pasado

Existen dos tiempos principales para hablar del pasado en inglés: el pretérito, el "verdadero" tiempo del pasado, que habla de un acontecimiento terminado, y el perfecto, que describe un pasado "relativo", es decir un acontecimiento terminado que tiene consecuencias medibles y palpables en el presente.

1. El pretérito indefinido

○ Formación

Las formas del pretérito de los verbos regulares son siempre iguales y corresponden a las del participio pasado.

○ Uso

El pretérito indefinido se utiliza cuando el acontecimiento pertenece por completo al pasado y existe una ruptura en relación con el momento presente. Corresponde al pretérito indefinido en español.

He broke his arm in an accident.
Se rompió el brazo en un accidente.

El pretérito indefinido se utiliza con indicaciones de tiempo precisas como la hora, la fecha o expresiones como *on Monday, last night, two years ago, yesterday,* etcétera.

We moved to the city two years ago.
Nos mudamos a la ciudad hace dos años.

2. El *present perfect* (pretérito perfecto)

○ Formación

have o *has* (tercera persona del singular) + participio pasivo.

○ Uso

El *present perfect* se utiliza cuando existe una relación entre un acontecimiento del pasado y la situación presente:

During the tournament our team has gotten better.
Durante el torneo, el equipo ha mejorado.

Con los verbos de estado, el *present perfect* expresa algo que comenzó en el pasado y continúa en el momento presente:

He has looked ill for quite a while.
Hace mucho que tiene cara de enfermo.

Se utiliza cuando el acontecimiento se sitúa en un pasado relativamente vago, sin indicaciones temporales:

Have you seen the latest Russell Crowe movie?
¿Has visto/Ya viste la última película de Russell Crowe?

Con expresiones como *so far, until now, yet, not yet, ever, never, already, recently*, este tiempo indica la idea de "hasta ahora":

I've never visited Japan.
Nunca he visitado Japón.

I haven't been to New York yet.
Todavía no he ido a Nueva York.

También se emplea para expresar desde cuándo ocurre cierta situación, lo cual corresponde en español al presente del indicativo + desde. "Desde" se traduce como *for* (para expresar la duración) o *since* (para expresar un punto de partida).

I have known Michelle for two years.
Conozco a Michelle desde hace dos años.

I have known Michelle since 2007.
Conozco a Michelle desde el 2007.

3. El *past perfect* o *pluperfect* (pluscuamperfecto)

○ Formación

had + participio pasivo.

○ Uso

El uso de este tiempo corresponde por lo general al del pluscuamperfecto en español: indica que un acontecimiento del pasado es anterior a otro también pasado.

> *He had already studied English for two years when he started at his new school.*
> Ya había estudiado inglés durante dos años cuando entró a su nueva escuela.

4. *Used to*

Esta expresión se traduce con el pretérito imperfecto en español.

Se emplea para hablar de algo que ocurrió en el pasado durante algún tiempo y que ya terminó. Expresa la idea de "antes" o "en otro tiempo".

> *She used to study Geography, but now she studies Biology.*
> Antes estudiaba geografía, pero ahora estudia biología

5. El participio pasado

Las formas del participio pasado de los verbos regulares son siempre iguales. Basta con agregar *–ed* a la base verbal:

finished, worked, talked, answered, looked, seemed. Cuidado, existen algunos verbos irregulares.

El futuro

En inglés no existe el futuro como tiempo gramatical, pero hay varias formas de expresar lo que ocurrirá en el porvenir.

Las diferentes maneras de expresar el futuro reflejan diferentes grados de probabilidad, o bien indican si se trata de un futuro más o menos próximo.

1. *will* o *shall* + base verbal

Will y *shall* se sustituyen a menudo con su contracción *–'ll*.

Shall sólo se utiliza en la primera persona (singular o plural).

> *I'll ask him to call you back.*
> Le pediré que te hable.

2. to be going to + base verbal

> *They're going to buy a new car.*
> Van a comprar un coche nuevo.

To be going to go a menudo se reduce a *to be going*:

> *We're going to Disneyland in July.*
> Vamos (a ir) a Disneylandia en julio.

3. to be about to + base verbal

> *The train is about to leave.*
> El tren está a punto de salir.

¡Atención!

En las subordinadas introducidas por *if*, *when* o *after* con valor de futuro, en inglés se utiliza el presente simple.
I'll go to the mall when I finish my homework. Iré al centro comercial cuando termine la tarea.

Los auxiliares

En inglés se utilizan auxiliares para expresar el tiempo, la voz, la negación, la interrogación y el modo.

To be se utiliza para formar la voz pasiva y las formas durativas. Fíjate en que la voz pasiva en inglés suele traducirse como voz activa en español.

> *The bread was bought this morning.*
> El pan fue comprado esta mañana/Se compró el pan esta mañana.

To have se utiliza para construir las formas compuestas de los tiempos:

His parents arrived when the game had finished.
Sus papás llegaron cuando ya había terminado el partido.

To do + base verbal se utiliza para formar las frases negativas, interrogativas o enfáticas.

En presente se emplea *do/does*. Para la forma negativa se emplea *don't/doesn't* (contracciones de *do/does not*).

It doesn't get any better.
Esto no mejora.

Do you know everybody?
¿Conoces a todos?

En pretérito se emplea *did* y *didn't* (contracción de *did not*).

Los auxiliares modales son *can, could, may, might, must, shall, should, will* y *would*. Se utilizan para expresar un punto de vista: la posibilidad o la probabilidad (*can, could, may,* y *might*, poder), lo que conviene hacer (*must, shall* y *should*, deber) o bien la voluntad (*will* y *would*, querer).

Could you help me to download a song?
¿Podrías ayudarme a descargar una canción?

May I leave the classroom?
¿Puedo salir del salón?

You must stop writing now.
Deben dejar de escribir ahora mismo.

Shall I close the window?
¿Quiere que cierre la ventana? (= ¿Debo cerrar la ventana?)

I think Jane should get a new cell.
Creo que Jane debería de conseguir un celular nuevo.

○ Uso

Los modales simplemente se anteponen a la base verbal:

Can you repeat that please?
¿Podrías repetirlo, por favor?

En presente tienen la misma forma en todas las personas:

You may/she may get a new laptop.
Puede que obtengas/obtenga un nuevo laptop.

She may return home tomorrow.

Puede que regrese mañana.

Algunos modales no pueden emplearse en pasado o futuro. En ese caso deben sustituirse con un equivalente:

I don't know if I'll be able to unlock the door.
No sé si podré abrir la puerta.

He had to stay home because he didn't feel well.
Tuvo que quedarse en casa porque no se sentía bien.

To be, to have, to do y los modales pueden contraerse, en especial si se combinan con la negación *not* que siempre se coloca detrás del auxiliar. (Ver las tablas al final de la gramática)

Hacer preguntas

1. Cómo formular las preguntas

Para hacer una pregunta en inglés debe utilizarse un auxiliar.

Si el verbo es un auxiliar, basta con hacer la inversión: auxiliar + sujeto.

Are you Mexican?
¿Eres mexicano?

Is she angry?
¿Está enojada?

Si el verbo principal no es un auxiliar, debe utilizarse la construcción: auxiliar + sujeto + verbo:

Have you visited the States?
¿Has estado en los Estados Unidos?

Could I use the bathroom?
¿Podría ir al baño?

Cuando no hay auxiliar, deben emplearse *do* o *does* en presente, y *did* en pretérito, seguidos por la base verbal.

Do you know everybody?
¿Conoces a todos?

Did you have a good trip?
¿Tuviste un buen viaje?

2. Las palabras interrogativas

○ Los pronombres interrogativos

Por lo general se colocan al inicio de una frase, pero pueden estar precedidos por una preposición.

> *Who lives next door?*
> ¿Quién vive en la casa de al lado?

> *Who do you see more often, Susie or Jane?*
> ¿A quién ves más a menudo, a Susie o a Jane?

> *Whose bag is this?*
> ¿De quién es esta bolsa?

> *Which one do you want?*
> ¿Cuál quieres?

○ Otras palabras interrogativas

> *How are you?*
> ¿Cómo estás?

> *How do you like your soda, with or without ice?*
> ¿Cómo te gusta el refresco, con o sin hielo?

> *When do they go on vacation?*
> ¿Cuándo se van de vacaciones?

> *Where does she live?*
> ¿Dónde vive?

> *Why does he go to Tlalpan every day?*
> ¿Por qué va todos los días a Tlalpan?

¡Atención!

En inglés, para preguntar cómo es alguien o algo, no puede utilizarse *how*, debe emplearse *what ... like*.

> *What's the new teacher like?*
> ¿Cómo es el nuevo profesor?

○ Cantidades

Para preguntar por una cantidad en inglés se utiliza *how much* + singular y *how many* + plural.

> *How much money do you have?*
> ¿Cuánto dinero tienes?

> *How many hours did you spend working on this project?*
> ¿Cuántas horas pasaste trabajando en este proyecto?

Los verbos con partícula o *phrasal verbs*

Los verbos compuestos en inglés son muy numerosos.

Existen los verbos preposicionales, que se forman con la base verbal seguida por una preposición y un complemento, y los verbos con partícula o *phrasal verbs*, es decir, los que se forman con la base verbal seguida por una partícula adverbial (*up*, *down*, *off*, etcétera) que forma parte integral del verbo y cambia su sentido original.

Por ejemplo, compara:

> *She always brings candy.*
> Siempre trae dulces.

> *She's bringing up three children under five.*
> Está criando tres hijos menores de cinco años.

> *He makes piñatas.*
> Hace piñatas.

> *He made the story up.*
> Inventó la historia.

> *I gave my brother an orange.*
> Le di una naranja a mi hermano.

> *Why did you give up?*
> ¿Por qué te diste por vencido?

Un mismo *phrasal verb* puede tener varios sentidos:

> *Turn the TV up.*
> Sube el volumen de la televisión.

> *They turned up late.*
> Ellos llegaron tarde.

La partícula es a menudo un adverbio de lugar que se coloca inmediatamente después de la base verbal:

> *Do sit down.*
> Siéntese.

Algunos phrasal verbs se construyen con una preposición y un complemento, lo cual otorga al verbo otro sentido. Compara:

To put up drapes (colgar las cortinas), *to put up a guest* (alojar a un invitado), *to put up with a situation* (soportar una situación).

¡Atención!

Cuando el complemento de objeto es un sustantivo, puede colocarse antes o después de la partícula:

Turn the radio off/Turn off the radio.
Apaga el radio.

Si es un pronombre, debe colocarse antes de la partícula:
Turn it off. Apágalo.

Cuando hay dos partículas, éstas permanecen pegadas al verbo:
She came up with a brilliant idea.
Tuvo una idea genial.

Cuando el phrasal verb va seguido de otro verbo, éste es un gerundio:
She gave up smoking.
Dejó de fumar.

Verbos irregulares más comunes

1. Primera categoría

El pretérito y el participio pasado de estos verbos tienen la misma forma. He aquí algunos de los más frecuentes:

bring	brought	mean	meant
build	built	pay	paid
buy	bought	read	read
dream	dreamed	say	said
feel	felt	sell	sold
find	found	send	sent
have	had	sit	sat
hear	heard	sleep	slept
hold	held	spend	spent
keep	kept	stand	stood
learn	learned	stick	stuck
leave	left	tell	told
lend	lent	think	thought
light	lit	understand	understood
lose	lost	win	won
make	made		
meet	met		

2. Segunda categoría

Entre estos verbos hay algunos que sólo

tienen una forma irregular (*to show, showed, shown*).

El pretérito y el participio pasado tienen formas diferentes.

He aquí una lista no exhaustiva de estos verbos:

Base verbal	Pretérito	Participio pasado
be	was/were	been
become	became	become
begin	began	begun
break	broke	broken
choose	chose	chosen
come	came	come
do	did	done
drink	drank	drunk
drive	drove	driven
eat	ate	eaten
fall	fell	fallen
fly	flew	flown
forbid	forbade	forbbiden
forget	forgot	forgotten
get	got	gotten
give	gave	given
go	went	gone
know	knew	known
ride	rode	ridden
ring	rang	rung
run	ran	run
see	saw	seen
show	showed	shown
sing	sang	sung
speak	spoke	spoken
steal	stole	stolen
swim	swam	swum
take	took	taken
wake	woke	woken
wear	wore	worn
write	wrote	written

3. Tercera categoría

Estos verbos, de una sola sílaba, terminan en −*d* o −*t* y tienen una misma forma para la base verbal, el pretérito y el participio pasado:

cost, cut, hit, hurt, let, put, said, shut.

La contracción

Las contracciones de *to be* y de los auxiliares se utilizan al hablar y al escribir, en un tono familiar. En las oraciones afirmativas, sólo *to be*, *to have*, *will/shall* y *would* poseen contracciones. Todos los auxiliares, salvo *may*, tienen contracciones que incorporan la negación *not*.

Las contracciones se utilizan en oraciones interrogativas negativas:

Can't you find it?
Doesn't he agree?

En las oraciones afirmativas, sólo las formas del presente tienen contracción:

I'm going; you're going; he's/she's/it's going; we're going; they're going.

En el caso de *to have*, las formas del presente y del pasado tienen contracciones:

They've agreed to come.
She's gone away.
I'd decided to go.

La contracción de *will* y *shall* es *'ll*:

I'll come tomorrow.
It'll be all right.

La contracción de *would* es *'d*:

He said he'd help me.
I'd rather have tea.

En las oraciones negativas, las contracciones de *to be*, *to have* y *to do* son las siguientes:

to be				
	contracción afirmativa		contracción negativa	
	singular	plural	singular	plural
1ª p.	*I'm*	*we're*	*I'm not*	*we're not/ we aren't*
2ª p.	*you're*	*you're*	*you're not/ you aren't*	*you're not/ you aren't*
3ª p.	*he's/ she's/ it's*	*they're he's/ she's/*	*it's not - he/she/it isn't*	*they're not/ they aren't*

Cuidado, en la primera persona del singular, la contracción se basa en *am* (*'m*) mientras que *not* permanece entero: *I'm not sure what to*

do. *Aren't* sólo se usa en oraciones interrogativas: *Why aren't I allowed to go?*

En el pasado se usa la forma *wasn't* para la 1ª y 3a persona en singular. Para la demás es *weren't*.

to have				
	contracción afirmativa		contracción negativa	
	singular	plural	singular	plural
1ª p.	*I've*	*we've*	*I haven't/ don't have*	*we haven't/ don't have*
2ª p.	*you've*	*you've*	*you haven't/ don't have*	*you haven't/ don't have*
3ª p.	*he's/ she's/it's*			*they haven't/ don't have*

En el pasado se usa la forma *hadn't* para todas las personas.

to do		
	sólo tiene contracción negativa	
	singular	plural
1ª p.	*I don't*	*we don't*
2ª p.	*you don't*	*you don't*
3ª p.	*he/she/it doesn't*	*they don't*

En el pasado se usa la forma *didn't* para todas las personas.

En el caso de los auxiliares modales *can*, *could*, *might*, *must*, *shall*, *should*, *will* y *would*, las contracciones son las siguientes:

can/can't (La forma negativa no contraída de *can* se escribe en una sola palabra: *cannot*.)

could/couldn't

might/mightn't

must/mustn't

shall/shan't

should/shouldn't

will/won't

would/wouldn't.

Guía Práctica

Numerales/*Numerals*

Cardinales *Cardinal numbers*

0	zero	cero		25	twenty-five	veinticinco
1	one	uno		26	twenty-six	veintiséis
2	two	dos		27	twenty-seven	veintisiete
3	three	tres		28	twenty-eight	veintiocho
4	four	cuatro		29	twenty-nine	veintinueve
5	five	cinco		30	thirty	treinta
6	six	seis		31	thirty-one	treinta y uno
7	seven	siete		32	thirty-two	treinta y dos
8	eight	ocho		40	forty	cuarenta
9	nine	nueve		50	fifty	cincuenta
10	ten	diez		60	sixty	sesenta
11	eleven	once		70	seventy	setenta
12	twelve	doce		80	eighty	ochenta
13	thirteen	trece		90	ninety	noventa
14	fourteen	catorce		100	one hundred	cien
15	fifteen	quince		101	one hundred and one	ciento uno
16	sixteen	dieciséis		500	five hundred	quinientos
17	seventeen	diecisiete		700	seven hundred	setecientos
18	eighteen	dieciocho		1000	one thousand	mil
19	nineteen	diecinueve		1020	one thousand and twenty	mil veinte
20	twenty	veinte		1606	one thousand six hundred and six	mil seiscientos seis
21	twenty-one	veintiuno		2000	two thousand	dos mil
22	twenty-two	veintidós		1.000.000	one million	un millón
23	twenty-three	veintitrés				
24	twenty-four	veinticuatro				

Ordinales *Ordinal numbers*

1st	1°	first	primero		16th	16°	sixteenth	decimosexto
2nd	2o	second	segundo		17th	17°	seventeenth	decimoséptimo
3rd	3°	third	tercero		18th	18°	eighteenth	decimoctavo
4th	4°	fourth	cuarto		19th	19°	nineteenth	decimonoveno
5th	5°	fifth	quinto		20th	20°	twentieth	vigésimo
6th	6°	sixth	sexto		21st	21°	twenty-first	vigésimo primer(o)
7th	7°	seventh	séptimo		22nd	22°	twenty-second	vigésimo segundo
8th	8°	eighth	octavo		23nd	23°	twenty-third	vigésimo tercero
9th	9°	ninth	noveno		30th	30°	thirtieth	trigésimo
10th	10°	tenth	décimo		100th	100°	hundredth	centésimo
11th	11°	eleventh	undécimo		101st	101°	hundred and first	centésimo primero
12th	12°	twelfth	decimosegundo		1000th	1000°	thousandth	milésimo
13th	13°	thirteenth	decimotercero					
14th	14°	fourteenth	decimocuarto					
15th	15°	fifteenth	decimoquinto					

Las matemáticas/*Mathematical operations*

Fracciones y decimales *Fractions and decimals*

1/2	one half	medio
2/3	two thirds	dos tercios
1/10	one tenth	un décimo/una décima parte
1/100	one hundredth	un centésimo/una centésima parte
0.1	(zero) point one	cero punto uno
2.5	two point five	dos punto cinco
6.03	six point zero three	seis punto cero tres
- 1	minus one	menos uno

Las operaciones *Mathematical operations*

8+2=10	eight plus two equals ten	ocho más dos igual a diez
9-3=6	nine minus three equals six	nueve menos tres igual a seis
7x3=21	seven times three equals twenty-one/ seven multiplied by three equals twenty-one	siete por tres igual a veintiuno
20 / 4 =5	twenty divided by four equals five	veinte entre cuatro igual a cinco
$\sqrt{9}=3$	the square root of nine is three	la raíz cuadrada de nueve es tres
$5^2=25$	five squared equals twenty-five	cinco al cuadrado igual a veinticinco

Los porcentajes *Percentages*

10%	ten percent	el diez por ciento

75%	seventy-five percent	75% of students have a computer.	El 75% de los estudiantes tiene un ordenador.
0.2%	zero point two percent	The unemployment rate has risen 0.2%.	El paro ha aumentado un 0,2%.

Los números de teléfono/*Phone numbers*

– Hello? Is this 718 323 6083? (seven one eight, three two three, six oh eight three)	–¿Bueno? ¿Es el 718 323 6083? (siete uno ocho, tres dos tres, seis cero ocho tres)
– No, you have the wrong number.	– No, está equivocado.

Unidades monetarias/*Currency*

La moneda estadounidense *US currency*

Monedas *Coins*

1c	one cent	un centavo
5c	five cents/a nickel	cinco centavos
10c	ten cents/a dime	diez centavos
25c	twenty-five cents/a quarter	veinticinco centavos

Billetes *Banknotes*

$1	one dollar	un dólar
$5	five dollars	cinco dólares
$10	ten dollars	diez dólares
$20	twenty dollars	veinte dólares
$50	fifty dollars	cincuenta dólares
$100	one hundred dollars	cien dólares

Pesos y medidas/*Weights and measures*

Longitud *Length*

mm	millimeter	milímetro
cm	centimeter	centímetro
m	meter	metro
km	kilometer	kilómetro
in	inch	pulgada
ft	foot	pie
yd	yard	yarda
mi	mile	milla

Capacidad *Capacity*

dl	deciliter	decilitro
l	liter	litro
1 oz	ounce	onza
1 pt	pint	pinta
gal	gallon	galón

Superficie *Area*

cm^2	square centimeter	centímetro cuadrado
m^2	square meter	metro cuadrado
km^2	square kilometer	kilómetro cuadrado
ha	hectare (=10.000m²)	hectárea
in^2	square inch	pulgada cuadrada
ft^2	square foot	pie cuadrado
yd^2	square yard	yarda cuadrada
mi^2	square mile	milla cuadrada

Velocidad *Speed*

m/s	meters per second	metro(s) por segundo
km/h	kilometers per hour	kilómetro(s) por hora
mph	miles per hour	milla(s) por hora

Peso *Weight*

mg	milligram	miligramo
g	gram	gramo
kg	kilo(gram)	kilo(gramo)
t	ton	tonelada
1 oz	ounce	onza
1 lb	pound	libra

Volume *Volume*

cm^3	cubic centimeter	centímetro cúbico
m^3	cubic meter	metro cúbico
ft^3	cubic foot	pie cúbico
yd^3	cubic yard	yarda cúbica

Temperatura *Temperature*

°C		degree Celsius	grados Celsius/centígrados
°F		degree Fahrenheit	grados Fahrenheit
100°	212°F	Water boils at two hundred and twelve degrees.	El agua hierve a 100 grados.
12°	55°F	Today it's fifty-five degrees.	Hoy estamos a 12 grados.
40°	104°F	My temperature was one hundred and four.	Tuve 40 de fiebre.

Informática *IT*

KB	kilobyte	kilobyte
MB	megabyte (=1024 KB)	megabyte
GB	gigabyte (=1024 MB)	gigabyte
Kbps	kilobyte per second	kilobyte por segundo

La hora/*Time*

11:30	las once y media	half past eleven
12:00	las doce del día	noon/twelve a.m./midday
01:00	la una de la madrugada/de la mañana	one a.m.
24:00	las doce de la noche	twelve p.m./midnight
05:00	las cinco	five o'clock
12:30	las doce y media	half past twelve/twelve thirty
07:05	las siete y cinco	five past seven
08:10	las ocho y diez	ten past eight
09:15	las nueve y cuarto	a quarter after nine
10:20	las diez y veinte	twenty after ten
13:00	la una	one p.m.
14:00	las dos	two o'clock

15:45	cuarto para las cuatro	a quarter of four / fifteen forty five
17:23	las cinco y veintitrés	five twenty-three

– ¿Qué hora es?	"What time is it?"
– Es la una/son las ocho y treinta y cinco.	"It's one o'clock/eight thirty-five."
– ¿A qué hora abre?	"When does it open?"
– A/hacia/sobre las once.	"About elevenish."
– Hace media hora.	"Half an hour ago."
– Dentro de tres cuartos de hora.	"In three quarters of an hour."
– ¿Tiene hora?	"Do you have the time?"

La fecha/*Dates*

El calendario *Calendar*

10/16/2008	October sixteenth two-thousand and eight	el dieciséis de octubre del dos mil ocho
1492	fourteen ninety-two	mil cuatrocientos noventa y dos
1975	nineteen seventy-five	mil novecientos setenta y cinco
70s	the Seventies	los años setenta
18th C	the eighteenth century	el siglo XVIII
BC/AD	before/after Christ	antes/después de Cristo

– ¿Cuál es tu fecha de nacimiento?	"What's your date of birth?"
– ¿Cuándo es tu cumpleaños?	"When is your birthday?"
– El 30 de julio.	"July 30th."
– ¿En qué mes naciste?	"Which month were you born in?"
– ¿En qué año?	"In which year?"
– En mayo del 68.	"In May 1968."
– En el siglo XXI.	"In the twenty first Century."
– Nací en marzo.	"I was born in March."

Ayer, hoy, mañana... *Yesterday, today, tomorrow...*

hoy	today
mañana	tomorrow
ayer	yesterday
pasado mañana	the day after tomorrow
anteayer	the day before yesterday
el día siguiente	the following day
la víspera	the day before
esta mañana	this morning
esta tarde	this afternoon
mañana por la tarde	tomorrow afternoon
ayer por la noche	yesterday evening
el sábado por la noche	Saturday night
hace dos días	two days ago
la semana pasada	last week
el año que viene	next year
el próximo verano O el verano que viene	next summer
un día sí y otro no	every second day

– ¿Qué día es hoy? O ¿A qué día estamos?	– What day is it today?
– Hoy es 5 de mayo. O Hoy estamos a 5 de mayo.	– Today is the fifth of May.

Mensajes de texto/*Text messages*

A		
A3	Anytime, Anywhere, Anyplace	Cuando quieras, donde quieras
AFAIK	As Far As I Know	Que yo sepa
AFAIR	As Far As I Remember	Que recuerde
Alwz	Always	Siempre
AMBW	All My Best Wishes	Mis mejores deseos
ASAP	As Soon As Possible	Tan pronto como posible
ATB	All The Best	Mis mejores deseos
ATM	At the moment	En este momento

B		
B	Be	Ser/estar
B4	Before	Antes (de)
BBL	Be Back Later	Luego vuelvo
BCNU	Be Seeing You	Nos vemos
BBS	Be Back Soon	Vuelvo en seguida
BF	Boyfriend	Novio
BFN o B4N	Bye For Now	Hasta el rato
BHL8	Be Home late	Llego tarde
BN	Been	Estado
BOL	Best Of Luck	Buena suerte
BRB	Be Right Back	Vuelvo en seguida
BRT	Be Right There	Llego en seguida
BT	Between	Entre
BTW	By The Way	A propósito

C		
C	See	Ver
COZ	Because	Porque
CU	See You	Hasta luego
CUB L8R	Call You Back Later	Te hablo después
CU@	See You At	Nos vemos en...
CYA	See You Around/ See ya	Hasta luego
CMi	Call me	Háblame
CMON	Come On	Órale

CUL8R	See You Later	Nos vemos
CYR BRO	Call Your Brother	Háblale a tu hermano
CYR SIS	Call Your Sister	Háblale a tu hermana

D		
Dk	Don't know	No sé
DNR	Dinner	La comida
doN	Doing	Haciendo

E		
EVRY1	Everyone	Todo el mundo
EZ/EZY	Easy	Fácil

F		
F2F	Face to Face	Cara a cara
F2T	Free to Talk	Te escucho
FC	Fingers Crossed	Cruz cruz
F?	Friends?	¿Amigos?
FYEO	For Your Eyes Only	Ni una palabra
FYI	For Your Information	Para que estés enterado

G		
GAL	Get A Life	Haz algo de provecho
GF	Girlfriend	Novia
GMTA	Great Minds Think Alike	Estoy de acuerdo contigo
GR8	Great!	¡Padre!
GTG	Got To Go	Tengo que irme

H		
h2cus	Hope to See You Soon	Espero que nos veamos pronto
H8	Hate	Odio
HAGN	Have A Good Night	Buenas noches
HAK o H&K	Hugs And Kisses	Un fuerte abrazo
HAND	Have A Nice Day	Que te vaya bien
HRU	How Are You?	¿Cómo estás?

I		
IAC	In Any Case	De todas formas
IAD8	It's A date	Ya quedamos
IC	I See	Ya veo

IDK	I Don't Know	No sé
ILU	I Love You	Te quiero
ILU2	I Love You too	Yo también te quiero
ILUA	I Love You Alot	Te quiero mucho
IM 4 U	I Am for You	Soy tuyo/tuya
IMI	I Mean It	Va en serio
IOU	I Owe You	Te lo debo
IRL	In Real Life	En la vida real
IYD	In Your Dreams	Sigue soñando
J		
J4F	Just for Fun	Justo para divertirse
JFK	Just For Kicks	Justo para divertirse
JK	Just Kidding	Es chiste
K		
KC	Keep Cool	Mantén la calma
KHUF	(I) Know How You Feel	Sé cómo te sientes
KIT	Keep In Touch	Mantente en contacto
KOTL	Kiss On The Lips	Beso en la boca
L		
L8	Late	Tarde
L8r	Later	Más tarde
LOL	Lots of love/ Laughing Out Loud	Besos/Doblado de la risa
LTNS o LTNC	Long Time No See	¡Cuánto hace que no nos vemos!
LUV o LV	Love	Besos
lyN	Lying	Mentiroso/ mentirosa
M		
MU	Miss You	Te extraño
MUSM	Miss You So Much	Te extraño tanto
MYOB	Mind Your Own Business	No te metas en lo que no te importa
N		
NBD	No Big Deal	Nada serio
NC	No Comment	Sin ts
NE	Any	Algún
NE1	Anyone	Cualquiera
NITING	Anything	Cualquier cosa
Njoy	Enjoy	Disfruta

No1	No one	Nadie
NP	No Problem	No hay problema
nufN	Nothing	Nada
NWO	No Way Out	Sin salida
O		
OIC	Oh, I see	Ah, ya veo
OMG	Oh, My God	O Dios mío
OTOH	On The Other Hand	Por otro lado
O4U	Only for You	Solo para ti
P		
PCM o PCME	Please Call Me	Háblame por favor
PLS	Please	Por favor
PPL	People	Gente
po$bl	Possible	Posible
PRT	Party	Fiesta
PRW	Parents are Watching	Los papás están viendo
PTB	Please Text Back	Contéstame por sms, por favor
Q		
QPSA?	What's up?	¿Qué pasa?
QT	Cutie	Chulo/chula
R		
R	Are	Son
ROFL	Rolling On the Floor Laughing	jajaja
RU?	Are You?	¿Estás?
RUOK?	Are You OK?	¿Estás bien?
S		
SC	Stay Cool	No pierdas la calma
Sry	Sorry	Lo siento
SUM1	Someone	Alguien
T		
T+	Think positive	Sé positivo
T2Go	Time to go	Hora de irse
T2ul	Talk to You Later	Te hablo después
Tnx o tks	Thanks	Gracias
THNQ	Thank you	Gracias
TMB	Text Me Back	Contéstame por sms
TTYL	Talk To You Later	Te hablo después
TUL	Tell You Later	Te lo digo después

TXT BAC	Text Back	Contéstame por sms
TYVM	Thank You Very Much	Muchas gracias
U		
U	You	Tú
U2	You too	Tú también/a ti también
UR	You are	Tú eres
URT1	You Are The One	Tú eres el único/la única que necesito
U4E	Yours forever	Tuyo/tuya por siempre
V		
VBG	Very Big Grin	Sonrisa muy grande
VRI	Very	Muy
W		
W	With	Con
W@	What	Que
W4u	Waiting for You	Te espero
W8	Wait	Espérate
W84M	Wait for Me	Espérame
W8N	Waiting	Te espero
WAN2	Want to	Quieres/quiero
WB	Welcome Back	Qué bueno que estés de regreso
WKND	Weekend	Weekend
WOT	What	Que
WRU	Where Are You?	¿Dónde estás?
WTG	Way To Go	Así es cómo se hace
WTH	What The Hell	Ni modo
WUF	Where Are You From?	¿De dónde eres?
WUWH	Wish You Were Here	¡Cómo no estás aquí!
X		
X!	Typical woman	¡Así son las mujeres!

X	Kiss	Beso
XO	Kiss and a hug	Beso y abrazo
XLNT	Excellent	Excelente
Y		
Y	Why?	¿Por qué?
Y!	Typical man	¡Así son los hombres!
YBS	You'll Be Sorry	Te vas a arrepentir
YGM	You Got Mail	Tienes correo
YR	Your	Tu
Z		
Z	the	El/La/Los
1		
10Q	Thank You	Gracias
1DAY	One day	Un día
1NC	Once	Una vez
2		
2	To/Two/Too	Hacia/dos/también
2DAY	Today	Hoy
2d4	To die for	Morir por
2l8	Too late	Demasiado tarde
2MORO	Tomorrow	Mañana
2NITE	Tonight	Hoy en la noche
4		
4	For	Por/para
4e	Forever	Para siempre
4gv	Forgive	Perdóname
4gvn	Forgiven	Perdonado
4yeo	For Your Eyes Only	Para tus ojos únicamente
8		
8	Ate	Ya comí
9		
911	Emergency/Call me	Emergencia/Háblame

Verbos irregulares/*Irregular verbs*

Infinitivo	Presente	Pretérito	Participio pasado	Traducción
arise	I/you arise he/she/it arises	arose	arisen	*surgir*
awake	I/you awake he/she/it awakes	awoke	awoken	*despertarse*
be	I am/you are he is	was/were	been	*ser estar*
bear	I/you bear he/she/it bears	bore	borne	*llevar soportar*
beat	I/you beat he/she/it beats	beat	beaten	*pegar golpear*
become	I/you become he/she/it becomes	became	became	*hacerse*
begin	I/you begin he/she/it begins	began	begun	*empezar*
bend	I/you bend he/she/it bends	bent	bent	*doblar*
bet	I/you bet he/she/it bets	bet/betted	bet/betted	*apostar*
bid	I/you bid he/she/it bids	bade	bidden	*ofrecer pujar*
bind	I/you bind he/she/it binds	bound	bound	*atar unir*
bite	I/you bite he/she/it bites	bit	bitten	*morder*
bleed	I/you bleed he/she/it bleeds	bled	bled	*sangrar*
blow	I/you blow he/she/it blows	blew	blown	*soplar*
break	I/you break he/she/it breaks	broke	broken	*romper*
breed	I/you breed he/she/it breeds	bred	bred	*criar procrear*
bring	I/you bring he/she/it brings	brought	brought	*traer*
build	I/you build he/she/it builds	built	built	*construir*
burn	I/you burn he/she/it burns	burnt/burned	burnt/burned	*quemar*
burst	I/you burst he/she/it bursts	burst	burst	*reventar*
buy	I/you buy he/she/it buys	bought	bought	*comprar*
can	I/you can he/she/it cans	could	–	*poder saber*
cast	I/you cast he/she/it casts	cast	cast	*lanzar*
catch	I/you catch he/she/it catches	caught	caught	*agarrar*
choose	I/you choose he/she/it chooses	chose	chosen	*escoger*

Infinitivo	Presente	Pretérito	Participio pasado	Traducción
come	I/you come he/she/it comes	came	come	*venir*
cost	I/you cost he/she/it costs	cost	cost	*costar*
creep	I/you creep he/she/it creeps	crept	crept	*deslizarse*
cut	I/you cut he/she/it cuts	cut	cut	*cortar*
deal	I/you deal he/she/it deals	dealt	dealt	*dar, repartir*
dig	I/you dig he/she/it digs	dug	dug	*cavar*
do	I/you do he/she/it does	did	done	*hacer*
draw	I/you draw he/she/it draws	drew	drawn	*dibujar* *descorrer*
dream	I/you dream he/she/it dreams	dreamt/dreamed	dreamt/dreamed	*soñar*
drink	I/you drink he/she/it drinks	drank	drunk	*beber*
drive	I/you drive he/she/it drives	drove	driven	*conducir*
eat	I/you eat he/she/it eats	ate	eaten	*comer*
fall	I/you fall he/she/it falls	fell	fallen	*caer*
feed	I/you feed he/she/it feeds	fed	fed	*alimentar*
feel	I/you feel he/she/it feels	felt	felt	*sentir* *tocar*
fight	I/you fight he/she/it fights	fought	fought	*pelearse* *luchar*
find	I/you find he/she/it finds	found	found	*encontrar*
fling	I/you fling he/she/it flings	flung	flung	*lanzar*
fly	I/you fly he/she/it flies	flew	flown	*volar* *pilotar*
forbid	I/you forbid he/she/it forbids	forbad	forbidden	*prohibir*
forget	I/you forget he/she/it forgets	forgot	forgotten	*olvidar*
forgive	I/you forgive he/she/it forgives	forgave	forgiven	*perdonar*
freeze	I/you freeze he/she/it freezes	froze	frozen	*helar* *congelar*
get	I/you get he/she/it gets	got	gotten	*recibir*
give	I/you give he/she/it gives	gave	given	*dar*
go	I/you go he/she/it goes	went	gone	*ir*
grind	I/you grind he/she/it grinds	ground	ground	*moler*

Infinitivo	Presente	Pretérito	Participio pasado	Traducción
grow	I/you grow he/she/it grows	grew	grown	crecer cultivar
hang	I/you hang he/she/it hangs	hung/hanged	hung/hanged	colgar
have	I/you have he/she/it haves	had	had	tener
hear	I/you hear he/she/it hears	heard	heard	escuchar
hide	I/you hide he/she/it hides	hid	hidden	esconder(se)
hit	I/you hit he/she/it hits	hit	hit	pegar
hold	I/you hold he/she/it holds	held	held	tener
hurt	I/you hurt he/she/it hurts	hurt	hurt	hacer daño a doler
keep	I/you keep he/she/it keeps	kept	kept	guardar seguir
kneel	I/you kneel he/she/it kneels	knelt/kneeled	knelt /kneeled	arrodillarse
know	I/you know he/she/it knows	knew	known	conocer saber
lay	I/you lay he/she/it lays	laid	laid	colocar poner
lead	I/you lead he/she/it leads	led	led	encabezar
lean	I/you lean he/she/it leans	leant/leaned	leant/leaned	apoyar(se)
leap	I/you leap he/she/it leaps	leapt/leaped	leapt/leaped	saltar
learn	I/you learn he/she/it learns	learnt/learned	learnt/learned	aprender
leave	I/you leave he/she/it leaves	left	left	dejar irse
lend	I/you lend he/she/it lends	lent	lent	prestar
let	I/you let he/she/it lets	let	let	dejar
lie	I/you lie he/she/it lies	lay	lain	mentir echarse
light	I/you light he/she/it lights	lit/lighted	lit/lighted	encender iluminar
lose	I/you lose he/she/it loses	lost	lost	perder
make	I/you make he/she/it makes	made	made	hacer
may	I/you may he/she/it mays	might	–	poder
mean	I/you mean he/she/it means	meant	meant	querer decir significar
meet	I/you meet he/she/it meets	met	met	encontrar(se)
mistake	I/you mistake he/she/it mistakes	mistook	mistaken	equivocar

Infinitivo	Presente	Pretérito	Participio pasado	Traducción
mow	I/you mow he/she/it mows	mowed	mown/mowed	*cortar*
pay	I/you pay he/she/it pays	paid	paid	*pagar*
put	I/you put he/she/it puts	put	put	*poner*
quit	I/you quit he/she/it quits	quit/quitted	quit/quitted	*dejar* *salir (Inform)*
read	I/you read he/she/it reads	read	read	*leer*
rid	I/you rid he/she/it rids	rid/ridded	rid/ridded	*deshacerse de*
ride	I/you ride he/she/it rides	rode	ridden	*montar en*
ring	I/you ring he/she/it rings	rang	rung	*sonar*
rise	I/you rise he/she/it rises	rose	risen	*salir (el sol)* *subir (precios)*
run	I/you run he/she/it runs	ran	run	*correr* *dirigir (proyecto)*
saw	I/you saw he/she/it saws	sawed	sawn/sawed	*serrar*
say	I/you say he/she/it says	said	said	*decir*
see	I/you see he/she/it sees	saw	seen	*ver*
seek	I/you seek he/she/it seeks	sought	sought	*buscar*
sell	I/you sell he/she/it sells	sold	sold	*vender(se)*
send	I/you send he/she/it sends	sent	sent	*enviar*
set	I/you set he/she/it sets	set	set	*poner(se)*
sew	I/you sew he/she/it sews	sewed	sown	*coser*
shake	I/you shake he/she/it shakes	shook	shaken	*sacudir* *tremblar*
shall	I/you shall he/she/it shalls	should	–	*(verbo auxiliar para formar tiempos en el futuro)*
shed	I/you shed he/she/it sheds	shed	shed	*perder* *deshacerse de*
shine	I/you shine he/she/it shines	shone	shone	*brillar*
shoot	I/you shoot he/she/it shoots	shot	shot	*disparar*
show	I/you show he/she/it shows	showed	shown	*mostrar* *verse*
shrink	I/you shrink he/she/it shrinks	shrank/shrunk	shrunk/shrunken	*encoger*
shut	I/you shut he/she/it shuts	shut	shut	*cerrar(se)*

Infinitivo	Presente	Pretérito	Participio pasado	Traducción
sing	I/you sing he/she/it sings	sang	sung	*cantar*
sink	I/you sink he/she/it sinks	sank	sunk	*hundir*
sit	I/you sit he/she/it sits	sat	sat	*sentarse*
sleep	I/you sleep he/she/it sleeps	slept	slept	*dormir*
slide	I/you slide he/she/it slides	slid	slid	*deslizar(se)*
sling	I/you sling he/she/it slings	slung	slung	*tirar*
smell	I/you smell he/she/it smells	smelt/smelled	smelt/smelled	*oler*
sow	I/you sow he/she/it sows	sowed	sown/sowed	*sembrar*
speak	I/you speak he/she/it speaks	spoke	spoken	*hablar*
speed	I/you speed he/she/it speeds	sped/speeded	sped/speeded	*ir a toda velocidad*
spell	I/you spell he/she/it spells	spelt/spelled	spelt/spelled	*deletrear*
spend	I/you spend he/she/it spends	spent	spent	*gastar*
spill	I/you spill he/she/it spills	spilt/spilled	spilt/spilled	*derramar*
spin	I/you spin he/she/it spins	spun	spun	*girar dar vueltas*
spit	I/you spit he/she/it spits	spat/spit	spat/spit	*escupir*
split	I/you split he/she/it splits	split	split	*rasgar*
spoil	I/you spoil he/she/it spoils	spoilt/spoiled	spoilt/spoiled	*estropear mimar*
spread	I/you spread he/she/it spreads	spread	spread	*extender untar*
spring	I/you spring he/she/it springs	sprang	sprung	*saltar*
stand	I/you stand he/she/it stands	stood	stood	*poner(se) de pie*
steal	I/you steal he/she/it steals	stole	stolen	*robar*
stick	I/you stick he/she/it sticks	stuck	stuck	*meter pegar*
sting	I/you sting he/she/it stings	stung	stung	*picar*
stink	I/you stink he/she/it stinks	stank	stunk	*apestar*
strike	I/you strike he/she/it strikes	struck	struck/stricken	*pegar*
swear	I/you swear he/she/it swears	swore	sworn	*jurar*
sweep	I/you sweep he/she/it sweeps	swept	swept	*barrer*

Infinitivo	Presente	Pretérito	Participio pasado	Traducción
swell	I/you swell he/she/it swells	swelled	swollen/swelled	*aumentar*
swim	I/you swim he/she/it swims	swam	swum	*nadar*
swing	I/you swing he/she/it swings	swung	swung	*balancear(se)*
take	I/you take he/she/it takes	took	taken	*tomar, agarrar*
teach	I/you teach he/she/it teaches	taught	taught	*enseñar ser profesor(a)*
tear	I/you tear he/she/it tears	tore	torn	*rasgar(se)*
tell	I/you tell he/she/it tells	told	told	*decir*
think	I/you think he/she/it thinks	thought	thought	*pensar*
throw	I/you throw he/she/it throws	threw	thrown	*lanzar*
tread	I/you tread he/she/it treads	trod	trodden	*andar*
wake	I/you wake he/she/it wakes	woke/waked	woken/waked	*despertar(se)*
wear	I/you wear he/she/it wears	wore	worn	*llevar*
weave	I/you weave he/she/it weaves	wove	woven	*tejer*
weep	I/you weep he/she/it weeps	wept	wept	*llorar*
win	I/you win he/she/it wins	won	won	*ganar*
wind	I/you wind he/she/it winds	wound	wound	*serpentear enrollar*
wring	I/you wring he/she/it wrings	wrung	wrung	*escurrir*
write	I/you write he/she/it writes	wrote	written	*escribir*

⊙ OBSERVACIÓN

No olvides que los verbos compuestos que terminan en un verbo irregular también varían.
Mira los siguientes ejemplos.

Infinitivo	Presente	Pretérito	Participio pasado	Traducción
overdo	I/you over**do** he/she/it over**does**	over**did**	over**done**	*pasarse con*
understand	I/you under**stand** he/she/it under**stands**	under**stood**	under**stood**	*entender*

INGLÉS - ESPAÑOL

a¹, A [eɪ] *s* a; A
■ **A** *s* ❶ *MÚSICA* la ❷ *EDUCACIÓN* ≃ sobresaliente
Dos plurales: as o a's; As o A's.

a²
◆ *artículo indeterminado*

acento atónico [ə], *acento tónico* [eɪ], *antes de vocal o "h" muda: "an", acento atónico* [ən], *acento tónico* [æn]

❶ [*se utiliza delante de un nombre sobre el que hay cierta indefinición*]
• **I bought a car** compré un coche
• **she ate an orange for breakfast** se comió una naranja para el desayuno
❷ [*se utiliza con nombres de profesiones*]
• **he is a doctor/lawyer/plumber** es médico/abogado/plomero
❸ [*se utiliza como número*]
• **there were three men and a woman** había tres hombres y una mujer
• **it costs a hundred/thousand dollars** cuesta cien/mil dólares
❹ [*para expresar frecuencia, precio o velocidad*]
• **he plays tennis twice a week/month** juega tenis dos veces por semana/mes
• **it costs 20 cents a kilo** cuesta 20 centavos el kilo
• **$10 an hour** $10 por hora
• **the speed limit is 75 kilometers an hour** el límite de velocidad es de 75 kilómetros por hora
❺ [*se utiliza a veces delante de nombres cuando no se conoce a la persona*]
• **there's a Ms. Jones to see you** hay una tal señorita Jones que quiere verte

AAA (*abreviatura de* American Automobile Association) *s*
▸ asociación automovilística estadounidense
aback [əˈbæk] *adv* • **to be taken aback** quedarse desconcertado, da
abandon [əˈbændən] ◆ *vt* abandonar ◆ *s* • **with abandon** con desenfreno
abattoir [ˈæbətwɑːr] *s* rastro
abbey [ˈæbɪ] *s* abadía

abbreviate [əˈbriːvɪeɪt] *vt* abreviar
abbreviation [əˌbriːvɪˈeɪʃn] *s* abreviatura
ABC *s literal & figurado* abecé
abdicate [ˈæbdɪkeɪt] ◆ *vi* abdicar ◆ *vt* abdicar de
abdomen [ˈæbdəmen] *s* abdomen
abduct [əbˈdʌkt] *vt* raptar
aberration [ˌæbəˈreɪʃn] *s* aberración
abide [əˈbaɪd] *vt* soportar; aguantar
■ **abide by** *vt* *El objeto siempre va después de la preposición al final.* ❶ acatar ❷ atenerse a
ability [əˈbɪlətɪ] *s* capacidad
abject [ˈæbdʒekt] *adj* ❶ vil; indigente ❷ sumiso, sa ❸ humillante (*disculpa*)
able [ˈeɪbl] *adj* ❶ • **to be able to do something a)** poder hacer algo **b)** saber hacer algo • **to feel able to do something** sentirse capaz de hacer algo ❷ capaz; competente
ably [ˈeɪblɪ] *adv* competentemente
abnormal [æbˈnɔːml] *adj* anormal
aboard [əˈbɔːd] ◆ *adv* a bordo ◆ *preposición* ❶ a bordo de (*barco, avión*) ❷ en (*camión, tren*)
abode [əˈbəʊd] *s formal* • **of no fixed abode** sin domicilio fijo
abolish [əˈbɒlɪʃ] *vt* abolir
abolition [ˌæbəˈlɪʃn] *s* abolición
aborigine [ˌæbəˈrɪdʒənɪ] *s* aborigen de Australia
abort [əˈbɔːt] *vt* ❶ abortar ❷ provocar el aborto a ❸ *INFORMÁTICA* abortar
abortion [əˈbɔːʃn] *s* aborto • **to have an abortion** abortar

about [əˈbaʊt]
◆ *adv*
❶ [*indica aproximación*]
• **she has got about 200 books** tiene unos 200 libros
• **let's meet at about five o'clock** nos vemos como a las cinco
• **I'm just about ready** estoy casi listo

❷ [*indica dispersión*]
• **he left his books lying about** dejó sus libros tirados

❸ [*indica una acción inminente*]
• **to be about to do something** estar a punto de hacer algo

◆ *preposición*

❶ [*indica un tema, un asunto*]
• **I'm reading a book about magic** estoy leyendo un libro sobre magia
• **what is it about?** ¿de qué se trata?

❷ [*indica proximidad en el espacio*]
• **I parked about a block away** me estacioné como a una cuadra

❸ [*indica dispersión*]
• **his belongings were scattered about the room** sus pertenencias estaban desperdigadas por el cuarto

❹ [*después de "how" o "what", expresa sugerencia*]
• **what about going to the movies?** ¿qué tal si vamos al cine?

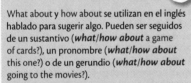

about

What about y how about se utilizan en el inglés hablado para sugerir algo. Pueden ser seguidos de un sustantivo (*what/how about* a game of cards?), un pronombre (*what/how about* this one?) o de un gerundio (*what/how about* going to the movies?).

Be about to se utiliza para expresar que algo va a ocurrir dentro de poco (the train's *about to* leave *el tren está a punto de salir*).

above [əˈbʌv] ◆ *adv* **❶** arriba • **the apartment above** el departamento de arriba • **see above** véase más arriba **❷** • **you can win with a score of 70 or above** puedes ganar con un puntaje de 70 o más • **children aged five and above** niños de cinco años en adelante ◆ *preposición* **❶** encima de **❷** por encima de • **temperatures above 90 degrees** temperaturas de más de 90 grados • **children above the age of 15** niños mayores de 15 años
■ **above all** *adv* sobre todo

aboveboard [ə,bʌvˈbɔːd] *adj* limpio, pia

abreast [əˈbrest] ◆ *adv* • **they were walking four abreast** caminaban en fila de a cuatro ◆ *preposición* • **to keep abreast of** mantenerse al día de

abroad [əˈbrɔːd] *adv* en el extranjero • **to go abroad** ir al extranjero

abrupt [əˈbrʌpt] *adj* **❶** repentino, na **❷** brusco, ca

abscess [ˈæbsɪs] *s* absceso

abscond [əbˈskɒnd] *vi* • **to abscond (with/from)** escaparse o fugarse (con/de)

abseil [ˈæbseɪl] *vi* • **to abseil (down something)** descolgarse o descender haciendo rápel (por algo)

abseiling [ˈæbseɪɪŋ] *s* rappel

absence [ˈæbsəns] *s* **❶** ausencia **❷** falta

absent [ˈæbsənt] *adj* ausente • **to be absent from** faltar a

absentee [ˌæbsənˈtiː] *s* ausente • **absentee ballot** voto por correo

absent-minded [-ˈmaɪndɪd] *adj* **❶** despistado, da **❷** distraído, da

absolute [ˈæbsəluːt] *adj* absoluto, ta • **that's absolute nonsense!** ¡qué tontería es eso!

absolutely [ˈæbsəluːtlɪ] ◆ *adv* absolutamente; completamente • **it was absolutely delicious** estuvo riquísimo ◆ *exclamación* ¡desde luego!

absolve [əbˈzɒlv] *vt* • **to absolve somebody (from)** absolver a alguien (de)

absorb [əbˈsɔːb] *vt* absorber • **to be absorbed in something** *figurado* estar absorto o embebido en algo

absorbent [əbˈsɔːbənt] *adj* absorbente • **absorbent cotton** algodón absorbente

absorption [əbˈsɔːpʃn] *s* absorción

abstain [əbˈsteɪn] *vi* • **to abstain (from)** abstenerse (de)

abstention [əbˈstenʃn] *s* abstención

abstract ◆ *adj* [ˈæbstrækt] abstracto, ta ◆ *s* [ˈæbstrækt] resumen; sinopsis

absurd [əbˈsɜːd] *adj* absurdo, da

abundant [əˈbʌndənt] *adj* abundante

abuse ◆ *s* [əˈbjuːs] ※ *incontable* **❶** insultos **❷** abuso ◆ *vt* [əˈbjuːz] **❶** insultar **❷** abusar de

abusive [əˈbjuːsɪv] *adj* **❶** grosero, ra **❷** insultante

abysmal [əˈbɪzml] *adj* pésimo, ma; nefasto, ta

abyss [əˈbɪs] *s* abismo

AC (*abreviatura de* alternating current) *s* CA

academic [ˌækəˈdemɪk] ◆ *adj* **❶** académico, ca **❷** estudioso, sa **❸** • **that's completely academic** eso carece por completo de relevancia ◆ *s* **❶** profesor universitario; profesora universitaria **❷** académico, ca

academy [əˈkædəmɪ] *s* academia

accelerate [əkˈseləreɪt] *vi* **❶** acelerar **❷** acelerarse

acceleration [əkˌseləˈreɪʃn] *s* aceleración

accelerator [əkˈseləreɪtər] *s* acelerador

accent [ˈæksent] *s* literal & figurado acento

accept [əkˈsept] *vt* **❶** aceptar **❷** asimilar (situación, problema) **❸** asumir (derrota, culpa, responsabilidad) **❹** • **to accept that** admitir que **❺** admitir (monedas, fichas)

acceptable [əkˈseptəbl] *adj* aceptable

acceptance [əkˈseptəns] *s* **❶** aceptación **❷** aprobación **❸** reconocimiento (de derrota, culpa, responsabilidad) **❹** admisión (de persona)

access [ˈækses] *s* **❶** acceso **❷** libre acceso • **to have access to** tener acceso a

accessible [əkˈsesəbl] *adj* **❶** accesible **❷** asequible **❸** para discapacitados

accessory [ək'sesərɪ] *s* accesorio
■ **accessories** *spl* complementos
accident ['æksɪdənt] *s* accidente • **to have an accident a)** tener un accidente **b)** tener un accidente de coche • **it was an accident** fue sin querer • **by accident a)** por casualidad **b)** sin querer
accidental [,æksɪ'dentl] *adj* accidental
accidentally [,æksɪ'dentəlɪ] *adv* ❶ por casualidad ❷ sin querer
accident-prone *adj* propenso, sa a los accidentes
acclaim [ə'kleɪm] ◆ *s* 🔆 *incontable* elogios; alabanza ◆ *vt* elogiar; alabar
acclimatize [ə'klaɪmətaɪz]**, acclimate** ['æklɪmeɪt] *vi* • **to acclimatize (to)** aclimatarse (a)
accolade ['ækəleɪd] *s* ❶ elogio; halago ❷ galardón
accommodate [ə'kɒmədeɪt] *vt* ❶ alojar ❷ albergar ❸ complacer
accommodations [ə,kɒmə'deɪʃnz] *spl* alojamiento
accompany [ə'kʌmpənɪ] *vt* acompañar
accomplice [ə'kʌmplɪs] *s* cómplice
accomplish [ə'kʌmplɪʃ] *vt* ❶ conseguir; alcanzar ❷ realizar
accomplished [ə'kʌmplɪʃt] *adj* ❶ competente; experto, ta ❷ logrado, da
accomplishment [ə'kʌmplɪʃmənt] *s* ❶ realización ❷ logro
accord [ə'kɔːd] ◆ *s*
expresión **to do something of your own accord** hacer algo por propia voluntad ▸ **the situation improved of its own accord** la situación mejoró por sí sola
◆ *vt* • **to accord somebody something, to accord something to somebody** conceder algo a alguien
accordance [ə'kɔːdəns] *s* • **in accordance with** de acuerdo con; conforme a
according [ə'kɔːdɪŋ] ■ **according to** *preposición* ❶ según ▸ **to go according to plan** ir según lo planeado ❷ de acuerdo con; conforme a
accordingly [ə'kɔːdɪŋlɪ] *adv* ❶ como corresponde ❷ por lo tanto
accordion [ə'kɔːdjən] *s* acordeón
accost [ə'kɒst] *vt* abordar
account [ə'kaʊnt] *s* ❶ cuenta ❷ relato ❸ informe ❹ cuenta; cliente
expresiones **to take account of something, to take something into account** tener en cuenta algo ▸ **of no account** sin importancia ▸ **it is of no account to me** me es indiferente ▸ **on no account** bajo ningún pretexto o concepto
■ **accounts** *spl* cuentas
■ **by all accounts** *adv* a decir de todos; según todo el mundo
■ **on account of** *preposición* debido a
■ **account for** *vt* 🔆 *El objeto siempre va después de la preposición al final.* ❶ justificar ❷ representar

accountable [ə'kaʊntəbl] *adj* • **accountable (for)** responsable (de)
accountancy [ə'kaʊntənsɪ] *s* contabilidad
accountant [ə'kaʊntənt] *s* contador, ra
accrue [ə'kruː] *vi* acumularse
accumulate [ə'kjuːmjʊleɪt] ◆ *vt* acumular ◆ *vi* ❶ acumularse ❷ amontonarse
accuracy ['ækjʊrəsɪ] *s* ❶ veracidad ❷ precisión ❸ exactitud
accurate ['ækjʊrət] *adj* ❶ veraz ❷ preciso, sa ❸ exacto, ta
accurately ['ækjʊrətlɪ] *adv* ❶ verazmente ❷ con precisión
accusation [,ækjuː'zeɪʃn] *s* ❶ acusación ❷ DERECHO denuncia
accuse [ə'kjuːz] *vt* • **to accuse somebody of something/of doing something** acusar a alguien de algo/ de hacer algo
accused [ə'kjuːzd] *s* DERECHO • **the accused** el acusado; la acusada

El plural de **accused** es **accused**.

accustomed [ə'kʌstəmd] *adj* • **accustomed to** acostumbrado, da a • **to grow accustomed to** acostumbrarse a
ace [eɪs] ◆ *s* ❶ as ❷ ace
expresión **to be within an ace of** *figurado* estar al borde de
◆ *vt* • **to ace an exam** pasar un examen
ache [eɪk] ◆ *s* dolor ◆ *vi* doler • **my back aches** me duele la espalda • **aches and pains** dolores
achieve [ə'tʃiːv] *vt* ❶ alcanzar; lograr ❷ realizar
achievement [ə'tʃiːvmənt] *s* ❶ logro; éxito ❷ consecución; realización
Achilles' tendon [ə'kɪliːz-] *s* tendón de Aquiles
acid ['æsɪd] ◆ *adj* ❶ QUÍMICA ácido, da ❷ agrio, agria ❸ *figurado* mordaz ◆ *s* ácido
acid house *s* acid house
acknowledge [ək'nɒlɪdʒ] *vt* ❶ reconocer ❷ saludar ❸ • **to acknowledge receipt of** acusar recibo de ❹ • **to acknowledge somebody as** reconocer a alguien como
acknowledg(e)ment [ək'nɒlɪdʒmənt] *s* ❶ reconocimiento ❷ acuse de recibo
■ **acknowledg(e)ments** *spl* agradecimientos
acne ['æknɪ] *s* acné
acorn ['eɪkɔːn] *s* bellota
acoustic [ə'kuːstɪk] *adj* acústico, ca
■ **acoustics** *spl* acústica
acquaintance [ə'kweɪntəns] *s* conocido, da • **to make somebody's acquaintance** *formal* conocer a alguien
acquire [ə'kwaɪər] *vt* ❶ adquirir ❷ procurarse
acquisitive [ə'kwɪzɪtɪv] *adj* consumista
acquit [ə'kwɪt] *vt* ❶ DERECHO • **to acquit somebody of something** absolver a alguien de algo ❷ • **to acquit yourself well/badly** hacer un buen/mal papel

A

acquittal [ə'kwɪtl] *s* Derecho absolución

acre ['eɪkər] *s* acre

acrimonious [ˌækrɪ'məʊnjəs] *adj* ❶ áspero, ra ❷ enconado, da

acrobat ['ækrəbæt] *s* acróbata

acronym ['ækrənɪm] *s* siglas

across [ə'krɒs] ◆ *adv* ❶ de un lado a otro ❷ • **the river is 2 km across** el río tiene 2 kms de ancho ◆ *preposición* ❶ a través de; de un lado a otro de • **there's a bridge across the river** hay un puente que atraviesa el río • **I walked across the street** crucé la calle • **to look across something** mirar hacia el otro lado de algo ❷ al otro lado de
■ **across from** *preposición* enfrente de

acrylic [ə'krɪlɪk] ◆ *adj* acrílico, ca ◆ *s* acrílico

act [ækt] ◆ *s* ❶ acto; acción ❷ farsa ❸ ley ❹ Teatro acto ◆ *vi* ❶ actuar • **to act as a)** hacer de **b)** actuar como ❷ • **to act (as if/like)** comportarse (como si/como) ❸ *figurado* fingir ◆ *vt* interpretar
expresión **to catch somebody in the act** coger a alguien con las manos en la masa

acting ['æktɪŋ] ◆ *adj* en funciones ◆ *s* actuación • **I like acting** me gusta actuar

action ['ækʃn] *s* ❶ acción • **to take action** tomar medidas ❷ acto; acción ❸ Derecho demanda
expresiones **to put something into action** poner algo en práctica ❶ **out of action a)** fuera de combate **b)** averiado, da ❶ **an action movie** una película de acción

activate ['æktɪveɪt] *vt* ❶ activar ❷ poner en funcionamiento

active ['æktɪv] *adj* ❶ activo, va ❷ en actividad *(volcán)* ❸ activado, da *(bomba)* • **on active duty** Militar en servicio activo

actively ['æktɪvlɪ] *adv* activamente

activity [æk'tɪvətɪ] *s* ❶ actividad ❷ afición

actor ['æktər] *s* actor; actriz

actress ['æktrɪs] *s* actriz

actual ['æktʃʊəl] *adj* • **the actual cost is $10** el coste real es de 10 dólares • **the actual spot where it happened** el sitio mismo en que ocurrió

actually ['æktʃʊəlɪ] *adv* ❶ • **do you actually like him?** ¿de verdad que te gusta? • **no-one actually saw her** en realidad, nadie la vio ❷ • **actually, I was there yesterday** pues yo estuve ayer por allí

acumen ['ækjʊmen] *s* • **business acumen** vista para los negocios

acute [ə'kjuːt] *adj* ❶ agudo, da ❷ extremo, ma ❸ perspicaz ❹ muy fino, na

ad [æd] *(abreviatura de* advertisement*) s* anuncio

AD *(abreviatura de* Anno Domini*)* d. C

adamant ['ædəmənt] *adj* • **to be adamant (that)** insistir (en que)

Adam's apple ['ædəmz-] *s* nuez de Adán

adapt [ə'dæpt] ◆ *vt* adaptar ◆ *vi* • **to adapt (to)** adaptarse (a)

adaptable [ə'dæptəbl] *adj* adaptable

adapter, adaptor [ə'dæptər] *s* ❶ Electricidad ladrón ❷ adaptador

add [æd] *vt* ❶ • **to add something (to something)** añadir algo (a algo) ❷ sumar
■ **add on** *vt* :ℚ: *El objeto se puede colocar antes o después de la preposición.* • **to add something on (to something)** añadir o incluir algo (en algo)
■ **add to** *vt* :ℚ: *El objeto siempre va después de la preposición al final.* aumentar; acrecentar
■ **add up** ◆ *vt* :ℚ: *El objeto se puede colocar antes o después de la preposición.* sumar ◆ *vi familiar* • **it doesn't add up** no tiene sentido

adder ['ædər] *s* víbora

addict ['ædɪkt] *s* ❶ adicto, ta ❶ **drug addict** drogadicto, ta; toxicómano, na ❷ *figurado* fanático, ca

addicted [ə'dɪktɪd] *adj* ❶ • **addicted (to)** adicto, ta (a) ❷ *figurado* • **to be addicted (to)** ser un fanático (de)

addiction [ə'dɪkʃn] *s* ❶ • **addiction (to)** adicción (a) ❷ *figurado* • **addiction (to)** vicio (por)

addictive [ə'dɪktɪv] *adj literal & figurado* adictivo, va

addition [ə'dɪʃn] *s* ❶ Matemáticas suma ❷ adición; añadido ❸ incorporación • **in addition** además • **in addition to** además de

additional [ə'dɪʃənl] *adj* adicional

additive ['ædɪtɪv] *s* aditivo

address [ə'dres] ◆ *s* ❶ dirección; domicilio ❷ Informática dirección ❸ discurso ◆ *vt* ❶ • **to address something to** dirigir algo a ❷ dirigirse a *(reunión, congreso)* ❸ abordar • **to address yourself to something** abordar algo

address book *s* agenda de direcciones

adept ['ædept] *adj* • **to be adept (at something/at doing something)** ser experto, ta (en algo/en hacer algo)

adequate ['ædɪkwət] *adj* ❶ suficiente ❷ aceptable

adhere [əd'hɪər] *vi* ❶ • **to adhere (to)** adherirse (a) ❷ • **to adhere to** respetar; observar

adhesive [əd'hiːsɪv] ◆ *adj* adhesivo, va; adherente ◆ *s* adhesivo

adhesive tape *s* cinta adhesiva

adjacent [ə'dʒeɪsənt] *adj* • **adjacent (to)** adyacente o contiguo, gua (a)

adjective ['ædʒɪktɪv] *s* adjetivo

adjoining [ə'dʒɔɪnɪŋ] ◆ *adj* ❶ adyacente ❷ contiguo, gua ◆ *preposición* junto a

adjourn [ə'dʒɜːn] *vt* ❶ levantar *(sesión)* ❷ interrumpir *(reunión)*

adjudicate [ə'dʒuːdɪkeɪt] *vi* actuar como juez • **to adjudicate on something** emitir un fallo o un veredicto sobre algo

adjust [ə'dʒʌst] ◆ *vt* ❶ ajustar ❷ arreglarse ◆ *vi* • **to adjust (to)** adaptarse o amoldarse (a)

adjustable [ə'dʒʌstəbl] *adj* regulable

adjustment [ə'dʒʌstmənt] *s* ❶ modificación; reajuste • **to make an adjustment to something** hacer un reajuste a algo ❷ ☺ *incontable* • **adjustment (to)** adaptación o amoldamiento (a)

ad lib [ˌæd'lɪb] ◆ *adj* improvisado, da ◆ *adv* ❶ improvisando ❷ a voluntad

■ **ad-lib** *vi* improvisar

administer [əd'mɪnɪstər] *vt* ❶ administrar ❷ aplicar *(castigo)*

administration [ədˌmɪnɪ'streɪʃn] *s* ❶ administración ❷ aplicación *(de castigo)*

■ **Administration** *s* • **the Administration** la Administración

administrative [əd'mɪnɪstrətɪv] *adj* administrativo, va

admirable ['ædmərəbl] *adj* admirable

admiral ['ædmərəl] *s* almirante

admiration [ˌædmə'reɪʃn] *s* admiración

admire [əd'maɪər] *vt* • **to admire somebody (for)** admirar a alguien (por)

admirer [əd'maɪərər] *s* admirador, ra

admission [əd'mɪʃn] *s* ❶ admisión; ingreso ❷ entrada ❸ reconocimiento • **by his/her** ETC **own admission** como el mismo/ella misma ETC reconoce

admit [əd'mɪt] ◆ *vt* ❶ • **to admit (that)** admitir o reconocer (que) • **to admit doing something** reconocer haber hecho algo • **to admit defeat** *figurado* darse por vencido ❷ admitir • 'admits two' válido para dos (personas)' ❸ internar *(en el hospital)* ◆ *vi* • **to admit to something** confesar algo

admittance [əd'mɪtəns] *s* • **to gain admittance to** conseguir entrar en • 'no admittance' 'prohibido el paso'

admittedly [əd'mɪtɪdlɪ] *adv* sin duda

ado [ə'duː] *s* • **without further** o **more ado** sin más preámbulos; sin mayor dilación

adolescence [ˌædə'lesns] *s* adolescencia

adolescent [ˌædə'lesnt] ◆ *adj* ❶ adolescente ❷ *despectivo* pueril ◆ *s* adolescente

adopt [ə'dɒpt] *vt* & *vi* adoptar

adoption [ə'dɒpʃn] *s* adopción

adore [ə'dɔːr] *vt* ❶ adorar ❷ • **I adore chocolate** me encanta el chocolate

adorn [ə'dɔːn] *vt* adornar

adrenalin [ə'drenəlɪn] *s* adrenalina

adrift [ə'drɪft] ◆ *adj* a la deriva ◆ *adv* • **to go adrift** *figurado* irse a la deriva

adult ['ædʌlt] ◆ *adj* ❶ adulto, ta ❷ maduro, ra ❸ para adultos o mayores ◆ *s* adulto, ta

adultery [ə'dʌltərɪ] *s* adulterio

advance [əd'vɑːns] ◆ *s* ❶ avance ❷ anticipo ◆ *en compuestos* • **advance notice** o **warning** previo aviso • **advance booking** reserva anticipada ◆ *vt* ❶ promover ❷ adelantar ❸ • **to advance somebody something** adelantarle algo a alguien ◆ *vi* avanzar

■ **advances** *spl* • **to make advances to somebody a)** hacerle proposiciones a alguien; insinuarse a alguien **b)** hacerle una propuesta a alguien

■ **in advance** *adv* ❶ por adelantado ❷ con antelación ❸ de antemano

advanced [əd'vɑːnst] *adj* ❶ avanzado, da ❷ adelantado, da ❸ superior

advantage [əd'vɑːntɪdʒ] *s* • **advantage (over)** ventaja (sobre) • **to be to your advantage** ir en beneficio de uno • **to take advantage of something a)** aprovechar algo **b)** aprovecharse de algo • **to have** o **hold the advantage (over somebody)** tener o llevar ventaja (sobre alguien) • **advantage Federer** ventaja de Federer

advent ['ædvənt] *s* advenimiento

■ **Advent** *s* RELIGIÓN Adviento

adventure [əd'ventʃər] *s* aventura

adventurous [əd'ventʃərəs] *adj* ❶ aventurero, ra ❷ arriesgado, da

adverb ['ædvɜːb] *s* adverbio

adverse ['ædvɜːs] *adj* adverso, sa

advert ['ædvɜːt] *s* anuncio

advertise ['ædvətaɪz] ◆ *vt* anunciar ◆ *vi* anunciarse; poner un anuncio • **to advertise for** buscar *(mediante anuncio)*

advertisement [əd'vɜːtɪsmənt] *s* anuncio; aviso • **to be a great advertisement for** *figurado* hacerle una propaganda excelente a

advertising ['ædvətaɪzɪŋ] *s* publicidad

advice [əd'vaɪs] *s* ☺ *incontable* consejos • **to take somebody's advice** seguir el consejo de alguien • **a piece of advice** un consejo • **to give somebody advice** aconsejar a alguien

advisable [əd'vaɪzəbl] *adj* aconsejable

advise [əd'vaɪz] ◆ *vt* ❶ • **to advise somebody to do something** aconsejar a alguien que haga algo • **to advise somebody against something/against doing something** desaconsejar a alguien algo/que haga algo ❷ • **to advise somebody on something** asesorar a alguien en algo ❸ recomendar ❹ *formal* • **to advise somebody (of something)** informar a alguien (de algo) ◆ *vi* ❶ • **to advise against something** desaconsejar algo • **to advise against doing something** aconsejar no hacer algo ❷ • **to advise on** asesorar en (materia de)

advisor [əd'vaɪzər] *s* ❶ consejero, ra ❷ asesor, ra

advocate ◆ *s* ['ædvəkət] ❶ DERECHO abogado defensor ❷ defensor, ra ◆ *vt* ['ædvəkeɪt] abogar por

aerial ['eərɪəl] *adj* aéreo, a

aerobics [eə'rəubɪks] *s* ☺ *incontable* aerobics

aerodynamic [ˌeərəudaɪ'næmɪk] *adj* aerodinámico, ca

aerosol ['eərəsɒl] *s* aerosol

affable ['æfəbl] *adj* afable

affair [ə'feər] *s* ❶ asunto ❷ aventura (amorosa) ❸ acontecimiento

affect [ə'fekt] *vt* ❶ afectar ❷ fingir

affected [əˈfektɪd] *adj* afectado, da
affection [əˈfekʃn] *s* cariño; afecto
affectionate [əˈfekʃnət] *adj* cariñoso, sa
affirm [əˈfɜ:m] *vt* afirmar
affirmative action *s*

Affirmative action

Este término designa las medidas concebidas para combatir la discriminación de las minorías étnicas y de las mujeres en los Estados Unidos. Inicialmente fueron introducidas en la década de los sesenta para luchar por la igualdad de oportunidades laborales entre blancos y negros. La noción de "affirmative action" ha llegado a desatar más de una polémica, especialmente en el ámbito racial, donde sus detractores han considerado que dispensaba un trato preferencial a los negros y a los hispanos, y continúa siendo objeto de debate.

affix [əˈfɪks] *vt* fijar; pegar
afflict [əˈflɪkt] *vt* aquejar; afligir • **to be afflicted with something** estar aquejido de algo
affluence [ˈæfluəns] *s* prosperidad
affluent [ˈæfluənt] *adj* pudiente
afford [əˈfɔ:d] *vt* • **to be able to afford** poder permitirse (el lujo de) • **I can't afford a new car** no tengo dinero para comprarme un coche nuevo • **we can't afford to let this happen** no podemos permitirnos el lujo de dejar que esto ocurra
affront [əˈfrʌnt] *s* afrenta
Afghanistan [æfˈɡænɪstæn] *s* Afganistán
afloat [əˈfləʊt] *adj* literal & figurado a flote
afraid [əˈfreɪd] *adj* ❶ asustado, da • **to be afraid of somebody** tenerle miedo a alguien • **I'm afraid of them** me dan miedo • **to be afraid of something** tener miedo de algo • **to be afraid of doing** o **to do something** tener miedo de hacer algo ❷ • **to be afraid that** temerse que • **I'm afraid so** me temo que sí
afresh [əˈfreʃ] *adv* de nuevo
Africa [ˈæfrɪkə] *s* África
African [ˈæfrɪkən] ◆ *adj* africano, na ◆ *s* africano, na
African American *s* afroamericano, na
after [ˈɑ:ftər] ◆ *preposición* ❶ después de • **after all my efforts** después de todos mis esfuerzos • **after you!** ¡usted primero! • **day after day** día tras día • **the day after tomorrow** pasado mañana • **the week after next** no la semana que viene sino la otra ❷ familiar • **to be after something** buscar algo • **to be after somebody** andar detrás de alguien ❸ • **to call after somebody** llamar a alguien • **to run after somebody** correr tras alguien ❹ • **it's twenty after three** son las tres y veinte ◆ *adv* más tarde; después ◆ *conjunción* después (de) que • **after you had done it** después de que lo hubieras hecho

■ **after all** *adv* ❶ después de todo ❷ al fin y al cabo
afterlife [ˈɑ:ftəlaɪf] *s* más allá
El plural de **afterlife** es **afterlives** [ˈɑ:ftəlaɪvz].
aftermath [ˈɑ:ftəmæθ] *s* ❶ periodo posterior ❷ situación posterior
afternoon [ˌɑ:ftəˈnu:n] *s* tarde • **in the afternoon** por la tarde • **at three in the afternoon** a las tres de la tarde • **good afternoon** buenas tardes
■ **afternoons** *adv* por las tardes
aftershave [ˈɑ:ftəʃeɪv] *s* loción para después del afeitado
aftertaste [ˈɑ:ftəteɪst] *s* ❶ resabio ❷ figurado mal sabor de boca
afterthought [ˈɑ:ftəɔ:t] *s* idea a posteriori
afterward(s) [ˈɑ:ftəwəd(z)] *adv* después; más tarde
again [əˈgen] *adv* otra vez; de nuevo • **never again** nunca jamás • **he's well again now** ya está bien • **to do something again** volver a hacer algo • **to say something again** repetir algo
expresiones **again and again** una y otra vez ▶ **all over again** otra vez desde el principio ▶ **half as much again** la mitad otra vez ▶ **time and again** una y otra vez ▶ **twice as much again** dos veces lo mismo otra vez ▶ **then** o **there again** por otro lado; por otra parte

again

No hay que confundir los adverbios again y back; su significado es parecido pero se usan de forma distinta. Again significa *otra vez*, (don't do it *again* or you'll be in trouble *no vuelvas a hacerlo o vas a tener problemas*), mientras que back indica la vuelta a un lugar o estado anterior (put it *back* in the closet *vuélvelo al closet*). Back también sirve para expresar la idea de *regresar* algo a alguien (give it *back* to me right now! *¡regrésamelo ahora mismo!*).

against [əˈgenst] ◆ *preposición* contra • **I'm against it** estoy (en) contra (de) ello • **to lean against something** apoyarse en algo • **(as) against** a diferencia de ◆ *adv* en contra
age [eɪdʒ] ◆ *s* ❶ edad • **what age are you?** ¿qué edad tienes? • **to be forty years of age** tener cuarenta años (de edad) • **at the age of thirty** a los treinta años ❷ vejez
expresiones **to be of age** ser mayor de edad ▶ **to come of age** alcanzar la mayoría de edad ▶ **to be under age** ser menor (de edad)
◆ *vt* & *vi* envejecer
Formas irregulares de **age**: gerundio **ageing** o **aging**.
■ **ages** *spl* • **ages ago** hace siglos • **I haven't seen her for ages** hace siglos que no la veo • **it took ages to download** tardó muchísimo en descargar

AGE

En Estados Unidos uno puede votar a partir de los 18 años. Las personas pueden conducir a los 16, pero para beber bebidas alcohólicas en un bar o comprarlas en una tienda hay que esperar hasta los 21.

aged *spl* ['eɪdʒɪd] • **the aged** los ancianos

age group *s* (grupo de) edad

agency ['eɪdʒənsɪ] *s* ❶ agencia ❷ organismo; instituto

agenda [ə'dʒendə] *s* ❶ orden del día ❷ intenciones

agent ['eɪdʒənt] *s* ❶ agente ❷ COMERCIO representante *(de empresa)*

aggravate ['ægrəveɪt] *vt* ❶ agravar; empeorar ❷ irritar

aggregate ['ægrɪgət] ◆ *adj* total ◆ *s* total

aggressive [ə'gresɪv] *adj* ❶ agresivo, va ❷ audaz; emprendedor, ra

agile ['ædʒəl] *adj* ágil

agitate ['ædʒɪteɪt] *vt* inquietar

AGM *s abreviatura escrita de* **annual general meeting**

agnostic [æg'nɒstɪk] ◆ *adj* agnóstico, ca ◆ *s* agnóstico, ca

ago [ə'gəʊ] *adv* • **a long time/three days/three years ago** hace mucho tiempo/tres días/tres años • **how long ago did he die?** ¿cuánto hace que murió?

ago

Ago va siempre a final de frases que indican tiempo (half an hour *ago hace media hora*). Se puede usar con el pretérito (the bus left 20 minutes *ago el camión salió hace 20 minutos*), o el pasado continuo (I was living abroad five years *ago hace cinco años vivía fuera*).

En preguntas se usa how long ago (*how long ago did you start English classes? ¿cuánto hace que empezaste a tomar inglés?*).

agonizing ['ægənaɪzɪŋ] *adj* angustioso, sa

agony ['ægənɪ] *s* ❶ dolor muy intenso • **to be in agony** morirse de dolor ❷ angustia • **to be in agony** estar angustiado

agree [ə'griː] ◆ *vi* ❶ • **to agree (with somebody about something)** estar de acuerdo (con alguien acerca de algo) • **to agree on something** ponerse de acuerdo en algo; estar de acuerdo en algo ❷ • **to agree (to something)** acceder (a algo) ❸ • **to agree with something** estar de acuerdo con algo ❹ concordar ❺ • **to agree with somebody** sentarle bien a alguien ❻ GRAMÁTICA • **to agree (with)** concordar (con) ◆ *vt* ❶ acordar; convenir ❷ • **to agree that** estar de acuerdo en que ❸ • **to agree to do something** acordar

hacer algo; quedar en hacer algo • **I agreed to meet him at the movie theater** quedé en encontrarme con él en el cine ❹ • **to agree (that)** reconocer que

agreeable [ə'griːəbl] *adj* ❶ agradable ❷ • **to be agreeable to something/doing something** estar conforme con algo/hacer algo

agreed [ə'griːd] ◆ *adj* • **to be agreed on something** estar de acuerdo sobre algo • **at the agreed time** a la hora convenida ◆ *adv* de acuerdo que

agreement [ə'griːmənt] *s* ❶ acuerdo • **to be in agreement with** estar de acuerdo con ❷ aceptación ❸ correspondencia ❹ GRAMÁTICA concordancia

agricultural [ˌægrɪ'kʌltʃərəl] *adj* agrícola

agriculture ['ægrɪkʌltʃər] *s* agricultura

aground [ə'graʊnd] *adv* • **to run aground** encallar

ahead [ə'hed] *adv* ❶ delante ❷ adelante; hacia delante • **right** o **straight ahead** todo recto o de frente ❸ ir ganando ❹ por delante ❺ • **to look** o **think ahead** mirar hacia el futuro

expresión to get ahead abrirse camino ▶ go ahead! ¡por supuesto!

■ **ahead of** *preposición* ❶ frente a ❷ • **to be two points ahead of** llevar dos puntos de ventaja a ❸ por delante de ❹ con anterioridad a • **ahead of schedule** por delante de lo previsto

aid [eɪd] ◆ *s* ayuda • **medical aid** asistencia médica • **to go to the aid of somebody** o **to somebody's aid** ir en auxilio de alguien • **in aid of** a beneficio de ◆ *vt* ayudar

aide [eɪd] *s* POLÍTICA ayudante

AIDS, Aids [eɪdz] *(abreviatura de* acquired immune deficiency syndrome) ◆ *s* SIDA ◆ *en compuestos* • AIDS patient sidoso, sa

ailment ['eɪlmənt] *s* achaque; molestia

aim [eɪm] ◆ *s* ❶ objetivo ❷ puntería • **to take aim at** apuntar a ◆ *vt* ❶ • **to aim something at** apuntar algo a ❷ • **to be aimed at doing something** ir dirigido a hacer algo ❸ • **to aim something at somebody** dirigir algo a alguien ◆ *vi* ❶ • **to aim (at something)** apuntar (a algo) ❷ • **to aim at** o **for something** apuntar a o pretender algo • **to aim to do something** pretender hacer algo

aimless ['eɪmlɪs] *adj* sin un objetivo claro

ain't [eɪnt] *familiar* ❶ *(abreviatura de* am not) → **be** ❷ *(abreviatura de* are not) → **be** ❸ *(abreviatura de* is not) → **be** ❹ *(abreviatura de* have not) → **have** ❺ *(abreviatura de* has not) → **have**

air [eər] ◆ *s* aire • **into the air** al aire • **by air** en avión

expresión to clear the air *figurado* aclarar las cosas ▶ on the air RADIO & TELEVISIÓN en el aire

◆ *en compuestos* aéreo, a ◆ *vt* ❶ airear ❷ ventilar ❸ expresar ❹ emitir ◆ *vi* ❶ airearse ❷ ventilarse

airbag ['eəbæg] *s* AUTOMÓVILES airbag

airbase ['eəbeɪs] *s* base aérea

airborne ['eəbɔːn] *adj* ❶ aerotransportado, da ❷ aéreo, a ❸ en el aire; en vuelo

A

air-conditioned [-kən'dɪʃnd] *adj* climatizado, da; con aire acondicionado

air-conditioning [-kən'dɪʃnɪŋ] *s* aire acondicionado

aircraft ['eəkrɑːft] *s* ❶ avión ❷ aeronave
El plural de **aircraft** es **aircraft**.

aircraft carrier *s* portaaviones

airfield ['eəfiːld] *s* campo de aviación

airforce ['eəfɔːs] *s* • **the airforce** las fuerzas aéreas

airgun ['eəgʌn] *s* pistola de aire comprimido

airlift ['eəlɪft] ♦ *s* puente aéreo ♦ *vt* transportar por avión

airline ['eəlaɪn] *s* línea aérea

airliner ['eəlaɪnər] *s* avión (grande) de pasajeros

airmail ['eəmeɪl] *s* • **by airmail** por correo aéreo

airplane ['eəpleɪn] *s* avión

airport ['eəpɔːt] *s* aeropuerto

air raid *s* ataque aéreo

airsick ['eəsɪk] *adj* • **to be airsick** marearse

airspace ['eəspeɪs] *s* espacio aéreo

airstrip ['eəstrɪp] *s* pista de aterrizaje

air terminal *s* terminal aérea

airtight ['eətaɪt] *adj* hermético, ca

air-traffic controller *s* controlador aéreo, controladora aérea

airy ['eərɪ] *adj* ❶ espacioso, sa y bien ventilado, da ❷ ilusorio, ria ❸ despreocupado, da

aisle [aɪl] *s* ❶ nave lateral ❷ pasillo

ajar [ə'dʒɑːr] *adj* entreabierto, ta

aka (*abreviatura de* also known as) alias

alarm [ə'lɑːm] ♦ *s* ❶ alarma • **to raise** o **sound the alarm** dar la (voz de) alarma ❷ despertador ♦ *vt* alarmar; asustar

alarm clock *s* despertador

alarming [ə'lɑːmɪŋ] *adj* alarmante

alas [ə'læs] ♦ *adv* desgraciadamente ♦ *exclamación* literario ¡ay!

Albania [æl'beɪnjə] *s* Albania

Albanian [æl'beɪnjən] ♦ *adj* albanés, esa ♦ *s* ❶ albanés, esa ❷ albanés

albeit [ɔːl'biːɪt] *conjunción* formal aunque; si bien

album ['ælbəm] *s* ❶ álbum ❷ elepé

alcohol ['ælkəhɒl] *s* alcohol

alcoholic [ˌælkə'hɒlɪk] ♦ *adj* alcohólico, ca ♦ *s* alcohólico, ca

alcopop ['ælkəʊpɒp] *s* ▶ refresco gaseoso que contiene un cierto porcentaje de alcohol

alderman ['ɔːldəmən] *s* ≃ concejal, la
El plural de **alderman** es **aldermen** ['ɔːldəmen].

ale [eɪl] *s* ▶ tipo de cerveza

alert [ə'lɜːt] ♦ *adj* ❶ atento, ta ❷ despierto, ta ❸ • **to be alert to** ser consciente de ♦ *s* alerta • **to be on the**

alert estar alerta ♦ *vt* alertar • **to alert somebody to something** alertar a alguien de algo

algae ['ældʒiː] *spl* algas

algebra ['ældʒɪbrə] *s* álgebra

Algeria [æl'dʒɪərɪə] *s* Argelia

alias ['eɪlɪəs] ♦ *adv* alias ♦ *s* alias
El plural de **alias** es **aliases**.

alibi ['ælɪbaɪ] *s* coartada

alien ['eɪljən] ♦ *adj* ❶ extraterrestre ❷ extraño, ña; ajeno, na ♦ *s* ❶ extraterrestre ❷ DERECHO extranjero, ra

alienate ['eɪljəneɪt] *vt* ganarse la antipatía de

alight [ə'laɪt] ♦ *adj* ardiendo • **to set something alight** prender fuego a algo ♦ *vi* formal ❶ posarse ❷ • **to alight from** apearse de
Formas irregulares de **alight**: *pret & pp* **alighted**.

align [ə'laɪn] *vt* alinear

alike [ə'laɪk] ♦ *adj* parecido, da ♦ *adv* de la misma forma • **to look alike** parecerse

alive [ə'laɪv] *adj* ❶ vivo, va ❷ lleno, na de vida

alkali ['ælkəlaɪ] *s* álcali
Dos plurales: **alkalis** o **alkalies**.

all [ɔːl] ♦ *adj* ❶ ☿ con sustantivo en singular todo, da • **all the drink** toda la bebida • **all day** todo el día • **all night** toda la noche • **all the time** todo el tiempo ❷ ☿ con sustantivo en plural todos, das • **all the boxes** todas las cajas • **all men** todos los hombres • **all three died** los tres murieron ♦ *pronombre* ❶ ☿ sing todo, da • **she drank it all, she drank all of it** se lo bebió todo ❷ ☿ pl todos, das • **all of them came, they all came** vinieron todos ❸ ☿ con superlativo • **he's the cleverest of all** es el más listo de todos • **the most amazing thing of all** lo más impresionante de todo • **best/worst of all...** lo mejor/peor de todo es que... ♦ *adv* ❶ completamente • **I'd forgotten all about that** me había olvidado completamente de eso • **all alone** completamente solo, la • **all over** por todas partes • **we looked all over for the perfect dress** buscamos por todas partes el vestido perfecto ❷ • **the score is two all** el resultado es de empate a dos ❸ ☿ con comparativo • **to run all the faster** correr aun más rápido

■ **all but** *adv* casi

■ **all in all** *adv* en conjunto

■ **all that** *adv* • **she's not all that pretty** no es tan guapa

■ **in all** *adv* en total

all

No confundas all, each y every. All es el único de estos adjetivos que puede ir acompañado de sustantivos plurales o incontables (*all* students; *all* money *todos los estudiantes; todo el dinero*); también puede ir con sustantivos contables en singular cuando expresan un periodo de tiempo (*all* day *todo el día*). Each y every se utilizan sólo con sustantivos contables en singular (*each* person; *every* town *cada persona; cada ciudad*).

Tanto all como each son además pronombres (I want *all* of it *lo quiero todo entero*; we got one *each nos tocó uno a cada uno*), y ambos pueden ir detrás de pronombres personales como we, you, they, ETC (we *all* went swimming *todos nos bañamos*; I gave them one *each les di uno a cada uno*).

Ver también *cada* en el lado español-inglés del diccionario.

Allah ['ælə] *s* Alá

allay [ə'leɪ] *vt formal* ❶ despejar ❷ apaciguar

all clear *s* ❶ señal de cese de peligro ❷ *figurado* luz verde

allegation [,ælɪ'geɪʃn] *s* acusación

allege [ə'ledʒ] *vt* alegar • **to be alleged to have done/said** ser acusado de haber hecho/dicho

allegedly [ə'ledʒɪdlɪ] *adv* presuntamente

allegiance [ə'liːdʒəns] *s* lealtad

allergy ['ælədʒɪ] *s* alergia

alleviate [ə'liːvɪeɪt] *vt* aliviar

alley(way) ['ælɪ(weɪ)] *s* callejuela

alliance [ə'laɪəns] *s* alianza

allied ['ælaɪd] *adj* aliado, da

alligator ['ælɪgeɪtər] *s* caimán

Dos plurales: **alligator** o **alligators**.

all-important *adj* crucial

all in ◆ *adj familiar* hecho, cha polvo ◆ *adv* todo incluido

all-night *adj* ❶ que dura toda la noche ❷ abierto, ta toda la noche

allocate ['æləkeɪt] *vt* • **to allocate something to somebody a)** destinar algo a alguien **b)** asignar algo a alguien

allot [ə'lɒt] *vt* ❶ asignar ❷ destinar

allow [ə'laʊ] *vt* ❶ permitir; dejar • **to allow somebody to do something** permitirle a alguien hacer algo ❷ destinar (*dinero*); dejar (*tiempo*) ❸ conceder (*suj: persona*); admitir (*suj: ley*) ❹ • **to allow that** admitir o reconocer que

■ **allow for** *vt* ⚲ *El objeto siempre va después de la preposición al final.* contar con

allowance [ə'laʊəns] *s* ❶ subsidio ❷ dietas ❸ domingo ❹ • **to make allowances for something/somebody a)** disculpar algo/a alguien **b)** tener en cuenta algo/a alguien

alloy ['ælɔɪ] *s* aleación

all right ◆ *adv* ❶ bien ❷ (más o menos) bien ❸ okey; bueno ◆ *adj* ❶ bien ❷ • **it's all right, but...** no está mal, pero... ❸ • **sorry — that's all right** lo siento — no importa

all-terrain vehicle *s* todoterreno

all-time *adj* ❶ de todos los tiempos ❷ histórico, ca

allude [ə'luːd] *vi* • **to allude to** aludir a

allusion [ə'luːʒn] *s* alusión

ally *s* ['ælaɪ] aliado, da

almighty [ɔːl'maɪtɪ] *adj familiar* descomunal

almond ['ɑːmənd] *s* almendra

almost ['ɔːlməʊst] *adv* casi

aloft [ə'lɒft] *adv* en lo alto

alone [ə'ləʊn] ◆ *adj* solo, la • **to be alone with** estar a solas con ◆ *adv* ❶ solo, la ❷ sólo

expresión **to leave something/somebody alone** dejar algo/a alguien en paz ▶ **leave my computer alone!** ¡no toques mi computadora!

■ **let alone** *conjunción* y mucho menos

along [ə'lɒŋ] ◆ *adv* ❶ hacia delante • **to go along** avanzar • **she was walking along** iba andando ❷ • **to come along** venir • **to go along** ir ◆ *preposición* por; a lo largo de

■ **all along** *adv* todo el rato • **she knew all along** lo sabía desde el principio

■ **along with** *preposición* junto con

alongside [ə,lɒŋ'saɪd] ◆ *preposición* ❶ junto a ❷ junto con ◆ *adv* • **to come alongside** ponerse a la misma altura

aloof [ə'luːf] ◆ *adj* frío, a; distante ◆ *adv* distante • **to remain aloof (from)** mantenerse a distancia (de)

aloud [ə'laʊd] *adv* en alto; en voz alta

alphabet ['ælfəbet] *s* alfabeto

alphabetical [,ælfə'betɪkl] *adj* alfabético, ca • **in alphabetical order** en orden alfabético

Alps [ælps] *spl* • **the Alps** los Alpes

already [ɔːl'redɪ] *adv* ya

alright [,ɔːl'raɪt] = **all right**

Alsatian [æl'seɪʃn] *s* pastor alemán

also ['ɔːlsəʊ] *adv* también

altar ['ɔːltər] *s* altar

alter ['ɔːltər] ◆ *vt* alterar; modificar ◆ *vi* cambiar

alteration [,ɔːltə'reɪʃn] *s* ❶ alteración • **to make an alteration/alterations to** hacer una modificación/modificaciones en ❷ arreglo

alternate ['ɒːltənət] ◆ *adj* ❶ alterno, na ❷ • **on alternate days/weeks** cada dos días/semanas ◆ *s* sustituto, ta ◆ *vi* ['ɒːltəneɪt] • **to alternate (with/between)** alternar (con/entre)

alternative [ɔːl'tɜːnətɪv] ◆ *adj* alternativo, va ◆ *s* alternativa; opción • **to have no alternative (but to do something)** no tener más remedio (que hacer algo)

alternatively [ɔːl'tɜːnətɪvlɪ] *adv* o bien

alternative medicine [ɔːl'tɜːnətɪv 'medɪsɪn] *adv* la medicina alternativa

although [ɔːl'ðəʊ] *conjunción* aunque

altitude ['æltɪtjuːd] *s* altitud

A

alto ['æltəʊ] *s* contralto
El plural de **alto** es **altos**.

altogether [,ɔːltə'geðər] *adv* ❶ completamente • **not altogether** no del todo ❷ en conjunto ❸ en total

aluminum [ə'luːmɪnəm] *s* aluminio

aluminum foil [ə'luːmɪnəm 'fɔɪl] *s* papel de aluminio

always ['ɔːlweɪz] *adv* siempre

am [æm] *v* → **be**

a.m. (*abreviatura de* ante meridiem) • **at 3 a.m.** a las tres de la mañana

amateur ['æmətər] ◆ *adj* ❶ aficionado, da ❷ *despectivo* chapucero, ra ◆ *s* ❶ aficionado, da ❷ *despectivo* chapucero, ra

amateurish [,æmə'tɜːrɪʃ] *adj* chapucero, ra

amaze [ə'meɪz] *vt* asombrar

amazed [ə'meɪzd] *adj* asombrado, da

amazement [ə'meɪzmənt] *s* asombro

amazing [ə'meɪzɪŋ] *adj* ❶ asombroso, sa; increíble ❷ genial

Amazon ['æməzn] *s* ❶ • **the Amazon** el Amazonas ❷ • **the Amazon (Basin)** la cuenca amazónica • **the Amazon rainforest** la selva amazónica

ambassador [æm'bæsədər] *s* embajador, ra

amber ['æmbər] ◆ *adj* de color ámbar ◆ *s* ámbar

ambiguous [æm'bɪgjʊəs] *adj* ambiguo, gua

ambition [æm'bɪʃn] *s* ambición

ambitious [æm'bɪʃəs] *adj* ambicioso, sa

ambulance ['æmbjʊləns] *s* ambulancia

ambush ['æmbʊʃ] ◆ *s* emboscada ◆ *vt* emboscar

amend [ə'mend] *vt* ❶ enmendar ❷ corregir ❸ modificar
■ **amends** *spl* • **to make amends for something** reparar algo

amendment [ə'mendmənt] *s* ❶ enmienda ❷ corrección ❸ modificación

amenities [ə'miːnətɪz] *spl* ❶ facilidades ❷ comodidades

America [ə'merɪkə] *s* ❶ América ❷ Estados Unidos

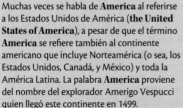

AMERICA
Muchas veces se habla de **America** al referirse a los Estados Unidos de América (**the United States of America**), a pesar de que el término **America** se refiere también al continente americano que incluye Norteamérica (o sea, los Estados Unidos, Canadá, y México) y toda la América Latina. La palabra **America** proviene del nombre del explorador Amerigo Vespucci quien llegó este continente en 1499.

American [ə'merɪkn] ◆ *adj* ❶ americano, na ❷ estadounidense ◆ *s* ❶ americano, na ❷ estadounidense

AMERICAN FOOTBALL
La versión estadounidense del futbol es más bien una adaptación del rugby. Generalmente se le llama sólo **football**, y es uno de los deportes más populares en los Estados Unidos. Todas las escuelas secundarias y universidades tienen equipo de futbol, y los partidos son eventos muy concurridos.

American Indian *s* amerindio, dia

THE AMERICAN REVOLUTION
Así se le llama a la guerra en que los habitantes de lo que serían los Estados Unidos se enfrentaron a los ingleses entre 1775 y 1783. Los americanos querían independizarse, sobre todo para no tener que seguir pagando impuestos a Inglaterra. El 4 de julio de 1776, el futuro presidente Thomas Jefferson firmó la Declaración de Independencia, la cual Inglaterra se negó a reconocer y la guerra continuó. George Washington, con la ayuda de soldados franceses, encabezó las tropas rebeldes y en 1783 se firmó el convenio de paz: los Estados Unidos habían nacido.

amiable ['eɪmjəbl] *adj* amable; agradable

amid(st) [ə'mɪd(st)] *preposición formal* entre; en medio de

amiss [ə'mɪs] ◆ *adj* • **something's amiss** algo va mal ◆ *adv* • **to take something amiss** tomarse algo a mal

ammonia [ə'məʊnjə] *s* amoniaco

ammunition [,æmjʊ'nɪʃn] *s* ☼ *incontable* MILITAR municiones

amnesia [æm'niːzjə] *s* amnesia

amnesty ['æmnəstɪ] *s* amnistía

amok [ə'mɒk], **amuck** *adv* • **to run amok** enloquecer atacando a gente de forma indiscriminada

among(st) [ə'mʌŋ(st)] *preposición* entre

amorous ['æmərəs] *adj* apasionado, da

amount [ə'maʊnt] *s* cantidad
■ **amount to** *vt* ☼ *El objeto siempre va después de la preposición al final.* ❶ ascender a ❷ venir a ser

amp [æmp] *s* ❶ amplificador ❷ amperio

amphibian [æm'fɪbɪən] *s* anfibio

ample ['æmpl] *adj* ❶ suficiente ❷ sobrado, da • **to have ample time** tener tiempo de sobra ❸ amplio, plia

amplifier ['æmplɪfaɪər] *s* amplificador

amputate ['æmpjʊteɪt] *vt* & *vi* amputar

Amtrak ['æmtræk] *s* ▸ organismo que regula y coordina las líneas férreas en Estados Unidos

amuck [ə'mʌk] = **amok**

amuse [ə'mju:z] *vt* ❶ divertir • **the joke amused Peter** el chiste le hizo gracia a Peter ❷ distraer; entretener • **to amuse yourself (by doing something)** distraerse (haciendo algo)

amused [ə'mju:zd] *adj* ❶ divertido, da • **I was not amused by that** no me hizo gracia eso ❷ • **to keep yourself amused** entretenerse; distraerse

amusement [ə'mju:zmənt] *s* ❶ regocijo; diversión ❷ atracción

amusement arcade *s* salón de juegos

amusement park *s* parque de atracciones

amusing [ə'mju:zɪŋ] *adj* divertido, da

an ☼ *acento tónico* [æn]*, acento atónico* [ən] → **a**

anabolic steroid [ˌænə'bɒlɪk-] *s* esteroide anabólico

analog ['ænəlɒg] *adj* analógico, ca

analysis [ə'næləsɪs] *s* ❶ análisis ❷ psicoanálisis
El plural de **analysis** es **analyses** [ə'næləsi:z].

analyst ['ænəlɪst] *s* ❶ analista ❷ psicoanalista

analytic(al) [ˌænə'lɪtɪk(l)] *adj* analítico, ca

analyze ['ænəlaɪz] *vt* analizar

anarchist ['ænəkɪst] *s* anarquista

anarchy ['ænəkɪ] *s* anarquía

anatomy [ə'nætəmɪ] *s* anatomía

ancestor ['ænsestər] *s* literal & figurado antepasado

anchor ['æŋkər] ◆ *s* NÁUTICA ancla ◆ *vt* ❶ sujetar ❷ TELEVISIÓN presentar

anchovy ['ænʧəvɪ] *s* ❶ anchoa ❷ boquerón
Dos plurales: **anchovy** o **anchovies**.

ancient ['eɪnʃənt] *adj* ❶ antiguo, gua ❷ *humorístico* vetusto, ta

ancillary [æn'sɪlərɪ] *adj* auxiliar

and ☼ *acento tónico* [ænd]*, acento atónico* [ən] *conjunción* ❶ y • **fish and chips** pescado con papas fritas • **faster and faster** cada vez más rápido • **it's nice and easy** es sencillito ❷ • **one hundred and eighty** ciento ochenta • **one and a half** uno y medio • **2 and 2 is 4** 2 y 2 son 4 ❸ • **try and come** intenta venir • **come and see the kids** ven a ver a los niños • **wait and see** espera a ver

■ **and so on, and so forth** *adv* etcétera; y cosas así

Andes ['ændi:z] *spl* • **the Andes** los Andes

anecdote ['ænɪkdəʊt] *s* anécdota

anemic [ə'ni:mɪk] *adj* anémico, ca

anesthetic [ˌænɪs'θetɪk] *s* anestesia

anesthetize [æ'ni:sθətaɪz] *s* anestesiar

anew [ə'nju:] *adv* de nuevo; nuevamente

angel ['eɪndʒəl] *s* ángel

anger ['æŋgər] ◆ *s* ira; furia • **he was shaking with anger** temblaba de rabia ◆ *vt* enfadar

angle ['æŋgl] *s* ❶ ángulo ❷ enfoque

angler ['æŋglər] *s* pescador, ra *(con caña)*

Anglican ['æŋglɪkən] ◆ *adj* anglicano, na ◆ *s* anglicano, na

angling ['æŋglɪŋ] *s* pesca con caña

Anglo-Saxon [ˌæŋgləʊ'sæksn] ◆ *adj* anglosajón, ona ◆ *s* ❶ anglosajón, ona ❷ anglosajón

angry ['æŋgrɪ] *adj* ❶ enojado, da; enfadado, da • **to be angry at** o **with somebody** estar enojado con alguien • **to get angry with somebody** enojarse con alguien ❷ furioso, sa; airado, da

anguish ['æŋgwɪʃ] *s* angustia

animal ['ænɪml] ◆ *adj* ❶ animal ❷ de los animales ◆ *s* animal

animate ['ænɪmət] *adj* animado, da

animated ['ænɪmeɪtɪd] *adj* animado, da

ankle ['æŋkl] ◆ *s* tobillo ■ *en compuestos* ▸ **ankle boots** botines ▸ **ankle socks** calcetines cortos

annex ['æneks] ◆ *s* edificio anejo ◆ *vt* anexionar

annihilate [ə'naɪəleɪt] *vt* aniquilar

anniversary [ˌænɪ'vɜ:sərɪ] *s* aniversario

announce [ə'naʊns] *vt* anunciar

announcement [ə'naʊnsmənt] *s* anuncio

announcer [ə'naʊnsər] *s* ▸ **radio/television announcer** presentador, ra de radio/televisión

annoy [ə'nɔɪ] *vt* fastidiar; molestar

annoyance [ə'nɔɪəns] *s* molestia

annoyed [ə'nɔɪd] *adj* • **to be annoyed at something/with somebody** estar molesto, ta por algo/con alguien • **to get annoyed at something/with somebody** molestarse por algo/con alguien

annoying [ə'nɔɪɪŋ] *adj* molesto, ta

annual ['ænjʊəl] ◆ *adj* anual ◆ *s* ❶ planta anual ❷ anuario

annual general meeting *s* asamblea general anual

annul [ə'nʌl] *vt* anular

anomaly [ə'nɒməlɪ] *s* anomalía

anonymous [ə'nɒnɪməs] *adj* anónimo, ma

anorexia (nervosa) [ˌænə'reksɪə(nɜ:'vəʊsə)] *s* anorexia

anorexic [ˌænə'reksɪk] ◆ *adj* anoréxico, ca ◆ *s* anoréxico, ca

another [ə'nʌðər] ◆ *adj* otro, tra • **another one** otro, tra • **in another few minutes** en unos minutos más ◆ *pronombre* otro, tra • **one after another** uno tras otro; una tras otra • **one another** el uno al otro; la una a la otra • **we love one another** nos queremos

answer ['ɑ:nsər] ◆ *s* ❶ respuesta • **in answer to** en respuesta a ❷ solución ◆ *vt* ❶ responder a; contestar a ❷ • **to answer the door** abrir la puerta • **to answer the phone** contestar el teléfono ◆ *vi* responder; contestar

A

■ **answer back** *vt* & *vi* ☼ *El objeto se coloca entre el verbo y la preposición.* replicar

■ **answer for** *vt* ☼ *El objeto siempre va después de la preposición al final.* ❶ responder por • **they have a lot to answer for** tienen mucho que explicar ❷ responder de

answerable ['ɑ:nsərəbl] *adj* • **answerable (to somebody/for something)** responsable (ante alguien/de algo)

answering machine ['ɑ:nsərɪŋ-] *s* contestador automático

ant [ænt] *s* hormiga

antagonize [æn'tægənaɪz] *vt* provocar la hostilidad de

Antarctic [æn'tɑ:ktɪk] ◆ *adj* antártico, ca ◆ *s* • **the Antarctic** el Antártico

Antarctica [æn'tɑ:ktɪkə] *s* (la) Antártida

antelope ['æntɪləʊp] *s* antílope

Dos plurales: **antelope** o **antelopes**.

antenna [æn'tenə] *s* ❶ (pl antennae [-ni:]) antena ❷ (pl antennas) antena

anthem ['ænθəm] *s* himno

anthology [æn'θɒlədʒɪ] *s* antología

antibiotic [ˌæntɪbaɪ'ɒtɪk] *s* antibiótico

antibody ['æntɪˌbɒdɪ] *s* anticuerpo

anticipate [æn'tɪsɪpeɪt] *vt* ❶ prever ❷ esperar ansiosamente ❸ adelantarse a

anticipation [æn,tɪsɪ'peɪʃn] *s* expectación • **in anticipation of** en previsión de

anticlimax [ˌæntɪ'klaɪmæks] *s* decepción

antics ['æntɪks] *spl* payasadas

antidepressant [ˌæntɪdɪ'presnt] *s* antidepresivo

antidote ['æntɪdəʊt] *s* literal & figurado • **antidote (to)** antídoto (contra)

antihistamine [ˌæntɪ'hɪstəmɪn] *s* antihistamínico

antiperspirant [ˌæntɪ'pɜ:spərənt] *s* antitranspirante

antique [æn'ti:k] ◆ *adj* antiguo, gua ◆ *s* antigüedad

antique shop *s* tienda de antigüedades

anti-Semitism [-'semɪtɪzm] *s* antisemitismo

antiseptic [ˌæntɪ'septɪk] ◆ *adj* antiséptico, ca ◆ *s* antiséptico

antisocial [ˌæntɪ'səʊʃl] *adj* ❶ antisocial ❷ poco sociable

anus ['eɪnəs] *s* ano

anvil ['ænvɪl] *s* yunque

anxiety [æŋ'zaɪətɪ] *s* ❶ ansiedad; inquietud ❷ preocupación ❸ afán; ansia

anxious ['æŋkʃəs] *adj* ❶ preocupado, da • **to be anxious about** estar preocupado por ❷ • **to be anxious that/to do something** estar ansioso, sa por que/por hacer algo

any ['enɪ]
◆ *adj*
❶ [*en frases negativas, expresa la ausencia de algo*]
• **I haven't got any money/tickets** no tengo dinero/boletos
• **he never does any work** nunca hace nada
❷ [*en frases interrogativas o condicionales*]
• **have you got any money?** ¿tienes dinero?
❸ [*cualquiera*]
• **any box will do** cualquier caja sirve
• **any other person would have refused** cualquier otro se habría negado
◆ *pronombre*
❶ [*en frases negativas*]
• **I didn't buy any (of them)** no compré ninguno
• **I didn't know any of the guests** no conocía a ninguno de los invitados
❷ [*en frases interrogativas*]
• **do you have any?** ¿tienes alguno?
❸ [*cualquiera*]
• **take any you like** llévate los que quieras
◆ *adv*
❶ [*en frases negativas*]
• **I can't see it any more** ya no lo veo
• **I can't stand it any longer** ya no aguanto más
❷ [*en frases interrogativas*]
• **do you want any more potatoes?** ¿quiere más papas?
• **is that any better/clearer?** ¿está mejor/más claro?

anybody ['enɪˌbɒdɪ] = **anyone**

anyhow ['enɪhaʊ] *adv* ❶ de todos modos ❷ de cualquier manera ❸ en cualquier caso

anyone ['enɪwʌn], **anybody** ['enɪˌbɒdɪ] *pronombre* ❶ ☼ *en oraciones negativas* nadie • **I don't know anyone** no conozco a nadie ❷ ☼ *en interrogativas* alguien • **is anybody home?** ¿hay alguien en casa? ❸ cualquiera • **anybody can do it** cualquiera puede hacerlo

anyplace ['enɪpleɪs] = **anywhere**

anything ['enɪθɪŋ] *pronombre* ❶ ☼ *en oraciones negativas* nada • **I don't want anything** no quiero nada ❷ ☼ *en interrogativas* algo • **would you like anything else?** ¿quiere algo más? ❸ cualquier cosa

anyway ['enɪweɪ] *adv* ❶ de todas formas ❷ en cualquier caso

anywhere ['enɪweər], **anyplace** ['enɪpleɪs] *adv* ❶ ☼ *en oraciones negativas* en ningún sitio • **I didn't go anywhere** no fui a ninguna parte ❷ ☼ *en interrogativas* en algún sitio • **did you go anywhere?** ¿fuiste a algún sitio? ❸ cualquier sitio • **anywhere you like** donde quieras

apart [ə'pɑ:t] *adv* ❶ • **they are two feet apart** hay 60 centímetros entre los dos • **we're living apart** vivimos separados ❷ aparte • **joking apart** bromas aparte
■ **apart from** *preposición* aparte de

apartment [ə'pɑ:tmənt] *s* departamento

apartment building *s* edificio de departamentos

apathy ['æpəθɪ] *s* apatía

ape [eɪp] ◆ *s* simio ◆ *vt despectivo* imitar

aperitif [əperə'tiːf] *s* aperitivo

aperture ['æpə,tjʊər] *s* abertura

apex ['eɪpeks] *s* vértice
Dos plurales: **apexes** o **apices.**

apices ['eɪpɪsiːz] *spl* → **apex**

apocalypse [ə'pɒkəlɪps] *s* apocalipsis

apologetic [ə,pɒlə'dʒetɪk] *adj* lleno, na de disculpas • **to be very apologetic (about)** no hacer más que disculparse (por)

apologize [ə'pɒlədʒaɪz] *vi* • **to apologize (to somebody for something)** disculparse (ante alguien por algo) • **I apologized to her** le pedí perdón

apology [ə'pɒlədʒɪ] *s* disculpa • **Tom sends his apologies** Tom se excusa por no poder asistir

apostle [ə'pɒsl] *s* RELIGIÓN apóstol

apostrophe [ə'pɒstrəfɪ] *s* apóstrofo

appall [ə'pɔːl] *vt* horrorizar

appalling [ə'pɔːlɪŋ] *adj* horroroso, sa

apparatus [,æpə'reɪtəs] *s* aparatos • **a piece of apparatus** un aparato
Dos plurales: **apparatus** o **apparatuses.**

apparel [ə'pærəl] *s* ropa

apparent [ə'pærənt] *adj* ❶ evidente; patente ❷ aparente

apparently [ə'pærəntlɪ] *adv* ❶ por lo visto ❷ aparentemente

appeal [ə'piːl] ◆ *vi* ❶ • **to appeal (to somebody for something)** solicitar (de alguien algo) ❷ DERECHO • **to appeal (against)** apelar (contra) ❸ • **to appeal (to)** atraer (a) ◆ *s* ❶ llamamiento; súplica ❷ campaña para recaudar fondos ❸ DERECHO apelación ❹ atractivo

appealing [ə'piːlɪŋ] *adj* atractivo, va

appear [ə'pɪər] *vi* ❶ aparecer ❷ • **to appear (to be/to do something)** parecer (ser/hacer algo) • **it would appear that…** parece que… ❸ • **to appear on TV/in a movie** salir en televisión/en una película ❹ DERECHO • **to appear (before)** comparecer (ante)

appearance [ə'pɪərəns] *s* ❶ aparición • **to make an appearance** aparecer ❷ actuación ❸ aspecto

appease [ə'piːz] *vt* aplacar; apaciguar

appendices [ə'pendɪsiːz] *spl* → **appendix**

appendicitis [ə,pendɪ'saɪtɪs] *s* ☿ *incontable* apendicitis

appendix [ə'pendɪks] *s* apéndice • **to have your appendix out** operarse de apendicitis
Dos plurales: **appendixes (de libro)** o **appendices (anatomía).**

appetite ['æpɪtaɪt] *s* ❶ apetito • **I no longer have any appetite for my food** ya no tengo ganas de comer ❷ *figurado* • **appetite for** entusiasmo por

appetizer ['æpɪtaɪzər] *s* aperitivo

appetizing ['æpɪtaɪzɪŋ] *adj* apetitoso, sa

applaud [ə'plɔːd] *vt* & *vi literal* & *figurado* aplaudir

applause [ə'plɔːz] *s* ☿ *incontable* aplausos

apple ['æpl] *s* manzana

apple pie *s* pay de manzana

apple tree *s* manzano

appliance [ə'plaɪəns] *s* aparato

applicable [ə'plɪkəbl] *adj* • **to be applicable (to)** aplicarse (a)

applicant ['æplɪkənt] *s* • **applicant (for)** solicitante (de)

application [,æplɪ'keɪʃn] *s* ❶ aplicación ❷ • **application (for)** solicitud (para) ❸ INFORMÁTICA aplicación

application form *s* impreso de solicitud

applied [ə'plaɪd] *adj* aplicado, da

apply [ə'plaɪ] ◆ *vt* ❶ aplicar • **to apply yourself (to something)** aplicarse (en algo) ❷ echar ◆ *vi* ❶ presentar una solicitud • **to apply to somebody for something** solicitar a alguien algo ❷ aplicarse • **to apply to** concernir a

appoint [ə'pɔɪnt] *vt* • **to appoint somebody (to something)** nombrar a alguien (para algo)

appointment [ə'pɔɪntmənt] *s* ❶ nombramiento ❷ puesto; cargo ❸ cita ❹ hora • **to have an appointment a)** tener una cita **b)** tener hora • **to make an appointment** concertar una cita

appraisal [ə'preɪzl] *s* evaluación

appreciate [ə'priːʃɪeɪt] *vt* ❶ apreciar ❷ darse cuenta de ❸ agradecer

appreciation [ə,priːʃɪ'eɪʃn] *s* ❶ aprecio ❷ entendimiento ❸ agradecimiento

appreciative [ə'priːʃjətɪv] *adj* ❶ agradecido, da ❷ entendido, da

apprehensive [,æprɪ'hensɪv] *adj* aprensivo, va

apprentice [ə'prentɪs] *s* aprendiz, za

apprenticeship [ə'prentɪʃɪp] *s* aprendizaje

approach [ə'prəʊtʃ] ◆ *s* ❶ llegada ❷ acceso ❸ enfoque ❹ • **to make approaches to somebody** hacerle propuestas a alguien ◆ *vt* ❶ acercarse a ❷ • **to approach somebody about something** dirigirse a alguien acerca de algo ❸ abordar ❹ aproximarse a ◆ *vi* acercarse

approachable [ə'prəʊtʃəbl] *adj* accesible

appropriate ◆ *adj* [ə'prəʊprɪət] apropiado, da; adecuado, da ◆ *vt* [ə'prəʊprɪeɪt] DERECHO apropiarse de

approval [ə'pruːvl] *s* ❶ aprobación ❷ visto bueno

approve [ə'pruːv] ◆ *vi* estar de acuerdo • **to approve of something/somebody** ver con buenos ojos algo/a alguien ◆ *vt* aprobar

approx. [ə'prɒks] (*abreviatura de* approximately) aprox

approximate *adj* [ə'prɒksɪmət] aproximado, da

A

approximately [ə'prɒksɪmətlɪ] *adv* aproximadamente

apricot ['eɪprɪkɒt] *s* chabacano

April ['eɪprəl] *s* abril ver también **September**

April Fools' Day *s* primero de abril, ≃ Día de los Santos Inocentes

apron ['eɪprən] *s* delantal; mandil
expresión **to be tied to somebody's apron strings** *familiar* estar pegado a las faldas de alguien

apt [æpt] *adj* acertado, da

aptitude ['æptɪtjuːd] *s* aptitud

aptly ['æptlɪ] *adv* apropiadamente

aqualung ['ækwəlʌŋ] *s* escafandra autónoma

aquarium [ə'kweərɪəm] *s* acuario
Dos plurales: **aquariums** o **aquaria** [ə'kweərɪə].

Aquarius [ə'kweərɪəs] *s* Acuario

aquatic [ə'kwætɪk] *adj* acuático, ca

aqueduct ['ækwɪdʌkt] *s* acueducto

Arab ['ærəb] ◆ *adj* árabe ◆ *s* árabe

Arabic ['ærəbɪk] ◆ *adj* árabe ◆ *s* árabe

Arabic numeral *s* número arábigo

arable ['ærəbl] *adj* cultivable

arbitrary ['ɑːbɪtrərɪ] *adj* arbitrario, ria

ARC (*abreviatura de* AIDS-related complex) *s* ▶ enfermedad relacionada con el sida

arcade [ɑː'keɪd] *s* ❶ galería comercial ❷ arcada; galería ❸ salón de juegos (de video)

arcade game *s* videojuego

arch [ɑːtʃ] ◆ *s* ❶ ARQUITECTURA arco ❷ puente ◆ *vt* arquear

archaeologist = archeologist

archaeology = archeology

archaic [ɑː'keɪɪk] *adj* arcaico, ca

archbishop [,ɑːtʃ'bɪʃəp] *s* arzobispo

archenemy [,ɑːtʃ'enɪmɪ] *s* peor enemigo; enemigo acérrimo

archeologist, archaeologist [,ɑːkɪ'ɒlədʒɪst] *s* arqueólogo, ga

archeology, archaeology [,ɑːkɪ'ɒlədʒɪ] *s* arqueología

archer ['ɑːtʃər] *s* arquero

archery ['ɑːtʃərɪ] *s* tiro con arco

archetypal [,ɑːkɪ'taɪpl] *adj* arquetípico, ca

architect ['ɑːkɪtekt] *s* arquitecto, ta

architecture ['ɑːkɪtektʃər] *s* arquitectura

archives ['ɑːkaɪvz] *spl* archivos

archway ['ɑːtʃweɪ] *s* ❶ arcada ❷ entrada en forma de arco

are ☼ *acento atónico* [ər], *acento tónico* [ɑːr] → **be**

area ['eərɪə] *s* ❶ zona; área • **in the area** en la zona ❷ zona; barrio ❸ *figurado* • **in the area of** del orden de; alrededor de ❹ superficie; área ❺ campo

area code *s* código de área; clave LADA

arena [ə'riːnə] *s* DEPORTE pabellón

aren't [ɑːnt] (*abreviatura de* are not) → **be**

Argentina [,ɑːdʒən'tiːnə] *s* (la) Argentina

Argentine ['ɑːdʒəntaɪn] *adj* argentino, na

Argentinian [,ɑːdʒən'tɪnɪən] ◆ *adj* argentino, na ◆ *s* argentino, na

arguably ['ɑːgjʊəblɪ] *adv* probablemente

argue ['ɑːgjuː] ◆ *vi* ❶ • **to argue (with somebody about something)** discutir (con alguien de algo) ❷ • **to argue (for)** abogar (por) • **to argue (against)** oponerse (a) ◆ *vt* • **to argue that** argumentar que

argument ['ɑːgjʊmənt] *s* ❶ discusión • **to have an argument (with)** tener una discusión (con) ❷ argumento

argumentative [,ɑːgjʊ'mentətɪv] *adj* propenso, sa a discutir

arid ['ærɪd] *adj literal & figurado* árido, da

Aries ['eəriːz] *s* Aries

arise [ə'raɪz] *vi* • **to arise (from)** surgir (de)
Formas irregulares de **arise**: *pretérito* **arose**, *pp* **arisen** [ə'rɪzn].

aristocrat [ə'rɪstəkræt] *s* aristócrata

aristocratic [ə,rɪstə'krætɪk] *adj* aristocrático, ca

arithmetic [ə'rɪəmətɪk] *s* aritmética

ark [ɑːk] *s* arca

arm [ɑːm] ◆ *s* ❶ brazo • **arm in arm** del brazo ❷ manga
expresión **to keep somebody at arm's length** *figurado* guardar las distancias con alguien
◆ *vt* armar ◆ *vi* armarse
■ **arms** *spl* armas

armaments ['ɑːməmənts] *spl* armamento

armband ['ɑːmbænd] *s* ❶ brazalete ❷ flotador

armchair ['ɑːmtʃeər] *s* sillón

armed [ɑːmd] *adj* ❶ armado, da ❷ *figurado* • **armed with** provisto, ta de

armed forces *spl* fuerzas armadas

armhole ['ɑːmhəʊl] *s* sisa

armor ['ɑːmər] *s* ❶ armadura ❷ blindaje

armored car [ɑːməd-] *s* MILITAR carro blindado

armpit ['ɑːmpɪt] *s* sobaco; axila

armrest ['ɑːmrest] *s* brazo

army ['ɑːmɪ] *s literal & figurado* ejército ◆ *en compuestos* del ejército; militar

aroma [ə'rəʊmə] *s* aroma

arose [ə'rəʊz] *pretérito* → **arise**

around [ə'raʊnd]
◆ *adv*
❶ [*indica proximidad en el espacio*]
• **have you seen him around?** ¿lo vieron por aquí?
• **she'll be around soon** llegará pronto
• **to walk around** pasear
• **to lie around** estar tirado

A

❷ [_alrededor_]
• **there was a yard with a fence all around** había un corral con una cerca alrededor

❸ [_con expresiones_]
• **to turn around** darse la vuelta

expresión he has been around _familiar_ tiene mucho mundo

◆ _preposición_

❶ [_alrededor de_]
• **they walked around the lake** pasearon alrededor del lago

❷ [_a través_]
• **all around the country** por todo el país

❸ [_expresa aproximación_]
• **I'll see you around 9 o'clock** le veré en torno a las 9
• **around here** por aquí

arouse [əˈraʊz] _vt_ ❶ excitar ❷ despertar _(sentimiento)_

arrange [əˈreɪndʒ] _vt_ ❶ colocar ❷ arreglar ❸ organizar • **to arrange to do something** acordar hacer algo • **we've arranged to meet at nine** hemos quedado a las nueve • **to arrange for somebody to do something** hacer lo necesario para que alguien haga algo ❹ MÚSICA arreglar

arrangement [əˈreɪndʒmənt] _s_ ❶ acuerdo • **to come to an arrangement** llegar a un acuerdo ❷ disposición ❸ arreglo ❹ MÚSICA arreglo

■ **arrangements** _spl_ preparativos

array [əˈreɪ] _s_ surtido

arrears [əˈrɪəz] _spl_ atrasos • **in arrears a)** con retraso **b)** atrasado en el pago

arrest [əˈrest] ◆ _s_ detención; arresto • **under arrest** detenido, da; arrestado • **you're under arrest** queda arrestado ◆ _vt_ detener; arrestar

arrival [əˈraɪvl] _s_ llegada • **late arrival** retraso ▶ **new arrival a)** recién llegado; recién llegada **b)** recién nacido; recién nacida

arrive [əˈraɪv] _vi_ llegar • **to arrive at** llegar a

arrogant [ˈærəgənt] _adj_ arrogante

arrow [ˈærəʊ] _s_ flecha

arson [ˈɑːsn] _s_ incendio premeditado

art [ɑːt] _s_ arte

■ **arts** _spl_ ❶ EDUCACIÓN & UNIVERSIDAD letras ❷ • **the arts** las bellas artes

■ **arts and crafts** _spl_ artesanía

artefact [ˈɑːtɪfækt] = **artifact**

artery [ˈɑːtərɪ] _s_ arteria

art gallery _s_ ❶ museo (de arte) ❷ galería (de arte)

arthritis [ɑːˈθraɪtɪs] _s_ artritis

artichoke [ˈɑːtɪʃəʊk] _s_ alcachofa

article [ˈɑːtɪkl] _s_ artículo • **article of clothing** prenda de vestir

articulate ◆ _adj_ [ɑːˈtɪkjʊlət] ❶ elocuente ❷ claro, ra; bien articulado, da ◆ _vt_ [ɑːˈtɪkjʊleɪt] expresar

artifact [ˈɑːtɪfækt] _s_ artefacto

artificial [ˌɑːtɪˈfɪʃl] _adj_ artificial

artillery [ɑːˈtɪlərɪ] _s_ artillería

artist [ˈɑːtɪst] _s_ artista

artiste [ɑːˈtiːst] _s_ artista

artistic [ɑːˈtɪstɪk] _adj_ ❶ artístico, ca ❷ • **to be artistic** tener sensibilidad artística

as
◆ _conjunción_

acento tónico [æz], acento atónico [əz]

❶ [_expresa simultaneidad_]
• **she rang (just) as I was leaving** me llamó (justo) cuando salía

❷ [_expresa cambio gradual_]
• **as time goes by** a medida que pasa el tiempo
• **he grew grumpier as he got older** se volvió más cascarrabias conforme envejecía

❸ [_expresa la causa_]
• **as it's snowing, we'd better stay at home** como está nevando, es mejor que nos quedemos en casa

❹ [_conforme_]
• **as you know, he is always late** como sabes, siempre llega tarde
• **do as I say** haz lo que te digo

❺ [_expresa oposición_]
• **long as it was, I didn't find the lesson boring** a pesar de que fue muy larga, la clase no me pareció aburrida

◆ _preposición_

❶ [_indica una función, un papel_]
• **she works as a nurse** trabaja de enfermera
• **I'm speaking as your friend** te hablo como amigo

❷ [_como_]
• **it could be used as evidence against him** podría ser usado como pruebas contra él

◆ _adv_

[_en una comparación_]
• **he's as tall as I am** es tan alto como yo
• **he runs as fast as his sister** corre tan rápido como su hermana
• **as much wine as** tanto vino como

■ **as for**
◆ _preposición_

• **as for dessert, there's some ice-cream in the freezer** en cuanto al postre, hay helado en el congelador

■ **as from, as of**
◆ _preposición_

[_indica un punto de partida en el tiempo_]
• **as of yesterday** a partir de ayer

A

• **your ticket is valid as of Monday** su boleto es válido a partir del lunes
■ **as if, as though**
◆ *conjunción*
como si
• **as if it mattered!** ¡como si tuviera alguna importancia!
• **it looks as if** o **as though it will rain** parece que va a llover
■ **as to**
◆ *preposición*
• **I'm still uncertain as to his motivation** todavía no tengo clara su motivación

---

as

As... se as se utiliza para construir el comparativo de igualdad. En el habla cotidiana puede ir seguido del pronombre de complemento me, him, her, ETC (she's *as* tall *as me*). En lenguaje formal, en cambio, debe ir con el pronombre de sujeto I, he, she, ETC, y además de un segundo verbo (she's not *as* tall *as I* am).

As if y as though significan lo mismo. Cuando el hablante tiene sus dudas de que la comparación sea cierta, o sabe que no lo es, as if y as though van seguidos de were (she went pale *as if/though* she *were* about to faint *se puso pálida como si fuera a desmayarse*).

---

a.s.a.p. (*abreviatura de* as soon as possible) a la mayor brevedad posible
asbestos [æs'bestəs] *s* asbesto
ascend [ə'send] ◆ *vt* subir ◆ *vi* ascender
ascent [ə'sent] *s* ❶ ascensión ❷ subida; cuesta
ash [æʃ] *s* ❶ ceniza ❷ fresno
ashamed [ə'ʃeɪmd] *adj* avergonzado, da; apenado, da • **I'm ashamed to do it** me da vergüenza hacerlo • **I'm ashamed of...** me da vergüenza...
ashore [ə'ʃɔːr] *adv* hasta la orilla (nadar) • **to go ashore** desembarcar
ashtray ['æʃtreɪ] *s* cenicero
Ash Wednesday *s* miércoles de ceniza
Asia ['eɪʒə] *s* Asia
Asian ['eɪʒn] ◆ *adj* asiático, ca • **Asian American** americano, na de origen asiático ◆ *s* asiático, ca
aside [ə'saɪd] *adv* ❶ a un lado • **to move aside** apartarse ❷ aparte • **aside from** aparte de
expresión **to brush** o **sweep something aside** dejar algo aparte o de lado
ask [ɑːsk] ◆ *vt* ❶ • **to ask a question** hacer una pregunta ❷ pedir • **to ask somebody (to do something)** pedir a alguien (que haga algo) • **to ask somebody for something** pedirle algo a alguien ❸ invitar ◆ *vi* ❶ preguntar ❷ pedir

■ **ask after** *vt* 💡 *El objeto siempre va después de la preposición al final.* preguntar por
■ **ask for** *vt* 💡 *El objeto siempre va después de la preposición al final.* ❶ preguntar por ❷ pedir
■ **ask out** *vt* 💡 *El objeto se coloca entre el verbo y la preposición.* invitar a salir
askew [ə'skjuː] *adj* torcido, da
asleep [ə'sliːp] *adj* dormido, da • **she's asleep** está durmiendo • **to fall asleep** quedarse dormido • **to be fast** o **sound asleep** estar profundamente dormido
asparagus [ə'spærəgəs] *s* espárragos
aspartame ['æspərteɪm] *s* aspartamo
aspect ['æspekt] *s* ❶ aspecto ❷ cariz; aspecto ❸ orientación
asphalt ['æsfælt] *s* asfalto
asphyxiate [əs'fɪksɪeɪt] *vt* asfixiar
aspiration [,æspə'reɪʃn] *s* aspiración
aspire [ə'spaɪər] *vi* • **to aspire to** aspirar a
aspirin ['æsprɪn] *s* aspirina
ass [æs] *s* ❶ asno, na ❷ *muy familiar* culo
assassin [ə'sæsɪn] *s* asesino, na
assassinate [ə'sæsɪneɪt] *vt* asesinar
assassination [ə,sæsɪ'neɪʃn] *s* asesinato
assault [ə'sɔːlt] ◆ *s* MILITAR • **assault (on)** ataque (contra) ◆ *vt* ❶ asaltar; agredir ❷ abusar de
assemble [ə'sembl] ◆ *vt* ❶ juntar; reunir ❷ montar ◆ *vi* reunirse
assembly [ə'semblɪ] *s* ❶ asamblea ❷ reunión ❸ montaje
assent [ə'sent] ◆ *s* consentimiento ◆ *vi* • **to assent (to)** asentir (a)
assert [ə'sɜːt] *vt* ❶ afirmar ❷ imponer
assertive [ə'sɜːtɪv] *adj* enérgico, ca
assess [ə'ses] *vt* evaluar
assessment [ə'sesmənt] *s* ❶ evaluación ❷ cálculo
asset ['æset] *s* ❶ cualidad positiva ❷ ventaja ❸ elemento importante
■ **assets** *spl* COMERCIO activo
assign [ə'saɪn] *vt* ❶ • **to assign something (to somebody)** asignar algo (a alguien) • **to assign somebody to something** asignar a alguien algo • **to assign somebody to do something** asignar a alguien que haga algo ❷ • **to assign something (to)** destinar algo (a)
assignment [ə'saɪnmənt] *s* ❶ misión ❷ EDUCACIÓN tarea
assimilate [ə'sɪmɪleɪt] *vt* ❶ asimilar ❷ • **to assimilate somebody (into)** integrar a alguien (en)
assist [ə'sɪst] ◆ *vt* • **to assist somebody (with something/in doing something)** ayudar a alguien (con algo/a hacer algo) ◆ *vi* ayudar
assistance [ə'sɪstəns] *s* ayuda; asistencia • **to be of assistance (to)** ayudar (a)
assistant [ə'sɪstənt] ◆ *s* ayudante ◆ *en compuestos* adjunto, ta ▸ **assistant manager** director

A

adjunto, directora adjunta ▶ **assistant referee** árbitro, tra asistente

associate ◆ *adj* [əˈsəʊʃɪət] asociado, da ◆ *s* [əˈsəʊʃɪət] socio, cia ◆ *vt* [əˈsəʊʃɪeɪt] asociar • **to associate something/somebody with** asociar algo/a alguien con • **to be associated with a)** estar relacionado con **b)** estar asociado con ◆ *vi* [əˈsəʊʃɪeɪt] • **to associate with somebody** relacionarse con alguien

association [əˌsəʊsɪˈeɪʃn] *s* ❶ asociación • **in association with** en colaboración con ❷ connotación

assorted [əˈsɔːtɪd] *adj* ❶ variado, da ❷ surtido, da

assortment [əˈsɔːtmənt] *s* surtido

assume [əˈsjuːm] *vt* ❶ suponer ❷ asumir

assuming [əˈsjuːmɪŋ] *conjunción* suponiendo que

assumption [əˈsʌmpʃn] *s* suposición

assurance [əˈʃʊərəns] *s* ❶ garantía ❷ seguridad de sí mismo ❸ seguro

assure [əˈʃʊər] *vt* asegurar; garantizar • **to assure somebody of something** garantizar a alguien algo • **to be assured of something** tener algo garantizado • **rest assured that...** ten por seguro que...

assured [əˈʃʊəd] *adj* seguro, ra

asterisk [ˈæstərɪsk] *s* asterisco

asthma [ˈæsmə] *s* asma

astonish [əˈstɒnɪʃ] *vt* asombrar

astonishment [əˈstɒnɪʃmənt] *s* asombro

astound [əˈstaʊnd] *vt* asombrar

astray [əˈstreɪ] *adv* • **to go astray** extraviarse • **to lead somebody astray** llevar a alguien por el mal camino

astride [əˈstraɪd] ◆ *adv* a horcajadas ◆ *preposición* a horcajadas en

astrology [əˈstrɒlədʒɪ] *s* astrología

astronaut [ˈæstrənɔːt] *s* astronauta

astronomical [ˌæstrəˈnɒmɪkl] *adj literal & figurado* astronómico, ca

astronomy [əˈstrɒnəmɪ] *s* astronomía

astute [əˈstjuːt] *adj* astuto, ta

asylum [əˈsaɪləm] *s* ❶ manicomio ❷ asilo

asylum seeker [əˈsaɪləmˈsiːkər] *s* peticionario, ria de asilo

at ☼*acento atónico* [ət], *acento tónico* [æt] *preposición* ❶ en • **at my father's** en casa de mi padre • **standing at the window** de pie junto a la ventana • **at the bottom of the hill** al pie de la colina • **at school/work/home** en la escuela/el trabajo/casa ❷ a • **to point at somebody** señalar a alguien ❸ • **at a more suitable time** en un momento más oportuno • **at midnight/noon/eleven o'clock** a medianoche/mediodía/las once • **at night** por la noche • **at Christmas/Easter** en Navidades/Semana Santa ❹ a • **at 100 kmh/high speed** a 100 kilómetros por hora/gran velocidad • **at $50 (a pair)** a 50 dólares (el par) ❺ • **at peace/war** en paz/guerra • **she's at lunch** está comiendo • **to work hard at something** trabajar duro en algo ❻ a • **at 52/**

your age a los 52/tu edad ❼ ☼*después de adjetivos* • **delighted at** encantado con • **experienced at** experimentado en • **puzzled/horrified at** perplejo/horrorizado ante • **he's good/bad at sport** se le dan bien/mal los deportes

■ **at all** *adv* ❶ ☼*con negativo* • **not at all a)** de nada **b)** en absoluto • **she's not at all happy** no está nada contenta ❷ • **anything at all will do** cualquier cosa valdrá • **do you know her at all?** ¿la conoces (de algo)?

at

No hay que confundir at, in y on, aunque las tres preposiciones se pueden usar para expresar tiempo.

At se usa con tiempos concretos (*at* nine o'clock; *at* lunch time), con los nombres de algunos periodos festivos (*at* Christmas; *at* New Year; *at* Easter), y con weekend y night (what did you do *at* the weekend? *¿qué hiciste el fin de semana?*; I do my homework *at* night *hago la tarea por la noche*.

In se utiliza con los meses (*in* September), los años (*in* 2009), los siglos (*in* the 19th century) y las estaciones (*in* spring). Además aparece con las palabras morning, afternoon y evening al referirse a ellas en general (*in* the evening we like to go out *nos gusta salir en la noche*; I'll call you *in* the afternoon *te llamaré en la tarde*).

Utilizamos on para referirnos a una fecha o día específicos (*on* Christmas Day; *on* March 8th, 1998; *on* Monday I went swimming *el lunes fui a nadar*), o a un día en general (*on* Sundays I visit my grandparents *los domingos voy a ver a mis abuelos*). También aparece con las palabras morning, afternoon y evening al referirnos a ellas más en particular (*on* Saturday morning *el sábado en la mañana*; *on* wet afternoons *en las tardes lluviosas*).

ate [eɪt] *pretérito* → **eat**

atheist [ˈeɪθɪɪst] *s* ateo, a

Athens [ˈæθɪnz] *s* Atenas

athlete [ˈæθliːt] *s* atleta

athletic [æθˈletɪk] *adj* atlético, ca

■ **athletics** *spl* atletismo

Atlantic [ətˈlæntɪk] ◆ *adj* atlántico, ca ◆ *s* ▶ **the Atlantic (Ocean)** el (océano) Atlántico

atlas [ˈætləs] *s* atlas

ATM (*abreviatura de* automatic teller machine) *s* cajero automático

atmosphere [ˈætməˌsfɪər] *s* ❶ atmósfera ❷ ambiente

A

atmospheric [ˌætməsˈferɪk] *adj* ❶ atmosférico, ca ❷ sugerente

atom [ˈætəm] *s FÍSICA* átomo

atom bomb, atomic bomb *s* bomba atómica

atomic [əˈtɒmɪk] *adj* atómico, ca

atomic bomb = atom bomb

atomizer [ˈætəmaɪzər] *s* atomizador

atone [əˈtəʊn] *vi* • to atone for reparar

A to Z *s* ❶ guía alfabética ❷ callejero

atrocious [əˈtrəʊʃəs] *adj* atroz

atrocity [əˈtrɒsətɪ] *s* atrocidad

attach [əˈtætʃ] *vt* ❶ • to attach something (to) sujetar algo (a) • a notice was attached to the window habían puesto un aviso en la ventana ❷ atar algo (a) ❸ *INFORMÁTICA* adjuntar ❹ • to attach something (to something) atribuir algo (a algo)

attaché case *s* maletín

attached [əˈtætʃt] *adj* • to be attached to tener cariño a

attachment [əˈtætʃmənt] *s* ❶ accesorio ❷ *INFORMÁTICA* archivo adjunto

attack [əˈtæk] ◆ *s* • attack (on) ataque (contra) • terrorist attack atentado terrorista • to be under attack estar siendo atacado ◆ *vt* ❶ atacar ❷ acometer ◆ *vi* atacar

attacker [əˈtækər] *s* atacante

attain [əˈteɪn] *vt* lograr; alcanzar

attempt [əˈtempt] ◆ *s* • attempt (at doing something) intento (de hacer algo) • attempt on somebody's life atentado contra la vida de alguien ◆ *vt* • to attempt something/to do something intentar algo/hacer algo

attend [əˈtend] ◆ *vt* asistir a ◆ *vi* asistir
■ **attend to** *vt* ☀️ *El objeto siempre va después de la preposición al final.* ❶ ocuparse de ❷ atender a ❸ asistir a

attendance [əˈtendəns] *s* asistencia • the attendance for the game was over 10,000 más de 10.000 personas asistieron al partido

attendant [əˈtendənt] *s* ❶ vigilante ❷ encargado, da

attention [əˈtenʃn] *s* ☀️ *incontable* ❶ atención • to bring something to somebody's attention, to draw somebody's attention to something llamar la atención de alguien sobre algo • to attract o catch somebody's attention atraer o captar la atención de alguien • to pay/pay no attention (to) prestar/no prestar atención (a) • for the attention of *COMERCIO* a la atención de • your attention please! ¡atención! ❷ asistencia

attentive [əˈtentɪv] *adj* atento, ta

attic [ˈætɪk] *s* desván

attitude [ˈætɪtjuːd] *s* ❶ actitud ❷ postura

attorney [əˈtɜːnɪ] *s* abogado, da

attorney general *s* fiscal general del estado
El plural de **attorney general** es **attorneys general**.

attract [əˈtrækt] *vt* ❶ atraer ❷ suscitar

attraction [əˈtrækʃn] *s* ❶ • attraction (to somebody) atracción (hacia o por alguien) ❷ atractivo

attractive [əˈtræktɪv] *adj* atractivo, va

attribute ◆ *vt* [əˈtrɪbjuːt] • to attribute something to atribuir algo a ◆ *s* [ˈætrɪbjuːt] atributo

auburn [ˈɔːbən] *adj* castaño rojizo

auction [ˈɔːkʃn] ◆ *s* subasta • to put something up for auction sacar algo a subasta ◆ *vt* subastar

auctioneer [ˌɔːkʃəˈnɪər] *s* subastador, ra

audacious [ɔːˈdeɪʃəs] *adj* ❶ audaz ❷ atrevido, da

audible [ˈɔːdəbl] *adj* audible

audience [ˈɔːdjəns] *s* ❶ público ❷ audiencia

audiovisual [ˈɔːdɪəʊ-] *adj* audiovisual

audit [ˈɔːdɪt] ◆ *s* auditoría ◆ *vt* auditar

audition [ɔːˈdɪʃn] *s* prueba *(a un artista)*

auditor [ˈɔːdɪtər] *s* auditor, ra

auditorium [ˌɔːdɪˈtɔːrɪəm] *s* auditorio
Dos plurales: **auditoriums** o **auditoria**

augur [ˈɔːgər] *vi* • to augur well/badly ser un buen/mal augurio

August [ˈɔːgəst] *s* agosto ver también **September**

aunt [ɑːnt] *s* tía

auntie, aunty [ˈɑːntɪ] *s familiar* tita

aural [ˈɔːrəl] *adj* auditivo, va

auspices [ˈɔːspɪsɪz] *spl* • under the auspices of bajo los auspicios de

auspicious [ɔːˈspɪʃəs] *adj* prometedor, ra

Aussie [ˈɒzɪ] *s familiar* australiano, na

austere [ɒˈstɪər] *adj* austero, ra

austerity [ɒˈsterətɪ] *s* austeridad

Australia [ɒˈstreɪljə] *s* Australia

Australian [ɒˈstreɪljən] ◆ *adj* australiano, na ◆ *s* australiano, na

Austria [ˈɒstrɪə] *s* Austria

Austrian [ˈɒstrɪən] ◆ *adj* austriaco, ca ◆ *s* austriaco, ca

authentic [ɔːˈθentɪk] *adj* auténtico, ca

author [ˈɔːθər] *s* ❶ escritor, ra ❷ autor, ra

authoritarian [ɔːˌθɒrɪˈteərɪən] *adj* autoritario, ria

authority [ɔːˈθɒrətɪ] *s* ❶ autoridad • to be an authority on ser una autoridad en ❷ autorización
■ **authorities** *spl* • the authorities las autoridades

authorize [ˈɔːθəraɪz] *vt* • to authorize (somebody to do something) autorizar (a alguien a hacer algo)

autism [ˈɔːtɪzm] *s* autismo

autistic [ɔːˈtɪstɪk] *adj* autista

auto [ˈɔːtəʊ] *s* coche
El plural irregular de **auto** es **autos**.

autobiography [ˌɔːtəbaɪˈɒgrəfɪ] *s* autobiografía

autograph [ˈɔːtəgrɑːf] ◆ *s* autógrafo ◆ *vt* autografiar

automate ['ɔːtəmeɪt] *vt* automatizar

automatic [ˌɔːtə'mætɪk] ◆ *adj* automático, ca ◆ *s* ❶ coche automático ❷ arma automática ❸ lavadora automática

automatically [ˌɔːtə'mætɪklɪ] *adv* automáticamente

automation [ˌɔːtə'meɪʃn] *s* automatización

automobile ['ɔːtəməbiːl] *s* coche; automóvil

autonomous [ɔː'tɒnəməs] *adj* autónomo, ma

autonomy [ɔː'tɒnəmɪ] *s* autonomía

autopsy ['ɔːtɒpsɪ] *s* autopsia

autumn ['ɔːtəm] *s* otoño

auxiliary [ɔːg'zɪljərɪ] ◆ *adj* auxiliar ◆ *s* auxiliar sanitario; auxiliar sanitaria

Av. (*abreviatura escrita de* avenue) Av.

avail [ə'veɪl] ◆ *s* • **to no avail** en vano ◆ *vt* • **to avail yourself of something** aprovechar algo

available [ə'veɪləbl] *adj* ❶ disponible • **this product is no longer available** ya no comercializamos este producto ❷ libre; disponible

avalanche ['ævəlɑːnʃ] *s literal & figurado* avalancha; alud

avant-garde [ˌævɒn'gɑːd] *adj* de vanguardia; vanguardista

avarice ['ævərɪs] *s* avaricia

Ave. (*abreviatura escrita de* avenue) Avda.

avenge [ə'vendʒ] *vt* vengar

avenue ['ævənjuː] *s* ❶ avenida ❷ *figurado* vía

average ['ævərɪdʒ] ◆ *adj* ❶ medio, dia ❷ regular ◆ *s* media; promedio • **on average** de media; como promedio ◆ *vt* alcanzar un promedio de

■ **average out** *vi* • **to average out at** salir a una media de

aversion [ə'vɜːʃn] *s* • **aversion (to)** aversión (a)

avert [ə'vɜːt] *vt* ❶ evitar; prevenir ❷ desviar

aviary ['eɪvjərɪ] *s* pajarera

avid ['ævɪd] *adj* • **avid (for)** ávido, da (de)

avocado [ˌævə'kɑːdəʊ] *s* ▶ **avocado (pear)** aguacate

Dos plurales: **avocados** o **avocadoes**.

avoid [ə'vɔɪd] *vt* • **to avoid (something/doing something)** evitar (algo/hacer algo) • **she's been avoiding me** ha estado esquivándome

avoidance [ə'vɔɪdəns] → **tax avoidance**

await [ə'weɪt] *vt* esperar; aguardar

awake [ə'weɪk] ◆ *adj* despierto, ta ◆ *vt literal & figurado* despertar ◆ *vi literal & figurado* despertarse

Formas irregulares de **awake**: *pretérito* **awoke** o **awaked**, *pp* **awoken**.

award [ə'wɔːd] ◆ *s* ❶ premio; galardón ❷ indemnización ◆ *vt* • **to award somebody something, to award something to somebody a)** conceder o otorgar algo a alguien **b)** adjudicar algo a alguien

aware [ə'weər] *adj* ❶ • **aware of** consciente de • **to become aware of** darse cuenta de ❷ informado, da; al

día • **aware of something** al día de algo • **to be aware that** estar informado de que

awareness [ə'weənɪs] *s* conciencia

away [ə'weɪ]
◆ *adv*
❶ [*expresa ausencia, distanciamento*]
• **I'll be away for two weeks** voy a estar fuera dos semanas
• **she moved away from him** se apartó de él
• **he looked away in disgust** miró hacia el otro lado con asco
❷ [*expresa la distancia*]
• **is the beach far away?** ¿queda muy lejos la playa?
• **we live four miles away (from here)** vivimos a quatro millas (de aquí)
❸ [*con expresiones de tiempo*]
• **the elections are a month away** falta un mes para las elecciones
❹ [*indica que algo ha sido colocado en su lugar*]
• **he put the dictionary away on the shelf** guardó el diccionario en la estantería
❺ [*expresa la desaparición*]
• **the music faded away as the lights went on** la música se desvaneció conforme las luces se encendían
• **I had two watches, so I gave one away** tenía dos relojes, por lo que di uno de ellos
❻ [*expresa la continuación*]
• **he was working away on a new project** trabajaba sin parar en un proyecto nuevo

awe [ɔː] *s* sobrecogimiento • **to be in awe of somebody** sentirse intimidado por alguien

awesome ['ɔːsəm] *adj* padrísimo, ma

awful ['ɔːfʊl] *adj* ❶ terrible; espantoso, sa • **I feel awful** me siento fatal ❷ *familiar* tremendo, da • **I like it an awful lot** me gusta muchísimo

awfully ['ɔːflɪ] *adv familiar* tremendamente • **it's awfully cold today** hoy hace un frío espantoso

awkward ['ɔːkwəd] *adj* ❶ torpe ❷ desgarbado, da ❸ incómodo, da ❹ difícil ❺ poco manejable ❻ inoportuno, na

awning ['ɔːnɪŋ] *s* toldo

awoke [ə'wəʊk] *pretérito* → **awake**

awoken [ə'wəʊkn] *participio pasado* → **awake**

awry [ə'raɪ] ◆ *adj* torcido, da; ladeado, da ◆ *adv* • **to go awry** salir mal

ax [æks] ◆ *s* hacha ◆ *vt* suprimir

axes ['æksiːz] *spl* → **axis**

axis ['æksɪs] *s* eje

El plural de **axis** es **axes**.

axle ['æksl] *s* eje

aye [aɪ] *adv* sí

Aztec ['æztek] ◆ *adj* azteca ◆ *s* azteca

B

b, B [bi:] *s* b; B
■ **B** *s* ❶ *MÚSICA* si ❷ *EDUCACIÓN* ≃ bien
Dos plurales: **b's o bs; B's o Bs.**

B & B *abreviatura escrita de* **bed and breakfast**

BA (*abreviatura de* Bachelor of Arts) *s* ▶ (titular de una) licenciatura de letras

babble ['bæbl] *vi* farfullar

babe [beɪb] *s familiar* ❶ cariño ❷ chica bonita

baboon [bə'bu:n] *s* babuino

baby ['beɪbɪ] ◆ *s* ❶ bebé ❷ niño ❸ *familiar* cariño
◆ *en compuestos* • **baby brother** hermanito • **baby sister** hermanita • **baby boy** niño • **baby girl** niña

baby boomer [-,bu:mər] *s* ▶ persona nacida durante el boom natalicio de los sesenta

baby buggy, baby carriage *s* carriola

baby food *s* papilla

baby-sit *vi* cuidar a niños

baby-sitter [-'sɪtər] *s* nana

bachelor ['bætʃələr] *s* soltero • **bachelor party** despedida de soltero

Bachelor of Arts *s* ≃ licenciado en Letras

Bachelor of Science *s* ≃ licenciado en Ciencias

---

back [bæk]
◆ *adv*
❶ [*indica un movimiento hacia atrás*]
• **stand back!** ¡atrás!
• **the company pushed back the offer until this week** la empresa amplió la oferta hasta el final de esta semana
❷ [*indica la vuelta a un lugar o estado anterior*]
• **I'll be back at five** volveré a las cinco
• **he drove me back home** me dio aventón hasta casa
• **don't forget to put the book back on the shelf!** ¡no te olvides de guardar el libro en la estantería!
• **to go back and forth** ir y venir
• **to go back to sleep** volverse a dormir
• **to be back (in fashion)** volver a estar de moda
• **to think back (to)** recordar

---

❸ [*expresa devolución*]
• **give it back to me** devuélvemelo
• **I'd like my money back** quiero mi dinero de vuelta
❹ [*expresa una acción en respuesta a otra*]
• **don't forget to call him back!** ¡no te olvides de llamarle!
• **if he hits you, hit him back** ¡si te pega, pégale tú también!
◆ *s*
❶ [*parte del cuerpo*] espalda
• **he's lying on his back** está tumbado de espaldas
❷ [*en el dorso de un documento*]
• **don't forget to write your name on the back of the envelope** no te olvides de escribir tu nombre al dorso del sobre
❸ [*de una silla*] respaldo
❹ [*el último, al fondo*]
• **she sat at the back of the car** se sentó en la parte de atrás del carro
• **the sugar's at the back of the cabinet** el azúcar está en el fondo del gabinete
❺ [*expresa el origen, la causa*]
• **the Parliament is at the back of all this** el Parlamento está por detrás de todo esto
expresión **he did it behind my back!** ¡lo hizo a mis espaldas! ▶ **I can't do anything! he's always on my back!** no puedo hacer nada, no me deja ni un instante
◆ *adj*
❶ [*de atrás, del final*]
• **the map is on the back seat** el mapa está en el asiento trasero
• **the back door is always closed** la puerta trasera siempre está cerrada
❷ [*atrasado, debido*]
• **he owes a back rent** debe un alquiler atrasado
◆ *vt*
❶ [*expresa un movimiento hacia atrás*]
• **she backed the car in the garage** entró en el garaje marcha atrás
❷ [*expresa apoyo*]
• **he backed the government** apoyó al gobierno

B

❸ [*para apostar*]
• **I'm backing the Dolphins to win** apuesto a que ganan los Dolphins
◆ *vi*
[*indica un movimiento hacia atrás*]
• **she backed quickly out of the room** salió retrocediendo rápidamente del cuarto

backache ['bækeɪk] *s* dolor de espalda

backbone ['bækbəʊn] *s* *literal & figurado* columna vertebral

back door *s* puerta trasera
expresión **the team qualified through the back door** *figurado* el equipo se clasificó por la puerta trasera

backfire [,bæk'faɪər] *vi* ❶ petardear ❷ • **it backfired on him** le salió el tiro por la culata

background ['bækgraʊnd] *s* ❶ fondo • **in the background a)** al fondo *(de cuadro,* ETC) **b)** en la sombra *(en el anonimato)* ❷ trasfondo ❸ origen • **family background** antecedentes familiares ❹ • **a background in** conocimientos de

backhand ['bækhænd] *s* revés

backing ['bækɪŋ] *s* ❶ apoyo ; respaldo ❷ MÚSICA acompañamiento

backlash ['bæklæʃ] *s* reacción violenta

backlog ['bæklɒg] *s* acumulación

back number, back issue *s* número atrasado

backpack ['bækpæk] *s* mochila

backpacker ['bækpækər] *s* mochilero, ra

backpacking ['bækpækɪŋ] *s* viajar de mochilero

backpedal [,bæk'pedl] *vi* *figurado* • **to backpedal (on something)** dar marcha atrás (con respecto a algo)

back seat *s* asiento trasero o de atrás
expresión **to take a back seat** *figurado* situarse en segundo plano

backside [,bæk'saɪd] *s* *familiar* trasero

backstage [,bæk'steɪdʒ] *adv* entre bastidores

backstroke ['bækstrəʊk] *s* espalda *(en natación)* • **to do the backstroke** nadar a espalda

backup ['bækʌp] ◆ *adj* ❶ de emergencia ❷ de apoyo ❸ INFORMÁTICA de seguridad ◆ *s* ❶ apoyo ❷ INFORMÁTICA copia de seguridad

backward ['bækwəd] ◆ *adj* ❶ hacia atrás ❷ atrasado, da ◆ *adv* ❶ hacia atrás • **I took a step backward** di un paso atrás ❷ al o del revés

backwards ['bækwədz] *adv* = **backward**

backyard [,bæk'jɑːd] *s* jardín (trasero)

bacon ['beɪkən] *s* bacon ; tocino

bacteria [bæk'tɪərɪə] *spl* bacterias

bad [bæd] *(comparativo* worse, *superlativo* worst) *adj*
❶ malo, la • **he's bad at French** se le da mal el francés • **to have a bad back** estar mal de la espalda • **to go bad** echarse a perder • **it's not bad (at all)** no está nada mal • **how are you? — not bad** ¿qué tal? — bien ❷ grave • **I was home with a bad cold** estaba en la

casa con un fuerte resfriado ❸ • **to feel bad about something** sentirse mal por algo
expresión **not bad** no está mal ▶ **too bad!** ¡mala suerte!

badge [bædʒ] *s* ❶ chapa ❷ insignia ❸ distintivo

badger ['bædʒər] ◆ *s* tejón ◆ *vt* • **to badger somebody (to do something)** ponerse pesado, da con alguien (para que haga algo)

badly ['bædlɪ] *(comparativo* worse, *superlativo* worst) *adv* ❶ mal ❷ gravemente • **I'm badly in need of help** necesito ayuda urgentemente
expresión **to think badly of somebody** pensar mal de alguien

badly-off *adj* ❶ apurado, da de dinero ❷ • **to be badly-off for something** andar mal de algo

bad-mannered [-'mænəd] *adj* maleducado, da

badminton ['bædmɪntən] *s* bádminton

bad-tempered [-'tempəd] *adj* ❶ • **to be bad-tempered** tener mal genio ❷ • **to be bad-tempered** estar malhumorado, da

baffle ['bæfl] *vt* desconcertar

bag [bæg] *s* ❶ bolsa ❷ bolso
expresión **to pack your bags** *literal & figurado* hacer las maletas
■ **bags** *spl* ❶ • **to have bags under your eyes** *familiar* tener ojeras ❷ • **bags of** *familiar* un montón de

bagel ['beɪgəl] *s* ▶ bollo de pan en forma de rosca

baggage ['bægɪdʒ] *s* ☿ *incontable* equipaje

baggage car *s* vagón de equipaje

baggage claim *s* reclamo de equipaje

baggy ['bægɪ] *adj* holgado, da • **she wore a baggy old sweatshirt** llevaba una sudadera ancha y vieja

bagpipes ['bægpaɪps] *spl* gaita

Bahamas [bə'hɑːməz] *spl* • **the Bahamas** las Bahamas

bail [beɪl] *s* ☿ *incontable* fianza • **on bail** bajo fianza
■ **bail out** *vt* ☿ *El objeto se puede colocar antes o después de la preposición.* ❶ obtener la libertad bajo fianza de ❷ sacar de apuros

bailiff ['beɪlɪf] *s* alguacil

bait [beɪt] ◆ *s* *literal & figurado* cebo
expresión **to rise to** o **take the bait** *figurado* picarse ; morder el anzuelo
◆ *vt* ❶ cebar ❷ hacer sufrir ; cebarse con

bake [beɪk] ◆ *vt* cocer al horno ◆ *vi* cocerse al horno

baked beans [beɪkt-] *spl* alubias cocidas en salsa de tomate

baked potato [beɪkt-] *s* patata asada o al horno

baker ['beɪkər] *s* panadero

bakery ['beɪkərɪ] *s* panadería

baking ['beɪkɪŋ] *s* cocción

baking soda *s* bicarbonato en polvo

balaclava (helmet) [bælə'klɑːvə-] *s* pasamontañas

B

balance [ˈbæləns] ◆ s ❶ equilibrio • **to keep/lose your balance** mantener/perder el equilibrio • **it caught me off balance** me agarró desprevenido, da ❷ balanza ❸ saldo
expresión **to be** o **hang in the balance** estar en el aire
◆ vt ❶ poner en equilibrio ❷ sopesar ◆ vi ❶ sostenerse en equilibrio ❷ cuadrar
■ **on balance** adv tras pensarlo detenidamente

balanced diet s dieta equilibrada

balance sheet s balance

balcony [ˈbælkənɪ] s ❶ terraza; balcón ❷ anfiteatro; galería

bald [bɔːld] adj calvo, va • **he's going bald** se está quedando calvo

bale [beɪl] s bala

Balearic Islands [ˌbælɪˈærɪk-], **Balearics** [ˌbælɪˈærɪks] spl • **the Balearic Islands** las Baleares

Balkans [ˈbɔːlkənz], **Balkan States** spl • **the Balkans** los Balcanes

ball [bɔːl] s ❶ pelota ❷ bola ❸ balón ❹ pulpejo ❺ baile ❻ ovillo
■ **balls** muy familiar ◆ spl pelotas ◆ s ·☀·**incontable** gilipolleces

ballad [ˈbæləd] s balada

ball boy s recogepelotas

ballerina [ˌbæləˈriːnə] s bailarina

ballet [ˈbæleɪ] s ballet

ballet dancer s bailarín, ina (de ballet)

ball game s partido de beisbol
expresión **it's a whole new ball game** es una historia totalmente distinta

balloon [bəˈluːn] s ❶ globo ❷ globo (aerostático) ❸ [en historietas] bocadillo

ballot [ˈbælət] ◆ s votación ◆ vt • **to ballot the members on an issue** someter un asunto a votación entre los afiliados

ballot box s urna • **to decide something at the ballot box** decidir algo en las urnas

ballot paper s boleta electoral

ballpoint (pen) [ˈbɔːlpɔɪnt-] s pluma (atómica)

ballroom [ˈbɔːlrʊm] s salón de baile

ballroom dancing s ·☀·**incontable** baile de salón

balm [bɑːm] s bálsamo

baloney [bəˈləʊnɪ] s ❶ ·☀·**incontable** familiar bobadas ❷ tipo de mortadela

Baltic [ˈbɔːltɪk] ◆ adj báltico, ca ◆ s • **the Baltic (Sea)** el (mar) Báltico

Baltic Republic s • **the Baltic Republics** las repúblicas bálticas

bamboo [bæmˈbuː] s bambú

bamboozle [bæmˈbuːzl] vt familiar camelar; engatusar

ban [bæn] ◆ s • **ban (on)** prohibición (de) ◆ vt • **to ban (somebody from doing something)** prohibir (a alguien hacer algo)

banana [bəˈnɑːnə] s plátano

band [bænd] s ❶ grupo ❷ banda ❸ cinta; tira ❹ franja
■ **band together** vi juntarse

bandage [ˈbændɪdʒ] ◆ s venda ◆ vt vendar

Band-Aid® s ≃ curita

b and b, B and B s abreviatura escrita de **bed and breakfast**

bandit [ˈbændɪt] s bandido, da

bandstand [ˈbændstænd] s quiosco de música

bandwagon [ˈbændwægən] s
expresión **to jump on the bandwagon** subirse al carro

bandy [ˈbændɪ] adj arqueado, da
■ **bandy about, bandy around** vt ·☀·*El objeto se puede colocar antes o después de la preposición.* sacar a relucir

bang [bæŋ] ◆ s ❶ golpe ❷ estampido; estruendo ◆ vt ❶ golpear ❷ golpearse ❸ cerrar de golpe ◆ vi golpear ◆ adv • **bang in the middle of** justo en mitad de • **bang on** muy acertado, da
■ **bangs** spl fleco

Bangladesh [ˌbæŋgləˈdeʃ] s Bangladesh

bangle [ˈbæŋgl] s brazalete

banish [ˈbænɪʃ] vt literal & figurado desterrar

banister [ˈbænɪstər] s barandilla; pasamanos

bank [bæŋk] ◆ s ❶ banco ❷ ribera; orilla ❸ loma ❹ masa ◆ vi ❶ FINANZAS • **to bank with** tener una cuenta en ❷ ladearse
■ **bank on** vt ·☀·*El objeto siempre va después de la preposición al final.* contar con

bank account s cuenta bancaria

bank balance s saldo bancario

bank charges spl comisiones bancarias

bank details spl datos bancarios

banker [ˈbæŋkər] s banquero, ra

banking [ˈbæŋkɪŋ] s banca

bank manager s director, ra de banco

bankrupt [ˈbæŋkrʌpt] ◆ adj quebrado, da; en quiebra • **to go bankrupt** quebrar ◆ vt llevar a la quiebra

bankruptcy [ˈbæŋkrəptsɪ] s quiebra; bancarrota

bank statement s extracto de cuenta

banner [ˈbænər] s ❶ pancarta ❷ banner; pancarta publicitaria

banquet [ˈbæŋkwɪt] s banquete

banter [ˈbæntər] s ·☀·**incontable** bromas

baptism [ˈbæptɪzm] s bautismo

baptize [ˈbæptaɪz] vt bautizar

bar [bɑːr] ◆ s ❶ • **a bar of chocolate** una tableta de chocolate ❷ barra ❸ lingote ❹ barrote ❺ barra (de metal) ❻ bar ❼ barra (en un bar) ❽ figurado barrera ❾ prohibición ❿ MÚSICA compás
expresión **to be behind bars** estar entre rejas

◆ *vt* ❶ atrancar ❷ • **to bar somebody's way** impedir el paso a alguien ❸ • **to bar somebody (from doing something)** prohibir a alguien (hacer algo) • **to bar somebody from somewhere** prohibir a alguien la entrada en un sitio ◆ *preposición* menos; salvo • **bar none** sin excepción

■ **Bar** *s Derecho* • **the Bar** la abogacía

barbaric [bɑːˈbærɪk] *adj* salvaje

barbecue [ˈbɑːbɪkjuː] *s* carne asada

barbed wire [bɑːbd-] *s* alambre de púas

barber [ˈbɑːbər] *s* peluquero

barbershop [ˈbɑːbəʃɒp] *s* peluquería

bar code *s* código de barras

bare [beər] ◆ *adj* ❶ desnudo, da ❷ descalzo, za ❸ esencial ❹ vacío, a ◆ *vt* descubrir • **to bare your teeth** enseñar los dientes

barefaced [ˈbeəfeɪst] *adj* descarado, da

barefoot(ed) [ˌbeəˈfʊt(ɪd)] *adj* & *adv* descalzo, za

barely [ˈbeəlɪ] *adv* apenas

bargain [ˈbɑːgɪn] ◆ *s* ❶ trato; acuerdo • **into the bargain** además ❷ ganga ◆ *vi* • **to bargain (with somebody for something)** negociar (con alguien para obtener algo)

■ **bargain for, bargain on** *vt* ☼ *El objeto siempre va después de la preposición al final.* contar con

barge [bɑːdʒ] ◆ *s* barcaza ◆ *vi familiar* • **to barge into a)** chocarse con **b)** irrumpir en

■ **barge in** *vi familiar* • **to barge in (on)** entrometerse (en)

baritone [ˈbærɪtəʊn] *s* barítono

bark [bɑːk] ◆ *s* ❶ ladrido ❷ corteza ◆ *vi* • **to bark (at)** ladrar (a)

barley [ˈbɑːlɪ] *s* cebada

barmaid [ˈbɑːmeɪd] *s* camarera

barman [ˈbɑːmən] *s* camarero; barman

El plural de **barman** es **barmen** [ˈbɑːmen].

barn [bɑːn] *s* granero

barometer [bəˈrɒmɪtər] *s* barómetro

baron [ˈbærən] *s* barón ▸ **press/oil baron** *figurado* magnate de la prensa/del petróleo

baroness [ˈbærənɪs] *s* baronesa

barrack [ˈbærək] ■ **barracks** *spl* cuartel

barrage [ˈbærɑːʒ] *s* ❶ descarga; fuego intenso de artillería ❷ aluvión; alud

barrel [ˈbærəl] *s* ❶ barril ❷ cañón

barren [ˈbærən] *adj* estéril

barrette [bəˈret] *s* broche

barricade [ˌbærɪˈkeɪd] ◆ *s* barricada ◆ *vt* levantar barricadas en

barrier [ˈbærɪər] *s literal & figurado* barrera

barring [ˈbɑːrɪŋ] *preposición* salvo • **barring a miracle** a menos que ocurra un milagro

barroom [ˈbɑːrʊm] *s* bar

barrow [ˈbærəʊ] *s* carrito

bartender [ˈbɑːtendər] *s* barman; cantinero, ra

barter [ˈbɑːtər] ◆ *s* trueque ◆ *vt* • **to barter (something for something)** trocar (algo por algo)

base [beɪs] ◆ *s* base ◆ *vt* ❶ • **to be based in** tener la base en • **the company is based in Detroit** la compañía tiene su sede en Detroit • **he's based in Paris** vive en París ❷ • **to base something on** basar algo en

baseball [ˈbeɪsbɔːl] *s* béisbol

baseball

El **béisbol** es el deporte preferido de los Estados Unidos. Hay dos equipos de nueve jugadores cada uno. Se juega con un bate largo, una pelota pequeña y unos guantes grandes de cuero. El campeonato de béisbol se llama **the World Series**. De los equipos más conocidos son los **New York Yankees**, los **Boston Red Sox**, los **Chicago Cubs** y los **Detroit Tigers**.

baseball cap *s* gorra de visera

basement [ˈbeɪsmənt] *s* sótano

bases [ˈbeɪsiːz] *spl* → **basis**

bash [bæʃ] *familiar* ◆ *s* juerga

expresión **to have a bash at something** intentar algo

◆ *vt* ❶ darle un porrazo a ❷ darse un porrazo en

bashful [ˈbæʃfʊl] *adj* ❶ vergonzoso, sa ❷ tímido, da

basic [ˈbeɪsɪk] *adj* básico, ca

■ **basics** *spl* ❶ principios básicos ❷ • **the basics** lo imprescindible

basically [ˈbeɪsɪklɪ] *adv* ❶ esencialmente ❷ en resumen

basil [ˈbæzl] *s* albahaca

basin [ˈbeɪsn] *s* ❶ lavabo ❷ *Geografía* cuenca

basis [ˈbeɪsɪs] *s* base • **on the basis of** de acuerdo con; a partir de • **on a weekly basis** semanalmente • **on a monthly basis** mensualmente

El plural de **basis** es **bases**.

bask [bɑːsk] *vi* • **to bask in the sun** tostarse al sol

basket [ˈbɑːskɪt] *s* ❶ cesta ❷ canasta

basketball [ˈbɑːskɪtbɔːl] *s* básquetbol

bass [beɪs] ◆ *adj* bajo, ja ◆ *s* ❶ bajo ❷ contrabajo ❸ graves

bass drum [beɪs-] *s* bombo

bass guitar [beɪs-] *s* bajo

bassoon [bəˈsuːn] *s* fagot

bastard [ˈbɑːstəd] *s* ❶ bastardo, da ❷ *muy familiar & despectivo* cabrón, ona

bat [bæt] ◆ *s* ❶ murciélago ❷ bate ❸ pala; paleta ◆ *vi* batear

batch [bætʃ] ◆ *s* ❶ hornada ❷ remesa ❸ montón ❹ lote

bath [bɑ:θ] ◆ s baño • **to have** o **take a bath** bañarse ◆ vt bañar

bathe [beɪð] ◆ vt lavar ◆ vi bañarse

bathing cap s gorra de natación

bathing suit s traje de baño

bathrobe ['bɑːðrəʊb] s bata

bathroom ['bɑːðrʊm] s ❶ baño (cuarto) ❷ baño (excusado)

bath towel s toalla de baño

bathtub ['bɑːðtʌb] s tina

baton ['bætən] s ❶ batuta ❷ estafeta

battalion [bə'tæljən] s batallón

batter ['bætər] ◆ s ❶ pasta para rebozar ❷ mezcla pastelera ❸ bateador ◆ vt ❶ pegar ❷ golpear
■ **batter down** vt ⚙ *El objeto se puede colocar antes o después de la preposición.* echar abajo

battered ['bætəd] adj ❶ maltratado, da ❷ abollado, da ❸ rebozado, da

battery ['bætərɪ] s ❶ pila ❷ batería (de coche)

battle ['bætl] ◆ s ❶ batalla ❷ **battle (for/against/with)** lucha (por/contra/con) ◆ vi • **to battle (for/against/with)** luchar (por/contra/con)

battlefield ['bætlfiːld], **battleground** ['bætlgraʊnd] s literal & figurado campo de batalla

battlements ['bætlmənts] spl almenas

battleship ['bætlʃɪp] s acorazado

bauble ['bɔːbl] s ❶ baratija ❷ bola de Navidad

bawl [bɔːl] vi ❶ vociferar ❷ berrear

bay [beɪ] s ❶ bahía ❷ zona de carga y descarga ❸ plaza
expresión **to keep something/somebody at bay** mantener algo/a alguien a raya

bay leaf s (hoja de) laurel

bazaar [bə'zɑːr] s bazar

BC (*abreviatura de* before Christ) a.C.

Bcc [,bi:si:'si:] (*abreviatura de* blind carbon copy) s Cco

be [bi:]
◆ *auxiliar*
❶ [*se usa con el gerundio para formar los tiempos progresivos*]
• **what is he doing?** ¿qué está haciendo?
• **it was snowing** estaba nevando; nevaba
• **they've been promising reform for years** llevan años prometiendo reformas
❷ [*se usa con el gerundio para formar el futuro*]
• **I'm going to Boston next week** voy a ir a Boston la próxima semana
• **I'll be coming back next Friday** volveré el próximo viernes
• **Paul's leaving tomorrow morning** Paul se va mañana por la mañana
❸ [*se usa con el participio pasado para formar la pasiva*] ser
• **to be loved** ser amado, a

❹ [*con las "coletillas"*]
• **the meal was delicious, wasn't it?** la cena estaba deliciosa, ¿no?
• **were you late? — no, I wasn't** ¿llegaste tarde? — no
❺ [*seguido de "to" + infinitivo*]
• **I'm to be promoted** me van a ascender
• **you're not to tell anyone** no se lo digas a nadie
• **there was no one to be seen** no había nadie
◆ v
❶ [*para describir algo o a alguien*] ser
• **to be a doctor** ser médico
• **she's attractive** es atractiva
• **he's fat** es gordo
• **she's Italian** es italiana
• **where are you from?** ¿de dónde eres?
❷ estar
• **how are you?** ¿cómo estás?
• **it's over there** está allá
• **Montreal is in Canada** Montreal está en Canadá
• **he's so fat I didn't recognize him** está tan gordo que no lo reconocí
❸ [*para describir un estado*] tener
• **she's hungry/thirsty** tiene hambre/sed
• **I'm hot/cold** tengo calor/frío
• **my hands are cold** tengo las manos frías
❹ [*con "there"*]
• **is there a café nearby?** ¿hay un café cerca?
❺ [*para expresar la edad*] tener
• **how old are you?** ¿cuántos años tienes?
• **I'm 20 (years old)** tengo 20 años
❻ [*para indicar el precio*] ser
• **how much was it?** ¿cuánto fue?
• **that will be $10, please** son 10 dólares, por favor
❼ [*para indicar la hora*] ser
• **it's two o'clock** son las dos
❽ [*para indicar la fecha*]
• **it's April first today** hoy es el primero de abril
❾ [*para hablar del tiempo*] hacer
• **it's hot/cold** hace calor/frío
• **it's windy** hace viento
❿ [*con "it", para identificar algo o a alguien*] ser
• **it's me/Paul** soy yo/Paul
⓫ [*en expresiones con "to have been to"*] estar
• **I've been to the movies** estuve en el cine
⓬ [*para indicar medida, distancia*]
• **how tall is he?** ¿cuánto mide?
• **the table is one meter long** la mesa tiene un metro de largo
• **it's 3 km to the next town** hay 3 km hasta el próximo pueblo
⓭ [*para dar una orden*]
• **be quiet!** ¡silencio!
• **be careful!** ¡cuidado!
expresión **be that as it may** así y todo • **there you are** ahí tienes

be

Presente: I am, you are, he/she/it is, we are, you are, they are.
Pretérito: I was, you were, he/she/it was, we were, you were, they were.
Gerundio: being.
Participio pasado: been.

Además de los significados que tiene como verbo normal, be funciona como verbo auxiliar, formando los tiempos continuos (why *are* you staring at me? *¿por qué me miras?*) y la voz pasiva de otros verbos (my suit *is being mended me están arreglando el traje*).

Hay que recordar que be puede traducirse por *ser* o *estar*.

No olvidemos tampoco que be suele traducirse por *tener* o *hacer* por ejemplo cuando el hablante se refiere a sensaciones y actitudes (I'm cold *tengo frío*; are you hungry? *¿tienes hambre?*; she's right *tiene razón*), o al clima (it's sunny *hace sol*).

Be to sirve para dar la idea de que alguien ha preparado un plan o una tarea para el sujeto de la oración (we're to meet at 10 o'clock *nos tenemos que reunir a las 10*). En pasado was to/were to, pueden expresar que algo estaba destinado a ocurrir (he *was to* become president at the age of 39 *iba a convertirse en presidente a los 39 años*).

Ver también go.

beach [biːtʃ] *s* playa

beacon ['biːkən] *s* **❶** almenara **❷** faro **❸** radiofaro

bead [biːd] *s* **❶** cuenta; abalorio **❷** gota

beak [biːk] *s* pico

beaker ['biːkər] *s* taza *(sin asa)*

beam [biːm] ◆ *s* **❶** viga **❷** rayo ◆ *vt* transmitir ◆ *vi* **❶** sonreír resplandeciente **❷** resplandecer

bean [biːn] *s* **❶** Cocina frijol • **green beans** ejotes **❷** grano

beansprout ['biːnspraʊt] *s* frijol germinado

bear [beər] ◆ *s* oso, sa ◆ *vt* **❶** soportar; aguantar **❷** cargar con *(responsabilidad)* **❸** llevar *(marca, insignia)* **❹** resistir; aguantar *(peso)* **❺** dar *(fruto, cultivo)* ◆ *vi* • **to bear left** torcer a la izquierda • **to bring pressure/influence to bear on** ejercer presión/influencia sobre

expresión to bear (something) in mind tener (algo) en cuenta

■ **bear up** *vi* resistir

■ **bear with** *vt* ☼ *El objeto siempre va después de la preposición al final.* tener paciencia con • **if you could just bear with me a moment...** si no le importa esperar un momento...

Formas irregulares de **bear**: *pretérito* **bore**, *pp* **borne**.

beard [bɪəd] *s* barba

bearer ['beərər] *s* **❶** portador, ra **❷** titular

bearing ['beərɪŋ] *s* **❶** • **bearing (on)** relación (con) **❷** rumbo

expresión to get your bearings orientarse ▶ to lose your bearings desorientarse

beast [biːst] *s literal & figurado* bestia

beat [biːt] ◆ *s* **❶** golpe **❷** latido **❸** Música ritmo **❹** golpe *(de compás)* **❺** ronda ◆ *vt* **❶** pegar; golpear; sacudir *(alfombra)* **❷** batir **❸** • **to beat somebody (at something)** ganar a alguien (a algo) **❹** ser mucho mejor que

expresión beat it! *familiar* ¡largo! ▶ it beats me *familiar* no me lo explico

◆ *vi* **❶** golpear **❷** latir **❸** redoblar

■ **beat up** *vt* ☼ *El objeto se puede colocar antes o después de la preposición.* *familiar* dar una paliza a

expresión to beat yourself up (about sth) castigarse (por algo)

■ **beat up on** *vt* ☼ *El objeto siempre va después de la preposición al final.* *familiar* dar una paliza a

Formas irregulares de **beat**: *pretérito* **beat**, *pp* **beaten**.

beating ['biːtɪŋ] *s* **❶** paliza **❷** derrota

beautiful ['bjuːtɪfʊl] *adj* **❶** bello, lla **❷** hermoso, sa **❸** *familiar* espléndido, da

beautifully ['bjuːtəflɪ] *adv* **❶** bellamente **❷** *familiar* espléndidamente

beauty ['bjuːtɪ] *s* belleza

beauty parlor, beauty salon *s* salón de belleza

beauty spot *s* **❶** bello paraje **❷** lunar

beaver ['biːvər] *s* castor

became [bɪˈkeɪm] *pretérito* → become

because [bɪˈkɒz] *conjunción* porque

■ **because of** *preposición* por; a causa de

beck [bek] *s*

expresión to be at somebody's beck and call estar siempre a disposición de alguien

beckon ['bekən] ◆ *vt* llamar (con un gesto) ◆ *vi* • **to beckon to somebody** llamar (con un gesto) a alguien

become [bɪˈkʌm] *vi* **❶** hacerse • **we've become great friends** nos hemos hecho muy amigos • **he's becoming more like his father** se parece cada vez más a su padre **❷** ponerse; volverse • **to become happy** ponerse contento • **to become suspicious** volverse receloso • **to become angry** enfadarse **❸** convertirse en • **he became president in 1991** en 1991 se convirtió en presidente

Formas irregulares de **become**: *pretérito* **became**, *pp* **become**.

bed [bed] *s* **❶** cama • **to get out of bed** levantarse • **to go to bed** irse a la cama • **to make the bed** hacer la cama • **to put somebody to bed** acostar a alguien **❷** macizo **❸** fondo **❹** lecho

expresión **a bed of roses** un lecho de rosas

bed and breakfast *s* **❶** cama y desayuno **❷** ≃ pensión

bedclothes ['bedkləʊðz] *spl* ropa de cama

bed linen *s* ropa de cama

bedraggled [bɪ'dræɡld] *adj* mojado y sucio, mojada y sucia

bedridden ['bed,rɪdn] *adj* postrado, da en cama

bedroom ['bedrʊm] *s* recámara

bedside ['bedsaɪd] *s* **❶** lado de la cama **❷** lecho

bedside table *s* buró

bedspread ['bedspred] *s* colcha

bedtime ['bedtaɪm] *s* hora de irse a la cama

bee [bi:] *s* abeja

beef [bi:f] *s* carne de res

■ **beef up** *vt* ⚡ *El objeto se puede colocar antes o después de la preposición. familiar* reforzar

beeline ['bi:laɪn] *s*

expresión **to make a beeline for** *familiar* irse derechito, ta hacia

been [bi:n] *participio pasado* → **be**

beer [bɪər] *s* cerveza

beet [bi:t] *s* **❶** betabel azucarero **❷** betabel

beetle ['bi:tl] *s* escarabajo

before [bɪ'fɔ:r] ◆ *adv* antes • **we went the year before** fuimos el año anterior ◆ *preposición* **❶** antes de • **I'll be back before midnight** volveré antes de la medianoche • **they arrived before us** llegaron antes que nosotros **❷** ante; delante de ◆ *conjunción* antes de • **before it's too late** antes de que sea demasiado tarde

beforehand [bɪ'fɔ:hænd] *adv* con antelación; de antemano

befriend [bɪ'frend] *vt* hacer amistad con

beg [beɡ] ◆ *vt* **❶** mendigar; pedir **❷** rogar • **to beg somebody to do something** rogar a alguien que haga algo • **to beg somebody for something** rogar algo a alguien ◆ *vi* **❶** • **to beg (for something)** pedir o mendigar (algo) **❷** • **to beg (for something)** rogar (algo)

expresión **I beg your pardon?** ¿perdón?

began [bɪ'ɡæn] *pretérito* → **begin**

beggar ['beɡər] *s* mendigo, ga

begin [bɪ'ɡɪn] ◆ *vt* • **to begin (doing** o **to do something)** empezar (a hacer algo) ◆ *vi* empezar; comenzar • **to begin with** para empezar; de entrada

Formas irregulares de **begin**: *pretérito* **began**, *pp* **begun**, *gerundio* **beginning**.

beginner [bɪ'ɡɪnər] *s* principiante

beginning [bɪ'ɡɪnɪŋ] *s* comienzo; principio • **at the beginning of the month** a principios de mes • **in the beginning** al principio

begrudge [bɪ'ɡrʌdʒ] *vt* **❶** • **to begrudge somebody something** envidiar a alguien algo **❷** • **to begrudge doing something** hacer algo de mala gana

begun [bɪ'ɡʌn] *participio pasado* → **begin**

behalf [bɪ'hɑ:f] *s* • **in behalf of** en nombre o en representación de • **he called in behalf of a friend** llamó de parte de un amigo

behave [bɪ'heɪv] ◆ *vt* • **to behave yourself** portarse bien ◆ *vi* **❶** comportarse; portarse • **how did he behave?** ¿cómo se portó? **❷** portarse bien • **to behave well/badly** portarse bien/mal

behavior [bɪ'heɪvjər] *s* comportamiento; conducta

behead [bɪ'hed] *vt* decapitar

behind [bɪ'haɪnd] ◆ *preposición* **❶** detrás de *(en el espacio, responsable de)* **❷** • **to be behind something/somebody** apoyar algo/a alguien **❸** • **to be behind schedule** ir retrasado, da ◆ *adv* **❶** detrás **❷** • **to be behind (with)** ir atrasado, da (con) **❸** por detrás *(con menos éxito)* ◆ *s familiar* trasero

beige [beɪʒ] *adj* beige

being ['bi:ɪŋ] *s* **❶** ser **❷** • **to come into being** ver la luz; nacer

belated [bɪ'leɪtɪd] *adj* tardío, a

belch [beltʃ] ◆ *vt* arrojar ◆ *vi* **❶** eructar **❷** brotar

Belgian ['beldʒən] ◆ *adj* belga ◆ *s* belga

Belgium ['beldʒəm] *s* Bélgica

belief [bɪ'li:f] *s* **❶** • **belief (in)** creencia (en) **❷** opinión

believe [bɪ'li:v] ◆ *vt* creer

expresión **believe it or not** lo creas o no

◆ *vi* • **to believe in** creer en

believer [bɪ'li:vər] *s* **❶** creyente **❷** • **believer in something** partidario, ria de algo

bell [bel] *s* **❶** campana **❷** campanilla **❸** timbre

bellhop ['belhɒp] *s* botones *(en hotel)*

belligerent [bɪ'lɪdʒərənt] *adj* **❶** beligerante **❷** belicoso, sa

bellow ['beləʊ] *vi* **❶** rugir **❷** bramar

bellows ['beləʊz] *spl* fuelle

belly ['belɪ] *s* barriga; vientre

bellyache ['belɪeɪk] *familiar* ◆ *s* dolor de barriga ◆ *vi* gruñir

belly button *s familiar* ombligo

belong [bɪ'lɒŋ] *vi* **❶** • **to belong to a)** pertenecer a **b)** ser miembro de **❷** • **where does this book belong?** ¿dónde va este libro? • **put it back where it belongs** vuélvelo a poner en su lugar • **he felt he didn't belong there** *figurado* sintió que no encajaba allí

belongings [bɪ'lɒŋɪŋz] *spl* pertenencias

beloved [bɪ'lʌvd] ◆ *adj* querido, da ◆ *s* amado, da

B

below [bɪ'ləʊ] ◆ *adv* ❶ abajo • **the apartment below** el departamento de abajo ❷ más abajo • **see below** véase más abajo ◆ *preposición* ❶ debajo de; bajo ❷ por debajo de *(con números)* ❸ • **thirty degrees below zero** treinta grados bajo cero

belt [belt] ◆ *s* ❶ cinturón ❷ TECNOLOGÍA cinta ❸ correa ◆ *vt familiar* arrear

beltway ['belt,weɪ] *s* carretera de circunvalación

bemused [bɪ'mju:zd] *adj* perplejo, ja

bench [bentʃ] ◆ *s* ❶ banca ❷ mesa de trabajo ❸ banca ◆ *vt* DEPORTE mandar a la banca

bend [bend] ◆ *s* curva ◆ *vt* doblar ◆ *vi* agacharse

expresión to bend over backwards for hacer todo lo humanamente posible por

Formas irregulares de **bend**: *pretérito & pp* **bent**.

beneath [bɪ'ni:θ] ◆ *adv* debajo ◆ *preposición* ❶ debajo de; bajo ❷ indigno, na de

beneficial [,benɪ'fɪʃl] *adj* • **beneficial (to)** beneficioso, sa (para)

beneficiary [,benɪ'fɪʃərɪ] *s* ❶ DERECHO beneficiario, ria ❷ beneficiado, da

benefit ['benɪfɪt] ◆ *s* ❶ ventaja • **for the benefit of** en atención a • **to be to somebody's benefit, to be of benefit to somebody** ir en beneficio de alguien ❷ ADMINISTRACIÓN subsidio ◆ *vt* beneficiar ◆ *vi* • **to benefit from** beneficiarse de

benign [bɪ'naɪn] *adj* ❶ bondadoso, sa ❷ MEDICINA benigno, na

bent [bent] ◆ *pretérito & participio pasado* → **bend** ◆ *adj* ❶ torcido, da ❷ encorvado, da ❸ • **to be bent on something/on doing something** estar empeñado, da en algo/en hacer algo

bereaved [bɪ'ri:vd] *s* • **the bereaved** la familia del difunto

El plural de **bereaved** es **bereaved**.

beret ['bereɪ] *s* boina

berm [bɜ:m] *s* acotamiento

Bermuda [bə'mju:də] *s* las Bermudas

berry ['berɪ] *s* baya

berserk [bə'zɜ:k] *adj* • **to go berserk** ponerse hecho, cha una fiera

berth [bɜ:θ] ◆ *s* ❶ amarradero; atracadero ❷ litera ◆ *vt & vi* atracar

beseech [bɪ'si:tʃ] *vt literario* • **to beseech (somebody to do something)** suplicar (a alguien que haga algo)

Formas irregulares de **beseech**: *pretérito & pp* **besought** o **beseeched**.

beset [bɪ'set] *adj* • **beset with** o **by** a) acosado, da por b) plagado, da de

Formas irregulares de **beset**: *pretérito & pp* **beset**.

beside [bɪ'saɪd] *preposición* ❶ al lado de; junto a ❷ comparado, da con

expresiones that's beside the point eso no importa ▶ to be beside yourself with rage estar fuera de sí ▶ to be beside yourself with joy estar loco, ca de alegría

besides [bɪ'saɪdz] ◆ *adv* además ◆ *preposición* aparte de

besiege [bɪ'si:dʒ] *vt literal & figurado* asediar

besought [bɪ'sɔ:t] *pretérito & participio pasado* → **beseech**

best [best] ◆ *adj* mejor • **best before...** consumir preferentemente antes de... ◆ *adv* mejor • **which did you like best?** ¿cuál te gustó más? ◆ *s* • **she's the best** es la mejor • **we're the best** somos los mejores • **to do your best** hacerlo lo mejor que uno puede

expresión to make the best of something sacarle el mayor partido posible a algo ▶ **for the best** para bien

■ **at best** *adv* en el mejor de los casos

best man *s* ≃ padrino de boda

best-seller *s* best seller; éxito editorial

bet [bet] ◆ *s* ❶ • **bet (on)** apuesta (a) ❷ *figurado* predicción

expresión to hedge your bets cubrirse; guardarse las espaldas

◆ *vt* apostar • **I bet you can't do it** apuesto a que no puedes hacerlo ◆ *vi* ❶ • **to bet (on)** apostar (a) ❷ • **to bet on something** contar con (que pase) algo

expresión you bet! *familiar* ¡ya lo creo!

Formas irregulares de **bet**: *pretérito & pp* **bet** o **betted**.

betray [bɪ'treɪ] *vt* ❶ traicionar ❷ revelar ❸ delatar

betrayal [bɪ'treɪəl] *s* ❶ traición ❷ revelación

better ['betər] ◆ *adj* ⚙ *comparativo de "good"* mejor • **to get better** mejorar ◆ *adv* ⚙ *comparativo de "well"* ❶ mejor • **I feel much better now** ahora me siento mucho mejor ❷ • **I like it better** me gusta más ❸ • **we had better be going** más vale que nos vayamos ya ◆ *s* mejor

expresión to get the better of somebody poder con alguien

◆ *vt* mejorar • **to better yourself** mejorarse

better off *adj* ❶ mejor de dinero ❷ • **you'd be better off not going** más te valdría no ir

betting ['betɪŋ] *s* ⚙ *incontable* apuestas

between [bɪ'twi:n] ◆ *preposición* entre • **closed between 1 and 2** cerrado de 1 a 2 ◆ *adv* • **(in) between** en medio; entremedio

beverage ['bevərɪdʒ] *s formal* bebida

beware [bɪ'weər] *vi* • **to beware (of)** tener cuidado (con) • **'beware of the dog!'** ¡cuidado con el perro!'

bewildered [bɪ'wɪldəd] *adj* desconcertado, da

beyond [bɪ'jɒnd] ◆ *preposición* más allá de • **beyond midnight** pasada la medianoche ◆ *adv* más allá

expresión it's beyond me! ¡no lo puedo entender!

bias ['baɪəs] *s* ❶ prejuicio ❷ tendencia; inclinación

biased ['baɪəst] *adj* parcial • **to be biased towards/against** tener prejuicios en favor/en contra de

bib [bɪb] *s* babero

Bible ['baɪbl] *s* • **the Bible** la Biblia

bicarbonate of soda [baɪˈkɑːbənət-] *s* bicarbonato sódico

biceps ['baɪseps] *s* bíceps

El plural de **biceps** es **biceps**.

bicker ['bɪkər] *vi* reñir

bicycle ['baɪsɪkl] ◆ *s* bicicleta ◆ *en compuestos* de bicicleta

bicycle path *s* ciclovía

bicycle pump *s* bomba de bicicleta

bid [bɪd] ◆ *s* ❶ • **bid (for)** intento (de hacerse con) ❷ puja ❸ • **bid (for something)** oferta (para adquirir algo) ◆ *vt* ❶ (*pretérito & pp* bid) ofrecer ❷ pujar

bide [baɪd] *vt* • **to bide your time** esperar el momento oportuno

bifocals [ˌbaɪˈfəʊklz] *spl* gafas bifocales

big [bɪg] *adj* ❶ grande • **a big problem** un gran problema ❷ mayor *(hermano, hermana)* ❸ popular

Big Apple

The Big Apple, que significa La Gran Manzana, es el apodo de la ciudad de Nueva York. Este nombre lo utilizaron originalmente los músicos de jazz de los años veinte, refiriéndose al éxito que podrían obtener en esta ciudad. Otras ciudades estadounidenses, como Chicago y Detroit, también tienen apodos: **the Windy City** apodo de la primera, por los fuertes vientos que soplan ahí, y **Motown** de la segunda, por el sello discográfico y la música del mismo nombre.

big deal *familiar* ◆ *s* • **it's no big deal** no tiene (la menor) importancia ◆ *exclamación* ¡y a mí qué!

bigheaded [ˌbɪgˈhedɪd] *adj familiar & despectivo* creído, da

bigot ['bɪgət] *s* intolerante

bigoted ['bɪgətɪd] *adj* intolerante

big time *familiar* ◆ *s* • **the big time** el éxito; la fama ◆ *adv* en grande • **they've messed it up big time** lo estropearon en grande

big toe *s* dedo gordo (del pie)

big top *s* carpa

bike [baɪk] *s* ❶ *familiar* bici ❷ moto

bikeway ['baɪkweɪ] *s* ciclovía

bikini [bɪˈkiːnɪ] *s* bikini

bilingual [baɪˈlɪŋgwəl] *adj* bilingüe

bill [bɪl] ◆ *s* ❶ • **bill (for)** a) cuenta (de) b) factura (de) ❷ proyecto de ley ❸ programa ❹ billete ❺ • 'post o stick no bills' 'prohibido fijar carteles' ❻ pico ◆ *vt* • **to bill somebody for** mandar la factura a alguien por

billboard ['bɪlbɔːd] *s* cartelera

billfold ['bɪlfəʊld] *s* cartera

billiards ['bɪljədz] *s* billar

billion ['bɪljən] *número* mil millones • **three billion dollars** tres mil millones de dólares

Bill of Rights *s* • **the Bill of Rights** las diez primeras enmiendas de la Constitución estadounidense

bimbo ['bɪmbəʊ] *s familiar & despectivo* niña tonta

Dos plurales: **bimbos** o **bimboes**.

bin [bɪn] *s* ❶ papelera ❷ depósito

bind [baɪnd] *vt* ❶ atar ❷ unir ❸ vendar ❹ encuadernar ❺ obligar

Formas irregulares de **bind**: *pretérito & pp* **bound**.

binder ['baɪndər] *s* carpeta

binding ['baɪndɪŋ] ◆ *adj* obligatorio, ria ◆ *s* cubierta; tapa

binge [bɪndʒ] *s familiar* • **to go on a binge** irse de juerga

bingo ['bɪŋgəʊ] *s* bingo

binoculars [bɪˈnɒkjʊləz] *spl* binoculares • **a pair of binoculars** unos binoculares

biochemistry [ˌbaɪəʊˈkemɪstrɪ] *s* bioquímica

biodegradable [ˌbaɪəʊdɪˈgreɪdəbl] *adj* biodegradable

biography [baɪˈɒgrəfɪ] *s* biografía

biological [ˌbaɪəˈlɒdʒɪkl] *adj* biológico, ca

biological mother *s* madre biológica

biology [baɪˈɒlədʒɪ] *s* biología

bioterrorism [ˌbaɪəʊˈterərɪzm] *s* bioterrorismo

biowarfare [ˌbaɪəʊˈwɔːfeər] *s* guerra biológica

bipolar disorder [baɪˈpəʊlədɪsˌɔːdər] *s* MEDICINA trastorno bipolar

birch [bɜːtʃ] *s* abedul

bird [bɜːd] *s* ave; pájaro

bird of prey *s* ave de rapiña

bird's-eye view *s* vista panorámica

bird-watcher [-ˌwɒtʃər] *s* observador, ra de pájaros

Biro® ['baɪərəʊ] *s* pluma atómica

birth [bɜːθ] *s* ❶ nacimiento • **by birth** de nacimiento ❷ parto • **to give birth (to)** dar a luz (a)

birth certificate *s* acta de nacimiento

birth control *s* metodo anticonceptivo

birthday ['bɜːθdeɪ] *s* cumpleaños • **happy birthday!** ¡feliz cumpleaños!

birthmark ['bɜːθmɑːk] *s* antojo

birth mother *s* madre biológica

birthrate ['bɜːθreɪt] *s* índice de natalidad

Biscay ['bɪskɪ] *s* • **the Bay of Biscay** el golfo de Vizcaya

biscuit ['bɪskɪt] *s* bisquet

bisect [baɪˈsekt] *vt* ❶ dividir en dos ❷ MATEMÁTICAS bisecar

bishop ['bɪʃəp] *s* ❶ obispo ❷ alfil

bison ['baɪsn] *s* bisonte

Dos plurales: **bison** o **bisons**.

B

bit [bɪt] ◆ *pretérito* → **bite** ◆ *s* ❶ trozo ; pedazo • **to take something to bits** desmontar algo ❷ • **a bit of** un poco de • **a bit of advice** un consejo • **a bit of news** una noticia • **a bit of shopping** algunas compras • **quite a bit of** bastante ❸ *INFORMÁTICA* bit

■ **a bit** ◆ *adv* un poco • **a bit easier** un poco más fácil • **wait a bit** espera un poco ◆ *pronombre* un poco • **do you want more soup? — just a bit, thanks** ¿quieres más sopa? — una poca, gracias

■ **bit by bit** *adv* poco a poco

a bit

A bit puede ser un adverbio (he's *a bit* shy es *un poco* tímido) o un pronombre (would you like some cake? — yes, just *a bit* ¿quieres pastel? — sí, *un poco*). Cuando va delante de un sustantivo se añade of (*a bit of* air *un poco de aire*).

A bit y a bit of significan lo mismo que a little, pero en un lenguaje menos formal.

bitch [bɪtʃ] ◆ *s* ❶ perra ❷ *muy familiar & despectivo* bruja ◆ *vi familiar* • **to bitch about** poner a parir a

bitchy ['bɪtʃɪ] *adj familiar* malicioso, sa

bite [baɪt] ◆ *s* ❶ mordisco ❷ picotazo ❸ *familiar* • **to have a bite (to eat)** comer algo ❹ mordedura ❺ piquete ◆ *vt* ❶ morder • **to bite your nails** comerse las uñas ❷ picar ◆ *vi* ❶ • **to bite (into something)** morder (algo) ❷ picar

> Formas irregulares de bite: *pretérito* bit, *pp* bitten.

biting ['baɪtɪŋ] *adj* ❶ gélido, da ; cortante ❷ mordaz

bitten ['bɪtn] *participio pasado* → bite

bitter ['bɪtər] *adj* ❶ amargo, ga ❷ gélido, da ❸ enconado, da ❹ amargado, da

bitter lemon *s* bíter de limón

bitterness ['bɪtənɪs] *s* ❶ amargor ❷ gelidez ❸ amargura

bizarre [bɪ'zɑːr] *adj* ❶ extravagante ❷ singular ; extraordinario, ria

blab [blæb] *vi familiar* irse de la lengua

black [blæk] ◆ *adj* negro, gra • **black and white** en blanco y negro • **a black coffee** un café negro
expresión **black and blue** amoratado, da

◆ *s* ❶ negro *(color)* ❷ negro, gra *(persona)*
expresión **in black and white** por escrito ▶ **to be in the black** tener saldo positivo

■ **black out** *vi* desmayarse

blackberry ['blækbərɪ] *s* ❶ mora ❷ zarzamora

blackbird ['blækbɜːd] *s* mirlo

blackboard ['blækbɔːd] *s* pizarrón

blackcurrant [ˌblæk'kʌrənt] *s* grosella negra

blacken ['blækn] *vt* ❶ ennegrecer ❷ manchar

black eye *s* ojo morado

blackhead ['blækhed] *s* barrillo

black ice *s* ▶ hielo transparente en las carreteras

blacklist ['blæklɪst] *s* lista negra

blackmail ['blækmeɪl] *literal & figurado* ◆ *s* chantaje ◆ *vt* chantajear

black market *s* mercado negro

blackout ['blækaʊt] *s* ❶ apagón ❷ censura ❸ desmayo

black sheep *s* oveja negra

blacksmith ['blæksmɪθ] *s* herrero

black spot *s* punto negro

bladder ['blædər] *s ANATOMÍA* vejiga

blade [bleɪd] *s* ❶ hoja ❷ aleta ; paleta ❸ brizna

blame [bleɪm] ◆ *s* culpa • **to take the blame for** hacerse responsable de • **to be to blame for** ser el culpable de • **who's to blame?** ¿quién tiene la culpa? ◆ *vt* echar la culpa a ; culpar • **to blame somebody for something** culpar a alguien de algo

bland [blænd] *adj* soso, sa

blank [blæŋk] ◆ *adj* ❶ en blanco ❷ virgen ❸ *figurado* vacío, a ◆ *s* ❶ espacio en blanco ❷ *MILITAR* cartucho de fogueo
expresión **my mind went blank** me quedé en blanco

blank cheque *s* cheque en blanco

blanket ['blæŋkɪt] *s* ❶ cobija ❷ manto

blare [bleər] *vi* resonar ; sonar

blasé [ˌblɑː'zeɪ] *adj* • **to be blasé about** ser indiferente a

blasphemy ['blæsfəmɪ] *s* blasfemia

blast [blɑːst] ◆ *s* ❶ explosión ❷ ráfaga • **we had a blast** la pasamos genial ◆ *vt* perforar *(con explosivos)*

■ **(at) full blast** *adv* a todo trapo

blasted ['blɑːstɪd] *adj familiar* maldito, ta

blast-off *s* despegue

blatant ['bleɪtənt] *adj* descarado, da

blaze [bleɪz] ◆ *s* ❶ incendio ❷ *figurado* explosión • **a blaze of publicity** una ola de publicidad ◆ *vi literal & figurado* arder

blazer ['bleɪzər] *s* ▶ chaqueta de sport generalmente con la insignia de un equipo, colegio, etc

bleach [bliːtʃ] ◆ *s* lejía ◆ *vt* ❶ blanquear ❷ desteñir

bleached [bliːtʃt] *adj* ❶ teñido, da de rubio ❷ desteñido, da

bleachers ['bliːtʃəz] *spl DEPORTE* gradas

bleak [bliːk] *adj* ❶ negro, gra ❷ sombrío, a ❸ desapacible

bleat [bliːt] *vi* balar

bleed [bliːd] *vi* sangrar

> Formas irregulares de bleed: *pretérito & pp* bled.

blemish ['blemɪʃ] *s* ❶ señal ; marca ❷ *figurado* mancha

blend [blend] ◆ *s* ❶ mezcla ❷ *INFORMÁTICA* degradado ◆ *vt* • **to blend (something with something)**

mezclar (algo con algo) ◆ *vi* • **to blend (with)** combinarse (con)

blender ['blendər] *s* licuadora

bless [bles] *vt* RELIGIÓN bendecir

expresión bless you! a) ¡salud! **b)** ¡gracias!

Formas irregulares de **bless**: *pretérito & pp* **blessed** o **blest.**

blessing ['blesıŋ] *s* ❶ RELIGIÓN bendición ❷ *figurado* aprobación

blest [blest] *pretérito* & *participio pasado* → **bless**

blew [blu:] *pretérito* → **blow**

blind [blaınd] ◆ *adj* ciego, ga • **a blind man** un ciego • **to go blind** quedarse ciego ◆ *s* persiana ◆ *spl* • **the blind** los ciegos ◆ *vt* ❶ dejar ciego, ga ❷ cegar • **to blind somebody to something** *figurado* no dejar a alguien ver algo

blind date *s* cita a ciegas

blinders ['blaındəz] *spl* anteojeras

blindfold ['blaındfəʊld] ◆ *adv* con los ojos vendados ◆ *s* venda ◆ *vt* vendar los ojos a

blindly ['blaındlı] *adv* ❶ a ciegas ❷ *figurado* a boleo ❸ ciegamente

blindness ['blaındnıs] *s literal & figurado* • **blindness (to)** ceguera (ante)

blind spot *s* ❶ ángulo muerto ❷ *figurado* punto débil

blink [blıŋk] ◆ *vt* ❶ • **to blink your eyes** parpadear ❷ AUTOMÓVILES • **to blink your lights** dar las luces (intermitentemente) ◆ *vi* parpadear

bliss [blıs] *s* gloria; dicha

blister ['blıstər] *s* ampolla

blizzard ['blızəd] *s* ventisca (de nieve)

blob [blɒb] *s* ❶ gota ❷ bulto borroso

block [blɒk] ◆ *s* ❶ bloque ❷ cuadra ❸ bloqueo ◆ *vt* ❶ bloquear *(carretera)* ❷ obstruir ❸ tapar • **my nose is blocked** tengo la nariz tapada ❹ tapar ❺ bloquear; obstaculizar ❻ INFORMÁTICA • **to block a stretch of text** seleccionar un bloque de texto

blockage ['blɒkıdʒ] *s* obstrucción

blockbuster ['blɒkbʌstər] *s* ❶ *familiar* (gran) éxito editorial ❷ (gran) éxito de taquilla

block capitals *spl* mayúsculas *(de imprenta)*

block letters *spl* mayúsculas *(de imprenta)*

blond [blɒnd] *adj* rubio, bia

blonde [blɒnd] ◆ *adj* rubia ◆ *s* rubia

blood [blʌd] *s* sangre

expresión in cold blood a sangre fría ▶ **new** o **fresh blood** savia nueva

blood cell *s* glóbulo

blood donor *s* donante de sangre

blood group *s* grupo sanguíneo

blood pressure *s* tensión arterial • **to have high/low blood pressure** tener la tensión alta/baja

bloodshed ['blʌdʃed] *s* derramamiento de sangre

bloodshot ['blʌdʃɒt] *adj* inyectado, da (de sangre)

bloodstream ['blʌdstri:m] *s* flujo sanguíneo

blood test *s* análisis de sangre

blood transfusion *s* transfusión de sangre

bloody ['blʌdı] *adj* ❶ sangriento, ta ❷ ensangrentado, da

bloom [blu:m] ◆ *s* flor • **in bloom** en flor ◆ *vi* florecer

blossom ['blɒsəm] ◆ *s* flor • **in blossom** en flor ◆ *vi literal & figurado* florecer

blot [blɒt] ◆ *s* ❶ borrón ❷ *figurado* mancha ◆ *vt* ❶ emborronar ❷ secar

blotting paper ['blɒtıŋ-] *s* ⚙*incontable* papel secante

blouse [blaʊz] *s* blusa

blow [bləʊ] ◆ *vi* ❶ soplar ❷ salir volando; volar ❸ fundirse ◆ *vt* ❶ hacer volar ❷ tocar; hacer sonar ❸ hacer *(burbujas)* ❹ mandar *(beso)* ❺ fundir ❻ • **to blow your nose** sonarse la nariz ❼ *familiar* despilfarrar *(dinero)* ❽ *familiar* echar a perder ◆ *s* golpe

■ **blow out** ◆ *vt* ⚙*El objeto se puede colocar antes o después de la preposición.* apagar ◆ *vi* ❶ apagarse ❷ reventar

■ **blow over** *vi* ❶ amainar ❷ calmarse

■ **blow up** ◆ *vt* ⚙*El objeto se puede colocar antes o después de la preposición.* ❶ inflar ❷ volar ❸ ampliar ◆ *vi* saltar por los aires; explotar

Formas irregulares de **blow**: *pretérito* **blew**, *pp* **blown.**

blow-dry *s* secado *(con secador)*

blown [bləʊn] *participio pasado* → **blow**

blowout ['bləʊaʊt] *s* pinchazo; reventón

blowtorch ['bləʊtɔ:tʃ] *s* soplete

blubber ['blʌbər] *vi despectivo* lloriquear

blue [blu:] ◆ *adj* ❶ azul ❷ *familiar* triste ❸ equis; porno ❹ colorado *(broma)* ◆ *s* azul • **out of the blue** en el momento menos pensado

■ **blues** *spl* • **the blues a)** MÚSICA el blues **b)** *familiar* la depre

blueberry ['blu:bərı] *s* arándano • **a blueberry pie** un pay de arándano

bluebottle ['blu:ˌbɒtl] *s* moscardón; moscón

blue cheese *s* queso azul

blue-collar *adj* • **blue-collar worker** obrero, ra

blue jeans *spl* jeans; pantalones de mezclilla

blueprint ['blu:prınt] *s figurado* proyecto

bluff [blʌf] ◆ *s* blof ◆ *vi* blofear

blunder ['blʌndər] ◆ *s* metida de pata ◆ *vi* ❶ meter la pata ❷ ir tropezando • **to blunder into something** tropezar con algo

blunt [blʌnt] *adj* ❶ desafilado, da ❷ romo, ma ❸ directo, ta; franco, ca

B

blur [blɜ:r] ◆ *s* imagen borrosa ◆ *vt* ❶ nublar ❷ desdibujar

blurb [blɜ:b] *s familiar* texto publicitario en la cubierta o solapa de un libro

blurt [blɜ:t] ■ **blurt out** *vt* ☼ *El objeto se puede colocar antes o después de la preposición.* espetar; decir de repente

blush [blʌʃ] ◆ *s* rubor ◆ *vi* ruborizarse; ponerse colorado, da

blusher ['blʌʃər] *s* colorete

BMX (*abreviatura de* bicycle motorcross) *s* ciclocross

BO (*abreviatura de* body odor) *s* � ● olor a sudor

boar [bɔ:r] *s* ❶ verraco ❷ jabalí

board [bɔ:d] ◆ *s* ❶ tabla ❷ tablero (*de anuncios, juegos*) ❸ pizarrón ❹ tablero de mensajes ❺ INFORMÁTICA placa ❻ ● **board (of directors)** junta directiva ❼ comité; junta ❽ • **on board a)** a bordo **b)** dentro **expresión above board** en regla ◆ *vt* ❶ embarcar en ❷ subirse a

boarder ['bɔ:dər] *s* ❶ huésped ❷ interno, na

board game *s* juego de mesa

boarding card ['bɔ:dɪŋ-] *s* tarjeta de embarque

boardinghouse ['bɔ:dɪŋhaʊs] *s* casa de huéspedes

boarding school ['bɔ:dɪŋ-] *s* internado

boardroom ['bɔ:drʊm] *s* sala de juntas

boardwalk ['bɔ:dwɔ:k] *s* ● paseo marítimo entarimado

boast [bəʊst] *vi* • **to boast (about)** alardear o jactarse (de)

boastful ['bəʊstfʊl] *adj* fanfarrón, ona

boat [bəʊt] *s* ❶ barco • **by boat** en barco ❷ lancha

bob [bɒb] ◆ *s* ❶ corte de chico ❷ = bobsleigh ◆ *vi* balancearse

bobby pin *s* pasador

bobsleigh ['bɒbsleɪ], **bob** *s* bobsleigh

bode [bəʊd] *vi literario* • **to bode ill/well for** traer malos/buenos presagios para

body ['bɒdɪ] *s* ❶ cuerpo ❷ cadáver ❸ entidad • **a body of thought/opinion** una corriente de pensamiento/opinión ❹ carrocería ❺ fuselaje ❻ body (*prenda*)

body building *s* fisiculturismo

bodyguard ['bɒdɪgɑ:d] *s* guardaespaldas; guarura

body language *s* lenguaje corporal

body odor *s* olor corporal

body piercing *s* piercing

bog [bɒg] *s* cenagal

bogged down [,bɒgd-] *adj* ❶ • **bogged down (in)** empantanado, da (en) ❷ • **bogged down in** atascado, da en

bogus ['bəʊgəs] *adj* falso, sa

boil [bɔɪl] ◆ *s* ❶ MEDICINA pústula ❷ • **to bring something to the boil** hacer que algo hierva • **to come to the boil** romper a hervir • **to boil the kettle** poner el agua a hervir ❷ cocer ◆ *vi* hervir

■ **boil down to** *vt* ☼ *El objeto siempre va después de la preposición al final.* reducirse a

boiled [bɔɪld] *adj* cocido, da • **boiled egg a)** huevo duro **b)** huevo pasado por agua

boiler ['bɔɪlər] *s* caldera

boiling ['bɔɪlɪŋ] *adj familiar* • **I'm boiling** estoy asado, da de calor • **it's boiling** hace un calor de muerte

boiling point *s* punto de ebullición

bold [bəʊld] *adj* ❶ audaz ❷ marcado, da ❸ vivo, va ❹ TIPOGRAFÍA • **bold type** o **print** negrita

Bolivia [bə'lɪvɪə] *s* Bolivia

Bolivian [bə'lɪvɪən] ◆ *adj* boliviano, na ◆ *s* boliviano, na

bollard ['bɒlɑ:d] *s* poste

bolt [bəʊlt] ◆ *s* ❶ cerrojo ❷ perno ◆ *adv* • **bolt upright** muy derecho, cha ◆ *vt* ❶ atornillar ❷ echar el cerrojo a ❸ tragarse ◆ *vi* salir disparado, da

bomb [bɒm] ◆ *s* ❶ bomba ❷ *familiar* desastre ◆ *vt* bombardear ◆ *vi familiar* fracasar estrepitosamente

bombard [bɒm'bɑ:d] *vt literal & figurado* • **to bombard (with)** bombardear (a)

bomb disposal squad *s* equipo de artificieros

bomber ['bɒmər] *s* ❶ bombardero ❷ terrorista que pone bombas

bombing ['bɒmɪŋ] *s* bombardeo

bomb scare *s* amenaza de bomba

bond [bɒnd] ◆ *s* ❶ lazo; vínculo ❷ FINANZAS bono ◆ *vt* ❶ adherir ❷ *figurado* unir

bone [bəʊn] ◆ *s* ❶ hueso ❷ raspa; espina **expresión to make no bones about doing something** no tener ningún reparo en hacer algo ◆ *vt* ❶ quitar las espinas a ❷ deshuesar

bonnet ['bɒnɪt] *s* toca

bonus ['bəʊnəs] *s* ❶ prima ❷ plus ❸ *figurado* beneficio adicional

El plural de **bonus** es **bonuses**.

bony ['bəʊnɪ] *adj* ❶ huesudo, da ❷ lleno, na de huesos ❸ espinoso, sa

boo [bu:] ◆ *exclamación* ¡bu! ◆ *s* abucheo ◆ *vt* & *vi* abuchear

El plural de **boo** es **boos**.

boob [bu:b] *s familiar* metedura de pata

boob tube *s familiar* caja idiota

booby trap ['bu:bɪ-] *s* bomba camuflada

book [bʊk] ◆ *s* ❶ libro ❷ librillo ❸ talonario ❹ librito (*de cerillos*) ◆ *vt* ❶ reservar • **to be fully booked** estar lleno ❷ *familiar* multar ◆ *vi* hacer reserva

■ **books** *spl* COMERCIO libros

expresión to be in somebody's good/bad books estar a bien/a mal con alguien

B

■ **book up** *vt* ☼ *El objeto se puede colocar antes o después de la preposición.* • **to be booked up** estar lleno

bookcase [ˈbʊkkeɪs] *s* librero

bookkeeping [ˈbʊk,kiːpɪŋ] *s* contabilidad

booklet [ˈbʊklɪt] *s* folleto

bookmaker [ˈbʊk,meɪkər] *s* corredor, ra de apuestas

bookmark [ˈbʊkmɑːk] ◆ *s* ❶ separador ❷ INFOR-MÁTICA marcador ◆ *vt* INFORMÁTICA añadir un marcador a

bookseller [ˈbʊk,selər] *s* librero, ra

bookshelf [ˈbʊkʃelf] *s* ❶ estante ❷ librero

El plural de bookshelf es bookshelves [ˈbʊkʃelvz].

bookstore [ˈbʊkstɔːr] *s* librería

boom [buːm] ◆ *s* ❶ estampido ❷ auge ; boom ◆ *vi* ❶ tronar ❷ ECONOMÍA estar en auge

boost [buːst] ◆ *s* ❶ incremento ❷ empujón ◆ *vt* ❶ incrementar ❷ levantar *(los ánimos)*

boot [buːt] ◆ *s* ❶ bota ❷ botín ◆ *vt* ❶ *familiar* dar una patada a ❷ INFORMÁTICA arrancar

■ **boot out** *vt* ☼ *El objeto se puede colocar antes o después de la preposición. familiar* correr ; poner (de patitas) en la calle

■ **boot up** *vt* ☼ *El objeto se puede colocar antes o después de la preposición.* INFORMÁTICA arrancar

booth [buːð] *s* ❶ puesto ❷ cabina

booty [ˈbuːtɪ] *s* ❶ botín ❷ *familiar* • **to get some booty** echarse un caldito

booze [buːz] *familiar* ◆ *s* ☼ *incontable* trago ◆ *vi* tomar ; empinar el codo

bop [bɒp] *familiar* ◆ *s* ❶ disco ❷ baile ◆ *vi* bailar

border [ˈbɔːdər] ◆ *s* ❶ frontera ❷ borde ❸ arriate ◆ *vt* ❶ limitar con ❷ bordear

■ **border on** *vt* ☼ *El objeto siempre va después de la preposición al final.* rayar en

borderline [ˈbɔːdəlaɪn] ◆ *adj* • **a borderline case** un caso dudoso ◆ *s figurado* límite

bore [bɔːr] ◆ *pretérito* → **bear** ◆ *s* ❶ *despectivo* pesado, da ❷ rollo ; lata ◆ *vt* ❶ aburrir ❷ taladrar

expresión **to bore somebody stiff** o **to tears** o **to death** aburrir a alguien muchísimo

bored [bɔːd] *adj* aburrido, da

expresión **to be bored stiff** o **to tears** o **to death** aburrirse muchísimo

boredom [ˈbɔːdəm] *s* aburrimiento

boring [ˈbɔːrɪŋ] *adj* aburrido, da

born [bɔːn] *adj* ❶ nacido, da • **to be born** nacer ❷ nato, ta

borne [bɔːn] *participio pasado* → **bear**

borough [ˈbʌrə] *s* ❶ distrito ❷ municipio

borrow [ˈbɒrəʊ] *vt* • **to borrow something from somebody** tomar algo prestado a alguien • **can I borrow your bike?** ¿me prestas tu bici? • **I had to bor-**

row the book from the library tuve que sacar el libro de la biblioteca

Bosnia [ˈbɒznɪə] *s* Bosnia

Bosnia-Herzegovina [-,hɜːtsəgəˈviːnə] *s* Bosnia-Hercegovina

Bosnian [ˈbɒznɪən] ◆ *adj* bosnio, nia ◆ *s* bosnio, nia

bosom [ˈbʊzəm] *s* busto ; pecho

boss [bɒs] ◆ *s* jefe, fa ◆ *vt despectivo* mangonear ; dar órdenes a

■ **boss about, boss around** *vt* ☼ *El objeto se puede colocar antes o después de la preposición. despectivo* mangonear ; dar órdenes a

bossy [ˈbɒsɪ] *adj* mandón, ona

botany [ˈbɒtənɪ] *s* botánica

botch [bɒtʃ] ■ **botch up** *vt* ☼ *El objeto se puede colocar antes o después de la preposición. familiar* estropear

both [bəʊθ] ◆ *adj* los dos ; las dos ; ambos, bas ◆ *pronombre* • **both (of them)** los dos, las dos ; ambos, bas • **both of us are coming** vamos los dos ◆ *adv* • **she is both pretty and intelligent** es linda e inteligente

both

Both funciona como adjetivo cuando va delante de un sustantivo contable en plural (*both girls are clever las dos niñas son inteligentes*), o de dos sustantivos contables en singular (*both my brother and my sister are coming ambos mi hermano y hermana vendrán*). En ambos casos el verbo va en plural.

Como adjetivo, both puede ir directamente delante del sustantivo (*both cars need repairs los dos coches necesitan ser arreglados*); del artículo the (*both the cars need repairs*); de posesivos como my, your, his, ETC (*both my cars need repairs*); o de los demostrativos this/these o that/those (*both these cars need repairs*).

Como pronombre, both puede ir solo (*I like them both me gustan los dos*; *both speak English los dos hablan inglés*), o con of y un pronombre de complemento como us, you o them (*both of them speak English*).

bother [ˈbɒðər] ◆ *vt* ❶ preocupar ❷ fastidiar ❸ molestar

expresión **I/she can't be bothered to do it** no tengo/tiene ganas de hacerlo

◆ *vi* • **to bother (doing** o **to do something)** molestarse (en hacer algo) • **to bother about** preocuparse por ◆ *s* ☼ *incontable* ❶ problemas ❷ molestia

bottle [ˈbɒtl] ◆ *s* ❶ botella ❷ bote ❸ frasco ❹ biberón ◆ *vt* embotellar

B

■ **bottle up** *vt* ☼ *El objeto se puede colocar antes o después de la preposición.* reprimir

bottle bank *s* contenedor de vidrio

bottleneck ['bɒtlnek] *s* embotellamiento

bottle-opener *s* abrebotellas

bottom ['bɒtəm] ◆ *adj* ❶ más bajo, ja; de abajo del todo ❷ peor ◆ *s* ❶ culo *(de vaso, botella)* ❷ fondo *(de bolsa, mina, mar)* ❸ pie *(de escalera, colina)* ❹ final *(de página, lista)* ❺ • **she's at the bottom of her class** es la última de su clase ❻ trasero
expresión **to get to the bottom of** llegar al fondo de

bottom line *s figurado* • **the bottom line is... a** fin de cuentas...

bought [bɔːt] *pretérito & participio pasado* → **buy**

boulder ['bəʊldəɾ] *s* roca grande y de forma redonda

bounce [baʊns] ◆ *vi* ❶ rebotar ❷ • **to bounce (on something)** dar botes (en algo) ❸ ser rechazado, da por el banco ◆ *vt* botar ◆ *s* bote

bouncer ['baʊnsəɾ] *s familiar* matón; gorila *(de un local)*

bound [baʊnd] ◆ *pretérito & participio pasado* → **bind** ◆ *adj* ❶ • **it's bound to happen** seguro que va a pasar ❷ • **bound (by something/to do something)** obligado, da (por algo/a hacer algo) • **I'm bound to say** tengo que decir ❸ • **to be bound for** ir rumbo a ◆ *s* salto ◆ *vi* ir dando saltos

■ **bounds** *spl* límites • **out of bounds** (en) zona prohibida

boundary ['baʊndərɪ] *s* ❶ límite ❷ frontera

bouquet [bəʊˈkeɪ] *s* ramo

bourbon ['bɜːbən] *s* bourbon; whisky americano

bourgeois ['bɔːʒwɑː] *adj* burgués, esa

bout [baʊt] *s* ❶ ataque; acceso ❷ racha ❸ combate

bow¹ [baʊ] ◆ *s* ❶ reverencia ❷ proa ◆ *vt* inclinar ◆ *vi* inclinarse

bow² [bəʊ] *s* ❶ arco ❷ moño

bowels ['baʊəlz] *spl literal & figurado* entrañas

bowl [bəʊl] *s* ❶ cuenco; bol ❷ plato *(de sopa)* ❸ barreño; balde

■ **bowl over** *vt* ☼ *El objeto se puede colocar antes o después de la preposición.* ❶ atropellar ❷ *figurado* dejar atónito, ta

bow-legged [ˌbəʊˈlegɪd] *adj* zambo, ba

bowler ['bəʊləɾ] *s* ▶ **bowler (hat)** bombín; sombrero hongo

bowling ['bəʊlɪŋ] *s* ☼ *incontable* boliche • **to go bowling** jugar boliche

bowling alley *s* boliche

bow tie [bəʊ-] *s* corbata de moño

box [bɒks] ◆ *s* ❶ caja ❷ estuche ❸ TEATRO palco ❹ casilla ◆ *vt* encajonar ◆ *vi* boxear

boxer ['bɒksəɾ] *s* boxeador; púgil

boxer shorts *spl* calzoncillos; boxers

boxing ['bɒksɪŋ] *s* boxeo

boxing glove *s* guante de boxeo

boxing ring *s* cuadrilátero

box office *s* taquilla

boy [bɔɪ] ◆ *s* ❶ chico; niño ❷ *familiar* chavo ◆ *exclamación* • **(oh) boy!** *familiar* ¡vaya, vaya!

boycott ['bɔɪkɒt] ◆ *s* boicot ◆ *vt* boicotear

boyfriend ['bɔɪfrend] *s* novio

boyish ['bɔɪɪʃ] *adj* juvenil

bra [brɑː] *s* sujetador; sostén

brace [breɪs] ◆ *s* ❶ aparato corrector ❷ par ◆ *vt* tensar • **to brace yourself (for)** *literal & figurado* prepararse (para)

bracelet ['breɪslɪt] *s* brazalete; pulsera

bracken ['brækn] *s* helechos

bracket ['brækɪt] ◆ *s* ❶ soporte ❷ corchete • **in brackets** entre corchetes ◆ *vt* poner entre corchetes

brag [bræg] *vi* fanfarronear; jactarse

braid [breɪd] ◆ *s* ❶ galón ❷ trenza ◆ *vt* trenzar

brain [breɪn] *s literal & figurado* cerebro

■ **brains** *spl* cerebro; seso • **he's got brains** es inteligente

brainstorm ['breɪnstɔːm] *s* idea genial; genialidad

brainwash ['breɪnwɒʃ] *vt* lavar el cerebro a

brainwave ['breɪnweɪv] *s* idea genial

brainy ['breɪnɪ] *adj familiar* listo, ta

brake [breɪk] ◆ *s literal & figurado* freno ◆ *vi* frenar

brake light *s* luz de freno

bramble ['bræmbl] *s* ❶ zarza; zarzamora ❷ mora

bran [bræn] *s* salvado

branch [brɑːntʃ] ◆ *s* ❶ rama ❷ ramal ❸ sucursal ◆ *vi* bifurcarse

■ **branch out** *vi* ❶ ampliar horizontes ❷ expandirse; diversificarse

brand [brænd] ◆ *s* ❶ marca ❷ *figurado* tipo; estilo ❸ hierro ◆ *vt* ❶ marcar (con hierro) ❷ *figurado* • **to brand somebody (as something)** tildar a alguien (de algo)

brandish ['brændɪʃ] *vt* ❶ blandir ❷ agitar

brand name *s* marca

brand-new *adj* flamante

brandy ['brændɪ] *s* coñac

brass [brɑːs] *s* ❶ latón ❷ MÚSICA • **the brass** el metal

brass band *s* banda de metal

brassiere [brəˈzɪr] *s* brasier

brat [bræt] *s familiar & despectivo* mocoso, sa

brave [breɪv] ◆ *adj* valiente ◆ *vt* ❶ desafiar ❷ hacer frente a

bravery ['breɪvərɪ] *s* valentía

brawl [brɔ:l] *s* gresca; reyerta

bray [breɪ] *vi* rebuznar

brazen ['breɪzn] *adj* ❶ descarado, da ❷ burdo, da

Brazil [brə'zɪl] *s* (el) Brasil

Brazilian [brə'zɪljən] ◆ *adj* brasileño, ña; brasilero, ra ◆ *s* brasileño, ña; brasilero, ra

brazil nut *s* nuez del Brasil

breach [bri:tʃ] ◆ *s* ❶ incumplimiento • **breach of confidence** abuso de confianza • **to be in breach of something** incumplir algo ▶ **breach of contract** incumplimiento de contrato ❷ brecha ◆ *vt* ❶ incumplir ❷ abrir (una) brecha en

breach of the peace *s* alteración del orden público

bread [bred] *s* ❶ pan • **bread and butter** pan con mantequilla ❷ *familiar* lana *(dinero)*

bread box *s* panera

breadcrumbs ['bredkrʌmz] *spl* ❶ migas (de pan) ❷ *COCINA* pan rallado

breadth [bretθ] *s* ❶ anchura ❷ *figurado* amplitud

breadwinner ['bred,wɪnər] *s* • **he's the breadwinner** es el que mantiene a la familia

break [breɪk] ◆ *s* ❶ claro ❷ corte *(de transmisión)* ❸ fractura ❹ • **break (from)** descanso (de) o **to have o take a break** tomarse un descanso ❺ recreo ❻ *familiar* oportunidad • **a lucky break** un golpe de suerte ◆ *vt* ❶ romper ❷ romperse *(el brazo, la pierna)* ❸ descomponer ❹ interrumpir *(viaje)* ❺ acabar con *(salud, costumbre)* ❻ reventar *(huelga)* ❼ violar *(ley, regla)* ❽ faltar a *(cita, la palabra)* ❾ batir *(récord)* ❿ • **to break the news (of something to somebody)** dar la noticia (de algo a alguien) ◆ *vi* ❶ romperse ❷ descomponerse ❸ parar ❹ cambiar *(el tiempo)* ❺ romper *(el día)*; estallar *(tormenta)* ❻ • **to break loose** o **free** escaparse ❼ cambiar *(la voz)* ❽ divulgarse *(noticia)*

expresión **to break even** salir sin pérdidas ni beneficios

■ **break away** *vi* escaparse • **to break away (from) a)** separarse (de) **b)** *POLÍTICA* escindirse (de)

■ **break down** ◆ *vt* ⚘: *El objeto se puede colocar antes o después de la preposición.* ❶ derribar; vencer *(oposición)* ❷ descomponer *(analizar)* ◆ *vi* ❶ venirse abajo ❷ descomponerse • **their car broke down** se les descompuso el coche ❸ perder el control ❹ descomponerse *(una sustancia)*

■ **break in** ◆ *vi* ❶ entrar por la fuerza ❷ • **to break in (on something/somebody)** interrumpir (algo/a alguien) ◆ *vt* ⚘: *El objeto se puede colocar antes o después de la preposición.* domar

■ **break into** *vt* ⚘: *El objeto siempre va después de la preposición al final.* ❶ entrar (por la fuerza) en ❷ forzar ❸ • **to break into song/a run** echarse a cantar/correr

■ **break off** ◆ *vt* ⚘: *El objeto se puede colocar antes o después de la preposición.* ❶ partir ❷ romper ❸ interrumpir ◆ *vi* ❶ partirse ❷ interrumpirse

■ **break out** *vi* ❶ desencadenarse ❷ estallar • **to break out (of)** escapar (de)

■ **break up** ◆ *vt* ⚘: *El objeto se puede colocar antes o después de la preposición.* ❶ hacer pedazos ❷ deshuesar ❸ romper *(relación)* ❹ poner fin a *(conversaciones, pelea)* ❺ disolver *(muchedumbre)* ◆ *vi* ❶ hacerse pedazos ❷ deshacerse *(relación)* • **to break up with somebody** romper con alguien ❸ concluir ❹ terminar ❺ disolverse *(muchedumbre)*

Formas irregulares de **break**: *pretérito* **broke**, *pp* **broken**.

breakage ['breɪkɪdʒ] *s* rotura

breakdown ['breɪkdaʊn] *s* ❶ avería ❷ ruptura *(de conversaciones, comunicación)* ❸ colapso *(del orden público)* ❹ desglose

breakfast ['brekfəst] *s* desayuno • **to have breakfast** desayunar

break-in *s* robo *(con allanamiento de morada)*

breakneck ['breɪknek] *adj* • **at breakneck speed** a (una) velocidad de vértigo

breakthrough ['breɪkθəru:] *s* avance

breakup ['breɪkʌp] *s* ruptura

breast [brest] *s* ❶ pecho *(de mujer)*; seno ❷ pecho *(de hombre)* ❸ pechuga

breast-feed *vt* & *vi* amamantar

breast milk *s* ⚘: *incontable* leche materna

breaststroke ['breststrəʊk] *s* estilo pecho

breath [breθ] *s* ❶ respiración • **to take a deep breath** respirar hondo ❷ aliento • **to be out of breath** quedarse sin aliento

expresión **to get your breath back** recuperar el aliento ▶ **to say something under your breath** decir algo en voz baja

breathalyze ['breθəlaɪz] *vt* hacer la prueba del alcohol a

breathe [bri:ð] ◆ *vi* respirar ◆ *vt* ❶ respirar ❷ despedir

■ **breathe in** *vt* & *vi* ⚘: *El objeto se puede colocar antes o después de la preposición.* aspirar

■ **breathe out** *vi* espirar

breather ['bri:ðər] *s familiar* respiro

breathing ['bri:ðɪŋ] *s* respiración

breathless ['breθlɪs] *adj* ❶ jadeante ❷ sin aliento *(por la emoción)*

breathtaking ['breθ,teɪkɪŋ] *adj* sobrecogedor, ra; impresionante

breed [bri:d] ◆ *s* raza ◆ *vt* ❶ criar ❷ cultivar ◆ *vi* reproducir

Formas irregulares de **breed**: *pretérito* & *pp* **bred** [bred].

breeding ['bri:dɪŋ] *s* ❶ cría ❷ cultivo ❸ educación

breeze [bri:z] ◆ *s* brisa ◆ *vi* • **to breeze in/out** entrar/salir como si tal cosa

breezy ['bri:zɪ] *adj* ❶ • **it's breezy** hace aire ❷ jovial; despreocupado, da

brew [bru:] ◆ *vt* ❶ elaborar ❷ preparar ◆ *vi* ❶ reposar ❷ fraguarse *(problemas)*

brewer [ˈbruːəɾ] *s* cervecero, ra

brewery [ˈbruərɪ] *s* fábrica de cerveza

bribe [braɪb] ◆ *s* soborno ◆ *vt* • **to bribe (somebody to do something)** sobornar (a alguien para que haga algo)

bribery [ˈbraɪbərɪ] *s* soborno

brick [brɪk] *s* ladrillo

bricklayer [ˈbrɪkˌleɪəɾ] *s* albañil

bridal [ˈbraɪdl] *adj* nupcial ▸ **bridal gown** vestido de novia

bride [braɪd] *s* novia • **the bride and groom** los novios

bridegroom [ˈbraɪdɡrʊm] *s* novio

bridesmaid [ˈbraɪdzmeɪd] *s* dama de honor

bridge [brɪdʒ] *s* ❶ puente ❷ puente de mando ❸ caballete ❹ bridge *(juego de naipes)*

bridle [ˈbraɪdl] *s* brida

brief [briːf] ◆ *adj* breve • **in brief** en resumen ◆ *vt* • **to brief somebody (on)** informar a alguien (acerca de)

■ **briefs** *spl* ❶ calzoncillos ❷ bragas

briefcase [ˈbriːfkeɪs] *s* maletín; portafolios

briefing [ˈbriːfɪŋ] *s* ❶ reunión informativa ❷ instrucciones

briefly [ˈbriːflɪ] *adv* ❶ brevemente ❷ en pocas palabras

brigade [brɪˈɡeɪd] *s* brigada

bright [braɪt] *adj* ❶ brillante ❷ luminoso, sa ❸ despejado, da ❹ vivo, va *(color)* ❺ radiante *(sonrisa)* ❻ listo, ta ❼ genial *(idea)* ❽ prometedor, ra

■ **brights** *spl familiar* altas

brighten [ˈbraɪtn] *vi* ❶ despejarse ❷ alegrarse

■ **brighten up** ◆ *vt* ⚲ *El objeto se puede colocar antes o después de la preposición.* animar; alegrar ◆ *vi* ❶ animarse ❷ despejarse

brilliance [ˈbrɪljəns] *s* ❶ brillantez ❷ brillo

brilliant [ˈbrɪljənt] *adj* ❶ genial ❷ vivo, va *(color)* ❸ brillante ❹ *familiar* fenomenal; genial

brim [brɪm] ◆ *s* ❶ borde ❷ ala *(de sombrero)* ◆ *vi* literal & figurado • **to brim with** rebosar de

bring [brɪŋ] *vt* traer • **I've brought you some flowers** te traje flores • **to bring something to an end** poner fin a algo

■ **bring about** *vt* ⚲ *El objeto se puede colocar antes o después de la preposición.* producir

■ **bring around, bring to** *vt* ⚲ *El objeto se coloca entre el verbo y la preposición.* reanimar

■ **bring back** *vt* ⚲ *El objeto se puede colocar antes o después de la preposición.* ❶ regresar ❷ traer de vuelta ❸ traer (a la memoria) ❹ volver a introducir *(costumbre)* ❺ volver a estar *(moda)*

■ **bring down** *vt* ⚲ *El objeto se puede colocar antes o después de la preposición.* ❶ bajar ❷ derribar ❸ derrocar ❹ reducir *(precios)*

■ **bring forward** *vt* ⚲ *El objeto se puede colocar antes o después de la preposición.* adelantar

■ **bring in** *vt* ⚲ *El objeto se puede colocar antes o después de la preposición.* ❶ implantar *(ley)* ❷ ganar

■ **bring off** *vt* ⚲ *El objeto se puede colocar antes o después de la preposición.* ❶ sacar adelante *(plan)* ❷ cerrar *(trato)*

■ **bring out** *vt* ⚲ *El objeto se puede colocar antes o después de la preposición.* ❶ sacar *(disco, libro)* ❷ revelar; despertar *(característica)*

■ **bring round, bring to** *vt* ⚲ *El objeto se coloca entre el verbo y la preposición.* = **bring around**

■ **bring up** *vt* ⚲ *El objeto se puede colocar antes o después de la preposición.* ❶ criar ❷ sacar a relucir ❸ devolver

Formas irregulares de **bring**: *pret* **brought**.

brink [brɪŋk] *s* • **on the brink of** al borde de

brisk [brɪsk] *adj* ❶ rápido, da ❷ enérgico, ca ❸ eficaz

bristle [ˈbrɪsl] ◆ *s* ❶ cerda ❷ pelillo ◆ *vi* ❶ erizarse; ponerse de punta ❷ • **to bristle (at)** enfadarse (por)

Brit [brɪt] *s familiar* británico, ca

Britain [ˈbrɪtn] *s* Gran Bretaña

British [ˈbrɪtɪʃ] ◆ *adj* británico, ca ◆ *spl* • **the British** los británicos

British Isles *spl* • **the British Isles** las Islas Británicas

Briton [ˈbrɪtn] *s* británico, ca

brittle [ˈbrɪtl] *adj* quebradizo, za; frágil

broach [brəʊtʃ] *vt* abordar

broad [brɔːd] ◆ *adj* ❶ ancho, cha ❷ amplio, plia ❸ general ❹ claro, ra *(indirecta)* ❺ cerrado, da *(acento)*

expresión in broad daylight a plena luz del día ◆ *s familiar* tipa

broad bean *s* haba

broadcast [ˈbrɔːdkɑːst] ◆ *s* emisión • **a live TV broadcast** un programa de televisión en vivo ◆ *vt* transmitir

Formas irregulares de **broadcast**: *pretérito & pp* **broadcast**.

broaden [ˈbrɔːdn] ◆ *vt* ❶ ensanchar ❷ ampliar ◆ *vi* ensancharse

broadly [ˈbrɔːdlɪ] *adv* ❶ en general ❷ abiertamente *(sonreír)*

Broadway

BROADWAY

Broadway es el nombre de una calle de Nueva York, en Manhattan, donde se encuentran muchos teatros. Centro de la cultura teatral estadounidense, Broadway se destaca sobre todo por sus obras musicales.

broccoli [ˈbrɒkəlɪ] *s* brócoli

brochure [ˈbrəʊʃəɾ] *s* folleto

broil [brɔɪl] *vt* asar bajo fuego directo

broiler ['brɔɪlər] *s* asador *(en horno)*

broke [brəʊk] ◆ *pretérito* → **break** ◆ *adj familiar* sin lana; sin un varo

broken ['brəʊkn] ◆ *participio pasado* → **break** ◆ *adj* ❶ roto, ta ❷ descompuesto, ta ❸ entrecortado, da ❹ discontinuo, nua *(viaje)*

broker ['brəʊkər] *s* ❶ corredor ❷ agente

bronchitis [brɒŋ'kaɪtɪs] *s* :☀: *incontable* bronquitis

bronze [brɒnz] *s* bronce • **he won the bronze medal** ganó la medalla de bronce • **the Bronze Age** la Edad de bronce

brooch [brəʊtʃ] *s* broche; alfiler

brood [bru:d] ◆ *s* nidada ◆ *vi* • **to brood (over** o **about)** dar vueltas (a)

brook [brʊk] *s* arroyo

broom [bru:m] *s* ❶ escoba ❷ retama

broomstick ['bru:mstɪk] *s* palo de escoba

Bros., bros. *(abreviatura de* brothers) Hnos

broth [brɒθ] *s* caldo

brothel ['brɒθl] *s* burdel

brother ['brʌðər] ◆ *s* hermano ◆ *exclamación familiar* ¡dios mío!

brother-in-law *s* cuñado

El plural de **brother-in-law** es **brothers-in-law**.

brought [brɔ:t] *pretérito* & *participio pasado* → **bring**

brow [braʊ] *s* ❶ frente ❷ ceja ❸ cima

brown [braʊn] ◆ *adj* ❶ café ❷ castaño, ña ❸ moreno, na ◆ *s* café

brownie ['braʊnɪ-] *s* ▶ pastel de chocolate con nueces

brown paper *s* :☀: *incontable* papel de estraza

brown rice *s* arroz integral

brown sugar *s* azúcar morena

browse [braʊz] ◆ *vi* ❶ echar un ojo; mirar • **to browse through** hojear ❷ INFORMÁTICA navegar ◆ *vt* INFORMÁTICA navegar por

bruise [bru:z] ◆ *s* moretón ◆ *vt* magullar

brunette [bru:'net] *s* morena

brunt [brʌnt] *s* • **to bear** o **take the brunt of** aguantar lo peor de

brush [brʌʃ] ◆ *s* ❶ cepillo ❷ brocha ❸ pincel ❹ escoba ◆ *vt* ❶ cepillar • **to brush your hair** cepillarse el pelo ❷ quitar; apartar ❸ rozar

■ **brush aside** *vt* :☀: *El objeto se puede colocar antes o después de la preposición.* hacer caso omiso de

■ **brush up** ◆ *vt* :☀: *El objeto se puede colocar antes o después de la preposición.* figurado repasar ◆ *vi* • **to brush up on** repasar

brushwood ['brʌʃwʊd] *s* leña

brusque [bru:sk] *adj* brusco, ca

Brussels ['brʌslz] *s* Bruselas

brussels sprout *s* col de Bruselas

brutal ['bru:tl] *adj* brutal

brute [bru:t] ◆ *adj* bruto, ta ◆ *s* ❶ bestia; bruto ❷ bestia

BS *(abreviatura de* Bachelor of Science) *s* ▶ (titular de una) licenciatura de ciencias

BTW *(abreviatura de* by the way) *adv* por cierto

bubble ['bʌbl] ◆ *s* ❶ burbuja ❷ pompa ◆ *vi* ❶ burbujear ❷ borbotar

bubble bath *s* espuma de baño

bubble gum *s* chicle (de globo)

buck [bʌk] ◆ *s* ❶ macho ❷ *familiar* dólar

expresión **to pass the buck to somebody** *familiar* echarle el muerto a alguien

◆ *vi* corcovear

■ **buck up** *familiar* ◆ *vt* :☀: *El objeto se puede colocar antes o después de la preposición.* mejorar ◆ *vi* ❶ darse prisa ❷ animarse

Dos plurales: **buck** o **bucks.**

bucket ['bʌkɪt] *s* cubeta

buckle ['bʌkl] ◆ *s* hebilla ◆ *vt* ❶ abrochar con hebilla ❷ combar ◆ *vi* ❶ combarse ❷ doblarse

bud [bʌd] ◆ *s* ❶ brote ❷ capullo ◆ *vi* brotar; echar brotes

Buddha ['bʊdə] *s* Buda

Buddhism ['bʊdɪzm] *s* budismo

budding ['bʌdɪŋ] *adj* en ciernes

buddy ['bʌdɪ] *s familiar* cuate

budge [bʌdʒ] ◆ *vt* mover ◆ *vi* ❶ moverse ❷ ceder

budgerigar ['bʌdʒərɪgɑ:r] *s* periquito

budget ['bʌdʒɪt] ◆ *adj* económico, ca ◆ *s* presupuesto

■ **budget for** *vt* :☀: *El objeto siempre va después de la preposición al final.* contar con

budgie ['bʌdʒɪ] *s familiar* periquito

buff [bʌf] ◆ *adj* color de ante ◆ *s familiar* aficionado, da

buffalo ['bʌfələʊ] *s* búfalo

Tres plurales: **buffalo** o **buffalos** o **buffaloes.**

buffer ['bʌfər] *s* ❶ defensa ❷ defensa; salvaguarda ❸ INFORMÁTICA búfer

buffet ['bʌfɪt] *vt* golpear

buffet car ['bʊfeɪ-] *s* coche restaurante

bug [bʌg] ◆ *s* ❶ bicho ❷ *familiar* virus ❸ *familiar* micrófono oculto ❹ INFORMÁTICA error ❺ manía ◆ *vt familiar* ❶ poner un micrófono oculto en ❷ fastidiar; jorobar

buggy ['bʌgɪ] *s* ❶ calesa ❷ carriola

bugle ['bju:gl] *s* corneta; clarín

build [bɪld] ◆ *vt* ❶ construir ❷ *figurado* crear ◆ *s* complexión; constitución

■ **build (up)on** ◆ *vt* :☀: *El objeto siempre va después de la preposición al final.* desarrollar ◆ *vt* :☀: *El objeto se puede colocar antes o después de la preposición.* fundar en

build up ◆ *vt* ☼ *El objeto se puede colocar antes o después de la preposición.* ❶ poner en pie ❷ fomentar ❸ fortalecer ◆ *vi* acumularse
Formas irregulares de build: *pretérito & pp* **built.**

builder ['bɪldər] *s* constructor, ra

building ['bɪldɪŋ] *s* ❶ edificio ❷ construcción

building and loan association *s* ≃ caja de ahorros

building site *s* obra

buildup ['bɪldʌp] *s* ❶ acumulación ❷ concentración

built [bɪlt] *pretérito & participio pasado* → build

built-in *adj* ❶ empotrado, da ❷ incorporado, da

built-up *adj* urbanizado, da

bulb [bʌlb] *s* ❶ bombilla ❷ bulbo

Bulgaria [bʌl'geərɪə] *s* Bulgaria

Bulgarian [bʌl'geərɪən] ◆ *adj* búlgaro, ra ◆ *s* ❶ búlgaro, ra ❷ búlgaro

bulge [bʌldʒ] ◆ *s* protuberancia; bulto ◆ *vi* • to bulge (with) rebosar (de); estar atestado, da (de)

bulk [bʌlk] ◆ *s* ❶ bulto; volumen ❷ • in bulk a granel ❸ • the bulk of la mayor parte de ◆ *adj* a granel

bulky ['bʌlkɪ] *adj* voluminoso, sa

bull [bʊl] *s* ❶ toro ❷ macho

bulldozer ['bʊldəʊzər] *s* bulldozer

bullet ['bʊlɪt] *s* ❶ bala ❷ topo *(en texto)*

bulletin ['bʊlətɪn] *s* ❶ boletín ❷ parte ❸ boletín; gaceta

bullfight ['bʊlfaɪt] *s* corrida (de toros)

bullfighter ['bʊl,faɪtər] *s* torero, ra

bullfighting ['bʊl,faɪtɪŋ] *s* toreo

bullock ['bʊlək] *s* buey; toro castrado

bullring ['bʊlrɪŋ] *s* ❶ plaza (de toros) ❷ ruedo

bull's-eye *s* diana

bully ['bʊlɪ] ◆ *s* abusón, ona; matón, ona ◆ *vt* intimidar • to bully somebody into doing something obligar a alguien con amenazas a hacer algo

bum [bʌm] *s familiar & despectivo* ❶ vagabundo, da ❷ vago, ga; flojo, ja

bum around *vi familiar* ❶ haraganear; flojear ❷ vagabundear

bumblebee ['bʌmblbi:] *s* abejorro

bump [bʌmp] ◆ *s* ❶ chichón ❷ bache ❸ golpe ◆ *vt* ❶ chocar con ❷ golpearse en • I bumped my head on the door me di con la cabeza en la puerta

bump into *vt* ☼ *El objeto siempre va después de la preposición al final.* toparse con

bumper ['bʌmpər] *s* ❶ AUTOMÓVILES defensa ❷ FERROCARRIL tope

bumpy ['bʌmpɪ] *adj* ❶ lleno, na de baches ❷ ajetreado

bun [bʌn] *s* ❶ bollo ❷ chongo

buns *spl familiar* trasero; nalgas

bunch [bʌntʃ] ◆ *s* ❶ grupo ❷ ramo ❸ racimo ❹ manojo ◆ *vi* agruparse

bunches *spl* coletas

bundle ['bʌndl] ◆ *s* ❶ lío; bulto ❷ fajo ❸ haz ❹ INFORMÁTICA paquete

expresión to be a bundle of nerves *figurado* ser un manojo de nervios
◆ *vt* empujar

bundle up *vt* ☼ *El objeto se puede colocar antes o después de la preposición.* liar

bung [bʌŋ] *s* tapón

bungalow ['bʌŋgələʊ] *s* bungalow

bungle ['bʌŋgl] *vt* chapucear

bunker ['bʌŋkər] *s* ❶ bunker ❷ carbonera

bunny ['bʌnɪ] *s* ▸ bunny (rabbit) conejito, ta

buoy ['bu:ɪ] *s* boya

buoy up *vt* ☼ *El objeto se puede colocar antes o después de la preposición.* alentar

burden ['bɜ:dn] ◆ *s literal & figurado* carga ◆ *vt* • to burden somebody with cargar a alguien con

bureau ['bjʊərəʊ] *s* ❶ departamento ❷ oficina ❸ cómoda
El plural de bureau es bureaux.

bureaucracy [bjʊə'rɒkrəsɪ] *s* burocracia

bureaux ['bjʊərəʊz] *spl* → bureau

burger ['bɜ:gər] *s* hamburguesa

burglar ['bɜ:glər] *s* ladrón, ona

burglar alarm *s* alarma antirrobo

burglarize ['bɜ:gləraɪz] *vt* robar; desvalijar *(una casa)*

burglary ['bɜ:glərɪ] *s* robo (de una casa)

burial ['berɪəl] *s* entierro

burly ['bɜ:lɪ] *adj* fornido, da

Burma ['bɜ:mə] *s* Birmania

burn [bɜ:n] ◆ *vt* ❶ quemar ❷ quemarse • I've burned my hand me quemé la mano ❸ INFORMÁTICA tostar; grabar ◆ *vi* ❶ arder ❷ estar encendido, da ❸ quemarse *(comida)* ❹ escocer ❺ quemarse *(por el sol)* ◆ *s* quemadura

burn down ◆ *vt* ☼ *El objeto se puede colocar antes o después de la preposición.* incendiar ◆ *vi* incendiarse
Formas irregulares de burn: *pretérito & pp* **burnt** o **burned.**

burner ['bɜ:nər] *s* quemador

burnt [bɜ:nt] *pretérito & participio pasado* → burn

burp [bɜ:p] *vi familiar* eructar

burrow ['bʌrəʊ] ◆ *s* madriguera ◆ *vi* ❶ escarbar (un agujero) ❷ *figurado* hurgar

burst [bɜ:st] ◆ *vi* ❶ reventarse ❷ romperse ❸ pincharse ❹ estallar ◆ *vt* ❶ reventar ❷ pinchar ◆ *s* estallido

burst into *vt* ☼ *El objeto siempre va después de la preposición al final.* ❶ • to burst into tears/song ponerse a llorar/cantar ❷ estallar en *(llamas)*

■ **burst out** *vi* • **to burst out laughing/crying** ponerse a reír/llorar

Formas irregulares de **burst**: *pretérito & pp* **burst.**

bursting ['bɜːstɪŋ] *adj* ❶ lleno, na a estallar ❷ • **bursting with** rebosando de ❸ • **to be bursting to do something** estar deseando hacer algo

bury ['berɪ] *vt* enterrar

bus [bʌs] ◆ *s* autobús; camión • **by bus** en camión ◆ *vt* • **to bus tables** recoger mesas

bush [bʊʃ] *s* ❶ arbusto ❷ • **the bush** el campo abierto; el monte

expresión **to beat about the bush** andarse por las ramas

bushy ['bʊʃɪ] *adj* poblado, da; espeso, sa

business ['bɪznɪs] *s* ❶ ☀ *incontable* negocios • **to be away on business** estar en viaje de negocios • **to go out of business** quebrar ❷ negocio; empresa ❸ oficio; ocupación • **to have no business doing** o **to do something** no tener derecho a hacer algo ❹ ☀ *incontable* asunto

expresiones **to mean business** *familiar* ir en serio ▶ **mind your own business!** *familiar* ¡no te metas donde no te llaman! ▶ **that's none of your business** eso no es asunto tuyo

business class *s* clase preferente

businesslike ['bɪznɪslaɪk] *adj* formal y eficiente

businessman ['bɪznɪsmæn] *s* empresario; hombre de negocios

El plural de **businessman** es **businessmen** ['bɪznɪsmen].

business studies *spl* empresariales

business trip *s* viaje de negocios

businesswoman ['bɪznɪsˌwʊmən] *s* empresaria; mujer de negocios

El plural de **businesswoman** es **businesswomen** ['bɪznɪsˌwɪmɪn].

bus-shelter *s* parada de camión

bus station *s* estación de camiones; central camionera

bus stop *s* parada *(de camión)*

bust [bʌst] ◆ *adj familiar* ❶ roto, ta ❷ • **to go bust** quebrar ◆ *s* busto ◆ *vt familiar* romper; estropear

Formas irregulares de **bust**: *pretérito & pp* **busted** o **bust.**

busy ['bɪzɪ] ◆ *adj* ❶ ocupado, da • **to be busy doing something** estar ocupado haciendo algo ❷ ajetreado, da ❸ concurrido, da ❹ con mucho tráfico ❺ activo, va ◆ *vt* • **to busy yourself (doing something)** ocuparse (haciendo algo)

busy signal *s* TELECOMUNICACIONES señal de ocupado • **I got a busy signal** el teléfono me sonaba ocupado

but [bʌt]
◆ *conjunción*
❶ [*expresa oposición*] pero
• **I'm sorry, but I don't agree** lo siento, pero no estoy de acuerdo
❷ [*expresa contradicción*] sino
• **he's not Chinese but Japanese** no es chino, sino japonés
◆ *preposición*
[*con "all", "every", "any", "no" y sus compuestos, expresa restricción*]
• **he has no one but himself to blame** él es el único culpable
• **Brazil won all but one of its matches** Brasil ganó todos los partidos menos uno
◆ *adv*
formal [*solamente*]
• **she's but a child** no es más que una niña
• **we can but try** por lo menos lo podemos intentar
• **had I but known!** ¡si lo hubiera sabido!
■ **but for**
◆ *preposición*
sin
• **but for you, I would never have succeeded** sin ti no habría tenido éxito

butcher ['bʊtʃər] ◆ *s* carnicero, ra • **butcher shop** carnicería ◆ *vt* ❶ matar ❷ *figurado* hacer una carnicería con

butler ['bʌtlər] *s* mayordomo

butt [bʌt] ◆ *s* ❶ colilla ❷ culata ❸ tina ❹ blanco *(de broma)* ❺ *familiar* trasero; culo ◆ *vt* topetar
■ **butt in** *vi* • **to butt in on somebody** interrumpir a alguien
■ **butt out** *vi* dejar de entrometerse

butter ['bʌtər] ◆ *s* mantequilla ◆ *vt* untar con mantequilla

buttercup ['bʌtəkʌp] *s* ranúnculo

butter dish *s* mantequera

butterfly ['bʌtəflaɪ] *s* ❶ mariposa ❷ (estilo) mariposa

buttocks ['bʌtəks] *spl* nalgas

button ['bʌtn] ◆ *s* ❶ botón ❷ prendedor ◆ *vt* = button up
■ **button up** *vt* ☀ *El objeto se puede colocar antes o después de la preposición.* abotonar; abrochar

buy [baɪ] ◆ *vt literal & figurado* comprar • **to buy something from somebody** comprar algo a alguien • **to buy somebody something** comprar algo a alguien; comprar algo para alguien ◆ *s* compra
■ **buy up** *vt* ☀ *El objeto se puede colocar antes o después de la preposición.* acaparar

Formas irregulares de **buy**: *pretérito & pp* **bought.**

buyer ['baɪər] *s* comprador, ra

buzz [bʌz] ◆ *s* ❶ zumbido ❷ *familiar* • **to give somebody a buzz** echar un fonazo a alguien ◆ *vi* ❶ zumbar ❷ *figurado* • **to buzz (with)** bullir (de)

buzzer ['bʌzər] *s* timbre
buzzword ['bʌzwɜːd] *s familiar* palabra de moda

by [baɪ]
◆ *preposición*
❶ [*en pasiva, introduce el complemento agente*] por
• **she was killed by a mad man** fue asesinada por un loco
❷ [*presenta el autor de una obra*] de
• **it's a poem by Shakespeare** es un poema de Shakespeare
❸ [*expresa el medio*]
• **I don't pay by check very often** no suelo pagar con cheque
• **he generally travels by bus** suele viajar en camión
• **by doing a lot of sport, you can keep fit** haciendo mucho deporte te puedes mantener en forma
❹ [*para describir a alguien*]
• **he's a lawyer by trade** es abogado de profesión
• **by nature, she's very patient** es muy paciente por naturaleza
❺ [*indica proximidad*] junto a
• **she lives by the sea** vive junto al mar
• **I sat by her bed** me senté junto a su cama
• **she passed by me** pasó a mi lado
❻ [*indica un límite temporal*]
• **I'll be there by eight** estaré ahí no más tarde de las ocho
❼ [*según*]
• **by my watch it's 9 o'clock** según mi reloj, son las nueve
• **by law** por ley
❽ [*para expresar opinión*]
• **if that's okay by you, I'd like to leave now** si no le importa, me gustaría irme ahora
• **that's fine by me** por mí no hay ningún problema
❾ [*con expresiones de cálculo, medida, cantidad*]
• **divide 20 by 2** divida 20 entre 2
• **multiply 10 by 5** multiplique 10 por 5
• **2 meters by 4** 2 por 4 metros
• **this fabric is sold by the yard** ≃ este tejido se vende por metros

• **the company decided to cut prices by 50%** la empresa decidió bajar los precios un 50%
❿ [*para expresar una diferencia, una distancia*]
• **she won by five points** ganó por cinco puntos
• **the bullet missed me by inches** la bala me pasó a pocos centímetros
⓫ [*para expresar frecuencia*]
• **the workers are paid by the day** los trabajadores cobran por día
⓬ [*para indicar un proceso gradual*]
• **she grew thinner day by day** fue adelgazando día a día
• **one by one, they told their amazing stories** uno a uno, contaron sus historias increíbles
⓭ [*para indicar los momentos de un viaje*]
• **we traveled by night and rested by day** viajábamos por la noche y descansábamos durante el día
expresión **(all) by yourself** (completamente) solo
▶ **by the way** a propósito

by
En la voz pasiva, el complemento agente — o sea, la persona o cosa que realiza la acción — va precedido de la preposición by (the tickets were booked *by* my mother *las entradas fueron reservadas por mi madre*; I was hurt *by* what he said *me sentó mal lo que me dijo*). El instrumento — aquello que se emplea para realizar la acción — va precedido de with (he was killed *with* a knife *fue asesinado con un cuchillo*).

bye (-bye) [baɪ(baɪ)] *exclamación familiar* ¡hasta luego!
bypass ['baɪpɑːs] ◆ *s* ❶ carretera de circunvalación ❷ MEDICINA ▶ **bypass (operation)** (operación de) by-pass ◆ *vt* evitar
by-product *s* ❶ subproducto ❷ consecuencia
bystander ['baɪˌstændər] *s* espectador, ra
byte [baɪt] *s* INFORMÁTICA byte

C

c¹, C [si:] *s* c; C

■ **C** *s* ❶ MÚSICA do ❷ (*abreviatura de* celsius, centigrade) C

Dos plurales: **c's** o **cs**; **C's** o **Cs**.

C² (*abreviatura escrita de* cent(s)) cént.

c. (*abreviatura de* circa) approx.

cab [kæb] *s* ❶ taxi ❷ cabina

cabbage ['kæbɪdʒ] *s* col; repollo

cabin ['kæbɪn] *s* ❶ camarote ❷ cabina ❸ cabaña

cabinet ['kæbɪnɪt] *s* ❶ armario ❷ vitrina ❸ POLÍTICA consejo de ministros; gabinete

cable ['keɪbl] *s* ❶ cable ❷ cablegrama

cable car *s* teleférico

cable television, cable TV *s* televisión por cable

cackle ['kækl] *vi* ❶ cacarear ❷ reírse

cactus ['kæktəs] *s* cactus

Dos plurales: **cactuses** o **cacti** ['kæktaɪ].

cadet [kə'det] *s* cadete

cafe, café ['kæfeɪ] *s* café

cafeteria [,kæfɪ'tɪərɪə] *s* (restaurante) autoservicio; cantina

caffeine ['kæfiːn] *s* cafeína

cage [keɪdʒ] *s* jaula

cake [keɪk] *s* ❶ pastel ❷ torta ❸ barra

caked [keɪkt] *adj* • **caked with mud** cubierto, ta de lodo seco

CAL (*abreviatura de* computer assisted learning, computer aided learning) (*abreviatura de*) *s* enseñanza asistida por computadora

calcium ['kælsɪəm] *s* calcio

calculate ['kælkjʊleɪt] *vt* ❶ calcular ❷ • **to be calculated to do something** estar pensado, da para hacer algo

calculating ['kælkjʊleɪtɪŋ] *adj despectivo* calculador, ra

calculation [,kælkjʊ'leɪʃn] *s* cálculo

calculator ['kælkjʊleɪtər] *s* calculadora

calendar ['kælɪndər] *s* calendario

calendar month *s* mes civil

calendar year *s* año civil

calf [kɑːf] *s* ❶ ternero, ra; becerro, rra ❷ cría ❸ pantorrilla

El plural de **calf** es **calves**.

caliber ['kælɪbər] *s* ❶ nivel ❷ calibre

call [kɔːl] ◆ *s* ❶ llamada *(grito)* ❷ reclamo ❸ TELECOMUNICACIONES llamada • **to give somebody a call** llamar a alguien ❹ visita • **to pay a call on somebody** hacerle una visita a alguien ❺ • **call for** llamamiento a *expresión* **on call** de guardia

◆ *vt* ❶ llamar • **I'm called Joan** me llamo Joan • **what is it called?** ¿cómo se llama? • **he called my name** me llamó por el nombre • **we'll call it $10** dejémoslo en 10 dólares ❷ anunciar *(vuelo)* ❸ convocar ◆ *vi* ❶ TELECOMUNICACIONES llamar • **who's calling?** ¿quién habla? ❷ pasar

■ **call at** *vt* ⚙ *El objeto siempre va después de la preposición al final.* efectuar parada en

■ **call back** ◆ *vt* ⚙ *El objeto se puede colocar antes o después de la preposición.* ❶ volver a llamar ❷ hacer volver ◆ *vi* ❶ volver a llamar ❷ volver a pasarse

■ **call for** *vt* ⚙ *El objeto siempre va después de la preposición al final.* ❶ ir a buscar ❷ pedir

■ **call in** *vt* ⚙ *El objeto se puede colocar antes o después de la preposición.* ❶ llamar ❷ exigir pago de *(préstamo)*

■ **call off** *vt* ⚙ *El objeto se puede colocar antes o después de la preposición.* ❶ suspender ❷ desconvocar ❸ llamar *(para que deje de atacar)*

■ **call on** *vt* ⚙ *El objeto siempre va después de la preposición al final.* visitar

■ **call out** ◆ *vt* ⚙ *El objeto se puede colocar antes o después de la preposición.* ❶ movilizar *(tropas)*; hacer intervenir *(policía, bomberos)* ❷ gritar ◆ *vi* gritar

■ **call up** *vt* ⚙ *El objeto se puede colocar antes o después de la preposición.* ❶ MILITAR llamar a filas ❷ llamar *(por teléfono)*

CALL (*abreviatura de* computer assisted (or aided) language learning) *s* enseñanza de idiomas asistida por computadora

call center *s* centro de atención telefónica

caller ['kɔːlər] *s* ❶ visita ❷ persona que llama

caller (ID) display *s* identificador de llamada

call-in *s* RADIO & TELEVISIÓN programa a micrófono abierto

calling card *s* tarjeta de visita

callous ['kæləs] *adj* despiadado, da

calm [kɑːm] ◆ *adj* **❶** tranquilo, la **❷** apacible **❸** en calma ◆ *s* calma ◆ *vt* calmar

■ **calm down** ◆ *vt* ☿ *El objeto se puede colocar antes o después de la preposición.* calmar ◆ *vi* calmarse

calorie ['kælərɪ] *s* caloría

calves [kɑːvz] *spl* → **calf**

Cambodia [kæm'bəʊdjə] *s* Camboya

camcorder ['kæm,kɔːdər] *s* camcorder; videocámara

came [keɪm] *pretérito* → **come**

camel ['kæml] *s* camello

camera ['kæmərə] *s* cámara

cameraman ['kæmərəmæn] *s* cámara *(persona)*

El plural de **cameraman** es **cameramen** ['kæmərəmen].

camouflage ['kæməflɑːʒ] ◆ *s* camuflaje ◆ *vt* camuflar

camp [kæmp] ◆ *s* **❶** campamento **❷** campo • **(summer) camp** campamento de verano **❸** bando ◆ *vi* acampar ◆ *adj familiar* amanerado, da

■ **camp out** *vi* acampar (al aire libre)

campaign [kæm'peɪn] ◆ *s* campaña ◆ *vi* • **to campaign (for/against)** hacer campaña (a favor de/en contra de)

camp bed *s* cama plegable

camper ['kæmpər] *s* **❶** campista **❷** ▸ **camper (van)** cámper

campground ['kæmpgraʊnd] *s* camping

camping ['kæmpɪŋ] *s* • **camping is not allowed in that park** no está permitido acampar en ese parque
• **to go camping** ir de campamento

camping site, campsite ['kæmpsaɪt] *s* camping

campus ['kæmpəs] *s* campus; ciudad universitaria

El plural de **campus** es **campuses**.

can¹ [kæn] ◆ *s* **❶** lata; bote **❷** lata ◆ *vt* enlatar

Formas irregulares de can: *pretérito & pp* **canned**, *gerundio* **canning**.

can²
◆ *v modal*

☿ *acento atónico* [kən], *acento tónico* [kæn], *condicional y pretérito "could"; forma negativa "cannot" y "can't"*

❶ [*expresa una posibilidad (con "can't", una imposibilidad)*] poder
• **can you come to lunch?** ¿puede venir a comer?
• **Peter can't come on Saturday** Peter no puede venir el sábado

❷ [*con verbos de percepción, no se traduce en español*]
• **can you see/hear/smell something?** ¿ven/oyen/huelen algo?

❸ [*indica una capacidad*]
• **can you drive?** ¿sabes manejar?
• **she can speak three languages** habla tres idiomas

❹ [*para pedir o dar permiso*]
• **you can use my car if you like** si quiere puede usar mi carro
• **can I speak to John, please?** quería hablar con John, por favor

❺ [*indica una probabilidad*]
• **what can she have done with it?** ¿qué puede haber hecho con él?
• **you can't be serious!** ¿no lo dirás en serio?

❻ [*con "could", indica una posibilidad de forma educada*]
• **I could see you tomorrow** lo podría ver mañana

can

En preguntas can sirve para pedir permiso, información, etc (*can* you tell me the way to the station? *¿me puede decir cómo llegar a la estación?*). Could sirve para lo mismo, sólo que es más cortés (*could* you help me with this, please? *¿podría ayudarme con esto, por favor?*).

Con verbos que se refieren a los sentidos, como hear (*escuchar*) o see (*ver*), cuando están en presente generalmente se coloca can o can't delante, pero no se traducen en español (*can* you hear something? *¿escuchas algo?*; I can't see the house from here *no veo la casa desde aquí*).

Asimismo, can y can't sirven para expresar si alguien sabe o no hacer algo I *can* speak English *sé hablar inglés* o I *can't* swim *no sé nadar*.

Ver también *poder* en el lado español-inglés del diccionario.

Canada ['kænədə] *s* (el) Canadá

Canadian [kə'neɪdjən] ◆ *adj* canadiense ◆ *s* canadiense

canal [kə'næl] *s* canal

canary [kə'neərɪ] *s* canario

Canary Islands, Canaries [kə'neərɪz] *spl* • **the Canary Islands** las (islas) Canarias

cancel ['kænsl] *vt* **❶** cancelar; suspender **❷** cancelar *(deuda, cheque)* **❸** anular *(pedido)*

■ **cancel out** *vt* ☿ *El objeto se puede colocar antes o después de la preposición.* anular • **the tax increase canceled out their profits** el aumento de impuestos les anuló los beneficios

C

cancellation [ˌkænsəˈleɪʃn] *s* suspensión

cancer [ˈkænsər] *s* cáncer

■ **Cancer** *s* Cáncer

candelabra [ˌkændɪˈlɑːbrə] *s* candelabro

candidate [ˈkændɪdət] *s* • **candidate (for)** candidato, ta (a)

candle [ˈkændl] *s* vela

candlelight [ˈkændllaɪt] *s* • **by candlelight** a la luz de una vela

candlelit [ˈkændllɪt] *adj* a la luz de las velas

candlestick [ˈkændlstɪk] *s* candelero

candy [ˈkændɪ] *s* ❶ ☼*incontable* dulces • **candy bar** chocolate • **candy store** tienda de dulces ❷ dulce

cane [keɪn] *s* ❶ ☼*incontable* caña; mimbre ❷ bastón ❸ • **the cane** la vara

canine [ˈkeɪnaɪn] ◆ *adj* canino, na ◆ *s* ▶ **canine (tooth)** (diente) canino; colmillo

canister [ˈkænɪstər] *s* ❶ bote ❷ lata ❸ tanque

cannabis [ˈkænəbɪs] *s* cannabis

canned [kænd] *adj* enlatado, da; en lata

cannibal [ˈkænɪbl] *s* caníbal

cannon [ˈkænən] *s* cañón

Dos plurales: **cannon** o **cannons.**

cannonball [ˈkænənbɔːl] *s* bala de cañón

cannot [ˈkænɒt] *formal (forma negativa de* can) → **can**

canoe [kəˈnuː] *s* ❶ canoa ❷ DEPORTE piragua

canoeing [kəˈnuːɪŋ] *s* piragüismo • **to go canoeing** hacer piragüismo

canon [ˈkænən] *s* canónigo

can opener *s* abrelatas

can't [kɑːnt] *(abreviatura de* cannot) → **can**

canteen [kænˈtiːn] *s* ❶ cantina ❷ (juego de) cubertería

canter [ˈkæntər] ◆ *s* medio galope ◆ *vi* ir a medio galope

Cantonese [ˌkæntəˈniːz] ◆ *adj* cantonés, esa ◆ *s* ❶ cantonés, esa ❷ cantonés

canvas [ˈkænvəs] *s* ❶ lona ❷ lienzo

canvass [ˈkænvəs] ◆ *vt* ❶ POLÍTICA solicitar el voto a ❷ pulsar ◆ *vi* ▶ solicitar votos yendo de puerta en puerta

canyon [ˈkænjən] *s* cañón

cap [kæp] ◆ *s* ❶ gorra ❷ gorro ❸ tapón ❹ tapa ❺ tope ◆ *vt* • **to be capped with** estar coronado, da de

expresión **to cap it all** para colmo

capability [ˌkeɪpəˈbɪlətɪ] *s* capacidad

capable [ˈkeɪpəbl] *adj* ❶ • **to be capable of something/of doing something** ser capaz de algo/de hacer algo ❷ competente

capacity [kəˈpæsɪtɪ] *s* ❶ • **capacity (for)** capacidad (de) • **seating capacity** aforo ❷ • **in your capacity as** en calidad de

cape [keɪp] *s* ❶ GEOGRAFÍA cabo ❷ capa

caper [ˈkeɪpər] *s* alcaparra

capital [ˈkæpɪtl] ◆ *adj* ❶ mayúscula ❷ capital ◆ *s* ❶ capital *(ciudad)* ❷ • **capital (letter)** mayúscula ❸ capital *(dinero)*

capitalism [ˈkæpɪtəlɪzm] *s* capitalismo

capitalist [ˈkæpɪtəlɪst] ◆ *adj* capitalista ◆ *s* capitalista

capitalize [ˈkæpɪtəlaɪz] *vi* • **to capitalize on something** aprovechar algo; capitalizar algo

capital punishment *s* ☼*incontable* pena capital

Capitol Hill [ˈkæpɪtl-] *s* el Capitolio

capitulate [kəˈpɪtjʊleɪt] *vi* • **to capitulate (to)** capitular (ante)

Capricorn [ˈkæprɪkɔːn] *s* Capricornio

capsize [kæpˈsaɪz] ◆ *vt* hacer volcar o zozobrar ◆ *vi* volcar; zozobrar

capsule [ˈkæpsjuːl] *s* cápsula

captain [ˈkæptɪn] *s* ❶ capitán, ana ❷ comandante

caption [ˈkæpʃn] *s* ❶ leyenda ❷ encabezamiento

captive [ˈkæptɪv] ◆ *adj* ❶ en cautividad ❷ *figurado* asegurado, da ◆ *s* cautivo, va

captivity [kæpˈtɪvətɪ] *s* • **in captivity** en cautividad; en cautiverio

captor [ˈkæptər] *s* apresador, ra

capture [ˈkæptʃər] ◆ *vt* ❶ capturar ❷ hacerse con ❸ tomar *(ciudad)* ❹ captar ❺ introducir ◆ *s* ❶ captura ❷ toma *(de ciudad)*

car [kɑːr] ◆ *s* ❶ coche; carro • **by car** en coche ❷ vagón; coche • **en compuestos** ❶ del coche ❷ IN-DUSTRIA del automóvil *(sector)* ❸ de automóvil *(accidente)* • **a car crash** un choque

car alarm *s* alarma de coche

caramel [ˈkærəmel] *s* ❶ caramelo (líquido); azúcar quemado ❷ caramelo

caravan [ˈkærəvæn] *s* caravana

carbohydrate [ˌkɑːbəʊˈhaɪdreɪt] *s* QUÍMICA hidrato de carbono

■ **carbohydrates** *spl* carbohidrato

carbon [ˈkɑːbən] *s* carbono

carbonated [ˈkɑːbəneɪtɪd] *adj* con gas

carbon copy *s figurado* calco

carbon dioxide [-daɪˈɒksaɪd] *s* dióxido de carbono

carbon monoxide [-mɒˈnɒksaɪd] *s* monóxido de carbono

carcass [ˈkɑːkəs] *s* ❶ cadáver (de animal) ❷ carcasa ❸ canal *(de res)*

card [kɑːd] ◆ *s* ❶ carta ❷ tarjeta ❸ documento de identificación ❹ postal ◆ *vt* pedir documento de identificación

■ **cards** *spl* las cartas • **they're playing cards** están jugando a las cartas

■ **in the cards** *adv familiar* más que probable

C

cardboard [ˈkɑːdbɔːd] ◆ s ☿ *incontable* cartón ◆ *en compuestos* de cartón

cardboard box s caja de cartón

cardiac [ˈkɑːdɪæk] *adj* cardíaco, ca

cardigan [ˈkɑːdɪɡən] s suéter abierto

cardinal [ˈkɑːdɪnl] ◆ *adj* capital *(pecado)* ◆ s RELIGIÓN cardenal

card stock s cartulina

care [keər] ◆ s ❶ cuidado • **medical care** asistencia médica • **in somebody's care** al cargo o cuidado de alguien • **to take care of a)** cuidar de **b)** cuidar **c)** encargarse de • **to take care (to do something)** tener cuidado (de hacer algo) ❷ preocupación

expresión **take care!** ¡nos vemos!, ¡cuídate!

◆ *vi* ❶ • **to care (about)** preocuparse (de o por) ❷ • **I don't care** no me importa

expresión **who cares?** ¿y a mí qué?

■ **care of** *preposición* al cuidado de; en casa de

■ **care for** *vt* ☿ *El objeto siempre va después de la preposición.* desusado • **I don't care for cheese** no me gusta el queso

career [kəˈrɪər] s carrera

careers adviser s asesor, ra de orientación profesional

carefree [ˈkeəfriː] *adj* despreocupado, da

careful [ˈkeəfʊl] *adj* ❶ cuidadoso, sa • **be careful!** ¡ten cuidado! • **to be careful to do something** tener cuidado de hacer algo ❷ prudente ❸ esmerado, da

carefully [ˈkeəflɪ] *adv* ❶ cuidadosamente; con cuidado ❷ detenidamente ❸ con esmero

careless [ˈkeəlɪs] *adj* ❶ descuidado, da ❷ despreocupado, da

caress [kəˈres] ◆ s caricia ◆ *vt* acariciar

car ferry s transbordador de coches

cargo [ˈkɑːɡəʊ] s carga; cargamento

Dos plurales: **cargoes o cargos.**

Caribbean [kəˈrɪbɪən] ◆ s • **the Caribbean (Sea)** el (mar) Caribe ◆ *adj* caribeño, ña

caring [ˈkeərɪŋ] *adj* solícito, ta; dedicado, da

carnage [ˈkɑːnɪdʒ] s carnicería

carnation [kɑːˈneɪʃn] s clavel

carnival [ˈkɑːnɪvl] s carnaval

carnivorous [kɑːˈnɪvərəs] *adj* carnívoro, ra

carol [ˈkærəl] s villancico

carousel [ˌkærəˈsel] s ❶ tiovivo ❷ cinta transportadora

carp [kɑːp] s carpa

Dos plurales: **carp o carps.**

carpenter [ˈkɑːpəntər] s carpintero, ra

carpentry [ˈkɑːpəntrɪ] s carpintería

carpet [ˈkɑːpɪt] ◆ s *literal & figurado* alfombra • **wall-to-wall carpet** alfombra

expresión **to sweep something under the carpet** *figurado* echar tierra a algo

◆ *vt* alfombrar

carpeting s alfombra • **wall-to-wall carpeting** alfombra

carport [ˈkɑːˌpɔːt] s cochera

car rental s renta de autos

carrier [ˈkærɪər] s ❶ COMERCIO transportista ❷ aerolínea ❸ portador, ra *(de enfermedad)*

carrot [ˈkærət] s ❶ zanahoria ❷ *familiar* aliciente

carry [ˈkærɪ] ◆ *vt* ❶ llevar • **she's carrying a large bag** está cargando una bolsa grande ❷ llevar encima ❸ ser portador de ❹ acarrear; conllevar ❺ estar embarazada de ❻ MATEMÁTICAS llevarse ◆ *vi* oírse

■ **carry away** *vt* ☿ *El objeto se coloca entre el verbo y la preposición.* • **to get carried away** exaltarse

■ **carry off** *vt* ☿ *El objeto se puede colocar antes o después de la preposición.* ❶ llevar a cabo ❷ llevarse *(premio)*

■ **carry on** *vt* ☿ *El objeto siempre va después de la preposición al final.* ❶ continuar; seguir • **to carry on doing something** continuar o seguir haciendo algo ❷ mantener *(conversación)*

■ **carry out** *vt* ☿ *El objeto se coloca entre el verbo y la preposición.* ❶ llevar a cabo ❷ cumplir

carryall [ˈkærɪɔːl] s bolsa de viaje

carry-out s comida para llevar

carsick [ˈkɑːˌsɪk] *adj* mareado, da *(al ir en coche)*

cart [kɑːt] ◆ s ❶ carro; carreta ❷ carrito *(de compras)* ◆ *vt familiar* acarrear

carton [ˈkɑːtn] s ❶ caja de cartón ❷ cartón; envase

cartoon [kɑːˈtuːn] s ❶ chiste (en viñeta); caricatura ❷ tira cómica ❸ caricatura; dibujos animados

cartridge [ˈkɑːtrɪdʒ] s ❶ cartucho o recambio

cartwheel [ˈkɑːtwiːl] s voltereta lateral

carve [kɑːv] *vt* ❶ tallar ❷ esculpir ❸ trinchar ❹ grabar

■ **carve out** *vt* ☿ *El objeto se puede colocar antes o después de la preposición.* conquistar

■ **carve up** *vt* ☿ *El objeto se puede colocar antes o después de la preposición.* repartir

carving [ˈkɑːvɪŋ] s ❶ tallado ❷ labrado ❸ talla

carving knife s cuchillo de trinchar

car wash s lavado de coches

case [keɪs] s ❶ caso • **to be the case** ser el caso • **in that/which case** en ese/cuyo caso • **as o whatever the case may be** según sea el caso • **in case of** en caso de ❷ argumentos • **the case for/against (something)** los argumentos a favor/en contra (de algo) ❸ DERECHO pleito; causa ❹ funda ❺ estuche ❻ cajón

■ **in any case** *adv* en cualquier caso

■ **in case** *conjunción & adv* por si acaso • **in case she doesn't come** por si no viene

cash [kæʃ] ◆ s ❶ (dinero) efectivo • **to pay (in) cash** pagar al contado o en efectivo ❷ *familiar* dinero ◆ *vt* cobrar; hacer efectivo

■ **cash in** *vi* • **to cash in on** *familiar* sacar partido de

cash card s tarjeta de cajero automático

cash dispenser [-dɪ'spensər] *s* cajero automático

cashew (nut) ['kæʃuː-] *s* nuez de la India

cashier [kæ'ʃɪər] *s* cajero, ra

cashless ['kæʃlɪs] *adj* sin dinero en efectivo

cash machine = cash dispenser

cashmere [kæʃ'mɪər] *s* cachemira

cash register *s* caja (registradora)

casino [kə'siːnəʊ] *s* casino

   El plural de **casino** es **casinos**.

cask [kɑːsk] *s* tonel; barril

casket ['kɑːskɪt] *s* ❶ estuche ❷ ataúd

casserole ['kæsərəʊl] *s* ❶ guiso ❷ cazuela; cacerola

cassette [kæ'set] *s* cinta; caset

cassette player *s* casetera

cassette recorder *s* casetera

cast [kɑːst] ◆ *s* reparto ◆ *vt* ❶ echar; lanzar ❷ irradiar ❸ proyectar ❹ arrojar; lanzar ❺ emitir *(voto)* ❻ fundir

   Formas irregulares de **cast**: *pretérito & pp* **cast**.

castanets [ˌkæstə'nets] *spl* castañuelas

castaway ['kɑːstəweɪ] *s* náufrago, ga

caste [kɑːst] *s* casta

casting vote *s* voto de calidad

cast iron *s* hierro fundido

castle ['kɑːsl] *s* ❶ castillo ❷ torre

castor oil *s* aceite de ricino

casual ['kæʒʊəl] *adj* ❶ despreocupado, da ❷ *despectivo* descuidado, da; *informal* ❸ ocasional *(visita)* ❹ casual *(comentario)* ❺ de sport; *informal* ❻ eventual *(trabajador)*

casually ['kæʒʊəlɪ] *adv* ❶ con aire despreocupado ❷ informalmente

casualty ['kæʒjʊəltɪ] *s* ❶ víctima ❷ MILITAR baja

cat [kæt] *s* ❶ gato, ta ❷ felino

Catalan ['kætə,læn] ◆ *adj* catalán, ana ◆ *s* ❶ catalán, ana ❷ catalán

catalog ['kætəlɒg] ◆ *s* catálogo ◆ *vt* ❶ catalogar ❷ *figurado* enumerar

Catalonia [ˌkætə'ləʊnɪə] *s* Cataluña

Catalonian [ˌkætə'ləʊnɪən] ◆ *adj* catalán, ana ◆ *s* catalán, ana

catalyst ['kætəlɪst] *s* *literal & figurado* catalizador

cataract ['kætərækt] *s* catarata

catarrh [kə'tɑːr] *s* ⚙ *incontable* catarro

catastrophe [kə'tæstrəfɪ] *s* catástrofe

catch [kætʃ] ◆ *vt* ❶ agarrar • she caught the flu pescó una gripa ❷ atrapar ❸ pescar ❹ parar ❺ tomar • I've got a train to catch tengo que tomar un tren ❻ entender; llegar a oír ❼ • to catch sight o a glimpse of alcanzar a ver ❽ atorarse *(la camisa)* ❾ machucarse *(el dedo)* ❿ golpear ◆ *vi* ❶ engancharse ❷ prenderse ◆ *s* ❶ parada ❷ pesca; captura ❸ pestillo ❹ cierre ❺ trampa *(inconveniente)*

■ **catch on** *vi* ❶ hacerse popular ❷ *familiar* • to catch on (to) caer en la cuenta (de)

■ **catch out** *vt* ⚙ *El objeto se puede colocar antes o después de la preposición.* pillar

■ **catch up** ◆ *vt* ⚙ *El objeto se puede colocar antes o después de la preposición.* alcanzar ◆ *vi* • we'll soon catch up pronto nos pondremos a la misma altura • to catch up on a) recuperar *(sueño)* b) ponerse al día con *(trabajo, lectura)*

■ **catch up with** *vt* ⚙ *El objeto siempre va después de la preposición al final.* ❶ alcanzar ❷ pillar; descubrir

   Formas irregulares de **catch**: *pret & pp* **caught**.

catching ['kætʃɪŋ] *adj* contagioso, sa

catchphrase ['kætʃfreɪz] *s* muletilla

catchy ['kætʃɪ] *adj* pegadizo, za

categorically [ˌkætɪ'gɒrɪklɪ] *adv* ❶ categóricamente ❷ rotundamente

category ['kætəgərɪ] *s* categoría

cater ['keɪtər] ◆ *vi* proveer comida ◆ *vt* dar el servicio de comida y bebida de

■ **cater to** *vt* ⚙ *El objeto siempre va después de la preposición al final.* complacer

caterer ['keɪtərər] *s* empresa de hostelería

catering ['keɪtərɪŋ] *s* ❶ servicio de banquetes ❷ hostelería

caterpillar ['kætəpɪlər] *s* oruga

cathedral [kə'θiːdrəl] *s* catedral

Catholic ['kæθlɪk] ◆ *adj* católico, ca ◆ *s* católico, ca

catsup ['kætsəp] *s* ketchup

cattle ['kætl] *spl* ganado (vacuno)

catwalk ['kætwɔːk] *s* pasarela

caucus ['kɔːkəs] *s* comité

■ **Caucus** *s* ▸ congreso de los principales partidos estadounidenses

caught [kɔːt] *pretérito & participio pasado* → catch

cauliflower ['kɒlɪ,flaʊər] *s* coliflor

cause [kɔːz] ◆ *s* ❶ causa ❷ • cause (for) motivo (para) • cause for complaint motivo de queja • cause to do something motivo para hacer algo ◆ *vt* causar • to cause somebody to do something hacer que alguien haga algo

caustic ['kɔːstɪk] *adj* ❶ QUÍMICA cáustico, ca ❷ mordaz; hiriente

caution ['kɔːʃn] ◆ *s* ❶ ⚙ *incontable* precaución; cautela ❷ advertencia ◆ *vt* ❶ prevenir ❷ advertir

cautious ['kɔːʃəs] *adj* prudente; cauto, ta

cavalry ['kævlrɪ] *s* caballería

cave [keɪv] *s* cueva

■ **cave in** *vi* hundirse

caveman ['keɪvmæn] *s* cavernícola

   El plural de **caveman** es **cavemen** [-men].

caviar(e) ['kævɪɑːr] *s* caviar

cavity ['kævətɪ] *s* ❶ cavidad ❷ caries

CB *s abreviatura escrita de* **Citizens' Band**

cc *s* ❶ (*abreviatura de* cubic centimeter) cc ❷ (*abreviatura escrita de* carbon copy) cc

CD *s* (*abreviatura de* compact disc) CD

CD burner *s* grabadora de CD

CD player *s* reproductor de CD

CD-R (*abreviatura de* compact disc recordable) *s* CD-R

CD-R drive *s* grabadora de CD-R

CD-ROM burner *s* grabadora de CD

CD-RW (*abreviatura de* compact disc rewritable) *s* CD-RW

CD tower *s* torre de almacenamiento de CDs

cease [si:s] *vt & vi formal* cesar

cease-fire *s* alto el fuego

cedar (tree) ['si:dər-] *s* cedro

ceiling ['si:lɪŋ] *s* ❶ techo ❷ tope; límite

celebrate ['selɪbreɪt] *vt & vi* celebrar

celebration [,selɪ'breɪʃn] *s* ❶ ⚬ *incontable* celebración ❷ fiesta; festejo

celebrity [sɪ'lebrətɪ] *s* celebridad

celery ['selərɪ] *s* apio

celibate ['selɪbət] *adj* célibe

cell [sel] *s* ❶ BIOLOGÍA & POLÍTICA célula ❷ INFORMÁTICA celda ❸ celda (*de preso, monja*) ❹ ELECTRICIDAD pila

cellar ['selər] *s* ❶ sótano ❷ bodega

cello ['ʧeləʊ] *s* violoncelo

El plural de **cello** es **cellos**.

Cellophane® ['seləfeɪn] *s* celofán®

cell phone ['selfəʊn], **cellular phone** ['səljʊlər-] *s* teléfono celular; celular

Celsius ['selsɪəs] *adj* centígrado, da • **20 degrees Celsius** 20 grados centígrados

Celt [kelt] *s* celta

Celtic ['keltɪk] ◆ *adj* celta ◆ *s* celta

cement [sɪ'ment] *s* cemento

cement mixer *s* hormigonera

cemetery ['semɪtrɪ] *s* cementerio

censor ['sensər] ◆ *s* censor, ra ◆ *vt* censurar

censorship ['sensəʃɪp] *s* censura

census ['sensəs] *s* censo

El plural de **census** es **censuses.**

cent [sent] *s* centavo

centennial [sen'tenjəl] *s* centenario

center ['sentər] ◆ *s* centro • **center of attention/gravity** centro de atención/gravedad • **the center** POLÍTICA el centro ◆ *adj* ❶ central ❷ POLÍTICA centrista ◆ *vt* centrar

center back, center half *s* FÚTBOL defensa central

center forward *s* FÚTBOL delantero, ra centro

center half = **center back**

centigrade ['sentɪgreɪd] *adj* centígrado, da • **20 degrees centigrade** 20 grados centígrados

centiliter ['sentɪ,li:tər] *s* centilitro

centimeter ['sentɪ,mi:tər] *s* centímetro

centipede ['sentɪpi:d] *s* ciempiés

central ['sentrəl] *adj* ❶ central • **central control** control central ❷ céntrico, ca

Central America *s* Centroamérica

Central Europe *s* Europa Central

central heating *s* calefacción central

centralize ['sentrəlaɪz] *vt* centralizar

central locking [-'lɒkɪŋ] *s* cierre centralizado

century ['senʧʊrɪ] *s* siglo

ceramic [sɪ'ræmɪk] *adj* de cerámica; cerámico, ca

■ **ceramics** *s* cerámica

cereal ['sɪərɪəl] *s* ❶ cereal ❷ cereales

ceremony ['serɪmənɪ] *s* ceremonia

expresión **to stand on ceremony** andarse con cumplidos o ceremonias

certain ['sɜːtn] *adj* ❶ seguro, ra • **he's certain to be late** (es) seguro que llega tarde • **to be certain (of)** estar seguro (de) • **to make certain (of)** asegurarse (de) • **for certain** con toda seguridad ❷ cierto, ta • **to a certain extent** hasta cierto punto ❸ • **a certain...** un, una tal...

certainly ['sɜːtnlɪ] *adv* desde luego • **certainly not!** ¡claro que no!

certainty ['sɜːtntɪ] *s* seguridad

certificate [sə'tɪfɪkət] *s* ❶ certificado ❷ EDUCACIÓN & UNIVERSIDAD diploma; título ❸ partida

certified ['sɜːtɪfaɪd] *adj* ❶ certificado, da ❷ diplomado, da

certified mail *s* correo certificado

certified public accountant *s* contador público, contadora pública

certify ['sɜːtɪfaɪ] *vt* ❶ certificar ❷ declarar demente

cervical smear *s* citología; frotis cervical

cervix ['sɜːvɪks] *s* cuello del útero

El plural de **cervix** es **cervices** ['sɜːvɪsiːz].

cesarean (section) [sɪ'zeərɪən-] *s* cesárea

cf. (*abreviatura de* confer) cf.; cfr.

Chad [ʧæd] *s* el Chad

chafe [ʧeɪf] *vt* rozar

chain [ʧeɪn] ◆ *s* cadena • **chain of mountains** cordillera; cadena montañosa • **chain of events** serie de acontecimientos ◆ *vt* encadenar

chain reaction *s* reacción en cadena

chain saw *s* motosierra; sierra mecánica

chain-smoke *vi* fumar un cigarrillo tras otro

chain store *s* tienda (*de una cadena*)

chair [ʧeər] ◆ *s* ❶ silla ❷ sillón ❸ cátedra ❹ presidencia ◆ *vt* presidir

chair lift *s* telesilla

chairman ['tʃeəmən] *s* presidente

El plural de **chairman** es **chairmen** ['tʃeəmen].

chairperson ['tʃeə,pɜ:sn] *s* presidente, ta

El plural de **chairperson** es **chairpersons**.

chalet ['ʃæleɪ] *s* chalé; chalet

chalk [tʃɔ:k] *s* ❶ gis • **a piece of chalk** un gis ❷ creta

chalkboard ['tʃɔ:kbɔ:d] *s* pizarrón

challenge ['tʃælɪndʒ] ♦ *s* desafío; reto ♦ *vt* ❶ • **to challenge somebody (to something/to do something)** desafiar a alguien (a algo/a que haga algo) ❷ poner en tela de juicio

challenging ['tʃælɪndʒɪŋ] *adj* ❶ estimulante • **a challenging task** una tarea que supone un reto ❷ desafiante

chamber ['tʃeɪmbər] *s* cámara

chambermaid ['tʃeɪmbəmeɪd] *s* camarera

chamber music *s* música de cámara

chamber of commerce *s* cámara de comercio

chameleon [kə'mi:ljən] *s* camaleón

champagne [,ʃæm'peɪn] *s* champán

champion ['tʃæmpjən] ♦ *s* ❶ campeón, ona ❷ defensor, ra ♦ *vt* defender

championship ['tʃæmpjənʃɪp] *s* campeonato

chance [tʃɑ:ns] ♦ *s* ❶ azar; suerte • **by chance** por casualidad ❷ posibilidad • **he has a good chance of winning** hay buenas posibilidades de que gane • **not to stand a chance (of)** no tener ninguna posibilidad (de) • **by any chance** por casualidad; acaso ❸ oportunidad ❹ riesgo • **to take a chance (on)** correr un riesgo o arriesgarse (con) ♦ *adj* fortuito, ta; casual ♦ *vt* arriesgar

expresión **to chance it** arriesgarse

chancellor ['tʃɑ:nsələr] *s* ❶ canciller ❷ UNIVERSIDAD ≃ rector

chandelier [,ʃændə'lɪər] *s* candelabro

change [tʃeɪndʒ] ♦ *s* ❶ cambio • **change of clothes** muda • **for a change** para variar ❷ cambio ❸ cambio; feria ❹ • **have you got change for $5?** ¿tienes cambio de 5 dólares? ♦ *vt* ❶ cambiar • **to change something into** transformar algo en • **to change dollars into pesos** cambiar dólares por pesos • **to change direction** cambiar de rumbo • **to change your mind** cambiar de idea o opinión ❷ cambiar de *(trabajo, marcha, tren)* • **to change hands** COMERCIO cambiar de mano • **to change your shirt** cambiarse de camisa • **to get changed** cambiarse de ropa ♦ *vi* ❶ cambiar • **to change into something** transformarse en algo ❷ cambiarse *(de ropa)* ❸ hacer transbordo

■ **change over** *vi* • **to change over to** cambiar a

changeable ['tʃeɪndʒəbl] *adj* variable

change machine *s* máquina de cambio

changeover ['tʃeɪndʒ,əʊvər] *s* • **changeover (to)** cambio (a)

change purse *s* monedero

changing ['tʃeɪndʒɪŋ] *adj* cambiante

changing room *s* ❶ DEPORTE vestidor ❷ probador

channel ['tʃænl] ♦ *s* canal ♦ *vt* literal & figurado canalizar

■ **Channel** *s* • **the (English) Channel** el Canal de la Mancha

■ **channels** *spl* conductos; medios

Channel tunnel *s* • **the Channel tunnel** el túnel del Canal de la Mancha

chant [tʃɑ:nt] ♦ *s* ❶ RELIGIÓN canto ❷ consigna ❸ cántico ♦ *vt* ❶ RELIGIÓN cantar ❷ corear

chaos ['keɪɒs] *s* caos

chaotic [keɪ'ɒtɪk] *adj* caótico, ca

chapel ['tʃæpl] *s* capilla

chaplain ['tʃæplɪn] *s* capellán

chapped [tʃæpt] *adj* agrietado, da

chapter ['tʃæptər] *s* literal & figurado capítulo

character ['kærəktər] *s* ❶ carácter • **to be out of/in character (for)** no ser/ser típico (de) ❷ personaje ❸ *familiar* tipo ❹ *familiar* • **to be a character** ser todo un carácter

characteristic [,kærəktə'rɪstɪk] ♦ *adj* característico, ca ♦ *s* característica

characterize ['kærəktəraɪz] *vt* caracterizar

charade [ʃə'rɑ:d] *s* farsa

■ **charades** *s* ⚙ *incontable* charadas

charcoal ['tʃɑ:kəʊl] *s* ❶ carbón (vegetal) ❷ carboncillo

charge [tʃɑ:dʒ] ♦ *s* ❶ precio • **free of charge** gratis • **will that be cash or charge?** ¿pagará en efectivo o con tarjeta? ❷ DERECHO cargo; acusación ❸ • **to have charge of something** tener algo al cargo de uno • **to take charge (of)** hacerse cargo (de) • **to be in charge** ser el encargado, la encargada • **in charge of** encargado, da de ❹ ELECTRICIDAD carga ❺ MILITAR carga *(de caballería)* ♦ *vt* ❶ cobrar • **to charge something to somebody** cargar algo en la cuenta de alguien ❷ cargar contra ❸ cargar *(pilas)* • **I need to charge my cellphone** tengo que cargar el celular ❹ • **to charge somebody (with something)** acusar a alguien (de algo) ♦ *vi* cargar • **to charge in/out** entrar/salir en tromba

charge card *s* tarjeta de compra

charger ['tʃɑ:dʒər] *s* cargador

chariot ['tʃærɪət] *s* carro; cuadriga

charisma [kə'rɪzmə] *s* carisma

charitable ['tʃærətəbl] *adj* ❶ caritativo, va ❷ benéfico, ca

charity ['tʃærətɪ] *s* ❶ caridad ❷ institución benéfica • **for charity** para un fin benéfico

charm [tʃɑ:m] ♦ *s* ❶ encanto ❷ hechizo ❸ dije; amuleto ♦ *vt* dejar encantado, da

charming ['tʃɑ:mɪŋ] *adj* encantador, ra

chart [tʃɑ:t] ♦ *s* ❶ gráfico ❷ carta ♦ *vt* ❶ representar en un mapa ❷ *figurado* trazar

■ **charts** *spl* • **the charts** la lista de éxitos

charter ['tʃɑ:tər] ♦ *s* carta ♦ *en compuestos* chárter ♦ *vt* fletar

charter flight *s* vuelo chárter

chase [ʧeɪs] ◆ *s* persecución ◆ *vt* ❶ perseguir ❷ ahuyentar ❸ ir detrás de

chassis ['ʃæsɪ] *s* chasis

  El plural de **chassis** es **chassis**.

chaste [ʧeɪst] *adj* casto, ta

chat [ʧæt] ◆ *s* charla ◆ *vi* ❶ charlar ❷ *INFORMÁTICA* chatear

chat line *s* línea compartida

chat room *s* *INFORMÁTICA* sala de chat

chatter ['ʧætər] ◆ *s* ❶ cháchara ❷ gorjeo ❸ chillidos ◆ *vi* ❶ parlotear ❷ castañetear

chatterbox ['ʧætəbɒks] *s familiar* parlanchín, ina

chatty ['ʧætɪ] *adj* ❶ dicharachero, ra ❷ informal *(carta)*

chauffeur ['ʃəʊfər] *s* chófer

chauvinist ['ʃəʊvɪnɪst] *s* ❶ sexista • **male chauvinist** machista ❷ chovinista

cheap [ʧi:p] ◆ *adj* ❶ barato, ta ❷ de mala calidad ❸ de mal gusto ❹ tacaño, ña ◆ *adv* barato

cheaply ['ʧi:plɪ] *adv* barato

cheat [ʧi:t] ◆ *s* tramposo, sa ◆ *vt* engañar ; estafar ◆ *vi* ❶ copiar ❷ hacer trampas

check [ʧek] ◆ *s* ❶ • **check (on)** inspección o control (de) • **to keep a check on** controlar ❷ • **check (on)** restricción (en) ❸ cheque • **he paid by check** pagó con un cheque ❹ cuenta • **can I have the check, please?** la cuenta, por favor ❺ señal de visto bueno ❻ cuadros ❼ jaque ◆ *vt* ❶ comprobar ❷ inspeccionar ❸ revisar ; controlar ❹ refrenar ◆ *vi* comprobar • **to check (for/on something)** comprobar (algo)

■ **check in** ◆ *vt* ☼ *El objeto se puede colocar antes o después de la preposición.* facturar ◆ *vi* ❶ registrarse ❷ documentarse

■ **check out** ◆ *vt* ☼ *El objeto se puede colocar antes o después de la preposición.* ❶ recoger ❷ comprobar ❸ *familiar* mirar • **check this out!** ¡checa esto! ◆ *vi* salir de un hotel

■ **check up** *vi* • **to check up (on something)** informarse (acerca de algo) • **to check up on somebody** hacer averiguaciones sobre alguien

checkbook ['ʧekbʊk] *s* chequera

checkers ['ʧekəz] *s* ☼ *incontable* damas

check guarantee card *s* tarjeta de identificación bancaria

check-in *s* documentación

check-in desk *s* mostrador de documentación

checking account ['ʧekɪŋ-] *s* cuenta corriente

checkmate ['ʧekmeɪt] *s* jaque mate

checkout ['ʧekaʊt] *s* caja *(de supermercado)*

checkpoint ['ʧekpɔɪnt] *s* control

checkup ['ʧekʌp] *s* chequeo

cheek [ʧi:k] *s* ❶ mejilla ❷ *familiar* descaro

cheekbone ['ʧi:kbəʊn] *s* pómulo

cheeky ['ʧi:kɪ] *adj* descarado, da

cheer [ʧɪər] ◆ *s* aclamación • **cheers** vítores • **three cheers for Donald!** ¡viva Donald! ◆ *vt* aclamar ◆ *vi* gritar con entusiasmo

■ **cheers** *exclamación* ¡salud!

■ **cheer up** ◆ *vt* ☼ *El objeto se puede colocar antes o después de la preposición.* animar ◆ *vi* animarse

cheerful ['ʧɪəfʊl] *adj* alegre

cheerleader ['ʧɪəli:dər] *s* porrista

cheerleading

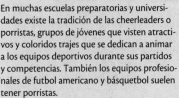

CHEERLEADING

En muchas escuelas preparatorias y universidades existe la tradición de las cheerleaders o porristas, grupos de jóvenes que visten atractivos y coloridos trajes que se dedican a animar a los equipos deportivos durante sus partidos y competencias. También los equipos profesionales de futbol americano y básquetbol suelen tener porristas.

cheese [ʧi:z] *s* queso

cheeseboard ['ʧi:zbɔ:d] *s* tabla de quesos

cheeseburger ['ʧi:z,bɜ:gər] *s* hamburguesa con queso

cheesecake ['ʧi:zkeɪk] *s* pastel o tarta de queso

cheetah ['ʧi:tə] *s* guepardo

chef [ʃef] *s* chef; jefe de cocina

chemical ['kemɪkl] ◆ *adj* químico, ca ◆ *s* sustancia química

chemist ['kemɪst] *s* químico, ca

chemistry ['kemɪstrɪ] *s* química

cherish ['ʧerɪʃ] *vt* ❶ abrigar *(esperanza, memoria)* ❷ apreciar ❸ tener mucho cariño a

cherry ['ʧerɪ] *s* cereza ▶ **cherry (tree)** cerezo

chess [ʧes] *s* ajedrez

chessboard ['ʧesbɔ:d] *s* tablero de ajedrez

chest [ʧest] *s* ❶ *ANATOMÍA* pecho ❷ baúl; cofre ❸ caja

expresión **to get something off your chest** *familiar* contar algo para desahogarse

chestnut ['ʧesnʌt] ◆ *adj* castaño, ña ◆ *s* castaña ▶ **chestnut (tree)** castaño

chest of drawers *s* cómoda

  El plural de **chest of drawers** es **chests of drawers.**

chew [ʧu:] *vt* ❶ masticar ❷ morderse *(las uñas)* ❸ morder

■ **chew up** ☼ *El objeto se puede colocar antes o después de la preposición.* ❶ masticar ❷ mordisquear

chewing gum ['ʧu:ɪŋ-] *s* chicle

chic [ʃi:k] *adj* chic ; elegante

chick [ʧɪk] *s* ❶ polluelo ❷ *familiar* nena

chicken ['ʧɪkɪn] *s* ❶ gallina ❷ pollo ❸ *familiar* gallina *(cobarde)*

C

C

■ **chicken out** *vi familiar* • **to chicken out (of something/of doing something)** rajarse (a la hora de algo/de hacer algo)

chickenpox ['ʧɪkɪnpɒks] *s* varicela

chickpea ['ʧɪkpiː] *s* garbanzo

chicory ['ʧɪkərɪ] *s* achicoria

chief [ʧiːf] ◆ *adj* principal ◆ *s* jefe, fa

Chief Executive *s* presidente, ta

chief executive officer *s* director, ra general

chiefly ['ʧiːflɪ] *adv* ❶ principalmente ❷ por encima de todo

child [ʧaɪld] *s* ❶ niño, ña ❷ hijo, ja
El plural de **child** es **children**.

childbirth ['ʧaɪldbɜːθ] *s* 🔆 *incontable* parto

childcare ['ʧaɪldkeər] *s* cuidado de los niños

childhood ['ʧaɪldhʊd] *s* infancia; niñez

childish ['ʧaɪldɪʃ] *adj despectivo* infantil

childlike ['ʧaɪldlaɪk] *adj* ❶ como un niño ❷ de niño

children ['ʧɪldrən] *spl* → **child**

children's home *s* hogar infantil

Chile ['ʧɪlɪ] *s* Chile

Chilean ['ʧɪlɪən] ◆ *adj* chileno, na ◆ *s* chileno, na

chili ['ʧɪlɪ] = **chilli**

chill [ʧɪl] ◆ *s* ❶ resfriado ❷ • **there's a chill in the air** hace un poco de fresco ◆ *vt* ❶ enfriar ❷ hacer sentir escalofríos

■ **chill out** *vi familiar* relajarse

chili ['ʧɪlɪ] *s* guindilla; chile
El plural de **chili** es **chilies**.

chilling ['ʧɪlɪŋ] *adj* escalofriante

chilly ['ʧɪlɪ] *adj* frío, a • **it's chilly** hace frío

chime [ʧaɪm] ◆ *s* ❶ campanada ❷ repique ◆ *vi* ❶ repicar ❷ sonar

chimney ['ʧɪmnɪ] *s* chimenea

chimneypot ['ʧɪmnɪpɒt] *s* cañón de chimenea

chimp [ʧɪmp], **chimpanzee** [ˌʧɪmpən'ziː] *s* chimpancé

chin [ʧɪn] *s* barbilla

china ['ʧaɪnə] *s* porcelana

China ['ʧaɪnə] *s* la China

Chinese [ˌʧaɪ'niːz] ◆ *adj* chino, na ◆ *s* ❶ chino, na ❷ chino ◆ *spl* • **the Chinese** los chinos

chink [ʧɪŋk] ◆ *s* ❶ grieta ❷ resquicio ❸ tintineo ◆ *vi* tintinear

chip [ʧɪp] ◆ *s* ❶ papa frita *(de bolsa)* ❷ pedacito; viruta; lasca ❸ despostilladura ❹ *INFORMÁTICA* chip ❺ ficha ◆ *vt* despostillar

■ **chip in** *vi* ❶ poner dinero ❷ intervenir *(en conversación)*

■ **chip off** *vt* 🔆 *El objeto se puede colocar antes o después de la preposición.* desconchar

chiropodist [kɪ'rɒpədɪst] *s* podólogo, ga; pedicuro, ra

chirp [ʧɜːp] *vi* ❶ piar ❷ chirriar

chisel ['ʧɪzl] *s* ❶ formón; escoplo ❷ cincel

chitchat ['ʧɪtʧæt] *s* 🔆 *incontable familiar* güirigüiri

chives [ʧaɪvz] *spl* cebolleta

chlorine ['klɔːriːn] *s* cloro

chock-a-block, chock-full *adj familiar* • **chock-a-block (with)** hasta los topes (de)

chocolate ['ʧɒkələt] ◆ *s* chocolate ◆ **en compuestos** de chocolate

choice [ʧɔɪs] ◆ *s* ❶ elección • **to do something by choice** elegir hacer algo ❷ preferido, da ❸ alternativa preferida ❹ surtido ◆ *adj* de primera calidad

choir ['kwaɪər] *s* coro

choirboy ['kwaɪəbɔɪ] *s* niño de coro

choke [ʧəʊk] ◆ *s* AUTOMÓVILES estárter ◆ *vt* ❶ estrangular; ahogar ❷ asfixiar ❸ hacer atragantarse ❹ atascar ◆ *vi* ❶ atragantarse ❷ ahogarse ❸ asfixiarse

cholera ['kɒlərə] *s* cólera

choose [ʧuːz] ◆ *vt* ❶ elegir; escoger ❷ • **to choose to do something** decidir hacer algo • **do whatever you choose** haz lo que quieras

expresión **there's little** o **not much to choose between them** no se sabe cuál es mejor
◆ *vi* elegir; escoger

Formas irregulares de **choose**: *pretérito* **chose**, *pp* **chosen**.

choos(e)y ['ʧuːzɪ] *(comparativo* **choosier,** *superlativo* **choosiest)** *adj* ❶ quisquilloso, sa ❷ exigente; remilgado, da

chop [ʧɒp] ◆ *s* ❶ COCINA chuleta ❷ hachazo ◆ *vt* ❶ picar ❷ cortar ◆ *vi*

expresión **to chop and change** cambiar cada dos por tres

■ **chop down** *vt* 🔆 *El objeto se puede colocar antes o después de la preposición.* talar

■ **chop up** *vt* 🔆 *El objeto se puede colocar antes o después de la preposición.* ❶ picar ❷ cortar

chopper ['ʧɒpər] *s* ❶ hacha ❷ cuchillo de carnicero ❸ *familiar* helicóptero

choppy ['ʧɒpɪ] *adj* picado, da

chopsticks ['ʧɒpstɪks] *spl* palillos

chord [kɔːd] *s* MÚSICA acorde

chore [ʧɔːr] *s* ❶ tarea; faena ❷ *familiar* lata

chorus ['kɔːrəs] *s* ❶ estribillo ❷ coro

chose [ʧəʊz] *pretérito* → **choose**

chosen ['ʧəʊzn] *participio pasado* → **choose**

Christ [kraɪst] *s* Cristo

christen ['krɪsn] *vt* bautizar

christening ['krɪsnɪŋ] *s* bautizo

Christian ['krɪsʧən] ◆ *adj* cristiano, na ◆ *s* cristiano, na

Christianity [ˌkrɪstɪ'ænətɪ] *s* cristianismo

Christian name *s* nombre de pila

Christmas ['krısməs] *s* Navidad • **what are you doing at Christmas?** ¿qué vas a hacer para la Navidad? • **happy** o **merry Christmas!** ¡Feliz Navidad!

CHRISTMAS

El 25 de diciembre en Estados Unidos la tradicional comida de Navidad incluye pavo al horno acompañado con relleno (**stuffing**) y verduras, junto con **cranberry sauce** o jalea de arándano. Durante la temporada navideña la gente manda **Christmas cards** (tarjetas de Navidad) a todos sus conocidos.

Christmas card *s* tarjeta de Navidad
Christmas carol *s* villancico
Christmas Day *s* día de Navidad
Christmas Eve *s* Nochebuena
Christmas tree *s* árbol de Navidad
chrome [krəum], **chromium** ['krəumıəm] ◆ *s* cromo ◆ *en compuestos* cromado, da
chronic ['krɒnık] *adj* ❶ crónico, ca ❷ empedernido, da
chrysanthemum [krı'sænəəməm] *s* crisantemo
chubby ['ʧʌbı] *adj* rechoncho, cha • **to have chubby cheeks** ser mofletudo, da
chuck [ʧʌk] *vt familiar* ❶ tirar; arrojar • **to chuck somebody out** echar a alguien ❷ dejar *(trabajo, novio)*
■ **chuck away, chuck out** *vt* ☼ *El objeto se puede colocar antes o después de la preposición. familiar* tirar
chuckle ['ʧʌkl] *vi* reírse entre dientes
chum [ʧʌm] *s* ❶ *familiar* cuate ❷ compañero, ra
chunk [ʧʌŋk] *s* trozo
church [ʧɜ:ʧ] *s* iglesia • **to go to church** ir a misa
Church of England *s* • **the Church of England** la Iglesia Anglicana
churchyard ['ʧɜ:ʧja:d] *s* cementerio; camposanto
churn [ʧɜ:n] ◆ *s* ❶ mantequera ❷ lechera ◆ *vt* agitar
■ **churn out** *vt* ☼ *El objeto se puede colocar antes o después de la preposición. familiar* hacer en cantidades industriales
chute [ʃu:t] *s* ❶ vertedor ❷ tobogán ❸ rampa
chutney ['ʧʌtnı] *s* ▶ salsa agridulce y picante de fruta y semillas
cider ['saıdər] *s* ❶ sidra ❷ jugo de manzana
cigar [sı'ga:r] *s* puro
cigarette [,sıgə'ret] *s* cigarro
cigarette paper *s* papel de fumar
Cinderella [,sındə'relə] *s* Cenicienta
cinema ['sınəmə] *s* cine
cinnamon ['sınəmən] *s* canela
circa ['sɜ:kə] *preposición* ❶ hacia ❷ aproximadamente

circle ['sɜ:kl] ◆ *s* ❶ círculo ❷ anfiteatro
expresión to go round in circles darle (mil) vueltas al mismo tema
◆ *vt* ❶ rodear con un círculo ❷ describir círculos alrededor de ◆ *vi* dar vueltas
circuit ['sɜ:kıt] *s* ❶ circuito ❷ vuelta
circular ['sɜ:kjʊlər] ◆ *adj* circular ◆ *s* circular
circulate ['sɜ:kjʊleıt] ◆ *vi* ❶ circular ❷ alternar ◆ *vt* hacer circular
circulation [,sɜ:kjʊ'leıʃn] *s* ❶ circulación ❷ tirada
circumcise ['sɜ:kəmsaız] *vt* circuncidar
circumference [sə'kʌmfərəns] *s* circunferencia
circumstance ['sɜ:kəmstəns] *s* circunstancia
• **circumstances** circunstancias • **under** o **in no circumstances** bajo ningún concepto • **in** o **under the circumstances** dadas las circunstancias
circus ['sɜ:kəs] *s* ❶ circo ❷ glorieta
cistern ['sıstən] *s* cisterna
cite [saıt] *vt* citar
citizen ['sıtızn] *s* ciudadano, na
Citizens' Band *s* ▶ banda de radio reservada para radioaficionados y conductores
citizenship ['sıtıznʃıp] *s* ciudadanía
citrus fruit ['sıtrəs-] *s* cítrico
city ['sıtı] *s* ciudad
city center *s* centro de la ciudad
city hall *s* ayuntamiento
civic ['sıvık] *adj* ❶ cívico, ca ❷ público, ca
civics ['sıvıks] *s* ☼ *incontable* EDUCACIÓN educación cívica
civil ['sıvl] *adj* ❶ civil ❷ cortés
civil engineering *s* ingeniería civil
civilian [sı'vıljən] ◆ *s* civil ◆ *en compuestos* ❶ civil ❷ de paisano
civilization [,sıvılaı'zeıʃn] *s* civilización
civilized ['sıvılaızd] *adj* civilizado, da
civil law *s* derecho civil
civil liberties *spl* libertades civiles
civil rights *spl* derechos civiles
civil servant *s* funcionario, ria público, ca
civil service *s* administración pública
civil war *s* guerra civil

THE AMERICAN CIVIL WAR

En la guerra civil o de secesión, que tuvo lugar entre 1861 y 1865, se enfrentaron los estados del sur, con su economía agrícola basada en gran parte en la esclavitud, y los estados industriales del norte, donde se oponían a la esclavitud. Los estados del norte, con más soldados y armas, ganaron finalmente y se abolió la esclavitud.

CJD (*abreviatura de* Creutzfeldt-Jakob disease) *s* enfermedad de Creutzfeldt-Jakob

claim [kleɪm] ◆ *s* ❶ reclamación ❷ reivindicación • **to have a claim on somebody** tener un derecho sobre alguien • **to lay claim to something** reclamar algo ❸ afirmación ◆ *vt* ❶ reclamar ❷ cobrar ❸ atribuirse ❹ • **to claim (that)** mantener que • **he claims to be famous** afirma que es famoso ◆ *vi* • **to claim on your insurance** reclamar al seguro

claimant ['kleɪmənt] *s* ❶ pretendiente ❷ solicitante ❸ DERECHO demandante

clam [klæm] *s* almeja

clammy ['klæmɪ] *adj* ❶ húmedo, da; pegajoso, sa ❷ bochornoso, sa

clamor ['klæmər] ◆ *s* ⚇ *incontable* ❶ clamor ❷ • **clamor (for)** demandas (de) ◆ *vi* • **to clamor for something** exigir a voces algo

clamp [klæmp] ◆ *s* abrazadera ◆ *vt* sujetar (con una abrazadera)

■ **clamp down** *vi* • **to clamp down on** poner freno a

clandestine [klæn'destɪn] *adj* clandestino, na

clang [klæŋ] *vi* hacer un ruido metálico

clap [klæp] ◆ *vt* • **to clap your hands** dar palmadas ◆ *vi* aplaudir

clapboard ['klæpbɔ:d] *s* tablilla

clapping ['klæpɪŋ] *s* ⚇ *incontable* aplausos

claret ['klærət] *s* burdeos

clarify ['klærɪfaɪ] *vt* aclarar

clarinet [,klærə'net] *s* clarinete

clarity ['klærətɪ] *s* claridad

clash [klæʃ] ◆ *s* ❶ conflicto ❷ choque *(de personalidades)* ❸ estruendo ◆ *vi* ❶ • **to clash (with)** enfrentarse (con) ❷ estar en desacuerdo ❸ • **to clash (with)** coincidir (con) ❹ • **to clash (with)** desentonar (con)

clasp [klɑ:sp] ◆ *s* ❶ broche ❷ cierre ◆ *vt* ❶ abrazar ❷ agarrar

class [klɑ:s] ◆ *s* clase ◆ *vt* • **to class somebody (as)** clasificar a alguien (de)

classic ['klæsɪk] ◆ *adj* clásico, ca ◆ *s* clásico

classical ['klæsɪkl] *adj* clásico, ca • **classical music** la música clásica

classified ['klæsɪfaɪd] *adj* reservado, da; secreto, ta

classified ad *s* anuncio por palabras

classify ['klæsɪfaɪ] *vt* clasificar

classmate ['klɑ:smeɪt] *s* compañero, ra de clase

classroom ['klɑ:srʊm] *s* aula; clase

classroom assistant *s* EDUCACIÓN ayudante del profesor

classy ['klɑ:sɪ] *adj familiar* con clase

clatter ['klætər] *s* ❶ estrépito ❷ ruido (de cacharros)

clause [klɔ:z] *s* ❶ cláusula ❷ GRAMÁTICA oración

claw [klɔ:] ◆ *s* ❶ garra ❷ uña *(de gato)* ❸ pinza ◆ *vi* • **to claw at something a)** arañar algo **b)** intentar agarrarse a algo

clay [kleɪ] *s* arcilla

clean [kli:n] ◆ *adj* ❶ limpio, pia ❷ en blanco ❸ no contaminante ❹ impecable ❺ sin multas *(permiso de conducir)* ❻ inocente *(chiste)* ❼ nítido, da ◆ *vt* & *vi* limpiar

■ **clean out** *vt* ⚇ *El objeto se puede colocar antes o después de la preposición.* ❶ limpiar el interior de ❷ *familiar* • **the burglars cleaned us out** (los ladrones) nos limpiaron la casa

■ **clean up** *vt* ⚇ *El objeto se puede colocar antes o después de la preposición.* ordenar; limpiar • **to clean yourself up** asearse

cleaner ['kli:nər] *s* ❶ limpiador, ra • **the cleaner comes twice a week** la mujer de la limpieza viene dos veces a la semana ❷ producto de limpieza

cleaning ['kli:nɪŋ] *s* limpieza

cleanliness ['klenlɪnɪs] *s* limpieza

cleanse [klenz] *vt* limpiar

cleanser ['klenzər] *s* crema o loción limpiadora

clean-shaven [-'ʃeɪvn] *adj* ❶ barbilampiño, ña ❷ bien afeitado, da

clear [klɪər] ◆ *adj* ❶ claro, ra • **to make something clear (to)** dejar algo claro (a) • **it's clear that...** está claro que... • **are you clear about it?** ¿lo entiendes? • **to make yourself clear** explicarse con claridad ❷ despejado, da ❸ transparente ❹ nítido, da ❺ terso, sa ❻ libre *(tiempo)* ❼ • **to be clear of the ground** no tocar el suelo ❽ entero, ra *(día, semana)* ❾ neto, ta *(beneficio)* ◆ *adv* • **stand clear!** ¡aléjense! • **to jump/step clear** saltar/dar un paso para hacerse a un lado ◆ *vt* ❶ despejar • **they cleared the area of mines** limpiaron el área de minas • **to clear a space** hacer sitio • **to clear the table** recoger la mesa ❷ talar ❸ destapar ❹ quitar ❺ saltar ❻ aprobar ❼ declarar inocente • **to be cleared of something** salir absuelto de algo ◆ *vi* despejarse

■ **clear away** *vt* ⚇ *El objeto se puede colocar antes o después de la preposición.* poner en su sitio

■ **clear out** *vt* ⚇ *El objeto se puede colocar antes o después de la preposición.* limpiar a fondo

■ **clear up** ◆ *vt* ⚇ *El objeto se puede colocar antes o después de la preposición.* ❶ limpiar ❷ recoger ❸ aclarar ❹ resolver ◆ *vi* ❶ despejarse ❷ desaparecer *(enfermedad, infección)* ❸ ordenar; recoger

clearance ['klɪərəns] *s* ❶ despeje; limpieza ❷ eliminación ❸ autorización; permiso ❹ distancia libre

clear-cut *adj* ❶ bien definido, da ❷ nítido, da

clearing ['klɪərɪŋ] *s* claro

clearly ['klɪəlɪ] *adv* ❶ claramente ❷ obviamente

cleavage ['kli:vɪdʒ] *s* escote

clef [klef] *s* clave

clench [klentʃ] *vt* apretar

clergy ['klɜ:dʒɪ] *spl* • **the clergy** el clero

clergyman ['klɜ:dʒɪmən] *s* clérigo

El plural de **clergyman** es **clergymen** ['klɜ:dʒɪmen].

clerical ['klerɪkl] *adj* ❶ de oficina ❷ administrativo, va

clerk [klɜːrk] *s* ❶ oficinista ❷ secretario *(de tribunal)* ❸ vendedor, ra

clever ['klevər] *adj* ❶ listo, ta; inteligente ❷ ingenioso, sa ❸ hábil

cliché ['kliːʃeɪ] *s* cliché

click [klɪk] ◆ *s* INFORMÁTICA clic ◆ *vt* ❶ INFORMÁTICA hacer clic en ❷ chasquear ◆ *vi* ❶ INFORMÁTICA • **to click (on something)** hacer clic (en algo) ❷ hacer clic ❸ *familiar* • **suddenly, it clicked** de pronto, caí en la cuenta

client ['klaɪənt] *s* cliente, ta

cliff [klɪf] *s* ❶ acantilado ❷ precipicio

climate ['klaɪmɪt] *s* ❶ clima ❷ *figurado* ambiente

climax ['klaɪmæks] *s* clímax; culminación

climb [klaɪm] ◆ *s* ❶ subida ❷ escalada ◆ *vt* ❶ subir ❷ trepar a ❸ escalar ◆ *vi* ❶ • **to climb over something** trepar por algo • **to climb into something** meterse en algo ❷ subir

climber ['klaɪmər] *s* ❶ montañista ❷ escalador, ra

climbing ['klaɪmɪŋ] *s* montañismo • **to go climbing** hacer montañismo

clinch [klɪntʃ] *vt* cerrar *(trato)*

cling [klɪŋ] *vi* ❶ • **to cling (to)** agarrarse (a) ❷ • **to cling (to)** pegarse (a)

Formas irregulares de **cling**: *pretérito & pp* **clung**.

clinic ['klɪnɪk] *s* clínica

clinical ['klɪnɪkl] *adj* ❶ MEDICINA clínico, ca ❷ frío, a

clink [klɪŋk] *vi* tintinear

clip [klɪp] ◆ *s* ❶ clip ❷ pasador ❸ fragmento; secuencias *(de película)* ❹ • **to give somebody's hair a clip** cortarle el pelo a alguien ◆ *vt* ❶ sujetar ❷ recortar ❸ picar

clipboard ['klɪpbɔːd] *s* ❶ tabloncillo con pinza sujetapapeles ❷ INFORMÁTICA portapapeles

clippers ['klɪpəz] *spl* ❶ cortaúñas ❷ maquinilla para cortar el pelo ❸ tijeras de podar

clipping ['klɪpɪŋ] *s* recorte

clique [kliːk] *s despectivo* camarilla

cloak [kləʊk] *s* capa

cloakroom ['kləʊkrʊm] *s* guardarropa

clock [klɒk] *s* ❶ reloj • **round the clock** las 24 horas ❷ cuentakilómetros

clockwise ['klɒkwaɪz] *adj & adv* en el sentido de las manecillas del reloj

clockwork ['klɒkwɜːk] *en compuestos* de cuerda

clog [klɒg] *vt* atascar; obstruir

■ **clogs** *spl* zuecos

■ **clog up** ◆ *vt* ☼ *El objeto se puede colocar antes o después de la preposición.* ❶ atascar ❷ congestionar ◆ *vi* atascarse

close¹ [kləʊs] ◆ *adj* ❶ cercano, na • **close to** cerca de • **close to tears/laughter** a punto de llorar/reír • **close up, close to** de cerca • **close by, close at hand** muy cerca ❷ íntimo, ma • **to be close to somebody** estar muy unido, da a alguien ❸ cercano, na *(pariente)* ❹ • **to bear a close resemblance to somebody** parecerse mucho a alguien ❺ estrecho, cha *(vínculo, cooperación)* ❻ minucioso, sa *(interrogación)* ❼ detallado, da *(examen)* ❽ de cerca • **to keep a close watch on** vigilar de cerca ❾ cargado, da *(ambiente)* ❿ bochornoso, sa ⓫ reñido, da ⓬ apretado, da *(resultado)*

expresión **we arrived on time, but it was a close shave o thing** llegamos a tiempo, pero por los pelos

◆ *adv* cerca • **close to** cerca de

■ **close on, close to** *preposición* cerca de *(casi)*

close² [kləʊz] ◆ *vt* ❶ cerrar ❷ clausurar ❸ terminar ❹ reducir *(distancia)* ❺ INFORMÁTICA cerrar ◆ *vi* ❶ cerrarse ❷ cerrar *(tienda)* ❸ terminar ◆ *s* final

■ **close down** ◆ *vt* ☼ *El objeto se puede colocar antes o después de la preposición.* cerrar (definitivamente) ◆ *vi* cerrarse (definitivamente)

closed [kləʊzd] *adj* cerrado, da

close-knit [ˌkləʊs-] *adj* muy unido, da

closely ['kləʊslɪ] *adv* ❶ estrechamente • **to be closely involved in something** estar muy metido en algo ❷ mucho *(parecerse)* ❸ atentamente

closeout ['kləʊzaʊt] *s* liquidación

closet ['klɒzɪt] ◆ *adj familiar* en secreto ◆ *s* clóset

expresión **to come out of the closet** salir del clóset

close-up ['kləʊs-] *s* primer plano

closing time *s* hora de cierre

closure ['kləʊʒər] *s* cierre

clot [klɒt] ◆ *s* coágulo ◆ *vi* coagularse

cloth [klɒθ] *s* ❶ ☼ *incontable* tela ❷ trapo

clothe [kləʊð] *vt formal* vestir

clothes [kləʊðz] *spl* ropa • **to put your clothes on** ponerse la ropa; vestirse • **to take your clothes off** quitarse la ropa; desvestirse

clothesline ['kləʊðzlaɪn] *s* tendedero

clothespin ['kləʊðzpɪn] *s* gancho (para la ropa)

clothing ['kləʊðɪŋ] *s* ropa

cloud [klaʊd] *s* nube

■ **cloud over** *vi literal & figurado* nublarse

cloudy ['klaʊdɪ] *adj* ❶ nublado, da ❷ turbio, bia

clove [kləʊv] *s* • **a clove of garlic** un diente de ajo

■ **cloves** *spl* clavos

clover¹ ['kləʊvər] *s* trébol

clown [klaʊn] *s* payaso

club [klʌb] ◆ *s* ❶ club ❷ discoteca ❸ porra; garrote ❹ ▶ **(golf) club** palo de golf ◆ *vt* apalear; aporrear

■ **clubs** *spl* tréboles

club car *s* FERROCARRIL vagón o coche club

cluck [klʌk] *vi* cloquear

clue [kluː] *s* ❶ pista ❷ pregunta; clave

C

expresión **not to have a clue (about)** no tener ni idea (de)

clump [klʌmp] *s* ❶ mata ❷ grupo

clumsy ['klʌmzɪ] *adj* torpe

clung [klʌŋ] *pretérito & participio pasado* → **cling**

cluster ['klʌstər] ◆ *s* grupo ◆ *vi* agruparse

clutch [klʌtʃ] ◆ *s* AUTOMÓVILES embrague ◆ *vt* ❶ estrechar ❷ agarrar ◆ *vi* • **to clutch at something** tratar de agarrarse a algo

clutter ['klʌtər] ◆ *s* desorden ◆ *vt* cubrir desordenadamente

cm (*abreviatura escrita de* centimeter) cm

CNG (*abreviatura de* compressed natural gas) *s* GNC; gas natural comprimido

c/o (*abreviatura escrita de* care of) c/d

Co. ❶ (*abreviatura escrita de* Company) Cía. ❷ (*abreviatura escrita de* County) = **county**

coach [kəutʃ] ◆ *s* ❶ autocar ❷ FERROCARRIL vagón ❸ carruaje ❹ DEPORTE entrenador, ra ❺ profesor, ra particular ❻ • **coach (class)** clase turista ◆ *vt* ❶ DEPORTE entrenar ❷ dar clases particulares a

coal [kəul] *s* carbón

coalition [ˌkəuə'lɪʃn] *s* coalición

coalmine ['kəulmaɪn] *s* mina de carbón

coarse [kɔ:s] *adj* ❶ áspero, ra ❷ basto, ta ❸ ordinario, ria

coast [kəust] ◆ *s* costa ◆ *vi* ❶ ir en punto muerto ❷ • **they coasted into the semifinals** se metieron en las semifinales sin ningún esfuerzo

coastal ['kəustl] *adj* costero, ra

coaster ['kəustər] *s* posavasos

coastguard ['kəustgɑ:d] *s* guardacostas

coastline ['kəustlaɪn] *s* litoral

coat [kəut] ◆ *s* ❶ abrigo ❷ chaqueta ❸ pelo; pelaje ❹ capa ◆ *vt* • **to coat something (with)** cubrir algo (de)

coat hanger *s* gancho *(de ropa)*

coat of arms *s* escudo de armas

El plural de **coat of arms** es **coats of arms**.

coax [kəuks] *vt* • **to coax somebody (to do** o **into doing something)** engatusar a alguien (para que haga algo)

cob [kɒb] → **corn**

cobbled ['kɒbld] *adj* adoquinado, da

cobbler ['kɒblər] *s* zapatero (remendón), zapatera (remendona)

cobbles ['kɒblz], **cobblestones** ['kɒblstəunz] *spl* adoquines

cobweb ['kɒbweb] *s* telaraña *(abandonada)*

cocaine [kəu'keɪn] *s* cocaína

cock [kɒk] ◆ *s* ❶ gallo ❷ macho ◆ *vt* ❶ amartillar ❷ ladear

cockerel ['kɒkrəl] *s* gallo joven

cockle ['kɒkl] *s* berberecho

cockpit ['kɒkpɪt] *s* cabina

cockroach ['kɒkrəutʃ] *s* cucaracha

cocktail ['kɒkteɪl] *s* cóctel

cocky ['kɒkɪ] *adj familiar* creído, da

cocoa ['kəukəu] *s* ❶ cocoa ❷ chocolate

coconut ['kəukənʌt] *s* coco

cod [kɒd] *s* bacalao

Dos plurales: **cod** o **cods**.

code [kəud] ◆ *s* ❶ código ❷ prefijo *(telefónico)* ◆ *vt* codificar; cifrar

coed [ˌkəu'ed] *adj* (*abreviatura de* coeducational) mixto, ta

coffee ['kɒfɪ] *s* café

coffee break *s* descanso para el café

coffeepot ['kɒfɪpɒt] *s* cafetera *(para servir)*

coffee shop *s* café

coffee table *s* mesa de centro

coffin ['kɒfɪn] *s* ataúd

cog [kɒg] *s* ❶ diente ❷ rueda dentada

cognac ['kɒnjæk] *s* coñac

coherent [kəu'hɪərənt] *adj* coherente

cohesive [kəu'hi:sɪv] *adj* unido, da

coil [kɔɪl] ◆ *s* ❶ rollo ❷ tirabuzón ❸ espiral ❹ ELECTRICIDAD bobina ◆ *vi* enrollarse; enroscarse ◆ *vt* enrollar; enroscar

■ **coil up** *vt* ☀️ *El objeto se puede colocar antes o después de la preposición.* enrollar

coin [kɔɪn] ◆ *s* moneda ◆ *vt* acuñar

coin-box *s* depósito de monedas

coincide [ˌkəuɪn'saɪd] *vi* • **to coincide (with)** coincidir (con)

coincidence [kəu'ɪnsɪdəns] *s* coincidencia

coincidental [kəuˌɪnsɪ'dentl] *adj* fortuito, ta

Coke® [kəuk] *s* Coca-Cola®

coke [kəuk] *s* coque

cola ['kəulə] *s* (bebida de) cola

colander ['kʌləndər] *s* colador; escurridor

cold [kəuld] ◆ *adj* frío, a • **it's cold** hace frío • **my hands are cold** tengo las manos frías • **I'm cold** tengo frío • **to get cold** enfriarse ◆ *s* ❶ resfriado; constipado • **to catch (a) cold** resfriarse; pescar un resfriado ❷ frío

cold-blooded [-'blʌdɪd] *adj* ❶ de sangre fría ❷ despiadado, da ❸ a sangre fría

cold sore *s* calentura

cold war *s* • **the cold war** la guerra fría

coleslaw ['kəulslɔ:] *s* ▶ ensalada de col, zanahoria, cebolla y mayonesa

colic ['kɒlɪk] *s* cólico

collaborate [kə'læbəreɪt] *vi* • **to collaborate (with)** colaborar (con)

collapse [kə'læps] ◆ *s* ❶ derrumbamiento *(de edificio, imperio)* ❷ hundimiento *(de techo)* ❸ fracaso *(de relación, sistema)* ❹ caída *(de gobierno)* ❺ MEDICINA colapso ◆ *vi* ❶ derrumbarse • **to collapse with laughter**

partirse de risa ❷ hundirse ❸ venirse abajo ❹ *MEDI-CINA* sufrir un colapso

collapsible [kə'læpsəbl] *adj* plegable

collar ['kɒlər] *s* ❶ cuello *(de ropa)* ❷ collar

collarbone ['kɒləbəʊn] *s* clavícula

collate [kə'leɪt] *vt* ❶ cotejar ❷ poner en orden

colleague ['kɒliːg] *s* colega

collect [kə'lekt] ◆ *vt* ❶ reunir; juntar ❷ coleccionar ❸ recaudar
expresión **to collect yourself** concentrarse
◆ *vi* ❶ congregarse; reunirse ❷ acumularse ❸ hacer una colecta ◆ *adv* *TELECOMUNICACIONES* • **to call (somebody) collect** llamar (a alguien) por cobrar

collect call *s* llamada por cobrar

collection [kə'lekʃn] *s* ❶ colección ❷ recopilación ❸ recogida ❹ recaudación ❺ colecta

collective [kə'lektɪv] ◆ *adj* colectivo, va ◆ *s* colectivo

collector [kə'lektər] *s* ❶ coleccionista ❷ recaudador, ra ❸ cobrador, ra

college ['kɒlɪdʒ] *s* ❶ universidad ❷ colegio

collide [kə'laɪd] *vi* • **to collide (with)** chocar (con)

collision [kə'lɪʒn] *s* colisión
expresión **to be on a collision course (with)** *figurado* estar al borde del enfrentamiento (con)

colloquial [kə'ləʊkwɪəl] *adj* coloquial

Colombia [kə'lɒmbɪə] *s* Colombia

Colombian [kə'lɒmbɪən] ◆ *adj* colombiano, na ◆ *s* colombiano, na

colon ['kəʊlən] *s* ❶ *ANATOMÍA* colon ❷ dos puntos

colonel ['kɜːnl] *s* coronel

colonize ['kɒlənaɪz] *vt* colonizar

colony ['kɒlənɪ] *s* colonia

color ['kʌlər] ◆ *s* color • **what color is it?** ¿de qué color es? ◆ *adj* a color • **a color photo** una foto a color ◆ *vt* ❶ dar color a ❷ colorear ❸ teñir ◆ *vi* ruborizarse

color-blind *adj* daltónico, ca

colored ['kʌləd] *adj* ❶ de colores ❷ • **maroon-colored** de color granate • **brightly-colored** de vivos colores

colorful ['kʌləfʊl] *adj* ❶ de vivos colores ❷ animado, da ❸ pintoresco, ca ❹ expresivo, va

coloring ['kʌlərɪŋ] *s* ❶ colorante ❷ tez ❸ color

color scheme *s* combinación de colores

colt [kəʊlt] *s* potro

column ['kɒləm] *s* ❶ columna ❷ hilera

columnist ['kɒləmnɪst] *s* columnista

coma ['kəʊmə] *s* coma

comb [kəʊm] ◆ *s* peine ◆ *vt* *literal & figurado* peinar • **he combed his hair** se peinó

combat ['kɒmbæt] ◆ *s* combate ◆ *vt* combatir

combination [ˌkɒmbɪ'neɪʃn] *s* combinación

combine ◆ *vt* [kəm'baɪn] • **to combine something (with)** combinar algo (con) ◆ *vi* [kəm'baɪn] combinarse ◆ *s* ['kɒmbaɪn] = **combine harvester**

combine harvester [-'hɑːvɪstər], **combine** *s* cosechadora

come [kʌm] *vi* ❶ venir ❷ llegar • **coming!** ¡ahora voy! • **the news came as a shock** la noticia constituyó un duro golpe ❸ pasar • **come what may** pase lo que pase ❹ • **to come true** hacerse realidad ❺ • **to come unstuck** despegarse • **my shoelaces have come undone** se me han desamarrado las agujetas ❻ • **to come to do something** llegar a hacer algo ❼ • **to come first/last in a race** llegar en primer/último lugar en una carrera • **she came second in the exam** quedó segunda en el examen • **P comes before Q** la P viene antes de la Q
expresión **he doesn't know whether he's coming or going** *figurado* no sabe si va o viene
■ **to come** *adv* • **in (the) days/years to come** en días/años venideros
■ **come about** *vi* pasar; ocurrir
■ **come along** *vi* ❶ aparecer; llegar ❷ surgir ❸ ir • **the project is coming along nicely** el proyecto va muy bien
■ **come apart** *vi* deshacerse
■ **come back** *vi* ❶ volver ❷ • **to come back to something** volver a algo ❸ • **to come back to somebody** volverle a la memoria a alguien
■ **come by** *vt* 🔅 *El objeto siempre va después de la preposición al final.* conseguir
■ **come down** *vi* ❶ bajar ❷ aterrizar ❸ caer *(lluvia)*
■ **come down to** *vt* 🔅 *El objeto siempre va después de la preposición al final.* reducirse a
■ **come down with** *vt* 🔅 *El objeto siempre va después de la preposición al final.* contagiarse de *(enfermedad)*
■ **come forward** *vi* presentarse
■ **come from** *vt* 🔅 *El objeto siempre va después de la preposición al final.* ❶ venir de ❷ ser de • **where do you come from?** ¿de dónde eres?
■ **come in** *vi* ❶ entrar; pasar • **come in!** ¡pase! ❷ llegar
■ **come in for** *vt* 🔅 *El objeto siempre va después de la preposición al final.* recibir; llevarse
■ **come into** *vt* 🔅 *El objeto siempre va después de la preposición al final.* ❶ heredar ❷ • **to come into being** nacer; ver la luz
■ **come off** ◆ *vi* ❶ descoserse ❷ despegarse ❸ soltarse ❹ quitarse *(mancha)* ❺ salir bien ◆ *vt* 🔅 *El objeto siempre va después de la preposición al final.* dejar de tomar *(medicamento)*
expresión **come off it!** *familiar* ¡venga ya!
■ **come on** *vi* ❶ empezar ❷ encenderse ❸ ir • **it's coming on nicely** va muy bien
expresión **come on! a)** ¡ándale! **b)** ¡venga ya!
■ **come out** *vi* ❶ caerse *(diente, tornillo)* ❷ quitarse *(mancha)* ❸ salir a la luz ❹ salir *(producto, libro, el sol)* ❺ estrenarse *(película)* ❻ ponerse en huelga ❼ declararse homosexual

■ **come over** ◆ *vt* ☿ *El objeto siempre va después de la preposición al final.* sobrevenir • **I don't know what has come over her** no sé qué le pasa ◆ *vi* pasarse; venir

■ **come round** *vi* ❶ pasarse; venir ❷ • **to come round (to something)** terminar por aceptar (algo) ❸ volver en sí

■ **come through** *vt* ☿ *El objeto siempre va después de la preposición al final.* ❶ pasar por ❷ sobrevivir a

■ **come to** ◆ *vt* ☿ *El objeto siempre va después de la preposición al final.* ❶ • **to come to an end** llegar al fin • **to come to a decision** alcanzar una decisión ❷ ascender a • **the plan came to nothing** el plan se quedó en nada ◆ *vi* volver en sí

■ **come under** *vt* ☿ *El objeto siempre va después de la preposición al final.* ❶ estar bajo ❷ • **to come under attack** ser atacado

■ **come up** *vi* ❶ surgir ❷ estar al llegar ❸ salir *(sol, luna)*

■ **come up against** *vt* ☿ *El objeto siempre va después de la preposición al final.* tropezarse o toparse con

■ **come up with** *vt* ☿ *El objeto siempre va después de la preposición al final.* ❶ salir con *(idea)* ❷ encontrar *(solución)*

Formas irregulares de **come:** *pretérito* **came,** *pp* **come.**

comeback ['kʌmbæk] *s* reaparición • **to make a comeback a)** volver (a ponerse de moda) **b)** hacer una reaparición **c)** recuperarse *(en un partido)*

comedian [kə'miːdjən] *s* cómico

comedy ['kɒmədɪ] *s* ❶ comedia ❷ serie de humor ❸ humorismo ❹ comicidad

comet ['kɒmɪt] *s* cometa

comfort ['kʌmfət] ◆ *s* ❶ comodidad ❷ consuelo ◆ *vt* consolar; confortar

comfortable ['kʌmftəbl] *adj* ❶ cómodo, da ❷ acomodado, da ❸ fácil ❹ amplio, plia

comfortably ['kʌmftəblɪ] *adv* ❶ cómodamente ❷ sin aprietos ❸ fácilmente

comforter ['kʌmfətər] *s* edredón

comic ['kɒmɪk] ◆ *adj* cómico, ca ◆ *s* ❶ cómico, ca ❷ comic ❸ cómic

■ **comics** *spl* sección de tiras cómicas

comical ['kɒmɪkl] *adj* cómico, ca

comic strip *s* tira cómica

coming ['kʌmɪŋ] ◆ *adj* próximo, ma ◆ *s* **expresión comings and goings** idas y venidas

comma ['kɒmə] *s* coma

command [kə'mɑːnd] ◆ *s* ❶ orden ❷ ☿ *incontable* mando ❸ dominio • **to have something at your command** dominar algo ❹ *INFORMÁTICA* comando ◆ *vt* ❶ • **to command somebody (to do something)** ordenar o mandar a alguien (que haga algo) ❷ *MILITAR* comandar

commander [kə'mɑːndər] *s* ❶ comandante ❷ capitán, ana de fragata

commandment [kə'mɑːndmənt] *s* RELIGIÓN mandamiento

commando [kə'mɑːndəʊ] *s* comando
Dos plurales: **commandos** o **commandoes.**

commemorate [kə'meməreɪt] *vt* conmemorar

commemoration [kə,memə'reɪʃn] *s* conmemoración

commence [kə'mens] *formal* ◆ *vt* • **to commence (doing something)** comenzar o empezar (a hacer algo) ◆ *vi* comenzar; empezar

commend [kə'mend] *vt* ❶ alabar ❷ • **to commend something (to)** recomendar algo (a)

comment ['kɒment] ◆ *s* comentario • **no comment** sin comentarios ◆ *vi* comentar • **to comment on** hacer comentarios sobre

commentary ['kɒmntrɪ] *s* ❶ comentarios ❷ comentario

commentator ['kɒmnteɪtər] *s* comentarista

commerce ['kɒmɜːs] *s* ☿ *incontable* comercio

commercial [kə'mɜːʃl] ◆ *adj* comercial ◆ *s* anuncio *(televisivo o radiofónico)*

commercial break *s* pausa publicitaria

commiserate [kə'mɪzəreɪt] *vi* • **I commiserated with her** le dije cuánto lo sentía

commission [kə'mɪʃn] ◆ *s* ❶ comisión ❷ encargo ◆ *vt* encargar • **to commission somebody (to do something)** encargar a alguien (que haga algo)

commit [kə'mɪt] *vt* ❶ cometer ❷ destinar *(dinero, recursos)* • **to commit yourself (to)** comprometerse (a) ❸ ingresar *(en manicomio)* • **to commit something to memory** aprender algo de memoria

commitment [kə'mɪtmənt] *s* compromiso

committee [kə'mɪtɪ] *s* comisión; comité

commodity [kə'mɒdətɪ] *s* producto básico

common ['kɒmən] *adj* ❶ • **common (to)** común (a) ❷ corriente; de la calle

■ **in common** *adv* en común

commonly ['kɒmənlɪ] *adv* generalmente; comúnmente

commonplace ['kɒmənpleɪs] *adj* corriente; común

common room *s* ❶ sala de estudiantes ❷ sala de profesores

common sense *s* sentido común

commotion [kə'məʊʃn] *s* alboroto

communal ['kɒmjʊnl] *adj* comunal

commune *s* ['kɒmjuːn] comuna

communicate [kə'mjuːnɪkeɪt] ◆ *vt* transmitir; comunicar ◆ *vi* • **to communicate (with)** comunicarse (con)

communication [kə,mjuːnɪ'keɪʃn] *s* ❶ comunicación ❷ comunicado

Communion [kə'mjuːnjən] *s* ☿ *incontable* RELIGIÓN comunión

communiqué [kə'mjuːnɪkeɪ] *s* comunicado

Communism ['kɒmjʊnɪzm] *s* comunismo

Communist ['kɒmjʊnɪst] ◆ *adj* comunista ◆ *s* comunista

community [kə'mju:nətɪ] *s* comunidad
community center *s* centro social
commute [kə'mju:t] ◆ *vt* DERECHO conmutar ◆ *vi*
▶ viajar diariamente al lugar de trabajo
commuter [kə'mju:tər] *s* ▶ persona que viaja diariamente al trabajo
compact ◆ *adj* [kəm'pækt] compacto, ta ◆ *s*
['kɒmpækt] ❶ polvera ❷ compacto
compact disc *s* compact disc
compact disc player *s* compact (disc); reproductor de discos compactos
companion [kəm'pænjən] *s* compañero, ra
companionship [kəm'pænjənʃɪp] *s* compañerismo
company ['kʌmpənɪ] *s* ❶ compañía ❷ empresa
expresión **to keep somebody company** hacer compañía a alguien ▶ **to part company (with)** separarse
(de)
comparable ['kɒmprəbl] *adj* • **comparable (to** o
with) comparable (a)
comparative [kəm'pærətɪv] ◆ *adj* ❶ relativo, va
❷ comparado, da ❸ GRAMÁTICA comparativo, va ◆ *s*
GRAMÁTICA comparativo
comparatively [kəm'pærətɪvlɪ] *adv*
relativamente
compare [kəm'peər] ◆ *vt* • **to compare something/**
somebody (with o **to)** comparar algo/a alguien (con)
• **compared with** o **to a)** comparado con **b)** en comparación con ◆ *vi* • **to compare (with)** compararse
(con) • **to compare favorably/unfavorably with** ser
mejor/peor que
comparison [kəm'pærɪsn] *s* comparación • **in comparison (with** o **to)** en comparación (con)
compartment [kəm'pɑ:tmənt] *s* ❶ compartimento
❷ FERROCARRIL departamento; compartimento
compass ['kʌmpəs] *s* brújula
■ **compasses** *spl* compás
compassion [kəm'pæʃn] *s* compasión
compassionate [kəm'pæʃənət] *adj*
compasivo, va
compatible [kəm'pætəbl] *adj* • **compatible (with)**
compatible (con)
compel [kəm'pel] *vt* obligar • **to compel somebody**
to do something obligar a alguien a hacer algo
compelling [kəm'pelɪŋ] *adj* ❶ convincente
❷ absorbente
compensate ['kɒmpenseɪt] ◆ *vt* • **to compensate somebody for something** indemnizar a alguien
por algo ◆ *vi* • **to compensate for something** compensar algo
compensation [ˌkɒmpen'seɪʃn] *s* ❶ • **compensation (for)** indemnización (por) ❷ • **compensation**
(for) compensación (por)
compete [kəm'pi:t] *vi* ❶ • **to compete (for/in)** competir (por/en) • **to compete (with** o **against)** competir (con) ❷ rivalizar
competence ['kɒmpɪtəns] *s* competencia

competent ['kɒmpɪtənt] *adj* competente;
capaz
competition [ˌkɒmpɪ'tɪʃn] *s* ❶ competencia
• **the competition** la competencia ❷ competición
❸ concurso
competitive [kəm'petətɪv] *adj* ❶ competitivo, va
❷ competidor, ra
competitor [kəm'petɪtər] *s* competidor, ra
compile [kəm'paɪl] *vt* recopilar
complacency [kəm'pleɪsnsɪ] *s* autocomplacencia
complacent [kəm'pleɪsnt] *adj* autocomplaciente
complain [kəm'pleɪn] *vi* ❶ • **to complain (about)**
quejarse (de) ❷ reclamar ❸ MEDICINA • **to complain**
of something sufrir algo
complaint [kəm'pleɪnt] *s* ❶ queja • **to make a**
complaint quejarse ❷ reclamación ❸ MEDICINA problema; dolencia
complement ◆ *s* ['kɒmplɪmənt] complemento
◆ *vt* ['kɒmplɪˌment] complementar
complementary [ˌkɒmplɪ'mentərɪ] *adj* ❶ complementario, ria ❷ alternativo, va
complete [kəm'pli:t] ◆ *adj* ❶ total • **I feel like a**
complete idiot me siento como un verdadero idiota
❷ completo, ta • **bathroom complete with shower**
baño con ducha ❸ terminado, da ◆ *vt* ❶ terminar
❷ rellenar ❸ completar
completely [kəm'pli:tlɪ] *adv* completamente
completion [kəm'pli:ʃn] *s* finalización;
terminación
complex ['kɒmpleks] ◆ *adj* complejo, ja ◆ *s*
complejo
complexion [kəm'plekʃn] *s* tez; cutis
compliance [kəm'plaɪəns] *s* • **compliance (with)**
cumplimiento (de); acatamiento (de)
complicate ['kɒmplɪkeɪt] *vt* complicar
complicated ['kɒmplɪkeɪtɪd] *adj* complicado, da
complication [ˌkɒmplɪ'keɪʃn] *s* complicación
compliment ◆ *s* ['kɒmplɪmənt] cumplido • **to pay**
somebody a compliment hacerle un cumplido a alguien • **my compliments to the cook** felicitaciones
a la cocinera ◆ *vt* ['kɒmplɪment] • **to compliment**
somebody (on) felicitar a alguien (por)
■ **compliments** *spl formal* saludos
complimentary [ˌkɒmplɪ'mentərɪ] *adj* ❶ elogioso, sa ❷ halagador, ra ❸ gratis
complimentary ticket *s* entrada gratuita
comply [kəm'plaɪ] *vi* • **to comply with something a)**
cumplir (con) algo **b)** acceder a algo **c)** acatar algo
component [kəm'pəʊnənt] *s* ❶ TECNOLOGÍA pieza
❷ elemento
compose [kəm'pəʊz] *vt* ❶ componer • **to be composed of** estar compuesto o componerse de ❷ componer ❸ • **to compose yourself** calmarse
composed [kəm'pəʊzd] *adj* tranquilo, la
composer [kəm'pəʊzər] *s* compositor, ra

composition [ˌkɒmpə'zɪʃn] *s* ❶ composición ❷ redacción

compost ['kɒmpəʊst] *s* abono

composure [kəm'pəʊʒər] *s* compostura; calma

compound *s* ['kɒmpaʊnd] ❶ compuesto ❷ recinto

comprehend [ˌkɒmprɪ'hend] *vt* comprender

comprehension [ˌkɒmprɪ'henʃn] *s* comprensión

comprehensive [ˌkɒmprɪ'hensɪv] *adj* ❶ completo, ta ❷ rotundo, da

compress [kəm'pres] *vt* ❶ comprimir ❷ reducir

comprise [kəm'praɪz] *vt* ❶ comprender ❷ constituir

compromise ['kɒmprəmaɪz] ◆ *s* arreglo; término medio ◆ *vt* comprometer ◆ *vi* llegar a un arreglo; transigir

compulsion [kəm'pʌlʃn] *s* ❶ ganas irrefrenables ❷ :ⓘ *incontable* obligación

compulsive [kəm'pʌlsɪv] *adj* ❶ empedernido, da ❷ compulsivo, va ❸ absorbente

compulsory [kəm'pʌlsərɪ] *adj* ❶ obligatorio, ria ❷ forzoso, sa *(despido, jubilación)*

computer [kəm'pju:tər] *s* computadora

computer game *s* juego de computadora

computer-generated [kəmˌpju:tə'dʒenəreɪtɪd] *adj* generado, da por computadora

computer graphics *spl* infografía

computerized [kəm'pju:təraɪzd] *adj* informatizado, da; computerizado, da

computing [kəm'pju:tɪŋ], **computer science** *s* informática

comrade ['kɒmreɪd] *s* camarada

con [kɒn] *familiar* ◆ *s* timo ◆ *vt* timar; estafar • **to con somebody out of something** timarle algo a alguien • **to con somebody into doing something** engañar a alguien para que haga algo

concave [ˌkɒn'keɪv] *adj* cóncavo, va

conceal [kən'si:l] *vt* ❶ ocultar • **to conceal something from somebody** ocultarle algo a alguien ❷ disimular

concede [kən'si:d] ◆ *vt* ❶ admitir; reconocer ❷ encajar *(gol)* ◆ *vi* ❶ ceder ❷ rendirse

conceited [kən'si:tɪd] *adj* engreído, da

conceive [kən'si:v] ◆ *vt* concebir ◆ *vi* ❶ MEDICINA concebir ❷ • **to conceive of something** imaginarse algo

concentrate ['kɒnsəntreɪt] ◆ *vt* concentrar ◆ *vi* • **to concentrate (on)** concentrarse (en)

concentration [ˌkɒnsən'treɪʃn] *s* concentración

concentration camp *s* campo de concentración

concept ['kɒnsept] *s* concepto

concern [kən'sɜ:n] ◆ *s* preocupación ◆ *vt* ❶ preocupar • **to be concerned about** preocuparse por ❷ concernir • **those concerned** los interesados • **to be concerned with** ocuparse de • **to concern yourself with something** preocuparse de o por algo • **as far as... is concerned** por lo que a... respecta

concerned [kən'sɜ:nd] *adj* ❶ preocupado, da ❷ de preocupación

concerning [kən'sɜ:nɪŋ] *preposición* en relación con

concert ['kɒnsət] *s* concierto

concerted [kən'sɜ:tɪd] *adj* conjunto, ta

concert hall *s* sala de conciertos

concerto [kən'tʃeətəʊ] *s* concierto

El plural de **concerto** es **concertos**.

concession [kən'seʃn] *s* concesión

concierge [ˌkɒnsɪ'ɛəʒ] *s* conserje

concise [kən'saɪs] *adj* conciso, sa

conclude [kən'klu:d] ◆ *vt* ❶ concluir; terminar ❷ • **to conclude (that)** concluir que ❸ llegar a *(acuerdo)* ❹ cerrar *(trato)* ❺ firmar *(tratado)* ◆ *vi* terminar; concluir

conclusion [kən'klu:ʒn] *s* ❶ conclusión ❷ conclusión; final ❸ cierre *(de trato)* ❹ firma *(de tratado, acuerdo)*

conclusive [kən'klu:sɪv] *adj* concluyente

concoction [kən'kɒkʃn] *s* ❶ brebaje ❷ mezcla *(comida)*

concourse ['kɒŋkɔ:s] *s* vestíbulo

concrete ['kɒŋkri:t] ◆ *adj* concreto, ta ◆ *s* concreto ◆ *en compuestos* de concreto

concur [kən'kɜ:r] *vi* • **to concur (with)** estar de acuerdo o coincidir (con)

concurrently [kən'kʌrəntlɪ] *adv* simultáneamente; al mismo tiempo

concussion [kən'kʌʃn] *s* conmoción cerebral

condemn [kən'dem] *vt* ❶ • **to condemn somebody (for/to)** condenar a alguien (por/a) ❷ declarar en ruinas

condensation [ˌkɒnden'seɪʃn] *s* ❶ condensación ❷ vaho

condense [kən'dens] ◆ *vt* condensar ◆ *vi* condensarse

condensed milk [kən'denst-] *s* leche condensada

condescending [ˌkɒndɪ'sendɪŋ] *adj* altivo, va; condescendiente

condition [kən'dɪʃn] ◆ *s* ❶ estado • **in good/bad condition** en buen/mal estado • **to be out of condition** no estar en forma ❷ condición • **on condition that** a condición de que • **on one condition** con una condición ❸ MEDICINA afección ◆ *vt* condicionar

conditional [kən'dɪʃənl] ◆ *adj* condicional • **to be conditional on** o **upon** depender de ◆ *s* • **the conditional** el condicional

conditioner [kən'dɪʃnər] *s* suavizante

condo ['kɒndəʊ] *familiar* *s* *abreviatura escrita de* **condominium**

condolences [kən'dəʊlənsɪz] *spl* pésame • **to offer your condolences** dar el pésame

condom ['kɒndəm] *s* preservativo; condón

condominium [,kɒndə'mɪnɪəm] *s* ❶ condominio ❷ edificio de condominios

condone [kən'dəʊn] *vt* perdonar

conducive [kən'dju:sɪv] *adj* • **conducive to** favorable para

conduct ◆ *s* ['kɒndʌkt] conducta ◆ *vt* [kən'dʌkt] ❶ llevar a cabo ❷ • **to conduct yourself well/badly** comportarse bien/mal ❸ *MÚSICA* dirigir ❹ *FÍSICA* conducir

conducted tour [kən'dʌktɪd-] *s* visita con guía

conductor [kən'dʌktər] *s* ❶ director, ra ❷ cobrador, ra

cone [kəʊn] *s* ❶ cono ❷ barquillo ❸ piña

confectioner [kən'fekʃnər] *s* dulcero, ra; confitero, ra

confectionery [kən'fekʃnərɪ] *s* ⚘ *incontable* dulces; golosinas • **confectionery store** dulcería

confederation [kən,fedə'reɪʃn] *s* confederación

confer [kən'fɜ:r] ◆ *vt formal* • **to confer something (on)** otorgar o conferir algo (a) ◆ *vi* • **to confer (with)** consultar (con)

conference ['kɒnfərəns] *s* congreso; conferencia

confess [kən'fes] ◆ *vt* confesar ◆ *vi* ❶ confesarse • **to confess to something** confesar algo ❷ • **to confess to something** admitir algo

confession [kən'feʃn] *s* confesión

confetti [kən'fetɪ] *s* confeti

confide [kən'faɪd] *vi* • **to confide (in)** confiarse (a)

confidence ['kɒnfɪdəns] *s* ❶ confianza o seguridad (en sí mismo/misma) ❷ confianza • **to have confidence in somebody** tener confianza en alguien ❸ • **in confidence** en secreto ❹ intimidad; secreto

confident ['kɒnfɪdənt] *adj* ❶ seguro de sí mismo, segura de sí misma; confiado, da ❷ • **confident (of)** seguro, ra (de)

confidential [,kɒnfɪ'denʃl] *adj* confidencial

confine [kən'faɪn] *vt* ❶ limitar; restringir • **to be confined to** limitarse a ❷ recluir; encerrar

confined [kən'faɪnd] *adj* reducido, da *(espacio)*

confinement [kən'faɪnmənt] *s* reclusión

confirm [kən'fɜ:m] *vt* confirmar

confirmation [,kɒnfə'meɪʃn] *s* confirmación

confirmed [kən'fɜ:md] *adj* ❶ inveterado, da ❷ empedernido, da

confiscate ['kɒnfɪskeɪt] *vt* confiscar

conflict ◆ *s* ['kɒnflɪkt] conflicto ◆ *vi* [kən'flɪkt] • **to conflict (with)** estar en desacuerdo (con)

conflicting [kən'flɪktɪŋ] *adj* contrapuesto, ta

conform [kən'fɔ:m] *vi* ❶ amoldarse a las normas sociales ❷ • **to conform (to** o **with) a)** corresponder (a) **b)** ajustarse (a)

confront [kən'frʌnt] *vt* ❶ hacer frente a ❷ presentarse a *(sujeto: problema, tarea)* ❸ enfrentarse con ❹ • **to confront somebody (with)** poner a alguien cara a cara (con)

confrontation [,kɒnfrʌn'teɪʃn] *s* enfrentamiento; confrontación

confuse [kən'fju:z] *vt* ❶ desconcertar; confundir ❷ • **to confuse (with)** confundir (con) ❸ complicar

confused [kən'fju:zd] *adj* ❶ confundido, da; desconcertado, da ❷ confuso, sa

confusing [kən'fju:zɪŋ] *adj* confuso, sa • **it's very confusing** es muy poco claro

confusion [kən'fju:ʒn] *s* ❶ confusión ❷ desconcierto

congeal [kən'dʒi:l] *vi* ❶ solidificarse ❷ coagularse

congested [kən'dʒestɪd] *adj* ❶ congestionado, da ❷ superpoblado, da

congestion [kən'dʒestʃn] *s* congestión

conglomerate [kən'glɒmərət] *s* *COMERCIO* conglomerado

congratulate [kən'grætʊleɪt] *vt* • **to congratulate somebody (on)** felicitar a alguien (por)

congratulations [kən,grætʊ'leɪʃənz] ◆ *spl* felicitaciones ◆ *exclamación* ¡enhorabuena!

congregation [,kɒŋgrɪ'geɪʃn] *s* *RELIGIÓN* feligreses

congress ['kɒŋgres] *s* congreso
■ **Congress** *s* • **(the) Congress** el Congreso

Congress

Por el artículo primero de la constitución estadounidense de 1789 se constituye el Congreso de EE. UU. ese mismo año, el cual está formado por dos instituciones: el Senado (**Senate**) o cámara alta y la Cámara de Representantes (**House of Representatives**) o cámara baja. Cada estado está representado por dos senadores, mientras que el número de diputados de la Cámara de Representantes varía según la población (hay un total de 435 diputados). El Senado debe ratificar todos los tratados con dos tercios de los votos. Los proyectos de ley son propuestos por la Cámara de Representantes pero han de ser aprobados por ambas cámaras (que tienen el mismo poder legislativo).

congressman ['kɒŋgresmən] *s* congresista
El plural de **congressman** es **congressmen** ['kɒŋgresmen].

congresswoman ['kɒŋgres,wʊmən] *s* congresista
El plural de **congresswoman** es **congresswomen** ['kɒŋgres,wɪmən].

conifer ['kɒnɪfər] *s* conífera

conjugate ['kɒndʒʊgeɪt] *vt* conjugar

conjugation [ˌkɒndʒʊ'geɪʃn] *s* conjugación

conjunction [kən'dʒʌŋkʃn] *s* ❶ GRAMÁTICA conjunción ❷ • **in conjunction with** juntamente con

conjure ['kʌndʒər] *vi* hacer juegos de manos

■ **conjure up** *vt* ☼: *El objeto se puede colocar antes o después de la preposición.* evocar

conjurer, conjuror ['kʌndʒərər] *s* prestidigitador, ra

conman ['kɒnmæn] *s* estafador; timador

El plural de **conman** es **conmen** ['kɒnmen].

connect [kə'nekt] ◆ *vt* ❶ • **to connect something (to)** conectar algo (a) • **to get connected** conectarse ❷ • **I'll connect you now** ahora le paso o pongo ❸ • **to connect something/somebody (with)** asociar algo/a alguien (con) ◆ *vi* • **to connect (with)** enlazar (con)

connected [kə'nektɪd] *adj* • **connected (with)** relacionado, da (con)

connection [kə'nekʃn] *s* ❶ • **connection (between/with)** conexión (entre/con) • **there's no connection between the two events** no hay ninguna relación entre ambos acontecimientos • **an Internet connection** una conexión a Internet • **in connection with** con respecto a ❷ enlace ❸ contacto • **to have good connections** tener palancas

connoisseur [ˌkɒnə'sɜːr] *s* entendido, da

conquer ['kɒŋkər] *vt* ❶ conquistar ❷ vencer

conqueror ['kɒŋkərər] *s* conquistador, ra

conquest ['kɒŋkwest] *s* conquista

cons [kɒnz] *spl* contra → **pro**

conscience ['kɒnʃəns] *s* conciencia

conscientious [ˌkɒnʃɪ'enʃəs] *adj* concienzudo, da

conscious ['kɒnʃəs] *adj* ❶ consciente • **to be conscious of** estar consciente de • **to become conscious of** darse cuenta de ❷ deliberado, da

consciousness ['kɒnʃəsnɪs] *s* ❶ conciencia ❷ conocimiento • **to lose/regain consciousness** perder/recobrar el conocimiento

conscript *s* recluta

conscription [kən'skrɪpʃn] *s* servicio militar obligatorio

consecutive [kən'sekjʊtɪv] *adj* consecutivo, va • **on three consecutive days** tres días seguidos

consent [kən'sent] ◆ *s* ☼: *incontable* ❶ consentimiento ❷ • **by common consent** de común acuerdo ◆ *vi* • **to consent (to)** consentir (en)

consequence ['kɒnsɪkwəns] *s* ❶ consecuencia • **in consequence** por consiguiente ❷ importancia

consequently ['kɒnsɪkwəntlɪ] *adv* por consiguiente

conservation [ˌkɒnsə'veɪʃn] *s* ❶ conservación ❷ protección del medio ambiente

conservative [kən'sɜːvətɪv] *adj* ❶ conservador, ra ❷ moderado, da

■ **Conservative** ◆ *adj* POLÍTICA conservador, ra ◆ *s* POLÍTICA conservador, ra

Conservative Party *s* • **the Conservative Party** el Partido Conservador

conserve ◆ *s* ['kɒnsɜːv] compota ◆ *vt* [kən'sɜːv] ❶ ahorrar ❷ conservar

consider [kən'sɪdər] *vt* ❶ considerar • **to consider doing something** considerar hacer algo • **to consider whether to do something** pensarse si hacer algo • **consider yourself lucky** considerarse afortunado, da ❷ tener en cuenta • **all things considered** teniéndolo todo en cuenta

considerable [kən'sɪdrəbl] *adj* considerable

considerably [kən'sɪdrəblɪ] *adv* considerablemente; sustancialmente

considerate [kən'sɪdərət] *adj* considerado, da

consideration [kənˌsɪdə'reɪʃn] *s* ❶ consideración ❷ factor

expresión **to take something into consideration** tener algo en cuenta

considering [kən'sɪdərɪŋ] ◆ *preposición* habida cuenta de ◆ *conjunción* después de todo

consign [kən'saɪn] *vt* • **to consign something/somebody to** relegar algo/a alguien a

consignment [kən'saɪnmənt] *s* remesa

consist [kən'sɪst] ■ **consist in** *vt* ☼: *El objeto siempre va después de la preposición al final.* consistir en ■ **consist of** *vt* ☼: *El objeto siempre va después de la preposición al final.* constar de

consistency [kən'sɪstənsɪ] *s* ❶ consecuencia; coherencia ❷ regularidad ❸ consistencia

consistent [kən'sɪstənt] *adj* ❶ constante ❷ • **consistent (with)** consecuente o coherente (con)

consolation [ˌkɒnsə'leɪʃn] *s* consuelo

console ◆ *s* ['kɒnsəʊl] consola ◆ *vt* [kən'səʊl] consolar

consonant ['kɒnsənənt] *s* consonante

consortium [kən'sɔːtjəm] *s* consorcio

Dos plurales: **consortiums** o **consortia** [kən'sɔːtjə].

conspicuous [kən'spɪkjʊəs] *adj* ❶ visible ❷ llamativo, va

conspiracy [kən'spɪrəsɪ] *s* conspiración

conspire [kən'spaɪər] ◆ *vt* • **to conspire to do something** conspirar para hacer algo ◆ *vi* • **to conspire (against/with)** conspirar (contra/con)

constant ['kɒnstənt] ◆ *adj* constante ◆ *s* constante

constantly ['kɒnstəntlɪ] *adv* constantemente

consternation [ˌkɒnstə'neɪʃn] *s* consternación

constipated ['kɒnstɪpeɪtɪd] *adj* estreñido, da

constipation [ˌkɒnstɪ'peɪʃn] *s* estreñimiento

constitute ['kɒnstɪtjuːt] *vt* constituir

constitution [ˌkɒnstɪ'tjuːʃn] *s* constitución

C

Constitution

La constitución estadounidense fue redactada tras la independencia, durante una convención extraordinaria celebrada en Filadelfia en 1787 y entró en vigor al año siguiente. Junto con la Declaración de Independencia y la Carta de Derechos, constituyó los cimientos de lo que puede considerarse el primer estado moderno.

construct *vt* [kən'strʌkt] *literal & figurado* construir

construction [kən'strʌkʃn] *s* construcción

constructive [kən'strʌktɪv] *adj* constructivo, va

consul ['kɒnsəl] *s* cónsul

consulate ['kɒnsjʊlət] *s* consulado

consult [kən'sʌlt] ◆ *vt* consultar ◆ *vi* • **to consult with somebody** consultar a o con alguien

consultant [kən'sʌltənt] *s* asesor, ra

consultation [ˌkɒnsəl'teɪʃn] *s* ❶ consulta ❷ discusión

consulting room [kən'sʌltɪŋ-] *s* consultorio; consulta

consume [kən'sju:m] *vt literal & figurado* consumir

consumer [kən'sju:mər] *s* consumidor, ra

consumption [kən'sʌmpʃn] *s* consumo

contact ['kɒntækt] ◆ *s* contacto • **in contact (with)** en contacto (con) • **to lose contact with** perder (el) contacto con • **to make contact with** ponerse en contacto con ◆ *vt* ponerse en contacto con

contact lens *s* lentilla; lente de contacto

contagious [kən'teɪdʒəs] *adj* contagioso, sa

contain [kən'teɪn] *vt* contener • **to contain yourself** contenerse

container [kən'teɪnər] *s* ❶ recipiente; envase ❷ contenedor

contaminate [kən'tæmɪneɪt] *vt* contaminar

cont'd (*abreviatura escrita de* continued) • **'cont'd page 30'** 'sigue en la página 30'

contemplate ['kɒntempleɪt] ◆ *vt* ❶ considerar; pensar en • **to contemplate doing something** contemplar la posibilidad de hacer algo ❷ *formal* contemplar ◆ *vi* reflexionar

contemporary [kən'tempərəri] ◆ *adj* contemporáneo, a ◆ *s* contemporáneo, a

contempt [kən'tempt] *s* • **contempt (for)** desprecio o desdén (por) • **to hold somebody in contempt** despreciar a alguien

contemptuous [kən'temptʃʊəs] *adj* despreciativo, va • **to be contemptuous of something** despreciar algo

contend [kən'tend] *vi* ❶ • **to contend with** enfrentarse a ❷ • **to contend for/against** competir por/contra

contender [kən'tendər] *s* ❶ contendiente ❷ aspirante

content ◆ *adj* [kən'tent] • **content (with)** contento, ta o satisfecho, cha (con) ◆ *s* ['kɒntent] contenido ◆ *vt* [kən'tent] • **to content yourself with something/with doing something** contentarse con algo/con hacer algo

■ **contents** *spl* ❶ contenido ❷ índice

contented [kən'tentɪd] *adj* satisfecho, cha; contento, ta

contention [kən'tenʃn] *s* • **to be in contention (for)** tener posibilidades (de ganar)

contest ◆ *s* ['kɒntest] ❶ concurso ❷ combate ❸ lucha ◆ *vt* [kən'test] ❶ presentarse como candidato, ta a ❷ disputar ❸ impugnar

contestant [kən'testənt] *s* ❶ concursante ❷ participante *(de carrera)* ❸ contrincante

context ['kɒntekst] *s* contexto

continent ['kɒntɪnənt] *s* continente

continental breakfast *s* desayuno continental

contingency plan *s* plan de emergencia

continual [kən'tɪnjʊəl] *adj* continuo, nua; constante

continually [kən'tɪnjʊəlɪ] *adv* continuamente; constantemente

continuation [kənˌtɪnjʊ'eɪʃn] *s* continuación

continue [kən'tɪnju:] ◆ *vt* • **to continue (doing** o **to do something)** continuar (haciendo algo) • **'to be continued'** 'continuará' ◆ *vi* • **to continue (with something)** continuar (con algo)

continuous [kən'tɪnjʊəs] *adj* continuo, nua

continuously [kən'tɪnjʊəslɪ] *adv* continuamente; ininterrumpidamente

contortion [kən'tɔ:ʃn] *s* contorsión

contour ['kɒnˌtʊər] *s* ❶ contorno ❷ curva de nivel

contraband ['kɒntrəbænd] ◆ *adj* de contrabando ◆ *s* contrabando

contraception [ˌkɒntrə'sepʃn] *s* anticoncepción

contraceptive [ˌkɒntrə'septɪv] ◆ *adj* anticonceptivo, va ◆ *s* anticonceptivo

contract ◆ *s* ['kɒntrækt] contrato ◆ *vt* [kən'trækt] ❶ • **to contract somebody (to do something)** contratar a alguien (para hacer algo) ❷ *formal* contraer ◆ *vi* [kən'trækt] contraerse

contraction [kən'trækʃn] *s* contracción

contractor [kən'træktər] *s* contratista

contradict [ˌkɒntrə'dɪkt] *vt* contradecir

contradiction [ˌkɒntrə'dɪkʃn] *s* contradicción

contraption [kən'træpʃn] *s* artilugio

contrary ['kɒntrəri] ◆ *adj* ❶ contrario, ria • **contrary to** en contra de ❷ [kən'treərɪ] latoso, sa ◆ *s* • **the contrary** lo contrario • **on the contrary** al contrario

■ **contrary to** *preposición* en contra de

contrast ◆ *s* ['kɒntrɑ:st] • **contrast (between)** contraste (entre) • **by** o **in contrast** en cambio • **to be a contrast (to** o **with)** contrastar (con) ◆ *vt* [kən'trɑ:st]

• **to contrast something with** contrastar algo con ◆ *vi* [kən'trɑːst] • **to contrast (with)** contrastar (con)

contravene [ˌkɒntrəˈviːn] *vt* contravenir

contribute [kənˈtrɪbjuːt] ◆ *vt* contribuir; aportar ◆ *vi* ❶ • **to contribute (to)** contribuir (a) ❷ • **to contribute to** colaborar con *(periódico, revista)*

contribution [ˌkɒntrɪˈbjuːʃn] *s* ❶ • **contribution (to)** contribución (a) ❷ colaboración ❸ cotización

contributor [kənˈtrɪbjʊtər] *s* ❶ contribuyente ❷ colaborador, ra *(de periódico, revista)*

contrived [kənˈtraɪvd] *adj* inverosímil

control [kənˈtrəʊl] ◆ *s* ❶ control • **beyond** o **outside your control** fuera del control de uno • **in control of** al mando de • **to be in control of the situation** dominar la situación • **to lose control (of)** perder el control (de) ❷ restricción *(del gasto)* ❸ dominio *(de emociones)*
expresión everything's under control todo está bajo control
◆ *vt* ❶ controlar • **to control yourself** dominarse; controlarse ❷ manejar ❸ regular *(calefacción)*
■ **controls** *spl* mandos

control panel *s* tablero de instrumentos o de mandos

controversial [ˌkɒntrəˈvɜːʃl] *adj* polémico, ca

controversy [ˈkɒntrəvɜːsɪ] *s* polémica; controversia

convalesce [ˌkɒnvəˈles] *vi* convalecer

convene [kənˈviːn] ◆ *vt* convocar ◆ *vi* reunirse

convenience [kənˈviːnjəns] *s* comodidad; conveniencia • **do it at your convenience** hágalo cuando le venga bien • **at your earliest convenience** en cuanto le sea posible

convenience store *s* tiendita *(que abre hasta tarde)*

convenient [kənˈviːnjənt] *adj* ❶ conveniente • **is Monday convenient?** ¿te viene bien el lunes? ❷ práctico, ca *(tamaño)* ❸ adecuado, da *(posición)* • **convenient for** bien situado, da para

convent [ˈkɒnvənt] *s* convento

convention [kənˈvenʃn] *s* convención

conventional [kənˈvenʃənl] *adj* convencional

converge [kənˈvɜːdʒ] *vi* literal & figurado • **to converge (on)** converger (en)

conversation [ˌkɒnvəˈseɪʃn] *s* conversación

conversational [ˌkɒnvəˈseɪʃənl] *adj* coloquial

conversely [kənˈvɜːslɪ] *adv* formal a la inversa

conversion [kənˈvɜːʃn] *s* RELIGIÓN conversión

convert ◆ *vt* [kənˈvɜːt] ❶ • **to convert something (to** o **into)** convertir algo (en) ❷ RELIGIÓN • **to convert somebody (to)** convertir a alguien (a) ◆ *s* [ˈkɒnvɜːt] converso, sa

convertible [kənˈvɜːtəbl] ◆ *adj* convertible ◆ *s* (coche) convertible

convex [kɒnˈveks] *adj* convexo, xa

convey [kənˈveɪ] *vt* ❶ formal transportar ❷ • **to convey something (to)** transmitir algo (a)

convict ◆ *s* [ˈkɒnvɪkt] presidiario, ria ◆ *vt* [kənˈvɪkt] • **to convict somebody of** condenar a alguien por

conviction [kənˈvɪkʃn] *s* ❶ convicción ❷ DERECHO condena

convince [kənˈvɪns] *vt* • **to convince somebody (of something/to do something)** convencer a alguien (de algo/para que haga algo)

convincing [kənˈvɪnsɪŋ] *adj* convincente

convulse [kənˈvʌls] *vt* • **to be convulsed with a)** retorcerse de *(dolor)* **b)** troncharse de *(risa)*

convulsion [kənˈvʌlʃn] *s* MEDICINA convulsión

coo [kuː] *vi* arrullar

cook [kʊk] ◆ *s* cocinero, ra ◆ *vt* ❶ cocinar; guisar ❷ preparar ◆ *vi* ❶ cocinar; guisar ❷ cocerse
■ **cook up** *vt* ☼ *El objeto se puede colocar antes o después de la preposición.* ❶ tramar; urdir ❷ inventarse *(excusa)*

cookbook [ˈkʊkbʊk] *s* libro de cocina

cookie [ˈkʊkɪ] *s* ❶ galleta ❷ INFORMÁTICA cookie

cooking [ˈkʊkɪŋ] *s* cocina • **to do the cooking** cocinar

cookout [ˈkʊkaʊt] *s* carne asada

cool [kuːl] ◆ *adj* ❶ fresco, ca • **it's cool** hace fresco ❷ tibio, bia ❸ tranquilo, la ❹ frío, a ❺ *familiar* padre; buena onda ◆ *vt* refrescar ◆ *vi* enfriarse ◆ *s*
expresión to keep/lose your cool mantener/perder la calma ▸ **to stay cool** no perder la calma
■ **cool down** ◆ *vi* ❶ enfriarse ❷ calmarse ◆ *vt* refrescar

cool box *s* nevera portátil

coop [kuːp] *s* gallinero
■ **coop up** *vt* ☼ *El objeto se puede colocar antes o después de la preposición.* familiar encerrar

cooperate [kəʊˈɒpəreɪt] *vi* • **to cooperate (with)** cooperar (con)

cooperation [kəʊˌɒpəˈreɪʃn] *s* cooperación

cooperative [kəʊˈɒpərətɪv] ◆ *adj* ❶ servicial ❷ cooperativo, va ◆ *s* cooperativa

coordinate ◆ *s* [kəʊˈɔːdɪnət] coordenada ◆ *vt* [kəʊˈɔːdɪneɪt] coordinar

coordination [kəʊˌɔːdɪˈneɪʃn] *s* coordinación

cop [kɒp] *s* familiar poli • **the cops** la policía

cope [kəʊp] *vi* arreglárselas • **to cope with a)** poder con *(trabajo)* **b)** hacer frente a *(problema, situación)*

copier [ˈkɒpɪər] *s* fotocopiadora

copper [ˈkɒpər] *s* cobre

coppice [ˈkɒpɪs], **copse** [kɒps] *s* bosquecillo

copy [ˈkɒpɪ] ◆ *s* ❶ copia ❷ ejemplar ◆ *vt* ❶ copiar • **to copy and paste** copiar y pegar ❷ fotocopiar

copyright [ˈkɒpɪraɪt] *s* ☼ *incontable* derechos de autor

coral [ˈkɒrəl] *s* coral

cord [kɔːd] *s* ❶ cuerda ❷ cordón ❸ cable ❹ pana
■ **cords** *spl* pantalones de pana

cordial [ˈkɔːdjəl] ◆ *adj* cordial ◆ *s* refresco *(hecho a base de concentrado de fruta)*

cordon ['kɔ:dn] *s* cordón
■ **cordon off** *vt* ⚙ *El objeto se puede colocar antes o después de la preposición.* acordonar
corduroy ['kɔ:dərɔɪ] *s* pana
core [kɔ:ɾ] ◆ *s* ❶ corazón ❷ núcleo ❸ meollo ◆ *vt* quitar el corazón de
coriander [,kɒrɪ'ændəɾ] *s* cilantro
cork [kɔ:k] *s* corcho
corkscrew ['kɔ:kskru:] *s* sacacorchos
corn [kɔ:n] *s* ❶ maíz ▸ **corn on the cob** elote ❷ callo
corner ['kɔ:nəɾ] ◆ *s* ❶ esquina • **just around the corner** a la vuelta de la esquina ❷ rincón ❸ curva ❹ comisura ❺ córner ◆ *vt* ❶ arrinconar ❷ acaparar
cornerstone ['kɔ:nəstəʊn] *s figurado* piedra angular
cornfield ['kɔ:nfi:ld] *s* milpa; maizal
cornflakes ['kɔ:nfleɪks] *spl* hojuelas de maíz; cornflakes
cornstarch ['kɔ:nstɑ:tʃ] *s* maizena®
coronary ['kɒrənrɪ] *s* infarto
coroner ['kɒrənəɾ] *s* ▸ juez de instrucción que investiga los casos de muerte sospechosa
Corp. *(abreviatura de* corporation) Corp.
corporal ['kɔ:pərəl] *s* cabo
corporal punishment *s* castigo corporal
corporate ['kɔ:pərət] *adj* ❶ corporativo, va ❷ empresarial ❸ colectivo, va
corporation [,kɔ:pə'reɪʃn] *s* ≃ sociedad anónima
corpse [kɔ:ps] *s* cadáver
correct [kə'rekt] ◆ *adj* ❶ exacto, ta ❷ correcto, ta • **you're completely correct** tienes toda la razón ❸ apropiado, da ◆ *vt* corregir
correction [kə'rekʃn] *s* corrección
correctly [kə'rektlɪ] *adv* ❶ correctamente • **I don't think I can have heard you correctly** no estoy segura de haberte oído bien ❷ apropiadamente
correlation [,kɒrə'leɪʃn] *s* • **correlation (between)** correlación (entre)
correspond [,kɒrɪ'spɒnd] *vi* ❶ • **to correspond (with o to)** corresponder (con o a) ❷ • **to correspond (with o to)** coincidir (con) ❸ • **to correspond (with)** cartearse (con)
correspondence [,kɒrɪ'spɒndəns] *s* • **correspondence (with/between)** correspondencia (con/entre)
correspondence course *s* curso por correspondencia
correspondent [,kɒrɪ'spɒndənt] *s* corresponsal
corridor ['kɒrɪdɔ:ɾ] *s* pasillo
corrode [kə'rəʊd] ◆ *vt* corroer ◆ *vi* corroerse
corrosion [kə'rəʊʒn] *s* corrosión
corrugated ['kɒrəgeɪtɪd] *adj* ondulado, da
corrugated iron *s* chapa ondulada

corrupt [kə'rʌpt] ◆ *adj* corrupto, ta ◆ *vt* corromper
corruption [kə'rʌpʃn] *s* corrupción
corset ['kɔ:sɪt] *s* corsé
Corsica ['kɔ:sɪkə] *s* Córcega
cosmetic [kɒz'metɪk] ◆ *s* cosmético ◆ *adj figurado* superficial
cosmopolitan [kɒzmə'pɒlɪtn] *adj* cosmopolita
cost [kɒst] ◆ *s* coste; costo • **at no extra cost** sin costo adicional • **at the cost of** a costa de **expresión at all costs** a toda costa
◆ *vt* ❶ costar • **it cost us $20/a lot of effort** nos costó 20 dólares/mucho esfuerzo • **how much does it cost?** ¿cuánto cuesta o vale? ❷ presupuestar; preparar un presupuesto de
Formas irregulares de **cost:** *pretérito & pp* **cost** o **costed**.
co-star ['kəʊ-] *s* coprotagonista
Costa Rica [,kɒstə'ri:kə] *s* Costa Rica
Costa Rican [,kɒstə'ri:kən] ◆ *adj* costarricense ◆ *s* costarricense
cost-effective *adj* rentable
costly ['kɒstlɪ] *adj* costoso, sa
cost of living *s* • **the cost of living** el costo de la vida
costume ['kɒstju:m] *s* ❶ traje ❷ traje de baño
costume jewelry *s* ⚙ *incontable* bisutería
cot [kɒt] *s* catre
cottage ['kɒtɪdʒ] *s* cabaña
cottage cheese *s* queso cottage
cotton ['kɒtn] *s* ❶ algodón ❷ hilo (de algodón)
■ **cotton on** *vi familiar* • **to cotton on (to)** caer en la cuenta (de)
cotton candy *s* algodón de azúcar
cotton swab *s* hisopo de algodón
couch [kaʊtʃ] *s* ❶ sofá ❷ diván
cough [kɒf] ◆ *s* tos • **to have a cough** tener tos ◆ *vi* toser
cough syrup *s* jarabe para la tos
could [kʊd] *pretérito* → **can**
couldn't ['kʊdnt] *(abreviatura de* could not) = **can**
could've ['kʊdəv] *(abreviatura de* could have) = **can**
council ['kaʊnsl] *s* ❶ ayuntamiento ❷ consejo ❸ junta *(reunión)*
councilor ['kaʊnsələɾ] *s* concejal, la
counsel ['kaʊnsəl] *s* ❶ ⚙ *incontable formal* consejo • **to keep your own counsel** reservarse su opinión ❷ abogado, da
counselor ['kaʊnsələɾ] *s* ❶ consejero, ra ❷ psicólogo, ga ❸ abogado, da
count [kaʊnt] ◆ *s* ❶ total ❷ recuento • **to keep/lose count of** llevar/perder la cuenta de ❸ conde ◆ *vt* ❶ contar ❷ calcular ❸ • **to count somebody as** considerar a alguien como ❹ incluir; contar ◆ *vi* contar

• **to count (up) to** contar hasta • **to count for nothing** no contar para nada

■ **count against** *vt* ☼ *El objeto siempre va después de la preposición al final.* perjudicar

■ **count (up)on** *vt* ☼ *El objeto siempre va después de la preposición al final.* contar con

■ **count up** *vt* ☼ *El objeto siempre va después de la preposición al final.* contar

countdown ['kaʊntdaʊn] *s* cuenta atrás

counter ['kaʊntər] ◆ *s* ❶ mostrador • **over the counter** sin receta médica ❷ ventanilla ❸ ficha ◆ *vt* • **to counter something with** responder a algo mediante • **to counter something by doing something** contrarrestar algo haciendo algo

■ **counter to** *adv* contrario a

counteract [ˌkaʊntəˈrækt] *vt* contrarrestar

counterattack [ˌkaʊntərəˈtæk] ◆ *s* contraataque ◆ *vt* & *vi* contraatacar

counterclockwise [ˌkaʊntəˈklɒkwaɪz] *adv* en sentido opuesto a las manecillas del reloj

counterfeit ['kaʊntəfɪt] ◆ *adj* falsificado, da ◆ *vt* falsificar

counterpart ['kaʊntəpɑːt] *s* homólogo, ga

counterproductive [ˌkaʊntəprəˈdʌktɪv] *adj* contraproducente

countess ['kaʊntɪs] *s* condesa

countless ['kaʊntlɪs] *adj* innumerables

country ['kʌntrɪ] ◆ *s* ❶ país ❷ • **the country** el pueblo ❸ • **the country** el campo ❹ terreno ◆ *en compuestos* campestre

country dancing *s* ☼ *incontable* baile tradicional

country house *s* casa solariega

countryman ['kʌntrɪmən] *s* compatriota

El plural de **countryman** es **countrymen** ['kʌntrɪmən].

countryside ['kʌntrɪsaɪd] *s* ❶ campo ❷ paisaje

county ['kaʊntɪ] *s* condado

coup [kuː] *s* ❶ • **coup (d'état)** golpe (de estado) ❷ éxito

couple ['kʌpl] ◆ *s* ❶ pareja ❷ • **a couple (of)** un par (de) ❸ • **a couple (of)** un par (de); unos, unas ◆ *vt* • **to couple something (to)** enganchar algo (con)

coupon ['kuːpɒn] *s* vale; cupón

courage ['kʌrɪdʒ] *s* valor

courageous [kəˈreɪdʒəs] *adj* valiente

courier ['kʊrɪər] *s* mensajero, ra

course [kɔːs] *s* ❶ curso • **course of treatment** MEDICINA tratamiento • **to change course** cambiar de rumbo • **to run** o **take its course** seguir su curso • **off course** fuera de su rumbo ▶ **course (of action)** camino (a seguir) • **in the course of** a lo largo de ❷ ciclo *(de conferencias)* ❸ UNIVERSIDAD carrera ❹ plato ❺ campo *(de golf)* ❻ circuito *(de carreras)*

■ **of course** *adv* ❶ naturalmente ❷ claro • **of course not** claro que no

coursebook ['kɔːsbʊk] *s* libro de texto

coursework ['kɔːswɜːk] *s* ☼ *incontable* trabajo realizado durante el curso

court [kɔːt] ◆ *s* ❶ tribunal • **he appeared in court** compareció ante el tribunal ❷ DEPORTE cancha; pista ❸ corte ◆ *vi desusado* cortejarse

courteous ['kɜːtjəs] *adj* cortés

courtesy ['kɜːtɪsɪ] ◆ *s* cortesía ◆ *en compuestos* de cortesía

■ **(by) courtesy of** *preposición* ❶ con permiso de ❷ por cortesía o gentileza de

courthouse ['kɔːthaʊs] ☼ *pl* **[-haʊzɪz]** *s* juzgado

court-martial *s* consejo de guerra

Dos plurales: **court-martials** o **courts-martial**.

courtroom ['kɔːtrʊm] *s* sala del tribunal

courtyard ['kɔːtjɑːd] *s* patio

cousin ['kʌzn] *s* primo, ma

cove [kəʊv] *s* cala; ensenada

cover ['kʌvər] ◆ *s* ❶ cubierta ❷ tapa ❸ funda ❹ cobija • **under the covers** debajo de las sábanas ❺ portada; contraportada ❻ refugio • **under cover** a cubierto • **to take cover** ponerse a cubierto ❼ tapadera • **under cover of** al amparo o abrigo de ❽ cobertura ◆ *vt* ❶ • **to cover something (with) a)** cubrir algo (de) **b)** tapar algo (con) • **Tom was covered with bruises** Tom estaba lleno de moretones ❷ abarcar ❸ informar sobre ❹ abarcar

■ **cover up** *vt* ☼ *El objeto se puede colocar antes o después de la preposición.* ❶ tapar ❷ encubrir

coverage ['kʌvərɪdʒ] *s* cobertura informativa

coveralls ['kʌvərɔːlz] *spl* overol

cover charge *s* cover

covering ['kʌvərɪŋ] *s* ❶ cubierta ❷ capa

cover letter *s* ❶ carta de presentación ❷ nota aclaratoria

covert ['kʌvət] *adj* ❶ encubierto, ta; secreto, ta ❷ furtivo, va

cover-up *s* encubrimiento

covet ['kʌvɪt] *vt* codiciar

cow [kaʊ] *s* ❶ vaca ❷ hembra

coward ['kaʊəd] *s* cobarde

cowardly ['kaʊədlɪ] *adj* cobarde

cowboy ['kaʊbɔɪ] *s* vaquero

cower ['kaʊər] *vi* encogerse

co-worker *s* compañero, ra de trabajo

cox [kɒks], **coxswain** ['kɒksən] *s* timonel

coy [kɔɪ] *adj* tímido, da

cozy ['kəʊzɪ] *adj* ❶ acogedor, ra • **it's cozy in here** qué rico se está aquí adentro ❷ agradable; amigable

CPA *s abreviatura escrita de* **certified public accountant**

crab [kræb] *s* cangrejo

crack [kræk] ◆ *s* ❶ grieta ❷ rajadura ❸ rendija ❹ chasquido ❺ crujido ❻ *familiar* • **to have a crack at something** intentar algo ❼ crack ◆ *adj* de primera ◆ *vt* ❶ romper; partir ❷ cascar ❸ chasquear ❹ • **to crack your head** golpearse la cabeza ❺ dar con la clave de *(código)* ❻ resolver *(problema)* ❼ *familiar* contar *(chiste)* ◆ *vi* ❶ agrietarse ❷ partirse ❸ hundirse ❹ chasquear ❺ crujir

■ **crack down** *vi* • **to crack down (on)** tomar medidas severas (contra)

■ **crack up** *vi* ❶ venirse abajo ❷ *familiar* partirse de risa

cracker ['krækəɾ] *s* galleta (salada)

crackle ['krækl] *vi* ❶ crujir; chasquear ❷ sonar con interferencias

cradle ['kreɪdl] ◆ *s* cuna ◆ *vt* acunar; mecer

craft [krɑːft] *s* ❶ oficio ❷ arte ❸ embarcación

Dos plurales: **crafts** [krɑːfts] en los primeros dos sentidos y **craft** en el tercero.

■ **crafts** *spl* artesanía

craftsman ['krɑːftsmən] *s* artesano

El plural de **craftsman** es **craftsmen** ['krɑːftsmən].

craftsmanship ['krɑːftsmənʃɪp] *s* ☼*incontable* ❶ destreza; habilidad ❷ artesanía

crafty ['krɑːftɪ] *adj* astuto, ta

crag [kræg] *s* peñasco

cram [kræm] ◆ *vt* ❶ embutir ❷ apiñar ❸ • **to cram something with** atiborrar o atestar algo de • **to be crammed (with)** estar repleto, ta (de) ◆ *vi* empollar

cramp [kræmp] *s* calambre • **stomach cramps** retortijones de vientre

cranberry ['krænbərɪ] *s* arándano (agrio) • **cranberry sauce** salsa de arándano (agrio)

crane [kreɪn] *s* ❶ grúa ❷ grulla

crank [kræŋk] ◆ *s* manivela ◆ *vt* girar

cranky ['kræŋkɪ] *(comparativo* crankier, *superlativo* crankiest) *adj familiar* refunfuñón, ona

cranny ['krænɪ] → **nook**

crap [kræp] *s* ☼*incontable muy familiar* mierda

crash [kræʃ] ◆ *s* ❶ choque ❷ estruendo ❸ FINANZAS crac ◆ *vt* estrellar ◆ *vi* ❶ chocar ❷ estrellarse • **to crash into something** estrellarse contra algo ❸ FINANZAS quebrar ❹ INFORMÁTICA colgarse; bloquearse ❺ *familiar* dormir

■ **crash out** *vi familiar* dormir

crash course *s* curso acelerado; cursillo intensivo de introducción

crash helmet *s* casco protector

crash-land *vi* realizar un aterrizaje forzoso

crate [kreɪt] *s* caja *(para embalaje o transporte)*

crater ['kreɪtəɾ] *s* cráter

crave [kreɪv] ◆ *vt* ansiar ◆ *vi* • **to crave for something** ansiar algo

crawl [krɔːl] ◆ *vi* ❶ andar a gatas ❷ arrastrarse ❸ avanzar lentamente ◆ *s* • **the crawl** el crol

crayon ['kreɪɒn] *s* (barra de) cera

craze [kreɪz] *s* moda

crazy ['kreɪzɪ] *adj familiar* ❶ loco, ca • **like crazy** como un loco • **to be crazy about** estar loco, ca por • **to drive someone crazy** volverle loco, ca a alguien ❷ disparatado, da *(idea)*

creak [kriːk] *vi* ❶ crujir ❷ chirriar

cream [kriːm] ◆ *adj* (color) crema ◆ *s* ❶ nata ❷ crema ❸ (color) crema ❹ • **the cream** la flor y nata; la crema

cream cheese *s* queso cremoso o blanco

crease [kriːs] ◆ *s* ❶ pliegue; raya ❷ arruga ◆ *vt* arrugar ◆ *vi* ❶ arrugarse ❷ fruncirse

create [kriːˈeɪt] *vt* ❶ crear ❷ producir

creation [kriːˈeɪʃn] *s* creación

creative [kriːˈeɪtɪv] *adj* ❶ creativo, va ❷ creador, ra ❿ **creative writing** creación literaria

creature ['kriːtʃəɾ] *s* criatura • **creatures from outer space** seres del espacio exterior

credentials [krɪˈdenʃlz] *spl* credenciales

credibility [ˌkredəˈbɪlətɪ] *s* credibilidad

credit ['kredɪt] ◆ *s* ❶ crédito • **on credit** a crédito ❷ ☼*incontable* reconocimiento ❸ saldo acreedor o positivo • **to be in credit** tener saldo acreedor o positivo

expresión **to do somebody credit** decir mucho en favor de alguien ❿ **to give somebody credit for** reconocer a alguien el mérito de

◆ *vt* ❶ FINANZAS abonar • **we'll credit your account** lo abonaremos en su cuenta ❷ creer ❸ • **to credit somebody with** atribuir a alguien el mérito de

■ **credits** *spl* títulos

credit card *s* tarjeta de crédito

creditor ['kredɪtəɾ] *s* acreedor, ra

creek [kriːk] *s* ❶ cala ❷ riachuelo

creep [kriːp] ◆ *vi* ❶ deslizarse; andar con sigilo ❷ arrastrarse *(insecto)* ❸ avanzar lentamente ◆ *s familiar* asqueroso, sa

■ **creeps** *spl*

expresión **to give somebody the creeps** *familiar* ponerle a alguien la piel de gallina

Formas irregulares de **creep**: *pretérito* & *pp* **crept**.

creepy ['kriːpɪ] *adj familiar* horripilante

cremate [krɪˈmeɪt] *vt* incinerar

crematory ['kremətrɪ] *s* crematorio

crepe [kreɪp] *s* crepa

crepe paper *s* ☼*incontable* papel crepé

crept [krept] *pretérito* & *participio pasado* → **creep**

crescendo [krɪˈʃendəʊ] *s* crescendo

El plural de **crescendo** es **crescendos**.

crescent ['kresnt] *s* ❶ medialuna ❷ calle en forma de medialuna

cress [kres] *s* berro

crest [krest] *s* ❶ cresta ❷ cima; cumbre ❸ blasón

Crete [kriːt] *s* Creta

cretin ['kretɪn] *s familiar* cretino, na

Creutzfeldt-Jakob disease [ˌkrɔɪtsfelt'jækɒb-] *s* enfermedad de Creutzfeldt-Jakob

crevice ['krevɪs] *s* grieta; hendidura

crew [kruː] *s* ❶ tripulación ❷ equipo *(de rodaje)*

crew cut *s* rapado; corte al cero

crew-neck(ed) [-nek(t)] *adj* con cuello redondo

crib [krɪb] *s* ❶ cuna ❷ *familiar* cantón

crick [krɪk] *s* tortícolis

cricket ['krɪkɪt] *s* ❶ cricket ❷ grillo

crime [kraɪm] ◆ *s* ❶ crimen ❷ delito ❸ criminalidad; delincuencia ◆ *en compuestos* • **crime novel** novela policíaca

criminal ['krɪmɪnl] ◆ *adj* ❶ DERECHO criminal; delictivo, va ❷ penal • **to have a criminal record** tener antecedentes penales ❸ criminalista ◆ *s* ❶ criminal ❷ delincuente

crimson ['krɪmzn] ◆ *adj* carmesí ◆ *s* carmesí

cringe [krɪndʒ] *vi* ❶ encogerse ❷ *familiar* sentir vergüenza ajena

cripple ['krɪpl] ◆ *s desusado & insultante* tullido, da ◆ *vt* ❶ MEDICINA dejar inválido, da ❷ paralizar *(país, industria)*

crisis ['kraɪsɪs] *s* crisis

El plural de **crisis** es **crises** ['kraɪsiːz].

crisp [krɪsp] *adj* ❶ crujiente ❷ fresco, ca ❸ directo, ta *(forma de ser)*

crisscross ['krɪskrɒs] *adj* entrecruzado, da

criterion [kraɪ'tɪərɪən] *s* criterio

Dos plurales: **criteria** [kraɪ'tɪərɪə] o **criterions**.

critic ['krɪtɪk] *s* crítico, ca

critical ['krɪtɪkl] *adj* ❶ crítico, ca • **to be critical of** criticar ❷ grave

critically ['krɪtɪklɪ] *adv* ❶ críticamente • **critically important** de vital importancia • **critically acclaimed** aclamado, da por la crítica ❷ gravemente *(enfermo)*

criticism ['krɪtɪsɪzm] *s* crítica

criticize ['krɪtɪsaɪz] *vt & vi* criticar

croak [krəʊk] *vi* ❶ croar ❷ graznar ❸ ronquear

Croat ['krəʊæt], **Croatian** [krəʊ'eɪʃn] ◆ *adj* croata ◆ *s* ❶ croata ❷ croata

Croatia [krəʊ'eɪʃə] *s* Croacia

Croatian = **Croat**

crochet ['krəʊʃeɪ] *s* ganchillo

crockery ['krɒkərɪ] *s* loza; vajilla

crocodile ['krɒkədaɪl] *s* cocodrilo

Dos plurales: **crocodile** o **crocodiles**.

crocus ['krəʊkəs] *s* azafrán *(planta)*

El plural de **crocus** es **crocuses**.

crook [krʊk] *s* ❶ ratero, ra ❷ *familiar* ladrón, ona; sinvergüenza ❸ cayado

crooked ['krʊkɪd] *adj* ❶ torcido, da ❷ encorvado, da ❸ sinuoso, sa ❹ *familiar* corrupto, ta

crop [krɒp] ◆ *s* ❶ cultivo ❷ cosecha ❸ fusta ◆ *vt* cortar (muy corto)

■ **crop up** *vi* surgir

croquette [krɒ'ket] *s* croqueta

cross [krɒs] ◆ *adj* enojado, da • **to get cross (with)** enojarse (con) ◆ *s* ❶ cruz ❷ cruce • **a cross between** una mezcla de ❸ DEPORTE centro ◆ *vt* ❶ cruzar ❷ DEPORTE centrar ❸ contrariar ❹ RELIGIÓN • **to cross yourself** santiguarse ◆ *vi* cruzarse

■ **cross off**, **cross out** *vt* ⚡: *El objeto se puede colocar antes o después de la preposición.* tachar

crossbar ['krɒsbɑːɾ] *s* ❶ travesaño ❷ barra *(de bicicleta)*

cross-country ◆ *adj & adv* a campo traviesa ◆ *s* cross

cross-eyed ['krɒsaɪd] *adj* bizco, ca

crossfire ['krɒsˌfaɪəɾ] *s* fuego cruzado

crossing ['krɒsɪŋ] *s* ❶ cruce; paso de peatones ❷ paso a nivel ❸ travesía

crossing guard *s* ▸ persona encargada de ayudar a cruzar la calle a los colegiales

cross-legged ['krɒslegd] *adv* con las piernas cruzadas

cross-purposes *spl* • **I think we're at cross-purposes** creo que estamos hablando de cosas distintas

cross-reference *s* remisión; referencia

crossroads ['krɒsrəʊdz] *s* cruce

El plural de **crossroads** es **crossroads**.

cross-section *s* ❶ sección transversal ❷ muestra representativa

crosswalk ['krɒswɔːk] *s* paso de peatones

crosswise ['krɒswaɪz] *adv* en diagonal

crossword (puzzle) ['krɒswɜːd-] *s* crucigrama

crotch [krɒtʃ] *s* entrepierna

crouch [kraʊtʃ] *vi* ❶ agacharse ❷ agazaparse

crow [krəʊ] ◆ *s* cuervo ◆ *vi* ❶ cantar ❷ *familiar* alardear

crowbar ['krəʊbɑːɾ] *s* palanca

crowd [kraʊd] ◆ *s* ❶ multitud; muchedumbre ❷ público ❸ gente • **I don't like that crowd** no me gusta esa gente ◆ *vi* agolparse; apiñarse • **to crowd in/out** entrar/salir en tropel ◆ *vt* ❶ llenar ❷ meter; apiñar

crowded ['kraʊdɪd] *adj* • **crowded (with)** repleto, ta o abarrotado, da (de)

crown [kraʊn] ◆ *s* ❶ corona ❷ copa ❸ coronilla ❹ cumbre; cima ◆ *vt* coronar

expresión **to crown it all** para colmo

crown jewels *spl* joyas de la corona

crown prince *s* príncipe heredero

crow's feet *spl* patas de gallo

crucial ['kruːʃl] *adj* crucial

crucifix ['kruːsɪfɪks] *s* crucifijo

Crucifixion [ˌkruːsɪ'fɪkʃn] *s* • **the Crucifixion** la Crucifixión

crude [kruːd] *adj* ❶ crudo, da ❷ basto, ta ❸ tosco, ca

crude oil *s* crudo

cruel [kruəl] *adj* ❶ cruel ❷ duro, ra *(golpe)*

cruelty ['kruəltı] *s* ⚲*incontable* crueldad

cruet ['kru:ıt] *s* vinagrera

cruise [kru:z] ◆ *s* crucero ◆ *vi* ❶ hacer un crucero ❷ ir a velocidad de crucero

cruiser ['kru:zəɾ] *s* ❶ crucero ❷ yate *(para cruceros)*

crumb [krʌm] *s* ❶ miga; migaja ❷ pizca *(de información)*

crumble ['krʌmbl] ◆ *vt* desmigajar ◆ *vi* ❶ desmoronarse ❷ caerse ❸ *figurado* venirse abajo

crumbly ['krʌmblı] *adj* que se desmigaja con facilidad

crumpet ['krʌmpıt] *s* ▶ bollo que se come tostado

crumple ['krʌmpl] *vt* ❶ arrugar ❷ estrujar

crunch [krʌntʃ] ◆ *s* crujido ◆ *vt* ronzar

crunchy ['krʌntʃı] *adj* crujiente

crusade [kru:'seıd] *s literal & figurado* cruzada

crush [krʌʃ] ◆ *s* ❶ gentío ❷ *familiar* • to have a crush on somebody estar loco, ca por alguien ◆ *vt* ❶ aplastar ❷ triturar ❸ picar *(hielo)* ❹ exprimir *(uvas)* ❺ demoler

crust [krʌst] *s* ❶ corteza ❷ masa *(de pay)*

crutch [krʌtʃ] *s* muleta

crux [krʌks] *s* • the crux of the matter el quid de la cuestión

cry [kraı] ◆ *s* ❶ llanto ❷ grito ◆ *vi* ❶ llorar ❷ gritar

crystal ['krıstl] *s* cristal

crystal clear *adj* ❶ cristalino, na ❷ claro, ra como el agua

cub [kʌb] *s* ❶ cachorro ❷ lobato boy scout de entre 8 y 11 años

Cuba ['kju:bə] *s* Cuba

Cuban ['kju:bən] ◆ *adj* cubano, na ◆ *s* cubano, na

cube [kju:b] ◆ *s* ❶ cubo ❷ terrón ◆ *vt* ❶ MATEMÁTICAS elevar al cubo ❷ cortar en dados

cubic ['kju:bık] *adj* cúbico, ca

cubicle ['kju:bıkl] *s* ❶ caseta *(de piscina)* ❷ probador ❸ cubículo

Cub Scout *s* lobato boy scout de entre 8 y 11 años

cuckoo ['kuku:] *s* cucú

cuckoo clock *s* reloj de cucú

cucumber ['kju:kʌmbəɾ] *s* pepino

cuddle ['kʌdl] ◆ *s* abrazo ◆ *vt* abrazar ◆ *vi* abrazarse

cuddly toy ['kʌdlı-] *s* muñeco de peluche

cue [kju:] *s* ❶ RADIO, TEATRO & TELEVISIÓN entrada • on cue justo en aquel instante ❷ *figurado* señal ❸ taco *(de billar)*

cuff [kʌf] *s* ❶ puño ❷ valenciana ❸ cachetada ▪ *expresión* off the cuff improvisado, da; sacado, da de la manga

cuff link *s* mancuernilla

cuisine [kwı'zi:n] *s* cocina

cul-de-sac ['kʌldəsæk] *s* callejón sin salida

cull [kʌl] *vt* sacrificar *(selectivamente)*

culminate ['kʌlmıneıt] *vi* • to culminate in culminar en

culmination [ˌkʌlmı'neıʃn] *s* culminación

culottes [kju:'lɒts] *spl* falda pantalón

culprit ['kʌlprıt] *s* culpable

cult [kʌlt] ◆ *s* RELIGIÓN culto ◆ en compuestos de culto

cultivate ['kʌltıveıt] *vt* cultivar

cultivated ['kʌltıveıtıd] *adj* ❶ culto, ta ❷ cultivado, da

cultivation [ˌkʌltı'veıʃn] *s* ⚲*incontable* cultivo

cultural ['kʌltʃərəl] *adj* cultural

culture ['kʌltʃəɾ] *s* ❶ cultura ❷ cultivo *(de bacteria)*

cultured ['kʌltʃəd] *adj* culto, ta

cumbersome ['kʌmbəsəm] *adj* ❶ abultado, da ❷ aparatoso, sa ❸ torpe

cunning ['kʌnıŋ] ◆ *adj* ❶ astuto, ta ❷ ingenioso, sa ◆ *s* ⚲*incontable* astucia

cup [kʌp] ◆ *s* ❶ taza ❷ copa ◆ *vt* ahuecar *(las manos)*

cupboard ['kʌbəd] *s* armario

cupcake ['kʌpkeık] *s* panquecitos

curator [ˌkjuə'reıtəɾ] *s* conservador, ra

curb [kɜ:b] ◆ *s* ❶ • curb (on) control o restricción (de) • to put a curb on something poner freno a algo ❷ bordo de la banqueta ◆ *vt* controlar; contener

curdle ['kɜ:dl] *vi* cuajarse

cure [kjuəɾ] ◆ *s* ❶ MEDICINA • cure (for) cura (para) ❷ • cure (for) remedio (a) ◆ *vt* ❶ curar ❷ remediar ❸ curtir

curfew ['kɜ:fju:] *s* toque de queda

curiosity [ˌkjuərı'ɒsətı] *s* curiosidad

curious ['kjuərıəs] *adj* curioso, sa • to be curious about sentir curiosidad por

curl [kɜ:l] ◆ *s* rizo ◆ *vt* ❶ rizar ❷ enroscar ◆ *vi* ❶ rizarse ❷ abarquillarse
■ curl up *vi* ❶ acurrucarse ❷ abarquillarse

curler ['kɜ:ləɾ] *s* rulo

curly ['kɜ:lı] *adj* ❶ rizado, da ❷ enroscado, da

currant ['kʌrənt] *s* pasa de Corinto

currency ['kʌrənsı] *s* FINANZAS moneda ▶ foreign currency divisa

current ['kʌrənt] ◆ *adj* ❶ actual ❷ en curso *(año)* ❸ último, ma *(número de revista)* ❹ corriente ◆ *s* corriente

current affairs *spl* asuntos de actualidad

currently ['kʌrəntlı] *adv* actualmente

curriculum [kə'rıkjələm] *s* plan de estudios; temario

Dos plurales: **curriculums** o **curricula** [kə'rıkjələ].

curry ['kʌrɪ] *s* curry

curse [kɜːs] ◆ *s* ❶ maldición ❷ palabrota ◆ *vt* maldecir ◆ *vi* decir palabrotas

cursor ['kɜːsər] *s* INFORMÁTICA cursor

curt [kɜːt] *adj* brusco, ca; seco, ca

curtail [kɜːˈteɪl] *vt* ❶ acortar *(visita)* ❷ reducir *(gasto)* ❸ restringir *(derechos)*

curtain ['kɜːtn] *s* ❶ cortina ❷ telón

curts(e)y ['kɜːtsɪ] ◆ *s* reverencia *(de mujer)* ◆ *vi* hacer una reverencia *(una mujer)*

Formas irregulares de **curtsy**: *pret & pp* **curtsied**.

curve [kɜːv] ◆ *s* curva ◆ *vi* ❶ hacer una curva ❷ curvarse

cushion ['kʊʃn] ◆ *s* ❶ cojín ❷ colchón ◆ *vt literal & figurado* amortiguar

cushy ['kʊʃɪ] *adj familiar* cómodo, da • **a cushy job** o **number** un chollo (de trabajo)

custard ['kʌstəd] *s* ☿*incontable* natillas

custody ['kʌstədɪ] *s* custodia • **to take somebody into custody** detener a alguien • **in custody** bajo custodia

custom ['kʌstəm] ◆ *s* ❶ costumbre ❷ ☿*incontable formal* clientela ◆ *adj* hecho, cha de encargo

■ **customs** *s* aduana • **to go through customs** pasar por la aduana

customary ['kʌstəmrɪ] *adj* acostumbrado, da; habitual

customer ['kʌstəmər] *s* ❶ cliente ❷ *familiar* tipo

customize ['kʌstəmaɪz] *vt* personalizar

customs officer *s* agente de aduanas

cut [kʌt] ◆ *s* ❶ corte ❷ • **cut (in)** reducción (de) • **wage cut** recorte salarial ❸ *familiar* parte *(de beneficios, ETC)* ◆ *vt* ❶ cortar • **to cut somebody's hair** cortarle el pelo a alguien • **to cut a hole** hacer un agujero ❷ cortarse *(el dedo ETC)* • **to cut yourself** cortarse ❸ reducir; recortar ❹ acortar ❺ *familiar* • **to cut class** faltar a clase ◆ *vi* cortar

■ **cut back** *vt* ☿ *El objeto se puede colocar antes o después de la preposición.* ❶ podar ❷ recortar

■ **cut down** ◆ *vt* ☿ *El objeto se puede colocar antes o después de la preposición.* ❶ cortar; talar ❷ reducir ◆ *vi* • **to cut down on smoking** o **cigarettes** fumar menos

■ **cut in** *vi* ❶ • **to cut in (on somebody)** cortar o interrumpir (a alguien) ❷ colarse

■ **cut off** *vt* ☿ *El objeto se puede colocar antes o después de la preposición.* ❶ cortar ❷ interrumpir • **we were cut off** se cortó la comunicación ❸ • **to be cut off (from)** quedarse incomunicado, da (de)

■ **cut out** *vt* ☿ *El objeto se puede colocar antes o después de la preposición.* ❶ recortar ❷ cortar ❸ • **to cut out smoking** o **cigarettes** dejar de fumar ❹ eliminar • **to cut somebody out of your will** desheredar a alguien

expresión **to be cut out for something** *figurado* estar hecho, cha para algo ▶ **cut it out!** *familiar* ¡basta ya!

■ **cut up** *vt* ☿ *El objeto se puede colocar antes o después de la preposición.* cortar; desmenuzar

Formas irregulares de **cut**: *pretérito & pp* **cut**.

cutback ['kʌtbæk] *s* • **cutback (in)** recorte o reducción (en)

cute [kjuːt] *adj* mono, na; lindo, da

cutlery ['kʌtlərɪ] *s* ☿*incontable* cubertería

cutlet ['kʌtlɪt] *s* chuleta

cut-price, cut-rate *adj* de oferta

cutting ['kʌtɪŋ] ◆ *adj* cortante; hiriente ◆ *s* ❶ esqueje ❷ recorte

cyanide ['saɪənaɪd] *s* cianuro

cybercafe ['saɪbəˌkæfeɪ] *s* cibercafé

cybercrime ['saɪbəkraɪm] *s* ciberdelito

cyberspace ['saɪbəspeɪs] *s* ciberespacio

cycle ['saɪkl] ◆ *s* ❶ bicicleta ❷ ciclo ◆ *vi* ir en bicicleta

cycling ['saɪklɪŋ] *s* ciclismo

cyclist ['saɪklɪst] *s* ciclista

cylinder ['sɪlɪndər] *s* ❶ cilindro ❷ tanque

cynic ['sɪnɪk] *s* cínico, ca

cynical ['sɪnɪkl] *adj* cínico, ca

cynicism ['sɪnɪsɪzm] *s* cinismo

cypress ['saɪprəs] *s* ciprés

Cypriot ['sɪprɪət] ◆ *adj* chipriota ◆ *s* chipriota

Cyprus ['saɪprəs] *s* Chipre

cyst [sɪst] *s* quiste

cystitis [sɪsˈtaɪtɪs] *s* cistitis

czar [zɑːr] *s* zar

Czech [tʃek] ◆ *adj* checo, ca ◆ *s* ❶ checo, ca ❷ checo

Czech Republic *s* • **the Czech Republic** la República Checa

D

d, D [di:] *s* d; D

■ **D** *s* ❶ MÚSICA re ❷ EDUCACIÓN ≃ aprobado ❸ *abreviatura escrita de* **Democrat**, *abreviatura escrita de* **Democratic**

Dos plurales: **d's** o **ds; D's** o **Ds**.

D.A. *s abreviatura escrita de* **district attorney**

dab [dæb] ◆ *s* ❶ toque ❷ pizca ◆ *vt* • **to dab something on** o **onto** aplicar algo sobre

dabble ['dæbl] *vi* • **to dabble (in)** pasar el tiempo (con)

dad [dæd], **daddy** ['dædɪ] *s familiar* papá

daffodil ['dæfədɪl] *s* narciso

dagger ['dægər] *s* puñal

daily ['deɪlɪ] ◆ *adj* diario, ria ◆ *adv* diariamente • **twice daily** dos veces al día ◆ *s* diario *(periódico)*

dainty ['deɪntɪ] *adj* delicado, da; fino, na

dairy ['deərɪ] *s* ❶ lechería ❷ central lechera ▶ **dairy products** productos lácteos

dairy products *spl* productos lácteos

daisy ['deɪzɪ] *s* margarita *(flor)*

dam [dæm] ◆ *s* presa ◆ *vt* represar

damage ['dæmɪdʒ] ◆ *s* • **damage (to)** daño (a) • **to cause damage to something** ocasionar daños a algo ◆ *vt* dañar

■ **damages** *spl* DERECHO daños y perjuicios

damn [dæm] ◆ *adj familiar* maldito, ta ◆ *adv familiar* muy • **don't be so damn stupid** no seas tan tonto ◆ *s*

expresión **I don't give** o **care a damn (about it)** *familiar* me importa un bledo

◆ *vt* ❶ condenar ❷ *muy familiar* • **damn it!** ¡maldita sea!

damning ['dæmɪŋ] *adj* condenatorio, ria

damp [dæmp] ◆ *adj* húmedo, da ◆ *s* humedad ◆ *vt* humedecer

dampen ['dæmpən] *vt* ❶ humedecer ❷ *figurado* apagar

dance [dɑːns] ◆ *s* baile ◆ *vt* bailar ◆ *vi* ❶ bailar ❷ agitarse; moverse

dancer ['dɑːnsər] *s* bailarín, ina

dancing ['dɑːnsɪŋ] *s* ☀*incontable* baile • **he has dancing lessons** tiene clases de baile

dandruff ['dændrʌf] *s* caspa

Dane [deɪn] *s* danés, esa

danger ['deɪndʒər] *s* • **danger (to)** peligro (para) • **in/out of danger** en/fuera de peligro • **to be in danger of doing something** correr el riesgo de hacer algo

dangerous ['deɪndʒərəs] *adj* peligroso, sa

dangle ['dæŋgl] ◆ *vt* ❶ colgar ❷ *figurado* • **to dangle something before somebody** tentar a alguien con algo ◆ *vi* colgar

Danish ['deɪnɪʃ] ◆ *adj* danés, esa ◆ *s* ❶ LINGÜÍSTICA danés ❷ = **Danish pastry** ◆ *spl* • **the Danish** los daneses

Danish pastry, Danish *s* ▶ panecillo de hojaldre con queso crema o manzana o almendras, etc.

dank [dæŋk] *adj* húmedo, da e insalubre

dapper ['dæpər] *adj* pulcro, cra

dare [deər] ◆ *vt* ❶ • **to dare to do something** atreverse a hacer algo; osar hacer algo ❷ • **to dare somebody to do something** desafiar a alguien a hacer algo

expresión **I dare say(...)** supongo o me imagino (que...)

◆ *vi* atreverse; osar

expresión **how dare you!** ¿cómo te atreves?

◆ *s* desafío; reto

daring ['deərɪŋ] ◆ *adj* atrevido, da; audaz ◆ *s* audacia

dark [dɑːk] ◆ *adj* oscuro, ra • **he has dark hair** tiene pelo oscuro • **dark blue pants** pantalones azul oscuro • **it's getting dark** está oscureciendo • **it was already dark** ya era de noche ◆ *s* ❶ • **the dark** la oscuridad ❷ • **before/after dark** antes/después del anochecer

expresión **to be in the dark about something** estar a oscuras sobre algo

darken ['dɑːkn] ◆ *vt* oscurecer ◆ *vi* oscurecerse

dark glasses *spl* anteojos oscuros

darkness ['dɑːknɪs] *s* oscuridad

darling ['dɑːlɪŋ] ◆ *adj* querido, da ◆ *s* encanto

dart [dɑːt] ◆ *s* dardo ◆ *vi* precipitarse
■ **darts** *s* 🔆 *incontable* dardos
expresión to play darts jugar a los dardos

dartboard ['dɑːtbɔːd] *s* blanco; diana

dash [dæʃ] ◆ *s* ❶ gotas; chorrito ❷ carrera ❸ guión ◆ *vt* ❶ *literario* arrojar ❷ frustrar; malograr ◆ *vi* ir de prisa • **he dashed into the room** entró corriendo al cuarto

dashboard ['dæʃbɔːd] *s* tablero de instrumentos

data ['deɪtə] *s* 🔆 *incontable* datos

database ['deɪtəbeɪs] *s* INFORMÁTICA base de datos

data management *s* INFORMÁTICA gestión de datos

data processing *s* proceso de datos

data protection *s* INFORMÁTICA protección de datos

date [deɪt] ◆ *s* ❶ fecha • **to date** hasta la fecha ❷ cita ❸ pareja *(con la que se sale)* ❹ dátil ◆ *vt* ❶ salir con ❷ datar ❸ fechar

dated ['deɪtɪd] *adj* anticuado, da

date of birth *s* fecha de nacimiento

daughter ['dɔːtər] *s* hija

daughter-in-law *s* nuera

El plural de **daughter-in-law** es **daughters-in-law.**

dawn [dɔːn] ◆ *s* ❶ amanecer ❷ albores ◆ *vi* amanecer
■ **dawn (up)on** *vt* 🔆 *El objeto siempre va después de la preposición al final.* • **it dawned on me that...** caí en la cuenta de que...

day [deɪ] *s* ❶ día • **I work an eight-hour day** trabajo una jornada de ocho horas • **the day before/after** el día anterior/siguiente • **the day before yesterday** antier • **the day after tomorrow** pasado mañana • **any day now** cualquier día de estos • **from day to day** de un día para otro ❷ • **in those days** en aquellos tiempos • **these days** hoy en día

daydream ['deɪdriːm] ◆ *s* sueño; ilusión ◆ *vi* soñar despierto, ta

daylight ['deɪlaɪt] *s* ❶ luz del día ❷ amanecer
expresión in broad daylight a plena luz del día

daytime ['deɪtaɪm] *s* 🔆 *incontable* día • *en compuestos* de día; diurno, na

day-to-day *adj* cotidiano, na

daze [deɪz] ◆ *s* • **in a daze** aturdido, da ◆ *vt* aturdir

dazzle ['dæzl] *vt* deslumbrar

DC *(abreviatura de* direct current) *s* CC; corriente continua

DEA *(abreviatura de* Drug Enforcement Administration) *s* ❱ organismo estadounidense para la lucha contra la droga

deactivate [ˌdiːˈæktɪveɪt] *vt* desactivar

dead [ded] ◆ *adj* ❶ muerto, ta • **a dead body** un cadáver • **to be dead on arrival** ingresar cadáver ❷ entumecido, da • **my arm has gone dead** se me durmió el brazo ❸ cortado, da ❹ descargado, da ◆ *adv* ❶ justo ❷ totalmente • **'dead slow'** 'al paso' ❸ *familiar* la mar de; muy ❹ • **to stop dead** parar en seco
expresión to be dead set on something estar decidido a hacer algo
◆ *spl* • **the dead** los muertos

deaden ['dedn] *vt* ❶ atenuar ❷ amortiguar

dead end *s* callejón sin salida

dead heat *s* empate

deadline ['dedlaɪn] *s* ❶ plazo ❷ fecha tope

deadlock ['dedlɒk] *s* punto muerto

deadly ['dedlɪ] ◆ *adj* ❶ mortal ❷ absoluto, ta ◆ *adv* ❶ terriblemente *(aburrido)* ❷ totalmente *(serio)*

deaf [def] ◆ *adj* sordo, da ◆ *spl* • **the deaf** los sordos

deafen ['defn] *vt* ensordecer

deafness ['defnɪs] *s* sordera

deal [diːl] ◆ *s* ❶ • **a good** o **great deal (of)** mucho ❷ acuerdo ❸ trato • **to do** o **strike a deal with somebody** hacer un trato con alguien ❹ *familiar* trato
expresiones it's a deal! ¡trato hecho! ❱ big deal! ¡vaya cosa! ❱ to get a good deal on something conseguir algo a un precio barato
◆ *vt* ❶ • **to deal somebody/something a blow, to deal a blow to somebody/something** asestar un golpe a alguien/algo ❷ repartir; dar *(cartas)* ◆ *vi* traficar con droga
■ **deal in** *vt* 🔆 *El objeto siempre va después de la preposición al final.* COMERCIO comerciar en
■ **deal out** *vt* 🔆 *El objeto se puede colocar antes o después de la preposición.* repartir
■ **deal with** *vt* 🔆 *El objeto siempre va después de la preposición al final.* ❶ hacer frente a; resolver; tratar con ❷ tratar de ❸ enfrentarse a
Formas irregulares de **deal:** *pretérito & pp* **dealt.**

dealer ['diːlər] *s* ❶ comerciante ❷ traficante ❸ repartidor, a

dealing ['diːlɪŋ] *s* comercio
■ **dealings** *spl* ❶ trato ❷ tratos

dealt [delt] *pretérito & participio pasado* → **deal**

dean [diːn] *s* ❶ ≃ decano ❷ deán

dear [dɪər] ◆ *adj* ❶ querido, da • **dear to somebody** preciado, da para alguien ❷ caro, ra ❸ • **Dear Sir** Estimado señor; Muy señor mío • **Dear Madam** Estimada señora • **Dear Daniela** Querida Daniela ◆ *s* • **my dear** cariño ◆ *exclamación* • **oh dear!** ¡Dios mío!

dearly ['dɪəlɪ] *adv* • **I love you dearly** te quiero muchísimo • **I would dearly love to...** me encantaría...

death [deθ] *s* muerte • **to frighten somebody to death** dar un susto de muerte a alguien

death certificate *s* certificado de defunción

deathly ['deθlɪ] ◆ *adj* sepulcral ◆ *adv* • **he was deathly pale** estaba pálido como un muerto

death penalty *s* pena de muerte

debate [dɪˈbeɪt] ◆ *s* debate
expresión that's open to debate eso es discutible

◆ *vt* & *vi* discutir; debatir

debit ['debɪt] ◆ *s* debe; débito ◆ *vt* • **to debit somebody's account with an amount** adeudar una cantidad en la cuenta de un alguien

debit card *s* tarjeta de débito

debris ['deɪbri:] *s* ❶ 💡 *incontable* escombros ❷ restos

debt [det] *s* deuda • **to be in debt (to somebody)** tener una deuda (con alguien) • **to get into debt** endeudarse • **to be in somebody's debt** *figurado* estar en deuda con alguien

debtor ['detər] *s* deudor, ra

debut ['deɪbju:] *s* debut

decade ['dekeɪd] *s* década

decadent ['dekədənt] *adj* decadente

decaffeinated [dɪ'kæfɪneɪtɪd] *adj* descafeinado, da

decathlon [dɪ'kæθlɒn] *s* decatlón

decay [dɪ'keɪ] ◆ *s* 💡 *incontable* ❶ caries ❷ descomposición ❸ *figurado* deterioro ◆ *vi* ❶ picarse ❷ pudrirse ❸ *figurado* deteriorarse

deceased [dɪ'si:st] *s formal* • **the deceased** el difunto, la difunta

El plural de **deceased** es **deceased**.

deceit [dɪ'si:t] *s* engaño

deceitful [dɪ'si:tfʊl] *adj* ❶ embustero, ra ❷ falso, sa

deceive [dɪ'si:v] *vt* engañar • **to deceive yourself** engañarse (a uno mismo/una misma)

December [dɪ'sembər] *s* diciembre ver también **September**

decency ['di:snsɪ] *s* ❶ decencia ❷ • **to have the decency to do something** tener la delicadeza de hacer algo

decent ['di:snt] *adj* decente

deception [dɪ'sepʃn] *s* engaño

deceptive [dɪ'septɪv] *adj* engañoso, sa

decide [dɪ'saɪd] ◆ *vt* ❶ • **to decide (to do something)** decidir (hacer algo) • **to decide (that)** decidir que ❷ hacer decidirse ❸ resolver ◆ *vi* decidir • **I couldn't decide** no me decidía • **I decided against doing it** decidí no hacerlo

■ **decide (up)on** *vt* 💡 *El objeto siempre va después de la preposición al final.* decidirse por

decidedly [dɪ'saɪdɪdlɪ] *adv* decididamente

decimal ['desɪml] ◆ *adj* decimal ◆ *s* (número) decimal

decimal point *s* punto decimal

decipher [dɪ'saɪfər] *vt* descifrar

decision [dɪ'sɪʒn] *s* decisión • **to make a decision** tomar una decisión

decisive [dɪ'saɪsɪv] *adj* ❶ decidido, da ❷ decisivo, va

deck [dek] *s* ❶ cubierta ❷ piso ❸ baraja ❹ entarimado *(junto a una casa)*

declaration [,deklə'reɪʃn] *s* declaración

Declaration of Independence *s* • **the Declaration of Independence** la declaración de independencia estadounidense de 1776

declare [dɪ'kleər] *vt* declarar

decline [dɪ'klaɪn] ◆ *s* declive • **in decline** en decadencia • **on the decline** en declive ◆ *vt* ❶ declinar ❷ denegar • **to decline to do something** rehusar hacer algo ◆ *vi* ❶ disminuir ❷ negarse

decompose [,di:kəm'pəʊz] *vi* descomponerse

decorate ['dekəreɪt] *vt* ❶ • **to decorate something (with)** decorar algo (de) ❷ pintar ❸ condecorar

decoration [,dekə'reɪʃn] *s* ❶ decoración ❷ adorno ❸ condecoración

decrease ◆ *s* ['di:kri:s] • **decrease (in)** disminución (de); reducción (de) ◆ *vt* & *vi* [dɪ'kri:s] disminuir

decree [dɪ'kri:] ◆ *s* ❶ decreto ❷ sentencia; fallo ◆ *vt* decretar

decrepit [dɪ'krepɪt] *adj* ❶ decrépito, ta ❷ deteriorado, da

dedicate ['dedɪkeɪt] *vt* ❶ dedicar • **to dedicate yourself to something** dedicarse a algo ❷ inaugurar

dedication [,dedɪ'keɪʃn] *s* ❶ dedicación ❷ dedicatoria

deduce [dɪ'dju:s] *vt* • **to deduce (something from something)** deducir (algo de algo)

deduct [dɪ'dʌkt] *vt* • **to deduct (from)** deducir (de); descontar (de)

deduction [dɪ'dʌkʃn] *s* deducción

deed [di:d] *s* ❶ acción; obra ❷ DERECHO escritura

deep [di:p] ◆ *adj* ❶ profundo, da • **to be 10 feet deep** tener 10 pies de profundidad ❷ hondo, da • **to take a deep breath** respirar hondo ❸ intenso, sa ❹ grave ◆ *adv* hondo

deepen ['di:pn] ◆ *vt* ahondar ◆ *vi* ❶ ahondarse ❷ agudizarse ❸ hacerse más intenso, sa

deeply ['di:plɪ] *adv* ❶ profundamente ❷ hondo

deep-sea *adj* • **deep-sea diving** buceo de profundidad

deer [dɪər] *s* venado

El plural de **deer** es **deer**.

default [dɪ'fɔ:lt] ◆ *s* ❶ incumplimiento ❷ incomparecencia (del contrario) • **by default** por incomparecencia ❸ INFORMÁTICA • **default (setting)** configuración por defecto ◆ *vi* incumplir un compromiso • **to default on something** incumplir algo

defeat [dɪ'fi:t] ◆ *s* derrota • **to admit defeat** darse por vencido, da ◆ *vt* ❶ derrotar ❷ rechazar ❸ frustrar

defect ◆ *s* ['di:fekt] defecto ◆ *vi* [dɪ'fekt] POLÍTICA desertar • **to defect to the other side** pasarse al otro bando

defective [dɪ'fektɪv] *adj* defectuoso, sa

defend [dɪ'fend] *vt* defender

defendant [dɪ'fendənt] *s* acusado, da

defender [dɪ'fendər] *s* ❶ defensor, ra ❷ DEPORTE defensa

D

defense [dɪˈfens] *s* defensa

defenseless [dɪˈfenslɪs] *adj* indefenso, sa

defensive [dɪˈfensɪv] ◆ *adj* ❶ defensivo, va ❷ • **to be defensive** ponerse a la defensiva ◆ *s* • **on the defensive** a la defensiva

defer [dɪˈfɜːr] ◆ *vt* aplazar ◆ *vi* • **to defer to somebody** deferir con o a alguien

defiance [dɪˈfaɪəns] *s* desafío • **in defiance of** en desafío de; a despecho de

defiant [dɪˈfaɪənt] *adj* desafiante

deficiency [dɪˈfɪʃnsɪ] *s* ❶ escasez ❷ deficiencia

deficient [dɪˈfɪʃnt] *adj* ❶ • **to be deficient in** ser deficitario, ria en; estar falto, ta de ❷ deficiente

deficit [ˈdefɪsɪt] *s* déficit

define [dɪˈfaɪn] *vt* definir

definite [ˈdefɪnɪt] *adj* ❶ definitivo, va ❷ indudable ❸ seguro, ra • **I am quite definite (about it)** estoy bastante seguro (de ello) ❹ tajante; concluyente

definitely [ˈdefɪnɪtlɪ] *adv* ❶ sin duda ❷ desde luego; con (toda) seguridad • **definitely not** desde luego que no

definition [ˌdefɪˈnɪʃn] *s* ❶ definición • **by definition** por definición ❷ nitidez

deflate [dɪˈfleɪt] ◆ *vt* ❶ desinflar ❷ *figurado* bajar los humos a ◆ *vi* desinflarse

deflect [dɪˈflekt] *vt* ❶ desviar ❷ soslayar

deformed [dɪˈfɔːmd] *adj* deforme

defraud [dɪˈfrɔːd] *vt* defraudar; estafar

defrost [ˌdiːˈfrɒst] ◆ *vt* ❶ descongelar ❷ desempañar ◆ *vi* descongelarse

defunct [dɪˈfʌŋkt] *adj* ❶ desaparecido, da ❷ desechado, da

defy [dɪˈfaɪ] *vt* ❶ desobedecer ❷ violar ❸ • **to defy somebody to do something** retar o desafiar a alguien a hacer algo ❹ hacer inútil • **to defy description** ser indescriptible • **to defy explanation** ser inexplicable

degenerate ◆ *adj* [dɪˈdʒenərət] degenerado, da ◆ *vi* [dɪˈdʒenəreɪt] • **to degenerate (into)** degenerar (en)

degrading [dɪˈgreɪdɪŋ] *adj* denigrante

degree [dɪˈgriː] *s* ❶ grado • **it was 90 degrees Fahrenheit in the shade** hacía 90 grados Fahrenheit a la sombra • **a degree of risk** un cierto riesgo • **by degrees** paulatinamente; poco a poco ❷ título universitario, ≈ licenciatura • **to have/take a degree (in something)** tener/hacer una licenciatura (en algo) ❸ ≈ carrera

deity [ˈdiːɪtɪ] *s* deidad

dejected [dɪˈdʒektɪd] *adj* abatido, da

delay [dɪˈleɪ] ◆ *s* retraso ◆ *vt* retrasar • **to delay starting something** retrasar el comienzo de algo ◆ *vi* • **to delay (in doing something)** retrasarse (en hacer algo)

delayed [dɪˈleɪd] *adj* • **to be delayed a)** retrasarse **b)** llevar retraso

delegate ◆ *s* [ˈdelɪgət] delegado, da ◆ *vt* [ˈdelɪgeɪt] • **to delegate something (to somebody)** delegar algo

(en alguien) • **to delegate somebody to do something** delegar a alguien para hacer algo

delegation [ˌdelɪˈgeɪʃn] *s* delegación

delete [dɪˈliːt] *vt* ❶ borrar; suprimir ❷ tachar

deli [ˈdelɪ] *s familiar abreviatura escrita de* **delicatessen**

deliberate ◆ *adj* [dɪˈlɪbərət] ❶ deliberado, da ❷ pausado, da ◆ *vi* [dɪˈlɪbəreɪt] *formal* deliberar

deliberately [dɪˈlɪbərətlɪ] *adv* ❶ adrede ❷ pausadamente

delicacy [ˈdelɪkəsɪ] *s* ❶ delicadeza ❷ manjar

delicate [ˈdelɪkət] *adj* ❶ delicado, da ❷ suave; sutil ❸ delicado, da; prudente ❹ sensible

delicatessen [ˌdelɪkəˈtesn] *s* ≈ charcutería

delicious [dɪˈlɪʃəs] *adj* delicioso, sa

delight [dɪˈlaɪt] ◆ *s* gozo; regocijo • **to our delight** para gran alegría nuestra • **to take delight in doing something** disfrutar haciendo algo ◆ *vt* encantar ◆ *vi* • **to delight in something/in doing something** disfrutar con algo/haciendo algo

delighted [dɪˈlaɪtɪd] *adj* encantado, da; muy contento, ta • **delighted by** o **with** encantado con • **to be delighted to do something/that** estar encantado de hacer algo/de que • **I'd be delighted (to come)** me encantaría (ir)

delightful [dɪˈlaɪtfʊl] *adj* ❶ encantador, ra ❷ delicioso, sa ❸ muy agradable

delinquent [dɪˈlɪŋkwənt] ◆ *adj* ❶ delictivo, va ❷ delincuente ◆ *s* delincuente

delirious [dɪˈlɪrɪəs] *adj* ❶ delirante ❷ *figurado* enfervorizado, da

deliver [dɪˈlɪvər] *vt* ❶ entregar ❷ repartir • **to deliver something to somebody** entregar algo a alguien ❸ pronunciar; transmitir; asestar ❹ prestar ❺ traer al mundo

delivery [dɪˈlɪvərɪ] *s* ❶ entrega ❷ reparto ❸ partida ❹ (estilo de) discurso ❺ parto

delude [dɪˈluːd] *vt* engañar • **to delude yourself** engañarse (a uno mismo/una misma)

deluge [ˈdeljuːdʒ] *s* ❶ diluvio ❷ *figurado* aluvión

delusion [dɪˈluːʒn] *s* espejismo; engaño

de luxe [dəˈlʌks] *adj* de lujo

demand [dɪˈmɑːnd] ◆ *s* ❶ exigencia; reclamación • **on demand** a petición ❷ *ECONOMÍA* • **demand for** demanda de • **in demand** solicitado, da ◆ *vt* ❶ exigir ❷ reivindicar; demandar • **to demand to do something** exigir hacer algo

demanding [dɪˈmɑːndɪŋ] *adj* exigente

demean [dɪˈmiːn] *vt* • **to demean yourself** humillarse; rebajarse

demeaning [dɪˈmiːnɪŋ] *adj* denigrante

demeanor [dɪˈmiːnər] *s* ⚠ *incontable formal* comportamiento

demented [dɪˈmentɪd] *adj* demente

demise [dɪˈmaɪz] *s formal* ❶ defunción ❷ desaparición

demo ['deməʊ] *s familiar* demo

democracy [dɪ'mɒkrəsɪ] *s* democracia

democrat ['deməkræt] *s* demócrata

■ **Democrat** *s* demócrata

democratic [demə'krætɪk] *adj* democrático, ca

■ **Democratic** *adj* demócrata

Democratic Party *s* Partido Demócrata

demolish [dɪ'mɒlɪʃ] *vt* ❶ demoler ❷ destrozar

demonstrate ['demənstreɪt] ◆ *vt* ❶ demostrar ❷ hacer una demostración de ◆ *vi* manifestarse • **to demonstrate for/against something** manifestarse a favor/en contra de algo

demonstration [demən'streɪʃn] *s* ❶ demostración ❷ manifestación

demonstrator ['demənstreɪtər] *s* manifestante

demoralized [dɪ'mɒrəlaɪzd] *adj* desmoralizado, da

demote [,di:'məʊt] *vt* descender de categoría

den [den] *s* guarida

denial [dɪ'naɪəl] *s* ❶ negación; rechazo • **she's in denial about her drink problem** se niega a aceptar que tiene un problema con la bebida ❷ desmentido ❸ denegación

denim ['denɪm] *s* mezclilla

Denmark ['denmɑ:k] *s* Dinamarca

denounce [dɪ'naʊns] *vt* denunciar

dense [dens] *adj* ❶ denso, sa ❷ tupido, da ❸ *familiar* bruto, ta

density ['densətɪ] *s* densidad

dent [dent] ◆ *s* abolladura ◆ *vt* abollar

dental ['dentl] *adj* dental

dental surgeon *s* odontólogo, ga

dentist ['dentɪst] *s* dentista • **to go to the dentist's** ir al dentista

deny [dɪ'naɪ] *vt* ❶ negar; rechazar • **to deny doing something** negar haber hecho algo ❷ desmentir ❸ *formal* • **to deny somebody something** denegar algo a alguien

deodorant [di:'əʊdərənt] *s* desodorante

depart [dɪ'pɑ:t] *vi formal* ❶ • **to depart (from)** salir (de) • **this train will depart from Platform 2** este tren efectuará su salida por la vía 2 ❷ • **to depart from something** apartarse de algo

department [dɪ'pɑ:tmənt] *s* ❶ departamento ❷ ministerio; secretaría

department store *s* tienda de departamentos

departure [dɪ'pɑ:tʃər] *s* ❶ salida *(de tren, avión)* ❷ marcha *(de persona)* ❸ • **departure (from)** abandono (de) • **a new departure** un nuevo enfoque

departure lounge *s* ❶ sala de embarque ❷ vestíbulo de salidas

depend [dɪ'pend] *vi* • **to depend on** depender de • **you can depend on me** puedes confiar en mí • **it depends** depende • **depending on** según; dependiendo de

dependable [dɪ'pendəbl] *adj* fiable

dependent [dɪ'pendənt] ◆ *adj* ❶ • **to be dependent (on)** depender (de) ❷ adicto, ta ◆ *s* • **my dependents** las personas a mi cargo

depict [dɪ'pɪkt] *vt* retratar

deplete [dɪ'pli:t] *vt* mermar; reducir

deplorable [dɪ'plɔ:rəbl] *adj* deplorable

deplore [dɪ'plɔ:r] *vt* deplorar

deploy [dɪ'plɔɪ] *vt* desplegar

deport [dɪ'pɔ:t] *vt* deportar

depose [dɪ'pəʊz] *vt* deponer

deposit [dɪ'pɒzɪt] ◆ *s* ❶ GEOLOGÍA yacimiento ❷ poso; sedimento ❸ depósito ❹ adelanto; fianza ◆ *vt* depositar

depot ['depəʊ] *s* ❶ almacén ❷ depósito ❸ cochera ❹ terminal

depress [dɪ'pres] *vt* ❶ deprimir ❷ desactivar ❸ reducir

depressed [dɪ'prest] *adj* deprimido, da

depressing [dɪ'presɪŋ] *adj* deprimente

depression [dɪ'preʃn] *s* ❶ depresión • **to suffer from depression** sufrir depresiones ❷ *formal* hueco

deprivation [,deprɪ'veɪʃn] *s* ❶ miseria ❷ privación

deprive [dɪ'praɪv] *vt* • **to deprive somebody of something** privar a alguien de algo

depth [depθ] *s* profundidad • **in depth** a fondo

expresión **to be out of your depth** no poder tocar el fondo ❯ **he was out of his depth with that job** ese trabajo le venía grande

■ **depths** *spl* • **in the depths of winter** en pleno invierno • **to be in the depths of despair** estar en un abismo de desesperación

deputize, deputise ['depjʊtaɪz] *vi* • **to deputize (for)** actuar en representación (de)

deputy ['depjʊtɪ] ◆ *adj* ❯ **deputy head** subdirector, ra ◆ *s* ❶ asistente; suplente ❷ POLÍTICA diputado, da ❸ ayudante del sheriff

derail [dɪ'reɪl] *vt* & *vi* descarrilar

derelict ['derəlɪkt] *adj* abandonado, da; en ruinas

deride [dɪ'raɪd] *vt* mofarse de

derisory [də'raɪzərɪ] *adj* ❶ irrisorio, ria ❷ burlón, ona

derivative [dɪ'rɪvətɪv] *s* derivado

derive [dɪ'raɪv] ◆ *vt* ❶ • **to derive something from something** encontrar algo en algo ❷ • **to be derived from** derivar de ◆ *vi* • **to derive from** derivar de

derogatory [dɪ'rɒgətrɪ] *adj* despectivo, va

descend [dɪ'send] ◆ *vt* formal descender por ◆ *vi* ❶ *formal* descender ❷ • **to descend (on something/somebody)** invadir (algo/a alguien) ❸ • **to descend to something/to doing something** rebajarse a algo/a hacer algo

descendant [dɪ'sendənt] *s* descendiente

descended [dɪ'sendɪd] *adj* • **to be descended from** ser descendiente de; descender de

descent [dɪ'sent] *s* ❶ descenso ; bajada ❷ ascendencia

describe [dɪ'skraɪb] *vt* describir • **to describe yourself as** definirse como

description [dɪ'skrɪpʃn] *s* ❶ descripción ❷ • **of all descriptions** de todo tipo

desert ◆ *s* ['dezət] GEOGRAFÍA desierto ◆ *vt* [dɪ'zɜːt] abandonar ◆ *vi* MILITAR desertar

deserted [dɪ'zɜːtɪd] *adj* desierto, ta

deserter [dɪ'zɜːtər] *s* desertor, ra

deserve [dɪ'zɜːv] *vt* merecer

deserving [dɪ'zɜːvɪŋ] *adj* encomiable • **deserving of** *formal* merecedor, ra de

design [dɪ'zaɪn] ◆ *s* ❶ diseño ❷ corte ❸ dibujo ❹ *formal* designio • **by design** adrede
expresión **to have designs on** tener las miras puestas en
◆ *vt* ❶ diseñar ❷ concebir

designate ◆ *adj* ['dezɪgnət] designado, da ◆ *vt* ['dezɪgneɪt] designar • **to designate somebody as something/to do something** designar a alguien algo/ para hacer algo

designer [dɪ'zaɪnər] ◆ *adj* ❶ de diseño ❷ de marca ◆ *s* ❶ diseñador, ra ❷ TEATRO escenógrafo, fa

desirable [dɪ'zaɪərəbl] *adj* ❶ *formal* deseable ; conveniente ❷ atractivo, va

desire [dɪ'zaɪər] ◆ *s* • **desire (for something/to do something)** deseo (de algo/de hacer algo) ◆ *vt* desear

desk [desk] *s* ❶ mesa ; escritorio ❷ pupitre ❸ ▸ **information desk** mostrador de información

desolate ['desələt] *adj* ❶ desolado, da ❷ desolador, ra

despair [dɪ'speər] ◆ *s* desesperación • **to do something in despair** hacer algo desesperadamente ◆ *vi* desesperarse • **to despair of somebody** desesperarse con alguien • **to despair of something/doing something** perder la esperanza de algo/hacer algo

despairing [dɪ'speərɪŋ] *adj* ❶ desesperado, da ❷ de desesperación

despatch [dɪ'spætʃ] = **dispatch**

desperate ['desprət] *adj* desesperado, da • **to be desperate for something** necesitar algo desesperadamente

desperately ['desprətlɪ] *adv* ❶ desesperadamente ❷ gravemente ❸ tremendamente

desperation [ˌdespə'reɪʃn] *s* desesperación • **in desperation** con desesperación

despicable [dɪ'spɪkəbl] *adj* despreciable

despise [dɪ'spaɪz] *vt* despreciar

despite [dɪ'spaɪt] *preposición* a pesar de ; pese a

despondent [dɪ'spɒndənt] *adj* descorazonado, da

dessert [dɪ'zɜːt] *s* postre

dessertspoon [dɪ'zɜːtspuːn] *s* cuchara de postre

destination [ˌdestɪ'neɪʃn] *s* destino

destined ['destɪnd] *adj* ❶ • **destined for something/to do something** destinado, da a algo/a hacer algo ❷ • **destined for** con destino a

destiny ['destɪnɪ] *s* destino

destitute ['destɪtjuːt] *adj* indigente

destroy [dɪ'strɔɪ] *vt* ❶ destruir ❷ aplastar ❸ matar ; sacrificar

destruction [dɪ'strʌkʃn] *s* destrucción

detach [dɪ'tætʃ] *vt* ❶ • **to detach something (from)** quitar o separar algo (de) ❷ • **to detach yourself from something** distanciarse de algo

detachable [dɪ'tætʃəbl] *adj* ❶ de quita y pon ❷ postizo, za

detached [dɪ'tætʃt] *adj* ❶ objetivo, va ❷ distante

detachment [dɪ'tætʃmənt] *s* ❶ objetividad ❷ distanciamiento ❸ MILITAR destacamento

detail ['diːteɪl] ◆ *s* ❶ detalle ❷ ⚙ *incontable* detalles • **to go into detail** entrar en detalles • **in detail** con detalle ❸ MILITAR destacamento ◆ *vt* detallar
■ **details** *spl* ❶ información ❷ datos

detailed ['diːteɪld] *adj* detallado, da

detain [dɪ'teɪn] *vt* ❶ retener ❷ detener

detect [dɪ'tekt] *vt* ❶ detectar ❷ notar ; percibir

detection [dɪ'tekʃn] *s* ⚙ *incontable* ❶ detección ❷ investigación ❸ descubrimiento

detective [dɪ'tektɪv] *s* ❶ detective ❷ agente

detective story *s* novela policíaca

detention [dɪ'tenʃn] *s* ❶ detención ; arresto ❷ castigo consistente en tener que quedarse en la escuela después de clase

deter [dɪ'tɜːr] *vt* • **to deter somebody (from doing something)** disuadir a alguien (de hacer algo)

detergent [dɪ'tɜːdʒənt] *s* detergente

deteriorate [dɪ'tɪərɪəreɪt] *vi* ❶ deteriorarse ❷ empeorar

determination [dɪˌtɜːmɪ'neɪʃn] *s* determinación

determine [dɪ'tɜːmɪn] *vt* determinar • **to determine to do something** *formal* decidir o resolver hacer algo

determined [dɪ'tɜːmɪnd] *adj* decidido, da • **determined to do something** decidido, da o resuelto, ta a hacer algo

deterrent [dɪ'terənt] *s* elemento de disuasión • **to serve as a deterrent** tener un efecto disuasorio • **nuclear deterrent** armas nucleares disuasorias

detest [dɪ'test] *vt* detestar

detonate ['detəneɪt] ◆ *vt* hacer detonar ◆ *vi* detonar

detour ['diːˌtʊər] *s* desvío • **to make a detour** dar un rodeo

detox ['diːtɒks] *s* desintoxicación

detract [dɪ'trækt] *vi* • **to detract from something a)** mermar algo ; aminorar algo **b)** restar importancia a algo

D

detriment ['detrɪmənt] *s* • **to the detriment of** en detrimento de

detrimental [,detrɪ'mentl] *adj* perjudicial

devaluation [,diːvæljʊ'eɪʃn] *s* devaluación

devastated ['devəsteɪtɪd] *adj* ❶ asolado, da ❷ *figurado* desolado, da

devastating ['devəsteɪtɪŋ] *adj* ❶ devastador, ra ❷ abrumador, ra ❸ desolador, ra ❹ imponente; irresistible

develop [dɪ'veləp] ◆ *vt* ❶ desarrollar ❷ urbanizar ❸ MEDICINA contraer ❹ • **to develop a fault** estropearse ❺ FOTOGRAFÍA revelar ◆ *vi* ❶ desarrollarse • **to develop into something** transformarse en algo ❷ presentarse

developing country [dɪ'veləpɪŋ-] *s* país en vías de desarrollo

development [dɪ'veləpmənt] *s* ⚬ *incontable* ❶ desarrollo ❷ elaboración ❸ urbanización ❹ (nuevo) acontecimiento • **recent developments** la evolución reciente ❺ avance

device [dɪ'vaɪs] *s* dispositivo

devil ['devl] *s* ❶ demonio ❷ • **the Devil** el diablo ❸ • **poor devil** pobre diablo • **you lucky devil!** ¡vaya suerte que tienes! • **who/where/why the devil...?** ¿quién/dónde/por qué demonios...?

devious ['diːvjəs] *adj* ❶ retorcido, da ❷ enrevesado, da ❸ sinuoso, sa

devise [dɪ'vaɪz] *vt* ❶ diseñar ❷ concebir

devoid [dɪ'vɔɪd] *adj formal* • **devoid of** desprovisto, ta de

devote [dɪ'vəʊt] *vt* • **to devote something to** dedicar o consagrar algo a

devoted [dɪ'vəʊtɪd] *adj* ❶ unido, da ❷ ferviente • **to be devoted to somebody** tenerle mucho cariño a alguien

devotion [dɪ'vəʊʃn] *s* ⚬ *incontable* ❶ • **devotion (to)** dedicación (a) ❷ devoción

devour [dɪ'vaʊər] *vt literal & figurado* devorar

devout [dɪ'vaʊt] *adj* RELIGIÓN devoto, ta

dew [djuː] *s* rocío

dexterity [dek'sterətɪ] *s* destreza

diabetes [,daɪə'biːtiːz] *s* diabetes

diabetic [,daɪə'betɪk] ◆ *adj* diabético, ca ◆ *s* diabético, ca

diabolic(al) [,daɪə'bɒlɪk(l)] *adj familiar* pésimo, ma

diagnose ['daɪəgnəʊz] *vt* MEDICINA diagnosticar • **she was diagnosed as having cancer** le diagnosticaron cáncer

diagnosis [,daɪəg'nəʊsɪs] *s* ❶ MEDICINA diagnóstico ❷ diagnosis

El plural de **diagnosis** es **diagnoses** [,daɪəg'nəʊsiːz].

diagonal [daɪ'ægənl] ◆ *adj* diagonal ◆ *s* diagonal

diagram ['daɪəgræm] *s* diagrama

dial ['daɪəl] ◆ *s* ❶ carátula ❷ cuadrante ◆ *vt* marcar

dialect ['daɪəlekt] *s* dialecto

dialog ['daɪəlɒg] *s* diálogo

dial tone *s* señal de marcar

diameter [daɪ'æmɪtər] *s* diámetro

diamond ['daɪəmənd] *s* ❶ diamante ❷ rombo
■ **diamonds** *spl* diamantes

diaper ['daɪpər] *s* pañal

diaphragm ['daɪəfræm] *s* diafragma

diarrhea [,daɪə'rɪə] *s* diarrea

diary ['daɪərɪ] *s* ❶ agenda ❷ diario

dice [daɪs] ◆ *s* dado ◆ *vt* cortar en cuadritos
El plural de **dice** es **dice**.

dictate *vt* [dɪk'teɪt] • **to dictate something (to somebody)** dictar algo (a alguien)

dictation [dɪk'teɪʃn] *s* dictado

dictator [dɪk'teɪtər] *s* dictador, ra

dictatorship [dɪk'teɪtəʃɪp] *s* dictadura

dictionary ['dɪkʃənrɪ] *s* diccionario

did [dɪd] *pretérito* → **do**

didn't ['dɪdnt] (*abreviatura de* did not) = **do**

die [daɪ] ◆ *vi* ❶ morir • **to be dying** estar muriéndose ❷ *literario* extinguirse
expresión to be dying for something/to do something morirse por algo/por hacer algo
◆ *s* (pl dice) dado
■ **die away** *vi* desvanecerse
■ **die down** *vi* ❶ amainar ❷ apaciguarse ❸ calmarse
■ **die out** *vi* extinguirse
Formas irregulares de **die**: *pret & pp* **died**, *gerundio* **dying**.

diesel ['diːzl] *s* diesel

diet ['daɪət] ◆ *s* ❶ dieta ❷ dieta • **to be on a diet** estar a dieta ◆ *en compuestos* light ◆ *vi* estar a dieta

differ ['dɪfər] *vi* ❶ ser diferente • **to differ from something** distinguirse o diferir de algo ❷ • **to differ with somebody (about something)** disentir o discrepar de alguien (en algo)

difference ['dɪfrəns] *s* diferencia • **it didn't make any difference** no cambió nada

different ['dɪfrənt] *adj* • **different (from)** diferente o distinto, ta (de)

differentiate [,dɪfə'renʃieɪt] ◆ *vt* • **to differentiate (something from something)** diferenciar o distinguir (algo de algo) ◆ *vi* • **to differentiate between** diferenciar o distinguir entre

difficult ['dɪfɪkəlt] *adj* difícil

difficulty ['dɪfɪkəltɪ] *s* dificultad • **to have difficulty in doing something** tener dificultad en o para hacer algo

diffident ['dɪfɪdənt] *adj* retraído, da

diffuse *vt* [dɪ'fjuːz] difundir

dig [dɪg] ◆ *vt* ❶ cavar; escarbar ❷ cavar en ❸ excavar ❹ • **to dig something into** clavar o hundir algo en ◆ *vi* ❶ cavar ❷ escarbar ❸ • **to dig into** clavarse o hundirse en ◆ *s* ❶ pulla ❷ ARQUEOLOGÍA excavación
■ **dig out** *vt* ☼*El objeto se puede colocar antes o después de la preposición.* familiar desempolvar; encontrar
■ **dig up** *vt* ☼*El objeto se puede colocar antes o después de la preposición.* ❶ desenterrar ❷ arrancar
Formas irregulares de **dig**: *pretérito & pp* **dug**.

digest ◆ *s* ['daɪdʒest] compendio ◆ *vt* [dɪ'dʒest] *literal & figurado* digerir

digestion [dɪ'dʒestʃn] *s* digestión

digit ['dɪdʒɪt] *s* ❶ dígito ❷ dedo

digital ['dɪdʒɪtl] *adj* digital

dignified ['dɪgnɪfaɪd] *adj* ❶ digno, na ❷ ceremonioso, sa

dignity ['dɪgnəti] *s* dignidad

digress [daɪ'gres] *vi* apartarse del tema • **to digress from** apartarse o desviarse de

dike, dyke [daɪk] *s* dique

dilapidated [dɪ'læpɪdeɪtɪd] *adj* ❶ derruido, da ❷ destartalado, da

dilate [daɪ'leɪt] *vi* dilatarse

dilemma [dɪ'lemə] *s* dilema

diligent ['dɪlɪdʒənt] *adj* diligente

dilute [daɪ'luːt] *vt* diluir

dim [dɪm] ◆ *adj* ❶ tenue ❷ sombrío, bría ❸ débil ❹ vago, ga ❺ *familiar* tonto, ta; torpe ◆ *vt* atenuar ◆ *vi* atenuarse

dime [daɪm] *s* ▶ moneda de diez centavos

dimension [dɪ'menʃn] *s* dimensión

diminish [dɪ'mɪnɪʃ] *vt & vi* disminuir

diminutive [dɪ'mɪnjʊtɪv] *formal* ◆ *adj* diminuto, ta ◆ *s* GRAMÁTICA diminutivo

dimple ['dɪmpl] *s* hoyuelo

din [dɪn] *s* familiar estrépito

dine [daɪn] *vi* formal cenar
■ **dine out** *vi* cenar fuera

diner ['daɪnər] *s* ❶ comensal ❷ restaurante barato; ≃ restaurante o parador de carretera

dinghy ['dɪŋgɪ] *s* ❶ bote ❷ lancha neumática

dingy ['dɪndʒɪ] *adj* ❶ lóbrego, ga ❷ deslustrado, da

dining room ['daɪnɪŋ-] *s* comedor

dinner ['dɪnər] *s* ❶ cena ❷ cena de gala; banquete

dinosaur ['daɪnəsɔːr] *s* dinosaurio

dip [dɪp] ◆ *s* ❶ pendiente ❷ salsa ❸ chapuzón • **to go for/take a dip** ir a darse/darse un chapuzón ◆ *vt* • **to dip something in** o **into something** mojar algo en algo ◆ *vi* descender suavemente

diploma [dɪ'pləʊmə] *s* diploma

diplomacy [dɪ'pləʊməsɪ] *s* diplomacia

diplomat ['dɪpləmæt] *s* ❶ diplomático, ca ❷ persona diplomática

diplomatic [ˌdɪplə'mætɪk] *adj* diplomático, ca

dire ['daɪər] *adj* ❶ grave ❷ serio, ria ❸ extremo, ma

direct [dɪ'rekt] ◆ *adj* directo, ta ◆ *vt* ❶ • **to direct something at somebody** dirigir algo a alguien ❷ • **to direct somebody (to)** indicar a alguien el camino (a) ❸ • **to direct somebody to do something** mandar a alguien hacer algo ◆ *adv* directamente

direct current *s* corriente continua

direction [dɪ'rekʃn] *s* dirección • **sense of direction** sentido de la orientación
■ **directions** *spl* ❶ señas; indicaciones ❷ modo de empleo

directly [dɪ'rektlɪ] *adv* ❶ directamente ❷ inmediatamente ❸ pronto; en breve

director [dɪ'rektər] *s* director, ra

directory [dɪ'rektərɪ] *s* ❶ guía (alfabética) ❷ INFORMÁTICA directorio

dirt [dɜːt] *s* ☼*incontable* ❶ suciedad ❷ tierra

dirty ['dɜːtɪ] ◆ *adj* ❶ sucio, cia • **to get dirty** ensuciarse ❷ colorado, da ❸ obsceno, na • **dirty word** palabrota ◆ *vt* ensuciar

disability [ˌdɪsə'bɪlətɪ] *s* discapacidad; minusvalía • **people with disabilities** los discapacitados; los minusválidos

disabled [dɪs'eɪbld] ◆ *adj* discapacitado, da; minusválido, da • **disabled toilet** servicio para discapacitados o minusválidos ◆ *spl* • **the disabled** los minusválidos; los discapacitados

disadvantage [ˌdɪsəd'vɑːntɪdʒ] *s* desventaja • **to be at a disadvantage** estar en desventaja

disagree [ˌdɪsə'griː] *vi* ❶ • **to disagree (with)** no estar de acuerdo (con) ❷ contradecirse; no concordar ❸ • **to disagree with somebody** sentar mal a alguien

disagreeable [ˌdɪsə'griːəbl] *adj* desagradable

disagreement [ˌdɪsə'griːmənt] *s* ❶ desacuerdo ❷ discusión

disallow [ˌdɪsə'laʊ] *vt* ❶ *formal* rechazar ❷ anular

disappear [ˌdɪsə'pɪər] *vi* desaparecer

disappearance [ˌdɪsə'pɪərəns] *s* desaparición

disappoint [ˌdɪsə'pɔɪnt] *vt* ❶ decepcionar ❷ defraudar

disappointed [ˌdɪsə'pɔɪntɪd] *adj* ❶ • **disappointed (in** o **with something)** decepcionado, da (con algo) ❷ defraudado, da

disappointing [ˌdɪsə'pɔɪntɪŋ] *adj* decepcionante

disappointment [ˌdɪsə'pɔɪntmənt] *s* decepción; desilusión • **to be a disappointment** ser decepcionante

disapproval [ˌdɪsə'pruːvl] *s* desaprobación

disapprove [ˌdɪsə'pruːv] *vi* ❶ estar en contra • **to disapprove of something** desaprobar algo ❷ •

disapprove of somebody no ver con buenos ojos a alguien

disarm [dɪs'ɑ:m] ◆ *vt* literal & figurado desarmar ◆ *vi* desarmarse

disarmament [dɪs'ɑ:məmənt] *s* desarme

disaster [dɪ'zɑ:stər] *s* ❶ desastre ❷ catástrofe

disastrous [dɪ'zɑ:strəs] *adj* desastroso, sa

disband [dɪs'bænd] ◆ *vt* disolver; disgregar ◆ *vi* disolverse; disgregarse

disbelief [ˌdɪsbɪ'li:f] *s* • in o with disbelief con incredulidad

discard [dɪ'skɑ:d] *vt* ❶ desechar ❷ descartar

discern [dɪ'sɜ:n] *vt* ❶ discernir ❷ percibir ❸ distinguir

discerning [dɪ'sɜ:nɪŋ] *adj* ❶ refinado, da ❷ entendido, da

discharge ◆ *s* ['dɪstʃɑ:dʒ] ❶ alta ❷ puesta en libertad ❸ licencia ❹ emisión ❺ MEDICINA supuración ❻ ELECTRICIDAD descarga ◆ *vt* [dɪs'tʃɑ:dʒ] ❶ dar de alta ❷ poner en libertad ❸ licenciar ❹ formal cumplir ❺ despedir ❻ descargar

disciple [dɪ'saɪpl] *s* discípulo, la

discipline ['dɪsɪplɪn] ◆ *s* disciplina ◆ *vt* ❶ disciplinar ❷ castigar

disc jockey *s* disk jockey; DJ

disclose [dɪs'kləʊz] *vt* revelar

disclosure [dɪs'kləʊʒər] *s* revelación

disco ['dɪskəʊ] *s* ❶ discoteca ❷ baile ❸ música disco

El plural de disco es discos.

discomfort [dɪs'kʌmfət] *s* ❶ incomodidad ❷ molestia

disconcert [ˌdɪskən'sɜ:t] *vt* desconcertar

disconnect [ˌdɪskə'nekt] ◆ *vt* ❶ quitar; separar ❷ desconectar; cortar el suministro a ❸ cortar la línea a ◆ *vi* desconectarse

discontent [ˌdɪskən'tent] *s* • discontent (with) descontento, ta (con)

discontented [ˌdɪskən'tentɪd] *adj* descontento, ta

discontinue [ˌdɪskən'tɪnju:] *vt* interrumpir

discord ['dɪskɔ:d] *s* ❶ discordia ❷ MÚSICA disonancia

discount ['dɪskaʊnt] ◆ *s* descuento • at a discount con descuento ◆ *vt* descartar

discourage [dɪ'skʌrɪdʒ] *vt* ❶ desanimar ❷ impedir ❸ ahuyentar • to discourage somebody from doing something disuadir a alguien de hacer algo

discover [dɪ'skʌvər] *vt* descubrir

discovery [dɪ'skʌvərɪ] *s* descubrimiento

discredit [dɪs'kredɪt] ◆ *s* descrédito ◆ *vt* ❶ desacreditar ❷ refutar

discreet [dɪ'skri:t] *adj* discreto, ta

discrepancy [dɪ'skrepənsɪ] *s* • discrepancy (in/between) discrepancia (en/entre)

discretion [dɪ'skreʃn] *s* incontable ❶ discreción ❷ criterio • at the discretion of a voluntad de

discriminate [dɪ'skrɪmɪneɪt] *vi* ❶ • to discriminate (between) discriminar o distinguir (entre) ❷ • to discriminate against somebody discriminar a alguien

discriminating [dɪ'skrɪmɪneɪtɪŋ] *adj* ❶ refinado, da ❷ entendido, da

discrimination [dɪˌskrɪmɪ'neɪʃn] *s* ❶ • discrimination (against) discriminación (hacia) ❷ (buen) gusto

discus ['dɪskəs] *s* disco (en atletismo) • the discus el lanzamiento de disco

discuss [dɪ'skʌs] *vt* hablar de; discutir • we discussed the book in class hablamos del libro en clase • she discussed the problem with him discutió el problema con él

discussion [dɪ'skʌʃn] *s* discusión • they had a long discussion on the subject tuvieron una larga discusión sobre el tema

disdain [dɪs'deɪn] formal ◆ *s* • disdain (for) desdén o desprecio (hacia) ◆ *vt* desdeñar; despreciar

disease [dɪ'zi:z] *s* literal & figurado enfermedad

disembark [ˌdɪsɪm'bɑ:k] *vi* desembarcar

disenchanted [ˌdɪsɪn'tʃɑ:ntɪd] *adj* • disenchanted (with) desencantado, da (con)

disfigure [dɪs'fɪgər] *vt* desfigurar

disgrace [dɪs'greɪs] ◆ *s* ❶ vergüenza • he's a disgrace to his family es una deshonra para su familia ❷ estar castigado, da ◆ *vt* deshonrar

disgraceful [dɪs'greɪsfʊl] *adj* vergonzoso, sa • it's disgraceful es una vergüenza

disgruntled [dɪs'grʌntld] *adj* disgustado, da

disguise [dɪs'gaɪz] ◆ *s* disfraz ◆ *vt* disfrazar

disgust [dɪs'gʌst] ◆ *s* ❶ • disgust (at) asco (hacia) ❷ indignación (ante) ◆ *vt* ❶ repugnar ❷ indignar

disgusting [dɪs'gʌstɪŋ] *adj* ❶ asqueroso, sa ❷ indignante

dish [dɪʃ] *s* ❶ plato ❷ platillo ❸ fuente
■ **dishes** *spl* platos • to do o wash the dishes lavar (los trastes)
■ **dish out** *vt* El objeto se puede colocar antes o después de la preposición. familiar repartir
■ **dish up** *vt* El objeto se puede colocar antes o después de la preposición. familiar servir

disheartened [dɪs'hɑ:tnd] *adj* descorazonado, da

disheveled [dɪ'ʃevəld] *adj* ❶ desaliñado, da ❷ despeinado, da

dishonest [dɪs'ɒnɪst] *adj* deshonesto, ta; nada honrado, da

dishonor [dɪs'ɒnər] formal ◆ *s* deshonra ◆ *vt* deshonrar

dish towel *s* trapo (de cocina)

dishwasher ['dɪʃˌwɒʃər] *s* ❶ lavadora de trastes (electrodoméstico) ❷ lavaplatos

disillusioned [ˌdɪsɪ'lu:ʒnd] *adj* desilusionado, da

disinfect [ˌdɪsɪn'fekt] *vt* desinfectar

disinfectant [,dɪsɪn'fektənt] *s* desinfectante

disintegrate [dɪs'ɪntɪgreɪt] *vi literal & figurado* desintegrarse

disinterested [,dɪs'ɪntrəstɪd] *adj* ❶ desinteresado, da ❷ *familiar* • **disinterested (in)** indiferente (a)

disjointed [dɪs'dʒɔɪntɪd] *adj* confuso, sa

disk [dɪsk] *s* INFORMÁTICA disco

disk drive *s* INFORMÁTICA unidad de disco

dislike [dɪs'laɪk] ◆ *s* • **dislike (for) a)** aversión (a) **b)** antipatía (por) • **to take a dislike to** agarrarle tirria a ❷ • **her likes and dislikes** las cosas que le gustan y las que no le gustan ◆ *vt* ❶ • **I dislike her** no me cae bien ❷ • **I dislike them** no me caen bien

dislocate ['dɪsləkeɪt] *vt* MEDICINA dislocar • **to dislocate your shoulder** dislocarse el hombro

dislodge [dɪs'lɒdʒ] *vt* • **to dislodge something/somebody (from)** sacar algo/a alguien (de)

disloyal [,dɪs'lɔɪəl] *adj* • **disloyal (to)** desleal (a)

dismal ['dɪzml] *adj* ❶ sombrío, a ❷ deprimente ❸ lamentable

dismantle [dɪs'mæntl] *vt* ❶ desmontar ❷ desmantelar

dismay [dɪs'meɪ] ◆ *s* ☿ *incontable* consternación • **to my/his** ETC **dismay** para mí/su ETC consternación ◆ *vt* consternar

dismiss [dɪs'mɪs] *vt* ❶ desechar ❷ • **to dismiss somebody (from)** despedir a alguien (de) ❸ • **to dismiss somebody** dar a alguien permiso para irse

dismissal [dɪs'mɪsl] *s* despido

dismount [,dɪs'maʊnt] *vi* • **to dismount (from something)** desmontar (de algo)

disobedience [,dɪsə'biːdjəns] *s* desobediencia

disobedient [,dɪsə'biːdjənt] *adj* • **disobedient (to)** desobediente (con)

disobey [,dɪsə'beɪ] *vt & vi* desobedecer

disorder [dɪs'ɔːdər] *s* ❶ • **in disorder** en desorden ❷ ☿ *incontable* disturbios ❸ MEDICINA afección; dolencia ❹ trastorno

disorderly [dɪs'ɔːdəlɪ] *adj* ❶ desordenado, da ❷ incontrolado, da

disorganized, disorganised [dɪs'ɔːgənaɪzd] *adj* desorganizado, da

disoriented [dɪs'ɔːrɪəntɪd] *adj* desorientado, da

disown [dɪs'əʊn] *vt* ❶ renegar de ❷ no reconocer como propio, pia

disparaging [dɪ'spærɪdʒɪŋ] *adj* menospreciativo, va

dispassionate [dɪ'spæʃnət] *adj* desapasionado, da

dispatch, despatch [dɪ'spætʃ] ◆ *s* ❶ despacho ❷ envío ◆ *vt* ❶ expedir ❷ enviar

dispel [dɪ'spel] *vt* disipar

dispense [dɪ'spens] *vt* ❶ ofrecer ❷ administrar ❸ despachar

■ **dispense with** *vt* ☿ *El objeto siempre va después de la preposición al final.* prescindir de

disperse [dɪ'spɜːs] ◆ *vt* dispersar ◆ *vi* dispersarse

dispirited [dɪ'spɪrɪtɪd] *adj* desanimado, da

displace [dɪs'pleɪs] *vt* reemplazar; sustituir

display [dɪ'spleɪ] ◆ *s* ❶ exposición; muestrario ❷ demostración ❸ exhibición • **on display** en exhibición ❹ INFORMÁTICA pantalla ◆ *vt* ❶ exponer ❷ demostrar ❸ mostrar

displease [dɪs'pliːz] *vt* ❶ disgustar ❷ enfadar

displeasure [dɪs'pleʒər] *s* ❶ disgusto ❷ enfado

disposable [dɪ'spəʊzəbl] *adj* desechable

disposal [dɪ'spəʊzl] *s* ❶ eliminación ❷ trituradora de basuras ❸ • **to have something at your disposal** disponer de algo

dispose [dɪ'spəʊz] ■ **dispose of** *vt* ☿ *El objeto siempre va después de la preposición al final.* ❶ deshacerse de ❷ quitarse de encima o de en medio

disposed [dɪ'spəʊzd] *adj* • **to be disposed to do something** estar dispuesto, ta a hacer algo

disposition [,dɪspə'zɪʃn] *s* carácter

disprove [,dɪs'pruːv] *vt* refutar

dispute [dɪ'spjuːt] ◆ *s* ❶ disputa ❷ ☿ *incontable* conflicto; desacuerdo • **in dispute a)** en desacuerdo **b)** en litigio; en entredicho ❸ INDUSTRIA conflicto laboral ◆ *vt* cuestionar

disqualify [,dɪs'kwɒlɪfaɪ] *vt* ❶ • **to disqualify somebody (from doing something)** incapacitar a alguien (para hacer algo) ❷ DEPORTE descalificar

disquiet [dɪs'kwaɪət] *s* inquietud

disregard [,dɪsrɪ'gɑːd] ◆ *s* • **disregard (for)** indiferencia (a); despreocupación (por) ◆ *vt* hacer caso omiso de

disreputable [dɪs'repjʊtəbl] *adj* ❶ de mala fama ❷ vergonzante

disrepute [,dɪsrɪ'pjuːt] *s* • **to bring something into disrepute** desprestigiar o desacreditar algo

disrupt [dɪs'rʌpt] *vt* ❶ interrumpir ❷ trastornar; perturbar ❸ revolucionar; enredar en

disruption [dɪs'rʌpʃn] *s* ❶ interrupción ❷ trastorno

dissatisfaction ['dɪs,sætɪs'fækʃn] *s* descontento

dissatisfied [,dɪs'sætɪsfaɪd] *adj* • **dissatisfied (with)** insatisfecho, cha o descontento, ta (con)

dissect [dɪ'sekt] *vt* ❶ MEDICINA diseccionar ❷ *figurado* analizar minuciosamente

dissent [dɪ'sent] ◆ *s* ❶ disconformidad; disentimiento ❷ DEPORTE • **he was booked for dissent** lo amonestaron por protestar ◆ *vi* • **to dissent (from)** disentir (de)

dissertation [,dɪsə'teɪʃn] *s* tesis

dissident ['dɪsɪdənt] *s* disidente

dissimilar [,dɪ'sɪmɪlər] *adj* • **dissimilar (to)** distinto, ta (de)

dissociate [dɪ'səʊʃɪeɪt] *vt* disociar

dissolute ['dɪsəlu:t] *adj* disoluto, ta

dissolve [dɪ'zɒlv] ◆ *vt* disolver ◆ *vi* ❶ disolverse ❷ *figurado* desvanecerse; desaparecer

dissuade [dɪ'sweɪd] *vt* • **to dissuade somebody (from doing something)** disuadir a alguien (de hacer algo)

distance ['dɪstəns] *s* distancia • **at a distance** a distancia • **from a distance** desde lejos • **in the distance** a lo lejos

distance learning *s* enseñanza a distancia

distant ['dɪstənt] *adj* ❶ lejano, na • **distant from** distante de ❷ frío, a; distante

distaste [dɪs'teɪst] *s* • **distaste (for)** desagrado (por)

distasteful [dɪs'teɪstfʊl] *adj* desagradable

distill [dɪ'stɪl] *vt* destilar

distillery [dɪ'stɪlərɪ] *s* destilería

distinct [dɪ'stɪŋkt] *adj* ❶ • **distinct (from)** distinto, ta (de) • **as distinct from** a diferencia de ❷ notable; visible; claro, ra

distinction [dɪ'stɪŋkʃn] *s* ❶ distinción ❷ sobresaliente

distinctive [dɪ'stɪŋktɪv] *adj* característico, ca; particular

distinguish [dɪ'stɪŋgwɪʃ] *vt* • **to distinguish something (from)** distinguir algo (de)

distinguished [dɪ'stɪŋgwɪʃt] *adj* distinguido, da

distinguishing [dɪ'stɪŋgwɪʃɪŋ] *adj* distintivo, va

distort [dɪ'stɔ:t] *vt* ❶ deformar ❷ distorsionar ❸ tergiversar

distracted [dɪ'stræktɪd] *adj* ausente

distraction [dɪ'strækʃn] *s* distracción

distraught [dɪ'strɔ:t] *adj* fuera de sí

distress [dɪ'stres] ◆ *s* ❶ angustia ❷ dolor ❸ peligro ◆ *vt* afligir; apenar

distressing [dɪ'stresɪŋ] *adj* angustioso, sa

distribute [dɪ'strɪbju:t] *vt* distribuir; repartir

distribution [ˌdɪstrɪ'bju:ʃn] *s* distribución

distributor [dɪ'strɪbjʊtər] *s* COMERCIO distribuidor, ra

district ['dɪstrɪkt] *s* ❶ zona; región; barrio ❷ distrito

district attorney *s* fiscal (del distrito); procurador, ra general

distrust [dɪs'trʌst] ◆ *s* desconfianza ◆ *vt* desconfiar de

disturb [dɪ'stɜ:b] *vt* ❶ molestar; perturbar ❷ inquietar ❸ alterar; desordenar

disturbance [dɪ'stɜ:bəns] *s* ❶ tumulto • **there were a number of minor disturbances throughout the night** se produjeron algunos disturbios durante la noche ❷ interrupción ❸ trastorno

disturbed [dɪ'stɜ:bd] *adj* ❶ trastornado, da ❷ inquieto, ta

disturbing [dɪ'stɜ:bɪŋ] *adj* inquietante

ditch [dɪtʃ] ◆ *s* ❶ zanja ❷ cuneta ◆ *vt familiar* ❶ romper con ❷ deshacerse de

dither ['dɪðər] *vi* vacilar

ditto ['dɪtəʊ] *adv* ídem

dive [daɪv] *vi* ❶ zambullirse; tirarse al agua; sumergirse ❷ bucear ❸ lanzarse; caer en picada ❹ • **to dive into** meter la mano en ◆ *s* ❶ zambullida ❷ inmersión ❸ salto; DEPORTE estirada • **it was a dive** se tiró un clavado ❹ descenso en picada

Formas irregulares de **dive**: *pretérito* **dived** o **dove**, *pp* **dived**.

diver ['daɪvər] *s* ❶ buceador, ra ❷ buzo ❸ clavadista

diverge [daɪ'vɜ:dʒ] *vi* ❶ • **to diverge (from)** divergir (de) ❷ discrepar

diversify [daɪ'vɜ:sɪfaɪ] ◆ *vt* diversificar ◆ *vi* diversificarse

diversion [daɪ'vɜ:ʃn] *s* ❶ desviación ❷ distracción

diversity [daɪ'vɜ:sətɪ] *s* diversidad

divert [daɪ'vɜ:t] *vt* ❶ desviar ❷ distraer

divide [dɪ'vaɪd] ◆ *vt* • **to divide something (between** o **among)** dividir algo (entre) • **to divide something into** dividir algo en • **to divide something by** dividir algo entre o por • **divide 3 into 89** divide 89 entre 3 ◆ *vi* ❶ bifurcarse ❷ dividirse

dividend ['dɪvɪdend] *s* ❶ FINANZAS dividendo ❷ beneficio

divine [dɪ'vaɪn] *adj* divino, na

diving ['daɪvɪŋ] *s* ☿ *incontable* ❶ clavados ❷ buceo

division [dɪ'vɪʒn] *s* ❶ división ❷ reparto

divorce [dɪ'vɔ:s] ◆ *s* divorcio ◆ *vt* divorciarse de ◆ *vi* divorciarse

divorced [dɪ'vɔ:st] *adj* divorciado, da

divorcee [dɪvɔ:'si:] *s* divorciado, da

divulge [daɪ'vʌldʒ] *vt* divulgar; revelar

DIY *abreviatura escrita de* **do-it-yourself**

dizzy ['dɪzɪ] *adj* ❶ mareado, da ❷ • **to feel dizzy** sentir vértigo

DJ *s abreviatura escrita de* **disc jockey**

DNA *(abreviatura de* deoxyribonucleic acid) *s* ADN

---

do [du:]

◆ *auxiliar*

❶ [*en frases negativas, cuando no hay otro auxiliar*]
• **don't leave it there** no lo dejes ahí

❷ [*en frases interrogativas, cuando no hay otro auxiliar*]
• **what did he want?** ¿qué quería?
• **do you think she'll come?** ¿te parece que vendrá?

❸ [*para repetir un verbo*]
• **she reads more than I do** ella lee más que yo

❹ [*con las "coletillas", cuando no hay otro auxiliar*]
• **so you think you can dance, do you?** así que te crees que sabes bailar, ¿no?

❺ [*para añadir énfasis*]
• **I did tell you but you've forgotten** sí que te lo dije, pero se te olvidó

❻ [*para contrastar*]
• **I am not very fond of the piano. I do like Chopin though** no me gusta mucho el piano, pero me gusta Chopin

❼ [*para invitar, incitar*]
• **do come in** entre, por favor

◆ *vt*

❶ [*para expresar la realización de una acción*]
• **she does the cooking, he does the housework** ella cocina y él se encarga de las tareas domésticas
• **she's doing her hair** se está peinando
• **they do fish very well in this restaurant** en este restaurante preparan el pescado muy bien
• **I did physics at school** estudié física en el colegio

❷ [*para preguntarle a alguien su profesión*]
• **what do you do?** ¿en qué trabajas?

❸ [*en expresiones*]
• **shall we do lunch?** *familiar* ¿qué tal si almorzamos?

◆ *vi*

❶ [*realizar una acción*] hacer
• **do as I tell you** haz como te digo

❷ [*para expresar una idea de éxito*]
• **they're doing really well** les va muy bien
• **he could do better** podría hacerlo mejor
• **how did you do in the exam?** ¿cómo te fue en el examen?

❸ [*para expresar que algo es suficiente*]
• **will six dollars do?** ¿te bastarán 6 dólares?
• **that will do** con eso será suficiente

■ **dos**

◆ *nombre proprio*

expresión **dos and don'ts** [*órdenes*] reglas básicas

■ **do away with**

◆ *vt* 🔆 *El objeto siempre va después de la preposición al final.*

❶ acabar con *(pobreza)*

❷ suprimir *(leyes)*

■ **do down**

◆ *vt* 🔆 *El objeto se puede colocar antes o después de la preposición.*

familiar
• **to do somebody down** menospreciar a alguien
• **to do yourself down** menospreciarse

■ **do over**

◆ *vt* 🔆 *El objeto se puede colocar antes o después de la preposición.*

volver a hacer

■ **do up**

◆ *vt* 🔆 *El objeto se puede colocar antes o después de la preposición.*

❶ amarrar ; abrochar
• **do your shoes up** amárrate los zapatos
• **do your coat up** abróchate el abrigo

❷ renovar ; redecorar
• **to do yourself up** arreglarse

❸ envolver *(regalo)*

■ **do with**

◆ *vt* 🔆 *El objeto siempre va después de la preposición al final.*

❶ [*necesitar*]
• **I could do with a break** no me vendría mal un descanso

❷ tener que ver (con)
• **that has nothing to do with it** eso no tiene nada que ver (con ello)

■ **do without**

◆ *vt* 🔆 *El objeto siempre va después de la preposición al final.*

pasar sin
• **I can do without your sarcasm** podrías ahorrarte tu sarcasmo

◆ *vi*

arreglárselas
• **they did without bread** se las arreglaron sin pan

do

Presente: I do, you do, he/she/it does, we do, you do, they do. *Pretérito*: I did, you did, he/she/it did, we did, you did, they did. *Gerundio*: doing. *Participio pasado*: done.

Además de los significados que tiene como un verbo normal, do funciona como verbo auxiliar, principalmente para formar oraciones interrogativas (*do* you watch much television? *¿ves mucho la televisión?*) y negativas (I *didn't* see him at school today *no lo vi en el colegio hoy*), cuando el verbo principal está en presente o pasado simples. Para otros tiempos utilizaremos be o have.

Do también sirve para añadir énfasis a la frase (you're wrong — I do know her *te equivocas; — sí que la conozco*).
Ver también *hacer* en el lado español-inglés del diccionario.

docile ['dɒsəl] *adj* dócil

dock [dɒk] ◆ *s* muelle ◆ *vi* **❶** atracar *(barco)* **❷** acoplarse *(nave espacial)*

doctor ['dɒktər] *s* **❶** médico, ca **❷** doctor, ra
expresión **to see a doctor** ir al médico

doctorate ['dɒktərət], **doctor's degree** *s* doctorado

doctrine ['dɒktrɪn] *s* doctrina

document *s* ['dɒkjʊmənt] documento

documentary [ˌdɒkjʊ'mentərɪ] ◆ *adj* documental ◆ *s* documental

dodge [dɒdʒ] ◆ *vt* esquivar ◆ *vi* echarse a un lado

doe [dəʊ] *s* ❶ cierva ❷ coneja

does ☀:*acento atónico* [dəz]*, acento tónico* [dʌz] *v* → do

doesn't ['dʌznt] (*abreviatura de* does not) = **do**

dog [dɒg] ◆ *s* perro ◆ *vt* ❶ seguir ❷ perseguir

dogged ['dɒgɪd] *adj* tenaz

doing ['du:ɪŋ] *s* • this is all your doing es de tu entera responsabilidad
■ **doings** *spl* actividades

do-it-yourself *s* hazlo tú mismo

doll [dɒl] *s* muñeca

dollar ['dɒlər] *s* dólar

dolphin ['dɒlfɪn] *s* delfín

domain [də'meɪn] *s* ❶ campo ❷ dominios ❸ *INFORMÁTICA* dominio

dome [dəʊm] *s* ❶ cúpula ❷ bóveda

domestic [də'mestɪk] ◆ *adj* ❶ nacional ❷ doméstico, ca ❸ casero, ra ◆ *s* criado, da

domestic appliance *s* electrodoméstico

dominant ['dɒmɪnənt] *adj* dominante

dominate ['dɒmɪneɪt] *vt* dominar

domineering [ˌdɒmɪ'nɪərɪŋ] *adj* dominante

dominion [də'mɪnjən] *s* ❶ ☀:*incontable* dominio ❷ dominios

domino ['dɒmɪnəʊ] *s* dominó
■ **dominoes** *spl* dominó
El plural de **domino** es **dominoes**.

donate [də'neɪt] *vt* donar

done [dʌn] ◆ *participio pasado* → do ◆ *adj* ❶ listo, ta ❷ hecho, cha • well-done muy hecho ◆ *adv* • done! ¡(trato) hecho!

donkey ['dɒŋkɪ] *s* burro
El plural de **donkey** es **donkeys**.

donor ['dəʊnər] *s* donante

don't [dəʊnt] (*abreviatura de* do not) = **do**

donut ['dəʊnʌt] *s* dona

doom [du:m] *s* perdición; fatalidad

doomed [du:md] *adj* condenado, da al fracaso

door [dɔ:r] *s* ❶ puerta ❷ entrada
expresión to open the door to *figurado* abrir la puerta a

doorbell ['dɔ:bel] *s* timbre (de la puerta)

doorman ['dɔ:mən] *s* portero
El plural de **doorman** es **doormen** ['dɔ:men].

doormat ['dɔ:mæt] *s* tapete de entrada

doorstep ['dɔ:step] *s* umbral de la puerta

doorway ['dɔ:weɪ] *s* entrada

dope [dəʊp] ◆ *s familiar* ❶ mota ❷ estimulante ❸ tonto, ta ◆ *vt* drogar; dopar

dormant ['dɔ:mənt] *adj* inactivo, va

dormitory ['dɔ:mətrɪ] *s* residencia de estudiantes

dose [dəʊs] *s literal & figurado* dosis

dot [dɒt] ◆ *s* punto • on the dot en punto ◆ *vt* salpicar

dotcom ['dɒtkɒm] *adj* puntocom

double ['dʌbl] ◆ *adj* ❶ doble ❷ repetido, da • it's double the price cuesta el doble • double three eight two treinta y tres, ochenta y dos ◆ *adv* ❶ el doble • to cost double costar el doble ❷ en dos • to bend double doblarse; agacharse ◆ *s* ❶ el doble ❷ doble ◆ *vt* doblar ◆ *vi* doblarse
■ **doubles** *spl* TENIS dobles

double bass [-beɪs] *s* contrabajo

double bed *s* cama matrimonial

double-breasted [-'brestɪd] *adj* cruzado, da

double-check *vt* & *vi* verificar dos veces

double chin *s* papada

double-click ◆ *s* INFORMÁTICA doble clic ◆ *vt* INFORMÁTICA hacer doble clic en ◆ *vi* INFORMÁTICA hacer doble clic

double-cross *vt* traicionar

double-decker [-'dekər] *s* camión de dos pisos

doubly ['dʌblɪ] *adv* doblemente

doubt [daʊt] ◆ *s* duda • there is no doubt that no cabe duda de que • without (a) doubt sin duda (alguna) • to be in doubt about something estar dudando acerca de algo • to cast doubt on poner en duda • no doubt sin duda ◆ *vt* ❶ dudar de ❷ dudar • I doubt it lo dudo • to doubt whether o if dudar que

doubtful ['daʊtfʊl] *adj* ❶ dudoso, sa ❷ incierto, ta • to be doubtful about o of tener dudas acerca de

dough [dəʊ] *s* ☀:*incontable* masa; pasta

doughnut ['dəʊnʌt] *s* dona

douse [daʊs] *vt* ❶ apagar ❷ empapar

dove[1] [dʌv] *s* paloma

dove[2] [dəʊv] *pretérito* → dive

down [daʊn] ◆ *adv* ❶ (hacia) abajo • to fall down caerse • to bend down agacharse • down here/there aquí/allí abajo ❷ hacia el sur • we're going down to Galveston vamos a Galveston ❸ • prices are coming down los precios van bajando ❹ • down to the last detail hasta el último detalle ◆ *preposición* ❶ • they ran down the hill corrieron cuesta abajo • he walked down the stairs bajó la escalera • rain poured down the window la lluvia resbalaba por la ventana ❷ • she was walking down the street iba andando por la calle ◆ *adj* ❶ deprimido, da ❷ • the computer is down again la computadora está descompuesta otra vez ◆ *s* ❶ plumón ❷ vello ❸ cada uno de los cuatro intentos de avance que tiene el equipo atacante ◆ *vt* ❶ derribar ❷ beberse de un trago
■ **down with** *exclamación* • down with the president! ¡abajo el presidente!

downcast ['daʊnkɑ:st] *adj formal* alicaído, da; triste

downfall ['daʊnfɔ:l] *s* ❶ ruina ❷ caída

downhearted [ˌdaʊn'hɑːtɪd] *adj* desanimado, da

downhill [ˌdaʊn'hɪl] ◆ *adj* cuesta abajo ◆ *adv* ❶ cuesta abajo ❷ • **to be going downhill** ir cuesta abajo ◆ *s* descenso

download ['daʊnləʊd] *vt* bajar

downpour ['daʊnpɔːr] *s* tromba de agua

downright ['daʊnraɪt] *adv* sumamente

downstairs [ˌdaʊn'steəz] ◆ *adj* de abajo ◆ *adv* abajo • **to come/go downstairs** bajar (la escalera)

downstream [ˌdaʊn'striːm] *adv* río abajo

down-to-earth *adj* realista

downtown [ˌdaʊn'taʊn] ◆ *adj* del centro (de la ciudad) ◆ *s* centro (urbano) ◆ *adv* ❶ en el centro ❷ al centro • **he gave me a lift downtown** me dio un aventón al centro

downturn ['daʊntɜːn] *s* bajón

downward ['daʊnwəd] ◆ *adj*❶ hacia abajo ❷ descendente ◆ *adv* = **downwards**

downwards ['daʊnwədz], **downward** *adv* hacia abajo • **face downwards** boca abajo

dowry ['daʊərɪ] *s* dote

doze [dəʊz] ◆ *s* siestecita • **to have a doze** echarse una dormidita ◆ *vi* dormitar

■ **doze off** *vi* quedarse dormido, da

dozen ['dʌzn] ◆ *adj numeral* • **a dozen eggs** una docena de huevos ◆ *s* docena • **50 pesos a dozen** 50 pesos la docena

■ **dozens** *spl familiar* • **dozens of** montones de

Dr. ❶ *(abreviatura escrita de* Doctor*)* Dr ❷ *(abreviatura de* Drive*)* ≃ c/

drab [dræb] *adj* ❶ apagado, da ❷ soso, sa ❸ monótono, na

draft [drɑːft] ◆ *s* ❶ borrador ❷ corriente de aire ❸ MILITAR • **the draft** la llamada a filas • **on draft** de barril ◆ *vt* ❶ redactar; hacer un borrador de ❷ MILITAR llamar a filas ❸ transferir

draft dodger [-dɒdʒər] *s* ▶ persona que se libra de alistarse en el ejército mediante subterfugios

draftee [ˌdrɑːf'tiː] *s* recluta

drafty ['drɑːftɪ] *adj* que tiene corrientes de aire • **it's drafty** hay una corriente

drag [dræg] ◆ *vt* ❶ arrastrar • **to drag and drop something** arrastrar y soltar algo ❷ dragar ◆ *vi* ❶ arrastrarse ❷ ir muy despacio ◆ *s familiar* ❶ rollo; pesado, da ❷ calada ❸ • **in drag** vestido de mujer

■ **drag on** *vi* ser interminable

dragon ['drægən] *s* dragón

dragonfly ['drægnflaɪ] *s* libélula

drain [dreɪn] ◆ *s* ❶ desagüe ❷ coladera ❸ alcantarilla ◆ *vt* ❶ drenar ❷ escurrir ❸ agotar ❹ apurar ◆ *vi* ❶ escurrirse ❷ desaparecer poco a poco

drainage ['dreɪnɪdʒ] *s* ❶ alcantarillado ❷ drenaje

drainboard ['dreɪnbɔːrd] *s* escurridor

drama ['drɑːmə] *s* ❶ drama ❷ teatro ❸ dramatismo

dramatic [drə'mætɪk] *adj* ❶ dramático, ca ❷ espectacular

dramatist ['dræmətɪst] *s* dramaturgo, ga

dramatize, dramatise ['dræmətaɪz] *vt* ❶ adaptar ❷ *despectivo* dramatizar

drank [dræŋk] *pretérito* → **drink**

drape [dreɪp] *vt* • **to drape something over something** cubrir algo con algo • **draped with** o **in** cubierto con

■ **drapes** *spl* cortinas

drastic ['dræstɪk] *adj* drástico, ca

draw [drɔː] ◆ *vt* ❶ dibujar ❷ sacar ❸ establecer ❹ atraer • **to be** o **feel drawn to** sentirse atraído, da a o por ◆ *vi*❶ dibujar ❷ moverse • **to draw away** alejarse • **to draw closer** acercarse • **to draw to an end** o **a close** llegar a su fin ❸ DEPORTE empatar (con) ◆ *s*❶ DEPORTE empate ❷ sorteo

■ **draw out** *vt* ☼ *El objeto se puede colocar antes o después de la preposición.* ❶ hacer hablar ❷ prolongar ❸ sacar

■ **draw up** ◆ *vt* ☼ *El objeto se puede colocar antes o después de la preposición.* preparar; redactar ◆ *vi* pararse

Formas irregulares de **draw**: *pretérito* **drew**, *pp* **drawn**.

drawback ['drɔːbæk] *s* inconveniente; desventaja

drawer [drɔːr] *s* cajón

drawing ['drɔːɪŋ] *s* dibujo

drawl [drɔːl] *s* ▶ manera lenta y poco clara de hablar, alargando las vocales

drawn [drɔːn] *participio pasado* → **draw**

dread [dred] ◆ *s* pavor ◆ *vt* • **to dread (doing something)** temer (hacer algo)

dreadful ['dredfʊl] *adj*❶ terrible ❷ horrible; fatal ❸ espantoso, sa

dreadfully ['dredfʊlɪ] *adv* terriblemente

dream [driːm] ◆ *s literal & figurado* sueño • **bad dream** pesadilla ◆ *adj* ideal ◆ *vt* • **to dream (that)** soñar que

expresión **I never dreamt this would happen** jamás creí que esto pudiera suceder

◆ *vi literal & figurado* • **to dream of doing something** soñar con hacer algo • **to dream (of** o **about)** soñar (con)

expresión **I wouldn't dream of it** ¡ni hablar!; ¡de ninguna manera!

■ **dream up** *vt* ☼ *El objeto se puede colocar antes o después de la preposición.* inventar; idear

Formas irregulares de **dream**: *pretérito & pp* **dreamed** o **dreamt**.

dreamt [dremt] *participio pasado* → **dream**

dreamy ['driːmɪ] *adj*❶ soñador, ra ❷ de ensueño

dreary ['drɪərɪ] *adj* ❶ triste ❷ monótono, na ❸ gris

dredge [dredʒ] *vt* dragar

■ **dredge up** *vt* ☼ *El objeto se puede colocar antes o después de la preposición.* ❶ sacar del agua *(al dragar)* ❷ *figurado* sacar a relucir

drench [drentʃ] *vt* empapar • **drenched to the skin** empapado, da hasta los huesos • **to be drenched in** o **with** estar empapado, da en

dress [dres] ◆ *s* ❶ vestido ❷ ☼ *incontable* traje ◆ *vt* ❶ vestir • **to be dressed in** ir vestido, da de • **to be dressed** estar vestido, da • **to get dressed** vestirse ❷ vendar ❸ COCINA aliñar ◆ *vi* ❶ vestirse ❷ vestir • **to dress well/badly** vestir bien/mal

dresser ['dresər] *s* cómoda

dressing ['dresɪŋ] *s* ❶ vendaje ❷ aderezo ❸ relleno

dressing room *s* ❶ TEATRO camerino ❷ DEPORTE vestidor

dress rehearsal *s* ensayo general

drew [druː] *pretérito* → draw

dribble ['drɪbl] ◆ *s* ❶ baba ❷ hilo ◆ *vt* DEPORTE driblar ◆ *vi* ❶ babear ❷ gotear; caer gota a gota

dried [draɪd] *adj* ❶ seco, ca ❷ en polvo

drier ['draɪər] = **dryer**

drift [drɪft] ◆ *s* ❶ movimiento; tendencia ❷ flujo ❸ sentido ❹ ventisquero; montículo ◆ *vi* ❶ ir a la deriva ❷ amontonarse

drill [drɪl] ◆ *s* ❶ taladro; broca; fresa; perforadora ❷ ejercicio; simulacro ◆ *vt* ❶ perforar ❷ entrenar; instruir • **to drill something into somebody** inculcar algo en alguien ◆ *vi* • **to drill into/for** perforar en/en busca de

drink [drɪŋk] ◆ *s* ❶ bebida • **a drink of water** un trago de agua ❷ copa • **would you like a drink?** ¿quieres tomar algo (de beber)? • **to have a drink** tomar algo; tomar una copa ◆ *vt* beber ◆ *vi* beber • **to drink to somebody/somebody's success** beber a la salud de alguien/por el éxito de alguien

Formas irregulares de **drink**: *pretérito* **drank**, *pp* **drunk**.

drinker ['drɪŋkər] *s* ❶ bebedor, ra ❷ • **tea/coffee drinker** persona que bebe té/café

drinking water ['drɪŋkɪŋ-] *s* agua potable

drip [drɪp] ◆ *s* ❶ gota ❷ goteo ❸ MEDICINA gota a gota ◆ *vi* gotear

drive [draɪv] ◆ *s* ❶ paseo (en coche) • **to go for a drive** ir a dar una vuelta en coche ❷ viaje (en coche) ❸ instinto ❹ campaña ❺ vigor; energía ❻ camino (de entrada) ❼ calle ❽ drive ❾ INFORMÁTICA unidad de disco ◆ *vt* ❶ manejar ❷ llevar (en coche) ❸ impulsar ❹ arrastrar; arrear • **it drove people from their homes** obligó a la gente a abandonar sus hogares ❺ motivar ❻ • **to drive somebody to do something** conducir o llevar a alguien a hacer algo • **to drive somebody to despair** hacer desesperar a alguien • **to drive somebody mad** o **crazy** volver loco a alguien ❼ clavar ◆ *vi* AUTOMÓVILES manejar • **I don't drive** no sé conducir • **I drove there** fui en coche

Formas irregulares de **drive**: *pretérito* **drove**, *pp* **driven**.

driven ['drɪvn] *participio pasado* → drive

driver ['draɪvər] *s* ❶ conductor, ra ❷ chofer ❸ piloto

driver's license *s* licencia de manejar

driveway ['draɪvweɪ] *s* camino (de entrada)

driving ['draɪvɪŋ] ◆ *adj* ❶ torrencial ❷ huracanado, da ◆ *s* ☼ *incontable* conducción; el conducir

driving lesson *s* clase de manejo

driving test *s* examen de manejo

drizzle ['drɪzl] ◆ *s* llovizna ◆ *v impersonal* lloviznar

droop [druːp] *vi* ❶ encorvarse ❷ cerrarse ❸ inclinarse ❹ marchitarse

drop [drɒp] ◆ *s* ❶ gota ❷ • **drop (in) a)** caída (de) **b)** descenso (de) **c)** disminución (en) ❸ caída ◆ *vt* ❶ dejar caer; lanzar ❷ reducir ❸ bajar ❹ dejar; retirar; abandonar; excluir; no seleccionar ❺ lanzar; soltar ❻ • **to drop somebody a line** mandar unas líneas a alguien ❼ bajar ◆ *vi* ❶ caer • **it dropped onto the ground** se cayó al suelo • **to drop to your knees** arrodillarse • **we walked until we dropped** estuvimos andando hasta no poder más ❷ ceder ❸ bajar; disminuir; amainar

■ **drops** *spl* MEDICINA gotas

■ **drop in** *vi familiar* • **to drop in on** pasarse por casa de

■ **drop off** ◆ *vt* ☼ *El objeto se puede colocar antes o después de la preposición.* dejar ◆ *vi* ❶ quedarse dormido, da ❷ bajar

■ **drop out** *vi* • **to drop out (of** o **from) a)** dejar de asistir (a) **b)** retirarse (de)

dropout ['drɒpaʊt] *s* ❶ marginado, da ❷ persona que ha dejado los estudios

droppings ['drɒpɪŋz] *spl* excrementos *(de animal)*

drought [draʊt] *s* sequía

drove [drəʊv] *pretérito* → drive

drown [draʊn] ◆ *vt* ahogar ◆ *vi* ahogarse

drowsy ['draʊzɪ] *adj* somnoliento, ta

drudgery ['drʌdʒərɪ] *s* ▸ trabajo pesado y monótono

drug [drʌg] ◆ *s* ❶ medicamento ❷ droga • **to be on** o **take drugs** drogarse ◆ *vt* ❶ drogar ❷ echar droga a

drug abuse *s* consumo de drogas

drug addict *s* drogadicto, ta

drugstore ['drʌgstɔːr] *s* farmacia *(que también vende productos de perfumería, periódicos, ETC)*

drum [drʌm] ◆ *s* ❶ tambor • **drums** batería ❷ barril; bidón ◆ *vt* tamborilear con ◆ *vi* golpetear

■ **drum up** *vt* ☼ *El objeto se puede colocar antes o después de la preposición.* intentar conseguir

drummer ['drʌmər] *s* ❶ tambor ❷ baterista

drumstick ['drʌmstɪk] *s* ❶ baqueta ❷ muslo

drunk [drʌŋk] ◆ *participio pasado* → drink ◆ *adj* borracho, cha • **to get drunk** emborracharse • **to be drunk** estar borracho, cha ◆ *s* borracho, cha

drunkard ['drʌŋkəd] *s* borracho, cha

D

drunk-driving *s* manejar borracho

drunken ['drʌŋkn] *adj* ❶ borracho, cha ❷ de borracho, cha

dry [draɪ] ◆ *adj* ❶ seco, ca ❷ sin lluvia ❸ árido, da ◆ *vt* ❶ secar ❷ secarse • **to dry yourself** secarse • **to dry your eyes** secarse las lágrimas ◆ *vi* secarse

■ **dry up** ◆ *vt* ☼: *El objeto se puede colocar antes o después de la preposición.* secar ◆ *vi* ❶ secarse ❷ agotarse ❸ quedarse mudo ❹ secar

dry cleaner *s* • **dry cleaner's (shop)** tintorería

dryer ['draɪər] *s* secadora

dry land *s* tierra firme

dual ['dju:əl] *adj* doble

dubbed [dʌbd] *adj* ❶ CINE doblado, da ❷ apodado, da

dubious ['dju:bjəs] *adj* ❶ sospechoso, sa; paradójico, ca ❷ dudoso, sa

duchess ['dʌtʃɪs] *s* duquesa

duck [dʌk] ◆ *s* ❶ pato, ta ❷ pato
expresión **to take to something like a duck to water** encontrarse en seguida en su salsa con algo
◆ *vt* ❶ agachar; bajar ❷ esquivar ◆ *vi* agacharse

duckling ['dʌklɪŋ] *s* patito

duct [dʌkt] *s* conducto

dud [dʌd] ◆ *adj* ❶ falso, sa ❷ que no estalla ❸ sin fondos ◆ *s* ▸ persona o cosa inútil

dude [dju:d] *s familiar* ❶ tipo ❷ wey; mano

due [dju:] ◆ *adj* ❶ esperado, da • **it's due out in May** saldrá en mayo • **she's due back soon** volverá dentro de poco • **the bus is due in half an hour** el autobús debe llegar dentro de media hora ❷ debido, da • **with all due respect** sin ganas de ofender • **in due course a)** a su debido tiempo **b)** al final ❸ pagadero, ra • **I'm due a bit of luck** ya sería hora que tuviera un poco de suerte • **to be due to** deberse a ◆ *s*
expresión **to give somebody their due** hacer justicia a alguien
◆ *adv* • **due north/south** derecho hacia el norte/sur

■ **dues** *spl* cuota

■ **due to** *preposición* debido a

duel ['dju:əl] *s* duelo

duet [dju:'et] *s* dúo

dug [dʌg] *pretérito* & *participio pasado* → **dig**

duke [dju:k] *s* duque

dull [dʌl] ◆ *adj* ❶ aburrido, da ❷ torpe ❸ apagado, da ❹ gris; triste ❺ sordo, da ◆ *vt* ❶ entorpecer ❷ aliviar ❸ enturbiar

duly ['dju:lɪ] *adv* ❶ debidamente ❷ como era de esperar

dumb [dʌm] *adj* ❶ mudo, da • **to be struck dumb** quedarse de una pieza ❷ *familiar* estúpido, da

dummy ['dʌmɪ] ◆ *adj* falso, sa ◆ *s* ❶ muñeco ❷ maniquí ❸ imitación ❹ DEPORTE amago ❺ *familiar* imbécil

dump [dʌmp] ◆ *s* ❶ basurero; tiradero ❷ depósito ❸ INFORMÁTICA volcado de memoria ❹ *familiar* casucha ◆ *vt* ❶ descargar; dejar ❷ deshacerse de

dumping ['dʌmpɪŋ] *s* tirado • **'no dumping'** 'prohibido tirar basura'

dumpling ['dʌmplɪŋ] *s* ▸ bola de masa que se guisa al vapor con carne y verduras

dune [dju:n] *s* duna

dung [dʌŋ] *s* ❶ excremento ❷ estiércol

dungeon ['dʌndʒən] *s* calabozo

duo ['dju:əʊ] *s* dúo

dupe [dju:p] ◆ *s* inocente ◆ *vt* • **to dupe somebody (into doing something)** embaucar a alguien (para que haga algo)

duplex ['dju:pleks] *s* ❶ penthouse ❷ dúplex

duplicate ◆ *adj* ['dju:plɪkət] duplicado, da ◆ *s* ['dju:plɪkət] copia; duplicado • **in duplicate** por duplicado ◆ *vt* ['dju:plɪkeɪt] duplicar

durable ['djʊərəbl] *adj* duradero, ra

duration [djʊ'reɪʃn] *s* duración • **for the duration of** durante

duress [djʊ'res] *s* • **under duress** bajo coacción

during ['djʊərɪŋ] *preposición* durante

dusk [dʌsk] *s* crepúsculo; anochecer

dust [dʌst] ◆ *s* polvo
expresión **to gather dust a)** cubrirse de polvo **b)** *figurado* quedar arrinconado, da
◆ *vt* ❶ sacudir ❷ • **to dust something (with)** espolvorear algo (con)

dustpan ['dʌstpæn] *s* recogedor

dusty ['dʌstɪ] *adj* polvoriento, ta

Dutch [dʌtʃ] ◆ *adj* holandés, esa ◆ *s* holandés ◆ *spl* • **the Dutch** los holandeses

dutiful ['dju:tɪfʊl] *adj* obediente; sumiso, sa

duty ['dju:tɪ] *s* ❶ ☼: *incontable* deber • **to do your duty** cumplir con su deber ❷ servicio ❸ impuesto

■ **duties** *spl* tareas

duty-free ◆ *adj* libre de impuestos ◆ *s* ☼: *incontable familiar* artículos libres de impuestos

DVD (*abreviatura de* Digital Versatile Disk) *s* DVD

DVD player *s* reproductor de DVD

DVD recorder *s* grabadora de DVD

DVD ROM (*abreviatura de* Digital Versatile Disk read only memory) *s* DVD ROM

dwarf [dwɔ:f] ◆ *s* enano, na ◆ *vt* achicar; empequeñecer

Dos plurales: **dwarfs** o **dwarves** [dwɔ:vz].

dwell [dwel] *vi literario* vivir; habitar

■ **dwell on** *vt* ☼: *El objeto siempre va después de la preposición al final.* darle vueltas a

Formas irregulares de **dwell**: *pretérito* & *pp* **dwelled** o **dwelt**.

dwelling ['dwelɪŋ] *s literario* vivienda
dwelt [dwelt] *pretérito* & *participio pasado*
→ **dwell**
dye [daɪ] ◆ *s* tinte ◆ *vt* teñir • **to dye your hair** pintarse el pelo
dying ['daɪɪŋ] ◆ *continuo* → **die** ◆ *adj* ❶ moribundo, da ❷ en vías de desaparición
dyke [daɪk] = **dike**
dynamic [daɪ'næmɪk] *adj* dinámico, ca

dynamite ['daɪnəmaɪt] *s literal* & *figurado*
dinamita
dynamo ['daɪnəməʊ] *s* dinamo
El plural de **dynamo** es **dynamics**.
dynasty ['daɪnəstɪ] *s* dinastía
dysfunctional [dɪs'fʌŋkʃənəl] *adj* disfuncional
dyslexia [dɪs'leksɪə] *s* dislexia
dyslexic [dɪs'leksɪk] *adj* disléxico, ca

D

E

e, E [iː] *s* e; E
■ **E** *s* ❶ *MÚSICA* mi ❷ *EDUCACIÓN* ≃ reprobado ❸ *(abreviatura de* east) E ❹ *familiar (abreviatura de* ecstasy) éxtasis

Dos plurales: **e's** o **es; E's** o **Es.**

each [iːtʃ] ◆ *adj* cada ◆ *pronombre* cada uno, una • **one each** uno cada uno • **each of us/the boys** cada uno de nosotros/los niños • **two of each** dos de cada (uno) • **each other** el uno al otro • **they kissed each other** se besaron • **we know each other** nos conocemos

eager ['iːgəʳ] *adj* ❶ entusiasta ❷ de entusiasmo • **to be eager for something/to do something** estar ansioso, sa por algo/por hacer algo

eagle ['iːgl] *s* águila

ear [ɪəʳ] *s* ❶ oreja ❷ oído ❸ espiga
expresión to have o **keep your ear to the ground** *familiar* mantenerse al corriente

earache ['ɪəreɪk] *s* dolor de oídos

eardrum ['ɪədrʌm] *s* tímpano

earl [ɜːl] *s* conde

earlier ['ɜːlɪəʳ] ◆ *adj* anterior ◆ *adv* antes • **earlier on** antes

earliest ['ɜːlɪəst] ◆ *adj* primero, ra ◆ *s* • **at the earliest** como muy pronto

early ['ɜːlɪ] ◆ *adj* ❶ temprano, na • **she was early** llegó temprano • **I'll take an early lunch** almorzaré pronto o temprano • **to get up early** madrugar ❷ • **early morning** la madrugada • **in the early 1950s** a principios de los años 50 ◆ *adv* ❶ temprano; pronto • **we got up early** nos levantamos temprano • **it arrived ten minutes early** llegó con diez minutos de adelanto ❷ • **as early as 1920** ya en 1920 • **early this morning** esta mañana temprano • **early in the year** a principios de año • **early on** temprano

early retirement *s* prejubilación; jubilación anticipada

earmark ['ɪəmɑːk] *vt* • **to be earmarked for** estar destinado, da a

earn [ɜːn] *vt* ❶ ganar ❷ generar ❸ *figurado* ganarse

earnest ['ɜːnɪst] *adj* ❶ serio, ria ❷ sincero, ra

■ **in earnest** *adv* en serio

earnings ['ɜːnɪŋz] *spl* ❶ ingresos ❷ ganancias

earphones ['ɪəfəʊnz] *spl* auriculares

earring ['ɪərɪŋ] *s* pendiente; arete

earshot ['ɪəʃɒt] *s* • **within/out of earshot** al alcance/fuera del alcance del oído

earth [ɜːθ] *s* ❶ tierra ❷ toma de tierra

earthenware ['ɜːθənweəʳ] *s* loza

earthquake ['ɜːθkweɪk] *s* terremoto

earthworm ['ɜːθwɜːm] *s* lombriz (de tierra)

ease [iːz] ◆ *s* 💡*incontable* ❶ facilidad • **with ease** con facilidad ❷ comodidad • **at ease** cómodo, da • **ill at ease** incómodo, da ◆ *vt* ❶ calmar; aliviar ❷ atenuar ❸ • **to ease something open** abrir algo con cuidado • **to ease yourself out of something** levantarse despacio de algo ◆ *vi* ❶ atenuarse ❷ calmarse ❸ amainar ❹ relajarse

■ **ease off** *vi* ❶ atenuarse ❷ calmarse ❸ amainar

■ **ease up** *vi* ❶ *familiar* • **to ease up on somebody** no ser tan duro, ra con alguien ❷ amainar ❸ tomarse las cosas con más calma

easel ['iːzl] *s* caballete

easily ['iːzɪlɪ] *adv* ❶ fácilmente ❷ sin lugar a dudas ❸ tranquilamente; relajadamente

east [iːst] ◆ *s* ❶ este ❷ • **the east** el este ◆ *adj* ❶ oriental ❷ del este ◆ *adv* • **east (of)** al este (de)
■ **East** *s* • **the East a)** *POLÍTICA* el Este **b)** el Oriente

Easter ['iːstəʳ] *s* ❶ Semana Santa ❷ Pascua

Easter egg *s* huevo de Pascua

easterly ['iːstəlɪ] *adj* del este

eastern ['iːstən] *adj* del este; oriental
■ **Eastern** *adj* ❶ del Este ❷ oriental

eastward ['iːstwəd] ◆ *adj* hacia el este ◆ *adv* = **eastwards**

eastwards ['iːstwədz], **eastward** *adv* hacia el este

easy ['iːzɪ] *adj* ❶ fácil ❷ cómodo, da ❸ relajado, da

easygoing [,iːzɪ'gəʊɪŋ] *adj* ❶ tolerante ❷ relajado, da

eat [iːt] *vt* & *vi* comer

■ **eat away** *vt* ☼ *El objeto se puede colocar antes o después de la preposición.* ❶ corroer ❷ mermar
Formas irregulares de eat: *pretérito* **ate**, *pp* **eaten**.

eaten ['iːtn] *participio pasado* → **eat**

eatery ['iːtərɪ] *s* restaurante

eavesdrop ['iːvzdrɒp] *vi* • **to eavesdrop (on)** escuchar secretamente (a)

ebb [eb] ◆ *s* reflujo ◆ *vi* bajar

ebony ['ebənɪ] *s* ébano

e-business *s* ❶ empresa electrónica ❷ comercio electrónico

e-cash *s* dinero electrónico

eccentric [ɪk'sentrɪk] ◆ *adj* excéntrico, ca ◆ *s* excéntrico, ca

echo ['ekəʊ] ◆ *s literal & figurado* eco ◆ *vt* ❶ repetir ❷ hacerse eco de ◆ *vi* resonar

eclipse [ɪ'klɪps] ◆ *s literal & figurado* eclipse • **a total/partial eclipse** un eclipse total/parcial ◆ *vt figurado* eclipsar

eco- ['iːkəʊ] *(abreviatura de* ecology or ecological) *prefijo* eco-

eco-friendly ['iːkəʊ'frendlɪ] *adj* ecológico, ca

ecological [ˌiːkə'lɒdʒɪkl] *adj* ❶ ecológico, ca ❷ ecologista

ecology [ɪ'kɒlədʒɪ] *s* ecología

economic [ˌiːkə'nɒmɪk] *adj* ❶ económico, ca ❷ rentable

economical [ˌiːkə'nɒmɪkl] *adj* económico, ca • **to be economical with the truth** no decir toda la verdad

economics [ˌiːkə'nɒmɪks] ◆ *s* ☼ *incontable* economía ◆ *spl* aspecto económico

economize [ɪ'kɒnəmaɪz] *vi* • **to economize (on)** economizar (en)

economy [ɪ'kɒnəmɪ] *s* economía

ecotourism [ˌiːkəʊ'tʊərɪzm] *s* ecoturismo

ecstasy ['ekstəsɪ] *s* éxtasis

ecstatic [ek'stætɪk] *adj* extático, ca

Ecuador ['ekwədɔːr] *s* (el) Ecuador

Ecuadoran [ˌekwə'dɔːrən], **Ecuadorian** [ˌekwə'dɔːrɪən] ◆ *adj* ecuatoriano, na ◆ *s* ecuatoriano, na

eczema ['eksɪmə] *s* eczema

edge [edʒ] ◆ *s* ❶ borde • **to be on the edge of** estar al borde de ❷ canto ❸ filo ◆ *vi* • **to edge away/closer** ir alejándose/acercándose poco a poco
■ **on edge** *adj* con los nervios de punta

edgeways ['edʒweɪz], **edgewise** ['edʒwaɪz] *adv* de lado

edgy ['edʒɪ] *adj* nervioso, sa

edible ['edɪbl] *adj* comestible

edit ['edɪt] *vt* ❶ corregir; revisar ❷ *INFORMÁTICA* editar ❸ editar ❹ *CINE, RADIO & TELEVISIÓN* montar ❺ dirigir

edition [ɪ'dɪʃn] *s* edición

editor ['edɪtər] *s* ❶ director, ra ❷ redactor, ra ❸ editor, ra ❹ *CINE, RADIO & TELEVISIÓN* montador, ra ❺ *INFORMÁTICA* editor

editorial [ˌedɪ'tɔːrɪəl] ◆ *adj* editorial • **editorial staff** redacción ◆ *s* editorial

educate ['edʒʊkeɪt] *vt* ❶ educar ❷ informar

education [ˌedʒʊ'keɪʃn] *s* ☼ *incontable* ❶ enseñanza ❷ educación

educational [ˌedʒʊ'keɪʃənl] *adj* ❶ educativo, va ❷ docente

eel [iːl] *s* anguila

effect [ɪ'fekt] ◆ *s* efecto • **to have an effect on** tener o surtir efecto en • **to do something for effect** hacer algo para causar efecto • **to take effect a)** entrar en vigor **b)** hacer efecto • **words to that effect** palabras por el estilo ◆ *vt* efectuar ; llevar a cabo
■ **effects** *spl* ▶ **(special) effects** efectos especiales

effective [ɪ'fektɪv] *adj* ❶ eficaz ❷ efectivo, va ❸ operativo, va

effectively [ɪ'fektɪvlɪ] *adv* ❶ eficazmente ❷ de hecho

effectiveness [ɪ'fektɪvnɪs] *s* eficacia

effeminate [ɪ'femɪnət] *adj despectivo* afeminado, da

effervescent [ˌefə'vesənt] *adj* efervescente

efficiency [ɪ'fɪʃənsɪ] *s* ❶ eficiencia ❷ rendimiento

efficient [ɪ'fɪʃənt] *adj* ❶ eficiente ❷ de buen rendimiento

effort ['efət] *s* ❶ esfuerzo • **to be worth the effort** merecer la pena • **to make the effort to do something** hacer el esfuerzo de hacer algo • **to make an/no effort to do something** hacer un esfuerzo/no hacer ningún esfuerzo por hacer algo ❷ *familiar* tentativa

e.g. *(abreviatura de* exempli gratia) *adv* p. ej.

egg [eg] *s* huevo
■ **egg on** *vt* ☼ *El objeto se puede colocar antes o después de la preposición.* incitar

eggplant ['egplɑːnt] *s* berenjena

eggshell ['egʃel] *s* cáscara de huevo

egg white *s* clara (de huevo)

egg yolk [-jəʊk] *s* yema (de huevo)

ego ['iːgəʊ] *s* ❶ amor propio ❷ ego
El plural de ego es egos.

egoism ['iːgəʊɪzm] *s* egoísmo

egoistic [ˌiːgəʊ'ɪstɪk] *adj* egoísta

egotistic(al) [ˌiːgə'tɪstɪk(l)] *adj* egotista

Egypt ['iːdʒɪpt] *s* Egipto

Egyptian [ɪ'dʒɪpʃn] ◆ *adj* egipcio, cia ◆ *s* egipcio, cia

eight [eɪt] *número* ocho ver también **six**

eighteen [ˌeɪ'tiːn] *número* dieciocho ver también **six**

eighth [eɪtə] *número* octavo, va ver también **sixth**

eighty ['eɪtɪ] *número* ochenta ver también **sixty**

Eire ['eərə] *s* Eire

either ['aɪðər] ['iːðər] ◆ *adj* ❶ cualquiera de los dos • she couldn't find either jumper no podía encontrar ninguno de los dos jerseys • you can do it either way lo puedes hacer como quieras • I don't care either way me da igual ❷ cada • on either side a ambos lados ◆ *pronombre* • either (of them) cualquiera de ellos, ellas • I don't like either (of them) no me gusta ninguno de ellos, ninguna de ellas ◆ *adv* ☼ *en oraciones negativas* tampoco • she can't and I can't either ella no puede y yo tampoco ◆ *conjunción* • either... or o... o • either you or me o tú o yo • I don't like either him or his wife no me cae bien ni él ni su mujer

either

Cuando es un adjetivo, either sólo se usa delante de sustantivos contables en singular (*either* dictionary; *either* alternative).

Cuando either es el sujeto de la oración, o cuando lo es el sustantivo que acompaña, el verbo siempre va en singular al contrario que en español (*either* movie *is* fine with me *cualquiera de las dos películas me van bien*).

Cuando el sujeto de la oración se encuentra entre either y or el verbo va siempre en singular al contrario que en español (*either* John *or* Deborah *has* taken it *o John o Deborah lo tomaron*).

eject [ɪ'dʒekt] *vt* ❶ expulsar ❷ • to eject somebody (from) expulsar a alguien (de)

eke [iːk] ■ eke out *vt* ☼ *El objeto se puede colocar antes o después de la preposición.* estirar

elaborate ◆ *adj* [ɪ'læbrət] ❶ complicado, da ❷ trabajado, da, ❸ detallado, da ◆ *vi* [ɪ'læbəreɪt] • to elaborate on something ampliar algo; explicar algo con más detalle

elapse [ɪ'læps] *vi* transcurrir

elastic [ɪ'læstɪk] ◆ *adj* ❶ elástico, ca ❷ *figurado* flexible ◆ *s* elástico

elated [ɪ'leɪtɪd] *adj* eufórico, ca

elbow ['elbəʊ] *s* codo

elder ['eldər] ◆ *adj* mayor ◆ *s* ❶ mayor ❷ anciano

elderly ['eldəli] ◆ *adj* mayor; anciano, na ◆ *spl* • the elderly los ancianos

eldest ['eldɪst] *adj* mayor

elect [ɪ'lekt] ◆ *adj* electo, ta • the president elect el presidente electo ◆ *vt* ❶ elegir • to elect somebody (as) something elegir a alguien (como) algo ❷ *formal* • to elect to do something optar por o decidir hacer algo

election [ɪ'lekʃn] *s* elección

ELECTIONS

Las elecciones presidenciales estadounidenses tienen lugar cada cuatro años. Por ley, el presidente no puede mantenerse en el cargo más de dos periodos consecutivos. Las elecciones se celebran el día después del primer lunes de noviembre.

elective [ɪ'lektɪv] *s* EDUCACIÓN & UNIVERSIDAD materia optativa

elector [ɪ'lektər] *s* elector, ra

electorate [ɪ'lektərət] *s* • the electorate el electorado

electric [ɪ'lektrɪk] *adj* eléctrico, ca

electrical [ɪ'lektrɪkl] *adj* eléctrico, ca

electrician [ˌɪlek'trɪʃn] *s* electricista

electricity [ˌɪlek'trɪsəti] *s* electricidad

electrify [ɪ'lektrɪfaɪ] *vt* ❶ electrificar ❷ *figurado* electrizar

electrocute [ɪ'lektrəkjuːt] *vt* electrocutar • to electrocute yourself, to be electrocuted electrocutarse

electron [ɪ'lektrɒn] *s* electrón

electronic [ˌɪlek'trɒnɪk] *adj* electrónico, ca

■ **electronics** ◆ *s* ☼ *incontable* electrónica ◆ *spl* sistema electrónico

elegant ['elɪgənt] *adj* elegante

element ['elɪmənt] *s* ❶ elemento ❷ toque ❸ resistencia

■ **elements** *spl* ❶ elementos ❷ • the elements los elementos

elementary [ˌelɪ'mentəri] *adj* elemental • elementary education enseñanza primaria

elementary school *s* escuela primaria

elephant ['elɪfənt] *s* elefante

elevator ['elɪveɪtər] *s* elevador

eleven [ɪ'levn] *número* once ver también six

eleventh [ɪ'levnθ] *número* onceavo, va ver también sixth

elicit [ɪ'lɪsɪt] *vt formal* ❶ • to elicit something (from somebody) provocar algo (en alguien) ❷ • to elicit something (from somebody) sacar algo (a alguien)

eligible ['elɪdʒəbl] *adj* elegible • to be eligible for something/to do something reunir los requisitos para algo/para hacer algo

eliminate [ɪ'lɪmɪneɪt] *vt* eliminar • to be eliminated from something ser eliminado, da de algo

elite [ɪ'liːt] ◆ *adj* selecto, ta ◆ *s* élite

elitist [ɪ'liːtɪst] *adj despectivo* elitista

elongated ['iːlɒŋgeɪtɪd] *adj* alargado, da

elope [ɪ'ləʊp] *vi* • to elope (with) fugarse (con)

eloquent ['eləkwənt] *adj* elocuente

El Salvador [ˌel'sælvədɔːr] *s* El Salvador

else [els] *adv* • anything else? ¿algo más? • I don't need anything else no necesito nada más • everyone else todos los demás, todas las demás • everywhere else en o a cualquier otra parte • **little else** poco más • **nothing/nobody else** nada/nadie más • **somebody/something else** otra persona/cosa • **somewhere else** en o a otro sitio • **who else?** ¿quién si no? • **who else came?** ¿quién más vino? • **what else?** ¿qué más? • **where else?** ¿en o a qué otro sitio?

■ **or else** *conjunción* si no; de lo contrario

elsewhere [els'weər] *adv* a o en otro sitio

elude [ı'lu:d] *vt* ❶ escaparse de; eludir a ❷ esquivar

elusive [ı'lu:sıv] *adj* ❶ esquivo, va ❷ difícil de encontrar

emaciated [ı'meıʃıeıtıd] *adj* demacrado, da

e-mail ◆ *s* INFORMÁTICA correo electrónico ▶ **e-mail account** cuenta de correo electrónico ▶ **e-mail address** dirección electrónica ◆ *vt* INFORMÁTICA enviar por correo eléctronico ◆ *vi* INFORMÁTICA escribir correo eléctronico

emanate ['emǝneıt] *vi formal* • **to emanate from** emanar de

emancipate [ı'mænsıpeıt] *vt* • **to emancipate somebody (from)** emancipar a alguien (de)

embankment [ım'bæŋkmǝnt] *s* ❶ FERROCARRIL terraplén ❷ dique

embark [ım'bɑ:k] *vi* embarcar • **to embark on** *figurado* embarcarse en

embarkation [,embɑ:'keıʃn] *s* ❶ embarque ❷ embarco

embarrass [ım'bærǝs] *vt* ❶ apenar • **it embarrasses me** me da pena ❷ poner en un aprieto

embarrassed [ım'bærǝst] *adj* ❶ apenado, da ❷ penoso, sa

embarrassing [ım'bærǝsıŋ] *adj* embarazoso, sa; penoso, sa • **how embarrassing!** ¡qué pena!

embarrassment [ım'bærǝsmǝnt] *s* pena

embassy ['embǝsı] *s* embajada

embedded [ım'bedıd] *adj* • **embedded (in)** incrustado, da (en)

embers ['embǝz] *spl* rescoldos

embezzle [ım'bezl] *vt* malversar

emblem ['emblǝm] *s* emblema

embody [ım'bɒdı] *vt* personificar; encarnar • **to be embodied in something** estar plasmado en algo

embossed [ım'bɒst] *adj* ❶ • **embossed (on)** estampado, da (en) ❷ repujado, da (en) ❸ • **embossed (with)** estampado, da (con) ❹ • **embossed (with)** repujado, da (con)

embrace [ım'breıs] ◆ *s* abrazo ◆ *vt* ❶ abrazar; dar un abrazo a ❷ *formal* convertirse en ❸ *formal* abarcar ◆ *vi* abrazarse

embroider [ım'brɔıdǝr] *vt* ❶ COSER bordar ❷ *despectivo* adornar

embroidery [ım'brɔıdǝrı] *s* ☀ *incontable* bordado

embryo ['embrıǝu] *s* embrión

El plural de **embryo** es **embryos**.

emerald ['emǝrǝld] ◆ *adj* esmeralda • **the Emerald Isle** Irlanda ◆ *s* esmeralda

emerge [ı'mɜ:dʒ] ◆ *vi* ❶ • **to emerge (from)** salir (de) ❷ surgir; emerger ◆ *vt* • **it emerged that...** resultó que...

emergence [ı'mɜ:dʒǝns] *s* surgimiento; aparición

emergency [ı'mɜ:dʒǝnsı] ◆ *adj* ❶ de emergencia ❷ de urgencia ❸ de reserva ❹ extraordinario, ria ◆ *s* emergencia

emergency exit *s* salida de emergencia

emergency landing *s* aterrizaje forzoso

emergency room *s* (sala de) urgencias

emergency services *spl* servicios de urgencia

emigrant ['emıgrǝnt] *s* emigrante

emigrate ['emıgreıt] *vi* • **to emigrate (to/from)** emigrar (a/de)

eminent ['emınǝnt] *adj* eminente

emission [ı'mıʃn] *s* emisión

emit [ı'mıt] *vt* ❶ emitir ❷ despedir

emoticon [ı'mǝutıkɒn] *s* INFORMÁTICA emoticono

emotion [ı'mǝuʃn] *s* emoción

emotional [ı'mǝuʃǝnl] *adj* ❶ emotivo, va ❷ emocional • **to get emotional** emocionarse

empathize, empathise ['empǝǝaız] *vi* • **to empathize (with)** identificarse (con)

emperor ['empǝrǝr] *s* emperador

emphasis ['emfǝsıs] *s* • **emphasis (on)** énfasis (en) • **to lay** o **place emphasis on** poner énfasis en; hacer hincapié en

El plural de **emphasis** es **emphases** ['emfǝsi:z].

emphasize, emphasise ['emfǝsaız] *vt* ❶ acentuar ❷ subrayar; hacer hincapié en • **to emphasize that...** subrayar que...

emphatic [ım'fætık] *adj* ❶ rotundo, da; categórico, ca ❷ convincente

emphatically [ım'fætıklı] *adv* ❶ rotundamente; enfáticamente ❷ convincentemente ❸ ciertamente

empire ['empaıǝr] *s* imperio

employ [ım'plɔı] *vt* ❶ emplear • **to be employed as** estar empleado, da de ❷ *formal* utilizar; emplear • **to employ something as something/to do something** utilizar algo de algo/para hacer algo

employee [ım'plɔıi:] *s* empleado, da

employer [ım'plɔıǝr] *s* ❶ patrono, na; empresario, ria ❷ • **one of the country's biggest employers** una de las empresas que más trabajadores tiene en el país

employment [ım'plɔımǝnt] *s* empleo • **to be in employment** tener trabajo

empress ['emprıs] *s* emperatriz

empty ['emptı] ◆ *adj* ❶ vacío, a ❷ desierto, ta ❸ *despectivo* vano, na ◆ *vt* vaciar ◆ *vi* vaciarse ◆ *s familiar* casco

E

E

empty-handed [-'hændɪd] *adv* con las manos vacías

enable [ɪ'neɪbl] *vt* INFORMÁTICA ejecutar

enact [ɪ'nækt] *vt* ❶ DERECHO promulgar ❷ representar

enamel [ɪ'næml] *s* ❶ esmalte ❷ pintura de esmalte

encampment [ɪn'kæmpmənt] *s* campamento

encase [ɪn'keɪs] *vt* • **encased in** revestido, da de

enchanted [ɪn'tʃɑːntɪd] *adj* • **enchanted (by** o **with)** encantado, da (con)

enchanting [ɪn'tʃɑːntɪŋ] *adj* encantador, ra

encircle [ɪn'sɜːkl] *vt* rodear

enclose [ɪn'kləʊz] *vt* ❶ rodear • **enclosed by** o **with** rodeado de • **an enclosed space** un espacio cerrado ❷ adjuntar • **'please find enclosed...'** 'envío adjunto...'

encore ['ɒŋkɔːr] ◆ *s* bis ◆ *exclamación* ¡otra!

encounter [ɪn'kaʊntər] ◆ *s* encuentro ◆ *vt formal* encontrarse con

encourage [ɪn'kʌrɪdʒ] *vt* ❶ • **to encourage somebody (to do something)** animar a alguien (a hacer algo) ❷ fomentar

encouragement [ɪn'kʌrɪdʒmənt] *s* ❶ aliento ❷ fomento

encrypt [ɪn'krɪpt] *vt* INFORMÁTICA encriptar

encyclop(a)edia [ɪn,saɪklə'piːdjə] *s* enciclopedia

end [end] ◆ *s* ❶ fin; final • **at the end of May/2012** a finales de mayo/2012 • **at the end of the week** al final de la semana • **to bring something to an end** poner fin a algo • **to come to an end** llegar a su fin • **my patience is at an end** se me está agotando la paciencia • **'the end'** 'FIN' ❷ extremo ❸ punta ❹ fondo ❺ lado • **end to end** extremo con extremo • **to turn something on its end** poner algo boca abajo ❻ *formal* fin
expresiones **at the end of the day** a fin de cuentas; al fin y al cabo ▸ **to be at the end of your rope** estar hasta la coronilla ▸ **in the end** al final
◆ *vt* • **to end something (with)** terminar algo (con)
◆ *vi* acabarse; terminarse

■ **on end** *adv* ❶ de punta; de pie ❷ • **for days on end** durante días y días

■ **end up** *vi* acabar; terminar • **to end up doing something** acabar o terminar por hacer algo/haciendo algo • **to end up in** ir a parar a

endanger [ɪn'deɪndʒər] *vt* poner en peligro

endearing [ɪn'dɪərɪŋ] *adj* simpático, ca

endeavor [ɪn'devər] *formal* ◆ *s* esfuerzo ◆ *vt* • **to endeavor to do something** procurar hacer algo

ending ['endɪŋ] *s* final; desenlace

endless ['endlɪs] *adj* ❶ interminable ❷ inagotable

endorse [ɪn'dɔːs] *vt* apoyar; respaldar

endorsement [ɪn'dɔːsmənt] *s* apoyo; respaldo

endow [ɪn'daʊ] *vt* ❶ *formal* • **to be endowed with** estar dotado, da de ❷ donar fondos a

endurance [ɪn'djʊərəns] *s* resistencia

endure [ɪn'djʊər] ◆ *vt* soportar; aguantar ◆ *vi formal* perdurar

enemy ['enɪmɪ] *s* enemigo, ga

energetic [,enə'dʒetɪk] *adj* ❶ enérgico, ca ❷ activo, va; vigoroso, sa

energy ['enədʒɪ] *s* energía

enforce [ɪn'fɔːs] *vt* ❶ hacer cumplir; aplicar ❷ imponer

enforced [ɪn'fɔːst] *adj* forzoso, sa

engage [ɪn'geɪdʒ] ◆ *vt* ❶ atraer • **to engage somebody in conversation** entablar conversación con alguien ❷ TECNOLOGÍA pisar; meter ❸ *formal* contratar • **to be engaged in** o **on** dedicarse a ◆ *vi* ❶ • **to engage in** dedicarse a ❷ entablar

engaged [ɪn'geɪdʒd] *adj* ❶ • **engaged (to)** prometido, da (con) • **to get engaged** prometerse ❷ ocupado, da • **engaged in something** ocupado en algo ❸ TELECOMUNICACIONES comunicando

engagement [ɪn'geɪdʒmənt] *s* ❶ compromiso ❷ noviazgo ❸ cita

engagement ring *s* anillo de compromiso

engaging [ɪn'geɪdʒɪŋ] *adj* atractivo, va

engender [ɪn'dʒendər] *vt formal* engendrar

engine ['endʒɪn] *s* ❶ motor ❷ FERROCARRIL locomotora; máquina

engineer [,endʒɪ'nɪər] ◆ *s* ❶ ingeniero, ra ❷ maquinista ◆ *vt* ❶ construir ❷ tramar

engineering [,endʒɪ'nɪərɪŋ] *s* ingeniería

England ['ɪŋglənd] *s* Inglaterra

English ['ɪŋglɪʃ] ◆ *adj* inglés, esa ◆ *s* inglés ◆ *spl* • **the English** los ingleses

Englishman ['ɪŋglɪʃmən] *s* inglés

El plural de **Englishman** es **Englishmen** ['ɪŋglɪʃmen].

English muffin *s* ≃ bísquet

Englishwoman ['ɪŋglɪʃ,wʊmən] *s* inglesa

El plural de **Englishwoman** es **Englishwomen** ['ɪŋglɪʃ,wɪmɪn].

engrave [ɪn'greɪv] *vt literal & figurado* • **to engrave something (on)** grabar algo (en)

engraving [ɪn'greɪvɪŋ] *s* grabado

engrossed [ɪn'grəʊst] *adj* • **to be engrossed (in)** estar absorto, ta (en)

enhance [ɪn'hɑːns] *vt* ❶ aumentar ❷ elevar ❸ realzar

enjoy [ɪn'dʒɔɪ] *vt* ❶ disfrutar de • **did you enjoy the film/book?** ¿te gustó la película/el libro? • **she enjoys reading** le gusta leer • **enjoy your meal!** ¡que aproveche!; ¡buen provecho! • **to enjoy yourself** pasarlo bien; divertirse ❷ *formal* gozar o disfrutar de

enjoyable [ɪn'dʒɔɪəbl] *adj* agradable

enjoyment [ɪn'dʒɔɪmənt] *s* placer

enlarge [ɪn'lɑːdʒ] *vt* POLÍTICA ampliar

enlargement [ɪn'lɑːdʒmənt] *s* POLÍTICA ampliación

enlighten [ɪn'laɪtn] *vt formal* iluminar

enlightened [ɪn'laɪtnd] *adj* amplio, plia de miras

enlightenment [ɪn'laɪtnmənt] *s* 🔦*incontable* aclaración

enlist [ɪn'lɪst] ◆ *vt* ❶ alistar; reclutar ❷ obtener ◆ *vi* MILITAR • **to enlist (in)** alistarse (en)

enormous [ɪ'nɔːməs] *adj* enorme

enough [ɪ'nʌf] ◆ *adj* bastante; suficiente • **do you have enough glasses?** ¿tienes suficientes vasos? ◆ *pronombre* bastante • **is this enough?** ¿basta con eso? • **more than enough** más que suficiente

expresión **to have had enough (of)** estar harto, ta (de)

◆ *adv* bastante; suficientemente • **I was stupid enough to believe her** fui lo bastante tonto como para creerla • **he was good enough to lend me his car** *formal* tuvo la bondad de dejarme su coche • **strangely enough** curiosamente

enough

Cuando enough acompaña a un adjetivo o a un adverbio, se coloca después y no antes de éste (he's *old enough* to understand *ya es lo suficientemente mayor para entenderlo*; *strangely enough*, she couldn't remember *curiosamente, no lo recordaba*).

enquire [ɪn'kwaɪər] *vi* informarse • **to enquire about something** informarse de algo • **to enquire when/how/whether...** preguntar cuándo/cómo/si...

■ **enquire into** *vt* 🔦*El objeto siempre va después de la preposición al final.* investigar

enquiry [ɪn'kwaɪərɪ] *s* ❶ pregunta • **'Enquiries'** 'Información' ❷ investigación

enraged [ɪn'reɪdʒd] *adj* enfurecido, da

enroll [ɪn'rəʊl] ◆ *vt* inscribir ◆ *vi* • **to enroll (in)** inscribirse (en)

en route [ˌɒn'ruːt] *adv* • **en route (from/to)** en el camino (de/a)

ensue [ɪn'sjuː] *vi* ❶ *formal* seguir ❷ sobrevenir

ensure [ɪn'ʃʊər] *vt* • **to ensure (that)** asegurar que

entail [ɪn'teɪl] *vt* conllevar; suponer

enter ['entər] ◆ *vt* ❶ entrar en ❷ ingresar en; matricularse en; alistarse en ❸ meterse en; inscribirse en ❹ • **to enter something/somebody for something** inscribir algo/a alguien en algo ❺ apuntar ❻ presentarse o aparecer en ◆ *vi* ❶ entrar ❷ • **to enter (for something)** inscribirse (en algo)

■ **enter into** *vt* 🔦*El objeto siempre va después de la preposición al final.* ❶ entrar en ❷ comprometerse a ❸ entablar

enterprise ['entəpraɪz] *s* ❶ empresa ❷ iniciativa

enterprising ['entəpraɪzɪŋ] *adj* emprendedor, ra

entertain [ˌentə'teɪn] *vt* ❶ divertir; entretener ❷ recibir (en casa) ❸ *formal* considerar

entertainer [ˌentə'teɪnər] *s* artista

entertaining [ˌentə'teɪnɪŋ] *adj* divertido, da; entretenido, da

entertainment [ˌentə'teɪnmənt] *s* ❶ 🔦*incontable* diversión ❷ espectáculo

enthrall [ɪn'ɔːl] *vt* embelesar

enthusiasm [ɪn'ɵjuːzɪæzm] *s* ❶ • **enthusiasm (for)** entusiasmo (por) ❷ pasión; interés

enthusiast [ɪn'ɵjuːzɪæst] *s* entusiasta

enthusiastic [ɪnˌɵjuːzɪ'æstɪk] *adj* ❶ entusiasta ❷ entusiástico, ca

entice [ɪn'taɪs] *vt* seducir; atraer • **nothing could entice me to do that** no haría eso de ninguna manera

entire [ɪn'taɪər] *adj* entero, ra • **the entire evening** toda la noche

entirely [ɪn'taɪəlɪ] *adv* completamente • **I'm not entirely sure** no estoy del todo seguro

entirety [ɪn'taɪrətɪ] *s formal* • **in its entirety** en su totalidad

entitle [ɪn'taɪtl] *vt* • **to entitle somebody to something** dar a alguien derecho a algo • **to entitle somebody to do something** autorizar a alguien a hacer algo

entitled [ɪn'taɪtld] *adj* ❶ • **to be entitled to something/to do something** tener derecho a algo/a hacer algo ❷ titulado, da

entrance ◆ *s* ['entrəns] • **entrance (to)** entrada (a o de) • **to gain entrance to a)** *formal* lograr acceso a **b)** lograr el ingreso en ◆ *vt* [ɪn'trɑːns] encantar; hechizar

entrance examination *s* examen de admisión

entrance fee *s* (precio de) entrada

entrant ['entrənt] *s* participante

entrepreneur [ˌɒntrəprə'nɜːr] *s* empresario, ria

entrust [ɪn'trʌst] *vt* • **to entrust something to somebody**, **to entrust somebody with something** confiar algo a alguien

entry ['entrɪ] *s* ❶ • **entry (into)** entrada (en) • **'no entry'** 'se prohibe la entrada'; 'prohibido el paso' ❷ *figurado* ingreso ❸ participante ❹ anotación ❺ partida

entry form *s* impreso de inscripción

entryway ['entrɪˌweɪ] *s* camino (de entrada)

envelope ['envələʊp] *s* sobre

envious ['envɪəs] *adj* ❶ envidioso, sa ❷ de envidia • **to be envious of** tener envidia de

environment [ɪn'vaɪərənmənt] *s* ❶ • **the environment** el medio ambiente ❷ entorno ❸ ambiente

environmental [ɪnˌvaɪərən'mentl] *adj* ❶ medioambiental • **environmental pollution** contaminación del medio ambiente ❷ ecologista

environmentally [ɪnˌvaɪərən'mentəlɪ] *adv* ecológicamente • **environmentally friendly** ecológico, ca

Environmental Protection Agency *s* ▸ agencia gubernamental de protección del medio ambiente

envoy ['envɔɪ] *s* enviado, da

E

E

envy ['envɪ] ◆ *s* envidia ◆ *vt* • **to envy (somebody something)** envidiar (algo a alguien)

epic ['epɪk] ◆ *adj* épico, ca ◆ *s* ❶ epopeya ❷ película épica

epidemic [,epɪ'demɪk] *s* epidemia

epileptic [,epɪ'leptɪk] ◆ *adj* epiléptico, ca ◆ *s* epiléptico, ca

episode ['epɪsəʊd] *s* ❶ episodio ❷ capítulo

epistle [ɪ'pɪsl] *s* epístola

epitaph ['epɪtɑːf] *s* epitafio

epitome [ɪ'pɪtəmɪ] *s* • **the epitome of a)** la personificación de **b)** el vivo ejemplo de

epitomize, epitomise [ɪ'pɪtəmaɪz] *vt* ❶ personificar ❷ representar el paradigma de

epoch ['iːpɒk] *s* época

equal ['iːkwəl] ◆ *adj* igual • **equal to** igual a • **to be equal to** estar a la altura de ◆ *s* igual • **to treat somebody as an equal** tratar a alguien de igual a igual ◆ *vt* ❶ *MATEMÁTICAS* ser igual a ❷ igualar

equality [iː'kwɒlətɪ] *s* igualdad

equalize, equalise ['iːkwəlaɪz] *vi* *DEPORTE* empatar

equalizer ['iːkwəlaɪzər] *s* *DEPORTE* gol del empate

equally ['iːkwəlɪ] *adv* ❶ igualmente • **equally important** de igual importancia ❷ a partes iguales; por igual ❸ de igual modo

equal opportunities *spl* igualdad de oportunidades

equate [ɪ'kweɪt] *vt* • **to equate something with** equiparar algo con

equation [ɪ'kweɪʒn] *s* ecuación

equator [ɪ'kweɪtər] *s* • **the Equator** el Ecuador

equilibrium [,iːkwɪ'lɪbrɪəm] *s* equilibrio

equip [ɪ'kwɪp] *vt* ❶ • **to equip something (with)** equipar algo (con) • **to equip somebody (with)** proveer a alguien (de) ❷ • **to be equipped for** estar preparado, da para

equipment [ɪ'kwɪpmənt] *s* ☀*incontable* equipo

equitable ['ekwɪtəbl] *adj* equitativo, va

equity ['ekwətɪ] *s* ❶ ☀*incontable* *FINANZAS* capital social ❷ fondos propios

■ **equities** *spl* *FINANZAS* acciones ordinarias

equivalent [ɪ'kwɪvələnt] ◆ *adj* equivalente • **to be equivalent to** equivaler a ◆ *s* equivalente

er [ɜːr] *exclamación* ¡ejem!

ER (*abreviatura de* Emergency Room) *s* (sala de) urgencias

era ['ɪərə] *s* era; época

eradicate [ɪ'rædɪkeɪt] *vt* erradicar

erase [ɪ'reɪz] *vt* *literal & figurado* borrar

eraser [ɪ'reɪzər] *s* goma de borrar

erect [ɪ'rekt] ◆ *adj* erguido, da ◆ *vt* ❶ erigir; levantar ❷ montar

erection [ɪ'rekʃn] *s* ❶ ☀*incontable* construcción ❷ erección

erode [ɪ'rəʊd] *vt* ❶ erosionar ❷ desgastar ❸ mermar

erosion [ɪ'rəʊʒn] *s* ❶ erosión ❷ desgaste ❸ merma

erotic [ɪ'rɒtɪk] *adj* erótico, ca

err [ɜːr] *vi* equivocarse; errar

errand ['erənd] *s* recado; mandado • **to go on** o **run an errand** hacer un recado

erratic [ɪ'rætɪk] *adj* irregular

error ['erər] *s* error • **to make an error** cometer un error • **spelling error** falta de ortografía • **in error** por equivocación

erupt [ɪ'rʌpt] *vi* ❶ entrar en erupción ❷ *figurado* estallar

eruption [ɪ'rʌpʃn] *s* ❶ erupción ❷ estallido

escalate ['eskəleɪt] *vi* ❶ intensificarse ❷ ascender

escalator ['eskəleɪtər] *s* escalera mecánica

escapade [,eskə'peɪd] *s* aventura

escape [ɪ'skeɪp] ◆ *s* ❶ fuga ❷ escape ◆ *vt* ❶ escapar a; eludir ❷ • **her name escapes me right now** ahora mismo no me sale su nombre ◆ *vi* ❶ • **to escape (from)** escaparse (de) ❷ escapar

escapism [ɪ'skeɪpɪzm] *s* ☀*incontable* evasión

escort ◆ *s* ['eskɔːt] ❶ escolta ❷ acompañante ◆ *vt* [ɪ'skɔːt] escoltar

especially [ɪ'speʃəlɪ] *adv* ❶ especialmente ❷ sobre todo

espionage ['espɪə,nɑːʒ] *s* espionaje

essay ['eseɪ] *s* ❶ *EDUCACIÓN* redacción ❷ *UNIVERSIDAD* trabajo ❸ *LITERATURA* ensayo

essence ['esns] *s* esencia

essential [ɪ'senʃl] *adj* ❶ • **essential (to** o **for)** esencial o indispensable (para) ❷ fundamental; esencial

■ **essentials** *spl* los elementos esenciales

essentially [ɪ'senʃəlɪ] *adv* esencialmente

establish [ɪ'stæblɪʃ] *vt* ❶ establecer ❷ verificar

establishment [ɪ'stæblɪʃmənt] *s* establecimiento

■ **Establishment** *s* • **the Establishment** el sistema

estate [ɪ'steɪt] *s* ❶ finca ❷ *DERECHO* herencia

esteem [ɪ'stiːm] ◆ *s* estima ◆ *vt* estimar; apreciar

estimate ◆ *s* ['estɪmət] ❶ cálculo; estimación ❷ presupuesto ◆ *vt* ['estɪmeɪt] estimar

estimation [,estɪ'meɪʃn] *s* ❶ juicio ❷ cálculo

Estonia [e'stəʊnɪə] *s* Estonia

estranged [ɪ'streɪndʒd] *adj* separado, da • **his estranged son** su hijo, con el que no se habla

estuary ['estjʊərɪ] *s* estuario

etc. (*abreviatura de* etcetera) etc.

eternal [ɪ'tɜːnl] *adj* ❶ eterno, na ❷ *figurado* perpetuo, tua

eternity [ɪ'tɜːnətɪ] *s* eternidad

ethic ['eθɪk] *s* ética

■ **ethics** ♦ s ☼ *incontable* ética ♦ *spl* moralidad
ethical ['eɵɪkl] *adj* ético, ca
Ethiopia [ˌiːɵɪ'əʊpɪə] s Etiopía
ethnic ['eɵnɪk] *adj* étnico, ca
ethos ['iːɵɒs] s código de valores
etiquette ['etɪket] s etiqueta
EU (*abreviatura de* European Union) s UE
euphemism ['juːfəmɪzm] s eufemismo
euphoria [juː'fɔːrɪə] s euforia
euro ['jʊərəʊ] s euro
Europe ['jʊərəp] s Europa
European [ˌjʊərə'piːən] ♦ *adj* europeo, a ♦ s europeo, a
European Union s • the European Union la Unión Europea
euthanasia [ˌjuːɵə'neɪzjə] s eutanasia
evacuate [ɪ'vækjʊeɪt] *vt* evacuar
evade [ɪ'veɪd] *vt* ❶ eludir ❷ evadir
evaluate [ɪ'væljʊeɪt] *vt* evaluar
evaporate [ɪ'væpəreɪt] *vi* ❶ evaporarse ❷ *figurado* desvanecerse
evaporated milk [ɪ'væpəreɪtɪd-] s leche evaporada
evasion [ɪ'veɪʒn] s ❶ evasión ❷ evasiva
evasive [ɪ'veɪsɪv] *adj* evasivo, va
eve [iːv] s • on the eve of en la víspera de

even ['iːvn]
♦ *adj*
❶ [*expresa uniformidad*]
• the surface is even la superficie es lisa
❷ [*expresa igualdad*]
• the teams are even los equipos están empatados
• the odds o chances are about even hay un cincuenta por ciento de posibilidades
❸ [*en matemáticas*]
• two is an even number dos es un número par
♦ *adv*
❶ [*expresa sorpresa, burla*]
• he can't even dance no sabe ni bailar
• even my little brother could do it incluso mi hermano pequeño podría hacerlo
• even now incluso ahora
• even then incluso entonces
❷ [*permite introducir una precisión, una aclaración*]
• she's always been very nice to me, even generous on occasion siempre ha sido muy simpática conmigo, incluso a veces generosa
❸ [*en una comparación, intensificando, añadiendo énfasis*]
• it's even better now ahora es incluso mejor
■ **even if**
♦ *conjunción*
aunque
• even if I knew, I wouldn't tell you aunque lo supiera, no te lo diría

■ **even so**
♦ *adv*
• yes, but even so sí, pero aun así
■ **even though**
♦ *conjunción*
aunque
• even though I asked politely, he still refused to help me aunque se lo pedí educadamente, se negó a ayudarme

evening ['iːvnɪŋ] s ❶ tarde; noche • in the evening por la tarde/noche ❷ velada
evenly ['iːvnlɪ] *adv* ❶ equitativamente ❷ regularmente
event [ɪ'vent] s ❶ acontecimiento ❷ DEPORTE prueba
expresión in any event en todo caso ▶ in the event of en caso de
eventual [ɪ'ventʃʊəl] *adj* final
eventuality [ɪ,ventʃʊ'ælətɪ] s eventualidad
eventually [ɪ'ventʃʊəlɪ] *adv* finalmente

ever ['evər]
♦ *adv*
❶ [*con preguntas en presente o pretérito perfecto, para preguntarle a alguien sobre sus experiencias*]
• have you ever been to New York? ¿has estado en Nueva York?
❷ [*con palabras que tienen un sentido negativo*]
• I hardly ever see him no lo veo casi nunca
• nothing ever happens here aquí nunca pasa nada
❸ [*en frases comparativas o superlativas*]
• it was more beautiful than ever era más hermoso que nunca
• it's the best movie I've ever seen es la mejor película que he visto jamás
❹ [*indica una permanencia, una continuidad*]
• the danger is ever present el peligro está siempre presente
• she is as cheerful as ever está tan alegre como siempre
■ **ever since**
♦ *adv*
[*indica un punto de partida en el tiempo*]
• she has loved him ever since lo ha amado desde entonces
♦ *conjunción*
desde que
• it's been raining ever since I arrived ha estado lloviendo desde que llegué
♦ *preposición*
desde
• he's known her ever since his childhood la conoce desde la infancia

every ['evrɪ] *adj* cada • every day cada día; todos los días • every week todas las semanas

E

■ **every now and then, every so often** *adv* de vez en cuando

■ **every other** *adj* • **every other day** un día sí y otro no; cada tercer día

■ **every which way** *adv* en todas direcciones; sin orden ni concierto

everybody ['evrɪ,bɒdɪ] = **everyone**

everyday ['evrɪdeɪ] *adj* diario, ria; cotidiano, na

everyone ['evrɪwʌn], **everybody** ['evrɪ,bɒdɪ] *pronombre* todo el mundo; todos, das

everyplace = **everywhere**

everything ['evrɪθɪŋ] *pronombre* todo • **money isn't everything** el dinero no lo es todo

everywhere ['evrɪweəɾ], **everyplace** ['evrɪ,pleɪs] *adv* ❶ en o por todas partes ❷ a todas partes • **everywhere you go** dondequiera que vayas

evict [ɪ'vɪkt] *vt* • **to evict somebody from** desalojar a alguien de

evidence ['evɪdəns] *s* ⚬ *incontable* ❶ pruebas ❷ *DERECHO* declaración • **to give evidence** dar testimonio

evident ['evɪdənt] *adj* evidente

evidently ['evɪdəntlɪ] *adv* ❶ por lo visto; al parecer ❷ evidentemente

evil ['iːvl] ◆ *adj* ❶ malo, la; malvado, da ❷ perverso, sa; vil ◆ *s* ❶ maldad ❷ mal

evocative [ɪ'vɒkətɪv] *adj* evocador, ra

evoke [ɪ'vəʊk] *vt* ❶ evocar ❷ producir

evolution [ˌiːvə'luːʃn] *s* *BIOLOGÍA* evolución

evolve [ɪ'vɒlv] ◆ *vt* desarrollar ◆ *vi* ❶ *BIOLOGÍA* • **to evolve (into/from)** evolucionar (en/de) ❷ desarrollarse

exact [ɪg'zækt] *adj* exacto, ta • **to be exact** para ser exactos

exacting [ɪg'zæktɪŋ] *adj* ❶ arduo, dua ❷ severo, ra ❸ exigente

exactly [ɪg'zæktlɪ] ◆ *adv* exactamente • **it's exactly ten o'clock** son las diez en punto

expresión **not exactly a)** no precisamente **b)** no exactamente

◆ *exclamación* ¡exacto!

exaggerate [ɪg'zædʒəreɪt] *vt* & *vi* exagerar

exaggeration [ɪgˌzædʒə'reɪʃn] *s* exageración

exam [ɪg'zæm] (*abreviatura de* examination) *s* examen

examination [ɪgˌzæmɪ'neɪʃn] *s* ❶ = **exam** ❷ inspección; examen ❸ *MEDICINA* reconocimiento ❹ estudio

examine [ɪg'zæmɪn] *vt* ❶ examinar ❷ *MEDICINA* reconocer ❸ estudiar ❹ *DERECHO* interrogar

examiner [ɪg'zæmɪnəɾ] *s* examinador, ra

example [ɪg'zɑːmpl] *s* ejemplo • **for example** por ejemplo

expresión **to make an example of somebody** imponer un castigo ejemplar a alguien

exasperate [ɪg'zæspəreɪt] *vt* exasperar

exasperation [ɪgˌzæspə'reɪʃn] *s* exasperación

excavate ['ekskəveɪt] *vt* excavar

exceed [ɪk'siːd] *vt* ❶ exceder; sobrepasar ❷ rebasar

excel [ɪk'sel] *vi* • **to excel (in** o **at)** sobresalir (en)

excellence ['eksələns] *s* excelencia

excellent ['eksələnt] *adj* excelente

except [ɪk'sept] *preposición* & *conjunción* • **except (for)** excepto; salvo

exception [ɪk'sepʃn] *s* excepción

exceptional [ɪk'sepʃənl] *adj* excepcional

excerpt ['eksɜːpt] *s* • **excerpt (from)** extracto (de)

excess ◆ *adj* [ɪk'ses] excedente ◆ *s* ['ekses] exceso

excess baggage, excess luggage *s* exceso de equipaje

excessive [ɪk'sesɪv] *adj* excesivo, va

exchange [ɪks'tʃeɪndʒ] ◆ *s* intercambio • **in exchange (for)** a cambio (de) ◆ *vt* ❶ intercambiar ❷ cambiar • **to exchange something for something** cambiar algo por algo • **to exchange something with somebody** intercambiar algo con alguien

exchange rate *s* *FINANZAS* tipo de cambio

excite [ɪk'saɪt] *vt* ❶ emocionar ❷ despertar

excited [ɪk'saɪtɪd] *adj* emocionado, da

excitement [ɪk'saɪtmənt] *s* emoción

exciting [ɪk'saɪtɪŋ] *adj* emocionante

exclaim [ɪk'skleɪm] ◆ *vt* exclamar ◆ *vi* • **to exclaim (at)** exclamar (ante)

exclamation [ˌekskləˈmeɪʃn] *s* exclamación

exclamation point *s* signo de exclamación

exclude [ɪk'skluːd] *vt* • **to exclude something/somebody (from)** excluir algo/a alguien (de)

excluding [ɪk'skluːdɪŋ] *preposición* sin incluir; con excepción de

exclusive [ɪk'skluːsɪv] *adj* ❶ exclusivo, va ❷ selecto, ta

excruciating [ɪk'skruːʃɪeɪtɪŋ] *adj* insoportable

excursion [ɪk'skɜːʃn] *s* excursión

excuse ◆ *s* [ɪk'skjuːs] excusa • **to make an excuse** dar una excusa; excusarse ◆ *vt* [ɪk'skjuːz] ❶ • **to excuse yourself (for doing something)** excusarse o disculparse (por haber hecho algo) ❷ • **to excuse somebody (from)** dispensar a alguien (de)

expresión **excuse me a)** oiga (por favor) **b)** con permiso **c)** perdone **d)** ¿perdón?; ¿cómo?

execute ['eksɪkjuːt] *vt* ejecutar

execution [ˌeksɪ'kjuːʃn] *s* ejecución

executioner [ˌeksɪ'kjuːʃnəɾ] *s* verdugo

executive [ɪg'zekjʊtɪv] ◆ *adj* ejecutivo, va ◆ *s* ❶ ejecutivo, va ❷ ejecutiva; órgano ejecutivo

exempt [ɪg'zempt] ◆ *adj* • **exempt (from)** exento, ta (de) ◆ *vt* • **to exempt something/somebody (from)** eximir algo/a alguien (de)

exercise ['eksəsaɪz] ◆ s ❶ ejercicio ❷ *MILITAR* maniobra ◆ *vi* hacer ejercicio

exert [ɪg'zɜ:t] *vt* ejercer • **to exert yourself** esforzarse

exertion [ɪg'zɜ:ʃn] *s* esfuerzo

exhale [eks'heɪl] ◆ *vt* exhalar ◆ *vi* espirar

exhaust [ɪg'zɔ:st] ◆ *s* ☼ *incontable* gases de combustión ▸ **exhaust (pipe)** tubo de escape ◆ *vt* agotar

exhausted [ɪg'zɔ:stɪd] *adj* agotado, da

exhausting [ɪg'zɔ:stɪŋ] *adj* agotador, ra

exhaustion [ɪg'zɔ:stʃn] *s* agotamiento

exhaustive [ɪg'zɔ:stɪv] *adj* exhaustivo, va

exhibit [ɪg'zɪbɪt] ◆ *s* ❶ *ARTE* objeto expuesto ❷ exposición ❸ *DERECHO* prueba (instrumental) ◆ *vt* ❶ *formal* mostrar; manifestar ❷ *ARTE* exponer

exhibition [ˌeksɪ'bɪʃn] *s* ❶ *ARTE* exposición ❷ manifestación

exhilarating [ɪg'zɪləreɪtɪŋ] *adj* estimulante

exile ['eksaɪl] ◆ *s* ❶ exilio • **in exile** en el exilio ❷ exiliado, da ◆ *vt* • **to exile somebody (from/to)** exiliar a alguien (de/a)

exist [ɪg'zɪst] *vi* existir

existence [ɪg'zɪstəns] *s* existencia • **to be in existence** existir • **to come into existence** nacer

existing [ɪg'zɪstɪŋ] *adj* existente; actual

exit ['eksɪt] ◆ *s* salida ◆ *vi* salir

exodus ['eksədəs] *s* éxodo

exotic [ɪg'zɒtɪk] *adj* exótico, ca

expand [ɪk'spænd] ◆ *vt* ampliar ◆ *vi* ❶ extenderse; ampliarse ❷ expandirse; dilatarse

■ **expand (up)on** *vt* ☼ *El objeto siempre va después de la preposición al final.* desarrollar

expanse [ɪk'spæns] *s* extensión

expansion [ɪk'spænʃn] *s* expansión

expect [ɪk'spekt] ◆ *vt* ❶ esperar • **to expect somebody to do something** esperar que alguien haga algo • **to expect something (from somebody)** esperar algo (de alguien) • **to expect the worst** esperarse lo peor • **as expected** como era de esperar ❷ imaginarse; suponer • **I expect so** supongo que sí ◆ *vi* ❶ • **to expect to do something** esperar hacer algo ❷ • **to be expecting** estar embarazada

expectancy → **life expectancy**

expectant [ɪk'spektənt] *adj* expectante

expectant mother *s* futura madre

expectation [ˌekspek'teɪʃn] *s* esperanza • **against all expectation** o **expectations, contrary to all expectation** o **expectations** contrariamente a lo que se esperaba • **to live up to/fall short of expectations** estar/no estar a la altura de lo esperado

expedition [ˌekspɪ'dɪʃn] *s* expedición

expel [ɪk'spel] *vt* ❶ • **to expel somebody (from)** expulsar a alguien (de) ❷ • **to expel something (from)** expeler algo (de)

expend [ɪk'spend] *vt* • **to expend something (on)** emplear algo (en)

expendable [ɪk'spendəbl] *adj* reemplazable

expenditure [ɪk'spendɪtʃəɾ] *s* ☼ *incontable* gasto

expense [ɪk'spens] *s* ☼ *incontable* gasto • **to go to great expense (to do something)** incurrir en grandes gastos (para hacer algo) • **at the expense of** a costa de

expresión **at somebody's expense** *literal & figurado* a costa de alguien ▸ **to spare no expense** no repararse en gastos

■ **expenses** *spl* *COMERCIO* gastos

expensive [ɪk'spensɪv] *adj* caro, ra

experience [ɪk'spɪərɪəns] ◆ *s* experiencia ◆ *vt* experimentar

experienced [ɪk'spɪərɪənst] *adj* • **experienced (at** o **in)** experimentado, da (en)

experiment [ɪk'sperɪmənt] ◆ *s* experimento ◆ *vi* • **to experiment (with/on)** experimentar (con); hacer experimentos (con)

expert ['ekspɜ:t] ◆ *adj* • **expert (at something/ at doing something)** experto, ta (en algo/en hacer algo) • **expert advice** la opinión de un experto ◆ *s* experto, ta

expertise [ˌekspɜ:'ti:z] *s* ☼ *incontable* pericia

expiration [ˌɪk'spirɪʃn] *s* ❶ caducación ❷ vencimiento

expire [ɪk'spaɪəɾ] *vi* ❶ caducar ❷ vencer

explain [ɪk'spleɪn] ◆ *vt* • **to explain something (to somebody)** explicar algo (a alguien) ◆ *vi* explicar • **to explain to somebody about something** explicarle algo a alguien

explanation [ˌeksplə'neɪʃn] *s* • **explanation (for)** explicación (de)

explicit [ɪk'splɪsɪt] *adj* explícito, ta

explode [ɪk'spləʊd] ◆ *vt* ❶ hacer explotar ❷ volar ❸ *figurado* reventar ◆ *vi* *literal & figurado* estallar

exploit ◆ *s* ['eksplɔɪt] hazaña ◆ *vt* [ɪk'splɔɪt] explotar

exploitation [ˌeksplɔɪ'teɪʃn] *s* ☼ *incontable* explotación

exploration [ˌeksplə'reɪʃn] *s* exploración

explore [ɪk'splɔ:ɾ] *vt & vi literal & figurado* explorar

explorer [ɪk'splɔ:rəɾ] *s* explorador, ra

explosion [ɪk'spləʊʒn] *s* explosión

explosive [ɪk'spləʊsɪv] ◆ *adj* explosivo, va ◆ *s* explosivo

export ◆ *s* ['ekspɔ:t] ❶ exportación ❷ artículo de exportación ◆ *en compuestos* de exportación ◆ *vt* [ɪk'spɔ:t] *COMERCIO & INFORMÁTICA* exportar

exporter [ek'spɔ:təɾ] *s* exportador, ra

expose [ɪk'spəʊz] *vt* ❶ exponer • **to be exposed to something** estar expuesto a algo ❷ descubrir

exposed [ɪk'spəʊzd] *adj* expuesto, ta; al descubierto

E

exposure [ɪk'spəʊʒər] *s* ❶ exposición ❷ *MEDICINA* congelación ❸ publicidad

express [ɪk'spres] ◆ *adj* rápido, da ◆ *s* expreso ◆ *vt* expresar • **to express yourself** expresarse

expression [ɪk'spreʃn] *s* expresión

expressive [ɪk'spresɪv] *adj* expresivo, va

expressway [ɪk'spresweɪ] *s* autopista

exquisite [ɪk'skwɪzɪt] *adj* exquisito, ta

ext., extn. (*abreviatura escrita de* extension) ext.

extend [ɪk'stend] ◆ *vt* ❶ extender ❷ ampliar ❸ prolongar ❹ prorrogar ❺ brindar; conceder ◆ *vi* ❶ extenderse ❷ sobresalir

extension [ɪk'stenʃn] *s* ❶ extensión ❷ ampliación ❸ prolongación ❹ prórroga ❺ *ELECTRICIDAD* ▶ **extension (lead)** alargador

extension cable *s* alargador

extensive [ɪk'stensɪv] *adj* ❶ extenso, sa ❷ profundo, da ❸ amplio, plia

extensively [ɪk'stensɪvlɪ] *adv* ❶ extensamente ❷ profundamente • **to use something extensively** hacer (un) gran uso de algo

extent [ɪk'stent] *s* ❶ extensión ❷ alcance ❸ • **to what extent...?** ¿hasta qué punto...? • **to the extent that a)** en la medida en que **b)** hasta tal punto que • **to some/a certain extent** hasta cierto punto • **to a large** o **great extent** en gran medida

exterior [ɪk'stɪərɪər] ◆ *adj* exterior ◆ *s* exterior

exterminate [ɪk'stɜ:mɪneɪt] *vt* exterminar

external [ɪk'stɜ:nl] *adj* externo, na

extinct [ɪk'stɪŋkt] *adj* extinto, ta

extinguish [ɪk'stɪŋgwɪʃ] *vt* ❶ *formal* extinguir ❷ apagar

extinguisher [ɪk'stɪŋgwɪʃər] *s* extintor

extn. = ext.

extort [ɪk'stɔ:t] *vt* • **to extort something from somebody a)** arrancar algo a alguien **b)** sacar algo a alguien

extortionate [ɪk'stɔ:ʃnət] *adj* desorbitado, da; exorbitante

extra ['ekstrə] ◆ *adj* ❶ adicional ❷ de más • **take extra care** pon sumo cuidado ◆ *s* ❶ extra ❷ suplemento ❸ *CINE & TEATRO* extra ◆ *adv* extra • **to pay/ charge extra** pagar/cobrar un suplemento

extra- ['ekstrə] *prefijo* extra-

extract ◆ *s* ['ekstrækt] ❶ fragmento ❷ *QUÍMICA* extracto ◆ *vt* [ɪk'strækt] • **to extract something (from) a)** extraer algo (de) **b)** arrancar algo (de)

extraordinary [ɪk'strɔ:dnrɪ] *adj* extraordinario, ria

extravagance [ɪk'strævəgəns] *s* ❶ ☀:*incontable* derroche; despilfarro ❷ extravagancia

extravagant [ɪk'strævəgənt] *adj* ❶ derrochador, ra ❷ caro, ra ❸ extravagante

extreme [ɪk'stri:m] ◆ *adj* extremo, ma ◆ *s* extremo

extremely [ɪk'stri:mlɪ] *adv* sumamente; extremadamente

extremist [ɪk'stri:mɪst] ◆ *adj* extremista ◆ *s* extremista

extricate ['ekstrɪkeɪt] *vt* • **to extricate something from** lograr sacar algo de • **to extricate yourself from** lograr salirse de

extrovert ['ekstrəvɜ:t] ◆ *adj* extrovertido, da ◆ *s* extrovertido, da

exultant [ɪg'zʌltənt] *adj* ❶ jubiloso, sa ❷ de júbilo

eye [aɪ] ◆ *s* ojo

expresiones before my ETC (very) eyes ante mis ETC propios ojos ▶ to have an eye for something tener buen ojo para algo ▶ to keep your eyes open for, to keep an eye out for estar atento, ta a
◆ *vt* mirar

Formas irregulares de eye: *gerundio* eyeing o eying.

eyeball ['aɪbɔ:l] *s* globo ocular

eyebrow ['aɪbraʊ] *s* ceja

eyebrow pencil *s* delineador de cejas

eyeglasses ['aɪglasɪz] *s* lentes

eyelash ['aɪlæʃ] *s* pestaña

eyelid ['aɪlɪd] *s* párpado

eyeliner ['aɪˌlaɪnər] *s* lápiz de ojos

eye-opener *s* ❶ *familiar* revelación ❷ sorpresa

eye shadow *s* sombra de ojos

eyesight ['aɪsaɪt] *s* vista

eye test *s* revisión ocular

eyewitness [ˌaɪ'wɪtnɪs] *s* testigo ocular

F

f, F [ef] *s* f; F

■ **F** ◆ *s* ❶ *MÚSICA* fa ❷ *EDUCACIÓN* ≃ muy deficiente ◆ *adj (abreviatura de* Fahrenheit) F

Dos plurales: **f's o fs; F's o Fs.**

fable ['feɪbl] *s* fábula

fabric ['fæbrɪk] *s* ❶ tela ❷ estructura

fabulous ['fæbjʊləs] *adj familiar* fabuloso, sa

facade [fə'sɑːd] *s* fachada

face [feɪs] ◆ *s* ❶ cara ❷ carátula ❸ aspecto ❹ superficie

expresiones face down boca abajo ▶ face time tiempo de contacto personal ▶ face to face cara a cara ▶ face up boca arriba ▶ in the face of ante ▶ to look somebody in the face mirar a alguien a la cara ▶ to lose face quedar mal ▶ to save face salvar las apariencias ▶ on the face of it a primera vista

◆ *vt* ❶ mirar a ❷ hacer frente a ❸ *familiar* aguantar

expresión let's face it no nos engañemos

◆ *vi* • to face forwards/south mirar hacia delante/ al sur

■ **face up to** *vt* ☀: *El objeto siempre va después de la preposición al final.* hacer frente a

face cream *s* crema facial

facet ['fæsɪt] *s* faceta

facetious [fə'siːʃəs] *adj* guasón, ona

face value *s* valor nominal

expresión to take something at face value tomarse algo literalmente

facility [fə'sɪlətɪ] *s* prestación

■ **facilities** *spl* ❶ instalaciones ❷ servicios

facing ['feɪsɪŋ] *adj* opuesto, ta

facsimile [fæk'sɪmɪlɪ] *s* facsímil

fact [fækt] *s* ❶ dato ❷ hecho • to know something for a fact saber algo a ciencia cierta ❸ ☀: *incontable* realidad

■ **in fact** *conjunción* & *adv* de hecho; en realidad

fact of life *s* • it's a fact of life es un hecho indiscutible

■ **facts of life** *spl* eufemismo • to tell somebody (about) the facts of life contar a alguien cómo nacen los niños

factor ['fæktər] *s* factor

factory ['fæktərɪ] *s* fábrica

factual ['fæktʃʊəl] *adj* basado, da en hechos reales

faculty ['fækltɪ] *s* ❶ facultad ❷ • the faculty el profesorado

fad [fæd] *s* ❶ moda pasajera ❷ capricho

fade [feɪd] ◆ *vt* descolorar; desteñir ◆ *vi* ❶ descolorarse; desteñirse ❷ marchitarse ❸ irse apagando ❹ desvanecerse

Fahrenheit ['færənhaɪt] *adj* Fahrenheit

fail [feɪl] ◆ *vt* ❶ reprobar ❷ • to fail to do something no lograr hacer algo ❸ • to fail to do something no hacer algo ❹ fallar ◆ *vi* ❶ fracasar • if all else fails en último extremo ❷ reprobar ❸ fallar ❹ debilitarse

failing ['feɪlɪŋ] ◆ *s* fallo ◆ *preposición* a falta de • failing that en su defecto

failure ['feɪljər] *s* ❶ fracaso ❷ fracasado, da ❸ fallo ❹ • her failure to do it el que no lo hiciera

faint [feɪnt] ◆ *adj* ❶ débil ❷ impreciso, sa ❸ vago, ga ❹ leve ❺ reducido, da ❻ mareado, da ◆ *vi* desmayarse

fair [feər] ◆ *adj* ❶ justo, ta • it's not fair! ¡no hay derecho! ❷ considerable ❸ bastante bueno, na • 'fair' *EDUCACIÓN* 'regular' ❹ rubio, bia ❺ claro, ra ❻ bueno, na ❼ *literario* hermoso, sa ◆ *s* feria ◆ *adv* limpio

fair-haired [-'heəd] *adj* rubio, bia

fairly ['feəlɪ] *adv* ❶ bastante ❷ justamente

fairness ['feənɪs] *s* justicia

fair play *s* juego limpio

fairy ['feərɪ] *s* hada

fairy tale *s* cuento de hadas

faith [feɪθ] *s* fe • in good/bad faith de buena/mala fe

faithful ['feɪθfʊl] ◆ *adj* fiel ◆ *spl RELIGIÓN* • the faithful los fieles

faithfully ['feɪθfʊlɪ] *adv* fielmente

fake [feɪk] ◆ *adj* falso, sa ◆ *s* ❶ falsificación ❷ impostor, ra ◆ *vt* ❶ falsificar ❷ fingir ◆ *vi* fingir

falcon ['fɔ:lkən] *s* halcón

fall [fɔ:l] ◆ *vi* ❶ caer • **he fell off the chair** se cayó de la silla • **she fell backwards** se cayó hacia atrás • **to fall to bits** o **pieces** hacerse pedazos ❷ bajar ❸ • **to fall asleep** dormirse • **to fall ill** ponerse enfermo, ma • **to fall in love** enamorarse

expresión **to fall flat** *figurado* no causar el efecto deseado

◆ *s* ❶ caída ❷ • **a fall of snow** una nevada ❸ • **fall (in)** descenso (de) ❹ otoño
■ **falls** *spl* cataratas

■ **fall apart** *vi* ❶ romperse ❷ *figurado* desmoronarse

■ **fall back** *vi* echarse atrás; retroceder

■ **fall back on** *vt* ☼: *El objeto siempre va después de la preposición al final.* recurrir a

■ **fall behind** *vi* ❶ quedarse atrás ❷ retrasarse

■ **fall for** *vt* ☼: *El objeto siempre va después de la preposición al final.* ❶ *familiar* enamorarse de ❷ tragarse

■ **fall off** *vi* ❶ desprenderse ❷ disminuir

■ **fall out** *vi* ❶ • **his hair is falling out** se le está cayendo el pelo ❷ pelearse; discutir

■ **fall over** *vi* caerse

■ **fall through** *vi* fracasar

Formas irregulares de **fall**: *pretérito* **fell**, *pp* **fallen**.

fallen ['fɔ:ln] *participio pasado* → **fall**

fall guy *s familiar* el que paga el pato

false [fɔ:ls] *adj* ❶ falso, sa ❷ postizo, za

false alarm *s* falsa alarma

false teeth *spl* dentadura postiza

falsify ['fɔ:lsɪfaɪ] *vt* falsificar

falter ['fɔ:ltər] *vi* vacilar

fame [feɪm] *s* fama

familiar [fə'mɪljər] *adj* ❶ familiar; conocido, da • **to be familiar to somebody** serle familiar a alguien ❷ • **familiar with** familiarizado, da con • **to be on familiar terms with somebody** tener trato informal con alguien ❸ *despectivo* demasiado amistoso, sa

familiarity [fə,mɪlɪ'ærətɪ] *s* ☼: *incontable* • **familiarity with** conocimiento de

familiarize [fə'mɪljəraɪz] *vt* • **to familiarize yourself/somebody with something** familiarizarse/familiarizar a alguien con algo

family ['fæmlɪ] *s* familia

family doctor *s* médico de cabecera

family planning *s* planificación familiar

famine ['fæmɪn] *s* hambruna

famous ['feɪməs] *adj* • **famous (for)** famoso, sa (por)

fan [fæn] ◆ *s* ❶ abanico ❷ ventilador ❸ fan; admirador, ra ❹ aficionado, da ❺ *FÚTBOL* hincha ◆ *vt* ❶ abanicar ❷ avivar

■ **fan out** *vi* desplegarse en abanico

fanatic [fə'nætɪk] *s* fanático, ca

fanciful ['fænsɪfʊl] *adj* extravagante

fancy ['fænsɪ] ◆ *vt* ❶ *familiar* • **I fancy a lemonade** se me antoja un agua de limón ❷ *familiar* • **do you fancy her?** ¿te gusta? ❸ • **fancy that!** ¡imagínate!; ¡mira por dónde! ◆ *s* capricho • **to take a fancy to** encapricharse con ◆ *adj* ❶ elaborado, da ❷ de lujo; caro, ra ❸ exorbitante

fang [fæŋ] *s* colmillo

fanny pack *s* cangurera

fantasize ['fæntəsaɪz] *vi* fantasear • **to fantasize about something/about doing something** soñar con algo/con hacer algo

fantastic [fæn'tæstɪk] *adj* fantástico, ca

fantasy ['fæntəsɪ] *s* fantasía

fao (*abreviatura de* for the attention of) a/a

far [fɑ:r] ◆ *adv* ❶ lejos • **is it far?** ¿está lejos? • **how far is it?** ¿a qué distancia está? • **how far is it to Mérida?** ¿a qué distancia queda Mérida? • **so far** por ahora; hasta ahora • **far and wide** por todas partes • **as far as** hasta ❷ • **how far have you got?** ¿hasta dónde llegaste? • **as far as I know** que yo sepa • **as far as I'm concerned** por o en lo que a mí respecta • **as far as possible** en (la medida de) lo posible • **far and away, by far** con mucho • **far from it** en absoluto; todo lo contrario • **so far a)** hasta el momento **b)** hasta un cierto punto ◆ *adj* (*comparativo* farther o further, *superlativo* farthest o furthest) extremo, ma

faraway ['fɑ:rəweɪ] *adj* ❶ lejano, na ❷ ausente

fare [feər] *s* ❶ (precio del) boleto ❷ tarifa ❸ pasajero, ra *(de taxi)*

Far East *s* • **the Far East** el Extremo Oriente

farewell [,feə'wel] ◆ *s* despedida ◆ *exclamación literario* ¡vaya con Dios!

farm [fɑ:m] ◆ *s* ❶ granja ❷ rancho ◆ *vt* ❶ cultivar ❷ criar

farmer ['fɑ:mər] *s* ❶ granjero, ra ❷ agricultor, ra

farmhouse ['fɑ:mhaʊs] *s* granja

farming ['fɑ:mɪŋ] *s* ☼: *incontable* ❶ *AGRICULTURA & INDUSTRIA* agricultura ❷ cultivo; cría; crianza

farmland ['fɑ:mlænd] *s* ☼: *incontable* tierras de labranza

farm worker = **farmhand**

farmyard ['fɑ:mjɑ:d] *s* corral

far-reaching [-'ri:tʃɪŋ] *adj* trascendental; de amplio alcance

farsighted [,fɑ:'saɪtɪd] *adj* ❶ con visión de futuro ❷ de vista cansada

farther ['fɑ:ðər] *comparativo* → **far**

farthest ['fɑ:ðəst] *superlativo* → **far**

fascinate ['fæsɪneɪt] *vt* fascinar

fascinating ['fæsɪneɪtɪŋ] *adj* fascinante

fascination [,fæsɪ'neɪʃn] *s* fascinación

fascism ['fæʃɪzm] *s* fascismo

fashion ['fæʃn] ◆ s ❶ moda ❷ manera ◆ vt formal ❶ elaborar ❷ figurado forjar

fashionable ['fæʃnəbl] adj de moda

fashion show s pase o desfile de modelos

fast [fɑːst] ◆ adj ❶ rápido, da ❷ • her watch is two minutes fast su reloj va dos minutos adelantado ❸ que no destiñe ◆ adv ❶ rápido; rápidamente • how fast were they going? ¿a qué velocidad iban? ❷ • stuck fast bien pegado, da • to hold fast to something a) agarrarse fuerte a algo b) mantenerse fiel a algo • fast asleep profundamente dormido ◆ s ayuno ◆ vi ayunar

fasten ['fɑːsn] vt ❶ sujetar ❷ abrochar • he fastened his coat se abrochó el abrigo ❸ • to fasten something to something fijar algo a algo

fast food s ⚥ incontable comida rápida

fastidious [fə'stɪdɪəs] adj quisquilloso, sa

fat [fæt] ◆ adj ❶ gordo, da • to get fat engordar ❷ con mucha grasa ❸ grueso, sa ◆ s ❶ grasa ❷ manteca

fatal ['feɪtl] adj ❶ mortal ❷ fatal; funesto, ta

fatality [fə'tælətɪ] s víctima mortal

fate [feɪt] s ❶ destino ❷ suerte; final
expresión to tempt fate tentar a la suerte

fateful ['feɪtful] adj fatídico, ca

fat-free adj sin grasas

father ['fɑːðər] s literal & figurado padre

father-in-law s suegro
Dos plurales: father-in-laws o fathers-in-law.

fatherly ['fɑːðəlɪ] adj paternal

fatigue [fə'tiːg] s fatiga

fatten ['fætn] vt engordar

fattening ['fætnɪŋ] adj que engorda

fatty ['fætɪ] adj graso, sa

fatuous ['fætjuəs] adj necio, cia

faucet ['fɔːsɪt] s llave

fault [fɔːlt] s ❶ culpa • it's my fault es culpa mía • to be at fault tener la culpa ❷ defecto • to find fault with encontrar defectos a ❸ GEOLOGÍA falla ❹ falta

faultless ['fɔːltlɪs] adj impecable

faulty ['fɔːltɪ] adj ❶ defectuoso, sa ❷ imperfecto, ta

favor ['feɪvər] ◆ s favor • in favor a favor • in somebody's favor a favor de alguien • to be in/out of favor (with) ser/dejar de ser popular (con) ◆ vt ❶ preferir ❷ favorecer

favorable ['feɪvrəbl] adj favorable

favorite ['feɪvrɪt] ◆ adj favorito, ta ◆ s favorito, ta

fawn [fɔːn] ◆ adj beige ◆ s cervato; cervatillo ◆ vi • to fawn on somebody adular a alguien

fax [fæks] ◆ s fax ◆ vt ❶ mandar un fax a ❷ enviar por fax

fax machine, facsimile machine s fax

FBI (abreviatura de Federal Bureau of Investigation) s FBI

fear [fɪər] ◆ s ❶ miedo; temor • for fear of por miedo a ❷ peligro ◆ vt ❶ temer ❷ temerse • to fear (that)... temerse que...

fearful ['fɪəful] adj ❶ formal temeroso, sa ❷ terrible

fearless ['fɪəlɪs] adj intrépido, da

feasible ['fiːzəbl] adj factible; viable

feast [fiːst] ◆ s banquete; festín ◆ vi • to feast on o off something darse un banquete a base de algo

feat [fiːt] s hazaña

feather ['feðər] s pluma

feature ['fiːtʃər] ◆ s ❶ característica ❷ rasgo ❸ GEOGRAFÍA accidente geográfico ❹ artículo de fondo ❺ RADIO & TELEVISIÓN programa especial ◆ vt ❶ tener como protagonista a ❷ tener como atracción principal a ◆ vi • to feature (in) aparecer o figurar (en)

February ['februərɪ] s febrero ver también **September**

feces ['fiːsiːz] spl heces

fed [fed] pretérito & participio pasado → **feed**

Fed [fed] ◆ s familiar ❶ (abreviatura de Federal Reserve Board) órgano de control del banco central estadounidense ❷ agente del FBI ◆ s ❶ abreviatura escrita de **federal** ❷ abreviatura escrita de **federation**

federal ['fedrəl] adj federal

federation [ˌfedə'reɪʃn] s federación

fed up adj • fed up (with) harto, ta (de)

fee [fiː] s honorarios • membership fee cuota de socio • entrance fee entrada • school fees (precio de) matrícula

feeble ['fiːbəl] adj ❶ débil ❷ pobre; flojo, ja

feed [fiːd] ◆ vt ❶ alimentar ❷ dar de comer a ◆ vi comer ◆ s ❶ toma ❷ pienso
Formas irregulares de **feed**: pretérito & pp **fed**.

feedback ['fiːdbæk] s ⚥ incontable ❶ reacciones ❷ INFORMÁTICA & ELECTRICIDAD retroalimentación ❸ feedback

feel [fiːl] ◆ vt ❶ tocar ❷ sentir • I felt myself blushing noté que me ponía colorado ❸ creer • to feel (that) creer o pensar que
expresión not to feel yourself no encontrarse bien
◆ vi ❶ • to feel hot/cold/sleepy tener calor/frío/sueño • how do you feel? ¿cómo te encuentras? ❷ • to feel safe/happy sentirse seguro/feliz ❸ parecer (al tacto) ❹ • to feel like something buscar algo a tientas ❺ • do you feel like going to the movies? ¿se te antoja ir al cine? ◆ s ❶ tacto; sensación ❷ atmósfera
Formas irregulares de **feel**: pretérito & pp **felt**.

feeling ['fiːlɪŋ] s ❶ sentimiento ❷ sensación ❸ presentimiento ❹ opinión

feet [fiːt] spl → **foot**

fell [fel] ◆ vt talar ◆ pretérito → **fall**

fellow ['feləu] ◆ adj • fellow students compañeros de clase • fellow citizens conciudadanos ◆ s ❶ des-

usado tipo ❷ camarada ❸ miembro ❹ miembro del claustro de profesores

fellowship ['feləʊʃɪp] _s_ ❶ camaradería ❷ asociación ❸ beca de investigación

felony ['felənɪ] _s_ DERECHO crimen ; delito grave

felt [felt] ◆ _pretérito_ & _participio pasado_ → **feel** ◆ _s_ ※ _incontable_ fieltro

felt-tip pen _s_ rotulador

female ['fiːmeɪl] ◆ _adj_ ❶ hembra ❷ femenino, na ◆ _s_ ❶ hembra ❷ mujer

feminine ['femɪnɪn] ◆ _adj_ femenino, na ◆ _s_ GRAMÁTICA femenino

feminist ['femɪnɪst] _s_ feminista

fence [fens] ◆ _s_ valla

expresión to sit on the fence _figurado_ nadar entre dos aguas
◆ _vt_ cercar

fencing ['fensɪŋ] _s_ DEPORTE esgrima

fend [fend] _vi_ • **to fend for yourself** valerse por sí mismo, ma
■ **fend off** _vt_ ※ _El objeto se puede colocar antes o después de la preposición._ ❶ defenderse de ; desviar ❷ eludir

ferment ◆ _s_ ['fɜːment] agitación ◆ _vi_ [fə'ment] fermentar

fern [fɜːn] _s_ helecho

ferocious [fə'rəʊʃəs] _adj_ feroz

ferry ['ferɪ] ◆ _s_ ❶ transbordador ; ferry ❷ barca ◆ _vt_ llevar ; transportar

fertile ['fɜːtaɪl] _adj_ fértil

fertilizer ['fɜːtɪlaɪzər] _s_ abono

fervent ['fɜːvənt] _adj_ ferviente

festival ['festəvl] _s_ festival

fetch [fetʃ] _vt_ ❶ ir a buscar ❷ _familiar_ venderse por

fetching ['fetʃɪŋ] _adj_ atractivo, va

fetus ['fiːtəs] _s_ feto

feud [fjuːd] ◆ _s_ enfrentamiento duradero ◆ _vi_ pelearse

feudal ['fjuːdl] _adj_ feudal

fever ['fiːvər] _s_ literal & figurado fiebre • **to have a fever** tener fiebre

feverish ['fiːvərɪʃ] _adj_ literal & figurado febril

---

few [fjuː]
◆ _adj_
• **few people come here** poca gente viene aquí
• **the first few pages were interesting** las primeras páginas eran interesantes
expresión few and far between muy de vez en cuando
◆ _pronombre_
• **few of them agree** pocos están de acuerdo
• **quite a few** o **a good few** unos cuantos
■ **a few**

◆ _adj_
• **I need a few books** necesito unos cuantos libros
◆ _pronombre_
• **a few of them are wearing hats** unos pocos llevan sombreros

---

few

No hay que confundir few (_pocos(as)_) y a few (_algunos(as)_).

Few puede ir delante de sustantivos contables en plural (_few_ women). Con sustantivos incontables usaremos little (_little_ water).

No confundamos tampoco a few y a little. A little va con sustantivos incontables (_a little_ sugar, _a little_ patience) mientras que a few va con sustantivos contables en plural (_a few_ good ideas _algunas buenas ideas_). A little puede también ser adverbio, al contrario de a few.

En oraciones negativas generalmente usaremos not many en vez de few, y not much en lugar de little.

Ver también little.

---

fewer ['fjuːər] ◆ _adj_ menos ◆ _pronombre_ menos

fewest ['fjuːəst] _adj_ menos

fiancé [fɪ'ɒnseɪ] _s_ prometido

fiancée [fɪ'ɒnseɪ] _s_ prometida

fiasco [fɪ'æskəʊ] _s_ fiasco

El plural de **fiasco** es **fiascoes**.

fib [fɪb] _s familiar_ mentirilla

fiber ['faɪbər] _s_ fibra

fiberglass ['faɪbəglɑːs] _s_ ※ _incontable_ fibra de vidrio

fickle ['fɪkl] _adj_ voluble

fiction ['fɪkʃn] _s_ ❶ (literatura de) ficción ❷ ficción

fictional ['fɪkʃənl] _adj_ ❶ novelesco, ca ❷ ficticio, cia

fictitious [fɪk'tɪʃəs] _adj_ ficticio, cia

fiddle ['fɪdl] _s_ violín

fidget ['fɪdʒɪt] _vi_ no estarse quieto, ta

field [fiːld] _s_ campo • **in the field** sobre el terreno

fiendish ['fiːndɪʃ] _adj_ ❶ malévolo, la ❷ _familiar_ endiablado, da

fierce [fɪəs] _adj_ ❶ feroz ❷ endiablado, da ❸ ferviente ❹ asfixiante

fifteen [fɪf'tiːn] _número_ quince ver también **six**

fifth [fɪfθ] _número_ quinto, ta ver también **sixth**

fifty ['fɪftɪ] _número_ cincuenta ver también **sixty**

fifty-fifty ◆ *adj* al cincuenta por ciento • **a fifty-fifty chance** unas posibilidades del cincuenta por ciento ◆ *adv* • **to go fifty-fifty** ir a medias

fig [fɪg] *s* higo

fight [faɪt] ◆ *s* ❶ pelea ❷ *figurado* lucha • **to have a fight (with)** pelearse (con) • **to put up a fight** oponer resistencia ◆ *vt* ❶ luchar contra ❷ pelearse con ❸ librar ❹ luchar en ◆ *vi* ❶ pelearse ❷ luchar ❸ *figurado* • **to fight (for/against)** luchar (por/contra) ❹ • **to fight (about** o **over)** pelearse o discutir (por)

■ **fight back** *vi* defenderse

Formas irregulares de **fight**: pretérito & pp **fought.**

fighter ['faɪtər] *s* ❶ caza ❷ combatiente ❸ púgil ❹ luchador, ra

fighting ['faɪtɪŋ] *s* ❶ ⚙ *incontable* peleas ❷ combates

figure ['fɪgjər] ◆ *s* ❶ cifra ❷ figura

expresión to put a figure on something dar un número exacto de algo

◆ *vt* figurarse; suponer ◆ *vi* figurar

■ **figure out** *vt* ⚙ *El objeto se puede colocar antes o después de la preposición.* ❶ figurarse ❷ resolver ❸ calcular • **to figure out how to do something** dar con la manera de hacer algo

file [faɪl] ◆ *s* ❶ expediente • **on file, on the files** archivado ❷ *INFORMÁTICA* archivo ❸ lima ❹ • **in single file** en fila india ◆ *vt* ❶ archivar ❷ *DERECHO* presentar ❸ limar ◆ *vi* ir en fila

filing cabinet ['faɪlɪŋ-] *s* archivero

Filipino [ˌfɪlɪ'piːnəʊ] ◆ *adj* filipino, na ◆ *s* filipino, na

El plural de **Filipino** es **Filipinos.**

fill [fɪl] ◆ *vt* ❶ • **to fill something (with)** llenar algo (de) ❷ rellenar ❸ tapar ❹ cubrir ❺ ocupar ◆ *s*

expresión to eat your fill comer hasta hartarse ▸ to have had your fill of something estar hasta la coronilla de algo

■ **fill in** *vt* ⚙ *El objeto se puede colocar antes o después de la preposición.* ❶ rellenar ❷ • **to fill somebody in (on)** poner a alguien al corriente (de)

■ **fill out** *vt* ⚙ *El objeto se puede colocar antes o después de la preposición.* rellenar

■ **fill up** ◆ *vt* ⚙ *El objeto se puede colocar antes o después de la preposición.* llenar (hasta arriba) ◆ *vi* llenarse

fillet ['fɪleɪ] ◆ *s* filete ◆ *vt* cortar en filetes

fillet steak *s* filete

filling ['fɪlɪŋ] ◆ *adj* que llena mucho ◆ *s* relleno

film [fɪlm] ◆ *s* ❶ película ❷ ⚙ *incontable* cine ◆ *vt* & *vi* filmar; rodar

filter ['fɪltər] ◆ *s* filtro ◆ *vt* filtrar

filth [fɪlθ] *s* ⚙ *incontable* ❶ suciedad ❷ obscenidades

filthy ['fɪlθɪ] *adj* ❶ mugriento, ta; sucísimo, ma ❷ obsceno, na

fin [fɪn] *s* aleta

final ['faɪnl] ◆ *adj* ❶ último, ma ❷ final ❸ definitivo, va ◆ *s* final

finalize, finalise ['faɪnəlaɪz] *vt* finalizar

finally ['faɪnəlɪ] *adv* ❶ por fin ❷ finalmente; por último

finance ◆ *s* ['faɪnæns] ⚙ *incontable* ❶ finanzas ❷ fondos ◆ *vt* [faɪ'næns] financiar

■ **finances** *spl* finanzas

financial [fɪ'nænʃl] *adj* financiero, ra

find [faɪnd] ◆ *vt* ❶ encontrar ❷ darse cuenta de; descubrir ❸ *DERECHO* • **to be found guilty/not guilty (of)** ser declarado, da culpable/inocente (de) ◆ *s* hallazgo; descubrimiento

■ **find out** *vi* ❶ enterarse ❷ informarse ◆ *vt* ⚙ *El objeto se puede colocar antes o después de la preposición.* ❶ descubrir ❷ averiguar

Formas irregulares de **find**: pretérito & pp **found.**

findings ['faɪndɪŋz] *spl* conclusiones

fine [faɪn] ◆ *adj* ❶ excelente ❷ • **it's/that's fine** está bien • **how are you? — fine thanks** ¿qué tal? — muy bien ❸ bueno, na ❹ fino, na ❺ sutil ◆ *adv* ❶ bien ❷ muy bien ◆ *s* multa ◆ *vt* multar

fine arts *spl* bellas artes

finger ['fɪŋgər] ◆ *s* dedo ◆ *vt* acariciar con los dedos

fingernail ['fɪŋgəneɪl] *s* uña *(de las manos)*

fingerprint ['fɪŋgəprɪnt] *s* huella digital

fingertip ['fɪŋgətɪp] *s* punta del dedo

finish ['fɪnɪʃ] ◆ *s* ❶ final ❷ meta ❸ acabado ◆ *vt* • **to finish something/doing something** acabar o terminar algo/de hacer algo ◆ *vi* terminar

■ **finish off** *vt* ⚙ *El objeto se puede colocar antes o después de la preposición.* acabar o terminar del todo

■ **finish up** *vi* acabar; terminar

finishing line ['fɪnɪʃɪŋ-] *s* línea de meta

finite ['faɪnaɪt] *adj* finito, ta

Finland ['fɪnlənd] *s* Finlandia

Finn [fɪn] *s* finlandés, esa

Finnish ['fɪnɪʃ] ◆ *adj* finlandés, esa ◆ *s* finlandés

fir [fɜːr], **fir tree** *s* abeto

fire ['faɪər] ◆ *s* ❶ fuego • **on fire** en llamas • **to catch fire** prender • **to open fire (on somebody)** abrir fuego (contra alguien) • **to set fire to** prender fuego a ❷ incendio ◆ *vt* ❶ disparar • **to fire a shot** disparar ❷ despedir ◆ *vi* • **to fire (on** o **at)** disparar (contra)

fire alarm *s* alarma antiincendios

firearm ['faɪərɑːm] *s* arma de fuego

fire department *s* cuerpo de bomberos

fire door *s* puerta cortafuegos

fire engine *s* coche de bomberos

fire escape *s* escalera de incendios

fire exit *s* salida de incendios

fire extinguisher *s* extinguidor

firefighter ['faɪəfaɪtər] *s* bombero, era

firehouse ['faɪəhaʊs] *s* estación de bomberos
fireman ['faɪəmən] *s* bombero
El plural de **fireman** es **firemen** ['faɪəmen].

fireplace ['faɪəpleɪs] *s* chimenea
fire station *s* estación de bomberos
firewood ['faɪəwʊd] *s* leña
firework ['faɪəwɜːk] *s* fuego artificial
■ **fireworks** *spl* fuegos artificiales
firing ['faɪərɪŋ] *s* ☼ *incontable* MILITAR disparos
firing squad *s* pelotón de ejecución o fusilamiento
firm [fɜːm] ◆ *adj* ❶ firme • **to stand firm** mantenerse firme ❷ FINANZAS estable ◆ *s* empresa
first [fɜːst] ◆ *adj* primero, ra • **the first day** el primer día • **for the first time** por primera vez • **first thing (in the morning)** a primera hora (de la mañana) ◆ *adv* ❶ primero • **to come first** quedar en primer lugar • **first of all** en primer lugar ❷ por primera vez ◆ *s* ❶ primero, ra ❷ acontecimiento sin precedentes
■ **at first** *adv* al principio
■ **at first hand** *adv* de primera mano
first aid *s* ❶ ☼ *incontable* primeros auxilios ❷ socorrismo
first-aid kit *s* botiquín de primeros auxilios
first-class ◆ *adj* ❶ de primera ❷ de primera clase ◆ *adv* en primera clase
first-degree *adj* ❶ MEDICINA ▶ **first-degree burn** quemadura de primer grado ❷ DERECHO ▶ **first-degree murder** homicidio en primer grado
first floor *s* planta baja
firsthand [ˌfɜːst'hænd] ◆ *adj* de primera mano ◆ *adv* directamente
first lady *s* primera dama
firstly ['fɜːstlɪ] *adv* en primer lugar
first name *s* nombre de pila
first-rate *adj* de primera
firtree ['fɜːtriː] = **fir**
fish [fɪʃ] ◆ *s* ❶ pez ❷ ☼ *incontable* pescado ◆ *vt* pescar en ◆ *vi* • **to fish (for something)** pescar (algo)
El plural de **fish** es **fish**.

fisherman ['fɪʃəmən] *s* pescador
El plural de **fisherman** es **fishermen** ['fɪʃəmen].

fishing ['fɪʃɪŋ] *s* pesca • **to go fishing** ir de pesca
fishing boat *s* barco pesquero
fishing line *s* sedal
fishing net *s* red de pesca
fishing rod *s* caña de pescar
fishy ['fɪʃɪ] *adj* ❶ a pescado ❷ *familiar* sospechoso, sa
fist [fɪst] *s* puño
fit [fɪt] ◆ *adj* ❶ • **to see** o **think fit to do something** creer conveniente hacer algo • **do as you think fit** haz lo que te parezca conveniente ❷ en forma • **to keep fit** mantenerse en forma ◆ *s* ❶ • **it's a good fit**

le/te ETC sienta o va bien ❷ ataque • **in fits and starts** a tropezones
expresión **he had a fit** *literal & figurado* le dio un ataque
◆ *vt* ❶ quedar bien a; ir bien a ❷ • **to fit something into** encajar algo en ❸ • **to fit something with** equipar algo con • **to have an alarm fitted** poner una alarma ❹ corresponder a ◆ *vi* ❶ quedar bien de talla ❷ • **this bit fits in here** esta pieza encaja aquí ❸ caber
■ **fit in** ◆ *vt* ☼ *El objeto se puede colocar antes o después de la preposición.* hacer un hueco a ◆ *vi* ❶ • **to fit in (with)** adaptarse (a) ❷ • **it doesn't fit in with our plans** no encaja con nuestros planes
fitness ['fɪtnɪs] *s* ☼ *incontable* ❶ buen estado físico ❷ • **fitness (for)** idoneidad (para)
fitting ['fɪtɪŋ] ◆ *adj* *formal* adecuado, da ◆ *s* ❶ accesorio ❷ prueba
■ **fittings** *spl* accesorios
fitting room *s* probador
five [faɪv] *número* cinco ver también **six**
fix [fɪks] ◆ *vt* ❶ fijar • **to fix something (to)** fijar algo (a) ❷ arreglar ❸ *familiar* amañar ❹ preparar ◆ *s* *familiar* • **to be in a fix** estar en un aprieto
■ **fix up** *vt* ☼ *El objeto se puede colocar antes o después de la preposición.* ❶ • **to fix somebody up with** proveer a alguien de ❷ organizar; preparar
fixation [fɪk'seɪʃn] *s* • **fixation (on** o **about)** fijación (con)
fixed [fɪkst] *adj* fijo, ja
fixture ['fɪkstʃər] *s* ❶ instalación fija ❷ rasgo característico ❸ encuentro
fizz [fɪz] *vi* burbujear
fizzle ['fɪzl] ■ **fizzle out** *vi* ❶ apagarse ❷ disiparse
fizzy ['fɪzɪ] *adj* ❶ gaseoso, sa ❷ con gas
flabby ['flæbɪ] *adj* fofo, fa
flag [flæg] ◆ *s* bandera ◆ *vi* decaer
■ **flag down** *vt* ☼ *El objeto se puede colocar antes o después de la preposición.* parar
flagpole ['flægpəʊl] *s* asta (de bandera)
flair [fleər] *s* ❶ don • **to have a flair for something** tener un don para algo ❷ estilo
flake [fleɪk] ◆ *s* ❶ escama ❷ copo ◆ *vi* descascararse
flaky ['fleɪkɪ] (*comparativo* flakier, *superlativo* flakiest) *adj* ❶ con escamas ❷ descascarado, da ❸ *familiar* raro, ra
flamboyant [flæm'bɔɪənt] *adj* ❶ extravagante ❷ vistoso, sa
flame [fleɪm] *s* llama • **in flames** en llamas
flamingo [flə'mɪŋgəʊ] *s* flamingo
Dos plurales: **flamingos** o **flamingoes**.

flammable ['flæməbl] *adj* inflamable
flank [flæŋk] ◆ *s* ❶ costado ❷ flanco ◆ *vt* • **to be flanked by** estar flanqueado, da por
flannel ['flænl] *s* franela

flap [flæp] ◆ *s* solapa ◆ *vt* ❶ agitar ❷ batir ◆ *vi* ❶ ondear ❷ aletear

flare [fleər] ◆ *s* bengala ◆ *vi* ❶ • **to flare (up)** llamear ❷ • **to flare (up)** estallar

flash [flæʃ] ◆ *s* ❶ destello • **a flash of lightning** un relámpago ❷ *FOTOGRAFÍA* flash ❸ momento ❹ acceso • **in a flash** en un instante ◆ *vt* ❶ dirigir ❷ encender intermitentemente ❸ lanzar ❹ mostrar; emitir ◆ *vi* ❶ destellar ❷ brillar ❸ • **to flash by** o **past** pasar como un rayo

flashback ['flæʃbæk] *s* flashback

flashlight ['flæʃlaɪt] *s* linterna

flashy ['flæʃɪ] *adj despectivo* ostentoso, sa

flask [flɑːsk] *s* ❶ **termo**® ❷ matraz ❸ petaca

flat [flæt] ◆ *adj* ❶ llano, na ❷ plano, na ❸ bajo, ja ❹ desinflado, da; ponchado, da ❺ rotundo, da ❻ flojo, ja ❼ monótono, na ❽ soso, sa ❾ *MÚSICA* desafinado, da ❿ bemol ⓫ único, ca ⓬ muerto, ta ⓭ descargado, da ◆ *adv* ❶ • **to lie flat** estar totalmente extendido, da • **to fall flat on your face** caerse de bruces ❷ • **in five minutes flat** en cinco minutos justos ◆ *s* ❶ ponchadura ❷ *MÚSICA* bemol
■ **flat out** *adv* a toda velocidad

flatly ['flætlɪ] *adv* ❶ de plano; rotundamente ❷ monótonamente

flatten ['flætn] *vt* ❶ allanar; aplanar ❷ alisar ❸ arrasar
■ **flatten out** ◆ *vi* allanarse; nivelarse ◆ *vt* ⌯ *El objeto se puede colocar antes o después de la preposición.* allanar

flatter ['flætər] *vt* ❶ adular; halagar ❷ favorecer

flattering ['flætərɪŋ] *adj* ❶ halagador, ra ❷ favorecedor, ra

flattery ['flætərɪ] *s* ⌯ *incontable* halagos

flatware ['flætweər] *s* ⌯ *incontable* cubiertos

flaunt [flɔːnt] *vt* ostentar; hacer gala de

flavor ['fleɪvər] ◆ *s* ❶ sabor ❷ *figurado* aire; sabor ◆ *vt* condimentar

flavoring ['fleɪvərɪŋ] *s* ⌯ *incontable* condimento • **artificial flavoring** aromatizante artificial

flaw [flɔː] *s* desperfecto

flawless ['flɔːlɪs] *adj* impecable

flea [fliː] *s* pulga

fled [fled] *pretérito & participio pasado* → **flee**

flee [fliː] ◆ *vt* huir de ◆ *vi* • **to flee (from/to)** huir (de/a)
Formas irregulares de **flee**: *pretérito & pp* **fled**.

fleece [fliːs] ◆ *s* ❶ vellón ❷ forro polar ◆ *vt familiar* desplumar

fleet [fliːt] *s* flota

fleeting ['fliːtɪŋ] *adj* fugaz

Flemish ['flemɪʃ] ◆ *adj* flamenco, ca ◆ *s* flamenco ◆ *spl* • **the Flemish** los flamencos

flesh [fleʃ] *s* ❶ carne • **in the flesh** en persona ❷ pulpa

flew [fluː] *pretérito* → **fly**

flex [fleks] ◆ *s* *ELECTRICIDAD* cable; cordón ◆ *vt* flexionar

flexible ['fleksəbl] *adj* flexible

flick [flɪk] ◆ *s* golpe rápido ◆ *vt* apretar; mover
■ **flick through** *vt* ⌯ *El objeto siempre va después de la preposición al final.* hojear

flicker ['flɪkər] *vi* parpadear

flight [flaɪt] *s* ❶ vuelo • **flight of fancy** o **of the imagination** vuelo de la imaginación ❷ tramo ❸ fuga

flight attendant *s* sobrecargo

flight crew *s* tripulación de vuelo

flight deck *s* ❶ cabina del piloto ❷ cubierta de vuelo

flight recorder *s* caja negra

flimsy ['flɪmzɪ] *adj* ❶ muy ligero, ra ❷ débil; poco sólido, da ❸ flojo, ja

flinch [flɪntʃ] *vi* ❶ estremecerse • **without flinching** sin pestañear ❷ • **to flinch (from something/from doing something)** retroceder (ante algo/ante hacer algo) • **without flinching** sin inmutarse

fling [flɪŋ] *vt* arrojar
Formas irregulares de **fling**: *pretérito & pp* **flung**.

flint [flɪnt] *s* ❶ sílex ❷ piedra

flip [flɪp] *vt* ❶ dar la vuelta a • **to flip something open** abrir algo de golpe ❷ pulsar
■ **flip through** *vt* ⌯ *El objeto siempre va después de la preposición al final.* hojear

flip-flop *s* chancla

flippant ['flɪpənt] *adj* frívolo, la

flipper ['flɪpər] *s* aleta

flirt [flɜːt] ◆ *s* coqueto, ta ◆ *vi* • **to flirt (with)** coquetear (con)

flirtatious [flɜːˈteɪʃəs] *adj* coqueto, ta

flit [flɪt] *vi* revolotear

float [fləʊt] ◆ *s* ❶ corcho ❷ flotador ❸ carro alegórico ❹ cambio ◆ *vt* hacer flotar ◆ *vi* flotar

flock [flɒk] *s* ❶ rebaño ❷ bandada ❸ *figurado* multitud; tropel

flog [flɒg] *vt* azotar

flood [flʌd] *s* ❶ inundación ❷ avalancha

flooding ['flʌdɪŋ] *s* ⌯ *incontable* inundación

floodlight ['flʌdlaɪt] *s* foco

floor [flɔːr] ◆ *s* ❶ suelo ❷ pista ❸ fondo ❹ piso; planta ◆ *vt* ❶ derribar ❷ desconcertar; dejar perplejo, ja

floorboard ['flɔːbɔːd] *s* tabla (del suelo)

floor lamp *s* lámpara de pie

flop [flɒp] *s* *familiar* fracaso

floppy ['flɒpɪ] *adj* aguado, da; flojo, ja

florist ['flɒrɪst] *s* florista • **florist's (shop)** florería

flounce [flaʊns] ◆ *s* *COSER* volante ◆ *vi* • **to flounce out** salir airadamente

flounder ['flaʊndər] *vi* ❶ debatirse ❷ titubear

flour ['flaʊər] *s* harina

flourish ['flʌrɪʃ] ◆ *vi* florecer ◆ *vt* agitar ◆ *s* • **to do something with a flourish** hacer algo exageradamente

flout [flaʊt] *vt* desobedecer

flow [fləʊ] ◆ *s* flujo • **traffic flow** circulación ◆ *vi* ❶ fluir; correr ❷ ondear

flow chart, flow diagram *s* organigrama; cuadro sinóptico

flower ['flaʊər] ◆ *s* literal & figurado flor ◆ *vi* literal & figurado florecer

flowerbed ['flaʊəbed] *s* macizo de flores

flowerpot ['flaʊəpɒt] *s* maceta

flowery ['flaʊərɪ] *adj* ❶ de flores; floreado, da ❷ despectivo florido, da

flown [fləʊn] *participio pasado* → **fly**

flu [fluː] *s* gripa

fluctuate ['flʌktʃʊeɪt] *vi* fluctuar

fluency ['fluːənsɪ] *s* soltura; fluidez

fluent ['fluːənt] *adj* ❶ • **to be fluent in French, to speak fluent French** dominar el francés ❷ fluido, da

fluff [flʌf] *s* pelusa

fluffy ['flʌfɪ] *adj* ❶ esponjoso, sa ❷ de peluche

fluid ['fluːɪd] ◆ *s* fluido; líquido ◆ *adj* ❶ fluido, da ❷ incierto, ta

fluke [fluːk] *s* familiar chiripa • **by a fluke** por o de chiripa

flung [flʌŋ] *pretérito* & *participio pasado* → **fling**

fluorescent [flʊə'resnt] *adj* fluorescente

fluoride ['flʊəraɪd] *s* fluoruro

flurry ['flʌrɪ] *s* ❶ ráfaga ❷ torbellino

flush [flʌʃ] ◆ *adj* • **flush with** nivelado, da con ◆ *s* ❶ rubor ❷ arrebato ◆ *vt* ❶ jalar ❷ • **to flush somebody out** hacer salir a alguien ◆ *vi* ruborizarse

flushed [flʌʃt] *adj* ❶ encendido, da ❷ • **flushed (with)** enardecido, da (por)

flustered ['flʌstəd] *adj* aturdido, da

flute [fluːt] *s* MÚSICA flauta

flutter ['flʌtər] ◆ *s* ❶ aleteo ❷ pestañeo ❸ familiar arranque ◆ *vi* ❶ aletear ❷ ondear

flux [flʌks] *s* • **to be in a state of flux** cambiar constantemente

fly [flaɪ] ◆ *s* ❶ mosca ❷ bragueta ◆ *vt* ❶ pilotar ❷ hacer volar ❸ transportar en avión ❹ ondear ◆ *vi* ❶ volar ❷ ir en avión ❸ pilotar ❹ ondear

expresión **to send something/somebody flying, to knock something/somebody flying** familiar mandar algo/a alguien por los aires

■ **fly away** *vi* irse volando

Formas irregulares de **fly**: *pretérito* **flew**, *pp* **flown**.

flying ['flaɪɪŋ] ◆ *adj* volador, ra; volante ◆ *s* • **I hate/love flying** odio/me encanta ir en avión • **her hobby is flying** es aficionada a la aviación

flying saucer *s* platillo volador

flying start *s* • **to get off to a flying start** empezar con muy buen pie

flying visit *s* visita relámpago

FM (abreviatura de frequency modulation) FM

foal [fəʊl] *s* potro

foam [fəʊm] ◆ *s* ❶ espuma ❷ ▶ **foam (rubber)** hule espuma ◆ *vi* hacer espuma

fob [fɒb] ■ **fob off** *vt* ☼ *El objeto se puede colocar antes o después de la preposición.* • **to fob somebody off (with something)** quitarse a alguien de encima (con algo) • **to fob something off on somebody** endosar a alguien algo

focal point ['fəʊkl-] *s* punto focal o central

focus ['fəʊkəs] ◆ *s* foco • **in focus** enfocado • **out of focus** desenfocado ◆ *vt* ❶ enfocar ❷ fijar; centrar ◆ *vi* ❶ • **to focus (on something)** enfocar (algo) ❷ • **to focus on something** centrarse en algo

fodder ['fɒdər] *s* forraje

foe [fəʊ] *s* literario enemigo, ga

fog [fɒg] *s* niebla

foggy ['fɒgɪ] *adj* de niebla

expresión **it's foggy** hay niebla

fog lamp *s* faro antiniebla

foil [fɔɪl] ◆ *s* ☼ *incontable* papel aluminio ◆ *vt* frustrar

fold [fəʊld] ◆ *vt* ❶ doblar ❷ plegar • **to fold your arms** cruzar los brazos ◆ *vi* ❶ plegarse ❷ familiar venirse abajo ◆ *s* pliegue

■ **fold up** *vt* ☼ *El objeto se puede colocar antes o después de la preposición.* ❶ doblar ❷ plegar ◆ *vi* ❶ doblarse ❷ plegarse ❸ venirse abajo

folder ['fəʊldər] *s* fólder

folding ['fəʊldɪŋ] *adj* ❶ plegable ❷ de tijera

foliage ['fəʊlɪɪdʒ] *s* follaje

folk [fəʊk] ◆ *adj* popular ◆ *spl* gente ◆ *s* = **folk music**

■ **folks** *spl* familiar padres

folklore ['fəʊklɔːr] *s* folclore

folk music *s* ❶ música folclórica o popular ❷ música folk

folk song *s* ❶ canción popular ❷ canción folk

folksy ['fəʊksɪ] (comparativo folksier, superlativo folksiest) *adj* familiar campechano, na

follow ['fɒləʊ] ◆ *vt* ❶ seguir ❷ comprender ◆ *vi* ❶ seguir ❷ ser lógico, ca • **it follows that** se deduce que ❸ comprender

■ **follow up** *vt* ☼ *El objeto se puede colocar antes o después de la preposición.* ❶ hacer un seguimiento de ❷ • **to follow something up with** proseguir algo con

follower ['fɒləʊər] *s* partidario, ria

following ['fɒləʊɪŋ] ◆ *adj* siguiente ◆ *s* ❶ partidarios ❷ afición ◆ *preposición* tras

folly ['fɒlɪ] *s* ☼ *incontable* locura

fond [fɒnd] *adj* ❶ afectuoso, sa; cariñoso, sa ❷ • **to be fond of somebody** tener cariño a alguien • **to be**

F

fond of something/of doing something ser aficionado, da a algo/a hacer algo

fondle ['fɒndl] *vt* acariciar

font [fɒnt] *s* ❶ pila bautismal ❷ *INFORMÁTICA* fuente

food [fu:d] *s* comida

food poisoning [-'pɔɪznɪŋ] *s* intoxicación alimenticia

food processor [-ˌprəʊsesər] *s* procesador de alimentos

food stamp *s* ▸ cupón estatal canjeable por comida

fool [fu:l] ◆ *s* idiota; imbécil • **to act** o **play the fool** hacer el tonto ◆ *vt* engañar • **to fool somebody into doing something** embaucar a alguien para que haga algo ◆ *vi* bromear

■ **fool about, fool around** *vi* • **to fool about (with something)** hacer el tonto (con algo)

foolish ['fu:lɪʃ] *adj* tonto, ta

foolproof ['fu:lpru:f] *adj* infalible

foot [fʊt] *s* ❶ (pl feet) pie ❷ pata • **to be on your feet** estar de pie • **to get to your feet** levantarse • **on foot** a pie; andando ❸ (pl feet) pie *(30,48 cm)*

expresión **to put your foot in it** meter la pata ▸ **to put your feet up** descansar

footage ['fʊtɪdʒ] *s* ⚡*incontable* secuencias

football ['fʊtbɔ:l] *s* ❶ futbol; futbol americano ❷ balón

football field *s* campo de futbol americano

football game *s* partido de futbol americano

foothold ['fʊthəʊld] *s* punto de apoyo para el pie

expresión **to get a foothold** encontrar un punto de apoyo

footing ['fʊtɪŋ] *s* ❶ equilibrio • **to lose your footing** perder el equilibrio ❷ base • **on an equal footing (with)** en pie de igualdad (con)

footlights ['fʊtlaɪts] *spl* candilejas

footnote ['fʊtnəʊt] *s* nota a pie de página

footpath ['fʊtpɑ:θ] ⚡*pl* [-pɑ:ðz] *s* sendero; vereda

footprint ['fʊtprɪnt] *s* huella; pisada

footstep ['fʊtstep] *s* ❶ paso ❷ pisada

expresión **to follow in somebody's footsteps** seguir los pasos de alguien

footwear ['fʊtweər] *s* calzado

---

for [fɔr]

◆ *preposición*

❶ [*expresa objetivo, intención*] para

• **let's meet for a game of soccer** vamos a vernos para jugar futbol

• **what's it for?** ¿para qué es?

❷ [*expresa la causa*] por

• **for various reasons** por varias razones

❸ [*introduce el destino, el destinatario*]

• **the plane for Acapulco has already left** el vuelo de Acapulco ya salió

• **this is for him** esto es para él

❹ [*expresa la duración*]

• **she'll be away for a month** va a estar fuera un mes

• **I've lived here for 3 years** llevo viviendo aquí 3 años; vivo aquí desde hace tres años

❺ [*expresa un plazo*]

• **I can do it for you for tomorrow** te lo podría hacer para mañana

❻ [*expresa la distancia*]

• **this medical centre is the only one for 50 kilometers** este centro médico es el único que hay en 50 kilómetros a la redonda

• **I walked for miles** caminé muchas millas

❼ [*a favor de*]

• **he voted for his friend** votó a favor de su amigo

❽ [*indica una ocasión, un acontecimiento*]

• **she's coming home for Christmas** viene a casa por Navidad

• **what are you doing for your birthday?** ¿qué vas a hacer para tu cumpleaños?

❾ [*en lugar de*]

• **let me do that for you** déjame que lo haga por ti

❿ [*indica una equivalencia*]

• **P for Peter** P de Peter

• **what's the Greek for 'mother'?** ¿cómo se dice 'madre' en griego?

⓫ [*con un precio*]

• **they're 50 pesos for ten** son 50 pesos por cada diez

• **I bought/sold it for ten pesos** lo compré/vendí por 10 pesos

---

for

No hay que confundir for y during. For se utiliza como respuesta a la pregunta how long? (*¿cuánto tiempo?; ¿por cuánto tiempo?*) (I went to Boston *for* three weeks *Fui a Boston por tres semanas*), mientras que during responde a la pregunta when? (*¿cuándo?*) (I went to Boston *during* the holidays *Fui a Boston en las vacaciones*).

---

forbad [fə'bæd], **forbade** [fə'beɪd] *pretérito* → **forbid**

forbid [fə'bɪd] *vt* • **to forbid somebody (to do something)** prohibir a alguien (hacer algo)

Formas irregulares de **forbid**: *pretérito* **forbade** o **forbad**, *pp* **forbid** o **forbidden**.

forbidden [fə'bɪdn] *adj* prohibido, da

forbidding [fə'bɪdɪŋ] *adj* ❶ inhóspito, ta ❷ severo, ra; austero, ra

force [fɔ:s] ◆ *s* fuerza ▸ **sales force** personal de ventas ▸ **security forces** fuerzas de seguridad • **by force** a la fuerza • **to be in/come into force** estar/entrar en vigor • **in force** en masa; en gran número ◆ *vt* forzar • **to force your way through/into** abrirse paso a la fuerza a través de/para entrar en

■ **forces** *spl* • **the forces** las fuerzas armadas
expresión to join forces (with) unirse (con)

forceful [ˈfɔːsful] *adj* ❶ fuerte ❷ enérgico, ca ❸ contundente

forcibly [ˈfɔːsəblɪ] *adv* ❶ por la fuerza ❷ convincentemente

ford [fɔːd] *s* vado

forearm [ˈfɔːrɑːm] *s* antebrazo

forecast [ˈfɔːkɑːst] ◆ *s* ❶ predicción; previsión ❷ pronóstico ◆ *vt* ❶ predecir ❷ pronosticar
Formas irregulares de **forecast**: *pretérito & pp* **forecast** o **forecasted**.

forefinger [ˈfɔːˌfɪŋgər] *s* (dedo) índice

forefront [ˈfɔːfrʌnt] *s* • **in** o **at the forefront of** en o a la vanguardia de

forego [fɔːˈgəʊ] = **forgo**

foregone conclusion [ˈfɔːgɒn-] *s* • **it's a foregone conclusion** es un resultado conocido de antemano

foreground [ˈfɔːgraʊnd] *s* primer plano

forehead [ˈfɔːhed] *s* frente

foreign [ˈfɒrən] *adj* ❶ extranjero, ra ❷ exterior; en el extranjero ❸ extraño, ña ❹ • **foreign (to somebody/something)** ajeno, na (a alguien/algo)

foreigner [ˈfɒrənər] *s* extranjero, ra

foreman [ˈfɔːmən] *s* ❶ encargado ❷ presidente
El plural de **foreman** es **foremen** [ˈfɔːmen].

foremost [ˈfɔːməʊst] ◆ *adj* primero, ra ◆ *adv* • **first and foremost** ante todo; por encima de todo

forerunner [ˈfɔːˌrʌnər] *s* precursor, ra

foresee [fɔːˈsiː] *vt* prever
Formas irregulares de **foresee**: *pretérito* **foresaw** [fɔːˈsɔː], *pp* **foreseen**.

foreseeable [fɔːˈsiːəbl] *adj* previsible • **for** o **in the foreseeable future** en un futuro próximo

foreseen [fɔːˈsiːn] *participio pasado* → **foresee**

foreshadow [fɔːˈʃædəʊ] *vt* presagiar

foresight [ˈfɔːsaɪt] *s* ☞*incontable* previsión

forest [ˈfɒrɪst] *s* bosque

forestall [fɔːˈstɔːl] *vt* anticiparse a

foretell [fɔːˈtel] *vt* predecir
Formas irregulares de **foretell**: *pret & pp* **foretold**.

forever [fəˈrevər] *adv* ❶ para siempre ❷ *familiar* siempre; continuamente

forewarn [fɔːˈwɔːn] *vt* prevenir

foreword [ˈfɔːwɜːd] *s* prefacio

forfeit [ˈfɔːfɪt] ◆ *s* ❶ precio ❷ prenda ◆ *vt* renunciar a; perder

forgave [fəˈgeɪv] *pretérito* → **forgive**

forge [fɔːdʒ] ◆ *s* fragua ◆ *vt* ❶ fraguar ❷ falsificar

■ **forge ahead** *vi* hacer grandes progresos

forger [ˈfɔːdʒər] *s* falsificador, ra

forgery [ˈfɔːdʒərɪ] *s* falsificación

forget [fəˈget] ◆ *vt* • **to forget (to do something)** olvidar (hacer algo) ◆ *vi* • **to forget (about something)** olvidarse (de algo)
Formas irregulares de **forget**: *pretérito* **forgot**, *pp* **forgotten**.

forgetful [fəˈgetful] *adj* olvidadizo, za

forgive [fəˈgɪv] *vt* • **to forgive somebody (for something/for doing something)** perdonar a alguien (algo/por haber hecho algo)
Formas irregulares de **forgive**: *pretérito* **forgave**, *pp* **forgiven**.

forgiveness [fəˈgɪvnɪs] *s* perdón

forgo, forego [fɔːˈgəʊ] *vt* sacrificar; renunciar a
Formas irregulares de **forgo/forego**: *pretérito* **forwent**, *pp* **forgone** [fɔːˈgɒn].

forgot [fəˈgɒt] *pretérito* → **forget**

forgotten [fəˈgɒtn] *participio pasado* → **forget**

fork [fɔːk] ◆ *s* ❶ tenedor ❷ horca ❸ bifurcación ◆ *vi* bifurcarse

■ **fork out** *vi familiar* • **to fork out for something** soltar pelas para algo

forklift truck [ˈfɔːklɪft-] *s* carretilla elevadora

form [fɔːm] ◆ *s* ❶ forma • **in the form of** en forma de ❷ • **in form** en forma • **off form** en baja forma ❸ impreso; formulario ❹ figura ◆ *vt* ❶ formar ❷ concebir ◆ *vi* formarse

formal [ˈfɔːml] *adj* ❶ formal ❷ convencional ❸ de etiqueta

formality [fɔːˈmælətɪ] *s* formalidad

format [ˈfɔːmæt] ◆ *s* ❶ formato ❷ plan ◆ *vt* INFORMÁTICA formatear

formation [fɔːˈmeɪʃn] *s* formación

formative [ˈfɔːmətɪv] *adj* formativo, va

former [ˈfɔːmər] ◆ *adj* ❶ antiguo, gua • **in former times** antiguamente ❷ primero, ra ◆ *s* • **the former** el primero, la primera/los primeros, las primeras

formerly [ˈfɔːməlɪ] *adv* antiguamente

formidable [ˈfɔːmɪdəbl] *adj* ❶ imponente; temible ❷ formidable

formula [ˈfɔːmjʊlə] *s* ❶ fórmula ❷ leche maternizada
Dos plurales: **formulas** o **formulae** [ˈfɔːmjʊliː].

formulate [ˈfɔːmjʊleɪt] *vt* formular

forsake [fəˈseɪk] *vt literario* abandonar
Formas irregulares de **forsake**: *pretérito* **forsook**, *pp* **forsaken**.

forsaken [fəˈseɪkn] *adj* abandonado, da

forsook [fəˈsʊk] *pretérito* → **forsake**

fort [fɔːt] *s* fuerte; fortaleza
expresión to hold the fort (for somebody) quedarse al cargo (en lugar de alguien).

Fort Knox

La base militar de **Fort Knox**, en Kentucky, alberga los lingotes de las reservas de oro de EE. UU. El nombre Fort Knox se emplea a menudo en sentido figurado para dar a entender que un lugar está celosamente vigilado o es inexpugnable: "their house has so many burglar alarms it's like Fort Knox" ("su casa tiene tantas alarmas que parece Fort Knox").

forte ['fɔːtɪ] *s* fuerte

forthcoming [fɔːθ'kʌmɪŋ] *adj* ❶ próximo, ma ❷ de próxima aparición ❸ abierto, ta

forthright ['fɔːθraɪt] *adj* directo, ta; franco, ca

fortify ['fɔːtɪfaɪ] *vt* ❶ MILITAR fortificar ❷ fortalecer

fortnight ['fɔːtnaɪt] *s* quincena • **in a fortnight** en quince días

fortnightly ['fɔːt,naɪtlɪ] ♦ *adj* quincenal ♦ *adv* quincenalmente

fortress ['fɔːtrɪs] *s* fortaleza

fortunate ['fɔːtʃnət] *adj* afortunado, da

fortunately ['fɔːtʃnətlɪ] *adv* afortunadamente

fortune ['fɔːtʃuːn] *s* ❶ fortuna ❷ • **to tell somebody's fortune** decir a alguien la buenaventura

fortune-teller [-,telər] *s* adivino, na

forty ['fɔːtɪ] *número* cuarenta ver también **sixty**

forward ['fɔːwəd] ♦ *adj* ❶ hacia adelante ❷ delantero, ra ❸ • **forward planning** planificación (de futuro) ❹ • **we're no further forward** no hemos adelantado (nada) ♦ *adv* hacia adelante • **to go** o **move forward** avanzar ♦ *s* DEPORTE delantero, ra ♦ *vt* remitir • **'please forward'** 'remítase al destinatario'

forwarding address ['fɔːwədɪŋ-] *s* nueva dirección *(para reenvío de correo)*

forwards ['fɔːwədz] *adv* = **forward**

forward slash *s* TIPOGRAFÍA barra inclinada

forwent [fɔː'went] *pretérito* → **forgo**

fossil ['fɒsl] *s* fósil

foster ['fɒstər] *vt* ❶ acoger ❷ promover

foster child *s* menor en régimen de acogida

foster parents *spl* familia de acogida

fought [fɔːt] *pretérito & participio pasado* → **fight**

foul [faʊl] ♦ *adj* ❶ fétido, da; asqueroso, sa; sucio, cia ❷ horrible • **to fall foul of somebody** ponerse a mal con alguien ♦ *s* falta ♦ *vt* ❶ ensuciar ❷ DEPORTE cometer una falta contra

found [faʊnd] ♦ *pretérito & participio pasado* → **find** ♦ *vt* • **to found something (on)** fundar algo (en)

foundation [faʊn'deɪʃn] *s* ❶ fundación ❷ fundamento; base ❸ ▸ **foundation (cream)** crema base
■ **foundations** *spl figurado* CONSTRUCCIÓN cimientos

founder ['faʊndər] *s* fundador, ra

fountain ['faʊntɪn] *s* ❶ fuente ❷ chorro

four [fɔːr] *número* cuatro • **on all fours** a gatas ver también **six**

foursome ['fɔːsəm] *s* grupo de cuatro personas

fourteen [,fɔː'tiːn] *número* catorce ver también **six**

fourth [fɔːθ] *número* cuarto, ta ver también **sixth**

Fourth of July *s* • **the Fourth of July** el cuatro de julio, día de la independencia de los Estados Unidos

THE FOURTH OF JULY

F

El 4 de julio o **Fourth of July**, también llamado **Independence Day**, es una de las fiestas nacionales de mayor importancia en los Estados Unidos; conmemora el momento en que los Estados Unidos declaró su independencia de Inglaterra en el año 1776. Como parte de los festejos se organizan desfiles por las calles, y por la noche se encienden castillos de fuegos artificiales en los que predominan los colores rojo, blanco y azul. Los edificios se decoran con adornos de estos mismos colores o con banderas estadounidenses.

four-way stop *s* cruce *(de cuatro stops)*

fowl [faʊl] *s* ave de corral
Dos plurales: **fowl** o **fowls**.

fox [fɒks] ♦ *s* zorro ♦ *vt* dejar perplejo, ja

foyer ['fɔɪeɪ] *s* vestíbulo

fraction ['frækʃn] *s* ❶ MATEMÁTICAS quebrado; fracción ❷ fracción

fractionally ['frækʃnəlɪ] *adv* ligeramente

fracture ['fræktʃər] ♦ *s* fractura ♦ *vt* fracturar

fragile ['frædʒaɪl] *adj* frágil

fragment *s* ['frægmənt] ❶ fragmento ❷ trozo

fragrance ['freɪgrəns] *s* fragancia

fragrant ['freɪgrənt] *adj* fragante

frail [freɪl] *adj* frágil

frame [freɪm] ♦ *s* ❶ marco ❷ armazón ❸ base ♦ *vt* ❶ enmarcar ❷ expresar ❸ *familiar* tender una trampa a; amañar la culpabilidad de

framework ['freɪmwɜːk] *s* ❶ armazón; esqueleto ❷ marco

France [frɑːns] *s* Francia

frank [fræŋk] *adj* franco, ca

frankly ['fræŋklɪ] *adv* francamente

frantic ['fræntɪk] *adj* frenético, ca

fraternity [frə'tɜːnətɪ] *s* ❶ asociación de estudiantes que suele funcionar como club social ❷ ⚲ *incontable formal* fraternidad

FRATERNITY

Los clubes de estudiantes masculinos (**fraternities**) son un elemento sobresaliente de la vida social universitaria estadounidense. Cada club posee su propio nombre, constituido por letras del alfabeto griego y tiene su sede en el edificio donde reside la mayoría de sus miembros. Estos clubes realizan trabajos para instituciones de asistencia social, pero también son famosas sus juergas con alcohol y sus ceremonias secretas. Algunas universidades han decidido prohibirlos porque sus ceremonias de iniciación incluían novatadas crueles y peligrosas.

fraud [frɔːd] s ❶ :ᵍ: *incontable* fraude ❷ *despectivo* farsante

fraught [frɔːt] *adj* • **fraught with** lleno, na o cargado, da de

fray [freɪ] ◆ *vt figurado* crispar; poner de punta ◆ *vi* ❶ deshilacharse ❷ *figurado* crisparse

frayed [freɪd] *adj* deshilachado, da

freak [friːk] ◆ *adj* imprevisible ◆ *s* ❶ monstruo; estrafalario, ria ❷ anormalidad; caso insólito ❸ *familiar* • **fitness freak** fanático, ca del ejercicio
■ **freak out** *vi familiar* espantarse

freckle ['frekl] *s* peca

free [friː] ◆ *adj* (*comparativo* freer, *superlativo* freest) ❶ • **free (from** o **of)** libre (de) • **to be free to do something** ser libre de hacer algo • **feel free!** ¡adelante!; ¡cómo no! • **to set free** liberar ❷ gratis; gratuito, ta • **free of charge** gratis ❸ suelto, ta ◆ *adv* ❶ • (**for) free** gratis ❷ libremente ❸ • **to pull/cut something free** soltar algo jalando/cortando ◆ *vt* ❶ liberar; libertar • **to free somebody of something** librar a alguien de algo ❷ dejar libre ❸ rescatar; soltar

freedom ['friːdəm] *s* libertad • **freedom from** indemnidad ante o de

free-for-all *s* refriega

free gift *s* obsequio

freehand ['friːhænd] *adj & adv* a pulso

free kick *s* tiro libre

freely ['friːlɪ] *adv* ❶ sin reparos; fácilmente ❷ abiertamente; francamente ❸ libremente ❹ liberalmente

free-range *adj* de granja

freestyle ['friːstaɪl] *s* estilo libre

free trade *s* libre cambio

freeway ['friːweɪ] *s* autopista

freewheel [ˌfriːˈwiːl] *vi* ❶ andar sin pedalear ❷ ir en punto muerto

free will *s* libre albedrío
expresión **to do something of your own free will** hacer algo por voluntad propia

freeze [friːz] ◆ *vt* ❶ helar ❷ congelar ❸ bloquear ◆ *vi* ❶ helarse ❷ INFORMÁTICA bloquearse ◆ *v impersonal* METEOROLOGÍA helar ◆ *s* ❶ helada ❷ congelación

Formas irregulares de **freeze**: *pretérito* **froze**, *pp* **frozen**.

freezer ['friːzər] *s* congelador

freezing ['friːzɪŋ] *adj* ❶ helado, da ❷ muy frío, a • **it's freezing in here** hace un frío espantoso aquí

freezing point *s* punto de congelación

freight [freɪt] *s* :ᵍ: *incontable* ❶ mercancías; flete ❷ transporte

French [frentʃ] ◆ *adj* francés, esa ◆ *s* francés ◆ *spl* • **the French** los franceses

French bean *s* ejote

French bread *s* :ᵍ: *incontable* pan de barra

French dressing *s* vinagreta

French fries, fries *spl* papas fritas *(de sartén)*

Frenchman ['frentʃmən] *s* francés
El plural de **Frenchman** es **Frenchmen** ['frentʃmen].

Frenchwoman ['frentʃwʊmən] *s* francesa
El plural de **Frenchwoman** es **Frenchwomen** ['frentʃwɪmɪn].

frenetic [frəˈnetɪk] *adj* frenético, ca

frenzy ['frenzɪ] *s* frenesí

frequency ['friːkwənsɪ] *s* frecuencia

frequent ◆ *adj* ['friːkwənt] frecuente ◆ *vt* [frɪˈkwent] frecuentar

frequently ['friːkwəntlɪ] *adv* a menudo

fresh [freʃ] *adj* ❶ fresco, ca ❷ refrescante *(sabor)* ❸ • **fresh bread** pan del día ❹ dulce *(agua)*

freshen ['freʃn] *vt* refrescar
■ **freshen up** *vi* refrescarse

freshly ['freʃlɪ] *adv* recién

freshman ['freʃmən] *s* estudiante de primer año
El plural de **freshman** es **freshmen** ['freʃmen].

freshness ['freʃnɪs] *s* :ᵍ: *incontable* ❶ frescura ❷ novedad ❸ frescor

freshwater ['freʃˌwɔːtər] *adj* de agua dulce

fret [fret] *vi* preocuparse

friction ['frɪkʃn] *s* fricción

Friday ['fraɪdɪ] *s* viernes ver también **Saturday**

fried [fraɪd] *adj* frito, ta

friend [frend] *s* amigo, ga • **to be friends with somebody** ser amigo de alguien • **to make friends (with)** hacerse amigo (de); trabar amistad (con)

friendly ['frendlɪ] *adj* ❶ amable; simpático, ca ❷ amistoso, sa *(partido, relación)*
expresión **to be friendly with somebody** llevarse bien con alguien

friendship ['frendʃɪp] *s* amistad

fries [fraɪz] = **French fries**

fright [fraɪt] *s* ❶ miedo ❷ susto
expresión **to take fright** espantarse; asustarse

frighten ['fraɪtn] *vt* asustar • **to frighten somebody into doing something** atemorizar a alguien para que haga algo

frightened ['fraɪtnd] *adj* asustado, da • **to be frightened of something/of doing something** tener miedo a algo/a hacer algo

frightening ['fraɪtnɪŋ] *adj* aterrador, ra; espantoso, sa

frightful ['fraɪtfʊl] *adj* desusado terrible

frigid ['frɪdʒɪd] *adj* frígido, da

frill [frɪl] *s* ❶ volante ❷ familiar adorno

fringe [frɪndʒ] ◆ *s* ❶ flecos ❷ periferia ❸ margen ◆ *vt* bordear

frisk [frɪsk] *vt* cachear; registrar

frisky ['frɪskɪ] *adj* familiar juguetón, ona

fritter ['frɪtər] *s* buñuelo

■ **fritter away** *vt* ☼: *El objeto se puede colocar antes o después de la preposición.* • **to fritter money/time away on something** malgastar dinero/tiempo en algo

frivolous ['frɪvələs] *adj* frívolo, la

frog [frɒg] *s* rana

from
◆ *preposición*

☼: *acento atónico* [frəm], *acento tónico* [frɒm]

❶ [indica el origen] de
• **where are you from?** ¿de dónde eres?
• **she's from Italy** es italiana; es de Italia

❷ [indica la procedencia]
• **I got a letter from her today** recibí una carta suya ayer
• **the 10 o'clock flight from Paris has just arrived** el vuelo de las 10 de París acaba de llegar

❸ [indica un punto de partida en el tiempo]
• **we worked from 2 pm to** o **till 6 pm** trabajamos de 2 de la tarde a 6 de la tarde
• **from the moment I saw him, I was in love** me enamoré desde el momento en el que lo vi

❹ [indica un punto de partida en el espacio]
• **it's 60 km from here** está a 60 km de aquí
• **seen from above/below, it seems much smaller** visto desde arriba/abajo, parece mucho más pequeño
• **he ran away from home** se escapó de casa

❺ [indica un punto de partida de forma más general]
• **prices start from 50 pesos** los precios comienzan a partir de los 50 pesos
• **you must translate from Spanish into English** tienes que traducir del español al inglés
• **he started drinking from a glass very early** comenzó a beber en vaso desde muy temprano

❻ [indica una protección, un impedimento]
• **a tree gave us shelter from the rain** un árbol nos protegía de la lluvia
• **he prevented her from coming** le impidió venir

❼ [indica una diferencia]
• **he is quite different from the others** es bastante diferente de los otros
• **the two sisters are so similar it's almost impossible to tell one from another** las dos hermanas son tan parecidas que es imposible diferenciarlas

❽ [indica un cambio, una modificación]
• **the price went up from $100 to $150** el precio pasó de 100 a 150 dólares
• **things got from bad to worse** las cosas fueron de mal en peor

❾ [indica el material]
• **it's made from wood/plastic** es de madera/plástico

❿ [introduce la causa]
• **too many people still suffer from cold/hunger** demasiada gente todavía sigue pasando frío/hambre
• **he died from his injuries** murió de las heridas recibidas

⓫ [introduce una referencia, un punto de vista]
• **from what I have heard, this is a very arduous task** por lo que he oído, es un trabajo muy arduo
• **from his point of view, she'll never help you** desde su punto de vista, ella nunca te ayudará

front [frʌnt] ◆ *s* ❶ parte delantera ❷ fachada ❸ principio ❹ parte de delante ❺ METEOROLOGÍA, MILITAR & POLÍTICA frente ❻ fachada ◆ *adj* ❶ delantero, ra ❷ primero, ra

■ **in front** *adv* ❶ delante ❷ ganando

■ **in front of** *preposición* delante de

front door *s* puerta principal

frontier [frʌn'tɪər] *s* literal & figurado frontera

front-runner *s* favorito, ta

frost [frɒst] *s* ❶ escarcha ❷ helada

frostbite ['frɒstbaɪt] *s* ☼: *incontable* MEDICINA congelación

frosting ['frɒstɪŋ] *s* glaseado; betún

frosty ['frɒstɪ] *adj* ❶ de helada ❷ escarchado, da ❸ figurado glacial

froth [frɒθ] ◆ *s* espuma ◆ *vi* hacer espuma

frown [fraʊn] *vi* fruncir el ceño

■ **frown (up)on** *vt* ☼: *El objeto siempre va después de la preposición al final.* desaprobar

froze [frəʊz] *pretérito* → freeze

frozen [frəʊzn] ◆ *participio pasado* → freeze ◆ *adj* ❶ helado, da ❷ congelado, da

frugal ['fruːgl] *adj* frugal

fruit [fruːt] *s* ❶ fruta ❷ fruto
Dos plurales: **fruit** o **fruits.**

fruitcake ['fruːtkeɪk] *s* pastel de frutas

fruitful ['fruːtfʊl] *adj* fructífero, ra

fruition [fruː'ɪʃn] *s* • **to come to fruition a)** realizarse **b)** cumplirse

fruit juice *s* jugo de fruta

fruitless ['fruːtlɪs] *adj* infructuoso, sa

fruit salad *s* ensalada (de frutas)

frustrate [frʌ'streɪt] *vt* frustrar

frustrated [frʌ'streɪtɪd] *adj* frustrado, da

frustration [frʌ'streɪʃn] *s* frustración

F

fry [fraɪ] ◆ *vt* freír ◆ *vi* freírse

frying pan ['fraɪɪŋ-] *s* sartén

ft. *abreviatura escrita de* **foot**

fudge [fʌdʒ] *s* ✑ *incontable* dulce de azúcar, leche y mantequilla

fuel [fjʊəl] ◆ *s* combustible ◆ *vt* ❶ alimentar ❷ agravar

Formas irregulares de **fuel**: *pretérito & pp* **fueled**, *gerundio* **fueling**.

fuel tank *s* depósito de gasolina

fugitive ['fjuːdʒətɪv] *s* fugitivo, va

fulfill [fʊl'fɪl] *vt* ❶ cumplir *(promesa, obligación)* ❷ realizar *(ambición, deseo)* ❸ cumplir con *(deber)* ❹ desempeñar *(papel)* ❺ satisfacer *(requisitos)*

fulfillment [fʊl'fɪlmənt] *s* ❶ satisfacción; realización *(propia)* ❷ cumplimiento *(de promesa, obligación)* ❸ realización *(de ambición, deseo)* ❹ desempeño *(de papel)* ❺ satisfacción *(de requisitos)*

full [fʊl] ◆ *adj* ❶ • **full (of)** lleno, na (de) • **I'm full!** ¡no puedo más! ❷ completo, ta ❸ pleno, na; completo, ta; detallado, da; numerario, ria • **three full weeks** tres semanas enteras ❹ máximo, ma • **at full speed** a toda velocidad ❺ grueso, sa ❻ holgado, da; amplio, plia ◆ *adv* • **to know something full well** saber algo perfectamente ◆ *s* • **to pay in full** pagar el total • **write your name in full** escriba su nombre y apellidos

full board *s* pensión completa

full moon *s* luna llena

full-scale *adj* ❶ de tamaño natural ❷ a gran escala

full-size(d) *adj* AUTOMÓVILES ▶ **full-sized car** sedán

full stop *s* punto

full-time *adj* & *adv* a tiempo completo

full up *adj* lleno, na

fully ['fʊlɪ] *adv* ❶ completamente ❷ detalladamente

fumble ['fʌmbl] *vi* hurgar

fume [fjuːm] *vi* rabiar

■ **fumes** *spl* humo

fumigate ['fjuːmɪgeɪt] *vt* fumigar

fun [fʌn] *s* ✑ *incontable* ❶ diversión • **my uncle/ parachuting is great fun** mi tío/el paracaidismo es muy divertido • **to have fun** divertirse • **have fun!** ¡que te diviertas! • **for fun, for the fun of it** por diversión ❷ • **he's full of fun** le encanta todo lo que sea diversión ❸ • **to make fun of somebody, to poke fun at somebody** reírse o burlarse de alguien

function ['fʌŋkʃn] ◆ *s* ❶ función ▶ **function key** INFORMÁTICA tecla de función ❷ acto ◆ *vi* funcionar • **to function as** hacer de

functional ['fʌŋkʃnəl] *adj* ❶ funcional ❷ en funcionamiento

fund [fʌnd] ◆ *s* fondo ◆ *vt* financiar

■ **funds** *spl* fondos

fundamental [ˌfʌndə'mentl] *adj* • **fundamental (to)** fundamental (para)

funding ['fʌndɪŋ] *s* ❶ financiación ❷ fondos

funeral ['fjuːnərəl] *s* funeral

funeral parlor *s* funeraria

funfair ['fʌnfeəʳ] *s* feria

fungus ['fʌŋgəs] *s* hongo

Dos plurales: **fungi** ['fʌŋgaɪ] o **funguses**.

funnel ['fʌnl] *s* ❶ embudo ❷ chimenea

funny ['fʌnɪ] *adj* ❶ divertido, da • **I don't think that's funny** no me cae en gracia ❷ raro, ra

fur [fɜːʳ] *s* ❶ pelaje; pelo ❷ (prenda de) piel

fur coat *s* abrigo de piel o pieles

furious ['fjʊərɪəs] *adj* ❶ furioso, sa ❷ frenético, ca

furnace ['fɜːnɪs] *s* horno

furnish ['fɜːnɪʃ] *vt* ❶ amueblar ❷ *formal* proveer; aducir • **to furnish somebody with something** proporcionar algo a alguien

furnished ['fɜːnɪʃt] *adj* amueblado, da

furnishings ['fɜːnɪʃɪŋz] *spl* mobiliario

furniture ['fɜːnɪtʃəʳ] *s* ✑ *incontable* muebles; mobiliario • **a piece of furniture** un mueble

furrow ['fʌrəʊ] *s* *literal & figurado* surco

furry ['fɜːrɪ] *adj* ❶ peludo, da ❷ de peluche

further ['fɜːðəʳ] ◆ *comparativo* → **far** ◆ *adv* ❶ más lejos • **how much further is it?** ¿cuánto queda? • **further on** más adelante ❷ más • **further on/back** más adelante/atrás ❸ además ◆ *adj* otro, tra • **until further notice** hasta nuevo aviso • **nothing further** nada más ◆ *vt* promover; fomentar

furthermore [ˌfɜːðə'mɔːʳ] *adv* lo que es más

furthest ['fɜːðɪst] ◆ *superlativo* → **far** ◆ *adj* ❶ más lejano, na ❷ extremo, ma ◆ *adv* ❶ más lejos ❷ más

furtive ['fɜːtɪv] *adj* furtivo, va

fury ['fjʊərɪ] *s* furia

fuse [fjuːz] ◆ *s* ❶ ELECTRICIDAD fusible ❷ mecha ◆ *vt* fundir ◆ *vi* fundirse

fuse-box *s* caja de fusibles

fused [fjuːzd] *adj* con fusible

fuselage ['fjuːzəlɑːʒ] *s* fuselaje

fuss [fʌs] ◆ *s* ✑ *incontable* ❶ alboroto • **to make a fuss** armar un escándalo ❷ protestas ◆ *vi* apurarse; angustiarse

fussy ['fʌsɪ] *adj* ❶ quisquilloso, sa • **I'm not fussy** me da lo mismo ❷ recargado, da

futile ['fjuːtaɪl] *adj* inútil; vano, na

futon ['fuːtɒn] *s* futón

future ['fjuːtʃəʳ] ◆ *s* futuro • **in future** de ahora en adelante • **in the future** en el futuro • **in the not too distant future** en un futuro próximo ▶ **future (tense)** futuro ◆ *adj* futuro, ra

fuzzy ['fʌzɪ] *adj* ❶ crespo, pa ❷ borroso, sa

G

g¹, G [dʒiː] *s* g; G

■ **G** *s* CINE *(abreviatura escrita de* general (audience)) para todos los públicos

■ **G** *s* ❶ MÚSICA sol ❷ *(abreviatura escrita de* good) B.

Dos plurales: g's o gs; G's o Gs.

g² *s* *(abreviatura escrita de* gram) g.

gadget ['gædʒɪt] *s* artilugio; aparato

gag [gæg] ♦ *s* ❶ mordaza ❷ *familiar* chiste ♦ *vt* amordazar

gage [geɪdʒ] ♦ *s* ❶ indicador ❷ calibrador ❸ calibre ❹ FERROCARRIL ancho de vía ♦ *vt* *literal & figurado* calibrar

gain [geɪn] ♦ *s* ❶ beneficio; ganancia ❷ mejora ❸ aumento ♦ *vt* ganar ♦ *vi* ❶ • **to gain in something** ganar algo ❷ • **to gain (from** o **by)** beneficiarse (de) ❸ adelantarse

■ **gain on** *vt* ⚙ *El objeto siempre va después de la preposición al final.* ganar terreno a

gal. *abreviatura escrita de* **gallon**

gala ['gɑːlə] *s* fiesta

galaxy ['gæləksɪ] *s* galaxia

gale [geɪl] *s* vendaval

gallant *adj* ❶ ['gælənt] valiente; valeroso, sa ❷ [gə'lænt] ['gælənt] galante

gallery ['gælərɪ] *s* ❶ museo ❷ galería ❸ tribuna

galley ['gælɪ] *s* ❶ galera ❷ cocina

El plural de galley es galleys.

gallon ['gælən] *s* galón *(3,785 litros)*

gallop ['gæləp] ♦ *s* galope ♦ *vi* *literal & figurado* galopar

gallows ['gæləʊz] *s* horca

El plural de gallows es gallows.

gamble ['gæmbl] ♦ *s* riesgo ♦ *vi* ❶ jugar • **to gamble on a)** apostar a **b)** jugar a ❷ • **to gamble on** contar de antemano con que

gambler ['gæmblər] *s* jugador, ra

gambling ['gæmblɪŋ] *s* ⚙ *incontable* juego

game [geɪm] ♦ *s* ❶ juego ❷ partido ❸ partida ❹ caza ♦ *adj* ❶ valiente ❷ • **game (for something/to do something)** dispuesto, ta (a algo/a hacer algo)

■ **games** ♦ *s* ⚙ *incontable* deportes ♦ *spl* juegos

games console *s* consola de juegos

gaming ['geɪmɪŋ] *s* ⚙ *incontable* juegos

gang [gæŋ] *s* ❶ banda ❷ pandilla

■ **gang up** *vi* *familiar* • **to gang up (on somebody)** confabularse (contra alguien)

gangster ['gæŋstər] *s* gángster

gap [gæp] *s* ❶ hueco ❷ claro ❸ espacio en blanco ❹ intervalo ❺ *figurado* laguna ❻ brecha

gape [geɪp] *vi* mirar boquiabierto, ta

gaping ['geɪpɪŋ] *adj* ❶ boquiabierto, ta ❷ abierto, ta ❸ enorme

garage ['gærɑːdʒ] [gə'rɑːʒ] *s* ❶ garage ❷ taller

garbage ['gɑːbɪdʒ] *s* ⚙ *incontable* ❶ basura ❷ *familiar* tonterías

garbage can *s* bote de la basura

garbage truck *s* camión de la basura

garden ['gɑːdn] *s* jardín

gardener ['gɑːdnər] *s* jardinero, ra

gardening ['gɑːdnɪŋ] *s* jardinería • **to do some gardening** trabajar en el jardín

gargle ['gɑːgl] *vi* hacer gárgaras

garish ['geərɪʃ] *adj* chillón, ona

garland ['gɑːlənd] *s* guirnalda

garlic ['gɑːlɪk] *s* ajo

garlic bread *s* pan de ajo

garment ['gɑːmənt] *s* prenda (de vestir)

garnish ['gɑːnɪʃ] *vt* guarnecer

garrison ['gærɪsn] *s* guarnición

gas [gæs] ♦ *s* ❶ gas ❷ gasolina ♦ *vt* asfixiar con gas

Dos plurales: gases o gasses.

gash [gæʃ] ♦ *s* raja ♦ *vt* rajar

gasoline ['gæsəliːn] *s* gasolina

gasp [gɑːsp] ♦ *s* ❶ resuello ❷ grito ahogado ♦ *vi* ❶ resollar; jadear ❷ ahogar un grito

gas pedal *s* acelerador

gas station *s* gasolinera

gas stove *s* cocina de gas

gas tank *s* depósito de gasolina

gas tap *s* llave del gas

gastronomy [gæs'trɒnəmı] *s* gastronomía

gate [geɪt] *s* **①** puerta **②** verja **③** *DEPORTE* taquilla **④** sala de abordar

gatecrash ['geɪtkræʃ] *vi familiar* colarse

gateway ['geɪtweɪ] *s* **①** puerta; pórtico **②** *INFOR-MÁTICA* pasarela

gather ['gæðər] ◆ *vt* **①** recoger • **to gather together** reunir **②** llenarse de **③** ganar; cobrar **④** • **to gather (that)** deducir que **⑤** fruncir ◆ *vi* **①** reunirse **②** acumularse

gathering ['gæðərɪŋ] *s* reunión

gaudy ['gɔ:dɪ] *adj* chillón, ona; llamativo, va

gaunt [gɔ:nt] *adj* **①** demacrado, da **②** adusto, ta

gauntlet ['gɔ:ntlɪt] *s* guante

expresión **to run the gauntlet of something** exponerse a algo ▸ **to throw down the gauntlet (to somebody)** arrojar el guante (a alguien)

gauze [gɔ:z] *s* gasa

gave [geɪv] *pretérito* → **give**

gay [geɪ] ◆ *adj* **①** gay; homosexual **②** alegre ◆ *s* gay

gaze [geɪz] ◆ *s* mirada fija ◆ *vi* • **to gaze (at something/somebody)** mirar fijamente (algo/a alguien)

gear [gɪər] ◆ *s* **①** velocidad • **in gear** con una velocidad metida • **out of gear** en punto muerto • **to change gear** cambiar de velocidad **②** ☀️ *incontable* equipo ◆ *vt* • **to gear something to** orientar o encaminar algo hacia

■ **gear up** *vi* • **to gear up for something/to do something** hacer preparativos para algo/para hacer algo

gearbox ['gɪəbɒks] *s* caja de velocidades

gear shift *s* palanca de velocidades

geek [gi:k] *s familiar* matadito, ta

geese [gi:s] *spl* → **goose**

gel [dʒel] *s* gel

gem [dʒem] *s* **①** gema **②** joya

Gemini ['dʒemɪnaɪ] *s* Géminis

gender ['dʒendər] *s* **①** *GRAMÁTICA* género **②** sexo

gene [dʒi:n] *s* gen

general ['dʒenərəl] ◆ *adj* general ◆ *s* general

■ **in general** *adv* **①** en general **②** por lo general

general election *s* elecciones generales

generalization [ˌdʒenərəlaɪ'zeɪʃn] *s* generalización

general knowledge *s* cultura general

generally ['dʒenərəlı] *adv* en general

general public *s* • **the general public** el gran público

generate ['dʒenəreɪt] *vt* generar

generation [ˌdʒenə'reɪʃn] *s* generación

generator ['dʒenəreɪtər] *s* generador

generosity [ˌdʒenə'rɒsətı] *s* generosidad

generous ['dʒenərəs] *adj* **①** generoso, sa **②** amplio, plia

genetic [dʒɪ'netɪk] *adj* genético, ca

■ **genetics** *s* ☀️ *incontable* genética

genetically modified [dʒɪ'netɪkəlɪ'mɒdɪfaɪd] *adj* modificado, da genéticamente; transgénico, ca

genial ['dʒi:njəl] *adj* cordial; afable

genitals ['dʒenɪtlz] *spl* genitales

genius ['dʒi:njəs] *s* genio

gentle ['dʒentl] *adj* **①** tierno, na; dulce **②** suave **③** ligero, ra **④** sutil

gentleman ['dʒentlmən] *s* **①** caballero **②** señor; caballero

El plural de **gentleman** es **gentlemen** ['dʒentlmən].

gently ['dʒentlɪ] *adv* **①** dulcemente **②** suavemente **③** con cuidado

genuine ['dʒenjuɪn] *adj* **①** auténtico, ca **②** sincero, ra

geography [dʒɪ'ɒgrəfı] *s* geografía

geology [dʒɪ'ɒlədʒı] *s* geología

geometric(al) [ˌdʒɪə'metrɪk(l)] *adj* geométrico, ca

geometry [dʒɪ'ɒmətrı] *s* geometría

geranium [dʒɪ'reɪnjəm] *s* geranio

geriatric [ˌdʒerɪ'ætrɪk] ◆ *adj* geriátrico, ca ◆ *s* **①** *MEDICINA* anciano, na **②** *familiar* vejestorio

germ [dʒɜ:m] *s* **①** *figurado BIOLOGÍA* germen **②** *MEDICINA* microbio

German ['dʒɜ:mən] ◆ *adj* alemán, ana ◆ *s* **①** alemán, ana **②** alemán

German measles *s* rubeola

Germany ['dʒɜ:mənı] *s* Alemania

germinate ['dʒɜ:mıneɪt] *vt* & *vi literal* & *figurado* germinar

gerund ['dʒerənd] *s* gerundio

gesticulate [dʒes'tɪkjuleɪt] *vi* gesticular

gesture ['dʒestʃər] ◆ *s* gesto ◆ *vi* • **to gesture to** o **towards somebody** hacer gestos a alguien

get [get]
◆ *vt*

① [*recibir, obtener*]
• **what did you get for your birthday?** ¿qué te dieron para tu cumpleaños?
• **you need to get permission from the head teacher** tienes que tener permiso del director

② [*tener*]
• **do you get the feeling he doesn't like us?** ¿no tienes la impresión de que no le gustamos?
• **I got a chance to see my cousin when I was in Veracruz** tuve la ocasión de ver a mi primo cuando estaba en Veracruz

③ [*encontrar*]
• **they can't get work** no encuentran trabajo
• **it's difficult to get good players** es difícil encontrar buenos jugadores

❹ [*tener, coger, hablando de una enfermedad*]
• **he never gets the flu** nunca le da gripa

❺ [*ir a buscar*]
• **can I get you something to eat?** ¿te puedo traer algo para comer?
• **call me when you arrive and I'll go down and get you** llámame cuando llegues y bajaré a buscarte

❻ [*entender*]
• **I don't get it** *familiar* no lo entiendo
• **I don't get the joke** no entiendo el chiste

❼ [*hacer que hagan*]
• **I'll get my sister to help** haré que mi hermana nos ayude
• **I got my bike fixed** me arreglaron la bici

❽ [*indica un cambio de estado*]
• **your driving almost got us killed!** ¡tu forma de manejar casi nos mata!
• **I can't get the car started** no consigo que arranque el carro

◆ *vi*

❶ [*indica un cambio de estado*]
• **he got suspicious when he heard police sirens** comenzó a sospechar cuando oyó las sirenas de la policía
• **I'm getting cold/bored** me estoy enfriando/ aburriendo
• **it's getting late** se está haciendo tarde

❷ [*llegar, volver, en sentido literal*]
• **I got back yesterday** volví ayer
• **how do you get to the beach from here?** ¿cómo se va a la playa desde aquí?

❸ [*llegar, volver, en sentido figurado*]
• **did you get to see him?** ¿llegaste a verlo?
• **how far have you got?** ¿hasta dónde llegaste?

expresión **we're getting nowhere** no estamos progresando

◆ *auxiliar*

[*indica un cambio de estado*]
• **my dog gets excited when I come home** se emociona mi perro cuando llego a la casa
• **no one got hurt** nadie resultó herido
• **let's get going** o **moving** venga; vamos

■ **get along**
◆ *vi*
❶ arreglárselas

❷ [*progresar*]
• **how are you getting along?** ¿cómo te va?

❸ [*llevarse bien*]
• **to get along (with somebody)** llevarse bien (con alguien)

■ **get around, get round**
◆ *vt* :Q: *El objeto siempre va después de la preposición al final.*
[*superar - problema*] evitar; [*- obstáculo*] sortear
◆ *vi*
difundirse

■ **get at**
◆ *vt* :Q: *El objeto siempre va después de la preposición al final.*
❶ llegar a; alcanzar
❷ referirse a
❸ *familiar* [*criticar*]
• **stop getting at me!** ¡deja ya de meterte conmigo!

■ **get away**
◆ *vi*
❶ salir; irse
❷ escaparse

■ **get away with**
◆ *vt* :Q: *El objeto siempre va después de la preposición al final.*
salir impune de
• **she lets him get away with everything** ella se lo consiente todo

■ **get back**
◆ *vt* :Q: *El objeto se puede colocar antes o después de la preposición.*
recuperar
◆ *vi*
❶ echarse atrás; apartarse
❷ volver

■ **get back to**
◆ *vt* :Q: *El objeto siempre va después de la preposición al final.*
❶ volver a
❷ *familiar* [*por teléfono*]
• **I'll get back to you later** te llamo de vuelta más tarde

■ **get by**
◆ *vi*
arreglárselas

■ **get down**
◆ *vt* :Q: *El objeto se puede colocar antes o después de la preposición.*
❶ deprimir
❷ bajar
❸ anotar

■ **get down to**
◆ *vt* :Q: *El objeto siempre va después de la preposición al final.*
• **to get down to doing something** ponerse a hacer algo

■ **get in**
◆ *vi*
❶ entrar
❷ llegar

■ **get into**
◆ *vt* :Q: *El objeto siempre va después de la preposición al final.*
❶ subir a
❷ meterse en

G

G

❸ [*en situación, estado*]
• **to get into a panic** o **state** ponerse nerviosísimo, ma
• **to get into trouble** meterse en líos
• **to get into the habit of doing something** adquirir el hábito o coger la costumbre de hacer algo

❹ [*universidad*]
• **she managed to get into Oxford** consiguió entrar en Oxford

■ **get off**
◆ *vt* ☀ *El objeto se coloca entre el verbo y la preposición.*

❶ quitar
❷ librar
◆ *vt* ☀ *El objeto siempre va después de la preposición al final.*

❶ irse o salirse de
• **get off my land!** ¡fuera de mis tierras!
❷ bajarse de
◆ *vi*

❶ bajarse; desembarcarse
❷ escaparse; librarse
• **he got off lightly** salió bien librado
❸ irse; salir

■ **get on**
◆ *vt* ☀ *El objeto siempre va después de la preposición al final.*
subirse a
◆ *vi*

❶ subirse; montarse
❷ llevarse bien
❸ [*progresar*]
• **how are you getting on?** ¿cómo te va?
❹ seguir
• **to get on with something** seguir o continuar con algo
❺ triunfar

■ **get out**
◆ *vt* ☀ *El objeto se puede colocar antes o después de la preposición.*

❶ [*objeto*] sacar
❷ [*mancha*] quitar
❸
• **she got a pen out of her bag** sacó una pluma de la bolsa
◆ *vi*

❶ salir
• **get out!** ¡vete de aquí!
❷ bajarse
❸ difundirse; filtrarse

■ **get out of**
◆ *vt* ☀ *El objeto siempre va después de la preposición al final.*

❶ bajar de
❷ [*la cama*] levantarse de
❸ escapar o huir de

❹ [*evitar*]
• **to get out of (doing) something** librarse de (hacer) algo

■ **get over**
◆ *vt* ☀ *El objeto siempre va después de la preposición al final.*

❶ recuperarse de
❷ superar
◆ *vt* ☀ *El objeto se puede colocar antes o después de la preposición.*
hacer comprender

■ **get round**
◆ *vt*
= **get around**

■ **get through**
◆ *vt* ☀ *El objeto siempre va después de la preposición al final.*

❶ terminar
❷ aprobar
❸ consumir
❹ sobrevivir a
◆ *vi*
TELECOMUNICACIONES conseguir comunicar

■ **get to**
◆ *vt* ☀ *El objeto siempre va después de la preposición al final.*
familiar fastidiar; molestar
◆ *vi*
ir a parar

■ **get together**
◆ *vt* ☀ *El objeto se puede colocar antes o después de la preposición.*
organizar *(proyecto)*; montar; juntar *(equipo)*; preparar *(informe)*
◆ *vi*
juntarse; reunirse

■ **get up**
◆ *vi*
levantarse
◆ *vt* ☀ *El objeto siempre va después de la preposición al final.*
preparar; organizar

■ **get up to**
◆ *vt* ☀ *El objeto siempre va después de la preposición al final.*
familiar hacer; montar

---

get

En la lengua hablada, get se utiliza con más frecuencia que be en las oraciones pasivas que describen una acción más bien que un estado (they *got* married on Saturday *se casaron el sábado*; the window *got* broken last night *la ventana se rompió ayer*). También se usa a menudo para hablar de una acción que se hace a uno mismo (he *got* washed *se lavó*), o para decir que algo inesperado ha sucedido (he *got* left behind *se quedó atrás*). Hay gente que todavía considera este uso de get demasiado informal.

Formas irregulares de **get**: *pp* **gotten**.

getaway ['getəweɪ] *s* fuga; huida • **to make your getaway** darse a la fuga

get-together *s familiar* reunión

geyser ['giːzər] *s* géiser

Ghana ['gɑːnə] *s* Ghana

ghastly ['gɑːstlɪ] *adj* ❶ *familiar* horrible; espantoso, sa ❷ horripilante ❸ fatal

gherkin ['gɜːkɪn] *s* pepinillo

ghetto ['getəʊ] *s* gueto

  Dos plurales: **ghettos** o **ghettoes**.

ghost [gəʊst] *s* fantasma

giant ['dʒaɪənt] ◆ *adj* gigantesco, ca ◆ *s* gigante

gibberish ['dʒɪbərɪʃ] *s* tonterías

giddy ['gɪdɪ] *adj* mareado, da • **to be giddy** tener vértigo

gift [gɪft] *s* ❶ regalo; obsequio ❷ don • **to have a gift for something/for doing something** tener un don especial para algo/para hacer algo

gift certificate *s* vale o cupón para regalo

gifted ['gɪftɪd] *adj* ❶ dotado, da ❷ superdotado, da

gig [gɪg] *s familiar* concierto

gigabyte ['gaɪgəbaɪt] *s* INFORMÁTICA gigabyte

gigantic [dʒaɪ'gæntɪk] *adj* gigantesco, ca

giggle ['gɪgl] ◆ *s* risita; risa tonta ◆ *vi* soltar risitas

gimmick ['gɪmɪk] *s despectivo* truco ▶ **advertising gimmick** reclamo publicitario

gin [dʒɪn] *s* ginebra

ginger ['dʒɪndʒər] *s* jengibre

gingerly ['dʒɪndʒəlɪ] *adv* con mucho tiento

gipsy, gypsy ['dʒɪpsɪ] *adj* gitano, na

giraffe [dʒɪ'rɑːf] *s* jirafa

  Dos plurales: **giraffe** o **giraffes**.

girl [gɜːl] *s* ❶ niña ❷ chica ❸ *familiar* • **the girls** las amigas; las chicas

girlfriend ['gɜːlfrend] *s* ❶ novia ❷ amiga

girl scout *s* niña scout

gist [dʒɪst] *s* • **the gist of** lo esencial de • **to get the gist (of something)** entender el sentido (de algo)

give [gɪv] ◆ *vt* ❶ dar ❷ dedicar ❸ prestar ❹ • **to give somebody something, to give something to somebody** regalar algo a alguien ❺ • **to give somebody something, to give something to somebody** entregar o dar algo a alguien ◆ *vi* ❶ romperse; ceder ❷ dar de sí

■ **give or take** *preposición* más o menos • **in half an hour give or take five minutes** dentro de media hora, cinco minutos más o cinco minutos menos

■ **give away** *vt* ⚲ *El objeto se puede colocar antes o después de la preposición.* ❶ regalar ❷ revelar; descubrir ❸ llevar al altar

■ **give back** *vt* ⚲ *El objeto se puede colocar antes o después de la preposición.* devolver; regresar

■ **give in** *vi* ❶ rendirse; darse por vencido, da ❷ • **to give in to something** ceder ante algo

■ **give off** *vt* ⚲ *El objeto siempre va después de la preposición al final.* despedir

■ **give out** ◆ *vt* ⚲ *El objeto se puede colocar antes o después de la preposición.* repartir; distribuir ◆ *vi* ❶ agotarse; acabarse ❷ fallar

■ **give up** ◆ *vt* ⚲ *El objeto se puede colocar antes o después de la preposición.* ❶ abandonar • **to give up chocolate** dejar de comer chocolate ❷ dejar ◆ *vi* rendirse; darse por vencido, da

  Formas irregulares de **give**: *pretérito* **gave**, *pp* **given**.

given ['gɪvn] ◆ *adj* ❶ dado, da ❷ • **to be given to something/to doing something** ser dado, da a algo/a hacer algo ◆ *preposición* dado, da • **given that** dado que

given name *s* nombre de pila

glacier ['glæsjər] *s* glaciar

glad [glæd] *adj* ❶ alegre; contento, ta • **to be glad about/that** alegrarse de/de que ❷ • **to be glad to do something** tener gusto en hacer algo

gladly ['glædlɪ] *adv* ❶ alegremente ❷ con mucho gusto

glamor ['glæmər] *s* encanto; atractivo; sofisficación

glamorous ['glæmərəs] *adj* atractivo, va; lleno, na de encanto

glance [glɑːns] ◆ *s* mirada; vistazo • **to cast** o **take a glance at something** echar un vistazo a algo • **at a glance** de un vistazo • **at first glance** a primera vista ◆ *vi* • **to glance at somebody** lanzar una mirada a alguien • **to glance at** o **through something** hojear algo

■ **glance off** *vt* ⚲ *El objeto siempre va después de la preposición al final.* rebotar en

gland [glænd] *s* glándula

glare [gleər] ◆ *s* ❶ mirada asesina ❷ resplandor; deslumbramiento ❸ ⚲ *incontable figurado* foco ◆ *vi* brillar

glaring ['gleərɪŋ] *adj* ❶ flagrante ❷ deslumbrante

glass [glɑːs] ◆ *s* ❶ vidrio; cristal ❷ vaso ❸ copa ◆ *en compuestos* de vidrio o cristal

■ **glasses** *spl* anteojos; lentes

glassware ['glɑːsweər] *s* ⚲ *incontable* cristalería

glassy ['glɑːsɪ] *adj* ❶ cristalino, na ❷ vidrioso, sa

glaze [gleɪz] ◆ *s* ❶ vidriado ❷ glaseado ◆ *vt* ❶ vidriar ❷ glasear ❸ acristalar

gleam [gliːm] ◆ *s* ❶ destello ❷ rayo ◆ *vi* relucir

gleaming ['gliːmɪŋ] *adj* reluciente

glean [gliːn] *vt* ❶ recoger ❷ extraer

glee [gliː] *s* ⚲ *incontable* alegría; regocijo

glide [glaɪd] *vi* ❶ deslizarse ❷ planear

glider ['glaɪdər] *s* planeador

gliding ['glaɪdɪŋ] *s* vuelo sin motor

glimmer ['glɪmər] *s* ❶ luz tenue ❷ *figurado* atisbo ❸ rayo

glimpse [glɪmps] ◆ *s* ❶ vislumbre • **to catch a glimpse of something/somebody** entrever algo/a alguien ❷ asomo; atisbo ◆ *vt* entrever; vislumbrar

glint [glɪnt] ◆ *s* ❶ destello ❷ brillo ◆ *vi* destellar

glisten ['glɪsn] *vi* relucir; brillar

glitter ['glɪtər] *vi* relucir; brillar

gloat [gləʊt] *vi* • **to gloat (over something)** regodearse (con algo)

global ['gləʊbl] *adj* mundial; global

globalization [ˌgləʊbəlaɪˈzeɪʃn] *s* globalización

global warming [-ˈwɔːmɪŋ] *s* calentamiento global

globe [gləʊb] *s* ❶ globo ❷ globo (terráqueo)

gloom [gluːm] *s* ⚡ *incontable* ❶ penumbra ❷ pesimismo; melancolía

gloomy ['gluːmɪ] *adj* ❶ oscuro, ra ❷ melancólico, ca ❸ pesimista; desalentador, ra

glorious ['glɔːrɪəs] *adj* magnífico, ca

glory ['glɔːrɪ] *s* ❶ gloria ❷ esplendor

■ **glory in** *vt* ⚡ *El objeto siempre va después de la preposición al final.* disfrutar de; regocijarse con

gloss [glɒs] *s* ❶ lustre; brillo ❷ ▶ **gloss (paint)** pintura esmalte

■ **gloss over** *vt* ⚡ *El objeto siempre va después de la preposición al final.* tocar muy por encima

glossary ['glɒsərɪ] *s* glosario

glossy ['glɒsɪ] *adj* ❶ lustroso, sa ❷ de papel satinado

glove [glʌv] *s* guante

glow [gləʊ] ◆ *s* resplandor ◆ *vi* brillar

glower ['glaʊər] *vi* • **to glower (at something/somebody)** mirar con furia (algo/a alguien)

glucose ['gluːkəʊs] *s* glucosa

glue [gluː] ◆ *s* ❶ pegamento ❷ goma ◆ *vt* pegar (con pegamento)

expresión **to be glued to something** estar pegado, da a algo

Formas irregulares de **glue**: *gerundio* **glueing** o **gluing**

glum [glʌm] *adj* sombrío, a

glut [glʌt] *s* superabundancia

glutton ['glʌtn] *s* glotón, ona

expresión **to be a glutton for punishment** ser un masoquista

GM [dʒiːˈem] *adj* transgénico, ca; modificado, da genéticamente • **GM foods** alimentos transgénicos • **GM products** productos modificados genéticamente

GM foods *spl* alimentos transgénicos

GMO (*abreviatura de* genetically modified organism) *s* OMG

gnarled [nɑːld] *adj* nudoso, sa

gnat [næt] *s* mosquito

gnaw [nɔː] *vt* roer • **to gnaw (away) at somebody** corroer a alguien

gnome [nəʊm] *s* gnomo

go [gəʊ] ◆ *vi* ❶ ir • **where are you going?** ¿adónde vas? • **he's gone to Toluca** fue a Toluca • **we went by bus/metro** fuimos en autobús/metro • **to go and do something** ir a hacer algo • **where does this path go?** ¿adónde lleva este camino? • **to go right/left** girar a la derecha/izquierda • **to go swimming/shopping** ir a nadar/de compras • **to go for a walk/run** ir a dar un paseo/a correr ❷ irse; marcharse; salir • **I must go, I have to go** tengo que irme • **it's time we went** es hora de irse ❸ pasar • **the time went slowly/quickly** el tiempo pasaba lentamente/rápido ❹ salir • **to go well/badly** salir bien/mal ❺ caber; pertenecer • **it won't go into the suitcase** no cabe en la maleta ❻ ponerse • **to go grey** encanecer • **to go mad** volverse loco, ca • **to go blind** quedarse ciego, ga ❼ • **what are you going to do now?** ¿qué vas a hacer ahora? • **he said he was going to be late** dijo que llegaría tarde • **it's going to rain/snow** va a llover/nevar ❽ • **to go (with)** ir bien (con) • **this blouse goes well with the skirt** esta blusa va muy bien o hace juego con la falda ❾ funcionar ❿ sonar ⓫ empezar ⓬ estropearse • **the fuse must have gone** debe haberse fundido el fusible ⓭ • **her sight/hearing is going** está perdiendo la vista/el oído

expresión **let's go!** ¡vámonos! ▶ **how's it going?** *familiar* ¿qué tal?

◆ *s* turno • **it's my go** me toca a mí

expresión **to have a go at somebody** *familiar* regañar a alguien ▶ **to be on the go** *familiar* no parar

■ **to go** *adv* • **there are only three days to go** sólo quedan tres días

■ **go about** ◆ *vt* ⚡ *El objeto siempre va después de la preposición al final.* ❶ hacer; realizar • **to go about your business** ocuparse uno de sus asuntos ❷ • **to go about doing something** arreglárselas para hacer algo • **how do you intend going about it?** ¿cómo piensas hacerlo? ◆ *vi* = **go around**

■ **go ahead** *vi* ❶ • **to go ahead (with something)** seguir adelante (con algo) • **go ahead!** ¡adelante! ❷ celebrarse ❸ ponerse por delante

■ **go along** *vi* • **as you go along** a medida que lo vayas haciendo

■ **go along with** *vt* ⚡ *El objeto siempre va después de la preposición al final.* estar de acuerdo con

■ **go around, go round, go about** *vi* correr (por ahí)

■ **go away** *vi* ❶ irse • **go away!** ¡vete! ❷ desaparecer

■ **go back** *vi* volver; regresar

■ **go back on** *vt* ⚡ *El objeto siempre va después de la preposición al final.* faltar a

■ **go back to** *vt* ⚡ *El objeto siempre va después de la preposición al final.* ❶ continuar o seguir con • **to go back to sleep** volver a dormir ❷ remontarse a

■ **go by** ◆ *vi* pasar ◆ *vt* ⚡ *El objeto siempre va después de la preposición al final.* ❶ guiarse por ❷ • **going by her accent, I'd say she was French** a juzgar por su acento yo diría que es francesa

■ **go down** ◆ *vi* ❶ bajar ❷ • **to go down well/badly** tener una buena/mala acogida ❸ ponerse ❹ desinflarse ❺ descender ◆ *vt* ☿ *El objeto siempre va después de la preposición al final.* bajar

■ **go for** *vt* ☿ *El objeto siempre va después de la preposición al final.* ❶ decidirse por ❷ lanzarse sobre; atacar ❸ ir por

■ **go in** *vi* entrar

■ **go in for** *vt* ☿ *El objeto siempre va después de la preposición al final.* ❶ presentarse a ❷ *familiar* • **I don't really go in for classical music** no me va la música clásica

■ **go into** *vt* ☿ *El objeto siempre va después de la preposición al final.* ❶ entrar en ❷ investigar ❸ dedicarse a

■ **go off** ◆ *vi* ❶ estallar; dispararse ❷ sonar ❸ estropearse; cortarse ❹ apagarse ◆ *vt* ☿ *El objeto siempre va después de la preposición al final.* *familiar* perder el gusto a o el interés en o por

■ **go on** ◆ *vi* ❶ pasar; ocurrir ❷ • **to go on (doing something)** seguir (haciendo algo) ❸ • **to go on (about)** no parar de hablar (de) ◆ *exclamación* ¡venga!; ¡vamos!

■ **go out** *vi* ❶ salir • **to go out for a meal** cenar fuera ❷ apagarse

■ **go over** *vt* ☿ *El objeto siempre va después de la preposición al final.* ❶ repasar ❷ repetir

■ **go round** *vi* girar; dar vueltas ; = **go around**

■ **go through** *vt* ☿ *El objeto siempre va después de la preposición al final.* ❶ atravesar ❷ pasar por; experimentar ❸ registrar • **she went through his pockets** le miró en los bolsillos

■ **go through with** *vt* ☿ *El objeto siempre va después de la preposición al final.* llevar a cabo

■ **go towards** *vt* ☿ *El objeto siempre va después de la preposición al final.* contribuir a

■ **go under** *vi* *literal* & *figurado* hundirse

■ **go up** ◆ *vi* ❶ subir ❷ levantarse; construirse ◆ *vt* ☿ *El objeto siempre va después de la preposición al final.* subir

■ **go without** ◆ *vt* ☿ *El objeto siempre va después de la preposición al final.* prescindir de ◆ *vi* arreglárselas

---

go

Para describir actividades físicas o deportivas o pasatiempos es bastante común usar go seguido de gerundio (*to go* dancing/running *ir a bailar/correr*). I like swimming (= I like to be in the water *me gusta nadar*) y I like going swimming (= I like going to the swimming pool *me gusta ir a nadar*).

Cuando a go le sigue un infinitivo, en lugar de usar to se usa and y I'll *go and* see what's happening y no: I'll *go to* see what's happening *voy a ver lo qué pasa*.

Ver también *ir* en el lado español-inglés del diccionario.

Formas irregulares de go: *pretérito* **went**, *pp* **gone**.

goad [gəʊd] *vt* aguijonear; incitar

go-ahead ◆ *adj* dinámico, ca ◆ *s* ☿ *incontable* luz verde

goal [gəʊl] *s* ❶ DEPORTE gol ❷ portería ❸ objetivo; meta

goalkeeper ['gəʊl,kiːpər] *s* portero, ra

goalpost ['gəʊlpəʊst] *s* poste (de la portería)

goat [gəʊt] *s* cabra

gobble ['gɒbl] *vt* engullir; tragar

■ **gobble down, gobble up** *vt* ☿ *El objeto se puede colocar antes o después de la preposición.* engullir; tragar

god [gɒd] *s* dios

■ **God** ◆ *s* Dios

expresiones God knows sabe Dios ▶ for God's sake ¡por el amor de Dios! ▶ thank God ¡gracias a Dios!

◆ *exclamación*

expresión (my) God! ¡Dios (mío)!

godchild ['gɒdtʃaɪld] *s* ahijado, da

El plural de **godchild** es **godchildren** [gɒd,tʃɪldrən].

goddaughter ['gɒd,dɔːtər] *s* ahijada

goddess ['gɒdɪs] *s* diosa

godfather ['gɒd,fɑːðər] *s* padrino

godmother ['gɒd,mʌðər] *s* madrina

godson ['gɒdsʌn] *s* ahijado

goes [gəʊz] → **go**

goggles ['gɒglz] *spl* goggles; gogles

going ['gəʊɪŋ] ◆ *adj* actual ◆ *s* ☿ *incontable* ❶ marcha ❷ condiciones

gold [gəʊld] ◆ *adj* dorado, da ◆ *s* oro ◆ *en compuestos* de oro

golden ['gəʊldən] *adj* ❶ de oro ❷ dorado, da

goldfish ['gəʊldfɪʃ] *s* pez dorado

El plural de **goldfish** es **goldfish**.

gold medal *s* medalla de oro

golf [gɒlf] *s* golf

golf club *s* ❶ club de golf ❷ palo de golf

golf course *s* campo de golf

golfer ['gɒlfər] *s* golfista

gone [gɒn] ◆ *participio pasado* → **go** ◆ *adj* • **those days are gone** esos tiempos ya pasaron ◆ *preposición* • **it was gone six already** ya eran las seis pasadas

good [gʊd] ◆ *adj* (*comparativo* better, *superlativo* best) ❶ bueno, na • **it's good to see you** me alegro de verte • **she's good at it** se le da bien • **he's a very good singer** canta muy bien • **to be good with** saber manejárselas con • **it's good for you** es bueno; es beneficioso • **to feel good** sentirse fenomenal • **it's good that...** está bien que... • **to look good** a) estar muy guapo, pa b) tener buena pinta • **it looks good on you** te queda bien • **good looks** atractivo • **be good!** ¡sé bueno!; ¡pórtate bien! • **good!** ¡muy bien!; ¡estupendo! ❷ amable • **to be good to somebody** ser amable con alguien • **to be good enough to do something** ser tan amable de hacer algo • **that was very good of him** fue muy amable de su parte ◆ *s* ❶ 🔅 *incontable* bien • **it will do him good** le hará bien ❷ beneficio; provecho • **what's the good of...?** ¿de o para qué sirve...? • **it's no good** no sirve para nada ❸ el bien • **to be up to no good** estar tramando algo malo ◆ *adv* ❶ estupendo ◆ *familiar* bien

■ **goods** *spl* ❶ COMERCIO productos; mercancías ❷ ECONOMÍA bienes

■ **as good as** *adv* casi; prácticamente • **it's as good as new** está como nuevo

■ **for good** *adv* para siempre

■ **good afternoon** *exclamación* ¡buenas tardes!

■ **good evening** *exclamación* ❶ ¡buenas tardes! ❷ ¡buenas noches!

■ **good morning** *exclamación* ¡buenos días!; ¡buen día!

■ **good night** *exclamación* ¡buenas noches!

goodbye [ˌgʊdˈbaɪ] ◆ *exclamación* ¡adiós! • **to say goodbye** despedirse ◆ *s* adiós

Good Friday *s* Viernes Santo

good-humored [-ˈhjuːməd] *adj* jovial

good-looking [-ˈlʊkɪŋ] *adj* guapo, pa

good-natured [-ˈneɪtʃəd] *adj* bondadoso, sa

goodness [ˈgʊdnɪs] ◆ *s* 🔅 *incontable* ❶ bondad ❷ alimento ◆ *exclamación*

expresiones **(my) goodness!** ¡Dios mío! ▶ **for goodness' sake!** ¡por Dios! ▶ **thank goodness** ¡gracias a Dios!

goodwill [ˌgʊdˈwɪl] *s* buena voluntad

goof [guːf] *familiar* ◆ *s* metedura de pata ◆ *vi* meter la pata

goose [guːs] *s* ganso; oca

El plural de **goose** es **geese**.

goosebumps [ˈguːsbʌmps] *familiar spl* = **gooseflesh**

gooseflesh [ˈguːsfleʃ] *s* carne de gallina

gore [gɔːr] ◆ *s literario* sangre (derramada) ◆ *vt* cornear

gorge [gɔːdʒ] ◆ *s* cañón ◆ *vt* • **to gorge yourself on** o **with** atracarse de

gorgeous [ˈgɔːdʒəs] *adj* magnífico, ca; espléndido, da

gorilla [gəˈrɪlə] *s* gorila

gory [ˈgɔːrɪ] *adj* ❶ sangriento, ta ❷ escabroso, sa

gospel [ˈgɒspl] *s* evangelio

gossip [ˈgɒsɪp] ◆ *s* ❶ chisme ❷ chismoso, sa ◆ *vi* cotillear

got [gɒt] *pretérito* & *participio pasado* → **get**

gotten [ˈgɒtn] *participio pasado* → **get**

gourmet [ˈgʊəmeɪ] ◆ *s* gastrónomo, ma ◆ *en compuestos* para o de gastrónomos

govern [ˈgʌvən] ◆ *vt* ❶ POLÍTICA gobernar ❷ dictar ◆ *vi* POLÍTICA gobernar

governess [ˈgʌvənɪs] *s* institutriz

government [ˈgʌvnmənt] ◆ *s* gobierno ◆ *en compuestos* gubernamental

governor [ˈgʌvənər] *s* ❶ POLÍTICA gobernador, ra ❷ director, ra

gown [gaʊn] *s* ❶ vestido; traje ❷ toga

grab [græb] ◆ *vt* ❶ arrebatar • **to grab something off somebody** arrebatar algo a alguien ❷ agarrar; asir ❸ *familiar* seducir ◆ *vi* • **to grab at something** intentar agarrar algo

grace [greɪs] ◆ *s* ❶ 🔅 *incontable* elegancia; gracia ❷ 🔅 *incontable* prórroga ❸ • **to say grace** bendecir la mesa ◆ *vt formal* ❶ honrar ❷ adornar; embellecer

graceful [ˈgreɪsfʊl] *adj* ❶ elegante ❷ cortés

gracious [ˈgreɪʃəs] ◆ *adj* ❶ cortés ❷ elegante ◆ *exclamación*

expresión **(good) gracious!** ¡Dios mío!

grade [greɪd] ◆ *s* ❶ clase; calidad ❷ curso; clase ❸ calificación ◆ *vt* ❶ clasificar ❷ calificar

grade crossing *s* paso a nivel

grade school *s* escuela primaria

gradient [ˈgreɪdjənt] *s* pendiente

grad school *s* escuela de posgrado

gradual [ˈgrædʒʊəl] *adj* gradual

gradually [ˈgrædʒʊəlɪ] *adv* gradualmente

graduate ◆ *s* [ˈgrædʒʊət] ❶ licenciado, da; egresado, da ❷ ≃ bachiller ◆ *vi* [ˈgrædʒʊeɪt] ❶ • **to graduate (from)** licenciarse (en); egresar (de) ❷ • **to graduate (from)** ≃ obtener el título de bachiller (en)

GRADUATE SCHOOL

Muchos estudiantes universitarios en Estados Unidos continúan sus estudios en una **graduate school** tras alcanzar la licenciatura. Allí pueden obtener primero la maestría y después el doctorado. Para ingresar a la **graduate school** hay que presentar el GRE, un examen que requieren las universidades para admisión a los programas de posgrado. Aunque continuar los estudios puede resultar muy caro, el título de posgrado casi se ha convertido en requerimiento para trabajar en ciertos campos.

graduation [ˌgrædʒʊˈeɪʃn] *s* graduación

graft [grɑːft] *s* ❶ MEDICINA & BOTÁNICA injerto ❷ *familiar* chanchullos

grain [greɪn] *s* ❶ grano ❷ 🔅 *incontable* cereales ❸ *figurado* pizca ❹ veta

gram, gramme [græm] *s* gramo

grammar [ˈgræmər] *s* gramática

grammar checker *s* INFORMÁTICA corrector de gramática

grammar school *s* escuela primaria

grammatical [grəˈmætɪkl] *adj* ❶ gramatical ❷ (gramaticalmente) correcto, ta

grand [grænd] ♦ *adj* ❶ grandioso, sa ❷ ambicioso, sa ❸ distinguido, da ♦ *s familiar* • **a grand** mil dólares • **five grand** cinco mil dólares

grandchild ['græntʃaɪld] *s* nieto, ta
El plural de **grandchild** es **grandchildren** ['græn,tʃɪldrən].

grand(d)ad ['grændæd] *s familiar* abuelito

granddaughter ['græn,dɔːtər] *s* nieta

grandeur ['grændʒər] *s* ❶ grandiosidad ❷ grandeza

grandfather ['grænd,fɑːðər] *s* abuelo

grand jury *s* jurado de acusación

grandma ['grænmɑː] *s familiar* abuelita

grandmother ['græn,mʌðər] *s* abuela

grandpa ['grænpɑː] *s familiar* abuelito

grandparents ['græn,peərənts] *spl* abuelos

grand piano *s* piano de cola

grandson ['grænsʌn] *s* nieto

grandstand ['grændstænd] *s* tribuna

grand total *s* ❶ cantidad total ❷ importe total

granite ['grænɪt] *s* granito

granny ['grænɪ] *s familiar* abuelita

granola [grə'nəʊlə] *s* muesli de avena

grant [grɑːnt] ♦ *s* ❶ subvención ❷ beca ♦ *vt formal* ❶ conceder ❷ admitir ; aceptar
expresión **to take something/somebody for granted** no apreciar algo/a alguien en lo que vale ▸ **it is taken for granted that...** se da por sentado que...

grape [greɪp] *s* uva

grapefruit ['greɪpfruːt] *s* toronja
Dos plurales: **grapefruit** o **grapefruits**.

graph [grɑːf] *s* gráfica

graphic ['græfɪk] *adj literal & figurado* gráfico, ca
■ **graphics** *spl* ❶ ilustraciones ❷ INFORMÁTICA gráficos

graphite ['græfaɪt] *s* grafito

graph paper *s* ☒ *incontable* papel cuadriculado

grapple ['græpl] ■ **grapple with** *vt* ☒ *El objeto siempre va después de la preposición al final.* ❶ forcejear con ❷ esforzarse por resolver

grasp [grɑːsp] ♦ *s* ❶ agarre ❷ comprensión • **to have a good grasp of something** dominar algo ♦ *vt* ❶ agarrar ❷ comprender ❸ aprovechar

grasping ['grɑːspɪŋ] *adj despectivo* avaro, ra

grass [grɑːs] *s* ❶ hierba ; pasto ❷ césped ❸ pasto • **'keep off the grass'** 'prohibido pisar el césped'

grasshopper ['grɑːs,hɒpər] *s* chapulín

grass roots ♦ *spl* bases ♦ *en compuestos* de base

grate [greɪt] ♦ *s* parrilla ; rejilla ♦ *vt* rallar ♦ *vi* rechinar ; chirriar • **to grate on somebody's nerves** poner a alguien los nervios de punta

grateful ['greɪtfʊl] *adj* ❶ agradecido, da ❷ de agradecimiento • **to be grateful to somebody (for something)** estar agradecido a alguien (por algo) • **I'm very**

grateful to you te lo agradezco mucho • **I'd be grateful if you could do it by tomorrow** te agradecería que lo hicieras para mañana

grater ['greɪtər] *s* rallador

gratify ['grætɪfaɪ] *vt* ❶ • **to be gratified** estar satisfecho, cha ❷ satisfacer

grating ['greɪtɪŋ] ♦ *adj* chirriante ♦ *s* reja ; enrejado

gratitude ['grætɪtjuːd] *s* ☒ *incontable* • **gratitude (to somebody for)** agradecimiento o gratitud (a alguien por)

grave [greɪv] ♦ *adj* grave ♦ *s* sepultura ; tumba

gravel ['grævl] *s* grava ; gravilla

gravestone ['greɪvstəʊn] *s* lápida (sepulcral)

graveyard ['greɪvjɑːd] *s* cementerio

gravity ['grævətɪ] *s* gravedad

gravy ['greɪvɪ] *s* ❶ ☒ *incontable* salsa o jugo de carne ❷ *muy familiar* dinero fácil

gray [greɪ] ♦ *adj literal & figurado* gris • **a grey hair** una cana ♦ *s* gris

graze [greɪz] ♦ *vt* ❶ pastar en ❷ rasguñar ❸ rozar ♦ *vi* pastar ♦ *s* rasguño

grease [griːs] ♦ *s* grasa ♦ *vt* engrasar

greasy ['griːzɪ] *adj* ❶ grasiento, ta ❷ grasoso, sa

great [greɪt] ♦ *adj* ❶ grande ❷ intenso, sa • **with great care** con mucho cuidado • **a great deal of...** un montón de... ❸ *familiar* estupendo, da ; fenomenal • **we had a great time** lo pasamos en grande • **great!** ¡estupendo! ♦ *adv* • **great big** enorme ♦ *s* grande

Great Britain *s* Gran Bretaña

great-grandchild *s* bisnieto, ta

great-grandfather *s* bisabuelo

great-grandmother *s* bisabuela

greatly ['greɪtlɪ] *adv* enormemente

greatness ['greɪtnɪs] *s* grandeza

Greece [griːs] *s* Grecia

greed [griːd] *s* ☒ *incontable* • **greed (for) a)** gula **b)** codicia (de) **c)** ambición (de)

greedy ['griːdɪ] *adj* ❶ goloso, sa ❷ • **greedy for** codicioso, sa o ávido, da de

Greek [griːk] ♦ *adj* griego, ga ♦ *s* ❶ griego, ga ❷ griego

green [griːn] ♦ *adj* ❶ verde ❷ verde ; ecologista ❸ *familiar* novato, ta ❹ *familiar* pálido, da ♦ *s* ❶ verde ❷ green
■ **greens** *spl* verdura

greenback ['griːnbæk] *s familiar* billete *(dólar estadounidense)*

Green Beret *s familiar* • **the Green Berets** los boinas verdes

green card *s* permiso de trabajo

Green Card

Para vivir y trabajar en Estados Unidos, todo ciudadano extranjero necesita el documento llamado **Green Card** ("tarjeta verde"), si bien en la actualidad ya no es de dicho color. El proceso para obtener este permiso de residencia permanente es largo y complicado. Se puede conceder a familiares directos de ciudadanos estadounidenses (como por ejemplo, esposos), a refugiados o asilados políticos que lo hayan sido desde hace al menos un año y a trabajadores con un contrato indefinido (o patrocinados por su empresa). Asimismo, existe el sistema llamado informalmente "Green Card Lottery", que, mediante un programa informático aleatorio, concede 50.000 permisos a ciudadanos de países con un nivel bajo de inmigración a EE.UU.

greenhorn ['gri:nhɔːn] s ❶ recién llegado, da ❷ novato, ta

greenhouse ['gri:nhaʊs] ·Ö· *pl* [-haʊzɪz] *s* invernadero

greenhouse effect *s* • the greenhouse effect el efecto invernadero

greenhouse gas *s* gas invernadero

Greenland ['gri:nlənd] *s* Groenlandia

greet [gri:t] *vt* ❶ saludar ❷ recibir

greeting ['gri:tɪŋ] *s* saludo

greeting card *s* tarjeta de felicitación

grenade [grə'neɪd] *s* ▶ **(hand) grenade** granada (de mano)

grew [gru:] *pretérito* → **grow**

greyhound ['greɪhaʊnd] *s* galgo

grid [grɪd] *s* ❶ reja; enrejado ❷ cuadrícula

griddle ['grɪdl] *s* plancha

gridiron ['grɪd,aɪən] *s* ❶ parrilla ❷ futbol americano ❸ campo de futbol americano

gridlock ['grɪdlɒk] *s* embotellamiento; atasco

grief [gri:f] *s* ·Ö· *incontable* ❶ dolor; pesar ❷ *familiar* problemas

expresión **to come to grief a)** sufrir un percance **b)** irse al traste ▶ **good grief!** ¡madre mía!

grievance ['gri:vns] *s* (motivo de) queja

grieve [gri:v] *vi* • **to grieve (for)** llorar (por)

grievous bodily harm *s* ·Ö· *incontable* lesiones graves

grill [grɪl] ◆ *s* ❶ grill ❷ parrilla ❸ parrillada ◆ *vt* ❶ asar al grill ❷ asar a la parrilla ❸ *familiar* someter a un duro interrogatorio

grille [grɪl] *s* ❶ rejilla ❷ reja

grim [grɪm] *adj* ❶ adusto, ta ❷ inexorable ❸ desolador, ra

grimace [grɪ'meɪs] ◆ *s* mueca ◆ *vi* hacer una mueca

grime [graɪm] *s* mugre

grimy ['graɪmɪ] *adj* mugriento, ta

grin [grɪn] ◆ *s* sonrisa (abierta) ◆ *vi* • **to grin (at)** sonreír (a)

grind [graɪnd] ◆ *vt* moler ◆ *vi* rechinar; chirriar ◆ *s* rutina

■ **grind up** *vt* ·Ö· *El objeto se puede colocar antes o después de la preposición.* pulverizar

Formas irregulares de **grind**: *pret* & *pp* **ground**.

grinder ['graɪndər] *s* molinillo

grip [grɪp] ◆ *s* ❶ • **to have a grip (on something/somebody)** tener (algo/a alguien) bien agarrado ❷ • **grip on** control de; dominio de • **in the grip of something** en las garras de algo; dominado, da por algo ❸ sujeción; adherencia ❹ asidero ❺ bolsa de viaje

expresiones **to get to grips with** llegar a controlar ▶ **to get a grip on yourself** calmarse; controlarse ▶ **to lose your grip** *figurado* perder el control

◆ *vt* ❶ agarrar; asir ❷ apretar ❸ empuñar ❹ apoderarse de ◆ *vi* adherirse

gripping ['grɪpɪŋ] *adj* apasionante

grisly ['grɪzlɪ] *adj* espeluznante

grit [grɪt] *s* ❶ grava ❷ arena

■ **grits** *spl* granos de maíz molidos

groan [grəʊn] ◆ *s* gemido ◆ *vi* gemir

grocer ['grəʊsər] *s* abarrotero, ra

groceries ['grəʊsərɪz] *spl* comestibles; abarrotes

grocery ['grəʊsərɪ], **grocery store** *s* tienda de abarrotes

groin [grɔɪn] *s* ingle

groom [gru:m] ◆ *s* ❶ mozo de cuadra ❷ novio ◆ *vt* ❶ cepillar ❷ • **to groom somebody (for something)** preparar a alguien (para algo)

groove [gru:v] *s* ❶ ranura ❷ surco

gross [grəʊs] ◆ *adj* ❶ bruto, ta ❷ *formal* grave ❸ basto, ta; vulgar ❹ *familiar* obeso, sa ❺ *familiar* asqueroso, sa ◆ *s* gruesa ◆ *vt* ganar en bruto

Dos plurales: **gross** o **grosses**.

grossly ['grəʊslɪ] *adv* enormemente

grotesque [grəʊ'tesk] *adj* grotesco, ca

grotto ['grɒtəʊ] *s* gruta

Dos plurales: **grottoes** o **grottos**.

ground [graʊnd] ◆ *pretérito* & *participio pasado* → **grind** ◆ *s* ❶ suelo ❷ tierra • **above/below ground** sobre/bajo tierra • **on the ground** en el suelo ❸ terreno ❹ *DEPORTE* campo

expresión **to break fresh** o **new ground** abrir nuevas fronteras ▶ **to gain/lose ground** ganar/perder terreno

◆ *vt* ❶ • **to be grounded on** o **in something** basarse en algo ❷ hacer permanecer en tierra ❸ *familiar* castigar sin salir ❹ *ELECTRICIDAD* • **to be grounded** estar conectado, da a tierra

■ **grounds** *spl* ❶ • **grounds (for something/for doing something)** motivos (para algo/para hacer algo) • **on**

the grounds that aduciendo que; debido a que ❷ jardines ❸ terrenos ❹ posos

---

Ground zero

Ground Zero es el nombre que se le ha dado al lugar donde estaban las torres gemelas del **World Trade Center** antes de los atentados del 11 de septiembre de 2001.

---

ground beef *s* carne molida

ground crew, ground staff *s* personal de tierra

ground floor *s* planta baja • **ground floor flat** (piso) bajo

grounding ['graʊndɪŋ] *s* • **grounding (in)** base (de); conocimientos básicos (de)

groundless ['graʊndlɪs] *adj* infundado, da

groundwork ['graʊndwɜːk] *s* ☼ *incontable* trabajo preliminar

group [gruːp] ◆ *s* grupo ◆ *vt* agrupar ◆ *vi* • **to group (together)** agruparse

grove [grəʊv] *s* arboleda

grovel ['grɒvl] *vi literal & figurado* • **to grovel (to)** arrastrarse (ante)

Formas irregulares de **grovel**: *pretérito & pp* **groveled**, *gerundio* **groveling**.

grow [grəʊ] ◆ *vi* ❶ crecer ❷ volverse; ponerse • **to grow dark** oscurecer • **to grow old** envejecer ◆ *vt* ❶ cultivar ❷ dejarse crecer

■ **grow on** *vt* ☼ *El objeto siempre va después de la preposición al final. familiar* • **it's growing on me** me gusta cada vez más

■ **grow out of** *vt* ☼ *El objeto siempre va después de la preposición al final.* ❶ • **he has grown out of his clothes** se le ha quedado pequeña la ropa ❷ perder • **he'll grow out of it** ya se le pasará

■ **grow up** *vi* crecer • **when I grow up** cuando sea mayor • **grow up!** ¡no seas niño!

Formas irregulares de **grow**: *pretérito* **grew**, *pp* **grown**.

grower ['grəʊər] *s* cultivador, ra

growl [graʊl] *vi* ❶ gruñir ❷ rugir

grown [grəʊn] ◆ *participio pasado* → **grow** ◆ *adj* adulto, ta

grown-up *s* persona mayor

growth [grəʊθ] *s* ❶ • **growth (of** o **in)** crecimiento (de) ❷ *MEDICINA* tumor

grubby ['grʌbɪ] *adj* sucio, cia; mugriento, ta

grudge [grʌdʒ] ◆ *s* rencor • **to bear somebody a grudge, to bear a grudge against somebody** guardar rencor a alguien ◆ *vt* • **to grudge somebody something** conceder algo a alguien a regañadientes • **to grudge doing something** hacer algo a regañadientes

grueling ['grʊəlɪŋ] *adj* agotador, ra

gruesome ['gruːsəm] *adj* horripilante

gruff [grʌf] *adj* ❶ bronco, ca ❷ hosco, ca

grumble ['grʌmbl] *vi* ❶ quejarse; refunfuñar ❷ gruñir; hacer ruido

grumpy ['grʌmpɪ] *adj familiar* gruñón, ona

grunt [grʌnt] *vi* gruñir

guarantee [,gærən'tiː] ◆ *s* garantía ◆ *vt* garantizar

guard [gɑːd] ◆ *s* ❶ guardia ❷ carcelero, ra ❸ guardia • **to be on/stand guard** estar de/hacer guardia ❹ protector; cubierta protectora

expresión to catch somebody off guard coger a alguien desprevenido

◆ *vt* ❶ guardar ❷ vigilar

guard dog *s* perro guardián

guarded ['gɑːdɪd] *adj* cauteloso, sa

guardian ['gɑːdjən] *s* ❶ tutor, ra ❷ guardián, ana; protector, ra

guardrail ['gɑːdreɪl] *s* barrera de protección

Guatemala [,gwɑːtə'mɑːlə] *s* Guatemala

Guatemalan [,gwɑːtə'mɑːlən] ◆ *adj* guatemalteco, ca ◆ *s* guatemalteco, ca

guerrilla [gə'rɪlə] *s* guerrillero, ra

guerrilla warfare *s* ☼ *incontable* guerra de guerrillas

guess [ges] ◆ *s* suposición; conjetura • **to take a guess** intentar adivinar ◆ *vt* adivinar

expresión guess what? ¿sabes qué?

◆ *vi* ❶ adivinar • **to guess at something** tratar de adivinar algo • **to guess right** acertar • **to guess wrong** equivocarse ❷ • **I guess (so)** supongo o me imagino que sí

expresión to keep somebody guessing tener a alguien en la incertidumbre

guesswork ['geswɜːk] *s* ☼ *incontable* conjeturas; suposiciones

guest [gest] *s* ❶ invitado, da ❷ huésped

guesthouse ['gesthaʊs] ☼ *pl* [-haʊzɪz] *s* casa de huéspedes

guestroom ['gestrʊm] *s* cuarto de los invitados

guidance ['gaɪdəns] *s* ☼ *incontable* ❶ orientación ❷ dirección

guide [gaɪd] ◆ *s* ❶ guía ❷ guía ◆ *vt* ❶ guiar ❷ conducir; dirigir ❸ • **to be guided by** guiarse por

guide book *s* guía

guidelines ['gaɪdlaɪnz] *spl* directrices

guild [gɪld] *s* ❶ *HISTORIA* gremio ❷ corporación

guile [gaɪl] *s* ☼ *incontable* astucia

guilt [gɪlt] *s* ❶ culpa ❷ *DERECHO* culpabilidad

guilty ['gɪltɪ] *adj* • **guilty (of)** culpable (de)

guinea pig ['gɪnɪ-] *s literal & figurado* conejillo de Indias

guise [gaɪz] *s formal* apariencia

guitar [gɪ'tɑːr] *s* guitarra

guitarist [gɪ'tɑːrɪst] *s* guitarrista

gulch [gʌltʃ] *s* barranco

G

gulf [gʌlf] *s* ❶ golfo ❷ sima; abismo ❸ • **gulf (between)** abismo (entre)
■ **Gulf** *s* • **the Gulf** el Golfo
gull [gʌl] *s* gaviota
gullet ['gʌlɪt] *s* esófago
gullible ['gʌləbl] *adj* crédulo, la
gully ['gʌlɪ] *s* barranco
gulp [gʌlp] ◆ *s* trago ◆ *vt* ❶ tragarse ❷ engullir ◆ *vi* tragar saliva
■ **gulp down** *vt* ⚲ *El objeto se puede colocar antes o después de la preposición.* ❶ tragarse ❷ engullir
gum [gʌm] ◆ *s* ❶ chicle ❷ pegamento ❸ ANATOMÍA encía ◆ *vt* pegar; engomar
gun [gʌn] *s* ❶ pistola ❷ escopeta; fusil ❸ cañón ❹ pistola
■ **gun down** *vt* ⚲ *El objeto se puede colocar antes o después de la preposición.* abatir (a tiros)
gunfire ['gʌnfaɪər] *s* ⚲ *incontable* disparos; tiroteo
gunman ['gʌnmən] *s* pistolero
El plural de **gunman** es **gunmen** ['gʌnmen].
gunpoint ['gʌnpɔɪnt] *s* • **at gunpoint** a punta de pistola
gunpowder ['gʌn,paʊdər] *s* pólvora
gunshot ['gʌnʃɒt] *s* tiro; disparo

gunsmith ['gʌnsmɪθ] *s* armero
gurgle ['gɜ:gl] *vi* ❶ gorgotear ❷ gorjear
guru ['gʊru:] *s literal & figurado* gurú
gush [gʌʃ] ◆ *s* chorro ◆ *vi* ❶ chorrear; manar ❷ *despectivo* ser muy efusivo, va
gust [gʌst] *s* ráfaga; racha
gusto ['gʌstəʊ] *s* • **with gusto** con deleite
gut [gʌt] ◆ *s* MEDICINA intestino ◆ *vt* ❶ destripar ❷ limpiar ❸ destruir el interior de
■ **guts** *spl familiar* ❶ tripas ❷ agallas
gutter ['gʌtər] *s* ❶ cuneta ❷ canalón
gutter press *s despectivo* prensa amarilla o sensacionalista
guy [gaɪ] *s familiar* tipo; tío; chavo
guy rope *s* viento; cuerda *(de tienda de campaña)*
guzzle ['gʌzl] ◆ *vt* zamparse ◆ *vi* zampar
gym [dʒɪm] *s familiar* ❶ gimnasio ❷ gimnasia
gymnasium [dʒɪm'neɪzjəm] *s* gimnasio
gymnast ['dʒɪmnæst] *s* gimnasta
gymnastics [dʒɪm'næstɪks] *s* ⚲ *incontable* gimnasia
gynecologist [,gaɪnə'kɒlədʒɪst] *s* ginecólogo, ga
gynecology [,gaɪnə'kɒlədʒɪ] *s* ginecología
gypsy ['dʒɪpsɪ] = **gipsy**

G

h, H [eɪʧ] *s* h; H
   Dos plurales: **h's** o **hs**; **H's** o **Hs**.

habit ['hæbɪt] *s* ❶ costumbre; hábito • **to make a habit of something** tomar algo por costumbre • **to make a habit of doing something** tener por costumbre hacer algo ❷ hábito *(de monja)*

habitat ['hæbɪtæt] *s* hábitat

habitual [hə'bɪʧʊəl] *adj* ❶ habitual; acostumbrado, da ❷ empedernido, da

hack [hæk] ♦ *s* ❶ *despectivo* escritorzuelo, la ❷ gacetillero, ra ♦ *vt* cortar en tajos; acuchillar
■ **hack into** *vt* ⚙ *El objeto siempre va después de la preposición al final.* piratear

hacker ['hækəɾ] *s* ❱ **(computer) hacker** pirata informático

hackneyed ['hæknɪd] *adj despectivo* trillado, da;

hacksaw ['hæksɔ:] *s* sierra para metales

had ⚙ *acento atónico* [həd]*, acento tónico* [hæd] *pretérito* & *participio pasado* → **have**

hadn't ['hædnt] *(abreviatura de* had not) = **have**

haemorrhage ['hemərɪdʒ] = **hemorrhage**

haggard ['hægəd] *adj* ojeroso, sa

haggle ['hægl] *vi* • **to haggle (with somebody over** o **about something)** regatear (algo con alguien)

hail [heɪl] ♦ *s* ❶ Meteorología granizo; pedrisco ❷ *figurado* lluvia ♦ *vt* ❶ llamar ❷ parar ❸ • **to hail somebody as something** aclamar a alguien algo • **to hail something as something** ensalzar algo catalogándolo de algo ♦ *v impersonal* • **it's hailing** está granizando

hailstone ['heɪlstəʊn] *s* granizo; piedra

hair [heəɾ] *s* ❶ ⚙ *incontable* pelo • **to do your hair** arreglarse el pelo ❷ vello

hairbrush ['heəbrʌʃ] *s* cepillo (para el pelo)

haircut ['heəkʌt] *s* corte de pelo

hairdo ['heədu:] *s familiar* peinado
   El plural de **hairdo** es **hairdos**.

hairdresser ['heə,dresəɾ] *s* peluquero, ra • **hairdresser's (salon)** peluquería

hairdryer ['heə,draɪəɾ] *s* secador (de pelo)

hair gel *s* gel para el pelo

hairpin ['heəpɪn] *s* pasador

hairpin bend *s* curva muy cerrada

hair-raising [-,reɪzɪŋ] *adj* espeluznante

hair remover [-rɪ,muːvəɾ] *s* depilatorio

hairspray ['heəspreɪ] *s* laca (para el pelo)

hairstyle ['heəstaɪl] *s* peinado

hairy ['heərɪ] *adj* ❶ peludo, da ❷ *familiar* espeluznante; espantoso, sa

Haiti ['heɪtɪ] *s* Haití

half [hɑːf] ♦ *adj* medio, dia • **half a dozen/mile** media docena/milla • **half an hour** media hora ♦ *adv* ❶ • **half Mexican** medio mexicano • **half full/open** medio lleno/abierto • **half and half** mitad y mitad ❷ • **half as big (as)** la mitad de grande (que) ❸ • **half past nine, half after nine** las nueve y media ♦ *s* ❶ (pl halves) mitad • **one half of the group** una mitad del grupo • **in half** por la mitad; en dos ❷ (pl halfs) medio ❸ (pl halves) tiempo; mitad
expresión to go halves (with somebody) ir a medias (con alguien)
   ♦ *pronombre* la mitad • **half of it/them** la mitad

halfback ['hɑːfbæk] *s* medio

half-hearted [-'hɑːtɪd] *adj* poco entusiasta

half hour *s* media hora

half-mast *s* • **at half-mast** a media asta

half moon *s* media luna

half note *s* Música blanca

half-price *adj* a mitad de precio

half time *s* ⚙ *incontable* descanso

halfway [hɑːf'weɪ] ♦ *adj* intermedio, dia ♦ *adv* ❶ • **I was halfway down the street** llevaba la mitad de la calle andada ❷ • **the film was halfway through** la película iba por la mitad

hall [hɔːl] *s* ❶ vestíbulo ❷ pasillo ❸ sala ❹ mansión

hallmark ['hɔːlmɑːk] *s* ❶ sello distintivo ❷ contraste

Hallowe'en [,hæləʊ'iːn] *s* ❱ fiesta celebrada la noche del 31 de octubre

HALLOWEEN

Se pensaba que el 31 de octubre, víspera del Día de Todos los Santos, los espíritus de los muertos venían a visitar a los vivos. Hoy en día, los niños se disfrazan de brujas y fantasmas y van de puerta en puerta, llamando **trick or treat!** para pedir dulces.

hallucinate [hə'lu:sɪneɪt] *vi* alucinar
hallway ['hɔ:lweɪ] *s* ❶ vestíbulo ❷ pasillo
halo ['heɪləʊ] *s* halo; aureola

Dos plurales: **haloes** o **halos**.

halt [hɔ:lt] ◆ *s*
expresión **to grind to a halt a)** ir parando lentamente **b)** paralizarse ▶ **to call a halt to** poner fin a
◆ *vt* ❶ parar; detener ❷ interrumpir ◆ *vi* ❶ pararse; detenerse ❷ interrumpirse
halve [hæv] *vt* ❶ reducir a la mitad ❷ partir en dos
halves [hævz] *spl* → half
ham [hæm] ◆ *s* jamón ◆ *en compuestos* de jamón
hamburger ['hæmbɜ:gər] *s* ❶ hamburguesa ❷ *incontable* carne molida
hammer ['hæmər] ◆ *s* martillo ◆ *vt* ❶ martillear ❷ golpear ❸ *familiar* dar una paliza a ◆ *vi* • **to hammer (on something)** golpear (algo)
■ **hammer out** *vt* *El objeto siempre va después de la preposición al final.* alcanzar con esfuerzo
hammock ['hæmək] *s* hamaca
hamper ['hæmpər] ◆ *s* canasta ◆ *vt* obstaculizar
hamster ['hæmstər] *s* hámster
hamstring ['hæmstrɪŋ] *s* tendón de la corva
hand [hænd] ◆ *s* ❶ mano • **to hold hands** ir cogidos de la mano • **hand in hand** (cogidos) de la mano • **by hand** a mano • **in the hands of** en manos de ❷ influencia ❸ bracero; peón; tripulante ❹ manecilla; aguja ❺ letra ❻ • **a big hand** un gran aplauso
expresiones **to force somebody's hand** apretar las tuercas a alguien ▶ **to get** o **lay your hands on something** hacerse con algo ▶ **to get** o **lay your hands on somebody** pillar a alguien ▶ **to give somebody a free hand** dar carta blanca a alguien ▶ **to go hand in hand** ir de la mano ▶ **to have your hands full** estar muy ocupado, da ▶ **to have time in hand** tener tiempo de sobra ▶ **to overplay your hand** *figurado* extralimitarse ▶ **to take somebody in hand** hacerse cargo o ocuparse de alguien ▶ **to have a hand in something/in doing something** intervenir en algo/al hacer algo
◆ *vt* • **to hand something to somebody, to hand somebody something** dar o entregar algo a alguien
■ **(close) at hand** *adv* cerca
■ **on hand** *adv* al alcance de la mano
■ **on the other hand** *conjunción* por otra parte
■ **out of hand** *adv* terminantemente
■ **to hand** *adv* a mano

■ **hand back** *vt* *El objeto se puede colocar antes o después de la preposición.* devolver
■ **hand down** *vt* *El objeto se puede colocar antes o después de la preposición.* ❶ dejar en herencia ❷ transmitir
■ **hand in** *vt* *El objeto se puede colocar antes o después de la preposición.* ❶ entregar ❷ presentar
■ **hand out** *vt* *El objeto se puede colocar antes o después de la preposición.* repartir; distribuir
■ **hand over** ◆ *vt* *El objeto se puede colocar antes o después de la preposición.* ❶ entregar ❷ ceder ◆ *vi* • **to hand over (to)** dar paso (a)
handbag ['hændbæg] *s* bolsa
handball ['hændbɔ:l] *s* balonmano
handbook ['hændbʊk] *s* manual
handcuffs ['hændkʌfs] *spl* esposas
handful ['hændfʊl] *s* puñado
handgun ['hændgʌn] *s* pistola
handheld PC ['hændheld-] *s* computadora de bolsillo; asistente personal
handicap ['hændɪkæp] ◆ *s* ❶ discapacidad; minusvalía ❷ desventaja; obstáculo ❸ *Deporte* hándicap ◆ *vt* estorbar
handicapped ['hændɪkæpt] ◆ *adj* discapacitado, da; minusválido, da ◆ *spl* • **the handicapped** los discapacitados; los minusválidos
handicraft ['hændɪkrɑ:ft] *s* artesanía
handiwork ['hændɪwɜ:k] *s* *incontable* obra
handle ['hændl] ◆ *s* ❶ mango ❷ manija ❸ asa ❹ empuñadura ◆ *vt* ❶ manejar ❷ encargarse de ❸ conducir ❹ tratar
handlebars ['hændlbɑ:z] *spl* manillar
handmade [,hænd'meɪd] *adj* hecho, cha a mano
handout ['hændaʊt] *s* ❶ donativo ❷ hoja (informativa) ❸ notas
handrail ['hændreɪl] *s* pasamano
handset ['hændset] *s* auricular *(de teléfono)* • **to lift/replace the handset** descolgar/colgar (el teléfono)
hands free kit *s* kit manos libres
handshake ['hændʃeɪk] *s* apretón de manos
handsome ['hænsəm] *adj* ❶ guapo; atractivo ❷ bella ❸ considerable
handstand ['hændstænd] *s* pino
handwriting ['hænd,raɪtɪŋ] *s* letra; caligrafía
handy ['hændɪ] *adj* *familiar* ❶ práctico, ca • **to come in handy** venir bien ❷ mañoso, sa ❸ a mano; cerca • **to keep something handy** tener algo a mano
handyman ['hændɪmæn] *s* • **a good handyman** un manitas

El plural de **handyman** es **handymen** ['hændɪmen].

hang [hæŋ] ◆ *vt* ❶ *(pret & pp* hung*)* colgar ❷ tender ❸ poner ❹ *(pret & pp* hung o hanged*)* ahorcar
expresión **to hang yourself** ahorcarse
◆ *vi* ❶ *(pret & pp* hung*)* colgar; pender ❷ *(pret & pp* hung o hanged*)* ser ahorcado, da ❸ *(pret & pp* hung*)*

familiar • **I'm going to hang with my friends tonight** voy a ir por ahí esta noche con los amigos ❹ INFORMÁTICA colgarse ◆ *s*

expresión **to get the hang of something** *familiar* agarrarle el modo a algo

■ **hang about, hang around, hang round** *vi* ❶ pasar el rato • **they didn't hang about** se pusieron en marcha sin perder un minuto ❷ esperar • **hang about!** ¡un momento!

■ **hang on** *vi* ❶ • **to hang on (to)** agarrarse (a) ❷ *familiar* esperar; aguardar ❸ resistir

■ **hang out** *vi familiar* pasar el rato

■ **hang round** *vi* = **hang about**

■ **hang up** ◆ *vt* ⚡*El objeto se puede colocar antes o después de la preposición.* colgar ◆ *vi* colgar

■ **hang up on** *vt* ⚡*El objeto siempre va después de la preposición al final.* • **to hang up on somebody** colgarle a alguien

hanger ['hæŋər] *s* gancho

hang gliding *s* vuelo con ala delta

hangover ['hæŋ,əʊvər] *s* resaca

hang-up *s familiar* complejo

hankie, hanky ['hæŋkɪ] (*abreviatura de* handkerchief) *s familiar* pañuelo

haphazard [,hæp'hæzəd] *adj* caótico, ca

happen ['hæpən] *vi* ❶ pasar; ocurrir • **to happen to somebody** pasarle o sucederle a alguien ❷ • **I happened to be looking out of the window...** dio la casualidad de que estaba mirando por la ventana... • **do you happen to have a pen on you?** ¿no tendrás una pluma por casualidad? • **as it happens...** da la casualidad de que...

happily ['hæpɪlɪ] *adv* ❶ alegremente; felizmente ❷ con mucho gusto ❸ afortunadamente

happiness ['hæpɪnɪs] *s* ❶ felicidad ❷ alegría

happy ['hæpɪ] *adj* ❶ feliz • **happy Christmas/birthday!** ¡feliz navidad/cumpleaños! ❷ contento, ta • **to be happy with/about something** estar contento con algo ❸ alegre ❹ feliz; oportuno, na ❺ • **to be happy to do something** estar más que dispuesto, ta a hacer algo • **I'd be happy to do it** yo lo haría con gusto

harass ['hærəs] *vt* acosar

harbor ['hɑːbər] ◆ *s* puerto ◆ *vt* ❶ abrigar (*sentimientos*) ❷ dar refugio a; encubrir

hard [hɑːd] ◆ *adj* ❶ duro, ra • **to go hard** endurecerse • **to be hard on somebody/something a)** ser duro con alguien/algo **b)** perjudicar a alguien/algo (*trabajo*) **c)** ser inmerecido, da para alguien/algo (*resultado*) ❷ difícil ❸ fuerte (*golpe, escarcha*) ❹ concreto, ta

expresión **hard of hearing** duro de oído

◆ *adv* ❶ mucho (*intentar, llover*) ❷ duro (*trabajar*) ❸ atentamente (*escuchar*) ❹ detenidamente (*reflexionar*) ❺ fuerte; con fuerza (*golpear, empujar*)

expresión **to be hard pushed** o **put** o **pressed to do something** vérselas y deseárselas para hacer algo ▶ **to feel hard done by** sentirse tratado injustamente

hardback ['hɑːdbæk] *s* edición en pasta dura

hardball ['hɑːdbɔːl] *s* beisbol • **to play hardball (with somebody)** ponerse duro, ra (con alguien); adoptar una línea dura (con alguien)

hardboard ['hɑːdbɔːd] *s* madera conglomerada

hard-boiled *adj literal & figurado* duro, ra

hard cash *s* dinero contante y sonante

hard copy *s* INFORMÁTICA copia impresa

hard disk *s* INFORMÁTICA disco duro

hard drive *s* INFORMÁTICA unidad de disco duro

harden ['hɑːdn] ◆ *vt* ❶ endurecer ❷ reforzar ◆ *vi* ❶ endurecerse ❷ reforzarse

hard labor *s* ⚡*incontable* trabajos forzados

hard-liner *s* partidario, ria de la línea dura

hardly ['hɑːdlɪ] *adv* apenas • **hardly ever/anything** casi nunca/nada • **that's hardly fair** eso no es justo • **I'm hardly a communist, am I?** ¡pues sí que tengo yo mucho que ver con el comunismo!

hardness ['hɑːdnɪs] *s* ❶ dureza ❷ dificultad

hardship ['hɑːdʃɪp] *s* ❶ ⚡*incontable* privaciones ❷ infortunio

hard up *adj familiar* • **to be hard up** andar mal de dinero • **to be hard up for something** andar escaso, sa de algo

hardware ['hɑːdweər] *s* ⚡*incontable* ❶ artículos de ferretería ❷ INFORMÁTICA hardware

hardware store *s* ferretería

hardworking [,hɑːd'wɜːkɪŋ] *adj* trabajador, ra

hardy ['hɑːdɪ] *adj* ❶ fuerte; robusto, ta ❷ resistente

hare [heər] *s* liebre

harm [hɑːm] ◆ *s* daño • **it won't do him any harm** no le hará ningún daño • **there's no harm in trying/asking** no se pierde nada por intentarlo/preguntar

expresión **to come to no harm a)** salir sano y salvo **b)** no dañarse ▶ **to be out of harm's way** estar a salvo

◆ *vt* hacer daño a; dañar

harmful ['hɑːmfʊl] *adj* • **harmful (to) a)** perjudicial o dañino, na (para) **b)** nocivo, va (para)

harmless ['hɑːmlɪs] *adj* inofensivo, va

harmonica [hɑː'mɒnɪkə] *s* armónica

harmonize ['hɑːmənaɪz] ◆ *vi* • **to harmonize (with)** armonizar (con) ◆ *vt* armonizar

harmony ['hɑːmənɪ] *s* armonía

harness ['hɑːnɪs] ◆ *s* arreos; guarniciones ◆ *vt* ❶ enjaezar ❷ aprovechar

harp [hɑːp] *s* arpa

■ **harp on** *vi* • **to harp on (about something)** insistir (con algo)

harpsichord ['hɑːpsɪkɔːd] *s* clavicémbalo

harsh [hɑːʃ] *adj* ❶ duro, ra (*vida, condiciones, invierno*) ❷ severo, ra (*castigo, decisión, persona*) ❸ áspero, ra (*textura, voz*) ❹ violento, ta (*luz, sonido*)

harvest ['hɑːvɪst] ◆ *s* ❶ cosecha; pizca ❷ vendimia ◆ *vt* cosechar

has

has ☼ *acento atónico* [həz]*, acento tónico* [hæz]
☼ *tercera persona del singular* → **have**

hash [hæʃ] *s* ❶ picadillo *(de carne)* ❷ *familiar* hachís

hash browns *spl* ▶ papas ralladas, fritas y servidas en forma de croqueta

hashish ['hæʃiːʃ] *s* hashish

hasn't ['hæznt] *(abreviatura de* has not*)* = **have**

hassle ['hæsl] *familiar* ◆ *s* ☼ *incontable* rollo; lío ◆ *vt* dar la lata a

haste [heist] *s* prisa • **to make haste** *desusado* darse prisa; apresurarse

hasten ['heisn] *formal* ◆ *vt* acelerar ◆ *vi* • **to hasten (to do something)** apresurarse (a hacer algo)

hastily ['heistili] *adv* ❶ de prisa; precipitadamente ❷ a la ligera; sin reflexionar

hasty ['heisti] *adj* ❶ apresurado, da; precipitado, da ❷ irreflexivo, va

hat [hæt] *s* sombrero

hatch [hætʃ] ◆ *vi* romper el cascarón; salir del huevo ◆ *vt* ❶ incubar ❷ *figurado* tramar ◆ *s* escotilla

hatchback ['hætʃ,bæk] *s* (coche con) 3/5 puertas

hatchet ['hætʃit] *s* hacha

hatchway ['hætʃ,wei] *s* escotilla

hate [heit] ◆ *s* odio ◆ *vt* odiar • **to hate doing something** odiar hacer algo

hatred ['heitrid] *s* odio

hat trick *s* DEPORTE tres tantos marcados por un jugador en el mismo partido

haughty ['hɔːti] *adj* altanero, ra; altivo, va

haul [hɔːl] ◆ *s* ❶ botín ❷ alijo ❸ • **long haul** largo camino; largo trayecto ◆ *vt* tirar; arrastrar

haulage ['hɔːlidʒ] *s* transporte

hauler ['hɔːlər] *s* transportista

haunch [hɔːntʃ] *s* ❶ asentaderas • **to squat on your haunches** ponerse en cuclillas ❷ pernil

haunt [hɔːnt] ◆ *s* sitio favorito ◆ *vt* ❶ aparecer en; aparecerse a *(suj: fantasma)* ❷ atormentar *(suj: memoria, miedo, problema)*

have [hæv]
◆ *auxiliar*
• **she has already eaten** ya comió
• **I was out of breath, having run all the way** estaba sin aliento, después de haber corrido hasta ahí
• **she hasn't gone yet, has she?** todavía no se fue, ¿no?
• **I have made a mistake** cometí un error
◆ *vt*
❶ [*para expresar la posesión, la obligación*] tener
• **I don't have any money, I have no money** no tengo dinero
• **Rosie has blue eyes** o **Rosie has got blue eyes** Rosie tiene los ojos azules
• **I have things to do** tengo cosas que hacer

❷ [*con enfermedades*] tener
• **to have the flu** tener gripa

❸ [*obtener, recibir*]
• **I had some news from her yesterday** recibí noticias suyas ayer

❹ [*se utiliza con acciones en el lugar de un verbo específico*]
• **I have a bath every morning** me baño todas las mañanas
• **I'll have some coffee** tomaré café
• **he always has a cigarette after dinner** siempre se fuma un cigarrillo después de cenar

❺ [*dar a luz*]
• **my cousin has just had a baby** mi prima acaba de tener un bebé

❻ [*hacer que alguien haga*]
• **to have somebody do something** hacer que alguien haga algo
• **I had him mow the lawn** hice que cortara el césped
• **to have something done** mandar hacer algo
• **he had his hair cut** se cortó el pelo
• **I had my car stolen** me robaron el coche

expresiones **to be had** *familiar* ser engañado • **I hate being had** odio que me engañen ▶ **to have it in for somebody** tenerla tomada con alguien ▶ **to have had it** estar para el arrastre

◆ *v modal*
❶ [*expresa obligación, necesidad*]
• **do you have to go?** ¿tienes que irte?
• **I've got to go to work** tengo que irme a trabajar

❷ [*expresa certeza*]
• **he has to be ready by now** a estas horas ya debe de estar listo
• **you've got to be joking!** ¡no hablarás en serio!

■ **have off**
◆ *vt* ☼ *El objeto se puede colocar antes o después de la preposición.*
tener libre *(día, tiempo)*

■ **have on**
◆ *vt* ☼ *El objeto se coloca entre el verbo y la preposición.*
❶ llevar (puesto)
❷ tomar el pelo a
❸ [*actividad, compromiso*]
• **to have something on** hacer algo
• **have you got anything on Friday?** ¿estás libre o haces algo el viernes?

■ **have out**
◆ *vt* ☼ *El objeto se coloca entre el verbo y la preposición.*
operarse de; sacar
• **to have your tonsils out** operarse de las amígdalas

Formas irregulares de **have:** *pretérito+pp* **had.**

have

Presente: I have, you have, he/she/it has, we have, you have, they have. *Pretérito*: I had, you had, he/she/it had, we had, you had, they had. *Gerundio*: having. *Participio pasado*: had.

Además de los significados que tiene como un verbo normal have funciona como verbo auxiliar, principalmente para formar tiempos compuestos (I *have* always *liked* you *siempre me has gustado*; I wish they *had told* me before *me gustaría que me lo hubiesen dicho antes*).

También aparece en construcciones pasivas (he *had* his bike *stolen* the other day *le robaron la bicicleta el otro día*). A veces se puede utilizar el verbo have para indicar que otra persona ejerce la acción del verbo sobre el sujeto (she's *having* the house *painted le están pintando la casa*; he *had* his hair *cut se cortó el pelo*).

Cuando significa *tener* o *poseer* have funciona como un verbo normal en inglés americano; es decir, utiliza do para formar oraciones negativas o interrogativas (I don't have any money *no tengo dinero*; do you have any money? *¿tienes dinero?*).

Ver también must, need.

haven ['heɪvn] *s figurado* refugio; asilo
haven't ['hævnt] *(abreviatura de* have not*)* = **have**
havoc ['hævək] *s ☼ incontable* estragos
Hawaii [hə'waɪɪ] *s* Hawai
hawk [hɔːk] *s literal & figurado* halcón
expresión to watch somebody like a hawk observar a alguien con ojos de lince
hay [heɪ] *s* heno
hay fever *s ☼ incontable* fiebre del heno
haystack ['heɪˌstæk] *s* almiar
hazard ['hæzəd] ◆ *s* riesgo; peligro ◆ *vt* aventurar
hazardous ['hæzədəs] *adj* peligroso, sa
haze [heɪz] *s* neblina
hazel ['heɪzl] *adj* color avellana
hazelnut ['heɪzl,nʌt] *s* avellana
hazy ['heɪzɪ] *adj* ❶ neblinoso, sa ❷ vago, ga; confuso, sa
he [hiː] ◆ *pronombre personal* él • **he's tall/happy** es alto/feliz • **he can't do it** él no puede hacerlo • **there he is** allí está ◆ *en compuestos* • **he-goat** macho cabrío

he

He es el pronombre personal que se usa para hablar de hombres y animales de compañía de sexo masculino (there's my brother — *he*'s a teacher *ahí está mi hermano* — *es profesor*; there's my cat — isn't *he* funny? *ahí está mi gato* — *¿verdad que es gracioso?*). Su equivalente femenino es she (there's my sister — *she*'s a nurse *ahí está mi hermana* — *es enfermera*). It designa lo que carece de sexo, las ideas y los animales en general (there's my car — *it*'s a Ford *ahí está mi coche* — *es un Ford*).

Con nombres de animales o con algunas palabras referidas a personas, como baby, se puede usar it si se desconoce el sexo (listen to that baby — I wish *it* would be quiet! *¿escuchas al bebé? — Ojalá se callase*).

head [hed] ◆ *s* ❶ ANATOMÍA & *INFORMÁTICA* cabeza • **a** o **per head** por persona; por cabeza ❷ talento; aptitud • **she has a head for figures** se le dan bien las cuentas ❸ cabeza *(parte de arriba)* ❹ cabecera ❺ cabezuela ❻ espuma *(de cerveza)* ❼ jefe, fa ❽ director, ra *(de colegio)*
expresiones to be soft in the head estar mal de la sesera ▶ to be out of your head estar como una cabra ▶ it was over my head no me enteré de nada ▶ it went to her head se le subió a la cabeza ▶ to keep/lose your head no perder/perder la cabeza ▶ to laugh your head off reír a mandíbula batiente
◆ *vt* ❶ encabezar ❷ dirigir ❸ *FÚTBOL* cabecear ◆ *vi* • **to head north/for home** dirigirse hacia el norte/a casa
■ **heads** *spl* cara • **heads or tails?** ¿cara o cruz?
■ **head for** *vt ☼ El objeto siempre va después de la preposición al final.* ❶ dirigirse a ❷ *figurado* ir camino de
headache ['hedeɪk] *s* ❶ *MEDICINA* dolor de cabeza • **I have a headache** me duele la cabeza ❷ *figurado* quebradero de cabeza
headband ['hedbænd] *s* cinta; banda *(para el pelo)*
header ['hedər] *s* ❶ *FÚTBOL* cabezazo ❷ *TIPOGRAFÍA* encabezamiento
headfirst [ˌhed'fɜːst] *adv* de cabeza
heading ['hedɪŋ] *s* encabezamiento
headlight ['hedlaɪt] *s* faro
headline ['hedlaɪn] *s* titular
headlong ['hedlɒŋ] *adv* ❶ de cabeza ❷ precipitadamente
headmaster [ˌhed'mɑːstər] *s* director *(de colegio)*
headmistress [ˌhed'mɪstrɪs] *s* directora *(de colegio)*
head office *s* oficina central
head of state *s* jefe de Estado
head-on ◆ *adj* de frente; frontal ◆ *adv* de frente
headphones ['hedfəʊnz] *spl* auriculares

H

headquarters [ˌhedˈkwɔːtəz] *spl* ❶ (oficina) central; sede ❷ MILITAR cuartel general

headrest [ˈhedrest] *s* reposacabezas

headscarf [ˈhedskɑːf] *s* pañuelo *(para la cabeza)*
Dos plurales: **headscarves** [ˈhedskɑːvz] o **headscarfs**.

headset [ˈhedset] *s* auriculares con micrófono

head start *s* • **head start (on** o **over)** ventaja (con respecto a)

head waiter *s* capitán de meseros

headway [ˈhedweɪ] *s* • **to make headway** avanzar; hacer progresos

headwind [ˈhedwɪnd] *s* viento de proa

heal [hiːl] ◆ *vt* ❶ curar ❷ cicatrizar ❸ *figurado* remediar ◆ *vi* cicatrizar

healing [ˈhiːlɪŋ] *s* curación

health [helθ] *s* ❶ salud ❷ *figurado* buen estado *(de país, organización)*

health care *s* asistencia sanitaria

health center *s* clínica; centro de salud

health food *s* comida naturista

health food store *s* tienda naturista

healthy [ˈhelθɪ] *adj* ❶ sano, na ❷ saludable ❸ pingüe *(beneficio)*

heap [hiːp] ◆ *s* montón; pila ◆ *vt* • **to heap something (on** o **onto something)** amontonar algo (sobre algo)
■ **heaps** *spl familiar* montones

hear [hɪər] ◆ *vt* ❶ oír • **I hear (that...)** me dicen que... ❷ DERECHO ver ◆ *vi* oír • **have you heard about that job yet?** ¿sabes algo del trabajo ese? • **to hear from somebody** tener noticias de alguien
expresión **to have heard of** haber oído hablar de ▶ **I won't hear of it!** ¡de eso ni hablar!
Formas irregulares de **hear**: *pret & pp* **heard** [hɜːd].

hearing [ˈhɪərɪŋ] *s* ❶ oído • **in** o **within somebody's hearing** al alcance del oído de alguien ❷ DERECHO vista
expresión **to give somebody a fair hearing** *figurado* dar a alguien la oportunidad de que se exprese

hearing aid *s* audífono

hearsay [ˈhɪəseɪ] *s* ☼ *incontable* habladurías

hearse [hɜːs] *s* coche fúnebre

heart [hɑːt] *s* ❶ corazón • **from the heart** con toda sinceridad ❷ • **I didn't have the heart to tell her** no tuve valor para decírselo • **to lose heart** descorazonarse ❸ quid ❹ centro *(de ciudad)* ❺ cogollo *(de lechuga)*
■ **hearts** *spl* corazones
■ **at heart** *adv* en el fondo
■ **by heart** *adv* de memoria

heart attack *s* infarto

heartbeat [ˈhɑːtbiːt] *s* latido

heartbroken [ˈhɑːtˌbrəʊkn] *adj* desolado, da; abatido, da

heartburn [ˈhɑːtbɜːn] *s* ardor de estómago

heart failure *s* paro cardíaco

heartfelt [ˈhɑːtfelt] *adj* sincero, ra; de todo corazón

hearth [hɑːθ] *s* hogar

hearty [ˈhɑːtɪ] *adj* ❶ bonachón, ona ❷ cordial ❸ fuertote, ta ❹ abundante *(comida)* ❺ bueno, na *(apetito)* ❻ profundo, da *(antipatía, recelo)*

heat [hiːt] ◆ *s* ❶ calor ❷ temperatura ❸ *figurado* tensión ❹ serie; prueba eliminatoria
expresión **in the heat of the moment** en el calor del momento
◆ *vt* calentar
■ **heat up** ◆ *vt* ☼ *El objeto se puede colocar antes o después de la preposición.* calentar ◆ *vi* calentarse

heated [ˈhiːtɪd] *adj* ❶ climatizado, da *(piscina)* ❷ acalorado, da *(discusión)*

heater [ˈhiːtər] *s* calentador; estufa

heath [hiːθ] *s* brezal

heathen [ˈhiːðn] *s* pagano, na

heather [ˈheðər] *s* brezo

heating [ˈhiːtɪŋ] *s* calefacción

heatstroke [ˈhiːtstrəʊk] *s* ☼ *incontable* insolación

heat wave *s* ola de calor

heave [hiːv] ◆ *vt* ❶ tirar de; arrastrar ❷ empujar ◆ *vi* ❶ tirar ❷ palpitar *(pecho)*

heaven [ˈhevn] *s* el cielo
expresión **it was heaven** fue divino
■ **heavens** *spl* • **the heavens** *literario* los cielos
expresión **(good) heavens!** ¡cielos!

heavenly [ˈhevnlɪ] *adj* divino, na

heavily [ˈhevɪlɪ] *adv* ❶ mucho *(fumar, beber)* ❷ con fuerza *(llover)* • **heavily in debt** con muchas deudas ❸ • **heavily built** corpulento, ta ❹ profundamente *(suspirar)* ❺ pesadamente *(moverse, caerse)*

heavy [ˈhevɪ] *adj* ❶ pesado, da • **how heavy is it?** ¿cuánto pesa? • **heavy build** corpulencia ❷ sólido, da ❸ grueso, sa *(abrigo)* ❹ intenso, sa *(tráfico, lluvia, combate)* ❺ • **to be a heavy smoker/drinker** ser un fumador/bebedor empedernido ❻ grande *(pérdidas, responsabilidad)* ❼ duro, ra *(golpe, multa, derrota, trabajo)* ❽ apretado, da ❾ cargado, da *(tiempo)*

heavy cream *s* crema para batir

heavyweight [ˈhevɪweɪt] ◆ *adj* DEPORTE de los pesos pesados ◆ *s* DEPORTE peso pesado

Hebrew [ˈhiːbruː] ◆ *adj* hebreo, a ◆ *s* ❶ hebreo, a ❷ hebreo

heck [hek] *exclamación* • **what/where/why the heck...?** ¿qué/dónde/por qué demonios...? • **a heck of a lot of** la mar de

heckle [ˈhekl] *vt & vi* interrumpir con exabruptos

hectic [ˈhektɪk] *adj* ajetreado, da

he'd [hiːd] ❶ *(abreviatura de* he had*)* = **have** ❷ *(abreviatura de* he would*)* = **would**

hedge [hedʒ] *s* seto

hedgehog [ˈhedʒhɒg] *s* erizo

heed [hi:d] ◆ *s* • **to pay heed to somebody** hacer caso a alguien • **to take heed of something** tener algo en cuenta ◆ *vt formal* tener en cuenta

heel [hi:l] *s* ❶ talón ❷ tacón

hefty ['heftɪ] *adj familiar* ❶ fornido, da ❷ considerable; importante

height [haɪt] *s* ❶ altura • **5 meters in height** 5 metros de altura • **to gain/lose height** ganar/perder altura ❷ estatura • **she's of average height** es de estatura mediana ❸ • **the height of a)** el punto álgido de **b)** el colmo de

heighten ['haɪtn] ◆ *vt* intensificar; aumentar ◆ *vi* intensificarse; aumentar

heir [eər] *s* heredero

heiress ['eərɪs] *s* heredera

heirloom ['eəlu:m] *s* reliquia de familia

heist [haɪst] *s familiar* robo

held [held] *pretérito* & *participio pasado* → **hold**

helicopter ['helɪkɒptər] *s* helicóptero

hell [hel] ◆ *s* infierno • **one** o **a hell of a mess** *familiar* un lío de mil demonios • **it was hell** *familiar* fue un infierno • **neighbors from hell** *familiar* vecinos infernales

expresiones **to do something for the hell of it** *familiar* hacer algo porque sí ▶ **to give somebody hell** *familiar* hacérselas pasar canutas a alguien ▶ **go to hell!** *muy familiar* ¡vete al infierno!

◆ *exclamación familiar* ¡hostias!

he'll [hi:l] ❶ (*abreviatura de* he will) = **will** ❷ (*abreviatura de* he shall) = **shall**

hellish ['helɪʃ] *adj familiar* diabólico, ca

hello, hallo [hə'ləʊ] *exclamación* ❶ ¡hola! ❷ ¡bueno! *(al contestar el teléfono)* ¡oiga! *(al llamar a alguien por teléfono, para llamar la atención)*

helm [helm] *s literal* & *figurado* timón

helmet ['helmɪt] *s* casco

help [help] ◆ *s* ❶ ayuda • **with the help of** con la ayuda de • **to be a help** ser una ayuda • **to be of help** ayudar ❷ *incontable* socorro; ayuda • **to help somebody (to) do something/with something** ayudar a alguien (a hacer algo/con algo) • **can I help you?** ¿en qué puedo servirle? ❸ • **I can't help it/feeling sad** no puedo evitarlo/evitar que me dé pena **expresión** **it can't be helped** ¿qué se le va a hacer? ▶ **to help yourself (to something)** servirse (algo)

◆ *vi* • **to help (with)** ayudar (con) ◆ *exclamación* ¡socorro!; ¡auxilio!

■ **help out** ◆ *vt* ❖ *El objeto se puede colocar antes o después de la preposición.* echar una mano a ◆ *vi* echar una mano

helper ['helpər] *s* ❶ ayudante ❷ mujer o señora de la limpieza

helpful ['helpfʊl] *adj* ❶ servicial; atento, ta ❷ útil

helping ['helpɪŋ] *s* porción • **would you like a second helping?** ¿quiere repetir?

helpless ['helplɪs] *adj* ❶ indefenso, sa ❷ impotente *(mirada, gesto)*

helpline ['helplaɪn] *s* servicio de asistencia telefónica

help menu *s* INFORMÁTICA menú de ayuda

hem [hem] *s* bastilla; dobladillo

■ **hem in** *vt* ❖ *El objeto se puede colocar antes o después de la preposición.* rodear; cercar

hemisphere ['hemɪˌsfɪər] *s* hemisferio

hemline ['hemlaɪn] *s* bajo *(de falda* ETC*)*

hemorrhage, haemorrhage ['hemərɪdʒ] *s* hemorragia

hen [hen] *s* ❶ gallina ❷ hembra

hence [hens] *adv formal* ❶ por lo tanto; así pues ❷ • **five years hence** de aquí a cinco años

henceforth [ˌhens'fɔ:θ] *adv formal* de ahora en adelante

henchman ['hentʃmən] *s despectivo* esbirro

El plural de **henchman** es **henchmen** ['hentʃmen].

henpecked ['henpekt] *adj despectivo* • **a henpecked husband** un mandilón

hepatitis [ˌhepə'taɪtɪs] *s* hepatitis

her [hɜ:r] ◆ *pronombre personal* ❶ ❖ *directo - acentuado* la • **I know her** la conozco • **I like her** me gusta ❷ ❖ *directo - no acentuado* ella • **it's her** es ella • **if I were** o **was her** si (yo) fuera ella • **you can't expect her to do it** no esperarás que ella lo haga ❸ ❖ *cuando se refiere a un barco, coche, etc* lo • **fill her up!** AUTO-MÓVILES ¡llénemelo!; ¡lleno, por favor! ❹ ❖ *indirecto - generalmente* le • **he sent her a letter** le mandó una carta • **we spoke to her** hablamos con ella ❺ ❖ *indirecto - con otros pronombres de tercera persona* se • **I gave it to her** se lo di ❻ ❖ *tras preposición, en comparaciones, etc* ella • **I'm shorter than her** yo soy más bajo que ella ◆ *adj posesivo* su; sus ❖ *pl* • **her coat** su abrigo • **her children** sus niños • **her name is Sarah** se llama Sarah • **it wasn't her fault** no fue culpa suya • **she washed her hair** se lavó el pelo

her
No olvidemos que al hablar de las partes del cuerpo se usa el adjetivo posesivo *her* en lugar del artículo *the* (she put *her* hand up *alzó la mano*; she broke *her* leg *se rompió la pierna*).

herald ['herəld] ◆ *vt formal* ❶ anunciar ❷ proclamar ◆ *s* ❶ heraldo ❷ anuncio

herb [ɜ:rb] *s* hierba *(aromática o medicinal)*

herd [hɜ:d] ◆ *s* ❶ rebaño ❷ manada *(de elefantes)* ◆ *vt figurado* conducir (en grupo) bruscamente

here [hɪər]
◆ *adv*
❶ [*en este lugar*] aquí
• **I've lived here for 5 years** llevo cinco años viviendo aquí

- **come here!** ¡ven aquí!
- **he's not here today** hoy no está aquí
❷ [para indicar donde se está]
- **Jenny Cooper? — here!** ¿Jenny Cooper? — ¡presente!
❸ [para presentar algo]
- **here is what I want** aquí está lo que quiero
❹ [para presentar a alguien] aquí
- **here he is/they are** aquí está/están
- **here comes John** aquí está John

hereabout [ˌhɪərə'baʊt] *adv* por aquí

hereafter [ˌhɪər'ɑːftər] *adv* ❶ *formal* de ahora en adelante ❷ más tarde

hereby [ˌhɪə'baɪ] *adv formal* ❶ por la presente ❷ • **I hereby declare you the winner** desde este momento te declaro vencedor

hereditary [hɪ'redɪtrɪ] *adj* hereditario, ria

heresy ['herəsɪ] *s figurado* RELIGIÓN herejía

heritage ['herɪtɪdʒ] *s* patrimonio

hermetically [hɜː'metɪklɪ] *adv* • **hermetically sealed** cerrado, da herméticamente

hermit ['hɜːmɪt] *s* ermitaño, ña

hero ['hɪərəʊ] *s* ❶ héroe ❷ ídolo ❸ torta hecha con una barra de pan rellena de varios ingredientes
El plural de **hero** es **heroes**.

heroic [hɪ'rəʊɪk] *adj* heroico, ca

heroin ['herəʊɪn] *s* heroína *(droga)* • **heroin addict** heroinómano, na

heroine ['herəʊɪn] *s* heroína *(persona)*

heron ['herən] *s* garza
Dos plurales: **heron** o **herons**.

herring ['herɪŋ] *s* arenque
Dos plurales: **herring** o **herrings**.

hers [hɜːz] *pronombre posesivo* suyo, suya • **that money is hers** ese dinero es suyo • **those keys are hers** esas llaves son suyas • **it wasn't his fault, it was hers** no fue culpa de él sino de ella • **a friend of hers** un amigo suyo; un amigo de ella • **mine is good, but hers is bad** el mío es bueno pero el suyo es malo

herself [hɜː'self] *pronombre* ❶ ☼ *reflexivo* se • **she's washing herself** se está lavando ❷ ☼ *tras preposición* sí misma • **with herself** consigo misma ❸ ☼ *para enfatizar* ella misma • **she did it herself** lo hizo ella sola ⸢**expresión**⸣ **by herself** sola

he's [hiːz] ❶ *(abreviatura de he is)* = **be** ❷ *(abreviatura de he has)* = **have**

hesitant ['hezɪtənt] *adj* ❶ indeciso, sa; inseguro, ra ❷ vacilante

hesitate ['hezɪteɪt] *vi* vacilar; dudar

hesitation [ˌhezɪ'teɪʃn] *s* vacilación

heterosexual [ˌhetərəʊ'sekʃʊəl] ◆ *adj* heterosexual ◆ *s* heterosexual

hey [heɪ] *exclamación* ¡eh!; ¡oye!

heyday ['heɪdeɪ] *s* apogeo; auge

hi [haɪ] *exclamación familiar* ¡hola!

hibernate ['haɪbəneɪt] *vi* hibernar

hiccough, hiccup ['hɪkʌp] ◆ *s* ❶ hipo • **to have (the) hiccoughs** tener hipo ❷ *figurado* contratiempo ◆ *vi* hipar

hid [hɪd] *pretérito* → hide

hidden ['hɪdn] ◆ *participio pasado* → hide ◆ *adj* oculto, ta

hide [haɪd] ◆ *vt* ❶ esconder; ocultar • **to hide something (from somebody)** esconder o ocultar algo (a alguien) ❷ tapar ◆ *vi* esconderse ◆ *s* ❶ piel *(de animal)* ❷ puesto *(para observar animales, aves)*
Formas irregulares de **hide**: *pretérito* **hid**, *pp* **hidden**.

hide-and-seek *s* escondite *(juego)*

hideaway ['haɪdəweɪ] *s familiar* escondite *(lugar)*

hideous ['hɪdɪəs] *adj* horrible

hiding ['haɪdɪŋ] *s* ❶ • **in hiding** escondido, da ❷ *familiar* • **to give somebody/get a (good) hiding** darle a alguien/recibir una (buena) paliza

hiding place *s* escondite

hierarchy ['haɪərɑːkɪ] *s* jerarquía

hi-fi ['haɪfaɪ] ◆ *adj* de alta fidelidad ◆ *s* equipo de alta fidelidad

high [haɪ] ◆ *adj* ❶ alto, ta • **it's 6 meters high** tiene 6 metros de alto • **how high is it?** ¿cuánto mide? • **temperatures in the high 20s** temperaturas cercanas a los 30 grados • **at high speed** a gran velocidad ❷ grande *(altitud, riesgo, calidad)* ❸ fuerte *(viento)* ❹ elevado, da *(ideales, principios)* ❺ agudo, da *(voz, sonido)* ❻ *familiar* colocado, da *(de droga)* ◆ *adv* alto • **he threw the ball high in the air** lanzó la pelota muy alto ◆ *s* ❶ punto álgido ❷ anticiclón ❸ máxima

highball ['haɪbɔːl] *s* jaibol

high chair *s* silla alta

high-class *adj* de (alta) categoría

higher ['haɪər] *adj* superior

higher education *s* enseñanza superior

high jump *s* salto de altura

Highlands ['haɪləndz] *spl* • **the Highlands** las Tierras Altas de Escocia

highlight ['haɪlaɪt] ◆ *s* punto culminante ◆ *vt* ❶ resaltar; marcar *(con rotulador)* ❷ destacar; resaltar
■ **highlights** *spl* ❶ luces; rayos ❷ mejores momentos

highlighter (pen) ['haɪlaɪtər-] *s* plumón fluorescente

highly ['haɪlɪ] *adv* ❶ muy • **highly paid** bien pagado, da ❷ • **to speak highly of somebody** hablar muy bien de alguien • **to think highly of somebody** tener a alguien en mucha estima

Highness ['haɪnɪs] *s* • **His/Her/Your (Royal) Highness** Su Alteza (Real) • **their (Royal) Highnesses** Sus Altezas (Reales)

high-pitched [-'pɪtʃt] *adj* agudo, da

high point *s* momento o punto culminante

high-powered [-'pauəd] *adj* ❶ de gran potencia ❷ prestigioso, sa *(actividad, trabajo)* ❸ de altos vuelos *(persona)*

high-ranking [-'ræŋkɪŋ] *adj* ❶ de alta graduación ❷ • **high-ranking official** alto cargo

high-rise *adj* • **high-rise building** torre

high school *s* ≈ instituto de bachillerato

high season *s* temporada alta

high tech, hi-tech [-'tek] *adj* de alta tecnología

high tide *s* marea alta

highway ['haɪweɪ] *s* carretera; autopista

hijack ['haɪdʒæk] *vt* secuestrar

hijacker ['haɪdʒækər] *s* secuestrador, ra *(de un avión)*

hike [haɪk] ◆ *s* caminata • **to go for** o **on a hike** ir de excursión ◆ *vi* ir de excursión

hiker ['haɪkər] *s* excursionista

hiking ['haɪkɪŋ] *s* excursionismo • **to go hiking** ir de excursión

hilarious [hɪ'leərɪəs] *adj* desternillante

hill [hɪl] *s* ❶ colina ❷ cuesta

hillbilly ['hɪl,bɪlɪ] *s despectivo* palurdo, da de las montañas

hillside ['hɪlsaɪd] *s* ladera

hilly ['hɪlɪ] *adj* montañoso, sa

hilt [hɪlt] *s* puño; empuñadura

him [hɪm] *pronombre personal* ❶ ☼:*directo - no acentuado* lo; le • **I know him** lo o le conozco • **I like him** me gusta ❷ ☼:*directo - acentuado* él • **it's him** es él • **if I were** o **was him** si (yo) fuera él • **you can't expect him to do it** no esperarás que él lo haga ❸ ☼:*indirecto - generalmente* le • **she sent him a letter** le mandó una carta ❹ ☼:*indirecto - con otros pronombres de tercera persona* se • **we spoke to him** hablamos con él • **I gave it to him** se lo di ❺ ☼:*tras preposición, en comparaciones, etc* él • **I'm shorter than him** yo soy más bajo que él

Himalayas [,hɪmə'leɪəz] *spl* • **the Himalayas** el Himalaya

himself [hɪm'self] *pronombre* ❶ ☼:*reflexivo* se • **he's washing himself** se está lavando ❷ ☼:*tras preposición* sí mismo • **with himself** consigo mismo ❸ ☼:*para enfatizar* él mismo • **he did it himself** lo hizo él solo

expresión **by himself** solo

hind [haɪnd] *adj* trasero, ra

hinder ['hɪndər] *vt* ❶ estorbar ❷ entorpecer

Hindi ['hɪndɪ] *s* hindi

hindrance ['hɪndrəns] *s* ❶ obstáculo; impedimento ❷ estorbo

hindsight ['haɪndsaɪt] *s* • **with the benefit of hindsight** ahora que se sabe lo que pasó

Hindu ['hɪndu:] ◆ *adj* hindú ◆ *s* hindú
El plural de **Hindu** es **Hindus**.

hinge [hɪndʒ] *s* bisagra

hint [hɪnt] ◆ *s* ❶ indirecta • **to drop a hint** lanzar una indirecta ❷ consejo ❸ asomo ❹ pizca *(de color)* ◆ *vi* • **to hint at something** insinuar algo ◆ *vt* • **to hint that** insinuar que

hip [hɪp] ◆ *s* ANATOMÍA cadera ◆ *adj* familiar moderno, na

hippie, hippy ['hɪpɪ] *s* hippy

hippopotamus [,hɪpə'pɒtəməs] *s* hipopótamo
Dos plurales: **hippopotamuses** o **hippopotami** [,hɪpə'pɒtəmaɪ].

hippy ['hɪpɪ] = **hippie**

hire ['haɪər] ◆ *s* ☼:*incontable* alquiler • **for hire** libre • **'boats for hire'** 'se alquilan barcos' ◆ *vt* ❶ alquilar ❷ contratar

■ **hire out** *vt* ☼:*El objeto se puede colocar antes o después de la preposición.* ❶ alquilar ❷ ofrecer *(servicios)*

his [hɪz] ◆ *adj posesivo* su; sus ☼:*pl* • **his house** su casa • **his children** sus niños • **his name is Joe** se llama Joe • **it wasn't his fault** no fue culpa suya • **he washed his hair** se lavó el pelo ◆ *pronombre posesivo* suyo, suya • **that money is his** ese dinero es suyo • **those keys are his** esas llaves son suyas • **it wasn't her fault, it was his** no fue culpa de ella sino de él • **a friend of his** un amigo suyo; un amigo de él • **mine is good, but his is bad** el mío es bueno pero el suyo es malo

his

No olvidemos que al hablar de las partes del cuerpo se usa el adjetivo posesivo **his** en lugar del artículo **the** (he put ***his*** hand up *alzó la mano*; he broke ***his*** leg *se rompió la pierna*).

Hispanic [hɪ'spænɪk] ◆ *adj* hispánico, ca ◆ *s* hispano, na

hiss [hɪs] ◆ *s* ❶ bisbiseo; siseo ❷ silbido ◆ *vi* ❶ bisbisear; sisear ❷ silbar

historic [hɪ'stɒrɪk] *adj* histórico, ca

historical [hɪ'stɒrɪkəl] *adj* histórico, ca

history ['hɪstərɪ] ◆ *s* ❶ historia ❷ historial ◆ *en compuestos* de historia

hit [hɪt] ◆ *s* ❶ golpe ❷ impacto ❸ éxito ❹ INFORMÁTICA visita ◆ *en compuestos* de éxito ◆ *vt* ❶ pegar; golpear • **I hit my knee on the table** me golpeé la rodilla en la mesa ❷ chocar contra o con ❸ alcanzar ❹ dar en *(el blanco)* ❺ afectar

expresión **the solution hit me** se me ocurrió la solución
Formas irregulares de **hit**: *pretérito & pp* **hit**.

hitch [hɪtʃ] ◆ *s* problema; pega ◆ *vt* ❶ • **to hitch a lift** conseguir un aventón ❷ • **to hitch something on** o **onto something** enganchar algo a algo ◆ *vi* pedir aventón

■ **hitch up** *vt* ☼:*El objeto se puede colocar antes o después de la preposición.* subirse *(el pantalón)*

hitchhike ['hɪtʃhaɪk] *vi* pedir aventón

hitchhiker ['hɪtʃhaɪkər] *s* autoestopista

hi-tech [ˌhaɪ'tek] = **high tech**

hitherto [ˌhɪðə'tuː] *adv formal* hasta ahora

HIV (*abreviatura de* human immunodeficiency virus) *s* VIH • **to be HIV-positive** ser seropositivo, va

hive [haɪv] *s* colmena

expresión **a hive of activity** un enjambre; un centro de actividad

■ **hive off** *vt* ☀️ *El objeto se puede colocar antes o después de la preposición.* transferir

HMO (*abreviatura de* health maintenance organization) *s* ▶ organización para la administración de los servicios médicos bajo un seguro

hoard [hɔːd] ◆ *s* acopio ◆ *vt* ❶ acumular ❷ acaparar

hoarse [hɔːs] *adj* ❶ ronco, ca ❷ afónico, ca

hoax [həʊks] *s* engaño • **hoax call** falsa alarma telefónica

hobble ['hɒbl] *vi* cojear

hobby ['hɒbɪ] *s* hobby; afición

hobo ['həʊbəʊ] *s* vagabundo, da

Dos plurales: **hoboes** o **hobos**.

hockey ['hɒkɪ] *s* ❶ hockey sobre hielo ❷ hockey sobre pasto

hoe [həʊ] ◆ *s* azada ◆ *vt* remover con la azada

hog [hɒg] ◆ *s* cerdo; puerco

expresión **to go the whole hog** *figurado* tirar la casa por la ventana

◆ *vt familiar* acaparar

hoist [hɔɪst] *vt* izar

hokum ['həʊkəm] *s familiar* palabrería

hold [həʊld] ◆ *vt* ❶ tener cogido, da • **I was holding the key in my hand** tenía la llave en la mano ❷ sujetar ❸ sostener; aguantar ❹ abrazar ❺ detener ❻ guardar ❼ mantener (*el interés, una conversación*) ❽ poseer ❾ contener; tener cabida para ❿ celebrar (*congreso, reunión*); realizar (*investigación*) ⓫ • **please hold the line** no cuelgue por favor ⓬ MILITAR ocupar; tener

expresiones **hold it** o **everything!** ¡para!; ¡espera! ▶ **to hold your breath** contener la respiración ▶ **to hold something dear** apreciar mucho algo ▶ **to hold your own** defenderse

◆ *vi* ❶ continuar así (*suerte, tiempo*) ❷ seguir en pie (*promesa, oferta*) • **to hold still** o **steady** estarse quieto ❸ esperar (*al teléfono*) ◆ *s* ❶ • **to have a firm hold on something** tener algo bien agarrado • **to take hold of something** agarrar algo ❷ bodega (*de avión, barco*) ❸ dominio

expresión **to get hold of something** hacerse con algo; conseguir algo

■ **hold back** *vt* ☀️ *El objeto se puede colocar antes o después de la preposición.* ❶ contener; reprimir ❷ ocultar

■ **hold down** *vt* ☀️ *El objeto se puede colocar antes o después de la preposición.* conservar (*puesto de trabajo*)

■ **hold off** *vt* ☀️ *El objeto se puede colocar antes o después de la preposición.* rechazar

■ **hold on** *vi* ❶ esperar ❷ no colgar ❸ • **to hold on (to something)** agarrarse (a algo)

■ **hold out** ◆ *vt* ☀️ *El objeto se puede colocar antes o después de la preposición.* ❶ tender ❷ extender ◆ *vi* durar

■ **hold up** ◆ *vt* ☀️ *El objeto se puede colocar antes o después de la preposición.* ❶ levantar; alzar ❷ retrasar ❸ atracar ◆ *vi* tenerse en pie

Formas irregulares de **hold**: *pretérito & pp* **held**.

holder ['həʊldər] *s* ❶ soporte ❷ candelero ❸ titular ❹ poseedor, ra

holding ['həʊldɪŋ] *s* ❶ participación ❷ propiedad; terreno de cultivo

holdup ['həʊldʌp] *s* ❶ retraso ❷ atraco a mano armada

hole [həʊl] *s* ❶ agujero ❷ hoyo ❸ madriguera ❹ cuchitril

holiday ['hɒlɪdeɪ] *s* fiesta; día festivo

■ **holidays** *s* • **the holidays** las fiestas o vacaciones (de Navidad) • **happy holidays!** ¡felices fiestas!

Holidays

En Estados Unidos cada estado tiene sus propios días festivos, además de las fiestas nacionales. Estas son **Christmas Day**, **New Year's Day**, **Labor Day** (primer lunes de septiembre), **Columbus Day** (segundo lunes de octubre) y **Thanksgiving** (cuarto jueves de noviembre). En otras dos se conmemoran aniversarios de líderes importantes: **Martin Luther King Day** (tercer lunes de enero) y **Presidents' Day** (tercer lunes de febrero, aniversario de los presidentes Lincoln y Washington). Por último, también se celebran eventos relacionados con distintas guerras: **Memorial Day** (en memoria de las víctimas de guerra, último lunes de mayo), **Independence Day** (4 de julio) y **Veteran's Day** (11 de noviembre).

holistic [həʊ'lɪstɪk] *adj* holístico, ca

Holland ['hɒlənd] *s* Holanda

holler ['hɒlər] *vt* & *vi familiar* gritar

hollow ['hɒləʊ] ◆ *adj* ❶ hueco, ca ❷ hundido, da (*ojos, mejillas*) ❸ sonoro, ra; resonante ❹ vano, na (*promesa, palabras*) ◆ *s* ❶ hueco ❷ depresión

■ **hollow out** *vt* ☀️ *El objeto se puede colocar antes o después de la preposición.* ❶ dejar hueco, ca ❷ hacer ahuecando

holly ['hɒlɪ] *s* acebo

Hollywood

HOLLYWOOD

Hollywood es una zona de Los Ángeles, California, donde se produce la mayor parte de las películas estadounidenses desde hace casi un siglo, y donde viven muchas celebridades. Las primeras productoras cinematográficas se establecieron allí en 1908, donde el clima privilegiado permitía rodar en exteriores todo el año.

holocaust [ˈhɒləkɔːst] *s* holocausto
■ **Holocaust** *s* • **the Holocaust** el Holocausto
holster [ˈhəʊlstər] *s* pistolera
holy [ˈhəʊlɪ] *adj* ❶ sagrado, da ❷ bendito, ta *(agua)* ❸ santo, ta

Holy Ghost, Holy Spirit *s* • **the Holy Ghost** o **Spirit** el Espíritu Santo

homage [ˈhɒmɪdʒ] *s* ☿ *incontable formal* homenaje • **to pay homage to** rendir homenaje a
home [həʊm] ◆ *s* ❶ casa • **away from home** fuera de casa • **to make your home somewhere** establecerse en algún sitio ❷ tierra ❸ ciudad natal ❹ hogar • **to leave home** independizarse; irse de casa ❺ residencia *(de ancianos* ETC*)*
expresión it's a home away from home me siento como en mi propia casa
    ◆ *adj* ❶ nacional ❷ casero, ra ❸ familiar *(vida)* ❹ en la casa *(reformas)* ❺ a domicilio *(entrega)* ❻ DEPORTE de casa ◆ *adv* ❶ a casa • **she took me home** me llevó a mi casa • **to go home** irse a casa • **to get home** llegar a casa ❷ en casa
■ **at home** *adv* ❶ en casa ❷ • **at home (with)** a gusto (con) ❸ en mi país
expresión to make yourself at home acomodárse
▶ **make yourself at home!** estás en tu casa
home address *s* domicilio particular
home brew *s* cerveza casera
homecoming [ˈhəʊmˌkʌmɪŋ] *s* EDUCACIÓN & UNIVERSIDAD recepción para antiguos alumnos
home computer *s* computadora doméstica
home economics *s* ☿ *incontable* economía doméstica
homeland [ˈhəʊmlænd] *s* tierra natal; patria
homeless [ˈhəʊmlɪs] *adj* sin hogar
homely [ˈhəʊmlɪ] *adj* ❶ feúcho, cha ❷ sencillo, lla
homemade [ˌhəʊmˈmeɪd] *adj* ❶ casero, ra ❷ de fabricación casera
homeopathy [ˌhəʊmɪˈɒpəθɪ] *s* homeopatía
home page *s* página inicial o de inicio
home run *s* jonrón
home school *vt* educar en casa
homesick [ˈhəʊmsɪk] *adj* nostálgico, ca • **to be homesick** tener morriña • **she was homesick for most of the trip** extrañó a su familia durante la mayor parte del viaje
hometown [ˈhəʊmtaʊn] *s* pueblo/ciudad natal
homeward [ˈhəʊmwəd] ◆ *adj* de regreso o vuelta (a casa) ◆ *adv* = **homewards**
homewards [ˈhəʊmwədz], **homeward** *adv* hacia casa

homework [ˈhəʊmwɜːk] *s* ☿ *incontable literal & figurado* tarea
homey, homy [ˈhəʊmɪ] ◆ *adj* confortable; agradable ◆ *s familiar* cuate
homicide [ˈhɒmɪsaɪd] *s* homicidio
homosexual [ˌhɒməˈsekʃʊəl] ◆ *adj* homosexual ◆ *s* homosexual
homy = **homey**
Honduran [hɒnˈdjʊərən] ◆ *adj* hondureño, ña ◆ *s* hondureño, ña
Honduras [hɒnˈdjʊərəs] *s* Honduras
honest [ˈɒnɪst] *adj* ❶ honrado, da ❷ franco, ca; sincero, ra • **to be honest...** si he de serte franco...
honestly [ˈɒnɪstlɪ] ◆ *adv* ❶ honradamente ❷ de verdad; en serio ◆ *exclamación* ¡será posible!
honesty [ˈɒnɪstɪ] *s* ❶ honradez ❷ sinceridad • **in all honesty...** si he de serte franco...
honey [ˈhʌnɪ] *s* ❶ miel ❷ cielo; mi vida
honeycomb [ˈhʌnɪkəʊm] *s* panal
honeymoon [ˈhʌnɪmuːn] *s* ❶ luna de miel ❷ *figurado* periodo idílico
honk [hɒŋk] ◆ *vi* ❶ tocar el claxon ❷ graznar ◆ *vt* tocar
honor [ˈɒnər] ◆ *s* honor; honra • **in honor of** en honor de ◆ *vt* ❶ cumplir *(promesa, acuerdo)* ❷ satisfacer *(deuda)* ❸ pagar; aceptar *(cheque)* ❹ *formal* honrar
■ **honors** *spl* honores
honorable [ˈɒnrəbl] *adj* ❶ honroso, sa ❷ honorable
honorary [ɒnəˈreərɪ] *adj* ❶ honorario, ria ❷ honorífico, ca
honor roll *s* lista de honor
hooch [huːtʃ] *s familiar* alcohol *(destilado clandestinamente)*
hood [hʊd] *s* ❶ capuchón ❷ campana (extractora) ❸ cofre
hoodlum [ˈhuːdləm] *s familiar* matón
hoof [huːf] [hʊf] *s* ❶ casco ❷ pezuña
  Dos plurales: **hoofs** o **hooves**.
hook [hʊk] ◆ *s* ❶ gancho • **off the hook** descolgado, da ❷ anzuelo ❸ corchete ◆ *vt* ❶ enganchar ❷ pescar
■ **hook up** *vt* ☿ *El objeto se puede colocar antes o después de la preposición.* ❶ • **to hook something up to something** conectar algo a algo ❷ • **to hook up with somebody** reunirse o juntarse con alguien; ligar con alguien
hooked [hʊkt] *adj* ❶ aguileño, ña ❷ *familiar* • **to be hooked (on)** estar enganchado, da (a)
hooker [ˈhʊkər] *s familiar* puta
hook(e)y [ˈhʊkɪ] *s familiar* • **to play hookey** irse de pinta
hooligan [ˈhuːlɪgən] *s* vándalo
hoop [huːp] *s* aro
hooray [hʊˈreɪ] = **hurray**

H

hoot [huːt] ◆ *s* ❶ grito *(de tecolote)*; ululato ❷ bocinazo ❸ • **a hoot of laughter** una carcajada ◆ *vi* ❶ ulular ❷ sonar *(bocina)* ❸ • **to hoot with laughter** reírse a carcajadas ◆ *vt* tocar *(bocina)*

hooter [ˈhuːtər] *s* claxon®; bocina

hooves [huːvz] *spl* → hoof

hop [hɒp] ◆ *vi* ❶ saltar a la pata coja ❷ dar saltitos ❸ ponerse de un brinco • **he hopped over the ditch** brincó por encima de la zanja • **she hopped in the car and drove off** se subió al coche y se fue ◆ *vt familiar* subirse a

■ **hops** *spl* lúpulo

hope [həʊp] ◆ *vi* • **to hope (for something)** esperar (algo) • **I hope so** espero que sí • **I hope not** espero que no ◆ *vt* • **to hope (that)** esperar que ◆ *s* esperanza • **in the hope of** con la esperanza de

expresión **to raise somebody's hopes** dar esperanzas a alguien

hope chest *s* ajuar

hopeful [ˈhəʊpfʊl] *adj* ❶ optimista • **to be hopeful of something/of doing something** tener esperanzas de algo/hacer algo ❷ prometedor, ra

hopefully [ˈhəʊpfəlɪ] *adv* ❶ esperanzadamente ❷ con suerte • **hopefully not** espero que no

hopeless [ˈhəʊplɪs] *adj* ❶ desesperado, da ❷ imposible ❸ *familiar* inútil • **he's hopeless at sports** es negado para los deportes

hopelessly [ˈhəʊplɪslɪ] *adv* ❶ desesperadamente ❷ totalmente

horizon [həˈraɪzn] *s* horizonte

expresión **on the horizon a)** en el horizonte **b)** *figurado* a la vuelta de la esquina

horizontal [ˌhɒrɪˈzɒntl] *adj* horizontal

hormone [ˈhɔːməʊn] *s* hormona

horn [hɔːn] *s* ❶ cuerno ❷ *MÚSICA* trompa ❸ **claxon**®; bocina ❹ sirena ❺ *familiar* teléfono

horny [ˈhɔːnɪ] *adj muy familiar* cachondo, da; caliente

horoscope [ˈhɒrəskəʊp] *s* horóscopo

horrendous [hɒˈrendəs] *adj* horrendo, da

horrible [ˈhɒrəbl] *adj* ❶ horrible ❷ malo, la

horrid [ˈhɒrɪd] *adj* horroroso, sa

horrific [hɒˈrɪfɪk] *adj* horrendo, da

horrify [ˈhɒrɪfaɪ] *vt* horrorizar

horror [ˈhɒrər] *s* horror • **to have a horror of something** tener horror a algo

horror movie *s* película de terror o de miedo

horse [hɔːs] *s* caballo

horseback [ˈhɔːsbæk] ◆ *adj* • **horseback riding** equitación ◆ *s* • **on horseback** a caballo

horseman [ˈhɔːsmən] *s* jinete

El plural de **horseman** es **horsemen** [ˈhɔːsmen].

horsepower [ˈhɔːsˌpaʊər] *s* ⚙*incontable* caballos de vapor

horse racing *s* ⚙*incontable* carreras de caballos

horseradish [ˈhɔːsˌrædɪʃ] *s* rábano silvestre

horserider [ˈhɔːsraɪdər] *s* jinete, amazona

horse riding *s* equitación • **to go horse riding** montar a caballo

horseshoe [ˈhɔːsʃuː] *s* herradura

horsewoman [ˈhɔːsˌwʊmən] *s* amazona

El plural de **horsewoman** es **horsewomen** [ˈhɔːsˌwɪmɪn].

hose [həʊz], **hosepipe** [ˈhəʊzpaɪp] *s* manguera

hospice [ˈhɒspɪs] *s* hospital para enfermos terminales

hospitable [hɒˈspɪtəbl] *adj* hospitalario, ria

hospital [ˈhɒspɪtl] *s* hospital

hospitality [ˌhɒspɪˈtælətɪ] *s* hospitalidad

host [həʊst] ◆ *s* ❶ anfitrión, ona ❷ presentador, ra ❸ *RELIGIÓN* hostia ❹ *INFORMÁTICA* host; anfitrión ◆ *vt* ❶ presentar ❷ ser el anfitrión de ❸ *INFORMÁTICA* albergar; hospedar

hostage [ˈhɒstɪdʒ] *s* rehén • **to be taken/held hostage** ser tomado, da/mantenido, da como rehén

hostel [ˈhɒstl] *s* albergue

hostess [ˈhəʊstes] *s* ❶ anfitriona ❷ chica de alterne

host family *s* familia de acogida

hostile [ˈhɒstl] *adj* ❶ • **hostile (to)** hostil (hacia) ❷ adverso, sa

hostility [hɒˈstɪlətɪ] *s* hostilidad

■ **hostilities** *spl* hostilidades

hot [hɒt] *adj* ❶ caliente • **I'm hot** tengo calor ❷ caluroso, sa • **it's (very) hot** hace (mucho) calor ❸ picante; picoso, sa ❹ *familiar* • **hot on** o **at** experto, ta en ❺ caliente; último, ma *(noticia)* ❻ vivo, va *(genio)* ❼ *familiar* sexy

hot-air balloon *s* aeróstato; globo

hot dog *s* perrito caliente

hotel [həʊˈtel] *s* hotel

hot flash *s* sofoco

hothouse [ˈhɒthaʊs] *s* invernadero

hot line *s* teléfono rojo

hotly [ˈhɒtlɪ] *adv* ❶ acaloradamente ❷ • **we were hotly pursued** nos pisaban los talones

hotplate [ˈhɒtpleɪt] *s* ❶ placa ❷ calientaplatos

hot-tempered *adj* iracundo, da

hot-water bottle *s* bolsa de agua caliente

hound [haʊnd] ◆ *s* perro de caza; sabueso ◆ *vt* ❶ acosar ❷ • **to hound somebody out (of somewhere)** conseguir echar a alguien (de algún sitio) acosándolo

hour [ˈaʊər] *s* hora • **half an hour** media hora • **a quarter of an hour** un cuarto de hora • **70 kilometers per** o **an hour** 70 kilómetros por hora • **to pay by the hour** pagar por horas • **on the hour** a la hora en punto cada hora

■ **hours** *spl* horas *(de tienda, negocio)*

hourly [ˈaʊəlɪ] *adj & adv* ❶ cada hora ❷ por hora

house ◆ *s* [haʊs] ☼*pl* ['haʊzɪz] **❶** casa **❷** POLÍ-TICA cámara
expresión to bring the house down *familiar* ser un exitazo; ser muy aplaudido, da ▸ it's on the house la casa invita; es cortesía de la casa
◆ *vt* [haʊz] **❶** alojar **❷** albergar ◆ *adj* **❶** de la empresa **❷** de la casa *(vino)*
housebroken ['haʊs,brəʊkn] *adj* entrenado, da *(animal de compañía)*
housecoat ['haʊskəʊt] *s* bata
household ['haʊshəʊld] ◆ *adj* **❶** doméstico, ca; de la casa **❷** conocido, da por todos ◆ *s* hogar
housekeeper ['haʊs,kiːpər] *s* ama de llaves
housekeeping ['haʊs,kiːpɪŋ] *s* ☼*incontable* **❶** quehaceres domésticos **❷** ▸ housekeeping (money) dinero para los gastos de la casa
house music *s* música house
House of Representatives *s* • the House of Representatives la Cámara de (los) Representantes

THE HOUSE OF REPRESENTATIVES

La Cámara de Representantes (**House of Representatives**) constituye, junto con el Senado, el organismo legislativo estadounidense. Cada dos años se elige a sus 435 miembros, cuyo número es proporcional con la población de cada estado. De esta manera, el estado de Delaware tiene sólo 2 representantes mientras que California tiene 52. Todas las leyes nuevas deben ser ratificadas por ambas cámaras del Congreso.

houseplant ['haʊsplɑːnt] *s* planta interior
Houses of Parliament *s* • the Houses of Parliament el Parlamento británico
housewarming (party) ['haʊs,wɔːmɪŋ-] *s* fiesta de inauguración de una casa
housewife ['haʊswaɪf] *s* ama de casa
El plural de **housewife** es **housewives** ['haʊswaɪvz].
housework ['haʊswɜːk] *s* ☼*incontable* quehaceres domésticos
housing ['haʊzɪŋ] *s* **❶** vivienda **❷** alojamiento
housing project *s* ▸ urbanización generalmente de protección oficial, ≃ fraccionamiento
hover ['hɒvər] *vi* cernerse
hovercraft ['hɒvəkrɑːft] *s* aerodeslizador
Dos plurales: **hovercraft** o **hovercrafts**.
how [haʊ] *adv* **❶** cómo • **how do you do it?** ¿cómo se hace? • **I found out how he did it** averigüé cómo lo hizo • **how are you?** ¿cómo estás? **❷** • **how high is it?** ¿cuánto mide de alto? • **he asked how high it was** preguntó cuánto medía de alto • **how expensive is it?** ¿qué precio tiene?; ¿es muy caro? • **how far is**

it to Boston? ¿a qué distancia está Boston de aquí? • **how long have you been waiting?** ¿cuánto llevas esperando? • **how many people came?** ¿cuánta gente vino? • **how old are you?** ¿qué edad o cuántos años tienes? **❸** qué • **how nice/awful!** ¡qué bonito/horrible! • **how pretty you look!** ¡qué linda te ves! • **how I hate doing it!** ¡cómo odio tener que hacerlo!
expresión how do you do? mucho gusto
■ **how about** *adv* • **how about a drink?** ¿qué tal una copa? • **how about you?** ¿qué te parece?; ¿y tú?
■ **how much** ◆ *pronombre* cuánto, ta • **how much does it cost?** ¿cuánto cuesta? ◆ *adj* cuánto, ta • **how much bread?** ¿cuánto pan?
however [haʊ'evər] ◆ *adv* **❶** sin embargo; no obstante **❷** • **however difficult it may be** por (muy) difícil que sea • **however many times I told her** por mucho que se lo dijera **❸** cómo • **however did you know?** ¿cómo lo sabías? ◆ *conjunción* comoquiera que • **however you want** como quieras
howl [haʊl] ◆ *s* **❶** aullido **❷** alarido; grito • **a howl of laughter** una carcajada ◆ *vi* **❶** aullar **❷** gritar • **to howl with laughter** reírse a carcajadas **❸** bramar
hp *(abreviatura de* horsepower) CV; cv
HQ *s abreviatura escrita de* **headquarters**
hub [hʌb] *s* **❶** cubo **❷** centro; eje
hubcap ['hʌbkæp] *s* tapacubos
huddle ['hʌdl] *vi* **❶** acurrucarse **❷** apretarse unos contra otros; amontonarse
huff [hʌf] *s* • **in a huff** mosqueado, da
hug [hʌg] ◆ *s* abrazo ◆ *vt* **❶** abrazar **❷** ceñirse o ir pegado a
huge [hjuːdʒ] *adj* enorme
hull [hʌl] *s* casco *(de barco)*
hum [hʌm] ◆ *vi* **❶** zumbar **❷** canturrear; tararear ◆ *vt* tararear; canturrear
human ['hjuːmən] ◆ *adj* humano, na ◆ *s* ▸ human (being) (ser) humano
humane [hjuː'meɪn] *adj* humano, na
humanitarian [hjuː,mænɪ'teərɪən] *adj* humanitario, ria
humanity [hjuː'mænətɪ] *s* humanidad
■ **humanities** *spl* • **the humanities** las humanidades
human race *s* • **the human race** la raza humana
human rights *spl* derechos humanos
humble ['hʌmbl] ◆ *adj* humilde ◆ *vt formal* humillar
humid ['hjuːmɪd] *adj* húmedo, da
humidity [hjuː'mɪdətɪ] *s* humedad
humiliate [hjuː'mɪlɪeɪt] *vt* humillar
humiliation [hjuː,mɪlɪ'eɪʃn] *s* humillación
humility [hjuː'mɪlətɪ] *s* humildad
humor ['hjuːmər] ◆ *s* **❶** humor • **in good/bad humor** *formal* de buen/mal humor **❷** gracia ◆ *vt* complacer
humorous ['hjuːmərəs] *adj* **❶** gracioso, sa **❷** humorístico, ca

H

hump [hʌmp] *s* ❶ montículo ❷ joroba; giba

hunch [hʌntʃ] ◆ *s familiar* presentimiento ◆ *vt* encorvar

hunchback ['hʌntʃbæk] *s* jorobado, da

hunched [hʌntʃt] *adj* encorvado, da

hundred ['hʌndrəd] *número* cien • **a o one hundred** cien • **a o one hundred and eighty** ciento ochenta • **three hundred** trescientos • **five hundred** quinientos ver también **six**
■ **hundreds** *spl* cientos

hundredth ['hʌndrətə] ◆ *adj numeral* centésimo, ma ◆ *sustantivo numeral* centésimo • **a hundredth of a second** una centésima ver también **sixth**

hung [hʌŋ] *pretérito* & *participio pasado* → **hang**

Hungarian [hʌŋ'geərıən] ◆ *adj* húngaro, ra ◆ *s* ❶ húngaro, ra ❷ húngaro

Hungary ['hʌŋgərı] *s* Hungría

hunger ['hʌŋgər] *s* ❶ hambre ❷ *literario* sed *(de aprender* ETC*)*
■ **hunger after, hunger for** *vt* ☼ *El objeto siempre va después de la preposición al final.* literario anhelar; ansiar

hunger strike *s* huelga de hambre

hung over *adj familiar* • **to be hung over** tener resaca

hungry ['hʌŋgrı] *adj* hambriento, ta • **to be/go hungry** tener/pasar hambre

hung up *adj familiar* acomplejado, da

hunk [hʌŋk] *s* ❶ pedazo; trozo ❷ *familiar* cuero

hunt [hʌnt] ◆ *s* ❶ caza ❷ busca; búsqueda ◆ *vi* cazar ◆ *vt* ❶ cazar ❷ perseguir

hunter ['hʌntər] *s* cazador, ra

hunting ['hʌntıŋ] *s* caza • **to go hunting** ir de caza o cacería

hurdle ['hɜːdl] ◆ *s* ❶ valla *(de carrera)* ❷ obstáculo ◆ *vt* saltar

hurl [hɜːl] *vt* ❶ lanzar; arrojar ❷ proferir; soltar *(insultos)*

hurray, hooray [hʊ'reı] *exclamación* ¡hurra!

hurricane ['hʌrıkən] *s* huracán

hurried ['hʌrıd] *adj* apresurado, da

hurriedly ['hʌrıdlı] *adv* apresuradamente

hurry ['hʌrı] ◆ *s* prisa • **to be in a hurry** tener prisa • **to do something in a hurry** hacer algo a toda prisa
expresión **to be in no hurry to do something** no tener ningunas ganas de hacer algo
◆ *vt* ❶ meter prisa a ❷ apresurar ◆ *vi* • **to hurry (to do something)** apresurarse (a hacer algo)
■ **hurry up** *vi* darse prisa • **hurry up!** ¡apúrate!

hurt [hɜːt] ◆ *vt* ❶ hacer daño a; hacerse daño en • **I hurt my leg** me hice daño en la pierna • **nobody was hurt** nadie resultó herido • **to hurt yourself** lastimarse ❷ herir • **to hurt somebody's feelings** herir los sentimientos de alguien ❸ perjudicar ◆ *vi* ❶ doler • **my head hurts** me duele la cabeza ❷ lastimar ◆ *adj* ❶ herido, da ❷ dolido, da
Formas irregulares de **hurt**: *pretérito* & *pp* **hurt**.

hurtful ['hɜːtfʊl] *adj* hiriente

husband ['hʌzbənd] *s* marido

hush [hʌʃ] ◆ *s* silencio ◆ *exclamación* ¡silencio!; ¡a callar!

husk [hʌsk] *s* cáscara

husky ['hʌskı] ◆ *adj* ronco, ca ◆ *s* husky; perro esquimal

hustle ['hʌsl] ◆ *vt* • **to hustle somebody into doing something** presionar a alguien para que haga algo ◆ *s*
▶ **hustle (and bustle)** ajetreo; bullicio

hut [hʌt] *s* ❶ cabaña; choza ❷ cobertizo

hutch [hʌtʃ] *s* conejera

hyacinth ['haıəsınə] *s* jacinto

hydroelectric [ˌhaıdrəʊı'lektrık] *adj* hidroeléctrico, ca

hydrofoil ['haıdrəfɔıl] *s* embarcación con hidroala

hydrogen ['haıdrədʒən] *s* hidrógeno

hyena [haı'iːnə] *s* hiena

hygiene ['haıdʒiːn] *s* higiene

hygienic [haı'dʒiːnık] *adj* higiénico, ca

hymn [hım] *s* himno

hype [haıp] *s familiar* bombo; publicidad exagerada

hyperactive [ˌhaıpər'æktıv] *adj* hiperactivo, va

hyperlink ['haıpə,lıŋk] *s* INFORMÁTICA hiperenlace

hypermarket ['haıpə,mɑːkıt] *s* hipermercado

hyphen ['haıfn] *s* guión

hypnosis [hıp'nəʊsıs] *s* hipnosis

hypnotize ['hıpnətaız] *vt* hipnotizar

hypochondriac [ˌhaıpə'kɒndriæk] *s* hipocondríaco, ca

hypocrisy [hı'pɒkrəsı] *s* hipocresía

hypocrite ['hıpəkrıt] *s* hipócrita

hypocritical [ˌhıpə'krıtıkl] *adj* hipócrita

hypothesis [haı'pɒəsıs] *s* hipótesis
El plural de **hypothesis** es **hypotheses** [haı'pɒəsiːz].

hypothetical [ˌhaıpə'əetıkl] *adj* hipotético, ca

hysteria [hıs'tıərıə] *s* histeria

hysterical [hıs'terıkl] *adj* ❶ histérico, ca ❷ *familiar* tronchante

hysterics [hıs'terıks] *spl* ❶ histeria; histerismo ❷ *familiar* • **to be in hysterics** partirse de risa

H

i, I [aɪ] *s* i; I

Dos plurales: **i's** o **is**, **I's** o **Is**.

I [aɪ] *pronombre personal* yo • **I'm happy** soy feliz • **I'm leaving** me voy • **she and I were at college together** ella y yo fuimos juntos a la universidad • **it is I** *formal* soy yo • **I can't do that** yo no puedo hacer eso

ice [aɪs] ◆ *s* hielo ◆ *vt* COCINA glasear; alcorzar

■ **ice over, ice up** *vi* helarse

iceberg ['aɪsbɜːg] *s* iceberg

icebox ['aɪsbɒks] *s* refrigerador

ice cream *s* helado

ice cube *s* cubito de hielo

ice hockey *s* hockey sobre hielo

Iceland ['aɪslənd] *s* Islandia

Icelandic [aɪs'lændɪk] ◆ *adj* islandés, esa ◆ *s* islandés

ice pick *s* pico para el hielo

ice rink *s* pista de (patinaje sobre) hielo

ice skate *s* patín de cuchilla

■ **ice-skate** *vi* patinar sobre hielo

ice-skating *s* patinaje sobre hielo

icicle ['aɪsɪkl] *s* carámbano

icing ['aɪsɪŋ] *s* glaseado

icon, ikon ['aɪkɒn] *s* INFORMÁTICA & RELIGIÓN icono

icy ['aɪsɪ] *adj* ❶ helado, da • **the road is icy** la calle está cubierta de hielo ❷ *figurado* glacial

ID *s* *abreviatura escrita de* **identification**

I'd [aɪd] ❶ (*abreviatura de* I had) = **have** ❷ (*abreviatura de* I would) = **would**

idea [aɪ'dɪə] *s* ❶ idea • **to have an idea of something** tener (alguna) idea de algo • **to have no idea** no tener ni idea • **to get the idea** *familiar* captar la idea; hacerse una idea ❷ sensación; impresión • **to have an idea (that)...** tener la sensación de que...

ideal [aɪ'dɪəl] ◆ *adj* • **ideal (for)** ideal (para) ◆ *s* ideal

ideally [aɪ'dɪəlɪ] *adv* ❶ idealmente ❷ perfectamente ❸ a ser posible

identical [aɪ'dentɪkl] *adj* idéntico, ca • **identical twins** gemelos idénticos

identification [aɪˌdentɪfɪ'keɪʃn] *s* ❶ • **identification (with)** identificación (con) ❷ documentación

identify [aɪ'dentɪfaɪ] ◆ *vt* identificar • **to identify somebody with something** relacionar a alguien con algo ◆ *vi* • **to identify with somebody/something** identificarse con alguien/algo

identity [aɪ'dentətɪ] *s* identidad

identity card, ID card *s* documento de identidad; credencial de identidad

ideology [ˌaɪdɪ'ɒlədʒɪ] *s* ideología

idiom ['ɪdɪəm] *s* locución; modismo

idiomatic [ˌɪdɪə'mætɪk] *adj* natural

idiosyncrasy [ˌɪdɪə'sɪŋkrəsɪ] *s* rareza; manía

idiot ['ɪdɪət] *s* idiota • **what an idiot!** ¡qué idiota!

idiotic [ˌɪdɪ'ɒtɪk] *adj* idiota

idle ['aɪdl] ◆ *adj* ❶ perezoso, sa; vago, ga ❷ parado, da (*máquina, fábrica*) ❸ desocupado, da; sin trabajo ❹ vano, na (*amenaza*) ◆ *vi* estar en punto muerto

■ **idle away** *vt* ☀ *El objeto se puede colocar antes o después de la preposición.* desperdiciar

idol ['aɪdl] *s* ídolo

idolize ['aɪdəlaɪz] *vt* idolatrar

idyllic [ɪ'dɪlɪk] *adj* idílico, ca

i.e. (*abreviatura de* id est) i.e.; es decir

if [ɪf] *conjunción* ❶ si • **if I were you** yo que tú; yo en tu lugar ❷ aunque • **he's clever, if a little arrogant** es listo, aunque algo arrogante

■ **if not** *conjunción* ❶ si no; de lo contrario ❷ por no decir • **it was cheeky, if not downright rude of him** fue mucha caradura de su parte, por no decir grosería

■ **if only** ◆ *conjunción* ❶ aunque sólo sea • **at least he got me a present, if only a little one** por lo menos me ha comprado un regalo, aunque sea pequeño ❷ si • **if only I'd been quicker!** ¡ojalá hubiera sido más rápido! ◆ *exclamación* ¡ojalá!

igloo ['ɪgluː] *s* iglú

El plural de **igloo** es **igloos**.

ignite [ɪg'naɪt] ◆ *vt* encender ◆ *vi* encenderse

ignition [ɪgˈnɪʃn] s ❶ ignición ❷ encendido • **to switch on the ignition** arrancar (el motor)

ignition key s llave de contacto

ignorance [ˈɪgnərəns] s ignorancia

ignorant [ˈɪgnərənt] adj ❶ ignorante ❷ formal • **to be ignorant of something** ignorar algo

ignore [ɪgˈnɔːr] vt ❶ no hacer caso de; ignorar ❷ no hacer caso a; ignorar

ill [ɪl] adj ❶ enfermo, ma • **to feel ill** encontrarse mal • **to be taken** o **to fall ill** caer o ponerse enfermo, ma ❷ malo, la

I'll [aɪl] ❶ (abreviatura de I will) = **will** ❷ (abreviatura de I shall) = **shall**

ill-advised [-ədˈvaɪzd] adj ❶ poco aconsejable ❷ imprudente

ill at ease adj incómodo, da

illegal [ɪˈliːgl] adj ilegal

illegible [ɪˈledʒəbl] adj ilegible

illegitimate [ˌɪlɪˈdʒɪtɪmət] adj ilegítimo, ma

ill-equipped [-ɪˈkwɪpt] adj • **to be ill-equipped to do something** estar mal preparado, da para hacer algo

ill feeling s resentimiento

ill health s mala salud

illicit [ɪˈlɪsɪt] adj ilícito, ta

illiteracy [ɪˈlɪtərəsɪ] s analfabetismo

illiterate [ɪˈlɪtərət] ◆ adj analfabeto, ta ◆ s analfabeto, ta

illness [ˈɪlnɪs] s enfermedad

illogical [ɪˈlɒdʒɪkl] adj ilógico, ca

ill-suited adj • **ill-suited (for)** poco adecuado, da (para)

ill-treat vt maltratar

illuminate [ɪˈluːmɪneɪt] vt ❶ iluminar ❷ ilustrar; aclarar

illumination [ɪˌluːmɪˈneɪʃn] s alumbrado; iluminación

illusion [ɪˈluːʒn] s ❶ ilusión • **to be under the illusion that** creer equivocadamente que ❷ truco de ilusionismo

illustrate [ˈɪləstreɪt] vt ilustrar

illustration [ˌɪləˈstreɪʃn] s ilustración

ill will s rencor; animadversión • **to bear somebody ill will** guardar rencor a alguien

I'm [aɪm] (abreviatura de I am) = **be**

image [ˈɪmɪdʒ] s imagen

imaginary [ɪˈmædʒɪnrɪ] adj imaginario, ria

imagination [ɪˌmædʒɪˈneɪʃn] s imaginación

imaginative [ɪˈmædʒɪnətɪv] adj imaginativo, va

imagine [ɪˈmædʒɪn] vt ❶ imaginar • **imagine never having to work!** ¡imagina que nunca tuvieras que trabajar! • **I can't imagine what he means** no tengo ni idea de qué quiere decir • **imagine (that)!** ¡imagínate! ❷ • **to imagine (that)** imaginarse que

imbalance [ˌɪmˈbæləns] s desequilibrio

imbecile [ˈɪmbɪsiːl] s imbécil

IMHO (abreviatura de in my humble opinion) adv familiar en mi humilde opinión

imitate [ˈɪmɪteɪt] vt imitar

imitation [ˌɪmɪˈteɪʃn] ◆ s imitación ◆ adj de imitación • **imitation jewellery** bisutería

immaculate [ɪˈmækjʊlət] adj ❶ inmaculado, da ❷ exquisito, ta ❸ impecable

immature [ˌɪməˈtjʊər] adj ❶ inmaduro, ra ❷ joven

immediate [ɪˈmiːdjət] adj ❶ inmediato, ta • **in the immediate future** en un futuro inmediato • **in the immediate vicinity** en las inmediaciones ❷ más cercano, na (familia)

immediately [ɪˈmiːdjətlɪ] ◆ adv ❶ inmediatamente ❷ directamente ◆ conjunción en cuanto

immense [ɪˈmens] adj inmenso, sa

immerse [ɪˈmɜːs] vt ❶ • **to immerse something in something** sumergir algo en algo ❷ • **to immerse yourself in something** enfrascarse en algo

immigrant [ˈɪmɪgrənt] s inmigrante

immigration [ˌɪmɪˈgreɪʃn] s inmigración

imminent [ˈɪmɪnənt] adj inminente

immobilize [ɪˈməʊbɪlaɪz] vt inmovilizar

immoral [ɪˈmɒrəl] adj inmoral

immortal [ɪˈmɔːtl] adj inmortal

immune [ɪˈmjuːn] adj ❶ • **immune (to)** inmune (a) ❷ • **immune (from)** exento, ta (de)

immunity [ɪˈmjuːnətɪ] s ❶ • **immunity (to)** inmunidad (a) ❷ • **immunity (from)** exención (de)

immunize [ˈɪmjuːnaɪz] vt • **to immunize somebody (against something)** inmunizar a alguien (contra algo)

impact ◆ s [ˈɪmpækt] impacto • **to make an impact on** causar impacto en ◆ vt [ɪmˈpækt] influenciar

impair [ɪmˈpeər] vt ❶ dañar; debilitar ❷ entorpecer (movimiento) ❸ mermar (capacidad, eficiencia) ❹ perjudicar (perspectivas)

impartial [ɪmˈpɑːʃl] adj imparcial

impassable [ɪmˈpɑːsəbl] adj intransitable; impracticable

impatience [ɪmˈpeɪʃns] s impaciencia

impatient [ɪmˈpeɪʃnt] adj impaciente • **to be impatient to do something** estar impaciente por hacer algo • **to be impatient for something** esperar algo con impaciencia • **to get impatient** impacientarse

impeachment [ɪmˈpiːtʃmənt] s proceso de destitución

impede [ɪmˈpiːd] vt dificultar

impediment [ɪmˈpedɪmənt] s ❶ impedimento; obstáculo ❷ defecto

impending [ɪmˈpendɪŋ] adj inminente

imperative [ɪmˈperətɪv] ◆ adj apremiante • **it is imperative that...** es imprescindible que... ◆ s imperativo

imperfect [ɪm'pɜ:fɪkt] ◆ *adj* imperfecto, ta ◆ *s* GRA-MÁTICA ▶ **imperfect (tense)** (pretérito) imperfecto

imperial [ɪm'pɪərɪəl] *adj* ❶ imperial ❷ • **imperial system** sistema anglosajón de medidas

imperialism [ɪm'pɪərɪəlɪzm] *s* imperialismo

impersonate [ɪm'pɜ:səneɪt] *vt* ❶ hacerse pasar por ❷ imitar

impersonation [ɪm,pɜ:sə'neɪʃn] *s* ❶ imitación • **to do impersonations (of)** imitar (a); hacer imitaciones (de) ❷ • **charged with impersonation of a policeman** acusado de hacerse pasar por policía

impertinent [ɪm'pɜ:tɪnənt] *adj* impertinente; insolente

impetuous [ɪm'petʃʊəs] *adj* impetuoso, sa

impetus ['ɪmpɪtəs] *s* ◌ *incontable* ❶ ímpetu ❷ impulso

implant ◆ *s* ['ɪmplɑ:nt] implante ◆ *vt* [ɪm'plɑ:nt] MEDICINA • **to implant something in** o **into** implantar algo en

implausible [ɪm'plɔ:zəbl] *adj* inverosímil

implement ◆ *s* ['ɪmplɪmənt] herramienta ◆ *vt* ['ɪmplɪment] llevar a cabo; poner en práctica

implication [,ɪmplɪ'keɪʃn] *s* consecuencia 𝗲𝘅𝗽𝗿𝗲𝘀𝗶ó𝗻 **by implication** de forma indirecta

implicit [ɪm'plɪsɪt] *adj* ❶ • **implicit (in)** implícito, ta (en) ❷ absoluto, ta *(creencia)*

imply [ɪm'plaɪ] *vt* ❶ insinuar; dar a entender ❷ implicar; suponer

impolite [,ɪmpə'laɪt] *adj* maleducado, da; descortés

import ◆ *s* ['ɪmpɔ:t] importación ◆ *vt* [ɪm'pɔ:t] importar

importance [ɪm'pɔ:tns] *s* importancia

important [ɪm'pɔ:tnt] *adj* • **important (to)** importante (para) • **it's not important** no importa

importer [ɪm'pɔ:tər] *s* importador, ra

impose [ɪm'pəʊz] ◆ *vt* • **to impose something (on)** imponer algo (a) ◆ *vi* • **to impose (on)** abusar (de); molestar (a)

imposing [ɪm'pəʊzɪŋ] *adj* imponente; impresionante

imposition [,ɪmpə'zɪʃn] *s* ❶ imposición ❷ molestia

impossible [ɪm'pɒsəbl] *adj* ❶ imposible ❷ inaguantable; insufrible

impostor, imposter [ɪm'pɒstər] *s* impostor, ra

impotent ['ɪmpətənt] *adj* impotente

impoverished [ɪm'pɒvərɪʃt] *adj* empobrecido, da

impracticable [ɪm'præktɪkəbl] *adj* impracticable; irrealizable

impractical [ɪm'præktɪkl] *adj* poco práctico, ca

impregnate ['ɪmpregneɪt] *vt* ❶ • **to impregnate something (with)** impregnar o empapar algo (de) ❷ *formal* fecundar

impress [ɪm'pres] ◆ *vt* ❶ impresionar • **I was favorably impressed** me causó buena impresión ❷ • **to impress something on somebody** hacer comprender a alguien la importancia de algo ◆ *vi* ❶ causar buena impresión ❷ impresionar

impression [ɪm'preʃn] *s* ❶ impresión • **to make an impression** impresionar • **to make a good/bad impression** causar una buena/mala impresión • **to be under the impression that** tener la impresión de que ❷ imitación

impressive [ɪm'presɪv] *adj* impresionante

imprint ['ɪmprɪnt] *s* huella; impresión

imprison [ɪm'prɪzn] *vt* encarcelar

improbable [ɪm'prɒbəbl] *adj* ❶ improbable ❷ inverosímil

impromptu [ɪm'prɒmptju:] *adj* improvisado, da

improper [ɪm'prɒpər] *adj* ❶ impropio, pia ❷ indebido, da ❸ indecoroso, sa

improve [ɪm'pru:v] ◆ *vi* mejorar • **to improve on something** mejorar algo ◆ *vt* mejorar

improvement [ɪm'pru:vmənt] *s* ❶ • **improvement (in/on)** mejora (en/con respecto a) • **to be an improvement on something** ser mejor que algo ❷ mejoría *(de salud)* ❸ reforma *(en casa)*

improvise ['ɪmprəvaɪz] *vt* & *vi* improvisar

impudent ['ɪmpjʊdənt] *adj* insolente

impulse ['ɪmpʌls] *s* impulso • **on impulse** sin pensar

impulsive [ɪm'pʌlsɪv] *adj* impulsivo, va

impurity [ɪm'pjʊərətɪ] *s* impureza

---

in [ɪn]
◆ *preposición*
❶ [*indica una localización*] en
• **the key is in a box/bag** la llave está en una caja/bolsa
• **they live in the country** viven en el campo
• **he is in the hospital** está en el hospital
• **they sat in the sun** se sentaron al sol
❷ [*con términos geográficos*]
• **they live in Boston** viven en Boston
• **they arrived in Mexico this morning** llegaron a México esta mañana
❸ [*indica una fecha, una temporada, un momento del día*]
• **they went to Italy in 2004** fueron a Italia en 2004
• **he will start working in April** comenzará a trabajar en abril
• **you should visit Montreal in (the) spring** deberías visitar Montreal en primavera
• **I'll meet you at two o'clock in the afternoon** nos veremos a las dos de la tarde
• **I'll call you in the morning** te voy a llamar en la mañana
❹ [*indica la duración*]
• **he learned to type in two weeks** aprendió a escribir a máquina en dos semanas

• **I'll be ready in five minutes** estaré listo en cinco minutos

• **it's my first decent meal in weeks** es mi primera comida decente en mucha semanas

❺ [*con la ropa*]

• **he was dressed in a suit** llevaba un traje

❻ [*indica las condiciones de vida*]

• **many people still live/die in poverty** mucha gente todavía vive/muere en la pobreza

• **she was in danger/difficulty** estaba en peligro/dificultades

❼ [*indica un área profesional*]

• **he's in computers** trabaja con informática

❽ [*expresa el modo, la forma*]

• **you should write in pencil/ink** debes escribir con lápiz/tinta

• **he spoke to me in a loud/soft voice** me habló en una voz fuerte/suave

• **speak in English!** ¡habla en inglés!

❾ [*expresa la causa*]

• **in anger, he slammed the door shut** enojado, dio un portazo

❿ [*indica una persona o una categoría de personas*]

• **pollen allergies are rare in adults** las alergias al polen son raras entre adultos

• **the theme of irony is even stronger in Shakespeare** el tema de la ironía es incluso más fuerte en Shakespeare

• **in him, the party sees a great leader** el partido ve en él a un gran líder

⓫ [*con cantidades, números*]

• **don't buy in large/small quantities** no compres en grandes/pequeñas cantidades

• **letters of support arrived in (their) thousands** llegaban millares de cartas de apoyo

• **she's in her sixties** tiene sesenta y tantos años

⓬ [*indica la distribución, el reparto*]

• **good things come in twos** las buenas cosas llegan en pares

• **they were standing in a row/circle** estaban de pie formando una fila/círculo

⓭ [*indica una proporción*]

• **one child in ten suffers from malnutrition** uno de cada diez niños sufre de desnutrición

⓮ [*después de un superlativo*]

• **it is the longest river in the world** es el río más largo del mundo

⓯ [*seguido del gerundio*]

• **in doing something** al hacer algo

• **in saying this, I would not suggest that the task is easy** al decir esto, no quiero sugerir que la tarea sea fácil

◆ *adv*

❶ [*indica la presencia*]

• **is Judith in?** ¿está Judith?

• **nobody was in** no había nadie

• **I'm staying in tonight** hoy por la noche me voy a quedar en casa

❷ [*indica un movimiento hacia el interior*]

• **the door opened and they all rushed in** la puerta se abrió y todos entraron corriendo

• **she opened the safe and put the money in** abrió la caja fuerte y guardó el dinero

❸ [*hablando de un tren*]

• **the train is in** el tren ya llegó

❹ [*hablando de la marea*]

• **the tide's in** la marea está alta

expresión **you're in for a shock** te vas a llevar una sorpresa ▶ **we're in for some bad weather** se nos viene encima mal tiempo

◆ *adj*

❶ [*en los deportes*]

• **the umpire said that the ball was in** el árbitro dijo que la pelota había entrado

❷ *familiar* [*de moda*]

• **long skirts are in this year** las faldas largas están de moda este año

■ **ins**

◆ *spl*

expresión **the ins and outs** los pormenores

■ **in all**

◆ *adv*

en total

• **there are 30 in all** hay 30 en total

■ **in between**

◆ *preposición*

❶ [*sentido espacial*] entre

• **the house is located in between two streets** la casa está situada entre dos calles

❷ [*sentido temporal*]

• **in between customers, we chatted about our plans** entre un cliente y otro, platicábamos sobre nuestros planes

◆ *adv*

• **a row of bushes with clumps of flowers in between** una fila de arbustos con matas de flores intercaladas

in. *abreviatura escrita de* **inch**

inability [ˌɪnəˈbɪlətɪ] *s* • **inability (to do something)** incapacidad (de hacer algo)

inaccessible [ˌɪnəkˈsesəbl] *adj* inaccesible

inaccurate [ɪnˈækjʊrət] *adj* inexacto, ta

inadequate [ɪnˈædɪkwət] *adj* ❶ insuficiente ❷ incapaz

inadvertently [ˌɪnədˈvɜːtəntlɪ] *adv* sin querer; accidentalmente

inadvisable [ˌɪnədˈvaɪzəbl] *adj* poco aconsejable

inappropriate [ˌɪnəˈprəʊprɪət] *adj* ❶ impropio, pia ❷ inoportuno, na

inarticulate [ˌɪnɑːˈtɪkjʊlət] *adj* ❶ que no se expresa bien ❷ mal pronunciado, da o expresado, da *(discurso)*

inasmuch [ˌɪnəzˈmʌtʃ] ■ **inasmuch as** *conjunción* en la medida en que

inauguration [ɪˌnɔːgjʊˈreɪʃn] *s* ❶ investidura ❷ inauguración

in-between *adj* intermedio, dia

inborn [ˌɪnˈbɔːn] *adj* innato, ta

inbound [ˈɪnbaʊnd] *adj* de llegada

in-box *s* buzón de entrada

inbuilt [ˌɪnˈbɪlt] *adj* ❶ innato, ta ❷ inherente

inc. (*abreviatura escrita de* inclusive) inclus.

Inc. [ɪŋk] (*abreviatura de* incorporated) ≃ S.A.

incapable [ɪnˈkeɪpəbl] *adj* ❶ • **to be incapable of something/of doing something** ser incapaz de algo/de hacer algo ❷ incompetente

incapacitated [ˌɪnkəˈpæsɪteɪtɪd] *adj* incapacitado, da

incendiary device [ɪnˈsendjərɪ-] *s* artefacto incendiario

incense ◆ *s* [ˈɪnsens] incienso ◆ *vt* [ɪnˈsens] enfurecer; indignar

incentive [ɪnˈsentɪv] *s* incentivo

incentivize [ɪnˈsentɪvaɪz] *vt* incentivar

inception [ɪnˈsepʃn] *s formal* inicio

incessant [ɪnˈsesnt] *adj* incesante; constante

incessantly [ɪnˈsesntlɪ] *adv* incesantemente; constantemente

incest [ˈɪnsest] *s* incesto

inch [ɪntʃ] ◆ *s* pulgada *(2,54 cm)*

expresión to be within an inch of doing something estar en un tris de hacer algo

◆ *vi* • **to inch forward** avanzar poco a poco

incidence [ˈɪnsɪdəns] *s* índice

incident [ˈɪnsɪdənt] *s* incidente; suceso

incidental [ˌɪnsɪˈdentl] *adj* accesorio, ria

incidentally [ˌɪnsɪˈdentəlɪ] *adv* por cierto; a propósito

incinerate [ɪnˈsɪnəreɪt] *vt* incinerar

incisive [ɪnˈsaɪsɪv] *adj* ❶ incisivo, va ❷ penetrante

incite [ɪnˈsaɪt] *vt* incitar • **to incite somebody to do something** incitar a alguien a que haga algo

inclination [ˌɪnklɪˈneɪʃn] *s* ❶ ☼ *incontable* inclinación; propensión ❷ • **inclination to do something** tendencia a hacer algo

incline ◆ *s* [ˈɪnklaɪn] pendiente ◆ *vt* [ɪnˈklaɪn] inclinar; ladear

inclined [ɪnˈklaɪnd] *adj* ❶ • **to be inclined to something** ser propenso, sa a algo • **to be inclined to do something** tener tendencia a hacer algo • **I'm inclined to agree** creo que estoy de acuerdo ❷ *formal* • **to be inclined to do something** estar dispuesto, ta a hacer algo ❸ inclinado, da

include [ɪnˈkluːd] *vt* ❶ incluir ❷ adjuntar

included [ɪnˈkluːdɪd] *adj* incluido, da

including [ɪnˈkluːdɪŋ] *preposición* incluyendo • **six died, including a child** murieron seis personas, incluyendo a un niño

inclusive [ɪnˈkluːsɪv] *adj* ❶ inclusivo, va • **one to nine inclusive** uno a nueve inclusive ❷ • **inclusive of sales tax** con el IVA incluido • **$150 inclusive** 150 dólares todo incluido

inclusivity [ˌɪnkluːˈsɪvɪtɪ] *s* política de inclusión

incoherent [ˌɪnkəʊˈhɪərənt] *adj* incoherente

income [ˈɪŋkʌm] *s* ☼ *incontable* ❶ ingresos ❷ renta ❸ réditos

income tax *s* impuesto sobre la renta

incompatible [ˌɪnkəmˈpætɪbl] *adj* • **incompatible (with)** incompatible (con)

incompetent [ɪnˈkɒmpɪtənt] *adj* incompetente; incapaz

incomplete [ˌɪnkəmˈpliːt] *adj* incompleto, ta

incomprehensible [ɪnˌkɒmprɪˈhensəbl] *adj* incomprensible

inconclusive [ˌɪnkənˈkluːsɪv] *adj* ❶ poco convincente ❷ sin conclusión clara

incongruous [ɪnˈkɒŋgrʊəs] *adj* incongruente

inconsiderable [ˌɪnkənˈsɪdərəbl] *adj* • **not inconsiderable** nada despreciable

inconsiderate [ˌɪnkənˈsɪdərət] *adj* desconsiderado, da

inconsistency [ˌɪnkənˈsɪstənsɪ] *s* ❶ inconsecuencia ❷ falta de correspondencia ❸ contradicción

inconsistent [ˌɪnkənˈsɪstənt] *adj* ❶ • **inconsistent (with)** incoherente o incongruente (con) ❷ inconsecuente ❸ irregular; desigual

inconspicuous [ˌɪnkənˈspɪkjʊəs] *adj* discreto, ta

inconvenience [ˌɪnkənˈviːnjəns] ◆ *s* ❶ molestia; incomodidad • **we apologize for any inconvenience caused** disculpen las molestias ❷ inconveniente ◆ *vt* incomodar

inconvenient [ˌɪnkənˈviːnjənt] *adj* ❶ inoportuno, na • **that date is inconvenient** esa fecha no me viene bien ❷ incómodo, da *(lugar)*

incorporate [ɪnˈkɔːpəreɪt] *vt* ❶ • **to incorporate something/somebody (in** o **into)** incorporar algo/a alguien (en) ❷ incluir; comprender

incorporated [ɪnˈkɔːpəreɪtɪd] *adj* COMERCIO • **incorporated company** sociedad anónima

incorrect [ˌɪnkəˈrekt] *adj* incorrecto, ta

increase ◆ *s* [ˈɪnkriːs] ❶ • **increase (in)** aumento (de) • **to be on the increase** ir en aumento ❷ • **increase (in) a)** subida (de) ◆ *vt* [ɪnˈkriːs] ❶ aumentar; incrementar ❷ subir ◆ *vi* [ɪnˈkriːs] ❶ aumentar ❷ subir

increasing [ɪnˈkriːsɪŋ] *adj* creciente

increasingly [ɪnˈkriːsɪŋlɪ] *adv* cada vez más

incredible [ɪnˈkredəbl] *adj* increíble

incredibly [ɪnˈkredəblɪ] *adv* increíblemente

incriminating [ɪnˈkrɪmɪneɪtɪŋ] *adj* comprometedor, ra

incubator [ˈɪnkjʊbeɪtər] *s* incubadora

incumbent [ɪnˈkʌmbənt] *formal* ◆ *adj* • **to be incumbent on somebody to do something** incumbir a alguien hacer algo ◆ *s* titular

incur [ɪnˈkɜːr] *vt* incurrir en

indebted [ɪnˈdetɪd] *adj* ❶ • **indebted (to)** en deuda (con) ❷ • **indebted (to)** endeudado, da (con)

indecent [ɪn'diːsnt] *adj* ❶ indecente ❷ desmedido, da

indecent assault *s* abusos deshonestos

indecent exposure *s* exhibicionismo

indecisive [ˌɪndɪ'saɪsɪv] *adj* ❶ indeciso, sa ❷ no decisivo, va

indeed [ɪn'diːd] *adv* ❶ ciertamente • **are you coming? — indeed I am** ¿vienes tú? — por supuesto que sí ❷ de hecho ❸ realmente • **very big indeed** grandísimo, ma • **very few indeed** poquísimos, mas ❹ • **indeed?** ¿ah sí? ❺ es más

indefinite [ɪn'defɪnɪt] *adj* ❶ indefinido, da ❷ impreciso, sa ❸ GRAMÁTICA indeterminado, da; indefinido, da

indefinitely [ɪn'defɪnətlɪ] *adv* ❶ indefinidamente ❷ de forma imprecisa

indent [ɪn'dent] ♦ *s* sangrado ♦ *vt* sangrar

independence [ˌɪndɪ'pendəns] *s* independencia • **to gain independence** independizarse

Independence Day *s* el Día de la Independencia

independent [ˌɪndɪ'pendənt] *adj* • **independent (of)** independiente (de)

in-depth *adj* a fondo; exhaustivo, va

indestructible [ˌɪndɪ'strʌktəbl] *adj* indestructible

index ['ɪndeks] *s* índice

Dos plurales: **indexes** o **indices**.

index card *s* ficha

index finger *s* (dedo) índice

India ['ɪndjə] *s* (la) India

Indian ['ɪndjən] ♦ *adj* ❶ indio, dia ❷ hindú ♦ *s* ❶ indio, dia ❷ hindú

Indian Ocean *s* • **the Indian Ocean** el océano Índico

indicate ['ɪndɪkeɪt] ♦ *vt* indicar ♦ *vi* • **to indicate left/right** indicar a la izquierda/derecha

indication [ˌɪndɪ'keɪʃn] *s* ❶ indicación ❷ indicio

indicative [ɪn'dɪkətɪv] ♦ *adj* • **indicative of something** indicativo, va de algo ♦ *s* GRAMÁTICA indicativo

indicator ['ɪndɪkeɪtər] *s* ❶ indicador ❷ intermitente

indices ['ɪndɪsiːz] *spl* → **index**

indict [ɪn'daɪt] *vt* • **to indict somebody (for)** acusar a alguien (de)

indictment [ɪn'daɪtmənt] *s* ❶ DERECHO acusación ❷ crítica severa

indifference [ɪn'dɪfrəns] *s* indiferencia

indifferent [ɪn'dɪfrənt] *adj* ❶ • **indifferent (to)** indiferente (a) ❷ mediocre

indigenous [ɪn'dɪdʒɪnəs] *adj* indígena

indigestion [ˌɪndɪ'dʒestʃn] *s* 🔅 *incontable* indigestión

indignant [ɪn'dɪgnənt] *adj* • **indignant (at)** indignado, da (por)

indigo ['ɪndɪgəʊ] ♦ *adj* (color) añil ♦ *s* añil

indirect [ˌɪndɪ'rekt] *adj* indirecto, ta

indiscreet [ˌɪndɪ'skriːt] *adj* indiscreto, ta

indiscriminate [ˌɪndɪ'skrɪmɪnət] *adj* indiscriminado, da

indispensable [ˌɪndɪ'spensəbl] *adj* indispensable; imprescindible

indisputable [ˌɪndɪ'spjuːtəbl] *adj* incuestionable

indistinct [ˌɪndɪ'stɪŋkt] *adj* ❶ confuso, sa *(memoria)* ❷ imperceptible *(palabras)* ❸ borroso, sa *(imagen, marca)*

indistinguishable [ˌɪndɪ'stɪŋgwɪʃəbl] *adj* • **indistinguishable (from)** indistinguible (de)

individual [ˌɪndɪ'vɪdʒʊəl] ♦ *adj* ❶ individual ❷ particular *(clases)* ❸ personal *(estilo, enfoque)* ♦ *s* individuo

individually [ˌɪndɪ'vɪdʒʊəlɪ] *adv* individualmente; por separado

indoctrination [ɪnˌdɒktrɪ'neɪʃn] *s* adoctrinamiento

Indonesia [ˌɪndə'niːzjə] *s* Indonesia

indoor ['ɪndɔːr] *adj* ❶ interior • **indoor shoes** zapatos de andar por casa • **indoor plants** plantas de interior ❷ en pista cubierta *(deportes)* • **indoor swimming pool** alberca cubierta

indoors [ˌɪn'dɔːz] *adv* ❶ dentro • **to go/come indoors** entrar ❷ en casa

induce [ɪn'djuːs] *vt* ❶ • **to induce somebody to do something** inducir o persuadir a alguien a que haga algo ❷ provocar

induction [ɪn'dʌkʃn] *s* introducción

induction course *s* curso introductorio

indulge [ɪn'dʌldʒ] ♦ *vt* ❶ satisfacer ❷ consentir ♦ *vi* • **to indulge in something** permitirse algo

indulgence [ɪn'dʌldʒəns] *s* ❶ indulgencia ❷ capricho

indulgent [ɪn'dʌldʒənt] *adj* indulgente

industrial [ɪn'dʌstrɪəl] *adj* industrial

industrial action *s* huelga • **to take industrial action** declararse en huelga

industrialist [ɪn'dʌstrɪəlɪst] *s* industrial

industrial park *s* parque industrial

industrial relations *spl* relaciones laborales

industrial revolution *s* revolución industrial

industrious [ɪn'dʌstrɪəs] *adj* diligente; trabajador, ra

industry ['ɪndəstrɪ] *s* industria • **the tourist industry** el sector turístico

inebriated [ɪ'niːbrɪeɪtɪd] *adj formal* ebrio, ebria

inedible [ɪn'edɪbl] *adj* ❶ no comestible ❷ incomible

ineffective [ˌɪnɪ'fektɪv] *adj* ineficaz; inútil

ineffectual [ˌɪnɪ'fektʃʊəl] *adj* inútil

inefficiency [ˌɪnɪ'fɪʃnsɪ] *s* ineficiencia

inefficient [ˌɪnɪ'fɪʃnt] *adj* ineficiente

ineligible [ɪnˈelɪdʒəbl] *adj* inelegible • **to be ineligible for** no tener derecho a

inept [ɪˈnept] *adj* inepto, ta • **inept at** incapaz para

inequality [ˌɪnɪˈkwɒlətɪ] *s* desigualdad

inert [ɪˈnɜːt] *adj* inerte

inertia [ɪˈnɜːʃə] *s* inercia

inevitable [ɪnˈevɪtəbl] *adj* inevitable

inevitably [ɪnˈevɪtəblɪ] *adv* inevitablemente

inexcusable [ˌɪnɪkˈskjuːzəbl] *adj* inexcusable; imperdonable

inexpensive [ˌɪnɪkˈspensɪv] *adj* barato, ta; económico, ca

inexperienced [ˌɪnɪkˈspɪərɪənst] *adj* inexperto, ta

inexplicable [ˌɪnɪkˈsplɪkəbl] *adj* inexplicable

infallible [ɪnˈfæləbl] *adj* infalible

infamous [ˈɪnfəməs] *adj* infame

infancy [ˈɪnfənsɪ] *s* primera infancia

expresión **to be in its infancy** dar sus primeros pasos

infant [ˈɪnfənt] *s* ❶ bebé ❷ niño pequeño, niña pequeña

infantry [ˈɪnfəntrɪ] *s* infantería

infatuated [ɪnˈfætjʊeɪtɪd] *adj* • **infatuated (with)** encaprichado, da (con)

infatuation [ɪnˌfætjʊˈeɪʃn] *s* • **infatuation (with)** encaprichamiento (con)

infect [ɪnˈfekt] *vt* infectar

infection [ɪnˈfekʃn] *s* ❶ infección ❷ contagio

infectious [ɪnˈfekʃəs] *adj* ❶ infeccioso, sa ❷ contagioso, sa

infer [ɪnˈfɜːr] *vt* ❶ • **to infer (that)** deducir o inferir que • **to infer something (from something)** deducir o inferir algo (de algo) ❷ insinuar

inferior [ɪnˈfɪərɪər] ◆ *adj* • **inferior (to)** inferior (a) ◆ *s* inferior

inferiority [ɪnˌfɪərɪˈɒrətɪ] *s* inferioridad

inferiority complex *s* complejo de inferioridad

inferno [ɪnˈfɜːnəʊ] *s* infierno • **the building was an inferno** el edificio sufría un pavoroso incendio

El plural de **inferno** es **infernos**.

infertile [ɪnˈfɜːtaɪl] *adj* estéril

infested [ɪnˈfestɪd] *adj* • **infested with** infestado, da de

infighting [ˈɪnˌfaɪtɪŋ] *s* ☿ *incontable* disputas internas

infiltrate [ˈɪnfɪltreɪt] *vt* infiltrar

infinite [ˈɪnfɪnət] *adj* infinito, ta

infinitive [ɪnˈfɪnɪtɪv] *s* infinitivo • **in the infinitive** en infinitivo

infinity [ɪnˈfɪnətɪ] *s* ❶ MATEMÁTICAS infinito ❷ • **an infinity (of)** infinidad (de)

infirm [ɪnˈfɜːm] ◆ *adj* achacoso, sa ◆ *spl* • **the infirm** los enfermos

infirmary [ɪnˈfɜːmərɪ] *s* ❶ hospital ❷ enfermería

inflamed [ɪnˈfleɪmd] *adj* MEDICINA inflamado, da

inflammable [ɪnˈflæməbl] *adj* inflamable

inflammation [ˌɪnfləˈmeɪʃn] *s* MEDICINA inflamación

inflatable [ɪnˈfleɪtəbl] *adj* inflable; hinchable

inflate [ɪnˈfleɪt] ◆ *vt* inflar; hinchar ◆ *vi* inflarse; hincharse

inflation [ɪnˈfleɪʃn] *s* ECONOMÍA inflación

inflationary [ɪnˈfleɪʃnrɪ] *adj* ECONOMÍA inflacionista

inflict [ɪnˈflɪkt] *vt* • **to inflict something on somebody** infligir algo a alguien

influence [ˈɪnflʊəns] ◆ *s* • **influence (over somebody/on something)** influencia (sobre alguien/en algo) • **to be a bad influence on somebody** tener mala influencia en alguien • **under the influence of a)** bajo la influencia de *(persona, grupo)* **b)** bajo los efectos de *(alcohol, droga)* ◆ *vt* influenciar

influential [ˌɪnflʊˈenʃl] *adj* influyente

influenza [ˌɪnflʊˈenzə] *s formal* gripe

influx [ˈɪnflʌks] *s* afluencia

inform [ɪnˈfɔːm] *vt* • **to inform somebody (of/about something)** informar a alguien (de/sobre algo)

■ **inform on** *vt* ☿ *El objeto siempre va después de la preposición al final.* delatar

informal [ɪnˈfɔːml] *adj* ❶ informal ❷ familiar

informant [ɪnˈfɔːmənt] *s* ❶ delator, ra ❷ informante

information [ˌɪnfəˈmeɪʃn] *s* ☿ *incontable* • **information (on o about)** información o datos (sobre) • **a piece of information** un dato • **for your information** para tu información

information desk *s* (mostrador de) información

information technology *s* informática

informative [ɪnˈfɔːmətɪv] *adj* informativo, va

informer [ɪnˈfɔːmər] *s* delator, ra

infrared [ˌɪnfrəˈred] *adj* infrarrojo, ja

infrastructure [ˈɪnfrəˌstrʌktʃər] *s* infraestructura

infringe [ɪnˈfrɪndʒ] ◆ *vt* ❶ infringir ❷ vulnerar ◆ *vi* • **to infringe on something** vulnerar algo

infringement [ɪnˈfrɪndʒmənt] *s* ❶ infracción ❷ violación

infuriating [ɪnˈfjʊərɪeɪtɪŋ] *adj* exasperante

ingenious [ɪnˈdʒiːnjəs] *adj* ingenioso, sa

ingenuity [ˌɪndʒɪˈnjuːətɪ] *s* ingenio; inventiva

ingot [ˈɪŋgət] *s* lingote

ingrained [ˌɪnˈgreɪnd] *adj* ❶ incrustado, da ❷ arraigado, da

ingredient [ɪnˈgriːdjənt] *s* ingrediente

inhabit [ɪnˈhæbɪt] *vt* habitar

inhabitant [ɪnˈhæbɪtənt] *s* habitante

inhale [ɪnˈheɪl] ◆ *vt* inhalar ◆ *vi* ❶ inspirar ❷ tragarse el humo *(fumador)*

inhaler [ɪn'heɪlər] *s MEDICINA* inhalador

inherent [ɪn'hɪərənt] [ɪn'herənt] *adj* • **inherent (in)** inherente (a)

inherently [ɪn'hɪərəntlɪ] [ɪn'herəntlɪ] *adv* intrínsecamente

inherit [ɪn'herɪt] *vt* • **to inherit something (from somebody)** heredar algo (de alguien)

inheritance [ɪn'herɪtəns] *s* herencia

inhibit [ɪn'hɪbɪt] *vt* ❶ impedir ❷ cohibir

inhibition [ˌɪnhɪ'bɪʃn] *s* inhibición

inhospitable [ˌɪnhɒ'spɪtəbl] *adj* ❶ inhospitalario, ria ❷ inhóspito, ta

in-house ◆ *adj* ❶ de circulación interna *(revista, informe)* ❷ de plantilla *(trabajador)* ❸ en el lugar de trabajo *(formación)* ◆ *adv* en la misma empresa

inhuman [ɪn'hjuːmən] *adj* ❶ inhumano, na ❷ infrahumano, na

initial [ɪ'nɪʃl] ◆ *adj* inicial ◆ *vt* poner las iniciales a
■ **initials** *spl* iniciales

initially [ɪ'nɪʃəlɪ] *adv* inicialmente

initiate [ɪ'nɪʃɪeɪt] *vt* iniciar

initiative [ɪ'nɪʃətɪv] *s* iniciativa

inject [ɪn'dʒekt] *vt MEDICINA* • **to inject somebody with something, to inject something into somebody** inyectarle algo a alguien

injection [ɪn'dʒekʃn] *s* inyección • **to give somebody an injection** ponerle una inyección a alguien

injunction [ɪn'dʒʌŋkʃn] *s* interdicto

injure [ɪn'dʒər] *vt* ❶ herir ❷ *DEPORTE* lesionar • **he has injured his leg** se lesionó la pierna

injured ['ɪndʒəd] *adj* ❶ herido, da ❷ *DEPORTE* lesionado, da

injury ['ɪndʒərɪ] *s* ❶ herida ❷ lesión ❸ ☀️*incontable* lesiones

injury time *s* (tiempo de) descuento

injustice [ɪn'dʒʌstɪs] *s* injusticia
expresión to do somebody an injustice ser injusto, ta con alguien

ink [ɪŋk] *s* tinta

ink-jet printer *s INFORMÁTICA* impresora de chorro de tinta

inkling ['ɪŋklɪŋ] *s* • **to have an inkling of something** tener una vaga idea de algo

inland ◆ *adj* ['ɪnlənd] interior ◆ *adv* [ɪn'lænd] ❶ hacia el interior ❷ en el interior

in-laws *spl* suegros

inlet ['ɪnlet] *s* ❶ entrante *(de agua)* ❷ entrada; admisión

in-line skating *s DEPORTE* patinaje en línea

inmate ['ɪnmeɪt] *s* ❶ preso, sa ❷ interno, na *(de manicomio)*

inn [ɪn] *s* fonda

innate [ˌɪ'neɪt] *adj* innato, ta

inner ['ɪnər] *adj* ❶ interior ❷ íntimo, ma *(sentimientos)* ❸ interno, na *(miedo, dudas, significado)*

inner city *s* núcleo urbano deprimido

inner tube *s* cámara (de aire)

inning ['ɪnɪŋ] *s* entrada; inning

innocence ['ɪnəsəns] *s* inocencia

innocent ['ɪnəsənt] ◆ *adj* • **innocent (of)** inocente (de) ◆ *s* inocente

innocuous [ɪ'nɒkjuəs] *adj* inocuo, cua

innovation [ˌɪnə'veɪʃn] *s* innovación

innovative ['ɪnəvətɪv] *adj* innovador, ra

innuendo [ˌɪnju:'endəu] *s* ❶ insinuación; indirecta ❷ ☀️*incontable* insinuaciones; indirectas
Dos plurales: **innuendos** o **innuendoes**.

inoculate [ɪ'nɒkjuleɪt] *vt* • **to inoculate somebody (against something)** inocular a alguien (contra algo)

in-patient *s* paciente interno, paciente interna

input ['ɪnput] ◆ *s* ❶ aportación; contribución ❷ *INFORMÁTICA & ELECTRICIDAD* entrada ◆ *vt INFORMÁTICA* introducir
Formas irregulares de **input**: *pretérito & pp* **input** o **inputted**.

inquest ['ɪnkwest] *s* investigación judicial

inquire [ɪn'kwaɪər] ◆ *vi* informarse; preguntar • **to inquire about something** informarse de algo ◆ *vt* • **to inquire when/if/how...** preguntar cuándo/si/cómo...
■ **inquire after** *vt* ☀️*El objeto siempre va después de la preposición al final.* preguntar por
■ **inquire into** *vt* ☀️*El objeto siempre va después de la preposición al final.* investigar

inquiry [ɪn'kwaɪərɪ] *s* ❶ consulta; pregunta • **'Inquiries'** 'Información' ❷ investigación

inquiry desk *s* (mostrador de) información

inquisitive [ɪn'kwɪzətɪv] *adj* curioso, sa

inroads ['ɪnrəudz] *spl* • **to make inroads into** mermar *(ahorros, reservas)*; abrirse paso en *(mercado)*

insane [ɪn'seɪn] *adj* ❶ demente ❷ *figurado* loco, ca • **to drive somebody insane** volver loco a alguien • **to go insane** volverse loco

insanity [ɪn'sænətɪ] *s* ❶ *MEDICINA* demencia ❷ locura

inscription [ɪn'skrɪpʃn] *s* ❶ inscripción ❷ dedicatoria

insect ['ɪnsekt] *s* insecto

insecticide [ɪn'sektɪsaɪd] *s* insecticida

insect repellent *s* loción antiinsectos

insecure [ˌɪnsɪ'kjuər] *adj* ❶ inseguro, ra ❷ poco seguro, ra

insensitive [ɪn'sensətɪv] *adj* • **insensitive (to)** insensible (a)

inseparable [ɪn'seprəbl] *adj* • **inseparable (from)** inseparable (de)

insert ◆ *vt* [ɪn'sɜ:t] • **to insert something (in** o **into) a)** introducir algo (en) **b)** insertar algo (en) ◆ *s* ['ɪnsɜ:t] PRENSA encarte

insertion [ɪn'sɜ:ʃn] *s* inserción

inshore ◆ *adj* ['ɪnʃɔ:r] costero, ra ◆ *adv* [ɪn'ʃɔ:r] hacia la orilla o la costa

inside [ɪn'saɪd] ◆ *preposición* dentro de • **inside three months** en menos de tres meses ◆ *adv* ❶ dentro ❷ adentro • **to come/go inside** entrar ❸ *figurado* por dentro ◆ *adj* interior • **inside leg measurement** medida de la entrepierna ◆ *s* interior • **from the inside** desde dentro • **to overtake on the inside** adelantar por dentro • **inside out** al revés • **to turn something inside out** dar la vuelta a algo

expresión to know something inside out conocer algo de arriba abajo o al dedillo

■ **insides** *spl familiar* tripas

■ **inside of** *preposición* dentro de

inside lane *s* ❶ AUTOMÓVILES carril de dentro ❷ DEPORTE calle de dentro

insight ['ɪnsaɪt] *s* ❶ ☿ *incontable* perspicacia ❷ idea

insignificant [,ɪnsɪg'nɪfɪkənt] *adj* insignificante

insincere [,ɪnsɪn'sɪər] *adj* insincero, ra

insinuate [ɪn'sɪnjʊeɪt] *vt despectivo* • **to insinuate (that)** insinuar (que)

insipid [ɪn'sɪpɪd] *adj despectivo* soso, sa ; insípido, da

insist [ɪn'sɪst] ◆ *vt* • **to insist that** insistir en que ◆ *vi* • **to insist on something** exigir algo • **to insist (on doing something)** insistir (en hacer algo)

insistent [ɪn'sɪstənt] *adj* ❶ insistente • **to be insistent on something** insistir en algo ❷ persistente

insofar [,ɪnsəʊ'fɑ:r] ■ **insofar as** *conjunción* en la medida en que

insole ['ɪnsəʊl] *s* plantilla

insolent ['ɪnsələnt] *adj* insolente

insolvent [ɪn'sɒlvənt] *adj* insolvente

insomnia [ɪn'sɒmnɪə] *s* insomnio

inspect [ɪn'spekt] *vt* ❶ inspeccionar ; examinar ❷ pasar revista a

inspection [ɪn'spekʃn] *s* inspección • **on closer inspection** tras un examen más detallado

inspector [ɪn'spektər] *s* ❶ inspector, ra ❷ revisor, ra

inspiration [,ɪnspə'reɪʃn] *s* ❶ inspiración ❷ • **inspiration (for)** fuente de inspiración (para)

inspirational [,ɪnspə'reɪʃnl] *adj* inspirador, ra

inspire [ɪn'spaɪər] *vt* ❶ • **to inspire somebody (to do something)** alentar o animar a alguien (a hacer algo) ❷ • **to inspire somebody with something, to inspire something in somebody** inspirar algo a alguien

instal [ɪn'stɔ:l] *vt* instalar

installation [,ɪnstə'leɪʃn] *s* instalación

installment [ɪn'stɔ:lmənt] *s* ❶ plazo • **in installments** a plazos ❷ TELEVISIÓN & RADIO episodio

instance ['ɪnstəns] *s* ejemplo • **for instance** por ejemplo • **in the first instance** *formal* en primer lugar • **in this instance** en este caso

instant ['ɪnstənt] ◆ *adj* instantáneo, a • **the album was an instant success** el disco fue un éxito inmediato ◆ *s* instante • **at that** o **the same instant** en aquel mismo instante • **the instant (that)...** en cuanto... • **this instant** ahora mismo

instantly ['ɪnstəntlɪ] *adv* en el acto

instead [ɪn'sted] *adv* en cambio • **I came instead** yo vine en su lugar • **if you haven't got any sugar, use honey instead** si no tiene azúcar, utilice miel en su lugar

■ **instead of** *preposición* en lugar de ; en vez de • **I came instead of her** yo vine en su lugar

instep ['ɪnstep] *s* empeine

instigate ['ɪnstɪgeɪt] *vt* iniciar • **to instigate somebody to do something** instigar a alguien a hacer algo

instill [ɪn'stɪl] *vt* • **to instil something in** o **into somebody** inculcar algo a alguien

instinct ['ɪnstɪŋkt] *s* instinto • **my first instinct was...** mi primer impulso fue...

instinctive [ɪn'stɪŋktɪv] *adj* instintivo, va

institute ['ɪnstɪtju:t] *s* instituto

institution [,ɪnstɪ'tju:ʃn] *s* ❶ institución ❷ asilo ❸ hospital psiquiátrico

institutional racism, institutionalized racism *s* racismo institucional

instruct [ɪn'strʌkt] *vt* ❶ • **to instruct somebody to do something** mandar o ordenar a alguien que haga algo ❷ • **to instruct somebody (in something)** instruir a alguien (en algo)

instruction [ɪn'strʌkʃn] *s* instrucción

■ **instructions** *spl* instrucciones

instructor [ɪn'strʌktər] *s* ❶ instructor, ra ❷ monitor, ora *(de esquí)* ❸ profesor, ra

instrument ['ɪnstrʊmənt] *s* instrumento

instrumental [,ɪnstrʊ'mentl] *adj* ❶ instrumental ❷ • **to be instrumental in something** jugar un papel fundamental en algo

instrument panel *s* tablero de instrumentos

insubstantial [,ɪnsəb'stænʃl] *adj* ❶ endeble ❷ poco sustancioso, sa

insufficient [,ɪnsə'fɪʃnt] *adj* • **insufficient (for)** insuficiente (para)

insular ['ɪnsjʊlər] *adj* estrecho, cha de miras

insulate ['ɪnsjʊleɪt] *vt* aislar

insulation [,ɪnsjʊ'leɪʃn] *s* ❶ aislamiento ❷ aislamiento térmico

insulin ['ɪnsjʊlɪn] *s* insulina

insult ◆ *vt* [ɪn'sʌlt] ❶ insultar ❷ ofender ◆ *s* ['ɪnsʌlt] ❶ insulto ❷ ofensa

insurance [ɪn'ʃʊərəns] *s* ❶ • **insurance (against)** seguro (contra) ❷ *figurado* • **insurance (against)** prevención (contra)

insurance policy *s* póliza de seguros

insure [ɪn'ʃʊər] ♦ *vt* **❶** • **to insure something/ somebody (against)** asegurar algo/a alguien (contra) **❷** asegurar ♦ *vi* • **to insure (against)** prevenir o prevenirse (contra)

insurer [ɪn'ʃʊərər] *s* asegurador, ra

insurmountable [ˌɪnsə'maʊntəbl] *adj formal* infranqueable; insuperable

intact [ɪn'tækt] *adj* intacto, ta

intake ['ɪnteɪk] *s* **❶** ingestión **❷** inspiración **❸** número de ingresos

integral ['ɪntɪgrəl] *adj* integrante • **to be integral to** ser parte integrante de

integrate ['ɪntɪgreɪt] ♦ *vi* • **to integrate (with** o **into)** integrarse (en) ♦ *vt* • **to integrate something/ somebody with something, to integrate something/ somebody into something** integrar algo/a alguien en algo

integrity [ɪn'tegrətɪ] *s* integridad

intellect ['ɪntəlekt] *s* intelecto; inteligencia

intellectual [ˌɪntə'lektjʊəl] ♦ *adj* intelectual ♦ *s* intelectual

intelligence [ɪn'telɪdʒəns] *s* ⚫ *incontable* **❶** inteligencia **❷** información secreta **❸** servicio secreto o de espionaje

intelligent [ɪn'telɪdʒənt] *adj* inteligente

intend [ɪn'tend] *vt* pretender • **to intend doing** o **to do something** tener la intención de hacer algo • **what do you intend to do?** ¿qué piensas hacer? • **later than I had intended** más tarde de lo que había pensado • **to be intended for/as something** estar pensado para/como algo • **the flowers were intended for you** las flores eran para ti

intended [ɪn'tendɪd] *adj* pretendido, da

intense [ɪn'tens] *adj* **❶** intenso, sa **❷** muy serio, ria

intensely [ɪn'tenslɪ] *adv* **❶** enormemente **❷** intensamente; profundamente

intensify [ɪn'tensɪfaɪ] ♦ *vt* intensificar ♦ *vi* intensificarse

intensity [ɪn'tensətɪ] *s* intensidad

intensive [ɪn'tensɪv] *adj* intensivo, va

intensive care *s* ⚫ *incontable* • **(in) intensive care** (bajo) cuidados intensivos

intent [ɪn'tent] ♦ *adj* **❶** • **to be intent on doing something** estar empeñado, da en hacer algo **❷** atento, ta ♦ *s formal* intención

expresión **to all intents and purposes** para todos los efectos

intention [ɪn'tenʃn] *s* intención • **to have no intention of** no tener la menor intención de

intentional [ɪn'tenʃənl] *adj* deliberado, da; intencionado, da • **it wasn't intentional** fue sin querer

interact [ˌɪntər'ækt] *vi* **❶** • **to interact (with somebody)** relacionarse (con alguien) **❷** • **to interact (with something)** interaccionar (con algo)

interactive [ˌɪntər'æktɪv] *adj* interactivo, va

intercept [ˌɪntə'sept] *vt* interceptar

interchange ♦ *s* ['ɪntəʧeɪndʒ] **❶** intercambio **❷** enlace ♦ *vt* [ˌɪntə'ʧeɪndʒ] intercambiar

interchangeable [ˌɪntə'ʧeɪndʒəbl] *adj* • **interchangeable (with)** intercambiable (con)

intercity [ˌɪntə'sɪtɪ] *adj* interurbano, na

intercom ['ɪntəkɒm] *s* **❶** intercom **❷** interfono

intercourse ['ɪntəkɔːs] *s* ⚫ *incontable* ▶ **sexual intercourse** relaciones sexuales; coito

interest ['ɪntrəst] ♦ *s* **❶** • **interest (in)** interés (en o por) • **that's of no interest** eso no tiene interés **in the interest** o **interests of a)** en interés de **b)** en pro de • **that's of no interest** eso no tiene interés • **to lose interest in something** perder interés en algo • **it's in your best interest to finish your degree** te conviene terminar tus estudios de grado **❷** *FINANZAS* interés • **to pay the interest on a loan** pagar los intereses de un préstamo **❸** afición ♦ *vt* interesar • **to interest somebody in something/in doing something** interesar a alguien en algo/en hacer algo

interested ['ɪntrəstɪd] *adj* interesado, da • **I'm not interested** no me interesa • **to be interested in something/in doing something** estar interesado en algo/en hacer algo • **I'm interested in that subject** me interesa el tema

interesting ['ɪntrəstɪŋ] *adj* interesante

interest rate *s* tipo de interés

interface *s* *INFORMÁTICA* interfaz; interface

interfere [ˌɪntə'fɪər] *vi* **❶** • **to interfere (with** o **in something)** entrometerse o interferir (en algo) • **don't interfere!** ¡no te metas! **❷** interferir • **to interfere with something a)** interferir en algo *(carrera, rutina)* **b)** interferir con algo *(trabajo, rendimiento)*

interference [ˌɪntə'fɪərəns] *s* ⚫ *incontable* **❶** • **interference (with** o **in)** intromisión o interferencia (en) **❷** interferencia

interim ['ɪntərɪm] ♦ *adj* **❶** parcial *(informe)* **❷** provisional *(medida)* **❸** interino, na *(gobierno)* ♦ *s* • **in the interim** entre tanto

interior [ɪn'tɪərɪər] ♦ *adj* **❶** interior **❷** *POLÍTICA* del Interior ♦ *s* interior

interior decorator, interior designer *s* interiorista

interlude ['ɪntəluːd] *s* **❶** intervalo **❷** intermedio

intermediary [ˌɪntə'miːdjərɪ] *s* intermediario, ria

intermediate [ˌɪntə'miːdjət] *adj* intermedio, dia

intermission [ˌɪntə'mɪʃn] *s* **❶** descanso **❷** entreacto

intermittent [ˌɪntə'mɪtənt] *adj* intermitente

intern ♦ *vt* [ɪn't3ːn] recluir; internar ♦ *s* ['ɪnt3ːn] médico interno residente

internal [ɪn't3ːnl] *adj* **❶** interno, na **❷** interior; nacional ▶ **internal flight** vuelo nacional

internally [ɪn't3ːnəlɪ] *adv* **❶** internamente **❷** a nivel nacional

Internal Revenue Service *s* • **the Internal Revenue Service** ≃ la Secretaría de Hacienda

international [ˌɪntəˈnæʃənl] *adj* internacional

Internet [ˈɪntənet] *s* • **the Internet** Internet • **on the Internet** en Internet

Internet access *s* acceso a Internet

Internet access provider *s* proveedor de acceso a Internet

Internet café *s* cibercafé

Internet connection *s* conexión a Internet

Internet radio *s* radio por Internet

Internet Service Provider *s* proveedor de servicios Internet

Internet television, Internet TV *s* televisión por Internet

interpret [ɪnˈtɜ:prɪt] ♦ *vt* interpretar ♦ *vi* hacer de intérprete

interpreter [ɪnˈtɜ:prɪtər] *s* intérprete

interrogate [ɪnˈterəgeɪt] *vt* interrogar

interrogation [ɪnˌterəˈgeɪʃn] *s* interrogatorio

interrogation mark *s* signo de interrogación

interrogative [ˌɪntəˈrɒgətɪv] *adj* GRAMÁTICA interrogativo, va

interrupt [ˌɪntəˈrʌpt] *vt* & *vi* interrumpir

interruption [ˌɪntəˈrʌpʃn] *s* interrupción

intersect [ˌɪntəˈsekt] ♦ *vi* cruzarse ♦ *vt* cruzar

intersection [ˌɪntəˈsekʃn] *s* cruce ; intersección

intersperse [ˌɪntəˈspɜ:s] *vt* • **to be interspersed with** o **by** estar entremezclado con

interstate [ˈɪntəsteɪt] *s* autopista interestatal

interval [ˈɪntəvl] *s* • **interval (between)** intervalo (entre) • **at intervals** a ratos • **at regular intervals** a intervalos regulares • **at monthly/yearly intervals** a intervalos de un mes/un año

intervene [ˌɪntəˈvi:n] *vi* ❶ • **to intervene (in)** intervenir (en) ❷ interponerse • **the war intervened** sobrevino la guerra ❸ transcurrir

intervention [ˌɪntəˈvenʃn] *s* intervención

interview [ˈɪntəvju:] ♦ *s* ❶ entrevista ❷ interrogatorio ♦ *vt* ❶ entrevistar ❷ interrogar

interviewer [ˈɪntəvju:ər] *s* entrevistador, ra

intestine [ɪnˈtestɪn] *s* intestino

intimacy [ˈɪntɪməsɪ] *s* • **intimacy (between/with)** intimidad (entre/con)

intimate *adj* [ˈɪntɪmət] ❶ íntimo, ma ❷ profundo, da *(conocimiento)*

intimidate [ɪnˈtɪmɪdeɪt] *vt* intimidar

into [ˈɪntʊ] *preposición* ❶ en • **to go into a room** entrar en una habitación • **to put something into something** meter algo en algo • **to get into a car** subir a un coche ❷ con • **to bump/crash into** tropezar/chocar con ❸ • **to turn** o **develop into** convertirse en • **to translate something into Spanish** traducir algo al español ❹ en relación con • **research into electronics** investigación en torno a la electrónica ❺ • **fifteen minutes into the game** a los quince minutos de empezar el partido • **well into the spring** hasta bien en-

trada la primavera ❻ MATEMÁTICAS • **to divide 4 into 8** dividir 8 entre 4

intolerance [ɪnˈtɒlərəns] *s* intolerancia

intolerant [ɪnˈtɒlərənt] *adj* intolerante

intoxicated [ɪnˈtɒksɪkeɪtɪd] *adj* ❶ embriagado, da ❷ *figurado* • **intoxicated (by** o **with)** ebrio, ebria (de)

intransitive [ɪnˈtrænzətɪv] *adj* intransitivo, va

intravenous [ˌɪntrəˈvi:nəs] *adj* intravenoso, sa

in-tray *s* bandeja de entrada

intricate [ˈɪntrɪkət] *adj* intrincado, da

intrigue [ɪnˈtri:g] ♦ *s* intriga ♦ *vt* intrigar

intriguing [ɪnˈtri:gɪŋ] *adj* intrigante

intrinsic [ɪnˈtrɪnsɪk] *adj* intrínseco, ca

introduce [ˌɪntrəˈdju:s] *vt* ❶ • **to introduce something (to** o **into)** introducir algo (en) ❷ presentar • **to introduce somebody (to somebody)** presentar a alguien (a alguien) • **to introduce yourself** presentarse ❸ • **to introduce somebody to something** iniciar a alguien en algo

introduction [ˌɪntrəˈdʌkʃn] *s* ❶ • **introduction (to something)** introducción (a algo) ❷ • **introduction (to somebody)** presentación (a alguien)

introductory [ˌɪntrəˈdʌktrɪ] *adj* ❶ introductorio, ria ❷ preliminar *(comentario)* ❸ de lanzamiento *(precio, oferta)*

introvert [ˈɪntrəvɜ:t] *s* introvertido, da

introverted [ˈɪntrəvɜ:tɪd] *adj* introvertido, da

intrude [ɪnˈtru:d] *vi* ❶ • **to intrude (on** o **upon somebody)** inmiscuirse (en los asuntos de alguien) • **to intrude (on** o **upon something)** inmiscuirse (en algo) ❷ molestar

intruder [ɪnˈtru:dər] *s* intruso, sa

intrusive [ɪnˈtru:sɪv] *adj* ❶ entrometido, da ❷ indeseado, da

intuition [ˌɪntju:ˈɪʃn] *s* intuición

inundate [ˈɪnʌndeɪt] *vt* ❶ *formal* inundar ❷ desbordar • **to be inundated with** verse desbordado por

invade [ɪnˈveɪd] *vt* invadir

invalid ♦ *adj* [ɪnˈvælɪd] ❶ nulo, la ❷ que no es válido, da ♦ *s* [ˈɪnvəlɪd] inválido, da

invaluable [ɪnˈvæljʊəbl] *adj* • **invaluable (to) a)** inestimable (para) *(información, consejos)* **b)** valiosísimo, ma (para) *(persona)*

invariably [ɪnˈveərɪəblɪ] *adv* siempre ; invariablemente

invasion [ɪnˈveɪʒn] *s* invasión

invent [ɪnˈvent] *vt* inventar

invention [ɪnˈvenʃn] *s* ❶ invención ❷ inventiva

inventive [ɪnˈventɪv] *adj* ❶ inventivo, va ❷ ingenioso, sa

inventor [ɪnˈventər] *s* inventor, ra

inventory [ˈɪnventrɪ] *s* ❶ inventario ❷ existencias

invert [ɪnˈvɜ:t] *vt* invertir

invest [ɪnˈvest] ◆ *vt* • **to invest something (in)** invertir algo (en) ◆ *vi literal & figurado* • **to invest (in)** invertir (en)

investigate [ɪnˈvestɪgeɪt] *vt & vi* investigar

investigation [ɪnˌvestɪˈgeɪʃn] *s* • **investigation (into)** investigación (en)

investment [ɪnˈvestmənt] *s* inversión

investor [ɪnˈvestər] *s* inversor, ra

invigorating [ɪnˈvɪgəreɪtɪŋ] *adj* ❶ vigorizante ❷ estimulante

invincible [ɪnˈvɪnsɪbl] *adj* invencible

invisible [ɪnˈvɪzɪbl] *adj* invisible

invitation [ˌɪnvɪˈteɪʃn] *s* invitación • **an invitation to something/to do something** una invitación a algo/a hacer algo

invite [ɪnˈvaɪt] *vt* ❶ • **to invite somebody (to something/to do something)** invitar a alguien (a algo/a hacer algo) ❷ buscarse *(problemas)*

inviting [ɪnˈvaɪtɪŋ] *adj* tentador, ra

invoice [ˈɪnvɔɪs] ◆ *s* factura ◆ *vt* ❶ mandar la factura a ❷ facturar

involuntary [ɪnˈvɒləntrɪ] *adj* involuntario, ria

involve [ɪnˈvɒlv] *vt* ❶ • **to involve something/doing something** conllevar algo/hacer algo • **it involves working weekends** supone oimplica trabajar los fines de semana ❷ afectar a • **to be involved in something** verse envuelto en algo

involved [ɪnˈvɒlvd] *adj* ❶ enrevesado, da ❷ • **involved in** metido, da en • **he didn't want to get involved** no quería tener nada que ver ❸ • **to be/get involved with somebody** estar liado, da/liarse con alguien

involvement [ɪnˈvɒlvmənt] *s* ❶ • **involvement (in)** a) implicación (en) b) participación (en) ❷ • **involvement (in)** compromiso (con) ❸ 💡 *incontable* relación sentimental

inward [ˈɪnwəd] ◆ *adj* ❶ interno, na ❷ hacia el interior ◆ *adv* = **inwards**

inwards, inward [ˈɪnwədz] *adv* hacia dentro

in-your-face *adj familiar* impactante

iodine [ˈaɪədaɪn] *s* yodo

IOU *(abreviatura de* I owe you) *s* pagaré

IQ *(abreviatura de* intelligence quotient) *s* C.I.

Iran [ɪˈrɑːn] *s* (el) Irán

Iranian [ɪˈreɪnjən] ◆ *adj* iraní ◆ *s* iraní

Iraq [ɪˈrɑːk] *s* (el) Irak

Iraqi [ɪˈrɑːkɪ] ◆ *adj* iraquí ◆ *s* iraquí

irate [aɪˈreɪt] *adj* iracundo, da; airado, da

Ireland [ˈaɪələnd] *s* Irlanda

iris [ˈaɪərɪs] *s* ❶ lirio ❷ iris

El plural de **iris** es **irises**

Irish [ˈaɪrɪʃ] ◆ *adj* irlandés, esa ◆ *s* irlandés ◆ *spl* • **the Irish** los irlandeses

Irishman [ˈaɪrɪʃmən] *s* irlandés

El plural de **Irishman** es **Irishmen** [ˈaɪrɪʃmen].

Irish Sea *s* • **the Irish Sea** el mar de Irlanda

Irishwoman [ˈaɪrɪʃˌwʊmən] *s* irlandesa

El plural de **Irishwoman** es **Irishwomen** [ˈaɪrɪʃˌwɪmɪn].

iron [ˈaɪən] ◆ *adj literal & figurado* de hierro ◆ *s* ❶ hierro ❷ plancha ◆ *vt & vi* planchar

■ **iron out** *vt* 💡 *El objeto se puede colocar antes o después de la preposición. figurado* resolver *(problemas)*

ironic(al) [aɪˈrɒnɪk(l)] *adj* irónico, ca

ironing [ˈaɪənɪŋ] *s* ❶ planchado ❷ ropa para planchar

ironing board *s* burro de planchar

irony [ˈaɪrənɪ] *s* ironía

irrational [ɪˈræʃənl] *adj* irracional

irregular [ɪˈregjʊlər] *adj* irregular

irrelevant [ɪˈreləvənt] *adj* irrelevante • **that's irrelevant** eso no viene al caso

irreplaceable [ˌɪrɪˈpleɪsəbl] *adj* irreemplazable; insustituible

irrepressible [ˌɪrɪˈpresəbl] *adj* ❶ irreprimible ❷ imparable

irresistible [ˌɪrɪˈzɪstəbl] *adj* irresistible

irrespective [ˌɪrɪˈspektɪv] ■ **irrespective of** *preposición* independientemente de

irresponsible [ˌɪrɪˈspɒnsəbl] *adj* irresponsable

irrigate [ˈɪrɪgeɪt] *vt* regar; irrigar

irrigation [ˌɪrɪˈgeɪʃn] *s* riego

irritable [ˈɪrɪtəbl] *adj* ❶ irritable ❷ irritado, da

irritate [ˈɪrɪteɪt] *vt* irritar

irritating [ˈɪrɪteɪtɪŋ] *adj* irritante

irritation [ˌɪrɪˈteɪʃn] *s* ❶ irritación ❷ motivo de irritación

IRS *(abreviatura de* Internal Revenue Service) *s* • **the IRS** ≃ la Secretaría de Hacienda

is [ɪz] *v* → **be**

ISDN *(abreviatura de* Integrated Services Delivery Network) *s* INFORMÁTICA RDSI

Islam [ˈɪzlɑːm] *s* el islam

Islamic fundamentalist *s* fundamentalista islámico, ca

Islamist [ˈɪzləmɪst] *adj & s* islamista

island [ˈaɪlənd] *s* ❶ isla ❷ isleta

islander [ˈaɪləndər] *s* isleño, ña

isle [aɪl] *s* ❶ isla ❷ *literario* ínsula

Isle of Man *s* • **the Isle of Man** la isla de Man

Isle of Wight [-waɪt] *s* • **the Isle of Wight** la isla de Wight

isn't [ˈɪznt] *(abreviatura de* is not) → **be**

isolate [ˈaɪsəleɪt] *vt* • **to isolate somebody (from)** a) aislar a alguien (de) b) marginar a alguien (de)

isolated [ˈaɪsəleɪtɪd] *adj* aislado, da

ISP *(abreviatura de* Internet Service Provider) *s* PSI

Israel [ˈɪzreɪəl] *s* Israel

Israeli [ɪzˈreɪlɪ] ◆ *adj* israelí ◆ *s* israelí

issue ['ɪʃuː] ◆ *s* ❶ cuestión; tema • **at issue** en cuestión • **to avoid the issue** evitar el tema • **to make an issue of something** darle demasiada importancia a algo ❷ número *(de periódico, revista)* ❸ emisión *(de billetes, acciones)* ◆ *vt* ❶ hacer público, ca ❷ promulgar ❸ emitir *(billetes, acciones)* ❹ • **to issue something to somebody, to issue somebody with something a)** expedir algo a alguien **b)** proporcionar algo a alguien

it [ɪt] *pronombre* ❶ él, ella *(sujeto)*; lo, la *(complemento directo)*; le *(complemento indirecto)* • **it is in my hand** está en mi mano • **did you find it?** ¿lo encontraste? • **give it to me** dámelo • **he gave it a kick** le dio una patada ❷ :☼: *con preposiciones* él, ella • **in it** dentro • **have you been to it before?** ¿has estado antes? • **on it** encima • **to talk about it** hablar de él/ella/ello • **under/beneath it** debajo • **beside it** al lado • **from/ of it** de él/ella/ello • **over it** por encima ❸ ello • **as if his life depended on it** como si le fuera la vida en ello ❹ :☼: *uso impersonal* • **it was raining** llovía • **it is cold today** hace frío hoy • **it's two o'clock** son las dos • **who is it? — it's Mary/me** ¿quién es? — soy Mary/yo • **what day is it?** ¿a qué (día) estamos hoy? • **it's Monday** es lunes • **it says here that...** aquí dice que...

it

It es el pronombre personal que se usa para referirse a los que carecen de sexo, las ideas y los animales en general (there's my car — *it*'s a Ford *ahí está mi carro — es un Ford*).

También se puede usar it con nombres de animales o con algunas palabras referidas a personas como baby — si se desconoce el sexo (listen to that baby — I wish *it* would be quiet! *¿escuchas al bebé? — Ojalá se callase*).

No olvidemos que no hay un pronombre posesivo que corresponde a it. Its es sólo un adjetivo (*its* fur is wet *tiene la piel mojada*).

Los verbos que hablan del tiempo meteorológico van siempre en tercera persona del singular con el sujeto it.

IT *s abreviatura escrita de* **information technology**
Italian [ɪ'tæljən] ◆ *adj* italiano, na ◆ *s* ❶ italiano, na ❷ italiano
italic [ɪ'tælɪk] *adj* cursiva
■ **italics** *spl* cursiva • **in italics** en cursiva
Italy ['ɪtəlɪ] *s* Italia
itch [ɪtʃ] ◆ *s* picor; picazón ◆ *vi* ❶ tener picazón; picar • **my arm is itching** me pica el brazo ❷ *figurado* • **to be itching to do something** estar deseando hacer algo
itchy ['ɪtʃɪ] *adj* • **this hat is itchy** este sombrero pica • **I've got an itchy arm** me pica el brazo

it'd ['ɪtəd] ❶ *(abreviatura de* it had) → **have** ❷ *(abreviatura de* it would) → **would**
item ['aɪtəm] *s* ❶ artículo ❷ punto *(en lista, orden del día)* ❸ artículo *(de prensa)* • **news item** noticia
itinerary [aɪ'tɪnərərɪ] *s* itinerario
it'll [ɪtl] ❶ *(abreviatura de* it will) → **will** ❷ *(abreviatura de* it shall) → **shall**
its [ɪts] *adj posesivo* su; sus :☼: *pl* • **the dog broke its leg** el perro se rompió la pata

its

El adjetivo posesivo que va con sustantivos como government, team y school puede ser tanto its, como their. Hay que asegurarse de que el verbo concuerde con el pronombre en singular o plural (the government *has* made up *its* mind = the government *have* made up *their* minds *el gobierno se ha decidido*).

No olvidemos que al hablar de las partes del cuerpo se usa el adjetivo posesivo its en lugar del artículo the (the cat was licking *its* paws *el gató se lamía las patas*).

it's [ɪts] ❶ *(abreviatura de* it is) → **be** ❷ *(abreviatura de* it has) → **have**
itself [ɪt'self] *pronombre* ❶ :☼: *reflexivo* se • **the cat is washing itself** el gato se está lavando ❷ :☼: *tras preposición* sí mismo, ma • **by itself** solo • **the door closed by itself** la puerta se cerró sola • **with itself** consigo mismo, ma ❸ :☼: *para enfatizar* • **the town itself is lovely** el pueblo en sí es muy bonito • **in itself** en sí • **it's simplicity itself** es la sencillez misma
I've [aɪv] *(abreviatura de* I have) → **have**
ivory ['aɪvərɪ] *s* marfil
ivy ['aɪvɪ] *s* hiedra
Ivy League *s* ▶ grupo de ocho prestigiosas universidades del este de los EE.UU.

IVY LEAGUE

El término **Ivy League** se utiliza en Estados Unidos para referirse al colegio universitario de Dartmouth y a las universidades de **Brown**, **Columbia, Cornell, Harvard, Pensilvania, Princeton** y **Yale**, que son algunos de los centros académicos más antiguos del país. El nombre de la liga alude a la hiedra, **ivy**, que suele trepar por las paredes de los añosos edificios que albergan estas universidades. Un título de la **Ivy League** es un aval para el éxito profesional.

j

j, J [dʒeɪ] *s* j; J
  Dos plurales: **j's o js; J's o Js.**

jab [dʒæb] ◆ *s* ❶ codazo ❷ golpe corto *(en boxeo)* ◆ *vt* • **to jab something into** clavar algo en • **to jab something at** apuntarle algo a

jack [dʒæk] *s* ❶ gato *(para vehículos)* ❷ Electricidad clavija ❸ clavijero ❹ ≃ jota ❺ ≃ sota
  ■ **jack up** *vt* ☼ *El objeto se puede colocar antes o después de la preposición.* ❶ levantar con gato ❷ subir

jackal ['dʒækəl] *s* chacal

jacket ['dʒækɪt] *s* ❶ chaqueta; saco ❷ sobrecubierta ❸ cubierta *(de disco)*

jacket potato *s* papa asada con piel

jackhammer ['dʒæk,hæmər] *s* martillo neumático

jack-knife *vi* • **the truck jack-knifed** derrapó la parte delantera del camión

jackpot ['dʒækpɒt] *s* (premio) gordo

jagged ['dʒægɪd] *adj* dentado, da

jail, gaol [dʒeɪl] ◆ *s* cárcel • **in jail** en la cárcel ◆ *vt* encarcelar

jailer ['dʒeɪlər] *s* carcelero, ra

jam [dʒæm] ◆ *s* ❶ mermelada ❷ embotellamiento; atasco ❸ Música sesión improvisada de jazz o rock ❹ *familiar* • **to get into/be in a jam** meterse/estar en un apuro ◆ *vt* ❶ meter a la fuerza ❷ sujetar • **jam the door shut** atranca la puerta ❸ apiñar ❹ abarrotar; atestar ❺ Telecomunicaciones bloquear ❻ atascar • **it's jammed** se ha atascado ❼ Radio interferir ◆ *vi* ❶ atascarse ❷ Música improvisar

Jamaica [dʒə'meɪkə] *s* Jamaica

jam-packed [-'pækt] *adj* *familiar* a tope

jangle ['dʒæŋgl] *vi* tintinear

janitor ['dʒænɪtər] *s* conserje; portero

January ['dʒænjʊərɪ] *s* enero ver también **September**

Japan [dʒə'pæn] *s* (el) Japón

Japanese [,dʒæpə'niːz] ◆ *adj* japonés, esa ◆ *s* japonés ◆ *spl* • **the Japanese** los japoneses
  El plural de **Japanese** es **Japanese.**

jar [dʒɑːr] ◆ *s* tarro ◆ *vt* sacudir ◆ *vi* ❶ • **to jar (on somebody)** poner los nervios de punta (a alguien) ❷ discordar ❸ desentonar

jargon ['dʒɑːgən] *s* jerga

jaundice ['dʒɔːndɪs] *s* ictericia

javelin ['dʒævlɪn] *s* jabalina

jaw [dʒɔː] *s* mandíbula

jawbone ['dʒɔːbəʊn] *s* mandíbula; maxilar

jaywalker ['dʒeɪwɔːkər] *s* peatón imprudente

jazz [dʒæz] *s* Música jazz
  ■ **jazz up** *vt* ☼ *El objeto se puede colocar antes o después de la preposición.* *familiar* alegrar; avivar

jazzy ['dʒæzɪ] *adj* llamativo, va

jealous ['dʒeləs] *adj* ❶ • **to be jealous (of)** tener celos o estar celoso, sa (de) ❷ • **to be jealous (of)** ser celoso, sa (de)

jealousy ['dʒeləsɪ] *s* ☼ *incontable* celos

jeans [dʒiːnz] *spl* pantalones de mezclilla; jeans

jeep [dʒiːp] *s* jeep; campero

jeer [dʒɪər] ◆ *vt* ❶ abuchear ❷ mofarse de ◆ *vi* • **to jeer (at somebody) a)** abuchear (a alguien) **b)** mofarse (de alguien)

Jehovah's Witness [dʒɪ'həʊvəz-] *s* testigo de Jehová

Jell-O® ['dʒeləʊ] *s* gelatina

jelly ['dʒelɪ] *s* mermelada

jellyfish ['dʒelɪfɪʃ] *s* medusa
  El plural de **jellyfish** es **jellyfish** o **jellyfishes.**

jelly roll *s* niño envuelto

jeopardize ['dʒepədaɪz] *vt* poner en peligro; arriesgar

jerk [dʒɜːk] ◆ *s* ❶ movimiento brusco ❷ tirón ❸ sacudida ❹ *muy familiar* idiota; pendejo, ja ◆ *vi* ❶ saltar ❷ dar sacudidas

jerky ['dʒɜːkı] *s* tasajo; cecina

jersey ['dʒɜːzı] *s* ❶ jersey ❷ maillot

El plural de **jersey** es **jerseys**.

jest [dʒest] *s* • **in jest** en broma

Jesus (Christ) ['dʒiːzəs-] ◆ *s* Jesús; Jesucristo ◆ *exclamación familiar* ¡Santo Dios!

jet [dʒet] *s* ❶ reactor ❷ avión ❸ chorro ❹ boquilla

jet-black *adj* negro, gra azabache

jet engine *s* reactor

jetfoil ['dʒetfɔıl] *s* hidroplano

jet lag *s* desfase horario

jetty ['dʒetı] *s* embarcadero

Jew [dʒuː] *s* judío, a

jewel ['dʒuːəl] *s* ❶ piedra preciosa ❷ joya

jewel case *s* caja *(de CD)*

jeweler ['dʒuːələr] *s* joyero, ra • **jeweler's (store)** joyería

jewelry ['dʒuːəlrı] *s* ☼ *incontable* joyas; alhajas

Jewish ['dʒuːıʃ] *adj* judío, a

jibe [dʒaıb] *s* pulla; burla

jiffy ['dʒıfı] *s familiar* • **in a jiffy** en un segundo

jig [dʒıg] *s* giga

jigsaw (puzzle) ['dʒıgsɔː-] *s* rompecabezas; puzzle

jilt [dʒılt] *vt* dejar plantado, da

jingle ['dʒıŋgl] ◆ *s* ❶ tintineo ❷ sintonía *(de anuncio publicitario)* ◆ *vi* tintinear

jinx [dʒıŋks] *s* gafe

jitters ['dʒıtəz] *spl familiar* • **to have the jitters** estar como un flan

jive [dʒaıv] ◆ *s familiar* palabrería ◆ *vi* bailar el swing

job [dʒɒb] *s* ❶ trabajo; empleo ❷ tarea • **to make a good job of something** hacer un buen trabajo con algo • **we had a job doing it** nos costó mucho hacerlo ❸ cometido

jobless ['dʒɒblıs] *adj* desempleado, da

jobsharing ['dʒɒbʃeərıŋ] *s* ☼ *incontable* empleo compartido

jockey ['dʒɒkı] ◆ *s* jockey; jinete ◆ *vi* • **to jockey for position** competir por colocarse en mejor posición

El plural de **jockey** es **jockeys**.

jodhpurs ['dʒɒdpəz] *spl* pantalón de montar

jog [dʒɒg] ◆ *s* trote • **to go for a jog** salir a correr ◆ *vt* golpear ligeramente ◆ *vi* correr

jogging ['dʒɒgıŋ] *s* correr; jogging

john [dʒɒn] *s familiar* baño

John Hancock [-'hænkɒk] *s familiar* firma

join [dʒɔın] ◆ *s* juntura ◆ *vt* ❶ unir; juntar ❷ reunirse con • **can I join you?** ¿puedo sentarme contigo? ❸ afiliarse a; hacerse socio de; alistarse en ❹ unirse a • **to join the line** meterse en la cola ◆ *vi* ❶ confluir ❷ unirse; juntarse ❸ afiliarse; hacerse socio; alistarse

■ **join in** ◆ *vt* ☼ *El objeto siempre va después de la preposición al final.* participar en; tomar parte en ◆ *vi* participar; tomar parte

■ **join up** *vi* MILITAR alistarse

joiner ['dʒɔınər] *s* carpintero

joinery ['dʒɔınərı] *s* carpintería

joint [dʒɔınt] ◆ *adj* ❶ compartido, da ▸ **joint owner** copropietario, ria ❷ conjunto, ta ◆ *s* ❶ ANATOMÍA articulación ❷ juntura ❸ *familiar & despectivo* antro ❹ *familiar* churro

joint account *s* cuenta conjunta

jointly ['dʒɔıntlı] *adv* conjuntamente

joke [dʒəʊk] ◆ *s* ❶ chiste ❷ broma • **to play a joke on somebody** hacerle una broma a alguien

expresión **to be a joke a)** ser un inútil **b)** ser una tomadura de pelo ▸ **it's no joke** no es (nada) fácil

◆ *vi* bromear • **you're joking** estás de broma • **I'm not joking** hablo en serio

joker ['dʒəʊkər] *s* ❶ bromista ❷ inútil ❸ comodín

jolly ['dʒɒlı] *adj* ❶ alegre ❷ divertido, da

jolt [dʒəʊlt] ◆ *s* sacudida ◆ *vt* sacudir; zarandear

Jordan ['dʒɔːdn] *s* Jordania

jostle ['dʒɒsl] ◆ *vt* empujar; dar empujones a ◆ *vi* empujar; dar empujones

jot [dʒɒt] *s* pizca

■ **jot down** *vt* ☼ *El objeto se puede colocar antes o después de la preposición.* apuntar; anotar

jotter ['dʒɒtər] *s* bloc

journal ['dʒɜːnl] *s* ❶ revista; boletín ❷ diario

journalism ['dʒɜːnəlızm] *s* periodismo

journalist ['dʒɜːnəlıst] *s* periodista

journey ['dʒɜːnı] ◆ *s* viaje ◆ *vi* viajar

El plural de **journey** es **journeys**.

joy [dʒɔı] *s* ❶ alegría; regocijo ❷ placer

joyful ['dʒɔıfʊl] *adj* alegre

joyous ['dʒɔıəs] *adj* jubiloso, sa

joyride ['dʒɔıraıd] ◆ *s* vuelta en un coche robado ◆ *vi* darse una vuelta en un coche robado

Formas irregulares de **joyride**: *pretérito* **joyrode**, *pp* **joyridden**.

joystick ['dʒɔıstık] *s* ❶ palanca de mando ❷ joystick

Jr. *(abreviatura escrita de* Junior) jr • **Mark Andrews Jr.** Mark Andrews, hijo

jubilant ['dʒuːbılənt] *adj* ❶ jubiloso, sa ❷ alborozado, da

jubilee ['dʒuːbıliː] *s* aniversario

judge [dʒʌdʒ] ◆ *s* juez • **to be a good judge of character** tener buen ojo para la gente ◆ *vt* ❶ juzgar ❷ calcular ◆ *vi* juzgar

judg(e)ment ['dʒʌdʒmənt] *s* ❶ DERECHO fallo; sentencia • **to pass judgement (on somebody)** pronunciar sentencia (sobre alguien) ❷ juicio • **against my better judgement** en contra de lo que me dicta el juicio

JK

judiciary [dʒuː'dɪʃərɪ] *s* • **the judiciary a)** el poder judicial **b)** la judicatura

judo ['dʒuːdəʊ] *s* judo

jug [dʒʌg] *s* jarra

juggle ['dʒʌgl] ◆ *vt* ❶ hacer juegos malabares con ❷ jugar con ◆ *vi* hacer juegos malabares

juggler ['dʒʌglər] *s* malabarista

jugular (vein) ['dʒʌgjʊlər-] *s* yugular

juice [dʒuːs] *s* jugo

juicer ['dʒuːsər] *s* exprimidor

juicy ['dʒuːsɪ] *adj* ❶ jugoso, sa ❷ *familiar* picante

jukebox ['dʒuːkbɒks] *s* máquina de discos

July [dʒuː'laɪ] *s* julio ver también **September**

jumble ['dʒʌmbl] ◆ *s* revoltijo ◆ *vt* • **to jumble (up)** revolver

jumbo jet ['dʒʌmbəʊ-] *s* jumbo

jumbo-sized ['dʒʌmbəʊsaɪzd] *adj* gigante

jump [dʒʌmp] ◆ *s* ❶ salto ❷ sobresalto ❸ incremento; salto ◆ *vt* ❶ saltar ❷ asaltar ❸ saltarse ◆ *vi* ❶ saltar ❷ sobresaltarse • **you made me jump** me asustaste ❸ aumentar de golpe

■ **jump at** *vt* ⚙ *El objeto siempre va después de la preposición al final.* no dejar escapar *(oportunidad)*

jumper ['dʒʌmpər] *s* jumper

jumper cables *spl* cables de arranque *(de batería)*

jumpsuit ['dʒʌmpsuːt] *s* mono

junction ['dʒʌŋkʃn] *s* ❶ cruce ❷ empalme

June [dʒuːn] *s* junio ver también **September**

jungle ['dʒʌŋgl] *s literal & figurado* selva

jungle gym *s* ▶ estructura para que trepen los niños en un parque

junior ['dʒuːnjər] ◆ *adj* ❶ de menor antigüedad; júnior ❷ subalterno, na ❸ • **Mark Andrews junior** Mark Andrews, hijo ❹ *Deporte* • **the junior tennis championship** el campeonato de tenis de menores ◆ *s* ❶ subalterno, na ❷ • **he's my junior** soy mayor que él ❸ *Educación & Universidad* alumno de penúltimo año

junior college *s* ▶ colegio universitario para los dos primeros años

junior high school *s* ≃ secundaria *(13-15 años)*

junk [dʒʌŋk] *s* ⚙ *incontable familiar* trastos • **it's a piece of junk!** ¡es basura!

junk food *s despectivo* comida chatarra

junkie ['dʒʌŋkɪ] *s familiar* drogadicto

junk mail *s* ⚙ *incontable despectivo* propaganda *(por correo)*

junk shop *s* tienda de objetos usados

Jupiter ['dʒuːpɪtər] *s* Júpiter

jurisdiction [,dʒʊərɪs'dɪkʃn] *s* jurisdicción

juror ['dʒʊərər] *s* jurado

jury ['dʒʊərɪ] *s* jurado

expresión **the jury is still out on that** eso está por ver

just [dʒʌst] ◆ *adv* ❶ • **he has just left/moved** acaba de salir/mudarse ❷ • **we were just leaving when...** justo íbamos a salir cuando... • **I'm just about to do it** voy a hacerlo ahora • **I couldn't do it just then** no lo podía hacer en aquel momento • **just as I was leaving** justo en el momento en que salía • **just recently** hace muy poco • **just yesterday** ayer mismo ❸ sólo; solamente • **he's just a child** no es más que un niño • **'just add water'** 'simplemente añada un poco de agua' • **if you need help, just ask** si necesitas ayuda, no tienes más que pedirla • **just a minute** o **moment** o **second** un momento ❹ apenas • **I (only) just did it** conseguí hacerlo por muy poco ❺ • **I just know it!** ¡estoy seguro! • **just imagine!** ¡imagínate! • **just look what you've done!** ¡mira lo que has hecho! ❻ exactamente; precisamente • **just what I need** justo lo que necesito • **we're just in time!** ¡estamos justo a tiempo! • **just here/there** aquí/allí mismo ❼ • **could you just open your mouth?** ¿podrías abrir la boca un momento, por favor? ◆ *adj* justo, ta

■ **just about** *adv* ❶ casi ❷ más o menos

■ **just as** *adv* • **just as... as** tan... como; igual de... que

■ **just now** *adv* ❶ hace un momento ❷ justo ahora; ahora mismo

justice ['dʒʌstɪs] *s* justicia

expresión **to do justice to something a)** estar a la altura de algo *(un trabajo)* **b)** hacerle los honores a algo *(una comida)*

justify ['dʒʌstɪfaɪ] *vt* ❶ • **to justify (something/ doing something)** justificar (algo/el haber hecho algo) ❷ *Tipografía* justificar

jut [dʒʌt] *vi* • **to jut (out)** sobresalir

juvenile ['dʒuːvənaɪl] ◆ *adj* ❶ *Derecho* juvenil ❷ *despectivo* infantil ◆ *s* *Derecho* menor (de edad)

juxtapose [,dʒʌkstə'pəʊz] *vt* • **to juxtapose something (with)** yuxtaponer algo (a)

K

k, K [keɪ] *s* k; K

■ **K** *s* ❶ *(abreviatura de* kilobyte(s)*)* K ❷ abreviatura escrita de **thousand**

Dos plurales: **k's** o **ks** **K's** o **Ks**

kaleidoscope [kə'laɪdəskəʊp] *s literal & figurado* caleidoscopio

kangaroo [,kæŋgə'ruː] *s* canguro

kaput [kə'pʊt] *adj familiar* dado, da al cuás

karaoke [kɑːrəˈəʊkɪ] *s* karaoke

karat ['kærət] *s* quilate

karate [kə'rɑːtɪ] *s* kárate

kayak ['kaɪæk] *s* kayac

Kb *s* *Informática* Kb

kebab [kɪ'bæb] *s* brocheta

keel [kiːl] *s* quilla

expresión **on an even keel** en equilibrio estable

JK

keen [kiːn] *adj* ❶ entusiasta • **to be keen on something** ser aficionado, da a algo • **I'm keen on you** tú le gustas • **I'm not keen on the idea** no me entusiasma la idea • **to be keen to do** o **on doing something** tener ganas de hacer algo ❷ profundo, da *(interés, deseo)*; reñido, da *(competencia)* ❸ agudo, da *(olfato, vista, mente)*; fino, na *(ojos, oídos)*

keep [kiːp] ◆ *vt* ❶ mantener • **to keep somebody waiting/awake** tener a alguien esperando/despierto • **to keep somebody talking** darle conversación a alguien ❷ quedarse con • **keep the change** quédese con la vuelta ❸ guardar • **to keep something for somebody** guardar algo para alguien ❹ detener ❺ • **to keep somebody from doing something** impedir que alguien haga algo ❻ acudir a *(cita)* ❼ cumplir *(promesa)* ❽ • **to keep something from somebody** ocultar algo a alguien • **to keep something to yourself** no contarle algo a nadie • **to keep a secret** guardar un secreto ❾ llevar *(cuenta, registro)*; escribir *(diario)*; tomar *(nota)* ❿ tener *(tienda, animales)* ◆ *vi* ❶ mantenerse • **to keep calm** mantener la calma • **to keep quiet** callarse • **to keep still** estarse quieto ❷ • **to keep doing something a)** no dejar de hacer algo **b)** continuar o seguir haciendo algo • **to keep going** seguir adelante ❸ continuar; seguir • **to keep left/right** circular por la izquierda/derecha ❹ conservarse *(alimentos)* ◆ *s* • **to earn your keep** ganarse el pan

■ **keeps** *s* • **for keeps** para siempre

■ **keep back** ◆ *vt* 🔅 *El objeto se puede colocar antes o después de la preposición.* ❶ ocultar *(información)* ❷ retener *(dinero, sueldo)* ◆ *vi* no acercarse

■ **keep off** *vt* 🔅 *El objeto siempre va después de la preposición al final.* 'evitar' • **'keep off the grass'** 'prohibido pisar el pasto'

■ **keep on** ◆ *vi* ❶ • **to keep on doing something a)** continuar o seguir haciendo algo **b)** no dejar de hacer algo ❷ • **to keep on (about)** seguir a voy y voy (con) ◆ *vt* 🔅 *El objeto se coloca entre el verbo y la preposición.* mantener en el puesto

■ **keep out** ◆ *vt* 🔅 *El objeto se puede colocar antes o después de la preposición.* no dejar pasar ◆ *vi* • **'keep out'** 'prohibida la entrada'

■ **keep to** *vt* 🔅 *El objeto siempre va después de la preposición al final.* ❶ ceñirse a ❷ cumplir

■ **keep up** ◆ *vt* 🔅 *El objeto se puede colocar antes o después de la preposición.* mantener ◆ *vi* mantener el ritmo • **to keep up with somebody/something** seguir el ritmo de alguien/algo

Formas irregulares de **keep**: *pretérito & pp* **kept**.

keeper [ˈkiːpər] *s* guarda

keeping [ˈkiːpɪŋ] *s* ❶ • **in somebody's keeping** al cuidado de alguien • **in safe keeping** en lugar seguro ❷ • **in/out of keeping (with)** de acuerdo/en desacuerdo (con)

kennel [ˈkenl] *s* caseta del perro

Kenya [ˈkenjə] *s* Kenia

Kenyan [ˈkenjən] ◆ *adj* keniano, na ◆ *s* keniano, na

kept [kept] *pretérito* & *participio pasado* → **keep**

kernel [ˈkɜːnl] *s* pepita

kestrel [ˈkestrəl] *s* cernícalo

ketchup [ˈketʃəp] *s* catsup

kettle [ˈketl] *s* tetera para hervir • **to put the kettle on** poner el agua a hervir

key [kiː] ◆ *s* ❶ llave ❷ tecla ❸ clave • **the key (to)** la clave (de) ❹ MÚSICA tono • **off key** desafinado, da ◆ *adj* clave

keyboard [ˈkiːbɔːd] *s* teclado

keyboard shortcut *s* atajo de teclado

key card *s* tarjeta de acceso

keyhole [ˈkiːhəʊl] *s* ojo de la cerradura

keypad [ˈkiːpæd] *s* teclado numérico

key ring *s* llavero

kg *(abreviatura escrita de* kilogram) kg

khaki [ˈkɑːkɪ] ◆ *adj* caqui ◆ *s* caqui

■ **khakis** *spl* pantalones de caqui

kick [kɪk] ◆ *s* ❶ patada; puntapié ❷ coz ❸ *familiar* • **to do something for kicks** hacer algo para divertirse ◆ *vt* ❶ patear ❷ patear ❸ *familiar* dejar *(costumbre, adicción)* ◆ *vi* ❶ patalear ❷ patear

■ **kick back** *vi* relajarse

■ **kick in** *vi* surtir efecto

■ **kick off** *vi* hacer el saque inicial

■ **kick out** *vt* 🔅 *El objeto se puede colocar antes o después de la preposición.* *familiar* echar; poner de patitas en la calle

kid [kɪd] ◆ *s* ❶ *familiar* crío, a ❷ *familiar* chico, ca; chaval, la ❸ cabrito ❹ cabritilla ◆ *en compuestos familiar* menor *(hermano, hermana)* ◆ *vt familiar* ❶ tomar el pelo a ❷ • **to kid yourself** hacerse ilusiones ◆ *vi familiar* • **to be kidding** estar de broma

kidnap [ˈkɪdnæp] *vt* secuestrar; raptar

kidnapping [ˈkɪdnæpɪŋ] *s* secuestro; rapto

kidney [ˈkɪdnɪ] *s* ANATOMÍA & COCINA riñón

El plural de **kidney** es **kidneys**.

kidney bean *s* frijol o poroto rojo *(con forma de riñón)*

kill [kɪl] ◆ *vt* ❶ matar • **he was killed in an accident** murió en un accidente ❷ *figurado* poner fin a ❸ • **to kill time** matar el tiempo ◆ *vi* matar ◆ *s* • **we watched the wolves move in for the kill** vimos cómo los lobos se preparaban para caer sobre su presa

killer [ˈkɪlər] *s* asesino, na

killing [ˈkɪlɪŋ] *s* asesinato

kiln [kɪln] *s* horno

kilo [ˈkiːləʊ] *(abreviatura de* kilogram) *s* kilo

El plural de **kilo** es **kilos**.

kilobyte [ˈkɪləbaɪt] *s* kilobyte

kilogram [ˈkɪləɡræm] *s* kilogramo

kilohertz [ˈkɪləhɜːtz] *s* kilohercio

El plural de **kilohertz** es **kilohertz**.

kilometer [kɪˈlɒmɪtər] *s* kilómetro

kilowatt [ˈkɪləwɒt] *s* kilovatio

kilt [kɪlt] *s* falda escocesa

kind [kaɪnd] ◆ *adj* ❶ amable ❷ considerado, da ◆ *s* tipo; clase • **what kind of plant is it?** ¿qué especie de planta es? • **a kind of** una especie de • **all kinds of** todo tipo de • **kind of** *familiar* bastante • **nothing of the kind** nada por el estilo • **they're two of a kind** son tal para cual

kindergarten [ˈkɪndəˌgɑːtn] *s* kinder; preprimaria

kind-hearted [-ˈhɑːtɪd] *adj* bondadoso, sa

kindly [ˈkaɪndlɪ] ◆ *adj* amable; bondadoso, sa ◆ *adv* ❶ amablemente • **to look kindly on something/somebody** mirar algo/a alguien con buenos ojos ❷ • **will you kindly...?** ¿sería tan amable de...?

kindness [ˈkaɪndnɪs] *s* ❶ amabilidad ❷ favor

king [kɪŋ] *s* rey

kingdom [ˈkɪŋdəm] *s* reino

kingfisher [ˈkɪŋˌfɪʃər] *s* martín pescador

king-size(d) [-saɪz(d)] *adj* ❶ extralargo *(cigarrillo)* ❷ gigante *(paquete)* ❸ extragrande *(cama)*

kinky [ˈkɪŋkɪ] *adj familiar* morboso, sa; pervertido, da

kiosk [ˈkiːɒsk] *s* quiosco

kipper [ˈkɪpər] *s* arenque ahumado

kiss [kɪs] ◆ *s* beso ◆ *vt* besar • **to kiss somebody goodbye** dar un beso de despedida a alguien ◆ *vi* besarse

kiss of life *s* • **the kiss of life** la respiración boca a boca

kit [kɪt] *s* ❶ equipo ❷ modelo para armar; kit

kit bag *s* macuto; petate

kitchen [ˈkɪtʃɪn] *s* cocina

kitchen sink *s* fregadero

kitchen unit *s* módulo de cocina

kite [kaɪt] *s* papalote

kitesurfing [ˈkaɪtsɜːfɪŋ] *s* kitesurf

kitten [ˈkɪtn] *s* gatito

kitty [ˈkɪtɪ] *s* ❶ fondo común ❷ bote; puesta *(en juegos de naipes)*

kiwi (fruit) *s* kiwi

km *(abreviatura escrita de* kilometer*)* km

km/h *(abreviatura escrita de* kilometers per hour*)* km/h

knack [næk] *s* • **it's easy once you've got the knack** es fácil cuando le agarras la onda • **he has the knack of appearing at the right moment** tiene el don de aparecer en el momento adecuado

knapsack [ˈnæpsæk] *s* mochila

knead [niːd] *vt* amasar

knee [niː] ◆ *s* rodilla ◆ *vt* dar un rodillazo a

kneecap [ˈniːkæp] *s* rótula

kneel [niːl] *vi* ❶ arrodillarse ❷ estar de rodillas

■ **kneel down** *vi* arrodillarse

Formas irregulares de **kneel**: *pretérito* & *pp* **knelt** o **kneeled**.

knelt [nelt] *pretérito* & *participio pasado* → **kneel**

knew [njuː] *pretérito* → **know**

knick-knack [ˈnɪknæk] *s* baratija

knife [naɪf] ◆ *s* cuchillo ◆ *vt* acuchillar
El plural de **knife** es **knives**.

knight [naɪt] *s* ❶ HISTORIA caballero ❷ caballo *(en ajedrez)*

knighthood [ˈnaɪthʊd] *s* HISTORIA título de caballero

knit [nɪt] ◆ *vt* tejer ◆ *vi* ❶ tejer ❷ soldarse
Formas irregulares de **knit**: *pretérito* & *pp* **knit** o **knitted** (regular).

knitting [ˈnɪtɪŋ] *s* ☞*incontable* ❶ tejido ❷ punto; tejido

knitting needle *s* aguja de tejer

knitwear [ˈnɪtweər] *s* ☞*incontable* género o ropa de punto

knives [naɪvz] *spl* → **knife**

knob [nɒb] *s* ❶ perilla ❷ botón

knock [nɒk] ◆ *s* ❶ golpe ❷ *familiar* revés ◆ *vt* ❶ golpear • **I knocked my head on the shelf** me golpeé la cabeza con el estante • **he knocked the nail into the wall** clavó el clavo en la pared ❷ hacer; abrir *(agujero)* ❸ *familiar* poner por los suelos ◆ *vi* • **to knock (at** o **on)** llamar (a)

■ **knock down** *vt* ☞ *El objeto se puede colocar antes o después de la preposición.* ❶ atropellar ❷ derribar

■ **knock off** *vi familiar* dejar de trabajar

■ **knock out** *vt* ☞ *El objeto se puede colocar antes o después de la preposición.* ❶ dejar sin conocimiento ❷ dejar fuera de combate ❸ dejar dormido a ❹ eliminar *(de competición)*

■ **knock over** *vt* ☞ *El objeto se puede colocar antes o después de la preposición.* ❶ hacer caer ❷ atropellar

knocker [ˈnɒkər] *s* aldaba

knockout [ˈnɒkaʊt] *s* K.O.

knot [nɒt] ◆ *s* nudo • **to tie/untie a knot** hacer/deshacer un nudo
expresión **to tie the knot** *familiar* casarse ◆ *vt* anudar

know [nəʊ] ◆ *vt* ❶ • **to know (that)** saber (que) • **to know how to do something** saber hacer algo • **to get to know something** enterarse de algo • **to let somebody know (about)** avisar a alguien (de) ❷ saber hablar ❸ conocer • **to get to know somebody** llegar a conocer a alguien
expresión **to know something backwards** saberse algo al dedillo
◆ *vi* saber • **he's Italian — yes, I know** es italiano — sí, lo sé • **to know about something** saber de algo • **how should I know?** ¿cómo quieres que sepa? ◆ *s* • **to be in the know** estar enterado, da
Formas irregulares de **know**: *pretérito* **knew**, *pp* **known**.

know-how *s* conocimientos; know-how

JK

knowingly ['nəʊɪŋlɪ] *adv* ❶ con complicidad ❷ a sabiendas

knowledge ['nɒlɪdʒ] *s* ☼ *incontable* ❶ conocimiento • **to the best of my knowledge** por lo que yo sé ❷ conocimientos

knowledgeable ['nɒlɪdʒəbl] *adj* entendido, da

known [nəʊn] *participio pasado* → **know**

knuckle ['nʌkl] *s* ❶ nudillo ❷ codillo

kook [kuːk] *s familiar* loco, ca; chiflado, da

kooky ['kuːkɪ] (*comparativo* kookier *superlativo* kookiest) *adj familiar* loco, ca; chiflado, da

Koran [kɒ'rɑːn] *s* • **the Koran** el Corán

Korea [kə'rɪə] *s* Corea

Korean [kə'rɪən] ◆ *adj* coreano, na ◆ *s* ❶ coreano, na ❷ coreano

kosher ['kəʊʃər] *adj* ❶ kosher; permitido, da por la religión judía ❷ *familiar* limpio, pia; legal

Kurd [kɜːd] *s* kurdo, da

JK

l¹, L [el] *s* l; L
Dos plurales: **l's o ls; L's o Ls.**

l² (*abreviatura escrita de* liter) l

lab [læb] *familiar* = **laboratory**

label ['leɪbl] ◆ *s* ❶ etiqueta ❷ sello discográfico ◆ *vt* etiquetar

labor ['leɪbər] ◆ *s* ❶ trabajo ❷ esfuerzo ❸ mano de obra ❹ parto ◆ *vi* ❶ trabajar ❷ • **to labor at** o **over** trabajar afanosamente en

■ **Labor** *adj* Política laborista

laboratory ['læbrəˌtɔ:rɪ], **lab** *s* laboratorio • **a chemistry lab** un laboratorio de química

Labor Day *s* Día del Trabajador

Labor Day

El **Labor Day** es una fiesta celebrada en honor de los trabajadores. Su origen se remonta a la huelga general iniciada el 1 de mayo de 1886 en los EE. UU. para reclamar la jornada laboral de ocho horas, por lo que es también una ocasión para reivindicar y rendir homenaje a "los mártires de Chicago", ejecutados por haber participado en aquellas jornadas de lucha. Curiosamente, en los Estados Unidos esta conmemoración --que es fiesta federal desde 1894-- no se celebra el primero de mayo sino el primer lunes de septiembre. Para la mayor parte de los norteamericanos esta fecha marca el final del verano, y las playas y otros populares lugares de recreo están abarrotados de gente; asimismo, muchas escuelas empiezan las clases tras este largo fin de semana, lo que representa el inicio del año escolar.

laborer ['leɪbərər] *s* obrero, ra
labor union *s* sindicato
labyrinth ['læbərɪnθ] *s* laberinto

lace [leɪs] ◆ *s* ❶ encaje ❷ cordón ◆ *vt* ❶ amarrar (*zapatos*) ❷ • **coffee laced with brandy** café con unas gotas de coñac

■ **lace up** *vt* ☼ *El objeto se puede colocar antes o después de la preposición.* amarrar

lack [læk] ◆ *s* falta • **for** o **through lack of** por falta de • **there was no lack of excitement** no faltó emoción ◆ *vt* carecer de ◆ *vi* • **to be lacking** faltar • **to be lacking in** carecer de

lacquer ['lækər] *s* laca

lad [læd] *s familiar* chaval • **come on lads!** ¡vamos chicos!

ladder ['lædər] *s* escalera

laden ['leɪdn] *adj* • **laden (with)** cargado, da (de)

ladies' room *s* lavabo de señoras

ladle ['leɪdl] ◆ *s* cucharón ◆ *vt* servir con cucharón

lady ['leɪdɪ] ◆ *s* ❶ señora • **ladies' clothes** ropa de mujer • **Ladies and Gentlemen!** ¡señoras y señores! ❷ dama ◆ *en compuestos* mujer ▸ **lady doctor** doctora

■ **Lady** *s* lady

ladybug ['leɪdɪbʌg] *s* mariquita

ladylike ['leɪdɪlaɪk] *adj* elegante; propio, pia de una señora

lag [læg] ◆ *vi* ❶ • **to lag (behind)** rezagarse ❷ • **to lag (behind)** andar a la zaga ◆ *s* retraso; demora

lager ['lɑ:gər] *s* cerveza rubia

lagoon [lə'gu:n] *s* laguna

laid [leɪd] *pretérito & participio pasado* → **lay**

laid-back *adj familiar* relajado, da; tranquilo, la

lain [leɪn] *participio pasado* → **lie**

lake [leɪk] *s* lago

lamb [læm] *s* cordero

lambswool ['læmzwʊl] ◆ *s* lana de cordero ◆ *en compuestos* de lana de cordero

lame [leɪm] *adj* ❶ cojo, ja ❷ pobre (*excusa, argumento*)

lame duck *s* ❶ inútil ❷ fracaso (*negocio*) ❸ presidente saliente

lament [lə'ment] ◆ *s* lamento ◆ *vt* lamentar

laminated ['læmɪneɪtɪd] *adj* ❶ laminado, da ❷ plastificado, da

lamp [læmp] *s* lámpara

lamppost ['læmppəʊst] *s* farol

lampshade ['læmpʃeɪd] *s* pantalla *(de lámpara)*

lance [lɑːns] ◆ *s* lanza ◆ *vt* abrir con lanceta

land [lænd] ◆ *s* ❶ tierra • **a piece of land** un terreno ❷ tierras; finca ◆ *vt* ❶ desembarcar ❷ hacer aterrizar ❸ pescar ❹ *familiar* conseguir ❺ *familiar* • **to land somebody in something** meter a alguien en algo • **to land somebody with somebody/something** cargar a alguien con alguien/algo ◆ *vi* ❶ aterrizar; tomar tierra ❷ desembarcar ❸ caer ❹ ir a parar

■ **land up** *vi familiar* • **to land up (in)** ir a parar (a)

landfill site ['lændfɪl-] *s* vertedero de basuras

landing ['lændɪŋ] *s* ❶ rellano ❷ aterrizaje ❸ desembarco

landing card *s* tarjeta de desembarque

landing gear *s* ☿ *incontable* tren de aterrizaje

landing stage *s* desembarcadero

landing strip *s* pista de aterrizaje

landlady ['lænd,leɪdɪ] *s* ❶ casera ❷ patrona

landlord ['lændlɔːd] *s* ❶ dueño; casero ❷ patrón

landmark ['lændmɑːk] *s* ❶ punto de referencia ❷ *figurado* hito

landowner ['lænd,əʊnər] *s* terrateniente

landscape ['lændskeɪp] *s* paisaje

landslide ['lændslaɪd] *s* ❶ desprendimiento de tierras ❷ POLÍTICA victoria arrolladora o aplastante

lane [leɪn] *s* ❶ camino ❷ callejuela; callejón ❸ carril *(de autopista)* ❹ calle *(de piscina, pista)* ❺ ruta

language ['læŋgwɪdʒ] *s* ❶ idioma; lengua ❷ lenguaje

language laboratory *s* laboratorio de idiomas

languish ['læŋgwɪʃ] *vi* ❶ languidecer ❷ pudrirse

lank [læŋk] *adj* lacio, cia

lanky ['læŋkɪ] *adj* larguirucho, cha

lantern ['læntən] *s* farol

lap [læp] ◆ *s* ❶ regazo ❷ vuelta *(de carrera)* ◆ *vt* ❶ beber a lengüetadas ❷ doblar *(en carrera)* ◆ *vi* romper con suavidad *(olas)*

lapel [lə'pel] *s* solapa

Lapland ['læplænd] *s* Laponia

lapse [læps] ◆ *s* ❶ fallo; lapsus ❷ desliz ❸ lapso; periodo ◆ *vi* ❶ caducar ❷ cumplir; expirar ❸ bajar momentáneamente ❹ extinguirse *(tradición)* ❺ • **to lapse into** terminar cayendo en

lap-top (computer) *s* INFORMÁTICA computadora portátil

lard [lɑːd] *s* manteca de cerdo

larder ['lɑːdər] *s* despensa

large [lɑːdʒ] *adj* ❶ grande ❷ numeroso, sa *(familia)* ❸ importante *(cantidad)*

■ **at large** *adv* ❶ en general ❷ suelto, ta *(preso, animal)*

■ **by and large** *adv* en general

largely ['lɑːdʒlɪ] *adv* ❶ en gran parte ❷ principalmente

lark [lɑːk] *s* ❶ alondra ❷ *familiar* broma

laryngitis [,lærɪn'dʒaɪtɪs] *s* ☿ *incontable* laringitis

larynx ['lærɪŋks] *s* laringe

lasagna, lasagne [lə'zænjə] *s* ☿ *incontable* lasaña

laser ['leɪzər] *s* láser

laser printer *s* INFORMÁTICA impresora láser

lash [læʃ] ◆ *s* ❶ pestaña ❷ latigazo ◆ *vt* ❶ *literal & figurado* azotar ❷ • **to lash something (to)** amarrar algo (a)

■ **lash out** *vi* • **to lash out at somebody a)** soltar un golpe a alguien **b)** arremeter contra alguien

lass [læs] *s* chavala; muchacha

lasso [læ'suː] *s* lazo

El plural de **lasso** es **lassos**

last [lɑːst] ◆ *adj* último, ma • **last month/Tuesday** el mes/martes pasado • **last March** en marzo del año pasado • **last night** anoche • **last but one** penúltimo, ma • **last but two** antepenúltimo, ma ◆ *adv* ❶ por última vez • **when I last called him** la última vez que lo llamé ❷ en último lugar • **he arrived last** llegó el último • **last but not least** por último, pero no por ello menos importante ◆ *pronombre* • **the year/Saturday before last** no el año/sábado pasado, sino el anterior • **the night before last** anteanoche • **the time before last** la vez anterior a la pasada • **the last but one** el penúltimo, la penúltima • **to leave something till last** dejar algo para el final ◆ *s* • **the last I saw/heard of him** la última vez que lo vi/que oí de él ◆ *vi* ❶ durar ❷ conservarse

■ **at (long) last** *adv* por fin

last-ditch *adj* último, ma; desesperado, da

lasting ['lɑːstɪŋ] *adj* duradero, ra

lastly ['lɑːstlɪ] *adv* ❶ por último ❷ al final

last-minute *adj* de última hora

latch [lætʃ] *s* pestillo

■ **latch onto** *vt* ☿ *El objeto siempre va después de la preposición al final.* ❶ *familiar* pegarse o engancharse a ❷ pillar *(una idea)*

late [leɪt] ◆ *adj* ❶ con retraso • **to be late (for)** llegar tarde (a) • **the flight is twenty minutes late** el vuelo lleva veinte minutos de retraso • **the bus was an hour late** el autobús llegó con una hora de retraso ❷ • **in the late afternoon** al final de la tarde • **in late December** a finales de diciembre • **it's getting late** se está haciendo tarde ❸ tardío, a • **we had a late breakfast** desayunamos tarde ❹ • **the late president** el ex-presidente ❺ difunto, ta ◆ *adv* ❶ tarde • **they are open late** abren hasta tarde ❷ • **late in the day** al final del día • **late in August** a finales de agosto

■ **of late** *adv* últimamente

---

late 🌀

Lately y late no significan lo mismo bien que los dos sean adverbios (late también es adjetivo). Lately equivale a *últimamente*. Comparemos los dos ejemplos he arrived *late* (*llegó tarde*) y we haven't spoken *lately* (*no hemos hablado últimamente*).

---

latecomer ['leɪt,kʌmər] *s* persona que llega tarde

lately ['leɪtlɪ] *adv* últimamente

later ['leɪtər] ◆ *adj* ❶ posterior ❷ • in the later 15th century a finales del siglo XV ◆ *adv* • later (on) más tarde; después • no later than Friday el viernes como muy tarde

expresión see you later! ¡hasta luego!

latest ['leɪtɪst] ◆ *adj* último, ma ◆ *s* • at the latest a más tardar; como muy tarde

lather ['lɑːðər] ◆ *s* espuma (de jabón) ◆ *vt* enjabonar

Latin ['lætɪn] ◆ *adj* ❶ latino, na ❷ de latín ◆ *s* latín

Latin America *s* América Latina; Latinoamérica

Latin American ◆ *adj* latinoamericano, na ◆ *s* latinoamericano, na

latitude ['lætɪtjuːd] *s* GEOGRAFÍA latitud

latter ['lætər] ◆ *adj* ❶ último, ma ❷ segundo, da ◆ *s* • the latter éste, ta

latterly ['lætəlɪ] *adv* últimamente

lattice ['lætɪs] *s* enrejado; celosía

Latvia ['lætvɪə] *s* Letonia

laugh [lɑːf] ◆ *s* ❶ risa ❷ *familiar* • to have a laugh divertirse • to do something for laughs o a laugh hacer algo para divertirse ◆ *vi* reírse

■ **laugh at** *vt* ☿ *El objeto siempre va después de la preposición al final.* reírse de

■ **laugh off** *vt* ☿ *El objeto se puede colocar antes o después de la preposición.* tomarse a risa

laughable ['lɑːfəbl] *adj despectivo* ridículo, la; risible

laughing stock ['lɑːfɪŋ-] *s* hazmerreír

laughter ['lɑːftər] *s* ☿ *incontable* risa; risas

launch [lɔːntʃ] ◆ *s* ❶ botadura ❷ lanzamiento ❸ lancha ◆ *vt* ❶ botar ❷ lanzar ❸ fundar

launch(ing) pad ['lɔːntʃ(ɪŋ)-] *s* plataforma de lanzamiento

launder ['lɔːndər] *vt* ❶ lavar ❷ *familiar* blanquear *(dinero)*

Laundromat ® ['lɔːndrəmæt] *s* lavandería (automática)

laundry ['lɔːndrɪ] *s* ❶ colada; ropa sucia • to do the laundry lavar la ropa sucia ❷ ropa limpia ❸ lavandería

lava ['lɑːvə] *s* lava

lavatory ['lævətrɪ] *s* ❶ excusado ❷ baño

lavender ['lævəndər] *s* ❶ lavanda ❷ color lavanda

lavish ['lævɪʃ] ◆ *adj* ❶ pródigo, ga • to be lavish with a) ser pródigo en b) ser desprendido, da con ❷ muy generoso, sa ❸ espléndido, da; suntuoso, sa ◆ *vt* • to lavish something on a) prodigar algo a b) gastar algo en

law [lɔː] *s* ❶ ley • against the law ilegal • to break the law infringir o violar la ley ▶ law and order el orden público ❷ derecho

law-abiding [-ə,baɪdɪŋ] *adj* observante de la ley

law court *s* tribunal de justicia

law enforcement officer *s* agente de policía

law firm *s* bufete de abogados

lawful ['lɔːfʊl] *adj formal* legal; lícito, ta

lawn [lɔːn] *s* césped; pasto

lawnmower ['lɔːn,məʊər] *s* cortacésped

lawn party *s* recepción al aire libre

law school *s* facultad de derecho • he went to law school estudió derecho

lawsuit ['lɔːsuːt] *s* pleito

lawyer ['lɔːjər] *s* abogado, da

lax [læks] *adj* ❶ relajado, da *(disciplina)* ❷ negligente *(persona)* ❸ poco riguroso, sa *(seguridad)*

laxative ['læksətɪv] *s* laxante

lay [leɪ] ◆ *pretérito* → **lie** ◆ *vt* ❶ colocar; poner • to lay yourself open to something exponerse a algo ❷ poner *(ladrillos)*; tender *(trampa, cables)*; echar *(cimientos)* • to lay the table poner la mesa ❸ poner *(huevos)* ❹ • to lay something on somebody echar algo a alguien *(la culpa, una maldición)* ◆ *adj* ❶ laico, ca ❷ lego, ga

■ **lay aside** *vt* ☿ *El objeto se puede colocar antes o después de la preposición.* ❶ guardar; ahorrar ❷ dejar a un lado

■ **lay down** *vt* ☿ *El objeto se puede colocar antes o después de la preposición.* ❶ imponer; establecer ❷ deponer; entregar *(armas)*; dejar *(herramientas)*

■ **lay off** ◆ *vt* ☿ *El objeto se puede colocar antes o después de la preposición.* despedir ◆ *vt* ☿ *El objeto siempre va después de la preposición al final. familiar* • to lay off (doing something) dejar de (hacer algo) ◆ *vi familiar* • lay off! ¡déjame en paz!

■ **lay on** *vt* ☿ *El objeto se puede colocar antes o después de la preposición.* ❶ organizar ❷ preparar *(comida)*

■ **lay out** *vt* ☿ *El objeto se puede colocar antes o después de la preposición.* ❶ disponer ❷ diseñar el trazado de

Formas irregulares de **lay**: *pretérito & pp* **laid**.

layer ['leɪər] *s* ❶ capa ❷ *figurado* nivel

layman ['leɪmən] *s* ❶ lego, ga ❷ RELIGIÓN laico, ca

El plural de **layman** es **laymen** ['leɪmen].

layout ['leɪaʊt] *s* ❶ diseño ❷ presentación; composición

layover ['leɪəʊvər] *s* ❶ parada ❷ escala *(de avión)*

L

laze [leɪz] *vi* • **to laze (about** o **around)** gandulear; holgazanear

lazy ['leɪzɪ] *adj* ❶ perezoso, sa; vago, ga ❷ lento, ta *(paseo, gesto)* ❸ ocioso, sa

lazybones ['leɪzɪbəʊnz] *s familiar* gandul, la
El plural de **lazybones** es **lazybones.**

lb *(abreviatura escrita de* pound) lb

LCD *s abreviatura escrita de* **liquid crystal display**

lead¹ [li:d] ◆ *s* ❶ delantera • **to be in** o **have the lead** llevar la delantera; ir en cabeza • **to take the lead** ponerse a la cabeza ❷ ventaja • **to have a lead of...** llevar una ventaja de... ❸ ejemplo • **to take the lead** tomar la delantera ❹ TEATRO • **(to play) the lead** (hacer) el papel principal ❺ pista ❻ correa *(de perro)* ❼ cable ◆ *adj* ❶ principal ❷ solista ❸ más destacado, da *(artículo de prensa)* ◆ *vt* ❶ encabezar ❷ conducir ❸ dirigir ❹ moderar ❺ llevar *(una vida)* ❻ • **to lead somebody to do something** llevar a alguien a hacer algo • **we were led to believe that...** nos dieron a entender que...

expresión **to lead the way** mostrar el camino

◆ *vi* ❶ • **to lead (to)** conducir o llevar (a) ❷ • **to lead (to** o **into)** dar (a) *(puerta)* ❸ ir en cabeza • **Brazil is leading 3 goals to 2** Brasil va ganando por 3 goles a 2 ❹ • **to lead to** conducir a ❺ salir *(en juegos de naipes)*

■ **lead up to** *vt* ☼: *El objeto siempre va después de la preposición al final.* ❶ conducir a; preceder ❷ apuntar a
Formas irregulares de **lead:** *pretérito & pp* **led.**

lead² [led] *s* ❶ plomo ❷ mina *(de lápiz)*

leader ['li:dər] *s* líder

leadership ['li:dəʃɪp] *s* ☼: *incontable* ❶ • **the leadership** los líderes ❷ liderazgo ❸ dotes de mando

lead guitar *s* guitarra solista

leading ['li:dɪŋ] *adj* ❶ destacado, da ❷ principal ❸ que va en cabeza

leading lady *s* primera actriz

leading man *s* primer actor

leaf [li:f] *s* ❶ hoja ❷ hoja abatible *(de mesa)*

■ **leaf through** *vt* ☼: *El objeto siempre va después de la preposición al final.* hojear
El plural de **leaf** es **leaves.**

leaflet ['li:flɪt] *s* ❶ folleto ❷ octavilla

league [li:g] *s* liga

expresión **to be in league with** estar confabulado con

leak [li:k] ◆ *s* ❶ agujero; gotera ❷ escape; fuga ❸ filtración *(de información)* ◆ *vt* filtrar *(información)* ◆ *vi* ❶ tener un agujero ❷ tener goteras ❸ calar *(botas)* ❹ salirse; escaparse • **to leak (out) from** salirse de

■ **leak out** *vi* escaparse

leakage ['li:kɪdʒ] *s* fuga; escape

lean [li:n] ◆ *adj* ❶ delgado, da ❷ magro, gra ❸ de escasez *(invierno, año)* ◆ *vt* • **to lean something against** apoyar algo contra ◆ *vi* ❶ inclinarse • **he leaned forward** se inclinó hacia delante • **to lean out of the win-**

dow asomarse a la ventana ❷ • **to lean on/against** apoyarse en/contra
Formas irregulares de **lean:** *pretérito & pp* **leant** o **leaned** (regular).

leaning ['li:nɪŋ] *s* • **leaning (towards)** inclinación (hacia o por)

leant [lent] *pretérito & participio pasado* → **lean**

leap [li:p] ◆ *s* salto ◆ *vi* saltar • **to leap to your feet** ponerse de pie de un salto
Formas irregulares de **leap:** *pretérito & pp* **leapt** o **leaped** (regular).

leapfrog ['li:pfrɒg] ◆ *s* burro ◆ *vt* saltar

leapt [lept] *pretérito & participio pasado* → **leap**

leap year *s* año bisiesto

learn [lɜ:n] ◆ *vt* ❶ aprender • **to learn (how) to do something** aprender a hacer algo ❷ • **to learn (that)** enterarse de (que) ◆ *vi* aprender
Formas irregulares de **learn:** *pretérito & pp* **learned** o **learnt** (regular).

learned ['lɜ:nɪd] *adj* erudito, ta

learner ['lɜ:nər] *s* ❶ principiante ❷ estudiante

learner (driver) *s* conductor principiante o en prácticas

learner's permit *s* carné de conducir provisional

learning ['lɜ:nɪŋ] *s* saber; erudición

learning disability *s* discapacidad para el aprendizaje

learnt [lɜ:nt] *pretérito & participio pasado* → **learn**

lease [li:s] ◆ *s* DERECHO contrato de arrendamiento; arriendo

expresión **to give somebody a new lease on life** darle nueva vida a alguien

◆ *vt* arrendar • **to lease something from/to somebody** arrendar algo de/a alguien

leash [li:ʃ] *s* correa

least [li:st] ☼: *superlativo de little* ◆ *adj* menor • **I don't have the least idea** no tengo la menor idea • **he earns the least money** es el que menos dinero gana ◆ *pronombre* • **the least** lo menos • **it's the least (that) he can do** es lo menos que puede hacer • **not in the least** en absoluto • **to say the least** por no decir otra cosa ◆ *adv* menos

■ **at least** *adv* por lo menos

■ **least of all** *adv* y menos (todavía)

■ **not least** *adv* sobre todo

leather ['leðər] ◆ *s* piel; cuero ◆ *en compuestos* ❶ de cuero ❷ de piel

leave [li:v] ◆ *vt* ❶ dejar • **he left it to her to decide** dejó que ella decidiera ❷ irse de; salir de; • **to leave home** irse de casa ❸ abandonar *(cónyuge)* ❹ dejarse ❺ • **to leave somebody something, to leave something to somebody** dejarle algo a alguien

expresión to leave somebody alone dejar a alguien en paz
◆ *vi* ❶ salir ❷ irse; marcharse ◆ *s* licencia • to be on leave estar de licencia
■ leave behind *vt* 🔅 *El objeto se puede colocar antes o después de la preposición.* ❶ dejar ❷ dejarse ❸ • to get left behind quedarse atrás
■ leave out *vt* 🔅 *El objeto se puede colocar antes o después de la preposición.* ❶ omitir ❷ excluir
Formas irregulares de leave: *pretérito & pp* left.
leave of absence *s* excedencia
leaves [li:vz] *spl* → leaf
Lebanon ['lebənən] *s* • (the) Lebanon (el) Líbano
lecherous ['letʃərəs] *adj* lascivo, va
lecture ['lektʃər] ◆ *s* ❶ clase (*en universidad*); conferencia (*en congreso*) • to give a lecture (on) a) dar una clase (sobre) b) dar una conferencia (sobre) ❷ sermón ◆ *vt* echar un sermón a ◆ *vi* • to lecture (on/in) a) dar clases (de/en) b) dar una conferencia (sobre/en)
lecturer ['lektʃərər] *s* profesor, ra de universidad
led [led] *pretérito & participio pasado* → lead¹
ledge [ledʒ] *s* ❶ alféizar ❷ saliente
leech [li:tʃ] *s literal & figurado* sanguijuela
leek [li:k] *s* puerro
leer [lɪər] *vi* • to leer at somebody mirar lascivamente a alguien
leeway ['li:weɪ] *s* libertad (de acción o movimientos)
left [left] ◆ *adj* ❶ izquierdo, da ❷ • to be left quedar • there's no wine left no queda vino ◆ *adv* a la izquierda ◆ *s* izquierda • on o to the left a la izquierda
■ Left *s* POLÍTICA • the Left la izquierda
left-hand *adj* izquierdo, da • the left-hand side el lado izquierdo; la izquierda
left-handed [-'hændɪd] ◆ *adj* ❶ zurdo, da ❷ para zurdos ❸ con doble sentido (*cumplido*) ◆ *adv* con la (mano) izquierda
leftover ['leftəʊvər] *adj* sobrante
■ leftovers *spl* sobras
left wing *s* POLÍTICA izquierda
■ left-wing *adj* izquierdista
lefty ['leftɪ] *s* zurdo, da
leg [leg] *s* ❶ pierna • Colin has broken his leg Colin se quebró una pierna ❷ pata ❸ pernera; pierna (*de pantalón*) ❹ muslo (*de pollo*) ❺ etapa ❻ partido
expresión to pull somebody's leg tomarle el pelo a alguien
legacy ['legəsɪ] *s literal & figurado* legado
legal ['li:gl] *adj* ❶ legal ❷ jurídico, ca; legal
legalize ['li:gəlaɪz] *vt* legalizar
legal tender *s* moneda de curso legal
legend ['ledʒənd] *s literal & figurado* leyenda
leggings ['legɪŋz] *spl* mallas
legible ['ledʒəbl] *adj* legible
legislation [ˌledʒɪs'leɪʃn] *s* legislación

legislature ['ledʒɪsleɪtʃər] *s* asamblea legislativa
legitimate [lɪ'dʒɪtɪmət] *adj* legítimo, ma
legroom ['legrʊm] *s* 🔅*incontable* espacio para las piernas
leisure ['li:ʒər] *s* ocio • do it at your leisure hazlo cuando tengas tiempo
leisure center *s* centro deportivo y cultural
leisurely ['li:ʒərlɪ] *adj* lento, ta
leisure time *s* tiempo libre
lemon ['lemən] *s* limón
lemonade [ˌlemə'neɪd] *s* limonada
lemon juice *s* jugo de limón
lemon sole *s* mendo limón
lemon squeezer [-'skwi:zər] *s* exprimidor; exprimelimones
lemon tea *s* té con limón
lend [lend] *vt* ❶ prestar; dejar • to lend somebody something, to lend something to somebody prestarle algo a alguien ❷ • to lend something (to somebody) prestar algo (a alguien) • to lend itself to something prestarse a algo
expresión to lend somebody a hand echar una mano a alguien
Formas irregulares de lend: *pretérito & pp* lent.
length [leŋθ] *s* ❶ longitud; largo • what length is it? ¿cuánto mide de largo? • it's a meter in length tiene un metro de largo ❷ extensión ❸ duración ❹ largo (*de alberca*) ❺ trozo (*de cuerda, madera*); largo (*de tela*)
■ at length *adv* ❶ por fin ❷ largo y tendido (*hablar*); con detenimiento (*debatir*)
lengthen ['leŋθən] ◆ *vt* alargar ◆ *vi* alargarse
lengthy ['leŋθɪ] *adj* ❶ extenso, sa ❷ prolongado, da
lenient ['li:njənt] *adj* indulgente
lens [lenz] *s* ❶ lente ❷ lente; objetivo (*de cámara*) ❸ lente de contacto
lent [lent] *pretérito & participio pasado* → lend
Lent [lent] *s* Cuaresma
lentil ['lentɪl] *s* lenteja
Leo ['li:əʊ] *s* Leo
leopard ['lepəd] *s* leopardo
leotard ['li:ətɑːd] *s* malla
leper ['lepər] *s* leproso, sa
leprosy ['leprəsɪ] *s* lepra
lesbian ['lezbɪən] *s* lesbiana
less [les] 🔅 *comparativo de little* ◆ *adj* menos • less... than menos... que • less and less... cada vez menos... ◆ *pronombre* menos • it costs less than you think cuesta menos de lo que piensas • the less you work, the less you earn cuanto menos trabajas, menos ganas • no less than nada menos que ◆ *adv* menos • less than five menos de cinco • less often menos • less and less cada vez menos ◆ *preposición* menos
lessen ['lesn] ◆ *vt* aminorar; reducir ◆ *vi* aminorarse; reducirse

L

lesson ['lesn] s ❶ clase ❷ lección

expresión to teach somebody a lesson darle una buena lección a alguien

let [let] vt ❶ • to let somebody do something dejar a alguien hacer algo • to let somebody know something avisar a alguien de algo ❷ • let's go! ¡vamos! • let's see veamos • let him wait! ¡déjale que espere! ❸ alquilar; arrendar • 'to let' 'se alquila'

expresiones to let go of something/somebody soltar algo/a alguien ▸ to let something/somebody go liberar algo/a alguien; soltar algo/a alguien ▸ to let yourself go a) soltarse el pelo b) abandonarse

■ **let alone** adv ni mucho menos

■ **let down** vt ⚙ *El objeto se puede colocar antes o después de la preposición.* ❶ desinflar ❷ fallar; defraudar

■ **let in** vt ⚙ *El objeto se puede colocar antes o después de la preposición.* ❶ dejar entrar ❷ dejar pasar

■ **let off** vt ⚙ *El objeto se puede colocar antes o después de la preposición.* ❶ • to let somebody off something eximir a alguien de algo ❷ perdonar ❸ hacer estallar *(bomba)*; disparar *(arma de fuego)* ❹ despedir *(gas)*

■ **let on** vi • don't let on! ¡no cuentes nada!

■ **let out** vt ⚙ *El objeto se puede colocar antes o después de la preposición.* ❶ dejar salir ❷ soltar *(sonido, grito)*

■ **let up** vi ❶ amainar ❷ parar

Formas irregulares de **let**: *pretérito* & *pp* **let.**

lethal ['li:θl] adj letal; mortífero, ra

lethargic [lə'θɑ:dʒɪk] adj ❶ letárgico, ca ❷ aletargado, da ❸ apático, ca

let's [lets] *(abreviatura de* let us*)* → **let**

letter ['letər] s ❶ carta ❷ letra • to the letter *figurado* al pie de la letra

letter bomb s carta bomba

letter carrier s cartero, ra

letter-perfect adj impecable

lettuce ['letɪs] s lechuga

letup ['letʌp] s tregua; respiro

leukemia [luː'kiːmɪə] s leucemia

level ['levl] ◆ adj ❶ igualado, da • they are level van igualados ❷ nivelado, da • the pictures aren't level los cuadros no están derechos • to be level (with something) estar al mismo nivel (que algo) ❸ liso, sa; llano, na ◆ s ❶ nivel ❷ piso ❸ nivel de burbuja de aire

expresión to be on the level *familiar* ser de fiar ◆ vt ❶ allanar ❷ derribar *(edificio)*; arrasar *(bosque)*

■ **level off, level out** vi ❶ estabilizarse ❷ nivelarse ❸ enderezarse

■ **level with** vt ⚙ *El objeto siempre va después de la preposición al final.* *familiar* ser sincero, ra con

lever ['levər] s palanca

levy ['levɪ] ◆ s • levy (on) a) contribución (a o para) b) tasa o impuesto (sobre) ◆ vt ❶ imponer ❷ recaudar

lewd [lju:d] adj ❶ lascivo, va ❷ obsceno, na ❸ verde *(chiste)*

liability [ˌlaɪə'bɪlətɪ] s ❶ • liability (for) responsabilidad (de o por) ❷ estorbo

■ **liabilities** spl FINANZAS pasivo

liable ['laɪəbl] adj ❶ • that's liable to happen eso pueda que ocurra ❷ • to be liable to ser propenso, sa a ❸ • to be liable (for) ser responsable (de)

liaise [lɪ'eɪz] vi • to liaise (with) estar en contacto (con)

liaison [lɪ'eɪzɒn] s • liaison (with/between) coordinación (con/entre); enlace (con/entre)

liar ['laɪər] s mentiroso, sa

libel ['laɪbl] ◆ s libelo ◆ vt calumniar

liberal ['lɪbərəl] ◆ adj ❶ liberal ❷ generoso, sa ◆ s liberal

■ **Liberal** ◆ adj POLÍTICA liberal ◆ s POLÍTICA liberal

liberate ['lɪbəreɪt] vt liberar

liberation [ˌlɪbə'reɪʃn] s liberación

liberty ['lɪbətɪ] s libertad • at liberty en libertad • to be at liberty to do something ser libre de hacer algo

Libra ['liːbrə] s Libra

librarian [laɪ'breərɪən] s bibliotecario, ria

library ['laɪbrərɪ] s biblioteca

El plural de **library** es **libraries.**

Libya ['lɪbɪə] s Libia

lice [laɪs] spl → **louse**

licence number s AUTOMÓVILES número de licencia

license, licence ['laɪsəns] ◆ s ❶ permiso; licencia • under license con autorización o permiso oficial ❷ AUTOMÓVILES licencia de manejar o conducir ◆ vt ❶ dar licencia a ❷ autorizar

licensed ['laɪsənst] adj ❶ • to be licensed to do something estar autorizado, da para hacer algo ❷ registrado, da; con licencia

license plate s placa

lick [lɪk] ◆ s *familiar* • a lick of paint una mano de pintura ◆ vt *literal* & *figurado* lamer

licorice ['lɪkərɪʃ] ['lɪkərɪs] s ⚙ *incontable* regaliz

lid [lɪd] s ❶ tapa ❷ párpado

lie [laɪ] ◆ s mentira • to tell lies contar mentiras; mentir ◆ vi ❶ *(pretérito* lied, *pp* lied, *gerundio* lying*)* mentir • to lie to somebody mentirle a alguien ❷ *(pretérito* lay, *pp* lain, *gerundio* lying*)* tumbarse; echarse ❸ yacer • to be lying estar tumbado, da ❹ *(pretérito* lay, *pp* lain, *gerundio* lying*)* hallarse • there is snow lying on the ground hay nieve en el suelo • he is lying in fourth place se encuentra en cuarto lugar ❺ *(pretérito* lay, *pp* lain, *gerundio* lying*)* hallarse; encontrarse *(solución, atractivo)*

expresión to lie low permanecer escondido, da

■ **lie about, lie around** vi estar o andar tirado, da

■ **lie down** vi acostarse; echarse

expresión not to take something lying down no quedarse cruzado de brazos ante algo

lieutenant [lu:'tenənt] *s* ➊ MILITAR teniente ➋ lugarteniente ➌ oficial de policía

life [laɪf] *s* vida • **that's life!** ¡así es la vida! • **for life** de por vida; para toda la vida

expresión to breathe life into something infundir una nueva vida a algo

El plural de **life** es **lives**.

lifeboat ['laɪfbəʊt] *s* ➊ bote salvavidas ➋ lancha de salvamento

life buoy *s* flotador; salvavidas

life cycle *s* ciclo vital

life expectancy *s* experanza de vida

lifeguard ['laɪfɡɑ:d] *s* socorrista

life imprisonment [-ɪm'prɪznmənt] *s* cadena perpetua

life insurance *s* incontable seguro de vida

lifeless ['laɪflɪs] *adj* ➊ sin vida ➋ insulso, sa

lifelike ['laɪflaɪk] *adj* realista; natural

lifeline ['laɪflaɪn] *s* ➊ cuerda o cable (de salvamento) ➋ cordón umbilical

lifelong ['laɪflɒŋ] *adj* de toda la vida

life preserver [-prɪ,zɜ:vər] *s* ➊ chaleco salvavidas ➋ flotador; salvavidas

life raft *s* balsa salvavidas

lifesaver ['laɪf,seɪvər] *s* socorrista

life sentence *s* (condena a) cadena perpetua

life-size(d) [-saɪz(d)] *adj* (de) tamaño natural

lifespan ['laɪfspæn] *s* vida

lifestyle ['laɪfstaɪl] *s* estilo de vida

life-support system *s* aparato de respiración artificial

lifetime ['laɪftaɪm] *s* vida

lift [lɪft] ◆ *s* aventón • **to give somebody a lift (somewhere)** dar (un) aventón a alguien (a algún sitio) ◆ *vt* ➊ levantar • **to lift something down** bajar algo • **to lift something out of something** sacar algo de algo ➋ copiar ◆ *vi* disiparse *(neblina)*

lift-off *s* despegue

light [laɪt] ◆ *adj* ➊ ligero, ra ➋ fino, na *(lluvia)* ➌ simple *(deberes, responsabilidades)* ➍ suave *(trabajo)* ➎ leve *(castigo)* ➏ light ➐ luminoso, sa; lleno, na de luz • **it's growing light** se hace de día ➑ claro, ra *(color)* • **a light green shirt** una camisa verde claro ◆ *s* ➊ luz ➋ fuego; lumbre • **have you got a light?** ¿tienes fuego?

expresiones to see something/somebody in a different light ver algo/a alguien de otra manera distinta ▶ to bring something to light sacar algo a la luz ▶ to come to light salir a la luz (pública) ▶ to set light to prender fuego a ▶ to throw o cast o shed light on arrojar luz sobre

◆ *vt* ➊ encender ➋ iluminar ◆ *vi* prenderse ◆ *adv* • **to travel light** viajar con poco equipaje

■ **light up** ◆ *vt* El objeto se puede colocar antes o después de la preposición. iluminar ◆ *vi* ➊ iluminarse; encenderse ➋ *familiar* encender un cigarrillo

Formas irregulares de **light**: *pretérito & pp* **lit**.

light bulb *s* foco

light cream *s* crema líquida

lighten ['laɪtn] ◆ *vt* ➊ iluminar ➋ aligerar ◆ *vi* aclararse

lighter ['laɪtər] *s* encendedor; mechero

light-headed [-'hedɪd] *adj* ➊ mareado, da ➋ exaltado, da

light-hearted [-'hɑ:tɪd] *adj* ➊ alegre ➋ frívolo, la

lighthouse ['laɪthaʊs] *pl* [-haʊzɪz] *s* faro

lighting ['laɪtɪŋ] *s* iluminación ▶ **street lighting** alumbrado público

lightly ['laɪtlɪ] *adv* ➊ suavemente ➋ ligeramente ➌ a la ligera

lightning ['laɪtnɪŋ] *s* incontable • **it was struck by lightning** lo alcanzó un rayo ▶ **a flash of lightning** un relámpago ▶ **a bolt of lightning** un rayo

expresión as quick as lightning como un rayo

lightweight ['laɪtweɪt] ◆ *adj* ligero, ra ◆ *s* peso ligero

likable, likeable ['laɪkəbl] *adj* simpático, ca

like [laɪk] ◆ *preposición* ➊ como ➋ en preguntas directas o indirectas cómo • **what did it taste like?** ¿a qué sabía? • **what did it look like?** ¿cómo era? • **tell me what it's like** dime cómo es • **something like $100** algo así como cien dólares • **something like that** algo así; algo por el estilo ➌ como; igual que • **like this/ that** así • **do it like this** hazlo como este ➍ propio, pia o típico, ca de • **it's not like them** no es su estilo ◆ *vt* ➊ • **I like cheese** me gusta el queso • **I like it/them** me gusta/gustan • **I don't like it/them** no me gusta/gustan • **he likes doing** o **to do something** (a él) le gusta hacer algo ➋ querer • **would you like some more?** ¿quieres un poco más? • **I would like** o **I'd like** quisiera • **I'd like a cup of tea** quisiera una taza de té • **I'd like to come tomorrow** querría o me gustaría venir mañana • **I'd like you to come to dinner** me gustaría que vinieras a cenar • **I'd like a kilo of apples** póngame un kilo de manzanas • **I don't like to bother her** no quiero molestarla • **if you like** si quieres • **whenever you like** cuando quieras ◆ *s* • **the like of some-body/something** alguien/algo del estilo

■ **likes** *spl* gustos; preferencias

likeable ['laɪkəbl] = **likable**

likelihood ['laɪklɪhʊd] *s* probabilidad

likely ['laɪklɪ] *adj* ➊ probable • **rain is likely** es probable que llueva • **he's likely to come** es probable que venga ➋ indicado, da

liken ['laɪkn] *vt* • **to liken something/somebody to** comparar algo/a alguien con

likeness ['laɪknɪs] *s* ➊ • **likeness (to)** parecido (con) ➋ retrato

likewise ['laɪkwaɪz] *adv* de la misma forma • **to do likewise** hacer lo mismo

liking ['laɪkɪŋ] *s* • **to have a liking for something** tener afición por o a algo • **to take a liking to somebody** tomar o coger cariño a alguien • **to be to somebody's liking** ser del gusto de alguien • **for my/his** ETC **liking** para mi/su ETC gusto

lilac ['laɪlək] ◆ *adj* lila ◆ *s* lila

lily ['lɪlɪ] *s* lirio; azucena

limb [lɪm] *s* miembro

limber ['lɪmbər] ■ **limber up** *vi* desentumecerse

limbo ['lɪmbəʊ] *s* ⚘ *incontable* • **to be in limbo** estar en un estado de incertidumbre

lime [laɪm] *s* ❶ lima ❷ ▶ **lime (juice)** jugo de lima ❸ *QUÍMICA* cal

limelight ['laɪmlaɪt] *s* • **in the limelight** en (el) candelero

limestone ['laɪmstəʊn] *s* ⚘ *incontable* (piedra) caliza

limey ['laɪmɪ] *s familiar* término peyorativo que designa a un inglés

limit ['lɪmɪt] ◆ *s* límite

expresión **off limits** en zona prohibida

◆ *vt* limitar

limitation [,lɪmɪ'teɪʃn] *s* limitación

limited ['lɪmɪtɪd] *adj* limitado, da • **to be limited to** estar limitado a

limited (liability) company *s* sociedad limitada

limousine ['lɪməzi:n] *s* limusina

limp [lɪmp] ◆ *adj* flojo, ja ◆ *vi* cojear ◆ *s* • **to have a limp** cojear

line [laɪn] ◆ *s* ❶ línea ❷ fila • **in a line** en fila ❸ cola *(de personas esperando)* • **to stand in line** hacer cola ❹ camino • **what's his line of business?** ¿a qué negocios se dedica? ❺ cuerda; sedal; hilo ❻ *TELECOMUNICACIONES* ▶ **(telephone) line** línea (telefónica) • **hold the line, please** no cuelgue, por favor • **the line is busy** está comunicando • **it's a bad line** hay interferencias • **your wife is on the line for you** su mujer al teléfono ❼ línea; renglón ❽ verso ❾ arruga ❿ límite

expresión **to drop somebody a line** *familiar* mandar unas letras a alguien

◆ *vt* ❶ forrar ❷ cubrir el interior de *(cajón)*

■ **out of line** *adv* • **to be out of line** estar fuera de lugar

■ **line up** ◆ *vt* ⚘ *El objeto se puede colocar antes o después de la preposición.* ❶ alinear ❷ programar; organizar ◆ *vi* alinearse

lined [laɪnd] *adj* ❶ • **lined paper** papel de rayas ❷ arrugado, da

line dancing *s* ▶ baile en el que los participantes se colocan en fila y se mueven al mismo tiempo que los otros

linen ['lɪnɪn] *s* ❶ lino ❷ ropa blanca o de hilo ▶ **bed linen** ropa de cama

liner ['laɪnər] *s* transatlántico

linesman ['laɪnzmən] *s* juez de línea

El plural de **linesman** es **linesmen** ['laɪnzmen].

lineup ['laɪnʌp] *s* ❶ alineación ❷ rueda de identificación

linger ['lɪŋgər] *vi* ❶ entretenerse ❷ rezagarse ❸ persistir

lingerie ['lænʒərɪ] *s* ropa interior femenina

lingo ['lɪŋgəʊ] *s* ❶ *familiar* idioma ❷ jerga

El plural de **lingo** es **lingoes**

linguist ['lɪŋgwɪst] *s* ❶ lingüista ❷ • **he's a good linguist** tiene facilidad para las lenguas

linguistics [lɪŋ'gwɪstɪks] *s* ⚘ *incontable* lingüística

lining ['laɪnɪŋ] *s* forro

link [lɪŋk] ◆ *s* ❶ eslabón ❷ conexión; enlace • **links (between/with)** lazos (entre/con); vínculos (entre/con) ◆ *vt* ❶ comunicar *(ciudades)*; conectar *(computadoras)*; relacionar *(hechos)* • **to link something with** o **to** relacionar o asociar algo con ❷ enlazar *(brazos)* ◆ *vi* *INFORMÁTICA* • **to link to sth** enlazar con algo

■ **link up** *vt* ⚘ *El objeto se puede colocar antes o después de la preposición.* • **to link something up (with)** conectar algo (con)

links [lɪŋks] *s* campo de golf *(cerca del mar)*

El plural de **links** es **links**

lion ['laɪən] *s* león

lioness ['laɪənes] *s* leona

lip [lɪp] *s* ❶ labio ❷ borde *(de taza)* ❸ pico *(de jarra)*

lip-read *vi* leer los labios

lip service *s*

expresión **to pay lip service to something** hablar en favor de algo sin hacer nada al respeto

lipstick ['lɪpstɪk] *s* ❶ lápiz o barra de labios ❷ carmín

liqueur [lɪ'kjʊər] *s* licor

liquid ['lɪkwɪd] ◆ *adj* líquido, da ◆ *s* líquido

liquidation [,lɪkwɪ'deɪʃn] *s* liquidación • **to go into liquidation** ir a la quiebra

liquid crystal display *s* pantalla de cristal líquido

liquor ['lɪkər] *s* ⚘ *incontable* alcohol; bebida alcohólica

liquor store *s* vinatería

lisp [lɪsp] ◆ *s* ceceo ◆ *vi* cecear

list [lɪst] ◆ *s* lista ◆ *vt* ❶ hacer una lista de ❷ enumerar ◆ *vi* *NÁUTICA* escorar

listen ['lɪsn] *vi* ❶ • **to listen (to something/somebody)** escuchar (algo/a alguien) • **to listen for** estar atento a ❷ • **to listen (to somebody/something)** hacer caso (a alguien/de algo) • **to listen to reason** atender a razones

listener ['lɪsnər] *s* radioyente

lit [lɪt] *pretérito* & *participio pasado* → **light**

liter ['li:tər] *s* litro

literacy ['lɪtərəsɪ] *s* alfabetización

literal ['lɪtərəl] *adj* literal

literally ['lɪtərəlɪ] *adv* literalmente

literary ['lɪtərərɪ] *adj* literario, ria

literate ['lɪtərət] *adj* ❶ alfabetizado, da ❷ culto, ta; instruido, da

literature ['lɪtrətʃər] *s* ❶ literatura ❷ publicaciones ❸ documentación

lithe [laɪð] *adj* ágil

Lithuania [ˌlɪθjʊˈeɪnɪə] *s* Lituania

litigation [ˌlɪtɪˈɡeɪʃn] *s formal* litigio

litter [ˈlɪtər] ◆ *s* ❶ basura ❷ camada ◆ *vt* • **to litter something (with)** ensuciar algo (de) • **papers littered the floor** había papeles esparcidos por el suelo

little [ˈlɪtl] ◆ *adj* ❶ pequeño, ña • **a little dog** un perrito • **her little sister** su hermanita • **you poor little thing!** ¡pobrecillo! ❷ corto, ta • **a little while** un ratito ❸ *(comparativo* less, *superlativo* least*)* poco, ca • **a little bit** un poco • **he speaks little English** habla poco inglés • **he speaks a little English** habla un poco de inglés ◆ *pronombre* • **I understood very little** entendí muy poco • **a little** un poco • **a little under half** algo menos de la mitad ◆ *adv* poco • **little by little** poco a poco

little

A little es lo mismo que a bit y a bit of, pero tiene un matiz algo más formal. Recordemos que a little al contrario de a bit no lleva of cuando va justo delante del sustantivo (would you like *a little* bread with your soup? *¿quiere un poco de pan con la sopa?*).

Al igual que a bit, a little también funciona como adverbio (he seems *a little* better *parece que está algo mejor*; I slept *a little* this afternoon *dormí algo esta tarde*).

Ver también few.

little finger *s* dedo meñique

live¹ [lɪv] ◆ *vi* vivir ◆ *vt* vivir • **to live a quiet life** llevar una vida tranquila

■ **live down** *vt* ⚙ *El objeto se puede colocar antes o después de la preposición.* lograr hacer olvidar

■ **live off** *vt* ⚙ *El objeto siempre va después de la preposición al final.* ❶ vivir de ❷ vivir a costa de

■ **live on** ◆ *vt* ⚙ *El objeto siempre va después de la preposición al final.* vivir de ◆ *vi* permanecer ; perdurar

■ **live together** *vi* vivir juntos

■ **live up to** *vt* ⚙ *El objeto siempre va después de la preposición al final.* estar a la altura de

■ **live with** *vt* ⚙ *El objeto siempre va después de la preposición al final.* ❶ vivir con ❷ aceptar *(situación, dificultad)*

live² [laɪv] *adj* ❶ vivo, va ❷ sin explotar *(bomba)* ❸ real *(munición)* ❹ ELECTRICIDAD cargado, da ❺ en vivo ; en directo

livelihood [ˈlaɪvlɪhʊd] *s* sustento ; medio de vida

lively [ˈlaɪvlɪ] *adj* ❶ animado, da • **she's very lively** está llena de vida ❷ agudo, da ; perspicaz *(mente)* ❸ vivo, va *(colores)*

liven [ˈlaɪvn] ■ **liven up** ◆ *vt* ⚙ *El objeto se puede colocar antes o después de la preposición.* animar ◆ *vi* animarse

liver [ˈlɪvər] *s* hígado

lives [laɪvz] *spl* → **life**

livestock [ˈlaɪvstɒk] *s* ganado

livid [ˈlɪvɪd] *adj* furioso, sa

living [ˈlɪvɪŋ] ◆ *adj* ❶ vivo, va ❷ contemporáneo, a ◆ *s* ❶ • **what do you do for a living?** ¿cómo te ganas la vida? • **to earn a living** ganarse la vida ❷ vida

living conditions *spl* condiciones de vida

living room *s* sala de estar ; salón

living standards *spl* nivel de vida

lizard [ˈlɪzəd] *s* ❶ lagartija ❷ lagarto

llama [ˈlɑːmə] *s* llama

> Dos plurales: **llama** o **llamas**.

load [ləʊd] ◆ *s* ❶ carga ❷ • **a heavy/light load** mucho/poco trabajo ❸ • **loads/a load of** *familiar* montones o un montón de ◆ *vt* • **to load something/somebody (with)** cargar algo/a alguien (de) • **to load a camera** ponerle rollo a la cámara

■ **load up** *vt & vi* ⚙ *El objeto se puede colocar antes o después de la preposición.* cargar

loaded [ˈləʊdɪd] *adj* ❶ trucado, da *(dado)* ❷ con doble sentido o intención *(pregunta, afirmación)* ❸ *familiar* forrado, da *(rico)*

loaf [ləʊf] *s* pan • **a loaf of bread** un pan

> El plural de **loaf** es **loaves**.

loan [ləʊn] ◆ *s* préstamo • **on loan** prestado, da ◆ *vt* prestar • **to loan something to somebody, to loan somebody something** prestar algo a alguien

loath, loth [ləʊθ] *adj* • **to be loath to do something** ser reacio, cia a hacer algo

loathe [ləʊð] *vt* • **to loathe (doing something)** aborrecer o detestar (hacer algo)

loaves [ləʊvz] *spl* → **loaf**

lob [lɒb] *s* TENIS lob

lobby [ˈlɒbɪ] ◆ *s* ❶ vestíbulo ❷ grupo de presión ; lobby ◆ *vt* ejercer presión (política) sobre

> Formas irregulares de **lobby**: *pret & pp* **lobbied**.

lobster [ˈlɒbstər] *s* langosta

local [ˈləʊkl] ◆ *adj* local ◆ *s familiar* ❶ • **the locals a)** los lugareños **b)** los vecinos del lugar ❷ ómnibus

local call *s* llamada local

local government *s* gobierno municipal

locally [ˈləʊkəlɪ] *adv* ❶ en el lugar ❷ por la zona

locate [ˈləʊkeɪt] ◆ *vt* ❶ localizar ❷ ubicar ◆ *vi* establecerse

location [ləʊˈkeɪʃn] *s* ❶ ubicación ; situación ❷ localización ❸ CINE • **on location** en exteriores

lock [lɒk] ◆ *s* ❶ cerradura ❷ candado ❸ esclusa ❹ *literario* mechón ◆ *vt* ❶ cerrar con llave ❷ cerrar con candado ❸ poner bajo llave ◆ *vi* ❶ cerrarse ❷ bloquearse

■ **lock in** *vt* ⚙ *El objeto se puede colocar antes o después de la preposición.* encerrar

■ **lock out** *vt* ⚙ *El objeto se puede colocar antes o después de la preposición.* ❶ dejar fuera al cerrar acci-

dentalmente la puerta • **to lock yourself out** quedarse fuera *(por olvidarse la llave dentro)* ❷ dejar fuera a
■ **lock up** *vt* ☼ *El objeto se puede colocar antes o después de la preposición.* ❶ encerrar ❷ internar ❸ cerrar (con llave)

locker ['lɒkər] *s* casillero; locker

locker room *s* vestidor

locomotive ['ləʊkə,məʊtɪv] *s* locomotora

locum ['ləʊkəm] *s* interino, na

> El plural de **locum** es **locums**.

locust ['ləʊkəst] *s* langosta *(insecto)*

lodge [lɒdʒ] ◆ *s* ❶ portería ❷ casa del guarda ❸ refugio ◆ *vi* alojarse ◆ *vt formal* presentar *(apelación, queja)*

lodger ['lɒdʒər] *s* huésped

lodgings ['lɒdʒɪŋz] *spl* habitación (alquilada)

loft [lɒft] *s* ❶ desván ❷ pajar ❸ almacén reformado y convertido en apartamento

log [lɒg] ◆ *s* ❶ tronco ❷ leño ❸ diario de a bordo ❹ *INFORMÁTICA* registro ◆ *vt* registrar
■ **log in** *vi INFORMÁTICA* entrar
■ **log off** *vi INFORMÁTICA* salir
■ **log on** *vi INFORMÁTICA* entrar
■ **log out** *vi INFORMÁTICA* salir

logbook ['lɒgbʊk] *s* ❶ diario de a bordo ❷ diario de vuelo ❸ documentación *(de vehículo)*

logic ['lɒdʒɪk] *s* lógica

logical ['lɒdʒɪkl] *adj* lógico, ca

logistics [lə'dʒɪstɪks] ◆ *s* ☼ *incontable* logística ◆ *spl* logística

logo ['ləʊgəʊ] *s* logotipo

> El plural de **logo** es **logos**.

logrolling ['lɒgrəʊlɪŋ] *s* ☼ *incontable* acción de alabar o respaldar el trabajo de alguien para recibir después el mismo trato

loin [lɔɪn] *s* lomo

loiter ['lɔɪtər] *vi* ❶ merodear ❷ vagar

lollipop ['lɒlɪpɒp] *s* paleta

London ['lʌndən] *s* Londres

Londoner ['lʌndənər] *s* londinense

lone [ləʊn] *adj* solitario, ria

loneliness ['ləʊnlɪnɪs] *s* soledad

lonely ['ləʊnlɪ] *adj* ❶ solo, la ❷ solitario, ria

lonesome ['ləʊnsəm] *adj familiar* ❶ solo, la ❷ solitario, ria

long [lɒŋ] ◆ *adj* largo, ga • **the table is 5 feet long** la mesa mide 150 cm de largo • **two days long** de dos días de duración • **the journey is 50km long** el viaje es de 50 km • **the book is 500 pages long** el libro tiene 500 páginas • **a long time** mucho tiempo • **a long way from** muy lejos de ◆ *adv* mucho tiempo • **how long will it take?** ¿cuánto se tarda? • **how long will you be?** ¿cuánto tardarás? • **how long have you been waiting?** ¿cuánto tiempo llevas esperando? • **how long have you known them?** ¿cuánto hace que los conoces? • **how long is the journey?** ¿cuánto hay de

viaje? • **I'm no longer young** ya no soy joven • **I can't wait any longer** no puedo esperar más • **I'll wait as long as you like** esperaré todo el tiempo que quieras • **as long as a week** hasta una semana • **before long** pronto • **for long** mucho tiempo

> *expresión* **so long** *familiar* hasta luego o pronto

◆ *vt* • **to long to do something** desear ardientemente hacer algo
■ **as long as, so long as** *conjunción* mientras • **as long as you do it, so will I** siempre y cuando tú lo hagas, yo también lo haré
■ **long for** *vt* ☼ *El objeto siempre va después de la preposición al final.* desear ardientemente

long-distance *adj* de fondo *(corredor)*

long-distance call *s* llamada de larga distancia

longhand ['lɒŋhænd] *s* escritura a mano

long-haul *adj* de larga distancia

longing ['lɒŋɪŋ] ◆ *adj* anhelante ◆ *s* ❶ anhelo; deseo ❷ nostalgia; añoranza ❸ • **(a) longing (for)** (un) ansia (de)

longitude ['lɒndʒɪtjuːd] *s* longitud

long jump *s* salto de longitud

long-life *adj* de larga duración

long-range *adj* ❶ de largo alcance *(misil)* ❷ a largo plazo

longshoreman ['lɒŋʃɔːmən] *s* estibador

long shot *s* posibilidad remota

longsighted [,lɒŋ'saɪtɪd] *adj* présbita

long-standing *adj* antiguo, gua

long term *s* • **in the long term** a largo plazo

long wave *s* ☼ *incontable* onda larga

longwearing [,lɒŋ'weərɪŋ] *adj* resistente

long weekend *s* puente

longwinded [,lɒŋ'wɪndɪd] *adj* prolijo, ja

look [lʊk] ◆ *s* ❶ mirada • **to give somebody a look** mirar a alguien • **to take** o **have a look (at something)** mirar algo • **let her have a look** déjale ver • **to have a look through something** ojear algo ❷ • **to have a look (for something)** buscar (algo) ❸ aspecto • **his new look** su nuevo look • **I don't like the look of it** no me gusta nada • **by the look** o **looks of it, it has been here for ages** parece que hace años que está aquí ◆ *vi* ❶ • **to look (at something/somebody)** mirar (algo/a alguien) ❷ • **to look (for something/somebody)** buscar (algo/a alguien) ❸ • **to look (out) onto** dar a ❹ verse ❺ parecer • **it looks as if it's going to snow** parece que va a nevar ◆ *vt* ❶ mirar ❷ • **to look your age** representar la edad que se tiene
■ **looks** *spl* belleza
■ **look after** *vt* ☼ *El objeto siempre va después de la preposición al final.* ❶ cuidar ❷ encargarse de
■ **look around** ◆ *vt* ☼ *El objeto siempre va después de la preposición al final.* ❶ echar un vistazo a ❷ visitar ◆ *vi* ❶ voltear la cabeza ❷ mirar *(en una tienda)*
■ **look at** *vt* ☼ *El objeto siempre va después de la preposición al final.* ❶ mirar ❷ examinar ❸ echar un vistazo a ❹ ver

■ **look down on** *vt* ☼: *El objeto siempre va después de la preposición al final.* despreciar

■ **look for** *vt* ☼: *El objeto siempre va después de la preposición al final.* buscar

■ **look forward to** *vt* ☼: *El objeto siempre va después de la preposición al final.* esperar (con ilusión) • **to be looking forward to doing something** estar deseando hacer algo

■ **look into** *vt* ☼: *El objeto siempre va después de la preposición al final.* ❶ estudiar ❷ investigar

■ **look on** *vi* mirar; observar

■ **look out** *vi* tener cuidado • **look out!** ¡cuidado!

■ **look out for** *vt* ☼: *El objeto siempre va después de la preposición al final.* estar atento, ta a

■ **look over** *vt* ☼: *El objeto se puede colocar antes o después de la preposición.* mirar por encima

■ **look to** *vt* ☼: *El objeto siempre va después de la preposición al final.* ❶ recurrir a ❷ pensar en

■ **look up** ◆ *vt* ☼: *El objeto se puede colocar antes o después de la preposición.* ❶ buscar *(en un libro)* ❷ ir a ver o visitar ◆ *vi* mejorar

■ **look up to** *vt* ☼: *El objeto siempre va después de la preposición al final.* respetar; admirar

lookout ['lʊkaʊt] *s* ❶ puesto de observación ❷ centinela ❸ • **to be on the lookout for** estar al acecho de

loom [luːm] ◆ *s* telar ◆ *vi* surgir o aparecer amenazante

■ **loom up** *vi* divisarse sombríamente

loony ['luːnɪ] *familiar* ◆ *adj* loco, ca ◆ *s* loco, ca

loop [luːp] ◆ *s* ❶ lazo ❷ INFORMÁTICA bucle
expresión **to be out of the loop** no estar al corriente
◆ *vt* • **to loop something round something** pasar algo alrededor de algo ◆ *vi* hacer un lazo

loophole ['luːphəʊl] *s* laguna

loose [luːs] ◆ *adj* ❶ flojo, ja • **to come loose** aflojarse ❷ suelto, ta ❸ suelto, ta *(ropa)* ❹ impreciso, sa
expresión **to stay loose** *familiar* estar tranqui
◆ *s* ☼: *incontable* • **to be on the loose** andar suelto, ta

loose change *s* (dinero) suelto; feria

loose end *s* • **to be at loose ends** no tener nada que hacer

loosely ['luːslɪ] *adv* ❶ holgadamente; sin apretar ❷ vagamente

loosen ['luːsn] *vt* aflojar

■ **loosen up** *vi* ❶ desentumecerse ❷ *familiar* relajarse

loot [luːt] ◆ *s* botín ◆ *vt* saquear

looting ['luːtɪŋ] *s* saqueo

lop [lɒp] *vt* podar

■ **lop off** *vt* ☼: *El objeto se puede colocar antes o después de la preposición.* cortar

lop-sided [-'saɪdɪd] *adj* ladeado, da; torcido, da

Lord [lɔːd] *s* ❶ RELIGIÓN • **the Lord** el Señor ❷ lord ❸ • **my Lord a)** su Señoría

Lordship ['lɔːdʃɪp] *s* • **your/his Lordship** su Señoría

lose [luːz] ◆ *vt* perder • **to lose your way** perderse • **my watch has lost ten minutes** mi reloj se ha atrasado diez minutos • **to lose yourself in something** *figurado* quedarse absorto, ta en algo ◆ *vi* perder
Formas irregulares de **lose**: *pretérito & pp* **lost**.

loser ['luːzər] *s* ❶ perdedor, ra • **he's a bad loser** es un mal perdedor ❷ *familiar & despectivo* desgraciado, da

loss [lɒs] *s* ❶ pérdida • **to make a loss** sufrir pérdidas ❷ derrota

lost [lɒst] ◆ *pretérito & participio pasado* → **lose** ◆ *adj* ❶ perdido, da • **to get lost** perderse ❷ extraviado, da; perdido, da
expresión **get lost!** *familiar* ¡vete a la porra!

lost-and-found office *s* oficina de objetos perdidos

lot [lɒt] *s* ❶ • **a lot of, lots of** mucho, cha • **a lot of people** mucha gente; muchas personas • **a lot of problems** muchos problemas • **the lot** todo ❷ lote ❸ destino; suerte ❹ terreno ❺ aparcamiento
expresión **to draw lots** echar a suerte
■ **a lot** *adv* mucho • **quite a lot** bastante • **such a lot** tanto

---

lot

Lots y lots of son de un registro algo más informal que a lot y a lot of.

En las oraciones interrogativas y negativas, muchas veces se reemplaza a lot (of) y lots (of) con much (con incontables) y many (con plurales) (I haven't got **much** time *no tengo mucho tiempo*; were there **many** people at the party? *¿había mucha gente en la fiesta?*). A lot (of) y lots of se pueden utilizar para dar énfasis a lo que se está expresando (there's not *a lot* to do here *no hay mucho que hacer aquí*; lots of people don't agree *hay mucha gente que no está de acuerdo*).

---

lotion ['ləʊʃn] *s* loción

lottery ['lɒtərɪ] *s* lotería

lottery ticket *s* billete de lotería

loud [laʊd] ◆ *adj* ❶ alto, ta *(voz, música)* ❷ fuerte *(explosión, ruido)* ❸ ruidoso, sa ❹ chillón, ona *(colores)* ◆ *adv* fuerte *(hablar)* • **out loud** en voz alta

loudly ['laʊdlɪ] *adv* ❶ a voz en grito *(gritar)* ❷ en voz alta *(hablar)* ❸ con colores chillones

loudspeaker [ˌlaʊd'spiːkər] *s* altavoz

lounge [laʊndʒ] ◆ *s* sala de espera ◆ *vi* flojear

louse [laʊs] *s* (pl lice) piojo

lousy ['laʊzɪ] *adj familiar* fatal; pésimo, ma

lout [laʊt] *s* gamberro

louver ['luːvər] *s* persiana

love [lʌv] ◆ s ❶ amor • **the love she felt for her children** el amor que sentía por sus hijos • **to be in love (with)** estar enamorado, da (de) • **to fall in love with somebody** enamorarse de alguien • **to make love** hacer el amor ❷ abrazo • **give her my love** dale un abrazo de mi parte • **love from** un abrazo de • **she sends her love** te manda recuerdos ❸ pasión • **a love of** o **for** una pasión por ❹ *familiar* cariño *(en apelativos)* ❺ TENIS • **30 love** 30 a nada ◆ vt ❶ amar ❷ querer ❸ • **I love golf** me encanta el golf • **I love going to the theater** me encanta ir al teatro

love affair s aventura amorosa

love life s vida amorosa

lovely ['lʌvlɪ] adj ❶ encantador, ra ❷ precioso, sa ❸ estupendo, da • **we had a lovely time** lo pasamos muy bien

lover ['lʌvər] s amante

love song s canción de amor

loving ['lʌvɪŋ] adj cariñoso, sa

low [ləʊ] ◆ adj ❶ bajo, ja • **in the low twenties** 20 y algo ❷ escaso, sa *(reservas)* ❸ malo, la *(opinión)*; poco, ca *(estima)* ❹ tenue *(luz)* ❺ escotado, da ❻ deprimido, da ◆ adv ❶ bajo • **the batteries are running low** las pilas están acabándose • **morale is running very low** la moral está por los suelos • **low paid** mal pagado ❷ en voz baja ◆ s ❶ punto más bajo ❷ METEOROLOGÍA área de bajas presiones ❸ mínima

low-calorie adj light; bajo, ja en calorías

low-cut adj escotado, da

lower ['ləʊər] ◆ adj inferior ◆ vt ❶ bajar ❷ arriar ❸ reducir

low-fat adj bajo, ja en grasas

low-lying adj bajo, ja

loyal ['lɔɪəl] adj leal; fiel

loyalty ['lɔɪəltɪ] s lealtad

lozenge ['lɒzɪndʒ] s ❶ pastilla ❷ rombo

LP *(abreviatura de* long-playing record*)* s LP

Ltd, ltd *(abreviatura escrita de* limited*)* S.L.

lubricant ['luːbrɪkənt] s lubricante

lubricate ['luːbrɪkeɪt] vt lubricar

lucid ['luːsɪd] adj ❶ claro, ra ❷ lúcido, da

luck [lʌk] s suerte • **good/bad luck** buena/mala suerte • **good luck!** ¡suerte! • **bad** o **hard luck!** ¡mala suerte! • **to be in luck** estar de suerte • **to try your luck at something** probar suerte con algo • **with (any) luck** con un poco de suerte

■ **luck out** vi *familiar* tener suerte

luckily ['lʌkɪlɪ] adv afortunadamente

lucky ['lʌkɪ] adj ❶ afortunado, da • **to be lucky** tener suerte • **it's lucky he came** fue una suerte que llegara ❷ oportuno, na ❸ • **to be lucky** dar suerte • **horseshoes are lucky** las herraduras dan suerte • **a lucky charm** un amuleto

lucrative ['luːkrətɪv] adj lucrativo, va

ludicrous ['luːdɪkrəs] adj absurdo, da

lug [lʌg] vt *familiar* arrastrar

luggage rack s portaequipajes

lukewarm ['luːkwɔːm] adj ❶ tibio, bia; templado, da ❷ indiferente

lull [lʌl] ◆ s

expresión **the lull before the storm** la calma antes de la tormenta

◆ vt • **to lull somebody into a false sense of security** infundir una sensación de falsa seguridad a alguien • **to lull somebody to sleep** adormecer a alguien

lullaby ['lʌləbaɪ] s nana; canción de cuna

lumber ['lʌmbər] s ⚙ *incontable* maderas

lumberjack ['lʌmbədʒæk] s leñador, ra

lumbermill ['lʌmbəˌmɪl] s aserradero; serrería

lump [lʌmp] ◆ s ❶ trozo ❷ terrón ❸ grumo ❹ bulto ◆ vt • **to lump something together a)** amontonar algo **b)** agrupar o juntar algo

lump sum s cantidad global

lumpy ['lʌmpɪ] *(comparativo* lumpier, *superlativo* lumpiest*)* adj grumoso, sa

lunatic ['luːnətɪk] s ❶ *despectivo* idiota ❷ loco, ca

lunch [lʌntʃ] ◆ s comida • **to have lunch** comer • **what did you have for lunch?** ¿qué comiste? • **why don't we do lunch some time?** ¿por qué no comemos juntos algún día de estos? ◆ vi comer

lunch hour s hora de la comida

lunchtime ['lʌntʃtaɪm] s hora del almuerzo

lung [lʌŋ] s pulmón

lunge [lʌndʒ] vi lanzarse • **to lunge at somebody** arremeter contra alguien

lurch [lɜːtʃ] ◆ s ❶ bandazo ❷ tumbo

expresión **to leave somebody in the lurch** dejar a alguien en la estacada

◆ vi ❶ dar bandazos ❷ tambalearse

lure [ljʊər] vt atraer

lurid ['ljʊərɪd] adj ❶ chillón, ona ❷ espeluznante ❸ escabroso, sa

lurk [lɜːk] vi ❶ estar al acecho ❷ ocultarse *(peligro, miedo)*

luscious ['lʌʃəs] adj *literal & figurado* apetitoso, sa

lush [lʌʃ] ◆ adj exuberante ◆ s *familiar* borracho, cha

lust [lʌst] s ❶ lujuria ❷ • **lust for something** ansia de algo

■ **lust after, lust for** vt ⚙ *El objeto siempre va después de la preposición al final.* ❶ codiciar ❷ desear

Luxembourg ['lʌksəmˌbɜːg] s Luxemburgo

luxurious [lʌgˈʒʊərɪəs] adj ❶ lujoso, sa ❷ de lujo

luxury ['lʌkʃərɪ] ◆ s lujo ◆ *en compuestos* de lujo

LW *(abreviatura de* long wave*)* s OL

Lycra® ['laɪkrə] s lycra®

lying ['laɪɪŋ] ◆ adj mentiroso, sa ◆ s ⚙ *incontable* mentiras

lynch [lɪntʃ] vt linchar

lyrics ['lɪrɪks] spl letra *(de canción)*

M

m¹, M [em] *s* m; M

Dos plurales: **m's** o **ms; M's** o **Ms.**

m² ❶ *(abreviatura escrita de* meter) m ❷ *(abreviatura escrita de* million) m ❸ *abreviatura escrita de* **mile**

MA *s abreviatura escrita de* **Master of Arts**

macaroni [ˌmækəˈrəʊnɪ] *s* ☼ *incontable* macarrones

machine [məˈʃiːn] *s* máquina

machinegun [məˈʃiːngʌn] *s* ❶ ametralladora ❷ metralleta

machinery [məˈʃiːnərɪ] *s literal & figurado* maquinaria

macho [ˈmætʃəʊ] *adj familiar* macho

mackerel [ˈmækrəl] *s* caballa

Dos plurales: **mackerel** o **mackerels.**

mad [mæd] *adj* ❶ loco, ca • **to be mad about somebody/something** estar loco, ca por alguien/algo • **to go mad** volverse loco ❷ disparatado, da ❸ furioso, sa • **to be mad at somebody** estar furioso con alguien ❹ desenfrenado, da

madam [ˈmædəm] *s* ❶ señora ❷ madam

madden [ˈmædn] *vt* volver loco, ca

made [meɪd] *pretérito & participio pasado* → **make**

made-up *adj* ❶ maquillado, da; pintado, da ❷ inventado, da

madly [ˈmædlɪ] *adv* enloquecidamente • **madly in love** locamente enamorado

madman [ˈmædmən] *s* loco

El plural de **madman** es **madmen** [ˈmædmən].

madness [ˈmædnɪs] *s* locura

Mafia [ˈmæfɪə] *s* • **the Mafia** la mafia

magazine [ˌmægəˈziːn] *s* revista

maggot [ˈmægət] *s* gusano; larva

magic [ˈmædʒɪk] ◆ *adj* mágico, ca ◆ *s* magia • **a magic trick** un truco de magia

magical [ˈmædʒɪkl] *adj literal & figurado* mágico, ca

magician [məˈdʒɪʃn] *s* ❶ prestidigitador, ra ❷ mago

magic wand *s* varita mágica

magistrate [ˈmædʒɪstreɪt] *s* juez de primera instancia

magnesium [mægˈniːzɪəm] *s* magnesio

magnet [ˈmægnɪt] *s* imán

magnetic [mægˈnetɪk] *adj* ❶ magnético, ca ❷ *figurado* carismático, ca

magnificent [mægˈnɪfɪsənt] *adj* ❶ grandioso, sa ❷ magnífico, ca

magnify [ˈmægnɪfaɪ] *vt* aumentar; ampliar

magnifying glass [ˈmægnɪfaɪɪŋ-] *s* lupa

magpie [ˈmægpaɪ] *s* urraca

mahogany [məˈhɒgənɪ] *s* caoba

maid [meɪd] *s* ❶ criada ❷ recamarera *(de hotel)*

maiden [ˈmeɪdn] ◆ *adj* inaugural ◆ *s literario* doncella

maiden name *s* nombre de soltera

mail [meɪl] ◆ *s* ❶ correo • **by mail** por correo ❷ correspondencia ❸ correo electrónico; mail • **you have mail** tienes mails ◆ *vt* ❶ mandar por correo ❷ echar al buzón

mailbox [ˈmeɪlbɒks] *s* buzón

mailing list [ˈmeɪlɪŋ-] *s* ❶ lista de distribución de publicidad o información ❷ INFORMÁTICA lista de correo

mailman [ˈmeɪlmən] *s* cartero

El plural de **mailman** es **mailmen** [ˈmeɪlmən].

mail order *s* venta por correo

mailshot [ˈmeɪlʃɒt] *s* folleto de publicidad (por correo)

maim [meɪm] *vt* mutilar

main [meɪn] ◆ *adj* principal ◆ *s* ❶ tubería principal ❷ cable principal

expresión **in the main** por lo general

■ **mains** *spl* • **the mains** la tubería principal

main course *s* plato principal

mainland [ˈmeɪnlənd] ◆ *adj* continental • **mainland Spain** la Península ◆ *s* • **on the mainland** en tierra firme

mainly [ˈmeɪnlɪ] *adv* principalmente

main road *s* carretera principal

mainstream ['meɪnstriːm] ◆ *adj* ❶ predominante ❷ corriente ❸ convencional ◆ *s* • **the mainstream** la tendencia general

maintain [meɪn'teɪn] *vt* ❶ mantener ❷ sostener • **to maintain (that)** sostener que

maintenance ['meɪntənəns] *s* ❶ mantenimiento ❷ pensión alimenticia

maisonette [ˌmeɪzə'net] *s* dúplex

maize [meɪz] *s* maíz

majestic [mə'dʒestɪk] *adj* majestuoso, sa

Majesty ['mædʒəstɪ] *s* • **His/Her/Your Majesty** Su Majestad

major ['meɪdʒər] ◆ *adj* ❶ importante • **of major importance** de gran importancia ❷ principal ❸ MÚSICA mayor ◆ *s* ❶ MILITAR comandante ❷ especialidad; asignatura principal ◆ *vi* • **to major in** especializarse en

majority [mə'dʒɒrətɪ] *s* mayoría

make [meɪk]
◆ *vt*
❶ [*producir*] hacer
• **she makes her own clothes** se hace su propia ropa
• **to make a meal** hacer una comida
❷ [*con sustantivos*]
• **to make a speech** dar un discurso
• **to make a decision** tomar una decisión
• **to make a mistake** cometer un error
• **to make a payment** efectuar un pago
• **to make the bed** hacer la cama
❸ [*con emociones*]
• **it makes me sick** me pone enfermo
• **it makes me want to...** me da ganas de...
• **it made him angry** hizo que se enfadara
• **you made me jump!** ¡vaya susto que me has dado!
• **to make somebody happy** hacer a alguien feliz
• **to make somebody sad** poner a alguien triste
❹ [*forzar*]
• **to make somebody do something** hacer que alguien haga algo; obligar a alguien a hacer algo
❺ [*indicando material, construcción*]
• **it's made of wood/metal** es de madera/metal; está hecho de madera/metal
• **made in China** fabricado en China
❻ MATEMÁTICAS ser
• **2 and 2 make 4** 2 y 2 son 4
❼ [*con cantidades, la hora*] calcular
• **I make it 50/six o'clock** calculo que serán 50/las seis
• **what time do you make it?** ¿qué hora tienes?
❽ [*dinero, ganancia*] ganar
• **to make a profit** obtener beneficios
• **to make a loss** sufrir pérdidas
❾ [*indicando calidades*] ser
• **she'd make a good doctor** seguro que sería una buena doctora

❿ [*indicando relaciones, amistades*]
• **to make friends with somebody** hacerse amigo de alguien

expresiones **to make do** arreglárselas ▶ **to make do with something** conformarse con algo ▶ **to make it a)** conseguir llegar a tiempo **b)** alcanzar el éxito **c)** venir/ir *(a una fiesta, cita)* **d)** vivir
◆ *s*
marca
■ **make for**
◆ *vt* ☼ *El objeto siempre va después de la preposición al final.*
dirigirse a o hacia
■ **make into**
◆ *vt* ☼ *El objeto se coloca entre el verbo y la preposición.*
• **to make something into something** convertir algo en algo
■ **make of**
◆ *vt* ☼ *El objeto siempre va después de la preposición al final.*
❶ [*comprender*] entender
• **what do you make of this word?** ¿qué entiendes tú por esta palabra?
❷ [*opinión*] opinar de
■ **make off**
◆ *vi*
darse a la fuga
■ **make out**
◆ *vt* ☼ *El objeto se puede colocar antes o después de la preposición.*
❶ *familiar* distinguir
❷ entender; oír
❸ *familiar* descifrar *(número, palabra)*; comprender *(actitud)*
❹ rellenar *(formulario)*; extender *(cheque, factura)*; hacer *(lista)*
❺ *familiar* [*fingir*]
• **to make yourself out to be something** dárselas de algo
■ **make up**
◆ *vt* ☼ *El objeto se puede colocar antes o después de la preposición.*
❶ componer; constituir
❷ inventar
❸ maquillar
❹ preparar *(paquete, receta médica)*
❺ completar *(cantidad)*; cubrir *(diferencia)*; recuperar *(déficit, tiempo perdido)*
expresión **to make up your mind** decidirse
◆ *vi*
reconciliarse
◆ *s*
examen que se realiza más tarde si no se pudo hacer en su día

■ **make up for**
◆ *vt* ⌖ *El objeto siempre va después de la preposición al final.*
compensar
• **to make up for lost time** recuperar el tiempo perdido
Formas irregulares de **make**: *pretérito* & *pp* **made.**

make-believe *s* ⌖ *incontable* fantasías

makeover ['meɪkəʊvər] *s* ❶ cambio de imagen ❷ reforma completa

maker ['meɪkər] *s* ❶ creador, ra ❷ fabricante

makeshift ['meɪkʃɪft] *adj* ❶ provisional ❷ improvisado, da

make-up *s* ❶ maquillaje • **to wear make-up** maquillarse ❯ **make-up remover** loción desmaquilladora ❷ carácter ❸ estructura ❹ composición *(de un equipo)*

making ['meɪkɪŋ] *s* ❶ fabricación ❷ rodaje
expresiones **your problems are of your own making** tus problemas te los has buscado tú mismo ❯ **to be the making of somebody/something** ser la causa del éxito de alguien/algo ❯ **to have the makings of** tener madera de

malaria [məˈleərɪə] *s* malaria

Malaysia [məˈleɪzɪə] *s* Malaisia

male [meɪl] ◆ *adj* ❶ macho ❷ masculino, na; varón ◆ *s* ❶ macho ❷ varón

male nurse *s* enfermero

malfunction [mælˈfʌŋkʃn] ◆ *s* fallo ◆ *vi* averiarse

malice ['mælɪs] *s* malicia

malicious [məˈlɪʃəs] *adj* malicioso, sa

malignant [məˈlɪɡnənt] *adj* MEDICINA maligno, na

mall [mɔːl] *s* • **(shopping) mall** centro comercial

mallet ['mælɪt] *s* mazo

malnutrition [ˌmælnjuːˈtrɪʃn] *s* malnutrición

malt [mɔːlt] *s* ❶ malta ❷ whisky de malta ❸ leche malteada con helado

mammal ['mæml] *s* mamífero

mammogram ['mæməɡræm] *s* MEDICINA mamografía

mammoth ['mæməθ] ◆ *adj* descomunal ◆ *s* mamut

man [mæn] ◆ *s* ❶ hombre • **an old man** un viejo • **a young man** un joven • **el hombre**
expresión **the man in the street** el hombre de la calle
❯ **to be man enough to do something** ser lo suficientemente hombre para hacer algo
◆ *vt* ❶ manejar ❷ tripular • **manned 24 hours a day** en servicio las 24 horas del día
El plural de **man** es **men** [men].

manage ['mænɪdʒ] ◆ *vi* ❶ poder • **I can manage by myself** puedo solo ❷ arreglárselas • **tendrán que arreglárselas** they'll just have to manage ◆ *vt* ❶ • **to manage to do something** conseguir hacer algo ❷ dirigir; llevar *(una empresa)* ❸ administrar; manejar

(dinero) ❹ representar *(famoso, músico)* ❺ organizar *(el tiempo)* ❻ poder con • **can you manage that box?** ¿puedes con la caja?

manageable ['mænɪdʒəbl] *adj* ❶ factible; posible ❷ controlable

management ['mænɪdʒmənt] *s* ❶ gestión ❷ dirección

management studies *spl* administración de empresas

manager ['mænɪdʒər] *s* ❶ director, ra; gerente ❷ jefe, fa; encargado, da ❸ manager ❹ DEPORTE ≃ director técnico

manageress [ˌmænɪdʒəˈres] *s* jefa

managerial [ˌmænɪˈdʒɪərɪəl] *adj* directivo, va

managing director ['mænɪdʒɪŋ-] *s* director, ra gerente

mandarin ['mændərɪn] *s* mandarina

mandate ['mændeɪt] *s* ❶ mandato • **to have a mandate to do something** tener autoridad para hacer algo ❷ misión

mandatory ['mændətrɪ] *adj* obligatorio, ria

mane [meɪn] *s* ❶ crin ❷ melena *(de león)*

maneuver [məˈnuːvər] ◆ *s literal & figurado* maniobra ◆ *vt* maniobrar ◆ *vi* maniobrar

manfully ['mænfʊlɪ] *adv* valientemente

mangle ['mæŋɡl] *vt* ❶ aplastar ❷ despedazar

mango ['mæŋɡəʊ] *s* mango
Dos plurales: **mangoes** o **mangos.**

mangy ['meɪndʒɪ] *adj* sarnoso, sa

manhandle ['mæn,hændl] *vt* • **they manhandled her into the van** la metieron en el camión a empujones

Manhattan

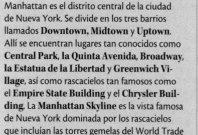

MANHATTAN

Manhattan es el distrito central de la ciudad de Nueva York. Se divide en los tres barrios llamados **Downtown**, **Midtown** y **Uptown**. Allí se encuentran lugares tan conocidos como **Central Park, la Quinta Avenida, Broadway, la Estatua de la Libertad y Greenwich Village**, así como rascacielos tan famosos como el **Empire State Building** y el **Chrysler Building**. La **Manhattan Skyline** es la vista famosa de Nueva York dominada por los rascacielos que incluían las torres gemelas del World Trade Center, hasta la destrucción de éstas en los ataques terroristas del 11 de septiembre del 2001.

manhole ['mænhəʊl] *s* boca (del alcantarillado)

manhood ['mænhʊd] *s* ❶ virilidad ❷ edad adulta

mania ['meɪnjə] *s* ❶ • **mania (for)** pasión (por) ❷ PSICOLOGÍA manía

M

maniac ['meɪnɪæk] *s* ❶ maníaco, ca ❷ fanático, ca

manic ['mænɪk] *adj* maníaco, ca

manicure ['mænɪˌkjʊər] *s* manicura

manifesto [ˌmænɪ'festəʊ] *s* manifiesto
Dos plurales: **manifestos** o **manifestoes**.

manipulate [mə'nɪpjʊleɪt] *vt* ❶ manipular ❷ manejar

mankind [mæn'kaɪnd] *s* la humanidad

manly ['mænlɪ] *adj* varonil; viril

man-made *adj* ❶ producido, da por el hombre ❷ artificial ❸ sintético, ca

manner ['mænər] *s* ❶ manera • **she treated me in a decent manner** me trató de manera amable ❷ actitud

■ **manners** *spl* modales • **good/bad manners** buenos/malos modales • **it's good/bad manners to do something** es de buena/mala educación hacer algo

mannerism ['mænərɪzm] *s* costumbre (típica de uno)

manor ['mænər] *s* casa solariega

manpower ['mæn,paʊər] *s* ❶ mano de obra ❷ personal

mansion ['mænʃn] *s* ❶ casa solariega ❷ casa grande

manslaughter ['mæn,slɔ:tər] *s* homicidio involuntario

mantelpiece ['mæntlpi:s] *s* repisa (de la chimenea)

manual ['mænjʊəl] *adj* & *s* manual

manual worker *s* obrero, ra

manufacture [ˌmænjʊ'fæktʃər] ◆ *s* fabricación ◆ *vt* fabricar

manufacturer [ˌmænjʊ'fæktʃərər] *s* fabricante

manure [mə'njʊər] *s* estiércol

manuscript ['mænjʊskrɪpt] *s* ❶ manuscrito ❷ hoja de examen

many ['menɪ] ◆ *adj* (comparativo more, superlativo most) muchos, chas • **many people** muchas personas; mucha gente • **how many?** ¿cuántos, tas? • **I wonder how many people went** me pregunto cuánta gente fue • **too many** demasiados, das • **I ate too many chocolates** comí demasiados chocolates • **there weren't too many students** no había muchos estudiantes • **as many... as** tantos, tas... como • **they have three times as many soldiers as us** tienen el triple de soldados que nosotros • **so many** tantos, tas • **I've never seen so many people** nunca había visto tanta gente • **a good o great many** muchísimos, mas ◆ *pronombre* muchos, chas • **twice as many** el doble • **four times as many** cuatro veces esa cantidad • **take as many as you like** toma todos los que quieras

many

Many se emplea principalmente en oraciones interrogativas (were there *many* people at the party? *¿había mucha gente en la fiesta?*) y negativas (I didn't get *many* presents for my birthday *no tuve muchos regalos por el cumpleaños*). En oraciones afirmativas, se suele usar a lot (of) o lots (of), si bien many sirve para construir expresiones como too many, how many y so many.
Ver también lot, plenty.

map [mæp] *s* ❶ mapa ❷ plano

■ **map out** *vt* ☀️ *El objeto se puede colocar antes o después de la preposición.* planear; planificar

maple ['meɪpl] *s* maple

maple syrup *s* miel de maple

marathon ['mærəθən] *s* maratón

marble ['mɑ:bl] *s* ❶ mármol ❷ canica

march [mɑ:tʃ] ◆ *s* ❶ MILITAR marcha ❷ avance (progreso) ◆ *vi* ❶ marchar ❷ • **to march up to somebody** abordar a alguien decididamente ◆ *vt* llevar por la fuerza

March [mɑ:tʃ] *s* marzo ver también **September**

marcher ['mɑ:tʃər] *s* manifestante

mare [meər] *s* yegua

margarine [ˌmɑ:dʒə'ri:n] [ˌmɑ:gə'ri:n] *s* margarina

margin ['mɑ:dʒɪn] *s* margen

marginal ['mɑ:dʒɪnl] *adj* marginal

marginally ['mɑ:dʒɪnəlɪ] *adv* ligeramente

marigold ['mærɪgəʊld] *s* caléndula

marihuana, marijuana [ˌmærɪ'wɑ:nə] *s* marihuana

marine [mə'ri:n] ◆ *adj* marino, na ◆ *s* infante de marina

expresión go tell it to the marines! *familiar* ¡cuéntaselo a tu abuela!

marital ['mærɪtl] *adj* matrimonial

marital status *s* estado civil

maritime ['mærɪtaɪm] *adj* marítimo, ma

mark [mɑ:k] ◆ *s* ❶ mancha ❷ marca ❸ señal ❹ nota (en examen) ❺ punto ❻ • **once past the half-way mark** una vez llegado a medio camino ❼ huella ◆ *vt* ❶ manchar ❷ marcar ❸ señalar ❹ puntuar; calificar ❺ conmemorar

■ **mark off** *vt* ☀️ *El objeto se puede colocar antes o después de la preposición.* poner una marca en

marked [mɑ:kt] *adj* ❶ notable (mejora) ❷ acusado, da (diferencia)

marker ['mɑ:kər] *s* ❶ señal ❷ DEPORTE marcador, ora

marker pen *s* rotulador

market ['mɑ:kɪt] ◆ *s* mercado ◆ *vt* comercializar

market garden *s* huerta

marketing ['mɑ:kɪtɪŋ] *s* ❶ marketing ❷ comercialización

marketplace ['mɑːkɪtpleɪs] *s literal & figurado* mercado

market research *s* estudio de mercados

marking ['mɑːkɪŋ] *s* ❶ corrección ❷ *DEPORTE* marcaje

■ **markings** *spl* ❶ pintas *(de flor, animal)* ❷ señales *(en carretera)*

marksman ['mɑːksmən] *s* tirador

El plural de **marksman** es **marksmen** ['mɑːksmen].

marmalade ['mɑːməleɪd] *s* mermelada *(de cítricos)*

maroon [mə'ruːn] *adj* granate

marooned [mə'ruːnd] *adj* incomunicado, da; aislado, da

marquee [mɑː'kiː] *s* ❶ carpa; toldo grande ❷ marquesina

marriage ['mærɪdʒ] *s* ❶ boda ❷ matrimonio

marriage certificate *s* certificado de matrimonio

marriage guidance *s* asesoría matrimonial

married ['mærɪd] *adj* ❶ casado, da • **a married couple** un matrimonio ❷ matrimonial

marrow ['mærəʊ] *s* médula

marry ['mærɪ] ◆ *vt* ❶ casarse con • **to get married** casarse ❷ casar ◆ *vi* casarse

Mars [mɑːz] *s* Marte

marsh [mɑːʃ] *s* ❶ zona pantanosa ❷ pantano

marshal ['mɑːʃl] ◆ *s* ❶ *MILITAR* mariscal ❷ oficial; miembro del servicio de orden ❸ jefe, fa de policía ◆ *vt* dirigir; conducir

martial arts [ˌmɑːʃl-] *spl* artes marciales

martyr ['mɑːtər] *s* mártir

martyrdom ['mɑːtədəm] *s* martirio

marvel ['mɑːvl] ◆ *s* maravilla ◆ *vi* • **to marvel (at)** maravillarse o asombrarse (ante)

marvelous ['mɑːvələs] *adj* maravilloso, sa

Marxism ['mɑːksɪzm] *s* marxismo

Marxist ['mɑːksɪst] *adj & s* marxista

marzipan ['mɑːzɪpæn] *s* mazapán

mascara [mæs'kɑːrə] *s* rímel

masculine ['mæskjʊlɪn] *adj* ❶ masculino, na ❷ hombruno, na

mash [mæʃ] *vt* hacer puré

mashed potatoes [mæʃt] *spl* puré de patatas

mask [mɑːsk] ◆ *s literal & figurado* máscara ◆ *vt* ❶ enmascarar ❷ ocultar; disfrazar

masochist ['mæsəkɪst] *s* masoquista

mason ['meɪsn] *s* ❶ cantero ❷ masón

masonry ['meɪsnrɪ] *s* albañilería

mass [mæs] ◆ *s* ❶ masa ❷ montón ❸ misa ◆ *adj* ❶ masivo, va *(paro)* ❷ de masas *(comunicación)* ◆ *vi* agruparse; concentrarse

■ **masses** *spl* ❶ *familiar* montones ❷ • **the masses** las masas

massacre ['mæsəkər] ◆ *s* matanza; masacre ◆ *vt* masacrar

massage [mə'sɑːʒ] ◆ *s* masaje ◆ *vt* dar un masaje a

massive ['mæsɪv] *adj* ❶ enorme ❷ aplastante *(mayoría)*

mass media *s & spl* • **the mass media** los medios de comunicación de masas

mass production *s* producción o fabricación en serie

mast [mɑːst] *s* ❶ mástil ❷ *RADIO & TELEVISIÓN* poste; torre

master ['mɑːstər] ◆ *s* ❶ amo; dueño ❷ señor *(de la casa)* ❸ original *(de una grabación)* ◆ *adj* maestro, tra ◆ *vt* ❶ dominar ❷ superar

mastermind ['mɑːstəmaɪnd] ◆ *s* cerebro ◆ *vt* ser el cerebro de; dirigir

Master of Arts *s* ❶ máster en Letras ❷ licenciado, da con máster en Letras

El plural de **Master of Arts** es **Masters of Arts**.

Master of Science *s* ❶ máster en Ciencias ❷ licenciado, da con máster en Ciencias

El plural de **Master of Science** es **Masters of Science**.

masterpiece ['mɑːstəpiːs] *s literal & figurado* obra maestra

master's degree *s* máster

mat [mæt] *s* ❶ alfombrilla ❷ posavasos ❸ salvamanteles ❹ felpudo ❺ tapete; colchoneta *(para hacer gimnasia)*

match [mætʃ] ◆ *s* ❶ partido ❷ cerilla ❸ • **to be a match for** estar a la altura de • **to be no match for** no poder competir con ◆ *vt* ❶ coincidir con ❷ • **to match something (to)** emparejar algo (con) ❸ competir con ❹ hacer juego con ◆ *vi* ❶ coincidir ❷ hacer juego; combinar

matchbox ['mætʃbɒks] *s* caja de cerillas

matching ['mætʃɪŋ] *adj* a juego

mate [meɪt] ◆ *s* ❶ *familiar* amigo, ga; compañero, ra ❷ esposo, sa ❸ macho, hembra ◆ *vi* • **to mate (with)** aparearse (con)

material [mə'tɪərɪəl] ◆ *adj* material ◆ *s* ❶ material ❷ materia ❸ tela ❹ tejido ❺ ⚲ *incontable* información; documentación

■ **materials** *spl* • **building materials** materiales de construcción • **writing materials** objetos de escritorio • **cleaning materials** productos de limpieza

materialistic [mə,tɪərɪə'lɪstɪk] *adj* materialista

maternal [mə'tɜːnl] *adj* ❶ maternal ❷ materno, na

maternity [mə'tɜːnətɪ] *s* maternidad

maternity dress *s* vestido premamá

maternity hospital *s* hospital de maternidad

maternity leave *s* baja por maternidad

math [mæθ] *(abreviatura de* mathematics*) s* ⚲ *incontable* mate

M

mathematical [ˌmæθə'mætɪkl] *adj* matemático, ca

mathematics [ˌmæθə'mætɪks] *s* ☼ *incontable* matemáticas

matinée ['mætɪneɪ] *s* ❶ primera sesión ❷ función de tarde

matrices ['meɪtrɪsi:z] *spl* → **matrix**

matriculation [məˌtrɪkjʊ'leɪʃn] *s* matrícula

matrimony ['mætrɪmənɪ] *s* ☼ *incontable* matrimonio

matrix ['meɪtrɪks] *s* matriz

Dos plurales: **matrices** o **matrixes**.

matte [mæt] *adj* mate

matted ['mætɪd] *adj* enmarañado, da

matter ['mætər] ◆ *s* ❶ asunto • **the fact** o **truth of the matter is (that)...** la verdad es que... • **that's another** o **a different matter** es otra cuestión • **as a matter of course** automáticamente • **to make matters worse** para colmo de desgracias • **a matter of opinion/time** una cuestión de opiniones/tiempo ❷ • **what's the matter (with it/her)?** ¿qué (le) pasa? • **something's the matter with my computer** algo le pasa a mi computadora • **there's nothing the matter** no pasa nada ❸ FÍSICA materia ❹ ☼ *incontable* material ◆ *vi* importar • **of course it matters** claro que importa • **it doesn't matter** no importa

expresiones **as a matter of fact** en realidad ▸ **for that matter** de hecho ▸ **no matter** • **no matter how hard I try** por mucho que lo intente • **no matter what he does** haga lo que haga ▸ **no matter what** • **we must win, no matter what** tenemos que ganar como sea

matter-of-fact *adj* pragmático, ca

mattress ['mætrɪs] *s* colchón

mature [mə'tjʊər] ◆ *adj* ❶ maduro, ra ❷ curado, da *(queso)* ◆ *vi* ❶ madurar ❷ envejecer *(vino)*

mauve [məʊv] *adj* malva

max. [mæks] *(abreviatura escrita de* maximum) máx.

maximum ['mæksɪməm] ◆ *adj* máximo, ma ◆ *s* máximo • **at the maximum** como máximo

Dos plurales: **maxima** o **maximums**.

---

may [meɪ]
◆ *v modal*

❶ [*expresa una probabilidad*]
• **it may rain** puede que llueva
• **she may have phoned** puede que haya llamado

❷ [*para pedir o dar permiso*] poder
• **may I come in?** ¿puedo entrar?
• **you may sit down** se puede sentar

❸ [*para expresar contraste*]
• **he may be fat, but he can still run fast** puede que esté gordo, pero aún así corre rápido
• **be that as it may** así y todo

❹ *formal* [*para expresar una posibilidad*] poder
• **on a clear day the coast may be seen** en un día claro se puede ver la costa

❺ *formal* [*para formular un deseo*]
• **may they be happy!** ¡que sean felices!
• **may he rest in peace!** ¡descanse en paz!

❻ [*en expresiones*]
• **may I go home now? — you may as well** ¿me puedo ir a casa? — no veo por qué no
• **we may as well play another game** ya puestos, podríamos jugar otro partido

---

may

May en el sentido de *tener permiso para* no se puede utilizar cuando hablamos del pasado o del futuro. En estos casos utilizaremos be allowed to en su lugar (she *wasn't allowed to* see him again *no la dejaron volver a verlo*; I hope that I'll *be allowed to* go *espero que me dejen ir*).
Ver también might.

May [meɪ] *s* mayo ver también **September**

maybe ['meɪbɪ] *adv* ❶ quizás; tal vez • **maybe she'll come** tal vez venga • **maybe not** quizás no ❷ más o menos

mayonnaise [ˌmeɪə'neɪz] *s* mayonesa

mayor [meər] *s* alcalde, esa

mayoress ['meərɪs] *s* alcaldesa

maze [meɪz] *s* literal & figurado laberinto

MB *(abreviatura escrita de* megabyte) MB

MD *s abreviatura escrita de* **managing director**

me [mi:] *pronombre personal* ❶ ☼ *directo, indirecto* me • **can you see/hear me?** ¿me ves/oyes? • **it's me** soy yo • **they spoke to me** hablaron conmigo • **she gave it to me** me lo dio • **give it to me!** ¡dámelo! ❷ ☼ *tras preposición* mí • **they went with/without me** fueron conmigo/sin mí ❸ ☼ *en comparaciones, para enfatizar* yo • **she's shorter than me** (ella) es más baja que yo • **you can't expect me to do it** no esperarás que lo haga yo

meadow ['medəʊ] *s* prado; pradera

meager ['mi:gər] *adj* miserable; escaso, sa

meal [mi:l] *s* comida • **enjoy your meal!** ¡buen provecho!

mealtime ['mi:ltaɪm] *s* hora de la comida

mean [mi:n] ◆ *vt* ❶ significar; querer decir • **what does that word mean?** ¿qué quiere decir esa palabra? • **it means nothing to me** no significa nada para mí ❷ querer decir; referirse a • **what do you mean?** ¿qué quieres decir? • **do you know what I mean?** ¿sabes? • **to be meant for** estar destinado, da a • **to be meant to do something** deber hacer algo • **that's not meant to be there** eso no debería estar allí • **it was meant to be a surprise** se suponía que era una sorpresa • **it was meant to be a joke** era solamente una broma ❸ • **I mean it** hablo o lo digo en serio ❹ significar *(ser importante)* • **it means a lot to us** significa mucho para nosotros ❺ suponer; implicar

expresión to mean well tener buenas intenciones ▸ I **mean** quiero decir; o sea
◆ *adj* ❶ tacaño, ña ❷ mezquino, na; malo, la • **to be mean to somebody** ser malo con alguien ❸ medio, dia ◆ *s* promedio; media
Formas irregulares de **mean**: pretérito & pp **meant**.

meander [mɪˈændər] *vi* ❶ serpentear ❷ vagar ❸ divagar

meaning [ˈmiːnɪŋ] *s* ❶ significado ❷ intención; sentido ❸ propósito; razón de ser

meaningful [ˈmiːnɪŋfʊl] *adj* ❶ significativo, va ❷ profundo, da

meaningless [ˈmiːnɪŋlɪs] *adj* ❶ sin sentido ❷ irrelevante

means [miːnz] ◆ *s* medio • **a means of transport** un medio de transporte • **we have no means of doing it** no tenemos manera de hacerlo • **by means of** por medio de • **by legal means** legalmente ◆ *spl* recursos
expresión by all means por supuesto ▸ by no means en absoluto

meant [ment] *pretérito* & *participio pasado* → **mean**

meantime [ˈmiːnˌtaɪm] *s* • **in the meantime** mientras tanto

meanwhile [ˈmiːnˌwaɪl] *adv* mientras tanto

measles [ˈmiːzlz] *s* • **(the) measles** (el) sarampión

measure [ˈmeʒər] ◆ *s* ❶ medida ❷ • **a measure of** una muestra de ❸ MÚSICA compás ◆ *vt* ❶ medir ❷ determinar; evaluar ◆ *vi* medir • **the room measures 2 feet by 3 feet** la habitación mide 2 pies por 3 pies

measurement [ˈmeʒəmənt] *s* medida

MEASUREMENTS

En Estados Unidos no se usa comúnmente el sistema métrico, sino que se emplean las medidas del antiguo sistema inglés. Las unidades más comunes son: **inches** - pulgadas; **feet** - pies; **yards** - yardas; **miles** - millas; **ounces** - onzas; **pounds** - libras; **degrees Fahrenheit** - grados Fahrenheit. 1 inch = 2,54cm, 1 foot = 30,48cm, 1 yard = 91,44cm, 1 mile = 1,6km, 1 ounce = 28,35g, 1 pound = 0,453kg, 1 degree Fahrenheit = -17,22 grados centígrados.

---

meat [miːt] *s* carne • **cold meat** fiambre

meatball [ˈmiːtbɔːl] *s* albóndiga

meaty [ˈmiːtɪ] *adj figurado* sustancioso, sa

Mecca [ˈmekə] *s* ❶ GEOGRAFÍA La Meca ❷ *figurado* meca

mechanic [mɪˈkænɪk] *s* mecánico, ca
■ **mechanics** ◆ *s* ⚲ *incontable* mecánica ◆ *spl figurado* mecanismos

mechanical [mɪˈkænɪkl] *adj* mecánico, ca

mechanism [ˈmekənɪzm] *s literal* & *figurado* mecanismo

---

medal [ˈmedl] *s* medalla

medallion [mɪˈdæljən] *s* medallón

meddle [ˈmedl] *vi* • **to meddle (in)** entrometerse (en) • **to meddle with something** manosear algo

media [ˈmiːdjə] ◆ *spl* → **medium** ◆ *s* & *spl* • **the media** los medios de comunicación

mediaeval [ˌmedɪˈiːvl] = **medieval**

median [ˈmiːdjən] ◆ *adj* mediano, na ◆ *s* mediana

mediate [ˈmiːdɪeɪt] *vi* • **to mediate (for/between)** mediar (por/entre)

mediator [ˈmiːdɪeɪtər] *s* mediador, ra

Medicaid [ˈmedɪkeɪd] *s* ▸ sistema estatal de ayuda médica

Medicaid/Medicare

En 1965 se establecieron en Estados Unidos dos programas de atención sanitaria: **Medicare** y **Medicaid**. El primero, dirigido a mayores de 65 años, se financia por medio de contribuciones a la seguridad social y una prima mensual individual. Además hay que pagar un pequeño suplemento cada vez que se utiliza un servicio médico. El número de beneficiarios de **Medicare** está en continuo aumento, por lo que el programa se enfrenta a problemas financieros y tendrá que ser renovado para satisfacer la demanda. Por su parte, **Medicaid**, que también debe afrontar problemas presupuestarios, está dirigido a personas con ingresos bajos o alguna discapacidad y se financia a través del gobierno federal y los distintos gobiernos estatales.

---

medical [ˈmedɪkl] ◆ *adj* médico, ca ◆ *s* reconocimiento médico

medical examiner *s* forense

Medicare [ˈmedɪkeər] *s* ▸ ayuda médica estatal para ancianos

medicine [ˈmedsɪn] *s* ❶ medicina ▸ **Doctor of Medicine** UNIVERSIDAD doctor, ra en medicina ❷ medicamento

medieval, mediaeval [ˌmedɪˈiːvl] *adj* medieval

mediocre [ˌmiːdɪˈəʊkər] *adj* mediocre

meditate [ˈmedɪteɪt] *vi* • **to meditate (on** o **upon)** meditar (sobre)

Mediterranean [ˌmedɪtəˈreɪnjən] ◆ *s* • **the Mediterranean (Sea)** el (mar) Mediterráneo ◆ *adj* mediterráneo, a

medium [ˈmiːdjəm] ◆ *adj* mediano, na ◆ *s* ❶ (pl media) medio ❷ (pl mediums) médium

medium-sized [-saɪzd] *adj* de tamaño mediano

medium wave *s* onda media

meet [miːt] ◆ *vt* ❶ encontrarse con ❷ conocer • **pleased to meet you** encantado de conocerlo ❸ reunirse con ❹ ir/venir a buscar ❺ satisfacer *(necesi-*

M

dad, demanda) ❻ cumplir con *(objetivo)* ❼ cumplir *(plazo)* ❽ hacer frente a *(problema)* ❾ pagar *(deudas)* ❿ darse contra ⓫ juntarse con ◆ *vi* ❶ encontrarse; verse • **we met by chance in the street** nos encontramos por casualidad en la calle • **let's meet in front of the movie theater** encontrémonos frente al cine • **shall we meet at eight?** ¿quedamos a las ocho? ❷ reunirse *(en trabajo)* ❸ conocerse • **have you met Lisa's brother?** ¿conoces al hermano de Lisa? ❹ buscar • **I'm going to meet them at the airport** voy a buscarlos al aeropuerto ❺ chocar ❻ tocar ❼ • **their eyes met** sus miradas se cruzaron ❽ juntarse ❾ enfrentarse *(en deporte)* ◆ *s* encuentro

■ **meet up** *vi* • **to meet up (with somebody)** quedar (con alguien) • **we're meeting up for lunch** hemos quedado para comer

■ **meet with** *vt* ☼ *El objeto siempre va después de la preposición al final.* ❶ • **to meet with refusal** ser rechazado, da • **to meet with success** tener éxito • **to meet with failure** fracasar ❷ reunirse con

Formas irregulares de **meet**: *pretérito & pp* **met**.

meeting ['mi:tɪŋ] *s* ❶ reunión ❷ encuentro ❸ cita ❹ entrevista

megabyte ['megəbaɪt] *s* INFORMÁTICA megabyte; mega

megaphone ['megəfəʊn] *s* megáfono

mellow ['meləʊ] ◆ *adj* suave ◆ *vi* ❶ suavizarse ❷ ablandarse

melody ['melədɪ] *s* melodía

melon ['melən] *s* melón

melt [melt] ◆ *vt* ❶ derretir ❷ *figurado* ablandar ◆ *vi* ❶ derretirse ❷ *figurado* ablandarse ❸ • **to melt away a)** esfumarse **b)** desvanecerse

■ **melt down** *vt* ☼ *El objeto se puede colocar antes o después de la preposición.* fundir

member ['membər] *s* ❶ miembro ❷ afiliado, da ❸ socio, cia

Member of Congress *s* miembro del Congreso *(de los Estados Unidos)*

El plural de **Member of Congress** es **Members of Congress.**

membership ['membəʃɪp] *s* ❶ afiliación ❷ calidad de socio ❸ número de afiliados ❹ • **the membership a)** los miembros **b)** los afiliados **c)** los socios

membership card *s* ❶ carnet de afiliado, da ❷ carnet de socio, cia

memento [mɪ'mentəʊ] *s* recuerdo

memo ['meməʊ] *s* memorándum

memoirs ['memwɑ:z] *spl* memorias

memorial [mɪ'mɔ:rɪəl] ◆ *adj* conmemorativo, va ◆ *s* monumento conmemorativo ▸ **war memorial** monumento a los caídos

MEMORIAL DAY

En Estados Unidos, **Memorial Day** es el día en que se conmemora a todos los soldados que participaron y murieron en las guerras. Hay desfiles de soldados y veteranos y las calles y las casas se decoran con banderas y listones de los colores nacionales: rojo, blanco y azul. **Memorial Day** se celebra el último lunes de mayo y se considera el comienzo informal del verano.

memorize ['meməraɪz] *vt* memorizar; aprender de memoria

memory ['memərɪ] *s* ❶ memoria ❷ recuerdo • **from memory** de memoria

men [men] *spl* → **man**

menace ['menəs] ◆ *s* ❶ amenaza ❷ peligro ◆ *vt* amenazar

menacing ['menəsɪŋ] *adj* amenazador, ra

mend [mend] ◆ *s*

expresión **to be on the mend** *familiar* ir recuperándose

◆ *vt* ❶ arreglar ❷ zurcir ❸ remendar

meningitis [ˌmenɪn'dʒaɪtɪs] *s* ☼ *incontable* meningitis

menopause ['menəpɔ:z] *s* • **the menopause** la menopausia

men's room *s* • **the men's room** el baño de caballeros

menstruation [ˌmenstrʊ'eɪʃn] *s* menstruación

menswear ['menzweər] *s* ropa de caballeros

mental ['mentl] *adj* mental

mental hospital *s* hospital psiquiátrico

mentality [men'tælətɪ] *s* mentalidad

mentally handicapped ['mentəlɪ-] *spl* • **the mentally handicapped** los disminuidos psíquicos

mention ['menʃn] ◆ *vt* • **to mention something (to)** mencionar algo (a) • **not to mention** sin mencionar; además de

expresión **don't mention it!** ¡de nada!; ¡no hay de qué!

◆ *s* mención

menu ['menju:] *s* ❶ carta ❷ INFORMÁTICA menú

meow, mew [mɪ'aʊ] ◆ *s* maullido ◆ *vi* maullar

mercenary ['mɜ:sɪnrɪ] *s* mercenario, ria

merchandise ['mɜ:tʃəndaɪz] *s* ☼ *incontable* mercancías; géneros

merchant ['mɜ:tʃənt] ◆ *adj* mercante ◆ *s* comerciante

merchant marine *s* marina mercante

merciful ['mɜ:sɪfʊl] *adj* ❶ compasivo, va ❷ afortunado, da

merciless ['mɜ:sɪlɪs] *adj* despiadado, da

mercury ['mɜ:kjʊrɪ] *s* mercurio

Mercury ['mɜ:kjʊrɪ] *s* Mercurio

mercy ['mɜ:sɪ] *s* ❶ compasión • **to have mercy on** apiadarse de • **to beg for mercy** pedir clemencia • **at the mercy of** *figurado* a merced de ❷ suerte

mere [mɪər] *adj* simple; mero, ra • **she's a mere child** no es más que una niña

merely['mɪəlɪ] *adv* simplemente; sólo

merge[mɜ:dʒ] ◆ *vt* ❶ mezclar ❷ *COMERCIO & INFOR-MÁTICA* fusionar ◆ *vi* ❶ • **to merge (with)** a) fusionarse (con) b) unirse o convergir (con) ❷ fundirse • **to merge into** confundirse con

merger['mɜ:dʒər] *s* *COMERCIO* fusión

meringue[məˈræŋ] *s* merengue

merit ['merɪt] ◆ *s* mérito ◆ *vt* merecer; ser digno, na de
■ **merits** *spl* ventajas • **to judge something on its merits** evaluar o juzgar algo según sus méritos

mermaid['mɜ:meɪd] *s* sirena

merry ['merɪ] *adj* ❶ alegre • **Merry Christmas!** ¡feliz Navidad! ❷ animado, da *(fiesta)* ❸ *familiar* achispado, da

merry-go-round *s* tiovivo

mesh[meʃ] ◆ *s* malla ◆ *vi* *figurado* encajar

mesmerize ['mezməraɪz] *vt* • **to be mesmerized (by)** estar fascinado, da (por)

mess[mes] *s* ❶ desorden • **what a mess!** ¡qué desorden! • **to make a mess** dejar un desastre • **to make a mess of something** hacer algo muy mal ❷ lío
■ **mess about, mess around** *familiar* ◆ *vt* ⚲ *El objeto se coloca entre el verbo y la preposición.* vacilar ◆ *vi* ❶ pasar el rato; perder el tiempo ❷ hacer el tonto ❸ • **to mess about with something** manosear algo • **don't mess around with my guitar** ¡deja mi guitarra tranquila!
■ **mess up** *vt* ⚲ *El objeto se puede colocar antes o después de la preposición.* *familiar* ❶ ensuciar ❷ desordenar ❸ echar a perder

message['mesɪdʒ] *s* mensaje

messenger['mesɪndʒər] *s* mensajero, ra

Messrs.['mesəz] *(abreviatura de* messieurs) Sres.

messy['mesɪ] *adj* ❶ sucio, cia ❷ desordenado, da

met[met] *pretérito* & *participio pasado* → **meet**

metal['metl] ◆ *s* metal ◆ *en compuestos* de metal; metálico, ca

metallic [mɪˈtælɪk] *adj* ❶ metálico, ca ❷ metalizado, da

metalwork['metlwɜ:k] *s* metalistería

metaphor['metəfər] *s* metáfora

meteor['mi:tɪər] *s* bólido

meteorology[ˌmi:tjəˈrɒlədʒɪ] *s* meteorología

meter['mi:tər] *s* ❶ metro ❷ contador

method['meθəd] *s* método

methodical[mɪˈɒdɪkl] *adj* metódico, ca

Methodist ['meθədɪst] ◆ *adj* metodista ◆ *s* metodista

meticulous [mɪˈtɪkjʊləs] *adj* meticuloso, sa; minucioso, sa

metric['metrɪk] *adj* métrico, ca

metronome['metrənəʊm] *s* metrónomo

metropolitan [ˌmetrəˈpɒlɪtn] *adj* metropolitano, na

mew[mju:] = **meow**

Mexican ['meksɪkn] ◆ *adj* mexicano, na ◆ *s* mexicano, na

Mexico['meksɪkəʊ] *s* México

mezzanine ['metsəni:n] *s* ❶ entresuelo ❷ primer palco

mice[maɪs] *spl* → **mouse**

microchip['maɪkrəʊʃɪp] *s* *INFORMÁTICA* microchip

microphone['maɪkrəfəʊn] *s* micrófono

micro scooter *s* patinete

microscope['maɪkrəskəʊp] *s* microscopio

microscopic [ˌmaɪkrəˈskɒpɪk] *adj* *literal & figurado* microscópico, ca

microwave['maɪkrəweɪv] ◆ *s* • **microwave (oven)** microondas ◆ *vt* cocinar en el microondas

mid- [mɪd] *prefijo* medio, dia • **(in) mid-morning** a media mañana • **(in) mid-August** a mediados de agosto • **(in) mid-winter** en pleno invierno • **she's in her mid-twenties** tiene unos 25 años

midair[mɪdˈeər] *s* • **in midair** en el aire

midday['mɪddeɪ] *s* mediodía

middle['mɪdl] ◆ *adj* del medio • **he sat in the middle chair** se sentó en la silla del medio ◆ *s* ❶ medio; centro • **in the middle of the month/the 19th century** a mediados del mes/del siglo XIX • **in the middle of the week** a mitad de semana • **to be in the middle of doing something** estar haciendo algo • **in the middle of the night** en plena noche ❷ cintura

middle-aged *adj* de mediana edad

Middle Ages *spl* • **the Middle Ages** la Edad Media

middle-class *adj* de clase media

middle classes *spl* • **the middle classes** la clase media

Middle East *s* • **the Middle East** el Oriente Medio

middle name *s* segundo nombre *(en un nombre compuesto)*

middleweight['mɪdlweɪt] *s* peso medio

middling['mɪdlɪŋ] *adj* regular

midfield[ˌmɪdˈfi:ld] *s* *FÚTBOL* centro del campo

midge[mɪdʒ] *s* (tipo de) mosquito pequeño

midget['mɪdʒɪt] *s* enano, na

midi system['mɪdɪ-] *s* minicadena

midnight['mɪdnaɪt] *s* medianoche

midst[mɪdst] *s* • **in the midst of** en medio de

midsummer['mɪdˌsʌmər] *s* pleno verano

midway[ˌmɪdˈweɪ] *adv* ❶ • **midway (between)** a medio camino (entre) ❷ • **midway (through)** a la mitad (de)

midweek ◆ *adj* [mɪdˈwi:k] de entre semana ◆ *adv* ['mɪdwi:k] entre semana

midwife['mɪdwaɪf] *s* comadrona
El plural de **midwife** es **midwives**['mɪdwaɪvz].

midwifery['mɪdˌwɪfərɪ] *s* obstetricia

M

might [maɪt]
◆ *v modal*
❶ [*expresa una eventualidad o una probabilidad, con poca certeza*]
• **the criminal might be armed** puede que el criminal esté armado
• **she might have gotten lost** puede que se haya perdido
❷ [*expresa un reproche*]
• **you might at least say "thank you"** por lo menos podrías haber dicho "gracias"
❸ *formal* [*en el discurso indirecto, es el equivalente de "may"*]
• **he asked if he might leave the room** preguntó si podía salir del cuarto
◆ *s*
fuerza
• **with all your might** con todas sus fuerzas

---

might

May y might pueden emplearse para dar la idea de que existe una posibilidad real, pero might, expresa un mayor grado de incertidumbre. Comparemos you *may* be right but I'll have to check *puede que tengas razón pero tendré que comprobarlo*; if you phone now, you *might* catch him in his office *si llamas ahora, a lo mejor lo agarras en la oficina*.

---

mighty ['maɪtɪ] ◆ *adj* ❶ fuerte ❷ poderoso, sa ◆ *adv* muy • **that was mighty kind of you** ha sido muy amable de tu parte

migraine ['miːgreɪn] ['maɪgreɪn] *s* migraña

migrant ['maɪgrənt] ◆ *adj* inmigrante ◆ *s* emigrante

migrate ['maɪgreɪt] *vi* emigrar

mike [maɪk] (*abreviatura de* microphone) *s familiar* micro

mild [maɪld] *adj* ❶ suave ❷ leve ❸ apacible ❹ sereno, na ❺ templado, da

mildew ['mɪldjuː] *s* ❶ moho ❷ añublo

mildly ['maɪldlɪ] *adv* ligeramente; levemente • **to put it mildly** por no decir más

mile [maɪl] *s* milla • **I walked for miles** caminé millas y millas • **it's miles away** está muy lejos

expresión **to be miles away** estar en la luna

mileage ['maɪlɪdʒ] *s* distancia en millas

mileometer, milometer [maɪ'lɒmɪtər] *s* cuentamillas, ≃ cuentakilómetros

milestone ['maɪlstəʊn] *s* ❶ mojón ❷ *figurado* hito

militant ['mɪlɪtənt] ◆ *adj* militante ◆ *s* militante

military ['mɪlɪtrɪ] ◆ *adj* militar ◆ *s* • **the military** los militares; las fuerzas armadas

militia [mɪ'lɪʃə] *s* milicia

milk [mɪlk] ◆ *s* leche ◆ *vt* ❶ ordeñar ❷ sacar todo el jugo a • **they milked him for every penny he had** le chuparon hasta el último centavo

milk chocolate *s* chocolate con leche

milkman ['mɪlkmən] *s* lechero

El plural de **milkman** es **milkmen** ['mɪlkmen].

milk shake *s* batido

Milky Way *s* • **the Milky Way** la Vía Láctea

mill [mɪl] ◆ *s* ❶ molino ❷ fábrica ❸ molinillo ◆ *vt* moler
■ **mill about, mill around** *vi* arremolinarse

millennium [mɪ'lenɪəm] *s* milenio

El plural de **millennium** es **millennia** [mɪ'lenɪə].

miller ['mɪlər] *s* molinero, ra

milligram(me) ['mɪlɪgræm] *s* miligramo

millimeter ['mɪlɪˌmiːtər] *s* milímetro

million ['mɪljən] *s* millón • **four million dollars** cuatro millones de dólares

millionaire [ˌmɪljə'neər] *s* millonario

milometer [maɪ'lɒmɪtər] = **mileometer**

mime [maɪm] ◆ *s* mímica ◆ *vt* describir con gestos ◆ *vi* hacer mímica

mimic ['mɪmɪk] ◆ *s* imitador, ra ◆ *vt* imitar

Formas irregulares de **mimic**: *pretérito & pp* **mimicked**, *gerundio* **mimicking**.

min. [mɪn] ❶ (*abreviatura escrita de* minute) min ❷ (*abreviatura escrita de* minimum) mín.

mince [mɪns] ◆ *vt* picar ◆ *vi* andar con afectación

mind [maɪnd] ◆ *s* ❶ mente • **state of mind** estado de ánimo • **to calculate something in your mind** calcular algo mentalmente • **to cross somebody's mind** pasársele a alguien por la cabeza • **it never even crossed my mind** ni se me pasó por la cabeza • **the first thing that came into my mind** lo primero que me vino a la mente • **to have something on your mind** estar preocupado por algo • **to keep an open mind** tener una actitud abierta • **that was a load** o **weight off my mind** me quité un peso de encima • **are you out of your mind?** ¿estás loco? ❷ atención • **to put your mind to something** poner empeño en algo ❸ • **to change your mind** cambiar de opinión • **to my mind** en mi opinión ❹ memoria ❺ • **to have something in mind** tener algo en mente • **to have a mind to do something** estar pensando en hacer algo • **nothing could be further from my mind** nada más lejos de mis intenciones

expresiones **to make your mind up** decidirse ▸ **to be in two minds about something** no estar seguro, ra de algo ▸ **to speak your mind** hablar sin rodeos

◆ *vi* • **do you mind?** ¿te importa? • **I don't mind...** no me importa... • **which do you want? — I don't mind** ¿cuál prefieres? — me da igual

expresión **never mind a)** no te preocupes **b)** no importa

◆ *vt* ❶ • **do you mind if I leave?** ¿te molesta si me voy? • **I don't mind waiting** no me importa esperar ❷ cuidar

expresiones I **wouldn't mind...** me vendría bien... • **I wouldn't mind some soup** me vendría bien una sopa ‣ **mind you a)** te advierto que... **b)** tener cuidado con • **mind you don't fall** ten cuidado no te vayas a caer • **he's a bit deaf; mind you, he is old** está un poco sordo; te advierto que es ya mayor ‣ **mind your own business!** *muy familiar* ¡métete en tus asuntos!

mindless ['maɪndlɪs] *adj* ❶ absurdo, da; sin sentido ❷ aburrido, da

mine¹ [maɪn] *pronombre posesivo* mío, mía • **that money is mine** ese dinero es mío • **his car hit mine** su coche chocó contra el mío • **it wasn't your fault, it was mine** la culpa no fue tuya sino mía • **a friend of mine** un amigo mío

mine² [maɪn] ◆ *s* mina ◆ *vt* ❶ extraer *(minerales)* ❷ minar

minefield ['maɪnfiːld] *s literal & figurado* campo de minas

miner ['maɪnər] *s* minero, ra

mineral ['mɪnərəl] ◆ *adj* mineral ◆ *s* mineral

mineral water *s* agua mineral

mingle ['mɪŋgl] *vi* ❶ • **to mingle (with)** mezclarse (con) ❷ • **to mingle (with)** alternar (con)

miniature ['mɪnətʃər] ◆ *adj* en miniatura ◆ *s* ❶ miniatura ❷ botellín de licor en miniatura

minibus ['mɪnɪbʌs] *s* microbús

El plural de **minibus** es **minibuses**.

minima ['mɪnɪmə] *spl* → **minimum**

minimal ['mɪnɪml] *adj* mínimo, ma

minimum ['mɪnɪməm] ◆ *adj* mínimo, ma ◆ *s* mínimo

Dos plurales: **minimums** o **minima**.

minimum wage *s* salario mínimo

mining ['maɪnɪŋ] ◆ *s* minería ◆ *adj* minero, ra

miniskirt ['mɪnɪskɜːt] *s* minifalda

minister ['mɪnɪstər] *s* ❶ Política • **minister (for)** ministro, tra (de) ❷ Religión pastor, ra

ministry ['mɪnɪstri] *s* ❶ Política ministerio ❷ Religión • **the ministry** el clero

mink [mɪŋk] *s* visón

El plural de **mink** es **mink**.

minnow ['mɪnəʊ] *s* pececillo (de agua dulce)

minor ['maɪnər] ◆ *adj* ❶ menor ❷ leve *(herida)* ◆ *s* ❶ menor (de edad) ❷ subespecialidad ◆ *vi* estudiar una subespecialidad

minority [maɪˈnɒrəti] *s* minoría • **to be in a** o **the minority** estar en la minoría; ser minoría

mint [mɪnt] ◆ *s* ❶ menta; hierbabuena ❷ pastilla de menta

expresión **in mint condition** flamante; como nuevo, va

◆ *vt* acuñar

minus ['maɪnəs] ◆ *preposición* ❶ Matemáticas • **4 minus 2 is 2** 4 menos 2 es 2 ❷ • **it's minus 5°C** estamos a 5 grados bajo cero ◆ *s* ❶ Matemáticas signo (de) menos ❷ desventaja

El plural de **minus** es **minuses**.

minus sign *s* signo (de) menos

minute¹ ['mɪnɪt] *s* minuto • **at any minute** en cualquier momento • **at the minute** en este momento • **just a minute** un momento • **this minute** ahora mismo

■ **minutes** *spl* acta • **to take (the) minutes** levantar o tomar acta

minute² [maɪˈnjuːt] *adj* diminuto, ta

miracle ['mɪrəkl] *s literal & figurado* milagro

miraculous [mɪˈrækjʊləs] *adj* milagroso, sa

mirage [mɪˈrɑːʒ] *s literal & figurado* espejismo

mirror ['mɪrər] ◆ *s* ❶ espejo ❷ retrovisor ◆ *vt* reflejar

misappropriation ['mɪsəˌprəʊprɪˈeɪʃn] *s* • **misappropriation (of)** malversación (de)

misbehave [ˌmɪsbɪˈheɪv] *vi* portarse mal

miscalculate [ˌmɪsˈkælkjʊleɪt] *vt & vi* calcular mal

miscarriage [ˌmɪsˈkærɪdʒ] *s* aborto (natural)

miscarriage of justice *s* error judicial

miscellaneous [ˌmɪsəˈleɪnjəs] *adj* diverso, sa

mischief ['mɪstʃɪf] *s* 💡 *incontable* ❶ picardía ❷ travesuras

mischievous ['mɪstʃɪvəs] *adj* ❶ lleno, na de picardía ❷ travieso, sa

misconception [ˌmɪskənˈsepʃn] *s* concepto erróneo

misconduct [ˌmɪsˈkɒndʌkt] *s* mala conducta

miscount [ˌmɪsˈkaʊnt] *vt & vi* contar mal

misdemeanor [ˌmɪsdɪˈmiːnər] *s formal* delito menor

miser ['maɪzər] *s* avaro, ra

miserable ['mɪzrəbl] *adj* ❶ infeliz; triste ❷ miserable ❸ horrible *(el tiempo)* ❹ lamentable

miserly ['maɪzəli] *adj* miserable; mezquino, na

misery ['mɪzəri] *s* ❶ desdicha ❷ sufrimiento

misfire [ˌmɪsˈfaɪər] *vi* ❶ no arrancar *(motor)* ❷ fracasar *(plan)*

misfit ['mɪsfɪt] *s* inadaptado, da

misfortune [mɪsˈfɔːtʃuːn] *s* ❶ mala suerte ❷ desgracia

misgivings [mɪsˈgɪvɪŋz] *spl* recelos

misguided [ˌmɪsˈgaɪdɪd] *adj* ❶ descaminado, da ❷ equivocado, da

mishandle [ˌmɪsˈhændl] *vt* ❶ maltratar *(persona, animal)* ❷ llevar mal *(asunto)*

mishap ['mɪshæp] *s* contratiempo

misinterpret [ˌmɪsɪnˈtɜːprɪt] *vt* malinterpretar

misjudge [ˌmɪsˈdʒʌdʒ] *vt* ❶ calcular mal ❷ juzgar mal

mislay [ˌmɪsˈleɪ] *vt* extraviar

Formas irregulares de **mislay**: *pretérito & pp* **mislaid**.

M

mislead [ˌmɪsˈliːd] *vt* engañar
Formas irregulares de **mislead**: *pretérito & pp* **misled**.

misleading [ˌmɪsˈliːdɪŋ] *adj* engañoso, sa

misled [ˌmɪsˈled] *pretérito & participio pasado* → **mislead**

misnomer [ˌmɪsˈnəʊmər] *s* término equivocado

misplace [ˌmɪsˈpleɪs] *vt* extraviar

misprint [ˈmɪsprɪnt] *s* errata; error de imprenta

miss [mɪs] ◆ *vt* ❶ perderse *(programa, película)* ❷ no ver *(error, persona)* • **it's a big house, you can't miss it** es una casa grande, la vas a ver enseguida ❸ no oír ❹ saltarse *(omitir)* ❺ fallar *(tiro)* ❻ no dar a *(balón, pelota)* ❼ echar de menos o en falta • **I miss you** te extraño ❽ perder; dejar pasar *(oportunidad)* ❾ pasarse *(calle)* ❿ perder *(tren, camión)* ⓫ faltar a *(cita)* ⓬ no cumplir *(plazo)* ⓭ evitar ◆ *vi* fallar ◆ *s* fallo
expresión **to give something a miss** *familiar* pasar de algo

■ **miss out** ◆ *vt* ☼ *El objeto se puede colocar antes o después de la preposición.* pasar por alto ◆ *vi* • **to miss out (on something)** perderse *(algo)*

Miss [mɪs] *s* señorita • **Miss Brown** la señorita Brown

missile [ˈmɪsaɪl] *s* ❶ misil ❷ proyectil

missing [ˈmɪsɪŋ] *adj* ❶ perdido, da; extraviado, da ❷ ausente • **there's something missing** falta algo • **fill in the missing words** llene las palabras que faltan ▸ **missing person** persona desaparecida

mission [ˈmɪʃn] *s* misión

missionary [ˈmɪʃənrɪ] *s* misionero, ra

mist [mɪst] *s* ❶ neblina ❷ bruma
■ **mist over, mist up** *vi* empañarse

mistake [mɪˈsteɪk] ◆ *s* error • **to make a mistake** equivocarse; cometer un error • **by mistake** por error; por equivocación ◆ *vt* ❶ entender mal ❷ • **to mistake somebody for somebody else** confundir a alguien con alguien
Formas irregulares de **mistake**: *pretérito* **mistook**, *pp* **mistaken**.

mistaken [mɪˈsteɪkn] ◆ *participio pasado* → **mistake** ◆ *adj* equivocado, da • **to be mistaken about somebody/something** estar equivocado respecto a alguien/algo

mister [ˈmɪstər] *s familiar* amigo
■ **Mister** *s* señor • **mister Brown** el señor Brown

mistletoe [ˈmɪsltəʊ] *s* muérdago

mistook [mɪˈstʊk] *pretérito* → **mistake**

mistreat [ˌmɪsˈtriːt] *vt* maltratar

mistress [ˈmɪstrɪs] *s* ❶ amante ❷ señora

mistrust [ˌmɪsˈtrʌst] ◆ *s* desconfianza; recelo ◆ *vt* desconfiar de

misty [ˈmɪstɪ] *adj* ❶ neblinoso, sa ❷ brumoso, sa

misunderstand [ˌmɪsʌndəˈstænd] *vt & vi* entender mal

Formas irregulares de **misunderstand**: *pretérito & pp* **misunderstood**.

misunderstanding [ˌmɪsʌndəˈstændɪŋ] *s* malentendido

misunderstood [ˌmɪsʌndəˈstʊd] *pretérito & participio pasado* → **misunderstand**

misuse ◆ *s* [ˌmɪsˈjuːs] uso indebido ◆ *vt* [ˌmɪsˈjuːz] hacer uso indebido de

mitt [mɪt] *s* ❶ manopla ❷ guante

mitten [ˈmɪtn] *s* manopla

mix [mɪks] ◆ *vt* • **to mix something (with)** mezclar algo (con) ◆ *vi* ❶ mezclarse ❷ ir bien juntos, tas ❸ • **to mix with** alternar con ◆ *s* mezcla
■ **mix up** *vt* ☼ *El objeto se puede colocar antes o después de la preposición.* ❶ confundir ❷ mezclar

mixed [mɪkst] *adj* ❶ surtido, da; variado, da ❷ mixto, ta

mixed grill *s* parrillada mixta

mixed up *adj* ❶ confuso, sa • **to get mixed up** confundirse ❷ • **mixed up in** involucrado, da en

mixer [ˈmɪksər] *s* ❶ batidora ❷ mesa de mezclas ❸ refresco para mezclar con bebidas alcohólicas

mixture [ˈmɪkstʃər] *s* ❶ mezcla ❷ surtido *(de caramelos)*

mix-up *s familiar* confusiónó**mm** *(abreviatura escrita de* millimeter*)* mm

moan [məʊn] ◆ *s* gemido ◆ *vi* ❶ gemir ❷ *familiar* • **to moan (about)** quejarse (de)

moat [məʊt] *s* foso

mob [mɒb] ◆ *s* muchedumbre ◆ *vt* asediar

mobile [ˈməʊbaɪl] ◆ *adj* móvil ◆ *s* móvil

mobile home *s* caravana

mobile phone *s* teléfono celular

mobilize [ˈməʊbɪlaɪz] *vt* movilizar

mock [mɒk] ◆ *adj* fingido, da ◆ *vt* burlarse de ◆ *vi* burlarse

mockery [ˈmɒkərɪ] *s* burlas • **to make a mockery of something** poner en ridículo algo

mode [məʊd] *s* modo

model [ˈmɒdl] ◆ *s* ❶ modelo ❷ maqueta ◆ *adj* ❶ modelo ❷ en miniatura ◆ *vt* ❶ modelar ❷ lucir *(en pase de modelos)* ❸ • **to model yourself on somebody** tener a alguien como modelo ❹ *INFORMÁTICA* simular por computadora ◆ *vi* trabajar de modelo

modem [ˈməʊdem] *s INFORMÁTICA* módem

moderate ◆ *adj* [ˈmɒdərət] moderado, da ◆ *s* [ˈmɒdərət] *POLÍTICA* moderado, da ◆ *vt* [ˈmɒdəreɪt] moderar ◆ *vi* [ˈmɒdəreɪt] hacer de moderador

moderation [ˌmɒdəˈreɪʃn] *s* moderación • **in moderation** con moderación

modern [ˈmɒdən] *adj* moderno, na

modernize [ˈmɒdənaɪz] ◆ *vt* modernizar ◆ *vi* modernizarse

modern languages *spl* lenguas modernas

modest [ˈmɒdɪst] *adj* ❶ modesto, ta ❷ ligero, ra *(mejora)* ❸ módico, ca *(precio)*

M

modesty ['mɒdɪstɪ] *s* modestia
modify ['mɒdɪfaɪ] *vt* modificar
module ['mɒdju:l] *s* módulo
moist [mɔɪst] *adj* húmedo, da
moisten ['mɔɪsn] *vt* humedecer
moisture ['mɔɪstʃər] *s* humedad
moisturizer ['mɔɪstʃəraɪzər] *s* (crema) hidratante
molar ['məʊlər] *s* muela
molasses [mə'læsɪz] *s* ⚬*incontable* melaza
mold [məʊld] ◆ *s* ❶ moho ❷ molde ◆ *vt literal & figurado* moldear
moldy ['məʊldɪ] *adj* mohoso, sa
mole [məʊl] *s* ❶ topo ❷ lunar
molecule ['mɒlɪkju:l] *s* molécula
molest [mə'lest] *vt* ❶ abusar sexualmente de ❷ molestar
mollusk ['mɒləsk] *s* molusco
molt [məʊlt] *vi* ❶ mudar la pluma ❷ mudar el pelo
mom [mɒm] *s familiar* mamá
moment ['məʊmənt] *s* momento • **at any moment** de un momento a otro • **at the moment** en este momento • **for the moment** de momento
momentarily ['məʊməntərɪlɪ] *adv* ❶ pronto ❷ momentáneamente
momentary ['məʊməntrɪ] *adj* momentáneo, a
momentous [mə'mentəs] *adj* trascendental
momentum [mə'mentəm] *s* ⚬*incontable* ❶ FÍSICA momento ❷ *figurado* ímpetu; impulso • **to gather momentum** cobrar intensidad
momma ['mɒmə], **mommy** ['mɒmɪ] *s* mamá
monarch ['mɒnək] *s* monarca
monarchy ['mɒnəkɪ] *s* ❶ monarquía ❷ • **the monarchy** la familia real
monastery ['mɒnəstrɪ] *s* monasterio
Monday ['mʌndɪ] *s* lunes ver también **Saturday**
money ['mʌnɪ] *s* dinero • **to make money** hacer dinero • **we got our money's worth** sacamos provecho a nuestro dinero
expresión **for my money** en mi opinión
money belt *s* cinturón monedero
moneybox ['mʌnɪbɒks] *s* hucha
money order *s* giro postal
mongrel ['mʌŋgrəl] *s* perro cruzado
monitor ['mɒnɪtər] ◆ *s* monitor ◆ *vt* ❶ controlar ❷ escuchar
monk [mʌŋk] *s* monje
monkey ['mʌŋkɪ] *s* mono
El plural de **monkey** es **monkeys**.
monkey nut *s* cacahuete
monkey wrench *s* llave inglesa
mono ['mɒnəʊ] ◆ *adj* mono ◆ *s familiar* mononucleosis infecciosa

monolog ['mɒnəlɒg] *s* monólogo
mononucleosis ['mɒnəʊ,nju:klɪ'əʊsɪs] *s* mononucleosis infecciosa
monopolize [mə'nɒpəlaɪz] *vt* monopolizar
monopoly [mə'nɒpəlɪ] *s* • **monopoly (on** o **of)** monopolio (de)
monotonous [mə'nɒtənəs] *adj* monótono, na
monotony [mə'nɒtənɪ] *s* monotonía
monsoon [mɒn'su:n] *s* monzón
monster ['mɒnstər] *s* monstruo
monstrosity [mɒn'strɒsətɪ] *s* monstruosidad
monstrous ['mɒnstrəs] *adj* ❶ monstruoso, sa ❷ gigantesco, ca
month [mʌnθ] *s* mes
monthly ['mʌnθlɪ] ◆ *adj* mensual ◆ *adv* mensualmente
monument ['mɒnjʊmənt] *s* monumento
monumental [,mɒnjʊ'mentl] *adj* ❶ monumental ❷ descomunal *(error)*
moo [mu:] *vi* mugir
mood [mu:d] *s* ❶ humor • **in a (bad) mood** de mal humor • **in a good mood** de buen humor ❷ disposición *(de público, votantes)*
moody ['mu:dɪ] *adj despectivo* ❶ de humor variable; temperamental ❷ malhumorado, da
moon [mu:n] *s* luna
moonlight ['mu:nlaɪt] *s* luz de la luna
moonlighting ['mu:nlaɪtɪŋ] *s* pluriempleo
moonlit ['mu:nlɪt] *adj* ❶ de luna *(noche)* ❷ iluminado, da por la luna
moor [mɔ:r] ◆ *vt* amarrar ◆ *vi* echar las amarras
Moor [mɔ:r] *s* moro, ra
Moorish ['mɔ:rɪʃ] *adj* moro, ra; morisco, ca
moose [mu:s] *s* alce
El plural de **moose** es **moose**.
mop [mɒp] ◆ *s* ❶ fregona ❷ *familiar* pelambrera ◆ *vt* ❶ pasar la fregona por ❷ enjugar
■ **mop up** *vt* ⚬*El objeto se puede colocar antes o después de la preposición.* limpiar
mope [məʊp] *vi despectivo* estar deprimido, da
moped ['məʊped] *s* ciclomotor; motoneta
moral ['mɒrəl] ◆ *adj* moral ◆ *s* moraleja
■ **morals** *spl* moral
morale [mə'rɑ:l] *s* ⚬*incontable* moral
morality [mə'rælətɪ] *s* ❶ moralidad ❷ moral
morbid ['mɔ:bɪd] *adj* morboso, sa
more [mɔ:r] ◆ *adv* más • **more important (than)** más importante (que) • **we were more hurt than angry** más que enfadados estábamos heridos • **I couldn't agree more** estoy completamente de acuerdo ◆ *adj* más • **more food than drink** más comida que bebida • **more than 70 people died** más de 70 personas murieron • **have some more tea** toma un poco más de té • **I finished two more chapters today** acabé otros dos capítulos hoy ◆ *pronombre* más • **more than**

M

five más de cinco • **he's got more than I have** él tiene más que yo • **I don't want any more** no quiero más • **there's no more (left)** no queda nada (más) *expresiones* **(and) what's more** (y lo que) es más ▶ **more and more** cada vez más ▶ **more or less** más o menos

moreover [mɔːˈrəʊvər] *adv formal* además

morgue [mɔːg] *s* depósito de cadáveres

Mormon [ˈmɔːmən] *s* mormón, ona

morning [ˈmɔːnɪŋ] *s* ➊ mañana • **in the morning** en la mañana • **six o'clock in the morning** las seis de la mañana • **on Monday morning** el lunes por la mañana • **every morning** todas las mañanas • **yesterday morning** ayer en la mañana • **tomorrow morning** mañana en la mañana ➋ madrugada
■ **mornings** *adv* por la mañana

Moroccan [məˈrɒkən] ◆ *adj* marroquí ◆ *s* marroquí

Morocco [məˈrɒkəʊ] *s* Marruecos

moron [ˈmɔːrɒn] *s familiar* imbécil

morphine [ˈmɔːfiːn] *s* morfina

Morse (code) [mɔːs-] *s* (código) morse

morsel [ˈmɔːsl] *s* bocado

mortal [ˈmɔːtl] ◆ *adj* mortal ◆ *s* mortal

mortality [mɔːˈtælətɪ] *s* mortalidad

mortar [ˈmɔːtər] *s* ➊ argamasa ➋ mortero

mortgage [ˈmɔːgɪdʒ] ◆ *s* hipoteca ◆ *vt* hipotecar

mortician [mɔːˈtɪʃn] *s* director, ra de funeraria

mortified [ˈmɔːtɪfaɪd] *adj* muerto, ta de vergüenza

mortuary [ˈmɔːtʃʊərɪ] *s* depósito de cadáveres

mosaic [məˈzeɪɪk] *s* mosaico

Moslem [ˈmɒzləm] = **Muslim**

mosque [mɒsk] *s* mezquita

mosquito [məˈskiːtəʊ] *s* mosquito; zancudo
Dos plurales: **mosquitoes** o **mosquitos**.

moss [mɒs] *s* musgo

most [məʊst] ☀ *superlativo de many* ◆ *adj* ➊ la mayoría de • **most people** la mayoría de la gente ➋ • **(the) most** más • **who has got (the) most money?** ¿quién es el que tiene más dinero? ◆ *pronombre* ➊ • **most (of)** la mayoría (de) • **most are women** la mayoría son mujeres • **most of the time** la mayor parte del tiempo • **I spent most of the day in bed** me pasé la mayor parte del día en cama ➋ • **I earn (the) most** soy el que más dinero gana • **the most I've ever won** lo máximo que he ganado • **at most** como mucho
expresión **to make the most of something** sacarle el mayor partido a algo
◆ *adv* ➊ • **(the) most** el/la/lo más • **the most handsome man** el hombre más guapo • **he's the most experienced player on the team** es el jugador con más experiencia del equipo • **what I like most** lo que más me gusta • **most often** más a menudo ➋ *formal* muy • **most certainly** con toda seguridad ➌ casi

most

Fíjate que cuando most significa *la mayoría* o *la mayoría de* nunca lleva el artículo the delante (*most* people don't go to work on Sundays *la mayoría de la gente no trabaja el domingo*).

mostly [ˈməʊstlɪ] *adv* ➊ principalmente ➋ normalmente

motel [məʊˈtel] *s* motel

moth [mɒθ] *s* polilla

mother [ˈmʌðər] ◆ *s* madre ◆ *vt despectivo* mimar

motherhood [ˈmʌðəhʊd] *s* maternidad

mother-in-law *s* suegra
Dos plurales: **mothers-in-law** o **mother-in-laws**.

motherly [ˈmʌðəlɪ] *adj* maternal

mother-of-pearl *s* nácar

Mother's Day *s* el Día de la Madre

mother tongue *s* lengua materna

motif [məʊˈtiːf] *s* ARTE & MÚSICA motivo

motion [ˈməʊʃn] ◆ *s* ➊ movimiento ➋ moción
expresión **to go through the motions (of doing something)** (hacer algo para) cubrir el expediente
◆ *vt* • **to motion somebody to do something** indicar a alguien con un gesto que haga algo ◆ *vi* • **to motion to somebody** hacer una señal (con la mano) a alguien

motionless [ˈməʊʃənlɪs] *adj* inmóvil

motion picture *s* película

motivated [ˈməʊtɪveɪtɪd] *adj* motivado, da

motivation [ˌməʊtɪˈveɪʃn] *s* motivación

motive [ˈməʊtɪv] *s* ➊ motivo ➋ móvil

motor [ˈməʊtər] ◆ *adj* de automóviles ◆ *s* motor

motorbike [ˈməʊtəbaɪk] *s* moto

motorboat [ˈməʊtəbəʊt] *s* lancha motora

motorcar [ˈməʊtəkɑːr] *s* automóvil

motorcycle [ˈməʊtəˌsaɪkl] *s* motocicleta

motorcyclist [ˈməʊtəˌsaɪklɪst] *s* motociclista

motoring [ˈməʊtərɪŋ] *s* automovilismo

motorist [ˈməʊtərɪst] *s* automovilista; conductor, ra

motor lodge *s* motel

motor racing *s* ☀ *incontable* carreras de coches; automovilismo deportivo

motor scooter *s* **Vespa**®; escúter

motorsport [ˈməʊtəspɔːt] *s* carreras de coches

motor vehicle *s* vehículo de motor

motto [ˈmɒtəʊ] *s* lema
Dos plurales: **mottos** o **mottoes**.

mound [maʊnd] *s* ➊ montículo ➋ montón

M

mount [maʊnt] ◆ *s* ❶ montura ❷ marco *(de foto)* ❸ monte ▸ **Mount Rushmore** el Monte Rushmore ◆ *vt* ❶ subirse a; montar en ❷ lanzar *(un ataque)* ❸ enmarcar *(foto)* ◆ *vi* aumentar

MOUNT RUSHMORE

Se trata de un gigantesco relieve de los bustos de los presidentes estadounidenses **Washington, Jefferson, Lincoln** y **Theodore Roosevelt**, excavado en un lado del monte **Rushmore** (Dakota del Sur). Es un monumento nacional y una popular atracción turística. Los bustos se esculpieron utilizando taladros neumáticos y miden 28 metros de altura.

mountain ['maʊntɪn] *s* *literal & figurado* montaña

mountain bike *s* bicicleta de montaña

mountaineer [,maʊntɪ'nɪər] *s* montañero, ra; andinista

mountaineering [,maʊntɪ'nɪərɪŋ] *s* montañismo; andinismo

mountainous ['maʊntɪnəs] *adj* montañoso, sa

mourn [mɔːn] ◆ *vt* ❶ llorar por ❷ lamentarse de ◆ *vi* • **to mourn for somebody** llorar la muerte de alguien

mourner ['mɔːnər] *s* doliente

mourning ['mɔːnɪŋ] *s* luto • **in mourning** de luto

mouse [maʊs] *s* ZOOLOGÍA & INFORMÁTICA ratón

El plural de **mouse** es **mice**.

mouse pad *s* INFORMÁTICA tapete para el ratón

mousse [muːs] *s* mousse

mouth *s* [maʊθ] ❶ boca ❷ desembocadura

mouthful ['maʊθfʊl] *s* ❶ bocado ❷ trago

mouthorgan ['maʊθ,ɔ:gən] *s* armónica

mouthpiece ['maʊθpiːs] *s* ❶ micrófono *(de teléfono)* ❷ boquilla *(de instrumento)* ❸ portavoz

mouthwash ['maʊθwɒʃ] *s* enjuague bucal

mouth-watering [-,wɔ:tərɪŋ] *adj* muy apetitoso, sa

move [muːv] ◆ *s* ❶ movimiento • **on the move a)** viajando **b)** en marcha ❷ mudanza ❸ cambio *(de trabajo)* ❹ jugada • **it's your move** te toca a ti jugar ❺ medida • **selling that stock was a wise move** vender esas acciones fue un paso acertado

expresión **to get a move on** *familiar* espabilarse; darse prisa

◆ *vt* ❶ mover • **to move something closer** acercar algo ❷ mudarse de ❸ cambiar de *(trabajo)* ❹ trasladar ❺ conmover ❻ proponer *(una moción)* ❼ • **to move somebody to do something** mover o llevar a alguien a hacer algo ◆ *vi* ❶ moverse • **move closer** acércate • **come on, get moving!** ¡vamos, muévete! ❷ mudarse ❸ cambiar de trabajo

■ **move about, move around** *vi* ❶ ir de aquí para allá ❷ viajar

■ **move along** ◆ *vt* ☀ *El objeto se puede colocar antes o después de la preposición.* dispersar ◆ *vi* ❶ hacerse a un lado ❷ circular

■ **move around** *vi* = **move about**

■ **move away** *vi* ❶ apartarse ❷ marcharse *(para vivir en otro lugar)*

■ **move in** *vi* ❶ instalarse ❷ intervenir

■ **move on** *vi* ❶ marcharse ❷ avanzar

■ **move out** *vi* mudarse • **my girlfriend moved out yesterday** mi novia se fue a vivir a otra casa ayer

■ **move over** *vi* hacer sitio • **move over, I don't have enough room** córrete, no tengo suficiente espacio

■ **move up** *vi* hacer sitio

movement ['muːvmənt] *s* movimiento

movie ['muːvɪ] *s* película • **the movies** el cine • **I went to the movies with a friend** fui al cine con un amigo

movie camera *s* cámara cinematográfica

moviegoer ['muːvɪ,gəʊər] *s* ▸ persona que va mucho al cine

movie star *s* estrella de cine

movie theater *s* cine

moving ['muːvɪŋ] *adj* ❶ conmovedor, ra ❷ móvil

mow [məʊ] *vt* cortar *(el pasto)*

■ **mow down** *vt* ☀ *El objeto se puede colocar antes o después de la preposición.* acribillar

Formas irregulares de **mow**: *pp* **mown**

mower ['məʊər] *s* cortacésped

mown [məʊn] *participio pasado* → **mow**

MPEG *(abreviatura de* Moving Pictures Expert Group) *s* MPEG

mpg *(abreviatura de* miles per gallon) millas/galón

mph *(abreviatura de* miles per hour) mph

Mr ['mɪstər] *s* Sr. • **Mr Jones** el Sr. Jones

Mrs ['mɪsɪz] *s* Sra. • **Mrs Jones** la Sra. Jones

MRSA [,ema:res'eɪ] *(abreviatura de* methicillin resistant Staphylococcus aureus) *s* MEDICINA estafilococo áureo resistente a la meticilina

Ms [mɪz] *s* ▸ abreviatura utilizada delante de un apellido de mujer cuando no se quiere especificar si está casada o no

MS, ms *s* *abreviatura escrita de* **multiple sclerosis**

MSc *(abreviatura de* Master of Science) *s* (titular de un) máster en Ciencias

msg [emes'dʒiː] *(abreviatura de* message) *s* msj

much [mʌtʃ]

◆ *adj* (comparativo more, superlativo most)

☀ *se usa generalmente con nombres incontables en singular*

• **there isn't much rice left** no queda mucho arroz

• **as much money as...** tanto dinero cuanto...

• **too much** demasiado

• **how much...?** ¿cuánto... ?

M

- **how much do you earn?** ¿cuánto ganas?
- **so much** tanto
- **he got into so much trouble at school** se metió en tantos problemas en la escuela
◆ *pronombre*
- **I don't think much of his new house** no me parece que su casa nueva sea nada del otro mundo
- **I'm not much of a cook** no soy un gran cocinero
- **have as much as you like** toma todo lo que quieras
- **too much** demasiado
expresión **I thought as much** ya me imaginaba
▶ **so much for all my hard work** todo mi trabajo duro para nada
◆ *adv*
- **I don't go out much** no salgo mucho
- **it doesn't interest me much** no me interesa mucho
- **thank you very much** muchas gracias
- **I missed you so much** te eché tanto de menos
- **without so much as...** sin ni siquiera...
■ **much as**
◆ *conjunción*
- **much as I wanted to go, I had to stay in and finish my homework** aunque me apetecía mucho ir, me tuve que quedar y acabar la tarea

much

Much se emplea principalmente en oraciones interrogativas (is there **much** traffic in town today? **¿hay mucho tráfico en el centro hoy?**) y negativas (I don't have **much** money **no tengo mucho dinero**); para las afirmativas se suelen utilizar a lot (of) y lots (of) aunque much sirve para construir expresiones como too much, how much y so much.
Ver también lot, plenty.

muck [mʌk] *s ☿ incontable familiar* **①** mugre; porquería **②** estiércol
■ **muck about** *vi* hacer el tonto

mucky ['mʌkɪ] *adj* mugriento, ta

mucus ['mjuːkəs] *s* mucosidad

mud [mʌd] *s* barro; lodo

muddle ['mʌdl] ◆ *s* **①** desorden **②** lío; confusión
- **to be in a muddle** estar hecho un lío • **to get into a muddle** hacerse un lío ◆ *vt* **①** desordenar **②** liar; confundir
■ **muddle up** *vt ☿ El objeto se puede colocar antes o después de la preposición.* **①** desordenar **②** liar; confundir

muddy ['mʌdɪ] *adj* **①** lleno, na de barro **②** cenagoso, sa

mudguard ['mʌdgɑːd] *s* guardabarros

muff [mʌf] *s* manguito

muffin ['mʌfɪn] *s* ▶ especie de magdalena de varios sabores

muffle ['mʌfl] *vt* amortiguar

mug [mʌg] ◆ *s* **①** taza (alta) **②** *familiar* jeta ◆ *vt* asaltar; atracar

mugging ['mʌgɪŋ] *s* atraco

muggy ['mʌgɪ] *adj* bochornoso, sa

mule [mjuːl] *s* mula

mulled wine [mʌld-] *s* ▶ vino caliente con azúcar y especias

multicolored [ˌmʌltɪ'kʌləd] *adj* multicolor

multifaith ['mʌltɪfeɪθ] *adj* multiconfesional

multigym [ˌmʌltɪ'dʒɪm] *s* multiestación (de musculación)

multinational [ˌmʌltɪ'næʃənl] *s* multinacional

multiple ['mʌltɪpl] ◆ *adj* múltiple ◆ *s* múltiplo

multiple sclerosis [-sklɪ'rəʊsɪs] *s* esclerosis múltiple

multiplex ['mʌltɪpleks] *s* (cine) multisalas

multiplication [ˌmʌltɪplɪ'keɪʃn] *s* multiplicación

multiply ['mʌltɪplaɪ] ◆ *vt* multiplicar • **what's 3 multiplied by 7?** ¿cuánto es 3 multiplicado por 7? ◆ *vi* multiplicarse

multistory [ˌmʌltɪ'stɔːrɪ] *adj* de varias plantas

multitude ['mʌltɪtjuːd] *s* multitud

multi-user *adj* INFORMÁTICA multiusuario

mumble ['mʌmbl] ◆ *vt* mascullar ◆ *vi* musitar; hablar entre dientes

mummy ['mʌmɪ] *s* momia

mumps [mʌmps] *s ☿ incontable* paperas

munch [mʌntʃ] *vt & vi* masticar

municipal [mjuː'nɪsɪpl] *adj* municipal

municipality [mjuːˌnɪsɪ'pælətɪ] *s* municipio

murder ['mɜːdər] ◆ *s* asesinato ◆ *vt* **①** asesinar **②** *familiar* dar una paliza a

murderer ['mɜːdərər] *s* asesino

murky ['mɜːkɪ] *adj* turbio, bia

murmur ['mɜːmər] ◆ *s* murmullo ◆ *vt & vi* murmurar

muscle ['mʌsl] *s* MEDICINA músculo
■ **muscle in** *vi* entrometerse

muscular ['mʌskjʊlər] *adj* **①** muscular **②** musculoso, sa

museum [mjuː'ziːəm] *s* museo

mushroom ['mʌʃrʊm] ◆ *s* **①** champiñón **②** seta **③** BOTÁNICA hongo ◆ *vi* extenderse rápidamente

music ['mjuːzɪk] *s* música

musical ['mjuːzɪkl] ◆ *adj* **①** musical **②** con talento para la música ◆ *s* musical

musical instrument *s* instrumento musical

music center *s* cadena (musical)

musician [mjuː'zɪʃn] *s* músico, ca

Muslim, Moslem ['mʊzlɪm] ◆ *adj* musulmán, ana ◆ *s* musulmán, ana

muss [mʌs] *vt* • **to muss something (up) a)** despeinar algo *(pelo)* **b)** arrugar algo *(ropa)*

mussel ['mʌsl] *s* mejillón

must [mʌst]

◆ *v modal*

❶ [*expresa obligación*] tener que
• **I must go** tengo que irme
• **you must come and visit** tienes que venir y visitarnos
• **you must always read the instructions** siempre hay que leer las instrucciones

❷ [*en forma negativa, expresa prohibición*]
• **you mustn't talk during the lesson** no debes hablar durante la clase

❸ [*expresa una fuerte probabilidad, una deducción lógica*] deber (de)
• **Paul is not here today, he must be ill** Paul no está aquí hoy, debe (de) estar enfermo
• **I must have made a mistake** debo (de) haberme equivocado
• **they must have known** debían (de) saberlo
• **you must be kidding!** ¡no lo dices en serio!

❹ [*expresa énfasis*]
• **I must say, he's really stupid** realmente, es verdaderamente estúpido

◆ *s*
familiar
• **a must** un deber; una obligación
• **this movie's a must** esta película no hay que perdérsela

---

must

Cuando se expresa una obligación must significa lo mismo que have to (I *must* get up early tomorrow = I *have to* get up early tomorrow *tengo que levantarme temprano mañana*). Sin embargo, must no se suele utilizar con este significado en preguntas (*Do I have to/ have I got to* get up early tomorrow? *¿tengo que levantarme temprano mañana?*), o para expresar acciones cotidianas o reiteradas (I *have to* get up early every morning *tengo que levantarme temprano por la mañana*). Must tampoco tiene tiempo pasado (I *had to* get up early yesterday *tuve que levantarme temprano ayer*).

No hay que confundir frases como she *mustn't* leave (*no debe irse*) y she *doesn't have to* leave (*no tiene por qué irse*) ya que significan cosas bien distintas.

Ver también need

---

mustache ['mʌstæʃ] *s* bigote

mustard ['mʌstəd] *s* mostaza

must've ['mʌstəv] *(abreviatura de* must have) → must

musty ['mʌstɪ] *adj* ❶ que huele a cerrado ❷ que huele a viejo

mute [mjuːt] ◆ *adj* mudo, da ◆ *s* mudo, da

mutilate ['mjuːtɪleɪt] *vt* mutilar

mutiny ['mjuːtɪnɪ] ◆ *s* motín ◆ *vi* amotinarse

mutter ['mʌtər] ◆ *vt* musitar; mascullar ◆ *vi* murmurar

mutton ['mʌtn] *s* (carne de) carnero

mutual ['mjuːtʃʊəl] *adj* ❶ mutuo, tua ❷ común

mutually ['mjuːtʃʊəlɪ] *adv* mutuamente

muzzle ['mʌzl] ◆ *s* ❶ hocico; morro ❷ bozal ❸ boca *(de arma de fuego)* ◆ *vt* poner bozal a

MW *(abreviatura escrita de* medium wave) OM

my [maɪ] *adj posesivo* mi; mis ☼ *pl* • **my house/sister** mi casa/hermana • **my children** mis hijos • **my name is Sarah** me llamo Sarah • **it wasn't my fault** no fue culpa mía omi culpa • **I washed my hair** me lavé el pelo • **my Lord** milord • **my Lady** milady

---

my

No olvidemos que al hablar de las partes del cuerpo se usa el adjetivo posesivo my en lugar del artículo the (I closed *my* eyes *cerré los ojos*. I washed *my* hair *me lavé el pelo*).

---

myself [maɪ'self] *pronombre* ❶ ☼ *reflexivo* me • **I'm washing myself** me estoy lavando ❷ ☼ *tras preposición* mí mismo, ma • **with myself** conmigo mismo ❸ ☼ *para enfatizar* yo mismo, ma • **I did it myself** lo hice yo solo, la • **by myself** solo

mysterious [mɪ'stɪərɪəs] *adj* misterioso, sa

mystery ['mɪstərɪ] *s* misterio

mystical ['mɪstɪkl] *adj* místico, ca

mystified ['mɪstɪfaɪd] *adj* desconcertado, da; perplejo, ja

mystifying ['mɪstɪfaɪɪŋ] *adj* desconcertante

mystique [mɪ'stiːk] *s* misterio

myth [mɪθ] *s* mito

mythical ['mɪθɪkl] *adj* ❶ mítico, ca ❷ falso, sa

mythology [mɪ'θɒlədʒɪ] *s* mitología

M

N

n, N [en] *s* n; N

■ **N** *abreviatura* *(abreviatura escrita de* north) N
Dos plurales: **n's** o **ns; N's** o **Ns.**

n/a, N/A *(abreviatura escrita de* not applicable) ▸ no corresponde

nag [næg] *vt* dar la lata a

nagging ['nægɪŋ] *adj* ❶ persistente *(pensamiento, duda)* ❷ gruñón, ona

nail [neɪl] ◆ *s* ❶ clavo ❷ uña ◆ *vt* • **to nail something to something** clavar algo en o a algo

■ **nail down** *vt* ⚙ *El objeto se puede colocar antes o después de la preposición.* clavar

nailbrush ['neɪlbrʌʃ] *s* cepillo de uñas

nail file *s* lima de uñas

nail polish *s* esmalte para las uñas

nail scissors *spl* tijeras para las uñas

nail varnish *s* esmalte para las uñas

nail varnish remover [-rɪ'muːvəɾ] *s* quitaesmaltes

naive, naïve [naɪ'iːv] *adj* ingenuo, nua

naked ['neɪkɪd] *adj* ❶ desnudo, da • **naked flame** llama sin protección ❷ • **with the naked eye** a simple vista

Nam [næm] *(abreviatura de* Vietnam) *s familiar* Vietnam

name [neɪm] ◆ *s* ❶ nombre • **what's your name?** ¿cómo te llamas? • **my name is John** me llamo John • **by name** por el nombre • **it's in my wife's name** está a nombre de mi mujer • **in the name of** en nombre de ❷ apellido

expresión **to call somebody names** llamar de todo a alguien ▸ **to have a good name** tener buena fama

◆ *vt* ❶ poner nombre a • **we named him Jim** le llamamos Jim • **to name somebody for somebody** poner a alguien el nombre de alguien ❷ nombrar ❸ poner; decir *(fecha, precio)*

nameless ['neɪmlɪs] *adj* anónimo, ma

namely ['neɪmlɪ] *adv* a saber

namesake ['neɪmseɪk] *s* tocayo, ya

nanny ['nænɪ] *s* niñera

nanometer ['nænəʊˌmiːtəɾ] *s* nanómetro

nap [næp] ◆ *s* siesta • **to take** o **have a nap** echar una siesta ◆ *vi*

expresión **we were caught napping** *familiar* nos pillaron desprevenidos

nape [neɪp] *s* • **nape of the neck** nuca

napkin ['næpkɪn] *s* servilleta

narcotic [nɑː'kɒtɪk] ◆ *adj* narcótico, ca ◆ *s* narcótico

narrative ['nærətɪv] ◆ *adj* narrativo, va ◆ *s* ❶ narración ❷ narrativa

narrator ['næreɪtəɾ] *s* narrador, ra

narrow ['nærəʊ] ◆ *adj* ❶ estrecho, cha ❷ estrecho, cha de miras ❸ por un estrecho margen *(victoria, derrota)* ❹ escaso, sa *(mayoría)* ❺ por muy poco ◆ *vi* ❶ estrecharse ❷ entornarse *(los ojos)* ❸ reducirse *(distancia)*

■ **narrow down** *vt* ⚙ *El objeto se puede colocar antes o después de la preposición.* reducir

narrowly ['nærəʊlɪ] *adv* por muy poco

narrow-minded [-'maɪndɪd] *adj* estrecho, cha de miras

nasty ['nɑːstɪ] *adj* ❶ malintencionado, da • **she was nasty to him** fue muy mala con él ❷ desagradable ❸ horrible *(tiempo)* ❹ peliagudo, da ❺ doloroso, sa ❻ grave *(accidente)* ❼ malo, la *(caída)*

nation ['neɪʃn] *s* nación

national ['næʃənl] ◆ *adj* nacional ◆ *s* ciudadano, na

national anthem *s* himno nacional

National Guard *s* • **the National Guard** la Guardia Nacional estadounidense

nationalism ['næʃnəlɪzm] *s* nacionalismo

nationalist ['næʃnəlɪst] ◆ *adj* nacionalista ◆ *s* nacionalista

nationality [ˌnæʃə'nælətɪ] *s* nacionalidad

nationalize ['næʃnəlaɪz] *vt* nacionalizar

national park *s* parque nacional

nationwide ['neɪʃənwaɪd] ◆ *adj* de ámbito nacional ◆ *adv* ❶ por todo el país ❷ a todo el país *(transmitir)*

native ['neɪtɪv] ◆ *adj* ❶ natal ❷ nativo, va *(hablante)* • **native language** lengua materna ❸ • **native (to)** originario, ria (de) ◆ *s* natural; nativo, va

Native American *s* indio americano; india americana

NATIVE AMERICAN

Las tribus de aborígenes americanos que poblaban Estados Unidos antes de la llegada de los europeos reciben el nombre de **Native American**. Cada una poseía su propia lengua y modo de vida. Muchos indios murieron combatiendo a los colonos europeos o bien por haber contraído alguna de las enfermedades que estos trajeron a América. Otros muchos fueron obligados a vivir en reservas, territorios apartados especialmente para ellos. A lo largo del siglo XX, el gobierno estadounidense procuró conceder más derechos a los grupos étnicos nativos de Estados Unidos; también ha ido mostrando cada vez mayor interés por su historia y su cultura tradicional.

Nativity [nə'tɪvətɪ] *s* • **the Nativity** la Natividad

NATO ['neɪtəʊ] *(abreviatura de* North Atlantic Treaty Organization*) s* la OTAN

natural ['nætʃrəl] *adj* ❶ natural ❷ nato, ta

natural disaster *s* desastre natural

natural gas *s* gas natural

naturalize ['nætʃrəlaɪz] *vt* naturalizar • **to be naturalized** naturalizarse

naturally ['nætʃrəlɪ] *adv* ❶ naturalmente ❷ con naturalidad ❸ por naturaleza • **to come naturally to somebody** ser innato en alguien

nature ['neɪtʃər] *s* ❶ naturaleza • **I'm a nature lover** soy un amante de la naturaleza • **matters of this nature** asuntos de esta índole ❷ modo de ser; carácter • **by nature** por naturaleza

nature reserve *s* reserva natural

naughty ['nɔːtɪ] *adj* ❶ travieso, sa; malo, la • **they've been very naughty** se han portado muy mal ❷ verde *(chiste)*

nausea ['nɔːsjə] *s* náuseas

nautical ['nɔːtɪkl] *adj* náutico, ca; marítimo, ma

naval ['neɪvl] *adj* naval

nave [neɪv] *s* nave

navel ['neɪvl] *s* ombligo

navigate ['nævɪgeɪt] ◆ *vt* ❶ pilotar; gobernar ❷ surcar; navegar por ◆ *vi* ❶ dirigir; gobernar ❷ dar direcciones *(en automóvil)*

navigation [,nævɪ'geɪʃn] *s* navegación

navigator ['nævɪgeɪtər] *s* oficial de navegación; navegante

navy ['neɪvɪ] ◆ *s* marina; armada ◆ *adj* azul marino

navy blue *adj* azul marino

Nazi ['nɑːtsɪ] ◆ *adj* nazi ◆ *s* nazi

NB *(abreviatura de* nota bene*)* N.B.

near [nɪər] ◆ *adj* ❶ cercano, na • **the near side** el lado más cercano • **in the near future** en un futuro próximo • **she's the nearest thing to a mother I ever had** es lo más cercano a una madre que yo he tenido ❷ próximo, ma

expresión **it was a near thing** poco le faltó

◆ *adv* ❶ cerca • **to draw** o **come near** acercarse • **nowhere near** ni de lejos; ni mucho menos ❷ casi

◆ *preposición* ❶ • **near (to)** cerca de • **to go near something** acercarse a algo ❷ • **it's getting near (to) Christmas** ya estamos casi en Navidades • **near the end** casi al final • **nearer the time** cuando se acerque la fecha ❸ • **near (to)** al borde de ◆ *vt* acercarse o aproximarse a ◆ *vi* acercarse; aproximarse

nearby [nɪə'baɪ] ◆ *adj* cercano, na ◆ *adv* cerca

nearly ['nɪəlɪ] *adv* casi • **I nearly fell** por poco me caigo

near miss *s* ❶ • **it was a near miss** falló por poco ❷ incidente aéreo *(sin colisión)*

nearsighted [,nɪə'saɪtɪd] *adj* miope; corto, ta de vista

neat [niːt] *adj* ❶ pulcro, cra ❷ arreglado, da *(casa, habitación, persona)* ❸ esmerado, da *(caligrafía)* ❹ hábil ❺ solo, la *(bebida alcohólica)* ❻ familiar chido

neatly ['niːtlɪ] *adv* ❶ con pulcritud ❷ con esmero ❸ hábilmente

necessarily [,nesə'serəlɪ] *adv* necesariamente

necessary ['nesəsrɪ] *adj* ❶ necesario, ria ❷ inevitable

necessity [nɪ'sesətɪ] *s* necesidad • **of necessity** por fuerza; por necesidad

■ **necessities** *spl* artículos de primera necesidad

neck [nek] *s* ❶ cuello ❷ pescuezo

necklace ['neklɪs] *s* collar

neckline ['neklaɪn] *s* escote

necktie ['nektaɪ] *s* corbata

nectarine ['nektərɪn] *s* nectarina

née [neɪ] *adj* de soltera

---

need [niːd]

◆ *s*

[*expresa una necesidad*]

• **need for something/to do something** necesidad de algo/de hacer algo

• **there's no need to get up** no hace falta levantarse

• **there's no need for such language** no hace falta que uses ese lenguaje

• **to be in** o **have need of something** *formal* necesitar algo

• **if need be** si hiciera falta; si fuera necesario

• **in need** necesitado

◆ *vt*

❶ [*expresa una necesidad*] necesitar
• **he needs new shoes** necesita nuevos zapatos
• **the kitchen needs repainting** o **to be repainted** hace falta volver a pintar la cocina

❷ [*expresa una obligación*]
• **to need to do something** tener que hacer algo
• **I need to leave right away** me tengo que ir ahora mismo

◆ *v modal* 🔅 *funciona como verbo auxiliar*

• **need we go?** ¿tenemos que ir?
• **it need not happen** no tiene que ocurrir
• **you needn't shout!** ¡no hace falta que grites!

---

need

Need se puede usar con gerundio: my car *needs* wash*ing* (= my car needs to be washed *a mi coche le hace falta una lavada*). Esta construcción es muy común.

El uso de need en preguntas como need we finish this today? (*¿tenemos que terminar esto hoy?*) es muy formal. En el habla normal, need se suele sustituir por have to (*do we have to finish this today?*).

La forma negativa, needn't quiere decir *no es necesario que..., no hace falta que...* (you *needn't* get up early tomorrow *no hace falta que te levantes temprano mañana*). Es, por tanto, diferente de mustn't, que quiere decir *es necesario que no...* (you *mustn't* make so much noise, you'll wake the baby *no debes hacer tanto ruido que vas a despertar al bebé*). Ver también must.

---

needle ['niːdl] *s* aguja

needless ['niːdlɪs] *adj* innecesario, ria • **needless to say...** está de más decir que...

needlework ['niːdlwɜːk] *s* ❶ bordado ❷ 🔅 *incontable* costura

needn't ['niːdnt] (*abreviatura de* need not) → **need**

needy ['niːdɪ] *adj* necesitado, da

negative ['negətɪv] ◆ *adj* negativo, va ◆ *s* ❶ FOTOGRAFÍA negativo ❷ LINGÜÍSTICA negación • **to answer in the negative** decir que no

neglect [nɪ'glekt] ◆ *s* ❶ descuido • **a state of neglect** un estado de abandono ❷ incumplimiento (*del deber*) ◆ *vt* ❶ desatender ❷ no cumplir con (*deber, trabajo*)

neglectful [nɪ'glektfʊl] *adj* descuidado, da; negligente • **to be neglectful of something/somebody** desatender algo/a alguien

negligee ['neglɪʒeɪ] *s* salto de cama

negligence ['neglɪdʒəns] *s* negligencia

negligible ['neglɪdʒəbl] *adj* insignificante

negotiate [nɪ'gəʊʃɪeɪt] ◆ *vt* ❶ negociar ❷ salvar; franquear ❸ tomar (*una curva*) ◆ *vi* • **to negotiate** (**with somebody for something**) negociar (con alguien algo)

negotiation [nɪ,gəʊʃɪ'eɪʃn] *s* negociación
■ **negotiations** *spl* negociaciones

Negress ['niːgrɪs] *s* negra

Negro ['niːgrəʊ] ◆ *adj* negro, gra ◆ *s* negro, gra
El plural de **Negro** es **Negroes**.

neigh [neɪ] *vi* relinchar

neighbor ['neɪbər] *s* vecino, na

neighborhood ['neɪbəhʊd] *s* ❶ barrio; vecindad ❷ • **in the neighborhood of** alrededor de

neighboring ['neɪbərɪŋ] *adj* vecino, na

neither ['naɪðər,] ['niːðər] ◆ *adv* • **I don't drink — me neither** no bebo — yo tampoco • **he doesn't know and neither does she** él no sabe y ella tampoco • **she can't swim — neither can I** ella no sabe nadar — yo tampoco • **the food was neither good nor bad** la comida no era ni buena ni mala

expresión **to be neither here nor there** no tener nada que ver

◆ *pronombre* ninguno, na • **neither of us/them** ninguno de nosotros/ellos ◆ *adj* • **neither cup is blue** ninguna de las dos tazas es azul ◆ *conjunción* • **neither... nor...** ni... ni... • **she could neither eat nor sleep** no podía ni comer ni dormir

---

neither

Como adjetivo, neither sólo va delante de sustantivos contables en singular (*neither* dictionary *ninguno de los dos diccionarios*; *neither* alternative *ninguna de las dos alternativas*).

Cuando neither es el sujeto de la oración, o cuando lo es el sustantivo al que acompaña, el verbo siempre va en singular (*neither* movie appeals to me; *neither* appeals to me *ninguno de los dos me atrae*). Fíjate en que el verbo va en afirmativa.

Neither of puede ir seguido de un verbo en singular o plural (*neither of* us *like/likes* blue *a ninguno de nosotros nos gusta el azul*).

Cuando el sujeto de la oración se encuentra entre neither y nor el verbo va siempre en singular, al contrario que en español (*neither* John *nor* Deborah *is* coming tonight *ni John ni Deborah vendrán esta noche*).

---

neon ['niːɒn] *s* neón

neon light *s* luz de neón

nephew ['nefjuː] *s* sobrino

Neptune ['neptjuːn] *s* Neptuno

nerve [nɜːv] *s* ❶ ANATOMÍA nervio ❷ valor • **to keep your nerve** mantener la calma; no perder los nervios • **to lose your nerve** echarse atrás; perder el valor

❸ cara • **to have the nerve to do something** tener la cara de hacer algo

■ **nerves** *spl* nervios

expresión **to get on somebody's nerves** sacar de quicio a alguien

nerve-racking [-ˌrækɪŋ] *adj* crispante

nervous ['nɜːvəs] *adj* **❶** ANATOMÍA & PSICOLOGÍA nervioso, sa • **going to the dentist makes me nervous** me pone nervioso ir al dentista **❷** inquieto, ta; aprensivo, va

nervous breakdown *s* crisis nerviosa

nest [nest] ◆ *s* nido • **wasps' nest** avispero ◆ *vi* anidar

net [net] ◆ *adj* neto, ta ◆ *s* red ◆ *vt* **❶** coger con red **❷** embolsarse

Net [net] *s* • **the Net** la Red • **to surf the Net** navegar por la Red

Netherlands ['neðələndz] *spl* • **the Netherlands** los Países Bajos

netting ['netɪŋ] *s* red; malla

nettle ['netl] *s* ortiga

network ['netwɜːk] ◆ *s* **❶** red **❷** RADIO & TELEVISIÓN cadena ◆ *vt* INFORMÁTICA conectar a la red

neurotic [ˌnjʊə'rɒtɪk] ◆ *adj* neurótico, ca ◆ *s* neurótico, ca

neuter ['njuːtər] ◆ *adj* neutro, tra ◆ *vt* castrar

neutral ['njuːtrəl] ◆ *adj* **❶** neutro, tra **❷** neutral ◆ *s* AUTOMÓVILES punto muerto

neutrality [njuː'trælətɪ] *s* neutralidad

never ['nevər] *adv* **❶** nunca; jamás • **I've never done it** no lo he hecho nunca • **never again** nunca más • **never ever** nunca jamás; nunca en la vida **❷** *familiar* no • **I never knew** no lo sabía • **you never did!** ¡no (me digas)!

expresión **well I never!** ¡vaya!; ¡caramba!

never-ending *adj* inacabable

nevertheless [ˌnevəðə'les] *adv* sin embargo; no obstante

new [njuː] *adj* **❶** nuevo, va • **to be new to something** ser nuevo, va en algo • **as good as new** como nuevo • **what's new?** ¿qué hay de nuevo? **❷** recién nacido, recién nacida

newborn ['njuːbɔːn] *adj* recién nacido, recién nacida

newcomer ['njuːˌkʌmər] *s* • **newcomer (to)** recién llegado, recién llegada (a)

New Delhi *s* Nueva Delhi

new-found *adj* **❶** recién descubierto, recién descubierta **❷** reciente *(amigo)*

newly ['njuːlɪ] *adv* recién

newlyweds ['njuːlɪwedz] *spl* recién casados

new moon *s* luna nueva

news *s* ⚙ *incontable* noticias • **a piece of news** una noticia • **I have some good news** tengo buenas noticias • **the news a)** las noticias **b)** el telediario

expresión **that's news to me** me coge de nuevas

▶ **to break the news to somebody** dar la noticia a alguien

newscaster ['njuːzkɑːstər] *s* presentador, ra; locutor, ra

newsdealer ['njuːzdiːlər] *s* vendedor, ra de periódicos

newsflash ['njuːzflæʃ] *s* noticia de última hora

newsletter ['njuːzˌletər] *s* boletín

newspaper ['njuːzˌpeɪpər] *s* **❶** periódico **❷** diario **❸** papel de periódico

newsreader ['njuːzˌriːdər] *s* presentador, ra; locutor, ra

newsstand ['njuːzstænd] *s* quiosco de periódicos

newt [njuːt] *s* tritón

new technology *s* nueva tecnología

New Year *s* Año Nuevo • **Happy New Year!** ¡Feliz Año Nuevo!

New Year's Day *s* el día de Año Nuevo

New Year's Eve *s* la noche de Fin de Año

New York [-'jɔːk] *s* **❶** • **New York (City)** Nueva York **❷** • **New York (State)** (el estado de) Nueva York

New Zealand [-'ziːlənd] *s* Nueva Zelanda

New Zealander [-'ziːləndər] *s* neozelandés, esa

next [nekst] ◆ *adj* **❶** próximo, ma • **the next day** el día siguiente • **next Tuesday/year** el martes/el año que viene • **next week** la semana próxima o que viene • **the next week** los próximos siete días **❷** siguiente *(página)*; de al lado *(casa, habitación)* ◆ *pronombre* el siguiente, la siguiente • **who's next?** ¿quién es el siguiente? • **next, please!** ¡el siguiente, por favor! • **the day after next** pasado mañana • **the week after next** la semana que viene no, la otra ◆ *adv* **❶** después • **what should I do next?** ¿qué hago ahora? • **it's my go next** ahora me toca a mí **❷** de nuevo • **when do they next play?** ¿cuándo vuelven a tocar? **❸** • **next best/biggest** ETC el segundo mejor/más grande ETC ◆ *preposición* al lado de; junto a

■ **next to** *preposición* al lado de; junto a

expresión **next to nothing** casi nada ▶ **in next to no time** en un abrir y cerrar de ojos

next door *adv* (en la casa de) al lado

■ **next-door** *adj* • **next-door neighbor** vecino, na de al lado

next of kin *s* pariente más cercano, pariente más cercana

nib [nɪb] *s* plumilla

nibble ['nɪbl] *vt* mordisquear

Nicaragua [ˌnɪkə'rægjʊə] *s* Nicaragua

Nicaraguan [ˌnɪkə'rægjʊən] ◆ *adj* nicaragüense ◆ *s* nicaragüense

nice [naɪs] *adj* **❶** lindo, da • **you look nice** estás linda **❷** bueno, na • **it smells nice** huele bien **❸** amable • **that was nice of you** fue muy amable de tu parte **❹** agradable; simpático, ca • **to be nice to somebody** ser bueno con alguien **❺** agradable • **to have**

a nice time pasarla bien • **have a nice time!** ¡que la pases bien!

nice-looking [-'lʊkɪŋ] *adj* ❶ guapo, pa ❷ bonito, ta

nicely ['naɪslɪ] *adv* ❶ bien • **that will do nicely** esto irá de perlas ❷ educadamente; con educación • **ask nicely!** ¡pide con buenos modales!

niche [niːʃ] *s* ❶ nicho ❷ hueco *(en la vida)*

nick [nɪk] ◆ *s* ❶ cortecito ❷ muesca

expresión **in the nick of time** justo a tiempo
◆ *vt* ❶ cortar ❷ mellar

nickel ['nɪkl] *s* ❶ níquel ❷ moneda de cinco centavos

nickname ['nɪkneɪm] ◆ *s* apodo ◆ *vt* apodar

nicotine ['nɪkətiːn] *s* nicotina

niece [niːs] *s* sobrina

Nigeria [naɪ'dʒɪərɪə] *s* Nigeria

Nigerian [naɪ'dʒɪərɪən] ◆ *adj* nigeriano, na ◆ *s* nigeriano, na

night [naɪt] ◆ *adj* nocturno, na ◆ *s* ❶ noche • **last night** anoche; ayer por la noche • **tomorrow night** mañana por la noche • **on Monday night** el lunes por la noche • **at night** por la noche; de noche • **good night!** ¡buenas noches! • **night and day, day and night** noche y día; día y noche • **to have an early/a late night** irse a dormir pronto/tarde ❷ tarde

■ **nights** *adv* por las noches

nightclub ['naɪtklʌb] *s* club nocturno

nightdress ['naɪtdres] *s* camisón

nightfall ['naɪtfɔːl] *s* anochecer

nightgown ['naɪtgaʊn] *s* camisón

nightie ['naɪtɪ] *s familiar* camisón

nightlife ['naɪtlaɪf] *s* vida nocturna

nightly ['naɪtlɪ] ◆ *adj* nocturno, na; de cada noche ◆ *adv* cada noche

nightmare ['naɪtmeəʳ] *s literal & figurado* pesadilla

night porter *s* recepcionista del turno de noche

night school *s* ⚙*incontable* escuela nocturna

night shift *s* turno de noche

nightshirt ['naɪtʃɜːt] *s* camisa de dormir (masculina)

nightstick ['naɪtstɪk] *s* porra

nighttime ['naɪttaɪm] *s* noche • **at nighttime** de noche

nil [nɪl] *s* nada

Nile [naɪl] *s* • **the Nile** el Nilo

nimble ['nɪmbl] *adj* ágil

nine [naɪn] *número* nueve ver también **six**

nineteen [ˌnaɪn'tiːn] *número* diecinueve ver también **six**

ninety ['naɪntɪ] *número* noventa ver también **sixty**

ninth [naɪnθ] *número* noveno, na ver también **sixth**

nip [nɪp] *vt* ❶ pellizcar ❷ mordisquear

nipple ['nɪpl] *s* ❶ pezón ❷ tetilla

nit [nɪt] *s* liendre

nitpicking ['nɪtpɪkɪŋ] *s* ⚙*incontable familiar* • **that's just nitpicking** no son más que nimiedades

nitrogen ['naɪtrədʒən] *s* nitrógeno

no [nəʊ] ◆ *adv* no • **do you like seafood? — no, I don't** ¿te gustan los mariscos? — no • **to say no** decir que no • **you're no better than me** tú no eres mejor que yo ◆ *adj* no • **I have no time** no tengo tiempo • **there are no taxis** no hay taxis • **a woman with no money** una mujer sin dinero • **that's no excuse** esa no es excusa que valga • **he's no fool** no es ningún tonto • **she's no friend of mine** no es amiga mía • '**no smoking/parking/cameras**' 'prohibido fumar/aparcar/hacer fotos' ◆ *s* no

expresión **he/she won't take no for an answer** no acepta una respuesta negativa

El plural de **no** es **noes**.

no

Como adjetivo, **no** puede ir con sustantivos contables o incontables (*no* bread; *no* books).

Es importante recordar que cuando se usa **no** como adjetivo, el resto de la oración va en afirmativa (*no* changes **have** occurred *no ha habido cambios*; that's *no* problem *no hay ningún problema*).

Por último, tengamos presente que **no** nunca es pronombre; **none** es su forma correspondiente (there are *no* cookies left — there are *none* left *no quedan galletas — no queda ninguna*).

Ver también **some**.

No., no. (*abreviatura escrita de* number) n.°

nobility [nə'bɪlətɪ] *s* nobleza

noble ['nəʊbl] ◆ *adj* noble ◆ *s* noble

nobody ['nəʊbədɪ], **no one** ◆ *pronombre* nadie ◆ *s despectivo* don nadie

no-brainer ['nəʊ'breɪnəʳ] *s familiar* • **it's a no-brainer** es pan comido

nocturnal [nɒk'tɜːnl] *adj* nocturno, na

nod [nɒd] ◆ *vt* • **to nod your head a)** asentir con la cabeza **b)** indicar con la cabeza **c)** saludar con la cabeza ◆ *vi* ❶ asentir con la cabeza ❷ indicar con la cabeza ❸ saludar con la cabeza

■ **nod off** *vi* quedarse dormido, da

noise [nɔɪz] *s* ruido • **to make a noise** hacer ruido

noisy ['nɔɪzɪ] *adj* ruidoso, sa • **it was very noisy** había mucho ruido

nominate ['nɒmɪneɪt] *vt* ❶ • **to nominate somebody (for o as)** proponer a alguien (por o como) ❷ • **to nominate somebody (to something)** nombrar a alguien (algo)

nomination [ˌnɒmɪ'neɪʃn] *s* ❶ nominación
❷ • **nomination (to something)** nombramiento (a algo)

nominee [ˌnɒmɪ'niː] *s* candidato, ta

non- [nɒn] *prefijo* no

nonalcoholic [ˌnɒnælkə'hɒlɪk] *adj* sin alcohol

nonchalant [ˌnɒnʃə'lɑːnt] *adj* despreocupado, da

nonconformist [ˌnɒnkən'fɔːmɪst] ◆ *adj* inconformista ◆ *s* inconformista

nondescript [ˌnɒndɪ'skrɪpt] *adj* anodino, na; soso, sa

none [nʌn] ◆ *pronombre* ❶ nada • **there is none left** no queda nada • **it's none of your business** no es asunto tuyo ❷ ninguno, na • **none of us/the books** ninguno de nosotros/de los libros • **I had none** no tenía ninguno ◆ *adv* • **I'm none the worse/better** no me ha perjudicado/ayudado en nada • **I'm none the wiser** no me ha aclarado nada
expresión **none too soon** justo a tiempo

none

No hay que olvidar que none jamás es adjetivo.
Hay que usar no en ese caso (there are *none* left
— there are *no* cookies left *no queda ninguna*
— *no quedan galletas*).

En oraciones donde none es un pronombre, el
verbo va en la forma afirmativa (*none* of this *is*
your fault *nada de esto es tu culpa*).

Ver también no, some.

nonetheless [ˌnʌnðə'les] *adv* sin embargo; no obstante

nonexistent [ˌnɒnɪg'zɪstənt] *adj* inexistente

nonfiction [ˌnɒn'fɪkʃn] *s* no ficción

no-nonsense *adj* práctico, ca

nonreturnable [ˌnɒnrɪ'tɜːnəbl] *adj* no retornable; sin retorno

nonsense ['nɒnsəns] ◆ *s* ☼*incontable* ❶ tonterías • **it is nonsense to suggest that...** es absurdo sugerir que... ❷ galimatías ◆ *exclamación* ¡tonterías!

nonsensical [nɒn'sensɪkl] *adj* disparatado, da; absurdo, da

nonsmoker [ˌnɒn'sməʊkər] *s* no fumador, no fumadora

nonstick [ˌnɒn'stɪk] *adj* antiadherente

nonstop [ˌnɒn'stɒp] ◆ *adj* ❶ continuo, nua; incesante ❷ sin escalas *(vuelo)* ◆ *adv* sin parar

noodles ['nuːdlz] *spl* fideos

nook [nʊk] *s* • **every nook and cranny** todos los recovecos

noon [nuːn] *s* mediodía

no one *pronombre* = **nobody**

noose [nuːs] *s* ❶ nudo corredizo ❷ soga

no-place = **nowhere**

nor [nɔːr] *conjunción* ❶ → **neither** ❷ ni • **I don't smoke — nor do I** no fumo — yo tampoco • **I don't know, nor do I care** ni lo sé, ni me importa

norm [nɔːm] *s* norma • **the norm** lo normal

normal ['nɔːml] ◆ *adj* normal • **at the normal time** a la hora de siempre ◆ *s* • **above normal** por encima de lo normal • **to return to normal** volver a la normalidad

normality [nɔː'mælɪtɪ], **normalcy** ['nɔːmlsɪ] *s* normalidad

normally ['nɔːməlɪ] *adv* normalmente

north [nɔːθ] ◆ *s* ❶ norte ❷ • **the North** el norte ◆ *adj* del norte • **North Boston** el norte de Boston • **the north coast** la costa norte ◆ *adv* hacia el norte • **north (of)** al norte (de)

North Africa *s* África del Norte

North America *s* Norteamérica

North American ◆ *adj* norteamericano, na ◆ *s* norteamericano, na

northeast [ˌnɔːθ'iːst] ◆ *s* ❶ nordeste ❷ • **the Northeast** el nordeste ◆ *adj* del nordeste ◆ *adv* hacia el nordeste • **northeast (of)** al nordeste (de)

northerly ['nɔːðəlɪ] *adj* del norte

northern ['nɔːðən] *adj* del norte; norteño, ña • **northern Canada** el norte de Canadá

Northern Ireland *s* Irlanda del Norte

northernmost ['nɔːðənməʊst] *adj* más septentrional o al norte

North Korea *s* Corea del Norte

North Pole *s* • **the North Pole** el Polo Norte

North Sea *s* • **the North Sea** el Mar del Norte

northward ['nɔːθwəd] ◆ *adj* hacia el norte ◆ *adv* = **northwards**

northwards ['nɔːθwədz], **northward** *adv* hacia el norte

northwest [ˌnɔːθ'west] ◆ *s* ❶ noroeste ❷ • **the Northwest** el noroeste ◆ *adj* del noroeste ◆ *adv* hacia el noroeste • **northwest (of)** al noroeste (de)

Norway ['nɔːweɪ] *s* Noruega

Norwegian [nɔː'wiːdʒən] ◆ *adj* noruego, ga ◆ *s* ❶ noruego, ga ❷ noruego

nose [nəʊz] *s* ❶ nariz • **to blow your nose** sonarse la nariz ❷ hocico ❸ morro *(de avión, vehículo)*
expresiones **to keep your nose out of something** no meter las narices en algo ▶ **to poke** o **stick your nose in** *familiar* meter las narices ▶ **to turn up your nose at something** hacerle ascos a algo

nosebleed ['nəʊzbliːd] *s* hemorragia nasal

nosey ['nəʊzɪ] = **nosy**

no-smoking *adj* ❶ para no fumadores *(zona)* ❷ de no fumadores *(vuelo)* • **no-smoking flights** vuelos de no fumadores

nostalgia [nɒ'stældʒə] *s* • **nostalgia (for)** nostalgia (de)

nostril ['nɒstrəl] *s* ventana de la nariz

N

nosy ['nəʊzɪ], **nosey** *adj* fisgón, ona ; entrometido, da

not [nɒt] *adv* no • **this is not the first time** no es la primera vez • **it's green, isn't it?** es verde, ¿no? • **not me** yo no • **I hope/think not** espero/creo que no • **not a chance** de ninguna manera • **not even a...** ni siquiera un, una... • **not all** o **every** no todos, das • **not always** no siempre • **not that...** no es que... • **not at all a)** en absoluto **b)** de nada

notable ['nəʊtəbl] *adj* notable • **to be notable for something** destacar por algo

notably ['nəʊtəblɪ] *adv* ❶ especialmente ❷ marcadamente

notary ['nəʊtərɪ] *s* ▶ **notary (public)** notario, ria

notch [nɒtʃ] *s* muesca

note [nəʊt] ◆ *s* ❶ nota • **to make a note of something** tomar nota de algo ❷ billete ❸ tono ◆ *vt* ❶ notar • **please note that...** tenga en cuenta que... ❷ mencionar
■ **notes** *spl* ❶ apuntes • **to take notes** tomar apuntes ❷ notas

■ **note down** *vt* ☼: *El objeto se puede colocar antes o después de la preposición.* anotar ; apuntar

notebook ['nəʊtbʊk] *s* ❶ libreta ; cuaderno ❷ INFORMÁTICA • **notebook (computer)** computadora portátil

noted ['nəʊtɪd] *adj* destacado, da • **to be noted for** distinguirse por

notepad ['nəʊtpæd] *s* bloc de notas

notepaper ['nəʊtpeɪpər] *s* papel de escribir o de cartas

noteworthy ['nəʊt,wɜːðɪ] *adj* digno, na de mención

nothing ['nʌθɪŋ] ◆ *pronombre* nada • **I've got nothing to do** no tengo nada que hacer • **for nothing a)** gratis **b)** en vano ; en balde • **he's nothing if not generous** otra cosa no será pero desde luego generoso sí que es • **nothing but** tan sólo ◆ *adv* • **to be nothing like somebody/something** no parecerse en nada a alguien/algo • **I'm nothing like finished** no he terminado ni mucho menos

notice ['nəʊtɪs] ◆ *s* ❶ cartel ❷ anuncio ❸ atención • **to take notice (of)** hacer caso (de) ; prestar atención (a) • **he didn't take a blind bit of notice** no hizo ni el más mínimo caso ❹ aviso • **at short notice** casi sin previo aviso • **until further notice** hasta nuevo aviso • **without notice** sin previo aviso ❺ • **to be given your notice** ser despedido, da • **to hand in your notice** presentar la dimisión ◆ *vt* ❶ notar ❷ fijarse en ; ver • **to notice somebody doing something** fijarse en alguien que está haciendo algo ❸ darse cuenta de ◆ *vi* darse cuenta

noticeable ['nəʊtɪsəbl] *adj* notable

notice board *s* tablón de anuncios

notify ['nəʊtɪfaɪ] *vt* • **to notify somebody (of something)** notificar o comunicar (algo) a alguien

notion ['nəʊʃn] *s* noción
■ **notions** *spl* artículos de mercería

notorious [nəʊ'tɔːrɪəs] *adj* famoso, sa ; célebre

notwithstanding [,nɒtwɪə'stændɪŋ] *formal* ◆ *preposición* a pesar de ◆ *adv* sin embargo

nougat ['nuːgɑː] *s* ▶ dulce hecho a base de nueces y frutas

nought [nɔːt] *número* cero

noun [naʊn] *s* nombre ; sustantivo

nourish ['nʌrɪʃ] *vt* nutrir

nourishing ['nʌrɪʃɪŋ] *adj* nutritivo, va

nourishment ['nʌrɪʃmənt] *s* alimento ; sustento

novel ['nɒvl] ◆ *adj* original ◆ *s* novela

novelist ['nɒvəlɪst] *s* novelista

novelty ['nɒvltɪ] *s* ❶ novedad ❷ baratija (poco útil)

November [nə'vembər] *s* noviembre ver también **September**

novice ['nɒvɪs] *s* ❶ principiante ❷ RELIGIÓN novicio, cia

now [naʊ] ◆ *adv* ❶ ahora • **do it now** hazlo ahora • **he's been away for two weeks now** lleva dos semanas fuera • **any day now** cualquier día de éstos • **any time now** en cualquier momento • **for now** por ahora ; por el momento • **now and then** o **again** de vez en cuando • **right now** ahora mismo ❷ hoy día ❸ entonces ❹ vamos a ver ◆ *conjunción* • **now (that)** ahora que ; ya que ◆ *s* ahora • **five days from now** de aquí a cinco días • **from now on** a partir de ahora • **they should be here by now** ya deberían estar aquí • **up until now** hasta ahora

nowadays ['naʊədeɪz] *adv* hoy en día ; actualmente

nowhere ['nəʊweər], **no-place** *adv* ❶ en ninguna parte • **nowhere else** en ninguna otra parte • **to appear out of** o **from nowhere** salir de la nada • **(to be) nowhere near (as... as...)** (no ser) ni mucho menos (tan... como...) ❷ a ninguna parte • **to be getting nowhere** no estar avanzando nada ; no ir a ninguna parte

nozzle ['nɒzl] *s* boquilla

nuance [nju:'ɑːns] *s* matiz

nuclear ['nju:klɪər] *adj* nuclear

nuclear bomb *s* bomba atómica

nuclear disarmament *s* desarme nuclear

nuclear energy, nuclear power *s* energía nuclear

nuclear power station *s* central nuclear

nuclear reactor *s* reactor nuclear

nucleus ['nju:klɪəs] *s literal & figurado* núcleo

El plural de **nucleus** es **nuclei** ['nju:klɪaɪ].

nude [nju:d] ◆ *adj* desnudo, da ◆ *s* ARTE desnudo • **in the nude** desnudo, da

nudge [nʌdʒ] *vt* dar un codazo a

nudist ['nju:dɪst] *s* nudista

nudity ['nju:dətɪ] *s* desnudez

nugget ['nʌgɪt] *s* pepita (de oro)

nuisance['nju:sns] *s* ❶fastidio; molestia ❷pesado •**to make a nuisance of yourself** dar la lata

null[nʌl] *adj* •**null and void** nulo, la y sin efecto

numb[nʌm] ◆*adj* entumecido, da •**to be numb with cold** estar helado, da de frío •**to be numb with fear** estar paralizado, da de miedo ◆*vt* entumecer

number['nʌmbəɾ] ◆*s* ❶número •**a number of** varios, rias •**a large number of** gran número de •**large numbers of** grandes cantidades de •**any number of** la mar de ❷matrícula ◆*vt* ❶ascender a ❷numerar

number one ◆*adj* principal; número uno ◆*s* familiar uno mismo, una misma

numeral['nju:mərəl] *s* número; cifra

numerous['nju:mərəs] *adj* numeroso, sa

nun[nʌn] *s* monja

nurse[nɜ:s] ◆*s* ❶ *MEDICINA* enfermero, ra ❷niñera ◆*vt* ❶cuidar; atender ❷amamantar

nursery['nɜ:sərɪ] *s* ❶cuarto de los niños ❷guardería ❸vivero

nursery rhyme *s* poema o canción infantil

nursery school *s* jardín de niños; kinder

nursing['nɜ:sɪŋ] *s* ❶profesión de enfermera ❷asistencia; cuidado

nursing home *s* ❶clínica de reposo (privada) ❷clínica (privada) de maternidad

nurture['nɜ:ʧəɾ] *vt* ❶criar *(niño, planta)* ❷alimentar *(sentimientos)*

nut [nʌt] *s* ❶ nuez ❷ tuerca ❸ *familiar* chiflado, da

expresión **the nuts and bolts** *figurado* lo esencial; lo básico

■ **nuts** ◆*adj familiar* •**to be nuts** estar loco, ca ◆*exclamación* ¡maldita sea!

nutcrackers['nʌt,krækəz] *spl* cascanueces

nutmeg['nʌtmeg] *s* nuez moscada

nutritious[nju:'trɪʃəs] *adj* nutritivo, va

nutshell['nʌtʃel] *s*

expresión **in a nutshell** en una palabra

nylon ['naɪlɒn] ◆*s* nylon ◆*en compuestos* de nylon

N

o, O [əʊ] *s* ❶ o; O ❷ cero
Dos plurales: o's o os; O's o Os.

oak [əʊk] ◆ *s* roble ◆ *en compuestos* de roble

oar [ɔːr] *s* remo

expresión to put o stick your oar in entrometerse

oasis [əʊ'eɪsɪs] *s literal & figurado* oasis
El plural de oasis es oases [əʊ'eɪsiːz].

oath [əʊθ] *s* ❶ juramento • on o under oath bajo juramento ❷ palabrota

oatmeal ['əʊtmiːl] *s* ❶ copos de avena ❷ avena

oats [əʊts] *spl* avena

obedience [ə'biːdjəns] *s* • obedience (to somebody) obediencia (a alguien)

obedient [ə'biːdjənt] *adj* obediente

obese [əʊ'biːs] *adj formal* obeso, sa

obey [ə'beɪ] *vt* & *vi* obedecer

obituary [ə'bɪtʃʊərɪ] *s* nota necrológica ; necrología

object ◆ *s* ['ɒbdʒɪkt] ❶ objeto ❷ propósito ❸ *GRA-MÁTICA* complemento ◆ *vt* [ɒb'dʒekt] objetar ◆ *vi* • to object (to something/to doing something) oponerse (a algo/a hacer algo) • I object to that comment me parece muy mal ese comentario

objection [əb'dʒekʃn] *s* objeción; reparo • to have no objection (to something/to doing something) no tener inconveniente (en algo/en hacer algo)

objective [əb'dʒektɪv] ◆ *adj* objetivo, va ◆ *s* objetivo

obligation [,ɒblɪ'geɪʃn] *s* ❶ obligación • to be under an obligation to do something tener la obligación de hacer algo ❷ deber

obligatory [ə'blɪgətrɪ] *adj* obligatorio, ria

oblige [ə'blaɪdʒ] *vt* ❶ • to oblige somebody to do something obligar a alguien a hacer algo ❷ *formal* hacer un favor a • I would be much obliged if... le estaría muy agradecido si...

oblique [ə'bliːk] ◆ *adj* ❶ indirecto, ta ❷ oblicuo, cua ◆ *s* *TIPOGRAFÍA* barra

obliterate [ə'blɪtəreɪt] *vt* arrasar

oblivion [ə'blɪvɪən] *s* olvido

oblivious [ə'blɪvɪəs] *adj* inconsciente • to be oblivious to o of something no ser consciente de algo

oblong ['ɒblɒŋ] ◆ *adj* rectangular ; oblongo, ga ◆ *s* rectángulo

obnoxious [əb'nɒkʃəs] *adj* detestable

oboe ['əʊbəʊ] *s* oboe

obscene [əb'siːn] *adj* obsceno, na

obscure [əb'skjʊər] ◆ *adj literal & figurado* oscuro, ra ◆ *vt* ❶ oscurecer ❷ esconder

observance [əb'zɜːvns] *s* observancia ; cumplimiento

observant [əb'zɜːvnt] *adj* observador, ra

observation [,ɒbzə'veɪʃn] *s* ❶ vigilancia ❷ observación ❸ comentario

observatory [əb'zɜːvətrɪ] *s* observatorio

observe [əb'zɜːv] *vt* ❶ observar ❷ cumplir con

observer [əb'zɜːvər] *s* observador, ra

obsess [əb'ses] *vt* obsesionar • to be obsessed by o with estar obsesionado con

obsessive [əb'sesɪv] *adj* obsesivo, va

obsolete ['ɒbsəliːt] *adj* obsoleto, ta

obstacle ['ɒbstəkl] *s* ❶ obstáculo ❷ estorbo

obstetrics [ɒb'stetrɪks] *s* obstetricia

obstinate ['ɒbstənət] *adj* ❶ obstinado, da ; terco, ca ❷ tenaz

obstruct [əb'strʌkt] *vt* ❶ obstruir ; bloquear ❷ estorbar

obstruction [əb'strʌkʃn] *s* ❶ obstrucción ❷ atasco

obtain [əb'teɪn] *vt* obtener ; conseguir

obtainable [əb'teɪnəbl] *adj* disponible

obtuse [əb'tjuːs] *adj literal & figurado* obtuso, sa

obvious ['ɒbvɪəs] *adj* obvio, via ; evidente

obviously ['ɒbvɪəslɪ] *adv* ❶ evidentemente ; obviamente • obviously not claro que no ❷ claramente

occasion [ə'keɪʒn] *s* ❶ vez ; ocasión • on one occasion una vez ; en una ocasión • on several occasions varias veces ; en varias ocasiones ❷ acontecimiento

expresión to rise to the occasion ponerse a la altura de las circunstancias

occasional [ə'keɪʒənl] *adj* ❶ esporádico, ca ❷ ocasional

occasionally [ə'keɪʒnəlɪ] *adv* de vez en cuando

occupant ['ɒkjʊpənt] *s* ❶ inquilino, na ❷ ocupante

occupation [ˌɒkjʊ'peɪʃn] *s* ❶ empleo; ocupación ❷ pasatiempo ❸ MILITAR ocupación

occupational therapy *s* terapia ocupacional

occupier ['ɒkjʊpaɪər] *s* inquilino, na

occupy ['ɒkjʊpaɪ] *vt* ❶ ocupar ❷ habitar ❸ • **to occupy yourself** entretenerse

occur [ə'kɜːr] *vi* ❶ ocurrir; suceder ❷ encontrarse ❸ • **it never occurred to me to call** nunca se me ocurrió llamar

occurrence [ə'kʌrəns] *s* acontecimiento

ocean ['əʊʃn] *s* océano

o'clock [ə'klɒk] *adv* • **it's one o'clock** es la una • **it's two/three o'clock** son las dos/las tres • **at one/two o'clock** a la una/las dos

octave ['ɒktɪv] *s* octava

October [ɒk'təʊbər] *s* octubre ver también **September**

octopus ['ɒktəpəs] *s* pulpo

Dos plurales: **octopi** ['ɒktəpaɪ] o **octopuses**.

OD *abreviatura escrita de* **overdose**

odd [ɒd] *adj* ❶ raro, ra; extraño, ña ❷ sin pareja *(guante, calcetín)* ❸ impar ❹ *familiar* sobrante ❺ *familiar* • **I play the odd game** juego alguna que otra vez ❻ *familiar* • **30 odd years** 30 y tantos años

■ **odds** *spl* ❶ • **the odds a)** las probabilidades **b)** las apuestas • **the odds are that...** lo más probable es que... • **against all odds** contra viento y marea ❷ • **odds and ends** cosillas

expresión **to be at odds with something** no concordar con algo ▸ **to be at odds with somebody** estar reñido con alguien

odd jobs *spl* chapuzas

oddly ['ɒdlɪ] *adv* extrañamente • **oddly enough** aunque parezca mentira

odds-on ['ɒdz-] *adj familiar* • **the odds-on favorite** el favorito indiscutible

odometer [əʊ'dɒmɪtər] *s* odómetro

odor ['əʊdər] *s* ❶ olor ❷ fragancia

of ⚙️ *acento atónico* [əv], *acento tónico* [ɒv] *preposición* ❶ de • **the cover of a book** la portada de un libro • **a cousin of mine** un primo mío • **both of us** nosotros dos; los dos • **the worst of them** el peor de ellos • **to die of something** morir de algo ❷ • **thousands of people** miles de personas • **there are three of us** somos tres • **how many cups are there? — there are seven of them** ¿cuántas tazas hay? — hay siete • **a cup of coffee** un café; una taza de café ❸ • **a child of five** un niño de cinco (años) • **at the age of five** a los cinco años • **an increase of 6%** un incremento del 6% • **the 12th of February** el 12 de febrero ❹ • **a dress of silk** un vestido de seda • **to be made of something** estar hecho de algo; ser de algo ❺ • **fear of ghosts** miedo a los fantasmas • **love of good food** amor por

la buena mesa • **it was very kind of you** fue muy amable de o por tu parte

off [ɒf]

◆ *adv*

❶ [*indica alejamiento en el espacio*]
• **we're off to Japan today** nos vamos hoy a Japón
• **the station is 16 kilometers off** la estación está a 16 kilómetros

❷ [*indica alejamiento en el tiempo*]
• **my vacation is two days off** me voy de vacaciones dentro de dos días

❸ [*indica una separación*]
• **take your coat off** quítate la chamarra
• **the lid was off** no tenía la tapa puesta

❹ [*indica una interrupción o un fallo*]
• **don't forget to switch off the light** no te olvides de apagar la luz
• **the TV is off** la televisión está apagada
• **turn the faucet off** cierra la llave

❺ [*con precios, expresa una rebaja*]
• **I had $10 off** me descontaron 10 dólares
• **she gave me 30% off** me dio un descuento del 30%

❻ [*para hablar de las vacaciones*]
• **I've got the afternoon off** tengo la tarde libre
• **she's got a week off next month** tiene una semana de vacaciones el próximo mes

❼ [*expresa una idea de haber terminado*]
• **I'll finish off this work over the weekend** terminaré el trabajo este fin de semana
• **climate change killed off a variety of mammals** el cambio climático mató a una variedad de mamíferos

◆ *preposición*

❶ [*expresa un movimiento de arriba abajo*]
• **he got off the bus at the next stop** se bajó del camión en la siguiente parada
• **he stood up and took a book off the shelf** se levantó y tomó un libro de la estantería

❷ [*indica proximidad en el espacio*]
• **the hotel is located off the main street** el hotel está cerca de la calle principal
• **the island is just off the coast** la isla está justo al lado de la costa

❸ [*para indicar ausencia*]
• **he's off work today** hoy no trabaja
• **she's been off school for weeks** hace semanas que no va a la escuela

❹ [*indica rechazo, abandono*]
• **she's off her food** no está comiendo
• **he's off the drugs now** ya no se droga

❺ [*en expresiones*]
• **to buy something off somebody** *familiar* comprar algo a alguien

◆ *adj*

❶ [*expresa deterioro*]
• **the milk is off** la leche está cortada
• **this meat is off** la carne está mala

O

❷ [*expresa una interrupción o fallo*]
• **are the lights off?** ¿están apagadas las luces?

❸ [*expresa una anulación*]
• **the match is off** el partido ha sido cancelado

❹ [*indica una ausencia*]
• **he's off this week** esta semana no viene

offal ['ɒfl] *s* 🔆 *incontable* asaduras

off-chance *s* • **on the off-chance** por si acaso

off colour *adj* indispuesto, ta

off duty *adj* ❶ fuera de servicio ❷ de permiso *(soldado)*

offend [ə'fend] *vt* ofender

offender [ə'fendər] *s* ❶ delincuente ❷ culpable

offense [ə'fens] *s* ❶ delito ❷ ofensa • **to cause somebody offense** ofender a alguien • **to take offense** ofenderse ❸ ['ɒfens] DEPORTE ataque

offensive [ə'fensɪv] ◆ *adj* ❶ ofensivo, va ❷ atacante ◆ *s* MILITAR ofensiva

offer ['ɒfər] ◆ *s* oferta • **on offer a)** disponible **b)** en oferta ◆ *vt* ❶ ofrecer • **to offer something to somebody, to offer somebody something** ofrecer algo a alguien ❷ • **to offer to do something** ofrecerse a hacer algo ◆ *vi* ofrecerse

off-guard *adj* desprevenido, da

offhand [ˌɒf'hænd] ◆ *adj* frío, a; indiferente ◆ *adv* de improviso

office ['ɒfɪs] *s* ❶ oficina • **he's at the office** está en la oficina ❷ despacho ❸ consulta; consultorio ❹ cargo • **in office a)** en el poder *(partido)* **b)** en el cargo *(persona)* • **to take office a)** subir al poder *(partido)* **b)** asumir el cargo *(persona)*

office block *s* bloque de oficinas

office building *s* edificio de oficinas

office hours *spl* horas de oficina

officer ['ɒfɪsər] *s* ❶ MILITAR oficial ❷ delegado, da *(sindical)* ❸ agente *(de policía)*

office worker *s* oficinista

official [ə'fɪʃl] ◆ *adj* oficial ◆ *s* ❶ funcionario, ria ❷ representante *(sindical)*

offing ['ɒfɪŋ] *s* • **to be in the offing** estar al caer o a la vista

off-line ◆ *adj* ❶ desconectado, da ❷ fuera de línea ◆ *adv* • **to go off-line** desconectarse

off-peak *adj* ❶ de tarifa reducida *(electricidad, llamada, viajes)* ❷ económico, ca *(periodo)*

off-putting [-ˌputɪŋ] *adj* ❶ repelente ❷ • **it's very off-putting** me distrae mucho

off-ramp *s* carril de salida

off season *s* • **the off season** la temporada baja

offset ['ɒfset] *vt* compensar; contrarrestar

Formas irregulares de **offset**: *pretérito & pp* **offset**.

offshoot ['ɒfʃuːt] *s* retoño

offshore ['ɒfʃɔːr] ◆ *adj* ❶ costero, ra *(viento)* ❷ de bajura *(pesca)* ❸ marítimo, ma *(plataforma)* ❹ en ban-cos extranjeros ◆ *adv* mar adentro • **two miles offshore** a dos millas de la costa

offside ◆ *adj* [ˌɒf'saɪd] DEPORTE fuera de juego ◆ *adv* [ˌɒf'saɪd] DEPORTE fuera de juego

offspring ['ɒfsprɪŋ] *s* ❶ *formal & humorístico* descendiente; descendencia ❷ crías

El plural de **offspring** es **offspring**

offstage [ˌɒf'steɪdʒ] *adj & adv* entre bastidores

off-the-record ◆ *adj* extraoficial ◆ *adv* extraoficialmente

off-white *adj* blancuzco, ca

often ['ɒfn] ['ɒftn] *adv* a menudo • **how often do you go?** ¿cada cuánto o con qué frecuencia vas? • **I don't often see him** no lo veo mucho • **I don't do it as often as I used to** no lo hago tanto como antes

expresiones **as often as not** muchas veces ▶ **every so often** cada cierto tiempo ▶ **more often than not** la mayoría de las veces

oh [əʊ] *exclamación* ❶ ¡ah! • **oh really?** ¿de verdad? ❷ ¡oh! • **oh no!** ¡no!

oil [ɔɪl] ◆ *s* ❶ aceite ❷ petróleo ◆ *vt* engrasar

oilfield ['ɔɪlfiːld] *s* yacimiento petrolífero

oil-fired [-ˌfaɪəd] *adj* de fuel-oil

oil painting *s* (pintura al) óleo

oilrig ['ɔɪlrɪg] *s* plataforma petrolífera

oilskins ['ɔɪlskɪnz] *spl* impermeable; chubasquero

oil slick *s* marea negra

oil tanker *s* ❶ petrolero ❷ camión cisterna

oil well *s* pozo petrolífero o de petróleo

oily ['ɔɪlɪ] *adj* ❶ aceitoso, sa ❷ grasiento, ta ❸ graso, sa

ointment ['ɔɪntmənt] *s* pomada; ungüento

OK, okay [ˌəʊ'keɪ] ◆ *adj* • **I'm OK** estoy bien • **the food was OK** la comida no estuvo mal • **is it OK with you?** ¿te parece bien? ◆ *exclamación* ❶ okey; de acuerdo ❷ bien ◆ *vt* dar el visto bueno a

Formas irregulares de **OK**: *pretérito & pp* **OKed**, *gerundio* **OKing**

old [əʊld] ◆ *adj* ❶ viejo, ja • **how old are you?** ¿cuántos años tienes?; ¿qué edad tienes? • **I'm 20 years old** tengo 20 años • **an old woman** una vieja • **old people** las personas mayores • **when I'm older** cuando sea mayor ❷ antiguo, gua • **that's my old school** ése es mi antiguo colegio ◆ *spl* • **the old** los ancianos

old age *s* la vejez

old-fashioned [-'fæʃnd] *adj* ❶ pasado, da de moda; anticuado, da ❷ tradicional

old people's home *s* residencia o hogar de ancianos

olive ['ɒlɪv] *s* aceituna; oliva ▶ **olive tree** olivo

olive oil *s* aceite de oliva

Olympic [ə'lɪmpɪk] *adj* olímpico, ca

■ **Olympics** *spl* • **the Olympics** los Juegos Olímpicos

O

Olympic Games *spl* • **the Olympic Games** los Juegos Olímpicos

omelet(te) ['ɒmlɪt] *s* tortilla

omen ['əumen] *s* presagio

ominous ['ɒmɪnəs] *adj* siniestro, tra ; de mal agüero

omission [ə'mɪʃn] *s* omisión

omit [ə'mɪt] *vt* ❶ omitir • **to omit to do something** no hacer algo ❷ pasar por alto

omnibus ['ɒmnɪbəs] *s* antología

on [ɒn]

♦ *preposición*

❶ [*indica una localización*]
• **your book is on the chair** tu libro está en la silla
• **there were posters on the walls** había afiches en las paredes
• **the information is on disk** la información está en un disco
• **the museum is on the left/right** el museo está a la izquierda/derecha
• **I don't have any money on me** no llevo dinero encima

❷ [*hablando de medios de comunicación o de telecomunicaciones*]
• **the video was shown on TV** el video fue exhibido en televisión
• **I heard it on the radio** lo oí en la radio
• **you're on the air** está en el aire
• **she's on the telephone at the moment** ahora mismo está al teléfono

❸ [*para indicar un medio de transporte*]
• **they traveled on a bus/train/ship** viajaron en camión/tren/barco
• **I was on the bus** estaba en el camión
• **on foot** a pie

❹ [*indica un tema, un asunto*]
• **he's fond of books on astronomy** le encantan los libros de astronomía
• **have you heard him on this project?** ¿le has oído hablar sobre este proyecto?

❺ [*introduce una fecha*]
• **I have an appointment on Thursday** tengo una cita el jueves
• **she goes swimming on Tuesdays** hace natación los martes
• **on the 10th of February, we will fly to Cuba** el 10 de febrero volaremos a Cuba
• **it was snowing on my birthday** nevó en mi cumpleaños

❻ [*seguido de gerundio, expresa la casi simultaneidad*]
• **on hearing the news, she burst into tears** al oír las noticias, se echó a llorar

❼ [*indica un medio de subsistencia o dependencia*]
• **you can't live on water alone** no se puede vivir sólo del agua
• **the bird lives on fruit** el pájaro se alimenta de frutas

• **the car runs on gas** el carro funciona con gasolina
• **he's on tranquilizers** está tomando tranquilizantes
• **I think she's on drugs again** me parece que se está drogando de nuevo

❽ [*para hablar de ingresos*]
• **how much are you on?** ¿cuánto ganas?
• **he's on $25,000 a year** gana 25.000 dólares por año
• **people on a low income** la gente que gana poco dinero
• **his mother is on welfare** su madre cobra subsidios del Estado

❾ [*indica una proporción*]
• **25 cents on the dollar** 25 centavos por dólar

❿ [*con instrumentos de música*]
• **he played the tune on the violin/flute** tocó la melodía con el violín/la flauta

⓫ *familiar* [*indica quién paga*]
• **the drinks are on me** las bebidas corren por mi cuenta
• **we had a drink on the house** la casa nos invitó a una bebida

♦ *adv*

❶ [*indica que algo está en su lugar*]
• **I left the lid on the pot** dejé la tapa en la olla

❷ [*hablando de ropa*]
• **it's cold outside, you should put a sweater on** hace frío fuera, deberías ponerte un suéter
• **what did she have on?** ¿qué vestía?
• **he had nothing on** no llevaba nada puesto

❸ [*indica el encendido o la conexión*]
• **switch the light on, please** prende la luz, por favor
• **turn the power on** da la corriente

❹ [*expresa la continuación*]
• **if you read on, you'll find this book very interesting** si continúas leyendo, descubrirás que el libro es muy interesante
• **they walked on for hours** caminaron durante horas

❺ [*indica una evolución*]
• **send my mail on (to me)** hazme llegar el correo

❻ [*en expresiones*]
• **later on** más tarde
• **earlier on** antes

expresiones **from... on** [*indica tiempo*] • **from now on** de ahora en adelante ; a partir de ahora
• **from then on** desde entonces ▶ **on and off** • **I worked on and off for about a year** trabajé intermitentemente durante cerca de un año

♦ *adj*

❶ [*indica el encendido, el funcionamiento*]
• **the radio was on** la radio estaba encendida
• **the washing machine is on** la lavadora está encendida
• **the lights are on** las luces están encendidas
• **the faucet is on** la llave está abierta

O

O

❷ [*para hablar de la celebración de algún acontecimiento*]
• **there's a conference on next week** hay una conferencia la próxima semana
• **it's on at the local movie theater** pasa en el cine local
• **your favourite TV program is on tonight** hoy por la noche pasa tu programa favorito de televisión
• **is our deal still on?** ¿nuestro acuerdo sigue en pie?
❸ *familiar* [*indica una posibilidad*]
• **we'll never be ready by tomorrow: it just isn't on** no vamos a conseguir estar listos mañana, es completamente imposible
• **are you still on for dinner?** ¿sigue en pie la cena?
• **shall we say $10? — you're on!** ¿qué te parece 10 dólares? — ¡hecho!

once [wʌns] ◆ *adv* ❶ una vez • **once a week** una vez a la semana • **once again** o **more** otra vez • **for once** por una vez • **more than once** más de una vez • **once and for all** de una vez por todas • **once or twice** alguna que otra vez • **once in a while** de vez en cuando ❷ en otro tiempo; antiguamente • **this part of the city was once a village** esta parte de la ciudad era antes una aldea
expresión **once upon a time** érase una vez
◆ *conjunción* una vez que • **once you have done it** una vez que lo hayas hecho
■ **at once** *adv* ❶ en seguida; inmediatamente ❷ a la vez; al mismo tiempo • **all at once** de repente; de golpe

one [wʌn] ◆ *número* un, una; uno • **I only want one** sólo quiero uno • **one fifth** un quinto; una quinta parte • **one of my friends** uno de mis amigos • **(number) one** el uno ◆ *adj* ❶ único, ca • **it's her one ambition** es su única ambición ❷ • **one of these days** un día de éstos ◆ *pronombre* ❶ uno, una • **I want the red one** yo quiero el rojo • **the one with the blond hair** la del pelo rubio • **which one do you want?** ¿cuál quieres? • **this one** éste, ésta • **that one** ése, ésa • **another one** otro, otra • **she's the one I told you about** es ésa de la que te hablé ❷ *formal* uno, una • **to do one's duty** cumplir uno con su deber
■ **for one** *adv* • **I for one remain unconvinced** yo, por mi parte, sigo poco convencido

---

one

No se debe confundir el artículo indeterminado (a/an) con el numeral **one**. En la frase *an ice box is no good — you need a deep freeze un refrigerador no sirve; necesitas un congelador,* ice box se opone a deep freeze pero en *one ice box is no good — we've got enough food to fill three un refrigerador no sirve; tenemos comida para llenar tres,* one se opone a three.

El uso del pronombre one para hablar de uno mismo o de la gente en general es muy formal

(**how does one spell "focused"?** ¿cómo se escribe "focused"?). Generalmente en estos casos se emplea you (**how do you spell "focused"?**).

---

one-armed bandit *s* (máquina) tragaperras
one-off *familiar* ◆ *adj* excepcional ◆ *s* caso excepcional
one-on-one *adj* ❶ entre dos *(relación)* ❷ cara a cara ❸ individual *(clase)*
one-parent family *s* familia monoparental
oneself [wʌn'self] *pronombre* ❶ 🔆 *reflexivo, tras preposición* uno mismo, una misma • **to buy presents for oneself** hacerse regalos a sí mismo • **to take care of oneself** cuidarse ❷ 🔆 *para enfatizar* • **by oneself** solo, la
one-sided [-'saɪdɪd] *adj* ❶ desigual ❷ parcial
one-touch dialing *s* marcación automática
one-way *adj* ❶ de dirección única *(calle)* ❷ sencillo *(boleto)*
ongoing ['ɒn,gəʊɪŋ] *adj* ❶ en curso ❷ pendiente
onion ['ʌnjən] *s* cebolla
online ['ɒnlaɪn] ◆ *adj* INFORMÁTICA en línea • **to be online** estar conectado a Internet ◆ *adv* en línea • **to go online** conectarse a Internet
online banking *s* banca en línea
online shopping *s* compras en línea
onlooker ['ɒn,lʊkər] *s* espectador, ra
only ['əʊnlɪ] ◆ *adj* único, ca ▸ **only child** hijo único ◆ *adv* sólo; solamente • **I was only too willing to help** estaba encantado de poder ayudar • **I only wish I could!** ¡ojalá pudiera! • **it's only natural** es completamente normal • **it's only to be expected** no es de sorprender • **not only... but** no sólo... sino • **only just** apenas ◆ *conjunción* sólo que • **I would go, only I'm too tired** iría, lo que pasa es que estoy muy cansado
on-ramp *s* carril de aceleración o de incorporación
onset ['ɒnset] *s* comienzo
onshore ['ɒnʃɔːr] *adj* ❶ procedente del mar *(viento)* ❷ en tierra firme *(producción petrolera)*
onslaught ['ɒnslɔːt] *s* *literal & figurado* acometida
onward ['ɒnwəd] ◆ *adj* ❶ hacia delante ❷ progresivo, va ◆ *adv* ❶ adelante; hacia delante • **read from page 50 onward** lean de la página 50 en adelante ❷ • **from now/then onward** de ahora/allí en adelante
ooze [uːz] ◆ *vt* *figurado* rebosar ◆ *vi* • **to ooze (from** o **out of)** rezumar (de) • **to ooze with something** *figurado* rebosar o irradiar algo
opaque [əʊ'peɪk] *adj* opaco, ca
open ['əʊpn] ◆ *adj* ❶ abierto, ta ❷ descorrido, da ❸ despejado, da ❹ • **to be open to a)** estar abierto a *(ideas, sugerencias)* **b)** prestarse a *(críticas)* ❺ sincero, ra; franco, ca ❻ • **to be open to somebody** estar dispo-

nible para alguien ◆ *s* ❶ • **in the open** al aire libre
❷ *Deporte* open; abierto

expresión **to bring something out into the open**
sacar a luz algo

◆ *vt* ❶ abrir • **to open fire** abrir fuego ❷ correr
(las cortinas) ❸ inaugurar ❹ entablar ◆ *vi* ❶ abrirse
❷ abrir *(tienda, oficina)* ❸ dar comienzo

■ **open on to** *vt* ⚙ *El objeto siempre va después de
la preposición al final.* dar a

■ **open up** ◆ *vi* ⚙ *El objeto se puede colocar antes o
después de la preposición.* abrir ◆ *vi* ❶ surgir *(oportunidad)* ❷ abrir

opener ['əʊpnəɾ] *s* ❶ abridor ❷ abrelatas
❸ abrebotellas

opening ['əʊpnɪŋ] ◆ *adj* inicial ◆ *s* ❶ comienzo;
principio ❷ abertura ❸ oportunidad ❹ puesto
vacante

opening hours *spl* horario (de apertura)

openly ['əʊpənlɪ] *adv* abiertamente

open-minded [-'maɪndɪd] *adj* sin prejuicios

opera ['ɒpərə] *s* ópera

opera house *s* teatro de la ópera

operate ['ɒpəreɪt] ◆ *vt* ❶ hacer funcionar *(máquina)* ❷ dirigir *(negocio, sistema)* ❸ proporcionar *(un
servicio)* ◆ *vi* ❶ operar; actuar ❷ funcionar ❸ *Medicina* • **to operate (on somebody/something)** operar
(a alguien/de algo)

operating room ['ɒpəreɪtɪŋ-] *s* quirófano

operation [ˌɒpə'reɪʃn] *s* ❶ operación ❷ administración ❸ funcionamiento **a)** estar
funcionando *(máquina)* **b)** estar en vigor *(ley, sistema)*
❹ *Medicina* operación; intervención quirúrgica • **to
have an operation (for/on)** operarse (de)

operator ['ɒpəreɪtəɾ] *s* ❶ *Telecomunicaciones* opera-
dor, ra; telefonista ❷ operario, ria ❸ operadora

opinion [ə'pɪnjən] *s* opinión • **to be of the opinion that** opinar o creer que • **in my opinion** a mi juicio; en mi opinión • **what is her opinion of...?** ¿qué
opina de...?

opinion poll *s* sondeo; encuesta

opponent [ə'pəʊnənt] *s* ❶ *Política* adversario, ria
❷ opositor, ora ❸ *Deporte* contrincante

opportunist [ˌɒpə'tjuːnɪst] *s* oportunista

opportunity [ˌɒpə'tjuːnətɪ] *s* oportunidad; ocasión • **to take the opportunity to do** o **of doing something** aprovechar la ocasión o para hacer algo

oppose [ə'pəʊz] *vt* oponerse a

opposed [ə'pəʊzd] *adj* opuesto, ta • **to be opposed
to** oponerse a; estar en contra de • **as opposed to** en
vez de; en lugar de • **I like beer as opposed to wine**
me gusta la cerveza y no el vino

opposing [ə'pəʊzɪŋ] *adj* opuesto, ta;
contrario, ria

opposite ['ɒpəzɪt] ◆ *adj* ❶ de enfrente *(casa)*;
opuesto, ta *(parte)* • **on the opposite side of the street**
al otro lado de la calle ❷ • **opposite (to)** opuesto, ta o
contrario, ria (a) ◆ *adv* enfrente ◆ *preposición* enfrente de ◆ *s* contrario • **he always does the oppo-

site of what he is told** siempre hace lo contrario de
lo que le dicen

opposite number *s* homólogo, ga

opposition [ˌɒpə'zɪʃn] *s* ❶ oposición ❷ • **the opposition** los contrincantes

oppress [ə'pres] *vt* oprimir

oppressive [ə'presɪv] *adj* ❶ tiránico, ca; opresivo, va ❷ agobiante; sofocante

opt [ɒpt] ◆ *vt* • **to opt to do something** optar por
o elegir hacer algo ◆ *vi* • **to opt for something** optar
por o elegir algo

■ **opt in** *vi* • **to opt in (to something)** decidir participar (en algo)

■ **opt out** *vi* • **to opt out (of something)** decidir no
participar (en algo)

optical ['ɒptɪkl] *adj* óptico, ca

optician [ɒp'tɪʃn] *s* óptico, ca • **the optician's** la
óptica

optimist ['ɒptɪmɪst] *s* optimista

optimistic [ˌɒptɪ'mɪstɪk] *adj* optimista

optimum ['ɒptɪməm] *adj* óptimo, ma

option ['ɒpʃn] *s* opción • **to have the option to do** o
of doing something tener la opción o la posibilidad de
hacer algo • **to have no option** no tener otra opción

optional ['ɒpʃənl] *adj* facultativo, va; optativo, va
• **optional extra** extra opcional

or [ɔːɾ] *conjunción* ❶ o • **or (else)** de lo contrario;
si no ❷ ⚙ *tras negativo* • **he cannot read or write** no
sabe ni leer ni escribir

oral ['ɔːrəl] ◆ *adj* ❶ oral ❷ bucal ◆ *s* examen
oral

orally ['ɔːrəlɪ] *adv* ❶ oralmente ❷ por vía oral

orange ['ɒrɪndʒ] ◆ *adj* naranja ◆ *s* naranja ❱ **an
orange tree** un naranjo

orange juice *s* jugo de naranja

orbit ['ɔːbɪt] ◆ *s* órbita • **to put something into
orbit (around)** poner algo en órbita (alrededor de)
◆ *vt* girar alrededor de

orchard ['ɔːtʃəd] *s* huerto

orchestra ['ɔːkɪstrə] *s* ❶ orquesta ❷ platea o patio
de butacas

orchid ['ɔːkɪd] *s* orquídea

ordeal [ɔː'diːl] *s* calvario

order ['ɔːdəɾ] ◆ *s* ❶ orden • **he gave me an order** me
dio una orden • **in order** en orden • **out of order** desordenado, da • **in order of importance** por orden de
importancia ❷ *Comercio* pedido • **made to order** hecho
por encargo ❸ ración *(en restaurante)* ❹ • **in working
order** en funcionamiento • **'out of order'** 'no funciona'
• **to be out of order a)** estar estropeado, da **b)** ser improcedente • **in order** en regla ◆ *vt* ❶ • **to order somebody (to do something)** ordenar a alguien (que haga
algo) • **to order that** ordenar que ❷ pedir ❸ *Comercio*
encargar ❹ ordenar

■ **in order that** *conjunción* para que

■ **in order to** *conjunción* para

■ **on the order of** *preposición* del orden de

O

■ **order about, order around** *vt* ☼ *El objeto se puede colocar antes o después de la preposición.* mangonear

order form *s* hoja de pedido

orderly ['ɔːdəlɪ] ◆ *adj* ❶ disciplinado, da ❷ ordenado, da ◆ *s* auxiliar sanitario

ordinarily ['ɔːdənrəlɪ] *adv* normalmente

ordinary ['ɔːdənrɪ] ◆ *adj* ❶ corriente; normal ❷ *despectivo* mediocre; ordinario, ria ◆ *s* • **out of the ordinary** fuera de lo común

ore [ɔːr] *s* mineral

organ ['ɔːgən] *s* MÚSICA órgano

organic [ɔː'gænɪk] *adj* ❶ orgánico, ca ❷ biológico, ca; orgánico, ca *(comida)*

organization [ˌɔːgənaɪ'zeɪʃn] *s* organización

organize ['ɔːgənaɪz] *vt* organizar

organizer ['ɔːgənaɪzər] *s* organizador, ra

orgasm ['ɔːgæzm] *s* orgasmo

oriental [ˌɔːrɪ'entl] *adj* oriental

orienteering [ˌɔːrɪən'tɪərɪŋ] *s* deporte de orientación

origami [ˌɒrɪ'gɑːmɪ] *s* papiroflexia

origin ['ɒrɪdʒɪn] *s* origen • **country of origin** país de origen

■ **origins** *spl* origen

original [ə'rɪdʒənl] ◆ *adj* original • **the original owner** el primer propietario ◆ *s* original

originally [ə'rɪdʒənəlɪ] *adv* ❶ originariamente ❷ originalmente

originate [ə'rɪdʒəneɪt] *vi* • **to originate (in)** nacer o surgir (de) • **to originate from** nacer o surgir de

ornament ['ɔːnəmənt] *s* adorno

ornamental [ˌɔːnə'mentl] *adj* ornamental; decorativo, va

ornate [ɔː'neɪt] *adj* ❶ recargado, da ❷ muy vistoso, sa

orphan ['ɔːfn] ◆ *s* huérfano, na ◆ *vt* • **to be orphaned** quedarse huérfano

orphanage ['ɔːfənɪdʒ] *s* orfelinato

orthodox ['ɔːθədɒks] *adj* ortodoxo, xa

orthopedic [ˌɔːθə'piːdɪk] *adj* ortopédico, ca

ostensible [ɒ'stensəbl] *adj* aparente

ostentatious [ˌɒstən'teɪʃəs] *adj* ostentoso, sa

osteopath ['ɒstɪəpæθ] *s* osteópata

ostracize ['ɒstrəsaɪz] *vt* ❶ marginar; hacer el vacío a ❷ POLÍTICA condenar al ostracismo

ostrich ['ɒstrɪtʃ] *s* avestruz

other ['ʌðər] ◆ *adj* otro, otra • **the other one** el otro, la otra • **the other three** los otros tres • **the other day** el otro día • **the other week** hace unas semanas ◆ *pronombre* ❶ • **others** otros, otras ❷ • **the other** el otro, la otra • **the others** los otros, las otras; los demás, las demás • **one after the other** uno tras otro • **one or other** uno u otro • **to be none other than** no ser otro sino

■ **something or other** *pronombre* una cosa u otra
■ **somehow or other** *adv* de una u otra forma
■ **other than** *conjunción* excepto; salvo • **other than that** por lo demás

otherwise ['ʌðəwaɪz] ◆ *adv* ❶ si no ❷ por lo demás ❸ de otra manera • **deliberately or otherwise** adrede o no ◆ *conjunción* si no; de lo contrario

otter ['ɒtər] *s* nutria

ouch [aʊtʃ] *exclamación* ¡ay!

ought [ɔt]
◆ *v modal*
❶ [*para realizar una recomendación*]
• **you ought to see a doctor** deberías ver a un médico
• **I really ought to go** realmente me tengo que ir
❷ [*para realizar un reproche*]
• **you ought not to have done that** no deberías haber hecho eso
• **you ought to look after your children better** deberías cuidar mejor de tus niños
❸ [*para expresar una probabilidad*]
• **she ought to be here soon** debería llegar enseguida
• **she ought to pass her exam** debería aprobar el examen

ought

Ought to seguido del participio pasado expresa la idea de lamentar no haber hecho algo (I *ought to have called* on her birthday *debería haberla llamado por el cumpleaños*) y también se utiliza en reproches (you *ought to have been* more careful *deberías haber tenido más cuidado*).

ounce [aʊns] *s* ▸ = 28,35g, ≈ onza

our ['aʊər] *adj posesivo* nuestro, tra; nuestros, tras ☼ *pl* • **our money** nuestro dinero • **our house** nuestra casa • **our children** nuestros hijos • **it wasn't our fault** no fue culpa nuestra • **we washed our hair** nos lavamos el pelo

our

No olvidemos que al hablar de las partes del cuerpo se usa el adjetivo posesivo our en lugar del artículo the (we washed *our* hair *nos lavamos el pelo*).

ours ['aʊəz] *pronombre posesivo* nuestro, tra • **that money is ours** ese dinero es nuestro • **those keys are ours** esas llaves son nuestras • **it wasn't their fault, it was ours** no fue culpa de ellos sino de nosotros • **a friend of ours** un amigo nuestro • **their car hit ours** su coche chocó contra el nuestro

ourselves [aʊəˈselvz] *pronombre* ❶ ☿*reflexivo* nos ❷ ☿*tras preposición* nosotros, nosotras ❸ ☿*para enfatizar* nosotros mismos, nosotras mismas • **we did it by ourselves** lo hicimos nosotros solos • **by ourselves** solos

out [aʊt] *adv* ❶ fuera • **we all went out** todos salimos fuera • **it's hot out** afuera está caluroso • **I'm going out for a walk** voy a salir a dar un paseo • **they ran out** salieron corriendo • **he poured the water out** sirvió el agua • **John's out at the moment** John está fuera ahora mismo ❷ apagado, da • **the fire went out** el fuego se apagó ❸ • **the tide had gone out** la marea estaba baja ❹ pasado, da de moda ❺ publicado, da *(libro)* • **they've a new record out** han sacado un nuevo disco ❻ en flor ❼ *familiar* en huelga

■ **out of** *preposición* ❶ fuera de • **to go out of the room** salir de la habitación ❷ por • **out of spite/love** por rencor/amor ❸ de • **a page out of a book** una página de un libro • **to get information out of somebody** sacar información a alguien ❹ sin • **we're out of sugar** estamos sin azúcar ❺ hecho de • **it's made out of plastic** está hecho de plástico; es de plástico ❻ a resguardo de ❼ • **one out of ten people** una de cada diez personas • **ten out of ten** diez sobre diez *(nota)*

outback [ˈaʊtbæk] *s* • **the outback** los llanos del interior de Australia

outbreak [ˈaʊtbreɪk] *s* ❶ comienzo *(de guerra)* ❷ ola *(de delincuencia)* ❸ epidemia ❹ erupción

outburst [ˈaʊtbɜːst] *s* ❶ explosión; arranque ❷ estallido

outcast [ˈaʊtkɑːst] *s* marginado, da

outcome [ˈaʊtkʌm] *s* resultado

outcry [ˈaʊtkraɪ] *s* protestas

outdated [ˌaʊtˈdeɪtɪd] *adj* anticuado, da; pasado, da de moda

outdo [ˌaʊtˈduː] *vt* aventajar; superar

Formas irregulares de **outdo** pretérito **outdid**, pp **outdone** [ˌaʊtˈdʌn].

outdoor [ˈaʊtdɔːr] *adj* ❶ al aire libre *(vida)* ❷ descubierta *(alberca)* ❸ de calle *(ropa)*

outdoors [aʊtˈdɔːz] *adv* al aire libre

outer [ˈaʊtər] *adj* exterior; externo, na

outer space *s* espacio exterior

outfit [ˈaʊtfɪt] *s* conjunto; traje

outgoing [ˈaʊtˌgəʊɪŋ] *adj* ❶ saliente ❷ extrovertido, da

outgrow [ˌaʊtˈgrəʊ] *vt* ❶ • **he has outgrown his shirts** las camisas se le han quedado pequeñas ❷ ser demasiado mayor para

Formas irregulares de **outgrow**: pretérito **outgrew**, pp **outgrown**.

outing [ˈaʊtɪŋ] *s* excursión

outlaw [ˈaʊtlɔː] ◆ *s* proscrito, ta ◆ *vt* ilegalizar

outlay [ˈaʊtleɪ] *s* desembolso

outlet [ˈaʊtlet] *s* ❶ punto de venta ❷ ELECTRICIDAD toma de corriente ❸ salida ❹ desagüe

outline [ˈaʊtlaɪn] ◆ *s* ❶ esbozo; resumen ❷ contorno ◆ *vt* esbozar; resumir

outlive [ˌaʊtˈlɪv] *vt* sobrevivir a

outlook [ˈaʊtlʊk] *s* ❶ enfoque; actitud ❷ perspectiva (de futuro)

outlying [ˈaʊtˌlaɪŋ] *adj* ❶ lejano, na; remoto, ta ❷ periférico, ca

outnumber [ˌaʊtˈnʌmbər] *vt* exceder en número

out-of-date *adj* ❶ anticuado, da; pasado, da de moda ❷ caducado, da

out of doors *adv* al aire libre

out-of-the-way *adj* remoto, ta

outpatient [ˈaʊtˌpeɪʃnt] *s* paciente externo, paciente externa

output [ˈaʊtpʊt] *s* ❶ producción; rendimiento ❷ INFORMÁTICA salida; impresión

outrage [ˈaʊtreɪdʒ] ◆ *s* ❶ indignación ❷ atrocidad; escándalo ◆ *vt* ultrajar

outrageous [aʊtˈreɪdʒəs] *adj* ❶ indignante; escandaloso, sa ❷ extravagante *(ropa)* ❸ exorbitante *(precio)*

outright ◆ *adj* [ˈaʊtraɪt] ❶ categórico, ca ❷ completo, ta *(desastre)* ❸ indiscutible *(victoria, ganador)* ◆ *adv* [ˌaʊtˈraɪt] ❶ abiertamente ❷ categóricamente ❸ totalmente *(prohibir, ganar)* ❹ en el acto *(morir)*

outset [ˈaʊtset] *s* • **at the outset** al principio • **from the outset** desde el principio

outside ◆ *adj* [ˈaʊtsaɪd] ❶ exterior ❷ independiente *(opinión, críticas)* ❸ remoto, ta *(posibilidad)* ◆ *adv* [ˌaʊtˈsaɪd] fuera • **to go/run/look outside** ir/correr/mirar fuera ◆ *preposición* [ˈaʊtsaɪd] fuera de • **we live half an hour outside Miami** vivimos a media hora de Miami ◆ *s* [ˈaʊtsaɪd] exterior

■ **outside of** *preposición* aparte de

outside lane *s* carril de adelantamiento

outsider [ˌaʊtˈsaɪdər] *s* ❶ forastero, ra ❷ caballo, persona o equipo que no es uno de los favoritos en un concurso

outsize [ˈaʊtsaɪz] *adj* ❶ enorme ❷ de talla muy grande

outskirts [ˈaʊtskɜːts] *spl* • **the outskirts** las afueras

outsource [ˈaʊtsɔːs] *vt* COMERCIO externalizar

outspoken [ˌaʊtˈspəʊkn] *adj* franco, ca

outstanding [ˌaʊtˈstændɪŋ] *adj* ❶ destacado, da ❷ pendiente

outstay [ˌaʊtˈsteɪ] *vt* • **to outstay your welcome** quedarse más tiempo de lo debido

outstrip [ˌaʊtˈstrɪp] *vt* literal & figurado aventajar; dejar atrás

outward [ˈaʊtwəd] ◆ *adj* ❶ de ida *(viaje)* ❷ aparente *(compasión, calma)* ❸ visible; exterior *(señal, prueba)* ◆ *adv* hacia fuera

outwardly [ˈaʊtwədlɪ] *adv* aparentemente; de cara al exterior

outwards [ˈaʊtwədz] *adv* hacia fuera

outwit [ˌaʊtˈwɪt] *vt* ser más listo, ta que

O

oval ['əʊvl] ◆ *adj* oval ; ovalado, da ◆ *s* óvalo

Oval Office *s* • **the Oval Office** el Despacho Oval oficina que tiene el presidente de Estados Unidos en la Casa Blanca

ovary ['əʊvərɪ] *s* ovario

ovation [əʊ'veɪʃn] *s* ovación • **a standing ovation** una ovación de gala (con el público en pie)

oven ['ʌvn] *s* horno

ovenproof ['ʌvnpruːf] *adj* refractario, ria

over ['əʊvər]
◆ *preposición*
❶ [*indica una localización*]
• **there's a lamp over the table** hay una lámpara sobre la mesa
• **it would be nicer if you put a cloth over the table** quedaría más bonito si pusieras un mantel sobre la mesa
• **they live over the road** viven al otro lado de la calle
❷ [*indica que se franquea o supera algo*]
• **he jumped over the fence** saltó por encima de la valla
• **the water came over his waist** el agua le llegaba hasta la cintura
• **to go over the border** pasar la frontera
• **she's over forty** tiene más de 40 años
❸ [*indica un tema, un asunto*]
• **they argued over the price** discutieron por el precio
• **they fell out over politics** se pelearon por asuntos de política
❹ [*indica un periodo, una duración*]
• **it happened over the Christmas vacation** pasó durante las vacaciones de Navidad
• **I haven't seen him much over the last few years** no le he visto mucho en los últimos años
◆ *adv*
❶ [*indica un movimiento de acercamiento o de alejamiento*]
• **they flew over to Europe** volaron a Europa
• **we invited them over** los invitamos a casa
• **over here** aquí
• **over there** allá
❷ [*indica la superación de un límite*]
• **I would recommend this book to children aged 7 and over** recomendaría este libro a niños de más de 6 años
❸ [*expresa una noción de exceso*]
• **don't be over-anxious** no estés excesivamente preocupado
❹ [*se usa para hablar de lo que queda*]
• **there is some meat over** queda algo de carne
• **there's nothing (left) over** no queda nada
❺ [*en matemáticas*]
• **three into twenty-two goes seven and one over** veintidós entre tres igual a siete y sobra uno
❻ [*indica un movimiento efectuado para derribar algo o a alguien*]
• **don't knock the bottle over** no derribes la botella

• **he pushed me and I fell over** me empujó y me caí
❼ [*expresa una repetición*]
• **he did it ten times over** lo repitió diez veces
• **over and over again** una y otra vez
❽ [*expresa una idea de atención, cuidado*]
• **think it over** piénsalo bien
• **you'd better read it over** sería mejor que lo leyeras con atención
◆ *adj*
[*indica el final, la consecución de algo*]
• **to be over** terminar
• **the party's over** la fiesta ha terminado
• **after the war was over** después del final de la guerra
• **I'll be glad when this is all over** me alegraré mucho cuando todo estoy haya acabado
■ **all over**
◆ *preposición*
• **all over the world** por todo el mundo
◆ *adv*
• **the house was painted green all over** la casa estaba pintada toda de verde
◆ *adj*
acabado, da ; terminado, da
• **that's all over now** ya se ha acabado

overall ◆ *adj* ['əʊvərɔːl] global ; total ◆ *adv* [,əʊvər'ɔːl] en conjunto ◆ *s* ['əʊvərɔːl] ❶ guardapolvo ❷ overol
■ **overalls** *spl* ❶ overol ❷ pantalones de peto

overbalance [,əʊvə'bæləns] *vi* perder el equilibrio

overbearing [,əʊvə'beərɪŋ] *adj despectivo* despótico, ca

overboard ['əʊvəbɔːd] *adv* • **to fall overboard** caer al agua o por la borda
expresión **to go overboard (about somebody/something)** *familiar* ponerse como loco, ca (con alguien/ algo)

overcame [,əʊvə'keɪm] *pretérito* → **overcome**

overcast ['əʊvəkɑːst] *adj* cubierto, ta ; nublado, da

overcharge [,əʊvə'tʃɑːdʒ] *vt* • **to overcharge somebody (for something)** cobrar a alguien en exceso (por algo)

overcoat ['əʊvəkəʊt] *s* abrigo

overcome [,əʊvə'kʌm] *vt* vencer ; superar
Formas irregulares de **overcome**: *pretérito* **overcame** [,əʊvə'keɪm], *pp* **overcome**.

overcrowded [,əʊvə'kraʊdɪd] *adj* ❶ atestado, da de gente ❷ superpoblado, da

overcrowding [,əʊvə'kraʊdɪŋ] *s* ❶ superpoblación ❷ hacinamiento

overdo [,əʊvə'duː] *vt* ❶ *despectivo* exagerar ❷ hacer demasiado *(esfuerzo)*
Formas irregulares de **overdo**: *pretérito* **overdid** [,əʊvə'dɪd], *pp* **overdone** [,əʊvə'dʌn].

O

overdone [ˌəʊvə'dʌn] ◆ *participio pasado* → **overdo** ◆ *adj* muy hecho, cha

overdose ◆ *s* ['əʊvədəʊs] sobredosis ◆ *vi* [əʊvə'dəʊs] • **to overdose (on something)** tomar una sobredosis (de algo)

overdraft ['əʊvədrɑːft] *s* ❶ saldo deudor ❷ (giro en) descubierto

overdrawn [ˌəʊvə'drɔːn] *adj* • **to be overdrawn** tener un saldo deudor

overdue [ˌəʊvə'djuː] *adj* ❶ • **to be overdue a)** ir con retraso (*tren*) **b)** estar con el plazo de préstamo caducado (*libro de biblioteca*) • **I'm overdue (for) a bit of luck** va siendo hora de tener un poco de suerte ❷ • **(long) overdue** (largamente) esperado, da; ansiado, da ❸ vencido, da y sin pagar

overestimate [ˌəʊvər'estɪmeɪt] *vt* sobreestimar

overflow ◆ *vi* [ˌəʊvə'fləʊ] ❶ rebosar • **to be overflowing (with)** rebosar (de) ❷ desbordarse (*río*) ◆ *s* ['əʊvəfləʊ] cañería de desagüe

overgrown [ˌəʊvə'grəʊn] *adj* cubierto, ta de matojos

overhaul ◆ *s* ['əʊvəhɔːl] ❶ revisión ❷ repaso general ◆ *vt* [ˌəʊvə'hɔːl] revisar

overhead ◆ *adj* ['əʊvəhed] aéreo, a ◆ *adv* [ˌəʊvə'hed] por lo alto; por encima ◆ *s* ['əʊvəhed] ❶ ☼ *incontable* gastos generales ❷ transparencia

overhead projector *s* retroproyector

overhear [ˌəʊvə'hɪər] *vt* oír por casualidad
Formas irregulares de **overhear**: *pretérito & pp* **overheard** [ˌəʊvə'hɜːd].

overheat [ˌəʊvə'hiːt] *vi* recalentarse

overjoyed [ˌəʊvə'dʒɔɪd] *adj* • **to be overjoyed (at something)** estar encantado, da (con algo)

overkill ['əʊvəkɪl] *s* exageración; exceso

overladen [ˌəʊvə'leɪdn] *participio pasado* → **overload**

overland ['əʊvəlænd] ◆ *adj* terrestre ◆ *adv* por tierra

overlap [ˌəʊvə'læp] *vi* superponerse

overleaf [ˌəʊvə'liːf] *adv* al dorso

overload [ˌəʊvə'ləʊd] *vt* sobrecargar
Formas irregulares de **overload**: *pp* **overladen**.

overlook [ˌəʊvə'lʊk] *vt* ❶ mirar o dar a ❷ pasar por alto ❸ perdonar

overnight ◆ *adj* ['əʊvənaɪt] ❶ de noche; nocturno, na ❷ para una noche ❸ súbito, ta ◆ *adv* [ˌəʊvə'naɪt] ❶ durante la noche ❷ de la noche a la mañana

overpass ['əʊvəpɑːs] *s* paso elevado

overpower [ˌəʊvə'paʊər] *vt* ❶ vencer; subyugar ❷ *figurado* sobreponerse a

overran [ˌəʊvə'ræn] *pretérito* → **overrun**

overrated [ˌəʊvə'reɪtɪd] *adj* sobreestimado, da

override [ˌəʊvə'raɪd] *vt* ❶ predominar sobre ❷ desautorizar

Formas irregulares de **override**: *pretérito* **overrode** [ˌəʊvə'rəʊd], *pp* **overridden** [ˌəʊvə'rɪdn].

overriding [ˌəʊvə'raɪdɪŋ] *adj* predominante

overrode [ˌəʊvə'rəʊd] *pretérito* → **override**

overrule [ˌəʊvə'ruːl] *vt* ❶ desautorizar ❷ anular ❸ denegar

overrun [ˌəʊvə'rʌn] ◆ *vt* ❶ MILITAR apabullar; arrasar ❷ ocupar; invadir ❸ *figurado* • **to be overrun with** estar invadido, da de ◆ *vi* rebasar el tiempo previsto
Formas irregulares de **overrun**: *pretérito* **overran**, *pp* **overrun**.

oversaw [ˌəʊvə'sɔː] *pretérito* → **oversee**

overseas ◆ *adj* ['əʊvəsiːz] ❶ exterior (*mercado*); al extranjero (*ventas, ayuda*); en el extranjero (*red, filial*) ❷ extranjero, ra ◆ *adv* [ˌəʊvə'siːz] ❶ al extranjero ❷ en el extranjero

oversee [ˌəʊvə'siː] *vt* supervisar
Formas irregulares de **oversee**: *pretérito* **oversaw**, *pp* **overseen** [ˌəʊvə'siːn].

overshadow [ˌəʊvə'ʃædəʊ] *vt* ❶ • **to be overshadowed by** ser eclipsado, da por ❷ • **to be overshadowed by something** ser ensombrecido, da por algo

overshoot [ˌəʊvə'ʃuːt] *vt* pasarse
Formas irregulares de **overshoot**: *pretérito & pp* **overshot**.

oversight ['əʊvəsaɪt] *s* descuido

oversleep [ˌəʊvə'sliːp] *vi* no despertarse a tiempo; quedarse dormido, da
Formas irregulares de **oversleep**: *pretérito & pp* **overslept** [-'slept].

overstep [ˌəʊvə'step] *vt* pasar de
expresión **to overstep the mark** pasarse de la raya

overt ['əʊvɜːt] *adj* abierto, ta; evidente

overtake [ˌəʊvə'teɪk] *vt* AUTOMÓVILES adelantar
Formas irregulares de **overtake**: *pretérito* **overtook**, *pp* **overtaken** [ˌəʊvə'teɪkn].

overthrow *vt* [ˌəʊvə'θrəʊ] derrocar
Formas irregulares de **overthrow**: *pretérito* **overthrew**, *pp* **overthrown**.

overtime ['əʊvətaɪm] ◆ *s* ☼ *incontable* ❶ horas extra ❷ DEPORTE tiempo extra ◆ *adv* • **to work overtime** trabajar horas extra

overtook [ˌəʊvə'tʊk] *pretérito* → **overtake**

overturn [ˌəʊvə'tɜːn] ◆ *vt* ❶ volcar ❷ rechazar ◆ *vi* ❶ volcar ❷ zozobrar

overweight [ˌəʊvə'weɪt] *adj* gordo, da

overwhelm [ˌəʊvə'welm] *vt* ❶ abrumar ❷ aplastar (*derrotar*)

overwhelming [ˌəʊvə'welmɪŋ] *adj* ❶ abrumador, ra ❷ aplastante

overwork [ˌəʊvə'wɜːk] *vt* hacer trabajar demasiado

owe [əʊ] *vt* • **to owe something to somebody, to owe somebody something** deber algo a alguien

O

owing ['əʊɪŋ] *adj* que se debe
■ **owing to** *preposición* debido a
owl [aʊl] *s* búho; lechuza
own [əʊn] ◆ *adj* • **my/your/his** ᴇᴛᴄ **own car** mi/tu/su ᴇᴛᴄpropio coche ◆ *pronombre* • **my own** el mío, la mía • **his/her own** el suyo, la suya • **a house of my/his own** mi/su propia casa • **on your own** solo, la
expresión **to get your own back** tomarse la revancha; desquitarse
◆ *vt* poseer; tener
■ **own up** *vi* • **to own up (to something)** confesar (algo)

owner ['əʊnər] *s* propietario, ria
ownership ['əʊnəʃɪp] *s* propiedad
ox [ɒks] *s* buey

El plural de **ox** es **oxen**

oxtail soup ['ɒksteɪl-] *s* sopa de rabo de buey
oxygen ['ɒksɪdʒən] *s* oxígeno
oxygen mask *s* máscara de oxígeno
oyster ['ɔɪstər] *s* ostra
oz. *abreviatura escrita de* **ounce**
ozone ['əʊzəʊn] *s* ozono
ozone layer *s* capa de ozono

O

P

p¹, P [piː] *s* p; P
Dos plurales: **p's** o **ps**; **P's** o **Ps.**

p² (*abreviatura escrita de* page) p.; pág.

pa [pɑː] *s familiar* papá

p.a. (*abreviatura escrita de* per annum) p.a.

pace [peɪs] ◆ *s* paso; ritmo • **to keep pace (with somebody)** seguir el ritmo (a alguien) • **to keep pace (with something)** mantenerse al corriente (de algo) (*cambios, eventos*) ◆ *vi* • **to pace (up and down)** pasearse de un lado a otro

pacemaker [ˈpeɪsˌmeɪkər] *s* ❶ MEDICINA marcapasos ❷ liebre (*en carrera*)

pacesetter [ˈpeɪsˌsetər] *s* liebre (*en carrera*)

Pacific [pəˈsɪfɪk] ◆ *adj* del Pacífico ◆ *s* • **the Pacific (Ocean)** el (océano) Pacífico

pacifier [ˈpæsɪfaɪər] *s* chupete

pacifist [ˈpæsɪfɪst] *s* pacifista

pacify [ˈpæsɪfaɪ] *vt* calmar; apaciguar

pack [pæk] ◆ *s* ❶ lío; fardo ❷ mochila ❸ paquete ❹ baraja ❺ jauría (*de lobos*) ❻ manada (*de lobos*)
■ *expresión* **a pack of lies** una sarta de mentiras
◆ *vt* ❶ hacer (*las maletas*); meter (en la maleta) ❷ empaquetar ❸ envasar ❹ llenar; abarrotar • **to be packed into something** estar apretujados dentro de algo ◆ *vi* hacer las maletas
■ **pack in** *vi familiar* estropearse
■ **pack off** *vt* ☼ *El objeto se puede colocar antes o después de la preposición. familiar* enviar; mandar

package [ˈpækɪdʒ] ◆ *s* paquete ◆ *vt* envasar

package tour *s* vacaciones con todo incluido

packaging [ˈpækɪdʒɪŋ] *s* envasado

packed [pækt] *adj* • **packed (with)** repleto, ta (de)

packet [ˈpækɪt] *s* ❶ paquete ❷ bolsa (*de caramelos, papas fritas*)

packing [ˈpækɪŋ] *s* ❶ embalaje ❷ • **to do the packing** hacer las maletas

pact [pækt] *s* pacto

pad [pæd] ◆ *s* ❶ almohadilla ❷ tampón ❸ bloc (*de papel*) ◆ *vt* acolchar; rellenar

padding [ˈpædɪŋ] *s* ☼ *incontable* relleno

paddle [ˈpædl] ◆ *s* ❶ remo ❷ raqueta (*de tenis de mesa*) ◆ *vi* ❶ remar ❷ pasear por la orilla

paddle boat, paddle steamer *s* vapor de paletas

paddock [ˈpædək] *s* ❶ potrero; corral ❷ paddock

paddy field [ˈpædɪ-] *s* arrozal

paddy wagon [ˈpædɪ-] *s* camioneta para el transporte de presos

padlock [ˈpædlɒk] ◆ *s* candado ◆ *vt* cerrar con candado

pagan [ˈpeɪɡən] *adj* & *s* pagano, na

page [peɪdʒ] ◆ *s* página ◆ *vt* ❶ llamar por megafonía ❷ llamar por el busca

pageant [ˈpædʒənt] *s* desfile

paid [peɪd] ◆ *pretérito* & *participio pasado* → **pay** ◆ *adj* ❶ pagado, da • **badly/well paid** mal/bien pagado ❷ remunerado, da

pail [peɪl] *s* cubo

pain [peɪn] *s* ❶ dolor • **to be in pain** sufrir dolor ❷ pena; sufrimiento ❸ *familiar* pesado, da (*persona*); lata (*cosa*) • **what a pain to have to do it again** ¡qué lata tener que hacerlo otra vez!
■ **pains** *spl* esfuerzos • **to be at pains to do something** afanarse por hacer algo

painful [ˈpeɪnful] *adj* ❶ dolorido, da (*cuerpo*) ❷ doloroso, sa (*memoria*)

painfully [ˈpeɪnfulɪ] *adv* ❶ dolorosamente ❷ terriblemente

painkiller [ˈpeɪnˌkɪlər] *s* analgésico

painless [ˈpeɪnlɪs] *adj* ❶ indoloro, ra ❷ sin complicaciones

painstaking [ˈpeɪnzˌteɪkɪŋ] *adj* meticuloso, sa; minucioso, sa

paint [peɪnt] ◆ *s* pintura ◆ *vt* pintar • **to paint the ceiling white** pintar el techo de blanco • **to paint your lips/nails** pintarse los labios/las uñas ◆ *vi* pintar

paintbrush [ˈpeɪntbrʌʃ] *s* ❶ ARTE pincel ❷ brocha

painter [ˈpeɪntər] *s* pintor, ra

painting ['peɪntɪŋ] s ❶ cuadro; pintura ❷ ☀ *incontable* pintura *(arte, actividad)*

pair [peǝr] s ❶ par ❷ • **a pair of scissors** unas tijeras • **a pair of pants** unos pantalones ❸ pareja

pajamas [pǝ'dʒɑːmǝz] *spl* piyama • **a pair of pajamas** un piyama

Pakistan [,pækɪ'stæn] s (el) Paquistán

Pakistani [,pækɪ'stæni] ◆ *adj* paquistaní ◆ s paquistaní

pal [pæl] s *familiar* amigo, ga; colega

palace ['pælɪs] s palacio

palate ['pælǝt] s paladar

pale [peɪl] ◆ *adj* ❶ claro, ra *(color)* ❷ tenue *(luz)* ❸ pálido, da *(piel)* • **to turn pale** palidecer ◆ *vi* palidecer

Palestine ['pælɪ,staɪn] s Palestina

Palestinian [,pælǝ'stɪnɪǝn] ◆ *adj* palestino, na ◆ s palestino, na

palette ['pælǝt] s paleta

palings ['peɪlɪŋz] *spl* empalizada

palm [pɑːm] s ❶ palmera ❷ palma • **to read somebody's palm** leerle la mano a alguien

■ **palm off** *vt* ☀ *El objeto se puede colocar antes o después de la preposición. familiar* • **to palm something off on somebody** endosar algo a alguien • **to palm something off as** hacer pasar algo por

palm tree s palmera

paltry ['pɔːltrɪ] *adj* mísero, ra

pamper ['pæmpǝr] *vt* mimar

pamphlet ['pæmflɪt] s ❶ folleto ❷ panfleto

pan [pæn] ◆ s ❶ cazuela; cacerola ❷ sartén ❸ molde ◆ *vt familiar* poner por los suelos ◆ *vi* CINE • **the camera pans right/left** la cámara se mueve hacia la derecha/la izquierda

■ **pan out** *vi familiar* resultar; salir

Panama ['pænǝ,mɑː] s Panamá

Panama Canal s • **the Panama Canal** el canal de Panamá

pancake ['pænkeɪk] s hot cake

panda ['pændǝ] s panda

Dos plurales: **panda** o **pandas.**

pane [peɪn] s (hoja de) cristal

panel ['pænl] s ❶ panel *(de metal, jueces)* ❷ mesa *(en debates)* ❸ tablero *(de máquina)*

paneling ['pænǝlɪŋ] s ❶ ☀ *incontable* artesonado ❷ paneles

pang [pæŋ] s punzada

panic ['pænɪk] ◆ s pánico • **to be in a panic about something** ponerse muy nervioso por algo ◆ *vi* aterrarse • **don't panic** que no cunda el pánico

Formas irregulares de **panic:** *pretérito & pp* **panicked,** *gerundio* **panicking**

panicky ['pænɪkɪ] *adj* • **he feels panicky** tiene pánico • **she got panicky** le entró el pánico

panic-stricken *adj* preso, sa o víctima del pánico

panorama [,pænǝ'rɑːmǝ] s panorama

pant [pænt] *vi* jadear

panther ['pænθǝr] s pantera

Dos plurales: **panther** o **panthers.**

panties ['pæntɪz] *spl* calzones • **a pair of panties** unos calzones

pantihose ['pæntɪhǝʊz] = **panty hose**

pants [pænts] *spl* pantalones • **a pair of pants** unos pantalones

panty hose, pantihose ['pæntɪ-] *spl* pantimedias; medias

papa ['pæpǝ] s papá

paper ['peɪpǝr] ◆ s ❶ ☀ *incontable* papel • **piece of paper a)** hoja de papel **b)** trozo de papel ❷ periódico ❸ estudio; trabajo; ponencia ◆ *adj* de papel

■ **papers** *spl* documentación

paperback ['peɪpǝbæk] s libro en rústica

paper clip s clip

paperweight ['peɪpǝweɪt] s pisapapeles

paperwork ['peɪpǝwɜːk] s papeleo

par [pɑːr] s ❶ • **on a par with** al mismo nivel que ❷ GOLF par • **under/over par** bajo/sobre par

parable ['pærǝbl] s parábola

parachute ['pærǝʃuːt] s paracaídas

parade [pǝ'reɪd] ◆ s desfile • **on parade** MILITAR pasando revista ◆ *vt* ❶ hacer desfilar ❷ pasear ❸ *figurado* hacer alarde de ◆ *vi* desfilar

paradise ['pærǝdaɪs] s *figurado* paraíso

paradox ['pærǝdɒks] s paradoja

paradoxically [,pærǝ'dɒksɪklɪ] *adv* paradójicamente

paraffin ['pærǝfɪn] s parafina

paragliding ['pærǝ,glaɪdɪŋ] s parapente

paragraph ['pærǝgrɑːf] s párrafo

Paraguay ['pærǝgwaɪ] s (el) Paraguay

Paraguayan [,pærǝ'gwaɪǝn] ◆ *adj* paraguayo, ya ◆ s paraguayo, ya

parallel ['pærǝlel] ◆ *adj* • **parallel (to** o **with)** paralelo, la (a) ◆ s ❶ paralela ❷ • **to have no parallel** no tener precedente ❸ semejanza ❹ GEOGRAFÍA paralelo

paralysis [pǝ'rælɪsɪs] s parálisis

El plural de **paralysis** es **paralyses** [pǝ'rælisiːz].

paralyze ['pærǝlaɪz] *vt literal & figurado* paralizar

paramedic [,pærǝ'medɪk] s paramédico; paramédica

parameter [pǝ'ræmɪtǝr] s parámetro

paramount ['pærǝmaʊnt] *adj* vital; fundamental • **of paramount importance** de suma importancia

paranoid ['pærǝnɔɪd] *adj* paranoico, ca

parasite ['pærǝsaɪt] s parásito, ta

paratrooper ['pærǝtruːpǝr] s paracaidista *(del ejército)*

parcel ['pɑːsl] s paquete

P

parched [pɑːʧt] *adj* ❶ muy seco, ca *(boca, garganta)* ❷ quemado, da ❸ *familiar* • **I'm parched** me muero de sed

parchment ['pɑːʧmənt] *s* pergamino

pardon ['pɑːdn] ◆ *s* ❶ DERECHO perdón; indulto ❷ perdón

expresión **I beg your pardon?** ¿perdón?; ¿cómo (dice)? ▶ **I beg your pardon** le ruego me disculpe; perdón ◆ *vt* ❶ • **to pardon somebody (for something)** perdonar a alguien (por algo) • **pardon?** ¿perdón?; ¿cómo (dice)? • **pardon me a)** discúlpeme; perdón **b)** con permiso ❷ DERECHO indultar

parent ['peərənt] *s* padre; madre
■ **parents** *spl* padres

parental [pə'rentl] *adj* de los padres

parenthesis [pə'renθɪsɪs] *s* paréntesis • **in parenthesis** entre paréntesis

El plural de **parenthesis** es **parentheses** [pə'renθɪsiːz].

parish ['pærɪʃ] *s* parroquia

parity ['pærətɪ] *s* • **parity (with/between)** igualdad (con/entre)

park [pɑːk] ◆ *s* parque ◆ *vt* & *vi* estacionar

parking ['pɑːkɪŋ] *s* estacionamiento • **'no parking'** 'prohibido estacionarse'

parking brake *s* freno de mano

parking garage *s* estacionamiento *(en edificio)*

parking light *s* luz de estacionamiento

parking lot *s* estacionamiento (al aire libre)

parking meter *s* parquímetro

parking ticket *s* multa por estacionamiento indebido

parkway ['pɑːkweɪ] *s* avenida

parliament ['pɑːləmənt] *s* ❶ parlamento ❷ legislatura

parliamentary [ˌpɑːlə'mentərɪ] *adj* parlamentario, ria

parlor ['pɑːlər] *s* desusado salón

parochial [pə'rəʊkjəl] *adj* ❶ *despectivo* de miras estrechas ❷ • **parochial school** colegio privado religioso

parody ['pærədɪ] ◆ *s* parodia ◆ *vt* parodiar

parole [pə'rəʊl] *s* libertad condicional (bajo palabra) • **on parole** en libertad condicional

parrot ['pærət] *s* loro

parsley ['pɑːslɪ] *s* perejil

part [pɑːt] ◆ *s* ❶ parte • **the best** o **better part of** la mayor parte de • **for the most part** en su mayoría ❷ pieza ❸ TEATRO papel ❹ • **part (in)** participación (en) • **to play an important part (in)** desempeñar o jugar un papel importante (en) • **to take part (in)** tomar parte (en) ❺ raya *(en el pelo)* ◆ *adv* en parte ◆ *vt* ❶ abrir ❷ peinar con raya ◆ *vi* ❶ separarse ❷ abrirse
■ **part with** *vt* 🔆 *El objeto siempre va después de la preposición al final.* separarse de

partial ['pɑːʃl] *adj* ❶ parcial ❷ • **partial to** amigo, ga de; aficionado, da a

participant [pɑː'tɪsɪpənt] *s* participante

participate [pɑː'tɪsɪpeɪt] *vi* • **to participate (in)** participar (en)

participation [pɑːˌtɪsɪ'peɪʃn] *s* participación

participle ['pɑːtɪsɪpl] *s* participio

particle ['pɑːtɪkl] *s* partícula

particular [pə'tɪkjʊlər] *adj* ❶ en particular o especial • **did you want any particular color?** ¿quería algún color en particular? ❷ especial ❸ exigente
■ **particulars** *spl* ❶ datos ❷ detalles
■ **in particular** *adv* en particular

particularly [pə'tɪkjʊlərlɪ] *adv* especialmente

parting ['pɑːtɪŋ] *s* despedida

partisan [ˌpɑːtɪ'zæn] ◆ *adj* partidista ◆ *s* partisano, na

partition [pɑː'tɪʃn] ◆ *s* ❶ tabique ❷ separación ❸ INFORMÁTICA partición ◆ *vt* ❶ dividir con tabiques ❷ dividir ❸ INFORMÁTICA crear particiones en

partly ['pɑːtlɪ] *adv* en parte

partner ['pɑːtnər] *s* ❶ pareja ❷ compañero, ra ❸ socio, cia ❹ colega

partnership ['pɑːtnəʃɪp] *s* ❶ asociación ❷ sociedad

part-time ◆ *adj* a tiempo parcial ◆ *adv* a tiempo parcial

party ['pɑːtɪ] *s* ❶ fiesta • **to have a party** hacer una fiesta ❷ POLÍTICA partido ❸ grupo • **a party of ten** un grupo de diez

pass [pɑːs] ◆ *s* ❶ pase ❷ • **travel pass** tarjeta o abono de transportes ❸ puerto *(en montañas)* ◆ *vt* ❶ pasar ❷ pasar por (delante de) • **to pass somebody in the street** cruzarse con alguien ❸ AUTOMÓVILES rebasar ❹ sobrepasar ❺ aprobar *(examen, ley)* ❻ formular *(opinión)* ❼ dictar *(sentencia)* ◆ *vi* ❶ pasar ❷ AUTOMÓVILES rebasar ❸ aprobar ❹ transcurrir
■ **pass as, pass for** *vt* 🔆 *El objeto siempre va después de la preposición al final.* pasar por
■ **pass away, pass on** *vi* fallecer
■ **pass by** ◆ *vt* 🔆 *El objeto se puede colocar antes o después de la preposición.* pasar desapercibido, da a ◆ *vi* pasar cerca
■ **pass for** *vt* = **pass as**
■ **pass on** ◆ *vt* 🔆 *El objeto se puede colocar antes o después de la preposición.* • **to pass something on (to)** pasar algo (a) ◆ *vi* ❶ continuar ❷ = **pass away**
■ **pass out** *vi* desmayarse
■ **pass over** *vt* 🔆 *El objeto siempre va después de la preposición al final.* pasar por alto
■ **pass up** *vt* 🔆 *El objeto se puede colocar antes o después de la preposición.* dejar pasar o escapar

passage ['pæsɪdʒ] *s* ❶ pasillo ❷ pasaje *(de novela)* ❸ *formal* paso *(del tiempo)*

passageway ['pæsɪdʒweɪ] *s* pasillo

passenger ['pæsɪndʒər] *s* pasajero, ra

passerby [ˌpɑːsə'baɪ] *s* transeúnte

P

El plural de **passerby** es **passersby** [,pɑːsəzˈbaɪ].

passing ['pɑːsɪŋ] ◆ adj ❶ pasajero, ra ❷ de pasada ◆ s transcurso
■ **in passing** adv de pasada

passion ['pæʃn] s • **passion (for)** pasión (por)

passionate ['pæʃənət] adj apasionado, da

passive ['pæsɪv] adj pasivo, va

passport ['pɑːspɔːt] s pasaporte • **passport to something** figurado pasaporte a algo

password ['pɑːswɜːd] s contraseña

past [pɑːst] ◆ adj ❶ anterior ❷ último, ma • **over the past week** durante la última semana ❸ terminado, da ◆ adv por delante • **to walk/run past** pasar andando/corriendo ◆ s ❶ • **the past** el pasado ❷ pasado ◆ preposición ❶ • **it's five/half/a quarter past ten** son las diez y cinco/media/cuarto ❷ por delante de • **to walk/run past something** pasar algo andando/corriendo ❸ más allá de • **it's past the bank** está pasando el banco

pasta ['pæstə] s ☼ incontable pasta

paste [peɪst] ◆ s ❶ pasta ❷ paté ❸ engrudo ◆ vt pegar

pasteurize, pasteurise ['pɑːstʃəraɪz] vt pasteurizar

pastime ['pɑːstaɪm] s pasatiempo

past participle s participio pasado

pastry ['peɪstrɪ] s ❶ pasta; masa ❷ pastel

past tense s • **the past tense** el pasado

pasture ['pɑːstʃər] s pasto

pat [pæt] ◆ s palmadita ◆ vt ❶ golpear ligeramente ❷ acariciar • **to pat somebody on the back/hand** darle a alguien una palmadita en la espalda/la mano

patch [pætʃ] ◆ s ❶ remiendo ❷ parche ❸ área ❹ periodo ◆ vt remendar
■ **patch up** vt ☼ El objeto se puede colocar antes o después de la preposición. ❶ reparar ❷ salvar
expresión **we have patched things up** hemos hecho las paces

patchy ['pætʃɪ] adj ❶ irregular; desigual ❷ deficiente; incompleto, ta ❸ irregular

pâté ['pæteɪ] s paté

patent ['pætənt] ◆ adj patente; evidente ◆ s patente ◆ vt patentar

patent leather s charol

paternal [pə'tɜːnl] adj ❶ paternal ❷ paterno, na (abuelo)

paternity [pə'tɜːnətɪ] s paternidad

path [pɑːθ] ☼ pl [pɑːðz] s ❶ camino ❷ trayectoria; rumbo ❸ curso

pathetic [pə'θetɪk] adj ❶ patético, ca ❷ inútil ❸ malísimo, ma

pathological [,pæθə'lɒdʒɪkl] adj patológico, ca

pathology [pə'θɒlədʒɪ] s patología

pathos ['peɪθɒs] s patetismo

pathway ['pɑːθweɪ] s camino; sendero

patience ['peɪʃns] s paciencia

patient ['peɪʃnt] ◆ adj paciente ◆ s paciente

patriot ['peɪtrɪət] s patriota

patriotic [,peɪtrɪ'ɒtɪk] adj patriótico, ca

patriotism ['peɪtrɪətɪzm] s patriotismo

patrol [pə'trəʊl] ◆ s patrulla ◆ vt patrullar

patrol car s patrulla

patrolman [pə'trəʊlmən] s policía; guardia
El plural de **patrolman** es **patrolmen** [pə'trəʊlmen].

patrol wagon s patrulla

patron ['peɪtrən] s ❶ mecenas ❷ formal cliente

patronize ['pætrənaɪz] vt ❶ despectivo tratar con aire paternalista o condescendiente ❷ formal patrocinar

patronizing ['pætrənaɪzɪŋ] adj despectivo paternalista; condescendiente

pattern ['pætən] s ❶ diseño ❷ estructura ❸ desarrollo ❹ patrón ❺ modelo

patty ['pætɪ] s ❶ empanada ❷ hamburguesa

pause [pɔːz] ◆ s pausa ◆ vi ❶ hacer una pausa ❷ detenerse

pave [peɪv] vt pavimentar
expresión **to pave the way for** preparar el terreno para

pavement ['peɪvmənt] s calzada

pavilion [pə'vɪljən] s pabellón

paving ['peɪvɪŋ] s ☼ incontable pavimento

paving stone s losa

paw [pɔː] s ❶ pata ❷ zarpa

pawn [pɔːn] ◆ s ❶ peón ❷ títere ◆ vt empeñar

pay [peɪ] ◆ vt ❶ pagar • **to pay somebody for something** pagar a alguien por algo • **he paid $20 for it** pagó 20 dolares por ello ❷ hacer ❸ ofrecer ❹ prestar ❺ rendir ◆ vi ❶ pagar • **to pay by credit card** pagar con tarjeta de crédito • **it pays well** está bien pagado ❷ ser rentable
expresión **to pay dearly for something** pagar caro (por) algo
◆ s sueldo; paga
■ **pay back** vt ☼ El objeto se puede colocar antes o después de la preposición. ❶ devolver; reembolsar ❷ devolver el dinero a ❸ • **to pay somebody back (for something)** hacer pagar a alguien (por algo)
■ **pay for** vt ☼ El objeto siempre va después de la preposición al final. pagar
■ **pay off** ◆ vt ☼ El objeto se puede colocar antes o después de la preposición. ❶ liquidar; saldar ❷ despedir con indemnización ◆ vi dar fruto
■ **pay up** vi pagar
Formas irregulares de **pay**: pretérito & pp **paid**.

payable ['peɪəbl] adj ❶ pagadero, ra ❷ • **payable to** a favor de

pay-as-you-go s pago por uso

payday ['peɪdeɪ] s día de paga

payee [peɪ'iː] s beneficiario, ria

payment ['peɪmənt] s pago

pay rise s aumento de sueldo

payroll ['peɪrəʊl] s nómina

pay station s teléfono público

pc (*abreviatura escrita de* per cent) p.c.

PC (*abreviatura de* personal computer) s PC

PDF (*abreviatura de* portable document format) s IN-FORMÁTICA PDF

PE (*abreviatura de* physical education) s educación física

pea [piː] s chícharo

peace [piːs] s ❶ paz ❷ calma; tranquilidad • **peace and quiet** paz y tranquilidad ❸ orden

expresión to make (your) peace (with) hacer las paces (con)

peaceable ['piːsəbl] *adj* pacífico, ca

peaceful ['piːsfʊl] *adj* ❶ tranquilo, la ❷ pacífico, ca

peach [piːtʃ] ◆ *adj* de color durazno ◆ s ❶ durazno ❷ color durazno

peacock ['piːkɒk] s pavo real

peak [piːk] ◆ s ❶ pico; cima ❷ apogeo ❸ visera ◆ *adj* ❶ alto, ta ❷ perfecto, ta ◆ *vi* alcanzar el máximo

peak rate s tarifa máxima

peal [piːl] ◆ s repique • **peal (of laughter)** carcajada ◆ *vi* repicar

peanut ['piːnʌt] s cacahuate

peanut butter s mantequilla de cacahuate

pear [peər] s pera

pearl [pɜːl] s perla

peasant ['peznt] s campesino, na

peat [piːt] s turba

pebble ['pebl] s guijarro

peck [pek] ◆ s ❶ picotazo ❷ besito ◆ *vt* & *vi* picotear

peculiar [pɪ'kjuːljər] *adj* ❶ singular; extraño, ña ❷ • **to be peculiar to** ser propio, pia de

peculiarity [pɪ,kjuːlɪ'ærətɪ] s ❶ extravagancia ❷ peculiaridad

pedal ['pedl] ◆ s pedal ◆ *vi* pedalear

pedantic [pɪ'dæntɪk] *adj despectivo* puntilloso, sa

peddler ['pedlər] s traficante (de drogas)

pedestal ['pedɪstl] s pedestal

pedestrian [pɪ'destrɪən] ◆ *adj despectivo* pedestre ◆ s peatón

pediatrics, paediatrics [,piːdɪ'ætrɪks] s pediatría

pedigree ['pedɪgriː] ◆ *adj* de raza ◆ s ❶ pedigrí ❷ linaje

peek [piːk] *familiar* ◆ s mirada; ojeada ◆ *vi* mirar a hurtadillas

peel [piːl] ◆ s ❶ piel ❷ cáscara ◆ *vt* pelar ◆ *vi* ❶ descarapelarse ❷ pelarse

peep [piːp] ◆ s ❶ mirada; ojeada ❷ *familiar* pío ◆ *vi* mirar furtivamente

■ **peep out** *vi* asomar

peer [pɪər] ◆ s ❶ coetáneo; coetánea ❷ igual ◆ *vi* mirar con atención

peer group s ▸ grupo generacional o social

peeved [piːvd] *adj familiar* disgustado, da

peg [peg] s ❶ estaca ❷ gancho

pejorative [pɪ'dʒɒrətɪv] *adj* peyorativo, va; despectivo, va

pelican ['pelɪkən] s pelícano

El plural de **pelican** es **pelican** o **pelicans**.

pellet ['pelɪt] s ❶ bolita ❷ perdigón

pelt [pelt] ◆ s piel ◆ *vt* • **to pelt somebody with something** acribillar a alguien con algo; arrojar algo a alguien ◆ *vi* ❶ • **it was pelting down** o **with rain** llovía a cántaros ❷ correr a toda velocidad

pelvis ['pelvɪs] s pelvis

pen [pen] s ❶ pluma ❷ plumón ❸ redil; corral

penal ['piːnl] *adj* penal

penalize ['piːnəlaɪz] *vt* ❶ penalizar ❷ DEPORTE penalizar; castigar

penalty ['penltɪ] s ❶ pena ❷ multa ❸ FÚTBOL penal • **to win on penalties** ganar por/en penales ▸ **penalty (kick)** penal

expresión to pay the penalty (for something) *figurado* pagar las consecuencias (de algo)

penalty ['penltɪ] s ❶ pena ❷ multa ❸ DEPORTE penalty ▸ **penalty (kick) a)** FÚTBOL penalti

expresión to pay the penalty (for something) *figurado* pagar las consecuencias (de algo)

penance ['penəns] s penitencia

pencil ['pensl] s lápiz • **in pencil** a lápiz

pencil case s estuche

pencil sharpener s sacapuntas

pendant ['pendənt] s colgante

pending ['pendɪŋ] *formal* ◆ *adj* ❶ pendiente ❷ inminente ◆ *preposición* a la espera de

pendulum ['pendjʊləm] s péndulo

penetrate ['penɪtreɪt] *vt* ❶ atravesar ❷ penetrar en ❸ infiltrarse en

penguin ['peŋgwɪn] s pingüino

penicillin [,penɪ'sɪlɪn] s penicilina

peninsula [pə'nɪnsjʊlə] s península

penitentiary [,penɪ'tenʃərɪ] s penitenciaría

penknife ['pennaɪf] s navaja

El plural de **penknife** es **penknives** ['pennaɪvz].

pen name s seudónimo

penniless ['penɪlɪs] *adj* sin dinero

penny ['penɪ] s centavo

pen pal s *familiar* amigo, ga por correspondencia

pension ['penʃn] s ❶ pensión ❷ subsidio

pensioner ['penʃənər] s pensionado, ada

pensive ['pensɪv] *adj* pensativo, va

pentagon ['pentəgən] s pentágono

■ **Pentagon** s • **the Pentagon** el Pentágono

P

THE PENTAGON

El edificio del Pentágono, nombrado así por su forma, y que se encuentra en las afueras de la ciudad de Washington, es la sede de la secretaría de la defensa estadounidense. Muchas veces se habla del Pentágono para referirse al poder militar de los Estados Unidos en general. Parte del Pentágono fue destruida en los ataques terroristas del 11 de septiembre del 2001.

pent up ['pent-] *adj* reprimido, da

people ['pi:pl] ◆ *s* pueblo ◆ *spl* ❶ gente • **people say that...** dice la gente que... ❷ personas • **a table for eight people** una mesa para ocho personas • **young people** los jóvenes ❸ habitantes ❹ *POLÍTICA* • **the people** el pueblo ◆ *vt* • **to be peopled by** o **with** estar poblado, da de

pepper ['pepər] *s* ❶ pimienta ❷ pimiento ▶ **red/ green pepper** pimiento rojo/verde

peppermint ['pepəmɪnt] *s* ❶ pastilla de menta ❷ menta

per [pɜ:r] *preposición* por • **per hour/kilo/person** por hora/kilo/persona • **per day** al día • **as per instructions** de acuerdo con las instrucciones

per annum *adv* al o por año

per capita [pə'kæpɪtə] ◆ *adj* per cápita ◆ *adv* por cabeza

perceive [pə'si:v] *vt* ❶ percibir; apreciar ❷ advertir; apreciar ❸ • **to perceive something/somebody as** ver algo/a alguien como

per cent *adv* por ciento • **fifty per cent of the population** el cincuenta por ciento de la población

percentage [pə'sentɪdʒ] *s* porcentaje

perception [pə'sepʃn] *s* ❶ percepción ❷ perspicacia ❸ idea

perceptive [pə'septɪv] *adj* perspicaz

perch [pɜ:tʃ] ◆ *s* percha; vara ◆ *vi* • **to perch (on) a)** posarse (en) **b)** sentarse (en)

percussion [pə'kʌʃn] *s* *MÚSICA* percusión

perfect ◆ *adj* ['pɜ:fɪkt] perfecto, ta • **he's a perfect stranger to me** me es completamente desconocido ◆ *s* ['pɜ:fɪkt] *GRAMÁTICA* ▶ **the perfect (tense)** el perfecto ◆ *vt* [pə'fekt] perfeccionar

perfection [pə'fekʃn] *s* perfección • **to perfection** a la perfección

perfectionist [pə'fekʃənɪst] *s* perfeccionista

perfectly ['pɜ:fɪktlɪ] *adv* ❶ absolutamente • **perfectly well** perfectamente bien ❷ perfectamente

perforate ['pɜ:fəreɪt] *vt* perforar

perform [pə'fɔ:m] ◆ *vt* ❶ llevar a cabo ❷ cumplir ❸ interpretar ❹ representar ◆ *vi* ❶ funcionar; desenvolverse ❷ actuar ❸ interpretar

performance [pə'fɔ:məns] *s* ❶ realización ❷ cumplimiento ❸ representación ❹ rendimiento

performer [pə'fɔ:mər] *s* intérprete

perfume ['pɜ:fju:m] *s* perfume

perfunctory [pə'fʌŋktərɪ] *adj* superficial

perhaps [pə'hæps] *adv* ❶ quizás • **perhaps she'll do it** quizás ella lo haga • **perhaps so/not** tal vez sí/no ❷ • **perhaps you could help?** ¿te importaría ayudar? • **perhaps you should start again** ¿por qué no empiezas de nuevo? ❸ aproximadamente

peril ['perɪl] *s literario* peligro

perimeter [pə'rɪmɪtər] *s* perímetro

period ['pɪərɪəd] ◆ *s* ❶ período; periodo ❷ *HISTORIA* época ❸ *EDUCACIÓN* clase; hora ❹ período • **to be on your period** tener el período ❺ punto ❻ *DEPORTE* tiempo ◆ *en compuestos* de época

periodic [,pɪərɪ'ɒdɪk], **periodical** *adj* periódico, ca

periodical [,pɪərɪ'ɒdɪkl] ◆ *adj* = **periodic** ◆ *s* revista

peripheral [pə'rɪfərəl] ◆ *adj* ❶ marginal ❷ periférico, ca ◆ *s* *INFORMÁTICA* periférico

perish ['perɪʃ] *vi* ❶ perecer ❷ deteriorarse

perishable ['perɪʃəbl] *adj* perecedero, ra

■ **perishables** *spl* productos perecederos

perjury ['pɜ:dʒərɪ] *s* *DERECHO* perjurio

perk [pɜ:k] *s familiar* extra; beneficio adicional

■ **perk up** *vi* animarse

permanent ['pɜ:mənənt] ◆ *adj* ❶ permanente ❷ fijo, ja ❸ constante ◆ *s* permanente

permeate ['pɜ:mɪeɪt] *vt* impregnar

permissible [pə'mɪsəbl] *adj* permisible

permission [pə'mɪʃn] *s* • **permission (to do something)** permiso (para hacer algo)

permit ◆ *vt* [pə'mɪt] permitir • **to permit somebody something/to do something** permitir a alguien algo/hacer algo ◆ *vi* [pə'mɪt] • **if time permits** si hay tiempo ◆ *s* ['pɜ:mɪt] permiso

perpendicular [,pɜ:pən'dɪkjʊlər] ◆ *adj* ❶ *MATEMÁTICAS* • **perpendicular (to)** perpendicular (a) ❷ vertical ◆ *s* *MATEMÁTICAS* perpendicular

perpetual [pə'petʃʊəl] *adj* ❶ *despectivo* constante ❷ perpetuo, tua

perplex [pə'pleks] *vt* dejar perplejo, ja

perplexing [pə'pleksɪŋ] *adj* desconcertante

persecute ['pɜ:sɪkju:t] *vt* perseguir

perseverance [,pɜ:sɪ'vɪərəns] *s* perseverancia

persevere [,pɜ:sɪ'vɪər] *vi* • **to persevere (with something/in doing something)** perseverar (en algo/en hacer algo)

Persian ['pɜ:ʃn] *adj* persa

persist [pə'sɪst] *vi* ❶ persistir ❷ • **to persist in doing something** empeñarse en hacer algo

persistence [pə'sɪstəns] *s* ❶ persistencia ❷ perseverancia

persistent [pə'sɪstənt] *adj* ❶ continuo, nua ❷ persistente

person ['pɜ:sn] *s formal* ❶ persona • **in person** en persona ❷ • **to have something about your person**

P

llevar algo encima ❸ GRAMÁTICA persona • **in the first person** en primera persona

Dos plurales: **people** o **persons**.

personal ['pɜːsənl] ◆ *s* anuncio personal (por palabras) ◆ *adj* ❶ personal ❷ privado, da ❸ *despectivo* ofensivo, va • **to be personal** hacer alusiones personales

personal computer *s* computadora personal

personality [ˌpɜːsəˈnælətɪ] *s* personalidad

personally ['pɜːsnəlɪ] *adv* ❶ personalmente ❷ en persona

personal property *s* 💡 *incontable* bienes muebles

personify [pəˈsɒnɪfaɪ] *vt* personificar

personnel [ˌpɜːsəˈnel] ◆ *s* 💡 *incontable* departamento de personal ◆ *spl* personal

perspective [pəˈspektɪv] *s* perspectiva • **to get something in perspective** *figurado* poner algo en perspectiva

perspiration [ˌpɜːspəˈreɪʃn] *s* sudor

persuade [pəˈsweɪd] *vt* • **to persuade somebody (of something/to do something)** persuadir a alguien (de algo/a hacer algo) • **to persuade somebody that** convencer a alguien (de) que

persuasion [pəˈsweɪʒn] *s* ❶ persuasión ❷ creencia

persuasive [pəˈsweɪsɪv] *adj* persuasivo, va

perturb [pəˈtɜːb] *vt formal* perturbar

Peru [pəˈruː] *s* (el) Perú

Peruvian [pəˈruːvjən] ◆ *adj* peruano, na ◆ *s* peruano, na

perverse [pəˈvɜːs] *adj* ❶ perverso, sa ❷ puñetero, ra

perversion [pəˈvɜːrʒn] *s* ❶ perversión ❷ tergiversación

pervert ◆ *s* ['pɜːvɜːt] pervertido, da ◆ *vt* [pəˈvɜːt] ❶ tergiversar ❷ pervertir

pessimist ['pesɪmɪst] *s* pesimista

pessimistic [ˌpesɪˈmɪstɪk] *adj* pesimista

pest [pest] *s* ❶ insecto nocivo ❷ animal nocivo ❸ *familiar* pesado, da ❹ lata

pester ['pestər] *vt* dar lata a

pet [pet] ◆ *adj* ❶ preferido, da ❷ • **pet peeve** • **my pet peeve is seeing kids smoking** lo que más detesto es ver a los chavos fumando ◆ *s* ❶ mascota ❷ preferido, da ◆ *vt* acariciar ◆ *vi* fajar

petal ['petl] *s* pétalo

peter ['piːtər] ■ **peter out** *vi* ❶ agotarse ❷ desaparecer

petite [pəˈtiːt] *adj* chiquita

petition [pɪˈtɪʃn] ◆ *s* petición ◆ *vi* DERECHO • **petition for divorce** pedir el divorcio

petrified ['petrɪfaɪd] *adj* petrificado, da

petroleum [pɪˈtrəʊljəm] *s* petróleo

petting zoo ['petɪŋˈzuː] *s* ▸ parque zoológico en el que los niños pueden acariciar y dar de comer a los animales

petty ['petɪ] *adj* ❶ mezquino, na ❷ insignificante

phantom ['fæntəm] ◆ *adj* ilusorio, ria ◆ *s* fantasma

pharmaceutical [ˌfɑːməˈsjuːtɪkl] *adj* farmacéutico, ca

pharmacist ['fɑːməsɪst] *s* farmacéutico, ca

pharmacy ['fɑːməsɪ] *s* farmacia

phase [feɪz] ◆ *s* fase ◆ *vt* escalonar

■ **phase in** *vt* 💡 *El objeto se puede colocar antes o después de la preposición.* introducir progresivamente

■ **phase out** *vt* 💡 *El objeto se puede colocar antes o después de la preposición.* retirar progresivamente

PhD (*abreviatura de* Doctor of Philosophy) *s* ❶ doctorado ❷ doctor, ra

pheasant ['feznt] *s* faisán

Dos plurales: **pheasant** o **pheasants**.

phenomena [fɪˈnɒmɪnə] *spl* → **phenomenon**

phenomenal [fɪˈnɒmɪnl] *adj* extraordinario, ria

phenomenon [fɪˈnɒmɪnən] *s literal & figurado* fenómeno

El plural de **phenomenon** es **phenomena**.

philanthropist [fɪˈlænθrəpɪst] *s* filántropo, pa

Philippine ['fɪlɪpiːn] *adj* filipino, na

■ **Philippines** *spl* • **the Philippines** las Filipinas

philistine ['fɪlɪstiːn] *s figurado* inculto, ta

philosopher [fɪˈlɒsəfər] *s* filósofo, fa

philosophical [ˌfɪləˈsɒfɪkl] *adj* filosófico, ca

philosophy [fɪˈlɒsəfɪ] *s* filosofía

phobia ['fəʊbjə] *s* fobia • **to have a phobia about something** tener fobia a algo

phone [fəʊn] ◆ *s* teléfono • **to be on the phone a)** estar al teléfono • **to talk about something on the phone** discutir algo por teléfono ◆ *vt & vi* hablar; telefonear

■ **phone in** *vi* llamar

■ **phone up** *vt & vi* llamar

phone book *s* guía telefónica

phone booth *s* teléfono público

phone call *s* llamada telefónica • **to make a phone call** hacer una llamada

phonecard ['fəʊnkɑːd] *s* tarjeta telefónica

phone-in *s* RADIO & TELEVISIÓN programa con llamadas de los oyentes

phone number *s* número de teléfono

phonetics [fəˈnetɪks] *s* 💡 *incontable* fonética

phony ['fəʊnɪ] ◆ *adj* (*comparativo* phonier, *superlativo* phoniest) *familiar* falso, sa ◆ *s* farsante

photo ['fəʊtəʊ] *s* foto • **to take a photo (of)** sacar una foto (de)

photocopier ['fəʊtəʊˌkɒpɪər] *s* fotocopiadora

photocopy ['fəʊtəʊˌkɒpɪ] ◆ *s* fotocopia ◆ *vt* fotocopiar

photograph ['fəʊtəgrɑːf] ◆ *s* fotografía • **to take a photograph (of)** sacar una fotografía (de) ◆ *vt* fotografiar

photographer [fə'tɒgrəfər] *s* fotógrafo, fa

photography [fə'tɒgrəfɪ] *s* ☼ *incontable* fotografía

photoshoot ['fəʊtəʊʃuːt] *s* sesión fotográfica

phrasal verb ['freɪzl-] *s* verbo con preposición

phrase [freɪz] ◆ *s* locución; expresión ◆ *vt* ❶ expresar ❷ redactar

phrasebook ['freɪzbʊk] *s* guía de conversación

physical ['fɪzɪkl] ◆ *adj* físico, ca ◆ *s* examen médico

physical education *s* educación física

physically ['fɪzɪklɪ] *adv* físicamente

physically challenged *spl* • **the physically challenged** los discapacitados físicos

physician [fɪ'zɪʃn] *s* médico

physicist ['fɪzɪsɪst] *s* físico, ca

physics ['fɪzɪks] *s* ☼ *incontable* física

physiotherapy [,fɪzɪəʊ'θerəpɪ] *s* fisioterapia

physique [fɪ'ziːk] *s* físico

pianist ['pɪənɪst] *s* pianista

piano [pɪ'ænəʊ] *s* piano

El plural de **piano** es **pianos**

pick [pɪk] ◆ *s* ❶ pico ❷ púa ❸ • **take your pick** escoge el que quieras ❹ • **the pick of** lo mejor de ◆ *vt* ❶ seleccionar ❷ elegir • **to pick your way across** o **through** andar con tiento por ❸ recoger ❹ • **to pick something off something** quitar algo de algo ❺ hurgarse ❻ arrancarse ❼ • **to pick a fight/quarrel (with)** buscar pelea/bronca (con) ❽ forzar *(cerradura)*

■ **pick on** *vt* ☼ *El objeto siempre va después de la preposición al final.* meterse con

■ **pick out** *vt* ☼ *El objeto se puede colocar antes o después de la preposición.* ❶ reconocer ❷ identificar ❸ escoger

■ **pick up** ◆ *vt* ☼ *El objeto se puede colocar antes o después de la preposición.* ❶ recoger ❷ levantar ❸ descolgar ❹ adquirir • **to pick up speed** cobrar velocidad ❺ contraer; adquirir ❻ aprender; adquirir ❼ RADIO & TELECOMUNICACIONES captar ❽ reanudar

expresión **to pick up the pieces** volver a la normalidad

◆ *vi* ❶ mejorar ❷ seguir ❸ aumentar

pickax ['pɪkæks] *s* pico

picket ['pɪkɪt] ◆ *s* piquete ◆ *vt* formar piquetes en

pickpocket ['pɪk,pɒkɪt] *s* carterista

pick-up *s* camioneta

picnic ['pɪknɪk] ◆ *s* picnic ◆ *vi* hacer un picnic

Formas irregulares de **picnic** pretérito & pp **picnicked**, gerundio **picnicking**

picture ['pɪktʃər] ◆ *s* ❶ cuadro ❷ dibujo ❸ foto ❹ ilustración ❺ imagen *(en televisión)* ❻ situación

expresión **to get the picture** *familiar* entenderlo ▸ **to be**

in/out of the picture estar/no estar en el ajo

◆ *vt* ❶ imaginarse ❷ • **to be pictured** aparecer en la foto

picturesque [,pɪktʃə'resk] *adj* pintoresco, ca

pie [paɪ] *s* ❶ pie ❷ pastel

piece [piːs] *s* ❶ trozo; pedazo • **to come to pieces** deshacerse • **to take something to pieces** desmontar algo • **to tear something to pieces** hacer trizas algo • **in pieces** en pedazos ❷ ☼ *con sustantivo incontable* • **piece of furniture** mueble • **piece of clothing** prenda de vestir • **piece of fruit** fruta • **piece of luggage** bulto de equipaje • **piece of advice** consejo • **piece of news** noticia • **a piece of information** una información • **piece of luck** golpe de suerte ❸ pieza ❹ ficha ❺ artículo

expresión **to go to pieces** *figurado* venirse abajo

■ **piece together** *vt* ☼ *El objeto se puede colocar antes o después de la preposición.* componer

pie chart *s* gráfica de pie

pier [pɪər] *s* embarcadero

pierce [pɪəs] *vt* ❶ perforar • **to have your ears pierced** hacerse agujeros en las orejas ❷ romper

piercing ['pɪəsɪŋ] *adj* ❶ desgarrador, ra *(grito)* ❷ agudo, da *(voz)* ❸ cortante *(viento)* ❹ penetrante *(mirada)*

piety ['paɪətɪ] *s* piedad

pig [pɪg] *s* ❶ cerdo ❷ *familiar & despectivo* tragón, ona

pigeon ['pɪdʒɪn] *s* paloma

Dos plurales: **pigeon** o **pigeons**

pigeonhole ['pɪdʒɪnhəʊl] ◆ *s* casilla ◆ *vt* encasillar

pigment ['pɪgmənt] *s* pigmento

pigpen ['pɪgpen], **pigsty** ['pɪgstaɪ] *s* *literal & figurado* pocilga

pigtail ['pɪgteɪl] *s* ❶ trenza ❷ coleta

Pilates [pɪ'lɑːtiːz] *s* Pilates

pile [paɪl] ◆ *s* ❶ montón ❷ pila ❸ pelo *(de alfombra)* ◆ *vt* amontonar

■ **pile into** *vt* ☼ *El objeto siempre va después de la preposición al final.* *familiar* meterse atropelladamente en

■ **pile up** ◆ *vt* ☼ *El objeto se puede colocar antes o después de la preposición.* amontonar ◆ *vi* ❶ amontonarse ❷ acumularse

pileup ['paɪlʌp] *s* accidente en cadena

pilgrim ['pɪlgrɪm] *s* peregrino, na

pilgrimage ['pɪlgrɪmɪdʒ] *s* peregrinación

pill [pɪl] *s* MEDICINA pastilla

pillar ['pɪlər] *s* *literal & figurado* pilar

pillow ['pɪləʊ] *s* ❶ almohada ❷ cojín

pillowcase ['pɪləʊkeɪs], **pillowslip** ['pɪləʊslɪp] *s* funda de almohada

pilot ['paɪlət] ◆ *s* ❶ AERONÁUTICA & NÁUTICA piloto ❷ TELEVISIÓN programa piloto ◆ *en compuestos* piloto; de prueba ◆ *vt* AERONÁUTICA & NÁUTICA pilotar

pilot burner, pilot light *s* piloto; luz indicadora

pilot study *s* estudio piloto

pimple ['pɪmpl] *s* grano

pin [pɪn] ◆ *s* ❶ alfiler ▸ **pins and needles** hormigueo ❷ clavija ❸ *INFORMÁTICA* pin ❹ *TECNOLOGÍA* clavija ◆ *vt* ❶ • **to pin something to** o **on a)** clavar con alfileres algo en **b)** prender algo en ❷ • **to pin somebody against** o **to** inmovilizar a alguien contra ❸ • **to pin something on** o **upon somebody** cargar algo a alguien

■ **pin down** *vt* ⚡ *El objeto se puede colocar antes o después de la preposición.* determinar; identificar

pinball ['pɪnbɔːl] *s* millón; flíper

pincers ['pɪnsəz] *spl* ❶ tenazas ❷ pinzas

pinch [pɪntʃ] ◆ *s* ❶ pellizco ❷ pizca ◆ *vt* ❶ pellizcar ❷ apretar ◆ *vi* apretar

■ **in a pinch** *adv* si no hay más remedio

pine [paɪn] ◆ *s* pino ◆ *vi* • **to pine for** suspirar por

■ **pine away** *vi* morirse de pena

pineapple ['paɪnæpl] *s* piña

pinetree ['paɪntriː] *s* pino

ping [pɪŋ] *s* sonido metálico

pink [pɪŋk] ◆ *adj* rosa ◆ *s* ❶ rosa ❷ clavel

pinkie ['pɪŋkɪ] *s* dedo meñique

pinnacle ['pɪnəkl] *s* ❶ cumbre *(de carrera)* ❷ cima *(de montaña)* ❸ pináculo *(de torre)*

pinpoint ['pɪnpɔɪnt] *vt* determinar; identificar

pint [paɪnt] *s* ▸ = 0,473 litros, ≃ pinta

pinto ['pɪntəʊ] ◆ *adj* pinto, ta ◆ *s* caballo pinto

pioneer [ˌpaɪə'nɪər] *s* pionero, ra

pious ['paɪəs] *adj* ❶ piadoso, sa ❷ *despectivo* santurrón, na

pip [pɪp] *s* pepita

pipe [paɪp] ◆ *s* ❶ tubería ❷ pipa ◆ *vt* conducir por tuberías

■ **pipes** *spl MÚSICA* gaita

■ **pipe down** *vi familiar* cerrar la boca

■ **pipe up** *vi familiar* • **to pipe up with a suggestion** saltar con una sugerencia

pipeline ['paɪplaɪn] *s* ❶ tubería ❷ gasoducto ❸ oleoducto

pirate ['paɪrət] ◆ *adj* pirata ◆ *s* pirata ◆ *vt* piratear

pirouette [ˌpɪrʊ'et] *s* pirueta

Pisces ['paɪsiːz] *s* Piscis

pissed *adj vulgar* • **to be pissed (off)** estar encabronado, da

pistol ['pɪstl] *s* pistola

piston ['pɪstən] *s* pistón

pit [pɪt] ◆ *s* ❶ hoyo ❷ marca *(en metal, vidrio)* ❸ mina ❹ hueso *(de fruta)* ◆ *vt* • **to be pitted against** ser enfrentado, da con

pitch [pɪtʃ] ◆ *s* ❶ *DEPORTE* campo ❷ *MÚSICA* tono ❸ grado; punto ◆ *vt* ❶ lanzar ❷ • **to be pitched**

in order to do something estar diseñado para hacer algo ❸ montar; poner ◆ *vi* • **to pitch forwards** precipitarse hacia delante

pitch-black *adj* negro, gra como boca de lobo

pitcher ['pɪtʃər] *s* ❶ jarra ❷ pitcher

pitfall ['pɪtfɔːl] *s* peligro; escollo

pithy ['pɪθɪ] *adj* conciso, sa y contundente

pitiful ['pɪtɪfʊl] *adj* ❶ lamentable *(excusa, esfuerzo)* ❷ penoso, sa *(aspecto)*

pitiless ['pɪtɪlɪs] *adj* despiadado, da

pittance ['pɪtəns] *s* miseria

pity ['pɪtɪ] ◆ *s* ❶ compasión ❷ pena; lástima • **what a pity!** ¡qué pena! • **to take** o **have pity on** compadecerse de ◆ *vt* compadecerse de; sentir pena por

pivot ['pɪvət] *s* ❶ *TECNOLOGÍA* pivote; eje ❷ *figurado* eje

pizza ['piːtsə] *s* pizza

placard ['plækɑːd] *s* pancarta

placate [plə'keɪt] *vt* aplacar; apaciguar

place [pleɪs] ◆ *s* ❶ lugar • **place of birth** lugar de nacimiento • **it's good in places** tiene algunas partes buenas ❷ casa • **let's go to my place** vamos a mi casa ❸ plaza *(en curso)* ❹ papel • **to have an important place in** desempeñar un papel importante en

expresiones **all over the place** por todas partes ▸ **in place** en su sitio; en marcha ▸ **in place of** en lugar de ▸ **in the first place** desde el principio ▸ **in the first place... and in the second place...** en primer lugar... y en segundo lugar... ▸ **out of place** fuera de lugar ▸ **to put somebody in their place** poner a alguien en su lugar ▸ **to put yourself in somebody's place** ponerse en el lugar de alguien ▸ **to take place** tener lugar ▸ **to take the place of** sustituir a

◆ *vt* ❶ colocar; poner ❷ • **to place emphasis on** poner énfasis en • **to place pressure on** ejercer presión sobre ❸ • **I recognize the face, but I can't place her** me suena su cara, pero no sé de qué ❹ hacer *(pedido, apuesta)*

place mat *s* mantel individual

placement ['pleɪsmənt] *s* colocación

placid ['plæsɪd] *adj* ❶ apacible ❷ tranquilo, la

plagiarize, plagiarise ['pleɪdʒəraɪz] *vt* plagiar

plague [pleɪg] ◆ *s* ❶ peste ❷ • **(the) plague** la peste ❸ plaga

expresión **to avoid somebody/something like the plague** huir de alguien/algo como de la peste

◆ *vt* • **to plague somebody with a)** acosar a alguien con **b)** acribillar a alguien a • **to be plagued by a)** estar acosado de **b)** estar atormentado de

plain [pleɪn] ◆ *adj* ❶ liso, sa ❷ sencillo, lla; natural *(yogur)* ❸ evidente; claro, ra • **to make something plain to somebody** dejar algo bien claro a alguien ❹ franco, ca *(explicación)* ❺ auténtico, ca ❻ sin atractivo ◆ *adv familiar* completamente ◆ *s GEOGRAFÍA* llanura; planicie

plain-clothes *adj* vestido, da de civil

plainly ['pleɪnlɪ] *adv* ❶ evidentemente ❷ claramente ❸ francamente ❹ sencillamente

plaintiff ['pleɪntɪf] *s* demandante

plan [plæn] ◆ *s* ❶ plan • **to go according to plan** salir según lo previsto ❷ esquema ❸ plano ◆ *vt* ❶ planear ❷ planificar ❸ trazar un esquema o boceto de ◆ *vi* hacer planes
■ **plans** *spl* planes • **to have plans for** tener planes para
■ **plan on** *vt ⚲ El objeto siempre va después de la preposición al final.* • **to plan on doing something** pensar hacer algo

plane [pleɪn] *s* ❶ avión ❷ *Geometría* plano ❸ cepillo de carpintero

planet ['plænɪt] *s* planeta

plank [plæŋk] *s* tablón; tabla

planning ['plænɪŋ] *s* planificación

plant [plɑːnt] ◆ *s* ❶ *Botánica* planta ❷ planta; fábrica ❸ maquinaria ◆ *vt* ❶ • **to plant something (in)** plantar algo (en) ❷ colocar secretamente

plantation [plæn'teɪʃn] *s* plantación

plaque [plɑːk] *s* placa

plaster ['plɑːstər] ◆ *s* yeso ◆ *vt* enyesar

plastic ['plæstɪk] ◆ *adj* de plástico ◆ *s* plástico

plastic surgery *s* cirugía plástica

plastic wrap *s* plástico transparente *(para envolver alimentos)*

plate [pleɪt] ◆ *s* ❶ plato ❷ placa ❸ *⚲ incontable* • **gold/silver plate** chapa de oro/plata ❹ lámina ❺ dentadura postiza
expresión **to hand something on a plate to somebody** ponerle algo a alguien en bandeja de plata
◆ *vt* • **to be plated (with)** estar chapado, da (en o de)

plateau ['plætəʊ] *s* meseta
Dos plurales: plateaus o plateaux ['plætəʊz].

platform ['plætfɔːm] *s* ❶ plataforma ❷ estrado ❸ tribuna ❹ *Ferrocarril* andén • **platform 12** la vía 12 ❺ *Política* programa electoral

platinum ['plætɪnəm] *s* platino

platoon [plə'tuːn] *s* pelotón

platter ['plætər] *s* fuente

plausible ['plɔːzəbl] *adj* plausible; admisible

play [pleɪ] ◆ *s* ❶ *⚲ incontable* juego • **at play** jugando ❷ obra ❸ • **play on words** juego de palabras ◆ *vt* ❶ jugar ❷ • **to play somebody (at something)** jugar contra alguien (a algo) ❸ • **to play a dirty trick on** jugar una mala pasada a ❹ representar • **to play a part o role in** *figurado* desempeñar un papel en • **to play the fool** hacer el tonto ❺ tocar ❻ poner
expresión **to play it safe** actuar sobre seguro
◆ *vi* • **to play (with/against)** jugar (con/contra) • **to play for somebody/a team** jugar para alguien/con un equipo ❷ representarse; exhibirse ❸ *Música* tocar; sonar
■ **play along** *vi* • **to play along (with)** seguir la corriente (a)

■ **play down** *vt ⚲ El objeto se puede colocar antes o después de la preposición.* quitar importancia a
■ **play up** ◆ *vt ⚲ El objeto se puede colocar antes o después de la preposición.* hacer resaltar ◆ *vi* dar guerra

play-act *vi* fingir; hacer comedia

player ['pleɪər] *s* ❶ jugador, ra ❷ *Música* intérprete ❸ *Teatro* actor, actriz ❹ protagonista

playful ['pleɪfʊl] *adj* juguetón, ona

playground ['pleɪgraʊnd] *s* ❶ patio de recreo ❷ zona de juegos

playgroup ['pleɪgruːp] *s* jardín de infancia; guardería

playhouse ['pleɪhaʊs] *⚲ pl* [-haʊzɪz] *s* ▸ casita de juguete del tamaño de un niño

playing card ['pleɪɪŋ-] *s* naipe; carta

playing field ['pleɪɪŋ-] *s* campo de juego

playmate ['pleɪmeɪt] *s* compañero, ra de juego

play-off *s* partido de desempate

playschool ['pleɪskuːl] *s* jardín de niños; kinder

plaything ['pleɪθɪŋ] *s* *literal & figurado* juguete

playtime ['pleɪtaɪm] *s* recreo

playwright ['pleɪraɪt] *s* dramaturgo, ga

plea [pliː] *s* ❶ súplica; petición ❷ *Derecho* declaración • **a plea of guilty/not guilty** una declaración de culpabilidad/inocencia

plead [pliːd] ◆ *vt* ❶ *Derecho* defender ❷ pretender ◆ *vi* ❶ • **to plead (with somebody to do something)** rogar o implorar (a alguien que haga algo) • **to plead for something** pedir algo ❷ *Derecho* declarar
Formas irregulares de plead: pretérito & pp pleaded o pled.

pleasant ['pl<span></span>eznt] *adj* ❶ agradable ❷ grato, ta ❸ simpático, ca

please [pliːz] ◆ *vt* complacer; agradar • **he always pleases himself** siempre hace lo que le da la gana • **please yourself!** ¡como quieras! ◆ *vi* ❶ satisfacer; agradar ❷ • **to do as one pleases** hacer como a uno le parezca ◆ *adv* por favor

pleased [pliːzd] *adj* • **to be pleased (about/with)** estar contento, ta (por/con) • **to be pleased for somebody** alegrarse por alguien • **to be very pleased with yourself** estar muy satisfecho de sí mismo • **pleased to meet you!** ¡encantado, da de conocerle!; ¡mucho gusto!

pleasing ['pliːzɪŋ] *adj* agradable; grato, ta

pleasure ['pleʒər] *s* ❶ gusto ❷ diversión ❸ placer • **it's a pleasure, my pleasure** no hay de qué

pleat [pliːt] ◆ *s* pliegue ◆ *vt* plisar

pled [pled] *pretérito & participio pasado* → plead

pledge [pledʒ] ◆ *s* ❶ promesa ❷ señal; prenda ◆ *vt* ❶ prometer ❷ • **to pledge somebody to something** hacer jurar a alguien algo • **to pledge yourself to** comprometerse a ❸ empeñar

Pledge of Allegiance

La **Pledge of Allegiance** ("jura de lealtad") tiene su origen en 1892 durante las celebraciones que sirivieron para conmemorar el 400 aniversario del descubrimiento de América por parte de Cristóbal Colón. Hoy en día forma parte del ritual diario que se lleva a cabo en todas las escuelas estadounidenses: los alumnos recitan la **Pledge of Allegiance** con la mano derecha sobre el corazón y prometen lealtad a la bandera y a la nación americana.

plentiful ['plentɪfʊl] *adj* abundante

plenty ['plentɪ] ◆ *s* ⚡ *incontable* abundancia ◆ *adv* ❶ muy ❷ mucho ◆ *pronombre* • **we've got plenty** tenemos de sobra • **that's plenty** es más que suficiente • **plenty of** mucho, cha

plenty

En las oraciones interrogativas y negativas, plenty (of) se sustituye por much (con incontables) o many (con sustantivos en plural) (I've plenty of time — I haven't *much* time *tengo bastante tiempo* — *no tengo mucho tiempo*; there were plenty of people I knew at the party — were there *many* people you knew at the party? *conocía bastante gente en la fiesta* — *¿conocías mucha gente en la fiesta?*).

pliable ['plaɪəbl], **pliant** ['plaɪənt] *adj* flexible

pliers ['plaɪəz] *spl* alicates

plight [plaɪt] *s* grave situación

plod [plɒd] *vi* ❶ caminar con paso lento ❷ • **to plod away at something** trabajar pacientemente en algo

plot [plɒt] ◆ *s* ❶ complot; conspiración ❷ argumento; trama ❸ parcela ◆ *vt* ❶ tramar; urdir ❷ trazar ◆ *vi* • **to plot (to do something)** tramar (hacer algo) • **to plot against** conspirar contra

plotter ['plɒtər] *s* ❶ conspirador, ra ❷ *INFORMÁ-TICA* plotter

plow [plaʊ] ◆ *s* arado ◆ *vt* arar

■ **plow into** ◆ *vt* ⚡ *El objeto se puede colocar antes o después de la preposición.* invertir ◆ *vt* ⚡ *El objeto siempre va después de la preposición al final.* chocar contra

ploy [plɔɪ] *s* táctica; estratagema

pls (*abreviatura de* please) *adv* pf

pluck [plʌk] ◆ *vt* ❶ recoger ❷ arrancar ❸ desplumar ❹ depilar ❺ puntear ◆ *s desusado* valor

■ **pluck up** *vt* ⚡ *El objeto siempre va después de la preposición al final.* • **to pluck up the courage to do something** armarse de valor para hacer algo

plug [plʌg] ◆ *s* ❶ *ELECTRICIDAD* enchufe ❷ tapón ◆ *vt* ❶ tapar ❷ *familiar* dar publicidad a

■ **plug in** *vt* ⚡ *El objeto se puede colocar antes o después de la preposición.* enchufar

plughole ['plʌghəʊl] *s* desagüe

plumber ['plʌmər] *s* plomero, ra

plumbing ['plʌmɪŋ] *s* ⚡ *incontable* ❶ tuberías ❷ plomería

plume [pluːm] *s* ❶ pluma ❷ penacho

plummet ['plʌmɪt] *vi* caer en picado

plump [plʌmp] *adj* rechoncho, cha

■ **plump for** *vt* ⚡ *El objeto siempre va después de la preposición al final.* optar o decidirse por

plunder ['plʌndər] ◆ *s* ❶ saqueo; pillaje ❷ botín ◆ *vt* saquear

plunge [plʌndʒ] ◆ *s* zambullida

expresión **to take the plunge a)** dar el paso decisivo **b)** lanzarse

◆ *vt* • **to plunge something into** hundir algo en; sumergir algo en ◆ *vi* ❶ zambullirse ❷ bajar vertiginosamente

pluperfect [ˌpluːˈpɜːfɪkt] *s* ▶ **the pluperfect (tense)** el (pretérito) pluscuamperfecto

plural ['plʊərəl] ◆ *adj* plural ◆ *s* plural • **in the plural** en plural

plus [plʌs] ◆ *adj* • **35-plus** 35 o más ◆ *s* ❶ *MA-TEMÁTICAS* signo más ❷ ventaja ◆ *preposición* más ◆ *conjunción* además

Dos plurales: **pluses** o **plusses**.

plush [plʌʃ] *adj* lujoso, sa

plus sign *s* signo más

Pluto ['pluːtəʊ] *s* Plutón

plutonium [pluːˈtəʊnɪəm] *s* plutonio

ply [plaɪ] ◆ *vt* ❶ ejercer ❷ • **to ply somebody with something a)** acosar a alguien con algo **b)** no parar de ofrecer a alguien algo ◆ *vi* navegar

plywood ['plaɪwʊd] *s* triplay

p.m., pm (*abreviatura de* post meridiem) • **at 3 p.m.** a las tres de la tarde

PM *s abreviatura escrita de* **prime minister**

pneumatic [njuːˈmætɪk] *adj* neumático, ca

pneumonia [njuːˈməʊnjə] *s* ⚡ *incontable* pulmonía

poach [pəʊtʃ] ◆ *vt* ❶ cazar furtivamente ❷ pescar furtivamente ❸ plagiar ❹ *COCINA* cocer ❺ escalfar ◆ *vi* ❶ cazar furtivamente ❷ pescar furtivamente

poacher ['pəʊtʃər] *s* ❶ cazador furtivo, cazadora furtiva ❷ pescador furtivo, pescadora furtiva

poaching ['pəʊtʃɪŋ] *s* ❶ caza furtiva ❷ pesca furtiva

pocket ['pɒkɪt] ◆ *s* ❶ bolsillo ❷ bolsa ❸ foco ❹ tronera

expresión **to be $10 out of pocket** salir perdiendo 10 dólares ▶ **to pick somebody's pocket** vaciar a alguien el bolsillo

◆ *vt* ❶ meterse en el bolsillo ❷ birlar ◆ *adj* de bolsillo

P

pocketbook ['pɒkɪtbʊk] *s* ❶ libreta ❷ bolsa ❸ cartera

pocketknife ['pɒkɪtnaɪf] *s* navaja (de bolsillo)
El plural de **pocketknife** es **pocket-knives** ['pɒkɪtnaɪvz].

pocket money *s* ❶ domingo ❷ dinero para gastar

pod [pɒd] *s* vaina

podgy ['pɒdʒɪ], **pudgy** *adj familiar* gordinflón, ona

podium ['pəʊdɪəm] *s* podio

poem ['pəʊɪm] *s* poema; poesía

poet ['pəʊɪt] *s* poeta

poetic [pəʊ'etɪk] *adj* poético, ca

poetry ['pəʊɪtrɪ] *s* poesía

poignant ['pɔɪnjənt] *adj* patético, ca; conmovedor, ra

point [pɔɪnt] ◆ *s* ❶ punto ❷ momento • **at that point** en ese momento ❸ punta ❹ • **to make a point** hacer una observación • **to have a point** tener razón ❺ • **the point is...** lo fundamental es... • **that's the whole point** de eso se trata • **to miss the point of** no captar el sentido de • **to get** o **come to the point** ir al grano • **it's beside the point** no viene al caso ❻ aspecto • **weak/strong point** punto débil/fuerte ❼ sentido • **what's the point?** ¿para qué? • **there's no point in it** no tiene sentido
expresiones **a sore point** un asunto espinoso o delicado ▶ **on the point of doingsomething** a punto de hacer algo ▶ **to make a point of doing something** preocuparse de hacer algo ▶ **up to a point** hasta cierto punto
◆ *vt* • **to point a gun at something/somebody** apuntar a algo/alguien con una pistola • **to point your finger at something/somebody** señalar algo/a alguien con el dedo ◆ *vi* ❶ • **to point at something/somebody, to point to something/somebody** señalar algo/a alguien con el dedo ❷ *figurado* • **everything points to her guilt** todo indica que ella es la culpable
■ **point out** *vt* ☼ *El objeto se puede colocar antes o después de la preposición.* ❶ señalar; indicar ❷ hacer notar

point-blank *adv* ❶ categóricamente ❷ a quemarropa

pointed ['pɔɪntɪd] *adj* ❶ en punta; puntiagudo, da ❷ intencionado, da

pointer ['pɔɪntər] *s* ❶ consejo ❷ aguja ❸ *INFOR-MÁTICA* puntero

pointless ['pɔɪntlɪs] *adj* sin sentido • **it's pointless** no tiene sentido

point of view *s* ❶ punto de vista ❷ perspectiva
El plural de **point of view** es **points of view.**

poise [pɔɪz] *s* ❶ aplomo; serenidad ❷ elegancia

poised [pɔɪzd] *adj* ❶ • **to be poised for something** estar preparado, da para algo ❷ sereno, na

poison ['pɔɪzn] ◆ *s* veneno ◆ *vt* envenenar; intoxicar

poisoning ['pɔɪznɪŋ] *s* ❶ envenenamiento ❷ intoxicación

poisonous ['pɔɪznəs] *adj* ❶ tóxico, ca ❷ venenoso, sa

poke [pəʊk] ◆ *vt* ❶ empujar ❷ dar un codazo a ❸ • **to poke somebody in the eye** meter el dedo en el ojo de alguien ❹ • **to poke something into** meter algo en ◆ *vi* • **to poke out of something** sobresalir por algo
■ **poke about, poke around** *vi familiar* fisgonear; hurgar

poker ['pəʊkər] *s* ❶ póker ❷ atizador

poker-faced [-ˌfeɪst] *adj* con cara inexpresiva

poky ['pəʊkɪ] *adj despectivo* • **a poky little room** un cuartucho

Poland ['pəʊlənd] *s* Polonia

polar ['pəʊlər] *adj* polar

pole [pəʊl] *s* ❶ poste o palo ❸ *ELECTRICIDAD & GEOGRAFÍA* polo • **to be poles apart** *figurado* ser polos opuestos

Pole [pəʊl] *s* polaco, ca

pole vault *s* • **the pole vault** el salto con garrocha

police [pə'li:s] ◆ *spl* • **the police** la policía ◆ *vt* mantener el orden en; vigilar

police car *s* patrulla

police department *s* jefatura de policía

police force *s* cuerpo de policía

policeman [pə'li:smən] *s* policía
El plural de **policeman** es **policemen** [pə'li:smen].

police officer *s* agente de policía

police record *s* • **(to have a) police record** (tener) antecedentes policiales

police station *s* delegación

policewoman [pə'li:sˌwʊmən] *s* policía • **she's a policewoman** es policía
El plural de **policewoman** es **policewomen** [pə'li:sˌwɪmɪn].

policy ['pɒləsɪ] *s* ❶ política ❷ póliza

polio ['pəʊlɪəʊ] *s* polio

polish ['pɒlɪʃ] ◆ *s* ❶ cera ❷ grasa ❸ abrillantador ❹ esmalte ❺ brillo; lustre ❻ *figurado* refinamiento ◆ *vt* ❶ pulir ❷ encerar ❸ limpiar ❹ sacar brillo a
■ **polish off** *vt* ☼ *El objeto se puede colocar antes o después de la preposición.* *familiar* ❶ zamparse ❷ despachar

Polish ['pəʊlɪʃ] ◆ *adj* polaco, ca ◆ *s* polaco ◆ *spl* • **the Polish** los polacos

polished ['pɒlɪʃt] *adj* ❶ refinado, da ❷ esmerado, da

polite [pə'laɪt] *adj* educado, da; cortés

political [pə'lɪtɪkl] *adj* político, ca

P

political parties
En los Estados Unidos existen básicamente sólo dos partidos políticos: el partido demócrata

(the Democratic Party) y el partido republicano (the Republican Party). Los demócratas tienen tendencias más liberales, mientras que los republicanos son más bien conservadores.

political correctness

Political correctness
Lo políticamente correcto nació en los campus de las universidades estadounidenses en la década de los años 80, en un clima más liberal con respecto al multiculturalismo y la enseñanza de las humanidades. Se recomendaba un nuevo código lingüístico en el que no tuvieran cabida los términos que pudieran parecer racistas, sexistas u ofensivos para determinadas minorías sociales y étnicas. Así pues, expresiones como "American Indian" o "Black" fueron sustituidas por "Native American" y "African American" respectivamente. No obstante, ciertas expresiones políticamente correctas — "vertically challenged" ("persona con un reto vertical") en lugar de "short" ("bajo") — han suscitado controversia por su naturaleza excesivamente eufemística, y el movimiento de lo políticamente correcto ha sido objeto de burlas y críticas por el carácter extremista e intolerante de alguno de sus postulados.

politically correct [pə,lıtıklı-] *adj* políticamente correcto, ta

politician [,pɒlı'tıʃn] *s* político, ca

politics ['pɒlətıks] ◆ *s* :ᗴ̣:*incontable* política ◆ *spl* ❶ ideas políticas ❷ política

polka dot *s* lunar *(en un vestido)*

poll [pəʊl] ◆ *s* ❶ votación ❷ encuesta ◆ *vt* ❶ sondear ❷ obtener
■ **polls** *spl* • **the polls** las urnas

pollen ['pɒlən] *s* polen

polling place ['pəʊlıŋ-] *s* casilla electoral

pollute [pə'lu:t] *vt* contaminar

pollution [pə'lu:ʃn] *s* :ᗴ̣:*incontable* ❶ contaminación ❷ sustancias contaminantes

polo ['pəʊləʊ] *s* polo

pompous ['pɒmpəs] *adj* ❶ presumido, da ❷ ostentoso, sa

pond [pɒnd] *s* estanque

ponder ['pɒndər] *vt* considerar

pony ['pəʊnı] *s* pony

ponytail ['pəʊnıteıl] *s* cola (de caballo)

poodle ['pu:dl] *s* caniche; poodle

pool [pu:l] ◆ *s* ❶ charco ❷ estanque ❸ alberca ❹ *Comercio* fondo común ❺ billar; pool ◆ *vt* ❶ juntar ❷ poner en común

poor [pɔːr] ◆ *adj* ❶ pobre • **poor old John!** ¡el pobre de John! • **you poor thing!** ¡pobrecito! ❷ malo, la ❸ escaso, sa ◆ *spl* • **the poor** los pobres

poorly ['pɔːlı] *adv* mal • **poorly off** pobre

pop [pɒp] ◆ *s* ❶ (música) pop ❷ *familiar* papá ❸ pequeña explosión ◆ *vt* pinchar ◆ *vi* ❶ reventar ❷ salirse de las órbitas ❸ • **her ears popped** se le destaparon los oídos ❹ • **I'm just popping round to the shop** voy un momento a la tienda
■ **pop in** *vi* entrar un momento
■ **pop up** *vi* aparecer de repente

pop concert *s* concierto de música pop

popcorn ['pɒpkɔːn] *s* palomitas (de maíz)

pope [pəʊp] *s* papa • **the Pope** el Papa

pop group *s* grupo (de música) pop

poplar ['pɒplər] *s* álamo

poppy ['pɒpı] *s* amapola

Popsicle® ['pɒpsıkl] *s* paleta

popular ['pɒpjʊlər] *adj* ❶ popular ❷ generalizado, da

popularize, popularise ['pɒpjʊləraız] *vt* ❶ popularizar ❷ vulgarizar

population [,pɒpjʊ'leıʃn] *s* población

porcelain ['pɔːsəlın] *s* porcelana

porch [pɔːtʃ] *s* porche; terraza

porcupine ['pɔːkjʊpaın] *s* puerco espín

pore [pɔːr] *s* poro
■ **pore over** *vt* :ᗴ̣: *El objeto siempre va después de la preposición al final.* estudiar esmeradamente

pork [pɔːk] *s* carne de cerdo

pornography [pɔː'nɒgrəfı] *s* pornografía

porous ['pɔːrəs] *adj* poroso, sa

port [pɔːt] *s* ❶ puerto ❷ *Náutica* babor ❸ oporto

portable ['pɔːtəbl] *adj* portátil

porter ['pɔːtər] *s* ❶ conserje ❷ mozo

porthole ['pɔːthəʊl] *s* portilla

portion ['pɔːʃn] *s* ❶ porción ❷ ración

portrait ['pɔːtrıt] *s* ❶ retrato ❷ *Informática* formato vertical

portray [pɔː'treı] *vt* ❶ representar ❷ describir ❸ retratar

Portugal ['pɔːtʃʊgl] *s* Portugal

Portuguese [,pɔːtʃʊ'giːz] ◆ *adj* portugués, esa ◆ *s* portugués ◆ *spl* • **the Portuguese** los portugueses

posh [pɒʃ] *adj familiar* de lujo; elegante

position [pə'zıʃn] ◆ *s* ❶ posición ❷ lugar ❸ puesto ❹ situación • **to be in a/no position to do something** estar/no estar en condiciones de hacer algo ◆ *vt* colocar

positive ['pɒzətıv] *adj* ❶ positivo, va ❷ • **to be positive (about)** estar seguro, ra (de); ser optimista (respecto a) ❸ decisivo, va; categórico, ca ❹ irrefutable; concluyente

possess [pə'zes] *vt* ❶ poseer ❷ adueñarse de

P

possession [pə'zeʃn] *s* posesión • **to have something in your possession, to be in possession of something** tener (posesión de) algo
■ **possessions** *spl* bienes

possessive [pə'zesɪv] *adj* ❶ posesivo, va ❷ *despectivo* egoísta

possibility [,pɒsə'bɪlətɪ] *s* posibilidad • **there's a possibility that...** es posible que...

possible ['pɒsəbl] *adj* ❶ posible • **as soon as possible** cuanto antes • **as much as possible a)** todo lo posible **b)** en la medida de lo posible • **I go as often as possible** voy siempre que puedo • **it's possible that she'll come** es posible que venga ❷ viable; factible

possibly ['pɒsəblɪ] *adv* ❶ posiblemente; quizás ❷ • **could you possibly help me?** ¿te importaría ayudarme? ❸ • **how could he possibly do that?** ¿cómo demonios pudo hacer eso? ❹ • **I can't possibly do it** no puedo hacerlo de ninguna manera

possum ['pɒsəm] *s* zarigüeya

post [pəʊst] ◆ *s* ❶ • **the post** el correo • **by post** por correo ❷ poste ❸ puesto ◆ *vt* ❶ mandar por correo ❷ destinar ❸ poner

postage ['pəʊstɪdʒ] *s* franqueo; porte

postal ['pəʊstl] *adj* postal

postcard ['pəʊstkɑ:d] *s* postal

poster ['pəʊstər] *s* cartel; póster

postgraduate [,pəʊst'grædʒʊət] *s* posgraduado, da

postmark ['pəʊstmɑ:k] *s* matasellos

postmortem [,pəʊst'mɔ:təm] *s* autopsia

post office *s* ❶ • **the Post Office** ≃ Correos ❷ oficina de correos

postpone [,pəʊst'pəʊn] *vt* posponer

postscript ['pəʊstskrɪpt] *s* ❶ posdata ❷ *figurado* nota final

posture ['pɒstʃər] *s literal & figurado* postura • **posture on something** postura hacia algo

postwar [,pəʊst'wɔ:r] *adj* de (la) posguerra

pot [pɒt] *s* ❶ olla ❷ tetera ❸ cafetera ❹ bote ❺ maceta
expresión **to go to pot** ir al traste

potassium [pə'tæsɪəm] *s* potasio

potato [pə'teɪtəʊ] *s* papa
El plural de **potato** es **potatoes**.

potent ['pəʊtənt] *adj* ❶ poderoso, sa ❷ fuerte ❸ potente

potential [pə'tenʃl] ◆ *adj* potencial; posible ◆ *s* ⚲ *incontable* potencial • **to have potential** tener posibilidades; prometer

potentially [pə'tenʃəlɪ] *adv* en potencia

pothole ['pɒthəʊl] *s* ❶ bache ❷ cueva

potion ['pəʊʃn] *s* poción

potshot ['pɒt,ʃɒt] *s* • **to take a potshot (at something/somebody)** disparar (a algo/alguien) sin apuntar

pottery ['pɒtərɪ] *s* ❶ cerámica; alfarería ❷ fábrica de cerámica

pouch [paʊtʃ] *s* bolsa pequeña

poultry ['pəʊltrɪ] ◆ *s* carne de ave ◆ *spl* aves de corral

pounce [paʊns] *vi* • **to pounce (on** o **upon)** abalanzarse (sobre)

pound [paʊnd] ◆ *s* ❶ libra ❷ depósito (de coches) ❸ perrera ◆ *vt* ❶ golpear; aporrear ❷ machacar ◆ *vi* ❶ • **to pound on something** golpear o aporrear algo ❷ palpitar • **her heart was pounding** le palpitaba el corazón

pour [pɔ:r] ◆ *vt* • **to pour something (into)** echar o verter algo (en) • **can I pour you a cup of coffee?** ¿quieres que te sirva una taza de café? ◆ *vi* ❶ chorrear ❷ salir a borbotones ◆ *v impersonal* llover a cántaros • **it's pouring (down)** está lloviendo a cántaros
■ **pour in** *vi* llegar a raudales
■ **pour out** ◆ *vt* ⚲ *El objeto se puede colocar antes o después de la preposición.* ❶ echar; vaciar ❷ servir ◆ *vi* salir en manada

pouring ['pɔ:rɪŋ] *adj* torrencial

pout [paʊt] *vi* hacer pucheros

poverty ['pɒvətɪ] *s literal & figurado* pobreza

powder ['paʊdər] *s* polvo

powdered ['paʊdəd] *adj* en polvo

powdered sugar *s* azúcar glas

power ['paʊər] ◆ *s* ❶ ⚲ *incontable* poder • **to have power over somebody** tener poder sobre alguien • **to come to/take power** llegar al/hacerse con el poder • **to be in power** estar en el poder ❷ facultad • **it isn't within my power to do it** no está dentro de mis posibilidades hacerlo • **I'll do everything in my power to help** haré todo lo que pueda por ayudar ❸ autoridad; competencia • **to have the power to do something** tener autoridad para hacer algo ❹ fuerza ❺ energía ❻ corriente ❼ potencia ◆ *vt* impulsar

power failure *s* apagón

powerful ['paʊəfʊl] *adj* ❶ poderoso, sa ❷ potente ❸ conmovedor, ra

powerless ['paʊələs] *adj* ❶ impotente ❷ • **to be powerless to do something** no poder hacer algo

power outage *s* apagón

power station *s* central eléctrica

practicable ['præktɪkəbl] *adj* factible

practical ['præktɪkl] ◆ *adj* ❶ práctico, ca ❷ hábil ◆ *s* práctica

practicality [,præktɪ'kælətɪ] *s* viabilidad

practical joke *s* broma pesada

practically ['præktɪklɪ] *adv* ❶ de manera práctica ❷ prácticamente; casi

practice¹ ['præktɪs] ◆ *vt* ❶ *DEPORTE* entrenar ❷ *MÚSICA & TEATRO* ensayar ❸ practicar ❹ ejercer ◆ *vi* ❶ practicar; *DEPORTE* entrenarse ❷ practicar ❸ ejercer

practice² ['præktɪs] *s* ❶ práctica ❷ *DEPORTE* entrenamiento ❸ *MÚSICA* ensayo • **I'm out of practice** me falta práctica ❹ • **to put something into practice** llevar algo a la práctica ❺ costumbre ❻ ejercicio ❼ consulta; bufete; despacho

expresión practice makes perfect se aprende a base de práctica

practicing *adj* ❶ practicante ❷ en ejercicio ❸ activo, va

practitioner [præk'tɪʃnər] *s* • medical practitioner médico, ca

prairie ['preərɪ] *s* pradera

praise [preɪz] ◆ *s* ⚇*incontable* elogio; alabanza ◆ *vt* elogiar; alabar

praiseworthy ['preɪz,wɜ:ðɪ] *adj* encomiable

prank [præŋk] *s* travesura • to play a prank on somebody gastarle una broma pesada a alguien

pray [preɪ] *vi* rezar; orar • to pray to somebody rogar a alguien

prayer [preər] *s* ❶ RELIGIÓN oración ❷ *figurado* ruego; súplica

preach [pri:tʃ] ◆ *vt* ❶ predicar ❷ dar ◆ *vi* ❶ RELIGIÓN • to preach (to) predicar (a) ❷ *despectivo* • to preach (at) sermonear (a)

preacher ['pri:tʃər] *s* ❶ predicador, ra ❷ pastor, ra

precarious [prɪ'keərɪəs] *adj* precario, ria

precaution [prɪ'kɔ:ʃn] *s* precaución

precede [prɪ'si:d] *vt* preceder

precedence ['presɪdəns] *s* • to take precedence over tener prioridad sobre

precedent ['presɪdənt] *s* precedente

precinct ['pri:sɪŋkt] *s* distrito

■ **precincts** *spl* recinto

precious ['preʃəs] *adj* ❶ precioso, sa ❷ preciado, da ❸ *irónico* • I've heard enough about your precious dog! ¡ya estoy cansado de tu dichoso perro!

precipice ['presɪpɪs] *s literal & figurado* precipicio

precipitate *vt* [prɪ'sɪpɪteɪt] precipitar

précis ['preɪsi:] *s* resumen

precise [prɪ'saɪs] *adj* preciso, sa; exacto, ta

precisely [prɪ'saɪslɪ] *adv* ❶ exactamente ❷ precisamente ❸ • precisely! ¡eso es!; ¡exactamente!

precision [prɪ'sɪʒn] *s* precisión

preconceived [,pri:kən'si:vd] *adj* preconcebido, da

precondition [,pri:kən'dɪʃn] *s formal* • precondition (for) requisito previo (para)

predator ['predətər] *s* ❶ depredador, ra ❷ *figurado* buitre

predecessor ['pri:dɪsesər] *s* antecesor, ra

predicament [prɪ'dɪkəmənt] *s* apuro

predict [prɪ'dɪkt] *vt* predecir; pronosticar

predictable [prɪ'dɪktəbl] *adj* ❶ previsible ❷ poco original

prediction [prɪ'dɪkʃn] *s* pronóstico

predispose [,pri:dɪs'pəʊz] *vt* • to be predisposed to something/to do something estar predispuesto, ta a algo/a hacer algo

predominant [prɪ'dɒmɪnənt] *adj* predominante

predominantly [prɪ'dɒmɪnəntlɪ] *adv* fundamentalmente

preempt [,pri:'empt] *vt* adelantarse a

preemptive [,pri:'emptɪv] *adj* preventivo, va

preface ['prefɪs] *s* • preface (to) prólogo o prefacio (a)

prefer [prɪ'fɜ:r] *vt* • to prefer something (to) preferir algo (a) • to prefer to do something preferir hacer algo

preferable ['prefrəbl] *adj* • to be preferable (to) ser preferible (a)

preferably ['prefrəblɪ] *adv* preferentemente

preference ['prefərəns] *s* • preference (for) preferencia (por) • to give somebody preference, to give preference to somebody dar preferencia a alguien

preferential [,prefə'renʃl] *adj* preferente

prefix ['pri:fɪks] *s* prefijo

pregnancy ['pregnənsɪ] *s* embarazo

pregnant ['pregnənt] *adj* embarazada • she's seven months pregnant está embarazada de siete meses

prehistoric [,pri:hɪ'stɒrɪk] *adj* prehistórico, ca

prejudice ['predʒʊdɪs] ◆ *s* • prejudice (against) prejuicio (contra) • prejudice in favor of predisposición a favor de ◆ *vt* ❶ • to prejudice somebody (in favour of/against) predisponer a alguien (a favor de/en contra de) ❷ perjudicar

prejudiced ['predʒʊdɪst] *adj* parcial • to be prejudiced in favour of/against estar predispuesto a favor de/en contra de

preliminary [prɪ'lɪmɪnərɪ] *adj* preliminar

prelude ['prelju:d] *s* • prelude (to) preludio (a)

premature ['premə,tjʊər] *adj* prematuro, ra

premeditated [,pri:'medɪteɪtɪd] *adj* premeditado, da

premier ['premjər] ◆ *adj* primero, ra ◆ *s* primer ministro, primera ministra

premiere ['premɪeər] *s* estreno

premise ['premɪs] *s* premisa

■ **premises** *spl* local • on the premises en el local

premium ['pri:mjəm] *s* prima

expresión to put o place a high premium on something dar gran importancia a algo

premonition [,premə'nɪʃn] *s* premonición

prenatal [,pri:'neɪtl] *adj* prenatal

preoccupied [pri:'ɒkjʊpaɪd] *adj* • preoccupied (with) preocupado, da (por)

preparation [,prepə'reɪʃn] *s* preparación

■ **preparations** *spl* preparativos • to make preparations for hacer los preparativos para

preparatory [prɪ'pærətrɪ] *adj* preparatorio, ria; preliminar

P

prepare [prɪ'peər] ◆ *vt* preparar ◆ *vi* • **to prepare for something/to do something** prepararse para algo/para hacer algo

prepared [prɪ'peəd] *adj* ❶ preparado, da • **to be prepared for something** estar preparado para algo ❷ • **to be prepared to do something** estar dispuesto, ta a hacer algo

preposition [,prepə'zɪʃn] *s* preposición

preposterous [prɪ'pɒstərəs] *adj* absurdo, da

preppy ['prepɪ] *familiar* ◆ *adj* fresa ◆ *s* niño, ña bien

prerequisite [,priː'rekwɪzɪt] *s* • **prerequisite (for)** requisito (para)

prerogative [prɪ'rɒgətɪv] *s* prerrogativa

preschool ['priː,skuːl] ◆ *adj* preescolar ◆ *s* jardín de niños; kínder

prescribe [prɪ'skraɪb] *vt* ❶ MEDICINA recetar ❷ ordenar; mandar

prescription [prɪ'skrɪpʃn] *s* receta • **on prescription** con receta médica

presence ['prezns] *s* presencia • **to make your presence felt** hacer sentir la presencia de uno

presence of mind *s* aplomo

present ◆ *adj* ['preznt] ❶ actual ❷ presente • **to be present at something** asistir a algo; estar presente en algo ◆ *s* ['preznt] ❶ • **the present** el presente • **at present** actualmente ❷ LINGÜÍSTICA ▸ **the present (tense)** el presente ❸ regalo • **to give somebody a present** dar un regalo a alguien ◆ *vt* [prɪ'zent] ❶ presentar • **to present somebody with something, to present something to somebody** representar algo para alguien • **to present somebody to somebody** presentar a alguien a alguien • **to present yourself** presentarse ❷ • **to present somebody with something, to present something to somebody a)** obsequiar algo a alguien **b)** entregar algo a alguien ❸ representar

presentable [prɪ'zentəbl] *adj* presentable • **to look presentable** tener un aspecto presentable • **to make yourself presentable** arreglarse

presentation [,preznˈteɪʃn] *s* ❶ presentación ❷ entrega *(de premio)* ❸ representación

present day *s* • **the present day** el presente
■ **present-day** *adj* de hoy en día

presently ['prezntlɪ] *adv* ❶ dentro de poco ❷ actualmente

preservation [,prezə'veɪʃn] *s* preservación; conservación

preservative [prɪ'zɜːvətɪv] *s* conservante

preserve [prɪ'zɜːv] ◆ *vt* conservar ◆ *s* mermelada
■ **preserves** *spl* ❶ confituras ❷ conserva

president ['prezɪdənt] *s* presidente, ta

PRESIDENT'S DAY

President's Day, que se festeja el tercer lunes de febrero, es la fecha en que se conmemoran los cumpleaños de dos de los presidentes estadounidenses más destacados, George Washington y Abraham Lincoln. Dado que ambos hombres nacieron en el mes de febrero, se designó un día para celebrarlos a los dos.

presidential [,prezɪ'denʃl] *adj* presidencial

press [pres] ◆ *s* ❶ • **to give something a press** apretar algo ❷ • **the press** la prensa ❸ planchado
expresión to get a good/bad press tener buena/mala prensa
◆ *vt* ❶ apretar • **to press something against something** apretar algo contra algo ❷ prensar ❸ planchar ❹ • **to press somebody for something** presionar a alguien en busca de algo ❺ insistir en • **to press charges against somebody** DERECHO demandar a alguien ◆ *vi* ❶ • **to press (on something)** apretar (algo) ❷ • **to press forward** empujar hacia adelante

■ **press for** *vt* 🔆 *El objeto siempre va después de la preposición al final.* exigir; reclamar

■ **press on** *vi* • **to press on (with)** seguir adelante (con)

press agency *s* agencia de prensa

press conference *s* rueda de prensa

press corps *s* • **the press corps** la prensa

pressing ['presɪŋ] *adj* apremiante

press officer *s* jefe, fa de prensa

press release *s* comunicado de prensa

pressure ['preʃər] *s* presión

pressurize, pressurise ['preʃəraɪz] *vt* TECNOLOGÍA presurizar

prestige [pre'stiːʒ] *s* prestigio

presumably [prɪ'zjuːməblɪ] *adv* • **presumably you've read it** supongo que los has leído

presume [prɪ'zjuːm] *vt* suponer • **he is presumed dead** se supone que está muerto

presumption [prɪ'zʌmpʃn] *s* ❶ suposición ❷ presunción ❸ 🔆 *incontable* presunción; osadía

presumptuous [prɪ'zʌmptʃuəs] *adj* presuntuoso, sa

pretend [prɪ'tend] ◆ *vt* • **to pretend to do something** fingir hacer algo • **she pretended not to notice** hizo como si no se hubiera dado cuenta • **don't pretend you didn't know!** ¡no finjas que no lo sabías! ◆ *vi* fingir; simular ◆ *adj familiar* de mentira

pretense [prɪ'tens] *s* fingimiento; simulación • **to make a pretense of doing something** fingir hacer algo • **under false pretenses** con engaños; con falsos pretextos

pretension [prɪ'tenʃn] *s* pretensión • **to have pretensions to something** tener pretensiones de algo

pretentious [prɪ'tenʃəs] *adj* pretencioso, sa

pretext ['priː'tekst] *s* pretexto • **on** o **under the pretext that .../of doing something** con el pretexto de que.../de hacer algo

pretty ['prɪtɪ] ◆ *adj* bonito, ta ◆ *adv* bastante • **pretty much** más o menos • **pretty well** casi

prevail [prɪ'veɪl] *vi* ❶ predominar; imperar ❷ • **to prevail (over)** prevalecer (sobre) ❸ • **to prevail on** o **upon somebody to do something** persuadir a alguien para que haga algo

prevailing [prɪ'veɪlɪŋ] *adj* predominante

prevalent ['prevələnt] *adj* predominante

prevent [prɪ'vent] *vt* ❶ impedir ❷ evitar • **to prevent something (from) happening** impedir o evitar que algo pase • **to prevent somebody (from) doing something** impedir a alguien que haga algo

preventive [prɪ'ventɪv] *adj* preventivo, va

preview ['pri:vju:] *s* ❶ avance ❷ preestreno

previous ['pri:vjəs] *adj* previo, via; anterior

previously ['pri:vjəslɪ] *adv* ❶ anteriormente ❷ • **two years previously** dos años antes

prewar [ˌpri:'wɔ:r] *adj* de antes de la guerra

prey [preɪ] *s* presa; víctima

expresión **a bird of prey** un ave rapaz

■ **prey on** *vt* ☀ **El objeto siempre va después de la preposición al final.** ❶ cazar; alimentarse de ❷ • **to prey on somebody's mind** atormentar a alguien

price [praɪs] ◆ *s* literal & figurado precio • **to go up/down in price** subir/bajar de precio • **you can't put a price on health** la salud no tiene precio • **to pay the price for something** pagar el precio de algo • **at any price** a toda costa; a cualquier precio • **at a price** a un alto precio

expresión **to pay a high price for something** pagar algo caro

◆ *vt* poner precio a • **to be wrongly priced** tener el precio equivocado

priceless ['praɪslɪs] *adj* literal & figurado que no tiene precio; inestimable

price list *s* lista de precios

price tag *s* etiqueta (del precio)

pricey ['praɪsɪ] (*comparativo* pricier, *superlativo* priciest) *adj* caro, ra

prick [prɪk] ◆ *s* pinchazo ◆ *vt* ❶ pinchar ❷ picar

■ **prick up** *vt* ☀ **El objeto siempre va después de la preposición al final.** • **to prick up your ears a)** levantar las orejas **b)** aguzar el oído

prickle ['prɪkl] ◆ *s* ❶ espina ❷ comezón ◆ *vi* picar

prickly ['prɪklɪ] *adj* ❶ espinoso, sa ❷ figurado susceptible; enojadizo, za

pride [praɪd] ◆ *s* orgullo ◆ *vt* • **to pride yourself on something** enorgullecerse de algo

priest [pri:st] *s* sacerdote

priestess ['pri:stɪs] *s* sacerdotisa

priesthood ['pri:sthʊd] *s* ❶ • **the priesthood** el sacerdocio ❷ • **the priesthood** el clero

primarily ['praɪmərɪlɪ] *adv* principalmente

primary ['praɪmərɪ] ◆ *adj* ❶ principal ❷ EDUCACIÓN primario, ria ◆ *s* POLÍTICA primaria

primary election *s* primaria

primary school *s* escuela primaria

primate ['praɪmeɪt] *s* ZOOLOGÍA primate

prime [praɪm] ◆ *adj* ❶ primero, ra; principal ❷ excelente ❸ primero, ra ◆ *s* • **to be in your prime** estar en la flor de la vida ◆ *vt* ❶ preparar ❷ cebar

prime minister *s* primer ministro, primera ministra

primeval, primaeval [praɪ'mi:vl] *adj* primitivo, va

primitive ['prɪmɪtɪv] *adj* ❶ primitivo, va ❷ rudimentario, ria

primrose ['prɪmrəʊz] *s* primavera; prímula

prince [prɪns] *s* príncipe

princess [prɪn'ses] *s* princesa

principal ['prɪnsəpl] ◆ *adj* principal ◆ *s* EDUCACIÓN director, ra

principle ['prɪnsəpl] *s* ❶ principio • **to be against somebody's principles** ir contra los principios de alguien ❷ ☀ *incontable* principios • **on principle, as a matter of principle** por principio

■ **in principle** *adv* en principio

print [prɪnt] ◆ *s* ❶ ☀ *incontable* caracteres (de imprenta) • **in print a)** disponible **b)** en letra impresa • **to be out of print** estar agotado ❷ grabado ❸ reproducción ❹ fotografía ❺ estampado ❻ huella ◆ *vt* ❶ TIPOGRAFÍA imprimir ❷ tirar (*periódicos*) ❸ publicar (*artículo*) ❹ estampar ❺ escribir con letra de imprenta ◆ *vi* imprimir

■ **print out** *vt* ☀ **El objeto se puede colocar antes o después de la preposición.** INFORMÁTICA imprimir

printer ['prɪntər] *s* ❶ impresor, ra ❷ imprenta ❸ impresora

printing ['prɪntɪŋ] *s* ❶ ☀ *incontable* impresión ❷ imprenta

printout ['prɪntaʊt] *s* INFORMÁTICA salida de impresora

prior ['praɪər] *adj* previo, via • **without prior notice** sin previo aviso • **to have prior commitments** tener compromisos previos

■ **prior to** *preposición* antes de • **prior to doing something** con anterioridad a hacer algo

priority [praɪ'ɒrɪtɪ] *s* prioridad • **to have** o **take priority (over)** tener prioridad (sobre)

prise [praɪz] *vt* • **to prise something open/away** abrir/separar algo haciendo palanca

prison ['prɪzn] ◆ *s* cárcel; prisión • **to be in prison** estar en la cárcel • **to be sentenced to 5 years in prison** ser condenado a cinco años de cárcel ◆ *en compuestos* • **to be given a prison sentence** ser condenado a una pena de cárcel • **a prison officer** un funcionario de prisiones

prisoner ['prɪznər] *s* ❶ preso, sa ❷ prisionero, ra

prisoner of war *s* prisionero, ra de guerra

El plural de **prisoner of war** es **prisoners of war**.

privacy ['praɪvəsɪ] *s* intimidad

private ['praɪvɪt] ◆ *adj* ❶ privado, da ❷ personal (*llamada*) ❸ particular (*clase*) ❹ secreto, ta (*vida*) • **a private joke** un chiste entre amigos ❺ retirado, da

⑥ reservado, da ◆ *s* **❶** soldado raso **❷** • **(to do something) in private** (hacer algo) en privado

private education *s* ☼*incontable* enseñanza privada

private enterprise *s* ☼*incontable* empresa privada

privately ['praɪvɪtlɪ] *adv* **❶** de forma privada • **privately owned** de propiedad privada **❷** en privado

private property *s* propiedad privada

private school *s* escuela privada

privatize, privatise ['praɪvɪtaɪz] *vt* privatizar

privilege ['prɪvɪlɪdʒ] *s* privilegio

prize [praɪz] ◆ *adj* de primera ◆ *s* premio ◆ *vt* • **to be prized** ser apreciado, da

prizewinner ['praɪz,wɪnər] *s* premiado, da

pro [prəʊ] *s* **❶** *familiar* profesional **❷** ▸ **the pros and cons** los pros y los contras

El plural de **pro** es **pros.**

probability [,prɒbə'bɪlətɪ] *s* probabilidad

probable ['prɒbəbl] *adj* probable • **it is not very probable that it will happen** no es muy probable que ocurra

probably ['prɒbəblɪ] *adv* probablemente

probation [prə'beɪʃn] *s* **❶** libertad condicional • **to put somebody on probation** poner a alguien en libertad condicional **❷** periodo de prueba • **to be on probation** estar en periodo de prueba

probe [prəʊb] ◆ *s* **❶** • **probe (into)** investigación (sobre) **❷** MEDICINA & AERONÁUTICA sonda ◆ *vt* **❶** investigar **❷** sondar **❸** hurgar en

problem ['prɒbləm] *s* problema • **no problem!** *familiar* ¡por supuesto! ; ¡desde luego!

procedure [prə'si:dʒər] *s* procedimiento

proceed *vi* [prə'si:d] **❶** • **to proceed to do something** proceder a hacer algo **❷** *formal* avanzar

■ **proceeds** *spl* ['prəʊsi:dz] ganancias ; beneficios

proceedings [prə'si:dɪŋz] *spl* **❶** acto **❷** proceso • **to start proceedings against somebody** entablar proceso contra alguien

process ['prəʊses] ◆ *s* proceso • **in the process** en el intento ◆ *vt* **❶** procesar **❷** tramitar

processing ['prəʊsesɪŋ] *s* **❶** procesamiento **❷** tramitación

procession [prə'seʃn] *s* **❶** desfile **❷** procesión

proclaim [prə'kleɪm] *vt* **❶** proclamar **❷** promulgar

prod [prɒd] *vt* dar empujoncitos a

prodigy ['prɒdɪdʒɪ] *s* prodigio • **a child prodigy** un niño prodigio

produce ◆ *s* ['prɒdju:s] ☼*incontable* productos agrícolas • **'produce of France'** 'producto de Francia' ◆ *vt* [prə'dju:s] **❶** producir **❷** engendrar **❸** mostrar ; enseñar **❹** TEATRO poner en escena

producer [prə'dju:sər] *s* **❶** productor, ra **❷** TEATRO director, ra de escena

product ['prɒdʌkt] *s* producto

production [prə'dʌkʃn] *s* **❶** producción • **to put/go into production** TEATRO empezar a fabricar/fabricarse **❷** ☼*incontable* TEATRO puesta en escena

production line *s* cadena de producción

productive [prə'dʌktɪv] *adj* **❶** productivo, va **❷** provechoso, sa

productivity [,prɒdʌk'tɪvətɪ] *s* productividad

profession [prə'feʃn] *s* profesión • **by profession** de profesión

professional [prə'feʃənl] ◆ *adj* profesional ◆ *s* profesional

professor [prə'fesər] *s* profesor, ra (de universidad)

proficiency [prə'fɪʃənsɪ] *s* • **proficiency (in)** competencia (en)

profile ['prəʊfaɪl] *s* perfil • **high profile** notoriedad

profit ['prɒfɪt] ◆ *s* **❶** beneficio ; ganancia • **to make a profit** sacar un beneficio • **to sell something at a profit** vender algo con beneficios **❷** provecho ◆ *vi* • **to profit (from** o **by)** sacar provecho (de)

profitability [,prɒfɪtə'bɪlɪtɪ] *s* rentabilidad

profitable ['prɒfɪtəbl] *adj* **❶** rentable **❷** provechoso, sa

profound [prə'faʊnd] *adj* profundo, da

profusely [prə'fju:slɪ] *adv* profusamente • **to apologise profusely** pedir disculpas cumplidamente

profusion [prə'fju:ʒn] *s* profusión

program ['prəʊɡræm] ◆ *s* programa ◆ *vt* INFORMÁTICA programar • **to programme something (to do something)** programar algo (para que haga algo) ◆ *vi* INFORMÁTICA programar

Formas irregulares de **program**: *pretérito* & *pp* **programed**, *gerundio* **programing**.

programmer ['prəʊɡræmər] *s* INFORMÁTICA programador, ra

programming ['prəʊɡræmɪŋ] *s* programación

progress ◆ *s* ['prəʊɡres] **❶** progreso • **in progress** en curso • **to make progress** hacer progresos **❷** avance ◆ *vi* [prə'ɡres] **❶** progresar • **as the year progressed** conforme avanzaba el año **❷** hacer progresos **❸** avanzar

progressive [prə'ɡresɪv] *adj* **❶** progresista **❷** progresivo, va

prohibit [prə'hɪbɪt] *vt* prohibir • **to prohibit somebody from doing something** prohibirle a alguien hacer algo • **fishing is prohibited** prohibido pescar

project ◆ *s* ['prɒdʒekt] **❶** proyecto **❷** EDUCACIÓN • **project (on)** estudio o trabajo (sobre) **❸** • **the projects** fraccionamiento de viviendas de interés social ◆ *vt* [prə'dʒekt] **❶** proyectar **❷** dar una imagen de ◆ *vi* [prə'dʒekt] proyectarse

projection [prə'dʒekʃn] *s* **❶** proyección **❷** saliente

projector [prə'dʒektər] *s* proyector

prologue, prolog ['prəʊlɒg] *s* prólogo • **to be the** o **a prologue to something** *figurado* ser el prólogo a algo

prolong [prə'lɒŋ] *vt* prolongar

prom [prɒm] *s* baile de gala (en la escuela)

PROM

Prom es el baile formal que se celebra cada primavera en las escuelas secundarias de Estados Unidos. Es indudablemente el evento social más importante del año escolar. Muchos jóvenes gastan mucho dinero en sus vestidos y trajes y en el alquiler de limusinas para esa noche.

prominent ['prɒmɪnənt] *adj* ❶ destacado, da ; importante ❷ prominente

promise ['prɒmɪs] ◆ *s* promesa ◆ *vt* • **to promise (to do something)** prometer (hacer algo) • **to promise somebody something** prometer a alguien algo ◆ *vi* • **I promise** te lo prometo

promising ['prɒmɪsɪŋ] *adj* prometedor, ra

promote [prə'məʊt] *vt* ❶ fomentar ; promover ❷ promocionar ❸ • **to promote somebody (to something)** ascender a alguien (a algo) ❹ DEPORTE • **to be promoted** subir

promoter [prə'məʊtər] *s* ❶ organizador, ra ❷ promotor, ra

promotion [prə'məʊʃn] *s* ❶ ascenso • **to get** o **be given promotion** conseguir un ascenso ❷ promoción ❸ campaña de promoción

prompt [prɒmpt] ◆ *adj* rápido, da • **the injury requires prompt treatment** las heridas requieren un tratamiento inmediato • **to be prompt in doing something** hacer algo con prontitud ◆ *adv* en punto • **at 2 o'clock prompt** a las dos en punto ◆ *vt* ❶ • **to prompt somebody (to do something)** inducir o impulsar a alguien (a hacer algo) ❷ TEATRO apuntar ◆ *s* TEATRO apunte

promptly ['prɒmptlɪ] *adv* ❶ inmediatamente ; rápidamente ❷ puntualmente

prone [prəʊn] *adj* ❶ • **to be prone to something/ to do something** ser propenso, sa a algo/a hacer algo ❷ boca abajo

prong [prɒŋ] *s* diente ; punta

pronoun ['prəʊnaʊn] *s* pronombre

pronounce [prə'naʊns] ◆ *vt* ❶ pronunciar ❷ declarar ◆ *vi* • **to pronounce on something** pronunciarse sobre algo

pronounced [prə'naʊnst] *adj* pronunciado, da ; marcado, da

pronouncement [prə'naʊnsmənt] *s* declaración

pronunciation [prə‚nʌnsɪ'eɪʃn] *s* pronunciación

proof [pruːf] ◆ *s* prueba ◆ *adj* • **proof against** a prueba de

prop [prɒp] ◆ *s* ❶ puntal ; apoyo ❷ *figurado* sostén ◆ *vt* • **to prop something on** o **against something** apoyar algo contra algo
■ **props** *spl* utilería
■ **prop up** *vt* ☼ *El objeto se puede colocar antes o después de la preposición.* ❶ apuntalar ❷ *figurado* apoyar

propaganda [‚prɒpə'gændə] *s* propaganda

propel [prə'pel] *vt* propulsar ; impulsar

propeller [prə'pelər] *s* hélice

proper ['prɒpər] *adj* ❶ de verdad ❷ correcto, ta ; adecuado, da

properly ['prɒpəlɪ] *adv* ❶ bien ❷ correctamente

property ['prɒpətɪ] *s* ❶ propiedad ❷ finca ❸ *formal* inmueble

property owner *s* propietario, ria de un inmueble

prophecy ['prɒfɪsɪ] *s* profecía

prophesy ['prɒfɪsaɪ] *vt* profetizar

prophet ['prɒfɪt] *s* profeta

proportion [prə'pɔːʃn] *s* ❶ parte ❷ proporción ❸ • **out of proportion** desproporcionado, da • **to get things out of proportion** *figurado* sacar las cosas fuera de proporción • **to keep things in proportion** *figurado* no exagerar • **sense of proportion** *figurado* sentido de la medida

proportional [prə'pɔːʃənl] *adj* • **proportional (to)** proporcional (a) ; en proporción (a)

proportionate [prə'pɔːʃnət] *adj* • **proportionate (to)** proporcional (a)

proposal [prə'pəʊzl] *s* ❶ propuesta ❷ proposición

propose [prə'pəʊz] ◆ *vt* proponer • **to propose doing something** proponer hacer algo • **to propose to do something** tener la intención de hacer algo ◆ *vi* declararse

proposition [‚prɒpə'zɪʃn] *s* propuesta • **to make somebody a proposition** hacer una propuesta a alguien

proprietor [prə'praɪətər] *s* propietario, ria

prose [prəʊz] *s* ☼ *incontable* LITERATURA prosa

prosecute ['prɒsɪkjuːt] ◆ *vt* procesar ; enjuiciar ◆ *vi* ❶ entablar una acción judicial ❷ representar al demandante

prosecution [‚prɒsɪ'kjuːʃn] *s* ❶ procesamiento ❷ • **the prosecution** la acusación

prosecutor ['prɒsɪkjuːtər] *s* fiscal

prospect ◆ *s* ['prɒspekt] ❶ perspectiva • **it was a pleasant prospect** era una perspectiva agradable • **they were faced with the prospect of losing their jobs** tenían que hacer frente a la perspectiva de perder sus trabajos ❷ posibilidad ◆ *vi* [prə'spekt] • **to prospect (for)** hacer prospecciones (de)
■ **prospects** *spl* • **prospects (for)** perspectivas (de) • **job prospects** perspectivas laborales

prospecting [prə'spektɪŋ] *s* ☼ *incontable* prospecciones

P

prospective [prə'spektɪv] *adj* posible

prospectus [prə'spektəs] *s* prospecto; folleto informativo

prosper ['prɒspər] *vi* prosperar

prosperity [prɒ'sperətɪ] *s* prosperidad

prosperous ['prɒspərəs] *adj* próspero, ra

prostitute ['prɒstɪtjuːt] *s* prostituta

prostrate *adj* ['prɒstreɪt] postrado, da

protagonist [prə'tægənɪst] *s* protagonista

protect [prə'tekt] *vt* • **to protect something/somebody (against/from)** proteger algo/a alguien (contra/de)

protection [prə'tekʃn] *s* • **protection (against/from)** protección (contra/de)

protective [prə'tektɪv] *adj* protector, ra • **to feel protective towards somebody** tener sentimientos protectores hacia alguien

protein ['prəutiːn] *s* proteína

protest ◆ *s* ['prəutest] protesta • **under protest** bajo protesta • **without protest** sin protestar ◆ *vt* [prə'test] ❶ • **to protest that** quejarse de ❷ manifestar; aseverar ; **he protested his innocence** declaró su inocencia ❸ protestar en contra de ◆ *vi* [prə'test] • **to protest (about/against/at)** protestar (por/en contra de/por)

Protestant ['prɒtɪstənt] ◆ *adj* protestante ◆ *s* protestante

protester [prə'testər] *s* manifestante

protocol ['prəutəkɒl] *s* protocolo

prototype ['prəutətaɪp] *s* prototipo

protrude [prə'truːd] *vi* • **to protrude (from)** sobresalir (de)

protruding [prə'truːdɪŋ] *adj* ❶ prominente ❷ salido, da ❸ saltón, ona

protuberance [prə'tjuːbərəns] *s* protuberancia

proud [praud] *adj* ❶ orgulloso, sa • **to be proud of** estar orgulloso, sa de • **that's nothing to be proud of!** ¡yo no estaría orgulloso de eso! • **to be proud of yourself** estar orgulloso de uno mismo • **to be proud to do something** tener el honor de hacer algo ❷ *despectivo* soberbio, bia; arrogante

prove [pruːv] ◆ *vt* ❶ probar; demostrar ❷ • **to prove yourself to be something** resultar ser algo • **to prove yourself** demostrar (uno) sus cualidades ◆ *vi* resultar • **to prove (to be) interesting/difficult** resultar interesante/difícil

Formas irregulares de **prove**: *pp* **proved** o **proven**.

proven ['pruːvn] ['prəuvn] ◆ *participio pasado* → **prove** ◆ *adj* probado, da

proverb ['prɒvɜːb] *s* refrán

provide [prə'vaɪd] *vt* proporcionar; proveer • **to provide somebody with something** proporcionar a alguien algo • **to provide something for somebody** ofrecer algo a alguien

■ **provide for** *vt* 🔆 *El objeto siempre va después de la preposición al final.* ❶ mantener ❷ *formal* tomar medidas para

provided [prə'vaɪdɪd], **providing** ■ **provided (that), providing (that)** *conjunción* con tal (de) que • **you should pass, provided you work hard** aprobarás, con tal de que trabajes duro

providing [prə'vaɪdɪŋ] ■ **providing (that)** *conjunción* = **provided**

province ['prɒvɪns] *s* ❶ provincia ❷ campo; competencia

provincial [prə'vɪnʃl] *adj* ❶ provincial ❷ *despectivo* provinciano, na

provision [prə'vɪʒn] *s* ❶ suministro ❷ disposición

■ **provisions** *spl* víveres

provisional [prə'vɪʒənl] *adj* provisional

proviso [prə'vaɪzəu] *s* condición • **with the proviso that...** con la condición de que...

El plural de **proviso** es **provisos**.

provocative [prə'vɒkətɪv] *adj* ❶ provocador, ra ❷ provocativo, va

provoke [prə'vəuk] *vt* provocar • **to provoke somebody to do something** o **into doing something** provocar a alguien a que haga algo

prow [prau] *s* proa

prowess ['prauɪs] *s formal* proezas

prowl [praul] ◆ *s* • **on the prowl** merodeando ◆ *vt* merodear por ◆ *vi* merodear

prowler ['praulər] *s* merodeador, ra

prudent ['pruːdnt] *adj* prudente

prune [pruːn] ◆ *s* ciruela pasa ◆ *vt* podar

pry [praɪ] *vi* fisgonear

PS (*abreviatura de* postscript) *s* P.D.

psalm [sɑːm] *s* salmo

psychiatric [ˌsaɪkɪ'ætrɪk] *adj* psiquiátrico, ca

psychiatrist [saɪ'kaɪətrɪst] *s* psiquiatra

psychiatry [saɪ'kaɪətrɪ] *s* psiquiatría

psychoanalysis [ˌsaɪkəuə'næləsɪs] *s* psicoanálisis

psychoanalyst [ˌsaɪkəu'ænəlɪst] *s* psicoanalista

psychological [ˌsaɪkə'lɒdʒɪkl] *adj* psicológico, ca

psychologist [saɪ'kɒlədʒɪst] *s* psicólogo, ga

psychology [saɪ'kɒlədʒɪ] *s* psicología

psychopath ['saɪkəpæθ] *s* psicópata

psychotic [saɪ'kɒtɪk] ◆ *adj* psicótico, ca ◆ *s* psicótico, ca

pt ❶ *abreviatura escrita de* **pint** ❷ *abreviatura escrita de* **point**

PTO ❶ (*abreviatura de* parent-teacher organization) ≃ APA ❷ (*abreviatura de* please turn over) sigue

puberty ['pjuːbətɪ] *s* pubertad

public ['pʌblɪk] ◆ *adj* público, ca ◆ *s* público • **in public** en público • **the public** el gran público

publication [ˌpʌblɪ'keɪʃn] *s* publicación

public holiday *s* fiesta nacional

publicity [pʌb'lɪsɪtɪ] *s* publicidad

P

publicize, publicise[ˈpʌblɪsaɪz] *vt* divulgar

public opinion *s* ☼*incontable* opinión pública

public prosecutor *s* fiscal del Estado

public relations ◆ *s* ☼*incontable* relaciones públicas ◆ *spl* relaciones públicas

public school *s* escuela pública

public-spirited *adj* con sentido cívico

public transport *s* transporte público

publish [ˈpʌblɪʃ] *vt* ❶ publicar ❷ hacer público, ca

publisher[ˈpʌblɪʃər] *s* ❶editor, ra ❷editorial

publishing[ˈpʌblɪʃɪŋ] *s* ☼*incontable* industria editorial

pudding[ˈpʊdɪŋ] *s* ❶pudín ❷pastel

puddle[ˈpʌdl] *s* charco

Puerto Rico[ˌpwɜːtəʊˈriːkəʊ] *s* Puerto Rico

puff[pʌf] ◆ *s* ❶jadeo ❷soplo ❸bocanada ◆ *vt* echar ◆ *vi* jadear

■ **puff out** *vt* ☼*El objeto se puede colocar antes o después de la preposición.* ❶ hinchar ❷ ahuecar ❸echar

puffed[pʌft] *adj* • **puffed (up)** hinchado, da

puffy[ˈpʌfɪ] *adj* hinchado, da

pull[pʊl] ◆ *vt* ❶jalar ❷apretar ❸sacar y apuntar ◆ *vi* jalar ◆ *s* ❶jalón ❷ ☼*incontable* influencia

■ **pull apart** *vt* ☼*El objeto se puede colocar antes o después de la preposición.* ❶desmontar ❷hacer pedazos

■ **pull at** *vt* ☼*El objeto siempre va después de la preposición al final.* dar jalones en

■ **pull away** *vi* alejarse (de la acera)

■ **pull down** *vt* ☼*El objeto se puede colocar antes o después de la preposición.* derribar

■ **pull in** *vi* pararse • **the train pulled into the station** el tren llegó a la estación

■ **pull off** *vt* ☼*El objeto se puede colocar antes o después de la preposición.* conseguir llevar a cabo

■ **pull out** ◆ *vt* ☼*El objeto se puede colocar antes o después de la preposición.* ❶ retirar ❷ sacar ◆ *vi* ❶alejarse (de la acera) ❷retirarse

■ **pull over** *vi* AUTOMÓVILES hacerse a un lado

■ **pull through** *vi* recobrarse

■ **pull together** *vt* ☼*El objeto se puede colocar antes o después de la preposición.* • **to pull yourself together** calmarse; serenarse

■ **pull up** ◆ *vt* ☼*El objeto se puede colocar antes o después de la preposición.* acercar ◆ *vi* parar; detenerse

pulley[ˈpʊlɪ] *s* polea

El plural de **pulley** es **pulleys**

pulp[pʌlp] *s* ❶papilla ❷pulpa

pulpit[ˈpʊlpɪt] *s* púlpito

pulsate[pʌlˈseɪt] *vi* palpitar

pulse [pʌls] ◆ *s* ❶pulso • **to take somebody's pulse** tomarle el pulso a alguien ❷ TECNOLOGÍA impulso ◆ *vi* latir

■ **pulses** *spl* legumbres

puma[ˈpjuːmə] *s* puma

Dos plurales: **puma** o **pumas**

pump [pʌmp] ◆ *s* ❶ bomba ❷ surtidor ◆ *vt* bombear

■ **pump up** *vt* inflar

pumpkin[ˈpʌmpkɪn] *s* calabaza

pun[pʌn] *s* juego de palabras

punch[pʌntʃ] ◆ *s* ❶puñetazo ❷punzón; máquina para picar billetes ❸ponche ◆ *vt* ❶dar un puñetazo a ❷picar ❸perforar

■ **punch in** *vi* fichar (a la entrada)

■ **punch out** *vi* fichar (a la salida)

punch line *s* remate *(de un chiste)*

punctual[ˈpʌŋktʃʊəl] *adj* puntual

punctuation[ˌpʌŋktʃʊˈeɪʃn] *s* puntuación

punctuation mark *s* signo de puntuación

puncture[ˈpʌŋktʃər] ◆ *s* ❶ponchadura • **to have a puncture** ponchar ❷ punción ◆ *vt* ponchar

punish[ˈpʌnɪʃ] *vt* • **to punish somebody (for something/for doing something)** castigar a alguien (por algo/por haber hecho algo)

punishing[ˈpʌnɪʃɪŋ] *adj* penoso, sa

punishment[ˈpʌnɪʃmənt] *s* castigo

punk[pʌŋk] *adj* punk ◆ *s* ❶ • **punk (rock)** punk ❷ *familiar* vándalo

puny[ˈpjuːnɪ] *adj* ❶enclenque; raquítico, ca ❷penoso, sa; lamentable

pup[pʌp] *s* ❶cachorro ❷cría

pupil [ˈpjuːpl] *s* ❶ alumno, na ❷ pupilo, la ❸pupila

puppet[ˈpʌpɪt] *s* *literal & figurado* títere

puppy[ˈpʌpɪ] *s* cachorro; perrito

purchase[ˈpɜːtʃəs] *formal* ◆ *s* compra; adquisición ◆ *vt* comprar; adquirir

purchaser[ˈpɜːtʃəsər] *s* comprador, ra

purchasing power [ˈpɜːtʃəsɪŋ-] *s* poder adquisitivo

pure[pjʊər] *adj* puro, ra

puree[ˈpjʊəreɪ] *s* puré • **tomato puree** concentrado de tomate

purely[ˈpjʊəlɪ] *adv* puramente • **purely and simply** pura y simplemente

purge [pɜːdʒ] ◆ *s* POLÍTICA purga ◆ *vt* • **to purge something (of)** purgar algo (de)

purify[ˈpjʊərɪfaɪ] *vt* purificar

purity[ˈpjʊərətɪ] *s* pureza

purple[ˈpɜːpl] *adj* morado, da

purpose[ˈpɜːpəs] *s* propósito • **what is the purpose of your visit?** ¿cuál es el objeto de tu visita? • **for your own purposes** por su propio interés • **it serves no purpose** carece de sentido • **it has served its purpose** ya sirvió • **to no purpose** en vano

■ **on purpose** *adv* a propósito; adrede

purposeful[ˈpɜːpəsfʊl] *adj* resuelto, ta

P

purr [pɜːɼ] *vi* ❶ ronronear ❷ zumbar

purse [pɜːs] ◆ *s* bolsa ◆ *vt* fruncir (con desagrado) • **she pursed her lips** frunció los labios

purse snatcher [-ˌsnætʃəɼ] *s* ladrón que roba dando un jalón

pursue [pəˈsjuː] *vt* ❶ perseguir ❷ *formal* llevar a cabo ❸ ir en pos de; buscar ❹ profundizar en ❺ dedicarse a

pursuer [pəˈsjuːəɼ] *s* perseguidor, ra

pursuit [pəˈsjuːt] *s* ❶ ☿*incontable formal* búsqueda ❷ persecución ❸ ocupación • **leisure pursuit** pasatiempo

pus [pʌs] *s* pus

push [pʊʃ] ◆ *vt* ❶ empujar • **to push something into something** meter algo en algo • **to push something open/shut** abrir/cerrar algo empujándolo ❷ apretar; pulsar ❸ • **to push somebody (to do something)** empujar a alguien (a hacer algo) ❹ • **to push somebody (into doing something)** obligar a alguien (a hacer algo) ❺ *familiar* promocionar ◆ *vi* ❶ empujar ❷ apretar ◆ *s literal & figurado* empujón • **at the push of a button** con sólo apretar un botón • **at a push** apurando mucho

expresión **to give somebody the push a)** *familiar* dar calabazas a alguien **b)** dar la patada a alguien

■ **push around** *vt* ☿ *El objeto se puede colocar antes o después de la preposición. familiar* mandonear

■ **push for** *vt* ☿ *El objeto siempre va después de la preposición al final.* reclamar

■ **push in** *vi* colarse

■ **push off** *vi familiar* largarse

■ **push on** *vi* seguir adelante sin parar

■ **push through** *vt* ☿ *El objeto se puede colocar antes o después de la preposición.* conseguir que se apruebe

pushed [pʊʃt] *adj familiar* • **to be pushed for something** andar corto, ta de algo

expresión **to be hard pushed to do something** tenerlo difícil para hacer algo

push-up *s* flexión

pushy [ˈpʊʃɪ] *adj despectivo* agresivo, va ; insistente

puss [pʊs]**, pussy (cat)** [ˈpʊsɪ-] *s familiar* gatito; minino

put [pʊt] *vt* ❶ poner • **to put something into something** meter algo en algo ❷ colocar ❸ meter ❹ expresar; formular • **to put it bluntly** hablando claro ❺ hacer; presentar ❻ • **to put something at** calcular algo en ❼ • **to put money into an account** ingresar dinero en una cuenta • **to put a lot of effort into something** esforzarse mucho con algo ❽ • **to put pressure on** presionar a

expresión **to put it to somebody that...** sugerir a alguien que...

■ **put across, put over** *vt* ☿ *El objeto se puede colocar antes o después de la preposición.* transmitir • **to put yourself across** hacerse entender

■ **put away** *vt* ☿ *El objeto se puede colocar antes o después de la preposición.* poner en su sitio; guardar

■ **put back** *vt* ☿ *El objeto se puede colocar antes o después de la preposición.* ❶ devolver a su sitio ❷ aplazar ❸ retrasar ❹ atrasar

■ **put by** *vt* ☿ *El objeto se puede colocar antes o después de la preposición.* ahorrar

■ **put down** *vt* ☿ *El objeto se puede colocar antes o después de la preposición.* ❶ dejar ❷ colgar ❸ sofocar; reprimir ❹ apuntar

■ **put down to** *vt* ☿ *El objeto se coloca entre el verbo y la preposición.* achacar a

■ **put forward** *vt* ☿ *El objeto se puede colocar antes o después de la preposición.* ❶ proponer ❷ presentar ❸ adelantar

■ **put in** *vt* ☿ *El objeto se puede colocar antes o después de la preposición.* ❶ dedicar ❷ presentar ❸ instalar

■ **put off** *vt* ☿ *El objeto se puede colocar antes o después de la preposición.* ❶ posponer; aplazar ❷ hacer esperar ❸ distraer ❹ disuadir ❺ • **to put somebody off something** quitarle a alguien las ganas de algo

■ **put on** *vt* ☿ *El objeto se puede colocar antes o después de la preposición.* ❶ ponerse ❷ representar ❸ hacer (exposición) ❹ organizar (transporte) ❺ • **to put on weight** engordar ❻ encender (luz, radio) • **to put on the brakes** frenar ❼ poner ❽ empezar a hacer o cocinar • **to put the kettle on** poner el agua a hervir ❾ apostar por ❿ añadir ⓫ fingir

■ **put out** *vt* ☿ *El objeto se puede colocar antes o después de la preposición.* ❶ sacar ❷ hacer público ❸ apagar ❹ extender (mano, pierna) ; sacar (lengua) ❺ • **to be put out** estar disgustado, da ❻ causar molestias a

■ **put through** *vt* ☿ *El objeto se coloca entre el verbo y la preposición.* TELECOMUNICACIONES poner • **to put somebody through to somebody** poner a alguien con alguien

■ **put up** ◆ *vt* ☿ *El objeto se puede colocar antes o después de la preposición.* ❶ construir ❷ abrir ❸ levantar ❹ fijar ❺ colgar (cuadro) ❻ poner (dinero, fondos) ❼ proponer (candidato) ❽ subir; aumentar ◆ *vt* ☿ *El objeto siempre va después de la preposición al final.* ofrecer • **to put up a fight** ofrecer resistencia

■ **put up with** *vt* ☿ *El objeto siempre va después de la preposición al final.* aguantar

Formas irregulares de **put**: *pretérito & pp* **put**.

putter [ˈpʌtəɼ] *s* putter

■ **putter about, putter around** *vi* entretenerse

puzzle [ˈpʌzl] ◆ *s* ❶ rompecabezas ❷ misterio; enigma ◆ *vt* dejar perplejo; desconcertar ◆ *vi* • **to puzzle over something** romperse la cabeza con algo

■ **puzzle out** *vt* ☿ *El objeto se puede colocar antes o después de la preposición.* descifrar

puzzling [ˈpʌzlɪŋ] *adj* desconcertante

pylon [ˈpaɪlən] *s* torre (de conducción eléctrica)

pyramid [ˈpɪrəmɪd] *s* pirámide

python [ˈpaɪɵn] *s* pitón

Dos plurales: **python** o **pythons**.

q, Q [kjuː] *s* q; Q

Dos plurales: **q's o qs; Q's o Qs.**

quack [kwæk] *s* ❶ graznido *(de pato)* ❷ *familiar* matasanos

quadruple [kwɒˈdruːpl] ◆ *vt* cuadruplicar ◆ *vi* cuadruplicarse

quadruplets [ˈkwɒdrʊplɪts] *spl* cuatrillizos, zas

quads [kwɒdz] *spl familiar* cuatrillizos, zas

quaint [kweɪnt] *adj* ❶ pintoresco, ca ❷ singular

quake [kweɪk] ◆ *s familiar* terremoto ◆ *vi* temblar; estremecerse

qualification [ˌkwɒlɪfɪˈkeɪʃn] *s* ❶ título ❷ aptitud ❸ condición

qualified [ˈkwɒlɪfaɪd] *adj* ❶ cualificado, da • **to be qualified to do something** estar cualificado para hacer algo ❷ limitado, da

qualify [ˈkwɒlɪfaɪ] ◆ *vt* ❶ matizar ❷ • **to qualify somebody to do something** capacitar a alguien para hacer algo ◆ *vi* ❶ sacar el título ❷ • **to qualify (for)** tener derecho (a) ❸ DEPORTE clasificarse

quality [ˈkwɒlətɪ] ◆ *s* ❶ calidad ❷ cualidad ◆ *en compuestos* de calidad

qualms [kwɑːmz] *spl* escrúpulos

quandary [ˈkwɒndərɪ] *s* • **to be in a quandary about** o **over something** estar en un dilema sobre algo

quantify [ˈkwɒntɪfaɪ] *vt* cuantificar

quantity [ˈkwɒntətɪ] *s* cantidad

quarantine [ˈkwɒrəntiːn] *s* cuarentena

quarrel [ˈkwɒrəl] ◆ *s* pelea

expresión **to have no quarrel with somebody/something** no tener nada en contra de alguien/algo

◆ *vi* pelearse • **to quarrel with somebody** pelearse con alguien • **to quarrel with something** no estar de acuerdo con algo

Formas irregulares de **quarrel:** *pretérito & pp* **quarreled,** *gerundio* **quarreling.**

quarry [ˈkwɒrɪ] *s* ❶ cantera ❷ presa

quart [kwɔːt] *s* cuarto de galón

quarter [ˈkwɔːtər] *s* ❶ cuarto ❷ • **quarter after two** las dos y cuarto ❸ trimestre ❹ moneda de 25 centavos ❺ cuatro onzas ❻ barrio ❼ lugar; parte

■ **quarters** *spl* residencia; alojamiento

■ **at close quarters** *adv* muy de cerca

quarterback [ˈkwɔːtəbæk] *s* mariscal de campo

quarterfinal [ˌkwɔːtəˈfaɪnl] *s* cuarto de final

quarterly [ˈkwɔːtəlɪ] ◆ *adj* trimestral ◆ *adv* trimestralmente ◆ *s* trimestral

quartermaster [ˈkwɔːtəˌmɑːstər] *s* oficial de intendencia

quarter note *s* MÚSICA negra

quartet [kwɔːˈtet] *s* cuarteto

quartz [kwɔːts] *s* cuarzo

quartz watch *s* reloj de cuarzo

quash [kwɒʃ] *vt* ❶ anular; invalidar ❷ reprimir; sofocar

quasi- [ˈkweɪzaɪ] *prefijo* cuasi-

quaver [ˈkweɪvər] ◆ *s* MÚSICA corchea ◆ *vi* temblar

quay [kiː] *s* muelle

quayside [ˈkiːsaɪd] *s* muelle

queasy [ˈkwiːzɪ] *adj* mareado, da

queen [kwiːn] *s* ❶ reina ❷ dama

queer [kwɪər] ◆ *adj* ❶ raro, ra; extraño, ña ❷ *familiar & despectivo* marica ◆ *s familiar & despectivo* marica

quell [kwel] *vt* ❶ sofocar; reprimir ❷ dominar; contener

quench [kwentʃ] *vt* apagar

query [ˈkwɪərɪ] ◆ *s* pregunta; duda ◆ *vt* poner en duda

quest [kwest] *s literario* • **quest (for)** búsqueda (de)

question [ˈkwestʃn] ◆ *s* ❶ pregunta ❷ duda • **to bring something into question** hacer reflexionar sobre algo • **to call something into question** poner algo en duda • **without question** sin duda • **beyond question** fuera de toda duda ❸ cuestión; asunto

expresión **it is a question of staying calm** se trata de mantener la calma ▶ **there's no question of...** es imposible que...

◆ *vt* ❶ preguntar ❷ interrogar ❸ cuestionar

■ **in question** *adv* • **the matter in question** el asunto en cuestión

■ **out of the question** *adv* imposible • **that's out of the question!** ¡ni hablar!

questionable ['kwestʃənəbl] *adj* ❶ cuestionable ❷ dudoso, sa

question mark *s* (signo de) interrogación

questionnaire [ˌkwestʃə'neəɾ] *s* cuestionario

quibble ['kwɪbl] *vi despectivo* quejarse por tonterías • **to quibble over** o **about** quejarse tontamente por o de

quiche [kiːʃ] *s* quiche

quick [kwɪk] ◆ *adj* ❶ rápido, da • **be quick!** ¡date prisa! • **could we have a quick word?** ¿podríamos hablar un momento? ❷ espabilado, da; agudo, da ❸ • **a quick temper** un genio vivo ◆ *adv* rápidamente

quicken ['kwɪkn] ◆ *vt* apretar; acelerar ◆ *vi* acelerarse

quickly ['kwɪklɪ] *adv* ❶ rápidamente; de prisa ❷ rápidamente; en seguida

quicksand ['kwɪksænd] *s* arenas movedizas

quick-witted [-'wɪtɪd] *adj* agudo, da

quiet ['kwaɪət] ◆ *adj* ❶ silencioso, sa; tranquilo, la • **to be quiet** no hacer ruido • **be quiet!** ¡cállate! • **in a quiet voice** en voz baja ❷ callado, da ❸ tranquilo, la ❹ privado, da; íntimo, ma
expresión **to keep quiet about something** guardar silencio sobre algo ❱ **to go quiet** callarse
◆ *s* tranquilidad; silencio • **on the quiet** a escondidas ◆ *vt* tranquilizar

■ **quiet down** ◆ *vt* ☼ *El objeto se puede colocar antes o después de la preposición.* tranquilizar ◆ *vi* tranquilizarse

quieten ['kwaɪətn] *vt* tranquilizar

■ **quieten down** ◆ *vt* ☼ *El objeto se puede colocar antes o después de la preposición.* tranquilizar ◆ *vi* tranquilizarse

quietly ['kwaɪətlɪ] *adv* ❶ silenciosamente; sin hacer ruido • **to speak quietly** hablar en voz baja ❷ sin moverse ❸ tranquilamente ❹ discretamente

quilt [kwɪlt] *s* edredón

quinine [kwɪ'niːn] *s* quinina

quintet [kwɪn'tet] *s* quinteto

quints [kwɪnts] *spl familiar* quintillizos, zas

quintuplets [kwɪn'tjuːplɪts] *spl* quintillizos, zas

quip [kwɪp] *s* ocurrencia; salida

quirk [kwɜːk] *s* ❶ manía; rareza ❷ extraña coincidencia

quit [kwɪt] ◆ *vt* ❶ dejar; abandonar ❷ • **to quit doing something** dejar de hacer algo ❸ *INFORMÁTICA* salir de ◆ *vi* ❶ dimitir ❷ *INFORMÁTICA* salir

Formas irregulares de **quit**: *pretérito & pp* **quit**.

quite [kwaɪt] *adv* ❶ totalmente; completamente ❷ bastante • **quite a lot of people** bastante gente ❸ • **it's not quite big enough** no es todo lo grande que tendría que ser • **I'm not quite sure** no estoy del todo seguro • **I don't quite understand/know** no entiendo/sé muy bien ❹ • **quite a...** todo un, toda una... • **quite the opposite** todo lo contrario ❺ • **quite (so)!** ¡efectivamente!; ¡desde luego!

quite

Quite confunde porque puede significar *totalmente* y *bastante*. Pero resulta fácil distinguir estos dos usos cuando vemos el tipo de adjetivo que le sigue. Compara it's *quite* cold today; the movie was *quite* good (*hoy hace bastante frío; la película era bastante buena*) y he's *quite* right; the tree seems *quite* dead (*tiene toda la razón; el árbol parece totalmente muerto*).

quits [kwɪts] *adj familiar* • **to be quits (with somebody)** estar en paz (con alguien)
expresión **to call it quits** dejarlo así

quiver ['kwɪvəɾ] *vi* temblar; estremecerse

quiz [kwɪz] ◆ *s* ❶ concurso ❷ *EDUCACIÓN* control ◆ *vt* • **to quiz somebody (about)** interrogar a alguien (sobre)

El plural de **quiz** es **quizzes**.

quizzical ['kwɪzɪkl] *adj* burlón, ona

quota ['kwəʊtə] *s* cuota

quotation [kwəʊ'teɪʃn] *s* ❶ cita ❷ *COMERCIO* presupuesto

quotation marks *spl* comillas

quote [kwəʊt] ◆ *s* ❶ cita ❷ comillas • **in quotes** entre comillas ❸ *COMERCIO* presupuesto ◆ *vt* ❶ citar ❷ dar • **he quoted $100** fijó un precio de 100 dólares ◆ *vi* ❶ • **to quote (from)** citar (de) ❷ *COMERCIO* • **to quote for** dar un presupuesto por

Q

r, R [ɑːɾ] *s* r; R

Dos plurales: **r's** o **rs**; **R's** o **Rs**.

■ **R** *abreviatura* ❶ *(abreviatura de* restricted*)* no recomendada para menores ❷ *abreviatura escrita de* **Republican**

rabbit ['ræbɪt] *s* conejo

rabble ['ræbl] *s* chusma; populacho

rabies ['reɪbiːz] *s* rabia

race [reɪs] ◆ *s* ❶ *literal & figurado* carrera ❷ raza ◆ *vt* ❶ competir con *(corriendo)* • **they raced each other to the door** echaron una carrera hasta la puerta ❷ hacer carreras de ❸ hacer correr ◆ *vi* ❶ ir corriendo ❷ acelerarse

race car *s* coche de carreras

racecourse ['reɪskɔːs] *s* hipódromo

race driver *s* piloto de carreras

racehorse ['reɪshɔːs] *s* caballo de carreras

racetrack ['reɪstræk] *s* ❶ hipódromo ❷ circuito

racial ['reɪʃl] *adj* racial

racial discrimination *s* discriminación racial

racing ['reɪsɪŋ] *s* carreras • **motor racing** carreras de coches

racism ['reɪsɪzm], **racialism** *s* racismo

racist ['reɪsɪst] ◆ *adj* racista ◆ *s* racista

rack [ræk] *s* ❶ revistero ❷ escurridor ❸ percha ❹ portaequipajes

racket, racquet ['rækɪt] *s* ❶ DEPORTE raqueta ❷ alboroto ❸ estafa ❹ negocio sucio

racquet ['rækɪt] *s* = **racket**

radar ['reɪdɑːɾ] *s* radar

radiant ['reɪdjənt] *adj* ❶ radiante ❷ *literario* resplandeciente

radiate ['reɪdɪeɪt] ◆ *vt literal & figurado* irradiar ◆ *vi* ❶ ser irradiado, da ❷ salir; extenderse

radiation [ˌreɪdɪ'eɪʃn] *s* radiación

radiator ['reɪdɪeɪtər] *s* radiador

radical ['rædɪkl] ◆ *adj* radical ◆ *s* POLÍTICA radical

radically ['rædɪklɪ] *adv* radicalmente

radii ['reɪdɪaɪ] *spl* → **radius**

radio ['reɪdɪəʊ] ◆ *s* radio ◆ *en compuestos* de radio; radiofónico, ca

El plural de **radio** es **radios**.

radioactive [ˌreɪdɪəʊ'æktɪv] *adj* radiactivo, va

radio alarm *s* radiodespertador

radiology [ˌreɪdɪ'ɒlədʒɪ] *s* radiología

radiotherapy [ˌreɪdɪəʊ'θerəpɪ] *s* radioterapia

radish ['rædɪʃ] *s* rábano

radius ['reɪdɪəs] *s* radio

El plural de **radius** es **radii**.

raffle ['ræfl] ◆ *s* rifa; sorteo ◆ *en compuestos* • **raffle ticket** boleto ◆ *vt* rifar

raft [rɑːft] *s* balsa

rafter ['rɑːftər] *s* viga *(de armadura de tejado)*

rag [ræg] *s* ❶ trapo ❷ *despectivo* periodicucho

■ **rags** *spl* trapos; harapos

rage [reɪdʒ] ◆ *s* ❶ rabia; ira ❷ *familiar* • **it's all the rage** es la última moda ◆ *vi* ❶ estar furioso, sa ❷ enfurecerse ❸ hacer estragos ❹ continuar con violencia

ragged ['rægɪd] *adj* ❶ andrajoso, sa; harapiento, ta ❷ hecho, cha jirones

raid [reɪd] ◆ *s* ❶ incursión ❷ asalto; redada ◆ *vt* ❶ atacar por sorpresa ❷ asaltar ❸ hacer una redada en

raider ['reɪdər] *s* invasor, ra

rail [reɪl] *s* ❶ barandilla ❷ barra • **towel rail** toallero ❸ 🔎 *incontable* ferrocarril • **by rail** por ferrocarril ❹ carril; riel

railing ['reɪlɪŋ] *s* reja

railroad ['reɪlrəʊd] *s* ❶ ferrocarril ❷ línea de ferrocarril

railway *s* ferrocarril

rain [reɪn] ◆ *s* lluvia

expresión **in the rain** bajo la lluvia

◆ *v impersonal* METEOROLOGÍA llover

rainbow ['reɪnbəʊ] *s* arco iris

rain check *s*

expresión **I'll take a rain check (on that)** no ahora, pero igual me apunto la próxima vez

raincoat ['reɪnkəʊt] *s* impermeable

raindrop ['reɪndrɒp] *s* gota de lluvia

rainfall ['reɪnfɔːl] *s* precipitación

rain forest *s* selva tropical

rainy ['reɪnɪ] *adj* lluvioso, sa

raise [reɪz] ◆ *vt* ❶ levantar ❷ aumentar *(voz, nivel)* • **to raise your voice** levantar la voz ❸ mejorar *(calidad)* ❹ traer *(recuerdos)* ❺ criar *(educar)* ❻ cultivar ❼ plantear *(cuestión)* ❽ construir ◆ *s* aumento

raisin ['reɪzn] *s* pasa

rake [reɪk] ◆ *s* rastrillo ◆ *vt* rastrillar

rally ['rælɪ] ◆ *s* ❶ mitin ❷ rally ❸ peloteo ◆ *vt* reunir ◆ *vi* ❶ reunirse ❷ recuperarse

ram [ræm] ◆ *s* carnero ◆ *vt* ❶ embestir ❷ embutir

RAM [ræm] *(abreviatura de* random access memory) *s* INFORMÁTICA RAM

ramble ['ræmbl] ◆ *s* paseo por el campo ◆ *vi* ❶ pasear ❷ divagar

■ **ramble on** *vi* divagar sin parar

rambling ['ræmblɪŋ] *adj* ❶ laberíntico, ca ❷ incoherente

ramp [ræmp] *s* ❶ rampa ❷ AUTOMÓVILES salida; entrada • **the ramp was blocked** la entrada/salida estaba cerrada

rampage [ræm'peɪdʒ] *s* • **to go on the rampage** desbandarse

rampant ['ræmpənt] *adj* desenfrenado, da

ramparts ['ræmpɑːts] *spl* murallas

ramshackle ['ræm,ʃækl] *adj* destartalado, da

ran [ræn] *pretérito* → **run**

ranch [rɑːntʃ] *s* rancho

rancher ['rɑːntʃər] *s* ranchero, ra

ranch house *s* ❶ hacienda; estancia ❷ rancho

rancid ['rænsɪd] *adj* rancio, cia

rancor ['ræŋkər] *s* rencor

random ['rændəm] ◆ *adj* ❶ hecho, cha al azar ❷ TECNOLOGÍA aleatorio, ria ◆ *s* • **at random** al azar

random access memory *s* INFORMÁTICA memoria de acceso aleatorio

rang [ræŋ] *pretérito* → **ring**

range [reɪndʒ] ◆ *s* ❶ alcance ❷ • **to be out of/within range** estar fuera del/al alcance • **at close range** de cerca ❸ gama ❹ escala ❺ cordillera ❻ campo de tiro ❼ registro ◆ *vt* alinear ◆ *vi* • **to range from... to...,** **to range between... and...** oscilar o fluctuar entre... y... • **prices rangeing from $20 to $100** precios que van desde veinte hasta cien dólares

ranger ['reɪndʒər] *s* guardabosques

rank [ræŋk] ◆ *adj* ❶ absoluto, ta; flagrante ❷ pestilente ◆ *s* ❶ grado; rango ❷ clase; categoría ▸ **the rank and file** las bases ❸ fila ◆ *vt* • **to be ranked** estar clasificado, da ◆ *vi* • **to rank as** estar considerado, da (como) • **to rank among** encontrarse entre

■ **ranks** *spl* ❶ MILITAR • **the ranks** los soldados rasos ❷ *figurado* filas

ranking ['ræŋkɪŋ] ◆ *s* clasificación ◆ *adj* de alta graduación

ransack ['rænsæk] *vt* ❶ registrar a fondo ❷ saquear

ransom ['rænsəm] *s* rescate

expresión **to hold somebody to ransom** *figurado* hacer chantaje a alguien

rant [rænt] *vi* despotricar

rap [ræp] ◆ *s* ❶ golpecito ❷ rap ❸ acusación • **rap sheet** antecedentes penales ◆ *vt* dar un golpecito en

rape [reɪp] ◆ *s* ❶ violación ❷ BOTÁNICA colza ◆ *vt* violar

rapid ['ræpɪd] *adj* rápido, da

■ **rapids** *spl* rápidos

rapidly ['ræpɪdlɪ] *adv* rápidamente

rapist ['reɪpɪst] *s* violador, ra

rapport [ræ'pɔːr] *s* compenetración

rapture ['ræptʃər] *s* arrobamiento

expresión **to go into raptures over** o **about** deshacerse en elogios a

rapturous ['ræptʃərəs] *adj* muy entusiasta

rare [reər] *adj* ❶ poco común; raro, ra ❷ poco frecuente; raro, ra ❸ raro, ra; excepcional ❹ COCINA poco hecho, cha

rarely ['reəlɪ] *adv* raras veces

raring ['reərɪŋ] *adj*

expresión **to be raring to go** estar ansioso, sa por empezar

rarity ['reərətɪ] *s* rareza

rascal ['rɑːskl] *s* pícaro, ra

rash [ræʃ] ◆ *adj* precipitado, da ◆ *s* ❶ MEDICINA erupción (cutánea); sarpullido ❷ aluvión

rasher ['ræʃər] *s* rebanada de tocino

raspberry ['rɑːzbərɪ] *s* frambuesa

rat [ræt] *s* rata

rate [reɪt] ◆ *s* ❶ ritmo • **at this rate** a este paso ❷ índice ❸ tasa ❹ precio; tarifa ❺ tipo *(de interés)* ◆ *vt* ❶ • **to rate something/somebody (as/among)** considerar algo/a alguien (como/entre) ❷ merecer

■ **at any rate** *adv* ❶ al menos ❷ de todos modos

rather ['rɑːðər] *adv* ❶ bastante ❷ muy ❸ algo • **he's rather like you** se parece algo a ti ❹ • **I would rather wait** preferiría esperar • **I'd rather not stay** prefiero no quedarme • **would you like to come? — I'd rather not** ¿quieres venir? — mejor no ❺ • **or rather...** o más bien...; o mejor dicho... ❻ • **(but) rather...** (sino) más bien o por el contrario...

■ **rather than** *conjunción* en vez de

rather

Rather than puede ir seguido de un sustantivo (it's a comedy **rather than** an action movie *es una comedia más que una película de acción*) o de un verbo (I prefer to go on my own *rather than* going with my brother *prefiero ir solo que con mi hermano).* Observa que el verbo tiene que ir en gerundio.

Would *rather* se suele acortar a *-'d rather.* Fíjate en que va seguido del infinitivo sin *to* (I'*d rather stay* a bit longer *preferiría quedarme algo más).*

rating ['reitɪŋ] *s* clasificación

ratio ['reiʃiəʊ] *s* proporción; relación

El plural de **ratio** es **ratios**.

ration ['ræʃn] ◆ *s* ración ◆ *vt* racionar
■ **rations** *spl* víveres

rational ['ræʃənl] *adj* racional

rationale [,ræʃə'nɑ:l] *s* lógica; razones

rationalize, rationalise ['ræʃənəlaɪz] *vt* racionalizar

rattle ['rætl] ◆ *s* ❶ traqueteo ❷ crujido ❸ tintineo ❹ repiqueteo ❺ sonaja ◆ *vt* ❶ hacer sonar ❷ desconcertar ◆ *vi* ❶ golpetear ❷ crujir ❸ tintinear

rattlesnake ['rætlsneɪk], **rattler** ['rætlər] *s* víbora de cascabel

raucous ['rɔ:kəs] *adj* ronco, ca y estridente

ravage ['rævɪdʒ] *vt* estragar; asolar
■ **ravages** *spl* estragos

rave [reɪv] ◆ *s* macrofiesta tecno ◆ *vi* ❶ • **to rave at somebody** increpar a alguien • **to rave against somebody/something** despotricar contra alguien/algo ❷ • **to rave about something** deshacerse en alabanzas sobre algo

raven ['reɪvn] *s* cuervo

ravenous ['rævənəs] *adj* ❶ famélico, ca ❷ voraz

ravine [rə'vi:n] *s* barranca

raving ['reɪvɪŋ] *adj* ❶ de atar ❷ delirante

ravioli [,rævɪ'əʊlɪ] *s* ☼ *incontable* raviolis

ravishing ['rævɪʃɪŋ] *adj* ❶ de ensueño ❷ bellísimo, ma

raw [rɔ:] *adj* ❶ crudo, da ❷ sin tratar; sin refinar ❸ en carne viva ❹ novato, ta

raw deal *s* • **to get a raw deal** recibir un trato injusto

raw material *s* materia prima

ray [reɪ] *s* rayo • **ray of hope** resquicio de esperanza

raze [reɪz] *vt* arrasar

razor ['reɪzər] *s* ❶ navaja ❷ rasuradora

razor blade *s* hoja de rasurar

Rd *abreviatura escrita de* **road**

re [ri:] *preposición* Ref.

reach [ri:tʃ] ◆ *s* alcance • **he has a long reach** tiene los brazos largos • **within (somebody's) reach a)** al alcance (de alguien) **b)** a poco distancia (de alguien) • **out of** o **beyond somebody's reach** fuera del alcance de alguien ◆ *vt* ❶ alcanzar; llegar a ❷ localizar ◆ *vi*

• **I can't reach** no llego • **to reach out/across** alargar la mano • **to reach down** agacharse

react [rɪ'ækt] *vi* ❶ • **to react (to)** reaccionar (a o ante) ❷ • **to react against** reaccionar en contra de ❸ QUÍMICA • **to react with** reaccionar con

reaction [rɪ'ækʃn] *s* • **reaction (to/against)** reacción (a/contra)

reactionary [rɪ'ækʃənrɪ] ◆ *adj* reaccionario, ria ◆ *s* reaccionario, ria

reactor [rɪ'æktər] *s* reactor

read [ri:d] ◆ *vt* ❶ leer • **she can't read my writing** no entiende mi letra ❷ poner; decir ❸ marcar ❹ interpretar ◆ *vi* ❶ leer ❷ • **to read to somebody** leerle a alguien ❸ • **to read well** estar bien escrito
■ **read out** *vt* ☼ *El objeto se puede colocar antes o después de la preposición.* leer en voz alta
■ **read through** *vt* ☼ *El objeto se puede colocar antes o después de la preposición.* leer
■ **read up on** *vt* ☼ *El objeto siempre va después de la preposición al final.* leer o documentarse sobre

Formas irregulares de **read** *pretérito* & *pp* **read** [red].

readable ['ri:dəbl] *adj* ameno, na

reader ['ri:dər] *s* ❶ lector, ra ❷ INFORMÁTICA lector

readership ['ri:dəʃɪp] *s* lectores

readily ['redɪlɪ] *adv* ❶ de buena gana ❷ fácilmente

reading ['ri:dɪŋ] *s* ❶ lectura ❷ recital

readjust [,ri:ə'dʒʌst] ◆ *vt* reajustar ◆ *vi* • **to readjust (to)** volverse a adaptar (a)

ready ['redɪ] ◆ *adj* ❶ listo, ta; preparado, da • **to be ready for something/to do something** estar listo para algo/para hacer algo • **to get ready)** prepararse **b)** arreglarse ❷ • **to be ready to do something** estar dispuesto, ta a hacer algo ❸ • **to be ready for something** necesitar algo ❹ • **to be ready to do something** estar a punto de hacer algo ◆ *vt* preparar • **to ready yourself for something** prepararse para algo

ready-made *adj* ❶ hecho, cha ❷ confeccionado, da

ready money *s* dinero contante

real ['rɪəl] ◆ *adj* ❶ real • **for real** de verdad • **in real terms** en términos reales ❷ auténtico, ca
expresión **the real thing** lo auténtico ▸ **a real friend** un amigo de verdad
◆ *adv* muy

real estate *s* propiedad inmobiliaria

real estate agent *s* agente inmobiliario, agente inmobiliaria

realign [,ri:ə'laɪn] *vt* volver a alinear

realism ['rɪəlɪzm] *s* realismo

realistic [,rɪə'lɪstɪk] *adj* realista

reality [rɪ'ælətɪ] *s* realidad

realization [,rɪəlaɪ'zeɪʃn] *s* ❶ comprensión ❷ consecución

R

realize, realise ['rıəlaız] *vt* ❶ darse cuenta de ❷ realizar

really ['rıəlı] ◆ *adv* ❶ de verdad • **really good** buenísimo • **did you like it? — not really** ¿te gustó? — la verdad es que no ❷ realmente ❸ en realidad ◆ *exclamación* ❶ • **really? a)** ¿ah sí? **b)** ¿ah no? ❷ • **really?** ¿de verdad?; ¿seguro?

realm [relm] *s* ❶ campo; esfera ❷ reino

realtor ['rıəltər] *s* agente inmobiliario, agente inmobiliaria

reap [ri:p] *vt literal & figurado* cosechar

reappear [,ri:ə'pıər] *vi* reaparecer

rear [rıər] ◆ *adj* trasero, ra; de atrás ◆ *s* parte de atrás
expresión **to bring up the rear** cerrar la marcha
◆ *vt* criar ◆ *vi* • **to rear (up)** encabritarse

rearrange [,ri:ə'reındʒ] *vt* ❶ colocar de otro modo ❷ reorganizar ❸ volver a concertar

rearview mirror ['rıəvju:-] *s* (espejo) retrovisor

reason ['ri:zn] ◆ *s* ❶ • **reason (for)** razón (de) • **I don't know the reason why** no sé por qué • **by reason of** *formal* a causa de • **for some reason** por alguna razón ❷ • **to have reason to do something** tener motivos para hacer algo
expresión **to listen to reason** avenirse a razones ▸ **it stands to reason** es lógico
◆ *vt* & *vi* razonar
■ **reason with** *vt* ☼ *El objeto siempre va después de la preposición al final.* razonar con

reasonable ['ri:znəbl] *adj* razonable

reasonably ['ri:znəblı] *adv* razonablemente

reasoning ['ri:znıŋ] *s* razonamiento

reassess [,ri:ə'ses] *vt* reconsiderar

reassurance [,ri:ə'ʃʊərəns] *s* ☼ *incontable* palabras tranquilizadoras ❷ promesa

reassure [,ri:ə'ʃʊər] *vt* tranquilizar

reassuring [,ri:ə'ʃʊərıŋ] *adj* tranquilizador, ra

rebate ['ri:beıt] *s* ❶ devolución ❷ bonificación

rebel ◆ *s* ['rebl] rebelde ◆ *vi* [rı'bel] • **to rebel (against)** rebelarse (contra); alebrestarse (contra)

rebellion [rı'beljən] *s* rebelión

rebellious [rı'beljəs] *adj* rebelde

rebound ◆ *s* ['ri:baʊnd] • **on the rebound** de rebote ◆ *vi* [,rı'baʊnd] rebotar

rebuff [rı'bʌf] *s* ❶ desaire ❷ negativa

rebuild [,ri:'bıld] *vt* reconstruir
Formas irregulares de **rebuild**: *pretérito* & *pp* **rebuilt**.

rebuke [rı'bju:k] ◆ *s* reprimenda ◆ *vt* • **to rebuke somebody (for)** reprender a alguien (por)

recall [rı'kɔ:l] ◆ *s* memoria ◆ *vt* ❶ recordar; acordarse de ❷ retirar ❸ retirar del mercado

recap ['ri:kæp] *familiar* ◆ *s* resumen; recapitulación ◆ *vt* & *vi* recapitular; resumir

recapitulate [,ri:kə'pıtjʊleıt] *vt* & *vi* recapitular; resumir

recede [ri:'si:d] *vi* ❶ alejarse ❷ retroceder ❸ *figurado* esfumarse

receding [rı'si:dıŋ] *adj* • **to have a receding hairline** tener entradas

receipt [rı'si:t] *s* recibo • **to acknowledge receipt** acusar recibo
■ **receipts** *spl* recaudación

receive [rı'si:v] *vt* ❶ recibir • **I received a fine** me pusieron una multa ❷ tener ❸ sufrir ❹ • **to be well/ badly received** tener una buena/mala acogida

receiver [rı'si:vər] *s* ❶ auricular ❷ receptor

recent ['ri:snt] *adj* reciente

recently ['ri:sntlı] *adv* recientemente

receptacle [rı'septəkl] *s* receptáculo

reception [rı'sepʃn] *s* ❶ recepción ❷ recibimiento

reception desk *s* recepción

receptionist [rı'sepʃənıst] *s* recepcionista

recess ['ri:ses] *s* ❶ periodo vacacional; receso ❷ *EDUCACIÓN* recreo ❸ nicho; hueco

recession [rı'seʃn] *s* recesión

recharge [,ri:'tʃɑ:dʒ] *vt* recargar

recipe ['resıpı] *s figurado COCINA* receta

recipient [rı'sıpıənt] *s* destinatario, ria

reciprocal [rı'sıprəkl] *adj* recíproco, ca

recital [rı'saıtl] *s* recital

recite [rı'saıt] *vt* ❶ recitar ❷ enumerar

reckless ['reklıs] *adj* ❶ imprudente ❷ temerario, ria

reckon ['rekn] *vt* ❶ *familiar* • **to reckon (that)** pensar que ❷ • **to be reckoned to be something** ser considerado, da algo ❸ calcular
■ **reckon on** *vt* ☼ *El objeto siempre va después de la preposición al final.* contar con
■ **reckon with** *vt* ☼ *El objeto siempre va después de la preposición al final.* contar con

reckoning ['rekənıŋ] *s* cálculo

reclaim [rı'kleım] *vt* ❶ reclamar ❷ recuperar • **to reclaim land from the sea** ganarle tierra al mar

recline [rı'klaın] *vi* reclinarse

reclining [rı'klaınıŋ] *adj* reclinable

recluse [rı'klu:s] *s* solitario, ria

recognition [,rekəg'nıʃn] *s* reconocimiento • **to have changed beyond** o **out of all recognition** estar irreconocible • **in recognition of** en reconocimiento a

recognizable ['rekəgnaızəbl] *adj* reconocible

recognize, recognise ['rekəgnaız] *vt* reconocer

recoil ◆ *vi* [rı'kɔıl] retroceder; echarse atrás ◆ *s* ['ri:kɔıl] retroceso

recollect [,rekə'lekt] *vt* & *vi* recordar

recollection [,rekə'lekʃn] *s* recuerdo

recommend [,rekə'mend] *vt* recomendar

recompense ['rekəmpens] ◆ *s* • **recompense (for)** compensación o indemnización (por) ◆ *vt* • **to rec-**

R

ompense somebody (for) recompensar a alguien (por)

reconcile ['rekənsaɪl] *vt* ❶conciliar ❷reconciliar • **to be reconciled with somebody** reconciliarse con alguien ❸ • **to reconcile yourself to** resignarse a

reconditioned [ˌriːkən'dɪʃnd] *adj* reparado, da

reconnaissance [rɪ'kɒnɪsəns] *s* reconocimiento

reconnoiter [ˌrekə'nɔɪtər] ◆ *vt* reconocer ◆ *vi* hacer un reconocimiento

reconsider [ˌriːkən'sɪdər] *vt* & *vi* reconsiderar

reconstruct [ˌriːkən'strʌkt] *vt* reconstruir

record ◆ *s* ['rekɔːd] ❶registro ❷actas • **to go/ be on record as saying that...** declarar/haber declarado públicamente que... • **off the record** confidencial ❸disco ❹récord ❺resultados ❻ Historia historial • **criminal record** antecedentes penales ◆ *vt* [rɪ'kɔːd] ❶anotar ❷documentar ❸grabar ◆ *vi* [rɪ'kɔːd] grabar ◆ *adj* ['rekɔːd] récord

recording [rɪ'kɔːdɪŋ] *s* grabación

recount ◆ *s* ['riːkaʊnt] segundo recuento ◆ *vt* ❶[rɪ'kaʊnt] narrar ❷[ˌriː'kaʊnt] volver a contar

recover [rɪ'kʌvər] ◆ *vt* ❶recuperar ❷recobrar ◆ *vi* • **to recover (from)** recuperarse (de)

recovery [rɪ'kʌvərɪ] *s* recuperación

recreation [ˌrekrɪ'eɪʃn] *s* esparcimiento; recreo

recruit [rɪ'kruːt] ◆ *s* recluta ◆ *vt* ❶reclutar • **to recruit somebody (for something/to do something)** reclutar a alguien (para algo/para hacer algo) ❷contratar ◆ *vi* buscar empleados nuevos

recruitment [rɪ'kruːtmənt] *s* ❶reclutamiento ❷contratación

rectangle ['rek,tæŋgl] *s* rectángulo

rectangular [rek'tæŋgjʊlər] *adj* rectangular

rectify ['rektɪfaɪ] *vt* rectificar

recuperate [rɪ'kuːpəreɪt] ◆ *vt* recuperar ◆ *vi* • **to recuperate (from)** recuperarse (de)

recur [rɪ'kɜːr] *vi* repetirse

recurrence [rɪ'kʌrəns] *s* repetición

recurrent [rɪ'kʌrənt] *adj* que se repite

recycle [ˌriː'saɪkl] *vt* reciclar

red [red] ◆ *adj* rojo, ja

expresión **to go red** ponerse colorado, da ◆ *s* rojo

expresión **to be in the red** *familiar* estar en números rojos

red card *s*

expresión **to show somebody the red card** Futbol mostrarle a alguien (la) tarjeta roja

red carpet *s*

expresión **to roll out the red carpet for somebody** recibir a alguien con todos los honores

Red Cross *s* • **the Red Cross** la Cruz Roja

redeem [rɪ'diːm] *vt* ❶salvar; rescatar ❷ Religión redimir ❸*formal* desempeñar

redeeming [rɪ'diːmɪŋ] *adj* • **his only redeeming feature** lo único que le salva

red-haired [-'heəd] *adj* pelirrojo, ja

redhead ['redhed] *s* pelirrojo, ja

red-hot *adj* al rojo (vivo)

redid [ˌriː'dɪd] *pretérito* → **redo**

redirect [ˌriːdɪ'rekt] *vt* ❶redirigir ❷desviar ❸reexpedir

rediscover [ˌriːdɪs'kʌvər] *vt* ❶volver a descubrir ❷ • **to be rediscovered** ser descubierto, ta de nuevo

red light *s* semáforo rojo

redneck ['rednek] *s* ▶término despectivo para un sureño racista y reaccionario, de baja extracción social

redo [ˌriː'duː] *vt* ❶volver a hacer ❷ Informática rehacer

> Formas irregulares de **redo** *pretérito* **redid**, *pp* **redone**.

redouble [ˌriː'dʌbl] *vt* • **to redouble your efforts (to do something)** redoblar esfuerzos (para hacer algo)

redraft [ˌriː'drɑːft] *vt* volver a redactar

redress [rɪ'dres] *formal* ◆ *s* ⚇ *incontable* reparación ◆ *vt* • **to redress the balance (between)** equilibrar la balanza (entre)

red tape *s* *figurado* papeleo

reduce [rɪ'djuːs] ◆ *vt* reducir • **to be reduced to doing something** verse rebajado o forzado a hacer algo • **it reduced me to tears** me hizo llorar ◆ *vi* (intentar) adelgazar

reduction [rɪ'dʌkʃn] *s* ❶ • **reduction (in)** reducción (de) ❷ Comercio • **reduction (of)** descuento (de)

redundant [rɪ'dʌndənt] *adj* innecesario, ria; redundante

reef [riːf] *s* arrecife

reek [riːk] *vi* • **to reek (of)** apestar (a)

reel [riːl] ◆ *s* ❶carrete ❷rollo ◆ *vi* ❶tambalearse ❷ • **to reel from something** quedarse atónito, ta por algo

■ **reel in** *vt* ⚇ *El objeto se puede colocar antes o después de la preposición.* sacar enrollando el carrete (en pesca)

■ **reel off** *vt* ⚇ *El objeto se puede colocar antes o después de la preposición.* recitar al corrido

reenact [ˌriːɪn'ækt] *vt* representar de nuevo

ref [ref] *s* ❶ *familiar* Deporte (abreviatura de referee) árbitro ❷ Administración (abreviatura escrita de referees) ref.

refer [rɪ'fɜːr] *vt* ❶ • **to refer somebody to** a)enviar a alguien a b)remitir a alguien a ❷ • **to refer something to** remitir algo a

■ **refer to** *vt* ⚇ *El objeto siempre va después de la preposición al final.* ❶referirse a ❷consultar

referee [ˌrefə'riː] ◆ *s* Deporte árbitro ◆ *vt* & *vi* Deporte arbitrar

reference ['refrəns] *s* ❶ • **to make reference to** hacer referencia a • **with reference to** *formal* con referencia a ❷ ⚇ *incontable* • **reference (to)** consulta (a) ❸referencia; persona que proporciona referencias de alguien para un trabajo

referendum [,refə'rendəm] *s* referéndum
Dos plurales: **referendums** o **referenda** [,refə'rendə]

refill ◆ *s* ['ri:fɪl] ❶ recambio ❷ *familiar* • **would you like a refill?** ¿te apetece otra copa? ◆ *vt* [,ri:'fɪl] volver a llenar

refine [rɪ'faɪn] *vt* ❶ refinar ❷ pulir

refined [rɪ'faɪnd] *adj* ❶ refinado, da ❷ perfeccionado, da

refinement [rɪ'faɪnmənt] *s* ❶ • **refinement (on)** mejora (de) ❷ ⚙ *incontable* refinamiento

reflect [rɪ'flekt] ◆ *vt* ❶ reflejar ❷ • **to reflect that...** considerar que... ◆ *vi* • **to reflect (on** o **upon)** reflexionar (sobre)

reflection [rɪ'flekʃn] *s* ❶ reflejo ❷ • **reflection on** crítica de ❸ reflexión • **on reflection** pensándolo bien

reflector [rɪ'flektər] *s* reflector

reflex ['ri:fleks] *s* ▶ **reflex (action)** reflejo

reflexive [rɪ'fleksɪv] *adj* GRAMÁTICA reflexivo, va

reform [rɪ'fɔ:m] ◆ *s* reforma ◆ *vt* reformar ◆ *vi* reformarse

reformer [rɪ'fɔ:mər] *s* reformador, ra

refrain [rɪ'freɪn] *s* estribillo

refresh [rɪ'freʃ] *vt* refrescar • **to refresh somebody's memory** refrescarle la memoria a alguien

refreshed [rɪ'freʃt] *adj* descansado, da

refreshing [rɪ'freʃɪŋ] *adj* ❶ refrescante ❷ vigorizante

refreshments [rɪ'freʃmənts] *spl* refrigerio

refrigerator [rɪ'frɪdʒəreɪtər] *s* nevera ; refrigerador

refuel [,ri:'fjʊəl] ◆ *vt* llenar de carburante ◆ *vi* repostar
Formas irregulares de **refuel:** *pretérito & pp* **refueled,** *gerundio* **refueling.**

refuge ['refju:dʒ] *s* refugio • **to seek** o **take refuge (in)** *figurado* buscar refugio (en)

refugee [,refjʊ'dʒi:] *s* refugiado, da

refund ◆ *s* ['ri:fʌnd] reembolso ◆ *vt* [rɪ'fʌnd] • **to refund something to somebody, to refund somebody something** reembolsar algo a alguien

refurbish [,ri:'fɜ:bɪʃ] *vt* ❶ restaurar ❷ renovar

refusal [rɪ'fju:zl] *s* ❶ • **refusal (to do something)** negativa (a hacer algo) ❷ denegación ❸ • **to meet with refusal** ser rechazado, da

refuse[1] [rɪ'fju:z] *vt* ❶ • **to refuse somebody something, to refuse something to somebody** denegar a alguien algo ❷ rechazar ❸ • **to refuse to do something** negarse a hacer algo ◆ *vi* negarse

refuse[2] ['refju:s] *s* basura

refuse collection ['refju:s-] *s* recogida de basuras

refute [rɪ'fju:t] *vt formal* refutar

regain [rɪ'geɪn] *vt* ❶ recuperar ❷ recobrar

regal ['ri:gl] *adj* regio, gia

regard [rɪ'gɑ:d] ◆ *s* ❶ *formal* • **regard (for)** estima o respeto (por) • **to hold something/somebody in high regard** tener algo/a alguien en gran estima ❷ • **in this/that regard** a este/ese respecto ❸ • **with no regard for** sin ninguna consideración por ◆ *vt* ❶ • **to regard yourself as something** considerarse algo • **to be highly regarded** estar muy bien considerado ❷ • **to regard somebody/something with** ver a alguien/algo con
■ **regards** *spl* recuerdos • **give them my regards** salúdales de mi parte
■ **as regards** *preposición* en cuanto a ; por lo que se refiere a
■ **in regard to, with regard to** *preposición* respecto a ; en cuanto a

regarding [rɪ'gɑ:dɪŋ] *preposición* respecto a ; en cuanto a

regardless [rɪ'gɑ:dlɪs] *adv* a pesar de todo
■ **regardless of** *preposición* sin tener en cuenta • **regardless of the cost** cueste lo que cueste

regime [reɪ'ʒi:m] *s* régimen

regiment ['redʒɪmənt] *s* MILITAR regimiento

region ['ri:dʒən] *s* región • **in the region of** alrededor de

regional ['ri:dʒənl] *adj* regional

register ['redʒɪstər] ◆ *s* ❶ registro ❷ lista ◆ *vt* ❶ registrar; matricular ❷ mostrar; reflejar ◆ *vi* ❶ • **to register (as/for)** inscribirse (como/para) ❷ registrarse ; inscribirse ❸ *familiar* • **I told him but it didn't seem to register** se lo dije, pero no pareció que lo captara

registered ['redʒɪstəd] *adj* ❶ inscrito, ta oficialmente ❷ certificado, da

registered trademark *s* marca registrada

registrar ['redʒɪstrɑ:r] *s* ❶ registrador, ra oficial ❷ UNIVERSIDAD secretario, ria general ❸ médico, ca de hospital

registration [,redʒɪ'streɪʃn] *s* ❶ registro ❷ AUTOMÓVILES = **registration number**

registration number, registration *s* ❶ AUTOMÓVILES número de matrícula ❷ INFORMÁTICA número de registro

registry ['redʒɪstrɪ] *s* registro

regret [rɪ'gret] *s* ❶ *formal* pesar ❷ • **I've no regrets about it** no lo lamento en absoluto

regretfully [rɪ'gretfʊlɪ] *adv* con pesar • **regretfully, we have to announce...** lamentamos tener que anunciar...

regrettable [rɪ'gretəbl] *adj* lamentable

regular ['regjʊlər] ◆ *adj* ❶ regular ❷ habitual *(cliente)* ❸ acostumbrado, da *(lugar, hora)* ❹ usual ; normal *(problema)* ❺ normal ; mediano, na *(tamaño)* ◆ *s* cliente habitual

regularly ['regjʊləlɪ] *adv* ❶ con regularidad ❷ de manera uniforme

regulate ['regjʊleɪt] *vt* regular

regulation [,regjʊ'leɪʃn] *s* ❶ regla ; norma ❷ ⚙ *incontable* regulación

rehabilitate [,ri:ə'bɪlɪteɪt] *vt* rehabilitar

rehearsal [rɪˈhɜːsl] *s* ensayo

rehearse [rɪˈhɜːs] *vt* ensayar

reign [reɪn] *literal & figurado* ◆ *s* reinado ◆ *vi* • **to reign (over)** reinar (sobre)

reimburse [ˌriːɪmˈbɜːs] *vt* • **to reimburse somebody (for something)** reembolsar a alguien (algo)

rein [reɪn] *s*

expresión to keep a tight rein on somebody/something *figurado* tener muy controlado, da a alguien/algo

■ **reins** *spl* riendas

reindeer [ˈreɪnˌdɪər] *s* reno

El plural de **reindeer** es **reindeer**.

reinforce [ˌriːɪnˈfɔːs] *vt* reforzar

reinforcement [ˌriːɪnˈfɔːsmənt] *s* refuerzo

■ **reinforcements** *spl* refuerzos

re-install *vt* reinstalar

reinstate [ˌriːɪnˈsteɪt] *vt* ❶ restituir o reintegrar en su puesto a ❷ restablecer

reissue [riːˈɪʃuː] *vt* ❶ reeditar ❷ reestrenar

reject ◆ *s* [ˈriːdʒekt] • **rejects** artículos defectuosos ◆ *vt* [rɪˈdʒekt] rechazar

rejection [rɪˈdʒekʃn] *s* rechazo

rejoice [rɪˈdʒɔɪs] *vi* • **to rejoice (at** o **in)** alegrarse o regocijarse (con)

rejuvenate [rɪˈdʒuːvəneɪt] *vt* rejuvenecer

relapse [rɪˈlæps] ◆ *s* recaída ◆ *vi* • **to relapse into** volver a caer en

relate [rɪˈleɪt] ◆ *vt* ❶ • **to relate something (to)** relacionar algo (con) ❷ contar; relatar ◆ *vi* ❶ • **to relate to** estar relacionado, da con ❷ • **to relate to** referirse a ❸ • **to relate (to somebody)** tener mucho en común (con alguien)

■ **relating to** *preposición* concerniente o referente a

related [rɪˈleɪtɪd] *adj* ❶ emparentado, da • **to be related to somebody** ser pariente de alguien ❷ relacionado, da

relation [rɪˈleɪʃn] *s* ❶ • **relation (to/between)** relación (con/entre) • **to bear no relation to** no tener nada que ver con ❷ pariente; familiar

■ **relations** *spl* relaciones

relationship [rɪˈleɪʃnʃɪp] *s* ❶ relación ❷ parentesco

relative [ˈrelətɪv] ◆ *adj* relativo, va ◆ *s* pariente; familiar

■ **relative to** *preposición formal* con relación a

relatively [ˈrelətɪvlɪ] *adv* relativamente

relax [rɪˈlæks] ◆ *vt* ❶ relajar ❷ aflojar ◆ *vi* ❶ relajarse • **relax, everything will be fine** tranquilo, todo va a estar bien ❷ aflojarse

relaxation [ˌriːlækˈseɪʃn] *s* ❶ relajación; esparcimiento ❷ relajación *(de disciplina)*

relaxed [rɪˈlækst] *adj* relajado, da

relaxing [rɪˈlæksɪŋ] *adj* relajante

relay [ˈriːleɪ] ◆ *s* DEPORTE ❱ **relay (race)** carrera de relevos ◆ *vt* *(pretérito & pp* relayed*)* retransmitir

release [rɪˈliːs] ◆ *s* ❶ puesta en libertad; liberación ❷ comunicado ❸ escape *(de gas)*; emisión *(de calor, presión)* ❹ estreno *(de película)*; publicación *(de disco)* • **a new release** una nueva película; un nuevo disco ◆ *vt* ❶ • **to release somebody from** liberar a alguien de ❷ entregar *(fondos, recursos)* ❸ soltar ❹ aflojar ❺ disparar ❻ despedir *(gas, calor)* ❼ estrenar *(película)*; sacar *(disco)*

relegate [ˈrelɪɡeɪt] *vt* • **to relegate something/somebody (to)** relegar algo/a alguien (a)

relentless [rɪˈlentlɪs] *adj* implacable

relevant [ˈreləvənt] *adj* ❶ • **relevant (to)** pertinente (a) ❷ • **relevant (to)** importante o relevante (para) ❸ oportuno, na

reliable [rɪˈlaɪəbl] *adj* ❶ fiable • **he's very reliable** es muy cumplidor ❷ fidedigno, na

reliably [rɪˈlaɪəblɪ] *adv* ❶ sin fallar ❷ • **to be reliably informed about something** saber algo de fuentes fidedignas

reliant [rɪˈlaɪənt] *adj* • **to be reliant on somebody/something** depender de alguien/de algo

relic [ˈrelɪk] *s* ❶ reliquia ❷ vestigio

relief [rɪˈliːf] *s* ❶ alivio ❷ ayuda ❸ ☀ *incontable* subsidio

relieve [rɪˈliːv] *vt* ❶ aliviar ❷ • **to relieve somebody of something** liberar a alguien de algo

religion [rɪˈlɪdʒn] *s* religión

religious [rɪˈlɪdʒəs] *adj* religioso, sa

relinquish [rɪˈlɪŋkwɪʃ] *vt* renunciar a

relish [ˈrelɪʃ] ◆ *s* ❶ • **with (great) relish** con (gran) deleite ❷ salsa rojiza agridulce con pepinillo etc ◆ *vt* disfrutar con

relocate [ˌriːləʊˈkeɪt] ◆ *vt* trasladar ◆ *vi* trasladarse

reluctance [rɪˈlʌktəns] *s* reticencia

reluctant [rɪˈlʌktənt] *adj* reacio, cia • **to be reluctant to do something** estar poco dispuesto a hacer algo

reluctantly [rɪˈlʌktəntlɪ] *adv* con desgana; de mala gana

rely [rɪˈlaɪ] ■ **rely on** *vt* ☀ *El objeto siempre va después de la preposición al final.* ❶ contar con • **to be able to rely on somebody/something to do something** poder estar seguro de que alguien/algo hará algo • **it's a car you can rely on** es un coche en el que se puede confiar ❷ • **to rely on somebody/something for something** depender de alguien/algo para algo

remain [rɪˈmeɪn] ◆ *vt* continuar como • **to remain the same** continuar siendo igual ◆ *vi* ❶ quedarse; permanecer ❷ quedar; continuar

■ **remains** *spl* restos

remainder [rɪˈmeɪndər] *s* ❶ • **the remainder** el resto ❷ MATEMÁTICAS resto

remaining [rɪˈmeɪnɪŋ] *adj* restante

remand [rɪˈmɑːnd] ◆ *s* DERECHO • **on remand** detenido, da en espera de juicio ◆ *vt* DERECHO • **to be remanded in custody** estar bajo custodia

R

remark[rɪˈmɑːk] ◆ *s* comentario ◆ *vt* • **to remark (that)** comentar que

remarkable[rɪˈmɑːkəbl] *adj* ❶ extraordinario, ria ❷ sorprendente

remarry[ˌriːˈmærɪ] *vi* volver a casarse

remedial [rɪˈmiːdjəl] *adj* ❶ de refuerzo *(clase, profesor)* ❷ atrasado, da *(alumno)* ❸ correctivo, va

remedy [ˈremədɪ] ◆ *s literal & figurado* • **remedy (for)** remedio (para) ◆ *vt* remediar

remember [rɪˈmembər] ◆ *vt* recordar ; acordarse de • **to remember to do something** acordarse de hacer algo • **to remember doing something** recordar o acordarse de haber hecho algo ◆ *vi* recordar ; acordarse • **she reminds me of my sister** me recuerda a mi hermana

remembrance[rɪˈmembrəns] *s formal* • **in remembrance of** en conmemoración de

remind[rɪˈmaɪnd] *vt* • **to remind somebody (about something/to do something)** recordar a alguien (algo/que haga algo) • **she reminds me of my sister** me recuerda a mi hermana

reminder[rɪˈmaɪndər] *s* ❶ recordatorio ; recuerdo ❷ notificación ; aviso

reminisce[ˌremɪˈnɪs] *vi* • **to reminisce (about something)** rememorar (algo)

reminiscent[ˌremɪˈnɪsnt] *adj* • **to be reminiscent of** evocar ; recordar a

remnant [ˈremnənt] *s* ❶ resto ❷ retal

remorse [rɪˈmɔːs] *s* ⚲ *incontable* remordimientos

remorseful [rɪˈmɔːsfʊl] *adj* lleno, na de remordimientos

remorseless [rɪˈmɔːslɪs] *adj* ❶ despiadado, da ❷ implacable

remote [rɪˈməʊt] *adj* ❶ remoto, ta ❷ • **remote (from)** apartado, da o alejado, da (de)

remote control *s* control (remoto)

remotely[rɪˈməʊtlɪ] *adv* ❶ • **not remotely** ni remotamente ; en lo más mínimo ❷ muy lejos

removable [rɪˈmuːvəbl] *adj* ❶ separable ❷ extraíble *(disco duro)*

removal [rɪˈmuːvl] *s* ❶ ⚲ *incontable* separación ; extracción ❷ supresión *(de cláusula, amenaza)*

remove [rɪˈmuːv] *vt* ❶ • **to remove something (from)** quitar algo (de) ❷ quitarse *(ropa, zapatos)* ❸ • **to remove somebody (from)** destituir a alguien (de) ❹ eliminar

remuneration [rɪˌmjuːnəˈreɪʃn] *s formal* remuneración

render[ˈrendər] *vt* ❶ • **to render somebody speechless** dejar a alguien boquiabierto ❷ prestar *(ayuda, servicio)*

rendezvous [ˈrɒndɪvuː] *s* cita

El plural de **rendezvous** es **rendezvous**.

renew [rɪˈnjuː] *vt* ❶ reemprender *(intento, ataque)* ❷ reanudar *(relación)* ❸ renovar *(pasaporte, licencia)* ❹ reavivar *(interés)*

renewable [rɪˈnjuːəbl] *adj* renovable

renewal [rɪˈnjuːəl] *s* ❶ reanudación ❷ renovación

renounce [rɪˈnaʊns] *vt* renunciar a

renovate [ˈrenəveɪt] *vt* reformar ; renovar

renowned [rɪˈnaʊnd] *adj* • **renowned (for)** célebre (por)

rent [rent] ◆ *s* alquiler • **for rent** se alquila ; se renta ◆ *vt* alquilar ; rentar ◆ *vi* alquilarse • **this apartment rents for $300 a month** este departamento se alquila por 300 dólares al mes

rental [ˈrentl] ◆ *adj* de alquiler ◆ *s* alquiler

reorganize [ˌriːˈɔːgənaɪz] *vt* reorganizar

rep [rep] *s abreviatura escrita de* **representative**

Rep. ❶ *(abreviatura de* Representative) = **representative** ❷ *abreviatura escrita de* **Republican**

repaid [riːˈpeɪd] *pretérito & participio pasado* → **repay**

repair[rɪˈpeər] ◆ *s* reparación ; refacción ◆ *vt* reparar ; refaccionar

repatriate [ˌriːˈpætrɪeɪt] *vt* repatriar

repay[riːˈpeɪ] *vt* ❶ devolver *(dinero)* ❷ pagar *(deuda, persona)* ❸ devolver el favor a

Formas irregulares de **repay**: *pret & pp* **repaid**.

repayment [riːˈpeɪmənt] *s* ❶ devolución ❷ pago

repeal [rɪˈpiːl] ◆ *s* revocación ; abrogación ◆ *vt* revocar ; abrogar

repeat[rɪˈpiːt] ◆ *vt* ❶ repetir ❷ volver a emitir *(programa)* ◆ *s* ❶ repetición ❷ reposición *(de programa)*

repeatedly [rɪˈpiːtɪdlɪ] *adv* repetidamente

repel [rɪˈpel] *vt* repeler

repellent [rɪˈpelənt] ◆ *adj* repelente ◆ *s* espray antiinsectos

repent [rɪˈpent] ◆ *vt* arrepentirse de ◆ *vi* arrepentirse

repercussions [ˌriːpəˈkʌʃnz] *spl* repercusiones

repertoire [ˈrepətwɑːr] *s* repertorio

repetition [ˌrepɪˈtɪʃn] *s* repetición

repetitious [ˌrepɪˈtɪʃəs], **repetitive** [rɪˈpetɪtɪv] *adj* repetitivo, va

replace [rɪˈpleɪs] *vt* ❶ sustituir ❷ • **to replace something (with)** cambiar algo (por) ❸ • **to replace somebody (with)** sustituir a alguien (por) ❹ • **they replaced it** me dieron otro ❺ poner en su sitio • **replace the book on the shelf** vuelve a poner el libro en la repisa

replacement[rɪˈpleɪsmənt] *s* ❶ sustitución ❷ • **replacement (for)** sustituto, ta (para) ❸ • **replacement (for)** sustituto, ta o suplente (de) ❹ • **they gave me a replacement** me dieron otro

replay ◆ *s* [ˈriːpleɪ] repetición ◆ *vt* [ˌriːˈpleɪ] volver a poner *(película, disco)*

replenish [rɪˈplenɪʃ] *vt* • **to replenish something (with)** reaprovisionar o reponer algo (de)

replica [ˈreplɪkə] *s* réplica

reply [rɪ'plaɪ] ◆ *s* • **reply (to)** respuesta (a) ◆ *vt* responder; contestar ◆ *vi* • **to reply (to somebody/ something)** responder (a alguien/algo)

report [rɪ'pɔːt] ◆ *s* ❶ informe ❷ reportaje ❸ información *(en televisión, radio)* ◆ *vt* ❶ • **to report that** informar que; reportar que • **to report something (to)** informar de algo (a); reportar algo (a) ❷ anunciar *(pérdidas)* ❸ denunciar • **to report somebody (to somebody for something)** denunciar a alguien (a alguien por algo); reportar a alguien (a alguien por algo) ❹ dar parte de ◆ *vi* ❶ • **to report on** informar sobre ❷ • **please report to my office** por favor, preséntese en mi oficina

report card *s* boletín de evaluación; boletín de calificaciones

reportedly [rɪ'pɔːtɪdlɪ] *adv* según se afirma

reporter [rɪ'pɔːtər] *s* reportero, ra

repossess [ˌriːpə'zes] *vt* requisar la posesión de

represent [ˌreprɪ'zent] *vt* ❶ representar ❷ representar a

expresión to be well o strongly represented estar bien representado, da

representation [ˌreprɪzen'teɪʃn] *s* representación

representative [ˌreprɪ'zentətɪv] ◆ *adj* • **representative (of)** representativo, va (de) ◆ *s* representante

repress [rɪ'pres] *vt* reprimir

repression [rɪ'preʃn] *s* represión

reprieve [rɪ'priːv] *s* ❶ tregua ❷ indulto

reprimand ['reprɪmɑːnd] ◆ *s* reprensión ◆ *vt* reprender

reprisal [rɪ'praɪzl] *s* represalia

reproach [rɪ'prəʊtʃ] ◆ *s* reproche ◆ *vt* • **to reproach somebody (for** o **with something)** reprochar a alguien (algo)

reproachful [rɪ'prəʊtʃfʊl] *adj* de reproche

reproduce [ˌriːprə'djuːs] ◆ *vt* reproducir ◆ *vi* BIOLOGÍA reproducirse

reproduction [ˌriːprə'dʌkʃn] *s* reproducción

reptile ['reptaɪl] *s* reptil

Repub. *abreviatura escrita de* **Republican**

republic [rɪ'pʌblɪk] *s* república

republican [rɪ'pʌblɪkən] ◆ *adj* republicano, na ◆ *s* republicano, na

■ **Republican** ◆ *adj* republicano, na ▶ **the Republican Party** el partido republicano ◆ *s* republicano, na

repulsive [rɪ'pʌlsɪv] *adj* repulsivo, va

reputable ['repjʊtəbl] *adj* de buena fama o reputación

reputation [ˌrepjʊ'teɪʃn] *s* reputación • **to have a reputation for something/for being something** tener fama de algo/de ser algo

repute [rɪ'pjuːt] *s formal* • **of good/ill repute** de buena/mala fama

reputed [rɪ'pjuːtɪd] *adj* supuesto, ta • **to be reputed to be/do something** tener fama de ser/hacer algo

reputedly [rɪ'pjuːtɪdlɪ] *adv* según se dice

request [rɪ'kwest] ◆ *s* • **request (for)** petición (de) • **on request** a petición del interesado • **at somebody's request** a petición de alguien ◆ *vt* solicitar; pedir • **to request somebody to do something** rogar a alguien que haga algo

require [rɪ'kwaɪər] *vt* ❶ necesitar; requerir ❷ requerir • **to require somebody to do something** exigir a alguien que haga algo

requirement [rɪ'kwaɪəmənt] *s* requisito

rerun *s* ['riːˌrʌn] ❶ reposición *(de programa, película)* ❷ repetición

rescind [rɪ'sɪnd] *vt* ❶ DERECHO rescindir ❷ revocar

rescue ['reskjuː] ◆ *s* rescate • **to go** o **come to somebody's rescue** ir o acudir al rescate de alguien ◆ *vt* • **to rescue somebody/something (from)** rescatar a alguien/algo (de)

rescuer ['reskjʊər] *s* rescatador, ra

research [ˌrɪ'sɜːtʃ] ◆ *s* 💡 *incontable* • **research (on** o **into)** investigación (de o sobre) ▶ **research and development** investigación y desarrollo ◆ *vt* investigar

researcher [rɪ'sɜːtʃər] *s* investigador, ra

resemblance [rɪ'zembləns] *s* parecido; semejanza

resemble [rɪ'zembl] *vt* parecerse a

resent [rɪ'zent] *vt* • **to resent somebody** tener celos de alguien • **I resent the fact that...** me sienta mal que...

resentful [rɪ'zentfʊl] *adj* ❶ resentido, da ❷ de resentimiento *(mirada)*

resentment [rɪ'zentmənt] *s* resentimiento

reservation [ˌrezə'veɪʃn] *s* ❶ reserva ❷ • **without reservation** sin reserva

■ **reservations** *spl* reservas

reserve [rɪ'zɜːv] ◆ *s* ❶ reserva • **in reserve** en reserva ❷ DEPORTE suplente ◆ *vt* ❶ reservar ❷ • **to reserve the right to do something** reservarse el derecho a hacer algo

reserved [rɪ'zɜːvd] *adj* reservado, da

reservoir ['rezəvwɑːr] *s* pantano; embalse

reset [ˌriː'set] *vt* ❶ poner en hora ❷ reinicializar

Formas irregulares de **reset**: *pretérito & pp* **reset**.

reside [rɪ'zaɪd] *vi formal* residir

residence ['rezɪdəns] *s* ❶ *formal* residencia ❷ • **to be in residence (at)** residir (a)

residence permit *s* permiso de residencia

resident ['rezɪdənt] ◆ *adj* residente ◆ *s* residente

residential [ˌrezɪ'denʃl] *adj* en régimen de internado

residential area *s* zona residencial

residue ['rezɪdjuː] *s* residuo

resign [rɪ'zaɪn] ◆ *vt* ❶ dimitir de; renunciar a ❷ • **to resign yourself to something** resignarse a algo ◆ *vi* • **to resign (from)** dimitir (de)

R

resignation [ˌrezɪgˈneɪʃn] *s* ❶ dimisión ❷ resignación

resigned [rɪˈzaɪnd] *adj* • **resigned (to)** resignado, da (a)

resilient [rɪˈzɪlɪənt] *adj* resistente; fuerte

resin [ˈrezɪn] *s* resina

resist [rɪˈzɪst] *vt* ❶ resistir *(tentación)* ❷ oponerse a *(rechazar)* ❸ resistir a *(luchar contra)*

resistance [rɪˈzɪstəns] *s* • **resistance (to)** resistencia (a)

resolute [ˈrezəluːt] *adj* resuelto, ta; determinado, da

resolution [ˌrezəˈluːʃn] *s* ❶ resolución ❷ propósito

resolve [rɪˈzɒlv] ◆ *s* ☼ *incontable* resolución ◆ *vt* ❶ • **to resolve that** resolver que • **to resolve to do something** resolver hacer algo ❷ resolver *(problema)*

resort [rɪˈzɔːt] *s* lugar de vacaciones

expresión **as a** o **in the last resort** como último recurso

■ **resort to** *vt* ☼ *El objeto siempre va después de la preposición al final.* recurrir a

resound [rɪˈzaʊnd] *vi* resonar • **the room resounded with laughter** la risa resonaba por la habitación

resounding [rɪˈzaʊndɪŋ] *adj* ❶ retumbante; estruendoso, sa ❷ clamoroso, sa

resource [rɪˈsɔːs] *s* recurso

resourceful [rɪˈsɔːsfʊl] *adj* ❶ de recursos *(persona)* ❷ ingenioso, sa *(solución)*

respect [rɪˈspekt] ◆ *s* ❶ • **respect (for)** respeto (por) • **with respect** con respeto ❷ aspecto • **in this respect** a este respecto • **in that respect** en cuanto a eso ◆ *vt* respetar • **to respect somebody for something** respetar a alguien por algo

■ **respects** *spl*

expresión **to pay your respects (to)** presentar sus respetos (a)

■ **with respect to** *preposición* con respecto a

respectable [rɪˈspektəbl] *adj* respetable

respectful [rɪˈspektfʊl] *adj* respetuoso, sa

respective [rɪˈspektɪv] *adj* respectivo, va

respectively [rɪˈspektɪvlɪ] *adv* respectivamente

respiratory [ˈrespərətɒːrɪ] *adj* respiratorio, ria

respite [ˈrespaɪt] *s* ❶ respiro ❷ aplazamiento

respond [rɪˈspɒnd] *vi* • **to respond (to)** responder (a)

response [rɪˈspɒns] *s* respuesta

responsibility [rɪˌspɒnsəˈbɪlətɪ] *s* • **responsibility (for)** responsabilidad (de) • **to claim responsibility for something** reivindicar algo

responsible [rɪˈspɒnsəbl] *adj* ❶ responsable • **responsible (for)** responsable (de) ❷ • **responsible to somebody** responsable ante alguien ❸ de responsabilidad *(puesto, cargo)*

responsibly [rɪˈspɒnsəblɪ] *adv* de manera responsable

responsive [rɪˈspɒnsɪv] *adj* ❶ • **to be responsive** responder muy bien ❷ • **responsive (to)** sensible o perceptivo, va (a)

rest [rest] ◆ *s* ❶ • **the rest (of)** el resto (de) • **the rest of us** los demás ❷ descanso • **to have a rest** descansar ❸ respaldo *(para la cabeza)* ◆ *vt* ❶ descansar ❷ apoyar ◆ *vi* ❶ descansar ❷ apoyarse

expresión **rest assured that...** tenga la seguridad de que...

restaurant [ˈrestərɒnt] *s* restaurante

rest home *s* ❶ asilo de ancianos ❷ casa de reposo

restless [ˈrestlɪs] *adj* ❶ impaciente; desasosegado, da ❷ inquieto, ta; agitado, da

restoration [ˌrestəˈreɪʃn] *s* restauración

restore [rɪˈstɔːr] *vt* ❶ restablecer ❷ restaurar ❸ • **to restore somebody to something** restaurar a alguien en algo • **to restore something to something** volver a poner algo en algo ❹ devolver

restrain [rɪˈstreɪn] *vt* controlar • **to restrain yourself from doing something** contenerse para no hacer algo

restrained [rɪˈstreɪnd] *adj* comedido, da

restraint [rɪˈstreɪnt] *s* ❶ restricción ❷ control

restrict [rɪˈstrɪkt] *vt* restringir; limitar • **to restrict yourself to something** limitarse a algo

restriction [rɪˈstrɪkʃn] *s* restricción

restrictive [rɪˈstrɪktɪv] *adj* restrictivo, va

rest room *s* aseos

result [rɪˈzʌlt] ◆ *s* resultado • **as a result** como resultado ◆ *vi* ❶ • **to result (in something)** tener como resultado (algo) ❷ • **to result (from)** resultar (de)

resume [rɪˈzjuːm] ◆ *vt* reanudar ◆ *vi* volver a empezar

résumé [ˈrezjuːmeɪ] *s* ❶ resumen ❷ currículum (vitae)

resumption [rɪˈzʌmpʃn] *s* reanudación

resurgence [rɪˈsɜːdʒəns] *s* resurgimiento

resurrection [ˌrezəˈrekʃn] *s* resurrección

resuscitate [rɪˈsʌsɪteɪt] *vt* resucitar

retail [ˈriːteɪl] ◆ *s* venta al por menor ◆ *vt* vender al por menor ◆ *vi* • **to retail for** tener un precio de venta al público de ◆ *adv* al por menor

retailer [ˈriːteɪlər] *s* minorista; detallista

retail price *s* precio de venta al público

retain [rɪˈteɪn] *vt* retener

retaliate [rɪˈtælɪeɪt] *vi* ❶ responder ❷ tomar represalias

retaliation [rɪˌtælɪˈeɪʃn] *s* ☼ *incontable* represalias

retarded [rɪˈtɑːdɪd] *adj* retrasado, da

retch [retʃ] *vi* tener arcadas

reticent [ˈretɪsənt] *adj* reservado, da

retina [ˈretɪnə] *s* retina

Dos plurales: **retinas** o **retinae** [ˈretɪniː].

retire [rɪ'taɪər] *vi* ❶ jubilarse ❷ *formal* retirarse

retired [rɪ'taɪəd] *adj* jubilado, da

retirement [rɪ'taɪəmənt] *s* ❶ jubilación ❷ retiro

retiring [rɪ'taɪərɪŋ] *adj* retraído, da

retort [rɪ'tɔ:t] ◆ *s* réplica ◆ *vt* • **to retort (that)** replicar (que)

retrace [rɪ'treɪs] *vt* • **to retrace your steps** desandar lo andado

retract [rɪ'trækt] ◆ *vt* ❶ retractarse de ❷ retraer *(garras)* ◆ *vi* ❶ meterse; retraerse *(garras)* ❷ replegarse *(ruedas)*

retrain [ˌri:'treɪn] *vt* reciclar *(trabajador)*

retraining [ˌri:'treɪnɪŋ] *s* reciclaje *(de trabajador)*

retreat [rɪ'tri:t] ◆ *s* ❶ MILITAR • **retreat (from)** retirada (de) ❷ refugio ◆ *vi* • **to retreat (from) a)** retirarse (de) **b)** apartarse (de)

retribution [ˌretrɪ'bju:ʃn] *s* 🔅 *incontable* castigo merecido

retrieval [rɪ'tri:vl] *s* recuperación

retrieve [rɪ'tri:v] *vt* ❶ recobrar ❷ INFORMÁTICA recuperar

retriever [rɪ'tri:vər] *s* perro cobrador

retrospect ['retrəspekt] *s* • **in retrospect** retrospectivamente; mirando hacia atrás

retrospective [ˌretrə'spektɪv] *adj* ❶ retrospectivo, va ❷ con efecto retroactivo

return [rɪ'tɜ:n] ◆ *s* ❶ 🔅 *incontable* vuelta; regreso ❷ ganancia; rendimiento ◆ *vt* ❶ devolver ❷ corresponder a *(cumplido)* ❸ devolver a su sitio ◆ *vi* • **to return (from/to)** volver (de/a)

■ **returns** *spl* COMERCIO réditos

expresión **many happy returns (of the day)!** ¡feliz cumpleaños!

■ **in return** *adv* a cambio

■ **in return for** *preposición* a cambio de

return (key) *s* INFORMÁTICA tecla de retorno

reunion [ˌri:'ju:njən] *s* reunión

reunite [ˌri:ju:'naɪt] *vt* • **to be reunited with** volver a encontrarse con

rev [rev] *familiar* ◆ *s* *(abreviatura de* revolution) revolución (motriz) ◆ *vt* • **to rev something (up)** acelerar algo ◆ *vi* • **to rev (up)** acelerar el motor

revamp [ˌri:'væmp] *vt* *familiar* renovar

reveal [rɪ'vi:l] *vt* revelar

revealing [rɪ'vi:lɪŋ] *adj* ❶ revelador, ra ❷ atrevido, da *(prenda)*

revel ['revl] *vi* • **to revel in** deleitarse en

revelation [ˌrevə'leɪʃn] *s* revelación

revenge [rɪ'vendʒ] *s* venganza • **to get revenge** vengarse • **to take revenge (on somebody)** vengarse (de alguien)

revenue ['revənju:] *s* ingresos

reverberate [rɪ'vɜ:bəreɪt] *vi* resonar

reverberations [rɪˌvɜ:bə'reɪʃnz] *spl* reverberaciones

revere [rɪ'vɪər] *vt* venerar

reverence ['revərəns] *s* reverencia

Reverend ['revərənd] *s* reverendo

reversal [rɪ'vɜ:sl] *s* ❶ cambio total ❷ contratiempo

reverse [rɪ'vɜ:s] ◆ *adj* inverso, sa ◆ *s* ❶ AUTOMÓVILES ▶ **reverse (gear)** marcha atrás ❷ • **the reverse** lo contrario ❸ • **the reverse a)** el revés **b)** el reverso *(de moneda)* **c)** el dorso *(de hoja de papel)* ◆ *vt* ❶ AUTOMÓVILES dar marcha atrás a ❷ invertir ❸ cambiar completamente ◆ *vi* AUTOMÓVILES dar marcha atrás

revert [rɪ'vɜ:t] *vi* • **to revert to** volver a

review [rɪ'vju:] ◆ *s* ❶ revisión ❷ reseña ◆ *vt* ❶ revisar ❷ reconsiderar ❸ reseñar ❹ repasar

reviewer [rɪ'vju:ər] *s* crítico, ca

revise [rɪ'vaɪz] *vt* ❶ revisar ❷ modificar; corregir

revision [rɪ'vɪʒn] *s* corrección; modificación

revitalize [ˌri:'vaɪtəlaɪz] *vt* revivificar

revival [rɪ'vaɪvl] *s* ❶ resucitación ❷ reactivación *(de economía)* ❸ reposición *(de obra de teatro)*

revive [rɪ'vaɪv] ◆ *vt* ❶ resucitar ❷ reactivar *(economía)* ❸ restablecer *(tradición, memorias)* ❹ reponer *(obra de teatro)* ◆ *vi* reponerse

revolt [rɪ'vəʊlt] ◆ *s* rebelión ◆ *vt* repugnar ◆ *vi* • **to revolt (against)** rebelarse o sublevarse (contra)

revolting [rɪ'vəʊltɪŋ] *adj* repugnante; asqueroso, sa

revolution [ˌrevə'lu:ʃn] *s* revolución

revolutionary [revə'lu:ʃnərɪ] ◆ *adj* revolucionario, ria ◆ *s* revolucionario, ria

revolve [rɪ'vɒlv] *vi* girar • **to revolve around** o **round** *literal & figurado* girar en torno a

revolver [rɪ'vɒlvər] *s* revólver

revolving door *s* puerta giratoria

revue [rɪ'vju:] *s* revista (teatral)

revulsion [rɪ'vʌlʃn] *s* asco; repugnancia

reward [rɪ'wɔ:d] ◆ *s* recompensa ◆ *vt* • **to reward somebody (for/with)** recompensar a alguien (por/con)

rewarding [rɪ'wɔ:dɪŋ] *adj* gratificador, ra

rewind [ˌri:'waɪnd] *vt* rebobinar

Formas irregulares de **rewind** *pret* & *pp* **rewound**

rewire [ˌri:'waɪər] *vt* cambiar la instalación eléctrica de

reword [ˌri:'wɜ:d] *vt* expresar de otra forma

rewound [ˌri:'waʊnd] *pretérito* & *participio pasado* → **rewind**

rewritable [ˌri:'raɪtəbl] *adj* INFORMÁTICA regrabable

rewrite [ˌri:'raɪt] *vt* volver a escribir

Formas irregulares de **rewrite**: *pretérito* **rewrote** [ˌri:'rəʊt], *pp* **rewritten** [ˌri:'rɪtn].

rhetoric ['retərɪk] *s* retórica

rhetorical question [rɪ'tɒrɪkl-] *s* pregunta retórica *(a la que no se espera contestación)*

R

rheumatism ['ruːmətɪzm] *s* reumatismo

Rhine [rain] *s* • **the Rhine** el Rin

rhino ['raɪnəʊ], **rhinoceros** [raɪ'nɒsərəs] *s* rinoceronte

Dos plurales: **rhino** o **rhinos; rhinoceros** o **rhinoceroses.**

rhododendron [,rəʊdə'dendrən] *s* rododendro

rhubarb ['ruːbɑːb] *s* ruibarbo

rhyme [raɪm] ◆ *s* ❶ rima ❷ poesía; versos ◆ *vi* • **to rhyme (with)** rimar (con)

rhythm ['rɪðm] *s* ritmo

rib [rɪb] *s* ANATOMÍA costilla

ribbed [rɪbd] *adj* de canalé

ribbon ['rɪbən] *s* cinta

rice [raɪs] *s* arroz

rice pudding *s* arroz con leche

rich [rɪtʃ] ◆ *adj* ❶ rico, ca ❷ • **to be rich in** abundar en ❸ fértil ❹ pesado, da *(comida)* ◆ *spl* • **the rich** los ricos

■ **riches** *spl* ❶ riquezas ❷ riqueza

richly ['rɪtʃlɪ] *adv* copiosamente • **richly rewarded** generosamente compensado • **richly deserved** muy merecido

richness ['rɪtʃnɪs] *s* ❶ riqueza ❷ fertilidad *(de tierra)* ❸ pesadez *(de comida)*

rickety ['rɪkətɪ] *adj* desvencijado, da

ricochet ['rɪkəʃeɪ] ◆ *s* rebote ◆ *vi* • **to ricochet (off)** rebotar (de)

Formas irregulares de **ricochet:** *pretérito* **ricocheted** o **ricochetted,** *gerundio* **ricocheting** o **ricochetting.**

rid [rɪd] *vt* • **to get rid of** deshacerse de

Formas irregulares de **rid:** *pretérito* **rid** o **ridded,** *pp* **rid,** *gerundio* **ridding.**

ridden ['rɪdn] *participio pasado* → **ride**

riddle ['rɪdl] *s* ❶ acertijo ❷ enigma

riddled ['rɪdld] *adj* • **to be riddled with mistakes** estar plagado, da de errores

ride [raɪd] ◆ *s* ❶ paseo • **it's a short car ride away** está a poca distancia en coche **b)** darse un paseo a caballo **b)** darse un paseo en bicicleta **c)** darse una vuelta en coche • **to give somebody a ride** llevar a alguien ❷ viaje ❸ atracción

expresión **to take somebody for a ride** *familiar* embaucar a alguien

◆ *vt* ❶ montar a *(caballo)* ❷ montar en *(bici, moto)* • **he rode his bike to the station** fue a la estación en bici ❸ ir en *(colectivo, tren)* ❹ subir/bajar en *(ascensor)* ❺ recorrer ◆ *vi* ❶ montar a caballo • **she rode over to see me** vino a verme a caballo ❷ ir en bici ❸ ir en moto ❹ • **we rode to San Francisco in a jeep** fuimos a San Francisco en jeep

Formas irregulares de **ride:** *pretérito* **rode,** *pp* **ridden.**

rider ['raɪdər] *s* ❶ jinete, amazona ❷ ciclista ❸ motorista

ridge [rɪdʒ] *s* ❶ cresta ❷ rugosidad

ridicule ['rɪdɪkjuːl] ◆ *s* ☼ *incontable* burlas ◆ *vt* burlarse de

ridiculous [rɪ'dɪkjʊləs] *adj* ridículo, la

riding ['raɪdɪŋ] *s* equitación • **to go riding** ir a montar a caballo

riding school *s* escuela de equitación

rifle ['raɪfl] *s* fusil; rifle

rift [rɪft] *s* ❶ GEOLOGÍA hendidura; grieta ❷ desavenencia ❸ POLÍTICA • **rift between/in** escisión entre/en

rig [rɪg] ◆ *s* ❶ ▶ **(oil) rig a)** torre de perforación **b)** plataforma petrolífera ❷ camión ◆ *vt* amañar; falsificar

rigging ['rɪgɪŋ] *s* cordaje

right [raɪt] ◆ *adj* ❶ correcto, ta • **to be right (about)** tener razón (respecto a) • **that's right** sí; así es • **to get something right** acertar en algo ❷ bien • **to be right to do something** hacer bien en hacer algo • **something isn't right with it** le pasa algo ❸ apropiado, da, • **it's just right** es perfecto • **the right moment** el momento oportuno ❹ derecho, cha ◆ *s* ❶ ☼ *incontable* el bien • **to be in the right** tener razón ❷ derecho • **by rights** en justicia ❸ derecha • **on the right** a la derecha ◆ *adv* ❶ bien; correctamente ❷ a la derecha ❸ • **right here** aquí mismo • **right at the top** arriba del todo • **right in the middle** justo en el medio • **she crashed right into the tree** chocó de frente contra el árbol ❹ completamente ❺ • **I'll be right back** ahora mismo vuelvo • **right before/after (something)** justo antes/después (de algo) • **right now** ahorita • **right away** en seguida; luego ❻ • **right?** ¿verdad? • **you're Kathy, right?** tú eres Kathy, ¿verdad? ◆ *vt* ❶ corregir; rectificar ❷ enderezar ◆ *exclamación* ¡bien!

■ **Right** *s* POLÍTICA • **the Right** la derecha

right angle *s* ángulo recto • **at right angles (to)** en ángulo recto (con)

rightful ['raɪtful] *adj* legítimo, ma

right-hand *adj* derecho, cha • **the right-hand side** el lado derecho; la derecha • **it's on the right-hand side** está a mano derecha

right-handed [-'hændɪd] *adj* diestro, tra

right-hand man *s* brazo derecho

rightly ['raɪtlɪ] *adv* ❶ correctamente ❷ debidamente; bien ❸ con razón

right of way *s* ❶ AUTOMÓVILES prioridad ❷ derecho de paso

right-on *familiar* ◆ *adj* muy acertado, da ◆ *exclamación* ¡exacto!

right wing *s* • **the right wing** la derecha

■ **right-wing** *adj* derechista

rigid ['rɪdʒɪd] *adj* ❶ rígido, da ❷ inflexible

rigmarole ['rɪgmərəʊl] *s familiar & despectivo* ❶ ritual ❷ galimatías

rigor ['rɪgər] *s* rigor

rigorous ['rɪgərəs] *adj* riguroso, sa

rile [raɪl] *vt* irritar; sacar de quicio

rim [rɪm] *s* ❶borde ❷montura *(de anteojos)*

rind [raɪnd] *s* ❶corteza *(de beicon, queso)* ❷cáscara *(de naranja, limón)*

ring [rɪŋ] ◆*s* ❶ •**to give somebody a ring** llamar a alguien *(por teléfono)* ❷timbrazo ❸anillo ❹aro ❺anilla ❻círculo; corro ❼cuadrilátero *(en boxeo)* ❽pista *(en el circo)* ❾red *(de delincuentes)* ◆*vt* ❶*(pretérito* rang, *pp* rung*)* tocar *(el timbre)* ❷*(pretérito & pp* ringed*)* señalar con un círculo ❸*(pretérito* rang,*pp* rung*)* rodear ◆*vi* ❶sonar *(timbre, teléfono)* ❷ •**to ring (for)** llamar (para) ❸ •**to ring with** resonar con

Formas irregulares de **ring** *pretérito* **rang** *pp* **rung**

ring binder *s* archivador

ringing ['rɪŋɪŋ] *s* ❶repique; tañido ❷zumbido

ringing tone *s* tono de llamada

ringleader ['rɪŋ,li:dər] *s* cabecilla

ring-pull *s* anilla

ring tone *s* melodía *(de móvil)*

rink [rɪŋk] *s* pista

rinse [rɪns] *vt* ❶enjuagar •**to rinse your mouth out** enjuagarse la boca ❷aclarar

riot ['raɪət] ◆*s* disturbio

expresión **to run riot** desbocarse
◆*vi* amotinarse

rioter ['raɪətər] *s* amotinado, da

riot police *spl* cuerpo de granaderos

rip [rɪp] ◆*s* rasgón ◆*vt* ❶rasgar; desgarrar ❷quitar de un jalón ◆*vi* rasgarse; romperse

RIP *(abreviatura de* rest in peace*)* RIP

ripe [raɪp] *adj* maduro, ra

expresión **to be ripe (for something)** estar listo (para algo)

ripen ['raɪpn] *vt & vi* madurar

rip-off *s familiar* estafa

ripple ['rɪpl] *s* ❶onda; rizo *(en el agua)* ❷murmullo *(de risa, aplausos)*

rise ◆*s* ascenso

expresión **to give rise to something** dar origen a algo
◆*vi* [raɪz] ❶elevarse ❷subir *(precios, temperaturas)* ❸salir *(sol, luna)* ❹levantarse ❺ •**to rise to** reaccionar ante ❻sublevarse ❼ascender •**to rise to power/ fame** ascender al poder/a la gloria

Formas irregulares de **rise** *pretérito* **rose**, *pp* **risen** ['rɪzn].

rising ['raɪzɪŋ] *adj* ❶ascendente ❷creciente ❸en aumento *(temperatura, precios)* ❹en alza *(estrella)*

risk [rɪsk] ◆*s* ❶riesgo •**to run the risk of something/of doing something** correr el riesgo de algo/ de hacer algo •**to take a risk** arriesgarse •**at your own risk** bajo tu cuenta y riesgo ❷peligro •**a health risk** un peligro para la salud •**at risk** en peligro ◆*vt* ❶arriesgar ❷ •**to risk doing something** correr el riesgo de hacer algo

risky ['rɪskɪ] *adj* peligroso, sa; arriesgado, da

risqué ['ri:skeɪ] *adj* subido, da de tono

ritual ['rɪtʃʊəl] ◆*adj* ritual ◆*s* ritual

rival ['raɪvl] ◆*adj* rival ◆*s* rival ◆*vt* rivalizar con

rivalry ['raɪvlrɪ] *s* rivalidad

river ['rɪvər] *s* río

river bank *s* orilla ○margen del río

riverbed ['rɪvəbed] *s* cauce ○lecho del río

riverside ['rɪvəsaɪd] *s* ribera ○orilla del río

rivet ['rɪvɪt] ◆*s* remache ◆*vt figurado* •**to be riveted by something** estar fascinado, da con algo

Riviera [,rɪvɪ'eərə] *s* •**the French Riviera** la Riviera francesa

roach [rəʊtʃ] *s* cucaracha

road [rəʊd] *s* ❶carretera ❷calle ❸camino

expresión **on the road a)** en circulación **b)** de viaje **c)** de gira ▶ **to be on the road to recovery** estar en vías de recuperación

roadblock ['rəʊdblɒk] *s* control

road map *s* mapa de carreteras

road rage *s* violencia en carretera

road safety *s* seguridad en carretera

roadside ['rəʊdsaɪd] *s* borde de la carretera

road sign *s* señal de tráfico

roadtrip ['rəʊdtrɪp] *s* viaje hecho en automóvil

roadway ['rəʊdweɪ] *s* calzada

road works *spl* obras

roam [rəʊm] ◆*vt* vagar por ◆*vi* ❶vagar ❷viajar *(con teléfono móvil)*

roaming ['rəʊmɪŋ] *s* itinerancia *(con teléfono móvil)*

roar [rɔ:r] ◆*vi* rugir

expresión **to roar with laughter** reírse a carcajadas
◆*vt* rugir; decir a voces ◆*s* ❶fragor ❷rugido

roaring ['rɔ:rɪŋ] *adj* ❶clamoroso, sa ❷muy vivo *(fuego)* ❸ •**to do a roaring trade in something** vender algo como rosquillas

roast [rəʊst] ◆*adj* asado, da ◆*s* asado ◆*vt* ❶asar ❷tostar

roast beef *s* rosbif

rob [rɒb] *vt* ❶robar •**to rob somebody of something** *literal & figurado* robar a alguien algo ❷asaltar

robber ['rɒbər] *s* ❶ladrón, ona ❷asaltante

robbery ['rɒbərɪ] *s* ❶robo ❷asalto

robe [rəʊb] *s* ❶albornoz ❷sotana ❸bata

robin ['rɒbɪn] *s* ❶robín (americano) ❷petirrojo

robot ['rəʊbɒt] *s* robot

robust [rəʊ'bʌst] *adj* robusto, ta; fuerte

rock [rɒk] ◆*s* ❶ ♺*incontable* roca ❷piedra ❸peñasco ❹MÚSICA rock ◆*en compuestos* de rock *(grupo)* ◆*vt* mecer; balancear ◆*vi* mecerse

■ **on the rocks** *adv* ❶con hielo *(whisky)* ❷ •**their marriage is on the rocks** su matrimonio va mal

rock and roll, rock'n'roll *s* rock and roll

R

rock bottom *s* • **to hit rock bottom** tocar fondo
■ **rock-bottom** *adj* • **rock-bottom prices** precios muy bajos

rock dash *s* enguijarrado

rocket ['rɒkɪt] *s* ❶ cohete ❷ roqueta

rocking chair ['rɒkɪŋ-] *s* mecedora

rocking horse ['rɒkɪŋ-] *s* caballo de balancín

rock'n'roll [,rɒkən'rəʊl] = **rock and roll**

Rocky Mountains *spl* • **the Rocky Mountains** las montañas Rocosas

ROCKY MOUNTAINS

Las **Rocky Mountains**, o las Montañas Rocosas, es la cordillera que corre desde Canadá hasta México y atraviesa los Estados Unidos de norte a sur en la zona oeste del país. Se les conoce por su gran belleza natural y son la sede de populares centros de esquí como Vail y Aspen.

rod [rɒd] *s* ❶ vara ❷ barra ❸ caña *(de pescar)*

rode [rəʊd] *pretérito* → **ride**

rodent ['rəʊdənt] *s* roedor

rogue [rəʊg] *s* pícaro, ra

role [rəʊl] *s* *figurado* TEATRO papel

role model *s* modelo a seguir

roll [rəʊl] ◆ *s* ❶ rollo ❷ fajo *(de billetes)* ❸ bolillo ❹ lista ❺ redoble *(de tambor)* ❻ retumbo *(de truenos)* ◆ *vt* ❶ hacer rodar ❷ enrollar ❸ liar *(cigarrillo)* ❹ tirar *(dados)* ◆ *vi* ❶ rodar ❷ ir; avanzar *(vehículo)* ❸ redoblar

■ **roll about, roll around** *vi* • **to roll about** o **around (on)** rodar (por)

■ **roll over** *vi* darse la vuelta

■ **roll up** ◆ *vt* ☀ *El objeto se puede colocar antes o después de la preposición.* ❶ enrollar ❷ remangarse ◆ *vi* llegar *(vehículo)*

roll call *s* • **to take a roll call** pasar lista

roller ['rəʊlər] *s* ❶ rodillo ❷ rulo

rollerblade ['rəʊləbleɪd] *vi* patinar *(con patines en línea)*

Rollerblades ® ['rəʊlə,bleɪdz] *spl* patines en línea

rollerblading ['rəʊlə,bleɪdɪŋ] *s* patinaje *(con patines en línea)* • **to go rollerblading** ir a patinar

roller coaster *s* montaña rusa

roller skate *s* patín de ruedas

rollerskating ['rəʊlə,skeɪtɪŋ] *s* patinaje *(sobre ruedas)* • **to go rollerblading** ir a patinar *(sobre ruedas)*

rolling ['rəʊlɪŋ] *adj*
expresión **to be rolling in it** *familiar* nadar en la abundancia

rolling pin *s* rodillo (de cocina)

roll-on *s* desodorante de bola

ROM [rɒm] *(abreviatura de* read only memory) *s* ROM

Roman ['rəʊmən] ◆ *adj* romano, na ◆ *s* romano, na

Roman Catholic ◆ *adj* católico (romano), católica (romana) ◆ *s* católico (romano), católica (romana)

romance [rəʊ'mæns] ◆ *s* ❶ lo romántico ❷ amorío ❸ novela romántica ◆ *adj* • **Romance Languages** lenguas romances

Romania, Rumania [ru:'meɪnjə] *s* Rumanía

Romanian, Rumanian [ru:'meɪnjən] ◆ *adj* rumano, na ◆ *s* ❶ rumano, na ❷ rumano *(idioma)*

Roman numerals *spl* números romanos

romantic [rəʊ'mæntɪk] *adj* romántico, ca

roof [ru:f] *s* ❶ tejado ❷ techo ❸ paladar
expresión **to go through** o **hit the roof** subirse por las paredes

roof rack *s* portaequipajes

rooftop ['ru:ftɒp] *s* tejado

rook [rʊk] *s* torre *(de ajedrez)*

rookie ['rʊkɪ] *s* *familiar* novato, ta

room [ru:m] [rʊm] ◆ *s* ❶ habitación ❷ sala ❸ cuarto; dormitorio ❹ ☀ *incontable* espacio • **there isn't enough room** no hay suficiente espacio ◆ *vi* • **to room with somebody** compartir alojamiento con alguien

rooming house ['ru:mɪŋ-] *s* casa de huéspedes; pensión

roommate ['ru:mmeɪt] *s* compañero, ra de cuarto

room service *s* servicio de habitación

roomy ['ru:mɪ] *adj* espacioso, sa; amplio, plia

rooster ['ru:stər] *s* gallo

root [ru:t] ◆ *s* *literal & figurado* raíz ◆ *vi* hurgar; escarbar

■ **root for** *vt* ☀ *El objeto siempre va después de la preposición al final.* *familiar* apoyar a

■ **root out** *vt* ☀ *El objeto se puede colocar antes o después de la preposición.* desarraigar

root beer *s* ▶ cerveza sin alcohol hecha de raíces

rope [rəʊp] ◆ *s* ❶ cuerda ❷ soga ❸ NÁUTICA maroma; cable
expresión **to know the ropes** saber de qué va el asunto ▶ **to show somebody the ropes** poner a alguien al tanto
◆ *vt* atar con cuerda

■ **rope in** *vt* ☀ *El objeto se puede colocar antes o después de la preposición.* *familiar* arrastrar o enganchar a • **to rope somebody in to do something** liar a alguien para hacer algo

rose [rəʊz] ◆ *pretérito* → **rise** ◆ *adj* rosa; color de rosa ◆ *s* rosa

rosé ['rəʊzeɪ] *s* rosado

rose bush *s* rosal

rosemary ['rəʊzmərɪ] *s* romero

roster ['rɒstər] *s* lista

rosy ['rəʊzɪ] *adj* ❶ sonrosado, da ❷ prometedor, ra

rot [rɒt] ◆ *s* ☼*incontable* podredumbre ◆ *vt* pudrir ◆ *vi* pudrirse

rota ['rəʊtə] *s* lista (de turnos)

rotary ['rəʊtərɪ] ◆ *adj* giratorio, ria; rotativo, va ◆ *s* glorieta; cruce de circulación giratoria

rotate [rəʊ'teɪt] ◆ *vt* hacer girar; dar vueltas a ◆ *vi* girar; dar vueltas

rotation [rəʊ'teɪʃn] *s* rotación

rotten ['rɒtn] *adj* ❶ podrido, da ❷ *familiar* malísimo, ma; fatal ❸ *familiar* despreciable ❹ *familiar* • to feel rotten sentirse fatal o muy mal

rouge [ru:ʒ] *s* colorete

rough [rʌf] ◆ *adj* ❶ áspero, ra ❷ desigual *(terreno)* ❸ bruto, ta ❹ grosero, ra; tosco, ca ❺ precario, ria *(refugio)* ❻ a grandes rasgos; aproximado, da • to write a rough draft of something escribir un borrador de algo ❼ duro, ra; difícil ❽ picado, da *(mar)* ❾ tormentoso, sa ❿ peligroso, sa *(barrio)*; violento, ta *(persona)* ◆ *adv* • to sleep rough dormir al raso ◆ *s* ❶ GOLF • the rough el rough ❷ • in rough en borrador ◆ *vt*
expresión to rough it vivir sin comodidades

rough and ready *adj* tosco, ca

roughly ['rʌflɪ] *adv* ❶ más o menos ❷ brutalmente ❸ toscamente

roughneck ['rʌfnek] *s* ❶ trabajador en una explotación petrolífera ❷ *familiar* matón; duro

roulette [ru:'let] *s* ruleta

round [raʊnd] ◆ *adj* redondo, da ◆ *preposición* ❶ alrededor de • the reeds round the pond las cañas alrededor del estanque • round (and round) the park alrededor del parque • she put her arm round his shoulder le puso el brazo al hombro ❷ cerca de • round here por aquí ❸ por todo, da • to go round sth dar la vuelta a algo • we went round the museum dimos la vuelta al museo • they were waiting round the corner esperaban a la vuelta de la esquina • to drive round the corner doblar la esquina ❹ • she's 30 inches round the waist mide 30 pulgadas de cintura ❺ • to drive/walk round something conducir/caminar esquivando algo ◆ *adv* ❶ • all round por todos lados ❷ • round about alrededor; en las proximidades ❸ • to travel round viajar por ahí ❹ • to pass something round pasar algo • she passed round a plate of cookies pasó un plato de galletas • round (and round) en redondo • to go o spin round girar ❺ • to come/go round to see somebody venir/ir a ver a alguien • he came round to see us vino a vernos ◆ *s* ❶ ronda • a round of toast una tostada • a round of applause una salva de aplausos ❷ vuelta *(de competición, en golf)* ❸ visitas *(de médico)* ❹ recorrido *(de cartero, lechero)* ❺ cartucho ❻ asalto *(en boxeo)* ◆ *vt* doblar

■ **rounds** *spl* visitas *(de médico)* • he's out on his rounds está visitando pacientes

expresión to do o go the rounds a) divulgarse *(rumor, chiste)* b) estar rodando *(enfermedad)*

■ **round off** *vt* ☼ *El objeto se puede colocar antes o después de la preposición.* terminar

■ **round up** *vt* ☼ *El objeto se puede colocar antes o después de la preposición.* ❶ recoger ❷ reunir ❸ MATEMÁTICAS redondear al alza

roundly ['raʊndlɪ] *adv* rotundamente

round trip *s* viaje redondo ▸ **round trip ticket** boleto redondo

roundup ['raʊndʌp] *s* ❶ resumen • **news roundup** resumen informativo ❷ redada *(de criminales)*

rouse [raʊz] *vt* ❶ *formal* despertar ❷ • to rouse somebody/yourself to do something animar a alguien/animarse a hacer algo ❸ excitar • it roused his interest le despertó el interés

rousing ['raʊzɪŋ] *adj* conmovedor, ra

rout [raʊt] ◆ *s* derrota aplastante ◆ *vt* derrotar; aplastar

route [raʊt] *s* ❶ ruta ❷ línea; recorrido *(de colectivo)* ❸ rumbo *(de barco)* ❹ reparto *(de periódicos)* • **Billy has a paper route** Billy hace un reparto de periódicos ❺ carretera principal

route map *s* plano (del camino)

routine [ru:'ti:n] ◆ *adj* rutinario, ria • to have a routine checkup hacerse un reconocimiento médico rutinario ◆ *s* rutina

row¹ [rəʊ] ◆ *s* ❶ fila; hilera ❷ serie • three in a row tres seguidos ◆ *vt* remar ◆ *vi* remar • to row across the river cruzar el río a remo

row² [raʊ] ◆ *s* ❶ pelea; bronca ❷ *familiar* estruendo; ruido ◆ *vi* reñir; pelearse

rowboat ['rəʊbəʊt] *s* bote de remos

rowdy ['raʊdɪ] *adj* ❶ ruidoso, sa ❷ pendenciero, ra

row house [rəʊ-] *s* casa adosada

rowing ['rəʊɪŋ] *s* remo

royal ['rɔɪəl] ◆ *adj* real ◆ *s* *familiar* miembro de la familia real

royal family *s* familia real

royalty ['rɔɪəltɪ] *s* realeza

■ **royalties** *spl* derechos de autor

RSVP *(abreviatura de* répondez s'il vous plaît*)* s.r.c.

rub [rʌb] ◆ *vt* • to rub something (against o on) frotar algo (en o contra) • to rub something on o onto frotar algo en

expresión to rub somebody the wrong way sacar a alguien de quicio

◆ *vi* • to rub (against something) rozar (algo) • to rub (together) rozarse • to rub your hands together frotarse las manos

■ **rub off on** *vt* ☼ *El objeto siempre va después de la preposición al final.* influir en

■ **rub out** *vt* ☼ *El objeto se puede colocar antes o después de la preposición.* borrar

rubber ['rʌbər] *s* ❶ goma; caucho ❷ *familiar* goma *(condón)* ❸ partido

rubber band *s* liga

rubber boot *s* bota de agua

rubberneck ['rʌbənek] *vi* *familiar* curiosear

rubber stamp *s* sello de goma

R

■ **rubber-stamp** *vt* aprobar oficialmente

rubbish ['rʌbɪʃ] *s* ☼*incontable* ❶ basura ❷ *familiar & figurado* porquería ❸ *familiar* tonterías • **don't talk rubbish** no digas tonterías

rubble ['rʌbl] *s* ☼*incontable* escombros

ruby ['ru:bɪ] *s* rubí

rucksack ['rʌksæk] *s* mochila

rudder ['rʌdər] *s* timón

ruddy ['rʌdɪ] *adj* rojizo, za

rude [ru:d] *adj* ❶ grosero, ra • **it's rude to talk with your mouth full** es de mala educación hablar con la boca llena ❷ verde *(chiste)*

rueful ['ru:fʊl] *adj* arrepentido, da

ruffian ['rʌfjən] *s* rufián

ruffle ['rʌfl] *vt* ❶ despeinar ❷ encrespar ❸ poner nervioso, sa a

rug [rʌg] *s* ❶ alfombra ❷ manta de viaje

rugged ['rʌgɪd] *adj* ❶ escabroso, sa ❷ fuerte • **his rugged good looks** sus rasgos recios

ruin ['ru:ɪn] ◆ *s* ruina ◆ *vt* ❶ arruinar ❷ estropear

■ **in ruin(s)** *adv* en ruinas

rule [ru:l] ◆ *s* ❶ regla; norma • **to break the rules** violar las normas • **to be against the rules** ir contra las reglas • **the rule** la regla; la norma ❷ dominio • **it was under Roman rule** estuvo bajo dominio romano ❸ regla *(para medir)* ◆ *vt* ❶ gobernar ❷ *formal* regir ❸ • **to rule that** decidir o ordenar que ◆ *vi* ❶ decidir; fallar ❷ *formal* ser primordial ❸ gobernar

■ **rule out** *vt* ☼ *El objeto se puede colocar antes o después de la preposición.* descartar

ruled [ru:ld] *adj* rayado, da

ruler ['ru:lər] *s* ❶ regla *(para medir)* ❷ gobernante ❸ soberano, na

ruling ['ru:lɪŋ] ◆ *adj* • **the ruling party** el partido en el poder ◆ *s* fallo; decisión

rum [rʌm] *s* ron

Rumania [ru:'meɪnjə] = **Romania**

Rumanian [ru:'meɪnjən] = **Romanian**

rumble ['rʌmbl] ◆ *s* ❶ estruendo ❷ ruido *(del estómago)* ❸ *familiar* riña callejera ◆ *vi* ❶ retumbar ❷ hacer ruido *(el estómago)*

rummage ['rʌmɪdʒ] *vi* hurgar; rebuscar • **to rummage around in something** revolver en algo

rummage sale *s* ▸ venta de objetos usados con fines benéficos

rumor ['ru:mər] *s* rumor • **there's a rumor going around that...** corre el rumor que...

rumored ['ru:məd] *adj* • **to be rumored** rumorearse • **she is rumored to be very rich** se rumorea que es muy rica

rump [rʌmp] *s* ❶ grupa; ancas ❷ *familiar* trasero

rump steak *s* filete de lomo

rumpus room *s* cuarto de juegos

run [rʌn] ◆ *s* ❶ carrera • **to go for a run** ir a correr • **on the run** en fuga ❷ paseo o vuelta *(en coche)* • **to**

go for a run ir a dar una vuelta; viaje *(en barco, avión)* ❸ serie *(de victorias, catástrofes)* ❹ TEATRO • **the play had a 6-week run** la obra estuvo en cartelera 6 semanas ❺ • **a run on something** una gran demanda de algo ❻ pista *(de esquí)* ◆ *vt* ❶ correr ❷ dirigir; administrar *(negocio)* ❸ organizar *(congreso)* ❹ poner *(programa, máquina, película)* ❺ hacer funcionar *(vehículo)* ❻ abrir *(grifo)* • **to run a bath** llenar la bañera ❼ publicar *(artículo)* ◆ *vi* ❶ correr ❷ • **to run (for)** presentarse como candidato, ta (a) • **he's running for president** se presenta a la presidencia ❸ funcionar *(máquina)* ❹ estar encendido, da *(motor)* • **to run on** ○ **off something** funcionar con algo • **to run smoothly** ir bien ❺ circular *(colectivo, tren)* ❻ gotear *(grifo)* • **somebody has left the faucet running** alguien se ha dejado la llave abierta ❼ moquear • **my nose is running** me moquea la nariz ❽ llorar *(los ojos)* ❾ desteñir *(ropa, color)*

■ **run across** *vt* ☼ *El objeto siempre va después de la preposición al final.* encontrarse con

■ **run away** *vi* • **to run away (from)** huir o fugarse (de)

■ **run down** ◆ *vt* ☼ *El objeto se puede colocar antes o después de la preposición.* ❶ atropellar ❷ hablar mal de ◆ *vi* acabarse *(pila)*

■ **run into** *vt* ☼ *El objeto siempre va después de la preposición al final.* ❶ encontrar *(problema)* ❷ tropezarse con ❸ chocar con

■ **run off** ◆ *vt* ☼ *El objeto se puede colocar antes o después de la preposición.* sacar *(copias)* ◆ *vi* • **to run off (with)** fugarse (con)

■ **run out** *vi* ❶ acabarse ❷ caducar

■ **run out of** *vt* ☼ *El objeto siempre va después de la preposición al final.* quedarse sin

■ **run over** *vt* ☼ *El objeto se puede colocar antes o después de la preposición.* atropellar • **to get run over** ser atropellado

■ **run through** *vt* ☼ *El objeto siempre va después de la preposición al final.* ❶ recorrer; atravesar ❷ ensayar ❸ echar un vistazo a

■ **run to** *vt* ☼ *El objeto siempre va después de la preposición al final.* ascender a • **the bill ran to thousands** la cuenta subía a varios miles

■ **run up** *vt* ☼ *El objeto siempre va después de la preposición al final.* incurrir en • **he ran up a huge bill** acumuló una factura enorme

■ **run up against** *vt* ☼ *El objeto siempre va después de la preposición al final.* tropezar con

Formas irregulares de **run**: *pretérito* **ran**, *pp* **run**

runaway ['rʌnəweɪ] ◆ *adj* ❶ fugitivo, va ❷ desbocado, da *(caballo)* ❸ fuera de control *(tren)* ❹ desenfrenado, da *(inflación)* ❺ fácil *(victoria)* ◆ *s* fugitivo, va

rundown ['rʌndaʊn] *s* informe; resumen • **to give somebody a rundown on something** poner a alguien al tanto de algo

■ **run-down** *adj* ❶ en ruinas ❷ agotado, da • **to feel run-down** sentirse débil

rung [rʌŋ] ◆ *participio pasado* → **ring** ◆ *s literal & figurado* peldaño

runner ['rʌnər] *s* corredor, ra

runner-up *s* subcampeón, ona

El plural de **runner-up** es **runners-up**.

running ['rʌnɪŋ] ◆ *adj* ❶ continuo, nua ❷ seguidos, das • **four days running** cuatro días consecutivos ❸ corriente *(agua)* ◆ *s* ❶ el correr • **to go running** salir a correr ❷ DEPORTE carreras ❸ dirección; organización ❹ funcionamiento

expresión **to be in/out of the running (for something)** tener/no tener posibilidades (de algo)

running mate *s* candidato, ta a vicepresidente

runny ['rʌnɪ] *adj* ❶ derretido, da ❷ • **I have a runny nose** me gotea la nariz ❸ lloroso, a

run-of-the-mill *adj* común y corriente

run-up *s* ❶ periodo previo • **the run-up to the elections** el periodo previo a las elecciones ❷ DEPORTE carrerilla

runway ['rʌnweɪ] *s* pista

rupture ['rʌptʃər] ◆ *s* MEDICINA hernia ◆ *vt* romper

rural ['ruərəl] *adj* rural

rush [rʌʃ] ◆ *s* ❶ apuro • **to be in a rush** estar apurado • **what's the rush?** ¿qué apuro hay? ❷ hora punta ❸ ráfaga; torrente ❹ • **to make a rush for something** ir en desbandada hacia algo • **there was a rush for the exit** la gente salió apresuradamente ◆ *vt* ❶ apresurar • **to rush somebody into doing something** apresurar a alguien para que haga algo ❷ llevar rápidamente • **he**

was rushed to hospital lo llevaron al hospital a toda prisa ◆ *vi* ❶ apurarse; correr • **to rush into something** meterse de cabeza en algo • **there's no need to rush** no hay ninguna prisa • **he rushed to help her** corrió a ayudarla ❷ precipitarse

■ **rushes** *spl* BOTÁNICA juncos

rush hour *s* hora pico

Russia ['rʌʃə] *s* Rusia

Russian ['rʌʃn] ◆ *adj* ruso, sa ◆ *s* ❶ ruso, sa ❷ ruso

rust [rʌst] ◆ *s* óxido ◆ *vi* oxidarse

rustle ['rʌsl] ◆ *vt* ❶ hacer crujir ❷ robar *(ganado)* ◆ *vi* ❶ susurrar ❷ crujir

rusty ['rʌstɪ] *adj* *literal & figurado* oxidado, da • **my French is a bit rusty** hace mucho que no practico el francés

rut [rʌt] *s* rodada

expresión **to get into/be in a rut** *figurado* caer/estar metido en una rutina ❱ **to get out of a rut** salir de la rutina

rutabaga [ˌruːtəˈbeɪgə] *s* nabo sueco

ruthless ['ruːθlɪs] *adj* despiadado, da

RV *(abreviatura de* recreational vehicle) *s* casa remolque

rye [raɪ] *s* centeno

rye bread *s* pan de centeno

R

S

s, S [es] *s* s; S

Dos plurales: **ss** o **s's; Ss** o **S's.**

■ **S** *abreviatura* (*abreviatura escrita de* south) S

Sabbath ['sæbəə] *s* • **the Sabbath a)** el domingo **b)** el sábado (*judío*)

sabotage ['sæbətɑ:ʒ] ♦ *s* sabotaje ♦ *vt* sabotear

saccharin(e) ['sækərɪn] *s* sacarina

sachet ['sæʃeɪ] *s* bolsita

sack [sæk] *s* saco

sacred ['seɪkrɪd] *adj* *literal & figurado* sagrado, da

sacrifice ['sækrɪfaɪs] *figurado* ♦ *s* RELIGIÓN sacrificio • **to make sacrifices** sacrificarse ♦ *vt* RELIGIÓN sacrificar

sacrilege ['sækrɪlɪdʒ] *s figurado* RELIGIÓN sacrilegio

sad [sæd] *adj* triste

sadden ['sædn] *vt* entristecer

saddle ['sædl] ♦ *s* ❶ montura; silla (de montar) ❷ asiento ♦ *vt* ❶ ensillar ❷ *figurado* • **to saddle somebody with something** cargar a alguien con algo • **she was saddled with an elderly patient** le encajaron un paciente anciano

sadistic [sə'dɪstɪk] *adj* sádico, ca

sadly ['sædlɪ] *adv* ❶ tristemente ❷ lamentablemente

sadness ['sædnɪs] *s* tristeza

safari [sə'fɑːrɪ] *s* safari

safe [seɪf] ♦ *adj* ❶ seguro, ra • **a safe place** un lugar seguro • **is this ladder safe?** ¿es segura esta escalera? • **it's safe to swim here** aquí se puede nadar sin peligro • **he's a safe driver** es un conductor prudente • **safe and sound** sano y salvo, sana y salva ❷ sano y salvo, sana y salva ❸ • **it's safe to say that...** se puede afirmar con seguridad que... • **to be on the safe side** por mayor seguridad ❹ digno, na de confianza ♦ *s* caja (de caudales)

safeguard ['seɪfgɑːd] ♦ *s* salvaguardia; protección • **as a safeguard** como protección • **a safeguard against something** una protección contra algo ♦ *vt* • **to safeguard something/somebody (against something)** salvaguardar o proteger algo/a alguien (contra algo)

safekeeping [ˌseɪf'kiːpɪŋ] *s* • **she gave me the letter for safekeeping** me dio la carta para que se la guardara en un lugar seguro

safely ['seɪflɪ] *adv* ❶ con seguridad ❷ seguramente ❸ sano y salvo, sana y salva ❹ • **I can safely say that...** puedo decir con toda confianza que...

safe sex *s* sexo sin riesgo

safety ['seɪftɪ] *s* seguridad

safety belt *s* cinturón de seguridad

safety island *s* refugio

safety pin *s* seguro

saffron ['sæfrən] *s* azafrán

sag [sæg] *vi* hundirse; combarse

sage [seɪdʒ] ♦ *adj* sabio, bia ♦ *s* ❶ salvia ❷ sabio

Sagittarius [ˌsædʒɪ'teərɪəs] *s* Sagitario

Sahara [sə'hɑːrə] *s* • **the Sahara (Desert)** el (desierto del) Sáhara

said [sed] *pretérito & participio pasado* → **say**

sail [seɪl] ♦ *s* ❶ vela • **to set sail** zarpar ❷ paseo en barco de vela • **to go for a sail** salir a hacer una excursión en barco de vela ♦ *vt* ❶ gobernar (*barco*) ❷ cruzar (*mar*) ♦ *vi* ❶ navegar ❷ • **the ship sailed across the ocean** el barco cruzó el océano ❸ zarpar

■ **sail through** *vt* ⚙ *El objeto siempre va después de la preposición al final.* hacer con facilidad

sailboat ['seɪlbəʊt] *s* barco de vela

sailing ['seɪlɪŋ] *s* ❶ ⚙ *incontable* DEPORTE vela ❷ travesía

sailing ship *s* (buque) velero

sailor ['seɪlər] *s* marinero, ra

saint [seɪnt] *s figurado* RELIGIÓN santo, ta ▶ **Saint Patrick's Day** el día de San Patricio

expresión **to have the patience of a saint** tener más paciencia que un santo

sake [seɪk] *s* • **for the sake of** por (el bien de) • **do it for my sake** hazlo por mí

expresión **for God's** o **heaven's sake** ¡por el amor de Dios!

salad ['sæləd] *s* ensalada

salad bowl *s* ensaladera

salad dressing *s* aliño (para la ensalada)

salami [sə'lɑ:mɪ] *s* salami

salary ['sælərɪ] *s* sueldo

sale [seɪl] *s* ❶ venta • **on sale** en venta • **(up) for sale** en venta • **'for sale'** 'se vende' ❷ liquidación; saldo • **Bloomingdale's is having a sale** hay rebajas en Bloomingdale's

■ **sales** *spl* ❶ ECONOMÍA ventas ❷ • **the sales** las rebajas

sales assistant ['seɪlz-]**, salesclerk** ['seɪlzklɜ:rk] *s* dependiente, ta

salesman ['seɪlzmən] *s* ❶ dependiente; vendedor ❷ viajante

El plural de **salesman** es **salesmen** ['seɪlzmen].

sales rep *s familiar* comercial; vendedor

sales slip *s* recibo

saleswoman ['seɪlz‚wʊmən] *s* ❶ dependienta; vendedora ❷ viajante

El plural de **saleswoman** es **saleswomen** ['seɪlz‚wɪmɪn].

saliva [sə'laɪvə] *s* saliva

salmon ['sæmən] *s* salmón

Dos plurales: **salmon** o **salmons.**

salmonella [‚sælmə'nelə] *s* salmonelosis

salon ['sælɒn] *s* salón

saloon [sə'lu:n] *s* ❶ bar ❷ salón

salt [sɔ:lt] [sɒlt] ◆ *s* sal

expresión **to take something with a pinch of salt** considerar algo con cierta reserva

◆ *vt* ❶ salar ❷ echar sal en *(las carreteras* ETC *para evitar que se hielen)*

salt shaker [-‚ʃeɪkər] *s* salero

saltwater ['sɔ:lt‚wɔ:tər] *adj* de agua salada

salty ['sɔ:ltɪ] *adj* salado, da; salobre

salute [sə'lu:t] ◆ *s* ❶ saludo ❷ MILITAR salva ◆ *vt* MILITAR saludar

Salvadorean, Salvadorian [‚sælvə'dɔ:rɪən] ◆ *adj* salvadoreño, ña ◆ *s* salvadoreño, ña

salvage ['sælvɪdʒ] ◆ *s* ⚙️ *incontable* ❶ salvamento ❷ objetos recuperados o rescatados ◆ *vt literal & figurado* • **to salvage something (from)** salvar algo (de)

salvation [sæl'veɪʃn] *s* salvación

same [seɪm] ◆ *adj* mismo, ma • **the same color as his** el mismo color que el suyo • **at the same time a)** al mismo tiempo **b)** aún así • **one and the same** el mismo, la misma ◆ *pronombre* • **the same** el mismo, la misma • **she did the same** hizo lo mismo • **the ingredients are the same** los ingredientes son los mismos o iguales • **his car is the same as yours** su coche es el mismo que el tuyo • **to look the same** parecerse • **I'll have the same (again)** tomaré lo mismo (que antes) • **all** o **just the same** de todos modos • **it's all the same to me** me da igual • **it's not the same** no es lo mismo • **happy Christmas! — the same to you!** ¡feliz Navidad! — ¡igualmente! ◆ *adv* • **the same** lo mismo

sample ['sɑ:mpl] ◆ *s* muestra ◆ *vt* probar

sanctimonious [‚sæŋktɪ'məʊnjəs] *adj despectivo* santurrón, ona

sanction ['sæŋkʃn] ◆ *s* sanción ◆ *vt* sancionar

sanctuary ['sæŋktʃʊərɪ] *s* ❶ reserva • **a bird sanctuary** una reserva de aves ❷ refugio ❸ santuario

sand [sænd] ◆ *s* arena ◆ *vt* lijar

sandal ['sændl] *s* sandalia • **a pair of sandals** unas sandalias

sandbox ['sændbɒks] *s* cuadro de arena

sandcastle ['sænd‚kɑ:sl] *s* castillo de arena

sand dune *s* duna

sandpaper ['sænd‚peɪpər] ◆ *s* ⚙️ *incontable* papel de lija ◆ *vt* lijar

sandstone ['sændstəʊn] *s* piedra arenisca

sandwich ['sænwɪdʒ] ◆ *s* ❶ bocadillo ❷ sandwich frío • **a cheese sandwich** un sandwich de queso ◆ *vt figurado* apretujar • **she was sandwiched between two businessmen** quedó atrapada entre dos hombres de negocios

sandy ['sændɪ] *adj* ❶ arenoso, sa ❷ rojizo, za

sane [seɪn] *adj* ❶ cuerdo, da ❷ prudente; sensato, ta

sang [sæŋ] *pretérito* → **sing**

sanitary ['sænɪtrɪ] *adj* ❶ sanitario, ria ❷ higiénico, ca

sanitary napkin, sanitary pad *s* compresa; toalla higiénica

sanitation [‚sænɪ'teɪʃn] *s* sanidad

sanitation worker *s* basurero, ra

sanity ['sænətɪ] *s* ❶ cordura ❷ sensatez

sank [sæŋk] *pretérito* → **sink**

Santa (Claus) ['sæntə(‚klaʊz)] *s* Papá Noel

sap [sæp] ◆ *s* ❶ savia ❷ *familiar* primo, ma ◆ *vt* minar

sapling ['sæplɪŋ] *s* árbol nuevo; arbolito

sapphire ['sæfaɪər] *s* zafiro

Saran wrap® [sə'ræn-] *s* plástico transparente *(para envolver alimentos)*

sarcastic [sɑ:'kæstɪk] *adj* sarcástico, ca

sardine [sɑ:'di:n] *s* sardina

expresión **to be packed in like sardines** ir como sardinas en lata

SASE *s abreviatura escrita de* **self-addressed stamped envelope**

sash [sæʃ] *s* faja

sassy ['sæsɪ] *adj familiar* descarado(da); fresco(ca)

sat [sæt] *pretérito & participio pasado* → **sit**

SAT [sæt] *s* ▸ examen de ingreso a la universidad en Estados Unidos

S

SAT

El **SAT** (anteriormente llamado "Scholastic Aptitude Test") es el examen de acceso a la universidad más extendido en Estados Unidos. Desde 2005 cuenta con tres partes: una escrita, una lectura crítica y una matemática. Este examen tiene lugar varias veces al año y los estudiantes tienen la oportunidad de presentarse más de una vez para intentar mejorar la calificación. Como criterio de admisión, las universidades estadounidenses tienen en cuenta los resultados del **SAT**, el expediente académico del alumno, sus actividades extraescolares, una carta de motivación escrita por él y, en ocasiones, referencias de profesores.

Satan ['seɪtn] *s* Satanás

satchel ['sætʃəl] *s* cartera

satellite ['sætəlaɪt] *s literal & figurado* satélite

satellite dish *s* antena parabólica

satellite TV *s* televisión por satélite

satin ['sætɪn] ◆ *s* satén; raso ◆ *en compuestos* de satén; de raso

satire ['sætaɪər] *s* sátira

satisfaction [,sætɪs'fækʃn] *s* satisfacción • **to do something to somebody's satisfaction** hacer algo a la satisfacción o al gusto de alguien

satisfactory [,sætɪs'fæktərɪ] *adj* satisfactorio, ria

satisfied ['sætɪsfaɪd] *adj* satisfecho, cha • **you're never satisfied!** ¡nunca te conformas con nada! • **a satisfied smile** una sonrisa de satisfacción

satisfy ['sætɪsfaɪ] *vt* ❶ satisfacer ❷ convencer ❸ cumplir

satisfying ['sætɪsfaɪɪŋ] *adj* ❶ satisfactorio, ria ❷ sustancioso, sa *(comida)*

satsuma [,sæt'su:mə] *s* satsuma

saturate ['sætʃəreɪt] *vt* ❶ • **to saturate something (with)** empapar algo (de) ❷ saturar

Saturday ['sætədɪ] ◆ *s* sábado • **what day is it? — it's Saturday** ¿a qué estamos hoy? — estamos a sábado • **on Saturday** el sábado • **on Saturdays** los sábados • **last Saturday** el sábado pasado • **this Saturday** este sábado; el sábado que viene • **next Saturday** el sábado de la semana que viene • **every Saturday** todos los sábados • **every other Saturday** cada dos sábados; un sábado sí y otro no • **the Saturday before** el sábado anterior • **the Saturday after next** no este sábado sino el siguiente • **the Saturday before last** hace dos sábados ◆ *en compuestos* del sábado

Saturn ['sætən] *s* Saturno

sauce [sɔ:s] *s* COCINA salsa

saucepan ['sɔ:spən] *s* ❶ cacerola ❷ cazo

saucer ['sɔ:sər] *s* platillo

saucy ['sɔ:sɪ] *adj familiar* descarado, da; fresco, ca

Saudi Arabia [,saudɪə'reɪbjə] *s* Arabia Saudí

Saudi (Arabian) ['saudɪ-] ◆ *adj* saudí; saudita ◆ *s* saudí; saudita

sauna ['sɔ:nə] *s* sauna

sausage ['sɒsɪdʒ] *s* salchicha

sauté [səʊ'teɪ] *vt* saltear

Formas irregulares de **sauté**: *pretérito & pp* **sautéed** o **sautéd**.

savage ['sævɪdʒ] ◆ *adj* feroz; salvaje ◆ *s despectivo* salvaje ◆ *vt* embestir; atacar

save [seɪv] ◆ *vt* ❶ salvar; rescatar • **to save somebody from something** salvar a alguien de algo ❷ ahorrar • **save your strength for later** ahorra fuerzas para más tarde • **to save time** ahorrar tiempo ❸ guardar • **why don't you save some of your candy for later?** ¿por qué no te guardas algunos caramelos para más tarde? • **will you save me some soup?** ¿me guardarás algo de sopa? ❹ evitar • **it saves having to go to the bank** ahorra tener que ir al banco • **to save somebody from doing something** evitar a alguien (el) hacer algo ❺ DEPORTE parar ❻ INFORMÁTICA guardar

expresión **to save face** salvar las apariencias

◆ *vi* ahorrar ◆ *s* DEPORTE parada ◆ *preposición formal* • **save (for)** excepto

■ **save up** *vi* ahorrar

savings ['seɪvɪŋz] *spl* ahorros

savings account *s* cuenta de ahorros

savings bank *s* ≃ caja de ahorros

savior ['seɪvjər] *s* salvador, ra

savor ['seɪvər] *vt literal & figurado* saborear

savory ['seɪvərɪ] ◆ *adj* ❶ salado, da ❷ sabroso, sa ◆ *s* comida de aperitivo

saw [sɔ:] ◆ *pretérito* → **see** ◆ *s* sierra ◆ *vt* serrar

sawdust ['sɔ:dʌst] *s* serrín

sawed-off shotgun [sɔ:d-] *s* arma de cañones recortados

saxophone ['sæksəfəʊn] *s* saxofón

say [seɪ] ◆ *vt* ❶ decir • **she said that...** dijo que... • **you should have said so!** ¡haberlo dicho! • **to say something again** repetir algo • **you can say that again!** ¡ya lo creo! • **to say yes** decir que sí • **he's said to be good** se dice que es bueno • **let's say you were to win** pongamos que ganaras • **shall we say 9.30?** ¿qué tal a las 9.30? • **to say the least** por no decir otra cosa ❷ marcar *(suj: reloj, indicador)*

expresiones **that goes without saying** ni que decir tiene ▶ **I'll say this for him/her...** hay que decir o admitir que él/ella... ▶ **it has a lot to be said for it** tiene muy buenos puntos en su favor

◆ *s* • **to have a/no say in something** tener/no tener voz y voto en algo • **let me have my say** déjame decir lo que pienso

■ **that is to say** *adv* es decir

Formas irregulares de **say**: *pretérito & pp* **said**.

saying ['seɪɪŋ] *s* dicho

scab [skæb] *s* MEDICINA costra

scaffold ['skæfəʊld] *s* ❶ andamio ❷ cadalso

scaffolding ['skæfəldɪŋ] *s* ⚲ *incontable* andamios; andamiaje

scald [skɔ:ld] *vt* escaldar

scale [skeɪl] ◆ *s* ❶ escala • **to scale** a escala • **not drawn to scale** no hecho, cha a escala ❷ tamaño; dimensiones • **on a large scale** a gran escala ❸ escama ◆ *vt* ❶ escalar ❷ escamar

■ **scales** *spl* ❶ balanza ❷ báscula ▶ **bathroom scales** báscula de baño

■ **scale down** *vt* ☀️ *El objeto siempre va después de la preposición al final.* reducir

scale model *s* maqueta

scallion ['skæljən] *s* cebolleta

scallop ['skɒləp] *s ZOOLOGÍA* vieira

scalp [skælp] ◆ *s* cuero cabelludo ◆ *vt* cortar la cabellera a

scalpel ['skælpəl] *s* bisturí

scan [skæn] ◆ *s* ❶ escáner ❷ ecografía ◆ *vt* ❶ examinar ❷ dar un vistazo a ❸ *ELECTRÓNICA & TELEVISIÓN* escanear

scandal ['skændl] *s* ❶ escándalo ❷ habladurías

scandalize ['skændəlaɪz] *vt* escandalizar

Scandinavia [,skændɪ'neɪvjə] *s* Escandinavia

Scandinavian [,skændɪ'neɪvjən] ◆ *adj* escandinavo, va ◆ *s* escandinavo, va

scant [skænt] *adj* escaso, sa

scanty ['skæntɪ] *adj* ❶ escaso, sa ❷ ligero, ra *(ropa)* ❸ insuficiente *(comida)*

scapegoat ['skeɪpgəʊt] *s* cabeza de turco

scar [skɑːr] *s* cicatriz

scarce ['skeəs] *adj* escaso, sa

scarcely ['skeəslɪ] *adv* apenas • **scarcely anyone/ever** casi nadie/nunca

scare [skeər] ◆ *s* ❶ susto ❷ temor ❸ • **there was a bomb scare** hubo una amenaza de bomba ◆ *vt* asustar

■ **scare away, scare off** *vt* ☀️ *El objeto se puede colocar antes o después de la preposición.* ahuyentar

scarecrow ['skeəkrəʊ] *s* espantapájaros

scared ['skeəd] *adj* ❶ asustado, da • **don't be scared** no te asustes ❷ • **to be scared that** tener miedo que

expresión to be scared stiff o to death estar muerto de miedo

scarf [skɑːf] ◆ *s* ❶ bufanda ❷ pañuelo de cabeza ◆ *vt* • **scarf (down)** zamparse

Dos plurales: **scarfs** o **scarves**

scarlet ['skɑːlət] *adj* color escarlata

scarlet fever *s* escarlatina

scarves [skɑːvz] *spl* → **scarf**

scathing ['skeɪðɪŋ] *adj* mordaz • **to be scathing about something/somebody** criticar duramente algo/a alguien

scatter ['skætər] ◆ *vt* esparcir; desparramar ◆ *vi* dispersarse

scatterbrained ['skætəbreɪnd] *adj familiar* atolondrado, da

scavenger ['skævɪndʒər] *s* ❶ carroñero, ra ❷ persona que rebusca en las basuras

scenario [sɪ'nɑːrɪəʊ] *s* ❶ situación hipotética ❷ resumen del argumento

El plural de **scenario** es **scenarios**

scene [siːn] *s* ❶ escena • **behind the scenes** entre bastidores ❷ panorama; paisaje ❸ lugar • **the scene of the crime** el lugar del crimen ❹ escándalo

expresión to set the scene a) describir la escena b) crear el ambiente propicio

scenery ['siːnərɪ] *s* ☀️ *incontable* ❶ paisaje ❷ *TEATRO* decorado

scenic ['siːnɪk] *adj* ❶ pintoresco, ca ❷ turístico, ca *(viaje)*

scent [sent] *s* ❶ fragancia ❷ rastro *(de animal)* ❸ perfume ❹ *figurado* pista • **to throw somebody off the scent** burlar a alguien

schedule ['skedʒʊl] ◆ *s* ❶ programa; plan • **I have a busy schedule** tengo el calendario muy apretado • **on schedule** sin retraso • **ahead of schedule** con adelanto • **behind schedule** con retraso ❷ lista ❸ horario ◆ *vt* • **to schedule something (for)** fijar algo (para)

scheduled flight ['skedʒʊld-] *s* vuelo regular

scheme [skiːm] ◆ *s* ❶ plan; proyecto ❷ *despectivo* intriga ❸ • **color scheme** combinación de colores ◆ *vi despectivo* • **to scheme (to do something)** intrigar (para hacer algo)

schizophrenic [,skɪtsə'frenɪk] *adj* esquizofrénico, ca

schmuck [ʃmʌk] *s familiar* tonto, ta

scholar ['skɒlər] *s* ❶ erudito, ta ❷ *desusado* alumno, na

scholarship ['skɒləʃɪp] *s* ❶ beca ❷ erudición

school [skuːl] *s* ❶ colegio; escuela • **to go to school** ir al colegio; ir a la escuela • **the children are at school** los niños están en el colegio • **art school** escuela de arte • **driving school** autoescuela • **law/medical school** facultad de derecho/medicina ❷ universidad

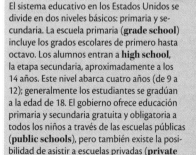

SCHOOL

El sistema educativo en los Estados Unidos se divide en dos niveles básicos: primaria y secundaria. La escuela primaria (**grade school**) incluye los grados escolares de primero hasta octavo. Los alumnos entran a **high school**, la etapa secundaria, aproximadamente a los 14 años. Este nivel abarca cuatro años (de 9 a 12); generalmente los estudiantes se gradúan a la edad de 18. El gobierno ofrece educación primaria y secundaria gratuita y obligatoria a todos los niños a través de las escuelas públicas (**public schools**), pero también existe la posibilidad de asistir a escuelas privadas (**private schools**).

school age *s* edad escolar

schoolbook ['skuːlbʊk] *s* libro de texto

schoolboy ['skuːlbɔɪ] *s* colegial

S

schoolchild ['sku:ltʃaɪld] *s* colegial, la
El plural de **schoolchild** es **schoolchildren**
['sku:ltʃɪldrən].

schooldays ['sku:ldeɪz] *spl* años de colegio

schoolgirl ['sku:lgɜ:l] *s* colegiala

schooling ['sku:lɪŋ] *s* educación escolar

schoolmaster ['sku:l,mɑ:stər] *s* ❶ *desusado* maestro ❷ profesor

schoolmistress ['sku:l,mɪstrɪs] *s* ❶ *desusado* maestra ❷ profesora

school of thought *s* corriente de opinión

schoolteacher ['sku:l,ti:tʃər] *s* ❶ maestro, tra ❷ profesor, ra

school year *s* año escolar

science ['saɪəns] *s* ciencia • **his best subject is science** su mejor asignatura son las ciencias

science fiction *s* ciencia ficción

scientific [,saɪən'tɪfɪk] *adj* científico, ca

scientist ['saɪəntɪst] *s* científico, ca

scissors ['sɪzəz] *spl* tijeras • **a pair of scissors** unas tijeras

sclerosis = multiple sclerosis

scold [skəʊld] *vt* regañar; reñir

scoop [sku:p] ◆ *s* ❶ cucharita plana; pinzas *(de helado)*; paleta *(de harina)* ❷ bola *(de helado)* ◆ *vt* ❶ recoger ❷ recoger con cucharilla

■ **scoop out** *vt* ⚙ *El objeto se puede colocar antes o después de la preposición.* sacar con cuchara

scooter ['sku:tər] *s* ❶ patinete ❷ Vespa® ; motoneta

scope [skəʊp] *s* ⚙ *incontable* ❶ posibilidades • **there is scope for improvement** se puede mejorar ❷ alcance

scorch [skɔ:tʃ] *vt* ❶ chamuscar ❷ quemar

scorching ['skɔ:tʃɪŋ] *adj familiar* abrasador, ra

score [skɔ:r] ◆ *s* ❶ calificación; nota ❷ puntuación • **to keep (the) score?** llevar el tanteo ❸ DEPORTE resultado • **what's the score?** ¿cómo van? • **the final score was 2 all** el resultado final fue empate a dos ❹ *desusado* veintena ❺ MÚSICA partitura ❻ • **on that score** a ese respecto; por lo que se refiere a eso

expresión **to have a score to settle with somebody** tener una cuenta que saldar con alguien ▶ **to know the score** conocer el percal

◆ *vt* ❶ DEPORTE marcar ❷ obtener *(éxito, victoria)* ❸ grabar ◆ *vi* ❶ DEPORTE marcar ❷ obtener una puntuación • **you scored well in part one** obtuviste una buena puntuación en la primera parte

scoreboard ['skɔ:bɔ:d] *s* marcador

scorer ['skɔ:rər] *s* ❶ tanteador, ra ❷ goleador, ra ❸ marcador, ra

scorn [skɔ:n] ◆ *s* menosprecio; desdén • **to pour scorn on something/somebody** despreciar algo/a alguien ◆ *vt* menospreciar; desdeñar

scornful ['skɔ:nful] *adj* despectivo, va

Scorpio ['skɔ:pɪəʊ] *s* Escorpión

El plural de **Scorpio** es **Scorpios**.

scorpion ['skɔ:pjən] *s* alacrán

Scot [skɒt] *s* escocés, esa

Scotch [skɒtʃ] *s* whisky escocés

Scotch tape® *s* cinta **Scotch®**

Scotland ['skɒtlənd] *s* Escocia

Scots [skɒts] ◆ *adj* escocés, esa ◆ *s* escocés

Scotsman ['skɒtsmən] *s* escocés

El plural de **Scotsman** es **Scotsmen** ['skɒtsmen].

Scotswoman ['skɒtswʊmən] *s* escocesa

El plural de **Scotswoman** es **Scotswomen** ['skɒts,wɪmɪn].

Scottish ['skɒtɪʃ] *adj* escocés, esa

scoundrel ['skaʊndrəl] *s desusado* sinvergüenza; canalla

scour [skaʊər] *vt* ❶ fregar; restregar ❷ registrar; batir

scout [skaʊt] *s* MILITAR explorador

■ **Scout** *s* explorador

scowl [skaʊl] *vi* fruncir el ceño

scramble ['skræmbl] ◆ *s* pelea ◆ *vi* ❶ trepar ❷ • **to scramble to your feet** levantarse rápidamente y tambaleándose

scrambled eggs ['skræmbld-] *spl* huevos revueltos

scrap [skræp] ◆ *s* ❶ trozo; pedazo ❷ ⚙ *incontable* chatarra ❸ *familiar* pelea • **to have a scrap** pelearse ◆ *vt* desechar; descartar

■ **scraps** *spl* sobras

scrapbook ['skræpbʊk] *s* álbum de recortes

scrape [skreɪp] ◆ *s* ❶ chirrido ❷ apuro ◆ *vt* ❶ • **to scrape something off something** raspar algo de algo ❷ rayar ❸ rasguñar ◆ *vi* • **to scrape against/on something** rozar contra/en algo

■ **scrape through** *vt* ⚙ *El objeto siempre va después de la preposición al final.* aprobar por los pelos

scraper ['skreɪpər] *s* raspador

scrapyard ['skræpjɑ:d] *s* ❶ depósito de chatarra ❷ cementerio de coches

scratch [skrætʃ] ◆ *s* ❶ arañazo; rasguño ❷ rayón

expresión **to do something from scratch** hacer algo partiendo desde el principio ▶ **to be up to scratch** estar a la altura requerida

◆ *vt* ❶ arañar; rasguñar ❷ rayar ❸ rascar • **he scratched his head** se rascó la cabeza ◆ *vi* rascarse

scratchpad ['skrætʃpæd] *s* bloc de notas

scratch paper *s* ⚙ *incontable* papel usado

scrawl [skrɔ:l] ◆ *s* garabatos ◆ *vt* garabatear

scrawny ['skrɔ:nɪ] *adj* flaco, ca

scream [skri:m] ◆ *s* ❶ grito; chillido ❷ chirrido ◆ *vt* vociferar ◆ *vi* chillar • **to scream at somebody** gritar a alguien

screech [skri:tʃ] ◆ *s* ❶ chillido ❷ chirrido ◆ *vt* gritar ◆ *vi* ❶ chillar ❷ chirriar

S

screen [skri:n] ◆ s ❶ TELEVISIÓN, CINE & INFORMÁTICA pantalla ❷ biombo ◆ vt ❶ proyectar ❷ emitir ❸ examinar • **to screen somebody for something** hacer un chequeo a alguien para algo

screening ['skri:nɪŋ] s ❶ proyección *(en cine)* ❷ emisión *(en televisión)* ❸ examen *(de seguridad)* ❹ MEDICINA chequeo

screenplay ['skri:npleɪ] s guión

screen saver s INFORMÁTICA protector de pantalla

screenshot ['skri:nʃɒt] s pantallazo; captura de pantalla

screw [skru:] ◆ s tornillo ◆ vt ❶ • **to screw something to** atornillar algo a ❷ enroscar • **I screwed the top on the bottle** enrosqué la tapa en la botella

■ **screw up** vt ☼ *El objeto se puede colocar antes o después de la preposición.* ❶ arrugar ❷ entornar ❸ *muy familiar* fastidiar

screwball ['skru:bɔ:l] s loco, ca ‣ **screwball comedy** comedia disparatada

screwdriver ['skru:ˌdraɪvər] s desarmador

screwy ['skru:ɪ] adj familiar pirado, da

scribble ['skrɪbl] ◆ s garabato ◆ vt & vi garabatear

script [skrɪpt] s ❶ guión ❷ escritura ❸ letra

Scriptures ['skrɪptʃəz] spl • **the Scriptures** las Sagradas Escrituras

scriptwriter ['skrɪptˌraɪtər] s guionista

scroll [skrəʊl] ◆ s rollo de pergamino/papel ◆ vt INFORMÁTICA desplazar

■ **scroll down** vi INFORMÁTICA desplazarse hacia abajo

■ **scroll up** vi INFORMÁTICA desplazarse hacia arriba

scrounge [skraʊndʒ] vt familiar gorronear

scrounger ['skraʊndʒər] s familiar gorrón, ona

scrub [skrʌb] ◆ s ❶ restregón • **give it a good scrub** dale un buen fregado ❷ maleza ◆ vt restregar

scruff [skrʌf] s • **to have/get somebody by the scruff of the neck** tener/tomar a alguien por el pescuezo

scruffy ['skrʌfɪ] adj ❶ dejado, da ❷ andrajoso, sa ❸ desordenado, da

scruples ['skru:plz] spl escrúpulos

scrutinize ['skru:tɪnaɪz] vt escudriñar

scrutiny ['skru:tɪnɪ] s ☼ *incontable* escrutinio; examen

scuff [skʌf] vt pelar *(zapatos)*; rayar *(mueble, suelo)*

scuffle ['skʌfl] s refriega; reyerta • **there were scuffles between the police and demonstrators** hubo enfrentamientos entre la policía y los manifestantes

sculptor ['skʌlptər] s escultor, ra

sculpture ['skʌlptʃər] s escultura

scum [skʌm] s ☼ *incontable* ❶ espuma ❷ *muy familiar & despectivo* escoria

scupper ['skʌpər] vt hundir

scurry ['skʌrɪ] vi • **to scurry off** o **away** escabullirse

scuttle ['skʌtl] ◆ s cubo del carbón ◆ vi • **to scuttle off** o **away** escabullirse

scythe [saɪð] s guadaña

sea [si:] s mar • **at sea** en el mar • **by sea** en barco • **by the sea** a orillas del mar • **out to sea a)** mar adentro **b)** hacia el mar

expresión **to be all at sea** estar totalmente perdido, da

seabed ['si:bed] s lecho marino

seaboard ['si:bɔ:d] s litoral

sea breeze s brisa marina

seafood ['si:fu:d] s ☼ *incontable* mariscos

seafront ['si:frʌnt] s paseo marítimo

seagull ['si:gʌl] s gaviota

seal [si:l] ◆ s ❶ foca ❷ sello ❸ precinto

expresión **to put** o **set the seal on something** sellar algo ‣ **to give something your seal of approval** dar el visto bueno a algo

◆ vt ❶ sellar; cerrar ❷ tapar; cerrar

■ **seal off** vt ☼ *El objeto se puede colocar antes o después de la preposición.* ❶ cerrar ❷ acordonar

sea level s nivel del mar

sea lion s león marino

seam [si:m] s COSER costura

seaman ['si:mən] s marinero

El plural de **seaman** es **seamen** ['si:men].

seaplane ['si:pleɪn] s hidroavión

seaport ['si:pɔ:t] s puerto de mar

search [sɜ:tʃ] ◆ s ❶ búsqueda • **search for something** búsqueda de algo • **in search of** en busca de ❷ registro ❸ cacheo ◆ vt registrar • **to search something for something** buscar algo en algo ◆ vi • **to search (for something/somebody)** buscar (algo/a alguien)

search engine s INFORMÁTICA buscador; motor de búsqueda

searching ['sɜ:tʃɪŋ] adj ❶ agudo, da *(pregunta)* ❷ penetrante *(mirada)*

searchlight ['sɜ:tʃlaɪt] s reflector

search party s grupo de rescate

search warrant s mandamiento de registro

seashell ['si:ʃel] s concha (marina)

seashore ['si:ʃɔ:r] s la orilla del mar

seasick ['si:sɪk] adj mareado, da • **to be/feel seasick** estar/sentirse mareado • **to get seasick** marearse

seaside ['si:saɪd] s • **the seaside** la playa

seaside resort s lugar de veraneo (en la playa)

season ['si:zn] ◆ s ❶ estación • **the four seasons** las cuatro estaciones ❷ temporada • **the soccer season** la temporada de fútbol • **the season** la temporada de vacaciones • **to book a vacation out of season** reservar unas vacaciones fuera de temporada ❸ época • **the planting season** la época de plantar ❹ • **out of/ in season** fuera de/en sazón • **plums are in season** las ciruelas están en temporada ◆ vt sazonar • **to season with salt and pepper** salpimentar

seasonal ['siːzənl] *adj* ❶ temporal ❷ estacional

seasoned ['siːznd] *adj* veterano, na • **to be a seasoned traveller** ser un viajero experimentado

seasoning ['siːznɪŋ] *s* condimento

season ticket *s* abono

seat [siːt] ◆ *s* ❶ asiento • **is this seat taken?** ¿está ocupado este asiento? • **take a seat, please** siéntese, por favor ❷ localidad *(en teatro)* ❸ trasero *(de pantalón, falda)* ❹ POLÍTICA escaño ❺ sede • **the seat of government** la sede del gobierno ◆ *vt* ❶ sentar • **be seated!** ¡siéntese! ❷ tener cabida para

seat belt *s* cinturón de seguridad

seating ['siːtɪŋ] *s* ☿ *incontable* asientos

seawater ['siː‚wɔːtər] *s* agua de mar

seaweed ['siːwiːd] *s* ☿ *incontable* alga marina

sec. *(abreviatura de* second) seg.

secluded [sɪ'kluːdɪd] *adj* apartado, da

seclusion [sɪ'kluːʒn] *s* aislamiento • **to live in seclusion** vivir aislado, da

second ['sekənd] ◆ *s* ❶ segundo • **can you wait a second?** ¿podrías esperar un momento? ❷ segunda *(marcha)* ◆ *número* segundo, da • **to ask for a second chance/opinion** pedir una segunda oportunidad/opinión • **Elizabeth the Second** Isabel II ◆ *vt* secundar ver también **sixth**

■ **seconds** *spl* ❶ COMERCIO artículos defectuosos ❷ • **to have seconds** repetir *(en una comida)* • **are there any seconds?** ¿se puede repetir?

secondary ['sekəndrɪ] *adj* ❶ EDUCACIÓN secundario, ria *(escuela)*; medio, dia *(enseñanza)* ❷ secundario, ria *(menos importante)*

secondary school *s* escuela secundaria

second-class ['sekənd-] ◆ *adj* de segunda clase **expresión** **to be a second-class citizen** ser un ciudadano de segunda (clase)

◆ *adv* • **to travel second-class** viajar en segunda

second floor ['sekənd-] *s* primer piso

second hand ['sekənd-] *s* segundero

second-hand ['sekənd-] ◆ *adj* de segunda mano ◆ *adv* de segunda mano

secondly ['sekəndlɪ] *adv* en segundo lugar

second-rate ['sekənd-] *adj* *despectivo* de segunda categoría; mediocre

second thought ['sekənd-] *s* • **to have second thoughts about something** tener dudas acerca de algo • **on second thought** pensándolo bien

secrecy ['siːkrəsɪ] *s* ☿ *incontable* secreto • **to be shrouded in secrecy** estar rodeado de un gran secreto

secret ['siːkrɪt] ◆ *adj* secreto, ta ◆ *s* secreto • **in secret** en secreto • **to keep a secret** guardar un secreto • **to tell somebody a secret** contar a alguien un secreto • **to make no secret of something** no ocultar algo • **the secret of happiness** la clave de la felicidad

secretarial [‚sekrə'teərɪəl] *adj* ❶ de secretariado ❷ administrativo, va

secretary ['sekrə‚terɪ] *s* ❶ secretario, ria ❷ POLÍTICA ministro

Secretary of State *s* ministro estadounidense de Asuntos Exteriores

secretive ['siːkrətɪv] *adj* ❶ reservado, da ❷ secreto, ta

secretly ['siːkrɪtlɪ] *adv* ❶ secretamente ❷ en secreto • **she was secretly pleased** aunque no lo expresara, estaba contenta

sect [sekt] *s* secta

section ['sekʃn] *s* sección

sector ['sektər] *s* sector

secure [sɪ'kjʊər] ◆ *adj* seguro, ra ◆ *vt* ❶ conseguir; obtener ❷ proteger ❸ cerrar bien

security [sɪ'kjʊərətɪ] *s* seguridad

■ **securities** *spl* FINANZAS valores

security guard *s* guardia jurado o de seguridad

sedan [sɪ'dæn] *s* (coche) utilitario

sedate [sɪ'deɪt] ◆ *adj* sosegado, da ◆ *vt* sedar

sedative ['sedətɪv] *s* sedante

sediment ['sedɪmənt] *s* sedimento

seduce [sɪ'djuːs] *vt* seducir • **to seduce somebody (into doing something)** seducir a alguien (a hacer algo)

seductive [sɪ'dʌktɪv] *adj* seductor, ra

see [siː] ◆ *vt* ❶ ver • **see you soon/later/tomorrow!** ¡hasta pronto/luego/mañana! • **see you!** ¡hasta luego! • **see below/p 10** véase más abajo/pág. 10 ❷ ir a ver; visitar ❸ • **to see somebody to the door** acompañar a alguien a la puerta ❹ • **to see (to it) that...** encargarse de que... ◆ *vi* ❶ ver • **I can't see** no veo • **to see if you can do something** ver si uno puede hacer algo • **let's see, let me see** vamos a ver; veamos • **you see...** verás, es que... • **I see** ya veo • **we'll see** veremos ❷ entender

■ **seeing as, seeing that** *conjunción* *familiar* como

■ **see about** *vt* ☿ *El objeto siempre va después de la preposición al final.* encargarse de

■ **see off** *vt* ☿ *El objeto se puede colocar antes o después de la preposición.* despedir

■ **see through** *vt* ☿ *El objeto siempre va después de la preposición al final.* • **I can see right through her** veo claramente sus intenciones

■ **see to** *vt* ☿ *El objeto siempre va después de la preposición al final.* ocuparse de

Formas irregulares de **see**: pretérito **saw**, pp **seen**.

seed [siːd] *s* semilla

seek [siːk] *vt* *formal* ❶ buscar ❷ solicitar

Formas irregulares de **seek**: pretérito & pp **sought**.

seem [siːm] ◆ *vi* parecer • **it seems (to be) good** parece (que es) bueno • **I can't seem to do it** no puedo hacerlo (por mucho que lo intente) ◆ *v impersonal* • **it seems (that)** parece que • **it seems to me that** me parece que

seemingly ['siːmɪŋlɪ] *adv* aparentemente

seen [siːn] *participio pasado* → **see**

seep [siːp] *vi* rezumar; filtrarse

seesaw ['si:sɔ:] *s* balancín

seethe [si:ð] *vi* **❶** rabiar **❷** • **to be seething with** estar a rebosar de

see-through *adj* transparente

segment ['segmənt] *s* **❶** segmento **❷** gajo

segregate ['segrɪgeɪt] *vt* segregar

Seine [seɪn] *s* • **the (River) Seine** el (río) Sena

seize [si:z] *vt* **❶** agarrar **❷** tomar; hacerse con *(poder, control, ciudad)* **❸** detener *(arrestar)* **❹** aprovechar *(oportunidad)*

■ **seize up** *vi* agarrotarse

seizure ['si:ʒər] *s* MEDICINA ataque

seldom ['seldəm] *adv* raramente

select [sɪ'lekt] ◆ *adj* selecto, ta ◆ *vt* **❶** elegir; escoger **❷** DEPORTE & INFORMÁTICA seleccionar

selection [sɪ'lekʃn] *s* **❶** selección **❷** elección **❸** surtido

selective [sɪ'lektɪv] *adj* selectivo, va

self [self] *s* uno mismo, una misma • **she wasn't her usual self** no estaba como de costumbre • **the self** el yo

El plural de **self** es **selves**.

self-addressed stamped envelope [-ə,drest'stæmpt-] *s* ▶ sobre con sus señas y franqueo

self-assured *adj* seguro de sí mismo, segura de sí misma

self-catering *adj* sin pensión • **a self-catering vacation/chalet** unas vacaciones/un chalet sin servicio de comidas

self-centered [-'sentəd] *adj* egocéntrico, ca

self-confessed [-kən'fest] *adj* confeso, sa

self-confident *adj* **❶** seguro de sí mismo, segura de sí misma **❷** lleno, na de seguridad

self-conscious *adj* cohibido, da

self-contained [-kən'teɪnd] *adj* independiente • **a self-contained apartment** un apartamento independiente

self-control *s* control de sí mismo/misma

self-defense *s* defensa propia • **in self-defense** en defensa propia

self-discipline *s* autodisciplina

self-employed [-ɪm'plɔɪd] *adj* autónomo, ma

self-esteem *s* amor propio

self-evident *adj* evidente; patente

self-explanatory *adj* evidente

self-important *adj* despectivo engreído, da

self-indulgent *adj* despectivo autocomplaciente

self-interest *s* ⚇ *incontable* despectivo interés propio

selfish ['selfɪʃ] *adj* egoísta

selfishness ['selfɪʃnɪs] *s* egoísmo

selfless ['selflɪs] *adj* desinteresado, da

self-made *adj* • **a self-made man** un hombre hecho a sí mismo

self-pity *s* despectivo lástima de uno mismo/una misma

self-portrait *s* autorretrato

self-reliant *adj* independiente

self-respect *s* amor propio

self-respecting [-rɪs'pektɪŋ] *adj* que se precie; digno, na • **no self-respecting person would eat this rubbish** nadie con un mínimo de dignidad se comería esa basura

self-restraint *s* dominio de sí mismo/misma

self-righteous *adj* despectivo santurrón, ona

self-rising flour *s* harina con levadura

self-sacrifice *s* abnegación

self-satisfied *adj* **❶** despectivo satisfecho de sí mismo, satisfecha de sí misma **❷** lleno, na de suficiencia

self-service *en compuestos* de autoservicio • **a self-service restaurant** un autoservicio

self-sufficient *adj* • **self-sufficient (in)** autosuficiente (en)

self-taught *adj* autodidacta

sell [sel] ◆ *vt* vender • **to sell something to somebody, to sell somebody something** vender algo a alguien • **to sell something for** vender algo por ◆ *vi* **❶** vender **❷** venderse • **this model sells well** este modelo se vende muy bien • **to sell (for o at)** venderse (a)

■ **sell off** *vt* ⚇ *El objeto se puede colocar antes o después de la preposición.* liquidar; vender

■ **sell out** ◆ *vt* ⚇ *El objeto se puede colocar antes o después de la preposición.* • **to have sold out** estar agotado, da • **all the tickets are sold out** las entradas están agotadas ◆ *vi* **❶** • **to sell out (of something)** agotar las existencias (de algo) • **we're sold out of coffee** se nos terminó el café **❷** venderse

Formas irregulares de **sell**: pretérito & pp **sold**.

seller ['selər] *s* vendedor, ra

selling price *s* precio de venta

sell-out *s* lleno *(partido, actuación, sesión)*

selves [selvz] *spl* → **self**

semen ['si:men] *s* semen

semester [sɪ'mestər] *s* semestre

semicircle ['semɪ,sɜ:kl] *s* semicírculo

semicolon [,semɪ'kəʊlən] *s* punto y coma

semifinal [,semɪ'faɪnl] *s* semifinal

seminar ['semɪnɑ:r] *s* seminario

seminary ['semɪnərɪ] *s* RELIGIÓN seminario

semiskilled [,semɪ'skɪld] *adj* semicualificado, da

semitrailer [,semɪ'treɪlər] *s* camión articulado

semolina [,semə'li:nə] *s* sémola

Senate ['senɪt] *s* POLÍTICA • **the (United States) Senate** el Senado (de los Estados Unidos)

S

SENATE

El Senado (**Senate**) constituye, junto con la Cámara de Representantes, el organismo legislativo estadounidense. Se elige a sus 100 miembros cada seis años. Cada uno de los 50 estados tiene 2 senadores. Todas las leyes nuevas deben ser ratificadas por ambas cámaras del Congreso.

senator ['senətər] *s* senador, ra

send [send] *vt* ❶ mandar • **to send somebody something, to send something to somebody** mandar a alguien algo • **send them my best wishes** mándales saludos de mi parte ❷ enviar; mandar • **she sent her son to the store for some bread** envió a su hijo a comprar pan en la tienda • **he was sent to prison** fue encarcelado

■ **send for** *vt* ⚙ *El objeto siempre va después de la preposición al final.* • **I sent for the doctor** mandé a buscar al médico

■ **send in** *vt* ⚙ *El objeto se puede colocar antes o después de la preposición.* mandar; enviar

■ **send off** *vt* ⚙ *El objeto se puede colocar antes o después de la preposición.* ❶ mandar (por correo) ❷ DEPORTE expulsar

■ **send off for** *vt* ⚙ *El objeto siempre va después de la preposición al final.* pedir; encargar

sender ['sendər] *s* remitente

send-off *s* despedida

senile ['si:naɪl] *adj* senil

senior ['si:njər] ◆ *adj* ❶ superior; de rango superior • **senior people in the government** altos personajes del gobierno ❷ EDUCACIÓN mayor *(alumno)* ❸ de los mayores *(clase)* ▶ **senior year** último curso de la enseñanza secundaria y de la universidad en Estados Unidos ◆ *s* ❶ EDUCACIÓN estudiante del último año ❷ • **I'm five years his senior** le llevo cinco años ❸ • **he's my senior** es mi superior ❹ persona de la tercera edad

senior citizen *s* ciudadano, na de la tercera edad

senior high school *s* ≃ preparatoria (16-18 años)

sensation [sen'seɪʃn] *s* sensación • **to cause a sensation** causar sensación

sensational [sen'seɪʃənl] *adj* sensacional

sensationalist [sen'seɪʃnəlɪst] *adj despectivo* sensacionalista

sense [sens] ◆ *s* ❶ sentido • **to make sense** tener sentido • **what you say doesn't make sense** lo que dices no tiene sentido • **to make sense of something** entender algo ❷ sentimiento ❸ sensación; noción ❹ • **business sense** talento para los negocios • **sense of humor/style** sentido del humor/estilo ❺ juicio; sentido común • **you have no sense** no tienes sentido común

expresión **there's no** o **little sense in arguing** no tiene sentido discutir

◆ *vt* sentir; percibir • **to sense (that)** percibir o sentir que

■ **in a sense** *adv* en cierto sentido

senseless ['senslɪs] *adj* ❶ sin sentido ❷ inconsciente • **the blow knocked him senseless** el golpe lo dejó inconsciente

sensible ['sensəbl] *adj* ❶ sensato, ta ❷ práctico, ca *(ropa)*

sensitive ['sensɪtɪv] *adj* ❶ sensible • **sensitive to heat/light** sensible al calor/a la luz ❷ • **sensitive (to)** comprensivo, va (hacia) ❸ • **sensitive (to/about)** susceptible (a/acerca de) • **she's sensitive about her weight** no le gusta que hagan comentarios sobre su peso ❹ delicado, da *(tema)*

sensual ['sensjʊəl] *adj* sensual

sensuous ['sensjʊəs] *adj* sensual

sent [sent] *pretérito & participio pasado* → **send**

sentence ['sentəns] ◆ *s* ❶ frase; oración ❷ DERECHO sentencia ▶ **prison sentence** condena de cárcel ◆ *vt* • **to sentence somebody (to)** condenar a alguien (a) • **he was sentenced to death/3 years** lo condenaron a muerte/tres años de cárcel

sentimental [,sentɪ'mentl] *adj* sentimental

sentry ['sentrɪ] *s* centinela

separate ◆ *adj* ['seprət] ❶ • **separate (from)** separado, da (de) • **put it in a separate envelope** ponlo en un sobre aparte ❷ distinto, ta ◆ *vt* ['sepəreɪt] ❶ • **to separate something/somebody (from)** separar algo/a alguien (de) ❷ • **to separate something/somebody from** diferenciar algo/a alguien de ❸ • **to separate something/somebody into** dividir algo/a alguien en ◆ *vi* ['sepəreɪt] ❶ • **to separate (from)** separarse (de) ❷ • **to separate (into)** dividirse (en)

separately ['seprətlɪ] *adv* ❶ independientemente ❷ por separado

separation [,sepə'reɪʃn] *s* separación

September [sep'tembər] *s* septiembre • **1 September 2007** 1 de septiembre de 2007 • **by/in September** para/en septiembre • **last/this/next September** en septiembre del año pasado/de este año/del año que viene • **every September** todos los años en septiembre • **during September** en septiembre; durante el mes de septiembre • **at the beginning/end of September** a principios/finales de septiembre • **in the middle of September** a mediados de septiembre

septic ['septɪk] *adj* séptico, ca

sequel ['si:kwəl] *s* ❶ • **sequel (to)** continuación (de) *(libro, película)* ❷ • **sequel (to)** secuela (de)

sequence ['si:kwəns] *s* ❶ secuencia ❷ sucesión

Serb = **Serbian**

Serbia ['sɜ:bjə] *s* Serbia

Serbian ['sɜ:bjən], **Serb** [sɜ:b] ◆ *adj* serbio, bia ◆ *s* ❶ serbio, bia ❷ serbio

sergeant ['sɑ:dʒənt] *s* MILITAR sargento

sergeant major *s* sargento mayor

serial ['sɪərɪəl] *s* serial

serial killer *s* asesino, na en serie

serial number *s* número de serie

S

series ['sɪəriːz] *s* serie • **a TV series** una serie televisiva

El plural de **series** es **series**.

serious ['sɪərɪəs] *adj* ❶ serio, ria • **are you serious?** ¿hablas en serio? ❷ grave

seriously ['sɪərɪəslɪ] *adv* ❶ en serio ❷ gravemente • **to be seriously ill** estar gravemente enfermo ❸ seriamente

expresión to take something/somebody seriously tomar algo/a alguien en serio

seriousness ['sɪərɪəsnɪs] *s* ❶ gravedad ❷ seriedad

sermon ['sɜːmən] *s despectivo* RELIGIÓN sermón

servant ['sɜːvənt] *s* sirviente, ta

serve [sɜːv] ◆ *vt* ❶ servir • **to serve something to somebody, to serve somebody something** servir algo a alguien • **to serve to do something** servir para hacer algo ❷ • **to serve a purpose** cumplir un propósito ❸ abastecer ❹ despachar; servir • **are you being served?** ¿lo atienden? ❺ cumplir *(condena)* ❻ ejercer *(cargo)* ❼ DEPORTE sacar; servir

expresión that serves you right! ¡bien merecido lo tienes!

◆ *vi* ❶ servir ❷ • **to serve as** servir de ❸ despachar ❹ DEPORTE sacar ◆ *s* DEPORTE saque

■ **serve out, serve up** *vt* ☼ *El objeto se puede colocar antes o después de la preposición.* servir

service ['sɜːvɪs] ◆ *s* ❶ servicio • **in service** en funcionamiento • **out of service** fuera de servicio • **bus/ train service** servicio de autobús/tren ❷ revisión *(de vehículo)* ❸ RELIGIÓN oficio; servicio • **to hold a service** celebrar un oficio ❹ servicio; juego • **dinner service** servicio de mesa ❺ DEPORTE saque ❻ • **the service** las fuerzas armadas ❼ • **to be of service (to somebody)** servir (a alguien) ◆ *vt* revisar

■ **services** *spl* servicios

service charge *s* servicio

serviceman ['sɜːvɪsmən] *s* militar

El plural de **serviceman** es **servicemen** ['sɜːvɪsmen].

service provider *s* proveedor de servicios

service station *s* estación de servicio

serving dish *s* fuente

sesame ['sesəmɪ] *s* sésamo

session ['seʃn] *s* ❶ sesión • **in session** en sesión ❷ trimestre

set [set] ◆ *adj* ❶ fijo, ja ❷ establecido, da *(método, patrón)* ❸ • **set (for something/to do something)** listo, ta (para algo/para hacer algo) ◆ *s* ❶ juego *(colección)* ❷ serie *(de timbres)* ❸ aparato ❹ TEATRO decorado ❺ CINE foro ❻ TENIS set ❼ marcado *(estilo de pelo)* ◆ *vt* ❶ poner; colocar ❷ • **to set something in** o **into** montar algo en ❸ • **to set free** poner en libertad • **to set fire to** prender fuego a • **to set somebody thinking** hacer pensar a alguien ❹ poner *(trampa, la mesa, trabajo, alarma)* ❺ fijar *(tiempo, salario, objetivo)* ❻ dar *(ejemplo)* • **to set a good example** dar ejemplo ❼ establecer *(récord)* ❽ sentar *(precedente)* ❾ imponer; dic-

tar *(moda, tendencia)* ❿ MEDICINA componer ⓫ situar; ambientar • **the series is set in San Francisco** la serie está ambientada en San Francisco ◆ *vi* ❶ ponerse *(el sol)* ❷ cuajarse ❸ secarse

■ **set about** *vt* ☼ *El objeto siempre va después de la preposición al final.* comenzar *(tarea)*; atacar *(problema)* • **to set about doing something** ponerse a hacer algo

■ **set aside** *vt* ☼ *El objeto se puede colocar antes o después de la preposición.* ❶ reservar ❷ dejar de lado

■ **set back** *vt* ☼ *El objeto se puede colocar antes o después de la preposición.* retrasar

■ **set off** ◆ *vt* ☼ *El objeto se puede colocar antes o después de la preposición.* ❶ provocar ❷ hacer estallar *(bomba)* ❸ tirar *(fuegos artificiales)* ❹ hacer sonar *(alarma)* ◆ *vi* salir; ponerse en camino

■ **set out** ◆ *vt* ☼ *El objeto se puede colocar antes o después de la preposición.* disponer ◆ *vi* ❶ salir; ponerse en camino ❷ • **to set out to do something** proponerse hacer algo

■ **set up** *vt* ☼ *El objeto se puede colocar antes o después de la preposición.* ❶ poner; montar *(negocio)* ❷ crear *(comité, organización)* ❸ establecer *(procedimiento)* ❹ organizar *(entrevista, reunión)* • **to set up house** o **home** instalarse ❺ levantar *(control de carretera)* ❻ preparar ❼ instalar *(computadora)* ❽ *familiar* tender una trampa a

Formas irregulares de **set**: *pretérito* & *pp* **set**.

setback ['setbæk] *s* revés; contratiempo

set menu *s* menú del día

settee [se'tiː] *s* sofá

setting ['setɪŋ] *s* ❶ escenario ❷ posición *(de selector, mando)*

settle ['setl] ◆ *vt* ❶ resolver • **that settles it, she can move out!** ¡no se hable más, que se vaya! ❷ ajustar; saldar *(deuda, cuenta)* ❸ tranquilizar • **this should settle your stomach** esto te asentará el estómago ◆ *vi* ❶ instalarse • **they settled in Canada** se establecieron en Canadá ❷ acomodarse ❸ depositarse • **the snow has settled** la nieve ha cuajado ❹ calmarse

■ **settle down** *vi* ❶ • **to settle down (for something)** prepararse (para algo) ❷ sentar la cabeza ❸ calmarse ❹ acomodarse

■ **settle for** *vt* ☼ *El objeto siempre va después de la preposición al final.* conformarse con

■ **settle in** *vi* ❶ instalarse ❷ adaptarse

■ **settle on** *vt* ☼ *El objeto siempre va después de la preposición al final.* decidirse por

■ **settle up** *vi* • **to settle up (with somebody)** ajustar las cuentas (con alguien)

settlement ['setlmənt] *s* ❶ acuerdo ❷ poblado

settler ['setlər] *s* colono

set-up *s familiar* ❶ sistema ❷ trampa

seven ['sevn] *número* siete ver también **six**

seventeen [ˌsevn'tiːn] *número* diecisiete ver también **six**

seventeenth [ˌsevn'tiːnə] *número* decimoséptimo, ma ver también **sixth**

S

seventh ['sevnθ] *número* séptimo, ma ver también **sixth**

seventy ['sevntɪ] *número* setenta ver también **sixty**

sever ['sevər] *vt* ❶ cortar ❷ romper *(relaciones)*

several ['sevrəl] ◆ *adj* varios, rias ◆ *pronombre* varios, rias

severe [sɪ'vɪər] *adj* ❶ severo, ra ❷ fuerte; agudo, da *(dolor)*

severity [sɪ'verətɪ] *s* ❶ gravedad ❷ severidad

sew [səʊ] *vt* & *vi* coser

■ **sew up** *vt* ☀ *El objeto se puede colocar antes o después de la preposición.* coser

Formas irregulares de **sew**: *pp* **sewed** o **sewn**.

sewage ['suːɪdʒ] *s* ☀ *incontable* aguas residuales

sewer ['sʊər] *s* alcantarilla; cloaca

sewing ['səʊɪŋ] *s* ☀ *incontable* ❶ labor de costura ❷ costura

sewing machine *s* máquina de coser

sewn [səʊn] *participio pasado* → **sew**

sex [seks] *s* sexo • **to have sex** tener relaciones sexuales

sexist ['seksɪst] ◆ *adj* sexista ◆ *s* sexista

sexual ['sekʃʊəl] *adj* sexual

sexual harassment *s* acoso sexual

sexual intercourse *s* ☀ *incontable* relaciones sexuales

sexy ['seksɪ] *adj familiar* sexi

shabby ['ʃæbɪ] *adj* ❶ desastrado, da ❷ de aspecto abandonado ❸ andrajoso, sa

shack [ʃæk] *s* chabola

shade [ʃeɪd] ◆ *s* ❶ ☀ *incontable* sombra • **in the shade** a la sombra ❷ pantalla *(de lámpara)* ❸ matiz ❹ persiana ❺ • **a shade too big** un poquito grande ◆ *vt* dar sombra a • **the car was shaded from the sun** el coche estaba protegido del sol

■ **shades** *spl familiar* lentes oscuros

shadow ['ʃædəʊ] ◆ *s* ❶ sombra ❷ oscuridad
expresión **there's not a shadow of a doubt** no hay la menor duda

◆ *vt* seguir

shady ['ʃeɪdɪ] *adj* ❶ sombreado, da ❷ *familiar* sospechoso, sa *(hombre de negocios)*; turbio, bia *(trato)*

shaft [ʃɑːft] *s* ❶ pozo ❷ hueco *(de ascensor)* ❸ rayo ❹ asta

shaggy ['ʃægɪ] *adj* peludo, da

shake [ʃeɪk] ◆ *vt* ❶ sacudir • **to shake somebody's hand** dar o estrechar la mano a alguien • **to shake hands** darse o estrecharse la mano • **he shook hands with her** le dio la mano • **to shake your head a)** negar con la cabeza **b)** mover la cabeza mostrando incredulidad • **to shake your fist at somebody** amenazar a alguien con el puño ❷ agitar • **shake well before using** agitar bien antes de usar ❸ trastornar; conmocionar ◆ *vi* ❶ temblar • **to shake with fear** temblar de miedo ❷ *familiar* • **let's shake on it** venga esa mano

■ **shake off** *vt* ☀ *El objeto se puede colocar antes o después de la preposición.* ❶ deshacerse de *(perseguidor)* ❷ quitarse de encima *(resfriado)*

■ **shake up** *vt* ☀ *El objeto se puede colocar antes o después de la preposición.* ❶ agitar ❷ • **she wasn't hurt, just a bit shaken up** no resultó herida, sólo un poco conmocionada

Formas irregulares de **shake**: *pretérito* **shook**, *pp* **shaken**.

shaken ['ʃeɪkn] *participio pasado* → **shake**

shaky ['ʃeɪkɪ] *adj* ❶ tembloroso, sa • **to feel shaky** encontrarse nervioso ❷ incierto, ta *(actuación, comienzo)* ❸ poco sólido, da *(argumento)* ❹ inestable

---

shall

◆ *auxiliar*

☀ *acento atónico* [ʃəl], *acento tónico* [ʃæl]

❶ [*para expresar el futuro (1ª pers. sing & 1ª pers. pl)*]
• **I shall be in Ohio next week** la próxima semana estaré en Ohio
• **we shall not** o **shan't be there before 6** no estaremos allí antes de las 6

❷ [*para sugerir algo (1ª pers. sing & 1ª pers. pl)*]
• **let's go, shall we?** ¿nos vamos?
• **shall we have lunch now?** ¿qué tal si almorzamos?

❸ [*en preguntas*]
• **where shall I put this?** ¿dónde pongo esto?

❹ [*para dar una orden*]
• **you shall tell me!** ¡me lo dices a mí!
• **thou shalt not kill** no matarás

---

shall

Se puede emplear shall con I y we en oraciones interrogativas que sugieren algo (*shall* I make you a cup of tea? *¿quieres una taza de té?*), hacen una invitación (*shall* we go for a picnic on Sunday? *¿te apetece hacer un picnic el domingo?*) o piden consejo (what *shall* I wear? *¿qué me pongo?*).

Aparte de esto, shall no se usa mucho, especialmente en inglés americano. Shan't la forma negativa, se usa aún menos. Should cumple la función de pasado de shall.

---

shallow ['ʃæləʊ] *adj* ❶ poco profundo, da ❷ *despectivo* superficial

sham [ʃæm] *s* farsa

shame [ʃeɪm] ◆ *s* ❶ ☀ *incontable* pena ❷ • **to bring shame on** o **upon somebody** deshonrar a alguien ❸ • **what a shame!** ¡qué pena o lástima! • **it's a shame** es una pena o lástima ◆ *vt* ❶ apenar ❷ • **to shame somebody into doing something** conseguir que alguien haga algo avergonzándolo

shameful ['ʃeɪmfʊl] *adj* vergonzoso, sa

shameless [ˈʃeɪmlɪs] *adj* desvergonzado, da
shampoo [ʃæmˈpuː] ◆ *s* champú ◆ *vt* lavar (con champú)

El plural de **shampoo** es **shampoos.**

shamrock [ˈʃæmrɒk] *s* trébol
shandy [ˈʃændɪ] *s* cerveza con gaseosa
shan't [ʃɑːnt] (*abreviatura de* shall not) → **shall**
shantytown [ˈʃæntɪtaʊn] *s* ciudad perdida
shape [ʃeɪp] ◆ *s* ❶ forma • it's oval in shape tiene forma ovalada • cookies in the shape of stars galletas con forma de estrellas ❷ figura ❸ configuración ❹ • to be in good/bad shape estar/no estar en forma *(persona)*; estar en buen/mal estado *(negocio)* • to get back in shape ponerse en forma
expresión to take shape tomar forma ▸ to lick o knock somebody into shape poner a alguien a punto
◆ *vt* ❶ • to shape something (into) dar a algo forma (de) ❷ desarrollar
■ **shape up** *vi* desarrollarse
-shaped [ˈʃeɪpt] *sufijo* • egg/star-shaped en forma de huevo/estrella
shapely [ˈʃeɪplɪ] *adj* bien hecho, cha
share [ʃeəʳ] ◆ *s* ❶ • share (of o in) parte (de) ❷ • to have/do your share of something tener/hacer la parte que a uno le toca de algo ◆ *vt* • to share something (with) compartir algo (con) • we share a love of opera nos une la pasión por la ópera ◆ *vi* compartir
■ **shares** *spl* acciones
■ **share out** *vt* ⚙ *El objeto se puede colocar antes o después de la preposición.* repartir; distribuir
shareholder [ˈʃeəˌhəʊldəʳ] *s* accionista
shark [ʃɑːk] *s* ❶ tiburón ❷ *figurado* estafador, ra

Dos plurales: **shark** o **sharks.**

sharp [ʃɑːp] ◆ *adj* ❶ afilado, da ❷ puntiagudo, da ❸ definido, da *(silueta)*; nítido, da *(foto)*; marcado, da *(contraste)* ❹ listo, ta ❺ penetrante *(vista)*; fino, na *(oído)* ❻ brusco, ca ❼ seco, ca *(golpe)* ❽ cortante *(comentario, respuesta)* ❾ agudo, da *(grito, dolor)*; penetrante *(frío, viento)* ❿ ácido, da ⓫ MÚSICA desafinado, da • F sharp fa sostenido ◆ *adv* ❶ • at seven o'clock sharp a las siete en punto ❷ bruscamente ◆ *s* MÚSICA sostenido
sharpen [ˈʃɑːpn] *vt* ❶ afilar ❷ sacar punta a ❸ agudizar
sharpener [ˈʃɑːpnəʳ] *s* ❶ sacapuntas ❷ afilador
sharply [ˈʃɑːplɪ] *adv* ❶ claramente ❷ repentinamente ❸ duramente
shat [ʃæt] *pretérito* & *participio pasado* → **shit**
shatter [ˈʃætəʳ] ◆ *vt* ❶ hacer añicos ❷ echar por tierra ◆ *vi* hacerse añicos
shattered [ˈʃætəd] *adj* destrozado, da
shave [ʃeɪv] ◆ *s* rasurada • to have a shave rasurarse ◆ *vt* ❶ rasurar ❷ • to shave your legs rasurarse las piernas ❷ raspar ◆ *vi* rasurarse
shaver [ˈʃeɪvəʳ] *s* rastrillo eléctrico
shaving brush [ˈʃeɪvɪŋ-] *s* brocha de afeitar

shaving cream [ˈʃeɪvɪŋ-] *s* espuma para rasurar; crema de afeitar
shaving foam [ˈʃeɪvɪŋ-] *s* espuma para rasurar
shavings [ˈʃeɪvɪŋz] *spl* virutas
shawl [ʃɔːl] *s* chal
she [ʃiː] ◆ *pronombre personal* ❶ ella • she's tall es alta • I don't like it, but she does no me gusta, pero a ella sí • she can't do it ella no puede hacerlo • there she is allí está ❷ • she's a fine ship es un buen barco ◆ *en compuestos* • she-elephant elefanta • she bear osa

she

She es el pronombre personal que se utiliza para hablar de mujeres y animales de compañía de sexo femenino (there's my sister — *she*'s a nurse *allí está mi hermana — es enfermera*; there's my cat — isn't *she* funny? *allí esta mi gata — ¿verdad que es graciosa?*); he es el equivalente masculino (there's my brother — *he*'s a teacher *allí está mi hermano — es profesor*). It designa lo que carece de sexo, las ideas y los animales en general (there's my car — *it*'s a Ford *allí está mi coche — es un Ford*).

She se emplea a veces para referirse a un barco (the Titanic was new but *she* sank the first time *she* left port *el Titánico era nuevo pero se hundió la primera vez que se hizo al mar*).

Varios sustantivos ingleses se utilizan tanto para hombres como mujeres, p. ej. doctor, cousin, friend. El pronombre que se utiliza en esos casos depende del sexo de la persona (there's my boss — do you know *him/her*? *allí está mi jefe/jefa — ¿lo/la conoces?*). Con nombres de animales o con algunas palabras referidas a personas como baby se puede usar it si se desconoce el sexo (listen to that baby — I wish it would be quiet! *¿escuchas al bebé? Ojalá se callase*).

Cuando no se conoce el sexo de la persona, lo normal en el lenguaje hablado es usar el pronombre masculino (if a student is sick, *he* must have a note from his parents *si un alumno está enfermo, debe presentar un justificante de sus padres*). También se usa they (if a student is sick, *they* must have a note from their parents). En el lenguaje escrito o formal, se usan los dos pronombres, el masculino y el femenino (if a student is sick, *he or she* must have a note from his or her parents).

shear [ʃɪəʳ] *vt* esquilar
■ **shears** *spl* tijeras de podar
■ **shear off** *vi* romperse

Formas irregulares de **shear**: *pp* **sheared** o **shorn.**

S

sheath [ʃiːθ] *s* vaina

El plural de **sheath** es **sheaths**.

shed [ʃed] ◆ *s* cobertizo ◆ *vt* ❶ mudar de *(piel)* ❷ despojarse de *(hojas)* ❸ derramar *(lágrimas, sangre)*

Formas irregulares de **shed**: *pretérito & pp* **shed**.

she'd ʒ: *acento atónico* [ʃɪd], *acento tónico* [ʃiːd] ❶ *(abreviatura de* she had*)* → **have** ❷ *(abreviatura de* she would*)* → **would**

sheep [ʃiːp] *s* oveja

El plural de **sheep** es **sheep**.

sheepdog ['ʃiːpdɒg] *s* perro pastor

sheepskin ['ʃiːpskɪn] *s* piel de carnero

sheer [ʃɪəʳ] *adj* ❶ puro, ra ❷ escarpado, da ❸ vertical ❹ transparente *(medias)*

sheet [ʃiːt] *s* ❶ sábana ❷ hoja ❸ lámina

sheik(h) [ʃeɪk] *s* jeque

shelf [ʃelf] *s* repisa

El plural de **shelf** es **shelves**.

shell [ʃel] ◆ *s* ❶ cáscara ❷ caparazón ❸ concha ❹ esqueleto *(de edificio)* ❺ MILITAR proyectil ◆ *vt* ❶ desvainar ❷ quitar la cáscara a ❸ MILITAR bombardear

she'll [ʃiːl] ❶ *(abreviatura de* she will*)* → **will** ❷ *(abreviatura de* she shall*)* → **shall**

shellfish ['ʃelfɪʃ] *s* ❶ crustáceo ❷ ʒ: *incontable* mariscos

El plural de **shellfish** es **shellfish**.

shelter ['ʃeltəʳ] ◆ *s* refugio • **to take shelter (from)** refugiarse (de) • **to run for shelter** correr a refugiarse ◆ *vt* ❶ • **to be sheltered by/from** estar protegido, da por/de ❷ dar asilo o cobijo a ❸ proteger; esconder ◆ *vi* • **to shelter from/in** resguardarse de/en; protegerse de/en

sheltered ['ʃeltəd] *adj* protegido, da

shelve [ʃelv] *vt* dar carpetazo a

shelves [ʃelvz] *spl* → **shelf**

shepherd ['ʃepəd] ◆ *s* pastor ◆ *vt figurado* acompañar

sherbet ['ʃɜːbət] *s* sorbete

sheriff ['ʃerɪf] *s* sheriff

sherry ['ʃerɪ] *s* jerez

she's [ʃiːz] ❶ *(abreviatura de* she is*)* → **be** ❷ *(abreviatura de* she has*)* → **have**

shield [ʃiːld] ◆ *s* escudo ◆ *vt* • **to shield somebody (from)** proteger a alguien (de)

shift [ʃɪft] ◆ *s* ❶ cambio ❷ turno • **the night shift** el turno de noche ◆ *vt* ❶ cambiar de sitio; mover ❷ cambiar de *(actitud)* ◆ *vi* ❶ moverse ❷ cambiar ❸ AUTOMÓVILES cambiar de marcha

shifty ['ʃɪftɪ] *adj* ❶ *familiar* con pinta deshonesta ❷ sospechoso, sa ❸ huidizo, za

shin [ʃɪn] *s* espinilla

shinbone ['ʃɪnbəʊn] *s* espinilla

shine [ʃaɪn] ◆ *s* brillo ◆ *vt* dirigir *(lámpara, linterna)* ◆ *vi* brillar

Formas irregulares de **shine**: *pretérito & pp* **shone**.

shingle ['ʃɪŋgl] *s* ❶ ʒ: *incontable* guijarros ❷ placa con el nombre

expresión **to hang out your shingle** abrir un despacho/consultorio

■ **shingles** *s* ʒ: *incontable* herpes

shin pad *s* espinillera

ship [ʃɪp] ◆ *s* barco; buque ◆ *vt* ❶ despachar ❷ enviar por barco

shipbuilding ['ʃɪp,bɪldɪŋ] *s* construcción naval

shipment ['ʃɪpmənt] *s* envío

shipping ['ʃɪpɪŋ] *s* ʒ: *incontable* ❶ envío; transporte ❷ barcos; buques

shipwreck ['ʃɪprek] ◆ *s* ❶ naufragio ❷ barco náufrago ◆ *vt* • **to be shipwrecked** naufragar

shipyard ['ʃɪpjɑːd] *s* astillero

shirk [ʃɜːk] *vt* eludir

shirt [ʃɜːt] *s* camisa

shirtsleeves ['ʃɜːtsliːvz] *spl* • **to be in (your) shirtsleeves** ir en mangas de camisa

shit [ʃɪt] *vulgar* ◆ *s* ❶ mierda ❷ ʒ: *incontable* pendejadas ◆ *vi* cagar ◆ *exclamación* ¡mierda!

shiver ['ʃɪvəʳ] ◆ *s* escalofrío • **it sent shivers down her spine** le puso los pelos de punta

expresión **to give somebody the shivers** dar escalofríos a alguien

◆ *vi* • **to shiver (with) a)** temblar o estremecerse (de) **b)** tiritar (de)

shoal [ʃəʊl] *s* banco *(de peces)*

shock [ʃɒk] ◆ *s* ❶ susto • **it came as a shock** fue un duro golpe ❷ ʒ: *incontable* MEDICINA • **to be suffering from shock, to be in shock** estar en un estado de choque ❸ choque ❹ descarga o sacudida (eléctrica) • **to get a shock from something** recibir una descarga de algo ◆ *vt* ❶ conmocionar ❷ escandalizar

shocking ['ʃɒkɪŋ] *adj* ❶ pésimo, ma ❷ escandaloso, sa ❸ de escándalo *(precios)*

shod [ʃɒd] ◆ *pretérito & participio pasado* → **shoe** ◆ *adj* calzado, da

shoddy ['ʃɒdɪ] *adj* ❶ de mala calidad ❷ de pacotilla

shoe [ʃuː] ◆ *s* zapato ◆ *vt (gerundio* shoeing*)* herrar

Formas irregulares de **shoe**: *pretérito & pp* **shod** o **shoed**.

shoebrush ['ʃuːbrʌʃ] *s* cepillo para los zapatos

shoelace ['ʃuːleɪs] *s* cordón del zapato

shoe polish *s* betún

shoe store *s* zapatería

shone [ʃɒn] *pretérito & participio pasado* → **shine**

shoo [ʃuː] ◆ *vt* ❶ espantar; ahuyentar • **he shooed the cat away** echó al gato ❷ mandar a otra parte ◆ *exclamación* ¡fuera!

shook [ʃʊk] *pretérito* → **shake**

shoot [ʃuːt] ◆ *s* brote; retoño ◆ *vt* ❶ disparar contra ❷ herir a tiros • **he was shot in the leg** le pegaron un tiro en la pierna ❸ matar a tiros • **to shoot yourself** pegarse un tiro ❹ disparar *(flecha)* ❺ CINE rodar; filmar

expresión **to shoot the breeze** estar de cháchara

◆ *vi* ❶ • **to shoot (at)** disparar (contra) ❷ • **to shoot in/out/past** entrar/salir/pasar disparado, da ❸ CINE rodar; filmar ❹ DEPORTE chutar • **he shot at goal** chutó a puerta

■ **shoot down** *vt* ❖ *El objeto se puede colocar antes o después de la preposición.* ❶ derribar ❷ matar a tiros

■ **shoot up** *vi* ❶ crecer rápidamente ❷ dispararse *(precios)*

Formas irregulares de **shoot**: *pretérito & pp* **shot**.

shooting ['ʃuːtɪŋ] *s* ❶ asesinato *(a tiros)* ❷ ❖ *incontable* caza; cacería

shooting star *s* estrella fugaz

shop [ʃɒp] ◆ *s* tienda ◆ *vi* comprar; hacer compras

shop floor *s* • **the shop floor** los trabajadores de producción

shopkeeper ['ʃɒpˌkiːpər] *s* tendero, ra

shoplifting ['ʃɒpˌlɪftɪŋ] *s* ❖ *incontable* robo en una tienda

shopper ['ʃɒpər] *s* comprador, ra

shopping ['ʃɒpɪŋ] *s* ❖ *incontable* ❶ compras ❷ compra • **to do some/the shopping** hacer algunas compras/la compra • **to go shopping** ir de compras

shopping bag *s* bolsa de la compra

shopping cart *s* ❶ carrito de la compra ❷ cesta de la compra *(en Internet)*

shopping mall, shopping plaza [-ˌplɑːzə] *s* centro comercial

shop window *s* aparador

shore [ʃɔːr] *s* ❶ orilla ❷ • **on shore** en tierra

shorn [ʃɔːn] ◆ *participio pasado* → **shear** ◆ *adj* ❶ corto, ta *(pelo)* ❷ rapado, da

short [ʃɔːt] ◆ *adj* ❶ corto, ta • **a short time ago** hace poco ❷ bajo, ja ❸ • **to be short (with somebody)** ser seco, ca (con alguien) • **to have a short temper** tener mal genio ❹ escaso, sa • **to be short on something** no andar sobrado de algo • **to be short of** estar o andar mal de ❺ • **to be short for** ser el diminutivo de ◆ *adv* ❶ • **we are running short of water** se nos está acabando el agua ❷ • **to cut something short** interrumpir algo • **we had to cut short our trip to Bolivia** tuvimos que interrumpir nuestro viaje a Bolivia

expresión **to bring** o **pull somebody up short** hacer a alguien parar en seco ❭ **to stop short** parar en seco

◆ *s* cortometraje

■ **shorts** *spl* ❶ pantalones cortos ❷ calzoncillos

■ **for short** *adv* para abreviar

■ **in short** *adv* en resumen

■ **nothing short of** *preposición* • **it was nothing short of madness/a disgrace** fue una auténtica locura/vergüenza

■ **short of** *preposición* ❶ cerca de ❷ • **short of asking, I can't see how you'll find out** salvo que preguntes, no sé cómo lo vas a averiguar

shortage ['ʃɔːtɪdʒ] *s* falta; escasez

short-change *vt* dar mal el cambio a

short circuit *s* cortocircuito

shortcomings ['ʃɔːtˌkʌmɪŋz] *spl* defectos

short cut *s* ❶ atajo • **to take a short cut** tomar un atajo ❷ método rápido

shorten ['ʃɔːtn] ◆ *vt* acortar ◆ *vi* acortarse

shortfall ['ʃɔːtfɔːl] *s* • **shortfall (in** o **of)** déficit (de)

shorthand ['ʃɔːthænd] *s* taquigrafía

shortly ['ʃɔːtlɪ] *adv* dentro de poco • **shortly before/after** poco antes/después de

shortsighted [ˌʃɔːt'saɪtɪd] *adj* ❶ miope; corto, ta de vista ❷ *figurado* corto de miras

shortstop ['ʃɔːtstɒp] *s* ❭ jugador que intenta interceptar bolas entre la segunda y tercera base

short story *s* cuento

short-tempered [-'tempəd] *adj* de mal genio

short-term *adj* a corto plazo

short wave *s* ❖ *incontable* onda corta

shot [ʃɒt] ◆ *pretérito & participio pasado* → **shoot** ◆ *s* ❶ tiro; disparo ❷ tirador, ra • **to be a good shot** ser un buen tirador ❸ chut; tiro *(en fútbol)* ❹ golpe *(en golf, tenis)* • **good shot!** ¡buen golpe! ❺ foto ❻ CINE plano; toma ❼ *familiar* intento • **go on, have a shot** venga, inténtalo • **to have a shot at (doing) something** intentar (hacer) algo ❽ inyección

expresión **like a shot** disparado, da

shotgun ['ʃɒtɡʌn] *s* escopeta

---

should [ʃʊd]

◆ *v modal*

❶ [*para dar un consejo, expresar lo que sería deseable*]
• **you should go** deberías ir
• **should I go too?** ¿yo también debería ir?
• **we should leave now** deberíamos irnos ahora

❷ [*expresa una deducción, una probabilidad*]
• **she should be home soon** debe llegar a casa enseguida
• **that should be her** esa debe ser ella

❸ [*seguido de "have" + participio pasado expresa arrepentimiento, reproche*]
• **they should have won the match** deberían haber ganado el partido
• **you should have helped your sister** deberías haber ayudado a tu hermana

❹ [*con valor condicional*]
• **I should be very sorry if they couldn't come** lo sentiría mucho si no pudieran venir
• **I should like to come with you** me gustaría ir contigo
• **I should deny everything** negaré todo

S

❺ [*después de "if", para expresar una eventualidad*]
• **if anyone should call, please let met know** si llamara alguien, avísame

should

Cuando should have va seguido de un participio pasado puede expresar arrepentimiento (I *should have phoned* on her birthday *debería haberle llamado por su cumpleaños*) o reproche (you *should have been* more careful *deberías haber tenido más cuidado*).

Ver también shall.

shoulder ['ʃəʊldər] ◆ *s* ❶ hombro ❷ *COCINA* espaldilla; paleta ◆ *vt* • **to shoulder the blame** asumir la responsabilidad

shoulder blade *s* omóplato

shoulder strap *s* ❶ tirante; bretel ❷ correa; bandolera

shouldn't ['ʃʊdnt] (*abreviatura de* should not) → **should**

should've ['ʃʊdəv] (*abreviatura de* should have) → **should**

shout [ʃaʊt] ◆ *s* grito • **to let out a shout** lanzar un grito ◆ *vt* gritar ◆ *vi* • **to shout (at)** gritar (a)

shouting ['ʃaʊtɪŋ] *s* ☼ *incontable* gritos

shove [ʃʌv] ◆ *s* • **(to give something/somebody) a shove** (dar a algo/a alguien) un empujón ◆ *vt* empujar • **to shove something/somebody in** meter algo/a alguien a empujones

shovel ['ʃʌvl] ◆ *s* pala ◆ *vt* remover con la pala o a paletadas • **to shovel food into your mouth** zamparse la comida

show [ʃəʊ] ◆ *s* ❶ demostración • **a show of strength** una demostración de fuerza ❷ espectáculo *(teatral)*; programa *(televisivo)* ❸ función ❹ exposición ◆ *vt* ❶ mostrar ❷ • **to show somebody to the door** llevar o acompañar a alguien hasta la puerta • **he showed us to our seats** nos llevó a nuestros asientos ❸ dejar ver • **white clothes show the dirt** la ropa blanca deja ver la suciedad • **come on, show yourself!** venga, ¡déjate ver! ❹ arrojar; registrar *(beneficio, pérdida, aumento)* ❺ dar *(película)*; dar *(programa)* ◆ *vi* ❶ indicar; mostrar ❷ verse • **does it show?** ¿se ve? ❸ • **it is showing at the Odeon** lo ponen en el Odeon

■ **show off** ◆ *vt* ☼ *El objeto se puede colocar antes o después de la preposición.* lucir; presumir de ◆ *vi* presumir

■ **show out** *vt* ☼ *El objeto se puede colocar antes o después de la preposición.* acompañar hasta la puerta

■ **show up** ◆ *vt* ☼ *El objeto se puede colocar antes o después de la preposición.* poner en evidencia ◆ *vi* ❶ resaltar ❷ aparecer

Formas irregulares de **show:** *pp* **shown** [ʃəʊn] o **showed.**

show business *s* ☼ *incontable* el mundo del espectáculo

showdown ['ʃəʊdaʊn] *s* • **to have a showdown with** enfrentarse abiertamente a o con

shower ['ʃaʊər] ◆ *s* ❶ ducha ❷ • **to have** o **take a shower** ducharse ❸ chubasco; chaparrón ❹ fiesta con regalos organizada en honor de una mujer por sus amigas ◆ *vt* ❶ rociar ❷ • **to shower somebody with something, to shower something on** o **upon somebody a)** colmar a alguien de algo *(regalos, cumplidos)* **b)** acribillar a alguien a algo *(insultos)* ◆ *vi* ducharse

shower cap *s* gorro de ducha

showing ['ʃəʊɪŋ] *s* pase; proyección

show jumping [-ˌdʒʌmpɪŋ] *s* concurso hípico de salto

shown [ʃəʊn] *participio pasado* → **show**

show-off *s familiar* presumido, da

showroom ['ʃəʊrʊm] *s* salón o sala de exposición

shrank [ʃræŋk] *pretérito* → **shrink**

shred [ʃred] ◆ *s* ❶ jirón ❷ pedacito • **to be in shreds** *literal & figurado* estar hecho, cha pedazos ❸ *figurado* pizca • **there isn't a shred of truth in what he says** no hay una pizca de verdad en lo que dice ◆ *vt* ❶ hacer trizas ❷ rallar

shredder ['ʃredər] *s* destructora

shrewd [ʃruːd] *adj* astuto, ta

shriek [ʃriːk] ◆ *s* chillido; grito ◆ *vi* • **to shriek (with** o **in)** chillar (de)

shrill [ʃrɪl] *adj* estridente; agudo, da

shrimp [ʃrɪmp] *s* gamba; camarón

shrine [ʃraɪn] *s* santuario

shrink [ʃrɪŋk] ◆ *vt* encoger ◆ *vi* ❶ encoger ❷ *figurado* disminuir ❸ • **to shrink away from** retroceder o arredrarse ante ❹ • **to shrink from something** eludir algo

Formas irregulares de **shrink:** *pretérito* **shrank** [ʃræŋk], *pp* **shrunk** [ʃrʌŋk].

shrivel ['ʃrɪvl] *vi* • **to shrivel (up)** secarse; marchitarse

Shrove Tuesday ['ʃrəʊv-] *s* martes de carnaval

shrub [ʃrʌb] *s* arbusto

shrug [ʃrʌg] ◆ *vt* • **to shrug your shoulders** encogerse de hombros ◆ *vi* encogerse de hombros

shrunk [ʃrʌŋk] *participio pasado* → **shrink**

shucks [ʃʌks] *exclamación familiar* ❶ ¡no es nada! ❷ ¡chin!

shudder ['ʃʌdər] *vi* • **to shudder (with)** estremecerse (de)

shuffle ['ʃʌfl] *vt* ❶ arrastrar *(los pies)* ❷ barajar *(cartas)* ❸ revolver *(papeles)*

shun [ʃʌn] *vt* rehuir; esquivar

shut [ʃʌt] ◆ *adj* cerrado, da ◆ *vt* cerrar ◆ *vi* ❶ cerrarse ❷ cerrar

■ **shut away** *vt* ☼ *El objeto se puede colocar antes o después de la preposición.* guardar bajo llave

■ **shut down** *vt* & *vi* cerrar *(negocio, computadora)*

S

■ **shut out** *vt* ☀ *El objeto se puede colocar antes o después de la preposición.* dejar fuera a
■ **shut up** *familiar* ◆ *vt* ☀ *El objeto se puede colocar antes o después de la preposición.* hacer callar ◆ *vi* callarse • **shut up!** ¡cállate!

Formas irregulares de **shut**: *pretérito* & *pp* **shut**.

shutter ['ʃʌtər] *s* ❶ postigo ❷ obturador

shuttle ['ʃʌtl] ◆ *adj* • **shuttle service a)** puente aéreo **b)** servicio regular ◆ *s* avión (de puente aéreo)

shy [ʃaɪ] ◆ *adj* tímido, da ◆ *vi* espantarse

sibling ['sɪblɪŋ] *s* hermano, na

Sicily ['sɪsɪlɪ] *s* Sicilia

sick [sɪk] *adj* ❶ enfermo, ma ❷ • **to feel sick** marearse ❸ • **to be sick of something/of doing something** estar harto, ta de algo/de hacer algo • **to be sick and tired of (doing) something** estar hasta la coronilla de (hacer) algo ❹ de mal gusto *(chiste, broma)*

sickbay ['sɪkbeɪ] *s* enfermería

sicken ['sɪkn] *vt* poner enfermo, ma; asquear

sickening ['sɪknɪŋ] *adj* ❶ asqueroso, sa ❷ exasperante

sick leave *s* ☀ *incontable* baja por enfermedad

sickly ['sɪklɪ] *adj* ❶ enfermizo, za ❷ nauseabundo, da

sickness ['sɪknɪs] *s* enfermedad

sick pay *s* ☀ *incontable* paga por enfermedad

side [saɪd] ◆ *s* ❶ lado • **at** o **by your side** al lado de uno • **on every side, on all sides** por todos los lados • **from side to side** de un lado a otro • **side by side** juntos; uno al lado de otro ❷ costado ❸ ijada ❹ lado; borde ❺ falda; ladera ❻ orilla ❼ cara *(de página)* ❽ lado; bando ❾ DEPORTE equipo ❿ punto de vista • **you should try to see both sides** deberías considerar las dos caras de la situación • **to take somebody's side** ponerse del lado o de parte de alguien • **to take sides** tomar partido • **to be on somebody's side** estar del lado o de parte de alguien ⓫ aspecto • **it does have its comical side** tiene su lado cómico
expresión **to be on the safe side** para estar seguro ▶ **to put something to** o **on one side** poner algo a un lado
◆ *adj* lateral
■ **side with** *vt* ☀ *El objeto siempre va después de la preposición al final.* ponerse de parte de

sideboard ['saɪdbɔːd] *s* aparador

sideburns ['saɪdbɜːnz] *spl* patillas

side effect *s* efecto secundario

sideline ['saɪdlaɪn] *s* ❶ negocio suplementario ❷ línea lateral *(en cancha de tenis)* ❸ línea de banda

sidelong ['saɪdlɒŋ] *adj* & *adv* de reojo o soslayo • **to give somebody a sidelong glance** mirar a alguien de reojo o soslayo

sideshow ['saɪdʃəʊ] *s* barraca o caseta de feria

sidestep ['saɪdstep] *vt* ❶ regatear ❷ *figurado* esquivar

side street *s* calle lateral

sidetrack ['saɪdtræk] *vt* • **to be sidetracked** desviarse o salirse del tema • **I keep getting sidetracked** me distraigo continuamente

sidewalk ['saɪdwɔːk] *s* banqueta

sideways ['saɪdweɪz] ◆ *adj* hacia un lado • **a sideways glance** una mirada de soslayo ◆ *adv* ❶ de lado ❷ de reojo

siding ['saɪdɪŋ] *s* vía muerta

sidle ['saɪdl] ■ **sidle up** *vi* • **to sidle up to** acercarse furtivamente a

siege [siːdʒ] *s* ❶ sitio; cerco ❷ cerco policial

sieve [sɪv] ◆ *s* colador
expresión **to have a head** o **memory like a sieve** tener muy mala memoria
◆ *vt* ❶ colar ❷ tamizar

sift [sɪft] ◆ *vt* ❶ tamizar ❷ *figurado* examinar cuidadosamente ◆ *vi* • **to sift through something** examinar cuidadosamente algo

sigh [saɪ] ◆ *s* suspiro ◆ *vi* suspirar

sight [saɪt] ◆ *s* ❶ vista • **in sight** a la vista • **to catch sight of something** ver algo • **to disappear out of sight** perderse de vista • **to lose sight of** perder de vista • **at first sight** a primera vista • **it was love at first sight** fue un flechazo • **I know him by sight** lo conozco de vista ❷ • **her first sight of the sea** la primera vez que vio el mar • **he faints at the sight of blood** se desmaya de sólo ver sangre ❸ espectáculo • **it's not a pretty sight** no es muy agradable de ver ❹ mira *(de arma)*
expresión **to set your sights on something** echarle el ojo a algo
◆ *vt* divisar; avistar
■ **sights** *spl* atracciones turísticas

sightseeing ['saɪtˌsiːɪŋ] *s* ☀ *incontable* recorrido turístico • **to go sightseeing** hacer turismo

sightseer ['saɪtˌsiːər] *s* turista

sign [saɪn] ◆ *s* ❶ señal ❷ signo ▶ **sign of the zodiac** signo del zodiaco ❸ letrero ❹ cartel ◆ *vt* firmar ◆ *vi* firmar
■ **sign on** *vi* • **to sign on (for) a)** alistarse (en) **b)** firmar el contrato (de) **c)** matricularse (en)
■ **sign up** ◆ *vt* ☀ *El objeto se puede colocar antes o después de la preposición.* ❶ contratar ❷ alistar ◆ *vi* • **to sign up (for) a)** alistarse (en) **b)** firmar el contrato (de) **c)** matricularse (en)

signal ['sɪgnl] ◆ *s* señal ◆ *vt* ❶ indicar ❷ • **to signal somebody (to do something)** hacer señas a alguien (para que haga algo) ◆ *vi* ❶ AUTOMÓVILES señalizar ❷ • **to signal for something** pedir algo por señas

signature ['sɪgnətʃər] *s* firma

signature tune *s* sintonía

significance [sɪgˈnɪfɪkəns] *s* trascendencia; importancia • **to attach significance to something** atribuir importancia a algo • **to be of little/great/no significance** ser de poca/mucha/ninguna importancia

significant [sɪgˈnɪfɪkənt] *adj* ❶ significativo, va ❷ trascendente

signpost ['saɪnpəʊst] *s* letrero indicador

S

Sikh [si:k] ◆ *adj* sij ◆ *s* sij

silence ['saɪləns] ◆ *s* silencio ◆ *vt* acallar

silent ['saɪlənt] *adj* ❶ silencioso, sa ❷ • **to be silent about** quedar en silencio respecto a • **to remain silent** permanecer callado, da ❸ *CINE & LINGÜÍSTICA* mudo, da • **a silent movie** una película muda • **a silent b** una b muda

silhouette [,sɪlu:'et] *s* silueta

silicon chip [,sɪlɪkən-] *s* chip de silicio

silk [sɪlk] ◆ *s* seda ◆ *en compuestos* de seda • **a silk blouse** una blusa de seda

sill [sɪl] *s* alféizar

silly ['sɪlɪ] *adj* estúpido, da • **that was a silly thing to say** qué tontería has dicho

silver ['sɪlvər] ◆ *adj* ❶ plateado, da ❷ de plata ◆ *s* ☀ *incontable* ❶ plata ❷ monedas plateadas

silver-plated [-'pleɪtɪd] *adj* plateado, da

silverware ['sɪlvəweər] *s* ☀ *incontable* ❶ plata ❷ cubertería de plata

similar ['sɪmɪlər] *adj* • **similar (to)** parecido, da o similar (a)

similarly ['sɪmɪləlɪ] *adv* ❶ asimismo ❷ igualmente

simmer ['sɪmər] *vt* & *vi* hervir a fuego lento

simple ['sɪmpl] *adj* ❶ sencillo, lla ❷ simple ❸ mero, ra; puro, ra

simple-minded [-'maɪndɪd] *adj* simple

simplicity [sɪm'plɪsətɪ] *s* sencillez

simplify ['sɪmplɪfaɪ] *vt* simplificar

simply ['sɪmplɪ] *adv* ❶ sencillamente; simplemente ❷ de manera sencilla

simulate ['sɪmjʊleɪt] *vt* simular

simulation [sɪmjʊ'leɪʃn] *vt* simulación

simultaneous [,saɪməl'teɪnjəs] *adj* simultáneo, a

sin [sɪn] ◆ *s* pecado ◆ *vi* • **to sin (against)** pecar (contra)

---

since [sɪns]
◆ *adv*
[*para indicar un punto de partida en el tiempo*] desde entonces
• **he left home at 5.00 on Tuesday and we haven't heard from him since** se marchó de casa a las 5 del martes y no hemos sabido nada de él desde entonces
◆ *preposición*
[*para indicar un punto de partida en el tiempo*] desde
• **I haven't seen her since Christmas** no la vi desde Navidades
• **since then** desde entonces
◆ *conjunción*
❶ [*para indicar un punto de partida en el tiempo*] desde que

---

• **she hasn't stopped crying since you left her** no paró de llorar desde que la dejaste
❷ [*introduce la causa*] ya que
• **since you are ill, you should stay at home** ya que estás enfermo, deberías quedarte en casa

---

since

Fíjate en los tiempos que se emplean con since cuando es una preposición: we *have been* friends *since* school (perfecto) *hemos sido amigas desde la escuela*; we *had been working* together *since* the summer (pluscuamperfecto continuo) *habíamos trabajado juntos desde el verano; we had been* in contact *since* 1985 (pluscuamperfecto) *habíamos estado en contacto desde 1985.*

Fíjate en los tiempos que se emplean con since cuando es una conjunción: I haven't read much *since I left* school (pretérito) *no he leído mucho desde que acabé la escuela*; his books sell very well *since he's become* famous (perfecto) *sus libros se venden muy bien desde que se hizo famoso.*

---

sincere [sɪn'sɪər] *adj* sincero, ra

sincerely [sɪn'sɪəlɪ] *adv* sinceramente • **Yours sincerely** atentamente

sinew ['sɪnju:] *s* tendón

sinful ['sɪnfʊl] *adj* ❶ pecador, ra ❷ pecaminoso, sa

sing [sɪŋ] *vt* & *vi* cantar • **to sing along with somebody** cantar a coro con alguien

Formas irregulares de **sing** *pretérito* **sang**, *pp* **sung**

Singapore [,sɪŋə'pɔ:r] *s* Singapur

singe [sɪndʒ] *vt* chamuscar

singer ['sɪŋər] *s* cantante • **she's a good singer** canta muy bien

singing ['sɪŋɪŋ] *s* ☀ *incontable* canto

single ['sɪŋgl] ◆ *adj* ❶ solo, la • **not a single person was there** no había ni una sola persona ❷ • **every single cent** todos y cada uno de los centavos ❸ soltero, ra ◆ *s MÚSICA* sencillo; single

■ **singles** *spl TENIS* (partido) individual • **the men's singles** los individuales masculinos

■ **single out** *vt* ☀ *El objeto se puede colocar antes o después de la preposición.* • **to single somebody out (for)** escoger a alguien (para)

single bed *s* cama individual

single-breasted [-'brestɪd] *adj* recto, ta

single-click ◆ *s* clic ◆ *vi* hacer clic ◆ *vt* hacer clic en

single file *s* • **in single file** en fila india

single-handed [-'hændɪd] *adv* sin ayuda

single-minded [-'maındıd] *adj* resuelto, ta
single parent *s* padre soltero; madre soltera
single-parent family *s* familia monoparental
single room *s* habitación individual
singular ['sıŋgjʊlər] ◆ *adj* singular ◆ *s* singular • **in the singular** en singular
sinister ['sınıstər] *adj* siniestro, tra
sink [sıŋk] ◆ *s* ❶ fregadero ❷ lavabo ◆ *vt* ❶ hundir ❷ • **to sink something into a)** clavar algo en *(cuchillo, garras)* **b)** hincar algo en *(dientes)* ◆ *vi* ❶ hundirse • **she sank into a chair** se desplomó en una silla ❷ bajar
■ **sink in** *vi* hacer mella • **it hasn't sunk in yet** todavía no lo tengo/tiene asumido

Formas irregulares de **sink**: *pretérito* **sank**, *pp* **sunk**.

sink board *s* escurridero
sink unit *s* fregadero (con mueble debajo)
sinner ['sınər] *s* pecador, ra
sinus ['saınəs] *s* seno

El plural de **sinus** es **sinuses**.

sip [sıp] ◆ *s* sorbo ◆ *vt* beber a sorbos
siphon, syphon ['saıfn] *s* sifón
■ **siphon off** *vt* ☼: *El objeto se puede colocar antes o después de la preposición.* ❶ sacar con sifón ❷ *figurado* desviar *(fondos)*
sir [sɜ:ʳ] *s* ❶ señor • **Dear sir,...** Estimado Señor,... ❷ • **Sir Philip Holden** Sir Philip Holden
siren ['saıərən] *s* sirena
sirloin (steak) ['sɜ:lɔın] *s* solomillo
sister ['sıstər] *s* hermana
sister-in-law *s* cuñada

Dos plurales: **sisters-in-law** o **sister-in-laws**.

sit [sıt] *vi* ❶ sentarse • **to be sitting** estar sentado ❷ • **to sit on a committee** ser miembro de un comité ❸ reunirse
■ **sit about, sit around** *vi* estar sentado, da sin hacer nada
■ **sit down** *vi* sentarse • **she was sitting down** estaba sentada
■ **sit in on** *vt* ☼: *El objeto siempre va después de la preposición al final.* estar presente en *(sin tomar parte)*
■ **sit through** *vt* ☼: *El objeto siempre va después de la preposición al final.* aguantar *(hasta el final)*
■ **sit up** *vi* ❶ incorporarse • **sit up straight!** siéntate derecho ❷ quedarse levantado, da

Formas irregulares de **sit**: *pretérito & pp* **sat**.

sitcom ['sıtkɒm] *s* comedia de situación
site [saıt] ◆ *s* ❶ lugar; escenario ❷ obra ❸ sitio web ◆ *vt* situar
sitting ['sıtıŋ] *s* ❶ turno (para comer) ❷ sesión
sitting room *s* sala de estar
situated ['sıtjʊeıtıd] *adj* • **to be situated** estar situado, da
situation [,sıtjʊ'eıʃn] *s* situación
six [sıks] ◆ *adj numeral* seis • **she's six (years old)** tiene seis años ◆ *sustantivo numeral* ❶ seis • **two**

hundred and six doscientos seis • **six comes before seven** el seis va antes que el siete ❷ • **it's six (thirty)** son las seis (y media) • **we arrived at six** llegamos a las seis ❸ • **six Peyton Place** Peyton Place número seis ❹ • **six-nil** seis a cero ◆ *pronombre numeral* seis • **there are six of us** somos seis
six-shooter [-'ʃu:tər] *s* revólver de seis tiros
sixteen [sıks'ti:n] *número* dieciséis ver también **six**
sixteenth [sıks'ti:nθ] *número* decimosexto, ta ver también **sixth**
sixth [sıksθ] ◆ *adj numeral* sexto, ta ◆ *adv numeral* sexto, ta ◆ *pronombre numeral* sexto, ta ◆ *s* ❶ • **a sixth** o **one sixth of** un sexto de; la sexta parte de ❷ • **the sixth** el (día) seis • **the sixth of September** el seis de septiembre
sixty ['sıkstı] *número* sesenta • **sixty-two** sesenta y dos ver también **six**
■ **sixties** *spl* ❶ • **the sixties** los años sesenta ❷ • **to be in your sixties** estar en los sesenta
size [saız] *s* ❶ tamaño ❷ talla • **what size do you take?** ¿cuál es su talla? • **I'm a size 16** uso la talla 16 ❸ número • **what size shoes do you take?** ¿qué número calza?
■ **size up** *vt* ☼: *El objeto se puede colocar antes o después de la preposición.* ❶ evaluar ❷ calar *(una persona)*
sizeable ['saızəbl] *adj* considerable
sizzle ['sızl] *vi* chisporrotear
skate [skeıt] ◆ *s* ❶ (pl skates) patín ❷ (pl skate) raya ◆ *vi* patinar
skateboard ['skeıtbɔ:d] *s* monopatín
skater ['skeıtər] *s* patinador, ra
skating ['skeıtıŋ] *s* patinaje • **to go skating** ir a patinar
skating rink *s* pista de patinaje
skeleton ['skelıtn] *s* ANATOMÍA esqueleto
expresión **to have a skeleton in the cupboard** guardar un secreto vergonzante
skeleton staff *s* personal mínimo
skeptic ['skeptık] *s* escéptico, ca
skeptical ['skeptıkl] *adj* escéptico, ca • **to be skeptical about** tener muchas dudas acerca de
sketch [sketʃ] ◆ *s* ❶ esbozo; bosquejo ❷ sketch ◆ *vt* esbozar; hacer un bosquejo de
sketchbook ['sketʃbʊk] *s* cuaderno de dibujo
sketchpad ['sketʃpæd] *s* bloc de dibujo
sketchy ['sketʃı] *adj* incompleto, ta
skewer ['skjʊər] *s* brocheta
ski [ski:] ◆ *s* esquí ◆ *vi* esquiar

Formas irregulares de **ski**: *pretérito & pp* **skied**, *gerundio* **skiing**.

ski boots *spl* botas de esquí
skid [skıd] ◆ *s* patinazo ◆ *vi* patinar
skid row [-rəʊ] *s familiar* barrio bajo
skier ['ski:ər] *s* esquiador, ra

S

skies [skaɪz] *spl* → **sky**

skiing ['ski:ɪŋ] *s* ☀ *incontable* esquí • **to go skiing** ir a esquiar

ski lift *s* telesilla

skill [skɪl] *s* ☀ *incontable* habilidad; destreza ❷ técnica

skilled [skɪld] *adj* ❶ habilidoso, sa • **to be skilled (in** o **at doing something)** ser experto, ta (en hacer algo) ❷ cualificado, da

skillet ['skɪlɪt] *s* sartén

skillful ['skɪlfʊl] *adj* hábil

skim [skɪm] ♦ *vt* ❶ desnatar ❷ volar rozando ♦ *vi* • **to skim through something** hojear algo, leer algo por encima

skim milk *s* leche desnatada

skimp [skɪmp] ♦ *vt* escatimar ♦ *vi* • **to skimp on something** escatimar algo

skimpy ['skɪmpɪ] *adj* ❶ muy corto y estrecho, muy corta y estrecha *(ropa)* ❷ escaso, sa

skin [skɪn] ♦ *s* ❶ piel • **a banana skin** una cáscara de plátano ❷ cutis ❸ nata *(de leche)* ❹ capa; película *(de pintura)*
expresión **to save** o **protect your own skin** salvar el pellejo
♦ *vt* ❶ despellejar ❷ rasguñarse

skincare ['skɪnkeər] *s* ☀ *incontable* cuidado de la piel

skin diving *s* buceo; submarinismo (sin traje ni escafandra)

skinny ['skɪnɪ] ♦ *adj familiar* flaco, ca ♦ *s* • **the skinny** información confidencial

skin-tight *adj* muy ajustado, da

skip [skɪp] ♦ *s* brinco; saltito ♦ *vt* saltarse • **to skip class** faltar a clase ♦ *vi* ir dando brincos

ski pants *spl* pantalones de esquí

ski pole *s* bastón para esquiar

skipper ['skɪpər] *s* NÁUTICA & DEPORTE capitán, ana

skirmish ['skɜ:mɪʃ] *s* *literal & figurado* escaramuza

skirt [skɜ:t] ♦ *s* ❶ falda ❷ ▸ **(bed) skirt** volante ♦ *vt* ❶ rodear; bordear ❷ sortear; esquivar ❸ eludir
■ **skirt round** *vt* ☀ *El objeto siempre va después de la preposición al final.* ❶ sortear ❷ evitar; eludir

skull [skʌl] *s* ❶ calavera ❷ ANATOMÍA cráneo

skunk [skʌŋk] *s* mofeta

sky [skaɪ] *s* cielo

sky blue *adj* (azul) celeste

skylight ['skaɪlaɪt] *s* claraboya

sky marshal *s* ▸ policía destinado en un avión para evitar secuestros

skyscraper ['skaɪ,skreɪpər] *s* rascacielos

slab [slæb] *s* ❶ losa ❷ pedazo ❸ tableta *(de chocolate)*

slack [slæk] *adj* ❶ flojo, ja ❷ inactivo, va *(negocio)* ❸ descuidado, da

slacken ['slækn] ♦ *vt* ❶ reducir *(el ritmo)* ❷ aflojar ♦ *vi* reducirse *(el ritmo)*

slain [sleɪn] *participio pasado* → **slay**

slam [slæm] ♦ *vt* ❶ cerrar de golpe • **she slammed the door** dio un portazo ❷ • **to slam something on** o **onto something** dar un golpe con algo contra algo violentamente • **he slammed his fist on the desk** dio un puñetazo en la mesa ♦ *vi* cerrarse de golpe

slander ['slɑ:ndər] ♦ *s* calumnia; difamación ♦ *vt* calumniar; difamar

slang [slæŋ] *s* argot; jerga

slant [slɑ:nt] ♦ *s* ❶ inclinación ❷ enfoque ♦ *vi* inclinarse

slanting ['slɑ:ntɪŋ] *adj* inclinado, da

slap [slæp] ♦ *s* ❶ bofetada ❷ palmada • **he gave him a slap on the back** le dio una palmadita en la espalda
expresión **it was a slap in the face** fue una bofetada
♦ *vt* ❶ abofetear • **she slapped him round the face** lo abofeteó; le dio una bofetada ❷ dar una palmada a ❸ • **he slapped the folder on the desk** dejó la carpeta en la mesa dando un golpetazo ♦ *adv familiar* de narices • **he walked slap into a lamp post** se dio de lleno con una farola

slash [slæʃ] ♦ *s* ❶ raja; tajo ❷ barra oblicua ▸ **forward slash** barra inclinada ♦ *vt* ❶ rasgar • **she slashed her wrists** se cortó las venas ❷ *familiar* recortar drásticamente

slasher movie *s familiar* película sanguinaria

slate [sleɪt] ♦ *s* pizarra ♦ *vt* poner por los suelos

slaughter ['slɔ:tər] ♦ *s literal & figurado* matanza ♦ *vt* matar

slaughterhouse ['slɔ:təhaʊs] *s* matadero
El plural de **slaughterhouse** es **slaughterhouses** ['slɔ:təhaʊzɪz].

slave [sleɪv] ♦ *s* esclavo, va
expresión **to be a slave to something** ser un esclavo de algo
♦ *vi* trabajar como un negro
expresión **to slave over a hot stove** *humorístico* pasarse el día bregando en la cocina

slavery ['sleɪvərɪ] *s literal & figurado* esclavitud

Slavic ['slɑ:vɪk] *adj* eslavo, va

slay [sleɪ] *vt literario* asesinar; matar
Formas irregulares de **slay**: *pretérito* **slew**, *pp* **slain**.

sleaze [sli:z] *s* corrupción

sleazy ['sli:zɪ] *adj* ❶ de mala muerte ❷ corrupto, ta

sled [sled] *s* trineo

sledgehammer ['sledʒ,hæmər] *s* almádena

sleek [sli:k] *adj* ❶ suave y brillante *(pelo)* ❷ lustroso, sa *(piel)* ❸ de línea depurada

sleep [sli:p] ♦ *s* sueño • **I need some sleep** necesito dormir • **to go to sleep** dormirse ♦ *vi* dormir
■ **sleep in** *vi* levantarse tarde

■ **sleep with** *vt* 💡 *El objeto siempre va después de la preposición al final. eufemismo* acostarse con

Formas irregulares de **sleep**: *pretérito & pp* **slept**.

sleeper ['sli:pər] *s* ❶ • **to be a heavy/light sleeper** tener el sueño profundo/ligero ❷ coche-cama ❸ tren nocturno (con literas)

sleeping bag ['sli:pɪŋ-] *s* saco de dormir

sleeping car ['sli:pɪŋ-] *s* coche-cama; coche dormitorio

sleeping pill ['sli:pɪŋ-] *s* pastilla para dormir

sleepless ['sli:plɪs] *adj* • **a sleepless night** una noche en blanco

sleepover ['sli:p,əuvər] *s* ▶ fiesta en la que los niños pasan la noche en casa de un amigo

sleepwalk ['sli:pwɔ:k] *vi* ❶ ser sonámbulo, la ❷ andar mientras uno duerme

sleepy ['sli:pɪ] *adj* soñoliento, ta • **to be** o **feel sleepy** tener sueño

sleet [sli:t] ◆ *s* aguanieve ◆ *v impersonal* • **it's sleeting** cae aguanieve

sleeve [sli:v] *s* ❶ manga ❷ cubierta *(de disco)*

expresión **to have something up your sleeve** guardar una carta en la manga

sleigh [sleɪ] *s* trineo

slender ['slendər] *adj* ❶ esbelto, ta ❷ escaso, sa

slept [slept] *pretérito & participio pasado* → sleep

slew [slu:] *pretérito* → slay

slice [slaɪs] ◆ *s* ❶ rebanada ❷ rodaja ❸ parte ◆ *vt* ❶ cortar ❷ rebanar

slick [slɪk] *adj* ❶ logrado, da ❷ *despectivo* de labia fácil

slide [slaɪd] ◆ *s* ❶ descenso ❷ FOTOGRAFÍA diapositiva ❸ resbaladilla; tobogán ◆ *vt* deslizar ◆ *vi* ❶ resbalar ❷ deslizarse ❸ caer

Formas irregulares de **slide**: *pret & pp* **slid** [slɪd].

sliding door [,slaɪdɪŋ-] *s* puerta corredera

slight [slaɪt] ◆ *adj* ❶ ligero, ra • **not in the slightest** *formal* en absoluto ❷ superficial *(herida)* ❸ menudo, da ◆ *s* desaire ◆ *vt* menospreciar; desairar

slightly ['slaɪtlɪ] *adv* ligeramente • **I feel slightly better** me siento un poco mejor

slim [slɪm] ◆ *adj* ❶ delgado, da ❷ remoto, ta *(posibilidad)* ◆ *vi* (intentar) adelgazar

slime [slaɪm] *s* ❶ lodo; cieno ❷ baba

slimming ['slɪmɪŋ] *s* adelgazamiento

sling [slɪŋ] ◆ *s* ❶ cabestrillo ❷ braga; honda ◆ *vt* ❶ colgar descuidadamente ❷ *familiar* tirar

Formas irregulares de **sling**: *pretérito & pp* **slung**.

slingshot ['slɪŋʃɒt] *s* tirachinas

slip [slɪp] ◆ *s* ❶ descuido; desliz ❷ papelito; hoja ❸ fondo

expresión **a slip of the pen/tongue** un lapsus ▶ **to give somebody the slip** *familiar* dar esquinazo a alguien

◆ *vt* • **to slip something into** meter algo rápidamente en ◆ *vi* ❶ resbalar; patinar ❷ escurrirse; resbalar ❸ empeorar

■ **slip up** *vi* cometer un error (poco importante)

slipper ['slɪpər] *s* pantufla

slippery ['slɪpərɪ] *adj* resbaladizo, za

slip-up *s familiar* desliz

slit [slɪt] ◆ *s* ranura; hendidura ◆ *vt* abrir; cortar (a lo largo)

Formas irregulares de **slit**: *pretérito &pp* **slit**.

slither ['slɪðər] *vi* deslizarse

sliver ['slɪvər] *s* ❶ esquirla ❷ astilla ❸ tajada muy fina

slog [slɒg] *familiar* ◆ *s* chamba; trabajo pesado ◆ *vi* • **to slog (away) at** trabajar sin descanso en

slogan ['sləugən] *s* eslogan

slope [sləup] ◆ *s* cuesta; pendiente ◆ *vi* inclinarse • **the road slopes down to the beach** la carretera desciende hasta la playa

sloping ['sləupɪŋ] *adj* ❶ inclinado, da ❷ en pendiente

sloppy ['slɒpɪ] *adj* ❶ descuidado, da ❷ chapucero, ra ❸ dejado, da

slot [slɒt] *s* ❶ ranura ❷ muesca ❸ espacio (en calendario)

slot machine *s* ❶ máquina automática *(de bebidas, cigarrillos, ETC)* ❷ máquina tragaperras

slouch [slautʃ] *vi* ir con los hombros caídos

Slovakia [slə'vækɪə] *s* Eslovaquia

slovenly ['slʌvnlɪ] *adj* ❶ desaliñado, da ❷ descuidado, da

slow [sləu] ◆ *adj* ❶ lento, ta ❷ • **to be slow to do something** tardar en hacer algo ❸ atrasado, da *(reloj)* • **my watch is a few minutes slow** mi reloj va atrasado unos cuantos minutos ❹ corto, ta (de alcances) ◆ *adv* despacio • **we're going slow** vamos despacio ◆ *vt* aminorar; ralentizar ◆ *vi* ir más despacio

■ **slow down, slow up** ◆ *vt* 💡 *El objeto se puede colocar antes o después de la preposición.* ❶ retrasar ❷ reducir la velocidad de ◆ *vi* ❶ ir más despacio ❷ reducir la velocidad ❸ tomarse las cosas con calma

slowdown ['sləudaun] *s* ralentización

slowly ['sləulɪ] *adv* despacio; lentamente

slow motion *s* • **in slow motion** a cámara lenta

sludge [slʌdʒ] *s* ❶ 💡 *incontable* fango; lodo ❷ aguas residuales

slug [slʌg] *s* ❶ babosa ❷ *familiar* bala

sluggish ['slʌgɪʃ] *adj* ❶ lento, ta ❷ aturdido, da

slum [slʌm] *s* barrio bajo

slumber party ['slʌmbər-] *s* ▶ fiesta en la que los niños pasan la noche en casa de un amigo

slump [slʌmp] ◆ *s* ❶ • **slump (in)** bajón (en) ❷ ECONOMÍA crisis económica ◆ *vi* ❶ dar un bajón ❷ desplomarse; dejarse caer

slung [slʌŋ] *pretérito & participio pasado* → sling

S

slur [slɜːɾ] ◆ *s* agravio ◆ *vt* mascullar

slush [slʌʃ] *s* nieve medio derretida

slut [slʌt] *s* ❶ *familiar* marrana ❷ *muy familiar* piruja

sly [slaɪ] (*comparativo* slyer o slier, *superlativo* slyest o sliest) *adj* ❶ furtivo, va ❷ astuto, ta

smack [smæk] ◆ *s* ❶ cachete ❷ golpe ◆ *vt* ❶ pegar; dar un cachete a • **she smacked him on the bottom** le dio una nalgada ❷ tirar de golpe ◆ *vi* • **to smack of something** oler a algo

small [smɔːl] *adj* ❶ pequeño, ña • **to make somebody feel small** hacer que alguien se sienta muy poca cosa • **to get smaller** empequeñecer ❷ bajo, ja ❸ de poca importancia

small change *s* cambio

small hours *spl* primeras horas de la madrugada • **in the small hours** en la madrugada

smallpox ['smɔːlpɒks] *s* viruela

small print *s* • **the small print** la letra pequeña

small talk *s* ☿ *incontable* conversación trivial

smart [smɑːt] ◆ *adj* ❶ elegante ❷ inteligente ❸ rápido, da ◆ *vi* ❶ escocer ❷ sentir resquemor

■ **smarts** *s* coco

smarten ['smɑːtn] ■ **smarten up** *vt* ☿ *El objeto se puede colocar antes o después de la preposición.* arreglar • **to smarten yourself up** arreglarse

smash [smæʃ] ◆ *s* ❶ estrépito ❷ *familiar* accidente ❸ TENIS mate; smash ◆ *vt* romper; hacer pedazos ◆ *vi* ❶ romperse; hacerse pedazos ❷ • **to smash through something** romper algo atravesándolo • **to smash into something** chocar violentamente con algo

smattering ['smætərɪŋ] *s* nociones • **he has a smattering of Spanish** tiene nociones de español

smear [smɪəɾ] ◆ *s* ❶ mancha ❷ citología; Papanicolau ◆ *vt* ❶ manchar ❷ • **to smear something onto something** untar algo con algo • **the screen was smeared with grease** la pantalla estaba embadurnada de grasa

smell [smel] ◆ *s* ❶ olor ❷ olfato ◆ *vt* literal & figurado oler ◆ *vi* ❶ oler • **to smell of/like** oler a/como • **to smell good/bad** oler bien/mal ❷ apestar; oler mal

Formas irregulares de **smell**: *pret* & *pp* **smelled** o **smelt**.

smelly ['smelɪ] *adj* maloliente

smelt [smelt] *pretérito* & *participio pasado* → smell

smile [smaɪl] ◆ *s* sonrisa ◆ *vi* sonreír • **to smile at somebody** sonreírle a alguien

smirk [smɜːk] *s* sonrisa desdeñosa

smog [smɒg] *s* niebla baja; smog

smoke [sməʊk] ◆ *s* humo

expresión **to go up in smoke** ser consumido, da por las llamas

◆ *vt* ❶ fumar • **to smoke a pipe** fumar en pipa ❷ ahumar ◆ *vi* ❶ fumar ❷ echar humo

smoked [sməʊkt] *adj* ahumado, da

smoker ['sməʊkəɾ] *s* fumador, ra • **he's a heavy smoker** fuma mucho

smoke shop *s* tabaquería

smoking ['sməʊkɪŋ] *s* el tabaquismo • **smoking is bad for you** fumar es malo para la salud • **to give up smoking** dejar de fumar • **'no smoking'** 'prohibido fumar'

smoky ['sməʊkɪ] *adj* ❶ lleno, na de humo ❷ ahumado, da

smolder ['sməʊldəɾ] *vi* ❶ arder sin llama ❷ *figurado* arder

smooth [smuːð] ◆ *adj* ❶ liso, sa ❷ terso, sa ❸ sin grumos ❹ suave ❺ tranquilo, la *(vuelo, viaje)* ❻ *despectivo* meloso, sa ❼ sin problemas ◆ *vt* alisar

■ **smooth out** *vt* ☿ *El objeto se puede colocar antes o después de la preposición.* ❶ alisar ❷ allanar *(problemas)*

smother ['smʌðəɾ] *vt* ❶ • **to smother something in** o **with** cubrir algo de ❷ asfixiar ❸ sofocar; apagar

SMS (*abreviatura de* short message service) *s* INFORMÁTICA SMS

smudge [smʌdʒ] ◆ *s* ❶ mancha ❷ borrón ◆ *vt* ❶ emborronar ❷ manchar

smug [smʌg] *adj despectivo* pagado, da o satisfecho, cha de sí mismo, ma

smuggle ['smʌgl] *vt* pasar de contrabando

smuggler ['smʌgləɾ] *s* contrabandista

smuggling ['smʌglɪŋ] *s* ☿ *incontable* contrabando

smutty ['smʌtɪ] *adj familiar* & *despectivo* guarro, rra

snack [snæk] ◆ *s* botana ◆ *vi* picar

snack bar *s* bar; cafetería

snag [snæg] ◆ *s* pega ◆ *vi* • **to snag (on)** engancharse (en)

snail [sneɪl] *s* caracol

expresión **at a snail's pace** a paso de tortuga

snail mail *s* correo caracol

snake [sneɪk] *s* ❶ serpiente ❷ culebra

snap [snæp] ◆ *adj* repentino, na *(decisión)* ◆ *s* ❶ crujido; chasquido ❷ *familiar* foto ❸ broche de presión ◆ *vt* ❶ partir (en dos) ❷ • **to snap something open** abrir algo de golpe ◆ *vi* ❶ partirse (en dos) ❷ • **to snap at something/somebody** intentar morder algo/a alguien ❸ • **to snap (at somebody)** contestar bruscamente o de mala manera a alguien

■ **snap up** *vt* ☿ *El objeto se puede colocar antes o después de la preposición.* no dejar escapar

snappy ['snæpɪ] *adj familiar* ❶ con estilo ❷ rápido, da • **make it snappy!** ¡date prisa! ❸ arisco, ca

snapshot ['snæpʃɒt] *s* foto

snare [sneəɾ] *s* trampa

snatch [snætʃ] ◆ *s* fragmento ◆ *vt* agarrar • **to snatch something from somebody** arrebatarle algo a alguien

sneak [sni:k] ◆ *vt* pasar a escondidas • **she tried to sneak the cakes out of the pantry** intentó sacar los pasteles de la despensa a escondidas • **she sneaked him into the house** lo metió en la casa a escondidas ◆ *vi* • **to sneak in/out** entrar/salir a escondidas • **he sneaked in without paying** se coló sin pagar • **don't try and sneak off!** ¡no intentes escabullirte!

Formas irregulares de **sneak**: *pretérito* **snuck**.

sneakers ['sni:kəz] *spl* tenis

sneer [snɪər] *vi* sonreír con desprecio

sneeze [sni:z] *vi* estornudar

snide [snaɪd] *adj* sarcástico, ca

sniff [snɪf] ◆ *vt* ❶ oler ❷ esnifar ◆ *vi* sorber por la nariz

snigger ['snɪgər] ◆ *s* risa disimulada ◆ *vi* reírse por lo bajo

snip [snɪp] ◆ *s familiar* ganga ◆ *vt* cortar con tijeras

snippet ['snɪpɪt] *s* retazo • **snippet of information** un dato aislado

snivel ['snɪvl] *vi* lloriquear

Formas irregulares de **snivel**: *pret & pp* **sniveled**, *gerundio* **sniveling**.

snob [snɒb] *s* esnob

snobbish ['snɒbɪʃ], **snobby** ['snɒbɪ] *adj* esnob

snoop [snu:p] *vi familiar* • **to snoop (around)** fisgonear

snooty ['snu:tɪ] *adj* engreído, da

snooze [snu:z] ◆ *s* cabezada • **to have a snooze** echar una cabezada ◆ *vi* dormitar

snore [snɔ:r] ◆ *s* ronquido ◆ *vi* roncar

snoring ['snɔ:rɪŋ] *s* 🔆 *incontable* ronquidos

snorkel ['snɔ:kl] *s* tubo para buceo

snort [snɔ:t] ◆ *s* resoplido ◆ *vi* resoplar

snout [snaʊt] *s* hocico

snow [snəʊ] ◆ *s* nieve ◆ *v impersonal* nevar • **it's snowing** está nevando

snowball ['snəʊbɔ:l] ◆ *s* bola de nieve ◆ *vi figurado* aumentar rápidamente

snowboard ['snəʊbɔ:d] *s* snowboard

snowboarding ['snəʊbɔ:dɪŋ] *s* snowboard • **to go snowboarding** hacer snowboard

snowbound ['snəʊbaʊnd] *adj* bloqueado, da por la nieve

snowdrift ['snəʊdrɪft] *s* montón de nieve

snowfall ['snəʊfɔ:l] *s* nevada

snowflake ['snəʊfleɪk] *s* copo de nieve

snowman ['snəʊmæn] *s* muñeco de nieve

El plural de **snowman** es **snowmen** ['snəʊmen].

snow pea *s* chícharo chino

snowplow ['snəʊplaʊ] *s* quitanieves

snowshoe ['snəʊʃu:] *s* raqueta de nieve

snowstorm ['snəʊstɔ:m] *s* tormenta de nieve

Snr, snr (*abreviatura de* senior) sén.

snub [snʌb] ◆ *s* desaire ◆ *vt* desairar

snuck [snʌk] *pretérito* → **sneak**

snug [snʌg] *adj* ❶ cómodo y calentito, cómoda y calentita ❷ acogedor, ra ❸ ajustado, da

snuggle ['snʌgl] *vi* • **to snuggle up to somebody** arrimarse a alguien acurrucándose

so [səʊ] ◆ *adv* ❶ tan • **so difficult (that)** tan difícil (que) • **don't be so stupid!** ¡no seas bobo! • **I wish he wouldn't talk so much** ojalá no hablara tanto • **I've never seen so much money/many cars** en mi vida he visto tanto dinero/tantos carros • **thank you so much** muchísimas gracias • **it's about so high** es así de alto ❷ • **so what's the point then?** entonces ¿qué sentido tiene? • **so you knew already?** ¿así que ya lo sabías? • **I don't think so** no creo; me parece que no • **I'm afraid so** me temo que sí • **if so** si es así • **is that so?** ¿es cierto? ❸ también • **so can I** y yo (también puedo) • **so do I** y yo (también) • **she speaks French and so does her husband** ella habla francés y su marido también ❹ • **(like) so** así; de esta forma ❺ • **so there is!** ¡pues (sí que) es verdad! • **so I see** ya lo veo ❻ • **they pay us so much a week** nos pagan tanto a la semana • **it's not so much the money as the time involved** no es tanto el dinero como el tiempo que conlleva • **they didn't so much as say thank you** ni siquiera dieron las gracias • **or so** más o menos ◆ *conjunción* ❶ así que ❷ (bueno) pues • **so what have you been up to?** bueno, ¿y qué has estado haciendo? • **so that's who she is!** ¡anda! ¡o sea que ella!

expresiones **so long!** ¡adiós! ▶ **so what?** *familiar* ¿y qué? ▶ **so there** *familiar* ¡(y si no te gusta,) te chinchas!

■ **and so on, and so forth** *adv* y cosas por el estilo

■ **so as** *conjunción* para • **we didn't knock so as not to disturb them** no llamamos para no molestarlos

■ **so far** *conjunción* hasta ahora • **so far, so good** por ahora todo bien

■ **so that** *conjunción* para que • **he lied so that she would go free** mintió para que ella saliera en libertad

soak [səʊk] ◆ *vt* ❶ poner en remojo ❷ empapar ◆ *vi* ❶ • **to leave something to soak, to let something soak** dejar algo en remojo ❷ • **to soak into** o **through something** calar algo

■ **soak up** *vt* 🔆 *El objeto se puede colocar antes o después de la preposición.* absorber

soaking ['səʊkɪŋ] *adj* empapado, da • **to be soaking wet** estar empapado

so-and-so *s familiar* ❶ fulano, na de tal ❷ hijo, ja de tal

soap [səʊp] *s* ❶ 🔆 *incontable* jabón ❷ TELEVISIÓN telenovela

soap opera *s* telenovela

soap powder *s* jabón en polvo

soapy ['səʊpɪ] *adj* jabonoso, sa

soar [sɔ:r] *vi* ❶ remonta el vuelo ❷ elevarse ❸ dispararse

sob [sɒb] ◆ *s* sollozo ◆ *vi* sollozar

sober ['səʊbər] *adj* ❶ sobrio, bria ❷ serio, ria

■ **sober up** *vi* pasársele a uno la borrachera

S

sobering ['səʊbərɪŋ] *adj* que hace reflexionar • **it was a sobering thought** dio mucho que pensar

so-called [-kɔːld] *adj* ❶ mal llamado, da ❷ así llamado, da

soccer ['sɒkər] *s* ⚗️*incontable* futbol

SOCCER

Soccer es la palabra que se utiliza en Estados Unidos para referirse al deporte mundialmente conocido como futbol. Ha ganado mucha popularidad en años recientes y hoy en día muchos niños y niñas estadounidenses practican este deporte.

sociable ['səʊʃəbl] *adj* sociable

social ['səʊʃl] *adj* social

social club *s* club social

socialism ['səʊʃəlɪzm] *s* socialismo

socialist ['səʊʃəlɪst] ◆ *adj* socialista ◆ *s* socialista

socialize, socialise ['səʊʃəlaɪz] *vi* • **to socialize (with)** alternar (con)

social security *s* seguridad social

social services *spl* servicios sociales

social worker *s* asistente, ta social

society [sə'saɪətɪ] *s* ❶ sociedad ❷ asociación

sociology [ˌsəʊsɪ'ɒlədʒɪ] *s* sociología

sock [sɒk] *s* media

socket ['sɒkɪt] *s* ❶ *ELECTRICIDAD* enchufe ❷ cuenca

soda ['səʊdə] *s* ❶ soda ❷ refresco

soda water *s* soda

sodden ['sɒdn] *adj* empapado, da

sodium ['səʊdɪəm] *s* sodio

sofa ['səʊfə] *s* sofá

soft [sɒft] *adj* ❶ blando, da • **to go soft** ablandarse ❷ suave

soft drink *s* refresco

soften ['sɒfn] ◆ *vt* suavizar ◆ *vi* ❶ ablandarse ❷ suavizarse

softhearted [ˌsɒft'hɑːtɪd] *adj* de buen corazón

softly ['sɒftlɪ] *adv* ❶ con delicadeza ❷ suavemente ❸ con indulgencia

soft-spoken *adj* de voz suave

software ['sɒftweər] *s* *INFORMÁTICA* software

soggy ['sɒgɪ] *adj* *familiar* empapado, da

soil [sɔɪl] ◆ *s* tierra ◆ *vt* ensuciar

soiled [sɔɪld] *adj* sucio, cia

solar ['səʊlər] *adj* solar • **solar eclipse** eclipse de sol

solar energy *s* energía solar

solar power *s* energía solar

sold [səʊld] *pretérito & participio pasado* → **sell**

soldier ['səʊldʒər] *s* soldado

sold out *adj* agotado, da • **the theater was sold out** se agotaron las localidades • **all the shops were sold out of lemons** se habían agotado los limones en todas las tiendas

sole [səʊl] ◆ *adj* ❶ único, ca ❷ exclusivo, va ◆ *s* ❶ (pl soles) planta ❷ suela ❸ (pl sole) lenguado

solemn ['sɒləm] *adj* solemne

solid ['sɒlɪd] ◆ *adj* ❶ sólido, da ❷ macizo, za ❸ serio, ria ❹ sin interrupción • **it rained for two solid weeks** llovió sin parar durante dos semanas ◆ *s* sólido • **to be on solids** estar tomando alimentos sólidos

solidarity [ˌsɒlɪ'dærətɪ] *s* solidaridad

solitaire [ˌsɒlɪ'teər] *s* solitario

solitary ['sɒlɪtrɪ] *adj* solitario, ria

solitude ['sɒlɪtjuːd] *s* soledad

solo ['səʊləʊ] ◆ *adj* & *adv* a solas ◆ *s* solo

El plural de **solo** es **solos**.

soloist ['səʊləʊɪst] *s* solista

soluble ['sɒljʊbl] *adj* soluble

solution [sə'luːʃn] *s* • **solution (to)** solución (a)

solve [sɒlv] *vt* resolver

solvent ['sɒlvənt] ◆ *adj* *FINANZAS* solvente ◆ *s* disolvente

somber ['sɒmbər] *adj* sombrío, a

some [sʌm]
◆ *adj*
❶ [*con incontables en singular o contables en plural*]
• **there is some milk left** queda algo de leche
• **I've brought you some sweets** te traje unos caramelos
❷ [*en frases interrogativas*]
• **will you have some more meat?** ¿quieres más carne?
❸ [*indica una intensidad o una cantidad relativamente importante*]
• **I had some difficulty getting here** tuve dificultades para llegar aquí
• **I've known him for some years** lo conozco desde hace unos años
❹ [*expresa un contraste*]
• **some jobs are better paid than others** algunos trabajos están mejor pagados que otros
• **some people like his music** a algunos les gusta su música
❺ [*para hablar de una persona desconocida o no especificada*]
• **she married some writer or other** se casó con no sé cuál escritor
❻ *familiar* [*en frases exclamativas, para expresar entusiasmo o admiración*]
• **that was some party!** ¡qué fiesta!
• **she's some girl!** ¡es una chica genial!

S

◆ *pronombre*
• **can I have some?** ¿puedo probarlo?
• **some (of them) left early** algunos se marcharon pronto
• **some of it is mine** una parte es mía
◆ *adv*
[*expresa una aproximación*]
• **there were some 7,000 people there** había unas 7.000 personas

somebody ['sʌmbədɪ] *pronombre* alguien • **somebody came to see you** alguien vino a verte • **somebody or other** alguien • **somebody else** otra persona

someday ['sʌmdeɪ] *adv* algún día

somehow ['sʌmhaʊ], **someway** ['sʌmweɪ] *adv* ❶ de alguna manera • **I'll do it somehow** lo haré de alguna manera • **somehow or other** de un modo u otro ❷ por alguna razón

someone ['sʌmwʌn] *pronombre* alguien • **someone or other** alguien, no sé quien

someplace ['sʌmpleɪs] *adv* en alguna parte; a alguna parte • **it's someplace in the kitchen** está en alguna parte de la cocina • **it's someplace else** está en otra parte • **shall we go someplace else?** ¿nos vamos a otra parte?

somersault ['sʌməsɔːlt] *s* ❶ salto mortal ❷ voltereta

something ['sʌmθɪŋ] ◆ *pronombre* algo • **I have something in my eye** tengo algo en el ojo • **or something** *familiar* o algo así • **something or other** alguna cosa
expresión **that was something else!** ¡eso fue genial!
❿ **he's something else!** ¡es fuera de serie!
◆ *adv* • **something like, something in the region of** algo así como

sometime ['sʌmtaɪm] *adv* en algún momento • **I'll see you sometime next week** te veré en algún momento la semana que viene • **sometime or other** en algún momento • **sometime next week** durante la semana que viene

sometimes ['sʌmtaɪmz] *adv* a veces

---

some

El adjetivo o pronombre **some** sólo se usa en frases afirmativas (there are **some** cookies left *quedan algunas galletas;* **some** of my old school friends are married *algunos de mis antiguos compañeros de clase están casados*). Para las negativas se usa el adjetivo no o el pronombre none (there are **no** cookies left; **none** of my school friends are married). Si el verbo de la oración principal está en negativa se usa any a cambio (I **don't** know if there are **any** cookies left; there **aren't** any cookies left).

Para hacer preguntas podemos usar some si la respuesta esperada es yes (would you like **some**

soup?). De lo contrario usaremos any (are there **any** cookies left?).

Ver también no, none.

someway = somehow
somewhat ['sʌmwɒt] *adv formal* algo
somewhere ['sʌmpleɪs] *adv* ❶ en alguna parte; a alguna parte • **I need somewhere to spend the night** necesito un lugar donde pasar la noche ❷ • **somewhere between five and ten** entre cinco y diez • **somewhere around 20** alrededor de 20 • **he's somewhere in his fifties** tiene cincuenta años y pico

son [sʌn] *s* hijo

song [sɒŋ] *s* ❶ canción ❷ canto
expresión **to make a song and dance about something** *familiar* armar la de Dios es Cristo sobre algo

son-in-law *s* yerno

Dos plurales: **sons-in-law** o **son-in-laws**.

sonnet ['sɒnɪt] *s* soneto
sonny ['sʌnɪ] *s familiar* hijo
soon [suːn] *adv* pronto • **he'll soon be here** estará aquí pronto • **how soon will it be ready?** ¿para cuándo estará listo? • **soon after** poco después • **as soon as** tan pronto como • **as soon as possible** cuanto antes • **see you soon** hasta pronto

sooner ['suːnər] *adv* ❶ antes • **you should have come sooner** deberías haber venido antes • **no sooner did he arrive than...** apenas había llegado cuando... • **no sooner said than done** dicho y hecho • **sooner or later** (más) tarde o (más) temprano • **the sooner the better** cuanto antes mejor ❷ • **I'd sooner (not)...** preferiría (no)...

soothe [suːð] *vt* ❶ aliviar ❷ calmar
sophisticated [səˈfɪstɪkeɪtɪd] *adj* sofisticado, da
sophomore ['sɒfəmɔːr] *s* estudiante del segundo curso

sopping ['sɒpɪŋ] *adj* • **sopping (wet)** chorreando
soppy ['sɒpɪ] *adj familiar & despectivo* sentimentaloide

soprano [səˈprɑːnəʊ] *s* soprano

El plural de **soprano** es **sopranos**.

sorbet ['sɔːbeɪ] *s* sorbete • **lemon sorbet** sorbete de limón

sorcerer ['sɔːsərər] *s* brujo, ja
sordid ['sɔːdɪd] *adj* ❶ obsceno, na ❷ sórdido, da
sore [sɔːr] ◆ *adj* ❶ dolorido, da • **to have a sore throat** tener dolor de garganta ❷ enfadado, da • **to get sore** enfadarse ◆ *s* llaga

sorority [səˈrɒrətɪ] *s* ❿ club de estudiantes universitarios

sorrow ['sɒrəʊ] *s* pesar

sorry ['sɒrɪ] ◆ *adj* ❶ • **to be sorry about something** sentir algo • **I'm sorry for what I did** siento lo que hice • **I'm sorry** lo siento • **I'm sorry if I'm disturbing you** o **to disturb you** siento molestarte ❷ • **to be sorry that** sentir que • **we were sorry about his resignation** sentimos que dimitiera • **to be sorry for** arrepentirse de **❸** • **I'm sorry to have to say that...** siento tener que decir que... **❹** • **to be** o **feel sorry for yourself** sentir lástima de uno mismo, una misma **❺** • **I'm sorry, but...** perdón, pero... **❻** lamentable • **it was a sorry sight** tenía un aspecto lamentable ◆ *exclamación* **❶** • **sorry!** ¡perdón! **❷** • **sorry?** ¿perdón? **❸** • **a girl, sorry, a woman** una chica, perdón, una mujer

sort [sɔːt] ◆ *s* tipo • **what sort of computer have you got?** ¿qué tipo de computadora tienes? • **she did nothing of the sort** no hizo nada por el estilo • **all sorts of** todo tipo de • **sort of** más o menos • **a sort of** una especie de ◆ *vt* clasificar

■ **sort out** *vt* 🔆 *El objeto se puede colocar antes o después de la preposición.* **❶** ordenar • **I'm going to sort out all my papers** voy a ordenar todos mis papeles **❷** solucionar • **he managed to sort the problem out** logró solucionar el problema

SOS (*abreviatura de* save our souls) *s* SOS • **to send an SOS** lanzar un SOS

so-so *adj* & *adv familiar* así así

sought [sɔːt] *pretérito* & *participio pasado* → **seek**

soul [səʊl] *s* **❶** alma **❷** soul

soulful ['səʊlfʊl] *adj* lleno, na de sentimiento

sound [saʊnd] ◆ *adj* **❶** sano, na **❷** sólido, da **❸** fiable ◆ *adv* • **to be sound asleep** estar profundamente dormido, da ◆ *s* **❶** sonido **❷** ruido
expresión by the sound of it por lo que parece
◆ *vt* hacer sonar ◆ *vi* **❶** sonar **❷** • **it sounds interesting** parece interesante • **it sounds like fun** suena divertido

■ **sound out** *vt* 🔆 *El objeto se puede colocar antes o después de la preposición.* • **to sound somebody out (on** o **about)** sondear a alguien (sobre)

sound barrier *s* barrera del sonido

sound card *s* INFORMÁTICA tarjeta de sonido

sound effects *spl* efectos sonoros

soundly ['saʊndlɪ] *adv* **❶** totalmente **❷** profundamente

soundproof ['saʊndpruːf] *adj* insonorizado, da

soundtrack ['saʊndtræk] *s* banda sonora

soup [suːp] *s* **❶** sopa **❷** caldo

soup plate *s* plato hondo

soup spoon *s* cuchara sopera

sour [saʊər] ◆ *adj* **❶** ácido, da **❷** agrio, gria • **the milk has gone sour** la leche está cortada ◆ *vt* agriar

source [sɔːs] *s* **❶** fuente **❷** origen

sour grapes *s* 🔆 *incontable familiar* • **it's sour grapes!** ¡están verdes!

south [saʊθ] ◆ *s* **❶** sur **❷** • **the South** el sur ◆ *adj* del sur ◆ *adv* • **south (of)** al sur (de)

South Africa *s* • **(the Republic of) South Africa** (la República de) Sudáfrica

South African ◆ *adj* sudafricano, na ◆ *s* sudafricano, na

South America *s* Sudamérica

South American ◆ *adj* sudamericano, na ◆ *s* sudamericano, na

southeast [,saʊθ'iːst] ◆ *s* **❶** sudeste **❷** • **the Southeast** el sudeste ◆ *adj* del sudeste ◆ *adv* • **southeast (of)** hacia el sudeste (de)

southerly ['sʌðəlɪ] *adj* del sur

southern ['sʌðən] *adj* del sur • **the southern hemisphere** el hemisferio sur

South Korea *s* Corea del Sur

South Pole *s* • **the South Pole** el polo Sur

southward ['saʊθwəd] ◆ *adj* sur ◆ *adv* = **southwards**

southwards ['saʊθwədz], **southward** *adv* hacia el sur

southwest [,saʊθ'west] ◆ *s* **❶** suroeste **❷** • **the Southwest** el suroeste ◆ *adj* del suroeste ◆ *adv* • **southwest (of)** hacia el suroeste (de)

souvenir [,suːvə'nɪər] *s* recuerdo

sovereign ['sɒvrɪn] ◆ *adj* soberano, na ◆ *s* soberano, na

Soviet Union *s* • **the (former) Soviet Union** la (antigua) Unión Soviética

sow¹ [səʊ] *vt literal* & *figurado* sembrar
Formas irregulares de **sow**: *pretérito* **sowed**, *pp* **sown** o **sowed**.

sow² [saʊ] *s* chancha

sown [səʊn] *participio pasado* → **sow**

soya ['sɔɪə] *s* soja

soy(a) bean ['sɔɪ(ə)-] *s* frijol de soja

spa [spɑː] *s* balneario

spa bath *s* bañera de hidromasaje

space [speɪs] ◆ *s* espacio • **there isn't enough space for it** no hay suficiente espacio para ello • **who was the first man in space?** ¿quién fue el primer hombre en el espacio? • **in the space of 30 minutes** en el espacio de 30 minutos • **can you make a space for me?** ¿puedes hacerme un lugar? ◆ *vt* espaciar

■ **space out** *vt* 🔆 *El objeto se puede colocar antes o después de la preposición.* espaciar

spacecraft ['speɪskrɑːft] *s* nave espacial
El plural de **spacecraft** es **spacecraft**.

spaceman ['speɪsmæn] *s familiar* astronauta
El plural de **spaceman** es **spacemen** ['speɪsmen].

spaceship ['speɪsʃɪp] *s* nave espacial

space shuttle *s* transbordador espacial

spacesuit ['speɪssuːt] *s* traje espacial

spacing ['speɪsɪŋ] *s* TIPOGRAFÍA espacio • **double spacing** doble espacio

spacious ['speɪʃəs] *adj* espacioso, sa

spade [speɪd] *s* pala

■ **spades** *spl* picas

spaghetti [spə'getɪ] *s* 🔆 *incontable* espaguetis

Spain [speɪn] *s* España

spam [spæm] ◆ *s* INFORMÁTICA correo basura ◆ *vt* INFORMÁTICA enviar correo basura a

spammer ['spæmər] *s* INFORMÁTICA spammer

spamming ['spæmɪŋ] *s* ☼ *incontable* INFORMÁTICA envío de correo basura

span [spæn] ◆ *pretérito* → **spin** ◆ *s* ❶ periodo ❷ gama ❸ envergadura ◆ *vt* ❶ abarcar ❷ cruzar

Spaniard ['spænjəd] *s* español, la

Spanish ['spænɪʃ] ◆ *adj* español, la, ◆ *s* español ◆ *spl* • **the Spanish** los españoles

spank [spæŋk] *vt* zurrar

spanner ['spænər] *s* llave inglesa

spare [speər] ◆ *adj* ❶ de sobra • **I've got a spare pen you can borrow** tengo una pluma de sobra que te puedo prestar ❷ libre • **there's a spare seat at the back** hay un asiento libre en el fondo ◆ *s* • **I always carry a spare** siempre llevo uno de sobra ❷ *familiar* refacción ◆ *vt* ❶ conceder ❷ dejar • **can you spare a minute?** ¿tienes un minuto? • **we can't spare any time/money** no tenemos tiempo/dinero • **to spare** de sobra ❸ perdonar • **they spared his life** le perdonaron la vida; salvar ❹ ahorrar *(molestia)* • **to spare somebody something** ahorrarle a alguien algo • **you've spared me the trouble** me has ahorrado la molestia ❺ • **to spare no expense/effort** no escatimar gastos/esfuerzos

spare part *s* AUTOMÓVILES refacción

spare time *s* tiempo libre

spare tire *s* llanta de refacción

sparing ['speərɪŋ] *adj* • **to be sparing with** o **of** ser parco, ca en

sparingly ['speərɪŋlɪ] *adv* con moderación

spark [spɑːk] *s* literal & figurado chispa

sparkle ['spɑːkl] ◆ *s* ☼ *incontable* ❶ destello ❷ brillo ◆ *vi* ❶ centellear ❷ brillar

sparkling wine ['spɑːklɪŋ-] *s* vino espumoso

spark plug *s* bujía

sparrow ['spærəʊ] *s* gorrión

sparse [spɑːs] *adj* escaso, sa

spasm ['spæzm] *s* ❶ MEDICINA espasmo ❷ MEDICINA acceso

spat [spæt] *pretérito & participio pasado* → **spit**

spate [speɪt] *s* cadena

spatter ['spætər] *vt* salpicar

spawn [spɔːn] ◆ *s* ☼ *incontable* huevas ◆ *vt* figurado engendrar ◆ *vi* desovar

speak [spiːk] ◆ *vt* ❶ decir ❷ hablar • **can you speak French?** ¿hablas francés?

expresión **to speak your mind** decir lo que se piensa ◆ *vi* hablar • **speak more slowly** habla más despacio • **who's speaking?** ¿quién habla? • **this is Kate speaking** habla Kate • **to speak to** o **with** hablar con • **to speak to somebody (about)** hablar con alguien (de) • **to speak about** hablar de • **we aren't speaking** no nos hablamos

expresión **nobody/nothing to speak of** nadie/nada especial

■ **so to speak** *adv* por así decirlo

■ **speak for** *vt* ☼ *El objeto siempre va después de la preposición al final.* hablar en nombre de

■ **speak up** *vi* • **to speak up for** salir en defensa de ❷ hablar más alto

Formas irregulares de **speak**: *pretérito* **spoke**, *pp* **spoken.**

speaker ['spiːkər] *s* ❶ persona que habla ❷ orador, ra; conferenciante ❸ hablante • **English speakers** angloparlantes ❹ parlante

speaking ['spiːkɪŋ] ◆ *adv* • **generally speaking** en general • **legally speaking** desde una perspectiva legal ◆ *adj* • **we are not on speaking terms** no nos dirigimos la palabra

spear [spɪər] ◆ *s* ❶ lanza ❷ jabalina ◆ *vt* ❶ atravesar ❷ pinchar

spearhead ['spɪəhed] *vt* encabezar

special ['speʃl] *adj* especial

special delivery *s* correo urgente

specialist ['speʃəlɪst] ◆ *adj* ❶ especialista ❷ especializado, da ◆ *s* especialista

speciality [,speʃɪ'ælətɪ], **specialty** ['speʃltɪ] *s* especialidad

specialize, specialise ['speʃəlaɪz] *vi* • **to specialize (in)** especializarse (en)

specially ['speʃəlɪ] *adv* especialmente

special needs *spl* • **special needs children** niños con necesidades especiales

specialty = **speciality**

species ['spiːʃiːz] *s* especie

El plural de **species** es **species.**

specific [spə'sɪfɪk] *adj* ❶ determinado, da ❷ específico, ca • **specific to** específico, ca de

specifically [spə'sɪfɪklɪ] *adv* ❶ expresamente ❷ específicamente

specify ['spesɪfaɪ] *vt* • **to specify (that)** especificar (que)

specimen ['spesɪmən] *s* ❶ espécimen ❷ muestra

speck [spek] *s* ❶ manchita ❷ mota

speckled ['spekld] *adj* • **speckled (with)** moteado, da (de)

spectacle ['spektəkl] *s* espectáculo • **to make a spectacle of yourself** dar el espectáculo

spectacular [spek'tækjʊlər] *adj* espectacular

spectator [spek'teɪtər] *s* espectador, ra

spectrum ['spektrəm] *s* ❶ espectro ❷ figurado gama

El plural de **spectrum** es **spectra** ['spektrə].

speculation [,spekjʊ'leɪʃn] *s* especulación

sped [sped] *pretérito & participio pasado* → **speed**

speech [spiːtʃ] *s* ❶ habla ❷ discurso • **to give** o **make a speech (on something to somebody)** pronunciar un discurso (sobre algo a alguien) ❸ manera de hablar ❹ dialecto

speechless ['spiːtʃlɪs] *adj* • **to be speechless (with)** enmudecer (de)

S

speed [spi:d] ◆ s ❶ velocidad • **at a speed of 30 mph** a una velocidad de 30 millas por hora • **at top speed** a toda velocidad ❷ rapidez ◆ vi ❶ • **to speed along/away** ir/alejarse a toda velocidad • **to speed by** pasar volando ❷ *Automóviles* conducir con exceso de velocidad

■ **speed up** ◆ vt ⚡ *El objeto se puede colocar antes o después de la preposición.* ❶ acelerar ❷ meter prisa a ◆ vi ❶ acelerar ❷ darse prisa

Formas irregulares de **speed**: *pret & pp* **speeded** o **sped**.

speedboat ['spi:dbəʊt] s lancha motora

speed-dial button s botón de marcado abreviado

speed-dialing s ⚡*incontable Telecomunicaciones* marcado rápido

speeding ['spi:dɪŋ] s ⚡*incontable* exceso de velocidad

speed limit s límite de velocidad

speedometer [spɪ'dɒmɪtər] s velocímetro

speedway ['spi:dweɪ] s ❶ ⚡*incontable Deporte* carreras de moto ❷ autopista

speedy ['spi:dɪ] *adj* rápido, da

spell [spel] ◆ s ❶ temporada • **to go through a good/bad spell** pasar una buena/mala racha ❷ intervalo • **sunny spells** intervalos de sol ❸ hechizo • **to cast** o **put a spell on somebody** hechizar a alguien ◆ vt ❶ deletrear • **how do you spell that?** ¿cómo se escribe eso? ❷ *figurado* significar • **to spell trouble** augurar problemas ◆ vi escribir correctamente • **I can't spell** cometo muchas faltas de ortografía

■ **spell out** vt ⚡ *El objeto se puede colocar antes o después de la preposición.* ❶ deletrear ❷ • **to spell something out (for** o **to somebody)** decir algo por las claras (a alguien)

Formas irregulares de **spell**: *pretérito & pp* **spelled**.

spellbound ['spelbaʊnd] *adj* hechizado, da • **to hold somebody spellbound** tener hechizado, da a alguien

spellcheck ['speltʃek] vt *Informática* pasar el corrector ortográfico a

spellchecker ['speltʃekər] s *Informática* corrector ortográfico

spelling ['spelɪŋ] s ortografía • **the right/wrong spelling** la grafía correcta/incorrecta • **to be good at spelling** tener buena ortografía • **spelling mistake** falta de ortografía

spend [spend] vt ❶ gastar • **to spend something on** gastar algo en ❷ pasar • **to spend your time doing something** pasar el tiempo haciendo algo

Formas irregulares de **spend**: *pretérito & pp* **spent**.

spendthrift ['spendθrɪft] s derrochador, ra

spent [spent] ◆ *pretérito & participio pasado* → **spend** ◆ *adj* ❶ usado, da ❷ agotado, da

sperm [spɜ:m] s esperma

Dos plurales: **sperm** o **sperms**.

spew [spju:] vt arrojar

sphere [sfɪər] s ❶ esfera ❷ círculo

spice [spaɪs] s *Cocina* especia

spicy ['spaɪsɪ] *adj* ❶ *figurado* picante ❷ con muchas especias

spider ['spaɪdər] s araña

spike [spaɪk] s ❶ punta ❷ clavo ❸ pincho

spill [spɪl] ◆ vt derramar ◆ vi derramarse

Formas irregulares de **spill**: *pretérito & pp* **spilled**.

spin [spɪn] ◆ s ❶ vuelta ❷ *Aeronáutica* barrena ❸ *familiar* vuelta • **to go for a spin** ir a dar una vuelta ◆ vt ❶ girar ❷ centrifugar ◆ vi girar • **to spin out of control** comenzar a dar trompos • **my head is spinning** la cabeza me da vueltas

■ **spin out** vt ⚡ *El objeto se puede colocar antes o después de la preposición.* ❶ alargar ❷ estirar

Formas irregulares de **spin**: *pretérito* **span** o **spun**, *pp* **spun**.

spinach ['spɪnɪdʒ] s ⚡*incontable* espinacas

spinal column ['spaɪnl-] s columna vertebral

spinal cord s médula espinal

spine [spaɪn] s ❶ *Anatomía* espina dorsal ❷ lomo ❸ espina

spinning top s peonza

spin-off s subproducto

spinster ['spɪnstər] s soltera

spiral ['spaɪərəl] ◆ *adj* en espiral ◆ s espiral ◆ vi moverse en espiral

Formas irregulares de **spiral**: *pret & pp* **spiraled**, *gerundio* **spiraling**.

spiral staircase s escalera de caracol

spire [spaɪər] s aguja

spirit ['spɪrɪt] s ❶ espíritu ❷ vigor

■ **spirits** spl ❶ humor • **to be in high/low spirits** estar exultante/alicaído ❷ licores

spirited ['spɪrɪtɪd] *adj* enérgico, ca

spiritual ['spɪrɪtʃʊəl] *adj* espiritual

spit [spɪt] ◆ s ❶ saliva ❷ asador ◆ vi escupir

Formas irregulares de **spit**: *pretérito & pp* **spit**.

spite [spaɪt] ◆ s rencor ◆ vt fastidiar

■ **in spite of** *preposición* a pesar de

spiteful ['spaɪtfʊl] *adj* ❶ rencoroso, sa ❷ malintencionado, da

splash [splæʃ] ◆ s ❶ chapoteo ❷ mancha ◆ vt salpicar ◆ vi ❶ • **to splash about** o **around** chapotear ❷ • **to splash on** o **against something** salpicar algo

■ **splash out** vi *familiar* • **to splash out (on something)** gastar un dineral (en algo)

splashguard ['splæʃgɑ:d] s alfombra salpicadero

spleen [spli:n] s ❶ *Anatomía* bazo ❷ *figurado* cólera

splendid ['splendɪd] *adj* ❶ espléndido, da ❷ magnífico, ca

splint [splɪnt] s tablilla

splinter ['splɪntər] ◆ s ❶ astilla ❷ fragmento ◆ vi astillarse

split [splɪt] ◆ s ❶ grieta ❷ desgarrón ❸ • split (in) escisión (en) ❹ • split (between) diferencia (entre) ◆ vt ❶ desgarrar ❷ agrietar ❸ partir ❹ escindir ❺ repartir ◆ vi ❶ bifurcarse; partirse ❷ escindirse ❸ agrietarse ❹ desgarrarse ❺ familiar largarse
■ **split off** ◆ vt • to split something off (from) separar algo (de) ◆ vi • to split off (from) desprenderse (de)
■ **split up** ◆ vt • to split something up (into) dividir algo (en) ◆ vi separarse
■ **splits** spl • to do the splits hacer split saltar y caer al suelo con las piernas abiertas
Formas irregulares de **split:** pretérito & pp **split.**

split second s fracción de segundo • for a split second por una fracción de segundo

spoil [spɔɪl] vt ❶ estropear ❷ mimar
■ **spoils** spl botín
Formas irregulares de **spoil:** pretérito & pp **spoiled** o **spoilt.**

spoiled [spɔɪld] = spoilt

spoilsport ['spɔɪlspɔːt] s aguafiestas

spoilt [spɔɪlt] ◆ pretérito & participio pasado → spoil ◆ adj mimado, da

spoke [spəʊk] ◆ pretérito → speak ◆ s radio

spoken ['spəʊkn] participio pasado → speak

spokesman ['spəʊksmən] s portavoz
El plural de **spokesman** es **spokesmen** ['spəʊksmen].

spokeswoman ['spəʊks,wʊmən] s portavoz
El plural de **spokeswoman** es **spokeswomen** ['spəʊks,wɪmɪn].

sponge [spʌndʒ] ◆ s ❶ esponja ❷ bizcocho ◆ vt limpiar con una esponja ◆ vi familiar • to sponge off vivir a costa de
Formas irregulares de **sponge:** gerundio **sponging**

sponge cake s bizcocho

sponsor ['spɒnsər] ◆ s patrocinador, ra ◆ vt ❶ patrocinar ❷ respaldar

sponsored walk [,spɒnsəd-] s marcha benéfica

sponsorship ['spɒnsəʃɪp] s patrocinio

spontaneous [spɒn'teɪnjəs] adj espontáneo, a

spook [spuːk] vt asustar

spooky ['spuːkɪ] adj familiar escalofriante

spoon [spuːn] s ❶ cuchara ❷ cucharada

spoon-feed vt dar de comer con cuchara a

spoonful ['spuːnfʊl] s cucharada
Dos plurales: **spoonfuls** o **spoonsful** ['spuːnzfʊl].

sporadic [spə'rædɪk] adj esporádico, ca

sport [spɔːt] s deporte

sporting ['spɔːtɪŋ] adj literal & figurado deportivo, va
expresión to give somebody a sporting chance dar a alguien la oportunidad de ganar

sports car ['spɔːts-] s carro sport

sports jacket ['spɔːts-] s chaqueta de esport

sportsman ['spɔːtsmən] s deportista
El plural de **sportsman** es **sportsmen** ['spɔːtsmen].

sportsmanship ['spɔːtsmənʃɪp] s deportividad

sports utility vehicle s todoterreno utilitario

sportswear ['spɔːtsweər] s ropa deportiva

sportswoman ['spɔːts,wʊmən] s deportista
El plural de **sportswoman** es **sportswomen** ['spɔːts,wɪmɪn].

sporty ['spɔːtɪ] adj familiar aficionado, da a los deportes

spot [spɒt] ◆ s ❶ mancha ❷ punto ❸ grano ❹ gota ❺ familiar pizca ❻ lugar • on the spot en el lugar ❼ RADIO & TELEVISIÓN espacio
expresión to do something on the spot hacer algo en el acto
◆ vt notar

spot check s control aleatorio

spotless ['spɒtlɪs] adj ❶ inmaculado, da ❷ intachable

spotlight ['spɒtlaɪt] s foco
expresión to be in the spotlight ser el centro de atención

spotted ['spɒtɪd] adj de lunares

spouse [spaʊs] s cónyuge

spout [spaʊt] ◆ s ❶ pitorro ❷ pico ◆ vi • to spout from o out of a) salir a chorros de b) salir incesantemente de

sprain [spreɪn] ◆ s torcedura ◆ vt torcerse • to sprain your ankle torcerse el tobillo

sprang [spræŋ] pretérito → spring

sprawl [sprɔːl] vi ❶ repantigarse ❷ echarse

spray [spreɪ] ◆ s ❶ rociada ❷ espray ❸ atomizador; pulverizador ◆ vt rociar

spread [spred] ◆ s ❶ • cheese spread queso para untar ❷ propagación ◆ vt ❶ extender • to spread something over something extender algo por algo ❷ desplegar (mapa) ❸ estirar (dedos) ❹ untar (mantequilla) ❺ repartir (pegamento, pintura) ❻ propagar (enfermedad) ❼ difundir (noticia) ◆ vi ❶ extenderse (enfermedad, fuego) ❷ esparcirse (gas)
■ **spread out** vi diseminarse
Formas irregulares de **spread:** pret & pp **spread.**

spreadsheet ['spredʃiːt] s INFORMÁTICA hoja de cálculo

spree [spriː] s • a killing spree una matanza • to go on a shopping spree salir a comprar a lo loco

spring [sprɪŋ] ◆ s ❶ primavera ❷ muelle ❸ salto ❹ manantial ◆ vi ❶ saltar ❷ moverse de repente • to spring into action o to life entrar inmediatamente en acción
■ **spring up** vi surgir de repente
Formas irregulares de **spring:** pretérito **sprang,** pp **sprung**

springboard ['sprɪŋbɔːd] s literal & figurado trampolín

S

spring-clean *vt* limpiar a fondo

springtime ['sprɪŋtaɪm] *s* • **in (the) springtime** en primavera

sprinkle ['sprɪŋkl] *vt* rociar • **to sprinkle something over** o **on something, to sprinkle something with something** rociar algo sobre algo

sprinkler ['sprɪŋklər] *s* aspersor

sprint [sprɪnt] ◆ *s* ❶ *Deporte* esprint ❷ carrera ◆ *vi* ❶ *Deporte* esprintar ❷ correr a toda velocidad

sprout [spraʊt] ◆ *s* ❶ *Cocina* ❱ **(Brussels) sprouts** coles de Bruselas ❷ brote ◆ *vt* echar ◆ *vi* ❶ crecer ❷ brotar

spruce [spruːs] *adj* pulcro, cra

■ **spruce up** *vt* ☼ *El objeto se puede colocar antes o después de la preposición.* arreglar

sprung [sprʌŋ] *participio pasado* → **spring**

spun [spʌn] *pretérito & participio pasado* → **spin**

spur [spɜːr] ◆ *s* ❶ • **spur (to something)** estímulo (para conseguir algo) ❷ espuela ◆ *vt* • **to spur somebody to do something** animar a alguien a hacer algo

■ **on the spur of the moment** *adv* sin pensarlo dos veces

■ **spur on** *vt* ☼ *El objeto se puede colocar antes o después de la preposición.* • **to spur somebody on** animar a alguien

spurious ['spʊərɪəs] *adj* falso, sa

spurt [spɜːt] ◆ *s* ❶ chorro ❷ llamarada ❸ arranque *(esfuerzo)* ❹ acelerón ◆ *vi* • **to spurt (out of** o **from) a)** salir a chorros de **b)** salir incesantemente de

spy [spaɪ] ◆ *s* espía ◆ *vt familiar* divisar ◆ *vi* • **to spy (on)** espiar (a)

spying ['spaɪɪŋ] *s* espionaje

Sq., sq. *abreviatura escrita de* **square**

squabble ['skwɒbl] ◆ *s* riña ◆ *vi* • **to squabble (about** o **over)** reñir (por)

squad [skwɒd] *s* ❶ brigada *(de policía)* ❷ *Militar* pelotón *(del ejército)* ❸ *Deporte* plantilla; seleccionado • **the England squad** el equipo inglés

squad car *s* auto patrulla

squadron ['skwɒdrən] *s* ❶ escuadrilla *(de aviones)* ❷ escuadra *(de barcos)* ❸ escuadrón *(de soldados)*

squalid ['skwɒlɪd] *adj* miserable

squalor ['skwɒlər] *s* ☼ *incontable* miseria

squander ['skwɒndər] *vt* ❶ desaprovechar ❷ despilfarrar ❸ malgastar

square [skweər] ◆ *adj* ❶ cuadrado, da • **4 square meters** 4 metros cuadrados • **the kitchen is 4 meters square** la cocina mide 4 metros por 4 ❷ • **we're square now** ya estamos en paz ◆ *s* ❶ cuadrado ❷ plaza ◆ *vt* ❶ *Matemáticas* elevar al cuadrado ❷ • **how can you square that with your principles?** ¿cómo encajas esto con tus principios?

■ **square up** *vi* • **to square up with** saldar cuentas con

squarely ['skweəlɪ] *adv* justo

square meal *s* comida satisfactoria

squash [skwɒʃ] ◆ *s* ❶ squash ❷ cucurbitácea ◆ *vt* aplastar

squat [skwɒt] ◆ *adj* achaparrado, da ◆ *vi* • **to squat (down)** agacharse; ponerse en cuclillas

squawk [skwɔːk] *s* graznido

squeak [skwiːk] *s* ❶ chillido ❷ chirrido

squeal [skwiːl] *vi* ❶ chillar ❷ chirriar

squeamish ['skwiːmɪʃ] *adj* aprensivo, va

squeeze [skwiːz] ◆ *s* apretón ◆ *vt* ❶ apretar ❷ sacar (estrujando); exprimir ❸ • **to squeeze something into something a)** conseguir meter algo en algo **b)** arreglárselas para hacer algo en algo

squid [skwɪd] *s* ❶ *Zoología* calamar ❷ ☼ *incontable* calamares

  Dos plurales: **squid** o **squids**.

squint [skwɪnt] ◆ *s* estrabismo ◆ *vi* • **to squint at** mirar con los ojos entrecerrados

squirm [skwɜːm] *vi* retorcerse

squirrel ['skwɜːrəl] *s* ardilla

squirt [skwɜːt] ◆ *vt* sacar a chorro de ◆ *vi* • **to squirt out of** salir a chorro

Sr *abreviatura escrita de* **senior**

St ❶ (*abreviatura escrita de* saint) Sto., Sta. ❷ (*abreviatura escrita de* Street) c/

stab [stæb] ◆ *s* ❶ puñalada ❷ *familiar* • **to have a stab (at something)** probar (a hacer algo) ❸ punzada ◆ *vt* ❶ apuñalar ❷ pinchar

stable ['steɪbl] ◆ *adj* ❶ estable ❷ fijo, ja ❸ *Medicina* estacionario, ria ◆ *s* establo

stack [stæk] ◆ *s* pila ◆ *vt* apilar

stadium ['steɪdjəm] *s* estadio

  Dos plurales: **stadiums** o **stadia** ['steɪdjə].

staff [stɑːf] ◆ *s* personal ◆ *vt* • **the shop is staffed by women** la tienda está llevada por una plantilla de mujeres

stag [stæg] *s* ciervo

  Dos plurales: **stag** o **stags**.

stage [steɪdʒ] ◆ *s* ❶ etapa • **at this stage** a estas alturas ❷ escenario ❸ • **the stage** el teatro ◆ *vt* ❶ *Teatro* representar ❷ organizar

stagger ['stægər] ◆ *vt* ❶ dejar atónito, ta • **to be staggered by something** quedarse pasmado, da por algo ❷ escalonar ◆ *vi* tambalearse

stagnant ['stægnənt] *adj* *literal & figurado* estancado, da

stagnate [stæg'neɪt] *vi* estancarse

stag party *s* despedida de soltero

stain [steɪn] ◆ *s* mancha ◆ *vt* manchar

stained glass [,steɪnd-] *s* ☼ *incontable* vidrio de color • **stained glass window** vidriera

stainless steel [,steɪnlɪs-] *s* acero inoxidable

stain remover [-rɪ,muː'vər] *s* quitamanchas

stair [steər] *s* peldaño

■ **stairs** *spl* escaleras

staircase ['steəkeɪs] *s* escalera

stairway ['steəweɪ] *s* escalera

stairwell ['steəwel] *s* hueco de la escalera

stake [steɪk] ◆ *s* ❶ interés • **to have a stake in** tener intereses en ❷ estaca ❸ apuesta ◆ *vt* ❶ • **to stake something (on** o **upon)** arriesgar algo (en) ❷ apostar

■ **at stake** *adv* • **to be at stake** estar en juego

stale [steɪl] *adj* ❶ duro, ra ❷ pasado, da ❸ viciado, da

stalemate ['steɪlmeɪt] *s* ❶ punto muerto ❷ AJE-DREZ tablas

stalk [stɔːk] ◆ *s* ❶ tallo ❷ rabillo ◆ *vt* acechar ◆ *vi* • **to stalk in/out** entrar/salir con paso airado

stall [stɔːl] ◆ *s* puesto ◆ *vt* AUTOMÓVILES calar ◆ *vi* ❶ AUTOMÓVILES calarse ❷ andar con evasivas

stamina ['stæmɪnə] *s* resistencia

stammer ['stæmər] ◆ *s* tartamudeo ◆ *vi* tartamudear

stamp [stæmp] ◆ *s* ❶ timbre ❷ tampón ◆ *vt* ❶ timbrar ❷ • **to stamp your feet** patear ◆ *vi* ❶ patalear ❷ • **to stamp on something** pisotear o pisar algo

stamp album *s* álbum de timbres

stamp collecting [-kə,lektɪŋ] *s* filatelia

stampede [stæm'piːd] ◆ *s literal & figurado* estampida ◆ *vi* salir de estampida

stance [stæns] *s* ❶ postura ❷ • **stance (on)** postura (ante)

stand [stænd] ◆ *s* ❶ puesto ❷ quiosco ❸ soporte • **coat stand** perchero ❹ DEPORTE tribuna • **the stands** las gradas ❺ • **to make a stand** resistir al enemigo ❻ postura ◆ *vt* ❶ colocar (verticalmente) ❷ soportar • **I can't stand that woman** no soporto a esa mujer • **he can't stand being beaten** odia perder ◆ *vi* ❶ estar parado *(persona)*; estar *(objeto)* • **try to stand still** procura no moverte • **to stand in line** hacer cola ❷ ponerse de pie ❸ reposar *(líquido, comida)* ❹ seguir vigente *(documento)* ❺ AUTOMÓVILES • **'no standing'** 'prohibido aparcar'

expresiones **as things stand** tal como están las cosas ▶ **to know where you stand** saber a qué atenerse ▶ **to stand a chance** tener posibilidades • **he doesn't stand a chance of winning** no tiene la más mínima posibilidad de ganar ▶ **to stand in somebody's way** interponerse a alguien • **he doesn't let anything stand in his way** no deja que nada se interponga en su camino ▶ **to stand on your own two feet** valerse por sí mismo

■ **stand back** *vi* echarse para atrás

■ **stand by** ◆ *vt* 💡 *El objeto siempre va después de la preposición al final.* ❶ seguir al lado de ❷ mantener ◆ *vi* ❶ • **to stand by (for something/to do something)** estar preparado, da (para algo/para hacer algo) ❷ quedarse sin hacer nada

■ **stand down** *vi* retirarse

■ **stand for** *vt* 💡 *El objeto siempre va después de la preposición al final.* ❶ significar • **PTO stands for "please turn over"** PTO quiere decir "sigue en la página siguiente" ❷ aguantar • **I won't stand for it!** ¡no pienso aguantarlo!

■ **stand in** *vi* • **to stand in for somebody** sustituir a alguien

■ **stand out** *vi* sobresalir

■ **stand up** ◆ *vt* 💡 *El objeto se puede colocar antes o después de la preposición. familiar* dejar plantado, da ◆ *vi* levantarse

■ **stand up for** *vt* 💡 *El objeto siempre va después de la preposición al final.* salir en defensa de

■ **stand up to** *vt* 💡 *El objeto siempre va después de la preposición al final.* ❶ resistir ❷ hacer frente a

Formas irregulares de **stand**: *pretérito & pp* **stood**.

standard ['stændəd] ◆ *adj* ❶ corriente ❷ establecido, da ◆ *s* ❶ nivel • **to be of a high standard** ser de un excelente nivel • **it's below standard** está por debajo del nivel exigido ❷ criterio; norma ❸ estandarte

■ **standards** *spl* valores morales

standard of living *s* nivel de vida

El plural de **standard of living** es **standards of living.**

standby ['stændbaɪ] ◆ *s* • **to be on standby** estar preparado, da ◆ *en compuestos* • **standby ticket** billete en lista de espera

El plural de **standby** es **standbys.**

stand-in *s* ❶ doble ❷ sustituto, ta

standing ['stændɪŋ] ◆ *adj* permanente ◆ *s* ❶ reputación ❷ duración • **friends of 20 years' standing** amigos desde hace 20 años

standing order *s* débito bancario

standing room *s* ❶ 💡 *incontable* sitio para ir parado ❷ localidades de pie

standpoint ['stændpɔɪnt] *s* punto de vista

standstill ['stændstɪl] *s* • **at a standstill a)** parado, da **b)** *figurado* en un punto muerto • **to come to a standstill a)** pararse **b)** *figurado* llegar a un punto muerto

stand-up *adj* • **a stand-up guy** un tipo decente

stank [stæŋk] *pretérito* → **stink**

staple ['steɪpl] ◆ *adj* básico, ca ◆ *s* ❶ grapa ❷ producto básico ◆ *vt* grapar

stapler ['steɪplər] *s* grapadora

star [stɑːr] ◆ *s* estrella ◆ *en compuestos* estelar ◆ *vi* • **to star (in)** hacer de protagonista en

■ **stars** *spl* horóscopo

starboard ['stɑːbəd] ◆ *adj* de estribor ◆ *s* • **to starboard** a estribor

starch [stɑːtʃ] *s* ❶ almidón ❷ fécula

stardom ['stɑːdəm] *s* estrellato

stare [steər] ◆ *s* mirada fija ◆ *vi* • **to stare (at something/somebody)** mirar fijamente (algo/a alguien)

stark [stɑːk] ◆ *adj* ❶ austero, ra ❷ crudo, da ◆ *adv* • **stark naked** en cueros

starry ['stɑːrɪ] *adj* estrellado, da

S

starry-eyed [-'aɪd] *adj* ❶ iluso, sa ❷ encandilado, da

Stars and Stripes *s* • **the Stars and Stripes** la bandera de las barras y estrellas

Stars and Stripes

Es el apelativo con que se conoce a la bandera nacional estadounidense. Toma su nombre de las 50 estrellas, que representan los 50 estados americanos, y de las 13 barras, que representan las 13 colonias que lucharon por la independencia de EEUU, y que forman el diseño de la misma. También se conoce a la bandera por el sobrenombre "Star-spangled banner" (bandera de estrellas centelleantes), que es además el título del himno nacional estadounidense.

start [stɑːt] ◆ *s* ❶ principio • **at the start of the year** a principios de año ❷ sobresalto ❸ salida ❹ ventaja • **to have a start on somebody** llevar ventaja a alguien ◆ *vt* ❶ empezar • **to start doing** o **to do something** empezar a hacer algo ❷ poner en marcha; arrancar ❸ formar ❹ montar ◆ *vi* ❶ empezar • **to start with somebody/something** empezar por alguien/algo • **don't start!** *familiar* ¡no empieces! ❷ ponerse en marcha ❸ arrancar ❹ ponerse en camino

■ **start off** ◆ *vt* ☼ *El objeto se puede colocar antes o después de la preposición.* ❶ desencadenar ❷ empezar ❸ • **this should be enough to start you off** con esto tienes suficiente para empezar ◆ *vi* ❶ empezar ❷ ponerse en camino

■ **start out** *vi* ❶ empezar • **she started out as a journalist** empezó como periodista ❷ salir/ponerse en camino

■ **start up** ◆ *vt* ☼ *El objeto se puede colocar antes o después de la preposición.* ❶ montar *(negocio)* ❷ poner *(tienda)* ❸ arrancar *(motor)* ◆ *vi* ❶ empezar ❷ arrancar

starting point ['stɑːtɪŋ-] *s literal & figurado* punto de partida

startle ['stɑːtl] *vt* sobresaltar

start-up *s* nueva empresa

starvation [stɑːˈveɪʃn] *s* hambre

starve [stɑːv] ◆ *vt* privar de comida ◆ *vi* pasar hambre • **to starve to death** morirse de hambre
expresión **I'm starving!** *familiar* ¡me muero de hambre!

state [steɪt] ◆ *s* estado • **not to be in a fit state to do something** no estar en condiciones de hacer algo
expresión **to be in a state a)** tener los nervios de punta **b)** estar hecho un asco
◆ *en compuestos* ❶ oficial ❷ estatal ◆ *vt* ❶ indicar ❷ plantear *(razón)* ❸ exponer *(caso)* ❹ fijar *(hora, fecha)*

■ **State** *s* • **the State** el Estado

■ **States** *spl* • **the States** los Estados Unidos

State of the Union Address

La constitución estadounidense estipula que el presidente debe mantener informado al Congreso sobre el estado de la nación. Por ello, cada año el presidente pronuncia un discurso que es radiotelevisado, en el que recoge los puntos principales de su gestión y las medidas que su administración tiene previsto adoptar en el futuro.

State Department *s* ≈ Ministerio de Asuntos Exteriores

statement ['steɪtmənt] *s* ❶ declaración ❷ extracto de cuenta

state of mind *s* estado de ánimo
El plural de **state of mind** es **states of mind**.

stateside ['steɪtsaɪd] ◆ *adj* estadounidense ◆ *adv* ❶ hacia Estados Unidos ❷ en Estados Unidos

statesman ['steɪtsmən] *s* estadista
El plural de **statesman** es **statesmen** ['steɪtsmen].

static ['stætɪk] ◆ *adj* estático, ca ◆ *s* ☼ *incontable* interferencias

static electricity *s* electricidad estática

station ['steɪʃn] ◆ *s* ❶ estación ❷ RADIO emisora ◆ *vt* ❶ situar ❷ MILITAR estacionar

stationary ['steɪʃnərɪ] *adj* inmóvil

stationer's (shop) ['steɪʃnərz] *s* papelería

stationery ['steɪʃnərɪ] *s* ☼ *incontable* artículos de escritorio

station house *s* comisaría (de policía)

stationmaster ['steɪʃn,mɑːstər] *s* jefe de estación

station wagon *s* ranchera

statistic [stəˈtɪstɪk] *s* estadística

■ **statistics** *s* ☼ *incontable* estadística

statistical [stəˈtɪstɪkl] *adj* estadístico, ca

statue ['stætʃuː] *s* estatua • **the Statue of Liberty** la estatua de la Libertad

THE STATUE OF LIBERTY

Se trata de un monumento regalado por el gobierno de Francia a los Estados Unidos en 1886 en reconocimiento de la alianza forjada entre éstos durante la revolución americana. La estatua mide 93 metros de altura y se encuentra en una isla (**Liberty Island**), en el puerto de Nueva York. Con el tiempo se convirtió en un símbolo de bienvenida a los inmigrantes que llegaban al país provenientes de todo el mundo. Actualmente es una popular atracción turística.

stature ['stætʃər] *s* ❶ estatura ❷ categoría

status ['steɪtəs] *s* ☼*incontable* ❶ condición ❷ prestigio

status bar *s* INFORMÁTICA barra de estado

status symbol *s* símbolo de prestigio

statute ['stætjuːt] *s* estatuto

statutory ['stætjʊtrɪ] *adj* reglamentario, ria

staunch [stɔːnʧ] ◆ *adj* fiel ◆ *vt* restañar

stave [steɪv] *s* MÚSICA pentagrama

■ **stave off** *vt* ☼*El objeto se puede colocar antes o después de la preposición.* ❶ retrasar ❷ aplacar temporalmente

> Formas irregulares de **stave off**: *pret* & *pp* **staved** o **stove**.

stay [steɪ] ◆ *vi* ❶ permanecer • **to stay put** permanecer en el mismo sitio • **to stay out of something** mantenerse al margen de algo • **stay here!** ¡quédate aquí! ❷ alojarse ◆ *s* estadía

■ **stay in** *vi* quedarse en casa

■ **stay on** *vi* permanecer

■ **stay out** *vi* quedarse fuera

■ **stay up** *vi* quedarse levantado, da

steadily ['stedɪlɪ] *adv* ❶ constantemente ❷ normalmente ❸ fijamente; con tranquilidad

steady ['stedɪ] ◆ *adj* ❶ gradual ❷ constante ❸ firme ❹ sereno, na ❺ fijo, ja ❻ estable ❼ formal • **a steady job** un trabajo fijo ❽ sensato, ta ◆ *vt* ❶ mantener firme • **to steady yourself** dejar de temblar ❷ dominar • **to steady yourself** controlar los nervios

steak [steɪk] *s* ❶ ☼*incontable* bistec ❷ filete

steal [stiːl] ◆ *vt* ❶ robar ❷ apropiarse de ◆ *vi* moverse sigilosamente • **he stole into the bedroom** entró sigilosamente en el dormitorio

> Formas irregulares de **steal**: *pretérito* **stole**, *pp* **stolen**.

steam [stiːm] ◆ *s* ☼*incontable* vapor ◆ *vt* COCINA cocer al vapor ◆ *vi* echar vapor

■ **steam up** ◆ *vt* ☼*El objeto se puede colocar antes o después de la preposición.* empañar ◆ *vi* empañarse

steamboat ['stiːmbəʊt] *s* buque de vapor

steam engine *s* máquina de vapor

steamer ['stiːmər] *s* buque de vapor

steamroller ['stiːmˌrəʊlər] *s* apisonadora

steamy ['stiːmɪ] *adj* ❶ lleno, na de vaho ❷ *familiar* caliente

steel [stiːl] *s* acero

steelworks ['stiːlwɜːks] *s* fundición de acero

> El plural de **steelworks** es **steelworks**.

steep [stiːp] ◆ *adj* ❶ empinado, da ❷ considerable ❸ *familiar* muy caro, ra ◆ *vt* remojar

steeplechase ['stiːplʧeɪs] *s* carrera de obstáculos

steer ['stɪər] ◆ *vt* ❶ conducir ❷ dirigir ◆ *vi* • **the car steers well** el carro se conduce bien

expresión **to steer clear of something/somebody** evitar algo/a alguien

steering ['stɪərɪŋ] *s* ☼*incontable* dirección

steering wheel *s* volante

stem [stem] ◆ *s* ❶ tallo ❷ pie ❸ GRAMÁTICA raíz ◆ *vt* ❶ contener ❷ restañar

■ **stem from** *vt* ☼*El objeto siempre va después de la preposición.* derivarse de

stem cell *s* MEDICINA célula madre

stench [stenʧ] *s* hedor

stencil ['stensl] ◆ *s* plantilla *(en dibujo)* ◆ *vt* estarcir

> Formas irregulares de **stencil**: *pretérito* & *pp* **stenciled**, *gerundio* **stenciling**.

stenographer [stəˈnɒgrəfər] *s* taquígrafo, fa

step [step] ◆ *s* ❶ paso • **step by step** paso a paso ❷ medida ❸ peldaño ◆ *vi* ❶ dar un paso • **she took one step backwards** dio un paso atrás • **he stepped off the bus** se bajó del autobús ❷ • **to step on something** pisar algo • **to step in something** meter el pie en algo

■ **steps** *spl* escaleras

■ **step down** *vi* renunciar

■ **step in** *vi* intervenir

■ **step up** *vt* ☼*El objeto se puede colocar antes o después de la preposición.* aumentar

stepbrother ['stepˌbrʌðər] *s* hermanastro

stepdaughter ['stepˌdɔːtər] *s* hijastra

stepfather ['stepˌfɑːðər] *s* padrastro

stepladder ['stepˌlædər] *s* escalera de tijera

stepmother ['stepˌmʌðər] *s* madrastra

stepsister ['stepˌsɪstər] *s* hermanastra

stepson ['stepsʌn] *s* hijastro

stereo ['sterɪəʊ] ◆ *adj* estéreo ◆ *s* ❶ equipo estereofónico ❷ estéreo

> El plural de **stereo** es **stereos**.

stereotype ['sterɪətaɪp] *s* estereotipo

sterile ['steraɪl] *adj* ❶ esterilizado, da ❷ estéril

sterilize, sterilise ['sterəlaɪz] *vt* esterilizar

sterling ['stɜːlɪŋ] ◆ *adj* ❶ FINANZAS esterlina ❷ excelente ◆ *s* ☼*incontable* libra esterlina

stern [stɜːn] ◆ *adj* severo, ra ◆ *s* popa

steroid ['stɪərɔɪd] *s* esteroide

stethoscope ['steθəskəʊp] *s* estetoscopio

stew [stjuː] ◆ *s* estofado; guisado ◆ *vt* ❶ estofar; guisar ❷ hacer una compota de

steward ['stjʊəd] *s* ❶ auxiliar de vuelo ❷ camarero

stewardess ['stjʊədɪs] *s* auxiliar de vuelo; azafata

stick [stɪk] ◆ *s* ❶ palo ❷ cartucho *(de pólvora)* ❸ bastón ◆ *vt* ❶ • **to stick something through something** atravesar algo con algo ❷ *familiar* meter ◆ *vi* ❶ • **to stick (to)** pegarse (a) ❷ atrancarse

■ **stick out** ◆ *vt* ☼*El objeto se puede colocar antes o después de la preposición.* ❶ sacar • **to stick your tongue out** sacar la lengua ❷ aguantar ◆ *vi* sobresalir

S

■ **stick to** *vt* ☼ *El objeto siempre va después de la preposición al final.* ❶ seguir ❷ ser fiel a ❸ cumplir con ❹ atenerse a

■ **stick up** *vi* salir; sobresalir

■ **stick up for** *vt* ☼ *El objeto siempre va después de la preposición al final.* defender

Formas irregulares de **stick**: *pretérito & pp* **stuck**.

sticker ['stɪkər] *s* pegatina

sticking plaster ['stɪkɪŋ-] *s* esparadrapo

stick shift *s* palanca de cambios

stick-up *s familiar* atraco a mano armada

sticky ['stɪkɪ] *adj* ❶ pegajoso, sa ❷ adhesivo, va ❸ *familiar* engorroso, sa

stiff [stɪf] ◆ *adj* ❶ rígido, da ❷ atascado, da ❸ agarrotado, da • **to have a stiff neck** tener tortícolis • **to be stiff** tener agujetas ❹ severo, ra ❺ duro, ra ◆ *adv familiar* • **bored/frozen stiff** muerto, ta de aburrimiento/frío

stiffen ['stɪfn] *vi* ❶ endurecerse ❷ entumecerse *(huesos)* ❸ agarrotarse *(músculos)* ❹ intensificarse

stifle ['staɪfl] *vt* ❶ ahogar; sofocar ❷ reprimir

stifling ['staɪflɪŋ] *adj* sofocante

---

still [stɪl]
◆ *adv*

❶ [*indica que un estado continúa*]
• **he was still sleeping when I arrived** cuando llegué todavía estaba durmiendo
• **she still lives in New York** todavía vive en Nueva York

❷ [*introduce la idea de que queda algo*]
• **I've still got 5 dollars left** todavía me quedan 5 dólares
• **we still have time** todavía tenemos tiempo
• **there are many questions still to be answered** todavía quedan mucha preguntas sin respuesta

❸ [*expresa oposición*]
• **you may not approve of what he did, still he is your brother** aunque no apruebes lo que hizo, sigue siendo tu hermano
• **even though she didn't have much time, she still offered her help** aunque no tenía mucho tiempo, se ofreció a ayudar

❹ [*con los comparativos, para enfatizar*]
• **he was angrier still after we talked** después de conversar estaba todavía más enojado
• **still more worrying is the problem of corruption** incluso más preocupante es el problema de la corrupción

◆ *adj*

❶ [*expresa la ausencia de movimiento*]
• **the lizard was perfectly still** la lagartija estaba completamente quieta
• **it's difficult to stand still** es difícil quedarse quieto

❷ [*expresa la ausencia de ruido*]
• **all was still** reinaba la calma

---

stillborn ['stɪlbɔːn] *adj* nacido muerto, nacida muerta

still life *s* bodegón; naturaleza muerta
El plural de **still life** es **still lifes**.

stilted ['stɪltɪd] *adj* forzado, da

stilts [stɪlts] *spl* ❶ zancos ❷ pilotes

stimulate ['stɪmjʊleɪt] *vt* ❶ estimular ❷ excitar

stimulating ['stɪmjʊleɪtɪŋ] *adj* ❶ estimulante ❷ interesante

stimulus ['stɪmjʊləs] *s* estímulo
El plural de **stimulus** es **stimuli** ['stɪmjʊlaɪ].

sting [stɪŋ] ◆ *s* ❶ picadura ❷ aguijón ❸ escozor
expresión **to take the sting out of something** suavizar algo
◆ *vt* ❶ picar ❷ escocer ◆ *vi* picar
Formas irregulares de **sting**: *pretérito & pp* **stung**.

stingy ['stɪndʒɪ] *adj familiar* tacaño, ña

stink [stɪŋk] ◆ *s* peste ◆ *vi* apestar
Formas irregulares de **stink**: *pretérito* **stank** o **stunk**, *pp* **stunk**.

stinking ['stɪŋkɪŋ] *familiar & figurado* ◆ *adj* asqueroso, sa ◆ *adv* • **to have a stinking cold** tener un resfriado horrible

stipulate ['stɪpjʊleɪt] *vt* estipular

stir [stɜːr] ◆ *s* revuelo • **to cause a stir** causar revuelo ◆ *vt* ❶ remover ❷ agitar ❸ conmover ◆ *vi* moverse

■ **stir up** *vt* ☼ *El objeto se puede colocar antes o después de la preposición.* ❶ levantar ❷ provocar

stirrup ['stɪrəp] *s* estribo

stitch [stɪtʃ] ◆ *s* ❶ COSER puntada ❷ MEDICINA punto (de sutura) ❸ • **to have a stitch** sentir pinchazos (en el estómago) ◆ *vt* ❶ COSER coser ❷ MEDICINA suturar

stoat [stəʊt] *s* armiño

stock [stɒk] ◆ *s* ❶ reserva ❷ ☼ *incontable* COMERCIO existencias • **in stock** en existencia; en almacén • **out of stock** agotado, da ❸ FINANZAS capital • **stocks and shares** acciones ❹ COCINA caldo ❺ ganado
expresión **to take stock (of something)** evaluar (algo)
◆ *adj* estereotipado, da ◆ *vt* ❶ COMERCIO abastecer de ❷ llenar ❸ repoblar

■ **stock up** *vi* • **to stock up (with)** abastecerse (de)

stockbroker ['stɒk,brəʊkər] *s* corredor, ra de bolsa

stock company *s* ≃ sociedad anónima

stock exchange *s* bolsa

stockholder ['stɒk,həʊldər] *s* accionista

stocking ['stɒkɪŋ] *s* media

stock market *s* bolsa; mercado de valores

stocky ['stɒkɪ] *adj* corpulento, ta; robusto, ta

stodgy ['stɒdʒɪ] *adj* indigesto, ta

stoke [stəʊk] *vt* avivar; alimentar

stole [stəʊl] *pretérito* → **steal**

stolen ['stəʊln] *participio pasado* → **steal**

stomach ['stʌmək] ◆ s ❶ estómago • **to do something on an empty stomach** hacer algo con el estómago vacío ❷ vientre ◆ vt tragar • **I can't stomach him** no lo trago

stomachache ['stʌməkeɪk] s dolor de estómago

stomach upset [-'ʌpset] s trastorno gástrico

stone [stəʊn] ◆ s ❶ piedra ❷ hueso ◆ vt apedrear

El plural de **stone** es **stones.**

stone-cold adj helado, da

stonewashed ['stəʊnwɒʃt] adj lavado, da a la piedra

stood [stʊd] pretérito & participio pasado → stand

stool [stuːl] s taburete

stoop [stuːp] ◆ s • **to walk with a stoop** caminar encorvado, da ◆ vi ❶ inclinarse ❷ encorvarse

stop [stɒp] ◆ s parada

expresión to put a stop to something poner fin a algo

◆ vt ❶ parar • **to stop doing something** dejar de hacer algo ❷ impedir ❸ detener ◆ vi ❶ pararse ❷ cesar

expresión to stop at nothing (to do something) no reparar en nada (para hacer algo)

■ **stop off** vi hacer una parada

■ **stop up** vt ⚲ *El objeto se puede colocar antes o después de la preposición.* taponar

stoplight ['stɒplaɪt] s semáforo

stopover ['stɒp,əʊvər] s ❶ parada ❷ escala

stoppage ['stɒpɪdʒ] s paro; huelga

stopper ['stɒpər] s tapón

stop press s noticias de última hora

stopwatch ['stɒpwɒtʃ] s cronómetro

storage ['stɔːrɪdʒ] s almacenamiento

store [stɔːr] ◆ s ❶ tienda ❷ provisión; reserva ❸ almacén ◆ vt ❶ almacenar ❷ guardar

■ **store up** vt ⚲ *El objeto se puede colocar antes o después de la preposición.* ❶ almacenar ❷ acumular

storekeeper ['stɔː,kiːpər] s tendero, ra

storeroom ['stɔːrʊm] s ❶ almacén ❷ despensa

stork [stɔːk] s cigüeña

storm [stɔːm] ◆ s tormenta ◆ vt MILITAR asaltar ◆ vi ❶ • **to storm out** salir echando pestes ❷ vociferar

stormy ['stɔːmɪ] adj ❶ tormentoso, sa ❷ acalorado, da ❸ tempestuoso, sa

story ['stɔːrɪ] s ❶ cuento ❷ historia ❸ artículo ❹ planta *(de edificio)*

storyteller ['stɔːrɪ,telər] s narrador, ra; cuentista

stout [staʊt] adj ❶ corpulento, ta ❷ fuerte ❸ firme

stove [stəʊv] ◆ pretérito & participio pasado → stave ◆ s ❶ estufa ❷ cocina

stow [stəʊ] vt • **to stow something (away)** guardar algo

stowaway ['stəʊəweɪ] s polizón

straddle ['strædl] vt sentarse a horcajadas sobre

straggle ['strægl] vi ❶ desparramarse ❷ rezagarse

straight [streɪt] ◆ adj ❶ recto, ta • **sit up straight!** ¡siéntate derecho! ❷ liso, sa ❸ sincero, ra ❹ arreglado, da ❺ simple ❻ solo, la ◆ adv ❶ directamente; recto, ta • **straight ahead** todo recto • **it was heading straight for me** venía directo hacia mí ❷ directamente ❸ inmediatamente • **come straight home** ven directamente a casa ❹ francamente ❺ solo, la

expresión let's get things straight vamos a aclarar las cosas ▸ **to go straight** dejar la mala vida

■ **straight off** adv en el acto

■ **straight out** adv sin tapujos

straight away [,streɪtə'weɪ] adv en seguida

straighten ['streɪtn] vt ❶ ordenar; poner bien ❷ poner recto, ta; enderezar

■ **straighten out** vt ⚲ *El objeto se puede colocar antes o después de la preposición.* ❶ arreglar ❷ resolver

straight face s

expresión to keep a straight face aguantar la risa

straightforward [,streɪt'fɔːwəd] adj ❶ sencillo, lla ❷ directo, ta; sincero, ra

strain [streɪn] ◆ s ❶ peso ❷ presión ❸ tensión nerviosa • **to be under a lot of strain** estar muy agobiado, da ❹ torcedura ◆ vt ❶ estirar ❷ • **to strain your eyes/ears** aguzar la vista/el oído ❸ cansar; torcerse ❹ colar ◆ vi • **to strain to do something** esforzarse por hacer algo

strained [streɪnd] adj ❶ preocupado, da ❷ tirante ❸ forzado, da

strainer ['streɪnər] s colador

strait [streɪt] s estrecho

■ **straits** spl

expresión in dire o desperate straits en un serio aprieto

straitjacket ['streɪt,dʒækɪt] s camisa de fuerza

straitlaced [,streɪt'leɪst] adj *despectivo* mojigato, ta

strand [strænd] s hebra • **a strand of hair** un pelo del cabello

stranded ['strændɪd] adj ❶ varado, da ❷ colgado, da

strange [streɪndʒ] adj ❶ raro, ra; extraño, ña ❷ desconocido, da

stranger ['streɪndʒər] s ❶ extraño, ña; desconocido, da ❷ forastero, ra

expresión to be a/no stranger to something no estar/ estar familiarizado con algo

strangle ['stræŋgl] vt estrangular

stranglehold ['stræŋglhəʊld] s *figurado* dominio absoluto

strap [stræp] ◆ s ❶ correa ❷ tirante ◆ vt atar con correa

strapping ['stræpɪŋ] adj robusto, ta

strategic [strə'tiːdʒɪk] adj estratégico, ca

S

strategy ['strætɪdʒɪ] *s* estrategia

straw [strɔ:] *s* ❶ *AGRICULTURA* paja ❷ popote

expresión **the last straw** el colmo

strawberry ['strɔ:bərɪ] ◆ *s* fresa ◆ *en compuestos* de fresa

stray [streɪ] ◆ *adj* ❶ callejero, ra; extraviado, da ❷ perdido, da ◆ *vi* ❶ desviarse ❷ extraviarse ❸ perderse

streak [stri:k] ◆ *s* ❶ mechón • **to have streaks in your hair** tener un mechón en el pelo ❷ rayo ❸ vena *(en carácter)* ◆ *vi* ir como un rayo

stream [stri:m] ◆ *s* ❶ riachuelo ❷ chorro ❸ raudal ❹ corriente ❺ torrente ❻ serie ◆ *vi* ❶ • **to stream into** entrar a raudales en • **to stream out of** brotar de ❷ • **to stream into** entrar atropelladamente en • **to stream out of** salir atropelladamente de ❸ • **to have a streaming cold** tener un resfriado horrible

streamer ['stri:mər] *s* serpentina

streamlined ['stri:mlaɪnd] *adj* ❶ aerodinámico, ca ❷ racional

street [stri:t] *s* calle • **to be on the streets** estar en la calle

streetcar ['stri:tkɑ:r] *s* tranvía

street lamp, street light *s* farola

street plan *s* plano (de la ciudad)

streetwise ['stri:twaɪz] *adj familiar* espabilado, da

strength [streŋθ] *s* ❶ fuerza ❷ poder ❸ punto fuerte ❹ solidez ❺ intensidad; potencia ❻ peso *(de argumento)*

strengthen ['streŋθən] *vt* ❶ fortalecer ❷ reforzar ❸ acentuar ❹ estrechar

strenuous ['strenjʊəs] *adj* agotador, ra

stress [stres] ◆ *s* ❶ • **stress (on)** énfasis (en) ❷ estrés ❸ • **stress (on)** presión (en) ❹ *LINGÜÍSTICA* acento ◆ *vt* ❶ recalcar; subrayar ❷ *familiar* estresar ❸ *LINGÜÍSTICA* acentuar ◆ *vi familiar* estresarse

■ **stress out** *vt familiar* estresar

stressful ['stresfʊl] *adj* estresante

stretch [stretʃ] ◆ *s* ❶ extensión ❷ tramo; trecho ❸ periodo ❹ • **to have a stretch** estirarse ◆ *vt* ❶ estirar • **I'm going to stretch my legs** voy a estirar las piernas ❷ extender ❸ hacer rendir al máximo

■ **stretch out** ◆ *vt* ⚥ *El objeto se puede colocar antes o después de la preposición.* ❶ estirar ❷ alargar ◆ *vi* ❶ tumbarse ❷ estirarse

stretcher ['stretʃər] *s* camilla

stricken ['strɪkn] *adj* • **to be stricken by** o **with a)** estar aquejado, da de **b)** estar asolado, da por **c)** estar afligido, da por **d)** estar atenazado, da por • **she was stricken with remorse** le remordía la conciencia

strict [strɪkt] *adj* estricto, ta

strictly ['strɪktlɪ] *adv* ❶ severamente ❷ terminantemente *(prohibido)*; absolutamente ❸ estrictamente • **strictly speaking** en el sentido estricto de la palabra ❹ exclusivamente • **this is strictly between you and me** esto debe quedar exclusivamente entre tú y yo

stride [straɪd] ◆ *s* zancada

expresión **to take something in your stride** tomarse algo con calma

◆ *vi* • **to stride along** andar a zancadas • **he strode off down the road** marchó calle abajo dando grandes zancadas

Formas irregulares de **stride**: *pretérito* **strode**, *pp* **stridden** ['strɪdn].

strife [straɪf] *s* ⚥ *incontable formal* conflictos

strike [straɪk] ◆ *s* ❶ huelga • **to be (out) on strike** estar en huelga • **to go on strike** declararse en huelga ❷ *MILITAR* ataque ◆ *vt* ❶ *formal* golpear; chocar contra ❷ asolar ❸ fulminar • **she was struck by lightning** le alcanzó un rayo ❹ cerrar ❺ encender ◆ *vi* ❶ estar en huelga ❷ *formal* • **to strike against** chocar contra ❸ sobrevenir ❹ caer ❺ *formal* atacar ❻ dar la hora • **the clock struck six** el reloj dio las seis

■ **strike down** *vt* ⚥ *El objeto se puede colocar antes o después de la preposición.* fulminar

■ **strike out** *vt* ⚥ *El objeto se puede colocar antes o después de la preposición.* tachar

■ **strike up** *vt* ⚥ *El objeto siempre va después de la preposición al final.* ❶ trabar ❷ entablar ❸ empezar a tocar

Formas irregulares de **strike**: *pretérito* & *pp* **struck**.

striker ['straɪkər] *s* ❶ huelguista ❷ *FUTBOL* delantero, ra

striking ['straɪkɪŋ] *adj* ❶ chocante ❷ llamativo, va

string [strɪŋ] *s* ❶ cuerda *(cordel, de instrumento)* • **a (piece of) string** un cordel ❷ sarta ❸ serie

expresión **to pull strings** utilizar uno sus influencias

■ **strings** *spl MÚSICA* • **the strings** los instrumentos de cuerda

■ **string out** *vt* ⚥ *El objeto siempre va después de la preposición al final.* • **to be strung out** alinearse

■ **string together** *vt* ⚥ *El objeto se puede colocar antes o después de la preposición.* encadenar

stringent ['strɪndʒənt] *adj* estricto, ta; severo, ra

strip [strɪp] ◆ *s* ❶ tira ❷ franja ◆ *vt* ❶ desnudar ❷ quitar ◆ *vi* desnudarse

■ **strip off** *vi* desnudarse

stripe [straɪp] *s* ❶ raya; franja ❷ galón

striped [straɪpt] *adj* a rayas

strive [straɪv] *vi formal* • **to strive for something** luchar por algo • **to strive to do something** esforzarse por hacer algo

Formas irregulares de **strive**: *pretérito* **strove**, *pp* **striven** ['strɪvn].

strode [strəʊd] *pretérito* → **stride**

stroke [strəʊk] ◆ *s* ❶ *MEDICINA* apoplejía; derrame cerebral ❷ trazo *(de pluma)* ❸ pincelada ❹ estilo *(natación)* ❺ golpe *(en tenis, golf)* ❻ campanada *(de reloj)* ❼ • **a stroke of genius** una genialidad • **a stroke of luck** un golpe de suerte • **at a stroke** de una vez; de golpe ◆ *vt* acariciar

stroll [strəʊl] ◆ *s* paseo • **to go for a stroll** dar un paseo ◆ *vi* pasear

stroller ['strəυlər] *s* sillita (de niño)

strong [strɒŋ] *adj* ❶ fuerte ❷ sólido, da; resistente ❸ profundo, da *(sentimiento)* ❹ firme *(oposición)* ❺ marcado, da *(acento)* ❻ convincente *(argumento)* ❼ • **the crowd was 2,000 strong** la multitud constaba de 2.000 personas ❽ • **your strong point** el punto fuerte de uno ❾ concentrado, da

expresión **to be still going strong a)** conservarse bien **b)** seguir en la brecha **c)** estar todavía en forma

strongbox ['strɒŋbɒks] *s* caja fuerte

stronghold ['strɒŋhəυld] *s* *figurado* bastión

strongly ['strɒŋlɪ] *adv* ❶ fuertemente ❷ intensamente ❸ • **to support/oppose something strongly** apoyar/oponerse a algo totalmente • **I feel very strongly about that** eso me preocupa muchísimo

strong room *s* cámara acorazada

strove [strəυv] *pretérito* → **strive**

struck [strʌk] *pretérito* & *participio pasado* → **strike**

structure ['strʌktʃər] *s* ❶ estructura ❷ construcción

struggle ['strʌgl] ◆ *s* ❶ • **struggle (for something/ to do something)** lucha (por algo/por hacer algo) ❷ forcejeo ◆ *vi* ❶ • **to struggle (for something/to do something)** luchar (por algo/por hacer algo) ❷ • **to struggle free** forcejear para soltarse

strung [strʌŋ] *pretérito* & *participio pasado* → **string**

stub [stʌb] ◆ *s* ❶ colilla ❷ cabo *(de lápiz)* ❸ resguardo *(de boleto)* ❹ matriz *(de cheque)* ◆ *vt* • **to stub your toe on** darse con el pie en

■ **stub out** *vt* ◌ *El objeto se puede colocar antes o después de la preposición.* apagar

stubble ['stʌbl] *s* ❶ ◌ *incontable* rastrojo ❷ barba incipiente o de tres días

stubborn ['stʌbən] *adj* terco, ca; testarudo, da

stuck [stʌk] ◆ *pretérito* & *participio pasado* → **stick** ◆ *adj* ❶ atascado, da ❷ atascado, da • **to get stuck** atascarse

stuck-up *adj* *familiar* & *despectivo* engreído, da

stud [stʌd] *s* ❶ tachón ❷ pendiente

student ['stjuːdnt] ◆ *s* estudiante ◆ *en compuestos* estudiantil

studio ['stjuːdɪəυ] *s* estudio

El plural de **studio** es **studios**.

studio apartment *s* estudio

studious ['stjuːdjəs] *adj* estudioso, sa

study ['stʌdɪ] ◆ *s* estudio ◆ *vt* ❶ estudiar ❷ examinar ◆ *vi* estudiar

■ **studies** *spl* estudios

stuff [stʌf] ◆ *s* ◌ *incontable familiar* cosas • **what's all this stuff on the table?** ¿qué hacen todas estas cosas en la mesa? • **what's that stuff in your pocket?** ¿qué es eso que llevas en el bolsillo? ◆ *vt* ❶ meter ❷ • **to stuff something (with) a)** llenar algo (de) **b)** rellenar algo (de) ❸ *Cocina* rellenar

stuffed [stʌft] *adj* ❶ • **stuffed with** atestado, da de ❷ *familiar* lleno, na ❸ *Cocina* relleno, na ❹ disecado, da

stuffing ['stʌfɪŋ] *s* ◌ *incontable* relleno

stuffy ['stʌfɪ] *adj* ❶ cargado, da ❷ mal ventilado, da

stumble ['stʌmbl] *vi* tropezar

■ **stumble across, stumble on** *vt* ◌ *El objeto siempre va después de la preposición al final.* ❶ dar con ❷ encontrarse con

stumbling block ['stʌmblɪŋ-] *s* obstáculo; escollo

stump [stʌmp] ◆ *s* ❶ tocón ❷ muñón ◆ *vt* ❶ dejar perplejo, ja • **I'm stumped** no tengo ni idea • **he was stumped for an answer** no sabía qué contestar ❷ *Política* recorrer en campaña electoral

stun [stʌn] *vt* *literal* & *figurado* aturdir

stung [stʌŋ] *pretérito* & *participio pasado* → **sting**

stunk [stʌŋk] *pretérito* & *participio pasado* → **stink**

stunning ['stʌnɪŋ] *adj* ❶ imponente ❷ pasmoso, sa

stunt [stʌnt] *s* ❶ truco publicitario ❷ *Cine* escena arriesgada o peligrosa

stunt man *s* especialista; doble

stupefy ['stjuːpɪfaɪ] *vt* ❶ aturdir; atontar ❷ dejar estupefacto, ta

stupid ['stjuːpɪd] *adj* estúpido, da

stupidity [stjuː'pɪdətɪ] *s* ◌ *incontable* estupidez

sturdy ['stɜːdɪ] *adj* ❶ fuerte ❷ firme; sólido, da

stutter ['stʌtər] ◆ *vi* tartamudear ◆ *vt* decir tartamudeando

sty [staɪ] *s* pocilga

style [staɪl] ◆ *s* ❶ estilo ❷ ◌ *incontable* clase ◆ *vt* peinar

stylish ['staɪlɪʃ] *adj* elegante; con estilo

stylist ['staɪlɪst] *s* peluquero, ra

styrofoam® ['staɪrəfəυm] *s* poliestireno

suave [swɑːv] *adj* ❶ afable; amable ❷ zalamero, ra

sub [sʌb] *s* *familiar* *Deporte* *(abreviatura de* substitute) reserva

S

subconscious [,sʌb'kɒnʃəs] *adj* subconsciente

subcontract [,sʌbkən'trækt] *vt* subcontratar

subdivide [,sʌbdɪ'vaɪd] *vt* subdividir

subdue [səb'djuː] *vt* ❶ sojuzgar ❷ contener

subdued [səb'djuːd] *adj* ❶ apagado, da ❷ tenue

subject ◆ *adj* ['sʌbdʒekt] • **subject to a)** sujeto, ta a **b)** proclive a ❶ ['sʌbdʒekt] tema • **don't change the subject** no cambies de tema ❷ *Gramática* sujeto ❸ *Educación* & *Universidad* asignatura ❹ súbdito, ta ◆ *vt* [səb'dʒekt] someter; dominar

■ **subject to** *preposición* dependiendo de

subjective [səb'dʒektɪv] *adj* subjetivo, va

subject matter ['sʌbdʒekt-] *s* ☼ *incontable* tema; contenido

subjunctive [səb'dʒʌŋktɪv] *s GRAMÁTICA* ▶ **subjunctive (mood)** (modo) subjuntivo

sublet [ˌsʌb'let] *vt* & *vi* subarrendar

Formas irregulares de **sublet**: *pret* & *pp* **sublet**.

sublime [sə'blaɪm] *adj* sublime

submachine gun [ˌsʌbmə'ʃiːn-] *s* metralleta

submarine [ˌsʌbmə'riːn] *s* ❶ submarino ❷ sándwich hecho con una barra de pan larga y estrecha

submerge [səb'mɜːdʒ] ◆ *vt* ❶ sumergir ❷ *figurado* ▪ **to submerge yourself in something** dedicarse de lleno a algo ◆ *vi* sumergirse

submission [səb'mɪʃn] *s* ❶ sumisión ❷ presentación

submissive [səb'mɪsɪv] *adj* sumiso, sa

submit [səb'mɪt] ◆ *vt* presentar ◆ *vi* ▪ **to submit (to somebody)** rendirse (a alguien) ▪ **to submit (to something)** someterse (a algo)

subnormal [ˌsʌb'nɔːml] *adj* subnormal

subordinate ◆ *adj* [sə'bɔːdɪnət] *formal* ▪ **subordinate (to)** subordinado, da (a) ◆ *s* subordinado, da

subscribe [səb'skraɪb] *vi* ❶ ▪ **to subscribe (to)** suscribirse (a) ❷ ▪ **to subscribe to** estar de acuerdo con

subscriber [səb'skraɪbər] *s* ❶ suscriptor, ra ❷ abonado, da

subscription [səb'skrɪpʃn] *s* ❶ suscripción ▪ **to take out a subscription to something** suscribirse a algo ❷ abono ❸ cuota

subsequent ['sʌbsɪkwənt] *adj* subsiguiente; posterior ▪ **subsequent to this** con posterioridad a esto

subsequently ['sʌbsɪkwəntlɪ] *adv* posteriormente

subservient [səb'sɜːvjənt] *adj* ▪ **subservient (to somebody)** servil (ante alguien)

subside [səb'saɪd] *vi* ❶ apaciguarse ❷ pasarse; calmarse *(dolor)* ❸ amainar *(tormenta)* ❹ bajar; descender *(río)*

subsidence [səb'saɪdns] ['sʌbsɪdns] *s CONSTRUCCIÓN* hundimiento

subsidiary [səb'sɪdjərɪ] ◆ *adj* secundario, ria ◆ *s* ▶ **subsidiary (company)** filial

subsidize, subsidise ['sʌbsɪdaɪz] *vt* subvencionar

subsidy ['sʌbsɪdɪ] *s* subvención

substance ['sʌbstəns] *s* ❶ sustancia ❷ esencia

substantial [səb'stænʃl] *adj* ❶ sustancial; considerable ❷ abundante ❸ sólido, da

substantially [səb'stænʃəlɪ] *adv* ❶ sustancialmente; considerablemente ❷ esencialmente ❸ en gran parte

substitute ['sʌbstɪtjuːt] ◆ *s* ❶ ▪ **substitute (for)** sustituto, ta (de) ❷ *DEPORTE* suplente; reserva ◆ *vt* ▪ **to substitute something/somebody for** sustituir algo/a alguien por

substitute teacher *s* profesor, ra suplente

subtitle ['sʌb,taɪtl] *s* subtítulo

subtle ['sʌtl] *adj* ❶ sutil ❷ delicado, da ❸ ingenioso, sa

subtlety ['sʌtltɪ] *s* ❶ sutileza ❷ delicadeza ❸ ingenio

subtract [səb'trækt] *vt* ▪ **to subtract something (from)** restar algo (de)

subtraction [səb'trækʃn] *s* resta

suburb ['sʌbɜːb] *s* barrio residencial

■ **suburbs** *spl* ▪ **the suburbs** los barrios de las afueras

suburban [sə'bɜːbn] *adj* ❶ de los barrios residenciales ❷ *despectivo* convencional; burgués, esa

suburbia [sə'bɜːbɪə] *s* ☼ *incontable* barrios residenciales

subversive [səb'vɜːsɪv] ◆ *adj* subversivo, va ◆ *s* subversivo, va

subway ['sʌbweɪ] *s* metro

succeed [sək'siːd] ◆ *vt* suceder a ▪ **to succeed somebody to the throne** suceder a alguien en el trono ◆ *vi* ❶ tener éxito ❷ ▪ **to succeed in something/in doing something** conseguir algo/hacer algo ❸ salir bien ❹ triunfar

succeeding [sək'siːdɪŋ] *adj formal* sucesivo, va

success [sək'ses] *s* ❶ éxito ▪ **to be a success** tener éxito ❷ triunfo

successful [sək'sesful] *adj* ❶ de éxito ❷ logrado, da

succession [sək'seʃn] *s* sucesión ▪ **to follow in quick** o **close succession** sucederse rápidamente

successive [sək'sesɪv] *adj* sucesivo, va ▪ **he won on 3 successive years** ganó durante tres años consecutivos

succinct [sək'sɪŋkt] *adj* sucinto, ta

such [sʌtʃ] ◆ *adj* ❶ semejante; tal ▪ **such stupidity** tal estupidez ▪ **there's no such thing** no existe nada semejante ▪ **such as** como ❷ ▪ **have you got such a thing as a tin opener?** ¿tendrías acaso un abrelatas? ▪ **such words as "duty" and "honor"** palabras (tales) como "deber" y "honor" ❸ ▪ **there are such differences that...** las diferencias son tales que... ▪ **such... that** tal... que ◆ *adv* tan ▪ **such a lot of books** tantos libros ▪ **such nice people** una gente tan amable ▪ **such a good car** un coche tan bueno ▪ **such a long time** tanto tiempo ◆ *pronombre* ▪ **and such (like)** y otros similares o por el estilo

■ **as such** *pronombre* propiamente dicho, cha

■ **such and such** *adj* ▪ **at such and such a time** a tal hora

such

Cuando such es adjetivo siempre va delante del sustantivo. Such a/an se emplea delante de sustantivos contables en singular (*such a* fool; *such an* awful person); y such delante de incontables (*such* energy; *such* amazing stupidity) y de contables en plural such (*such* fools; *such* expensive tastes).

suck [sʌk] ◆ *vt* ❶ chupar ❷ aspirar ◆ *vi muy familiar* • **that really sucks!** ¡es una mierda!

sucker ['sʌkəɾ] *s* ❶ ventosa ❷ *familiar* primo, ma; ingenuo, nua • **to be a sucker for punishment** ser un masoquista

suction ['sʌkʃn] *s* ❶ succión ❷ aspiración

sudden ['sʌdn] *adj* ❶ repentino, na ❷ inesperado, da • **all of a sudden** de repente

suddenly ['sʌdnlı] *adv* de repente

sue [su:] *vt* • **to sue somebody (for)** demandar a alguien (por)

suede [sweɪd] *s* ❶ ante ❷ cabritilla

suffer ['sʌfəɾ] ◆ *vt* sufrir ◆ *vi* ❶ sufrir ❷ salir perjudicado, da ❸ Mᴇᴅɪᴄɪɴᴀ • **to suffer from** sufrir o padecer de

sufferer ['sʌfrəɾ] *s* enfermo, ma • **cancer sufferer** enfermo de cáncer • **hay fever sufferer** persona que padece fiebre del heno

suffering ['sʌfrıŋ] *s* ❶ sufrimiento ❷ dolor

sufficient [sə'fıʃnt] *adj formal* suficiente; bastante

suffocate ['sʌfəkeɪt] ◆ *vt* asfixiar; ahogar ◆ *vi* asfixiarse; ahogarse

sugar ['ʃugəɾ] ◆ *s* azúcar ◆ *vt* echar azúcar a

sugar beet *s* remolacha (azucarera)

sugarcane ['ʃugəkeın] *s* ☼ *incontable* caña de azúcar

sugary ['ʃugərı] *adj* azucarado, da; dulce

suggest [sə'dʒest] *vt* ❶ sugerir • **to suggest doing something** sugerir hacer algo ❷ insinuar

suggestion [sə'dʒestʃn] *s* ❶ sugerencia ❷ insinuación • **there was no suggestion of murder** no había nada que indicara que fue un asesinato

suggestive [sə'dʒestıv] *adj* provocativo, va; insinuante

suicide ['su:ısaıd] *s literal & figurado* suicidio • **to commit suicide** suicidarse

suit [su:t] ◆ *s* ❶ traje; traje de chaqueta ❷ palo ◆ *vt* ❶ favorecer; sentar bien a • **it suits you** te favorece; te sienta bien ❷ convenir • **that suits me fine** por mí, estupendo • **suit yourself!** ¡haz lo que quieras! ❸ ser adecuado, da para • **that job suits you perfectly** ese trabajo te va de perlas

suitable ['su:təbl] *adj* adecuado, da • **the most suitable person** la persona más indicada

suitably ['su:təblı] *adv* adecuadamente

suitcase ['su:tkeıs] *s* petaca

suite [swi:t] *s* ❶ suite ❷ juego • **dining-room suite** comedor

suited ['su:tıd] *adj* • **suited to/for** adecuado, da para • **the couple are ideally suited** forman una pareja perfecta

sulfate *s* sulfato

sulfur ['sʌlfəɾ] *s* azufre

sulfuric acid [sʌl'fjuərık'æsıd] *s* ácido sulfúrico

sulk [sʌlk] *vi* estar de mal humor

sulky ['sʌlkı] *adj* malhumorado, da

sullen ['sʌlən] *adj* hosco, ca; antipático, ca

sultry ['sʌltrı] *adj* bochornoso, sa; sofocante

sum [sʌm] *s* suma

■ **sum up** *vt* & *vi* ☼ *El objeto se puede colocar antes o después de la preposición.* resumir

summarize ['sʌməraız] *vt* & *vi* resumir

summary ['sʌmərı] *s* resumen

summer ['sʌməɾ] ◆ *s* verano ◆ *en compuestos* de verano

summerhouse ['sʌməhaus] ☼ *pl* [-hauzız] *s* cenador

summer school *s* escuela de verano

summertime ['sʌmətaım] *s* • **(the) summertime** (el) verano

summit ['sʌmıt] *s* ❶ cima; cumbre ❷ cumbre

summon ['sʌmən] *vt* ❶ llamar ❷ convocar

■ **summon up** *vt* ☼ *El objeto se puede colocar antes o después de la preposición.* armarse de • **to summon up the strength to do something** reunir fuerzas para hacer algo

sumptuous ['sʌmptʃuəs] *adj* suntuoso, sa

sun [sʌn] *s* sol • **in the sun** al sol

expresión **everything under the sun** todo lo habido y por haber

sunbathe ['sʌnbeıð] *vi* tomar el sol

sunbed ['sʌnbed] *s* camilla de rayos ultravioletas

sunburn ['sʌnbɜ:n] *s* ☼ *incontable* quemadura de sol

sunburned ['sʌnbɜ:nd], **sunburnt** ['sʌnbɜ:nt] *adj* quemado, da por el sol

Sunday ['sʌndı] *s* domingo ver también **Saturday**

Sunday school *s* catequesis

sundial ['sʌndaıəl] *s* reloj de sol

sundown ['sʌndaun] *s* anochecer

sunflower ['sʌn,flauəɾ] *s* girasol

sung [sʌŋ] *participio pasado* → **sing**

sunglasses ['sʌn,glɑ:sız] *spl* gafas de sol

sunk [sʌŋk] *participio pasado* → **sink**

sunlight ['sʌnlaıt] *s* luz del sol • **in direct sunlight** a la luz directa del sol

sunny ['sʌnı] *adj* ❶ de sol • **sunny side up** frito ❷ soleado, da ❸ alegre

sunrise ['sʌnraız] *s* ❶ ☼ *incontable* amanecer ❷ salida del sol

sunroof ['sʌnru:f] *s* ❶ techo corredizo ❷ azotea

sunset ['sʌnset] *s* ❶ ☼ *incontable* anochecer ❷ puesta del sol

sunshade ['sʌnʃeıd] *s* sombrilla

sunshine ['sʌnʃaın] *s* (luz del) sol

sunstroke ['sʌnstrəuk] *s* ☼ *incontable* insolación • **to get sunstroke** coger una insolación

suntan ['sʌntæn] ◆ *s* bronceado • **to have a suntan** estar bronceado, da • **to get a suntan** broncearse ◆ *en compuestos* bronceador, ra

S

sunup ['sʌnʌp] *s* ⚙ *incontable familiar* salida del sol

super ['su:pər] ◆ *adj* ❶ *familiar* fenomenal ❷ superior ◆ *s familiar* portero, ra

superb [su:'pɜːb] *adj* excelente; magnífico, ca

Super Bowl *s* • **the Super Bowl** la final del campeonato estadounidense de futbol americano

THE SUPER BOWL

El **Super Bowl** es un partido de futbol americano en el que se enfrentan los campeones de las dos ligas o **conferences** más importantes del futbol profesional en Estados Unidos. Tiene lugar al final de la temporada de juegos — a fines de enero de cada año — y una gran cantidad de gente en Estados Unidos y otros países presencian este encuentro por televisión.

superficial [ˌsuːpə'fɪʃl] *adj* superficial

superfluous [su:'pɜːfluəs] *adj* superfluo, flua

superhuman [ˌsuːpə'hjuːmən] *adj* sobrehumano, na

superimpose [ˌsuːpərɪm'pəuz] *vt* • **to superimpose something on** superponer o sobreponer algo a

superintendent [ˌsuːpərɪn'tendənt] *s* ❶ *formal* supervisor, ra ❷ *familiar* portero, ra

superior [su:'pɪərɪər] ◆ *adj* ❶ • **superior (to)** superior (a) ❷ *despectivo* altanero, ra; arrogante ◆ *s* superior

superlative [su:'pɜːlətɪv] ◆ *adj* supremo, ma ◆ *s* GRAMÁTICA superlativo

supermarket ['suːpəˌmaːkɪt] *s* supermercado

supernatural [ˌsuːpə'nætʃrəl] *adj* sobrenatural

superpower ['suːpəˌpauər] *s* superpotencia

supersonic [ˌsuːpə'sɒnɪk] *adj* supersónico, ca

superstitious [ˌsuːpə'stɪʃəs] *adj* supersticioso, sa

superstore ['suːpəstɔːr] *s* hipermercado

supertanker ['suːpəˌtæŋkər] *s* superpetrolero

supervise ['suːpəvaɪz] *vt* ❶ vigilar ❷ supervisar

supervisor ['suːpəvaɪzər] *s* ❶ supervisor, ra ❷ director, ra

supper ['sʌpər] *s* cena

supple ['sʌpl] *adj* flexible

supplement ◆ *s* ['sʌplɪmənt] suplemento ◆ *vt* ['sʌplɪment] complementar

supplementary [ˌsʌplɪ'mentərɪ] *adj* suplementario, ria

supplier [sə'plaɪər] *s* proveedor, ra

supply [sə'plaɪ] ◆ *s* ❶ suministro ❷ surtido ❸ ⚙ *incontable* ECONOMÍA oferta • **supply and demand** la oferta y la demanda ◆ *vt* • **to supply something (to)** suministrar o proveer algo (a) • **to supply something with something** suministrar a algo de algo

■ **supplies** *spl* ❶ MILITAR pertrechos ❷ provisiones ❸ material

support [sə'pɔːt] ◆ *s* ❶ ⚙ *incontable* apoyo • **in support of** en apoyo de ❷ ⚙ *incontable* ayuda ❸ ⚙ *incontable* respaldo ❹ TECNOLOGÍA soporte ◆ *vt* ❶ sostener ❷ apoyar ❸ mantener; financiar • **to support yourself** ganarse la vida ❹ DEPORTE seguir

supporter [sə'pɔːtər] *s* ❶ partidario, ria ❷ DEPORTE hincha

support group *s* grupo de apoyo

suppose [sə'pəuz] ◆ *vt* suponer ◆ *vi* suponer • **I suppose (so)** supongo (que sí) • **I suppose not** supongo que no

supposed [sə'pəuzd] *adj* ❶ supuesto, ta ❷ • **he was supposed to be here at eight** debería haber estado aquí a las ocho ❸ • **it's supposed to be very good** se supone o se dice que es muy bueno

supposedly [sə'pəuzɪdlɪ] *adv* supuestamente

supposing [sə'pəuzɪŋ] *conjunción* • **supposing your father found out?** ¿y si se entera tu padre?

suppress [sə'pres] *vt* ❶ reprimir ❷ contener

supreme [su'priːm] *adj* supremo, ma

Supreme Court *s* • **the Supreme Court** el Tribunal Supremo (de los Estados Unidos)

surcharge ['sɜːtʃaːdʒ] *s* • **surcharge (on)** recargo (en)

sure [ʃuər] ◆ *adj* ❶ seguro, ra • **I'm not sure why he said that** no estoy seguro de por qué dijo eso ❷ • **to be sure of** poder estar seguro, ra de • **make sure (that) you do it** asegúrate de que lo haces ❸ • **to be sure of yourself** estar seguro, ra de uno mismo ◆ *adv* ❶ *familiar* por supuesto; pues claro ❷ realmente

■ **for sure** *adv* a ciencia cierta • **I don't know for sure** no lo sé con total seguridad

■ **sure enough** *adv* efectivamente

■ **sure thing** *adv familiar* por supuesto; claro

surely ['ʃuəlɪ] *adv* sin duda • **surely you remember him?** ¡no me digas que no te acuerdas de él!

surf [sɜːf] ◆ *s* espuma *(de las olas)* ◆ *vt* INFORMÁTICA • **to surf the Net** navegar por Internet

surface ['sɜːfɪs] ◆ *s* ❶ superficie ❷ *figurado* • **on the surface** a primera vista • **below o beneath the surface** debajo de las apariencias ◆ *vi* salir a la superficie

surface mail *s* correo por vía terrestre/marítima

surfboard ['sɜːfbɔːd] *s* plancha o tabla de surf

surfeit ['sɜːfɪt] *s formal* exceso

surfing ['sɜːfɪŋ] *s* surf

surge [sɜːdʒ] ◆ *s* ❶ oleada *(de mar, gente)* ❷ sobrecarga momentánea ❸ arrebato *(de emoción)* ❹ aumento súbito *(de interés, ventas)* ◆ *vi* ❶ avanzar en masa ❷ encresparse • **the angry mob surged forward** la multitud encolerizada avanzó en tropel

surgeon ['sɜːdʒən] *s* cirujano, na

surgery ['sɜːdʒərɪ] *s* ❶ ⚙ *incontable* MEDICINA cirugía ❷ consulta

surgical ['sɜːdʒɪkl] *adj* quirúrgico, ca

surly ['sɜːlɪ] *adj* hosco, ca; malhumorado, da

S

surmount [sɜ:'maunt] *vt* superar

surname ['sɜ:neɪm] *s* apellido

surpass [sə'pɑ:s] *vt formal* superar; sobrepasar

surplus ['sɜ:pləs] ◆ *adj* excedente; sobrante ◆ *s* ❶ excedente; sobrante ❷ superávit

surprise [sə'praɪz] ◆ *s* sorpresa
expresión **to take somebody by surprise** coger a alguien desprevenido
◆ *vt* sorprender

surprised [sə'praɪzd] *adj* sorprendido, da • **we were really surprised** nos quedamos sorprendidos • **I'm surprised you're still here** me sorprende que todavía estés aquí • **she was surprised to find the house empty** se sorprendió al encontrar la casa vacía

surprising [sə'praɪzɪŋ] *adj* sorprendente

surrender [sə'rendər] ◆ *s* rendición ◆ *vi literal & figurado* • **to surrender (to)** rendirse (a)

surrogate ['sʌrəgeɪt] ◆ *adj* sustitutorio, ria ◆ *s* sustituto, ta

surrogate mother *s* madre de alquiler

surround [sə'raund] *vt literal & figurado* rodear • **to be surrounded by** estar rodeado, da de

surrounding [sə'raundɪŋ] *adj* ❶ circundante ❷ relacionado, da

surroundings [sə'raundɪŋz] *spl* ❶ alrededores ❷ entorno

surveillance [sɜ:'veɪləns] *s* vigilancia

survey ◆ *s* ['sɜ:veɪ] ❶ encuesta ❷ medición ❸ inspección ◆ *vt* [sə'veɪ] ❶ contemplar ❷ hacer un estudio de ❸ medir; inspeccionar

survival [sə'vaɪvl] *s* supervivencia

survive [sə'vaɪv] ◆ *vt* sobrevivir a ◆ *vi* ❶ sobrevivir • **how are you? — surviving** ¿cómo estás? — voy tirando ❷ perdurar

survivor [sə'vaɪvər] *s* superviviente • **there were no survivors** no hubo supervivientes

susceptible [sə'septəbl] *adj* ❶ • **susceptible (to)** sensible (a) ❷ MEDICINA • **susceptible (to)** propenso, sa (a)

suspect ◆ *adj* ['sʌspekt] sospechoso, sa ◆ *s* ['sʌspekt] sospechoso, sa ◆ *vt* [sə'spekt] ❶ sospechar ❷ imaginar • **I suspect he's right** imagino que tiene razón ❸ • **to suspect somebody (of)** considerar a alguien sospechoso, sa (de)

■ **suspected** *participio pasado* • **to have a suspected heart attack** haber sufrido un posible infarto • **the suspected culprits** los presuntos culpables

suspend [sə'spend] *vt* ❶ suspender ❷ interrumpir ❸ expulsar temporalmente

suspended sentence [sə'spendɪd-] *s* condena condicional

suspenders [sə'spendəz] *spl* tirantes

suspense [sə'spens] *s* ❶ incertidumbre ❷ CINE suspenso • **to keep somebody in suspense** mantener a alguien en vilo

suspension [sə'spenʃn] *s* ❶ suspensión ❷ expulsión temporal

suspension bridge *s* puente colgante

suspicion [sə'spɪʃn] *s* ❶ sospecha • **on suspicion of** bajo sospecha de • **to be under suspicion** estar bajo sospecha • **to arouse suspicion** levantar sospechas ❷ pizca

suspicious [sə'spɪʃəs] *adj* ❶ receloso, sa ❷ sospechoso, sa

sustain [sə'steɪn] *vt* ❶ sostener ❷ *formal* sufrir

sustenance ['sʌstɪnəns] *s* 💡 *incontable formal* sustento

SW (*abreviatura escrita de* short wave) OC

swab [swɒb] *s* (trozo de) algodón

swagger ['swægər] *vi* pavonearse

swallow ['swɒləʊ] ◆ *s* golondrina ◆ *vt* tragar
■ **swallow up** *vt* 💡 *El objeto se puede colocar antes o después de la preposición.* tragarse

swam [swæm] *pretérito* → **swim**

swamp [swɒmp] ◆ *s* pantano; ciénaga ◆ *vt* ❶ hundir; inundar ❷ • **to swamp something (with)** inundar algo (de) • **to swamp somebody (with)** agobiar a alguien (con) • **we were swamped with applications** nos vimos inundados de solicitudes

swan [swɒn] *s* cisne

swap [swɒp], **swop** *vt* ❶ • **to swap something (for/with)** cambiar algo (por/con) ❷ *figurado* intercambiar

swarm [swɔ:m] ◆ *s* ❶ enjambre ❷ *figurado* multitud ◆ *vi* ❶ *figurado* ir en tropel ❷ *figurado* • **to be swarming (with)** estar abarrotado, da (de)

swarthy ['swɔ:ðɪ] *adj* moreno, na

swastika ['swɒstɪkə] *s* esvástica; cruz gamada

swat [swɒt] *vt* aplastar

sway [sweɪ] ◆ *vt* convencer ◆ *vi* balancearse

swear [sweər] ◆ *vt* • **I could have sworn I saw him** juraría que lo vi ◆ *vi* ❶ jurar • **I couldn't swear to it** no me atrevería a jurarlo ❷ decir palabrotas; jurar • **to swear at somebody** insultar a alguien

Formas irregulares de **swear**: *pretérito* **swore**, *pp* **sworn**.

swearword ['sweəwɜ:d] *s* palabrota

sweat [swet] ◆ *s* sudor ◆ *vi* sudar ◆ *vt* ❶ MEDICINA • **to sweat out a cold** quitarse un resfriado sudando ❷ • **to sweat it out** aguantar

sweater ['swetər] *s* suéter

sweatshirt ['swetʃɜ:t] *s* sudadera

sweatsuit ['swetsu:t] *s* pants

sweaty ['swetɪ] *adj* ❶ sudoroso, sa ❷ sudado, da

Swede [swi:d] *s* sueco, ca

Sweden ['swi:dn] *s* Suecia

Swedish ['swi:dɪʃ] ◆ *adj* sueco, ca ◆ *s* sueco ◆ *spl* • **the Swedish** los suecos

sweep [swi:p] ◆ *s* barrido; movimiento o gesto amplio ◆ *vt* ❶ barrer ❷ rastrear ❸ recorrer ◆ *vi* ❶ • **to sweep over** o **across something** azotar algo ❷ • **to sweep past** pasar como un rayo

S

■ **sweep away** *vt* ⊙: *El objeto se puede colocar antes o después de la preposición.* destruir completamente

■ **sweep up** *vt* & *vi* ⊙: *El objeto se puede colocar antes o después de la preposición.* barrer

Formas irregulares de **sweep**: *pretérito* & *pp* **swept.**

sweeping ['swiːpɪŋ] *adj* ❶ radical *(cambio)* ❷ generalizado *(comentario)* ❸ amplio, plia *(curva, gesto)*

sweet [swiːt] ◆ *adj* ❶ dulce ❷ azucarado, da ❸ perfumado, da *(olor)* ❹ melodioso, sa *(sonido)* ❺ amable *(carácter)* ◆ *exclamación familiar* genial

sweet corn *s* elote

sweeten ['swiːtn] *vt* endulzar

sweetheart ['swiːthɑːt] *s* ❶ cariño ❷ amor ; novio, via

sweetness ['swiːtnɪs] *s* ❶ dulzura ❷ dulzor

sweet pea *s* chícharo de olor

swell [swel] ◆ *vi* ❶ • **to swell (up)** hincharse ❷ aumentar ◆ *vt* aumentar ◆ *s* oleaje ◆ *adj familiar* estupendo, da

Formas irregulares de **swell**: *pp* **swollen** o **swelled.**

swelling ['swelɪŋ] *s* hinchazón • **the swelling has gone down** ha bajado la hinchazón

sweltering ['sweltərɪŋ] *adj* ❶ abrasador, ra ; sofocante ❷ achicharrado, da

swept [swept] *pretérito* & *participio pasado* → **sweep**

swerve [swɜːv] *vi* virar bruscamente

swift [swɪft] *adj* ❶ rápido, da ❷ pronto, ta

swig [swɪg] *s familiar* trago • **to take a swig of something** tomar un trago de algo

swim [swɪm] ◆ *s* baño • **to go for a swim** ir a nadar o a darse un baño ◆ *vi* ❶ nadar ❷ dar vueltas ◆ *vt* • **to swim the English Channel** cruzar el canal de la Mancha a nado • **I swam 20 lengths** nadé veinte largos

Formas irregulares de **swim**: *pretérito* **swam**, *pp* **swum.**

swimmer ['swɪmər] *s* nadador, ra • **she's a good swimmer** nada bien

swimming ['swɪmɪŋ] *s* natación • **to go swimming** ir a nadar

swimming cap *s* gorro de baño

swimming pool *s* alberca

swimming trunks *spl* bañador

swimsuit ['swɪmsuːt] *s* traje de baño

swindle ['swɪndl] ◆ *s* estafa ; timo ◆ *vt* estafar ; timar • **to swindle somebody out of something** estafar a alguien algo

swine [swaɪn] *s familiar* & *despectivo* cerdo, da ; canalla

swing [swɪŋ] ◆ *s* ❶ columpio ❷ viraje • **a swing towards the Conservatives** un giro hacia los conservadores ❸ meneo ; balanceo

expresión to be in full swing estar en plena marcha

◆ *vt* ❶ balancear ❷ hacer virar bruscamente ◆ *vi* ❶ balancearse ; oscilar ❷ girar ❸ • **to swing (round)** volverse ; girarse

Formas irregulares de **swing** *pret* & *pp* **swung.**

swipe [swaɪp] ◆ *vt familiar* birlar ◆ *vi* • **to swipe at something** intentar golpear algo

swirl [swɜːl] *vi* arremolinarse

swish [swɪʃ] *vt* agitar

Swiss [swɪs] ◆ *adj* suizo, za ◆ *s* suizo, za ◆ *spl* • **the Swiss** los suizos

switch [swɪtʃ] ◆ *s* ❶ interruptor ❷ cambio completo ◆ *vt* ❶ cambiar de • **to switch your attention to something** dirigir la atención a o hacia algo ❷ intercambiar

■ **switch off** *vt* ⊙: *El objeto se puede colocar antes o después de la preposición.* ❶ apagar ❷ parar

■ **switch on** *vt* ⊙: *El objeto se puede colocar antes o después de la preposición.* ❶ encender ❷ poner en marcha

switchblade ['swɪtʃbleɪd] *s* navaja automática

switchboard ['swɪtʃbɔːd] *s* conmutador

Switzerland ['swɪtsələnd] *s* Suiza

swivel ['swɪvl] ◆ *vt* hacer girar ◆ *vi* girar

Formas irregulares de **swivel**: *pret* & *pp* **swiveled**, *gerundio* **swiveling.**

swivel chair *s* silla giratoria

swollen ['swəʊln] ◆ *participio pasado* → **swell** ◆ *adj* ❶ hinchado, da • **my eyes were swollen** tenía los ojos hinchados ❷ crecido, da

swop [swɒp] = **swap**

sword [sɔːd] *s* espada

swordfish ['sɔːdfɪʃ] *s* pez espada

Dos plurales: **swordfish** o **swordfishes.**

swore [swɔːr] *pretérito* → **swear**

sworn [swɔːn] ◆ *participio pasado* → **swear** ◆ *adj* Derecho jurado, da

swum [swʌm] *participio pasado* → **swim**

swung [swʌŋ] *pretérito* & *participio pasado* → **swing**

syllable ['sɪləbl] *s* sílaba

syllabus ['sɪləbəs] *s* programa (de estudios)

Dos plurales: **syllabuses** o **syllabi** ['sɪləbaɪ].

symbol ['sɪmbl] *s* símbolo

symbolize, symbolise ['sɪmbəlaɪz] *vt* simbolizar

symmetry ['sɪmətrɪ] *s* simetría

sympathetic [ˌsɪmpə'θetɪk] *adj* ❶ comprensivo, va ❷ favorable • **sympathetic to** bien dispuesto, ta hacia

sympathize, sympathise ['sɪmpəθaɪz] *vi* ❶ • **to sympathize (with)** compadecerse (de) ❷ • **to sympathize (with something)** comprender (algo) ❸ • **to sympathize with something** apoyar algo

sympathizer, sympathiser ['sɪmpəθaɪzər] *s* simpatizante

sympathy ['sɪmpəθɪ] *s* ❶ • **sympathy (for) a)** comprensión (hacia) **b)** compasión (por) ❷ solidaridad

■ **sympathies** *spl* pésame

symphony ['sɪmfənɪ] *s* sinfonía

symptom ['sɪmptəm] *s* *literal & figurado* síntoma

synagogue ['sɪnəɡɒɡ] *s* sinagoga

syndrome ['sɪndrəʊm] *s* síndrome

synonym ['sɪnənɪm] *s* • **synonym (for** o **of)** sinónimo (de)

synopsis [sɪ'nɒpsɪs] *s* sinopsis

El plural de **synopsis** es **synopses** [sɪ'nɒpsiːz].

syntax ['sɪntæks] *s* sintaxis

synthesis ['sɪnθəsɪs] *s* síntesis

El plural de **synthesis** es **syntheses** ['sɪnθəsiːz].

synthetic [sɪn'θetɪk] *adj* ❶ sintético, ca ❷ *despectivo* artificial

syphon ['saɪfn] = **siphon**

syringe [sɪ'rɪndʒ] *s* jeringa; jeringuilla

syrup ['sɪrəp] *s* ⚙ *incontable* ❶ Cocina almíbar ❷ Medicina jarabe • **cough syrup** jarabe para la tos

system ['sɪstəm] *s* ❶ sistema ❷ instalación

expresión **to get something out of your system** *familiar* sacarse algo de encima

systematic [ˌsɪstə'mætɪk] *adj* sistemático, ca

systems analyst ['sɪstəmz-] *s* Informática analista de sistemas

S

T

t, T [tiː] *s* t; T

Dos plurales: **t's** o **ts**; **T's** o **Ts**.

tab [tæb] *s* **❶** etiqueta **❷** lengüeta **❸** cuenta • **to pick up the tab** *familiar* pagar la cuenta

expresión **to keep tabs on somebody** vigilar de cerca a alguien

table ['teɪbl] ◆ *s* **❶** mesa • **to set the table** poner la mesa **❷** mesilla **❸** tabla ◆ *vt* aplazar; posponer

tablecloth ['teɪblklɒθ] *s* mantel

table lamp *s* lámpara de mesa

tablemat ['teɪblmæt] *s* salvamanteles

tablespoon ['teɪblspuːn] *s* **❶** cuchara grande **❷** cucharada (grande)

tablet ['tæblɪt] *s* **❶** pastilla **❷** lápida

table tennis *s* tenis de mesa

table wine *s* vino de mesa

tabloid ['tæblɔɪd] *s* ▶ **tabloid (newspaper)** periódico sensacionalista • **the tabloids** los periódicos sensacionalistas

tacit ['tæsɪt] *adj formal* tácito, ta

tack [tæk] ◆ *s* **❶** tachuela **❷** *figurado* táctica ◆ *vt* fijar con tachuelas ◆ *vi* NÁUTICA virar

tackle ['tækl] ◆ *s* **❶** FÚTBOL entrada **❷** ☀*incontable* equipo; aparejos ◆ *vt* **❶** emprender; abordar **❷** FÚTBOL entrar **❸** atacar

tacky ['tækɪ] *adj* **❶** *familiar* chafa **❷** naco, ca **❸** pegajoso, sa

tact [tækt] *s* ☀*incontable* tacto; discreción

tactful ['tæktfʊl] *adj* discreto, ta

tactic ['tæktɪk] *s* táctica

■ **tactics** *s* ☀*incontable* MILITAR táctica

tactical ['tæktɪkl] *adj* **❶** estratégico, ca **❷** táctico, ca

tactless ['tæktlɪs] *adj* indiscreto, ta

tadpole ['tædpəʊl] *s* renacuajo

taffy ['tæfɪ] *s* caramelo de melaza

tag [tæg] *s* etiqueta • **price tag** etiqueta del precio

■ **tag question** *s* cláusula final interrogativa

■ **tag along** *vi familiar* • **to tag along (with)** pegarse (a); engancharse (a)

tail [teɪl] ◆ *s* **❶** cola **❷** faldón ◆ *vt familiar* seguir de cerca

■ **tails** *spl* **❶** frac **❷** sol • **heads or tails?** ¿águila o sol?

■ **tail off** *vi* **❶** ir debilitándose **❷** ir disminuyendo

tailcoat ['teɪlˌkəʊt] *s* frac

tail end *s* parte final

tailgate ['teɪlgeɪt] ◆ *s* puerta trasera de un vehículo ◆ *vt* conducir pegado a

tailor ['teɪlər] ◆ *s* sastre ◆ *vt* adaptar • **it can be tailored to your needs** se puede adaptar a sus necesidades

tailor-made *adj* hecho, cha a la medida

tail pipe *s* tubo de escape

tainted ['teɪntɪd] *adj* **❶** manchado, da **❷** estropeado, da

take [teɪk] ◆ *vt* **❶** tomar • **do you take sugar?** ¿tomas azúcar? • **to take control/command** tomar control/el mando • **to take a photo** hacer una foto • **to take a walk** dar un paseo • **to take a bath** bañarse • **to take a test** hacer un examen • **to take pity on somebody** compadecerse de alguien • **to take offence** ofenderse • **to be taken ill** ponerse enfermo • **take the second turning on the right** toma el segundo giro a la derecha **❷** llevar **❸** quitar; robar **❹** quedarse con • **I'll take the red one** me quedo con el rojo **❺** alquilar **❻** capturar • **to take somebody prisoner** capturar a alguien **❼** aceptar *(oferta, crítica, consejo)*; seguir; asumir *(responsabilidad)* • **the machine only takes 50p pieces** la máquina sólo admite monedas de 50 peniques • **take my word for it, take it from me** créeme **❽** tener cabida para **❾** soportar; aguantar • **some people can't take a joke** hay gente que no sabe aguantar una broma **❿** requerir; costar • **it will take a week/three hours** llevará una semana/tres horas • **it only took me 5 minutes** sólo me llevó cinco minutos • **it takes guts to do that** hay que tener agallas para hacer eso • **it took 5 people to move the piano** hicieron falta 5 personas para mover el piano **⓫** tomar *(tren, camión)* **⓬** calzar *(número)*; usar *(talla)* **⓭** considerar • **now, take John for instance...** tomemos a John, por ejemplo... • **to take somebody for a fool/a policeman** tomar a alguien por tonto/por un policía **⓮** • **I take it (that)...** supongo que... ◆ *s* CINE toma

■ **take after** *vt* ☿ *El objeto siempre va después de la preposición al final.* parecerse a

■ **take apart** *vt* ☿ *El objeto se puede colocar antes o después de la preposición.* desmontar

■ **take away** *vt* ☿ *El objeto se puede colocar antes o después de la preposición.* ❶ quitar ❷ restar ; sustraer

■ **take back** *vt* ☿ *El objeto se puede colocar antes o después de la preposición.* ❶ devolver ❷ aceptar la devolución de ❸ retirar ❹ ● **it takes me back to when I was a teenager** me hace volver a mi adolescencia

■ **take down** *vt* ☿ *El objeto se puede colocar antes o después de la preposición.* ❶ desmontar ❷ tomar nota de

■ **take in** *vt* ☿ *El objeto se puede colocar antes o después de la preposición.* ❶ engañar ● **to be taken in by somebody** ser engañado por alguien ❷ comprender ; asimilar ● **I can't take it all in** no consigo asimilarlo todo ❸ incluir ; abarcar ❹ acoger

■ **take off** ◆ *vt* ☿ *El objeto se puede colocar antes o después de la preposición.* ❶ quitarse ❷ tomarse ◆ *vi* ❶ despegar ❷ irse ; marcharse

■ **take on** *vt* ☿ *El objeto se puede colocar antes o después de la preposición.* ❶ aceptar ; asumir ❷ emplear ; coger ❸ desafiar

■ **take out** *vt* ☿ *El objeto se puede colocar antes o después de la preposición.* sacar

■ **take over** ◆ *vt* ☿ *El objeto se puede colocar antes o después de la preposición.* ❶ absorber ; adquirir ❷ apoderarse de ❸ asumir ◆ *vi* ❶ tomar el poder ❷ entrar en funciones

■ **take to** *vt* ☿ *El objeto siempre va después de la preposición al final.* ❶ coger cariño a ; aficionarse a ❷ ● **to take to doing something** empezar a hacer algo

■ **take up** *vt* ☿ *El objeto se puede colocar antes o después de la preposición.* ❶ ● **to take up singing** dedicarse a cantar ❷ aceptar ; tomar ❸ ocupar ; requerir

Formas irregulares de **take**: pretérito **took**, pp **taken**.

taken ['teɪkn] *participio pasado* → **take**

takeoff ['teɪkɒf] *s* despegue

takeout ['teɪkaʊt] *s* comida para llevar

takeover ['teɪk,əʊvər] *s* adquisición

takings *spl* ❶ venta ❷ recaudación

talc [tælk]**, talcum (powder)** ['tælkəm-] *s* talco

tale [teɪl] *s* ❶ cuento ❷ anécdota

talent ['tælənt] *s* ● **talent (for something)** talento (para algo)

talented ['tæləntɪd] *adj* con talento

talk [tɔːk] ◆ *s* ❶ conversación ; plática ● **to have a talk** conversar ❷ ☿ *incontable* habladurías ❸ charla ; plática ● **to give a talk on something** dar una charla sobre algo ◆ *vi* ❶ hablar ● **to talk to/of** hablar o platicar con/de ● **talking of Sarah, I met her mum yesterday** hablando de Sarah, ayer me encontré a su madre ● **to talk on** o **about** hablar o platicar acerca de ● **they aren't talking to each other** no se hablan ❷ chismorrear ◆ *vt* hablar de

■ **talks** *spl* conversaciones

■ **talk into** *vt* ☿ *El objeto se coloca entre el verbo y la preposición.* ● **to talk somebody into doing something** convencer a alguien para que haga algo

■ **talk out of** *vt* ☿ *El objeto se coloca entre el verbo y la preposición.* ● **to talk somebody out of doing something** disuadir a alguien de que haga algo

■ **talk over** *vt* ☿ *El objeto se puede colocar antes o después de la preposición.* discutir ; hablar de

talkative ['tɔːkətɪv] *adj* hablador, ra

talk show *s* programa de entrevistas

talk time *s* ☿ *incontable* tiempo de conversación

tall [tɔːl] *adj* alto, ta ● **she's 2 metres tall** mide 2 metros ● **how tall is he?** ¿cuánto mide?

tall story *s* cuento (increíble)

tally ['tælɪ] ◆ *s* cuenta ● **to keep a tally** llevar la cuenta ◆ *vi* concordar

talon ['tælən] *s* garra

tambourine [,tæmbə'riːn] *s* pandereta

tame [teɪm] ◆ *adj* ❶ doméstico, ca ❷ *despectivo* soso, sa ◆ *vt* ❶ domesticar ❷ dominar

tamper ['tæmpər] ■ **tamper with** *vt* ☿ *El objeto siempre va después de la preposición al final.* ❶ intentar forzar ❷ falsear ❸ manipular

tampon ['tæmpɒn] *s* tampón

tan [tæn] ◆ *adj* de color marrón claro ◆ *s* bronceado ● **to get a tan** broncearse ◆ *vi* broncearse

tang [tæŋ] *s* ❶ olor fuerte ❷ sabor fuerte

tangent ['tændʒənt] *s* GEOMETRÍA tangente
<img> **expresión** **to go off at a tangent** salirse por la tangente

tangerine [,tændʒə'riːn] *s* mandarina

tangible ['tændʒəbl] *adj* tangible

tangle ['tæŋgl] *s* ❶ maraña ❷ *figurado* enredo ; embrollo

tank [tæŋk] *s* ❶ depósito ; tanque ❷ MILITAR tanque ; carro de combate

tanker ['tæŋkər] *s* ❶ barco cisterna ; petrolero ❷ camión cisterna

tanned [tænd] *adj* bronceado, da

Tannoy® ['tænɔɪ] *s* (sistema de) altavoces ● **his name was called out over the Tannoy** su nombre sonó por megafonía

tantrum ['tæntrəm] *s* rabieta ● **to throw a tantrum** coger una rabieta

El plural de **tantrum** es **tantrums**

tap [tæp] ◆ *s* ❶ llave ❷ golpecito ◆ *vt* ❶ golpear ligeramente ❷ utilizar ; usar ❸ intervenir

tap dancing *s* claqué

tape [teɪp] ◆ *s* ❶ cinta ❷ cinta adhesiva ◆ *vt* ❶ grabar ❷ pegar con cinta adhesiva

tape measure *s* cinta métrica

tape recorder *s* magnetófono

T

tapestry ['tæpɪstrɪ] *s* ❶ tapiz ❷ tapicería

tar [tɑːɾ] *s* alquitrán

target ['tɑːgɪt] *s* ❶ objetivo ❷ blanco • **to be on target to do something** llevar el ritmo adecuado para hacer algo

tariff ['tærɪf] *s* tarifa

Tarmac® ['tɑːmæk] *s* alquitrán

■ **tarmac** *s* AERONÁUTICA • **the tarmac** la pista

tarnish ['tɑːnɪʃ] *vt* ❶ deslustrar ❷ *figurado* empañar; manchar

tart [tɑːt] ◆ *adj* agrio, agria ◆ *s* tarta

tartar(e) sauce ['tɑːtəɾ-] *s* salsa tártara

task [tɑːsk] *s* tarea

task force *s* MILITAR destacamento de fuerzas

taste [teɪst] ◆ *s* ❶ gusto • **in bad/good taste** de mal/buen gusto ❷ sabor ❸ • **have a taste** pruébalo ❹ *figurado* • **taste (for)** afición (a); gusto (por) ❺ *figurado* experiencia ◆ *vt* ❶ notar un sabor a • **I can't taste the lemon in it** no noto el sabor a limón ❷ probar ❸ *figurado* conocer ◆ *vi* saber • **to taste of** o **like** saber a

tasteful ['teɪstfʊl] *adj* de buen gusto

tasteless ['teɪstlɪs] *adj* ❶ de mal gusto ❷ insípido, da; soso, sa

tasty ['teɪstɪ] *adj* sabroso, sa

tatters ['tætəz] *spl* • **in tatters a)** andrajoso, sa **b)** *figurado* por los suelos

tattoo [tə'tuː] ◆ *s* tatuaje ◆ *vt* tatuar

El plural de **tattoo** es **tattoos**.

taught [tɔːt] *pretérito* & *participio pasado* → **teach**

Taurus ['tɔːrəs] *s* Tauro

tax [tæks] ◆ *s* impuesto ◆ *vt* ❶ gravar ❷ imponer contribuciones a ❸ poner a prueba

taxable ['tæksəbl] *adj* imponible

tax allowance *s* desgravación fiscal

taxation [tæk'seɪʃn] *s* ☿*incontable* ❶ sistema tributario ❷ impuestos

tax avoidance [-ə'vɔɪdəns] *s* evasión fiscal

tax collector *s* recaudador, ra de impuestos

tax evasion *s* fraude fiscal; evasión de impuestos

tax-exempt *adj* exento, ta de impuestos

taxi ['tæksɪ] ◆ *s* taxi ◆ *vi* rodar por la pista

taxi driver *s* taxista

tax inspector *s* ≃ inspector de Hacienda

taxi stand *s* parada de taxis

taxpayer ['tæks,peɪəɾ] *s* contribuyente

tax relief *s* ☿*incontable* desgravación fiscal

tax return *s* declaración de renta

TB *s* *abreviatura escrita de* **tuberculosis**

tea [tiː] *s* té

teabag ['tiːbæg] *s* bolsita de té

teach [tiːtʃ] ◆ *vt* ❶ dar clases a • **to teach somebody something** enseñar algo a alguien • **to teach**

(somebody) that inculcar a alguien que • **that will teach you a lesson!** ¡eso te enseñará! ❷ dar clases de ◆ *vi* ser profesor, ra

Formas irregulares de **teach**: *pretérito* & *pp* **taught**.

teacher ['tiːtʃəɾ] *s* ❶ maestro, tra ❷ profesor, ra

teachers college *s* escuela normal

teaching ['tiːtʃɪŋ] *s* enseñanza

tea cozy *s* cubretetera

teacup ['tiːkʌp] *s* taza de té

team [tiːm] *s* equipo

teammate ['tiːmmeɪt] *s* compañero, ra de equipo

teamster ['tiːmstəɾ] *s* camionero, ra

teamwork ['tiːmwɜːk] *s* ☿*incontable* trabajo en equipo

teapot ['tiːpɒt] *s* tetera

tear¹ [tɪəɾ] *s* lágrima • **in tears** llorando

tear² [teəɾ] ◆ *vt* ❶ rasgar; romper ❷ arrancar • **she tore a page out of her exercise book** arrancó una página de su libro de ejercicios

expresión **to tear something to pieces** *figurado* poner algo por los suelos

◆ *vi* ❶ romperse; rasgarse ❷ *familiar* • **he tore out of the house** salió de la casa a toda pastilla • **they were tearing along** iban a toda pastilla ◆ *s* rasgón; desgarrón

■ **tear apart** *vt* ☿*El objeto se puede colocar antes o después de la preposición.* ❶ despedazar ❷ desgarrar

■ **tear down** *vt* ☿*El objeto se puede colocar antes o después de la preposición.* echar abajo

■ **tear up** *vt* ☿*El objeto se puede colocar antes o después de la preposición.* hacer pedazos

Formas irregulares de **tear**: *pretérito* **tore**, *pp* **torn**.

teardrop ['tɪədrɒp] *s* lágrima

tearful ['tɪəfʊl] *adj* lloroso, sa

tear gas [tɪəɾ-] *s* ☿*incontable* gas lacrimógeno

tearoom ['tiːrʊm] *s* salón de té

tease [tiːz] *vt* ❶ • **to tease somebody (about)** tomar el pelo a alguien (acerca de) ❷ cardarse

tea service, tea set *s* servicio o juego de té

teaspoon ['tiːspuːn] *s* ❶ cucharilla ❷ cucharadita

teat [tiːt] *s* ❶ tetilla ❷ tetina

tea towel *s* paño de cocina

technical ['teknɪkl] *adj* técnico, ca

technicality [,teknɪ'kælətɪ] *s* detalle técnico

technically ['teknɪklɪ] *adv* ❶ técnicamente ❷ teóricamente; en teoría

technician [tek'nɪʃn] *s* técnico, ca

technique [tek'niːk] *s* técnica

techno ['teknəʊ] *s* MÚSICA tecno

technological [,teknə'lɒdʒɪkl] *adj* tecnológico, ca

technology [tek'nɒlədʒɪ] *s* tecnología

technophobe ['teknəfəʊb] *s* tecnófobo, ba

teddy ['tedɪ] *s* ▸ **teddy (bear)** oso de peluche

tedious ['tiːdjəs] *adj* tedioso, sa

teem [tiːm] *vi* ❶ llover a cántaros ❷ • **to be teeming with** estar inundado, da de

teenage ['tiːneɪdʒ] *adj* adolescente

teenager ['tiːnˌeɪdʒər] *s* adolescente

teens [tiːnz] *spl* adolescencia • **he's in his teens** es adolescente

tee-shirt *s* camiseta

teeter ['tiːtər] *vi literal & figurado* tambalearse

teeter-totter *s* balancín; subibaja

teeth [tiːθ] *spl* → **tooth**

teethe [tiːð] *vi* echar los dientes

teething troubles ['tiːðɪŋ-] *spl figurado* problemas iniciales

teetotaler [tiːˈtəʊtlər] *s* abstemio, mia

tel. (*abreviatura escrita de* telephone) tel.

telebanking ['telɪbæŋkɪŋ] *s* FINANZAS banca telefónica

telecommunications ['telɪkəˌmjuːnɪˈkeɪʃnz], **telecoms** ['telɪkɒmz] *spl* telecomunicaciones

telegram ['telɪɡræm] *s* telegrama

telegraph ['telɪɡrɑːf] *s* telégrafo

telegraph pole *s* poste de telégrafos

telepathy [tɪˈlepəθɪ] *s* telepatía

telephone ['telɪfəʊn] ◆ *s* teléfono ◆ *vt & vi* telefonear

telephone banking *s* banca telefónica

telephone book *s* guía telefónica

telephone booth *s* teléfono público

telephone call *s* llamada telefónica; llamado telefónico

telephone directory *s* guía telefónica

telephone number *s* número de teléfono

telephoto lens [ˌtelɪˈfəʊtəʊ-] *s* teleobjetivo

telescope ['telɪskəʊp] *s* telescopio

teletext ['telɪtekst] *s* teletexto

televideo [telɪˈvɪdɪəʊ] *s* televídeo

televise ['telɪvaɪz] *vt* televisar

television ['telɪˌvɪʒn] *s* televisión • **to watch television** ver la televisión

television set *s* televisor; (aparato de) televisión

teleworker ['telɪwɜːkər] *s* teletrabajador, ra

tell [tel] ◆ *vt* ❶ decir • **to tell somebody (that)** decir a alguien que • **to tell somebody something, to tell something to somebody** decir a alguien algo ❷ contar ❸ • **to tell what somebody is thinking** saber en qué está pensando alguien • **to tell the time** decir la hora ❹ • **to tell the difference between A and B** distinguir entre A y B • **it's hard to tell one from another** son difíciles de distinguir ◆ *vi* surtir efecto

■ **tell apart** *vt* ⚙ *El objeto se coloca entre el verbo y la preposición.* distinguir • **I can't tell them apart** no consigo distinguirlos

■ **tell off** *vt* ⚙ *El objeto se puede colocar antes o después de la preposición.* reñir; reprender

Formas irregulares de **tell**: *pretérito & pp* told.

telling ['telɪŋ] *adj* revelador, ra

telltale ['telteɪl] ◆ *adj* revelador, ra ◆ *s* chivato, ta; acusica

temp [temp] *vi* • **she's temping** tiene un trabajo temporal

temper ['tempər] *s* ❶ humor • **to keep your temper** mantener la calma ❷ • **to be in a temper** estar de mal humor ❸ temperamento

expresión **to lose your temper** enfadarse; perder la paciencia

temperament ['temprəmənt] *s* temperamento

temperamental [ˌtemprəˈmentl] *adj* temperamental

temperate ['temprət] *adj* templado, da

temperature ['temprətʃər] *s* temperatura • **to take somebody's temperature** tomarle a alguien la temperatura • **to have a temperature** tener fiebre

tempestuous [temˈpestjʊəs] *adj literal & figurado* tempestuoso, sa

template ['templɪt] *s* plantilla

temple ['templ] *s* ❶ RELIGIÓN templo ❷ ANATOMÍA sien

temporarily [ˌtempəˈrerəlɪ] *adv* temporalmente; provisionalmente

temporary ['tempərərɪ] *adj* ❶ temporario; provisional ❷ pasajero, ra

tempt [tempt] *vt* • **to be** o **feel tempted to do something** estar o sentirse tentado de hacer algo

temptation [tempˈteɪʃn] *s* tentación

tempting ['temptɪŋ] *adj* tentador, ra

ten [ten] *número* diez *ver también* **six**

tenancy ['tenənsɪ] *s* alquiler; arrendamiento

tenant ['tenənt] *s* ❶ inquilino, na ❷ arrendatario, ria

tend [tend] *vt* ❶ cuidar ❷ • **to tend bar** atender en el bar

tendency ['tendənsɪ] *s* inclinación

tender ['tendər] ◆ *adj* ❶ tierno, na ❷ dolorido, da ◆ *s* ❶ COMERCIO propuesta; oferta ❷ • **(legal) tender** moneda de curso legal ◆ *vt formal* presentar

tendon ['tendən] *s* tendón

tennis ['tenɪs] *s* tenis

tennis ball *s* pelota de tenis

tennis court *s* pista de tenis

tennis match *s* partido de tenis

tennis player *s* tenista

tennis racket *s* raqueta de tenis

tenor ['tenər] *s* tenor

T

tense [tens] ◆ *adj* tenso, sa ◆ *s* tiempo ◆ *vt* tensar

tension ['tenʃn] *s* tensión

ten-spot *s* billete de diez dólares

tent [tent] *s* carpa

tentacle ['tentəkl] *s* tentáculo

tentative ['tentətɪv] *adj* ❶ indeciso, sa ❷ vacilante ❸ provisional

tenterhooks ['tentəhʊks] *spl* • **to be on tenterhooks** estar sobre ascuas

tenth [tenθ] *número* décimo, ma ver también **sixth**

tent peg *s* estaca

tent pole *s* mástil de tienda

tenuous ['tenjʊəs] *adj* ❶ flojo, ja ❷ débil; insignificante ❸ ligero, ra

tepid ['tepɪd] *adj* tibio, bia

term [tɜːm] ◆ *s* ❶ término ❷ EDUCACIÓN & UNIVERSIDAD trimestre ❸ POLÍTICA mandato • **term of office** mandato ❹ periodo • **in the long/short term** a largo/corto plazo ◆ *vt* • **to term something something** calificar algo de algo

■ **terms** *spl* ❶ condiciones ❷ • **on equal** o **the same terms** en condiciones de igualdad

expresión **to be on speaking terms (with somebody)** hablarse (con alguien) ❱ **to come to terms with something** aceptar algo

■ **in terms of** *preposición* por lo que se refiere a

terminal ['tɜːmɪnl] ◆ *adj* MEDICINA incurable; terminal ◆ *s* ❶ terminal ❷ INFORMÁTICA terminal

terminate ['tɜːmɪneɪt] ◆ *vt* ❶ *formal* poner fin a ❷ interrumpir ◆ *vi* ❶ finalizar el trayecto ❷ terminarse

termini ['tɜːmɪnaɪ] *spl* → **terminus**

terminus ['tɜːmɪnəs] *s* (estación) terminal

Dos plurales: **terminni** o **terminuses**.

terrace ['terəs] *s* terraza

■ **terraces** *spl* FÚTBOL • **the terraces** las gradas

terraced ['terəst] *adj* ❶ a terrazas ❷ adosado, da

terrain [te'reɪn] *s* terreno

terrible ['terəbl] *adj* ❶ terrible; espantoso, sa ❷ fatal

terribly ['terəblɪ] *adv* ❶ malísimamente ❷ terriblemente

terrific [tə'rɪfɪk] *adj* ❶ estupendo, da ❷ enorme

terrified ['terɪfaɪd] *adj* aterrorizado, da • **to be terrified (of)** tener terror (a)

terrifying ['terɪfaɪɪŋ] *adj* aterrador, ra

territory ['terətrɪ] *s* ❶ territorio ❷ terreno ❸ esfera

terror ['terər] *s* terror • **to live in terror** vivir aterrorizado, da • **they ran out of the house in terror** salieron de la casa aterrorizados

terrorism ['terərɪzm] *s* terrorismo

terrorist ['terərɪst] *s* terrorista

terrorize, terrorise ['terəraɪz] *vt* aterrorizar

terse [tɜːs] *adj* seco, ca

test [test] ◆ *s* ❶ prueba • **to put something to the test** poner algo a prueba ❷ examen; prueba ❸ MEDICINA análisis ❹ revisión ◆ *vt* ❶ probar; poner a prueba ❷ examinar • **to test somebody on** examinar a alguien de

testament ['testəmənt] *s* testamento

test-drive *vt* someter a prueba de carretera

testicles ['testɪklz] *spl* testículos

testify ['testɪfaɪ] ◆ *vi* ❶ DERECHO prestar declaración ❷ • **to testify to something** dar fe de o atestiguar algo ◆ *vt* • **to testify that** declarar que

testimony ['testəməʊnɪ] *s* DERECHO testimonio; declaración

testing ['testɪŋ] *adj* duro, ra

test pilot *s* piloto de pruebas

test tube *s* probeta

test-tube baby *s* bebé probeta

tetanus ['tetənəs] *s* tétanos

tether ['teðər] ◆ *vt* atar ◆ *s*

expresión **to be at the end of your tether** estar uno que ya no puede más

text [tekst] ◆ *s* ❶ texto ❷ libro de texto ❸ mensaje de texto; SMS ◆ *vt* enviar un mensaje de texto a ◆ *vi* enviar mensajes de texto

textbook ['tekstbʊk] *s* libro de texto

textile ['tekstaɪl] *s* textil; tejido

texting ['tekstɪŋ] *s familiar* mensajes de texto

text message *s* mensaje de texto

text messaging [-'mesɪdʒɪŋ] *s* mensajería de texto

texture ['tekstʃər] *s* textura

Thai [taɪ] ◆ *adj* tailandés, esa ◆ *s* ❶ tailandés, esa ❷ tailandés

Thailand ['taɪlænd] *s* Tailandia

than ⬥ *acento atónico* [ðən], *acento tónico* [ðæn]
◆ *preposición* que • **you're older than me** eres mayor que yo • **you're older than I thought** eres mayor de lo que pensaba ◆ *conjunción* que • **I'd sooner read than sleep** prefiero leer que dormir • **no sooner did he arrive than she left** tan pronto llegó él, ella se fue • **more than three/once** más de tres/de una vez • **rather than stay, he chose to go** en vez de quedarse, prefirió irse

than

Para realizar comparaciones se utiliza than seguido normalmente del pronombre de complemento me, him, them, ETC (he's bigger *than me*, Keith has a faster car *than me*). En el lenguaje formal se prefiere el pronombre de sujeto (I, he, they, ETC) incluso si se omite el verbo que le sigue (he's bigger *than I*, Keith has a faster car *than I*).

thank [θæŋk] *vt* • **to thank somebody (for something)** dar las gracias a alguien (por algo); agradecer a alguien (algo)

expresión **thank God** o **goodness** o **heavens!** ¡gracias a Dios!

■ **thanks** ◆ *spl* agradecimiento • **they left without a word of thanks** se marcharon sin dar las gracias ◆ *exclamación* ¡gracias! • **thanks a lot** muchas gracias • **would you like a biscuit? — no thanks** ¿quieres una galleta? — no, gracias • **thanks for** gracias por

■ **thanks to** *preposición* gracias a

thankful ['θæŋkfʊl] *adj* ❶ aliviado, da ❷ • **thankful (for)** agradecido, da (por)

thankless ['θæŋklɪs] *adj* ingrato, ta

Thanksgiving ['θæŋks,gɪvɪŋ] *s* Día de Acción de Gracias *(el cuarto jueves de noviembre)*

Thanksgiving

Con la celebración del Thanksgiving, el cuarto jueves de noviembre, se conmemora el asentamiento de los primeros colonos en Norteamérica. Se suele celebrar con una cena en familia, que consiste tradicionalmente en un pavo asado con salsa de arándanos, acompañado por camotes al horno como guarnición, y el tradicional pay de calabaza como postre.

thank you *exclamación* ¡gracias! • **thank you very much** muchas gracias • **thank you for** gracias por • **to say thank you (for something)** dar gracias (por algo) • **tea? — no thank you** ¿té? — no, gracias

that
◆ *pronombre*

🖙 *acento atónico* [ðæt]*, acento tónico* [ðət]*,* [ðæt]

❶ [*en contraste con "this", se usa para referirse a elementos que están lejos del hablante*]
• **who's that?** ¿quién es ese?
• **is that Maureen?** ¿esa es Maureen?
• **what's that?** ¿qué es eso?
• **which shoes are you going to wear, these or those?** ¿qué zapatos te vas a poner, estos o esos?

❷ [*para introducir una especificación*]
• **we came to a path that led into the woods** llegamos a un camino que llevaba al bosque
• **show me the book that you bought** enséñame el libro que compraste
• **it started raining on the day that we left** comenzó a llover el día que nos fuimos

❸ [*en expresiones*]
• **that's a shame** qué pena

◆ *adj*

❶ [*en contraste con "this", se usa para referirse a elementos que están lejos del hablante*]
• **those chocolates are delicious** estos bombones están deliciosos

• **he arrived later that day** llegó ese mismo día más tarde
• **I prefer that book** prefiero ese libro
• **I'll have that one** quiero aquel

❷ [*para expresar exasperación*]
• **that man again! we're sick of him!** ¡otra vez ese hombre! ¡estamos hartos de él!

❸ [*en expresiones*]
• **it's just one of those things** son cosas que pasan
◆ *adv*

[*para expresar un nivel*]
• **I can't go that far** no puedo ir tan lejos
• **it wasn't that bad/good** no fue tan bueno/malo

■ **that** [ðət]
◆ *conjunción*

• **tell him that I'm sick** dile que estoy enfermo
• **he recommended that I phone you** recomendó que te llamara

■ **that is (to say)**
◆ *adv*

esto es

• **approximately 50,000 people have visited the museum, that is to say an average of 500 people a day** han visitado el museo aproximadamente 50.000 personas, esto es, un promedio de 500 por día

El plural de **that** es **those** [ðəʊz].

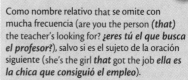

that

Como nombre relativo **that** se omite con mucha frecuencia (**are you the person (that) the teacher's looking for?** ¿eres tú el que busca el profesor?), salvo si es el sujeto de la oración siguiente (**she's the girl *that* got the job** *ella es la chica que consiguió el empleo*).

También muy a menudo se omite la conjunción **that** tras verbos como **believe, say, think** y **tell** (**he said *(that)* he liked her** *dijo que le gustaba*; **she told him *(that)* she was getting married** *le dijo que se iba a casar*).

Ver también **this**.

that's [ðæts] *(abreviatura de* that is*)* = **that**
thaw [θɔː] ◆ *vt* ❶ derretir ❷ descongelar ◆ *vi* ❶ derretirse ❷ descongelarse ◆ *s* deshielo

the
◆ *artículo determinado*

🖙 *acento atónico* [ðə]*, antes de vocal* [ðɪ]*, acento tónico* [ðiː]

❶ [*indica un elemento definido o ya mencionado*]
• **the book you bought is very interesting** el libro que compraste es muy interesante
• **we were getting fed up with the situation** estábamos hartándonos de la situación

T

• **the Joneses are coming to supper** los Jones vienen a cenar

❷ [*hablando de una cosa única*]
• **the world is not flat** la Tierra no es plana
• **the sun is shining** brilla el sol

❸ [*para expresar una generalidad*]
• **the lion is a wild animal** el león es un animal salvaje

❹ [*para indicar una oposición*]
• **the English drink a lot of tea, the French rather drink coffee** los ingleses beben mucho té, los franceses prefieren beber café

❺ [*delante de adjetivos sustantivados*]
• **the old/young** los viejos/jóvenes
• **the impossible** lo imposible

❻ [*con instrumentos de música*]
• **he plays the piano very well** toca el piano muy bien

❼ [*con expresiones de tiempo*]
• **the fourth of July is the American celebration of independence** el 4 de julio es la celebración de la independencia americana
• **the forties were the golden age for movies** los cuarenta fueron la era de oro del cine

❽ [*en su forma acentuada, indica el carácter único o excepcional de algo o alguien*]
• **it's THE book just now** es el libro imperdible del momento
• **are you talking about THE Professor Baxter?** ¿te refieres al famoso profesor Baxter?
• **he's THE specialist** es el gran especialista

❾ [*en una correlación*]
• **the more he talks, the more I feel like listening** cuanto más habla, más me apetece escucharlo
• **the more I see him, the less I like him** cuanto más lo veo, menos me gusta
• **the sooner the better** cuanto antes, mejor

❿ [*con el nombre de un rey o emperador*]
• **Alexander the Great** Alejandro Magno
• **Attila the Hun** Atila, rey de los hunos

the

The no se coloca delante de sustantivos incontables (work, beer, money) o de contables en plural (children, cats, houses), cuando se refieren a cosas en general (money isn't important to me *no me importa el dinero*; I don't like modern houses *no me gustan las casas modernas*).

The se omite a veces delante de sustantivos que hablan de un lugar en general (to go to school/church *ir a la escuela/a misa*; to be in bed/the hospital/prison *estar en la cama/el hospital/la cárcel*; to come home *volver a casa*). Sin embargo, debe usarse the si nos referimos a un ejemplo concreto de estos lugares (we go to the school at *the* end of the road *vamos a la*

escuela al final de la calle; the church is very pretty *la iglesia es muy bonita*).

The también se suele omitir con las comidas del día (to have breakfast *desayunar*; to meet for lunch *quedar para comer*) así como con las estaciones (in spring *en la primavera*; y los periodos de tiempo next year *el año que viene*; last semester *el semestre pasado*).

The no se coloca delante de nombres propios de persona (President Kennedy *el presidente Kennedy*; Doctor Allen *el doctor Allen*).

theater ['θɪətər] *s* ❶ teatro ❷ cine
theatergoer ['θɪətə.gəʊər] *s* aficionado, da al teatro
theatrical [θɪ'ætrɪkl] *adj literal & figurado* teatral
theft [θeft] *s* ❶ robo ❷ hurto
their [ðeər] *adj posesivo* su; sus ☼ *pl* • **their house** su casa • **their children** sus hijos • **it wasn't their fault** no fue culpa suya o su culpa • **they washed their hair** se lavaron el pelo

their

No olvidemos que al hablar de las partes del cuerpo se usa el adjetivo posesivo their en lugar del artículo the (they had *their* ears pierced *se hicieron agujeros en las orejas*).

Ver también its.

theirs [ðeəz] *pronombre posesivo* suyo, suya • **that money is theirs** ese dinero es suyo • **our car hit theirs** nuestro coche chocó contra el suyo • **it wasn't our fault, it was theirs** no fue culpa nuestra sino suya o de ellos • **a friend of theirs** un amigo suyo o de ellos
them ☼ *acento átono* [ðəm], *acento tónico* [ðem] *pronombre personal pl* ❶ ☼ *complemento directo* los; las • **I know them** los conozco • **I like them** me gustan • **if I were o was them** si (yo) fuera ellos ❷ ☼ *complemento indirecto - generalmente* les ❸ ☼ *con pronombres de la 3ª persona* • **she sent them a letter** les mandó una carta • **we spoke to them** hablamos con ellos • **I gave it to them** se lo di (a ellos) ❹ ☼ *acento tónico, tras preposición, en comparaciones, etc* ellos; ellas • **you can't expect them to do it** no esperarás que **ellos** lo hagan • **with/without them** con/sin ellos • **a few of them** unos pocos • **some of them** algunos • **all of them** todos ellos • **we're not as wealthy as them** no somos tan ricos como ellos
theme [θiːm] *s* ❶ tema ❷ sintonía
theme tune *s* tema musical
themselves [ðem'selvz] *pronombre* ❶ ☼ *reflexivo* se • **they enjoyed themselves** se divirtieron ❷ ☼ *tras preposición* sí • **they were talking amongst themselves** hablaban entre sí o ellos ❸ ☼ *para dar énfasis* ellos mismos; ellas mismas • **they did it themselves** lo hicieron ellos mismos ❹ solos, las • **they organized**

it (by) themselves lo organizaron ellas solas ❺ • **the boys aren't themselves today** hoy los chicos no se están portando como de costumbre

then [ðen] ◆ *adv* ❶ entonces • **it starts at 8 — I'll see you then** empieza a las 8 — hasta las 8, entonces • **up until then he had always trusted her** hasta entonces siempre había confiado en ella • **from then on** desde entonces • **then it must have been her!** ¡entonces tiene que haber sido ella! ❷ luego; después • **I had dinner then I went to bed** cené y luego me fui a acostar ❸ pues • **I'll do it straight away then** pues lo hago ahora mismo • **all right then** de acuerdo, pues ❹ además ◆ *adj* entonces • **the then headmistress** la entonces directora

expresión **then again** pero por otra parte

theoretical [θɪəˈretɪkl] *adj* teórico, ca

theorize, theorise [ˈθɪəraɪz] *vi* • **to theorize (about something)** teorizar (sobre algo)

theory [ˈθɪərɪ] *s* teoría • **in theory** en teoría

therapeutic cloning *s* MEDICINA clonación terapéutica

therapist [ˈθerəpɪst] *s* terapeuta

therapy [ˈθerəpɪ] *s* terapia

---

there [ðeəɾ]
◆ *pronombre*
[*para introducir una frase*]
• **there is/are** hay
• **there's somebody at the door** hay alguien llamando a la puerta
• **there are some nice flowers** hay alguna flores bonitas
• **there was a good movie on TV yesterday evening** hubo una buena película en la televisión ayer por la noche
• **there must be some mistake** debe haber un error
◆ *adv*
❶ [*para referirse a un lugar lejano*]
• **I'm going there next week** voy a ir allí la próxima semana
• **he lives over there** vive allá
• **is anybody there?** ¿hay alguien ahí?
• **is John there, please?** ¿está John, por favor?
❷ [*para expresar la llegada de algo o alguien*]
• **there it is** ahí está
• **there he is!** ¡ahí está!
◆ *exclamación*
• **there, I knew he'd turn up!** ¡ves, ¡sabía que aparecería!
• **there, there, stop crying now!** ¡venga, vamos, para de llorar!
■ **there again**
◆ *adv*
por otra parte
• **but there again, no one really knows** por otra parte, nadie lo sabe
■ **there and then, then and there**
◆ *adv*
en el acto

• **I liked the bike so much when I saw it in the shop, that I bought it there and then** o **then and there** me gustó tanto la bici cuando la vi en la tienda que la compré en el acto

thereabouts [ˌðeərəˈbaʊts], **thereabout** [ˌðeərəˈbaʊt] *adv* • **or thereabouts** o por ahí

thereafter [ˌðeərˈɑːftəɾ] *adv formal* después; a partir de entonces

therefore [ˈðeəfɔːɾ] *adv* por lo tanto

there's [ðeəz] (*abreviatura de* there is) → **there**

thermal [ˈθɜːml] *adj* térmico, ca

thermometer [θəˈmɒmɪtəɾ] *s* termómetro

Thermos (flask)® [ˈθɜːməs-] *s* termo

thesaurus [θɪˈsɔːrəs] *s* diccionario de sinónimos y voces afines

El plural de **thesaurus** es **thesauruses**.

these [ðiːz] *pronombre pl* → **this**

thesis [ˈθiːsɪs] *s* tesis

El plural de **thesis** es **theses** [ˈθiːsiːz].

they [ðeɪ] *pronombre personal pl* ❶ ellos; ellas • **they're pleased** (ellos) están satisfechos • **they're pretty earrings** son unos pendientes bonitos • **they can't do it** ellos no pueden hacerlo • **there they are** allí están ❷ • **they say it's going to snow** dicen que va a nevar

they'd [ðeɪd] ❶ (*abreviatura de* they had) → **have** ❷ (*abreviatura de* they would) → **would**

they'll [ðeɪl] ❶ (*abreviatura de* they will) → **will** ❷ (*abreviatura de* they shall) → **shall**

they're [ðeəɾ] (*abreviatura de* they are) → **be**

they've [ðeɪv] (*abreviatura de* they have) → **have**

thick [θɪk] ◆ *adj* ❶ grueso, sa • **it's 3 cm thick** tiene 3 cm de grueso • **how thick is it?** ¿qué espesor tiene? ❷ espeso, sa ❸ *familiar* necio, cia ◆ *s*

expresión **to be in the thick of** estar en el centro o meollo de

thicken [ˈθɪkn] ◆ *vt* espesar ◆ *vi* espesarse

thickness [ˈθɪknɪs] *s* espesor

thief [θiːf] *s* ladrón, ona

El plural de **thief** es **thieves**.

thieves [θiːvz] *spl* → **thief**

thigh [θaɪ] *s* muslo

thimble [ˈθɪmbl] *s* dedal

thin [θɪn] *adj* ❶ delgado, da; fino, na ❷ delgado, da; flaco, ca ❸ claro, ra; aguado, da ❹ poco denso, poco densa (*vegetación*); ralo, la (*pelo*)

■ **thin down** *vt* ⚗️ *El objeto se puede colocar antes o después de la preposición.* aclarar

thing [θɪŋ] *s* ❶ cosa • **he has a lot of things to do** tiene muchas cosas que hacer • **the next thing on the list** lo siguiente de la lista • **the (best) thing to do would be...** lo mejor sería... • **first thing in the morning** a primer hora de la mañana • **last thing at night** a última hora de la noche • **the main thing** lo principal • **the whole thing is a shambles** es un auténtico desastre • **it's a good thing you were there** menos

T

mal que estabas allí • **I thought the same thing** lo mismo pensé yo ❷ • **not a thing** nada • **I didn't do a thing** no hice nada **expresiones** **the thing is...** el caso es que... ▶ **to make a thing (out) of something** *familiar* exagerar algo ▶ **poor thing!** ¡pobrecito!

■ **things** *spl* ❶ cosas • **things aren't what they used to be** las cosas ya no son lo que eran ❷ *familiar* • **how are things?** ¿qué tal (van las cosas)?

think [θɪŋk] ◆ *vt* ❶ • **to think (that)** creer o pensar que • **I think so** creo que sí • **I don't think so** creo que no • **do you think you could help me?** ¿cree que podría ayudarme? ❷ pensar • **what are you thinking?** ¿en qué piensas? • **I didn't think to ask her** no se me ocurrió preguntárselo ❸ entender • **I can't think what might have happened to them** no quiero ni pensar lo que les podría haber ocurrido • **I thought so** ya me lo imaginaba ◆ *vi* ❶ pensar • **to think aloud** pensar en voz alta ❷ • **what do you think of o about his new movie?** ¿qué piensas de su nueva película? **expresión** **to think a lot of something/somebody** tener en mucha estima algo/a alguien ▶ **to think twice** pensárselo dos veces

■ **think about** *vt* 💡 *El objeto siempre va después de la preposición al final.* pensar en • **I'll have to think about it** tendré que pensarlo

■ **think of** *vt* 💡 *El objeto siempre va después de la preposición al final.* ❶ • **to think of doing something** pensar en hacer algo ❷ acordarse de ❸ pensar en • **how did you think of (doing) that?** ¿cómo se te ocurrió (hacer) esto?

■ **think out, think through** *vt* 💡 *El objeto se puede colocar antes o después de la preposición.* ❶ elaborar ❷ examinar

■ **think over** *vt* 💡 *El objeto se puede colocar antes o después de la preposición.* pensarse

■ **think up** *vt* 💡 *El objeto se puede colocar antes o después de la preposición.* idear

Formas irregulares de **think**: *pret* & *pp* **thought**.

think tank *s* ▶ grupo de expertos (convocados por una organización para aconsejar sobre un tema determinado)

third [θɜːd] ◆ *adj numeral* tercer, ra ◆ *sustantivo numeral* ❶ tercio ❷ tercero, ra ver también **sixth**

thirdly ['θɜːdlɪ] *adv* en tercer lugar

third party insurance *s* seguro a terceros

third-rate *adj despectivo* de poca categoría

Third World *s* • **the Third World** el Tercer Mundo

thirst [θɜːst] *s literal & figurado* • **thirst (for)** sed (de)

thirsty ['θɜːstɪ] *adj* • **to be o feel thirsty** tener sed

thirteen [,θɜː'tiːn] *número* trece ver también **six**

thirty ['θɜːtɪ] *número* treinta ver también **sixty**

this [ðɪs] ◆ *pronombre* ❶ éste; ésta; éstos; éstas • **this is Daphne Logan a)** ésta es o te presento a Daphne Logan *(en presentaciones)* **b)** soy Daphne Logan *(al teléfono)* ❷ *indefinido* esto • **this is/these are for you** esto es/éstos son para ti • **this can't be true** esto no puede ser cierto • **do you prefer these or those?** ¿prefieres éstos o aquéllos? • **what's this?** ¿qué es eso? ◆ *adj* ❶ este, esta; estos, estas 💡 *pl* • **this country** este país • **these thoughts** estos pensamientos • **I prefer this one** prefiero éste • **this morning/week** esta mañana/semana • **this Sunday/summer** este domingo/verano ❷ *familiar* un, una • **there's this woman I know** hay una tipa que conozco ◆ *adv* • **it was this big** era así de grande • **you'll need about this much** te hará falta un tanto así

El plural de **this** es **these**.

this

This y these se refieren a cosas cercanas en el espacio o tiempo (is *this* your coat on the floor here? *¿éste es tu abrigo aquí en el suelo?*; this music is excellent *esta música es excelente*). Están relacionados con here y con now. That y those se emplean con cosas que nos parecen más alejadas (isn't *that* your father over there? *ése de allí ¿no es tu padre?*; he was born in 1915 — *that*'s a long time ago *nació en el 1915 — eso sí que hace mucho tiempo*). Están emparentados con there y then.

En ocasiones this/these y that/those se utilizan juntos para comparar cosas (which skirt should I wear? — *this one* or *that one?* *¿cuál falda me pongo? — ¿ésta o ésa?*), pero si se quiere realizar el contraste entre dos posibilidades es más común emplear this/these y the other/the others (Nadal is serving from *this* end and Murray receiving at *the other* *Nadal saca de este lado y Murray recibe del otro.*).

Como pronombre, únicamente those (y no this/these o that) puede referirse directamente a personas. En este caso, those suele ir seguido de una frase especificativa (*those* of you who agree, please put up your hands *los que estén de acuerdo que levanten la mano*).

thong [θɒŋ] *s* ❶ correa ❷ tanga ❸ chancleta

thorn [θɔːn] *s* espina

thorough ['θʌrə] *adj* ❶ exhaustivo, va ❷ minucioso, sa

thoroughbred ['θʌrəbred] *s* pura sangre

thoroughly ['θʌrəlɪ] *adv* ❶ a fondo ❷ completamente

those [ðəʊz] *pronombre pl* → **that**

though, tho' [ðəʊ] ◆ *conjunción* aunque • **even though** aunque • **as though** como si ◆ *adv* sin embargo • **she still likes him though** y sin embargo le sigue gustando

thought [θɔːt] ◆ *pretérito* & *participio pasado* → **think** ◆ *s* ❶ idea ❷ • **after much thought** después de pensarlo mucho ❸ pensamiento

■ **thoughts** *spl* ❶ reflexiones ❷ opiniones • **what are your thoughts on the subject?** ¿qué piensas sobre el tema?

thoughtful ['θɔːtfʊl] *adj* ❶ pensativo, va ❷ considerado, da • **that was thoughtful of her** fue muy considerada

thoughtless ['θɔːtlɪs] *adj* desconsiderado, da

thousand ['θaʊznd] *número* mil • **a** o **one thousand** mil • **two thousand** dos mil • **thousands of** miles de • **they came in their thousands** vinieron miles de ellos ver también **six**

thousandth ['θaʊzntθ] ◆ *adj numeral* milésimo, ma ◆ *sustantivo numeral* milésima ver también **sixth**

thrash [θræʃ] *vt literal & figurado* dar una paliza a

thread [θred] ◆ *s* ❶ hilo ❷ rosca ◆ *vt* enhebrar

threat [θret] *s* • **threat (to/of)** amenaza (para/de) • **they were just empty threats** no eran más que amenazas vanas

threaten ['θretn] ◆ *vt* amenazar • **to threaten somebody (with)** amenazar a alguien (con) ◆ *vi* amenazar

three [θriː] *número* tres ver también **six**

three-dimensional [-dɪ'menʃənl] *adj* tridimensional

threefold ['θriːfəʊld] ◆ *adj* triple ◆ *adv* tres veces

three-piece *adj* de tres piezas • **three-piece suite** tresillo

threshold ['θreʃhəʊld] *s* ❶ umbral ❷ límite • **the pain threshold** el umbral del dolor

threw [θruː] *pretérito* → **throw**

thrift shop *s* ▸ tienda de una entidad benéfica en la que se venden productos de segunda mano donados por simpatizantes

thrifty ['θrɪftɪ] *adj* ❶ ahorrativo, va ❷ frugal

thrill [θrɪl] ◆ *s* ❶ estremecimiento ❷ • **it was a thrill to see it** fue emocionante verlo ◆ *vt* entusiasmar

thrilled [θrɪld] *adj* • **thrilled (with something/to do something)** encantado, da (de algo/de hacer algo)

thriller ['θrɪlər] *s* novela/película/obra de suspenso

thrilling ['θrɪlɪŋ] *adj* emocionante

thrive [θraɪv] *vi* ❶ crecer mucho ❷ rebosar de salud ❸ prosperar

Formas irregulares de **thrive**: *pretérito* **throve**.

throat [θrəʊt] *s* garganta • **to have a sore throat** tener dolor de garganta

throb [θrɒb] *vi* ❶ latir ❷ palpitar ❸ vibrar; resonar

throes [θrəʊz] *spl* • **to be in the throes of** estar en medio de

throne [θrəʊn] *s* trono • **to be on the throne** ocupar el trono

through, thru [θruː] ◆ *adj* • **to be through with something** haber terminado algo ◆ *adv* ❶ de parte a parte; de un lado a otro • **they let us through** nos

dejaron pasar • **I read it through** lo leí hasta el final ❷ hasta el final ◆ *preposición* ❶ a través de • **to cut/travel through something** cortar/viajar por algo ❷ durante • **all through the night** durante toda la noche • **to go through an experience** pasar por una experiencia ❸ a causa de; por ❹ gracias a; por medio de • **I got it through a friend** lo conseguí a través de un amigo ❺ • **Monday through Friday** de lunes a viernes

■ **through and through** *adv* de pies a cabeza

throughout [θruː'aʊt] ◆ *preposición* ❶ a lo largo de; durante todo, durante todo, da ◆ *adv* ❶ todo el tiempo ❷ por todas partes

throve [θrəʊv] *pretérito* → **thrive**

throw [θrəʊ] ◆ *vt* ❶ tirar; aventar ❷ lanzar *(pelota)* ❸ *figurado* desconcertar

expresión **to throw yourself into something** *figurado* meterse de lleno en algo
◆ *s* lanzamiento; tiro

■ **throw away** *vt* ◌ **El objeto se puede colocar antes o después de la preposición.** ❶ tirar ❷ *figurado* desperdiciar

■ **throw out** *vt* ◌ **El objeto se puede colocar antes o después de la preposición.** ❶ tirar ❷ echar

■ **throw up** *vi familiar* vomitar

Formas irregulares de **throw**: *pretérito* **threw**, *pp* **thrown**.

throwaway ['θrəʊə,weɪ] *adj* ❶ desechable ❷ hecho, cha como quien no quiere la cosa

thrown [θrəʊn] *participio pasado* → **throw**

thru [θruː] *familiar* = **through**

thrust [θrʌst] *s* ❶ estocada *(con espada)* ❷ cuchillada ❸ arremetida *(de tropas)* ❹ TECNOLOGÍA (fuerza de) propulsión

thruway ['θruː,weɪ] *s* autopista

thug [θʌg] *s* matón

thumb [θʌm] ◆ *s* pulgar ◆ *vt familiar* • **to thumb a lift** hacer dedo

■ **thumb through** *vt* ◌ **El objeto siempre va después de la preposición al final.** hojear

thumbs down [,θʌmz-] *s* • **to get** o **be given the thumbs down a)** ser rechazado, da **b)** ser recibido, da con descontento

thumbs up [,θʌmz-] *s* • **we got** o **were given the thumbs up** nos dieron luz verde o el visto bueno

thumbtack ['θʌmtæk] *s* chincheta

thump [θʌmp] ◆ *s* ❶ puñetazo ❷ golpe seco ◆ *vt* dar un puñetazo a ◆ *vi* latir con fuerza

thunder ['θʌndər] ◆ *s* ◌ **incontable** ❶ METEOROLOGÍA truenos ❷ *figurado* estruendo ◆ *v impersonal* METEOROLOGÍA tronar ◆ *vi* retumbar

thunderbolt ['θʌndəbəʊlt] *s* rayo

thunderclap ['θʌndəklæp] *s* trueno

thunderstorm ['θʌndəstɔːm] *s* tormenta

thundery ['θʌndərɪ] *adj* tormentoso, sa

Thursday ['θɜːzdɪ] *s* jueves ver también **Saturday**

thus [ðʌs] *adv formal* ❶ por consiguiente; así que ❷ así; de esta manera

T

thwart [θwɔ:t] *vt* frustrar

thyroid ['θaɪrɔɪd] *s* tiroides

Tibet [tɪ'bet] *s* (el) Tibet

tic [tɪk] *s* tic

tick [tɪk] ◆ *s* ❶ marca o señal de visto bueno ❷ tic-tac ❸ *familiar* • **on tick** a crédito ◆ *vt* marcar (con una señal) ◆ *vi* hacer tictac

■ **tick off** *vt* ⚡ *El objeto se puede colocar antes o después de la preposición.* ❶ marcar (con una señal de visto bueno) ❷ • **to tick somebody off (for something)** echar una bronca a alguien (por algo) ❸ *familiar* fastidiar

ticked [tɪkd] *adj* enfadado, da; afectado, da

ticket ['tɪkɪt] *s* ❶ boleto ❷ entrada ❸ multa

ticket machine *s* máquina de boletos

ticket office *s* boletería

tickle ['tɪkl] *vt* ❶ hacer cosquillas a ❷ *figurado* divertir

ticklish ['tɪklɪʃ] *adj* • **to be ticklish** tener cosquillas

tick-tack-toe *s* tres en raya

tidal wave *s* maremoto

tidbit ['tɪdbɪt] *s* ❶ golosina ❷ *figurado* noticia breve e interesante

tide [taɪd] *s* ❶ marea • **high/low tide** marea alta/baja • **the tide is in/out** ha subido/bajado la marea • **the tide is coming in/going out** la marea está subiendo/bajando ❷ *figurado* oleada • **the rising tide of crime** la creciente oleada de crímenes

tidy ['taɪdɪ] ◆ *adj* ❶ ordenado, da ❷ arreglado, da ◆ *vt* ordenar; arreglar

■ **tidy up** *vt* ⚡ *El objeto se puede colocar antes o después de la preposición.* ordenar; arreglar

tie [taɪ] ◆ *s* ❶ corbata ❷ atadura *(con cordel)* ❸ vínculo; lazo ❹ DEPORTE empate ◆ *vt* ❶ • **to tie something (to o onto something)** atar algo (a algo) • **to tie something round/with something** atar algo a/con algo ❷ atar; hacer ❸ *figurado* • **to be tied to** estar ligado, da a ◆ *vi* • **to tie (with)** empatar (con)

■ **tie down** *vt* ⚡ *El objeto se puede colocar antes o después de la preposición.* *figurado* atar

■ **tie in with** *vt* ⚡ *El objeto siempre va después de la preposición al final.* concordar con

■ **tie up** *vt* ⚡ *El objeto se puede colocar antes o después de la preposición.* ❶ atar ❷ *figurado* inmovilizar ❸ *figurado* • **to be tied up with** estar ligado, da a

⬛ Formas irregulares de **tie**: *pretérito & pp* **tied**, *gerundio* **tying**.

tiebreak(er) ['taɪbreɪk(ər)] *s* ❶ TENIS muerte súbita; tiebreak ❷ pregunta adicional para romper un empate

tier [tɪər] *s* ❶ hilera *(en gradas)* ❷ piso *(de pastel)*

tiger ['taɪgər] *s* tigre

tight [taɪt] ◆ *adj* ❶ apretado, da ❷ estrecho, cha *(zapatos)* ❸ tirante *(cordel, piel)* ❹ ajustado, da *(presupuesto)* ❺ riguroso, sa *(normas)* ❻ cerrado, da *(curva)* ❼ reñido, da *(partido)* ❽ *familiar* agarrado, da *(per-*

sona) ◆ *adv* ❶ con fuerza • **to hold tight** agarrarse (fuerte) • **to shut** o **close something tight** cerrar algo bien ❷ de modo tirante

■ **tights** *spl* medias

tighten ['taɪtn] ◆ *vt* ❶ • **to tighten your hold** o **grip on something** coger con más fuerza algo ❷ tensar *(cuerda)* ❸ apretar *(nudo)* ❹ apretarse *(cinturón)* ❺ intensificar *(normas, sistema)* ◆ *vi* tensarse *(cuerda)*

tightfisted [ˌtaɪt'fɪstɪd] *adj familiar & despectivo* agarrado, da

tightly ['taɪtlɪ] *adv* ❶ con fuerza ❷ bien ❸ apretadamente

tightrope ['taɪtrəʊp] *s* cuerda floja

expresión **to be on** o **walking a tightrope** andar o bailar en la cuerda floja

tile [taɪl] *s* ❶ teja ❷ baldosa ❸ azulejo

tiled [taɪld] *adj* ❶ tejado, da ❷ embaldosado, da ❸ alicatado, da

till [tɪl] ◆ *preposición* hasta • **till now/then** hasta ahora/entonces ◆ *conjunción* hasta que • **wait till he arrives** espera hasta que llegue ◆ *s* caja (registradora)

tilt [tɪlt] ◆ *vt* inclinar ◆ *vi* inclinarse

timber ['tɪmbər] *s* ❶ ⚡ *incontable* madera *(para la construcción)* ❷ cuaderna; viga

time [taɪm] ◆ *s* ❶ tiempo • **in good time** con tiempo • **to take time** llevar tiempo • **on time** puntualmente • **ahead of time** temprano • **it's (about) time to...** ya es hora de... ❷ hora • **what time is it?, what's the time?** ¿qué hora es? • **the time is three o'clock** son las tres • **in a week's/year's time** dentro de una semana/un año ❸ rato; tiempo • **it was a long time before he came** pasó mucho rato antes de que viniera • **for a time** durante un tiempo ❹ época • **at that time** en aquella época ❺ vez • **three times a week** tres veces a la semana • **from time to time** de vez en cuando ❻ MÚSICA compás • **to keep time** llevar el compás

expresiones **to have no time for** no poder con; no aguantar ▶ **to pass the time** pasar el rato ▶ **to play for time** intentar ganar tiempo

◆ *vt* ❶ programar ❷ cronometrar ❸ elegir el momento oportuno para

■ **times** ◆ *s* • **four times as much as me** cuatro veces más que yo ◆ *preposición* MATEMÁTICAS • **4 times 5** 4 por 5

■ **about time** *adv* • **it's about time** ya va siendo hora

■ **at a time** *adv* • **for months at a time** durante meses seguidos • **one at a time** de uno en uno

■ **at times** *adv* a veces

■ **at the same time** *adv* al mismo tiempo

■ **for the time being** *adv* de momento

■ **in time** *adv* ❶ • **in time (for)** a tiempo (para) ❷ con el tiempo

time bomb *s* ❶ bomba de relojería ❷ *figurado* bomba

timeless ['taɪmlɪs] *adj* eterno, na

time limit *s* plazo

timely ['taɪmlɪ] *adj* oportuno, na

time off *s* tiempo libre

time out *s* DEPORTE tiempo muerto

timer ['taɪmər] *s* temporizador

timetable ['taɪm,teɪbl] *s* ❶ horario ❷ programa

time zone *s* huso horario

timid ['tɪmɪd] *adj* tímido, da

timing ['taɪmɪŋ] *s* ☼ *incontable* ❶ • she made her comment with perfect timing su comentario fue hecho en el momento más oportuno ❷ • the timing of the election is crucial es crucial que las elecciones se celebren en el momento oportuno

tin [tɪn] *s* estaño • **tin plate** hojalata

tin can *s* lata

tinfoil ['tɪnfɔɪl] *s* ☼ *incontable* papel de estaño

tinge [tɪndʒ] *s* ❶ matiz ❷ ligera sensación

tinged [tɪndʒd] *adj* • **tinged with** con un toque de

tingle ['tɪŋgl] *vi* • **my feet are tingling** siento hormigueo en los pies

tinker ['tɪŋkər] *vi* hacer chapuzas • **to tinker with** enredar con

tinkle ['tɪŋkl] *vi* tintinear

tint [tɪnt] *s* tinte; matiz

tinted ['tɪntɪd] *adj* tintado, da; ahumado, da

tiny ['taɪnɪ] *adj* diminuto, ta; pequeñito, ta

tip [tɪp] ◆ *s* ❶ punta ❷ propina ❸ consejo ◆ *vt* ❶ inclinar; ladear ❷ vaciar; verter ❸ dar una propina a ◆ *vi* ❶ inclinarse; ladearse ❷ derramarse

■ **tip over** ◆ *vt* ☼ *El objeto se puede colocar antes o después de la preposición.* volcar ◆ *vi* volcarse

tip-off *s* información (confidencial)

tipsy ['tɪpsɪ] *adj familiar & desusado* alegre

tiptoe ['tɪptəʊ] *s* • **on tiptoe** de puntillas

tire ['taɪər] ◆ *s* llanta ◆ *vt* cansar ◆ *vi* • **to tire (of)** cansarse (de)

tired ['taɪəd] *adj* • **tired (of something/of doing something)** cansado, da (de algo/de hacer algo)

tireless ['taɪələs] *adj* incansable

tire pressure *s* presión de las llantas

tiresome ['taɪəsəm] *adj* pesado, da

tiring ['taɪərɪŋ] *adj* cansado, da

tissue ['tɪʃuː] *s* ❶ pañuelo de papel ❷ ☼ *incontable* BIOLOGÍA tejido

tissue paper *s* ☼ *incontable* papel de seda

tit for tat [-'tæt] *s* • **it's tit for tat** donde las dan las toman

title ['taɪtl] *s* título

title deed *s* título de propiedad

title role *s* papel principal

titter ['tɪtər] *vi* reírse por lo bajo

TM *abreviatura escrita de* **trademark**

to
◆ *preposición*

☼ *acento tónico* [tuː], *acento atónico antes de consonante* [tə], *acento atónico antes de vocal* [tʊ]

❶ [*indica una dirección*]
• **she went to New York/to Mexico/to school** se fue a Nueva York/México/la escuela
• **I'm going to the butcher's** voy a la carnicería
• **turn to the left/right** gira a la izquierda/derecha

❷ [*indica un destinatario*]
• **to give something to somebody** dar algo a alguien
• **I'm writing a letter to my daughter** estoy escribiéndole una carta a mi hija

❸ [*para expresar una emoción*]
• **to my delight/surprise, my parcel arrived very quickly** para mi deleite/sorpresa, el paquete llegó muy rápido

❹ [*para expresar una opinión*]
• **to me, it is a real miracle** para mí, es un auténtico milagro
• **it seemed quite unnecessary to me/him** me/le pareció bastante innecesario

❺ [*hasta*]
• **she can already count to 10** sabe contar hasta 10
• **we work from 9 to 5** trabajamos de 9 a 5
• **I didn't stay to the end of the movie** no me quedé hasta el final de la película
• **she sang the baby to sleep** arrulló al bebé

❻ [*expresa un contacto físico*]
• **they were dancing cheek to cheek** bailaban muy agarrados
• **stand back to back** poneros dándoos las espaldas

❼ [*para dar la hora*]
• **it's ten to three/quarter to one** son las tres menos diez/la una menos cuarto

❽ [*indica una proporción*]
• **this car does 40 miles to the gallon** ≃ este carro consumo 7 litros cada cien kilómetros
• **there are 200 people to the square kilometer** hay 200 habitantes por km2
• **the odds against it happening are a million to one** las probabilidades de que eso ocurra son de una en un millón

❾ [*indica una relación entre dos elementos*]
• **he gave me the key to his car** me dio la llave de su carro

◆ **+** *infinitivo*

❶ [*después de ciertos verbos*]
• **I'd like to be on holiday** me gustaría estar de vacaciones
• **she tried to help her brother** intentó ayudar a su hermano
• **she wants to go to the movies** quiere ir al cine

T

❷ [*después de ciertos adjetivos*]
• **it's difficult to do** es difícil de hacer
• **we're ready to go** estamos listos para irnos
❸ [*para expresar el objetivo*]
• **he worked hard to pass his exam** trabajó duro para aprobar el examen
• **they left early to catch the train** se fueron pronto para coger el tren
• **to be honest,...** para serte sincero,...
• **to sum up,...** en resumen,...
❹ [*sustituye una proposición subordinada conjuntiva*]
• **he told me to leave** me dijo que me fuera
❺ [*para referirse a una acción anterior*]
• **I meant to call him but I forgot to** tenía intención de llamarle pero me olvidé

to

No olvidemos que to lleva el sustantivo directamente después sin the en algunas expresiones (he's gone **to** work/school/prison/hospital/bed/church).

Por el contrario to no debe utilizarse con la palabra home en frases como I'm going home *me voy a casa*.

toad [təʊd] *s* sapo

toadstool ['təʊdstuːl] *s* seta venenosa

toast [təʊst] ◆ *s* ❶ ☼ *incontable* pan tostado • **a slice of toast** una tostada ❷ brindis ◆ *vt* ❶ tostar ❷ brindar por

toasted sandwich [ˌtəʊstɪd-] *s* sándwich tostado

toaster ['təʊstər] *s* tostador, ra

tobacco [tə'bækəʊ] *s* tabaco

toboggan [tə'bɒgən] *s* trineo; tobogán

today [tə'deɪ] ◆ *s* ❶ hoy • **today's date** la fecha de hoy • **what is today's date?** ¿qué día es hoy? • **today's paper** el periódico de hoy • **as from today** a partir de hoy ❷ hoy (en día) ◆ *adv* ❶ hoy • **what's the date today?, what date is it today** ¿qué fecha es hoy? • **today is the 6th of January** hoy es el 6 de enero • **what day is it today?** ¿qué día es hoy? • **it's Sunday today** hoy es domingo • **a week ago today** hoy hace una semana • **a week (from) today** de aquí a una semana ❷ hoy (en día)

toddler ['tɒdlər] *s* niño pequeño, niña pequeña (que empieza a andar)

to-do *s familiar* jaleo

El plural de to-do es to-dos.

toe [təʊ] ◆ *s* ❶ dedo (del pie) ❷ punta ❸ puntera ◆ *vt* • **to toe the line** acatar las normas

toenail ['təʊneɪl] *s* uña del dedo del pie

toffee ['tɒfɪ] *s* caramelo

together [tə'geðər] *adv* ❶ juntos, tas • **all together** todos juntos • **to stick together** pegar • **to go (well) together** combinar bien ❷ a la vez; juntos, tas
■ **together with** *preposición* junto con

toilet ['tɔɪlɪt] *s* ❶ excusado • **to go to the toilet** ir al baño ❷ baño

toilet bag *s* neceser

toilet paper *s* ☼ *incontable* papel higiénico

toiletries ['tɔɪlɪtrɪz] *spl* artículos de tocador

toilet roll *s* rollo de papel higiénico

toilet water *s* (agua de) colonia

token ['təʊkn] ◆ *adj* simbólico, ca ◆ *s* ❶ vale ❷ ficha ❸ muestra; símbolo • **as a token of our appreciation** como muestra de nuestro agradecimiento
■ **by the same token** *adv* del mismo modo

told [təʊld] *pretérito* & *participio pasado* → **tell**

tolerable ['tɒlərəbl] *adj* tolerable; pasable

tolerance ['tɒlərəns] *s* tolerancia

tolerant ['tɒlərənt] *adj* tolerante

tolerate ['tɒləreɪt] *vt* ❶ soportar; tolerar ❷ tolerar

toll [təʊl] ◆ *s* ❶ • **death toll** número de víctimas ❷ peaje
expresión to take its toll hacer mella
◆ *vi* tocar; doblar

toll-free *adv* • **to call a number toll-free** llamar a un número gratis

tomato [tə'meɪtəʊ] *s* jitomate

El plural de tomato es tomatoes.

tomb [tuːm] *s* tumba; sepulcro

tomboy ['tɒmbɔɪ] *s* niña poco feminina

tombstone ['tuːmstəʊn] *s* lápida

tomcat ['tɒmkæt] *s* gato (macho)

tomorrow [tə'mɒrəʊ] ◆ *s* *literal & figurado* mañana • **tomorrow is Sunday** mañana es domingo • **the day after tomorrow** pasado mañana • **tomorrow night** mañana por la noche • **he was drinking like there was no tomorrow** bebía como si se fuera a acabar el mundo • **tomorrow's world** el futuro ◆ *adv* mañana • **see you tomorrow** hasta mañana • **a week (from) tomorrow** dentro de una semana, a partir de mañana • **it happened a year ago tomorrow** mañana hará un año que ocurrió

ton [tʌn] *s* tonelada (= 1000 kg)
■ **tons** *spl familiar* • **tons (of)** un montón (de)

Dos plurales: ton o tons.

tone [təʊn] *s* ❶ tono ❷ señal
■ **tone down** *vt* ☼ *El objeto se puede colocar antes o después de la preposición.* suavizar; moderar
■ **tone up** *vt* ☼ *El objeto se puede colocar antes o después de la preposición.* poner en forma

tone-deaf *adj* que no tiene (buen) oído

tongs [tɒŋz] *spl* ❶ tenazas; pinzas; tenacillas

tongue [tʌŋ] *s* ❶ lengua ❷ lengüeta

tongue-in-cheek *adj* • **it was only tongue-in-cheek** no iba en serio

tongue-tied [-,taɪd] *adj* incapaz de hablar *(por timidez o nervios)*

tongue twister [-,twɪstər] *s* trabalenguas

tonic ['tɒnɪk] *s* ❶ tónico ❷ tónica

tonic water *s* agua tónica

tonight [tə'naɪt] ◆ *s* esta noche ◆ *adv* esta noche

tonne [tʌn] *s* tonelada (métrica)

Dos plurales: **tonne** o **tonnes**.

tonsil ['tɒnsl] *s* amígdala • **to have your tonsils out** operarse de las amígdalas

tonsillitis [,tɒnsɪ'laɪtɪs] *s* 🔆 *incontable* amigdalitis

too [tu:] *adv* ❶ también • **me too** yo también ❷ demasiado • **too much** demasiado • **too many things** demasiadas cosas • **it finished all** o **only too soon** terminó demasiado pronto • **I'd be only too happy to help** me encantaría ayudarte • **not too...** no muy...

took [tʊk] *pretérito* → **take**

tool [tu:l] *s* herramienta • **garden tools** útiles del jardín

tool bar *s* INFORMÁTICA barra de herramientas

tool box *s* caja de herramientas

tool kit *s* juego de herramientas

toot [tu:t] ◆ *s* bocinazo ◆ *vi* tocar la bocina

tooth [tu:θ] *s* diente • **to brush your teeth** cepillarse o lavarse los dientes • **he had a tooth out** le sacaron un diente

El plural de **tooth** es **teeth**.

toothache ['tu:θeɪk] *s* dolor de muelas

toothbrush ['tu:θbrʌʃ] *s* cepillo de dientes

toothpaste ['tu:θpeɪst] *s* pasta de dientes

toothpick ['tu:θpɪk] *s* palillo

top [tɒp] ◆ *adj* ❶ de arriba; de encima ❷ importante • **to be a top model** ser top model • **she got the top mark** sacó la mejor nota ❸ máximo, ma • **at top speed** a máxima velocidad • **to be top secret** ser altamente confidencial ◆ *s* ❶ parte superior o de arriba ❷ cabeza; principio ❸ copa ❹ cumbre; cima • **at the top of the stairs** en lo alto de la escalera • **from top to bottom** de pies a cabeza • **on top** encima ❺ tapa; tapón; capuchón ❻ superficie ❼ blusa ❽ camiseta ❾ parte de arriba ❿ cabeza

expresión **at the top of your voice** a voz en grito ◆ *vt* ❶ estar a la cabeza de ❷ superar ❸ exceder

■ **on top of** *preposición* ❶ encima de • **to be feeling on top of the world** estar en la gloria ❷ además de

■ **top off** *vt* 🔆 *El objeto se puede colocar antes o después de la preposición.* volver a llenar

top floor *s* último piso

topic ['tɒpɪk] *s* tema; asunto

topical ['tɒpɪkl] *adj* actual

topless ['tɒplɪs] *adj* en topless

top-level *adj* de alto nivel

topmost ['tɒpməʊst] *adj* más alto, ta

top-of-the-line *adj* de gama alta

topping ['tɒpɪŋ] *s* capa • **with a topping of cream** cubierto de nata

topple ['tɒpl] ◆ *vt* ❶ derribar ❷ derrocar ◆ *vi* venirse abajo

top-secret *adj* sumamente secreto, sumamente secreta

top-up *s* • **can I give you a top-up?** ¿quieres que te ponga más?

top-up card *s* tarjeta de recarga

torch [tɔ:tʃ] *s* antorcha

tore [tɔ:r] *pretérito* → **tear**

torment ◆ *s* [ˈtɔ:ment] tormento • **she waited in torment** esperaba atormentada ◆ *vt* [tɔ:ˈment] ❶ atormentar ❷ fastidiar

torn [tɔ:n] *participio pasado* → **tear**

tornado [tɔ:ˈneɪdəʊ] *s* tornado

Dos plurales: **tornadoes** o **tornados**.

torpedo [tɔ:ˈpi:dəʊ] *s* torpedo

El plural de **torpedo** es **torpedoes**.

torrent ['tɒrənt] *s* torrente

torrid ['tɒrɪd] *adj* ❶ tórrido, da ❷ *figurado* apasionado, da

tortoise ['tɔ:təs] *s* tortuga (de tierra)

torture ['tɔ:tʃər] ◆ *s* tortura ◆ *vt* torturar

toss [tɒs] ◆ *vt* ❶ tirar ❷ sacudir *(cabeza)* ❸ remover *(ensalada)* ❹ voltear en el aire *(hot cake)*

expresión **to toss a coin** echarse un volado ◆ *vi* • **to toss and turn** dar vueltas (en la cama)

■ **toss up** *vi* echarlo a águila o sol

total ['təʊtl] ◆ *adj* total ◆ *s* total ◆ *vt* ❶ sumar ❷ *familiar* dejar hecho una ruina ◆ *vi* ascender a

Formas irregulares de **total**: *pretérito & pp* **totaled**, *gerundio* **totaling**.

totalitarian [,təʊtælɪ'teərɪən] *adj* totalitario, ria

totally ['təʊtəlɪ] *adv* totalmente

tote bag [təʊt-] *s* bolsa (de la compra)

touch [tʌtʃ] ◆ *s* ❶ tacto ❷ toque • **to put the finishing touches to something** dar el último toque a algo ❸ • **to get/keep in touch (with)** ponerse/mantenerse en contacto (con) • **to lose touch (with)** perder el contacto (con) • **to be out of touch with** no estar al tanto de ❹ DEPORTE • **in touch** fuera de banda ❺ • **a touch (of)** un poquito (de) ◆ *vt* ❶ tocar • **you haven't touched your food** no has tocado la comida ❷ conmover ❸ igualar • **nobody can touch her for professionalism** nadie la iguala en profesionalismo ◆ *vi* tocarse

■ **touch down** *vi* aterrizar

■ **touch on** *vt* 🔆 *El objeto siempre va después de la preposición al final.* tratar por encima

touch-and-go *adj* dudoso, sa; poco seguro, poco segura

touchdown ['tʌtʃdaʊn] *s* ❶ aterrizaje ❷ ensayo

touched [tʌtʃt] *adj* emocionado, da

touching ['tʌtʃɪŋ] *adj* conmovedor, ra

touchline ['tʌtʃlaɪn] *s* línea de banda

T

touchscreen ['tʌtʃskriːn] *s* pantalla táctil

touchy ['tʌtʃɪ] *adj* ❶ • **touchy (about)** susceptible (con) ❷ delicado, da

tough [tʌf] *adj* ❶ fuerte ❷ resistente *(material)* ❸ duro, ra *(carne, norma)* ❹ difícil ❺ peligroso, sa

toughen ['tʌfn] *vt* endurecer

toupee ['tuːpeɪ] *s* peluquín

tour [tʊər] ◆ *s* ❶ viaje; recorrido • **to go on a tour of Germany** hacer un recorrido por Alemania ❷ gira ❸ visita ◆ *vt* ❶ visitar ❷ recorrer; viajar por ◆ *vi* estar de gira

touring ['tʊərɪŋ] *s* viajes turísticos

tourism ['tʊərɪzm] *s* turismo

tourist ['tʊərɪst] *s* turista

tourist (information) office *s* oficina de turismo

tournament ['tɔːnəmənt] *s* torneo

tour operator *s* touroperador

tout [taʊt] ◆ *s* revendedor, ra ◆ *vt* revender ◆ *vi* • **to tout for something** solicitar algo • **to tout for business** tratar de captar clientes

tow [təʊ] ◆ *s* • **to give somebody a tow** remolcar a alguien • **in tow with somebody** acompañado de alguien ◆ *vt* remolcar

toward [tə'wɔːd] *preposición* ❶ hacia ❷ para

towaway zone ['təʊəweɪ-] *s* ≃ zona de estacionamiento prohibido

towel ['taʊəl] *s* toalla

toweling ['taʊəlɪŋ] *s* ⚙ *incontable* (tejido de) toalla

towel rail *s* toallero

tower ['taʊər] ◆ *s* torre ◆ *vi* • **to tower over somebody** ser mucho más alto, ta que alguien

towering ['taʊərɪŋ] *adj* altísimo, ma

town [taʊn] *s* ❶ ciudad ❷ pueblo ❸ centro (de la ciudad)

expresión **to go out on the town** irse de juerga ▶ **to go to town** a) *figurado* emplearse a fondo b) tirar la casa por la ventana

town center *s* centro (de la ciudad)

town council *s* ayuntamiento

town hall *s* delegación

town plan *s* plano de la ciudad

town planning *s* urbanismo

township ['taʊnʃɪp] *s* ≃ municipio

tow truck *s* (coche) grúa

toxic ['tɒksɪk] *adj* tóxico, ca

toy [tɔɪ] *s* juguete

■ **toy with** *vt* ⚙ *El objeto siempre va después de la preposición al final.* ❶ acariciar ❷ jugetear con

toy shop *s* juguetería

trace [treɪs] ◆ *s* ❶ rastro; huella • **there's no trace of her** no hay rastro de ella ❷ pizca ◆ *vt* ❶ localizar; encontrar ❷ describir ❸ calcar

track [træk] ◆ *s* ❶ sendero ❷ *DEPORTE* pista ❸ *FERROCARRIL* vía ❹ rastro; huella ❺ canción

expresión **to be on the right/wrong track** ir por el buen/mal camino

◆ *vt* seguir la pista de

■ **track down** *vt* ⚙ *El objeto se puede colocar antes o después de la preposición.* localizar

track record *s* historial • **to have a good track record** tener un buen historial

traction ['trækʃn] *s* tracción • **to have your leg in traction** tener la pierna escayolada en alto

tractor ['træktər] *s* tractor

tractor-trailer *s* camión articulado

trade [treɪd] ◆ *s* ❶ ⚙ *incontable* comercio ❷ oficio • **by trade** de oficio ◆ *vt* • **to trade something (for) something** cambiar algo (por) algo ◆ *vi* ❶ *COMERCIO* • **to trade (with)** comerciar (con) ❷ • **to trade at** o **with** hacer sus compras en

■ **trade in** *vt* ⚙ *El objeto se puede colocar antes o después de la preposición.* dar como entrada

trade fair *s* feria de muestras

trademark ['treɪdmɑːk] *s* *COMERCIO* marca comercial

trade name *s* *COMERCIO* nombre comercial

trader ['treɪdər] *s* comerciante

tradesman ['treɪdzmən] *s* ❶ comerciante ❷ tendero

El plural de **tradesman** es **tradesmen** ['treɪdzmən].

trading ['treɪdɪŋ] *s* ⚙ *incontable* comercio

tradition [trə'dɪʃn] *s* tradición

traditional [trə'dɪʃənl] *adj* tradicional

traffic ['træfɪk] ◆ *s* ❶ tráfico ❷ • **traffic (in)** tráfico (de) ◆ *vi* • **to traffic in** traficar con

Formas irregulares de **traffic**: *pret* & *pp* **trafficked**, *gerundio* **trafficking**.

traffic circle *s* rotonda

traffic jam *s* embotellamiento

trafficker ['træfɪkər] *s* • **trafficker (in)** traficante (de)

traffic lights *spl* semáforos

tragedy ['trædʒədɪ] *s* tragedia

tragic ['trædʒɪk] *adj* trágico, ca

trail [treɪl] ◆ *s* ❶ sendero; camino ❷ rastro; huellas • **a trail of smoke** un rastro de humo • **they left a trail of clues** dejaron un rastro de pistas • **they are hot on his trail** le están pisando los talones

expresión **to blaze a trail** *figurado* marcar la pauta ▶ **to be on the trail of somebody/something** seguir la pista de alguien/algo

◆ *vt* ❶ arrastrar ❷ ir por detrás de ◆ *vi* ❶ arrastrarse ❷ andar con desgana ❸ ir perdiendo

■ **trail away, trail off** *vi* apagarse

trailer ['treɪlər] *s* ❶ remolque ❷ roulotte; caravana ❸ *CINE* trailer

T

trailer park *s* camping para roulottes o caravanas

train [treɪn] ◆ *s* ❶ *FERROCARRIL* tren • **to go by train** ir en tren ❷ cola ◆ *vt* ❶ • **to train somebody (to do something)** enseñar a alguien (a hacer algo) • **to train somebody in something** preparar a alguien para algo ❷ • **to train somebody (as something)** formar o preparar a alguien (como algo) ❸ amaestrar ❹ *DEPORTE* • **to train somebody (for)** entrenar a alguien (para) ❺ apuntar ◆ *vi* ❶ estudiar • **to train as** formarse o prepararse como • **to train to be a teacher** estudiar para ser profesor ❷ *DEPORTE* • **to train (for)** entrenarse (para)

trained [treɪnd] *adj* cualificado, da

trainee [treɪ'ni:] *s* aprendiz, za

trainer ['treɪnər] *s* ❶ amaestrador, ra ❷ *DEPORTE* entrenador, ra

training ['treɪnɪŋ] *s* ☼ *incontable* ❶ • **training (in)** formación o preparación (para) ❷ *DEPORTE* entrenamiento • **to be in training (for something)** estar entrenando para algo

training college *s* escuela normal

train station *s* estación de ferrocarril

trait [treɪt] *s* rasgo ; característica

traitor ['treɪtər] *s* • **traitor (to)** traidor, ra (a)

trajectory [trə'dʒektərɪ] *s* trayectoria

tramp [træmp] *s* ❶ vagabundo, da ❷ *familiar* fulana

trample ['træmpl] *vt* pisar ; pisotear • **to be trampled underfoot** ser pisoteado, da

trampoline ['træmpəli:n] *s* cama elástica

trance [trɑ:ns] *s* trance • **to go into a trance** entrar en trance

tranquil ['træŋkwɪl] *adj* *literario* tranquilo, la ; apacible

tranquilizer ['træŋkwɪlaɪzər] *s* tranquilizante

transaction [træn'zækʃn] *s* transacción • **money transactions** transacciones de dinero

transcend [træn'send] *vt* *formal* ir más allá de

transcript ['trænskrɪpt] *s* expediente académico

transfer ◆ *s* ['trænsfɜ:r] ❶ transferencia ❷ traslado *(por empleo)* ❸ *DEPORTE* traspaso ❹ calcomanía *(dibujo)* ❺ billete válido para transbordar a otro camión, tren, etc ◆ *vt* [træns'fɜ:ɒr] ❶ trasladar ❷ transferir ◆ *vi* [træns'fɜ:ɒr] • **he transferred to a different department** lo trasladaron a otro departamento

transfix [træns'fɪks] *vt* paralizar • **transfixed with** paralizado, da por

transform [træns'fɔ:m] *vt* • **to transform something/somebody (into)** transformar algo/a alguien (en)

transfusion [træns'fju:ʒn] *s* transfusión

transient ['trænzɪənt] ◆ *adj* *formal* transitorio, ria ; pasajero, ra ◆ *s* viajero, ra de paso

transistor [træn'zɪstər] *s* transistor

transit ['trænsɪt] *s* transporte • **in transit** en tránsito

transition [træn'zɪʃn] *s* • **transition (from something to something)** transición (de algo a algo)

transitive ['trænzɪtɪv] *adj* *GRAMÁTICA* transitivo, va

transitory ['trænzɪtrɪ] *adj* transitorio, ria

translate [træns'leɪt] *vt* traducir

translation [træns'leɪʃn] *s* traducción

translator [træns'leɪtər] *s* traductor, ra

transmission [trænz'mɪʃn] *s* transmisión

transmit [trænz'mɪt] *vt* transmitir

transmitter [trænz'mɪtər] *s* *ELECTRÓNICA* transmisor

transparency [trans'pærənsɪ] *s* ❶ transparencia ❷ diapositiva

transparent [træns'pærənt] *adj* ❶ transparente ❷ claro, ra

transplant *s* ['trænsplɑ:nt] trasplante • **he had a heart transplant** le hicieron un trasplante de corazón

transport ◆ *s* ['trænspɔ:t] transporte ◆ *vt* [træn'spɔ:t] transportar

transportation [,trænspɔ:'teɪʃn] *s* transporte

trap [træp] *s* trampa • **to lay a trap (for)** tender una trampa (a) ◆ *vt* ❶ coger con trampa ❷ atrapar ; engañar ❸ • **she trapped her fingers in the door** se pilló los dedos en la puerta

trapdoor [,træp'dɔ:r] *s* trampa

trash [træʃ] *s* *literal & figurado* basura

trashcan ['træʃkæn] *s* cubo de la basura

traumatic [trɔ:'mætɪk] *adj* traumático, ca

travel ['trævl] ◆ *s* ☼ *incontable* viajes ◆ *vt* ❶ viajar por ❷ recorrer ◆ *vi* viajar

Formas irregulares de **travel**: *pretérito & pp* **traveled**, *gerundio* **traveling**.

travel agency *s* agencia de viajes

travel agent *s* empleado, da de una agencia de viajes • **travel agent's** agencia de viajes

traveler ['trævlər] *s* viajero, ra

traveling ['trævlɪŋ] *adj* ambulante

traveller's check *s* cheque de viajero

travelsick ['trævəlsɪk] *adj* que se marea al viajar • **to be** o **feel travelsick** estar mareado, da

trawler ['trɔ:lər] *s* trainera

tray [treɪ] *s* bandeja

treacherous ['tretʃərəs] *adj* ❶ traicionero, ra ❷ traidor, ra ❸ peligroso, sa

treachery ['tretʃərɪ] *s* traición

tread [tred] ◆ *s* ❶ banda ❷ pasos ◆ *vi* andar **expresión** **to tread carefully** *figurado* andar con pies de plomo

Formas irregulares de **tread**: *pretérito* **trod**, *pp* **trodden**.

treason ['tri:zn] *s* traición

treasure ['treʒər] ◆ *s* *literal & figurado* tesoro ◆ *vt* guardar como oro en paño

T

treasurer ['treʒərər] s tesorero, ra

treat [tri:t] ◆ *vt* ❶ tratar • **to treat somebody well/badly** tratar bien/mal a alguien • **to treat something as a joke** tomarse algo como si fuera broma • **to treat somebody for something** MEDICINA tratar a alguien de algo ❷ • **to treat somebody (to)** invitar a alguien (a) ◆ *s* regalo • **it's my treat** yo invito • **he took me out to dinner as a treat** me invitó a cenar

treatise ['tri:tɪs] *s formal* • **treatise (on)** tratado (sobre)

treatment ['tri:tmənt] s ❶ MEDICINA • **treatment (for)** tratamiento (para) ❷ trato

treaty ['tri:tɪ] s tratado

treble ['trebl] ◆ *adj* ❶ MÚSICA de tiple ❷ triple ◆ *vt* triplicar ◆ *vi* triplicarse

treble clef s clave de sol

tree [tri:] s BOTÁNICA & INFORMÁTICA árbol

tree-hugger s *familiar, humorístico & despectivo* ecologista

treetop ['tri:tɒp] s copa (de árbol)

tree-trunk s tronco (de árbol)

trek [trek] s viaje largo y difícil

tremble ['trembl] *vi* temblar • **to tremble with cold/fear** temblar de frío/miedo

tremendous [trɪ'mendəs] *adj* ❶ tremendo, da ❷ *familiar* estupendo, da

tremor ['tremər] s ❶ estremecimiento ❷ temblor

trench [trentʃ] s ❶ zanja ❷ MILITAR trinchera

trend [trend] s ❶ tendencia ❷ moda • **to set a trend** establecer una moda

trendy ['trendɪ] *adj familiar* ❶ moderno, na ❷ de moda

trepidation [ˌtrepɪ'deɪʃn] s *formal* • **in** o **with trepidation** con ansiedad o agitación

trespass ['trespəs] *vi* entrar ilegalmente • **to trespass on** entrar ilegalmente en • **'no trespassing'** prohibido el paso'

trespasser ['trespəsər] s intruso, sa • **'trespassers will be prosecuted'** los intrusos serán sancionados por la ley'

trial ['traɪəl] s ❶ DERECHO juicio; proceso • **to be on trial (for)** ser procesado, da (por) • **to be brought to trial** ser llevado, da a juicio ❷ prueba • **on trial** de prueba • **by trial and error** a base de probar

triangle ['traɪæŋgl] s ❶ GEOMETRÍA & MÚSICA triángulo ❷ escuadra; cartabón

tribe [traɪb] s tribu

tribunal [traɪ'bju:nl] s tribunal

tributary ['trɪbjʊtrɪ] s afluente

tribute ['trɪbju:t] s ❶ tributo • **to be a tribute to** hacer honor a ❷ ⚡ *incontable* • **to pay tribute (to)** rendir homenaje (a)

trice [traɪs] s • **in a trice** en un dos por tres

trick [trɪk] ◆ *s* ❶ truco ❷ trampa ❸ broma • **to play a trick on somebody** gastarle una broma a alguien ❹ juego (de manos) ❺ truco

expresión **that should do the trick** eso es lo que necesitamos

◆ *vt* engañar • **to trick somebody into doing something** engañar a alguien para que haga algo

trickery ['trɪkərɪ] s ⚡ *incontable* engaño

trickle ['trɪkl] ◆ *s* hilo ◆ *vi* ❶ resbalar *(formando un hilo)* ❷ • **to trickle in/out** llegar/salir poco a poco

tricky ['trɪkɪ] *adj* difícil

tricycle ['traɪsɪkl] s triciclo

tried [traɪd] *adj* • **tried and tested** probado, da

trifle ['traɪfl] s nadería

■ **a trifle** *adv formal* ligeramente

trifling ['traɪflɪŋ] *adj despectivo* trivial

trigger ['trɪgər] s gatillo

■ **trigger off** *vt* ⚡ *El objeto se puede colocar antes o después de la preposición.* desencadenar

trill [trɪl] s trino

trim [trɪm] ◆ *adj* ❶ limpio y arreglado, limpia y arreglada ❷ esbelto, ta ◆ *s* recorte ◆ *vt* ❶ recortar ❷ • **to trim something (with)** adornar algo (con)

trimmings ['trɪmɪŋz] *spl* ❶ adornos ❷ guarnición

trinket ['trɪŋkɪt] s baratija

trio ['tri:əʊ] s trío

El plural de **trio** es **trios**.

trip [trɪp] ◆ *s* viaje • **to be (away) on a trip** estar de viaje • **a trip to London** un viaje a Londres ◆ *vt* poner la zancadilla a ◆ *vi* tropezar • **to trip over something** tropezar con algo

■ **trip up** *vt* ⚡ *El objeto se puede colocar antes o después de la preposición.* poner la zancadilla a

tripe [traɪp] s ⚡ *incontable* ❶ COCINA mondongo ❷ *familiar* tonterías

triple ['trɪpl] ◆ *adj* triple ◆ *adv* • **triple the quantity** el triple ◆ *vt* triplicar ◆ *vi* triplicarse

triple jump s • **the triple jump** el triple salto

triplets ['trɪplɪts] *spl* trillizos, zas

triplicate ['trɪplɪkət] s • **in triplicate** por triplicado

tripod ['traɪpɒd] s trípode

trite [traɪt] *adj despectivo* trillado, da

triumph ['traɪəmf] ◆ *s* triunfo ◆ *vi* • **to triumph (over)** triunfar (sobre)

trivia ['trɪvɪə] s ⚡ *incontable* trivialidades

trivial ['trɪvɪəl] *adj despectivo* trivial

trod [trɒd] *pretérito* → **tread**

trodden ['trɒdn] *participio pasado* → **tread**

trolley ['trɒlɪ] s tranvía

El plural de **trolley** es **trolleys**.

trolley case s maleta tipo carrito

trombone [trɒm'bəʊn] s trombón

troop [tru:p] ◆ *s* grupo; bandada ◆ *vi* ir en grupo

■ **troops** *spl* tropas

■ **troop in** *vi* entrar en tropel

■ **troop out** *vi* salir en tropel

trooper ['tru:pər] *s* ❶ *MILITAR* soldado de caballería ❷ miembro de la policía estatal

trophy ['trəʊfɪ] *s DEPORTE* trofeo

tropical ['trɒpɪkl] *adj* tropical

tropics ['trɒpɪks] *spl* • **the tropics** el trópico

trot [trɒt] ◆ *s* ❶ trote ❷ paso rápido ◆ *vi* ❶ trotar ❷ andar con pasos rápidos

■ **on the trot** *adv familiar* • **three times on the trot** tres veces seguidas

trouble ['trʌbl] ◆ *s* :ᄋ̈:*incontable* ❶ molestia ❷ problema • **to tell somebody your troubles** contarle a alguien sus problemas • **what seems to be the trouble?** ¿cuál es el problema? • **would it be too much trouble to ask you to...?** ¿tendría inconveniente en...? • **to be in trouble** tener problemas • **to have trouble doing something** tener problemas haciendo algo ❸:ᄋ̈:*incontable* dolor ❹ enfermedad • **heart trouble** problemas cardiacos • **back trouble** problemas de espalda • **I'm having trouble with my leg** me está molestando la pierna ❺ :ᄋ̈:*incontable* problemas ◆ *vt* ❶ preocupar ❷ molestar

■ **troubles** *spl* ❶ problemas ❷ *POLÍTICA* conflicto

troubled ['trʌbld] *adj* ❶ preocupado, da ❷ agitado, da; turbulento, ta

troublemaker ['trʌbl,meɪkər] *s* alborotador, ra

troublesome ['trʌblsəm] *adj* molesto, ta

troupe [tru:p] *s* compañía

trousers ['traʊzəz] *spl* pantalones

trout [traʊt] *s* trucha

Dos plurales: **trout** o **trouts**.

trowel ['traʊəl] *s* ❶ desplantador ❷ paleta

truant ['tru:ənt] *s* alumno, na que se va de pinta • **to play truant** irse de pinta

truce [tru:s] *s* • **truce (between)** tregua (entre)

truck [trʌk] ◆ *s* ❶ camión ❷ *FERROCARRIL* vagón de mercancías ◆ *vt* transportar en camión

truck driver *s* camionero, ra

trucker ['trʌkər] *s* camionero, ra

truck farm *s* ▸ puesto de verduras y frutas para la venta

trucking ['trʌkɪŋ] *s* transporte por camión

truck stop *s* restaurante de carretera

true [tru:] *adj* ❶ verdadero, ra • **it's true** es verdad • **to come true** hacerse realidad ❷ auténtico, ca ❸ de verdad ❹ exacto, ta

truffle ['trʌfl] *s* trufa

truly ['tru:lɪ] *adv* verdaderamente

expresión yours truly le saluda atentamente

trump [trʌmp] *s* triunfo *(en cartas)*

trumped-up ['trʌmpt-] *adj despectivo* inventado, da

trumpet ['trʌmpɪt] *s* trompeta

truncheon ['trʌntʃən] *s* porra

trundle ['trʌndl] *vi* rodar lentamente • **he trundled along to the post office** se arrastró lentamente hasta correos

trunk [trʌŋk] *s* ❶ tronco ❷ trompa ❸ baúl ❹ cajuela *(de coche)*

■ **trunks** *spl* traje de baño (de hombre)

trunk road *s* ≃ carretera nacional

trust [trʌst] ◆ *vt* ❶ confiar en ❷ • **to trust somebody to do something** confiar en alguien para que haga algo ❸ • **to trust somebody with something** confiar algo a alguien ❹ fiarse de ◆ *s* ❶ :ᄋ̈:*incontable* • **trust (in)** confianza (en) • **to put** o **place your trust in** confiar en ❷ *FINANZAS* trust • **in trust** en fideicomiso

trusted ['trʌstɪd] *adj* de confianza

trustee [trʌs'ti:] *s FINANZAS & DERECHO* fideicomisario, ria

trust fund *s* fondo de fideicomiso

trusting ['trʌstɪŋ] *adj* confiado, da

trustworthy ['trʌst,wɜ:ðɪ] *adj* digno, na de confianza

truth [tru:θ] *s* verdad • **in (all) truth** en verdad; verdaderamente

truthful ['tru:θfʊl] *adj* ❶ sincero, ra ❷ verídico, ca

try [traɪ] ◆ *vt* ❶ intentar • **to try to do something** tratar de o intentar hacer algo ❷ probar ❸ *DERECHO* ver ❹ juzgar; procesar ❺ acabar con la paciencia de; acabar con ◆ *vi* intentar ◆ *s* ❶ intento; tentativa • **to have a try at something** intentar hacer algo ❷ • **to give something a try** probar algo

■ **try on** *vt* :ᄋ̈: *El objeto se puede colocar antes o después de la preposición.* probarse

■ **try out** *vt* :ᄋ̈: *El objeto se puede colocar antes o después de la preposición.* ❶ probar ❷ poner a prueba • **to try something out on somebody** probar algo con alguien • **to try out for** presentarse a una prueba de selección para

---

try

En el lenguaje hablado, el verbo try suele ir seguido de and y luego del infinitivo del verbo sin el 'to' (*try and* come tonight *trata de venir esta noche* en vez de *try to* come tonight).

---

trying ['traɪɪŋ] *adj* difícil; pesado, da

T-shirt *s* playera

T-square *s* escuadra en forma de T

tub [tʌb] *s* ❶ bote; tina ❷ *familiar* bañera

tubby ['tʌbɪ] *adj familiar* regordete, ta

tube [tju:b] *s* ❶ tubo ❷ *ANATOMÍA* conducto

tuberculosis [tju:,bɜ:kjʊ'ləʊsɪs] *s* tuberculosis

tubing ['tju:bɪŋ] *s* :ᄋ̈:*incontable* tubos

tubular ['tju:bjʊlər] *adj* tubular

tuck [tʌk] *vt* meter

■ **tuck away** *vt* :ᄋ̈: *El objeto se puede colocar antes o después de la preposición.* guardar

■ **tuck in** ◆ *vt* ☼ *El objeto se puede colocar antes o después de la preposición.* ❶ arropar ❷ meterse ◆ *vi familiar* comer con apetito

■ **tuck up** *vt* ☼ *El objeto se puede colocar antes o después de la preposición.* arropar • **to tuck somebody up in bed** arropar a alguien en la cama

Tuesday ['tju:zdɪ] *s* martes ver también **Saturday**

tuft [tʌft] *s* ❶ mechón ❷ manojo

tug [tʌg] ◆ *s* ❶ tirón ❷ remolcador ◆ *vt* tirar de ◆ *vi* • **to tug (at)** tirar (de)

tuition [tju:'ɪʃn] *s* enseñanza • **private tuition** clases particulares

tulip ['tju:lɪp] *s* tulipán

tumble ['tʌmbl] ◆ *vi* caerse (rodando) ◆ *s* caída

tumbledown ['tʌmbldaʊn] *adj* ruinoso, sa

tumble-dryer [-,draɪər] *s* secadora

tumbler ['tʌmblər] *s* vaso

tummy ['tʌmɪ] *s familiar* barriga

tumor ['tju:mər] *s* tumor

tuna ['tu:nə] *s* atún

Dos plurales: **tuna** o **tunas.**

tune [tju:n] ◆ *s* ❶ melodía ❷ • **in tune** Música afinado, da • **out of tune** Música desafinado, da ◆ *vt* ❶ Música afinar ❷ Radio & Televisión sintonizar ❸ poner a punto

■ **tune in** *vi* Radio & Televisión • **to tune in (to something)** sintonizar (algo)

■ **tune up** *vi* Música afinar los instrumentos

tuneful ['tju:nful] *adj* melodioso, sa

tuner ['tju:nər] *s* ❶ Radio & Televisión sintonizador ❷ Música afinador, ra

tunic ['tju:nɪk] *s* túnica

tuning fork ['tju:nɪŋ-] *s* diapasón

tunnel ['tʌnl] ◆ *s* túnel ◆ *vi* hacer un túnel

Formas irregulares de **tunnel:** *pretérito & pp* **tunneled,** *gerundio* **tunneling.**

turban ['tɜ:bən] *s* turbante

turbine ['tɜ:baɪn] *s* turbina

turbocharged ['tɜ:bəʊtʃɑ:dʒd] *adj* turbo

turbodiesel [,tɜ:bəʊ'di:zl] *s* turbodiésel

turbulence ['tɜ:bjʊləns] *s* ☼ *incontable literal & figurado* turbulencia

turbulent ['tɜ:bjʊlənt] *adj literal & figurado* turbulento, ta

tureen [tə'ri:n] *s* sopera

turf [tɜ:f] *s* césped

■ **turf out** *vt* ☼ *El objeto se puede colocar antes o después de la preposición.* tirar

Dos plurales: **turfs** o **turves.**

Turk [tɜ:k] *s* turco, ca

turkey ['tɜ:kɪ] *s* pavo

El plural de **turkey** es **turkeys.**

Turkey ['tɜ:kɪ] *s* Turquía

Turkish ['tɜ:kɪʃ] ◆ *adj* turco, ca ◆ *s* turco ◆ *spl* • **the Turkish** los turcos

turmoil ['tɜ:mɔɪl] *s* confusión; alboroto • **the country was in turmoil** reinaba la confusión en el país

turn [tɜ:n] ◆ *s* ❶ curva ❷ vuelta *(de rueda, perilla)* ❸ cambio ❹ turno *(en juegos)* • **it's my turn** me toca a mí • **in turn** sucesivamente • **to take (it in) turns (to do something)** turnarse (en hacer algo)

expresión **to do somebody a good turn** hacerle un favor a alguien

◆ *vt* ❶ dar la vuelta a ❷ girar ❸ doblar ❹ • **to turn something to** dirigir algo hacia ❺ • **to turn something into** convertir o transformar algo en ❻ • **the cold turned his fingers blue** se le pusieron los dedos azules por el frío • **to turn something inside out** volver algo del revés ◆ *vi* ❶ girar ❷ torcer ❸ volverse; darse la vuelta ❹ dar vueltas ❺ • **turn to page two** pasen a la página dos ❻ • **to turn to** dirigirse hacia ❼ • **to turn to somebody/something** buscar consuelo en alguien/algo • **she has nobody to turn to** no tiene a quien acudir ❽ • **to turn into** convertirse o transformarse en ❾ • **it turned black** se volvió negro

■ **turn around** ◆ *vt* ☼ *El objeto se puede colocar antes o después de la preposición.* ❶ dar la vuelta a ❷ hacer girar ◆ *vi* darse la vuelta; volverse

■ **turn away** *vt* ☼ *El objeto se puede colocar antes o después de la preposición.* no dejar entrar

■ **turn back** ◆ *vt* ☼ *El objeto se puede colocar antes o después de la preposición.* hacer volver ◆ *vi* volver; volverse

■ **turn down** *vt* ☼ *El objeto se puede colocar antes o después de la preposición.* ❶ rechazar ❷ bajar

■ **turn off** ◆ *vt* ☼ *El objeto siempre va después de la preposición al final.* ❶ desviarse de *(carretera)* ❷ apagar *(radio, calentador)* ❸ parar *(motor)* ❹ cerrar *(llave, gas)* ◆ *vi* desviarse

■ **turn on** ◆ *vt* ☼ *El objeto se puede colocar antes o después de la preposición.* ❶ encender ❷ abrir ◆ *vt* ☼ *El objeto siempre va después de la preposición al final.* atacar

■ **turn out** ◆ *vt* ❶ apagar ❷ vaciar ◆ *vt* ☼ *El objeto siempre va después de la preposición al final.* • **to turn out to be** resultar ser ◆ *vi* ❶ salir ❷ • **to turn out (for)** venir o presentarse (a)

■ **turn over** ◆ *vt* ☼ *El objeto se puede colocar antes o después de la preposición.* ❶ dar la vuelta a ❷ volver ❸ darle vueltas a ❹ • **to turn something/somebody over (to)** entregar algo/a alguien (a) ◆ *vi* darse la vuelta

■ **turn up** ◆ *vt* ☼ *El objeto se puede colocar antes o después de la preposición.* subir ◆ *vi familiar* aparecer

turning point *s* momento decisivo

turnip ['tɜ:nɪp] *s* nabo

turnout ['tɜ:naʊt] *s* número de asistentes; asistencia

turnpike ['tɜ:npaɪk] *s* autopista de cuota

turnstile ['tɜ:nstaɪl] *s* torniquete

turn-up *s*

expresión **a turn-up for the books** *familiar* una auténtica sorpresa

turpentine ['tɜ:pəntaɪn] *s* aguarrás

turquoise ['tɜːkwɔɪz] *adj* & *s* turquesa

turret ['tʌrɪt] *s* torreta; torrecilla

turtle ['tɜːtl] *s* tortuga (marina)
Dos plurales: **turtle** o **turtles**.

turtleneck ['tɜːtlnek] *s* cuello alto; cuello (de) tortuga

tusk [tʌsk] *s* colmillo

tussle ['tʌsl] ◆ *s* lucha; pelea ◆ *vi* • **to tussle (over)** pelearse (por)

tutor ['tjuːtər] *s* profesor particular, profesora particular; tutor, ra

tutorial [tjuːˈtɔːrɪəl] *s* tutoría

tuxedo [tʌkˈsiːdəʊ] *s* esmoquin
El plural de **tuxedo** es **tuxedos**.

TV (*abreviatura de* television) *s* televisión • **on TV** en la televisión

TV movie *s* telefilm

twang [twæŋ] *s* ❶ tañido ❷ sonido vibrante ❸ gangueo; acento nasal

tweenage ['twiːneɪdʒ] *adj familiar* preadolescente

tweezers ['twiːzəz] *spl* pinzas

twelfth [twelfθ] *número* duodécimo, ma ver también **sixth**

twelve [twelv] *número* doce ver también **six**

twentieth ['twentɪəθ] *número* vigésimo, ma ver también **sixth**

twenty ['twentɪ] *número* veinte ver también **sixty**

twenty-one [twentɪˈwʌn] *s* veintiuna

twice [twaɪs] *adv numeral* dos veces • **twice a week** dos veces por semana • **twice as big** el doble de grande • **it costs twice as much** cuesta el doble • **he's twice her age** le dobla en edad • **think twice** piénsalo dos veces

twiddle ['twɪdl] ◆ *vt* dar vueltas a
expresión **to twiddle your thumbs** holgazanear
◆ *vi* • **to twiddle with** juguetear con

twig [twɪg] *s* ramita

twilight ['twaɪlaɪt] *s* crepúsculo

twin [twɪn] ◆ *adj* gemelo, la ◆ *s* gemelo, la

twin-bedded [-ˈbedɪd] *adj* de dos camas

twinge [twɪndʒ] *s* ❶ punzada ❷ remordimiento

twinkle ['twɪŋkl] *vi* ❶ centellear ❷ brillar

twin room *s* habitación con dos camas

twin town *s* ciudad hermanada

twirl [twɜːl] ◆ *vt* dar vueltas a ◆ *vi* dar vueltas rápidamente

twist [twɪst] ◆ *s* ❶ vuelta; recodo ❷ giro ❸ espiral ❹ *figurado* giro imprevisto ◆ *vt* ❶ retorcer *(trapo, cuerda)* ❷ enroscar *(pelo)* ❸ torcer *(cara, boca)* ❹ desenroscar ❺ volver *(cabeza)* ❻ torcerse *(tobillo, rodilla)* • **to twist your ankle** torcerse el tobillo ❼ tergiversar ◆ *vi* ❶ retorcerse ❷ serpentear ❸ contorsionarse ❹ torcerse ❺ volverse

twister ['twɪstər] *s familiar* tornado

twitch [twɪtʃ] ◆ *s* contorsión • **nervous twitch** tic (nervioso) ◆ *vi* contorsionarse

two [tuː] *número* dos • **to break in two** partirse en dos • **to do something in twos** hacer algo en pares
expresión **to put two and two together** atar cabos ver también **six**

two-bit *adj despectivo* de tres al cuarto

two-door *adj* de dos puertas

twofaced [,tuːˈfeɪst] *adj despectivo* hipócrita

twofold ['tuːfəʊld] ◆ *adj* doble • **a twofold increase** un incremento del doble ◆ *adv* • **to increase twofold** duplicarse

two-piece *adj* de dos piezas

twosome ['tuːsəm] *s familiar* pareja

two-way *adj* ❶ en ambas direcciones ❷ mutuo, tua

two-way street *s* calle de doble sentido

tycoon [taɪˈkuːn] *s* magnate • **an oil tycoon** un magnate del petróleo

type [taɪp] ◆ *s* ❶ tipo ❷ ☼ *incontable* TIPOGRAFÍA tipo; letra • **in bold/italic type** en negrita/cursiva ◆ *vt* ❶ escribir a máquina; mecanografiar ❷ escribir en la computadora • **to type something into something** escribir algo en algo ◆ *vi* escribir a máquina

typecast ['taɪpkɑːst] *vt* • **to typecast somebody (as)** encasillar a alguien (como)
Formas irregulares de **typecast**: *pretérito* **typecast**.

typeface ['taɪpfeɪs] *s* tipo; letra

typewriter ['taɪpˌraɪtər] *s* máquina de escribir

typhoid (fever) ['taɪfɔɪd-] *s* fiebre tifoidea

typhoon [taɪˈfuːn] *s* tifón

typical ['tɪpɪkl] *adj* • **typical (of)** típico, ca (de)

typing ['taɪpɪŋ] *s* mecanografía

typist ['taɪpɪst] *s* mecanógrafo, fa

typography [taɪˈpɒɡrəfɪ] *s* tipografía

tyranny ['tɪrənɪ] *s* tiranía

tyrant ['taɪrənt] *s* tirano, na

T

U

u, U [ju:] *s* u; U

Dos plurales: **u's** o **us**, **U's** o **Us**

U-bend *s* sifón

udder ['ʌdər] *s* ubre

UFO (*abreviatura de* unidentified flying object) *s* OVNI

ugh [ʌg] *exclamación* ¡puf!

ugly ['ʌglɪ] *adj* ❶ feo, a ❷ *figurado* desagradable

UHF (*abreviatura de* ultra-high frequency) UHF

UK (*abreviatura de* United Kingdom) *s* RU • **the UK** el Reino Unido

ulcer ['ʌlsər] *s* úlcera

ulcerated ['ʌlsəreɪtɪd] *adj* ulceroso, sa

ulterior [ʌl'tɪərɪər] *adj* • **ulterior motive** motivo oculto

ultimata [,ʌltɪ'meɪtə] *spl* → ultimatum

ultimate ['ʌltɪmət] ◆ *adj* ❶ final; definitivo, va ❷ máximo, ma ◆ *s* • **the ultimate in** el colmo de

ultimately ['ʌltɪmətlɪ] *adv* finalmente; a la larga

ultimatum [,ʌltɪ'meɪtəm] *s* ultimátum • **to issue an ultimatum to somebody** dar un ultimátum a alguien

Dos plurales: **ultimatums** o **ultimata**,

ultrasound ['ʌltrəsaund] *s* ultrasonido

ultraviolet [,ʌltrə'vaɪələt] *adj* ultravioleta

umbilical cord [ʌm'bɪlɪkl-] *s* cordón umbilical

umbrella [ʌm'brelə] ◆ *s* ❶ paraguas ❷ parasol ❸ • **under the umbrella of** *figurado* bajo la protección de ◆ *adj* que engloba a otros, otras

umpire ['ʌmpaɪər] *s* árbitro

umpteen [,ʌmp'ti:n] *adj numeral familiar* • **umpteen times** la tira de veces

umpteenth [,ʌmp'ti:nθ] *adj numeral familiar* enésimo, ma • **for the umpteenth time** por enésima vez

UN (*abreviatura de* United Nations) *s* • **the UN** la ONU

unable [ʌn'eɪbl] *adj* • **to be unable to do something** no poder hacer algo

unacceptable [,ʌnək'septəbl] *adj* inaceptable

unaccompanied [,ʌnə'kʌmpənɪd] *adj* ❶ que no va acompañado, da ❷ desatendido, da ❸ sin acompañamiento

unaccounted [,ʌnə'kauntɪd] *adj* • **12 people are unaccounted for** hay 12 personas aún sin localizar

unaccustomed [,ʌnə'kʌstəmd] *adj* • **to be unaccustomed to** no estar acostumbrado, da a

unadulterated [,ʌnə'dʌltəreɪtɪd] *adj* ❶ sin adulterar ❷ completo, ta; absoluto, ta

unanimous [ju:'nænɪməs] *adj* unánime

unanimously [ju:'nænɪməslɪ] *adv* unánimemente

unanswered [,ʌn'ɑ:nsəd] *adj* sin contestar

unappetizing [,ʌn'æpɪtaɪzɪŋ] *adj* poco apetitoso, sa

unarmed [,ʌn'ɑ:md] *adj* desarmado, da

unashamed [,ʌnə'ʃeɪmd] *adj* descarado, da

unassuming [,ʌnə'sju:mɪŋ] *adj* sin pretensiones

unattached [,ʌnə'tætʃt] *adj* ❶ independiente • **unattached to** que no está ligado a ❷ libre; sin compromiso

unattended [,ʌnə'tendɪd] *adj* desatendido, da • **to leave something unattended** dejar algo desatendido

unattractive [,ʌnə'træktɪv] *adj* poco atractivo, va

unauthorized, unauthorised [,ʌn'ɔ:θəraɪzd] *adj* no autorizado, da

unavailable [,ʌnə'veɪləbl] *adj* • **to be unavailable** no estar disponible • **he was unavailable for comment** no quiso hacer ningún comentario

unavoidable [,ʌnə'vɔɪdəbl] *adj* inevitable; ineludible • **unavoidable delays** retrasos inevitables

unaware [,ʌnə'weər] *adj* inconsciente • **to be unaware of** no ser consciente de

unawares [,ʌnə'weəz] *adv*

expresión to catch o take somebody unawares pillar a alguien desprevenido, da

unbalanced [,ʌn'bælənst] *adj* desequilibrado, da

unbearable [ʌn'beərəbl] *adj* insoportable; inaguantable

unbeatable [ˌʌn'biːtəbl] *adj* ❶ insuperable ❷ inmejorable

unbelievable [ˌʌnbɪ'liːvəbl] *adj* increíble

unbias(s)ed [ˌʌn'baɪəst] *adj* imparcial

unborn [ˌʌn'bɔːn] *adj* no nacido, da aún

unbreakable [ˌʌn'breɪkəbl] *adj* irrompible

unbutton [ˌʌn'bʌtn] *vt* desabrochar

uncalled-for [ˌʌn'kɔːld-] *adj* injusto, ta ; inmerecido, da

uncanny [ʌn'kænɪ] *adj* extraño, ña

unceremonious ['ʌnˌserɪ'məʊnjəs] *adj* brusco, ca

uncertain [ʌn'sɜːtn] *adj* ❶ incierto, ta ❷ indeciso, sa • **it's uncertain whether they will accept the proposals** no se sabe si aceptarán las propuestas • **in no uncertain terms** de forma vehemente

unchanged [ˌʌn'tʃeɪndʒd] *adj* sin alterar

unchecked [ˌʌn'tʃekt] ◆ *adj* desenfrenado, da ◆ *adv* libremente ; sin restricciones

uncivilized [ˌʌn'sɪvɪlaɪzd] *adj* ❶ incivilizado, da ❷ inculto, ta

uncle ['ʌŋkl] *s* tío

unclear [ˌʌn'klɪər] *adj* poco claro, ra • **to be unclear about something** no tener claro algo

uncomfortable [ˌʌn'kʌmftəbl] *adj* ❶ incómodo, da ❷ *figurado* inquietante ; desagradable

uncommon [ʌn'kɒmən] *adj* poco común ; raro, ra

uncompromising [ˌʌn'kɒmprəmaɪzɪŋ] *adj* inflexible ; intransigente

unconcerned [ˌʌnkən'sɜːnd] *adj* indiferente

unconditional [ˌʌnkən'dɪʃənl] *adj* incondicional

unconscious [ʌn'kɒnʃəs] ◆ *adj* inconsciente • **to be unconscious of something** ser inconsciente de algo • **he was knocked unconscious by a falling brick** un ladrillo que caía lo dejó inconsciente ◆ *s* inconsciente

unconsciously [ʌn'kɒnʃəslɪ] *adv* inconscientemente

uncontrollable [ˌʌnkən'trəʊləbl] *adj* ❶ incontrolable ❷ irrefrenable *(deseo)* ❸ incontenible *(risa)*

unconventional [ˌʌnkən'venʃənl] *adj* poco convencional

unconvinced [ˌʌnkən'vɪnst] *adj* • **to remain unconvinced** seguir sin convencerse

uncouth [ʌn'kuːθ] *adj* grosero, ra

uncover [ʌn'kʌvər] *vt* ❶ descubrir ❷ destapar

undecided [ˌʌndɪ'saɪdɪd] *adj* ❶ indeciso, sa ❷ pendiente

undeniable [ˌʌndɪ'naɪəbl] *adj* innegable

under ['ʌndər] ◆ *preposición* ❶ debajo de ; abajo de ❷ bajo ; debajo de • **put it under the table** ponlo debajo o bajo la mesa • **they walked under the bridge** pasaron bajo o por debajo del puente ❸ • **under the circumstances** dadas las circunstancias • **under dis-**cussion en proceso de discusión • **he has 20 men under him** tiene 20 hombres a su cargo ❹ menor de • **children under the age of 14** niños menores de 14 años ❺ según ❻ • **he filed it under "D"** lo archivó en la "D" ❼ • **under an alias** bajo nombre supuesto ◆ *adv* ❶ debajo ❷ • **children of 12 years and under** niños menores de 13 años • **$5 or under** cinco dólares o menos ❸ bajo el agua

expresión **to go under** irse a pique

underage [ʌndər'eɪdʒ] *adj* ❶ menor de edad ❷ en menores de edad

underbrush ['ʌndəbrʌʃ] *s* 💡*incontable* maleza ; monte bajo

undercarriage ['ʌndəˌkærɪdʒ] *s* tren de aterrizaje

undercharge [ˌʌndə'tʃɑːdʒ] *vt* cobrar menos del precio estipulado a

underclothes ['ʌndəkləʊðz] *spl* ropa interior

undercover ['ʌndəˌkʌvər] *adj* secreto, ta

undercurrent ['ʌndəˌkʌrənt] *s figurado* sentimiento oculto

undercut [ˌʌndə'kʌt] *vt* vender más barato que
Formas irregulares de **undercut**: *pretérito & pp* **undercut.**

underdeveloped [ˌʌndədɪ'veləpt] *adj* subdesarrollado, da

underdog ['ʌndədɒg] *s* • **the underdog** el que lleva las de perder

underdone [ˌʌndə'dʌn] *adj* poco hecho, cha

underestimate *vt* [ˌʌndər'estɪmeɪt] subestimar

underexposed [ˌʌndərɪk'spəʊzd] *adj* FOTOGRAFÍA subexpuesto, ta

underfed ['ʌndə'fed] *adj* desnutrido, da

underfoot [ˌʌndə'fʊt] *adv* debajo de los pies • **it's wet underfoot** el suelo está mojado

undergo [ˌʌndə'gəʊ] *vt* ❶ sufrir ; experimentar ❷ someterse a
Formas irregulares de **undergo**: *pretérito* **underwent**, *pp* **undergone.**

undergraduate [ˌʌndə'grædʒʊət] *s* estudiante universitario no licenciado, estudiante universitaria no licenciada

underground ◆ *adj* ['ʌndəgraʊnd] ❶ subterráneo, a ❷ *figurado* clandestino, na ◆ *adv* [ˌʌndə'graʊnd] • **to go underground** pasar a la clandestinidad ◆ *s* ['ʌndəgraʊnd] movimiento clandestino

undergrowth ['ʌndəgrəʊθ] *s* 💡*incontable* maleza

underhand [ˌʌndə'hænd] *adj* turbio, bia ; poco limpio, pia

underline [ˌʌndə'laɪn] *vt* subrayar

underlying [ˌʌndə'laɪɪŋ] *adj* subyacente

undermine [ˌʌndə'maɪn] *vt figurado* minar ; socavar • **to undermine somebody's confidence/authority** minar la confianza/autoridad de alguien

U

underneath [ˌʌndəˈniːθ] ◆ *preposición* ❶ debajo de ❷ bajo ◆ *adv* debajo ◆ *adj familiar* inferior; de abajo ◆ *s* • **the underneath** la superficie inferior

underpaid *adj* [ˈʌndəpeɪd] mal pagado, da

underpants [ˈʌndəpænts] *spl* calzoncillos

underpass [ˈʌndəpɑːs] *s* paso subterráneo

underprivileged [ˌʌndəˈprɪvɪlɪdʒd] *adj* desvalido, da; desamparado, da

underrated [ˌʌndəˈreɪtɪd] *adj* subestimado, da; infravalorado, da

undershirt [ˈʌndəʃɜːt] *s* camiseta

underside [ˈʌndəsaɪd] *s* • **the underside** la superficie inferior

underskirt [ˈʌndəskɜːt] *s* enaguas

understand [ˌʌndəˈstænd] ◆ *vt* ❶ comprender; entender • **is that understood?** ¿queda claro? ❷ entender de ❸ *formal* • **to understand that** tener entendido que ❹ • **it is understood that...** se entiende que... ◆ *vi* comprender; entender

Formas irregulares de **understand**: *pretérito & pp* **understood**.

understandable [ˌʌndəˈstændəbl] *adj* comprensible

understanding [ˌʌndəˈstændɪŋ] ◆ *s* ❶ entendimiento; comprensión ❷ comprensión mutua ❸ acuerdo • **we have a little understanding** tenemos un pequeño acuerdo ◆ *adj* comprensivo, va

understatement [ˌʌndəˈsteɪtmənt] *s* • **it's an understatement to say he's fat** decir que es gordo es quedarse corto

understood [ˌʌndəˈstʊd] *pretérito* & *participio pasado* → **understand**

understudy [ˈʌndəstʌdɪ] *s* suplente

undertake [ˌʌndəˈteɪk] *vt* ❶ emprender ❷ asumir; tomar ❸ • **to undertake to do something** comprometerse a hacer algo

Formas irregulares de **undertake**: *pretérito* **undertook**, *pp* **undertaken**.

undertaking [ˌʌndəˈteɪkɪŋ] *s* ❶ tarea; empresa ❷ promesa

undertone [ˈʌndətəʊn] *s* ❶ voz baja • **in an undertone** en voz baja ❷ matiz

undertook [ˌʌndəˈtʊk] *pretérito* → **undertake**

underwater [ˌʌndəˈwɔːtər] ◆ *adj* submarino, na ◆ *adv* bajo el agua

underwear [ˈʌndəweər] *s* ropa interior

underwent [ˌʌndəˈwent] *pretérito* → **undergo**

underworld [ˈʌndəwɜːld] *s* • **the underworld** el hampa; los bajos fondos

undid [ˌʌnˈdɪd] *pretérito* → **undo**

undies [ˈʌndɪz] *spl familiar* paños menores

undisputed [ˌʌndɪˈspjuːtɪd] *adj* indiscutible

undistinguished [ˌʌndɪˈstɪŋgwɪʃt] *adj* mediocre

undo [ˌʌnˈduː] *vt* ❶ desatar *(nudo)*; desabrochar *(botón, cinturón)* ❷ anular ❸ *INFORMÁTICA* deshacer

Formas irregulares de **undo**: *pretérito* **undid**, *pp* **undone**.

undoing [ˌʌnˈduːɪŋ] *s* ☀ *incontable formal* perdición • **it was his undoing** fue su perdición

undone [ˌʌnˈdʌn] ◆ *participio pasado* → **undo** ◆ *adj* ❶ desabrochado, da ❷ desatado, da • **to come undone** desatarse

undoubted [ʌnˈdaʊtɪd] *adj* indudable

undoubtedly [ʌnˈdaʊtɪdlɪ] *adv formal* indudablemente; sin duda (alguna)

undress [ˌʌnˈdres] ◆ *vt* desnudar ◆ *vi* desnudarse

unearth [ˌʌnˈɜːθ] *vt* ❶ desenterrar ❷ *figurado* descubrir

unearthly [ʌnˈɜːθlɪ] *adj familiar* intempestivo, va

unease [ʌnˈiːz] *s* malestar

uneasy [ʌnˈiːzɪ] *adj* ❶ intranquilo, la ❷ inseguro, ra

uneconomic [ˈʌnˌiːkəˈnɒmɪk] *adj* poco rentable

uneducated [ˌʌnˈedjʊkeɪtɪd] *adj* ignorante; inculto, ta

unemployed [ˌʌnɪmˈplɔɪd] ◆ *adj* desempleado, da ◆ *spl* • **the unemployed** los desempleados

unemployment [ˌʌnɪmˈplɔɪmənt] *s* desempleo

unemployment compensation *s* subsidio de desempleo

uneven [ˌʌnˈiːvn] *adj* ❶ lleno, na de baches; escabroso, sa ❷ desigual

unexpected [ˌʌnɪkˈspektɪd] *adj* inesperado, da

unexpectedly [ˌʌnɪkˈspektɪdlɪ] *adv* inesperadamente

unfailing [ʌnˈfeɪlɪŋ] *adj* indefectible

unfair [ˌʌnˈfeər] *adj* injusto, ta

unfaithful [ˌʌnˈfeɪθfʊl] *adj* infiel

unfamiliar [ˌʌnfəˈmɪljər] *adj* ❶ desconocido, da ❷ • **to be unfamiliar with something/somebody** desconocer algo/a alguien

unfashionable [ˌʌnˈfæʃnəbl] *adj* ❶ pasado, da de moda ❷ poco popular

unfasten [ˌʌnˈfɑːsn] *vt* ❶ desabrochar ❷ desatar; soltar ❸ abrir

unfavorable [ˌʌnˈfeɪvrəbl] *adj* desfavorable

unfeeling [ʌnˈfiːlɪŋ] *adj* insensible

unfinished [ˌʌnˈfɪnɪʃt] *adj* sin terminar

unfit [ˌʌnˈfɪt] *adj* ❶ lesionado, da ❷ que no está en forma ❸ impropio, pia; • **unfit to** incapaz de • **unfit for** no apto para

unfold [ʌnˈfəʊld] ◆ *vt* ❶ desplegar; desdoblar ❷ revelar ◆ *vi* revelarse

unforeseen [ˌʌnfɔːˈsiːn] *adj* imprevisto, ta

unforgettable [ˌʌnfəˈgetəbl] *adj* inolvidable

unforgivable [ˌʌnfəˈgɪvəbl] *adj* imperdonable

unfortunate [ʌnˈfɔːtʃnət] *adj* ❶ desgraciado, da; desdichado, da ❷ inoportuno, na

unfortunately [ʌnˈfɔːʧnətlɪ] *adv* desgraciadamente; desafortunadamente

unfounded [ˌʌnˈfaʊndɪd] *adj* infundado, da

unfriendly [ˌʌnˈfrendlɪ] *adj* poco amistoso, sa

unfurnished [ˌʌnˈfɜːnɪʃt] *adj* desamueblado, da

ungodly [ˌʌnˈgɒdlɪ] *adj familiar* intempestivo, va • **at an ungodly hour** a una hora intempestiva

ungrateful [ʌnˈgreɪtfʊl] *adj* desagradecido, da; ingrato, ta

unhappy [ʌnˈhæpɪ] *adj* ❶ triste ❷ desdichado, da; infeliz ❸ • **to be unhappy (with** o **about)** estar inquieto, ta (por) ❹ *formal* desafortunado, da

unharmed [ˌʌnˈhɑːmd] *adj* ❶ ileso, sa ❷ indemne • **he escaped unharmed** salió ileso

unhealthy [ʌnˈhelθɪ] *adj* ❶ enfermizo, za ❷ insalubre ❸ *figurado* morboso, sa

unheard-of [ʌnˈhɜːd-] *adj* ❶ inaudito, ta ❷ sin precedente

unhook [ˌʌnˈhʊk] *vt* ❶ desabrochar ❷ desenganchar

unhurt [ˌʌnˈhɜːt] *adj* ileso, sa

unhygienic [ˌʌnhaɪˈdʒiːnɪk] *adj* antihigiénico, ca

unidentified flying object *s* objeto volador no identificado

unification [ˌjuːnɪfɪˈkeɪʃn] *s* unificación

uniform [ˈjuːnɪfɔːm] ◆ *adj* uniforme ◆ *s* uniforme

unify [ˈjuːnɪfaɪ] *vt* unificar; unir

unilateral [ˌjuːnɪˈlætərəl] *adj* unilateral

unimportant [ˌʌnɪmˈpɔːtənt] *adj* sin importancia; insignificante

uninhabited [ˌʌnɪnˈhæbɪtɪd] *adj* deshabitado, da

uninjured [ˌʌnˈɪndʒəd] *adj* ileso, sa

uninstall [ˌʌnɪnˈstɔːl] *vt* desinstalar

unintelligent [ˌʌnɪnˈtelɪdʒent] *adj* poco inteligente

unintentional [ˌʌnɪnˈtenʃənl] *adj* involuntario, ria

union [ˈjuːnjən] ◆ *s* ❶ sindicato ❷ unión ◆ *en compuestos* sindical

Union Jack *s* • **the Union Jack** la bandera del Reino Unido

union shop *s* ▸ fábrica donde todos los empleados tienen que pertenecer a un sindicato

unique [juːˈniːk] *adj* ❶ único, ca ❷ *formal* • **unique to** peculiar de

unison [ˈjuːnɪzn] *s* unísono

unit [ˈjuːnɪt] *s* ❶ unidad ❷ módulo; elemento

unite [juːˈnaɪt] ◆ *vt* ❶ unir ❷ unificar ◆ *vi* unirse; juntarse

united [juːˈnaɪtɪd] *adj* unido, da

United Kingdom *s* • **the United Kingdom** el Reino Unido

United Nations *s* • **the United Nations** las Naciones Unidas

United States *s* • **the United States (of America)** los Estados Unidos (de América)

unity [ˈjuːnətɪ] *s* ◌ *incontable* unidad

universal [ˌjuːnɪˈvɜːsl] *adj* universal

universe [ˈjuːnɪvɜːs] *s* • **the universe** el universo

university [ˌjuːnɪˈvɜːsətɪ] ◆ *s* universidad ◆ *en compuestos* universitario, ria • **university student** (estudiante) universitario, (estudiante) universitaria

unjust [ˌʌnˈdʒʌst] *adj* injusto, ta

unkempt [ˌʌnˈkempt] *adj* ❶ desaseado, da ❷ despeinado, da ❸ descuidado, da

unkind [ʌnˈkaɪnd] *adj* poco amable; cruel

unknown [ˌʌnˈnəʊn] *adj* desconocido, da • **unknown to him** sin que él lo supiera

unlawful [ˌʌnˈlɔːfʊl] *adj* ilegal; ilícito, ta

unleaded [ˌʌnˈledɪd] *adj* sin plomo

unless [ənˈles] *conjunción* a menos que • **unless I say so** a menos que yo lo diga • **unless I'm mistaken** si no me equivoco

unlike [ˌʌnˈlaɪk] *preposición* ❶ distinto, ta a; diferente a ❷ a diferencia de ❸ poco característico, ca de • **that's unlike him** no es propio de él

unlikely [ʌnˈlaɪklɪ] *adj* ❶ poco probable • **it's unlikely that he'll come now, he's unlikely to come now** ahora es poco probable que venga • **to be highly unlikely** ser muy poco probable ❷ inverosímil

unlisted [ʌnˈlɪstɪd] *adj* que no figura en la guía telefónica

unload [ˌʌnˈləʊd] *vt* descargar

unlock [ˌʌnˈlɒk] *vt* abrir (con llave)

unlucky [ʌnˈlʌkɪ] *adj* ❶ desgraciado, da • **to be unlucky** tener mala suerte ❷ de la mala suerte • **to be unlucky** traer mala suerte

unmarried [ˌʌnˈmærɪd] *adj* soltero, ra

unmetered [ʌnˈmiːtəd] *adj* ilimitado, da

unmistakable [ˌʌnmɪˈsteɪkəbl] *adj* inconfundible

unmitigated [ʌnˈmɪtɪgeɪtɪd] *adj* absoluto, ta

unnatural [ʌnˈnæʧrəl] *adj* ❶ anormal ❷ afectado, da

unnecessary [ʌnˈnesəsərɪ] *adj* innecesario, ria

unnoticed [ˌʌnˈnəʊtɪst] *adj* inadvertido, da; desapercibido, da • **to go unnoticed** pasar desapercibido, da

unobtainable [ˌʌnəbˈteɪnəbl] *adj* inasequible

unofficial [ˌʌnəˈfɪʃl] *adj* extraoficial

unorthodox [ˌʌnˈɔːθədɒks] *adj* poco ortodoxo, xa

unpack [ˌʌnˈpæk] ◆ *vt* ❶ desempaquetar; desembalar ❷ deshacer ❸ sacar (de la maleta) ◆ *vi* deshacer las maletas

unpalatable [ʌnˈpælətəbl] *adj* ❶ incomible ❷ imbebible ❸ *figurado* desagradable

U

unplug [ʌn'plʌg] *vt* desenchufar; desconectar

unpopular [ˌʌn'pɒpjʊlər] *adj* poco popular • **she was unpopular with the other girls** las otras chicas no le tenían mucho aprecio

unprecedented [ʌn'presɪdəntɪd] *adj* sin precedentes; inaudito, ta

unpredictable [ˌʌnprɪ'dɪktəbl] *adj* imprevisible

unprofessional [ˌʌnprə'feʃənl] *adj* poco profesional

unqualified [ˌʌn'kwɒlɪfaɪd] *adj* ❶ sin título; no cualificado, da ❷ incondicional

unquestionable [ʌn'kwestʃənəbl] *adj* incuestionable; indiscutible

unreal [ˌʌn'rɪəl] *adj* irreal

unrealistic [ˌʌnrɪə'lɪstɪk] *adj* ❶ poco realista ❷ impracticable

unreasonable [ʌn'ri:znəbl] *adj* ❶ poco razonable ❷ excesivo, va

unrelated [ˌʌnrɪ'leɪtɪd] *adj* • **to be unrelated (to)** no tener conexión (con)

unrelenting [ˌʌnrɪ'lentɪŋ] *adj* implacable; inexorable

unreliable [ˌʌnrɪ'laɪəbl] *adj* que no es de fiar

unreserved [ˌʌnrɪ'zɜ:vd] *adj* incondicional; absoluto, ta

unresolved [ˌʌnrɪ'zɒlvd] *adj* sin resolver; pendiente

unrest [ˌʌn'rest] *s* ☼ *incontable* malestar; inquietud

unrivaled [ʌn'raɪvld] *adj* incomparable; sin par

unroll [ˌʌn'rəʊl] *vt* desenrollar

unruly [ʌn'ru:lɪ] *adj* ❶ revoltoso, sa ❷ rebelde

unsafe [ˌʌn'seɪf] *adj* ❶ inseguro, ra ❷ arriesgado, da

unsaid [ˌʌn'sed] *adj* • **to leave something unsaid** dejar algo sin decir

unsatisfactory [ˈʌnˌsætɪs'fæktərɪ] *adj* insatisfactorio, ria

unsavory [ˌʌn'seɪvərɪ] *adj* desagradable

unscathed [ˌʌn'skeɪðd] *adj* ileso, sa

unscheduled [ˌʌn'skedʒʊld] *adj* imprevisto, ta

unscrew [ˌʌn'skru:] *vt* ❶ abrir ❷ desatornillar

unscrupulous [ʌn'skru:pjʊləs] *adj* desaprensivo, va; poco escrupuloso, sa

unselfish [ˌʌn'selfɪʃ] *adj* altruista

unsettle [ˌʌn'setl] *vt* perturbar

unsettled [ˌʌn'setld] *adj* ❶ nervioso, sa; intranquilo, la ❷ variable ❸ pendiente ❹ inestable

unshak(e)able [ʌn'ʃeɪkəbl] *adj* inquebrantable

unshaven [ˌʌn'ʃeɪvn] *adj* sin afeitar

unsightly [ʌn'saɪtlɪ] *adj* ❶ feo, a ❷ desagradable

unskilled [ˌʌn'skɪld] *adj* ❶ no cualificado, da ❷ no especializado, da

unsociable [ʌn'səʊʃəbl] *adj* poco sociable

unsocial [ˌʌn'səʊʃl] *adj* • **to work unsocial hours** trabajar a horas intempestivas

unsound [ˌʌn'saʊnd] *adj* ❶ erróneo, a ❷ defectuoso, sa

unspeakable [ʌn'spi:kəbl] *adj* ❶ incalificable ❷ indecible

unstable [ˌʌn'steɪbl] *adj* inestable

unsteady [ˌʌn'stedɪ] *adj* ❶ inestable ❷ tembloroso, sa ❸ vacilante

unstoppable [ˌʌn'stɒpəbl] *adj* irrefrenable

unstuck [ˌʌn'stʌk] *adj*
expresión **to come unstuck a)** despegarse; desprenderse **b)** *figurado* fracasar

unsubscribe [ˌʌnsəb'skraɪb] *vi* • **to unsubscribe (from sth)** cancelar la suscripción (de algo)

unsuccessful [ˌʌnsək'sesfʊl] *adj* ❶ fracasado, da ❷ infructuoso, sa • **to be unsuccessful** no tener éxito

unsuccessfully [ˌʌnsək'sesfʊlɪ] *adv* sin éxito; en vano

unsuitable [ˌʌn'su:təbl] *adj* inadecuado, da; inapropiado, da • **he is unsuitable for the job** no es la persona indicada para el trabajo • **I'm afraid 3 o'clock would be unsuitable** lo siento, pero no me va bien a las 3

unsure [ˌʌn'ʃɔ:r] *adj* ❶ • **to be unsure of yourself** sentirse inseguro, ra ❷ • **to be unsure (about o of)** no estar muy seguro (de)

unsympathetic [ˈʌnˌsɪmpə'θetɪk] *adj* • **unsympathetic to** indiferente a

untangle [ˌʌn'tæŋgl] *vt* desenmarañar

untenable [ˌʌn'tenəbl] *adj* insostenible

unthinkable [ʌn'θɪŋkəbl] *adj* impensable; inconcebible

untidy [ʌn'taɪdɪ] *adj* ❶ desordenado, da ❷ desaliñado, da

untie [ˌʌn'taɪ] *vt* desatar

Formas irregulares de **untie**: *gerundio* **untying**.

until [ən'tɪl] ◆ *preposición* hasta • **until now/then** hasta ahora/entonces ◆ *conjunción* ❶ hasta que • **wait until everybody is there** espera a que haya llegado todo el mundo ❷ ☼ *después de negativo* • **don't leave until you've finished** no te vayas hasta que hayas terminado

untimely [ʌn'taɪmlɪ] *adj* ❶ prematuro, ra ❷ inoportuno, na

untold [ˌʌn'təʊld] *adj* ❶ incalculable ❷ indecible

untoward [ˌʌntə'wɔ:d] *adj* ❶ adverso, sa ❷ fuera de lugar

untrue [ˌʌn'tru:] *adj* falso, sa

unused *adj* ❶ [ˌʌn'ju:zd] nuevo, va; sin usar ❷ [ʌn'ju:st] • **to be unused to something/to doing something** no estar acostumbrado, da a algo/a hacer algo

unusual [ʌn'ju:ʒl] *adj* insólito, ta; poco común

U

unusually [ʌn'juːʒəlɪ] *adv* ❶ extraordinariamente • **the exam was unusually difficult** el examen fue extraordinariamente difícil ❷ sorprendentemente

unveil [ˌʌn'veɪl] *vt* ❶ descubrir ❷ *figurado* revelar

unwanted [ˌʌn'wɒntɪd] *adj* ❶ superfluo, flua ❷ no deseado, da

unwelcome [ʌn'welkəm] *adj* inoportuno, na

unwell [ˌʌn'wel] *adj* • **to be/feel unwell** estar/sentirse mal

unwieldy [ʌn'wiːldɪ] *adj* ❶ abultado, da ❷ poco manejable ❸ *figurado* poco eficiente

unwilling [ˌʌn'wɪlɪŋ] *adj* • **to be unwilling to do something** no estar dispuesto a hacer algo

unwind [ˌʌn'waɪnd] ◆ *vt* desenrollar ◆ *vi figurado* relajarse

Formas irregulares de **unwind**: *pretérito & pp* **unwound**.

unwise [ˌʌn'waɪz] *adj* imprudente

unwitting [ʌn'wɪtɪŋ] *adj formal* inconsciente

unworkable [ˌʌn'wɜːkəbl] *adj* impracticable

unworthy [ʌn'wɜːðɪ] *adj* • **to be unworthy of** no ser digno, na de

unwound [ˌʌn'waʊnd] *pretérito & participio pasado* → **unwind**

unwrap [ˌʌn'ræp] *vt* ❶ desenvolver ❷ desempaquetar

---

up [ʌp]
◆ *adv*

❶ [*indica un movimiento hacia arriba*]
• **we walked up to the top** subimos hasta la cima
• **she's up in her bedroom** está arriba en su cuarto
• **up there** ahí arriba

❷ [*indica un movimiento de levantarse*]
• **stand up!** ¡levántate!
• **what time did you get up?** ¿a qué hora te levantaste?

❸ [*indica un punto situado en el norte o un desplazamiento hacia el norte*]
• **up north** hacia el norte
• **I'm coming up to New York next week** subo a Nueva York la próxima semana

❹ [*más lejos*]
• **their house is up the street from us** su casa está en la misma calle que la nuestra

❺ [*expresa una idea de haber conseguido algo*]
• **eat up your soup!** ¡acábate la sopa!

❻ [*expresa intensidad*]
• **speak up!** ¡habla más alto!

◆ *preposición*

❶ [*indica un lugar elevado*]
• **he lives up a hill/mountain** vive en lo alto de una colina/montaña
• **he was up a ladder picking cherries** estaba subido a una escalera cogiendo cerezas

❷ [*más lejos*]
• **they live up the road from us** viven en la misma calle que nosotros

❸ [*indica un movimiento hacia el nacimiento de un río*]
• **they sailed up the Amazon** remontaron el Amazonas en barco

◆ *adj*

❶ [*levantarse, estar levantado*]
• **I was up at six today** hoy estaba levantado a las seis
• **he was up all night playing video games** se pasó toda la noche levantado jugando con los videojuegos

❷ [*expresa una subida*]
• **petrol is up again** volvió a subir la gasolina

❸ [*expresa una idea de haber conseguido algo*]
• **his leave is up** su permiso se acabó
• **time's up** se terminó el tiempo

❹ *familiar* [*para preguntar qué está pasando*]
• **what's up?** ¿qué pasa?
• **is something up?** ¿pasa algo?

❺ [*en expresiones*]
• **the road is up** la carretera está en obras
• **his blood is up** está furioso

◆ *s*
• **ups and downs** altos y bajos

■ **up and down**
◆ *adv*
• **to jump up and down** saltar
• **to walk up and down** caminar de arriba a abajo
◆ *preposición*
• **we walked up and down the avenue** recorrimos la avenida de arriba a abajo

■ **up to**
◆ *preposición*

❶ [*hasta*]
• **it could take up to six weeks** podría llevar hasta seis semanas

❷ [*expresa capacidad*]
• **to be up to doing something** ser capaz de hacer algo
• **my French isn't up to much** mi francés no es ninguna maravilla

❸ *familiar* [*hacer, combinar*]
• **what are you up to?** ¿qué estás haciendo?
• **they're up to something** están tramando algo

❹ [*para nombrar a la persona responsable de algo*]
• **it's not up to me to decide** no me toca a mí decidir
• **it's up to you** depende de ti

■ **up until**
◆ *preposición*
hasta
• **up until last year, I worked for myself** hasta el año pasado, era autónomo

up-and-coming *adj* prometedor, ra

upbringing ['ʌpˌbrɪŋɪŋ] *s* educación

update [ˌʌp'deɪt] *vt* actualizar

upheaval [ʌp'hi:vl] *s* trastorno; agitación

upheld [ʌp'held] *pretérito* & *participio pasado* → **uphold**

uphill [ˌʌp'hɪl] ◆ *adj* ❶ empinado, da; cuesta arriba ❷ *figurado* arduo, dua; difícil ◆ *adv* cuesta arriba

uphold [ʌp'həʊld] *vt* sostener; apoyar

Formas irregulares de **uphold**: *pret* & *pp* **upheld**.

upholstery [ʌp'həʊlstərɪ] *s* tapicería

upkeep ['ʌpki:p] *s* mantenimiento

uplifting [ʌp'lɪftɪŋ] *adj* inspirador, ra

up-market *adj* de clase superior

upon [ə'pɒn] *preposición formal* en; sobre • **upon entering the room** al entrar en el cuarto • **question upon question** pregunta tras pregunta • **summer is upon us** ya tenemos el verano encima

upper ['ʌpər] ◆ *adj* superior ◆ *s* empeine

upper class *s* • **the upper class** la clase alta

■ **upper-class** *adj* de clase alta

upper hand *s* • **to have/gain the upper hand (in)** llevar/empezar a llevar la ventaja (en)

uppermost ['ʌpəməʊst] *adj* ❶ más alto, ta ❷ • **to be uppermost in your mind** ser lo más importante para uno

upright ['ʌpraɪt] ◆ *adj* ❶ derecho, cha ❷ vertical ❸ *figurado* recto, ta; honrado, da ◆ *adv* erguidamente ◆ *s* poste

uprising ['ʌp,raɪzɪŋ] *s* sublevación

uproar ['ʌprɔ:r] *s* ❶ ☿ *incontable* alboroto ❷ escándalo

uproot [ʌp'ru:t] *vt* ❶ desplazar; mudar ❷ BOTÁNICA desarraigar

upset [ʌp'set] ◆ *adj* ❶ disgustado, da • **to get upset** disgustarse ❷ MEDICINA • **to have an upset stomach** sentirse mal del estómago ◆ *s* • **to have a stomach upset** sentirse mal del estómago ◆ *vt* ❶ disgustar; perturbar ❷ dar al traste con ❸ volcar

Formas irregulares de **upset**: *pretérito* & *pp* **upset**.

upside down [ˌʌpsaɪd-] ◆ *adj* al revés ◆ *adv* al revés

expresión **to turn something upside down** revolver algo; desordenar algo

upstairs [ˌʌp'steəz] ◆ *adj* de arriba ◆ *adv* arriba ◆ *s* el piso de arriba

upstart ['ʌpstɑ:t] *s* advenedizo, za

upstate [ˌʌp'steɪt] ◆ *adj* • **upstate New York** la parte norteña del Estado de Nueva York ◆ *adv* en/hacia el norte del Estado

upstream [ˌʌp'stri:m] *adv* río arriba

upsurge ['ʌps3:dʒ] *s* • **upsurge of** o **in** aumento considerable de

uptake ['ʌpteɪk] *s* • **to be quick on the uptake** cogerlas al vuelo • **to be slow on the uptake** ser un poco torpe

uptight [ʌp'taɪt] *adj familiar* tenso, sa; nervioso, sa

up-to-date *adj* ❶ moderno, na ❷ actual; al día ❸ • **to keep up-to-date with** mantenerse al día de

uptown [ˌʌp'taʊn] ◆ *adj* alejado, da del centro ◆ *adv* ❶ en las afueras ❷ a las afueras

upturn ['ʌpt3:n] *s* • **upturn (in)** mejora (de)

upward ['ʌpwəd] ◆ *adj* hacia arriba ◆ *adv* = **upwards**

upwards ['ʌpwədz], **upward** *adv* hacia arriba

■ **upwards of** *preposición* más de

uranium [jʊ'reɪnjəm] *s* uranio

Uranus ['jʊərənəs] *s* Urano

urban ['3:bən] *adj* urbano, na

urbane [3:'beɪn] *adj* cortés; urbano, na

urge [3:dʒ] ◆ *s* impulso; deseo • **to have an urge to do something** desear ardientemente hacer algo ◆ *vt* ❶ • **to urge somebody to do something** instar a alguien a hacer algo ❷ recomendar encarecidamente

urgency ['3:dʒənsɪ] *s* ☿ *incontable* urgencia

urgent ['3:dʒənt] *adj* ❶ urgente ❷ apremiante

urinal [ˌjʊə'raɪnl] *s* ❶ urinario ❷ orinal

urinate ['jʊərɪneɪt] *vi* orinar

urine ['jʊərɪn] *s* orina

URL (*abreviatura de* uniform resource locator) *s* INFORMÁTICA URL

urn [3:n] *s* urna

Uruguay ['jʊərəgwaɪ] *s* Uruguay

Uruguayan [ˌjʊərə'gwaɪən] ◆ *adj* uruguayo, ya ◆ *s* uruguayo, ya

us [ʌs] *pronombre personal* ❶ ☿ *directo, indirecto* nos • **can you see/hear us?** ¿puedes vernos/oírnos? • **it's us** somos nosotros • **he sent us a letter** nos mandó una carta • **she gave it to us** nos lo dio ❷ ☿ *acento tónico, tras preposición, en comparaciones* nosotros, tras • **you can't expect us to do it** no esperarás que lo hagamos nosotros • **with/without us** con/sin nosotros • **they are more wealthy than us** son más ricos que nosotros • **all of us** todos (nosotros) • **some of us** algunos de nosotros

US (*abreviatura de* United States) *s* EEUU

USA (*abreviatura de* United States of America) *s* EEUU

usage ['ju:zɪdʒ] *s* uso

USB port *s* INFORMÁTICA puerto USB

---

use

◆ *s* [ju:s]

❶ [*indica un uso*]

• **this machine is in use every day** utilizamos esta máquina todos los días

• **this machine is out of use** esta máquina no funciona

• **nowadays this word is out of use** hoy en día esta palabra ya no se usa

❷ [*indica la posibilidad de usar algo*]

• **I have the use of his garage** me deja usar su garaje

- **he gave me the use of his car** me deja usar su carro
- **he's lost the use of his left arm** se le quedó el brazo izquierdo inutilizado

❸ [*expresa la utilidad*]
- **to be of use** ser útil
- **it's no use crying** de nada sirve llorar
- **what's the use (of doing something)?** ¿de qué sirve(hacer algo)?

expresión **to make use of something** utilizar algo

◆ *auxiliar* [ju:s]

💡 **solo en pretérito** [*indica una acción habitual en el pasado que ya no ocurre en el presente*]
- **I used to live in London** antes vivía en Londres
- **there used to be a tree here** (antes) solía haber un árbol aquí

◆ *vt* [ju:z]

❶ [*indica un uso*]
- **he used scissors to open the parcel** usó tijeras para abrir el paquete
- **we used the money to buy a new car** usamos el dinero para comprar un coche nuevo
- **somebody is using the bathroom** hay alguien en el baño

❷ *despectivo* [*indica un abuso*]
- **he used me** me usó

■ **use up**

◆ *vt* 💡 *El objeto se puede colocar antes o después de la preposición.*

agotar

---

use 🌀

Used to tiene tres usos distintos que no conviene confundir.

En primer lugar, used to se utiliza seguido de infinitivo sin to para hablar de una acción que ocurría de forma habitual u ocurrió durante un periodo de tiempo en el pasado (they *used to live* next door but they've moved now *vivían al lado pero ya se mudaron*).

En segundo lugar, used to se emplea seguido de un gerundio para expresar la costumbre de

hacer algo (I don't mind leaving at 6 o'clock tomorrow morning — I'm *used to getting up* early *no me importa salir mañana a las seis; estoy acostumbrada a madrugar*).

Por último, used to puede formar parte de una construcción pasiva que exprese intención o finalidad (this part *is used to increase* the speed of the engine *esta pieza sirve para aumentar la velocidad del motor*). En este caso suele ir precedido del verbo be y seguido de infinitivo sin to.

used *adj* ❶ [ju:zd] usado, da ❷ [ju:st] • **to be used to** estar acostumbrado, da a • **to get used to** acostumbrarse a

useful ['ju:sfʊl] *adj* ❶ útil ❷ valioso, sa

useless ['ju:slɪs] *adj* ❶ inútil ❷ *familiar* incompetente

user ['ju:zər] *s* usuario, ria

user-friendly *adj* fácil de utilizar

usual ['ju:ʒəl] *adj* habitual • **as usual a)** como de costumbre **b)** como siempre

usually ['ju:ʒəlɪ] *adv* por regla general • **we usually go to church on Sunday** solemos ir a misa el domingo

utensil [ju:'tensl] *s* utensilio

uterus ['ju:tərəs] *s* útero

Dos plurales: **uteri** ['ju:təraɪ] o **uteruses**.

utility [ju:'tɪlətɪ] *s* ❶ utilidad ❷ servicio público
■ **utilities** *s* empresa de servicios públicos

utility room *s* trascocina

utilize, utilise ['ju:təlaɪz] *vt* utilizar

utmost ['ʌtməʊst] ◆ *adj* mayor; supremo, ma ◆ *s*
- **to do your utmost** hacer lo imposible • **to the utmost** al máximo; a más no poder

utter ['ʌtər] ◆ *adj* puro, ra; completo, ta ◆ *vt* ❶ pronunciar ❷ emitir

utterly ['ʌtəlɪ] *adv* completamente

U-turn *s literal & figurado* giro de 180° • **to do a U-turn a)** cambiar de sentido **b)** *figurado* dar un giro radical

v¹, V [viː] *s* v; V

Dos plurales: **v's** o **vs; V's** o **Vs.**

v² ❶ (*abreviatura escrita de* verse) v ❷ (*abreviatura escrita de* volt) v ❸ *abreviatura escrita de* **versus**

vacancy ['veɪkənsɪ] *s* ❶ vacante ❷ habitación libre • **'no vacancies'** 'completo'

vacant ['veɪkənt] *adj* ❶ libre ❷ vacante ❸ distraído, da

vacant lot *s* terreno disponible

vacate [vəˈkeɪt] *vt* ❶ dejar vacante ❷ desocupar

vacation [vəˈkeɪʃn] ◆ *s* vacaciones • **to be on vacation** estar de vacaciones ◆ *vi* pasar las vacaciones

vacationer [vəˈkeɪʃənər] *s* • **summer vacationer** veraneante

vaccinate ['væksɪneɪt] *vt* • **to vaccinate somebody (against something)** vacunar a alguien (de o contra algo)

vaccine [vækˈsiːn] *s* vacuna

vacuum ['vækjʊəm] ◆ *s* ❶ *figurado* TECNOLOGÍA vacío ❷ aspiradora ◆ *vt* pasar la aspiradora por

vacuum cleaner *s* aspiradora

vacuum-packed *adj* envasado, da al vacío

vagina [vəˈdʒaɪnə] *s* vagina

vagrant ['veɪɡrənt] *s* vagabundo, da

vague [veɪɡ] *adj* ❶ vago, ga; impreciso, sa ❷ poco claro, ra ❸ leve *(sentimiento)* ❹ evasivo, va

vaguely ['veɪɡlɪ] *adv* ❶ vagamente ❷ levemente

vain [veɪn] *adj* ❶ *despectivo* vanidoso, sa ❷ vano, na

■ **in vain** *adv* en vano

valentine card ['væləntaɪn-] *s* ▶ tarjeta que se manda el Día de los Enamorados

valid ['vælɪd] *adj* ❶ válido, da ❷ en vigor • **to be valid for six months** ser válido, da durante seis meses

valley ['vælɪ] *s* valle

valuable ['væljʊəbl] *adj* valioso, sa

■ **valuables** *spl* objetos de valor

valuation [ˌvæljʊˈeɪʃn] *s* ❶ valuación ❷ valoración

value ['væljuː] ◆ *s* valor

expresiones **to be good value** estar muy bien de precio ▶ **to be value for money** estar muy bien de precio ▶ **to take something/somebody at face value** tomarse algo/a alguien en su sentido literal

◆ *vt* ❶ valorar; tasar • **a necklace valued at $300** un collar valorado en 300 dólares ❷ apreciar

■ **values** *spl* valores morales

valued ['væljuːd] *adj* apreciado, da

valve [vælv] *s* válvula

vamoose [vəˈmuːs] *vi familiar* • **vamoose!** ¡largo o fuera de aquí!

van [væn] *s* AUTOMÓVILES furgoneta; camioneta

vandal ['vændl] *s* vándalo

vandalism ['vændəlɪzm] *s* vandalismo

vandalize, vandalise ['vændəlaɪz] *vt* destrozar

vanguard ['vænɡɑːd] *s* vanguardia • **in the vanguard of** a la vanguardia de

vanilla [vəˈnɪlə] *s* vainilla

vanish ['vænɪʃ] *vi* desaparecer

vanity ['vænətɪ] *s despectivo* vanidad

vantage point ['vɑːntɪdʒˌpɔɪnt] *s* posición ventajosa

vapor ['veɪpər] *s incontable* vapor

variable ['veərɪəbl] *adj* variable

variance ['veərɪəns] *s formal* • **at variance (with)** en desacuerdo (con)

variation [ˌveərɪˈeɪʃn] *s* • **variation (in/on)** variación (en/sobre)

varicose veins ['værɪkəʊs-] *spl* varices

varied ['veərɪd] *adj* variado, da

variety [vəˈraɪətɪ] *s* ❶ variedad • **for a variety of reasons** por razones varias ❷ *incontable* TEATRO variedades

variety show *s* espectáculo de variedades

various ['veərɪəs] *adj* ❶ varios, rias ❷ diversos, sas

varnish ['vɑːnɪʃ] ◆ *s* barniz ◆ *vt* ❶ barnizar ❷ pintar

vary ['veərɪ] ◆ *vt* variar ◆ *vi* • **to vary (in/with)** variar (de/con)

vase [veɪz] *s* florero

Vaseline® ['væsəliːn] *s* vaselina®

vast [vɑːst] *adj* enorme; inmenso, sa

vat [væt] *s* tina

Vatican ['vætɪkən] *s* • **the Vatican** el Vaticano

vault [vɔːlt] *s* ❶ cámara acorazada ❷ cripta ❸ bóveda

VCR (*abreviatura de* video cassette recorder) *s* grabadora de video

VDU (*abreviatura de* visual display unit) *s* monitor

veal [viːl] *s* 🔆 *incontable* ternera

vegan ['viːgən] *s* ❱ vegetariano que no consume ningún producto que provenga de un animal, como huevos, leche, etc

vegetable ['vedʒtəbl] ◆ *s* ❶ BOTÁNICA vegetal ❷ hortaliza; legumbre • **vegetables** verduras ◆ *adj* vegetal

vegetarian [ˌvedʒɪ'teəriən] ◆ *adj* vegetariano, na ◆ *s* vegetariano, na

vegetation [ˌvedʒɪ'teɪʃn] *s* vegetación

veggieburger ['vedʒɪbɜːgər] *s* hamburguesa vegetariana

vehement ['viːəmənt] *adj* ❶ vehemente ❷ violento, ta

vehicle ['viːəkl] *s* vehículo

veil [veɪl] ◆ *s* *literal & figurado* velo ◆ *vt* cubrir con un velo

vein [veɪn] *s* ❶ ANATOMÍA & BOTÁNICA vena ❷ filón; veta

velocity [vɪ'lɒsətɪ] *s* velocidad

velvet ['velvɪt] *s* terciopelo

vending machine ['vendɪŋ-] *s* máquina expendedora

vendor ['vendɔːr] *s* vendedor, ra

veneer [və'nɪər] *s* ❶ chapa ❷ *figurado* apariencia • **a veneer of** una apariencia de

venetian blind *s* persiana veneciana

Venezuela [ˌvenɪz'weɪlə] *s* Venezuela

Venezuelan [ˌvenɪz'weɪlən] ◆ *adj* venezolano, na ◆ *s* venezolano, na

vengeance ['vendʒəns] *s* venganza • **with a vengeance** con creces

venison ['venɪzn] *s* carne de venado

venom ['venəm] *s* ❶ veneno ❷ *figurado* malevolencia

vent [vent] ◆ *s* ❶ abertura de escape ❷ rejilla de ventilación

expresión **to give vent to something** dar rienda suelta a algo

◆ *vt* • **to vent something (on)** desahogar algo (contra)

ventilate ['ventɪleɪt] *vt* ventilar

ventilator ['ventɪleɪtər] *s* ventilador

venture ['ventʃər] ◆ *s* empresa ◆ *vt* aventurar • **to venture an opinion** aventurarse a dar una opinión

• **to venture to do something** aventurarse a hacer algo ◆ *vi* ❶ • **she ventured outside** se atrevió a salir ❷ • **to venture into** lanzarse a

venue ['venjuː] *s* lugar; local

Venus ['viːnəs] *s* Venus

veranda(h) [və'rændə] *s* porche

verb [vɜːb] *s* verbo

verbal ['vɜːbl] *adj* verbal

verdict ['vɜːdɪkt] *s* DERECHO veredicto; fallo • **a verdict of guilty/not guilty** un veredicto de culpabilidad/inocencia

verge [vɜːdʒ] *s* ❶ borde ❷ • **on the verge of something** al borde de algo • **to be on the verge of doing something** estar a punto de hacer algo

■ **verge (up)on** *vt* 🔆 *El objeto siempre va después de la preposición al final.* rayar en

verify ['verɪfaɪ] *vt* ❶ verificar; comprobar ❷ confirmar

veritable ['verɪtəbl] *adj* *humorístico & formal* verdadero, ra

vermin ['vɜːmɪn] *spl* ❶ bichos ❷ alimañas

vermouth ['vɜːməθ] *s* vermut

versa → **vice versa**

versatile ['vɜːsətaɪl] *adj* ❶ polifacético, ca ❷ que tiene muchos usos

verse [vɜːs] *s* ❶ 🔆 *incontable* poesía ❷ estrofa ❸ versículo

versed [vɜːst] *adj* • **well versed in** versado, da en

version ['vɜːʃn] *s* versión

versus ['vɜːsəs] *preposición* DEPORTE contra

vertebra ['vɜːtɪbrə] *s* vértebra

El plural de **vertebra** es **vertebrae** ['vɜːtɪbriː].

vertical ['vɜːtɪkl] *adj* vertical

vertigo ['vɜːtɪgəʊ] *s* vértigo

verve [vɜːv] *s* brío; entusiasmo

very ['verɪ] ◆ *adv* ❶ muy • **he's not very intelligent** no es muy inteligente • **very much** mucho • **I don't go out very often** o **much** no salgo mucho • **is it good?** — **not very** ¿es bueno? — no mucho ❷ • **the very same/next day** justo ese mismo día/al día siguiente • **the very first** el primero de todos • **the very best** el mejor (de todos) • **at the very least** como muy poco • **a house of my very own** mi propia casa ◆ *adj* • **in the very middle of the picture** en el mismísimo centro del cuadro • **the very thing I was looking for** justo lo que estaba buscando • **the very thought makes me ill** sólo con pensarlo me pongo enfermo • **fighting for his very life** luchando por su propia vida • **the very idea!** ¡vaya idea!

■ **very well** *adv* muy bien • **you can't very well stop him now** es un poco tarde para impedírselo

vessel ['vesl] *s* *formal* ❶ nave ❷ vasija; recipiente

vest [vest] *s* chaleco

vested interest ['vestɪd-] *s* • **vested interest (in)** intereses creados (en)

V

vestibule ['vestɪbjuːl] *s* **❶** *formal* vestíbulo **❷** fuelle

vestige ['vestɪdʒ] *s formal* vestigio

vet [vet] *s (abreviatura de* veteran) excombatiente

veteran ['vetrən] *s* veterano, na

veterinarian [ˌvetərɪˈneərɪən] *s* veterinario, ria

veto ['viːtəʊ] ◆ *s* veto ◆ *vt* vetar
El plural de **veto** es **vetoes**.

vg *(abreviatura escrita de* very good) MB

VHF *(abreviatura de* very high frequency) VHF

VHS *(abreviatura de* video home system) *s* VHS

via ['vaɪə] *preposición* **❶** vía **❷** a través de; por

viable ['vaɪəbl] *adj* viable

vibrate [vaɪˈbreɪt] *vi* vibrar

vice [vaɪs] *s* **❶** vicio **❷** torno de banco

vice-chairman *s* vicepresidente

vice-chancellor *s* UNIVERSIDAD rector, ra

vice-president *s* vicepresidente, ta

vice versa [ˌvaɪsɪˈvɜːsə] *adv* viceversa

vicinity [vɪˈsɪnətɪ] *s* • **in the vicinity (of)** cerca (de)

vicious ['vɪʃəs] *adj* **❶** furioso, sa *(perro)* **❷** cruel **❸** despiadado, da *(ataque, crítica)*

vicious circle *s* círculo vicioso

victim ['vɪktɪm] *s* víctima

victimize, victimise ['vɪktɪmaɪz] *vt* **❶** tomar represalias contra **❷** mortificar

victorious [vɪkˈtɔːrɪəs] *adj* victorioso, sa

victory ['vɪktərɪ] *s* • **victory (over)** victoria (sobre)

video ['vɪdɪəʊ] ◆ *s* **❶** video **❷** videocasete ◆ *vt* **❶** grabar en video **❷** hacer un video de
El plural de **video** es **videos**.

video camera *s* videocámara

video cassette *s* videocasete

videoconference ['vɪdɪəʊˌkɒnfərəns] *s* videoconferencia

videoconferencing ['vɪdɪəʊˌkɒnfərənsɪŋ] *s* 🔆 *incontable* videoconferencias

video game *s* videojuego

video on demand *s* 🔆 *incontable* TELEVISIÓN video a la carta

videorecorder ['vɪdɪəʊrɪˌkɔːdər] *s* video

video shop *s* tienda de videos

videotape ['vɪdɪəʊteɪp] *s* videocinta

vie [vaɪ] *vi* • **to vie (with somebody for something/to do something)** competir (con alguien por algo/para hacer algo)
Formas irregulares de **vie:** *pretérito & pp* **vied,** *gerundio* **vying.**

Vietnam [ˌvjetˈnɑːm] *s* (el) Vietnam

Vietnamese [ˌvjetnəˈmiːz] ◆ *adj* vietnamita ◆ *s* vietnamita

view [vjuː] ◆ *s* **❶** parecer; opinión • **in my view** en mi opinión **❷** • **view (of)** actitud (frente a) **❸** vista; panorama **❹** vista • **to come into view** aparecer ◆ *vt* **❶** ver; considerar **❷** *formal* observar; visitar; ver
■ **in view of** *preposición* en vista de
■ **with a view to** *conjunción* con miras o vistas a

viewer ['vjuːər] *s* **❶** espectador, ra **❷** visualizador

viewfinder ['vjuːˌfaɪndər] *s* visor

viewpoint ['vjuːpɔɪnt] *s* **❶** punto de vista **❷** mirador

vigil ['vɪdʒɪl] *s* vigilia • **to keep (a) vigil** observar vigilia

vigilante [ˌvɪdʒɪˈlæntɪ] *s* ▸ persona que extraoficialmente patrulla un área para protegerla, tomándose la justicia en sus manos

vigorous ['vɪgərəs] *adj* enérgico, ca

vile [vaɪl] *adj* **❶** vil; infame *(persona, acción)* **❷** repugnante *(olor)* **❸** de perros *(humor)*

villa ['vɪlə] *s* **❶** villa **❷** chalet

village ['vɪlɪdʒ] *s* aldea; pueblecito

villager ['vɪlɪdʒər] *s* aldeano, na

villain ['vɪlən] *s* malo, la

vinaigrette [ˌvɪnɪˈgret] *s* vinagreta

vindicate ['vɪndɪkeɪt] *vt* justificar

vindictive [vɪnˈdɪktɪv] *adj* vengativo, va

vine [vaɪn] *s* **❶** vid **❷** parra

vinegar ['vɪnɪgər] *s* vinagre

vineyard ['vɪnjəd] *s* viña; viñedo

vintage ['vɪntɪdʒ] ◆ *adj* **❶** añejo, ja **❷** clásico, ca **❸** • **a vintage year** un año excepcional ◆ *s* cosecha *(de vino)*

vintage wine *s* vino añejo

vinyl ['vaɪnɪl] *s* vinilo

viola [vɪˈəʊlə] *s* viola

violate ['vaɪəleɪt] *vt* **❶** violar; infringir **❷** invadir

violence ['vaɪələns] *s* violencia

violent ['vaɪələnt] *adj* **❶** violento, ta **❷** intenso, sa • **to have a violent dislike for somebody** sentir una enorme antipatía hacia alguien

violet ['vaɪələt] ◆ *adj* violeta; violado, da ◆ *s* violeta

violin [ˌvaɪəˈlɪn] *s* violín

violinist [ˌvaɪəˈlɪnɪst] *s* violinista

VIP *(abreviatura de* very important person) *s* VIP

viper ['vaɪpər] *s* víbora

virgin ['vɜːdʒɪn] *adj* & *s* virgen

Virgo ['vɜːgəʊ] *s* Virgo

virile ['vɪraɪl] *adj* viril

virtually ['vɜːtʃʊəlɪ] *adv* prácticamente

virtual reality *s* realidad virtual

virtue ['vɜːtjuː] *s* **❶** virtud **❷** ventaja
■ **by virtue of** *preposición formal* en virtud de

virtuous ['vɜːtʃʊəs] *adj* virtuoso, sa

virus ['vaɪrəs] *s* INFORMÁTICA & MEDICINA virus

visa ['viːzə] *s* visa

viscose ['vɪskəʊs] *s* viscosa

vise [vaɪs] *s* torno de banco

visibility [ˌvɪzɪ'bɪlətɪ] *s* visibilidad

visible ['vɪzəbl] *adj* visible

vision ['vɪʒn] *s* ❶ ☀*incontable* visión; vista ❷ *figurado* clarividencia ❸ visión

visit ['vɪzɪt] ◆ *s* visita • **to pay somebody a visit** hacer una visita a alguien • **on a visit** de visita ◆ *vt* visitar ■ **visit with** *vt* ❶ hablar o charlar con ❷ visitar; ir a ver

visiting hours ['vɪzɪtɪŋ-] *spl* horas de visita

visitor ['vɪzɪtər] *s* ❶ visita • **we've got visitors** tenemos visitas ❷ visitante

visitors' book *s* libro de visitas

visor ['vaɪzər] *s* visera

vista ['vɪstə] *s* ❶ vista; perspectiva ❷ *figurado* perspectiva

visual ['vɪʒʊəl] *adj* ❶ visual ❷ ocular

visual aids *spl* medios visuales

visual display unit *s* monitor

visualize, visualise ['vɪʒʊəlaɪz] *vt* visualizar • **to visualize (somebody) doing something** imaginar (a alguien) haciendo algo

vital ['vaɪtl] *adj* ❶ vital ❷ enérgico, ca

vitally ['vaɪtəlɪ] *adv* sumamente

vital statistics *spl familiar* medidas *(del cuerpo de la mujer)*

vitamin ['vaɪtəmɪn] *s* vitamina • **vitamin C** vitamina C

vitamin pill *s* pastilla vitamínica

vivacious [vɪ'veɪʃəs] *adj* vivaz

vivid ['vɪvɪd] *adj* ❶ vivo, va ❷ vívido, da

vividly ['vɪvɪdlɪ] *adv* ❶ con colores muy vivos ❷ vívidamente

vixen ['vɪksn] *s* zorra

V-neck *s* jersey con cuello de pico

vocabulary [və'kæbjʊlərɪ] *s* vocabulario

vocal ['vəʊkl] *adj* ❶ vociferante ❷ vocal

vocal cords *spl* cuerdas vocales

vocalist ['vəʊkəlɪst] *s* ❶ vocalista ❷ cantante

vocation [vəʊ'keɪʃn] *s* vocación

vocational [vəʊ'keɪʃənl] *adj* profesional

vodka ['vɒdkə] *s* vodka

vogue [vəʊg] *s* moda • **in vogue** en boga; de moda

voice [vɔɪs] ◆ *s* voz • **to give voice to** expresar ◆ *vt* expresar

voice mail *s* correo de voz • **to send/receive voice mail** mandar/recibir un mensaje de correo de voz • **to check your voice mail** verificar el correo de voz

void [vɔɪd] ◆ *adj* ❶ inválido, da ; → **null** ❷ *formal* • **void of** falto, ta de ◆ *s literario* vacío

volatile ['vɒlətl] *adj* ❶ volátil ❷ voluble

volcano [vɒl'keɪnəʊ] *s* volcán

Dos plurales: **volcanoes** o **volcanos**.

volley ['vɒlɪ] ◆ *s* ❶ ráfaga ❷ *figurado* torrente ❸ DEPORTE volea ◆ *vt* volear

volleyball ['vɒlɪbɔːl] *s* voleibol

volt [vəʊlt] *s* voltio

voltage ['vəʊltɪdʒ] *s* voltaje

voluble ['vɒljʊbl] *adj formal* locuaz

volume ['vɒljuːm] *s* volumen

expresión **to speak volumes** decir mucho

voluntarily [ˌvɒlən'terəlɪ] *adv* voluntariamente

voluntary ['vɒləntrɪ] *adj* voluntario, ria • **voluntary organization** organización benéfica

volunteer [ˌvɒlən'tɪər] ◆ *s* voluntario, ria ◆ *vi* ❶ • **to volunteer to do something** ofrecerse para hacer algo ❷ dar; ofrecer ◆ *vi* ❶ • **to volunteer (for)** ofrecerse (para) ❷ MILITAR alistarse

vomit ['vɒmɪt] ◆ *s* vómito ◆ *vi* vomitar

vote [vəʊt] ◆ *s* ❶ voto ❷ votación • **to put something to the vote, to take a vote on something** someter algo a votación ❸ • **the vote** los votos ◆ *vt* ❶ elegir ❷ • **to vote to do something** votar hacer algo ◆ *vi* • **to vote (for/against)** votar (a favor de/ en contra de)

voter ['vəʊtər] *s* votante

voting ['vəʊtɪŋ] *s* votación

vouch [vaʊtʃ] ■ **vouch for** *vt* ☀*El objeto siempre va después de la preposición al final.* ❶ responder por ❷ dar fe de

voucher ['vaʊtʃər] *s* vale

vow [vaʊ] ◆ *s* ❶ RELIGIÓN voto ❷ promesa solemne ◆ *vt* • **to vow to do something** jurar hacer algo • **to vow that** jurar que

vowel ['vaʊəl] *s* vocal

voyage ['vɔɪɪdʒ] *s* viaje

vs abreviatura escrita de **versus**

vulgar ['vʌlgər] *adj* ❶ ordinario, ria ❷ grosero, ra

vulnerable ['vʌlnərəbl] *adj* • **vulnerable (to)** vulnerable (a)

vulture ['vʌltʃər] *s literal & figurado* buitre

V

w, W ['dʌblju:] *s* w; W

■ **W** *abreviatura* ❶ (*abreviatura de* west) O ❷ (*abreviatura de* watt) w

Dos plurales: **w's** o **ws; W's** o **Ws.**

wad [wɒd] *s* ❶ taco (*de papel*) ❷ fajo (*de billetes*) ❸ bola (*de algodón*))

waddle ['wɒdl] *vi* caminar como un pato

wade [weɪd] *vi* caminar por el agua

■ **wade through** *vt* ☼ *El objeto siempre va después de la preposición al final. figurado* • **he was wading through the documents** le costaba mucho leer los documentos

wading pool ['weɪdɪŋ-] *s* chapoteadero

wafer ['weɪfər] *s* oblea

waffle ['wɒfl] ◆ *s* COCINA waffle ◆ *vi* cambiar de opinión continuamente • **to waffle about something** cambiar de opinión sobre algo

wag [wæg] ◆ *vt* menear • **the dog was wagging its tail** el perro meneaba la cola ◆ *vi* menearse

wage [weɪdʒ] ◆ *s* ❶ salario ❷ jornal ◆ *vt* • **to wage war** hacer la guerra

■ **wages** *spl* ❶ salario ❷ jornal

wage earner [-,ɜːnər] *s* asalariado, da

wager ['weɪdʒər] *s* apuesta

waggle ['wægl] *vt familiar* menear

waggon ['wægən] = **wagon**

wagon, waggon ['wægən] *s* carro

wail [weɪl] ◆ *s* lamento; gemido ◆ *vi* lamentarse; gemir

waist [weɪst] *s* cintura

waistcoat ['weɪskəʊt] *s* chaleco

waistline ['weɪstlaɪn] *s* cintura; talle

wait [weɪt] ◆ *s* espera • **to lie in wait for somebody** estar al acecho de alguien ◆ *vi* • **to wait (for something/somebody)** esperar (algo/a alguien) • **keys cut while you wait** se hacen llaves en el acto

expresión to wait and see esperar y ver lo que pasa ▶ **wait a minute** o **second** o **moment! a)** ¡espera un minuto o segundo o momento! **b)** ¡espera!

■ **wait for** *vt* ☼ *El objeto siempre va después de la preposición al final.* esperar

■ **wait on** *vt* ☼ *El objeto siempre va después de la preposición al final.* servir

■ **wait up** *vi* ❶ quedarse despierto, ta esperando ❷ • **wait up!** ¡un momento!

waiter ['weɪtər] *s* camarero

waiting list ['weɪtɪŋ-] *s* lista de espera

waiting room ['weɪtɪŋ-] *s* sala de espera

waitress ['weɪtrɪs] *s* camarera

wake [weɪk] ◆ *s* estela • **in the wake of** *figurado* tras ◆ *vt* despertar ◆ *vi* despertarse

■ **wake up** ◆ *vt* ☼ *El objeto se puede colocar antes o después de la preposición.* despertar ◆ *vi* despertarse

Formas irregulares de **wake:** pretérito **woke** o **waked,** pp **woken** o **woked.**

waken ['weɪkən] *formal* ◆ *vt* despertar ◆ *vi* despertarse

Wales [weɪlz] *s* (el país de) Gales

walk [wɔːk] ◆ *s* ❶ andar; paseo ❷ paseo • **to go for a walk** dar un paseo • **it's ten minutes' walk away** está a diez minutos andando ◆ *vt* ❶ pasear ❷ andar por ❸ recorrer; andar ◆ *vi* ❶ andar; caminar ❷ pasear

■ **walk out** *vi* ❶ salirse ❷ declararse en huelga

■ **walk out on** *vt* ☼ *El objeto siempre va después de la preposición al final.* abandonar

walker ['wɔːkər] *s* caminante; paseante

walkie-talkie [,wɔːkɪ'tɔːkɪ] *s* walki-talki

walk-in *adj* ❶ • **walk-in closet** vestidor ❷ fácil

walking ['wɔːkɪŋ] ◆ *s* ❶ ☼ *incontable* marcha ❷ andar • **he does a lot of walking** camina mucho ◆ *adj* • **he's a walking disaster** *humorístico* es un desastre andante

walking shoes *spl* zapatos para caminar

walking stick *s* bastón

Walkman® ['wɔːkmən] *s* walkman®

walk of life *s* • **people from all walks of life** gente de toda condición

El plural de **walk of life** es **walks of life.**

walkout ['wɔːkaʊt] *s* huelga

walkover ['wɔːk,əʊvər] *s* victoria fácil

walkup ['ːwɔːkʌp] *s* edificio sin ascensor

walkway ['wɔːkweɪ] *s* ❶ pasarela ❷ paso

wall [wɔːl] *s* ❶ pared ❷ muro

ɛxpresión it's like talking to a brick wall le entra por un oído y le sale por el otro ▸ to drive somebody up the wall volver loco a alguien

wallchart ['wɔːltʃɑːt] *s* (gráfico) mural

walled [wɔːld] *adj* amurallado, da

wallet ['wɒlɪt] *s* cartera; billetera

wallop ['wɒləp] *vt familiar* ❶ pegar una torta a ❷ golpear fuerte

wallpaper ['wɔːl,peɪpər] ◆ *s* ❶ papel pintado ❷ *INFORMÁTICA* papel tapiz ◆ *vt* empapelar

Wall Street *s* Wall Street

walnut ['wɔːlnʌt] *s* ❶ nuez ❷ nogal

walrus ['wɔːlrəs] *s* morsa

Dos plurales: **walrus** o **walruses**.

waltz [wɔːls] ◆ *s* vals ◆ *vi* bailar el vals

wand [wɒnd] *s* • **(magic) wand** varita mágica

wander ['wɒndər] *vi* vagar • **my mind kept wandering** se me iba la mente en otras cosas

wane [weɪn] *vi* disminuir; decrecer

wangle ['wæŋgl] *vt familiar* agenciarse

want [wɒnt] ◆ *s formal* ❶ necesidad ❷ falta • **for want of** por o a falta de ❸ indigencia; miseria ◆ *vt* querer • **to want to do something** querer hacer algo • **to want somebody to do something** querer que alguien haga algo

want ad *s familiar* anuncio por palabras

wanted ['wɒntɪd] *adj* • **to be wanted (by the police)** ser buscado, da (por la policía)

WAP [wæp] *(abreviatura de* wireless application protocol*) s* WAP

war [wɔːr] ◆ *s literal & figurado* guerra • **to be at war** estar en guerra • **the war on drugs** la guerra contra las drogas ◆ *vi* estar en guerra

ward [wɔːd] *s* ❶ sala ❷ *DERECHO* pupilo, la

■ **ward off** *vt* ☼ *El objeto siempre va después de la preposición al final.* protegerse de

warden ['wɔːdn] *s* ❶ guarda ❷ • **(traffic) warden** ≃ guardia de tráfico ❸ director, ra

warder ['wɔːdər] *s* carcelero, ra

wardrobe ['wɔːdrəʊb] *s* ❶ armario ❷ guardarropa; vestuario

warehouse ['weəhaʊs] ☼ *pl* [-haʊzɪz] *s* almacén

warfare ['wɔːfeər] *s* ☼ *incontable* guerra

warhead ['wɔːhed] *s* ojiva; cabeza

warily ['weərəlɪ] *adv* con cautela

warm [wɔːm] ◆ *adj* ❶ caliente; caluroso, sa ❷ tibio, bia; templado, da • **it's/I'm warm** hace/tengo calor • **to get warm** calentarse • **they tried to keep warm** intentaron mantenerse calientes ❸ que abriga ❹ cálido, da ❺ afectuoso, sa; efusivo, va ◆ *vt* calentar

■ **warm up** ◆ *vt* ☼ *El objeto se puede colocar antes o después de la preposición.* calentar ◆ *vi* ❶ entrar en calor ❷ calentarse ❸ calentar

warm-hearted [-'hɑːtɪd] *adj* afectuoso, sa

warmly ['wɔːmlɪ] *adv* ❶ • **to dress warmly** vestirse con ropa de abrigo ❷ calurosamente

warmth [wɔːmθ] *s* ❶ calor ❷ abrigo ❸ cordialidad

warn [wɔːn] *vt* advertir • **to warn somebody of something** advertir a alguien de algo • **to warn somebody not to do something, warn somebody against doing something** advertir a alguien que no haga algo

warning ['wɔːnɪŋ] *s* aviso; advertencia • **to give somebody a warning** hacer una advertencia a alguien • **without warning** sin previo aviso

warning light *s* piloto *(luz)*

warp [wɔːp] *vi* combarse; alabearse

warrant ['wɒrənt] *s* orden o mandamiento judicial

warranty ['wɒrəntɪ] *s* garantía • **to be under warranty** estar en garantía

warren ['wɒrən] *s* red de madrigueras

warrior ['wɒrɪər] *s* guerrero, ra

warship ['wɔːʃɪp] *s* buque de guerra

wart [wɔːt] *s* verruga

wartime ['wɔːtaɪm] *s* tiempos de guerra

wary ['weərɪ] *adj* • **wary (of)** receloso, sa (de)

was ☼ *acento atónico* [wəz], *acento tónico* [wɒz] *pretérito* → **be**

wash [wɒʃ] ◆ *s* ❶ lavado • **to have a wash** lavarse • **to give something a wash** lavar algo ❷ ropa sucia ❸ estela ◆ *vt* ❶ lavar ❷ lavarse • **she's washing her hair** se está lavando el pelo ❸ arrastrar • **it was washed ashore** el mar lo arrastró hasta la costa ◆ *vi* ❶ lavarse ❷ • **to wash over something** bañar algo

■ **wash away** *vt* ☼ *El objeto se puede colocar antes o después de la preposición.* ❶ llevarse; barrer ❷ quitar

■ **wash up** *vi* lavarse

washable ['wɒʃəbl] *adj* lavable

washbowl ['wɒʃbəʊl] *s* lavabo

washcloth ['wɒʃ,klɒθ] *s* toallita para lavarse la cara

washer ['wɒʃər] *s* *TECNOLOGÍA* arandela

washing ['wɒʃɪŋ] *s* ☼ *incontable* ❶ colada • **to do the washing** hacer la colada ❷ ropa sucia o para lavar; colada • **to hang up the washing** tender la colada

washing line *s* tendedero

washing machine *s* lavadora

Washington ['wɒʃɪŋtən] *s* • **Washington D.C.** Washington DC

washing-up *s* fregado • **to do the washing-up** fregar los platos

washout ['wɒʃaʊt] *s familiar* desastre

washroom ['wɒʃrʊm] *s* aseos

wasn't [wɒznt] *(abreviatura de* was not*)* → **be**

wasp [wɒsp] *s* avispa
Wasp

WASP

Este término se usa en Estados Unidos, a veces con tono despectivo, para referirse a una persona de raza blanca con antepasados protestantes originarios del norte de Europa, principalmente del Reino Unido. A pesar de la imagen de crisol de culturas que proyecta el país americano, los WASP han constituido tradicionalmente la élite social y política, manteniendo el monopolio del poder. Tanto ha sido así que la victoria de John F. Kennedy, católico de origen irlandés, en las elecciones a la presidencia de 1962, fue vista como un hito histórico, signo de que las personas de un origen social o étnico distinto ya no eran ciudadanos de segunda.

---

waste [weɪst] ◆ *adj* ❶ yermo, ma ❷ de desecho ◆ *s* ❶ desperdicio; derroche • **a waste of time** una pérdida de tiempo ❷ ☀ *incontable* desperdicios ❸ residuos ◆ *vt* ❶ perder ❷ malgastar; derrochar ❸ desperdiciar

wastebasket = **wastepaper basket**

waste disposal unit *s* triturador de basuras

wasteful ['weɪstful] *adj* derrochador, ra

waste ground *s* ☀ *incontable* descampados

wastepaper basket [ˌweɪst'peɪpər-], **wastebasket** ['weɪstˌbɑ:skɪt] *s* papelera

watch [wɒtʃ] ◆ *s* ❶ reloj ❷ • **to keep watch** estar de guardia • **to keep watch on something/somebody** vigilar algo/a alguien ❸ *MILITAR* guardia ◆ *vt* ❶ mirar; contemplar; ver ❷ vigilar ❸ tener cuidado con • **watch what you say** ten cuidado con lo que dices ◆ *vi* mirar; observar

■ **watch out** *vi* tener cuidado

watchdog ['wɒtʃdɒg] *s* ❶ perro guardián ❷ *figurado* comisión de vigilancia

watchful ['wɒtʃful] *adj* atento, ta

watchmaker ['wɒtʃˌmeɪkər] *s* relojero, ra

watchman ['wɒtʃmən] *s* vigilante

El plural de **watchman** es **watchmen** ['wɒtʃmen].

water ['wɔːtər] ◆ *s* agua ◆ *vt* regar ◆ *vi* ❶ • **my eyes are watering** me lloran los ojos ❷ • **my mouth is watering** se me hace la boca agua

■ **waters** *spl* aguas

■ **water down** *vt* ☀ *El objeto se puede colocar antes o después de la preposición.* diluir; aguar

water bottle *s* cantimplora

watercolor ['wɔːtəˌkʌlər] *s* acuarela

watercress ['wɔːtəkres] *s* berro

waterfall ['wɔːtəfɔːl] *s* cascada; salto de agua

water heater *s* calentador de agua

watering can ['wɔːtərɪŋ-] *s* regadera

water level *s* nivel del agua

water lily *s* nenúfar

waterline ['wɔːtəlaɪn] *s* *NÁUTICA* línea de flotación

waterlogged ['wɔːtəlɒgd] *adj* inundado, da

water main *s* cañería principal

watermark ['wɔːtəmɑːk] *s* filigrana

watermelon ['wɔːtəˌmelən] *s* sandía

water polo *s* water-polo

waterproof ['wɔːtəpruːf] ◆ *adj* impermeable ◆ *s* impermeable

watershed ['wɔːtəʃed] *s* *figurado* momento decisivo

water skiing *s* esquí acuático

water tank *s* reserva de agua

watertight ['wɔːtətaɪt] *adj* hermético, ca

waterway ['wɔːtəweɪ] *s* vía navegable

waterworks ['wɔːtəwɜːks] *s* central de agua

El plural de **waterworks** es **waterworks**.

watt [wɒt] *s* vatio

wave [weɪv] ◆ *s* ❶ señal (con la mano) ❷ ola ❸ oleada *(de delitos)* ❹ onda *(de luz, calor)* ❺ ondulación *(en pelo)* ◆ *vt* ❶ agitar ❷ hacer señales o señas a • **she waved them in** les hizo una señal para que entraran ◆ *vi* ❶ saludar con la mano; decir adiós con la mano • **to wave at** o **to somebody** saludar a alguien con la mano • **he waved hello to us** nos saludó con la mano ❷ ondear ❸ agitarse

wavelength ['weɪvleŋθ] *s* longitud de onda

expresión **to be on the same wavelength** estar en la misma onda

wavy ['weɪvɪ] *adj* ondulado, da

wax [wæks] ◆ *s* cera ◆ *vt* encerar

wax paper *s* papel encerado

way [weɪ] ◆ *s* ❶ manera; modo • **in the same way** del mismo modo • **this/that way** así • **in a way** en cierto modo • **to be in a bad way** estar bastante mal ❷ camino • **to lose your way** perderse • **to find your way around** orientarse • **the way back** o **home** el camino de vuelta a casa • **way in** entrada • **way out** salida • **it's out of my way** no me pilla de camino • **it's out of the way** está algo aislado • **on the** o **on your way** de camino • **I'm on my way** voy de camino • **across** o **over the way** enfrente • **to be under way** estar en marcha • **to get under way** ponerse en marcha • **to get in the way** ponerse en medio • **to get out of the way** quitarse de en medio ❸ dirección • **come this way** ven por aquí • **go that way** ve por ahí • **which way do we go?** ¿hacia dónde vamos? • **which way is it to the cathedral?** ¿por dónde se va a la catedral? • **the wrong way up** o **round** al revés • **the right way up** o **round** del derecho ❹ • **all the way** todo el camino o trayecto • **it's a long way away** está muy lejos • **we have a long way to go** queda mucho camino por recorrer • **we've come a long way since then** *figurado* hemos avanzado mucho desde entonces

expresiones **no way!** ¡ni hablar! ▸ **to be in the way** estar en medio ▶ **to get something out of the way** quitarse algo de encima ▶ **to go out of your way to do something** tomarse muchas molestias para hacer algo ▶ **to keep out of the way** mantenerse alejado ▶ **to make way for** dar paso a ▶ **to go a long way towards doing something** contribuir enormemente a hacer algo ▶ **to give way** ceder

◆ *adv familiar* mucho • **it's way too big** está demasiado grande

■ **ways** *spl* costumbres; hábitos
■ **by the way** *adv* por cierto

WC (*abreviatura de* water closet) WC

we [wi:] *pronombre personal* nosotros, tras • **we can't do it** nosotros no podemos hacerlo • **here we are** aquí estamos • **as we say in France** como decimos en Francia • **we British** nosotros los británicos

weak [wi:k] *adj* ❶ débil • **to grow weak** debilitarse ❷ frágil ❸ flojo, ja

weaken ['wi:kn] ◆ *vt* debilitar ◆ *vi* ❶ ceder; flaquear ❷ debilitarse

weakling ['wi:klɪŋ] *s despectivo* enclenque

weakness ['wi:knɪs] *s* ❶ debilidad • **to have a weakness for something** tener debilidad por algo ❷ defecto

wealth [welθ] *s* ❶ riqueza ❷ profusión; abundancia • **a wealth of something** abundancia de algo

wealthy ['welθɪ] *adj* rico, ca

weapon ['wepən] *s* arma

weaponry ['wepənrɪ] *s* 🔆 *incontable* armamento

weapons of mass destruction *spl* armas de destrucción masiva

wear [weəʳ] ◆ *s* 🔆 *incontable* ❶ uso • **I've had a lot of wear out of this jacket** le he sacado mucho partido a esta chaqueta ❷ desgaste • **wear and tear** desgaste ❸ ropa • **children's wear** ropa de niños • **evening wear** ropa de noche

expresión **to be the worse for wear a)** estar deteriorado **b)** estar hecho un trapo

◆ *vt* ❶ llevar ❷ calzar • **to wear red** vestirse de rojo ❸ desgastar • **to wear a hole in something** acabar haciendo un agujero en algo ◆ *vi* ❶ desgastarse ❷ • **to wear well/badly** durar mucho/poco

■ **wear away** ◆ *vt* 🔆 *El objeto se puede colocar antes o después de la preposición.* desgastar ◆ *vi* desgastarse

■ **wear down** *vt* 🔆 *El objeto se puede colocar antes o después de la preposición.* ❶ desgastar ❷ agotar

■ **wear off** *vi* desaparecer

■ **wear out** ◆ *vt* 🔆 *El objeto se puede colocar antes o después de la preposición.* ❶ gastar ❷ agotar ◆ *vi* gastarse

Formas irregulares de **wear:** *pretérito* **wore,** *pp* **worn.**

weary ['wɪərɪ] *adj* fatigado, da; cansado, da • **to be weary of something/of doing something** estar cansado de algo/de hacer algo

weasel ['wi:zl] *s* comadreja

weather ['weðəʳ] *s* tiempo • **what's the weather like?** ¿qué tal tiempo hace?

expresión **to make heavy weather of something** complicar algo innecesariamente ▶ **to be under the weather** no encontrarse muy bien

weathercock ['weðəkɒk] *s* veleta

weather forecast *s* parte meteorológico

weatherman ['weðəmæn] *s* hombre del tiempo

El plural de **weatherman** es **weathermen** ['weðəmen].

weather vane [-veɪn] *s* veleta

weave [wi:v] ◆ *vt* tejer ◆ *vi* • **to weave through** colarse por entre • **to weave in and out of the traffic** avanzar zigzagueando en el tráfico

Formas irregulares de **weave:** *pretérito* **wove,** *pp* **woven.**

web [web] *s* ❶ telaraña ❷ *figurado* urdimbre ❸ INFORMÁTICA • **the Web** la Web

web browser *s* INFORMÁTICA navegador

webcam ['webkæm] *s* cámara web

web designer *s* diseñador, ra de páginas Web

web page *s* página web

web site *s* sitio Web

we'd [wi:d] ❶ (*abreviatura de* we had) → **have** ❷ (*abreviatura de* we would) → **would**

wedding ['wedɪŋ] *s* boda; casamiento

wedding anniversary *s* aniversario de boda

wedding cake *s* tarta nupcial

wedding dress *s* traje de novia

wedding ring *s* anillo de boda; argolla

wedge [wedʒ] *s* ❶ cuña ❷ porción; trozo

Wednesday ['wenzdɪ] *s* miércoles ver también **Saturday**

wee [wi:] ◆ *s familiar* pipí • **to do a wee** hacer pipí ◆ *vi familiar* hacer pipí

weed [wi:d] *s* mala hierba

weedkiller ['wi:d,kɪləʳ] *s* herbicida

week [wi:k] *s* semana • **a week on Saturday, Saturday week** del sábado en ocho días • **this/next week** esta/la próxima semana • **in 2 weeks' time** en dos semanas • **we haven't seen him for weeks** hace semanas que no lo vemos

weekday ['wi:kdeɪ] *s* día laborable

weekend [,wi:k'end] *s* fin de semana

weekly ['wi:klɪ] ◆ *adj* semanal ◆ *adv* semanalmente ◆ *s* semanario

weep [wi:p] ◆ *vt* derramar ◆ *vi* llorar

Formas irregulares de **weep:** *pretérito & pp* **wept.**

weeping willow [,wi:pɪŋ-] *s* sauce llorón

weigh [weɪ] *vt* ❶ pesar ❷ sopesar • **she weighed her words** sopesó sus palabras

■ **weigh down** *vt* 🔆 *El objeto se puede colocar antes o después de la preposición.* ❶ sobrecargar ❷ • **to be weighed down by** o **with** estar abrumado, da de o por

W

■ **weigh up** *vt* ☼: *El objeto se puede colocar antes o después de la preposición.* ❶ sopesar ❷ hacerse una idea de

weight [weɪt] *s* ❶ peso • **to put on** o **gain weight** engordar • **to lose weight** adelgazar ❷ pesa

expresión **to pull your weight** poner (uno) de su parte

weightlifting ['weɪt,lɪftɪŋ] *s* levantamiento de pesos; halterofilia

weighty ['weɪtɪ] *adj* de peso

weir [wɪər] *s* presa; dique

weird [wɪəd] *adj* raro, ra; extraño, ña

welcome ['welkəm] ◆ *adj* ❶ bienvenido, da • **to make somebody welcome** acoger bien a alguien ❷ • **you're welcome to come** si quieres, puedes venir ❸ • **to be welcome** ser de agradecer ❹ • **you're welcome** de nada ◆ *s* bienvenida • **to give somebody a warm welcome** dar una calurosa bienvenida a alguien ◆ *vt* ❶ dar la bienvenida a ❷ recibir bien ◆ *exclamación* ¡bienvenido, da!

weld [weld] ◆ *s* soldadura ◆ *vt* soldar

welfare ['welfeər] *s* ❶ bienestar ❷ subsidio de la seguridad social • **to be on welfare** recibir un subsidio

well [wel] ◆ *adj* (comparativo better, superlativo best) bien • **to be well** estar bien (de salud) • **I don't feel well** no me siento bien • **to get well** mejorarse • **all is well** todo va bien • **(it's) just as well** menos mal • **it would be as well to check first** sería mejor comprobar primero ◆ *adv* ❶ bien • **well done!** ¡muy bien! • **to go well** ir bien • **he's doing very well at his new school** le va muy bien en el nuevo colegio • **well and truly** completamente ❷ claramente; definitivamente • **it was well worth it** sí que valió la pena ❸ • **you know perfectly well (that)** sabes de sobra (que) ❹ • **it could well rain** es muy posible que llueva

expresión **to be well out of something** *familiar* tener la suerte de haberse salido de algo

◆ *s* pozo ◆ *exclamación* ❶ bueno • **oh well!** ¡en fin! ❷ ¡vaya!

■ **as well** *adv* también

expresión **you may** o **might as well (do it)** ¿y por qué no (lo haces)?

■ **as well as** *conjunción* además de

■ **well up** *vi* brotar

we'll [wi:l] ❶ (abreviatura de we will) → **will** ❷ (abreviatura de we shall) → **shall**

well-advised [-əd'vaɪzd] *adj* sensato, ta • **you would be well-advised to do it** sería aconsejable que lo hicieras

well-behaved [-bɪ'heɪvd] *adj* formal; bien educado, da • **to be well-behaved** portarse bien

wellbeing [,wel'bi:ɪŋ] *s* bienestar

well-built *adj* fornido, da

well-done *adj* muy hecho, cha

well-dressed [-'drest] *adj* bien vestido, da

well-earned [-'ɜ:nd] *adj* bien merecido, da

wellington boots ['welɪŋtən-], **wellingtons** ['welɪŋtənz] *spl* botas de agua

well-kept *adj* ❶ bien cuidado, da ❷ bien guardado, da

well-known *adj* conocido, da

well-mannered [-'mænəd] *adj* de buenos modales

well-meaning *adj* bienintencionado, da

well-off *adj* acomodado, da; rico, ca

well-read [-'red] *adj* instruido, da; culto, ta

well-rounded [-'raundɪd] *adj* completo, ta

well-timed *adj* oportuno, na

well-to-do *adj* adinerado, da

wellwisher ['wel,wɪʃər] *s* simpatizante (que da muestras de apoyo)

Welsh [welʃ] ◆ *adj* galés, esa ◆ *s* galés ◆ *spl* • **the Welsh** los galeses

Welshman ['welʃmən] *s* galés

El plural de **Welshman** es **Welshmen** ['welʃmen].

Welshwoman ['welʃ,wumən] *s* galesa

El plural de **Welshwoman** es **Welshwomen** ['welʃ,wɪmɪn].

went [went] *pretérito* → **go**

wept [wept] *pretérito* & *participio pasado* → **weep**

were [wɜ:r] *pretérito* → **be**

we're [wɪər] (abreviatura de we are) → **be**

weren't [wɜ:nt] (abreviatura de were not) = **be**

west [west] ◆ *s* ❶ oeste ❷ • **the West** el Oeste ◆ *adj* del oeste ◆ *adv* • **west (of)** al oeste (de)

■ **West** *s* POLÍTICA • **the West** Occidente

West Bank *s* • **the West Bank** Cisjordania

westerly ['westəlɪ] *adj* del oeste

western ['westən] ◆ *adj* occidental ◆ *s* película del oeste; western

West Indian *adj* & *s* antillano, na

West Indies [-'ɪndi:z] *spl* • **the West Indies** las Antillas

westward ['westwəd] ◆ *adj* hacia el oeste ◆ *adv* = **westwards**

westwards ['westwədz], **westward** *adv* hacia el oeste

wet [wet] ◆ *adj* ❶ mojado, da • **to get wet** mojarse ❷ húmedo, da ❸ lluvioso, sa ❹ fresco, ca (pintura) *expresión* **wet paint** recién pintado, da

◆ *vt* ❶ mojar ❷ humedecer

Formas irregulares de **wet**: *pret* & *pp* **wet** o **wetted**.

wet blanket *s familiar* & *despectivo* aguafiestas

wet suit *s* traje de submarinista

we've [wi:v] (abreviatura de we have) = **have**

whack [wæk] *familiar* ◆ *s* castañazo ◆ *vt* ❶ pegar; zurrar ❷ dar un porrazo a ❸ liquidar

whale [weɪl] *s* ballena

W

wharf [wɔːf] *s* muelle; embarcadero

Dos plurales: **wharfs** o **wharves** [wɔːvz].

what [wɒt] ◆ *adj* ❶ ☼ *en interrogativas directas e indirectas* qué • **what kind of car does she have?** ¿qué carro tiene? • **what shape is it?** ¿qué forma tiene? • **what color is it?** ¿de qué color es? • **he asked me what shape it was** me preguntó qué forma tenía • **I don't know what to do** no sé qué hacer ❷ ☼ *en exclamaciones* qué • **what a surprise!** ¡qué sorpresa! • **what a stupid idea!** ¡qué idea más tonta! ◆ *pronombre* ❶ ☼ *interrogativo* qué • **what are they doing?** ¿qué hacen? • **she asked me what they were doing** me preguntó qué estaban haciendo • **what are they talking about?** ¿de qué están hablando? • **what is it called?** ¿cómo se llama? • **what does it cost?** ¿cuánto cuesta? • **what is it like?** ¿cómo es? • **what's the Spanish for "book"?** ¿cómo se dice "book" en español? • **what is this for?** ¿para qué es esto? • **what about another drink/going out for a meal?** ¿qué tal otra copa/si salimos a comer? • **what about me?** ¿y yo qué? • **what if nobody comes?** ¿y si no viene nadie, qué? ❷ ☼ *relativo* lo que • **I saw what happened/he did** yo vi lo que ocurrió/hizo • **what we need is...** lo que nos hace falta es... ◆ *exclamación* ¿qué? • **what, no milk!** ¿cómo? ¿que no hay leche?

what

No se deben confundir which y what. Which se utiliza cuando hay un número limitado de posibilidades de elección (*which* is your car? *¿cuál es tu coche?*; *which* one do you want? *¿cuál quieres?*), mientras que what sugiere un abanico de posibilidades mucho mayor (*what* is that? *¿qué es eso?*; *what* songs do you know? *¿qué canciones sabes?*).

En el lenguaje coloquial, what for significa lo mismo que why (*what* did she tell me that *for*? *¿por qué me dijo eso?*; I don't know *what* she told me that *for no sé por qué me dijo eso*).

Conviene recordar que en preguntas what va al principio de la oración, y que si lleva alguna preposición (about, for, ETC), ésta permanece en su lugar habitual después del verbo (*what* are you thinking *about*? *¿en qué piensas?*; *what* did you do that *for*? *¿porqué hiciste eso?*).

What about y how about se usan en el inglés hablado para proponer o sugerir algo. Pueden ir seguidos de un sustantivo what/how about a game of cards? *¿qué tal si jugamos a la baraja?*, de un pronombre what/how about this one? *¿qué tal éste?* o de un verbo en gerundio what/how about going to the movies? *¿quieres ir al cine?*

whatever [wɒt'evər] ◆ *adj* cualquier • **eat whatever food you find** come lo que encuentres • **no chance**

whatever ni la más remota posibilidad • **nothing whatever** nada en absoluto ◆ *pronombre* ❶ • **whatever they may offer** ofrezcan lo que ofrezcan • **whatever you like** lo que (tú) quieras • **don't touch this, whatever you do** hagas lo que hagas, no toques esto • **whatever happens** pase lo que pase • **whatever the weather** haga el tiempo que haga ❷ • **whatever do you mean?** ¿qué quieres decir? ❸ • **he told me to get a D.R.V., whatever that is** o **may be** me dijo que consiguiera un D.R.V., sea lo que sea eso • **or whatever** o lo que sea

whatsoever [ˌwɒtsəʊ'evər] *adj* • **nothing whatsoever** nada en absoluto • **none whatsoever** ni uno

wheat [wiːt] *s* trigo

wheel [wiːl] ◆ *s* ❶ rueda ❷ volante • **to be at the wheel** estar al volante ◆ *vt* empujar *(algo sobre ruedas)* ◆ *vi* ❶ dar vueltas ❷ • **to wheel round** darse la vuelta

wheelbarrow ['wiːlˌbærəʊ] *s* carretilla

wheelchair ['wiːlˌtʃeər] *s* silla de ruedas

wheelclamp ['wiːlˌklæmp] *s* cepo

wheeze [wiːz] *vi* resollar

when [wen] ◆ *adv* ☼ *en interrogativas directas e indirectas* cuándo • **when does the plane arrive?** ¿cuándo llega el avión? • **he asked me when I would be in London** me preguntó cuándo estaría en Londres • **I don't know when I'll be back** no sé cuándo volveré • **that was when I knew for sure that...** fue entonces cuando me di cuenta que... • **say when!** ¡di basta! ◆ *conjunción* cuando • **tell me when you've read it** avísame cuando lo hayas leído • **on the day when it happened** el día (en) que pasó • **use less oil when frying food** utiliza menos aceite al freír comida • **how can I buy it when I can't afford it?** ¿cómo voy a comprarlo si no tengo dinero?

whenever [wen'evər] ◆ *conjunción* ❶ cuando • **whenever you like** cuando quieras ❷ cada vez que • **whenever I call him he runs away** siempre que le llamo se marcha corriendo ◆ *adv* cuando sea

where [weər] ◆ *adv* ☼ *en interrogativas directas e indirectas* dónde • **where do you live?** ¿dónde vives? • **do you know where he lives?** ¿sabes dónde vive? • **where are you from?** ¿de dónde eres? • **where are we going?** ¿adónde vamos? • **I don't know where to start** no sé por dónde empezar ◆ *conjunción* ❶ donde • **this is where...** es aquí donde... • **go where you like** vete (a) donde quieras ❷ • **where possible** siempre que sea posible

whereabouts ◆ *adv* [ˌweərə'baʊts] (por) dónde ◆ *spl* ['weərəbaʊts] paradero • **to know somebody's whereabouts** conocer el paradero de alguien

whereas [weər'æz] *conjunción* mientras que

whereby [weə'baɪ] *conjunción formal* por el/la cual

wherever [weər'evər] ◆ *conjunción* dondequiera que • **wherever you go** dondequiera que vayas • **sit wherever you like** siéntate donde quieras ◆ *adv* ❶ en cualquier parte ❷ • **wherever did you hear that?** ¿dónde habrás oído eso?

whet [wet] *vt* • **to whet somebody's appetite (for something)** despertar el interés de alguien (por algo)

whether ['weðər] *conjunción* ❶ si • **she doesn't know whether to go or stay** no sabe si quedarse o marcharse • **I doubt whether she'll do it** dudo que lo haga ❷ • **whether I want to or not** tanto si quiero como si no; quiera o no quiera

which [wɪtʃ] ◆ *adj* ❶ ☼: *en interrogativas directas e indirectas* qué • **which house is yours?** ¿cuál es tu casa?; ¿qué casa es la tuya? • **which one?** ¿cuál? • **which ones?** ¿cuáles? ❷ • **in which case** en cuyo caso • **we won't arrive until 6, by which time it will be dark** no llegaremos hasta la 6, hora a la cual ya será de noche ◆ *pronombre* ❶ ☼: *en interrogativas directas e indirectas* cuál; cuáles ☼: *pl* • **which do you prefer?** ¿cuál prefieres? • **I can't decide which to have** no sé cuál coger ❷ ☼: *en oraciones subordinadas relativas en lugar del sustantivo* que • **the table, which was made of wood,...** la mesa, que o la cual era de madera,... • **the world in which we live** el mundo en que o en el cual vivimos ❸ ☼: *para referirse a una oración previa* lo cual • **she denied it, which surprised me** lo negó, lo cual me sorprendió • **before which** antes de lo cual

which

Cuando which es el sujeto de la oración es invariable. El verbo que lo acompaña irá en singular o plural según el contexto (*which is* the right answer? *¿cuál es la respuesta correcta?*; *which are* our presents? *¿cuáles son nuestros regalos?*).

Conviene recordar que en las preguntas which va al principio de la oración y que si lleva alguna preposición (to, in, ETC), ésta aparece en su lugar habitual después del verbo (*which* movie are you going to tonight?; *¿qué película vas a ver esta noche?*; which department do you work in? *¿en qué departamento trabajas?*).

Ver también what.

whichever [wɪtʃ'evər] ◆ *adj* ❶ • **whichever route you take** vayas por donde vayas ❷ • **whichever color you prefer** el color que prefieras ◆ *pronombre* el que, la que; los que, las que ☼: *pl* • **take whichever you like** coge el que quieras

whiff [wɪf] *s* olorcillo • **she caught a whiff of his aftershave** le llegó el olorcillo de su aftershave

while [waɪl] ◆ *s* rato • **it's a long while since I did that** hace mucho que no hago eso • **for a while** un rato • **after a while** después de un rato • **in a while** dentro de poco • **once in a while** de vez en cuando ◆ *conjunción* ❶ mientras ❷ mientras que ❸ aunque

whilst [waɪlst] *conjunción formal* ❶ mientras ❷ mientras que ❸ aunque

whim [wɪm] *s* capricho

whimper ['wɪmpər] *vt* & *vi* gimotear

whimsical ['wɪmzɪkl] *adj* ❶ fantasioso, sa ❷ juguetón, ona

whine [waɪn] *vi* ❶ gemir ❷ ulular

whip [wɪp] ◆ *s* ❶ látigo ❷ fusta ◆ *vt* ❶ azotar ❷ • **to whip something out/off** sacar/quitar algo rápidamente ❸ batir

whipped cream [wɪpt-] *s* nata montada

whirl [wɜːl] ◆ *s figurado* torbellino ◆ *vt* • **to whirl somebody/something round** hacer dar vueltas a alguien/algo ◆ *vi* ❶ arremolinarse ❷ girar vertiginosamente

whirlpool ['wɜːlpuːl] *s* remolino

whirlpool bath *s* bañera de hidromasaje

whirlwind ['wɜːlwɪnd] *s* torbellino

whirr [wɜːr] *vi* zumbar

whisk [wɪsk] ◆ *s* COCINA varilla ◆ *vt* ❶ • **to whisk something away/out** llevarse/sacar algo rápidamente • **we were whisked off to visit the museum** nos llevaron rápidamente a visitar el museo ❷ COCINA batir

whisker ['wɪskər] *s* (pelo del) bigote

■ **whiskers** *spl* ❶ patillas ❷ bigotes

whiskey ['wɪskɪ] *s* whisky

El plural de **whiskey** es **whiskeys**.

whisper ['wɪspər] ◆ *vt* susurrar ◆ *vi* cuchichear

whistle ['wɪsl] ◆ *s* ❶ silbido; pitido ❷ silbato; pito ◆ *vt* silbar ◆ *vi* ❶ silbar; chiflar ❷ pitar ❸ piar

white [waɪt] ◆ *adj* ❶ blanco, ca • **to go** o **turn white** ponerse blanco ❷ con leche ◆ *s* ❶ blanco ❷ blanco, ca ❸ clara

white-collar *adj* de oficina • **white-collar worker** oficinista

white elephant *s figurado* mamotreto *(caro e inútil)*

white-hot *adj* incandescente

White House *s* • **the White House** la Casa Blanca

WHITE HOUSE

La Casa Blanca (**the White House**) es la residencia oficial y lugar de trabajo del presidente de los Estados Unidos. Se encuentra en Washington D.C., que además de ser la capital del país es la sede del gobierno federal. La Casa Blanca es un símbolo tanto de la presidencia, como del ramo ejecutivo del gobierno estadounidense.

white lie *s* mentira piadosa

whiteness ['waɪtnɪs] *s* blancura

white paper *s* POLÍTICA libro blanco

white sauce *s* (salsa) bechamel

whitewash ['waɪtwɒʃ] ◆ *s* ❶ ☼ *incontable* blanqueo; lechada (de cal) ❷ *despectivo* encubrimiento ◆ *vt* blanquear

whiting ['waɪtɪŋ] *s* pescadilla

Dos plurales: **whiting** o **whitings**.

whittle ['wɪtl] *vt* • **to whittle down** o **away** reducir gradualmente

whiz, whizz [wɪz] *vi* • **to whiz past** o **by** pasar muy rápido o zumbando

whiz(z) kid *s familiar* genio; prodigio

who [huː] *pronombre* ❶ ☼ *en interrogativas directas e indirectas* quién; quiénes ☼ *pl* • **who are you?** ¿quién eres tú? • **who is it?** ¿quién es? • **who did you see?** ¿a quién viste? • **I didn't know who she was** no sabía quién era ❷ ☼ *en oraciones subordinadas relativas* que • **he's the doctor who treated me** es el médico que me atendió • **those who are in favor** los que están a favor

---

who

Cuando who es el sujeto de la oración es invariable. El verbo irá en singular o plural según el contexto (*who is* coming to the concert? ¿*quién viene* al concierto?, *who are* they? ¿*quiénes son?*).

Conviene recordar que en las preguntas who va al principio de la oración y que si lleva alguna preposición (at, from, ETC), ésta permanece en su lugar habitual después del verbo (*who* are you staring *at*? ¿*a quién miras tan fijamente?*, *who* did you get the money *from*? ¿*quién te dio el dinero?*).

Who como pronombre relativo, se puede omitir si no es el sujeto de la oración siguiente (I just met some friends (*who*) I know from university *acabo de encontrarme con unos amigos de la universidad*). Sin embargo, cuando es el sujeto no se puede suprimir (I have a brother *who* is a teacher *tengo un hermano que es profesor*).

---

who'd [huːd] ❶ (*abreviatura de* who had) = **have** ❷ (*abreviatura de* who would) = **would**

whodunnit [ˌhuːˈdʌnɪt] *s familiar* historia policíaca de misterio

whoever [huːˈevər] *pronombre* ❶ quienquiera • **whoever finds it** quienquiera que lo encuentre ❷ quienesquiera ☼ *pl* • **tell whoever you like** díselo a quien quieras ❸ • **whoever can that be?** ¿quién podrá ser? ❹ • **come in, whoever you are** pasa, seas quién seas

whole [həʊl] ◆ *adj* ❶ entero, ra • **we've had enough of the whole thing** ya estamos hartos de todo esto ❷ • **a whole lot taller** muchísimo más alto • **a whole new idea** una idea totalmente nueva ◆ *s* ❶ • **the**

whole of the school/summer el colegio/verano entero ❷ todo

■ **as a whole** *adv* en conjunto

■ **on the whole** *adv* en general

whole-hearted [-ˈhɑːtɪd] *adj* incondicional

whole note *s* semibreve

wholesale ['həʊlseɪl] ◆ *adj* ❶ COMERCIO al por mayor ❷ *despectivo* indiscriminado, da ◆ *adv* ❶ COMERCIO al por mayor ❷ *despectivo* indiscriminadamente

wholesaler ['həʊl,seɪlər] *s* mayorista

wholesome ['həʊlsəm] *adj* sano, na

whole wheat *adj* integral

who'll [huːl] ❶ (*abreviatura de* who will) = **will** ❷ (*abreviatura de* who shall) = **shall**

wholly ['həʊlɪ] *adv* completamente

whom [huːm] *pronombre* ❶ ☼ *en interrogativas directas e indirectas formal* quién; quiénes ☼ *pl* • **from whom did you receive it?** ¿de quién lo recibiste? • **for/ of/to whom** por/de/a quién ❷ ☼ *en oraciones subordinadas relativas* que • **the man whom I saw** el hombre que vi • **the man to whom I gave it** el hombre al que se lo di • **several people came, none of whom I knew** vinieron varias personas, de las que no conocía a ninguna

---

whom

Whom se puede omitir cuando funciona como pronombre relativo (I just met some friends (*whom*) I know from university *acabo de encontrarme con unos amigos que conozco de la universidad*) salvo que vaya acompañado de alguna preposición como to, with, ETC, en cuyo caso no se puede suprimir (these are the friends *with whom* I went to the theatre *estos son los amigos con quienes fui al teatro*).

Ver también quién del lado español-inglés del diccionario.

---

whooping cough ['huːpɪŋ-] *s* tos ferina

whopping ['wɒpɪŋ] *familiar* ◆ *adj* enorme ◆ *adv* • **a whopping great truck/lie, a whopping big truck/ lie** un camión/una mentira enorme

whore [hɔːr] *s despectivo* puta

who're ['huːər] (*abreviatura de* who are) = **be**

whose [huːz] ◆ *pronombre* ☼ *en interrogativas directas e indirectas* de quién; de quiénes ☼ *pl* • **whose is this?** ¿de quién es esto? • **I wonder whose they are** me pregunto de quién serán ◆ *adj* ❶ ☼ *en interrogativas directas e indirectas* de quién; de quiénes ☼ *pl* • **whose car is that?** ¿de quién es ese coche? ❷ ☼ *en oraciones subordinadas relativas* cuyo, ya; cuyos, yas ☼ *pl* • **that's the boy whose father's a lawyer** ese es el chico cuyo padre es abogado • **the woman whose daughters are twins** la mujer cuyas hijas son gemelas

who've [huːv] (*abreviatura de* who have) = **have**

W

why [waɪ] ◆ *adv* por qué • **why did you lie to me?** ¿por qué me mentiste? • **why don't you all come?** ¿por qué no venís todos? • **why not?** ¿por qué no? ◆ *conjunción* por qué • **I don't know why he said that** no sé por qué dijo eso ◆ *pronombre* • **there are several reasons why he left** hay varias razones por las que se marchó • **that's why she did it** eso es por lo que lo hizo • **I don't know the reason why** no se por qué razón ◆ *exclamación* ¡hombre!; ¡vaya!

why

Why seguido de not o don't sirve para sugerir algo (*why don't* we try again? *¿por qué no lo intentamos otra vez?*) o dar un consejo (*why not* take a little more exercise? *¿y si hicieras un poco más de ejercicio?*).

wick [wɪk] *s* mecha

wicked ['wɪkɪd] *adj* ❶ malvado, da ❷ travieso, sa

wide [waɪd] ◆ *adj* ❶ ancho, cha • **how wide is it?** ¿cuánto mide de ancho? • **it's 50 cm wide** tiene 50 cm de ancho ❷ amplio, plia ❸ grande; considerable ❹ desviado, da ◆ *adv* ❶ • **to open/spread something wide** abrir/desplegar algo completamente ❷ • **to go o be wide** salir desviado

wide-angle lens *s* gran angular

wide awake *adj* completamente despierto, ta

widely ['waɪdlɪ] *adv* ❶ extensamente • **to be widely read/travelled** haber leído/viajado mucho ❷ generalmente • **there is a widely held view that…** existe la creencia generalizada de que… ❸ mucho

widen ['waɪdn] *vt* ❶ ampliar ❷ ensanchar

wide open *adj* ❶ abierto, ta de par en par ❷ completamente abierto, ta

wide-ranging [-'reɪndʒɪŋ] *adj* ❶ de gran alcance *(cambios, consecuencias)* ❷ de gran variedad *(actividades, intereses)* ❸ amplio, plia *(variedad, selección)*

widescreen ['waɪdskriːn] *adj* de pantalla ancha

widescreen TV ['waɪdskriːn-] *s* televisor panorámico; televisor de pantalla ancha

widespread ['waɪdspred] *adj* extendido, da; general

widow ['wɪdəʊ] *s* viuda

widowed ['wɪdəʊd] *adj* viudo, da

widower ['wɪdəʊər] *s* viudo

width [wɪdθ] *s* ❶ anchura • **it's 50 cm in width** tiene 50 cm de ancho ❷ ancho

wield [wiːld] *vt* ❶ manejar; esgrimir *(arma)* ❷ ejercer *(poder)*

wife [waɪf] *s* mujer; esposa

El plural de **wife** es **wives**.

wig [wɪg] *s* peluca

wiggle ['wɪgl] *vt familiar* ❶ menear ❷ contonear

wild [waɪld] *adj* ❶ salvaje *(animal)* ❷ silvestre *(flor)* ❸ agreste *(paisaje)* ❹ frenético, ca *(aplauso)* ❺ alborotado, da *(pelo)* ❻ descabellado, da *(plan)*

wilderness ['wɪldənɪs] *s* ❶ yermo; desierto ❷ jungla

wildlife ['waɪldlaɪf] *s* ☼ *incontable* fauna

wildly ['waɪldlɪ] *adv* ❶ frenéticamente ❷ a lo loco ❸ extremadamente

will¹ [wɪl] *s* ❶ voluntad ❷ testamento • **to make a will** hacer testamento

will² [wɪl]
◆ *v modal*

❶ [*expresa una idea de futuro*]
• **I will see you next week** te veré la próxima semana
• **when will you have finished it?** ¿cuándo lo tendrás acabado?
• **will you be here next week? — yes I will/no I won't** ¿estarás aquí la próxima semana? — sí/no

❷ [*expresa un deseo, una decisión*]
• **will you have some more tea?** ¿quieres más té?
• **I won't do it** no lo haré

❸ [*para dar una orden*]
• **you will leave this house at once!** ¡te vas a marchar de esta casa ahora mismo!
• **close that window, will you?** cierra esa ventana, por favor
• **will you be quiet!** ¡te quieres callar!

❹ [*expresa una posibilidad, una capacidad*]
• **the hall will hold up to 1,000 people** en la sala cabrá un máximo de 1.000 personas

❺ [*expresa una deducción, una certeza casi total*]
• **that'll be your father** ese debe ser tu padre
• **I can't tell you myself but he will know** yo no te lo puedo decir pero él lo debe saber

❻ [*expresa una acción habitual, con un tanto de obstinación*]
• **he will ask silly questions!** ¡hace cada pregunta más tonta!
• **she will talk all the time** ¡no para de hablar!

expresión **boys will be boys** los chicos, chicos son

will

Existe un uso especial de will, que nos permite describir costumbres cotidianas o hacer afirmaciones genéricas (cats *won't* eat vegetables *los gatos no comen verduras*). Con frecuencia, este uso tiene un matiz de enojo (he *will* call when we're in the middle of dinner *siempre tiene que llamar a la mitad de la cena*). En preguntas con you, will puede servir para solicitar algo (*will* you cook dinner this evening? *¿haces tú la cena esta noche?*). Would se puede usar de la misma forma, sólo que es más cortés (*would* you cook dinner this evening? *¿podrías hacer tú la cena esta noche?*).

willful ['wɪlfʊl] *adj* ❶ terco ❷ deliberado, da

W

willing ['wɪlɪŋ] *adj* servicial • **to be willing to do something** estar dispuesto a hacer algo

willingly ['wɪlɪŋlɪ] *adv* de buena gana

willow (tree) ['wɪləʊ-] *s* sauce

willpower ['wɪl,paʊər] *s* fuerza de voluntad

willy-nilly [,wɪlɪ'nɪlɪ] *adv* a la buena de Dios

wilt [wɪlt] *vi* ❶ marchitarse ❷ desfallecer; extenuarse

wimp [wɪmp] *s familiar & despectivo* blandengue

win [wɪn] ◆ *s* victoria; triunfo ◆ *vt & vi* ganar • **she won the race** ganó la carrera

expresión **you/I** ETC **can't win** no hay manera

■ **win over, win round** *vt* ☼*El objeto se puede colocar antes o después de la preposición.* convencer

Formas irregulares de **win** *pretérito & pp* **won**

wince [wɪns] *vi* hacer una mueca de dolor • **to wince at/with something** estremecerse ante/de algo

winch [wɪntʃ] *s* torno

wind¹ [wɪnd] ◆ *s* ❶ METEOROLOGÍA viento ❷ aliento ❸ ☼*incontable* gases • **to break wind** *eufemismo* ventosear ◆ *vt* dejar sin aliento

wind² [waɪnd] ◆ *vt* ❶ enrollar • **to wind something around something** enrollar algo alrededor de algo ❷ dar cuerda a ◆ *vi* serpentear

■ **wind down** ◆ *vt* ☼*El objeto se puede colocar antes o después de la preposición.* ❶ bajar ❷ cerrar poco a poco ◆ *vi* relajarse; descansar

■ **wind up** ◆ *vt* ☼*El objeto se puede colocar antes o después de la preposición.* ❶ finalizar; concluir ❷ liquidar *(negocio)* ❸ dar cuerda a *(reloj)* ❹ subir *(ventanilla)* ◆ *vi familiar* terminar; acabar • **to wind up doing something** acabar haciendo algo

Formas irregulares de **wind** *pretérito & pp* **wound**

windfall ['wɪndfɔːl] *s* dinero llovido del cielo

wind farm [wɪnd-] *s* parque eólico

winding ['waɪndɪŋ] *adj* tortuoso, sa

wind instrument [wɪnd-] *s* instrumento de viento

windmill ['wɪndmɪl] *s* molino de viento

window ['wɪndəʊ] *s* ❶ ventana ❷ AUTOMÓVILES ventanilla ❸ escaparate

window box *s* jardinera (de ventana)

window cleaner *s* limpiacristales

window pane *s* cristal (de la ventana)

window shade *s* persiana

windpipe ['wɪndpaɪp] *s* tráquea

windscreen washer *s* lavaparabrisas

windscreen wiper *s* limpiaparabrisas

windshield ['wɪndʃiːld] *s* parabrisas

windsurfing ['wɪnd,sɜːfɪŋ] *s* windsurf

windswept ['wɪndswept] *adj* azotado, da por el viento

wind turbine [wɪnd-] *s* aerogenerador

windy ['wɪndɪ] *adj* ❶ ventoso, sa; de mucho viento • **it's windy** hace viento ❷ expuesto, ta al viento

wine [waɪn] *s* vino • **red/white wine** vino tinto/blanco

wine cellar *s* bodega

wineglass ['waɪnglɑːs] *s* copa o vaso (de vino)

wine list *s* lista de vinos

wine tasting [-,teɪstɪŋ] *s* cata de vinos

wine waiter *s* sommelier

wing [wɪŋ] *s* ❶ ala ❷ AUTOMÓVILES guardabarros ❸ DEPORTE banda ❹ extremo

winger ['wɪŋər] *s* DEPORTE extremo

wing mirror *s* retrovisor

wink [wɪŋk] *s* guiño

expresión **not to sleep a wink, not to get a wink of sleep** *familiar* no pegar ojo

Winnebago® [,wɪnɪ'beɪgəʊ] *s* autocaravana

winner ['wɪnər] *s* ganador, ra

winning ['wɪnɪŋ] *adj* ❶ vencedor, ra ❷ de la victoria ❸ premiado, da ❹ atractivo, va

■ **winnings** *spl* ganancias

winning post *s* meta

winter ['wɪntər] ◆ *s* ☼*incontable* invierno ◆ *en compuestos* de invierno; invernal

winter sports *spl* deportes de invierno

wintertime ['wɪntətaɪm] *s* ☼*incontable* invierno

wint(e)ry ['wɪntrɪ] *adj* ❶ de invierno; invernal ❷ con nieve

wipe [waɪp] ◆ *s* • **give the table a wipe** pásale un trapo a la mesa ◆ *vt* ❶ limpiar; pasar un trapo a ❷ secar

■ **wipe out** *vt* ☼*El objeto se puede colocar antes o después de la preposición.* ❶ borrar ❷ aniquilar

■ **wipe up** *vt* ☼*El objeto se puede colocar antes o después de la preposición.* empapar; limpiar

wire ['waɪər] ◆ *s* ❶ alambre ❷ ELECTRICIDAD cable ❸ telegrama ◆ *vt* ❶ ELECTRICIDAD poner la instalación eléctrica de; conectar el cable a ❷ enviar un telegrama a

wiring ['waɪərɪŋ] *s* ☼*incontable* instalación eléctrica

wiry ['waɪərɪ] *adj* ❶ estropajoso, sa ❷ nervudo, da

wisdom ['wɪzdəm] *s* ❶ sabiduría ❷ sensatez

wisdom tooth *s* muela del juicio

wise [waɪz] *adj* ❶ sabio, bia ❷ prudente

expresión **she's no wiser** o **none the wiser** sigue sin entender

■ **wise up** *vi* enterarse; ponerse al tanto

wisecrack ['waɪzkræk] *s despectivo* broma; chiste

wish [wɪʃ] ◆ *s* deseo • **to do something against somebody's wishes** hacer algo en contra de los deseos de alguien ◆ *vt* desear • **to wish to do something** *formal* desear hacer algo • **to wish somebody something** desear a alguien algo • **I wish (that) you had told me before!** ¡ojalá me lo hubieras dicho antes! • **I wish (that)**

you would shut up ¿por qué no te callas? ◆ *vi* • **to wish for something** pedir (como deseo) algo ■ **wishes** *spl* • **(with) best wishes** muchos recuerdos

wish

Cuando wish va seguido del verbo be, se puede usar la forma hipotética were en vez de was (I *wish* I was/were rich ¡*ojalá fuese rica!*). Were es más formal que was.

wishful thinking [,wɪʃfʊl-] *s* ≥ *incontable* • **it's just wishful thinking** no son más que (vanas) ilusiones

wishy-washy ['wɪʃɪ,wɒʃɪ] *adj familiar & despectivo* soso, sa; insípido, da

wisp [wɪsp] *s* ❶ mechón ❷ brizna ❸ nubecilla ❹ voluta

wit [wɪt] *s* ❶ ingenio; agudeza ❷ • **to have the wit to do something** tener el buen juicio de hacer algo ■ **wits** *spl*

expresión **to be scared out of your wits** *familiar* estar muerto de miedo

witch [wɪtʃ] *s* bruja

with [wɪð] *preposición* ❶ con • **we stayed with them for a week** estuvimos con ellos una semana • **with me** conmigo • **with you** contigo • **I washed it with detergent** lo lavé con detergente • **with my luck, I'll probably lose** con la suerte que tengo seguro que pierdo • **"all right", she said with a smile** "vale" dijo con una sonrisa • **he's very mean with money** es muy tacaño con el dinero • **with the weather as it is,...** con el tiempo como está,... ❷ de • **filled with wine** lleno de vino • **covered with mud** cubierto de barro • **she was trembling with fear** temblaba de miedo • **the woman with the black hair/big dog** la señora del pelo negro/perro grande

expresión **are you with me?** ¿me sigues? ▶ **I'm with you/dad on this** en eso estoy contigo/con papá

withdraw [wɪð'drɔː] ◆ *vt* ❶ • **to withdraw something (from)** retirar algo (de) ❷ sacar ◆ *vi* • **to withdraw (from/to)** retirarse (de/a) • **to withdraw into yourself** encerrarse en uno mismo

Formas irregulares de **withdraw**: *pretérito* **withdrew**, *pp* **withdrawn**.

withdrawal [wɪð'drɔːəl] *s* ❶ retirada ❷ retractación ❸ *FINANZAS* reintegro

withdrawal symptoms *spl* síndrome de abstinencia

withdrawn [wɪð'drɔːn] ◆ *participio pasado* → **withdraw** ◆ *adj* reservado, da

withdrew [wɪð'druː] *pretérito* → **withdraw**

wither ['wɪðər] *vi* ❶ marchitarse ❷ debilitarse

withhold [wɪð'həʊld] *vt* ❶ retener ❷ negar

Formas irregulares de **withhold**: *pretérito & pp* **withheld** [wɪð'held].

within [wɪ'ðɪn] ◆ *preposición* ❶ dentro de • **within reach** al alcance de la mano • **within sight of** a la vista de ❷ a menos de; en menos de • **it's within walking distance** se puede ir andando • **he was within five seconds of the leader** estaba a cinco segundos del líder • **within the next six months** en los próximos seis meses • **it arrived within a week** llegó en menos de una semana ◆ *adv* dentro

without [wɪð'aʊt] ◆ *preposición* sin • **without something/doing something** sin algo/hacer algo • **without making any mistakes** sin cometer ningún error • **it happened without my realizing** pasó sin que me diera cuenta ◆ *adv*

expresión **to go** o **do without something** pasar sin algo

withstand [wɪð'stænd] *vt* resistir; aguantar

Formas irregulares de **withstand**: *pretérito & pp* **withstood** [wɪð'stʊd].

witness ['wɪtnɪs] ◆ *s* ❶ testigo • **to be witness to something** ser testigo de algo ❷ • **to bear witness to something** atestiguar algo; dar fe de algo ◆ *vt* ❶ presenciar ❷ firmar (como testigo)

witness stand *s* tribuna (de los testigos)

witticism ['wɪtɪsɪzm] *s* ocurrencia

witty ['wɪtɪ] *adj* ingenioso, sa; ocurrente

wives [waɪvz] *spl* → **wife**

wizard ['wɪzəd] *s* ❶ mago *(en cuentos)* ❷ genio

wobble ['wɒbl] *vi* ❶ tambalearse ❷ cojear ❸ temblar

woe [wəʊ] *s literario* aflicción

woke [wəʊk] *pretérito* → **wake**

woken ['wəʊkn] *participio pasado* → **wake**

wolf [wʊlf] *s ZOOLOGÍA* lobo

El plural de **wolf** es **wolves**.

wolves ['wʊlvz] *spl* → **wolf**

woman ['wʊmən] ◆ *s* ❶ mujer ❷ la mujer ◆ *en compuestos* • **woman doctor** médica

El plural de **woman** es **women**.

womanly ['wʊmənlɪ] *adj* femenino, na

womb [wuːm] *s* matriz; útero

women ['wɪmɪn] *spl* → **woman**

won [wʌn] *pretérito & participio pasado* → **win**

wonder ['wʌndər] ◆ *s* ❶ asombro; admiración ❷ • **it's a wonder (that)...** es un milagro que... ❸ maravilla

expresión **to work** o **do wonders** hacer maravillas o milagros

◆ *vt* • **to wonder (if** o **whether)** preguntarse (si) ❷ • **I wonder if** o **whether I could ask you a question?** ¿le importaría que le hiciera una pregunta? ❸ • **I wonder (that) she hasn't left him** me pregunto cómo es que todavía no lo ha dejado ◆ *vi* • **I was only wondering** preguntaba sólo por curiosidad • **to wonder about something** preguntarse por algo

wonderful ['wʌndəfʊl] *adj* maravilloso, sa ; estupendo, da

wonderfully ['wʌndəfʊlɪ] *adv* ❶ estupendamente ❷ extremadamente

won't [wəʊnt] (*abreviatura de* will not) = **will**

woo [wuː] *vt* ❶ *literario* cortejar ❷ granjearse el apoyo de

wood [wʊd] *s* ❶ madera ❷ leña ❸ bosque

■ **woods** *spl* bosque

wooden ['wʊdn] *adj* ❶ de madera ❷ *despectivo* acartonado, da

woodpecker ['wʊd,pekər] *s* pájaro carpintero

woodwind ['wʊdwɪnd] *s* • **the woodwind** los instrumentos de viento de madera

woodwork ['wʊdwɜːk] *s* carpintería

woodworm ['wʊdwɜːm] *s* carcoma

wool [wʊl] *s* lana

expresión to pull the wool over somebody's eyes *familiar* dar a alguien gato por liebre

woolen ['wʊlən] *adj* de lana

■ **woollens** *spl* géneros de lana

woolly ['wʊlɪ] *adj* ❶ de lana ❷ *familiar* confuso, sa

word [wɜːd] ◆ *s* ❶ LINGÜÍSTICA palabra • **we couldn't understand a word he said** no entendimos ni una sola palabra de lo que dijo • **word for word** palabra por palabra • **in other words** en otras palabras • **in a word** en una palabra ❷ ◌ *incontable* noticia • **there is no word from them** no hemos tenido noticias de ellos • **word has it that...** se rumorea que... ❸ palabra

expresiones she doesn't mince her words no tiene pelos en la lengua ▶ I couldn't get a word in edgeways no pude meter baza ▶ to be as good as your word, to be true to your word cumplir lo prometido

◆ *vt* redactar ; expresar

wording ['wɜːdɪŋ] *s* ◌ *incontable* términos ; forma (de expresión)

word processor [-'prəʊsesər] *s* procesador de textos

wore [wɔːr] *pretérito* → **wear**

work [wɜːk] ◆ *s* ❶ ◌ *incontable* trabajo ; empleo • **to be out of work** estar desempleado • **at work** en el trabajo ❷ trabajo • **at work** trabajando ❸ (*ARTE*) obra ❹ obra • **it was the work of a psychopath** fue obra de un psicópata

expresión to have your work cut out doing something o to do something tenerlo muy difícil para hacer algo

◆ *vt* ❶ hacer trabajar • **she works herself too hard** trabaja demasiado ❷ manejar ; operar ❸ trabajar

◆ *vi* ❶ • **to work (on something)** trabajar (en algo) • **he works as a gardener** trabaja de jardinero • **to work for somebody** trabajar para alguien ❷ funcionar ❸ surtir efecto ❹ • **to work loose** soltarse • **to work free** desprenderse

■ **works** *s* fábrica

■ **work on** *vt* ◌ *El objeto siempre va después de la preposición al final.* ❶ trabajar en ❷ partir de

■ **work out** ◆ *vt* ◌ *El objeto se puede colocar antes o después de la preposición.* ❶ elaborar ❷ calcular ❸ dar con ◆ *vi* • **to work out at** salir a ❷ resolverse ❸ salir bien ❹ hacer ejercicio

■ **work up** *vt* ◌ *El objeto se puede colocar antes o después de la preposición.* ❶ • **to work yourself up into a frenzy** ponerse frenético, ca ❷ despertar • **I can't work up much enthusiasm** no consigo entusiasmarme • **to work up an appetite** abrir el apetito

workable ['wɜːkəbl] *adj* factible ; viable

workaholic [,wɜːkə'hɒlɪk] *s* adicto, ta al trabajo

workday ['wɜːkdeɪ], **working day** *s* día laborable

worked up [,wɜːkt-] *adj* nervioso, sa • **to get worked up** alterarse

worker ['wɜːkər] *s* ❶ trabajador, ra • **a hard/fast worker** una persona que trabaja mucho/a prisa • **office worker** oficinista ❷ obrero, ra

workforce ['wɜːkfɔːs] *s* mano de obra

working ['wɜːkɪŋ] *adj* ❶ funcionando ❷ empleado, da • **a working mother** una madre trabajadora ❸ laboral ; laborable

■ **workings** *spl* mecanismo

working class *s* • **the working class** la clase obrera

■ **working-class** *adj* obrero, ra

working order *s* • **to be in (good) working order** funcionar (bien)

workload ['wɜːkləʊd] *s* cantidad de trabajo

workman ['wɜːkmən] *s* obrero

El plural de **workman** es **workmen** ['wɜːkmen].

workmanship ['wɜːkmənʃɪp] *s* artesanía

workmate ['wɜːkmeɪt] *s* compañero, ra de trabajo ; colega

work permit [-,pɜːmɪt] *s* permiso de trabajo

workplace ['wɜːkpleɪs] *s* lugar de trabajo

workshop ['wɜːkʃɒp] *s* taller

workspace ['wɜːkspeɪs] *s* INFORMÁTICA espacio de trabajo

workstation ['wɜːk,steɪʃn] *s* INFORMÁTICA estación de trabajo

world [wɜːld] ◆ *s* mundo • **the best in the world** el mejor del mundo • **the highest mountain in the world** la montaña más alta del mundo • **all over the world** por todo el mundo • **to see the world** ver mundo • **the antique world** el mundo antiguo • **what is the world coming to?** ¿a dónde vamos a ir a parar? • **to have all the time in the world** tener todo el tiempo del mundo

expresiones to think the world of somebody apreciar a alguien enormemente ▶ a world of difference una diferencia enorme ▶ it's a small world el mundo es un pañuelo ▶ they are worlds apart hay un abismo entre ellos

◆ *en compuestos* mundial

W

WORLD SERIES

La **World Series** o Serie Mundial es un conjunto de hasta siete partidos de béisbol en los que se enfrentan, al final de la temporada, los campeones de las dos ligas principales: la **National League** y la **American League**. Se proclama campeón el primero en obtener cuatro victorias. Éste es uno de los acontecimientos deportivos anuales de mayor importancia en los Estados Unidos; la tradición marca que sea el presidente de la nación quien lance la primera bola del encuentro.

world-class *adj* de primera categoría

world-famous *adj* famoso, sa en el mundo entero

worldly ['wɜːldlɪ] *adj literario* mundano, na

World Trade Organization *s* Organización Mundial del Comercio

World War I *s* la Primera Guerra Mundial

World War II *s* la Segunda Guerra Mundial

worldwide ['wɜːldwaɪd] ◆ *adj* mundial ◆ *adv* en todo el mundo

World Wide Web *s* • the World Wide Web la (World Wide) Web

worm [wɜːm] *s* ❶ gusano ❷ lombriz (de tierra)

worn [wɔːn] ◆ *participio pasado* → **wear** ◆ *adj* ❶ gastado, da ❷ agotado, da

worn-out *adj* ❶ • to be worn-out estar ya para tirar ❷ agotado, da

worried ['wʌrɪd] *adj* preocupado, da • to be worried about somebody o something estar preocupado por alguien o algo

worry ['wʌrɪ] ◆ *s* preocupación ◆ *vt* preocupar ◆ *vi* • to worry (about) preocuparse (por)

expresión not to worry! ¡no importa!

worrying ['wʌrɪɪŋ] *adj* preocupante

worrywort ['wɜːrɪwɔːrt] *s familiar* angustiado, da

worse [wɜːs] ◆ *adj* peor • to get worse empeorar • to get worse and worse ir cada vez peor • to go from bad to worse ir de mal en peor • to make things worse empeorar las cosas • they are none the worse for their adventure se sienten perfectamente a pesar de su aventura ◆ *adv* peor • you could do worse than marry him no harías tan mal casándote con él

expresión worse off a) en peor situación b) peor económicamente

◆ *s* • worse was to come lo peor estaba aún por venir • a change for the worse un cambio para peor • to take a turn for the worse empeorar

worsen ['wɜːsn] *vt* & *vi* empeorar

worship ['wɜːʃɪp] ◆ *vt literal & figurado* adorar ◆ *s literal & figurado* • worship (of) culto (a); adoración (por)

■ **Worship** *s* • Your/Her/His Worship su señoría • his Worship the Mayor el Excelentísimo Señor alcalde

Formas irregulares de **worship**: *pretérito & pp* **worshiped**, *gerundio* **worshiping**.

worst [wɜːst] ◆ *adj* peor • the worst thing is... lo peor es que... • worst of all lo peor de todo ◆ *adv* peor • the worst affected area la región más afectada ◆ *s* • the worst a) lo peor b) el peor, la peor • this is communism at its worst esto es la peor manifestación del comunismo • to fear the worst temer lo peor • to bring out the worst in somebody sacar lo peor de alguien

expresión if the worst comes to the worst en último extremo

■ **at (the) worst** *adv* en el peor de los casos

worth [wɜːθ] ◆ *preposición* ❶ • it's worth $50 vale 50 dólares • how much is it worth? ¿cuánto vale? • it isn't worth that much no vale tanto ❷ digno, na de • the museum is worth visiting o a visit, it's worth visiting the museum el museo merece una visita • it's not worth it no vale la pena • it's worth a try vale la pena intentarlo • for what it's worth, I think that... por si mi opinión sirve de algo, creo que... ◆ *s* • $5,000 worth of antiques antigüedades por valor de 50.000 dólares • a month's worth of groceries provisiones para un mes

worthless ['wɜːθlɪs] *adj* ❶ sin valor ❷ despreciable

worthwhile [,wɜːθ'waɪl] *adj* ❶ que vale la pena ❷ noble; digno, na

worthy ['wɜːðɪ] *adj* ❶ digno, na ❷ encomiable

would [wʊd]
◆ *v modal*

❶ [*en estilo indirecto*]
• she said she would come dijo que vendría

❷ [*expresa el condicional*]
• what would you do? ¿que harías tú?
• what would you have done? ¿qué habrías hecho tú?
• he would do anything for her haría cualquier cosa por ella
• I would be most grateful te lo agradecería sumamente

❸ [*con "if", para dar un consejo*]
• I wouldn't worry if I were you yo en tu lugar no me preocuparía
• I would report it if I were you yo en tu lugar lo denunciaría

❹ [*para expresar la voluntad*]
• she wouldn't go no quería ir
• I tried to explain the situation to him but he wouldn't listen to me intenté explicarle la situación pero no quiso escucharme

❺ [*con peticiones corteses*]
• would you like a drink? ¿quiere una bebida?
• would you mind closing the window? ¿le importaría cerrar la ventana?

W

❻ [*para indicar una característica, una costumbre*]
• **he would say that** no me sorprende nada que dijera eso
• **you would go and tell her!** ¡tenías que contárselo!

❼ [*para expresar una acción que era habitual en el pasado*]
• **he would smoke a cigar after dinner** se fumaba un habano después de cenar
• **she would often complain about the neighbors** solía quejarse mucho de los vecinos
• **the dinner would always be ready when they arrived home** la cena siempre estaba lista cuando llegaban a casa

❽ [*para expresar una posibilidad*]
• **he'd be about 50 but he doesn't look it** debe tener unos 50 años, pero no lo parece

would-be *adj* • **a would-be author** un aspirante a literato

wouldn't ['wʊdnt] (*abreviatura de* would not) = **would**

would've ['wʊdəv] (*abreviatura de* would have) = **would**

wound¹ [wuːnd] ◆ *s* herida ◆ *vt* *literal & figurado* herir

wound² [waʊnd] *pretérito & participio pasado* → **wind**

wove [wəʊv] *pretérito* → **weave**

woven ['wəʊvn] *participio pasado* → **weave**

wrangle ['ræŋgl] ◆ *s* disputa ◆ *vi* • **to wrangle (with somebody over something)** discutir o pelearse (con alguien por algo)

wrap [ræp] ◆ *vt* ❶ envolver • **to wrap something in something** envolver algo en algo • **to wrap something around something** amarrar algo alrededor de algo ❷ • **he wrapped his hands around it** lo rodeó con sus manos ◆ *s* ❶ chal ❷ tipo de sánwich servido en una tortilla de harina de trigo y enrollado
expresión **to keep something under wraps** mantener algo en secreto

■ **wrap up** ◆ *vt* ☀ *El objeto se puede colocar antes o después de la preposición.* envolver ◆ *vi* • **wrap up well** abrígate bien

wrapper ['ræpər] *s* envoltorio

wrapping ['ræpɪŋ] *s* envoltorio

wrapping paper *s* ☀ *incontable* papel de envolver

wrath [rɒθ] *s* *literario* ira; cólera

wreak [riːk] *vt* causar • **to wreak havoc** hacer estragos

wreath [riːθ] *s* corona (de flores)

wreck [rek] ◆ *s* ❶ restos del siniestro ❷ restos del naufragio ❸ *familiar* guiñapo • **to be a nervous wreck** estar hecho un manojo de nervios ◆ *vt* ❶ destrozar ❷ NÁUTICA hacer naufragar • **to be wrecked** naufragar ❸ dar al traste con ❹ acabar con

wreckage ['rekɪdʒ] *s* ❶ ☀ *incontable* restos ❷ escombros

wrecker ['rekər] *s* camión grúa

wrench [rentʃ] ◆ *s* ❶ llave inglesa ❷ torcedura ◆ *vt* ❶ • **to wrench something (off)** arrancar algo • **to wrench something open** abrir algo de un tirón ❷ torcer

wrestle ['resl] *vi* *literal & figurado* • **to wrestle (with)** luchar (con)

wrestler ['reslər] *s* luchador, ra

wrestling ['reslɪŋ] *s* lucha libre

wretch [retʃ] *s* desgraciado, da

wretched ['retʃɪd] *adj* ❶ miserable ❷ *familiar* maldito, ta

wring [rɪŋ] *vt* ❶ estrujar; escurrir ❷ retorcer

Formas irregulares de **wring** *pret & pp* **wrung**

wrinkle ['rɪŋkl] ◆ *s* arruga ◆ *vt* arrugar ◆ *vi* arrugarse

wrist [rɪst] *s* muñeca

wristwatch ['rɪstwɒtʃ] *s* reloj de pulsera

write [raɪt] ◆ *vt* ❶ escribir • **to write somebody a letter** escribirle una carta a alguien ❷ escribir a • **you never write your grandmother** nunca le escribes a la abuela ◆ *vi* escribir

■ **write away** *vi* • **to write away for something** escribir pidiendo algo

■ **write back (to)** *vt & vi* ☀ *El objeto siempre va después de la preposición al final.* contestar

■ **write down** *vt* ☀ *El objeto se puede colocar antes o después de la preposición.* apuntar

■ **write off** *vt* ☀ *El objeto se puede colocar antes o después de la preposición.* ❶ abandonar ❷ cancelar; anular ❸ considerar un fracaso

■ **write up** *vt* ☀ *El objeto se puede colocar antes o después de la preposición.* redactar

Formas irregulares de **write**: *pretérito* **wrote**, *pp* **written**

write-off *s* • **the car was a write-off** el carro quedó totalmente destrozado

writer ['raɪtər] *s* ❶ escritor, ra ❷ autor, ra

writing ['raɪtɪŋ] *s* ❶ ☀ *incontable* letra; caligrafía ❷ escrito • **to put something in writing** poner algo por escrito ❸ escritura

writing paper *s* ☀ *incontable* papel de carta

written ['rɪtn] ◆ *participio pasado* → **write** ◆ *adj* ❶ escrito, ta ❷ por escrito

wrong [rɒŋ] ◆ *adj* ❶ malo, la • **the clock's wrong** el reloj anda mal • **what's wrong?** ¿qué pasa? • **there's nothing wrong** no pasa nada • **there's nothing wrong with me** no me pasa nada ❷ equivocado, da • **he has given me the wrong change** me ha dado el cambio equivocado • **I think we've gone the wrong way** creo que nos hemos equivocado de camino • **to be wrong** equivocarse • **to be wrong about something/somebody** equivocarse con respecto a algo/alguien • **to be wrong to do something** cometer un error al hacer algo ❸ inoportuno, na ❹ incorrecto, ta • **I always seem to say the wrong thing** parece que siempre digo lo que no debo ❺ malo, la • **it's wrong to**

W

steal/lie robar/mentir está mal • **what's wrong with being a communist?** ¿qué tiene de malo ser comunista? ◆ *adv* mal • **to get something wrong** entender mal algo ◆ *s* **❶** mal • **to be in the wrong** haber hecho mal **❷** injusticia

wrongly ['rɒŋlɪ] *adv* equivocadamente

wrote [rəʊt] *pretérito* → **write**

wrung [rʌŋ] *pretérito* & *participio pasado* → **wring**

WTO [ˌdʌbljuːtiːˈəʊ] (*abreviatura de* World Trade Organization) *s* OMC

WWW (*abreviatura de* World Wide Web) *s* WWW

X

x, X [eks] *s* x; X
  Dos plurales: **x's** o **xs**, **X's** o **Xs**,
xenophobia [ˌzenə'fəʊbjə] *s* xenofobia
Xmas ['eksməs] *s* Navidad
XML [ˌeksem'el] (*abreviatura de* Extensible Markup Language) *s* INFORMÁTICA XML
X-ray ◆ *s* ❶ rayo X ❷ radiografía • **to have a chest X-ray** hacerse una radiografía ◆ *vt* examinar con rayos X; radiografiar
xylophone ['zaɪləfəʊn] *s* xilofón

Y

y, Y [waɪ] *s* y; Y
  Dos plurales: **y's** o **ys** **Y's** o **Ys**
yacht [jɒt] *s* yate
yachting ['jɒtɪŋ] *s* vela
yachtsman ['jɒtsmən] *s* navegante; tripulante
  El plural de **yachtsman** es **yachtsmen** ['jɒtsmen].
yam [jæm] *s* batata
Yank [jæŋk] *s familiar & despectivo* yanqui
Yankee ['jæŋkɪ] *s* ▸ término usado para designar a una persona del noreste de los EE.UU.

Yankee
En sus orígenes, el término inglés **Yankee** o **Yank** se refería a los inmigrantes holandeses que se establecieron principalmente en el noreste de los Estados Unidos. Más tarde se utilizó para referirse a cualquier persona procedente del noreste, por lo que durante la Guerra de Secesión se llamaba "yanquis" (**Yankees**) a los soldados que luchaban en el bando de los estados del norte. En nuestros días, algunos etadounidenses sureños aún utilizan el término en tono despectivo para referirse a la gente del norte. Los no norteamericanos también lo emplean, generalmente con sentido peyorativo, para designar a cualquier persona de nacionalidad norteamericana.

yard [jɑːd] *s* ❶ yarda *(91.44 cm)* ❷ patio; jardín ❸ astillero • **builder's/goods yard** depósito de materiales/de mercancías
yarn [jɑːn] *s* estambre
yawn [jɔːn] ◆ *s* bostezo ◆ *vi* ❶ bostezar ❷ abrirse
yd *abreviatura escrita de* **yard**
yeah [jeə] *adv familiar* sí
year [jɪər] *s* ❶ año • **he's 25 years old** tiene 25 años • **all (the) year round** todo el año • **over the years** con los años ❷ EDUCACIÓN curso • **he's in (his) first year** está en primero
  ■ **years** *spl* años • **it's years since I last saw you** hace siglos que no te veo
yearbook

Yearbook
Al final de cada año académico los centros de enseñanza de Estados Unidos publican un **yearbook** (anuario) que resume lo ocurrido a los alumnos del último curso e incluye sus respectivas fotografías y a menudo predicciones sobre su futuro. Últimamente los **yearbooks** han comenzado a aparecer en sitios Web, con lo que se facilita su actualización y permite a los antiguos alumnos mantenerse en contacto.

yearly ['jɪəlɪ] ◆ *adj* anual ◆ *adv* ❶ una vez al año ❷ cada año

yearn [jɜːn] *vi* • **to yearn for something/to do something** ansiar algo/hacer algo

yearning [ˈjɜːnɪŋ] *s* • **yearning (for somebody/something)** anhelo (de alguien/algo)

yeast [jiːst] *s* levadura

yell [jel] ♦ *s* grito; alarido ♦ *vt* & *vi* gritar

yellow [ˈjeləʊ] ♦ *adj* amarillo, lla ♦ *s* amarillo

yellow card *s* FUTBOL tarjeta amarilla

yelp [jelp] ♦ *s* aullido ♦ *vi* aullar

yes [jes] ♦ *adv* sí • **to say yes** decir que sí • **to say yes to something** consentir algo • **does he speak English? — yes, he does** ¿habla inglés? — sí • **he doesn't speak English — yes he does!** no habla inglés — sí, sí que habla ♦ *s* sí

yesterday [ˈjestədɪ] ♦ *s* ayer ♦ *adv* ayer • **yesterday afternoon** ayer por la tarde • **the day before yesterday** anteayer; antier

---

yet [jet]
♦ *adv*

❶ [*en forma negativa, indica una acción que todavía no ha ocurrido*]
• **he hasn't arrived yet** todavía no ha llegado
• **I have had no response to my ad as yet** todavía no me ha contestado nadie al anuncio

❷ [*en preguntas, para saber si una acción ya ha ocurrido*]
• **have they finished yet?** ¿ya terminaron?
• **are we there yet?** ¿ya llegamos?

❸ [*con un comparativo, con papel intensificador*]
• **she needs yet more time** necesita todavía más tiempo
• **yet more people arrived at the party** llegó todavía más gente a la fiesta
• **she told us a yet sadder tale** nos contó una historia todavía más triste
• **yet again** una vez más

❹ [*con un superlativo*]
• **it's the best film we've seen yet** es la mejor película que hemos visto hasta ahora
• **it's the greatest book yet written** es el mejor libro escrito jamás
♦ *conjunción*

[*introduce una oposición*]
• **they can't sing or play their instruments yet everyone buys their records** no saben ni cantar ni tocar y aun así la gente compra sus discos

---

yield [jiːld] ♦ *s* ❶ AGRICULTURA cosecha ❷ FINANZAS rédito ♦ *vt* ❶ producir; dar ❷ ceder ♦ *vi* ❶ ceder ❷ *formal* rendirse • **to yield to somebody/something** claudicar ante alguien/algo

expresión 'yield' AUTOMÓVILES 'ceda el paso'

yippee [ˈjɪpɪ] *exclamación* ¡yupi!

YMCA (*abreviatura de* Young Men's Christian Association) *s* ▶ asociación internacional de jóvenes cristianos

yoga [ˈjəʊgə] *s* yoga

yogurt [ˈjəʊgət] *s* yogurt

---

yolk [jəʊk] *s* yema

you [juː] *pronombre personal* ❶ ☼ *como sujeto en singular* tú; usted • **you're a good cook** eres/usted es un buen cocinero • **are you Mexican?** ¿eres/es usted mexicano? • **you idiot!** ¡imbécil! • **there you are a)** ¡ya estás/está usted aquí! **b)** ahí tienes/tiene • **that jacket isn't really you** esa chaqueta no te/le sienta bien ❷ ☼ *como sujeto en plural* ustedes • **¿fueron ustedes?** was it you? ❸ ☼ *como complemento directo - acento atónico - en singular* te; lo; la • **yes, Madam, I understand you** sí, señora, la comprendo ❹ ☼ *como complemento directo - acento atónico - en plural* los; las • **I can see you** los/las veo ❺ ☼ *como complemento directo - acento tónico* • **I don't expect you to do it** no te voy a pedir que **tú** lo hagas ❻ ☼ *como complemento indirecto en singular* te; le • **she gave it to you** te lo dio • **can I get you a chair, sir?** ¿le traigo una silla, señor? ❼ ☼ *como complemento indirecto en plural* les • **I called you yesterday** les llamé ayer ❽ ☼ *después de preposición* ti; usted; ustedes • **we shall go with/without you** iremos con/sin ustedes ❾ ☼ *en comparaciones* tú; usted; ustedes • **I'm shorter than you** soy más bajo que tú o ustedes ❿ ☼ *uso impersonal* se • **you wouldn't have thought so** no se lo hubiera imaginado • **exercise is good for you** el ejercicio es bueno (para uno)

---

you

You sirve tanto para el singular como para el plural. Además, se usa con independencia del grado de familiaridad que haya con nuestro interlocutor.

You sirve para hablar de la gente en general, p. ej. para dar o pedir instrucciones (how do *you* get to the station? *¿cómo se llega a la estación?*). También se puede usar el pronombre one (how does *one* get to the station?) pero suena muy formal.

---

you'd [juːd] ❶ (*abreviatura de* you had) → **have** ❷ (*abreviatura de* you would) → **would**

you'll [juːl] ❶ (*abreviatura de* you will) → **will** ❷ (*abreviatura de* you shall) → **shall**

young [jʌŋ] ♦ *adj* joven • **his younger sister** su hermana pequeña • **I'm younger than her** soy más joven que ella • **I'm two years younger than her** soy dos años menor que ella • **the younger generation** la generación más joven ♦ *spl* ❶ • **the young** los jóvenes ❷ crías

youngster [ˈjʌŋstər] *s* joven

your [jɔːr] *adj posesivo* ❶ ☼ *al referirse a una persona* tu; tus (*con plurales*); su; sus (*uso formal*) • **your dog** tu/su perro ❷ ☼ *al referirse a más de una persona* su; sus • **your house** su casa • **your children** sus niños • **what's your name?** ¿cómo te llamas? • **it wasn't your fault** no fue culpa tuya/suya ❸ ☼ *uso impersonal* • **your attitude changes as you get older** la actitud de uno cambia con la vejez • **your average**

American el americano medio ❹ ☿ *con partes del cuerpo* te ; se • **you didn't wash your hair** no te lavaste el pelo • **it's good for your teeth/hair** es bueno para los dientes/el pelo

your

Your sirve tanto para el singular como para el plural. Además, se usa con independencia del grado de familiaridad que haya con nuestro interlocutor.

No olvidemos que al hablar de las partes del cuerpo se usa el adjetivo posesivo your en lugar del artículo the (have you washed *your* hair? *¿te lavaste la cabeza?*).

you're [jɔːɾ] (*abreviatura de* you are) → **be**

yours [jɔːz] *pronombre posesivo* ❶ ☿ *al referirse a una persona* tuyo, tuya ; suyo, suya • **that money is yours** ese dinero es tuyo/suyo • **my car hit yours** mi coche chocó contra el tuyo/el suyo • **it wasn't her fault, it was yours** no fue culpa de ella sino **tuya/suya** ❷ ☿ *al referirse a más de una persona* suyo, suya • **is this yours?** ¿esto es suyo? • **those keys are yours** esas llaves son suyas • **a friend of yours** un amigo suyo ■ **Yours** *adv* • **Yours faithfully/sincerely** atentamente

yours

Yours sirve tanto para el singular como para el plural. Además, se usa con independencia del grado de familiaridad que haya con nuestro interlocutor (that desk is yours *ese escritorio es tuyo/suyo/vuestro*).

yourself [jɔːˈself] *pronombre* ❶ ☿ *como reflexivo en singular* te ; le ; se • **did you hurt yourself?** ¿te hiciste/se hizo daño? ❷ ☿ *como reflexivo en plural* les ❸ ☿ *tras preposición en singular* ti mismo, ti misma ; usted mismo, usted misma • **with yourself** contigo mismo/misma ❹ ☿ *tras preposición en plural* ustedes mismos, ustedes mismas ❺ ☿ *para dar énfasis* • **you yourself** tú mismo, tú misma ; usted mismo, ma • **you yourselves** ustedes mismos, ustedes mismas ❻ solo, la *(sin ayuda)* • **did you do it (by) yourself?** ¿lo hiciste solo?

El plural de **yourself** es **yourselves** [jɔːˈselvz].

youth [juːθ] *s* ❶ juventud • **in his youth** en su juventud ❷ joven

youth club *s* club juvenil

youthful [ˈjuːθfʊl] *adj* juvenil

youth hostel *s* albergue juvenil

you've [juːv] (*abreviatura de* you have) → **have**

YWCA (*abreviatura de* Young Women's Christian Association) *s* ▶ asociación internacional de jóvenes cristianas

Z

z, Z [ziː] *s* z ; Z

Dos plurales: **z's** o **zs**, **Z's** o **Zs**

zany [ˈzeɪnɪ] *adj* ❶ *familiar* disparatado, da ❷ loco, ca

zebra [ˈziːbrə] *s* cebra

Dos plurales: **zebra** o **zebras**

zenith [ˈziːnəθ] *s* *figurado* ASTRONOMÍA cenit

zero [ˈzɪərəʊ] ◆ *adj* cero ; nulo, la ◆ *s* cero • **below zero** bajo cero

Dos plurales: **zero** o **zeroes**

zest [zest] *s* ☿ *incontable* ❶ entusiasmo • **her zest for life** su entusiasmo por vivir ❷ cáscara

zigzag [ˈzɪɡzæɡ] ◆ *s* zigzag ◆ *vi* zigzaguear

zilch [zɪltʃ] *s* *familiar* ❶ cerapio ❷ nada

zinc [zɪŋk] *s* cinc ; zinc

zip [zɪp] *s* INFORMÁTICA comprimir ■ **zip up** *vt* ☿ *El objeto se puede colocar antes o después de la preposición.* cerrar el zíper de

zip code *s* código postal

zipper [ˈzɪpəɾ] *s* zíper

zodiac [ˈzəʊdɪæk] *s* • **the zodiac** el zodiaco

zone [zəʊn] *s* zona

zoo [zuː] *s* zoo

zoology [zəʊˈɒlədʒɪ] *s* zoología

zoom [zuːm] *vi* *familiar* • **to zoom past** pasar zumbando

zoom lens *s* zoom

zucchini [zuːˈkiːnɪ] *s* calabacita

El plural de **zucchini** es **zucchini**